The New Everyman
DICTIONARY
OF MUSIC

originally compiled by
ERIC BLOM

Sixth edition by
DAVID CUMMINGS

Fitzhenry & Whiteside
Toronto, Ottawa, Halifax
Winnipeg, Edmonton
Vancouver

Fitzhenry & Whiteside Limited
195 Allstate Parkway
Markham, Ontario L3R 4T8

ISBN 0-88902-8761

Blom, Eric, 1888–1959.
   The new Everyman dictionary of music

6th ed./rev. by David Cummings.
Previous eds. published under title: Everyman's dictionary of music.

ISBN 0-88902-876-1
1. Music - Dictionaries. I. Cummings, David.
II. Title.   III. Title: Everyman's dictionary of music.

ML100.B56 1988   780'.3'21   C88-093706-8

CONTENTS

PREFACE

The dictionary was first published in 1947, under the editorship of Eric Blom. Seven years later the nine-volume fifth edition of *Grove's Dictionary* appeared, also edited by Eric Blom, and in many ways *Everyman* was Blom's 'dry run' for *Grove*. After revisions by Eric Blom in 1954 and 1958 *Everyman's Dictionary* was further revised, by Sir Jack Westrup, in 1962 and 1971.

The interests of Eric Blom and Sir Jack Westrup lay largely with Classical and earlier music. Without wishing to disturb unduly the excellent work of my predecessors, I have attempted to bring *Everyman* into line with modern requirements. To this end, most of my 1500 new and 1000 substantially revised entries are concerned in some way with twentieth-century music. They include musical terms, with appropriate examples, leading orchestras, individual works and many composers and performing artists (there are new entries for musicians who were born after Eric Blom's death). Although the present edition of the dictionary is 100 pages longer than that of 1971, it has been necessary to make room for new material by deleting many entries for minor turn-of-the-century figures.

A lexicographer is like a detective; he is only as good as his sources. I have brought to *Everyman* the experience I gained in working for the American dictionary, *Baker's Biographical Dictionary of Musicians, The Oxford Dictionary of Music*, and two forthcoming *Grove*-related reference books; I am therefore particularly indebted to the four editors concerned, Nicolas Slonimsky and Dennis McIntire (*Baker's*), Michael Kennedy and Stanley Sadie. David Fallows has revised many early composers and provided some technical terms. Advice and information from Desmond Shawe-Taylor is also gratefully acknowledged. I am indebted to Karl-Josef Kutsch for much information on singers which appears here for the first time in English.

The following notes are intended as a guide to users of the dictionary:

Alphabetical order: The system used by Eric Blom has been followed, i.e. 'all entries consisting of more than one word are arranged in such a way as to make the first word alone the key to their place in the alphabet'; thus all names starting with La as a separate word are grouped together at the beginning of letter L. For hyphenated names the second part of the name is taken as the Christian name; thus Fischer-Dieskau appears before Edwin Fischer.

Dates: For the first time in *Everyman* dates are given to many works listed under important composers. Unless otherwise indicated, stage works are given years of première and other pieces years of composition (or completion). Dates of birth and death for East Europeans are rendered in new style, i.e. according to the Gregorian calendar. Deaths have been recorded up to the end of 1987, but readers are invited to contribute any which have been missed.

Cross references: Important references are indicated with *q.v.* Works given separate entries are not referenced under the composers concerned. A titled work by a major composer is likely to have a separate entry (this applies particularly to twentieth-century composers).

Titles and translations: Except where East European and Scandinavian languages are concerned, titles of works are usually given in the original language. Translations have been provided sparingly, largely because to the intelligent reader they are often unnecessary; help is surely not needed with Messiaen's *Couleurs de la cité céleste* or *Visions de l'Amen*.

Work lists: For major composers works are grouped in separate paragraphs, under stage, choral, orchestral, chamber, instrumental, etc. The same order is usually followed in single-paragraph listings for lesser composers, although the order here and for some major modern composers whose output is difficult to define by *genre* is sometimes chronological.

Performers: Performers in general and singers in particular have not been favoured in previous single-volume dictionaries; I have therefore made a particular effort to include singers. Their entries range alphabetically from Emma Abbott to Teresa Zylis-Gara and historically from Andreana Basile (Monteverdi's favourite prima donna) to Aprile Millo (born 1958). For reasons of space it is not possible to give composer and/or opera every time a role is mentioned, but the list at the back of the dictionary provides the necessary information.

Performers other than singers have not been neglected. New entries for conductors range from Claudio Abbado to Fritz Zweig; violinists begin with Salvatore Accardo and end with Paul Zukovsky; there are plenty of pianists between Dmitri Alexeev and Krystian Zimerman.

The dictionary has benefited over the years from the comments and corrections sent in by readers who, I hope, will write to me care of the publishers with suggestions for the next edition.

Harrow, 1988   David Cummings

ABBREVIATIONS

abbr.	abbreviated, abbreviation	Brit. Mus.	British Museum
Acad.	Academy	bsn.	bassoon
accomp.	accompanied, accompaniment, accompany	Bulg.	Bulgaria, Bulgarian
		BWV	Bach-Werke-Verzeichnis (Schmieder catalogue no. of J.S. Bach's works)
addit.	addition, additional		
Add. MS.	Additional Manuscript	c	circa (about)
Ala.	Alabama	Calif.	California
Alsat.	Alsatian	CB	Companion of the Order of the Bath
altern.	alternate, alternating		
Amer.	America, American	CBE	Commander of the Order of the British Empire
Angl.	Anglican		
anon.	anonymous	CBS	Columbia Broadcasting System
app.	appointed, appointing	CBSO	City of Birmingham Symphony Orchestra
appt.	appointment		
Arg.	Argentine, Argentinian	cent.	century
		cf.	confer (compare)
Armen.	Armenia, Armenian	CG	Royal Opera House, Covent Garden, London
arr.	arranged, arrangement, arranger		
		Chin.	Chinese
		choreog.	choreographer, choreographic, choreography
assoc.	associated, association		
asst.	assistant, assisted	clar.	clarinet
attrib.	attributed	Co.	Company, County
Aus.	Austria, Austrian	co-ed.	co-editor
Austral.	Australia, Australian	Col.	Colorado
autobiog.	autobiographical, autobiography	Coll.	College
		comp.	compose composed, composer, composing, composition
b	born		
bap.	baptized	conc.	concerto
bar.	baritone	cond.	conducted, conducting, conductor
BBC	British Broadcasting Corporation		
		Conn.	Connecticut
B.C.	Before Christ	Cons.	Conservatoire, Conservatorio, Conservatorium, Conservatory
Beds.	Bedfordshire		
Belg.	Belgian, Belgium		
Bibl.	Bibliothek, Bibliothèque		
		contrib.	contributed, contribution, contributor
bibliog.	bibliographer, bibliography		
		Ct.	Canton
B.Mus.	Bachelor of Music	Cz.	Czech, Czechoslovakia
biog.	biographer, biographical, biography		
BNOC	British National Opera Company	D	Deutsch catalogue no. (Schubert's works)
Boh.	Bohemia	d	died
Brit.	Britain, British	db.	double bass
Brit. Lib.	British Library		

DBE	Dame Commander of the Order of the British Empire
DC	District of Columbia
ded.	dedicated, dedication
Den.	Denmark
dept.	department
dir.	director, directed
D.Mus.	Doctor of Music
do.	ditto
E.	East
eccles.	ecclesiastical
ECO	English Chamber Orchestra
ed.	edited, editing, edition, editor
educ.	educated, education
e.g.	*exempli gratia* (for example)
elec.	electric, electronic
Eng.	English
ENO	English National Opera
ens.	ensemble
EOG	English Opera Group
esp.	especially
estab.	establish, established, establishing, establishment
etc.	*et cetera* (and so on)
Eur.	Europe, European,
ex.	example
Fin.	Finland, Finnish
fig.	figurative, figuratively
fl.	*floruit* (he/she flourished)
fl.	flute
Fla.	Florida
Flem.	Flemish
fp	first performance, first performed
Fr.	France, French
Ger.	German, Germany
Gk.	Greek
Glam.	Glamorgan
Glos.	Gloucestershire
GSM	Guildhall School of Music and Drama, London
Gvt.	Government
hist.	historian, historical, history
Hol.	Holland
hon.	honorary
Hung.	Hungarian, Hungary
i.e.	*id est* (that is)

Ill.	Illinois
Imp.	Imperial
IMS	International Musical Society
incid.	incidental
incl.	include, included, includes, including
Ind.	Indiana
inst.	instrument, instrumental, instrumentation
internat.	international, internationally
intro.	introduce, introduced, introducing, introduction
Ir.	Ireland, Irish
IRCAM	Institut de recherche et de co-ordination acoustique musique
ISCM	International Society for Contemporary Music
ISM	Incorporated Society of Musicians
It.	Italian, Italy
Jap.	Japan, Japanese
jun.	junior
K	Köchel catalogue no. (Mozart's works)
Kans.	Kansas
La.	Louisana
LA	Los Angeles
Lat.	Latin
lib.	librettist, libretto
lit.	literally, literary
Litt.D.	Doctor of Letters
LPO	London Philharmonic Orchestra
LSO	London Symphony Orchestra
maj.	major
Mass.	Massachusetts
Md.	Maryland
Me.	Maine
Met	Metropolitan Opera House
Mex.	Mexican, Mexico
Mich.	Michigan
min.	minor
Minn.	Minnesota
MIT	Massachusetts Institute of Technology
misc.	miscellaneous
Miss.	Mississippi
M.Mus.	Master of Music
Mo.	Missouri
Morav.	Moravian

movt.	movement	prod.	produced, producer,
MS.	manuscript		producing,
munic.	municipal		production
Mus.B.	Bachelor of Music	prof.	professor
Mus.D.	Doctor of Music	Prov.	Provençal
		prov.	province, provincial
N.	North	Prus.	Prussia, Prussian
nat.	national	pseud.	pseudonym
NBC	National Broadcasting	pub.	publication, published,
	Company		publisher, publishing
Nev.	Nevada		
NC	North Carolina	q.v.	quod vide (which see)
NDR	Norddeutscher		
	Rundfunk	RAM	Royal Academy of
	(North German Radio)		Music, London
NH	New Hampshire	RCM	Royal College of
NJ	New Jersey		Music, London
no.	number	ref.	reference, referring
norm.	normal, normally	rep.	repertory
Northants.	Northamptonshire	repub.	republished
Norw.	Norway	Rest.	Restoration
	Norwegian	rev.	revised,
Notts.	Nottinghamshire	RIAM	Royal Irish Academy
nr.	near		of Music.
NSW	New South Wales	RLPO	Royal Liverpool
NY	New York		Philharmonic Orchestra
NZ	New Zealand	RMCM	Royal Manchester
			College of Music
ob.	oboe	RMA	Royal Musical Association
Okla.	Oklahoma	RNCM	Royal Northern College of
Ont.	Ontario		Music, Manchester
onomat.	onomatopoeic	RPO	Royal Philharmonic
op.	opus		Orchestra
orch.	orchestra, orchestrated,	Rum.	Rumania, Rumanian
	orchestration	Rus.	Russia, Russian
org.	organ		
orig.	original, originally,	S.	South
	originated	S.A.	South Africa
ov.	overture	Salop	Shropshire
Oxon.	Oxfordshire	SC	South Carolina
		Scand.	Scandinavia,
partic.	particular, particularly		Scandinavian
perc.	percussion	Scot.	Scotland, Scottish
perf.	performance,	sec.	secretary
	performed, performer	sen.	senior
pf.	piano	SIM	Société internationale
Phil.	Philharmonic		de musicologie
PO	Philharmonic	SO	Symphony Orchestra
	Orchestra	son.	sonata
Pol.	Poland, Polish	sop.	soprano
Port.	Portugal,	Span.	Spanish
	Portuguese	SS.	Saints
poss.	possibly	SW	Sadler's Wells
posth.	posthumous, posthumously		Theatre, London
prec.	preceded, preceding	Swed.	Sweden, Swedish
pres.	president	Switz.	Switzerland
prin.	principal	symph.	symphonic,
prob.	probably		symphony

TCM	Trinity College of Music, London	vol.	volume
theoret.	theoretical	W.	West
tpt.	trumpet	Wash.	Washington
trans.	translated, translation, translator	Wilts.	Wiltshire
		Wis.	Wisconsin
		WNO	Welsh National Opera
tromb.	trombone		
TV	television	WoO	Werk ohne Opuszahl (work without opus no.)
UCLA	University of California at Los Angeles	W. Va.	West Virginia
unaccomp.	unaccompanied	Yorks.	Yorkshire
univ.	university		
unpub.	unpublished	Z	Zimmerman catalogue no. (Purcell's works)
US(A)	United States (of America)		
		4tet	quartet
v.	voice	5tet	quintet
Va.	Virginia	6tet	sextet
var.	variety, variation, various	7tet	septet
		8tet	octet
vers.	version	8ve	octave
vla.	viola	9et	nonet
vln.	violin		

A

A, the 6th note, or submediant, of the scale of C major. The note

to which an orch. tunes, is estab. by international agreement at a pitch of 440 cycles a second although 415 cycles is often now used for Baroque music.

A battuta (It. = at the beat, with the beat), a direction indicating that after a free passage the strict time is to be resumed.

A cappella (It.), also **Alla cappella** (lit. at or in the chapel), a term used now only to designate unaccomp. music for a vocal ensemble.

A due (It.) = in 2 parts; generally written 'a 2'. The term is also used in the opposite sense in orchestral scores where pairs of instruments are to play in unison.

A la manière de . . . (*In the manner of . . .*), 2 sets of pf. pieces by Casella and Ravel imitating the styles of Wagner, Fauré, Brahms, Debussy, R. Strauss, Franck, Borodin, d'Indy, Chabrier and Ravel. Only the Borodin and Chabrier pieces are by Ravel.

A piacere (It. = at pleasure), a direction indicating that a passage may be played or sung in any way the perf. desires, esp. in regard to tempo.

A tempo (It. = in time), a direction indicating a return to the principal pace of a comp. after a temporary alteration.

Aaron (Aron), Pietro (b Florence, *c* 1480; d Bergamo, *c* 1550), Italian monk and contrapuntist. Wrote on hist. and science of music. Worked in Imola and Venice, entered monastery of San Leonardo, Bergamo, 1536.

Aavik, Juhan (b Reval, 29 Jan 1884; d Stockholm, 26 Nov 1982), Estonian conductor and composer. Studied at the St Petersburg Cons. and became a cond. at Wanemuine in 1911, later director of the Dorpat Cons. and choral cond. at Reval. Settled in Sweden in 1944.

Works incl. cantata *Homeland*, unaccomp. choruses; pf. sonata in C min.; songs; 2 symphs., cello concerto (1949); Requiem (1959).

Abaco, Evaristo and **Joseph dall'**. *See* **Dall' Abaco**.

Abbà-Cornaglia, Pietro (b Alessandria, Piedmont, 20 Mar 1851; d Alessandria, 2 May 1894), Italian composer. Studied at the Milan Cons. and later became a teacher and music historian.

Works incl. operas *Isabella Spinola* (Milan, 1877), *Maria di Warden, Una partita di scacchi* (Pavia, 1892); Requiem; chamber music.

Abbado, Claudio (b Milan, 26 Jun 1933), Italian conductor. He studied with Hans Swarowsky and won the 1958 Koussevitzky competition, Tanglewood; cond. NY PO in 1963. Wider recognition came in 1965, when he made his Brit. debut (Hallé Orch.), and appeared at Salzburg, Vienna and Milan. He first cond. at La Scala in 1967, became music dir. 1971 and brought the co. to CG, London, in 1976: his debut at CG had been in 1968 (*Don Carlos*). He took the LSO to Salzburg in 1973 and was prin. cond. 1979–87; often heard in modern music and has given works by Nono, Ligeti and Stockhausen (series of concerts with the LSO, 1985, *Mahler, Vienna and the 20th Cent.*). In 1986 he left his post at La Scala and became dir. of the Vienna Opera.

Abbado, Marcello (b Milan, 7 Oct 1926), Italian composer and pianist, brother of prec. He studied with Ghedini at the Milan Cons., and since 1951 has held teaching posts in Venice, Piacenza, Pesaro and Milan.

Works incl. *Ciapo*, cantata (1945); *Costruziono* for 5 small orchs. (1964), concerto for vln., pf. and 2 chamber orchs. (1967), 3 string 4tets (1947, 1953, 1969), concerto for pf., 4tet and orch. (1969).

Abbatini, Antonio Maria (b Tiferno, now Città di Castello, *c* 1595; d Tiferno, 1679), Italian composer and church musician. Held various posts at churches in Rome.

Works incl. 3 operas, Masses, motets, psalms, madrigals.

Abbellimenti (It. lit. embellishments) = Ornaments, esp. florid passages introduced into vocal music.

Abbey, John (b Whilton, Northants., 22 Dec 1785; d Versailles, 19 Feb 1859), English organ builder. Worked in Paris from 1826 and built many organs in Fr. and S. America.

Abbott, Emma (b Chicago, 9 Dec 1850; d Salt Lake City, 5 Jan 1891), American soprano. Studied with Achille Errani in NY, later in Milan and Paris, with Mathilde Marchesi and others. She 1st appeared at CG 1876 as Donizetti's Marie; NY Met, 1877, same role. Formed an operatic co. in America, managed by Eugene Wetherell, whom she had married in 1875. Her best role was Marguerite.

Abegg Variations, Schumann's op. 1, for pf., a set of variations on a theme constructed on the notes A.B(♭). E.G.G. and bearing the ded. 'à Mlle. Pauline, Comtesse d'Abegg', who did not exist, though there was a family of that name. The existence of Meta Abegg has yet to be proved. The work was comp. in 1830 and pub. in 1832.

Abeille, Johann Christian Ludwig (b Bayreuth, 20 Feb 1761; d Stuttgart, 2 Mar 1838), German composer, pianist and organist. In the service of the Duke of Württemberg in Stuttgart.

Works incl. *Singspiele,* songs and keyboard music.

Abel, Carl Friedrich (b Cöthen, 22 Dec 1723; d London, 20 Jun 1787), German harpsichord and vla. da gamba player. Worked under Hasse at Dresden 1743–58. From 1759 resident in London, where he was app. chamber musician to Queen Charlotte. Abel was joint promoter with Johann Christian Bach of the Bach-Abel Concerts (1765–81). Wrote a large quantity of instrumental music, of which the works for vla. da gamba are perhaps the most notable.

Abel, Christian Ferdinand (b Hanover, *c* 1683; d Cöthen, 1737), German cellist and vla. da gamba player, father of prec. Served at Cöthen under J.S. Bach, whose unaccomp. cello suites were probably written for him.

Abel, Leopold August (b Cöthen, 24 Mar 1718; d Ludwigslust, 25 Aug 1794), German violinist and composer, son of prec.

Abélard, Pierre (b Pallet nr. Nantes, 1079; d Saint-Marcel nr. Châlon-sur-Saône, 21 Apr 1142), French scholar and musician. Comp. songs for his beloved, Héloïse, Lat. Lamentations, etc.

Abell, John (b Aberdeenshire, 1653; d Cambridge, 1724), Scottish counter-tenor and lutenist. Possibly a boy chorister at the Chapel Royal in London, of which he became a Gentleman in 1679. Married Frances Knollys, sister of the Earl of Banbury, travelled much abroad, was intendant at Kassel, 1698–9, and returned to Eng. as a stage singer. Pub. some collections of songs.

Abencérages, Les, ou L'Étendard de Grenade (*The Abencerrages, or The Standard of Granada*), opera by Cherubini (lib. by V.J.E. de Jouy, based on a novel by Jean-Pierre de Florian), prod. Paris, Opéra, 6 Apr 1813.

Abendmusik(en) (Ger. = evening music(s)), music evening perfs. of semi-sacred charac-

ter estab. by Tunder at Lübeck in the 1640s and becoming so famous there that they were imitated by other N. German towns, esp. Hamburg. They were held mainly during Advent.

Abert, Hermann (b Stuttgart, 25 March 1871; d Stuttgart, 13 Aug 1927), German musicologist of Czech descent. Prof. of music at Leipzig Univ. in succession to Riemann from 1920 and at Berlin from 1923. Wrote many hist. works, incl. a greatly enlarged ed. of Jahn's *Mozart.*

Abgesang (Ger. = after-song). *See* **Bar.**

Abingdon, Henry. *See* **Abyngdon.**

Abondante, Giulio. Italian 16th-cent. lutenist and composer. Pub. several books of lute pieces.

Abos, Girolamo (b Valetta, 16 Nov 1715; d Naples, Oct 1760), Maltese (?) composer, principally of Italian opera and church music.

Abraham, Gerald (b Newport, Isle of Wight, 9 Mar 1904), English musicologist, specialist in Russian music. Prof. of music at Liverpool Univ. 1947–62; Assistant Controller, Music, BBC, 1962–7. Ed. of vols. iv, viii and ix of the *New Oxford History of Music* and co-ed. of vol. iii; wrote *Concise Oxford History of Music,* 1979. CBE, 1974

Abraham and Isaac, Canticle II by Britten for alto, tenor and pf. Comp. 1952 for Ferrier and Pears and perf. by them Nottingham, 21 Jan 1952.

Sacred ballad for bar. and chamber orch. by Stravinsky (Hebrew text); comp. 1962–4, fp Jerusalem 23 Aug 1964.

Abramsky, Alexander (b Moscow, 22 Jan 1898; d Moscow, 29 Aug 1985), Russian composer. Studied at the Moscow Cons. He turned to Soviet ideology by writing an opera on the subject of life on a collective farm (*Laylikhon and Anarkhon,* 1943). Other works incl. piano concerto (1941) and cantata, *Land of the Silent Lake* (1971).

Ábrányi, Emil (b Budapest, 22 Sep 1882; d Budapest, 11 Feb 1970), Hungarian conductor and composer. Cond. of the Opera at Budapest from 1911. His operas, prod. there, incl. *Monna Vanna* (after Maeterlinck), *Paolo and Francesca* (after Dante, 1912), and *Don Quixote* (after Cervantes, 1917).

Ábrányi, Kornél (b Szentgyörgy-Ábrány, 15 Oct 1822; d Budapest, 20 Dec 1903), Hungarian critic, father of prec. Partfounder of the music paper *Zenészeti Lapok,* 1860, and prof. at Budapest Acad. of Music from 1875. Wrote the lib. for his son's *Monna Vanna.*

Abravanel, Maurice (b Thessaloniki, 6 Jan 1903), Greek-born American conductor. He studied at Lausanne Univ. and with Weill in Berlin. He was in Paris during the 1930s, where he gave several works by Weill, and moved to NY in 1936; gave *Samson et Dalila, Lakmé* and *Lohengrin* at the Met and then worked on Broadway. He cond. several theatre works by Weill and in 1947 became cond. of the Utah SO. Well known in music by Mahler, Vaughan Williams and Mozart. Retired 1979.

Abreise, Die, opera by d'Albert (lib. by F. von Sporck, based on a play by August von Steigentesch), prod. Frankfurt, 20 Oct 1898).

Absil, Jean (b Péruwelz, Hainault, 23 Oct 1893; d Brussels, 2 Feb 1974), Belgian composer. Studied at the Brussels Cons., where he became prof. in 1931, after being app. director of Etterbeek Music Acad. in 1923.

Works incl. opera *Peau d'âne* (1937); ballet *Le Miracle de Pan*; radio opera *Ulysse et les Sirennes*; 5 symphs. (1920–70); 4 string 4tets (1929–41); 3 string trios and other chamber music.

Absolute Music, broadly speaking, any music not set to words and not based on any kind of literary, pictorial, descriptive or other extra-musical subject or idea.

Absolute Pitch. Those who can identify by ear any note heard without ref. to music are said to possess the faculty of absolute pitch.

Abstrakte Oper no. 1, opera by Blacher (lib. by Werner Egk), fp Frankfurt (concert), 28 Jun 1953; prod. Mannheim, 17 Oct 1953. Text consists largely of nonsense words.

Abt, Franz (b Eilenburg, 22 Dec 1819; d Wiesbaden, 31 Mar 1885), German composer and conductor. Studied at St Thomas's and Univ., Leipzig; later cond. at Bernburg Zurich and Brunswick. Wrote an enormous number of songs and part-songs.

Abu Hassan, opera by Weber (lib. by F.C. Hiemer), prod. Munich, 4 Jun 1811.

Abyngdon, Henry (b *c* 1418; d *c* 1497), English musician. In the service of the Duke of Gloucester, 1445; app. succentor of Wells Cathedral, 1447; Master of the Children of the Chapel Royal, 1456; was the 1st to receive a music degree at Cambridge (B. Mus., 1463); master of St Catherine's Hospital, Bristol, 1478, in which year he was succeeded by Gilbert Banastre at the Chapel Royal.

Academic Festival Overture (*Akademische Fest-Ouvertüre),* Brahms's op. 80, comp. 1880 and fp at Breslau, 4 Jan 1881, in acknowledgment of the hon. degree of doc-tor of philosophy, conferred on him by Breslau Univ. in 1879. The thematic material is taken from Ger. students' songs. The *Tragic Overture* was written as a companion-piece.

Academie (or Akademie), 18th-cent. German term for a concert.

Académie de Musique, the official title of the Paris Opéra, though never actually called so after 1671. It was first so styled in letters-patent granted by Louis XIV, 28 Jun 1669. It became the Académie des Opera [*sic*] in 1671 and the Académie Royale de Musique in 1672 until the Revolution more than a cent. later; after that, at various times, according to the political situation: Théâtre de l'Opéra, Opéra National, Théâtre des Arts, Théâtre de la République et des Arts, Théâtre Impérial de l'Opéra, Théâtre de la Nation, Académie Nationale de Musique, Théâtre National de l'Opéra.

Academy of St Martin-in-the-Fields, chamber orch. founded 1958 by (Sir) Neville Marriner. At first based in London church; dir., from 1978, Iona Brown.

Acante et Céphise, *pastorale-héroïque* by Rameau (lib. by Marmontel), prod. Paris, Opéra, 18 Nov 1751.

Accademia (It. = academy, from Plato's *Academia),* an Italian society for the encouragement and furtherance of science and/ or the arts. An 'Accademia di Platone' was founded, on Plato's model, at the Medici court of Florence in 1470. The earliest academy of any importance devoted primarily to music was the 'Accademia Filarmonica' of Verona (1543); later ones included the 'Accademia di Santa Cecilia' at Rome (1584) and the 'Accademia Filarmonica' at Bologna (1666). In France the movement began with the foundation of the 'Académie de poésie et de musique' by Baïf and Thibaut at Paris in 1570, with the aim of promoting the ideals of *musique mesurée.*

Accardo, Salvatore (b Turin, 26 Sep 1941), Italian violinist and conductor. First winner Paganini Comp. 1958; has given many perfs. of the Paganini concertos, incl. the first in modern times of the E min. concerto (*c* 1815).

Accelerando (It.) = accelerating; quickening the pace.

Accents. Accents have much the same function in music as in prosody, being the metrical or rhythmic stresses of music. Normally the main accent is on the 1st beat after the bar-line, and in any music divided into bars of more than 3 beats there is usually a secondary accent, less strongly stressed. But accents are frequently displaced by being marked on a weak beat, transferred by syncopation or omitted on the main beat by the replacement of a rest for a note or chord. Strong accents are marked by the sign > or by the abbreviations *sf* (*sforzando*) or *fz* (*forzando*).

Acciaccatura (It., from *acciaccare* = to crush), term now generally used for the short Appoggiatura. In old keyboard music it is an ornament consisting of a discordant note struck together with that immediately above, but at once released while the principal note is held on, e.g.:

Bach, *Partita No.3*

Accidentals, the signs by which notes are chromatically altered by being raised or lowered by a semitone or whole tone. The ♯ raises and the ♭ (flat) lowers the note by a semitone: the × (double sharp) raises and the ♭♭ (double flat) lowers it by a whole tone; the ♮ (natural) contradicts a ♯ or ♭ in the key signature or restores a note previously sharpened or flattened to its orig. position.

Accompagnato. *See* **Recitativo accompagnato**.

Accompanied Recitative. *See* **Recitativo accompagnato**.

Accompaniment, the instrumental part or parts forming a background to the melodic line of a solo voice or instrument, generally played by a keyboard instrument or by the orch. The accompaniment may also be improvised or ed. by the setting out of additional parts where the comp.'s harmony has been left incomplete or indicated only by a figured bass.

Accompaniment to a Film Scene (*Begleitungsmusik zu einer Lichtspielszene*), orch. work by Schoenberg, op.34. Comp. 1929–30; fp Berlin, 6 Nov 1930, cond. Klemperer. The 3 movts. are for imaginary scenes. (Title '*Begleitmusik*' etc. is incorrect.)

Accordatura (It.), the notes to which a string instrument is tuned.

Accordion, an instrument prod. its sound by means of tuned reeds through which wind is driven by pleated bellows opened and closed by the player's hands. The reeds speak when opened by the pressing of buttons and sometimes by the playing of one hand on a keyboard similar to that of the pf.

Achille, Italian opera by Paer (lib. by G. di Gamera), prod. Vienna, Kärntnertortheater, 6 Jun 1801. Contains a funeral march said to have been admired by Beethoven.

Achille et Polyxène, opera by Lully and Colassse (lib. by J.G. de Campistron), prod. Paris, Opéra, 7 Nov 1687. Left unfinished at Lully's death and completed by his pupil Colasse.

Achille in Sciro (*Achilles in Scyros*), opera by Caldara (lib. by Metastasio), prod. Vienna, Burgtheater, 13 Feb 1739.

Opera by Naumann (lib. do.), prod. Palermo, 5 Sep 1767.

Also settings by Jommelli (Vienna, 1749), Hasse (Naples, 1759), Paisiello (St Petersburg, 1778), Pugnani (Turin, 1785).

Achucarro, Joaquin (b Bilbao, 1 Nov 1936), Spanish pianist. He studied with Gieseking and Magaloff. Won Liverpool International Pf. Competition 1959; London debut same year.

Acide, festa teatrale by Haydn (lib. G.A. Migliavacca), prod. Eisenstadt, 11 Nov 1763.

Aci, Galatea e Polifemo, Italian serenata by Handel, comp. Naples, 1708. *See also* following.

Acis and Galatea, masque for soloists, chorus and orch. by Handel (lib. by John Gay, with additions by Hughes, Pope and Dryden), comp. *c* 1718, perf. Cannons, nr. Edgware; 1st public perf. London, King's Theatre, 10 Jun 1732. A composite, bilingual version of this and the prec. It. serenata (1708) received several perfs. in 1732.

Acis et Galatée (*Acis and Galatea*), opera by Lully (lib. by J.G. de Campistron), prod. at Anet at an entertainment given for the Dauphin by the Duke of Vendôme, 6 Sep 1686, fp Paris, 17 Sep 1686.

Ackté, Aïno (b Helsinki, 23 Apr 1876; d Nummela, 8 Aug 1944), Finnish soprano. Debut Paris, 1897, as Marguerite; Met 1904, same role. First Salome in Brit. (CG 1910, cond. Beecham).

Acoustics, the physical science of all matters pertaining to sound, esp. the generation and reception of sound-waves; also, more loosely, the properties of sound-transmission in the interior of buildings.

Act Tune, a term used in 17th-cent. England for a musical intermezzo or entr'acte perf. between the acts of a play.

Action, the mechanism intervening between the player and an instrument, esp. in stringed keyboard instruments, organs and harps (in the last case pedals only).

Action musicale (Fr.), a term used by d'Indy

for some of his operas, evidently on the model of Wagner's 'Handlung für Musik'.

Actus Tragicus, name often given Bach's church cantata no. 106, *Gottes Zeit ist die allerbeste Zeit*. Comp. *c* 1707 for a funeral.

Ad lib. (abbr. of Lat. *ad libitum* = at pleasure), a direction indicating that a passage may be played freely according to the perf.'s fancy. The term also applies to an instrumental part that may be added or omitted in the perf. of a work.

Adagietto (It. lit. a little Adagio), a tempo direction indicating a pace slightly quicker than *adagio*. Best known ex. is the 4th movt. of Mahler's 5th symph.

Adagio (It. *ad agio* = at ease, comfortably) = at a slow pace. The word is also used as a noun for a slow piece or movement.

Adam, 15th-cent. composer. Three *ronddeaux* by him are in the Oxford MS. Canonici misc. 213.

Adam, Adolphe (Charles) (b Paris, 24 Jul 1803; d Paris, 3 May 1856), French composer. Allowed to study at the Paris Cons. only as an amateur. Wrote about 20 vaudeville pieces for 3 Paris theatres, 1824–9, then prod. an operetta, *Pierre et Catherine,* at the Opéra-Comique in 1829 and his first opera, *Danilowa,* in 1830. Comp. a great deal for the stage and in 1847 started a new operatic venture, the Théâtre National. Member of the Institut, 1844, and prof. of comp. at the Cons., 1849.

Works incl. operas *Le 'Châlet* (1834), *Le Postillon de Lonjumeau* (1836), *La Poupée de Nuremberg, Si j'etais roi* (1852), *Falstaff* (1856), *Richard en Palestine* (after Scott), etc.; ballets *Faust* (1833), *Giselle* (1841).

Adam de la Halle. See **La Halle.**

Adam, Theo (b Dresden, 1 Aug 1926), German bass-baritone. Debut Dresden 1949. Berlin and Bayreuth from 1952; CG 1967 (Wotan), NY Met 1969 (Sachs). Sang title roles in Cerha's *Baal,* Salzburg 1981 and Berio's *Un re in ascolto,* Salzburg 1984. Other roles incl. Wozzeck, Ochs and Don Giovanni.

Adam und Eva, opera by Theile (lib. by C. Richter), prod. Hamburg, at the opening of the 1st estab. Ger. opera house, Theater beim Gänsemarkt, 12 Jan 1678.

Adam Zero, ballet by Bliss (scenario by M. Benthall, choreography by Robert Helpmann), prod. London, CG, 8 Apr 1946.

Adamberger, Valentin (b Munich, 6 Jul 1743; d Vienna, 24 Aug 1804), German tenor. Studied and sang in It., appeared in London in 1777 and went to Vienna, becoming a member of the Ger. opera in 1780 and

of the Imperial Chapel in 1789. Sang Belmonte in the fp of Mozart's *Entführung*.

Adams, Charles (b Charlestown, Mass., 9 Feb 1843; d Charlestown, 4 Jul 1900), American tenor. He sang in Haydn's *Creation* at Boston, in 1856. Between 1867 and 1876 1st tenor at the Opera in Vienna; made his 1st real success in USA in 1877 (1st US Rienzi, Academy of Music, 1878).

Adams, John (b Worcester, Mass., 15 Feb 1947), American composer and conductor. Studied at Harvard under Kirchner and Del Tredici. Head of comp., San Francisco Cons., 1971–81. Composer-in-residence with the San Francisco SO. A leading member of the minimalist school of composers, his best-known piece is *Grand Pianola Music,* for 2 pfs., 2 sops. and mezzo (fp 1982). Other works incl. opera *Nixon in China* (1987), *Common Tones in Simple Time* for orch. (1979), *Harmonium* for chorus and orch. (texts by Donne and Dickinson, 1981), *Shaker Loops* for strings (1978) and *Bridge of Dreams* for orch. (1982–3).

Adams, Suzanne (b Cambridge, Mass., 28 Nov 1872; d London, 5 Feb 1953), American soprano. Debut Paris, Opéra, 1895, Juliette; CG 1898 in same role. Created Hero in Stanford's *Much Ado about Nothing,* CG 1901. She married the cellist Leo Stern.

Added Sixth, a term invented by Rameau (*sixte ajoutée*) to describe the addition of a 6th from the bass to a subdominant chord when it is followed by the tonic chord, e.g. in the key of C major:

Addinsell, Richard (b Oxford, 13 Jan 1904; d London, 14 Nov 1977), English composer. Studied law at Hertford Coll., Oxford, but became interested in theatre music and studied at the RCM in London. In 1929–32 he studied abroad, mainly in Berlin and Vienna; in 1933 he visited the USA and wrote film music in Hollywood.

Works incl. much incid. music for films, theatre (incl. plays by Clemence Dane) and radio. His greatest success was music for the film *Dangerous Moonlight,* which incl. the *Warsaw* concerto for pf. and orch. He also composed light music and songs for theatre revues.

Addison, John (b London, *c* 1766; d London, 30 Jan 1844), English double bass player and composer. His wife (*née* Willems) sang at Vauxhall Gardens in London; then both went to Liverpool and Dublin, returning to London in 1796 and proceeding to Bath, Dublin and Manchester. From 1805, when he wrote music for Skeffington's *Sleeping Beauty*, he had a number of stage successes in London.

Additional Accompaniments, amplifying orchestral parts added to old oratorios and other works left by the comps. in an incomplete state, to be amplified orig. by the continuo player at the organ or harpsichord. The most familiar exs. are Mozart's additional accompaniments for Handel's *Messiah*.

Adelaide, song by Beethoven to words by Friedrich von Matthisson, comp. in 1795–1796 and ded. to the poet.

'Adélaïde' Concerto, a vln. concerto ed. by Marius Casadesus in the early 1930s from a sketch supposedly written by Mozart and ded. to Princess Adélaïde of Fr. in 1766. It was in fact comp. by Casadesus.

Adelson e Salvini, opera by Bellini (his first) with lib. by A.L. Tottola. Prod. Naples, San Sebastiano Cons., early 1825; revised 1826 with recitative replacing dialogue.

Adeney, Richard (b London, 25 Jan 1920), English flautist. First concert 1938, *St Matthew Passion* under Vaughan Williams. Prin. flautist LPO 1941–50 and 1960–69; has played with the Melos Ensemble and the ECO; often heard as soloist.

Adenez (Adam Le Roy), French 13th-cent. minstrel. Lived at the court of Henry III, Duke of Brabant; wrote trouvère songs, some of which are preserved.

Adieux, l'absence et le retour, Les (*Farewell, Absence and Return*), title given by Beethoven's pub. for his pf. sonata in E♭ maj., op. 81a, comp. in 1809–10 and ded. to the Archduke Rudolph to commemorate his absence from Vienna during the occupation by the French.

Adler, Guido (b Eibenschütz, Moravia, 1 Nov 1855; d Vienna, 15 Feb 1941), Czech-German musicologist and editor. Studied in Vienna; app. prof. of musicology at Prague Univ., 1885, and prof. in Vienna, 1898, in succession to Hanslick. Wrote many books on music inc. studies of Wagner (1904) and Mahler (1916) and ed. *Handbuch der Musikgeschichte*, 1924.

Adler, Kurt (b Neuhaus, Bohemia, 1 Mar 1907; d Butler, NJ, 21 Sep 1977), American pianist and conductor. He studied at Vienna; worked at the Berlin Staatsoper 1927–9 and at the German Opera, Prague, 1929–32. He conducted at the Kiev Opera and with the Stalingrad PO after the Nazis came to power; in 1938 moved to the USA. Worked first as a pianist and cond. at the NY Met 1951–73 (debut with *Die Zauberflöte*). Ed. of var. vocal editions.

Adler, Kurt Herbert (b Vienna, 2 Apr 1905), American conductor and manager of Austrian birth. He studied in Vienna and cond. there until leaving for the USA in 1938; Chicago Opera 1938–43, then engaged by the San Francisco Opera. He became general dir. in 1956 and did much to raise standards of opera performance on the West Coast.

Adler, Larry (Lawrence) (b Baltimore, 10 Feb 1914), American harmonica virtuoso, settled in UK since 1949. Won a competition aged 13, and has since travelled widely, incl. command perfs. before King George VI, King Gustav of Sweden, Presidents Roosevelt and Truman. Learned to read music in 1940 and studied with Toch. Many comps. have written for him, incl. Milhaud and Vaughan Williams.

Adler, Peter Hermann (b Jablonec, 2 Dec 1899), Czech-born American conductor. He studied at Prague with Zemlinsky and cond. in Brno, Bremen and Kiev; left for USA in 1938. He assisted Fritz Busch in founding the New Opera Company NY (1941) and from 1949 was dir. NBC television opera; founded NET opera 1969 and gave the 1st US perf. of Janáček's *From the House of the Dead*. Music dir. Baltimore SO 1959–67. Retired 1972.

Adler, Samuel (b Mannheim, 4 Mar 1928), American composer of German birth. He moved to the USA aged 11 and studied with Piston and Thompson at Harvard and with Copland and Koussevitzky at Tanglewood. Prof. of comp. at Eastman School, Rochester, from 1966.

Works incl. operas *The Outcasts of Poker Flat* (1962) and *The Wrestler* (1972); *The Disappointment*, reconstruction of an American ballad opera of 1767; 5 symphs. (1953–75), organ concerto (1970), Concerto for orch. (1977), flute concerto (1977); 6 string 4tets (1945–75), 3 vln. sonatas (1948–65); *From out of Bondage*, cantata (1969), *The Vision of Isaiah* for bass, chorus and orch. (1963).

Adlgasser, Anton Cajetan (b Inzel, Bavaria, 1 Oct 1729; d Salzburg, 22 Dec 1777), German organist and composer. A pupil of Eberlin in Salzburg, he was 1st organist of the cathedral there from 1750. His church music was highly valued by Mozart. Wrote oratorio, *Christus am Ölberg*, perf. Salzburg 1754.

Adlung, Jakob (b Bindersleben nr. Erfurt, 14 Jan 1699; d Erfurt, 5 Jul 1762), German organist and scholar. Organist in Erfurt from 1727, and prof. at the *Gymasium* there from 1741. Author of important music treatises.

Admeto, rè di Tessaglia (*Admetus, King of Thessaly*), opera by Handel (lib. N.F. Haym or P.A. Rolli), prod. London, King's Theatre, Haymarket, 31 Jan 1727.

Adni, Daniel (b Haifa, 6 Dec 1951), Israeli pianist. Debut Haifa 1963; studied with Perlemuter in Paris and Anda in Zurich. London debut 1970; tours of Europe and USA in Romantic repertory.

Adolfati, Andrea (b Venice, c 1721; d Genoa, 28 Oct 1760, Italian composer. Pupil of Galuppi at Venice. Held church posts there and wrote several operas, incl. *Artaserse, Arianna, Adriano in Siria* and *La clemenza di Tito*.

Adorno, Theodor Wiesengrund (b Frankfurt, 11 Sep 1903; d Geneva, 6 Aug 1969), German writer on music. Studied with Sekles in Frankfurt and Alban Berg in Vienna. Music critic in Frankfurt and taught at the univ. Emigrated to USA in 1934, working in connection with radio research at Princeton (1938–41). In 1950 returned to Frankfurt and became prof. at the univ. His writings, which have influenced the younger generation of comps., include *Philosophie der neuen Musik* (1949), *Klangfiguren* (1959). He was a champion of Schoenberg and was consulted by Thomas Mann for the novel *Dr. Faustus*.

Adrastus (b Philippi, Macedonia, ?), Greek 4th-cent. B.C. philosopher. Pupil of Aristotle; wrote a treatise on acoustics, *Harmonicon biblia tria*.

Adriaensen, Emmanuel (b Antwerp, c 1554; d Antwerp, buried 27 Feb 1604), 16th-cent. lutenist. Pub. books of lute pieces. Also known as Hadrianus.

Adriana Lecouvreur, opera by Cilea (lib. by A. Colautti, based on the play *Adrienne Lecouvreur* by Scribe and E. Legouvé), prod. Milan, Teatro Lirico, 6 Nov 1902.

Adriano in Siria (*Hadrian in Syria*), opera by Pergolesi (lib. by Metastasio), prod. Naples, Teatro San Bartolommeo, with the intermezzi *Livietta e Tracollo*, 25 Oct 1734. Also settings by Caldara (Vienna, 1732), Galuppi (Turin, 1740), Hasse (Dresden, 1752), J.C. Bach (London, 1765), Holzbauer (Mannheim, 1768), Anfossi (Padua, 1777), Cherubini (Livorno, 1782), Mayr (Venice, 1798).

Adson, John (d London, c 1640), English musician and composer. He was a member of Charles I's household and pub. *Courtly Masquing Ayres* for various instruments in 1611.

Aegidius de Murino. *See* Murino.

Aegyptische Helena (Strauss). *See* Ägyptische Helena.

Aenéas, ballet with chorus by Roussel. Comp. 1935, fp Brussels 31 Jul 1935.

Aeneas i Carthago, opera by J.M. Kraus (lib. by J.H. Kellgren), prod. Stockholm, 18 Nov 1799.

Aeolian Harp, an instrument played by no human performer, but by currents of air blown across its strings when it is hung up in the open. It was first recorded in the 17th cent., but the principle dates back to antiquity.

Aeolian Mode, the scale represented by the white keys of the pf. beginning on the note A. *See also* **Ionian Mode.**

Aeoliphone. *See* **Wind Machine.**

Aerophor (or **Aerophon**), a German instrument invented by Bernhard Samuel and patented in 1911, with the aid of which wind instruments can sustain notes indefinitely. R. Strauss used it in the *Alpensinfonie* and *Festliches Praeludium.*

Aeschylus (525–456 B.C.), Greek dramatist, *See* **Halévy** (*Prometheus*), **Hauer** (do.), **Honegger** (*Prometheus* and *Les Suppliantes*), **Meyerbeer** (*Eumenides*), **Milhaud** (*Agamemnon, Choéphares* and *Eumenides*), **Oresteia** (Taneiev), **Parry** (H.) (*Agamemnon*), **Pizzetti** (do.), **Prométhée** (Fauré), **Prometheus** (Orff), **Schillings** (*Orestes*).

Aetherophone (from Gk.), an electrophonic instrument invented by Lev Theremin of Leningrad in 1924, prod. notes from the air the pitch of which was determined by movements of the hand but could not be definitely fixed according to the normal chromatic scale, the transitions between the notes producing a sliding wail like that of a siren. But *see* **Theremin.**

Affektenlehre (German, doctrine of affections), 18th-cent. aesthetic theory, associated partic. with J.J. Quantz and C.P.E. Bach, according to which music should be directly expressive of partic. emotions. *See* **Empfindsamer Stil.**

Affettuoso (It.) = affectionate, feeling (adv. *affettuosamente*).

Affré, Agustarello (b St Chinian, 23 Oct 1858; d Cagnes-sur-Mer, 27 Dec 1931), French tenor. He was discovered by the dir. of the Paris Opéra, Pierre Gailhard, and made his debut in 1890, as Edgardo; remained at the Opéra until 1911, singing in the fp of Massenet's *Le Mage* and the 1st local perf. of *Pagliacci*. At CG he sang Faust and Samson; appeared in San Francisco, New Orleans and Havana, 1911–13, often as Gounod's Roméo, and sang for Fr. troops during the war.

Affrettando (It.) = urging, hastening. The term is often used to indicate emotional pressure as well as increase in speed.

Agnus Dei (Lat. 'Lamb of God'), the 5th and last item of the Ordinary of the Mass. Orig. a part of the Litany, it was 1st intro. into the Roman Mass towards the end of the 7th cent. It is not present in the Ambrosian rite. Its text is tripartite in structure, and its music in its simplest form consists of three statements of the same melody (*see* illustration).

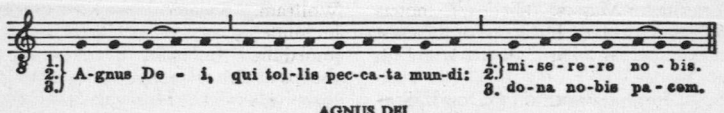

AGNUS DEI

Afranio Albonese (b Pavia, *c* 1480; d ? Ferrara, *c* 1560), Italian priest. Canon at Ferrara, inventor of the Phagotus.

Africaine, L' (*The African Girl*; orig. title *Vasco da Gama*), opera by Meyerbeer (lib. by Scribe), prod. Paris, Opéra, 28 Apr1865, after Meyerbeer's death.

Agazzari, Agostino (b Siena, 2 Dec 1578; d Siena, ? 10 Apr 1640), Italian composer. Held various church posts in Rome, but returned to Siena in 1630 as *maestro di cappella* of the cathedral.

Works incl. pastoral *Eumelio*, madrigals, Masses and other church music, and 2 books on music.

Age of Gold, The (*Zoloty vek*), ballet by Shostakovich, op. 22. Prod. Leningrad, 26 Oct 1930; choreog. by E. Kaplan and V. Vaynonen; concerns activities of a Stalinist football team.

Agitato (It.) = agitated, precipitate, restless.

Agnelli, Salvatore (b Palermo, 1817; d Marseilles, 1874), Italian composer. Pupil of Donizetti and Zingarelli at Naples. He worked at Marseilles and Paris in later life.

Works incl. operas, incl. *Léonore de Médicis* (1855), ballets, church music, etc.

Agnes von Hohenstaufen, opera by Spontini (lib. by E. Raupach), prod. Berlin, Opera, 12 Jun 1829.

Agnese di Fitz-Henry, opera by Paer (lib. by L. Buonavoglia, based on Amelia Opie's novel *Father and Daughter*), prod. Ponte d'Altaro nr. Parma, Oct 1809.

Agnesi, Luigi (real name Louis Ferdinand Léopold Agniez) (b Erhent, Namur, 17 Jul 1833; d London, 2 Feb 1875), Belgian bass. Made his 1st appearance in Merelli's It. opera company in Ger. and Hol. and went to the Théâtre Italien in Paris, 1864, as Assur, and to London in 1865. After his successes in Rossini's operas he also became a concert singer in Eng. 1871–4.

More complex plainsong settings exist and in the later Middle Ages numerous additional melodies were written. The Agnus Dei is naturally incl. in polyphonic settings of the Mass Ordinary, and in later settings of the same series of texts. *See* **Mass**.

Agogic Accent. An accent which lends a note prominence by means of increased length rather than greater volume or higher pitch.

Agon (Gk. = Contest), ballet for 12 dancers by Stravinsky; comp. 1953–7 fp (concert) Los Angeles, 17 Jun 1957; prod. NY, 1 Dec 1957, choreog. Balanchine.

Agostini, Paolo (b Valerano, *c* 1583; d Rome, 3 Oct 1629), Italian composer. Pupil and son-in-law of B. Nanini in Rome. After various posts in Rome, he became master of the Vatican chapel in 1627. Wrote Masses and other church music.

Agostini, Pietro Simone (b Rome, *c* 1635; d Parma, 1 Oct 1680), Italian composer. *Maestro di cappella to* the Duke of Parma. Wrote 5 operas, incl. *Il ratto delle Sabine*, oratorios, church music.

Agrell, Johan Joachim (b Löth, 1 Feb 1701; d Nuremberg, 19 Jan 1765), Swedish composer. Studied at Linköping and Uppsala, was app. court musician at Kassel in 1723 and music director at Nuremberg in 1746. Works incl. harpsichord concertos, sonatas, etc.

Agricola, Alexander (Alexander Ackerman) (b ? 1446; d nr. Valladolid, late Aug 1506), Flemish composer. His epitaph (printed by Rhaw in 1538) states that he died at the age of 60, the date of death being estab. by his disappearance from the court rolls of Philip the Handsome, Duke of Austria (Philip I of Spain from 1504). He served at the court of Galeazzo Maria Sforza, Duke of Milan, during the early 1470s, as well as with Lorenzo the Magnificent in Florence.

After a brief period at Mantua he returned to the Low Countries, his name appearing in the Accounts of Cambrai Cathedral for 1475–6. After a 2nd visit to Italy he entered in 1500 the service of Philip, whom he accomp. on journeys to Paris and Spain. During his 2nd visit to Spain Philip died of fever, Agricola apparently dying at the same time.

Works incl. 9 Masses, 2 Credos, 25 motets and 93 secular pieces. He is one of the most florid continental comps. of the late 15th cent.

Agricola, Johann Friedrich (b Dobitz, Saxony, 4 Jan 1720; d Berlin, 2 Dec 1774), German composer. Studied with Bach at Leipzig, afterwards with Hasse at Dresden and Quantz and Graun in Berlin. Director of the Hofkapelle there from 1759 to his death. Married the singer Benedetta Molteni in 1751.

Works incl. operas, psalms, hymns and other church music. It. secular cantatas.

Agricola, Martin (Martin Sore) (b Schwiebus, 6 Jan 1486; d Magdeburg, 10 Jun 1556), German theorist and composer. His most important treatise was a work on musical instruments, *Musica instrumentalis deudsch* (1528, based on Virdung's *Musica getutscht* of 1511, but in verse), and he contributed 3 pieces to Georg Rhaw's *Newe deudsche geistliche Gesenge* (1544).

Agrippina, opera by Handel (lib. by V. Grimani), prod. Venice, Teatro San Giovanni Crisostomo, 26 Dec 1709.

Aguiar, Alexandra de (b Oporto; d nr. Talavéra, 12 Dec 1605), Portuguese lutenist and poet. In the service of King Sebastian and later of Philip II of Spain.

Works incl. Lamentations for Holy Week.

Aguiari (Agujari), Lucrezia (b Ferrara, 1743; d Parma, 18 May 1783), Italian soprano. Made her 1st appearance at Florence in 1764. In a letter of 24 Mar 1770 Mozart wrote down a remarkably high and florid passage he heard her sing. She married the comp. and cond. Giuseppe Colla in 1780; from 1769 had sung in several fps of Colla's operas. Known as 'La Bastardella' (*q.v.*)

Aguilera de Heredia, Sebastián (b Huesca, Aragon, *c* 1565; d Saragossa, 16 Dec 1627), Spanish organist and composer. For many years from 1603 organist at the old cathedral of Saragossa.

Works incl. Magnificats and other church music.

Ägyptische Helena, Die (*The Egyptian Helen*), opera by R. Strauss (lib. by H. von Hofmannsthal), prod. Dresden, 6 Jun 1928.

Ahle, Johann Georg (b Mühlhausen, Thuringia, bap. 12 Jun 1651; d Mühlhausen, 2 Dec 1706), German composer. Organist at the church of St Blasius, Mühlhausen. Like his father (Johann Rudolf, 1625–73) he wrote hymn tunes.

Ahlersmeyer, Mathieu (b Cologne, 29 Jun 1896; d Garmisch, 23 Jul 1979), German baritone. Debut Mönchengladbach 1929, as Wolfram. Appeared at the Kroll Opera, Berlin, under Klemperer, 1930–31 and in 1934 joined the Dresden Staatsoper: sang there in the fps of *Die schweigsame Frau* (1935) and Joseph Haas's *Die Hochzeit des Jobs* (1944). At the Berlin Staatsoper he created Egk's Peer Gynt (1938) in a prod. admired by Hitler, and at the 1947 Salzburg Festival co-created the title role in Einem's *Dantons Tod*. He sang with the Hamburg Staatsoper 1945–73 and in 1952 appeared with the co. at the Edinburgh Festival as Matthias Grunewald, in the Brit. stage première of Hindemith's *Mathis der Maler.*

Ahlin, Čvetka (b Ljubljana, 28 Sep 1928; d Hamburg, 30 Jun 1985), Yugoslav mezzo. She sang with the Hamburg Staatsoper from 1955, as Orpheus, Azucena, Marina and Amneris. Visited Edinburgh and London (1966) with the co. and from 1963 sang at Salzburg: from 1967 appeared in *The Ring*, under Karajan. Guest appearances in Fr., It. and Israel.

Ahna, Pauline de (b Ingolstadt, 4 Feb 1863; d Garmisch, 13 May 1950), German soprano. She studied at Munich. Debut Weimar 1890, as Pamina; later roles there incl. Eva, Elsa and Donna Elvira. She sang at Karlsruhe 1890–91 as Agathe, Leonore and Donna Anna. In 1894 she created Freihild in Strauss's *Guntram;* she married the comp. the same year. He ded. several sets of songs to her, incl. 4 Lieder op. 27, and portrayed her in *Ein Heldenleben*, the *Symphonia domestica* and *Intermezzo*. Bayreuth 1891, Elisabeth.

Ahronovich, Yury (b Leningrad, 13 May 1932), Israeli conductor of Russian birth. Moscow Radio SO 1964–72; left Russia 1972 and settled in Israel. Has cond. in Cologne from 1973. CG debut 1974 (*Boris Godunov*).

Aiblinger, Johann Kaspar (b Wasserburg, Bavaria, 23 Feb 1779; d Munich, 6 May 1867), German composer and conductor. Music director of the Munich opera, 1819–23, but as a comp. devoted mainly to church music.

Aich, Arnt von (Arnt of Aachen) (b ?1474; d Cologne, *c* 1530), German music publisher.

His *Liederbuch* (Cologne, *c* 1510) contained 75 4-part songs, sacred and secular, and is possibly the 1st printed ed. of its kind.

Aichinger, Gregor (b Regensburg, *c* 1564; d Augsburg, 21 Jan 1628), German priest and musician. Organist to the Fugger family at Augsburg, pub. books of sacred music at Venice in 1590 and 1603 and visited Rome for further music study in 1599.

Aida, opera by Verdi (lib. by A Ghislanzoni, based on a scenario by F.A.F. Mariette and outlined in Fr. by C. Du Locle), prod. Cairo, 24 Dec 1871; fp in It., Milan, La Scala, 8 Feb 1872.

Aiglon, L' (*The Eaglet*), opera by Honegger and Ibert (lib. by H. Cain, based on Rostand's play), prod. Monte Carlo, 11 Mar 1937.

Aimon, (Pamphile Léopold) François (b L'Isle nr. Avignon, 4 Oct 1779; d Paris, 2 Feb 1866), French cellist and composer. He cond. at Marseilles in his youth and in Paris from 1821.

Works incl. *Jeux floraux* (1818), *Michel et Christine, Les Sybarites* (1831) and chamber music.

Aitken, Robert (b Kentville, Nova Scotia, 28 Aug 1939), Canadian flautist and composer. He has played the flute in several Canadian orchs. and has organised new music concerts in Toronto.

Works incl. Concerto for 12 solo insts (1964), *Spectra* for 4 chamber groups (1969), *Spiral* for orch. with amplified woodwind insts (1975).

Ajo nell'imbarazzo, L' (*The Tutor in a Fix*), opera by Donizetti (lib. by J. Ferretti), prod. Rome, Teatro Valle, 4 Feb 1824.

Akeroyde, Samuel (b Yorkshire), English 17th-cent. composer. Musician in Ordinary to James II in 1687 and later to William and Mary. Contrib. many songs to var. collections and to the 3rd part of Durfey's *Don Quixote* in 1696, the music to the 1st 2 of which had been written by Purcell the year before his death.

Akhnaten, opera by Philip Glass (lib. by the comp. with S. Goldman, R. Israel and R. Riddell), prod. Stuttgart, 24 Mar 1984. The story is based on the hermaphrodite, monotheist Pharaoh of the 18th dynasty.

Akimenko, Feodor Stepanovich (b Kharkov, 20 Feb 1876; d Paris, 3 Jan 1945), Russian composer. Pupil of Balakirev and Rimsky-Korsakov in St Petersburg. Taught in the court choir, where he had been a chorister, but lived in Fr. from 1903 to 1906 and settled there after the Rus. Revolution. He was Stravinsky's first comp. teacher.

Works incl. opera, *The Queen of the Alps* (1914); orchestral and chamber music; sonatas; numerous pf. works incl. *Sonate fantastique.*

Akutagawa, Yasushi (b Tokyo, 12 Jul 1925), Japanese composer. He has been active in Tokyo as a cond. and in promoting new music.

Works incl. the opera *L'Orphée in Hiroshima* (1967), 4 ballets, incl. *Paradise Lost* (1951); *Ostinato Sinfonica* (1967), *Rhapsody* for orch. (1971).

Al (It. masc. = 'at the', 'to the'). The word is used in var. combinations with nouns, as below.

Al fine (It.) = 'to the end'. The term is used in cases where an earlier portion of a comp. is to be repeated (*da capo*) and indicates that it is to be played over again to the end, not to some earlier place, which would otherwise be marked with a special sign, the appropriate direction being then *al segno*.

Al rovescio. (It.) = 'backwards'. *See* **Cancrizans.**

Ala, Giovanni Battista (b Monza, *c* 1598; d Milan, *c* 1630), Italian composer. Organist of the church of the Servitori at Milan, he wrote canzonets, madrigals, etc.

Alain, Jehan (Ariste) (b St Germain-en-Laye, 3 Feb 1911; d Saumur, 20 Jun 1940), French composer. Studied at the Paris Cons. organ with Dupré and comp. with Dukas and Roger-Ducasse. He became a church organist in Paris in 1935, but served in World War II and was killed in action.

Works incl. numerous choral comps. mainly sacred; 3 dances for orch.; chamber music; pf. and organ works; songs.

Alain, Marie-Claire (b St Germain-en-Laye, 10 Aug 1926), French organist, sister of prec. She studied with Duruflé and Dupré; Paris debut 1950. She has toured in Europe and US; noted in Bach and the music of her brother.

Alba, type of troubadour-trouvère song, in which the singer watches for daybreak on behalf of two lovers (e.g. *Reis glorios,* by Guiraut de Bornelh). As used by the Minnesinger it was called *Tagelied.*

Albanese, Licia (b Bari, 22 Jul 1913), American soprano of Italian origin. Studied in Milan and made her first stage appearance at the Teatro Lirico there in 1934, as Madam Butterfly, followed in the same year by an appearance at La Scala. From 1940 she was a member of the NY Met. She was chosen by Toscanini for his recorded broadcasts of *La Bohème* and *La Traviata.* Her other roles incl. Donna Anna, Manon and Aida.

Albani (orig. Lajeunesse), **(Marie Louise Cécile) Emma** (b Chambly nr. Montreal, 1 Nov 1847; d London, 3 Apr 1930), Canadian soprano. Studied with Duprez in Paris and Lamperti at Milan. Debut at Messina, 1870, and in London at CG, 1872, both as Amina; she was the 1st London Elsa (1875) and Elisabeth (1876), and was often heard in oratorio. Lived in London, but toured widely. DBE, 1925.

Albéniz, Isaac (Manuel Francisco) (b Camprodón, Catalonia, 29 May 1860; d Cambo-les-Bains, Pyrenees, 18 May 1909), Spanish composer. He made his appearance as an infant prodigy both as pianist and comp. at Barcelona, a *pasodoble*, written at the age of 7, being played by a military band there. Later he appeared in Paris as a child-pupil of Marmontel and afterwards studied at the Madrid Cons., where he received a grant from the king to enable him to go to Brussels. There he studied comp. with Gevaert and pf. with Brassin, and later went to Liszt at Weimar for pf. and to Jadassohn and Reinecke at Leipzig for comp. After touring successfully, he settled as pf. teacher 1st at Barcelona and then at Madrid, from c 1880, but left before long and spent the rest of his life mainly in London and Paris. He had married in 1883. In London he prod. operas and began a trilogy on Arthurian legends to a libretto by Francis Money-Coutts (Lord Latymer), who financed him, but he did not progress far.

Works incl. operas *The Magic Opal* (London, 1893), *Henry Clifford* (Barcelona, 1895), *Pepita Jiménez, San Antonio de la Florida, Merlin* (unfinished 1st part of Arthurian cycle); zarzuelas *Cuanto más viejo, Los Catalanes en Grecia;* contribution to Millöcker's operetta *Der arme Jonathan* for the London prod. 1893, *Catalonia,* orch. with the aid of Dukas; c 250 pf. pieces, incl. *Catalonia, La Vega, Navarra, Azulejos* and the cycle of 12 entitled *Iberia;* 13 songs.

Albéniz, Mateo Pérez de (b c 1755; d San Sebastian, 23 Jun 1831), Spanish composer of church and keyboard music. *Maestro de capilla* at Logroño and San Sebastian.

Albéniz, Pedro (b Logroño, 14 Apr 1795; d Madrid, 12 Apr 1855), Spanish pianist and composer, son of prec. He was organist at var. towns from the age of 13 and in 1830 became prof. of pf. at Madrid Cons. and 1st organist at the royal chapel in 1834. App. pf. teacher to Queen Isabella and the Infanta Maria Luisa in 1841. Wrote a method for pf., c 70 pf. works and some songs.

Albergati, Pirro Capacelli, Count (b Bolog-

na, 20 Sep 1663; d Bologna, 22 Jun 1735), nobleman and amateur composer. Works incl. operas *Gli amici* (Bologna, 1699), *Il principe selvaggio* (Bologna, 1712); oratorios *Giobbe, L'innocenza di Santa Eufemia, Il convito di Baldassare;* church music, comps. for var. instruments.

Albert de Sisteron (b Gapençois; d Sisteron), French 12th–13th-cent. troubadour, c 20 of whose songs exist although only 3 melodies survive.

Albert, Eugen (Eugène Francis Charles) d' (b Glasgow, 10 Apr 1864; d Riga, 3 Mar 1932), French–English (later Germanized) composer and pianist, son of C.L.N. d'Albert. Although born in Scotland, he came from Newcastle upon Tyne, and after being well taught by his father as a very precociously gifted child, he went as Newcastle scholar to the Nat. Training School in London (later the RCM), where he learnt pf. from Pauer and theory from Stainer, Prout and Sullivan. He appeared with great success as pianist and comp. in London and later went to Vienna for further study, finishing with a course under Liszt. In 1892 he married Teresa Carreño, but they were divorced in 1895 (d'Albert married 6 times). In 1907 he succeeded Joachim as director of the Hochschule für Musik in Berlin. During World War I he repudiated his Brit. birth, declaring himself to be entirely Ger. Of his 20 operas, only *Tiefland* (1903) has had any real success. The rest of his considerable output has largely fallen into neglect.

Works incl. operas *Der Rubin* (after Hebbel) (Karlsruhe, 1893), *Ghismonda, Gernot, Die Abreise* (Frankfurt, 1898), *Kain, Der Improvisator, Tiefland, Flauto solo, Tragaldabas (Der geborgte Ehemann), Izeÿl* (Hamburg, 1909), *Die verschenkte Frau, Liebesketten* (Vienna, 1912), *Die toten Augen* (Dresden, 1916), *Der Stier von Olivera* (Leipzig, 1918), *Revolutionshochzeit, Scirocco, Mareika von Nymwegen, Der Golem, Die schwarze Orchidee* (Leipzig, 1928), *Die Witwe von Ephesus, Mister Wu* (unfinished, completed by Blech); *Der Mensch und das Leben,* choral work in 6 parts; symph. in F; overtures *Esther* and *Hyperion;* 2 string 4tets; pf. suite and sonata.

Albert, Heinrich (b Lobenstein, Saxony, 8 Jul 1604; d Königsberg, 6 Oct 1651), German poet, organist and composer. Studied music at Dresden with Schütz, who was his uncle. His parents, however, compelled him to read law at Leipzig Univ.; but in 1626 he set out for Königsberg, was taken prisoner by the Swedes, and at last reached that city in

1628, resuming music studies with Stobäus. In 1631 he was app. organist at the Old Church there, and became member of the Königsberg school of poets.

Works incl. Te Deum, many hymns to words of his own, secular songs.

Albert Herring, opera by Britten (lib. by E. Crozier, based on Maupassant's story *Le Rosier de Madame Husson*), prod. Glyndebourne, 20 Jun 1947.

Alberti Bass, a conventional broken-chord accomp. common in 18th-cent. keyboard music, taking its name from Domenico Alberti, who made much use of it. Many familiar examples of the device can be found in the works of Haydn, Mozart and Beethoven, e.g. the opening of Mozart's little C maj sonata (*see* illustration).

Albertus, Magister, Parisian composer of early 12th cent. A *Benedicamus Domino* trope, *Congaudeant catholici*, is ascribed to him in the Codex Calixtinus of Compostela (*c* 1125), and is the earliest known 3-part comp.

Albicastro, Enrico (It. from Hainz Weissenburg), Swiss 17th-cent. composer and violinist. He was a captain of the Swiss horse, serving in the Span. war in the Netherlands as a mercenary. Works incl. 8 op. nos. of solo and trio sonatas and 1 of concertos.

Albinoni, Tommaso (b Venice, 8 Jun 1671; d Venice, 17 Jan 1751), Italian violinist and composer. Wrote operas and instrumental music. Bach used some of his themes.

Works incl. 55 operas, incl. *Radamisto* (Venice, 1698), *Griselda* (Florence, 1703),

Mozart, *Piano Sonata K.545*

ALBERTI BASS

Alberti, Domenico (b Venice, *c* 1710; d Rome, 14 Oct 1746), Italian singer, harpsichordist and composer, pupil of Lotti. The charact. left-hand accomp. figuration in his keyboard music has given his name to the 'Alberti Bass'.

Alberti, Gasparo (b Padua, *c* 1480; d Bergamo, *c* 1560), Italian composer, singer at S Maria Maggiore, Bergamo, from 1508. He was one of the earliest exponents of *cori spezzati*. Works incl. 5 Masses, 3 Passions and other church music.

Alberti, Giuseppe Matteo (b Bologna 1685; d Bologna, 20 Sep 1751), Italian violinist and composer. Wrote mainly for strings.

Alberti, Innocenzo di (b Tarvisio, *c* 1535; d 15 Jun 1615), Italian composer. In the service of Alfonso, Duke of Ferrara. In 1568 he ded. a book of 46 madrigals to Henry, Earl of Arundel.

Works incl. madrigals, penitential psalms, secular songs.

Albertini, Gioacchino (b Pesaro, 1751; d Rome—or Warsaw?—Apr 1811), Italian composer, resident much of his life in Poland. Works include 2 Pol. operas, *Don Juan* and *Kapelmajster Polski*, also It. and Ger. operas.

Pimpinone (Venice, 1708) and *L'impresario delle Canarie* (Venice, 1725); 9 op. nos. for instrumental chamber combinations.

Albion and Albanius, opera by Grabu (lib. by Dryden), prod. London, Duke's Theatre, 3 Jun 1685.

Alboni, Marietta (b Città di Castello, 6 Mar 1823; d Ville d'Avray, 23 Jun 1894), Italian contralto. Pupil of Rossini; 1st appearance Bologna, 1842, in Pacini's *Saffo*. Sang with much success in Paris and London, where she was heard as Arsace, Urbain, Cherubino, Zerlina and Fides.

Alborada (Span., from *alba* = dawn) = morning song, in the same sense that a serenade is an evening song; *cf.* Fr. *aubade*. Orig. the alborada is a popular instrumental piece of NW. Spain, usually played on bagpipes.

Alborada del gracioso (Span., *The Jester's Morning Song*), a pf. piece by Ravel, No. 4 of the set entitled *Miroirs*, comp. 1905. Vers. for orch. perf. Paris, 17 May 1919.

Albrecht, Gerd (b Essen, 19 Jul 1935), German conductor. Study at Hamburg was followed by cond. posts at the opera houses of Mainz, Lübeck and Kassel (1963–72). Appeared as guest cond. with the Berlin PO and gave the 1967 fp of Henze's *Telemanniana* with the orch. Princ. cond. Berlin,

Deutsche Opera, 1972–9 (fp Fortner's *Elisabeth Tudor*, 1972). He has worked with the Zurich Tonhalle orch. from 1975: fp Henze's *Barcarola*, 1980. At the 1982 Munich Festival he gave *Moses und Aron* and in 1986 *Der fliegende Holländer* at CG and the fp of Reimann's *Troades* at Munich.

Albrechtsberger, Johann Georg (b Klosterneuburg nr. Vienna, 3 Feb 1736; d Vienna, 7 Mar 1809), Austrian theorist, composer and teacher. Court organist in Vienna and *Kapellmeister* of St Stephen's Cathedral. Renowned as a contrapuntist, he was for a short time Beethoven's teacher. Prolific comp. of church music and instrumental music, much of it in a contrapuntal style

Albrici, Bartolomeo (b Rome, *c* 1640; d London, after 1687), Italian 17th-cent. organist. In the service of Queen Christina of Sweden, organist at Dresden until 1663, in the service of Charles II from 1664 and James II from 1685. Also active as a private teacher in London.

Albrici, Vincenzo (b Rome, 26 Jun 1631; d Prague, 8 Aug 1696), Italian composer and organist, brother of prec. Pupil of Carissimi. Director of the Queen of Sweden's It. musicians, 1652–3; *Kapellmeister* at Dresden from 1654; in the service of Charles II in London, 1664–7; returned to Dresden, 1667; organist of St Thomas's, Leipzig, 1681–2; finally *Kapellmeister* at Prague, St Augustin.

Works incl. Masses, psalms, concertos and madrigals.

Albumblatt (Ger. = album leaf), the title often given to a short piece, usually for pf., suggesting an inscription in an autograph album.

Alceste. *See also* **Alkestis.**

Opera by Gluck (lib. by R. Calzabigi). It. version prod. Vienna, Burgtheater, 26 Dec 1767. Fr. version, revised by the comp. (lib. by C.L.G.L. du Roullet), prod. Paris, Opéra, 23 Apr 1776.

Opera by Schweitzer (lib. by Wieland), prod. Weimar, at court, 28 May 1773. The 1st Ger. opera in the manner of Metastasio.

Opera by Strungk (lib. by P. Thiemich, based on Aurelio Aureli's *Antigona delusa da Alceste*), prod. Leipzig, 18 May 1693. Written for the opening of the Leipzig opera-house.

Incid. music by Handel (later used for *The Choice of Hercules*) to a play by Tobias Smollett, comp. for a prod. in London, C G, in 1750, which did not take place.

Alceste, ou Le Triomphe d'Alcide, opera by Lully (lib. by Quinault), prod. Paris, Opéra, 19 Jan 1674.

Alchemist, The, incid. music by Handel, partly adapted from *Rodrigo*, for a revival of Ben Jonson's play, prod. London, Drury Lane Theatre, 7 Mar 1732.

Opera by Cyril Scott (lib. by comp.), prod. in Ger. trans., Essen, 28 May 1925.

Alchymist, Der, opera by Spohr (lib. by K. Pfeiffer, based on a story by Washington Irving), prod. Kassel, 28 Jul 1830.

Alcidor, opera by Spontini (lib. by G.M. Théaulon de Lambert), prod. Berlin, 23 May 1825.

Alcina, opera by Handel (lib. by A. Marchi), prod. London, CG, 16 Apr 1735.

Alcione, opera by Marais (lib. by A.H. de la Motte), prod. Paris, Opéra, 18 Feb 1706.

Alcock, John (b London, 11 Apr 1715; d Lichfield, 23 Feb 1806), English organist and composer. Organist at var. parish churches in London and Warwicks., and for a time at Lichfield Cathedral. D. Mus. Oxford, 1761.

Works incl. church music, glees and catches, harpsichord music.

Alcoke (Alcock), Philip, English mid-16th-cent. composer of a *Salve Regina* (*c* 1555).

Alcôve, L', operetta by Offenbach (lib. by P.A.A.P. de Forges and A.de Leuven), prod. Paris, Salle de la Tour d'Auvergne, 24 Apr 1847. Offenbach's 1st operetta.

Alcuin (b ?York, *c* 753; d Tours, 19 May 804), poet, statesman, musician and adviser to Charlemagne. He may also have written about music.

Alda, Frances (b Christchurch, 31 May 1883; d Venice, 18 Sep 1952), New Zealand soprano. Stage debut Melbourne; sang Manon at the Paris Opéra-Comique, 1904. In Dec 1908 she sang Gilda at the NY Met, opposite Caruso; she appeared in NY until Dec 1929, as Mimi, Butterfly and Manon Lescaut, and in the fps of operas by Victor Herbert and Walter Damrosch. She married the manager of the Met, Gatti-Casazza, and was admired by Toscanini: at La Scala in 1908 she appeared under him as the first local Louise.

Aldeburgh Festival, annual festival held at Aldeburgh, Suffolk, since 1948. Content of programmes has largely reflected tastes of co-founders, Benjamin Britten and Peter Pears, although visiting foreign comps. have incl. Henze, Lutosławski and Takemitsu. The Maltings concert hall, Snape, and nearby Orford Parish Church have seen many Britten premières, e.g. the church parables, the 3rd string 4tet and *Phaedra*. Artistic dirs.

since Britten's death have incl. Rostropovich and Murray Perahia. A feature of recent festivals has been the posthumous fps of works by Britten which were withdrawn by the comp. and subsequently 'lost'.

Aldenhoff, Bernd (b Duisburg, 14 Jun 1908; d Munich, 8 Oct 1959), German tenor. After engagements at Cologne, Darmstadt and Erfurt he sang at Düsseldorf 1938–44; Dresden 1944–52, as Herod, Max and Walther; Bayreuth 1951–2 and 1957, as Siegfried; NY Met, 1954–5, debut as Tannhäuser, and appeared as guest at La Scala, Paris and Zurich; sang in the *Ring* cycles cond. by Furtwängler in Milan.

Aldrich, Richard (b Providence, Rhode Island, 31 Jul 1862; d Rome, 2 Jun 1937), American music critic. After var. activities he became music ed. of the *New York Times*. His works incl. 2 Wagnerian guide-books.

Aleatory (from Lat. *alea*, a die, plur. *aleae*, dice), a term applied to music in which the details of perf. or the actual notes are left wholly or in part to the players or singers. Most strictly the word is used for works such as Stockhausen's *Klavierstück XI*, in which the choice is between specific alternatives.

Aleko, opera by Rakhmaninov (lib. by V.I. Nemirovich-Danchenko, based on Pushkin's poem *The Gypsies*), prod. Moscow, 9 May 1893.

Alembert, Jean Le Rond d' (b Paris, 16 Nov 1717; d Paris, 29 Oct 1783), French author, philosopher and mathematician. His books incl. many studies of musical subjects, incl. acoustics, opera, the theories of Rameau, etc., and he contrib. music articles to the *Encyclopédie*. One of the adherents of Gluck against Piccinni.

Alen, William, English 16th-cent. composer. His *Gaude virgo mater Christi* is in Cambridge, Peterhouse part-books (1540–47).

Alessandri, Felice (b Rome, 24 Nov 1747; d Casalbino, 15 Aug 1798), Italian conductor and composer. Studied at Naples and 1st worked at Turin and Paris; prod. his 1st opera at Venice in 1767 and went to London the following year, and in 1786 to St Petersburg in search of a court app., which he failed to secure. From 1789 to 1792 he was 2nd *Kapellmeister* at the Berlin Opera.

Works incl. *c* 35 operas, incl. *Ezio* (Verona, 1767), *Alcina* (Turin, 1775), *Artaserse* (Naples, 1783) *Il ritorno d'Ulisse* (Potsdam, 1790), *Armida* (Padua, 1794), an oratorio, several symphs., sonatas.

Alessandro, opera by Handel (lib. by P.A. Rolli), prod. London, King's Theatre, Haymarket, 5 May 1726.

Alessandro della Viola. *See* **Merlo.**

Alessandro nell' Indie (*Alexander in India*). *See also* **Cleofide** and **Poro.**

Opera by Johann Christian Bach (lib. by Metastasio), prod. Naples, Teatro San Carlo, 20 Jan 1762.

Opera by Francesco Corselli (*c* 1700–78) (lib. do.), prod. Madrid, Palacio Real Buen Retiro, 9 May 1738, at the wedding of Charles IV of Naples and Princess Maria Amalia of Saxony. The 1st It. opera prod. there.

Opera by Galuppi (lib. do.), prod. Mantua, Teatro Nuovo, Carnival 1738.

Opera by Pérez (lib. do.), prod. Genoa, Teatro Sant' Agostino, 26 Dec 1745.

Opera by Piccinni (lib. do.), prod. Naples, Teatro San Carlo, 12 Jan 1774.

Opera by Sacchini (lib. do.), prod. Venice, Teatro San Salvatore, spring 1763.

Opera by Vinci (lib. do.), prod. Rome, Teatro delle Dame, 26 Dec 1729. (This was the 1st setting of the lib.)

Alessandro Romano. *See* **Merlo.**

Alessandro Severo, opera by Lotti (lib. by A. Zeno), prod. Venice, Teatro San Giovanni Crisostomo, 26 Dec 1716.

Alessandro Stradella, opera by Flotow (lib., in Ger., by F.W. Riese, pseud. 'W. Friedrich'), prod. Hamburg, 30 Dec 1844. It deals with doubtful incidents in the life of Stradella, and is based on a play with music, some by Flotow, by P.A.A.P. de Forges and P. Dupert.

Alessandro vincitor di se stesso (*Alexander, Victor over himself*), opera by Cavalli (lib. by F. Sbarra), prod. Venice, Teatro Santi Giovanni e Paolo, prob. 20 Jan 1651.

Alexander Balus, oratorio by Handel (lib by T. Morell), prod. London, CG, 23 Mar 1748.

Alexander, Der Wilde, German 13th-cent. Minnesinger, 6 of whose songs have been preserved.

Alexander Nevsky, film music by Prokofiev, comp. 1938. Later arr. as Cantata, op.78, for mezzo, chorus and orch. fp Moscow, 17 May 1939.

Alexander's Feast, Dryden's ode set to music by Handel (words arr. and added to by Newburgh Hamilton), prod. London, CG, 19 Feb 1736.

Alexander, Carlos (b Utica, NY, 15 Oct 1915), American bass-baritone. He studied in Berlin and with Friedrich Schorr in NY. Debut St Louis 1941, as Masetto. He sang widely in N. and S. Amer. in the 1940s and in Ger. from 1955. In 1961 he sang Mandryka at Florence and was Gregor Mittenhoffer in the Brit. fp of Henze's *Elegy for Young Lovers*, at Glyndebourne. Bayreuth 1963–4, as Beckmesser. At the Stuttgart Staatsoper he took part in the 1968 fp of Orff's *Prometheus*. He taught at the Salzburg Mozarteum.

Alexander, John (b Meridian, Miss., 21 Oct 1923), American tenor. Debut Cincinnati 1952, Faust. NY City 1957, Alfredo: Met 1961, Ferrando. He sang Rudolfo and Korngold's Paul in Vienna and in 1970 was Pollione at CG. In 1973, at the Boston Opera, he took the title role in the 1st complete stage perf. of Verdi's *Don Carlos*. He was Idreno in the Sutherland recording of *Semiramide*. Other roles incl. Bacchus, Walther, and Percy in *Anna Bolena*.

Alexandrov, Anatol Nicolaievich (b Plakhino, 25 May 1888; d Moscow, 16 Apr 1982), Russian composer. Studied under Taneiev and at the Moscow Cons., later comp. under Vassilenko and Ilyinski. Prof. at Moscow Cons.

Works incl. operas *Two Worlds, The Forty-First, Bela* (Moscow, 1946), *The Wild Girl* (1957); incid. music for Maeterlinck's *Ariane et Barbe-bleue*, Scribe's *Adrienne Lecouvreur*, etc.; music for film *Thirteen*; overture on popular Rus. themes and 2 suites for orch.; 4 string 4tets (1921–53); 14 pf. sonatas, pf. pieces; *Three Goblets*, for baritone and orch.; songs, folksong arrs.

Alexeev, Dmitri (b Moscow, 10 Aug 1947), Russian pianist. He studied at the Moscow Cons. and in 1975 became the first Russian to win the Leeds International Competition. London debut 1975, and has appeared with all the leading British orchs. US debut 1976, with Giulini and the Chicago SO; Carnegie Hall, NY, 1978. Well known in recital and has recorded works by Chopin, Brahms and Prokofiev. Appeared with the Concertgebouw Orch. and the Berlin PO in 1986.

Aleyn (Alanus), John, English 14th–15th cent. composer whose identity is uncertain, possibly a canon of Windsor who died in 1373 or a minor canon of St Paul's who died in 1437. A motet praising the skill of Eng. musicians in MS. 1047 of the Musée Condé, Chantilly, is ascribed to Johannes Alanus, while a *Gloria* in the Old Hall MS. is ascribed to Aleyn. A Jean Alain was one of John of Gaunt's musicians in 1396, together with three Fr. minstrels.

Alfano, Franco (b Posillipo, nr. Naples, 8 Mar 1875; d San Remo, 27 Oct 1954), Italian composer. Studied 1st at the Naples Cons. and afterwards at that of Leipzig, under Jadassohn. He had some pf. pieces pub. in Ger. before the end of the cent. and in 1896 wrote his 1st opera, *Miranda*, on a subject from Fogazzaro. The ballet *Napoli*, prod. Paris 1900, was his first big success, and was followed by the still greater success of his 3rd opera, *Risurrezione*, prod. 1904, a work in the *verismo* tradition. His first symph. was perf. at San Remo in 1910. In 1919 he was app. director of the Liceo Musicale Rossini at Bologna and in 1923 of the Cons. at Turin. After Puccini's death in 1924 he completed the unfinished *Turandot*, finishing the final scenes from Puccini's sketches.

Works incl. operas *Miranda, La fonte di Enschir* (Breslau, 1898) *Risurrezione* (based on Tolstoy) (Turin, 1904), *Il principe Zilah, L'ombra di Don Giovanni* (Naples, 1930), *Sakuntala* (after Kalidasa), *L'ultimo Lord, Cyrano de Bergerac* (Rome, 1936) (after Rostand), *Il dottor Antonio*; ballet *Napoli*; 2 symphs., *Suite romantica* for orch.; pf. tet, 3 string 4tets; sonata for cello and pf.; songs incl. 3 settings of Tagore and a cycle *Dormiveglia*.

Alfonso X (King of Castile and Leon, 1252–84), known as *El Sabio* (the Wise). He assembled a collection of 400 songs in Galician-Portug., known as the *Cantigas de Santa Maria.*

Alfonso und Estrella, opera by Schubert (lib. by F. von Schober), comp. 1821–2, but never perf. in Schubert's lifetime; prod. Weimar, by Liszt, 24 Jun 1854.

Alford, John, English 16th-cent. lutenist. He lived in London and in 1568 pub. a trans. of Adrien Le Roy's book on the lute, *A Briefe and Easye Instruction to learne . . . the Lute.*

Alfred, masque by Arne (words by J. Thomson and D. Mallet), perf. at Cliveden, Bucks., the residence of Frederick, Prince of Wales, 1 Aug 1740. It contains 'Rule, Britannia'.

Opera by Dvořák, his first (lib. by K.T. Korner). Comp. 1870; prod. Olomouc, 10 Dec 1938.

Alfred, König der Angelsachsen (*Alfred, King of the Anglo-Saxons*), incidental music by Haydn for a drama by J.W. Cowmeadow. Perf. Eisenstadt, Sep 1796.

Alfvén, Hugo (b Stockholm, 1 May 1872; d Uppsala, 8 May 1960), Swedish violinist and composer. Studied under Lindegren at the Stockholm Cons., and began his career as violinist in the court orch. From 1910 to 1939 he was music director at the Univ. of Uppsala.

Works incl. 5 symphs., 2 symph. poems and Swed. rhapsody *Midsommarvaka*

(1903) and 2 others for orch.; *Sten Sture* for chorus and orch.; *The Bells* for solo voice and orch.; a cantata; 2 marches; pieces for pf. and for vln.; songs.

Algarotti, Francesco, Count (b Venice, 11 Dec 1712; d Pisa, 3 May 1764), Italian scholar. Among many learned works he wrote a treatise on the reform of opera, *Saggio sopra l'opera in musica,* pub. 1755.

Algarotti, Giovanni Francesco (b Novara, *c* 1536; d 8 May 1596), Italian composer. Pub. books of madrigals at Venice in 1567 and 1569.

Alghisi, Paris Francesco (b Brescia, 19 Jun 1666; d Brescia, 29 Mar 1743), Italian composer. Studied under Polarolo and was engaged for some time at the Pol. court. Two operas were prod. at Venice: *Amor di Curzio per la patria,* 1690, and *Il trionfo della continenza,* 1691. He also wrote several oratorios and other works.

Ali Baba, ou Les Quarante Voleurs (. . . *or The Forty Thieves*), opera by Cherubini (lib. by Scribe and A.H.J. Mélesville), prod. Paris, Opéra, 22 Jul 1833. A new version of *Koukourgi,* comp. 1793, but not perf.

Alina, Regina di Golconda, opera by Donizetti (lib. by F. Romani), prod. Genoa, 12 May 1828.

Aline, Reine de Golconde, opera by Berton (lib. by J.B.C. Vial and E.G.F. de Favières, based on Sedaine's older lib.), prod. Paris, Opéra-Comique, 2 Sep 1803.

Opera by Monsigny (lib. by J.M. Sedaine), prod. Paris, Opéra, 15 Apr 1766.

Aliquot Parts (from Lat. *aliquot* = some), parts contained by the whole, integral factors: in music the parts of a fundamental note vibrating separately as Overtones.

Aliquot Scaling }
Aliquot Strings } additional strings, vibrating with those struck by the hammers, introd. into the upper registers of Blüthner's pfs., evidently on the old principle of the sympathetic strings in bowed string instruments.

Alkan, Charles-Valentin, (actually Morhange) (b Paris, 30 Nov 1813; d Paris, 29 Mar 1888), French pianist and composer. He was so precocious as a player as to be admitted to the Paris Cons. at the age of 6. After a visit to London in 1833, he settled in Paris as teacher of the pf. In his works he cultivated an advanced, immensely difficult and often very modern technique.

Works incl. 2 pf. concertos; pf trio; pf. sonatas, numerous pf. studies (incl. 1 for the right hand and 1 for the left), charact. pieces; 4 op. nos, of pieces for pedal pf.

Alkestis, opera by Boughton (lib. taken from Gilbert Murray's Eng. trans. of the tragedy by Euripides), prod. Glastonbury, 26 Aug 1922.

Opera by Wellesz (lib. by H. von Hofmannsthal, after Euripides), prod. Mannheim, 20 Mar 1924.

Alkmene, opera by Klebe (lib. by comp., after Kleist), prod. Berlin, 25 Sep 1961.

All' ottava (It. = at the octave), a direction that a passage, so far as it is marked by a dotted line over it, is to be played an octave higher than it is written; it is usually represented by the symbol 8*va*. If the dotted line is below, it means an octave lower.

Alla (It. fem. = 'at the', in the manner of, = Fr. *à la*). The word is used in various ways in combination with nouns, e.g. *alla marcia* = march-like, *alla francese* = in the Fr. manner, etc. (also abbr. *all'* with nouns beginning with a vowel).

Alla breve (It. = with the breve [as unit of the beat, instead of the semibreve]), a term used for a tempo direction indicating that the time is twice as fast as the note-values would suggest, though not necessarily a rapid tempo. The normal *alla breve* time-signature is ₵.

Allargando (It.) = becoming broader, slowing down.

Allegranti, Maddalena (b Venice, 1754; d ?Ireland, *c* 1802), Italian soprano. Made her 1st appearance in Venice in 1770. Appeared in operas by Gassmann, Sacchini and Salieri in It. and Ger. before her 1781 London debut, in Anfossi's *I Viaggiatori Felici*.

Allegretto (It. dim. of *allegro*) = a little fast, i.e. not as fast as *allegro,* although in certain cases, esp. in France *c.* 1800, faster than allegro.

Allegri, Domenico (b Rome, 1585; d Rome, 5 Sep 1629), Italian composer. *Maestro di cappella* at Santa Maria Maggiore in Rome, 1610–29. Works incl. motets and music for voices and strings.

Allegri, Gregorio (b Rome, 1582; d Rome, 7 Feb 1652), Italian priest and composer. Pupil of the Nanini brothers in Rome, where he sang tenor in the Papal Chapel from 1629. His famous *Miserere* is still sung there; Mozart, as a boy of 14, wrote it down from memory after hearing it in Rome. Allegri also wrote Magnificats, motets and other church music.

Allegri Quartet, British string quartet founded in 1953 with Eli Goren as leader. Since 1983 members have been Peter Carter and David Roth (vlns.), Keith Lovell (vla.) and Bruno Schrecker (cello). Has given perfs. of

4tets by Maconchy, LeFanu, Goehr, Britten and Bridge.

Allegro (It. lit. cheerful, sprightly). In music the term, although orig. doubtless describing the character of a piece, now indicates merely speed: a fast but not very fast pace.

Allegro Barbaro, work for solo pf. by Bartók, comp. 1911 but not perf. until 27 Feb 1921, in Budapest.

Allegro, il Penseroso ed il Moderato, L' (*The Cheerful, the Thoughtful and the Moderate Man*), oratorio by Handel (lib. Parts i and ii by Milton, Part iii by Charles Jennens), prod. London, Lincoln's Inn Fields Theatre, 27 Feb 1740.

Alleluia, the 3rd chant of the Proper of the Mass, sung immediately after the Gradual. The word is Hebrew (= praise ye Jehova), and was sung in many contexts in Jewish life, but especially in connection with the singing of the Psalms. It was taken over unchanged by the Christian Church and sung both alone and as an addition to chants of various kinds, especially during the Easter season. As a Mass-chant of the Roman rite it was originally sung alone, at first during Eastertide only and, after the time of Gregory I, during the whole year except from Septuagesima to Easter. At some time before 750 one or more verses were added, in which form it became a responsorial chant, the choir singing the alleluia at the beginning and end, and the soloists the verse or verses in between.

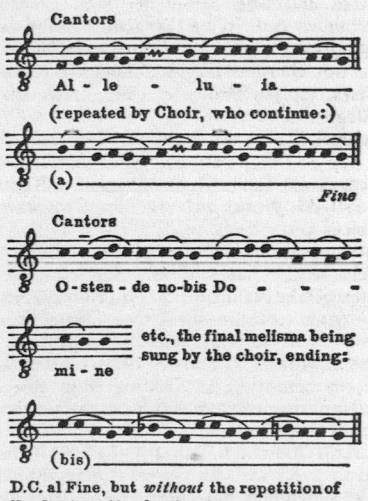

D.C. al Fine, but *without* the repetition of the first section by the choir.

ALLELUIA

The exact form as sung since the Middle Ages may be illustrated from the alleluia for the 1st Sunday of Advent (*see* illustration).

The alleluia of the Ambrosian chant, possibly retaining more of its original oriental characteristics, is even more florid in character.

Allemande (Fr. fem. = German) (1) A dance in moderate 4–4 time, divided into 2 sections, each repeated, and usually beginning with a short upbeat. It occurs in most classical suites, where it takes 1st place unless they open with a prelude. (2) = Deutscher Tanz.

Allen, Henry Robinson (b Cork, 1809; d London, 27 Nov 1876), Irish baritone. He first became known in London in 1842 when he sang Damon in a perf. of *Acis and Galatea* at Drury Lane and made a great reputation as an operatic artist, but retired early to devote himself to teaching and the comp. of songs, incl. 'When we two parted'.

Allen, Perceval (b Ripley, 1880; d London, Dec 1955), English soprano. She studied with William Shakespeare and sang in concert with the LSO, 1905. Successful in oratorio and appeared at CG 1908–10, as Brünnhilde, under Richter, and as Lia in a stage vers. of Debussy's *L'Enfant prodigue* (1910). Toured in N. America with the Quinlan co. and was heard in Chicago, Philadelphia and Boston as Brünnhilde, Brangaene, Erda, and Rebecca in Sullivan's *Ivanhoe*.

Allen, Thomas (b Seaham Harbour, Co. Durham, 10 Sep 1944), English baritone. Opera debut 1969, with WNO. CG from 1971, Glyndebourne from 1973. Noted as Papageno, Pelléas and Don Giovanni; also concert singer. In 1985 he sang Ulysses in the Salzburg fp of Monteverdi's *Il ritorno di Ulisse*, arranged by Henze. At the London Coliseum in 1986 he was Faust in the 1st Brit. stage perf. of Busoni's opera.

Allende, Pedro Humberto (b Santiago, 29 Jun 1885; d Santiago, 17 Aug 1959), Chilean composer and educationist. Studied at the Nat. Cons. of Chile.

Works incl. *Tres Tonadas, Escenas campesinas chilenas* (1913) and *La voz de la calles* (1921) for orch.; concertos for cello (1915), vln. (1942), pf. (1945).

Allin, Norman (b Ashton-under-Lyme, 19 Nov 1884; d London, 27 Oct 1973), English bass. He studied at the RMCM and from 1916 sang with the Beecham co. as Dosifey, Méphistophélès and Marke; CG 1919–20, as Konchak and Gurnemanz. BNOC 1922–9, as leading bass and director, and sang Bartolo in the 1934 prod. of *Figaro* which inaugurated the Glyndebourne Festival. Prof. RAM, 1935–60. CBE 1958.

Allison (Alison, Aloyson), Richard, English 16th–17th-cent. composer. He first appeared as a contrib. to East's *Whole Book of Psalms* in 1592 and pub. a collection of church melodies set for voices and instruments, *The Psalmes of David in Meter,* in 1599. Other works incl. lute music and 24 songs for voices and instruments, *An Howres Recreation . . .,* pub. 1606.

Almahide, opera by ? Giovanni Bononcini (lib. by?, after Dryden's *Almanzor and Almahide*), prod. London, Queen's Theatre, Haymarket, 10 Jan 1710. According to Burney, the 1st opera performed in Eng. wholly in It.

Almeida, Fernando de (b Lisbon, *c* 1600; d Thomar, 21 Mar 1660), Portuguese monk and composer. Pupil of Lobo; entered the monastery of Thomar in 1638; wrote Masses and other church music.

Almeida, Francisco Antonio de (b *c* 1702; d Lisbon, 1755), Portuguese 18th-cent. composer. Prob. studied in Rome and was the 1st Port. to write It. operas, incl. *La Spinalba* (1739) and *La pazienza di Socrate* (1733).

Almeida, Ignácio Antonio de (b Guimarães, 18 Feb 1760; d S. Pedro de Penedono, 25 Oct 1825), Portuguese priest and composer. His works incl. a Requiem, a *Stabat Mater* and other church music.

Almérie, a kind of lute invented in the 18th cent. by Jean Lemaire, on whose name its own is an anagram.

Almira, opera by Handel (lib. by F.C. Feustking), prod. Hamburg, Theater beim Gänsemarkt, 8 Jan 1705.

Alpaerts, Flor (b Antwerp, 12 Sep 1876; d Antwerp, 5 Oct 1954), Belgian conductor and composer. Studied with Benoit and Blockx at the Antwerp Cons., in 1903 became prof. there and in 1934–41 was its director. In 1919 he also became cond. of the Antwerp Zoo Orch. and in 1922–3 he directed the Royal Flem. Opera.

Works incl. opera *Shylock* (after Shakespeare); incid. music for plays; church music, *Spring* symph., symph. poem *Psyche* and other orchestral works; vln. concerto; chamber music. pf. works; songs.

Alpensinfonie, Eine (*An Alpine Symph.*) symph. by R. Strauss, op. 64, fp Berlin 28 Oct 1915.

Also sprach Zarathustra (*Thus spake Zoroaster*), symph. poem by R. Strauss, op. 30, based on Nietzsche, comp. 1896, fp Frankfurt, 27 Nov 1896.

Altenberglieder, 5 songs for voice and orch.

to picture-postcard texts by 'Peter Altenberg' (i.e. Richard Englander, 1862–1919), by Berg. At fp in Vienna of 2 of the songs, 1913, a riot caused the concert to be abandoned. First complete perf. Rome, 24 Jan 1953, cond. Horenstein.

Alternatim (Lat.), a manner of performance in which singers or players are heard in alternation, e.g. between two sides of a choir, between choir and organ, etc. It can also be applied to alternation between music styles, e.g. plainsong and polyphony.

Alternativo (It.), a contrasting section, much the same as the trio in a minuet or scherzo, but often in a piece of a different character, and there may be more than one alternativo in a single piece. Familiar exs. appear in Schumann.

Althouse, Paul (b Reading, Penn., 2 Dec 1889; d New York, 6 Feb 1954), American tenor. Debut NY, with Philadelphia co., 1911 (Faust); Met from 1913, as Dmitri and in the fps of works by Herbert, Giordano, de Koven and Cadman. Appeared in Europe from 1929 and after study at Bayreuth sang Tristan at the 1935 Salzburg Festival; returned to the Met 1934 and sang Tristan and Siegmund, opposite Flagstad. Among his pupils were Richard Tucker and Leopold Simoneau.

Altmeyer, Jeannine (b Pasadena, 4 May 1948), American soprano of German-Italian parentage. She studied with Lotte Lehmann and in Salzburg. NY Met 1971, Chicago 1972. Salzburg and Zurich from 1973. Sang Sieglinde at Bayreuth, 1979, and Brünnhilde in first compact disc recording of *The Ring* (cond. Janowski). She sang Isolde at Bayreuth in 1986.

Altnikol, Johann Christoph (b Berna, Silesia, Oct 1719; d Naumburg, buried 25 Jul 1759), German harpsichordist, organist and composer. Pupil of Bach in Leipzig from 1744. App. organist at Niederwiesa nr. Greifenberg early in 1748, and later the same year at Naumburg. Married Bach's daughter Elisabetha Juliane Frederica (1726–81) in 1749. Known primarily as a copyist of Bach's music.

Alto (It. = high) (1) Properly an extension of the highest male-voice register, prod. by Falsetto, used in Angl. church choirs and in male-voice 4tets and choral societies, partic. in glees and part-songs. (2) = Contralto. (3) (Fr.) = Viola. (4) As a prefix to an instrument = a size larger than the soprano, e.g. alto saxophone.

Alto Clef, the C clef so used as to indicate that middle C stands on the central line of the stave; not now used in vocal music, but still in use for the vla.:

Alto Rhapsody (Brahms). *See* **Rhapsodie.**

Alva, Luigi (Luis) (b Lima, 10 Apr 1927), Peruvian tenor. Began his career with Radio Lima and in 1953 went to It., singing at La Scala in 1954. He specializes in operatic lyric roles, and has sung at most of the great opera-houses and festivals. CG from 1960; NY Met debut 1964, as Fenton. Other roles incl. Alfredo, Almaviva and Ferrando.

Alvarez, Albert (b Bordeaux, 1860; d Nice, 26 Feb 1933), French tenor. Debut Ghent, 1887, Faust; repeated the role at the Paris Opéra in 1892. He became associated with the operas of Isidore de Lara and created Leicester in *Amy Robsart* (CG, Jul 1893) and Helion in *Messaline* (Monte Carlo, Mar 1899). Massenet was also favoured: created Nicias in *Thaïs* (Paris, 1894) and Aragui in *La Navarraise* (London, 1894). Met debut Dec 1899, as Gounod's Roméo.

Alvary, Max (b Düsseldorf, 3 May 1856; d Gross-Tabarz, Thuringia, 7 Nov 1898), German tenor. Debut Weimar, 1879. NY Met 1885, as Don José; first US Loge, Siegfried and Adolar. Sang in CG *Ring* under Mahler, 1892, as Siegfried. Other roles incl. Max, Tristan and Spontini's Cortez.

Alwin, Karl (b Königsberg, 15 Apr 1891; d Mexico City, 15 Oct 1945), German conductor, pianist and composer. He studied at Berlin with Humperdinck; cond. opera at Halle, Düsseldorf and Hamburg 1913–20, and worked at the Vienna Staatsoper 1920–38: during this period he was married to Elisabeth Schumann. Appeared widely as guest, and at CG in 1924 gave the 1st local perf. of *Ariadne auf Naxos*, rev. vers., with Schumann and Lotte Lehmann. Cond., National Opera, Mexico City, from 1941.

Alwyn, William (b Northampton, 7 Nov 1905; d Southwold, 11 Sep 1985 English composer. Entered the RAM in London as a student for fl., pf. and comp., studying the last under McEwen and obtaining the Costa Scholarship. Later he became prof. of comp. there, was elected to the Collard Fellowship of the Worshipful Co. of Musicians in 1937 and became an Hon. Freeman of that Co. in 1940. Prof. of comp. RAM 1926–56. CBE 1976.

Works incl. opera, *Miss Julie* (1961–76), music for films, *Our Country, The Lost*

Illusion, and many others; 5 preludes, concerto grosso, overture to a masque, and 5 symphs. for orch.; pf. concerto, vln. concerto, *Pastoral Fantasia* for vla. and strings; 2 string 4tets, Rhapsody for pf. 4tet; Sonata-Impromptu for vln. and vla., sonatina for vla. and pf.; pf. pieces; Divertimento for solo fl.

Alyabyev, Alexander Alexandrovich (b Tobolsk, 15 Aug 1787; d Moscow, 6 Mar 1851), Russian composer. He was an army officer who fought as a hussar against Napoleon; cultivated music as an amateur from 1823.

Works incl. two operas after Shakespeare: *Burya* (*The Tempest*, 1835) and *The Enchanted Night* (*A Midsummer Night's Dream*, 1839). His song *The Nightingale* was used by Patti and Viardot for the letter scene in *Il Barbiere di Siviglia.*

Alypios, 4th-cent. Greek theorist to whom our knowledge of ancient Greek notation is due.

Alzira, opera by Verdi (lib. by S. Cammarano, based on Voltaire's play *Alzire*), prod. Naples, Teatro San Carlo, 12 Aug 1845.

Amadei, Filippo (b Reggio, *c* 1670; d after 1729), Italian cellist and composer. His 1st opera, *Teodosio il giovane,* was prod. in Rome in 1711. *See also* **Mattei (F.).**

Amadeus Quartet, British string quartet; members from its foundation in 1948 were Norbert Brainin and Sigmund Nissel (vlns.), Peter Schidlof (vla.) and Martin Lovett (cello). Gave fp of Britten's 3rd 4tet in 1975 but mostly associated with the Classical repertory. Brainin, OBE, 1960; other members, 1973. The 4tet was disbanded in 1987 on the death of Peter Schidlof.

Amadigi di Gaula (*Amadis of Gaul*), opera by Handel (lib. adapted from A.H. de la Motte's *Amadis de Grèce,* set by Destouches, 1699), prod. London, King's Theatre, Haymarket, 25 May 1715.

Amadis, opera by Lully (lib. by Quinault, based on the old Iberian romance *Amadis de Gaula*), prod. Paris, Opéra, 18 Jan 1684.

Opera by Massenet (lib. by J. Claretie), comp. *c* 1895 and perf. posth. in Monte Carlo, 1 Apr 1922.

Amadis de Gaule, opera by J.C. Bach (lib by Quinault, altered by A.M.D. de Vismes), prod. Paris, Opéra, 14 Dec 1779.

Amadori, Giuseppe (b *c* 1670; d after 1730), Italian composer. *Maestro di cappella* in Rome, where his oratorio, *Il martirio di Sant' Adriano,* was prod. in 1702. He also wrote Masses and other church music.

Amahl and the Night Visitors, opera in 1 act by Menotti (lib. by the comp., after Bosch's painting *The Adoration of the Magi*), prod. on NBC Television 24 Dec 1951. It is the 1st opera esp. written for TV.

Amar, Licco (b Budapest, 4 Dec 1891; d Freiburg, 19 Jul 1959), Hungarian violinist. He was leader of the Berlin Phil. 1915–20 and in 1921 formed the Amar string quartet, with Hindemith as violist: gave frequent fps. of modern works, incl. Hindemith's string 4tets nos. 2, 3 and 4.

Amara, Lucine (b Hartford, Conn., 1 Mar 1927), American soprano. Her career began in California and she made her NY Met debut in Nov 1950, on the opening night of Rudolf Bing's regime; later sang there as Aida, Mimi, Donna Anna and Eurydice. Glyndebourne 1955–8, as Ariadne and Donna Elvira. She recorded Musetta with Beecham and Elsa with Leinsdorf.

Amarus, lyric cantata by Janáček for sop., tenor, bar., chorus and orch.; comp. *c* 1897, rev. 1901 and 1906. Fp Kroměříž, 2 Dec 1900.

Amat, Juan Carlos (b Monistrol nr. Barcelona, *c* 1572; d Monistrol, 10 Feb 1642), Spanish scientist and author. He wrote *Guitarra española. . .*, the earliest known treatise on the subject, pub. prob. 1586.

Amati, Italian 16th–17th-cent. family of vln. makers at Cremona:

Andrea A. (b before 1511; d Cremona, before 1580).

Antonio A. (b 1550; d 1638).

Girolamo (or Geronimo) A. (b 1561; d 1630).

Nicolo A. (b 3 Dec 1596; d 12 Apr 1684).

Girolamo A. (b 26 Feb 1649; d 21 Feb 1740).

Amato, Pasquale (b Naples, 21 Mar 1878; d Jackson Heights, Long Island, NY, 12 Aug 1942), Italian baritone. Made his 1st appearance in Eng. in 1904 as Amonasro at CG and later had much success in opera in USA. He sang at the NY Met 1908–21 and created Jack Rance in *La Fanciulla del West*, 1910. Other roles incl. Valentin, Escamillo, Kurwenal and Amfortas.

Ambiela, Miguel (b Saragossa, 29 Sep 1666; d Toledo, 29 Mar 1733), Spanish priest and composer. Music director of the new cathedral at Saragossa, 1700–7, and *maestro de capilla* at Toledo, 1710–33.

Works incl. Masses, *Stabat Mater* and other church music.

Ambleto (*Hamlet*), opera by Gasparini (lib. by A. Zeno and P. Pariati), prod. Venice, Teatro San Cassiano, Carnival 1705.

Opera by D. Scarlatti (lib. do.), prod. Rome, Teatro Capranica, Carnival 1715.

Ambros, August Wilhelm, (b Vysoké Myto, 17 Nov 1816; d Vienna, 28 Jun 1876), Czech (Germanized) musicologist. Studied at Prague Univ. His life's work was a hist. of music which at his death reached only the 4th vol. and the early 17th cent. He also comp. a Cz. opera, *Bratislav and Jitka*, overtures to Shakespeare's *Othello* and Calderón's *Mágico prodigioso*, etc.

Ambrose, John, English 15th–16th-cent. composer of an untitled keyboard piece (Oxford, Christ Church MS. 1034) and a wordless canon in Brit. Royal App. 58. An 'Ambros' was a clerk of King's College, Cambridge, 1481–2.

Ambrosian Chant, the music of the Milanese rite associated with St Ambrose (340–397), Bishop of Milan from 374. The music as we now have it is mostly preserved in late medieval MSS. and probably differs considerably from that heard in Ambrosian times; nor can any of the extant tunes to the few authentic hymns of St Ambrose be definitely considered to be of the same date. The rite itself belongs to the Gallican family, containing oriental features not preserved in that of Rome; while the chant, even in its present form, shows Eastern influences to a greater degree than 'Gregorian' chant.

Amelia al Ballo (*Amelia goes to the Ball*), opera by Menotti (lib. by the comp.), prod. Philadelphia, 1 Apr 1937.

Ameling, Elly (b Rotterdam, 8 Feb 1934), Dutch soprano. She sang in Amsterdam from 1961; London debut 1966. Sang with Netherlands Opera in 1973 but has most often been heard in Lieder and oratorio. She took part in the 1959 fp of Martin's *Mystère de la Nativité* and has been heard in the cantatas and Passions of Bach, songs by Satie and Schubert and concert music by Mahler and Mendelssohn.

Amener (Fr., prob. from *à mener* = to lead), a French dance of the 17th cent. in triple time and moderate pace, with charact. 6-bar phrases. It occurs in French instrumental suites and thence passed to some extent into Ger. and It. music.

Amengual, René (b Santiago, 2 Sep 1911; d Santiago, 2 Aug 1954), Chilean composer. Works incl. piano concerto (1942), harp concerto; 2 string 4tets (1941, 1950), wind 6tet (1953).

America, epic rhapsody by Bloch in 3 movts. (1. 1620; 2. 1861–5; 3. 1926), comp. 1926–7. Fp 20 Dec 1928 and then on 21 Dec 1928 simultaneously in 7 Amer. cities. It won the prize offered by *Musical America* for the best Amer. symph. work.

American Musical Terminology. The main differences from Brit. usage are nearly all direct translations from Ger. Whole note, half note, quarter note, etc. (for semibreve, minim, crotchet, etc.); concert master for leader, and so on. The most potentially confusing is the word 'tone' meaning Brit. 'pitch': hence Americans tend to use 'tone row' for Brit. 'note row', 'neighbour tone' for 'auxiliary note', 'whole step' and 'half step' for Brit. 'tone' and 'semitone'. Other details in which usage tends to cross the Atlantic in both directions include 'flutist' (flautist), and 'measure' (bar).

American Organ, an instrument similar to the harmonium, differing from the latter in some details, partic. in sucking in the wind through its reeds instead of expelling it. Its principle was discovered by a workman attached to Jacob Alexandre (1804–1876), an instrument maker in Paris, but he took it to Amer. and the 1st important instruments of the kind were made by Mason & Hamlin of Boston *c* 1860.

Amériques, work for orch. by Varèse; insts. incl. sleighbells, steamboat whistle and hand siren as used by NY Fire Dept; comp. 1918–22, fp Philadelphia, 9 Apr 1926, cond. Stokowski.

Amfiparnaso, L' (*The Amphi-Parnassus*), madrigal opera by Orazio Vecchi, prod. Modena, 1594, and pub. Venice, 1597, described as a *commedia harmonica*. It consists of 3 acts and a prologue, and the characters are the stock figures of the *commedia dell' arte*, but the musical setting of their speech is in the form of madrigals for mixed voices. It has been supposed that the action was prod. in dumb-show while the madrigals were sung behind the scenes, but a passage in the text which says that 'the spectacle is to enter by the ear, not by the eye' gives good reason to doubt this. The same subject was treated earlier in a smaller form by Lassus.

Amicis, Anna Lucia de. *See* **De Amicis, Anna Lucia.**

Amico Fritz, L', opera by Mascagni (lib. by P. Suardon, based on Erckmann-Chatrian's novel *L'Ami Fritz*), prod. Rome, Teatro Costanzi, 31 Oct 1891.

Amid Nature (or *In Nature's Realm*), concert overture by Dvořák, op. 91, comp. 1891 and forming, with *Carnival* and *Othello*, a cycle with thematic connections, orig. called *Nature, Life and Love*.

Amirov, Fikret Dzhamll (b Kirovabad, 22

Nov 1922; d Baku, 20 Feb 1984), Azerbaijani composer. Works incl. opera *Sevil* (1953); double concerto for vln., pf. and orch. (1948); *The Pledge of the Korean Guerrilla Fighter* for voice and orch. (1951); piano concerto (1957).

Amitié à l'épreuve, L' (*Friendship on Trial*), opera by Grétry (lib. by C.S. Favart and C.H. F. de Voisenon, based on a story by Marmontel), prod. Fontainebleau, at court, 13 Nov 1770; 1st Paris perf., Comédie-Italienne, 24 Jan 1771.

Amleto (*Hamlet*), opera by Faccio (lib. by Boito, after Shakespeare), prod. Genoa, Teatro Carlo Felice, 30 May 1865.

Opera by Mercadante (lib. by Romani, after Shakespeare), prod. Milan, La Scala, 26 Dec 1822.

Ammerbach (Amerbach), Elias Nikolaus (b Naumberg, *c* 1530; d Leipzig, buried 29 Jan 1597), German organist and composer. Was organist of St Thomas, Leipzig, from 1560 and pub. 2 books of music in organ tablature containing important explanations of ornaments and modes of perf.

Amner, John (b Ely, bap. 24 Aug 1579; d Ely, buried 28 Jul 1641), English organist and composer. He became organist and choirmaster at Ely Cathedral in 1610; wrote services, anthems and *Sacred Hymns*.

Amon, Johann Andreas (b Bamberg, 1763; d Wallerstein, Bavaria, 29 Mar 1825), German horn player, composer and conductor. Toured in Fr. and Ger. and had comp. lessons from Sacchini in Paris in 1781; became music director at Heilbronn in 1789 and *Kapellmeister* to the Prince of Oettingen-Wallerstein in 1817.

Works incl. 2 *Singspiele*, Masses, symphs., chamber music.

Amor brujo, El (*Love, the Magician*), ballet by Falla, comp. 1913–14, fp Madrid, Teatro de Lara, 15 Apr 1915.

Amor coniugale, L', opera by Mayr (lib. G. Rossi, after Bouilly), prod. Padua, 26 Jul 1805 (4 months before *Fidelio*, which is based on the same source).

Amor vuol sofferenza (*Love means Suffering*), opera by Leo (lib. by G.A. Federico), prod. Naples, Teatro Nuovo, autumn 1739.

Amore artigiano, L' (*Love among the Artisans*), opera by Gassmann (lib. by Goldoni), prod. Vienna, Burgtheater, 26 Apr 1767.

Opera by Latilla (lib. do.), prod. Venice, Teatro Sant' Angelo, 26 Dec 1760.

Amore dei tre re, L' (*The love of the Three Kings*), opera by Montemezzi (lib. by S. Benelli, from his play of the same title), prod. Milan, La Scala, 10 Apr 1913.

Amorevoli, Angelo (b Venice, 16 Sep 1716; d Dresden, 15 Nov 1798), Italian tenor. He sang in It. 1730–41, in operas by Porpora, Hasse, Leo and G. Scarlatti. Spent most of his time at the court of Dresden in operas by Hasse, 1745–64, and sang in London 1741–3.

Amoroso (It. = amorous), a direction indicating an emotional and tender manner of perf.

Amour médecin, L', comédie-ballet by Lully (lib. by Molière), prod. Versailles, 16 Sep 1665.

Amours d'Antoine et de Cléopâtre, Les (*The Loves of A. and C.*), ballet by R. Kreutzer (choreog. by J.P. Aumer, based on Shakespeare), prod. Paris, Opéra, 8 Mar 1808.

Amram, David (b Philadelphia, 17 Nov 1930), American composer and horn player. Studied at the Manhattan School of Music and with Charles Mills. Has written incid. music for Shakespeare's plays, films and jazz bands.

Works incl. operas *The Final Ingredient* (ABC TV, 1965), *Twelfth Night* (1968); *Shakespearean Concerto* (1960), *King Lear Variations* for wind, perc. and pf. (1967), concertos for horn, jazz 5tet, bassoon and vln. (1968–80); string 4tet (1961), sonata for solo vln. (1964), wind 5tet (1968); cantatas *The American Bell, A Year in our Land* and *Let us Remember* (1962–5).

Amy, Gilbert (b Paris, 29 Aug 1936), French composer of advanced tendencies. Studied with Milhaud, Messiaen and Boulez. Dir of the Concerts du Domaine Musical, specializing in new music. His comps. show influences of oriental music, total serialism and also aleatory techniques.

Works incl. *Messe* for soloists, chorus and orch. (1983); *Mouvements* for chamber orch. (1958), *Adagio et Stretto* for orch. (1978); *Alpha-Beth* for 6 wind instruments (1964), *Cycles* for perc.; *Epigrammes* for pf.

Amy Robsart, opera by Isidore de Lara (lib. by A. Harris, based on Scott's *Kenilworth*), prod. in French (trans. by Paul Milliet), London, CG, 20 Jul 1893.

An die ferne Geliebte (*To the Distant Beloved*), song cycle by Beethoven (6 songs), op. 98, to poems by A. Jeitteles, comp. 1816. It is the 1st Ger. set of songs intended to form a connected cycle.

Ana, Francesco d' (b ? Venice, c 1460; d Venice, c 1503), Italian composer. At St Mark's, Venice, 1490; comp. *frottole*, Lamentations, etc.

Anacréon, *acte de ballet* by Rameau (lib. by

P.-J. Bernard), prod. Fontainebleau, 23 Oct 1754; rev. and prod. Paris, Opéra, 10 Oct 1758.

Anacréon, ou L'Amour fugitif, *opera-ballet* by Cherubini (lib. by R. Mendouze), prod. Paris, Opéra, 4 Oct 1803.

Anacrusis, in prosody an unstressed syllable at the beginning of a verse or line; in music the literary term is borrowed as a synonym for Upbeat.

Anakreontika, Greek songs for mezzo and inst. ens. by Peter Maxwell Davies; fp London, 17 Sep 1976.

Analysis. As recently as the 1950s, the analysis of music was widely understood to denote any kind of description with some technical component. But for more than a cent. there has been a growing academic discipline which attempts to explain musical phenomena by means as rigorous and logical as possible, to approach formal models of how music works, or to break down the organism of musical structures into smaller components. Pure musical analysis often eschews value judgment, which is more the province of the critic or aesthetician. *See* Keller, Meyer (L.), Nattiez, Reti, Schenker.

Ančerl, Karel (b Tučapy, Bohemia, 11 Apr 1908; d Toronto, 3 Jul 1973), Czech conductor. Studied with Křička and Alois Hába at the Prague Cons. (1925–9). Asst. to Scherchen in Berlin (1929–31). His public career began in 1931 as a theatre cond. and with Czech radio. Cond. at ISCM festivals, 1933–7. Imprisoned in World War II, he resumed his career in 1945, becoming prof. at the Academy of Musical Arts in Prague (1950). Cond. Cz. PO 1950–68; music dir. Toronto SO from 1969.

Anchieta, Juan de (b Azpeitia nr. San Sebastián, 1462; d Azpeitia, 30 Jul 1523), Spanish composer. He became a court musician in 1489 and a canon of Granada 10 years later. From 1500 he was rector of the parish church in his native place. Wrote church music and secular songs.

Ancona, Mario (b Livorno, 28 Feb 1860; d Florence, 23 Feb 1931), Italian baritone. Debut Trieste 1890, as Scindia in Massenet's *Roi de Lahore*. In 1893 he was Tonio in the 1st local perfs. of *Pagliacci* at CG and the NY Met. He sang Le Cid at La Scala in 1890 and Bellini's Riccardo at the opening night of the Manhattan Opera House, NY, 1906. Other roles incl. Don Giovanni, Amonasro, Iago, Sachs and Escamillo.

Anda, Géza (b Budapest, 19 Nov 1921; d Zurich, 14 Jun 1976), Hungarian pianist and conductor. Studied at the Royal Music

Acad. in Budapest with Dohnányi, winning the Liszt Prize. Left Hung. in World War II and lived in Switzerland. He was best known as an exponent of Brahms, Liszt, Bartók and Mozart, all of whose pf. concertos he recorded.

Andamento (It.) = a fugue subject of more than usual length and often in 2 contrasted sections.

Andante (It. = going), a tempo direction indicating a 'walking pace', i.e. a moderate tempo.

Andantino (It. dim. of prec.), orig. intended to indicate a slower pace than *andante*, i.e. a dim. of 'walking'; but since *andante* is now taken to mean a slow pace, the dim. suggests an only moderately slow, i.e. slightly quicker tempo.

Anday, Rosette (b Budapest, 22 Dec 1903; d Vienna, 28 Sep 1977), Hungarian-born mezzo. She studied vln. with Jenö Hubay at Budapest and made her stage debut there in 1920; sang at the Vienna Staatsoper 1921–61, and was popular there and at Salzburg as Carmen, Orpheus, Dorabella, Clytemnestra and Weber's Fatima. At Salzburg in 1947 she sang in the fp of Einem's *Dantons Tod*. She appeared as guest in London and in N. and S. America.

Anders, Peter (b Essen, 1 Jul 1908; d Hamburg, 10 Sep 1954), German tenor. Made his debut in Berlin in 1931 in *La Belle Hélène*, and from 1936 to 1948 sang at the Berlin Staatsoper. Brit. debut in 1950 at the Edinburgh Festival, as Bacchus. CG 1951 as Walther. Other roles incl. Tamino, Lohengrin and Florestan. He was killed in a car crash.

Anderson, Emily (b Galway, Ir., 17 Mar 1891; d London, 26 Oct 1962), English musicologist. Although employed in the Foreign Office, she ed. and trans. the complete letters of Mozart and his family (2 vols., 1938) and those of Beethoven (3 vols., 1962).

Anderson, June (b Boston, 30 Dec 1952), American soprano. Debut NY City Opera 1978, Queen of Night; other NY roles incl. Lucia, Cleopatra and Olympia. European debut 1982, Rome, as Semiramide. In 1985–6 she sang Amina at La Scala and Isabelle in *Robert le Diable* at the Paris Opéra. Her spectacular coloratura was much applauded in a concert perf. of *Semiramide* at CG. Other roles incl. Gilda, Violetta, Rossini's Desdemona and Bellini's Elvira.

Anderson, Marian (b Philadelphia, 17 Feb 1902), American contralto. Won competition to appear with NY PO in 1925; studied

in Europe 1933–5. Heard largely in concert rep. but in 1955 became first black singer to appear at NY Met (Ulrica).

Andrade, Francisco d' (b Lisbon, 11 Jan 1859; d Berlin, 8 Feb 1921), Portuguese baritone. Made his 1st appearance in 1882 in San Remo, as Amonasro; sang all over Europe; CG 1886–90 as Rigoletto and Don Giovanni.

André, Johann (b Offenbach, 28 Mar 1741; d Offenbach, 18 Jun 1799), German music publisher and composer. Prod. his first successful *Singspiel* in 1773 and set Goethe's *Erwin und Elmire* in 1775. Estab. his publishing firm in 1774. His opera *Belmont und Constanze* of 1781 preceded Mozart's *Entführung*, on the same subject.

André, Johann Anton b Offenbach, 6 Oct 1775; d Offenbach, 6 Apr 1842), German music publisher, violinist, pianist and composer, son of prec. He followed his father in business, acquired Mozart's MSS. from Constanze in 1799 and with Senefelder applied the principle of lithography to music publishing.

André, Maurice (b Alès nr. Nîmes, 24 May 1933), French trumpeter. Debut 1954; has won competitions in Geneva and Munich. Best known in Baroque and contemporary music.

Andrea Chénier, opera by Giordano (lib. by L. Illica), prod. Milan, La Scala, 28 Mar 1896.

Andreae, Volkmar (b Berne, 5 Jul 1879; d Zurich, 18 Jun 1962), Swiss composer and conductor. Studied at Berne and Cologne, in 1900 became asst. cond. at the Munich Opera, in 1902 choral cond. at Zurich and Winterthur, later cond. of the Zurich symph. concerts. From 1914 to 1916 he lectured at Zurich Univ. and from 1914 to 1939 was director of the Zurich Cons.

Works incl. operas *Ratcliff* (based on Heine's tragedy, prod. Duisburg, 1914) and *Abenteuer des Casanova* (prod. Dresden, 1924); 2 symphs.; several concertos; choral works; chamber music.

Andreozzi, Gaetano (b Naples, 1763; d Paris, 21 Dec 1826), Italian composer. Pupil and relation of Jommelli; wrote 45 operas, incl. *L'Olimpiade* (Pisa, 1782), *Giovanna d' Arco* (Vicenza, 1789) and *Piramo e Tisbe* (1803), 3 oratorios, chamber music and songs.

Andrésen, Ivar (b Oslo, 27 Jul 1896; d Stockholm, 24 Nov 1940), Norwegian bass. Debut Stockholm, 1919. Dresden and Berlin 1925–36; Bayreuth 1927–36 as Gurnemanz, King Marke and Pogner.

Glyndebourne 1935 as Sarastro and Osmin.

Andricu, Michel (b Bucharest, 3 Jan 1895; d Bucharest, 4 Feb 1974), Rumanian composer. Studied at the Bucharest Cons. and later became prof. at the Royal Acad. there, gaining the Enescu Prize for comp. in 1924. From 1926 to 1959 he was prof. at the Bucharest Cons.

Works incl. ballet *Taina*; 11 symphs. (1944–70), 13 sinfoniettas (1945–73), 9 orch. suites (1924–58), serenade, 3 *Tableaux symphoniques, Suite pittoresque, Suite brève, Poem*, etc., for orch.; string 4tet (1931), *Novellettes* for pf. 5tet and other chamber music; sonatina, *Suite lyrique* and other pf. works.

Andriessen, Hendrik (b Haarlem, 17 Sep 1892; d Heemstede, 12 Apr 1981), Dutch organist and composer. Studied under Zweers at the Amsterdam Cons. Later became director of the Utrecht Cons. and choirmaster at the Roman Catholic cathedral there.

Works incl. operas *Philomela* (1950) and *The Mirror from Venice* (1964); 8 Masses and *Te Deum*; 4 symphs. (1930–54), variations for orch.; songs for voice and orch.; chamber music; cello and pf. sonata; organ works.

Andriessen, Louis (b Utrecht, 6 Jun 1939), Dutch composer, son of prec. He studied with his father and with Berio, in Milan. Cage, Ives and Stravinsky are among the composers to whom he owes allegiance.

Works incl. *Anachronie*, in memory of Ives, for orch. (1966), *Reconstructie*, anti-imperialist theatre piece (1969), *What it's Like* for electronics and 52 strings (1970), *Uproar* for 16 wind, 6 perc. and electronics (1970), *The 9 Symphonies of Beethoven* for ens. and ice-cream bell (1970), *Il Principe*, after Machiavelli (1974), *Orpheus*, theatre piece (1977), *Matthew Passion* (1977), *George Sand*, theatre piece (1980), *Velocity* for orch. (1983).

Andriessen, Willem (b Haarlem, 25 Oct 1887; d Amsterdam, 29 Mar 1964), Dutch pianist and composer. Studied at the Amsterdam Cons., of which he became director in 1937 in succession to Dresden, after teaching at The Hague and Rotterdam.

Works incl. Mass for solo voices, chorus and orch.; scherzo for orch (1912); pf. concerto (1908); pf. sonata.

Andrieu Contredit d'Arras (b Arras, *c* 1180; d Arras, 1248), French trouvère, 18 of whose songs survive.

Andrieu, F. Late 14th-cent. composer. He

set a double *ballade* by Eustace Deschamps on the death of Machaut.

Andromaque (*Andromache*), opera by Grétry (lib. by L.G. Pitra, based on Racine's tragedy), prod. Paris, Opéra, 6 Jun 1780.

Anerio, Felice (b Rome, *c* 1560; d Rome, 27 Sep 1614), Italian composer. Chorister in the Papal Chapel as a boy, later *maestro di cappella* at the Eng. Coll. in Rome, which he left for the service of Cardinal Aldobrandini. App. comp. to the Papal Chapel on the death of Palestrina in 1594.

Works incl. Masses, motets, hymns and other church music; madrigals, canzonets.

Anerio, Giovanni Francesco (b Rome, *c* 1567; d Graz, buried 12 Jun 1630), Italian composer, brother of prec. He was *maestro di cappella* at the cathedral of Verona in 1609, and from 1613 to 20 was music instructor at the Seminario Romano and *maestro di cappella* of the church of the Madonna de' Monti in Rome. In the service of Sigismund III of Poland 1624–28.

Works incl. Masses, Requiem, Te Deum and other church music.

Anet, Jean-Jacques-Baptiste (b Paris, 2 Jan 1676; d Lunéville, 14 Aug 1755), French violinist and composer. He travelled in Fr. and It., studying with Corelli in Rome, and made a great reputation in Paris from 1701 to 35, at the Concert Spirituel with the Violons du Roy. He retired to the court of the ex-king of Pol., Stanislas Leszcsinski, at Lunéville in 1738. Wrote sonatas and other works for his instrument.

Anfossi, Pasquale (b Taggia nr. Naples, 25 Apr 1727; d Rome, Feb 1797), Italian composer. Pupil of Piccinni at Naples. Wrote operas from 1763, but had his 1st real success with *L'incognita perseguitata* (Rome, 1773). Later prod. operas in Paris, London, Berlin and Prague. In 1762 he became *maestro di cappella* of St John Lateran in Rome.

Works incl. operas *Armida* (Turin, 1770), *L'incognita perseguitata, La finta giardiniera, Il geloso in cimento, L'avaro* (Venice, 1775), *Gengis-Kan* (Turin, 1777), *La vera costanza, Il curioso indiscreto, I viaggiatori felici* (Venice, 1780), *Le gelosie fortunate*, church music.

Angecourt, Perrin d', French 13th-cent. trouvère. He was at the court of Charles of Anjou. 53 of his songs have survived.

Angeles, Victoria de los. *See* **Los Angeles.**

Angélique, opera in 1 act by Ibert (lib. by Nino), prod. Paris, Théâtre Fémina, 28 Jan 1927.

Angiolina, ossia Il matrimonio per susurro (*Angiolina, or The Marriage by Noise*), opera by Salieri (lib. by C.P. Defranceschi, based on Ben Jonson's *Epicoene*), prod. Vienna, Kärntnertortheater, 22 Oct 1800. *See also* **Schweigsame Frau** (Strauss).

Anglaise (Fr.), a dance-form similar to that of the country dance, which in France became the *contredanse* in the 18th cent., when the name of anglaise was sometimes given to it instead to show its Eng. origin unmistakably.

Anglebert, Jean Henri d' (b Paris, 1635; d Paris, 23 Apr 1691), French harpsichordist and composer. Pupil of Chambonnières. Became organist to the Duke of Orleans in 1661 and chamber musician to Louis XIV in 1664. He wrote harpsichord and org. pieces and arr. many instrumental pieces from Lully's operas for harpsichord.

Anglican Chant. *See* **Chant.**

Ängstlich (Ger. = anxiously, apprehensively). Beethoven used the term as a direction for the singing of the recitative in the 'Agnus Dei' section of his *Missa solemnis*.

Aniara, opera by Blomdahl (lib. by E. Lindegren, after H. Martinson's epic poem), prod. Stockholm, 31 May 1959. The action is set on board a space-ship.

Anima del filofoso ossia Orfeo ed Euridice (*The Philosopher's Stone, or Orpheus and Eurydice*), Haydn's last opera; comp. 1791 in London but not perf. First known performance. Florence, 10 Jun 1951, cond. E. Kleiber, with Callas and Christoff.

Animato (It. = animated), a direction orig. intended to suggest a spirited perf. but later generally the quickening of a passage.

Animuccia, Giovanni (b Florence, c 1500; d Rome, 25 Mar 1571), Italian composer. Studied under Goudimel in Rome; *maestro di cappella* at the Vatican from 1555 until his death. A friend of St Philip Neri, for whom he comp. a series of *Laude*. He also wrote Masses, other church music and madrigals.

Animuccia, Paolo (b Florence, c 1500; d ? Urbino, c 1570), Italian composer, brother of prec. *Maestro di cappella* at St John Lateran in Rome 1550–52 before Lassus. Wrote madrigals and church music.

Anitúa, Fanny (b Durango, 22 Jan 1887; d Mexico City, 4 Apr 1968), Mexican mezzo. Debut Rome 1909, as Gluck's Orpheus. La Scala from 1910; took part in the 1915 fp of Pizzetti's *Fedra* and sang under Toscanini 1925–7 as Orpheus and Azucena. She sang regularly in S. Amer. 1911–37; last role at Buenos Aires as Mistress Quickly. She toured N. Amer. in 1913, and was heard in Parma and Pesaro as Rosina and Cenerentola. Later taught in Mexico City.

Aniuta, Russian opera adapted from music by Piccinni, Grétry and others, prod. St Petersburg, 1772. Formerly wrongly attributed to Fomin.

Anna Amalia, Princess of Prussia (b Berlin, 9 Nov 1723; d Berlin, 30 Mar 1787), sister of Frederick the Great and amateur musician. With her *Kapellmeister* Kirnberger she was a champion of the works of Bach and Handel in Berlin, and collected a valuable library of old music. She was also a composer.

Anna Bolena (*Anne Boleyn*), opera by Donizetti (lib. by F. Romani), prod. Milan, Teatro Carcano, 26 Dec 1830.

Anna Karenina, opera by Hubay (lib., in Hung., by S. Góth, based on Tolstoy's novel), prod. Budapest, 10 Nov 1923.

Opera by Iain Hamilton (lib. by comp.), prod. London, Coliseum, 7 May 1981.

Années de pèlerinage, 4 sets of pf. pieces by Liszt, mainly recording his travels in Switzerland and It.—*1re Année: En Suisse*, comp. 1835–6, pub. 1855: 1. *Chapelle de Guillaume Tell*. 2. *Au Lac de Wallenstadt*. 3. *Pastorale*. 4. *Au Bord d'une source*. 5. *Orage*. 6. *Vallée d'Obermann* (inspired by Senancour's *Obermann*; the valley is an imaginary or unidentified one in the canton of Valais). 7. *Eglogue*. 8. *Le Mal du pays*. 9. *Les Cloches de Genève*. (Nos. 1, 2, 4, 6 and 9 orig. formed part of an *Album d'un voyageur* for pf. pub. in 1836: they were revised for the pub. of the *A. d. p.* in 1855.—*2me Année: En Italie*, comp. 1838–9, pub. 1846: 1. *Sposalizio* (after Raphael's picture in the Brera at Milan). 2. *Il pensieroso* (after Michelangelo's statue of Giuliano dei Medici in the Medici mausoleum at San Lorenzo, Florence). 3. *Canzonetta del Salvator Rosa*. 4. *Sonetto No. 47 del Petrarca*. 5. *Sonetto No. 104 del Petrarca*. 6. *Sonetto No. 123 del Petrarca* (Nos. 4–6 are transcriptions of settings of these Petrarch sonnets for voice and pf.). 7. *Après une lecture du Dante: Fantasia quasi Sonata* ('Dante Sonata').—*3me Année*, comp. 1872–7, pub. 1883: 1. *Angelus: Prière aux anges gardiens*. 2. *Aux Cyprès de la Villa d'Este*. 3. do.: *Thrénodie*. 4. *Les Jeux d'eau de la Villa d'Este*. 5. *'Sunt lacrymae rerum' en mode hongrois*. 6. *Marche funèbre* (in memory of the Emperor Maximilian I of Mex., d 19 Jun 1867). 7. *Sursum corda*.—Supplement to Vol. II: *Venezia e Napoli*, comp. 1859, pub. 1861: 1. *Gondoliera* (on a canzona by Cavaliere Peruchini). 2. *Canzone* (on the gondolier's song in Rossini's *Otello*). 3. *Tarantella* (on some canzoni by Guillaume Louis Cottrau). (This set is partly a revision of an earlier one of the same title comp. in 1840, but not pub.)

Annibale (Il Padovano) (b Padua, 1527; d Graz, Mar 1575), Italian contrapuntist and composer. Organist at St Mark's, Venice, 1552–66, and then *maestro di cappella* to the Archduke Carl at Graz. Wrote church and organ music, madrigals.

Annibali, Domenico (b Macerata, c 1705; d ? Rome, 1779 or later), Italian male soprano. He 1st appeared at Rome in 1725 and later went to Dresden, where he remained till 1764, singing the soprano lead in many of Hasse's operas. He sang for Handel in London in 1736–7, incl. the fps of *Arminio, Giustino* and *Berenice*.

Ansani, Giovanni (b Rome, 11 Feb 1744; d Florence, 15 Jul 1826), Italian tenor. Sang with great success in Copenhagen and London, as well as It.; created roles in operas by Paisiello, Cimarosa and Anfossi. Retired to Naples at the age of 50 to teach singing.

Ansermet, Ernest (b Vevey, 11 Nov 1883; d Geneva, 20 Feb 1969), Swiss conductor. Originally a prof. of mathematics, 1906–10, he studied music with Bloch, Mottl and Nikisch. From 1915 to 1923 he was assoc. with Diaghilev's ballet company. In 1918 he founded the Orchestre de la Suisse Romande, which he cond. until 1967. He pub. a book criticizing certain aspects of modern, esp. serial, music in 1961. Ansermet was well known for his perfs. of Stravinsky's earlier music and gave the fps of *The Soldier's Tale* (1918), *Pulcinella* (1920) and *Renard* (1922)

Ansseau, Fernand (b Boussu-Bois, 6 Mar 1890; d Brussels, 1 May 1972), Belgian tenor. Debut Brussels 1913 in *Hérodiade*; successful in Belg. until 1939 as Masaniello, Tannhäuser, Alvaro and in Puccini. CG debut 1919, as Massenet's Des Grieux. In Paris he was heard as Lohengrin and Gluck's Orpheus and Admète. Chicago 1923–8.

Answer, in Fugue, the 2nd entry of the subject, brought in while the 1st entry continues with a counterpoint to it (*see* illustration).

Antar, a programme symph. by Rimsky-Korsakov, op. 9, based on Senkovsky's oriental story of that name, comp. 1868 as '2nd Symph.', rev. 1875, fp St Petersburg, Russian Music Soc., Jan 1876, repub. in 1903 as 'symph. suite'. The titles of the movements are I. Introduction; II. 'Joy of Revenge'; III. 'Joy of Power'; IV. 'Joy of Love'.

Antechrist, work for chamber ens. by Peter Maxwell Davies; comp. 1967, fp London, 30 May 1967.

Antegnati, Costanzo (b Brescia, 9 Dec 1549; d Brescia, 14 Nov 1624), Italian composer and member of a family of organ-builders famous in N. Italy from 1470 to 1642. He wrote Masses, motets and madrigals, and organ and other instrumental music.

Antheil, George (b Trenton, NJ, 8 Jul 1900; d New York, 12 Feb 1959), American composer. Studied with Bloch, later in Europe. His music of the 1920s is aggressively 'modern' (the *Ballet mécanique* of 1924 incl. 8 pianos, aeroplane propellers, motor horns, anvils, etc.) but his later work is much more restrained and classical in character. In 1939 he became associated with the film industry in Hollywood.

Works incl. operas *Transatlantic* (Frankfurt, 1930), *Helen Retires* (New York, 1934) and *Volpone* (Los Angeles, 1953); ballets *Ballet mécanique* and *Dreams*; 6 symphs. (1920–50), *Zingaresca, Capriccio* and *Archipelago* for orch. (1935); 3 string 4tets; 2 vln. and pf. sonatas.

Anthem, a comp. for church choir, with or without solo voices and accomp., sung in the course of Morning or Evening Service in the Anglican Church. There are 2 kinds: the full anthem is a species sung by the choir throughout, the verse anthem is written for solo voices, with or without sections for the choir.

Bach, '48', Bk.I, no.1

ANSWER

Anthonello da Caserta. *See* **Caserta.**

Anthony, Cristofferus, 15th-cent. composer, prob. English, of a Magnificat and other pieces from the Trent Codices.

Anticipation, the occurrence of a note or notes from a chord before the rest of the chord is sounded, e.g.:

Beethoven, *Piano Sonata, Op.27, No.2*

Antico, Andrea de, Italian composer and music publisher who worked mainly in Rome and then Venice during the 1st half of the 16th cent. His most important pub. was probably *Frottole intabulate da sonar organi* (Rome, 1517), the first known printed ed. of keyboard music in Italy.

Antifone, work for orch. by Henze; comp. 1960, fp Berlin, 20 Jan 1962, cond. Karajan.

Antigonae, play with music by Orff (text by Hölderlin, after Sophocles), prod. Salzburg, 9 Aug 1949.

Antigone, incid. music to Sophocles' tragedy by Mendelssohn, prod. at the New Palace, Potsdam, 28 Oct 1841, and repeated at the Berlin Opera, 13 Apr 1842.

Opera by Honegger (lib. by Cocteau, after Sophocles), prod. Brussels, Théâtre de la Monnaie, 28 Dec 1927.

Opera by Zingarelli (lib. by J.F. Marmontel), prod. Paris, Opéra, 30 Apr 1790.

Antigono, opera by Gluck (lib. by Metastasio), prod. Rome, Teatro Argentina, 9 Feb 1756.

Opera by Hasse (lib. do.), prod. Hubertusburg nr. Dresden, 10 Oct 1743.

Antinori, Luigi (b Bologna, *c* 1697), Italian tenor. First appeared in London 1725 and sang in the fps of Handel's *Scipione* and *Alessandro*. Later sang in Venice, Genoa and Florence in operas by Porpora, Pergolesi and A. Scarlatti.

Antiphon (Gk. = 'answering sound'), in Gregorian chant a refrain sung before and after a psalm, and orig. between verses as well. Its name prob. derives from its use in connection with antiphonal, or alternative, choir singing. The earliest antiphons are often merely a single verse of the psalm itself, which in that case is not necessarily repeated.

The tone of the psalm always corresponds numerically to the mode of the antiphon, while its ending is chosen to link up with the beginning of the antiphon. The bulk of the repertory consists of biblical texts set to non-psalmodic melodies. A basic repertory of nearly 50 themes in the 8 modes is used for many thousands of texts. Their structure is often quite regular, and they may even have been sung metrically.

The Introit and Communion of the Mass are antiphons orig. sung with a complete psalm. The final stage in its history occurs when the antiphon becomes an independent piece in its own right (e.g. votive and processional antiphons). Originally they were borrowed from antiphons to psalms, but later they were newly comp. and often achieved considerable complexity.

Antiquis, Giovanni de, Italian 16th-cent. composer. Music director at the church of San Niccolo at Bari; ed. 2 books of *Villanelle alla napolitana* by musicians of Bari, incl. himself, pub. at Venice, 1574.

Antoni, Antonio d' (b Palermo, 25 Jun 1801; d Trieste, 18 Aug 1859), Italian conductor and composer. Prod. a Mass at the age of 12 and became cond. at the Palermo Theatre in 1817; settled at Trieste and founded the Società Filarmonica there, 1829.

Works incl. operas *Un duello* (Palermo, 1817), *Amina* (Trieste, 1825) and *Amazilda e Zamoro* (Florence, 1826).

Antonio e Cleopatra, opera by Malipiero (lib. by comp., based on Shakespeare), prod. Florence, Teatro Comunale, 4 May 1938.

Antony and Cleopatra, opera by Barber (lib. by comp., after Shakespeare), perf. on opening night of NY Met in Lincoln Center, 16 Sep 1966; rev. and prod. at Juilliard School, NY, 6 Feb 1975.

Anvil, an orch. perc. instrument imitating the sound of a blacksmith's anvil, but constructed of small steel bars struck by a mallet of wood or metal. It can be so made as to prod. notes of definite pitch, as in Wagner's *Rheingold*, but is usually indeterminate in sound.

Ap Rhys, Philip. *See* **Rhys, Philip ap.**

Apel, Nikolaus (b Königshofen, *c* 1475; d Leipzig, 1537), compiler of a large MS. in choirbook form (Leipzig, Univ. Bibl. 1494) containing sacred and secular music of the late 15th and early 16th cents. It has been pub. in full by Rudolf Gerber (*Das Erbe deutscher Musik*, xxxii–xxxiv).

Apel, Willi (b Konitz, 10 Oct 1893), German, later American, musicologist. Studied mathematics at Bonn, Munich and Berlin Univs., and also pf. under Edwin Fischer, Martienssen and others. Settled in the USA in 1936. Taught at the Longy School of Music, Cambridge, Mass., 1936–43, and Harvard Univ., 1938–42. Prof. at Indiana Univ., 1950–63. His pubs. incl. *The Notation of Polyphonic Music* (5th ed. 1961), *Harvard Dictionary of Music* (rev. ed., 1969), *Gregorian Chant* (1958) and *A History of Keyboard Music.* (1972). Joint ed. (with A.T. Davison) of *Historical Anthology of Music* (2 vols., 1946 and 1960).

Aperto (It., lit. open, frank, straightforward). Mozart used the adj. in conjunction with *allegro* in some early works, e.g. the A maj. vln. concerto, K219. The meaning is not clear, but may be taken to suggest an energetic delivery strictly in time.

Apiarius, Matthias (b Berchingen, *c* 1500; d Berne, 1554), German music publisher. He worked in partnership with Peter Schöffer in Strasbourg, 1543–7, and independently in Berne, 1537–54.

Aplvor, Denis (b Collinstown, Ir., 14 Apr 1916), Irish composer of Welsh stock. Was chorister at Hereford Cathedral, later at Christ Church, Oxford, and studied comp. with Patrick Hadley and Rawsthorne.

Works incl. operas *She Stoops to Conquer* (lib. by comp. after Goldsmith) (1947), *Yerma* (1959), *Ubu Roi* (1966); *The Hollow Men* (T.S. Eliot) for baritone, chorus and orch. (1939); pf. concerto; 2 symphs., 2 vln. concertos; Chaucer songs with string 4tet (1936), sonata for clar., pf. and perc., vln. and pf. sonata; songs with words by F. García Lorca and others.

Apollo e Dafne, Italian cantata by Handel, for sop., bar. and chamber ens.; comp. *c* 1708.

Apollo et Hyacinthus, Lat. intermezzo by Mozart K38 (lib. by Rufinus Widl), prod. Salzburg Univ., 13 May 1767.

Apollo Musagetes (*Apollo, Leader of the Muses*), ballet for string orch. by Stravinsky; comp. 1927–8, prod. Washington DC, 27 Apr 1928 (choreog. A. Bolm).

Apollonicon, a large organ playable both by hand and mechanically by barrels, built by Flight & Robson in London and exhib. by them in 1817.

Apostel, Hans Erich (b Karlsruhe, 22 Jan 1901; d Vienna, 30 Nov 1972), Austrian composer of German birth. Entered Karlsruhe Cons. in 1916. He later studied with Schoenberg and Berg in Vienna, where he lived from 1921. In 1937 his *Requiem* won the Hertzka Prize.

Works incl. *Requiem* (text by Rilke) for 8-part chorus and orch.; *Variations on a theme of Haydn* for orch. (1949); pf. concerto; 2 string 4tets; songs with pf. or orch. on texts by Trakl and Hölderlin.

Apostles, The, oratorio by Elgar, op. 49 (lib. compiled from the Bible by the comp.), Part I of a trilogy of which II is *The Kingdom* and III was never completed. Fp Birmingham Festival, 14 Oct 1903.

Appalachia, variations for orch. with chorus by Delius, comp. 1902, fp Elberfeld, 1904, first London perf. 22 Nov 1907. The title is the old Red Indian name for N. Amer.; the theme is a Negro folk song.

Appalachian Spring, ballet by Copland (choreog. Martha Graham), prod. Washington DC, 30 Oct 1944. Orch. suite from ballet perf. NY, 4 Oct 1945, cond Rodzinski.

Appassionata (It. = impassioned), the name commonly used for Beethoven's F min. pf. sonata of 1804–5, op. 57, but not authorized by himself.

Appenzeller, Benedictus (b *c* 1485; d after 1558), Flemish 16th-cent. composer. Pupil of Josquin des Prés. In the service of Mary of Hung. dowager regent of the Netherlands.

Works incl. *chansons*, church music, a *Nenia* on the death of Josquin, etc.

Applausus, Latin allegorical oratorio by Haydn for soloists, chorus and orch. perf. Zwettl, 17 Apr 1768.

Appleby, Thomas (b ? Lincoln, 1488; d Lincoln, *c* 1562), English organist and composer. App. organist of Lincoln Cathedral in 1538, the next year organist at Magdalen Coll., Oxford, but returned to Lincoln in 1541; was succeeded by Byrd there in 1563. Wrote church music.

Appoggiatura (It., from *appoggiare* = to lean), a note of varying length, dissonant with the harmony against which it is heard but resolving on to a harmony note. Various symbols have been used in the past to indicate it, the commonest of which is a note in smaller type, e.g.:

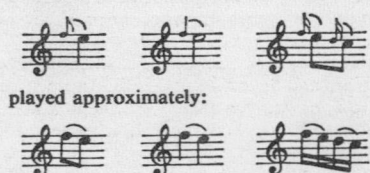

played approximately:

Where the appoggiatura is short it may in certain contexts occur before the beat. In much Baroque music, esp. in recitatives, the appoggiatura is understood without being written, i.e. where a phrase ends with two notes on the same pitch, the first of them should often be sung on the pitch of the preceding note (if it is a 4th higher), or performed a note higher (or sometimes lower than written.

Apprenti sorcier, L' (The Sorcerer's Apprentice), scherzo for orch. by Dukas on Goethe's ballad *Der Zauberlehrling*; fp Paris, Société Nationale de Musique, 18 May 1897.

Après-midi d'un faune (Debussy). *See* **Prélude à L'Après-midi d'un faune.**

Aprile, Giuseppe (b Martina Franca, Apulia, 28 Oct 1732; d Martina Franca, 11 Jan 1813), Italian male alto and singing teacher. He 1st appeared in 1753 and sang many times in It. and elsewhere in operas by Jommelli. Later a teacher of Cimarosa.

Arabella, opera by R. Strauss (lib. by H. von Hofmannsthal, based on his story *Lucidor*), prod. Dresden, 1 Jul 1933. Hofmannsthal's last lib. for Strauss.

Arabesk, An, work by Delius for bar., chorus and orch. (text by J.P. Jacobsen); comp. 1911 and perf. Newport, 1920. 1st London perf. 18 Oct 1929.

Arabeske (Ger.) ⎱ orig. a term applied
Arabesque (Fr.) ⎰
to ornamentation in Arabic or Moorish architecture; used by some comps. (e.g. Schumann, Debussy) for pieces probably meant to be regarded as decorative rather than emotionally expressive.

Aragall, Giacomo (b Barcelona, 6 Jun 1939), Spanish tenor. Debut 1963, Venice, as Gaston in first modern perf. of Verdi's *Jérusalem*; sang Romeo in Bellini's *I Capuleti*, La Scala 1966. CG 1966 and NY Met 1968, both as Duke of Mantua. Other roles incl. Alfredo, Cavaradossi and Roland in *Esclarmonde*.

Aragonaise (Fr.), a Spanish dance of Aragon, i.e. the *Jota aragonesa*.

Araia (Araja), Francesco (b Naples, 25 Jun 1709; d Bologna, *c* 1770), Italian composer. He prod. his 1st opera in 1729. From 1735 he was for 24 years opera director to the Russian court in St Petersburg, where he prod. several of his own works, e.g. *Il finto Nino* (1737), *Artaserse* (1738), *Scipione* (1745), *Mitridate* (1747) and *Bellerofonte* (1750). Another was *Cephalus and Procris* (1755), the first opera given in Russia known to have been sung in Russian and not in Italian.

Araiza, Francisco (b Mexico City, 4 Oct 1950), Mexican tenor. He sang in concert and oratorio from 1968 and in 1973 was heard as Massenet's Des Grieux and Rodolfo

in Mexico City. His European debut was in Karlsruhe, 1974, and he has since appeared in Munich, Salzburg, Aix, London and Vienna; successful in operas by Mozart, Massenet and Donizetti and as Gounod's Faust.

Aranaz, Pedro (b Tudela, bap. 2 May 1740; d Cuença, 24 Sep 1820), Spanish priest and composer. App. *maestro de capilla* at Saragossa Cathedral in 1766, having been a choir-boy there. After a year at Zamora he went to Cuença Cathedral in 1769.
Works incl. church music with orchestral accomp., secular songs (*tonadillas* and *villancicos*).

Arányi, Jelly d' (b Budapest, 30 May 1893; d Florence, 30 Mar 1966), Hungarian violinist. Debut Vienna 1909; became British citizen and gave the fps in London of both Bartók's vln. sonatas, with the composer (1922, 1923). Ravel's *Tzigane* and Vaughan Williams's *Concerto Accademico* are ded. to her. Gave first Brit. perf. of the Schumann concerto (1938), after claiming that the comp. had appeared to her in a dream with his neglected MS. Many concerts with her sister Adila Fachiri (*q.v.*).

Arbeau, Thoinot (anag. on real name of Jehan Tabourot) (b Dijon, 17 Mar 1520; d Langres, 23 Jul 1595), French priest and author. Wrote a book on dancing, *Orchésographie*, pub. 1589, containing a large number of dance tunes current in 16th-cent. France.

Arbore di Diana, L' (*Diana's Tree*), opera by Martín y Soler (lib. by da Ponte), prod. Vienna, Burgtheater, 1 Oct 1787.

Arbre enchanté, L', ou Le Tuteur dupé (*The Enchanted Tree, or The Tutor Duped*), comic opera by Gluck (lib. by P.L. Moline, after J.J. Vadé), prod. Vienna, Schönbrunn Palace, at court, 3 Oct 1759.

Arcadelt, Jacob (b *c* 1505; d ? Paris, 14 Oct 1568), Flemish composer. Became a singer at the court of the Medici at Florence before 1539, in which year he was app. singing-master to the boys at St Peter's in Rome, entering the college of papal singers the following year. Many of his madrigals were pub. in his lifetime.
Works incl. Masses, motets, madrigals, etc. (The *Ave Maria* attributed to him is a spurious adaptation of his 3-part *chanson Nous voyons que les hommes font tous vertu d'aimer*.)

Arcadia in Brenta, L', opera by Galuppi (lib. by Goldoni), prod. Venice, Teatro Sant' Angelo, 14 May 1749. The 1st comic opera by Galuppi written in collaboration with Goldoni.

Arcana, work for large orch. by Varèse; comp. 1925–7, fp Philadelphia, 8 Apr 1927, cond. Stokowski.

'Archduke' Trio, the name sometimes given to Beethoven's pf. trio in B♭ maj., op. 97, comp. in 1811 and ded. to the Archduke Rudolph of Austria.

Archlute, a large Lute of the theorbo type with 2 sets of strings, the pegs of which were set at different distances in the double neck; the longer bass strings had no fingerboard and could therefore not be altered in pitch during perf.

Arco (It. = bow), a direction (sometimes **col arco**) in music for bowed string instruments, indicating that the bow is to be resumed after a passage of plucked notes.

Arden muss sterben (*Arden must die*), opera by A. Goehr (lib. by E. Fried, after the anon. Elizabethan play *Arden of Faversham*), prod. Hamburg, 5 Mar 1967.

Arditti Quartet, British string quartet founded in 1974; members are Irvine Arditti and Alexander Balanescu (vlns.), Levine Andrade (vla.) and Rohan de Saram (cello). Perfs. in Brit. and all over Europe of contemporary works, incl. 4tets by Boulez, Carter, Ferneyhough, Ligeti and Henze; novel techniques incl. amplification with raad instruments.

Arensky, Anton Stepanovich (b Novgorod, 12 Jul 1861; d Terioki, Finland, 25 Feb 1906), Russian composer. Pupil of Rimsky-Korsakov for a time, but belonged to the eclectic rather than the nationalist school. App. prof. at the Moscow Cons. in 1882.

Works incl. operas *A Dream on the Volga* (on Ostrovsky's *Voyevoda*) (1891), *Raphael* (1894), *Nal and Damayanti*; ballet, *Egyptian Nights* (1908); incid. music for Shakespeare's *Tempest*; 2 symphs. (1883 and 1889); pf. concerto; chamber music; numerous pf. pieces; choruses, songs, church music.

Argento, Dominick (b York, Penn. 27 Oct 1927), American composer. He studied with Hovhaness and Hanson at the Eastman School and with Dallapiccola in Italy.

Works incl. operas *Sicilian Limes* (1954), *The Boor* (1957), *Christopher Sly* (1963), *The Masque of Angels* (1964), *The Shoemaker's Holiday* (1967), *The Voyage of Edgar Allan Poe* (1976), *Miss Havisham's Fire* (1978) and *Casanova's Homecoming* (1985); oratorio *Jonah and the Whale* (1973); *A Ring of Time*, for orch. (1972); choral music and song-cycles, incl. *6 Elizabethan Songs* for voice and ens. (1958).

Argerich, Martha (b Buenos Aires, 5 Jun 1941), Argentine pianist. Studied with Magaloff and Gulda; 1st prize Chopin Int. Competition Warsaw, 1965. London debut 1964. Admired in Romantic repertory.

Aria (It. = air), a vocal piece, esp. in opera or oratorio, formally more highly organized than a song: in the late 17th and early 18th cent. as a rule in 3 sections, the 3rd being a repetition of the 1st and the 2nd a contrasting strain (*da capo aria*); later often var. modifications of the instrumental sonata form. In the late 18th cent. arias were conventionally classified as follows:

A. all' unisono, an aria in which the voice and instrumental parts have the tune in octave unison, without harmony, at any rate so far as the comp.'s writing went, though chords may have been added by the *continuo* player at the harpsichord.

A. cantabile, an aria with a slow, sustained melody.

A. concertata, an aria making a feature of an elaborate instrumental solo part in the accomp.

A. d'agilità = aria di bravura.

A. d'imitazione, an aria in which either the voice or some instruments, or both, gave a more or less realistic imitation of some other musical or non-musical sounds.

A. di bravura, an aria containing a more than usual amount of brilliant and difficult passages.

A. di mezzo carattere, an aria 'of indeterminate character' which could be almost anything that could not be classified under any other species, but had as a rule an elaborate accomp.

A. di portamento, an aria requiring a slow and full-toned delivery and laying great stress on the display of a beautiful voice at the expense of the accomp.

A. parlante, an aria of a declamatory kind, intended less to display the voice than the singer's verbal eloquence and dramatic expression.

A. senza accompagnamento. A wholly unaccomp. aria, which was rarely used.

See also **Parable Aria.**

Ariadne, opera in 1 act by Martinů (lib. by comp. after G. Neveux), prod. Gelsenkirchen, 2 Mar 1961.

Ariadne auf Naxos, play with music (melodrama) by G. Benda (text by J.C. Brandes), prod. Gotha, 27 Jan 1775.

Opera by R. Strauss (lib. by H. von Hofmannsthal), orig. a 1-act opera played after a shortened version of Molière's *Le Bourgeois gentilhomme*, with incid. music by Strauss, prod. Stuttgart, 25 Oct 1912; 2nd version, with a new operatic 1st act, prod. Vienna, Opera, 4 Oct 1916.

Ariane et Barbe-bleue (*A. and Bluebeard*), opera by Dukas (lib. Maeterlinck's play with slight alterations), prod. Paris, Opéra-Comique, 10 May 1907.

Ariane, ou Le Mariage de Bacchus, opera by Grabu (lib. by P. Perrin, previously set by Cambert), prod. London, Drury Lane Theatre, 30 Mar 1674.

Arianna, opera by Marcello (lib. V. Cassani), comp. 1727, never perf. in Marcello's lifetime; ed. by O. Chilesotti, 1885, prod. Venice, Liceo Benedetto Marcello, 27 Apr 1913.
Opera by Handel (lib. adapted from P. Pariati's *Arianna e Teseo*), prod. London, King's Theatre, Haymarket, 26 Jan 1734.

Arianna, L', opera by Monteverdi (lib. by O. Rinuccini), prod. Mantua, at the ducal court, for the wedding of the Hereditary Prince Francesco Gonzaga with Margherita, Princess of Savoy, 28 May 1608. Most of the music is lost; only the *Lamento d'Arianna* (Ariadne's Lament) survives.

Arianna a Naxos (*Ariadne on Naxos*), cantata by Haydn for sop. and keyboard; comp. 1790.

Arianna e Teseo (*Ariadne and Theseus*), opera by Porpora (lib. by P. Pariati), prod. Vienna, 1 Oct 1714.

Aribo Scholasticus, Flemish 11th-cent. monk and music theorist. His treatise *De Musica* is important in the development of modal theory in the West, with its emphasis on melodic formulae as well as scales in the definition of mode.

Arietta (It. = little air), a shorter and simpler kind of Aria, usually of a lighter character.

Ariette (Fr. = little aria or air). Now the same as an *arietta*, but in early 18th-cent. Fr. opera an elaborate aria (sometimes with Italian words) and in late 18th-cent. *opéra comique* a song introduced into a scene in dialogue. *See also* **Debussy** (*Ariettes oubliées*).

Arlodant, opera by Méhul (lib. by F.-B. Hoffman, after Ariosto's poem *Orlando Furioso* (1516), prod. Paris, Théâtre Favart, 11 Oct 1799.

Ariodante, opera by Handel (lib. by A.Salvi, based on Ariosto's *Orlando furioso*), prod. London, CG, 8 Jan 1735.

Ariosi, work by Henze for sop., vln. and orch., to poems by Tasso; comp. for Wolfgang Schneiderhan and Irmgard Seefried and perf. by them Edinburgh, 23 Aug 1964.

Arioso (It. = song-like), a vocal or instrumental piece or passage of a declamatory or recitative character, to be sung or played in a melodic manner.

Ariosti, Attilo (b Bologna, 5 Nov 1666; d England, ? 1729), Italian composer. Prod. his 1st opera at Venice in 1696. Court comp. in Berlin, 1697–1703. Later visited Vienna, London and Bologna.
Works incl. operas *La più gloriosa fatica d'Ercole* (Vienna, 1703), *Amor tra nemici, La fede ne' tradimenti* (Berlin, 1701), *Coriolano* (London, 1723), *Vespasiano* (London, 1724), *Artaserse, Dario, Lucio Vero,* etc.; oratorio *Nabucodonosor,* Passion oratorio and others, cantatas; lessons for vla. d'amore.

Ariosto, Lodovico (1474–1533), Italian poet. *See* **Ariodant** (*Orlando furioso,* Méhul), **Ariodante** (do., Handel), **Holmès** (do.), **Orlando** (Handel), **Roussel** (*Enchantements d'Alcine*), **Vivaldi** (*Orlando furioso*.)

Aristoxenus of Tarentum, Greek philosopher of 4th cent. B.C. His treatise on *Harmonics* (i.e. acoustics and music theory) has the merit of being based on the music practice of his day rather than being purely speculative.

Arkhipova, Irina (b Moscow, 2 Dec 1925), Russian mezzo. Moscow, Bolshoy, debut 1956 as Carmen; has sung Eboli and Amneris there. La Scala, 1965, with Bolshoy co. as Marfa and Marina. CG 1975, Azucena. Other roles incl. Charlotte and Prokofiev's Helen.

Arlecchino, opera in 1 act by Busoni (lib. by the comp.), prod. Zurich, 11 May 1917.

Arlesiana, L' (*The Girl from Arles*), opera by Ciléa (lib. by L. Marenco, based on Alphonse Daudet's play, *L'Arlésienne*), prod. Milan, Teatro Lirico, 27 Nov 1897.

Arlésienne, L' (*The Girl from Arles*), incid. music by Bizet for Daudet's play, prod. Paris, 1 Oct 1872. Bizet afterwards extracted an orchestral suite from it. (The 2nd suite was arr. by Guiraud.)

Arme Heinrich, Der (*Poor Heinrich*), opera by Pfitzner (lib. by J. Grun), prod. Mainz, 2 Apr 1895. Pfitzner's 1st opera.

Armenian Chant, the music of the Church in Armenia from its estab. in 303. It pursued an independent path after the separation from the Greek Church in 536. Its original, alphabetical notation was replaced in the 12th cent. by a neumatic system (in which the only MSS. have survived), which cannot now be deciphered. The Church's collection of hymns (the *Sharakan*) is arr. according to the 8 modes or *echoi,* apparently defined by melodic formulae rather than by scale.

Armida, opera by Anfossi (lib. by J. Durandi, based on Tasso's *Gerusalemme liberata*) prod. Turin, Teatro Regio, Carnival 1770.

Opera by Dvořák (lib. by J. Vrchlický, based on his Cz. trans. of Tasso), prod. Prague, Cz. Theatre, 25 Mar 1904.

Opera by Haydn (lib. by J. Durandi), prod. Eszterháza, 26 Feb 1784.

Opera by Mysliveček (lib. by G.A. Migliavacca, an It. version of Quinault), prod. Milan, La Scala, 26 Dec 1779.

Opera by Naumann (lib. by G. Bertati, based on Tasso), prod. Padua, Jun 1773.

Opera by Rossini (lib. by G. Schmidt, after Tasso), prod. Naples, Teatro San Carlo, 11 Nov 1817.

Opera by Sacchini (lib. by G. de Gamerra), prod. Milan, Teatro Regio Ducal, Carnival 1772.

Opera by Salieri (lib. by M. Coltellini, based on Tasso), prod. Vienna, Burgtheater, 2 Jun 1771.

Opera by Traetta (lib. by Count G. Durazzo, based on Quinault), prod. Vienna, Burgtheater, 3 Jan 1761.

Armida abbandonata, Italian cantata by Handel for sop., 2 vlns. and cont.; comp. 1707.

Armide, opera by Gluck (lib. by Quinault, based on Tasso's *Gerusalemme liberata*), prod. Paris, Opéra, 23 Sep 1777.

Opera by Lully (lib. do.), prod. Paris, Opéra, 15 Feb 1686.

Arminio, opera by Handel (lib. by A. Salvi), prod. London, CG, 12 Jan 1737.

2 operas by Hasse: I. (lib. by G.C. Pasquini), prod. Dresden, at court, 7 Oct 1745; II. (lib. by Salvi), prod. Milan, 28 Aug 1730.

Opera by A. Scarlatti (lib. by Salvi), prod. Villa Medici, Pratolino, Sep 1703.

Armonica, an instrument also called Glass Harmonica, the notes of which are prod. by friction on a series of tuned glasses, either with the fingers or mechanically.

Armourer of Nantes, The, opera by Balfe (lib. by G.V. Bridgeman, based on Victor Hugo's *Marie Tudor*), prod. London, CG 12 Feb 1863.

Armstrong, Karan (b Horne, Mont., 14 Dec 1941), American soprano. Sang in US from 1969 before European debut in Strasbourg, 1976, as Salome; Bayreuth 1979, Elsa. In 1981 sang Lulu at CG in first Brit. perf. of 3-act vers. of Berg's opera; in the same year she created the title role in Giuseppe Sinopoli's opera *Lou Salomé*, at Munich. Often appears in the prods. of her husband, Götz Friedrich (*q.v.*).

Armstrong, Richard (b Leicester, 1 Jul 1943), English conductor. Studied Cambridge; CG staff 1966–8, asst. cond. WNO 1968–73, music director 1973–86; cond. several Janáček prods. CG debut 1982 (*Billy Budd*); in 1986 he led WNO in *The Ring* at CG.

Armstrong, Sheila (b Ashington, 13 Aug 1942), English soprano. Opera debut SW 1965; Glyndebourne 1966, CG 1973. Roles incl. Pamina, Zerlina, Despina and Fiorilla. Also heard in concert.

Arne, Michael (b London, *c* 1741; d London, 14 Jan 1786), English singer and composer, illegitimate (?) son of Thomas Augustine A. He made his first appearance as a singer in 1750, and a collection of songs, *The Flow'ret*, was pub. the same year. In 1761 he prod. his 1st opera, *Edgar and Emmeline*. He also collaborated with other comps. in the prod. of works for the stage, e.g. *A Midsummer Night's Dream* (with Burney and others, 1763) and *Almena* (with Battishill, 1764). He married the singer Elizabeth Wright on 5 Nov 1766, and the next year wrote the music for Garrick's *Cymon*, his most successful work. In 1771–2 he toured Ger., where he cond. the first Ger. perf. of *Messiah*. He was also interested in alchemy; his search for the 'philosophers' stone' twice ruined him.

Arne, Susanna Maria (b London, Feb 1714; d London, 30 Jan 1766), English singer and actress, sister of Thomas Augustine A. First appeared on the London stage in 1732. Married Theophilus Cibber in 1734, and sang under her married name.

Arne, Thomas Augustine (b London, bap. 28 May 1710; d London, 5 Mar 1778), English composer. He was educ. at Eton and intended for the law, but practised secretly on a muffled harpsichord and learnt the vln. from Festing, until his father at length allowed him to make music his career. He also taught his sister Susanna singing, and she appeared in his first opera, a setting of Addison's *Rosamond*, in 1733. Many successful works for the stage followed, incl. *Alfred*, containing 'Rule, Britannia', which was prod. at the residence of Frederick, Prince of Wales, at Cliveden in 1740. He married the singer Cecilia Young in 1736. In 1742–4 he and his wife worked successfully in Dublin, which they twice revisited in the 1750s. In 1745 Arne was app. comp. to Vauxhall Gardens. D.Mus. Oxford, 1759. In 1760, after a quarrel with Garrick, he gave up his post as comp. to Drury Lane Theatre and went over to Covent Garden, where in 1762 he prod. his opera

Artaxerxes, trans. by himself from Metastasio and comp. in the It. manner. Two years later he set the same librettist's *Olimpiade* in the orig. language.

Works incl. OPÉRAS AND PLAYS WITH MUSIC: *Rosamond* (1733), *The Opera of Operas, or Tom Thumb the Great* (adapted from Fielding), *Love and Glory, The Fall of Phaeton* (1736), *An Hospital for Fools, The Blind Beggar of Bethnal Green* (1741), *Eliza, Britannia* (1755), *The Temple of Dullness, King Pepin's Campaign, Harlequin's Incendiary, or Columbine, The Triumph of Peace* (1748), *Henry and Emma* (after M. Prior), *Don Saverio, The Prophetess, Thomas and Sally* (1760), *Artaxerxes* (1762), *Love in a Village, The Birth of Hercules, The Guardian Outwitted, L'Olimpiade* (1765), *The Ladies' Frolic, The Fairy Prince, Squire Badger* (later *The Sot*), *The Cooper* (1772), *The Rose, Achilles in Petticoats, May Day, Phoebe at Court*.

MASQUES: *Dido and Aeneas, Comus* (Milton adapted by Dalton), *The Judgment of Paris, Alfred* (1770)

INCID. MUSIC to Aaron Hill's *Zara*, Shakespeare's *As You Like It* (1740), *Twelfth Night, The Merchant of Venice, The Tempest, Romeo and Juliet* (1750), *Cymbeline*, Mason's *Elfrida* and *Caractacus*.

ORATORIOS: *The Death of Abel* and *Judith* (1761).

Ode on Cheerfulness, Ode to Shakespeare; c 25 books of songs; Masses and motets; 8 overtures for orch.; 6 concertos for keyboard (organ or harpsichord); 7 sonatas for 2 vlns. and bass; 8 harpsichord sonatas.

Arneiro, José Augusto Ferreira Veiga d' (b Macao, China, 22 Nov 1838; d San Remo, 7 Jul 1903), Portuguese composer.

Works incl. operas *Elisir di giovinezza* (Milan, 1877), *La derelitta* (after Ann Radcliffe) and *Don Bibas* (1885); ballet *Gina*; Te Deum and other church music.

Arnell, Richard (Anthony Sayer) (b London, 15 Sep 1917), English composer. Studied with John Ireland at the RCM in London and took the Farra Prize in 1938. From 1939 to 1947 he lived in NY, where he was consultant to the BBC's N. American service.

Works incl. operas *Love in Transit* (1958), *The Petrified Princess* (1959); ballets *Punch and the Child, Harlequin in April* and *The Great Detective* (after Conan Doyle) (1953); film music; symphs., symph. poem *Lord Byron* and other orchestral music; vln. concerto; 5 string 4tets; pf. and organ music.

Arnold, Denis (Midgley) (b Sheffield, 15

Dec 1926; d Budapest, 28 Apr 1986), English critic, teacher and musicologist. Studied at Sheffield Univ. and taught at Hull and Nottingham Univs. 1964–75; prof. of music at Oxford from 1975. He was a specialist in Renaissance and Baroque music. Author of book on Monteverdi; ed., *New Oxford Companion to Music* (1983).

Arnold, Malcolm (Henry) (b Northampton, 21 Oct 1921), English composer, formerly trumpeter. Studied at the RCM in London with a scholarship, 1938–41, then joined the LPO, becoming 1st trumpet in 1942. In 1945 he became 2nd trumpet of the BBC SO; he rejoined the LPO later as principal (1946–8). He later took up the career of a full-time comp. Hon. D.Mus., Exeter, 1969, CBE 1970.

Works incl. ballets *Homage to the Queen* (1953), *Rinaldo and Armida* (1955) and *Solitaire*; more than 80 film scores, incl. *The Bridge on the River Kwai*; incid. music for Shakespeare's *Tempest*; overture *Beckus the Dandipratt* for orch.; symph. for strings; 8 symphs. (1951–79); concertos for horn, clar. (2), fl. (2), ob., pf. duet and mouth organ; 2 string 4tets (1951, 1975); vln. and pf. sonata, vla. and pf. sonata; pf. works.

Arnold, Samuel (b London, 10 Aug 1740; d London, 22 Oct 1802), English composer. Chorister at the Chapel Royal under Gates and Nares; was engaged by Beard as comp. to Covent Garden Theatre in 1765, where he prod. the pasticcio *The Maid of the Mill* that year. Ed. a collection of *Cathedral Music* and the works of Handel. D.Mus., Oxford, 1773, and organist of the Chapel Royal, 1783. Founder of the Glee Club with Callcott in 1787. Organist of Westminster Abbey, 1793.

Works incl. operas and plays with music *The Maid of the Mill* (1765), *The Portrait* (1770), *The Castle of Andalusia, Gretna Green, Peeping Tom of Coventry* (1784), *Inkle and Yarica, The Enraged Musician* (on Hogarth's picture), *The Surrender of Calais* (1791), *Harlequin, Dr. Faustus* (1766), *The Mountaineers, The Shipwreck, Obi, or Three-fingered Jack* and many others; oratorios *Elisha, The Cure of Saul, The Resurrection* (1770), *The Prodigal Son* (1773); church music; overture for orch.; odes for chorus; harpsichord music; songs.

Arnoldson, Sigrid (b Stockholm, 20 Mar 1861; d Stockholm, 7 Feb 1943), Swedish soprano. Daughter of the tenor Oscar A. Studied with Maurice Strakosch and Désirée Artôt-Padilla, made her debut at Prague, 1885, as Rosina, and appeared in London

1887–94; other roles incl. Charlotte and Carmen.

Arnould, Madeleine Sophie (b Paris, 13 Feb 1740; d Paris, 22 Oct 1802), French soprano and actress. She made her debut in 1757. Sang Iphigenia in the fp of Gluck's *Iphigénie en Aulide* in Paris, 1774, and Eurydice in the Fr. version of his *Orfeo* the same year.

Aroldo, opera by Verdi (lib. by Piave), prod. Rimini, Teatro Nuovo, 16 Aug 1857. A revision of *Stiffelio* (1850).

Aronowitz, Cecil (b King William's Town, 4 Mar 1916; d Ipswich, 7 Sep 1978), South African-born British viola player. He studied at the RCM and played vln. in various London orchs. until the war. From 1949 he was princ. vla. successively of the Goldsbrough Orch. (later ECO), London Mozart Players and EOG: Britten's church parables at Aldeburgh. He was a founder member of the Melos Ensemble, in 1950, and was often heard in string 5tets with the Amadeus Quartet. Prof., RCM, 1948–75.

Arpeggio (It. *arpeggiare,* to play the harp), the notes of a chord played in rapid succession, either in regular time (as in instrumental and vocal exercises) or freely as an interpretation of the foll. sign:

played approximately:

Arpeggione, a 6-stringed instrument invented by G. Staufer of Vienna in 1823; a hybrid between a cello and a guitar, played with a bow and with a fretted fingerboard. Schubert wrote a sonata for it in 1824.

Arpicordo (It. = Harpsichord), another and much rarer It. name for the harpsichord.

Arquimbau, Domingo (b *c* 1758; d Seville, 26 Jan 1829), Spanish composer. Music dir. of Seville Cathedral, 1795–1829. Wrote a Mass, motets and sacred *villancicos.*

Arrangement, an adaptation of a melody or musical work for some other medium than that orig. intended. In some music of the 17th cent. and earlier, it can involve merely the spelling out of one of the possible versions implied in a relatively unspecific musical text. *See also* **Realization.**

Arrau, Claudio (b Chillán, 6 Feb 1903), Chilean pianist. First played in public aged 5, and in 1910 was sent to study in Berlin, where he settled from 1925 to 1940. Since 1941 he has lived in the USA. He is best known for his perfs. of the Romantic pf. repertory. London debut 1922; still active 1986.

Arriaga y Balzola, Juan Crisóstomo Antonio (b Bilbao, 27 Jan 1806; d Paris, 17 Jan 1826), Spanish violinist and composer. Played and comp. as a child and was sent to the Paris Cons. in 1821. His early death cut short a remarkable career.

Works incl. *Los esclavos felices* (The Happy Slaves, 1820), symph. in D and 3 string 4tets.

Arrieta y Corera, (Pascual Juan) Emilio (b Puente la Reina, Navarre, 21 Oct 1823; d Madrid, 11 Feb 1894), Spanish composer. Studied under Vaccai at the Milan Cons. and prod. his 1st opera there in 1845, returning to Spain the following year. Prof. of comp. at the Madrid Cons. from 1857 and director from 1868.

Works incl. It. operas *Ildegonda* (Milan, 1825), *La conquista di Granada* (1850; rev. as *Isabella la Católica,* 1855); zarzuelas *El dómino azul, El grumete, La Estrella de Madrid, Marina and c* 50 others.

Arrigoni, Carlo (b Florence, 5 Dec 1697; d Florence, 19 Aug 1744), Italian lutenist and composer. Gave concerts with Sammartini in London 1732–3, and pub. *10 Cantate da camera* there in 1732.

Arroyo, Martina (b Harlem, NY, 2 Feb 1936), American soprano. Debut NY, Carnegie Hall, 1958, and sang in Europe 1963–5 before Aida at NY Met 1965; later sang other Verdi roles, and Elsa and Donna Anna. CG from 1968. Concert perfs. in Varèse and Dallapiccola; she gave the fp of Stockhausen's *Momente* (Cologne, 1962).

Ars antiqua (Lat. = the old art), music of the late 12th and 13th cents., before the intro. of the *ars nova* in the 14th cent. A term originally used by 14th-cent. writers of the music immediately preceding their own time.

Ars nova (Lat. = the new art), the title of a treatise (*c* 1322) by Philippe de Vitry. It described a new and wider range of note-values which can be seen as the main difference between 14th-cent. music and that of the 13th cent. Hence the word is often used as a descriptive term for all 14th-cent. music, though stricter usage confines it to Fr. music of that cent. (for the It. repertory *see* **Trecento**); the most literal usage restricts it to Fr. works of the first few decades of the cent. (for the slightly later repertory, *see* **Ars subtilior**).

Ars subtilior (Lat. = the more refined art). A term found in the writings of Philipottus de

Caserta to describe a late 14th-cent. style of great notational and rhythmic complexity. Certain works by comps. such as Philipottus, Senleches, Ciconia and Asproys include cross-rhythms of a baffling complexity that has no parallels until the 20th cent.

Arsilda, Regina di Ponto, opera by Vivaldi (lib. by D. Lalli), prod. Venice, Teatro San Angelo, autumn 1716.

Art of Fugue, The. See **Kunst der Fuge.**

Artamene, opera by Albinoni (lib. by B. Vitturi), prod. Venice, Teatro di Sant' Angelo, 26 Dec 1740.

Opera by Gluck (lib. do.), prod. London, King's Theatre, Haymarket, 4 Mar 1746.

Artaria, Viennese firm of music pubs, founded in Mainz, 1765; moved to Vienna, 1766; closed in 1858. Prominent in the pub. of works by Haydn, Mozart and Beethoven.

Artaserse (*Artaxerxes*), opera by Abos (lib. by Metastasio), prod. Venice, Teatro di San Giovanni Grisostomo, Carnival 1746.

Opera by Gluck (lib. do.), prod. Milan, Teatro Regio Ducal, 26 Dec 1741. Gluck's 1st opera.

Opera by Graun (lib. do.), prod. Berlin, Opera, 2 Dec 1743.

Opera by Hasse (lib. do.), prod. Venice, Teatro San Giovanni Grisostomo, Feb 1730.

Opera by Jommelli (lib. do.), prod. Rome, Teatro Argentina, 4 Feb 1749.

Opera by Terradellas (lib. do.), prod. Venice, Teatro San Giovanni Grisostomo, Carnival 1744.

Opera by Vinci (lib. do.), prod. Rome, Teatro delle Dame, 4 Feb 1730.

Artaxerxes, opera by Arne (lib. by comp., trans. from Metastasio's *Artaserse*), prod. London, CG 2 Feb 1762.

Arteaga, Esteban (b Moraleja (Segovia), 26 Dec 1747; d Paris, 30 Feb 1799), Spanish scholar. He was a Jesuit priest, but after the suppression of the Order went to It. where he worked for many years with Padre Martini in Bologna. 5 treatises on music survive, the most important of them being that on opera, *Rivoluzioni del teatro musicale italiano,* pub. 1733–8.

Artôt, (Marguerite Josephine) Désirée (Montagney) (b Paris, 21 Jul 1835; d Berlin, 3 Apr 1907), Belgian mezzo. Pupil of Pauline Viardot-García. First sang at concerts in Belg. and Eng., but joined the Paris Opéra in 1858, debut as Fides. Other roles incl. Leonora (*Trovatore*), Rosina and Angelina. Later appeared in It., Ger. and Rus. Married Mariano Padilla in 1869.

Arts Council of Great Britain, a nat. organization formed in 1940 as the Council for the Encouragement of Music and the Arts (CEMA), whose charter was renewed under the new title, 9 Aug 1946. New charter 1967. Council also administers the Contemporary Music Network (frequent concerts promoted on country-wide basis).

Artusi, Giovanni Maria (b c 1540; d Bologna, 18 Aug 1613), Italian composer and theorist. His 4-part canzonets appeared in 1598, and his *L'Arte del Contrapunto* in 1586–9. Apart from his polemical works against Zarlino, Galilei and Bottrigari, his *L'Artusi, overo delle Imperfettioni della musica moderna* (1600) singles out 9 as yet unpub. madrigals by Monteverdi for special attack, to which the comp. replied in the preface to his 5th book of madrigals (1605). Here he promised a treatise, never completed, to be entitled *Seconda Prattica overo delle perfettioni della moderna musica,* in contradistinction to the 'Prima prattica' of the conservatives. The controversy was continued in two more works by Artusi, pub. under a pseud. (1606 and 1608), and by Monteverdi's brother Giulio Cesare in the preface to the *Scherzi musicali* of 1607.

Arundell, Dennis (b London, 22 Jul 1898), English actor, producer and composer. Educated at Tonbridge School and Cambridge, he prod. many operas and music plays, trans. several It. and Fr. libs. and wrote a book on Purcell (1927). In Cambridge and London he prod. the *Fairy Queen, Semele, Katya Kabanová* and *The Soldier's Tale.* He taught at the RNCM from 1974.

Ascanio, opera by Saint-Saëns (lib. by L. Gallet, after P. Meurice), prod. Paris, Opéra, 21 Mar 1890.

Ascanio in Alba, opera by Mozart (lib. by G. Parini), prod. Milan, Teatro Regio Ducal, 17 Oct 1771.

Ascension, L', work for orch. in 4 movts. by Messiaen; comp. 1933, vers. for organ 1934. Orch. version perf. Paris, Feb 1935.

Ashkenazy, Vladimir (b Gorky, 6 Jul 1937), Russian-born pianist and conductor. Toured US 1958; joint winner Tchaikovsky Comp., Moscow, 1963; moved to Brit. 1963 and became Icelandic citizen 1972. World tours in Romantic rep.; prin. cond. Philharmonia Orch. from 1981. He succeeded André Previn as music dir. of the RPO in 1986.

Ashwell, Thomas (Ashewell, Hashewell) (b c 1478; d after 1513), English composer. In 1508 he was *informator choristarum,* Lincoln Cathedral, and in 1513 held the equivalent post in Durham. His surviving works incl. four Masses, two (*God save King*

Harry and *Sancte Cuthberte*) in a fragmentary state and two (*Ave Maria* and *Jesu Christe*) complete.

Asioli, Bonifazio (b Correggio, 30 Aug 1769; d Correggio, 18 May 1832), Italian music scholar and composer. Worked in his native town at the beginning and end of his career, but in between was at Turin, Venice, Milan and Paris. Wrote much church, stage, vocal and instrumental music and several theoretical treatises.

Askenase, Stefan (b Lwów, 10 Jul 1896; d Cologne, 18 Oct 1985), Belgian pianist of Polish birth. He studied at Vienna with Emil von Sauer; debut 1919. He toured widely in Europe and S. America and was best known in Chopin. Belgian citizen from 1950; taught at Brussels Cons. 1954–61.

Asola, Giovanni Matteo (b Verona, *c* 1532; d Venice, 1 Oct 1609), Italian priest and composer. *Maestro di cappella* successively at Treviso (1577) and Vincenza (1578). Wrote church music, madrigals.

Aspelmayr, Franz (b Vienna, bap. 2 Apr 1728; d Vienna, 29 Jul 1786), Austrian composer attached to the Viennese court.

Works incl. melodrama *Pygmalion* (after Rousseau, 1776), *Singspiele*, ballets, incl. *Agamemnon vengé* (1771), *Acis et Galathée* (1773), *Ifigenie* (1773), symphs., chamber music.

Asproys (Hasprois), Johannes, French composer, one of the singers of the anti-pope at Avignon in 1394. Some of his *chansons* are in an early 15th-cent. MS. now at Oxford, Bodleian Library, Canonici misc. 213.

Asrael, symph. by Josef Suk (his second); written in memory of his wife and of Dvořák, his father-in-law. Fp Prague, 3 Feb 1907.

Assafiev, Boris Vladimirovich (b St Petersburg, 29 Jul 1884; d Moscow, 27 Jan 1949), Russian composer and critic. Studied philosophy at St Petersburg Univ. and music at the Cons., where he later became prof. Author of numerous books on composers, incl. Glinka, Tchaikovsky, Skriabin and Stravinsky, on Rus. and Cz. music etc., written under the name of Igor Glebov.

Works incl. OPERAS (9) incl. *Cinderella* (1906), *The Treasurer's Wife* (after Lermontov), *The Storm* (after Ostrovsky), *A Feast in Time of Plague* (Pushkin) (1940), *The Bronze Horseman* (Pushkin).

BALLETS (27) incl. *Solveig* (based on Grieg) (1918), *The Fountain of Bakhchisserai* (after Pushkin), *Lost Illusions* (after Balzac) (1935), *The Beauty is Happy* (after Gorky's story *Makar Chudra*), *Christmas Eve* (after Gogol).

INCID. MUSIC to Shakespeare's *Macbeth, Merchant of Venice* and *Othello,* Tirso de Molina's *Seducer of Seville* (*Don Juan*), Sophocles' *Oedipus Rex,* Schiller's *Fiesco* and *Don Carlos.*

ORCH. AND CHAMBER: 4 symphs. (1938–42), sinfonietta for orch., Suvarov Suite for wind insts.; pf. concerto; string 4tet; vla. solo sonata, sonata for tpt. and pf.; 6 Arias for cello and pf.; pf. works; choruses; songs.

Assai (It.) = much, very.

Assassinio nella cattedrale, L' (*Murder in the Cathedral*), opera by Pizzetti (lib. by comp. after T.S. Eliot's dramatic poem), prod. Milan, La Scala, 1 Mar 1958.

Assmayr, Ignaz (b Salzburg, 11 Feb 1790; d Vienna, 31 Aug 1862), Austrian organist and composer. Held several organist's posts at Salzburg and Vienna, was cond. of the Vienna Music Society and wrote oratorios and much church and other music.

Astaritta, Gennaro (b Naples, *c* 1745; d after 1803), Italian composer of *c* 40 operas, 1765–93, incl. the popular *Circe ed Ulisse,* and *L'isola disabitata* (Florence, 1773), *Armida* (Venice, 1777), *Rinaldo d'Asti* (St Petersburg, 1796).

Astarto, opera by G. Bononcini (lib. by P.A. Rolli, based on one by Zeno and P. Pariati), prod. London, King's Theatre, Haymarket, 19 Nov 1720.

Aston, Hugh (b *c* 1480; d Nov 1558), English composer. He took the B.Mus. at Oxford, 1510, and was *magister choristarum* at Newarke College, Leicester, 1525–48. His works include 6 votive antiphons and 2 Masses, a 'Hornepype' for keyboard, and possibly other keyboard music also. There are works on a ground bass of his by Whytbroke (for viols) and Byrd (for keyboard).

Astorga, Emanuele (Gioacchino Cesare Rincón) d' (b Augusta, Sicily, 20 Mar 1680; d Lisbon or Madrid, ? 1757), Italian nobleman and composer of Spanish descent. His opera, *Dafni,* was prod. in Genoa and Barcelona in 1709. His most famous work is a *Stabat Mater* (*c* 1707). He also wrote a number of chamber cantatas. From *c* 1721 he seems to have lived mainly in Spain and Portugal.

Astuzie femminili, Le (*Women's Wiles*), opera by Cimarosa (lib. by G. Palomba), prod. Naples, Teatro del Fondo, 16 Aug 1794.

At the Boar's Head, opera by Holst (lib. by comp., drawn from Shakespeare's *Henry IV*), prod. Manchester, 3 Apr 1925.

Atalanta, opera by Handel (lib. adapted

from *La caccia in Etolia* by B. Valeriani), prod. London, CG, 12 May 1736.

Atem gibt das Leben, (*Breathing gives Life*), work for chorus by Stockhausen; perf. Hamburg, 16 May 1975.

Athalia, oratorio by Handel (words by S. Humphreys), prod. Oxford, 10 Jul 1733.

Athalie, incid. music for Racine's tragedy by Mendelssohn, op. 74; choruses comp. 1843, overture 1844–5, prod. Charlottenburg, 1 Dec 1845.

The choruses were also set by Moreau (Saint-Cyr, 5 Jan 1691), Gossec (1785), Vogler (1786), J.A.P. Schulz (1786) and Boieldieu (1836).

Atherton, David (b Blackpool, 3 Jan 1944), English conductor. Conducted opera at Cambridge, and *Il Trovatore* at CG in 1967; 1976 fp Henze's *We Come to the River*. In 1968 gave fp Birtwistle's *Punch and Judy* (Aldeburgh) and became the youngest cond.

ever at Promenade Concerts. Also founded London Sinfonietta in 1968 and gave frequent perfs. of modern music. Music dir. San Diego SO from 1981. Guest cond. BBC SO.

Atlantida, L', scenic oratorio by Falla (text by comp., after J. Verdaguer); sketched 1926–46 and completed by E. Halffter; prod. Milan, La Scala, 18 Jun 1962

Atmosphères, work for orch. by Ligeti; fp Donaueschingen, 22 Oct 1961, cond. Rosbaud.

Atonality, the lack of a tonal centre. In its broadest sense it can be used for passages of free-flowing chromaticism which lose touch with tonality, as occasionally encountered in the music of Liszt and Wagner. More specifically it concerns the conscious attempt to compose without any tonal reference. It was in attempting to achieve this that Schoenberg devised **Serialism** (*q.v.*).

Universal Edition
(Alfred A. Kalmus Ltd)

Schoenberg, *3 Piano Pieces*,
op. 11 (1909)

ATONAL MUSIC

Attacca (It. imper. = attack, begin), a direction placed at the end of a movement indicating that the next movement is to be started without a pause.

Attacco (It. = attack), a short musical figure or phrase treated by imitation.

Attaingnant, Pierre (d Paris, 1552), French 16th-cent. music printer. He pub. many important music books between 1525 and his death, and his widow (*née* Pigouchet), whose father he had succeeded, continued after 1553.

Atterberg, Kurt (Magnus) (b Göteborg, 12 Dec 1887; d Stockholm, 15 Feb 1974), Swedish composer and conductor. First trained as a civil engineer, he studied music at the RAM in Stockholm under Hallén, and later at Munich, Berlin and Stuttgart. Music critic of *Stockholms Tidningen* from 1919. Cond. much in Europe.

Works incl. 5 operas; pantomime-ballets; incid. music for plays; Requiem (1914), *Järnbäraland* (*The Land of Iron-Carriers*), for chorus and orch. (1919); 9 symphs. (1 in memory of Schubert), 9 suites, *Swed. Rhapsody*, symph. poem *Le Fleuve, Rondeau rétrospectif* and *The Song* for orch.; symph. poem for baritone and orch.; concertos for vln., cello, pf. and horn; 3 string 4tets; cello and pf. sonata.

Attey, John (d Ross, Herefordshire, 1640), English composer. His vol. of 'Ayres' (1622) marks the virtual end of the lute-song in England.

Attila, opera by Verdi (lib. by T. Solera), prod. Venice, Teatro La Fenice, 17 Mar 1846.

Attwood, Thomas (b London, bap. 23 Nov 1765; d London, 24 Mar 1838), English organist and composer. He was a chorister at the Chapel Royal; later studied in Naples and Vienna, where he was a pupil of Mozart 1785–7. Organist of St Paul's Cathedral and comp. to the Chapel Royal from 1796 to his death. One of the original members of the Phil. Society in 1813, and a prof. at the RAM on its foundation in 1823. He was also a friend of Mendelssohn, whose 3 Preludes and Fugues for organ, op. 37, were dedicated to him.

Works incl. over 30 dramatic comps.; coronation anthems for George IV and William IV, service settings, anthems and other church music; songs, etc. His harmony and counterpoint exercises for Mozart also survive, with Mozart's corrections.

Atys, opera by Lully (lib. by Quinault), prod. at Saint-Germain, 10 Jan 1676 and fp Paris, Apr 1676

Opera by Piccinni (lib. do., altered by J.F. Marmontel), prod. Paris, Opéra, 22 Feb 1780.

Atzmon, Moshe (b Budapest, 30 Jul 1931), Israeli conductor. Won Liverpool Int. Competition 1964; cond. in Sydney and Hamburg 1969–76. Opera debut Berlin, 1969. Prin. cond. Basle SO from 1972.

Aubade (Fr. from *aube* = dawn) = morning song, in the same sense that a serenade is an evening song; cf. Span. *Alborada*.

Choreographic concerto by Poulenc, for pf. and 18 insts.; fp Paris, 18 Jun 1929.

Auber, Daniel François Esprit (b Caen, 29 Jan 1782; d Paris, 12 May 1871), French composer. Began to comp. early, but went to London as a young man to follow a commercial career. He attracted attention with his songs, however, and on his return to Paris in 1804 wrote cello concertos for the cellist Lamarre and a vln. concerto for Mazas. In 1805 he appeared with a comic opera, *L'Erreur d'un moment*, the lib. of which had previously been set by Dezède, but he did not prod. an opera in public until 1813 (*Le Séjour militaire*) and had no real success until 1820 (*La Bergère châtelaine*). In 1842 he became dir. of the Paris Cons. and in 1857 of the Imp. chapel.

Works incl. nearly 50 operas, e.g. *Emma* (1821), *Leicester, Le Maçon, La Muette de Portici (Masaniello)* (1828), *La Fiancée, Fra Diavolo* (1830), *Le Dieu et la Bayadère, Le Philtre, Le Serment, Gustave III, Le Cheval de bronze* (2 versions) (1835 and 1857), *Actéon, L'Ambassadrice, Le Domino noir* (1837), *Les Diamants de la couronne, La Part du diable, Haydée* (1847), *Marco Spada* (with a later ballet version), *Jenny Bell, Manon Lescaut* (1856), *La Circassienne.*

Aubert, Jacques (b Paris, 30 Sep 1689; d Belleville, 17 or 18 May 1753), French violinist and composer. Pupil of Senaillé; member of the king's 24 vlns. from 1727 and of the Paris Opéra orch. from 1728. Wrote numerous vln. concertos, concert suites and other instrumental works.

Aubert, Louis (b Paris, 15 May 1720; d Paris, after 1783), French violinist and composer, son of prec. He was violinist and 2nd cond. at the Paris Opéra, 1731–74. Wrote sonatas and other works for his instrument.

Aubin, Tony (Louis Alexandre) (b Paris, 8 Dec 1907; d Paris, 21 Sep 1981), French composer. Studied at the Paris Cons., where Dukas was his comp. master. Took the Prix de Rome in 1930. In 1939 he was app. head of the music dept. of the Paris-Mondial radio station and in 1946 prof. at the Paris Cons.

Works incl. suite *Cressida* for solo voices, chorus and orch. (1935); cantata *Actéon* (1930); *Symphonie romantique* and *Le Sommeil d'Iskander* for orch.; string 4tet; sonata and *Prélude, Récitatif et Final* for pf.; 6 Verlaine songs.

Aubry, Pierre (b Paris, 14 Feb 1874; d Dieppe, 31 Aug 1910), French musicologist and orientalist. Lectured on music hist. at the École des Hautes Études Sociales in Paris; did important research on Fr. medieval music.

Aucassin et Nicolete, a 13th-cent. French narrative in prose and verse. Its verse sections show a technique similar to that employed in the *chanson de geste*, in that each pair of lines is sung to the same tune constantly repeated, each section being rounded off by a single line sung to a different tune. Its alternation between prose and verse, however, classifies it as a *chante-fable*.

Aucassin et Nicolette, ou Les Mœurs du bon vieux temps, opera by Grétry (lib. by J.M. Sedaine, based on the French 13th-cent. tale), prod. Versailles, at court, 30 Dec 1779, 1st Paris perf., Comédie-Italienne, 3 Jan 1780.

Audefroi le Bastart (*fl.* 1190–1230), French poet and musician now known from 10 courtly *chansons* and 6 *chansons de toile*.

Auden, W(ystan) H(ugh) (1907–73), American poet of English birth. *See* **Bassarids** (Henze), **Bernstein** (*Age of Anxiety*), **Britten** (*Ascent of F.6, Ode to St Cecilia,* and *On this Island*), **Elegy for Young Lovers** (Henze), **Henze** (*Moralities,* 3 Auden poems), **Nabokov** (*Love's Labour Lost*), **Paul Bunyan** (Britten) **Our Hunting Fathers** (do.) **Rake's Progress** (Stravinsky).

Audran, Edmond (b Lyons, 12 Apr 1840; d Tierceville, 17 Aug 1901), French composer. Studied at Niedermeyer's school in Paris and 1st made his mark as a church organist and comp. at Marseilles and Paris, prod. a Mass; but later with operettas, the 1st of which, *L'Ours et le Pacha,* was prod. at Marseilles in 1862. His 1st prod. in Paris (1879) was *Les Noces d'Olivette.* Others incl. *La Mascotte* (1880), *Gillette de Narbonne* (based on Boccaccio) (1882), *La Cigale et la Fourmi* (based on La Fontaine) (1886), *La Poupée, Monsieur Lohengrin.*

Auer, Leopold (b Veszprém, 7 Jun 1845; d Loschwitz, 15 Jul 1930), Hungarian violinist. Pupil of Dont in Vienna and Joachim at Hanover. Prof. at the St Petersburg Cons. from 1868; he declined the ded. of Tchaikovsky's violin concerto but after revision of the solo part played it in the year of T.'s death. Went to USA after the Rus. Revolution.

Aufforderung zum Tanz (*Invitation to the Dance*), a pf. piece by Weber, op. 65, which he calls a *rondeau brillant,* in waltz form with a slow intro. and epilogue, comp. in 1819. Usually heard today in orch. version by Berlioz.

Aufgesang (Ger. = Fore-song). *See* **Bar.**

Aufstieg und Fall der Stadt Mahagonny (*Rise and Fall of the City of Mahoganny*), opera by Weill (lib. by Brecht), prod. Leipzig, 9 Mar 1930.

Auftakt (Ger.) = Upbeat.

Auftrittslied (Ger. = entry song), a song or air in a musical play or opera, esp. a German *Singspiel,* by which a character introduces and describes himself to the audience, either directly or by addressing another character or characters; e.g. Papageno's 1st song in Mozart's *Die Zauberflöte.*

Augenarzt, Der (*The Oculist*), opera by Gyrowetz (lib. by J.E. Veith), prod. Vienna, Kärntnertortheater, 1 Oct 1811.

Augenlicht, Das, work for chorus and orch. by Webern (text by H. Jone); comp. 1935, fp London, 17 Jun 1938, cond. Scherchen.

Augmentation, the enlargement of a musical figure or phrase by lengthening, usually doubling, the note-values.

Augmented, said of intervals normally 'perfect' (4th, 5ths, 8ves) or 'major' (2nds, 3rds, 6ths, 7ths) which have been made wider by a semitone:

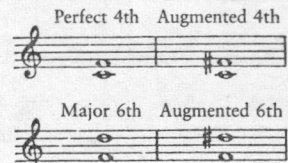

Augmented 6th chords. A group of chords that stand as the springboard for much of the more colourful harmonic style of the 19th cent. They depend for their effect on the interval of an augmented 6th between the flattened 6th degree and the sharpened 4th degree of the diatonic scale. Almost invariably their logical progression is to the dominant (V) or to a second inversion triad on the dominant (I$^6_4$) which in turn leads to the dominant.

The earliest of these, occasionally found even in the 17th cent., is the 'Italian 6th', a 3-note chord as follows (in C major):

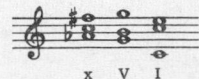

Aulen

Of the 4-note forms, the 'German 6th' first became a firm favourite at the end of the 18th cent. and was used with particular force by Beethoven. Since its structure (in equal temperament) is identical with that of the dominant 7th, the German 6th is extremely useful for modulation to distant keys:

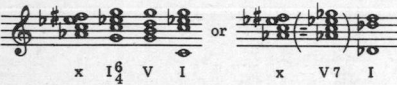

Less common is the 'French 6th', with its 2 middle notes a major 2nd apart:

Finally, it may be noted that from the middle of the 19th cent. many other variants of the principle appear. One possible analysis of the famous opening chord of Wagner's *Tristan und Isolde* is as an augmented 6th like the French 6th but with the 3rd flattened, thus sometimes called the 'Tristan 6th' (here transposed from A minor to C minor for comparison):

Aulen, Johannes, German 15th-cent. composer of a motet printed by Petrucci in 1505 and of a 3-voice Mass.

Auletta, Pietro (b Sant, Angelo a Scala nr. Avellino, 1698; d Naples, Sep 1771), Italian composer. He made his debut as an opera comp. at Naples in 1725 with *Il trionfo d'amore,* in which year he also received the title of *maestro di cappella* to the Prince of Belvedere. Several comic and then some serious operas followed. His most popular work, *Orazio* (1737), eventually became debased into a pasticcio by the addition of music by other comps., and was pub. in Paris as *Il maestro di musica* in 1753 under the name of Pergolesi.

Aulos, an ancient Gr. double-reed instrument, the equivalent of the Latin *tibia* and akin to the modern oboe. The double aulos often seen in pictures and sculpture would have enabled the melody to be accompanied by a drone.

Aureliano in Palmira, opera by Rossini (lib. by F. Romani), prod. Milan, La Scala, 26 Dec 1813. The overture was afterwards used for *Elisabetta regina d'Inghilterra,* and later for *Il barbiere di Siviglia.* Other parts of the music also appear in the latter work.

Auric, Georges (b Lodève, Hérault, 15 Feb 1899; d Paris, 23 Jul 1983), French composer. Studied at the Paris Cons. and the Schola Cantorum. Member of the group 'Les Six' and influenced by Satie and later by Stravinsky.

Works incl. comic opera *Sous le masque* (lib. by L. Laloy) (1907), ballets *Les Noces de Gamache* (from *Don Quixote*), *Les Matelots, La Pastorale, La Concurrence, Les Imaginaires;* incid. music to *Les Fâcheux* (Molière), *The Birds* (Aristophanes) (1928), *Volpone* (Ben Jonson) (1927), *Le Mariage de Figaro* (Beaumarchais), *Le 14 Juillet* (Rolland) (1931), with 9 others; film music *À nous la liberté* (René Clair), *Caesar and Cleopatra* (after Bernard Shaw); symph., suite, overture, *Fox-trot* and *Nocturne* for orch.; pf. concerto; pf. sonata and sonatina, *3 Pastorales* for pf.; *Chandelles romaines* for pf. duet; trio for ob., clar. and bassoon; vln. and pf. sonata; several song cycles.

Aus Italien (*From Italy*), symph. by R. Strauss, op. 16, comp. 1885–6 during and after a visit to It., fp Munich, 2 Mar 1887. The 4 movements are entitled *On the Campagna, The Ruins of Rome, On the Shore of Sorrento* and *Neapolitan Folk Life,* and the last contains a quotation of Denza's *Funiculì funiculà,* which Strauss took for a folksong.

Aus meinem Leben (*From my Life*), subtitle of Smetana's string 4tet in E min. (1876). Slow movt. depicts Smetana's love of his wife, and a sustained high note on the vln. in the finale suggests his tinnitus.

Austin, Frederic (b London, 30 Mar 1872; d London, 10 Apr 1952), English baritone and composer. Began his career as organist and music teacher at Liverpool, but appeared as a singer in 1902 and in opera at CG, London, in 1908. Artistic director of the BNOC from 1924. He arr. *The Beggar's Opera* for the revival at the Lyric Theatre, Hammersmith, London, in 1920, and the sequel, *Polly,* for that at the Kingsway Theatre, in 1922. Stage works incl. setting of Congreve's *The Way of the World.*

Austral (real name Wilson), **Florence** (b Melbourne, 26 Apr 1894; d Newcastle, NSW, 16 May 1968), Australian soprano. Entered Melbourne Cons. in 1914 and in 1918 studied in NY. She made her debut at

CG in 1922 as Brünnhilde. She was known as a leading Wagner singer, touring both Europe and America.

Auxcousteaux, Artus (or **Arthur**) (d 1656), French singer and composer. He was a singer in Louis XIII's chapel *c* 1613–27 and (?) at Noyon; later music master at the cathedral of Saint-Quentin and singer in the Sainte-Chapelle in Paris, becoming chaplain, precentor and canon at later dates.

Works incl. Masses, Magnificats, *Noëls* and other church music.

Avison, Charles (b Newcastle upon Tyne, bap. 16 Feb 1709; d Newcastle, 10 May 1770), English organist and composer. Pupil of Geminiani. He is chiefly remembered for his treatise *An Essay on Musical Expression* (1752), but also wrote a quantity of instrumental music, incl. 48 concertos for chamber orch. and (with John Garth) edited Marcello's Psalms in 1757.

Avolio (Avoglio), Signora, Italian 18th-cent. soprano, who sang in the fps of *Messiah* (1742), *Samson* (1743) and *Semele* (1744).

Avondano, Pedro Antonio (b Lisbon, bap. 16 Apr 1714; d Lisbon, 1782), Portuguese composer and violinist of Italian descent.

Works incl. comic opera *Il mondo della luna* (1765); sacred dramas *Il voto di Jefte* and *Adamo ed Eva* (1772); *Sinfonia* for strings; ? church music and harpsichord pieces destroyed in the Lisbon earthquake of 1755.

Ax, Emanuel (b Lwów, 8 Jun 1949), Polish-born American pianist. Studied Warsaw and in NY; debut there 1973. Won the 1st Rubinstein Comp., Israel, 1974. London from 1977. Admired in Romantic music, also plays Bartók and Schoenberg. Plays in trio with Yo-Yo Ma (*q.v.*) and Young Uck Kim.

Axman, Emil (b Rataje, Moravia, 3 Jun 1887; d Prague, 25 Jan 1949), Czech composer. Studied at Prague Univ. and was a comp. student of Novák.

Works incl. melodrama *Just Once*; cantatas and other choral works; 6 symphs., symph. poem *Sorrow and Hope*; suite, sinfonietta, suite *From the Beskides*, Morav. dances for orch.; vln. concerto; 4 string 4tets (1924–46), pf. trio, vln. and pf. sonata, cello and pf. sonata; 3 pf. sonatas, sonatina and other pf. works.

Axur (Salieri). *See* **Tarare**

Aylward, Theodore (b *c* 1730; d London, 27 Feb 1801), English organist and composer. Organist at several London churches. D. Mus. Oxford; app. prof. of music at Gresham Coll., London, 1771.

Works incl. incid. music for Shakespeare's *Cymbeline* and *Midsummer Night's Dream* (with M. Arne, Battishill and Burney) (1765); lessons for organ; canzonets for 2 voices; glees, catches and songs.

Ayre (Old Eng.), a 16th–17th-cent. song with predominantly melodic, as distinct from harmonic or contrapuntal, interest.

Ayrton, Edmund (b Ripon, bap. 19 Nov 1734; d London, 22 May 1808), English organist and composer. Studied with Nares at York Minster, became organist and choirmaster at Southwell Minster in 1754, vicar-choral at St Paul's Cathedral in London, 1767, and lay clerk at Westminster Abbey in 1780, also Master of the Children at the Chapel Royal. Mus.D., Cambridge, 1784. Comp. services and anthems.

Azione sacra (It. = sacred action), a 17th–18th-cent. term for a sacred drama with music or acted oratorio, e.g. Mozart's *La Betulia Liberata*.

Azione teatrale (It. = theatrical action), a 17th-cent. term for an opera or musical festival play.

Azzaiolo, Filippo, Italian 16th-cent. composer of *villotte*, popular madrigal-like part-songs. Byrd wrote a keyboard piece on the bass of his popular *Chi passa*.

B

B, the 7th note, or leading note, of the scale of C major. In Ger. B = B♭, and B♮ is represented by H.

B.A.C.H., a musical theme formed of the notes B♭, A, C, B♮ in German nomenclature (*see* above) and used by var. comps. as a ref. to Bach, who was himself the 1st to use it. Here are some exs.:

Albrechtsberger, Fugue for keyboard.

Bach, one of the subjects of the final fugue (unfinished) in *Die Kunst der Fugue* (4 organ fugues are prob. spurious).

Bach, J.C., Fugue for clavier or organ.

Busoni, *Fantasia contrappuntistica* for pf. and for 2 pfs.

Casella, *Ricercari sul nome di Bach* for pf.

Eisler, Trio on a 12-note row.

Honegger, *Prélude, arioso et Fughette* for piano.

d'Indy, *Beuron* in *Tableaux de voyage* for pf.

Karg-Elert, *Basso ostinato* in organ pieces *Sempre semplice*, op. 143; Passacaglia and Fugue, op. 150 for organ: Sonata, B♭ min., op. 46, for Kunstharmonium.

Koechlin, *Offrande musicale* for organ (later orch.).

Liszt, Fantasy and Fugue for organ.

Nielsen (R.), Ricercare, Chorale and Toccata for pf.

Piston, Chromatic Study for organ.

Reger, Fantasy and Fugue for organ.

Rimsky-Korsakov, Fugue in *Chopsticks* Vars. for pf. by var. comps.; 6 variations for pf., op. 10.

Schoenberg, Variations for orch., op. 31.

Schumann, 6 Fugues for organ or pedal pf.

BBC. See **British Broadcasting Corporation.**

B-la-F Quartet, a string 4tet on the name of Belaiev by Rimsky-Korsakov, Liadov, Borodin and Glazunov, perf. on M. P. Belaiev's 50th birthday, 22 Feb 1886. It is constructed on the notes B♭, A, F.

B Minor Mass. Bach's great setting of the Latin text begins in B min., but as a whole centres on D maj. The work was not comp. in one piece, however, but in four sections, some of them intended for separate perf. The *Kyrie* and *Gloria* (constituting in themselves a complete Lutheran short Mass) were written in 1733, and used to support Bach's application for the title of Court Comp. to the Elector of Saxony; the *Symbolum Nice-*

num (Creed) *c* 1748; *Sanctus* 1724; finally, the movements from *Osanna* to *Dona nobis pacem c* 1748. Several of the movements were adapted from earlier works, viz. church cantatas Nos. 11, 12, 29, 46, 120 and 171 and the secular cantata *Preise dein Glücke*.

Baal, opera by Friedrich Cerha (lib. by the comp. after Brecht), prod. Salzburg, 7 Aug 1981.

Baal Shem, 3 Pictures of Chassidic Life, for vln. and pf., by Bloch (1923). Vers. for vln. and orch., 1939; fp NY, 19 Oct 1941, with Szigeti.

Baaren, Kees van (b Enschede, 22 Oct 1906; d Oegstgeest, 2 Sep 1970), Dutch composer. Studied with Pijper. He was a leading Dutch exponent of serial music, and also very active as a teacher. From 1957 he was director of the Royal Cons. in The Hague.

Works incl. *The Hollow Men* (words by T.S. Eliot), cantata for chorus and orch. (1948); *Variazioni per Orchestra* (1959); a string 4tet and a wind 5tet (*Sovraposizione I and II*) (1963).

Babbitt, Milton (b Philadelphia, 10 May 1916), American composer. Studied at univs. of New York and Princeton, and also privately with Sessions. In 1938 he was app. to the music faculty at Princeton, where from 1943 to 1945 he also taught mathematics. His early work is much influenced by Webern, and later he turned to total serialism and electronic music.

Works incl. *Composition for 12 Instruments* (1948); *Composition for 4 Instruments, Composition for Vla. and Pf.; Composition for Synthesizer* (1961); *Vision and Prayer* (words by Dylan Thomas) with electronic tape accomp.; *Du*, a song cycle; var. electronic and film scores; an opera, *Kräfte* (1975); *A Solo Requiem* for sop. and 2 pfs. (1977).

Babell, William (b *c* 1690; d London, 23 Sep 1723), English harpsichordist, violinist and composer. Member of the royal band in London and for some years organist at All Hallows Church.

Works incl. chamber music; harpsichord pieces, airs from operas arr. for harpsichord.

Babin, Victor (b Moscow, 13 Dec 1908; d Cleveland, 1 Mar 1972), American pianist and composer of Russian birth. He studied with Schnabel and Schreker in Berlin and in 1933 married his pf. duettist partner, Vitya Vronsky; moved to the US 1937. He was dir. Cleveland Inst. of Music from 1961 and comp. 2 concertos for 2 pfs. and orch., which he gave with his wife.

Babi-Yar, sub-title of symph. no. 13 in Bb min., for bass, male chorus and orch. by Shostakovich (text by Yevtushenko). Comp. 1961 fp Moscow, 18 Dec 1962. Babi-Yar is site of World War II massacre of Rus. Jews by the Germans.

Babini, Matteo (b Bologna, 19 Feb 1754; d Bologna, 22 Sep 1816), Italian tenor. Began his career in the service of Frederick the Great and Catherine II of Rus.; afterwards sang in Vienna, London, It. and again in Berlin.

Baccaloni, Salvatore (b Rome, 14 Apr 1900; d New York, 31 Dec 1969), Italian bass. Sang as a boy in the choir of the Sistine Chapel. Studied with Kaschmann. As an adult made his 1st appearance in opera in Rome in 1922 as Rossini's Bartolo. A member of the opera co. at La Scala, Milan, from 1927. He sang also at CG, Glyndebourne and the NY Met (1940–62). He specialized in *buffo* roles, such as Dulcamara, Don Pasquale and Leporello.

Bacchantinnen, Die (*The Bacchantes*), opera by Wellesz (lib. by the comp., based on Euripides), prod. Vienna, Opera, 20 Jun 1931.

Baccusi, Ippolito (b Mantua, *c* 1550; d Verona, 1609), Italian composer. His works incl. madrigals, Masses, motets, psalms and Magnificats.

Bacewicz, Grazyna (b Łódź, 5 Feb 1909; d Warsaw, 17 Jan 1969), Polish composer and violinist. She studied composition at the Warsaw Cons. under Sikorski and later in Paris with Nadia Boulanger. Taught at Łódź Cons. 1934–5, returning to Paris in 1945. Her 4th string 4tet won 1st prize at the International Competition, Liège, in 1951.

Works incl. 4 symphs. (1945–53); 7 vln. concertos (1937–65); cello concerto; pf. concerto; concerto for string orch.; 7 string 4tets; 2 pf. 5tets; 6 vln. sonatas and various vln. pieces.

Bach, German 16th–18th-cent. family of musicians:

1. Veit B. (b ? Pressburg; d Wechmar nr. Gotha, before 1577).

2. Hans B. (b *c* 1550; d Wechmar, 1626), son of prec.

3. Lips (Philippus) B. (b Wechmar; d ? Wechmar, 10 Oct 1620), grandson of 1.

4. Johannes B. (b Wechmar, 26 Nov 1604; d Erfut, buried 13 May 1673), son of 2.

5. Christoph b. (b Wechmar, 19 Apr 1613; d Arnstadt, 12 Sep 1661), brother of prec.

6. Heinrich B. (b Wechmar, 16 Sep 1615; d Arnstadt, 10 Jul 1692), brother of prec.

7. Johann Christian B. (b Erfurt, bap. 17 Aug 1640; d Erfurt, buried 1 Jul 1682), son of 4.

8. Georg Christoph B. (b Erfurt, 6 Sep 1642; d Schweinfurt, 24 Apr 1697), son of 5.

9. Johann Christoph B. (b Arnstadt, bap. 8 Dec 1642; d Eisenach, 31 Mar 1703), son of 6.

10. Johann Aegidius B. (b Erfurt, 9 Feb 1645; d Erfurt, buried 22 Nov 1716), son of 4, brother of 7.

11. Johann Christoph B. (b Erfurt, 22 Feb 1645; d Arnstadt, 25 Aug 1693) son of 5.

12. Johann Ambrosius B. (b Erfurt, 22 Feb 1645; d Eisenach, 20 Feb 1695), son of 5, twin brother of 11, father of 25.

13. Johann Michael B. (b Arnstadt, bap. 9 Aug 1648; d Gehren, 17 May 1694), son of 6, father of 24.

14. Johann Günther B. (b Arnstadt, bap. 17 Jul 1653; d Arnstadt, 8 Apr 1683), son of 6.

15. Johann Nikolaus B. (b Eisenach, 10 Oct 1669; d Jena, 4 Nov 1753), son of 9.

16. Johann Christoph B. (b Erfurt, 16 Jun 1671; d Ohrdruf, 22 Feb 1721), son of 12, brother of 25.

17. Johann Christoph B. (b Eisenach, bap. 29 Aug 1676; d ? London, 1740), son of 9.

18. Johann Friedrich B. (b Eisenach, *c* 1682; d Mühlhausen, buried 8 Feb 1730), brother of prec.

19. Johann Michael B. (b Eisenach, bap. 1 Aug 1685; d ?), brother of prec.

20. Johann Bernhard B. (b Erfurt, bap. 25 Nov 1676; d Eisenach, 11 Jun 1749), son of 10.

21. Johann Ludwig B. (b Thal nr. Eisenach, 4 Feb 1677; d Meiningen, buried 1 May 1731), great-grandson of 3.

22. Johann Jakob B. (b Eisenach, 9 Feb 1682; d Stockholm, 16 Apr 1722), son of 12, brother of 25.

23. Johann Ernst B. (b Arnstadt, 5 Aug 1683; d Arnstadt, 21 Mar 1739), son of 11.

24. Maria Barbara B. (b Gehren, 20 Oct 1684; d Cöthen, Jul 1720), daughter of 13, 1st wife of 25.

25. Johann Sebastian B. (b Eisenach, 21 Mar 1685; d Leipzig, 28 Jul 1750), son of 12, husband of 24 and 28.

26. Johann Christoph B. (b Erfurt, bap. 17 Aug 1685; d Erfurt, buried 15 May 1740), son of 10.

27. Johann Lorenz B. (b Schweinfurt, 10

Sep 1695; d Lahm, 14 Dec 1773), grandson of 8.

28. Anna Magdalena B. (*née* Wilcke) (b 22 Sep 1701; d 27 Feb 1760), 2nd wife of 25.

29. Johann Elias B. (b Schweinfurt, 12 Feb 1705; d Schweinfurt, 30 Nov 1755), grandson of 8, brother of 27.

30. Samuel Anton B. (b Meiningen, 26 Apr 1713; d Meiningen, 1781), son of 21.

31. Johann Ernst B. (b Eisenach, bap. 30 Jan 1722; d Eisenach, 1 Sep 1777), son of 20.

32. Johann Michael B. (b Struth, 9 Nov 1745; d Elberfeld, 1820).

Children of Johann Sebastian Bach (25) by 24:

33. Catharina Dorothea B. (b Weimar, bap. 29 Dec 1708; d Leipzig, 14 Jan 1774).

34. Wilhelm Friedemann B. (b Weimar, 22 Nov 1710; d Berlin, 1 Jul 1784).

35. Johann Christoph B. (b and d Weimar, 23 Feb 1713), twin.

36. Maria Sophie B. (b and d Weimar, 23 Feb 1713), twin.

37. Carl Philipp Emanuel B. (b Weimar, 8 Mar 1714; d Hamburg, 14 Dec 1788).

38. Johann Gottfried Bernhard B. (b Weimar, 11 May 1715; d Jena, 27 May 1739).

39. Leopold Augustus B. (b Cöthen, 15 Nov 1718; d Cöthen, buried 28 Sep 1719).

Children of Johann Sebastian Bach (25) by 28:

40. Christiane Sophie Henrietta B. (b Cöthen or Leipzig, 1723; d Leipzig, 29 Jun 1726.

41. Gottfried Heinrich B. (b Leipzig, 26 Feb 1724; d Naumburg, buried 12 Feb 1763).

42. Christian Gottlieb B. (b Leipzig, bap. 14 Apr 1725; d 21 Sep 1728).

43. Elisabetha Juliane Frederica B. (b Leipzig, bap. 5 Apr 1726; d Naumburg, 24 Aug 1781), married Johann Christoph Altnikol.

44. Ernestus Andreas B. (b Leipzig, bap. 30 Oct 1727; d Leipzig, 1 Nov 1727).

45. Regine Johanne B. (b Leipzig, bap. 10 Oct 1728; d Leipzig, 25 Apr 1733).

46. Christiane Benedicta B. (b Leipzig, 31 Dec 1729; d Leipzig, 4 Jan 1730).

47. Christiane Dorothea B. (b Leipzig, bap. 18 Mar 1731; d Leipzig, 31 Aug 1732).

48. Johann Christoph Friedrich B. (b Leipzig, 21 Jun 1732; d Bückeburg, 26 Jan 1795).

49. Johann August Abraham B. (b Leipzig, 4 Nov 1733; d Leipzig, 6 Nov 1733).

50. Johann Christian B. (b Leipzig, 5 Sep 1735; d London, 1 Jan 1782).

51. Johanne Caroline B. (b Leipzig, bap. 30 Oct 1737; d 18 Aug 1781).

52. Regine Susanna B. (b Leipzig, bap. 22 Feb 1742; d 14 Dec 1809)

Bach, Carl Philipp Emanuel (b Weimar, 8 Mar 1714; d Hamburg, 14 Dec 1788), German harpsichordist and composer (37 above), 2nd son of J. S. and Maria Barbara B. (25 and 24 above). Educ. at St Thomas's School, Leipzig, and at the univs. of Leipzig (1731–4) and Frankfurt an der Oder(1734–8), where he studied law. His musical training, according to himself, he received entirely from his father. He was connected with the household of the Crown Prince of Prussia from 1738, and in 1740, on the latter's accession as King Frederick II, he was app. harpsichordist to the court at Berlin and Potsdam. In 1744 he married Johanna Maria Dannemann, and in 1747 his father visited him at court. His most important works at this time were keyboard pieces, which contributed much to the development of a more homophonic style and modern formal procedures. His treatise on keyboard playing (*Versuch uber die wahre Art das Clavier zu spielen*, 1753 and 1762) is a valuable guide to contemporary practice. Bach found Berlin restricting, partly because his duties involved only harpsichord playing, partly because of the stiff-necked conservatism of the king, and in 1768 he moved to Hamburg as municipal director of music at the 5 principal churches. Burney visited him there in 1772, and commented on his remarkable improvising. In Hamburg Bach had wider scope, directing concerts, etc., with great success, and there he wrote most of his music for large forces, e.g. oratorios.

Works incl. oratorios *Die Israeliten in der Wüste* (1769) and *Die Auferstehung und Himmelfahrt Jesu* (1780); Magnificat (1749), *Heilig (Sanctus)* for double choir, Passions and other church music; 19 symphs.; 50 keyboard concertos; c 200 keyboard pieces (sonatas, fantasias, rondos, etc.), odes, songs, etc.

Bach, Johann Ambrosius (b Erfurt, 22 Feb 1645; d Eisenach, 20 Feb 1695), German organist and composer (12 above). Born as the twin of Johann Christoph B. (11 above) and taught by his father Christoph B. (5 above). He became town musician at Erfurt in 1667, marrying Elisabeth Lämmerhirt there on 8 Apr 1668. In 1671 he was app. town musician at Eisenach. His wife died on 3 May 1694 and he married Barbara Margaretha Keul on 27 Nov but died himself 3 months later.

Bach, Johann (John) Christian (b Leipzig, 5 Sep 1735; d London, 1 Jan 1782), German clavier player and composer (50 above), youngest son of J.S. and Anna Magdalena B. (25 and 28 above). Pupil of his father and, after the latter's death in 1750, of his brother Carl Philipp Emanuel (37 above) in Berlin. In 1756 he went to Italy, studying under Padre Martini in Bologna; embraced Roman Catholicism, wrote much Lat. church music, and in 1760 was app. organist of Milan Cathedral. His 1st opera, *Artaserse*, was prod. at Turin in 1760. Two years later he went to London, where he remained for the rest of his life. In 1763 he prod. his 1st opera for London, *Orione,* and was app. music master to Queen Charlotte. In 1764 he founded with C.F. Abel a series of subscription concerts which continued till 1781, and in the same year befriended the young Mozart on his visit to London. Bach visited Mannheim in 1772 and 1776, and Paris in 1778, where his last opera was prod. in 1779. His popularity in London declined in his last years and he died in obscurity.

Works incl. operas *Artaserse* (1760), *Catone in Utica* (1761), *Alessandro nell' Indie* (all Metastasio), *Orione ossia Diana vendicata, Zanaida* (1763), *Adriano in Siria* (1765), *Carattaco* (1767), *Temistocle* (1772), *Lucio Silla* (1774), *La Clemenza di Scipione* (1778), *Amadis de Gaule*; oratorio *Gioas rè di Giuda*; church music; over 90 symphs. and similar works for orch.; *c* 40 concertos and over 30 sonatas for clavier; chamber music; Eng. and It. cantatas, arias, songs; serenata *Endimione* (after Metastasio), perf. King's Theatre, London, 6 Apr 1772.

Bach, Johann Christoph (b Arnstadt, bap. 8 Dec 1642; d Eisenach, 31 Mar 1703), German organist and composer (9 above). Became organist at Eisenach in 1665 and remained there to the end of his life. Comp. motets, church cantatas, chorale preludes for organ and harpsichord music.

Bach, Johann Christoph (b Erfurt, 16 Jun 1671; d Ohrdruf, 22 Feb 1721), German organist (16 above). Pupil of Pachelbel at Erfurt. In Oct 1694 he married Dorothea von Hof, and the next year he took his young brother Johann Sebastian (25 above) into his house after their parents' death.

Bach, Johann Christoph Friedrich (b Leipzig, 21 Jun 1732; d Bückeburg, 26 Jan 1795), German composer (48 above), son of J.S. and Anna Magdalena B. (25 and 28 above). Educ. at St Thomas's School and Leipzig Univ., where he studied law. Received his music training from his father, and in 1750 was app. chamber musician to Count Wilhelm of Schaumburg-Lippe in Bückeburg, where he remained for the rest of his life, becoming *Konzertmeister* in 1759. He married the court singer Elisabeth Münchhausen in 1755. In 1778 he visited his brother Johann Christian in London.

Among his most notable works are the oratorios on words by Johann Gottfried Herder (attached to the court at Bückeburg 1771–4), *Die Kindheit Jesu* and *Die Auferweckung Lazarus*; a third oratorio and an opera, *Brutus*, both on words by the same poet, are lost. Other works incl. Passion oratorio *Der Tod Jesu* (words by Ramler); cantatas (some with Herder); 20 symphs.; keyboard concertos and sonatas; chamber music.

Bach, Johann Michael (b Arnstadt, bap. 9 Aug 1648; d Gehren, 17 May 1694), German organist, instrument maker and composer (13 above). Organist and parish clerk at Gehren from 1673. Comp. motets, sacred arias, etc.

Bach, Johann Sebastian (b Eisenach, 21 Mar 1685; d Leipzig, 28 Jul 1750), German organist and composer (25 above). After his father's death in 1695 he was a pupil of his brother Johann Christoph in Ohrdruf. At 15 he became a chorister in Lüneburg, where he may have had organ lessons from Böhm. App. violinist in the court orch. of the Duke of Weimar in 1703, but left the same year to become organist in Arnstadt, from where in 1705 he took leave to travel to Lübeck, to hear Buxtehude play. In 1707 moved to Mühlhausen, where he married his cousin Maria Barbara Bach. A year later returned to Weimar as court organist, remaining there for nine years. In 1717 app. *Kapellmeister* to the court of Prince Leopold of Anhalt-Cöthen. His wife died in 1720, and he married Anna Magdalena Wilcke in 1721. At Cöthen Bach had little opportunity for church music and there he wrote mainly instrumental works, but in 1723 he returned to church work when he succeeded Kühnau as Cantor of St Thomas's in Leipzig, where he remained for the rest of his life. In 1747, with his eldest son, Wilhelm Friedemann, he visited the court of Frederick the Great at Potsdam, where his second son, Carl Philipp Emanuel, was court harpsichordist. Two years later his eyesight failed; an operation in 1750 was unsuccessful, and he spent his last months totally blind.

Works incl. CHURCH CANTATAS: 200 are extant. Among those most frequently perf. are no. 1 *Wie schön leuchtet der Morgenstern* (1725), no. 4 *Christ lag in Todesbanden* (1708), no. 6 *Bleib bei uns, denn es will Abend werden* (1725), no. 8 *Liebster Gott, wann werd ich Sterben?* (1724), no. 11 *Lobet Gott in seinen Reichen* (*Ascension Oratorio*, 1735), no. 12 *Weinen, Klagen, Sorgen, Zagen* (1714), no. 20 *O Ewigkeit, du Donnerwort* (1724), no. 21 *Ich hatte viel Bekümmernis* (*c* 1714), no. 29 *Wir danken dir, Gott* (1731), no. 34 *O ewiges Feuer, O Ursprung der Liebe* (*c* 1740), no. 36 *Schwingt freudig euch empor* (1731), no. 51 *Jauchzet Gott in allen Landen* (1730), no. 55 *Ich armer Mensch, ich Sündenknecht* (1726), no. 56 *Ich will den Kreuzstab gerne tragen* (1726), no. 57 *Selig ist der Mann* (1725), no. 61 *Nun komm der Heiden Heiland* (1714), no. 63 *Christen, ätzet diesen Tag* (*c* 1716), no. 68 *Also hat Gott die Welt geliebt* (1725), no. 76 *Die Himmel erzählen die Ehre Gottes*, no. 80 *Ein feste Burg ist unser Gott* (1724), no. 82 *Ich habe genug* (1727), no. 106 *Gottes Zeit ist die allerbeste Zeit* (*c*. 1707), no. 132 *Bereitet die Wege, bereitet die Bahn* (1715), no 140 *Wachet auf, ruft uns die Stimme* (1731), no. 147 *Herz und Mund und Tat und Leben* (1723), no. 152 *Tritt auf die Glaubensbahn* (1714), no. 158 *Der Friede sei mit dir*, no. 169 *Gott soll allein mein Herze haben* (1726), no. 191 *Gloria in excelsis Deo* (*c*. 1740).

SECULAR CANTATAS: no. 201 *Der Streit zwischen Phoebus und Pan* (1729), no. 202 *Weichet nur, betrübte Schatten* (*c* 1720), no. 208 *Was mir behagt ist nur die muntre Jagd* (1713), no. 209 *Non sa che sia dolore*, no. 211 *Schweigt stille, plaudert nicht* (*Coffee Cantata*, 1734), no. 213 *Hercules auf dem Scheidewege* (1733: most of the music later adapted for use in the *Christmas Oratorio*).

OTHER CHURCH MUSIC: Mass in B min., BWV 232, assembled *c* 1748 from music previously composed by Bach; 4 *Missae breves*, in F, A, G min. and G (late 1730s); 5 settings of the *Sanctus*; *Magnificat* in E♭ BWV 243 (1723, including 4 Christmas texts; rev. *c* 1730, in D, without Christmas texts); *St Matthew Passion* (11 Apr 1727 or 15 Apr 1729); *St John Passion* (7 Apr 1724, later rev.); *Christmas Oratorio* BWV 248, 6 cantatas for Christmas to Epiphany (perf. 1734–5); 6 motets BWV 225–30, *Singet dem Herrn ein neues Lied, Der Geist hilft unser Schwachheit auf, Jesu, meine Freude, Fürchte dich nicht, Komm, Jesu, komm!*

Lobet den Herrn; Easter Oratorio (1 Apr 1725) BWV 249.

ORGAN: 19 preludes and fugues, incl. E♭, ('St Anne') (1739) and E min. ('Wedge') (*c* 1730) BWV 548; 6 trio sonatas BWV 525–30, E♭, C min., D min., E min., C and G); Toccata and Fugue in D min. ('Dorian') BWV 538 and D min. BWV 565 (now doubtful); Fantasia and Fugue in C min. BWV 562 and G min. BWV 542; Toccata, Adagio and Fugue in C BWV 564; 6 concertos BWV 592–7, all transcriptions from other composers, including Vivaldi; 4 duets BWV 802–5; 4 fantasias, in B min., G and C(2); *Pastorale* in F BWV 590 (*c* 1710); 134 chorale preludes BWV 599–768, some of the best known being *Allein Gott in der Höh' sei Ehr* BWV 711, *An Wasserflüssen Babylon* BWV 653, *Ein feste Burg* BWV 720, *In dulci jubilo* BWV 729, *Jesu, meine Freude* BWV 713, *Komm Gott Schöpfer* BWV 667, *Liebster Jesu, wir sind hier* BWV 706, *Vom Himmel hoch* BWV 700, *Wachet auf* BWV 645; 3 Chorale partitas BWV 766–8.

OTHER KEYBOARD: The Well-tempered Clavier, Books 1 (1722) and 2 (*c* 1740), 24 preludes and fugues in each, BWV 846–93; 16 concertos BWV 972–87 (Weimar, 1708–17), all arrs. of works by other composers; Capriccio in B♭, on the departure of a beloved brother BWV 992; Chromatic Fantasia and Fugue in D min. BWV 903 (1720); 6 English Suites BWV 806–11 in A, A min., G min., F, E min. and D min.; 6 French Suites BWV 812–17 in D min., C min., B min., E♭, G and E; *Goldberg Variations* BWV 988; 15 Inventions BWV 772–86; 15 Sinfonias BWV 787–801; *Italian Concerto* BWV 971; 6 partitas BWV 825–30, in B♭, C min., A min., D, G and E min.; 7 toccatas BWV 910–16, in F♯ min., C min., D, D min., E min., G min. and G, 9 fugues, 3 on themes by Albinoni.

CHAMBER: 3 Partitas for solo vln., in B min., D min. and E, and 3 Sonatas for solo vln., in G min., A min. and C BWV 1001–6 (Cöthen, *c* 1720); 6 Sonatas for vln. and harpsichord in B min., A, E, C min., F min. and G BWV 1014–19; 6 Suites for solo cello, in G, D min., C, E♭, C min. and D BWV 1007–12 (*c* 1720); 3 Sonatas for viola da gamba and clavier, in G, D and G min. BWV 1027–9 (*c*1720); Partita in A min. for solo flute BWV 1013 (early 1720s); *The Musical Offering* BWV 1079 (1747) for fl., vln. and continuo; *The Art of Fugue* BWV 1080 (*c* 1745–50), for keyboard.

ORCHESTRAL: concertos, 6 Brandenburg, in F, F, G, G, D and B♭ BWV 1046–51 (1721), for vln. in A min. and E, for two vlns.

in D min., for fl., vln. and harpsichord in A min., 7 for harpsichord and strings BWV 1052–8, 3 for two harpsichords, 2 for three and 1 for four; 4 orch. suites in C, B min., D and D BWV 1066–9; concerto in D min. for vln. oboe and strings is a reconstruction from the C min. concerto for 2 harpsichords.

'Bach' Trumpet, a special brass wind instrument of the tpt. type invented by Kosleck of Berlin and improved by Walter Morrow of London, so devised as to be capable of playing the high clarino parts in the works of Bach and his contemporaries and forerunners; first heard at Eisenach in 1884.

Bach, Wilhelm Friedemann (b Weimar, 22 Nov 1710; d Berlin, 1 Jul 1784), German organist and composer (34 above), eldest son of J.S. and Maria Barbara B. (25 and 24 above). Educ. at St Thomas's School and Leipzig Univ.; received his musical training from his father. App. organist of St Sophia's, Dresden, in 1723, and in 1746 succeeded Zachau as organist of St Mary's, Halle. Married Dorothea Elisabeth Georgi in 1751. He resigned his post in Halle in 1764, and never held another permanent position, living an unsettled life and attempting to support his family mainly by teaching. In 1770 he moved to Brunswick, and in 1774 finally to Berlin. There his remarkable organ playing could still arouse astonishment, but his last years were spent in increasing poverty.

Works incl. cantatas and other church music; 9 symphs.; keyboard conertos; 9 sonatas, 12 fantasias, and other works for keyboard; organ music.

Bachauer, Gina (b Athens, 21 May 1913; d Athens, 22 Aug 1976), Greek pianist of Austrian parentage. Won Medal of Honour at an international competition in Vienna, 1933, and from 1933 to 1935 took occasional lessons with Rakhmaninov. Made her professional debut in Athens in 1935; London debut 1947, NY 1950.

Bachianas Brasileiras, 9 pieces for various inst. combinations by Villa-Lobos, in which Brazilian rhythms are treated in the spirit of Bach's counterpoint (1930–44).

Bachmann, Hermann (b Kottbus, 7 Oct 1864; d Berlin, 5 Jul 1937), German baritone. He sang at Halle 1890–94 and Nuremberg 1894–7. From 1897 he was a leading member of the Berlin Hofoper; worked also as a prod. from 1910 and taught singing after his retirement in 1917. He appeared as Kothner at the 1892 Bayreuth Festival and sang Wotan in the *Ring* cycles cond. by Felix Mottl in 1896. Recorded Escamillo in 1909.

Bachofen, Johann Caspar (b Zurich, 26 Dec 1695; d Zurich, 23 Jun 1755), Swiss composer. Cantor of the grammar school in Zurich, 1720, and of the *Grossmünster*, 1742. He compiled and partly comp. several books of hymns and sacred songs, and in 1759 wrote a setting of the Passion oratorio by Brockes.

Bachrich, Sigismund (b Zsambokreth, 23 Jan 1841; d Vienna, 16 Jul 1913), Hungarian violinist and composer. Studied at the Vienna Cons. Played and cond. in Vienna and Paris, became prof. at the Vienna Cons. and played vla. in the Phil. and Opera Orch. and with the Rosé 4tet.

Works incl. operas *Muzzedin* (1883) and *Heini von Steier* (1884), operetta *Der Fuchs-Major*; ballet *Sakuntala* (after Kalidasa), etc.

Bäck, Sven-Erik (b Stockholm, 16 Sep 1919), Swedish composer and violinist. Studied comp. with Rosenberg at the Stockholm Cons., 1940–44, and later at the Schola Cantorum, Basle.

Works incl. *Ett Spel om Maria*; a scenic oratorio; vln. concerto; 2 string 4tets; string 5tet; songs and pf. music.

Backfall = Appoggiatura (taken from the note above).

Backhaus, Wilhelm (b Leipzig, 26 Mar 1884; d Villach, 5 Jul 1969), German pianist. Studied at the Leipzig Cons. under A. Reckendorf until 1899, and then with d'Albert in Frankfurt. In 1905 he taught at the RMCM, winning the Rubinstein Prize in the same year. He then began his professional concert career. Backhaus excelled in the standard repertory, esp. the sonatas of Beethoven.

Bacon, Ernst (b Chicago, 26 May 1898), American pianist, conductor and composer. Studied music at Chicago and in Vienna, later in the USA with Bloch and Eugene Goossens. In 1925 he was app. pf. prof. at the Eastman School of Music, Rochester, NY; in 1945 director of the music school of the Univ. of Syracuse, NY.

Works incl. musical comedy *Take your Choice*; musical play *A Tree on the Plains*; cantatas *Ecclesiastes* and *From Emily's Diary* (Emily Dickinson); *Dr. Franklin*, musical play (1976); 3 symphs. (1932, 1937, 1961), 2 suites and other orchestral musical; settings of Dickinson and Whitman for voice and orch.; pf. 5tet.

Bacquier, Gabriel (b Béziers, 17 May 1924), French baritone. Debut Nice, 1950. Brussels from 1953, Paris from 1956. Glyndebourne 1962, CG 1964, both as Mozart's Count. Other roles incl. Scarpia, Don Giovanni and Falstaff.

Bachus et Ariane, ballet in 2 acts by Roussel, scenario by A. Hermant; prod. Paris, Opéra, 22 May 1931. Suite no. 1 for orch. perf. Paris, 2 Apr 1933, cond. Munch; Suite no. 2 perf. Paris, 2 Feb 1934, cond. Monteux.

Badescu, Dinu (b Craiova, 17 Oct 1904), Rumanian tenor. Debut Cluj, 1931, as Germont (baritone). Tenor debut as Alessandro Stradella. Bucharest Opera 1934–61, in Verdi and Puccini. In 1937 he sang Calaf and Faust at the Warsaw Opera, with Shalyapin; appeared in It. 1938 and throughout occupied Europe during the war. Vienna Staatsoper from 1948, in about 50 roles; E. Europe 1955–61.

Badinerie (Fr., lit. teasing, frivolity, playfulness), a title given, sometimes as *Badinage*, by Fr. and Ger. comps. of the 18th cent. to light, playful pieces in quick 2–4 time (e.g. final movement of Bach's B min. Orch. Suite for fl. and strings).

Badings, Henk (Hendrik Herman) (b Bandoeng, Java, 17 Jan 1907; d Maarheeze, 26 Jun 1987), Dutch composer. Began his career as a mining engineer, but studied music with Pijper and in 1935 abandoned science entirely for music. Prof. at the Music Lyceum, Amsterdam, and the Rotterdam Cons. Director of the Royal Cons. at The Hague, 1941.

Works incl. opera *The Night Watch* (after Rembrandt) (1942); ballets and incid. music for plays; a cantata; 14 symphs. (1932–68); symph. variations; *Heroic Overture*; vln. concerto, cello concerto, concerto for 2 vlns. and orch.; recitations with orch.; 4 string 4tets; vln. and cello sonatas; pf. pieces. From 1956 he comp. electronic music, incl. 2 operas (*Salto mortale*, 1959).

Badini, Ernesto (b San Colombano, 14 Sep 1876; d Milan, 6 Jul 1937), Italian baritone. Debut 1895, Rossini's Figaro. He sang under Toscanini at La Scala and took part there in the fps of Giordano's *La cena delle beffe* (1924) and Wolf-Ferrari's *Sly* (1927); he had created Gianni Schicchi there in 1922 and repeated the role at CG, 1924. At the Teatro Costanzi, Rome, he sang in the 1921 fp of Mascagni's *Il piccolo Marat*. Other roles incl. Beckmesser, Ford, Colline and Malatesta.

Badura-Skoda, Paul (b Vienna, 6 Oct 1927), Austrian pianist. He studied with Edwin Fischer in Vienna, and made his debut there in 1948; NY debut 1953. He has pub. books on the piano music of Mozart and Beethoven, and excells as a perf. of these comps. as well as of Schubert.

Bagatelle (Fr. = trifle), a short piece, generally of a light or humorous character.
Bagatelles. Beethoven pub. 3 sets: 7, op. 33, comp. 1782–1802; 11, op. 119, comp. 1821; 6, op. 126, comp. 1824.

Bagpipe, an instrument prod. its sound by wind stored up in a bag filled by the player through a mouthpiece; the melody is fingered on a pipe attached to that bag, called the chaunter, while a drone-bass is sounded continually by 2 or 3 additional pipes giving out fixed notes. In some types the wind was supplied by bellows.

Bahr-Mildenburg, Anna (b Vienna, 29 Nov 1872; d Vienna, 27 Jan 1947), Austrian mezzo and soprano. Made her 1st appearance at Hamburg in 1895 as Brünnhilde, under Mahler, with whom she had an affair. She became a noted Wagner and Strauss singer and sang in London between 1906 and 1913; 1st Clytemnestra in London, 1910. Bayreuth 1897–1914, as Kundry and Ortrud. Other roles inc. Reiza, Waltraute, Norma, Adriano, Amneris and Isolde.

Bailey, Norman (b Birmingham, 23 Mar 1933), English baritone. Debut Vienna, 1959, and sang in Ger. during the 1960s (Hans Sachs in Bremerhaven, 1967) before Sachs with the SW Co. in 1968; also sang this role in his debuts at Bayreuth (1969) and NY Met (1976). Specialist in Wagner rep. and sang in fp of Goehr's *Behold the Sun* (Duisburg, 1985).

Baillie, Isobel (b Hawick, 9 Mar 1895; d Manchester, 24 Sep 1983), Scottish soprano. Debut Manchester, 1921. Sang in Lieder and oratorio in Eng. and US (1000 perfs. of *Messiah*). One of 16 singers in Vaughan Williams's *Serenade to Music*, 1938. DBE 1978; autobiog., *Never Sing Louder than Lovely* (1982).

Baillot, Pierre (Marie François de Sales) (b Passy nr. Paris, 1 Oct 1771; d Paris, 15 Sep 1842), French violinist. Studied in Rome and later under Catel, Cherubini and Reicha in Paris; joined Napoleon's private band, 1802, and began to give chamber concerts in 1814. Was prof. at the Cons. and wrote works for his instrument and chamber music.

Bainbridge, Simon (b London, 30 Aug 1952), English composer. He studied at the RCM and has taught there.

Works incl. *Music to Oedipus Rex* (1969); *Heterophony* for orch. (1970); *Spirogyra* for chamber orch. (1970); wind quintet (1971); string 4tet; vla. concerto (1977); *Landscape and Woods* for sop. and chamber ens. (1981).

Bainton, Edgar L(eslie) (b London, 14 Feb 1880; d Sydney, 8 Dec 1956), English composer and teacher. Studied at the RCM in London and in 1901 was app. prof. of pf. and comp. at the Cons. of Newcastle upon Tyne, of which he became principal in 1912. In 1934 he went to Australia as director of the State Cons. at Sydney (1934–47). He wrote operas and orch. and chamber music.

Baird, Tadeusz (b Grodzisk Masowiecki, 26 Jul 1928; d Warsaw, 2 Sep 1981), Polish composer. Studied at Łódź Cons. Imprisoned in World War II. His music is influenced by serialism, esp. by Berg.

Works incl. opera *Jutro (Tomorrow,* after Conrad) (1966); 3 symphs.; *Cassation for Orch.*; *4 Essays for Orch.*; *Expressions* for vln. and orch. (1959); pf. concerto; other orchestral music; *Goethe Letters,* for bar., chorus and orch. (1970).

Bairstow, Edward C(uthbert) (b Huddersfield, 22 Aug 1874; d York, 1 May 1946), English organist, conductor and composer. After var. organist's posts he took the D.Mus. at Durham in 1901 and became organist and choirmaster at York Minster in 1913. Ed. *The Eng. Psalter* and wrote *The Evolution of Musical Form* and (with Plunket Greene) *Singing Learnt from Speech.* Prof. of music at Durham Univ., 1929–46. Knighted 1932.

Works incl. services, anthems; org. music; vars. for 2 pfs.

Baiser de la fée, Le (Stravinsky). *See* Fairy's Kiss.

Baiser et la quittance, Le (*The Kiss and the Receipt*), opera by Boieldieu, Isouard, R. Kreutzer and Méhul (lib. by L. Picard, M. Dieulafoy and C. de Longchamps), prod. Paris, Opéra-Comique, 18 Jun 1803.

Baker, (Dame) Janet (b York, 23 Mar 1933), English mezzo. Opera debut 1959, Oxford. Sang with Handel Opera Society and EOG and in Birmingham before international career; CG and US from 1966. Roles incl. Ariodante, Rameau's Aricie, Dorabella, Berlioz's Dido, Cavalli's Callisto and Monteverdi's Penelope and Poppaea. Retired from opera 1982, singing Mary Stuart and Gluck's Alceste in London and Orpheus at Glyndebourne. Sings Bach, Britten and Mahler in concert. DBE 1976.

Bakfark, Balint Valentin (b Brasso [Kronstadt], 1507; d Padua, 22 Aug 1576), Hungarian, later Polish, lutenist and composer also known by name of Greff. He went into royal service, learnt the lute, later lived in France and in 1549–66 was at the Pol. court. He pub. a lute book with Moderne of Lyons

in 1552 and a second with Andreae of Kraków in 1565.

Baklanov, Georgy (b Riga, 4 Jan 1881; d Basle, 6 Dec 1938), Russian baritone. He sang Amonasro and Rubinstein's Demon at Kiev in 1903. Bolshoy and St Petersburg 1905–9, in operas by Rakhmaninov. He appeared widely in Europe until the war: CG (1910 as Rigoletto and Scarpia), at Berlin (1911) and at Monte Carlo in the 1914 fp of Ponchielli's *I Mori di Valenzia*. Boston 1911–14; Chicago 1917–26 in operas by Février and Rimsky-Korsakov and as Méphistophélès, Prince Igor, Ruslan and Scarpia.

Balakirev, Mily Alexeievich (b Nizhny-Novgorod, 2 Jan 1837; d St Petersburg, 29 May 1910), Russian composer. He taught music by his mother, but learnt most of what he knew as a youth in the house of Ulibishev, on whose estate he was able to use the music library and gain experience with the private orch. At 18 he went to St Petersburg, full of enthusiasm for national music, and won the approval of Glinka. In 1861 he began to form the group of nationalist musicians of which he became the leader, although he was not the oldest. Cui became his 1st disciple, Mussorgsky, Rimsky-Korsakov and Borodin following later, and he even influenced Tchaikovsky to some extent at first. In 1862 he helped to estab. the Free School of Music with the choral cond. Lomakin, and in connection with it cond. progressive symph. concerts.

In 1871 he had a grave nervous breakdown and withdrew from public life, feeling that he had been defeated by the 'official' musicians; he was forced to become a minor railway official to earn a modest living and he turned to religious mysticism. Not till 1876 did he begin to take some interest in composition again, and only in 1883, when he was app. director of the Imp. Chapel, did he fully emerge once more. He retired in 1895 with a pension and took up comp. anew, but again lived in seclusion and was almost wholly forgotten by his former friends.

Works incl. incid. music for Shakespeare's *King Lear* (1860); 2 symphs., symph. poems *Russia* and *Tamara,* overtures on a Span. march, on 3 Rus. themes, to *King Lear* and on Cz. themes; pf. concerto (finished by Liapunov); many pf. works, incl. sonata in Bb min., *Islamey* fantasy (1869), scherzos, mazurkas, nocturnes, waltzes, etc.; 43 songs; 2 books of folk-songs; 6 anthems for unaccomp. chorus; cantata for the unveiling of the Glinka monument.

Balalaika, a Russian instrument similar to the guitar, but as a rule with a triangular body. It is made in var. sizes, so that bands of instruments ranging from treble to bass can be organized.

Balanchine, George (b St Petersburg, 22 Jan 1904; d New York, 30 Apr 1983), Russian-American choreographer. After leaving Rus. in 1924 he was engaged by Diaghilev as choreog. for the Ballets Russes; worked on the 1st Paris perf. of *Apollo Musagetes* and was later choreog. for Stravinsky's *Orpheus, Jeu de Cartes* and *Agon*. From 1948 was artistic dir. NY City Ballet.

Balassa, Sandor (b Budapest, 20 Jan 1935), Hungarian composer. He studied in Budapest and is music dir. Hung. Radio.

Works incl. vln. concerto (1964); 7tet for brass; *The Golden Age,* cantata (1965); *Xenia,* 9et (1970); *Iris* for orch.; opera *Beyond the Threshold* (1976); *Calls and Cries* for orch. (1982).

Balbi, Lodovico (b Venice, 1545; d Venice, Dec 1604), Italian monk, singer and composer. Pupil of Porta; singer at St Mark's, Venice, c 1570; later at Verona Cathedral. Afterwards worked at Venice and Padua, and retired to the Minorite monastery at Venice.

Works incl. Masses, motets and other church music; madrigals.

Baldassari, Benedetto, Italian 18th-cent. tenor. Appeared in London, 1719–22, and took part in the fps of Handel's *Radamisto* and *Floridante*.

Baldwin, John (b before 1560; d London, 28 Aug 1615), English singer and composer. At var. times singer in St George's Chapel, Windsor, and a gentleman of the Chapel Royal in London. He copied out much music, esp. into a book for his own use, which preserves many valuable works and incl. instrumental pieces and sacred and secular works for several voices. He also completed the Sextus part-book of the Forrest-Heyther collection of Tudor Masses, and wrote out My Ladye Nevells Booke, a beautifully copied anthology of keyboard music by Byrd, dated 1591.

Baldwyn, John, English 15th-cent. musician. Took the Mus.B. at Cambridge, 1470 or 1471; prob. the composer of a Magnificat (lost) in the Eton Choirbook.

Balfe, Michael (William) (b Dublin, 15 May 1808; d Rowney Abbey, Herts., 20 Oct 1870), Irish composer and singer. Son of a dancing-master, who removed to Wexford in 1810. On the death of his father in 1823, he was sent to London as a pupil of C.E.

Horn; there he appeared as a violinist and played in the orch. at Drury Lane Theatre. Next he studied comp. with C.F. Horn and appeared as a singer in Weber's *Freischütz* at Norwich. In 1825 Count Mazzara became his patron and took him to It., where he introduced him to Cherubini. He then went to Paris, met Rossini, and in 1827 appeared as Figaro in *Barbiere* at the Théâtre Italien.

Three years later he sang at Palermo and prod. his 1st opera there, *I rivali di se stessi*. At Milan he sang with Malibran and at Bergamo he met the Hung. singer Lina Rosa, whom he married. Early in 1833 he returned to London and appeared at concerts. His 1st Eng. opera, *The Siege of Rochelle,* was prod. at Drury Lane in 1835 and the next year Malibran sang in *The Maid of Artois*. In 1842 he went to live in Paris for some years and worked there with great success, though in 1843 he returned for a time to prod. *The Bohemian Girl* in London. Triumphant visits to Berlin in 1849 and St Petersburg in 1852 followed, and in 1854 he prod. *Pittore e Duca* at Trieste. That year he finally returned to Eng.; he had bought property in Hertfordshire, where he took to farming.

Works incl. 29 operas, among which are *Un avvertimento ai gelosi* (Pavia, 1830), *The Siege of Rochelle* (1835), *The Maid of Artois, Joan of Arc* (1837), *Falstaff* (1838), *Le Puits d'amour, The Bohemian Girl, Les Quatre Fils Aymon* (Paris, 1844), *The Bondman, The Maid of Honour, The Sicilian Bride, The Rose of Castile, Satanella* (1858), *The Armourer of Nantes* (1863), *Il Talismano;* operetta *The Sleeping Queen;* ballet *La Pérouse;* 3 cantatas, incl. *Mazeppa;* many songs, etc.

Ballabene, Gregorio (b Rome, 1720; d Rome, c 1803), Italian composer. One of the latest adherents of the *stile antico,* wrote unaccomp. church music often of considerable complexity, incl. a 48-part Mass.

Ballabile (It. = in a dancing manner, accent on 2nd syll.), a term applicable to any piece in the form or character of a dance.

Ballad, a narrative song either traditional or written in traditional style. Applied in the late 19th and early 20th cents. to a sentimental, drawing-room song.

Ballad Opera, an English light operatic entertainment the fashion for which was set by John Gay's *The Beggar's Opera* in 1728 and continuing its vogue until the 1760s. The most distinctive feature of its music is that it consists mainly of short songs interspersed with dialogue and that they are not specially comp. for the piece, but chosen from popular songs of the day.

Ballad of Blanik, The (*Balada blanická*), symph. poem by Janáček after a poem by J. Vrchický; perf. Brno, 21 Mar 1920.

Ballade (Fr.). (1) A form of medieval French verse, often set to music by trouvères and 14th-cent. comps., in which each stanza is in AAB form with a refrain line at the end. (2) In the 19th and 20th cents. an instrumental piece, often of a lyrical and romantic character.

Ballard, French 16th–18th-cent. family of music printers. The founder was Guillaume Le Bé, 1540, and the chief members were:

1. Robert B. (b *c* 1525; d Paris, buried 8 Jul 1588), son-in-law of Le Bé.

2. Lucrèce B. (*née* Le Bé), his wife, who continued after his death.

3. Pierre B. (b Paris, *c* 1580; d Paris, 4 Oct 1639), their son.

4. Robert B. (b *c* 1575; d Paris, *c* 1679), son of 3.

5 Christophe B. (b 12 Apr 1641; d Paris, 1715), son of 4.

6. Jean-Baptiste Christophe B. (b *c* 1663; d Paris, May 1750), son of 5.

7. Christophe Jean François B. (b *c* 1701; d Paris, 5 Sep 1765), son of 6.

8. Pierre Robert Christophe B. (d Paris, ? 1788), son of 7.

Ballata (It.), a 14th-cent. verse form, often set to music, in which the refrain precedes and follows each stanza. The term implies an association with dancing.

Ballet (*see also* **Ballett**), a stage entertainment consisting entirely of dancing and therefore requiring exclusively instrumental music from the comp., although vocal features have been intro. by some modern musicians and were a feature in French ballet of the 18th cent., where the term was often short for *opéra-ballet* and the ballet proper was called *ballet-pantomime*.

Ballet comique de la royne, stage entertainment perf. in Paris, 15 Oct 1581, at the marriage of the Duc de Joyeux and Mlle. de Vaudemont, under the supervision of Balthasar de Beaujoyeulx. The verse was by the Sieur de la Chesnaye, the scenery by Patin, and the music by the bass singer Lambert de Beaulieu, Jacques Salmon and others. It is in effect the 1st of the *ballets de cour*.

Ballet de Cour (Fr. = court ballet), a 16th–17th-cent. French stage entertainment with music developing from the older tourneys and masquerades, containing vocal and dance movements specially comp. Guédron and Boësset were its chief exponents. The

species developed later into the *opéra-ballet* and the opera.

Ballet-pantomime. See **Ballet.**

Ballett (or **Ballet**), a type of 16th–17th-cent. composition for several voices, resembling a madrigal, but in a lighter, more dance-like style.

Balletti (It.), pieces of music intended for dancing, esp. on the stage.

Balling, Michael (b Heidingsfeld, 27 Aug 1866; d Darmstadt, 1 Sep 1925), German conductor. Associated with the Wagner festivals at Bayreuth (1904–25, *Parsifal, Tristan, Ring*) and cond. of the Hallé Orch., Manchester, 1912–14; Darmstadt from 1919. He prod. an incomplete ed. of Wagner's music (1912–29).

Ballo (It. = dance), usually used in comb., e.g. *tempo di ballo.*

Ballo delle Ingrate, Il, ballet-opera in 1 act by Monteverdi (lib. by O. Rinuccini), prod. Mantua, 1608. The work was pub. in *Madrigali guerrieri et amorosi*, 1638. The 'Ingrate' of the title are ladies who have declined the attentions of their suitors. The ungrateful spirits are summoned from Hades and perform a melancholy dance.

Ballo in maschera, Un (*A Masked Ball*), opera by Verdi (lib. by A. Somma, based on Scribe's *Gustave III* set by Auber), prod. Rome, Teatro Apollo, 17 Feb 1859.

Balsam, Artur (b Warsaw, 8 Feb 1906), Polish-born American pianist. He studied at the Łódź Cons. and in Berlin; settled in US 1933. Active in chamber music and as soloist in standard rep.; has pub. cadenzas for Mozart's piano concertos.

Baltsa, Agnes (b Lefkas, 19 Nov 1944), Greek mezzo. Debut Frankfurt, 1968, Cherubino; Octavian in Vienna, 1970. La Scala and CG from 1976; Romeo in Bellini's *I Capuleti* at CG 1984. Other roles incl. Berlioz's Dido, Dorabella and Carmen.

Baltzar, Thomas (b Lübeck, *c* 1630; d London, buried 27 Jul 1663), German or Swedish violinist. In the service of Queen Christina of Sweden 1653–5 and violinist to Charles II from 1661.

Bampton, Rose (b Lakewood, Ohio, 28 Nov 1908), American soprano orig. mezzo. Sang Laura at the NY Met in 1932 and made her soprano debut in 1937 as Leonora in *Trovatore*. Admired as Donna Anna and Alceste, and from the 1940s as Sieglinde, Kundry and Strauss's Daphne. CG 1937, as Amneris. Taught at Juilliard School from 1974.

Banchieri, Adriano (b Bologna, 3 Sep 1568; d Bologna, 1634), Italian organist, theorist and composer. A pupil of Gioseffo Guami, he was a Benedictine monk. In 1596 he became organist at the monastery of San Michele in Bosco (Monte Oliveto) nr. Bologna, to which he returned in 1609, remaining there until shortly before his death; from 1600 to 1604 he was organist at Santa Maria in Regola at Imola. He helped to found the Accademia dei Floridi at Bologna in 1615, and wrote theoretical works, esp. on figured bass.

Works incl. Masses; sacred symphs. and concertos; comic intermezzi for the stage; organ works.

Banda (It. = band), a military band, in particular a band used on the stage or behind the scene in an opera, e.g. in Verdi's *Macbeth*.

Bandurria (Span. = Pandora), a string instrument of the Cittern type, with 6 double strings which are plucked with the fingers or with a plectrum.

Banestre, Gilbert (b c 1445; d London, Aug 1487), English composer. Master of the Children in the Chapel Royal in succession to Abyngdon, 1478; wrote sacred and secular vocal music.

Banister, John (b London, c 1625; d London, 3 Oct 1679), English violinist and concert promoter. Lived in London; sent to Fr. by Charles II in 1661. Leader of the King's vlns. 1662–7. Comp. music for Davenant's *Circe* and Wycherley's *Gentleman Dancing-Master* and contrib. songs to various collections.

Banister, John (b London; d London, ? 1725), English violinist and teacher of his instrument, son of prec. Wrote for the stage.

Banjo, an American string instrument of the Guitar type with a hollow body covered with stretched parchment and 5 strings, which are plucked with the fingers; the neck is fretted. The 5-stringed instrument is now the normal type but previously there were up to 9 strings.

Bánk-Bán, opera by Erkel (lib. by B. Egressy, based on a play by József Katona), prod. Budapest, 9 Mar 1861.

Banks, Don (b Melbourne, 25 Oct 1923; d Sydney, 5 Sep 1980), Australian composer. Studied at Melbourne Cons. and later (1950) with Seiber in London and Dallapiccola in Florence (1953). Settled in London.

Works incl. horn concerto (1960); divertimento for fl. and string trio; duo for vln. and cello; vln. sonata; 3 studies for cello and pf.; 3 Episodes for fl. and pf.; film music.

Bänkelsänger (Ger.), a singer of ballads, esp. at fairs, a chapman singing the songs he sold.

Banti (*née* **Giorgi**), **Brigitta** (b Crema, c 1757; d Bologna, 18 Feb 1806), Italian soprano. She sang in the streets of Venice and the cafés of Paris at first, but was engaged for the Paris Opéra in 1776 and had much success in London from 1779 to 1802 in operas by Paisiello, Zingarelli and Anfossi. Described by Da Ponte as ignorant and insolent.

Bantock, Granville (b London, 7 Aug 1868; d London, 16 Oct 1946), English composer. Son of a doctor; educ. for the civil service, but entered the RAM in 1889, where some of his earliest works were perf., and Lago prod. the opera *Cædmar* at the Olympic Theatre in 1892. After some experience in theatrical cond. he gave a concert of modern Eng. music in 1896. The next year he was app. cond. at the Tower, New Brighton, where he intro. much contemporary music. In Feb 1900 he gave a concert of new Eng. music at Antwerp and in Sep. was app. principal of the Birmingham and Midland Inst. School of Music. He remained in Birmingham until 1933, and became prof. of music at the Univ. in 1908, succeeding Elgar. Knighted in 1930.

Works incl. STAGE: operas *Cædmar* (1892), *Pearl of Iran* (1894), *The Seal Woman* (1924); 5 ballets; incid. music for Sophocles' *Electra* (1909), Shakespeare's *Macbeth* (1926), Wilde's *Salome*, etc.

ORCHESTRAL: *Processional* and *Jaga-Naut* (from 24 projected symph. poems on Southey's *Curse of Kehama*), *Helena* variations, comedy overtures *The Pierrot of the Minute* (after Ernest Dowson) (1908) and *Circus Life*, orchestral ballad *The Sea Reivers*, *Overture to a Gk. Tragedy*, symph. poem *Dante and Beatric*, *Fifine at the Fair* (after Browning) (1901), overture to *The Frogs* (Aristophanes), *Hebridean Symph.* (1915), *A Pagan Symph.* (1926), serenade *From the Far West*, *Scenes from the Scottish Highlands*, *The Land of Gael* for string orch.; *Elegiac Poem, Sapphic Poem, Dramatic Poem* for cello and orch. (1914).

CHORUS AND ORCH. (with or without solo voices): *The Fire-Worshippers* (1892), *The Time-Spirit, Sea Wanderers* (1906), *Christ in the Wilderness, Omar Khayyám* (setting of FitzGerald's trans. in 3 parts, 1909), *Gethsemane, The Great God Pan, Song of Songs,* oratorio *The Pilgrim's Progress* (Bunyan) (1928).

UNACCOMP. CHORUS: choral symphs. *Atlanta in Calydon* (Swinburne) (1911), and *Vanity of Vanities* (Ecclesiastes), suite *A*

Pageant of Human Life (1913) and many smaller works and part-songs.

SONGS: incl. cycles *Songs of the East* (6 vols.), *Songs of the Seraglio, Six Jester Songs, Five Ghazals of Hafiz, Ferishtah's Fancies* (Browning), *Sappho, Songs from the Chinese Poets* (8 sets).

CHAMBER: Vla. sonata (1919), 3 cello sonatas (1924, 1940, 1945), 3 vln. sonatas (1929, 1932, 1940).

Bar (Eng.). (1) Originally the line drawn through the music stave or staves to indicate the metrical divisions of a comp., now called 'bar-line' in Brit. (2) The space between two bar-lines, called 'measure' in America.

Bar (Ger.), a medieval German musical form (*Barform*) of song, used by the Minne-singer and Meistersinger. Each stanza consists of two similar phrases or periods (*Stollen,* together called the *Aufgesang*), followed by a different but relevant one (*Abgesang*).

Barabas, Sari (b Budapest, 14 Mar 1918), Hungarian soprano. Debut Budapest, 1939, as Gilda. She remained in Hung. during the war and sang at Munich from 1949; appeared as guest in Vienna, Fr. and It. Glyndebourne, 1953–7, as Constanze, Adèle (also recorded) and Zerbinetta. She was heard in San Francisco as the Queen of Night (1950).

Barbaia, Domenico (old spelling Barbaja) (b Milan, ? 1778; d Posillipo nr. Naples, 19 Oct 1841), Italian impresario. Was 1st a waiter, then a circus proprietor and finally the most popular of operatic managers. In 1821–8, coming from the Teatro San Carlo at Naples, he managed the Kärntnertortheater and the Theater an der Wien in Vienna, introducing Rossini and Bellini and commissioning *Euryanthe* from Weber.

Barbé, Anton (d Antwerp, 2 Dec 1564), Flemish composer and 1st of a line of Antwerp musicians. From 1527 to 1562 he was *Kapellmeister* at Antwerp Cathedral. He pub. Masses, motets and *chansons,* and contributed a Dutch song to Susato's *Het ierste musyck boexken* (1551).

Barbe-bleue (*Bluebeard*), operetta by Offenbach (lib. by H. Meilhac and L. Halévy), prod. Paris, Théâtre des Variétés, 5 Feb 1866.

Barbella, Emanuele (b Naples, 14 Apr 1718; d Naples, 1 Jan 1777), Italian violinist and composer. Studied at Naples and wrote sonatas and duets for vln., trio sonatas, also an opera in collaboration with Logroscino, *Elmira generosa* (Naples, 1753).

Barber of Baghdad, The (Cornelius). *See* **Barbier von Bagdad.**

Barber of Seville, The (Paisiello, Rossini). *See* **Barbiere di Siviglia.**

Barber, Robert, English 16th-cent. composer. *Informator choristarum,* Winchester Coll., 1541–2. A *Dum transisset sabbatum* is in the Gyffard part-books.

Barber, Samuel (b West Chester, Penn., 9 Mar 1910; d New York, 23 Jan 1981), American composer. Entered Curtis Institute of Music in 1924, winning a prize with a vln. sonata in 1928. In the following years he won several more prizes, incl. the American Prix de Rome, 1935. In 1964 he was commissioned to write an opera for the opening of the new NY Met house, and prod. *Antony and Cleopatra.*

Works incl. operas, *Vanessa* (1958), *A Hand of Bridge* and *Antony and Cleopatra* (after Shakespeare) (1966, rev. 1974); 2 symphs. (1936 and 1944), 2 Essays, overture to Sheridan's *School for Scandal,* music for a scene from Shelley for orch.; Adagio for strings (from string 4tet of 1936); vln. concerto (1940), cello concerto (1945), pf. concerto (1962), *Capricorn Concerto* for fl., ob., tpt. and strings; string 4tet, cello and pf. sonata, vln. and pf. sonata, pf. sonata, *Excursions* for pf.

VOCAL: *Dover Beach* (Matthew Arnold) for baritone and string 4tet (1933); works for unaccomp. chorus to words by Helen Waddell, Emily Dickinson, James Stephens and Stephen Spender; song cycle from James Joyce's *Chamber Music* and songs to words by James Stephens, A.E. Housman, Gerard Manley Hopkins and Yeats.

Barberiis, Melchiore de, Italian 16th-cent. lutenist. Lived at Padua and pub. several books of pieces in lute tablature, 1546–9.

Barbetta, Giulio Cesare (b ? Padua, *c* 1540; d after 1603), Italian 16th-cent. lutenist. Lived at Padua and pub. 4 books of music in lute tablature, 1569–1603.

Barbi, Alice (b Modena, 1 Jun 1862; d Rome, 4 Sep 1948), Italian mezzo and violinist. Made her 1st appearance as singer in 1882 at Milan. She toured widely and became a favourite interpreter of Brahms.

Barbier, Jules. *See* **Carré, Michel.**

Barbier von Bagdad, Der (*The Barber of Baghdad*), opera by Cornelius (lib. by comp.), prod. Weimar, 15 Dec 1858.

Barbiere di Siviglia, Il, ossia La precauzione inutile (*The Barber of Seville, or Vain Precaution*; orig. title: *Almaviva, ossia L'inutile precauzione*), opera by Rossini (lib. by C. Sterbini, based on Beaumarchais' *Le Barbier de Séville*), prod. Rome, Teatro Argentina, 20 Feb 1816.

Barbiere di Siviglia, Il, ovvero La pre-cauzione inutile (*The Barber of Seville, or Vain Precaution*), opera by Paisiello (lib. by G. Petrosellini, based on Beaumarchais' *Le Barbier de Séville*), prod. St Petersburg, Hermitage, at court, 26 Sep 1782.

Barbieri, Fedora (b Trieste, 4 Jun 1920), Italian mezzo. Debut Florence, 1940, and in 1953 sang there in the fp of the revision of Prokofiev's *War and Peace*. NY Met 1950–75, debut as Eboli. CG 1950–58 as Mistress Quickly, Azucena and Amneris. Also sang Carmen and Orpheus.

Barbieri-Nini, Marianna (b Florence, 18 Feb 1818, d Florence, 27 Nov 1887), Italian soprano. Debut La Scala, 1840, in *Belisario*; not successful until she masked her ugly face. She appeared widely in Italy as Lucrezia Borgia, Anna Bolena and Semiramide; created Verdi's Lady Macbeth and roles in *I due Foscari* and *Il Corsaro*.

Barbingant (*fl.* 1460–80), French composer of polyphonic songs and Mass cycles, formerly confused with Barbireau.

Barbireau, Jacob (b 1455–6; d Antwerp, 8 Aug 1491), Flemish composer. Singer at 's-Hertogenbosch and Antwerp. 2 Masses and var. other works by him survive.

Barbirolli, John (b London, 2 Dec 1899; d London, 29 Jul 1970), English conductor. Studied at Trinity College, London (1911–12) and the RAM (1912–17). He made his debut as a cellist, aged 11, and joined the Queen's Hall Orch. in that capacity in 1915. Achieved recognition as a cond. in 1926, later succeeding Toscanini as chief cond. of the NY PO in 1937. He returned to England in 1943, where he took over the Hallé Orch. In 1949 he was knighted and in 1950 received the Royal Phil. Society's gold medal. With the Hallé gave the fps of Vaughan Williams's 7th and 8th symphs. Guest cond. Berlin PO, Boston SO and Chicago SO. He was married to the oboist Evelyn Rothwell (1939). Barbirolli excelled in the Romantic repertory, esp. the symphs. of Elgar, Sibelius and Mahler. He conducted Gluck's *Orfeo* and *Tristan* at CG (1953–4); recorded *Otello* and *Butterfly*.

Barcarola, work for orch. by Henze; it depicts a journey across the river Styx and quotes the Eton Boating Song. Fp Zurich, 22 Apr 1980, cond. Albrecht.

Barcarolle (Fr. from It. *barcaruola*), a boating-song, esp. of the type sung by the gondoliers at Venice. A piece or song in that style, generally in 6–8 time and a moderate tempo with a swaying rhythm.

Barcroft, George (b Ely; d Ely), English 16th–17th-cent. organist and composer. Studied at Cambridge and was minor canon and organist at Ely Cathedral, 1579–1610. Comp. church music.

Barcroft, Thomas (d Ely), English 16th-cent. organist and composer, ? father of prec. Organist at Ely. Wrote church music.

Bardi, Giovanni, Count of Vernio (b Florence, 5 Feb 1534; d Rome, Sep 1612), Italian nobleman and amateur musician. Patron of the *camerata* at Florence. Works by Caccini, Galilei, Peri and others were perf. at his house. He wrote madrigals himself.

Barenboim, Daniel (b Buenos Aires, 15 Nov 1942), Israeli pianist and conductor. Debut as soloist Paris, 1955. Has worked as cond.-soloist in Eng. and USA. London from 1956, NY from 1957. Music dir. Orchestre de Paris from 1975 and began a series of Berlioz recordings. Opera debut Edinburgh, 1973, with *Don Giovanni*, and cond. *Tristan* at Bayreuth in 1981. Also active in chamber music with Zukerman, Perlman and, before her illness, his wife, Jacqueline du Pré. As a pianist he is particularly well known in the sonatas of Beethoven. On 31 Jul 1986 he gave a Liszt concert at the Bayreuth Festspielhaus, to mark the cent. of Liszt's death.

Bärenhäuter, Der (*The bear skinner*), opera by Siegfried Wagner (lib. by comp.), prod. Munich, 21 Jan 1899.

Bariolage (Fr.), The alteration on a string instrument of the same note on an open string and a stopped string. Also the playing of high notes on a string instrument in high positions on the lower strings to obtain a different tone-colour or to facilitate the perf. of rapid high passages without changing to lower positions.

Baritone (from Gk. *barutonos* = deep-sounding). (1) A male voice midway between tenor and bass, with approximately the foll. compass:

(2) A brass instrument of the Saxhorn family, of the same pitch as the Euphonium but with a smaller bore and only 3 valves.

(3) Applied to instruments of moderately low compass, e.g. baritone ob., baritone saxophone.

Barlow, David (b Rothwell, Northants., 20 May 1927; d Newcastle upon Tyne 9 Jun 1975), English composer. He studied with Gordon Jacob at the RCM and with Boulanger in France. His early music is Romantic in style but from 1963 he adopted serial technique.

Works incl. church operas *David and Bathsheba* and *Judas Iscariot* (1969 and 1975); 2 symphs. (1950 and 1959), vars. for cello and orch. (1969), Sinfonietta concertante for clar. and orch. (1972); *The Lambton Worm* for narrator and orch. (1969); string trio, string 4tet (1969), brass 5tet (1972); *Passion Music* for organ.

Barlow, Wayne (Brewster) (b Elyria, Ohio, 6 Sep 1912), American composer. Studied with Howard Hanson at the Eastman School and with Schoenberg at the Univ. of Southern Calif. in 1935. Dir. of the electronic music studio at Eastman 1968–78.

Works incl. *Zion in Exile*, cantata (1937), *3 Moods for Dancing*, ballet (1940), *Nocturne* for 18 insts. (1946), pf. 5tet (1951), *Images* for harp and orch. (1961), *Vistas* for orch. (1963), *Moonflight*, for tape (1970), *Soundprints in Concrete* (1972), *Voices of Faith*, cantata (1976), *Divertissement* for fl. and chamber orch. (1980).

Bärmann, Heinrich Joseph (b Potsdam, 14 Feb 1784; d Munich, 11 Jun 1847), German clarinettist. Member of the court orch. at Munich. Weber wrote several works for him.

Barnard, John (b ? 1591), English 17th-cent. musician. Minor canon at St Paul's Cathedral in London; pub. the 1st printed collection of English cathedral music in 1641.

Barnby, Joseph (b York, 12 Aug 1838; d London, 28 Jan 1896), English conductor, organist and composer. Held various organist's posts in London; precentor at Eton Coll. 1875–92, then principal of GSM. Distinguished as choral cond., he gave oratorios by Bach and Dvořák and the 1st Eng. perf. of *Parsifal* (concert, 1884). Knighted 1892.

Barnett, John (b Bedford, 15 Jul 1802; d nr. Cheltenham, 16 Apr 1890), English composer of German descent (orig. name Beer: Meyerbeer's family). Was a stage singer as a child and studied with C.E. Horn. In 1825 he prod. his 1st stage piece, which was followed by a large number of others, incl. *The Mountain Sylph*, prod. 25 Aug 1834.

Baron, Ernst Gottlieb (b Breslau, 17 Feb 1696; d Berlin, 12 Apr 1760), German author, lutenist and composer, pupil of Weiss. Travelled widely as a lutenist, wrote several theoretical works on the lute, and comp. for his instrument.

Baroni, Italian 17th-cent. family of singers and lutenists:

1. Andreana B. *See* **Basile, Andreana.**

2. Leonora B. (b Mantua, Dec 1611; d Rome, 6 Apr 1670), daughter of 1. Also played vla. da gamba and comp. Milton met her in Rome in 1638 and wrote 3 poems on her and her mother.

3. Catarina B. (b Mantua, after 1620; d ? Rome), sister of 2. Also played the harp and wrote poetry.

Baroque, the music of the years *c* 1600–1759, most easily described as the generations whose compositions were based on continuo practice. Before the late 19th cent. the term was one of denigration and practically confined to art history; but soon after the art-historian Heinrich Wölfflin demonstrated positive uses for the word (1888) it was adopted also for its current musical use.

Barraqué, Jean (b Paris, 17 Jan 1928; d Paris, 17 Aug 1973), French composer. Studied with Jean Langlais and Messiaen, later working in the experimental laboratories of the Radiodiffusion Française in Paris.

Works incl. *Séquence* for soprano and chamber ens., (after Nietzsche) (1955); *Le Temps restitué* for voices and orch. (1957); *Au delà du hasard* (based on Hermann Broch) for voices and instrumental groups (1959), *Chant après chant* for perc.; (1966); pf. sonata; *La mort de Virgile*, incomplete dramatic cycle.

Barraud, Henry (b Bordeaux, 23 Apr 1900), French composer. Studied 1st at Bordeaux and later at the Paris Cons. with Caussade, Dukas and Aubert. In 1937 he was in charge of the music at the Paris World Fair; he then joined the radio service, where he rose to the post of head of the national programme in 1948.

Works incl. operas *La Farce de Maître Pathelin* (1938), *Numance* and *Lavinia* (1959); ballets *La Kermesse* (1943) and *L'Astrologue dans le puits*; film and radio music; oratorio *Les Mystères des Saints Innocents* (1947), cantatas and other choral works; 3 symphs.; pf. concerto; woodwind trio, string trio, string 4tet (1940), vln. and pf. sonata; pf. music; songs.

Barré (Fr. lit. barred). A chord on string instruments with fretted fingerboards, partic. the guitar, is said to be played barré when a finger is laid horizontally across the whole fingerboard, thus raising all the strings in pitch by the same interval's distance from the fundamental tuning.

Barré, Antonio (d ? diocese of Langres), French 16th-cent. singer, music printer and composer. Alto in the choir of St Peter's in Rome in the middle of the cent. Wrote madrigals and pub. them, with those of many other comps., in 7 books printed by his own press, 1st in Rome and after 1564 at Milan.

Barrel Organ, a popular mechanical instrument prod. music by the mere turning of a handle, but sometimes actuated by clockwork. A cylinder (barrel) moves tongue-shaped keys by means of pins or studs arranged in such order that its turning prod. an ordered piece of music. The keys control pipes similar to those of the org., but restricted to a single range of tone-colour and limited in compass. Barrel organs were formerly used in small village churches that could not maintain an organ and organist and they mechanically played a number of hymn tunes. The barrel organ is often wrongly called Hurdy-gurdy, which is a totally different instrument.

Barrett, John (b c 1674; d London, ? Dec 1719), English organist, teacher and composer. Wrote incid. music for plays, many popular songs.

Barrientos, Maria (b Barcelona, 10 Mar 1883; d Ciboure, 8 Aug 1946), Spanish soprano. Debut Barcelona, 1898, as Meyerbeer's Ines. She sang in It. and Ger. from 1899; among her best roles were Meyerbeer's Marguerite de Valois and Dinorah (La Scala, 1904), Rosina and Lakmé. NY Met debut 1916, as Lucia; appeared as Norina opposite Caruso and was the Queen of Shemakha in the 1st local perf. of *The Golden Cockerel* (1918). She was well known as Amina and Bellini's Elvira and sang Stravinsky's Nightingale at Monte Carlo (1929). The foremost coloratura singer of her time.

Barshai, Rudolf (b Labinskaya, 28 Sep 1924), Russian violist and conductor. He founded the Moscow Chamber Orch. in 1956 and cond. it until he left Rus. for Israel in 1976. Prin. cond. Bournemouth SO from 1982. His transcriptions incl. Prokofiev's *Visions Fugitives*, for chamber orch., and Shostakovich's string 4tet no. 8, for string orch.

Barsova, Valeriya (b Astrakhan, 13 'Jun 1892; d Sochi, 13 Dec 1967), Russian soprano. Debut Moscow, 1917; sang Rosina at the Bolshoy, 1920. She appeared widely in Europe from 1929 and remained at the Bolshoy until 1948. Other roles incl. Ludmilla, Butterfly, Lakmé, Gilda and Violetta.

Barstow, Josephine (b Sheffield, 27 Sep 1940), English soprano. London debut 1967, SW; from 1969 at CG, where she took part in the fps of Tippett's *The Knot Garden* and *The Ice Break*, and Henze's *We Come to the River*. She sang Autonoe in the first Brit. stage perf. of *The Bassarids*, at the Col-

iseum; other roles there have incl. Salome, Emilia Marty and Prokofiev's Natasha. NY Met debut 1977, as Musetta. Bayreuth 1983, Gutrune. In 1986 she created Benigna in Penderecki's *Die schwarze Maske*, at Salzburg.

Bartered Bride, The (*Prodaná Nevěsta*), opera by Smetana (lib. by K. Sabina), prod., 1st version, Prague, Cz. Theatre, 30 May 1866); rev. version, 29 Jan 1869; final version (with recitatives), 25 Sep 1870.

Barth, Hans (b Leipzig, 25 Jun 1897; d Jacksonville, Florida, 9 Dec 1956), German pianist and composer who emigrated to the USA in 1907. A meeting with Busoni encouraged him to experiment with new scales, and in 1928 he invented a ¼-tone pf., for which he comp. a number of works. He also comp. ¼-tone chamber and instrumental music, as well as more conventional pieces.

Barthélémon, François Hippolyte (b Bordeaux, 27 Jul 1741; d London, 20 Jul 1808), French violinist and composer. Settled in London, 1765. A year later prod. *Pelopida*, the 1st of several successful dramatic works, and married the singer Mary Young, daughter of Charles Young and niece of Mrs. Arne and Mrs. Lampe. Comp. stage pieces for Garrick and visited Fr., Ger. and It. with his wife, who sang there. A friend of Haydn during the latter's visits to London, he is said to have suggested the subject of *The Creation*.

Works incl. the stage works *Pelopida* (1766), *The Judgement of Paris* (1768), *The Maid of the Oaks* (1774), *Belphegor* (1778); oratorio *Jefte in Masfa*; symphs.; concertos, sonatas, duets for vln.

Bartleman, James (b London, 19 Sep 1769; d London, 15 Apr 1821), English bass. Educ. at Westminster School and Abbey; a distinguished boy treble, he first appeared as a bass in 1788.

Bartlet, John, English 16th–17th-cent. lutenist and composer. Prob. in the service of Lord Hertford. Pub. a *Booke of Ayres* for voices and instruments in 1606.

Bartók, Béla (b Nagyszentmiklós, 25 Mar 1881; d New York, 26 Sep 1945), Hungarian composer and pianist. Son of a director of agriculture. His mother, a school-teacher, was a musician and taught him from an early age. He appeared in public as a pianist at the age of 10. Studied under László Erkel at Porzsony (now Bratislava) until 1899 and then the pf. under István Thomán and comp. under Koessler at the Budapest Cons. About 1905 he began to collect folk tunes, often with Zoltán Kodály, and they discovered that the true Magyar music differed greatly from that of the Hung. gypsies so far regarded as the only Hung. folk music. App. prof. of pf. at Budapest Cons. in 1907. After the war of 1914–18 he began to be known in Europe and Amer., and in 1922 was made an hon. member of the ISCM. In 1940 emigrated to the USA where he taught briefly at Columbia Univ. and Harvard. He was already suffering from leukaemia and he was not in demand as a pianist or, initially, as a comp. A 1943 commission from the Koussevitzky Foundation, for the *Concerto for Orchestra*, helped to alleviate his financial hardship. Bartók was one of the foremost comps. of the 20th cent. Much influenced by Hung. folk music, he never imitated it, but incorporated its rhythms and melodic characteristics into complex, subtle and effective forms.

Works incl. STAGE: *Duke Bluebeard's Castle*, 1-act opera (1911), prod. Budapest, 1918, cond. Tango; *The Wooden Prince*, 1-act ballet (1914–17; prod. Budapest, 1917, cond. Tango; *The Miraculous Mandarin*, 1-act pantomime (1918–23), prod. Cologne, 1926.

ORCH.: *Kossuth*, symph. poem (1903), Rhapsody, pf. and orch., op. 1 (1904), Scherzo (Burlesque), pf. and orch. (1904), Suite no. 1, op. 3 (1905, rev. 1920), Suite no. 2, op. 4 (1905–7), vln. concerto no. 1 (1907–8, fp Basle, 1958), *Two Portraits* (1907–11), *Two Pictures* (1910), *Four Pieces* op. 12 (1912–21), *The Wooden Prince*, suite from ballet (fp Budapest, 1931), *Rumanian Folkdances* (1917), *The Miraculous Mandarin*, suite from pantomime (fp Budapest 1928), *Dance Suite* (1923), pf. concerto no. 1 (1926, fp Frankfurt, 1927, with comp., cond. Furtwängler), 2 Rhapsodies for vln. and orch. (1928), pf. concerto no. 2 (1930–31, fp Frankfurt, 1933, with comp., cond. Rosbaud), *Transylvanian Dances* (1931), *Hung. Sketches* (1933), *Hung. Peasant Songs* (1933), *Music for Strings, Percussion and Celesta* (1936, fp Basle, 1937, cond. Sacher), vln. concerto no. 2 (1937–8, fp Amsterdam, 1939, with Székely, cond. Mengelberg), *Divertimento* for strings (1939, fp Basle, 1940, cond. Sacher), 2 pf. concerto (1940, fp London, 1942, with Kentner and Kabós, cond. Boult), *Concerto for Orch.* (1943–4, fp Boston, 1944, cond. Koussevitzky), pf. concerto no. 3 (1945, fp Philadelphia, 1946, cond. Ormandy), vla. concerto (completed by T. Serly, 1945).

VOCAL: *Three Village Scenes* for female

voices and orch. (1926), *Cantata Profana* for tenor, bar., chorus and orch. (1930), *Five Hung. Folk Songs* for low voice and orch. (1933); choruses on Hung. and Slovak folksongs; many solo songs, most based on Hung. folksongs.

CHAMBER: pf. 5tet (1903–4), 6 string 4tets (1908, 1917, 1927, 1928, 1934, 1939), 2 pf. and vln. sonatas (1921, 1922), 2 Rhapsodies for vln. and pf. (1928, also in vers. with orch.), Rhapsody for cello and pf. (1928), 44 Duos for 2 vlns. (1931), sonata for 2 pfs. and 2 perc. (1937, vers. with orch. 1940), *Contrasts* for vln., clar. and pf. (1938), sonata for solo vln. (1944).

PIANO: *14 Bagatelles*, op. 6 (1908), *85 Pieces for Children* (1909, rev. 1945), *Allegro barbaro* (1911), *Sonatina* (1915, orch. as *Transylvanian Dances*), Suite, op. 14 (1916), *15 Hungarian Peasant Songs* (1914–18), sonata (1926), *Out of Doors* (1926), *Mikrokosmos*, 153 'progressive pieces' in 6 vols. (1926, 1932–9); editions of keyboard music by B. Marcello, M. Rossi, Frescobaldi, Zipoli and Bach.

Bartoš, Jan Zdeněk (b Dvůr Králiové nad-Labem, 4 Jun 1908; d Prague, 1 Jun 1981), Czech composer and violinist. He played the vln. in orchs. and as a soloist pre-war; taught at the Prague Cons. from 1958.

Works incl. operas *Ripar's Wife* (1949) and *The Accursed Castle* (1949); 3 ballets; 7 cantatas; 7 symphs. (1949–78), 2 vla. concertos, vln. concerto (1970); 11 string 4tets (1940–73).

Bary, Alfred von (b Valetta, Malta, 18 Jan 1873; d Munich, 9 Sep 1926), German tenor. He studied medicine and became a neurologist at the Univ. of Leipzig; discovered by Nikisch, he made his debut at Dresden in 1903 as Lohengrin. The next year he sang Siegmund at Bayreuth; he returned there until 1914 as Parsifal, Tristan and Siegfried. Dresden until 1912, then 6 years at Munich.

Baryton, string instrument of the bass viol type with sympathetic strings which can be plucked by the hand. It was cultivated mainly in Ger. and Aus. Haydn's patron, Prince Nikolaus Esterházy, played it and Haydn wrote nearly 200 works for it.

Basile, Andreana (b Posillipo nr. Naples, *c* 1580; d Rome, *c* 1640), Italian singer and instrumentalist. Her career began in Rome and Naples; engaged for the Mantuan court in 1610 and sang there until 1624. Much admired by Monteverdi, she sang in several of his operas and became one of the first prima donnas. She sang widely in It. after

Basili

breaking with the Duke of Mantua, and from 1634 lived in Rome, where she played the guitar in musical soirées.

Basili (or **Basily**), **Francesco** (b Loreto, 31 Jan 1767; d Rome, 25 Mar 1850), Italian singer and composer. Became dir. of the Milan Cons. in 1827. *Maestro di cappella* at St Peter's in Rome from 1837.

Works incl. operas *La locandiera* (1789), *Achille nell'assedio di Troia, Ritorno d'Ulisse* (1798), *Antigona* (1799), *Achille, L'orfana egiziana* (1818); oratorio *Sansone* (1824); Requiem for Jannaconi; several settings of *Miserere*; symphs.

Basilius (*Der königliche Schäfer, oder Basilius in Arcadien: The Royal Shepherd, or Basil in Arcady*), opera by Keiser (lib. by F. C. Bressand), prod. Brunswick, ? 1693. The 1st of more than 100 operas by Keiser.

Basiola, Mario (b Annico nr. Cremona, 12 Jul 1892; d Annico, 3 Jan 1965), Italian baritone. After his 1918 debut he sang at Barcelona and Florence; 1923–5 with the San Carlo, Naples co. in N. Amer. NY Met, 1925–31 (debut as Amonasro). In 1930 he took part in the local fp of Rimsky-Korsakov's *Sadko*, cond. by Serafin. Returned to Italy 1933 and joined the La Scala co.; CG, 1939, as Iago and Scarpia. He toured Australia in 1946 and remained there until 1951 as a teacher. His son, **Mario jr.** (b 1935), made his debut at Venice in 1961 as Belcore and has toured widely in the Italian repertory and in operas by Berg, Dallapiccola and Penderecki.

Basiron, Philippe (Baziron, Philippon) (b ? Bourges, c 1450; d Bourges, 1491), French composer of Masses, motets and *chansons*.

Bass. (1) The lowest adult male voice, with approximately the following compass:

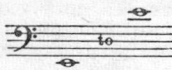

(2) Abbr. for Double Bass.

(3) Applied to instruments of a low compass, e.g. Bass Trumpet.

(4) The lowest part of a vocal or instrumental ensemble, often used as an abbr. for *Basso continuo*.

Bass Clarinet, a clar. with a range an octave lower than the ordinary instrument.

Bass Clef, the F clef on the 4th line of the stave:

Bass Drum, the largest of the drums not prod. notes of definite pitch. It is usually placed upright and struck sideways, prod. a dull thud. It is used both in the orch. and in military bands, and in the latter it is played in conjunction with the Cymbals, one of which is placed on it while the other is held in the player's hand not used to hold the drumstick.

Bass Flute, a fl. with a range a fourth lower than that of the ordinary instrument. It is a transposing instrument in G.

Bass Trumpet, a tpt. invented by Wagner, with a written compass an octave below that of the normal orchestral instrument.

Bass Viol. *See* **Viola da gamba.**

Bassani, Giovanni Battista (b Padua, c 1647; d Bergamo, 1 Oct 1716), Italian violinist and composer. Organist at Ferrara from 1667 and later in charge of the cathedral music at Bologna; returned to Ferrara as *maestro di cappella* in 1683. Comp. 12 oratorios, prod. 9 operas and brought out a large amount of church and instrumental music.

Bassano, Giovanni (b c 1558; d Venice, ? 1617), Venetian composer. Wrote instrumental music incl. ornamented transcriptions of vocal works by Gabrieli, Marenzio, etc.

Bassarids, The, 1-act opera with intermezzo by Henze (lib. by W.H. Auden and C. Kallman after *The Bacchae* of Euripides), prod. Salzburg, 6 Aug 1966; 1st Brit. stage perf. London, Coliseum, 10 Oct 1974, cond. Henze.

Bass Chantante (Fr. = singing-bass), a bass voice esp. suited to melodic delivery and lyrical parts.

Basse-Contre (Fr.), low bass, whether a voice, an instrument or an organ stop.

Basse Danse, a French dance of the 15th–16th cent. So called because the feet were kept low, not thrown up in the air as in some other dances.

Basset Horn, an alto instrument of the clar. family, with an extra key controlling notes below the normal range of instruments of this family. Mozart frequently wrote for it.

Bassi, Amadeo (b Florence, 20 Jul 1874; d Florence, 15 Jan 1949), Italian tenor. After his 1897 debut he sang in Florence and Venice and in 1908 sang Radames at the opening of the Teatro Colon, Buenos Aires. At CG he was heard from 1907 in operas by Franchetti, Catalani and Puccini. At Monte Carlo he sang in the fp of Mascagni's *Amica* (1905), at Chicago (1910–16) he was heard in operas by Leoncavallo and Wolf-Ferrari. La Scala 1921–6, as Loge, Parsifal and Siegmund.

Bassi, Carolina Manna (b Naples, 10 Jan 1781; d Cremona, 12 Dec 1862), Italian contralto. She sang at the Teatro San Carlo, Naples, from 1789. At Turin she sang in the fp of Meyerbeer's *Semiramide* (1819); in the following two seasons she was heard at La Scala in the fps of *Margherita d'Anjou* and *L'esule di Granata*. Also successful in operas by Rossini, Pacini and Mercadante.

Bassi, Luigi (b Pesaro, 5 Sep 1766; d Dresden, 13 Sep 1825), Italian baritone. Appeared in soprano parts at the age of 13 and went to Prague in 1784, where he made a great reputation, singing Count Almaviva in the 1st Prague prod. of *Le Nozze di Figaro* (1786). He was Mozart's 1st Don Giovanni there in 1787. He later sang in Leipzig, Vienna and Dresden; other Mozart roles incl. Guglielmo and Masetto.

Basso Cantante (It. = singing-bass), a bass voice esp. suited to melodic delivery and lyrical parts.

Basso continuo (It. = continuous bass). *See* **Continuo** and **Thorough-Bass.**

Basso Ostinato (It., lit. obstinate bass) = Ground Bass, a bass part in a comp. continually tracing the same melodic outline.

Bassoon, a double-reed instrument dating from the 16th cent. The normal compass is:

though a few higher notes are possible.

Bastardella, La, the nickname given to the singer Lucrezia Aguiari (*q.v.*), who was the illegitimate daughter of an Italian nobleman.

Bastianini, Ettore (b Siena, 24 Sep 1922; d Sirmione, 25 Jan 1967), Italian baritone. Debut, as a bass, Ravenna, 1945. Debut as bar. 1951, Germont. NY Met 1953–66; in 1953 sang Andrei in the fp of the revision of Prokofiev's *War and Peace*. La Scala from 1954. CG 1962. Other roles incl. Onegin, Renato and Posa.

Bastien und Bastienne, *Singspiel* by Mozart, K50 (lib. by F.W. Weiskern and A. Schachtner, based on Favart's parody of Rousseau's *Le Devin du Village*), prod. Vienna, at the house of Anton Mesmer, the hypnotist, Sep 1768.

Bastin, Jules (b Pont, 18 Aug 1933), Belgian bass. Théâtre de la Monnaie, Brussels, from 1960. Has sung in London, Chicago and NY, largely in Fr. rep., e.g. *Le Prophète, Pelléas et Mélisande, Benvenuto Cellini.* He sang the Banker in the fp of the 3-act version of Berg's *Lulu*, Paris, 1979.

Bataille, Gabriel (b ? Brie, 1575; d Paris, 17 Dec 1630), French lutenist and composer. Contrib. music to ballets danced at the court of Louis XIII. Between 1608 and 1623 he pub. many lute pieces and songs.

Bates, Joah (b Halifax, bap. 8 Mar 1740; d London, 8 Jun 1799), English organist, scholar and conductor. Cond. the Concert of Ancient Music in London from its foundation in 1776.

Bates, William, English 18th-cent. composer. Worked in London, where he prod. several stage pieces and wrote songs for the pleasure gardens, glees, catches, etc.

Bateson, Thomas (b Cheshire, c 1570; d Dublin, Mar 1630), English organist and composer. Prob. organist at Chester Cathedral until 1609, when he became vicar-choral and organist at Christ Church Cathedral, Dublin. 2 books of madrigals by him were pub. in 1604 and 1618.

Bathe, William (b Ireland, 2 Apr 1564; d Madrid, 17 Jun 1614), Irish priest and music scholar. In state service at first, he went to Spain and became a Jesuit priest in 1599. He wrote *Briefe Introductions to the True Art of Musick and the Skill of Song*, also *Janua linguarum.*

Baton (Fr.), the stick used by the cond. in orchestral and choral perfs. It orig. from a roll of music used in the 15th cent. and passed through a phase of a heavy stick beaten on the floor in the 17th (Lully died after striking himself on the foot with his baton; later conductors have favoured a lighter stick).

Battaglia di Legnano, La (*The Battle of L.*), opera by Verdi (lib. by S. Cammarano), prod. Rome, Teatro Argentina, 27 Jan 1849.

Battement (Fr.) = Mordent.

Batten, Adrian (b Salisbury, bap. 1 Mar 1591; d London, 1637), English organist and composer. Chorister at Winchester Cathedral as a boy. In 1614 he came to London as vicar-choral at Westminster Abbey and in 1626 became organist at St Paul's Cathedral.

Works incl. 11 services, c 50 anthems and other church music.

Batterie (Fr.). An 18th-cent. term for rapid broken accomp. figures. Also a collective term for the group of perc. instruments in the orchestra.

Battishill, Jonathan (b London, May 1738; d London, 10 Dec 1801), English harpsichordist, organist and composer. Chorister at St Paul's Cathedral. About 1762 became harpsichordist to Covent Garden Theatre, where he prod. in 1764 the opera *Almena*, written jointly with M. Arne. About the

same time he became organist of 3 city churches, and began to write church music. His
best-known pieces are the anthems *Call to
remembrance* and *O Lord, look down from
heaven.* Other works incl. music for the
stage, glees, catches, songs, etc.

Battistini, Mattia (b Rome, 27 Feb 1856; d
Colle Baccaro nr. Rieti, 7 Nov 1928), Italian
baritone. Made his 1st appearance in opera
in Rome, 1878, in *La Favorita.* London,
1883–1906, as Rigoletto, Valentin, Don
Giovanni, Amonasro and Onegin. Sang in
Russia 1888–1914 (Ruslan and Demon).
Other roles incl. Wolfram, Iago and Boccanegra. The leading It. baritone of his
time.

Battle, Kathleen (b Portsmouth, Ohio, 13
Aug 1948), American soprano. Studied at
the Univ. of Cincinnati and appeared with
the NY PO and Los Angeles SO from 1972.
NY Met debut 1978. At the 1979 Glyndebourne Festival she was heard as Nerina in
Haydn's *La fedeltà premiata.* In 1985 her
agile coloratura as Zerbinetta was much
acclaimed at CG.

Battle of Prague, The, a descriptive pf.
piece with vln., cello and drum *ad lib.* by
Franz Koczwara, comp. 1788, of no musical
value, but very popular in the early 19th
cent.

Battle of the Huns (Liszt). *See* **Hunnenschlacht.**

Battle of Vittoria, The, Beethoven's 'Battle
Symph.', op. 91, orig. entitled *Wellingtons
Sieg oder die Schlacht bei Vittoria,* fp 8 Dec
1813. An extravagantly descriptive piece,
orig. intended for a mechanical instrument,
it contains quotations from nat. songs, incl.
Rule, Britannia.

Batton, Désiré (Alexandre) (b Paris, 2 Jan
1798; d Versailles, 15 Oct 1855), French
composer. Studied at the Paris Cons. and
gained the Prix de Rome in 1817; went to
Rome and travelled after prod. his 1st comic
opera, *La Fenêtre secrète,* in 1818.

  Works incl. operas *Ethelwina* (1827), *Le
Prisonnier d'état, Le Champ du drap d'or*
(1828); church music; symph.

Battuta (It.) = Beat, often used loosely in the
plural (e.g. *ritmo di 3 battute*) to indicate a
change in the metrical scheme of bars — not
beats — grouped in unexpected numbers.

Baudo, Serge (b Marseilles, 16 Jul 1927),
French conductor. Debut 1950, with the
Concerts Lamoureux. Paris Opéra from
1962 and opera at La Scala and NY Met.
Chief cond. Orchestre de Paris 1967–9. He
gave the fps of Messiaen's *Et exspecto resurrectionem mortuorum* (Chartres, 1965) and

La Transfiguration (Lisbon, 1969). Founded Berlioz Festival, Lyons, 1979.

Baudrier, Yves (b Paris, 11 Feb 1906),
French composer. Originally a law student,
he formed the group of La Jeune France with
Jolivet, Lesur and Messiaen in 1936.

  Works incl. *Agnus Dei* for sop., chorus
and orch.; symph., symph. poem *Le Grand
Voilier* (1939); string 4tet (1944); pf. pieces,
songs.

Bauermeister, Mathilde (b Hamburg,
1849; d Herne Bay, 15 Oct 1926), German-
born soprano. After study at the RAM she
sang in Dublin, 1866. London, CG, 1868–
1905 (debut as Siebel). She made many tours
of the USA, from 1879, and sang at the NY
Met, 1891–1906 (debut as Thomas's Gertrude). Other roles incl. Marguerite de
Valois and Elvira.

Bauldeweyn, Noel (d *c* 1530), Flemish composer. *Maître de chapelle* of Notre Dame at
Antwerp, 1513–18. Comp. sacred and secular music incl. the Mass *Da Pacem* formerly
thought to be by Josquin.

Baum, Kurt (b Prague, 15 Mar 1908), Czech
tenor. Debut Zurich 1933, in the fp of Zemlinsky's *Der Kreidekreis.* He sang at the
German Theatre, Prague, 1934–9 and
appeared as Radames at Chicago in 1939.
NY Met, 1941–67, often in operas by Wagner. He sang Rossini's Arnold at the 1952
Florence Festival and the following year was
heard as Radames at CG.

Baumgartner, Rudolf (b Zurich, 14 Sep
1917), Swiss violinist and conductor. He
studied with Schneiderhan, with whom he
founded the Lucerne Festival Strings in
1956; he has toured world wide with the
orch. as cond. and has arr. for it Bach's
Musical Offering and *Art of Fugue.* From
1968 artistic dir. Lucerne Festival.

Bavarian Highlands, Scenes from the, 6
Choral Songs with pf., op. 27, by Elgar;
comp. 1895, fp Worcester, 21 Apr 1896.
Version with orch., 1896. Nos. 1, 3 and 6
were arr. for orch. alone as *Three Bavarian
Dances,* perf. Crystal Palace, 23 Oct 1897,
cond. August Manns.

Bax, Arnold (Edward Trevor) (b London, 8
Nov 1883; d Cork, 3 Oct 1953), English
composer. Entered the RAM in 1900, studying pf. with Matthay and comp. with F.
Corder. Stayed frequently in Ir. and travelled
in Rus. He never held any official music
position until he was app. Master of the
King's Music in 1942. Knighted 1937.

  Works incl. DRAMATIC: ballet *The Truth
about the Rus. Dancers* (J. M. Barrie)
(1920); film music for *Malta G.C.*

(documentary) and *Oliver Twist* (after Dickens).

CHORAL: incl. *Enchanted Summer* (1910), *Fatherland* (1907), *I sing of a Maiden, Mater ora Filium, St. Patrick's Breastplate, This Worldes Joie* (1922), *To the Name above every Name*; *Te Deum* and Nunc Dimittis for chorus and org.

ORCH.: 7 symphs. (1922–39), *Sinfonietta*, symph. poems *November Woods* (1917), *The Garden of Fand, The Happy Forest, Tintagel* (1919); overture *Work in Progress, Overture to a Picaresque Comedy* (1930), *Legend,* 2 *Northern Ballads* and other orch. works; concertos for vln. and orch. (1938), and for cello and orch. (1949), symph. variations and *Winter Legends* for pf. and orch.

CHAMBER MUSIC: incl. nonet, 8tet, 5tets for pf. and strings, ob. and strings, strings and harp, strings, 3 string 4tets (1916–36), pf. 4tet, trios for vln., vla. and pf., vln., cello and pf., and fl., vla. and harp; 3 sonatas for vln. and pf., sonata for vla. and pf., sonata for cello and pf., sonata for clar. and pf.; 4 pf. sonatas (1910–32) and numerous pf. pieces; sonata and 5 other works for 2 pfs.; many songs and a number of folksong arrs.

Baxevanos, Peter (b Salonika, 29 Sep 1908; d Vienna, 24 Jun 1982), Greek tenor. Debut 1934 in Wolf-Ferrari's *Sly*, at the Vienna Volksoper. He sang at Zurich until 1938 and was Alwa in the fp of Berg's *Lulu* (1937) and the Kardinal in the fp of Hindemith's *Mathis der Maler* (1938); returned to the Volksoper during the war and from 1945 appeared at the Staatsoper, Vienna, and in Italy as Manrico, Cavaradossi, Don Carlos, Don José and Florestan.

Bayer, Joseph (b Vienna, 6 Mar 1852; d Vienna, 12 Mar 1913), Austrian conductor and composer. Studied at the Vienna Cons., played the vln. at the Court Opera and from 1885 was director of the ballet music there.

Works incl. operettas *Der Chevalier von San Marco, Mr. Menelaus, Fräulein Hexe, Der Polizeichef* and others; ballets *Die Puppenfee* (1888) and many others, etc.

Bayreuth, the small town in Bavaria where Wagner built the festival theatre for the perf. of his works, opened in 1876 with the 1st prod. of *The Ring*. Theatre then closed until it re-opened in 1882, with the 1st prod. of *Parsifal*. Cosima Wagner was dir. 1883–1908, her son Siegfried 1908–30. Wieland and Wolfgang Wagner, the comp.'s grandsons, were dirs. 1951–66 and revolutionised the way in which the operas were presented; realism was replaced by abstraction. Wieland's 1951 prod. of *Parsifal* was well received, but later stagings have provoked controversy; the Chéreau prod. of *The Ring* (1976) was much discussed, but Peter Hall (1983) attempted some return to realism. Wieland Wagner has been artistic dir. from 1966.

Bazelon, Irwin (Allen) (b Evanston, Ill., 4 Jun 1922), American composer. Studied with Hindemith, Milhaud and Bloch. Experienced in film music and incid. music for Shakespeare's plays.

Works incl. 7 symphs. (1963–80), *Chamber Symph.* for 7 insts. (1957), *Symphonie Concertante* (1963), *Early American Suite* (1970), *Excursions* for orch. (1966), *Spirits of the Night* for orch. (1976), *Sound Dreams* for 6 insts. (1977), *Spires* for tpt and orch. (1981), pf. concerto (1984); 2 string 4tets, 3 pf. sonatas.

Beach (*née* **Cheney), Amy Marcy** (b Henniker, New Hampshire, 5 Sep 1867; d New York, 27 Dec 1944), American pianist and composer, known as Mrs. Henry Beach.

Works incl. Mass in E; *Christ in the Universe* for chorus and orch. (1931); *Gaelic Symph.* (1896, the first symph. work by an Amer. woman); pf. concerto; string 4tet, pf. trio; numerous songs.

Beak Flute (= Ger. *Schnabelflöte*) = Recorder.

Bear, The, nickname (*L'Ours*) of the 1st of Haydn's 'Paris' symphs., no. 82 in C, comp. 1786.

Opera by Walton (lib. by P. Dehn and the comp., based on Chekhov), prod. Aldeburgh, 3 Jun 1967.

Bearbeitung (Ger. = arrangement), partic. the adaptation of a work for a different performing medium.

Beard, John (b London, *c* 1717; d Hampton, 5 Feb 1791), English tenor. Chorister of the Chapel Royal under Gates, he later sang in the fps of many of Handel's oratorios. The tenor parts in *Israel in Egypt, Messiah, Samson, Judas Maccabeus* and *Jephtha* were comp. for him; also created roles in *Ariodante, Alcina, Atalanta, Berenice* and *Semele.*

Beat. (1) The unit of measurement in music, indicated in choral and orch. music by the cond. It is not necessarily synonymous with accent. (2) An Old Eng. name for a variety of ornaments.

Béatitudes, Les, oratorio by Franck for solo voices, chorus and orch. (words from the Bible), comp. 1869–79, fp privately by Franck's pupils at his house, 20 Feb 1879 (pf. acc.), and in public only after his death, Dijon, 15 Jun 1891.

Beatrice di Tenda, opera by Bellini (lib. by F. Romani), prod. Venice, Teatro La Fenice, 16 Mar 1833.

Béatrice et Bénédict (*Beatrice and Benedick*), opera by Berlioz (lib. by comp., based on Shakespeare's *Much Ado about Nothing*), prod. Baden-Baden, 9 Aug 1862.

Beatrix Cenci, opera in 2 acts by Ginastera (lib. by W. Shand and A. Girri after Shelley's *The Cenci*, 1819, and Stendhal's *Chroniques Italiennes*, 1837), prod. NY, City Opera, 14 Mar 1973.

Beats, in acoustics the clashing of soundwaves of slightly different frequencies prod., for ex., by 2 pf. strings for the same note not perfectly in tune with each other, or certain org. stops using 2 pipes for each note purposely kept slightly out of tune to prod. that wavering effect. Sensitive ears perceive beats as slight periodical swellings of the tone on sustained notes, and pf. tuners rely on beats to tell them whether the strings of any one note are in tune or not.

Beaujoyeulx, Balthasar de (Baldassare da Belgioioso, Baltazarini) (b before 1535; d *c* 1587), Italian violinist, sent to France *c* 1555 with a large band of string players by the Maréchal de Brissac to form the orch. of Catherine de' Medici. He supervised the perf. of the *Ballet comique de la royne*.

Beaulieu, Eustorg de (b Beaulieu-sur-Menoire, 1495–1500; d Basle, 8 Jan 1552), French poet and musician. He wrote a few *chansons*, but is better known for his verse, incl. a collection of early Protestant song texts.

Beaumarchais, Pierre Augustin Caron de (1732–99), French author and musician. He sang and played the fl. and harp, teaching the latter to the daughters of Louis XV. His comedy *Le Barbier de Séville* was at 1st to be a comic opera with music arr. by Beaumarchais from Span. songs and dances. *See also* Auric (*Marriage de Figaro*), Barbiere di Siviglia (Paisiello and Rossini), Benda (F.L.) (*Barbier von Sevilla*), Dittersdorf (*Hochzeit des F.*), Glière (*Figaro*), Morlacchi (*Barbiere di S.*), Nozze di Figaro (Mozart), Paer (*Nuovo Figaro*), Portugal (*Pazza giornata*), Ricci (L.) (do. and *Nozze di F.*), Schulz (*Barbier de Séville*), Shaporin (*Marriage of Figaro*), Shield (do.), Tarare (Salieri).

Beaux Arts Trio, American pf. trio, founded at the Berkshire Music Fest., Tanglewood, in 1955. Members until 1987: Menahem Pressler (pf.), Isadore Cohen (vln.) and Bernard Greenhouse (cello). Has toured widely in the Classical repertory. Peter Wiley cellist from 1987.

Bebung (Ger. = Trembling), an effect of tone-vibration obtainable on the clavichord by moving the finger up and down on the key, thereby varying the tension of the string.

Bechi, Gino (b Florence, 16 Oct 1913), Italian baritone. Debut Empoli, 1936, as Germont. He sang at Rome and La Scala from 1937 and created roles in operas by Rocca and Alfano; appeared as guest throughout Europe and S. Amer. and was admired as Nabucco, Amonasro, Gérard and Hamlet. London, 1950 and 1958, as Iago, Falstaff and William Tell. He sang in Chicago and San Francisco (1952) and appeared in films of *Aida, Ballo in Maschera* and *Cavalleria Rusticana*. Taught in Florence from 1965.

Becht, Hermann (b Karlsruhe, 1940), German bass-baritone. After engagements in Brunswick and Wiesbaden he sang at the Deustche Oper, Düsseldorf, from 1974. He is today's leading interpreter of Alberich and has sung the role in London, NY and at Bayreuth (from 1979). Other roles incl. Mandryka, Kurwenal, Amfortas, Falstaff and Pfitzner's Borromeo.

Beck, Conrad (b Lohn, Schaffenhausen, 16 Jun 1901), Swiss composer. After studying engineering, he became a student at the Zurich Cons. under Andreae and others; later in Berlin and Paris, where he lived in 1923–32 and was closely in touch with Roussel and Honegger. Awarded important prizes for comp. in 1954, 1956 and 1964.

Works incl. opera *La Grande Ourse* (1936); incid. music for Goethe's *Pandora* (1945) and other plays; oratorios *Angelus Silesius* and *Der Tod zu Basel*; Requiem; *Der Tod des Oedipus* for chorus and orch.; *Lyric Cantata* (Rilke) for female voices and orch.; chamber cantata (sonnets by Louise Labé); 5 symphs. (1925–30), *Sinfonietta, Innominata* and *Ostinato* for orch.; concerto for string 4tet and orch., *Konzertmusik* for ob. and strings, concerto, concertino and rhapsody for pf. and orch., cello concerto; 5 string 4tets (1922–52); org. and pf. works; *Liederspiel* cycle and other songs.

Beck, Franz (b Mannheim, 20 Feb 1734; d Bordeaux, 31 Dec 1809), German violinist and composer. A member of the Mannheim school of symphonists and a pupil of Johann Stamitz. He is said to have fled from Mannheim as the result of a duel; went to Italy and later settled in France.

Works incl. the operas *La belle jardinière* (Bordeaux, 1767) and *Pandore* (Paris, 1789); *c* 30 symphs., *Stabat Mater*, keyboard music.

Beddoe, Dan (b Ammanford, 16 Mar 1863; d New York, 26 Dec 1937), Welsh-born tenor. He emigrated to the USA after winning an Eisteddfod prize in 1882. Studied at Pittsburgh and New York, concert debut 1903. He sang the title role in a concert perf. of *Parsifal* cond. by Walter Damrosch (1904), and until 1934 was highly successful in Cincinnati and NY in oratorios by Mendelssohn and Handel; admired by Caruso for his *messa-di-voce* technique. He sang at Crystal Palace in a 1911 perf. of *Messiah* which celebrated the coronation of George V.

Bedford, David (b London, 4 Aug 1937), English composer. He studied at the RAM with Berkeley and in Venice with Nono.

Works incl. the school operas *The Rime of the Ancient Mariner* (1976) and *The Ragnarok* (1983); symph. for 12 players, *Sun Paints Rainbows on the Vast Waves* for orch. (1982); *Star Clusters, Nebulae and Places in Devon* for chorus and brass (1971); many pieces for inst. ensemble and voices and insts., many of which reflect the fact that he is a teacher and a one-time member of the pop music group *The Whole World*.

Bedford, Steuart (b London, 31 Jun 1939), English conductor. He studied at the RAM. Debut SW, 1967, with the English Opera Group; toured with the group in Europe and the USA. 1975–80, co-art. dir. the English Music Theatre (formerly EOG). Cond. fps of Britten's *Death in Venice* (1973) and *Phaedra* (1976), both at Aldeburgh.

Bedyngham, John (d London, *c* 1460), English composer. Wrote Masses, motets and *chansons*, possibly incl. *O rosa bella*, often ascribed to Dunstable. His music was widely known on the Continent.

Bee's Wedding, The. The English nickname of Mendelssohn's *Song without Words* in C maj. op. 67 no. 4, the Ger. being *Spinnerlied* (spinning-song).

Beecham, Thomas (b St Helens, Lancs., 29 Apr 1879; d London, 8 Mar 1961), English conductor. He was educated at Rossall School and Wadham Coll., Oxford. After cond. the Hallé Orch. at a concert at St Helens in 1899 he studied comp. with Charles Wood, intending to be a comp., but turned his attention to cond. and first appeared in London in 1905. From that time he rapidly became one of the most original and versatile English conds. From 1909 up to the 1914–18 war, and also during the war, he was responsible for intro. a number of unfamiliar operas to the public, incl.

Strauss's *Feuersnot, Ariadne auf Naxos* and *Rosenkavalier* (all 1st Brit. perfs.) . In 1929 he gave a festival of Delius's music in London, and in 1932 founded the LPO. During the 1939–45 war he was active as a cond. in Australia, Canada and USA. He founded the RPO in 1947. While excelling in Mozart, he was also passionately interested in the works of Romantic comps., particularly Delius: he cond. the fp of the opera *Irmelin* (Oxford, 1953). He was knighted in 1914 and succeeded to his father's baronetcy in 1916.

Beeson, Jack (Hamilton) (b Muncie, Ind., 15 Jul 1921), American composer. Studied with Howard Hanson at Rochester and with Bartók in NY, 1945; Prof. at Columbia Univ. from 1965. He is best known for his operas: *Jonah* (1950), *Hello, Out There* (1954), *The Sweet Bye and Bye* (1957), *Lizzie Borden* (1965), *Dr. Heidegger's Fountain of Youth* (after Hawthorne, 1978); also symph. in A (1959), *Transformations* for orch. (1959), 5 pf. sonatas, TV opera *My Heart's in the Highlands* (after Sorayan, 1970).

Beeth, Lola (b Kraków, 23 Nov 1860; d Berlin, 18 Mar 1940), German soprano. She studied with Pauline Viardot and Desirée Artôt. Debut Berlin, Hofoper, 1882, as Elsa; remained until 1888 and then sang at the Vienna Hofoper until 1895. She appeared at the NY Met 1895–6 (debut as Meyerbeer's Valentine). After guest appearances at CG, St Petersburg and Monte Carlo she returned to Vienna, 1898–1901, and often sang under Mahler.

Beethoven, Ludwig van (b Bonn, bap. 17 Dec 1770; d Vienna, 26 Mar 1827), German composer of Flemish descent. Son and grandson of musicians in the service of the Elector of Cologne in Bonn. Became pupil of C.G. Neefe in 1781. In 1783 was harpsichordist in the court orch., and the same year pub. 3 pf. sonatas. 2nd organist at court 1784, and 1789 also vla. player. A visit to Vienna in 1787 to study with Mozart was cut short after only a few weeks by his mother's fatal illness, and he continued as a court musician in Bonn, meeting Count Waldstein in 1788. In 1792 he returned to Vienna to be a pupil of Haydn, whom he had met in Bonn. He remained in Vienna for the rest of his life, scarcely leaving the city or its suburbs. From 1793 to 1796 he lived in the house of Prince Lichnowsky and estab. himself in the musical life of Vienna. Tuition with Haydn was not a success, and he took lessons from Schenk, Albrechtsberger and Salieri. In 1795 he pub. his op. 1, 3 pf. trios, and made his first public appearance in Vienna as a pianist and comp. He lived by playing and teaching, later increasingly by the pub. of his works. His 3rd symph. (*Eroica*) was ded. to Napoleon, but Beethoven changed the dedication when Napoleon proclaimed himself Emperor.

He refused to accept regular employment under the old system of patronage, but received support from the aristocracy: in 1808, for instance, 3 noblemen, the Archduke Rudolph, Prince Kinsky and Prince Lobkowitz, agreed to pay him an unconditional annuity; the 5th symph. dates from the same year. The deafness which had threatened from as early as *c* 1795 increased, and his despair gave rise to the suicidal 'Heiligenstadt Testament' in 1802; by 1806 he was forced to abandon public perf. altogether. More time was now available for comp.: there followed the Rasumovsky 4tets, the vln. concerto, *Pastoral*, 7th and 8th symphs. and the *Emperor* concerto. Prod. his only opera in 1805 (*Fidelio*, rev, 1806 and again 1814). In 1815, after his brother's death, became guardian to his nephew Karl, a task he took seriously and which caused him constant worry. By 1819 he was totally deaf, and communication with him was possible only in writing. He had begun work on the *Choral* symph. in 1817 and this was followed by the Missa Solemnis (1819–22) and the last 5 4tets (1822–6). He never recovered from an infection caught in 1826, and his death the following year was due to dropsy.

Works incl. STAGE: opera, *Fidelio*, (1805, rev. 1806 and 1814), incid. music for *Egmont* (Goethe, 1810), *The Ruins of Athens* (A. von Kotzebue, 1812), *King Stephen* (Kotzebue, 1812), *The Creatures of Prometheus*, ov., intro. and 16 nos. for a ballet prod. at the Burgtheater, Vienna, 1801.

CHORAL WITH ORCH.: *Cantata on the Death of the Emperor Joseph II* (1790), oratorio *Christus am Ölberge*, op. 85 (1803), Mass in C, op. 86 (1807), *Choral Fantasia*, for pf., chorus and orch., op. 80 (1808), Mass in D, (*Missa Solemnis*), op. 123 (1819–22).

SYMPHS: no. 1 in C, op. 21 (1800), no. 2 in D, op. 36 (1802), no. 3 in Eb (*Eroica*), op. 55 (1803), no. 4 in Bb, op. 60 (1806), no. 5 in C min., op. 67 (1808), no. 6 in F, (*Pastoral*), op. 68 (1808), no. 7 in A, op. 92 (1812), no. 8 in F, op. 93 (1812), no. 9 in D min. (*Choral*), op. 125 (1817–24); 'Battle Symph.', op. 91 (1813).

CONCERTOS: pf., no. 1 in C, op. 15 (1795), no. 2 in Bb, op. 19 (before 1793, rev. 1794–5, 1798), no. 3 in C min., op. 37 (? 1800), no. 4 in G, op. 58 (1806), no. 5 in Eb, (*Emperor*), op. 73 (1809); vln. concerto, op. 61 (1806), triple concerto for pf., vln. and cello, op. 56 (1804).

OVERTURES: *Leonora* 1–3, for the 1st and 2nd versions of *Fidelio* (1805, 1806), *Coriolan*, op. 62 (1807), *Namensfeier* (*Name-day*), op. 115 (1815), *Die Weihe des Hauses* (*The Consecration of the House*), op. 124 (1822).

CHAMBER: Septet in Eb op. 20 (1800); 2 5tets, for piano and wind in Eb (1796), for strings in C, op. 29 (1801); 16 string 4tets, op. 18 nos. 1–6, in F, G, D, C min., A and Bb (1798–1800), op. 59 nos. 1–3, *Rasumovsky*, in F, E min. and C (1806), op. 74 in Eb *Harp*, (1809), op. 95 in F min. (1810), op. 127 in Eb (1825), op. 130 in Bb (1826; present rondo finale replaces original *Grosse Fuge*, op. 133), op. 131 in C♯ min. (1826), op. 132 in A min. (1825), op. 135 in F (1826); 5 string trios: op. 3 in Eb (*c* 1794), op. 8, ('Serenade') in D (1797), op. 9 nos. 1–3, in G, D and C min. (1798); 6 pf. trios, op. 1 nos. 1–3, in Eb, G and C min. (1794), op. 70 nos. 1 and 2, in D (*Ghost*), and Eb (1808), op. 97 in Bb, (*Archduke*) (1811); 10 vln. sons: op. 12 nos. 1–3, in D, A and Eb (1798), op. 23 in A min. (1800), op. 24 in F, (*Spring*) (1801), op. 30 nos. 1–3, in A, C min. and G (1802), op. 47 in A, (*Kreutzer*) (1803), op. 96 in G (1812); 5 cello sons., op. 5 nos. 1 and 2, in F and G min. (1796), op. 69 in A (1808), op. 102 nos. 1 and 2, in C and D (1815).

PIANO: 32 sons., op. 2 nos. 1–3, in F min., A and C (1795), op. 7 in Eb (1796), op. 10 nos. 1–3, in C min., F and D (1798), op. 13 in C min. (*Pathétique*) (1799), op. 14 nos. 1 and 2 in E and G (1799), op. 22 in Bb (1800), op. 26 in Ab (1801), op. 27 nos. 1 and 2, in Eb and C♯ min. (*Moonlight*) (1801), op. 28 in D (*Pastoral*) (1801), op. 31 nos. 1–3, in G, D min. and Eb (1802), op. 49 nos. 1 and 2, in G min. and G (1802), op. 53 in C (*Waldstein*) (1804), op. 54 in F (1804), op. 57 in F min. (*Appassionata*) (1805), op. 78 in F♯ (1809), op. 79 in G (1809), op. 81a in Eb (*Les Adieux*) (1801), op. 90 in E min. (1814), op. 101 in A (1816), op. 106 in Bb (*Hammerklavier*) (1818), op. 109 in E (1820), op. 110 in Ab (1821), op. 111 in C min. (1822); 3 sets of bagatelles, op. 33 (1782–1802), op. 119 (1821), op. 126 (1824), 15 Vars. and Fugue on a theme from Prometheus, (*Eroica Variations*) in Eb

(1802), 33 *Variations on a Waltz by Diabelli*, op. 120 (1819–23).

SOLO VOICE: Scena and aria *Ah! Perfido!* for sop. and orch. (1796), *Adelaide* for tenor and pf. (1795–6), *An die ferne Geliebte* for tenor and pf. (1816), 37 Scottish songs with pf. trio accompaniment (1815–16).

Beffroy de Reigny, Louis Abel (b Lâon, 6 Nov 1757; d Paris, 17 Dec 1811), French playwright and composer. Known as 'Cousin Jacques', under which name he wrote satirical operettas popular during the Revolution, incl. *Nicodème dans la lune, Nicodème aux enfers* and *La Petite Nanette*.

Beggar's Opera, The, ballad opera, prod. London, Theatre in Lincoln's Inn Fields, 29 Jan 1728, consisting of a play by John Gay interspersed with songs. The music, popular tunes of the day but for the most part not folksongs, was arr. by John Christopher Pepusch, who also comp. the overture. Several modern realizations, incl. Britten (1948).

Beginning of a Novel, The (*Počátek románu*), opera in 1 act by Janáček (lib. by J. Tichý, after a story by G. Preissová), comp. 1891, prod. Brno, 10 Feb 1894.

Beglarian, Grant (b Tiflis, 1 Dec 1927), American composer of Russian birth. Emigrated to US in 1947 and studied with Ross Lee Finney at the Univ. of Michigan. Taught at the Univ. of Southern Calif., LA, 1969–82.

Works incl. string 4tet (1948), *Symphony in 2 Movements* (1950), *Divertimento* for orch. (1957), woodwind 5tet (1966), *Diversions* for vla., cello and orch. (1972), *Sinfonia* for strings (1974).

Begleitungsmusik (Schoenberg). *See* **Accompaniment to a Film Scene.**

Begnis, Giuseppe de (b Lugo, 1793; d New York, Aug 1849), Italian bass. Choirboy at Lugo; made his 1st operatic appearance at Modena in 1813; created Dandini in *La Cenerentola,* Rome 1817, and went to Paris and London with his wife, 1819 and 1822; sang there in operas by Rossini, Mayr and Pacini (*see also* **Ronzi de Begnis**).

Beheim (Behaim), Michel (b Sulzbach, 29 Sep 1416; d Sulzbach, ? 1474), German Meistersinger. Active as soldier and singer in the service of German, Danish and Hungarian princes. 11 of his melodies survive.

Behrens, Hildegard (b Varel, Oldenburg, 9 Feb 1937), German soprano. Debut Düsseldorf, 1971; rep. at this time incl. Fiordiligi, Marie and Katya Kabanová. CG 1976, Leonore; Salzburg 1977, Salome. A successful Brünnhilde at Bayreuth, 1983, and Isolde in the Bernstein rec. of *Tristan und Isolde.* Other roles incl. Tosca, Eva, Elsa and Agathe.

Being Beauteous, cantata by Henze for sop., harp and 4 cellos (text from Rimbaud), perf. Berlin, 12 Apr 1964.

Beirer, Hans (b Vienna, 23 Jun 1911), Austrian tenor. Debut Linz 1936. He sang at the Berlin Städtischen Oper, 1945–58; later sang with the Stuttgart Co. Bayreuth from 1958 as Parsifal, Tristan and Tannhäuser. He sang Siegfried at the Paris Opéra in 1955 and was often heard at the Vienna Staatsoper: fps of Einem's *Der Besuch der alten Dame* (1971) and *Kabale und Liebe* (1976). Sang Aegisthus in film version of *Elektra,* 1981.

Beinum, Eduard van (b Arnhem, 3 Sep 1901; d Amsterdam, 13 Apr 1959), Dutch conductor. Studied with his brother and comp. with Sem Dresden. After a post in Haarlem (1926) he became 2nd cond. of the Concertgebouw Orch. of Amsterdam (1931–8), an associate to Mengelberg in 1938 and his successor in 1945. He toured Europe and America, and in 1956 became cond. of the Los Angeles PO, but resigned and returned to Europe, where he died.

Bekker, Paul (b Berlin, 11 Sep 1882; d New York, 7 Mar 1937), German writer on music. Studied in Berlin and was at 1st a violinist in the Phil. Orch. there. In 1906 he began to devote himself to music journalism and became critic to several papers, later operatic manager at Kassel and Wiesbaden. The Nazi regime drove him to the USA. Wrote on Beethoven, Wagner, Mahler, opera and modern comps. He was a champion of Mahler, Schoenberg, Schreker and Hindemith.

Beklemmt (Ger. = oppressed), a term used by Beethoven in the Cavatina of the string 4tet op. 130.

Bel canto (It., lit. beautiful song), singing in the traditional It. manner, with beautiful tone, perfect phrasing, clean articulation, etc. The art of bel canto culminated in It. in the 19th cent.

Belaiev, Mitrofan Petrovich (b St Petersburg, 22 Feb 1836; d St Petersburg, 10 Jan 1904), Russian timber merchant and music amateur. Founded a pub. firm for the propagation of Rus. music in 1885.

Beldemandis, Prosdocimus de (b Padua, c 1375; d Padua, 1428), Italian music scholar. Prof. of mathematics and astronomy at Padua in 1422. Wrote treatises on music pub. between 1404 and 1413.

Belenoi, Aimeric de (b Lespare, Bordelais;

d Catalonia), French 13th-cent. troubadour, 22 of whose songs have been preserved.

Belfagor, opera by Respighi (lib. by C. Guastalla, based on a comedy by E.L. Morselli), prod. Milan, La Scala, 26 Apr 1923.

Belhomme, Hypolite (b Paris, 1854; d Nice, 16 Jan 1923), French bass. Debut Paris, Opéra-Comique, 1879, and sang there till 1916; appeared there in the fps of *Les Contes d'Hoffmann* (1881) and *Louise* (1913). He sang also at Marseilles and Brussels. Other roles incl. Pistol, Kecal and Benoit.

Belin, Julien (b Le Mans, *c* 1530; d after 1584), French lutenist and composer. Pub. a book of lute pieces in tablature, 1556.

Belisario, opera by Donizetti (lib. by S. Cammarano), prod. Venice, Teatro La Fenice, 4 Feb 1836.

'Bell Anthem', the name once given to Purcell's anthem *Rejoice in the Lord alway,* comp. *c* 1682–5. The instrumental introd. contains descending scales resembling the ringing of church bells.

Belle Hélène, La (*The Fair Helen*), operetta by Offenbach (lib. by H. Meilhac and L. Halévy), prod. Paris, Théâtre des Variétés, 17 Dec 1864.

Bellerofonte, Il, opera by Mysliveček (lib. by G. Bonechi), prod. Naples, Teatro San Carlo, 20 Jan 1767.

Opera by Terradellas (lib. by F. Vanneschi), prod. London, King's Theatre, Haymarket, 24 Mar 1747.

Bellérophon, opera by Lully (lib. by T. Corneille with (?) B. de Fontenelle and Boileau), prod. Paris, Opéra, 31 Jan 1679.

Belletti, Giovanni Battista (b Sarzana, 17 Feb 1813; d Sarzana, 27 Dec 1890), Italian baritone. Studied at Bologna and made his 1st stage appearance at Stockholm in 1834 as Rossini's Figaro under the patronage of the sculptor Byström, and then sang with Jenny Lind, London, Her Majesty's Theatre, 1848, in the first local perfs. of *Attila, L'Elisir d'Amore* and *Don Pasquale.*

Bell'haver, Vincenzo (d Venice, ? Sep 1587), Italian composer. From 30 Dec 1586 he was 2nd organist of St Mark's Venice, in succession to Andrea Gabrieli. His works incl. Magnificats, motets and madrigals.

Belli, Domenico (d Florence, buried 5 May 1627), Italian 16th–17th-cent. composer. Prob. in the service of the Duke of Parma; he taught at the church of San Lorenzo at Florence, 1610–13. Pub. a book of airs for 1 and 2 voices with chitarrone accomp., and another of 5 interludes for Tasso's *Aminta.*

Belli, Girolamo (b Argenta nr. Ferrara,

1552; d ? Argenta, *c* 1620), Italian composer. Pupil of Luzzaschi; singer at the Gonzaga court at Mantua; in Rome in 1582. Pub. several books of madrigals as well as Masses, psalms and *Sacrae cantiones.*

Belli, Giulio (b Longiano, *c* 1560; d ? Imola, *c* 1621), Italian monk and composer. Held various church apps. at Imola, Venice, Montagnana, Osimo, Forli and Padua. He returned to Imola in 1611. Wrote madrigals and other secular vocal works at first, but (?) only church music later, incl. numerous Masses, motets, psalms.

Bellincioni, Gemma (b Como, 18 Aug 1864; d Naples, 23 Apr 1950), Italian soprano. Made her 1st appearance at Naples in 1879 and sang with great success in Italy and on tour in Europe. In 1895 she 1st visited Eng., as Santuzza and Carmen, and in 1899 S. America. Other roles incl. Fedora, Tosca and Salome.

Bellini, Vincenzo (b Catania, Sicily, 3 Nov 1801; d Puteaux nr. Paris, 23 Sep 1835), Italian composer. His father, an organist, was enabled with the help of a Sicilian nobleman to send him to study with Zingarelli at the Naples Cons., where he met Donizetti and Mercadante. In 1825 his 1st opera (*Adelson e Salvini*) was prod., while he was still a student, and attracted the attention of Barbaia, who commissioned him to write a 2nd (*Bianca e Gernando*), which he prod. at the Teatro San Carlo in 1826. Its success induced Barbaia to ask for another opera (*Il pirata*) for the La Scala at Milan; this was prod. there in 1827 with Rubini in the cast. It was also successfully perf. in Paris, and 3 other operas followed, at Milan, Parma and Venice, before he attained full maturity in *La sonnambula,* brought out at Milan in 1831. *Norma* followed in Dec of the same year, with Pasta in the title-part. In 1833 Bellini went to London and Paris, where Rossini advised him to write a work for the Théâtre Italien. This was *I puritani,* prod. there in 1835, with Giulia Grisi, Rubini, Tamburini and Lablache in the cast. It was brought to London the same year for Grisi's benefit perf. Bellini went to stay with an Eng. friend at Puteaux, at whose house he was taken ill and died.

Works incl. operas *Adelson e Salvini, Bianca e Gernando, Il pirata, La straniera* (1829), *Zaira, I Capuleti e i Montecchi* (based on Shakespeare's sources for *Romeo and Juliet*), *La sonnambula, Norma, Beatrice di Tenda* (1833), *I puritani;* church music, songs; symphs.

Belloc, Teresa Giorgi (b San Benigno nr.

Turin, 2 Jul 1784; d San Giorgio Cavanese, 13 May 1855), Italian soprano of French descent. Made her 1st appearances at the Teatro Regio, Turin, in 1801 in operas by Pacini and Mayr. Later heard in Rossini roles, incl. Tancredi and Isabella.

Bells, The, poem for orch., chorus and soloists by Rakhmaninov, op. 35 (text by Edgar Allan Poe, trans. by K. Balmont); comp. 1913, fp St Petersburg, 30 Nov 1913. Rev. 1936 and perf. Sheffield, 21 Oct 1936, cond. Henry Wood.

Bells of Zlonice, The, symph. no. 1 in C min. by Dvořák; comp. 1865 as op. 3 but lost until 1923. Fp Prague, 4 Oct 1936.

Belly, the surface of string instruments, also sometimes the sound-board of the pf.

Belmont und Constanze, oder Die Entführung aus dem Serail, opera by André (lib. by C.F. Bretzner, based on I. Bickerstaffe's *The Captive*), prod. Berlin, 25 May 1781.

Opera by Christian Ludwig Dieter (1757–1822) (lib. do.), prod. Stuttgart, 27 Aug 1784.

For Mozart's opera on this subject *see* **Entführung.**

Belshazzar, oratorio by Handel (words by Charles Jennens), prod. London, King's Theatre, Haymarket, 27 Mar 1745.

Belshazzar's Feast, cantata by William Walton (words from the Bible arr. by O. Sitwell), prod. Leeds Festival, 8 Oct 1931. Incid. music by Sibelius for a play by H. Procopé, fp Helsinki, 7 Nov 1906. Orch. Suite op. 51 in 4 movts. fp Helsinki, 25 Sep 1907.

Bemberg, Herman (b Paris, 29 Mar 1859; d Berne, 21 Jul 1931), French composer. Pupil of Dubois and Massenet at the Paris Cons.

Works incl. operas *Le Baiser de Suzon* (1888) and *Elaine* (CG, 1892); cantata *La Mort de Jeanne d'Arc*; recitation with accomp. *La Ballade du désespéré*; many songs incl. *Aime-moi* and *Chant hindou*.

Bémol (Fr.) }
Bemolle (It.) } = Flat; the sign ♭.

Beňačková, Gabriela (b Bratislava, 25 Mar 1947), Czech soprano. Opera debut Prague, 1970, as Prokofiev's Natasha. She has sung Jenůfa and other roles by Janáček in Prague and Vienna. Tatyana in Moscow and at CG (debut 1979). In 1984 she was acclaimed as Smetana's Libuse, at the Nat. Theatre, Prague. Her Marguerite, in a prod. of *Faust* at the Vienna Staatsoper by Ken Russell, was well received.

Benda. Bohemian family of musicians:

1. Franz (František) B. (b Staré Benátky,

bap. 22 Nov 1709; d Nowawes nr. Potsdam, 7 Mar 1786), violinist and composer. After being a chorister in Prague he travelled widely in his youth until in 1733 he joined the service of the Crown Prince of Prussia. He succeeded J.G. Graun as *Konzertmeister* to the same patron, now Frederick II, in 1771. His daughter Juliane married Reichardt.

Works incl. trio-sonatas; concertos; sonatas, studies, etc., for vln.

2. Johann (Jan) Wenzl B. (b Staré Benátky, bap. 30 Aug 1713; d Berlin, 1752), violinist and composer, brother of prec. In the service of Frederick II in Potsdam.

3. Georg Anton (Jiří Antonín) B. (b Staré Benátky, bap. 30 Jun 1722; d Köstritz, 6 Nov 1795), harpsichordist, oboist and composer, brother of prec. Entered the service of Frederick II of Prussia in 1742, app. *Kapellmeister* to the Duke of Gotha 1750. He retired in 1778. His most influential works were the melodramas (spoken words to instrumental music) *Ariadne auf Naxos* (1775), *Medea* and *Pygmalion* (1779). Other works incl. *Singspiele: Der Dorfjahrmarkt, Romeo und Julia* (1776), *Walder, Der Holzhauer* (1778); symphs.; concertos; keyboard music.

4. Joseph B. (b Staré Benátky, bap 7 May 1724; d Berlin, 22 Feb 1804), violinist, brother of prec. Succeeded his brother Franz (1 above) as *Konzertmeister* to the Prussian court in 1786.

5. Friedrich Wilhelm Heinrich B. (b Potsdam, 15 Jul 1745; d Potsdam, 19 Jun 1814), violinist and composer, son of Franz (1 above). In the service of the Prussian court, 1765–1810, and wrote *Singspiele*, incl. *Orpheus* (1785) and *Alceste* (1786), concertos, sonatas.

6. Karl Hermann Heinrich B. (b Potsdam, 2 May 1748; d Berlin 15 Mar 1836), violinist and composer, son of Franz (1 above). Comp. little, mainly chamber music.

7. Friedrich Ernst B. (b Potsdam or Berlin, bap. 10 Oct 1749; d Berlin, 24 Feb 1785), violinist and harpsichordist, son of Joseph (4 above). One of the founders of the Berlin amateur concerts in 1770.

8. Friedrich Ludwig B. (b Gotha, bap. 4 Sep 1752; d Königsberg, 20 or 27 Mar 1792), violinist and composer, son of Georg (3 above). Director of music in Hamburg 1780–82, *Konzertmeister* at Königsberg from 1789.

Works incl. opera *Der Barbier von Seville* (based on Beaumarchais, 1776) and 2 others; oratorio; cantatas; inst. music.

Bender, Paul (b Driedorf, Westerwald, 28

Jul 1875; d Munich, 25 Nov 1947), German bass. From 1903 made a great reputation at the Munich Opera; 1st visited London in 1914, as Amfortas in the 1st stage perf. of *Parsifal* in Brit., and again, after World War I, from 1924 onwards. Afterwards he became a leading bass at the Met. Opera in NY, where he sang Hagen, Ochs and Osmin, but he returned to Munich to teach at the State School of Music.

Bendl, Karel (b Prague, 16 Apr 1838; d Prague, 20 Sep 1897), Bohemian composer and conductor. After var. posts in foreign countries as a cond. he worked in Prague from 1865 to 1878 and from 1881. He gave much encouragement to Dvořák. His works, partly in a traditional style and partly influenced by Smetana, incl. 11 operas, choral and orchestral works, and church and chamber music.

Benedetti, Michele (b Loreto, 17 Oct 1778), Italian bass. Debut Naples, 1811, in Spontini's *La Vestale*. He often sang in the fps of Rossini's operas for Naples and created Moses (1818); also appeared in *Otello*, *Armida, Ermione, La donna del lago* and *Zelmira*.

Benedict, Julius (b Stuttgart, 27 Nov 1804; d London, 5 Jun 1885), English conductor and composer of German birth. Pupil of Hummel and Weber, with the latter of whom he met Beethoven in Vienna in 1823, when he was app. cond. at the Kärntnertortheater. Next he went to Naples, where he prod. his 1st It. opera in 1829. In 1835 he went to Paris and to London, where he remained for the rest of his life. He cond. a great deal in London, both opera and concerts, and was cond. of the Norwich Festival, 1845–78, and of the Liverpool Phil. Soc., 1876–80. Knighted 1871.

Works incl. operas *Giacinta ed Ernesto, I Portoghesi in Goa* (1830), *Un anno ed un giorno* (1836), *The Gypsy's Warning, The Brides of Venice* (1844), *The Crusaders, The Lily of Killarney, The Bride of Song* (1864); 2 symphs.; 2 pf. concertos; 5 cantatas, etc.

Benedicite, work by Vaughan Williams for sop., chorus and orch.; comp. 1929, fp Dorking, 2 May 1930, cond. Vaughan Williams.

Benelli, Antonio Peregrino (b Forli, 5 Sep 1771; d Börnichen, Saxony, 16 Aug 1830), Italian tenor and composer. Pupil of Mattei in Bologna, 1st appeared as a singer in 1790 in Naples, where his opera *Partenope* was prod. in 1798. Other works incl. church music and a treatise on singing.

Benet, John, English 15th-cent. composer. Wrote Masses and other church music.

Benevoli, Orazio (b Rome, 19 Apr 1605; d Rome, 17 June 1672), Italian composer. Held appts. at the churches of San Luigi de' Francesi and Santa Maria Maggiore in Rome, the former with an interruption in 1644–6, when he was at the Aus. court in Vienna. In 1646 he became *maestro di cappella* at the Vatican.

Works incl. Masses, motets and other church music, much of it for several choirs in a large number of parts. The celebrated 53-part *Missa salisburgensis* formerly attrib. to him is probably by Biber.

Beni Mora, Oriental Suite in E min., op. 29 no. 1 for orch. by Holst. Comp. 1910 after a visit to Algeria: last of 3 movts. is titled 'In the Street of the Ouled Naïls'; fp London, 1 May 1912, cond. Holst.

Benjamin, Arthur (b Sydney, 18 Sep 1893; d London, 9 Apr 1960), Australian pianist and composer. Educ. at Brisbane and studied at the RCM in London, where later he became prof. After fighting in the 1914–18 war, he returned to Austral. to teach pf. at the Sydney Cons. in 1919–20, but having developed as a comp., settled in London. From 1930 to 1936 he lived in Vancouver.

Works incl. operas *The Devil take her* (1931), *Prima Donna* (1933), *A Tale of Two Cities* (after Dickens) (1950), *Tartuffe*; film music incl. *An Ideal Husband* (after Oscar Wilde); symph. suite *Light Music* and *Overture to an Italian Comedy* for orch.; *Romantic Fantasy* for vln., vla. and orch., vln. concerto (1932), concertino for pf. and orch., chamber music, songs.

Benjamin, George (b London, 31 Jan 1960), English composer and pianist. He studied with Messiaen and Yvonne Loriod in Paris from 1974, Paris Cons. 1977, and with Alexander Goehr at Cambridge. With *Ringed by the Flat Horizon* (1980) he became the youngest comp. ever to have a work perf. at the Prom concerts. At the 1983 Aldeburgh Festival he gave the fp of Britten's *Sonatina Romantica* (1940).

Other works incl. *At First Light*, for chamber orch. (1982); *A Mind of Winter*, for sop. and ens.; vln. son. (1977), octet (1978), duo for cello and pf. (1980); *Meditations on Haydn's Name*, for pf. (1982).

Bennet, John (b ? Lancashire), English 16th–17th-cent. composer. Pub. a book of madrigals in 1599 and contrib. others to collections, incl. *The Triumphes of Oriana*.

Bennett, Richard Rodney (b Broadstairs, Kent, 29 Mar 1936), English composer and pianist. Studied at the RAM with Lennox Berkeley and Howard Ferguson, and in Paris with Boulez. Influenced by Bartók, he has also used serial techniques but he writes in a lighter vein too.

Works incl. operas *The Ledge* (1961), *The Mines of Sulphur* (1963), *A Penny for a Song* (1966), *Victory* (after Conrad) (1970); symph.; *Aubade* for orch.; pf. concerto (1968), ob. concerto, *Anniversaries* for orch. (1982); *Love Songs* for ten. and orch. (texts by e.e. cummings) (1985); 4 string 4tets (1952–64); *Calendar* for chamber ensemble; vocal music, and film, radio and television music.

Bennett, Robert Russell (b Kansas City, 15 Jun 1894;. d New York, 17 Aug 1981), American pianist, conductor, composer and orchestrator. Studied with his parents and later with Nadia Boulanger in Paris. He played in his father's orch. as a youth and earned a living as arranger and orchestrator.

Works incl. opera *Maria Malibran* (1935); ballet-operetta *Endymion* (1927); film music *Sights and Sounds*; *Abraham Lincoln Symph.* (1931), *Charlestown Rhapsody* (1926), etc. for orch.; March for 2 pfs. and orch.

Bennett, William Sterndale (b Sheffield, 13 Apr 1816; d London, 1 Feb 1875), English pianist and composer. Chorister at King's Coll., Cambridge and student at the RAM in London. He then went to Leipzig, where he made friends with Mendelssohn. Schumann ded. his *Études symphoniques* for pf. to him. Prof. of music at Cambridge Univ., 1856–75. Principal of the RAM, 1866–75. Knighted 1871.

Works incl. incid. music to Sophocles' *Ajax* (1872); cantata *The May Queen* (1858), odes for the Internat. Exhib. (Tennyson) and the Cambridge Installation of Chancellor (Kingsley); anthems; 6 symphs. (1832–64), overtures *The Naiads* and *The Wood-Nymphs*, fantasy-overture on Moore's *Paradise and the Peri*; 5 pf. concertos (1832–8); pf. picccs, songs.

Benoît, Camille (b Roanne, Loire, 7 Dec 1851; d Paris, 1 Jul 1923), French writer on music and composer. Pupil of Franck and disciple of Wagner; arr. Berlioz's *Roméo et Juliette* for pf. duet. On the staff of the Louvre museum and curator from 1895.

Works incl. opera *Cléopâtre* (1889); symph. poem *Merlin l'enchanteur*; *Eleison* for solo voices, chorus and orch.; Epithalamium for Anatole France's *Noces corinthiennes*.

Benoit, Peter (Léonard Léopold) (b Har-

lebeke, 17 Aug 1834; d Antwerp, 8 Mar 1901), Belgian composer. Pupil of Fétis at the Brussels Cons. He became cond. at a Flem. theatre and was keenly interested in Flem. national music as distinct from that influenced by Fr. comps. He travelled in Ger. and visited Paris, but tended more and more towards an indigenous type of music. His 1st opera was prod. in 1857.

Works incl. French opera *Le Roi des aulnes* (on Goethe's *Erl King*) (1859); Flem. operas *The Mountain Village, Isa, Pompeja*; incid. music to Flem. plays; Te Deum, *Messe solennelle*, Requiem; oratorios *Lucifer* (1865) and *The Scheldt* (1868); *Petite Cantate de Noël* and many Flem. cantatas, etc.

Bentzon, Nils Viggo (b Copenhagen, 24 Aug 1919), Danish composer. Studied pf. with his mother and comp. with Jeppesen.

Works incl. 4 operas, incl. *Faust III* (after Goethe, Kafka and Joyce, 1964); 15 symphs. (1942–80); 8 pf. concertos, 4 vln. concertos, much chamber music, incl. chamber concerto, for 11 instruments, a chamber symph., 9 string 4tets (1940–76), sonata for solo cello; 11 pf. sonatas, *Propostae Novae* for 2 pfs.; vocal music, incl. *Bonjour Max Ernst*, cantata for chorus and orch. (1961).

Benucci, Francesco (b Florence, *c* 1745; d Florence, 5 Apr 1824), Italian bass. He was engaged for Vienna in 1783, and was Mozart's orig. Figaro there in 1786; also sang in operas by Salieri, Paisiello, Cimarosa and Galuppi.

Benvenuto Cellini, opera by Berlioz (lib. by L. de Wailly and A. Barbier, based on Cellini's autobiog.), prod. Paris, Opéra, 10 Sep 1838.

Berberian, Cathy (b Attleboro, Mass., 4 Jul 1925; d Rome, 6 Mar 1983), American soprano of Armenian parentage. She achieved first success in 1958 with a perf. of *Fontana Mix* by John Cage; soon became associated with *avant garde* music requiring unconventional vocal gymnastics; sang in many perfs. of works by Berio, to whom she was married 1950–66. In 1983 she sang her own version of the *Internationale* for It. TV to mark the cent. of the death of Karl Marx; her own works incl. *Stripsody* and *Morsicath(h)y*.

Berceuse (Fr.) = Cradle Song. Although strictly speaking a song, a berceuse may just as well be an instrumental piece.

Berceuse élégiaque, pf. piece by Busoni, comp. 1909 and added to the *Elegien* of 1907; orch. vers. of 1909 is subtitled *Des Mannes Wiegenlied am Sarge seine Mutter* (The man's lullaby at his mother's coffin): Busoni's mother died on 3 Oct 1909. Fp conducted by Mahler at his last concert, NY, 21 Feb 1911.

Berchem, Jachet de (b Berchem, c 1505; d ? Ferrara, c 1565), Flemish composer. Prob. organist to the ducal court at Ferrara in 1555. Wrote church music, madrigals for 4 and 5 voices, Fr. *chansons*, etc. Not to be confused with Jachet of Mantua.

Berenice, opera by Handel (lib. by A Salvi), prod. London, CG, 18 May 1737.

Opera by Perti (lib. do.), prod. Villa Pratolino nr. Florence, Sep 1709.

Berenice, che fai?, Italian cantata by Haydn for sop. and orch. (text from Metastasio's *Antigono*), comp. May 1795.

Berenstadt, Gaetano, Italian 17th–18th-cent. bass singer of German descent. The 1st record of his appearing in London dates from 1717. He sang in the fps of Handel's *Ottone, Flavio* and *Giulio Cesare.*

Beresford, Hugh (b Birkenhead, 17 Dec 1925), English baritone, later tenor. He studied at the RMCM, then with Dino Borgioli and Alfred Piccaver. Debut Linz, 1953, as Wolfram. From 1960 made guest appearances at CG, Vienna, Munich and the Paris Opéra. In 1966 he sang Mandryka at the Teatro Fenice, Venice; other roles incl. Rigoletto, Posa and Don Giovanni. Later developed as a tenor and sang Otello at Vienna and Tannhäuser at the 1973 Bayreuth Festival.

Berezovsky, Maximus Sosnovich (b Glukhov, 27 Oct 1745; d St Petersburg, 2 Apr 1777), Russian composer. Pupil at the academy in Kiev, later a singer in the service of the court. In 1765 went to It. to study under Martini. On his return to Rus., unable to secure an appointment, he finally cut his throat. His most important contrib. was to church music; he also wrote an opera, *Demofoonte* (1773), and other works.

Berezovsky, Nikolai (b St Petersburg, 17 May 1900; d New York, 27 Aug 1953), Russian (Americanized) violinist and composer. Learnt music in the Imperial Chapel at St Petersburg, became violinist in the opera orchs. at Saratov and Moscow and cond. at the School of Modern Art there; but emigrated to USA in 1922, continued his studies there, played in the NY SO, became a member of the Coolidge 4tet and appeared as concert and broadcasting cond.

Works incl. 4 symphs. (1931–43), *Sinfonietta* and *Hebrew Suite* for orch.; waltzes for string orch.; vln. concerto (1931), Fantasy for 2 pfs. and orch., *Concerto lirico* for cello and orch., *Toccata, Variations and Finale* for string 4tet and orch.; cantata *Gil-*

gamesh (1947); string 4tet, 2 woodwind 5tets, 6tet for clar., pf. and strings, suite for 7 brass instruments.

Berg, Alban (b Vienna, 9 Feb 1885; d Vienna, 24 Dec 1935), Austrian composer. Self-taught from the age of 15, he was a pupil of Schoenberg from 1904 to 1910. Schoenberg's influence on him was profound and Berg continued a devoted admirer to the end. The nature of this influence may be measured as Berg passes from the extended tonality of his early works to atonality and, later, serialism. His use of serial technique is distinctive in that he does not avoid tonal references (e.g. the vln. concerto). He was also a gifted writer. In 1911 he married Helene Nahowski. His first major work, the string 4tet op.3, dates from the same year. His music was known only to a small circle until the 1925 prod. of *Wozzeck*. The Chamber Concerto and Lyric Suite followed shortly after. He was a friend of Alma Mahler and the death of her daughter, Manon, occasioned his last completed work, the violin concerto. His second opera, *Lulu*, was begun in 1929 but left unfinished after his death.

Works incl. OPERAS: *Wozzeck* (after Büchner) (1917–22; prod. Berlin, 1925) and *Lulu* (after Wedekind) (1929–35; 2 acts prod. Zurich, 1937, act 3 realized by F. Cerha, perf. Paris, 1979).

SONGS, AND VOICE WITH ORCH.: 70 early Lieder, to texts by Ibsen, Altenberg, Rückert, Heine, Rilke and others; 7 *Early Songs* for voice and pf. (1905–8, orch. vers. 1928); 4 *Songs* op. 2 (1909–10); 5 *Altenberglieder* for voice and orch. (1912, fp Rome, 1953); 3 *Fragments from Wozzeck*, op. 7 (fp Frankfurt, 1924, cond. Scherchen); *Der Wein,* concert aria to text by Baudelaire (1929); *Lulu-Symphonie* for sop. and orch. (1934).

ORCH.: *Three Pieces*, op. 6 (1914–15, rev. 1929; fp Oldenburg, 1930); 3 *Movements from the Lyric Suite*, arr. for string orch. (1929; fp Berlin, 1929); Chamber Concerto for pf., vln. and 13 wind insts. (1923–4; fp Berlin, 1927); vln. concerto (1935; fp Barcelona 1936).

CHAMBER: pf. sonata op. 1 (1907–8); Variations on an original theme op. (1908); string 4tet op. 3 (1910); 4 *Pieces* for clar. and pf. (1913); *Lyric Suite* for string 4tet (1925–6; fp Vienna, 1927, perf. with vocal finale NY, 1979); adagio from Chamber Concerto arr. for vln., clar. and pf. (1935).

Berg, (Carl) Natanael (b Stockholm, 9 Feb 1879; d Stockholm, 14 Oct 1957), Swedish composer. Studied at the Stockholm Cons. and in Paris and Vienna.

Works incl. operas *Leila* (after Byron's *Giaour*) (1910), *Engelbrekt* (1928), *Judith* (after Hebbel's drama) (1935), *Birgitta*, *Genoveva* (1946); 5 symphs.; symph. pocms; vln. concerto; pf. concerto; 2 string 4tets, pf. 5tet.

Bergamasca, an Italian dance from Bergamo at least as old as the 16th cent., called Bergomask by Shakespeare.

Berganza, Teresa (b Madrid, 16 Mar 1935), Spanish mezzo. Debut Aix 1957, Dorabella. Glyndebourne 1958, Cherubino; CG 1960, Rosina, and 1976 with co. of La Scala as Cenerentola. US debut 1958, Dallas; NY Met from 1967. Edinburgh 1977 as Carmen. Other roles incl. Isabella, Octavia and Cesti's Orontea. Also successful in song recitals.

Berger, Arthur (b New York, 15 May 1912), American composer. Studied with Piston at Harvard Univ., with Pirro at the Sorbonne in Paris, also with Pierre Lalo and Paul Valéry there, and comp. with Nadia Boulanger. He became music ed. of the NY *Sun*.

Works incl. *Slow Dance* for strings; serenade for chamber orch. (1944); 3 pieces for string 4tet, wind 4tet, 2 movements for vln. and cello; ballet *Entertainment Piece* and other works for pf.; *Words for Music Perhaps* (Yeats) and other songs, etc.

Berger, Erna (b Dresden, 19 Oct 1900), German soprano. Debut Dresden, 1925. Salzburg 1932–54 as Blonde and Zerlina. CG 1934–51 as Queen of Night, Constanze, Sophie, Gilda. NY Met 1949–51. Sang Lieder until 1968, after retiring from stage in 1955.

Berger, Rudolf (b Brno, 17 Apr 1874; d New York, 27 Feb 1915), Czech baritone, later tenor. Debut Brno, 1896. He sang at the Berlin Hofoper from 1898 and appeared at Bayreuth 1901–8 as Amfortas, Klingsor and Gunther. After singing at CG, Vienna and Paris he made his NY Met debut in 1914, as Siegmund. Jochanaan was among his 96 baritone roles, and he had 18 tenor roles.

Berger, Theodor (b Traismauer, 18 May 1905), Austrian composer. Studied at the Vienna Academy; much influenced by his teachers, Korngold and Franz Schmidt. Works incl. *Malincolia* for strings (1938), *Homerische Symphonie* (1948), *La Parola* for orch. (1955), *Symphonischer Triglyph*, on themes by Schubert (1957), *Divertimento* for chorus, wind and perc. (1968), vln. concerto (1963); 2 string 4tets (1930–31).

Bergknappen, Die (*The Miners*), opera by Umlauf (lib. by P. Weidmann), prod. Vienna, Burgtheater, on the opening of its career as a national Ger. opera, 17 Feb 1778.

Berglund, Joel (b Torsåker, 4 Jun 1903), Swedish baritone. Debut Stockholm, 1929. Bayreuth 1942, Dutchman. NY Met 1946, Sachs. Other Wagner roles in Europe and N. and S. America were Wotan, Kurwenal and Gurnemanz. Also sang Boccanegra, Philip II and Scarpia. Dir. Stockholm Opera, 1949–52.

Berglund, Paavo (b Helsinki, 14 Apr 1929), Finnish conductor. After an early career as a violinist, co-founded the Helsinki Chamber Orch. in 1953; prin. cond. Helsinki Radio SO from 1962, Helsinki PO 1975–9. Has cond. the Bournemouth SO from 1964, music dir. 1972–9; assoc. with revival of Sibelius's early *Kullervo* Symphony. Prin. guest cond. Scottish National Orch. from 1981.

Bergmann, Carl (b Ebersbach, Saxony, 12 Apr 1821; d New York, 10 Aug 1876), German cellist and conductor. Went to USA in 1850 and did much to estab. orch. music there. He was cond. of the NY Phil. Society from 1866 until 1876.

Bergonzi, Italian family of vln. makers who worked in Cremona:

1. Carlo B. (b ? Cremona, *c* 1683; d Cremona, 1747). He began to work independently about 1716.

2. Michelangelo B. (b ? Cremona, 1722; d ? Cremona, after 1758), son of 1.

3. Nicola B. (b after 1746; d after 1796), son of 2.

Bergonzi, Carlo (b Parma, 13 Jul 1924), Italian tenor. Debut 1948 as Rossini's Figaro (a bar. role); tenor debut Bari, 1951, as Chénier. La Scala, Milan, from 1953. US debut 1955, Chicago; NY Met 1956, Radames. CG from 1962 as Alvaro, Manrico, Riccardo, Cavaradossi.

Bergsma, William (b Oakland, Calif., 1 Apr 1921), American composer. Studied at Stanford Univ. and the Eastman School of Music under Hanson and Bernard Rogers, and after winning many awards became teacher of comp. at the Juilliard School NY.

Works incl. opera *The Wife of Martin Guerre* (1956); ballets *Paul Bunyan* (1938) and *Gold and the Señor Commandante* (1941); choral symph.; choral works; symph. for chamber orch.; 4 string 4tets (1942–70); songs.

Berio, Luciano (b Oneglia, 24 Oct 1925), Italian composer. Studied with Ghedini in Milan and with Dallapiccola in USA. He is one of the most active comps. of electronic music and has worked with Boulez at IRCAM (*q.v.*). He has also employed graphic notation; many of his works leave the perf. a wide range of choices. He has been partic. concerned to explore the possibilities of language as developed in musical perf. He was at Darmstadt 1954–9 and was on the faculty at Juilliard, NY, 1965–72. He often wrote for his wife, the sop. Cathy Berberian.

Works incl. DRAMATIC: *Allez-Hop*, mimed story (Venice, 1959, rev. 1968), *Passaggio*, messa in scena (Milan, 1963), *Laborintus II* (Paris, 1970), *Opera* (Santa Fe, 1970, rev. 1979), *Recital I (for Cathy)* (Lisbon, 1972), *I trionfi del Petraca*, ballet (Florence, 1974), *Linea*, ballet (Grenoble, 1974), *La Vera Storia*, opera (Milan, 1982), *Un Re in Ascolto*, opera (Salzburg, 1984).

ORCH.: *Variazioni* (1954), *Nones* (1954), *Divertimento* (with Maderna) (1958), *Chemins I-IV*, after *Sequenze* for insts. (1965–75), *Tempi concertati* (1959), *Bewegung* (1971), Concerto for 2 pfs. and orch. (1973), *Still* (1973), *Eindrücke* (1974), *Points on the curve to find* . . . for pf. and 20 insts. (1974), *Après visage* for orch. and tape (1974), *Il ritorno degli Snovidenia* for cello and orch. (1977), pf. concerto (1977), *Entrata* (1980), *Accordo* for 4 wind bands (1981), *Corale* for vln. and orch. (1982), *Voci* for vla. and orch. (1984).

VOCAL: *Quattro canzoni populari* (1947), *Opus Number Zoo* for speaker and wind 5tet (1952, rev. 1970), *Chamber Music* (texts by Joyce) (1953), *Circles* for female v., harp and 2 perc. (texts by e.e. cummings) (1960), *Epifanie* for female v. and orch. (texts by Proust, Joyce, Brecht, etc.) (1961), *Sinfonia* for 8 solo voices and orch. (material from Mahler, Wagner, Strauss and Ravel is used in collage fashion) (1968–9), *Ora* (text after Virgil) (1971), *Bewegung II* for bar. and orch. (1971), *Cries of London*, for 8 solo voices (1973–5), *11 Folk Songs* for mezzo and orch. (1975), *Calmo (in memoriam Bruno Maderna)* for sop. and ens. (1974), *Coro* for 40 voices and orch. (1976), *Duo* for bar., 2 vlns., chorus & orch. (1982).

CHAMBER AND INST.: suite for pf. (1948), string 4tet (1956), *Serenata* for fl. and 14 insts. (1957), *Différences* for ens. (1959), *Sincronie* for string 4tet (1964), *Wasserklavier* for pf. (1964), *Erdenklavier* (1970), *Sequenze* (I–X) for solo fl., harp, voice, pf., trombone, vla., oboe, vln., clar., and trumpet (1958–85), *Duette per due violini* (1979–82).

ELECTRONIC: *Mutazioni* (1955), *Perspectives* (1957), *Thema (Omaggio a Joyce)* (1958), *Momenti* (1960), *Visage* (1961), *Chants parallèles* (1975).

Bériot, Charles (Auguste) de (b Louvain, 20 Feb 1802; d Brussels, 8 Apr 1870), Belgian violinist and composer. Played in public at the age of 9, but 10 years later went to Paris to perfect himself under Viotti and Baillot. He had a brilliant success in Paris and was app. chamber musician to the king. In 1826 he visited London for the 1st time. He travelled much in the company of Malibran, whom he married after her divorce from her 1st husband; but after her early death in 1836 he retired to Brussels until 1840, when he travelled again and married Marie Huber in Vienna. Prof. of vln. at the Brussels Cons., 1843–52.

Works incl. 10 vln. concertos, variations and studies for vln., pf. trios.

Berkeley, (Sir) Lennox (Randall Francis) (b Oxford, 12 May 1903), English composer. Did not study music until he left Oxford (Merton Coll.) in 1926, when he went to Paris until 1933 as a pupil of Nadia Boulanger. Works of his were heard at the ISCM festivals at Barcelona and London, 1936 and 1938, and at the Leeds and Worcester festivals, 1937–8. Hon. D.Mus., Oxford, 1970. Knighted 1974.

Works incl. operas *Nelson* (1954), *A Dinner Engagement* and *Ruth* (1956); ballet *The Judgment of Paris* (1938); incid. music for Shakespeare's *Tempest*; music for film *Hotel Reserve*; oratorio *Jonah* (1935); psalm *Domini est terra* for chorus and orch.; *Missa brevis*; 4 symphs. (1940–78); *Nocturne* and divertimento for orch.; pf. concerto (1947), vln. concerto; 3 string 4tets (1935–70); 2 vln. and pf. sonatas, sonata and pieces for pf.; *Polka* for 2 pfs.

Berkeley, Michael (b London, 29 May 1948), English composer, son of prec. He studied at the RAM with his father, and with Richard Rodney Bennett. In 1982 his oratorio *Or shall we Die?* was perf. in London: it contains a vivid protest at the threat of nuclear war. Composer-in-residence, London College of Music, 1987–8.

Other works incl. *Meditations*, for strings (1976), ob. concerto (1977), *Fantasia Concertante*, for chamber orch., symph. *Uprising* (1980), *Gregorian Vars.*, for orch. (1982), cello concerto (1982); *The Wild Winds*, for sop. and chamber orch. (1978), *At the Round Earth's Imagin'd Corners* (text by Donne) for soloists, chorus and organ (1980); string trio (1978), vln. son. (1980); string 4tet (1981), clar. 5tet (1983).

Berlin, Irving (orig. Israel Baline) (b Tyumen, 11 May 1888), American songwriter of Russian origin. He had no formal musical training and was unable to read music but became one of the most successful comps. of popular songs.

Works incl. songs for plays, films and revues, incl. *Music Box Revues*; popular songs, e.g. *Alexander's Ragtime Band*.

Berlin Philharmonic Orchestra, German orch. founded 1882. Early conductors were Franz Wüllner, Karl Klindworth, Hans von Bülow and Richard Strauss. Later conductors have incl. Arthur Nikisch, 1895–1922, Wilhelm Furtwängler, 1922–45 and Sergiu Celibidache, 1945–51. Herbert von Karajan has been prin. conductor since 1954. A new Philharmonic Hall was opened in 1963 with a perf. of the *Choral* symphony.

Berlioz, (Louis-)Hector (b Côte-Saint-André, Isère, 11 Dec 1803; d Paris, 8 Mar 1869), French composer. Son of a doctor who taught him the fl., but wished him to study medicine. As a boy he also learnt the guitar and picked up theoret. knowledge from books. Sent to the École de Médecine in Paris, 1821, he found the studies so distasteful that he decided to give them up for music. His parents made great difficulties, but Lesueur accepted him as a pupil in 1823, when he at once set to work on an opera and an oratorio, a Mass following the next year. Entered the Cons. in 1826, but failed several times to gain the Prix de Rome, obtaining it at last in 1830 with the cantata *La mort de Sardanapale*. In the meantime he had fallen in love with the Irish actress Harriet Smithson and expressed his feelings for her in the *Symph. fantastique*. Then, on the point of going to Rome, he became engaged to the pianist, Marie Moke, who during his absence married Camille Pleyel.

He wrote much in Rome and returned to Paris in 1832, this time meeting Harriet and marrying her in Oct. 1833. To add to his income he became a music critic. In 1838 Paganini sent him 20,000 francs to enable him to devote all his time to comp. He separated from Harriet in 1842 and started a liaison with the singer Marie Recio. He travelled much with her during the next few years, to Ger., Vienna, Prague, Budapest, Rus. and London. After Harriet's death he married Marie in 1854; meanwhile he had resumed his journalistic work. Marie died in 1862 and he suffered much ill health during the 1860s and was greatly depressed by the death of his son Louis in 1867. After another visit to Rus. he had a bad fall at Nice, where he had gone for his health in 1868, and he

grew gradually more infirm. He wrote 7 books, incl. *Traité de l'instrumentation* and *Mémoires*.

Works incl. OPERAS: *Benvenuto Cellini* (1834–7), *Les Troyens* (2 parts) (1856–8) and *Béatrice et Bénédict* (after Shakespeare's *Much Ado about Nothing*) (1860–62).

ORCH: The programme symphs., *Symphonie fantastique* (1830), *Harold en Italie* (with solo vla.)(1834), *Roméo et Juliette* (with voices) (1839) and *Symphonie funèbre et triomphale* (for military band, strings and chorus) (1840), 5 concert overtures, *Waverley* (1828), *King Lear* (1831), *Rob Roy* (1831), *Carnaval Romain* (1844), *Le Corsaire* (1844); 2 marches for orch.

CHORAL AND SONGS: *Messe des morts* (Requiem), *La Damnation de Faust* (1846), *Te Deum* (1849) and *L'Enfance du Christ* (1850–54); 6 smaller vocal works with orch. or pf.; 28 songs incl. the cycle *Nuits d'été*; *Lélio, ou Le Retour à la vie*, a lyric monodrama intended as a sequel to the *Symph. fantastique* (1832).

Berman, Lazar (b Leningrad, 26 Feb 1930), Russian pianist. He studied with Richter at the Moscow Cons. and made his debut in 1940; continued at the Cons. until 1957. London debut 1958, NY 1976, followed by US tour. Much praised in Liszt, Schumann, Tchaikovsky and Skriabin.

Bermudo, Juan (b Ecija nr. Seville, b *c* 1510; d Andalusia, *c* 1565), Spanish 16th-cent. friar and music theorist. Friend of Morales. He wrote 3 music treatises, pub. 1549–55.

Bernac (real name Bertin), **Pierre** (b Paris, 12 Jan 1899; d Villeneuve-les-Avignon, 17 Oct 1979), French baritone. From 1936 he specialized in recitals, frequently in association with Poulenc, many of whose songs he introduced.

Bernacchi, Antonio (b Bologna, 23 Jun 1685; d Bologna, 13 Mar 1756), Italian castrato and teacher. 1st heard in London in 1716; in the season 1729–30 he sang in the fps of Handel's *Lotario* and *Partenope*.

Bernardi, Francesco. *See* Senesino.

Bernardi, Steffano (b Verona, *c* 1585; d ? Salzburg, 1636), Italian priest and composer. Chaplain at Verona Cathedral, studied in Rome later and became *maestro di cappella* of the church of the Madonna dei Monti. In 1611 he became *maestro di cappella* at Verona Cathedral, and in 1622 went into the service of the Archduke Karl Josef, Bishop of Breslau, and soon afterwards to Salzburg Cathedral, which he helped to cocsecrate in 1628. He wrote a Te Deum for 12 choirs (now lost), and many Masses, motets, psalms, madrigals and instrumental works.

Bernasconi, Andrea (b Marseilles, 1706; d Munich, Jan 1784), Italian composer. *Kapellmeister* in Munich from 1755. He was stepfather of Antonia B. (below), who was his pupil.

Works incl. 25 operas, most to texts by Metastasio, one oratorio and a large quantity of church music.

Bernasconi, Antonia (b Stuttgart, 1741; d ? Vienna, 1803), German soprano, step-daughter of prec. She sang the title role in the 1st prod. of Gluck's *Alceste* (Vienna, 1767), also Aspasia in Mozart's *Mitridate* (Milan, 1770).

Berners, Lord (Sir Gerald Hugh Tyrwhitt-Wilson) (b Arley Park nr. Bridgnorth, 18 Sep 1883; d Faringdon House, Berks., 19 Apr 1950), English composer, painter and author. In the diplomatic service at first, he studied music at Dresden and Vienna, also sought the advice of Stravinsky and Casella. His operatic setting of Mérimée's comedy *Le Carrosse du Saint-Sacrement* was prod. in Paris in 1924, and the ballet *The Triumph of Neptune* in London in 1926; another, with words by Gertrude Stein, *The Wedding Bouquet*, at SW in 1937 with settings designed by himself.

Works incl. opera *Le Carrosse du Saint-Sacrement*; ballets *The Triumph of Neptune*, *Luna Park* (1930), *The Wedding Bouquet* (words by Gertrude Stein), *Cupid and Psyche* (1939); 3 pieces (*Chinoiserie*, *Valse sentimentale*, *Kasatchok*), *Fantaisie espagnole* (1920) and *Fugue* for orch. (1928); *Variations*, *Adagio and Hornpipe* for string orch.; *Le Poisson d'or*, *Trois Petites Marches funèbres* and *Fragments psychologiques* for pf.; *Valses bourgeoises* for pf. duet; songs incl. 3 sets in the Ger., Fr. and Eng. manners.

Bernier, Nicolas (b Mantes, 5 or 6 Jun 1665; d Paris, 6 Jul 1734), French composer. Studied in Rome. *Maître de chapelle* at Chartres and at the church of Saint-Germain-l'Auxerrois in Paris; then music master at the Sainte Chapelle there, 1704–26.

Works incl. 8 books of cantatas, 3 of motets, church music.

Bernstein, Leonard (b Lawrence, Mass., 25 Aug 1918), American conductor, composer, pianist, teacher and writer on music, of Russian parentage. He entered Harvard in 1935, graduated 1939. Studied with Fritz Reiner and Randall Thompson at Curtis Inst. from 1939; asst. to Koussevitzky at Tanglewood 1940–43. In Nov 1943 he deputised for Bruno Walter at a NY PO concert, achieving instant recognition; became sole cond. of the orch. 1958, cond. laureate for life 1969. Many guest appearances with Vienna SO, LSO and Israel PO. With the Boston SO he gave the 1949 fp of Messiaen's *Turangalîla Symphonie*, and at the Vienna Staatsoper has given *Falstaff* and his own opera *A Quiet Place* (1986). As a pianist he has been heard in the Mozart concertos, directing from the keyboard, and as accompanist to leading singers. At Tanglewood and Brandeis Univ. he was an inspirational teacher; on television and through his books has influenced several generations of young people. Partic. in his theatre pieces, Bernstein has attempted to reconcile the distinctions between 'serious' and popular music. A chance to reassess his orch. music came in 1986, with a series of concerts in London: the *Serenade* and *The Age of Anxiety* were given before the Queen. Bernstein's status as a composer is controversial; his stature as a performing musician, a supreme communicator, is beyond dispute.

Works incl. THEATRE PIECES: *Fancy Free*, ballet (1944), *On the Town*, musical comedy (1944), *Candide*, musical after Voltaire (1956, rev. 1982), *Facsimile*, ballet (1946), *Trouble in Tahiti*, 1-act opera (1952, rev. as *A Quiet Place*, 1983), *Wonderful Town*, musical comedy (1952), *West Side Story* (1957, also filmed), *Mass*, for chorus, boys' chorus, orch. and dancers (1971), *Dybbuk*, ballet (1974).

WORKS WITH ORCH.: symph. no. 1, *Jeremiah* (1944), symph. no. 2, with pf., *The Age of Anxiety* (1949), *Fugues and Riffs* for band (1949), *Serenade* for vln., strings and perc., after Plato's *Symposium* (1954), symph. no. 3, *Kaddish* for narrator, chorus and orch. (1963), *Chichester Psalms* for chorus and orch. (1965), *Songfest*, 12 pieces for 6 singers and orch. (1977), *Divertimento* for fl., strings and perc., in memory of Israeli war dead (1981), *Jubilee Games* (1985); chamber music and songs.

Béroff, Michel (b Epinal, 9 May 1950), French pianist. He studied at the Paris Cons. with Yvonne Loriod, the wife of Messiaen; has given many perfs. of M.'s music, notably the massive *Vingt regards sur L'Enfant Jésus*. Also heard in Bartók, Debussy, Prokofiev and Mozart.

Berry, Walter (b Vienna, 8 Apr 1929), Austrian bass-baritone. Vienna Staatsoper from 1950 as Mozart's Figaro, Leporello, Wozzeck and Ochs. Salzburg from 1952 as Masetto and in the fps of operas by Liebermann, Egk and Von Einem. NY Met since 1966 (debut as Barak). CG from 1976. Married to the mezzo Christa Ludwig 1957–70. Returned to CG 1986 (Waldner in *Arabella*).

Berselli, Matteo, 18th-cent. Italian soprano castrato. Went to London with Senesino in 1720, and sang in revivals of Handel's *Radamisto* and the pasticcio *Muzio Scevola*.

Bertali, Antonio (b Verona, Mar 1605; d Vienna, 17 Apr 1669), Italian violinist and composer. Played in the court chapel in Vienna from 1637 and became *Kapellmeister* in 1649. His opera *L'inganno d'amore* was prod. at the Diet of Regensburg in 1653.

Works incl. several operas, e.g. *Niobe* and *Theti* (both Mantua, 1652); equestrian ballet; 2 oratorios; Masses and other church music.

Berté, Heinrich (b Galgócz, 8 May 1857; d Vienna, 23 Aug 1924), Austro-Hungarian composer.

Works incl. operettas *Die Schneeflocke* (Prague, 1896), *Die Millionenbraut* (Munich, 1905), *Der Märchenprinz, Das Dreimäderlhaus* (*Lilac Time*, on music by Schubert, 1916) and others; ballets *Das Märchenbuch, Amor auf Reisen* (Vienna, 1895) and others.

Bertheaume, Isidore (b Paris, *c* 1752; d St Petersburg, 20 Mar 1802), French violinist and composer. Appeared at the Concert Spirituel in Paris, 1761, and became cond. in 1783, but left at the Revolution, going 1st to Eutin and then to St Petersburg, where he joined the Imp. band.

Works incl. 2 symphs.; vln. concerto and several for 2 vlns.; sonatas for pf. with vln. acc.

Bertini, Gary (b Brichevo, Bessarabia, 1 May 1927), Russian-born Israeli conductor and composer. He studied in Tel Aviv, Milan and Paris; founded Israel Chamber Orch. 1965, guest cond. with the Israel PO. Scottish Nat. Orch. from 1970, Detroit SO 1981–3. Chief cond. Cologne Radio SO from 1983. He has cond. the premières of 3 operas by Joseph Tal: *Ashmedai* (Hamburg, 1970), *Masada 967* (Jerusalem, 1973) and *Die Versuchung* (Munich, 1977).

Works incl. concerto for horn, strings and timp. (1952), solo vln. sonata (1953), ballet *The Unfound Door* (1962).

Bertini, Henri (b London, 28 Oct 1798; d Meylan, 1 Oct 1876), French pianist and composer. Pupil of his brother, Benoît Auguste B. (b 1780). Went on a continental tour at the age of 12, lived in Eng. and Scot., but settled in Paris in 1821. Wrote much for his instrument, incl. studies.

Bertoldo, Bertoldino e Cacasenno (also

Bertoldo or **Bertoldo alla corte**), comic opera by Ciampi (lib. by Goldoni), prod. Venice, Teatro San Moisè, 27 Dec 1748.

Bertolli, Francesca (b Rome; d Bologna, 9 Jan 1763), Italian 18th-cent. contralto. 1st heard in London in 1729, she sang in the 1st prods. of Handel's *Partenope*, *Ezio*, *Sosarme*, *Orlando* and *Berenice*, as well as in operas by Porpora.

Berton, Henri-Montan (b Paris, 17 Sep 1767; d Paris, 22 Apr 1844), French violinist and composer. Violinist at the Paris Opéra from 1782, prof. at the Cons. from 1795 and cond. at the Opéra-Comique from 1807. The 1st of his 48 operas was prod. in 1787.

Works incl. operas *Les Promesses de mariage, Les Rigueurs du cloître* (1790), *Ponce de Léon* (1797), *Montano et Stéphanie, Le Délire, Le Grand Deuil, Le Concert intérrompu* (1802), *Aline, Reine de Golconde* (1803), *Les Maris garçons, Virginie*; oratorios *Absalon* (1786), etc.; ballets; cantatas; instrumental music; also theoret. works.

Bertoni, Ferdinando Giuseppe (b Salò, Lake Garda, 15 Aug 1725; d Desenzano, Lake Garda, 1 Dec 1813), Italian composer. Pupil of Martini at Bologna. Organist at St Mark's, Venice, from 1752 and choirmaster at the Cons. dei Mendicanti from 1757. He prod. his 1st opera at Florence, 1745. In 1776 prod. his *Orfeo*, on the lib. by Calzabigi already set by Gluck in 1762; it contains many echoes of Gluck's music. He visited London to prod. operas in 1778–80 and 1781–3. In 1785 he succeeded Galuppi as *maestro di cappella* at St Mark's, Venice.

Works incl. operas *Cajetto* (1746), *Orazio Curiazo, Tancredi* (1766), *Orfeo ed Euridice, Quinto Fabio* (1778) and over 40 others; oratorios and Latin cantatas; string 4tets; keyboard music.

Bertram, Theodor (b Stuttgart, 2 Feb 1869; d Bayreuth, 24 Nov 1907), German baritone. Debut Ulm, 1889. Bayreuth 1892–1906; 1st Dutchman there, 1901; NY Met 1900, same role. Munich 1893–1900 and CG 1900–07 as Wotan, Amfortas and Pizarro. He committed suicide after the death of his wife.

Bertrand, Antoine de (b Fontanges, *c* 1535; d Toulouse, *c* 1581), French composer. In some of his settings of Ronsard's *Amours* he experimented with quarter-tones. Altogether he published 3 vols. of *chansons*, and a vol. of *Airs spirituels* appeared posthumously in 1582.

Berutti, Arturo (b San Juan, 27 Mar 1862; d Buenos Aires, 3 Jan 1938), Argentine composer. Studied at the Leipzig Cons. and in Paris and Milan, settling at Buenos Aires in 1896.

Works incl. operas *Vendetta* (1892), *Evangelina* (1893), *Taras Bulba* (after Gogol) (1895), *Pampa* (1892), *Yupanki*, *Khrysé*, *Horrida nox* (1908) and *Los heroes*.

Berwald, Franz Adolf (b Stockholm, 23 Jul 1796; d Stockholm, 3 Apr 1868), Swedish violinist and composer. Comp. several works before he studied in Berlin. He twice visited Vienna, where he had more success than at home, but settled at Stockholm in 1849 as director of music at the univ. and court *kapellmästare*.

Works incl. operas *Leonida* (1829), *The Traitor*, *Estrella di Soria* (1848, rev. 1862), *The Queen of Golconda* (1864, perf. 1968); operettas *I Enter a Convent*, *The Milliner*, *A Rustic Betrothal in Sweden* (1847); incid. music to plays.

4 symphs., no. 1 *Sérieuse* (1842), no. 2 *Capricieuse* (1842), no. 3 *Singulière* (1845), no. 4 (1845); vln. concerto (1820), pf. concerto (1855); orch. works incl. *Recollections of the Norwegian. Alps*; 3 string 4tets, 2 pf. 5tets and other chamber music; songs.

Besanzoni, Gabriella (b Rome, 20 Sep 1888; d Rome, 8 Jul 1962), Italian mezzo. She sang Ulrica at Rome in 1913 and appeared at Buenos Aires from 1918. NY Met 1919–20 as Amneris and Isabella. She appeared in Havana, with Caruso, and sang Orfeo and Carmen at La Scala, under Toscanini, 1923–32; guest at the Berlin Staatsoper. Other roles incl. Mignon, Adalgisa and Cenerentola.

Besard (Besardus), Jean-Baptiste (b Besançon, *c* 1567; d ? Augsburg, after 1617), French lutenist and composer. Studied law at the Univ. of Dôle, then the lute with Lorenzini in Rome. Later lived at Cologne and Augsburg. Pub. theoret. works and collections of lute music incl. his own.

Besseler, Heinrich (b Hörde, nr. Dortmund, 2 Apr 1900; d Leipzig, 25 Jul 1969). German musicologist. Studied at Freiburg i/B., Vienna and Göttingen, where later he became lecturer at the univ. Prof. at Jena, 1949, and at Leipzig from 1956. Wrote on medieval and Renaissance music.

Best, W(illiam) T(homas) (b Carlisle, 13 Aug 1826; d Liverpool, 10 May 1897), English organist. Studied at Liverpool and lived most of his life there as organist at St George's Hall, where he gave recitals that made him famous all over the world. He made many org. arrs. of famous works.

Besuch der Alten Dame, Der (*The Visit of the Old Lady*), opera by Gottfried von Einem (lib. by F. Dürrenmatt after his own drama), prod. Vienna, Staatsoper, 23 May 1971.

Béthune, Conon de (b *c* 1160; d 17 Dec 1219 or 1220), French trouvère. 10 of his poems, 9 with music, are preserved.

Betrothal in a Monastery, The (*Obrucheniye monastïre*), opera by Prokofiev (lib. by and M. Mendelssohn, after Sheridan's play *The Duenna*); comp. 1940–41, fp Leningrad, Kirov Theatre, 3 Nov 1946.

Bettoni, Vincenzo (b Melegnano, 1 Jul 1881; d Melegnano, 4 Nov 1954), Italian bass. After his 1902 debut he sang at La Scala from 1905 and at Buenos Aires from 1910. Gurnemanz in the 1st Spanish perf. of *Parsifal* (Barcelona, 1914). In 1926 he began a series of Rossini perfs., with Conchita Supervia. Don Alfonso in the 1st season at Glyndebourne, 1934, and the following year was heard at CG as Basilio, Don Magnifico and Mustafà.

Betulia Liberata, La (*Betulia Liberated*), oratorio in 2 acts by Mozart to a text by Metastasio, based on the story of Judith and Holofernes. The work was commissioned by a Paduan nobleman, Giuseppe Ximenes, Prince of Aragon, and comp. 1771 in Italy and Salzburg but not perf. in Mozart's lifetime. 1st Brit. perf. London, 6 Nov 1968, by Opera Viva. Metastasio's text was 1st set by Reutter (perf. Vienna, 8 Apr 1734). Later settings by Jommelli (Venice, 1734), Holzbauer (Mannheim, 1760), Gassmann (Vienna, 1772) and Schuster (Dresden, 1796).

Betz, Franz (b Mainz, 19 Mar 1835; d Berlin, 11 Aug 1900), German baritone. Made his 1st appearance at Hanover in 1856, as Heinrich in *Lohengrin*, was Wagner's 1st Hans Sachs at Munich in 1868, and the 1st Wotan at Bayreuth. Other roles incl. Amonasro, Falstaff, Don Giovanni, Marke and Wolfram. He sang at the Royal Opera, Berlin, 1859–97 (Valentin, Pizarro and Telramund).

Bevin, Elway (b *c* 1554; d Bristol, buried 19 Oct 1638), English organist and composer of Welsh descent. Possibly a pupil of Tallis, vicar-choral at Wells Cathedral, 1575–84, and organist at Bristol Cathedral after that. He wrote a *Briefe and Short Instruction in the Art of Musicke* (1631), Comp. services, anthems and other church music, keyboard pieces, etc.

Bevis (or Beves) of Hampton (or Hamtoun), Anglo-Norman 13th-cent. romance. *See* **Buovo d'Antona** (Traetta).

Bialas, Günter (b Bielschowitz, Silesia, 19 Jul 1907), German composer. He studied in Berlin, 1927–33, and has taught in Breslau, Weimar and Munich. His music shows a wide range of influences, incl. neoclassicism, twelve-tone technique and medieval polyphony.

Works incl. 3 operas, *Hero und Leander* (1966), *Die Geschichte von Aucassin und Nicolette* (1969), *Der gestiefelte Kater* (1974); vla. concerto (1940), vln. concerto (1949), cello concerto (1962), *Sinfonia piccola*; sacred and secular choral music; 3 string 4tets (1936, 1949, 1969); *Erwartung*, for org. (1972).

Bianca e Falliero, ossia Il consiglio di tre (. . . *or The Council of Three*), opera by Rossini (lib. by F. Romani, from Manzoni's tragedy *Il conte di Carmagnola*), prod. Milan, La Scala, 26 Dec 1819.

Bianca e Fernando, opera by Bellini (lib. by D. Gilardoni), prod. Naples, Teatro San Carlo, 30 May 1826. Bellini's 1st opera heard in public.

Bianca und Giuseppe, oder Die Franzosen vor Nizza (. . . *or The French before Nice*), opera by J.F. Kittl (lib. by Wagner), prod. Prague, 19 Feb 1848. Wagner had written the lib. for himself in 1836; it is based on a novel by Heinrich König.

Bianchi, Francesco (b Cremona, *c* 1752; d London, 27 Nov 1810), Italian composer, *Maestro al cembalo* at the Comédie Italienne in Paris 1775, where he worked under Piccinni and prod. 2 operas. In 1778 went to Florence, and in 1783 was app. 2nd *maestro di cappella* at Milan Cathedral. His most successful opera, *La villanella rapita*, was prod. the same year in Venice. In 1795 he went to London as comp. to the King's Theatre, and 3 years later to Dublin. He returned to London in 1801, where he remained till his death by suicide.

Works incl. 60 operas, oratorios, church music, trio-sonatas.

Biber, Heinrich Ignaz Franz von (b Wartenberg, Bohemia, 12 Aug 1644; d Salzburg, 3 May 1704), Bohemian violinist and composer. He was high steward and cond. at the archbishop's court at Salzburg.

Works incl. opera *Chi la dura, la vince* (1687), church music, several sets of vln. sonatas, partitas for 3 instruments; vespers for voices, strings and trombs., and possibly the 53-part *Missa salisburgensis*, perf. in Salzburg Cathedral in 1682 and formerly attrib. to Benevoli.

Biches, Les, ballet in 1 act with chorus by Poulenc; comp. 1923, prod. Monte Carlo, 6

Jan 1924, with choreog. by Nijinska. Orch. Suite in 5 movts. (1939–40).

Bierey, Gottlob Benedikt (b Dresden, 25 Jul 1772; d Breslau, 5 May 1840), German composer. Succeeded Weber as cond. at the opera of Breslau in 1808. He wrote numerous operas, operettas and musical plays, incl. *Rosette, das Schweizer Hirtenmädchen* (Leipzig, 1806), and *Wladimir, Fürst von Novgorod* (Vienna, 1807).

Biggs, E. Power (b Westcliff, Essex, 29 Mar 1906; d Boston, Mass., 10 Mar 1977), English-born American organist. Studied at the RAM and moved to the US in 1930. Gave weekly broadcasts in Baroque repertory (1942–58) and commissioned works from Howard Hanson, Roy Harris and Walter Piston.

Bigot (*née* **Kiene**), **Marie** (b Colmar, 3 Mar 1786; d Paris, 16 Sep 1820), Alsatian pianist, wife of the librarian to Count Rasumovsky in Vienna and a friend of Haydn and Beethoven; reportedly played the Appassionata son. from the MS. In 1809 she and her husband went to Paris, but he was taken prisoner at Milan in the war of 1812 and she had to give poorly paid lessons. Mendelssohn was her pupil in 1816.

Bihari, János (b Nagyabony, bap. 21 Oct 1764; d Pest, 26 Apr 1827), Hungarian violinist and composer. Of gypsy stock, he learnt the vln. early and acquired great virtuosity. After his marriage to a daughter of Banyák, a cimbalom player, he soon took up the leadership of his father-in-law's band. It travelled throughout Hung. and repeatedly visited Vienna. As a comp. Bihari cultivated the *verbunkos* style with great success.

Billet de loterie, Le (*The Lottery Ticket*), opera by Isouard (lib. by A.F.C. de Lesser and J.F. Roger), prod. Paris, Opéra-Comique, 14 Sep 1811.

Billings, William (b Boston, Mass., 7 Oct 1746; d Boston, 26 Sep 1800), American tanner and amateur composer. Wrote many hymn tunes and patriotic songs.

Billington (*née* **Weichsel**), **Elizabeth** (b London, *c* 1765; d nr. Venice, 25 Aug 1818), English soprano, daughter of Carl Weichsel, a German oboist settled in London. She was a pupil of J.C. Bach, and first appeared as a child pianist in 1774. Married the double-bass player James Billington in 1783. Made her debut as a singer in Dublin, and subsequently sang with great success in London, Paris and Naples. After her return to London in 1801 she continued to be in great demand until her retirement in 1811.

Billy Budd, opera by Britten (lib. by E.M.

Forster and E. Crozier, on Herman Melville's story), prod. London, CG 1 Dec 1951. Rev. 1960 and heard on BBC, 13 Nov 1960; prod. CG, 9 Jan 1964.

Billy the Kid, ballet by Copland, prod. NY, 24 May 1939.

Bilt, Peter van der (b Jakarta, 30 Aug 1936; d Amsterdam, 25 Sep 1983), Dutch baritone. Debut, Amsterdam 1960, as Dulcamara. He sang Rossini's Basilio at San Francisco in 1963 and the following year joined the Deutsche Oper, Düsseldorf; appeared as guest in Vienna, Munich and Los Angeles, with Scot. Opera and at Edinburgh. Other roles incl. Don Giovanni, Figaro, Varlaam, Beckmesser and Don Quichotte. Also well known in concert and oratorio.

Binary. A song or piece in 2 distinct sections is said to be in binary form. The sections are dependent on each other because the 1st does not close and the 2nd does not open in the principal key, so that each by itself would fail to give any impression of completeness. They are also usually based on the same or similar thematic material – alike, but not identical. The dances in Bach's suites are exs. of binary form.

Binchois, (Gilles de Bins) (b ? Mons, *c* 1400; d Soignies, 20 Sep 1460), Franco-Flemish composer. Chaplain to Philip, Duke of Burgundy, from *c* 1430 until 1453, when he became provost of Saint-Vincent, Soignies. He comp. Mass-movements, Magnificats and other liturgical works in a severely functional style; but his most charact. works are his *chansons*, mostly in 3 parts and in the form of *rondeau* or *ballade*.

Bindernagel, Gertrud (b Magdeburg 11 Jan 1894; d Berlin, 3 Nov 1932), German soprano. After engagements at Magdeburg, Breslau and Regensburg she sang in Berlin from 1920, chiefly in the Wagner repertory; appeared as guest in Barcelona, Munich and Hamburg. After a perf. of *Siegfried* she was shot by her jealous husband, a banker, and died of her wounds shortly after.

Binet, Jean (b Geneva, 17 Oct 1893; d Trélex-sur-Nyon, Switz., 24 Feb 1960), Swiss composer. Studied at the Jaques-Dalcroze Inst. at Geneva and with Barblan, Templeton Strong, Bloch and others. Lived in USA and Brussels for a time.

Works incl. 3 psalms for chorus and orch., *Cantate de Noël* for chorus and org.; ballets *L'Ile enchantée* and *Le Printemps* (1950); suites on Swiss and Eng. themes and dances for orch.; concertino for chamber orch.; string 4tet (1927) and other chamber music, songs, part-songs.

Bing (Sir) **Rudolf** (b Vienna, 9 Jan 1902), Austrian-born manager, nationalised British subject 1946. Held appts. in Darmstadt and Berlin, 1928–33, until moving with Carl Ebert to Glyndebourne; manager there 1935–49. He helped found the Edinburgh Festival and was dir. 1947–9. Gen. manager NY Met 1950–72. His experiences with prima donnas (male and female) are detailed in 2 vols. of autobiog.: *5,000 Nights at the Opera* (1972) and *A Knight at the Opera* (1981). Knighted 1971.

Bioni, Antonio (b Venice, 1698; d after 1739), Italian composer. Pupil of Porta. Prod. his 1st opera at Chioggia in 1721; worked at Breslau and Prague, 1726–34.

Works incl. *c* 25 operas, e.g. *Climene, Issipile*; serenata *La pace fra la virtù e la bellezza* (Metastasio); also church music.

Birthday Odes, works for soli, chorus and orch. written by Eng. comps. from the Restoration onwards to commemorate royal birthdays. Purcell wrote 6 for Queen Mary, consort of William III, as follows: 1. *Now does the glorious day appear* (1689), 2. *Arise my Muse* (1690), 3. *Welcome, welcome, glorious morn* (1691), 4. *Love's goddess sure was blind* (1692), 5. *Celebrate this festival* (1693), 6. *Come ye sons of art away* (1694).

Birtwistle, Harrison (b Accrington, Lancs., 15 Jul 1934), English composer. Studied at the RMCM and later at the RAM, London. As a comp. he combines violent sonorities with a strictly controlled serial technique. He makes extensive use of electronics; the tape for *The Mask of Orpheus* was prepared at IRCAM (*q.v.*).

Works incl. STAGE: *Punch and Judy*, opera in 1 act (1968), *Monodrama* for sop., speaker and inst. ens. (1967), *Down by the Greenwood Side*, dramatic pastoral (1969), incid. music for National Theatre prods. of *Hamlet* (1975) and *The Oresteia* (1981), *Frames, Pulses and Interruptions*, ballet (1977), *Bow Down*, music-theatre (1977), *The Mask of Orpheus*, opera (1973–5, 1981–4; prod. 1986), *Yan Tan Tethera*, TV opera (1986).

ORCH.: *Chorales* (1960–63), *3 Movements with Fanfares* (1964), *Nomos* (1968), *An Imaginary Landscape* (1971), *The Triumph of Time* (1972), *Grimethorpe Aria* for brass band (1973), *Melencolia 1* (1976), *Silbury Air* for small orch. (1977), *Still Movement* for 13 solo strings (1984), *Earth Dances* (1985), *Endless Parade* (1987).

VOCAL: *Monody for Corpus Christi* for sop. and ens. (1959), *Narration: a Description of the Passing Year* for chorus (1963),

Entr'actes and Sappho Fragments for sop. and ens. (1964), *Carmen paschale* for chorus and org. (1965), *Ring a Dumb Clarion* for sop., clar. and perc. (1965), *Cantata* for sop. and ens. (1969), *Nenia on the Death of Orpheus* for sop. and ens. (1970), *The Fields of Sorrow* for 2 sop., chorus and ens. (1971–2), *Meridian* for mezzo, chorus and ens. (1970–71), *Epilogue: Full Fathom Five* for bar. and ens. (1972), ... *agm* . . . . . for 16 solo voices and 3 inst. ens. (1979), *On the Sheer Threshold of the Night* for 4 solo voices and 12-part chorus (1980).

INSTRUMENTAL: *Refrains and Choruses* for wind 5tet (1957), *The World is Discovered* for chamber ens. (1960), *Tragoedia* for ens. (1965), *Verses for Ensembles* (1969), *Ut heremita solus*, arr. of Ockeghem (1969), *Hoquetus David*, arr. of Machaut (1969), *Medusa* for ens. (1970, rev. 1980), *Chronometer* for 8-track tape (1971), *Chorales from a Toyshop* (1967–74), *Carmen Arcadiae Mechanicae Perpetuum* for ens. (1977), *For O for O, the Hobby Horse is Forgot* for 6 perc. (1976), clar. 5tet (1980).

Bishop (*née* **Riviere**), **Anna** (b London, 9 Jan 1810; d New York 18 Mar 1884), English soprano. Taught singing by her father and pf. by Moscheles, also studied at the RAM, where she met Bishop, whom she married in 1831. She made her debut that year, but in 1839 went on a tour with Robert Bochsa, harpist, bigamist and forger, and soon afterwards eloped with him, never to return to her husband and 3 children.

Bishop, Henry (Rowley) (b London, 18 Nov 1786; d London, 30 Apr 1855), English conductor and composer. Studied under Bianchi and prod. *Angelina* (comp. with Lanza) at Margate in 1804 and the ballet *Tamerlan et Bajazet* at the King's Theatre in London, 1806. From that time on he brought out one or more stage pieces almost each year until 1840. In 1813 he was one of the founders of the Phil. Society and became one of its conds. Knighted in 1842; D.Mus. at Oxford in 1853. Prof. of music at Oxford, 1848. He was twice married to singers: Sarah Lyon on 30 Apr 1809 and Anna Riviere on 9 Jul 1831.

Works incl. over 100 pieces for the stage, e.g. *The Corsair, The Circassian Bride* (1809), *Guy Mannering* (after Scott) (1816), *The Burgomaster of Saardam, The Heart of Midlothian* (after Scott) (1819), *Montrose* (after Scott), *The Law of Java, Maid Marian, Clari, Cortez, Faustus* (1825), *Aladdin, The Fortunate Isles* (1840); incid. music for 3 tragedies, for adapts. of Scott, Byron and Shakespeare; oratorio *The Fallen Angel;* cantata *The Seventh Day;* 3 vols of nat. melodies with words by Moore and other collections of arrs.

Bishop-Kovacevich, Stephen (b Los Angeles, 17 Oct 1940), American pianist of Yugoslav parentage. Debut San Francisco, 1951. Moved to London in 1959 (study with Myra Hess) and made British debut with the Diabelli vars. by Beethoven; gave fp of R.R. Bennett's concerto, Birmingham, 1968, and is often heard in Bartók, Mozart and Schubert.

Bispham, David (Scull) (b Philadelphia, 5 Jan 1857; d New York, 2 Oct 1921), American baritone. Studied with Vannuccini and Lamperti at Milan and with W. Shakespeare in London, where he made his 1st concert appearance in 1890, and his debut on the stage in 1891; in 1892 he sang Kurwenal, under Mahler. 5 years later he appeared in NY, at the Met, and sang the Wagner bar. roles, as well as Masetto, Escamillo, Iago and Falstaff.

Bisser (Fr. verb from Lat. *bis*= twice) = to encore.

Bitonality, the writing of music in 2 keys at once, e.g. the fanfare in Stravinsky's *Petrushka*, played simultaneously in C maj. and F♯ maj., or the following (see illustration).

Ravel, *L'Enfant et les Sortilèges*

Bittner, Julius (b Vienna, 9 Apr 1874; d Vienna, 10 Jan 1939), Austrian composer. A lawyer at first, studied music with Josef Labor and Bruno Walter.

Works incl. operas *Die rote Gred* (1907), *Der Musikant*(1909), *Der Bergsee* (1910), *Der Abenteurer*, *Das höllisch Gold*, *Die Kohlhaymerin*, *Das Rosengärtlein* (1922), *Mondnacht* (1928), *Das Veilchen;* ballets *Der Markt der Liebe*, *Die Todes-tarantella*; *Missa Austriaca* for solo voices, chorus and orch.; chamber music, pf. pieces; songs.

Bizet, Georges (actually Alexandre César Léopold) (b Paris, 25 Oct 1838; d Bougival nr. Paris, 3 Jun 1875), French composer. His father, a teacher of singing, gave him his 1st instruction in music and at the age of 9, being exceptionally gifted, he was admitted to the Paris Cons., studying pf. under Marmontel, org. under Benoist and comp. under Zimmermann. In 1853, when Zimmermann died, he became a pupil of Halévy, having already taken a 1st prize for pf. In 1857 he won the Prix de Rome, but before he went to Rome he had already gained a prize in a competition for an operetta, *Le Docteur Miracle*, sponsored by Offenbach. He tied with Lecocq, whose setting was prod. alternately with his own at the Théâtre des Bouffes-Parisiens.

He wrote several works in Rome and on his return to Paris in 1860 he set out to capture the operatic stage; but although the Opéra-Comique accepted his 1-act opera, *La Guzla de l'Émir*, he withdrew it, destroying it later. The Théâtre Lyrique prod. his next work, *Les Pêcheurs de perles*, in 1863; *Ivan le Terrible*, written in 1865, said to have been burnt by him, was recovered in 1944 and perf. in Ger., at Mühringen Castle, Württemberg. In 1869 Pasdeloup for the 1st time gave him the chance to appear with an orchestral work, *Souvenirs de Rome*, perf. 28 Feb, which he later entitled *Roma*. The same year he married Geneviève Halévy, his former master's daughter.

In 1872 he was commissioned to write incid. music for Daudet's play, *L'Arlésienne*, prod. at the Vaudeville on 1 Oct. In 1874 Pasdeloup prod. his overture *Patrie* (unconnected with Sardou's play), but he had set to work before that on *Carmen*, which was prod. at the Opéra-Comique, with spoken dialogue, on 3 Mar 1875 and received 37 perfs; but just after the 33rd. perf. Bizet died, before the work had won through prejudice to a decided success.

Works incl. OPERAS *Don Procopio* (1859), *Les Pêcheurs de perles* (1863), *La*

Jolie Fille de Perth (after Scott) (1866), *Djamileh*, *Carmen* (after Mérimee) (1874); operetta *Le Docteur Miracle*; incid. music to Daudet's *L'Arlésienne* (1872); cantatas *David* and *Clovis et Clotilde*; completion of Halévy's opera *Noë*.

ORCH.: symph. in C maj. (1855), suite *Roma* (1868), overture *Patrie*, *Petite Suite* (*Jeux d'enfants*) and *Marche funèbre* for orch.; *Vasco de Gama*, symph. ode with chorus.

PF. AND SOLO VOCAL: *Chasse fantastique*, *Chants du Rhin*, *Trois Esquisses*, *Marine*, *Premier Nocturne*, *Variations chromatiques* for pf.; *Jeux d'enfants* suite for pf. duet; *Chanson du rouet* for vocal solo and chorus, *Le Golfe de Bahia* for solo voices and chorus; *Saint Jean de Pathmos* for unaccomp. male chorus, 4 vocal duets; a number of songs incl. *Feuilles d'album*.

Björner, Ingrid (b Kraakstad, 8 Nov 1927), Norwegian soprano. She sang Third Norn and Gutrune in a concert perf. of *Götterdämmerung* for Oslo Radio in 1956, later issued as the opera's 1st recording. Stage debut Donna Anna, 1957. Munich from 1960 as Strauss's Empress and Daphne; Isolde in the cent. prod. of the opera's 1865 première there. NY Met debut 1961, Elsa. CG from 1967 as Senta, Sieglinde and Leonore. A successful recitalist in the songs of Grieg.

Björling, Jussi (actually Johan) **(Jonaton)** (b Stors Tuna, Kopparbergs län, 5 Feb 1911; d Stockholm, 9 Sep 1960), Swedish tenor. Studied with his father at the Stockholm Cons., and at the Royal Opera School in Stockholm. 1st appeared as Don Ottavio in *Don Giovanni*, Stockholm, 1930. He sang at CG in 1939 as Manrico; NY Met from 1938 as Rodolfo, Faust, Verdi's Riccardo and Cavaradossi. One of the finest lyric tenors of his time.

Björling, Sigurd (b Stockholm, 2 Nov 1907; d Helsingborg, 8 Apr 1983), Swedish baritone. He studied with John Forsell at the Stockholm Cons.; debut 1934. US debut San Francisco 1950, Kurwenal; NY Met 1952, Telramund. CG 1951, Amfortas. Bayreuth 1952 as Wotan; sang this role until 1973 in Stockholm. Other roles incl. Balstrode and Hindemith's Mathis.

Blacher, Boris (b Niu-chang, China, 19 Jan 1903; d Berlin, 30 Jan 1975), German composer. Studied in Berlin and began his career under great difficulties during the Nazi rule, but later became very successful as a comp. of the *avant garde*, developing a system of variable metres following arithmetical progressions, upon which many of his works are based. In 1953 he became director of the Berlin Hochschule für Musik.

Works incl. operas *Fürstin Tarakanova* (1940), *Preussisches Märchen* (1949), *Abstrakte Oper no.1* (1953), *200,000 Taler* (1969), *Das Geheimnis* (1975), chamber operas *Romeo und Julia* (1943) (after Shakespeare) *Die Flut* (1946), *Die Nachtschwalbe* (1948); several ballets incl. *Harlekinade* (1939), *Lysistrata* (1950), *Hamlet* (1949), *Der Mohr von Venedig* (1955); scenic oratorio *Der Grossinquisitor* (after Dostoievsky (1947).

Symph., symph. poem *Hamlet* (after Shakespeare), variations on theme by Paganini and other orchestral works; 2 pf. concertos, via. concerto; 5 string 4tets(1930–67) and other chamber music pf. music, songs.

Blachut, Beno (b Ostrava-Vitkovice, 14 Jun 1913; d Prague, 10 Jan 1985), Czech tenor. Debut Olomouc, 1939, Jeník. Prague Nat. Theatre from 1941; British debut with the co. Edinburgh Fest., 1970, as Matej Brouček in the Brit. première of Janáček's *The Excursions of Mr. Brouček*. Other roles incl. Lača, Dalibor and the Prince in *Rusalka*. He sang in Vienna as guest.

Black, Andrew (b Glasgow, 15 Jan 1859; d Sydney, NSW, 15 Sep 1920), Scottish baritone. At first an organist, but studied singing in London and Milan. Appeared in Scot. with success and 1st sang in London in 1887. Best known in oratorios, e.g. *The Spectre's Bride* (Dvořák), *Elijah* and *The Apostles*.

'Black Key' Study. Chopin's pf. Study in Gb maj., op. 10 no. 5, written *c* 1831–2 and pub. in 1833. So called because the right hand plays only on the black keys throughout.

Black Knight, The, cantata for chorus and orch. by Elgar, op. 25, a setting of Longfellow's trans. of Uhland's ballad *Der schwarze Ritter*, fp Worcester Festival, 1893.

Bladder Pipe, an early bagpipe with an animal's bladder used for the bag.

Blades, James (b Peterborough, 9 Sep 1901), English timpanist and percussionist. Employed in dance bands and playing film music in the 1930s. He joined the LSO in 1960 and has been a member of the ECO and Melos Ens.; with the EOG for their prods. of Britten's 3 church parables. Prof. RAM from 1960, OBE 1972.

Blaise le savetier (*B. the Cobbler*), opera by Philidor (lib. by J.M. Sedaine, after La Fontaine), prod. Paris, Opéra-Comique, 9 Mar 1759.

Blake, David (Leonard) (b London, 2 Sep 1936), English composer. He studied at Cambridge, and with Hanns Eisler in Berlin; has taught at York Univ. from 1964. He has used serial technique, and has been influenced by the music of the Far East.

Works incl. the opera *Toussaint L'Ouverture* (1974–6, rev. 1982); chamber symph. (1966), 2 vln. concertos (1976 and 1983); 3 choruses to poems by Frost (1964), *Lumina*, cantata for sop., bar., chorus and orch., to text by Pound (1969), *From the Mattress Grave*, 12 Heine poems for sop. and 11 insts. (1978), *Rise, Dove*, for bar. and orch. (1982); 3 string 4tets (1962, 1973, 1982), Nonet for wind (1971), Capriccio, for wind, strings and pf. (1980).

Blake, William (1757–1827), English poet and painter. *See* **Bolcom** (*Songs of Innocence and Experience*), **Britten** (*Songs and Proverbs*), **Connolly** (*The Marriage of Heaven and Hell*), **Goehr, (A.)** (*5 poems and an Epigram*), **Job** (Vaughan Williams), **Parry** (*Jerusalem*), **Tippett** (*Song of Liberty*).

Blamont, François Colin de (b Versailles, 22 Nov 1690; d Versailles, 14 Feb 1760), French composer. Pupil of his father, who was in the royal band, and later of Lalande. He became in 1719 superintendent of the royal music and, after Lalande's death in 1726, master of the chamber music.

Works incl. stage pieces (mostly ballets and ballet-operas) *Les Festes grecques et romaines* (1723), *Le Retour des dieux sur la terre* (for the marriage of Louis XV, 1725), *Le Caprice d'Érato* (1730), *Endymion* (1731), *Les Caractères de l'Amour, Les Amours du printemps, Jupiter vainqueur des Titans* (1745), *Les Festes de Thétis* (1750); cantata *Circé* and 3 books of *Cantates françaises* for solo voice; motets with orch. accomp.

Blanc, Ernest (b Sanary-sur-Mer, 1 Nov 1923), French baritone. Debut Marseilles, 1950; Paris Opéra from 1954. Well known as Scarpia and Rigoletto and in Wagner roles: Bayreuth 1958–9, as Telramund. At Glyndebourne in 1960 as Don Giovanni and Bellini's Riccardo, opposite Sutherland. Guest at Milan, Vienna and in Chicago and San Francisco. Widely known in recordings of *Faust, Carmen, Hoffmann* and *Les Pêcheurs de perles*.

Blanchard, Henri Louis (b Bordeaux, 9 Apr. 1791; d Paris, 18 Dec 1858), French violinist, composer, music critic and playwright. Studied vln. under R. Kreutzer and comp. under Méhul and others. Was cond. and theatre director in Paris. Wrote 3 operas, incl. *Diane de Vernon* (after Scott's *Rob Roy*) (1831), chamber music and airs for vaudevilles.

Bland (*née* **Romanzini**), **Maria Theresa** (b 1769; d London, 15 Jan 1838), English ballad singer of Italian extraction. Sang with great success, esp. at Vauxhall and other London pleasure gardens as well as in opera at Drury Lane. Married Bland, a brother of Mrs. Jordan, the actress.

Blangini, (Giuseppe Marco Maria) Felice (b Turin, 18 Nov 1781; d Paris, 18 Dec 1841), Italian tenor and composer. Sang at Turin Cathedral as a child and learnt music there. In 1799 he went to Paris, where he finished an opera left incomplete by P.A.D. Della Maria and prod. one of his own. In 1809 he was called to Kassel as music director to King Jérôme; but he returned to Paris in 1814 and 2 years later became prof. of singing at the Cons.

Works incl. over 30 operas, e.g. *La Fausse Duègne* (finished by him), *Chimère et réalité* (1803), *Nephtali, ou Les Ammonites* (1806), *Encore un tour de Caliphe*, *Inez de Castro* (1810), *Les Fêtes lacédémoniennes* (1807), *Le Sacrifice d'Abraham* (1810); contrib. to *La Marquise de Brinvilliers*; cantata *Die letzten Augenblicke Werthers* (after Goethe); 174 songs.

Blaník (Smetana). *See* **Má Vlast**.

Blankenburg, Quirijn Gerbrandt van (b Gouda, 1654; d The Hague, 12 May 1739), Dutch organist and composer. Studied philosophy and medicine at Leyden, was organist there and later at The Hague. Wrote theoret. books, pub. harpsichord and organ accomps. to psalms and hymns and in honour of the betrothal of the Prince of Orange in 1677 wrote pieces in 2 parts to be sung normally or upside down, forwards or backwards.

Blankenheim, Toni (b Cologne, 12 Dec 1921), German baritone. He studied with Res Fischer. Debut Frankfurt, 1947, as Mozart's Figaro. From 1950 he was prin. bar. at the Hamburg Staatsoper; sang Berg's Wozzeck and Dr. Schön with the co. at SW, London, in 1962. Bayreuth 1954–60 as Donner, Klingsor, Beckmesser and Kothner. He has appeared widely in Europe, in Mexico and San Francisco and at the NY Met.

Blas de Castro, Juan (b Aragon, *c* 1560; d Madrid, 6 Aug 1631), Spanish composer. In the 1590s he was private musician to the Duke of Alba at Salamanca and in 1605 musician and usher to Philip III. Lope de Vega and Tirso de Molina mentioned him in their works. Only 20 songs for 3 and 4 voices survive.

Blass, Robert (b New York, 27 Oct 1867; d Berlin, 3 Dec 1930), American bass of German parentage. Debut Weimar, 1892, as King Henry; sang widely as guest incl. CG 1899 and appeared at Bayreuth in 1901 as Gurnemanz and Hagen, under Muck and Richter. NY Met 1900–10 (debut as the Landgrave). Gurnemanz at Amsterdam, in the local fp of *Parsifal* (1905).

Blauwaert, Emile (b St. Nikolaas, 15 Jun 1845; d Brussels, 2 Feb 1891), Belgian bass. Studied at the Brussels Cons.; made his debut in 1866; sang at Bayreuth in 1889 as Gurnemanz.

Blavet, Michel (b Besançon, 13 Mar 1700; d Paris, 28 Oct 1768), French flautist and composer. Works incl. *opéra comique Le Jaloux corrigé* (1752), ballets, sonatas and duets for fl.

Blech (Ger.) = Brass, an abbr. often used in scores for *Blechinstrumente*.

Blech, Leo (b Aachen, 21 Apr 1871; d Berlin, 24 Aug 1958), German conductor and composer. Pupil of Bargiel and Humperdinck, cond. in his native town, 1892–8; later at Prague and in 1906–37 cond. of the Berlin Opera.

Works incl. operas *Aglaja* (1893), *Cherubina* (1894), *Versiegelt* (Hamburg, 1908), *Das war ich* (Dresden, 1902), *Aschenbrödel, Alpenkönig und Menschenfeind* (after Raimund) (1903); 3 symph. poems; choral works with orch.

Blegen, Judith (b Missoula, Mont., 27 Apr 1941), American soprano. Opera debut Nuremberg, 1963; Mélisande at Spoleto in 1964. Vienna, Staatsoper, 1969, as Rosina; NY Met from 1970 as Papagena, Zerlina and Sophie. In the 1969 Santa Fe US première of Menotti's *Help! Help! the Globoniks!* she sang the role of Emily and played the violin. CG debut 1975, Despina.

Blessed Damozel, The (Debussy). *See* **Damoiselle élue**.

Blind Man's Buff, masque by Peter Maxwell Davies for high voice, mezzo, mime and stage band (text by Davies from Büchner's *Leonce und Lena*, et al.), fp London, 29 May 1972, cond. Boulez.

Blind Octaves, a trick of pf. writing: figures in 8ves rapidly alternating between the 2 hands where the thumbs trace a continuous melodic line while the outer notes fly off at broken intervals.

Bliss, Arthur (Drummond) (b London, 2 Aug 1891; d London, 27 Mar 1975), English composer. Educ. at Rugby and Pembroke

Coll., Cambridge, where he studied music under C. Wood. Entered the RCM in London, 1913, studying with Stanford, Vaughan Williams and Holst, but joined the army in 1914, serving all through the war until 1918. Prof. of comp. at RCM in 1921, but took wholly to comp. the next year, never holding any official post until he was app. music director of the BBC in 1941, an appt. he resigned to Hely-Hutchinson in 1945. He was knighted in 1950 and succeeded Bax as Master of the Queen's Music in 1953.

Works incl. DRAMATIC: operas, *The Olympians* (lib. by J.B. Priestley) (1949), and *Tobias and the Angel* (C. Hassall) (1960); ballets, *Checkmate, Miracle in the Gorbals* and *Adam Zero*; incid. music for Shakespeare's *Tempest*; film music for *Things to Come* (H.G. Wells), *Conquest of the Air, Caesar and Cleopatra* (G.B. Shaw).

ORCH: *A Colour Symph.* (1922), *Introduction and Allegro* (1926), *Hymn to Apollo, Meditations on a Theme by John Blow* (1955); concertos for pf. and 2 pfs.; march *Phoenix* for the liberation of Fr.; *Music for Strings*.

VOCAL: *Morning Heroes* for orator, chorus and orch. (1930), *Pastoral* for mezzo, chorus, fl., strings and drums, cantata *Mary of Magdala* for contralto, bass, chorus and orch., *Serenade* for bar. and orch. (1929), concerto for pf., tenor and chamber orch., *Rout* for voice and chamber orch. *Madam Noy* for voice and 6 instruments; several song cycles with var. instruments or pf., incl. *5 Amer. Songs* (Edna St Vincent Millay).

CHAMBER: *Conversations* for fl., ob., vln., vla. and cello; 2 string 4tets (1941, 1950), ob. 5tet, clar. 5tet; sonatas for vln. and pf. and vla. and pf.

Blitheman, John (b *c* 1525; d London, 23 May 1591), English organist and composer. Gentleman of the Chapel Royal from before Dec 1558 till his death. He was a famous organist and a teacher of Bull. Works incl. motets and 6 *In Nomines* for virginal.

Blitzstein, Marc (b Philadelphia, 2 Mar 1905; d Fort-de-France, Martinique, 22 Jan 1964), American pianist and composer. Appeared as solo pianist at the age of 15; studied comp. with Scalero in NY, Nadia Boulanger in Paris and Schoenberg in Vienna; also pf. with Siloti in Amer. His 1st great success was the light opera *The Cradle Will Rock*, prod. in NY 1937. He was a political radical and was killed after an argument with Amer. sailors.

Works incl. operas *Triple Sec* (1929), *Parabola and Circula* (1929), *The Harpies, The Cradle Will Rock* (1937); ballet *Cain*; incid. music for Shakespeare's *Julius Caesar*; film music for *Surf and Seaweed, The Spanish Earth, No for an Answer* (1941), *Chesapeake Bay Retriever*; choral opera *The Condemned*; radio song-play *I've got the Tune*, Children's Cantata; *The Airborne* for orch., chorus and narrator (1946); *Romantic Piece, Jigsaw* ballet suite, and variations for orch.; pf. concerto (1931), string 4tet and serenade for string 4tet; pf. sonata and *Percussion Music* for pf. (1929).

Bloch, Ernest (b Geneva, 24 Jul 1880; d Portland, Oregon, 15 Jul 1959), Swiss (Americanized) composer. Pupil of Jaques-Dalcroze at first, then of Ysaÿe and Rasse at the Brussels Cons., and later at the Hoch Cons. at Frankfurt where Iwan Knorr was his comp. master. His last teacher was Thuille at Munich, and he then went to live in Paris, where he began the opera *Macbeth* on a Fr. lib. by Edmond Fleg, having already written several important works. It was prod. in Paris in 1910, but he had in the meantime returned to Switz. to cond. subscription concerts at Lausanne and Neuchâtel. From 1911 to 1915 he was prof. of music aesthetics at the Geneva Cons. In 1917 he went to the USA and settled in NY as prof. at the David Mannes School of Music. A second opera *Jézabel*, begun there in 1918, was unfinished.

From 1920 to 1925 Bloch was director of the Cleveland Inst. of Music. In 1930 he retired to Switz. to live quietly in remote places. Some interest was shown in his work in Eng. and a good deal in It., where his *Sacred Service* was prod. (at Turin) and *Macbeth* was revived in an It. trans. at Naples, 5 Mar 1938. But the anti-Semitic movement encouraged by the Fascists put an end to this appreciation. As an American citizen he could no longer remain absent from USA without losing his adopted nationality, and he returned there at the end of 1938.

Works incl. opera *Macbeth* (1904–9), *Sacred Service (Avodath Hakodesh)* for baritone solo, chorus and orch.

ORCH.: *Israel* symph. for 5 voices and orch.; symph. in C♯ min. (1901), symph. poems *Hiver—Printemps, Trois Poèmes juifs* for orch., *America*, epic rhapsody for orch. (1926); *Helvetia*, symph. fresco (1928), *Evocations*, symph. suite (1938), suite: *Overture, Passacaglia and Finale*; vln. concerto (1938); *Concerto symphonique* for pf. and orch., *Schelomo* for cello and orch.

(1916), *Concerto grosso* for pf. and strings, *Voice in the Wilderness* for cello and orch. (1926), *Four Episodes* for chamber orch. (1926).

CHAMBER: 5 string 4tets (1916–56); 2 vln. and pf. sonatas, vla. and pf. suite, pf. 5tet, *Three Nocturnes* for pf. trio; *In the Mountains, Night, Three Landscapes* and *Recueillement* (prelude) for string 4tet.

VOCAL AND INSTRUMENTAL: *Poèmes d'automne* and 3 Psalms for voice and orch.; *Enfantines, 5 Sketches in Sepia, In the Night, Nirvana, Poems of the Sea* and sonata for pf.; *Baal Shem* (3 pieces), *Melody, Exotic Night* and *Abodah* for vln. and pf.; *From Jewish Life* (3 pieces) and *Méditation hébraïque* for cello and pf., song cycle *Historiettes au crépuscule* (1903) and other songs.

Block Harmony, a term used for a type of harmonic accomp. in which all the notes of the chords move simultaneously in 'blocks' without being made to depart from one another by means of figuration or counterpoint.

Blockflöte (Ger. lit. block fl.; actually Fipple Fl.) = Recorder.

Blockx, Jan (b Antwerp, 25 Jan 1851; d Antwerp, 26 May 1912), Belgian composer. Learnt music as a choir-boy and went to the Antwerp School of Music, later to the Leipzig Cons. In 1886 he became prof. and in 1901 director of the Antwerp Cons., succeeding Benoit, whom he followed as a Flem. music nationalist. Most of his operas and all his cantatas for solo voices, chorus and orch. are set to Flem. words.

Works incl. operas *Jets vergeten* (1877), *Maître Martin* (1892), *Herbergprinses* (1896), *Thyl Uilenspiegel* (1900), *De Bruid der Zee, De Kapel* (1903), *Baldie*; ballet *Milenka* (1887); cantatas *Op den Stroom, Een Droom van't Paradijs, Vredeszang, Klokke Roeland, De Scheldezang*; overture *Rubens*; Romance for vln. and orch.

Blodek, Vilém (b Prague, 3 Oct 1834; d Prague, 1 May 1874), Czech flautist, teacher and composer. Prod. the nat. opera *In the Well* at Prague in 1867, but his 2nd opera, *Zitek*, remained unfinished at his death; it was completed by F.X. Vana, and perf. in Prague on the cent. of Blodek's birth.

Blom, Eric (Walter) (b Berne, 20 Aug 1888; d London, 11 Apr 1959), English critic, of Danish origin. He was educated privately and 1st became known in England as assistant to Rosa Newmarch in providing programme notes for the Promenade concerts in 1919. He was London music critic of the *Manchester Guardian* from 1923 to 1931,

music critic of the *Birmingham Post* from 1931, and music critic of the *Observer* from 1949 to 1953. He also ed. *Music & Letters* from 1937 to 1950 and 1954 to 1959. His books incl. *The Limitations of Music, Mozart, Beethoven's Sonatas Discussed, Music in England* and the 1st eds. of this dictionary. He also trans. several foreign books and ed. the 5th ed. of *Grove's Dictionary of Music and Musicians* (1954). He was made CBE and Hon. D.Litt. of Birmingham Univ. in 1955.

Blomdahl, Karl-Birger (b Växjö, 19 Oct 1916; d Växjö, 14 Jun 1968), Swedish composer. Studied at Stockholm under var. masters, incl. Rosenberg and Wöldike. In 1960 he was app. prof. at the Stockholm Cons.

Works incl. opera *Aniara* (a space-ship drama) (1957–9); incid. music; 3 symphs. (1943, 1947, 1950), symph. dances, concert overture, *Concerto grosso* for orch.; vln. concerto (1946), vla. concerto, chamber concerto for pf., wind and perc.; 2 string 4tets, string trio, woodwind trio, suites for cello and pf. and bassoon and pf.; pf. pieces; trios for women's voices.

Blondel de Nesle (*fl.*1180–1200), French trouvère whose surviving songs (over 20) are exceptionally widely represented in the surviving sources and often formed the basis for later adaptations. The legend that he was associated with King Richard the Lionheart and was instrumental in rescuing him from prison has contributed to Blondel's subsequent fame.

Blow, John (b Newark, bap. 23 Feb 1649; d London, 1 Oct 1708), English organist and composer. He became one of the children in the Chapel Royal in London as soon as it was re-established after the Restoration (1660) and was taught by H. Cooke. He wrote 3 anthems in 1663 and took a share with Humfrey and Turner in the 'Club Anthem' *c* 1664. About the same time he set Herrick's 'Go, perjur'd man' in the style of Carissimi at Charles II's request. Hingston and C. Gibbons also had a share in Blow's musical educ. In 1668 he became organist at Westminster Abbey in succession to Albert Bryne; in Mar 1674 he was sworn a Gentleman of the Chapel Royal and the following Jul he became Master of the Children following Humfrey. In November he married Elizabeth Braddock. Mus.D. at Canterbury, 1677. In 1679 he was followed in the Westminster organist's post by Purcell, returning as organist after Purcell's death in 1695. In 1687 he succeeded Wise as almoner and choirmaster at St Paul's Cathedral (as yet unfinished). James II app. him a member of the royal band and confirmed a previous app. as Comp. in Ordinary. Towards the end of the cent. he bought a property at Hampton, but still retained a house at Westminster, where he died.

Works incl. *c* 12 services; over 100 Eng. anthems, 9 Lat. anthems; masque *Venus and Adonis* (*c* 1685); Act Songs for Oxford Univ.; at least 16 Welcome Songs, 5 for St Cecilia's Day, odes on the death of Queen Mary (1695) and of Purcell (1696); 3 coronation anthems for James II, 1 for William and Mary; anthem for the opening service at St Paul's Cathedral (1697); sonata for 2 vlns. and bass; harpsichord lessons, suites and pieces; some org. pieces; song collection *Amphion Anglicus*, songs and catches, etc.

Blue Notes, a device in Blues, the playing of certain notes, esp. the 3rd and 7th of the scale, deliberately out of tune, between maj. and min.

Bluebeard. *See* **Ariane et Barbe-bleue; Barbe-bleue; Ritter Blaubart.**

Bluebeard's Castle (Bartók). *See* **Duke Bluebeard's Castle.**

Blues. Song (lament) from black American jazz, usually in 3 groups of 4 bars, in maj. keys with flattened 3rds and 7ths ('blue notes'). Ravel (son. for vln. and pf.), Copland and Tippett have drawn on Blues style.

Blume, Friedrich (b Schlüchtern, Hesse, 5 Jan 1893; d Schlüchtern, 22 Nov 1975), German musicologist. Studied at Munich, Leipzig and Berlin. He was a prisoner in England for 3 years during the 1914–18 war. After teaching in Berlin from 1921 he became prof. at Kiel Univ. from 1934 to 1958. He was ed.-in-chief of the complete works of M. Praetorius and the series *Das Chorwerk*, and was ed. of the encyclopaedia *Die Musik in Geschichte und Gegenwart*. His books incl. a history of Protestant church music.

Blumine, original 2nd movt. of Mahler's 1st symph., in D, and heard in the work's fp, Budapest, 20 Nov 1889. The movt. was discarded in 1894 and not perf. again until 18 Jun 1976 at Aldeburgh, cond. Britten.

Blüthner, Julius Ferdinand (b Falkenhain, 11 Mar 1824; d Leipzig, 13 Apr 1910), German pf. manufacturer. Founded his firm at Leipzig in 1853.

Bluthochzeit, opera by Fortner (lib. by E. Beck after Lorca's *Bodas de Sangre*), comp. for the opening of the new opera house, Cologne, and perf. there 8 Jun 1957.

Opera by Szokolay (*Vérnász*, same source), prod. Budapest, 30 Oct 1964.

Boccabadati, Luigia (b Modena, 1800; d Turin, 12 Oct 1850), Italian mezzo. Made her 1st appearance at Parma in 1817. Her 3 daughters were also singers.

Boccherini, Luigi (b Lucca, 19 Feb 1743; d Madrid, 28 May 1805), Italian cellist and composer. Pupil of his father, a double-bass player, who sent him to Rome for further study in 1757. On his return to Lucca in 1761 he played cello in the theatre orch. With the violinist Manfredi he travelled widely on concert tours in Aus. and Fr. Particularly successful in Paris (1767–8), he pub. there his first chamber music. In 1769 he went to Madrid and settled there, being first in the service of the Infante Don Luis until 1785, when the latter died. In 1787 Boccherini was app. court comp. to Frederick William II of Prussia, who had the exclusive right to his works, but he seems to have maintained his residence in Madrid. After the king's death in 1797 he was apparently without a permanent post, for he spent his last years in increasing poverty, largely owing to inconsiderate treatment by his publishers.

Works incl. oratorios *Giuseppe riconosciuto* and *Gioas, rè di Giuda* (*c* 1765); *Stabat Mater* (1781), Mass (1800), cantatas, motets, etc.; zarzuela *La Clementina* (1780); concert arias, etc.; 26 symphs; 11 cello concertos and one each for fl., vln. and harpsichord; 91 string 4tets, 48 string trios, 125 string 5tets, 12 piano 5tets, 18 5tets for wind and strings, 16 6tets, 2 8tets; 27 vln. sonatas, 6 cello sonatas.

Bochsa, Robert Nicolas Charles (b Montmédi, 9 Aug 1789; d Sydney, NSW, 6 Jan 1856), French harpist, conductor and composer. Began as a comp. of opera, oratorio and ballet at Lyons and Bordeaux; entered the Paris Cons. in 1806; made a great name as harpist and opera comp., but fled to Eng. in 1817 when discovered in forgeries. Although condemned, he was able to live in London, where he made the harp extremely popular and became prof. of the instrument on the foundation of the RAM, but in 1827 had to leave owing to scandals, including bigamy. In 1839 he ran away with Bishop's wife, Anna Riviere. They went on a world tour together, during which he died.

Works incl. opera *Trajan* (Lyon, 1805) and 8 others; a ballet; oratorio *Le Déluge universel* (1806; perf. CG, 22 Feb 1822); Requiems for Louis XVI, which contains anticipations of Berlioz's *Symphonie funèbre et triomphale*); many pieces for harp.

Bockelmann, Rudolf (August Louis Wilhelm) (b Bodenteich nr. Lüneburg, 2 Apr 1890; d Dresden, 10 Oct 1958), German bass-baritone. He studied with Oscar Lassner and 1st appeared in *Lohengrin* at Leipzig, 1921; sang there in title role of Krenek's *Das Leben des Orest*, 1930. He sang regularly at Bayreuth 1928–42, as Gunther, Kurwenal, Sachs and the Dutchman, and frequently in London (CG 1929–38). After the 1939–45 war he settled as a teacher in Hamburg.

Bocklet, Carl Maria von (b Prague, 1801; d Vienna, 15 Jul 1881), Bohemian pianist and violinist. Settled in Vienna in 1820. Friend of Beethoven and Schubert.

Bockshorn, Samuel (Friedrich) (Capricornus) (b Žeržice nr. Mlada Boleslav, 21 Dec 1628; d Stuttgart, 10 Nov 1665), Bohemian composer. Music dir. at Pressburg, Nuremberg and Stuttgart.

Works incl. dramatic cantata *Raptus Proserpinae* (1662); sacred and secular works for voices and instruments; vocal table music, songs.

Bockstriller (Ger. = goat's trill), a kind of vocal shake of no artistic value, prod. by a rapid, bleating repetition of a single note. Wagner asks for this kind of shake from the tailors' chorus in the 3rd act of *Die Meistersinger*.

Bodanzky, Artur (b Vienna, 16 Dec 1877; d New York, 23 Nov 1939), Austrian conductor. Studied at the Vienna Cons. and after some minor apps. became asst. cond. to Mahler at the Imp. Opera. After several engagements at Ger. opera houses, he became cond. of the Ger. operas at the NY Met, 1915; cond. the Soc. of the Friends of Music from 1921. At CG in 1914 he cond. the 1st Brit. stage perf. of *Parsifal*.

Bode, Hannelore (b Berlin-Zehlendorf, 2 Aug 1941), German soprano. Debut Bonn, 1964. She sang in Basle 1967–8, then joined the Deutsche Oper, Düsseldorf; Wagner roles, e.g. Eva and Elisabeth. She sang Eva at Bayreuth 1973–4 and in 1975 recorded the role with Solti.

Bodenschatz, Erhard (b Lichtenberg, 1576; d Gross-Osterhausen, 1636), German theologian and musician. Ed. of various collections of sacred music, notably the *Florilegium Portense*, pub. in 2 parts (1603 and 1621).

Boehm, Theobald (b Munich, 9 Apr 1794; d Munich, 25 Nov 1881), German flautist and inventor. He wrote music for his instrument and made important changes in its fingering and mechanism.

Boëllmann, Léon (b Ensisheim, 25 Sep 1862; d Paris, 11 Oct 1897), French (Alsatian) organist and composer. Pupil of Gigout at Niedermeyer's school in Paris, later organist at the church of Saint-Vincent-de-Paul there.

Works incl. symph. in F maj.; *Fantasie dialoguée* for organ and orch., *Variations symph.* for cello and orch. (1893); pf. 4tet; pf. trio; cello and pf. sonata; church music, organ works incl. 2 suites (1st *Gothique*, 1895).

Boëly, Alexandre (Pierre François) (b Versailles, 19 Apr 1785; d Paris, 27 Dec 1858), French pianist, organist and composer. Organist at the church of Saint-Germain-l'Auxerrois, 1840–51, where he cultivated Bach's organ music.

Works incl. chamber music (5 string trios, 4 string 4tets); organ works; vln. and pf. sonatas; numerous pf. works incl. sonatas, caprices, studies, preludes and fugues.

Boësset, French 16th–17th-cent. family of musicians:

1. Antoine B., Sieur de Villedieu (b Blois, *c.* 1586; d Paris, 8 Dec 1643). Became Master of the King's Music to Louis XIII through his marriage to Guédron's daughter and held other important posts at court. Wrote 24 ballets and pub. 9 books of *Airs de cour* in 4 and 5 parts (Paris 1617–42); also wrote Masses and motets.

2. Jean-Baptiste B., Seigneur de Dehault (b Paris, 1614; d Paris, 1685), son of prec. Succeeded his father in 1644. Wrote opera *La Mort d'Adonis*, with words by Perrin, and ballets *Ballet du Temps* (1654), *Triomphe de Baccus* (*c* 1666) and *Alcidiane*; also vocal chamber mus.

3. Claude Jean-Baptiste B., Seigneur de Launay (b July 1664; d Paris, *c* 1701), brother of prec. Held some of his father's posts and titles from 1686, but was replaced by 1696 by Lully's son Jean-Baptiste and by Colasse.

Works incl. *Fruits d'automne*.

Boethius, Anicius Manlius Severinus (b Rome, *c* 480; d 524), Roman consul and senator, and philosopher. His most important work is the *De consolatione philosophiae* (some verses from which were set to music in Carolingian times), but he is also, in his *De institutione musica*, the interpreter of ancient musical theory to the Western world. In spite of some misconceptions and the irrelevancy of much of the Gk. system, his work remained the fundamental basis of almost all medieval and Renaissance musical theory.

Bogatirev, Anatoly Vassilevich (b Vitebsk, 13 Aug 1913), Russian composer. Studied at the Minsk Cons. under Zolotarev. Later studied folksong and became deputy director of the Cons. at Minsk.

Works incl. operas *The Two Foscari* (after Byron) and *In the Thick Woods of Polesye* (1939); incid. music for Romashev's *Stars Cannot be Dimmed*; *The Tale of a Bear* for solo voices, chorus and orch., cantata *To the People of Leningrad*; string 4tet, pf. trio; *Manfred* suite (after Byron) and variations for pf.; choruses, songs, folksong arrs. In 1957 he made a performing vers. from the sketches of Tchaikovsky's 7th symph.

Bohème, La (*Bohemian Life*), opera by Leoncavallo (lib. by comp., based on Murger's novel *Scènes de la vie de Bohème*), prod. Venice, Teatro La Fenice, 6 May 1897. Comp. at the same time as Puccini's work.

Opera by Puccini (lib. by G. Giacosa and L. Illica, based on Murger), prod. Turin, Teatro Regio, 1 Feb 1896.

Bohemian Girl, The, opera by Balfe (lib. by A. Bunn based on a ballet-pantomime, *La Gypsy*, by J.H.V. de Saint-Georges), prod. London, Drury Lane Theatre, 27 Nov 1843.

Böhm, Georg (b Hohenkirchen nr. Ohrdruf, 2 Sep 1661; d Lüneburg, 18 May 1733), German composer. Organist at Hamburg before 1698, then at St John's Church, Lüneburg. As comp. and organist an important forerunner of Bach; his works incl. a Passion, songs, organ and harpsichord music.

Böhm, Karl (b Graz, 28 Aug 1894; d Salzburg, 14 Aug 1981), Austrian conductor. Studied music and law in Vienna. He held posts in many of the chief European opera houses, incl. Dresden (1934–43) and Vienna (1943–5, 1954–6). Böhm was esp. well known for his perfs. of Mozart and of R. Strauss, the fps of whose *Schweigsame Frau* (1935) and *Daphne* (1938) he cond., both in Dresden; CG debut with the co. in 1936. NY Met 1957–74, Bayreuth 1962–70. He was a regular cond. of the Vienna PO.

Böhme, Kurt (b Dresden, 5 May 1908), German bass. Dresden 1930–50, where he took part in the fp of *Die schweigsame Frau*; sang with the co. CG in 1936 as the Commendatore. Bayreuth 1952–67, Pogner and Klingsor. At Salzburg he created roles in operas by Liebermann and Egk (*Irische Legende*, 1955). NY Met debut 1954, as Pogner. Sang Hunding, Hagen and Ochs – his best role – at CG 1956–70.

Bohnen, Michael (b Cologne, 2 May 1887; d Berlin, 26 Apr 1965), German bass-baritone. Made his debut in Düsseldorf in 1910 as Kaspar and then sang at the Berlin Hofoper from 1913 to 1921. From 1922 to 1932 he sang at the NY Met (US première of Krenek's *Jonny spielt auf,* 1929); in Berlin again from 1933 to 1945. Other roles incl. Hunding, Daland, Ochs and Sarastro.

Boieldieu, François Adrien (b Rouen, 16 Dec 1775; d Jarcy, 8 Oct 1834), French composer. Studied under Broche, the organist of Rouen Cathedral, and in 1793 brought out his 1st opera. *La Fille coupable*, there, with a lib. by his father, who was secretary to the archbishop. He also wrote many songs at that time, some of which were pub. in Paris. Having failed to estab. a school of music at Rouen on the model of the Paris Cons., he left for the capital, where in 1797 he prod. his 1st opera away from home, *La Famille suisse*, which was so successful that he brought out 4 more within 2 years. He also became pf. prof. at the Cons. in 1798. Being reproached by Cherubini for having attained too easy a success on very slender gifts, he placed himself under that master for a course in counterpoint. In 1802 he married the dancer Clotilde Mafleuray, with disastrous results, and in 1803 he left for St Petersburg as cond. of the Imp. Opera. There he wrote 9 operas between 1804 and 1810. He returned to Paris in 1811 and had a greater success than before because there was less competition and he did better work.

He collaborated by turns with Cherubini, Catel, Isouard, R. Kreutzer, Hérold, Berton, Paer and Auber, also with some of these and Batton, Blangini and Carafa in *La Marquise de Brinvilliers* of 1831; but his best works are among those he did alone. In *La Dame blanche*, to match the lib. from Scott, he used some Scot. folksongs. Soon after he began to suffer from tuberculosis contracted in Rus. and his fortune declined until he was granted a state pension. In 1827 he was married for the 2nd time, to the singer Jenny Philis-Bertin, with whom he had long been living and by whom he had a son, Adrien Louis Victor, in 1815, who also became a comp. Boieldieu lived at Geneva for a time not long before his death.

Works incl. operas *Le Calife de Bagdad* (1800), *Ma Tante Aurore* (1803), *Aline, Reine de Golconde* (1804), *La Jeune Femme colère, Télémaque* (1807), *Rien de trop, Jean de Paris* (1812), *La Fête du village voisin, Le Petit Chaperon rouge, La Dame blanche* (1825), *Les Deux Nuits* and others; incid.

music for Racine's *Athalie*; pf. concerto (1792), harp concerto (1801), pf. trio and other chamber music; duets for vln. and pf. and harp and pf., 6 pf. sonatas.

Boismortier, Joseph Bodin de (b Thionville, 23 Dec 1689; d Roissy-en-Brie, 28 Oct 1755), French composer. Wrote 3 opera-ballets, *Les voyages de L'Amour* (1736), *Don Quichote* (1743), *Daphnis et Chloé* (1747); 8 cantatas, in 2 books (1724 and 1737), over 50 instrumental works incl. many for musette and vielle.

Boito, Arrigo (b Padua, 24 Feb 1842; d Milan, 10 Jun 1918), Italian poet and composer. Studied at the Milan Cons. and prod. his Faust opera, *Mefistofele*, at La Scala there in 1868. Wrote libs. for several comps. as well as for himself, incl. those of Verdi's *Otello* and *Falstaff*. His *Nerone* was not prod. until after his death. He also wrote the opera *Ero e Leandro*, but destroyed the music (the lib. was set by Bottesini and later by Mancinelli) and he wrote a lib. on *Hamlet* for Faccio.

Bokor, Margit (b Losoncz, 1905; d New York, 9 Nov 1949), Hungarian soprano. Debut Budapest, 1928. She sang Leonora (*Trovatore*) in Berlin, 1930, and created Zdenka in *Arabella* at Dresden in 1933. The following year she was heard as Octavian at Salzburg. After singing at the Vienna Staatsoper 1935–8, she moved to the USA; appeared at Chicago, Philadelphia and NY Met.

Bolcom, William (Elden) (b Seattle, 26 May 1938), American composer and pianist. Studied at Stanford Univ. and the Paris Cons.; has taught at Univ. of Michigan from 1973. As a pianist he has been heard in popular early Amer. music, often with his wife, the mezzo Joan Morris. Works have been influenced by techniques of collage and microtonal electronics: theatre pieces *Dynamite Tonite* (1963), *Greatshot* (1969), *Theatre of the Absurd* (1970), *The Beggar's Opera* (adaptation of Gay, 1978); *Oracles*, symph. (1964), pf. concerto (1976), symph. for chamber orch. (1979), vln. concerto (1983); 8tet for wind, strings and pf. (1962), *Session*, works for various inst. groups, with drum play (1965–7), 14 piano rags (1967–70), pf. 4tet (1976), brass 5tet (1980); *Songs of Innocence and Experience*, 48 Blake settings for solo voices and choruses (1958–81; vers. with orch. perf. Stuttgart 1984).

Bolero, a Spanish dance in 3–4 with a characteristic rhythm that usually has a triplet on the 2nd half of the 1st beat.

Bolero, an orchestral work by Ravel, com-missioned as a ballet by Ida Rubinstein and 1st perf. by her in Paris, 22 Nov 1928. It consists entirely of a single theme of Spanish character, repeated over and over again with different orch. and in a gradual taut *crescendo*.

Bologna, Jacopo da (Jacobus de Bononia) (*fl.* 1340–60), Italian composer, 2nd only to Landini in stature. He belongs to the earliest generation of *trecento* comps.: all his known works are madrigals, and nearly all are for two voices. There is also a short treatise, *L'arte del biscanto misurato*.

Bolshakov, Nikolay (b Kharkov, 23 Nov 1874; d Leningrad, 20 Jun 1958), Russian tenor. Debut St Petersburg, 1899; member of Maryinsky co. 1906–29. London, Drury Lane, 1913, in the 1st of Beecham's Russian seasons; appeared as guest in Paris, Barcelona and Berlin. He was well known as Lensky, Hermann, Faust, Pinkerton and Don José.

Bolt, The, ballet in 3 acts by Shostakovich (scenario by V. Smirnov), perf. Leningrad, 8 Apr 1931. Ballet suite (no. 5) op. 27a, perf. 1933.

Bomarzo, opera by Ginastera (lib. by M.M. Láinez, set in 16th-cent. Italy), perf. Washington DC, 19 May 1967; banned in Ginastera's own country, Argentina, owing to alleged obscenities in the ballet. Cantata *Bomarzo*, for bar., speaker, chorus and orch., perf. Washington, 1 Nov 1964.

Bombard, the bass instrument of the Shawm family, a double reed wind instrument prec. the oboe, the bombard thus being a forerunner of the bassoon.

Bombardon (Fr.; *see also* **Saxhorn**), the name of a brass instrument of the Tuba variety, derived from Bombard (or Ger. *Pommer*), previously applied to var. instruments of the oboe and bassoon family. The bombardon takes the lowest bass parts in military and brass bands.

Bomtempo, João Domingos (b Lisbon, 28 Dec 1775; d Lisbon, 18 Aug 1842), Portuguese composer. Settled in Paris in 1802, but returned to Lisbon in 1815, founded a Phil. Society there in 1820 and became director of the Cons. in 1833.

Works incl. It. opera *Alessandro in Efeso*; Mass for the promulgation of the Port. Constitution (1821), Requiems for Maria I, Pedro IV and Camões; 2 symphs.; 4 pf. concertos; pf. 5tet; variations on a fandango and on *God Save the King* for pf.

Bona, Valerio (b Brescia, 1560; d Verona, after 1619), Italian composer and Franciscan friar. *Maestro di cappella* at various churches, incl. Vercelli, Milan, Brescia and Verona.

Works incl. Masses, motets and other church music; madrigals and cazonets.

Bonci, Alessandro (b Cesena nr. Rimini, 10 Feb 1870; d Viserba, 9 Aug 1940), Italian tenor. He studied with Delle Sedie in Paris. Debut Parma, 1896, Fenton; then sang Bellini's Arturo and Elvino at La Scala. He was considered a rival to Caruso and sang Rodolfo at CG in 1900. US debut 1906, as Arturo at the Manhattan Opera House; NY Met 1907–10, debut as the Duke of Mantua. Sang at Chicago and Rome before his retirement in 1925. Other roles incl. Alfredo, Riccardo and Faust.

Bonelli, Richard (b Port Byron, NY, 6 Feb 1887; d Los Angeles, 7 Jun 1980), American baritone. He studied with Jean de Reszke and made his NY debut (as Richard Bunn) in 1915, as Valentin. After appearances at La Scala and the Paris Opéra he sang at Chicago 1925–45 and at the NY Met 1932–45; debut, Germont. Other roles incl. Amonasro, Posa and Wolfram.

Boni, Guillaume (b Saint-Fleur; d after 1594), French 16th-cent. composer. *Maître de chapelle* at the church of Saint-Étienne at Toulouse. Comp. 2 books of sonnets by Ronsard, 1 of quatrains by Pibrac, *Psalmi Davidici*, etc.

Bonini, Severo (b Florence, 23 Dec 1582; d Florence, 5 Dec 1663), Italian composer. Organist at Forli. Set Rinuccini's *Lamento d'Arianna* in recitative style (1613), and wrote madrigals and spiritual canzonets for a single voice with continuo accomp. His *Discorsi e Regole* (c 1650) contains important information on early opera.

Boninsegna, Celestina (b Reggio Emilia, 26 Feb 1877; d Milan, 14 Feb 1947), Italian soprano. Debut Reggio Emilia, 1892, as Norina. At the Teatro Costanzi, Rome, she took part in the shared fp of Mascagni's *Le Maschere* (1901), and in 1904 sang Aida at CG. NY Met·debut 1906 as Aida, opposite Caruso. Was heard in London as Amelia and the *Trovatore* Leonora, and appeared as guest at Boston, Barcelona and St Petersburg.

Bonne Chanson, La, cycle of 9 songs by Fauré, set to poems from Verlaine's vol. of that name, comp. 1891–2, fp Paris, 20 Apr 1895.

Symph. poem by Loeffler, on the same source; comp. 1901, fp Boston, 11 Apr 1902.

Bonno, Giuseppe (b Vienna, 29 Jan 1711; d Vienna, 15 Apr 1788), Austrian composer of Italian extraction. Studied in Naples 1726–37. In 1739 app. comp. to the Aus. court, and in 1774 succeeded Gassmann as *Kapellmeister*.

Works incl. over 20 operas incl. *Trajano* (1736), *Il natale di Giove* (1740), *Il re pastore* (1751); 3 oratorios incl. *Il Giuseppe riconosciuto* (1774); Masses, Requiems and other church music.

Bononcini (or **Buononcini**). Italian 17th–18th-cent., family of musicians:

1. Giovanni Maria B. (b Montecorone nr. Modena, bap. 23 Sep 1642; d 18 Nov 1678), pupil of Bendinelli, *maestro di cappella* of Modena Cathedral. He wrote a treatise, *Musico prattico*.

Works incl. cantatas, sonatas, suites, etc.

2. Giovanni B. (b Modena, 18 Jul 1670; d Vienna, 9 Jul 1747), son of prec. Pupil of Colonna and of his father; *maestro de cappella* at San Giovanni in Monte at Modena. He prod. his 1st opera in Rome in 1692. Lived in Vienna, 1698–1711, in It. 1711–20, in London, 1720–32, later in Fr. and Vienna.

Works incl. operas *Tullo Ostilio* (1694), *Xerse*, *Endimione* (1706), *Astarto* (1715), *Crispo*, *Erminia* (1719), *Farnace*, *Calfurnia* (1724), *Astianatte*, *Griselda* (1733) and many others, incl. an act in *Muzio Scevola* with Handel and Amadei; 7 oratorios; funeral anthem for Marlborough; music for the Peace of Aix-la-Chapelle; Masses, Te Deum, psalms, *Laudate pueri*; chamber cantatas and duets.

3. Antonio Maria B. (b Modena, 18 Jun 1677; d Modena, 8 Jul 1726), brother of prec. Became *maestro di cappella* to the Duke of Modena in 1721.

Works incl. c 20 operas, oratorios, etc.

Bonporti, Francesco Antonio (b Trent, bap. 11 Jun 1672; d Padua, 19 Dec 1749), Italian composer. Trained for the priesthood in Rome from 1691 and studied music with Pitoni and Corelli. On his ordination he returned to Trent, and spent the next 40 years in hope of a canonry. He retired disappointed to Padua in 1740.

Works incl. motets; trio sonatas; concertos; 'Inventions' for solo vln.

Bontempi, Giovanni Andrea (b Perugia, c 1624; d nr. Perugia, 1 Jul 1705), Italian castrato, theorist and composer. He took the name of a patron, Cesare Bontempi, and sang in St Mark's, Venice, from 1643. At the end of the 1640s he went to Dresden, where he became asst. cond. to Schütz in 1666, but devoted himself to science and architecture the next year. He returned to It. in 1669 and after another visit to Dresden in 1671 settled down in his birthplace. He wrote 3 theoret. books.

Works incl. Italian operas *Paride* (1662), *Dafne* (1671) und *Jupiter and Io* (1673).

Bonynge, Richard. *See* **Sutherland, Joan.**

Boosey & Hawkes, London music publishers and instrument makers. Boosey founded 1816 as Brit. agents for Rossini, Hummel, Mercadante etc.; manufactured wind instruments from *c* 1850. Hawkes founded 1865, handling brass and military band music. Amalgamation in 1930. Catalogue includes many 20th-cent. comps., e.g. Strauss, Prokofiev, Stravinsky, Bartók, Mahler and Britten (1938–63). Contemporary comps. incl. Carter, Bernstein, Reich, Copland, Kurtág, Robin Holloway and Maxwell Davies.

Bordes, Charles (b La Roche-Corbon nr. Vouvray, 12 May 1863; d Toulon, 8 Nov 1909), French pianist, composer and scholar. Pupil of Marmontel for pf. and of Franck for comp. As *maître de chapelle* 1st at Nogent-sur-Marne and from 1890 at the church of Saint-Gervais in Paris, he devoted himself to research into old polyphonic music and gave perfs. with the Chanteurs de Saint-Gervais cond. by him. In 1889–90 he explored Basque folk music and in 1894 was one of the founders of the Schola Cantorum.

Works incl. unfinished opera *Les Trois Vagues* (1892–8), motets, choruses.

Bordogni, Giulio Marco (b Gazzaniga, 23 Jan 1789; d Paris, 31 Jul 1856), Italian tenor. He studied with Mayr and from 1813 was well known in Rossini's *Tancredi*. He sang at the Paris Théâtre Italien from 1819 and was highly regarded in operas by Paer and Mercadante and in the first local perfs. of Rossini's *Otello, Elisabetta, Mosè* and *La donna del lago*. Taught at the Paris Cons. from 1820 and retired in 1832.

Bordoni, Faustina (b Venice, 1700; d Venice, 4 Nov 1781), Italian mezzo, pupil of Gasparini. 1st appeared in Venice in 1716. For 2 seasons, 1726–8, sang for Handel in London, creating roles in *Admeto, Riccardo Primo, Siroe* and *Tolomeo*. Her rivalry with Cuzzoni at this time was satirized in *The Beggar's Opera*. Married the comp. Hasse in 1731 and sang at Dresden in at least 15 of her husband's operas.

Bore, the width of the tubing of wind instruments, which affects the character of their tone.

Boréades, Les, tragédie-lyrique in 5 acts by Rameau (lib. by L. de Cahusac), written for the court of Louis XV, 1764, but not perf. Fp (concert) London, 19 Apr 1975; 1st stage perf. Aix-en-Provence, 21 Jul 1982.

Boree, one of the old English names for the Bourrée, others being Borea, Bore and Borry.

Borg, Kim (b Helsinki, 7 Aug 1919), Finnish bass. Concert debut 1947, opera debut Åarhus 1951, Glyndebourne 1956 as Don Giovanni; returned in 1959, Pizarro, and 1968, Gremin. NY Met debut 1959, Almaviva. He has sung Boris at the Bolshoy, and other roles incl. Marke, Pimen, Berg's Schigolch and Nielsen's Saul.

Borgatti, Giuseppe (b Cento, 17 Mar 1871; d Reno, Lago Maggiore, 18 Oct 1950), Italian tenor. Debut Castelfranco, 1892, Faust. After singing at Madrid and St Petersburg he created Andrea Chénier at La Scala, in 1896; sang Tristan and Siegfried there, under Toscanini (1899–1900) and until 1914 was admired for his forceful interpretations of Wagnerian and verismo roles: Walther, Parsifal, Lohengrin, Des Grieux and Cavaradossi.

Borgioli, Armando (b Florence, 19 Mar 1898; d Codogno nr. Modena, 20 Jan 1945), Italian baritone. He sang Amonasro at Milan in 1925 and from 1927 was a member of La Scala: debut as Alfio. CG, London, 1927–39, and NY Met, 1932–5 (debut as Carlo). At Buenos Aires and Rio he was admired as Barnaba, Jack Rance and Enrico. Killed while travelling on a bus during an allied air attack.

Borgioli, Dino (b Florence, 15 Feb 1891; d Florence, 12 Sep 1960), Italian tenor. Debut Milan, 1914, as Bellini's Arturo; sang at La Scala from 1918. Much applauded in England and appeared at CG 1925–39 as Edgardo, Almaviva, the Duke of Mantua and Don Ramiro. Glyndebourne 1937–9, as Ernesto and Ottavio. NY Met debut 1934, as Rodolfo. Retired 1946 and taught in London.

Borgomastro di Saardam, Il (*The Burgomaster of Saardam*), comic opera by Donizetti (lib. by D. Gilardoni, based on a Fr. play by A.H.J. Mélesville, J.T. Merle and E. C. de Boirie), prod. Naples, Teatro del Fondo, 19 Aug 1827. The subject is that of Lortzing's *Zar und Zimmermann*.

Bori, Lucrezia (b Gandia, 24 Dec 1887; d New York, 14 May 1960), Spanish soprano. Debut Rome, 1908, Micaela. Paris 1910 as Manon Lescaut with the NY Met co. on tour, and repeated the role in her NY debut; sang there until 1936. In 1911 she was Octavian in the 1st Italian *Rosenkavalier*. Other roles incl. Mimi, Norina, Juliette.

Boris Godunov, opera by Mussorgsky (lib.

by comp. based on Pushkin's drama and N.M. Karamazin's *History of the Russian Empire*), comp. 1868–9; enlarged and rev. 1871–2; this later version cut and prod. St Petersburg, Imp. Opera, 8 Feb 1874, the orig. having been rejected in 1870. Rimsky-Korsakov's ed. prod. St Petersburg, Imp. Opera, 10 Dec 1896. Further rev. by Rimsky-Korsakov, 1908. The orig. prod. Leningrad, 16 Feb 1928.

Borkh, Inge (b Mannheim, 26 May 1917), German soprano. She sang in Switzerland 1940–51; Bayreuth 1952 as Freia and Sieglinde. US debut San Francisco, 1953. NY Met debut 1958, as Salome; repeated the role at CG 1959 and sang the Dyer's Wife there in 1976. Other roles: Eglantine, Leonore, Elektra, Lady Macbeth.

Born, Claire (b Vienna, 1898), Austrian soprano. At the Vienna Staatsoper, 1922–9, she was heard as Mozart's Countess and Pamina, Agathe and Rosalinde. Bayreuth 1924, as Eva and Gutrune; Salzburg 1925–6, as Elvira and Ariadne. She took part in the 1926 fp of Hindemith's *Cardillac*, at Dresden, and sang there until 1933. With the rise of the Nazis she moved to Eng., where she taught.

Borodin, Alexander Porphyrevich (b St Petersburg, 12 Sep 1833; d St Petersburg, 27 Feb 1887), Russian composer and chemist. Illegitimate son of Prince Gedeanov, who registered him as the son of one of his serfs. He tried to compose at the age of 9 and was given music lessons. In his studies at the Acad. of Medicine he distinguished himself esp. in chemistry, and while studying in Germany he met the pianist Ekaterina Protopopova, whom he married in 1863. The prec. year, having so far been self-taught in comp., he began to take lessons from Balakirev, who cond. his 1st symph. in 1869. He lectured on chemistry at the School of Medicine for Women from 1872 to his death and wrote important treatises on his subject.

Works incl. opera *Prince Igor* (unfinished) (1869–87); 3 symphs. (3rd unfinished); *In the Steppes of Central Asia* (1880) for orch.; 2 string 4tets (1874–9, 1881); *Serenata alla spagnuola* for string 4tet; *Serenade de quatre galants à une dame* for male-voice 4tet; *Petite Suite* for pf.; songs.

Borodin String Quartet, Russian ensemble founded 1946. Since 1974 the members have been Mikhail Kopelman (b 1948) and Andrei Abramenclov (b 1935), Dmitri Shebalin (b 1930) and Valentin Berlinsky (b 1925). Renowned for their technical skill and interpretive insight, they are today's

leading string quartet from E. Europe. Recorded the Shostakovich 4tets, 1985 and gave the complete cycle in London, 1986.

Boronat, Olimpia (b Genoa, 1867; d Warsaw, 1934), Italian soprano. She studied at Milan and sang in Italy and Latin America. After appearances at St Petersburg in the 1890s she married a Pol. nobleman and briefly retired. She returned to sing with much success in Pol., Rus. and from 1909 It. Retired 1922. She was best known as Thomas' Ophelia, Rosina, Violetta and Bellini's Elvira.

Borosini, Francesco (b Modena, c 1690), Italian tenor. He sang at the imperial court, Vienna, 1712–31, in oratorios by Caldara and operas by Fux, and went to London in 1724, singing in Handel's and Ariosti's operas in 1724–5; he created Grimoaldo in *Rodelinda* (1725).

Borosini (*née* d'Ambreville), **Rosa** (b Modena, 27 Jun 1698; d after 1740), Italian soprano, wife of prec. Made her debut in 1713. Sang in Prague in 1723, and married Francesco B., prob. after his return from London in 1725.

Børresen, Hakon (Axel Einar) (b Copenhagen, 2 Jun 1876; d Copenhagen, 6 Oct 1954), Danish composer. Pupil of Svendsen, he took a comp. prize in 1901. Later he held many important administrative posts in the musical life of Copenhagen.

Works incl. operas *The Royal Guest* (1919) and *Kaddara* (1921); ballet *Tycho Brahe's Dream* (1924); incid. music for plays; several symphs. and other orchestral works; chamber music incl. 2 string 4tets (1913, 1939), songs.

Borry, English corruption of the French Bourrée found in 17th-cent. music, e.g. Purcell.

Bortkievich, Sergei Eduardovich (b Kharkov, 28 Feb 1877; d Vienna, 25 Oct 1952), Russian composer. Studied law at St Petersburg and comp. under Liadov, later at Leipzig. Lived in Berlin until 1914, when he joined the Russian army, and at Constantinople after World War I. From 1922 till his death he lived in Vienna. He wrote a book about Tchaikovsky and Nadezhda von Meck (1938).

Works incl. opera *Acrobats* (1938); 2 symphs.; symph. poem *Othello*; 4 pf. concertos (1 for the left hand), 2 vln. concertos, cello concerto; pf. sonatas and pieces; songs.

Bortniansky, Dimitri Stepanovich (b Glukhov, Ukraine, 1752; d St Petersburg, 10 Oct 1825), Russian composer. Studied at

Moscow and in St Petersburg under Galuppi, whom he followed to It. in 1768 with a grant from Catherine II. Further studies at Bologna, Rome and Naples. He wrote motets and operas at Venice in 1776 and at Modena in 1778. In 1779 he returned to Rus. and became director of the Imp. church choir, which he reformed and turned into the Imp. Chapel in 1796.

Works incl. operas *Le Faucon* (1786), *Le Fils rival* (1787), *Creonte* and *Quinto Fabio* (1778); 35 sacred concertos, 10 concertos for double choir, Mass, chants.

Borwick, Leonard (b London, 26 Feb 1868; d Le Mans, 17 Sep 1925), English pianist. Pupil of Clara Schumann in 1883–9 at Frankfurt, where he made his 1st appearance, playing in London for the 1st time in 1890, at a Phil. Society concert. He also appeared in Vienna, frequently played with the most eminent artists in chamber music at the London St James's Hall and gave many recitals with Plunket Greene.

Boschi, Giuseppe (b ? Viterbo), Italian 17th–18th-cent. bass. Sang in Venice 1707–14. 1st appeared in London in 1710 and subsequently sang in many of Handel's operas; created Argante in *Rinaldo*, 1711, and was engaged at the Royal Academy 1720–28, appearing in 13 operas by Handel.

Bösendorfer, Ignaz (b Vienna, 28 Jul 1796; d Vienna, 14 Apr 1859), Austrian pf. manufacturer. Founded his firm in Vienna in 1828 and was succeeded in it by his son Ludwig (1835–1919) in 1859. *See also* **Pianola**.

Bosio, Angiolina (b Turin, 22 Aug 1830; d St Petersburg, 13 Apr 1859), Italian soprano. Studied at Milan under Cateneo and made her debut there in 1846 as Lucrezia in Verdi's *I due Foscari*. After many tours she 1st went to London in 1852 and appeared there as Gilda, Leonora (*Trovatore*) and Violetta.

Boskovsky, Willi (b Vienna, 16 Jun 1909), Austrian violinist and conductor. Vienna PO 1933–71; co-leader from 1939 and formed the Vienna Octet 1948. From 1954 to 1979 he cond. the New Year's Day concerts in Vienna.

Bossi, (Marco) Enrico (b Salò, 25 Apr 1861; d at sea, 20 Feb 1925), Italian organist and composer. Studied at the Liceo Musicale of Bologna and at the Milan Cons. After var. organist's and teaching apps. he became director of the principal music schools at Venice, Bologna and Rome in succession. Meanwhile he had become very famous as a concert organist, and it was when returning from a tour in USA that he died.

Works incl. operas *Paquita* (1881), *Il veggente* (1890) and *L'angelo della notte*; oratorios *Il Paradiso perduto* (after Milton) and *Giovanna d'Arco* (1914); Masses, motets and sacred cantatas; secular choral works with orch. or org. incl. *Il cieco, Inno di gloria* and *Cantico dei cantici* (1900); orchestral works; concerto for org. and orch.; chamber music, 50 org. works incl. suite *Res severa magnum gaudium*; pf. pieces; songs.

Bossi, Renzo (b Como, 9 Apr 1883; d Milan, 2 Apr 1965), Italian composer, son of prec. Studied under his father at the Liceo Benedetto Marcello in Venice and took a comp. prize in 1902, when he went to Leipzig, where he continued studying pf., org. and cond., the last under Nikisch. He was cond. of more than 1 Ger. opera house before he went to Milan as asst. cond. at La Scala. Prof. of comp. at Parma from 1913 and Milan from 1916.

Works incl. operas *Rosa rossa* (after Oscar Wilde) (Parma, 1940), *Passa la ronda!* (Milan, 1919), *La notte del mille, Volpino il calderaio* (after Shakespeare's *Taming of the Shrew*) (Milan, 1925) and *Proserpina*; symph., *Sinfoniale, Fantasia sinfonica* and *Bianco e nero* for orch.; vln. concerto; chamber music.

Boston Symphony Orchestra, American orch. founded 1881 by Henry Lee Higginson (1834–1919). Sir George Henschel was cond. 1881–4 and his successors have included Arthur Nikisch (1889–93), Emil Paur (1893–8), Karl Muck (1906–8 and 1912–18), Pierre Monteux (1919–24), Serge Koussevitsky (1924–49), Charles Munch (1949–62), Erich Leinsdorf (1962–9), William Steinberg (1969–72); Seiji Ozawa from 1973. Colin Davis was prin. guest cond. 1972–83.

Bottesini, Giovanni (b Crema, 22 Dec 1821; d Parma, 7 Jul 1889), Italian double bass player, conductor and composer. Was engaged at Havana, Paris, Palermo, Barcelona and Cairo.

Works incl. operas *Marion Delorme* (after Victor Hugo) (Palermo, 1862), *Ali Baba* (London, 1871) and *Ero e Leandro* (Turin, 1879); double bass concertos with orch.; much music for double bass and pf.

Bottrigari (Bottrigaro), **Ercole** (b Bologna, 24 Aug 1531; d San Alberto nr. Bologna, 30 Sep 1612), Italian theorist. His *Il Desiderio* (1594) deals with the problems of combining instruments of different families. From 1600 to 1604 he was involved in a controversy with Artusi.

Boucher, Alexandre (Jean) (b Paris, 11 Apr

1778; d Paris 29 Dec 1861), French violinist. Appeared in public at the age of 6, was court violinist at Madrid, 1787–1805, and toured Eur. from 1820 to 1844 with sensational success; notorious for his tastelessness, he was described as a charlatan by Spohr.

Boucourechliev, André (b Sofia, 28 Jul 1925), French composer and musicologist of Bulgarian birth. Studied in Sofia, Paris and Darmstadt. Has worked as music critic and written books on Schumann, Chopin and Beethoven. His works are influenced by Boulez and incl. the series *Archipel* (from 1967) which allows the perf. a wide range of interpretative choices. Other works: *Texte I* and *II* for tape (1959–60), *Grodek* for sop. and ens. (text by Trakl, 1963), *Musiques Nocturnes* for clar., harp and pf. (1966), *Ombres* for 11 strings (based on themes from Beethoven's late 4tets; fp Brussels 1970, cond. Boulez), *Amers* for orch. (1973), pf. concerto (1976).

Boughton, Rutland (b Aylesbury, 23 Jan 1878; d London, 25 Jan 1960), English composer. Studied at the RCM in London under Stanford and Walford Davies. But he left very soon, and prod. some early orchestral works, cond. for a time at the Haymarket Theatre. Idolizing Wagner, he determined to found an Eng. centre of opera on the same lines as Bayreuth and began in a very modest way at Glastonbury with a series of music dramas on the Arthurian legends; in Aug 1914 1st prod. *The Immortal Hour*. A special theatre was to be built at Glastonbury, but the project had to be abandoned. In 1922 *The Immortal Hour* had a long run in London, and *Alkestis* was prod. there by the BNOC in 1924.

Works incl. music dramas *The Birth of Arthur* (1908–9), *The Immortal Hour* (1914), *Bethlehem* (1913), *The Round Table, Alkestis* (1922), *The Queen of Cornwall* (1924), *The Lily Maid* (1934); ballets *Choral Dances, Snow White, The Moon Maiden*; dramatic scene *Agincourt* from Shakespeare's *Henry V*; works for chorus and orch. *The Skeleton in Armour* (Longfellow), *The Invincible Armada* (Schiller), *Midnight* (E. Carpenter), *Song of Liberty*; unaccomp. choral music, 2 string 4tets.

Bouhy, Jacques (Joseph André) (b Pepinster, 18 Jun 1848; d Paris, 29 Jan 1929), Belgian baritone. Studied at Liège and Paris, where he made his 1st appearance at the Opéra in 1871 as Méphistophélès. Director of NY Cons., 1885–9. Lived and taught in Paris from 1907. The 1st Escamillo in Bizet's *Carmen* and sang in the fps of operas by Massé, Massenet and Salvayre.

Bouilly, Jean-Nicolas (1763–1842), French writer. Administrator of a dept. nr. Tours during the Terror. Wrote libs. for a number of operas (*see* **Rescue Opera**) for var. comps., incl. Cherubini and Gaveaux. The lib. of Beethoven's *Fidelio* is based on his book for Gaveaux's *Léonore*.

Boulanger, Lili (Juliette Marie Olga) (b Paris, 21 Aug 1893; d Mézy, Seine-et-Oise, 15 Mar 1918), French composer. Pupil of her sister Nadia at first, then at the Paris Cons. Gained the Prix de Rome in 1913 (the 1st woman ever to do so), but suffered much ill health.

Works incl. incid. music for Maeterlinck's *La Princesse Maleine* (1918); 2 poems for orch.; cantata *Faust et Hélène* (after Goethe) (1913); psalms with orch.

Boulanger, Nadia (Juliette) (b Paris, 16 Sep 1887; d Paris, 22 Oct 1979), French composer and teacher, sister of prec. Student at the Paris Cons., where she taught later, as well as at the École Normale de Musique and the Amer. Cons. at Fontainebleau. She went to USA after the outbreak of war in 1939, returning in 1946. Many distinguished comps. were her pupils incl. L. Berkeley, Copland, Françaix and Piston. Hon. D.Mus., Oxford, 1968.

Works incl. incid. music to d'Annunzio's *La città morta* (with Pugno) (1911); cantata *La Sirène* (1908); orch. works; instrumental pieces, songs.

Boulevard Solitude, opera by Henze (lib. by the comp. and G. Weil), prod. Hanover, 17 Feb 1952. A modern version of the Manon story.

Boulez, Pierre (b Montbrison, 26 Mar 1925), French composer and conductor. After abandoning studies in mathematics, he studied with Messiaen at the Paris Cons, and later took a course in serial technique with Leibowitz (1946). In 1946 he worked for the Renaud-Barrault theatre co. and in 1953–4 founded the 'Domaine Musical' with Barrault, which specialized in new music. As a comp. he belongs to the *avant-garde*, writing in a style which has its roots in Debussy and Webern and also in the ideas of James Joyce and Mallarmé. He is one of the pioneers of total serialism, but later intro. freer elements into his music. Boulez is also a leading cond. of advanced new music. He was principal cond. of the BBC SO 1971–5; NY PO 1971–7. He cond. *Parsifal* at Bayreuth in 1966, and *The Ring* in 1976; gave 1st complete perf. *Lulu*, Paris 1979. From 1977 dir.

research inst. for techniques of modern music, Paris (IRCAM, *q.v.*).

Works incl. *Pli selón pli* for soprano and orch. (after Mallarmé, 1958–62); *Poésie pour pouvoir* for orch. and electronic tape after (Michaux, 1958); *Figures for Doubles-Prismes* for orch. (1963–6); . . . *explosante fixe* . . . (1971–3);, *Rituel in memoriam Bruno Maderna* (1974–5); *Répons* for 24 players, 6 inst. soloists, computerised electronics (1981); *Le Soleil des eaux* for solo voices, chorus and orch. (after Char); *Le Marteau sans maître* for alto and 6 instruments (after Char) (1952–7); *e.e. cummings ist der dichter* for 16 solo voices and 24 insts. (1970–; work in progress); fl. sonatine; 3 pf. sonatas (1946, 1948, 1957); *Structures* I, II for 2 pfs. (1952, 1961); *Livre* for string 4tet. (1948, rev. for string orch. 1968)

Boult, Adrian Cedric (b Chester, 8 Apr 1889; d London, 22 Feb 1983), English conductor. Educ. at Westminster School and Christ Church, Oxford, where he received a D.Mus. He then went to Leipzig to study cond. with Nikish (1912–13), also taking lessons from Reger. In 1914 he joined CG, making his debut as an orchestral cond. in 1918. Boult taught at the RCM in 1919 and was cond. of the CBSO, 1924–30. Later became cond. of the BBC SO and gave the 1st British (concert) perfs. of *Wozzeck* (1934) and Busoni's *Doktor Faust* (1937). He left the BBC in 1950 and became cond. of the LPO, 1951–7. Boult was best known for his perfs. of the standard repertory, although he helped to further the cause of modern (esp. Eng.) music; he gave the fps of Vaughan Williams's *Pastoral*, 4th and 6th symphs. Author of useful books on cond. Retired 1979. Knighted 1937; CH 1969.

Bourdin, Roger (b Paris, 14 Jun 1900; d Paris, 14 Sep 1973), French baritone. Debut Paris, Opéra-Comique, 1922, as Massenet's Lescaut; sang there for more than 30 years, appearing in the fps of operas by Pierné (*Sophie Arnould*), Ibert, Bondeville (*Madame Bovary*) and Milhaud (*Bolivar*). He sang as guest at the Paris Opéra and was Pelléas at CG in 1930. Sang further in operas by Rameau and Reynaldo Hahn.

Bourgault-Ducoudray, Louis (Albert) (b Nantes, 2 Feb 1840; d Vernouillet, 4 Jul 1910), French composer. A lawyer at first, he entered the Paris Cons. late and took a comp. prize in 1862. In 1869 he founded a choral society in Paris with which he gave perfs. of unfamiliar works. Collected and pub. Greek and Breton folksongs. Lectured on hist. of music at the Cons. from 1878.

Works incl. operas *L'Atelier de Prague* (1858), *Michel Colomb* (1887), *Bretagne*, *Thamara* (1891), *Myrdhin* (1905); satiric play *La Conjuration des fleurs*; *Stabat Mater*, *Symphonie religieuse* for unaccomp. chorus; *Fantaisie in Ut mineur*, *Carnaval d'Athènes*, *Rapsodie cambodgienne*, *L'Enterrement d'Ophélie* (after Shakespeare) for orch.

Bourgeois gentilhomme, Le (*The Bourgeois as Gentleman*), comedy-ballet by Molière with music by Lully, prod. Chambord, 14 Oct 1670.

Incid. music by R. Strauss to a shortened version of Molière's comedy trans. by H. von Hofmannsthal, prec. the 1-act opera *Ariadne auf Naxos*, prod. Stuttgart, 25 Oct 1912. Strauss afterwards dropped it for a new operatic 1st act and made a concert suite for orch. of the incid. music, adding a minuet by Lully (fp Vienna, 31 Jan 1920, cond. Strauss).

Bourgeois, Derek (David) (b Kingston upon Thames, 16 Oct 1941), English composer. He studied at Cambridge, and with Howells at the RCM; lecturer at Bristol Univ. from 1971.

Works incl. 2 symphs. (1960, 1968), vars. on a theme of Mozart, for db. and orch. (1967), symph. fantasy *The Astronauts* (1969); *Jabberwocky-Extravaganza*, for bar., chorus and orch. (1963); string 4tet (1962), 2 brass 5tets (1965, 1972).

Bourgeois, Louis (b Paris, c 1510; d Paris, c 1561), French musician. A Protestant, he went to Geneva to join Calvin's church, taking the place of Franc, who had gone to Lausanne, and working with Guillaume Fabri. He contrib. to the Genevan Psalter by selecting and harmonizing tunes. He also composed secular *chansons*.

Bourgeois, Thomas-Louis (b Fontaine-l'Évêque, Hainaut, 24 Oct 1676; d Paris, c 1750), French countertenor and composer. Choirmaster at Strasbourg 1703, alto at the Paris Opéra 1706–11, when he left to devote himself to comp. App. *maître de chapelle* at Toul c 1716.

Works incl. opera-ballets, solo cantatas, motet *Beatus vir*, etc.

Bourrée (Fr.), a French dance in quick 2–2 time beginning with an upbeat (in 17th-cent. Eng. 'borry') (*see* illustration).

Boutade (Fr. = whim, frolic), an 18th-cent. dance, or sometimes a whole ballet, in a style described by the title; also sometimes an instrumental piece of the same character.

Boutique fantastique, La (*The Fantastic Toyshop*), ballet by Respighi, arr. from

BOURRÉE
Bach, *Cello Suite no. 3*

music by Rossini (choreog. by Leonid Fedorovich Massin), prod. London, Alhambra
Theatre, 5 June 1919. The music consists
mainly of small pieces written by Rossini in
his retirement for the amusement of his
friends.

Boutmy, Flemish family of musicians.

1. Jacques-Adrien B. (b Ghent, 16 Jan
1683; d Brussels, 6 Sep 1719), organist.
Followed his father, Jacques B., as organist
of St Nicholas, Ghent, and in 1711 was app.
organist of the collegiate church of Ste.
Gudule in Brussels.

2. Josse B. (b Ghent, 1 Feb 1697; d Brussels, 27 Nov 1779), organist, harpsichordist
and composer, brother of prec. Went to
Brussels early, entered the service of Prince
Thurn and Taxis in 1736, taught at court
and was app. organist of the royal chapel in
1744. Works incl. a cantata and 3 books of
harpsichord pieces.

3. Guillaume B. (b Brussels, 15 Jun 1723;
d Brussels, 22 Jan 1791), composer, son of
prec. Also served Prince Thurn and Taxis
from 1752 and in 1760 was app. keeper of
keyboard instruments at court. Comp. sonatas for harpsichord.

4. Jean-Joseph B. (b Brussels, 29 Apr
1725; d Cleves, 1782), harpsichordist,
organist and composer, brother of prec.
Went to Ghent early, taught the harpsichord
there and in 1757 was app. organist at St
Baafs. In 1764 he settled at The Hague and
after 1775 at Cleves. Works incl. 6 *Divertissements* for harpsichord with vln. *ad lib.*,
and concertos for harpsichord and orch.

5. Laurent-François B. (b Brussels, 19 Jun
1756; d Brussels, 3 Nov 1838), harpsichordist, organist and composer, brother of prec.
Deputized for his ageing father, but failed to
succeed him and in 1779 settled at Rotterdam. In 1789 he went to Fr., but soon after
returned to Brussels after taking refuge in
London from the Fr. occupation. Works
incl. var. pf. pieces, some with vln. or fl.,
vocal works with var. accomps.

Bow, the stick with horsehair stretched
along it with which instruments of the viol
and vln. family are played. *See* **Tourte.**

Bowen, (Edwin) York (b London, 22 Feb
1884; d London, 23 Nov 1961), English
pianist, violinist, horn player and composer.
Studied at the RAM in London.
Works incl. 3 symphs., *Symph. Fantasia*
for orch.; 3 pf. concertos. (1904, 1906,
1908), vln. and vla. concertos; sonata for
vla. and pf.; numerous pf. works.

Bowing, the art of using a bow, or the
marking of scores and parts with indications
about how to bow. The main signs are ⊓
for a down-bow (that is, starting at the frog
and drawing the hand away from the instrument) and ⋁ for its opposite, the up-bow.
A slur in string-writing is normally an indication to take several notes under a single
bow.

Bowles, Paul (Frederic) (b New York, 30
Dec 1910), American composer. Pupil of
Aaron Copland, Virgil Thomson and Nadia
Boulanger. He lived by turns in Spain, Mex-
ico, Guatemala and N. Africa, but later re-
turned to USA. In 1949 he published a novel,
The Sheltering Sky, which established him as
a writer.
Works incl. operas *Denmark Vesey*
(1938) and *The Wind Remains* (1941–3).

Bowman, James (Thomas) (b Oxford, 6
Nov 1941), English countertenor. Stage de-
but London, 1967, as Britten's Oberon; the
Voice of Apollo in *Death in Venice* (Alde-
burgh, 1973) was written for him. Glynde-
bourne 1970–74 as Endimione in the
Cavalli-Leppard *Calisto.* He sang the Priest
Confessor and God the Father in the fp of
Maxwell Davies's *Taverner,* CG 1972, and
co-created the role of Astron in Tippett's
The Ice Break, 1977. Handel repertory incl.
Giulio Cesare, Tamerlano, Xerxes and Sci-
pione.

Bovy, Vina (b Ghent, 22 May 1900; d
Ghent, 16 May 1983), Belgian soprano. Debut Ghent, 1917, in *Hansel and Gretel.* She
sang at the Théâtre de la Monnaie, Brussels,
and in S. America, as Thaïs, Ophelia and
Juliette. NY Met debut 1936, as Violetta;
also sang Gilda, Lakmé and Manon in NY.
She sang in Paris during the war and was
dir. of Ghent Opera 1947–56, adding Elsa,

Desdemona and Pamina to her repertory.
Boyarina Vera Sheloga (Rimsky-Korsakov). *See* **Pskovitianka.**
Boyce, William (b London, Sep 1711; d London, 7 Feb 1779), English organist and composer. Chorister at St Paul's Cathedral and a pupil of Greene, whom he succeeded as Master of the King's Music in 1755. Meanwhile he held var. org. posts in London, was app. comp. to the Chapel Royal in 1736, and cond. of the Three Choirs Festival the following year. From 1758 he was organist of the Chapel Royal. Deafness forced him to give up much of his work during his later years.

Works incl. stage entertainments *The Chaplet* (1749) and *The Shepherd's Lottery* (1751); masque *Peleus and Thetis* (1740) and Dryden's *Secular Masque* (c 1746); incid. music for Shakespeare's *Tempest, Cymbeline* (1746)and *Romeo and Juliet* (1750); pantomime *Harlequin's Invasion* (with M. Arne and Aylward, and containing the song *Heart of Oak*); service settings and anthems; cantatas and odes.

20 symphs. and overtures; 12 triosonatas; keyboard music; songs, etc. He also completed a notable collection of earlier church music begun by Greene (pub. under the title *Cathedral Music* in 3 vols., 1760–73).
Boyhood's End, cantata for tenor and pf. by Tippett (text by W.H. Hudson), comp. 1943 and perf. London, 5 Jun 1943.
Bozay, Attila (b Balatonfőzfő, 11 Aug 1939), Hungarian composer. He studied in Budapest at the Bartók Cons. and with Ferenc Farkas. His music is influenced by serial technique and by Hung. folksongs.

Works incl. the opera *Queen Kungisz* (1969); *Pezzo concertato* for vla. and orch., *Pezzo sinfonico* for orch. (1967); *Trapeze and Bars,* cantata (1966); 2 string 4tets (1964, 1971), *Formations* for solo cello (1969).
Brace, a bracket connecting the 2 staves, e.g. in pf. and harp music, or a greater number of staves in a score.
Brack, Georg (Jörg), German 16th-cent. composer. His part-songs were pub. in collections printed by Schöffer (1513), Arnt von Aich (1519) and others.
Brade, William (b c 1560; d Hamburg, 26 Feb 1630), English violist and composer. Worked by turns at the court of Christian IV of Den., in the service of the Margraves of Brandenburg and the Duke of Schleswig-Gottorp, and at Halle, Berlin and Hamburg. Pub. instrumental music in several parts,

incl. pavans, galliards and other dances, *canzone,* concertos and fancies in 6 books at Hamburg, Lübeck, Antwerp and Berlin, 1609–21.
Braga, Gaetano (b Giulianova, 9 Jun 1829; d Milan, 21 Nov 1907), Italian cellist and composer. Studied at the Naples Cons., toured Eur. and lived mainly in Paris and London.

Works incl. opera *La Reginella* (1871) and 7 others; cantata; cello concerto; instrumental pieces incl. *Serenata.*
Braham (real name Abraham), **John** (b London, 20 Mar 1774; d London, 17 Feb 1856), English tenor and composer. Debut as a treble at CG in 1787. When his voice broke he taught the pf., but reappeared at Rauzzini's concerts at Bath in 1794 and in London in 1796. In 1798–1801 he appeared in Paris, It. and Ger. He then became attached to CG for many years and often interpolated his own songs, which became very popular, in operas. He also contrib. to operas prod. at the Lyceum and Drury Lane Theatres, incl. one on Shakespeare's *Taming of the Shrew.* Towards the end of his career he was the 1st Huon in Weber's *Oberon* (1826).
Brahms, Johannes (b Hamburg, 7 May 1833; d Vienna, 3 Apr 1897), German composer. Son of a double bass player, from whom he learnt the rudiments of music as a child. Although intended for an orch. player, he made such progress on the pf. that his parents decided to make a prodigy perf. of him when about 11; but his teachers wisely opposed this. He soon afterwards began to comp., but had to play in sailors' taverns and dancing-saloons at night to supplement his parents' earnings. He gave 2 concerts in 1848–9, but did not free himself from drudgery of playing and teaching until he went on a concert tour with Reményi in 1853, when he met Joachim, Liszt and other musicians of importance, partic. Schumann and Clara S., who took much interest in him. In 1857–60 he was intermittently engaged at the court of Lippe-Detmold, travelled as pianist and worked at Hamburg conducting a ladies' choir there.

1st visited Vienna in 1862 and settled there for good the following year. Entirely devoted to comp. from 1864, except for some concert tours, on which he played mainly his own works. His success as a comp. was firmly establ. during the 1860s, and he became known abroad; but he did not complete his 1st symph. until 1876. He wrote much during summer holidays in

Aus., Ger. and Switz., but hardly visited other countries except It. In 1877 he refused the Cambridge Mus.D. because he did not wish to go to receive it in person, but he accepted the Ph.D. from Breslau in 1879. The later years were uneventful except for the growing importance of his work. In 1896 he began to suffer seriously from cancer of the liver, the disease from which he died.

Works incl. CHORUS AND ORCH.: *Ein Deutsches Requiem* (texts from Luther's trans. of the Bible), with bar. and sop. soloists (1857–68), *Rinaldo*, for tenor, male chorus and orch. (1863–8), *Rhapsody* for contralto, male chorus and orch. (1869), *Schicksalslied* (1871), *Gesang der Parzen* (1882).

SYMPHONIES: no. 1 in C min., op. 68 (1855–76), no. 2 in D, op. 73 (1877), no. 3 in F, op. 90 (1883), no. 4 in E min., op. 98 (1884–5).

CONCERTOS: 2 for pf., no. 1 in D min., op. 15 (1854–8), no. 2 in B♭, op. 83 (1878–81); violin in D, op. 77 (1878); violin and cello in A min., op. 102 (1887).

OTHER ORCH.: 2 Serenades, no. 1 in D, op. 11 (1858), no. 2 in A, op. 16 (1859), *Variations on a theme by Haydn* in B♭, op. 56a (1873), *Academic Festival Overture* (1880), *Tragic Overture* (1880).

CHAMBER: 2 string 6tets, op. 18 in B♭ (1860), op. 36 in G (1865); 3 string 4tets, op. 51 nos. 1, 2, in C min. and A min. (1859–73), op. 67 in B♭ (1875); 2 string 5tets, op. 88 in F (1882), op. 111 in G (1890); 3 pf. 4tets, op. 25 in G min. (1861), op. 26 in A (1861), op. 60 (1855–75); pf. 5tet op. 34 in F min. (1864); clar. 5tet op. 115 in B min. (1891); 3 pf. trios, op. 8 in B (1854, rev. 1890), op. 87 in C (1880–82), op. 101 in C min. (1886); horn trio op. 40 in E♭ (1865); 2 cello sonatas, op. 38 in E min. (1862–5), op. 99 in F (1886); 3 vln. sonatas, op. 78 in G (1879), op. 100 in A (1886), op. 108 in D min. (1886–8); trio for clar., cello, pf. op. 114 in A min. (1891); 2 sonatas for vla. or clar. op. 120 in F min. and E♭ (1894).

SOLO PIANO: incl. 3 sonatas, op. 1–3, in C, F♯ min., F min. (1852–3); Vars. on themes by Schumann (op. 9, 1854), Handel (op. 24, 1861), Paganini (op. 35, 1863) and Haydn (vers. for 2 pfs. of work for orch., 1873); rhapsodies, intermezzos etc.

ORGAN: incl. 11 chorale preludes op. 122 (1896).

VOCAL: numerous part-songs, incl. *Zigeunerlieder* for 4 voices and pf. op. 103 (1887); the song cycles *Die Schöne Magelone* op. 33 (15 Romances to poems by L.

Tieck) and *Vier ernste Gesänge* for low voice and pf. op. 121 (texts from the New Testament); more than 200 Lieder, comp. 1852–86 to texts by Heyse, Möricke, Rückert and Brentano, among others.

Brain, Aubrey (Harold) (b London, 12 Jul 1893; d London, 20 Sep 1955), English horn player. He studied at the RCM; played for Beecham's touring opera co. from 1913, prin., BBC SO 1930–45. The foremost teacher of his inst. (RAM from 1923). His brother **Alfred** (1885–1966), also a horn player, was prin. of Wood's Queen's Hall Orch.; from 1923 prin. of the NY SO, then joined the Los Angeles PO.

Brain, Dennis (b London, 17 May 1921; d Hatfield, 1 Sep 1957), English horn player, son of prec. Studied under his father, played in orchs., formed a wind chamber-music group and became the most brilliant soloist on his instrument; Britten's *Serenade* and Hindemith's concerto were written for him. He was killed in a car accident on his way home from the Edinburgh Festival.

Brambilla, Marietta (b Cassano d'Adda, 6 Jun 1807; d Milan, 6 Nov 1875), Italian contralto. Debut London, 1827, as Rossini's Arsace; successful in such travesti roles as Adriano in *Il crociato* and Zingarelli's Romeo. For Donizetti she created roles in *Lucrezia Borgia* (Milan, 1833) and *Linda di Chamounix* (Vienna, 1842).

Brambilla, Teresa (b Cassano d'Adda, 23 Oct 1813; d Milan, 15 Jul 1895), Italian soprano, sister of prec. Debut Milan, 1831. She created Gilda at the Teatro Fenice, Venice, in 1851. Her other Verdi roles were Abigaille, Elvira and Luisa Miller.

Brambilla-Ponchielli, Teresina (b Cassano d'Adda, 15 Apr 1845; d Vercelli, 1 Jul 1921), Italian soprano, niece of the prec. She appeared in Ponchielli's *I promessi sposi* at Milan in 1872 and married the comp. in 1874. Well known as Gioconda, Aida, Elsa and the *Forza* Leonora.

Bramston, Richard (b *c* 1485; d Wells, 1554), English composer. He was instructor of the choristers and organist at Wells Cathedral, 1507–31, though apparently *in absentiis* from 1508 on. An antiphon, *Mariae virginis fecunda viscera*, survives.

Branchu, Alexandrine Caroline (b Cap Français, 2 Nov 1780; d Passy, 14 Oct 1850), French soprano. Debut Paris, 1799; sang at the Opéra 1801–26 and took part in the fps of Cherubini's *Anacréon* (1803) and *Les Abencérages* (1813). Highly regarded in operas by Gluck and as Piccinni's Didon.

Brand, Max (b Lwów, 26 Apr 1896; d

Langenzersdorf nr. Vienna, 5 Apr 1980), Austrian-Polish composer. Studied in Vienna under Schreker and Hába. Settled in US in 1940. His opera (fp 1929) is one of the outstanding works of the 'machinist' period of the 1920s; it was banned by the Nazis and not heard again complete until BBC, 1986. He also experimented with electronic music and wrote *The Astronauts, an Epic in Electronics* (1962). Returned to Aus. in 1975.

Works incl. opera *Maschinist Hopkins*; scenic oratorio *The Gate* (1944); symph. poems, chamber music.

Brandenburg Concertos, a series of 6 orchestral concertos by Bach, ded. in 1721 to the Margrave Christian Ludwig of Brandenburg: I, F, for 3 obs., 2 horns, bassoon, *violino piccolo*, strings and continuo; II, F, for recorder, ob., tpt., vln., strings and continuo; III, G, for 3 vlns., 3 vlas., 3 cellos, bass and continuo; IV, G, for 2 recorders, vln., strings and continuo; V, D, for fl., vln., harpsichord, strings and continuo; VI, B♭, for 2 vlas., 2 bass viols, cello, bass and continuo.

Brandenburgers in Bohemia, The (*Braniboři v Čechách*), opera by Smetana (lib. by K. Sabina), prod. Prague, Cz. Theatre, 5 Jan 1866.

Brandt-Forster, Ellen (b Vienna, 11 Oct 1866; d Vienna, 1921), Austrian soprano. Studied with Louise Dustmann; debut Danzig, 1885, as Marguerite. She appeared in Bayreuth in 1886 and the following year was engaged at the Vienna Hofoper; created Sophie in *Werther* there, 1892. Until her retirement in 1906 also sang in concert.

Brandt, Marianne (b Vienna, 12 Sep 1842; d Vienna, 9 Jul 1921), Austrian mezzo. Debut Olomouc, 1867, as Rachel; Berlin 1868–82, as Azucena and Amneris CG 1872, Leonore, and sang Brangaene in the 1st London perf. of *Tristan und Isolde*, Drury Lane 1882, under Richter. In 1876 she was Waltraute in the première of *Götterdämmerung*, at Bayreuth, and returned there in 1882 as Kundry. NY Met 1884–8 as Ortrud, Fides and Eglantine.

Brandts-Buys, Jan (b Zutphen, 12 Sep 1868; d Salzburg, 8 Dec 1933), Dutch composer. He won a state prize as a youth and studied at Frankfurt. Most of his operatic successes were prod. in Ger. and Aus.

Works incl. operas *Das Veilchenfest* (Berlin, 1909), *Le Carillon, Die Schneider von Schoenau* (Dresden, 1916), *Der Eroberer* (Dresden, 1918), *Mi-carême, Der Mann im Mond* (1922), *Traumland,Ulysses; Oberon Romancero* for orch.; 3 pf. concertos; suite

for strings, harp and horn; string 4tets, 5tet for fl. and strings, pf. trios; pf. works, songs.

Branle, a French dance in 2–2 or 3–2 time dating from the 15th cent. and cultivated until the 18th, called Brawl in Eng.

Brannigan, Owen (b Annitsford, Northumberland, 10 Mar 1908; d Newcastle, 9 May 1973), English bass. Studied at the GSM 1934–42, winning the GSM Gold Medal in 1942. From 1940 to 1947 he was principal bass at SW, and from 1947 to 1949 he sang at Glyndebourne. He also sang at CG, London and at many important festivals; took part in the fps of Britten's *Peter Grimes, Rape of Lucretia, Albert Herring* and *A Midsummer Night's Dream* (Bottom).

Brant, Henry Dreyfus (b Montreal, 15 Sep 1913), American composer, flautist and organist. Studied at McGill Univ. and Juilliard; also with Wallingford Riegger and Rubin Goldmark. Worked as orchestrator for various bands in 1930s, taught in NY 1945–54; moved to Santa Barbara, Calif., in 1982. Much influenced by Ives and as comp. and perf. has explored spatial effects: music emanates from various parts of the concert stage and auditorium.

Works incl. ballet *The Great American Goof* (1946), *Millenium I–IV* for brass insts. (1950–64), *Behold the Earth, Requiem Cantata* (1951), *Feuerwerk*, for fireworks, speaker and insts. (1961), *Solomon's Gardens* for 7 voices, chorus, 24 handbells and 3 insts. (1974), *Antiphony I* for 5 orch. groups and 5 conds. (1953; Stockhausen's *Gruppen* was written 1955–7), *Grand Universal Circus* (1956), *Violin Concerto with Lights* (1961), *Verticals Ascending* for 2 separate groups (1968), *Immortal Combat* for 2 bands (1972), *An American Requiem* (1974), *Homage to Ives* for bar. and 3 orch. groups (1975), *Antiphonal Responses* (1978), *Horizontals Extending* (1982).

Brant, Jobst vom (b Waldersdorf, 28 Oct 1517; d Brand, 22 Jan 1570), German composer. Contrib. songs to var. collections and also wrote psalms and German songs for several voices.

Branzell, Karin (b Stockholm, 24 Sep 1891; d Altadena, Calif., 15 Dec 1974), Swedish mezzo. Debut Stockholm, 1912, in D'Albert's *Izeÿl*; Berlin 1918–23. NY Met 1924–44 and in 1951 as Fricka and Brangaene. CG 1935–8, under Beecham. Other roles incl. Strauss's Nurse and Clytemnestra and Janáček's Kostelnička.

Braslau, Sophie (b New York, 16 Aug 1892; d New York, 22 Dec 1935), American contralto. She studied with Marcella Sembrich. NY Met 1914–20, as Carmen, Marina and in the fp of Giordano's *Mme. Sans-Gêne* (1915). She toured as a concert singer in the US and Europe from 1920.

Brassart, Johannes (de Leodio), Flemish 15th-cent. singer and comp. Master of the Imp. Chapel Choir, 1433–43, apparently then moving to Liège and Tongeren. Wrote sacred music and motets.

Braun, Carl (b Meisenheim, 2 Jun 1886; d Hamburg, 24 Apr 1960), German bass. He sang at Wiesbaden, Vienna and the Städtische Oper Berlin 1906–14. He was successful at the NY Met from 1912 but rejected as an enemy alien in 1917. At Bayreuth he had one of the longest careers of all singers who have appeared there: 1906–31, as Gurnemanz, Hagen, Wotan, Pogner and Hunding. He worked as a prod. in Berlin during the 1930s and was a concert agent from 1937.

Braun, Victor (b Windsor, Ontario, 4 Aug 1935), Canadian baritone. Debut 1961, Escamillo; European debut Frankfurt, 1963. He sang Hamlet in the 1st CG perf. of Searle's opera and other roles have incl. Don Giovanni, Almaviva, Germont, Posa and Onegin.

Braunfels, Walter (b Frankfurt, 19 Dec 1882; d Cologne, 19 Mar 1954), German pianist and composer. Studied at the Hoch Cons. at Frankfurt, later in Vienna and Munich.

Works incl. operas *Prinzessin Brambilla* (after a story by E.T.A. Hoffmann) (1906–8), *Till Eulenspiegel* (1913), *Die Vögel* (1913–19), *Don Gil von den grünen Hosen* (1921–3), *Der gläserne Berg* (1928), *Galatea*; incid. music to Shakespeare's *Twelfth Night* and *Macbeth*; Mass, Te Deum; orchestral variations and other works; pf. music; songs, etc.

Brautwahl, Die (*The Choice of a Bride*), opera by Busoni (lib. by comp., based on a story by E.T.A. Hoffmann), prod. Hamburg, 13 Apr 1912. Orch. suite in 5 movts. perf. Berlin, 2 Jan 1913.

Bravura (It., lit. courage, bravery, swagger). The term refers to passages in a comp. or feats in a perf. calling for virtuosity.

Break, the change in tone-quality between different registers of voices and of wind instruments, a natural defect which may be more or less successfully corrected by technical means.

Breaking, the 17th-cent. practice of varying a theme by dividing it into figurations of smaller note-values, as in Divisions (variations). Breaking the Ground was the same process if the theme was on a ground-bass.

Bream, Julian (Alexander) (b London, 15 Jul 1933), English guitarist and lutenist. Studied guitar with his father, also going to the RCM in London, where he studied pf. and cello as well. He was encouraged by Segovia, whose protégé he became. A brilliant perf. on many plucked instruments; Bream performs much modern music; Henze has comp. *Royal Winter Music* (2 sonatas after Shakespeare) for him.

Brecht, Bertolt (1898–1956), German poet and playwright. *See* **Aufstieg und Fall der Stadt Mahagonny, Baal, Dreigroschenoper, Lehrstück.**

Brehme, Hans (b Potsdam, 10 Mar 1904; d Stuttgart, 10 Nov 1957), German composer. Pupil of Robert Kahn in Berlin, he 1st attracted attention at the Bremen music festival.

Works incl. 3 operas *Triptychon* (variations on a theme by Handel) (1936) and *Concerto sinfonico* (1930) for orch.; pf. concerto; partita for string 4tet, etc.

Breitengraser, Wilhelm (b Nuremberg, c 1495; d Nuremberg, 23 Dec 1542), German composer. He wrote German part-songs and Masses.

Breitkopf & Härtel, pub. firm at Leipzig, founded 1719 by Bernhard Christoph Breitkopf (1695–1777). A West German branch was estab. at Wiesbaden in 1945, becoming independent in 1947.

Brema, Marie (real name Minny Fehrmann) (b Liverpool, 28 Feb 1856; d Manchester, 22 Mar 1925), English mezzo of German-American descent. 1st appearance in London, 1891. Sang at CG as Siebel and Stanford's Beatrice (1901). Bayreuth 1894–7, as Kundry, Ortrud and Fricka. NY Met 1895 as Brangaene. In 1902 she was the 1st Fr. Brünnhilde (*Götterdämmerung*), cond. Cortot. Prof. RMCM 1913–25.

Brendel, Alfred (b Wiesenberg, 5 Jan 1931), Austrian pianist. Studied with Steuermann and Edwin Fischer; debut Graz, 1948. He played with the Vienna PO at Salzburg in 1960; gave all the Beethoven sonatas for pf. in London 1962 and settled there in 1974. US debut 1963. Has played Bartók and Schoenberg but is heard most often in Liszt and the Viennese classics: he eschews Beethoven's own cadenzas for his concertos.

Brendel, Wolfgang (b Munich, 20 Oct 1947), German baritone. From 1971 he has been successful at Munich as Papageno, Wolfram, Germont and Pelléas. NY Met debut 1975, as Mozart's Count. CG 1985, as Luna. Other roles incl. Verdi's Miller (Chicago, 1983), Marcello and Mandryka.

Brenet, Michel (i.e. Marie Bobillier) (Lunéville, 12 Apr 1858; d Paris, 4 Nov 1918), French musicologist. Wrote studies of Ockeghem, Palestrina, Handel, Haydn, Grétry and Berlioz.

Brent, Charlotte (b London, c 1735; d London, 10 Apr 1802), English soprano. Pupil of Arne, in whose opera *Eliza* she made her 1st appearance, at Dublin in 1755. London from 1757; sang there in Arne's *Judith* (1761) and *Artaxerxes* (1762).

Bretón, Tomás (b Salamanca, 29 Dec 1850; d Madrid, 2 Dec 1923), Spanish composer. Director of Madrid Cons. from 1901.

Works incl. operas *Guzman el Bueno* (1875), *Garin, Raquel* (1900), *Farinelli, El certamen de Cremona, Tabaré* and *Don Gil* (1914); zarzuelas *Los amantes de Teruel, La Dolores, La verbena de la paloma* (1894) and c 30 others; oratorio *Apocalipsia* (1882); *Las escenas andalazas, Salamanca, En la Alhambra* for orch.; vln. concerto; 3 string 4tets, pf. 5tet, 6tet for wind, pf. trio.

Breuer, Hans (b Cologne, 27 Apr 1868; d Vienna, 11 Oct 1929), German tenor. He sang every year at Bayreuth 1896–1914, usually as Mime and David. NY Met debut 1900, as Erik. Member of the Vienna Hofoper 1900–29 and took part in the 1919 fp of *Die Frau ohne Schatten*. He sang at Salzburg from 1910 as Monostatos and Mozart's Basilio; later a prod. there.

Bréval, Lucienne (real name Berthe Agnès Lisette Schilling) (b Berlin, 4 Nov 1869; d Neuilly-sur-Sienne, 15 Aug 1935), French soprano of Swiss descent. Studied at the Conss. of Geneva and Paris. Made her 1st appearance at the Paris Opéra in 1892, as Selika, and remained there for nearly 30 years. She was the 1st *Walküre* Brünnhilde, Eva and Kundry at the Opéra; created Fauré's Pénélope (Monte Carlo, 1913). In 1906 she sang Armide in the 1st London perf. of Gluck's opera.

Breve (Lat. *brevis* = short), a square note equalling 2 semibreves in value: ≡. So called because it was originally a short note having one half or one third of the value of a Long (Lat. *longa*).

Bréville, Pierre (Onfroy) de (b Bar-le-Duc, 21 Feb 1861; d Paris, 24 Sep 1949), French composer. Was intended for the diplomatic service, but allowed to study with Dubois at the Paris Cons. He decided to devote himself to comp. and became a pupil of Franck. Later became prof. at the Schola Cantorum, a music critic and member of the committee of the Société Nationale de Musique.

Works incl. opera *Éros vainqueur* (1905);

incid. music for Maeterlinck's *Sept Princesses* and overture for his *La Princesse Maleine*; Mass and motets; *La Cloche fêlée* (after Baudelaire) for orch.; 2 vln. and pf. sonatas.

Brewer, Bruce (b San Antonio, 12 Oct 1944), American tenor. He studied at Texas Univ., Austin, and with Richard Bonynge. His career began in concert. Stage debut San Antonio, 1970, as Ottavio; later sang at Boston and San Francisco. He appeared at Düsseldorf and Berlin, and at the Aix Festival was heard in Campra; developed into Baroque specialist and has sung roles in Rameau's *Les Indes Galantes* and *Zoroastre*.

Brian, Havergal (b Dresden, Staffs., 29 Jan 1876; d Shoreham, 28 Nov 1972), English composer. Mainly self-taught as a comp., he became an organist and music teacher in Staffordshire and wrote criticism at Manchester from 1905. Later he moved to London, where he made a precarious living under great difficulties. Some of his early music was conducted by Wood and by Beecham, although he did not hear any of his 32 symphs. perf. until 1954 at the age of 78 (BBC, no. 8). The largest symph., no. 1 *The Gothic*, had its first prof. perf. in 1966.

Works incl. operas *The Tigers* (1916–29; fp BBC, 1983), *Turandot* (1950), *The Cenci* (1952), *Faust* (1956), *Agamemnon* (1957); 32 symphs. (1919–68); 3 *English Suites, Hero and Leander*, overtures *For Valour* (Whitman) and *Dr. Merryheart, Festal Dance, Fantastic Variations on Old Rhymes*, symph. poem *In Memoriam* for orch.; *By the Waters of Babylon, The Vision of Cleopatra* and a setting from Shelley's *Prometheus* for chorus and orch. (1937–44); Heine's *Pilgrimage to Kevlaar* for chorus and orch; songs; part-songs.

Bride of Messina, The (*Nevěsta Messinská*), opera by Fibich (lib. by O. Hostinský), based on Schiller's drama *Die Braut von Messina*), prod. Prague, Czech Theatre, 28 Mar 1884.

Bridge, the support over which the strings are stretched and kept away from the belly of string instruments.

Bridge, Frank (b Brighton, 26 Feb 1879; d Eastbourne, 10 Jan 1941), English composer. Student at the RCM, where Stanford was his comp. master. He also learnt the vln., vla. and cond. Later played vla. in var. 4tets and gained varied experience as operatic and concert cond. Won Cobbett Prizes for chamber music in 1905–15 and honourable mention for the E min. string 4tet at Bologna in

1906. His 3rd and 4th string 4tets (1927, 1937) show an advanced harmonic idiom, not far removed from the music of Berg. He was well known as a teacher; one of his pupils was Britten, whose *Variations on a theme of Frank Bridge* (1937) are based on a theme from his master's Idyll no. 2 for string 4tet (1906).

Works incl. opera *The Christmas Rose*, (1918–29; prod. London, 1932); symph. poem *Isabella* (1907), suite *The Sea* (1911), rhapsody *Enter Spring* (1927), tone-poem *Summer* for orch.; Lament for strings; *There is a willow grows aslant a brook* (on a passage in *Hamlet*); *Phantasm* for pf. and orch., (1931), *Oration* for cello and orch. 4 string 4tets (1901–37), 2 pf. trios, Fantasy 4tet and several smaller pieces for string 4tet, pf. 5tet, Fantasy Trio and 4tet for pf. and strings, string 6tet, Rhapsody for 2 vlns. and vla., *Divertimenti* for wind instruments, vln. and pf. sonata, cello and pf. sonata; numerous pf. works incl. sonata, 4 *Characteristic Pieces*, suite *A Fairy Tale*, 3 Improvisations for the left hand; vln., vla., cello and organ pieces; choruses; songs.

Bridge Passage, a transitional passage in a comp., esp. the transition between 1st and 2nd subjects in a sonata-form movement.

Bridgetower, George (Augustus Polgreen) (b Biala, Poland, 11 Oct 1778; d London, 28 Feb 1860), mulatto violinist, son of an African father and Polish mother. Met Beethoven in Vienna and Teplice and played the 'Kreutzer' sonata with him at its fp on 17 May 1803.

Briegel, Wolfgang Carl (b Nuremberg, May 1626; d Darmstadt, 19 Nov 1712), German composer. Organist at Schweinfurt and Gotha; from 1671 to his death music director at Darmstadt. Wrote operas and ballets, sacred works for several voices incl. 7 cantatas, *Evangelische Gespräch* and *Evangelischer Blumengarten* (1660–81), pieces for 3 and 4 instruments, convivial and funeral songs for several voices, hymns.

Briganti, I (*The Brigands*), opera by Mercadante (lib. by J. Crescini, based on Schiller's drama *Die Räuber*), prod. Paris, Théâtre Italien, 22 Mar 1836.

Brigg Fair (i.e. the fair at Brigg, Lincs.), rhapsody for orch. by Delius on a Lincolnshire folksong, actually a set of variations, or a kind of passacaglia, comp. 1907, perf. Basle, 1907; 1st Eng. perf. Liverpool, 18 Jan 1908.

Brighenti, Maria. *See* **Giorgi-Righetti, Geltrude,** for the singer's correct name.

Brilioth, Helge (b Växjo, 7 May 1931), Swedish tenor, formerly baritone. Debut Drottningholm, 1958, as Paisiello's Bartolo and sang further bar. roles in W. Ger. before tenor debut Stockholm, 1965, as Don José. He has sung Siegmund at Bayreuth and Siegfried at Salzburg; these roles and Tristan and Parsifal at CG since 1970. NY Met 1970, Parsifal; Glyndebourne 1971, Bacchus.

Brilliant (Fr.)
Brillante (It.) $\}$ = Brilliant, used either as an adj. in titles or as a direction showing how a partic. passage is to be perf.

Brimley, John, English 16th-cent. composer. He was a cantor at Durham Cathedral in 1536–7, and remained there as organist and choirmaster under the New Foundation until *c* 1576. Some Eng. church music has survived.

Brindisi (It. = a toast), drinking of someone's health, a drinking song, esp. in opera, e.g. in Donizetti's *Lucrezia Borgia*, Verdi's *Macbeth*, *Traviata* and *Otello* or Mascagni's *Cavalleria rusticana.*

Brio (It. = spirit, fire, brilliance). The word is often used in the direction *con* (with) *b.*

Brisé (Fr. = broken), an arpeggio in keyboard or harp music, détaché bowing in string music.

British Broadcasting Corporation, founded as the British Broadcasting Company Ltd. in 1922 and incorporated under a Royal Charter in 1927, when it took its present name. Now always known by its abbreviation, BBC.

British Broadcasting Corporation Symphony Orchestra (BBC SO), chief orch. of the BBC, founded in 1930 with Adrian Boult as prin. cond. Since 1950 conds. have been Malcolm Sargent (until 1957), Rudolf Schwarz (1957–62), Antal Dorati (1962–6), Colin Davis (1967–71), Pierre Boulez (1971–5), Rudolf Kempe (1975–6), Gennadi Rozhdestvensky (1978–81). John Pritchard from 1981. Unlike the other London orchs., the BBC SO is not dependent on box-office receipts: a much more adventurous repertory of works is therefore given, with many fps of British works. In recent years, the period with Boulez as prin. cond. was of partic. importance: many perfs. of works by Schoenberg, Stravinsky, Bartók, Berg and Boulez himself. Regional BBC orchs. are based in Manchester (BBC Philharmonic), Glasgow (Scottish) and Cardiff (Welsh).

Britten, (Edward) Benjamin (b Lowestoft, 22 Nov 1913; d Aldeburgh, 4 Dec 1976), English composer, conductor and pianist. Educ. at Gresham's School, Holt; studied pf.

with Harold Samuel, comp. with Frank Bridge; later, with a scholarship, at the RCM, London, under Benjamin and Ireland. He was represented at the ISCM festivals of 1934, 1936 and 1938. During the early war years he was in the USA. His talent showed itself early, and his first international success was the *Variations on a theme of Frank Bridge,* played at the Salzburg Festival of 1937. This was followed by a number of works which estab. him as the leading Eng. composer of the day, esp. the stark *Sinfonia da Requiem* (1940) and the *Serenade* (1943). In 1945 his 2nd opera, *Peter Grimes,* estab. him as a dramatist; it was succeeded by further operas, incl. the chamber opera *The Turn of the Screw* (1954). Much of Britten's music is inspired by words, as shown by the many song cycles, the *Spring Symphony* (1949) and the *Nocturne* (1958); most of his tenor songs and roles were written for his companion Peter Pears (1910–86). Close artistic assoc. with Shostakovich and Rostropovich from 1960. The *War Requiem* (1961) combines the liturgical text with poems by Wilfred Owen and was composed to mark the consecration of the new Coventry Cathedral (1962). Britten was an admired conductor and accompanist, often heard in partnership with Pears. OM 1965, life peer 1976. He was a founder of the Aldeburgh Festival, 1948.

Works incl. STAGE: operas *Paul Bunyan* (W.H. Auden, 1941, rev. 1974), *Peter Grimes* (M. Slater, after Crabbe, 1945), *The Rape of Lucretia* (R. Duncan, 1946), *Albert Herring* (E. Crozier, after Maupassant, 1947), *The Little Sweep* (Crozier, on Blake's poem *The Chimney Sweep,* 1949), *Billy Budd* (E.M. Forster and Crozier, after Melville, 1951, rev. 1960), *Gloriana* (W. Plomer, 1953), *The Turn of the Screw* (M. Piper, after James, 1954), *A Midsummer Night's Dream* (Shakespeare, 1960), *Owen Wingrave* (Piper, after James, 1971) and *Death in Venice* (Piper, after Mann, 1973); *Noye's Fludde* (children's opera, 1957); church parables *Curlew River* (1964), *The Burning Fiery Furnace* (1966) and *The Prodigal Son* (1968); ballet *The Prince of the Pagodas* (1957).

INCID. MUSIC: incl. Webster's *Duchess of Malfi,* Priestley's *Johnson over Jordan,* Auden and Isherwood's *Ascent of F.6* and *On the Frontier,* Duncan's *This Way to the Tomb.*

CHORAL: incl. *Hymn to St Cecilia* (Auden, 1942), *A Ceremony of Carols* (1942), cantatas *Rejoice in the Lamb* (C. Smart,

1943) and *Saint Nicolas* (Crozier, 1948), *Spring Symphony* (1949), *Cantata Academica* (1959), *War Requiem* (1961), *Cantata Misericordium* (1963).

ORCH.: incl. *Variations on a theme* of Frank Bridge for strings (1937), *Young Apollo* for pf. and strings (1939), *Sinfonia da Requiem* (1940), Prelude and Fugue for strings (1943), *The Young Person's Guide to the Orch.* (1946), concertos for pf. and for vln. (1938–9), *Diversions for pf.* (left hand) and orch. (1940, rev. 1954), *Scot. Ballad* for 2 pfs. and orch. (1941), cello symph. (1963).

VOICE AND ORCH: *Quatre chansons françaises* (1928), *Our Hunting Fathers* (Auden) for high voice and orch. (1936), *Les Illuminations* (A. Rimbaud, 1939) for high voice and strings, *Serenade* (var. poets) for tenor, horn and strings, *Nocturne* (var. poets, 1958).

CHAMBER AND INST: incl. 4 string 4tets (1931 rev. 1974; nos. 1–3, 1941, 1945, 1975), cello sonata, 3 suites for solo cello; *Lacrymae* on song by Dowland for vla. and pf. (also with strings); 6 *Metamorphoses after Ovid* for solo ob.; *Holiday Diary* and *Sonatina Romantica* for pf.; *Prelude and Fugue on a theme of Vittoria* for org.

SONG CYCLES: *On this Island* (Auden, 1937), 7 *Sonnets of Michelangelo* (1940), *The Holy Sonnets of John Donne* (1945), *A Charm of Lullabies* (var. poets, 1947), *Winter Words* (Hardy, 1953), 6 *Hölderlin-Fragmente* (1958), *Songs and Proverbs of William Blake* (1965), *The Poet's Echo* (Pushkin, 1965) 5 Canticles (1947–74).

Britton, Thomas (b Rushden nr. Higham Ferrers, 14 Jan 1644; d London, 27 Sep 1714), English coal dealer and music amateur. Began very poorly as a hawker, but acquired much knowledge in music and science and estab. weekly concerts in a room over his shop in London which soon had a great following.

Brixi, Franz Xaver (b Prague, 2 Jan 1732; d Prague, Oct 14 1771), Bohemian organist and composer. After var. church posts he became *Kapellmeister* of Prague Cathedral in 1756.

Works consist largely of church music; 105 Masses, incl. *Missa Pastoralis* (Christmas Mass); 263 offertories, hymns and motets; 11 Requiems; 24 Vespers; Litanies, etc.; also org. pieces (incl. 3 concertos), a sinfonia, etc.

Broadwood, British family of pf. manufacturers and music editors:

1. John B. (b Cockburnspath, Oct 1732; d London, 1812), worked with Shudi, married

his daughter Barbara in 1769 and was sole proprietor of Shudi & Broadwood from 1782.

2. James Shudi B. (b London, 20 Dec 1772; d London, 8 Aug 1851), son of prec., was taken into partnership in 1795, when the firm became John B. & Son.

3. Thomas B., brother of prec., was taken into partnership in 1807 and the name became John B. & Sons.

4. Henry Fowler B. (b London, 1811; d London, 1893), son of 2.

5. John B. brother of prec. One of the earliest folksong collectors.

6. Henry John Tschudi B. (d London, 8 Feb 1911), grandson of 4.

7. Lucy Etheldred B. (b Melrose, 8 Aug 1858; d London, 22 Aug 1929), daughter of 4. Collector and ed. of folksongs.

Brockes (Barthold) Heinrich (1680–1747), German poet. *See* **Handel** (Passion), **Telemann** (do.).

Brockway, Howard (b Brooklyn, 22 Nov 1870; d New York, 20 Feb 1951), American pianist and composer. Studied in NY and Berlin, taught privately in NY from 1895 and in 1903 joined the Peabody Cons. at Baltimore. Returning to NY in 1910 he taught comp. there privately and at the David Mannes Music School.

Works incl. symph. in D maj., Ballad, Scherzino, *Sylvan Suite* for orch. (1901); *Cavatina and Romanza* for vln. and orch., suite in E min. for cello and orch.; vln. and pf. sonata in G min.; pf. pieces.

Brodsky, Adolf (b Taganrog, 21 Mar 1851; d Manchester, 22 Jan 1929), Russian violinist. Pupil of Hellmesberger in Vienna; successively cond. at Kiev, prof. at the Leipzig Cons., leader of the Hallé Orch. in Manchester and principal of the RCM there from 1895. In 1881 he gave the fp of Tchaikovsky's violin concerto (Vienna, cond. Richter).

Broken Consort, term in use in England *c* 1600 for an ens. that performed well-known music with many embellishments or divisions. The view that the term referred to ens. of different kinds of instruments appears to be incorrect.

Broman, Sten (b Uppsala, 25 Mar 1902; d Lund, 29 Oct 1983), Swedish composer, vla. player and critic. Studied in Prague, Stockholm, Fribourg (Switz.) and Berlin, and in 1927 took a degree in music hist. at Lund Univ. He became music critic to the *Sydsvenska Dagbladet.*

Works incl. incid. music to Aristophanes' *Lysistrata*; fantasy for chorus and orch.; 9 symphs. (1962–77); *Acad. Festival Over-*

ture, Chorale Fantasy and concerto for orch.; prelude, *Gothic Suite* and Litany for string orch.; suite for vla. and strings; 3 string 4tets, keyboard music.

Bronsgeest, Cornelis (b Leiden, 24 Jul 1878; d Berlin, 22 Sep 1957), Dutch baritone. Debut Frankfurt, 1900; Berlin Hofoper from 1906 (debut as Amonasro). Toured in France and N. Amer. and in 1914 sang Papageno at Drury Lane, London, under Beecham. Worked 1924–33 to estab. music on Berlin Radio, and returned after the war to help rebuild opera performance there.

Bronskaya, Evgenia (b St Petersburg, 1 Feb 1888; d Leningrad, 12 Dec 1953), Russian soprano. Debut Tiflis, 1901; sang in Kiev and Moscow 1901–7, then toured It., Fr. and USA. She returned to Rus. in 1910 and was heard in the principal centres until 1950 in such coloratura roles as Lucia, Gilda, Musetta, Violetta and Rimsky-Korsakov's Snow Maiden. Also a recitalist.

Bros, Juan (b Tortosa, 5 Mar 1776; d Oviedo, 12 Mar 1852), Spanish composer, director by turns at the cathedrals of Málaga, León and Oviedo. Wrote church music.

Broschi, Carlo. *See* **Farinelli**

Brossard, Sébastien de (b Dompierre, bap. 12 Sep 1655; d Meaux, 10 Aug 1730), French composer. Studied philosophy and theology at Caen and was self-taught in music. He lived there until 1683, when he went to Paris and worked at Notre-Dame, later at Strasbourg. In 1687 he became *maître de chapelle* at the cathedral there and in 1698 music director at Meaux Cathedral. Although he was a prolific comp. he is more famous for his dictionary of music (1703).

Brott, Alexander (b Montreal, 17 Mar 1915), Canadian composer, conductor and violinist. Studied at Juilliard and McGill Univ., Montreal; taught there from 1939 and founded chamber orch., giving fps of Canadian works. He has made many arrs. of German Classical repertory.

Brott, Boris (b Montreal, 14 Mar 1944), Canadian conductor, son of prec. Cond. regional orchs. in N. Amer. and Brit. (BBC Welsh SO and Northern Sinfonia). Widely active as a music educator.

Brouwenstijn, Gré (Gerda Demphina) (b Den Helder, 26 Aug 1915), Dutch soprano. Studied under various teachers from childhood, becoming a leading singer at the Amsterdam opera. She later sang all over Eur., both in lyric and dramatic roles. CG 1951, Aida; Elisabeth de Valois 1958. Bayreuth 1954–6 as Elisabeth, Gutrune, Eva and Sieglinde. Glyndebourne 1959–63, as Leonore.

Brown, Earle (b Lunenburg, Mass., 26 Dec 1926), American composer of the *avant-garde*. Much influenced by the ideas of John Cage, and also by the visual arts (Calder, Pollock), he has developed a method of notating controlled improvisation by graphical means.

Works incl. *Available Forms I*; *Available' Forms II* for 98 players and 2 cond. (1961–2); 2 8tets for 8 magnetic tapes; *Light Music* for electric lights, electronic equipment and instruments; *Sign Sounds* for chamber ens. (1972), *Windsor Jambs* for sop. and orch. (1979).

Brown, Iona (b Salisbury, 7 Jan 1941), English violinist and conductor. She studied with Hugh Maguire and Henryk Szeryng. Philharmonia Orch. 1963–6. Joined Academy of St Martin-in-the-Fields 1964; dir. from 1978.

Browne, John (*fl. c* 1490), English composer who contrib. more pieces than anyone else to the Eton Choirbook and now seems the major Eng. comp. of his generation.

Browning, an English form of fancy for viols, similar to the 'In Nomine', but based on a folk-tune instead of a plainsong theme.

Brownlee, John (Donald Mackenzie) (b Geelong, 7 Jan 1900; d New York, 10 Jan 1969), Australian baritone. Educated at Geelong College, he was persuaded by Melba to take up singing seriously. He made his debut at her farewell concert in 1926 as Marcello, and in 1927 joined the Paris Opéra; sang there until 1936; Glyndebourne 1935–47 as Alfonso, Don Giovanni and Mozart's Count; NY Met 1937–56, debut role Rigoletto. In 1956 he became director of the Manhattan School of Music.

Bruch, Max (b Cologne, 6 Jan 1838; d Friedenau nr. Berlin, 2 Oct 1920), German composer. Learnt music as a child from his mother, a singer; later, with a scholarship, from Hiller, Reinecke and Breuning. He visited Leipzig, Munich and other musical centres to gain further experience and in 1863 prod. his opera *Loreley* at Mannheim, having obtained permission from Geibel to use the lib. orig. written for Mendelssohn. After 2 appts. at Koblenz and Sondershausen, he lived 1st in Berlin and then at Bonn, wholly devoted to comp. From 1880 to 1883 he was cond. of the Liverpool Phil. Society, and in 1881 he married the singer Clara Tuczek. From 1883 to 1890 he cond. at Breslau and in 1891 he became prof. of comp. at the Hochschule in Berlin, retiring to Friedenau in 1910.

Works incl. operas *Scherz, List und Rache*

(Goethe) (Cologne, 1858), *Die Loreley* (Mannheim, 1863) and *Hermione* (after Shakespeare's *Winter's Tale*) (Berlin 1872); works for solo voices, chorus and orch.: *Frithjof Scenen* (after Tegnér, 1864), *Schön Ellen*, *Odysseus* (after Homer, 1872), *Das Lied von de Glocke* (Schiller, 1879), *Achilleus* (after Homer), *Das Feuerkreuz* (after Scott's *Lay of the Last Minstrel*), *Moses*, *Gustav Adolf Damajanti, Die Macht des Gesangs* (Schiller, 1912).

ORCH. AND CHAMBER: 3 symphs.; 3 vln. concertos (1868, 1878, 1891), *Scottish Fantasia* for vln., harp and orch.; *Kol Nidrei* (1881) and *Ave Maria* for cello and orch.; Marfa's scene from Schiller's *Demetrius* for mezzo and orch. (1906); 2 string 4tets, pf. trio; many choruses; instrumental pieces; pf. music; songs.

Bruck, Arnold van (b Bruges, ? 1500; d Linz, 6 Feb 1554), Netherlands composer. 1st *Kapellmeister* to the emperor and dean of the Abbey of Laibach. Wrote motets and other church music, sacred and secular songs, esp. German songs.

Bruckner, Anton (b Ansfelden, 4 Sep 1824; d Vienna, 11 Oct 1896), Austrian composer and organist. Son of a country schoolmaster intended for the same calling and receiving little musical educ. On the early death of his father in 1837 he was taken in as a choir-boy by the monastery of St Florian. There he learnt the org. and was app. organist in 1845. By this time he had begun to compose, but was dissatisfied with his poor technique and went to study counterpoint with Sechter in Vienna, 1855. Cathedral organist at Linz, 1855–68, where he wrote much in his spare time and became an ardent Wagnerian on visiting Munich for the prod. of *Tristan* in 1865. The early progress of his work was hindered by his identification, in the minds of influential critics, with the music of Wagner. App. prof. at the Vienna Cons. in 1868, when his 1st symph. received its fp at Linz, and remained in the capital for the rest of his life, but visited Nancy, Paris and London as org. virtuoso in 1869 and 1871. His 3rd symph., strongly influenced by Wagner, had its fp at Vienna in 1873 but was a failure. Wide success came after the fp of the 7th symph. (1884). He was pensioned in 1891 and received an hon. doctor's degree from the univ of Vienna.

Works incl. SYMPHONIES: F min. (1863), D min. ('no. 0', *c* 1863–4, rev. 1869), no. 1 in C min. (1865, rev. 1868–84), no. 2 in C min. (1871, rev. 1873–7), no. 3 in D min. (1873, rev. 1874–7), no. 4 in E♭ ('Romantic'; 1874, new scherzo 1878, new finale 1880), no. 5 in B♭ (1875–6), no. 6 in A (1879–81), no. 7 in E (1881–3), no. 8 in C min. (1884–7 and 1889–90), no. 9 in D min. (1891–4).

CHORAL: Mass no. 1 in D min. (1864, rev. 1876–82), no. 2 in E min. with wind acc. (1866, rev. 1869–82), no. 3 in F min. (1867, rev. 1876–93); also Mass in F (1844), Requiem in D min. (1849), *Missa Solemnis* in B♭ (1852), Te Deum in C for soloists, chorus and orch. (1881–4), 5 Psalm settings (1852–92), many motets.

INST: string 4tet in C min. (1862), string 5tet in F (1879); organ music, piano pieces and songs.

Brudieu, Jean (or Juan or Joan) (b nr. Limoges, *c* 1520; d Urgell, Catalonia, 1591), French (Hispanicized) singer and composer. He visited Urgell in the Pyrenees to sing there at Christmas in 1538 and remained there as choirmaster until the 1570s, when he was at the church of Santa Maria del Mar at Barcelona, where he pub. a book of madrigals in 1585. He had returned to Urgell in 1579. Comp. church music as well as madrigals, incl. a *Missa defunctorum* (Requiem).

Brüggen, Frans (b Amsterdam, 30 Oct 1934), Dutch recorder player, flautist and conductor. He studied in Amsterdam and soon became the foremost recorder player of his time; also influential as a teacher. He favours original instruments, and has recorded much Baroque music. He has conducted *avant-garde* ensembles; from 1985 cond. symphonic music.

Bruhns, Nicolaus (b Schwabstedt, Slesvig, Advent 1665; d Husum, 29 Mar 1697), German organist, string player and composer. 1st employed in Copenhagen, then town organist at Husum, Slesvig-Holstein. Wrote cantatas, motets with orch. and organ music.

Brulé, Gace, French 12th-cent. trouvère. 90 songs are attrib. to him, but only some 30 are accepted as authentic.

Brüll, Ignaz (b Prossnitz, Moravia, 7 Nov 1846; d Vienna, 17 Sep 1907), Austrian pianist and composer. Studied in Vienna, where his family settled when he was 3, played there, toured, and prod. a number of comps. Later he taught the pf.

Works incl. operas *Die Bettler von Samarkand* (1864), *Das goldene Kreuz* (1875), *Der Landfriede* (1877), *Bianca, Königin Mariette* (1883), *Gloria, Das steinerne Herz, Gringoire, Schach dem König* (1893), *Der Husar;* ballet *Champagnermärchen* (1896); symph.; overture to Shakespeare's *Macbeth,*

serenade for orch.; 2 pf. concertos; vln. concerto; pf. trio and other chamber music; sonata for 2 pfs.; pf. music; songs.

Brumel, Antoine (b *c* 1460; d *c* 1515), French composer. Singer at Chartres Cathedral in 1483, canon at Laon in 1497, and from 1498 to 1501 choirmaster at Notre-Dame in Paris. Went to the court of the Duke of Ferrara in 1506, where he may have died. Wrote Masses, motets, Fr. *chansons.*

Bruna-Rasa, Lina (b Milan, 24 Sep 1907; d Milan, Oct 1984), Italian soprano. Debut La Scala, 1926, as Boito's Elena, under Toscanini; the following year took part in the fp of Wolf-Ferrari's *Sly.* Remained in Milan until 1940 as Venus, Loreley and Santuzza, and sang in the 1935 fp of Mascagni's *Nerone.* Appeared widely in Europe as Amelia, Tosca and Gioconda.

Bruneau, (Louis Charles Bonaventure) Alfred (b Paris, 3 Mar 1857; d Paris, 15 Jun 1934), French composer and critic. Son of a painter; learnt music incl. cello from his parents, who played vln. and pf., and took a cello prize at the Paris Cons. as a pupil of Franchomme. Afterwards studied comp. with Massenet and played in Pasdeloup's orch. In 1887 he prod. his 1st opera; the next 2 were based on works by Zola, who himself wrote the libs. for the next 3 stage works. The 1st of these, however, failed in 1897 because Bruneau and Zola were ardent supporters of Dreyfus. After Zola's death Bruneau wrote his own libs., some still based on Zola's work.

Works incl. operas *Kérim* (1887), *Le Rêve* and *L'Attaque du moulin* (after Zola, 1893), *Messidor, L'Ouragan* (1901) and *L'Enfant-roi* (libs. by Zola), *Lazare, Naïs Micoulin* and *Les Quatre Journées* (after Zola), *Le Tambour, Le Roi Candaule, Angélo, tyran de Padoue* (1928), *Virginie;* ballets *Les Bacchantes* (after Euripides, 1931) and *Le Jardin de Paradis;* incid. music to his adaptation of Zola's *La Faute de l'Abbé Mouret;* Requiem (1895), choral symphs. *Léda, La Belle au bois dormant* and *Penthésilée;* cantata *Geneviève de Paris; Ouverture héroïque* for orch.; vocal duets; songs *Chansons à danser* and 2 books of *Lieds de France* (all words by Catulle Mendès).

Brunelli, Antonio (b Bagnorea nr. Orvieto, *c* 1575; d Pisa, by 1630), Italian organist, music scholar and composer. Worked at Florence, both at churches and at the Tuscan court. Wrote 2 learned theoret. books.

Works incl. Masses, Requiems, sacred songs, psalms; a ballet; canzonets, madrigals.

Brunette (Fr. lit. a dark-haired girl), a light love-song of a type current in 17th–18th-cent. Fr., orig. so called because of the association of the words with dark girls.

Brunetti, Gaetano (b ? Fano, 1744; d nr. Madrid, 16 Dec 1798), Italian violinist and composer. Pupil of Nardini in Florence. Spent most of his life in Spain, in the service of the court and of the Duke of Alba, and there worked with Boccherini.

Works incl. symphs., serenades, 6tets, 5tets, trio sonatas, vln. duets.

Brunetti, Giovanni Gualberto (b Pistoia, 24 Apr 1706; d Pisa, 20 May 1787), Italian composer. Succeeded Clari as *maestro di cappella* of Pisa Cathedral in 1754.

Works incl. 7 operas incl. *Temistocle* (Lucca, 1776); Masses and other church music.

Brunskill, Muriel (b Kendall, Cumbria, 18 Dec 1899; d Bishops Tawton, Devon, Feb 1980), English contralto. Concert debut London, 1920; sang with BNOC 1922–9 as Geneviève, Erda and Boughton's Alceste. She appeared in N. Amer. from 1930 and toured Australia 1934–6. In 1934 she sang Amneris at CG, under Beecham. At the end of her career she perf. Gilbert and Sullivan. One of 16 solo singers in the fp of Vaughan Williams's *Serenade to Music* (1938).

Bruscantini, Sesto (b Porto Civitanova, 10 Dec 1919), Italian bass-baritone. Having originally studied law, he turned to singing and made his debut at La Scala, Milan, in 1949 in *Il Matrimonio segreto*. He was principally known as a *buffo* singer: Glyndebourne 1951–61 as Alfonso, Guglielmo, Dandini, both Figaros and Leporello. From 1962 sang Verdi.

Bruson, Renato (b Este nr. Padua, 13 Jan 1936), Italian baritone. Debut Spoleto, 1961, Luna; NY Met 1969 as Donizetti's Enrico. Brit. debut Edinburgh, 1972, as Ezio in *Attila*; CG 1976, Renato. In 1982 sang Falstaff under Giulini at San Francisco; later at CG.

Brussilovsky, Evgeny (b Rostov-on-Don, 12 Nov 1905; d Moscow, 9 May 1981), Russian composer. Having lost both his parents he joined the army at 16, but was released in 1922 in order to develop his talent at the Moscow Cons. He was expelled in 1924 for non-attendance, due to serious illness, but although very poor, managed to go to Leningrad and induced Steinberg to teach him at the cons. there. In 1933 he was commissioned to do research in Kazakh folk music and went to live at Alma-Ata, the capital of Kazakhstan. There he wrote operas in the nat. idiom.

Works incl. operas *Kiz-Ji-Bek* (1934), *Er-Targhin* (1937) and *Jalbir*; 8 symphs. (1931–72); instrumental pieces; pf. pieces; songs.

Brustad, Bjarne (b Oslo, 4 Mar 1895; d Oslo, 22 May 1978), Norwegian violinist, violist and composer. Studied at the Oslo Cons., later under Carl Flesch, and became active as violinist and cond. in Oslo.

Works incl. symph. poem *Atlantis* (1945), suite for orch., 9 symphs. (1948–73); *Nature morte* for string orch.; 4 vln. concertos (1922–61), *Rhapsody* for vln. and orch., concertino for vln. and chamber orch.; 3 string 4tets, suite for unaccomp. vln., suite for vla. and pf.; vln., vla. and pf. pieces.

Brygeman, William (d Bristol, 1524), English 16th-cent. composer. Singer at Eton, 1503–4; later at All Saints' Bristol. A fragmentary *Salve Regina* is in the Eton Choirbook.

Brymer, Jack (b South Shields, 27 Jan 1915), English clarinettist. Principal clar. RPO 1947–63; for most of this time under Beecham. BBC SO 1963–72, then principal clar. LSO; also active as broadcaster, soloist and chamber music player.

Bryn-Julson, Phyllis (b Bowdon, N. Dakota, 5 Feb 1945), American soprano of Norwegian parentage. She studied at Tanglewood and made her debut with the Boston SO in 1966 (Berg's *Lulu-Symphonie*). NY PO 1973, under Boulez; Brit. debut London, 1975, in his *Pli selon pli*. In 1976 she sang Malinche in the 1st US perf. of *Montezuma* by Sessions. Noted for her perfs. of Schoenberg's *Pierrot lunaire*, and in contemporary music.

Bryne, Albert (or Albertus Bryan) (b ? London *c* 1621; d London, 1671), English organist and composer. Organist of St Paul's Cathedral in London from 1638 and again after the Restoration. After the fire of London in 1666 he became organist of Westminster Abbey, a post in which he was succeeded by Blow in 1668. Wrote services, anthems, dances, etc.

Buccina. The Roman bugle horn, used in the army for signalling.

Bucenus, Paulus (b Holstein; *fl.* 1567–84), German composer. Worked as church musician at Riga where he may have died.

Works incl. a *St Matthew Passion* (1578), Masses, motets, *Sacrae Cantiones*.

Buch der hängenden Gärten, Das (*The Book of the Hanging Gardens*), 15 songs for sop. and pf. by Schoenberg, op. 15 (texts by Stefan George), comp. 1908–9, perf. Vienna, 14 Jan 1910.

Buch mit sieben Siegeln, Das (*The Book with Seven Seals*), oratorio by Franz Schmidt (text from the Apocalypse); comp. 1935–7, perf. Vienna, 15 Jun 1938.

Buchanan, Isobel (b Glasgow, 15 Mar 1954), Scottish soprano. She studied in Scotland and sang with Australian Opera from 1976; debut as Pamina. She repeated the role at Glyndebourne in 1978 and the same year was successful as Micaela, at the Vienna Staatsoper. She has sung Zerlina and Adina at Chicago and has appeared with the Chicago SO. CG debut 1979. Other roles incl. Susanna, Fiordiligi and Donna Elvira. Many concert perfs.

Buchardo, Carlos López (b Buenos Aires, 12 Oct 1881; d Buenos Aires, 21 Apr 1948), Argentine composer. Studied in Buenos Aires and with Roussel in Paris. On returning to Argentina he became director of the Nat. Cons. at Buenos Aires.

Works incl. opera *El sueño* de Alma (1914), *Escenas argentinas* for orch (1920); pf. pieces; songs.

Büchner, Georg (1813–37), German poet and playwright. *See* **Blind Man's Buff** (Davies, P.M.), **Dantons Tod** (Einem), **Müller-Hartmann** (*Leonce und Lena*), **Syberg** (do.), **Wagner-Régeny** (*Günstling*), **Weismann** (*Leonce und Lena*), **Wozzeck** (A. Berg and M. Gurlitt).

Buchner, Johann (Hans von Constantz) (b Ravensburg, Württemberg, 26 Oct 1483; d ? Konstanz, 1538), German composer. Prob. pupil of Hofhaimer. Worked at Konstanz Cathedral, but left in 1526, because of its growing Protestantism, for Überlingen. Wrote sacred and secular songs, org. pieces, etc. His *Fundamentum* is a didactic work incorporating org. music for the liturgical year.

Buckman, Rosina (b Blenheim, 1880; d London, 30 Dec 1948), New Zealand soprano. Debut Wellington, 1906; sang with Melba's co. in Australia. from 1911. In 1914 she was a Flowermaiden in the 1st Brit. stage perf. of *Parsifal*, at CG; later sang there with Beecham's co. as Musetta, Aida and Isolde. At the Shaftesbury Theatre she took part in the fp of Ethel Smyth's *The Boatswain's Mate* (1916); she returned to CG in 1919 for the 1st local perf. of de Lara's *Naïl*. Retired 1935. Recorded Butterfly with Goossens.

Budapest String Quartet, Hungarian ensemble founded 1917 by players from the Budapest Opera. From 1936 until its disbandment in 1967 the members were Rus. and Ukrainian: Joseph Roisman and Jac Gorodetzky (vlns.), Boris Kroyt (vla.) and

Mischa Schneider (cello). They were quartet-in-residence at the Library of Congress, Washington, 1938–62, and were highly regarded for their perfs. of Beethoven; joined by Milton Katims, then Walter Trampler, in the Mozart quintets.

Budavari Te Deum, work by Kodály for soloists, chorus and orch., perf. Budapest Cathedral, 11 Sep 1936.

Budden, Julian (Medforth) (b Hoylake, 9 Apr 1924), English musicologist and radio producer. He studied at Oxford and the RCM. Joined the BBC 1951 and was Chief Producer, Opera 1970–6; External Services Music Organizer 1976–83. Author of *The Operas of Verdi* (3 vols., 1973, 1978, 1981) and *Verdi* (1985). An internat. recognised authority on 19th-cent. Italian opera.

Buffo (It. 'comic', also 'comedian'), in music a singer of comic parts, used esp. as adj.; *tenore buffo, basso buffo.*

Bugle, a treble brass instrument with a wide conical bore, used mainly in the armed forces. Having no valves it can prod. only the natural harmonics. *See also* **Key Bugle.**

Bühnenweihfestspiel (Ger., from *Bühne* = stage, *Weihe* = consecration, *Fest* = festival, *Spiel* = play), the description given by Wagner to *Parsifal*, which he did not wish to call an 'opera' or a 'music drama'.

Bukofzer, Manfred (b Oldenburg, 27 Mar 1910; d Oakland, Calif., 7 Dec 1955), German-American musicologist. Studied at Heidelberg, Berlin and Basle, and went to USA in 1939, where after var. appts. he became prof. at Univ. of Calif., Berkeley. He specialized in medieval, partic. Eng., music and edited the complete works of Dunstable. His most important book is *Studies in Medieval and Renaissance Music.*

Bull, John (b c 1562; d Antwerp, 12–13 Mar 1628), English composer. He was a choir-boy in the Chapel Royal in London under Blitheman and became organist of Hereford Cathedral in 1582. On Blitheman's death in 1591 he became organist of the Chapel Royal. Mus.D., Cambridge, before 1592, and Oxford that year. In 1956 app. 1st prof. of music at Gresham Coll. In 1601 he travelled abroad, Thomas Byrd, son of William Byrd, acting as his deputy at Gresham Coll. Married Elizabeth Walter in 1607 and gave up his professorship, which could be held only by single men. In 1613 he left Eng., apparently to escape punishment for adultery, and became organist at the archducal chapel in Brussels. In 1617 he was app. organist at Antwerp Cathedral, where he remained to his death.

Works incl. anthems, incl. the 'Star' anthem *Almighty Lord*; secular vocal works for several voices; canons; a laud for the Blessed Virgin in Flem.; numerous org. and virginal pieces; some works for viols, etc.

Bull, Ole (Borneman) (b Bergen, 5 Feb 1810; d Lysø nr. Bergen, 17 Aug 1880), Norwegian violinist and composer. Was largely self-taught, his father insisting on his studying theology. In 1829 he visited Spohr at Kassel and in 1832 1st made his mark as a public player in Paris. He married a Fr. girl there, appeared with Chopin and Ernst, and visited It. with great success. Went to Eng. 1st in 1836 and to USA in 1843. Founded the Norse Theatre at Bergen in 1850. In 1870 he was married a 2nd time, to an American. Wrote 2 concertos and many other works for the vln.

Buller, John (b London, 7 Feb 1927), English composer. From 1959 he studied with Anthony Milner and in the 1970s prod. a series of works based on *Finnegans Wake*.

Works incl. *The Cave* for fl., clar., tromb., cello and tape (1970), 2 *Night Pieces* from *Finnegans Wake* for sop., clar., fl., pf. and cello (1971), *Finnegan's Floras* for chorus, perc. and pf. (1972), *Le Terraze* for 14 insts. and tape (1974), *Familiar*, string 4tet (1974), *The Theatre of Memory* for orch. (1981), *Towards Aquarius* for ens. (1983).

Bülow, Hans (Guido) Von (b Dresden, 8 Jan 1830; d Cairo, 12 Feb 1894), German pianist and conductor, 1st husband of Cosima Wagner (*née* Liszt). Studied law at Leipzig Univ. and pf. with Wieck there. At first exclusively a Wagnerian as a cond. and gave the fps of *Tristan und Isolde* (1865) and *Die Meistersinger* (1868), but after his wife went to live with Wagner became more enthusiastic about Brahms without abandoning Wagner; cond. the fp of Brahms's 4th symph. (1885). Made many tours both as cond. and pianist.

Bumbry, Grace (b St Louis, Miss., 4 Jan 1937), American mezzo and soprano. Debut Paris, Opéra, as Amneris; in 1961 became the first black singer to appear at Bayreuth (as Venus). CG 1963 and NY Met 1965, both as Eboli. Her Lady Macbeth at Salzburg, 1964, was her first soprano role. Other roles incl. Santuzza, Tosca, Carmen, Jenůfa and Dukas' Ariane. Her Salome at CG (1970) was a convincing visual and vocal display.

Bungert, August (b Mühlheim an der Ruhr, 14 Mar 1845; d Leutesdorf, 26 Oct 1915), German composer. Studied at Cologne Cons. and in Paris. Prod. his 1st (comic)

opera at Leipzig in 1884. His ambition was to build a special theatre for the prod. of his tetralogy on the model of Bayreuth.

Works incl. operas *Die Studenten von Salamanka* (Leipzig, 1884), tetralogy *Homerische Welt* (*Kirke, Nausicaa, Odysseus Heimkehr, Odysseus Tod*, prod. Dresden 1898–1903), 'mystery' *Warum? Woher? Wohin?*; incid. music to Goethe's *Faust*; symph. *Zeppelins erste grosse Fahrt*; *Tasso, Hohes Lied der Liebe, Auf der Wartburg* for orch.; pf. 4tet: pf. pieces; songs.

Buona figliuola, La (*The Good Girl*), also *La Cecchina*, opera by Piccinni (lib. by Goldoni, based on Richardson's *Pamela*), prod. Rome, Teatro delle Dame, 6 Feb 1760.

Buonamente, Giovanni Battista (b Mantua; d Assisi, 29 Aug 1642), Italian violinist and composer. Imp. court musician from 1622; *maestro di cappella* at the Franciscan monastery of Assisi from 1633. Wrote sonatas for 2 vlns. and bass, music for mixed teams of instruments, etc.

Buonamici, Giuseppe (b Florence, 12 Feb 1846; d Florence, 17 Mar 1914), Italian pianist, conductor and editor. Studied at home at first, then at the Munich Cons., pf. with Bülow and comp. with Rheinberger. Prof. there from 1870, but returned to Florence in 1873 as pf. prof., choral cond. and founder of a pf. trio. He did much to cultivate serious music.

Buovo d'Antona (*Bevis of Hampton*), opera by Traetta (lib. by Goldoni, based on the Anglo-Norman 13th-cent. romance), prod. Venice, Teatro San Moisè, 27 Dec 1758.

Burbero di buon cuore, Il (*The Good-hearted Grumbler*), opera by Martín y Soler (lib. by Lorenzo da Ponte, based on Goldoni's French comedy *Le Bourru bienfaisant*), prod. Vienna, Burgtheater, 4 Jan 1786. Mozart wrote 2 extra arias for it when it was revived, Vienna, 9 Nov 1789, and Haydn an addit. duet for its prod. in London, 1794.

Burck, Joachim à (Joachim Moller von Burck) (b Burg, 1546; d Mühlhausen, 24 May 1610), German organist and composer. Organist at various towns in Thuringia.

Works incl. 3 Passions, psalms; odes; songs.

Burden, in old vocal music the refrain sung at the end of each verse; in Eng. medieval carols, the refrain or chorus.

Burg, Robert (b Prague, 29 Mar 1890; d Dresden, 9 Feb 1946), German baritone. After engagements in Prague and Augsburg he joined the Hofoper, Dresden, in 1916 and remained until 1944; took part in the Verdi renaissance and created Busoni's Doktor

Faust (1925) and Hindemith's Cardillac (1926), both under Fritz Busch. Bayreuth 1933–42, as Kothner, Alberich and Klingsor. Also sang at Munich, Vienna, Berlin and Budapest.

Burgon, Geoffrey (b Hambledon, 16 Jul 1941), English composer. He studied with Peter Wishart and Lennox Berkeley at the GSM. His music shows a range of influences, incl. jazz and medieval French music. He is best known for his themes for successful TV series, e.g. *Brideshead Revisited*.

Works incl. ballets *The Golden Fish* (1964), *Ophelia* (1964), *Persephone* (1979); *Brideshead Variations* and *The World Again*, for orch. (1981 and 1983); *Think on Dredful Domesday* (1969), Magnificat (1970), *Veni Spiritus*, *Orpheus* and *Revelations*, all for soloists, chorus and orch. (1979–84); other works for chorus, and for voice and pf. or chamber ens.

Burgstaller, Alois (b Holzkirchen, 21 Sep 1871; d Gmund, 19 Apr 1945), German tenor. He made his Bayreuth debut in 1894 and in 1903 sang Siegmund at the NY Met; later the same year was Parsifal in the 1st staged US perf. of the opera: in spite of a ban on perfs. outside Bayreuth he continued to sing there until 1909.

Burian, Emil František (b Plzeň, 11 Apr 1904; d Prague, 9 Aug 1959), Czech singer, actor, author, stage manager and composer. Studied at the Prague Cons., joined the Dada Theatre in Prague and was director of the dramatic studio of the Brno Nat. Theatre in 1929–30; also founded a voice band, which sang to given rhythms without definite pitch, accomp. by percussion.

Works incl. operas *Alladine and Palomides* (after Maeterlinck, 1923), *Before Sunrise* (1924), *Bubu de Montparnasse, Mr Ipokras, Fear*; ballets *The Bassoon and the Flute* (1925), *Manège, Autobus*; choruses; chamber music, songs.

Burian, Karel (b Rousínov nr. Rakovník, 12 Jan 1870; d Senomaty, 25 Sep 1924), Czech tenor, uncle of prec. Debut Brno, 1891, Jeník. He sang Parsifal at Bayreuth in 1908 and in 1905 created Herod, in Dresden. CG from 1904 as Tristan and Lohengrin. NY Met 1903, as Tannhäuser, and sang there until 1913. Other roles incl. Manrico and Cavaradossi.

Burkhard, Willy (b Evilard-sur-Bienne, 17 Apr 1900; d Zurich, 18 Jun 1955), Swiss composer. Studied at the Berne School of Music, at Leipzig with Karg-Elert and Teichmüller and at Munich with Courvoisier, later in Paris. Became pf. prof. at the Berne

Cons. and cond. choirs and an amateur orch. Settled at Davos in 1937 to devote himself entirely to comp.

Works incl. opera *Die schwarze Spinne* (after Gotthelf, 1948); oratorios *Musikalische Uebung* (Luther, 1934) and *Das Gesicht Jesajas* (1933–5) Te Deum, choral suite *Neue Kraft*, festival cantata *Le Cantique de notre terre*, cantata *Das Jahr* and others, Psalm xciii for chorus and org.; *Christi Leidensverkündung* for tenor, chorus and org.; 2 symphs., *Ulenspiegel* variations for orch.; Fantasy, Little Serenade and concerto for string orch.; 2 vln. concertos, org. concerto (1945); 2 string 4tets, pf. trio, 2 triosonatas; Variations and Fantasy for org.; numerous song-cycles, incl. *Frage,* two on poems by Rilke, one on poems by Morgenstern.

Burla (It. = jest, trick, practical joke), in music a humorous piece, rather more boisterous than a scherzo.

Burleigh, Cecil (b Wyoming, NY, 17 Apr 1885; d Madison, Wis., 28 Jul 1980), American violinist and composer. Studied in USA, Berlin and finally at Chicago. After touring frequently and teaching in various places, he settled down as vln. prof. at Wis. Univ.

Works incl. symph. poem *Evangeline* (1918), *Mountain Pictures*, etc. for orch.; 3 vln. concertos; 2 vln. and pf. sonatas (*The Ascension* and *From the Life of St Paul*); numerous vln. pieces.

Burleigh, Henry T(hacker) (b Erie, Penn., 2 Dec 1866; d Stamford, Conn., 12 Apr 1949), black American singer and composer. Pupil of Dvořák at the Nat. Cons. in NY, where he intro. Negro tunes to his master.

Works incl. arrs. of Negro tunes, songs, etc.

Burlesca (It.) = Burla.

Burlesque, another name sometimes used for the Burletta in England.

Burletta (It. = a little joke), a form of light comic opera or operetta in 18th- and 19th-cent. England.

Burmeister, Joachim (b Lüneburg, 1564; d Rostock, 5 Mar 1629), German music theorist. In treatises pub. in 1599, 1601 and 1606 he codified as *figurae* the various technical and expressive devices used by 16th-cent. composers.

Burney, Charles (b Shrewsbury, 7 Apr 1726; d Chelsea, 12 Apr 1814), English organist, music historian and composer. Pupil of Arne, held org. posts in London (1749–51) and King's Lynn (1751–60). D.Mus., Oxford, 1769. Travelled extensively on the Continent 1770–72, collecting material for his 4-vol. *General History of Music* (pub. 1776–89). He also pub. those parts of his travel diaries relating to music. He was father of the novelist Fanny Burney, and a friend of Dr. Johnson, Reynolds, Garrick, etc. On his travels he made the acquaintance of many of the leading musicians of his day. His works incl. an Eng. version of Rousseau's *Le Devin du Village* under the title *The Cunning Man*, songs for a revival of *A Midsummer Night's Dream* (with M. Arne, Aylward and Battishill) and a quantity of instrumental music.

Burning Fiery Furnace, The, church parable by Britten (lib. by W. Plomer), prod. Orford Church, Suffolk, 9 Jun 1966.

Burrowes, Norma (b Bangor, 24 Apr 1944), Welsh soprano. She appeared in operas by Monteverdi and Puccini while at the RAM and from 1970 has sung at Glyndebourne, CG and the ENO: roles have incl. Zerlina, Susanna and Fiorilla; Janáček's Vixen at Glyndebourne, 1975. From 1979 she has sung Blondchen, Oscar and Sophie at the NY Met.

Burrows, Stuart (b Pontypridd, 7 Feb 1933), Welsh tenor. Opera debut with the WNO in 1963 as Verdi's Ismael; CG from 1967 as Beppe, Fenton and Elvino. US debut San Francisco, 1967, as Tamino; NY Met 1971, Don Ottavio. Other roles incl. Faust, Lensky, Ernesto and Rodolfo.

Burt, Francis (b London, 28 Apr 1926), English composer. He studied at the RAM and with Blacher in Berlin. Resident in Vienna from 1957; prof. of comp. Hochschule für Musik from 1973.

Works incl. operas *Volpone* (1960) and *Barnstaple, or Someone in the Attic* (1969); ballet *The Golem* (1962); *Iambics* (1953), *Espressione orchestrale* (1959) and *Fantasmagoria* (1963) for orch.; *Und Gott der Herr sprach*, for soloists, chorus and orch. (1983); string 4tet (1953).

Burton, Avery (b *c* 1470; d *c* 1543), English composer. On 29 Nov 1494 he was paid 20s. by Henry VII for composing a Mass; in 1509 he became a Gentleman of the Chapel Royal. On 20 Jun 1513 he went to France with the Chapel Royal, a Te Deum of his being sung after Mass at Tournai on 17 Sep; in Jun 1520 he was present at the Field of the Cloth of Gold. His name disappears from the records of the Chapel Royal after 1542. He is known as the composer of a Mass, *Ut re mi fa sol la*, in the Forrest-Heyther part-books (this is prob. not the Mass of 1494) and of a Te Deum for organ.

Burton, John (b Yorkshire, 1730; d Naples,

? 3 Sep 1782), English harpsichordist, organist and composer. Pupil of Keeble. Became a very famous player and had a great success in Ger. in 1754. Comp. concertos for both his instruments, sonatas, It. canzonets.

Burzio, Eugenia (b Milan, 20 Jun 1872; d Milan, 18 May 1922), Italian soprano. She sang at Parma and Palermo from 1904; La Scala 1906, as Katusha in Alfano's *Risurrezione*. The following year she had much success as Catalani's Loreley; often heard in verismo repertory, also as Pacini's Saffo, Gluck's Armide, and Norma. Her last role was as Ponchielli's Marion Delorme, at the Teatro Lirico, Milan, in 1919.

Busby, Thomas (b London, Dec 1755; d London, 28 May 1838), English organist and composer. Sang at Vauxhall as a boy with great success, later became a pupil of Battishill. Worked at a music dictionary with Arnold, was app. church organist at St Mary's, Newington, Surrey, *c* 1780. Mus. D. at Cambridge in 1801. Wrote several books on music.

Works incl. incid. music for Cumberland's *Joanna of Montfaucon* (an Eng. version of Kotzebue's *Johanna von M.*), Holcroft's *Tale of Mystery*, Anna Maria Porter's *Fair Fugitives* and Lewis's *Rugantino*; oratorios *The Prophecy* (from Pope's *Messiah*; *c* 1784, perf. Haymarket, 1799) and *Britannia*; settings of odes by Pope and Gay.

Busch, Adolf (b Siegen, Westphalia, 8 Aug 1891; d Guilford, Vermont, 9 Jun 1952), German violinist and composer. Studied at the Cologne Cons. and comp. with Hugo Grüters at Bonn. In 1918 he became vln. prof. at the Berlin Hochschule für Musik. In 1919 he formed a string 4tet with which he toured all over the world, and he was also famous as an interpreter of vln. and pf. sonatas with Rudolf Serkin. In 1933 he renounced Ger. citizenship as a protest against the Nazi rule; moved to US in 1939 and founded Marlboro School of Music, Vermont, 1950.

Works incl. choral, orchestral and much chamber music.

Busch, Fritz (b Siegen, Westphalia, 13 Mar 1890; d London, 14 Sep 1951), German conductor, brother of prec. Studied at the Cologne Cons. and after gaining experience at var. Ger. theatres and with orchs., he became cond. of the Stuttgart Opera in 1918 and music director of the Dresden Staatsoper in 1922. He cond. there the fps of Strauss's *Intermezzo* (1924) and *Die Ägyptische Helena* (1928), Busoni's *Doktor Faust* (1925) and Hindemith's *Cardillac* (1926).

Like his brother he renounced Ger. citizenship; went to Buenos Aires in 1933, cond. the Glyndebourne Opera from 1934 to his death and lived in Copenhagen as cond. of the State Radio.

Busch String Quartet, German ensemble formed 1919. From 1921–30 members were Adolf Busch and Gösta Andreasson (vlns.), Karl Doctor (vla.), Paul Grümmer (cello). In 1930 Grümmer was replaced by Hermann Busch. Toured widely in standard repertory, partic. admired in Beethoven. Moved to US 1939, disbanded 1952.

Busenello, Gian Francesco (b Venice, 24 Sep 1598; d Legnaro nr. Padua, 27 Oct 1659), Italian librettist and poet who is best known for his lib. for Monteverdi's *L'Incoronazione di Poppea* (1642); also libs. for Cavalli's *Gli amori d'Apollo e di Dafne* (1640), *Didone* (1641), and *Statira* (1655).

Bush, Alan (Dudley) (b London, 22 Dec 1900), English composer and teacher. Studied at the RAM in London and Berlin Univ., later with John Ireland. He also studied the pf. with Schnabel. He became prof. at the RAM, cond. of the London Labour Choral Union and in 1936 chairman of the Workers' Music Assoc.

Works incl. operas *The Press-Gang* (1946), *Wat Tyler* (1948–51), *The Spell Unbound* (1953), *Men of Blackmoor* (1955), *The Sugar Reapers* (1966) and *Joe Hill: the Man who Never Died* (1970); incid. music for Shakespeare's *Macbeth*, Sean O'Casey's *The Star Turns Red* and Patrick Hamilton's *The duke in Darkness*; choral work *The Winter Journey* (Randall Swingler) and others; symphs. (no. 2 'Nottingham' (1949), no. 3 *Byron* (1960), no. 4 *Lascaux* (1983) and other orch. music; pf. concerto with chorus (Swingler), vln. concerto, *Concert Suite* for cello and orch. (1952); string 4tet, pf. 4tet, *Dialectic* for string 4tet (1929); instrumental pieces with pf.; pf. and org. music, incl. 24 preludes for pf. (1977).

Bush, Geoffrey (b London, 23 Mar 1920), English composer. Became a choir-boy at Salisbury Cathedral in 1928, went to Lancing Coll. in 1933 and later to Balliol Coll., Oxford, where he gained the Nettleship Scholarship. B.Mus., Oxford, 1940, D.Mus. 1946. His studies were interrupted by war service at a hostel for abnormal evacuee children. He is mainly self-taught in comp., but had much valuable advice from his masters at Salisbury and Lancing, also from John Ireland and others later.

Works incl. 5 operas incl. *Spanish Rivals* (1948); *12th Night*, entertainment for chor-

us and orch.; overtures *In Praise of Salisbury* and *The Rehearsal* for orch., Divertimento for string orch., 2 symphs. (1954, 1957); concerto for pf. and strings, *Sinfonietta concertante* for cello and chamber orch., ob. concerto, rhapsody for clar. and string 4tet; sonatas for vln. and pf. and tpt. and pf.; 2 pf. sonatinas; *Portraits* and *La Belle Dame sans merci* (Keats) for unaccomp. chorus; songs.

Busnois, Antoine (b c 1430; d Bruges, 6 Nov 1492), French composer. Pupil of Ockeghem and later in the service of the Burgundian court until 1482, when (?) he became music director at the church of Saint-Sauveur at Bruges.

Works incl. Masses, motets, Magnificats; secular vocal pieces, songs.

Busoni, Ferruccio (Dante Michelangiolo Benvenuto) (b Empoli, 1 Apr 1866; d Berlin, 27 Jul 1924), German-Italian composer and pianist. Appeared as pianist in public at the age of 7; studied at Graz and Leipzig. Taught at the Helsinki Cons. in 1889; taught at Moscow in 1890 (where he married the Swede Gerda Sjöstrand) and in Amer. (at Boston), 1891–4. Settled in Berlin for good in 1894, but travelled widely as a pianist and during the war of 1914–18 lived 1st at Bologna as director of the Cons. and then at Zurich. At Bologna he hoped to influence It. music, and to prove that he was himself an It. comp., but was disappointed. He rejected the Teutonic past, as represented by Wagnerian music-drama, and sought to establish the ideals of neo-classicism and the *commedia dell'arte*. The Italians found him too intellectually rigorous, however. His opera *Doktor Faust* was completed by Jarnach and 1st perf. in 1925. His ideas on aesthetics, esp. his *Sketch of a New Aesthetic of Music* (1907), were attacked by conservatives such as Pfitzner.

Works incl. STAGE: operas *Sigune, oder Das vergessene Dorf* (1889), *Die Brautwahl* (1908–11; prod. Hamburg, 1912), *Arlecchino* and *Turandot* (1916–17; prod. in double bill, Zurich, 1917), *Doktor Faust* (1916–24; posth. prod. Dresden, 1925); incid. music to *Turandot* (prod. Berlin, 1911).

ORCH.: *Symphonische Suite* (1883), *Konzertstück* for pf. and orch. (1890), *Konzert-Fantasie* for pf. and orch. (1889; rev. as *Symphonisches Tongedicht*, 1892), Suite no. 2 for orch., *Geharnischte* (1895, rev. 1903), vln. concerto (1897), *Lustpielouvertüre* (1897, rev. 1904), pf. concerto with male chorus in finale (1903–4), *Turandot*, suite (1904), *Berceuse élégiaque* (1909), *Nocturne symphonique* (1912), *Indianische*

Fantasie for pf. and orch. (1913), *Die Braut-wahl*, suite (1912), *Rondò arlecchinesco* (1915), *Indianisches Tagebuch*, book 2, '*Gesang vom Reigen der Geister*' (1915), *Concertino* for clar. and orch. (1918), *Sara-bande und Cortège*, studies for *Doktor Faust* (1919), *Divertimento* for fl. and orch. (1920), *Tanzwalzer* (1920), *Romanza e scherzoso* for pf. and orch. (1921).

VOCAL: Mass (1879), *Le quattro stagioni* for male chorus and orch. (1882), *Il sabato del villaggio* for soloists, chorus and orch. (1883), *Unter den Linden* for sop. and orch. (1893), *Zigeunerlied* and *Schlechter Trost* for bar. and orch., texts by Goethe (1923), Lieder.

CHAMBER: *Serenata* for cello and pf. (1882), 2 string 4tets (1881, 1887), 2 vln. sonatas (1890, 1898), *Kleine Suite* for cello and pf. (1886).

PIANO: *Suite campestra* (1878), *Una festa di villaggio* (1882), 24 preludes (1879–81), 6 etudes (1883), *Macchiette medioevali* (1883), *Elegien*, 7 pieces (1907), *Indianis-ches Tagebuch*, book 1 (1915), *Fantasia contrappuntistica* (1910, as *Grosse Fuge*; rev. 1910 and 1912; vers. for 2 pfs. 1921), 6 sonatinas (1910–20), *Duettino concertante* on finale of Mozart's concerto K459 for 2 pfs. Also editions and arrangements of Bach for pf., incl. D min. Chaconne, and a concert vers. of Schoenberg's op. 11 no. 2 pf. piece.

Busser, (Paul) Henri (b Toulouse, 16 Jan 1872; d Paris, 30 Dec 1973), French conduc-tor and composer. Pupil of Guiraud at the Paris Cons. Gained the Prix de Rome in 1893. Successively organist at Saint-Cloud, cond. of the choral class at the Cons. and director of Niedermeyer's school. App. prof. of comp. at the cons. in 1921. He cond. Debussy's *Pelléas* at its 1st prod. (1902) and made an orch. vers. of *Printemps*.

Works incl. operas *Daphnis et Chloé* (1897), *Colomba* (after Mérimée), *Les Noces corinthiennes* (1922), *La Pie borgne*, *Le Carrosse du Saint-Sacrement* (Mérimée) (1948); Masses and motets; *Hercule au jar-din des Hespérides*, *Suite funambulesque* and other orchestral works; choruses, songs.

Bussotti, Sylvano (b Florence, 1 Oct 1931), Italian composer. Studied music in Florence and painting in Paris. After prod. some early works in a relatively traditional style, he turned to a graphical manner of composing which is influenced by Cage and attempts to suggest the type of improvisation required. Works incl. operas *Lorenzaccio* (1972) and *Nottetempo* (1976); *Torso* for voice and orch.; *Fragmentations* for harp; *5 pf. pieces*

for David Tudor (1959); *Pour clavier* for pf.; *Pearson Piece* for baritone and pf.; can-tata *Memoria* (1962); Requiem (1969); *Opus Cygne* for fl. and orch. (1979).

Bustini, Alessandro (b Rome, 24 Dec 1876; d Rome, 23 Jun 1970), Italian composer. Studied at the Acc. di Santa Cecilia in Rome, where he became prof. later.

Works incl. operas *Maria Dulcis* (based on a story in Berlioz's *Soirées de l'orchestre*) (Rome, 1902), *La città quadrata* and *L'in-cantesimo di Calandrino*; funeral Mass for Victor Emmanuel II; 2 symphs. (1899, 1909), symph. poem *Le tentazioni*; 2 string 4tets; sonatas for vln. and pf. and vla. and pf., pf. pieces.

Buths, Julius (b Wiesbaden, 7 May 1851; d Düsseldorf, 12 Mar 1920), German pianist and conductor. Worked at Düsseldorf from 1890, director of the cons. there and cond. of the Lower Rhine Festival, where he introd. Elgar's *Dream of Gerontius* in 1901.

Butler, Samuel (b Langar nr. Bingham, Notts., 4 Dec 1835; d London, 18 Jun 1902), English author, critic, biologist, pain-ter and amateur composer. He was a pas-sionate admirer of Handel and wrote 2 can-tatas, *Narcissus* and *Ulysses* (1897), in im-itation of Handel's oratorio style. *Narcissus*, a dramatic cantata on the Stock Exchange, was revived London, 1985.

Butt, Clara (b Steyning, Sussex, 1 Feb 1872; d North Stoke, Oxon, 23 Jan 1936), English contralto. Studied at RCM in London and in Paris. Made her 1st concert and stage appearance in 1892 as Orpheus. A great voice made her very popular, and having placed it at the disposal of war charities, she received the DBE in 1920. Elgar's *Sea Pictures* (Norwich, 1899) was comp. for her.

Butterfly (Puccini). *See* **Madama Butterfly**.

'Butterfly' (or 'Butterfly's Wing') Study, a nickname sometimes given to Chopin's pf. Study in G♭ maj. op. 25 no. 9.

Butterworth, George (Sainton Kaye) (b London, 12 Jul 1885; d Pozières, 5 Aug 1916), English composer. Educ. at Eton and Oxford, studied music briefly at the RCM in London. He collected folksongs, cultivated folk dancing and comp., but enlisted on the outbreak of war and was killed in action. He suggested the idea for Vaughan Williams's *London Symph.* (1911–13) and the work is ded. to his memory.

Works incl. Rhapsody *A Shropshire Lad* (1912) and Idyll *The Banks of Green Willow* (1913) for orch.; 2 song cycles on Hous-man's *Shropshire Lad*; Sussex folksongs arr.; carols set for chorus; a few other choral pieces and songs.

Butting, Max (b Berlin, 6 Oct 1888; d Berlin, 13 Jul 1976), German composer. Studied at Munich.

Works incl. unfinished Mass; 10 symphs. (1923–63), chamber symph.; cello concerto; 10 string 4tets (1914–71) and other chamber music; songs with small orch., etc.

Buttsett, Johann Heinrich (b Bindersleben nr. Erfurt, 25 Apr 1666; d Erfurt, 1 Dec 1727), German organist and composer. Pupil of Pachelbel. Organist of 2 Erfurt churches from 1684 and of the cathedral from 1691. Works incl. Masses and a vol. of keyboard music, *Musikalische Clavierkunst*.

Buus, Jachet (Jacques) (b ? Ghent, c 1500; d Vienna, Aug 1565), Flemish organist and composer. 1st pub. some work in Fr., but went to It. and in 1541 became organist at St Mark's in Venice, succeeding Baldassare da Imola. He went to Vienna on leave in 1550, but never returned and became organist at the court of Ferdinand I.

Works incl. motets, madrigals; Fr. *chansons; ricercari* for org.

Buxheimer Orgelbuch, large German MS. of keyboard music (not all of it necessarily for org.) dateable c 1470. It contains mostly ornamented arrangements of sacred and secular vocal works; also several versions of the *Fundamentum organisandi* by Paumann and some liturgical org. music. The upper part is written on a staff of (usually) 7 lines, the lower part(s) in letters. In some pieces the use of pedals is indicated.

Buxtehude, Dietrich (b ? Oldesloe, c 1637; d Lübeck, 9 May 1707), Danish composer and organist. Settled in Denmark and from 1668 organist of St Mary's Church, Lübeck. An important forerunner of Bach as organ composer; Bach is alleged to have walked 200 miles to hear him play.

Works incl. concerted works for chorus and orch. (*Abendmusiken*); church cantatas, all with German texts, except sequence of 7, *Membra Jesu nostri*, 1680; sonatas for strings; organ music, incl. chorale preludes; suites for harpsichord.

Buysine (or **Buzine**), in the early Middle Ages a large horn. From the 13th cent. a long tpt., Saracen in origin, which survived till the 16th cent. as a ceremonial instrument.

By an Overgrown Path (*Po zarostlém chodníčka*), work for pf. in 10 movts. by Janáček (1901–11). The movts. are titled: 1. Our evenings; 2. A blown-away leaf; 3. Come along with us; 4. The Virgin of Frýdek; 5. They chattered like swallows; 6. One cannot tell; 7. Good night; 8. In anguish; 9. In tears 10. The little owl continues screeching.

Byrd, William (b ? Lincoln, 1543; d Stondon Massey, Essex, 4 Jul 1623), English composer. After prob. studying under Tallis as one of the children of the Chapel Royal in London, he was app. organist of Lincoln Cathedral in 1563, at an unusually early age. He married Juliana Birley there, 14 Sep 1568, and on 22 Feb 1569 was elected a Gentleman of the Chapel Royal, but continued his duties at Lincoln until 1572, when he became organist of the Chapel Royal jointly with Tallis. In 1575 Queen Elizabeth granted the 2 an exclusive licence for printing and selling music and they dedicated to her their *Cantiones sacrae* pub. that year. Byrd married a 2nd time about 1587. In 1593 he bought Stondon Place nr. Stapleford-Abbott, Essex, where he remained for the rest of his life, as often as his duties in town would let him. He was frequently involved in litigation and was several times prosecuted for recusancy as a Roman Catholic, but remained in favour with the queen.

Works incl. 3 Masses; 17 Lat. motets in the *Cantiones sacrae* by Tallis and B.; 61 Lat. motets in 2 books of *Cantiones sacrae*; 99 Lat. motets in 2 books of *Gradualia*; c 50 motets in MS.; 4 Anglican services; c 61 anthems; some miscellaneous Eng. church music; *Psalmes, Sonets and Songs* (18 nos.); *Songs of Sundrie Natures* (47 nos.); *Psalmes, Songs and Sonnets* (32 nos.); 4 separate madrigals (others are in those 3 books); consort songs, canons; rounds; fantasies for strings, 7 In Nomines for strings, 10 pieces for strings on plainsong tunes, some miscellaneous music for strings; c 100 virginal pieces, among them fantasias, preludes, grounds, variations, pavans and galliards and other dances.

Byron, George Gordon, Lord (1788–1824), English poet. See **Corsaire** (Berlioz), **Corsaro** (Verdi), **Due Foscari** (Verdi), **Harold en Italie** (Berlioz) **Manfred** (incid. music, Schumann; symph., Tchaikovsky), **Marino Faliero** (Donizetti), **Mussorgsky** *(Destruction of Sennacherib)*, **Ode to Napoleon** (Schoenberg), **Parisina** (Donizetti), **Tasso** (Liszt), *also* **Vampyr** (Lindpainter and Marschner; subject attrib. to Byron, but actually from a story by John William Polidori).

Byttering (*fl. c* 1410; his name formerly misread as Gyttering), English composer represented in the Old Hall MS.

Byzantine Chant, the name given to the

Christian chant of the Gk.-speaking Orthodox Church. In 330 Constantine the Great
made Byzantium (henceforth Constantinople) capital of the Roman Empire; but only
in 527, with the coronation of Justinian I as
Emperor, did Byzantine liturgy, art and
music gain supremacy throughout the
Empire. Other important dates are 726–843
(the iconoclastic age), 1054 (the final break
from Roman Catholicism), and 1453 (the
sack of Constantinople by the Turks). During the course of the 11th cent. the introduction of new hymns was forbidden, and the
power of the Byzantine Empire was broken
with the estab. of the Lat. Empire (1204–
61). However, the restoration of the Eastern
Empire in 1261 led to a renaissance which
lasted for a century, followed by a gradual
deterioration until the end of the Empire.

Byzantine music and liturgy was dominated by its hymns, which adorned the Offices
rather than the Mass. The *troparion* (later
sticheron) was an intercalation between the
verses of a psalm. The *kontakion* was a
sermon in verse, sung after the reading of the
Gospel at the Morning Office. At the end of
the 7th cent. it was replaced by the *kanon*,
consisting of 9 odes of 9 stanzas each: each
ode had its own melody. Finally acclama-
tions to the Emperor were sung throughout
the period; unlike music actually sung in
church, these were accompanied by instruments, esp. the organ.

Byzantine music, notated in neumes, is
based on a system of eight modes (*echoi*),
defined by charact. melodic formulas as well
as by tonality. Like the verse itself (scanned
by stress, not quantity) it is Semitic in origin.
The comparative simplicity of earlier and
middle Byzantine music gave way, at the end
of the period, to a highly embellished style in
which the balance between verse and music
tended to be destroyed.

C

C, the keynote, or tonic, of the scale of C maj.

C Clef, the clef, derived from an ornamental letter C, which indicates that the line on which it is placed =

In the past it has been placed on all 5 lines of the stave (*see* illustration below).

Soprano	Mezzo-soprano	Alto	Tenor	

C CLEF

(The last of these has the same effect as the baritone F clef.) Only two C clefs are in use today: the Alto, for the viola, and the Tenor, for the tenor trombone and the upper register of the bassoon, cello and double bass.

Cabaletta (It. corrupt. from *cavatinetta*, dim. of *cavatina*), the quick and usually brilliant final section of an aria consisting of more than one movement.

Caballé, Montserrat (b Barcelona, 12 Apr 1933), Spanish soprano. Debut Basle, 1956. La Scala, Milan, from 1960 as Norma and Maria Stuarda. NY debut (concert) 1965, as Lucrezia Borgia; Met later that year as Marguerite. Glyndebourne 1965 as the Marschallin; CG debut 1972, Violetta. Other roles incl. Imogene and Elisabeth de Valois. She is noted for her fine technique. In a concert perf. of Salieri's *Les Danaïdes*, Perugia 1983, she sang Hypermestra.

Cabanilles, Juan (Bautista José) (b Algemesí Valencia, bap. 6 Sep 1644; d Valencia, 29 Apr 1712), Spanish organist and composer. In 1665 he was app. organist of Valencia Cathedral, a post he held till his death. He was regarded as one of the great organ comps. of his time.

Cabel, Marie-Josephe (b Liège, 31 Jan 1827; d Maisons-Laffitte, 23 May 1885), Belgian soprano. Debut Paris, Opéra-Comique, 1849. She sang in Brussels from 1850 and visited London with the co. of the Paris Théâtre-Lyrique, as Donizetti's Marie; returned to the Opéra-Comique and created

there leading roles in Meyerbeer's *Dinorah* and Thomas' *Mignon*. She was also heard in operas by Halévy and Auber.

Cabezón, Antonio de (b Castrillo de Matajudios nr. Burgos, 1510; d Madrid, 26 Mar 1566), Spanish organist and composer. Although blind from early childhood he studied with Tomás Gómez at Palencia and became chamber organist and harpsichordist to Charles V, remaining at court under Philip II, accomp. him to Eng. on his marriage to Mary I. Comp. organ, vihuela and other music.

Cabezón, Hernando de (b Madrid, bap. 7 Sep 1541; d Valladolid, 1 Oct 1602), Spanish organist and composer, son of prec. Studied under his father, whom he succeeded at court and whose works he ed. in 1578. Wrote organ music.

Cabo, Francisco Javier (b Nájara, Valencia, 1768; d Valencia, 21 Nov 1832), Spanish organist and composer. After some minor posts he was app. cantor at Valencia Cathedral in 1810, 1st organist in 1816 and *maestro de capilla* in 1830, succeeding Andrevi.

Works incl. church music, vocal music, with organ or orch., organ pieces.

Cabrette (Fr. dialect for *chevrette* = she-kid), a variety of musette from the Auvergnat region in France.

Caccia (It. = hunt), a 14th-cent. Italian composition in which 2 voices, with or without a supporting instrument, sang in canon. The texts, though always lively, were not confined to hunting. The corresponding form in Fr. was called *chace*.

Caccini, Francesca (b Florence, 18 Sep 1587; d Florence, *c* 1640), Italian singer and composer. Pupil of her father.

Works incl. opera *La liberazione di Ruggiero* (1625); ballets *Il ballo delle zigane* (1615) and *Rinaldo innamorato* (after Tasso); sacred and secular cantatas for 1 and 2 voices, etc.

Caccini, Giulio (b Rome, *c* 1545; d Florence, buried 10 Dec 1618), Italian singer, lutenist and composer, father of prec. Entered the service of the Medici at Florence in 1564. Visited Paris with his daughter in 1604–5. He wrote short vocal pieces in recitative style and sang them to the theorbo, which led to larger essays of the kind, set to scenes by Count Bardi, and eventually to Rinuccini's lib. for the opera *Euridice*, 1st set by Peri and immediately afterwards by Caccini in 1600.

Works incl. operas *Euridice* and *Il rapimento di Cefalo* (both 1600); *Nuove musiche* containing madrigals and arias for voice and continuo.

Cachucha (Span.), an Andalusian dance in quick, energetic 3–4 time.

Cadéac, Pierre, 16th-cent. French composer. He was master of the choir-boys at Auch (near Toulouse) in 1556. He composed Masses, motets and *chansons*, incl. perhaps the *Je suis désheritée* ascribed to him by Attaingnant in 1539 (but to 'Lupus' by the same pub. in 1533). This famous piece was used as the basis of numerous Masses in the 16th cent., incl. one by Palestrina.

Cadence (from Lat. *cado* = I fall).
(1) the fall of a melody to its final note.
(2) The harmonization of such a fall.
Traditional forms are, in the key of C major:

(*a*) Perfect (in Amer. Authentic): dominant to tonic:

(a)
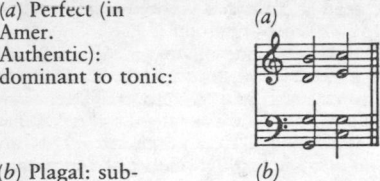

(*b*) Plagal: subdominant to tonic:

(b)
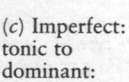

(*c*) Imperfect: tonic to dominant:

(c)
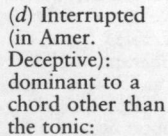

(*d*) Interrupted (in Amer. Deceptive): dominant to a chord other than the tonic:

(d)
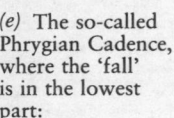

(*e*) The so-called Phrygian Cadence, where the 'fall' is in the lowest part:

(e)

derives its name from the Phrygian Mode. Apart from these traditional forms any harmonic progression which suggests finality, if only temporarily, is technically a cadence.

Cadence-Phrase, the final group in the exposition of a sonata movement, leading to the close in a key other than the tonic.

Cadenza (It. = Cadence). Orig. the cadenza was simply a cadence; but the custom gradually estab. itself of creating a feeling of suspense between the chords of a cadence by interpolating brilliant passages of greater or lesser extent and at the same time giving the perf. a chance to display technical gifts and inventiveness in improvisation. Cadenzas in concertos are now rarely improvised, but supplied either by the comp. himself or some other musician.

Cadi dupé, Le (*The Cadi Duped*), opera by Gluck (lib. by P.R. Lemonnier), prod. Vienna, Burgtheater, Dec 1761.

Opera by Monsigny (lib. do.), prod. Paris, Opéra-Comique, 4 Feb 1761.

Cadman, Charles Wakefield (b Johnstown, Penn., 24 Dec 1881; d Los Angeles, 30 Dec 1946), American composer. Studied at Pittsburgh and became organist, chorus cond. and critic there. He explored American Indian music and used it in some of his works. After a visit to Europe in 1910 he became organist at Denver and later settled at Los Angeles.

Works incl. operas *The Garden of Mystery* (1925), *The Land of Misty Water* (1909–12), *The Garden of Death, Shanewis* (*The Robin Woman*, 1918), *A Witch of Salem* (1926), *The Willow Tree*; cantatas for mixed and male voices; *Thunder-bird* suite (1914), *Oriental Rhapsody, Dark Dancers of the Mardi Gras* for orch.; *Amer. Suite* and *To a Vanishing Race* for string orch.; string 4tet (1917), pf. trio; vln. and pf. sonata, sonata and suite *Omar Khayyám* for pf.; songs.

Cadmus et Hermione, opera by Lully (lib. by Quinault), prod. Paris, Opéra, 27 Apr 1673.

Caduta de' giganti, La (*The Fall of the Giants*), opera by Gluck (lib. by F. Vanneschi), prod. London, King's Theatre, Haymarket, 7 Jan 1746.

Cafaro, Pasquale (b San Pietro in Galantina nr. Lecce, *c* 1715; d Naples, 23 or 25 Oct 1787), Italian composer. Pupil of Leo in Naples, app. director of the Conservatoria della Pietà in 1759, and supernumerary *maestro di cappella* to the court in 1770.

Works incl. operas *Ipermestra* (1751), *La Disfatta di Dario* (1756), etc.; oratorios *Il*

Figlio prodigo, Il trionfo di Davidde (1746), etc.; *Stabat Mater*, Masses, motets and other church music.

Caffarelli (real name **Gaetano Majorano**) (b Bitonto, 12 Apr 1710; d Naples, 31 Jan 1783), Italian castrato alto. Pupil of Porpora, made his operatic debut in Rome, 1726, in Sarro's *Valdemaro*. Sang for Handel in London, 1738, creating the title roles in *Faramondo* and *Serse*.

Cage, John (b Los Angeles, 5 Sep 1912), American composer. Studied pf. in Los Angeles and Paris and comp. with, among others, Cowell, Schoenberg and Varèse. Cage is the most prominent pioneer and exponent of such 'experimental' concepts as indeterminacy, chance, silence, etc., his ideas having had a very considerable influence in both Amer. and Eur. He has invented the 'prepared piano', in which different objects are inserted between the strings, altering the tone and the sound produced. Cage has also explored electronic music. Among his published writings, ideas and lectures on music is the collection *Silence* (1961).

Works incl. pf. concerto (1951); *Music of Changes* for pf.; *Winter Music* for 1–20 pfs.; *Music for Amplified Toy Piano* (1960); *Radio Music* for 1–8 radios; *Amores* for prepared pf.; *Imaginary Landscape No.5* for electronic tape; *4' 33"*, silent piece for different combinations; *Roaratorio*, after *Finnegans Wake* (1979); *Dance* for 4 orchs. and 4 conds. (1982); *Europera* (1987), a collage incl. arias from well-known operas.

Cagnoni, Antonio (b Godiasco, Voghera, 8 Feb 1828; d Bergamo, 30 Apr 1896), Italian composer. Studied at the Milan Cons., 1842–7. *Maestro di cappella* at Vigevano, 1856–63, then at Novara Cathedral, and from 1887 at the church of Santa Maria Maggiore at Bergamo.

Works incl. operas *Don Bucefalo* (1847), *Il testamento di Figaro, Amori e trappole* (1850), *Giralda, La valle d'Andorra, Il vecchio della Montagna* (1860), *La tombola, Un capriccio di donna, Papa Martin, Francesca da Rimini* (after Dante) (1878), etc.; motets and other church music.

Cahier, Mme **Charles** (b Nashville, 6 Jan 1870; d Manhattan Beach, Calif., 15 Apr 1951), American contralto. Studied with Jean de Reszke in Paris. Debut Nice, 1904; from 1906 she sang Carmen and other roles under Mahler at the Vienna Hofoper: took part in the 1911 fp of *Das Lied von der Erde*, under Walter. NY Met 1911–13, as Azucena, Amneris and Fricka. She taught in Swed., Salzburg and NY.

Cahill, Teresa (b Maidenhead, 30 Jul 1944), English soprano. Studied at the GSM. Debut 1967, Rosina with Phoenix Opera. From 1970 she has sung at Glyndebourne and CG, and later with WNO and Scottish Opera. In 1977 she was heard as Alice Ford at Glyndebourne. Has recorded roles in *Calisto, Cendrillon, Figaro* and *Rosenkavalier* (Sophie).

Caimo, Gioseppe (b Milan, *c* 1545; d Milan, 1584), Italian composer. Organist of Milan Cathedral, 1580 until his death. He wrote canzonets and madrigals, some of the latter employing the extremes of chromaticism favoured by Gesualdo.

Caix d'Hervelois, Louis de (b *c* 1670–80; d *c* 1760), French composer and vla. da gamba player. Wrote many pieces for vla. da gamba, duets for viols and fl. sonatas.

Calando (It. = lowering, decreasing, calming down), a direction similar to *diminuendo* and *rallentando*, capable of expressing both at once, i.e. weakening in tone as well as slowing down.

Calata (It.), an Italian lute dance of the early 16th cent., similar to the French *basse danse*. It was written in duple time, but had a triple rhythm of 3-bar groups.

Caldara, Antonio (b Venice, 1670; d Vienna, 28 Dec 1736), Italian composer. Pupil of Legrenzi at Venice. After travelling much and working in Rome and Madrid, he settled in Vienna as vice-cond. under Fux in 1716.

Works incl. *c* 100 operas and other stage works, e.g. *Ifigenia in Aulide* (1718), *Lucio Papirio, Gianguir* (1724), *Don Chisciotte* (1727), *La pazienza di Socrate con due moglie* (with Reutter, 1731), *Il Demetrio, Sancio Panza, Achille in Sciro* (1736); church music, oratorios, cantatas, madrigals, canons; trio sonatas, 4tets, 7tet.

Caldwell, Sarah (b Maryville, Mo., 6 Mar 1924), American conductor and producer. She staged her 1st opera while a student at Tanglewood; founded Boston Opera Co. 1957 and has given 1st US perfs. of *War and Peace, Moses und Aron* (prod.), *Benvenuto Cellini* and the original versions of *Boris Godunov* and *Don Carlos*. In 1976 she became the 1st woman cond. at the NY Met (*La Traviata*). 1st US perf. *The Ice Break* (1979).

Caledonica, an alto bassoon invented by the Scottish bandmaster Meik, *c* 1820. It was played with a clar. reed mouthpiece.

Calife de Bagdad, Le, opera by Boieldieu (lib. by C.G. de Saint-Just), prod. Paris, Opéra-Comique, 16 Sep 1800.

Calinda (or **Calenda**), a Negro dance intro. into the W. Indies and later cultivated in the southern states of USA, originally an African ritual dance accomp. by drums, which remained a feature of its music. Delius makes use of it in *Koanga*.

Calino casturame. *See* **Callino casturame.**

Calisto, La, opera by Cavalli (lib. by G. Faustini, after Ovid's *Metamorphoses*), prod. Venice, Teatro Sant' Apollinare, 1651; known today in a free realization by Raymond Leppard (Glyndebourne, 26 May 1970), and in an ed. by Paul Daniel.

Callas, Maria (real name Kalogeropoulos) (b New York, 3 Dec 1923; d Paris, 16 Sep 1977), American-born soprano of Greek descent. Aged 13, she went to Greece and studied at the Athens Cons., returning to NY in 1945. Italian debut, Verona, 1947, as Gioconda. In 1949 she married the It. industrialist G.B. Meneghini. Sang at La Scala 1950–58, cond. de Sabata, Giulini, Bernstein, Karajan. CG 1952–3, 1957–9. US debut, Chicago, 1954; NY Met debut (Norma) 1956. Although she sang many types of role, Callas is most remembered for her perfs. in 19th- and early 20th-cent. Romantic It. operas, incl. Cherubini's *Médée*, Spontini's *La Vestale* and Donizetti's *Anna Bolena*. Last app. in opera, CG, 5 Jul 1965, as Tosca.

Callcott, John (Wall) (b London, 20 Nov 1766; d Bristol, 15 May 1821), English organist and composer. Son of a bricklayer, he had no regular music teaching, but picked up much knowledge from Arnold and Cooke. Having obtained a deputy organist's post, he found time to compose and in 1785 gained 3 of the 4 prizes offered by the Catch Club. Two years later he took part in founding the Glee Club. When Haydn came to Eng. he studied instrumental writing under him, but he continued to write glees and catches with great success. D.Mus., Oxford, 1800. In 1809 he went insane. He died having reached letter P of a music dictionary, feeling unable to proceed further.

Works incl. setting of Joseph Warton's *Ode to Fancy* (1785); anthem for Arnold's funeral; scena on the death of Nelson; a book of psalms ed. with Arnold, with some new tunes; numerous glees, catches and canons.

Callino casturame (? corrupt. from Ir. 'Cailín ó chois tSiúire mé' = 'I am a girl from beside the [river] Suir'), a tune mentioned in Shakespeare's *Henry V* (IV.iv) and set by 16th-cent. comps. incl. Byrd.

Calm Sea and Prosperous Voyage (Beethoven and Mendelssohn). *See* **Meeresstille.**

Calvé, Emma (Rose Emma Calvet) (b Décazeville, 15 Aug 1858; d Millau, 6 Jan 1942), French soprano. 1st appeared in Brussels in 1881, as Marguerite, and appeared in Paris in 1884. La Scala, Milan, from 1887, as Thomas' Ophelia and in operas by Samara and Mascagni. She was famous as an interpreter of the role of Carmen. She created roles in Massenet's *La navarraise* (1894) and *Sapho* (1897).

Calvisius, Seth (b Gorsleben, Thuringia, 21 Feb 1556; d Leipzig, 24 Nov 1615), German scholar and musician. Cantor of St Thomas's School and music director of its church from 1594, and thus a predecessor of Bach. Wrote several learned books on music, compiled collections of vocal music and comp. motets, hymns, etc.

Calvocoressi, M(ichael) D(imitri) (b Marseilles, 2 Oct 1877; d London, 1 Feb 1944), English music critic of Greek descent. Studied in Paris, partic. music and languages, lectured there on music at the École des Hautes Études Sociales, 1905–14, and then settled in London, becoming naturalized. His books incl. studies of music criticism, Mussorgsky, etc.

Calzabigi, Raniero da (b Livorno, 23 Dec 1714; d Naples, Jul 1795), Italian literary critic and author. Lived in Paris and Vienna for a time. Wrote the libs. for Gluck's *Orfeo, Alceste* and *Paride ed Elena*. *See also* **Finta giardiniera** (Anfossi and Mozart), **Orfeo ed Euridice** (Bertoni) and **Orpheus og Euridice** (Naumann).

Cambert, Robert (b Paris, *c* 1628; d London, *c* Feb 1677), French composer. Studied harpsichord with Chambonnières, was organist at the church of Saint-Honoré in Paris and superintendent of the queen's music. He was ousted by Lully and sent to live in London in 1673. His *Pomone* (1671) was the 1st French opera to be staged in public. Most of his music is lost.

Works incl. comedy with music *La Muette ingrate* (1658); a pastoral perf. at Issy and another, *Les Peines et les plaisirs de l'amour* (1671); operas *Ariane, ou Le Mariage de Bacchus, Pomone* (1674); a trio for Brécourt's *Jaloux invisible*; *airs à boire*.

Cambiale di matrimonio, La (*The Marriage Contract*), opera by Rossini (lib. by G. Rossi, based on a comedy by C. Federici), prod. Venice, Teatro San Moisè, 3 Nov 1810. Rossini's 1st opera to be perf.

Cambini, Giovanni Giuseppe (b Livorno, 13 Feb 1746; d ? Paris, 1825), Italian violinist and composer. Pupil of Martini at Bologna. In 1770 he settled in Paris, where at first he had great success as both comp. and cond.

Later his fortunes declined, and he died in poverty.

Works incl. 19 operas, e.g. *Alcide* (1782), ballets, an oratorio, 60 symphs., 144 4tets and 5tets; church music.

Camden, Archie (Archibald) (b Newark, 9 Mar 1888; d Wheathampstead, Herts., 16 Feb 1979), English bassoonist. He became a principal with the Hallé Orch. in 1914, after study in Manchester, and joined the BBC SO in 1933; remained until 1946 and after a season with the RPO became a freelance. Well known as a soloist and an influential teacher (prof. at RMCM 1914–33, later at RCM).

Camera, Concerto da (It. = chamber
Camera, Sonata da ∫ concerto or sonata), a secular work written for perf. at home or at concerts, as distinct from a concerto or sonata *da chiesa* = for the church.

Camerata (It. = society), a group of intellectuals meeting for cultural exchanges, in particular one at Florence under Count Giovanni de' Bardi in *c* 1573–87 and strongly influenced by Girolamo Mei's research into ancient Gk. music. The earliest operas seem to have emerged from their deliberations.

Cameriera (It. = chambermaid), a term used in It. opera, esp. of the 17th and 18th cents., in the same way as *servetta* (servant-girl), for soubrette parts.

Cameron, Basil (b Reading, 18 Aug 1884; d Leominster, 26 Jun 1975), English conductor. He studied in Berlin 1902–6, and as cond. in Torquay adopted, but only up to the war, the name Basil Hindenburg in an attempt to negate the usual prejudice against conds. with Eng. names. Engaged with seaside orchs. 1912–30, then cond. orchs. in San Francisco and Seattle before return to Britain in 1938. He assisted Wood, then Boult, with the Prom. Concerts from 1940; in Sep 1945 he conducted the 1st Eur. perf. of Schoenberg's pf. concerto.

Camilla (Bononcini). *See* **Trionfo di C.**

Cammarano, Salvatore (b Naples, 19 Mar 1801; d Naples, 17 Jul 1852), Italian librettist. He wrote var. stage pieces before lib. for Donizetti's *Lucia di Lammermoor* in 1835; other libs. for him incl. *Roberto Devereux*, *Belisario* and *Poliuto*. His first lib. for Verdi was *Alzira*, in 1841; later *La battaglia di Legnano*, *Luisa Miller* and most of *Il Trovatore*. Also wrote the libs. for Pacini's *Saffo* and Mercadante's *La Vestale* and *Medea*.

Campagnoli, Bartolomeo (b Cento di Ferrara, 10 Sep 1751; d Neustrelitz, 7 Nov 1827), Italian violinist and composer. Pupil of Nardini; worked in It., Ger. and Paris; wrote concertos, sonatas, duets, etc. for vln.; fl. music; caprices for vla., etc.; also an important work on vln. playing, *Metodo per violino*.

Campana Sommersa, La (*The Sunken Bell*), opera by Respighi (lib. by C. Guastalla, after G. Hauptmann's *Die versunkene Glocke*); 1923–7, fp Hamburg, 24 Nov 1928.

Campanella, La, the 3rd of Liszt's *Études d'exécution transcendante d'après Paganini* for pf., comp. in 1838, already used by him in 1831–2 for the *Grande Fantaisie de bravoure sur la Clochette*. The theme is that of the finale of Paganini's vln. concerto in B min., op. 7, a rondo in which harmonics are combined with a bell.

Campanini, Cleofonte (b Parma, 1 Sep 1860; d Chicago, 19 Dec 1919), Italian conductor. Made his 1st appearance at Parma in 1883 and the same year went to USA, where he spent most of his life, apart from visits to It., Eng. and S. Amer. Cond. Manhattan Opera NY, 1906–9; Chicago Opera Co., 1910–19. Married Eva Tetrazzini, the sister of Louisa T. He cond. the premières of *Adriana Lecouvreur* (1902) and *Madama Butterfly* (1904).

Campanini, Italo (b Parma, 30 Jun 1845; d Corcagno nr. Parma, 22 Nov 1896), Italian tenor, brother of prec. Debut Parma 1863, as Gennaro; London debut 1872, same role. He was the 1st Italian Lohengrin (Bologna, 1871) and the 1st Don José in London and NY (1878). He sang Gounod's Faust in the inaugural perf. at the NY Met (1883) and was heard also in the *Faust* settings by Boito and Berlioz.

Campenhout, François van (b Brussels, 5 Feb 1779; d Brussels, 24 Apr 1848), Belgian tenor and composer. Sang in Belg., Hol. and Fr. until 1827. During the 1830 revolution he wrote the Belg. nat. anthem, *La Brabançonne*.

Works incl. operas *Grotius, Le Passepartout, L'Heureux Mensonge*; church music; choruses; songs.

Campian, Thomas *See* **Campion.**

Campiello, Il (*The Square*), opera by Wolf-Ferrari (lib. by M. Ghisalberti, after Goldoni), prod. Milan, La Scala, 12 Feb 1936.

Campioli (real name **Antonio Gualandi**) (b Germany), 18th-cent. Italian castrato alto. Made his operatic debut in Berlin, 1708, and sang in Handel's operas in London, 1731–2; he sang Argone in the fp of *Sosarme* (1732).

Campion (or Campian), Thomas (b London, bap 12 Feb 1567; d London, buried 1 Mar 1620), English physician, poet and composer. Was sent to Cambridge in 1581 and being a lawyer at 1st entered Gray's Inn in 1586; (?) took part in the siege of Rouen in 1591 and soon afterwards practised medicine in London. He pub. a 1st collection of airs to the lute with Rosseter in 1601 and 4 more followed between *c* 1613 and 1617, all the words of the songs being his own. In 1613 he pub. a book on counterpoint, and wrote the poetry for *Songs of Mourning* on the death of Prince Henry, set by Coprario. He also pub. poems and a book on poetry. His poem *Neptune's Empire* was set for chorus and orch. by Ernest Walker. Poems set as songs by W. Busch.

Works incl. 5 books of airs to the lute (over 100) and 3 separate earlier songs; songs for the prod. of 4 masques, 1607–13, incl. *The Mask of Flowers*

Campioni, Carlo Antonio (b Lunéville, 16 Nov 1720; d Florence, 12 Apr 1788), Italian composer. In the service of the Grand Duke of Tuscany at Florence and the King of Sardinia.

Wrote a Requiem and other church music, trio sonatas, duets for 2 vlns. and for vln. and cello; keyboard music.

Campora, Giuseppe (b Tortona, 30 Sep 1923), Italian tenor. Debut Bari, 1949, as Rodolfo. In 1951 he joined Serafin at La Scala and sang as guest all over Europe and N. and S. Amer. in the lyric repertory; from 1952 at Buenos Aires; NY Met debut 1954, as Rodolfo. Other roles incl. Radames, Enzo, Pinkerton and Gabriele Adorno.

Camporese, Violante (b Rome, 1785; d Rome, 1839), Italian soprano. She sang at La Scala 1817–30, in the fps of operas by Morlacchi, Gyrowetz and Rossini (*Bianca e Falliero*, 1819). At the King's Theatre, London, she was heard as Susanna, Donna Anna and Dorabella and in the 1st local perfs. of Rossini's *La gazza ladra*, *Mosè* and *Otello*. Retired 1829.

Campra, André (b Aix-en-Provence, bap. 4 Dec 1660; d Versailles, 29 Jun 1744), French composer of Italian descent. He held var. provincial organist's posts and settled in Paris in 1694, when he was app. music director at Notre-Dame, where his motets soon attracted large congregations; but he became equally famous as a stage comp.

Works incl. operas and opera-ballets *L'Europe galante* (1697), *Le Carnaval de Venise* (1699), *Hésione, Tancrède, Iphigénie en Tauride* (with Desmarets, 1704), *Alcine, Hippodamie* (1708), *Les Festes vénitiennes, Idoménée* (1712), *Le Jaloux trompé, Achille et Déidamie* (1735), etc.; pasticcios *Frag-*

ments de Lully and *Télémaque* (the latter with pieces by Charpentier, Colasse, Desmarets, Marais and Rebel sen.); entertainments *Amaryllis, Les Festes de Corinthe, Le Génie de la Bourgogne, Les Noces de Vénus* (1740), etc.; a Mass, cantatas, motets and psalms.

Canary (Eng.), also Canarie or Canaries, a dance in quick triple time with a dotted rhythm, possibly originating from the Canary Islands.

Cancan, a lively dance of a risqué nature fashionable in Paris from *c* the middle of the 19th cent. It is in very animated 2–4 time.

Cancel (Amer.) = Natural, ♮ .

Canción (Span.) = Song.

Cancionero (Span.), a song-book.

Cancrizans (from Lat. *cancer* = crab) = crab-wise, a term used for the device of repeating a musical phrase or theme backwards, note for note. 'Canon cancrizans' is a canon in which one part or more proceed normally while another one or more go backwards. In serial music the reversed form of the series is often called cancrizans.

Candeille, Amélie-Julie (b Paris, 31 Jul 1767; d Paris, 4 Feb 1834), French actress, singer, pianist and composer. Made her debut as a singer at the Paris Opéra in 1782, but left to become an actress. 10 years later sang in her 1st opera, for which she had written both words and music.

Works incl. operas *La Belle Fermière* (1792), *Bathilde ou le Duc* and *Ida ou l'Orpheline* (1807); chamber music; piano music; songs.

Candeille, Pierre Joseph (b Estaires, 8 Dec 1744; d Chantilly, 24 Apr 1827), French singer and composer, father of prec.

Wrote operas, incl. *Castor et Pollux* (1791); ballets, pantomime, incid. music.

Candide, comic operetta by Bernstein (lib. by L. Hellman, after Voltaire), prod. Boston, 29 Oct 1956; rev. 1973 and prod. NY, City Opera, 13 Oct 1982.

Caniglia, Maria (b Naples, 5 May 1905; d Rome, 16 Apr 1979), Italian soprano. Debut Turin, 1930, Chrysothemis. La Scala 1930–51; appeared with the co. at CG in 1950. NY Met 1938 as Aida. Other Verdi roles incl. all 3 Leonoras, Amelia and Alice Ford. Also sang Tosca, Fedora and Respighi's Lucrezia.

Canis, Corneille (Cornelis de Hond) (b ? Antwerp; d Prague, 15 Feb 1561), Flemish composer. Choirmaster of Charles V's imp. chapel in the Netherlands from 1548, later chaplain to the Emperor Ferdinand in Prague. Wrote church music, *chansons*, etc.

Cannabich, (Johann) Christian (b Mannheim, bap. 28 Dec 1731; d Frankfurt, 20 Jan 1798), German violinist, conductor and composer. Pupil of Stamitz in Mannheim and Jommelli in Rome, became *Konzertmeister* of the Mannheim orch. in 1758 and director of instrumental music in 1774. From 1778 he worked in Munich. His cond. was admired by Mozart, who taught his daughter Rosa C. in 1777 and wrote a pf. sonata for her.

Works incl. operas, ballets, e.g. *Renaud et Armide* (1768), symphs., chamber music.

Cannon, Philip (b Paris, 21 Dec 1929), English composer. Studied with Imogen Holst and later at the RCM with Gordon Jacob (comp.) and Pierre Tas (vln). This was followed by some study with Hindemith. After a period of lecturing at Sydney Univ. he returned to the RCM in 1952.

Works incl. string 4tet (1964) and other chamber music, vocal and choral music incl. *Lord of Light*, oratorio for soloists, chorus and orch. (1980), pf. comps.

Canon (Gk. *kanón* = rule) a polyphonic comp., or section of a comp., in which one part is imitated by one or more others which enter successively, so that the entries overlap (*see* illustration (*a*)).

If the imitation is exact the canon is termed 'strict'; if it is modified by the addition or omission of accidentals it is 'free as to intervals'. A canon may proceed (1) by inversion, with one part going up where the other goes down and *vice versa* (*see* illustration (*b*)); (2) by augmentation, with one part in notes twice or more the length of the other (*see* illustration (*c*)); (3) by diminution, with one part in notes half or less the length of the other; (4) by retrograde motion (*canon cancrizans*), with one part going backwards while the other goes forward. Var. combinations of these forms are also possible. A canon may be accomp. by one or more independent parts. Two or more canons can occur simultaneously.

Cantabile (It. = song-like, songful, singable). The direction is usually placed against phrases in instrumental rather than vocal music where the comp. desires an expressive delivery.

Cantata (It. = a sung piece). The definition has become narrowed in modern times to

(a)

f sempre legato

f

Clementi, *Piano Sonata in G major*

CANON

(b)

sempre legato dolce

con espress.

Clementi

CANON

(c)

Purcell, *Sonata no. 6*

CANON

short vocal works, sacred or secular, and for single voices or chorus, with instrumental accompaniment.

Work by Stravinsky for sop., tenor, female chorus and inst. ens. (7 texts from anon. Eng. lyrics, incl. *Tomorrow shall be my dancing day* and *Westron wind*); comp. 1951–2, fp Los Angeles, 11 Nov 1952.

Cantata Academica, work by Britten for soloists, chorus and orch., comp. 1959 on Latin texts, for the 500th anniv. of Basle Univ; fp Basle, 1 Jul 1960.

Cantata Misericordium, work by Britten for tenor, bar., small chorus and chamber orch. (text by P. Wilkinson), comp. for the cent. of the International Red Cross, fp Geneva, 15 Sep 1963, cond. Ansermet.

Cantata on the death of the Emperor Joseph II, work by Beethoven for soloists, chorus and orch. (text by S.A. Averdonk). The cantata was commissioned from B. in Bonn after the death of the Emperor on 20 Feb 1790, but was not perf. The MS. was probably seen by Haydn, on his return from his 1st visit to England, and led to his offering B. lessons in Vienna. Not perf. until 1884, the cantata contains an anticipation of a theme from the last scene of *Fidelio*.

Cantata Profana (*A kilenc csodaszarvas: The Nine Enchanted Stags*), work by Bartók for tenor, bar., chorus and orch., comp. 1930, fp in BBC concert, 25 May 1934.

Cantelli, Guido (b Novara, 27 Apr 1920; d Paris, 24 Nov 1956), Italian conductor. Studied at the Milan Cons. and, after escaping from a Ger. prison camp and a Fascist prison hospital in the war, began to cond. concerts with the Scala orch. in Milan. He then quickly made his way in It. and abroad as a cond. whose gifts were second only to Toscanini's. He cond. the NBC SO from 1949 and the Philharmonia, London, from 1951. He was killed in an air accident.

Canteloube (de Malaret), (Marie) Joseph (b Annonay, Ardèche, 21 Oct 1879; d Paris, 4 Nov 1957), French composer. Studied with d'Indy at the Schola Cantorum in Paris. In 1900 he began to collect and study French folksong, particularly of Auvergne, of which he pub. several collections. Lecturer on French music and folksong from 1923. He is best known for his folksong arrs. *Chants d'Auvergne* (4 vols., pub. 1923–30).

Works incl. operas *Le Mas* (1910–13) and *Vercingetorix* (prod. 1933); symph. poems *Vers la princesse lointaine* and *Lauriers*; *Pièces françaises* for pf. and orch.; *Poème* for vln. and orch.; *Dans la montagne* for vln.

and pf.; songs with orch. and with pf.; many folksong arrs.

Canterbury Pilgrims, The, opera by Stanford (lib. by G.A. à Beckett, after Chaucer), prod. London, Drury Lane Theatre, 28 Apr 1884.

Canti di Prigionia (*Songs of Captivity*), work by Dallapiccola for chorus, 2 pfs., 2 harps and perc. (texts by Mary Stuart, Boethius and Savanarola); comp. 1938–41 in protest against It. fascism, fp Rome, 11 Dec 1941.

Canticle. A category of sacred song, usually Biblical, used in Christian church services; incl. the Te Deum, Benedictus, Magnificat, Nunc Dimittis.

Canticles, series of 5 works by Britten: no. 1 *My beloved is mine* (text by F. Quarles), for high voice and pf., fp Aldeburgh, 1 Nov 1947; no. 2 *Abraham and Isaac* (text from Chester miracle play), for alto, tenor and pf., fp Nottingham, 21 Jan 1952; no. 3 *Still falls the rain* (text by E. Sitwell), for tenor, horn and pf., fp London, 28 Jan 1955; no. 4 *The Journey of the Magi* (text by T.S. Eliot), for countertenor, ten., bar. and pf., fp Aldeburgh, 26 Jun 1971; no. 5 *The Death of Narcissus* (text by Eliot), for tenor and harp., fp Schloss Elmau, 15 Jan 1975.

Canticum Sacrum (ad honorem Sancti Marci nominis), work by Stravinsky, in honour of St Mark's, Venice, for tenor, bar., chorus and orch.; comp. 1955, fp Venice, 13 Sep 1956.

Cantigas (Span. = canticles), Span. sacred songs for single voice of the 13th cent., mostly in honour of the Virgin Mary, allied in form to the Fr. Virelai and the It. Lauda.

Cantilena (It.) = a sustained, flowing melodic line, esp. when sung *legato* or played in the manner of such singing.

Cantillation, chanting in unison in the Jewish synagogue service.

Cantino (It.), the E string of the vln.

Cantiones Sacrae (Lat. = Sacred Songs), a title often given to collections of Latin motets in the 16th and 17th cents.

Canto (It. = song), in instrumental as much as in vocal music usually the part of a comp. which has the chief melody. The direction *marcato il canto* indicates that such a melody is to be emphasized.

Canto carnascialesco (It. carnival song), a Florentine part-song of the 15th–16th cents. with secular, often ribald, words, sung in carnival processions.

Canto fermo (It.). *See* **Cantus firmus.**

Cantor (Lat. = singer), a church singer, esp. the leader or director of a choir in a Lutheran church (e.g. Bach at Leipzig) or in a synagogue.

Cantoris. In English cathedrals and in churches where the choir is divided, the cantoris side is that on the north of the chancel, near the stall of the cantor or precentor, the other being the *Decani* side.

Cantus firmus (Lat. lit. 'fixed song'), a preexisting melody chosen by a comp. to envelop in contrapuntal parts of his own, either for exercise or for the prod. of a comp.

Canyons aux étoiles, Des (*From the Canyons to the Stars*), work by Messiaen for pf., horn and orch., comp. 1970–74, fp NY, 20 Nov 1974.

Canzone, Canzona (It. = song, ballad). (1) A part-song in the style of a madrigal but lighter in character and less elaborately polyphonic.

(2) An instrumental piece in a polyphonic style, orig. *canzone francese*.

Canzonet (from It. *canzonetta* = little song), light songs written in Eng. round about 1600, either for several voices with or without insts. or for a single voice with lute accomp. Later simply a song in England, e.g. Haydn's Eng. Canzonets).

Canzonetta (It. = little song), often synonymous with Canzone in 16th–17th-cent. It.; later a light song or short and simple air in an opera, etc.

Canzoniere (It.), a song-book.

Capecchi, Renato (b Cairo, 6 Nov 1923), Italian baritone. Debut Reggio Emilia, 1949, Amonasro. NY Met 1951 as Germont. CG 1962 and 1973 as Melitone and Rossini's Bartolo. Other roles incl. Dandini, Gianni Schicchi, Don Giovanni and Mozart's Figaro. Glyndebourne 1977 and 1980, Falstaff.

Capella, Martianus (b ? Madaura, N. Africa), 4th–5th-cent. philosopher. His *De musica* is the ninth and last book of his *De nuptiis Mercurii et Philologiae*. His treatise, deriving in part from Varro and Quintilian, had considerable influence on later medieval theorists.

Capirola, Vincenzo (b Brescia, 1474; d after 1548), Italian lutenist and composer. His collection of lute music (*c* 1517) is among the most important early MSS. of the repertory.

Caplet, André (b Le Havre, 23 Nov 1878; d Paris, 22 Apr 1925), French conductor and composer, much influenced by Debussy, of several of whose works he completed the orch.

Works incl. symph. study *Le Masque de la Mort rouge* (after Poe, 1909); *Epiphanie* for cello and orch. (1923); Mass for unaccomp.

voices; *Le Miroir de Jésus* for voices, string 5tet and harp (1924); *Le Pie Jésus* for voice and org.; *Suite persane* for 10 wind instruments; *Conte fantastique* (after Poe) for harp and string 4tet (an arr. of *Le Masque de la Mort rouge*); *Sonata da chiesa* for vln. and org.; children's suite for pf. duet; song cycles *Prières*, *La Croix douloureuse*, *3 Fables de La Fontaine*, *5 Ballades françaises*. He orch Debussy's *Children's Corner* and cond. the fp of *Le Martyre de Saint Sébastien* (1911).

Capoul, Victor (b Toulouse, 27 Feb 1839; d Pujaudran-du-Gers, 18 Feb 1924), French tenor. Debut Paris, Opéra-Comique, 1861, in Adam's *Le Chalet*. In 1871 he sang for the 1st time in London and NY; CG from 1875, Met from 1883. Among his best roles were Wilhelm Meister, Otello, Meyerbeer's Robert and Gounod's Roméo. Stage manager, Paris Opéra, from 1897.

Cappuccilli, Piero (b Trieste, 9 Nov 1929), Italian baritone. Debut Milan, 1957; La Scala from 1964. NY Met debut 1960 as Germont. CG from 1967 as Renato, Iago and Boccanegra; sang Posa at Salzburg in 1975. Chicago from 1969.

Capriccio (It. = whim), a name given to var. types of composition at different times in the 17th and 18th cent. to animated pieces in a fugal style, but not strictly fugues in form; by Bach to a harpsichord piece in several movements on the departure of his brother Johann Jakob; *c* from the middle of the 18th cent. to studies for the vln. (e.g. Paganini's); later still to fantasies for pf. on well-known themes; last of all to short pieces in a humorous or whimsical manner.

Capriccio, opera by R. Strauss (lib. by C. Krauss and the comp.), prod. Munich, Staatsoper, 28 Oct 1942. An elegant 'conversation piece'.

Work by Janáček in 4 movts. for pf. left hand and orch.; comp. 1926, fp Prague, 2 Mar 1928.

Work by Stravinsky for pf. and orch.; comp. 1929, fp Paris, 6 Dec 1929, cond. Ansermet.

Capriccio espagnol (*Span.* C.), orchestral work by Rimsky-Korsakov, written as a display piece for the St Petersburg Orch., finished 4 Aug and perf. St Petersburg, 17 Dec 1887. It contains brilliant solo parts for most of the principal instruments and for the brass in groups. It was orig. intended to be for vln. and orch., a companion-piece to Rimsky-Korsakov's *Rus. Fantasy*.

Capriccio italien (*It.* C.), orchestral work by Tchaikovsky, comp. during a visit to Rome in 1880 and 1st perf. Moscow, 18 Dec 1880.

Caprichos, Los, fantasia for orch. by Henze; comp. 1963, fp Duisburg, 6 Apr 1967.

Caproli (or Caprioli), Carlo (b Rome, *c* 1615; d Rome, *c* 1693), Italian violinist and composer. Was brought to Paris by Cardinal Mazarin and prod. the opera *Le nozze di Peleo e Teti* there in 1654. He wrote the oratorio *Davidde prevaricante* in 1683.

Capuana, Franco (b Fano, 29 Sep 1894; d Naples, 10 Dec 1969), Italian conductor. His early career was at Naples and Brescia; cond. at La Scala 1937–40, with fps of works by Refice and Bianchi, and took the co. to CG in 1946 (music dir. La Scala, 1949–52). He was noted for his wide repertory and gave 1st local perfs. of operas by Janáček and Hindemith, revivals of Verdi and Bellini and works by Strauss and Wagner. He died while conducting Rossini's *Mosè*.

Capuana, Maria (b Fano, 1891; d Cagliari, 22 Feb 1955), Italian contralto, sister of the prec. Debut Naples, 1918, as Urbain. From 1920 she was well known in Wagner roles: Brangaene at Turin, Ortrud and Fricka at La Scala (debut 1922). She appeared at Buenos Aires in 1925. Other roles incl. Herodias and Amneris.

Capuleti e i Montecchi, I (*The Capulets and Montagues*), opera by Bellini (lib. by F. Romani, based on Shakespeare's sources for *Romeo and Juliet*), prod. Venice, Teatro La Fenice, 11 Mar 1830.

Cara, Marchetto (b Verona, *c* 1470; d ? Mantua, after 1525), Italian lutenist and composer. In service at the ducal court of Mantua, 1495–1525. Wrote *frottole* and other songs.

Caractacus, cantata for solo voices, chorus and orch. by Elgar, op. 35 (lib. by H.A. Acworth), comp. in 1898 and prod. Leeds Festival, 5 Oct 1898.

Music by Arne for a dramatic poem by W. Mason (pub. 1759), perf. London CG, 6 Dec 1776.

Caradori-Allan (née de Munck), Maria (Caterina Rosalbina) (b Milan, 1800; d Surbiton, Surrey, 15 Oct 1865), Italian soprano. Was taught music entirely by her mother, whose name she took, and after a tour in Fr. and Ger. made her debut in London in 1822 as Cherubino. Other roles incl. Rosina, Zerlina and Amina. She married in Eng. and appeared also at concerts and festivals, incl. the fp of Mendelssohn's *Elijah* in 1846.

Carafa (di Colobrano), Michele Enrico (b Naples, 17 Nov 1787; d Paris, 26 Jul 1872), Italian composer. On the failure of his 1st

opera he enlisted in the bodyguard of Murat, then king of Naples, took part in the Russian campaign in 1812 and was decorated by Napoleon, after whose fall he returned to music. He prod. operas not only in Italy but in Vienna and Paris, where he settled in 1827 and became very popular. Prof. of composition at the Paris Cons., 1840–58.

Works incl. *c* 35 operas, e.g. *Il fantasma* (1805), *Il vascello d'occidente, Gabriella di Vergy* (1816), *Ifigenia, Berenice, Le Solitaire, La Violette* (1826), *La Fiancée de Lammermoor* and *Elisabetta in Derbyshire* (after Scott, 1818), *Masaniello* (competing with Auber's *Muette de Portici,* 1827), *La Prison d'Édimbourg* (after Scott's *Heart of Midlothian*), *Jeanne d'Arc* (after Schiller, 1821).

Carattaco, opera by J.C. Bach (lib. by G.G. Bottarelli), perf. London, King's Theatre, 14 Feb 1767.

Cardew, Cornelius (b Winchcombe, Glos., 7 May 1936; d London, 13 Dec 1981), English composer and pianist. Studied at the RAM with, among others, Howard Ferguson (comp.). In 1958 he went to Cologne to study electronic music, also working with Stockhausen until 1960. Cardew belonged at one time to the *avant-garde* school, whose ideas are much influenced by Cage, but later espoused Marxist principles and pub. a book, *Stockhausen Serves Imperialism* (1974). His works have been widely perf. in Europe.

Works incl. *Octet 1959; Autumn 60* for orch.; *A Bun* for orch.; *The East is Red* for vln. and pf. (1972) *The Old and the New,* for sop., chorus and orch. (1973); pf. music.

Cardillac, opera by Hindemith (lib. by F. Lion, based on E.T.A. Hoffmann's story *Das Fräulein von Scudéri*), prod. Dresden, 9 Nov 1926; rev. vers. prod. Zurich, 20 Jun 1952.

Cardoso, Manuel (b Fronteira nr. Portalegre, bap. 11 Dec 1566; d Lisbon, 24 Nov 1650), Portuguese monk, organist and composer. Studied at the seminary of Evora and became choirmaster of the cathedral there. Joined the Carmelite monastery at Lisbon in 1588 and became its music director.

Works incl. Masses, motets, Magnificats and other church music.

Cardus, (John Frederick) Neville (b Manchester, 3 Apr 1888; d London, 28 Feb 1975), English critic. Began to write for the *Daily Citizen* at Manchester in 1913 and in 1917 joined the *Manchester Guardian* as asst. critic to Samuel Langford, whom he succeeded in 1927. He wrote on cricket as well as music, but not on the latter in London until 1931, ed. Langford's writings and pub. a book on *Ten Composers* as well as several on cricket. In 1939–47 he lived in Australia. In 1948 he settled in London. Knighted 1967.

Carelli, Emma (b Naples, 12 May 1877; d Montefiascone nr. Rome, 17 Aug 1928), Italian soprano. Debut Altamura, 1895, in Mercadante's *La Vestale*. She appeared widely in Italy and in 1899 sang Desdemona at La Scala, opposite Tamagno; 1900 1st Italian Tatyana. She appeared as guest at Rio, Buenos Aires and all over Europe; managed the Teatro Costanzi, Rome, and sang there in 1912 as the 1st Italian Elektra. She was also renowned as Zazà and Iris.

Carena, Maria (b Turin, 1891; d Turin, 9 Oct 1966), Italian soprano. Debut Turin, 1917, *Trovatore* Leonora; she soon sang at Rome, Naples and Buenos Aires. La Scala debut 1922, as Suor Angelica; remained until 1932 and sang in the 1st prod. of Boito's *Nerone*, 1924. One of her best roles was Spontini's Vestale (Rome, 1932).

Carestini, Giovanni (b Ancona, *c* 1705; d *c* 1760), Italian castrato alto. 1st appeared in Rome, 1721, and sang in Handel's operas in London, 1733–5, creating roles in *Arianna in Creta*, *Ariodante* and *Alcina*.

Carey, Henry (b ? Yorkshire *c* 1689; d London, 5 Oct 1743), English poet, composer and dramatist. Pupil of Roseingrave and Geminiani. Wrote libs. for Lampe's operas *The Dragon of Wantley*, *Margery* and *Amelia*.

Works incl. cantatas and songs to his own words; ballad operas *The Contrivances* (1729), *A Wonder or the Honest Yorkshireman* (1735), *Nancy, or the Parting Lovers* (1739), etc.; songs for Vanbrugh and Cibber's *The Provok'd Husband*.

Carillon, a set of bells hung in a church steeple or specially built tower, controlled by a keyboard below and played like an org. on manuals and pedals. Carillons are found partic. in the Netherlands.

Carissimi, Giacomo (b Marino nr. Rome, bap. 18 Apr 1605; d Rome, 12 Jan 1674), Italian composer. *Maestro di cappella* at Assisi in 1628–9; then went to Rome, where he held a similar post at the church of Sant' Apollinare attached to the Ger. Coll. He cultivated the oratorio and cantata in their early stages.

Works incl. Masses, motets; *Lauda Sion* and *Nisi Dominus* for 8 voices; oratorios *History of Job*, *Baltazar*, *Abraham and Isaac*, *Jephtha*, (*c* 1650), *The Last Judgment*, *Jonah*; sacred cantatas; vocal duets.

Carl Rosa Opera Company, The Royal, founded by Carl Rosa in 1873 for the perf. of opera in Eng. (*See* **Rosa, Carl**).

Carlton, Nicholas (I), English 16th-cent. composer. Two keyboard works are in the Mulliner Book.

Carlton, Nicholas (II) (b *c* 1570; d Boeley, Worcs., 1630), English composer and friend of Thomas Tomkins. A few keyboard works survive, one of which is an *In nomine* for keyboard duet (four hands at one keyboard).

Carlton, Richard (b *c* 1558; d *c* 1638), English composer. Educ. at Cambridge; became vicar at St Stephen's Church, Norwich, and minor canon at the cathedral. Pub. a book of madrigals in 1601 and contrib. to *The Triumphes of Oriana*.

Carlyle, Joan (b Wirral, 6 Apr 1931), English soprano. Debut CG 1955, as Frasquita; remained until 1969 as Pamina, Sophie, Arabella, Desdemona and Tippett's Jenifer. Glyndebourne 1965, Mozart's Countess. She appeared as guest at Munich and Vienna and recorded Nedda with Karajan.

Carmen, opera by Bizet (lib. by H. Meilhac and L. Halévy, based on the story by Mérimée), prod. Paris, Opéra-Comique, 3 Mar 1875.

Carmen, Johannes (*fl.* Paris, *c* 1400–20), French composer later praised by Martin le Franc. Of his comps. only three motets survive.

Carmina Burana, a 13th-cent. collection of Latin poems and other material, of Bavarian origin. Some of the poems have been provided with music, but the notation is in neumes which cannot be read except by comparing them with other MSS.

A setting of the poems by Carl Orff for chorus, orch. and soloists (1937), fp 8 Jun 1937, Frankfurt. See also **Catulli Carmina** and **Trionfo di Afrodite**.

Carnaval (*Carnival*), suite of pf. pieces on the notes A. S. (Ger. Es = E♭ ; also As = A♭) C. H. (Ger. = B♮) by Schumann, op. 9, the letters representing the only musical ones in Schumann's surname and the town of Asch in Bohemia, the home of Ernestine von Fricken, with whom he was in love in 1834–5, when he wrote the work. She is alluded to in the piece entitled *Estrella*; other persons referred to are Clara Wieck in *Chiarina*, Chopin and Paganini under their own names, and Schumann himself in his 2 different imaginary characters of *Florestan* and *Eusebius*.

Ballet on Schumann's music, orch. by Glazunov and others (choreog. by Fokin), prod. Paris, Opéra, 4 Jun 1910.

Carnaval des animaux, Le (*The Carnival of the Animals*), suite ('grand zoological fantasy') by Saint-Saëns for chamber orch. with 2 pfs., privately perf. and not intended by the comp. to be pub. It contains a number of humorous musical allusions.

Carnaval romain, Le (*The Roman Carnival*), concert overture by Berlioz, op. 9, written in 1843 on material from the opera *Benvenuto Cellini* of 1834–8, fp Paris, 3 Feb 1844.

Carner, Mosco (b Vienna, 15 Nov 1904; d Cornwall, 3 Aug 1985), English critic and writer of Austrian origin. Studied at the New Vienna Cons. and musicology at the univ. under Adler, taking a Ph.D. degree there in 1928. He then became opera cond. in Vienna, Troppau and Danzig until 1933, when he settled in London, later becoming naturalized. He worked as critic, music correspondent to foreign journals and cond. and pub. books, incl. *A Study of 20th-cent. Harmony*, *Of Men and Music*, *Puccini, a Critical Biography*, *Alban Berg*, chapters on Schubert, Dvořák, etc.

Carnicer, Ramón (b Tárrega nr. Lérida, 24 Oct 1789; d Madrid, 17 Mar 1855), Spanish composer. Choir-boy at Urgel Cathedral, later went to Barcelona and in 1808 fled to Minorca when Spain was invaded by Fr. Later managed the It. opera at Barcelona and wrote It. works for it, into which he intro. Span. songs. In 1827 he was called by royal command to dir. the opera at Madrid.

Works incl. operas *Adele di Lusignano* (1819), *Elena e Constantino*, *Don Giovanni Tenorio, ossia Il convitato di pietra* (1822), *Elena e Malvina*, *Cristoforo Colombo* (1831), *Eufemio di Messina*, *Ismalia* (1838); *Missa solemnis*, 2 Requiems; symphs.

Carnival. (1) Concert overture by Dvořák, op. 92, comp. 1891 and forming, with *Amid Nature* and *Othello*, a cycle with thematic connections orig. called *Nature, Life and Love.*

(2) Suite by Schumann. *See* **Carnaval.**

Carol, orig. a round dance from France (*carole*), in which the participants sang a burden (formally a separate refrain) while dancing in a circle, alternating with stanzas sung by the leader while they remained still. In 15th-cent. Eng. it lost its orig. dance associations and became a polyphonic form, still charact. by the alternation of stanzas and burden, but frequently with a sacred text. It was only after the Reformation that the word lost its specifically formal connotation and became primarily a Christmas song, though even today common usage admits the possibility of secular carols and carols celebrating seasons other than Christmas.

Caron, Firminius (*fl.* 1450–80), ? Flemish composer, much praised by writers of the time. 5 Masses and nearly 20 *chansons* survive. He may have had some connection with the Burgundian court, although it has proved impossible to identify him firmly with any surviving documentation.

Caron (*née* Meuniez), **Rosa-Lucile** (b Monerville, Seine-et-Oise, 17 Nov 1857; d Paris, 9 Apr 1930), French soprano. Studied at the Paris Cons. where she became prof. of singing in 1902. Made her 1st stage appearance at Brussels in 1884 as Alice in *Robert le Diable*. Other roles incl. Sieglinde, Desdemona, Leonore and Reyer's Salammbô, which she created (1890).

Carosio, Margherita (b Genoa, 7 Jun 1908), Italian soprano. Debut Novi Ligure, 1926, as Lucia. She sang Musetta at CG in 1928 and was a regular at La Scala 1929–55 (debut as Oscar), where she sang in the fps of Mascagni's *Nerone* and Wolf-Ferrari's *Il Campiello*. At Salzburg she was heard as Rosina and Cimarosa's Carolina (1939, 1951); she returned to CG 1946 and 1950. Other roles incl. Violetta, Adina and Menotti's Amelia.

Caroso, Fabritio (b *c* 1530; d after 1605), Italian dancing master. Wrote 2 important treatises on dancing, *Il Ballarino* (1581) and *Nobiltà di Dame* (1600), both of which contain much music.

Caroubel, Pierre-Francisque (b Cremona; d Paris, summer 1611), French violinist and composer in the service of Henri III of Anjou from 1576. He wrote and harmonized numerous dance-tunes, including 78 from *Terpsichore musarum* by Michael Praetorius (1612).

Carpani, Giuseppe (Antonio) (b Villalbese nr. Como, 28 Jan 1752; d Vienna, 22 Jan 1825), Italian poet and writer on music. Settled in Vienna. Friend and biog. of Haydn. His book on the composer was plagiarised by Stendhal.

Carpenter, John Alden (b Park Ridge, Ill., 28 Feb 1876; d Chicago, 26 Apr 1951), American composer. Learnt music privately and studied with Paine while a student at Harvard Univ., and (briefly) with Elgar in Rome in 1906, later at Chicago with Bernhard Ziehn. Although a business man, he comp. much.

Works incl. ballets *Krazy-Kat* (prod. 1921), *Skyscrapers* and *The Birthday of the Infanta* (after Wilde, 1919); *Song of Faith* for chorus and orch.; symph., *Adventures in a Perambulator* (1915) and *Sea Drift* (after Whitman) for orch.; concertino for pf. and orch., vln. concerto; string 4tet (1927), pf. 5tet; many songs incl. *Gitanjali* cycle (Tagore).

Carré, work by Stockhausen for 4 orchs., 4 choruses, with 4 conds., fp Hamburg, 28 Oct 1960.

Carré, Marguerite (*née* **Marthe Giraud)** (b Cauborg, 16 Aug 1880; d Paris, 26 Dec 1947), French soprano. She sang at Nantes in 1899 and from 1902 appeared at the Paris Opéra-Comique. She created roles in operas by Charpentier, Leroux and Rabaud and was successful as Pamina, Butterfly, Manon and Mélisande but was alleged by the press to owe her career to her husband, Albert Carré, the dir. of the Opéra-Comique. They were divorced in 1924 but remarried on her retirement.

Carré, Michel (b Paris, 1819; d Argenteuil, 27 Jun 1872), French librettist. Collaborated with Jules Barbier (1822–1901) in texts for most French opera comps. of their time; Shakespeare, Goethe, Molière and Corneille were raided to provide material to suite the bourgeois tastes of contemporary audiences. *See* **Contes d'Hoffmann** (Offenbach), **Françoise de Rimini, Hamlet** and **Mignon** (Thomas), **Médecin malgré lui, Mireille, Reine de Saba** and **Roméo et Juliette** (Gounod), **Pardon de Ploëmerl** (Meyerbeer), **Pêcheurs de Perles** (Bizet).

Carreño, Teresa (b Caracas, 22 Dec 1853; d New York, 12 Jun 1917), Venezuelan pianist. Studied in NY and Paris, later under A. Rubinstein; made her debut in NY aged 9, later became an opera singer for a time, reappearing as pianist in 1889. She married Émile Sauret in 1872; later Giovanni Tagliapietra, d'Albert and second husband's brother; cond. opera in Venezuela.

Carreras, José (b Barcelona, 5 Dec 1936), Spanish tenor. Early roles incl. Verdi's Ismaele and Donizetti's Gennaro; London debut (concert) 1971 as Leicester in *Maria Stuarda*. NY debut with the City Opera as Pinkerton in 1972; Met as Cavaradossi, 1974. CG since 1974 as Alfredo, Nemorino and Oronte in *I Lombardi*; in 1984 he sang Andrea Chénier there.

Carrillo, Julián (b San Luis Potosí, 28 Jan 1875; d Mexico City, 9 Sep 1965), Mexican composer. Studied at the Nat. Cons. at Mex. City, gained a vln. prize and made further studies at Leipzig and Ghent Conss. Returning to Mexico in 1905, he was active as violinist and cond. as well as comp. He experimented in his later works with music

using small fractional divisions of the scale. Works incl. operas *Ossian* (1902), *Mexico in 1810* (1909) and *Xulitl* (1920, rev. 1947); 2 Masses, Requiem; 6 symphs., (1901–48), 3 suites, overture *8 de Septiembre*, symph. poem *Xochimilco* for orch.; fantasy for pf. and orch., concerto for fl., vln. and cello; 4 string 4tets, pf. 5tet, string 6tet; 4 vln. and pf. sonatas; 40 works in fractional scales, incl. *Ave Maria* for chorus, *Fantasía Sonido 13* for chamber orch., *Preludio a Cristobál Colón* for sop. and ens.

Carron, Arthur (b Swindon, 12 Dec 1900; d Swindon, 10 May 1967), English tenor. Debut London, 1929; sang with SW until 1935 as Tannhäuser, Manrico and Otello. NY Met 1936–46, as Siegmund, Tristan and Canio. He had appeared at CG in the 1930s and returned 1946–52. Sang widely as guest in N. and S. Amer.

Carrosse du Saint-Sacrement, Le (*The Coach of the Holy Sacrament*), opera by Lord Berners (lib. from Mérimée's play), prod. Paris, Théâtre des Champs-Élysées, 24 Apr 1924.

Carse, Adam (b Newcastle upon Tyne, 19 May 1878; d Gt Missenden, 2 Nov 1958), English music scholar and composer. Studied in Ger. and at the RAM. Asst. music master at Winchester Coll., 1909–22 and prof. at the RAM from 1923. He made a special study of instruments and orch. Left a collection of early wind instruments to the Horniman Museum.

Carter, Charles Thomas (b Dublin, *c* 1735; d London, 12 Oct 1804), Irish composer. Choir-boy at Christ Church Cathedral, Dublin, and organist at St Werburgh's Church there, 1751–69. He became very popular as a song-writer and settled in London in 1770. Prod. a comic opera, *Just in Time*, in 1792 and wrote lighter stage pieces, etc.

Carter, Elliott (b New York, 11 Dec 1908), American composer. Educ. at Harvard Univ., where he studied music with Piston; later a pupil of Nadia Boulanger in Paris. From 1960 to 1962 he was prof. of comp. at Yale Univ. and in 1960 was awarded the Pulitzer Prize. His music is many-layered and of extreme rhythmic complexity. Featured composer, Warsaw Autumn Festival 1986.

Works incl. STAGE: opera *Tom and Lily* (1934), ballets *Pocahontas* (1939) and *The Minotaur* (1947).

ORCH.: horn concerto (1937), *Prelude, Fanfare and Polka* (1938), symph. no.1 (1942, fp 1944), *Holiday Overture* (1944, fp

1948), *Variations* (1953–5, fp 1956), *Double Concerto* for pf., harpsichord and 2 chamber orchs. (1961), pf. concerto (1965, fp 1967), *Concerto for Orchestra* (1969, fp 1970), *A Symphony of 3 Orchestras* (1976, fp 1977), *Penthode* for chamber orch. (1985), *Fanfare* (1986).

CHORAL: *Tarantella* (1936), *To Music* (1937), *Heart not so Heavy as Mine* (1938), *The Defence of Corinth* (1941), *The Harmony of Morning* (1944), *Musicians Wrestle Everywhere* (1945), *Emblems* (1947).

SOLO VOCAL: *Warble for Lilac Time* for sop. and insts. (after Whitman, 1943, fp 1946), *A Mirror on Which to Dwell* for sop. and 9 players (6 settings of Elizabeth Bishop, 1975), *Syringa*, cantata for mezzo, bass and 11 insts. (1978), *In Sleep, in Thunder*, song cycle for tenor and 14 players (texts by Robert Lowell, 1981).

INST.: fl. sonata (1934), *Canonic Suite* for 4 saxophones (1939, rev. for 4 clar. 1956), *Pastorale* for ens. (1940), pf. sonata (1946), woodwind 5tet (1948), cello sonata (1948), *8 Etudes and a Fantasy* for woodwind 5tet (1950), 4 string 4tets (1951, 1959, 1971, 1986), sonata for, fl., ob., cello and harpsichord (1952), duo for vln. and pf. (1974), brass 5tet (1974), *Night Fantasies* for pf. (1980), *Triple Duo* for paired insts.: fl./clar., vln./cello, pf./perc. (1982), *Changes* for guitar (1983), *Esprit rude/Esprit doux* for fl. and clar. (60th birthday tribute to Pierre Boulez, 1985).

Cartier, Antoine (*fl.* Paris, 1552–88), French composer, organist of Saint-Séverin, Paris, 1570–88. His surviving works consist entirely of *chansons* for 3 and 4 voices.

Cartier, Jean-Baptiste (b Avignon, 28 May 1765; d Paris, 1841), French violinist and composer. Pupil of Viotti; held posts at court before and after the Revolution, during which he played in the Opéra orch. Comp. 2 operas, 2 symphs., vln. music and other works.

Caruso, Enrico (b Naples, 27 Feb 1873; d Naples, 2 Aug 1921), Italian tenor. Made his debut at Naples in 1894 and began to become famous when he sang in the prod. of Giordano's *Fedora* at Milan in 1898. He 1st sang in London, with Melba, in 1902 as the Duke of Mantua, and in Amer. in 1903 until 1920; sang Johnson in fp of *La Fanciulla del West*, NY Met, 1910. He appeared at the Met more than 600 times; through his many recordings became one of the most highly-paid opera singers of all time.

Caruso, Luigi (b Naples, 25 Sep 1754; d Perugia, 1822), Italian composer. Pupil of

Sala at Naples. *Maestro di cappella* at Perugia Cathedral from 1790. Comp. more than 60 operas, Masses, oratorios, cantatas, etc.

Carvalho, João de Sousa (b Estremoz, 22 Feb 1745; d Alentejo, 1798), Portuguese composer. Studied at Naples; taught at Lisbon on his return.

Works incl. 15 It. operas, e.g. *Perseo* (1779), *Testoride Argonauta* (1780), *Penelope* (1782), *L'Endimione* (1783); Masses and other church music with orch.; harpsichord sonatas.

Carvalho, Marie (Caroline Félix Miolan-) (b Marseilles, 31 Dec 1827; d Puys, 10 Jul 1895), French soprano. Studied under her father and at the Paris Cons.; debut in 1849 as Lucia di Lammermoor and was engaged by the Opéra-Comique in 1850. At the Théâtre-Lyrique she created Gounod's Marguerite, Baucis, Juliette and Mireille. She married in 1853 Léon Carvalho (1825–97), who later became manager of that theatre.

Carver, Robert (b *c* 1490; d after 1546), Scottish monk and composer. Canon of Scone Abbey.

Works incl. Masses (1 in 10 parts), motets (1 in 19 parts) and other church music.

Cary, Annie Louise (b Wayne, Me., 22 Oct 1841; d Norwalk, Conn., 3 Apr 1921), American contralto. Studied at Milan and later with Pauline Viardot. Made her debut in Copenhagen, 1869, as Azucena. Made her 1st appearance in London (CG 1870) as Maffio Orsini in *Lucrezia Borgia*. She was the 1st US Aida, 1873, and sang Ortrud there in 1877.

Cary, Tristram (Ogilvie) (b Oxford, 14 May 1925), English composer. He has been a pioneer in the perf. of electronic music in Brit. and has experimented with the concept of environmental sound; he founded his own electronic studio and has been an influential teacher at the RCM. Works incl. the cantata *Peccata mundi* (Cheltenham, 1972) and stage and film music.

Caryll, Ivan (actually Felix Tilkin) (b Liège, 12 May 1861; d New York, 29 Nov 1921), Belgian-American composer. Studied at the Liège Cons.

Works incl. operattas *The Duchess of Dantzic* (1903), *The Earl and the Girl, Our Miss Gibbs*.

Casadesus, Robert (Marcel) (b Paris, 7 Apr 1899; d Paris, 19 Sep 1972), French pianist and composer. As a boy he showed precocious ability. He studied at the Paris Cons., where he won prizes in 1913, 1919,

1921. He began his career as a concert pianist in 1922, and on the outbreak of World War II went to the USA, where he taught and lectured at Princeton Univ. From 1935 he was prof. at the Amer. Cons. at Fontainebleau, of which he became director in 1945. He comp. much for the pf., and was also a noted exponent of Fr. pf. music. He was often heard in Mozart's concertos.

Casali, Giovanni Battista (b Rome, c 1715; d Rome, 6 Jul 1792), Italian composer. *Maestro di cappella* of St John Lateran, 1759–92. Wrote much church music; also operas, e.g. *Candaspe* and *Antigona*; oratorios, e.g. *Santa Firmina, La Benedizione di Giacobb.*

Casals, Pablo (Pau) (b Vendrell, 29 Dec 1876; d Rio Piedras, Puerto Rico, 22 Oct 1973), Catalan cellist, conductor and composer. He studied at the Madrid Cons. and first appeared as a soloist in Paris in 1898. In 1905 he joined the pf. trio founded by Cortot and recorded the major trios of Schubert, Beethoven and Mendelssohn. In the early years of the cent. he did much to estab. the solo suites of Bach in the cellist's repertory. In 1919 he founded the Orquestra Pau Casals in Barcelona. After the Spanish Civil War he left Catalonia and made his home at Prades, in the Pyrenees, where he held an annual festival from 1950. He settled in Puerto Rico in 1956.

Works incl. oratorio *El Pessebre* (1943–60); church music; orch. works; works for cello and pf., vln. and pf.

Casanova, André (b Paris, 12 Oct 1919), French composer. Studied the 12-note technique with Leibowitz. Works incl. trio for fl., vla. and horn, pf. pieces, songs.

Casazza, Elvira (b Ferrara, 15 Nov 1887; d Milan, 26 Jan 1965), Italian mezzo. Debut Varese, 1909. La Scala 1915–42, as Amneris, Mistress Quickly and Ortrud, and in the fps of operas by Pizzetti and Zandonai. Buenos Aires 1916 and 1935; CG 1926 and 1931. Retired 1948 and taught at Pesaro and Rome.

Case, Anna (b Clinton, NJ, 29 Oct 1888; d New York, 7 Jan 1984), American soprano. NY Met from 1909 as Aida and Carmen; Feodor and Sophie in the 1st US perfs. of *Boris Godunov* and *Rosenkavalier* (both 1913).

Casella, Alfredo (b Turin, 25 Jul 1883; d Rome, 5 Mar 1947), Italian composer. Was sent to the Paris Cons. in 1896 to study pf. under Diémer and comp. under Fauré. He lived there until the 1914–18 war, when he went to Rome and taught pf. at the

Accademia di Santa Cecilia. In 1924 he founded, with d'Annunzio and Malipiero, an assoc. for the propagation of modern Italian music.

Works incl. operas *La donna serpente* (after Gozzi, 1928–31), *La favola d'Orfeo* (1932), *Il deserto tentato*; ballets *Il convento veneziano* and *La giara* (after Pirandello); 3 symphs., suite *Italia, Elegia eroica, Pagine di guerra, Introduzione, aria e toccata* (1933), *concerto* for orch.; *A notte alta, Partita* and *Scarlattiana* for pf. and orch.; concerto for vln., cello, org. and orch.; *Notte di maggio* for voice and orch. (1914); concerto and 5 pieces for string 4tet and other chamber music; cello and pf. sonata; many pf. works incl. sonatina and *Sinfonia, arioso e toccata*; 2 suites for pf. duet; numerous songs.

Caserta, Anthonello (Marotus) da (b ? Caserta, c 1365; d ? Naples, after 1410), Italian composer. His works include 8 Fr. songs, several in the most complex 3-voice style of the Ars Subtilior (*q.v.*), and 8 simpler It. songs, mostly in 2 voices.

Caserta, Philipottus da (b ? Caserta, c 1350; d after 1390), Italian composer and theorist. Comp. works for the Papal Court of Clement VII (1378–94) and for the Milanese court of Bernabò Visconti (1354–85) and probably taught Ciconia. Works incl. 1 Credo, 6 Fr. ballades (several in the most complex Ars Subtilior style), 3 treatises on music.

Casken, John (b Barnsley, 15 Jul 1949), English composer. He studied at Birmingham Univ. with John Joubert and Peter Dickinson. His work has been influenced by Polish music and serialism; lecturer, Durham Univ. from 1981. Featured composer at Bath Fest. 1980.

Works incl. pf. concerto (1980), *Masque* for ob., 2 horns and strings (1982); *Kagura* for 13 wind insts. (1973), *Amarantos* for 9 players (1978), *Fonteyn Fanfares* for 12 brass insts.; string 4tet (1982); *Ligatura* for organ.

Cassadó, Gaspar (b Barcelona, 30 Sep 1897; d Madrid, 24 Dec 1966), Spanish cellist, son of the composer Joaquín C. He made his 1st public appearance aged 9, and later studied with, among others, Casals. He joined Menuhin and Kentner in pf. trios. He was also a composer, mostly for strings and pf.

Cassandra, opera by Gnecchi (lib. by L. Illica), prod. Bologna, Teatro Comunale, 5 Dec 1905. In 1909 the It. critic Giovanni Tebaldini created a sensation by pointing out that Strauss's *Elektra*, which did not appear until that year, contained passages strikingly resembling Gnecchi's music.

Cassation, an 18th-cent. term, similar to divertimento and serenade, for a work in several movements suitable for open-air perf. The derivation of the word is uncertain.

Casse-Noisette (Tchaikovsky). See **Nutcracker.**

Cassily, Richard (b Washington, DC, 14 Dec 1927), American tenor. He sang on Broadway in Menotti's *The Saint of Bleecker Street* before his NY, City Opera, debut as Tchaikovsky's Vakula; Chicago 1959 as Laca, which he repeated on his CG debut in 1968. Other roles there have been Florestan, Tannhäuser, Siegmund and Otello. Vienna, Munich and La Scala debuts 1970; NY Met 1973 as Radames. In 1974 he sang Aaron in a London concert perf. of Schoenberg's *Moses und Aron.*

Cassiodorus, Flavius Magnus Aurelius (b *c* 487; d *c* 580), Roman senator, ecclesiastical historian and theologian. He wrote no specifically musical work, but the music theory contained in his *Institutiones* (*c* 560), deriving largely from Aristoxenus, caused him to be regarded, with Boethius and Isidore of Seville, as one of the three founding fathers of medieval music theory.

Castagna, Bruna (b Bari, 15 Oct 1905; d Pinamar, Argentina, 10 Jul 1983), Italian contralto. Debut Mantua, 1925; sang at La Scala 1925–34, under Serafin and Toscanini, as Isabella, Adalgisa and Laura. NY Met 1936–45 (debut as Amneris). Well known as Carmen in Australia, Chicago and Spain.

Castanets (from Span. *castañetas*), a perc. instrument, doubtless orig. made of chestnut wood (*castaña*), held between the fingers and made to strike against each other by motions of the hand. So used mainly by Span. dancers, but a simplified form is made for use in orchs. and bands.

Castelmary, Armand (b Toulouse, 16 Aug 1834; d New York, 10 Feb 1897), French bass. He sang at the Paris Opéra from 1863 and took part in the fps of *L'Africaine* and *Don Carlos.* CG 1889–96. NY Met debut 1893, as Vulcan in Gounod's *Philémon.* Often heard as Méphistophélès. As Sir Tristan he died on stage at the Met at the end of the 1st act of *Martha.* He was married to Marie Sass (Elisabeth in the fp of *Don Carlos*).

Castelnuovo-Tedesco, Mario (b Florence, 3 Apr 1895; d Hollywood, 16 Mar 1969), Italian composer. Studied at the Istituto

Musicale Cherubini at Florence and later with Pizzetti. At the age of 15 he wrote *Cielo di settembre* for pf. (later orch.) and in 1925 he gained a prize for his opera *La Mandragola* (after Machiavelli). He settled in USA in 1939, at 1st at Larchmont, NY, and then at Los Angeles.

Works incl. OPERAS *La Mandragola* (1926), *Bacco in Toscana, Aucassin et Nicolette* (1938), *The Merchant of Venice, All's Well that Ends Well* (both after Shakespeare, 1959, 1961), *The Importance of being Earnest* (after Wilde, 1962).

ORCH.: 7 Shakespearian concert overtures, *The Taming of the Shrew, The Merchant of Venice, Twelfth Night, Julius Caesar, A Winter's Tale, A Midsummer Night's Dream, King John*; 2 pf. concertos (1928, 1939), *Concerto italiano,* symph. variations and *The Prophets* for vln. and orch., concerto for cello and orch., concerto for guitar and orch.

CHAMBER AND INST: concertino for harp and 7 instruments; 3 string 4tets (1929, 1948, 1964); pf. trio; *Sonata quasi una fantasia* and suite on themes by Donizetti for vln. and pf., cello and pf. sonata; 6 illustrations for Voltaire's *Candide* and other pf. pieces.

VOCAL: settings of all the songs in Shakespeare's plays (in Eng.) for voice and pf., *Sonnets from the Portuguese* (Elizabeth Barrett Browning) and other songs.

Castiglioni, Niccolo (b Milan, 17 Jul 1932), Italian composer and pianist. Studied with Ghedini at the Milan Cons. He has also pursued a career as a concert pianist. His music is eclectic in style, influenced by Debussy, Messiaen, Webern and Cage, and remarkable for its frequently delicate textures.

Works incl. *Impromptus I–IV* for orch.; *Rondels* for orch.; *Movimento continuato* for pf. and small ensemble (1959), *Gymel* for fl. and pf.; *Inizio di movimento* for pf.; *A Solemn Music I* for soprano and chamber orch. (after Milton, 1963); *Sinfonia* (1969).

Castil-Blaze (François Henri Joseph Blaze) (b Cavaillon, 1 Dec 1784; d Paris, 11 Dec 1857), French critic, composer, trans. of opera libs. and author of books on music. Critic of the *Journal des Débats* before Berlioz. He prod. operas by Mozart, Weber and Rossini, in his own Fr. versions, in the 1820s.

Works incl. 3 operas, church music and chamber music.

Castileti, Johann (Jean Guyot) (b Châtelet nr. Liège, 1512; d Liège, 11 Mar 1588), Flemish composer. He wrote Masses, motets and *chansons*, and added a further 6 voices to Josquin's 6-part motet *Benedicta es caelorum regina*.

Castillo, Bernardo Clavijo del (b *c* 1549; d Madrid, 1 Feb 1626), Spanish organist and composer. Wrote motets and organ music.

Castor et Pollux, opera by Rameau (lib. by P.J.J. Bernard), prod. Paris, Opéra, 24 Oct 1737; rev. vers. prod. Jun 1754.

Castore e Polluce (*Castor and Pollux*), opera by Vogler (lib. based on one by C.I. Frugoni), prod. Munich, 12 Jan 1787. Weber wrote variations for pf. on an air from it, op. 5.

Castrati (It.), male singers of the 17th and 18th cents., mainly but not exclusively in It., who were mutilated in boyhood to prevent the breaking of their voices and to supply male sopranos and contraltos to the churches and theatres of the time. They eventually became fashionable and made their greatest and most sensational successes on the operatic stage. The last famous castrato was Velluti (1780–1861).

Castro, Jean de (b Liège, *c* 1540; d 1600), South Netherlands composer of Portuguese descent. Worked at Antwerp, Vienna, Cologne, etc. Wrote Masses, motets, madrigals, *chansons*.

Castro, Juan (José) (b Avellaneda, Buenos Aires, 7 Mar 1895; d Buenos Aires, 5 Sep 1968), Argentine conductor and composer. Studied in Buenos Aires and with d'Indy in Paris. On his return he formed a 5tet with himself as violinist and his brother as cellist, and in 1928 a chamber orch. In 1930–43 he was cond. at the Teatro Colón.

Works incl. opera, *Prosperina y el extranjero* (prod. La Scala, 1952); ballet *Mekhano*; 3 symphs., *Sinfonia Argentina* and *Sinfonia Biblica*, symph. poems *Dans le jardin des morts*, *A una madre* and *La Chellah*, etc. for orch.; *Suite brève* for chamber orch.; pf. concerto; songs.

Castrucci, Pietro (b Rome, 1679; d Dublin, 29 Feb 1752), Italian violinist, conductor and composer. Studied with Corelli in Rome and went to Eng. with Lord Burlington in 1715. He became leader in Handel's opera orch., but was replaced by Festing in 1737. In 1750 he settled at Dublin.

Works incl. 12 *Concerti grossi* and 3 books of vln. sonatas.

Castrucci, Prospero (b Rome; d ? London, 1760), Italian violinist, brother of prec. Prob. also studied with Corelli and went to Eng. with his brother or later. He is supposedly the orig. of Hogarth's 'Enraged Musician'. In 1739 he pub. 6 vln. sonatas.

'Cat's Fugue, The', popular name for D. Scarlatti's G min. harpsichord sonata (no. 30 in Kirkpatrick's list). Its bizarre subject has been taken to represent a cat picking its way along a keyboard. Experiment suggests that no cat would hit upon this particular succession of intervals.

Catalani, Alfredo (b Lucca, 19 Jun 1854; d Milan, 7 Aug 1893), Italian composer. Studied 1st with his father, an organist, and prod. a Mass at the age of 14. Went to the Paris Cons. in 1871 and then taught at the Milan Cons.

Works incl. operas *La Falce* (1875), *Elda* (1880), *Dejanice* (1883), *Edmea*, *Loreley* (1890) and *La Wally* (1892); Mass; symph. poem *Ero e Leandro*, etc.

Catalani, Angelica (b Sinigaglia, 10 May 1780; d Paris, 12 Jun 1849), Italian soprano. 1st appearance, Teatro La Fenice, Venice, 1795, in Mayr's *Lodoïska*. Went to Port. in 1804, to London in 1806 and sang until 1813 in operas by Portugal, Nasolini, Paisiello and Piccinni. She was the 1st London Susanna (1812). Was manager of the Italian Opera in Paris, 1814–17, after which she resumed her career as a singer.

Catalogue d'oiseaux, pf. work by Messiaen in 7 books based on his notations of birdsong, comp. 1956–8, fp Paris, 15 Apr 1959.

Catch, a part-song, in vogue in England from the early 17th to the 19th cent., in which the voices follow each other in the manner of a canon or round, with the difference in the most characteristic examples that the words, thus mixed up, acquire new and ludicrous meanings, often of an indecent nature in the 17th cent.

Catch Club, a society named The Noblemen and Gentlemen's Catch Club, founded in London in 1761 for sociable gatherings and the singing of catches. It still exists.

Catel, Charles Simon (b L'Aigle, Orne, 10 Jun 1773; d Paris, 29 Nov 1830), French composer. Pupil of Sacchini and Gossec in Paris. After working as teacher, he became chief musician with Gossec of the Garde Nationale, for which he wrote much military music, and accompanist at the Opéra in 1790. App. prof. of harmony at the Cons. on its foundation in 1795, and pub. a treatise on the subject in 1802.

Works incl. operas *Sémiramis* (1802), *L'Auberge de Bagnières* (1807), *Les Bayadères* (1810), etc.; *De Profundis*, *Hymn of Victory*; symphs. for wind instruments; choral pieces; chamber music; songs.

Caterina Cornaro, opera by Donizetti (lib.

by G. Sacchero), prod. Naples, Teatro San Carlo, 12 Jan 1844; revived in 1972 with a concert perf. in London and a prod. in Naples.

Catgut Strings. Although still often so called, such strings are not made of the bowels of cats but of sheep.

Catline (also **Catling, Catlin, Catleen**). In 16th cent. a kind of roped and polished gut string, partic. for low pitches on viols and lutes; by late 18th cent. could refer to any high gut string.

Catone in Utica, opera by Vinci (lib. by Metastasio), prod. Rome, Teatro delle Dame, 19 Jan 1728.

Opera by Hasse (lib. do.), prod. Turin, Teatro Regio, 26 Jan 1731.

Opera by Vivaldi (lib. do.), prod. Verona, Teatro Filharmonica, May 1737.

Opera by J.C. Bach (lib. do.), prod. Naples, Teatro San Carlo, 4 Nov 1761.

Opera by Paisiello (lib. do.), prod. Naples, Teatro San Carlo, 5 Feb 1789.

Catterall, Arthur (b Preston, Lancs., 25 May 1883; d London, 28 Nov 1943), English violinist. Studied in Manchester, became a member of the Queen's Hall Orch. in London in 1909, later of the Hallé Orch. in Manchester and in 1929 of the BBC SO, which he left in 1936. He founded a string 4tet in 1910.

Catulli Carmina, scenic cantata by Orff (text from poems by Catullus), the 2nd of three works together called *Trionfi* (other two are *Carmina Burana* and *Trionfo di Afrodite*), prod. Leipzig, 6 Nov 1943.

Caturla, Alejandro García (b Remedios, 7 Mar 1906; d Remedios, 12 Nov 1940), Cuban composer. Studied at Havana and with Nadia Boulanger in Paris. He married a black woman and was much influenced by Afro-Cuban folk music. He was assassinated.

Works incl. 3 *Danzas cubanas*, symph. poem *Yamba-O, La Rumba* for orch.; *Bembé* suite for 14 instruments, *Primera Suite cubana* for 6 wind instruments and pf., sonata and prelude for pf.; songs.

Caurroy, (François) Eustache du, Sieur de Saint-Frémin (b Gerberoy nr. Beauvais, bap. 4 Feb 1549; d Paris, 7 Aug 1609), French composer. Went to Paris c 1569 as a singer in a royal chapel, where he became master of the children in 1583. He became a canon in the Sainte-Chapelle and the title of Surintendant de la Musique du Roy was created for him in 1599.

Works incl. Requiem, motets, psalms, noëls, 2 books of *Preces ecclesiasticae*; in-strumental fantasies on sacred and secular tunes, etc.

Causton, Thomas (b c 1520; d London, 28 Oct 1569), English composer. Gentleman of the Chapel Royal in London. Wrote services, anthems, psalms, and contrib. to Day's *Certaine Notes*.

Cavaccio, Giovanni (b Bergamo, c 1556; d Bergamo, 11 Aug 1626), Italian composer. *Maestro di cappella* at Bergamo Cathedral in 1583 and later at the church of Santa Maria Maggiore there. Wrote a Requiem, Magnificats, psalms, madrigals, etc. and contributed psalms to a collection ded. to Palestrina.

Cavalieri, Catharina (b Währing nr. Vienna, 19 Feb 1760; d Vienna, 30 Jun 1801), Austrian soprano. Pupil and mistress of Salieri in Vienna, where she made her operatic debut in 1775 in Anfossi's *La finta giardiniera*. Mozart wrote for her the role of Constanze in *Die Entführung*, specially designing the virtuoso part, as he wrote to his father, for her 'flexible gullet'. She sang Donna Elvira in the first Viennese prod. of *Don Giovanni* (1788).

Cavalieri, Emilio de' (b Rome, c 1550; d Rome, 11 Mar 1602), Italian composer. He was long in the service of Ferdinando de' Medici at Florence. In 1589 he oversaw the prod. of a lavish series of *intermedi*, to celebrate the marriage of Ferdinando to Christine of Lorraine. He was in close touch with the *Camerata*, and with them worked towards the evolution of opera; in 1600 Cavalieri prod. *Euridice*, text by Rinuccini, music by Caccini and Peri, the 1st opera of which the music is extant. His own works were still dramatic pieces to be perf. in concert form. They incl. the following, all set to words by L. Guidiccioni: *Il satiro, La disperazione di Fileno* and *Il giuoco della cieca* (all lost), and *La rappresentatione di Anima, et di Corpo*, an allegory prod. in 1600.

Cavalieri, Lina (b Viterbo, 25 Dec 1874; d Florence, 7 Feb 1944), Italian soprano. Born of humble parents, she 1st sang in cafés, but later studied seriously and made her 1st appearance in opera at Lisbon in 1901 as Mimi. 1st visited England in 1908, when she sang Fedora, Manon Lescaut and Tosca, but her greatest successes were in USA. She was killed in an air raid, while attempting to retrieve the jewellery given her by many titled admirers.

Cavalleria rusticana (*Rustic Chivalry*), opera by Mascagni (lib. by G. Menasci and G. Targioni-Tozzetti, based on G. Verga's play), prod. Rome, Teatro Costanzi, 17 May 1890.

Cavalli (orig. **Caletti-Bruni**), **(Pietro) Francesco** (b Crema, 14 Feb 1602; d Venice, 14 Jan 1676), Italian composer. Became a singer under Monteverdi at St Mark's, Venice, in 1617, 2nd organist of that church in 1640, 1st organist in 1665 and *maestro di cappella* in 1668. His 1st opera was prod. in 1639, and in 1660 he was called to Paris to perform his *Serse* at Louis XIV's marriage. He wrote operas for the 5 theatres of Venice. In recent years his operas have been heard in free adaptations by Raymond Leppard (*q.v.*).

Works incl. operas *Le nozze di Teti e di Peleo* (1639), *Gli amori di Apollo e di Dafne* (1640), *La Didone*, *L'Egisto* (1643), *Ormindo* (1644), *Calisto* (1651), *Eritrea* (1652), *Erismena* (1656), *Il Giasone*, *L'Oristeo*, *Serse*, *Il Ciro*, *L'Hipermestra*, *Ercole amante* (1662), *Scipione affricano*, *Mutio Scevola*, *Il Coriolano* and *c* 20 others; *Vespers of the Annunciation* (1675), *Messa concertata*, motets, psalms, antiphons, Requiem (1676).

Cavata (It. lit. a thing carved or engraved, e.g. an epitaph), in music a short Arioso following a recitative, esp. in the early 18th cent.

Cavatina (It. poss. from *cavata*), in the 18th cent. a song in an opera less elaborate than an aria. Now normally used of a short, sustained piece or air.

Cavazzoni, Girolamo (b *c* 1525; d after 1577), Italian organist and composer. He was organist of the ducal church of Santa Barbara, Mantua, from 1565 until at least 1577. His two books of organ music (1543 and before 1549) contain *ricercari*, *chanson* arrangements (*canzoni*), hymns, Magnificats and Masses.

Cavazzoni, Marco Antonio (da Bologna, d'Urbino) (b Bologna, *c* 1490; d Venice, *c* 1560), Italian composer, father of prec. The 2 *ricercari* from his *Recerchari*, *Motetti*, *Canzoni* for organ. (Venice, 1523) are toccata-like pieces designed as preludes to the 2 motet arrs.; the *Canzoni* are arrs. of Fr. *chansons* and the forerunners of the It. instrumental *canzona*.

Cavendish, Michael (b ? Cavendish Overhall, Suffolk, *c* 1565; d London, *c* 5 Jul 1628), English composer. Belonging to a noble family, he seems to have held no appts. He contrib. to East's *Whole Booke of Psalmes* in 1592 and pub. a vol. of his own comps., ded. to Lady Arabella Stuart, his 2nd cousin, in 1598, containing 20 airs to the lute, or with 3 other voices, and 8 madrigals. He also contrib. a madrigal to *The Triumphes of Oriana*.

Caverne, La (*The Cave*), opera by Lesueur (lib. by P. Dercy, from an episode in Lesage's *Gil Blas*), prod. Paris, Théâtre Feydeau, 16 Feb 1793.

Cavos, Catterino (b Venice, 1775; d St Petersburg, 10 May 1840), Italian composer. Assisted his father, who was cond. at the Teatro La Fenice, later cond. at Padua and taught at Venice. In 1800 he went to Rus. with Astaritta's opera co., and in 1803 became director of the It. and Rus. operas there, for which he had to write works in both languages, as well as some in Fr. His Rus. opera, *Ivan Susanin*, prod. in 1815, was very successful.

Cazden, Norman (b New York, 23 Sep 1914; d Bangor, Me., 18 Aug 1980), American composer. Studied at Juilliard and with Walter Piston at Harvard. Worked as pianist with dance groups and collected folk music.

Works incl. *The Lonely Ones*, ballet (1944), symph. (1948), *Songs from the Catskills*, for band (1950), vla. concerto (1972); wind 5tet (1966) and other chamber music; songs.

Cazzatti, Maurizio (b Guastalla, *c* 1620; d Mantua, 1677), Italian organist and composer. Held successive posts at Mantua, Ferrara, Bergamo and Bologna. Comp. secular vocal and instrumental music as well as works for the church.

Ce qu'on entend sur la montagne (*What is heard on the Mountain*), symph. poem by Liszt, based on a poem by Victor Hugo; comp. 1848–9, fp Weimar, Feb 1850.

Cebell, a dance occurring in English 17th-cent. music, similar to the Gavotte.

Cebotari, Maria (b Kishinev, 10 Feb 1910; d Vienna, 9 Jun 1949), Austrian soprano of Russian birth. Debut Dresden, 1931, Mimi; created Aminta in *Die schweigsame Frau* (1935) and visited CG with Dresden co. in 1936. She returned to London in 1947 with the Vienna Opera and on both occasions was heard in operas by Strauss and Mozart. Also active in Salzburg, she created roles in operas by Sutermeister and Einem. Best known as Donna Anna, Salome, Arabella and Susanna.

Cecilia, Saint, the patron saint of music and the blind. A member of the early Christian church, she is said to have suffered martyrdom under Marcus Aurelius with her husband and other friends she had converted to Christianity and to have praised God by vocal and instrumental music. Her festival is 22 Nov.

Cédez (Fr. imper., lit. cede, give, surrender) = hold back, a direction used by Debussy and some other Fr. comps. to indicate a *ritenuto*.

Celesta, a keyboard instrument brought out by Mustel of Paris in the 1880s. The tone is prod. by hammers struck upon steel plates.

Celestina, La, opera by Pedrell (lib. based on an anon. 15th–16th-cent. Spanish dialogue novel, *La comedia de Calisto y Melibia*, sometimes attrib. to Fernando de Rojas), not prod.

Celibidache, Sergiu (b Rome, 28 Jun 1912), Rumanian conductor. He studied musicology and cond. in Berlin, 1939–45, becoming resident cond. of the Berlin PO in 1948. In 1948 he shared the orch. with Furtwängler on a tour of the USA. He has been a guest cond. with the LSO since 1977. He has also comp. 4 symphs. and a Requiem. Joined Curtis Inst. of Music, Philadelphia, in 1985.

Cello (It. dim. ending), the now accepted name of the Violoncello.

Cello Symphony, work by Britten for cello and orch., op. 68, comp. 1963 and perf. Moscow, 12 Mar 1964 by Rostropovich.

Cellone (It. lit. big cello). A modern cello of large size made by Stelzner of Dresden, capable of being played seated and intended to supply a double bass instrument for chamber music. It has 4 strings tuned in perfect 5ths 2 octaves below the vln.

Celos aun del ayre matan (*Jealousy, even of the air, is deadly*), opera on the subject of Cephalus and Procris by Juan Hidalgo (lib. by Calderón), prod. Madrid, Buen Retiro, 5 Dec 1660. The 1st Span. opera.

Cembalist. Harpsichord player. *See also* **Maestro al cembalo.**

Cembalo (It. abbr. for clavicembalo, accent on 1st syll.) = Harpsichord; also used to designate a Thorough-bass *continuo* part.

Cendrillon (*Cinderella*), opera by Isouard (lib. by C.G. Étienne, after Perrault), prod. Paris, Opéra-Comique, 22 Feb 1810.

Opera by Laruette (lib. by L. Anseaume, after Perrault), prod. Paris, Opéra-Comique, 21 Feb 1759.

Opera by Massenet (lib. by H. Cain, after Perrault), prod. Paris, Opéra-Comique, 24 May 1899.

Opera by Steibelt (lib. by Étienne), prod. St Petersburg, 26 Oct 1810.

Cenerentola (*Cinderella*), opera by Wolf-Ferrari (lib. by M. Pezzè-Pescolato, after Perrault), prod. Venice, Teatro La Fenice, 22 Feb 1900.

Cenerentola, La, ossia La bontà in trionfo (*Cinderella, or The Triumph of Goodness*), opera by Rossini (lib. by J. Ferretti, based on

Étienne's text for Steibelt's opera), prod. Rome, Teatro Valle, 25 Jan 1817.

Cent, in acoustics the unit by which musical intervals are measured, a cent being a hundredth part of a semitone in a tempered scale.

Céphale et Procris, opera by Grétry (lib. by Marmontel), prod. Versailles, at court, 30 Dec 1773; 1st Paris perf., Opéra, 2 May 1775.

Cephalus and Procris, opera by Araia (lib., in Rus., by A.P. Sumarokov), prod. St Petersburg, at court, 10 Mar 1755.

Ceremony of Carols, A, 11 settings by Britten for treble voices and harp; comp. 1942, fp Norwich, 5 Dec 1942.

Cererols, Joan (b Martorell, Catalonia, 9 Sep 1618; d Montserrat, 28 Aug 1676), Spanish composer. He joined the monastery at Montserrat as a choir-boy, became a novice in 1636 and remained to his death a dir. of music; a versatile musician as well as comp. His works are often for double chorus and incl. a *Missa de batalla*, for 12 voices, 2 Requiems, a Magnificat and the antiphon *Alma redemptoris mater*.

Cerha, Friedrich (b Vienna, 17 Feb 1926), Austrian composer and violinist. He studied musicology at Vienna Univ. and also comp. with Alfred Uhl. In 1958, with Kurt Schwertsik, he founded *Die Reihe*, an organization devoted to the perf. of new music. He became director of the electronic studios of the Vienna Music Academy, 1960. His completion of Act 3 of *Lulu* from Berg's short score was perf. Paris, 1979.

Works incl. *Espressioni Fondamentali* for orch.; *Relazioni Fragile* for harpsichord and chamber orch.; *Intersecazioni* for vln. and orch.; *Spiegel I–VII* (1960–68); concerto for vln., cello and orch. (1975); *Baal*, opera (1974–9; fp Salzburg, 1981).

Černohorský, Bohuslav Matěj (b Nymburk, Boh., ? 16 Feb 1684; d Graz, ? 1 Jul 1742), Bohemian composer, theorist and friar. Held church apps. at Padua and Assisi, where Tartini was his pupil. From 1739 he was director of music at St James's Church in Prague. He was a highly valued comp. of church and organ music, but most of his works were destroyed by fire in 1754.

Certon, Pierre (b ? Melun; d Paris, 23 Feb 1572), French composer. He was in the Sainte-Chapelle in Paris, 1532, and became choirmaster there before 1542 and chaplain in 1548. As a canon of Notre-Dame at Melun he founded an annual service there.

Works incl. Masses, *c* 50 motets, psalms, canticles, *c* 200 *chansons*.

Cervetto, Giacobbe Basevi (b Italy, *c* 1682; d London, 14 Jan 1783), Italian cellist and composer. Settled in London *c* 1738 and played in the orch. at Drury Lane, where he was later theatre manager. Wrote sonatas, etc. for his instrument, chamber music.

Cervetto, James (b London, 1747 or 1749; d London, 5 Feb 1837), English cellist and composer of Italian descent, son of prec. Pupil of his father. Comp. music for his instrument.

Cesaris, Johannes (*fl. c* 1385–*c* 1420). French organist and composer. Mentioned (with Carmen and Tapissier) by Martin le Franc in his poem *Le Champion des dames* (1441–2) as having 'astonished all Paris' in the recent past. One motet and several *chansons* survive.

Cesti, (Pietro) Antonio (b Arezzo, bap. 5 Aug 1623; d Florence, 14 Oct 1669), Italian composer. After serving as a choir-boy at Arezzo he became a Minorite friar in 1637. He was a pupil of Carissimi in Rome, and in 1645 was app. *maestro di cappella* at Volterra Cathedral. In 1653, having previously become a priest, he entered the service of the court at Innsbruck and remained there, with a brief interval as tenor in the papal chapel, for 13 years. From 1666 to 1669 he was vice-*Kapellmeister* in Vienna, where his spectacular opera *Il pomo d'oro* was perf. in 1667.

Works incl. operas *L'Orontea* (1649), *Il Cesare amante* (1651), *Alessandro il vincitor di se stesso*, *L'Argia*, *La Dori* (1657), *Tito, Nettuno e Fiora festeggianti* (1666), *Il pomo d'oro*, *Semiramide*, *Le disgrazie d'Amore* (1667); motets; cantatas.

Chabrier, (Alexis) Emmanuel (b Ambert, Puy-de-Dôme, 18 Jan 1841; d Paris, 13 Sep 1894), French composer. Studied law and was employed at the Ministry of the Interior, but cultivated music as a gifted amateur. Having prod. 2 operettas in 1877 and 1879, he devoted himself entirely to composition. After the prod. of *Le Roi malgré lui*, the run of which was interrupted by the fire of 25 May 1887 at the Opéra-Comique, he came under the influence of Wagner.

Works incl. operas *Le Roi malgré lui*, *Gwendoline* (1885) and *Briséis* (unfinished, 1 act perf. Paris, 1897); operettas *L'Étoile* and *Une Éducation manquée* (1879); rhapsody *España* (1883) and *Joyeuse Marche* for orch.; *La Sulamite* for mezzo, chorus and orch.; 10 *Pièces pittoresques*, *Habanera* and *Bourrée fantasque*, etc. for pf.; 3 *Valses romantiques* for 2 pfs.; songs.

Chace (old Fr. = *chasse* = chase, hunt), a 14th-cent. term for Canon, because the parts 'chase' each other.

Chaconne (Fr.), orig. a dance, prob. of Spanish provenance. Now a comp., generally in 3–4 time, on an unvarying ground-bass which goes on throughout the piece and over which, at each reappearance, the upper parts are freely varied in different ways. This definition applies even to Bach's Chaconne for unaccomp. vln., since the bass is always implied even when not actually heard.

Chacony (Eng.) = Chaconne.

Chadwick, George (Whitefield) (b Lowell, Mass., 13 Nov 1854; d Boston, 4 Apr 1931), American composer. Studied at Boston, Leipzig and Munich, in the last place under Rheinberger. Returned to Amer. in 1880, became organist at Boston, then prof. at the New England Cons. and its director in 1897.

Works incl. operas *Tabasco* (1894), *Judith*, *The Padrone* (1912), etc.; works for chorus and orch. *The Viking's Last Voyage*, *The Song of the Viking*, *Lovely Rosabelle*, *The Lily Nymph*, *Phoenix expirans*, etc.; 3 symphs. (1882–94), symph. poems *Cleopatra*, *Aphrodite*, *Angel of Death*, *Tam o' Shanter* (after Burns), overtures *Rip van Winkle*, *Thalia*, *Melpomene*, *Adonis* (after Shelley), *Euterpe*, etc., *Symph. Sketches*, *Sinfonietta*, *Suite symphonique*; 5 string 4tets (1878–98) pf. 5tet.; songs with orch. and with pf.; pf. and org. works; church music, partsongs.

Chagrin, Francis (b Bucharest, 15 Nov 1905; d London, 10 Nov 1972), Anglo-Rumanian composer. Studied at Zurich, Bucharest and, with Dukas and Nadia Boulanger, in Paris; later with Seiber in London, where he joined the Fr. section of the BBC Overseas Service in 1941. In 1943 he founded the Committee for the Promotion of New Music.

Works incl. incid. music for Shaw's *Heartbreak House* and Gozzi's *Re cervo*; music for films and broadcasts; Prelude and Fugue and suites for orch.; 2 symphs; pf. concerto; chamber music; pf. pieces; over 100 songs.

Chailly, Luciano (b Ferrara, 19 Jan 1920), Italian composer. He studied in Bologna and Milan and with Hindemith at Salzburg. Artistic dir. La Scala, Milan, 1968–71; Milan Cons. from 1969. His style is neo-classical, with some serial and electronic effects.

His operas incl. *Il canto del cigno* (Bologna, 1957), *Una demanda di matrimonio*, (after Chekhov; Milan, 1957), *Procedura penale* (Como, 1959; Eng. trans. by A. Jacobs as 'Trial by Tea-Party') *Il Mantello*, 'surrealist opera' (Florence, 1960), *L'Idiota* (after Dostoievsky; Rome, 1970).

Chailly, Riccardo (b Milan, 20 Feb 1953), Italian conductor, son of the prec. He studied in Milan and Sienna and became asst. cond. at La Scala in 1972 and in 1974 gave *Butterfly* in Chicago. With Henze founded the music school in Montepulciano. In 1978 he cond. *I Masnadieri* at La Scala and *Don Pasquale* at CG; NY Met debut 1982 with *Les Contes d'Hoffmann* and in the same year was app. chief cond. of RIAS (West Berlin Radio Orch.), and prin. guest cond. of the LPO. Dir. Concertgebouw Orch. from 1986.

Chalet, Le, opera by Adam (lib. by E. Scribe and A.H.J. Mélesville), prod. Paris, Opéra-Comique, 25 Sep 1834.

Chalumeau. A single-reed wind instrument, the forerunner of the clarinet. Also the name for the lowest register of the clar.

Chamber Music, properly music played in a private room, consisting of works assigning individual parts to a few players (more rarely singers). From the 19th cent. more and more 'chamber music' was composed for perf. in large concert halls and therefore carries the title only by virtue of its small ensemble and solo allocation. See also **String Quartet** *et seq.*

Chamber Opera, a type of opera written for few singers without chorus and a small orch. often consisting entirely of solo instruments.

Chamber Orchestra, a small orch. designed for the perf. of table music, serenades, etc. in domestic surroundings or small concert halls.

Chamber Organ, a small organ with 1 or 2 manuals, suitable for playing figured-bass accomps. or 18th-cent. solo concertos.

Chamber Pitch. *See* **Kammerton.**

Chamberlain, Houston Stewart (b Portsmouth, 9 Sep 1855; d Bayreuth, 9 Jan 1927), English writer, mainly on Wagner. Educ. at Cheltenham and in Switz. Married Wagner's daughter Eva in 1908 and became naturalized German. Great champion of Wagner and propagandist of Pan-German and proto-fascist theories.

Chambonnières, Jacques Champion, Sieur de (b Paris, *c* 1602; d Paris, 1672), French harpsichordist and composer. In the service of Louis XIII and XIV, also for a time in Swed. He taught several of the later harpsichordists and pub. 2 books of harpsichord pieces.

Chaminade, Cécile (Louise Stéphanie) (b Paris, 8 Aug 1857; d Monte Carlo, 18 Apr 1944), French pianist and composer. Stud-ied with var. masters, incl. Godard for comp. Began to comp. at the age of 8, and at 18 gave her 1st concert. Toured widely in Fr. and Eng.

Works incl. comic opera *La Sévillane*; ballet *Callirhoë* (1888); *Symphonie lyrique* for chorus and orch.; suites for orch.; *Concertstück* for pf. and orch (1896); 2 pf. trios; numerous light pf. pieces; songs.

Champein, Stanislas (b Marseilles, 19 Nov 1753; d Paris, 19 Sep 1830), French composer. Went to Paris *c* 1775 and prod. a comic opera in 1780, which was followed by some 50 other works for the stage, incl. (?) a setting of a Fr. prose trans. of Sophocles' *Electra*, rehearsed at the Opéra, but prohibited.

Works incl. operas *La Mélomanie* (1781), *Le Nouveau Don Quichotte* (1789), etc.; Masses and other church music, etc.

Chandos Anthems, 12 anthems by Handel, comp. *c* 1717–20 for the Earl of Carnarvon, later Duke of Chandos, for perf. in his private chapel at Canons nr. Edgware.

Chanson (Fr. = song). In a special technical sense the *chanson* is an old Fr. part-song cultivated in Fr. before and during the period when the madrigal occupied the comps. of the Netherlands, It. and Eng. Though it is often polyphonic in construction, many exs. approximate more closely to the lighter type of canzonet. Many such *chansons* were arranged for solo voice and lute.

Chanson de geste (Fr. = song of deeds, epic or heroic song), 11th–13th-cent. verse-chronicle recited to music by Jongleurs. The subject-matter might be secular or religious. In form it consisted of verse-paragraphs (*laisses*) of unequal length, the music being the same for each line of verse except the last.

Chanson de Toile (Fr. = cloth song), a French medieval song which tells its story or perf. its actions with reference to a female, not a male, character. Hence the name, which doubtless referred to spinning or weaving.

Chansons de Bilitis, Trois, songs for voice and pf. by Debussy (texts by P. Louÿs) comp. 1892, fp Paris, 17 Mar 1897 (vers. with orch. perf. Paris, 20 Feb 1926). Incid. music for 2 fl., 2 harps and celesta comp. 1900, fp Paris, 7 Feb 1901; arr. by Boulez with add. of reciter, perf. London, 23 Mar 1965.

Chansons madécasses, 3 songs by Ravel for voice, fl., cello and pf. (texts by E. Parny), comp. 1925–6, fp Paris, 13 Jun 1926.

Chant, in Catholic church music the singing of psalms, canticles, Masses, etc. in plainsong to Latin words; in Angl. church music the singing of the psalms to harmonized and measured tunes, the rhythm of which may, however, be modified or obscured by the necessity to fit longer or shorter psalm verses.

Chant-Fable (Fr. = song-fable), a 13th-cent. narrative interspersed with songs.

Chant du Rossignol, Le, symph. poem in 3 movts. by Stravinsky, based on music from his opera *The Nightingale*, arr. 1917, fp Geneva, 6 Dec 1919, cond. Ansermet; ballet vers. perf. Paris, Opéra, 2 Feb 1920.

Chanter, the pipe of the bagpipes on which the melody is played.

Chanterelle (Fr. lit. the singing one), the E string of the vln. or (less often) the highest string of any stringed instrument.

Chapel Royal, the English court chapel, incl. not only the building but the whole institution, dating back to the 12th cent. at the latest.

Chapí y Lorente, Ruperto (b Villena nr. Alicante, 27 Mar 1851; d Madrid, 25 Mar 1909), Spanish composer. Studied at the Madrid Cons. and in 1872 was given a musical post in the artillery. Lived in Rome for a time from 1873.

Works incl. operas *Margarita la Tornera* (1909), *La serenata*, *Roger de Flor*, *Circe* and 4 others, 155 zarzuelas; oratorio *Los Angeles*, *Veni Creator* for double chorus and orch.; symph. in D min., Moorish fantasy *La corte de Granada*, legend *Los gnomos de la Alhambra* and other orch. works; *Jota* for vln. and orch.; 4 string 4tets, pf. trio; pf. pieces; songs.

Chaplet, The, musical stage entertainment by Boyce (lib. by M. Mendez), prod. London, Drury Lane Theatre, 2 Dec 1749.

Char, René (b 1907), French poet. *See* **Boulez** (*Le Visage Nuptial*, *Le Soleil des eaux*, *Le Marteau sans maître*).

Charakterstück (Ger. = character or characteristic piece), a short instrumental piece outlining some definite mood, human character or literary conception.

Charpentier, Gustave (b Dieuze, Meurthe, 25 Jun 1860; d Paris, 18 Feb 1956), French composer. Went into business at Tourcoing at the age of 15, but studied music at the Lille and Paris Consrs., gaining at the latter the Prix de Rome as a pupil of Massenet in 1887. In 1902 he founded the Cons. de Mimi Pinson, providing free instruction in music for working-class girls.

Works incl. operas *Louise* (prod. 1900) and *Julien* (1913); cantata *Didon* (1887); symph. drama for solo voices, chorus and orch., *La Vie du poète* (afterwards used in

Julien); orch. suite *Impressions d'Italie* (1889); *Fête du couronnement de la Muse* (later used in *Louise*); *Impressions fausses* (Verlaine) and *Sérénade à Watteau* for voice and orch. (1896); *Poèmes chantés* and 5 poems from Baudelaire's *Fleurs du mal* for voice and pf.

Charpentier, Marc-Antoine (b Paris, *c* 1645; d Paris, 24 Feb 1704), French composer. Pupil of Carissimi in Rome. On his return he became domestic musician to Mlle. de Guise and comp. to the Comédie-Française, where he worked with Molière and continued after Molière's death. In 1679 he was app. church comp. to the Dauphin; later music master to a Jesuit college and comp. teacher to the Duke of Orleans. In 1698 he became *maître de chapelle* at the Sainte-Chapelle.

Works incl. operas *Les Amours d'Acis et Galatée* (1678), *La Descente d'Orphée aux enfers*, *Endimion*, *Médée* (1693), *David et Jonathas* (1688), *c* 12 others; incid. music for Molière's *La Comtesse d'Escarbagnas* and *Le Malade imaginaire* (1674), for P. Corneille's *Polyeucte* and *Andromède*, T. Corneille's *La Pierre philosophale*, T. Corneille and Visé's *Circé* and *L'Inconnu* and Visé's *Les Amours de Vénus et d'Adonis*; ballets, etc.; *c* 10 Masses, Requiem, motets, psalms and other church music, some with orch.; *Histoires sacrées*, *Tragédies spirituelles*; vocal chamber music, *Airs sérieux et à boire*; instrumental pieces.

Charton-Demeur (*née* **Charton**), **Anne Arsène** (b Saujon, 5 Mar 1824; d Paris, 30 Nov 1892), French soprano. Made her debut at Bordeaux in 1842 as Lucia. She sang the part of Dido in Berlioz's *Les Troyens à Carthage* in 1863; sang Béatrice in 1862. Other roles incl. Cassandre and Amina.

Chartreuse de Parme, La (*The Carthusian Monastery of Parma*), opera by Sauguet (lib. by A. Lunel, based on Stendhal's novel), prod. Paris, Opéra, 16 Mar 1939.

Chase, Gilbert (b Havana, 4 Sep 1906), American music critic. Studied in NY and Paris, where he lived in 1929–35 as music critic to the *Daily Mail*. In 1936 he settled in NY. Made a special study of Span. music and wrote *The Music of Spain*.

Chasse, La (*The Hunt*). Nickname of Haydn's symph. no. 73, in D maj., comp. in 1781; also of his string 4tet in B♭ maj., op. 1 no. 1, written *c* 1755.

Chasseur maudit, Le (*The Accursed Huntsman*), symph. poem by Franck, based on a ballad by Bürger, comp. 1882. Fp Paris, Soc. Nat., 31 Mar 1883.

Chausson, Ernest (b Paris, 20 Jan 1855; d Limay, 10 Jun 1899), French composer. Pupil of Massenet at the Paris Cons., then of Franck. He never held an official app., but helped to found the Société Nationale de Musique and was its sec. 1889–99. He was a pioneer of cyclic form, and the first person to die in a cycling accident.

Works incl. operas *Le Roi Arthus* (1886–95), *La Légende de Sainte Cécile* (1891), etc.; incid. music to Shakespeare's *Tempest*; symph. in B♭ maj. (1890), symph. poem *Viviane*; *Poème de l'amour et de la mer* for voice and orch. (1882–90); string 4tet (unfinished), concerto for vln. and pf. with string 4tet (1891), pf. trio, pf. 4tet, *Chanson perpétuelle* for voice, string 4tet and pf.; pf. and organ pieces; 10 op. nos. of songs.

Chávez, Carlos (b Mexico City, 13 Jun 1899; d Mexico City, 2 Aug 1978), Mexican composer of mixed Indian and Spanish descent. He was taught music as a child by his brother and 2 casual teachers, but later went to Europe and NY to gain experience. In 1928 he founded a Mex. symph. orch., of which he later became cond., and the same year he became director of the Nat. Cons. A post in the Dept. of Fine Arts enabled him to do still more for the country's music reorganization, and he did much to explore Mex. folk music.

Works incl. opera *Panfilo and Lauretta* (1953, prod. NY, 1957), ballets *El fuego nuevo*, *Los cuatro soles* and *H.P.*; *Sinfonía de Antígona*, *Sinfonía proletaria* and *Sinfonía India* for orch.; concertos for harp and for pf. and orch.; *Energía* for inst. ens. *El sol* for chorus and orch.; 3 string 4tets (1921, 1932, 1944); sonata for 4 horns; pf. pieces.

Checkmate, ballet by Bliss (choreog. by N. de Valois), prod. by Sadler's Wells Ballet, Paris, Théâtre des Champs-Élysées, 15 Jun 1937; 1st London perf. SW, 5 Oct 1937.

Chef d'attaque (Fr.), the leader of an orch., so called because great importance was always attached in Fr. to unanimity of bowing and attack in orch. string playing.

Chekker, a 14th–16th-cent. keyboard instrument used in England, France and Spain, in which latter countries it was called *échiquier* and *exaquir* (and similar names). Its Ger. name is properly *Schachtbrett*, from the old Flem. word *Schacht* (spring or quill), and has nothing to do with the modern *Schachbrett* (chessboard). The instrument is clearly a forerunner of the harpsichord or clavichord.

Chelard, Hippolyte (André Jean Baptiste) (b Paris, 1 Feb 1789; d Weimar, 12 Feb 1861), French conductor and composer. Studied at the Paris Cons., vln. under R. Kreutzer and comp. under Gossec, Méhul and Cherubini. Gained the Prix de Rome in 1811, studied church music in Rome under Baini and Zingarelli, afterwards opera with Paisiello and Fioravanti at Naples, where he prod. an It. comic opera in 1815. In 1816 he became violinist at the Paris Opéra, where he prod. *Macbeth* in 1827. After the 1830 Revolution he settled at Munich and remained in Ger. to the end of his life. In 1832 and 1833 he cond. Ger. opera in London, with Schröder-Devrient and Haitzinger as the chief singers. From 1835 to 1840 he was employed as cond. at Augsburg, finally becoming court music dir. at Weimar.

Works incl. operas *La casa da vendere* (1815), *Macbeth* (in Fr., lib. by R. de l'Isle (1827), *La Table et le logement* (later Ger. ver. *Der Student*), *Mitternacht*, *Die Hermannsschlacht* (1835).

Cherkassky, Shura (b Odessa, 7 Oct 1911), American pianist of Russian birth. He studied 1st with his mother and later with Josef Hofmann. As a child prodigy, he played before President Hoover in the USA in 1923. 1st European tour 1945, still active 1985.

Cherubini, Luigi (Carlo Zanobi Salvatore Maria) (b Florence, 8 or 14 Sep 1760; d Paris, 15 Mar 1842), Italian composer. Studied 1st under his father, a musician at the Teatro della Pergola at Florence, then under var. minor masters. At the age of 16 he had written an oratorio, Masses, etc. About 1778, with a grant from the Grand Duke, he went to study with Sarti at Venice and in 1780 he prod. his 1st opera, *Quinto Fabio*. In 1785 and 1786 he prod. *La finta principessa* and *Giulio Sabino* in London and was app. composer to the King, but left for Paris in the latter year. After a brief return to Italy he settled in Paris for good in 1788 and prod. his 1st Fr. opera, *Démophon*, there, to a lib. by Marmontel. He soon became very busy cond. and writing operas, but was not very successful. In 1795 he married Cécile Tourette. In 1806 he prod. *Faniska* in Vienna, where it had been specially commissioned, and met Beethoven, who admired his work and whose *Fidelio* was influenced by it. On his return to Fr. he lived retired and embittered at the Prince de Chimay's country residence and there wrote church music as well as more operas. In 1816 he and Lesueur became attached to the royal chapel with large salaries and in 1822 he became director of the Cons.

Works incl. operas *Armida abbandonata*

(1782), *Alessandro nell' Indie*, *Demetrio*, *Ifigenia in Aulide*, *Lodoïska* (Fr.), *Médée* (1797), *Les Deux Journées* (*The Water Carrier*) (1800), *Anacréon, ou L'Amour fugitif* (1803), *Faniska, Pimmalione, Les Abencérages* (1813), *Bayard à Mézières, Ali Baba, ou Les Quarante Voleurs* (1833); ballet-pantomime *Achille à Scyros*; 10 Masses and 2 coronation Masses, 2 Requiems (1 for male voices) and other choral works; symph. in D maj. and overture for orch.; 6 string 4tets (1834–7), string 5tet; songs.

Chest of Viols, a set of (usually 6) viols of var. sizes in a cupboard or chest, an article of furniture which was often found in households of well-to-do Eng. families of the 16th and 17th cents.

Chest Voice, one of the so-called 'registers' in singing, used or said to be used for the lower notes of the singer's range, and so called because its resonance gives the sensation of being lodged in the chest, not in the head, as in the case of the Head Voice.

Chevel be bronze, Le (*The Bronze Horse*), opera by Auber (lib. by E. Scribe), prod. Paris, Opéra-Comique, 23 Mar 1835.

Chevillard, (Paul Alexandre) Camille (b Paris, 14 Oct 1859; d Chatou, 30 May 1923), French conductor and composer. Pupil of Chabrier and son-in-law of Lamoureux, whose concerts he cond. after Lamoureux's retirement.

Works incl. incid. music for E. Schuré's play *La Roussalka* (1903), *Ballade symphonique*, symph. poem *Le Chêne et le Roseau* and *Fantaisie symphonique* for orch.; string 4tet, pf. 5tet, 4tet and trio (1882–4); sonatas for vln. and pf. and cello and pf.; variations and *Étude chromatique* for pf.; vln. and cello pieces.

Chevreuille, Raymond (b Watermael, 17 Nov 1901; d Montignies-le-Tilleul, 9 May 1976), Belgian composer. Mainly self-taught, although he took some courses at the Brussels Cons. His works are in a harmonically advanced idiom.

Works incl. chamber opera *Atta Troll* (1952), 3 ballets; symph. with vocal 4tet, *Évasions* for soprano and chamber orch., *Saisons* for baritone and chamber orch.; concerto for 3 woodwind instruments, cello concerto; 6 string 4tets (1930–45).

Chezy (*née* **von Klencke**), **Wilhelmine** (or **Helmina**) **von** (1783–1856), German dramatist and novelist. Wrote the lib. of Weber's *Euryanthe* and Schubert's *Rosamunde*.

Chiara, Maria (b Oderzo nr. Venice, 24 Nov 1939), Italian soprano. Debut Venice, 1965, as Desdemona. She sang Liù at Verona in

1969, with Domingo, and repeated the role on her CG debut (1973, returned for Desdemona, 1978). In 1970 she appeared at Munich and Vienna. NY Met debut 1977, Traviata. She opened the 1985–6 season at La Scala, as Aida. Other roles incl. Maria Stuarda, Anna Bolena, Elisabeth de Valois and Amelia Boccanegra.

Chiavette (It. lit. little keys, actually little clefs), were clefs other than those normal in 16th and early 17th cent. vocal music, used either to avoid leger-lines or to indicate transposition, e.g. the tenor clef might be used for a bass part, the treble clef for a soprano part, and so on.

Chicago Symphony Orchestra, American orch. founded 1891 by Theodore Thomas; cond. by Thomas until 1905 and by Frederick Stock until 1942. Other conds. incl. Rafael Kubelik 1950–53, Fritz Reiner 1953–63, Jean Martinon 1963–9; Georg Solti from 1969.

Child, William (b Bristol, *c* 1606; d Windsor, 23 Mar 1697), English composer and organist. Educ. at Bristol Cathedral and app. one of the organists at St George's Chapel, Windsor, in 1632. At the Restoration he received a court appt. and in 1663 he took the D.Mus. degree at Oxford.

Works incl. *c* 25 services, *c* 50 anthems, motet *O bone Jesu*, 20 psalms for 3 voices with *continuo*, chants, Magnificat, 'in Gamut', Te Deum and Jubilate and other church music; secular vocal pieces, catches and ayres; 2 suites of dances for viols.

Child of our Time, A, oratorio by Tippett for soloists, chorus and orch. comp. 1939–41, inspired by persecution of Jews following assassination of a Nazi envoy in Paris. Tippett's own text includes Negro spirituals; fp London, 19 Mar 1944.

Childhood of Christ (Berlioz). *See* **Enfance du Christ.**

Children's Corner, a set of pf. pieces, with English titles, by Debussy, comp. in 1906–8, ded. to his daughter Claude-Emma D. (Chouchou): 1. *Doctor Gradus ad Parnassum*; 2. *Jimbo's Lullaby*; 3. *Serenade for the Doll*; 4. *The Snow is Dancing*; 5. *The Little Shepherd*; 6. *Golliwogg's Cake-Walk*. Fp Paris, 18 Dec 1908; orch. vers. by André Caplet perf. NY, 1910.

Chinese Block (or Temple Block), a perc. instrument in the shape of a hollow wooden box on which a dry, rapping sound is prod.

Chinese Pavilion, an instrument shaped like a tree or pagoda and hung with brass plates and small bells, shaken to make a jingling noise and used in military bands, esp. in the 18th cent. It was popularly called 'Jingling Johnny' or 'Turkish Crescent'.

Chiroplast, Logier's apparatus invented in the early years of the 19th cent. to facilitate pf. practice by mechanically making the hands flexible.

Chisholm, Erik (b Glasgow, 4 Jan 1904; d Cape Town, 8 Jun 1965), Scottish pianist, organist, conductor and composer. Studied comp. under Tovey and in 1934 took the D.Mus. degree at Edinburgh Univ. After touring in Canada he returned to Glasgow as organist and cond., founded a society for the propagation of modern music in 1930 and became cond. of the Glasgow Grand Opera Co., with which he gave interesting perfs., partic. of Berlioz's operas (e.g. *Les Troyens*, 1935). In 1947 he became principal of the Cape Town School of Music.

Works incl. opera *Isle of Youth* (lib. by comp., 1941); ballets *The Forsaken Mermaid* (1942) and *The Pied Piper of Hamelin*; 2 symphs. etc.

Chitarrone (It. lit. big guitar, from *chitarra* with augment. ending), a very large double-necked lute or theorbo, used as a bass to the lute family in It. in the 17th cent.

Chlubna, Osvald (b Brno, 22 Jul 1893; d Brno, 30 Oct 1971), Czech composer. Pupil of Janáček and later prof. at the Brno Cons.

Works incl. operas *Catullus's Vengeance* (1917), *Alladine and Palomides* (after Maeterlinck) (1922), *Nura* and *The Day of Beginning*; cantatas *Lord's Prayer*, *Minstrel's Child* and others; *Symph. of Life and Love*, symph. poems *Dreams*, *Before I go dumb*, *Two Fairy Tales*, *Song of my Longing*; overture *Fairy Land*, 2 suites for orch.; *Sinfonietta* for chamber orch.; 5 string 4tets, pf. music, songs.

Choirbook, a large book in which the parts of a polyphonic comp., though written out separately, were collected together on the open page so that they could be read simultaneously by all the perfs. (If a piece was too long for one 'opening' the parts were copied so that the turn came simultaneously in all of them.) The format was first employed in motet MSS. of the 13th cent. (superseding score arr. to save space), was common in Eng. in the 15th and early 16th cents. (*see* **Eton Choirbook**), and was also used for chamber music and lute songs in Eng. in the later 16th and early 17th cents., the parts now being arranged so that the book could be placed flat on a table and the perfs. seated around it.

Choir Organ, formerly often a small instrument set apart from the principal organ in a church and used separately to accomp. the choir. It is now the name given to the lowest manual of an organ with three or more manuals, of which it forms an integral part.

Chopin, Frédéric (François) (orig. **Fryderyk Franciszek)** (b Żelazowa Wola, ? 1 Mar 1810; d Paris, 17 Oct 1849), Polish composer of French descent. The family moved to Warsaw later in 1810, Chopin's father becoming prof. of Fr. there. Chopin took pf. lessons at the age of 6, played at a musical evening at 7 and in public at 8; took comp. lessons with Elsner from 1822, made great progress in comp. and improvisation, and 1st pub. a work, a Polonaise in G min., at the age of 7. Left Warsaw Cons. in 1827 and played in Vienna in 1829. On his return he fell in love with the singer Konstancia Gładkowska, who appeared at the 3rd of his public concerts in 1830; but he left Pol. that year, playing in Vienna and Munich and visiting Stuttgart, where he heard of the taking of Warsaw by the Rus. Went to Paris in Oct 1831 and decided to remain there. He appeared frequently in public and gave private lessons, esp. in Fr. and Pol. aristocratic circles.

Met Maria Wodzińska at Dresden in 1835 and Marienbad in 1836, fell in love with and became secretly engaged to her, but the engagement was broken off by her family. In 1838 he visited George Sand at Nohant, where she held house-parties in the summer, and although she was 6 years older an intimacy developed between them. She took him to Majorca in Nov for his health, but the stay, until Feb 1839, was spoilt by bad weather and primitive living conditions. Most summers spent at Nohant until 1847, when a family quarrel between G. Sand and her children led to one with Chopin and they parted. He suffered from tuberculosis of the throat and gave his last public concert in Feb 1848, but continued to teach and play at private houses. His pupil Jane Stirling took him to Scot. in Aug 1848 for a rest at the country house of her brother-in-law, Lord Torphichen. He afterwards played at Manchester, Glasgow, Edinburgh, and returned to London in Nov. In Jan 1849 he was back in Paris in a critical state of health and finance, but was supported by wealthy friends until his death.

Works (nearly all for pf. solo) incl. 2 concertos in E min. and F min. (1829–30); 4 other works with orch. incl. *Andante Spianato* (1834); 50 Mazurkas in 13 sets (1830–49), 27 Studies, 26 Preludes (24 in all keys), op. 28 (1836–9), 19 Nocturnes, 14

Waltzes (1827–41), 16 Polonaises, 4 Ballades in G min., F, A♭, F min. (1831–42), 4 Impromptus, 4 Scherzos in B min., B♭ min., C♯ min., E (1831–9), 3 Rondos, 3 sonatas in C min. (1828), B♭ min. (1839), B min. (1844), *Barcarolle* in F ♯, *Berceuse, Bolero, Fantasy* in F min., *Tarantella* and other miscellaneous pf. pieces; pf. trio (1829); cello and pf. sonata (1832).

Chopsticks, a childish little waltz played on the pf. by children with the forefingers of each hand, to which the name refers by analogy with the 2 sticks with which the Chinese eat their food.

'Chopsticks' Variations, a set of variations for pf. (3 hands, the 2nd player playing a variant in 2–4 time of the above with 1 hand) by Borodin, Cui, Liadov and Rimsky-Korsakov, written before 1880, when a 2nd ed. appeared and Liszt contrib. a new variation of his own.

Choral (Ger.), **Chorale** (Eng.), Lutheran hymn. The German word was orig. used to mean the choral parts of Lat. chant, and by extension plainsong in general, a meaning which it still bears today. At the Reformation it took on the secondary meaning of the monophonic congregational singing of the Lutheran liturgy, many of the melodies being adaptations from the plainsong itself; hence the term *Choralbearbeitung* (chorale arr.) to denote any kind of setting of such melodies. The Eng. word is simply an adaptation of the Ger. in its Lutheran sense, the final 'e' being added to make the pronunciation clear and to avoid confusion with the adj. 'choral'.

'Choral Symphony', popular name for Beethoven's 9th symph. in D min., op. 125, on account of its last movement, a setting of Schiller's ode *An die Freude* ('To Joy') for solo 4tet, chorus and orch. Comp. *c* 1817–24, fp Vienna, 7 May 1824.

Chorale. *See* Choral.

Chorale Cantata, term used for a form of church cantata, esp. by Bach, which draws on the text and, usually, music of a Lutheran hymn. The chorale words and melody may (rarely) be present in each movement of the cantata (e.g. in *Christ lag in Todesbanden*), or some verses may be replaced by free paraphrases of the text or completely new material set as recitatives, arias, etc. Treatment varies from the simple harmonizations found as the last movement of many cantatas to the complexity of the massive fantasialike chorus which opens *Ein' feste Burg*.

Chorale Fantasy, a type of organ comp. in which a hymn-tune is freely treated.

Choral Prelude, a type of organ piece for church use e.g. by Bach; introducing the tune of the hymn about to be sung by the congregation and artistically elaborating it by contrapuntal treatment or by the provision of an orig. accomp.

Chord, the sounding together of 3 or more notes, though 2 notes may imply others.

Chording, a term used to designate either the spacing of the notes in a chord in comp. or the perf. of them strictly in tune in relation to each other.

Choreography, the invention, design and stage management of the dancing in a ballet.

Chorley, Henry F(othergill) (b Blackley Hurst, Lancs., 15 Dec 1808; d London, 16 Feb 1872), English music critic, librettist and author, contrib. to the *Athenaeum* from 1830.

Choron, Alexandre (Étienne) (b Caen, 21 Oct 1771; d Paris, 29 Jun 1834), French music scholar and composer. Among his books are a music encyclopaedia and treatises on music study, part-writing, plainsong, etc.

Comps. incl. a Mass, a *Stabat Mater*, psalms, hymns, etc.

Chorton (Ger. lit. choir-pitch), the pitch to which church organs in Ger. were tuned in the 17th–18th cent. It was higher, usually by a whole tone, than *Kammerton* (chamberpitch), and it is for this reason that Bach transposed the woodwind parts in his cantatas up, or alternatively transposed the org. parts down. The strings, could, as necessary, play at either pitch.

Chout (*The Buffoon*), ballet in 6 scenes, op. 21, by Prokofiev (scenario by the comp. from a story by A. Afansyev), comp. 1915, rev. 1920; prod. Paris, Ballets Russes, 17 May 1921. Symphonic Suite from the ballet arr. 1920, fp Brussels, 15 Jan 1924.

Christelflein, Das, opera by Pfitzner (lib. by I. von Stach and comp.) prod. Munich, 11 Dec 1906, cond. Mottl.

Christmas Concerto, Corelli's Concerto grosso, op. 6. no. 8.

Christmas Eve (*Notch Pered Rozhdestvom),* opera by Rimsky-Korsakov (lib. by comp., based on Gogol's story), prod. St Petersburg, 10 Dec 1895.

See also **Vakula the Smith.**

Christmas Oratorio, a series of six cantatas by Bach (1734) designed for separate perf. between Christmas and Epiphany. Not orig. intended for perf. as one composite work.

Christmas Symphony (Haydn). *See* **Lamentatione.**

Christoff, Boris (b Sofia, 18 May, 1914),

Bulgarian bass-baritone. Initially a law student, he later studied singing in Rome and Salzburg, making his debut in Rome in 1946 as Colline; sang Boris at CG in 1949 and Philip II in 1958. US debut San Francisco, 1956. Other roles incl. Marke, Gurnemanz, Ivan Susanin, Fiesco and Haydn's Pluto (Florence, 1951). He excels in the Rus. repertory (esp. *Boris Godunov*) and has also given numerous recitals.

Christophe Colomb opera by Milhaud (lib. by P. Claudel), prod. in Ger., Berlin, Staatsoper, 5 May 1930, cond. Kleiber. The work makes use of film.

Christophorus, oder Die Vision einer Oper, opera by Schreker (lib. by the comp.), comp. 1925–9 but orig. prod. was banned by the Nazis; fp Freiburg, 1 Oct 1978.

Christus, oratorio by Liszt (words from the Bible and the Roman Catholic liturgy), comp. 1855–66, fp Weimar, 29 May 1873.

Oratorio by Mendelssohn (words by Chevalier Bunsen), began 1844, resumed 1847, but left unfinished.

Christus am Oelberg (*Christ at the Mount of Olives*), oratorio by Beethoven, op. 85 (lib. by F.X. Huber), prod. Vienna, 5 Apr 1803.

Chromatic (from Gk. *chrōmatikos* = coloured). The Chromatic scale is one proceeding entirely by semitones, i.e. taking in all the notes available in normal western music (*see* illustration). Chromatic harmony consists of chords using notes not included in the scale of the prevailing key and thus, in notation, involving the use of many accidentals.

scale of C maj., the other the sharps or flats, like the white and black notes on the pf.

Chromatic Madrigal. (1) A madrigal making free use of chromatic harmony.

(2) In 16th-cent. It. a *madrigale cromatico* was one using black notes as the basis of measurement and hence moving at a brisk speed.

Chromaticism, composition with extensive use of non-diatonic notes, that is, pitches that are not part of the prevailing maj. or min. scale. This is obviously a relative term, but it is most often applied to music that is on the verges of atonality.

Chronochromie (*Time-colour*), work for orch. in 7 sections by Messiaen; comp. 1960, fp Donaueschingen, 16 Oct 1960, cond. Rosbaud.

Chrysander, (Karl Franz) Friedrich (b Lübtheen, Mecklenburg, 8 Jul 1826; d Bergedorf nr. Hamburg, 3 Sep 1901), German music scholar and ed. Lived in Eng. for some time to research into material for his great biography of Handel, pub. 1858–67, never completed. He also ed. Handel's complete works. Other works of his on old music are valuable, but he was violently opposed to all 'modern', i.e. post-Handelian, music.

Chung, Kyung-Wha (b Seoul, 26 Mar 1948), Korean violinist. She went to the US in 1961 and in 1967 shared first prize in the Leventritt Comp.; 1968 soloist with the NY PO. 1970 European debut with the LSO. Her sister, **Myung-Wha** (b Seoul, 19 Mar 1944), is a cellist who made her orch. debut in 1957 and her brother, **Myung-Whun** (b

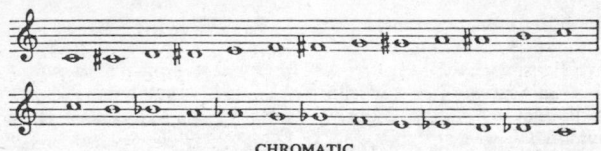

CHROMATIC

Chromatic Fantasy and Fugue. A keyboard work in D min. by Bach, written *c* 1720, rev. *c* 1730. The adj. refers to the harmonies of the Fantasy and the subject of the Fugue.

Chromatic Harp, a French type of harp which, instead of being tuned to the scale of Cb maj., like the normal harp, where each string can be raised in pitch by a semitone or a whole tone with the aid of pedals, has strings for all the notes of the chromatic scale. They are not all strung parallel, but slightly crossed, so that except where they actually intersect they stand away from each other in 2 ranges, one repres. the diatonic

Seoul, 22 Jan 1953), a pianist and cond.; won 2nd prize in Int. Tchaikovsky Comp., Moscow, 1974 and was asst. cond. of the Los Angeles PO 1978–81.

Chute de la Maison Usher, La (*The Fall of the House of Usher*), opera by Debussy (lib. by himself, based on E.A. Poe's story), worked at between 1908 and 1918, but never completed.

Ciampi, Vincenzo Legrenzio (b Piacenza, 1719; d Venice, 30 Mar 1762), Italian composer. Pupil of Durante. He was resident in London 1748–60, and from the latter year to his death *maestro di cappella* at the Ospizio degli Incurabili in Venice.

Works incl. 22 operas, e.g. *Bertoldo, Bertoldino e Cacasenno* (1748) and *Il negligente* (1749); 4 oratorios; church music; chamber music.

Cibber, Susanna Maria. *See* **Arne.**

Ciccimarra, Giuseppe (b Altamura, 22 May 1790; d Venice, 5 Dec 1836), Italian tenor. He was highly regarded as a Rossini singer at Naples; created Iago (1818) and took part in the fps of *Armida, Mosè, Erminione* and *Maometto II*. He taught in Vienna after his retirement from the stage.

Ciconia, Johannes (b Liège, ? *c* 1370; d Padua, Jun–Jul 1412), Liègeois composer and theorist. His only clearly documented activity is as choirmaster at Padua Cathedral from *c* 1401, though some believe that he was born *c* 1335 and was active earlier in Avignon. Perhaps the most important and influential comp. of his generation. Works incl. Mass movements, motets and secular works in both Fr. and It. There is also a treatise, *Nova musica*.

Cid, Der, opera by Cornelius (lib. by comp., based on Corneille's drama), prod. Weimar, 21 May 1865.

Cid, Le, opera by Massenet (lib. by A.P. d'Ennery, L. Gallet and É. Blau, based on Corneille's drama), prod. Paris, Opéra, 30 Nov 1885.

Cifra, Antonio (b nr. Terracina, 2 Oct 1629), Italian composer. Pupil of G.B. Nanini in Rome. He was *maestro di cappella* of the Ger. Coll. there in 1609, at Loreto from 1609 to 1622 and at the church of St John Lateran, Rome, from 1622 to 1625, returning to Loreto in 1626.

Works incl.Masses, motets, psalms, madrigals.

Cigna, Gina (b Paris, 6 Feb 1900), Italian soprano. Debut La Scala, 1927, as Freia; remained until the war as Abigaille, Gioconda and Turandot. CG 1933–9. NY Met debut 1936, as Aida. She appeared as guest in Chicago and San Francisco; taught in Toronto and Milan after the war.

Cikker, Ján (b Banská Bystrica, 29 Jul 1911), Slovak composer. Studied comp. with J. Kricka and Novák. He became prof. at Bratislava Cons. in 1951. His chief interest is in theatre comp., writing in an atonal, though romantically inclined, idiom.

Works incl. operas *Beg Bajazid* (1954), *Resurrection* (after Tolstoy, 1962), *Mr Scrooge* (after Dickens, 1963), *Coriolanus* (after Shakespeare, 1974).

Cilea, Francesco (b Palmi, Calabria, 26 Jul 1866; d Varazze, 20 Nov 1950), Italian composer. Studied at Naples and while still at the Cons. prod. his 1st opera there in 1889. The pub. Sonzogno then commissioned a second, prod. at Florence in 1892. Prof. at the Reale Istituto Musicale at Florence, 1896–1904.

Works incl. operas *Gina* (1889), *La Tilda*, *L'Arlesiana* (after Daudet), *Adriana Lecouvreur* (after Scribe, 1902), *Gloria*; cello and pf. sonata; numerous pf. works.

Cimador(o), Giovanni Battista (b Venice, 1761; d Bath, 27 Feb 1805), Italian composer. Successfully prod. dramatic works *Ati e Cibeli* (1789), *Il ratto di Proserpina* (Venice, 1791) and 'scena lyrica' *Pimmalione* in Italy, but settled in London 1791. Other works incl. concerto for double bass; vocal pieces.

Cimarosa, Domenico (b Dec Aversa nr. Naples, 17 Dec 1749; d Venice, 11 Jan 1801), Italian composer. Studied at Naples, among his masters being Sacchini and Piccinni, and prod. his 1st opera there in 1772. Later lived in Rome and Naples by turns, became famous with several operas, travelled much and in 1787 went to the court of Catherine II at St Petersburg. In 1791 the Emperor Leopold II invited him to Vienna, to succeed Salieri as court *Kapellmeister*. There he prod. his most successful opera, *Il matrimonio segreto*, in 1792. His engagement in Vienna ended the same year, when, on the death of Leopold, Salieri was re-app. Cimarosa returned to Naples, becoming *maestro di cappella* to the king. He was imprisoned because of his involvement in the Neapolitan rising of 1799. On his release he set out for St Petersburg, but died at Venice on the way.

Works incl. over 60 operas, e.g. *Le stravaganze del conte, L'Italiana in Londra* (1779), *Il pittore parigino, La ballerina amante* (1782), *L'Olimpiade, Artaserse* (1784), *L'impresario in augustie, Cleopatra* (1789), *Idalide, Il matrimonio segreto, Le astuzie femminili* (1794), *Il marito disperato, L'impegno superato, Gli Orazi ed i Curiazi, Penelope* (1795), *Achille all' assedio di Troia*; Masses, oratorios, cantatas.

Cimarrón, El, work by Henze for bar., fl., guitar and perc. (text from *The Autobiography of a Runaway Slave*, by E. Montejo), fp Aldeburgh, 22 Jun 1970.

Cimbalom, a Hungarian nat. instrument, descendant of the dulcimer, with strings stretched over a horizontal sound-board which are struck by hammers.

Cinderella. *See* **Cendrillon, Cenerentola.**

Cinesi, Le (*The Chinamen*), opera by Caldara (lib. by Metastasio), prod. Vienna, at court, Carnival 1735.

Opera by Gluck (lib. do.), prod. Schlosshof nr. Vienna, at court, 24 Sep 1754.

Cinquepace (from Fr. *cinq pas* = 5 steps; also colloq. 'Sink-a-pace'), a dance of the 16th cent. in quick 3–4 time and requiring movements in groups of 5 paces. The name was used both for the Galliard following the Pavan and for the Tordion concluding the Basse Danse. Shakespeare makes a pun on it in *Much Ado about Nothing*.

Cinti-Damoreau, Laure (Cinthie Montalant) (b Paris, 6 Feb 1801; d Paris, 25 Feb 1863), French opera singer. Studied at the Paris Cons. 1st appearance at the Théâtre Italien at the age of 14, in *Una Cosa rara*, and at the Opéra in 1826. She remained there until 1835 and sang leading roles in the fps of *Le Siège de Corinthe, Moïse, Le Comte Ory, Guillaume Tell* and *Robert le Diable*.

Ciphering, the escape of sound from organ pipes by a fault in or damage to the mechanism.

Circassian Bride, The, opera by Bishop (lib. by C. Ward), prod. London, Drury Lane Teatre, 23 Feb 1809.

Circe and Penelope, 2 parts of a cyclic opera, *Ulysses*, by Keiser (lib. by F.C. Bressand), prod. Brunswick, Feb 1696.

Circular Canon, a canon whose tune, instead of coming to an end, returns to the beginning and may be repeated *ad infinitum*. The round, e.g. *Three blind mice*, is a familiar example.

Circus Polka, work for pf. by Stravinsky, to accompany the elephants in the Ringling Bros. circus; scored for wind band by D. Raksin, 1942; arr. by the comp. for orch., fp Cambridge, Mass., 13 Jan 1944.

Ciro in Babilonia, o sia La caduta di Baldassarre (*Cyrus in Babylon or The Fall of Belshazzar*), opera by Rossini (lib. by F. Aventi), prod. Ferrara, 14 Mar 1812.

Cisneros, Eleanora de (b New York, 1 Nov 1878; d New York, 3 Feb 1934), American contralto. Debut NY, 1898, Siebel (as E. Broadfoot); appeared with Met co. in Chicago 1899 and NY 1900. Principal contralto with Manhattan co. 1906–11. She was the 1st Clytemnestra at La Scala (1909) and was heard in Paris as Brangaene (1914). From 1929 she taught in NY. Other roles incl. Herodias and Tchaikovsky's Countess.

Citole. Medieval plucked instrument, prob. with wire strings.

Cittern (or Cithren, Cither, Cythern, etc.), plucked instrument with a flat back, popular in 16th and 17th cents., possibly descended from the medieval gittern. It usually had 4

pairs of wire strings tuned either: or

The finger-board was fretted and the strings were played with a plectrum. The modern German and Austrian *Zither* derives its name from it, but is a different instrument.

Cividale del Friuli, Antonio da (Antonius de Civitate Austriae), Italian 14th–15th-cent. composer, active at Florence as well as in N. It. 5 motets, 3 Mass movements, 4 *chansons* and one *ballata* survive.

Civil, Alan (b Northampton, 13 Jun 1929), English horn player. He studied with Aubrey Brain and was prin. horn RPO 1952–5, co-prin. Philharmonia Orch. 1955–7, with Dennis Brain (prin. 1957–66). In 1966 he became prin. horn of the BBC SO and prof. at the RCM.

Clapisson, Antoine Louis (b Naples, 15 Sep 1808; d Paris, 19 Mar 1866), French violinist and composer. Violinist at the Paris Opéra, 1832–8, after which he made a great success with songs and comic operas. His collection of old instruments is in the Paris Cons.

Works incl. operas *La Figurante* (1838), *Le Code noir* (1842), *Gibby la Cornemuse, La Promise* (1854), *La Fanchonnette, Madame Grégoire,* etc.

Clapp, Philip Greeley (b Boston, Mass., 4 Aug 1888; d Iowa City, 9 Apr 1954), American composer. Graduated at Harvard Univ. and studied with Schillings at Stuttgart, and in London. After several academic appts. he became prof. of music at Univ. of Iowa.

Works incl. cantata *A Chant of Darkness* (H. Keller); 12 symphs. (1908–44), pf. concerto in B min., Fantasy on an Old Plainchant for cello and orch., *Dramatic Poem* for tromb. and orch.; songs with orch.; string 4tet, etc.

Clari, Giovanni Carlo Maria (b Pisa, 27 Sep 1677; d Pisa, 16 May 1754), Italian composer. *Maestro di cappella* successively at Pistoia (*c* 1712), Bologna (1720) and Pisa (1736). 5 of his vocal duets were used by Handel in *Theodora*.

Works incl. opera *Il Savio delirante* (1695); 11 oratorios; Masses, *Stabat Mater* and other church music.

Clari, or The Maid of Milan, opera by Bishop (lib. by J.H. Payne, based on Marmontel's story *Laurette*), prod. London, CG, May 1823. It contains the song *Home, sweet home*, not only as a song, but as a kind of

Leitmotiv or theme-song occurring in various forms.

Clarinet. A woodwind instrument with a single reed made in var. pitches, the most current being clars. in A and in B♭ (there is also a smaller clar. in E♭). It came into use later than the other woodwind instruments still current, and did not estab. itself regularly in the orch. until after the middle of the 18th cent. The sounding compass of the A clar. is:

of the B♭

of the E♭

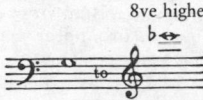

Other members of the family are the **Basset Horn**, the **Clarinette d'amour**, the **Bass Clarinet** and the **Contrabass** (or **Pedal**) **Clarinet** (with a compass 2 octaves below the ordinary **Clar.**).

Clarinette d'amour (Fr. = love clar.), a large clar. made in continental Europe between late 18th cent. and *c* 1820, usually a maj. 3rd or 4th lower than the clar. in C.

Clarino (It. = clarion), the name given to the tpt. in the 17th and 18th cents., also the name of the highest register of the instrument, from C above middle C upwards, which was regularly used for florid passages in the works of Bach and his contemporaries.

As a name for the instrument it = Tromba. In the early 18th cent. it sometimes = Clarinet, for which the normal It. term was *clarinetto*.

Clarke, Jeremiah (b ? London, *c* 1673; d London, 1 Dec 1707), English composer. Pupil of Blow at the Chapel Royal, organist at Winchester Coll., 1692–5, may have assisted Blow at St Paul's Cathedral in London. Sworn Gentleman-extraordinary of the Chapel Royal in 1700 and organist in 1704. He committed suicide, supposedly after an unhappy love affair.

Works incl. anthems; odes on the Assumption of the Blessed Virgin, in praise of Barbadoes and O *Harmony*; setting of Dryden's *Alexander's Feast* (1697); operas *The Island Princess* (with D. Purcell and Leveridge) (1699), *The World in the Moon* (Settle, with D. Purcell) (1697); incid. music for Shakespeare's *Titus Andronicus*, Sedley's *Antony and Cleopatra* and other plays; harpsichord music, incl. *The Prince of Denmark's March* ('Trumpet Voluntary').

Clarke, Rebecca (b Harrow, 27 Aug 1886; d New York, 13 Oct 1979), English vla. player and composer, born on the same day as Eric Coates. Studied at the RAM in London. In a competition in USA in 1919 for a work for vla. and pf. she won the prize with a sonata, 2nd only to Ernest Bloch's Suite. She settled in NY in 1944 and married James Friskin.

Works incl. Psalm for chorus; pf. trio (1921); vla. and pf. sonata, Rhapsody for cello and pf. (1923), duets for vla. and cello; songs for voice and vln. and for voice and pf.; instrumental pieces, etc.

Classical, a term commonly used to denote the period of Haydn, Mozart and Beethoven, as opposed to the later Romantic period.

Classical Symphony, symph. no. 1 in D, op. 25, by Prokofiev, written in emulation of Haydn, perf. Petrograd, 21 Apr 1918.

Claudel, Paul (1868–1955), French poet and dramatist. *See* **Christophe Colomb** (Milhaud), **Homme et son désir** (do.), **Honegger** (*Danse des morts, Soulier de satin*, 3 songs), **Jeanne d'Arc au bûcher** (Honegger), **Milhaud** (*Protée, Annonce faite à Marie,* Aeschylus transs. and songs).

Claudine von Villa Bella, play for music by Goethe.

Music by Ignaz von Beeck (1733–1803), prod. Vienna, Burgtheater, 13 Jun 1780.

Music by Johann Christoph Kienlen (1784–*c* 1830), prod. Munich, 9 Sep 1810.

Music by Reichardt, prod. Charlottenburg, Schlosstheater, at court, 29 Jul 1789; perf. Berlin, Opera, 3 Aug, 1789.

Music by Claus Schall (1757–1837) (lib. a Dan. trans. of Goethe's play by N.H. Weinwich), prod. Copenhagen, 29 Jan 1787.

Music by Schubert (lib. from Goethe's play); all 3 acts were comp. in 1815 but the MS. of Acts 2 and 3 were used as firelighters by the servants of Josef Hüttenbrenner. Ov. and Act 1 perf. Vienna, Gemeindehaus Wieden, 26 Apr 1913.

Clausula, an interpolation in regular rhythm into 12th- and 13th-cent. organum, without words, but either sung to the syllable of the text immediately preceding it or played by instruments or both together. The lowest (tenor) part, which in the main portions of the music is in very long notes, here moves at a quicker speed, the notes being arranged in a rhythmical pattern. Numerous clausulae were also designed apparently as independent pieces. In later usage the term meant 'cadential formula'.

Clavecin (Fr.) = Harpsichord (old spelling sometimes *clavessin*).

Clavicembalo (It.) = Harpsichord. The abbr. *cembalo* is often used.

Clavichord, a stringed keyboard instrument which differs in its tone-production from the harpsichord. The strings are not plucked, but struck by a tangent which presses against them as long as the key is held down by the finger and prod. a very faint note which can be made to vibrate by a gentle shaking of the finger. The pitch of the note is determined by the place at which the string is struck by the tangent, so that the same string can be used for 2 adjacent notes, which then can never be sounded simultaneously. Such instruments are called 'fretted' clavichords; those which have a separate string for each note are 'fretless'.

Clavicytherium (Lat.), a harpsichord whose wing-shaped body stood upright instead of being placed horizontally as in the grand pf.

Clavier (Fr. and Ger. = keyboard; Ger. also = harpsichord or pf.). In English the word may be used to designate any stringed keyboard instrument, esp. the harpsichord, clavichord and early pf. in cases where it is doubtful which was used in perf. or where the choice was at the player's discretion.

Clavierübung (Ger. lit. 'keyboard practice'). A collection of keyboard music by Bach, pub. in 4 parts: I (1731), 6 partitas; II (1735), It. concerto and Fr. overture; III (1739), org. prelude and fugue in Eb maj. framing 21 chorale preludes on the catechism and 4 manual *duetti*; IV (1741 or 1742), 'Goldberg' variations.

Claviorganum, an instrument combining harpsichord and organ mechanisms, dating from the late 16th cent. and made in various forms until the 18th.

Clay, Frederic (b Paris, 3 Aug 1838; d Great Marlow, 24 Nov 1889), English composer. Pupil of Molique and of Hauptmann at Leipzig. He began by writing light operas for amateurs, 1859–60, but prod. *Court and Cottage* at CG in London in 1862.

Works incl. light operas *Princess Toto, Don Quixote* (1876), *The Merry Duchess* (1883), *The Golden King*, etc.; incid. music for Shakespeare's *Twelfth Night*; cantatas

The Knights of the Cross and *Lalla Rookh* (Moore), the latter incl. 'I'll sing these songs of Araby'; songs 'She wandered down the mountainside', *The Sands of Dee*.

Clayton, Thomas (b ? 1660–70; d ? 1720–30), English composer and adapter. He set Addison's opera lib. of *Rosamond*, which proved a complete failure, in 1707. *Arsinoë*, prod. as his own opera in 1705, was a pasticcio of It. songs. In 1711 he prod. a setting of an altered version of Dryden's *Alexander's Feast.*

Clef, the sign in front of the key and time signatures at the begining of a comp. and repeated on each stave, determining the position of the notes shown on the stave; e.g. the C clef placed on the 3rd line indicates that the note on that line is middle C.

Clemens non Papa (Clément, Jacques) (b *c* 1510–*c* 1515; d ? Dixmuide, *c* 1556), Flemish composer. Worked at Bruges, (?) at Antwerp Cathedral and at the cathedral of 's Hertogenbosch. His nickname was long said to have distinguished him from Pope Clement VII, but it did not appear on pubs. until 14 years after that pope's death.

Works (over 400) incl. Masses, motets, psalms in Flem., *chansons.*

Clément, Félix (b Paris, 28 Mar 1867; d Nice, 24 Feb 1928), French tenor. Debut Paris, Opéra-Comique, 1889, in *Mireille*; remained there until 1910 and sang in the fps of operas by Bruneau, Saint-Saëns (*Phryné* and *Hélène*), Godard, Hahn and Erlanger. NY Met 1909–11. Other roles incl. Fenton, Pinkerton and Massenet's Des Grieux.

Clement, Franz (Joseph) (b Vienna, 17 Nov 1780; d Vienna, 3 Nov 1842), Austrian violinist. 1st appeared at the age of 7; leader of the orch. at the Theater an der Wien in Vienna in 1802–11 and 1817–21. Beethoven wrote his vln. concerto for him.

Clementi, Muzio (b Rome, 23 Jan 1752; d Evesham, 10 Mar 1832), Italian pianist, composer, pub. and pf. manufacturer. Showed early promise, and had comp. several works by the age of 14, when Peter Beckford took him to Eng. to complete his education. Pub. his 1st pf. sonatas in 1773, and appeared with spectacular success as virtuoso pianist and comp. He was cond. of the It. Opera in London 1777–80, after which he toured extensively on the Continent, in 1781 playing before the Viennese court in competition with Mozart (who thought little of him). Back in London, Cramer and John Field were his pupils. He was associated with the pubs. and pf. manufacturers Longman & Broderip, upon whose bankruptcy in 1798 he re-estab. the firm in partnership with Longman. His interest in the co. (trading under a constantly changing variety of names) continued to his death. He was again on tour in Europe 1802–10, taking Field with him to St Petersburg, where the latter remained. In 1807 he met Beethoven in Vienna. From 1810, apart from occasional further travels, he remained in England.

Works incl. 4 symphs.; *c* 60 pf. sonatas; 100 progressive pf. studies entitled *Gradus ad Parnassum*; capriccios and other pf. pieces; sonatas for various instruments and pf.; chamber music.

Clemenza di Scipione, La (*The Clemency of Scipio*), opera by J.C. Bach, prod. London, King's Theatre, Haymarket, 4 Apr 1778.

Clemenza di Tito, La (*The Clemency of Titus*). *See also* **Tito Vespasiano**.

Opera by Gluck (lib. by Metastasio), prod. Naples, Teatro San Carlo, 4 Nov 1752.

Opera by Mozart (lib. do., altered by Caterino Mazzolà), prod. Prague, to celebrate the coronation of the Emperor Leopold II as King of Bohemia, 6 Sep 1791.

Cleofide, opera by Hasse (lib. by M.A. Boccardi, based on Metastasio's *Alessandro nell'Indie*), prod. Dresden, at court, 13 Sep 1731.

Cleopatra (*Die betrogene Staats-Liebe, oder Die unglückselige Cleopatra, Königin von Egypten*), opera by Mattheson (lib. by F.C. Feustking), prod. Hamburg, Theatre beim Gänsemarkt, 20 Oct 1704.

Cleopatra e Cesare, opera by Graun (lib. by G.C. Bottarelli, based on Corneille's *La Mort de Pompée*), prod. Berlin, Opera, 7 Dec 1742. Written for the inauguration of that theatre.

Cléopâtre, opera by Massenet (lib. by L. Payen), prod. Monte Carlo, 23 Feb 1914.

Clérambault, Louis Nicolas (b Paris, 19 Dec 1676; d Paris, 26 Oct 1749), French organist and composer. Pupil of André Raison. Organist at var. Paris churches. Wrote cantatas and pieces for organ and for harpsichord.

Cleveland Orchestra, American orch. founded 1918 with Nikolay Sokoloff as prin. cond.; conductors since 1933 have been Arthur Rodzinski, until 1943; Erich Leinsdorf, 1943–4; George Szell, 1946–70; Lorin Maazel, 1972–82; Christoph von Dohnányi from 1984.

Cliburn, Van (b Shreveport, La., 12 Jul 1934), American pianist. In 1954 he graduated from Juilliard, and appeared with the NY PO; in 1958 became the first Amer. to win the Int. Tchaikovsky Comp., Moscow. Debut as cond. 1964. Estab. his own piano competition at Fort Worth, Texas, in 1962.

Clifford, James (b Oxford, 1622; d London, Sep 1698), English divine and musician. Chorister at Magdalen Coll., Oxford, 1632–42; app. minor canon at St Paul's Cathedral in London, 1661. Pub. a collection of the words of *Divine Services and Anthems*, 1663.

Clive (*née* **Raftor**), **Catherine (Kitty)** (b London 1711; d Twickenham, 6 Dec 1785), English actress and stage singer in ballad operas. Attached to Drury Lane Theatre in London, 1728–41.

Clochette, La (*The Little Bell*), opera by Duni (lib. by L. Anseaume), prod. Paris, Comedie-Italienne, 24 Jul 1766.

Clochette, La, ou Le Diable page (*The Little Bell, or The Devil as Page*), opera by Hérold (lib. by E.G.T. de Lambert), prod. Paris, Opéra-Comique, 18 Oct 1817. Schubert wrote 2 songs for the Vienna prod. in 1821.

'Clock Symphony', the nickname of Haydn's symph. no. 101, in D maj. (no. 9 of the 'Salomon' symphs.), written for London in 1794. The name derives from the ticking motion of the accomp. figuration in the slow movement.

Clori, Tirsi e Fileno, large-scale Italian cantata for 2 sops., alto and chamber ens. by Handel; comp. 1707. 1st modern revival, London, 1984.

Club Anthem, an anthem comp. jointly by Blow, Humfrey and W. Turner *c* 1664, when they were choir-boys at the Chapel Royal. It is a setting of the words 'I will always give thanks'.

Cluer, John (d London, Oct 1728), English music publisher. Worked in London early in the 18th cent. and was succeeded by his widow and later her 2nd husband, Thomas Cobb. He pub. some of Handel's operas, incl. *Giulio Cesare* and *Admeto*.

Cluytens, André (b Antwerp, 26 Mar 1905; d Paris, 3 Jun 1967), Belgian conductor. Studied pf. at Antwerp Cons. He 1st worked for his father as a chorus trainer at the Théâtre Royal in Antwerp, where he later cond. opera. He then held numerous posts in France, incl. director of the Paris Opéra Comique, 1947–9. In 1955 he cond. *Tannhäuser* at Bayreuth. US debut 1956, with the Vienna PO; Staatsoper from 1959.

Coates, Albert (b St Petersburg, 23 Apr 1882; d Milnerton nr. Cape Town, 11 Dec 1953), English conductor and composer (mother Russian). Sent to school in Eng. and entered Liverpool Univ., returned to Rus. to enter his father's business, but was sent to the Leipzig Cons. Studied cond. with Nikisch and cond. opera at several Ger. theatres before he was engaged at St Petersburg. He fled to Eng. during the Revolution in 1919 and settled in London for good.

Works incl. operas *Assurbanipal, Samuel Pepys, Pickwick* (CG, 1936), *Gainsborough's Duchess*; symph. poem *The Eagle*, Rus. Suite for orch.; pf. pieces.

Coates, Edith (b Lincoln, 31 May 1908; d Worthing, 7 Jan 1983), English mezzo. Studied TCM and with Dino Borgioli. SW 1931–46, in Rimsky-Korsakov's *Snow Maiden* and *Tsar Saltan*, and as Eboli, Carmen and Amneris. CG debut 1937; last appeared there in 1967. She was successful as Tchaikovsky's Countess and sang in the fps of Britten's *Peter Grimes* (1945) and *Gloriana* (1953).

Coates, Eric (b Hucknall, Notts., 27 Aug 1886; d Chichester, 23 Dec 1957), English composer. Studied at the RAM in London and became a vla. player in a 4tet and in the Queen's Hall Orch., but later devoted himself to the comp. of light and popular music. He is best known for the signature tune for BBC Radio's 'Desert Island Discs'.

Coates, John (b Girlington nr. Bradford, 29 Jun 1865; d Northwood nr. London, 16 Aug 1941), English tenor. He was trained for and began to make a career as a baritone, but made his 1st appearance as a tenor in 1899. He became equally famous in opera and oratorio, and was successful in Elgar's oratorios and as Siegfried, Tristan and Lohengrin. Later in life was one of the finest song recitalists.

Cobbett, W(alter) W(ilson) (b Blackheath, 11 Jul 1847; d London, 22 Jan 1937), English music amateur and editor. A wealthy business man, he did much valuable work for chamber music by offering prizes for new works by Brit. comps. e.g. Bridge, Bax and Britten, esp. 1-movement fantasies, and he ed. a *Cyclopaedia of Chamber Music* pub. in 1929 (rev. 1963).

Cobbold, William (b Norwich, 5 Jan 1560; d Beccles, 7 Nov 1639), English organist and composer. Organist at Norwich Cathedral, 1599–1608. He was one of the 10 musicians who harmonized the tunes in East's Psalter of 1592 and he contrib. a madrigal to *The Triumphes of Oriana* in 1601. Among his other few surviving works are 11 consort songs.

Cobelli, Giuseppina (b Maderno, 1 Aug 1898; d Barbarano di Salò, 10 Aug 1948), Italian soprano. Debut Piacenza, 1924, as Gioconda. La Scala 1925–42, as Sieglinde, Isolde, Kundry, Eboli and Adriana Lecouvreur. Buenos Aires 1925 and 1931. Other roles incl. Monteverdi's Octavia and Respighi's Silvana (*La Fiamma*).

Cocchi, Gioacchino (b ? Naples, *c* 1720; d ? Venice, after 1788), Italian composer. Worked at Naples, Rome and Venice until 1757, when he went to London as comp. to the King's Theatre, remaining there till 1773. He was also cond. of Mrs. Cornely's subscription concerts.

Works incl. over 40 operas, e.g. *La Maestra* (1747), *Li Matti per Amore* (1754), *Demetrio re di Siria.*

Coccia, Carlo (b Naples, 14 Apr 1782; d Novara, 13 Apr 1873), Italian composer. Pupil of Paisiello. He prod. many operas in Italy between 1807 and 1820, when he went 1st to Lisbon and then to London. He became cond. of the Opera there, also prof. of comp. at the RAM, and stayed until 1828, returning in 1833, but eventually settling at Novara as *maestro di cappella* in succession to Mercadante, 1840.

Works incl. *c* 40 operas, e.g. *Il matrimonio per cambiale* (1807), *Donna Caritea, Maria Stuarda* (1827), *Il lago delle fate*, 2 cantatas.

Coccia, Maria Rosa (b Rome, 4 Jan 1759; d Rome, Nov 1833), Italian composer. At the age of 16 she passed a severe examination at the Accademia di Santa Cecilia in Rome with brilliant success and an account of it was pub. In 1780 another eulogy of her was issued with letters from Martini, Metastasio and Farinelli.

Works incl. Magnificat for voices and organ, written at 15, *Dixit Dominus* and a cantata, but most are lost.

Cochlaeus, Johannes (Johann Dobnek) (b Wendelstein nr. Nuremberg, 10 Jan 1479; d Breslau, 10 Jan 1552), German cleric and music scholar. He was a Roman Catholic and an opponent of Luther, in office at Cologne, Worms, Mainz and Frankfurt. Wrote a treatise on music and wrote odes, etc.

Cockaigne (In London Town), concert overture by Elgar, op. 40, comp. 1900, fp London, Phil. Society, 20 Jun 1901.

Coclico (Coclicus), Adrianus Petit (b Flanders, 1499 or 1500; d Copenhagen, after Sep 1592), Flemish composer. He became a Protestant and went to Wittenberg in 1545. After var. posts in Ger. he went to the Dan. court at Copenhagen. Pub. a treatise entitled

Compendium musices and *Consolationes piae* (psalm settings).

Coda (It. = tail), the part of a musical comp. which forms a peroration, where it can be regarded, from the structural point of view, as a distinct and separate section. It is thus most clearly marked, for ex., in sonata form, where it appears as a 4th division after the exposition, working-out and recapitulation, or in a minuet or scherzo with trio, where it rounds off the movement after the restatement of the 1st section, usually with material based either on that or on the trio.

Codetta (It. = little tail), a small form of coda, not appearing as a rule at the end of a movement, but rather rounding off a section of such a movement, or a theme or group of themes, thus assuming the function of a bridge-passage.

Coelho, Rui (b Alcacer do Sal, 2 Mar 1892; d Lisbon, 5 May 1986), Portuguese composer. Studied at Lisbon and later with Humperdinck in Berlin. Became music critic of the *Diario de Noticias* at Lisbon and in 1924 won a prize with his 2nd opera.

Works incl. operas *Crisfal* (1919), *Belkiss* (1924), *Inés de Castro* (1925), *Tá-Mar* (1936), *Entre giestas* (1946); symph. poems *5 Sinfonias camoneanas, Promenade d'été,* etc.; chamber music; pf.; pieces; songs.

Coerne, Louis (Adolphe) (b Newark, NJ, 27 Feb 1870; d Boston, Mass., 11 Sep 1922), American conductor and composer. Studied in Europe and at Harvard Univ. After filling an organist's post at Buffalo and cond. there and at Columbus, he became assoc. prof. at Smith Coll., Northampton, Mass., and also taught at Harvard. Later he held other distinguished teaching posts and visited Ger., where some of his works were perf.

Works incl. operas *A Woman of Marblehead, Zenobia* (1902, prod. Bremen, 1905) and *Sakuntala* (after Kalidasa); incid. music to Euripides' *Trojan Women*; 6-part Mass; symph. poem *Hiawatha* (after Longfellow) and other works for orch.; vln. concerto, string 4tet in C min., 3 pf. trios in canon; songs.

Coffee Cantata, name given to J.S. Bach's secular cantata BWV 211 (*c* 1734–5), *Schweigt stille, plaudert nicht.* The lib. by Picander deals in a humorous way with the then new vogue for drinking coffee.

Cohen, Harriet (b London, 2 Dec 1895; d London, 13 Nov 1967), English pianist. Studied at the RAM and with T. Matthay, making her debut, aged 13, at the Queen's Hall, London. She did much for Eng. music, esp. that of Bax (whose mistress she was),

and also pub. a book, *Music's Handmaid,* on pf.-playing and interpretation. In 1937 she was awarded the CBE.

Col legno (It. = 'with the wood'), a direction indicating that a passage for a string instrument or a group of such instruments is to be played by striking the strings with the stick of the bow.

Colas Breugnon, opera by Kabalevsky (lib. by V. Bragin after R. Rolland's novel), prod. Leningrad, 22 Feb 1938); rev. 1953 and 1969.

Colasse, Pascal (b Rheims, bap. 22 Jan 1649; d Versailles, 17 Jul 1709), French composer. Studied at the Maîtrise de Saint-Paul and the Collège de Navarre in Paris, and *c* 1677 obtained an appt. at the Opéra from Lully, in whose works he wrote some of the subordinate parts. In 1683 he became one of the 4 superintendents of the royal chapel, each of whom had to direct the music for 3 months in the year, and 2 years later he shared with Lalande the appt. of royal chamber musician. *Maître de musique de chambre* from 1696.

Works incl. operas *Achille et Polyxène* (with Lully, 1687), *Thétis et Pélée* (1689), *Énée et Lavinie* (1690), *Jason, La Naissance de Vénus* (1696), *Polyxène et Pyrrhus,* etc.; motets, *Cantiques spirituels* and other church music.

Colbran, Isabella (Angela) (b Madrid, 2 Feb 1785; d Bologna, 7 Oct 1845), Spanish mezzo. Made her 1st appearance in Italy in 1806; married Rossini in 1822; she had already sung in the fps of his *Elisabetta, Otello, Armida, Mosè, La donna del lago, Maometto II* and *Zelmira.*

Coleman, Charles (d London, before 9 Jul 1664), English composer. Chamber musician to Charles I and after the Civil War music teacher in London. Mus.D., Cambridge, 1651; app. comp. to Charles II, 1662. With Cooke, Hudson, H. Lawes and Locke he contrib. music to Davenant's *Siege of Rhodes* (entertainment at Rutland House), 1656.

Coleman, Edward (b London; d Greenwich, 29 Aug 1669), English singer, lutenist and composer, son of prec. Both he and his wife sang in *The Siege of Rhodes* in 1656. He became a Gentleman of the Chapel Royal on its re-estab. in 1660 and succeeded Lanier in the royal band in 1662. Comp. incid. music to Shirley's *Contention of Ajax and Achilles* in 1653, contrib. songs to *Select Musicall Ayres and Dialogues* the same year, and pieces of his appeared in Playford's *Musical Companion* in 1672.

Coleridge-Taylor, Samuel (b London, 15 Aug 1875; d Croydon, 1 Sep 1912), English composer. Son of a black doctor and an Eng. mother. Sang at a church at Croydon as a boy, and entered the RCM as a vln. student in 1890, but also studied comp. under Stanford. He had works perf. while still at coll. and in 1899 he was represented at the N. Staffordshire Festival at Hanley. App. cond. of the Handel Society in 1904, and visited USA that year, as well as in 1906 and 1910; but otherwise devoted all his time to comp. and private teaching, with some teaching activity at the GSM in the last years of his life.

Works incl. opera *Thelma* (1907–9); settings for solo voices, chorus and orch. of portions from Longfellow's *Hiawatha* (3 parts, 1898), Coleridge's *Kubla Khan* (1905), Noyes's *A Tale of Old Japan*; 5 Choral Ballads (Longfellow), *Sea Drift* (Whitman) for chorus; oratorio *The Atonement*; incid. music for Shakespeare's *Othello* and Stephen Phillips's *Herod, Ulysses, Nero* and *Faust* (after Goethe); symph. in A min.; vln. concerto in G min.; nonet for strings and wind, pf. 5tet, clar. 5tet, string 4tet in D min. and other chamber music; pf. music, songs.

Coletti, Filippo (b Anagni, 11 May 1811; d Anagni, 13 Jan 1894), Italian baritone. Debut Naples, 1834; sang at the Teatro San Carlo in the fps of *Caterina Cornaro* and *Alzira*. At Her Majesty's, London, he created Francesco in *I Masnadieri* (1847). Well known as Boccanegra and in operas by Pacini and Bellini.

Colgrass, Michael (Charles) (b Chicago, 22 Apr 1932), American composer and percussionist. Studied with Milhaud, Lukas Foss and Ben Weber. Has worked in NY with various theatre ensembles.

Works incl. *Chamber Music* for 4 drums and string 4tet (1954), *Chant* for chorus and vibraphone (1954), *Divertimento* for 8 drums, pf. and strings (1960), *Seventeen* for orch. (1960), *Virgil's Dream*, theatre piece (1967), *The Earth's a Baked Apple* for chorus and orch. (1969), *Nightingale Inc.*, opera (1971), *Letter from Mozart*, collage for pf. and orch. (1976), *Concertmasters*, concerto for 3 vlns. and orch. (1976), *Theatre of the Universe* for solo voices, chorus and orch. (1976–7), pf. concerto (1982), vla. concerto (1984).

Colla, Giuseppe (b Parma, 4 Aug 1731; d Parma, 16 Mar 1806), Italian composer. *Maestro di musica* to the court at Parma, 1766, and to Ferdinand of Bourbon, 1785.

He married the singer Lucrezia Aguiari in 1780.

Works incl. operas *Adriano in Siria* (1762), *Enea in Cartagine* (1769), *Andromeda* and 6 others; also church music.

Colla parte (It. = 'with the part'), a direction indicating that the accomp. to a vocal or instrumental solo part is to follow the soloist in a passage perf. without strict adherence to the tempo.

Collegium Musicum (Lat. = musical fraternity), an assoc. for the perf. of chamber and orch. music in var. Ger. towns in the 18th cent. Now used in universities specifically for an ens. perf. early music.

Colles, H(enry) C(ope) (b Bridgnorth, 20 Apr 1879; d London, 4 Mar 1943), English music critic and scholar. Educ. at Oxford and the RCM in London. Asst. music critic to Fuller Maitland on *The Times* until 1911, when he became chief critic, and lecturer at the RCM from 1919. Pub. var. books on mus., incl. *Brahms, The Growth of Music, Voice and Verse*, etc., the 7th vol. of the *Oxford History of Music*, and ed. the 3rd and 4th eds. of *Grove's Dictionary of Music and Musicians*.

Collier, Marie (b Ballarat, 16 Apr 1927; d London, 8 Dec 1971), Australian soprano. She studied in Melbourne and Milan; CG debut 1956, as Musetta; among her best roles there were Tosca, Manon Lescaut and Jenůfa. She was the first Hecuba in Tippett's *King Priam*, and Katerina Izmaylova in the 1st stage perf. in Brit. of Shostakovich's opera (1963). Also admired as Emilia Marty and Katya Kabanová.

Collin, Heinrich Joseph von (1771–1811), Austrian poet. His chief connection with music is the drama *Coriolan* for which Beethoven wrote an overture. Stadler wrote incid. music for his tragedy *Polyxena*.

Collingwood, Lawrance (b London, 14 Mar 1887; d Killin, Perthshire, 19 Dec 1982), English conductor and composer. Chorister at Westminster Abbey and organ scholar at Exeter Coll., Oxford; lived in Rus. for a time and worked with Albert Coates at the St Petersburg Opera; married there and returned to England during the Revolution. Principal cond. SW 1931–46.

Works incl. opera *Macbeth* (1934), symph. poem for orch., 2 pf. sonatas, etc.

Colombe, La (*The Dove*), opera by Gounod (lib. by J. Barbier and M. Carré, after La Fontaine), prod. Baden-Baden, 3 Aug 1860.

Colonna, Giovanni Paolo (b Bologna, 16 Jun 1637; d Bologna, 29 Nov 1695), Italian composer. Studied in Rome with Carissimi,

Abbatini and Benevoli. Became organist of San Petronio at Bologna in 1659 and *maestro di cappella* in 1674.

Works incl. opera *Amilcare di Cipro* (1692) and other dramatic works; Masses, motets, psalms, litanies; oratorios.

Colonne, Édouard (actually Judas) (b Bordeaux, 23 Jul 1838; d Paris, 28 Mar 1910), French violinist and conductor. Founder of the Concerts Colonne. He was the 1st to popularize Berlioz and was well known for his perfs. of Wagner, Tchaikovsky and other comps. then unknown in Fr.

Color (Lat.), in medieval music = melodic figuration in general. Also a melodic unit repeated in the context of an isorhythmic structure. *See* **Isorhythmic.**

Coloratura (It. lit. colouring), florid singing, esp. in soprano parts containing elaborately decorative passages.

Colour, a word frequently used metaphorically for the different qualities of tone prod. by var. instruments and combinations of instruments. 'Tone-colour' is now generally current.

Colour Music, comps. referring to or using colour (light):

Bantock, *Atalanta in Calydon*, during the perf. of which the concert-room is to be lighted in a different colour for each movement.

Bliss, *Colour Symph.*, each movement of which bears the name of a colour as title.

Schoenberg, *Die glückliche Hand*, in which coloured light plays a part, as noted in the score.

Skriabin, *Prometheus*, which contains an optional part for the *tastiera per luce*, designed to throw differently coloured lights.

Colporteur, Le, ou L'Enfant du bûcheron (*The Pedlar, or The Woodcutter's Child*), opera by Onslow (lib. by F.A.E. de Planard), prod. Paris, Opéra-Comique, 22 Nov 1827.

Coltellini, Celeste (b Livorno, 26 Nov 1760; d Capodimonte nr. Naples, 24 Jul 1828), Italian mezzo. 1st appeared in 1780. Attached to the Teatro dei Fiorentini in Naples 1781–91, but made frequent appearances in Vienna; debut 1785 in Cimarosa's *La contadina in spirito*. Paisiello wrote *Nina* for her.

Combattimento di Tancredi e Clorinda, Il (*The Combat of T. and C.*), dramatic cantata by Monteverdi (text by Tasso, from Canto XII, *Gerusalemme liberata*), perf. Venice, Palazzo Mocenigo, 1624. Pub. in Monteverdi's *Madrigali guerrieri e amorosi*, 1638.

Combination Tones, the secondary sounds prod. by intervals of 2 notes struck at the

same time. There are 2 kinds of combination tone. Difference Tones, prod. by the difference between the 2 generating notes, which consequently sound below the generators, and Summation Tones, prod. by the sum of these 2 notes, which sound above. All combination tones are faint, and some are virtually inaudible. Tartini was the first to observe Difference Tones.

Come prima (It. = as at first), a direction indicating that the opening section of a movement is to be played again exactly as before, or that a passage is to be treated in the same manner as before.

Come sopra (It. = as above), a direction asking the player to repeat the manner of perf. of a passage heard earlier.

Come, thou monarch of the vine, song by Schubert, from Shakespeare's *Antony and Cleopatra*, trans. by F. von Mayerhofer as *Trinklied*, 'Bacchus', and comp. in German in 1826.

Come, ye sons of art, away, ode by Purcell for the birthday of Queen Mary II, 1694 (text by ? N. Tate).

Comédie lyrique (Fr.), an 18th-cent. French name for comic opera.

Comedy on a Bridge (*Veselohra na moste*), opera for radio in 1 act by Martinů (lib. by the comp., after V.K. Klicera), prod. Prague Radio, 18 Mar 1937.

Comes, Juan Bautista (b Valencia, c 1582; d Valencia, 5 Jan 1643), Spanish composer. *Maestro de capilla* at Lérida at first, later music director at Valencia Cathedral from 1613 and again from 1632 with an appt. at the royal chapel in Madrid and another at the Colegio del Patriarca at Valencia in between.

Works inc. much church music on a large scale; sacred music with Span. words, etc.

Commedia per musica (It. = comedy for music), a Neapolitan term of the 18th cent. for comic opera.

Common Chord, the non-technical term for the maj. or min. triad.

Common Time, a loose but widely current term for 4–4 time sometimes indicated by ⊂.

Communion, the last item of the Proper of the Rom. Mass. Orig. a psalm with antiphon before and after each verse, only the antiphon is now retained. In general style the Communion resembles the Introit.

Compact Disc, a form of gramophone record in which the music is digitally encoded and read by laser. *See* **Gramophone.**

Compass. The range of notes covered by a voice or instrument.

Compenius, German family of organ builders who also worked in Denmark:

1. Heinrich C. the elder (b *c* 1525; d Nordhausen, 2 May 1611).

2. Esaias C. (b Eisleben; d Hillerød, 1617), son of prec.

3. Heinrich C. the younger (b Eisleben; d Halle, 22 Sep 1631), brother of prec.

4. Ludwig C. (b Halle; d Erfurt, 11 Feb 1671), son of prec.

Heinrich C. the elder was also a theorist and comp. The organ at Frederiksborg Castle, built by Esaias C. in 1605–10, is still playable. His organ treatise (1615–16) was finished by Michael Praetorius (*c* 1619).

Compère, Loyset (b Hainaut, *c* 1445; d Saint-Quentin, 16 Aug 1518), French composer. At first a chorister, later a canon and chancellor of Saint-Quentin Cathedral.

Works incl. Masses, magnificats and other church music; also many secular songs with Fr. and It. words.

Compound Intervals, any Intervals exceeding the compass of an 8ve, so called, as distinct from Simple Intervals, because they differ from the latter only in width, not in character; e.g. a maj. 10th is essentially the same as a maj. 3rd, etc.

Compound Time, any musical metre in which the beats can be subdivided into three, e.g. 6–8, 9–8, 12–8, where there are respectively 2, 3 and 4 beats in the bar, each divisible into 3 quavers. In Simple Time, on the other hand, the beats are divisible into 2.

Computers in Music. Among the innumerable contributions of the 'new technology' to music may be mentioned (a) its use for electronic composition and performance, *see* **Synthesiser;** (b) its use for setting music in print; (c) its use for analysing music, particularly style characteristics or details of a particular performance.

Comte Ory, Le (*Count O.*), opera by Rossini (lib. by Scribe and C.G. Delestre-Poirson), prod. Paris, Opéra, 20 Aug 1828.

Comus, masque by Milton, with music by Henry Lawes, prod. Ludlow Castle, 29 Sep 1634.

The same with alterations by Dalton and music by Arne, prod. London, Drury Lane Theatre, 4 Mar 1738.

Con (It.) = with. The prep. is often used in directions indicating the manner of perf. of a piece or movement, e.g. *con brio* = with dash, *con molta espressione* = with much expression, etc.

Con amore (It. = with love, with affection), indicating an enthusiastic manner of perf.

Concento (It. = union, agreement), the playing of the notes of a chord exactly together.

Concert, orig., as in the English 'consort', the singing or playing together under any conditions; now a public perf. of music, except that of an opera or as a rule that given by a single perf., which is more often called a Recital.

Concert Spirituel, a musical institution founded in Paris by A. Philidor in 1725 for the prod. of sacred works, but afterwards widening its scope to incl. secular music, esp. symphs. and concertos. It lasted until 1791, but was later replaced by similar organizations.

Concertante (It. = concertizing), **concertant** (Fr.), an adj. used to designate instrumental or more rarely vocal parts in a comp. which are designed largely for the display of virtuosity. A *sinfonia concertante*, for ex., is a work with a prominent and brilliant solo part or several such parts.

Concertato (It. = concerted), a work or portion of a comp. written for several persons to perf. together.

Concerted Music, any music written for several soloists to perf. together. Any chamber music or a 4tet or other ensemble in an opera or oratorio is concerted music, but the opera or oratorio itself is not, neither is, for ex., a symph. or a choral part-song.

Concertgebouw Orchestra, Dutch orch. based in the Concertgebouw, Amsterdam, built in 1888. First cond. Willem Kes. Other conds. have incl. Willem Mengelberg, 1895–1945, Eduard van Beinum, 1945–59, Bernard Haitink and Eugen Jochum, jointly 1961–4; Haitink 1964–86. Present dir. is Riccardo Chailly.

Concertina, an instrument, patented in 1829, similar to the accordion, prod. its sound by means of metal reeds set vibrating by wind driven by pleated bellows opened and closed by the player's hands.

Concertino (It. = little concert or little concerto). In the former sense the concertino is a group of solo instruments playing alternately with the orchestra (*ripieno*) in a work of the *Concerto grosso* type; in the latter a concertino is a concerto for a solo instrument formally on a smaller scale.

Work by Janáček for pf., clar., horn, bassoon, 2 vlns., vla.; comp. 1925, fp Brno, 16 Feb 1926.

Work by Stravinsky for string 4tet, comp. 1920; rev. 1952 for 12 insts., fp Los Angeles, 11 Nov 1957.

Concertmaster (Amer.), the term used in

USA for the leader of an orch., derived from the Ger. *Konzertmeister*.

Concerto. Etymologically the word carries two implications: performing together (in 'concert') and fighting or struggling (from the Lat. 'concertare'). So the earliest common uses of the word appear in contexts such as the Ferrarese 'concerto delle donne' of the 16th cent., a superbly coordinated madrigal ensemble. Many concertos of the 17th and 18th cent. are simply ensemble pieces. From the early 18th cent. a concerto increasingly became an ensemble work in which a single performer was given the opportunity to display particular soloistic virtuosity; and from the time of Mozart the concerto has characteristically included a component of struggle between soloist and orchestra.

Concerto grosso (It. = grand or big concert), an orch. work of the 17th–18th cent. played by an orch. in which generally a group of solo instruments take a more or less prominent part. The group of soloists was called the *concertino* and the main orch. (*tutti*) the *ripieno*. Bach's Brandenburg Concertos are works of the concerto grosso type, although nos. 3 and 6 contain no *concertino* parts.

Concertstück (Ger., also *Konzertstück* = concerto piece), a title sometimes given to works of the concerto type for solo instrument and orch. which are not fully developed concertos. *Concertstücke* are often in 1 movement or in several connected sections. Although Ger., the title has been used by comps. in other countries, e.g. Chaminade and Pierné in Fr., Cowen in Eng.

Conchita, opera by Zandonai (lib., in Fr., by M. Vaucaire, trans. into It. by C. Zangarini, based on P. Louÿs's novel *La Femme et le pantin*), prod. Milan, Teatro dal Verme, 14 Oct 1911. The lib. was orig. written for Puccini.

Concord, the sounding together of notes in harmony that satisfies the ear as being final in itself and requiring no following chord to give the impression of resolution.

Concord Sonata, work for pf. by Ives in 4 movts.: *Emerson, Hawthorne, The Alcotts, Thoreau*, after the Concord, Mass., group of writers admired by Ives; comp. 1909–15, 1st complete perf. NY, 20 Jan 1939, by John Kirkpatrick.

Concrete Music. *See* **Musique Concrète.**

Conducting. Groups of more than about six performers have nearly always needed someone to ensure ensemble and consistency of interpretation, and there is iconographic evidence of conds. in Egypt and Sumeria from the 3rd millenium B.C., just as there is for medieval chant choirs. With the rise of written polyphony, however, ensembles tended to be small and musical direction normally lay in the hands of a leading performer – in the Baroque era often controlling the ensemble from an organ, harpsichord or (partic. in Classical music) from the violin. Cond. with a baton as an independent activity arose only in the 19th cent. partic. with Spontini, Spohr and Mendelssohn; and the earliest professional career cond. seems to have been Otto Nicolai (1810–49). But until the 20th cent. the main conds. were virtually all primarily composers.

Conductus, a 12th–13th-cent. vocal comp. originally processional in character and written for 1 or more voices. The basic melody of a *conductus* was generally a tune specially comp. A *conductus cum cauda* was a polyphonic comp. ending with an elaborate tail-piece without words (*cauda*, Lat. = tail). In the polyphonic *conductus* the parts normally move in the same rhythm.

Congreve, William (1670–1729), English dramatist and poet. *See* **Austin (F.)** (*The Way of the World*), **Eccles (J.)** (do., *Love for Love, Semele* and *Ode for St Cecilia's Day*), **Finger** (*Love for Love* and *Mourning Bride*), **Judgment of Paris** (J. Eccles, Finger, D. Purcell and Weldon), **Philidor (8)** (*Ode for St C.'s D.*), **Purcell** (*Double Dealer and Old Bachelor*), **Semele** (Handel), **Wellesz** (*Incognita*).

Connell, Elizabeth (b Port Elizabeth, S. Africa, 22 Oct 1946), Irish mezzo, later soprano. Debut as Varvara (*Katya Kabonová*) at Wexford in 1972. She then sang with Australian Opera and appeared as a mezzo with ENO 1975–80, as Eboli and Herodias. CG debut 1976, as Viclinda in *I Lombardi*. She sang Ortrud at Bayreuth in 1980; other mezzo roles incl. Lady Macbeth, Venus, Kundry and La Vestale. Geneva 1984, Norma. NY Met debut 1985, as Vitellia. She returned to CG in 1985–6 for the *Trovatore* Leonora and Leonore in *Fidelio*.

Connolly, Justin (Riveagh) (b London, 11 Aug 1933), English composer. He studied at the RCM with Fricker; prof. there since 1966. He taught at Yale Univ. in the early 1960s and his music has been influenced by Milton Babbitt and Elliott Carter.

Works incl. 6 sets of *Triads* (trios) for various inst. ens. (1964–74), 5 sets of *Obbligati* for var. chamber ens. (1965–81), *Antiphonies* for 36 insts. (1966), 2 sets of *Poems of Wallace Stevens* for sop., clar. and pf.

(1967–70), *Rebus* for orch. (1970), *Diaphony* for organ and orch. (1977), *Sentences* for chorus, brass and organ (to poems by Thomas Traherne, 1979),) oratorio *The Marriage of Heaven and Hell* (text by Blake).

Conradi, Johann Georg (d Oettingen, 22 May 1699), German composer. Music director at Ansbach, 1683–6, and director of the Hamburg opera 1690–93. One of the earliest comps. of Ger. operas, which incl. *Die schoene und getreue Ariadne* (1691), *Diogenes Cynicus, Numa Pompilius, Der tapffere Kayser Carolus Magnus* (1692), *Der Verstöhrung Jerusalem, Der wunderbar-vergnüte Pygmalion*; sacred music.

Consecration of the House (Beethoven). *See* **Weihe des Hauses.**

Consecutive, an adj. used to describe the progression of intervals of the same kind in similar motion.

Consequent, another term for the Answer in a Fugue.

Consorvatoire National Superieur de Musique, the chief school of music in Paris, opened in 1795 with Sarrette as director, having grown out of the École Royale du Chant, estab. in 1784 under the direction of Gossec. Later directors were Cherubini, Auber, A. Thomas, Dubois, Fauré, Rabaud, Delvincourt, M. Dupré and Loucheur.

Conservatorio (It.), later Conservatoire (Fr.), Conservatorium (Ger.), Conservatory (Eng., esp. Amer.), a school of music orig. in It., esp. Venice and Naples, an orphanage where children were 'conserved' to become useful citizens and at the same time trained as musicians.

Console, the part of an organ which is directly under the control of the player's hands and feet.

Consonance, the purely intoned sounding together of notes capable of prod. concord.

Consort. 16th- and 17th- cent. English term for Ensemble. The earliest uses are specifically associated with groups of diverse instruments, i.e. what until recently was thought of as Broken consort (*q.v.*).

Constant, Marius (b Bucharest, 7 Feb 1925), Rumanian-born French composer and conductor. He studied in Paris with Messiaen and Honegger; dir. Ballets de Paris, 1956–66, music dir. Ars Nova, an ens. promoting new music, 1963–71. His early works were impressionistic; later turned to serialism.

Works incl. operas *La Serrure* and *Le Souper* (both 1969), *La Tragédie de Carmen*

(1981); ballets *Jouer de flute* (1952), *Haut Voltage* (1956), *Cyrano de Bergerac* (1960), *Paradise Lost* (1967), *Candide* (1970), *Le Jeu de Sainte Agnes* ('ecclesistical action' for singers, dancers, actor, organ, elec. guitar, tromb. and perc.; 1974); pf. concerto (1954), *Turner,* 3 essays for orch. (1961), *Winds* for 13 wind insts. and db. (1968), *14 Stations* for 92 perc. insts. and ens. (1970), *103 Regards dans l'eau* for vln. and orch. (1981); *Pelléas and Mélisande Symphony* (1986).

Consul, The, opera by Menotti (lib. by the comp.), prod. Philadelphia, 1 Mar 1950.

Contano (It. = they count; accent on 1st syll.), a direction in a vocal or instrumental part of a work where the perfs. have a prolonged rest, warning them to count bars in order to make sure of coming in again at the proper moment.

Conte Caramella, Il, opera by Galuppi (lib. by Goldoni, partly based on Addison's comedy *The Drummer, or The Haunted House*), prod. Verona, 18 Dec 1749.

Contemporary Music Network. *See* **Arts Council of Great Britain.**

Contes d'Hoffmann, Les (*The Tales of Hoffmann*), opera by Offenbach (lib. by J. Barbier and M. Carré, based on a play of their own and farther back on stories by E.T.A. Hoffmann), prod. Paris, Opéra-Comique, 10 Feb 1881, after Offenbach's death. He did not finish it; the scoring is partly by Guiraud.

Contesa dei numi, La (*The Contest of the Gods*), opera by Gluck (lib. by Metastasio), prod. Copenhagen, at court, 9 Apr 1749, to celebrate the birth of Prince Christian, later Christian VII.

Opera by Vinci (lib. do.), prod. Rome, Cardinal Polignac's palace, 26 Nov 1729, to celebrate the birth of the Dauphin, son of Louis XV.

Conti, Carlo (b Arpino, 14 Oct 1796; d Arpino, 10 Jul 1868), Italian composer. Pupil of Zingarelli, later prof. at the Naples Cons., where he deputized as director in 1862 when Mercadante became blind.

Works incl. operas *Olimpia* and *Giovanna Shore* (after Rowe; 1829); 6 Masses, 2 Requiems, etc.

Conti, Francesco Bartolomeo (b Florence, 20 Jan 1681; d Vienna, 20 Jul 1732), Italian lutenist and composer. Theorbo player to the Aus. court in Vienna, 1701–5 and again from 1708; court comp. from 1713.

Works incl. operas *Alba Cornelia* (1714), *Clotilda, Il trionfo dell' Amore, I satiri in Arcadia, Don Chisciotte in Sierra Morena*

(1719), *L'Issipile, Pallade trionfante* (1722), etc., stage serenades; oratorios, cantatas.

Conti, Gioacchino. See **Gizziello.**

Continental Fingering, the fingering of pf. music now in universal use, with the fingers marked 1–5 from the thumb. This system has displaced the so-called English Fingering, marked + for the thumb and 1–4 for the other fingers, which however was by no means in use throughout the whole hist. of Eng. keyboard music.

Contino, Giovanni (b Brescia, *c* 1513; d *c* 1574), Italian composer. Active at Trent, perhaps teacher of Marenzio. From 1561 *maestro di cappella* to the Mantuan court. Composed Masses, Lamentations and motets.

Continuo (It. abbr. for *basso continuo*). A practice first written down shortly before 1600 by which the bass line of a work is perf. by one or more players who add chords above the line using an established set of principles often notated by **Thorough-bass** (*q.v.*; also called figured bass). Characteristically the continuo group consisted of a melody instrument or instruments (cello, bass, bassoon, trombone, viola da gamba) and chordal instruments (organ, harpsichord, chitarrone, harp, lute, etc). Much operatic music of the 17th and 18th cents., for example, was written purely as a melodic line with continuo: normally the harmonic structure was entirely clear from those two lines, and the function of the continuo players was not only to provide a firm basis against which the melody could be heard and to fill in the chords, but more partic. to provide variety of texture and rhythm. As time progressed the continuo group tended to become smaller: in chamber music from around 1680 it normally comprised only a keyboard instrument and a cello.

Contra (Lat. = against), a prefix used for org. stops denoting that the stop indicated by the word following it sounds an 8ve lower.

Contrabassoon. See **Double Bassoon.**

Contrafactum (Lat. = counterfeit), a vocal comp. in which the orig. words have been replaced by new ones, either secular words substituted for sacred, or vice versa. In the 16th cent. the Reformation was responsible for several changes of this kind, esp. from Lat. to vernacular words in the conversion of plainsong melodies to hymn-tunes.

Contralto, the lowest woman's voice, frequently abbreviated to *alto*, though this term is also used for the highest (falsetto) male voice and for a low boy's voice.

Contrapunctus (Lat.), counterpoint.

Contrary Motion. See **Motion.**

Contratenor, in the 14th and 15th cents. a voice in the same range as the Tenor but generally moving in far less conjunct fashion.

Contredanse (Fr.). See **Country Dance.**

Convenziene ed inconvenienze teatrali, II, 1-act opera (*farsa*) by Donizetti (lib. by the comp., after A.S. Sografi), perf. Naples, Teatro Nuovo, 21 Nov 1827. Sometimes given in modern revivals under the spurious title *Viva la Mama.*

Converse, Frederick (Shepherd) (b Newton, Mass., 5 Jan 1871; d Westwood, Mass., 8 Jun 1940), American composer. Although intended for a commercial career, he studied music at Harvard Univ. under Paine. Later he studied pf. with Carl Baermann and comp. with Chadwick at Boston, and took a finishing course at Munich. After his return to USA he held var. teaching posts at Boston and Harvard until 1907. From 1917 to 1919 he served in the army and in 1930 he became Dean of the New England Cons., a post which he held until 1938.

Works incl. operas *The Pipe of Desire* (1905), *The Sacrifice* (1910), *The Immigrants* (1914), and *Sinbad the Sailor*; *Job* for solo voices, chorus and orch., *Laudate Dominum* for male voices, brass and org.; 5 symphs. (1920–40), orch. tone-poems *Endymion's Narrative* (1901), *The Mystic Trumpeter* (after Whitman, 1905), *Ormazd, Ave atque vale, Song of the Sea, Flivver Ten Million,* romance *The Festival of Pan* for orch.; *Night and Day* for pf. and orch. (after Whitman); *Hagar in the Desert* for contralto and orch., *La Belle Dame sans merci* for baritone and orch. (Keats, 1902); 3 string 4tets; pf. trio; sonata and concerto for vln. and pf.; pf. pieces; songs.

Convitato di pietra, II (*The Stone Guest*), opera by Fabrizi (*c* 1765–?) (lib. by G.B. Lorenzi), prod. Rome, 1787.

Convitato di pietra, II, o sia II dissoluto, opera by Righini (lib. by ?), prod. Vienna, Kärntnertortheater, 21 Aug 1777.

Cook, Thomas (Aynsley) (b London, Jul 1831 or 1836; d Liverpool, 16 Feb 1894), English bass. Studied with Staudigl at Munich and sang at var. Bavarian theatres before he made his 1st stage appearance in Eng. at Manchester in 1856. The maternal grandfather of E. and L. Goossens.

Cooke, Arnold (b Gomersal, Yorks., 4 Nov 1906), English composer. Educ. at Repton School and Caius Coll., Cambridge, where he took the Mus.B. degree in 1929. From that year to 1932 he was a pupil of Hindemith in Berlin, and in 1933 was app. prof. of harmony and comp. at the RMCM. In 1938 he settled in London; app. prof. of comp. at TCM, 1947.

Works incl. operas *Mary Barton* (1949–54), *The Invisible Duke* (1976); cantata *Holderneth* for baritone, chorus and orch.; 6 symphs. (1946–84), 2 clar. concertos, concert overture for orch., Passacaglia, Scherzo and Finale for string orch., pf. concerto; 4 Shakespeare sonnets for voice and orch.; 5 string 4tets (1933–78), variations for string 4tet, pf. trio, 4tet for fl., vln., vla. and cello, 5tet for fl., clar., vln., cello and harp; duo for vln. and vla.; sonatas for vln. and pf., vla. and pf., cello and pf.; sonata for 2 pfs.; pf. sonata and suite.

Cooke, Benjamin (b London, 1734; d London, 14 Sep 1793), English organist and composer. Pupil of Pepusch, whom he succeeded in 1752 as cond. to the Academy of Ancient Music. In 1757 he was app. choirmaster at Westminster Abbey in succession to Gates. Mus.D., Cambridge, 1775, and Oxford, 1782, when he became organist of St Martin-in-the-Fields in London.

Works incl. services, anthems (some for special occasions), psalms, chants and hymns; ode for Delap's tragedy *The Captives*; *Ode on the Passions* (Collins), odes for Christmas Day, on Handel, on Chatterton and for the king's recovery, ode *The Syren's Song to Ulysses*; glees, catches and canons; orchestral concertos; organ pieces; harpsichord lessons.

Cooke, Deryck (b Leicester, 14 Sep 1919; d Thornton Heath, 26 Oct 1976), English musicologist. Studied privately and at Cambridge. From 1947 to 1959 he worked for the BBC, devoting much time to writing and broadcasting. His best-known works incl. the book *The Language of Music* (1959) and his performing vers. of Mahler's unfinished 10th symph., heard in London on 13 Aug 1964 (rev. 1972).

Cooke, Henry (b ? Lichfield, c 1615; d Hampton Court, 13 Jul 1672), English bass and composer. Pupil of the Chapel Royal; was a captain in the Duke of Northumberland's army during the Civil War. App. singer and Master of the Children at the Chapel Royal at the Restoration. With Charles Coleman, Hudson, H. Lawes and Locke be contrib. to Davenant's *Siege of Rhodes* (entertainment at Rutland House), 1656, and sang in it. His daughter married Humfrey.

Works incl. coronation music, hymn for the installation of Knights of the Garter,

anthems, songs for 1 and more voices, etc.

Cooke, Thomas (Simpson) (Tom), (b Dublin, 1782; d London, 26 Feb 1848), Irish tenor, violinist and composer. Learnt music from his father, Bartlett C., an oboist, played a vln. concerto in public at 7, learnt comp. from Giordani, was leader of the Crow Street Theatre orch. at 15 and kept a music shop in 1806–12. In 1813 he appeared in London with great success and settled there. For c 20 years he not only sang at Drury Lane Theatre, but led the orch., played 9 different instruments, managed the house and provided music stage pieces for it. He also taught singing with success.

Works incl. stage pieces *Frederick the Great* (1814), *The Wager, The Brigand, Peter the Great, King Arthur and the Knights of the Round Table* (1834); songs for Shakespeare's *Midsummer Night's Dream*; songs, glees, catches.

Coolidge, Elizabeth Sprague (b Chicago, 30 Oct 1864; d Cambridge, Mass., 4 Nov 1953), American music patron. In 1918 she estab. the Berkshire Festivals of Music and in 1925 created a foundation (named after her) to produce concerts, music festivals, to make awards, etc. She instituted the award of a gold medal (also named after her) for distinguished services to chamber music in 1932. The comps. from whom she commissioned works incl. Schoenberg, Webern, Stravinsky, Bartók, Prokofiev, Malipiero, Casella, Piston and Bridge.

Cooper, Emil (b Kherson, 20 Dec 1877; d New York, 19 Nov 1960), Russian conductor. After study at Odessa and Vienna he cond. in Russia and gave the fp of *The Golden Cockerel* (Moscow, 1909). Later gave the Rus. fp of *The Ring.* Chicago 1929–36. NY Met 1944–50 (*Peter Grimes* and *Khovanshchina*), Montreal Opera Guild from 1950.

Cooper, John. *See* **Coperario.**

Cooper, Martin (Du Pré) (b Winchester, 17 Jan 1910; d Richmond, Surrey, 16 Mar 1986), English writer on music. Educ. at Winchester Coll. and Oxford, studied music with Wellesz in Vienna. His work incl. books on Gluck, Bizet and Beethoven. He was chief music critic of *The Daily Telegraph* 1950–76 and was ed. of *The Musical Times* from 1953 to 1956.

Coperario, John (b c 1570–80; d ? London, 1626), English lutenist, violist and composer. Studied in It. and on his return, c 1604, adopted the Italianized name of Coperario or Coprario. He taught the children of James

I and was the master of W. and H. Lawes.

Works incl. *The Masque of the Inner Temple and Gray's Inn* (F. Beaumont), *The Masque of Flowers*; *Funeral Teares* on the death of the Earl of Devonshire, *Songs of Mourning* on the death of Prince Henry (words by Campion); anthems; works for viols and for viols and org; fancies for the organ based on It. madrigals; lute music; songs, etc.

Copland, Aaron (b Brooklyn, NY, 14 Nov 1900), American composer. Began to learn the pf. at the age of 13 and studied theory with Rubin Goldmark; later went to Fr. and became a pupil of Nadia Boulanger at the Fontainebleau School of Music. In 1924 a Guggenheim scholarship enabled him to spend 2 more years in Europe. He was represented for the 1st time at an ISCM festival at Frankfurt in 1927 and won a prize in Amer. music with his *Dance Symphony* in 1930. He has since done much propaganda work for Amer. music, and writes and lectures on music.

Works incl. opera *The Tender Land* (1952–4); ballets *Billy the Kid* (1938), *Rodeo*, *Appalachian Spring* (1943–4); school opera *The Second Hurricane*; music for films incl. *Of Mice and Men*; orch. works: 3 symphs., *Music for the Theatre*, *Symph. Ode*, *A Dance Symph.*, *Statements*, *El Salón México* (1933–6), *Music for the Radio*, *An Outdoor Overture*, *Quiet City* (1939), *Letter from Home*, *Danzón Cubano*; *Lincoln Portrait* for orator and orch. (1942), pf. concerto, clar. concerto, *Connotations* for orch. (1962), *Inscape* (1967), *3 Latin American Sketches* (1972).

The House on the Hill and *An Immorality* for female chorus; 2 pieces for string 4tet; 6tet for clar., strings and pf.; pf. 4tet; 9tet; vln. and pf. sonata; pf. sonata, pf. pieces.

Coppélia, ou La Fille aux yeux d'émail (*C., or The Girl with Enamel Eyes*), ballet by Delibes (scenario by C. Nuitter and A. Saint-Léon; choreog. by L. Mérante), prod. Paris, Opéra, 25 May 1870.

Coppola, Pier Antonio (b Castrogiovanni, Sicily, 11 Dec 1793; d Catania, 13 Nov 1877), Italian composer. Studied at Naples and prod. his 1st opera, *Il figlio del bandito*, there in 1816. He was at Lisbon in 1839–42 as cond. of the San Carlo Theatre and again in 1850–71.

Works incl. operas *La pazza per amore* (*Eva* in Fr., 1835), *Gli Illinesi*, *Inés de Castro* (1841), etc.; Masses, litanies and other church music.

Coprario, Giovanni. *See* **Coperario.**

Coptic Chant, the music of the Christian Church in Egypt, which from the middle of the 5th cent. has been Monophysite. There was a primitive system of notation by the 10th cent., but nothing definite is known about the chant in its orig. form. It still flourishes today, and is charact. by the use of perc. instruments.

Coq d'or (Rimsky-Korsakov). *See* **Golden Cockerel.**

Cor anglais. *See* **English Horn.**

Corbett, William (b *c* 1675; d ? London, 7 Mar 1748), English violinist and composer. At var. times leader of the orch. at the King's Theatre, Haymarket, director of Lincoln's Inn Fields Theatre, member of the royal band; lived for some time in It., where he toured as a violinist and collected instruments.

Works incl. incid. music to plays, e.g. Shakespeare's *Henry IV* (1699), orch. concertos and sonatas for var. instruments.

Cordatura (It.), the notes to which a string instrument is tuned, e.g. G, D, A, E for the vln. Any change in the normal tuning made temporarily is called *scordatura*.

Corder, Frederick (b London, 26 Jan 1852; d London, 21 Aug 1932), English teacher, conductor and composer. Studied at the RAM in London and under F. Hiller at Cologne. Prof. of comp. at RAM from 1888. 1st Eng. trans. of Wagner's *Ring*.

Works incl. opera *Nordisa* (1887), cantatas *The Bridal of Triermain* (after Scott) and *The Sword of Argantyr* (1889), overture *Prospero* (after Shakespeare's *Tempest*), Elegy for 24 vlns. and organ; recitations with music; songs, part-songs.

Cordier, Baude (*fl.* 1400 or shortly before), French composer. Recent research makes it seem likely that he was the harpist Baude Fresnel (d 1397–8), though certain features of his style make such an early death-date hard to accept. Of his 10 surviving *chansons* two are partic. famous because of their notation: *Belle, bonne*, written out in the form of a heart; and *Tout par compas*, written down in a circle.

Corelli, Arcangelo (b Fusignano, Imola, 17 Feb 1653; d Rome, 8 Jan 1713), Italian violinist and composer. Studied at Bologna, settled in Rome *c* 1685 and pub. his 1st vln. sonatas. He lived at the palace of his patron, Cardinal Pietro Ottoboni. Visited Modena and Naples, cond. at the Roman residence of Christina of Swed., collected pictures and taught many vln. pupils, incl. Geminiani and Locatelli.

Works incl. a set of 12 *Concerti grossi* op.

6, incl. no. 8 in G min., '*fatto per la notte di nattale*', i.e. Christmas; 5 sets of chamber sonatas.

Corelli, Franco (b Ancona, 8 Apr 1921), Italian tenor. Debut Spoleto, 1951, Don José; Milan, La Scala, since 1954. CG debut 1957, Cavaradossi; NY Met 1961, as Manrico. Paris, Opéra, and Vienna Staatsoper since 1970. Much admired as Calaf, Ernani, Radames and Raoul in *Les Huguenots*.

Corena, Fernando (b Geneva, 22 Dec 1916; d Lugano, 26 Nov 1984), Swiss bass. Debut Trieste, 1947, as Varlaam (after minor roles in Geneva pre-war). NY Met debut 1954, as Leporello. Edinburgh 1955 and 1963 as Falstaff and Don Pasquale. CG 1960 as Rossini's Bartolo. Other roles incl. Escamillo, Osmin, Dulcamara and Don Alfonso.

Corigliano, John (b New York, 16 Feb 1932), American composer. Studied with Otto Luening at Columbia Univ. and privately with Paul Creston; has taught at Lehmann Coll., NY, from 1973.

Works incl. vln. sonata (1963), *Elegy* for orch. (1966), pf. concerto (1968), clar. concerto (1977), *Hallucinations* for orch. (1981); incid. music for plays by Sophocles, Molière and Sheridan; *Naked Carmen*, arr. of Bizet for singers, pop and rock groups, synthesizer and instruments.

Coriolan, Beethoven's overture, op. 62, to the play of that name by Heinrich von Collin, comp. in 1807 and prod. with the play in March of that year. Apart from its subject the play has no connection with Shakespeare's *Coriolanus*.

Corkine, William (*fl.* 1610–12), English lutenist and composer. Pub. 2 books of airs to the lute and bass viol, followed by dances and other instrumental pieces; an anthem is also preserved. The 2nd book of airs contains settings of Donne's 'Go and catch a falling star'; *Break of Day*: ' 'Tis true, 'tis day'; *The Bait*: 'Come live with me, and be my love'.

Cornago, Johannes (*fl.* 1450–75), Spanish Franciscan friar and composer. He was at the Neapolitan court of Alfonso V and his son Ferrante I. His *Missa de la mapa mundi* has a *cantus firmus* with the text 'Ayo visto lo mappamundo'. His other works include a motet, and secular pieces to Span. words.

Corneille, Pierre (1606–84), French poet and dramatist. *See* Charpentier (M.-A.) (*Polyeucte* and *Andromède*), Cid (Cornelius and Massenet), Cleopatra e Cesare (Graun), Dukas (*Polyeucte* overture), Flavio (Handel), Lully (Œdipe), Martyrs

(Donizetti), Poliuto (Donizetti), Polyeucte (Gounod), Rieti (*Illusion comique*), Roberto Devereux (Mercadante), Sacchini (*Gran Cid*), Tito Vespasiano (Caldara and Hasse), Wagenaar (J.) (*Cid*).

Corneille, Thomas (1625–1709), French poet and dramatist, brother of prec. *See* Bellérophon (Lully), Charpentier (M.-A.) (*Pierre philosophale* and 2 plays with Visé), Médée (M.-A. Charpentier), Psyché (Lully).

Cornelius, Peter (b Mainz, 24 Dec 1824; d Mainz, 26 Oct 1874), German composer and author. Studied music after failing as an actor, 1st with Dehn in Berlin, 1845–50, and from 1852 with Liszt at Weimar, where he joined the new Ger. group of musicians and wrote eloquently about them in Schumann's *Neue Zeitschrift*, without however succumbing to Wagnerian influence in his own work. He sought out Wagner in Vienna in 1858 but declined to follow him to Munich in 1865.

Works incl. operas *Der Barbier von Bagdad* (1855–8), *Der Cid* (1860–62) and *Gunlöd* (unfinished); choral works *Trauerchöre* and *Vätergruft*; duets for soprano and baritone; songs incl. cycles *Liedercyclus*, *Weihnachtslieder* (1859), *Brautlieder* (1856–8), etc.

Cornelius, Peter (b Labjerggard, 4 Jan 1865; d Snekkersten, 30 Dec 1934), Danish tenor. He sang bar. roles from 1892, debut Copenhagen, as Escamillo. From 1902 he was heard in the Wagner heldentenor roles: Siegfried at Bayreuth, 1906, and in the 1st Eng.-language *Ring* perfs. at CG, 1908–9.

Cornelys (*née* Imer), T(h)eresa (b Venice, 1723; d London, 19 Aug 1797), Italian singer, married to the dancer Pompeati, but assumed the name of Cornelys when at Amsterdam. She made her 1st appearance in London in 1746 as Signora Pompeati, in Gluck's *Caduta de' giganti*, and in 1760 began to give usical entertainments at Carlisle House in Soho Square, continuing until 1771, when she was indicted for keeping it for immoral purposes, just possibly at the instigation of jealous rivals. A talented singer, she died in the Fleet prison, leaving a daughter by Casanova.

Cornet, a brass wind instrument derived from the coiled post-horn and fitted with valves to enable it to prod. all the chromatic notes within its compass. It is a regular member of the military band and the treble instrument of the brass band. It is also used in the orchestra as an addition to the tpts., less often as a substitute. Cornets are usually in A or Bb and transpose accordingly; a smaller cornet in Eb is standard in brass bands. To be distinguished from Cornett.

Cornett, wind instrument made of wood or ivory in the shape of a long, thin, slightly tapering tube, either straight or slightly curved, and covered with leather. Cornetts were often used as treble instruments with sackbuts (trombs.), frequently in church. The Serpent belongs to the same family.

Corno di bassetto (It.) = Basset Horn. (In 1888–9 Bernard Shaw wrote music criticism for *The Star* under the pseudonym of C.di B.)

Cornyshe, John (*fl.* 1500), English composer. His only surviving work is a setting of *Dicant nunc Judei.*

Cornyshe, William (d ? Hylden, Kent, *c* Oct 1523), English composer. Attached to the courts of Henry VII and Henry VIII, not only as musician, but as actor and prod. of interludes and pageants. Gentleman of the Chapel Royal from *c* 1496; succeeded Newark as Master of the Children in 1509. He wrote music for the court banquets and masques and officiated in Fr. at the Field of the Cloth of Gold in 1520.

Works incl. motets, Magnificats, *Ave Maria*; secular songs, some with satirical words, for instruments and voices, incl. a setting of (?) Skelton's *Hoyda, Jolly Rutterkin.*

A William C. senior (d *c* 1502), not to be confused with this composer, was the 1st recorded master of the choristers at Westminster Abbey (*c* 1480–90).

Coronach (Gael. = 'crying together'), a funeral cry, or in its more cultivated musical form a dirge.

Coronation Anthems, 4 anthems by Handel comp. for the coronation of George II and perf. at the ceremony in Westminster Abbey, 11 Oct 1727. 1. 'Zadok the Priest', 2. 'The King shall rejoice', 3. 'My heart is inditing', 4. 'Let thy hand be strengthened'. A number of other comps., from H. Cooke in the 17th cent. to Vaughan Williams in the 20th, have written anthems for coronations in England.

'Coronation' Concerto, the nickname of Mozart's pf. concerto in D, K537 (dated 24 Feb 1788), perf. by him at Frankfurt at the coronation festivities for Leopold II, 15 Oct 1790.

'Coronation' Mass, Mozart's Mass in C K317 (dated 23 Mar 1779), so called because it is said to have been written to commemorate the crowning in 1751 of a miraculous image of the Virgin Mary.

Coronation Ode, work by Elgar in 6 sec-

tions for soloists, chorus and orch., op. 44; comp. 1901–2, fp Sheffield, 2 Oct 1902. Finale is 'Land of Hope and Glory', based on tune from *Pomp and Circumstance* march no. 1.

Corregidor, Der (*The Magistrate*), opera by Wolf (lib. by R. Mayreder, based on P.A. de Alarcón's story *El sombrero de tres picos* = *The Three-cornered Hat*), prod. Mannheim, 7 Jun 1896.

Corrente (It.) = Courante.

Corrette, Michel (b Rouen, 1709; d Paris, 22 Jan 1795), French organist, teacher and composer. He held var. organist's posts from 1737, and between 1737 and 1784 pub. 17 methods on performing practice; these incl. *L'école d'orphée* (1738), for vln., *Les amusements du Parnasse* (1749, harpsichord), *Le parfait maître à chanter* (1758), *Les dons d'Apollon* (1762, guitar), *Les délices de la solitude* (1766, cello), *Nouvelle methode pour apprendre la harpe* (1774) and *Le berger galant* (1784, flute).

His comps. incl. ballets *Les âges* (1733) and *Le lys* (1752); sacred music, e.g. motets, Te Deum (1752), Laudate Dominum (1766), *Trois leçons de ténèbres* for low voice and organ (1784); secular vocal pieces incl. ariettes and cantatas; concertos for musette, vielle, fl. and vln.; sonatas, organ and harpsichord music.

Corri, Domenico (b Rome, 4 Oct 1746; d London, 22 May 1825), Italian conductor, publisher and composer. Pupil of Porpora. Settled at Edinburgh in 1771 as cond. of the Music Society, pub. and singing-master. He failed in business and settled in London *c* 1790, where he set up in partnership with Dussek, who married his daughter Sophia in 1792.

Works incl. operas *Alessandro nell' Indie* (1774) and *The Travellers* (1806); instrumental sonatas, rondos and other pieces; songs incl. *Six Canzones dedicated to Scots Ladies*, etc. He also wrote theoretical works, incl. a music dictionary.

Corri, Sophia. See Dussek.

Corsaire, Le, overture by Berlioz, op. 21, comp. in It., 1831, rewritten in Paris, 1844, fp Paris, 19 Jan 1845, as *La Tour de Nice*; final version (*Le Corsaire*) fp Brunswick, 8 Apr 1854.

Corsaro, Il (*The Corsair*), opera by Verdi (lib. by F.M. Piave, based on Byron's poem), prod. Trieste, 25 Oct 1848.

Corsi, Jacopo (b Florence, 17 Jul 1561; d Florence, 29 Dec 1602), Italian nobleman and amateur composer. Took part in the initiation of opera at Florence. Peri's *Dafne* was prod. at his house in 1598 and he took some share in its comp.

Corteccia, Francesco di Bernardo (b Florence, 27 Jul 1502; d Florence, 7 Jun 1571), Italian organist and composer. Organist at the church of San Lorenzo from 1531 and *maestro di cappella* from 1539 to Cosimo I de' Medici, for the marriage of whose son Francesco to Joanna of Aus. in 1565 he wrote music with Striggio, for Cini's intermezzo *Psiche ed Amore*.

Works incl. hymns in 4 parts, canticles and responses, madrigals, pieces for 4–8 voices and instruments.

Cortez, Viorica (b Bucium, 26 Dec 1935), Rumanian mezzo. After a concert career she sang Dalila at Toulouse in 1965. Her Carmen has been admired at CG (from 1968). NY Met debut 1971. In 1974 she was heard as Adalgisa at La Scala and as Dulcinea in Massenet's *Don Quichotte* at the Paris Opéra. Other roles incl. Amneris, Eboli and Charlotte.

Cortot, Alfred (Denis) (b Nyon, Switz., 26 Sep 1877; d Lausanne, 15 Jun 1962), French pianist and conductor. He studied at the Paris Cons., where he gained the *premier prix* in 1896. After serving as a *répétiteur* at Bayreuth he founded the Société des Festivals Lyriques at Paris and cond. the fp in Fr. of *Götterdämmerung* in 1902. In 1905 he formed a pf. trio with Jacques Thibaud and Pablo Casals. From 1907 to 1917 he taught at the Paris Cons. and in 1918 was joint founder of the École Normale de Musique. In addition to his continuous activity as a pianist and cond. he gave many lectures on pf. technique and interpretation and collected a valuable library of rare works.

Cosa rara (Martín y Soler). *See* **Una cosa rara**.

Così fan tutte, o sia La scuola degli amanti (*All women do it, or The School for Lovers*), opera by Mozart (lib. by L. da Ponte), prod. Vienna, Burgtheater, 26 Jan 1790.

Cossira, Emile (b Orthez, 1854; d Quebec, Feb 1923), French tenor. Debut Paris, Opéra-Comique, 1883; appeared at the Opéra 1888–91 and created Saint-Saëns's Ascanio (1889). At Brussels and Lyons he was the 1st local Tristan and Walther. CG 1891–1900 as Faust, Don José and Raoul.

Cossotto, Fiorenza (b Crescentino, Vercelli, 22 Apr 1935), Italian mezzo. Debut, Milan, La Scala, in the première of Poulenc's *Carmélites* (1957); roles at La Scala have incl. Azucena, Eboli, Adalgisa and Santuzza. CG since 1959, debut in Cherubini's *Médée*.

US debut Chicago, 1964; NY Met 1968, Amneris.

Cossutta, Carlo (b Trieste, 8 May 1932), Italian tenor. Sang small roles in Buenos Aires from 1956 before creating Ginastera's Don Rodrigo in 1964; CG debut same year, as Duke of Mantua. Other roles in London have incl. Otello, Manrico, Gabriele Adorno and Don Carlos. He sang Pollione at the NY Met in 1973 and Radames in Moscow with the La Scala co. on tour in 1974.

Costa, Michael (Michele Andrea Agniello) (b Naples, 4 Feb 1808; d Hove, 29 Apr 1884), Italian (anglicized) conductor and composer of Spanish descent. Studied in Naples and prod. his 1st 2 operas at the Cons. there in 1826–7, and wrote a Mass, 3 symphs. and other works. In 1829 he was sent to Birmingham by Zingarelli to cond. a work by that comp. at the Festival, but by a mistake was made to sing tenor instead. He then settled in London, wrote many ballets and operas and perfected the orch. at the Opera; in 1846 he was app. cond. of the Phil. Society and Covent Garden opera, and he became the most important festival cond. Knighted in 1869.

Works incl. operas *Il delitto punito*, *Il sospetto funesto*, *Il carcere d'Ildegonda*, *Malvina*, *Malek Adhel* (on M. Cottin's novel; for Paris, 1838), *Don Carlos* (London, 1844); ballets *Kenilworth* (after Scott), *Une Heure à Naples*, *Sir Huon*; oratorios *La passione*, *Eli*, *Naaman*; Mass for 4 voices, *Dixit Dominus*; symphs.; vocal 4tet *Ecco il fiero istante*.

Costanza e Fortezza (*Constancy and Fortitude*), opera by Fux (lib. by P. Pariati), prod. Prague, Hradžin Palace, at the coronation of the Emperor Charles VI as king of Bohemia, and birthday of the Empress Elizabeth Christina, 28 Aug 1723.

Costeley (Cauteley), Guillaume (b Fontagnes, Auvergne, *c* 1531; d Évreux, 28 Jan 1606), French organist and composer. He was organist to Henri II and Charles IV. 1st president of the St Cecilia society at Évreux estab. in 1570s. Wrote *chansons* for several voices, instrumental pieces.

Cosyn, Benjamin (b *c* 1570; d 1652 or later), English organist and composer. Organist at Dulwich Coll., 1622–4, and afterwards at the Charterhouse. Wrote church music and collected a book of virginal pieces by var. comps.

Cotrubas, Ileana (b Galati, 9 Jun 1939), Rumanian soprano. Debut as Debussy's Yniold, Bucharest, 1964. She sang in Frankfurt, Brussels and Salzburg before Glyndebourne, in 1969, as Mélisande; Callisto in the 1st modern perf. of Cavalli's opera in 1970. CG debut 1971, as Tatyana; other London roles have incl. Susanna, Violetta, Gilda, Antonia and Micaela. US debut in Chicago, as Mimi, in 1973; NY Met from 1977.

Cotton, John (also known as John of Afflighem), English or Flemish 12th-cent. music scholar. Author of a Latin treatise on music which seems to have been widely distributed in MS.; 6 copies are preserved in var. European libraries.

Couci, Le Chastelain de (Gui II) (d 1203), castellan, 1186–1201, of the Château de Coucy, N. of Soissons. He died in the crusade which was to lead to the estab. of the Lat. Empire in Constantinople (*see* **Byzantine Chant**). He was a *trouvère*; 15 of his poems with their music have come down to us.

Couleurs de la cité céleste, work by Messiaen for pf., 13 wind, xylophone, marimba and 4 perc.; comp. 1963, fp Donaueschingen, 17 Oct 1964, cond. Boulez.

members advocating the use of plainsong alone), correspondence between the music and the meaning of the words, etc. The opening of a Roman seminary for the training of priests was also decided, and this was opened in 1565 with Palestrina as music master.

Counter (verb), to perf. improvised variations on a tune in the 16th–17th cents.

Counter Subject, the name for a theme in a fugue which continues in the 1st voice at the point where the 2nd voice enters with the subject (*see* **Fugue**).

A regular counter subject recurs from time to time in association with the subject in the course of the comp.

Counterpoint, the art of combining 2 or more independent melodic lines. The general practice of counterpoint as a mode of comp. is called Polyphony. Double (or invertible) counterpoint is the term used where the top-and-bottom position of 2 melodies combined in counterpoint can be reversed (*see* illustration).

The principles of contrapuntal theory

Inversion:

COUNTERPOINT   Bach

Council of Trent, an eccles. council held at Trent (It. Trento, Ger. Trient) in S. Tyrol between 1545 and 1563 in 3 different periods each incl. a number of sessions. It was intended to introduce counter-reforms into the Roman Catholic Church to make the Reformation appear superfluous to Catholics who inclined to embrace Protestantism. Musical reforms were not discussed in detail until near the end, esp. at the meeting of 11 Nov 1563. They incl. the abolition of all Sequences except 4 (*Dies irae, Veni Sancte Spiritus, Victimae Paschali* and *Lauda Sion*), the expunging of all tunes with impious or lascivious associations used as *cantus firmi*, the simplifying of polyphony to make the words clearly audible (some

have remained more or less the same since the 13th cent.: the voices should proceed by contrary motion whenever possible and particularly in approaching a cadence; motion in parallel 5ths and 8ves is unacceptable; motion in parallel 3rds or 6ths should not last for more than a few notes; dissonances should be carefully prepared though passing notes give life to the structure; and (starting in practice in the 16th cent.) each line should have its own independent rhythmic life.

Countertenor, properly a high-pitched type of male voice which is prod. naturally in contrast to the *falsetto* of the male alto.

Country Dance, an English dance which became very popular in France in the 18th cent. and was called *Contredanse* there, having appeared as *Contredanse anglaise* in a pub. as early as 1699. It spread to other countries, being called *Contratanz* or *Kontretanz* in Ger. and Aus. It lost not only its rustic name but also its rustic nature on the Continent, where it was used for ballroom dancing and cultivated by comps of distinction, incl. Mozart and Beethoven.

Coup d'archet (Fr. = stroke of the bow), the bow attack in string playing.

Coup de glotte (Fr. = stroke of the glottis), a trick in singing whereby vowel sounds are preceded by a kind of click in the throat prod. by a momentary cutting off of the breath-stream. It is effective as an inflection and insisted on as a point of good technique by many singing-masters, while others consider it harmful to the voice.

Couperin. French 17th–18th-cent. family of musicians:

1. Louis C. (b Chaumes-en-Brie, c 1626; d Paris, 29 Aug 1661).

2. François C., Sieur de Crouilly (b Chaumes-en-Brie, c 1631; d Paris, c 1710), brother of prec.

3. Charles C. (b Chaumes-en-Brie, 9 Apr 1638; d Paris, Jan or Feb 1679), brother of prec.

4. François C. (b Paris, 10 Nov 1668; d Paris, 11 Sep 1733), son of prec.

5. Marguerite-Louise C. (b Paris, 1676 or 1679; d Versailles, 30 May 1728), daughter of 2.

6. Marie-Anne C. (b Paris, 11 Nov 1677; d ?), sister of prec.

7. Nicolas C. (b Paris, 20 Dec 1680; d Paris, 25 Jul 1748), brother of prec.

8. Marie-Madeleine-(Cécile) C. (b Paris, bap. 11 Mar 1690; d Maubuisson, 16 Apr 1742), daughter of 4.

9. Marguerite-Antoinette C. (b Paris, 19 Sep 1705; d Paris, c 1778), sister of prec.

10. Armand-Louis C. (b Paris, 25 Feb 1727; d Paris, 2 Feb 1789), son of 7.

11. Pierre-Louis C. (b Paris, 14 Mar 1755; d Paris, 10 Oct 1789), son of prec.

12. Gervais-François C. (b Paris, 22 May 1759; d Paris, 11 Mar 1826), brother of prec.

13. Céleste-Thérèse C. (b Paris, 1793; d Belleville, 14 Feb 1860), daughter of 12.

Couperin, Charles (b Chaumes-en-Brie, 9 Apr 1638; d Paris, Jan or Feb 1679), French organist and comp. (3 above). Succeeded his brother Louis as organist at the church of Saint-Gervais in Paris in 1661.

Couperin, François (b Paris, 10 Nov 1668; d Paris, 11 Sep 1733), French composer, harpsichordist and organist, son of prec. (4 above). The greatest member of a large musical family. Learnt music from his father and from Jacques-Denis Thomelin, organist of the king's chapel. App. organist at the church of Saint-Gervais in 1685, where he remained until his death. In 1693 he succeeded Thomelin as one of the organists to the king, and in 1717 received the title of Ordinaire de la Musique de la chambre du Roi. He had been connected with the court before and taught the royal children. In wider circles, too, he was famous as harpsichord teacher and laid down his system in the treatise *L'Art de toucher le clavecin*, pub. in 1716. He married Marie-Anne Ansault c 1689, and they had 2 daughters, the 2nd of whom, Marguerite-Antoinette (9 above), became a distinguished harpsichordist.

Works incl. 4 books of harpsichord pieces (c 230); 42 organ pieces; 4 *Concerts royaux* for harpsichord, strings and wind instruments; 10 chamber concertos *Les Goûts-réünis* (1724); 4 suites for strings and harpsichord *Les Nations* (1726); chamber sonatas *Le Parnasse, ou l'Apothéose de Corelli* and *L'Apothéose . . . de Lully* (1725); 2 suites of pieces for viols with figured bass; some miscellaneous chamber works; 12 songs for 1, 2 or 3 voices; church music, incl. *Laudate pueri Dominum*, *Leçons de Ténèbres* (c 1715), a number of motets, etc.

Couperin, Louis (b Chaumes-en-Brie, c 1626; d Paris, 29 Aug 1661), French composer, harpsichordist and organist, son of Charles C. (c 1595–1654) (1 above). He was sponsored by Chambonnières, musician at court, and was active in Paris from at least 1651; in 1653 he became the 1st of his family to hold the organist's post at St Gervais. He was a treble viol player at court and took part in several ballet perfs., incl. *Psyché* (1656). He is regarded as one of the finest keyboard comps. of the 17th cent.; among his 215 surviving pieces are allemandes, courantes, sarabandes, chaconnes and pasacailles for harpsichord, preludes, fugues and plainsong versets for organ, and fantaisies for chamber ensemble.

Coupler, an appliance whereby 2 manuals of an organ or a manual and the pedals can be so connected that while only 1 is being played the stops controlled by the other are brought into action. Special couplers can also be used to double the notes played automatically an octave above or below.

Couplet (Fr.), lit. a verse or stanza in a poem. In music a strophic song, generally of a light and often of a humorous type, in which the same music recurs for each verse.

Also the forerunner of the Episode in the Rondo form, occurring in the Fr. Rondeau as cultivated by Couperin and others, where a main theme returns again and again after statements of var. *couplets* between.

Courante (Fr.). (1) A dance in 3–2 time popular esp. in the 17th cent., whose name ('the running one', from *courir* = to run) suggests some affinity with the English 'running set'. It has 2 parts of equal length, each repeated, and its special feature is the rhythmic modification of the last bar of each section, where the notes appear in 2 groups of 3 instead of 3 groups of 2, as in the rest of the piece. (2) An It. dance (*corrente*) in brisk 3–4 or 3–8 time, with running passages.

Exs. of both types occur in Bach's suites and partitas.

Courses, sets of strings in instruments of the lute type used in pairs and prod. the same note, usually in unison, but sometimes in 8ves.

Courteville, English family of musicians, (?) of French descent:

1. Raphael C. (d ? London, 28 Dec 1675), Gentleman of the Chapel Royal under Charles I and again under Charles II after the Restoration.

2. Ralph (or Raphael) C. (b ? London; d ? London, *c* 1735), son of prec. Educ. in the Chapel Royal. App. organist of the church of St James, Westminster, in 1691.

Works incl. incid. music for Southerne's dramatic version of Aphra Behn's *Oroonoko* and for Part III of Durfey's *Don Quixote*; sonatas for 2 fls.; hymn-tune *St James*; many songs.

3. Raphael C (b ? London; d London, buried 10 Jun 1772), son of prec. whom (?) he succeeded at St James's Church, though he was active mainly as a political writer.

Covent Garden Theatre, London, 1st house opened 7 Dec 1732, burnt down 19 Sep 1808; 2nd opened 18 Sep 1809, burnt down 5 Mar 1856; 3rd opened 15 May 1858. The theatre did not become a regular opera house until 1847, though opera had long been perf. in it (e.g. Handel's 1st season there in 1734 and Weber's *Oberon* in 1826). The 1st work in 1847 was Rossini's *Semiramide*. It became the Royal Opera in 1892 and ran annual seasons, wholly in It. at first, but later in Fr. and Ger. also, until 1914, and again between the 2 world wars from 1919 to 1939. After being used as a dance hall from 1940 to 1945 it re-opened as a national opera house in 1946. At first opera only in English was attempted, but this impractical course was soon abandoned for prods. in the original language: a truly international house, under the administration of David Webster, then John Tooley, has therefore been developed. Jeremy Isaacs app. General Administrator in 1987, with effect from 1988.

Cowell, Henry (Dixon) (b Menlo Park, Cal., 11 Mar 1897; d Shady, NY, 10 Dec 1965), American composer and writer on music. Studied in NY, at California Univ. and in Berlin. Toured in Europe and Amer. as a pianist, lectured on music at univs. and colls. in USA and contrib. to many music papers. As early as 1912–13 he developed a technique using tone-clusters, played by striking the keyboard with the fist, forearm or elbow. He used these devices in, among other works, his pf. concerto (1929). He also employed sounds produced by plucking or stroking the strings inside the pf. With Lev Theremin he invented the Rhythmicon, an instrument allowing accurate performance of different, conflicting rhythms.

Works incl. opera *O'Higgins of Chile* (1949); ballets *The Building of Bamba* (1917) and *Atlantis*; 20 symphs. (1916–65), *Synchrony, Reel, Hornpipe, Sinfonietta, Scherzo*, etc. for orch.; 10 'tunes', 18 *Hymns and Fuguing Tunes, Exultation* and *Four Continuations* for strings; pf. concerto; 6 string 4tets (1915–62); Toccata for soprano (wordless), fl., cello and pf.; other chamber music; many pf. works.

Cowen, Frederic (Hymen) (b Kingston, Jamaica, 29 Jan 1852; d London, 6 Oct 1935), English composer and conductor. Studied in London, Leipzig and Berlin. Cond. by turns of the London Phil. Society, at Liverpool and Manchester. Knighted 1911.

Works incl. operas *Pauline* (1876), *Thorgrim, Signa* (1893) and *Harold* (1895); operettas and incid. music; oratorios *The Deluge* (1878), *St Ursula, Ruth* (1887), *The Veil*, etc.; cantatas *The Corsair, The Sleeping Beauty, St John's Eve, Ode to the Passions* (Collins), *John Gilpin* (Cowper); jubilee (1897) and coronation (1902) odes; cantatas for female voices, anthems, partsongs.

6 symphs. (1869–98: no. 3 *Scandinavian*, no. 4 *Welsh*, no. 6 *Idyllic*); 4 concert overtures, *Sinfonietta, Indian Rhapsody* and other works for orch.; concerto and *Concertstück* for pf. and orch.; string 4tet (1866), pf. trio; many pf. pieces; *c* 300 songs.

Cowie, Edward (b Birmingham, 17 Aug 1943), English composer. He studied with

Goehr, Fricker and Lutosławski and has taught in Eng., W. Ger. and Australia: several works based on the Australian criminal Ned Kelly. His interest in painting is reflected in the *Choral Symphony* of 1982, sub-titled *Symphs. of Rain, Sea and Speed.*

Works also incl. operas *Commedia* (1978) and *Kelly* (1980–); *Kate Kelly's Roadshow* for mezzo and ens. (1982); *Concerto for Orch. (1980), 2 symphs. (The American* and *The Australian*, 1980–82), 2 clar. concertos (1969, 1975), harp concerto (1982); *Endymion Nocturnes* for tenor and string 4tet (1973, rev. 1981), *Kelly Choruses* for voices and harp (1981); 4 string 4tets (1973–83), *Kelly Passacaglia* for string 4tet (1980).

Cowper, Robert (b *c* 1474; d between 1535 and 1540), English composer. Clerk of King's Coll., Cambridge, 1493–5. Wrote sacred pieces and carols, esp. in *XX songs ix of iii partes* and *xi of three partes* (1530).

Cox, Jean (b Gadsen, Ala., 16 Jan 1922), American tenor. He sang Lensky in Boston in 1951, then moved to Europe; Bayreuth debut 1956, and since 1967 as Lohengrin, Parsifal, and Siegfried. He sang Siegfried at CG in 1975 and returned in 1985 for Bacchus. Chicago from 1964; NY Met debut 1976, as Walther. Other roles incl. Janáček's Steva and Strauss's Apollo.

Crabbé, Armand (b Vandergoten, 23 Apr 1883; d Brussels, 24 Jul 1947), Belgian baritone. Debut Brussels, 1904, in *Le Jongleur de Notre Dame.* CG 1906–14, as Valentin, Silvio and Ford. La Scala debut 1914, as Rigoletto; 1929 in the fp of Giordano's *Il re.* Buenos Aires 1916–26, as Rossini's Figaro and Marouf. At Antwerp and Milan he was successful as Beckmesser.

Craft, Robert (b Kingston, NY, 20 Oct 1923), American conductor and writer on music. He studied at the Juilliard School and from 1948 was closely associated with Stravinsky: Craft was influential in his conversion to serial technique in the early 1950s. He collaborated with Stravinsky in recording his music, and was the first to record the complete works of Webern. At Santa Fe in 1963 he cond. the 1st US perf. of Berg's *Lulu* (2-act version); also recorded much of Schoenberg's music. With Stravinsky he compiled 6 vols. of 'conversations' (1959–69). Other books incl. *Stravinsky in Photographs and Documents* (1976).

Craig, Charles (b London, 3 Dec 1919), English tenor. He sang with the CG chorus from 1947 and in 1952 was heard in a London concert with Beecham, (Handel's *Ode for St Cecilia's Day*). CG debut 1959, as Pinkerton; sang in the 1st London perf. of Dvořák's *Russalka*, at SW, the same year. He was successful with the ENO as Otello, at the age of 65. As guest he has appeared at Chicago, Berlin, Paris and Vienna.

Cramer, Johann Baptist (b Mannheim, 24 Feb 1771; d London, 16 Apr 1858), German (anglicized) pianist, conductor and composer. Was taken to London at the age of 1, taught by his father and later went to Clementi for pf. study; 1st appeared in public in 1781. In 1824 he estab. a music pub. business. He lived abroad from 1835 to 1845.

Works incl. 9 pf. concertos; 2 pf. 4tets and 5tets; 124 pf. sonatas, 2 vols. of 42 studies each, 16 later studies, 100 daily exercises, etc.

Cramer, Wilhelm (b Mannheim, bap. 2 Jun 1746; d London, 5 Oct 1799), German violinist, father of prec. Member of the Mannheim Orch., 1757–72. Settled in London in 1772; leader of the royal band and of many important concert organizations. Works incl. 3 vln. concertos and chamber music.

Crawford (Seeger), Ruth (Porter) (b East Liverpool, Ohio, 3 Jul 1901; d Chevy Chase, Md., 18 Nov 1953), American composer. She studied at the Chicago Cons. and with Charles Seeger, whom she later married. Compiled many folksong anthologies, e.g. *American Folk Songs for Children* (1948) and wrote hundreds of her own pf. accompaniments. Her own comps. are regarded as anticipating certain later developments in music: they incl. suite for pf. and woodwind 5tet (1927), 9 pf. preludes (1924–8), string 4tet (1931), *Risselty, Rosselty* for small orch. (1941), 2 *Ricercari* for voice and pf. (1932).

Creation Mass (Haydn). *See* **Schöpfungsmesse.**

Creation, The (*Die Schöpfung*), oratorio by Haydn (lib. by Gottfried van Swieten after an Eng. model, now lost, based on Genesis and Milton's *Paradise Lost*), prod. Vienna, Schwarzenberg Palace, 29 Apr 1798.

Credo (Lat., 'I believe'), the 3rd item of the Ordinary of the Mass. Its text dates from the Council of Nicea (325), and its use was ordered in the Mozarabic and Gallican liturgies in 589. It was not introduced into the Roman liturgy until 1071. The example shows (i) the Mozarabic, (ii) the Gallican and (iii) the Roman forms of the chant (*see* illustration opposite).

Later medieval melodies are also known.

CREDO

Créquillon, Thomas (b between c 1480 and c 1500; d ? Béthune, 1557), Flemish composer. Choirmaster in Charles V's imperial chapel in the Netherlands. Wrote Masses, motets, Lamentations, *chansons*.

Crescendo (It. = growing), increasing in loudness.

Crescentini, Girolamo (b Urbania nr. Urbino, 2 Feb 1762; d Naples, 24 Apr 1846), Italian male soprano. Made his 1st appearance in Rome in 1783; sang in London in 1785–7. In Italy he sang in the fps of Rispoli's *Ipermestra* (1785), Cimarosa's *Gli Orazi* (1797), Zingarelli's *Meleagro* (1798) and Federici's *Ifigenia* (1809).

Crespin, Régine (b Marseilles, 23 Mar 1927), French soprano. Studied at the Paris Cons. After making her debut in the provinces, she appeared at the Paris Opéra in 1950 as Elsa. Bayreuth 1958–61, as Kundry and Sieglinde. Glyndebourne, 1959–60, as the Marschallin, the role of her NY Met debut, 1962.

Creston, Paul (real name **Joseph Guttovegio**) (b New York, 10 Oct 1906; d San Diego, 24 Aug 1985), American composer and teacher of Italian stock. Studied pf. and org., but was self-taught in harmony, theory and comp. He also did research in musicotherapy, aesthetics, acoustics and the history of music. In 1938 he was awarded a Guggenheim Fellowship. His music uses jazzy rhythms and a rich orch. palette.

Works incl. 6 symphs. (1941–82), a number of concertos, incl. 1 for 2 vlns., much orch. music; choral works, many based on texts by Whitman, chamber music, songs.

Cristofori, Bartolommeo di Francesco (b Padua, 4 May 1655; d Florence, 27 Jan 1731), Italian harpsichord maker. Worked 1st at Padua and then at Florence. Inventor of the pf., the 1st specimens of which he made in the earliest years of the 18th cent.

Critic, The, or An Opera Rehearsed, opera by Stanford (lib. by L.C. James, adapted from Sheridan's play), prod. London, Shaftesbury Theatre, 14 Jan 1916.

Criticism (from Gk. *kritein*, to judge), the evaluation and explanation of a work or a performance. In general parlance it concerns musical reporting in newspapers and journals. In more academic terms it follows the usage of, for example, literary criticism, in striving for a reasoned appreciation of a work or repertory taking the broadest possible account of its style, historical context and aesthetic impact.

Crivelli, Gaetano (b Brescia, 20 Oct 1768; d Brescia, 10 Jul 1836), Italian tenor. Appeared in Italy at a very early age and 1st went to Paris in 1811 and London in 1817; appeared in operas by Cimarosa, Paer and Mozart. In 1824 he created Adriano in Meyerbeer's *Il crociato in Egitto*.

Croce, Giovanni (b Chioggia nr. Venice, c 1557; d Venice, 15 May 1609), Italian priest and composer. Pupil of Zarlino, at Venice, where he worked at St Mark's and succeeded Donati as *maestro di cappella* in 1603. Wrote motets, psalms, madrigals, *capricci* for voices.

Croche, Monsieur, an imaginary character under whose name Debussy pub. a selection of his critical articles in 1917, the book being entitled *Monsieur Croche, antidilettante.*

Crociato in Egitto, Il (*The Crusader in Egypt*), opera by Meyerbeer (lib. by G. Rossi), prod. Venice, Teatro La Fenice, 7 Mar 1824.

Croesus (*Der hochmütige, gestürzte und wieder erhabne Croesus*), opera by Keiser (lib. by L. von Bostel after the It. of N. Minato), prod. Hamburg, Theater beim Gänsemarkt, Carnival, 1710.

Croft, William (b Nether Ettington, Warwicks, bap. 30 Dec 1678; d Bath, 14 Aug 1727), English organist and composer. Chorister of the Chapel Royal under Blow.

Organist of St Anne's, Soho, from 1700 and, with Clarke, of the Chapel Royal from 1704. Master of the Children there and organist of Westminster Abbey from 1708, succeeding Blow. D.Mus. Oxford, 1713. His most famous work is his setting of the Burial Service, which is still in use. Much other church music survives, incl. 2 vols. of anthems pub. under the title *Musica Sacra* in 1724.

Other works incl. theatrical pieces, keyboard music.

Croiza, Claire (b Paris, 14 Sep 1882; d Paris, 27 May 1946), French mezzo. Attached to the Opéra-Comique in Paris and appeared from 1906 at the Théâtre de la Monnaie in Brussels, where she sang Erda, Carmen, Berlioz's Dido, Clytemnestra and Charlotte. She was known mainly as a singer of modern French songs. In 1934 she became prof. of singing at the Paris Cons.

Crook, a detachable piece of tubing that can be fitted into brass wind instruments, esp. horns, to alter the length of the tube and thus change the tuning.

Crosdill, John (b London, 1755; d Eskrick, Yorks., Oct 1825), English cellist. The best Eng. player of his time, attached to the Concert of Antient Music, the Chapel Royal, etc. Chamber musician to Queen Charlotte.

Cross-Fingering, a method of fingering woodwind instruments which omits intermediate holes. It is often necessary for high notes and may also be convenient as an alternative.

Cross, Joan (b London, 7 Sep 1900), English soprano. She sang major roles with SW, London, from 1931 to 1946; created Ellen Orford there in 1945. Other Britten creations were the Female Chorus (1946), Lady Billows (1947), Elizabeth I (1953) and Mrs Grose (1954). She was a founder member of the EOG, 1945, and taught from 1955, esp. at the National School of Opera.

Cross-Rhythm, the device in composition of making the accentuation of a theme or melody conflict with (*a*) the normal strong beats of the bar or (*b*) the accents of another tune combined with it. For ex. a melodic shape in groups of 3 crotchets to the bar would be in cross-rhythm if it occurred in a piece with the time-signature of 6–8.

Crosse, Gordon (b Bury, 1 Dec 1937), English composer. He studied with Wellesz and Petrassi and has taught at Birmingham and Essex Univs.

Works incl. operas *Purgatory* (1969), *The Grace of Todd* (1969), *The Story of Vasco* (1974); 2 symphs. (1964 and 1976), 2 vln.

concertos (1962, 1969), *Dreamsongs* for orch. (1979), *Array* for tpt. and strings (1986); string 4tet (1980); pieces for children: *Meet my Folks* (Hughes), *Potter Thompson* and *Holly from the Bongs*.

Crossley, Paul (b Dewsbury, Yorks., 17 May 1944), English pianist and educator. He studied at Oxford and with Messiaen in Paris. London debut 1968. Tippett wrote for him the 3rd sonata (1973). Well known in Romantic and modern music; has played with the London Sinfonietta. In 1986 presented a successful series of TV programmes, on 20th cent. classics and played in the Brit. stage fp of Janáček's *Diary of One who Disappeared* (London Coliseum)..

Crotch, William (b Norwich, 5 Jul 1775; d Taunton, 29 Dec 1847), English composer. Played the organ in London at the age of 4, went to Cambridge at 11 to assist Randall at the organs of Trinity and King's Colls. and prod. an oratorio *The Captivity of Judah* there in 1789, having moved the prec. year to Oxford for theological studies. He turned to music finally in 1790 and was app. organist at Christ Church there. D.Mus., Oxford, 1799, having already succeeded Hayes as prof. in 1798. On the estab. of the RAM in London in 1822 he became its 1st principal.

Works incl. oratorios *Palestine* (1805–11) and *The Captivity of Judah* (2 settings); *Ode to Fancy* (J. Warton) and ode for the installation of Lord Grenville as Chancellor of Oxford Univ., ode for the accession of George IV; funeral anthem for the Duke of York; anthems and chants, motet *Methinks I hear*; glees; concertos and fugues for organ.

Crotchet, a note or rest taking half the time of a minim and forming the unit of any time-signature of which the lower figure is 4, also that marked C (= 4–4).

Crüger, Johann (b Gross-Breese, Prus., 9 Apr 1598; d Berlin, 23 Feb 1662), German theorist and composer. Cantor at St Nicholas's Church, Berlin, from 1622. Wrote several chorales afterwards used by Bach.

Works incl. *Praxis pietatis melica* containing hymn-tunes with bass, *Geistliche Kirchen-Melodien* containing hymn-tunes prescribed by Luther set for 4 voices with instruments (1649), Magnificats; secular songs.

Crumb, George (Henry) (b Charleston, W. Va., 24 Oct 1929), American composer. He studied in Berlin with Blacher and at the Univ. of Michigan with Ross Lee Finney. An early influence was Schoenberg, and aleatory techniques have also been employed.

Works incl. the orch. pieces *Variazoni*

(1959), *Echoes of Time and the River* (1967); *Star-Child* for sop., children's voices, male speaking choir, bell ringers and orch., perf. NY, 1977, cond. Boulez), *A Haunted Landscape* for inst. ens. (1984); *Night Music* for sop. and ens. (1963), 4 books of madrigals for sop., with various inst. ens. (1965–9), *11 Echoes of Autumn* for vln., fl., clar., pf. (1965), *Ancient Voices of Children* for sop. and ens. (1970), 4 books of *Makrokosmos* for amplified pf. and perc. (1972–9).

Crumhorn (or Cromorne), a woodwind instrument made of wood and bent, played with a double reed enclosed in a cap. It was used in the 16th and 17th cents., partic. in Ger. and mainly for dance music. It has a nutty, buzzing tone, somewhat reminiscent of a kaazoo.

Crusell, Bernhard Henrik (b Uusikaupunki nr. Turku, 15 Oct 1775; d Stockholm, 28 Jul 1838), Finnish composer and clarinettist. He was a member of the military band at Svaeborg castle, Finland, before moving to Stockholm in 1791; studied there with the Abbé Vogler. In 1798 he went to Berlin and in 1803 studied with Berton and Gossec in Paris. A leading clar. virtuoso of his day, he also worked at the Stockholm Opera; trans. and cond. for the 1st time in Sweden operas by Beethoven, Rossini, Meyerbeer and Auber.

Works incl. an opera *The Little Slave Girl* (*Den lilla slavinnan*, 1824); 3 clar. concertos (1811, 1818, 1828), Concertante for horn, bassoon, clar. and orch. (1816), Concertino for bassoon and orch.; 3 4tets for clar. and strings (1811, 1817, 1823), 3 clar. duos (1821), Div. for ob. and strings (1823); 37 songs for 4-part chorus.

Cruvilli (Crüwell), Johanne (Jeanne) Sophie Charlotte (b Bielefeld, 12 Mar 1826; d Monte Carlo, 6 Nov 1907), German soprano. Made her debut at Venice in 1847 as Odabella in *Attila*; 1st sang in Paris in 1851 and was engaged for the Opéra in 1854. She sang there in *Les Huguenots, La Vestale* and *La juive*; Hélène in the fp of *Les Vêpres Siciliennes*, 1855.

Cruz, Ivo (b Cidade de Corumba, Brazil, 19 May 1901; d Lisbon, 8 Sep 1983), Portuguese conductor and composer. Studied music and law at Lisbon, where later he founded the review *Renascimento musical*, resuming his studies at Munich in 1924. On his return he founded a choral society in 1930 and a chamber orch. in 1933. App. director of the Lisbon Cons. in 1938.

Works incl. *Nocturnos da Lusitania* and

Motivos lusitanos (1928) for orch., *Vexilla regis* for soprano and orch., sonatina for vln. and pf., pf. music, songs.

Crwth (Welsh = Crowd, also called Cruit, Crot, Crotta, Crotte or Rotte), an early bowed string instrument, ancestor of the vln. family.

Cry, work by Giles Swayne for 28 amplified voices, depicting the creation of the world; comp. 1978, fp London, 23 Jul 1980.

Csárdás (Hung.), a Hungarian dance consisting of a slow movement called *Lassú* and a quick one falled *Friss*.

Csermák, Antal György (b *c* 1774; d Veszprém, 25 Oct 1822), Hungarian violinist and composer. He became leader in a Budapest theatre orch., visited many noble houses and under the influence of Bihari began to cultivate a national style, esp. that of the *verbunkos*.

Cubana, La, oder Ein leben für die Kunst (*La Cubana, or a Life for the Arts*), vaudeville by Henze (text by M. Enzensberger, after M. Barnet); comp. 1973, fp NY, NET theatre, 4 Mar 1974; stage première Munich, Theater am Gärtnerplatz, 28 May 1975.

Cuckoo, a toy instrument. *See* **Toy Symphony.**

Cuclin, Demetre (b Galatz, 5 Apr 1885; d Bucharest, 7 Feb 1978), Rumanian composer. Studied at the Bucharest Cons. and later with Widor at the Cons. and d'Indy at the Schola Cantorum in Paris. In 1922–30 he taught in NY but returned to Rum. to become prof. at the Bucharest Cons.

Works incl. operas *Soria* (1911), *Agamemnon* (1922), *Trojan* and *Bellerophon* (1925); overture for chorus and orch., sacred and secular choruses; 20 symphs. (1910–72), symph. scherzo for orch.; vln. concerto; pf. trio; vln. and pf. sonatas, suites for vln. and pf. and cello and pf.; pf. pieces; songs.

Cue, a few notes printed in small music type in instrumental or vocal parts of a musical work, serving as a guide to show where the perf. is to come in after a lengthy rest.

Cuenod, Hugues (b Vevey, 26 Jun 1902), Swiss tenor. After a career as a concert singer sang also in opera from 1928. He created Stravinsky's Sellem (Venice, 1951). Glyndebourne 1954–84, in *Figaro, Falstaff, Calisto* and *The Cunning Little Vixen*. Active as a recitalist into his 80s.

Cui, César Antonovich (b Wilno, 18 Jan 1835; d Petrograd, 26 Mar 1918), Russian composer of French descent. Educ. at the High School of Wilno, where his father, a Fr.

officer left behind in the retreat from Moscow in 1812, was prof. of Fr. He had some lessons in music from Moniuszko, but was sent to the School of Military Engineering at St Petersburg in 1850, where he became sub-prof. in 1857. He became an authority on fortifications and remained an amateur in music. But he joined Balakirev's circle of Rus. nationalist comps. and became one of the 'Kutchka' group, though the least exclusively Rus. among them. He became a critic in 1864 and did much literary work for the cause.

Works incl. operas *The Mandarin's Son* (1859, prod. 1878), *The Captive in the Caucasus* (after Pushkin), *William Ratcliff* (after Heine, 1869), *Angelo* (after Hugo), *Le Flibustier* (lib. by J. Richepin), *The Saracen* (after Dumas sen., 1889), *A Feast in Time of Plague* (Pushkin, 1900), *Mam'zelle Fifi* (after Maupassant), *Matteo Falcone* (after Mérimée) and *The Captain's Daughter* (1911); works for chorus with and without orch.; 4 suites and other works for orch.; string 4tets in C min. (1890) and D (1907); 15 op. nos. of pf. pieces, 3 pieces for 2 pfs.; var. instrumental pieces; *c* 25 op. nos. of songs incl. settings of Pushkin, Lermontov, Nekrassov, Richepin and Mickiewicz.

cummings ist der Dichter (*c. is the poet*), work by Boulez for 16 voices and 24 insts.; comp. 1970, fp Stuttgart, 25 Sep 1970; work in progress. Title allegedly arose as the result of a misheard telephone conversation, concerning the name of the poet who provided the work's text (e.e. cummings).

cummings, e(dward) e(stlin) (1894–1962), American poet. *See* **Bennett (Richard R.)** (*Love Songs*), **Berio** (*Circles*), **Boulez** (*c. ist der Dichter*), **Dickinson** (songs), **Erb, (D.)** (*Cummings Cycle*), **Harper, (E.)** (*7 poems by e.e.c.*), **Smalley** (7tet for sop. and ens.).

Cunning Little Vixen, The (*Příhody lišky Bystroušky*), opera by Janáček (lib. by the comp., after R. Těsnohlídek's verses for a comic strip published serially in a Brno newspaper during 1920). Comp. 1921–3, prod. Brno, 6 Nov 1924.

Cupid and Death, masque by James Shirley with music by Locke and C. Gibbons, perf. London, before the Port. ambassador, Leicester Fields, 26 Mar 1653.

Curioso indiscreto, Il (*Indiscreet Curiosity*), opera by Anfossi (lib. by ?), prod. Rome, Teatro della Dame, Feb 1777. Mozart wrote 2 extra soprano arias for this when it was prod. in Vienna, 30 Jun 1783.

Curlew River, church parable in 1 act by Britten (lib. by W. Plomer after the Japanese

Noh play *Sumidagawa*), prod. Orford Church, Suffolk, 12 Jun 1964.

Curtain Tune, an old term sometimes used in the place of 'Act tune' for an Intermezzo or Entr'acte in the incid. music for a play.

Curtal(l), the 16th–17th-cent. English name for the bassoon and dulcian.

Curtis, Alan (b Mason, Mich., 17 Nov 1934), American conductor, harpsichordist and musicologist. He studied at Michigan and Illinois Univs. and with Gustav Leonhardt in Amsterdam. Prof. at Berkeley, Calif., since 1970. He is an authority on early keyboard music and has edited for recording and prod. several 17th-cent. operas, e.g. Monteverdi's *Poppea*, Cavalli's *Erismena* and Cesti's *Il Tito* (Innsbruck, 1983).

Curwen, English family of music educationists and publishers:

1. **John C.** (b Heckmondwike, Yorks., 14 Nov 1816; d Manchester, 26 May 1880), founded the Tonic Sol-fa method of music teaching, estab. the Tonic Sol-fa Assoc. in 1853 and the pub. firm in London in 1863.

2. **John Spencer C.** (b London, 30 Sep 1847; d London, 6 Aug 1916), son of prec., studied at the RAM under Macfarren, Sullivan and Prout, carried on his father's work and began the competition festival movement in England with the Stratford (E. London) Festival in 1882.

3. **Annie** (Jessy), *née* Gregg (b Dublin, 1 Sep 1845; d Matlock, 22 Apr 1932), wife of prec., studied at the RIAM, married in 1877 and wrote a number of books on a music teaching method of her own.

Curzon, Clifford (b London, 18 May 1907; d London, 1 Sep 1982), English pianist. Entered RAM in 1919, winning 2 scholarships and the Macfarren Gold Medal. He made his debut, aged 16, at the Queen's Hall, London. In 1926 he was appointed prof. at the RAM and in 1928 went to Berlin to study with Schnabel for 2 years. He later studied with Landowska and Nadia Boulanger, resigning his post at the RAM in 1932 to devote himself to concert work. He married in 1931. His great sensitivity and musical intelligence made him one of the finest pianists of the day, esp. in the work of Schubert, Brahms and Mozart. Knighted 1977.

Cusins, William (George) (b London, 14 Oct 1833; d Remonchamps, Ardennes, 31 Aug 1893), English pianist, violinist, organist, conductor and composer. Studied under Fétis at the Brussels Cons. and at the RAM in London. Was active in various musical organizations in London and at court. Knighted 1892.

Works incl. oratorio *Gideon* (1871); *Royal Wedding Serenata*; overture to Shakespeare's *Love's Labour's Lost* (1875); pf. concerto in A min., etc.

Cutting, Francis (*fl.* 1583–*c* 1603), English lutenist and composer. Virtually nothing is known of his life; he comp. much lute music, incl. 11 pieces in Barley's *A New Booke of Tabliture* (1596).

Cutting, Thomas English 16th–17th-cent. lutenist. In the service of Lady Arabella Stuart until 1607, then of Christian IV of Denmark at Copenhagen until 1611, when he returned and entered Prince Henry's private band.

Cuzzoni, Francesca (b Parma, *c* 1700; d Bologna, 1770), Italian soprano. Made her operatic debut in 1716, and sang 1723–8 in Handel's operas in London; created roles in *Ottone, Giulio Cesare, Tamerlano, Rodelinda* and *Alessandro*. Her rivalry with Faustina Bordoni became notorious, and they fought on stage during a perf. of Bononcini's *Astianatte* in 1727.

Cyclic Form. The form of a composition in several movements, usually a symph. or chamber work, in which one or more themes appear in at least 2 movements and lend organic unity to the whole.

Cyclic Mass. A misleading term for a setting of the Ordinary of the Mass in which there is some kind of thematic connection between the movements.

Cymbals. Plate-shaped brass percussion instruments a pair of which is struck together or 1 of which is made to sound in various ways by being touched with hard or soft drum-sticks. They have no fixed pitch, but there are ancient cymbals of smaller size which give out definite notes.

Cymon, opera by Michael Arne (lib. by D. Garrick, based on Dryden's *Cymon and Iphigenia*), prod. London, Drury Lane Theatre, 2 Jan 1767.

Cyrano, opera by W. Damrosch (lib. by W.J. Henderson, based on Rostand's play *Cyrano de Bergerac*), prod. NY Met, 27 Feb 1913.

Cyrano de Bergerac, opera by Alfano (lib. by H. Cain, based on Rostand's play), prod. in It. trans., Rome, Teatro Reale, 22 Jan 1936.

Cythère assiégée, La (*Cytherea Besieged*), opera by Gluck (lib. by C.S. Favart, based on Longus's *Daphnis and Chloe*), prod. Vienna, Burgtheater, spring 1759.

Czaar und Zimmermann (Lortzing). *See* **Zar und Zimmermann**

Czakan. A woodwind instrument, prob. originating from Transylvania but very fashionable in Vienna *c* 1830, of the fl. type, but made in the shape of a walking-stick and often used as such.

Czernohorsky. *See* **Černohorský.**

Czerny, Carl (b Vienna, 21 Feb 1791; d Vienna, 15 Jul 1857), Austrian pianist, teacher and composer. He was 1st taught the pf. by his father, played brilliantly at the age of 10 and became a pupil of Beethoven about that time; he also took advice from Hummel and Clementi. Not liking to appear in public, he took to teaching and soon had an enormous following of pupils, among which he chose only the most gifted. This left him enough leisure for comp., which he cultivated so assiduously as to prod. almost 1,000 works.

Works incl. 24 Masses, 4 Requiems, 300 graduals and offertories; many symphs., overtures; concertos; string 4tets and trios; choruses; songs and, most numerous of all, masses of pf. music, incl. studies, exercises, preludes and fugues in all the keys and endless arrs. of other composers' works.

Czerwenka, Oscar (b Linz, 5 Jul 1924), Austrian bass. Debut Graz, 1947, in *Der Freischütz*; Vienna Staatsoper since 1951, Salzburg since 1953. Glyndebourne debut 1959, as Ochs; NY Met 1960, as Rocco. Other roles incl. Osmin, Kečal and Abu Hassan in *Der Barbier von Bagdad*.

Cziffra, György (b Budapest, 5 Nov 1921), French pianist of Hungarian birth. He studied at the Liszt Academy, Budapest, with Dohnányi and was a recitalist before war service. He was a political prisoner during the early 1950s and escaped to Fr. in 1956. Best known in the music of Liszt, Chopin and Schumann.

Czyż, Henryk (b Grudziadz, 16 Jun 1923), Polish conductor and composer. He held posts with the orchs. of Łódź and Kraków, 1957–68, and in 1966 was in Munster to cond. the fp of Penderecki's *St Luke Passion*. In 1969 he gave the fp, in Hamburg, of Penderecki's opera *The Devils of Loudun*. Led the Düsseldorf orch. 1971–4 before returning to Łódź until 1980, when he became a prof. at the Warsaw Academy. US debut 1973, with the Minnesota Orch.

Works incl. *Etude* for orch. (1949), Symphonic Vars. (1952), and the comic opera *Kynolog w rosterce* (*The Dog-lover's Dilemma*; comp. 1964, prod. Kraków, 1967).

D

D, the 2nd note, or supertonic, of the scale of C major.

D. (abbr.) = **Deutsch,** followed by a number indicates listing of work by Schubert in the thematic catalogue by O.E. Deutsch (*q.v.*).

d, the Tonic note in any key in Tonic Sol-fa notation, pronounced Doh.

d', Fr. names with the prefix *de* abbr. to *d'* before a vowel appear under the principal surnames: e.g. Vincent d'Indy as Indy, Vincent d'.

D.C. (It. abbr.). *See* **Da capo.**

Da capo (It. = 'from the beginning'), a direction indicating that from the point at which it is marked the performer is to turn back to the beginning of the comp.

Da capo al fine (It. = 'from the beginning to the end'), as with the simple *da capo*, the perf. is asked to go back to the beginning, but the comp. is not in this case to be repeated as a whole, but only to the point where the word *fine* (end) appears.

Da capo Aria, a distinctive type of vocal piece for a single voice (though duets and other ensemble pieces may be in the same form) consisting of 3 sections, the 3rd of which is a repetition of the 1st, while the middle section is a contrast based sometimes on similar and sometimes on wholly different thematic material. The da capo aria was cultivated in the 2nd half of the 17th and 1st half of the 18th cent. (up to the earlier works of Gluck), notably by A. Scarlatti, Handel, Bach, Hasse, Jommelli, etc.

Da Ponte, Lorenzo. *See* **Ponte, Lorenzo da.**

Dabadie, Henri-Bernard (b Pau, 19 Jan 1797; d Paris, May 1853), French baritone. In 1819 he made his debut at the Paris Opéra, in Spontini's *La Vestale*, and remained until 1834; created leading roles in Rossini's *Moïse*, *Le Comte Ory* and *Guillaume Tell*. He sang in Italy and created Belcore in *L'elisir d'amore* (Milan, 1832).

Dafne, opera by Schütz (lib. by Martin Opitz, partly trans. from Rinuccini), prod. Torgau, Hartenfels Castle, at the wedding of Georg, Landgrave of Hesse, and Sophia Eleonora, Princess of Saxony, 23 Apr 1627. The music has not survived.

Dafne, La, opera by Gagliano (lib. by O. Rinuccini), prod. Mantua, at the ducal court, Jan 1608.

Opera by Peri (lib. do.), prod. Florence, Palazzo Corsi, Carnival 1597. The 1st Italian opera and 1st opera on record anywhere.

Dafni, opera by Astorga (lib. by E. Manfredi), prod. Genoa, Teatro Sant' Agostino, 21 Apr 1709.

Dagincourt (or d'Agincour), François (b Rouen, 1684; d Rouen, 30 Apr 1758), French organist and composer. App. organist to the royal chapel in Paris, 1714. Wrote organ and harpsichord pieces.

Dahl, Ingolf (b Hamburg, 9 Jun 1912; d Frutigen, nr. Berne, 6 Aug 1970), American composer of German birth. After study in Cologne and Zurich he moved to the USA in 1935, teaching at the Univ. of Southern Calif. from 1945. His earlier work was dissonant and expressionistic; later came under Stravinsky's influence.

Works incl. Concerto for saxophone and wind orch. (1949), Symphony Concertante for 2 clars. and orch. (1953), *The Tower of St Barbara* for orch. (1955), pf. 4tet (his 1st serial work, 1957), *Elegy Concerto* for vln. and orch. (1963), *Aria Sinfonica* (1965), *Intervals* for strings (1970).

Dahlhaus, Carl (b Hanover, 10 Jun 1928), German musicologist and editor. His early study, at Göttingen, was in Renaissance music. Later became a leading Wagner scholar, ed. complete edition, from 1970; pub. *Wagner's Music Dramas* (1971). From the early 1970s he was editor of the *Riemann Musik-Lexicon* and co-ed. of the *Neue Zeitschrift für Musik*.

Dal Monte, Toti (orig. name **Antonietta Meneghel**) (b Mogliano, Veneto, 27 Jun 1893; d Treviso, 26 Jan 1975), Italian soprano. Took up singing after her pf. studies had been interrupted by an accident. She made her debut at La Scala, Milan, in 1916, in Zandonai's *Francesca da Rimini*; sang Gilda there in 1921. NY Met debut 1924, as Lucia; Chicago 1924–8. London, CG, as Lucia and Rosina, in 1926. Other roles incl. Mimi, Butterfly and Stravinsky's Nightingale.

Dal segno . . . (It. = 'from the sign . . .'), a direction indicating that where a comp. is to be perf. over again from an earlier point, it is to be resumed, not at the beginning, as in an ordinary *da capo*, but from where a certain sign or 'signal' has been placed by the composer. The sign normally used is ·S·.

Dalayrac (orig. d'Alayrac), Nicholas (b Muret, 8 Jun 1753; d Paris, 26 Nov 1809), French composer. He was 1st intended for the law, then in 1774 sent to Versailles to embark on a military career. But his main interest was music and he took lessons from Langlé. In 1777 he pub. 6 string 4tets, and 2 small operas were perf. privately in 1781. The following year he made his debut with *L'Éclipse totale* at the Théâtre Italien. He changed his name from its aristocratic form during the Revolution.

Works incl. *c* 60 operas, e.g. *Nina ou la Folle par amour* (1786), *Les Deux petits Savoyards*, *Camille*, *Adolphe et Clara* (1799), *Maison à vendre* etc.; 36 string 4tets.

Dalberg, Frederick (b Newcastle on Tyne, 7 Jan 1908), English bass. He studied in Dresden and Leipzig, after a childhood in S. Africa, and made his debut in 1931. He sang at Leipzig, Berlin and Vienna, and from 1942 to 1951 at Bayreuth, where Hagen, Pogner and Fafner were his roles. Munich 1948–51 and CG during the 1950s: created Claggart in *Billy Budd* (1951); stage première in Brit. of *Wozzeck* (1952) and the fp of *Gloriana* (1953); within the space of 10 years he had sung for Hitler at Bayreuth and before Queen Elizabeth at CG. Glyndebourne 1952, Banquo. Mannheim from 1959.

Dalby, Martin (b Aberdeen, 25 Apr 1942), Scottish composer. He studied at the RCM with Herbert Howells (comp.) and Frederick Riddle (vla.). He has been influenced by jazz and by Spanish music; from 1965 has held admin. posts in London and Glasgow.

Works incl. symph. (1970), *Concerto Martin Pescatore*, for strings (1971), vla. concerto (1974), *Nozze di Primavera* for orch. (1984); *The Keeper of the Pass* for sop. and insts. (1971), *Orpheus* for chorus, narrator and 11 insts. (1972), *Call for the Hazel Tree*, for chorus and electronics (1979); *Yet still she is the Moon*, brass 7tet (1973), *Aleph* for 8 insts. (1975), *Man Walking*, 8tet for wind and strings (1980).

Dale, Benjamin (b London, 17 Jul 1885; d London, 30 Jul 1943), English composer. Studied at the RAM in London, where he later became prof. of comp. and warden.

Works incl. Cantata *Before the Paling of the Stars* (1912), and *Song of Praise* for chorus and orch (1923); vln. and pf. sonata.

Dalibor, opera by Smetana (lib. in Ger., by J. Wenzig, trans into Cz. by E. Špindler), prod. Prague, Cz. Theatre, 16 May 1868.

Dalis, Irene (b San José, Calif., 8 Oct 1925), American mezzo. She studied in New York and Milan and with Margarete Klose in Berlin. Debut Oldenburg, 1953; Berlin 1955–60. She sang Eboli at her NY Met debut in 1957 and first sang at CG in 1958. Bayreuth 1961–3 as Kundry and Ortrud.

Much admired as the Nurse in *Die Frau ohne Schatten* (SW 1966, in opera's 1st London perf.).

Dall' Abaco, Evaristo Felice (b Verona, 12 Jul 1675; d Munich 12 Jul 1742), Italian violinist and composer. Worked at Modena, Munich and Brussels; wrote chiefly string music. Like Torri, he followed the Elector Max Emanuel into exile at Brussels.

Dall' Abaco, Joseph Clemens Ferdinand (b Brussels, bap. 27 Mar 1710; d nr. Verona, 31 Aug 1805), Italian-German cellist and composer, son of prec. Worked at Bonn and played in London, Vienna, etc. Wrote sonatas for his instrument.

Dalla Rizza, Gilda (b Verona, 2 Oct 1892; d Milan, 4 Jul 1975), Italian soprano. Debut Bologna 1912, as Charlotte. She sang in Buenos Aires from 1915. Puccini wrote Magda for her (*La Rondine*, Monte Carlo, 1917) and she was successful as Lauretta, Suor Angelica and Minnie. At La Scala she sang from 1923 to 1939, often under Toscanini; appeared as Salud in the local fp of *La Vida Breve*, 1933. Other roles incl. Violetta, Arabella and Zandonai's Giulietta (creation, Rome, 1922). CG 1920, in Puccini.

Dallam, Thomas (b Lancashire, *c* 1570; d after 1614), English organ builder. Built organs for King's Coll., Cambridge, and Worcester Cathedral. Travelled to Constantinople in 1599–1600 with a mechanical organ, a present from Queen Elizabeth I to the Sultan. Robert D. (1602–65), Ralph D. (d 1673) and George D., also organ builders, were prob. members of the same family.

Dallapiccola, Luigi (b Pisino, Istria, 3 Feb 1904; d Florence, 19 Feb 1975), Italian composer. For political reasons his family were moved to Graz in 1917, where his decisive first contacts with music (esp. opera) were made. The famliy returned to Italy in 1921, where Dallapiccola studied at the Florence Cons. and in 1931 became prof. In 1956 he was app. prof. at Queen's Coll., NY. Dallapiccola's mature music while using serial techniques, modified them to allow for a more lyrical style than is usual, not avoiding tonal references, thematic structures and harmonic progressions.

Works incl. operas *Volo di notte* (after Saint-Exupéry, 1937–9), *Il Prigionero* (1944–1948), *Ulisse* (1960–8); ballet *Marsia* (1942–3)

VOICES AND ORCH.: *Canti di prigionera* (1941), *Canti di liberazione* (1955), *Parole di San Paolo* (1964), *Dalla mia terra*, *Laudi* (Jacopone da Todi). 2 lyrics from the *Kalevala*, 3 studies, rhapsody, *I cori di Michel-*

angelo Buonarroti il giovane, Tre laudi.

ORCH: partita; *Piccolo concerto* for pf. and orch. (1941), *Variations* (1954), *Tartiniana,* divertimento for vln. and chamber orch. (1951), *Piccola musica notturna* (1954; for chamber ens. 1961), *Dialoghi* for cello and orch. (1960).

Music for 3 pfs.; *Liriche anacreontiche Roncevals,* cycle of Gk. and other songs; *Commiato* for sop. and 15 insts. (1972); *Ciaccona, intermezzo e adagio* for solo collo (1945).

Dalmorès, Charles (b Nancy, 21 Dec 1871; d Los Angeles, 6 Dec 1939), French tenor. Debut Lyons 1899 as Loge, in a concert perf. of *Das Rheingold.* Brussels 1900–6, as Siegfried and in other Wagner roles. CG 1904–11; fp of Leoni's *L'Oracolo,* 1905. Bayreuth 1908, Lohengrin. At the Manhattan Opera House, 1906–10 he was admired in Massenet's *Thaïs* and *Grisélidis.* Chicago 1910–18.

Dalza, Joan Ambrosio (*fl.* 1508), Italian lutenist and composer, active in Milan. In 1508 he comp. and arr. a book of lute pieces for Ottaviano Petrucci (*q.v.*). Pieces in the collection incl. 42 dances (in 9 suites), ricercares and 4 arrs. of vocal pieces. Pavans appear here for the 1st time in print; each is followed by a saltarello (*q.v.*) and *piva* (a quick dance in triple-time, originally perf. to the accomp. of bagpipes).

Damascene, Alexander (d London, 14 Jul 1719), French composer of Italian descent. Settled in London, comp. to William III and Gentleman of the Chapel Royal after Purcell's death in 1695. Contrib. songs to several collections.

Dame blanche, La (*The White Lady*), opera by Boieldieu (lib. by Scribe, based on Scott's *Guy Mannering* and *The Monastery*), prod. Paris, Opéra-Comique, 10 Dec 1825. It contains some Scot. tunes.

Damett, Thomas (d *c* 1437), English composer. At the Chapel Royal, 1413–31; canon of Windsor, 1431 until his death. Works are incl. in the Old Hall MS.

Damnation de Faust, La, dramatic cantata by Berlioz (words by comp. and A. Gandonnière, based on Goethe's drama), comp. 1846, incorporating the *Huit Scènes de Faust* of 1828; fp Paris, Opéra-Comique, 6 Dec 1846; prod. as an opera, Monte Carlo, 18 Feb 1893.

Damoiselle élue, La (*The Blessed Damozel*), cantata for soprano, mezzo and female chorus and orch. by Debussy, set to Fr. trans. by Gabriel Sarrazin of Rossetti's poem in 1887–8. Fp Paris, Salle Erard, 8 Apr 1893.

Dämon, Der (*The Demon*) dance pantomime by Hindemith, scenario by M. Krell; comp. 1922 and perf. Darmstadt, 1 Dec 1923. Concert suite for small orch. arr. 1923.

Damoreau, Laure Cinthie Montalant. *See* **Cinti-Damoreau.**

Damping Pedal, the so-called 'soft' pedal of the pf., which on a grand pf. so shifts the hammers of the instrument that they touch only a single string for each note, instead of 2 or 3, for which reason its use is often indicated by the words *una corda* (1 string).

Damrosch, Leopold (b Posen, 22 Oct 1832; d New York, 15 Feb 1885), German, later American, conductor, violinist and composer. Studied medicine in Berlin, but gave it up for music. Appeared as violinist and became leader of the Weimar court orch. under Liszt. Having cond. at Breslau from 1850–71, he went to NY, where he did much to advance orchestral music and opera at the Met Opera House.

Damrosch, Walter (Johannes) (b Breslau, 30 Jan 1862; d New York, 22 Dec 1950), American conductor and composer, son of prec. Studied in Ger. and settled in USA in 1871; became cond. of the NY Oratorio and Symph. Societies in 1885. Director of the Damrosch Opera Co., 1894–9, giving the first US perfs. of several operas by Wagner.

Works incl. operas *The Scarlet Letter* (after Hawthorne, 1896), *Cyrano de Bergerac* (after Rostand, 1913), *The Dove of Peace, The Man without a Country* (1937); incid. music to Euripides' *Electra, Iphigenia in Aulis* and *Medea; Abraham Lincoln*'s *Song* for baritone solo, chorus and orch.; Te Deum; vln. and pf. sonata; songs.

Danaïdes, Les, opera by Salieri (lib. by F.L. du Roullet and L.T. de Tschudy, partly based on and trans. from Calzabigi's *Ipermestra* intended for Gluck, comp. by Millico), prod. Paris, Opéra, 26 Apr 1784.

Dance. Since the earliest known manifestations of music are almost all associated with dance, it follows that any serious consideration of the essence of music will take account of its physical aspect. For the earliest surviving written repertories of western music only vocal works survive, though in most cases it is possible to discern a dance background even here. From the 16th cent. dance music was increasingly written down; and it has been argued that there is very little in the music of the 17th and 18th cents. that is not best understood in terms of its relationship to the dance. Since about 1800, 'art-music' in the western world has increasingly separated itself from the dance. *See also* **Allemande, Ballata, Ballet, Ballet comique de la royne, Ballet de Cour, Ballett, Bergamasca, Branle, Calinda, Canary, Cancan, Chaconne, Courante, Deutsche Tänze, Écossaise, Gavotte, Jig, Mazurka, Minuet, Passacaglia, Passamezzo, Passepied, Pavan, Polka, Quadrille, Sarabande, Waltz.**

Dance Rhapsody, 2 works for orch. by Delius: no. 1 comp. 1908, fp Hereford Fest. 8 Sep 1909, cond. Delius; no. 2 comp. 1916, fp London, 23 Oct 1923, cond. Wood.

Dance Suite, work for orch. in 6 movts. by Bartók, comp. 1923 for 50th anniversary of the merging of Pest, Buda and Obuda into Budapest. Fp Budapest, 19 Nov 1925, cond. E. Dohnányi. Vers. for pf. 1925.

Dances of Galánta, orch. work by Kodály, comp. for the 80th anniversary of the Budapest Phil. Soc., fp Budapest, 11 Dec 1936.

Dances of Marosszék, work for pf. by Kodály, comp. 1927. Version for orch. fp Dresden, 28 Nov 1930, cond. F. Busch.

Danckerts, Ghiselin (b Tholen, Zeeland, *c* 1510; d after Aug 1565), Netherlands composer. Singer in the Papal Chapel in Rome, 1538–65. He acted as judge in the dispute between Vicentino and Lusitano. Wrote motets and madrigals.

Dancla, (Jean Baptiste) Charles (b Bagnères-de-Bigorre, 19 Dec 1817; d Tunis, 10 Nov 1907), French violinist. Pupil of Baillot at the Paris Cons., where he later became vln. prof. He comp. much music incl. educ. works for vln.

Danco, Suzanne (b Brussels, 22 Jan 1911), Belgian soprano. Studied at Brussels Cons. In 1936 she won an international singing competition in Venice. Debut Genoa, 1941, as Fiordiligi. London, CG, 1951 as Mimi; Glyndebourne as Donna Elvira same year. Other roles incl. Ellen Orford and Marie. She was a noted exponent of Ravel and Debussy.

Dandelot, Georges (Édouard) (b Paris, 2 Dec 1895; d St-Georges de Didonne, 17 Aug 1975), French composer. Studied at the Paris Cons. and in 1919 became prof. of comp. at the École Normale de Musique there.

Works incl. oratorio *Pax* (1937); pf. conc; *Trio en forme de suite*, string 4tet; waltzes for 2 pfs.; *Bilitis*: 17 songs (Pierre Louÿs).

Dandrieu (or d'Andrieu), Jean François (b Paris, 1682; d Paris, 17 Jan 1738), French organist and composer. Became organist of the church of Saint-Barthélemy in Paris in succession to his uncle, Pierre D., and in

1704 of that of Saint-Merry; member of the royal chapel in 1721; wrote a book on harpsichord accomp.

Works incl. a set of symphs. *Les Caractères de la guerre* (1718); trios for 2 vlns. and bass; vln. sonatas; org. pieces; 3 vols. of harpsichord pieces.

D'Angeri, Anna (orig. Anna von Angermayer) (b Vienna, 14 Nov 1853; d Trieste, 14 Dec 1907), Austrian soprano She studied in Vienna and sang at the Hofoper 1878–9; appeared as guest at CG 1874–7 and was the 1st London Ortrud and Venus (1875, 1876). Success in Wagner did not dissuade Verdi from inviting her to sing Amelia in the revision of *Simon Boccanegra* (1881).

Danican, Michel (b Dauphiné; d Paris, *c* 1659), French oboist in the service of Louis XIII, who bestowed on him the name of Philidor after the great oboist Filidori of Siena. (For all other members of the family *see* **Philidor.**)

Daniel, John. *See* **Danyel.**

Daniel-Leseur. *See* **Lesur, Daniel.**

Daniel, Play of (*Danielis Ludus*), a medieval liturgical music drama dealing with the story of Daniel in the lions' den. It was written by students of Beauvais between 1227 and 1234 and intended almost certainly for perf. after matins on the feast of the Circumcision (1 Jan).

Danning, Sophus Christian (b Copenhagen, 16 Jun 1867; d Odense, 7 Nov 1925), Danish conductor and composer. Studied in Copenhagen, Sondershausen and Leipzig. Travelled widely, lived for a time in Fin., then taught at Copenhagen and in 1899 went to Norway as theatre cond. at Bergen. In 1907–11 he was cond. at Oslo.

Works incl. operas *Gustav Adolf, Elleskudt* and *Kynthia*; operetta *Columbine*; incid. music to Oehlenschläger's *Aladdin* and other plays; symphs. (incl. *Dante*) and overtures for orch.; cantatas; vln. concerto; pf. pieces; songs.

Dannreuther, Edward (George) (b Strasbourg, 4 Nov 1844; d Hastings, 12 Feb 1905), German–English pianist, teacher and critic. Studied at Leipzig and went to live in London in 1863. Prof. at the RAM from 1895 and author of a valuable work on ornamentation.

Danse, La, last of 3 entrées which make up Rameau's opéra-ballet *Les fêtes d'Hébé* (lib. by A.G. de Montdorge), prod. Paris, Opéra, 21 May 1739. Often heard as a separate item.

Danse Sacrée et Danse Profane, work by Debussy for harp and strings; comp. 1903, fp Paris, 6 Nov 1904.

Danses Concertantes, work for chamber orch. by Stravinsky; comp. 1942, in Hollywood, fp Los Angeles, 8 Feb 1942.

Dante Alighieri (1265–1321), Italian poet. *See* **Dante Sonata** (Liszt), **Dante Symphony** (Liszt), **Francesca da Rimini** (operas, Goetz, Nápravník, Rakhmaninov, Zandonai; symph. fantasy, Tchaikovsky), **Françoise de Rimini** (opera, A. Thomas), **Generali** (*Francesca da Rimini)*, **Morlacchi**, (*Francesca da R.* and *Narration of Ugolino*), **Trittico** (*Gianni Schicchi*, Puccini), **Wolf-Ferrari** (*Vita Nuova*).

Dante and Beatrice, symph. poem by Bantock, fp London, Music Festival, 1911.

Dante Sonata, a 1-movement sonata by Liszt, entitled *Après une lecture du Dante*, in the It. vol. of his *Années de pèlerinage*, comp. 1837–9, revised 1849. Liszt called it a *sonata quasi fantasia*.

Dante Symphony, a symph. by Liszt based on Dante's *Divina commedia*, comp., 1855–6, fp Dresden, 7 Nov 1857. There are 2 movements, *Inferno* and *Purgatorio*.

Dantons Tod (*Danton's Death*), opera by Einem (lib. by Boris Blacher and comp., based on Georg Büchner's drama), prod. Salzburg, 6 Aug 1947.

Danyel (or **Daniel**), **John** (b Wellow, nr. Bath, bap. 6 Nov 1564; d ? London, *c* 1630), English lutenist and composer, brother of the poet Samuel D. When his brother died in 1619 he succeeded him as inspector of the Children of the Queen's Revels and later joined the royal company of musicians.

Danza, La, opera in 1 act by Gluck (lib. by Metastasio), perf. Vienna, Laxenberg, 5 May 1755.

Danzi, Franz (b Schwetzingen, 15 Jun 1763; d Karlsruhe, 13 Apr 1826), German cellist and composer. Pupil of Vogler; was a member of the court band at Mannheim and from 1778, at Munich. *Kapellmeister* to the court of Württemberg at Stuttgart, and later at Karlsruhe. A minor member of the Mannheim school of symphonists.

Works incl. operas *Die Mitternachtsstunde* (1788), *Turandot* (after Gozzi, 1817); church music; symphs, concertos and concertantes; chamber music.

Daphne, opera by R. Strauss (lib. by Joseph Gregor), prod. Dresden, 15 Oct 1938.

Daphnis et Alcimadure, pastoral by Mondonville (lib., in the Languedoc dialect, by the comp.), prod. Fontainebleau, at court, 4 Nov 1754, 1st Paris perf., Opéra, 29 Dec 1754.

Daphnis et Chloé, ballet by Ravel (scenario after Longus, choreography by Fokin), prod. Paris, Théâtre du Chatelet, 8 Jun 1912.

Daquin (or d'**Aquin**), **Louis Claude** (b Paris, 4 Jul 1694; d Paris, 15 Jun 1772), French organist, harpsichordist and composer. Pupil of Marchand. He played before Louis XIV as a child prodigy at the age of 6, and at 12 was app. organist of Petit St Antoine in Paris. In 1727 he was Rameau's successful rival for the post of organist of St Paul, and in 1739 succeeded Dandrieu at the Chapel Royal.

Works incl. cantata *La Rose*; harpsichord pieces incl. *Le Coucou*; *Noëls* for organ or harpsichord.

Darclée, Hariclea (b Braila, 10 Jun 1860; d Bucharest, 10 Jan 1939), Rumanian soprano. She studied with Faure in Paris and made her debut there in 1888 as Marguerite. La Scala, 1890, as Chimène in Massenet's *Le Cid*; she created Catalani's Wally at Milan in 1892 and Mascagni's Iris in 1898. The first Tosca, Rome 1900. Other roles incl. Juliette, Manon Lescaut, Santuzza, Ophelia, Aida and Desdemona.

Dardanus, opera by Rameau (lib. by C.A.L. de La Bruère), prod. Paris, Opéra, 19 Nov 1739).

Opera by Sacchini (lib. do., altered by N.F. Guillard), prod. Versailles, at court, 18 Sep 1784; 1st Paris perf., Opéra, 30 Nov 1784.

Dargason, an English country dance and folksong at least as old as the 16th cent. Holst used it in his *St Paul's Suite*.

Dargillières, Parisian family of instrument makers:

1. Anthoine D. (b *c* 1518; d 1572), 'faiseur d'orgues de la Chapelle du roi'; built various church organs in Paris.

2. Jehan D., prob. son of prec.

3. Gabriel D. Worked in various places near Paris; brother of prec.?

4. Roch D. (b 27 Jan 1559), another son of Anthoine; built numerous organs in the Paris neighbourhood, incl. those at Rouen (St Michael) and Chartres (cathedral).

Dargomizhsky, Alexander Sergeievich (b Troitskoye, Tula district, 14 Feb 1813; d St Petersburg, 17 Jan 1869), Russian composer. Studied music as an amateur at St Petersburg and after retiring from 4 years' government service in 1835 led the life of a dilettante. In 1833 he met Glinka, who lent him his notes taken during his studies with Dehn in Berlin, and he set to work on his 1st opera. After the next stage attempt he devoted himself mainly to songs between 1856 and 1860, incl. many of a satirical nature anticipating those of Mussorgsky. In 1864 he visited western Europe, but was able to gain a hearing only in Belg., where he perf. his orch. fantasies. On his return he associated himself with Balakirev's nationalist group, without actually joining it. He set Pushkin's *Stone Guest* as an opera word for word; it was orchestrated by Rimsky-Korsakov.

Works incl. operas *Esmeralda* (after Hugo, 1847), *Rusalka* (after Pushkin, 1856), *Rogdana* (unfinished). *The Stone Guest* (Pushkin, completed by Cui and Rimsky-Korsakov; prod. posth. 1872): ballet *Bacchus' Feast*: a duet for an opera *Mazeppa*; orchestral fantasies *Kazatchok*, *Baba-Yaga* and *Mummers' Dance*; *Tarantelle slave* for pf. duet; *c* 90 songs, vocal duets, trios, 4tets, choruses.

Darke, Harold (Edwin) (b London, 29 Oct 1888; d Cambridge, 28 Nov 1976), English organist and composer. Studied organ with Parratt and comp. with Stanford at the RCM in London. Organist at St Michael's, Cornhill, from 1916 to 1966.

Works incl. *The Kingdom of God* for soprano, chorus and orch., *Ring out ye crystal spheres* (Milton) for chorus, org. and orch., other choral works incl. *O Lord Thou art my God, Hymn of Heavenly Beauty* (Spenser); church music; organ works; songs.

Dart, (Robert) Thurston (b Kingston, Surrey, 3 Sep 1921; d London, 6 Mar 1971), English musicologist and harpsichordist. Studied at the RCM and London Univ. After further studies with C. van den Borren in Brussels he became lecturer in music at Cambridge in 1947 and prof. in 1962. Prof. of Music, London Univ. (King's Coll.) 1964–71. He was an expert continuo player and soloist on the harpsichord; author of *The Interpretation of Music* as well as learned articles.

Daser, Ludwig (b Munich, *c* 1525; d Stuttgart, 27 Mar 1589), German composer. He was *Kapellmeister* to the Bavarian court at Munich, 1552–9, when Lassus succeeded him, and held a similar post at the court of Württemberg at Stuttgart from 1572 to his death. Wrote Masses, motets, a passion, organ music.

Daughter of the Regiment (Donizetti). *See* **Fille du Régiment.**

Dauvergne, Antoine (b Moulins, 3 Oct 1713; d Lyons, 11 Feb 1797), French violinist and composer. Pupil of his father, Jacques D.; played at Clermont-Ferrand and went to Paris in 1739 as violinist in the court chamber music and in 1744 at the Opéra. In 1762 he became one of the directors of the Concert Spirituel and later manager of the Opéra.

Works incl. over 20 operas and other stage works, e.g. *Les Amours de Tempé* (1752), *Les Troqueurs* (1753); motets; symphs., divertimenti; vln. sonatas.

Davenant (or D'Avenant), William (1606–1668), English poet and playwright. *See* **Banister** (*Circe*), **Lawes (W.)** (*Triumph of the Prince d'Amour* and *Unfortunate Lovers*), **Locke** (*Macbeth*), **Pepys** ('Beauty retire'), **Siege of Rhodes** (Locke, H. Lawes, H. Cooke, Coleman and Hudson).

David, opera in 5 acts and 12 scenes by Milhaud (lib. by A. Lunel), written to celebrate the est. of Jerusalem as the capital of Judea, prod. Jerusalem, 1 Jun 1954.

David, Félicien (César) (b Cadenet, Vaucluse, 13 Apr 1810; d Saint-Germain-en-Laye, 29 Aug 1876), French composer. Entered the Paris Cons. in 1830, having been a chorister at Aix Cathedral and afterwards cond. at the theatre. In 1833 he travelled in the nr. East, returned in 1835, lived in. Igny for a time on finding that Paris neglected him, but settled in the capital in 1841 and made a great success with his oriental descriptive symph. *Le Désert* in 1844.

Works incl. operas *La Perle du Brésil* (1851), *Herculanum* (1859), *Lalla-Roukh* (after Moore, 1862), *Le Saphir* and *La Captive* (withdrawn); oratorio *Moïse au Sinaï*; mystery *Eden*; motets and hymns; descriptive symphs. *Le Désert* and *Christophe Colomb*; 4 symphs.; 4 string 4tets; 24 string 5tets, 2 nonets for wind; *Mélodies orientales* for pf.; songs.

David, Ferdinand (b Hamburg, 19 Jun 1810; d Klosters, Switz., 18 Jul 1873), German violinist and composer. Studied with Spohr and Hauptmann and made his 1st appearance at the Leipzig Gewandhaus in 1825, where he became leader under Mendelssohn in 1836; gave the fp of Mendelssohn's vln. concerto in 1845. Wrote 5 concertos and many other works for the vln.; chamber music.

David, Johann Nepomuk (b Eferding, 30 Nov 1895; d Stuttgart, 22 Dec 1977), Austrian composer. He was choir-boy at St Florian and studied at the Vienna Academy. He taught comp. successively at Leipzig, Salzburg and Stuttgart, and published analytical studies of classical comps.

Works incl. 8 symphs (1936–65), 2 partitas for orch., 2 concertos for string orch.; fl. concertos, 2 vln. concertos, *Requiem chorale* for soli, chorus and orch.; 3 string 4tets, 4 string trios and other chamber music; 3 cello sonatas; chorale preludes and other works for organ.

David, Karl Heinrich (b St Gall, 30 Dec 1884; d Nervi, 17 May 1951), Swiss conductor and composer. Studied at the Cologne and Munich Conss. Cond. at var. theatres, became prof. at the Basle Cons. in 1910 and settled at Zurich in 1917. Ed. of the *Schweizerische Musikzeitung* (1928–41).

Works incl. operas *Der Sizilianer* (after Molière, 1924), *Traumwandel* (after Turgenev, 1928); *Aschenputtel* play with music, Youth Festival Play; *Das hohe Lied Salomonis* for solo voices, chorus and orch.; festival drama for the Berne Exhibition of 1914; choral works with solo voices; concertos for vln., vla., cello and pf.; 6 string 4tets, string 5tet (1940), 2 string 6tets; songs.

Davidde penitente (*The Penitent David*), cantata by Mozart, K469 (lib. ? by L. da Ponte), made up in Mar 1785, mainly from portions of the unfinished C min. Mass, K427, of 1782–3. Only 2 arias are new.

Davide, Giacomo (b Presezzo nr. Bergamo, 1750; d Presezzo, 31 Dec 1830), Italian tenor. After many triumphs in Italy he 1st sang in Paris in 1785 and London in 1791. At La Scala he was heard 1782–1808 in operas by Mayr, Cimarosa and Sarti.

Davide, Giovanni (b Naples, 15 Sep 1790; d St Petersburg, 1864), Italian tenor and bass, son and pupil of prec. Made his 1st appearance at Brescia in 1810. He took part in the fps of Rossini's *Il turco in Italia*, *Otello*, *La donna del lago* and *Zelmira*.

Davidov, Karl (b Goldingen, Courland, 15 Mar 1838; d Moscow, 26 Feb 1889), Russian cellist and composer. Made his 1st appearance at the Leipzig Gewandhaus in 1859 and later became 1st cellist in its orch. and prof. at the Cons. In 1862 he was app. to a similar post at the St Petersburg Opera and was director of the Cons. there in 1876–86. Wrote 4 cello concertos and many other works for his instrument, etc.

Davidovsky, Mario (b Buenos Aires, 4 Mar 1934), Argentine composer. He studied at Buenos Aires and moved to US 1958; has worked at electronic studios of Columbia and Princeton Univs. Member of Columbia faculty from 1981.

Works incl. 2 string 4tets (1954, 1958), *Planos* for orch. (1961), 2 *Studies* for electronics (1961–2), *Contrasts* for strings (1962), *Inflexions* for 14 insts. (1965), *Synchronisms*, 7 pieces for various inst. groups (1963–74), *Chacona* for pf. trio (1972), *Scenes from Shir Hashirim*, cantata for 4 voices and chamber ens. (1976).

Davidsbund (Ger. = League of David), an assoc. formed in 1834 by Schumann and his friends to combat the musical 'Philistines'.

Davidsbündler (Ger.), the members of the above. They appear in the title of Schumann's *Davidsbündlertänze* and in the finale of his *Carnaval* in a 'marche contre les Philistins'.

Davidsbündlertänze (*Dances of the League of David*), a set of 18 pf. pieces by Schumann, op. 6, comp. in 1837, the title alluding to the above.

Davie, Cedric Thorpe (b Blackheath, 30 May 1913; d Dalry, Kirkcudbrightshire, 18 Jan 1983), Scottish composer and organist. Student at the Scot. Nat. Acad. of Mus., Glasgow, the RAM in London and later the RCM there, where he was a pupil of R.O. Morris, Vaughan Williams and Gordon Jacob, gaining the Cobbett and Sullivan Prizes in 1935. He also studied pf. with Egon Petri in Ger., and comp. with Kodály at Budapest and Kilpinen at Helsinki. Head of music at St Andrews Univ. from 1945.

Works incl. opera *Gammer Gurton's Needle*, ballad opera *The Forrigan Reel* (James Bridie); concerto for pf. and strings; string 4tet; vln. and pf. sonata, sonatinas for cello and pf. and fl. and pf.; 8 *Little Songs*.

Davies, Ben(jamin Grey) (b Pontardawe, nr. Swansea, 6 Jan 1858; d Bath, 28 Mar 1943), Welsh tenor. Studied at the RAM in London; made his 1st concert appearance at Dublin in 1879 and 1st sang in opera at Birmingham in 1881, in Balfe's *Bohemian Girl*. Successful in oratorio.

Davies, Cecilia (b ? London, c 1750; d London, 3 Jul 1836), English soprano. Sang at Dublin in 1763 and 1st appeared in London in 1767. The following year she went to Paris and Vienna with her sister Marianne (1744–?), a fl., harpsichord and harmonica player, where they had a great success, Hasse writing an ode for them to words specially provided by Metastasio; and in 1771–3 they were in It. where Cecilia became famous as 'L'Inglesina', and created Sacchini's Armida, Milan, 1772.

Davies, Dennis Russell (b Toledo, 16 Apr 1944), American conductor. He studied at Juilliard and founded the J. Ensemble, with Berio; in 1970 cond. the fp of Berio's *Opera*, at Santa Fe. Music dir. St Paul Chamber Orchestra 1973–80. Bayreuth debut 1978, *Der fliegende Holländer;* Württemberg Staatsoper, Stuttgart, from 1980. He has cond. the fps of works by Cage, Carter and Feldman, and in 1984 gave in Stuttgart the fp of Bolcom's *Songs of Innocence and Experience*.

Davies, Fanny (b Guernsey, 27 Jun 1861; d London, 1 Sep 1934), English pianist. Studied at Leipzig and under Clara Schumann at Frankfurt, making her 1st London appearance in 1885; often toured abroad and gave recitals with Casals.

Davies, (Albert) Meredith (b Birkenhead, 30 Jul 1922), English conductor and organist. Studied at the RCM, graduating in 1938, and then Keble Coll., Oxford, taking his B.Mus. in 1946. He took the post of organist at St Albans Cathedral in 1947 and Hereford in 1949, also conducting at the Three Choirs Festival. From 1956 to 1959 he was organist of New Coll., Oxford. He has since conducted frequently in Britain and abroad. Principal, TCL from 1979. CBE 1982.

Davies, (Sir) Peter Maxwell (b Manchester, 8 Sep 1934), English composer. Studied at the RMCM and in 1957 with Petrassi in Rome. From 1959 to 1962 he taught music at Cirencester Grammar School, and in 1962 went to the USA to study with Sessions at Princeton Univ. His music is strongly influenced by medieval techniques, which he uses in combination with serial devices. Many concerts with his ens., The Fires of London, 1970–87; stage works with Fires of London Productions from 1987. Since 1970 he has been based in Orkney. Music dir. Dartington Summer School, S. Devon, 1979–84. CBE 1981. Knighted 1987.

Works incl. STAGE: *Nocturnal Dances* (1970), *Blind Man's Buff*, masque (1972), *Taverner*, opera (1972), *The Martyrdom of St Magnus*, chamber opera (1977), *The 2 Fiddlers*, opera for children (1978), *Le Jongleur de Notre Dame*, masque (1978), *Salome*, ballet (1978), *The Lighthouse*, chamber opera (1980), *Cinderella*, pantomime (1980), *The Rainbow*, for children (1981), *The no. 11 Bus*, for vocal soloists, dancers, mime and ens. (1984).

The years given for the following works are of fp:

ORCH.: *St Michael*, Sonata for 17 wind insts. (1957), 2 *Fantasias on an In Nomine of John Taverner* (1962, 1964), *Antechrist*, for chamber ens. (1967), *Stedman Caters* (1968), *Worldes Blis* (1968), *Vesalii Icones* for dancer, cello. and ens. (1969), *Ave Maris Stella*, for chamber ens. (1975), 3 symphs. (1976, 1981 and 1985), *Image, Reflection, Shadow* (1981), Sinfonia Concertante (1983), Sinfonietta Accademica (1983), vln. concerto (1986).

VOCAL: *O Magnum Mysterium*, 4 carols a cappella (1960), *Leopardi Fragments* for sop., mezzo and insts. (1962), *Veni Sancte Spiritus* for soloists, chorus and orch. (1964), *The Shepherds' Calendar* for chorus and ens. (1965), *Revelation and Fall* for sop. and 16 insts. (1968), 8 *Songs for a Mad King* for voice and ens. (1969), *From Stone to Thorn* for mezzo and insts. (1971), *Hymn to St Magnus* for mezzo and insts. (1972), *Notre Dame des Fleurs* for soloists and ens. (1973), *Tenebrae super Gesualdo* for mezzo, guitar and ens., *Stone Litany* for mezzo and orch. (1973), *Miss Donnithorne's Maggot* for mezzo and ens. (1974), *Fiddlers at the Wedding* for mezzo and insts. (1974), *The Blind Fiddler* for sop. and ens. (1976), *Anakreontika* for mezzo and ens. (1976), *Westerlings* for chorus *a cappella* (1977), *Solstice of Light* for tenor, chorus and orch. (1979), *Black Pentecost* for mezzo, bar. and orch. (1982), *The Yellow Cake Revue* for singers and pf. (1980), *Into the Labyrinth*, cantata (1983). *Winterfold* for mezzo and ens. (1986).

CHAMBER AND INSTRUMENTAL: incl. Piano sonata (1981), Organ sonata (1982), Sea Eagle, for horn (1982), sonata for vln. and cimbalom (1984), guitar sonata (1984).

WORKS FOR CHILDREN: incl. *Kirkwall Shopping Songs* (1979), *Songs of Hoy* (1981), *First Ferry to Hoy* (1985).

Davies, Ryland (b Cwm, Ebbw Vale, 9 Feb 1943), Welsh tenor. He sang Paris in the Brit. première of Gluck's *Paride ed Elena* while still at the RMCM (1963). Prof. debut as Almaviva with the WNO, 1964. In 1968 he sang Belmonte at Glyndebourne, and at CG in 1969 Hylas in the first complete perf. of *Les Troyens* in French. US debut 1970, San Francisco; NY Met 1975 as Mozart's Ferrando. Other roles incl. Fenton, Ottavio and Lensky.

Davies, (Henry) Walford (b Oswestry, 6 Sep 1869; d Wrington, Som., 11 Mar 1941), English organist, educationist and composer. Educ. at St George's Chapel, Windsor, under Parratt, and at the RCM in London, where Stanford was his comp. master. Held var. organist's appts., took the Cambridge Mus.D. degree in 1898, when he was app. organist and choirmaster at the Temple Church. Prof. of Music at the Univ. of Wales, Aberystwyth, from 1919. Knighted 1922. He resigned from the Temple in 1923 and became organist at St George's, Windsor, in 1927 and Master of the King's Music in succession to Elgar in 1934. He wrote sacred music and pieces for children.

Davis, Andrew (b Ashridge, Herts., 2 Feb 1944), English conductor and keyboard player. He studied at Cambridge and in

Rome. First came to notice with the BBC SO in the *Glagolitic Mass* of Janáček. Associate cond. Philharmonia 1973, and led *Capriccio* at Glyndebourne the same year; has since given *Intermezzo* and *Schweigsame Frau* there. Prin. cond. Toronto SO from 1975; Royal Liverpool PO as guest cond. 1974–6. Has dir. his own ed. of *The Art of Fugue* from the harpsichord.

Davis, (Sir) **Colin** (b Weybridge, 25 Sep 1927), English conductor. Studied at the RCM. From 1957 to 1959 he was assistant cond. of the BBC Scot. Orch., becoming principal cond. at Sadler's Wells in 1961; he was also their music director, 1961–5. From 1967 to 1971 he was principal cond. of the BBC SO and music dir. at Covent Garden 1971–86. US debut 1960, with Minneapolis orch; principal guest cond. Boston SO 1972–83. NY Met debut 1967 (*Peter Grimes*). The first Briton to cond. at Bayreuth (*Tannhäuser*, 1977); Bavarian Radio SO from 1981. CBE 1965; knighted 1980. Admired in Mozart, Berlioz, Stravinsky and Tippett; cond. fps *The Knot Garden* (1970), *The Ice Break* (1977) and *The Mask of Time* (1984).

Davison, J(ames) W(illiam) (b London, 5 Oct 1813; d Margate, 24 Mar 1885), English critic attached to *The Times*, 1846–1879. Married the pianist Arabella Goddard.

Davy, Gloria (b New York, 29 Mar 1931), American soprano. She studied at Juilliard and was the Countess in the US fp of Strauss's *Capriccio*, 1954. She sang in Europe from 1957 and was the soloist in the fp of Henze's *Nachtstücke und Arien* at Donaueschingen, under Rosbaud. She made her NY Met and CG debuts as Aida (1958, 1960). Other roles incl. Purcell's Dido, Gluck's Armide and Santuzza.

Davy, John (b Upton Helions, nr. Exeter, 23 Dec 1763; d London, 22 Feb 1824), English composer. Pupil of Jackson at Exeter. Played in the CG orch. in London and wrote music for many plays, incl. Shakespeare's *Tempest*. His song *The Bay of Biscay* became famous.

Davy, Richard (*c* 1467; d ? Exeter, *c* 1507), English composer. Educ. at Magdalen Coll., Oxford, where he was organist and choirmaster in 1490–2. Chaplain to Anne Boleyn's grandfather and father in 1501–15. Wrote motets, Passion music for Palm Sunday, part-songs, etc.

De Amicis, Anna Lucia (b Naples, *c* 1733; d Naples, 1816), Italian soprano. She sang in comic operas on the continent before visiting London and taking part in the fp of J.C. Bach's *Orione* (King's Theatre, 1763). She

then sang in operas by Gluck and Jommelli in Venice and Naples. Highly regarded by Mozart, she sang Giunia in the fp of *Lucio Silla* (Milan, 1772).

De Angelis, Nazareno (b Rome, 17 Nov 1881; d Rome, 14 Dec 1962), Italian bass. Debut Aquila 1903, in *Linda di Chamounix*. He appeared at La Scala in 1905 and returned until 1933 as Mosè, Marke, Méphistophélès, Zaccaria and Hunding. At Buenos Aires in 1911 he was the 1st local Philip II. Other roles incl. Barnaba, Bartolo and Procida.

De Bassini, Achille (b Milan, 5 May 1819; d Cavadei Tirreni, 3 Jul 1881), Italian baritone. During the 1830s he was heard in operas by Bellini and Donizetti in the Italian provinces. A favourite bar. of Verdi, he took part in the premières of *I due Foscari* (1844), *Il Corsaro* (1848), *Luisa Miller* (1849) and *La Forza del Destino* (1862).

De Begnis, Giuseppe. *See* Begnis, de.

DeKoven, Reginald. *See* Koven, de.

De Lara, Isidore. *See* Lara, Isidore de.

De Luca, Giuseppe (b Rome, 25 Dec 1876; d New York, 26 Aug 1950), Italian baritone. Debut Piacenza, 1897 as Valentin; 1902–4 created the bar. leads in *Adriana Lecouvreur*, Giordano's *Siberia*; and *Madama Butterfly*. NY Met 1915–40; debut as Rossini's Figaro and created Paquiro in *Goyescas* by Granados (1916). London, CG, 1907, 1910 and 1935.

De Lucia, Fernando (b Naples, 11 Oct 1860; d Naples, 21 Feb 1925), Italian tenor. Debut Naples, 1885, as Faust. In 1891 he created the title role in Mascagni's *L'Amico Fritz* and repeated the role on his CG (1892) and NY Met (1894) debuts; also created roles in Mascagni's *I Rantzau* (1892), *Silvano* (1895) and *Iris* (1898). He sang in London, CG, until 1900: roles incl. Rodolfo, Turridu, Cavaradossi and Canio.

De Lussan *See* Lussan, de.

De natura sonoris, 2 works by Penderecki: no. 1 for orch., fp Royan, France, 7 Apr 1966; no. 2 for winds, perc. and strings, perf. New York, 3 Dec 1971.

De Reszke, Edouard (b Warsaw, 22 Dec 1853; d Garnek, 25 May 1917), Polish bass. Debut as Amonasro in the French première of *Aida* (Paris, 1876). CG 1880–4, as Alvise and Rossini's Basilio. Fiesco in the rev. of *Simon Boccanegra*, Milan 1881. He sang Frère Laurent on his NY Met debut and other roles incl. Gounod's Méphistophélès, Leporello, and, late in his career, Wagner's Daland, Sachs, Hagen and Wanderer.

De Reszke, Jean (b Warsaw, 14 Jan 1850;

d Nice, 3 Apr 1925), Polish tenor; brother of prec. Debut Venice, 1874, as Alfonso in *La favorite* (a bar. role). Debut as tenor Madrid, 1879, as Meyerbeer's Robert; created the title role in Massenet's *Le Cid*, Paris 1885, and sang Radames at Drury Lane, London, in 1887. CG roles incl. Meyerbeer's Vasco da Gama and Raoul, Faust and Riccardo. US debut Chicago 1891, as Lohengrin; sang Tristan and Siegfried in NY and retired 1902.

De Sabata, Victor (b Trieste, 10 Apr 1892; d Santa Margherita Ligure, 11 Dec 1967), Italian conductor and composer. Studied under his father, a chorus master at the Teatro alla Scala, Milan, and at the Cons. there, with Orefice and others. He became cond. at the Scala and at the Royal Opera in Rome, Monte Carlo from 1918 (fp *L'Enfant et les Sortilèges*, 1925). Visited USA in 1938, cond. at Bayreuth in 1939 (*Tristan*) and became known in London in 1946 ; with Scala co. 1950 (*Otello* and *Falstaff*).

Works incl. operas *Lisistrata* (after Aristophanes), *Il macigno*, *Mille e una notte* (1931); incid. music for Shakespeare's *Merchant of Venice*; symph. poems *Juventus*, *La notte di Platon*, *Gethsemani*, suite for orch.

Dean, Stafford (b Kingswood, Surrey, 20 Jun 1933), English bass. He studied at the RCM and sang minor roles at SW and Glyndebourne before Leporello at the Coliseum, 1968; repeated the role in San Francisco and Munich. CG debut 1969, Masetto. NY Met debut, as Mozart's Figaro, 1976. He is also heard in oratorio and the operas of Monteverdi.

Dean, Winton (Basil) (b Birkenhead, 18 Mar 1916), English writer on music, son of the producer Basil Dean. Educ. at Harrow and King's Coll., Cambridge; read classics and English, but studied music privately, trans. choruses, etc. from Aristophanes' *Frogs* for Walter Leigh and Weber's *Abu Hassan*. His books incl. *Bizet* (1948, rev. 1965), *Handel's Dramatic Oratorios* (1959) and *Handel's Operas, 1704—1726* (1987).

'Death and the Maiden' Quartet, Schubert's string 4tet in D min. D810, begun March 1824, finished or revised Jan 1826 and 1st perf. Vienna, 1 Feb 1826. It is so called because the 2nd movement is a set of variations on the introduction and the 2nd half of his song, *Der Tod und das Mädchen* (D531, 1817, text by M. Claudius), which consists of Death's quiet and reassuring answer to the girl's agitated plea to be spared. The work is sometimes heard today in an arr. for string orch. by Mahler.

Death and Transfiguration (Strauss). *See* **Tod und Verklärung.**

Death in Venice, opera by Britten (lib. by Myfanwy Piper, after Thomas Mann), prod. Snape, Maltings 16 Jun 1973).

Debora e Jaele (*Deborah and Jael*), opera by Pizzetti (lib. by comp.), prod. Milan, Teatro alla Scala, 16 Dec 1922.

Deborah, oratorio by Handel (words by S. Humphreys), prod. London, King's Theatre, Haymarket, 17 Mar 1733.

Debussy, (Achille) Claude (b Saint-Germain-en-Laye nr. Paris, 22 Aug 1862; d Paris 25 Mar 1918), French composer. Son of a shopkeeper, took his 1st pf. lessons at the age of 7, and from 1870 was taught for 3 years by Mme. Mauté de Fleurville, a former pupil of Chopin. Entered the Paris Cons. in 1873, studying with Lavignac and Marmontel, later with Émile Durand. At 17 he failed to win a pf. prize, but entered a comp. class in 1880. For the next 2 summers became domestic musician to Nadezhda von Meck, Tchaikovsky's former patroness, whose children he taught and who took him to Switz. and It. the 1st time and to Rus. the 2nd. Gained 1st Prix de Rome in 1884 and went to Rome the next year, but left in 1887 before the statutory 3 years were completed. Began to compose seriously in the new manner for which he became known with a Fr. trans. of Rossetti's *Blessed Damozel*, finished 1888. Influenced by Satie in 1891 and perf. his 1st important mature work, the prelude to Mallarmé's poem *L'Après-midi d'un faune*, in 1894. Married a dressmaker, Rosalie (Lili) Texier, in 1899; became music critic for the *Revue blanche* in 1901; prod. his only finished opera, a setting of Maeterlinck's *Pelléas et Mélisande*, 30 Apr 1902. Left his wife in 1904 for Mme. Emma Bardac; divorced 1905 and married to Mme. B. Growing success, abroad as well as in France during the last 10 years, but *c* 1909 he began to suffer from cancer.

Works incl. STAGE: opera *Pelléas et Mélisande* (1902); incid. music to d'Annunzio's *Le Martyre de Saint Sébastien* (1911); ballets *Jeux* (1913) and *Khamma*.

VOCAL: cantatas *L'Enfant prodigue* and *La Damoiselle élue*, 3 *Chansons de France* (Charles d'Orléans) for unaccomp. chorus; songs incl. sets *Cinq Poèmes de Baudelaire* (1890), *Ariettes oubliées* (Verlaine), 2 sets of *Fêtes galantes* (Verlaine), *Proses lyriques* (Debussy), 3 *Ballades de Villon*, *Chansons de Bilitis* (Pierre Louÿs) (1898), *Le Promenoir des deux amants* (Tristan Lhermite), *Trois Poèmes de Stéphane Mallarmé*.

ORCH.: *Printemps, Prélude à l'Après-midi d'un faune* (1895), *3 Nocturnes* (1899), *La Mer* (1905) and *3 Images* for orch. (1912); *Fantasie* for pf. and orch. (1889); *Danse sacrée et danse profane* for harp and strings (1904).

CHAMBER AND PIANO: string 4tet (1893); sonatas for cello and pf.; fl., vla. and harp; and vln. and pf. (1915–17) and some smaller chamber works for saxophone, clar. and fl.; many pf. pieces incl. *Suite bergamasque*, suite *Pour le Piano* (1901), *3 Estampes* (1903), *Masques, L'Île joyeuse* (1904), 2 sets of *3 Images*, suite *Children's Corner*, 2 sets of *12 Préludes* (1910, 1913), and 12 *Études* (1915); *Petite Suite, Marche écossaise, Six Épigraphes antiques* (on Pierre Louÿs's *Chansons de Bilitis*), etc. for pf. duet; *Lindaraja* and *En blanc et noir* (1915) for 2 pfs.

Decani. In English cathedrals and in churches where the choir is divided, the decani side is that on the south of the chancel, near the dean's stall, the other being the *Cantoris* side.

Decius, Nikolaus (b Hof, *c* 1485; d after 1546), German Lutheran pastor and theologian. He wrote the words and comp. or adapted the music of 3 chorales, anticipating even Luther in this field.

Decrescendo (It. = waning, decreasing), synonym of *diminuendo*, which is now more frequently used.

Dedekind, Constantin Christian (b Reinsdorf, Anhalt-Cöthen, 2 Apr 1628; d Dresden, 2 Sep 1715), German poet and composer. Studied at Dresden and in 1654 became a member of the Saxon court chapel and *Konzertmeister* in 1666. He arr. words for sacred music dramas.

Works incl. psalms, sacred and secular vocal music, concertos for voices and instruments.

Dedekind, Heinrich (or Enricius) (b Neustadt, Bavaria, Dec 1554; d Luneburg, 30 Nov 1619), German clergyman and composer. Cantor at St John's Church, Lüneburg. Wrote psalms and other sacred vocal works.

Dedekind, Henning (b Neustadt, 30 Dec 1562; d Gebsee, Thuringia, 28 Jul 1626), German composer, brother of prec. Held posts as cantor and preacher at Langensalza and Gebsee.

Works incl. Mass; secular vocal music.

Deering. *See* Dering.

Defesch, William (b Alkmaar, Aug 1687; d London, 3 Jan 1761), Flemish organist, violinist and composer. Organist and later choirmaster at Antwerp Cathedral until

1731, when he settled in London.

Works incl. Mass; oratorios *Judith* and *Joseph*; concertos and sonatas for var. insts.; cello pieces; songs.

Deidamia, opera by Handel (lib. by P.A. Rolli), prod. London, Theatre Royal, Lincoln's Inn Fields, 10 Jan 1741. Handel's last opera.

Del Mar, Norman (René) (b London, 31 Jul 1919), English conductor and writer on music. Studied at the RCM with R.O. Morris and Vaughan Williams. In 1944 he founded the Chelsea SO, and in 1947 became conductor of the Croydon SO. In the same year he was appointed assistant to Beecham with the RPO. He is esp. noted as a performer of complex modern scores, e.g. Busoni's pf. concerto and Mahler's symphs., and has written a 3-vol. study of the music of Richard Strauss. CBE 1975.

Del Monaco, Mario (b Florence, 27 Jul 1915; d Mestre, nr. Venice, 16 Oct 1982), Italian tenor. Studied at the Pesaro Cons. and made his debut in Milan in 1941 as Pinkerton, but later served in the It. army during World War II. From 1951 to 1959 he sang with the NY Met as Des Grieux, Don José, Cavaradossi, Manrico. A dramatic singer, one of his finest roles was that of Verdi's Otello, which he sang in London, CG, in 1962.

Del Tredici, David (b Cloverdale, Calif., 16 Mar 1937), American composer. He studied at Berkeley and with Roger Sessions at Princeton. His early music contains several settings of Joyce: *I Hear an Army*, for sop. and string 4tet (1964), *Night Conjure-Verse* for voices and insts. (1965), *Syzygy* for sop., horn, bells and chamber orch. (1968).

His recent music been concerned with Lewis Carroll: *Pop-Pourri*, for voices, rock group and orch. (1968), *The Lobster Quadrille* for sop., folk music ens. and orch. (1969, rev. 1974), *Vintage Alice* (1971; same forces), *An Alice Symphony* (1976), *Final Alice*, for orch. (1976), *Child Alice*, work for sop. & orch and in 4 parts: *In memory of a summer day, Happy Voices, All in the Golden afternoon* and *Quaint Events* (1977–81; perf. separately in St Louis, San Francisco, Philadelphia and Rotterdam, 1980–83. 1st complete perf. Aspen, 1984).

Delacôte, Jacques (b Remiremont, Vosges, 16 Aug 1942), French conductor. He studied at the Vienna Academy, with Swarowsky, and won the 1972 Mitropoulos Comp., NY; NY PO from 1973. Has cond. opera at Hamburg, Paris and London (CG) and appeared with the LSO, Cleveland SO and other orchs. in Mahler, Bruckner and Fr. music. Promenade Concerts, London, 1986.

Delage, Maurice (Charles) (b Paris, 13 Nov 1879; d Paris, 19 Sep 1961), French composer. Pupil of Ravel. He travelled to the east and incorporated exotic elements into his music.

Works incl. overture to a ballet *Les Bâtisseurs de ponts* (after Kipling), symph. poem *Conté par la mer* and other orchestral works; pf. pieces; songs.

Delannoy, Marcel (François Georges) (b Ferté-Alain, 9 Jul 1898; d Nantes, 14 Sep 1962), French composer. A painter and architect at first, he was mainly self-taught in music.

Works incl. operas *Le Poirier de misère* (1925), *Philippine* (1937), *Fête de la danse*, *Ginevra* (1942); ballet-cantata *Le Fou de la dame*, ballets *La Pantoufle de vair* and *L'Éventail de Jeanne* (with others); incid. music for Aristophanes' *Peace* and other plays; symph. and *Figures sonores* for orch., *Sérénade concertante* for vln. and orch.; string 4tets; many songs.

Delatre, Petit Jean (b ? Liège, c 1510; d Utrecht, 31 Aug 1569), Flemish composer of *chansons* and motels. He is not to be confused with the French composer Claude Petit Jehan (d Metz, 1589).

Delibes, (Clément Philibert) Léo (b Saint-Germain-du-Val, 21 Feb 1836; d Paris, 16 Jan 1891), French composer. Studied at the Paris Cons., where Adam was his composition master. He became accompanist at the Théâtre Lyrique in 1853 and was organist successively at 2 churches. Later he became accompanist and chorus master at the Opéra and in 1881 prof. of comp. at the Cons.

Works incl. operas *Maître Griffard* (1857), *Le Jardinier et son seigneur* (1863), *Le Roi l'a dit* (1873), *Jean de Nivelle*, *Lakmé* (1883), *Kassya* (unfinished); ballets *La Source* (with Minkus), *Coppélia* (on E.T.A. Hoffmann's story *Olympia*), *Sylvia*, *Le Pas des fleurs*; divertissement for Adam's ballet *Le Corsaire*; incid. music for Hugo's *Le Roi s'amuse*; operettas *Deux Sous de charbon* (1856), *Deux Vielles Gardes*, *L'Omelette à la Follembûche* (1859), *Le Serpent à plumes* (1864), *L'Écossais de Chatou* and others; Mass; cantata *Alger*; dramatic scene *La Mort d'Orphée*; songs; children's choruses.

Delius, Frederick (b Bradford, 29 Jan 1862; d Grez-sur-Loing, 10 Jun 1934), English composer of German descent. His father was a well-to-do business man and wished him to follow a commercial career; but music was cultivated in the home and although Delius had little systematic teaching until he went to Florida as an orange planter in 1884 and came under the influence of Thomas Ward, organist at Jacksonville, he worked steadily at music by himself. In 1886, after some teaching in USA, he went to the Leipzig Cons. for a short time, but found its conservative teaching uncongenial. In 1887 he visited Norway and made friends with Grieg, who persuaded his father to let him devote himself to comp. From 1889 he lived in Fr. mainly Paris, and in 1897 he married Jelka Rosen, a Ger. painter of Danish descent, and they settled at Grez-sur-Loing nr. Fontainebleau. A concert of his works was given in London in 1899 and he became known here and there in Germany. From 1907 important fps were given in England: Beecham gave *Paris* (1908) and *A Mass of Life* (1909) and Wood cond. *Sea Drift* in 1908. He contracted syphilis and in 1922 was attacked by paralysis, which gradually increased until 4 years later he was helpless and totally blind. In 1928 Eric Fenby volunteered to live in his house and act as amanuensis.

Works incl. OPERAS *Irmelin* (1890–2; prod. 1953), *The Magic Fountain* (1893–5; fp BBC 1977), *Koanga* (1896–8; prod 1904), *A Village Romeo and Juliet* (1900–1; prod. 1907), *Margot-la-Rouge* (1902; fp BBC, 1982), *Fennimore and Gerda* (1909–10; prod. 1919); incid. music for Heiberg's *Folkeraadet* and Flecker's *Hassan*.

ORCH. WORKS: *Florida* suite (1887), *Over the Hills and Far Away*, (c 1895), *Paris* (1899), *Life's Dance*, *Brigg Fair* (1907), *In a Summer Garden*, 2 *Dance Rhapsodies* (1908, 1916), *On hearing the first Cuckoo in Spring* (1911), *Summer Night on the River* (1913), *N. Country Sketches*, *Eventyr* (after Asbjørnsen's fairy-tales, 1917), *A Song before Sunrise*; concertos for pf., vln., cello and vln. and cello (1897, 1915, 1916, 1921).

CHAMBER MUSIC: string 4tet (1916); 3 vln. and pf. sonatas; sonata for cello and pf (1916).

CHORUS AND ORCH.: *Appalachia* (1898–1903), *Sea Drift*, *A Mass of Life* (1904–5), *Songs of Sunset*, *Arabesk* (1911), *A Song of the High Hills*, *Requiem* (1914–16). OTHER VOCAL: some part-songs, songs with orch. incl. cycle from Tennyson's *Maud*, 7 Dan. songs, Dowson's *Cynara*; c 40 songs with pf.

Della Casa, Lisa (b Burgdorf, Berne, 2 Feb 1919), Swiss soprano. Studied at the Berne Cons. and in Zurich, beginning her international career at the Salzburg Festival of

1947, as Zdenka; sang Donna Elvira there in 1953. She became known as one of the outstanding Mozart and Strauss singers of her day, also doing much to further the cause of Swiss music; NY Met debut 1953, as Mozart's Countess. London, CG, 1953 as Arabella. Retired 1974.

Delle Sedie, Enrico (b Livorno, 17 Jun 1822; d Paris, 28 Nov 1907), Italian baritone. After fighting as a volunteer in the war against Aus. he studied singing with Orazio Galeffi at Livorno and made his 1st appearance at Pistoia in 1851 as Nabucco. First London Renato, *Un ballo in maschera*, 1861. In 1867 he became prof. at the Paris Cons.

Deller, Alfred (b Margate, 31 May 1912; d Bologna, 16 Jul 1979), English countertenor. Entirely self-trained, he became a lay clerk at Canterbury Cathedral in 1940 and in 1947 joined the choir of St Paul's Cathedral. He was widely known as a soloist of outstanding musicianship, also frequently singing with the Deller Consort, which he formed in 1948.

Dello Joio, Norman (b New York, 24 Jan 1913), American composer. Studied at the Juilliard Graduate School in NY with Wagenaar, later with Hindemith at Yale School of Music. He joined the teaching staff of Sarah Lawrence Coll; Boston Univ. 1972–9.

Works incl. operas *The Ruby* (1953) and *The Triumph of St Joan* (1959), symph. ballet *On Stage*; *Western Star* for solo voices, narrator, chorus and orch.; sinfonietta, ballet suite *Duke of Sacramento* (1942), symph. movement *Silvermine* for orch. *Colonial Variations* for orch. (1976), concertos for pf., 2 pfs., harp and fl.; 4tet and trio for woodwind, trio for fl., cello and pf.; vln. and pf., sonata, *Duo concertante* for cello and pf., sonatina for cello solo; suite and *Duo concertante* for 2 pfs.; 2 sonatas, suite and 2 preludes for pf.

Delmas, Jean-Francois (b Lyons, 14 Apr 1861; d Saint-Alban de Monthel, 29 Sep 1933), French bass-baritone. At the Paris Opéra he was a leading singer 1886–1927; created Athanael in *Thaïs*, 1894, and was admired in Méhul's *Joseph*, Reyer's *Salammbô* and Dukas' *Ariane et Barbe-Bleue*. He was Hagen and Gurnemanz in the Opéra fps of *Götterdämmerung* and *Parsifal* (1908, 1914).

Delna, Marie (b Meudon, nr. Paris, 3 Apr 1875; d Paris, 23 Jul 1932), French contralto. Debut Paris, Opéra-Comique, 1892, as the Berlioz Dido; the following year she was Charlotte in the 1st French perf. of *Werther*.

Mistress Quickly, 1894. She sang at the Opéra 1898–1901 and in Milan 1898–1900; engaged by Toscanini for the NY Met in 1909 but did not repeat her European success. Retired from stage 1922 and gave concerts until 1930.

Demetrio (*Demetrius*), lib. by Metastasio.
Opera by Caldara, prod. Vienna, at court, 4 Nov 1731.
Opera by Gluck, prod. Venice, Teatro San Samuele, 2 May 1742.
Opera by Hasse, prod. Venice, Teatro San Giovanni Grisostomo, Jan 1732.
Opera by Jommelli, prod. Parma, spring 1749.
Opera by Pérez, prod. Venice, Teatro San Samuele, 13 Jun 1741.
Opera by Pescetti, prod. Florence, Teatro della Pergola, 26 Dec 1732.

Demofoonte, rè di Tracia (*Demophoon, King of Thrace*), lib. by Metastasio.
Opera by Caldara, prod. 4 Nov 1733.
Opera by Gluck, prod. Milan, Teatro Regio Ducal, 6 Jan 1743.
Opera by Graun, prod. Berlin, Opera, 17 Jan 1746. 3 airs are by Frederick II of Prussia.
Opera by Hasse, prod. Dresden, at court, 9 Feb 1748.
Opera by Jommelli, prod. Padua, 13 Jun 1743.

Demetrio e Polibio, opera by Rossini (lib. by V. Vigano-Mombelli). Rossini's 1st opera, it was written while he was a student at the Bologna Cons., from 1806; prod. Rome, Teatro Valle, 18 May 1812.

Demon, The, opera by A. Rubinstein (lib., in Rus., by P.A. Viskovatov, based on Lermontov's poem), prod. St Petersburg, 25 Jan 1875.

Démophoon, opera by Cherubini (lib. by Marmontel, based on Metastasio's *Demofoonte*), prod. Paris, Opéra, 5 Dec 1788. Cherubini's 1st French opera.

Demougeot, Marcelle (b Dijon, 18 Jun 1871; d Paris, 24 Nov 1931), French soprano. Debut Paris, Opéra, 1902, as Donna Elvira; 1909 Fricka in the local fp of *Das Rheingold* and sang in the Monte Carlo premiere of Saint-Saëns's *Déjanire*, 1911. She was successful as Elisabeth, Brünnhilde and Venus; sang Kundry in the Paris fp of *Parsifal*, 1914.

Dempsey, Gregory (b Melbourne, 20 Jul 1931), Australian tenor. He sang in Australia before joining the SW Co., London, in 1962; sang David in *The Mastersingers*, 1968, and Matej Brouček in the 1st prod. by a British co. of Janáček's *The Excursions* *of Mr. Brouček*; he sang Gregor in *The Makropoulos Case* on his US debut (San Francisco, 1966) and Steva in *Jenůfa* at CG in 1972. Other roles incl. Mime, Peter Grimes and Aeneas in *Les Troyens*.

Demus, Jörg (b St Polten, 2 Dec 1928), Austrian pianist. He studied with Gieseking and Kempff; debut Vienna, 1943, London 1950. Tours world-wide in classical rep. and has acc. leading singers and instrumentalists: piano duets with Paul Badura-Skoda. Plays from his own collection of historical instruments.

Demuth, Leopold (b Brno, 2 Nov 1861; d Czernowitz, 4 Mar 1910), Austrian baritone. Debut Halle 1889, as Hans Heiling; sang in Leipzig and Hamburg before going to Vienna, under Mahler, in 1898. Sang leading roles and took part in the fp of Goldmark's *Ein Wintermärchen* (based on *A Winter's Tale*, 1908). Bayreuth 1899 as Sachs and Gunther.

Demuth, Norman (b London, 15 Jul 1898; d Chichester, 21 Apr 1968), English composer and author. Educ. as a choir-boy at St George's Chapel, Windsor, and at Repton School. Studied music at the RCM in London and became prof. of comp. at the RAM there in 1930. His books include studies of Franck, Ravel and Roussel.

Works incl. 5 operas, incl. *Volpone* (after Jonson) and *The Oresteia* (Aeschylus); 5 ballets; 4 symphs, 2 pf. concertos; 3 sonatas for vln. and pf., string trio, string 4tet etc.

Density 21.5, work for solo flute by Varèse; fp NY, 16 Feb 1936. Title refers to the specific gravity of platinum.

Dent, Edward J(oseph) (b Ribston, Yorks, 16 Jul 1876; d London, 22 Aug 1957), English musicologist and composer. Educ. at Eton and Cambridge, Prof. of Music there from 1926 to 1941. President of the ISCM from its foundation in 1922 until 1938. A governor of Sadler's Wells Opera, for which he trans. many works. His books incl. works on A. Scarlatti, Mozart's operas, Eng. opera, Handel and Busoni, and his comps. polyphonic motets and a version of *The Beggar's Opera*. He was a member of the Editorial Board of the *New Oxford History of Music*.

Denza, Luigi (b Castellammare di Stabia, 24 Feb 1846; d London, 26 Jan 1922), Italian singing-teacher and composer. Studied at the Naples Cons. Settled in London in 1879, made a success with many of his light songs, esp. *Funiculì funiculà*, and was prof. of singing at the RAM from 1898.

Works incl. an opera on Schiller's *Wallenstein*, over 500 songs, etc.

Dering (or Deering), Richard (b *c* 1580; d London, buried 22 Mar 1630), English organist and composer. Became a Catholic and went to Brussels in 1617 as organist to the convent of Eng. nuns, but returned again to become organist to Henrietta Maria on her marriage to Charles I in 1625.

Works incl. *Cantiones sacrae* for several voices, motets, anthems; canzonets for 3 and 4 voices, quodlibets on street cries; fancies and other pieces for viols.

Dérivis, Henri Étienne (b Albi, 2 Aug 1780; d Livry, 1 Feb 1856), French bass. He sang at the Paris Opéra 1803–28 and was well known in operas by Spontini: created leading roles in *La Vestale* (1807), *Fernand Cortez* (1809) and *Olympie* (1819). In 1826 he sang the title role in Rossini's revision of *Maometto II* (*Le Siège de Corinthe*).

Dérivis, Prosper (b Paris, 28 Oct 1808; d Paris, 11 Feb 1880), French bass, son of the prec. He sang at the Paris Opéra 1831–41 and created roles in *Les Huguenots* (1836), *Benvenuto Cellini* (1838) and *Les Martyrs* (1840). In 1842 he was in Milan for the fp of *Nabucco* (Zaccaria) and in Vienna for the fp of Donizetti's *Linda di Chamounix*. Retired 1857.

Dermota, Anton (b Kropa, now in Yugoslavia, 4 Jun 1910), Austrian tenor. He sang Alfredo at the Vienna Staatsoper in 1936 and Florestan at the reopening of the house in 1955. Best known for his Mozart roles, he sang Ottavio under Furtwängler at Salzburg. Other roles incl. David, Lensky and Palestrina.

Dernesch, Helga (b Vienna, 3 Feb 1939), Austrian soprano, later mezzo. Debut Berne, 1961, as Marina. Bayreuth since 1965 as Elisabeth, Eva and Gutrune; Brünnhilde, Leonore and Isolde at Salzburg, from 1969, under Karajan. With Scottish Opera and in London CG, she has sung Leonore, the Marschallin, and Sieglinde. Mezzo roles from 1979, e.g. Fricka and Chrysothemis; (Adelaide in *Arabella*, CG 1986). She sang Hecuba in the fp of Reimann's *Troades* (Munich 1986).

Des Prés. *See* Josquin.

Descant. (a) A melodic line added to an existing melody, hence in general = counterpoint and was so used by older Eng. writers.

(2) The upper part of a polyphonic comp., whether vocal or instrumental; hence descant Recorder, Viol.

(3) In modern usage the addition of a treble part to a well-known tune, either by a

comp. or by improvisation: the word Faburden (or Fauxbourdon) is often used as an equivalent.

Descartes, René (b La Haye, 31 Mar 1596; d Stockholm, 11 Feb 1650), French philosopher. Wrote a book on music, *Compendium musicae* (1618), in which he outlined the relationship between the physical aspect of sound and its perception by the listener.

Deschamps-Jehin, Blanche (b Lyons, 18 Sep 1857; d Paris, Jun 1923), French contralto. In 1879 she sang Mignon at Brussels; created Massenet's Hérodiade there (1881) and Uta in Reyer's *Sigurd*, 1884. In 1885 she was at the Paris Opéra-Comique, in the fp of Massé's *Une Nuit de Cléopâtre*, and remained for the fps of *Le medicin malgré lui* (1886) and *Le Roi d'Ys* (1888). Carmen at CG in 1891, and the 1st local Dalila and *Walküre* Fricka, at the Paris Opéra, 1892–3.

Déserteur, Le, opera by Monsigny (lib. by J.M. Sedaine), prod. Paris, Comédie-Italienne, 6 Mar 1769.

Déserts, work by Varèse for wind insts., perc. and magnetic tapes *ad lib*; comp. 1953–4, fp Paris, 20 Dec 1954, cond. Scherchen. Early use is made here of electronic sound.

Desmarets, Henri (b Paris, Feb 1661; d Lunéville, 7 Sep 1741), French composer. Educ. at the court of Louis XIV. At the end of the cent. he secretly married the daughter of a dignitary at Senlis and fled to Spain, becoming music superintendent to Philip V in 1700. In 1708 he became music director to the Duke of Lorraine at Lunéville.

Works incl. operas and ballets *Didon* (1693), *Circé*, *Théagène et Chariclée* (on Heliodorus's *Aethiopica*, 1695), *Les Amours de Momus*, *Vénus et Adonis*, *Les Fêtes galantes* (1698), *Iphigénie en Tauride* (with Campra) and *Renaud ou La Suite d'Armide* (1722), motet and Te Deum for the marriage of Princess Élisabeth Thérèse to the King of Sardinia; church music written early in his career under the name of Goupillier.

Désormière, Roger (b Vichy, 13 Sep 1898; d Paris, 25 Oct 1963), French conductor. Studied at the Paris Cons. and in 1924 became cond. of the Swed. ballet. From 1925 to 1929 he worked with the Ballet Russe and from 1936 to 1944 cond. at the Opéra Comique; he gave *Pelléas et Mélisande* with the co. at CG in 1949. He became seriously ill in 1950 and was forced to give up his career.

Desprez. *See* **Josquin**.

Dessau, Paul (b Hamburg, 19 Dec 1894; d East Berlin, 28 Jun 1979), German composer. From 1910 he studied at the Klindworth-Scharwenka Cons. in Berlin and later in Hamburg, where in 1913 he became a coach at the opera. He cond. all over Germany, but was forced to leave and in 1939 went to NY. He returned to E. Ger. in 1948.

Works incl. operas *Das Verhör des Lukullus* (1949; prod. 1951), *Puntila* (1959; prod 1966), *Lanzelot* (1969), *Einstein* (1973); children's operas *Das Eisenbahnspiel, Tadel der Unzuverlässigkeit*; concertino for solo fl., clar., horn and vln.; a pf. sonata; much vocal and orchestral music, film and incid. music.

Dessus (Fr. = top of the viols), the treble viol.

Destinn (*née* **Kittl**) (later known as **Destinnova**), **Emmy** (b Prague, 26 Feb 1878; d České Budějovice, 28 Jan 1930), Czech soprano. Made her 1st appearance in Berlin in 1898 as Santuzza; 1st visited London (CG) in 1904 as Donna Anna. Later in London as Butterfly and Aida. Created Minnie in *La fanciulla del West*, NY Met 1910. She wrote poems and novels.

Destouches, André(-Cardinal) (b Paris, bap. 6 Apr 1672; d Paris, 7 Feb 1749), French composer. A sailor at first, and then a musketeer, he studied with Campra and prod. his 1st stage work, *Issé*, in 1697. He held various court appts. and was director of the Opéra in 1728–31.

Works incl. operas *Amadis de Crèce* (1699) *Marthésie*, *Omphale*, *Callirhoé*, *Télémaque et Calypso* (1714), *Sémiramis* (1718), *Les Stratagèmes de l'Amour*; heroic pastoral *Issé*; comedy-ballet *Le Carnaval et la folie*; ballet *Les Éléments* (with Lalande, 1721), cantatas Œnone and Sémélé.

Détaché (Fr. = detached, separated), a bowing style in string playing. In quick passages the bow changes direction so that each note is clearly separated, but without the sound being perceptibly interrupted, as in *staccato*.

Dettingen Te Deum, a Te Deum comp. by Handel to celebrate the victory of Dettingen won on 26 Jun 1743. fp London, Chapel Royal, 27 Nov 1743.

Deutekom, Cristina (b Amsterdam, 28 Aug 1932), Dutch soprano. Her coloratura was admired in Mozart's Queen of Night at her NY Met (1967) and CG (1968) debuts. She sang Bellini's Elvira at Buenos Aires in 1972 and returned to the Met for Verdi's Hélène, in 1974. Other roles incl. Rossini's Armida, Verdi's Odabella and Giselda and Mozart's Constanze.

Deuteromelia, the 2nd part of a collection of canons, rounds and catches pub. by Ravenscroft in London in 1609, the 1st part being *Pammelia*.

Deutsch, Otto Erich (b Vienna, 5 Sep 1883; d Vienna, 23 Nov 1967), Austrian music biographer and bibliographer. Made a special study of 1st eds. and of Schubert and other comps. After the *Anschluss* he took refuge in England and settled at Cambridge, but returned to Vienna in 1954. His pubs. incl. the complete Schubert, Handel and Mozart documents, a thematic catalogue of Schubert's works (1951), listing them in chronological order prefixed by 'D', a study of Mozart eds. (with C.B. Oldman), Leopold Mozart's later letters (with B. Paumgartner), the Harrow Replicas of various pubs., etc.

Deutsche Tänze (Ger. plur. = Ger. Dances), not an equivalent of the Allemande, but a type of country dance in 3–4 (slow waltz) time, cultivated by Mozart, Beethoven, Schubert and others. The adj. 'Deutsche' was frequently used alone in titles.

Deutsches Requiem (Brahms). *See* **German Requiem.**

Deux Avares, Les (*The Two Misers*), opera by Grétry (lib. by C.G.F. de Falbère), prod. Fontainebleau, at court, 27 Oct 1770; 1st Paris perf., Comédie-Italienne, 6 Dec 1770.

Deux Chasseurs et la Laitière, Les (*The Two Huntsmen and the Milkmaid*), opera by Duni (lib. by L. Anseaume, after La Fontaine), prod. Paris, Comédie-Italienne, 21 Jul 1763.

Deux Journées, Les (*The Two Days*: better known as *The Water-Carrier*), opera by Cherubini (lib. by J.N. Bouilly), prod. Paris, Théâtre Feydeau, 16 Jan 1800.

Deux Petits Savoyards, Les (*The Two Little Savoyards*), opera by Dalayrac (lib. by G.J. Marsollier), prod. Paris, Comédie-Italienne, 13 Jan 1789.

Development. *See* **Working-Out.**

Devienne, François (b Joinville, Haute-Marne, 31 Jan 1759; d Paris, 5 Sep 1803), French flautist, bassoonist, teacher and composer. After study with members of his family, he played the flute and bassoon in var. opera orchs. in Paris, from 1779. His wind concertos were perf. from 1780, notably at the *Loge Olympique* and Concert Spirituel concerts. The first of his opéras-comiques, *Le mariage clandestin*, was prod. at the Théâtre Feydeau in 1790; other works in the genre were *Les visitandines* (1792), *Agnès et Félix* (1795) and *Le valet de deux maîtres* (1799). The Revolutionary opera *Le congrés*

des rois was prod. at the Opéra-Comique in 1794. An influential method for the one-key flute was pub. in 1794, and the following year he was app. prof. of flute at the newly-founded Paris Cons. Devienne died in the mental asylum at Charenton.

Devil and Kate, The (*Čert a Káča*), opera by Dvořák (lib. by A. Wenig), prod. Prague, Cz. Theatre, 23 Nov 1899.

Devils of Loudun, The (*Diably z Loudun*), opera by Penderecki (lib. by comp., after John Whiting's play *The Devils*, based on a narrative by Aldous Huxley which describes a case of diabolic possession in a 17th cent. convent of Ursuline nuns), perf. Hamburg, 20 Jun 1969.

Devil's Opera, The, opera by Macfarren (lib. by G. Macfarren, the comp.'s father, a satire on the diabolic elements in works like Weber's *Freischütz*, Meyerbeer's *Robert le Diable*, Marschner's *Vampyr*, etc.), prod. London, Lyceum Theatre, 10 Sep 1838.

Devil's Trill (Tartini). *See* **Trillo del Diavolo.**

Devil's Wall, (*Certova stena*), the opera by Smetana (lib. by E. Krasnohorska), prod. Prague, Czech Theatre, 29 Jan 1882. Smetana's last completed opera.

Devin du village, Le (*The Village Soothsayer*), opera by Rousseau (lib. by comp.), prod. Fontainebleau, at court, 18 Oct 1752, with overture and recitatives by Pierre de Jélyotte (1713–87) and Francœur; Paris, Opéra, 1 Mar 1753, with music all by Rousseau.

Devisenarie (Ger. = device aria), a type of aria of the 17th and 18th cents. in which the 1st word or words occur separately in the voice-part, as though the singer were announcing a title, before the 1st line of the text or more is sung continuously, often after a further instrumental passage.

Devrient, Eduard (Philipp) (b Berlin, 11 Aug 1801; d Karlsruhe, 4 Oct 1877), German baritone and actor. A close friend of Mendelssohn, to whom he devoted a vol. of memoirs, and librettist of Marschner's *Hans Heiling* and other operas. He sang in operas by Gluck, Mozart, Spohr and Marschner; on 11 Mar 1829 he was Christus in the historic perf. of the *St Matthew Passion* in Berlin, under Mendelssohn.

Devrient, Wilhelmine. *See* **Schröder-Devrient.**

Di Murska, Ilma (b Zagreb, 4 Jan 1836; d Munich, 14 Jan 1889), Croatian soprano. Debut Florence 1862, as Martha; appeared widely on the continent and sang Lucia, in London in 1865. At Drury Lane in 1870 she was Senta in *Der fliegende Holländer*, the

1st Wagner production in Britain. Other roles incl. Amina, Constanze and the Queen of Night.

Di Stefano, Giuseppe (b nr. Catania, 24 Jul 1921), Italian tenor. Milan, La Scala from 1947. NY Met 1948–65, debut as Duke of Mantua. Edinburgh 1957 as Nemorino; CG 1961, as Cavaradossi. Sang in It. rep.; also Faust, Nadir, Massenet's Des Grieux and Don José. Made an ill-advised concert tour with Callas 1973–4. In his prime, noted for his discretion and vocal elegance.

Diabelli, Anton (b Mattsee nr. Salzburg, 5 Sep 1781; d Vienna, 8 Apr 1858), Austrian publisher and composer. Educ. for the priesthood, but studied music with M. Maydn. Went to Vienna as pf. and guitar teacher and joined Peter Cappi in his pub. firm in 1818; it became D. & Co. in 1824.

Works incl. operetta *Adam in der Klemme* (Vienna, 1809); Masses; many pf. pieces, incl. the little waltz on which Beethoven wrote the 33 variations op. 120, etc.

'Diabelli' Variations. *See above* and **Vaterländischer Künstlerverein.**

Diable à quatre, Le, ou La Double Métamorphose, ballad opera with airs arr. by F.A. Danican Philidor (lib. by J.M. Sedaine, based on Coffey's *Devil to Pay*), prod. Paris, Opéra-Comique, 19 Aug 1756.

Diable dans le beffroi, Le (*The Devil in the Belfry*), opera by Debussy (lib. by himself, based on Edgar Allan Poe's story), worked at in 1903 but not completed.

Diabolus in Musica (Lat. = the devil in music), a medieval warning against the use of the Tritone – the interval of the augmented 4th (e.g. C–F♯ or F–B), which was looked at askance as a melodic progression.

Diaghilev, Sergey Pavlovich (b Government of Novgorod, 31 Mar 1872; d Venice, 19 Aug 1929), Russian impresario. Studied law and music at St Petersburg, founded an art review there in 1899, prod. Rus. music in Paris from 1907 and in 1909 organized the Rus. Ballet there, which 1st visited London in 1911. He encouraged many comps to write for his co., incl. Stravinsky, Ravel, Debussy, Prokofiev, R. Strauss, de Falla, Poulenc, Milhaud, etc. and was thus directly responsible for some of the most important music of the 20th cent: works written for him by Stravinsky incl. *The Firebird* (1910), *Petrushka* (1911), *The Rite of Spring* (1913), *Pulcinella* (1920), *Les Noces* (1923) and *Oedipus Rex* (1927).

Dialogues des Carmélites, Les, opera by Poulenc (lib. by G. Bernanos), prod. Milan (La Scala), 26 Jan 1957.

Diamants de la Couronne, Les (*The Crown Diamonds*), opera by Auber (lib. by Scribe and J.H.V. de Saint-Georges), prod. Paris, Opéra-Comique 6 Mar 1841.

Diamond, David (Leo) (b Rochester, New York, 9 Jul 1915), American composer of Austrian descent. Studied at the Eastman School of Music at Rochester and later at Fontainebleau with Nadia Boulanger. After his return to Amer. he was awarded several comp. prizes. Juilliard School from 1973.

Works incl. 8 symphs. (1941–62), sinfonietta, serenade, variations, *Psalm, Elegy in Memory of Ravel* and ballet suite *Tom* for orch.; concerto and *Rounds* for string orch. (1944); vln. concerto (1936–67), *Hommage à Satie* and ballade for chamber orch., concertos for pf., cello and vln. (2) with chamber orch.; *A Night Litany* (Ezra Pound) for chorus and 3 madrigals for unaccomp. chorus (James Joyce); *A Secular Cantata* (1976); 10 string 4tets (1943–76), string trio; sonatina for vln. and pf., cello and pf. sonata, partita for bassoon and pf.; sonata and sonatina for pf.

Diapason (from Gk. = through all [the notes], hence interval of an octave; Fr. = a tuning-fork and hence pitch). The normal modern Eng. use of the term designates the foundation stops of the organ which produce the instrument's most distinctive and characteristic tone. There are 2 kinds of diapason pipes: open and stopped. The 4-ft. diapason is generally called Principal (or Octave) on Eng. organs.

Diapente (Gk.), the interval of the 5th. In old music canons at the 5th were called Epidiapente when answered in the 5th above and Subdiapente when answered below.

Diaphony (or Lat. Diaphonia), in Lat. 'dissonance', as distinct from *symphonia* = 'consonance'. Also the name given by some medieval theorists to early Organum.

Diary of a young man who disappeared (*Zápisník zmizelého*), cycle of 22 songs by Janáček for ten., mezzo, 3 women's voices and pf.; comp. 1917–21, perf. Brno, 18 Apr 1921.

Diastole (from Gk. = distinction, differentiation), an old term, in use to the middle of the 18th cent., for the divisions of music into sections or phrases.

Diatonic. The diatonic scale is, in a maj. key, one involving no accidentals (*see* illustration). In a min. key the diatonic scale has two forms, (*a*) melodic, (*b*) harmonic (*see* illustrations). Diatonic harmony is the opposite of chromatic harmony, using the notes proper to the prescribed maj. or min. scale only,

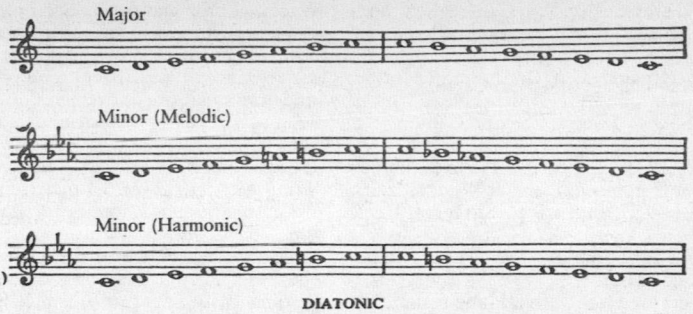

Major

Minor (Melodic)

Minor (Harmonic)

DIATONIC

without deviations to those marked with additional accidentals. Diatonic discords are those that occur in diatonic harmony.

Diaz, Justino (b San Juan, 29 Jan 1939), Puerto Rican bass. NY Met debut 1963, as Monterone; created Barber's Antony in 1966 and in the same year sang Escamillo at Salzburg, under Karajan. He sang Mahometo II in Rossini's *Assedio di Corinto* at La Scala in 1969. Among his other roles are Attila, Don Giovanni and Procida. CG debut 1976, Escamillo. He sang Iago in the 1986 film version of *Otello*, dir. Zeffirelli.

Dibdin, Charles (b Southampton, bap. 15 Mar 1745; d London, 25 Jul 1814), English singer, author and composer. Chorister at Winchester Cathedral, went to London at the age of 15. Made his stage debut in 1762, and shortly afterwards was engaged as a singing actor at CG, where his pastoral *The Shepherd's Artifice* was prod. in 1764. Over 100 dramatic works followed. In 1778 app. composer to Covent Garden Theatre, and during the 1780s dabbled in theatrical management with variable success. A projected journey to India came to nothing, but the fundraising travels which were to have financed it provided material for his *Musical Tour* (1788). In 1789 he began his series of 'Table Entertainments', in which he was author, comp., narrator, singer and accompanist. One of the most successful, *The Oddities*, contained the song *Tom Bowling*. Many other sea-songs achieved great popularity. Towards the end of his life a pub. venture made him bankrupt, and he was saved from destitution by a public subscription. He also wrote an account of his professional life and other literary works.

Works incl. over 100 dramatic pieces, e.g. *Lionel and Clarissa* (1768), *The Padlock, The Ephesian Matron, The Captive, The Ladle* (1773), *The Trip to Portsmouth, The Seraglio* (1776), *Rose and Colin, The Touchstone, The Milkmaid, Tom Thumb, Harvest Home* (1787); over 30 table entertainments containing innumerable songs.

Dichter, Mischa (b Shanghai, 27 Sep 1945), Chinese-born American pianist of Polish parentage. He was brought up in Los Angeles and studied at Juilliard. Silver medal at the 1966 Tchaikovsky Competition; US debut with Boston SO, same year. London debut 1967, with the New Philharmonia. He has often returned to Russia and is well known for his poetic interpretations of Chopin, Brahms and Beethoven.

Dichterliebe (*Poet's Love*), song cycle by Schumann, op. 48 (16 poems by Heine), comp. in 1840.

Dickie, Murray (b Bishopton, Renfrewshire, 3 Apr 1924), Scottish tenor. Debut London 1947, Almaviva. At CG he sang in the fp of Bliss's *Olympians* (1949). Glyndebourne 1950–4, as Pedrillo and Sellem and in the British fp of Busoni's *Arlecchino*. In 1951 he joined the Vienna Staatsoper (buffo roles, and the fp of Martin's *The Tempest*). NY Met 1962, David and Ottavio. In 1976 his prod. of *Eine Nacht in Venedig* was seen at the London Coliseum.

Dickinson, Peter (b Lytham St Annes, 15 Nov 1934), English composer and teacher. He studied at Cambridge and at the Juilliard School, NY; met Cage and Varèse in US, other influences have been Satie and Stravinsky. Prof. at Keele Univ. 1974–84.

Works incl. *Vitalitas*, ballet (1959), music-theatre piece *The Judas Tree* (1965); *Monologue* for strings (1959), *Transformations, Homage to Satie* for orch. (1970); pf. concerto (1978–84), vln. concerto (1986); settings of poems by Auden, Dylan Thomas, Alan Porter, e.e. cummings and Emily Dickinson for v. and pf. (1956–71); *Mass of the Apocalypse* for female chorus and 4 perc. (1984); 2 string 4tets; pf. and organ music.

Dido and Aeneas, opera by Purcell (lib. by

N. Tate, after Virgil), prod. Chelsea, London, Josias Priest's boarding school ('by young gentlewomen'), Dec 1689.

Dido, Königin von Carthago, opera by Graupner (lib. by Heinrich Hinsch), prod. Hamburg, Theater beim Gänsemarkt, spring 1707.

Didon (*Dido*), opera by Piccinni (lib. by Marmontel), prod. Fontainebleau, at court, 16 Oct 1783, 1st Paris perf., Opéra, 1 Dec 1783.

Didone abbandonata (*Dido Forsaken*), lib. by Metastasio:

Opera by Hasse, prod. Hubertusburg nr. Dresden, 7 Oct 1742.

Opera by Jommelli, prod. Rome, Teatro Argentina, 28 Jan 1747.

Opera by Sarro, prod. Naples, Teatro San Bartolommeo, 5 Feb 1724.

Opera by Traetta, prod. Venice, Teatro San Moisè, autumn 1757.

Didone, La (*Dido*), opera by Cavalli (lib. by G. Busenello), prod. Venice, Teatro San Cassiano, Carnival 1641.

Didur, Adam (b Wola Sekowa, nr. Sanok, 24 Dec 1874; d Katowice, 7 Jan 1946), Polish bass. After study in Lwów he made his debut at Rio in 1894, as Méphistophélès. La Scala from 1896, Warsaw Opera 1899–1903. He sang Colline and Leporello at CG in 1905. NY Met 1908–33; sang in the fps of *La Fanciulla del West* and *Königskinder*, and was the 1st Boris, Gremin and Konchak. Returned to Pol. in 1933 and taught at Katowice after the war.

Diepenbrock, Alphons (b Amsterdam, 2 Sep 1862; d Amsterdam, 5 Apr 1921), Dutch composer. At first a philologist, self-taught in music.

Works incl. incid. music for Aristophanes' *The Birds*, Sophocles' *Electra* (1920), Goethe's *Faust*, Vondel's *Gysbrecht van Amstel*; *Stabat Mater*, Te Deum for solo voices, chorus and orch., Mass; songs with orch.; chamber music; songs.

Dieren, Bernard van (b Rotterdam, 27 Dec 1887; d London, 24 Apr 1936), Dutch (anglicized) composer. Educ. for science, he had little musical experience, apart from vln. playing, before the age of 20, when he began to compose. In 1909 he settled in London as correspondent to foreign papers, after making serious music studies, which he continued in Ger. in 1912, when his real creative career began. He also prod. a book on the sculptor Epstein and a vol. of musical essays, *Down among the Dead Men*.

Works incl. opera *The Tailor* (R. Nichols, 1917); symph. on Chinese poems for solo voices, chorus and orch.; *Les Propous des beuveurs* (Rabelais) for chorus and orch.; *Beatrice Cenci*, orchestral epilogue to Shelley's drama (1909), overture *Anjou*; serenade for small orch., overture for chamber orch.; *Diafonia* for 17 instruments and baritone (Shakespeare sonnets, 1916), *Fayre eies* (Spenser) for baritone and chamber orch.; 6 string 4tets (1912–28); 3 unaccomp. choruses; sonata and 3 studies for unaccomp. vln., etc.

Dies irae (*Day of wrath*), the sequence from the Mass for the Dead orig. assoc. with a distinct plainsong theme which has been frequently used or quoted by var. composers, e.g.:

Bantock, Witches' Dance in incid. music to *Macbeth*.

Berlioz, Witches' Sabbath in *Fantastic Symph*, and Requiem.

Dallapiccola, *Canti di prigionia*.

Davies (Maxwell), *St Michael*.

Liszt, *Totentanz* for pf. and orch.

Miaskovsky, symph. No. 6

Rakhmaninov, Rhapsody on a Theme by Paganini for pf. and orch. and Symph. Dances, op. 45.

Respighi, *Impressioni brasiliane*.

Saint-Saëns, *Danse macabre* for orch.

Stevenson (Ronald), *Passacaglia on DSCH*.

Tchaikovsky, Theme and Variations in Suite No. 3 for orch. and song *In Dark Hell*.

Vaughan Williams, *Five Tudor Portraits* for chorus and orch. (lament for Philip Sparrow).

A recent theory claims the Dies Irae as the 'hidden' theme of Elgar's 'Enigma' Variations.

Dièse(or Dièze) (Fr.) = Sharp; the sign ♯.

Diesis (Gk.), in ancient Greece either the interval between a fourth and 2 'maj.' tones or a quarter-tone. In modern acoustics (*a*) the Great Diesis is the difference between 4 min. thirds and an octave; (*b*) the Enharmonic Diesis is the difference between an octave and 3 maj. thirds.

Dietrich, Albert (Hermann) (b Golk nr. Meissen, 28 Aug 1829; d Berlin, 20 Nov 1908), German composer and conductor. Court music director at Oldenburg from 1861. Wrote a vln. and pf. sonata jointly with Schumann and Brahms, 1853.

Works incl. opera *Robin Hood* (1879); incid. music to Shakespeare's *Cymbeline* (perf. London, 1896); symph. in D min.; choral and orchestral works; horn concertos; chamber music.

Dietrich, Sixt (b Augsburg, c 1491; d St

Gall, 21 Oct 1548), German composer. Studied at the Univs. of Freiburg i/B. and Wittenberg, holding appts. at Strasbourg and Konstanz between. Wrote Magnificats, antiphons and other vocal music.

Dietsch, (Pierre-)Louis(-Philippe) (b Dijon, 17 Mar 1808; d Paris, 20 Feb 1865), French conductor and composer. He comp. an unsuccessful opera to the orig. Fr. lib. of Wagner's *Flying Dutchman*, *Le Vaisseau fantôme*, prod. at the Paris Opéra in 1842. Cond. the disastrous perfs. of Wagner's *Tannhäuser* in 1861. Works incl. church and organ music.

Dieupart, Charles (b France; d London, c 1740), French violinist, harpsichordist and composer. Settled in London c 1700 and was involved in the promotion of It. opera at Drury Lane. Later abandoned opera, gave concerts and taught the harpsichord. Wrote suites, etc., for harpsichord.

Diminished, said of intervals normally 'perfect' (4ths, 5th, 8ves) or 'minor' (7nds, 3rds, 6ths, 7ths) which have been made a semitone narrower, e.g:

Perfect 5th   Diminished 5th

Minor 3rd   Diminished 3rd

Diminished 7th Chord, a chord of 3 superimposed min. 3rds, e.g.:

Diminuendo (It. = waning, lessening), a direction to decrease the sound of a note, chord or phrase, synonymous with *decrescendo* and now more frequently used.

Diminution, a shortening of a musical figure or phrase by its reduction to smaller notevalues.

Dimitri, opera by Dvořák (lib. by M Červinková-Riegerová), prod. Prague, Czech Theatre, 8 Oct 1882. The subject is the 'false Dimitri', the pretender who also figures in Mussorgsky's *Boris Godunov*.

Dinorah (Meyerbeer). See **Pardon de Ploërmel.**

Dioclesian (Purcell). See **Prophetess.**

Direct, a sign used in plainsong notation and often in old music in staff notation, indicating at the end of the stave the position of the first note at the beginning of the following one.

Dirge, a funeral composition, usually vocal, perf. at a burial or more rarely on a memorial occasion. The word derives from the Lat. *Dirige Domine*, the opening words of an antiphon from the Office for the Dead.

Diruta, Agostino (b Perugia; d Rome), Italian 16th–17th-cent. organist and composer. Organist at Venice, 1617, Asolo, 1620–2, and Rome, 1630–47.

    Works incl. Masses, motets, psalms, *Sacrae cantiones*, canticles and other vocal music.

Diruta, Girolamo (real name **Mancini**) (b Deruta nr. Perugia, c 1554; d ? after 1610), Italian Franciscan monk, organist and composer, uncle and master of prec. Pupil of Zarlino, Porta and Merulo. Organist at Chioggia and Gubbio Cathedrals. He was a famous player and wrote a treatise on organ playing, *Il Transilvano*, ded. to the Prince of Transylvania, Sigismund Bathori. Wrote organ music.

Discord, the opposite of concord: the sounding together of notes that do not satisfy the ear as being final in themselves and require a following chord to give the impression of resolution.

Diskantmesse (Ger.). See **Descant Mass.**

Dissoluto punito, Il (Mozart). See **Don Giovanni.**

Dissonance, the sounding together of notes which produces Discord.

Dissonance Quartet, string 4tet no. 19 in C, K465 by Mozart, comp. 1785. The dissonant intro. to the 1st movement gives the work its name.

Distler, Hugo (b Nuremberg, 24 Jun 1908; d Berlin, 1 Nov 1942), German organist and composer. Studied at Leipzig, became organist and cantor at Lübeck in 1921 and prof. of comp. at the Stuttgart Cons. in 1937. He died by committing suicide.

    Works incl. 52 motets entitled *Jahrkreis*, a Passion, oratorio *Nativity*; organ works; harpsichord concerto.

Distratto, Il, nickname of Haydn's symph. no. 60 in C maj., so called on account of its being an adaptation of the incid. music to *Der Zerstreute* (1775), a Ger. version of Regnard's *Le Distrait*.

Dital Harp. See **Harp Lute.**

Dittersdorf, Karl Ditters von (orig. simply Karl Ditters) (b Vienna, 2 Nov 1739; d Neuhof, Pilgram, Bohemia, 24 Oct 1799), Austrian composer and violinist. Educ. in the household of Prince Hildburghausen in Vienna, studied comp. with Bonno. Played in the orch. of the Imp. Opera in Vienna, 1761–3, when he travelled to Italy with

Gluck, winning great success as a violinist. In 1765 succeeded Michael Haydn as *Kapellmeister* to the Bishop of Grosswardein, and from 1769 to 1795 served the Prince Bishop of Breslau in the same capacity. But much of his time was spent in Vienna, where his most popular opera, *Doctor und Apotheker*, was prod. in 1786. He was ennobled in 1773, henceforth calling himself von Dittersdorf. Kelly's *Reminiscences* contain an account of Dittersdorf playing string 4tets with Haydn, Mozart and Vanhal. During his last years he was in the service of Baron Stillfried at Rothlhotta. His autobiography, dictated shortly before his death, was pub. in 1801.

Works incl. over 40 operas, e.g. *Amore in musica, Betrug durch Aberglauben, Doctor und Apotheker* (1786), *Hieronimus Knicker* (1789), *Das rothe Kaeppchen, Die Hochzeit des Figaro* (after Beaumarchais), etc.; oratorios *Isacco* (1766), *Davidde Penitente* (1771), *Esther, Giobbe* (1786); Masses and other church music; over 100 symphs., incl. 21 on Ovid's *Metamorphoses*; concertos; divertimenti, chamber music.

Diversions, work by Britten for pf., left hand, and orch.; comp. 1940, rev. 1954, fp Philadelphia, 16 Jan 1942, Paul Wittgenstein soloist.

Divertimento, a work for instrumental ensemble in several movements akin to the suite and predominantly light-hearted in character.

Divertissement, mainly a term connected with ballet, where it means a set of varied dances with no partic. plot. In music a suite, partic. of arrs. or pieces based on familiar tunes, an entertaining piece of any kind or a fantasy of a lighter sort, such as Schubert's *Divertissement à la hongroise*. In 18th-cent. French usage a dance interlude, with or without songs, in a play or opera; also sometimes a short play with dances and songs.

Divine Poem, The, title of symph. no. 3 in C min., op. 43 by Skriabin, fp Paris, 29 May 1905, cond. Nikisch. The work's 3 movts., titled 'Struggles', 'Delights' and 'Divine Play', reflect Skriabin's mystic beliefs.

Divisi (It. plur. = divided), a direction found in orchestral scores where string parts are intended to be distributed in such a way as to play in 2 or more parts within a single group of instruments which would normally play in unison.

Division Viol, a bass viol of moderate size on which divisions were often played in the 17th cent. Simpson, for ex., wrote for it.

Divisions, a term used in 17th-cent. Eng. for variations. It became current because variations then usually consisted of breaking up the melody of the theme into notes of smaller value.

Djamileh, opera by Bizet (lib. by L. Gallet, based on Musset's *Namouna*), prod. Paris, Opéra-Comique, 22 May 1872.

Djinns, Les (*The Genii*), symph. poem by Franck for pf. and orch., based on verses from Hugo's *Les Orientales*, comp. 1884; fp Paris, 15 Mar 1885.

Do, the old name for the note C (*see* **Solmization**), still used in Latin countries. In Tonic Sol-fa notation the Tonic note in any key, represented by the symbol d, pronounced Doh.

Dobbs, Mattiwilda (b Atlanta, 11 Jul 1925), American soprano. She studied with Lotte Lehmann and Pierre Bernac. Concert career from 1947; stage debut 1952, with Netherlands Opera. Glyndebourne 1953–61 as Zerbinetta, Constanze and the Queen of Night. CG 1954 as the Queen of Shemakha. NY Met debut 1956, as Gilda. She sang at Stockholm 1957–73. A secure coloratura technique.

Dobroven, Issay Alexandrovich (b Nizhny-Novgorod, 27 Feb 1891; d Oslo 9 Dec 1953), Russian conductor and composer. Studied with Taneiev and others at the Moscow Cons. and later took a pf. course with Godowsky in Vienna. He became prof. at the Moscow Cons. in 1917 and cond. of the Opera in 1919. Later he cond. Rus. opera on tour in Ger. and in 1927–8 he was cond. of the Bulgarian State Opera at Sofia. In the 1930s he cond. extensively in USA and Palestine.

Works incl. opera *A Thousand and One Nights* (perf. Moscow, 1922); incid. music to Verhaeren's *Philip II*; pf. concerto, vln. concerto; sonata and *Fairy Tales* for vln. and pf.; sonatas, studies and pieces for pf.; songs.

Docteur Ox, Le, opéra bouffe by Offenbach (lib. by P. Gille and A. Mortier, based on a Jules Verne story), prod. Paris, Théâtre des Variétés, 26 Jan 1877.

Doctor und Apotheker (*Doctor and Apothecary*), opera by Dittersdorf (lib. by G. Stephanie, jun.), prod. Vienna, Kärntnertortheater, 11 Jul 1786.

Dodecaphony, dodecaphonic, composition making equal use of all twelve notes of the chromatic octave. Normally this term is used only in reference to 12-note serialism, *see* **Twelve-Note Music.**

Dodgson, Stephen (b London, 17 Mar 1924), English composer and broadcaster. He studied at the RCM; taught there since

1964. Best known for his guitar concertos, he has also written for the clavichord and harpsichord. Other works incl. pf. 4tet, Symph. for wind (1974), *Epigrams from a Garden* for mezzo and clars. (1977), etc.

Doese, Helena (b Götenburg, 13 Aug 1946), Swedish soprano. Debut Götenburg 1971, as Aida. Berne 1972–5, as Jenufa, Micaela and Donna Anna. Royal Opera Stockholm from 1975, as Katya Kabanova and Eva. Glyndebourne from 1974, as Mozart's Countess and Fiordiligi. At CG she has been admired since 1974 as Mimi, Gutrune, Agathe and Amelia Boccanegra. US debut San Francisco, 1982. Other roles incl. Ariadne, the Marschallin, and Elisabeth de Valois.

Doh, the name for the Tonic note in any key in Tonic Sol-fa, so pronounced, but in notation represented by the symbol **d**.

Dohnányi, Christoph von (b Berlin, 8 Sep 1929), German born conductor, grandson of Ernö D. He studied in Munich, Florida and at Tanglewood; held opera posts in Frankfurt, Lübeck and Kassel, 1952–66, and was chief cond. Cologne Radio SO 1964–70. Hamburg Opera 1977–84, music dir. Cleveland Orch. from 1984. London debut 1965, with the LPO, and has cond. *Salome* and *Wozzeck* at CG. He gave the fps of Henze's *Der junge Lord* (Berlin, 1965) and *The Bassarids* (Salzburg, 1966); with his wife, the sop. Anja Silja, has given frequent perfs. of Schoenberg and Berg.

Dohnányi, Ernö (or **Ernst von**) (b Pozsony = Pressburg, 27 Jul 1877; d New York, 9 Feb 1960), Hungarian pianist and composer. Studied under Carl Forstner, the cathedral organist at his native town, until 1893, when he went to the Hungarian Acad. at Budapest, where he studied pf. under Stephan Thomán and comp. under Koessler. In 1897 he had some lessons from d'Albert and appeared as pianist in Berlin and Vienna. He visited Eng. in 1898 and USA in 1899, made many tours later, but eventually became better known as a comp. From 1908 to 1915 he was prof. of pf. at the Hochschule in Berlin and in 1919 became cond. of the Budapest PO and director of the city's Cons. As a pianist his powers were prodigious, while as a comp. he drew upon the classical Ger. tradition, esp. Brahms.

Works incl. operas *Aunt Simona* (Dresden, 1913), *The Tower of Voivod* (Budapest, 1922) and *The Tenor* (1929); ballet *Pierrette's Veil*; symphs. in F min., D min. and E maj., suite in F♯ min. and *Suite en valse* for orch.; 2 pf. concertos and *Varia-*

tions on a Nursery Song for pf. and orch. (1913); 2 vln. concertos, *Concertstück* for cello and orch.; 3 string 4tets, pf. 5tet, 6tet for vln., vla., cello, clar., horn and pf., serenade for string trio; sonatas for vln. and pf. and cello and pf.; 12 op. nos. of pf. music, incl. a passacaglia, 4 rhapsodies, *Humoresques in form of a Suite, Ruralia hungarica*; songs.

Doktor Faust, opera by Busoni (lib. by comp. based on the Faust legend and Marlowe's *Dr. Faustus* (1589); not based on Goethe), left unfinished at Busoni's death and completed by Jarnach: prod. Dresden, 21 May 1925. 1st prod. in Brit., London, Coliseum, 25 Apr 1986 (1st prod. anywhere with Busoni's fullest score).

Dolby, Charlotte. *See* **Sainton-Dolby.**

Dolce (It. = sweet), a direction indicating a suave and ingratiating perf., usually but not necessarily in a soft tone.

Dolcian, an early form of bassoon.

Doles, Johann Friedrich (b Steinbach, Saxe-Meiningen, 23 Apr 1715; d Leipzig, 8 Feb 1797), German organist and composer. Pupil of Bach at Leipzig from 1739. Cantor of St Thomas's School there from 1756 in succession to Harrer. Perf. Bach's motet *Singet dem Herrn* for Mozart, when the latter visited Leipzig in 1789.

Works incl. Passions, Masses, motets, cantatas and other church music.

Dolly, suite of 6 children's pieces for pf. duet by Fauré, op. 56, comp. in 1893, orch. for a ballet by Rabaud in 1896; 1st prod. Paris, 23 Jan 1913. It is ded. to the daughter of Mme. Emma Bardac, later Debussy's 2nd wife. As in the case of Debussy's *Children's Corner*, the title and 2 of the sub-titles seem to suggest some Eng. association: 1. *Berceuse*; 2 *Mi-a-ou*; 3. *Le Jardin de Dolly*; 4. *Kitty-Valse*; 5. *Tendresse*; 6. *Le Pas espagnol*.

Dolmetsch, Arnold (b Le Mans, 24 Feb 1858; d Haslemere, 28 Feb 1940), Swiss (anglicized) musicologist, instrument maker and perf. on old instruments. He studied vln. under Vieuxtemps at Brussels, but turned his interests to old music and instruments. Worked with the pf. firm of Chickering at Boston, 1902–9, and then with that of Gaveau in Paris until 1914, when he went to live in Eng. and set up his own workshop for harpsichords, viols, lutes, recorders, etc. at Haslemere, where he arr. periodical festivals of old music and brought up a family to take part in it with var. instruments. He ed. old music and wrote a book on interpretation. His second son, Carl, (b Fontenay-sous-

Bois, France, 23 Aug 1911), is a well-known recorder player.

Dom Sébastien, Roi de Portugal (*Dom Sebastian, King of Portugal*), opera by Donizetti (lib. by Scribe), prod. Paris, Opéra, 13 Nov 1843.

Domaine Musical, founded by Jean-Louis Barrault, Madeleine Renaud and Pierre Boulez in 1954 to promote concerts of new music, with Boulez as music director. The group had as its headquarters the Petit Marigny theatre.

Domaines, work by Boulez for solo clar. and 21 insts.; 1968, fp Brussels, 20 Dec 1968.

Domaninská, Libuše (b Brno, 4 Jul 1924), Czech soprano. She sang at Brno 1945–55, then joined the Prague National Theatre; visited Edinburgh with the Co. in 1964 and sang Milada in the 1st Brit. perf. of Smetana's *Dalibor*. Her best roles were Janáček's Vixen, Jenůfa and Katya Kabanova. She sang at the Vienna Staatsoper 1958–68.

Domestic Symphony (R. Strauss). *See* **Symphonia domestica.**

Domgraf-Fassbänder, Willi (b Aachen, 19 Feb 1897; d Nuremberg, 13 Feb 1978), German baritone. He studied in Berlin and Milan.'Debut Aachen, 1922; sang in Düsseldorf and Stuttgart before joining the Berlin Staatsoper in 1928; successful there in the prod. of Egk's *Peer Gynt* which was admired by Hitler. Glyndebourne 1934–7 as Figaro, Guglielmo and Papageno. Father of the mezzo, Brigitte Fassbaender.

Dominant. (1) The 5th note of the maj. or min. scale above the tonic or keynote, or the 4th below it. In classical harmony the dominant is the most conspicuous note in the scale apart from the tonic.

(2) the name often given to the reciting note of a psalm-tone or mode. *See* **Modes.**

Domingo, Placido (b Madrid, 21 Jan 1934), Spanish tenor. He spent his childhood in Mexico and sang in zarzuelas before opera debut as Alfredo in Monterrey, 1961; US debut same year, as Arturo, to Sutherland's *Lucia*, in Dallas. Israel Nat. Opera 1962–5; NY, City Opera, Pinkerton, 1965. NY Met from 1968 and London, CG, from 1971; debut as Cavaradossi. Other roles incl. Don José, Hoffmann, Dick Johnson, Radames, Otello, Samson and Aeneas in *Les Troyens*. He has sung Wagner's Walther on record and Lohengrin in NY and Hamburg. Debut as cond. *Attila*, Barcelona, 1973. Autobiog., *My First 40 Years* (1983). In terms of vocal consistency and range of repertory without a serious modern rival. Returned to CG 1987, Otello.

Dominguez, Oralia (b San Luis Potosi, 15 Oct 1928), Mexican contralto. Stage debut Mexico City 1950. She sang Cilea's Princesse de Bouillon at La Scala, in 1953. She was Sosostris in the 1955 fp of *The Midsummer Marriage*, at CG, and in the same year sang Mistress Quickly at Glyndebourne; she returned for Rossini's Isabella (1957) and was Arnalta in the Leppard-Monteverdi *Poppea* of 1962. Deutsche Oper, Düsseldorf, from 1960.

Domino noir, Le (*The Black Domino*), comic opera by Auber (lib. by Scribe) prod. Paris, Opéra-Comique, 2 Dec 1837.

Don Carlos, opera by Verdi in 5 acts (lib. by F.M. Méry and C. Du Locle, based on Schiller's drama), prod. Paris, Opéra, 11 Mar 1867. Verdi's 2nd Fr. opera. Revised in 4 acts, in Italian, and prod. Milan, La Scala, 10 Jan 1884.

Don Chisciotte della Mancia, opera by Paisiello (lib. by G.B. Lorenzi), perf. Naples, Teatro dei Fiorentini, summer 1769. Version by Henze perf. Montepulciano, 1 Aug 1976.

Don Chisciotte in corte della duchessa (*Don Quixote at the Duchess's Court*), opera by Caldara (lib. by G.C. Pasquini, based on Cervantes), prod. Vienna, 6 Feb 1727.

Don Chisciotte in Sierra Morena (*Don Quixote in the S.M.*), opera by Conti (lib. by Zeno and P. Pariati, based on Cervantes), prod. Vienna, 11 Feb 1719.

Don Giovanni (*Don Juan*), opera by Lattuada (lib. by A. Rossato, based on a Span. drama by José Zorilla), prod. Naples 18 May 1929.

Opera by Mozart (1st title: *Il dissoluto punito, ossia Il D.G.: The Rake Punished, or Don Juan*) (lib. by Lorenzo da Ponte), prod. Prague, 29 Oct 1787. In Vienna, with additions, Burgtheater, 7 May 1788.

Don Giovanni di Mañara (Alfano). *See* **Ombra di Don Giovanni.**

Don Giovanni Tenorio, ossia Il convitato di pietra (*Don Juan Tenorio, or The Stone Guest*), opera by Carnicer, prod. Barcelona, Teatro Principal, 20 Jun 1822. The 1st Don Juan opera by a Spanish composer, but set to Italian words.

Opera by Gazzaniga (lib. by G. Bertati, based on Tirso de Molina), prod. Venice, Teatro San Moisè, 5 Feb 1787.

Don Juan. *See also* **Convitato di pietra; Don Giovanni; Ombra di Don Giovanni; Stone Guest.**

Symph. poem by R. Strauss, op. 20, based on Lenau's poem, comp. 1887–8, fp Weimar, 11 Nov 1889.

Don Juan de Mañara, opera by Goossens (lib. by Arnold Bennett), prod. London, CG, 24 Jun 1937.

Don Juan legend. For musical treatments *see* **Albertini, Alfano** (*L'ombra di Don Giovanni*), **Assafiev** (*The Seducer of Seville*), **Carnicer, Convitato di pietra** (Fabrizi and Righini), **Dargomizhsky** (*Stone Guest*), **Don Giovanni** (Lattuada and Mozart), **Don G. Tenorio** (Carnicer and Gazzaniga), **Don Juan** (R. Strauss), **D.J. de Mañara** (Goossens), **Enna** (*D.J. Mañara*), **Ferreira, Graener** (*D.Js. letztes Abenteuer*), **Ombra di Don Giovanni** (Alfano), **Purcell** (Shadwell's *Libertine*), **Salazar** (*D.J. en los infiernos*), **Schulhoff (E.)** (opera), **Shebalin** (*Stone Guest*), **Tomasi** (*Don Juan de Mañara*).

Don Pasquale, comic opera by Donizetti (lib. by comp. and ?, based on Angelo Anelli's *Ser Marcantonio*, comp. by Pavesi in 1810), prod. Paris, Théâtre Italien, 3 Jan 1843.

Don Quichotte, opera by Massenet (lib. by H. Cain, based on Cervantes and Jacques Le Lorrain's comedy, *Le Chevalier de la longue figure*), prod. Monte Carlo, 19 Feb 1910.

Don Quixote. *See also* **Don Chisciotte; Retablo de Maese Pedro; Sancio Panza; Sancho Panza.**

Opera by Kienzl (lib. by comp., based on Cervantes), prod. Berlin, Opera, 18 Nov 1898.

Symph. poem by R. Strauss, op. 35, based on Cervantes, comp. 1897, fp Cologne, 8 Mar 1898. The work is described as 'Fantastic Variations on a theme of knightly character' and contains important solo parts for cello (Don Q.) and vla. (Sancho Panza).

Don Quixote, The Comical History of, play by Thomas Durfey, based on Cervantes, with music by Purcell and others, comp. parts i and ii, 1694, by Purcell and Eccles; Part iii, 1695, by Akeroyde, Courteville, Pack, Morgan and D. Purcell. i. prod. London, Dorset Gardens, May 1694; ii. do. Jun 1694; iii. London, Drury Lane Theatre, Nov 1695.

Donath, Helen (b Corpus Christi, 10 Jul 1940), American soprano. She sang in concert from 1958 and made her stage debut at Cologne in 1963; moved to Munich in 1967 and sang Pamina at Salzburg the same year. In 1971 she sang Sophie at San Francisco and the Bolshoy, Moscow. Among her recordings are *Freischütz, Dido and Aeneas, Palestrina* and operas by Schubert.

Donato (or Donati), Baldassare (b ? Venice, *c* 1530; d Venice, 1603), Italian organist, singer and composer. App. to St Mark's at Venice in 1550, he remained there in var. capacities all his life, becoming *maestro di cappella* in succession to Zarlino in 1590. He also taught singing at the seminary attached to St Mark's.

Works incl. motets, psalms; madrigals, *villanelle, canzoni*.

Donatoni, Franco (b Verona, 9 Jun 1927), Italian composer. He studied in Rome with Pizzetti; has been influenced by him, and has used serial and, more recently, aleatory techniques.

Works incl. Concerto for bassoon. and strings (1952), Divertimento for vln. and chamber orch. (1954), *Black and White,* for 37 strings (1964), *Doubles II* for orch. (1970), *Portrait* for harpsichord and orch. (1976); 4 string 4tets (1950–63), *Etwas ruhiger in Ausdruck,* for chamber ens. (1968; title from no. 2 of Schoenberg's pf. pieces op. 23). Vocal music incl. *The Book with 7 Seals,* oratorio for soloists, chorus and orch. (1951) and *Serenata* for sop. and 16 insts. (1959; text by Dylan Thomas).

Dönch, Karl (b Hagen, 8 Jan 1915), German bass-baritone. Debut Gorlitz 1936. Vienna Staatsoper from 1947; often heard as Beckmesser and sang in the fp of Martin's *Tempest,* 1956. He sang at Salzburg from 1951, as Alfonso and Berg's Doctor, and as Leiokritos in the 1954 fp of Liebermann's *Penelope.* NY Met 1959–67; guest at Milan and Buenos Aires.

Donington, Robert (b Leeds, 4 May 1907), English instrumentalist and musicologist. Educ. at St Paul's School, London, and Oxford, he studied early instruments and interpretation of early music with Dolmetsch at Haslemere. He has ed. early music, written learned articles, perf. with various teams on early instruments and prod. books on instruments and ornaments, incl. *The Interpretation of Early Music.* He has also pub. *Wagner's Ring and its Symbols* (1963) and *The Rise of Opera* (1981). OBE 1979.

Donizetti, Gaetano (Domenico Maria) (b Bergamo, 29 Nov 1797; d Bergamo, 8 Apr 1848), Italian composer. Studied at Bergamo and at the Liceo Filarmonico at Bologna. He entered the army to avoid following his father's trade and while at Venice in 1818 prod. his 1st opera, *Enrico di Borgogna,* there. After that, except in 1821, he prod. operas annually until 1844, when *Caterina Cornaro* came out as the last at Naples and his reason began to fail. In 1839–40 and 1843 he visited Paris and prod. operas there. He became paralysed in 1845.

Works incl. more than 70 operas. Among

those most frequently heard today are *Zoraida di Granata* (Rome, 1822), *L'ajo nell'imbarazzo* (Rome 1824), *Emilia di Liverpool* (Naples, 1824), *Gabriella di Vergy* (comp. 1826, perf. Naples, 1869), *Il borgomastro di Saardam* (Naples, 1827), *Le convenienze ed inconvenienze teatrali* (Naples, 1827), *Il Giovedi Grasso* (Naples, 1828), *Elisabetta, o Il castello di Kenilworth* (Naples, 1829), *Anna Bolena* (Milan, 1830), *Gianni di Parigi* (Milan, 1831), *Fausta* (Naples, 1832), *Ugo, conte di Parigi* (Milan, 1832), *L'elisir d'amore* (Milan 1832), *Il furioso all'isola di San Domingo* (Rome, 1833), *Torquato Tasso* (Rome, 1833), *Lucrezia Borgia* (Milan, 1833), *Rosmonda d'Inghilterra* (Florence, 1834), *Maria Stuarda* (Naples, 1834), *Gemma di Vergy* (Milan, 1834), *Marino Faliero* (Paris, 1835), *Lucia di Lammermoor* (Naples, 1835), *Belisario* (Venice, 1836), *Il campanello di notte* (Naples, 1836), *Pia de' Tolomei* (Venice, 1837), *Roberto Devereux* (Naples, 1837), *Maria di Rudenz* (Venice, 1838), *Poliuto* (Naples, 1848; comp. 1838 for Naples it was banned and prod. in Paris 1840 as *Les Martyrs*), *La fille du régiment* (Paris, 1840), *La favorite* (Paris, 1840), *Maria Padilla* (Milan, 1841), *Linda di Chamounix* (Vienna, 1842), *Caterina Cornaro* (Naples, 1842), *Don Pasquale* (Paris, 1843), *Maria di Rohan* (Vienna, 1843), *Dom Sébastien* (Paris, 1843). *Le duc d'Albe* was written for Paris in 1840 but not prod. The score was completed by M. Salvi and others and prod. Rome, Teatro Apollo, 22 Mar 1882.

Donna ancora è fedele, La (*The Lady is still Faithful*), opera by Pasquini (lib. by D.F. Contini), prod. Rome, Palazzo Colonna, 19 Apr 1676.

Donna del lago, La (*The Lady of the Lake*), opera by Rossini (lib. by A.L. Tottola, based on Scott's poem), prod. Naples, Teatro San Carlo, 24 Sep 1819.

Donna Diana, opera by Reznicek (lib. by comp., based on Moreto 's comedy), prod. Prague, Ger. Theatre, 16 Dec 1894.

Donna serpente, La (*The Serpent-Woman*), opera by Casella (lib. by C. Lodovici, based on Gozzi's comedy), prod. Rome, Teatro Reale, 17 Mar 1932. Wagner's *Die Feen* was on the same subject.

Donne curiose, Le (*The Inquisitive Ladies*), opera by Wolf-Ferrari (lib. by L. Sugano, based on Goldoni's comedy), prod. Munich, in Ger., 27 Nov 1903.

Donnerstag aus Licht (*Thursday from Light*), opera by Stockhausen from projected opera cycle **Licht.** The work is semi-

autobiographical: the 3 acts are titled *Michael's Youth, Michael's journey around the earth* (a huge concerto for trumpet and orch.) and *Michael's homecoming*; comp. 1978–80, prod. Milan, La Scala, 3 Apr 1981.

Donohoe, Peter (b Manchester, 18 Jun 1953), English pianist. He studied at the RMCM and with Yvonne Loriod in Paris. Debut 1979, Prom. Concerts. 1982 joint silver medal winner Tchaikovsky Int. Competition, Moscow; frequent visits to Rus. since. He plays modern works as well as the Romantic rep., and in 1983 gave the fp of Dominic Muldowney's pf. concerto.

Donzelli, Domenico (b Bergamo, 2 Feb 1790; d Bologna, 31 Mar 1873), Italian tenor. Made his 1st appearance in Italy 1816, and sang in Rossini's *Tancredi, Torvaldo e Dorliska* and *Cenerentola*; Paris, 1825, in the fp of *Il viaggio a Reims.* London, Drury Lane, 1829, in Bellini's *Il pirata,* and in 1831 created Pollione in *Norma* (La Scala). Also successful in operas by Donizetti, Auber and Mercadante.

Doppio Concerto, work by Henze for oboe, harp and strings, written for Heinz and Ursula Holliger and perf. by them Zurich, 2 Dec 1966.

Doppio movimento (It. = double movement), a direction indicating that a new tempo is to be exactly twice as fast as the one it displaces.

Doppler, Polish-Hungarian family of musicians:

   1. Albert Franz D. (b Lwów, 16 Oct 1821; d Baden nr. Vienna, 27 Jul 1883), flautist and composer. Taught at Pest and wrote operas, incl. *Judith* (1870), a ballet, overtures, fl. concertos, etc.

   2. Karl D. (b Lwów, 12 Sep 1825; d Stuttgart, 10 Mar 1900), flautist, conductor and composer, brother of prec. Toured widely and became cond. at the Pest Nat. Theatre. Wrote operas, incl. *Erzébeth* (1857) with Albert D. and Erkel, ballets, fl. music etc.

   3. Arpád D. (b Pest 5 Jun1857; d Stuttgart, 13 Aug 1927), pianist and composer, son of prec. Studied and taught at Stuttgart, and for a time in NY. Wrote a musical play *Halixula* (1891), orchestral works, pf. music, songs.

Dorati, Antal (b Budapest, 9 Apr 1906), American conductor of Hungarian birth. Studied at the Budapest Acad. of Music with Bartók and Kodály. He first cond. at the age of 18. In 1947 he became an Amer. citizen and in 1948 cond. of the Minneapolis SO.

From 1963 to 1967 he was chief cond. of the BBC SO; RPO 1975–8, Detroit SO 1977–81. Has recorded all the Haydn symphs. and most of the operas. He has also comp. and made a number of successful arrs. (e.g. *Graduation Ball*, after J. Strauss).

Dorfbarbier, Der (*The Village Barber*), comic opera by Schenk (lib. by J. and P. Weidmann), prod. Vienna, Burgtheater, 30 Oct 1796.

Dori, La, ovvero La schiava fedele (*Doris, or The Faithful Slave*), opera by Cesti (lib. by A. Apolloni), prod. Florence, Teatro dei Sorgenti, Carnival 1661.

Dorian Mode, the scale represented by the white keys on the pf. beginning on the note D.

'Dorian' Toccata and Fugue, org. work in D min. by Bach, so called on account of its notation without key-signature, the B♭ being inserted where necessary as an accidental.

Dorn, Heinrich (Ludwig Egmont) (b Königsberg, 14 Nov 1804; d Berlin, 10 Jan 1892), German composer, teacher and conductor. Pupil of Zelter in Berlin, teacher of Schumann at Leipzig, opera cond. at Hamburg and Riga, where he succeeded Wagner in 1839. Finally cond. at the Royal Opera and prof. in Berlin.

Works incl. operas, e.g. *Die Rolandsknappen* (1826), *Die Nibelungen* (1854), etc.; ballet *Amors Macht;* Requiem; cantatas; orchestral works; pf. music; songs.

Dostoievsky, Feodor Mikhailovich (b Moscow, 11 Nov 1821; d St Petersburg, 9 Feb 1881), Russian novelist. *See* **Chailly, R.** (*L'Idiota*), **From the House of the Dead** (Janáček), **Gambler** (Prokofiev), **Grossinquisitor** (Blacher), **Idiot** (Henze), **Rebikov** (*Christmas Tree*), **Ruyneman** (*Brothers Karamazov*), **Sutermeister** (*Raskolnikov*).

Dot. (1) Above or under a note normally indicates *staccato.* Uses other than this are: (*a*) in 18th-cent vln. music a series of dots with a slur indicates notes to be detached without changing the bow; (*b*) in 18th-cent. clavichord music a series of dots with a slur above or under a single note indicates repeated pressure on the key; (*c*) in older Fr. music dots above or under a succession of quavers or semi-quavers could mean the observance of equal note-values (*notes égales*), as opposed to the current fashion of lengthening or shortening such notes alternately (*notes inégales*)

(2) A dot to the right of a note normally lengthens it by half. *See* **Dotted Notes.**

Dot-way, a 17th-cent. system of notation

for recorders, with staves each line of which repres. a fingerhole, while dots placed over the lines showed which fingers were to be kept down for each note.

Dotted Notes, notes with a dot placed on their right, with the effect of prolonging them by half their orig. value. A double dot has the effect of adding another half of the smaller value to the orig. note, which is thus lengthened by three-quarters of its value. Double dots were intro. by Leopold Mozart, before whose time their effect could not be precisely indicated in notation, though it was often prod. at will by the interpreter, esp. in slow movements written in singly dotted rhythm, such as the slow intros. in Lully's and Handel's overtures.

Dotzauer, (Justus Johann) Friedrich (b Hildburghausen, 20 Jan 1783; d Dresden, 6 Mar 1860), German cellist. Played 1st in the court orch. at Meiningen, then at Leipzig, Berlin and Dresden. Wrote an opera, *Graziosa* (1841), a symph., chamber music and many cello works.

Double (Fr.), the old French name for a type of variation that was merely a more highly ornamented version of a theme previously played in plainer notes.

Double Bar, a pair of bar-lines placed very close together and marking off a principal section of a comp., such as the end of the exposition and beginning of the working-out in a sonata or symph. It may be prec. or followed by repeat signs, or both, in which case the music before and/or after it must be repeated.

Double Bass, the largest instrument of the vln. family, the bass of the string section in the orch. and occasionally in chamber music. It had 3 strings formerly, but now usually 4, tuned

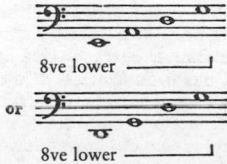

The first of these is the one in general use. The range can be artificially extended either by tuning down the bottom string or by the addition of a 5th string. In the latter case the instrument is normally tuned

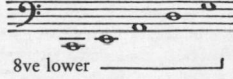

If the C string is tuned down to B, this will continue the tuning in 4ths.

Double Bass Viol. *See* **Violone.**

Double Bassoon, a bassoon with a range an 8ve lower than that of the ordinary instrument.

Double Chant, a chant in 2 sections used in the Anglican Church and covering 2 verses of a psalm.

Double Concerto, a concerto for 2 solo instruments: e.g. Bach's D min. for 2 vlns., Mozart's E♭ maj. for 2 pfs., Brahms's A min. for vln. and cello, Elliott Carter's for pf. and harpsichord, etc.

Double Counterpoint. *See* **Counterpoint.**

Double Dots. *See* **Dotted Notes.**

Double Flat, an accidental, ♭♭, lowering the note before which it stands by a whole tone.

Double Fugue. (1) A fugue on 2 subjects which appear simultaneously.

(2) A fugue in which a 2nd subject appears in the course of the comp.

Double Sharp, an accidental, ×, raising the note before which it stands by a whole tone.

Double Stopping, the prod. of 2 notes simultaneously on any string instrument.

Doucemelle (Fr.), a keyboard instrument of c the 15th cent.; a forerunner of the pf. Also = Dulcimer.

Douglas, Barry (b Belfast, 23 Apr 1960), British pianist. Made his professional debut 1977 and studied at RCM 1978–82. In 1986 became 1st Westerner since Van Cliburn (1958) to win the Tchaikovsky Competition, Moscow, outright.

Dowland, John (b ? London, 1563; d London, buried 20 Feb 1626), English lutenist and composer. He entered the service of the English ambassador, Sir Henry Cobham, in Paris in 1580, and was from 1583 in that of his successor, Sir Edward Stafford. He became a Roman Catholic, returned to Eng. soon after and married. In the 1590s he sought a place at Elizabeth's court, but was not admitted, and went to Ger. in the service of the Duke of Brunswick, then entered that of the Landgrave of Hesse and travelled to It., returning home towards the end of the cent. and turning to Protestantism again. In Nov 1598 he went to Denmark as court musician to Christian IV, returning in 1601 to buy instruments for the king and living in London again for a time in 1603, finally settling there in 1606 on being dismissed from Copenhagen. He complained of neglect after his successes abroad, but from 1612 to 1618 he was employed at court.

Works incl. 3 vols. of songs to the lute (1597–1603); a book of instrumental pavans entitled *Lachrymae*; a book of songs with lutes and viols, *A Pilgrimes Solace*; lute, viol and vocal music contrib. to Leighton's *Teares and Lamentacions*, East's Psalter and to a number of foreign collections, incl. Füllsack's and Fuhrmann's.

Dowland, Robert (b ? London, c 1591; d London, 1641), English lutenist and composer, son of prec. App. lutenist to Charles I on his father's death in 1626. Comp. lessons for the lute, etc. and pub. a book of airs by continental comps.

Down Bow, the movement of the bow in the playing of string instruments in the direction from the heel to the point.

Down by the Greenwood Side, dramatic pastoral in 1 act by Birtwistle (lib. by M. Nyman), for sop., 5 actors and chamber ens.; perf. Brighton, Pier Pavilion, 8 May 1969.

Downbeat, the downward motion of the cond.'s baton indicating the stressed beats of any bar. The corresponding upward motion is called the Upbeat.

Downes, Edward (b Birmingham, 17 Jun 1924), English conductor. He studied at the RCM and with Scherchen. He joined the CG staff in 1951 and in 1963 cond. the first stage prod. in Britain of Shostakovich's *Katerina Izmaylova*. In 1967 he gave the 1st post-war *Ring* cycle by a British cond.; fps of Bennett's *Victory* (1970) and Maxwell Davies's *Taverner* (1972). He gave *War and Peace* on the opening night of the Sydney Opera House (1973) and remained with Australian Opera until 1976. Princ. cond. BBC Philharmonic Orch. from 1980.

Draeseke, Felix (August Bernhard) (b Coburg, 7 Oct 1835; d Dresden, 26 Feb 1913), German composer. Studied at the Leipzig Cons. and with Liszt at Weimar, later taught at Dresden, Lausanne, Munich and Geneva, and finally settled at Dresden in 1876, becoming prof. of comp. at the Cons. in 1884.

Works incl. operas *Gudrun* (1884), *Herrat* and *Merlin* (1903–5); Requiem, trilogy of oratorios *Christus*, Easter scene from Goethe's *Faust* for solo voices, chorus and orch. (1907); 5 symphs., overtures for orch. incl. *Penthesilea* (after Kleist); concerto for pf., vln. and cello; 3 string 4tets, string 5tet; many pf. works incl. a sonata.

Drag, a stroke on the side-drum preceded by a group of grace-notes, usually 3 or 4.

Draghi, Antonio (b Rimini, c 1634; d Vienna, 16 Jan 1700), Italian composer. Began his career as a singer at Venice. Went to Vienna to take up a court app. in 1658, and app. *Hofkapellmeister* in 1682. He was also a librettist for other composers, incl. Bertali, Ziani and the Emperor Leopold I.

Works incl. 67 operas, incl. *Timone misantropo*, after Shakespeare, (1696), 116 smaller stage pieces, *c* 40 oratorios, cantatas, hymns, etc.

Draghi, Giovanni Battista (b *c* 1640; d London, 1708), Italian harpsichordist and composer. Settled in London; music master to the Princesses Mary and Anne and organist to Catherine of Braganza, wife of Charles II. Set Dryden's Ode for St Cecilia's Day, 1687, contrib. music to Durfey's *Wonders in the Sun*, 1706, and comp. many harpsichord lessons and songs.

Dragonetti, Domenico (b Venice, 10 Apr 1763; d London, 16 Apr 1846), Italian double bass player and composer. He was admitted to the opera orchs. at Venice from the age of 13 and soon began to compose concertos, sonatas and other works for his instrument. His 1st appearance abroad was in 1794 in London, where he spent most of the rest of his life with the cellist Lindley as partner. He led the double basses in the fp of the Choral Symph. (Vienna, 1824).

Drame lyrique, a modern French term for a serious opera.

Dramma giocoso (It. = jocular drama), name occasionally used for *opera buffa* in the later 18th cent. Mozart's orig. designation of *Don Giovanni*.

Dramma (per musica) (It. = drama [for music]), 18th-cent. term for opera; actually plays written especially for the purpose of being set to music.

Drátenik (*The Tinker*), opera by Škroup (lib. by J.K. Chmelenský), prod. Prague, 2 Feb 1826. The 1st Czech opera.

Drdla, František (b Žďár, Moravia, 28 Nov 1868; d Gastein, Sep 3 1944), Czech violinist and composer. Studied at the Prague and Vienna Conss., played vln. in the Vienna Court Opera orch. and toured Europe as a virtuoso.

Works incl. operettas *The Golden Net* (1916) and *The Shop Countess* (1917); many vln. pieces; pf. pieces; songs, etc.

Dream of Gerontius, The, oratorio by Elgar, op. 38 (words selected from Cardinal John Henry Newman's poem), fp Birmingham Festival, 3 Oct 1900.

Drei Pintos, Die (*The Three Pintos*), unfinished opera by Weber (lib. by T. Hell, based on Carl Ludwig Seidel's story *Der Brautkampf*), partly comp. 1821; prod. in an ed. completed by Mahler, Leipzig, 20 Jan 1888.

Dreigroschenoper, Die (*The Threepenny Opera*), operetta by Weill (lib. by B. Brecht, based on Elisabeth Hauptmann's German version of Gay's *Beggar's Opera*), prod. Berlin, Theater am Schiffbauerdamm, 31 Aug 1928.

Dresden, Sem (b Amsterdam, 20 Apr 1881; d The Hague, 31 Jul 1957), Dutch conductor and composer. Studied under Zweers at the Copenhagen Cons. and with Pfitzner in Ger. He became a choral cond., cultivating partic. motets and madrigals in Hol. Director of the Amsterdam Cons., 1924–37, and then of that at The Hague, in succession to Wagenaar. He was compelled to withdraw from public life during the Ger. occupation of Hol., but comp. much during that period. He wrote a book on *Dutch Music since 1880*.

Works incl. opera, *François Villon*, (prod. posth. Amsterdam, 1958); *Chorus tragicus* for chorus and orch.; variations for orch.; vln. concerto; *Symphonietta* for clar. and orch.; string 4tet, 6tet for strings and pf., 3 6tets for wind and pf.; sonatas for vln. and pf., cello and pf. and fl. and harp; duo for 2 pfs.; pf. pieces; songs.

Dressler, Ernst Christoph (b Greussen, Thuringia, 1734; d Kassel, 6 Apr 1779), German composer and singer. Worked as secretary and singer at Bayreuth and Gotha, later *Kapelldirektor* to Prince Fürstenberg at Wetzlar, finally opera singer in Vienna and Kassel. Beethoven's 1st pub. work was a set of variations (1782) on a march by D.

Dressler, Gallus (b Nebra, 16 Oct 1533; d Zerbst, *c* 1585), German composer. Wrote Lutheran psalms and hymns as well as Latin church music.

Drigo, Riccardo (b Padua, 30 Jun 1846; d Padua, 1 Oct 1930), Italian conductor and composer. He became ballet cond. at the St Petersburg Court Opera.

Works incl. ballet *Harlequin's Millions* (1900), many drawing-room pieces, etc.

Driscoll, Loren (b Wyoming, Minn., 14 Apr 1928), American tenor. Debut Boston 1954, in *Falstaff*. He sang at the NY City Opera 1958–9 and in 1962 joined the Deutsche Oper, Berlin; well known there as Ottavio, Flamand and Berg's Painter. In 1965 he created Lord Barrat in Henze's *Der Junge Lord* and in 1968 was Eumaus in the fp of Dallapiccola's *Ulisse*. At the 1966 Salzburg Festival he created Dionysus in *The Bassarids*. Glyndebourne 1962, Ferrando.

Drone, the 3 lower pipes of the bagpipe which prod. a fixed chord above which the melody is played on the chanter. The name was also given to a bowed instrument with a single string stretched on a stick over a bladder; this was also called Bumbass.

Drone Bass, an unvaryingly sustained bass on any composition resembling the drone of a bagpipe.

Druckman, Jacob (b Philadelphia, 26 Jun 1928), American composer. He studied at the Juilliard School and in Paris. He has dir. electronic music centres at Princeton and Yale Univs. Composer-in-residence, NY PO, from 1982.

Works incl. vln. concerto (1956), *Dark upon the Harp* for mezzo, brass 5tet and perc. (1962); *The Sound of Time* for sop. and orch. (1965); *Animus I–IV* for mezzo, insts. and tape (1966–77), *Windows* for orch. (1972); *Lamia* for sop. and orch. (1974); *Chiaroscuro* for orch. (1976); Vla. concerto 1978); *Aureole* for orch. (1979); *Prism*; 3 pieces for orch. after music from operas by M.A. Charpentier, Cavalli and Cherubini (1980); 2 string 4tets; *Athonor* for orch. (1985).

Drum Mass (Haydn). *See* **Paukenmesse.**

'Drum-Roll' Symphony (Ger. *S. mit dem Paukenwirbel*), nickname of Haydn's symph. no. 103 in Eb maj. (comp. for London, 1795), so called because it opens with a timpani roll.

Drums, percussion instruments on which the sound is prod. by beating a skin stretched tightly over a hollow space left open by a framework of var. patterns. *See* **Bass Drum, Kettledrums, Side Drum, Tabor, Tambourine, Tenor Drum.**

Dryden, John (1631–1700), English poet, dramatist and satirist. *See* **Acis and Galatea** (Handel), **Albion and Albanius** (Grabu), **Alexander's Feast** (Handel), **Almahide** (G. Bononcini), **Boyce** (*Secular Masque*), **Clarke** (J.) (*Alexander's Feast*), **Clayton** (do.), **Cymon** (M. Arne), **Draghi (G.B.)** (*Ode for St Cecilia's Day*), **Eccles (J.)** (*Spanish Friar*), **Humfrey** (*Conquest of Granada* and *Indian Emperor*), **Indian Queen** (Purcell), **King Arthur** (do.), **Ode for St Cecilia's Day** (Handel), **Purcell** (*Amphitryon, Aureng-Zebe, Cleomenes, Love Triumphant, Spanish Friar, Tyrannic Love* and *Oedipus*), **Staggins** (*Conquest of G. and Marriage à la Mode*).

Du Mage, Pierre (b Beauvais, bap. 23 Nov 1674; d Laon, 20 Oct 1751), French organist and composer. Pupil of Marchand in Paris, organist of the collegiate church at Saint-Quentin in 1703–1713. He played at the inauguration of the new organ at Notre-Dame in Paris. Pub. a vol. of organ pieces in 1708.

Du Pré, Jacqueline (b Oxford, 26 Jan 1945; d London, 19 Oct 1987), English cellist. She studied at the GSM with William Pleeth, and with Rostropovich and Tortelier. Debut recital Wigmore Hall, London, 1961; Elgar cello concerto at RFH, 1962, and on her US debut in NY, Carnegie Hall, in 1965. Married Daniel Barenboim, 1967, and gave orch. and chamber music concerts with him. Afflicted with multiple sclerosis from 1973, she taught and gave master classes. She was admired for her spirited interpretations. OBE 1976.

Du Puy, (Jean Baptiste) Edouard (b Corcelles, Neuchâtel, 1770 or 1; d Stockholm, 3 Apr 1822), Swiss baritone, violinist, pianist and composer. Studied pf. with Dussek in Paris and became a member of the orch. of Prince Henry of Prus. at Rheinsberg in 1785 and leader in 1787. In 1793 he settled at Stockholm, but was expelled in 1799, when he went to sing in opera at Copenhagen and taught singing to the wife of the future Christian VIII, with whom he was exiled for a love affair in 1809. In 1811 he returned to Stockholm and became court cond. and prof.

Works incl. operas *Ungdom og Galskab* (a Dan. version of the lib. of Méhul's *Une Folie,* 1806) and *Felicie* (1821); several ballets; funeral music for Charles XIII, etc.

Dua, Octave (b Ghent, 28 Feb 1888; d Brussels, 8 Mar 1952), Belgian tenor. Debut Brussels 1904, in *The Bartered Bride*. He appeared with Beecham at Drury Lane 1914–15 and regularly returned to London until 1937 (1919, 1st local perf. of *L'Heure Espagnole*. He sang at the NY Met 1919–21 and in 1921 was Truffaldino in the fp of *The Love for Three Oranges,* at Chicago.

Düben, German-Swedish family of musicians;

1. Andreas D. (b Lützen, 27 May 1558; d Leipzig, 19 Apr 1625), organist at St Thomas's Church, Leipzig.

2. Andreas D. (b ? Leipzig, *c* 1597; d Stockholm, 7 Jul 1662), organist and composer, son of prec. Pupil of Sweelinck at Amsterdam, 1614–20, went to Swed. in 1621, became organist at the Ger. church in Stockholm in 1625 and court music director in 1640. Comp. dances for viols, etc.

3. Gustaf D. (b Stockholm, *c* 1628; d Stockholm, 19 Dec 1690), organist and comp., son of prec. Succeeded his father in both his posts.

Works incl. church music, *concerti grossi,* symphs. and dances for strings, etc.

4. Gustaf D. (b Stockholm, 6 Aug 1659; d Stockholm, 5 Dec 1726), son of prec., whom

he succeeded as court music director.

5. Andreas D. (b Stockholm, 28 Aug 1673; d Stockholm, 23 Aug 1738), son of (3), whom he succeeded.

Dubois, (François Clément) Théodore (b Rosnay, Marne, 24 Aug 1837; d Paris, 11 Jun 1924), French composer. Studied at Rheims and then at the Paris Cons., where he took the Prix de Rome in 1861. Returning to Paris in 1866, he was active as organist and teacher, at last succeeding Saint-Saëns as organist at the Madeleine in 1877. From 1896 to 1905 he was director of the Cons.

Works incl. operas *La Guzla de l'Émir* (1873), *Le Pain bis* (1879), *Aben-Hamet*, *Xavière* (1895); ballet *La Farandole*; Requiem, *Messe de la Délivrance* and other Masses, motets and other church music; oratorios, *Les Sept Paroles du Christ* and *Paradis perdu*; orchestral works: *Divertissement*, *Pièces d'orchestre*, *Suite d'orchestre*, *Scènes symphoniques*, overture *Frithjof* (after Tegnér), symph. poem *Notre-Dame de la mer*.

Dubourg, Matthew (b London, 1703; d London, 3 Jul 1767), English violinist and composer. Pupil of Geminiani. Lived much of his life in Dublin, where he played in the first perf. of *Messiah* in 1742.

Ducasse, Roger. *See* **Roger-Ducasse.**

Ducis, Benedictus (b nr. Konstanz, *c* 1490; d Schalckstetten, nr. Ulm, 1544), German composer and Lutheran pastor. Wrote Lutheran psalms and hymns, Lat. church music, and Ger. part-songs.

Due Foscari, I (*The Two Foscari*), opera by Verdi (lib. by F.M. Piave, based on Byron's drama), prod. Rome, Teatro Argentina, 3 Nov 1844.

Due litiganti (Sarti). *See* **Fra due litiganti.**

Duenna, The, or The Double Elopement, opera by Thomas Linley, father and son (lib. by Sheridan), prod. London, CG 21 Nov 1775. Sheridan was son-in-law of Linley sen.

Duet, a comp. in 2 parts for voices or instruments. A duet may be in 2 single melodic parts only, or it may be accomp. by instruments in fuller harmony or it may be itself for 2 harmonic instruments or a single such instrument for 2 players (e.g. pf. duet).

Dufay, Guillaume (b ? Cambrai, *c* 1400; d Cambrai, 27 Nov 1474), Franco-Flemish composer. After being a choirboy at Cambrai Cathedral he travelled much, esp. in It., and was a member of the Papal choir, 1428–37. From 1439 to 1450 and from 1458 until his death he was resident as a canon of Cambrai, but had strong connections with the court of Burgundy and was at various times resident at the court of Savoy.

His 13 isorhythmic motets incl. *Nuper rosarum flores* for the dedication of Florence Cathedral (25 Mar 1436). Over 80 songs in Fr. and It. show an extraordinary range of techniques and musical emotions. His earlier sacred works often show a stark simplicity of style and he may well have been the inventor of Fauxbourdon. The Mass *Caput* is now thought to be by an anonymous English composer, not Dufay. But his grandest achievements are in the four cantus-firmus Mass cycles of his late years, works that pioneered the four-voice style that was to dominate sacred music for the next cent.: *Se la face ay pale*, prob. for the court of Savoy in the 1450s; *L'homme armé*, perhaps comp. for the court of Burgundy; *Ecce ancilla Domini* (? 1463); and *Ave regina caelorum*, prob. for the dedication of Cambrai Cathedral on 5 Jul 1472.

Dufranne, Hector (b Mons, 25 Oct 1870; d Paris, 4 May 1951), Belgian bass-baritone. Debut Brussels 1896, Valentin. At the Paris Opéra-Comique he sang in the fp of Massenet's *Grisélidis* and created Debussy's Golaud. Monte Carlo 1907, in the fp of Massenet's *Thérèse*. He sang in NY 1908–10 and in Chicago 1910–22; fp *The Love for Three Oranges*, 1921. Also heard in works by Strauss and Falla (fp *El retablo de Maese Pedro*, Paris 1923).

Dugazon (*née* **Lefèbvre**), **Louise Rosalie** (b Berlin, 18 Jun 1755; d Paris, 22 Sep 1821), French mezzo. Trained as a dancer, made her debut at the age of 12. Her voice was discovered by Grétry, in whose *Sylvain* she 1st appeared as a singer in 1774. Married the actor Dugazon in 1776. She created over 60 roles in Paris, and sang in operas by Dalayrac, Isouard and Boieldieu.

Dukas, Paul (b Paris, 1 Oct 1865; d Paris, 17 May 1935), French composer. Studied at the Paris Cons., among his masters being Dubois and Guiraud. Prof. of comp. there from 1913 to his death. From 1909 he taught orch. at the Paris Cons. and from 1913 comp. In 1926 he also began teaching at the École Normale. His best-known piece is the brilliant orch. scherzo *L'Apprenti sorcier* (1897), and his opera *Ariane et Barbe-bleue* (1907) is among the finest Fr. operas of its day.

Works incl. opera *Ariane et Barbe-bleue* (Maeterlinck, 1907); ballet *La Péri* (1912); symph. in C maj., (1896), overture to Corneille's *Polyeucte*, *L'Apprenti sorcier* (on Goethe's poem *Der Zauberlehrling*); sonata in E♭ min., *Variations on a theme by Rameau*, *Prélude élégiaque* on the name of

Haydn and *La Plainte, au loin, du faune* in memory of Debussy for pf.; *Sonnet de Ronsard* and *Vocalise* for voice and pf.; *Villanelle* for horn and pf., etc. (incl. unpub. overtures to Shakespeare's *King Lear* and Goethe's *Götz von Berlichingen*).

Duke Bluebeard's Castle (*A kékszakállú hercegvára*), opera in 1 act by Bartók (lib. by B. Balázs); comp. 1911, prod. Budapest, 24 May 1918, cond. Tango.

Dukelsky, Vladimir (b Parfianovka nr. Pskov, 10 Oct 1903; d Santa Monica, 16 Nov 1969), Russian-American composer. Studied at Moscow and Kiev, Glière being among his masters. Went to live in Constantinople in 1920 and settled in NY in 1922. Under the infuence of Gershwin he wrote light music under the name of Vernon Duke, but cultivated an advanced modern style under his own name. In 1924 Diaghilev heard his pf. concerto and commissioned him to write a work for the Rus. Ballet.

Works incl. operetta *Yvonne* (1926); ballets *Zéphir et Flore* and *Public Gardens*; oratorio *The End of St Petersburg* (1937); 4 symphs., *Dédicaces* for soprano, pf. and orch., pf. concerto; string 4tet; vln. sonata; song cycle *Triolets of the North* (Feodor Sologub); 3 Chinese songs and other songs.

Dulce Melos (Lat. = sweet Melody), another name for the Chekker.

Dulciana, an open Diapason organ stop of delicate tone. It may embrace 4ft., 8ft. or 16ft. pipes.

Dulcimer, an instrument akin to the psaltery, with a set of strings stretched over a sound-board which are struck by hammers. The Hung. Cimbalom is a descendant of it.

Dulcitone, a keyboard instrument prod. its sound on a set of tuning-forks, similar to the Celesta.

Dulichius, Philipp (b Chemnitz, 18 Dec 1562; d Stettin, 24 Mar 1631), German composer. Took the D.Phil. degree at Chemnitz and went to Stettin as music teacher at the Pädagogium in 1587.

Works incl. sacred and secular comps. for several voices.

Dumanoir, Guillaume (b Paris, 16 Nov 1615; d Paris, *c* 1697), French violinist and composer. As 'Roi des Violons' he came into conflict with the dancing-masters, whom he wished to compel to contribute to the violinists' guild of Saint-Julien, and being unsuccessful he wrote the abusive pamphlet *Le Mariage de la musique avec la danse* in 1664. He comp. dance music which was liked by Louis XIV, who app. him ballet master of the royal pages.

Dumanoir, Guillaume (Michel) (b Paris; d ? Paris, 1697), French violinist and composer, son of prec. Succeeded his father as head of the Confrérie de Saint-Julien and renewed the quarrel with the dancing masters, resigning in 1685. Before that he had quarrelled with Lully over the privilege of training orch. musicians and lost a law-suit against him in 1673. Wrote dance music.

Dumbarton Oaks, concerto in E♭ for chamber orch. by Stravinsky; comp. 1937–8, perf. Washington, DC, at D. Oaks, the private estate of R.W. Bliss, 8 May 1938. 1st public perf. Paris, 4 Jun 1938.

Dumka (Pol., Rus. and Cz.), a lament, which in music takes the form of a slow piece alternating with more animated sections, as e.g. in Dvořák's *Dumky* Trio.

Dumky, plur. of Dumka.

'Dumky' Trio, a pf. Trio by Dvořák, op. 90, based on music of the type of the above, comp. in 1891.

Dunhill, Thomas (Frederick) (b London, 1 Feb 1877; d Scunthorpe, Lincs., 13 Mar 1946), English composer. Entered the RCM in 1893, Stanford being his comp. master. He was asst. music master at Eton Coll. in 1899–1908 and organized concerts for chamber music and for the promotion of Brit. music in London during the early years of the cent. Prof. of comp. at the RCM. His 2nd ballet was prod. at Hamburg in 1937.

Works incl. operas *The Enchanted Garden* (1928), *Tantivy Towers* (A.P. Herbert, 1931) and *Happy Families*; ballets *Dick Whittington* and *Gallimaufry*; symph. in A min., *Elegiac Variations* in memory of Parry and overture *Maytime* for orch.; *Triptych* for vla. and orch.; pf. 4tet, 2 pf. trios, 5 5tets.

Duni, Egidio Romoaldo (b Matera nr. Naples, bap. 11 Feb 1708; d Paris, 11 Jun 1775), Italian-French composer. Pupil of Durante in Naples, where he prod. his 1st opera in 1731. Travelled widely, and settled in Paris in 1757, becoming a leading comp. of *opéras comiques*.

Operas incl. *Nerone* (1735), *Le Caprice amoureux, Le Peintre amoureux de son modèle* (1757), *L'Isle des fous, Le Milicien, Les Deux Chasseurs et la laitière* (1763), *La Fée Urgèle, La Clochette, Les Moissonneurs, Les Sabots* (1768).

Dunn, Mignon (b Memphis, 17 Jun 1932), American mezzo. She sang Carmen at the NY City Opera in 1956 and appeared at the Met from 1958; Azucena, and Anna in *Les Troyens*, 1973. Düsseldorf from 1965, as Eboli and Dalila.

Dunstable, John (b *c* 1390; d ? London, 24

Dec 1453), English mathematician, astrologer, and composer. Possibly connected with St Albans Cathedral, he was certainly in the Duke of Bedford's retinue during the English occupation of Normandy in the 1420s. As the most famous and most prolific Eng. composer of his time he was admired throughout Europe and considered to have had an important influence on the new musical style of Dufay and Binchois.

Works incl. Mass music, isorhythmic motets, service music and devotional pieces, though the widely admired song *O rosa bella* was probably composed by his younger contemporary Bedyngham.

Duparc, Elizabeth (d 1778), French soprano. She appeared in It. in her youth, where she was given the nickname of La Franccsina, under which name she sang in many of Handel's operas and oratorios in London from 1738; she sang in the fps of *Saul, Israel in Egypt, Imeneo, Deidamia, Semele* and *Belshazzar.*

Duparc, (Marie Eugène) Henri (Fouques-) (b Paris, 21 Jan 1848; d Mont de Marsan, 12 Feb 1933), French composer. Was taught the pf. as a child by Franck at the Jesuit Coll. of Vaugirard in Paris, and later became a comp. pupil of that master. He never took any share in official musical life, but continued to comp. at intervals until 1885, when he began to suffer from an incurable nervous complaint and retired to Switzerland.

Works incl. symph. poem *Lénore* (on Bürger's poem, 1875) and nocturne *Aux Etoiles;* motet *Benedicat vobis Dominus;* 15 songs incl. *Phydilé, Invitation au voyage, Soupir, La vague et la cloche, Extase, Le manoir de Rosemonde* and *Lamento;* and several afterwards destroyed.

Duple Time, 2 beats in a bar, e.g. 2–4 or 6–8.

Duplet, a group of 2 notes occupying the time of 3.

Duport, Jean Louis (b Paris, 4 Oct 1749; d Paris, 7 Sep 1819), French cellist. Made his 1st appearance at the Concert Spirituel in Paris in 1768. He went to the Prus. court in Berlin at the outbreak of the Revolution and there Beethoven played with him (or with his brother) his 2 cello sonatas, op. 5. He returned to Paris, 1806.

Duport, Jean Pierre (b Paris, 27 Nov 1741; d Berlin, 31 Dec 1818), French cellist, brother of prec. Made his 1st appearance at the Concert Spirituel in Paris in 1761, visited Eng. in 1769 and Spain in 1771, and in 1773 went to the court of Frederick II of Prus. in

Berlin. Mozart wrote pf. variations on a minuet of his (K573).

Dupré, Marcel (b Rouen, 3 May 1886; d Meudon, 30 May 1971), French organist and composer. Played Bach from memory at the age of 10, in 1898 was app. organist of the church of Saint-Vivien at Rouen and prod. an oratorio in 1901. After that he studied pf., organ and comp. at the Paris Cons. and gained the Prix de Rome in 1914 as a pupil of Widor. Organist at Notre-Dame in 1916–22 during the illness of Vierne. App. prof. of organ at the Paris Cons. in 1926 and organist at Saint-Sulpice in 1936, succeeding Widor. From 1954 to 1956 he was director of the Cons.

Works incl. oratorio *Le Songe de Jacob,* motets and *De Profundis;* 2 symphs.; concerto for org. and orch. (1934); vln and pf. sonata; cello pieces; songs; many organ works incl. *Symphonie-Passion,* 79 chorales, *Le Chemin de la Croix.*

Duprez, Gilbert (Louis) (b Paris, 6 Dec 1806; d Paris, 23 Sep 1896), French tenor and composer. 1st appeared at the Théâtre de l'Odéon in Paris, 1825. He sang in the fps of *Benvenuto Cellini,* Donizetti's *Les Martyrs, La favorite* and *Dom Sébastien* and Verdi's *Jérusalem.* Prof. at the Cons. 1842–50.

Dur (Ger., from Lat. *durus* = hard), the word for Major, because *B durum* meant B♮.

Durand, (Marie) Auguste (b Paris, 18 Jul 1830; d Paris, 31 May 1909), French publisher, organist and composer. Studied at the Paris Cons., was organist at var. churches and was a partner in the pub. firm of Durand & Fils. He wrote drawing-room music for pf., incl. popular waltzes.

Durand (Duranowski), Auguste Frédéric (b Warsaw, 1770; d Strasbourg, 1834), Polish-French violinist and composer. He was sent to Paris in 1787 to study under Viotti, travelled much in Ger. and It., joined the Fr. army and settled at Strasbourg in 1814. Wrote much superficial concert music for his instrument.

Durante, Francesco (b Fratta Maggiore, nr. Naples, 31 Mar 1684; d Naples, 30 Sep 1755), Italian composer. Educ. at Naples, where he later became *maestro di cappella* at the Cons. di S. Maria (1742) and S. Onofrio (1745). His pupils incl. Traetta, Paisiello, Sacchini, Pergolesi, Piccinni, etc. Unusually for a Neapolitan comp., he wrote no operas. His works consist largely of church music, also sonatas, toccatas, etc., for harpsichord.

Durastanti, Margherita (b *c* 1685), Italian

soprano. Visited London in 1720 and again in 1733, singing in several of Handel's operas. She created Agrippina (Venice, 1709) and in London took part in the fps of *Radamisto*, *Ottone*, *Flavio*, *Giulio Cesare* and *Arianna*.

Durazzo, Count Giacomo (b Genoa, 27 Apr 1717; d Venice, 15 Oct 1794), Italian nobleman. He was director of the Imp. Theatres in Vienna 1754–64, and played an influential role in the reform of music drama, particularly in connection with Gluck's *Orfeo*.

Durchführung (Ger. lit. through-leading), the German term for the development of working-out section of a movement in sonata form.

Durchkomponiert (Ger. lit. set throughout). A song is said in Ger. to be *durchkomponiert* if the words are set to music continuously, not strophically with the same music repeated for each verse.

Durey, Louis (b Paris, 27 May 1888; d St Tropez, 3 Jul 1979), French composer. He did not study music until the age of 22, and in 1914 he enlisted on the outbreak of war. In 1916, during leave, he came under the influence of Satie and joined the group of 'Les Six', but was the 1st to secede from it in 1921, and in 1923 he went to live in seclusion in the S. of Fr., writing very little.

Works incl. opera on Mérimée's *L'Occasion* (1925); incid. music to Hebbel's *Judith* (1918); 3 string 4tets, pf. trio, string trio; song cycles with chamber music or pf.

Durezza (It. = hardness). Up to the 17th cent. the term was used for discord in Italy; it is now used in the direction *con durezza* to indicate that a harsh or unyielding manner of perf. is required.

Durfey (D'Urfey), Thomas (1653–1723), English playwright and poet. *See* **Akeroyde** (*Don Quixote*), **Courteville**, 2 (do.), **Don Quixote, The Comical History of** (Purcell and others), **Draghi (G.B.)** (*Wonders in the Sun*), **Eccles (J.)** (*Don Q.*), **Locke** (*Fool turned Critic*), **Purcell (D.)** (*Cynthia and Endymion*), **Purcell** (*Fool's Preferment, Marriage-Hater Matched, ~ Richmond Heiress, Sir Barnaby Whigg* and *Virtuous Wife*), **Turner (Wm.)** (*Fond Husband* and *Madam Fickle*).

Durkó, Zsolt (b Szeged, 10 Apr 1934), Hungarian composer. He studied in Budapest and with Petrassi in Rome. His music breaks away from local influences and favours the avant-garde.

Works incl. opera *Moses* (prod. Budapest 1977); *Organismi* for vln. and orch. (1964),

Dartmouth Concerto for sop. and orch. (1966), *Fioriture* for orch. (1966), *Altimara* for chorus and orch. (1968), *Funeral Oration*, oratorio (1972), *Turner Illustrations* for orch. (1976); 2 string 4tets (1966, 1969), *Impromptus in F* for fl. and ens. (1984).

Durón, Sebastián (b Brihuega, Castile, bap. 19 Apr 1660; d Cambó, Pyrenees, 3 Aug 1716), Spanish composer. Was organist at Las Palmas, Canary Islands, and in 1691 became *maestro de capilla* at the court of Madrid until 1702. Not having supported the Bourbon succession, he seems to have gone into exile. He was an early exponent of Span. opera.

Works incl. operas and zarzuelas *Muerte en amor es la ausencia, Apolo y Dafne, Selva encantada de Amor, Las nuevas armas de Amor, La guerra de los gigantes, Salir el amor del mundo*; incid. music for a comedy, *Jupiter*; 2 ballets.

Dürr, Alfred (b Charlottenburg, Berlin, 3 Mar 1918), German musicologist. He studied at the Univ. of Göttingen. From 1953 he has ed. the *Bach-Jahrbuch* and has been prin. contributor to the Bach *Neue Ausgabe* (complete works). Bach's cantatas are at the centre of his research.

Dürr, Walter (b Berlin, 27 Mar 1932), German musicologist. He studied at Tübingen Univ. and has taught there from 1962; from 1965 he has been joint ed. of the *Neue Schubert-Ausgabe* at Tübingen. Other fields of study have been Mozart, and the Italian madrigal.

Duruflé, Maurice (b Louviers, Eure, 11 Jan 1902; d Paris, 24 Jun 1986), French organist and composer. Learnt music in the choirschool of Rouen Cathedral, 1912–18, and then studied at the Paris Cons. under Vierne, Tournemire and Dukas. App. organist at the church of Saint-Étienne-du-Mont in 1929.

Works incl. Requiem for chorus and orch. (1947); chorale on *Veni Creator*, suite and many other works for org.; *Prelude, Recitative and Variations* for fl., vla. and pf.; 3 dances for orch.

Dušek. *See also* **Dussek** and **Tuczek**.

Dušek, Franz (František Xaver) (b Choteborky, 8 Dec 1731; d Prague, 12 Feb 1799), Bohemian pianist and composer. Pupil of Wagenseil in Vienna; taught in Prague, master of many famous pupils. He and his wife were friends of Mozart, who worked ed on *Don Giovanni* at their home in Prague.

Dušek (née Hambacher), Josefa (b Prague, 6 Mar 1754; d Prague, 8 Jan 1824), Bohemian soprano, wife of prec. She travelled in Austria and Germany. Mozart wrote the concert aria *Bella mia fiamma* (K528) for her. She gave the fp of Beethoven's *Ah, perfido* (Leipzig, 1796).

Dushkin, Samuel (b Suwalki, 13 Dec 1891; d New York, 24 Jun 1976), American violinist of Polish birth. He studied in Paris and with Auer and Kreisler in NY. European tour 1918, US debut 1924. He advised Stravinsky on the comp. of the violin concerto and gave fp Berlin, 23 Oct 1931. He gave Stravinsky's *Duo Concertant* with S. in Berlin on 28 Oct 1932.

Dussek (or **Dušek, Dusík**)**, Jan Ladislav** (b Čáslav, 12 Feb 1760; d St Germain-en-Laye, Paris, 20 Mar 1812), Bohemian pianist and composer. Educ. at the Jesuit Coll. in Jihlav and Prague Univ., where he read theology. He had shown early promise, and *c* 1779 went to the Netherlands, holding organ posts at Malines and Bergen-op-Zoom. He gave up his organist's career *c* 1782, and won great success in Amsterdam and The Hague as a pianist and comp. Concert tours took him to Hamburg (where he studied with C.P.E. Bach), Berlin and St Petersburg, where he entered the service of Prince Radziwill, spending the next 2 years on the latter's estate in Lithuania. He played before Marie Antoinette in Paris in 1786, and after a visit to It. returned there in 1788. At the Revolution he fled to London, where he 1st appeared at one of Salomon's concerts in 1790. He married the singer and pianist Sophia Corri in 1792, and joined his father-in-law's firm of music pubs. The business failed, and he went to Hamburg to escape his creditors in 1800. More travels followed. He was with Prince Louis Ferdinand of Prus. 1803–6, then in the service of the Prince of Isenburg and, finally, Talleyrand.

Works incl. incid. music for *The Captive of Spilburg* (London, 1798) and Sheridan's *Pizarro* (both with Kelly); 3 overtures and serenade for orch.; Mass (1811); 3 string 4tets, 2 pf. 4tets, pf. 5tet. *c* 20 pf. trios; *c* 12 sonatas for pf. duet, sonata for 2 pfs.; pf. music; *c* 18 concertos, *c* 32 sonatas, *c* 25 rondos, *c* 20 sets of variations, var. miscellaneous pieces; *c* 65 sonatas with vln. or fl.

Dussek (or **Dusík, Dušek**)**, Sophia Giustina** (b Edinburgh, 1 May 1775; d London, 1847), English soprano of Italian descent. Daughter of Domenico Corri and wife of prec. Pupil of her father, she appeared as a pianist at Edinburgh at a very early age, and came out as a singer in London when the family moved there in 1788. She married in 1792.

Dutilleux, Henri (b Angers, 22 Jan 1916), French composer. He studied at the Paris Cons. and won the Prix de Rome in 1938; prof. at the Cons. since 1970. His music is regarded as being in the tradition of Ravel, Debussy and Messiaen.

Works incl. 2 symphs (perf. Paris, 1950 and Boston, 1959), *Salmacis*, ballet (1940), *La Giole* for voice and orch. (1944), *5 Métaboles* for orch. fp Cleveland, 1965), *Tout un monde lointain* for cello and orch. (1970), *Timbres, espaces, mouvement* for orch. (fp Washington, 1978), *Ainsi parle la nuit* for string 4tet (1976).

Dutoit, Charles (b Lausanne, 7 Oct 1936), Swiss conductor. Studied at the Lausanne Cons. and at Tanglewood. Debut with Berne SO 1964; chief cond. 1966–77. Guest cond. with Suisse Romande and Zurich Tonhalle Orchs. and the RPO, London. Music dir. Montreal SO from 1977; many perfs. of Haydn, Stravinsky and Debussy. The 2nd of his three wives was the pianist Martha Argerich (*q.v.*).

Duval, Denise (b Paris, 23 Oct 1921), French soprano. Debut Bordeaux 1941, as Lola. At the Paris Opéra-Comique she created Thérèse in Poulenc's *Les Mamelles de Tirésias*, 1947, and in 1959 was Elle in the fp of *La Voix Humaine*; at the Opéra she was Blanche in the 1st local perf. of the *Carmélites*. Glyndebourne, 1962, Mélisande. Other roles incl. Massenet's Salomé and Ravel's Concepcion. Retired 1965.

Duval, François (b Paris, *c* 1673; d Versailles, 27 Jan 1728), French violinist and composer. He was a member of Louis XIV's '24 violons du roi' and wrote vln. sonatas in the It. style and pub. as the 1st of the kind in 1704. Wrote numerous books of sonatas for vln. and bass and 2 vlns. and bass.

Dux, Claire (b Witkowicz, 2 Aug 1885; d Chicago, 8 Oct 1967), Polish soprano. Debut Cologne 1906, Pamina. Berlin Hofoper 1909–18, debut as Mimi. At CG in 1913 she sang Eva and was Sophie in the 1st London perf. of *Rosenkavalier* under Beecham. She had two brief marriages and sang in Chicago 1921–4; retired after her third marriage, to a millionaire meat-packer.

Dvořák, Antonín (b Nelahozeves, 8 Sep 1841; d Prague, 1 May 1904), Czech composer. Son of a village innkeeper and butcher. He heard only popular and simple church music as a child, but developed remarkable gifts. Sent to the organ school at Prague in 1857, began to comp. 2 years later and joined an orch. as violinist; later vla. in the orch. at the Cz. national theatre, under Smetana. In 1873 he married Anna Čermaková.

The next year he received for the 1st time the Aus. state prize for comp. and became a friend of Brahms, who was on the committee and intro. him to his pub., Simrock. 1st visit to Eng. in 1884 to cond. the *Stabat Mater* in London. In 1885 he bought the country estate of Vysoká, which remained his home. Hon.Mus.D. at Cambridge in 1891, when he was app. prof. at Prague Cons., of which he became director in 1901. In 1892–5 he was dir. of the new Nat. Cons. in NY, and spent some holidays at the Cz. colony of Spillville, Iowa. In 1896 he paid the last of his many visits to Eng., where he had prod. several works at the music festivals.

Works incl. OPERAS: (10) all except the 1st prod in Prague: *Alfred* (1870; prod Olomouc, 1938), *King and Coal Burner* (*Král a uhlíř*, 1874), *The pig-headed Peasants* (*Tvrdé palice*, 1881), *Vanda* (1876), *The Peasant A Rogue* (*Šelma sedlák*, 1878), *Dimitrij* (1882), *The Jacobin* (1889), *The Devil and Kate* (*Čert a Káča*, 1899), *Rusalka* (1901), *Armida* (1904).

ORCH: 9 symphonies: no. 1 in C min., *The Bells of Zlonice* (1865); no. 2 in B♭, (1865); no. 3 in E♭, op. 10 (1873); no. 4 in D min., (1874); no. 5 in F, op. 76 (1875); no. 6 in D, op. 60 (1880); no. 7 in D min., op. 70 (1885); no. 8 in G, op. 88 (1889); no. 9 in E min., 'From the New World', op. 95 (1893). 5 symph. poems *The Water-Sprite* (1896), *The Noon-day Witch* (1896), *The Golden Spinning-Wheel*, *The Wood-Dove*, *Hero's Song* (1897); 7 concert overtures incl. *Husitská* (1883) and the cycle *Amid Nature*, *Carnival* and *Othello* (1891–2); various orch. works incl. *Czech Suite* (1879), 3 *Slavonic Rhapsodies*, *Scherzo capriccioso* (1883), *Symph. Variations* (1877); 2 sets of Slavonic Dances; *Serenade* and *Notturno* for string orch.; concertos for pf., vln. and cello (1876, 1880, 1895); 4 smaller pieces for solo instruments and orch.

CHAMBER MUSIC: 14 string quartets: no. 1 in A, op. 2 (1862), no. 2 in B♭ (c 1870), no. 3 in D (c 1870), no. 4 in E min. (1870), no. 5 in F min. op. 9 (1873), no. 6 in A min., op. 12 (1873), no. 7 in A min. op. 16 (1874), no. 8 in E, op. 80 (1876), no. 9 in D min., op. 34 (1877), no. 10 in E♭, op. 51 (1879), no. 11 in C, op. 61 (1881), no. 12 in F, op. 96 (1893, American), no. 13 in G, op. 105 (1895), no. 14 in A♭, op. 106 (1895); 2 string 5tets: in G, op. 77, with db. (1875), in E♭, op. 97, with vla. (1893); string 6tet in A, op. 48 (1878); 4 piano trios: in B♭, op. 21 (1875), in G min., op. 26 (1876), in F min., op. 65 (1883), in E min., 'Dumky', op. 90

(1891); 2 piano 4tets in D, op. 23 (1875), in E♭, op. 87 (1889); Piano 5tet in A, op. 81 (1887). *Bagatelles* for 2 vlns., cello and harmonium (1878); *Terzetto* for 2 vlns. and vla. (1887); sonata (1880), sonatina (1893) and smaller pieces for vln. and pf.

CHORUS AND ORCH. (some with solo voices): *Stabat Mater* (1877), *The Spectre's Bride*, *St Ludmilla* (1886), Psalm cxlix, Mass in D maj., Requiem (1890); *The American Flag*, Te Deum; smaller choral works: *The Heirs of the White Mountain*, *Song of the Czechs*, *Hymn of the Czech Peasants*, *Hymnus*, *Festival Song*; several sets of part-songs; 4 sets of vocal duets; 68 songs.

PIANO: 14 op. nos. of pf. pieces, incl. Theme and Variations, *Poetic Tone-Pictures*, Suite and *Humoresques*, also some separate pf. pieces; 6 sets of pf. duets, incl. Slavonic Dances, *Legends* and *From the Bohemian Forest*.

Dvořákova, Ludmila (b Kolín, 11 Jul 1923), Czech soprano. Debut Ostrava 1949, Katya Kabanova. Sang in Bratislava, Prague and Vienna before Berlin debut 1960, as Octavian. Bayreuth 1965–71 as Gutrune, Venus, Kundry. London, CG, 1966–71 as Brünnhilde and Isolde. NY Met debut 1966 as Leonore. Other roles incl. Ortrud, the Marschallin, Ariadne and Jenůfa.

Dyck, Ernest (Marie-Hubert) van (b Antwerp, 2 Apr 1861; d Berlaer-les-Lierre, 31 Aug 1923), Belgian tenor. After studying law and working as a journalist, he learnt singing and made his 1st appearance in Paris in 1883. In 1887 he sang the 1st of the Wagnerian parts with which he was afterwards chiefly associated, Lohengrin in Paris, and the following year he was 1st engaged as Parsifal at Bayreuth. He also sang in Wagner's operas in London, Brussels, NY, etc. He created Massenet's Werther (Vienna, 1892). NY Met debut, 1898, Tannhäuser.

Dygon, John (b ? Canterbury, c 1485; d 1541), English cleric and composer. Took the B.Mus. at Oxford in 1512, (?) in 1521 went to Louvain to study with the Spanish humanist Juan Luis Vives, and became a prior at St Austin's Abbey, Canterbury. A motet of his is preserved and a treatise on proportions in Trinity Coll. library, Cambridge.

Dykes, John Bacchus (b Hull, 10 Mar 1823; d Ticehurst, Sussex, 22 Jan 1876), English church musician. Learnt music from an organist at Hull, graduated at Cambridge, where he studied music under Walmisley, and became curate at Malton, Yorks., becoming precentor and minor canon at Durham Cathedral in 1849–62. Wrote services, anthems and esp. many hymn-tunes, and took part in the compilation of *Hymns A. & M.*

Dynamics, the gradations of loudness and softness in music.

Dyson, George (b Halifax, 28 May 1883; d Winchester, 28 Sep 1964), English composer. Studied at the RCM in London and became music director at Winchester Coll. in 1924, having already held the appts. of music master at Osborne, Marlborough, Rugby and Wellington, serving in the 1914–18 war between. In 1937 he was app. director of the RCM in succession to Hugh Allen, retiring in 1952. Knighted 1941.

Works incl. *The Canterbury Pilgrims* (setting of Chaucer's prologue, 1931) and other comps. for solo voices, chorus and orch.; orch., chamber and pf. music; songs.

Dzerzhinsky, Ivan (b Tambov, 9 Apr 1909; d Leningrad, 18 Jan 1978), Russian composer. Studied at the Gnessin School of Music at Moscow and at the Leningrad Cons.

Works incl. operas *Quiet flows the Don, Ploughing the Fallows* (both after novels by Mikhail Sholokhov, 1934), *In the Days of Volochaiev, The Storm* (after Ostrovsky, 1940), *The Blood of the People*; incid. music for plays; film music: *Spring, Poem of the Dnieper* and *Rus. Overture* for orch.; 3 pf. concertos; pf. pieces; song cycles.

E

E, The third note, or mediant, of the scale of C maj.

Eadie, Noel (b Paisley, 10 Dec 1901; d London, 11 Apr 1950), Scottish soprano. Studied pf. at first, then singing with Esta d'Argo in London. She 1st appeared in London, at CG, in 1931, joined the BNOC and after an engagement at the Chicago Opera sang Constanze and the Queen of Night in the Mozart perfs. at Glyndebourne in 1935-6.

Eagles, Solomon. *See* **Eccles.**

Eames, Emma (b Shanghai, 13 Aug 1865; d New York, 13 Jun 1952), American soprano. She studied in Paris, and made her debut there in 1889 as Juliette. London, CG, 1891-1901 as Marguerite, Mireille, Elisabeth, Eva and Desdemona. NY Met 1891-1909 as Donna Anna, Pamina, Santuzza, Tosca and the 1st Alice Ford in the US. Concert tours only from 1911.

Ear Training, the development of the sense of pitch, the ready distinction of intervals, identification of var. types of chords, etc.

Early Reign of Oleg, The, Russian 'opera' or play with music (lib. by Catherine II), music by Pashkeievich, Canobbio and Sarti, prod. St Petersburg, at court, Hermitage Theatre, 26 Oct 1790.

Earth Dances, work for orch. by Birtwistle. Fp London, 14 Mar 1986.

Easdale, Brian (b Manchester, 10 Aug 1909), English composer. Educ. at Westminster Abbey choir-school and the RCM in London.

Works incl. operas *Rapunzel* (1927), *The Corn King* (1935) and *The Sleeping Children* (1951); incid. music for Eugene O'Neill's *Mourning Becomes Electra*; film music *The Red Shoes*; *Missa Coventrensis*, *Dead March*, *Tone Poem*, *Six Poems* for orch.; pf. concerto (1938); string trio; pieces for 2 pfs.; song cycles.

East, Michael (b London, *c* 1580; d Lichfield, 1648), English composer. He was apparently in the service of Lady Hatton in London early in the 17th cent. and from 1618 organist of Lichfield Cathedral.

Works incl. Evening Service, anthems; 6 books of madrigals (some with anthems) and a madrigal contrib. to *The Triumphes of Oriana*; music for viols.

East, Thomas (b *c* 1535; d London, 1608),

English publisher, ? father of prec. He worked in London and brought out several works by Byrd and the Elizabethan madrigalists.

Easter Music-Drama. *See* **Liturgical Drama**

Easter Oratorio (*Kommt, eilet und laufet*) work by J.S. Bach perf. as a church cantata in 1725 and rev. 1732-5 as an oratorio.

Easton, Florence (b Middlesbrough, 25 Oct 1882; d New York, 13 Aug 1955), English soprano. She was engaged in Berlin and Hamburg 1907-15 and made her NY Met debut in 1917; created Lauretta in 1918. Sang 35 of her 150 roles in NY, ending with Brünnhilde in 1936. London, CG, 1909 as Butterfly; 1927 and 1932 as Turandot, Brünnhilde and Isolde. Other roles incl. Carmen, the Marschallin and Tosca.

Eaton, John (b Bryn Mawr, Pa., 30 Mar 1935), American composer. Studied with Sessions and Babbitt at Princeton; has taught at Indiana Univ. from 1970. Works use microtones, serial techniques and synthesizer called syn-ket; operas *Ma Barker* (1957), *Heracles* (1968), *Myshkin* (1973), *The Tempest* (1985).

Eberl, Anton (b Vienna, 13 Jun 1765; d Vienna, 11 Mar 1807), Austrian pianist and composer. Friend and possibly pupil of Mozart, he toured as a pianist in Ger. with Mozart's widow and from 1796 to 1800 was *Kapellmeister* in St Petersburg.

Works incl. operas *La Marchande des modes* (1787), *Die Königen der schwarzen Inseln* (1801), etc.; melodrama *Pyramus und Thisbe* (1794); symphs.; pf. concertos; chamber music; sonatas, variations, etc. for pf.; songs. Much of his music was mistakenly ascribed to Mozart.

Eberlin, Johann Ernst (b Jettingen, 27 Mar 1702; d Salzburg, 19 Jun 1762), German organist and composer. Settled in Salzburg in 1724, where he became organist to the court and cathedral in 1729, and *Kapellmeister* in 1749. He was esteemed as a comp. of church music.

Works incl. several operas, to texts by Metastasio, over 50 Masses; 12 Requiems; offertories, etc.; several oratorios; organ music

Ebert, Carl (b Berlin, 20 Feb 1887; d Los Angeles, 14 May 1980), German opera producer and manager. He prod. *Le nozze di Figaro* in Darmstadt (1927) and worked in Berlin before leaving with Fritz Busch (1933; with Busch founded the Glyndebourne Festival in 1934. He was artistic dir. there until 1939 and again 1947-59; helped to create new standards in the perf. of

Mozart's operas. He staged the fp of *The Rake's Progress* (Venice, 1951) and worked again at the Berlin Städtische Oper 1954–61. His son **Peter** (b Frankfurt, 6 Apr 1918) has worked at Glyndebourne and Los Angeles and in W. Germany. Director of prods. Scottish Opera 1965–75; general administrator 1977–80.

Eberwein, Traugott Maximilian (b Weimar, 27 Oct 1775; d Rudolstadt, 2 Dec 1831), German violinist and composer. Son of a member of the Weimar court band, in which he played as a child. Through Zelter's influence he was much esteemed by Goethe. He went into the service of the Prince of Schwarzburg-Rudolstadt in 1797 and became music director there in 1817.

Works incl. operas *Claudine von Villa Bella* (1815) and *Der Jahrmarkt von Plundersweilen* (1818) (libs. by Goethe), *Preciosa* (P.A. Wolff) and 8 others; Mass; 3 cantatas; concertos, *Sinfonia concertante* for wind instruments; vocal 4tets; songs.

Ebony Concerto, work by Stravinsky for clar. and orch., comp. 1945 for Woody Herman and his band and perf. by them, NY, 25 Mar 1946.

Eccard, Johann (b Mühlhausen, Thuringia, 1553; d Berlin, 1611), German composer. Pupil of David Köler in the choir-school attached to the Weimar court chapel, 1567–71, and of Lassus at Munich. In the service successively of Jacob Fugger at Augsburg, at Königsberg, of the Margrave of Brandenburg-Ansbach and of the Elector Joachim Friedrich of Brandenburg in Berlin and his successor, Johann Sigismund. He was a follower of Lassus; his music was still printed 30 years after his death.

Works incl. motets, chorales (some harmonized, some newly comp. by him); sacred songs; secular Ger. songs for several voices, wedding songs, odes, festival songs.

Eccles (Eagles), English family of musicians:

1. Solomon E. (b *c* 1618, d London, 2 Jan 1682), descendant of a musical family, teacher of virginals and viols. He embraced Quakerism *c* 1660 and burnt all his music and instruments, but in 1667 pub. a book arguing for and against the moral justification of music. He went to the West Indies with George Fox to estab. Quakerism in 1671, was in New Eng. in 1672 and was prosecuted for sedition at Barbados in 1680.

2. Solomon E. (b *c* 1645; d Guildford, buried 1 Dec 1710), violinist and composer, (?) son of prec., musician at the courts of James II and William and Mary. Works incl.

music for plays by Aphra Behn and Otway.

3. John E. (b London, 1668; d Hampton Wick, 12 Jan 1735), composer, son of prec. Pupil of his father. Began to write music for the theatres *c* 1690. He became a member of the King's Band in 1694 and its Master in 1700 on the death of Staggins, and the same year gained the 2nd prize in a contest for the best comp. of Congreve's masque *The Judgment of Paris*, Weldon being 1st and D. Purcell and Finger 3rd and 4th. For *c* a quarter of a cent. he lived in retirement at Kingston, devoted mainly to fishing, though he continued to write odes for the royal household.

Works incl. music for many plays, e.g. *The Spanish Friar*(Dryden), *Love for Love* (Congreve), *Don Quixote* (Durfey, with Purcell), *The Stage Coach* (Farquhar), *Macbeth* (Shakespeare, 1694), *Europe's Revels for the Peace* (1697), *Rinaldo and Armida* (1698), *The Way of the World* and *Semele* (both Congreve), *The Biter* (Rowe); music for Queen Anne's coronation; Congreve's *Ode for St Cecilia's Day* (1701); many songs.

4. Henry E. (b London, *c* 1690; d Paris, ? 1742), violinist and composer, brother of prec. Member of the King's Band, 1689–1710, but went to Paris, considering himself neglected at home, and joined the royal band there. Wrote sonatas for vln. and for viol.

5. Thomas E. (b London, *c* 1672; d *c* 1745), violinist, son of 2. Pupil of his brother Henry (4), although highly gifted, secured no app., being a wastrel, but made such a living as he could by playing at taverns.

Échappée (Fr., short for *note échappée* = escaped note), a progression between 2 adjacent notes which deviates by at 1st taking a step in the opposite direction and then taking the 2nd note aimed at by an interval of a 3rd, e.g.:

Échelle de soie, L' (*The Silken Ladder*), opera by Gaveaux (lib. by F.A.E. de Planard), prod. Paris, Opéra-Comique, 22 Aug 1808. The orig. of Rossini's *Scala di seta*.

Echo. In comp. var. echo effects have been used in many ways at all times; e.g. Lassus's madrigal *Olà, che buon eco*, the witches' chorus in Purcell's *Dido and Aeneas*, the *Echo* piece in Bach's B min. clavier partita, the *Scène aux champs* in Berlioz's *Fantastic Symph.*, the 2nd act of Humperdinck's *Hänsel und Gretel*, etc.

Écho et Narcisse, opera by Gluck (lib. by L.T. de Tschudy), prod. Paris, Opéra, 24 Sep 1779.

Eck, Franz (b Mannheim, 1774; d Strasbourg, 1804), German violinist. Pupil of his brother Johann. Played in the court band at Munich as a youth, then travelled much and took Spohr to Rus. with him as his pupil.

Eck, Friedrich Johann (b Schwetzingen, 25 May 1767; d Schwetzingen, 22 Feb 1838), German violinist, conductor and composer, brother of prec. In the service of the court at Munich from 1778, *Konzertmeister* 1788, later opera cond. there. Left Munich 1800 and settled in France.

Works incl. 6 vln. concertos, *Concertante* for 2 vlns.

Eckardt, Johann Gottfried (b Augsburg, 21 Jan 1735; d Paris, 24 Jul 1809), German pianist, composer and miniature painter. Settled in Paris, 1758. Wrote sonatas, variations, etc. for pf.

Eckert, Carl (Anton Florian) (b Potsdam, 7 Dec 1820; d Berlin, 14 Oct 1879), German pianist, violinist, conductor and composer. Pupil of Mendelssohn at Leipzig. Accompanist at the Théâtre Italien in Paris and to Henriette Sontag in the USA, then cond. at the same theatre in Paris, director of the Court Opera in Vienna, *Kapellmeister* at Stuttgart in succession to Kücken, and successor of Dorn in Berlin.

Works incl. operas *Das Fischermädchen* (1830), *Wilhelm von Oranien*; oratorios *Ruth* (1833) and *Judith*; church music, symph.; cello concerto; pf. pieces; songs.

Éclat, work by Boulez for 15 insts.; fp Los Angeles, 26 Mar 1965. Expanded as *Éclat/Multiples* and perf. London, 21 Oct 1970; work in progress.

École d'Arcueil, a group of French composers gathered round Satie in his later years at his home in the Arcueil suburb of Paris, formed in 1923 and incl. Henri Cliquet-Pleyel, Roger Désormière, Maxime Jacob, Henri Sauguet and others.

Écossaise (Fr. fem. = lit. Scot. one), a dance long supposed to be of Scot. origin but no longer considered so. As a fashionable ballroom dance in the early 19th cent. it was in fairly animated 2–4 time, about half way between the polka and the galop in speed. Among the comps. who cultivated it were Beethoven, Schubert and Chopin. The Ger. *Schottisch* (usually written [in the plur.] *Schottische* in Eng.) is the same thing.

Ecuatorial, work by Varèse for bass voice, 8 brass, pf., organ, 2 ondes Martenots and 6 perc. (text is a Sp. trans. of a prayer from the sacred book of the Maya Quiché, the *Popul Vuh*), fp NY, 15 Apr 1934, cond. Nicolas Slonimsky.

Edelmann, Johann Friedrich (b Strasbourg, 5 May 1749; d Paris, 17 Jul 1794), Alsatian pianist and composer. He became famous in Paris through the patronage of his pupil, Baron Dietrich. He was a friend of Gluck, and Mozart thought well of his pf. comps. He apparently played a discreditable part during the Fr. Revolution, and died on the guillotine.

Works incl. operas *Ariane dans l'île de Naxos* (1782), *La Bergère des Alpes* (1781) and *Diane et l'Amour* (1802); symphs.; keyboard concertos and sonatas.

Edelmann, Otto (b Vienna, 5 Feb 1917), Austrian bass-baritone. Studied at the Vienna State Acad. of Music. His career was interrupted by World War II, but in 1947 he joined the Vienna Staatsoper, and in 1951 sang at Bayreuth, as Sachs; NY Met 1954, same role. Salzburg 1960 as Ochs. Other roles incl. Leporello, Amfortas, Gurnemanz and Dulcamara.

Edgar, opera by Puccini (lib. by F. Fontana, based on Musset's *La Coupe et les lèvres*), prod. Milan, La Scala, 21 Apr 1889.

Edinburgh Festival, annual festival of arts held in late summer in Scottish capital, founded 1947. Dirs.: Rudolf Bing (1947–9), Ian Hunter (1949–55), Robert Ponsonby (1955–60), Earl of Harewood (1961–5), Peter Diamond (1966–78), John Drummond (1979–83), Frank Dunlop from 1984. Until 1978 festival had strong musical emphasis. Many leading orchs. have perf., and visiting opera companies, incl. Glyndebourne, Hamburg and Prague, have given 1st Brit. perfs. of *The Rake's Progress*, *Mathis der Maler* and *The Excursions of Mr Brouček*. Maly Co., Leningrad, visited in 1986.

Edipo Re (*King Oedipus*), opera in 1 act by Leoncavallo (lib. by G. Forzano, after Sophocles), prod. Chicago, 13 Dec 1920.

Eduardo e Cristina, opera by Rossini (lib. by G. Schmidt, written for Pavesi, altered by A.L. Tottola and G. Bevilacqua-Aldovrandini), prod. Venice, Teatro San Benedetto, 24 Apr 1819.

Edwards, Richard (b nr. Yeovil, *c* 1522; d London, 31 Oct 1566), English composer. Pupil of the musician, physician and Gk. scholar George Etheridge of Thame, entered Corpus Christi Coll., Oxford in 1540, and transferred to Christ Church on its foundation in 1546. App. Master of the Children of the Chapel Royal in London in 1561 and wrote two plays for them. He was also a playwright, prod. *Palamon and Arcite* before Queen Elizabeth and also writing *Damon and Pithias*, etc., and a poet, compiling and contributing to a book of verse, *The Paradise of Dainty Devices*.

Works incl. music to his own *Damon and Pithias*; part-songs *In going to my naked bed* and *O the silly man*.

Egdon Heath, work for orch. by Holst, after the Dorset landscape described by Hardy in *The Return of the Native* (1878). Commissioned by the NY SO and perf. 12 Feb 1928 in NY.

Egge, Klaus (b Gransherad, Telemark, 19 Jul 1906; d Oslo, 7 Mar 1979), Norwegian composer. Studied under Valen and in Ger. He ed. *Tonekunst* in 1935–38.

Works incl. 5 symphs. (1945–69), 3 pf. concertos, trio for vln., cello and pf., vln. and pf. sonatas.

Egisto, L' (*Aegisthus*), opera by Cavalli (lib. by G. Faustini), prod. Venice, Teatro San Cassiano, autumn 1643. 1st modern revival Santa Fe 1974, in a free realization by Raymond Leppard.

Egk, Werner (b Auchsesheim, Bavaria, 17 May 1901; d Inning, nr. Munich, 10 Jul 1983), German composer. Mainly self-taught and spent some time in It. He began to comp. to broadcasting commissions. Settled nr. Munich and succeeded Graener as head of the faculty of comp. in the Nazi Reichsmusikkammer. From 1936 to 1940 he cond. at the Berlin Staatsoper and from 1950 to 1953 was director of the Hochschule für Musik in Berlin. He wrote music for the opening of the Berlin Olympics (1936).

Works incl. operas *Columbus* (1932; prod. 1942), *Die Zaubergeige* (1935), *Peer Gynt* (1938), *Circe* (1945), *Irische Legende* (after Yeats, 1953), *Der Revisor* (after Gogol, 1957), *Die Verlobung in San Domingo* (1963); ballets *Joan de Zarissa* and *Abraxas* (1948); dance suite *Georgica* for orch.; vln. concerto (*Geigenmusik*, 1936), Französische Suite, after Rameau (1949), *Spiegelzeit* for orch. (1979).

Egli, Johann Heinrich (b Seegraben nr. Zürich, 4 Mar 1742; d Zürich, 19 Dec 1810), Swiss composer. Pupil of Pastor Schmiedli at Wetzikon nr. Zurich and later music teacher at Zurich.

Wrote many songs which he pub. in several books.

Egmont, incid. music by Beethoven for Goethe's tragedy of that name, op. 84, written in 1809–10 for a revival at the Burgtheater in Vienna on 15 Jun 1810.

Egyptian Helen, The (R. Strauss), *See* **Ägyptische Helena.**

Ehrling, Sixten (b Malmö, 3 Apr 1918), Swedish conductor. He gave his 1st opera at the Stockholm Opera in 1940 and was music dir. there 1953–70; cond. the fp of Blomdahl's *Aniara* in 1959 and gave it soon after with the Stockholm co. in Edinburgh and London (CG). 1963–73 music dir. Detroit SO, and taught at the Juilliard School; prin. guest cond. Denver SO from 1979.

Eichendorff, Joseph von (1788–1857), German poet and novelist. *See* **Franz** (songs), **Lothar** (*Freier*), **Pfitzner** (*Von deutscher Seele*), **Schoeck** (*Schloss Dürande*, *Wanderprüche* and songs), **Schumann** (*Liederkreis*); 6 songs by **Brahms**, 16 by **Schumann**, 28 (incl. 8 early) by **H. Wolf.**

Eighteen-Twelve Overture (Tchaikovsky). *See* **Year 1812.**

Eighth-Note (Amer.) = Quaver.

Eilen (Ger.) = to hurry. *Nicht eilen* = do not hurry.

Eimert, Herbert (b Bad Kreuznach, 8 Apr 1897; d Cologne, 15 Dec 1972), German composer and critic. Studied music and musicology at Cologne Cons. and Univ. (1927–1933). Worked for Ger. radio and from 1936 to 1945 ed. the *Kölnische Zeitung*. In 1951 he founded an electronic studio at the Cologne branch of W. Ger. Radio and from 1955 edited *Die Reihe*. He wrote extensively on modern music.

Works incl. *Glockenspiel* (1953); *Etüden über Tongemische*; *Requiem für Aikichi Kuboyama* (1962); choral and chamber music and electronic pieces.

Ein musikalischer Spass (Mozart). *See* **Musikalischer Spass.**

Eine kleine Nachtmusik (Mozart). *See* **Kleine Nachtmusik.**

Einem, Gottfried von (b Berne, 24 Jan 1918), Austrian composer. Son of a military attaché at the Aus. embassy to Switz. The family moved to Plön in Holstein, where he went to school, and he 1st learned music from a pupil of Lamond. He worked at the Wagner theatre at Bayreuth and the Staatsoper in Berlin, studied further in London and Vienna. A plan to become Hindemith's pupil was frustrated by the latter's suspension by the Nazis in 1934, and Einem and his mother were themselves arrested by the Gestapo. After his release he studied with Boris Blacher, with whom he wrote the lib. for his

1st opera. In 1948 he was invited to help to direct the festival at Salzburg, where he later lived.

    Works incl. operas *Dantons Tod* (on Büchner's drama, 1947), *Der Prozess* (after Kafka, 1953), *Der Besuch der alten Dame* (after Dürrenmatt, 1971); *Kabale und Liebe* (after Schiller, 1976) and *Jesu Hochzeit* (1980); ballet *Prinzessin Turandot* (after Gozzi); *Capriccio* and concerto for orch.; 'Philadelphia' symph. (1960); pf. concerto; pf. pieces; Hafiz songs.

Einleitung (Ger.) = Introduction.

Einstein, Alfred (b Munich, 30 Dec 1880; d El Cerrito, Calif., 13 Feb 1952), German musicologist. Pupil of Sandberger, took his doctor's degree in 1903. Became ed. of the *Zeitschrift für Musikwissenschaft* in 1918, and was music critic of the *Berliner Tageblatt* from 1929, in 1933 went into exile from Ger., settling 1st in London, then at Florence and lastly in Northampton, Mass., where he was prof. at Smith Coll. He revised Riemann's *Musiklexicon* and Köchel's Mozart catalogue and wrote works on Ger. vla. da gamba music, on Gluck and Mozart, a short hist. of music and in partic. specialized in the study of the It. madrigal, on which he wrote a monumental book (1949).

Einstein on the Beach, opera by Philip Glass (text by Robert Wilson), prod. Avignon, 25 Jul 1976; NY Met 21 Nov 1976 (at Lincoln Center but not with Met Co.)

Eisinger, Irene (b Kosel, 8 Dec 1903), German soprano. She studied in Vienna. Debut Basle, 1926. Joined Klemperer at the Kroll Opera, Berlin, and was successful as Susanna (1931); sang at Prague 1933–7 and from 1934 was a leading perf. at Glyndebourne: Despina, Papagena, Blondchen, Susanna and Polly Peachum, until 1940. Despina in 1949. Lives in England.

Eisler, Hanns (b Leipzig, 6 Jul 1898; d Berlin, 6 Sep 1962), German composer. Studied with Schoenberg in Vienna and gained a comp. prize in 1924. In 1925–33 he taught in Berlin, but emigrated to USA when a price was put on his head for being interested in music for the proletariat and in anti-Nazi activities. He was app. prof. at the New School of Social Research there. He left the USA in 1948, living first in Vienna and then in E. Berlin.

    Works incl. operas *Galileo* (1947) and *Johannes Faustus* (1953), didactic plays *Mother* (after Gorky's novel, 1931), *Hangmen also die, For whom the bell tolls; The Roundheads and the Pointedheads* and others; music for numerous films; German

Symph. for solo voices, chorus and orch., cantatas, choral ballads, proletarian songs, etc.; orchestral suites on Rus. and Jewish folksongs; wind 5tet; chamber cantata *Palmström* for speech-song, fl., clar., vln. and cello; *Zeitungsausschnitte* for voice and pf.

Eisteddfod (Welsh, plur. Eisteddfodau, = a sitting of the learned), an annual gathering, now taking the form of a mainly music festival, but formerly a triennial assembly of Welsh bards, dating back to the 7th cent. at latest.

Eitner, Robert (b Breslau, 22 Oct 1832; d Templin nr. Berlin, 2 Feb 1905), German musicologist and bibliographer. Founder of the Gesellschaft für Musikforschung in 1868, ed. of the *Monatshefte für Musikgeschichte*, compiler of the *Quellen-Lexicon* (a catalogue of the contents of music libraries) and other bibliog. works.

Elder, Mark (b Hexham, 2 Jun 1947), English conductor. He studied at Cambridge and in 1970 was on the staff at Glyndebourne and CG; debut there 1976, *Rigoletto*. ENO, London, from 1974; prin. cond. from 1979 (fp of David Blake's *Toussaint* 1977). In 1980 he became princ. guest cond. of the London Mozart Players and in 1981 gave *Die Meistersinger* at Bayreuth. In Apr 1986 he gave the British stage premiere of Busoni's *Dr Faust* (London Coliseum).

Electrochord, an electrophonic pf. invented by Vierling of Berlin in 1929–33, prod. its notes by the conversion of electrical waves into audible sounds.

Electronde, an electrophonic instrument, invented by Martin Taubman of Berlin in 1929, prod. notes from the air graded according to the chromatic scale by means of a switch, not indeterminate in pitch like those of the Aetherophone or Theremin.

Electronic Music, music generated and composed by electronic means and performed primarily from a recording, usually a tape, (recent exs. incl. Stockhausen's *Donnerstag aus Licht* and Birtwistle's *The Mask of Orpheus* (1986). If original sounds are not electronic but simply modified by electronic means, it is normally called **Musique concrète.**

Electrophone, the class of musical instruments that generate their tone by electronic means., *See also* **Instruments, classification of.**

Elegy (from Gk. *elegeia*), in poetry a piece of sorrowful and usually commemorative character; in music either a vocal setting of such a poem or an instrumental piece suggesting the mood awakened by it.

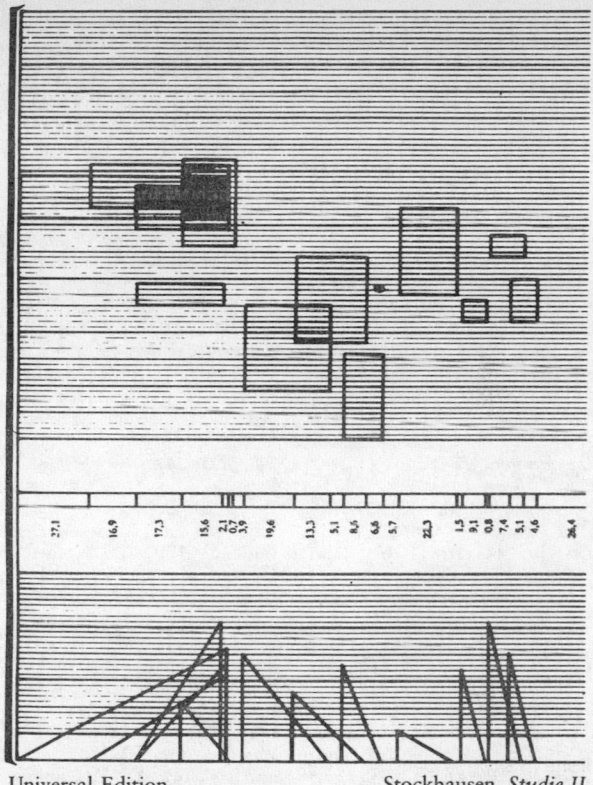

Universal Edition   Stockhausen, *Studie II*
(Alfred A. Kalmus Ltd)
ELECTRONIC MUSIC

Elegy for Young Lovers, opera by Henze (lib. by W.H. Auden and Chester Kallman), prod. Schwetzingen, Schlosstheater, 20 May 1961; first British prod. Glyndebourne, 13 Jul 1961.

Elektra, opera by R. Strauss (lib. by H. von Hofmannsthal, a much modernized re-interpretation of Sophocles), prod. Dresden, Royal Opera, 25 Jan 1909.

Elgar, Edward (William) (b Broadheath nr. Worcester, 2 Jun 1857; d Worcester, 23 Feb 1934), English composer. Son of a Worcester music dealer and organist at St George's Rom. Catholic Church. Self-taught as a comp. Wrote music for a little domestic play, *The Wand of Youth*, at the age of 12. Sent to a solicitor's office at 15, but preferred to help at his father's shop; joined a wind 5tet as bassoonist and the Worcester Glee Club, and at 17 became an orch. violinist. In 1879 he became cond. of the Worcester Glee Club

and of the band at the county lunatic asylum, for which he arr. much music. Also played organ at his father's church and became member of Stockley's orch. at Birmingham, which gave the 1st public perf. of a work of his, the *Sérénade mauresque*. Married Caroline Alice Roberts in 1889 and went to live in London.

In 1890 the Three Choirs Festival (at Worcester that year) for the 1st time played a work of his, the *Froissart* overture. Choral works, incl. *King Olaf* and *Caractacus*, were heard at festivals, and the *Enigma* variations for orch. were prod. by Hans Richter in Jun 1899. Setting of Cardinal Newman's *Dream of Gerontius* prod. at Birmingham Festival, 3 Oct 1900 and, in Ger., at the Lower Rhine Festival, Düsseldorf, in 1901 and 1902. An Elgar Festival at Covent Garden Theatre in London, Mar 1904, brought him greater recognition, and he was knighted on 5 Jul that year. Prof. of Music at Birmingham Univ., 1905–6. 1st symph. perf. by Richter, Manchester and London, Dec 1908, and vln. concerto by Kreisler, Nov 1910. During the war of 1914–18 he wrote much topical music and afterwards 3 chamber works. After the death of his wife in 1920 he wrote only some small pieces and incid. music. At his death he left unfinished a 3rd symph. and an opera, *The Spanish Lady*, based on Ben Jonson's *The Devil is an Ass*.

Works incl. incid. music for Yeats and George Moore's *Grania and Diarmid* (1901), Algernon Blackwood's *The Starlight Express* (1915) and other plays.

ORCH.: 2 symphs. (1908, 1911); concert overtures *Froissart* (1890), *Cockaigne* (1901), *In the South* (1904), *Polonia*; many misc. orch. works, incl. 2 suites from *The Wand of Youth* (1907–8), serenade for strings (1892), *Enigma* variations (1899), *Introduction and Allegro* for strings (1905), symph. study *Falstaff* (1902–13), *Dream Children* (after Lamb) for small orch., *Nursery Suite*; vln. concerto (1910), cello concerto (1919).

VOCAL: cantatas *The Black Knight* (1889–93), *King Olaf*, *The Banner of St. George*, *Caractacus* (1898), *The Music Makers* (1902–12); oratorios *The Light of Life*, *The Dream of Gerontius* (1900), *The Apostles*, *The Kingdom*.

CHAMBER: string 4tet, E min., pf. 5tet, A min. (1919), vln. and pf. sonata, E min. (1918); numerous smaller choral pieces and partsongs; songs for solo voice, incl. cycle *Sea Pictures* with pf. or orch. (1897–9); *Severn Suite* for brass band, etc.

Elijah (Ger. *Elias*), oratorio by Mendelssohn (words from the Old Testament), prod. 1st in the Eng. version at the Birmingham Festival, 26 Aug 1846; 1st Ger. perf., Hamburg, 7 Oct 1847.

Elisa, opera by Fux (lib., in It., by P. Pariati), prod. at court at Laxenburg Palace nr. Vienna, 25 Aug 1719.

Elisabetta regina d'Inghilterra (*Elizabeth, Queen of England*), opera by Rossini (lib. by G. Schmidt), prod. Naples, Teatro San Carlo, 4 Oct 1815. The overture was taken from *Aureliano in Palmira* and afterwards used for *Il barbiere di Siviglia*.

Elisir d'amore, L' (*The Love Potion*), opera by Donizetti (lib. by F. Romani, based on Scribe's *Le Philtre*, comp. by Auber), prod. Milan, Teatro della Canobbiana, 12 May 1832.

Eliza, ou Le voyage aux glaciers du Mont St Bernard, opera by Cherubini (lib. by J.A.

de R. Saint-Cyr), prod. Paris, Théâtre Feydeau, 13 Dec 1794.

Elizalde, Federico (b Manila, P.I., 12 Dec 1907; d Manila, 16 Jan 1979), Spanish conductor and composer. Educ. at Stanford Univ., California, and Cambridge; studied music with Pérez Casas in Madrid, Alfred Hertz and Bloch at San Francisco and E. Halffter in Paris.

Works incl. opera *Paul Gauguin* (1943); overture *La pájara pinta*; sinfonia concertante for pf. and orch.; vln. concerto; music for 15 solo instruments.

Elizza, Elise (b Vienna, 6 Jan 1870; d Vienna, 3 Jun 1926), Austrian soprano. Debut Vienna, Karltheater, 1892; Hofoper 1895–1919, debut as Ines, and sang a wide range of coloratura and dramatic roles: Elisabeth in *Tannhäuser* under Mahler. Retired 1923 and taught in Vienna.

Elleviou, Jean (b Rennes, 2 Dec 1769; d Paris, 6 May 1842), French tenor. Debut Paris 1790 in Monsigny's *Le Déserteur*, as a bass. He sang as a tenor at the Comédie Italienne 1797–1801, then moved to the Opéra-Comique, where he was heard as Blondel in Grétry's *Richard Coeur de Lion* and created Méhul's Joseph (1807) and Boieldieu's Jean de Paris (1812). A popular actor and singer, he retired in 1813, when he was refused a massive pay increase by Napoleon.

Ellis, David (b Liverpool, 10 Mar 1933), English composer. He studied at the RMCM and has worked as an administrator with the BBC since 1964.

Works incl. opera, *Crito* (1963); Sinfonietta (1953), vln. concerto, pf. concerto (1962), *Fanfares and Cadenzas* for orch. (1968), *February Music* for cello and chamber orch. (1977), *Circles* (1979); choral music incls. *Sequentia I-V* for soloists, chorus and orch. (1962–75); string trio (1954), wind 5tet (1956); pf. sonata (1956).

Elman, Mischa (b Talnoye, 20 Jan 1891; d New York, 5 Apr 1967), American violinist of Russian birth. Began serious studies at the age of 6 and in 1902 was accepted by Auer for his master class. He made his debut in 1904 in Berlin, later touring Europe and Amer. London debut 1905, NY 1908. Martinů wrote his 2nd vln. concerto for him and he gave the fp in Boston, 31 Dec 1943.

Elmendorff, Karl (b Düsseldorf, 25 Oct 1891; d Hofheim am Taunus, 21 Oct 1962), German conductor. After studying philology he entered the Cologne Cons. in 1913. He held var. cond. appts., incl. Berlin Staatsoper, Munich, Wiesbaden, Kassel, Mannheim and Dresden. From 1927–42 he was a regular guest cond. at Bayreuth (*Tristan, Meistersinger* and *The Ring*).

Eloy, Jean-Claude (b Mont-Saint-Aignan, 15 Jun 1938), French composer. Studied with Milhaud and Boulez; other influences incl Varèse, Webern and oriental music. Worked at electronic music studio, Cologne, with Stockhausen.
Works incl. *Étude III* for orch. (1962); *Equivalences* for wind and perc. (1963); *Polychronies* for chamber ens. (1964); *Kamakala* for chorus and 3 orch. groups (1971); *Kshara-Akshara* for sop., chorus and 3 orch. groups (1974); *Shanti* for 6 solo voices and electronics (1972–4).

Elsner, Ksawéry Jozef (b Grotków, Silesia, 1 Jun 1769; d Warsaw, 18 Apr 1854), Polish composer of Swedish descent. Being intended for medicine, he had little music teaching in his youth, but learnt the vln. and some harmony at Breslau and studied more assiduously on going to Vienna. In 1791 he became violinist at the Brno theatre and the next year cond. at Lwów. He went to Warsaw as theatre cond. in 1799, estab. a music society there in 1815 and became the 1st director of the Cons. opened in 1821. Among his pupils there was Chopin.
Works incl. 27 operas (22 in Pol., e.g. *Krol Lokietek* (1818), ballets and melodramas; *Stabat Mater*, church music; 11 symphs.; 6 string 4tets; instrumental pieces.

Elwes, Gervase (Cary) (b Northampton, 15 Nov 1866; d nr. Boston, USA, 12 Jan 1921), English tenor. Studied in Vienna, Munich, Paris and London. In Brit. diplomatic service, 1891–5. Made his 1st professional appearance in 1903. He sang in *The Dream of Gerontius* in London in 1904, and in 1909 gave the fp of Vaughan Williams's song cycle *On Wenlock Edge*. He was killed by a train, while on tour in America.

Embouchure (Fr., but used in Eng.), the position of the lips on the mouthpiece in wind instrument playing.

Emerald Isle, The, unfinished operetta by Sullivan, completed by German (lib. by B. Hood), prod. London, Savoy Theatre, 27 Apr 1901.

Emma di Resburgo (*Emma of Roxburgh*) opera by Meyerbeer (lib. by G. Rossi), prod. Venice, Teatro San Benedetto, 26 Jun 1819.

Emmanuel, (Marie François) Maurice (b Bar-sur-Aube, 2 May 1861; d Paris 14 Dec 1938), French musicologist and composer. Student at the Paris Cons. and pupil of Gevaert at Brussels. After var. appts. as historian and musician he became prof. of music hist. at the Cons. in succession to Bourgault-Ducoudray in 1907 and retained the post until 1936. He wrote several learned books on the musical idiom, Gk. music, modal accomp., Burgundian folksong, etc.
Works incl. operas *Prométhée enchaîné* (1916–18) and *Salamino* (1921–8, both after Aeschylus); operetta *Pierrot peintre* (1886); incid. music for Plautus's *Amphitryon*; 2 symphs., *Suite française, Ouverture pour un conte gai, Zingaresca* for orch.; *3 Odelettes anacréontiques* for voice, fl. and pf. (1911); vln. and pf. and cello and pf. sonatas; *Sonate bourguignonne* and 6 sonatinas for pf.; *In memoriam matris* and *Musiques* for voice and pf.

'Emperor' Concerto, nickname for Beethoven's Eb maj. pf. concerto, op. 73, given only in Brit. and USA, prob. invented by J.B. Cramer. There is nothing to justify it, though it suits the majestic work well enough.

Emperor Jones, opera by Gruenberg (lib. by K. de Jaffa, based on Eugene O'Neill's play), prod. NY, Met, 7 Jan 1933.

'Emperor' Quartet. *See* **Emperor's Hymn.**

Emperor's Hymn, The, *Gott erhalte Franz den Kaiser* (words by L.L. Haschka), comp. by Haydn and first sung to celebrate the Emperor's birthday, 12 Feb 1797. Also used by Haydn as a theme for variations in the string 4tet op. 76 no. 3 (known as the 'Emperor' 4tet). Later adopted as the Austrian national anthem. Well-known in England as a hymn-tune.

Empfindsamer Stil (Ger., sensitive style), term applied to music by some Ger. 18th-cent comps., esp. C.P.E. Bach, Quantz, etc., who sought to make their music directly expressive of feeling. *See* **Affektenlehre.**

En Saga (Sibelius). *See* **Saga, En.**

Encina, Juan del (b nr. Salamanca, 12 Jul 1468; d León, 1529), Spanish poet, playwright and composer. Studied at Salamanca Univ., entered the service of the Duke of Alba at Toledo, was app. archdeacon of Málaga in 1509, went to Rome in 1514 and to the Holy Land in 1519, and became prior of Laón. Prod. the *Farsa de Placida e Vittoriano* in Rome and comp. many songs for his own plays. His poems were pub. at Salamanca, 1496. Over 60 of his songs are contained in a MS. at Madrid, the *Cancionero Musical de Palacio*. He cultivated esp. the *villancico*, a form resembling the French *virelai*

Ende einer Welt, Das, (*The End of a World*) radio opera in 2 acts by Henze (lib. by W. Hildesheimer), perf. Hamburg, 4 Dec 1953; rev. for the stage 1964 and prod. Frankfurt, 30 Nov 1965.

Énée et Lavinie (*Aeneas and Lavinia*), opera by Colasse (lib. by B.de Fontenelle, after Virgil), prod. Paris, Opéra, 16 Dec 1690.
Opera by Dauvergne (lib. do.), prod. Paris, Opéra, 14 Feb 1758.

Enescu, George (b Dorohoiû, 19 Aug 1881; d Paris, 4 May 1955), Rumanian violinist and composer. Studied at the Vienna Cons., 1888–93, and then went to Paris to finish his vln. studies with Marsick and comp. with Massenet, Gedalge and Fauré. In 1899 he began his career as a virtuoso violinist and teacher of the instrument; Yehudi Menuhin was one of his pupils.
    Works incl. opera *Œdipe* (after Sophocles, 1921–31; prod. 1936); 5 symphs. (1905–41); *Poème roumain*, *Rumanian Rhapsodies*, suites and intermezzi, etc. for orch.; string octet (1900), wind decet (1906), 2 pf. 5tets (1894, 1940), 2pf 4tets (1909, 1943), 2 string 4tets (1920, 1953), 2 pf. trios (1897, 1916); 3 vln. and pf. sonatas (1897, 1899, 1926), 2 cello sonatas (1898, 1935); suites and other works for pf.; songs.

Enfance du Christ, L' (*The Childhood of Christ*), oratorio by Berlioz, op. 25, for solo voices, chorus and orch., comp. in 1850–4, fp Paris, 10 Dec 1854.

Enfant et les sortilèges, L' (*The Child and the Spells*), opera in 1 act by Ravel (lib. by Colette), prod. Monte Carlo, 21 Mar 1925.

Enfant prodigue, L' (*The Prodigal Son*), lyric scene by Debussy (lib. by E. Guinand), written for the Prix de Rome and pub. 1884; prod. as an opera, London, CG, 28 Feb 1910 with Perceval Allen, cond. by Pitt. *See also* Prodigal Son.

Engel, Karl (b Birsfeld, 1 Jun 1923), Swiss pianist. He studied in Bern and Paris with Bernhard Baumgartner and Cortot. A leading recitalist in the classical rep. since the early 1950s and has accomp. singers in Lieder, incl. Dietrich Fischer-Dieskau.

English Chamber Orchestra (ECO), orch. founded 1948 by Arnold Goldsborough, under his own name, to perf. Baroque music. Adopted present name in 1960 and has given fps of works by many British composers; since 1960 at the Aldeburgh Festival (fps *A Midsummer Night's Dream* and Britten's church parables in Suffolk, *Owen Wingrave* on TV, the *Cello Symph.* in Moscow.) No prin. cond. until 1985, when Jeffrey Tate (*q.v.*) was app.

English Horn (from Fr. *cor anglais*, a term which has not been satisfactorily explained), a woodwind instrument with double reed, belonging to the oboe family, played exactly like that instrument but standing a 5th lower in pitch and written for as a transposing instrument. Its tone is nasal, like that of the oboe, but darker in quality.

English National Opera. *See* Sadler's Wells.

English Opera Group, co. founded 1946 by Britten, John Piper and Eric Crozier. Many perfs. of operas by Britten and other Eng. composers at home and abroad. (e.g. Birtwistle, *Punch and Judy*, Aldeburgh 1968). Re-formed 1976 as English Music Theatre, under Colin Graham and Steuart Bedford. Disbanded 1980.

English Suites, 6 keyboard suites by Bach, comp. by 1724–5. In what respect they are 'English' has never been fully explained.

Enharmonic (adj.). In Greek music there were 3 *genera*: the diatonic, the chromatic and the enharmonic, and the last had divisions into degrees smaller than semitones. In modern usage the word enharmonic is applied to modulations made by means of changes of a note or notes between sharps and flats, e.g. C♯ becoming D♭, E♭ becoming D♯, etc. On the pf. or other instrument using the tempered scale these notes actually remain the same, but in string instruments there is, at least to the player's feeling, a minute difference between them.

Enigma Canon, a canon written down in a single part with no indication where the subsequent entries of the other parts are to occur, the perfs. being left to guess how the music fits by solving a riddle.

'Enigma' Variations, a set of orchestral variations by Elgar, op. 36, entitled *Variations on an Original Theme*, comp. 1898, fp London, 19 Jun 1899, cond. Richter. Each variation is a musical portrait of some person indicated only by initials or by a nickname, all of whom have, however, been identified. The word 'Enigma' appears over the theme. *See also* Potter.

Enigmatic Scale (Verdi's). *See* Scala enigmatica.

Enna, August (b Nakskov, 13 May 1859; d Copenhagen, 3 Aug 1939), Danish composer of Italian descent. The son of a cobbler, he was almost entirely self-taught. The family moved to Copenhagen in 1870. In 1888 Gade helped him to study in Ger. for year. He had already prod. an operetta by that time and become a provincial cond.
    Works incl. operas *Heksen* (*The Witch*, 1892), *Cleopatra*, *Aucassin and Nicolette* (1896), *The Little Match-Seller* and *The Princess on the Pea* (both after Andersen), *Komedianter* (*The Jesters*, after Hugo),

Gloria Arsena (after Dumas *père*), *Don Juan Mañara* (1922), etc.; operetta, *A Village Tale*; ballets; choral work *Mother-Love*; 2 symphs., Festival Overture, symph. pictures; vln. concerto.

Enoch Arden, melodrama for reciter and pf. by Strauss, op. 38 (a setting of Tennyson's poem in Ger. trans. by A. Strodtmann), fp Munich, 24 Mar 1897. (perf. in Vienna, 13 Jan 1899, with Zemlinsky at the pf.).

Ensalada (Span. lit. salad), a kind of burlesque madrigal cultivated in Spain in the 16th cent., in dramatic form, like Vecchi's *Amfiparnaso*, not intended for stage perf. Also a Quodlibet.

Ensemble (Fr. = together). The word is used in England for concerted singing or playing, esp. in critical descriptions of such singing or playing.

Entflieht auf leichten Kähnen, double canon for chorus *a cappella* by Webern, op. 2; comp. 1908, fp. Fürstenfeld, 10 Apr 1927.

Entführung aus dem Serail, Die (*The Elopement from the Harem,* known in Eng. as *The Seraglio,* in It. as *Il Ratto del serraglio*). *See also* **Belmont und Constanze,** Opera by Mozart (lib. by C.F. Bretzner [*Belmont und Constanze*] altered by G. Stephanie, jun.), prod. Vienna, Burgtheater, 16 Jul 1782.

Entr'acte (Fr.). *See* **Intermezzo.**

Entrée (Fr. = entrance, entry). In the 17th and 18th cents. a piece of music in a stately rhythm accomp. the entry of processions, etc. in ballets and other stage pieces; also, more generally, an intro. or prelude to any work, but more csp. a ballet or opera where it accomp. the rise of the curtain; an entrée could also be the beginning of each new scene in a ballet.

Entremont, Philippe (b Rheims, 6 Jun 1934), French pianist and conductor. He studied with Marguerite Long and at the Paris Cons.; has appeared internat. since the early 1950s in a wide rep. (won the Long-Thibaud Competition, Brussels in 1951). US debut, NY, 1953; music dir. New Orleans PO 1981–4. Vienna Chamber Orch. since 1976.

Entries, the appearances of the subject in the different parts of a fugue.

Entry, a 17th-18th-cent. English term for Prelude.

Éolides, Les, symph. poem for orch. by Franck, on a poem of the same name by Leconte de Lisle; comp. 1876, fp Paris, 13 May 1877.

Eötvös, Péter (b Székely-Udvarhely, 2 Jan 1944), Hungarian conductor and composer. He studied at Budapest and Cologne; resident W. Ger. from 1971. Music dir. Ensemble Intercontemporain, Paris, from 1979. In 1981 he gave the fp of Stockhausen's *Donnerstag aus Licht,* at La Scala. Prin. guest cond. BBC SO from 1985; with the orch. he gave the 1986 fp of Birtwistle's *Earth Dances.*

Ephesian Matron, The, comic serenata by Dibdin (lib. by I. Bickerstaffe), prod. London, Ranelagh House, 12 May 1769.

Epic of Gilgamesh, The, oratorio by Martinů for soloists, speaker, chorus and orch.; comp. 1954–5, fp Basle, 24 Jan 1958, cond. Sacher. The work's 3 sections are titled *Gilgamesh, The death of Enkidu* and *Invocation.*

Episode, an incid. passage in a comp. that may be described as a digression from the main theme or themes. It may or may not be derived from the chief thematic material: in a fugue it usually is so derived, whereas in a rondo it is as a rule an entirely new idea placed between 2 recurrences of the subject, but may assume the function of a 2nd subject, as in sonata form.

Equal Temperament, the tuning of an instrument, esp. the pf. or org., by dividing the 8ve into 12 semitones all divided by exactly the same ratio of vibrations, as distinct from Just Intonation, where the intervals vary slightly and the sharps and flats are not precisely the same in pitch.

Equale (It., plur. *Equali* = equals), a term used for instrumental pieces, esp. trombs. (e.g. Beethoven's equale), written for a group of similar instruments.

Equivoci, Gli (*The Doubles*), opera by Storace (lib. by L. da Ponte, based on Shakespeare's *Comedy of Errors*), prod. Vienna, Burgtheater, 27 Dec 1786).

Equivoci nel sembiante, Gli (*Dissimilarity in Similarity*), opera by A. Scarlatti (lib. by D.F. Contini), prod. Rome, Teatro Capranica, 5 Feb 1679. Scarlatti's 1st opera.

Érard, Pierre (b Paris, 1796; d Passy nr. Paris, 18 Aug 1855), French pf. and harp maker. Joined his uncle Sébastien É. in business.

Érard, Sébastien (b Strasbourg, 5 Apr 1752; d nr. Passy, 5 Aug 1831), French pf. and harp maker, uncle of prec., founder of the firm estab. *c* 1777.

Erb, Donald (b Youngstown, Ohio, 17 Jan 1929), American composer. Early career was as trumpeter in dance bands. Studied at Cleveland Inst. and with Boulanger in Paris. Has taught in Cleveland and Bloomington;

prof. of comp. Southern Methodist Univ. in Dallas from 1981.

Works influenced by jazz and neo-classical techniques; also employ electronics: *Symphony of Overtures* (1964), *The 7th Trumpet*, for orch. (1969), cello concerto (1975), trumpet concerto (1980); *The Last Quintet* for woodwinds (1982), *Fantasy for Cellist and Friends* (1983); *Cummings Cycle* for mixed chorus and orch. (1963), *New England's Prospect* for choruses and orch. (1974); electronic music incl. *The Purple-roofed Ethical Suicide Parlor* (1972) and *Autumnmusic* (1973).

Erb, Karl (b Ravensburg, 13 Jul 1877; d Ravensburg, 13 Jul 1958), German tenor. He was self-taught and after appearances in Stuttgart and Lübeck sang Lohengrin in Munich; created Pfitzner's Palestrina there in 1917. Other roles incl. Parsifal, Adolar, Pylades, Florestan and Belmonte (London, CG, 1927). From 1930 in Lieder and oratorio; often heard as the Evangelist in Bach's Passions and appears in Thomas Mann's novel *Dr Faustus* (1945) as Erbe, who sings in the fp of Adrian Leverkühn's *Apocalypse* oratorio, under the direction of Otto Klemperer.

Erba, Dionigi Italian 17th-cent. composer. *Maestro di cappella* at the church of San Francesco, Milan, in 1692. Wrote a Magnificat for double chorus from which Handel borrowed for *Israel in Egypt*.

Ercole amante (*Hercules as Lover*), opera by Cavalli (lib. by F. Buti), prod. Paris, Tuileries, 7 Feb 1662. The only opera specially written for Paris by Cavalli. The ballet music was by Lully. The title alludes to the marriage of Louis XIV.

Erede, Alberto (b Genoa, 8 Nov 1909), Italian conductor. He studied in Milan and with Weingartner and Fritz Busch; asst. to Busch at Glyndebourne from 1934 and cond. *Figaro* and *Don Giovanni* 1938–9. Returned 1955 for *Il barbiere di Siviglia*. Gave many perfs. at the Cambridge Theatre, 1946–8, with the New London Opera Co., and was engaged at the NY Met 1950–5. He cond. opera in Düsseldorf 1958–62 and in 1968 led *Lohengrin* at Bayreuth. Many recordings of It. opera.

Erismena, opera by Cavalli (lib. by A. Aureli), perf. Venice, Teatro San Apollinare, 1656. Modern eds. by L. Salter (BBC, 1967) and A. Curtis (1974).

Eritrea, opera by Cavalli (lib. by G. Faustini), perf. Venice, Teatro San Apollinare, 1652. An ed. by Jane Glover was cond. by her at the Wexford Festival in 1975.

Erkel, Ferenc (b Békésgyula, 7 Nov 1810; d Budapest, 15 Jun 1892), Hungarian composer. As a pianist and cond. he organized musical life at Kolozsvar in his early days. In 1825 he became music dir. of the Hung. theatre in Buda, in 1836 asst. cond. of the Ger. theatre in Pest, and in 1838 cond. of the Nat. Theatre. In 1845 he gained the prize in a competition for a Hung. nat. anthem. He founded the Budapest Phil. Society in 1853 and was dir. of the Acad. of Music in 1875–89. His operas were very popular for their patriotic subjects and nat. music.

Works incl. operas *Bátori Mária* (1840), *Hunyadi László* (1844), *Bánk Bán* (1861), *Dózsa György, Brankovics György* (1874), *Névtelen Hösök, István Király* (*King Stephen*); pf. music; songs, etc.

Erlanger, Camille (b Paris, 25 May 1863; d Paris, 24 Apr 1919), French composer. Studied at the Paris Cons. and gained the Prix de Rome in 1888.

Works incl. operas *Saint Julien l'Hospitalier* (after Flaubert), *Kermaria* (1897), *Le Juif polonais* (after Erckmann-Chatrian, 1900), *Aphrodite* (1906), *Bacchus triomphant* (1909), *La Sorcière, Le Fils de l'étoile* and *La Forfaiture*; cantata *Velléda* (1888); *Sérénade carnavalesque* for orch.; pf. pieces; *Poèmes russes* and other songs.

Erlanger, Frédéric d' (b Paris, 29 May 1868; d London, 23 Apr 1943), French (anglicized) banker and composer. He had only private lessons in music and was largely self-taught. Settled in London and became naturalized, but retained the Fr. title of Baron.

Works incl. operas *Jehan de Saintré* (1893), *Inez Mendo* (1897) and *Tess* (after Hardy's *Tess of the d'Urbervilles*, 1902): Requiem; *Suite symphonique* for orch.; *Concerto symphonique* for pf. and orch., vln. concerto; string 4tet, pf. 5tet; songs.

Erlkönig (*Erl* [actually Alder] *King*), a ballad by Goethe, set by Schubert in 1815 at the age of 18, 1st sung in public by Johann Michael Vogl, Vienna, 7 Mar 1821, pub. as op. 1 that year.

Ernani, opera by Verdi (lib. by F.M. Piave, based on Victor Hugo's drama *Hernani*), prod. Venice, Teatro La Fenice, 9 Mar 1844. The 1st of Verdi's operas prod. outside Milan.

Ernelinde, Princesse de Norvège, opera by Philidor (lib. by A.H.H. Poinsinet), prod. Paris, Opéra, 24 Nov 1767.

Ernst, Heinrich Wilhelm (b Brno, 6 May 1814; d Nice, 8 Oct 1865), Moravian violinist and composer. Pupil of Böhm, Seyfried

and Mayseder in Vienna. Lived in Paris from 1832 to 1838.
Works incl. concertos, fantasies, variations, an *Elégie*, etc. for vln., also, with Heller, *Pensées fugitives* for vln. and pf.

Ernste Gesänge (Brahms). *See* **Vier ernste Gesänge.**

Ernster, Deszö (b Pécs, 23 Nov 1898; d Zurich, 15 Feb 1981), Hungarian bass. Debut Düsseldorf 1925; Bayreuth 1931. On tour in US with Salzburg Opera Guild 1938–9; NY Met debut 1946, as King Marke (until 1963). Hagen at CG, London, 1949 and 1954; Glyndebourne 1952, Alfonso. Salzburg 1953 as the Commendatore, under Furtwängler. At the Kroll Opera, Berlin, he sang in the fp of Hindemith's *Neues vom Tage* (1929, under Klemperer).

Ero e Leandro (*Hero and Leander*), opera by Bottesini (lib. by Boito, at 1st intended for himself), prod. Turin, Teatro Regio, 11 Jan 1879.
Opera by Mancinelli (lib. do.), 1st prod. as a cantata, in Eng., Norwich Festival, 8 Oct 1896; 1st stage prod. Madrid, Teatro Real, 30 Nov 1897.

Eroe cinese, L' (*The Chinese Hero*), opera by Bonno (lib. by Metastasio), prod. Vienna, Schönbrunn Palace, at court, 13 May 1752.

'Eroica' Symphony, Beethoven's symph. No. 3 in Eb maj., op. 55, comp. 1803–4. It was to have been entitled *Bonaparte*, but on hearing that Napoleon had declared himself hereditary Emperor Beethoven renamed it *Sinfonia eroica, composta per festeggiare il souvenire di un grand' uomo* (Heroic symphony, composed to celebrate the memory of a great man).

'Eroica' Variations, Beethoven's pf. variations and fugue, op. 35 (comp. 1802), so called because they used the same theme as the finale of the 'Eroica' symph. The theme, however, was taken from one of Beethoven's dances, and the variations were written before the symph.

Erreur d'un moment, L', ou La Suite de Julie (*The Error of a Moment, or The Sequel to Julie*), opera by Dezède (lib. by J.M.B. de Monvel), prod. Paris, Comédie-Italienne, 14 Jun 1773.

Ershov, Ivan (b Novocherkassk, 20 Nov 1867; d Tashkent, 21 Nov 1943), Russian tenor. Studied Moscow and St Petersburg; debut 1893, as Faust. Sang at the Maryinsky Theatre 1895–1929 in Russian rep. and as Don José, Otello, Tristan, Siegfried and Lohengrin. Highly praised as an actor. Taught at Leningrad Cons. 1916–41.

Erwartung, monodrama for sop. and orch.

by Schoenberg (lib. by Marie Pappenheim), comp. 1909 but 1st prod. Prague, 6 Jun 1924, cond. Zemlinsky, with Marie Gutheil-Schoder (*q.v.*).

Es war einmal (*Once upon a time*), opera by Zemlinsky (lib. by Drachmann), prod. Vienna, Hofoper, 22 Jan 1900. The opera was cond. by Mahler, who assisted Zemlinsky in revising the work.

Eschenbach, Christoph (b Breslau, 20 Feb 1940), German pianist and conductor. He studied in Cologne and Hamburg and made his London debut in 1966. Gave the fp of Henze's 2nd pf. concerto (Bielefeld, 29 Aug 1968) and in 1969 made his US debut, with the Cleveland Orch. Debut as cond. 1973; plays Mozart's pf. concertos while cond. from the keyboard. CG debut 1984, *Così fan tutte.*

Esclarmonde, opera by Massenet (lib. by E. Blau and L. de Gramont), prod. Paris, Opéra-Comique, 15 May 1889.

Escobar, Pedro (b Oporto, *c* 1465; d ?) Évora, after 1535), Spanish composer, *maestro de capilla* at Seville early in the 16th cent. Comp. church music and secular pieces for 3 and 4 voices.

Escobedo, Bartolomeo (b Zamora, *c* 1500 d Segovia, 1563), Spanish composer. Entered the Papal Chapel in Rome in 1536, acted as judge in a dispute between Vicentino and Lusitano in 1551. In 1554 he returned to Spain as *maestro de capilla* at Segovia. Wrote Masses, motets, Magnificats, Miserere, etc.

Escribano, Juan (b ?Salamanca *c* 1480; d Spain, Oct 1557), Spanish singer and composer. Sang in the Papal Chapel in Rome, 1507–39. Wrote church music, *chansons* for several voices.

Escudier, Léon (b Castelnaudary, Aude, 17 Sep 1821; d Paris, 22 Jun 1881) and **Escudier, Marie** (b Castelnaudary, Aude, 29 Jun 1819; d Paris, 7 Apr 1880), French writers on music and publishers, brothers, who did most of their work jointly. It incl. biogs. of singers and of Rossini, a music dictionary; they founded *La France musicale* (1837). L. was dir. of the Théâtre Italien 1874–6.

Esmeralda, opera by Fabio Campana (1815–82) lib. by G.T. Cimino, based on Victor Hugo's novel, *Notre-Dame de Paris*), prod. St Petersburg, 30 Dec 1869.
Opera by Dargomizhsky (lib. by comp., trans. from Victor Hugo's lib. based on his *Notre-Dame de Paris*, and written for Louise Angélique Bertin [1805–77] for her opera prod. Paris, 1836), prod. Moscow, 17 Dec 1847.

España, rhapsody for orch. by Chabrier of Spanish tunes collected by the comp. during a visit to Spain in 1882–3; comp. 1883, fp Paris, 4 Nov 1883. Waldteufel later made a ballroom waltz of it.

Esplá, Oscar (b Alicante, 5 Aug 1886; d Madrid, 6 Jan 1976), Spanish composer. Studied civil engineering and took the degree of doctor of philosophy, but also worked at music and took a prize for an orchestral suite in Vienna in 1909. Settled at Brussels in 1936.

Works incl. ballets *El contrabandista* (1928) and *Ciclopes*; symph. poems *El sueño de Eros* (1904), *La vela de armas de Don Quixote* (1924) and *Los Cumbres*, *Poema de niños*, *Ambito de la danza* and *Levantine Suite* for orch.; 5tet; vln. and pf. sonata; sonata, scherzo and other works for pf.

Esposito, Michele (b Castellamare nr. Naples, 29 Sep 1855; d Florence, 26 Nov 1929), Italian pianist and composer. Studied at the Naples Cons., lived in Paris in 1878–82 and was then app. prof. of pf. at Dublin, where in 1899 he estab. the Dublin Orchestral Society, which he cond.

Works incl. operetta *The Postbag* (1902); incid. music for Douglas Hyde's *The Tinker and the Fairy* (1910); cantata *Deirdre*; Ir. Symph., overture to Shakespeare's *Othello*; 2 string 4tets; sonatas for vln. and pf. and cello and pf.

Esquivel, Juan (b Ciudad-Rodrigo, *c* 1565; d after 1613), Spanish composer. He was *maestro de capilla* at Salamanca Cathedral (1608) and at Ciudad-Rodrigo (1611–13). His Masses and motets were pub. (in 2 vols.) in 1608, and a vol. of misc. sacred works in 1613. An *Officium pro defunctis* survives in MS.

Essential Discord, a chord which is dissonant according to acoustic theory, but whose notes belong to the key in which a comp. or passage is written and has become sufficiently current to be intro. without preparation.

Esswood, Paul (b West Bridgford, Notts., 6 Feb 1942), English countertenor. He studied at the RCM. Debut 1965 (*Messiah*). Opera debut Berkeley, Calif., in Cavalli's *Erismena*, 1968. Has appeared all over Europe in operas by Monteverdi and has recorded many of the church cantatas of Bach.

Estampes (*Engravings*), a set of 3 pf. pieces by Debussy, comp. 1903; 1. *Pagodes*, 2. *Soirée dans Grenade*, 3. *Jardins sous la pluie*.

Estampida (Provençal), **Estampie** (Fr.), an instrumental dance form of the 13th and 14th cents. related to the troubadour/trouvère repertory. Its form consisted of several *puncta* (sections), each played twice, with 1st- and 2nd-time endings, called *ouvert* and *clos*. Frequently the *ouvert* and *clos* endings, which often comprised the greater part of each *punctum*, were the same throughout the piece, resulting in a great deal of repetition.

Estes, Simon (b Centreville, Iowa, 2 Mar 1938), American bass-baritone. He studied at Juilliard, NY, and engagements in Berlin and Hamburg soon followed; appeared in the USA from 1966; Met debut 1976, as Oroveso. Later NY roles have been Boris, Philip II and Amonasro. He sang the Dutchman at the 1978 Bayreuth festival, and returned as Amfortas, but was rejected for the 1983 Solti-Hall *Ring*, allegedly because he is black: sang Wotan with great success in a *Ring* prod. at Berlin, 1984–5; also heard in *Die Walküre* at NY Met, 1986. CG debut 1986, as the Dutchman. Also heard as concert singer.

Esther, oratorio by Handel. Fp as a masque entitled *Haman and Mordecai* (lib. prob. by Pope and Arbuthnot, after Racine), Canons, nr. Edgware, *c* 1720. Subsequently recast, with additional words by Samuel Humphreys, and perf. as an oratorio in London, at 1st privately to celebrate Handel's birthday and then at King's Theatre, Haymarket, 2 May 1732.

Oratorio by Dittersdorf (lib. by S.I. Pintus), perf. Vienna, 21 Dec 1773. During the interval of a revival of the work, 16 Dec 1785, Mozart's pf. concerto no. 22, K482 received its fp.

Estinto (It. = extinct, dead), a direction indicating that a passage is to be perf. in a toneless manner.

Estompé (Fr. lit. stumped, shaded off) = damped, muffled, a direction frequently used by Debussy where he asks for a veiled or dull tone.

Eszterháza, castle near Süttör, Hungary, built in 1766 in imitation of Versailles by the Princes Esterházy. The project was started by Paul Anton E., who engaged Haydn as vice–*Kapellmeister* in 1761, and completed by Nicolaus E. In 1766 Haydn took charge of the opera house and marionette theatre, as well as the castle's orchestra. He wrote orch. and instrumental music for his master and supervised frequent opera prods.: all his own operas from *Le pescatrici* (1770) to *Armida* (1784) were fp at E., but works by Anfossi, Salieri, Sacchini and Cimarosa were the staple fare. The musical activities at E.

were much reduced in 1790, and Haydn worked in Vienna and London, but between 1796 and 1802 he wrote 6 great masses for perf. at the castle. Beethoven's Mass in C was given its fp there on 13 Sep 1807.

Et exspecto resurrectionem mortuorum, work in 5 sections by Messiaen for 18 wood wind, 16 brass and 3 perc., comp. 1964 to commemorate the dead of two world wars. Fp Paris, Sainte-Chapelle, 7 May 1965, cond. Baudo.

Eternal Gospel, The (*Věčné evangelium*), legend by Janáček for sop., tenor, chorus and orch. (text by J. Vrchlický), comp. 1914, rev. 1924. Fp Prague, 5 Feb 1917.

Étoile, L', opéra bouffe by Chabrier (lib. by E. Leterrier and A. Vanloo), prod. Paris, Théâtre Bouffes-Parisiens, 28 Nov 1877.

Étoile du Nord, L' (*The North Star*), opera by Meyerbeer (lib. by Scribe), prod. Paris, Opéra-Comique, 16 Feb 1854).

Eton Choirbook (Eton Coll. Library, MS. 178), the most important source of English church music of the late 15th cent., containing works by John Browne, William Cornyshe, Walter Lambe, Richard Davy, Robert Fayrfax, and many others. The repertory reflects the statutes of the coll., which prescribed the singing of a polyphonic antiphon to the Virgin every evening (in Lent, the *Salve Regina*). The MS. orig. contained 67 antiphons to the Virgin and other saints (including 15 settings of the *Salve Regina*), 24 Magnificats, the St Matthew Passion by Davy, and a setting of the Apostles' Creed in the form of a 13-part round by Robert Wylkynson. The settings, except for this last, are for from 4 to 9 voices. About half the orig. contents are now lost, although some works can be recovered from other sources. The MS is pub. in *Musica Britannica*, vols. x–xii. For the format, *see* **Choirbook.**

Étouffé (Fr. = stifled, smothered), a direction to deaden the tone on instruments where it is liable to vibrate after being sounded, as on the harp or the kettledrums.

Étranger, L' (*The Stranger*), opera by d'Indy (lib. by comp.), prod. Brussels, Théâtre de la Monnaie, 7 Jan 1903.

Ettinger, Max (b Lwów, Pol., 27 Dec 1874; d Basle, 19 Jul 1951), German composer. Studied in Berlin and Munich and lived at both places until 1933, when he went into exile in Italian Switz.

Works incl. operas *Clavigo* (after Goethe, 1926), *Judith* (after Hebbel), *Frühlingserwachen* (after Frank Wedekind, 1928), *Juana* (after Georg Kaiser), *Dorlores* (1931); oratorios *Königin Esther*; *Moses, Weisheit*

des Orients (from Omar Khayyám) for solo voices, chorus and orch.; string 4tet (1945).

Étude (Fr. = study), a technical exercise for an instrumental (more rarely a vocal) perf., which may be as much an exercise in expression as in technique.

Études symphoniques, a set of 12 concert studies for pf. by Schumann, op. 13, at first entitled *Études en forme de variations*, comp. in 1834. They are variations on a theme by the father of Ernestine von Fricken, with whom Schumann was in love at that time, but they are ded. to Sterndale Bennett, in whose honour Schumann intro. into the finale a theme from Marschner's *Ivanhoe* opera *Der Templer und die Jüdin*: a song in praise of Eng. 5 further vars. are sometimes now given.

Etwas (Ger. – somewhat, rather).

Eugene Onegin, opera by Tchaikovsky (lib. by comp. and K.S. Shilovsky, based on Pushkin's poem-novel), prod., by students of the Cons., Moscow, 29 Mar 1879. 1st prof. perf. Moscow, Bolshoy, 23 Jan 1881.

Eulenburg, a pub. firm founded in Leipzig in 1874 by Ernst E. (1847–1926). In 1892 the firm took over the series of miniature scores issued by Albert Payne and extended its scope to cover a wide repertory of oratorios, operas, orchestral works and chamber music. The firm is now owned by Schott.

Eunuch Flute, an early wood-wind instrument with a mouthpiece containing a membrane vibrating when the player sang into it. It dates back to the 16th cent. at least, but it was never much more than a toy. *See also* **Mirliton.**

Eunuch Singers. *See* **Castrati.**

Euphonium (*see also* **Saxhorn**), a four-valved brass instrument of the Tuba family, used chiefly in military and brass bands. The compass is:

Euphony, suavity and harmoniousness of sound, the opposite of Cacophony.

Eurhythmics, a system of teaching musical, esp. rhythmic, perception by means of bodily movements, invented by Jaques-Dalcroze (1865–1950).

Euridice, L', opera by Caccini (lib. by Ottavio Rinuccini), prod. Florence, Palazzo Pitti, 5 Dec 1602.

Opera by Peri (lib. do.), prod. Florence, Palazzo Pitti, 6 Oct 1600.

Euripides (*c* 484–406 B.C.), Greek dramatist. *See* Alkestis (Boughton and Wellesz), Bassarids (Henze) Coerne (*Trojan Women*), Damrosch (W.) (*Electra, Iphigenia in Aulis, Medea*), Foulds (*Trojan Women*), Ghedini (*Baccanti, Ifigenia in Tauride*), Gray (C.) (*Trojan W.*), Ifigenia in Aulide (Caldara, Cherubini, Graun, Zingarelli), Ifigenia in Tauride (Galuppi, Maio and Traetta), Iphigénie en Aulide (Gluck), Iphigénie en Tauride (Campra, Gluck and Piccinni), Schürmann (*Getreue Alceste*), Senilov (*Hippolytus*), Slonimsky (*Orestes*), Taubert (*Medea*), Thomson (V.) (do.), Toch (*Bacchantes*), Troades (Reimann), Wood (C.) (*Ion* and *Iphigenia in T.*).

Europe Galante, L', opera-ballet by Campra (lib. by A.H. de la Motte), prod. Paris, Opéra, 24 Oct 1697. The works 4 entrées are titled *La France, L'Espagne, L'Italie, La Turquie*.

Euryanthe, opera by Weber (lib. by H. von Chézy), prod. Vienna, Kärntnertortheater, 25 Oct 1823.

Eusebius, one of the 2 imaginary characters, Florestan and Eusebius, used by Schumann as pseudonyms for his critical writings and also intro. into his music (*Carnaval, Davidsbündlertänze*) to personify what he felt to be his dual character as an artist. Florestan represents him as an impetuous romantic and Eusebius as a dreamer.

Euterpe, the Muse of lyric poetry in Gk. mythology, and since such poetry was sung, also the Muse of music which had no separate patroness among the 9 Muses.

Evans, Anne (b London, 20 Aug 1939), English soprano. Studied at the RCM and in Geneva: small roles at the Grand Théâtre there. She joined ENO in 1968 and sang Mimi, Tosca, Elsa, the Marschallin and Sieglinde at the Coliseum, London. With WNO she has sung Senta, Chrysothemis, the Empress and Donna Anna; her Brünnhilde in *The Ring* (1985) was repeated with great success at CG in 1986 when the co. visited London. At San Francisco she has been heard as Elsa and Elisabeth de Valois.

Evans, (Sir) Geraint (Llewellyn) (b Pontypridd, Glamorgan, 16 Feb 1922), Welsh baritone. Studied at the GSM and later in Hamburg, Geneva and in Italy. He made his debut at CG in 1948, and created roles in Britten's *Billy Budd* (1951) and *Gloriana* (1953); later sang all over Europe, incl. La Scala, Milan, in 1960 and the Vienna Staatsoper in 1961; both debuts as Mozart's Figaro. Glyndebourne 1950–61 as Gugliel-

mo, Masetto, Leporello and Papageno. NY Met debut 1964, as Falstaff. Last opera perf. London CG, 1984, as Dulcamara. Other roles incl. Beckmesser and Wozzeck. Knighted 1971.

Éventail de Jeanne, L' (*Joan's Fan*), ballet by Auric, Delannoy, Ferroud, Ibert, Milhaud, Poulenc, Ravel, Roland-Manuel, Roussel and Schmitt (choreography by Alice Bourgat), prod. Paris, in private, 16 Jun 1927; Opéra, 4 Mar 1929.

Eventyr (*Once upon a time*), ballad for orch. by Delius after fairy tales by P.C. Asbjørnsen (1812–85), comp. 1917 and ded. to Henry Wood, who gave the fp in London, 28 Jun 1919.

Everyman, incid. music for Hugo von Hofmannsthal's Ger. version of the 15th-cent Eng. morality play, *Jedermann*, by Sibelius, op. 83, comp. 1916, fp Helsinki, National Theatre, 5 Nov 1916. Six monologues from E. were set by Frank Martin for bar. and pf in 1943; orch. version 1949.

Évocations, 3 symph. poems by Roussel, comp. 1910–12: 1. *Les Dieux dans l'ombre des cavernes*; 2. *La Ville rose*; 3. *Aux bords du fleuve sacré*; fp Paris, Société Nat., 18 May 1912.

Evocations, symph. suite by Bloch, comp. 1937; fp San Francisco, 11 Feb 1938. 3 movts: *Contemplation, Houang* (God of War), *Renouveau*.

Ewen, David (b Lwów, Poland, 26 Nov 1907; d Miami, 28 Dec 1985), American writer on music. He moved to the USA in 1912 and studied in NY; Univ. of Miami from 1965. In 50 years he pub. more than 80 music reference books, e.g. *Dictators of the Baton* (1943), *Encyclopedia of the Opera* (1955, rev. 1971), *The World of 20th Century Music* (1968), *Composers Since 1900* (1969), *Musicians Since 1900* (1978) and *American Composers* (1982).

Ewing, Maria (b Detroit, 27 Mar 1950), American soprano. She studied in Cleveland with Eleanor Steber and Jennie Tourel; debut 1973 Ravinia Fest. with Chicago SO. In 1976 she sang Cherubino at the NY Met and Mélisande at La Scala, Milan. Glyndebourne 1978 and 1984–5 as Dorabella, Poppea and Carmen in prods. by her husband, Peter Hall.

Excursions of Mr. Brouček, The (*Výlety pana Broučka*), opera by Janáček (lib. by the comp. with F. Gellner, V. Dyke, F.S. Procházka and others, after 2 novels by S. Čech), prod. Prague, 23 Apr 1920. Not prod. in Brit. until Edinburgh, 5 Sep 1970, by the Prague Nat. Theatre Co. The work's 2 acts depict Mr. Brouček on the moon and in 15th cent. Prague.

Expert, Henri (b Bordeaux, 12 May 1863; d Tourrettes-sur-Loup, 18 Aug 1952), French musicologist. Studied, and later taught, at Niedermeyer's school in Paris, and was also a pupil of Franck and Gigout. Prof. of music at the École des Hautes Études Sociales and librarian of the Cons. library. Ed. series of old Fr. music, *Les Maîtres musiciens de la renaissance française* and *Monuments de la musique française*, of settings of Ronsard's poetry, old songs, church and harpsichord music.

'. . . . explosante-fixe . . . .' work by Boulez for unspecified forces. Given with flute, clar. and trumpet in London on 17 Jun 1971; with same forces, plus strings and computer-controlled electronics, NY PO, cond. Boulez, on 5 Jan 1973. Further rev. under Boulez, with the BBC SO in Rome, on 13 May 1973 . . . '. . . work in progress . . . .'

Exposition, the 1st setting forth of thematic material in a comp. In a fugue the exposition is the statement of the subject by its 1st entry in each voice; in a rondo the statement of the subject up to the 1st episode; in a sonata-form movement the whole 1st section up to the point at which the development (or working-out) section begins.

Expression Marks, all the indications by which the comp. indicates his wishes as to the manner of perf. of a work, esp. from the dynamic point of view (*forte, piano, crescendo, diminuendo*); but they may extend also to matters of speed and rhythm (e.g. *rallentando, rubato, accelerando*, etc.). Expression marks were little used before the 18th cent. and hardly at all before the 17th.

Expressionism, a term properly belonging to painting, esp. in Aus. and Ger. in the 1910s, but loosely applied to music aimed at a similar kind of interpretation, not of outward and visible things, but of moods and states of mind. Schoenberg's *Erwartung* (1909) is a familiar example.

Extemporization. See **Improvisation.**

Extravaganza (corrupt. from It. *stravaganza*), a word sometimes used for a comp. of a freakish nature, esp. for a light and fantastic stage piece with music, e.g. Gilbert and Sullivan's *Trial by Jury.*

Eybler, Joseph Leopold von (b Schwechat nr. Vienna, 8 Feb 1765; d Vienna, 24 Jul 1846), Austrian composer. Pupil of Albrechtsberger and, after holding various apps. in Vienna, chief *Kapellmeister* to the Aus. court from 1824 to 1833. He attempted to complete Mozart's Requiem (1791) and suffered a stroke while conducting it in 1833.

Works incl. opera *Das Zauberschwert* and others; oratorio *Die vier letzten Dinge* (1810), Requiem in C min. (1803, for Empress Maria Theresa), cantata *Die Hirten bei der Krippe*, 7 Te Deums, 32 Masses, offertories, graduals and other church music; symphs.; chamber music, pf. pieces, etc.

Ezio (*Aetius*). Lib. by Metastasio:

Opera by Gluck, prod. Prague, Carnival 1750.

Opera by Handel, prod. London, King's Theatre, Haymarket, 15 Jan 1732.

Opera by Hasse, prod. Dresden, at court, 20 Jan 1755.

Opera by Jommelli, prod. Bologna, Teatro Malvezzi, 29 Apr 1741. Other settings of *Ezio* by Jommelli were prod. Naples, Teatro San Carlo, 4 Nov 1748; Stuttgart, Ducal Theatre, 11 Feb 1759, and Lisbon, Ajuda Theatre, 20 Apr 1772.

F

F, the 4th note, or subdominant, of the scale of C major.

f, the subdominant note in any key in Tonic Sol-fa notation, pronounced Fah.

f (abbr.), the symbol commonly employed in music to indicate a loud (*forte*) tone. Progressively even louder dynamics are marked **ff, fff,** etc.

f Holes (or **ff Holes**), the sound-holes of instruments of the vln. family, so called because of their shape.

FRCO (abbr.) = Fellow of the Royal College of Organists.

Fa, the old name for the note F (*see* **Solmization**), still used in Lat. countries, and in Tonic Sol-fa notation the sub-dominant note in any key represented by the symbol **f,** pronounced Fa.

Fa-La, a light 16th–17th-cent. Eng. comp. for several voices of the ballett type. Its name derives from the syllables to which the refrain was sung.

Faber, Heinrich (b Lichtenfels, before 1500; d Olsnitz, 26 Feb 1552), German theorist and composer, author of a *Compendiolum musicae pro incipientibus* (Brunswick, 1548), which ran into numerous eds. There is some church music to Lat. and Ger. texts.

Fabliau (old Fr. = fable), a Troubadour ballad with narrative words, distinct from the love songs sung by the Troubadours.

Fabri, Annibale Pio (b Bologna, 1697; d Lisbon, 12 Aug 1760), Italian tenor. Pupil of Pistocchi. Sang in Handel's operas in London, 1729–31, and created roles in *Poro* and *Partenope.*

Fabricius, Werner (b Itzehoe, Holstein, 10 Apr 1633; d Leipzig, 9 Jan 1679), German organist and composer. Studied under his father, Albert F., organist at Flensburg and under Selle and Scheidemann at the Hamburg Gymnasium. After pursuing other studies at Leipzig Univ., incl. law, he became music dir. at St Paul's Church there in 1656 and, in addition, at St Nicolas' Church in 1658. He was also public notary.

Works incl. motets, hymn tunes; sacred and secular songs for several voices; suites for viols and other instruments, etc.

Fabritius, Albinus (b Görlitz, after 1550; d ? Bruck an der Murr, 19 Dec 1635), German composer. Wrote motets, 25 of which were pub. in 1595; many of them reissued in var. collections.

Faburden (Eng.). *See* **Fauxbourdon.**

Façade, diversion by Walton (poems by Edith Sitwell), privately prod. London, Chenil Gallery, Chelsea; 1st public perf. London, Aeolian Hall, 12 Jun 1923. 2 concert suites arr. later for enlarged orch. and for pf. duet. Prod. as a ballet (choreography by Frederick Ashton), London, Cambridge Theatre, 26 Apr 1931.

Faccio, Franco (b Verona, 8 Mar 1840; d Monza, 21 Jul 1891), Italian conductor and composer. Studied at the Milan Cons., prod. his 1st opera there and the 2nd at La Scala in 1863. App. prof. of harmony at the Cons. in 1868 and later cond. at the Carcano and Scala theatres. He was Verdi's cond. for *Aida* and *Otello* at Milan, 1872 and 1887. He also cond. the fps of the rev. versions of *Simon Boccanegra* (1881) and *Don Carlos* (1884) and the fp of *La Gioconda* (1876).

Works incl. operas *Le sorelle d'Italia, I profughi fiamminghi, Amleto* (after Shakespeare's *Hamlet*); symph. in F maj.

Fachiri (*née* **d'Aranyi), Adila** (b Budapest, 26 Feb 1886; d Florence, 15 Dec 1962), British violinist of Hungarian birth, a great-niece of Joachim, with whom she studied. She settled in London and appeared frequently as a soloist, often in double concertos with her sister, Jelly d'Aranyi (*q.v.*); they played the Bach concerto for the last time in 1960.

Fackeltanz (Ger.) = Torch Dance.

Fadinho, Fado (Port.), a type of popular song perf. in Port. towns, in the streets and cafés, accomp. by the guitar and enlivened by dancing.

Faenza Codex (Faenza, Bib. Comm., MS. 117), a large MS of keyboard music from the late 14th or early 15th cent., containing ornamented transcriptions of Fr. and It. secular vocal works (incl. some by Machaut and Landini), and some liturgical organ music. The notation is on two staves with regular barring. In the mid-15th cent. parts of the origin. contents were erased by Bonadies to make room for sacred vocal works by himself and others.

Fago, Nicola (b Taranto, 26 Feb 1677; d Naples, 18 Feb 1745), Italian composer, nicknamed Il Tarantino after his birthplace. Educ. at the Cons. della Pietà dei Turchini in Naples. *Maestro di cappella* at the Cons. di S. Onofrio, 1704–8, and at the Cons. della Pietà, 1705–40. His works consist mainly of church music but he also wrote 4 or more operas incl *Radamisto* (1707) and *Cassandra* (1711), oratorios, etc.

Fagott (Ger.) = Bassoon.

Fagotto (It. lit. fagot or bundle) = Bassoon.

Faignient, Noël (b Cambrai), Flemish 16th-cent. composer. From 1561 he lived in Antwerp. Wrote *chansons*, madrigals, songs to Dutch texts, and sacred Lat. works.

Fair Maid of Perth (Bizet). *See* **Jolie Fille de Perth.**

Fair Maid of the Mill (Schubert). *See* **Schöne Müllerin.**

Fair Melusina (Mendelssohn). *See* **Schöne Melusine.**

Fair of Sorotchintsy (Mussorgsky). *See* **Sorotchintsy Fair.**

Fairies, The, opera by John Christopher Smith (lib. by comp., based on Shakespeare's *A Midsummer Night's Dream*), prod. London, Drury Lane, 3 Feb 1755.

Fairy Queen, The, semi-opera by Purcell (lib. adapted from Shakespeare's *A Midsummer Night's Dream* ? by Elkanah Settle), prod. London, Dorset Gardens Theatre, Apr 1692.

Fairy Tale (*Pohádka*), work by Janáček for cello and pf., after the tale *Czar Berendei* by V.A. Zhukovsky, fp Brno, 13 Mar 1910, rev. *c* 1923

Fairy's Kiss, The (*Le Baiser de la fée*) ballet in 4 scenes by Stravinsky, based on songs and pf. pieces by Tchaikovsky, prod. Paris, Opéra, 27 Nov 1927, choreog. by Nijinska. Suite for orch., Divertimento, 1934.

Faisst, Immanuel (Gottlob Friedrich) (b Esslingen nr. Stuttgart, 13 Oct 1823; d Stuttgart, 5 Jun 1894), German organist and composer. Studied theology at Tübingen Univ., but gave it up, on Mendelssohn's advice, for music, in which he was self-taught. He travelled as organist and settled at Stuttgart, where he founded an organ school in 1847 and a society for the study of church music and was one of the founders of the Cons. He wrote on and edited music.

Works incl. cantata *Des Sängers Wiederkehr*, choral setting of Schiller's *Die Macht des Gesanges*; double fugue for pf.; organ works; vocal 4tets.

Falcon, (Marie) Cornélie (b Paris, 28 Jan 1812; d Paris, 25 Feb 1897), French soprano. Student at the Paris Cons. and pupil of Nourrit for operatic acting. 1st appearance 1832, at the Opéra, as Alice in *Robert le Diable*. She created Rachel in *La juive* (1835) and Valentine in *Les Huguenots* (1836). She gave her name to a particular kind of dramatic voice.

Falconieri, Andrea (b Naples, 1586; d Naples, 29 Jul 1656), Italian composer. Lived successively at Parma, Florence, Rome and Modena, and visited Spain. *Maestro di cappella* at Naples from 1650.

Works incl. motets, madrigals, instrumental pieces.

Fall, a Cadence (e.g. 'dying fall' in Shakespeare).

Fall, Leo (b Olomouc, 2 Feb 1873; d Vienna, 16 Sep 1925), Austrian composer. Studied at the Vienna Cons. and became cond. at Berlin, Hamburg and Cologne. Wrote *c* 25 works for the stage, chiefly operettas, incl. *Die Dollarprinzessin* (1907), *Eternal Waltz*, *Die geschiedene Frau* (*The Girl in the Train*), *Der liebe Augustin* (*Princess Caprice*), *Madame Pompadour.*

Falla, Manuel de (b Cádiz, 23 Nov 1876; d Alta Gracia, Argentina, 14 Nov 1946), Spanish composer. Began to study the pf. in Madrid at the age of 8 and prod. a zarzuela, *Los amores de Inés*, written with very little tuition in comp. in 1902. This had no success, and he studied comp. with Pedrell, 1902–4. In 1905 he gained 2 prizes for pf. playing and for his opera *La vida breve*. In 1907–14 he lived in Paris, becoming friendly with Debussy, Ravel and Dukas, but returned to Spain and settled in Madrid on the outbreak of war. The prod. of *La vida breve* at Nice and Paris in 1913 and of the ballet *The Three-cornered Hat* in London in 1919 spread his reputation. In 1921 he moved to Granada and became more exclusively a nationalist comp. again; but had later works perf. in Eng. Paris and NY. During the Span. Civil War he settled in S. Amer. and remained there.

Works incl. operas *La vida breve* (1904–5), *Fuego fatuo* (based on Chopin's music), *El retablo de maese Pedro* (for puppets after Cervantes's *Don Quixote*, 1923)), *L'Atlantida* (posth., completed by Ernesto Halffter, prod. La Scala, Milan, 1962); ballets *El amor brujo* (1915); *El sombrero de tres picos* (The Three-cornered Hat, on Alarcón's story).

INSTRUMENTAL AND SOLO VOCAL: *Noches en los jardines de España* for pf. and orch. (1911–15); *Psyché* for mezzo-soprano, fl., vln., vla., cello and harp (1924); concerto for harpsichord, fl., ob., clar., vln. and cello (1923–6); 4 Span. pieces, *Fantasia baetica* and *Pour le tombeau de Paul Dukas* for pf.; *Homenaje: pour le tombeau de Debussy* for guitar; 3 songs (Gautier), 7 popular Span. songs. *A Cordoba* (Góngora), for voice and harp.

False Relations, the simultaneous or closely adjacent occurrence in a comp. in several parts of 2 notes a semitone apart, at least 1 of which is foreign to the key of the passage in question. They often arise as a result of the independent movement of parts. 16th-cent. and early 17th-cent. comps. readily accepted simultaneous false relations and they were still being used by English composers in the latter half of the 17th cent., partly as a result of tradition and partly as a means of expression.

Falsetto (It.), the tone-prod. of male singers resulting in notes above their normal pitch and sounding like those of an unbroken voice. Falsetto is the voice normally cultivated by male altos.

Falsobordone (It.). *See* **Fauxbourdon.**

Falstaff. *See also* **At the Boar's Head; Lustigen Weiber von Windsor; Sir John in Love.**

Opera by Balfe (lib., in It., by S.M. Maggioni, based on Shakespeare's *Merry Wives of Windsor*), prod. London, Her Majesty's Theatre, 19 Jul 1838.

Opera by Verdi (lib. by Boito, based on Shakespeare's *Merry Wives of Windsor* and *King Henry IV*), prod. Milan, La Scala, 9 Feb 1893.

Symph. study by Elgar, op. 68 (based on Shakespeare's *King Henry IV* & refs. to Falstaff in *King Henry V*), comp. 1913, perf. Leeds Festival, 2 Oct 1913.

Falstaff, ossia Le tre burle (*Falstaff, or The Three Jests*), opera by Salieri (lib. by C.P. Defranceschi, after Shakespeare), prod. Vienna, Kärntnertortheater, 3 Jan 1799.

Fancelli, Giuseppe (b Florence 24 Nov 1833; d Florence, 23 Dec 1887), Italian tenor. Debut Milan 1860, in *Guillaume Tell.* At CG, 1866–72, Alfredo, Pollione and Elvino. In 1872 he was Radames in the 1st It. perf. of *Aida*, at La Scala. Other roles incl. Raoul, Vasco da Gama and Edgardo.

Fanciulla del West, La (*The Girl of the [Golden] West*), opera by Puccini (lib. by G. Civinini and C. Zangarini, based on David Belasco's play), prod. NY Met, 10 Dec 1910.

Fancy, the old Eng. term equivalent to the It. *fantasia,* i.e. a polyphonic comp. for a consort of viols or broken consort or keyboard instrument. Fancies had no definitely determined form, but always made considerable use of counterpoint and were generally divided into a number of sections, played without a break but not thematically connected.

Fandango, a Spanish dance in lively triple time, prob. S. Amer. in origin, with guitar and castanets prominent in the accomp. A slower, Basque, form also exists, which was adopted by Gluck in the ballet *Don Juan,* and subsequently by Mozart in *Figaro.*

Fanfare, a flourish of tpts., in Fr. also a brass band. Fanfares have also been written for other instruments, though usually wind and mainly brass, or imitated in any medium (e.g. strings in Purcell's *Dido and Aeneas* or pf. in Debussy's *Feux d'artifice* prelude). In opera Fanfares have frequently served as an excellent scenic effect (e.g. in Beethoven's *Fidelio,* Bizet's *Carmen,* Verdi's *Otello*).

Faniska, play with music by Cherubini (lib., in Ger., by Josef Sonnleithner), prod. Vienna, Kärntnertortheater, 25 Feb 1806.

Fantaisie, (Fr.), **Fantasia** (It.), **Fantasie** (Ger.) *See* **Fancy; Fantasy.**

Fantasia Concertante on a Theme of Corelli, work for strings by Tippett, based on C.'s Concerto Grosso op. 6 no. 2, comp. 1953 for the tercentenary of his birth. Fp Edinburgh, 29 Aug 1953.

Fantasia Contrappuntistica, work for pf. comp. 1910, with sub-title Grosse Fuge, by Busoni. Based on Contrapunctus XVIII of Bach's *The Art of Fugue* and completes the last unfinished fugue, with extra subject of Busoni's own. Two more versions for solo pf. by 1912 and vers. for 2 pfs. 1921, fp Berlin, 16 Nov 1921.

Fantasia on a Theme by Thomas Tallis, work for double string orch. and string 4tet by Vaughan Williams, based on no. 3 of 9 psalm tunes (1567) by Tallis, fp Gloucester, 6 Sep 1910.

Fantasia on a theme of Handel, work by Tippett for pf. and orch., comp. 1939–41. Fp London, 7 Mar 1942. Written while Tippett was in conflict with war-time government as a conscientious objector: just over a year after the fp he spent 3 months in Wormwood Scrubs prison.

Fantaisies symphoniques, title for Martinů's 6th and last symphony; comp. 1953 to celebrate the 75th anniv. of the founding of the Boston SO. Fp Boston, 12 Jan 1955, cond. Munch.

Fantasiestück (Ger. = Fantastic Piece). A short instrumental piece of a free or fantastic character, rather less extended as a rule than a fantasy and keeping to a single movement and mood, whereas the latter is usually in several connected sections.

Fantastic Symphony (Berlioz). *See* **Symphonie fantastique.**

Fantasy, an instrumental comp. of a free or fantastic character, in no particular form, usually in a number of linked-up but not thematically connected sections. A Fantasy may also be a comp. based on a chosen musical theme from another composer's work, a folksong, a popular tune, an operatic air, etc.

Faramondo, opera by Handel (lib. by A. Zeno, altered), prod. London, King's Theatre, Haymarket, 3 Jan 1738.

Farandole (Fr.), a dance of Provence, prob. of Gk. orig. It is danced by large groups of people in procession through the streets and accomp. by pipe and tabor. The music is in 6–8 time, so that the ex. in Bizet's *Arlésienne* music is not traditionally correct, though very evocative.

Farce (Eng. and Fr., from Lat. *farcire* = to stuff, to lard).In earlier Eng. the verb had the meaning it still has in Fr. of stuffing food with seasoning, and in music it was used for the practice of interpolating words in the *Kyrie eleison*. In 18th-cent. opera, a comic scene introduced into a serious work. Hence a complete comic opera so interpolated, or simply a comic opera in 1 act (It. *farsa*). The modern sense of the term in Eng. (an absurdly comic play) is derived from this.

Farewell, Absence and Return (Beethoven). *See* **Adieux, l'absence et le retour.**

'Farewell' Symphony, nickname of Haydn's symph. no. 45 in F♯ min., comp. in 1772 as a hint to Prince Esterházy that the orch. would welcome leave of absence. In the finale the players leave one by one until only 2 vlns. remain.

Farinelli (real name **Carlo Broschi**) (b Andria, 24 Jan 1705; d Bologna, 15 Jul 1782), Italian male soprano. Pupil of Porpora, in whose *Eumene* he made his debut in Rome in 1721. Sang with great success in many European cities, incl. Vienna and London. In the service of the European court court 1737–59. singing every night in private for Philip V, then Ferdinand VI. Retired to Bologna.

Farkas, Ferenc (b Nagykanizsa, 15 Dec 1905), Hungarian composer. Studied at the Budapest Cons. and with Respighi in Rome. After travelling to enlarge his experience and holding 2 posts at provincial schools of music he became prof. of comp. at the Acad. of Dramatic Art in Budapest in 1948.

Works incl. opera *The Magic Cupboard* (1942); ballet *Three Vagabonds*; incid. music (incl. Shakespeare's *Timon of Athens, As You Like It* and *Romeo and Juliet*); cantata *Fountain of St John*; symph. and other orch. works, chamber music, pf. music, songs.

Farkas, Ödön (b Jászmonostor, 1851; d Kolozsvár, 11 Sep 1912), Hungarian conductor and composer. Studied at the Acad. of Music in Budapest and in 1880 became

director of the Kolozsvár Cons. He had great influence as a teacher.

Works incl. 7 operas, an operetta; church music, choral and orch. works, 5 string 4tets and other chamber music, pf. music, songs.

Farmer, John (b *c* 1570), English 16th–17th-cent composer. He was organist of Christ Church Cathedral at Dublin from 1595 until 1599, when he went to London. He wrote a treatise on the polyphonic setting of plainsong tunes.

Works incl. psalm tunes set for 4 voices contrib. to East's Psalter; madrigals; instrumental pieces.

Farnaby, Giles (b *c* 1565; d London, buried 25 Nov 1640), English composer. He lived in London, where he married in 1587, and took the B.Mus. at Oxford in 1592.

Works incl. 20 canzonets for 4 and 1 for 8 voices, madrigals, psalm tunes set for 4 voices in East's Psalter; over 50 virginal pieces.

Farnaby, Richard (b London, *c* 1594; d ?), English composer, son of prec. In 1608 he became apprentice to Sir Nicholas Saunderson of Fillingham, Lincs.; in 1614 he married. 52 keyboard pieces were incl. in the Fitzwilliam Virginal Book (*q.v.*), compiled by Francis Tregian, who died in 1619.

Farncombe, Charles (b London, 29 Jul 1919), English conductor. Studied in London and in 1955 founded the Handel Opera Society; 1st prod. *Deidemia*, followed by many important revivals, incl. *Alcina, Semele, Rodelinda, Serse* and *Ottone*. He has taken the Soc. to several European festivals, incl. Drottningholm, where he has been music dir. since 1970. Trans. many Handel operas and has perf. them in a style which attempts to recreate 18th-cent. performing practice.

Farquhar, George (1678–1707), Irish dramatist. *See* **Eccles, (J.E.)**(*Stage Coach*), **Finger** (*Sir Harry Wildair*), **Leveridge** (*Constant Couple, Recruiting Officer, Love and a Bottle*), **Purcell (D.)** (*Beaux's Stratagem, Constant Couple, Inconstant*).

Farrant, John, English organist and composer. Organist of Ely Cathedral from 1567 to 1572, when he married Margaret Andras at Salisbury, where he became lay clerk and choirmaster at the cathedral. In 1587 he was app. organist but he was expelled in 1592 for an attack made on the dean. He then became organist of Hereford Cathedral, but lost that post too in 1593 because of his ungovernable temper. Wrote church music.

Farrant, John, (b Salisbury, 28 Sep 1575; d Salisbury, 1618), English organist and composer, son of prec. He became a choirboy at the cathedral under his father, and later organist, holding the post in 1598–1606 and 1611–16, prob. without any interruption between. Wrote church music.

Farrant, Richard (b c 1530; d London, 30 Nov 1580), English organist and composer. Gentleman of the Chapel Royal in London until 1564, when he became organist and choirmaster at St George's Chapel, Windsor. Also wrote music for the Blackfriar's theatre, London.

Works incl. Service in A min. (usually sung in G min.), anthems *Call to remembrance* and *Hide not Thou Thy face* and other church music, songs for plays prod. by him with the choir-boys before Queen Elizabeth; keyboard pieces in the Mulliner Book (*q.v.*).

Farrar, Geraldine (b Melrose, Mass., 28 Feb 1882; d Ridgefield, Conn., 11 Mar 1967), American soprano. Studied first in Boston and later in Paris and Berlin, making her debut in 1901. From 1906 to 1922 she sang at the NY Met, created Puccini's Suor Angelica there in 1918. On retiring from the stage became a concert singer. Her most famous role was that of Madame Butterfly.

Farrell, Eileen (b Willimantic, Conn., 13 Feb 1920), American soprano. She sang in concert and on radio from 1942 until her stage debut at Tampa in 1956, as Santuzza: she had already sung Berg's Marie and Cherubini's Medea in NY concert perfs. At Chicago she was heard as the *Trovatore* Leonora, in 1958. NY Met 1960, as Alceste. She also sang Brünnhilde and Isolde, in concert perfs. under Bernstein.

Farsa (or **Farsa per musica**) (It. = farce [for music]), an It. term of the early 19th cent. for a type of comic opera in 1 act, e.g. Rossini's *La cambiale di matrimonio.*

Farthyng, Thomas (d ? Dec 1520), English 15th–16th-cent. composer. At King's Coll., Cambridge as chorister, 1477–83, and as clerk, 1493–9. At the Chapel Royal, 1511–20. Wrote church music and secular songs.

Farwell, Arthur (b St Paul, 23 Apr 1872; d New York, 20 Jan 1952), American composer and educationist. Studied engineering, but afterwards went to Ger. as a pupil of Humperdinck and Pfitzner and to Guilmant in Paris. On returning to USA in 1899 he began to collect Indian folk music, and became a music lecturer, critic and pub. Prof. in the music dept. of the Michigan State Coll., 1927–39.

Works incl. masque *Caliban* for the Shakespeare tercentenary (1916), symph., Symbolistic Studies (no. 3 based on Whit-

man), suite *The Gods of the Mountain* (1928), *Prelude to a Spiritual Drama* and other orch. works; symph. song suite *Mountain Song* and other choral works; string 4tet, pf. 5tet; sonatas for vln. solo and for vln. and pf.; vln. pieces; pf. works.

Fasano, Renato (b Naples, 21 Aug 1902; d Rome, 3 Aug 1979), Italian composer and conductor. He studied in Naples and in 1948 founded the Collegium Musicum Italicum: in 1952 and 1957 this ens. developed into 2 groups ded. to the perf. of 18th-cent. It. music: I Virtuosi di Roma and Piccolo Teatro Musicale Italiano. The latter group toured in Europe and US with operas by Paisiello, Pergolesi and Galuppi. Fasano was dir. of the Rome Cons. 1960–72 and from 1972 was responsible for a complete ed. of the sacred works of Vivaldi.

Fasch, Carl Friedrich (Christian) (b Zerbst, 18 Nov 1736; d Berlin, 3 Aug 1800), German harpsichordist and composer. Pupil of his father and later of Hertel at Strelitz. App. 2nd harpsichordist (with C.P.E. Bach) to the court of Frederick the Great in 1756, but the outbreak of the Seven Years War (1756–63) cost him his position and forced him to live by teaching. Cond. of the court opera in Berlin 1774–6. In 1791 he founded the Berlin *Singakademie*, the choral society which he cond. until his death.

Works incl. oratorio *Giuseppe riconosciuto* (1774), Mass for 16 voices, cantatas, psalms and other church music; also some instrumental music.

Fasch, Johann Friedrich (b Büttelstedt nr. Weimar, 15 Apr 1688; d Zerbst, 5 Dec 1758), German organist and composer; father of prec. Pupil of Kuhnau at St Thomas's School, Leipzig. He founded the 'Collegium musicum' at Leipzig, travelled after 1714, held various posts at Gera, Greitz and in the service of Count Morzin at Lukaveč, Bohemia, and in 1722 was app. *Kapellmeister* at Zerbst.

Works incl. 4 operas e.g. *Die getreue Dido* (1712); Masses, a Requiem, church cantatas, motets, a Passion; overtures; trios, sonatas, etc.

Fasolo, Giovanni Battista (b Asti, c 1600; d ? Sicily, after 1659), Italian 17th-cent. monk, organist and composer. He became a Franciscan c 1645 and in 1659 was app. *maestro di cappella* to the Archbishop of Monreale at Palermo.

Works incl. *Arie spirituali*, cantatas, ariettas, sacred and secular songs; organ works; guitar pieces.

Fassbaender, Brigitte (b Berlin, 3 Jul

1939), German mezzo, daughter of Willi Domgraf-Fassbaender. She studied at the Nuremberg Cons. and made her debut in Munich, 1961, as Nicklaus; other roles have been Sextus, Eboli, Marina and the Countess Geschwitz. Salzburg 1970, Dorabella; Easter Festival 1973, as Fricka. Octavian was the role of her CG (1971) and NY Met (1974) debuts, and she is well-known as Carmen and Charlotte. Also successful as a concert singer (*Das Lied von der Erde*).

Fassbender, Zdenka (b Tetschen, 12 Dec 1879; d Munich, 14 Mar 1954), Czech soprano. She sang Halévy's Rachel at Karlsruhe in 1899. Munich 1906–32, as Elektra, Tosca and the Marschallin; at first with her husband, Felix Mottl. In 1913 she sang Isolde at CG, under Beecham.

Faun and Shepherdess, song-suite for mezzo and orch. by Stravinsky (text by Pushkin); comp. 1906, fp St Petersburg, 4 Feb 1908; in the same concert the Eb symph., ded. to Rimsky-Korsakov, was given its fp.

Fauré, Gabriel (Urbain) (b Pamiers nr. Foix, 12 May 1845; d Paris, 4 Nov 1924), French composer. Studied at Niedermeyer's school of music in Paris, 1854–66, and became church organist at Rennes in the latter year. Returned to Paris in 1870, became organist 1st at Saint-Sulpice and then at Saint-Honoré, and choirmaster at the Madeleine in 1877, being app. organist there in 1896, a post he held until 1905, when he became dir. of the Cons., where he had been prof. since 1896. He resigned in 1920. He had many distinguished comp. pupils.

Works incl. STAGE: music-drama *Prométhée* (1900), opera *Pénélope* (1913); incid. music *Caligula* (Dumas), *Shylock* (*Merchant of Venice*: Shakespeare), *La Voix du bonheur* (G. Clemenceau), *Pelléas et Mélisande* (Maeterlinck, 1898); ORCH: *Pavane*, suite *Masques et bergamasques* (1919); symph. (unpub.); *Ballade & Fantaisie* for pf. and orch.; *Romance* for vln. and orch.

CHAMBER: 2 pf. 5tets (D min., C min.), 2 pf. 4tets (C min, G min.); string 4tet; pf. trio; 2 sonatas for vln. and pf. (A maj., E min.), 2 sonatas for cello and pf.; pieces for vln. and pf., cello and pf. and fl. and pf.

VOCAL: *Cantique de Racine* and *Les Djinns* (Hugo) for chorus and orch.; *La Naissance de Vénus* for solo voices, chorus and orch.; *Madrigal* for vocal 4tet; Requiem for solo voices, chorus and orch. (1887–90); *Messe basse* for fem. voices and org.; 11 misc. religious vocal pieces.

SOLO PIANO: 34 op. nos. of pf. music incl. 3 *Romances sans paroles*, 5 Impromptus, 13 Barcarolles, 4 Valses-caprices, 8 Nocturnes, Theme and Variations, 8 *Pièces brèves*, 9 Preludes; *Dolly*, 6 pieces for pf. duet.

SOLO VOCAL: 96 songs incl. cycles *Poème d'un jour*, 5 *Mélodies de Verlaine*, *La Bonne Chanson* (Verlaine), *La Chanson d'Eve* (Charles van Lerberghe), *Le Jardin clos* (do.), *Mirages*, *L'Horizon chimérique*.

Faure, Jean-Baptiste (b Moulins, 15 Jan 1830; d Paris, 9 Nov 1914), French baritone. Studied at the Paris Cons. Made his 1st appearance at the Opéra-Comique in 1852 and from 1861 was attached for many years to the Opéra, where he created Nelusko in *L'Africaine*, Posa in *Don Carlos* and Thomas' Hamlet. London, CG, 1860–3.

Faust. See also **Adam (A.)** (ballet), **Arnold (S.)** (Dr. Faustus), **Bentzon** (*Faust III*), **Damnation de Faust** (Berlioz), **Doktor Faust** (Busoni), **Goethe**, **Mefistofele** (Boito), **Pousseur** (*Votre Faust*), **Reutter (H.)** (*Doktor F.*), **Szenen aus Goethes 'Faust'** (Schumann).

Episodes from Lenau's *Faust*: 2 orch. pieces by Liszt, *Night Procession* and *Dance in the Village Inn* (1st *Mephisto Waltz*), comp. c 1860, fp Weimar, 8 Mar 1861.

Opera by Gounod (lib. by J. Barbier and M. Carré, based on Goethe's drama), prod. Paris, Théâtre Lyrique, 19 Mar 1859.

Opera by Spohr (lib. by J.K. Bernard, founded on the Faust legend without ref. to Goethe's work, not completed at that time), prod. Prague, 1 Sep 1816. Rev. without spoken dialogue in 1852 and prod. London, CG, 4 Apr 1852.

Opera by Zöllner (lib. by comp., based on Goethe's drama), prod. Munich, 19 Oct 1887.

Overture by Wagner, not for Goethe's drama, but a kind of symph. poem on it, comp. Paris, 1839–40 after hearing Beethoven's symphs. at the Cons.; fp Dresden, 22 Jul 1844; rewritten 1854–5 and perf. at Zurich, 23 Jan 1855.

Faust-Symphonie, Eine, symph. by Liszt, based on Goethe's drama, 'in 3 character pictures': 1. *Faust*; 2. *Gretchen*; 3. *Mephistopheles*, with final chorus 'Alles Vergängliche ist nur ein Gleichnis'; finished without the chorus, 19 Oct 1854, chorus added 1857 and revised 1880; fp Weimar, Court Theatre, 5 Sep 1857, on the occasion of the unveiling of the Goethe-Schiller monument. The work is ded. to Berlioz. It was perf. at Bayreuth (cond. Barenboim) on the cent. of Liszt's death, 31 Jul 1986.

Fausta (i.e. Empress F., wife of Constantine I), opera by Donizetti (lib. by D. Gilardoni), prod. Naples, Teatro San Carlo, 12 Jan 1832.

Fausto (*Faust*), opera by Louise Angélique Bertin (1805–77) (lib. in It., by comp., based on Goethe's drama), prod. Paris, Théâtre Italien, 8 Mar 1831. The 1st *Faust* opera and the only one by a woman. Bertin was the sister of Berlioz's ed. of the *Journal des Débats*: Berlioz may have had a hand in the work; at any rate he probably suggested the subject.

Fauvel, Roman de, a satirical poem written in two parts (1310 and 1314) by Gervais de Bus. One MS. (Paris, Bibl. Nat., fr. 146) incorporates musical interpolations by Chaillou de Pesstain in 1316. The most important of these are 33 motets in 2 and 3 parts, but there are numerous other pieces, sacred and secular, polyphonic and monophonic. The collection is important as an anthology of music stretching back over a century (with many pieces newly adapted) and as the earliest source of works by Philippe de Vitry and his generation.

Faux Lord, Le (*The False Lord*), opera by Piccinni (lib. by G.M. Piccinni, the comp's son), prod. Paris, Comédie-Italienne, 6 Dec 1783.

Fauxbourdon (Fr.), **Faburden** (Eng.), **Falsobordone** (It.), lit. 'false bass', name given to a wide variety of technical procedures in the 15th–16th cents., usually involving improvisation. As originally used by Dufay and others, the term implied the use of chains of 6–3 chords, the middle part being 'improvised' by doubling the top part a 4th lower throughout; later, different techniques were employed to achieve the same effect. The Eng. used their version of the word for a similar process, the 3 parts being improvised straight from plainsong (at first in the middle, later in the top part). The fauxbourdon itself (i.e. the lowest part) was also used as the basis of entirely new compositions.

In the later 15th and early 16th cents. the use of the term in both France and England was enormously extended to include techniques in which the idea of 6–3 chords was entirely lost. It is to this final stage in its hist. that the It. use of the term belongs, meaning initially a kind of fauxbourdon in 4 parts with the 'true' bass supplied beneath the false one, and ultimately nothing more than simple declamatory comp. in note-against-note style.

Favart, Charles Simon (1710–92). French playwright and librettist. *See* **Bastien und Bastienne** (Mozart), **Cythère assiégée** (Gluck), **Lottchen am Hofe** (J.A. Hiller), **Moissonneurs** (Duni), **Rosina** (Shield), **Süssmayr** (*Soliman II*).

Favart (*née* Duronceray), **Marie Justine Benoîte** (b Avignon, 15 Jun 1727; d Paris, 21 Apr 1772), French dancer, actress and singer, wife of prec. After making her debut as a dancer in 1744, she married Favart in 1745 and in 1751 joined the Comédie-Italienne. In 1753 she appeared in her own *Bastien et Bastienne* (the direct model for Mozart's little opera), a parody of Rousseau's *Devin du village* with popular tunes in the style of a ballad opera.

Favero, Mafalda (b Ferrara, 6 Jan 1903; d Milan, 3 Sep 1981), Italian soprano. Debut Cremona 1925, Lola. She sang Liù at Parma in 1927 and in 1929 Eva at La Scala, under Toscanini; returned until 1950 as Manon, Mimi, Thaïs and in the fps of works by Lattuada and Wolf-Ferrari. CG 1937–9, NY Met 1938. Sang in concert from 1950.

Favola d'Orfeo, La (*The Story of Orpheus*), opera by Casella (lib. by C. Pavolini, after A. Ambrogini = Poliziano (1454–1494), prod. Mantua, ducal court, 18 Jul 1472, prod. Venice, Teatro Goldoni, 6 Sep 1932.

Opera by Monteverdi (lib. by A. Striggio), prod. Mantua, at the court of the Hereditary Prince Francesco Gonzaga, Carnival 1607.

Favola per musica (It. = story for music), an early It. term for opera of a legendary or mythological character; actually a story of that kind in dramatic form written for the purpose of being set to music.

Favorite, La, opera by Donizetti (lib., in Fr., by A. Royer and G. Vaëz, with Scribe's assistance), prod. Paris, Opéra, 2 Dec 1840.

Faydit, Gaucelm (b Uzerche, Limousin, *c* 1150; d *c* 1216), French troubadour. He went to the Holy Land with Richard Cœur de Lion.

Fayrfax, Robert (b Deeping Gate, Lincs., 23 Apr 1464; d St Albans, 24 Oct 1521), English composer. Lived for a time (?) at Bayford, Herts., and became organist and choirmaster at St Albans Cathedral before 1502. He took the D.Mus. degree at Oxford in 1504 for his Mass *O quam glorifica*; doctorate of music 1511. On the accession of Henry VIII in 1509 he was a Gentleman of the Chapel Royal, with which he attended at the Field of the Cloth of Gold in 1520.

Works incl. 6 Masses, motets, 2 Magnificats, *Stabat Mater*; songs for several voices, etc.

Feast at Solhaug, The, incid. music for Ibsen's play by H. Wolf for a prod. of a Ger. trans. by Emma Klingenfeld, Vienna, 21 Nov 1891.

Fedé, Jehan (b Douai, *c* 1415; d ?Paris ? 1477), French composer. He was vicar of Douai, 1439–40, a papal singer, 1443–5; at the Sainte Chapelle, 1449; at the court of Charles VII, 1452–3; at St Peter's Rome, 1466; and a member of Louis XI's chapel, 1473–4. He wrote sacred and secular music.

Fedele. *See* **Treu, Daniel Gottlieb.**

Fedeltà premiata, La, dramma pastorale giocoso by Haydn (lib. by G. Lorenzi), perf. Eszterháza, 25 Feb 1781; successfully revived in recent years at the Camden and Glyndebourne Festivals.

Fedora, opera by Giordano (lib. by A. Colautti, based on Sardou's play), prod. Milan, Teatro Lirico, 17 Nov 1898.

Fedra (*Phaedra*), opera by Pizzetti (lib. G. d'Annunzio's tragedy), prod. Milan, La Scala, 20 Mar 1915.

Opera by R. Romani (lib. A. Lenzoni), prod. Rome, Teatro Costanzi, 3 Apr 1915.

Fée Urgèle, La, ou Ce qui plaît aux dames (*The Fairy U., or What Pleases the Ladies*), opera by Duni (lib. by C.S. Favart, based on a story by Voltaire founded on Chaucer's *Tale of the Wife of Bath*), prod. Fontainebleau, at court, 26 Oct 1765; fp Paris, Comédie-Italienne, 4 Dec 1765.

Feen, Die (*The Fairies*), opera by Wagner (lib. by comp., based on Gozzi's comedy, *La Donna serpente*), comp. 1833 and not staged in Wagner's lifetime; prod. Munich, 29 Jun 1888; rehearsed by Richard Strauss, who was not allowed to cond. the perf. Dramatic ideas from *Die Feen* are developed in Strauss's opera *Die Frau ohne Schatten* (1919).

Feinhals, Fritz (b Cologne, 14 Dec 1869; d Munich, 30 Aug 1940), German baritone. After engagements in Essen and Mainz he sang at Munich 1898–1927; took part in the fp of Pfitzner's *Palestrina* there, 1917. CG 1898 and 1907; 1908 at the NY Met, in the 1st US perf. of *Tiefland*. He sang in operas by Verdi but was best known as Sachs; also appeared as Telramund, Amfortas and Wotan.

Fel, Marie (b Bordeaux, 24 Oct 1713; d Chaillot nr. Paris, 2 Feb 1794), French soprano. Made her 1st appearance at the Paris Opéra and at the Concert spirituel in 1734. She sang in the fps of Rameau's *Castor et Pollux* (both versions), *Les fêtes d'Hébé*, *Dardanus*, *Zaïs*, *Naïs*, *Zoroastre* and *Acante et Céphise*.

Felciano, Richard (b Santa Rosa, 7 Dec 1930), American composer. Studied with Milhaud and Dallapiccola; has worked at Univ. of Calif. at Berkeley. Works incl. opera

Sir Gawain and the Green Knight (1964); *Mutations* for orch. (1966), *Orchestra* (1980).

Feldman, Morton (b New York, 12 Jan 1926; d Buffalo, NY, 3 Sep 1987), American composer. Studied with Stefan Wolpe and Wallingford Riegger. Influenced by abstract expressionist painting, he intro. the element of chance into his music, indicating often only an approximation of what is to be played.

Works incl. *Durations I–V* (1960–1); *Extensions I–V* (1951–60); *Vertical Thoughts I–V* (1963); *Two Instruments* for cello and horn; *For Franz Kline* for soprano, vln., cello, horn, chimes and pf.; *De Kooning* for pf., cello, vln., horn and perc. (1963); ballet *Ixion*; *The Swallows of Salangan* for chorus and 76 instruments; *The Viola in my Life*, *I–IV* (1970–1); *The Rothko Chapel* for viola, chorus & perc. (1972); *Neither*, monodrama to text by Beckett for sop. and orch. (1977).

Feldpartie or Feldpartita (Ger. lit. field suite), an old Ger. term for suites written for wind instruments and played in the open on military or war-like occasions.

Felis, Stefano (b Bari, *c* 1550; d ? Bari, after 1603), Italian composer. Wrote Masses, motets, madrigals, *villanelle*.

Félix, ou L'Enfant trouvé (*Felix, or The Foundling*), opera by Monsigny (lib. by J.M. Sedaine), prod. Fontainebleau, at court, 10 Nov 1777; 1st Paris perf., Comédie-Italienne, 24 Nov 1777. Monsigny's last opera.

Félix, Benedict (b Budapest, 28 Sep 1860; d Vienna, 2 Mar 1912), Hungarian bass. He sang at the Karltheater, Vienna, in 1880 and at the Hofoper from 1882. Successful until his death in buffo roles, partic. as Dulcamara, but from 1897 suffered from the tyranny of the Hofoper's dir., Gustav Mahler. Other roles incl. Beckmesser, the Herald in *Lohengrin* and Johann in the fp of *Werther* (1892).

Fellowes, Edmund H(orace) (b London, 11 Nov 1870; d Windsor, 21 Dec 1951), English clergyman and musicologist. Educ. at Winchester Coll. and Oxford. Attached to St George's Chapel, Windsor, as minor canon from 1900. Hon. Mus.D., Dublin, 1917 and Oxford, 1938. Author of books on the English madrigal, Byrd and O. Gibbons; ed. of *The Eng. Madrigal School*, English lutenist songs, Byrd's works and co-ed of *Tudor Church Music*.

Felsenstein, Walter (b Vienna, 30 May 1901; d Berlin, 8 Oct 1975), Austrian opera producer. He studied in Graz and Vienna; worked in Cologne, Frankfurt and Zurich before moving to the Komische Oper, Berlin, in 1947 as dir. Gained wide recognition for his realistic and minutely rehearsed prods. of *Carmen, The Cunning Little Vixen* and *Otello*. Those who worked with him incl. Götz Friedrich and Joachim Herz.

Felsztynski, Sebastian (b Felsztyn nr. Przemysl, *c* 1490; d *c* 1544), Polish composer. Studied at Kraków Univ. He compiled a hymn-book for Sigismund I in 1522. Wrote church music.

Felton, William (b Drayton, 1715; d Hereford, 6 Dec 1769), English organist and composer. Educ. at Manchester and Cambridge, he became a clergyman, vicar-choral and later minor canon at Hereford Cathedral. He became famous as perf. on the organ and harpsichord, for which he wrote concertos and lessons. The celebrated *Felton's Gavotte* was a set of variations in one of the concertos.

Feminine Cadence, a cadence in which the conclusive tonic chord is reached on a weak beat of the bar.

Fenby, Eric (William) (b Scarborough, 22 Apr 1906), English composer. Became an organist at the age of 12 and studied music with A.E. Keeton. From 1928–34 he acted voluntarily as amanuensis to Delius, who was living blind and paralysed at Grez-sur-Loing, and helped him to commit *Songs of Farewell, A Song of Summer* and other late works to paper.

Works incl. symph., overture *Rossini on Ilkla Moor*, etc. He pub. a memoir, *Delius as I knew him*, in 1936.

Fennimore und Gerda, opera by Delius (lib., in Ger., by comp., based on P. Jacobsen's novel *Niels Lyhne*), prod. Frankfurt, 21 Oct 1919.

Fenton (real name Beswick), Lavinia (b London, 1708; d Greenwich, 24 Jan 1760), English soprano and actress. Made her 1st appearance at the King's Theatre in London in 1726 and was the 1st Polly in *The Beggar's Opera* in 1728. She retired at the end of the season and became the mistress of the Duke of Bolton, who married her on the death of his wife in 1751.

Feo, Francesco (b Naples, 1691; d Naples, 28 Jan 1761), Italian composer. Pupil of Gizzi and Fago at the Cons. della Pietà della Turchini in Naples, and later of Pitoni in Rome. Prod. his first opera, *L'amor tirannico*, in Naples, 1713. *Maestro di cappella* of the Cons. St Onofrio, 1723–8, and of the Cons. dei Poveri, 1739–43. Jommelli and

Pergolesi were among his pupils.

Works incl. operas *Siface* (1723), *Ipermestra, Arianna* (1728), *Andromaca* (1730), *Arsace* (1740) and others; Masses and other church music.

Feragut (or Feraguti), Beltrame (or Bertrand) (b Avignon, *c* 1385; d *c* 1450 ?), French composer who travelled in France and It. His motet *Excelsa civitas Vincencia* was written in honour of a new bishop of Vicenza, Francesco Malipiero, in 1433. A few other sacred works survive.

Feramors, opera by A. Rubinstein (lib. in Ger., by J. Rodenberg, based on Moore's *Lalla Rookh*), prod. Dresden, 24 Feb 1863.

Ferber, Albert (b Lucerne, 29 Mar 1911; d London, 11 Jan 1987), Swiss pianist. He studied with Gieseking and Marguerite Long. Toured widely and appeared with most leading orchs. His repertory was broad, but he often played Fauré, Debussy and Mozart. Resident in England from 1938.

Ferencsik, János (b Budapest, 18 Jan 1907; d Budapest, 12 Jun 1984), Hungarian conductor. He studied in Budapest and in 1953 became music dir. of the Opera and chief cond. of the Hungarian Nat. PO; in 1963 and 1973 brought the Opera Co. to Edinburgh for perfs. of Bartók's *Bluebeard's Castle*. US debut 1962 and cond. in Vienna, London and Salzburg.

Ferguson, Howard (b Belfast, 21 Oct 1908), Irish composer and pianist. Educ. at Westminster School and the RCM in London as a pupil of R.O. Morris.

Works incl. ballet *Chaunteclear* (1948); partita and 4 *Diversions on Ulster Airs* for orch.; concerto for pf. and strings (1951); octet; 2 vln. and pf. sonatas, 4 pieces for clar. and pf.; sonata and 5 bagatelles for pf.; 2 ballads for baritone and orch.; 3 *Medieval Carols* for voice and pf.

Fermata (It.) = pause, indicated by the sign ⌒, prolonging a note or rest beyond its normal length. For very short pauses a square sign was invented by Vincent d'Indy, but this device never found general acceptance.

In *da capo* arias the fermata sign over the final chord of the 1st section indicates where the aria is to end after the repeat.

In a chorale, or a chorale prelude, it indicates the end of a line.

Fernand Cortez, ou La Conquête de Mexique (*Hernán Cortés, or The Conquest of Mexico*), opera by Spontini (lib. by J.A. Esménard and V.J.E. de Jouy, based on a tragedy by Piron), prod. Paris, Opéra, 28 Nov 1809.

Fernando, operetta by Schubert (lib. by A. Stadler), comp. 1815; never perf. in Schubert's lifetime; prod. Magdeburg, 18 Aug 1918 (concert perf. Vienna, 1905).

Ferne Klang, Der (*The Distant Sound*), opera by Schreker (lib. by comp.), prod. Frankfurt, 18 Aug 1912.

Ferneyhough, Brian (b Coventry, 16 Jan 1943), English composer. He studied in Birmingham and with Lennox Berkeley at the RAM; further study in Amsterdam and with Klaus Huber in Basle. Since 1971 has taught at the Frankfurt Hochschule and lectured at Darmstadt. His music is of the advanced avant garde, incl. electronic devices.

Works incl. *Prometheus* for wind 6tet (1967), *Sonatas* for string 4tet, *Epicycle* for 20 strings (1969), *Missa Brevis* for 12 voices (1971), *Firecycle Beta* for orch. with 5 conds. (1971), *Sieben Sterne* for organ, *Transit* for 6 voices and chamber orch. (1975), *La Terre est un homme* for orch. (1978), *Funerailles* for strings and harp (2 versions), String 4tet no. 2 (1980), *Carceri d'Invenzione*, for chamber ens. (1982), for fl. and chamber orch. (1984), *Études transcendantales* for voices and ens. (1984).

Ferrabosco, English family of musicians, later members:

1. Alfonso F. (b ? Greenwich, c 1610, d ? London, before 1660), son of Alfonso, jun. Violist and wind player at court.

2. Henry F. (b ? Greenwich, c 1615; d ? Jamaica, c 1658), brother of prec. Succeeded his father as comp. to the King's Music.

3. John F. (b ? Greenwich, bap. 9 Oct 1626; d London, buried 15 Oct 1682), brother of prec. Wind player at court; app. organist at Ely Cathedral in 1662. Wrote services and anthems.

4. Elizabeth F. (b Greenwich, 1640), singer, daughter of 1.

Ferrabosco, Alfonso (b Bologna, bap. 18 Jan 1543; d Bologna, 12 Aug 1588), Italian composer. Settled in London before 1562; left the service of Queen Elizabeth in 1569, after becoming involved in a murder case, and returned to It. on leave, which he extended until 1572. In 1578 he left Eng. for good and entered the service of the Duke of Savoy at Turin. Many of his works appear in *Musica Transalpina*.

Works incl. motets, madrigals, etc.

Ferrabosco, Alfonso (b Greenwich, c 1575; d Greenwich, buried 11 Mar 1628), English composer of Italian descent, son of prec. He was left behind, being prob. illegitimate, when his father left Eng. in 1578. Trained in music at Queen Elizabeth's expense, he became one of James I's court musicians; succeeded Coprario as comp. to the King's Music in 1626.

Works incl. songs for masques (Ben Jonson) *The Masque of Blackness, Hymenaei, The Masque of Beauty, The Hue and Cry after Cupid, The Masque of Queens, Love freed from Ignorance and Folly*; fancies for viols; lessons for lyra viol; ayres with lute and bass viol.; contribs. to Leighton's *Teares or Lamentacions*.

Ferrabosco, Domenico Maria (b Bologna, 14 Nov 1513; d Bologna, Feb 1574), Italian composer, grandfather of prec. *Maestro di cappella* of the church of San Petronio at Bologna from 1547. App. to a similar post at the Vatican basilica in Rome, c 1548, was a singer in the Papal Chapel there, 1550–5; sacked for taking a wife.

Works incl. motets, madrigals.

Ferrani, Cesira (b Turin, 8 May 1863; d Pollone, nr. Biella, 4 May 1943), Italian soprano. Debut Turin 1887, Gilda. She was well known in operas by Puccini and created Manon Lescaut (1893) and Mimi (1896); sang at La Scala 1894–1911 and as guest in Spain, Russia and Egypt. Successful as Elsa and Elisabeth and chosen by Toscanini to be the 1st Mélisande in Italy (La Scala 1908).

Ferrarese del Bene (*née* Gabrieli), **Adrianna** (b Ferrara, c 1755; d ? Venice, after 1798), Italian soprano. Pupil of the Ospedaletto at Venice, married to one Del Bene and called La Ferrarese. Appeared in London in 1785–6 and in Vienna in 1788–91, debut in Martín y Soler's *L'arbore di Diana*; later in operas by Salieri, Guglielmi and Paisiello. The first Fiordiligi in Mozart's *Così fan tutte*, 1790. In the 1789 revival of *Figaro* she sang Susanna: Mozart replaced her 2 arias with K579 and K577.

Ferrari, Benedetto (b Reggio, c 1597; d Modena, 22 Oct 1681), Italian theorist, playwright and composer. Lived at Venice, where he began to prod. music dramas with words and music of his own in 1637. In 1645 he went to the court of Modena, where he remained until 1662, except for a visit to Vienna in 1651–3. He was then dismissed, but app. again in 1674. He may have comp. the duet at the end of Monteverdi's *L'incoronazione di Poppea*.

Works incl. operas *Armida* (1639), *La ninfa avara* (1641), *Il pastor regio* (1640), *Proserpina rapita* and others; oratorio *Sansone*; 3 books of *Musiche varie a voce sola.*

Ferrari, Domenico (b Piacenza, c 1722; d Paris, 1780), Italian violinist. Pupil of

Tartini. Won great acclaim on concert tours as one of the leading players of his time. Worked in Vienna and Stuttgart, and finally settled in Paris. Pub. 36 vln. sonatas, trio sonatas.

Ferrari-Fontana, Edoardo (b Rome, 8 Jul 1878; d Toronto, 4 Jul 1936), Italian tenor. After work in the diplomatic service he was encouraged to study by Serafin and sang Tristan at Turin in 1909. He took part in the 1913 fp of *L'amore dei tre re*, at La Scala, and at Beunos Aires sang Siegmund, Siegfried and Tannhäuser. He appeard in Boston, NY and Chicago 1913–16. Taught in Toronto from 1926.

Ferraris, Ines-Maria (b Bologna, 1882; d Milan, 11 Dec 1971), Italian soprano. Debut Bologna 1908, in *Mignon*. Cimarosa's Carolina at La Scala and the 1st Italian Sophie, in *Rosenkavalier* (both 1911). Sang in Buenos Aires, and in 1917 created Puccini's Lisette (*La Rondine*, Monte Carlo); remained at La Scala until 1934, often in operas by Verdi.

Ferras, Christian (b Le Touquet, 17 Jun 1933; d Paris, 15 Sep 1982), French violinist. He studied in Nice and Paris and made his debut in 1946 and in 1948 won the Marguerite Long-Jacques Thibaud Comp., Brussels. Many tours of Europe and the US: often heard in the Berg and Brahms concertos.

Ferreira, Manuel (d ? Madrid, 1797), Spanish composer and conductor. Attached to a Madrid theatre for which he wrote incid. music for plays and light operas which are early exs. of *tonadillas*.

Works incl. opera *El mayor triunfo de la mayor guerra*, numerous light operas, incid. music to plays by Calderón, Moreto, etc., incl. Antonio de Zamora's Don Juan play.

Ferretti, Giovanni (b c 1540; d Loreto, after 1609), Italian composer and priest. He was *maestro di capella* at Ancona Cathedral from 1575; then worked at the Santa Casa in Loreto. Apart from a few sacred works, he specialized in the lighter types of madrigal, publishing 5 books of *Canzoni alla Napolitana* (1573–1585).

Ferri, Baldassare (b Perugia, 9 Dec 1610; d Perugia, 18 Nov 1680), Italian castrato. In 1625 he went to the court of Pol. and later to that of the Emperors Ferdinand III and Leopold I.

Ferrier, Kathleen (b Higher Walton, Lancs., 22 Apr 1912; d London, 8 Oct 1953), English contralto. Studying the pf. at 1st and taking a diploma for it, she turned to singing in 1940 and sang in factories during the war. Made her operatic debut in the fp of Britten's *Rape of Lucretia* at Glyndebourne in 1946 and sang Gluck's Orpheus there and in Amsterdam and USA. She toured very extensively, sang at the Edinburgh and Salzburg Festivals, and gave song recitals accomp. by Bruno Walter. She was admired in *Das Lied von der Erde* and sang in the 1st Brit. perf. of Mahler's 3rd symph. (London, 1947). Received the CBE and sang in *Orfeo* again at CG on 20 Feb 1953, but was by then so ill that she had to withdraw.

Fervaal, opera by d'Indy (lib. by comp., based on and altered from Tegnér's *Axel*), prod. Brussels, Théâtre de la Monnaie, 12 Mar 1897.

Fesca, Friedrich Ernst (b Magdeburg, 15 Feb 1789; d Karlsruhe, 24 May 1826), German violinist and composer ? of Italian descent.

Works incl. operas *Cantemira* and *Leila*; *De profundis*; 3 symphs; 19 string 4tets.

Fesch, Willem de (b Alkmaar, 25 Aug 1687; d London, 3 Jan 1761), Dutch violinist and composer. *Maître de chapelle* at Antwerp Cathedral 1725–30, settled in London 1732, where he became known as a vln. teacher and comp. of oratorios.

Works incl. operetta *The London 'Prentice*, serenata *Love and Friendship*; oratorios *Judith* (1733) and *Joseph* (1745); sonatas for cello(s) and a large quantity of other chamber music.

Festa, Costanzo (b Piedmont, c 1490; d Rome, 10 Apr 1545), Italian composer. He prob. studied with Mouton in Paris, then became a member of the Papal choir in Rome, 1517, and later *maestro di cappella* at the Vatican. Comp. 4 Masses, 13 Magnificats, Litanies, 40 motets, Te Deum; madrigals.

Festa teatrale (It. = theatrical feast or festival), an 18th-cent. type of opera of a festive kind, esp. one expressly written for an occasion, such as a royal or princely patron's wedding. The subject of the lib. was usually mythological and allegorical. Mozart's *Ascanio in Alba* (1771) is an example.

Festes de l'Amour et de Bacchus, Les (*The Feasts of Cupid and Bacchus*), pastorale by Lully (lib. by Quinault, with Molière and I. de Benserade), prod. Paris, Opéra, 15 Nov 1672.

Festes de Thalie, Les (*Thalia's Feasts*), opera-ballet by Mouret (lib. by J. de Lafont), prod. Paris, Opéra, 19 Aug 1714.

Festes vénitiennes, Les (*The Venetian Feasts*), opera by Campra (lib. by A. Danchet), prod. Paris, Opéra, 17 Jun 1710. Revived Aix-en-Provence, 1975.

Festin de l'araignée, Le (*The Spider's Feast*), ballet by Roussel (choreography by G. de Voisins, based on Henri Fabre's *Souvenirs entomologiques*), prod. Paris, Théâtre des Arts, 3 Apr 1913.

Festing, Michael (Christian) (b *c* 1680; d London, 24 Jul 1752), English violinist and composer, ? of German birth or descent. Pupil of Geminiani in London. Made his 1st appearance there 1724 and became a member of the King's Band in 1735. Music director of the Italian Opera in 1737 and of Ranelagh Gardens from 1742.

Works incl. Paraphrase of the 3rd chapter of Habakkuk, Milton's *Song on May Morning* (1748), Addison's *Ode for St Cecilia's Day* and other odes, cantatas; symphs., concertos and sonatas for various instruments; songs.

Festschrift (Ger. = festival writing[s]), a vol. containing essays written by various authors as a tribute to an eminent colleague or master on some anniversary occasion.

Fêtes. *See also* **Festes.**

Fêtes d'Hébé, Les, ou Les Talens lyriques (*Hebe's Feasts, or The Lyrical Gifts*), opera-ballet by Rameau (lib. by A.M. de Montdorge), prod. Paris, Opéra, 21 May 1739.

Fétis, François Joseph (b Mons, 25 Mar 1784; d Brussels, 26 Mar 1871), Belgian musicologist. App. prof. at the Paris Cons., 1821, and librarian, 1827. Dir. of the Brussels Cons. from 1833. Author of a *Biographie universelle des musiciens* (1835–44), an *Histoire générale de la musique* (1869–71, unfinished) and many theoret. works. He also wrote several operas. This extraordinarily energetic man must count, among his innumerable other achievements, as the founder of modern musical lexicography and probably the most prolific musicologist ever, though his work is, perhaps understandably, often highly unreliable.

Feuermann, Emanuel (b Kolomyja nr. Lwów, 22 Nov 1902; d New York, 25 May 1942), Austrian cellist. Made his 1st appearance in Vienna, 1912, later travelled and studied with Klengel at Leipzig and became prof. at the Cologne Cons., at 16. In 1929–33 prof. in Berlin, in succession to Hugo Becker; driven to USA by the Nazi régime; taught at the Curtis Institute from 1941.

Feuersnot (*Fire Famine*), opera by R. Strauss (lib. by Ernst von Wolzogen), prod. Dresden, 21 Nov 1901.

Févin, Antoine de (b ? Arras, *c* 1474; d Blois, *c* 1512), French composer. Wrote 9 Masses, 20 motets, Magnificats, Lamentations, etc. He was a follower of Josquin.

Févin, Robert de (b Cambrai), French 15th–16th-cent. composer. In the service of the Duke of Savoy early in the 16th cent. Wrote Masses, etc.

Février, Henri (b Paris, 2 Oct 1875; d Paris, 8 Jul 1957), French composer. Studied under Massenet and Fauré at the Paris Con.

Works incl. operas *Monna Vanna* (after Maeterlinck, 1909), *Ghismonda* (1918), *La Damnation de Blanchefleur*, *La Femme nue* (1932), *L'Île désenchantée*, operetta *Sylvette* (with Delmas); comic operas *Le Roi aveugle*, *Agnès dame galante*, *Carmosine* (after Musset); songs. etc.

Ffrangcon-Davies, David (Thomas) (b Bethesda, Carnarvon, 11 Dec 1855; d London, 13 Apr 1918), Welsh baritone. Studied at GSM, London, and made his 1st appearance with the Carl Rosa Opera Co. in 1890, but later became mainly a concert singer. He sang in N. Amer. and Berlin 1896–1901. Gave up singing 1907 after a nervous breakdown.

Fiamma, La (*The Flame*), opera by Respighi (lib. by C. Guastalla after H.W. Jenssen), prod. Rome, Teatro Reale, 23 Jan 1934.

Fibich, Zdeněk (b Šebořice nr. Čáslav, 21 Dec 1850; d Prague, 15 Oct 1900), Czech composer. Very precociously gifted, he studied at the Leipzig Cons. under Carl Richter and Jadassohn, also Moscheles for the pf. Later in Paris and Mannheim. After teaching in Pol. for a time, he returned to Cz. in 1874 and cond. at the Nat. Theatre in Prague. He soon retired to devote himself entirely to comp. and wrote over 600 works of var. kinds.

Works incl. operas *Bukovin* (1874), *Blaník* (1881), *The Bride of Messina* (after Schiller, 1884), *The Tempest* (after Shakespeare), *Hedy* (after Byron's *Don Juan*), *Sarka* (1897), *Pad Arkuna*; melodramas *Christmas Eve*, *Eternity*, *The Water-Sprite*, *Queen Emma*, *Haakon* and the trilogy *Hippodamia* (1888–91); incid. music to Vrchlický's comedy *A Night at Karlstein*.

3 symphs., overtures, symph. poems *Othello* and *The Tempest* (both after Shakespeare) and 4 others; 2 string 4tets (1874, 1879), pf. 4tet, pf. trio, 5tet for pf., vln., cello, clar. and horn; pf. sonata, 350 pieces *Moods, Impressions and Memories* for pf.; songs, vocal duets.

Fida ninfa, La (*The faithful nymph*), opera by Vivaldi (lib. by S. Maffei, prod. Verona, Teatro Filarmonico, 6 Jan 1732. Pub. Cremona 1964 in an ed. by R. Monterosso.

Fiddle, a colloquial generic term for instruments of the vln. family. More specifically the word is used for chest-held bowed instrs. of the Middle Ages, partic. those with a flat back.

Fiddler's Child, The (*Šumařovo dítě*), ballad for orch. by Janáček, after a poem by S. Čech, comp. 1912. Fp Prague, 14 Nov 1917.

Fidelio, oder Die eheliche Liebe (*Fidelio, or Wedded Love*), opera by Beethoven (lib. by J. Sonnleithner, based on Bouilly's lib. of *Léonore, ou L'Amour conjugal* written for Gaveaux), prod. Vienna, Theater an der Wien, 20 Nov 1805, cond. Beethoven, with the overture *Leonora No. 2*; revised version, with overture *Leonora No. 3*, same theatre, 29 Mar 1806; overture *Leonora No. 1* written for the fp but abandoned as unsuitable; 2nd revision prod. Vienna Kärntnertortheater, 23 May 1814, with *Fidelio* overture in E maj.

Field, Helen (b Awyd, N. Wales, 14 May 1951), Welsh soprano. She has appeared with WNO since 1977 as Musetta, Poppea, Mimi and Tatyana. Much applauded as Janáček's Vixen and Jenůfa; Desdemona 1986. Mussorgsky's Emma at CG in 1982; appeared with the ENO at the NY Met as Gilda. Other roles incl. Pamina, Marenka, Marguerite and Tippett's Jenifer. In 1987 sang title role in 1st Brit. prod. of Strauss's *Daphne*.

Field, John (b Dublin, 26 Jul 1782; d Moscow, 23 Jan 1837), Irish pianist and composer. Son of a violinist at the Dublin theatre, he was taught music and the pf. by his grandfather, an organist. Having removed to Bath and then to London, his father apprenticed him to Clementi, who taught him and at whose pf. warehouse he was employed to show off the instruments by improvisation. He made his 1st public appearance at Giordani's concerts at Dublin in 1792 and in London in 1794. In 1802 Clementi took him to Paris, Ger. and Rus. leaving him behind at St Petersburg in 1803, where he became a pf. teacher. He married Mlle. Percheron in 1808. In 1822 he settled down at Moscow, where he had as great a success as he had had in the new capital. He travelled much as pianist, visited London in 1832, afterwards Paris, Switz. and It. At Naples he was taken ill and lay in hospital for months until a Rus. family took him back to Moscow, where he died soon after his return.

Works incl. 7 pf. concertos (1799–1822); 20 nocturnes, 4 sonatas and many rondos, fantasies, variations, etc., for pf.; pf. 5tet and other chamber music; works for pf. duet.

Field Mass, work by Martinů for bar., male chorus and orch., comp. 1939 in Paris. Fp Prague, 28 Feb 1946, cond. Kubelik.

Fielding, Henry (1707–54), English novelist and dramatist, author of ballad operas *The Intriguing Chambermaid*, *The Lottery*, *Miss Lucy in Town*, *Don Quixote in England* and others. *See* **Arne (T.A.)**, **Monro** (*Temple Beau*), **Tom Jones** (Philidor, 8).

Fierrabras (Span. *Fierabrás* = *The Braggart*), opera by Schubert (lib. by Kupelwieser, after Calderón, taken from A.W. von Schlegel's *Spanisches Theater*), comp. 1823, but not perf. during Schubert's lifetime; prod. Karlsruhe, 9 Feb 1897.

Fiery Angel, The (*Ogenny Angel*), opera in 5 acts by Prokofiev (lib. by comp. after novel by V. Bryusov), comp. 1919–27. Fp (concert) Paris, 25 Nov 1954; prod. Venice, 29 Sep 1955. Themes from the opera are used in Prokofiev's 3rd symph., in C min., op. 33; comp. 1928, fp Paris, 17 May 1929, cond. Monteux.

Fifara (It.), 17th-cent. name for the transverse flute.

Fife, a simple form of small transverse fl. with finger-holes and without keys, generally used in military bands in connection with drums. The name is now used for a military fl. in Bb with six finger-holes and several keys, used in drum and fife bands.

Fifine at the Fair, orchestral fantasy by Bantock on Browning's poem, comp. 1901, fp Birmingham Music Festival 1912.

Fifth, an interval covering 3 whole tones and a semitone, in which case it is a perfect fifth, e.g. D–A. If either of these notes is sharpened or flattened, the result is an augmented or a diminished fifth: D♭–A or D–A♯ is an augmented fifth, D♯–A or D–A♭ a diminished fifth.

Figaro (Mozart). *See* **Nozze di Figaro**.

Figlia del reggimento. *See* **Fille du Régiment**.

Figner, Medea (b Florence, 4 Apr 1859; d Paris, 8 Jul 1952), Russian mezzo, later soprano, of Italian birth. Debut Sinaluga 1874, Azucena. She sang widely as a mezzo, often as Carmen, until 1890; CG 1887, as Meyerbeer's Valentine and Leonore in *La favorite*. She married Nikolay Figner in 1899 (divorced 1904) and appeared with him at St Petersburg until 1912. She created Tchaikovsky's Lisa and Iolanta and was admired as Desdemona, Tatyana, Tosca, Elsa and Brünnhilde.

Figner, Nikolay (b nr. Kazan, 21 Feb 1857; d Kiev, 13 Dec 1918), Russian tenor. Debut Naples 1882, in Gounod's *Philémon*. He sang in Rio and Buenos Aires 1884–6, with perfs. under Toscanini, and sang Elvino and Ernani at CG in 1887. He then appeared at the Imperial Opera St Petersburg until 1907, as Hermann in the fp of *The Queen of Spades* (1890) and as Lensky, Don José, Werther, Lohengrin and Rubinstein's Nero.

Figuration, the persistent use of decorative or accomp. figures of similar type throughout a piece of music.

Figure, a short musical phrase, esp. one that assumes a distinctive character in the course of a comp.

Figured Bass. *See* **Thorough-Bass.**

Figured Chorale, a hymn-tune setting, esp. for organ, in which the plain notes of the melody are surrounded by more rapid patterns of notes, usually all of the same kind of formation.

Figures-Doubles-Prismes, work for orch. by Boulez, fp Strasbourg, 10 Jan 1964; an expansion of *Doubles* for orch., fp Paris, 16 Mar 1958.

Filar la voce (It.), **Filar il tuono** (It.), **Filer la voix** (Fr.), **Filer le son** (Fr.), spin the voice (tone), sustaining the voice in singing on a long-drawn soft note, without *crescendo* or *diminuendo.*

Fileuse (Fr. fem. = spinner, from *filer* = to spin), the name of a special type of instrumental piece with rapid figurations of var. kinds suggesting the motion of a spinning-wheel and often, in its melody, a spinning-song. There are familiar exs. by Raff and Fauré (in the latter's incid. music for *Pelléas et Mélisande*), and Mendelssohn's Song without Words, op. 67 No. 4, although not so entitled, conforms to the type, being in fact nicknamed *Spinnerlied* in Ger., though called *The Bee's Wedding* in Eng. The prototype of the fileuse was vocal, e.g. the spinning-choruses in Haydn's *Seasons* (Winter) and Wagner's *Flying Dutchman,* Schubert's song *Gretchen am Spinnrade.*

Fille du Régiment, La (*The Daughter of the Regiment*), opera by Donizetti (lib. by J.H.V. de Saint-Georges and J.F.A. Bayard), prod. Paris, Opéra-Comique, 11 Feb 1840. Donizetti's 1st Fr. opera.

Filosofo di campagna, Il (*The Country Philosopher*), opera by Galuppi (lib. by Goldoni), prod. Venice, Teatro San Samuele, 26 Oct 1754.

Filtz, Anton (Antonín Fils) (b Eichstätt, Bavaria, bap. 22 Sep 1733; d Mannheim, buried 14 Mar 1760), German cellist and composer. Entered the orch. at Mannheim in 1754 and became one of the early symphon-

ists attached to that court. Wrote *c* 40 symphs., overtures, a Mass, trios.

Final, the Tonic note of the Modes on which the scales of the authentic modes begin and end. In the plagal modes the final is on the 4th above the starting-note. *See* **Modes.**

Final (Fr.) = Finale.

Finale, the last movement of any instrumental work in several movements, also the last number in any act of an opera where the music is divided into more or less distinctly separated pieces, provided that this number is on a large scale (e.g. the great ensemble piece at the end of Act II of Mozart's *Figaro* is a finale, but the aria at the end of Act I is not).

Finck, Heinrich (b Bamberg, 1445; d Vienna, 9 Jun 1527), German composer. Educ. in the court chapel at Warsaw and at Leipzig Univ. and held apps. at the Pol. court *c* 1492–1506; then at the Court of Württemberg at Stuttgart until 1514. Later he lived at the Scot. monastery in Vienna, and worked at Salzburg cathedral.

Works incl. 4 Masses, motets, hymns and other church music, sacred and secular songs for several voices, songs to the lute.

Finck, Hermann (b Pirna, Saxony, 21 Mar 1527; d Wittenberg, 29 Dec 1558), German composer and theorist. Studied at the Univ. of Wittenberg, where he taught music from 1554. In 1557 he was app. organist, but he died the following year at the age of 31. He wrote a theoret. book, *Practica musica* in 5 vols. Works incl. motets, sacred songs and wedding songs for several voices.

Fine, Irving (b Boston, 3 Dec 1914; d Boston, 23 Aug 1962), American composer. He studied at Harvard with Walter Piston and in Paris with Boulanger; prof. at Harvard and Brandeis Univs. His music has reflected two of the major tendencies of the 20th cent. – neo-classicism and atonality.

Works incl. *Toccata concertante* (1948), *Partita* for wind 5tet., *Alice in Wonderland,* suite for chorus and orch. (1949), string 4tet (1952), *Diversions* for orch. (1958), *Symphony* (1962).

Fingal's Cave (also called **Hebrides**), concert overture by Mendelssohn, op. 26, comp. in recollection of a visit to the Hebrides in 1829, Rome, Dec 1830; revised version, London, summer 1832. The 1st score was entitled *Die einsame Insel* (*The Solitary Island*).

Finger, Gottfried (or **Godfrey**) (b Olomouc, *c* 1660; d Mannheim, buried 31 Aug 1730), Moravian composer. Nothing is known of his career until he went to London *c* 1685, working under the patronage of James II. He left in 1702, piqued at having gained only the 4th prize after Weldon, Eccles and D. Purcell for the comp. of Congreve's masque *The Judgment of Paris*, and went into the service of the Queen of Prus., Sophia Charlotte, in Berlin. Later he lived in the Palatinate and wrote some operas for Neuburg and Heidelberg.

Works incl. operas *The Virgin Prophetess* (Settle), *Sieg der Schönheit über die Helden* (1706), *L'amicizia in terzo* (in part); masques *The Loves of Mars and Venus* (Motteux, with Eccles) and *The Judgment of Paris* (Congreve, 1701); incid. music (some with D. Purcell) for Lee's *Rival Queens*, *The Wive's Excuse*, *Love for Love* and *The Mourning Bride* (both Congreve), *Love at a Loss*, *Love makes a Man* (Cibber), *The Humours of the Age* (Southerne), *Sir Harry Wildair* (Farquhar) and *The Pilgrim* (Vanbrugh); concertos and sonatas for var. instruments; pieces for vln. and fl. (with Banister), etc.

Fingerboard, the part of the neck of a string instrument to which the strings are pressed by the fingers in order to change their length and thus prod. different notes.

Fingered Tremolo. *See* **Tremolo.**

Fingering, the use of the fingers on any instrument to prod. the notes in var. ways; also the figures written above the notes indicating which finger is to be used to prod. this or that note.

Finite Canon, a Canon sung through once, without repetition of its phrases.

Finke, Fidelio (b Josefstal, Boh., 22 Oct 1891; d Dresden, 12 Jun 1968), German-Czech composer. Studied at the Prague Cons. with his uncle Romeo F. and with Novák for comp. He taught there from 1915, became inspector of the Ger. music schools in Cz. in 1920 and director of the Ger. Acad. of Music in Prague in 1927.

Works incl. opera *Die Jacobsfahrt* (1936); *Pan* symph., overture and other works for orch.; 2 string 4tets.

Finlandia, symph. poem for orch. by Sibelius, op. 26, comp. in 1899 (rev. 1900; fp Helsinki, 2 Jul 1900). It has become a work for national celebrations in Fin., being based on material sounding like Fin. patriotic songs, the whole of which, however, is the composer's own invention, not folk music.

Finney, Ross Lee (b Wells, Minnesota, 23 Dec 1906), American composer. Educ. at Carleton Coll., Minn., and studied music at Minn. Univ. and later in Paris and Vienna with Nadia Boulanger and Alban Berg, also

with Sessions at Harvard Univ. Prof. of Music and resident comp. at Univ. of Michigan.

Works incl. Overture to a Social Drama for orch.; 4 symphs. (1942–72); pf. concerto, vln. concerto; *John Brown* for tenor, male chorus and chamber orch.; 8 string 4tets. (1935–60), pf. trio.; vln. and pf. sonata; 4 pf. sonatas; 8 Poems for soprano, tenor and pf.

Finnissy, Michael (b London, 17 Mar 1946), English composer. He studied at the RCM with Bernard Stevens and Humphrey Searle. Music dept. London School of Contemp. Dance 1969–74.

Works incl. *Mysteries,* 8 separately performable music theatre pieces with Latin texts from the Bible: 1 *The Parting of Darkness,* 2 *The Earthly Paradise,* 3 *Noah and the Great Flood,* 4 *The Prophecy of Daniel,* 5 *The Parliament of Heaven,* 6 *The Annunciation,* 7 *The Betrayal and Crucifixion,* 8 *The Deliverance of Souls; Orfeo* for soloists and insts. (1975), *Mr. Punch* for voice and insts. (1977), *Vaudeville* for mezzo, bar., insts. and perc. (1983); 7 piano concertos (2 for pf. alone), *Offshore* for orch., *Pathways of Sun and Stars* for orch. (1976); *Jeanne d'Arc* for sop., tenor, cello and small orch. (1971), *Babylon* for mezzo and ens., *Sir Tristan* for sop. and ens. (1979), *Ngano* for mezzo, tenor, chorus, fl. and perc. (1984). Music for inst. ensemble, solo pf., solo insts.; string 4tet (1986).

Finta giardiniera, La (*The Pretended Garden-Girl*), opera by Anfossi (lib. by R. de Calzabigi), prod. Rome, Teatro delle Dame, Carnival 1774.

Opera by Mozart (lib. do.), prod. Munich, 13 Jan 1775.

Finta semplice, La (*The Pretended Simpleton*), opera by Mozart (lib. by M. Coltellini), comp. for Vienna, 1768, but not perf. there; prod. Salzburg, 1 May 1769).

Finte gemelle, Le (*The Pretended Twins*), opera by Piccinni (lib. by G. Petrosellini), prod. Rome, Teatro Valle, 2 Jan 1771.

Finto Stanislao, Il (*The False Stanislas*), opera by Gyrowetz (lib. by F. Romani), prod. Milan, La Scala, 5 Aug 1818. The lib. was used by Verdi in 1840 for *Un giorno di Regno.*

Finzi, Gerald (b London, 14 Jul 1901; d Oxford, 27 Sep 1956), English composer. Private pupil of Bairstow and R.O. Morris; prof. of comp. at the RAM in London, 1930–3, and afterwards went to live in the country to give his whole time to comp.

Works incl. incid. music for Shakespeare's

Love's Labour's Lost; festival anthem (Crashaw), *Intimations of Immortality* (Wordsworth, *c* 1938, rev. 1950) and *For St Cecilia* (Edmund Blunden) for chorus and orch.; 3 Elegies (Drummond) and 7 part-songs (Robert Bridges) for unaccomp. chorus.

New Year Music for orch., *Romance* for strings; *Introit* for vln. and small orch., concerto for clar. and strings (1949), cantata *Dies Natalis* (Traherne) for high voice and orch. (1926–39), *Farewell to Arms* (Ralph Knevet and George Peele) for tenor and small orch., 2 Sonnets by Milton for do.; *Interlude* for ob. and string 4tet, Prelude and Fugue for string trio; 5 Bagatelles for clar. and pf.; Thomas Hardy song cycles *By Footpath and Stile* for bar. and string 4tet (1922), *A Young Man's Exhortation* (1926–9), *Earth and Air and Rain* and *Before and After Summer*; 5 Shakespeare songs, *Let us Garlands Bring*.

Fiocco. Italian-Belgian family of musicians.

1. Pietro Antonio F. (b Venice, *c* 1650, d Brusssls, 3 Sep 1714), conductor and composer. He went to Brussels late in the 17th cent. and was app. cond. of the court band. Comp. prologues for several of Lully's operas; Masses, motets; *Sacri concerti*; cantata *Le Retour du printemps*, etc.

2. Jean-Joseph F. (b Brussels, bap. 15 Dec 1686; d Brussels, 30 Mar 1746), conductor, son of prec. Succeeded his father as cond. in 1714.

3. Joseph-Hector F. (b Brussels, 20 Jan 1703; d Brussels, 22 Jun 1741), conductor, harpsichordist and composer, brother of prec. He was cond. at Brussels in 1729, became choirmaster at Antwerp Cathedral in 1731 and at Sainte-Gudule at Brussels in 1737. Wrote harpsichord pieces, church music etc.

Fioravanti, Valentino (b Rome, 11 Sep 1764; d Capua, 16 Jun 1837), Italian composer. Pupil of Sala at one of the Naples Conss. Prod. his 1st opera in Rome in 1784. Cond. at Lisbon from 1803 and visited Paris in 1807, returning to It. to become *maestro di cappella* at St Peter's in Rome.

Works incl. operas *Le avventure di Bertoldino* (1784), *Le cantatrici villane* (1799), *I virtuosi ambulanti* (1807), *Ogni eccesso è vizioso* and 66 others; church music etc.

Fiorillo, Federigo (b Brunswick, 1 Jun 1755; d after 1823), Italian–German violinist and composer. Pupil of his father. Travelled on concert tours, and in 1782 was app. *Kapellmeister* in Riga. Visited Paris in 1785, and from 1788 to 1794 lived in London, where he appeared mostly as a vla. player.

Works incl. a large quantity of vln. music, incl. 36 *Caprices* (studies); string 4tets, 5tets and other chamber music, etc.

Fiorillo, Ignazio (b Naples, 11 May 1715; d Fritzlar, Hesse, Jun 1787), Italian composer, father of prec. Pupil of Leo and Durante at Naples. Prod. his 1st opera, *Mandane* at Venice in 1736; became court *Kapellmeister* at Brunswick in 1754 and at Kassel in 1762, retiring in 1780.

Works incl. 21 operas, most to texts by Metastasio; oratorio, *Isacco*; Requiem, 3 Te Deums; symphs.; sonatas.

Fioriture (It. lit. flowerings, flourishes, decorations), ornamental figures elaborating a plainer melodic passage, either according to the composer's notation or improvised according to the performer's fancy.

Fipple Flute, a generic term for a woodwind instrument held vertically and blown into through a mouptiece in which the air is diverted by an obstructive block called the 'fipple'. The recorder (Ger. *Blockflote*) is the chief member of the family.

Fire Symphony, a nickname of a symph. by Haydn, No. 59, in A maj., comp. *c* 1766–8.

Firebird, The (*Zhar Ptitsa*), ballet by Stravinsky (choreography by Fokin), prod. Paris, Opéra, 25 Jun 1910, cond. Gabriel Pierné.

Firenze, Ghiradello da. *See* **Gherardello.**

Fires of London, The, ensemble founded 1967 by Maxwell Davies and Harrison Birtwistle as the Pierrot Players; based on forces required for Schoenberg's *Pierrot lunaire* (*q.v.*) (Birtwistle left in 1970). Many fps of works by Davies, e.g. *8 Songs for a Mad King*, *The Martyrdom of St Magnus*, and other composers. Ens. disbanded 1987; Fires of London Productions formed same year for perf. of stage works.

Fireworks, fantasy for large orch. by Stravinsky, comp. 1908 to celebrate the marriage of Nadezhda Rimsky-Korsakov, his teacher's daughter, to Maximilian Steinberg, St Petersburg 17 Jun 1908. The score was rev. for smaller forces and perf. 22 Jan 1910.

Fireworks Music. Handel's *Music for the Royal Fireworks*, a suite of pieces originally for wind band, was comp. for the celebrations of the Peace of Aix-la-Chapelle, fp London, Green Park, 27 Apr 1749.

Firkušny, Rudolf (b Napajedlá, Morav., 11 Feb 1912), Czech pianist and composer. Studied at Brno Cons. with Vilem Kurz (pf.) and Janáček for comp. Later he studied with

Suk and Schnabel. Debut Prague, 1922. Eng. 1933, US, 1938. Well known in classics and modern music, esp. Janáček. His comps. incl. a pf. concerto and many pf. solos.

First-movement Form. The term is sometimes used for 'sonata form', but does not serve well, since there are some 1st sonata movements in other forms (e.g. variations) while there are any number of slow movements and still more of finales in regular sonata form.

First of May, The, symphony no. 3 in E♭, op. 20, by Shostakovich. The finale is a choral tribute to International Workers' Day (text by S. Kirsanov) but the fp in Leningrad on 21 Jan 1930 did not gain official approval. Shostakovich met with further trouble in his next work, *Lady Macbeth of the Mtsensk District*, denounced in Pravda and by Stalin.

Fischer, Annie (b Budapest, 5 Jul 1914), Hungarian pianist. She studied at the Budapest Academy with Dohnányi and in 1933 won the Int. Liszt Competition in Budapest. Her concert career had begun in 1928, and after war years spent in Swed. continued to tour world wide. Well known in Beethoven, Mozart, Brahms and Schubert.

Fischer-Dieskau, Dietrich (b Berlin, 28 May 1925), German baritone and conductor. Studied in Berlin with Georg Walter and with Weissenborn. Made his debut in 1947 and his first stage appearance in 1948 as Posa, in Berlin. London, 1951, in *A Mass of Life* by Delius. He has sung at most of the great opera houses and music centres of the world; CG 1965 as Mandryka, Bayreuth 1954–6 as Wolfram, Kothner and Amfortas; other Wagner roles have been Sachs, Kurwenal and the Dutchman. US debut Cincinnati, 1955. Conducting debut 1973. He sang in the fps of Henze's *Elegy for Young Lovers* (1961), Britten's *War Requiem* (1962) and Reimann's *Lear* (1978). An equally fine Lieder and opera singer, he is a musician of great intelligence, with a fine voice of remarkable range and flexibility and a perfect technique; highly regarded as Barak, Busoni's Faust, Hindemith's Mathis, Almaviva and Wozzeck.

Fischer, Edwin (b Basle, 6 Oct 1886; d Zurich, 24 Jan 1960), Swiss pianist and conductor. Studied at the Basle Cons., where he taught for several years. He returned to Switzerland in 1942. In addition to his activities as a soloist he also cond. orchs. in Lübeck, Munich and Berlin. He ed. a number of old keyboard works and wrote books on Bach and on Beethoven's pf. sonatas. A successful teacher in Lucerne and elsewhere.

Fischer, Emil (b Brunswick, 13 Jun 1838; d Hamburg, 11 Aug 1914), German bass-baritone. Debut Graz 1857 in Boieldieu's *Jean de Paris*. Appeared in var. Ger. centres and sang Sachs at CG in 1884. NY Met debut 23 Nov 1885; remained until 1890, taking part in the 1st US perfs. of *Meistersinger, Rienzi, Euryanthe, Tristan und Isolde* and *Der Ring des Nibelungen*.

Fischer, György (b Budapest, 12 Aug 1935), Austrian conductor and pianist of Hungarian birth. He studied in Budapest and Salzburg; asst. to Karajan at Vienna and conducted operas by Mozart there. Cologne Opera from 1973; many perfs. of Mozart, with the producer John Pierre Ponnelle. Brit. debut with WNO 1973, with *Die Zauberflöte*; has returned for *Die Entführung, Figaro* and *Così fan tutte*. London debut 1979, in a concert perf. of Mozart's *Mitridate*. ECO since 1980 and has given concerts widely in Europe and S. Amer. Often heard as an accompanist to leading singers. Formerly married to Lucia Popp.

Fischer, Ivan (b Budapest, 20 Jan 1951), Hungarian conductor. He studied in Budapest and with Swarowsky; conducted in Italy from 1975 and guest with the BBC SO from 1976. Opera debut Zurich 1977; gave *Agrippina* with Kent Opera in 1982 and became music dir. in 1984. *La Clemenza di Tito* with CG Opera at Manchester 1983. Music dir. Northern Sinfonia 1979–82. In 1983 he took the LSO to the Far East and was guest with the Los Angeles SO.

Fischer, Johann (b Augsburg, 25 Sep 1646; d Schwedt, Pomerania, *c* 1716), German violinist and composer. Studied with Bockshorn at Stuttgart and went to Paris, where he became copyist to Lully. Later he travelled, worked for a time at Augsburg and Schwerin, in Den. and Swed., and finally became *Kapellmeister* to the Margrave of Schwedt.

Works incl. *Feld und Helden Musik* describing the battle of Hochstadt, table music, overtures, dances and other pieces for vln. and for vla., some with *scordatura*.

Fischer, Johann Caspar Ferdinand (b *c* 1665; d Rastatt, 27 Mar 1746), German composer. *Kapellmeister* to the Margrave of Baden in Schlackenwerth (Bohemia) and Rastatt from 1692. His keyboard music includes *Ariadne musica* (1715), a series of 20 preludes and fugues, each in a different key, and thus a precursor of Bach's *Wohltemperierte Clavier*.

Other works incl. *Musicalisches Blumen-Büschlein* (a collection of keyboard suites in the French style), *Musicalischer Parnassus* (9 suites named after the Muses), *Blumenstrauss* (organ preludes and fugues on the 8 modes), *Le Journal de Printemps* (suite for orch. with tpts. *ad lib*), church music.

Fischer, Johann Christian (b Freiburg, Breisgau, 1733; d London, 29 Apr 1800), German oboist and composer. In the service of the Saxon court at Dresden, 1760–4. Concert tours took him in 1768 to London, where he settled, marrying Gainsborough's daughter in 1780. Played frequently at the concerts promoted by J.C. Bach and Abel (1768–81), and was a member of the queen's band. He was again on tour on the continent, 1786–90. Mozart, hearing him in Vienna in 1787, thought little of his playing, though he had already (1774) comp. pf. variations on a minuet by Fischer K179.

Works incl. 10 ob. concertos, divertimenti for 2 fls., fl. sonatas and 4tets, etc.

Fischer, Ludwig (b Mainz, 18 Aug 1745; d Berlin, 10 Jul 1825), German bass, the original Osmin in Mozart's *Die Entführung*. Sang with success in Paris, Prague, Dresden and London (Salomon concerts, 1794 and 1798).

Fischer, Michael Gotthard (b Albach nr. Erfurt, 3 Jun 1773; d Erfurt, 12 Jan 1829), German organist and composer. Pupil of Kittel at Erfurt and later organist of the Franciscan church there. Wrote organ music, symphs., string 4tets, pf. sonatas, songs.

Fischer, Res (b Berlin, 8 Nov 1896; d Stuttgart, 4 Oct 1974), German contralto. She studied in Prague and in Berlin with Lilli Lehmann. Basle 1927–35; Frankfurt 1935–41. Stuttgart from 1941. She was a friend of Carl Orff and created his Antigonae at Salzburg in 1949; returned for the fp of Wagner-Régeny's *Das Bergwerk zu Falun*, 1961. She sang Clytemnestra in a concert perf. of *Elektra* in London, 1955. Bayreuth 1959–61.

Fischietti, Domenico (b Naples, *c* 1720; d Salzburg, *c* 1810), Italian composer. Pupil of Durante and Leo in Naples, where he prod. his first opera in 1742. Worked as cond. in Prague, then became *Kapellmeister* at Dresden 1766–72, and at Salzburg Cathedral 1772–9.

Works incl. operas *Lo speziale* (with V. Pallavicini, 1754). *Il signor dottore, Il mercato di Malmantile, La ritornata di Londra* (all on libs. by Goldoni) and *c* 20 others; church music.

Fisher, John Abraham (b London, 1744; d ? London, May 1806), English violinist and composer. Pupil of Pinto, made his debut as

a violinist in 1765. His marriage in 1770 brought him a part-share in Covent Garden Theatre, and over the next ten years he comp. many dramatic works. On the death of his wife in 1780 he went on tour on the Continent. Married the singer Nancy Storace in Vienna in 1784, but his ill-treatment of her caused him subsequently to be banished from Austria. Later he spent some years in Dublin.

Works incl. oratorio *Providence* (1777); incid. music for Shakespeare's *Macbeth*; pantomimes; songs for Vauxhall Gardens, etc.; symphs. and other instrumental music.

Fisher, Sylvia (b Melbourne, 18 Apr 1910), Australian soprano. She sang in Melbourne from 1932 and appeared as Leonore at CG in 1949; returned until 1958 as Sieglinde, Gutrune, the Marschallin and the Kostelnička in the Brit. fp of *Jenůfa* (1956). She sang Britten roles with the EOG 1963–71; created Mrs Wingrave, on BBC TV, 1971. The title part in *Gloriana* was one of her best roles.

Fistoulari, Anatole (b Kiev, 20 Aug 1907), Russian-born conductor. Studied with his father and cond. Tchaikovsky's 6th symph. at the age of 8. From 1933 he was in Paris and in 1940 he settled in Eng.; he has cond. the LPO and cond. much ballet music.

Fitelberg, Jerzy (b Warsaw, 20 May 1903; d New York, 25 Apr 1951), Polish composer. He played perc. in his father's orch. as a boy and studied comp. at the Warsaw Cons. and under Schreker in Berlin; settled in Paris in 1933 and in NY in 1940.

Works incl. Concert Pieces, *Sinfonietta* (1946), *Pol. Pictures, Nocturne* and 2 suites for orch., symph. for strings, pf., harp and perc., concerto for strings; 2 pf. concertos (1929, 1934), 2 vln. concertos, cello concerto; 5 string 4tets (1926–45), string trio, woodwind 5tet; Suite for vln. and pf., sonatina for 2 vlns., duo for vln. and cello, sonata for cello solo; pf. sonata and pieces.

Fitzwilliam, Viscount (Richard Wentworth) (1745–1816), English collector and founder of the Fitzwilliam Museum at Cambridge, which houses his collection of MSS. and printed music, among other things left by him, incl. the old English church music pub. as *Fitzwilliam Music* by Vincent Novello in 1825 and Eng. virginal music ed. as the *Fitzwilliam Virginal Book* by J.A. Fuller-Maitland and W. Barclay Squire in 1899.

Fitzwilliam Virginal Book, a large MS of keyboard music written between 1609 and 1619 by Francis Tregian while in Fleet Prison, now in the Fitzwilliam Museum,

Cambridge. It is an important source of pieces by Byrd, Bull and Giles Farnaby.

'Five, The'. *See* **Kutchka.**

Five Movements for String Quartet, work by Webern; comp. 1909, fp Vienna, 8 Feb 1910. Vers. for string orch. 1929, fp Philadelphia, 26 Mar 1930.

Five Orchestral Pieces (*Fünf Orchesterstücke*), work for large orch. by Schoenberg, op.16, comp. 1909 rev. 1922; fp London, 3 Sep 1912, cond. Wood. Schoenberg gave the 5 pieces the titles *Premonitions, The Past, Chord-Colours, Peripetie, Endless Recitative.* Schoenberg's pupil, Webern, wrote Five Pieces for orch. 1911–13, fp Zurich, ISCM concert, 22 Jun 1926 (4 of the 5 pieces last for less than 1 minute). Webern's five posthumous pieces for orch. (1913) were perf. Cologne, 13 Jan 1969.

Five Tudor Portraits, choral suite by Vaughan Williams on poems by Skelton. 1. Ballad, *The Tunning of Elinor Rumming*; 2. Intermezzo, *My Pretty Bess*; 3. Burlesca, *Epitaph on John Jayberd of Diss*; 4. Romanza, *Jane Scroop: her Lament for Philip Sparrow*; 5. Scherzo, *Jolly Rutterkin.* For mezzosoprano, baritone, chorus and orch., fp Norwich Festival, 25 Sep 1936.

Flackton, William (b Canterbury, bap. Mar 1709; d Canterbury, 5 Jan 1798), English organist and composer. He was a bookseller, but played the organ and vln., taught and comp. harpsichord and string music, including works for vla.

Flagello, Ezio (b New York, 28 Jan 1933), American bass. He studied in NY with Friedrich Schorr. Stage debut Rome 1956, as Dulcamara. NY Met from 1957; debut as Leporello, created Barber's Enobarbus in the opening prod. at the new house, Lincoln Center, 1966. From 1968 he sang widely in the US and Europe. His recordings incl. *I Puritani, Lucrezia Borgia, Ernani, Luisa Miller* and *Alcina.*

Flagstad, Kirsten (Malfrid) (b Hamar, 12 Jul 1895; d Oslo, 7 Dec 1962), Norwegian soprano. She 1st appeared in opera at the Oslo Nat. Theatre in 1913 and continued to sing in Scandinavia (incl. operetta) until 1930. In 1933 she sang for the first time at Bayreuth and in 1934 sang Sieglinde and Gutrune there. For the next 17 years she enjoyed an international reputation as a Wagnerian soprano. NY Met 1935 as Sieglinde and Isolde. London, CG, 1936–7 as Isolde, Brünnhilde and Senta; returned 1948–51, to sing Wagner in English. The nobility and security of her singing are best displayed in her recording of Isolde (1953).

She sang in the fp of Strauss's *Four Last Songs* (London, 1950) and also appeared as Dido in Purcell's *Dido and Aeneas* 1951–3. From 1958–60 she was director of the Norwegian State Opera.

Flam, a double stroke, as distinct from a roll, on the Side Drum.

Flat, the sign ♭, which lowers a note by a semitone. Also an adj. describing out-of-tune intonation on the flat side.

Flautando (It. = fluting), flute-like tone prod. on the vln. by drawing the bow lightly over the strings near the end of the fingerboard.

Flautino (It. = little fl.), a small recorder, either the descant recorder or the flageolet, also called *flauto piccolo* in the early 18th cent. (e.g. in Handel's *Rinaldo*).

Flautist, the Eng. word for flute-player, der. from It. *flauto* and *flautista.*

Flauto traverso (It.), the transverse fl. distinguished from the Recorders and similar fls. played vertically.

Flavio, rè de' Longobardi (*Flavius, King of the Lombards*), opera by Handel (lib. by N.F. Haym, partly based on Corneille's *Cid*), prod. London, King's Theatre, Haymarket, 14 May 1723.

Flavius Bertaridus, König der Longobarden (*F.B., King of the Lombards*), opera by Telemann (lib. by C.G. Wendt), prod. Hamburg, Theater beim Gänsemarkt, 23 Nov 1729.

Flebile (It.; accent on 1st syll,), plaintive, mournful.

Flecha, Mateo (b Prades, Tarragona, 1481; d Poblet, *c* 1553), Spanish monk and composer. Pupil of Juan Castelló at Barcelona, *maestro de capilla* to the Infantas of Castile, the daughters of Charles V. Later became a Carmelite and settled in the monastery of Poblet.

Flecha, Mateo (b Prades, 1530; d Solsona, Lérida, 20 Feb 1604), Spanish monk and composer, nephew of prec. Pupil of his uncle. In the service of the Emperor Charles V until 1558 and of Philip II, then in Prague in that of the Emperor Maximilian, after whose death in 1576 he remained there until 1599, when he went to the abbey of Solsona as a Franciscan monk. A stage work of his, *El Parnaso*, (?) was perf. at Madrid in 1561.

Works by the 2 Flechas (not always distinguishable) incl. church music, madrigals, *ensaladas* (burlesque madrigals), etc.

Fledermaus, Die (*The Flittermouse, The Bat*), operetta by J. Strauss, jun. (lib. by C. Haffner and R. Genée, based on a Fr. vaudeville, *Le Réveillon*, by H. Meilhac and L.

Halévy, taken from a Ger. comedy, *Das Gefängnis*, by R. Benedix), prod. Vienna, Theater an der Wien, 5 Apr 1874.

Fleischer-Edel, Katharina (b Mülheim, 27 Sep 1873; d Dresden, 18 Jul 1928), German soprano. She sang at Dresden 1894–7 and was then engaged by Pollini for the Hamburg Opera; remained there until 1917, mainly in Wagnerian roles. Bayreuth 1904–8, as Elisabeth, Brangaene, Sieglinde and Elsa. Sang at CG 1905–7 and the NY Met 1906–7.

Fleischer, Edytha (b Falkenstein, 5 Apr 1898), German soprano. Debut Berlin 1918, as Constanze. Salzburg 1922, as Susanna and Zerlina. She toured Amer. 1922–4 and sang at the NY Met 1926–36 and in the 1st US perfs. of operas by Rossini, Rimsky-Korsakov and Puccini (*La Rondine* 1928). She was well known in concert and appeared at Buenos Aires 1936–49.

Fleisher, Leon (b San Francisco, 23 Jul 1928), American pianist and conductor. He studied with Schnabel and in NY; appeared with NY PO before the war and in 1952 won Queen Elisabeth Comp., Brussels. In the early 1960s lost the use of his right hand; learned the pf. left hand repertory and conducted major orchs. all over US. After surgery in 1981 he was able to resume his bimanual career as pf. soloist. From 1959 active as teacher, then cond. in Baltimore.

Flem, Paul Le. *See* **Le Flem.**

Flesch, Carl (b Moson, 9 Oct 1873; d Lucerne, 14 Nov 1944), Austro-Hungarian violinist and teacher. Studied in Vienna and Paris, where he was a pupil of Marsick with Kreisler. Made his 1st public appearance in Vienna, 1895, toured widely and taught by turns at Bucharest, Amsterdam, Philadelphia and Berlin. In 1934 he settled in London. Wrote books on vln. playing and comp. vln. studies. A bi-annual competition in his name has been held since 1945.

Fleta, Miguel (b Albalate de Cinca, 28 Dec 1893; d La Coruña, 30 May 1938), Spanish tenor. Debut Trieste 1919, as Zandonai's Paolo; Rome 1922, as Romeo in the fp of Zandonai's *Giulietta e Romeo*. He was soon heard in Rome, Vienna and Buenos Aires as Radames, the Duke of Mantua and Don José. NY Met debut 1923, as Cavaradossi; the following year returned to La Scala and created Calaf there in 1926. He fought for Franco during the Civil War and was sentenced to death by the Communists.

Fleury, Louis (b Lyons, 24 May 1878; d Paris, 11 Jun 1925), French flautist. Studied at the Paris Cons. From 1905 until his death

he was head of the Société Moderne d'Instruments à Vent. It was for him that Debussy comp. *Syrinx*.

Flicorno, an Italian brass instrument used in military bands corresponding to the Saxhorn and Flügelhorn.

Fliegende Holländer, Der (*The Flying Dutchman*), opera by Wagner (lib. by comp., based on Heine's *Memoiren des Herrn von Schnabelewopski*, ? Marryat's novel *The Phantom Ship* and other sources), prod. Dresden, 2 Jan 1843.

Flood, The, musical play by Stravinsky (text by Robert Craft from Genesis and the York and Chester miracle plays); comp. 1961–2, fp CBS TV, 14 Jun 1962. 1st stage perf. Hamburg, 30 Apr 1963, cond. Craft.

Floquet, Étienne Joseph (b Aix-en-Provence, 23 Nov 1748; d Paris, 10 May 1785), French composer. He received his musical educ. at the church of Saint-Sauveur at Aix, wrote a motet at the age of 10 and went to Paris 1767. In 1774, having come into conflict with Gluck's partisans, he went to Naples, where he studied under Sala, and to Bologna, where he sought further instruction from Martini, but returned to Paris in 1777.

Works incl. operas *Hellé* (1779), *Le Seigneur bienfaisant*, *La Nouvelle Omphale* (1782) and *Alceste* (Quinault, 1783); opera-ballets *L'Union de l'Amour et des Arts* and *Azolan*; 2 Requiems, ode *La Gloire du Seigneur* (J.B. Rousseau).

Florence (actually **Houghton**), **Evangeline** (b Cambridge, Mass., 12 Dec 1873; d London, 1 Nov 1928), American soprano. Made her 1st appearance at Boston in 1891. Later continued her studies in London and appeared much in England.

Florentinische Tragödie, Eine, opera in 1 act by Zemlinsky (text from the blank verse drama *A Florentine Tragedy* by Wilde, in Ger. trans. by M. Meyerfeld); comp. 1915–16, prod. Stuttgart, 30 Jan 1917, cond. Max von Schillings. Perf. in a Hamburg Opera prod. in 1983 at Edinburgh and in 1985 at CG.

Florestan, one of the 2 imaginary characters, Florestan and Eusebius, used by Schumann as pseudonyms for his critical writings and also introduced into his music (*Carnaval*, *Davidsbündlertänze*) to personify what he felt to be his dual character as an artist, Florestan representing him as an impetuous romantic and Eusebius as a dreamer.

Florida, suite for orch. by Delius, comp. 1886–7 and ded. to the people of Florida (it had been Delius's ambition to become an orange planter). Perf. privately in Leipzig 1888; 1st public perf. London, 1 Apr 1937, cond. Beecham. Not pub. until 1963. The 4 movts. are titled *Daybreak*, *By the river*, *Sunset* and *At Night*.

Floridante, Il, opera by Handel (lib. by R.A. Rolli), prod. London, King's Theatre, Haymarket, 9 Dec 1721.

Flos Campi (*Flower of the Field*) work by Vaughan Williams in 6 movements for viola, wordless chorus and small orch., fp London 10 Oct 1925, with Lionel Tertis, cond. Wood.

Floss der Medusa, Das (*The Raft of the 'Medusa'*), 'popular and military oratorio' by Henze (text by E. Schnabel), for soloists, chorus and orch., ded. to the memory of Ché Guevara. The projected fp in Hamburg on 9 Dec 1968 had to be cancelled when members of the chorus, revolting students and the police came into conflict. Fp (concert) Vienna 29 Jan 1971; stage prod. Nuremberg, 15 Apr 1972. The '*Medusa*' of the title was a French frigate abandoned at sea in 1816. The officers escaped in lifeboats and cut adrift the entire crew on a single raft.

Flothuis, Marius (b Amsterdam, 30 Oct 1914), Dutch composer. Studied with Hans Brandts-Buys.

Works incl. concertos for fl., horn, vln., chamber orch.; *Sinfonietta Concertante* for clar., saxophone and chamber orch.; cello sonata.

Flotow, Friedrich von (b Teutendorf, Mecklenburg-Schwerin, 27 Apr 1812; d Darmstadt, 24 Jan 1883), German composer. Son of a nobleman. Went to Paris in 1827 and studied music under Reicha and others. Began to prod. operas at aristocratic houses and wrote incid. music for the play *Alessandro Stradella* (enlarged into an opera, 1844) at the Palais-Royal in 1837. The next 2 years he contrib. musical numbers to Grisar's operas *Lady Melvill* and *L'Eau merveilleuse*, and in 1839 he made his 1st public stage success with *Le Naufrage de la Méduse*. He was intendant of the court theatre at Schwerin in 1856–63. He then returned to Paris, but went to live nr. Vienna in 1868.

Works incl. Fr., Ger. and It. operas, e.g. *Le Naufrage de la Méduse* (see above; 1839), *L'Esclave de Camoëns* (1843), *Stradella* (1844), *L'Âme en peine*, *Martha* (1847), *Rübezahl*, *L'Ombre*, *Il fior d'Harlem*, *Rob Roy* (after Scott); ballets *Lady Henriette* (with Burgmüller and Deldevez, on which *Martha* was based later), *Die Libelle* and *Tannkönig*; incid. music to Shakespeare's *Winter's Tale* (1859); *Fackeltanz*, overtures, etc. for orch.; chamber music, songs.

Flourish, lit., in old Eng., a Fanfare, but in modern music terminology a short figure used as an embellishment rather than as a theme.

Floyd, Carlisle (b Latta, S. Carolina, 11 Jun 1926), American composer. He studied at Syracuse Univ. and privately with Rudolf Firkušný. His 1st. opera, *Susannah*, was prod. at Univ. of Houston 1955 and at NY City Opera in 1956.

Other stage works incl. *Wuthering Heights* (Santa Fe, 1958), *The Passion of Jonathan Wade* (NY, 1962), *The Sojourner and Mollie Sinclair* (Raleigh, S. Carolina, 1963), *Markheim* (New Orleans, 1966), *Of Mice and Men*, after Steinbeck (Seattle, 1970), *Bilby's Doll* (Houston, 1976), *Willie Stark* (Houston, 1981), *All the King's Men* (1981).

Flügel (Ger. lit. wing), the Ger. name for the grand pf., which is wing-shaped.

Flügelhorn (Ger. lit. wing horn), a brass wind instrument akin to the keyed bugle and alto Saxhorn, still called by its Ger. name in England though spelt 'flugelhorn' (generally abbr. to 'flugel'). It is made in 3 pitches, soprano, alto and tenor, and used in military and brass bands. In England only the middle size (in Bb) is used, and normally only in brass bands.

Flute, a woodwind instrument played horizontally (*see also* **Bass Flute, Piccolo**). It is played through an open mouth-hole without reeds and the notes are controlled by keys, many more being obtainable, however, by overblowing and cross-fingering. It has the following compass:

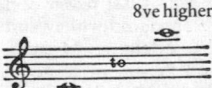

In the 17th cent. Flute normally meant Recorder, sometimes called the Eng. Flute.

Flûte à bec (Fr. = break fl.) = Fipple Fl., Flageolet, Recorder.

Flûte douce (Fr. lit. sweet fl.) = Recorder.

Flutter-Tonguing, a special kind of tone prod. used mainly in playing the fl. and clar., i.e. rolling an R while playing.

Flying Dutchman. See **Fliegende Holländer, Vaisseau-fantôme.**

Fodor-Mainvielle, Joséphine (b Paris, 13 Oct 1789; d Saint-Genis nr. Lyons, 14 Aug 1870), French soprano, daughter of the violinist and comp. Joseph Fodor (1751–1828). 1st appeared at the Opéra-Comique in Paris, 1814, in operas by Grétry and Berton. In London and Paris she was heard as Rossini's Elisabetta, Rosina and Ninetta (*La gazza ladra*). She retired in 1833.

Foerster. *See also* **Förster.**

Foerster, Josef (b Osenice, 22 Feb 1833; d Prague, 3 Jan 1907), Bohemian composer and organist. Wrote mainly church music. Organist at Prague Cathedral from 1887 and prof. at the Cons.

Foerster, Josef Bohuslav (b Dětenice, 30 Dec 1859; d Nový Vestec nr. Stará Boleslav, 29 May 1951), Czech composer, son of prec. Studied at Prague Organ School. Music teacher and critic at Hamburg, 1893–1903, and Vienna, 1903–18. Returned to Prague and was app. prof. at the Cons., and director in 1922.

Works incl. operas *Deborah* (1893), *Eva*, *Jessica* (on Shakespeare's *Merchant of Venice*, 1905), *The Invincibles*, *The Heart*, *The Fool*; incid. music for Vrchlický's *Samson*, Strindberg's *Lucky Peter's Journey*, Schiller's *Maria Stuart* and other plays; *Stabat Mater* and other works for chorus and orch.

5 symphs. (1887–1929), 6 suites, 4 symph. poems and 2 overtures for orch.; 2 vln. concertos; 5 string 4tets, 3 pf. trios, 5tet for wind instruments; 2 vln. and pf. sonatas, cello and pf. sonata; works for pf, org. and harmonium; 10 recitations with pf. accomp.; songs, part-songs.

Foerstrová-Lautererová, Berta (b Prague, 11 Jan 1869; d Prague, 9 Apr 1936), Czech soprano, wife of the prec. Debut Prague, 1887 as Agathe; created Julia in Dvořák's *Jacobin* (1889) and was heard as Tatyana by Tchaikovsky. Hamburg from 1893, under Mahler, and in 1900 followed him to the Hofoper, Vienna; roles there incl. Euryanthe, Nedda, Adalgisa, Mignon, Eva and Sieglinde.

Foggia, Francesco (b Rome *c* 1604; d Rome, 8 Jan 1688), Italian composer. Studied under Cifra, Nanini and Agostini; went into the service of the Elector of Cologne and Bavaria and the Archduke Leopold of Aus. in turn and after his return held var. church appts. in It. incl St John Lateran in Rome 1636–61, and Santa Maria Maggiore there from 1677.

Works incl. Masses, motets and other church music.

Fogliano, Giacomo (b Modena, 1468; d Modena, 10 Apr 1548), Italian composer of madrigals and *frottole*. Organist at Modena cathedral from 1489; influenced by Josquin.

Fogliano, Ludovico (b Modena; d after 1538), brother of prec. He sang in the papal chapel and was choirmaster at Modena

Cathedral. His *Musica Theorica* was pub. in 1529, and a single *frottola* was incl. in Petrucci's 9th book (1508).

Foldes, Andor (b Budapest, 21 Dec 1913), American pianist and conductor of Hungarian birth. Studied at Budapest Music Acad. with Dohnányi, winning the international Liszt Prize in 1933. He toured Eur. until 1939, when he went to the USA, becoming a citizen in 1948. He is well known as a performer of Bartók's music and for his playing of the classical repertory. He has conducted since 1960.

Foli (Foley), Allan James (b Cahir, Tipperary, 7 Aug 1835; d Southport, 20 Oct 1899), Irish bass. Studied at Naples and made his 1st appearance at Catania in 1862 in Rossini's *Otello*; in London in 1865. He sang Daland in *Der fliegende Holländer*, 1870; the 1st Wagner opera perf. in England. He sang regularly in oratorio as well as in opera.

Folia, La (*The Folly*), term used for melody found in popular dances and songs of the Baroque period. First mentioned by Francisco de Salinas in 1577, the melody was 1st used as the basis for variations in 1604 and later vars. have been by Corelli, Albicastro and Marais (*c* 1700), A. Scarlatti and C.P.E. Bach (1778). Liszt uses the theme in his *Rhapsodie Espagnole*, Rakhmaninov in his *Vars. on a theme of Corelli*, (ded. to Fritz Kreisler, fp Montreal, 12 Oct 1931), and Henze in *Aria de la folia española* (1977).

Folksong (*see also* **Volkslied**), a traditional song of often great but indeterminate antiquity the origins and comp. of which are unknown, but which has been preserved by being handed down aurally from generation to generation, often in several different versions or corruptions.

Folquet de Marseille (b Marseilles, *c* 1155; d Toulouse, 25 Dec 1231), French troubadour; he was a poet and musician 1179–93. He entered the Church at the end of the 12th cent. and d. as Bishop of Toulouse; much admired by Dante. 19 poems and 13 tunes of his songs are extant.

Fomin, Evstigney Ipatovich (b St Petersburg, 16 Aug 1761; d St Petersburg, 27 Apr 1800), Russian composer. Studied under Martini at Bologna and later became cond. in St Petersburg.

Works incl. operas *Boyeslav* (1786), *Orpheus* (1792), *Clorinda and Milo*, *The Americans* (1800), *The Golden Apple*, etc.

Fontaine, Pierre (b ? 1390; d *c* 1450), French singer and composer. Sang in the Papal Chapel in Rome 1420. Wrote *chansons*.

Fontana, Giovanni Battista (b Brescia, ?; d Padua, c 1631), Italian violinist and composer. Wrote sonatas for his instrument.

Fontanelli, Alfonso, Count (d Reggio d'Emilia, 15 Feb 1557; d Rome, 11 Feb 1622), Italian composer. Was in the service of the Duke of Modena at the end of the 16th cent. and in 1605 settled in Rome. Wrote madrigals.

Foote, Arthur (William) (b Salem, Mass., 5 Mar 1853; d Boston, 8 Apr 1937), American organist and composer. Studied at the New Eng. Cons. at Boston and later with Paine. For many years held organ appts. at Boston.

Works incl. cantatas on Longfellow's *The Farewell of Hiawatha* (1885), *The Wreck of the Hesperus* (1887) and *The Skeleton in Armour* (1891); overture *In the Mountains,* prologue to *Francesca da Rimini* and 3 suites for orch.; cello concerto; 3 string 4tets (1883–1901), pf. 4tet, pf. 5tet, 2 pf. trios; choral works; org. and pf. pieces; songs.

Forbes, Elizabeth (b Camberley, 3 Aug 1924), British critic and writer on music. She is well known as a journalist and has contributed to *Opera*, the *Financial Times* (1970–80) and the *Musical Times*. Her publications incl. *Mario and Grisi* (1985), and many entries on singers for the *New Grove Dictionary* (1980). Her transs. incl. operas by Spontini, Meyerbeer and Berwald for Nottingham Univ. and Max Brand's *Maschinist Hopkins* (BBC 1986).

Forbes, Sebastian (b Amersham, 22 May 1941), English composer and organist, son of Watson F., violist. Studied at RAM and King's College, Cambridge; later organist at Trinity.

Works incl. opera *Tom Cree* (1971); Chaconne and Symph. for orch.; pf. 5tet, pf. trio, 2 string 4tets; carols, madrigals and anthems for chorus; solo songs and organ music.

Ford, Thomas (b c 1580; d London, buried 17 Nov 1648), English lutenist and composer. He was in the service of Henry, Prince of Wales, in 1611 and app. one of the musicians to Charles I in 1626.

Works incl. *Musick of Sundrie Kindes* (1607) with airs to the lute (also to be perf. in 4 vocal parts), catches and rounds; 2 anthems contrib. to Leighton's *Teares and Lamentacions* and others incl. *Miserere my maker,* dances for lute.

Forefall = **Appoggiatura** (from below).

Forest, English composer, poss. the John F. who was canon and later dean of Wells, dying there in 1446. His motet *Qualis est dilectus tuus* was incl. (together with the beginning of *Ascendit Christus,* ascribed to Dunstable in a continental MS.), among the latest additions to the Old Hall MS. (*q.v.*). Other sacred music survives in continental sources.

Forkel, Johann Nikolaus (b Meeder, 22 Feb 1749); d Göttingen, 20 Mar 1818), German organist and music historian. Studied law at Göttingen, where he was dir. of music at the Univ. from 1779 to his death. Among his many writings his biog. of Bach (1802) is most notable—the first biog. of Bach and an important contrib. to the awakening interest in his music.

Forlana (or **Furlana**) (It.), an old Italian dance in 6–8 time. A classical ex. of its use is in Bach's Overture (Suite) in C for orch. and a modern one in Ravel's *Tombeau de Couperin.*

Form. The form of a composition is the course it is planned to take from beginning to end in such a way as to unfold itself logically. *See e.g.* **Binary, Fugue, Rondo, Sonata, Suite, Ternary, Variations.**

Formé, Nicolas (b Paris, 26 Apr 1567; d Paris, 27 May 1638), French composer. He was a clerk and singer in the Sainte-Chapelle in Paris, 1587–92, then became a countertenor in the royal chapel and succeeded Eustache du Caurroy as choirmaster and comp. there in 1609. Although almost dismissed from the Sainte-Chapelle for not conforming to the eccles. rules, he returned there in 1626 and, as a favourite musician of Louis XIII, enjoyed special privileges.

Works incl. Masses, motets, Magnificat and other church music.

Formes, Karl Johann (b Mülheim, 7 Aug 1816; d San Francisco, 15 Dec 1889), German bass. Debut Cologne 1842, Sarastro; created Flotow's Plunkett at Kärntnertortheater, Vienna, 1847. CG 1850–68 as Rocco, Leporello and in operas by Meyerbeer; sang in fp of the revised vers. of Spohr's *Faust* (1852). He appeared in NY from 1857, later taught at San Francisco.

Forqueray, French family of vla. da gamba players:

1. Antoine F. (b Paris, Sep 1672; d Mantes, 28 Jun 1745), pupil of his father. he played before Louis XIV at the age of 5. In 1689 he became a royal chamber musician.

2. Jean Baptiste Antoine F. (b Paris, 3 Apr 1699; d Paris, 15 Aug 1782), son of prec. His father's pupil. In the service of the Prince of Conti.

Forrest-Heyther Part-Books, a set of 6 books in the Bodleian Library, Oxford (Music School e. 376–81) containing 18 Masses of the early Tudor period; the books were started at Cardinal College, Oxford, and contain masses by Taverner. They belonged to a William Forrest in 1530 and subsequently to William Heyther, who may have written down the 3 Eng. anthems which the books also contain. The last part of the 6th book is in the hand of John Baldwin.

Forrester, Maureen (b Montreal, 25 Jul 1930), Canadian contralto. Debut (recital) Montreal, 1953. Appeared in Paris 1955 and made NY (Town Hall) debut in 1956. The following year she sang in Mahler's *Resurrection* Symph., under Bruno Walter, with the NY PO, and in the Verdi *Requiem* in London, under Sargent. Debut in opera Toronto 1961, as Gluck's Orpheus, and other roles incl. Ulrica, Brangaene, Cornelia in *Giulio Cesare* and La Cieca. In 1975 she made her belated NY Met debut, as the *Rheingold* Erda. Well-known in *Das Lied von der Erde* and as The Angel in *Gerontius*.

Forsell, John (b Stockholm, 6 Nov 1868; d Stockholm, 30 May 1941), Swedish baritone. Debut Stockholm 1896, Rossini's Figaro. In 1909–10 he was heard at the NY Met as Amfortas, Germont and Telramund. His best role was Don Giovanni, which he sang at CG in 1909 and at Salzburg in 1930. He was director of Stockholm Opera 1924–39. Other roles incl. Sachs, Beckmesser, Scarpia and Onegin.

Förster, (Emanuel) Aloys (b Niederstein, Silesia, 26 Jan 1748; d Vienna, 12 Nov 1823), German oboist and composer. After 2 years as a military bandsman, 1766–8, he lived as a freelance teacher and comp., first in Prague, then, from 1779, in Vienna. Author of a treatise on thorough-bass. Beethoven acknowledged his debt to Förster in the comp. of string 4tets.

Works incl. 48 string 4tets; 4 string 5tets; 6 pf. 4tets, and other chamber music; pf. concertos, sonatas, variations etc.

Forster, Georg (b Amberg/Oberpfalz, *c* 1510; d Nuremberg, 12 Nov 1568), German music pub. and composer. He pub. 5 sets of Ger. songs, the *Frische teutsche Liedlein*, 1539–56, some of which are by himself; he also comp. sacred and Lat. works.

Forte (It. lit. strong) = loud. Generally abbr. by the symbol *f*.

Forte, Allen (b Portland, 23 Dec 1926), American music theorist, known for his formulation of set-series, partic. to explain atonal music. His major works are *The Structure of Atonal Music* (1973) and *The Harmonic Organization of 'The Rite of Spring'* (1978).

Fortepiano (It. lit. loud-soft), the early It. name for the pf., given to the instrument because, unlike the harpsichord, it was capable of having varying intensities of tone prod. by the player's touch.

Forti, Anton (b Vienna, 8 Jun 1790; d Vienna, 18 Jul 1859), Austrian baritone and tenor. His career began at Eisenstadt and he sang at the Kärntnertortheater, Vienna, 1813–34; often heard in Mozart and created Pizarro in the final version of *Fidelio* (1814) and Weber's Lysiart (1823). Among his tenor roles were Max and Rossini's Otello. Appeared occasionally until 1841; sang also in operas by Isouard and Halévy.

Fortissimo (It. superl., lit. strongest) = loudest. Abbr. by *ff*.

Fortner, Wolfgang (b Leipzig, 12 Oct 1907; d Heidelberg, 11 Sep 1987), German composer. Studied with Hermann Grabner. From 1931 to 1954 he taught theory and comp. at the Evangelical Church Music Inst. in Heidelberg, where he founded and cond. a chamber orch. In 1954 he became prof. of comp. at the NW Ger. Music Acad. in Detmold, and in 1957 succeeded Genzmer at the Musikhochschule in Freiburg-im-Breisgau. His music shows the influence of Reger and Hindemith. He also used serial techniques in a personal way.

Works incl. *Bluthochzeit* (after Lorca, 1956; rev. 1963), *Corinna* (1958), *In seinem Garten liebt Don Pimperlin Belison* (after Lorca, 1962), *Elisabeth Tudor* (1972); ballet *Die Weisse Rose* (after Wilde); *Deutsche Liedmesse, Marianische Antiphonen* for unaccomp. chorus; symph., *Sinfonia concertante* for chamber orch.; concertos for var. instruments and small orch.; 4 string 4tets (1929–75), *Suite* for solo cello (1932), 5 *Bagatelles* for wind 5tet (1960).

Forty-Eight (Preludes and Fugues) (Bach). *See* **Wohltemperierte Clavier**.

Forza d'amor paterno, La (*The Force of Paternal Love*), opera by Stradella (lib. by ?), prod. Genoa, Teatro del Falcone, Carnival 1678.

Forza del destino, La (*The Force of Destiny*), opera by Verdi (lib. by F.M. Piave, based on the drama by A.P. de Saavedra, Duke of Rivas, *Don Alvaro, o La fuerza de sino*), prod. St Petersburg, 22 Nov 1862; fp in It., Rome, Teatro Apollo, 7 Feb 1863.

Foss (orig. **Fuchs**), **Lukas** (b Berlin, 15 Aug 1922), German, later American composer, conductor and pianist. Studied in Berlin with Julius Goldstein and from 1933 in Paris with Lazare Lévy (pf.) and Noel Gallon (comp.). In 1937 he went with his parents to the USA, studying at the Curtis Institute in Philadelphia. Later he studied with Hindemith at Yale Univ.; in 1944 he gave the Boston fp of Hindemith's *Four Temperaments* for pf. and strings. In 1945 he won a Guggenheim Fellowship and in 1950 a Fulbright Fellowship. He became prof. of comp. at California Univ. in 1953. He has composed much, in more recent years using an aleatory style. He was app. conductor of the Buffalo PO in 1964; music dir. Milwaukee SO from 1981. Featured composer, Aldeburgh Festival, 1987.

Works incl. operas *The Jumping Frog of Calaveras County* (after Mark Twain, 1950), *Griffelkin* (television opera, 1955), *Introductions and Goodbyes* (lib. by Foss and Menotti); ballet *Gift of the Magi*; cantata *The Prairie* (after Carl Sandberg), oratorio *A Parable of Death* (Rilke); 2 pf. concertos (1944, 1951); 2 symphs.; concerto for cello, ob. and clar.; 3 string 4tets; incid. music to *The Tempest*.

Fossa, Johannes de (b *c* 1540, d Munich, 1603), German or Flemish composer. He wrote 6 Masses and other sacred works. He succeeded Lassus as *Kapellmeister* at the Munich court in 1594.

Foster, Lawrence (b Los Angeles, 23 Oct 1941), American conductor. He studied in Los Angeles with Fritz Zweig and was asst. cond. of the LA PO 1965–8. Chief guest cond. RPO 1969–74; Houston SO 1971–8. In 1976 he led the revised vers. of Walton's *Troilus and Cressida* at CG. Music dir. Deutsche Oper am Rhein, Düsseldorf-Duisburg, from 1981. He is active on behalf of modern music and has given the fps of works by Birtwistle, Goehr and Crosse.

Foster, Stephen (Collins) (b nr. Pittsburgh, 4 Jul 1826; d New York, 13 Jan 1864), American composer. Almost wholly self-taught in music pub. his 1st song as early as 1842. He wrote *c* 175 popular songs, incl. *Old Folks at Home*, *My Old Kentucky Home*, *Massa's in the cold, cold ground*.

Fou Ts'ong (b Shanghai, 10 Mar 1934), British pianist of Chinese birth. Studied at Warsaw Cons.; prize in Chopin Comp. 1955. Settled in London from 1958. Widely heard in Debussy and Mozart.

Foulds, John (Herbert) (b Manchester, 2 Nov 1880; d Calcutta, 24 Apr 1939), English composer and conductor. He joined a theatre orch. in Manchester at the age of 14 and the Hallé Orch. in 1900. Worked at various opera-houses abroad, gave concerts for the forces during the 1914–18 war, and later cond. var. music societies in London.

Works incl. incid. music for Kalidasa's *Sakuntala*, Euripides' *Trojan Women* and several others; *A Vision of Dante* (concert opera 1905–8), *A World Requiem* for solo voices, chorus and orch. (1919–21); *Epithalamium*, *Keltic Suite* (1911) and *Suite fantastique* for orch.; *Holiday Sketches*, *Suite française* and *Gaelic Dream Song* for small orch.; *Idyll* for string orch.; *Mood Pictures* for vln. and pf.; Variations and *Essays in the Modes* for pf.

Four Last Songs (*Vier letzte Lieder*), sequence of songs for soprano and orch. by Strauss, comp. 1948; his last work. Fp London, 22 May 1950, with Flagstad and Furtwängler. First 3 texts are by Hermann Hesse; *Frühling*, *September*, *Beim Schlafengehen*. No. 4 by Eichendorff: *Im Abendrot*.

Four Saints in Three Acts, opera by Virgil Thomson (lib. by Gertrude Stein), prod. in concert form at Ann Arbor, Mich., 20 May 1933 and on the stage at Hartford, Conn., 8 Feb 1934.

Four Sea Interludes, concert work by Britten derived from his opera *Peter Grimes* (fp London, 1945). The 4 sections are titled *Dawn*, *Sunday Morning*, *Moonlight* and *Storm*; fp Cheltenham, 13 Jun 1945.

Four Seasons, The (*Le quattro Stagioni*), 4 vln. concertos by Vivaldi in E, G min., F and F min., depicting the seasons. The 1st 4 of 12 vln. concertos op. 8 pub. 1725 in Amsterdam as 'The contest between harmony and invention'.

Four Serious Songs (Brahms). *See* **Vier ernste Gesänge**.

Four Temperaments, The, title for symphony no. 2, op. 16, by Nielsen; comp. 1901–2, fp Copenhagen, 1 Dec 1902.

The Four Temperaments, Theme and Variations, work for pf. and string orch. by Hindemith. Commissioned by Balanchine and comp. 1940; fp (concert) Boston, 3 Sep 1944, Lukas Foss as soloist. Stage prod. NY, City Ballet, 20 Nov 1946. The 4 main sections are titled *Melancholy*, *Sanguine*, *Phlegmatic* and *Choleric*.

Fourestier, Louis (Félix André) (b Montpellier, 31 May 1892; d Boulogne-Billancourt, 30 Sep 1976), French conductor and composer. Pupil of Leroux, Gédalge, Vidal and d'Indy at the Paris Cons., and a follower of Dukas; took the Prix de Rome in 1925. He cond. much in Paris and also took charge of concerts at Angers, Cannes and Vichy, being app. cond. of the Paris Opéra in 1938.

Works incl. cantata *La Mort d'Adonis* (1927), symph. poem *Polynice* and *A Saint-*

Valéry for orch.; *Orchestique* (Paul Valéry); 4 poems by Tagore for voice and orch.; string 4tets.

Fournets, René (b Pau, 2 Dec 1858; d Paris, Dec 1926), French bass. Debut Paris, Opéra-Comique, 1884, as Gounod's Frère Laurent. At the Opéra he was successful 1892–9 as Méphistophélès, Wotan, Leporello and the Landgrave. At the Concerts Lamoureux he sang in the 1897 fp of Chabrier's *Briseïs*. He was highly regarded in operas by Massenet.

Fournier, Pierre (b Paris, 24 Jun 1906; d Geneva, 8 Jan 1986), French cellist. Studied at the Paris Cons., making his debut in 1925. He toured widely and was prof. of cello at the Paris Cons. 1941–9. Chamber music with Szigeti, Primrose and Badura-Skoda. He gave the fps of concertos by Roussel, Martin and Martinů.

Fourth, an interval which embraces 4 degrees of the diatonic scale. If perfect, it covers 2 tones and a semitone, e.g.:

It may be augmented or diminished, e.g.:

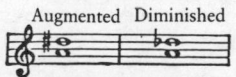

Fox Strangways A(rthur) H(enry) (b Norwich, 14 Sep 1859; d Dinton, nr. Salisbury, 2 May 1948), English musicologist, critic and editor. Educ. at Wellington Coll. and Balliol Coll., Oxford and studied music in Berlin. After teaching at Dulwich and Wellington Colls. until 1910, and visiting India, on the music of which he wrote a book, *The Music of Hindostan*, he became asst. critic of *The Times* in London in 1911 and chief critic of the *Observer* in 1925. Founded *Music & Letters* in 1920 and ed. it until 1936. He also wrote a biog. of Cecil Sharp and trans. many songs (some with Steuart Wilson, *q.v.*) by Schubert, Brahms, Wolf.

Fra Diavolo, ou L'Hôtellerie de Terracine (*Brother Devil, or the Inn at Terraccina*), opera by Auber (lib. by Scribe), prod. Paris, Opéra-Comique, 28 Jan 1830.

Fra due litiganti il terzo gode (*Between Two Litigants the Third makes Profit*), opera by Sarti (lib. altered from Goldoni's *Le nozze*), prod. Milan, La Scala, 14 Sep 1782. Mozart quotes a tune from it in the second-act finale of *Don Giovanni*: it was 1st prod. in Vienna, 28 May 1783.

Franc, Guillaume Le. *See* **Le Franc.**

Françaix, Jean (b Le Mans, 23 May 1912), French composer. Studied under his father, director of the Le Mans Cons. and Nadia Boulanger in Paris.

Works incl. operas *Le Diable boiteux* (1938), *La Main de gloire* (1950), *Paris à nous deux* (1954); ballets *Beach* and *Le Roi nu* (after Hans Andersen).

Symph., *Suite concertante*; *Divertissement* for string trio and orch.; pf. concerto and concertino, fl. concerto, Fantasy for cello and orch.; *Petit Quatuor* for strings, 5tet for fl., harp and strings.

Francesca da Rimini. *See also* **Françoise de Rimini; Paolo e Francesca.**

Opera by Generali (lib. by P. Pola, based on Dante), prod. Venice, Teatro La Fenice, 26 Dec 1829.

Opera by Nápravník (lib. by O.O. Paleček and E.P. Ponomarev, based on a play by Stephen Phillips, *Paolo and Francesca*, and farther back on Dante), prod. St Petersburg, 9 Dec 1902.

Opera by Rakhmaninov (lib. taken from scenes of Pushkin's play, with additions by Modest Tchaikovsky, based on Dante), prod. Moscow, 24 Jan 1906.

Opera by Zandonai (lib. by T. Ricordi, based on d'Annunzio's tragedy, and farther back on Dante), prod. Turin, Teatro Regio, 19 Feb 1914.

Symph. fantasy by Tchaikovsky, op. 32 (based on Dante), comp. 1876, fp Moscow, 9 Mar 1877.

Unfinished opera by Goetz, completed by Ernst Frank (lib. by comp.), prod. Mannheim, 30 Sep 1877.

Francescatti, Zino (b Marseilles, 9 Aug 1902), French violinist. Made his debut aged 5 and played the Beethoven vln. concerto aged 10. In 1926 he toured England with Ravel. US debut 1939, NY PO.

Francescina, La. *See* **Duparc, Elisabeth.**

Francesco Canova da Milano (b ? Monza, 18 Aug 1497; d Milan 15 Apr 1543), Italian lutenist and composer. Known as 'Il divino', he was the finest comp. of lute music before Dowland. In the service 1st of the Duke of Mantua, *c* 1510, and then of Pope Paul III from 1535. Pub. and contrib. to several books of lute pieces.

Franchetti, Alberto (b Turin, 18 Sep 1860; d Viareggio, 4 Aug 1942). Italian composer. Studied 1st in It., then with Draeseke at Dresden and at the Munich Cons. under Rheinberger. Director of the Cheubini Cons., Florence, 1926–8.

Works incl. operas *Asrael* (1888), *Cristoforo Colombo* (1892), *Fior d'Alpe*, *Signor di*

Pourceaugnac (after Molière, 1897), *Germania*, *La figlia di Jorio* (after d'Annunzio), *Notte di leggenda*, *Glauco* and (with Giordano) *Giove a Pompeii* (1921); symph. in E min.

Franchomme, Auguste (Joseph) (b Lille, 10 Apr 1808; d Paris, 21 Jan 1884), French cellist. Studied at the Paris Cons. He played in var. theatre orchs. and had much success as solo and 4tet player. Prof. at the Cons. from 1846. Chopin, whose friend he was, wrote the Polonaise for cello and pf., op. 3, for him, and Franchomme collaborated with him, as well as with Bertini and Osborne, in duos on operatic airs, Chopin's choice being Meyerbeer's *Robert le Diable*. He was the cellist in Alard's 4tet. Chopin's cello sonata is ded. to him.

Franci, Benvenuto (b Pienza, nr. Siena, 1 Jul 1891; d Rome, 27 Feb 1985), Italian baritone. Debut Rome, Teatro Costanzi, 1918, in Mascagni's *Lodoletta*; sang in the fp there of *Il piccolo Marat*, 1921. In 1923 he sang Amonasro at La Scala, under Toscanini, and in the following two seasons took part in the fps of operas by Giordano and Zandonai. CG 1925, 1931 and 1946, as Scarpia and Gerard. In 1940 he was Barak at La Scala, in the Italian fp of *Die Frau ohne Schatten*. Other roles incl. Macbeth, Barnaba and Telramund.

Francis of Assisi (1181 or 2–1226), Italian saint and poet. *See* **Inghelbrecht** (*Cantique des créatures*), **Loeffler** (*Canticum*), **Nobilissima Visione** (Hindemith), **Sigtenhorst Meyer** (*Hymn to the Sun*), **St François d'Assise** (Messiaen).

Francisque, Antoine (b Saint-Quentin, *c* 1570; d Paris, buried 5 Oct 1604), French lutenist and composer. He lived at Cambrai in 1596 and was married there, but went to Paris not long after, pub. a book of lute pieces, *Le Trésor d'Orphée* (1600), some comp. by himself, others arr. from popular dances.

Franck, César (Auguste) (b Liège, 10 Dec 1822; d Paris, 8 Nov 1890), Belgian composer. Precociously gifted, esp. as a pianist, he made a concert tour in Belg. at the age of 11. Sent to Paris in 1835 to study, he entered the Cons. in 1837. There he won prizes each year until he left in 1842. He returned to Belg., but settled permanently in Paris in 1844. In 1848 he married a young actress and was app. organist at the church of Saint-Jean-Saint-François in 1851. In 1853 he became choirmaster and in 1858 organist at Sainte-Clotilde. App. prof. of the organ at the Cons. in 1872. He became a chevalier of the Legion of Honour in 1885 and 2 years later, 30 Jan 1887, a festival of his music was held. 6 months before his death he was involved in a street accident.

Works incl. OPERAS: *Le Valet de ferme* (1851–3, unpub.), *Hulda* (1882–5), *Ghisèle*; symph. in D min. (1888); symph. poems, *Les Éolides* (1876), *Le Chasseur maudit* (after Burger), *Psyché* (with chorus); *Les Djinns* and *Variations symphoniques* for pf. and orch.

CHAMBER: 4 pf. trios (1834–42), pf. 5tet (1879), string 4tet; sonata for vln. and pf. (1886).

WORKS FOR CHORUS AND ORCH (some with solo voices): *Ruth*, *La Tour de Babel*, *Les Béatitudes* (1870), *Rédemption* (1874), *Rébecca*, Psalm cl; *Paris: chant patriotique* for tenor and orch.; *Messe solennelle* for bass and org.; Mass for 3 voices, org., harp, cello and double bass; 3 motets, 3 offertories and other small sacred vocal works.

KEYBOARD AND SONGS: *c* 16 works for pf., incl. *Prélude, Choral et Fugue* and *Prélude, Aria et Final*; 9 works for org., incl. 6 *Pièces pour Grand Orgue*, 44 *Petites Pièces*, 3 *Pièces pour Grand Orgue*, 3 *Chorals*; 5 works for harmonium; songs to poems by Chateaubriand, Hugo, Musset, Dumas, sen., Sully-Prudhomme, Joseph Méry, Jean-Pierre de Florian, Jean Reboul, Marceline Desbordes-Valmore.

Franck, Johann Wolfgang (b Unterschwaningen, bap. 17 Jun 1644; d ? London, *c* 1710), German composer. *Kapellmeister* at Ansbach between 1673 and 1679, when he killed a musician of the chapel and wounded his wife from jealousy and fled to Hamburg, where he prod. 17 operas in 1679–86. After 1690 he lived in London for some years, giving concerts with Robert King, contrib. songs to the *Gentleman's Journal* and writing one for Colley Cibber's *Love's Last Shift*, also music for a masque by Motteux added to Shadwell's adaptation of Shakespeare's *Timon of Athens*.

Franck, Melchoir (b Zittau, *c* 1579; d Coburg, 1 Jun 1639), German composer. Worked at Augsburg and briefly at Nuremberg, and in 1603 became *Kapellmeister* to the Duke of Coburg. He was influenced by Hassler and the Venetians.

Works incl. *Melodiae sacrae* for 3 to 12 voices, *Paradisus musicus* for 4 voices, church music, hymn-tunes; songs with instrumental accomp.; madrigals; instrumental pieces.

Franckenstein, Clemens von (b Wiesentheid, Bavaria, 14 Jul 1875; d Hechendorf,

Bavaria, 19 Aug 1942), German composer. Studied in Vienna and later at Munich with Thuille and at Frankfurt with Knorr. After a visit to USA he cond. the Moody-Manners Opera Co. in Eng., 1902–7, then worked at the court theatres of Wiesbaden and Berlin, and in 1912 became general intendant of the Munich court theatres.

Works incl. operas *Griseldis* (1898), *Rahab* (1911) and *Des Kaisers Dichter* (1920); ballet *Die Biene*; orchestral works: variations on a theme by Meyerbeer, Dance Suite, Serenade, Rhapsody, Praeludium, Symph. Suite, *Das alte Lied*, 4 Dances, *Festival Prelude*, chamber music; pf. works; songs.

Franco of Cologne, 13th-cent. music theorist, author of an *Ars cantus mensurabilis* surviving in 7 MSS. It expounds the system of notation in his day, now called 'Franconian'. An anon. monk of Bury St Edmunds, writing of Parisian music in the 13th cent., refers also to a 'Franco primus', apparently a Parisian, who also wrote on the same subject.

Francœur, François (b Paris, 21 Sep 1698; d Paris, 5 Aug 1787), French violinist and composer. Pupil of his father, Joseph F., he joined the Opéra orch. at the age of 15 and there met Rebel, with whom he worked for the rest of his life. In 1720 he pub. his 1st vln. sonatas, and in 1723 went with Rebel to Prague for the coronation of Charles VI. After his return to Paris in 1726 he gradually rose to the highest positions in Fr. music: comp. to the court 1727; member of the king's band 1730; 1743 Inspector, 1757 Director of the Opéra, 1760 Superintendent of the king's music (the last three jointly with Rebel). His nephew, Louis Joseph F. (1738–1804), was also a violinist and comp., and for a time Dir. of the Opéra.

Works incl. operas, comp. jointly with Rebel, beginning with *Pyrame et Thisbé* (1726), ballets, vln. sonatas, etc.

Françoise de Rimini (*Francesca da R.*), opera by A. Thomas (lib. by J. Barbier and M. Carré, based on Dante), prod. Paris, Opéra, 14 Apr 1882.

Francs-Juges, Les (*The Judges of the Secret Court*), unfinished opera by Berlioz (lib. by H. Ferrand), comp. 1827–8; fp of the overture Paris, 26 May 1828. The rest discarded or used elsewhere, e.g. in the *Symphonie fantastique*.

Frankel, Benjamin (b London, 31 Jan 1906; d London, 12 Feb 1973), English composer. He studied in Ger. and at 17 returned to London and picked up a precarious living as music teacher, café pianist and jazz-band violinist. He managed to attend the GSM in the daytime and gradually improved his living as orchestrator and theatre cond., finally succeeding as cond. and comp. of film music. An opera, *Marching Song* (lib. by H. Keller, after J. Whiting's play) was unfinished at his death; completed by Buxton Orr and perf. on BBC 1983.

Other works incl. music for many films, *Pezzo sinfonico* for orch., *Solemn Speech and Discussion* and *Music for Young Comrades* for string orch., *The Aftermath* (Robert Nichols) for tenor, strings, tpt. and drums; 8 symphs. (1952–72); vln. concerto; 5 string 4tets, 3 *Sketches* for string 4tet, string trio, trio for clar., cello and pf., *Early Morning Pieces* for ob., clar. and bassoon; vln. and pf. sonata, sonatas for unaccomp. vln. and vla., *Sonata ebraica* for cello and harp, *Élégie juive* for cello and pf.; Passacaglia for 2 pfs.; pf. pieces.

Frankl, Peter (b Budapest, 2 Oct 1935), British pianist of Hungarian birth. He studied in Budapest; debut there 1950. Won competitions in Paris, Munich and Rio de Janeiro in late 1950s. London debut 1962; British citizen from 1967. Has formed pf. trio with György Pauk (vln.) and Ralph Kirshbaum (cello).

Franklin, David (b London, 17 May 1908; d Evesham, Worcs., 22 Oct 1973), English bass. He sang at Glyndebourne 1936–9 as the Commendatore, Banquo and Sarastro. CG 1947–50 as Rocco, Ochs, Pimen, Pogner, Marke, and Mars in *The Olympians* by Bliss. After a throat operation in 1951 he was unable to sing but took speaking parts in *Ariadne auf Naxos* and *Die Entführung* at Glyndebourne, 1953–8.

Frantz, Ferdinand (b Kassel, 8 Feb 1906; d Munich, 26 May 1959), German bassbaritone. Debut Kassel 1927. He sang in Hamburg from 1938, until the opera house was destroyed, and in Munich from 1943; appeared in the major Wagner roles and sang Jupiter with the Munich co. at CG in the only prod. in Brit. to date of Strauss's *Die Liebe der Danae* (1953). NY Met debut 1949 as the *Walküre* Wotan and recorded the same role with Furtwängler. Often heard as Sachs and recorded role in *Die Meistersinger* with Kempe.

Franz (orig. **Knauth**), **Robert** (b Halle, 28 Jun 1815; d Halle, 24 Oct 1892), German composer. After much parental opposition he became a pupil of Schneider at Dessau in 1835, and after 2 years returned home, devoting himself to study and comp. without being able to secure a musical post. He became one of the best exponents of Ger. songs, the 1st of which he pub. in 1843 and which attracted the attention of Schumann, Mendelssohn, Liszt and others. He then became a church organist and choral cond., also lecturer at Halle Univ. Much troubled by increasing deafness and a nervous complaint, he had to retire in 1868, but did much work in ed. the older choral classics.

Works incl. more than 350 songs to texts by Burns, Eichendorff, Lenau, Geibel, Heine, Müller and Goethe; church music; part-songs.

Fraschini, Gaetano (b Pavia, 16 Feb 1816; d Naples, 23 May 1887), Italian tenor. Appeared as a church and opera singer at Pavia in 1837 in operas by Donizetti; sang in the fps of 6 operas by Pacini in Naples. Between 1845 and 1859 created roles in Verdi's *Alzira*, *Il corsaro*, *La battaglia di Legnano*, *Stiffelio* and *Un ballo in maschera*. London debut, 1847.

Fraser, Marjory Kennedy (b Perth, 1 Oct 1857; d Edinburgh, 22 Nov 1930), Scottish singer and folksong collector, daughter of David Kennedy. Studied under her father and Mathilde Marchesi in Paris and began to visit the Hebrides to collect folksongs in 1905. Pub. several collections of these songs and wrote the lib. for Bantock's opera *The Seal Woman*.

Frasi, Giulia, Italian singer. Made her London debut in 1743, the same year sang in *Roxana, or Alexander in India* (an adaptation of Handel's *Alessandro*), and subsequently in several of Handel's oratorios, incl. *Susanna, Solomon, Theodora* and *Jephtha*.

Frau ohne Schatten, Die (*The Woman without a Shadow*), opera by R. Strauss (lib. by H. von Hofmannsthal), prod. Vienna, Opera, 10 Oct 1919.

Frauenliebe und -Leben (*Woman's Love and Life*), song cycle by Schumann, op. 42 (8 poems by Adelbert von Chamisso), comp. in 1840.

Frauenlob (Heinrich von Meissen) (b Meissen; d Mainz, 1318), German *Minnesänger*. His songs belong to the end of the tradition of the *Minnesinger*, and in some ways foreshadow those of the *Meistersinger*.

Fredegunda, opera by Keiser (lib. by J.U. König, from the It. by Francesco Silvani), prod. Hamburg, Theater beim Gänsemarkt, Mar 1715.

Frederick II (Frederick the Great) (b Berlin, 24 Jan 1712; d Potsdam, 17 Aug 1786), king of Prussia, flautist and composer. Learnt music from Gottlob Hayne, the Berlin Cathedral organist, and in 1728 had fl. lessons from Quantz. In 1734 estab. a private band at his castle at Rheinsberg and on his accession in 1740 a court band at Berlin and Potsdam. Graun, Quantz and C.P.E. Bach were in his service.

Works incl. part of the opera *Il rè pastore* (Metastasio) and the libretti for several operas by Graun; over 120 instrumental works, many with prominent fl. parts.

Fredigundis, opera by Franz Schmidt (lib. by B. Warden and I.M. Welleminsky, after F. Dahn); comp. 1916–21, prod. Berlin, 19 Dec 1922.

Freischütz, Der (lit. *The Freeshooter*), opera by Weber (lib. by F. Kind, based on a story in Apel and Laun's *Gespensterbuch*), prod. Berlin, Schauspielhaus, 18 Jun 1821.

Freising, Eberhard von (Eberhardus Frisingensis) 9th-cent. author of a short treatise on the measurement of organ pipes.

Freitas Branco, Luiz (b Lisbon, 12 Oct 1890; d Lisbon 27 Nov 1955), Portuguese composer. Studied at Lisbon, with Humperdinck in Berlin, and in Paris. Taught scorereading at the Lisbon Cons. from 1916 and in 1930 took charge of the master-class in comp.

Works incl. oratorio, cantata; 4 symphs. (1924–52), 2 Port. suites for orch.; vln. concerto, Ballad for pf. and orch.; songs with orch.; string 4tet; 2 vln. and pf. sonatas; cello and pf. sonatas; pf. pieces; songs; madrigals to words by Camoens.

Freitas, Frederico de (b Lisbon, 15 Nov 1902; d Lisbon, 12 Jan 1980), Portuguese conductor and composer. Studied at the Lisbon Cons. He visited Brazil, Fr., Spain and Hol. as cond. and became broadcasting cond. at Lisbon.

Works incl. opera *Luzdor*; ballets *Ribatejo* and *Nazeré*; cantata *The Seven Words of Our Lady*; symph. poems *Lenda dos bailarins* and *Suite colonial*; poem on an eclogue by Virgil and prelude on a Lisbon street-cry for string orch.; *Quarteto Concertante* for 2 vlns., 2 cellos and string orch.; sonata for vln. and cello; instrumental works; pf. pieces; songs.

Fremstad, Olive (b Stockholm, 14 Mar 1871; d Irvington, NY, 21 Apr 1951), Swedish soprano. Adopted by an Amer. couple, who took her to Minnesota, she studied pf. in Minneapolis and then singing in NY in 1890. In 1893 she studied in Berlin with Lilli Lehmann, making her debut in 1895, in Cologne, as Azucena. She later sang at Bayreuth, Munich, Vienna and London, becoming a leading soprano at the NY Met from 1903 to 1914, where she was heard as Sieglinde, Kundry, Selika, Carmen, Salome and Armide in the fp of Gluck's opera in the US (1910). Her first Isolde, 1 Jan 1908, was on Mahler's debut as cond. at the Met. An outstanding Wagner singer, she also excelled in It. opera.

French Horn. See **Horn.**

French Overture. See **Overture.**

French Sixth. See **Augmented Sixth Chords.**

French Suites, 6 keyboard suites by Bach comp. mainly at Cöthen c 1722 and completed by c 1724. They differ from the Eng. Suites in having no preludes.

Freni, Mirella (b Modena, 27 Feb 1935), Italian soprano. Debut Modena 1955, Micaela. Glyndebourne 1960-2 as Zerlina, Susanna, Adina. London, CG, since 1961 as Nannetta and Violetta. US debut Chicago 1963 as Marguerite. Sang Mimi at La Scala, Milan in 1963 and on her NY Met debut in 1965. Toured the US with the Paris Opéra Co. in 1976. Other roles incl. Amelia Boccanegra, Elisabeth de Valois (Salzburg, with Karajan), Butterfly and Manon.

Frescobaldi, Girolamo (b Ferrara, Sep 1583; d Rome, 1 Mar 1643), Italian composer and organist. Studied at Ferrara under the cathedral organist Luzzaschi. Visited Brussels, 1607-8. App. organist at St Peter's in Rome, 1608. He was given leave of absence from 1628 to 1633, during which time he served as organist to Ferdinand II, Duke of Tuscany; also worked in Brussels, Mantua and Florence. Froberger was among his pupils.

Works incl. 2 Masses, a Magnificat, motets and madrigals; *ricercari, canzoni,* toccatas, etc. for organ and for harpsichord; fantasies for instruments in 4 parts; madrigals.

Frescoes of Piero della Francesca, The, work for orch. in 3 movts. by Martinů, depicting 3 of the frescoes by Piero at Arezzo; comp. 1955, fp Salzburg, 28 Aug 1956, cond. Kubelik.

Frets, the small strips of gut, wood or metal fixed on the fingerboard on certain string instruments (incl. the lute, viols, guitar, mandoline, banjo, ukelele and the Rus. balalaika), enabling the player to play in tune with certainty, the string being stopped by the finger at exactly the right spot, determined by the frets.

Freunde von Salamanka, Die (*The Friends of Salamanca*), operetta by Schubert (lib. by J. Mayrhofer), comp. 1815, but never perf.

in Schubert's lifetime; prod. with a new lib. by G. Ziegler, Halle, 6 May 1928.

Frezzolini, Erminia (b Orvieto, 27 Mar 1818; d Paris, 5 Nov 1884), Italian soprano. Made her 1st appearance in 1837 at Florence in Bellini's *Beatrice di Tenda.* Sang in Vienna, London, St Petersburg, Madrid, Paris, USA and Milan, where she sang in the fps of Verdi's *I Lombardi* and *Giovanna d'Arco.*

Friberth, Karl (b Wullersdorf, Lower Austria, 6 Jun 1736; d Vienna, 6 Aug 1816), Austrian tenor, author and composer. Studied with Bonno and Gassmann in Vienna and in 1759 joined the Esterházy household under Haydn, for whom he wrote the lib. of *L'incontro improvviso.* Returned to Vienna as *Kapellmeister* to the Jesuits and Minorites in 1776. Composed mainly church music.

Fricci, Antonietta (b Vienna, 8 Jan 1840; d Turin, 7 Sep 1912), Austrian soprano. Debut Pisa 1858, Violetta. La Scala 1865-73, as Norma, Lady Macbeth and Selika. In Jun 1867 she sang Eboli at CG, in the 1st Brit. perf. of *Don Carlos.*

Frick, Gottlob (b Olbronn, 28 Jul 1906), German bass. Debut Coburg 1934, as Daland. Dresden 1940-50; Munich and Vienna from 1953. Bayreuth 1957-64 as Pogner, Hagen and Hunding. London, CG 1957-67 in prods. of *Der Ring des Nibelungen;* from 1963 under Solti, with whom he recorded Hagen in the 1st stereo issue of *Götterdämmerung.* Gurnemanz at CG in 1971. NY Met debut 1961 as Fafner; a proposed debut in 1950 was vetoed by Rudolf Bing on account of Frick's alleged political past.

Fricker, Peter Racine (b London, 5 Sep 1920), English composer, partly of French descent. He studied at the RCM in London and later with Seiber. His wind 5tet won the Clements Prize in 1947 and his 1st symph. the Koussevitsky Award. Composer-in-residence Univ. of California at Santa Barbara from 1964.

Works incl. radio operas *The Death of Vivien* and *My Brother Died* (1954); ballet *Canterbury Prologue* (after Chaucer); oratorio *A Vision of Judgment* (1957-8); *Whispers at the Curtains* for bar., chorus and orch. (1984); 5 symphs. (1948-76); *Prelude, Elegy and Finale* for strings; vln. and vla. concertos, *Concertante* for 3 pfs. and strings; wind 5tet, 4 string 4tets (1947-76); vln. and pf. sonata; organ sonata.

Fricsay, Ferenc (b Budapest, 9 Aug 1914; d Basle, 20 Feb 1963), Hungarian conductor. He studied with Bartók and Kodály at the Budapest Academy, and was successively cond. at the Szeged Opera 1934–44, the Budapest Opera, 1945, and the Vienna Staatsoper, 1947; at the 1947 Salzburg Festival he cond. the fp of von Einem's *Dantons Tod*. From 1948 to 1952 he was director of the Berlin City Opera, and from 1956 to 1959 of the Munich Staatsoper. He appeared frequently as a guest cond. in England (debut 1950, Edinburgh, with Glyndebourne Opera, in *Figaro*), Italy, Holland and America; and made a large number of gramophone records.

Friderici, Daniel (b Eichstedt, Querfurt, 1584; d Rostock, 23 Sep 1638), German composer. Cantor at St Mary's Church, Rostock, from 1618 to his death. Pub. Morley's 3-part madrigals with German words in 1624.

Works incl. madrigals, German songs for 3–8 voices.

Friede auf Erden (*Peace on Earth*), work for chorus *a cappella* by Schoenberg (text by C.F. Mayer); comp. 1907, fp Vienna, 9 Dec 1911, cond. Schreker.

Friedenstag (*Peace Day*), opera by R. Strauss (lib. by J. Gregor, who 1st suggested it to Stefan Zweig, based on Calderón's play *La redención de Breda* and Velázquez's picture illustrating that), prod. Munich, 24 Jul 1938.

Friedlaender, Max (b Brieg, Silesia, 12 Oct 1852; d Eichkamp nr. Berlin, 2 Oct 1934), German baritone and writer of music. Studied under Garcia in London and Stockhausen at Frankfurt. Taught in Berlin and at Harvard Univ. Ed. songs by Schubert and Schumann and Ger. folksongs and wrote books on Ger. song and Brahms's songs.

Friedrich, Götz (b Naumburg, 4 Aug 1930), German opera producer. He assisted Felsenstein at the Komische Oper, Berlin, and prod. *Così fan tutte* in Weimar in 1958; dir. of prods. 1968. Hamburg from 1973, Deutsche Oper Berlin from 1980. Starting with his *Tannhäuser* at Bayreuth in 1972, and continuing with *Der Ring des Nibelungen* at CG, 1974–6, his prods. have been seen as reflecting his Marxist beliefs. He is married to the soprano Karan Armstrong (b 1941) and with her has worked on the Brit. fp of the 3-act version of Berg's *Lulu* (CG, 1981) and in 1985 Korngold's *Die tote Stadt* at the Vienna Staatsoper.

Friedrichs, Fritz (b Brunswick, 13 Jan 1849; d Königslutter, 15 May 1918), German baritone. After minor roles in Brunswick and elsewhere, from 1869 he moved to Nuremberg in 1883; well-known there and at Bremen as a Wagner singer. Bayreuth 1888–

1902 as Beckmesser, Alberich and Klingsor. He made guest appearances in Berlin, London and Vienna, and sang at the NY Met 1899–1900.

Friml, Rudolf (b Prague, 2 Dec 1879; d Hollywood, 12 Nov 1972), Czech composer and pianist. Studied at the Prague Cons. with Juranek (pf.) and Foerster (comp.). Toured for some time as accompanist to Jan Kubelík, remaining in Amer. after a tour in 1906. He appeared as a soloist with many orchs.

Works incl. operettas, *The Firefly*, *High Jinks*, *Katinka*, *Rose Marie* (1924), *The Vagabond King* (1925) and many others.

Friskin, James (b Glasgow, 3 Mar 1886; d New York, 16 Mar 1967), Scottish pianist and composer. Studied at the RCM in London. In 1914 he went to NY and became pf. prof. at the Inst. of Musical Art. He married Rebecca Clarke in 1944.

Works incl. 2 motets on Scot. psalm tunes; suite for orch.; pf. 5tet in C min.; phantasy string 4tet; cello and pf. sonata.

Froberger, Johann Jacob (b Stuttgart, bap. 19 May 1616; d Héricourt nr. Montbéliard, 7 May 1667), German organist and composer. Studied under his father, who was a singer, and later *Kapellmeister* at Stuttgart. App. court organist in Vienna on the accession of the Emperor Ferdinand III in 1637, remaining there until 1657, but spending 1637–41 in Italy as a pupil of Frescobaldi. In 1662 he went to London where he is said to have arrived destitute, having been twice robbed on the way. In later years he lived in the house of Sibylla, Dowager Duchess of Württemberg, at her retreat at Héricourt.

Works incl. harpsichord suites, many pieces for organ and harpsichord incl. toccatas, *ricercari*.

'Frog' Quartet, the nickname of Haydn's string 4tet in D maj., op. 50 No. 6, the finale of which is supposed to have a 'croaking' theme.

Fröhlich, Austrian family of musicians, 4 sisters, friends of Schubert:

1. **Anna (Nanette) F.** (b Vienna, 19 Nov 1793; d Vienna, 11 Mar 1880), pianist and soprano. Pupil of Hummel, Hauss and Siboni, singing teacher at the Vienna Cons. 1819–54. She gave the fps of several of Schubert's works.

2. **Barbara F.** (b Vienna, 30 Aug 1797; d Vienna, 30 Jun 1879), contralto and painter. Married Ferdinand Bogner, prof. of fl. at the Vienna Cons.

3. **Katharina F.** (b Vienna, 10 Jun 1800; d Vienna, 3 Mar 1879), intimate friend of

Grillparzer, who lived in the sisters' house until his death in 1872.

4. Josephine F. (b Vienna, 12 Dec 1803; d Vienna, 7 May 1878), soprano. Pupil of her sister Anna, made her 1st appearance in 1821 in *Die Entführung*, later went to Copenhagen to study under Siboni and sang with success in Scand., also, *c* 1829–31, in It. Grillparzer wrote texts of *Zögernd leise* (*Ständchen*) and *Mirjams Siegesgesang*, set by Schubert, for her.

Froissart, concert overture by Elgar, op. 19, comp. in 1890 and perf. at the Worcester Festival of that year on Sep 9, cond. Elgar. Title refers to the French historian Jean Froissart (1338–1404).

'From My Life' (Smetana). *See* **Aus meinem Leben.**

From the House of the Dead (Janáček). *See* **House of the Dead, From the.**

'From the New World' (Dvořák). *See* **'New World' Symphony.**

Fromm, Andreas (b Pänitz, Brandenburg, 1621; d Strahov, Prague, 16 Oct 1683), German composer. He was cantor and prof. at the Pädagogium of Stettin in the middle of the cent.

Works incl. oratorio (one of the earliest known in Ger.) *Vom reichen Mann und Lazarus* (1649); *Dialogus Pentecostalis.*

Frosch (Ger. = frog), the heel of the vln. bow. The direction 'am Frosch' found in Ger. scores means that a passage is to be bowed near the heel of the bow.

Frottola, an early 16th-cent. It. song, originating in Milan, for several voices or for solo voice and instruments, forerunner of the madrigal but less polyphonically elaborate.

The term is used in a general sense to cover numerous different forms: *strambotto, oda, capitolo,* etc., and also in a partic. sense, to mean a song in several stanzas with a refrain or burden (*ripresa*) sung complete at the beginning and (usually) curtailed, but often with a musical extension, after each stanza; the same music serves for both refrain and stanza.

Frühbeck de Burgos, Rafael (b Burgos, 15 Sep 1933), Spanish conductor of German parentage. Studied at Madrid and Munich. Madrid Nat. Orch. 1962–77. Guest cond. Philharmonia Orch., London. Düsseldorf SO 1966–71. US debut 1968; Washington SO from 1980.

Frye, Walter (d *c* 1475), 15th-cent. English composer. He wrote 3 Masses, *chansons* and antiphons; his *Ave regina caelorum mater regis* was copied into 13 continental MSS.

and is found in 3 arrs. for keyboard in the *Buxheimer Orgelbuch* (*q.v.*).

Fuchs, Eugen (b Nuremberg, *c* 1895; d Berlin, 3 Mar 1971), German baritone. He sang at Nuremberg, 1914–20, and after engagements at Breslau and Freiburg appeared at the Berlin Staatsoper, 1930–60. Guest in London, Rome and Paris and at Bayreuth, 1933–43, was heard as Beckmesser; returned there 1956–60. CG 1937, as Alberich.

Fuchs, Marta (b Stuttgart, 1 Jan 1898; d Stuttgart, 22 Sep 1974), German soprano. Debut Aachen 1928; Dresden from 1930 in mezzo roles. She sang Kundry at Bayreuth, 1933, and returned until 1942 as Isolde and Brünnhilde. London, CG, 1936 with Dresden co. as Donna Anna, Ariadne and the Marschallin.

Fuchs, Robert (b Frauenthal, 15 Feb 1847; d Vienna, 19 Feb 1927), Austrian composer. Prof. at the Vienna Cons. from 1875 to 1912.

Works incl. 2 operas, *Die Königsbraut* (1889) and *Die Teufelsglocke* (1893); Mass; symph. in C maj., 5 Serenades (4 for strings); pf. concerto; chamber music.

Fuenllana, Miguel de (b Navalcarnero, Madrid, *c* 1525; d after 1588), Spanish lutenist and vihuelist. Although blind, he became a great player, and in 1554 he pub. *Orphénica lyra,* a book of music for *vihuela* and similar instruments, incl. comps. of his own and many arrs. of works by Guerrero, Morales, Arcadelt, Verdelot and others.

Fuga (It. = flight) = Fugue; in earlier times one of the It. terms for Canon, another being Caccia.

Fuga ricercata. *See* **Ricercare.**

Fugato (It. = fugued), a passage written in the manner of a fugue, occurring merely incidentally in a comp.; or a piece in fugal style that cannot be considered to be in the form of a fugue.

Fugère, Lucien (b Paris, 22 Jul 1848; d Paris, 15 Jan 1935), French baritone. Having failed as a sculptor and made a living as a commercial traveller, he appeared at the Bata-clan café-concert in Paris in 1870 with Planquette's marching-song *Le Régiment de Sambre-et-Meuse* and made his 1st stage appearance at the Bouffes-Parisiens in 1874. 1st sang at the Opéra-Comique in 1877 and continued singing until he was 80. Roles incl. Papageno, Leporello, Schaunard and Massenet's Don Quichotte.

Fughetta (It. = little fugue). Unlike a *fugato,* a fughetta is formally a proper fugue, but much more condensed.

FUGUE

Bach, '48', Bk II, no. 17

Fugue, a contrapuntal comp. in 2 or more parts, based on a 'subject', short or long, which is introduced successively in imitation at the beginning and recurs in the course of the piece. The 2nd entry of the subject, generally at a level a 5th higher or a 4th lower (but sometimes a 4th higher or a 5th lower), is called the Answer. It does not necessarily imitate the subject exactly: it may be modified to preserve the tonality of the piece or to facilitate a 3rd entry. A 3rd entry is often deferred for a few bars, the intervening space being occupied by a Codetta.

The answer is accomp. by a counterpoint which, if it also recurs in the course of the piece, is called the Countersubject. After all the initial entries of the subject and answer there is generally an Episode, derived from the material already heard or completely independent, leading to a further entry of the subject. The remainder of the fugue is made up of an alternation of episodes and entries, which may incl. treatment of the subject in Canon. The illustration above shows the beginning of one of Bach's fugues.

A fugue may have more than one subject and more than one countersubject. It may be written for instruments or voices or for both combined and may occur as part of a large-scale work, such as a symph., opera or oratorio.

Fuhrmann, Georg Leopold, German 16th-17th cent. lutenist, engraver and bookseller. Worked at Nuremberg, where in 1615 he pub. a book of lute pieces, *Testudo Gallo-Germanica,* incl. some by J. and R. Dowland.

Fulda, Adam of (b *c* 1445; d Wittenberg, 1505), German monk, theorist and composer; Wrote a tract on music and composed motets, etc.

Fuleihan, Anis (b Kyrenia, Cyprus, 2 Apr 1900; d Stanford, Calif., 11 Oct 1970), American (naturalized) pianist and composer. Educ. at the Eng. School in Cyprus and studied music in USA, where he settled in 1915. Toured much in USA and the East, and lived at Cairo for 2 years. After his return to Amer. in 1928 he cond. and comp.

Works incl. opera *Vasco* (1958); several ballets; symph., suite *Mediterranean* and *Preface to a Child's Story-Book* for orch., suite for chamber orch.; 3 pf. concertos (1936–63), cello concerto, 2 vln. concertos, concerto for Theremin, Fantasy for vla. and orch.; 5 string 4tets (1940–65), clar. 5tet, horn 5tet; sonatas for vln., vla. and cello; 11 pf. sonatas.

Fuller-Maitland J(ohn) A(lexander) (b London, 7 Apr 1856; d Carnforth, Lancs., 30 Mar 1936), English critic, editor and writer on music. Educ. at Westminster School and Cambridge. Studied with Stanford, Dannreuther and Rockstro, became a music critic in London and was from 1889 to 1911 chief critic of *The Times*. Ed. old music esp. for the harpsichord, incl. the *Fitzwilliam Virginal Book* with W. Barclay Squire, and was ed. of the 2nd ed. of Grove's Dict. Among his books is the 4th vol. of the *Oxford History of Music*.

Füllsack, Zacharias (b *c* 1580; d Lübeck, buried 11 Jan 1621), German lutenist and trombonist. Worked at Hamburg until 1612 and later in the court chapel at Dresden. In 1607, with Christoph Hildebrand, he pub. a book of *Auserlesene Paduanen und Galliarden*, incl. many pieces by Engl. comps.

Functional Harmony. *See* **Harmonic Analysis.**

Fundamental Bass, an imaginary harmonic phenomenon expounded by Rameau. The fundamental bass is the Root bass of any chord occurring in a comp., and according to Rameau no comp. was aesthetically satisfying unless that bass, either actually present or implied, was in each chord used, proceeding from the one before it to the one after it in accordance with definite rules of musical logic.

Funeral March. *See* **March.**

Funeral Ode (Bach). *See* **Trauer-Ode.**

Furiant (Cz), a lively Czech dance in 3–4 time with a characteristic effect of crossrhythm, often used in place of a scherzo by Dvořák and other Cz. comps. of the nat. school.

Furlong, an old English name for the Forlana.

Fürstenau, Anton Bernhard (b Münster, 20 Oct 1792; d Dresden, 18 Nov 1852), German flautist and composer. In the court orch. at Dresden from 1820. Wrote 2 methods and many pieces for his instrument. He accomp. Weber to London in 1826.

Furtwängler, Wilhelm (b Berlin, 25 Jan 1886; d Baden-Baden, 30 Nov 1954), German conductor and composer. Studied at Munich with Rheinberger and Schillings, and early began gaining experience as cond. of concerts and opera at Zürich, Munich, Strasbourg (where he was a deputy to Pfitzner) and Lübeck. After an engagement at Mannheim he followed Nikisch at the Leipzig Gewandhaus, and in 1922 he became cond.-in-chief of the Berlin PO. In 1934 he was obliged to resign his post, when he supported Hindemith against the attacks of Goebbels and other Nazis. He toured infrequently but with great success, including Bayreuth (1931–44) and London (CG, 1935–8, *Tristan* and *The Ring*). He won renown for his measured, spacious recreations of Beethoven, Brahms and Bruckner, but was also active on behalf of modern music: gave the fps of works by Schoenberg, Bartók and Hindemith. Furtwängler was also active as a comp. prod. 3 symphs., a pf. concerto, a Te Deum and some chamber music. Thanks to re-issues of his recordings, many taken from live performances, Furtwängler's reputation remains as high as ever. His influence on later conductors has been considerable; Reginald Goodall and Daniel Barenboim are avowed disciples.

Fux, Johann Joseph (b Hirtenfeld, Styria, 1660; d Vienna, 14 Feb 1741), Austrian theorist and composer. Became organist to the Schottenstift in Vienna in 1696, court comp. 1698, 2nd *Kapellmeister* at St Stephen's Cathedral 1705 and 1st in 1712, vice-*Kapellmeister* to the court 1713, *Kapellmeister* 1715. His *Gradus ad Parnassum* (1725) was for many years the standard treatise on counterpoint, and was studied by Haydn and Beethoven among others.

Works incl. 18 operas, e.g. *Costanza e fortezza* (1723); 11 oratorios incl. *Gesù Cristo negato da Pietro* (1719); 70 Masses and quantities of other church music; 38 trio sonatas; partitas, etc., for orchestra; keyboard music.

fz. (abbr. for It. *forzando*), a direction which, placed against a note or chord, indicates that it should be strongly accentuated. The more usual word is *sforzando*, marked *sf*.

G

G, the 5th note, or dominant, of the scale of C major.

GSM (abbr.). *See* **Guildhall School of Music.**

Gabrieli, Adriana. *See* **Ferrarese del Bene.**

Gabrieli, Andrea (b Venice, *c* 1533; d Venice, 30 Aug 1585), Italian composer. Apparently a pupil of Lassus in Munich. Became 2nd organist at St Mark's, Venice, in 1566 and in 1584 1st organist. He was a famous teacher and had many distinguished pupils, It. and foreign, incl. his nephew Giovanni G. and the Germans Hassler and Aichinger; he visited Graz, Munich and Augsburg.

Works incl. Masses, motets and other church music with instruments; spiritual songs; madrigals, etc. for several voices; choruses for Sophocles' *Oedipus Tyrannus*; *ricercari* for organ.

Gabrieli, Giovanni (b Venice, *c* 1555; d Venice, 12 Aug 1612), Italian composer, nephew of prec. Pupil of his uncle, musician to the Duke of Bavaria under Lassus 1575–9; became 1st organist at St Mark's in Venice in 1585 in succession to Andrea G., like whom he had many famous It. and foreign pupils (Schütz 1609–12).

Works incl. church music for voices and instruments, often laid out antiphonally for choral and orchestral groups; *Sacrae symphoniae* in many vocal and instrumental parts pub. in 2 vols., 1597 and 1615; instrumental pieces of var. kinds; organ music and madrigals.

Gabrieli Quartet, British string quartet founded in 1966; members are Kenneth Sillito and Brendan O'Reilly (vlns.), Ian Jewel (vla.) and Keith Harvey (cello). Since 1967 has given a wide rep. of works, incl. the fps of 4tets by Alwyn, Crosse and Alan Bush. Foreign tours from 1975.

Gabrielli, Caterina (b Rome, 12 Nov 1730; d Rome, 16 Feb 1796), Italian soprano. Pupil of Garcia and Porpora, made her 1st appearance at Venice in 1755, and sang in Gluck's *Le cinesi, La danza* and *Il rè pastore*. From 1759 to 1772 sang in operas by Traetta in Parma and St Petersburg.

Gabrilovich, Ossip Salomonovich (b St Petersburg, 7 Feb 1878; d Detroit, 14 Sep 1936), Russian pianist, conductor and composer. Studied pf. with A. Rubinstein, later

at the St Petersburg Cons., where Liadov and Glazunov were among his masters, and finished his pf. studies with Leschetizky in Vienna, 1894–6, making his 1st appearance in Berlin in the latter year. He toured much in Europe and USA, married the contralto Clara Clemens, daughter of Mark Twain, in 1908 and settled in NY as an Amer. citizen in 1914. App. cond. of the Detroit SO in 1918.

Works incl. Overture-Rhapsody for orch.; Elegy for cello and pf.; many pf. pieces; songs.

Gade, Niels Vilhelm (b Copenhagen, 22 Feb 1817; d Copenhagen, 21 Dec 1890), Danish composer. Pupil of Berggreen, Weyse and others. He learnt var. instruments and became a violinist in the royal orch.; and having gained a comp. prize with the *Ossian* overture in 1841, was enabled to go to Leipzig for further study with a royal grant. There he came into touch with Mendelssohn, who prod. his 1st symph. in 1843 and engaged him to cond. the Gewandhaus concerts in his absence. He returned to Copenhagen in 1848 and worked as organist, cond. and teacher, becoming court music director in 1861.

Works incl. opera *Mariotta* (1849); cantatas *Baldurs Drom* (1858), *Comala, Erl King's Daughter, Zion, The Crusaders, Den Bjaergtagne* (1873), *Psyche*, etc.; 8 symphs. (1842–71), overtures *Echoes from Ossian, In the Highland, Hamlet* (after Shakespeare), *Michelangelo*, etc., suite *Holbergiana* for orch.

String 4tet, 5tet, string 8tet, pf. trios and other chamber music; 4 vln. and pf. sonatas; instrumental pieces; pf. sonata in E min. and pieces for pf. solo and duet; songs, partsongs.

Gadski, Johanna (b Anklam, Prussia, 15 Jun 1872; d Berlin, 22 Feb 1932), German soprano. Made her 1st appearance in Berlin in 1889. US debut with Damrosch Co. in NY, 1895, as Elsa. NY Met 1900–17, as Brünnhilde, Isolde and in Verdi rep. London, CG, 1898–1901, as Aida and Santuzza.

Gafori, Franchino (b Lodi, 14 Jan 1451; d Milan, 25 Jun 1522), Italian priest, composer and writer on music. *Maestro di cappella* at Monticello and Bergamo, and from 1484 attached to Milan Cathedral. Wrote several theoret. books, incl. *Practica musicae* (1496), and comp. Masses and other church music.

Gagliano (actually **Zenobi**), **Giovanni Battista da** (b Gagliano nr. Florence, 20 Dec 1584; d Florence, 8 Jan 1651), Italian composer. Instructor at the church of San Lorenzo at Florence in 1613 in succession to his brother and later musician to the Grand Duke of Tuscany.

Works incl. motets, psalms and other church music.

Gagliano, Marco da (Zenobi) (b Gagliano nr. Florence, 1 May 1582; d Florence, 25 Feb 1643), Italian composer, brother of prec. Studied organ and theorbo under Luca Bati at the church of San Lorenzo at Florence, where he became instructor in 1602 and *maestro di cappella* in 1608 and was a priest. In 1607 he founded the Accademia degl' Elevati for the cultivation of music and *c* 1610 became *maestro di cappella* to the Grand Duke of Tuscany. He was also in touch with the ducal family of Gonzaga at Mantua, where his opera *Dafne*, a setting of Rinuccini's lib., was prod. in 1608. He also wrote music for the wedding of the duke's son.

Works incl. operas *Dafne, La Flora, Il Medoro* (music lost); oratorio *La regina Santa Orsola* (1624, music lost); Masses, Offices for the Dead, *Sacrae cantiones*; madrigals.

Gagliarda (It.) = Galliard.

Gaigerova, Varvara (b Zuevo, 4 Oct 1903; d Moscow, 6 Apr 1944), Russian composer. She was a pupil of Miaskovsky at the Moscow Cons.

Works incl. 3 symphs. (1928, 1934, 1937), symph. suite on Caucasian themes; 2 string 4tets; pf. sonatas; songs to words by Pushkin, etc.

Gailhard, Pierre (b Toulouse, 1 Aug 1848; d Paris, 12 Oct 1918), French baritone. Studied at the Toulouse and Paris Conss. and made his 1st appearance in 1867 as Thomas's Falstaff, at the Opéra-Comique. He 1st appeared in London in 1879, and until 1883 his roles incl. Osmin and Méphistophélès. From 1884 to 1891, 1893 to 1899 and 1900 to 1905 he was joint manager of the Opéra, and from 1899 to 1900 and 1905 to 1908 sole manager. Responsible for several French fps of Wagner's operas.

Gaillarde. *See* **Galliard.**

Gál, Hans (b Brunn, nr. Vienna, 5 Aug 1890; d Edinburgh, 3 Oct 1987), Austrian composer and musicologist. Pupil of Mandyczewski in Vienna and lecturer at the Univ. there from 1918; later dir. of the Music Acad. at Mainz. After the *Anschluss* he took refuge at Edinburgh, where he was lecturer at the Univ. from 1945 to 1957.

Works incl. operas *Der Fischer, Der Arzt der Sobeide* (1919), *Ruth, Die heilige Ente* (1923), *Das Lied der Nacht* (1926), *Die*

beiden Klaus, Der Zauberspiegel; *Requiem für Mignon* (from Goethe's *Wilhelm Meister*, 1923) for chorus and orch. and other choral works; *Sinfonietta, Ballet Suite, Pickwickian Overture* (after Dickens), etc. for orch.; serenade for strings; pf. concerto, vln. concerto; 4 string 4tets (1916–71), 5 Intermezzi for string 4tet, serenade for string trio; pf. works.

Galant (Fr. and Ger. = courtly), an adj. used to designate a special musical style of the 18th cent., esp. that of C.P.E. Bach and the Mannheim school. Its main characts. are elegance, a certain superficiality of feeling, formality (the 1st approaches towards sonata form) and profuse ornamentation.

Galanterien (Ger.)⎱
Galanteries (Fr.)⎰ (lit. courtesies),
the extra dances or other pieces added to those which were normal in the classical Suite or Partita (Allemande, Courante, Sarabande and Gigue). The most frequently used galanteries were Bourrées, Minuets, Passepieds, Chaconnes and, among pieces other than dances, Airs.

Galatea, La, opera by Schürer (lib. by Metastasio), prod. Dresden, at court, 8 Nov 1746.

Galeffi, Carlo (b Malamocco, nr. Venice, 4 Jun 1884; d Rome, 22 Sep 1961), Italian baritone. Debut Rome 1903, Enrico. He was soon heard in Naples, as Amonasro and Rigoletto, and sang Posa at La Scala in 1912; remained until 1938, as Nabucco, Germont, Luna, often under Toscanini, and in the fps of Boito's *Nerone* and *L'amore dei tre re*. NY Met debut 1910, as Germont; the following year took part in the fp of Mascagni's *Isabeau*, at Buenos Aires. Other roles incl. Amfortas and Boccanegra.

Galilei, Vincenzo (b Santa Maria in Monte nr. Florence, *c* 1520; d Florence, buried 2 Jul 1591), Italian composer, lutenist and theorist. Studied under Zarlino at Venice. He took part in the discussions which led the Florentine *camerata* to opera after his death and wrote theoret. books. Galilei upheld Greek drama against the contemporary madrigal, becoming involved in controversy with Zarlino. Father of the astronomer Galileo Galilei.

Works incl. cantata *Il Conte Ugolino* from Dante, a setting of the Lamentations of Jeremiah (both lost, and both among the earliest music for a single voice with accomp.); 2 books of madrigals; pieces for 2 viols; a lute book in tablature; *Dialogo della musica antica et della moderna* (1581).

Galimat(h)ias (Fr. = gallimaufry, farrago,

gibberish). In music the term is found in Mozart's *Galimathias musicum* (K32) written by him at The Hague in 1766, at age of 10, for the coming of age of William of Orange. It contains the Dutch nat. air 'Wilhelmus van Nassouwe'.

Gall, Yvonne (b Paris, 6 Mar 1885; d Paris, 21 Aug 1972), French soprano. Debut Paris, Opéra, 1908 as Woglinde in *Götterdämmerung*; returned until 1935 and sang at the Opéra-Comique, 1921–34. In 1922 she was Daphné in the fp of Busser's *Les noces corinthiennes*. Chicago from 1918, incl. Ravel's Concepcion in 1920. CG 1924, as Tosca. Other roles incl. Rossini's Mathilde and Rameau's Phebé.

Gallenberg, Wenzel (Robert) von, Count (b Vienna, 28 Dec 1783; d Rome, 13 Mar 1839), Austrian composer. Studied with Albrechtsberger and married Countess Giulietta Guicciardi, a pupil of Beethoven. Works incl. *c* 50 ballets, e.g. *Wilhelm Tell* (1810), *Jeanne d' Arc* (1821), 3 overtures, 8 pieces for wind band, dances for orch. and for pf., contributions to periodical pubs.

Galli, Antonius (d Vienna, 2 Apr 1565), Flemish 16th-cent. composer, active in Bruges, 1544–50. Wrote much church music and a few *chansons*.

Galli, Caterina (b *c* 1723; d London, 1804), Italian mezzo-soprano. Lived in London from *c* 1742, and sang leading parts in several of Handel's oratorios, incl. *Joshua, Susanna, Solomon, Theodora* and *Jephtha*.

Galli-Curci, Amelita (b Milan, 18 Nov 1882; d La Jolla, Calif., 26 Nov 1963), Italian soprano. Studied pf. at Milan Cons. but mainly self-taught as a singer. She made her debut at Trani in 1906. Joined the Chica-go Opera Co. in 1916, when she sang Gilda, and sang subsequently in NY (Met debut 1921, Violetta). Other US roles incl. Rosina, Lakmé, Manon, Lucia and Dinorah. Concert tours in England from 1924. She retired through illness in 1930.

Galli, Filippo (b Rome, 1783; d Paris, 3 Jun 1853), Italian bass, at 1st a tenor. Made his 1st appearance as a tenor at Bologna in 1804 and as a bass at Venice in 1812. He created roles in Rossini's *L'inganno felice, L'italiana in Algeri, Maometto II* and *Semiramide*.

Galli-Marié, Marie (Célestine Laurence) (b Paris, Nov 1840; d Vence nr. Nice, 22 Sep 1905), French mezzo-soprano. Pupil of her father; made her 1st appearance at Strasbourg in 1859. She was the 1st Mignon (A. Thomas) and Carmen.

Galliard (Eng., from Fr. *Gaillarde* and It. *Gagliarda*), a sprightly dance dating from the early 16th cent., orig. in 3–2 time but later also in 2–2 time; often used in music as a contrast to the Pavan and frequently based on the same musical material (*see* illustration).

Galliard, Johann Ernst (John Ernest) (b Celle, *c* 1680; d London, 1749), anglicized oboist and composer of French-German origin. Pupil of J.B. Farinelli and Steffani, settled in Eng. *c* 1706 as oboist to Prince George of Denmark. Later active as a comp., esp. for the theatre, and also trans. Tosi's treatise on singing under the title *Observations on the Florid Song* (1742).

Works incl. operas *Calypso and Telemachus* (1712), *Pan and Syrinx* (1718) and *Oreste e Pilade* (unfinished); several pantomimes and other stage entertainments; choruses for the Earl of Buckingham's *Julius*

Pavane

Galliard

Byrd

GALLIARD

Caesar; The Hymn of Adam and Eve from Milton's *Paradise Lost*; church music; instrumental music, incl. piece for 24 bassoons and 4 double basses.

Gallican Chant, the Provençal plainsong in use in Fr. until the intro. of the Roman ritual in the 8th cent.

Galliculus (? Hähnel, Hähnlein), Joannes, German 16th-cent. theorist and composer, pupil of Isaac. Worked at Leipzig as a teacher, 1520–50; wrote a theoret. work *Isagoge* (later *Libellus*) *de compositione cantus* and comp. a Passion according to St Mark, 2 Magnificats, a psalm, liturgical works for Easter and Christmas.

Gallus, Jacobus. *See* **Handl.**

Gallus, Johannes (Jehan Le Cocq), Franco-Flemish 16th-cent. composer, not to be confused with Handl (Jacobus Gallus). Wrote *chansons.*

Galop (Fr. = gallop), a quick ballroom dance in 2–4 time 1st appearing under that name in Paris in 1829, but of older Ger. origin, its Ger. name (now *Galopp*) having been *Hopser* (hopper) or *Rutscher* (glider).

Galoubet (Prov.), a small wind instrument, the pipe used with the accomp. tabor (Fr. *tambourin*).

Galuppi, Baldassare (b Burano nr. Venice, 18 Oct 1706; d Venice, 3 Jan 1785), Italian composer. Pupil of his father and later, after the failure of his first opera in 1722, of Lotti in Venice. His operatic career proper began in 1728, after which he comp. a vast quantity of works. His *opere serie* met with indifferent success, but his comic operas are notable, esp. those on libretti by Goldoni, the most famous being *Il filosofo di campagna* (1754). Visited London 1741–3, where he prod. several operas. App. 2nd *maestro di cappella* at St Mark's, Venice, 1748; 1st *maestro* and Dir. of the Ospitale degl' Incurabili, 1762. Visited St Petersburg 1765. Thereafter comp. few operas and devoted himself chiefly to oratorios for the Incurabili.

Works incl. operas *Alessandro nell' Indie* (1738), *L'Olympiade, L'Arcadia in Brenta* (1749), *Il Conte Caramella, Il mondo della luna* (1750), *Il mondo alla roversa, La calamità de cuori, Il filosofo di campagna, Le nozze* (1755), *L'amante di tutte, Le tre amanti ridicoli, Il Marchese Villano* (1762), *Ifigenia in Tauride* (1768), etc. (over 90 in all); 27 oratorios; church music; instrumental music.

Galway, James (b Belfast, 8 Dec 1939), Irish flautist. He studied in London and with Jean-Pierre Rampal in Paris. Flautist with SW, then BBC SO, from 1960; prin. flautist RPO and LSO. Berlin PO 1969–75, under Karajan. Solo career from 1975; a popular performer on TV with his 18-carat gold flute. He arr. Vivaldi's *Four Seasons* for his instrument and pub. an autobiography in 1979.

Gamba (abbr.). *See* **Viola da gamba.**

Gambler, The (*Igrok*), opera in 4 acts by Prokofiev (lib. by comp. after the story by Dostoievsky); comp. 1915–17, rev. 1928, prod. Brussels, 29 Apr 1929; planned for perf. in St Petersburg, 1917, but cancelled at the outbreak of the Revolution. Orch. Suite *Portraits,* op. 49, in 4 movts.; fp Paris, 12 Mar 1932.

Gamma (Gk. = Letter Γ), the name of the lowest note of the musical scale known to medieval theory, G on the bottom line of the bass stave. Where the Hexachord was based on it, it received the name of 'gamma-ut' (hence 'Gamut'), and in France the name of the scale is still *gamme.*

Gamut, old English term for the scale or key of G, whether major or minor, and hence for a scale or range in general. It derives from the combination of *gamma* (Gk. = G) and *ut,* the name given in medieval theory to the note:

See **Hexachord, Solmization.**

Gamut-Way, a 17th-cent. term for music written in ordinary notation, as distinct from tablature.

Ganassi, Silvestro di (b Fontego nr. Venice, 1492; d Venice), Italian theorist, who pub. tutors for the recorder, incl. *Opera Intitulata Fontegara* (1535), and the viol (*Regola Rubertina,* 1542).

Ganne, (Gustave) Louis (b Buxière-les-Mines, Allier, 5 Apr 1862; d Paris, 14 Jul 1923), French composer. Pupil of Dubois and Franck. He cond. the Opéra balls in Paris and orchs. at Royan and Monte Carlo, and became very popular as a comp. of ballets and operettas.

Works incl. operettas *Rabelais, Les Colles des femmes, Les Saltimbanques* (1899) and *Hans le joueur de flûte* (1906); ballet *La Source du Nil* and several others; popular songs including *La Marche Lorraine* and *Le Père la Victoire;* dances *La Tsarine.*

Gänsbacher, Johann (b Sterzing, Tyrol, 8 May 1778; d Vienna, 13 Jul 1844), Austrian composer. Pupil of Vogler and Albrechtsberger. Became *Kapellmeister* of St Stephen's

Cathedral in Vienna, 1823.

Works incl. incid. music to Kotzebue's *Die Kreuzfahrer*; 35 Masses, 8 Requiems and other church music; a symph.; pf. music, songs.

Gapped Scales, any scales containing less than 7 notes, e.g. the Pentatonic scale, which has 5.

Garat, Pierre Jean (b Bordeaux, 26 Apr 1762; d Paris, 1 Mar 1823), French tenor-baritone. Pupil of Beck at Bordeaux. He became the favourite singer of Marie Antoinette, went to Hamburg and London during the Revolution. Prof. Paris Cons. from 1796.

Garbin, Edoardo (b Padua, 12 Mar 1865; d Brescia, 12 Apr 1943), Italian tenor. Debut Vicenza 1891, as Alvaro. He sang in Milan from 1893; created Fenton, in *Falstaff*, and in 1900 was heard in the fp of Leoncavallo's *Zazà*, under Toscanini. Guest in Vienna, Berlin and Barcelona; CG 1908. Often appeared with his wife, Adelina Stehle, the 1st Nannetta.

García, Spanish family of singers:

1. Manuel (del Popolo Vicente) G. (b Seville, 21 Jan 1775; d Paris, 9 Jun 1832), tenor, teacher and composer. Was a chorister at Seville Cathedral and became well known as singer, cond. and comp. in his teens. In 1808 he made his 1st appearance in Paris and in 1811 in It. At Naples. he comp. an opera, *Il Califfo di Bagdad*, not the 1st of a number of works for the stage. In 1816 he created Almaviva in *Il barbiere di Siviglia* He now sang much in Paris and London, in operas by Rossini and Mozart, and in 1825, took the 1st It. opera co., incl. himself, his son (2) and elder daughter (3), to NY, where they perf. in *Don Giovanni*. In 1826–8 was in Mex.

2. Manuel (Patricio Rodríguez) G. (b Madrid, 17 Mar 1805; d London, 1 Jul 1906), singing teacher, son of prec. Pupil of his father and of Fétis in music theory. He appeared early in opera, but in 1829 retired to devote himself to teaching only. App. prof. at the Paris Cons. in 1842 and at the RAM in London in 1848, where he remained to the end of his long life, retiring in 1895. He was the inventor of the laryngoscope.

3. Maria Felicità G. (b Paris, 24 Mar 1808; d Manchester, 23 Sep 1836), sister of prec. *See* **Malibran.**

4. (Michelle Ferdinande) Pauline G. (b Paris, 18 Jul 1821; d Paris, 17–18 May 1910), sister of prec. *See* **Viardot-Garcia.**

5. Gustave G. (b Milan, 1 Feb 1837; d London, 15 Jun 1925), baritone, son of 2. Appeared as an opera singer in London and then sang at Milan, but settled in London as teacher, at the RAM from 1880 and was prof. at the RCM from 1883.

García Robles, José (b Olot, 28 Jul 1835; d Barcelona, 28 Jan 1910), Spanish composer. Teacher at Barcelona, where he helped to found the Orfeó Català.

Works incl. opera *Julio César* (after Shakespeare, 1880); *Catalonia* for chorus and orch. and other choral works; chamber music.

Gardane, Antonio (b southern France, 1509; d Venice, 28 Oct 1569), Italian music printer, estab. at Venice from 1538. His sons Cipriano and Annibale continued the business, as well as 2 other relatives, Angelo and Alessandro G., until 1619.

Gardelli, Lamberto (b Venice, 8 Nov 1915), Italian conductor. He studied in Pesaro and was asst. to Serafin in Rome; debut there 1944, *La Traviata*. Swedish Opera, Stockholm, 1946–55. 1955–61 Danish Radio SO and cond. opera in Budapest and Berlin. Glyndebourne 1964–8, *Macbeth* and *Anna Bolena*. NY Met 1966, *Andrea Chénier*. Regular at CG since 1969; debut with *Otello; Norma* 1980. Bavarian Radio SO from 1983.

Garden, Mary (b Aberdeen, 20 Feb 1877; d Inverurie, 3 Jan 1967), Scottish soprano. Went to America as a child and first studied singing in Chicago. In 1895 she went to Paris, where she continued her studies under various teachers, making her debut in 1900 as Charpentier's Louise. She created the roles of Debussy's Mélisande in 1902 and Massenet's Chérubin in 1905. Other roles incl. Juliette, Ophelia, Carmen and Salome. In 1910 she joined the Chicago Opera and from 1921–2 was its director.

Garden of Fand, The, symph. poem by Bax, comp. 1913, fp Chicago, 29 Oct 1920. (Fand is a heroine of Ir. legend, but in this work the garden of F. is simply the sea, charged with Ir. legendry.)

Gardiner, H(enry) Balfour (b London, 7 Nov 1877; d Salisbury, 28 Jun 1950), English composer. Educ. at Charterhouse School and Oxford, and studied music under Knorr at Frankfurt. Became music master at Winchester Coll. for a short time, then devoted himself to composition. Financed and cond. series of concerts at Queen's Hall, 1912–13, incl. early perfs. of works by Brit. contemporaries.

Works incl. *News from Wydah* (Masefield) for chorus and orch. (1912); symph. in

D, *English Dance*, Fantasy and *Shepherd Fennel's Dance* (after Hardy) for orch.; string 4tet, string 5tet (1905) and other chamber music; *Noel*, 5 pieces, etc. for pf.; part-songs.

Gardiner, John Eliot (b Fontmell Magna, Dorset, 20 Apr 1943), English conductor. He founded the Monteverdi Choir while still at Cambridge and gave the Monteverdi Vespers in his own ed. at the Prom. Concerts, London, in 1968; founded Monteverdi Orch. the same year and later the English Baroque Soloists. He cond. Gluck's *Iphigénie en Tauride* at CG in 1973 and in 1975 gave in London a concert perf. of Rameau's opera *Les Boréades*, the MS. of which he had discovered in Paris; 1st stage prod. Aix, 1982. Artistic dir. Handel Festival, Göttingen, from 1981; music dir. Lyons Opera 1983.

Gardiner, William (b Leicester, 15 Mar 1770; d Leicester, 16 Nov 1853), English hosiery manufacturer, music amateur, writer and ed. Admirer of Haydn, to whom he sent 6 pairs of silk stockings with themes from Haydn's works woven into them. He adapted to English words music by Haydn, Mozart and Beethoven.

Gardner, John (Linton) (b Manchester, 2 Mar 1917), English composer. Educated at Wellington and Oxford, became music master at Repton School in 1939, and after doing war service appt. coach at CG in London. Chamber music of his was heard in London and Paris in the 1930s, but his first great success was the perf. of the 1st symph. at the Cheltenham Festival of 1951. Taught at Morley College 1952–76. CBE 1976.

Works incl. operas *The Moon and Sixpence* (after Somerset Maugham, 1957) and *Tobermory* (1977); symph. and Variations on a Waltz by Nielsen for orch. (1952); pf. concerto (1957), *An English Ballad* for orch. (1969); Mass in C (1965), *Cantata for Easter* (1970); string 4tet (1939), ob. 5tet; 2 pf. sonatas; *Intermezzo* for org.; songs.

Garland for the Queen, a set of songs for mixed voices ded. to Queen Elizabeth II on her coronation in 1953, with contribs. by Bax, Berkeley, Bliss, Finzi, Howells, Ireland, Rawsthorne, Rubbra, Tippett and Vaughan Williams.

Garlandia, Johannes de, 13th-cent. scholar and writer on music. Taught at the Univ. of Paris. His two treatises on plainsong and mensural music (*c* 1240), were among the most influential writings of their time.

Garrard, Don (b Vancouver, 31 Jul 1929), Canadian bass. He sang Don Giovanni for Canadian TV and in 1961 was heard at SW, London; roles with the co. (later ENO) have been Silva, Attila, Sarastro and the Wanderer. Glyndebourne from 1965 as Gremin, Trulove and Arkel; CG debut 1970. He has sung widely as guest in N. Amer. and Europe.

Garrigues, Malwina (b Copenhagen, 7 Dec 1825; d Karlsruhe, 8 Feb 1904), German soprano. Was engaged for the Opera at Karlsruhe, where she met the tenor Ludwig Schnorr von Carolsfeld, whom she married. In 1860 they were engaged by the Dresden Court Opera. In 1865 she was Wagner's 1st Isolde in the Munich prod. of *Tristan und Isolde*, to the Tristan of her husband, who died the following month.

Garsi, Santino (b 22 Feb 1542; d Parma, ? 17 Jan 1604), Italian composer, lute-player at the court of Parma from 1594 until his death. Wrote dance music for lute.

Gascongne, Matthieu, French 16th-cent. composer, priest in the diocese of Cambrai; he is mentioned in a document of 1518. Wrote numerous Masses, incl. one on de la Rue's *Pourquoi non*, motets and *chansons*.

Gaspar van Weerbeke. *See* Weerbeke.

Gaspard de la Nuit, 3 Poems for pf. by Ravel after Aloysius Bertrand; 1908, fp Paris, 9 Jan 1909. The movements are *Ondine*, *Le Gibet* and *Scarbo*.

Gasparini, Francesco (b Camaiore nr. Lucca, 5 Mar 1668; d Rome, 22 Mar 1727), Italian composer. Pupil of Corelli and Pasquini; choirmaster at the Ospedale della Pietà, Venice; app. *maestro di cappella* of St John Lateran, Rome, 1725. Author of *L'armonico pratico al cimbalo* (1708).

Works incl. 61 operas, e.g. *Il più fedel fra i vassalli*, *La fede tradita e vendicata* (1704), *Ambleto* (on Shakespeare's *Hamlet*, 1705); oratorios *Mosè liberato dal Nilo*, *La nascita di Cristo* and *Le nozze di Tobia* (1724); church music; cantatas.

Gasparini, Quirino (b Bergamo, 1721; d Turin, 30 Sep 1778), Italian cellist and composer, pupil of Padre Martini in Bologna. Worked at Turin, Brescia, Venice and Bergamo, and was *maestro dì cappella* at Turin cathedral from 1760.

Works incl. operas *Artaserse* (1756) and *Mitridate* (1767), instrumental music, church music.

Gasparo da Salò. *See* Salò.

Gassenhauer (Ger. lit. street-beater), a 16th-cent. term for a popular dance, which was very soon used to mean a popular song. It survived till the 20th cent. The modern term is *Schlager*.

Gassmann, Florian Leopold (b Brüx, 3 May 1729; d Vienna, 20 Jan 1774), Bohemian composer, pupil of Padre Martini in Bologna. Settled in Vienna as a ballet comp. in 1763. In 1771 he was instrumental in founding the *Tonkünstlersocietät* (Vienna's 1st music society). App. court *Kapellmeister* in succession to Reutter in 1772.

Works incl. 25 operas, e.g. *Gli uccellatori* (1759), *L'amore artigiano, La notte critica* (1768), *La contessina*; oratorio, *La Betulia liberata* (1772); over 50 symphs.; much church music; chamber music.

Gast, Peter (actually **Johann Heinrich Köselitz**) (b Annaberg, 10 Jan 1854; d Annaberg, 15 Aug 1918), German composer. Studied at the Leipzig Cons. and later went to Basle as a friend and disciple of Nietzsche, some of whose comps. he revised. Afterwards he lived at Venice and Weimar.

Works incl. operas *Wilbram* (1879), *Orpheus und Dionysos, König Wenzel, Die heimliche Ehe* (based on the lib. of Cimarosa's *Matrimonio segreto* and farther back on Colman and Garrick's *Clandestine Marriage*, 1891); festival play *Walpurgis* (1903), *Hosanna* for chorus and orch.; symph., symph. poem *Helle Nächte* and other orchestral works; string 4tet, 7tet, songs.

'Gastein' Symphony, a symph. in C maj., supposed to have been written by Schubert during a visit to Gastein in Autumn 1825, of which no trace is left. It has been suggested that it is identical with the Grand Duo for pf. duet, op. 140, but recent views identify it as the 'Great' C maj. symph. It must therefore have been composed in 1825, not as previously thought, in 1828.

Gastoldi, Giovanni Giacomo (b Caravaggio, c 1550; d 1622), Italian composer. *Maestro di cappella* at the church of Santa Barbara at Mantua from 1592 until 1608; then choirmaster at Milan Cathedral.

Works incl. a Magnificat and other church music; madrigals; *canzoni* and *balletti* for voices and instruments (those of 1591 influenced Morley and Weelkes).

Gaudentios, 2nd-cent. A.D. Greek theorist, the first to formulate a system of 8 *tonoi* (modes in the scalic sense) based on the idea of joining the interval of a 4th to that of a 5th with one note common to both.

Gaultier, the name of several French lutenists of the 17th cent.:

1. Ennemond G. (b ? Lyons, c 1575; d Villette, Dauphiné, 11 Dec 1651), taught Queen Marie de' Medici and Richelieu. Wrote lute pieces.

2. Jacques G., ? unrelated to prec. Fled to London, c 1617 and was attached to the court until 1647. Visited Hol. and Spain and comp. lute pieces and songs.

3. Denis G. (b ? Marseilles, c 1603; d Paris, 1672), nephew or cousin of 1. Wrote a large number of lute pieces.

4. Pierre G. (b Orléans; d after 1638), ? unrelated to prec. He was in Rome in 1638 and pub. lute pieces there.

Gavazzeni, Gianandrea (b Bergamo, 27 Jul 1909), Italian conductor and composer. Studied in Rome and Milan, and later became a comp. Pupil of Pizzetti and Pilati. He has also been active as a cond. and a critic; he cond. *Anna Bolena* at Glyndebourne in 1965. Music dir., La Scala, 1965–8.

Works incl. opera *Paolo e Virginia* (after Saint-Pierre, 1935); oratorio *Canti per Sant' Alessandro* (1934); choral triptych; Symph. Prelude, *Three Episodes*, etc. for orch.; concertos for vln. and for cello; chamber music.

Gaveau, Étienne (b Paris, 7 Oct 1872; d Paris, 26 May 1943), French pf. manufacturer. Followed his father Joseph G. (1824–1903) and built a factory at Fontenay-sous-Bois in 1896 and a concert hall (Salle G.) in Paris in 1907.

Gaveaux, Pierre (b Béziers, 9 Oct 1760; d Paris, 5 Feb 1825), French composer and tenor. Pupil of Beck at Bordeaux, where he 1st appeared as an opera singer; he then moved to Paris, where he was well known as a singer from c 1790.

Works incl. operas *Les Deux Suisses* (1792), *La Famille indigente, Le Petit Matelot* (1796), *Léonore, ou L'Amour conjugal* (1798), *Un Quart-d'heure de silence, Le Bouffe et le tailleur, Monsieur Deschalumeaux* (1806), *L'Enfant prodigue*; revolutionary hymn *Le Réveil du peuple*; It. canzonets and Fr. romances for voice and pf.

Gaviniès, Pierre (b Bordeaux, 11 May 1728; d Paris, 8 Sep 1800), French violinist and composer. Made his 1st appearance in Paris in 1741, at the Concert spirituel, of which he was cond. in 1773–7. Prof. of vln. at the Cons. from its foundation in 1795.

Works incl. opera *Le Prétendu* (1760); vln. concertos; sonatas for vln. and bass, vln. and pf., 2 vlns. and unaccomp. vln., vln. studies *Les Vingt-quatre Matinées*, vln. pieces incl. the *Romance de G.*

Gavotte (Fr.), a French dance in moderately animated 2–2 time, generally beginning on the 2nd beat, in 2 sections, each of which is repeated, the 1st ending usually in the dominant.

It often occurs in 18th-cent. suites, but is not a regular constituent of them. It may

Bach, *French Suite, No. 5*

GAVOTTE

have an alternative or trio section, sometimes in the character of a Musette (*see* illustration).

Gavrilov, Andrei (b Moscow, 21 Sep 1955), Russian pianist. In 1974 he won the Tchaikovsky Competition, Moscow. British debut 1976, and has since appeared with all the leading London orchs. NY debut Apr 1985. He is widely admired in Bach, Chopin, Prokofiev and Ravel. After defecting from Russia he decided to return in 1986, under an agreement in which he was allowed artistic freedom.

Gay, John (1685–1732), English poet and playwright. *See* **Acis and Galatea** (Handel), **Beggar's Opera**, **Busby** (odes), **Dreigroschenoper** (Weill), **Polly**.

Gay, Maria (b Barcelona, 13 Jul 1879; d New York, 29 Jul 1943), Spanish mezzosoprano. Studied sculpture and vln. as a girl, but was self-taught in singing. In 1902 Pugno engaged her to sing at his and Ysaÿe's concerts in Brussels and she appeared as Carmen at the Théâtre de la Monnaie at 5 days' notice. English debut in 1906. In 1913 she married the tenor Giovanni Zenatello. Roles incl. Carmen, Dalila and Amneris.

Gayarre, Julián (b Valle de Roncal, 9 Jan 1844; d Madrid, 2 Jan 1890), Spanish tenor. Debut Varese 1867, as Nemorino. London, CG, 1877–87 as Fernando in *La favorite*, Glinka's Sobinin (1887) and Faust. He created Enzo in *La gioconda* (Milan, 1876) and Marcello in the posthumous 1882 première of Donizetti's *Il duca d'Alba* (Rome). Retired 1889.

Gayer, Catherine (b Los Angeles, 11 Feb 1937), American soprano. After study in San Francisco and Berlin her debut was in the fp of Nono's *Intolleranza 60* (Venice 1961). She joined the Deutsche Oper Berlin and in 1968 created Nausikaa in Dallapiccola's *Ulisse*; she was Marie in Zimmermann's *Die Soldaten*, when the co. visited Edinburgh in 1972. At Schwetzingen she was heard in the fp of Reimann's *Melusine* (1971), and she appeared with Scottish Opera. Other roles

incl. Jenifer, Lulu and the Queen of Night (CG 1962).

Gaztambide y Garbayo, Joaquín (Romualdo) (b Tudela, Navarre, 7 Feb 1822; d Madrid, 18 Mar 1870), Spanish conductor and composer. Studied at Pamplona and the Madrid Cons. After a stay in Paris he became a theatre manager and cond. in Madrid.

Works incl. 44 *zarzuelas*, e.g. *La mensajera*, *El estreno de una artista*, *El valle de Andorra*, *Catalina*, *Los Magyares*, *El juramento*, *La conquista de Madrid*, etc.

Gazza ladra, La (*The Thieving Magpie*), opera by Rossini (lib. by G. Gherardini, based on the Fr. melodrama, *La Pie voleuse*, by J.-M.T.B. d'Aubigny and L.C. Caigniez), prod. Milan, La Scala, 31 May 1817.

Gazzaniga, Giuseppe (b Verona, 5 Oct 1743; d Crema, 1 Feb 1818), Italian composer, pupil of Porpora and Piccinni in Naples, where his first opera was prod. in 1768. Later lived chiefly in Venice, until his app. as *maestro di cappella* at Crema Cathedral in 1791. Of his 44 operas, *Don Giovanni o sia Il convitato di pietra* (1787) was an immediate forerunner of Mozart's opera with the same title (prod. later the same year in Prague). Other works incl. oratorios, a symph. and 3 pf. concertos.

Gazzelloni, Severino (b Roccasecca, Frosinone, 5 Jan 1919), Italian flautist. He studied in Rome, making his debut there in 1945. Often heard in Baroque music. He has developed new techniques for his inst. in perfs. of works by Maderna, Boulez, Berio and Nono.

Gebel, Georg (sen.) (b Breslau, 1685; d Breslau, *c* 1750), German organist and composer, pupil of Tiburtius Winckler in Breslau. App. organist in Brieg in 1709, but in 1713 returned to Breslau, where he became director of music at St Christoph the following year.

Works incl. Mass for double chorus; motets; cantatas; Passion oratorio; concertos; organ and harpsichord music.

Gebel, Georg (jun.) (b Brieg, 25 Oct 1709; d
Rudolstadt, 24 Sep 1755), German organist,
harpsichordist and composer, son of prec.
Pupil of his father, app. 2nd organist of St
Mary Magdalen in Breslau in 1729. After
apps. in Oels, Warsaw and Dresden, he became *Konzertmeister* to the court in Rudolstadt in 1747, and *Kapellmeister* 3 years
later.

Works incl. over 12 operas (none extant),
and large quantities of cantatas, symphs.,
chamber music, keyboard music.

Gebel, Georg Sigismund (b Breslau, *c*
1715; d Breslau, 1775), German organist,
harpsichordist and composer, brother of
prec. Organist of several churches at Breslau. Comp. organ music and cantatas.

Gebrauchsmusik (Ger. lit. utility music), a
term for a species of work written for practical use and best trans. as 'workaday music'.
It was common among German comps. in
the 1920s and 1930s. Hindemith's best
works of the kind (several are unpub.) are:
Spielmusik for strings, fls. and oboes (1927);
4 3-part *Songs for Singing Groups*; an educ.
work for concerted vlns. in 1st position
(1927); *Music to Sing or Play* (5 nos. for var.
vocal or instrumental combinations); *Lesson* for 2 male voices, narrator, chorus,
orch., a dancer, clowns and community singing (1929); *Let's Build a Town*, a musical
game for children (1930); *Plöner Musik-
tag* (1932; 4 nos. for var. vocal and instrumental combinations). Some other comps.,
e.g. Milhaud in Fr., Copland in USA, and
Weill and Orff in Ger., have done similar
work.

Geburtstag der Infantin, Der (*The Birthday
of the Infanta*), pantomime by Schreker after
the story by Wilde; comp. 1908, fp Vienna,
27 Jun 1908. Orch. in 1923 as a suite for
large orch. and perf. Amsterdam, 18 Oct
1923, cond. Mengelberg; new ballet scenario by Schreker, 1926, under title *Spanisches
Fest*, perf. Berlin 22 Jan 1927, cond. Leo
Blech. Wilde's story was set as an opera by
Zemlinsky in 1920–1; *see* **Der Zwerg**.

Gedackt (sometimes **Gedact**, Ger. properly
'gedeckt' = covered), an adj. used for stopped Diapason org. stops prod. a muted 8-ft
tone.

Gedämpft (Ger., lit. damped) = muted,
muffled (drums).

Gedda, Nicolai (b Stockholm, 11 Jul 1925),
Swedish tenor of Russian parentage. Studied
in Stockholm, making his debut there in
1952. In 1953 he sang in Paris and at CG in
1954 as the Duke of Mantua; has returned
as Benvenuto Cellini. In 1958 at the NY Met

he created Anatol in Barber's *Vanessa*.
Other roles incl. Tamino, Faust and Palestrina. First London song recital Apr 1986.

Geduldige Socrates, Der (*The Patient S.*),
opera by Telemann (lib. by J.Ü. von König,
after Minato), prod. Hamburg, 28 Jan
1721.

Geharnischte Suite, 2nd suite for orch. by
Busoni; comp. 1895, rev. 1903, fp Berlin, 1
Dec 1904. (G. = Armoured man).

Geheime Königreich, Das (*The Secret
Kingdom*), fairy tale opera in 1 act by
Krenek (lib. by comp.); 1926–7, prod. in a
triple bill with *Der Diktator* and *Schwergewicht*, Wiesbaden, 6 May 1928.

**Geheimnis des entwendeten Briefes,
Das**, chamber opera by Blacher (lib. by H.
Brauer after E.A. Poe's story *The Mystery
of the Purloined Letter*). The fp was
planned for 2 Feb 1975 but postponed after
Blacher's death on 30 Jan; prod. Berlin,
14 Feb 1975.

Geibel, Emanuel von (1815–84), German
poet. *See* **Jensen** (*Spanisches Liederbuch*),
Loreley (Bruch and Mendelssohn), **Schumann** (*Vom Pagen und der Königstochter*),
Spanisches Liederbuch (H. Wolf), **Volbach** (*Vom Pagen und der Königstochter*).

Geige (Ger. = fiddle), the familiar German
name of the vln.

Geisslerlieder (Ger. = flagellants' songs),
sacred German monophonic songs of the
Middle Ages in the It. *laude* tradition and
particularly cultivated at the time of the
Black Death in 1349. The chief MS. is the
Chronikon of Hugo von Reutlingen, which
also describes how the singing was accomp.
by penitential rites perf. by the *Geissler*
(flagellants).

Gellert Lieder, 6 songs by Beethoven for
voice and pf. to texts by C.F. Gellert, op. 48;
comp. *c* 1802. The titles are, 1. *Bitten*; 2. *Die
Liebe des Nächsten*; 3. *Vom Tode*; 4. *Die
Ehre Gottes aus der Natur*; 5. *Gottes Macht
und Vorsehung*; 6. *Busslied*.

Gelosie fortunate, Le (*The Fortunate
Jealousies*), opera by Anfossi (lib. by F.
Livigni), prod. Venice, Teatro San Samuele,
autumn 1786. Mozart added an aria to it on
its prod. in Vienna, 2 Jun 1788.

Gelosie villane, Le (*The Rustic Jealousies*),
opera by Sarti (lib. by T. Grandi, based on a
comedy by Goldoni), prod. Venice, Teatro
San Samuele, Nov 1776.

Gemel. *See* **Gymel.**

Geminiani, Francesco Saverio (b Lucca,
bap. 5 Dec 1687; d Dublin, 17 Sep 1762),
Italian violinist and composer, pupil of
Corelli in Rome. Went to Eng. in 1714,

where he had great success as a virtuoso. Apart from periods of residence in Dublin (1733–40 and 1759–62) and Paris, he remained there for the rest of his life. His teaching intro. modern vln. technique to Eng., and his *Art of Playing on the Vln.* (1751) was one of the earliest tutors on vln.-playing. He also wrote several other theoretical works.

Works. incl. *concerti grossi*, vln. sonatas, cello sonatas, trio sonatas, keyboard pieces.

Gemma di Vergy, opera by Donizetti (lib. by E. Bidera, based on the elder Dumas's play, *Charles VII chez ses grands vassaux*), prod. Milan, La Scala, 26 Dec 1834.

Gemshorn, a medieval recorder orig. made from a chamois horn, and hence an organ stop with soft, nasal tone.

Gencer, Leyla (b Istanbul, 10 Oct 1924), Turkish soprano. She sang Santuzza in Ankara, 1950 and in Naples, 1953, on her Italian debut. Milan, La Scala, since 1956; sang in the fp of Poulenc's *Carmélites*, 1957. US debut San Francisco, 1956. Glyndebourne 1962–5 as Countess Almaviva and Anna Bolena. Maria Stuarda and Rossini's Elisabetta at Edinburgh, 1969 and 1972. A specialist in the less-often heard It. operas of the 19th cent.

Genée, (Franz Friedrich) Richard (b Danzig, 7 Feb 1823; d Baden nr. Vienna, 15 Jun 1895), German conductor and composer. Studied medicine at first, but took to music and became cond. successively at Reval, Riga, Cologne, Aachen, Düsseldorf, Danzig, Mainz, Schwerin, Amsterdam, Prague and Vienna. He wrote or collaborated in many libs. for operettas by Viennese comps. Librettist of *Die Fledermaus*.

Works incl. operettas *Der Geiger aus Tirol* (1857); *Der Musikfeind, Die Generalprobe, Rosita, Der schwarze Prinz, Am Runenstein* (with Flotow), *Der Seekadett* (1876), *Nanon, Im Wunderlande der Pyramiden, Die letzten Mohikaner* (after Fenimore Cooper, 1879), *Nisida, Rosina* (1881), *Die Zwillinge* (1885), *Die Piraten, Die Dreizehn*; part-songs incl. the comic *Italienischer Salat*.

Generalbass (Ger. lit. general bass) = Thorough-Bass.

Generali (real name **Mercandetti**), **Pietro** (b Masserano, 23 Oct 1773; d Novara, 3 Nov 1832), Italian composer. Studied under Giovanni Masi in Rome and in 1802 prod. his 1st opera there. In 1817–21 he cond. opera at Barcelona, and later became *maestro di cappella* at Novara Cathedral.

Works incl. *c* 60 operas, e.g. *Gli amanti*

ridicoli, Il Duca Nottolone, La villana in cimento, Le gelosie di Giorgio, Pamela nubile (after Richardson, *via* Goldoni's comedy, 1804), *La calzolaia, Misantropia e pentimento* (after Kotzebue), *Gli effetti della somiglianza, Don Chisciotte* (after Cervantes), *Orgoglio ed umiliazione, L'idolo cinese, Lo sposo in bersaglio, Le lagrime di una vedova* (1808), *Adelina* (1810), *La moglie giudice del marito, I baccanali di Roma* (1816), *Francesca da Rimini* (after Dante). Masses and other church music; cantata *Roma liberata.*

Genet, Elzéar (Carpentras) (b Carpentras, *c* 1470; d Avignon, 14 Jun 1548), French composer. He was a papal singer to Julius II in 1508 and *maestro di cappella* under Leo X from 1513 to 1521, as well as being at the court of Louis XII some time between those dates. He wrote secular works to both It. and Fr. texts, and numerous sacred works (Masses, motets, hymns, Magnificats).

Genoveva, opera by Schumann (lib. by comp. altered from one by R. Reinick based on the dramas of Tieck and Hebbel), prod. Leipzig, 25 Jun 1850.

Gentle Shepherd, The, ballad opera (lib. by Allan Ramsay), prod. Edinburgh, Taylor's Hall, 29 Jan 1729. It was 1st pub. (1725) as a pastoral comedy, and is therefore not, as is sometimes said, the 1st ballad opera, since *The Beggar's Opera* (1728) was staged earlier.

Genzmer, Harald (b Blumental, nr. Bremen, 9 Feb 1909), German composer. Studied 1st in Marburg and later with Hindemith in Berlin. From 1946 to 1957 he was prof. of comp. at the Hochschule für Musik in Freiburg-im-Breisgau, and from 1957 prof. at the Hochschule für Musik in Munich.

Works incl. cantata *Racine* (1949); Mass in E; symph. no. 1, *Bremen* symph.; concertos for pf., cello, ob., fl. (2), trautonium (2); 2 string 4tets; sonatas for vln., fl. and other chamber music.

George, Stefan (1868–1933), German poet. *See* **Berg (A.)** (*Wein*), **Maler** (*cantata*), **Schoenberg** (*Buch der hängenden Gärten*), **Webern** (songs op. 3 and op. 4).

Gerber, Ernst Ludwig (b Sondershausen, 29 Sep 1746; d Sondershausen, 30 Jun 1819), German lexicographer and organist. His most important work was the dictionary of musicians, *Historisch-biographisches Lexicon der Tonkünstler* (2 vols., 1790–2), later much expanded as *Neues historisch-biographisches Lexikon* (4 vols., 1812–14).

Gerber, Heinrich Nicolaus (b Wenigen-Ehrich, 6 Sep 1702; d Wenigen, 6 Aug 1775), German organist and composer, father of prec. Studied at Leipzig Univ. and became a disciple of Bach there. Court organist at Sondershausen from 1731. Improved and invented instruments, incl. the *Strohfiedel*.

Works incl. a hymn-book with figured basses; variations on chorales for organ; music for harpsichord, organ, harp.

Gerbert, Martin (b Horb on Neckar, 12 Aug 1720; d St Blasien, 13 May 1793), German music historian. Entered the Benedictine monastery of St Blasien in 1737, ordained priest 1744, abbot 1764. Pub. a hist. of church music in 1774 under the title *De cantu et musica sacra*, and a collection of medieval music treatises in 1784.

Gerhard, Roberto (b Valls, Catalonia, 25 Sep 1896; d Cambridge, 5 Jan 1970), Spanish composer and pianist. Although a choirboy and a tentative pianist and comp. from an early age, he began serious music studies late, owing to parental opposition. But after 2 years' commercial studies in Switz., he studied pf. with Granados and comp. with Pedrell at Barcelona in 1915–22 and then comp. with Schoenberg in Vienna in 1923–8. In 1929–38 he lived and taught at Barcelona, was in charge of the music dept. of the Catalan Library, for which he ed. music by 18th-cent. Catalan comps., trans. var. music treatises into Spanish and contrib. to the literary weekly *Mirador*. Pedrell intro. him as a comp. and he began to make his way in Spain and Latin Amer. After the downfall of the Span. Republic he emigrated to Eng. and in 1939 settled at Cambridge with a research scholarship from King's College.

Works incl. opera *The Duenna* (after Sheridan, 1945–7); ballets *Ariel* (1934), *Soirées de Barcelone* (1938), *Don Quixote* (after Cervantes), *Alegrias* (1942) and *Pandora*; oratorio *The Plague* (after Camus, 1964); music for radio plays *Cristobal Colón* and *Adventures of Don Quixote* (Eric Linklater after Cervantes); 4 symphs. (1952–67, no. 3 *Collages* for orch. and magnetic tape); concerto for orch. (1965); *Epithalamion* for orch. (1966), vln. concerto (1943); *Cancionero de Pedrell, Serranillas* and *Cançons i Arietes* for voice and orch.

Hymnody for 11 players (1963); *Concert for 8*; nonet (1956), 2 string 4tets (1955, 1962); pf. trio (1918), wind 5tet; *Gemini* for vln. and pf.; cantata for solo voices, chorus and orch.; song cycle *L'infantament*

meravellós de Shaharazada (1917) and other songs; var. arrs. of old Spanish music.

Gerhardt, Elena (b Leipzig, 11 Nov 1883; d London, 11 Jan 1961), German mezzosoprano. Studied at the Leipzig Cons. with Marie Hedmont, making her debut in 1903. She owed much to the encouragement of Artur Nikisch, who accomp. her at many of her recitals. She excelled in the interpretation of Lieder. In 1933 she left Ger. and settled in London, where she was active in later years as a teacher.

Gerl, Barbara (*née* Reisinger) (b Vienna or Bratislava, 1770; d Mannheim, 25 May 1806), Austrian singer and actress. She perf. as a child in Moravia and Silesia from 1780; sang with Schikaneder's co. from 1789, appearing in operas by Guglielmi and her husband, Franz Xaver G. In 1791 she created Papagena, in *Die Zauberflöte*. After two years in Vienna she moved to Brno, then Mannheim.

Gerl, Franz Xaver (b Andorf, Upper Austria, 30 Nov 1764; d Mannheim, 9 Mar 1827), Austrian bass and composer. He studied with Leopold Mozart in Salzburg and by 1789 was a member of Schikaneder's opera co.; appeared in varied roles, incl. Figaro and Don Giovanni, and contributed as comp. to many Viennese *Singspiele: Don Quixotte und Sancho Pansa* (1790), and a series of pieces with the character Anton as hero. In 1791 he created Sarastro, in *Die Zauberflöte*, with his wife Barbara as Papagena.

Gerle, Hans (b Nuremberg, *c* 1500; d Nuremberg, 1570), German 16th-cent. lutenist, violist and lute-maker. Son of Conrad Gerle (d 1521), also a lute-maker. He pub. a book on viol and lute playing and 2 collections of lute pieces in tablature.

German, Edward (orig. **Edward German Jones**) (b Whitchurch, Salop., 17 Feb 1862; d London, 11 Nov 1936), English composer. Educ. at Chester. On his return home he organized and cond. a band and learnt the vln. Later he studied at Shrewsbury and the RAM in London. He became an orchestral violinist and in 1888 music director of the Globe Theatre, writing incid. music for Richard Mansfield's prods. In 1901 he completed *The Emerald Isle*, left unfinished by Sullivan. Knighted 1928.

Works incl. light operas *The Rival Poets* (1886, rev. 1901), *Merrie England* (1902), *The Princess of Kensington, Tom Jones* (after Fielding), *Fallen Fairies* (W. S. Gilbert); incid. music for Shakespeare's *Richard III, Henry VIII, Romeo and Juliet, As You Like*

It, Much Ado about Nothing, Anthony Hope's *Nell Gwyn*, etc.; 2 symphs., symph. suite in D min., symph. poem *Hamlet*, symph. suite *The Seasons*, *Welsh Rhapsody*, *Theme and 6 Diversions* and other orchestral works; Coronation March and Hymn for George V; chamber music and many songs.

German Flute, the name for the transverse fl. in Eng. in the 18th cent.

German Requiem, A. work for chorus, soprano and baritone solo and orch. by Brahms, op. 45, comp. in 1866–9, fp Leipzig, 18 Feb 1869, cond. Reinecke. The orig. name, *Ein deutsches Requiem*, means that Brahms did not set the liturgical Latin text, but a choice of his own from Luther's trans. of the Bible.

German Sixth. *See* **Augmented Sixth Chords.**

Germani, Fernando (b Rome, 5 Apr 1906), Italian organist and composer. Pupil of Respighi and others. He taught at the Curtis Inst. in Philadelphia, in Siena and at the Rome Cons., and was organist at St Peter's, Rome, from 1948. He travelled widely as a soloist and pub. a *Metodo per organo* and began an ed. of works by Frescobaldi, as well as pub. organ works of his own.

Gero, Jhan (*fl.* 1540–55), Franco-Flemish composer. He lived in Venice and was connected with the music printers Gardano and Scotto. Comp. motets, madrigals and a highly successful book of duos (1541).

Gershwin, George (b Brooklyn, NY, 26 Sep 1898; d Hollywood, 11 Jul 1937), American composer and pianist. Wrote a popular song at the age of 14, studied the pf. and had lessons in theory from R. Goldmark. From 1914 to 1917 he worked as pianist in a music publisher's office and wrote songs and a musical comedy. In 1924 at the invitation of Paul Whiteman, he wrote the *Rhapsody in Blue*. His musical comedies, mostly to lyrics by his brother Ira, were among Broadway's most successful in the 1920s and 1930s.

Works incl. opera *Porgy and Bess* (1935); many musical comedies incl. *Lady, be good* and *Of Thee I sing*; music for several films; *An American in Paris* (1928) and *Cuban Overture* (1932) for orch.; *Rhapsody in Blue* (1924) and concerto for pf. and orch.; a large number of popular songs.

Gerster, Etelka (b Kassán, Hung., 25 Jun 1855; d Pontecchio nr. Bologna, 20 Aug 1920), Hungarian-German soprano. Studied with Mathilde Marchesi in Vienna and made her 1st stage appearance at Venice in 1876 as Gilda. London 1877 as Amina, Lucia and Queen of Night. NY from 1878 in *Lohengrin* and *Les Huguenots*. She married the It. cond. Carlo Gardini.

Gerster, Ottmar (b Braunfels nr. Wetzlar, 29 Jun 1897; d Leipzig, 31 Aug 1969), German composer. Studied at the Hoch Cons. at Frankfurt and became vla. in the symph. orch. there. Later he taught at Essen, Weimar and Leipzig.

Works incl. opera *Enoch Arden* (after Tennyson, 1936) and others; 2 ballets; choral and orchestral works; concertos for pf., vln. and cello; chamber music.

Gertler, André (b Budapest, 26 Jul 1907), Hungarian, later Belgian, violinist. Studied with Hubay and Kodály. In 1928 he settled in Belg., and formed his own string 4tet in 1931. Since 1964 he has been a prof. at the Hanover Hochschule. He was well known as a perf. of 20th-cent. music, esp. Bartók.

Gervaise, Claude, 16th-cent. French musician who composed a considerable amount of dance music for var. instruments, and several books of *chansons*, 1541–57.

Gerville-Réache, Jeanne (b Orthez, Pyrenees, 26 Mar 1882; d New York, 5 Jan 1915), French contralto. She sang at the Paris Opéra-Comique, 1899–1903, creating Geneviève. At CG she was heard as Orpheus (1905) and from 1907 appeared with the Manhattan CO., NY; the 1st US Clytemnestra, 1910. Until the war she was heard widely in N. Amer. as Dalila and Hérodiade.

Gesang der Jünglinge (*The Song of the Youths*), work by Stockhausen for sung and spoken boys' voices, elec. processed and relayed through 5 loudspeakers; text from the *Book of Daniel*, on 3 Hebrew youths undergoing ordeal by fire in Babylon. Fp Cologne, 30 May 1956.

Geschöpfe des Prometheus, Die (*The Creatures of Prometheus*), ballet by Beethoven (choreog. by Salvatore Vigano), prod. Vienna, Burgtheater, 28 Mar 1801.

Gese (or Gesius), Bartholomäus (or Barthel Göss) (b Müncheberg nr. Frankfurt an der Oder 1562; d Frankfurt, Aug 1613), German theologian and composer. Cantor at Frankfurt from 1593.

Works incl. Masses (1 on themes by Lassus), motets, psalms, hymns, sacred songs, etc., all for the Lutheran Church; Passion according to St John; wedding and funeral music.

Gesellschaft der Musikfreunde (Ger. lit. Society of the Friends of Music = Phil. Society), a society formed in Vienna in 1812 for the promotion, perf. and collection of music.

Gesius. *See* **Gese.**

Gestalt (Ger. = shape, formation), a word

that has gained currency as a musical term in Ger.-speaking countries, used in music analysis and in philosophical or pseudo-philosophical discussions on music to designate a musical idea as it comes from the comp's. mind in what is supposed to be a kind of primeval or pre-existing form.

Gestopft (Ger. = stopped up, obstructed), notes on the horn played with the hand inserted into the bell to prod. an altered sound; formerly to obtain extra notes not in the series of natural harmonics, a device made unnecessary by the valve horn.

Gesualdo, Carlo, Prince of Venosa (b Naples, c 1560; d Gesualdo Avellino, 8 Sep 1613), Italian composer and lutenist. In spite of his position as a member of the nobility he took his music studies seriously in his youth and became a very accomplished lutenist. He married a noble Neapolitan lady in 1586, but assassinated her with her lover in 1590. In 1594 he went to the court of Ferrara and married Eleonora d'Este there, but returned to his estate at Naples. His work is notable for its chromatic harmony. In 1960 Stravinsky orch. 3 of Gesualdo's madrigals, to mark the 400th anniversary of his birth.

Works incl. 7 books of madrigals (the last posth. pub. of pieces comp. in 1594); 2 books of *Sacrae cantiones*, responds for 6 voices.

Geszty, Sylvia (b Budapest, 28 Feb 1934), Hungarian soprano. Debut, Budapest 1959; Amor at the Berlin Staatsoper, 1961. She sang the Queen of Night at CG in 1966 and repeated the role at Salzburg, 1967. After joining the Hamburg Opera she sang Zerbinetta at Glyndebourne (1971). At Buenos Aires and Los Angeles she was heard as Sophie. Other roles incl. Alcina, Constanze and Olympia.

Getreue Alceste, Die (*The Faithful Alcestis*), opera by Schürmann (lib. by J.U. König), prod. Brunswick, Feb 1719.

Gevaert, François Auguste (b Huysse nr. Oudenaarde, 31 Jul 1828; d Brussels, 24 Dec 1908), Belgian music historian, theorist and composer. Studied at Ghent and worked as organist there; later travelled in Spain, It. and Ger. Director of music at the Paris Opéra, 1867–70; of the Brussels Cons. from 1871. He wrote several treatises on history, plainsong and theory.

Works incl. operas *Hugues de Zomerghem* (1848), *La Comédie à la ville*, *Georgette* (1848), *Le Billet de Marguerite*, *Les Lavandières de Santarem* (1855), *Quentin Durward* (after Scott, 1858), *Le Diable au moulin*, *Château Trompette*, *La Poularde*

de Caux (1861), *Les Deux Amours*, *Le Capitaine Henriot*; Requiem for male voices and orch. (1853), Christmas cantata, psalm *Super flumina*, cantatas *De nationale verjaerdag* and *Le Retour de l'armée*; orchestral *Fantasia sobre motivos españoles*.

Gewandhaus (Ger. = Cloth Hall), orig. the hall of the clothmakers' guild at Leipzig, used for concerts from 1781 and rebuilt esp. as a concert hall in 1884. The 1st concert was conducted by J.A. Hiller. Mendelssohn was conductor of the Gewandhaus Orch. 1835–47; Julius Rietz 1854–60; Carl Reinecke 1860–95; Arthur Nikisch 1895–1920; Furtwängler 1922–9; Bruno Walter 1929–33; Franz Konwitschny 1949–62; Kurt Masur from 1970. The hall was destroyed in World War II, on 4 Dec 1943.

Gezeichneten, Die (*The Stigmatized*), opera by Schreker (lib. by comp.); comp. 1913–15, prod. Frankfurt, 25 Apr 1918.

Ghedini, Giorgio Federico (b Cuneo, Piedmont, 11 Jul 1892; d Nervi, 25 Mar 1965), Italian composer. Studied at Turin and Bologna, at first intended to be a cond., later taught at the conss. of Turin, Parma and Milan, but eventually devoted himself to comp.

Works incl. 8 operas, incl. *Le baccanti* (after Euripides, prod. Milan, 1948), and *Billy Budd* (after Melville, prod. Venice, 1949); incid. music for Euripides' *Iphigenia in Tauris*; 2 Masses and var. choral works; *Partita*, symph., *Concerto dell' Albatro* (after Melville's *Moby Dick*) for orch.; concertos for pf., 2 pfs., 2 cellos and vln.; concerto for vln. and fl. with chamber orch.; wind 5tet, pf. 4tet; 2 string 4tets and other chamber music; vln. and pf. sonata; pf. works; songs.

Gherardello da Firenze (b c 1320–5; d Florence, 1362 or 1363) Italian composer of sacred works and madrigals etc., famous esp. for his *caccia* (canonic hunting-song) 'Tosto che l'alba del bel giorno appare'.

Gherardeschi, Filippo Maria (b Pistoia, 1738; d Pisa, 1808), Italian composer, pupil of Padre Martini at Bologna, 1756–61. *Maestro di cappella* at the cathedrals of Volterra and Pistoia, and finally, from c 1766 to his death, at S. Stefano in Pisa. Also music director to the court of the Grand Duke of Tuscany.

Works incl. 7 operas, church music, keyboard music.

Gheyn, Matthias van den (b Tirlemont, 7 Apr 1721; d Louvain, 22 Jun 1785), Flemish harpsichordist, organist, carillonneur and composer. Son of a bell founder. The family moved to Louvain in 1725 and in 1741 Gheyn became organist at the church of Saint-Pierre there, having been (?) a pupil of Déodat Raick. In 1745 he was app. carillonneur to the city. Wrote organ, harpsichord and carillon music.

Ghiaurov, Nicolai (b Velingrad, 13 Sep 1929), Bulgarian bass. Debut, Sofia 1955, Rossini's Basilio. He sang Gounod's Méphistophélès on his Paris Opéra (1957), Italian (Bologna, 1958) and NY Met (1965) debuts. London, CG, and Vienna since 1962. His best roles are Boris Godunov, Philip II, Don Giovanni and Massenet's Don Quichotte.

Ghirardello da Firenze. See **Gherardello.**

Ghiselin (or **Verbonnet), Jean** (b c 1455; d ? Bergen op Zoom, c 1511), Flemish composer, active esp. in Ferrara. Petrucci of Venice pub. several of his works between 1501 and 1507. Comp. Masses (vol. pub. in 1503), motets, songs, etc.

Ghislanzoni, Antonio (b Lecco, 25 Nov 1824; d Caprino Bergamasco, 16 Jul 1893), Italian baritone, novelist, music ed. and librettist. He ed. the *Gazzetta musicale* of Milan and collaborated on the lib. for Verdi's *Aida*, as well as writing c 85 libs. of his own.

'Ghost' Trio, the nickname given to Beethoven's pf. trio in D maj., op. 70 no. 1, on account of its mysterious slow movement in D min., which has a mysterious, gloomy and haunting theme, accomp. frequently by string tremolos. Sketches for the work appear on the same sheet as sketches for a projected opera on Macbeth.

Ghro (or **Groh), Johann** (b Dresden, c 1575; d 1627), German 16th–17th-cent. organist and composer. Organist at Meissen in 1604–12 and later music director at Wesenstein.

Works incl. *intradas*, pavans, galliards etc. for several instruments; sacred music.

Giacobbi, Girolamo (b Bologna, bap. 10 Aug 1567; d Bologna, c 1629), Italian composer. *Maestro di cappella* at San Petronio at Bologna.

Works incl. operas and intermedi: *Andromeda (prod. Salzburg, 1618; perhaps 1st opera outside Italy), L'Aurora ingannata, Amor prigioniero, La selva dei mirti, Il Reno sacrificante*; motets, psalms and other church music.

Giacomelli, Geminiano (b Piacenza, c 1692; d Loreto, 25 Jan 1740), Italian composer. Pupil of Capelli at Parma and possibly later of A. Scarlatti. *Maestro di cappella* at Parma, 1719–27 and 1732–7; at Piacenza,

1727–1732; at Loreto from 1738.

Works incl. operas *Ipermestra* (1724), *Cesare in Egitto* (1735) and c 16 others; 2 orarorios, other sacred works; concert arias.

Giani, Nini (b 1904; d Milan, 16 Nov 1972), Italian mezzo. She sang in Italy from 1930 and in 1933 was heard at CG as Eboli and Amneris; La Scala 1933–45. Guest at Verona and in S. Amer. Later in her career she sang dramatic soprano roles, e.g. Santuzza.

Giannettini, Antonio (b prob. Fano, 1648; d Munich, 12 Jul 1721), Italian composer. He sang at St Mark's, Venice, c 1674–86, and was *maestro di cappella* at the ducal court of Modena from 1686. Prod. his 1st opera, *Medea in Atene*, at Venice in 1675.

Works incl. operas, e.g. *Temistocle* (1683), *Artaserse* (1705), oratorios, cantatas, motets, psalms.

Gianni Schicchi (Puccini). See **Trittico.**

Giannini, Dusolina (b Philadelphia, 19 Dec 1900; d Zurich, 26 Jun 1986), American soprano. Stage debut Hamburg, 1925, as Aida; CG 1929, same role. Donna Anna at Salzburg under Walter, and Alice Ford under Toscanini. NY Met 1936–41; NY City Opera 1941–4, as Carmen, Santuzza and Tosca. She sang Carmen at the Vienna Staatsoper in 1950 and retired in 1962.

'Giant' Fugue, the nickname of Bach's fugal chorale prelude on 'Wir glauben all', in Part III of the *Clavierübung*, so named because of a striding figure in the pedals.

Giardini, Felice de (b Turin, 12 Apr 1716; d Moscow, 8 Jun 1796), Italian violinist and composer. Choir-boy at Milan Cathedral and later pupil of Somis at Turin. Played in the opera orchs. at Rome and Naples, in 1748 visited Ger. and then settled in London, becoming leader of the It. opera orch. at the King's Theatre in 1752, succeeding Festing. He played and taught there until 1784, when he retired to It., but he reappeared in London in 1790 and died during a tour of Russia.

Works incl. operas *Enea e Lavinia* (1764), *Il rè pastore* (1765) and others; incid. music for Wm. Mason's *Elfrida*; oratorio *Ruth* (with Avison); 12 vln. concertos; 21 string 4tets, 6 string 5tets, 7 sets of string trios; sonatas for vln. and pf.; vln. duets.

Giasone (*Jason*), opera by Cavalli (lib. by G.A. Cicognini), prod. Venice, Teatro San Cassiano, prob. 5 Jan 1649.

Gibbons, English family of musicians:

1. **William G.** (b Oxford, c 1540; d Cambridge, Oct 1595), singer and/or player. Lived at Cambridge from 1567, but returned

to Oxford *c* 1579 and went back to Cambridge *c* 1587.

2. Edward G. (b Cambridge, Mar 1568; d ? Exeter, *c* 1650), organist and composer, son of prec. Graduated Mus.B. at Cambridge and later (1592) at Oxford. Lay clerk at King's Coll. chapel, Cambridge, and from *c* 1606 held an appt. at Exeter Cathedral.

Works incl. anthems, Kyrie and Creed; In Nomine in 5 parts, etc.

3. Ellis G. (b Cambridge, Nov 1573; d ? Cambridge, May 1603), composer, brother of prec.

Works incl. madrigals, etc.

4. Ferdinando G. (b Oxford, 1581), singer, brother of prec. Lived at Lincoln.

5. Orlando G. (b Oxford, bap. 25 Dec 1583; d Canterbury, 5 Jun 1625), composer and organist, brother of prec. Brought up at Cambridge, where he took the Mus.B. in 1606. Was a singer at the Chapel Royal from 1603 and organist from *c* 1615 until his death. Oxford conferred the D.Mus. on him in 1622. App. organist at Westminster Abbey in 1623. He died suddenly at Canterbury while waiting to officiate at Charles I's marriage service, for which he had written music.

Works incl. Angl. church music (5 services, *c* 13 full anthems, *c* 25 verse anthems); 20 madrigals; *Cries of London* for voices and strings, 30 fantasies for strings, 4 *In Nomine* for strings, 2 pavans and 2 galliards for strings; 16 keyboard fantasies, 6 sets of variations for keyboard and other keyboard pieces.

6. Christopher G. (b London, bap. 22 Aug 1615; d London, 20 Oct 1676), composer and organist, son of prec. Pupil of his father in the Chapel Royal, but (?) was adopted by his uncle Edward G. at Exeter on Orlando's death. App. organist at Winchester Cathedral in 1638. In 1646 he married Mary Kercher, who died in 1662, and later Elizabeth Ball. On the Restoration in 1600 he was app. private organist to Charles II, also organist at the Chapel Royal and Westminster Abbey. D.Mus., Oxford, 1663.

Works incl. music for Shirley's masque *Cupid and Death* (with Locke, 1659); anthems; many fantasies for strings; motets; organ music.

Gibbs, C(ecil) Armstrong (b Great Baddow, nr. Chelmsford, 10 Aug 1889; d Chelmsford, 12 May 1960), English composer. Educ. at Winchester Coll. and Trinity Coll., Cambridge, where he studied music with Dent, and later at the RCM in London, where he became a prof. of comp.

Works incl. incid. music to Maeterlinck's *The Betrothal* (1921); comic opera *The Blue Peter* (A.P. Herbert, 1923); play with music *Midsummer Madness* (Clifford Bax); Nativity play *The Three Kings*; cantata *The Birth of Christ* (1929), Passion according to St Luke, choral symph. *Odysseus*; *La Belle Dame sans merci* (Keats, 1928), *The Highwayman* (Alfred Noyes) and *Deborah and Barak* for chorus and orch.; symph. in E maj.; string 4tet in A maj.; songs.

Gibbs, Joseph (b ? Dedham, 23 Dec 1699; d Ipswich, 12 Dec 1788), English organist and composer. Organist at various Essex churches, finally from 1748 to his death at St Mary-le-Tower in Ipswich. His most important pub. is a set of 8 vln. sonatas (*c* 1746); 6 string 4tets (*c*1777) and organ music also survive.

Gibson, (Sir) Alexander (b Motherwell, 11 Feb 1926), Scottish conductor. He studied in Scotland and London; spent the 1950s with SW Opera and the BBC Scottish SO. Prin. cond. Scottish Nat. Orch. 1959–84. Co-founded Scottish Opera in 1962; *Les Troyens* (1969) and *Der Ring des Nibelungen* (1971) were notable achievements. US debut with Detroit SO 1970; prin. guest cond. Houston SO from 1981. Knighted 1977.

Gielen, Michael (b Dresden, 20 Jul 1927), Austrian conductor and composer. He studied in Buenos Aires and Vienna; worked at the Staatsoper 1951–60. Prin. cond. Stockholm Opera 1961–5; from 1965 in Cologne, where he gave the fp of Zimmermann's opera *Die Soldaten*. Netherlands Opera from 1972. Chief guest cond. BBC SO from 1978; frequent perfs. of modern music, esp. Second Viennese School: he gave a concert perf. of Schoenberg's *Moses und Aron* in Salzburg, later issued on record. Music dir. Cincinnati SO 1980–6.

Gieseking, Walter (b Lyons, 5 Nov 1895; d London, 26 Oct 1956), German pianist. Studied privately and at the Hanover Cons., and 1st appeared in 1915; London debut 1923. US debut 1926, with Hindemith's op. 36 no. 1. He won great fame by his sensitive perfs., esp. of modern Fr. music and Mozart.

Giga (It.). *See* **Jig.**

Gigault, Nicolas (b ? Paris, *c* 1625; d Paris, 20 Aug 1707), French organist and composer. Organist at var. Paris churches from 1646. Pub. two books of organ pieces in 1683 and 1685.

Gigli, Beniamino (b Recanati, 20 Mar 1890; d Rome, 30 Nov 1957), Italian tenor. Of humble parentage, he began to make his way with difficulty, but gained a scholarship to the Rome Liceo Musicale and in 1914 made his 1st stage appearance as Enzo, at Rovigo. NY Met debut 1920, as Boito's Faust. London, CG, 1930–46; debut as Andrea Chénier. Other roles incl. Rodolfo, Nadir, Lionel and Nemorino. A beautiful voice, not always used with taste or discretion. He won world-wide fame and was considered the successor of Caruso.

Gigout, Eugène (b Nancy, 23 Mar 1844; d Paris, 9 Dec 1925), French organist and composer. Studied music at Nancy Cathedral and the École Niedermeyer in Paris. He was a pupil of Saint-Saëns there and often deputized for him as organist at the Madeleine. Married one of Niedermeyer's daughters and became prof. at his school. App. organist of Saint-Augustin Church in 1863 and travelled much as organ virtuoso. In 1885 he founded an organ school. Organ prof. at Paris Cons. from 1911.

Works incl. church music; Meditation for vln. and orch.; pf. sonata; *c* 50 organ works for concert use and *c* 400 smaller organ pieces with pedals *ad lib.* for the church.

Gigue (Fr.). *See* **Jig.**

Gilbert, Anthony (b London, 26 Jul 1934), English composer. He studied at Morley College under Anthony Milner and Walter Goehr. Has taught in Manchester and London and has worked as a music ed.

Works incl. *Sinfonia* for chamber orch. (1965); *Regions* for 2 chamber orchs. (1969); *The Scene Machine*, 1-act opera prod. Kassel 1971; *Cantata* (1972); Symph. (1973); *The Chakravaka Bird*, song drama for radio (1977); *Towards Asavari* for pf. and small orch. (1978); *Vasanta with Dancing* for chamber ens. (1981).

Gilbert, Henry (Franklin Belknap) (b Somerville, Mass., 26 Sep 1868; d Cambridge, Mass., 19 May 1928), American composer. Studied at Boston and became a business man, but later devoted himself to comp. He often used Negro tunes for his thematic material.

Works incl. ballet *The Dance in Place Congo* (after G.W. Cable); symph. prologue to Synge's *Riders to the Sea* (1913); *Salammbô's Invocation to Tanith* (after Flaubert) for soprano and orch.; *Indian Sketches* and *Hymn to America* for chorus and orch.; *Americanesque, Comedy Overture on Negro Themes* (1906), 3 *American Dances, Negro Rhapsody, Legend* and *Negro Episode* for orch.; *The Island of Fay* (after Poe, 1923); *Indian Scenes* and *Negro Dances* for pf.; *Pirate Song* (Stevenson) for voice and pf.; ed. of 100 folksongs.

Gilbert, W(illiam) S(chwenck) (1836–1911), English playwright and librettist. Libs. for operettas with music by Sullivan, *see* **Gondoliers, Grand Duke, H.M.S. Pinafore, Iolanthe, Mikado, Patience, Pirates of Penzance, Princess Ida, Ruddigore, Sorcerer, Thespis, Trial by Jury, Utopia Limited, Yeomen of the Guard.**

Gilels, Emil (b Odessa, 19 Oct 1916; d Moscow, 14 Oct 1985), Russian pianist. Studied in Odessa and made his debut there in 1929. At the age of 16 he won 1st prize in the Soviet Pianists Competition and in 1936 2nd prize in the international pf. competition in Vienna. In 1938 he won 1st prize in the Brussels international pf. competition and began teaching at Moscow Cons. Paris and New York debuts 1955; London 1959. Well known in Rus. music and classical rep.

Giles, Nathaniel (b Worcestershire, *c* 1558; d Windsor, 24 Jan 1634), English organist and composer. Organist of Worcester Cathedral, 1581–5, when he became organist and choirmaster of St George's Chapel, Windsor, and also, in 1596, of the Chapel Royal in London, where he took the official titles of Gentleman and Master of the Children on the death of Hunnis in 1597; collaborated with Ben Jonson at Blackfriars Theatre from 1600. D.Mus., Oxford, 1622.

Works incl. services, anthems, motets; madrigal *Cease now, vain thoughts.*

Gilly, Dinh (b Algiers, 19 Jul 1877; d London, 19 May 1940), French-Algerian baritone. Pupil of Cotogni. Made his 1st appearance in London, at CG, in 1911 as Amonasro; also sang Jack Rance and Rigoletto. NY Met 1909–14 as Luna and Lescaut. Married the contralto Edith Furmedge.

Gilman, Lawrence (b Flushing, NY, 5 Jul 1878; d Franconia, NH, 8 Sep 1939), American critic. Self-taught in music, he wrote for various papers at first and in 1923 became music critic to the *New York Herald-Tribune* in succession to Krehbiel. Wrote books on MacDowell, Wagner, modern music, etc., and was a well-known programme annotator and radio commentator.

Gilson, Paul (b Brussels, 15 Jun 1865; d Brussels, 3 Apr 1942), Belgian composer. Pupil of Gevaert and others, he gained the Belg. Prix de Rome in 1889. App. prof. of harmony at the Cons. of Brussels in 1899 and of Antwerp in 1904. He was also music critic of *Le Soir*, 1906–14, and then of *Le Midi.*

Works incl. operas *Prinses Zonneschijn* and *Zeevolk* (1895); ballets *La Captive* and

Daphne; oratorio *Le Démon* (after Lermon-tov); *Francesca da Rimini* (after Dante) for solo voices, chorus and orch. (1892); *La mer* for reciter and orch. (1892).

Ginastera, Alberto (b Buenos Aires, 11 Apr 1916; d Geneva, 25 Jun 1983), Argentine composer. Studied with Athos Palma at the Nat. Cons. of Buenos Aires and graduated in 1938. Visited US, 1945–7. Taught from 1948 in Buenos Aires, where he was dir. of the Centre for Advanced Musical Studies from 1963. Lived in US from 1968 and Europe from 1970. Best known for his oper-as.

Works incl. operas *Don Rodrigo* (1964), *Bomarzo* (1967), *Beatrix Cenci* (1971); bal-lets *Panambi* (1940) and *Estancia*; psalms for chorus and orch.; *Variacones concer-tantes* for orch. (1953), *Concerto per corde* (1965), *Estudos sinfónicos* (1967), 2 pf. con-certos (1961, 1972), vln. concerto (1963), 2 cello concertos (1968, 1980).

3 string quartets (1948, 1953, 1973), 3 pf. sonatas (1952, 1981, 1982), pf. 5tet (1963), cello sonata (1979).

Cantata *Bomarzo* for narrator, bar. and orch. (1964).

Gines Pérez, Juan (b Orihuela, Oct 1548; d ? Orihuela, 1612), Spanish composer. He held a church appt. in his native town at the age of 14, in 1581–95 was *maestro di cap-pella* and dir. of the choir school at Valencia, and in 1595 returned home as canon at Orihuela Cathedral.

Works incl. motets, psalms; secular Span-ish songs; contributions to the Mystery play perf. annually at Elche nr. Alicante.

Ginguené, Pierre Louis (b Rennes, 25 Apr 1748; d Paris, 16 Nov 1816), French writer. In the controversy between the partisans of Gluck and Piccinni he sided with the latter and wrote his biog. Also pub. a music dic-tionary and other works on music.

Gintzler, Simon (b *c* 1500; d after 1550), German composer. His collection of lute music was published in Venice, 1547, and he also contrib. to Hans Gerle's *Eyn Newes . . . Lautenbuch* (Nuremberg, 1552).

Gioconda, La, opera by Ponchielli (lib. by Boito, based on Victor Hugo's *Angelo*), prod. Milan, La Scala, 8 Apr 1876.

Giocoso (It.) = playful, joking, humorous.

Gioielli della Madonna, I (*The Jewels of the Madonna*), opera by Wolf-Ferrari (lib. by E. Golisciani and C. Zangarini), prod., in Ger., Berlin, Kurfürsten-Oper, 23 Dec 1911.

Gioioso (It., formerly *giojoso*) = joyous, joyful.

Giordani, Italian family of musicians:

1. Carmine G. (b Cerreto Sannita, nr. Benevento, *c* 1685; d Naples, 1758), singer and composer. Prod. an opera, *La vittoria d'amor coniugale* at Naples in 1712. Other works incl. cantata for soprano, *Versetti* for organ.

2. Giuseppe G. (called Giordanello) (b Naples, 9 Dec 1743; d Fermo, 4 Jan 1798), composer, ? son of prec. Studied music at the Cons. di Loreto at Naples and brought out his 1st opera there in 1771. He became *maestro di cappella* at Fermo Cathedral in 1791.

Works incl. over 30 operas, e.g. *L'astuto in imbroglio* (1771); *La disfatta di Dario*, etc.; oratorios *La fuga in Egitto* (1775), *La morte d'Abele*, etc. The canzonetta 'Caro mio ben' is attrib. to him, but many of the works formerly supposed to be his are by Tommaso G.

Giordani, Tommaso (b Naples, *c* 1730; d Dublin, Feb 1806), Italian composer, unre-lated to the above family. Son of a travelling opera impresario, prod. his first opera with his father's co. in London in 1756. Subse-quently lived chiefly in London (1768–83, dir. at King's Theatre, Haymarket) and Dub-lin, comp. a large number of theatrical works for both capitals.

Works incl. operas *La comediante fatta cantatrice* (1756), *L'eroe cinese* (1766), *Love in Disguise* (1766), *Il padre e il figlio rivali*, *Artaserse*, *Il re pastore* (1778), *Phillis at Court* and others, *c* 50 in all; songs for Sheridan's *The Critic*; oratorio, *Isaac*; church music; concertos and sonatas for pf. and other instruments; string 4tets, trios; songs.

Giordano, Umberto (b Foggia, 28 Aug 1867; d Milan, 12 Nov 1948), Italian com-poser. Son of an artisan, he was allowed to learn music as best he could, but in the end studied at the Naples Cons. under Serrao. He attracted the attention of the pub. Son-zogno with the opera *Marina* and soon be-came very successful with a series of stage works.

Works incl. operas *Marina* (1889), *Mala vita* (1892), *Regina Diaz* (1894), *Andrea Chénier* (1896), *Fedora* (after Sardou, 1898), *Siberia* (1903), *Marcella*, *Mese Mariano*, *Madame Sans-Gêne* (after Sardou and Moreau, 1915), *Giove a Pompei* (with Franchetti), *La cena delle beffe* (1924), *Il rè*.

Giorgi-Righetti, Geltrude (b Bologna, 1792; d Bologna, 1862), Italian mezzo-soprano. Made her 1st appearance at Bolo-gna in 1814 and was Rossini's 1st Rosina in *Il Barbiere di Siviglia* in 1816. She pub. her reminiscences of Rossini in 1823. Retired 1836.

Giorgini, Aristodemo (b Naples, 1879; d Naples, 19 Jan 1937), Italian tenor. He sang Ernesto at La Scala in 1905 and in 1910 was heard there as Elvino. Guest in London, Barcelona, Poland and Russia. Other roles incl. Rodolfo and Boito's Faust.

Giorno di regno, Un, ossia Il finto Stanislao (*A Day's Reign, or The False Stanislas*), opera by Verdi (lib. by F. Romani, used earlier by Gyrowetz, *see* **Finto Stanislao**), prod. Milan, La Scala, 5 Sep 1840. Verdi's only comic opera except *Falstaff*.

Giornovichi, Giovanni (Mane) (known as Jarnowick) (b. Palermo, *c* 1740; d St Petersburg, 23 Nov 1804), Italian violinist and composer. Possibly a pupil of Lolli, made his 1st appearance at the Concert Spirituel in Paris in 1770. Having lived in Paris, Berlin, Aus., Rus. and Swed., he went to London in 1791, but left for Hamburg in 1796, whence he went to St Petersburg in 1802. He wrote *c* 20 vln. concertos, 3 string 4tets and much music for the vln.

Giovanna d'Arco (*Joan of Arc*), opera by Verdi (lib. by T. Solera, based on Schiller's drama *Die Jungfrau von Orleans*), prod. Milan, La Scala, 15 Feb 1845.

Giovanna di Guzman (Verdi). *See* **Vêpres siciliennes**.

Giovannelli, Ruggiero (b Velletri nr. Rome, *c* 1560; d Rome, 7 Jan 1625), Italian composer. After holding var. church apps. in Rome, he succeeded Palestrina as *maestro di cappella* at St Peter's in 1594 and became a member of the Sistine Chapel in 1599; *maestro di cappella* 1614. At the request of Pope Paul V he contributed to a new ed. of the Gradual. He retired in 1624.

Works incl. Masses, Miserere and other church music; 6 books of madrigals, 1 of *canzonette* and *villanelle*, etc.

Giovannini, ? de (d 1782), Italian composer. The customary identification of Giovannini with the Comte de St Germain remains without proof. The only works extant under the name Giovannini are a handful of songs (incl. 'Willst du dein Herz mir schenken' in Bach's Anna Magdalena Notebook) and 8 vln. sonatas.

Giove in Argo (*Jupiter in Argos*), opera by Lotti (lib. by A.M. Lucchini), prod. Dresden, Redoutensaal, 25 Oct 1717, the new opera-house not being ready. The latter was opened with the same work 3 Sep 1719. (An Eng. adaptation of the same lib., under the title *Jupiter in Argos*, was set by Handel, prod. London, King's Theatre, 1 May 1739).

Gioventù di Enrico V, La (*The Youth of Henry V*), opera by Pacini (lib. by J. Ferretti, partly based on Shakespeare's *Henry IV*), prod. Rome, Teatro Valle, 26 Dec 1820).

Gipps, Ruth (b Bexhill, 20 Feb 1921), English composer, pianist and oboist. Pupil of her mother, at the Bexhill School of Music and later at the RCM in London. In 1944–5 she was in the CBSO as 2nd ob. and Eng. horn. Prof. RCM from 1967.

Works incl. ballet *Sea Nymph*; 5 symphs. (1942–80), other orch. music and chamber works.

Giraldoni, Eugenio (b Marseilles, 20 May 1871; d Helsinki, 24 Jun 1924), Italian baritone, son of Leone G. Debut Barcelona, 1891, Escamillo. At the Teatro Constanzi, Rome, he created Scarpia (1900); repeated the role at La Scala and was heard there as Onegin and Gérard. NY Met debut 1904, as Barnaba. Widely known in the Italian repertory and in the role of Boris Godunov.

Giraldoni, Leone (b Paris, 1824; d Moscow, 1 Oct 1897), Italian baritone, father of prec. He sang in Italy from 1847 and in 1857 created Verdi's Simon Boccanegra (Venice). He was Renato in the 1859 fp of *Un Ballo in Maschera* and at the Teatro Apollo, Rome, sang the title role in the fp of Donizetti's posthumously prod. *Il duca d'Alba* (1882). Retired 1885.

Girardeau (*née* ? **Calliari**), **Isabella**, Italian 17th–18th-cent. soprano, Fr. by marriage. Made her 1st appearance in London in 1710 and created Almirena in Handel's *Rinaldo*.

Giraud, Fiorello (b Parma, 22 Oct 1868; d Parma, 28 Mar 1928), Italian tenor. Debut, Vercelli 1891, as Lohengrin; the following year he was Canio in the fp of *Pagliacci*, at Milan. In 1907 he sang Siegfried under Toscanini, at La Scala, and in 1908 was the first Italian Pelléas. In Barcelona, Lisbon and S. America he was well known in Puccini roles.

Girdlestone, C(uthbert) M(orton) (b Bovey-Tracey, 17 Sep 1895; d St Cloud, 10 Dec 1975), English scholar. Educ. at the Sorbonne in Paris and Cambridge, where he became lecturer in French. Prof. of French at King's Coll., Newcastle-on-Tyne, 1926–61. Author of *Mozart et ses concertos pour piano* and *Jean-Philippe Rameau*.

Girelli Aguilar, Antonia Maria, Italian 18th-cent. soprano. She sang in the fps of Gluck's *Il trionfo di Clelia* (1763) and *Le feste d'Apollo* (1769). Created Silvia in Mozart's *Ascanio in Alba* at Milan in 1771 and the following year appeared in London, succeeding Grassi at the King's Theatre.

Girl of the Golden West (Puccini). *See* **Fanciulla del West, La**

Giselle, ou Les Wilis, ballet by Adam (choreog. by Jean Coralli, on a story by Heine, adapted by Théophile Gautier), prod. Paris, Opéra, 28 Jun 1841.

Gismondi, Celeste (d London, 28 Oct 1735), Italian mezzo-soprano. Made her 1st appearance in London in 1732 and sang in the fps of *Orlando* and *Deborah*. Later in operas by Porpora. She married an Englishman named Hempson.

Gittern, the medieval guitar with 4 strings, played with a plectrum. It survived in Eng. until *c* 1400; the term was then applied to other members of the guitar family in the 16th–17th cents.

Giuliani, Mauro (Giuseppe Sergio Pantaleo) (b Bisceglie, nr. Bari, 27 Jul 1781; d Naples, 8 May 1829), Italian guitar virtuoso and composer. Settled in Vienna in 1806, and in 1808 gave the fp of the 1st of his 3 guitar concertos. He was widely active in Vienna as teacher, performer and comp., writing more than 200 works for his inst. Often appeared with Spohr, and in 1813 played the cello in the fp of Beethoven's 7th symp. Returned to Italy in 1819, working in Rome, then Naples. Played the lyre-guitar in his last years.

Giuliano, opera by Zandonai (lib. by A. Rossato, based on Flaubert's *Saint Julien l'Hospitalier*), prod. Naples, Teatro San Carlo, 4 Feb 1928.

Giulietta e Romeo (*Juliet and Romeo*), opera by Vaccai (lib. by F. Romani, after Shakespeare's sources for R. and J.), prod. Milan, Teatro della Canobbiana, 31 Oct 1825.

Opera by Zandonai (lib. by A. Rossato, after Shakespeare), prod. Rome, Teatro Costanzi, 14 Feb 1922.

Opera by Zingarelli (lib. by G.M. Foppa), prod. Milan, La Scala, 30 Jan 1796.

Giulini, Carlo Maria (b Barletta, 9 May 1914), Italian conductor. Studied at the Acad. of Santa Cecilia in Rome, vla. and cond. (Bustini). Later he studied cond. further with Casella and B. Molinari. From 1946 to 1951 he worked for It. Radio, in 1950 becoming cond. of Radio Milan. He made his debut at La Scala, Milan, during the 1951–2 season; prin. cond. from 1953. Brit. debut, Edinburgh 1955, with Glyndebourne Opera (*Falstaff*). *Don Carlos* at CG in 1958; after *Traviata* in 1967 gave concerts with Philharmonia, Vienna SO, Chicago SO; prin. cond. Los Angeles PO from 1978. Returned to opera 1982, with *Falstaff* in Los Angeles and London.

Giulio Cesare, opera by Malipiero (lib. by comp., based on Shakespeare's *Julius Caesar*), prod. Genoa, Teatro Carlo Felice, 8 Feb 1936.

Giulio Cesare in Egitto (*Julius Caesar in Egypt*), opera by Handel (lib. by N.F. Haym), prod. London, King's Theatre, Haymarket, 20 Feb 1724.

Giulio Sabino, opera by Sarti (lib. by P. Giovannini), prod. Venice, Teatro San Benedetto, Jan 1781.

Giuramento, Il (*The Vow*), opera by Mercadante (lib. by G. Rossi, based on Victor Hugo's *Angelo*), prod. Milan, La Scala, 10 Mar 1837.

Giustini, Lodovico (b Pistoia, 12 Dec 1685; d Pistoia, 7 Feb 1743), Italian composer and organist. Pub. in 1732 a book of sonatas, prob. the 1st pub. music specifically written for the pf., as distinct from music for keyboard instruments in general.

Giustinian, Leonardo (b Venice, *c* 1387; d Venice, 10 Nov 1446), Italian poet. He wrote love poems for musical settings, some of which he provided himself, which were called after him as late as the 16th cent *See also* **Justiniana**.

Giustino, opera by Handel (lib. altered by ? from Nicolo Beregani), prod. London, CG, 16 Feb 1737.

Giusto (It. = just, strict, suitable), a direction used, generally as an adj. with *tempo*, to indicate that a movement is to be taken at a suitable or reasonable pace.

Gizziello (so called after his teacher Domenico Gizzi, real name Gioacchino Conti) (b Arpino nr. Naples, 28 Feb 1714; d Rome, 25 Oct 1761), Italian male soprano. 1st appeared in Rome, 1730, and in London, 1736.

Glagolitic Mass, work by Janáček for soloists, chorus, organ and orch. (text by M. Weingart from Ordinary of the Mass in 9th-cent. Slavonic). 5 main sections are *Gospodi pomiluj, Slava, Veřuju, Svet, Agneče Boží*; comp. 1926, fp Brno, 5 Dec 1927.

Glanville-Hicks, Peggy (b Melbourne, 29 Dec 1912), Australian composer. Studied at the Melbourne Cons. and from the age of 19 under Vaughan Williams, Gordon Jacob and R.O. Morris at the RCM in London. She gained a scholarship in 1932 and another in 1935, which enabled her to travel and to study further with Wellesz in Vienna and Nadia Boulanger in Paris. In 1938 her choral suite was perf. at the ISCM festival in London and in 1939 she married Stanley Bate, with whom she went to US, living in NY until 1958 and Greece from 1959.

Works incl. operas *Cædmon* (1934), *The Glittering Gate* (1959), *Nausicaa* (1961), *Sappho* (1963); Sinfonietta, *Prelude* and *Scherzo*, *Span. Suite* and *Music for Robots* for orch.; choral suite (Fletcher) for women's voices, ob. and strings; pf. concerto, fl. concerto; *Concertino da camera* for fl., clar., bassoon and pf.; 6 Housman songs.

Glareanus, Henricus (real name **Heinrich Loris**) (b Mollis, Glarus, Jun 1488; d Freiburg i/B., 28 Mar 1563), Swiss theorist. Studied music at Berne and Cologne, taught at Basle from 1515 and again from 1522, after holding a professorship in Paris from 1517 on the recommendation of Erasmus of Rotterdam. In 1529 he moved to Ger., settling at Freiburg. He studied the relationship between the Gk. and the church modes and wrote treatises, notably *Isagoge in musicen* (1516) and *Dodecachordon* (1547), containing his new theory of 12 church modes.

Glasenapp, Carl Friedrich (b Riga, 3 Oct 1847; d Riga, 14 Apr 1915), German biographer. Author of the 1st large biog. of Wagner (1876–7) and of var. other unreliable works on him.

Gläser, Franz (b Horní Jiřetín, Obergeorgental, 19 Apr 1798; d Copenhagen, 29 Aug 1861), Bohemian composer. Studied in Prague; app. cond. at the Leopoldstadt Theatre in Vienna, 1817, at the Josephstadt Theatre, 1822, and at the Theater an der Wien, 1827. Later in Berlin and Copenhagen. Wrote mainly operas, e.g. *Des Adlers Horst* (1832), *Bryllupet ved Como-Søen* (after Manzoni's *Promessi sposi*, 1849) and 2 other Danish operas.

Glass Harmonica. *See* **Armonica**.

Glass, Philip (b Baltimore, 31 Jan 1937), American composer. He studied at the Juilliard School and with Boulanger in Paris. Under the influence of Indian and N. African music has evolved a technique whereby melodic ideas are not developed but endlessly repeated. The anti-intellectualism implied by such a formula (minimalism) has not hindered the success of the stage works: *Einstein on the Beach* (Avignon and NY Met, 1976); *Satyagraha* (Rotterdam, 1980); *The Photographer* (Amsterdam, 1982); *CIVIL WarS* (1982–4); *Akhnaten* (Stuttgart, 1984); *The Juniper Tree* (1985, with Philip Moran); also comp. instrumental ens. works.

Glaz, Herta (b Vienna, 16 Sep 1908), Austrian contralto. Debut, Breslau 1931. She fled Germany in 1933 and toured as a concert singer before visiting the USA in 1937 (Los Angeles, under Klemperer, in *Das Lied*

von der Erde and *St Matthew Passion*); she sang at Chicago, 1940–2, and made her NY Met debut in Dec 1942; often heard there as Octavian. Retired 1962.

Glazunov, Alexander Konstantinovich (b St Petersburg, 10 Aug 1865; d Paris, 21 Mar 1936), Russian composer. After being taught music at home as a child, he studied with Rimsky-Korsakov from 1880 and finished his course in 18 months, having a 1st symph. ready for perf. early in 1882. Belaiev arr. a concert of his works in 1884 and began to pub. them. Visited W. Europe, 1884. App. dir. of the St Petersburg Cons. in 1905 and wrote little after that to augment his enormous earlier output. He completed several of Borodin's unfinished works. He left Rus. in 1928 and settled in Paris.

Works incl. ballets, *Raymonda* (1897), *Les Ruses d'amour* (1898) and *The Seasons* (1899); incid. music for Romanov's play, *The King of the Jews* (1913); 8 symphs. (1881–1906); 5 concert overtures incl. 2 on Gk. themes and *Carnival*, symph. poems *Stenka Razin* (1885), *The Sea*, *The Kremlin* (1890), suite *From the Middle Ages*, 2 serenades, fantasy *The Forest*, *Introduction and Salome's Dance* (after Oscar Wilde), many miscellaneous orchestral works; vln. concerto (1904), 2 pf. concertos, concerto for saxophone.

INSTRUMENTAL AND VOCAL: 7 string 4tets (1881–1930), string 5tet, *Novelettes* and suite for string 4tet; many works for pf. incl. 2 sonatas and Theme and Variations; Fantasy for 2 pfs.; various small instrumental pieces; 21 songs; 3 cantatas; *Hymn to Pushkin* for female voices.

Glee, a part-song, usually for male voices, in not less than 3 parts, much cultivated by Eng. comps. in the 18th and early 19th cents. The word is derived from the Anglo-Saxon *gliw* = entertainment, partic. musical entertainment. Webbe, Stevens, Callcott, Horsley, Attwood, Battishill, Cooke and others cultivated the Glee.

Glee Club, a club formed in London in 1783 and existing until 1857, for the performance of glees, madrigals, motets, canons and catches at table after dinner at a member's house or in a tavern or coffee-house.

Gleichnisarie (Ger.). *See* **Parable Aria**.

Glière, Reinhold Moritzovich (b Kiev, 11 Jan 1875; d Moscow, 23 Jun 1956), Russian composer of Belgian descent. Learnt the vln. as a child, but soon began to comp. and was sent to the Kiev School of Music and later to the Moscow Cons., where he was a pupil of Arensky, Taneiev and Ippolitov-Ivanov.

Taught at the Gnessin School of Music in Moscow and at the Kiev Cons., of which he became director in 1914, but settled at Moscow in 1920 (prof. of comp. at Cons. until 1941). He made research into Azerbaijan, Uzbek and Ukrainian folksong and based some of his later works on it. In 1939 he became chairman of the Organizing Committee of USSR comps.

Works incl. operas *Shakh-Senem* (1926), *Leyli and Mejnun* (1937), *Rachel* (after Maupassant's *Mlle. Fifi*), *Ghulsara* (1949); ballet *The Red Poppy*, 1927; incid. music for Sophocles' *Oedipus Rex*, Aristophanes' *Lysistrata*, Beaumarchais's *Marriage of Figaro*, etc.; 3 symphs. (No. 3, *Ilia Muromets*, 1909–11), 3 symph. poems, concert overtures; harp concerto, concerto for soprano and orch.; fantasy for wind instruments; 4 string 4tets (1900–48); 3 string 6tets, string 8tet; many instrumental pieces; 18 op. nos. of pf. music, 22 op. nos. of songs.

Glinka, Mikhail Ivanovich (b Novospass-koye, Government of Smolensk, 1 Jun 1804; d Berlin, 15 Feb 1857), Russian composer. The son of a wealthy landowner, he was sent to school at St Petersburg, 1817–22. He took some pf. lessons from Field and others, also studied vln. and theory. At his father's wish he worked in the Ministry of Communications in 1824–8, but not being obliged to earn a living and wishing to devote himself to music he gave it up. He visited It., 1830–3, where he had lessons from Basili at Milan, and afterwards Vienna and Berlin, studying under Dehn in the latter city. On his father's death he returned to Rus., settled in St Petersburg and married in 1835. There he worked at *A Life for the Tsar* and succeeded in having it prod. in 1836. *Ruslan and Ludmilla* was delayed by domestic troubles and the separation from his wife in 1841. It was prod. in 1842. In 1844 he visited Paris and Spain, in 1848 Warsaw, and Fr. again in 1852–4. It was during a visit to Berlin, 1856–7, that he died. He was regarded as the founder of the Russian national school of music.

Works incl. operas *A Life for the Tsar* (formerly *Ivan Sussanin*) (1836) and *Ruslan and Ludmilla* (1842); incid. music to Count Kukolnik's *Prince Kholmsky*; orch. works: *Jota aragonesa* (*Capriccio brillante*), *A Night in Madrid* (1851), *Kamarinskaya* (1848), *Valse-Fantaisie*; string 4tet in F maj.; trio for clar., bassoon and pf.; 6tet for pf. and strings; *c* 40 pf. pieces; Pol. hymn and *Memorial Cantata* for chorus; *c* 85 songs; some vocal duets and 4tets.

Glissando (It. from Fr. *glisser* = to glide, slide), a direction for rapid scales played on the pf. or harp by sliding the fingers over the keys or strings. On the pf. only the C maj. and pentatonic scales can thus be played (on white and black keys respectively), and this applies also to the chromatic harp with its crossed strings, where however a chromatic scale can be played in addition if the strings are touched at the point of intersection. A glissando effect can also be obtained on string instruments by sliding the finger along the string, or by the voice by scooping, but in both cases the direction for this is more properly *portamento*. Trombs. can play glissando passages by not interrupting the breath while the slide is brought to another position.

Globokar, Vinko (b Anderny, Meurth-et-Moselle, 7 Jul 1934), Yugoslav composer and trombonist. He studied in Ljubljana and at the Paris Cons.; later with Leibowitz and Berio. From 1968 he has been prof. of trombone at the Cologne Musikhochschule. His avant-garde virtuosity encouraged Stockhausen, Kagel and Berio to write works for him. His own music includes *Voie* for narrator, chorus and orch. (1965); *Fluide* for 12 insts. (1967); *Traumdeutung* for 4 choruses and insts. (1967); *Concerto grosso* for 5 solo players, orch. and chorus (1970); *Ausstrahlungen* for soloists and 20 players (1971); *Carrousel* for 4 voices and 16 insts. (1977); *Discours I–VI* for var. insts. (1967–82).

Glock, (Sir) William (b London, 3 May 1908), English pianist, administrator and music critic. Studied with Boris Ord and Edward Dent at Cambridge in 1926–30 and with Schnabel in Berlin in 1930–3. He joined the *Observer* in 1934 and succeeded Fox Strangways as chief music critic in 1940, resigning in 1945. In 1948 he co-founded a summer school for advanced courses in music which is now held at Dartington Hall, Devon; remained as music dir. until 1979. He was BBC Controller of Music, 1959–73, and was knighted in 1970. He app. Boulez as conductor of the BBC SO in 1971; did much to improve the Promenade Concerts. Dir. of Bath Festival 1976–84.

Glockenspiel (Ger. = play of bells), a set of tuned steel bars played either with 2 hammers held one in each hand or with a pf. keyboard (e.g. Papageno's bells in Mozart's *Zauberflöte*). In the former case not more than 2 notes can be struck together.

Glogauer Liederbuch, an extensive MS. collection in 3 part-books of Latin pieces,

Ger. songs and instrumental pieces, dating from *c* 1480. It was in Berlin until the 2nd World War, but is now in Kraków. It is the earliest surviving set of part books.

Gloria (Lat., *Gloria in excelsis Deo* = 'Glory to God in the highest'), the 2nd item of the Ordinary of the Mass, following immediately upon the Kyrie. Although the Ambrosian Gloria is sung to an even simpler tone, the melody printed with Mass XV of the Vatican ed. is probably the oldest (*see illustration*).

Son of a forester, he left home in face of parental opposition to music and matriculated at Prague Univ. in 1731. In Vienna *c* 1735 entered the service of Prince Melzi, with whom he went to It. Possibly a pupil of Sammartini in Milan, where he made his debut as an opera comp. in 1741 with *Artaserse* (lib. by Metastasio). A number of operas followed, all in the conventional It. form. Went to Eng., perhaps with Prince Lobkowitz, in 1745, possibly visiting Paris

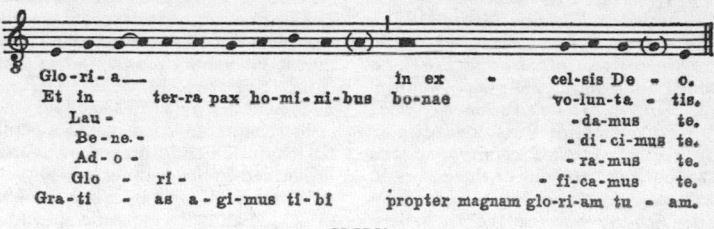

GLORIA

Gloriana, opera by Britten (lib. by William Plomer), prod. London, CG, 8 Jun 1953.
Glossop, Peter (b Sheffield, 6 Jul 1928), English baritone. He sang with SW, 1953–62, as Onegin, Scarpia and Luna. CG since 1961 as Demetrius, Posa, Iago and Boccanegra. NY Met debut 1967, as Rigoletto. Other roles incl. Falstaff, Billy Budd and Renato. His Iago was admired at Salzburg.
Glover, Jane (b Helmsley, Yorks., 13 May 1949), English conductor and musicologist. She studied at Oxford, Ph.D. on Cavalli, later issued as a book. Prof. debut as cond. Wexford Festival, 1975, with her own ed. of Cavalli's *Eritrea*, then in London, 1982. She started her Glyndebourne career as chorus mistress, then as cond. on tour; *Don Giovanni* at the Festival, 1982. Artistic dir. London Mozart Players from 1984. Presenter of music programmes on TV.
Gluck (*née* Fiersohn), Alma** (b Bucharest, 11 May 1884; d New York, 27 Oct 1938), Rumanian-American soprano. Was taken to USA as a child and worked as a stenographer in NY until her marriage to Bernard Gluck in 1906, when she began to study singing, making her 1st appearance in 1909 with the Met Opera Co. as Massenet's Sophie. Other roles incl. Gluck's Euridice, Marguerite, Venus, Gilda and Mimi. Concert career from 1913. In 1914 she married the violinist Efrem Zimbalist.
Gluck, Christoph Willibald (b Erasbach, Upper Palatinate, 2 Jul 1714; d Vienna, 15 Nov 1787), Bohemian-German composer.

on the way. In London, where he met Handel, prod. 2 operas and appeared as a perf. on the glass harmonica. In *c* 1747 joined the Mingotti touring opera company, of which he subsequently became *Kapellmeister,* and travelled widely.

Married in 1750, he settled in Vienna 2 years later, being connected with the court from 1754, though without official title (only in 1774 was he app. court comp.). Under the management of Count Durazzo the Viennese theatre moved away from conventional *opera seria,* and Gluck wrote a number of Fr. *opéras-comiques.* Dramatic ballet *Don Juan,* embodying Noverre's ideas on modern dance, prod. 1761.

Finally in *Orfeo* (1762) Gluck and his librettist Calzabigi realized in opera the current demands for greater dramatic truth in the theatre. The aims of this 'reform' were set out in the prefaces to *Alceste* (1767) and *Paride ed Elena* (1770). In many ways, e.g. prominent use of chorus and ballet, these works adopted features of Fr. opera, and Gluck now turned to Paris, where *Iphigénie en Aulide* was prod. in 1774, followed by Fr. versions of *Orfeo* and *Alceste* (1774 and 1776) and *Armide* (1777). Gluck was reluctantly involved in a squabble between his supporters and the partisans of Piccinni, but this was decisively closed by the triumph of his *Iphigénie en Tauride* (1779). His last opera for Paris, *Écho et Narcisse,* was unsuccessful, and he returned to Vienna, remaining there till his death.

Apart from a number of symphs., 8 trio sonatas, a setting of *De profundis* for chorus and orch., and settings of Klopstock's *Odes*, Gluck's works are almost entirely for the theatre, viz. *opere serie: Artaserse* (1741), *Demetrio, Demofoonte* (1743), *Il Tigrane, La Sofonisba* (1744), *Ipermestra, La caduta de' giganti* (1746), *Artamene, Le nozze d'Ercole e d'Ebe, Semiramide riconosciuta* (1748), *La Contesa dei numi, Ezio* (1750), *La clemenza di Tito* (1752), *Le Cinesi, Antigono, Il re pastore, Il Telemaco*, etc.; Fr. *opéras-comiques: L'Isle de Merlin* (1758), *La Cythère assiégée, L'Arbre enchanté, L'Yvrogne corrigé, Le Cadi dupé* (1761), *La Rencontre imprévue* (1764), etc.; 'reform' operas: *Orfeo, Alceste, Paride ed Elena* (1770); Fr. operas for Paris: *Iphigénie en Aulide* (1774), *Orphée et Euridice* and *Alceste* (both Fr. versions of the earlier It. operas), *Armide* (1777), *Iphigénie en Tauride, Écho et Narcisse* (1779); ballets: *Don Juan* (1761), *Semiramide* (1765); etc.

Glückliche Hand, Die (*The Lucky Hand*), opera by Schoenberg (lib. by comp.), comp. 1913, prod. Vienna, Volksoper, 14 Oct 1924.

Glyndebourne Festival Opera, a small private opera house opened by John Christie on his estate of Glyndebourne, Sussex, in 1934, for the perf. of opera in beautiful surroundings with an internat. company of singers. Musical dirs. have been Fritz Busch (1934–51), Vittorio Gui (1951–60), John Pritchard (1960–77) and Bernard Haitink. Until World War II the repertory was devoted almost wholly to Mozart, the only exceptions being Verdi's *Macbeth* and Donizetti's *Don Pasquale*. Since 1946 it has been considerably extended to include operas by Britten, Haydn, Rossini, Strauss, Henze, Janáček and Stravinsky. Mozart is still sometimes perf., however. The Glyndebourne Touring Co. was formed in 1968.

Glynne, Howell (b Swansea, 24 Jan 1906; d Toronto, 24 Nov 1969), Welsh bass. He sang with the Carl Rosa Co. in the 1930s in small roles. SW, 1946–64, as Kecal, Bartolo and Fiesco and in the Brit. fp of *I quattro rusteghi*. He sang in the 1949 fp of Bliss's *Olympians*, at CG, and was well-known there in the 1950s as Varlaam and Ochs.

Gnecchi, Vittorio (b Milan, 17 Jul 1876; d Milan, 5 Feb 1954), Italian composer. Studied music at Milan. His 1st opera, given at Bologna in 1905, was at the centre of great controversy in 1909, when Strauss's *Elektra* appeared and showed striking similarities to Gnecchi's music.

Works incl. operas *Cassandra* (after Homer's *Iliad*, 1905), and *La Rosiera* (1927); heroic poem for orch. *Notte nel campo di Holoferne*, etc.

Gnecco, Francesco (b Genoa, *c* 1769; d Milan, *c* 1810), Italian composer. Pupil (?) of Mariani and Cimarosa. *Maestro di cappella* at Savona Cathedral.

Works incl. 26 operas, e.g. *Carolina e Filandro* (1804) and *La prova d'un opera seria* (1803).

Gnessin, Mikhail Fabianovich (b Rostov-on-Don, 2 Feb 1883; d Moscow, 5 May 1957), Russian composer and teacher. Studied with Rimsky-Korsakov and Liadov at the St Petersburg Cons. and in Germany from 1911 to 1914. Settled at Rostov in 1914, at Moscow in 1923 and became prof. at the Leningrad Cons. in 1936; pupils incl. Khachaturian and Khrennikov. His work is influenced by Jewish music.

Works incl. operas *Youth of Abraham* (1921–3) and *The Maccabees*; incid. music for plays, incl. Sophocles' *Antigone* and *Oedipus Rex* (1915), Gogol's *The Revisor*, Blok's *The Rose and the Cross*, etc.; *The Conqueror Worm* (after Poe), 1905–17 for solo voices, chorus and orch. (1926); *Symph. Fragment* (after Shelley), *Song of Adonis* and *Fantasia in the Jewish Style* for orch.; *Requiem* for pf. 5tet, *Variations on Jewish Themes* and *Azerbaijan Folksongs* for string 4tet, 6tet *Adygeya*; vln. and pf. sonata in G min., *Sonata-Ballade* for cello and pf.; songs with orch.; song cycles to words by Alexander Blok, Sologub, etc.; Jewish folksong arrs.

Gobbi, Tito (b Bassano del Grappa, 24 Oct 1915; d Rome, 5 Mar 1984), Italian baritone. Orig. studied law, then sang in Rome with Crimi, making his debut in Rome in 1938. He first appeared at La Scala, Milan, in 1942 as Belcore; Wozzeck same season. London, CG, 1950–74. US debut, San Francisco 1948; NY Met 1956, as Scarpia. Gobbi had a huge repertory of some 102 roles, and was especially outstanding as a Verdi and Puccini singer. Other roles incl. Posa, Almaviva, Don Giovanni, Germont and Boccanegra. Active as opera prod., in London, Chicago and elsewhere. He was also a fine actor and made many films.

God save the Queen (or **King**), the British national anthem. A tune of possibly remote but uncertain ancestry, appearing in *Harmonia anglicana* in 1744; earliest known perf in 1745, when it became very popular as a royalist song attacking the Young Pretender. The tune has been adopted in several other countries.

Godard, Benjamin (Louis Paul) (b Paris, 18 Aug 1849; d Cannes, 10 Jan 1895), French composer. Studied vln. and comp. at the Paris Cons. He became a vla. player in chamber music. In 1878 he tied with Dubois in gaining the prize in a competition organized by the municipality of Paris with the dramatic symph. *Le Tasse* for solo voices, chorus and orch. In 1885 he estab. a series of 'modern concerts' without success.

Works incl. operas *Pedro de Zalamea* (1884), *Jocelyn* (1888), *Le Dante* (1890), *La Vivandière*, *Les Guelfes*; incid. music to Shakespeare's *Much Ado about Nothing* and Fabre's *Jeanne d'Arc*; *Scènes poétiques* (1879), dramatic poem *Diane, Symphonie-Ballet, Symphonie gothique, Symphonie orientale* and *Symphonie légendaire* for orch.; 2 vln. concertos, 2 pf. concertos; 3 string 4tets (1883–93), 2 pf. trios; 5 vln. and pf. sonatas; pf. pieces; over 100 songs.

Goddard, Arabella (b Saint-Servan, Saint-Malo, 12 Jan 1836; d Boulogne, 6 Apr 1922), English pianist. Pupil of Kalkbrenner in Paris and later of Thalberg in Eng. Made her 1st public appearance in London in 1850. She studied the classics with the critic J.W. Davison, whom she married in 1859.

Godfrey, Dan(iel Eyers) (b London, 20 Jun 1868; d Bournemouth, 20 Jul 1939), English conductor. Son of the bandmaster Daniel G. (1831–1903). Studied at the RCM in London and 1st cond. a military band and opera, and in 1892 became cond. of a small seaside orch. at Bournemouth, which in time he raised to a full symph. orch.; frequent fps of British works. He was knighted in 1922 and retired in 1934.

Godowsky, Leopold (b Wilno, 13 Feb 1870; d New York, 21 Nov 1938), Polish (Americanized) pianist and composer. Very precociously gifted, he appeared in public at the age of 9, made a tour of Pol. and Ger., and then entered the Hochschule für Musik in Berlin, studying with Bargiel and Rudorff. He 1st visited the USA in 1884, where he settled in 1901 and later became director of the Chicago Cons. In 1909–14 he taught in Vienna. He made many arrs. for pf. and comp. studies, concert pieces.

Goehr, Alexander (b Berlin, 10 Aug 1932), English composer. Studied at the RMCM and at the Paris Cons. with Messiaen. He writes frequently in a free serial technique. Prof., Leeds Univ., 1971–6; prof., Cambridge Univ., from 1976.

Works incl. STAGE: operas *Arden muss sterben* (Arden must Die, 1967) and *Behold the Sun* (1985); ballet *La Belle dame sans*

merci (1958); *Triptych*, music theatre in 3 parts: *Naboth's Vineyard, Shadowplay, Sonata about Jerusalem* (1968–70).

CHORAL AND SOLO VOCAL: *The Deluge*, cantata after da Vinci (1958), *Sutter's Gold*, cantata for bar., chorus and orch. (1960), *5 Poems and an Epigram of William Blake* for chorus and trumpet (1964), *Psalm IV* for sop., mezzo, women's voices, vla. and organ (1976), *Babylon the Great is Fallen* for chorus and orch. (1979), *Das Gesetz der Quadrille* for bar. and pf., to texts from Kafka (1979), *Behold the Sun*, concert aria from the opera (1981).

ORCH.: *Fantasia* (1954), *Hecuba's Lament* (1961), vln. concerto (1962), *Little Symphony* (1963), *Little Music for Strings* (1963), *Pastorals* (1965), *Romanza* for cello and orch. (1968), *Symphony in 1 movement* (1970), Concerto for 11 insts. (1970), pf. concerto (1971), *Chaconne* for 19 wind insts. (1974), *Metamorphosis/Dance* (1974), *Sinfonia* (1980), *Deux Etudes* (1981), *A musical offering* (JSB 1985), *Symph. with Chaconne*.

CHAMBER: pf. sonata (1952), *Suite* for ens. (1961), pf. trio (1966), 3 string 4tets. (1957, 1967, 1976), *Lyric Pieces* for wind septet and db. (1974).

Goehr, Walter (b Berlin, 28 May 1903; d Sheffield, 4 Dec 1960), British conductor and composer of German birth, father of prec. Studied with Schoenberg in Berlin, cond. Radio Orch. there, 1925–31. Moved to London 1933 and was music dir. of the Columbia Graphophone Co. until 1939. Cond., Morley College concerts from 1943. Gave fps of Britten's *Serenade* and Tippett's *A Child of our Time*. Made eds. of Monteverdi's *Vespers* of 1610 and *Poppea*. Works incl. symph., radio opera, incid. and chamber music.

Goethe, Johann Wolfgang von (1749–1832), German poet, novelist, dramatist and philosopher. See **André (J.)** (*Erwin und Elmire*), **Apprenti sorcier** (Dukas), **Benoit (P.)** (*Roi des aulnes*), **Bentzon** (*Faust III*), **Blangini** (*Letzten Augenblicke Werthers*), **Brahms** (*Gesang der Parzen, Rinaldo*), **Claudine von Villa Bella** (5 comps.), **Dukas** (*Apprenti sorcier* and *Götz von Berlichingen*), **Eberwein** (*Claudine von V.B.* and *Jahrmarkt von Plundersweilen*), **Egmont** (Beethoven), **Erlkönig** (Schubert), **Ettinger** (*Clavigo*), **Gál** (*Requiem für Mignon*), **Goldmark (C.)** (*Götz von B.* and *Meeresstille und glückliche Fahrt*), **Hoffmann (E.T.A.)** (*Scherz, List und Rache*), **Hüttenbrenner (A.)** (*Erlkönig*), **Kienlen** (*Claudine von V.B.* and *Scherz, L. und R.*), **Koechlin** (*Nuit de*

Walpurgis classique), Krenek (*Triumph der Empfindsamkeit*), Lassen (*Faust* and *Pandora*), Loewe (C.) (*Erlkönig*), Marx (A.B.) (*Jery und B.*), Medtner (songs), Meeresstille (Beethoven and Mendelssohn), Mendelssohn (A.) (*Werther*), Mendelssohn (*Erste Walpurgisnacht*), Mignon (A.Thomas), Pugnani (*Werther* symph.), Rauzzini (V.) (*Werther*), Reichardt (*Claudine von V.B., Erwin und E.* and *Jery und B.*), Rhapsodie (Brahms), Rietz (J.) (*Jery und B.* and incid. music for plays), Rinaldo (Brahms), Rubinstein (Anton) (*Wilhelm Meister*), Scherz, List und Rache (Bruch), Schoeck (*Erwin und Elmire, Dithyrambe* and songs), Schröter (C.) (*Fischerin, Neue Amadis* and *Erlkönig*), Schubert (*Claudine von V.B.* and 20 Lieder), Schumann (*Requiem für Mignon*), Stiehl (*Jery und B.*), Streicher (T.) (*Mignons Exequien*), Tasso (Liszt), Tomášek (songs), Unger (H.) (*Gott und Bajadere*), Veilchen (Mozart), Vogler (*Erwin und E.*), Vrieslander (songs), Webern (2 choral songs), Wellesz (*Scherz, L. und R.,*), Werther (Massenet), Winter (*Scherz, L. und R.* and *Jery und B.*), Wolf (E.W.) (*Erwin und Elmire.*), Zelter (songs), Zumsteeg (*Clavigo*).

5 songs by Brahms, 1 by Mozart (*Veilchen*), 71 by Schubert, 19 by Schumann, 60 (incl. 9 early) by Wolf.

See also Faust and Faust Symphonie.

Goetz. *See* **Götz.**

Gogol, Nikolai Vassilievich (1809–52), Russian novelist. *See* Assafiev (*Christmas Eve*), Berutti (*Taras Bulba*), Christmas Eve (Rimsky-Korsakov), Gnessin (*Revisor*), Kashperov (V.N.) (*Taras Bulba*), The Marriage (Mussorgsky and Martinů), May Night (Rimsky-Korsakov), Nose, (Shostakovich), Revisor (Egk), Searle (*Diary of a Madman*), Serov (*Christmas Eve Revels*), Soloviev (*Vakula the Smith*), Sorotchintsy Fair (Mussorgsky), Taras Bulba (Janáček), Vakula the Smith (Tchaikovsky), Weis (K.) (*Revisor*).

Göhringer, Franzilla. *See* Pixis.

Goldberg, Johann Gottlieb (b Danzig, bap. 14 Mar 1727; d Dresden, buried 15 Apr 1756), German harpsichordist, possibly pupil of W.F. and J.S. Bach. The latter allegedly wrote for him (aged only 15) the 'Goldberg Variations', pub. in 1741/2.

'Goldberg Variations' (Bach). *See above.*

Goldberg, Reiner (b Grostau, 17 Oct 1939), German tenor. He studied in Dresden and made his debut there in 1966. Joined Dresden Opera in 1973 and visited Tokyo with the Co. in 1980. London, CG, debut

1982 as Walther. Has visited Vienna, Hamburg, Berlin and Leningrad in roles of Bacchus, Tannhäuser, Max, Siegmund and Florestan. He sang the title role on the soundtrack of the Syberberg film version of *Parsifal*, while the part was being mimed onscreen by a woman. Recorded Strauss's Guntram 1985.

Golden Age (Shostakovich). *See* **Age of Gold.**

Golden Cockerel, The (*Zolotoy Petushok*), opera by Rimsky-Korsakov. (lib. V.I. Bielsky, based on Pushkin's satirical fairy-tale), prod. Moscow, 7 Oct 1909, after Rimsky-Korsakov's death. It is his last opera.

Golden Legend, The, oratorio by Sullivan (on Longfellow's poem), prod. Leeds Festival, 1886; revived at Leeds, 15 Mar 1986, cond. Mackerras.

'Golden Sonata', the nickname given to the 9th (F maj.) of Purcell's 10 *Sonatas of IV Parts* for 2 vlns., cello and continuo, pub. posthumously in 1697.

Goldene Bock, Der, chamber opera by Krenek (lib. by comp.), prod. Hamburg, 16 Jun 1964.

Goldmark, Carl (b Keszthely, 18 May 1830; d Vienna, 2 Jan 1915), Austro-Hungarian composer. Son of a poor Jewish cantor, who managed to enter him at the Sopron school of music in 1842. He studied vln. and made such rapid progress that he was sent to Vienna the next year and entered the cons. in 1847. During the 1848 Revolution he played at the theatre at Györ in Hung. and was nearly shot as a rebel. In 1850 he returned to Vienna, where he eventually settled as a teacher.

Works incl. operas *Die Königin von Saba* (1875), *Merlin* (1886), *Das Heimchen am Herd* (after Dickens's *Cricket on the Hearth*, 1896), *Die Kriegsgefangene, Götz von Berlichingen* (after Goethe, 1902), and *Ein Wintermärchen* (after Shakespeare's *Winter's Tale*, 1908); symph. poem *Rustic Wedding* and 2 symphs.; 2 Scherzos for orch. and overtures *Sakuntala* (after Kalidasa), *Penthesilea* (after Kleist), *Im Frühling, Der gefesselte Prometheus, Sappho, In Italien* and *Aus Jugendtagen*, symph. poem *Zrinyi*; *Meeresstille und glückliche Fahrt* (Goethe) for male chorus and horns, other choral works; 2 vln. concertos.

String 4tet (1860), pf. 5tet, 3 pf. trios and other chamber music; 2 suites and sonata for vln. and pf., cello and pf. sonata; pf. pieces; songs.

Goldmark, Rubin (b New York, 15 Aug 1872; d New York, 6 Mar 1936), American composer of Austro-Hungarian descent, nephew of prec. Studied at the Vienna Cons. and the Nat. Cons. in NY, where Dvořák was his comp. master. He was director of the Colorado Coll. Cons. in 1895–1901, but returned to NY in 1902 and settled as private pf. and comp. teacher, until in 1924 he was app. to the Juilliard Graduate School there.

Works incl. *Hiawatha* (after Longfellow, 1900), *Samson* (1914), *Requiem* (on Lincoln's address at Gettysburg), *Negro Rhapsody* and *The Call of the Plains* for orch.; string 4tet in A maj.; pf. trio in D min.; vln. and pf. sonata; vln. pieces; pf. music, songs; choruses, etc.

Goldoni, Carlo (b Venice, 25 Feb 1707; d Paris, 6 or 7 Feb 1793), Italian playwright and librettist. See **Amore artigiano** (Gassmann and Latilla), **Arcadia in Brenta** (Galuppi), **Buovo d'Antona** (Traetta), **Burbero di buon cuore** (Martín y Soler), **Conte Caramella** (Galuppi), **Donne curiose** (Wolf-Ferrari), **Filosofo di campagna** (Galuppi), **Fischietti** (4 operas), **Fra due litiganti** (Sarti), **Gelosie villane** (Sarti), **Generali** (*Pamela nubile*, after Richardson), **Isola disabitata** (G. Scarlatti), **Lottchen am Hofe** (J.A. Hiller), **Malipiero** (3 operas), **Mondo alla roversa** (Galuppi), **Mondo della luna** (do. and Haydn), **Paisiello** (*Ciarlone*), **Pallavicini (V.)** (*Speziale*), **Pescatrici** (Bertoni and Haydn), **Piccinni** (*Vittorina*), **Quattro rusteghi** (Wolf-Ferrari), **Scarlatti** (6) (*Portentosi effetti*), **Sinigaglia** (*Baruffe chiozzotte*), **Speziale** (Haydn), **Tigrane** (Gluck), **Uccellatori** (Gassmann), **Usiglio** (*Donne curiose*), **Vendemmia** (Gazzaniga), **Wagenaar (J.)** (*Philos. Princess*), **Wolf (E.W.)** (*Dorfdeputierten*).

Goldschmidt, Adalbert von (b Vienna, 5 May 1848; d Vienna, 21 Dec 1906), Austrian composer. He devoted himself as an amateur to the comp. of large-scale works, the 1st of which, prod. in Berlin in 1876, showed remarkable affinities with Wagner's *Ring*, not heard until later in the year at Bayreuth.

Works incl. music-dramas *Die sieben Todsünden* (1876), *Helianthus, Gaea* (trilogy), opera *Die fromme Helene* (after Wilhelm Busch); symph. poem; *c* 100 songs, etc.

Goldschmidt, Berthold (b Hamburg, 18 Jan 1903), English conductor and composer of German birth. Studied in Berlin, became asst. cond. of the Staatsoper there in 1926 and cond. at the Darmstadt Opera in 1927. In 1931–3 he cond. on the Berlin Radio and

was artistic adviser to the munic. opera there. But the Nazi régime drove him to Eng. In 1964 he cond. the fp of Deryck Cooke's performing vers. of Mahler's 10th symphony.

Works incl. operas *Der gewaltige Hahnrei* (after Crommelynck) and *Beatrice Cenci* (after Shelley, 1949–50); ballet *Chronica*; overture to Shakespeare's *Comedy of Errors*, symph. and other orchestral works; vln., cello and harp concertos, chamber music.

Goldschmidt, Otto (b Hamburg, 21 Aug 1829; d London, 24 Feb 1907), German pianist and composer. Studied at the Leipzig Cons. under Mendelssohn and in 1848 went to Paris intending to study with Chopin. In 1849 he went to London, where he settled in 1858. Accompanist and husband of Jenny Lind. Founder of the Bach Choir.

Works incl. oratorio *Ruth* (1867), cantata *Music* for soprano and female voices (1898); pf. concerto; pf. trio; 2 duets for 2 pfs.; studies and pieces for pf.; songs.

Golgotha, oratorio by Frank Martin for 5 soloists, chorus and orch. (text from the Bible and St Augustine); comp. 1945–8, fp Geneva, 29 Apr 1949.

Goltermann, Georg (Eduard) (b Hanover, 19 Aug 1824; d Frankfurt, 29 Dec 1898), German cellist, conductor and composer. Studied at Munich and began to tour as a cello virtuoso in 1850. In 1853 he became 2nd and in 1874 1st cond. at the Frankfurt theatre. Comp. a symph., a cello concerto and many other cello pieces.

Goltz, Christel (b Dortmund, 8 Jul 1912), German soprano. She studied in Munich and sang Agathe there in 1935. Dresden 1936–50; Berlin, Vienna and Munich from 1947 in Strauss roles, Tosca and Leonore. London, CG, from 1951; in 1952 sang Marie there in the 1st Brit. stage prod. of *Wozzeck*. NY Met debut, Dec 1954, as Salome. Other roles incl. Isolde, the Dyer's Wife and Orff's Antigonae.

Gombert, Nicolas (b *c* 1495; d ? Tournai, *c* 1556), Flemish composer. Pupil of Josquin des Prés. He was in service at the Emperor Charles V's chapel in Flanders from 1526 and became *maître des enfants* in 1529; later he became a canon at Tournai and in 1537 went to Spain with 20 singers and held a post in the imp. chapel in Madrid; exiled in 1540 for gross indecency with his choirboys.

Works incl. 10 Masses, 160 motets, psalms; *c* 80 *chansons*.

Gomes, (Antônio) Carlos (b Campinas, 11 Jul 1836; d Belém, 16 Sep 1896), Brazilian composer of Portuguese descent. Studied with Lauro Rossi in Milan. In 1895 he was app. director of the Cons. at Pará, but he was delayed at Lisbon by illness and died soon after his arrival.

Works incl. operas *A noite do castello* (1861), *Joana di Flandres*, *Il Guarany* (1870), *Fosca*, *Salvator Rosa* (1874), *Maria Tudor* (on Victor Hugo's play, 1879), *Lo schiavo*, *Condor* (1891); revues *Se sa minga* and *Nella luna*; ode *Il saluto del Brasil* (Philadelphia Exhibition, 1876) and cantata *Colombo* (Columbus Festival, 1892).

Gomez, Jill (b New Amsterdam, British Guiana, 21 Sep 1942), British soprano. She studied in London; sang Mélisande at Glyndebourne in 1969 and returned as Calisto and Anne Trulove. She created Flora in *The Knot Garden* at CG (1970); other London roles have been Tippett's Jenifer, Tytania and Ilia. With Scottish Opera she has been heard as Pamina, Fiordiligi and Henze's Elizabeth Zimmer. Often heard in concert, and at Lausanne in 1985 sang in Handel's *Belshazzar*.

Gomis, José Melchor (b Onteniente, Valencia, 6 Jan 1791; d Paris, 26 Jul 1836), Spanish composer. Bandmaster at Barcelona, moved to Madrid *c* 1817 and in 1823 went to Paris for political reasons. In 1826–9 he taught singing in London, where he pub. many Spanish songs, and then returned to Paris, where he prod. comic operas.

Works incl. Span. monodrama *Sensibilidad y prudencia, ó La aldeana*, Fr. comic operas *Le Diable à Séville* (1831), *Le Revenant* (after Scott, 1835), *Le Portefaix* and *Rock le barbu* (1836); *L'inverno* for 4 voices and orch.; songs.

Gondoliers, The, or The King of Barataria, operetta by Sullivan (lib. by W. S. Gilbert), prod. London, Savoy Theatre, 7 Dec 1889.

Gong, an oriental bronze disc with turneddown rims. It is struck with a mallet covered with var. materials according to the quality of sound required. Also called tam-tam.

Gonzaga, Guglielmo, Duke of Mantua (b Mantua, 24 Apr 1538; d Mantua, 14 Aug 1587). He succeeded to the duchy in 1556, became a great patron of music and was himself a comp., pub. anonymously a book of madrigals and 1 of *Sacrae cantiones*.

Goodall, (Sir) **Reginald** (b Lincoln, 13 Jul 1901), English conductor. He studied at the RCM and in Germany. After minor appts. pre-war he cond. the fp of *Peter Grimes* at SW, London, in 1945. On staff at CG from 1946, but gifts were not properly recognised. Major success came with *The Master-*

singers at SW in 1968. His broad tempi and intensity of expression were regarded as belonging to the best traditions of German conductors. *Parsifal* at CG 1971. *The Ring* at the London Coliseum 1973; *Tristan* with the WNO 1979. Also conducts Bruckner's symphonies. Knighted 1985.

Good-Humoured Ladies, The, ballet by Tommasini on music by D. Scarlatti (choreography by Massin), prod. Rome, Teatro Costanzi, 12 Apr 1917.

Goodman, Benny (b Chicago, 30 May 1909; d New York, 16 Jun 1986), American clarinettist, composer and band-leader. He played in various jazz and dance bands from 1921. In 1938 recorded the Mozart 5tet with the Budapest Quartet and commissioned Bartók's *Contrasts* (fp 1939). Copland and Hindemith wrote concertos for him (both fps 1950).

Goossens, Eugene (b London, 26 May 1893; d Hillingdon, 13 Jun 1962), English conductor and composer of Belgian descent, grandson of Eugène G. (1845–1906) and son of Eugène G. (1867–1958), both conds. of the Carl Rosa Opera Co. After study at Bruges, Liverpool and the RCM he played vln. in the Queen's Hall Orch., 1911–15, and then, until 1920, cond. some of Beecham's operatic prods. After that he formed an orch. of his own, giving early English perfs. of works by Stravinsky, and cond. the Russian Ballet. From 1923 he cond. the PO at Rochester, USA. In 1931 he was app. cond. of the Cincinnati SO and continued to live there until he was app. cond. of the Sydney Orch. and director of the Cons. there (1947–56). Knighted 1955.

Works incl. operas *Judith* (1929) and *Don Juan de Mañara* (1937); ballet *L'École en crinoline*; 2 symphs. (1940, 1944), sinfonietta; *Silence* for chorus and orch.; Fantasy Concerto for pf. and orch., ob. concerto (1927), vln. concerto; 2 string 4tets (1915, 1940).

Goossens, Léon (b Liverpool, 12 Jun 1897; d Tunbridge Wells, 12 Feb 1988), English oboist, brother of prec. From 1913 he was 1st ob. of the Queen's Hall Orch., afterwards playing with the RPO and with CG Opera. Taught at the RAM and the RCM. Elgar, Vaughan Williams and Gordon Jacob wrote works for him.

Goovaerts, Alphonse (Jean Marie André) (b Antwerp, 25 May 1847; d Brussels, 25 Dec 1922), Belgian composer and writer on music. Studied at the Jesuit Coll. of Antwerp and at the age of 15 was obliged by financial losses to take a commercial career; but he studied music thoroughly by himself and in 1866 obtained a post at the Antwerp town library. In 1869 his *Messe solennelle* was perf. In 1874 he was app. music secretary to Antwerp Cathedral where he estab. a special choir for which he copied a vast quantity of old motets of var. schools. He began to write on the reform of church music and in 1898 was app. keeper of the royal archives in Brussels.

Works incl. motets, *Petite Messe, Messe solennelle* and other church music; songs, part-songs.

Gopak (or **Hopak**), a Russian folk dance with music of a lively character in quick 2–4 time.

Gorczycki, Grzegorz (b Bytom, Silesia, *c* 1664; d Kraków, 30 Apr 1734), Polish composer. *Magister capellae* at Kraków Cathedral from 1698. Wrote motets and other church music.

Gordigiani, Luigi (b Modena, 21 Jun 1806; d Florence, 1 May 1860), Italian composer. Pupil of his father, Antonio G., who died when he was 14, so that he had to make a living by writing pf. pieces under German names. The Rus. Prince Nikolai Demidov and the Pol. Prince Joseph Poniatowski discovered his great gifts and patronized him, the latter providing him with the lib. for his opera *Filippo*, prod. at Florence in 1840.

Works incl. 10 operas; *Canzonette, Canti popolari* and other songs (*c* 300 in all); duets for female voices; Tuscan airs with pf. accomp.

Górecki, Henryk (b Czernica, 6 Dec 1933), Polish composer. Studied with Szabelski in Katowice. He tends toward strict serialism, but is also influenced by neo-classicism.

Works incl. cantata *Epitafium*; *Symph. no. 1* (1959), *No. 2* for sop., bar., chorus and orch. (1972), *No. 3* for sop. and orch. (1973); *Scontri* for orch.; *Genesis*, trilogy for sop. and insts. (1962–3); toccata for 2 pfs.; sonata for 2 vlns. (1957); *Cantata* for organ (1968).

Goritz, Otto (b Berlin, 8 Jun 1873; d Berlin, 16 Apr 1929), German baritone. Debut Neustrelitz 1895, in *Fra Diavolo*. After engagements at Breslau and Hamburg he sang at the NY Met 1903–17; appeared in the local fps of *Fledermaus, Hansel and Gretel, Rosenkavalier* (Ochs, 1911) and in the fp of *Parsifal* outside Bayreuth.

Görner, Johann Gottlieb (b Penig, Saxony, bap. 16 Apr 1697; d Leipzig, 15 Feb 1778), German organist and composer. Educ. in Leipzig and held various org. posts there: St Paul (1716), St Nikolai (1721) and St Tho-

mas (1729). In 1723 he founded a Collegium Musicum. Wrote church music.

Gorr, Rita (b Ghent, 18 Feb 1926), Belgian mezzo. Debut, Antwerp 1949 as Fricka; sang this role and Ortrud at Bayreuth 1958–9. She sang Charlotte at her Paris, Opéra-Comique, debut and she was also known as Massenet's Hérodiade. Often heard in the Verdi rep.; Amneris was the role of her CG (1959) and NY Met (1962) debuts. Also a distinguished Eboli, Azucena and Ulrica.

Gorzanis, Giacomo (b Apulia, *c* 1525; d ? Trieste, after 1575), blind Italian composer. He pub. 4 books of lute music incl. numerous dance-suites in 2 or 3 movements. One of these, consisting of a *passo e mezzo* and *padovana* (1561), provides an early example of 'sonata' used as a title.

Göss, Barthel. *See* **Gese, Bartholomäus.**

Goss, John (b Fareham, Hants., 27 Dec 1800; d London, 10 May 1880), English organist and composer. Studied under his father, organist at Fareham, then under J. S. Smith at the Chapel Royal in London and finally under Attwood. After holding several organ appts., he succeeded Attwood as organist of St Paul's Cathedral in 1838 and in 1856 became one of the comps. to the Chapel Royal in succession to Knyvett. Knighted in 1872 and Mus.D., Cambridge, in 1876.

Works incl. services, anthems, chants, psalms; orchestral pieces; glees; songs.

Gossec, François Joseph (b Vergnies, Hainaut, 17 Jan 1734; d Passy nr. Paris, 16 Feb 1829), Belgian-French composer. Chorister at Antwerp Cathedral, went to Paris in 1751, where with Rameau's help he obtained a post in La Pouplinière's private orch. in 1754. Later music director to the Prince of Condé. Founded the Concert des Amateurs in 1770, and in 1773 took over the direction of the Concert Spirituel. On the foundation of the Paris Cons. in 1795 he became one of its directors and prof. of comp. As one of the leading comps. of the Fr. Revolution he wrote many works for public ceremonies, often using vast forces. After 1800 he wrote little.

Works incl. OPERAS *Le Tonnelier* (1765), *Le Faux Lord, Les Pêcheurs, Toinon et Toinette* (1767), *Le Double Déguisement, Hilas et Silvie, Sabinus* (1773), *Alexis et Daphné, Philémon et Baucis* (1775), *La Fête de village, Thésée* (1782), *Rosine* (1786), etc.; ballets *Les Scythes enchaînés*, added to Gluck's *Iphigénie en Tauride* (1779), *La Reprise de Toulon, Mirsa* and *Callisto*;

incid. music for Racine's *Athalie* and Rochefort's *Électre*.

ORATORIOS: *La Nativité* (1774), *Saül* and *L'Arche d'alliance*; Requiem (1760), *Dixit Dominus, Exaudiat, Dernière Messe des vivants*, motets, etc.; funeral music for Mirabeau, *Le Chant du 14 juillet, L'Offrande à la liberté, Le Triomphe de la République* and other music for the Revolution. *c* 50 symphs. (1756–1809), overtures and other orchestral works; 12 string 4tets, trios and other chamber music.

Gossett, Philip (b New York, 27 Sep 1941), American musicologist. He studied at Princeton (Ph.D. 1970) and has taught at the Univ. of Chicago since 1968. Gen. ed of the critical edition of Verdi's works; joint ed. of the Rossini edition.

Gosswin, Antonius (b Liège, *c* 1540; d *c* 1597), Flemish composer, a pupil of Lassus in Munich; worked there in 1570s. Wrote Ger. songs, madrigals, motets and 7 Masses, 4 modelled on Lassus.

Gostona, Giovanni Battista dalla (b Genoa, *c* 1540; d Genoa, Dec 1598), Italian composer. Pupil of Philippe de Monte, *maestro di cappella* at Genoa Cathedral from 1584 to 1598, when his nephew, Molinaro, succeeded him.

Works incl. motets and other church music; 4 books of madrigals, 2 of *canzonette*; 25 fantasies for lute.

Gostling, John (b East Malling, Kent, *c* 1650; d London, 17 Jul 1733), English cleric and bass. Became a Gentleman of the Chapel Royal in London, 1679, and later held var. clerical posts in and out of the capital. Purcell's anthems afford evidence of his remarkable compass.

Gothic Symphony, the first by Havergal Brian, for soloists, children's choruses, brass band and orch. of 180; last of 4 movts is a setting of the Te Deum. Comp. 1919–27, fp by amateur forces, London, 24 Jun 1961; 1st. prof. perf. London, 30 Oct 1966, to mark Brian's 90th birthday. Broadcast live to the US by satellite, 25 May 1980.

Gotovac, Jakov (b Split, 11 Oct 1895; d Zagreb, 16 Oct 1982), Yugoslav conductor and composer. Studied at his home town, at Zagreb and in Vienna. In 1923 he became cond. of the Croatian Opera at Zagreb, also of a Balkan choral society, with which he travelled in Europe.

Works incl. operas *Morana* (1930) and *Ero the Joker* (1935); incid. music for pastoral play *Dubravka* (1928); choral works; *Symph. Kolo* and *The Ploughers* for orch.; chamber music; songs.

Götterdämmerung. *See* **Ring des Nibelungen, Der.**

Gottschalk, Louis Moreau (b New Orleans, 8 May 1829; d Rio de Janeiro, 18 Dec 1869), American pianist and composer. He studied in Paris and had much success there as a pianist from his debut in 1844; admired by Chopin and Berlioz. He toured throughout Europe and, from 1853, N. and S. America; died of yellow fever on tour in Brazil. His works are noted for their virtuosic exhibition of various American musical idioms.

Escenas campestres for sop., ten., bar. and orch. (1860); 2 symph. poems, *La nuit des tropiques* and *Montevideo*; numerous pf. pieces incl. *The Dying Poet* and *Grand Fantasy on the Brazilian National Anthem.*

Götz, Hermann (b Königsberg, 7 Dec 1840; d Hottingen nr. Zurich, 3 Dec 1876), German composer. At first he studied music only incidentally when a student at Königsberg Univ., but later went to the Stern Cons. in Berlin. In 1863 he went to Switz. as organist at Winterthur and in 1867 he settled at Zurich. From 1870 he devoted himself wholly to comp.

Works incl. operas *Der Widerspänstigen Zähmung* (on Shakespeare's *Taming of the Shrew*, 1874) and *Francesca da Rimini* (unfinished, prod. Mannheim, 1877); *Nänie* (Schiller) and Psalm cxxxvii for solo voices, chorus and orch.; cantata for male voices and orch.; symph. in F maj., *Spring* overture for orch.; vln. concerto in G maj. (1868), pf. concerto in Bb maj.; pf. 5tet, pf. 4tet, pf. trio; sonata for pf. duet; sonatina, *Genrebilder* and other works for pf.; songs.

Goudimel, Claude (b Besançon, *c* 1514; d Lyons, 28 Aug 1572), French composer. 1st appeared as comp. in Paris in 1549. About 1557, having become a Huguenot, he went to live at Metz with the Protestant colony there, but about 10 years later left for Besançon, and afterwards for Lyons where he died in the massacre of the Huguenots.

Works incl. 5 Masses, 3 Magnificats, psalms in motet form and other works for the Catholic Church; psalms, incl. a complete psalter, for the Protestant Church; sacred songs and numerous secular *chansons* for several voices.

Gould, Glenn (b Toronto, 25 Sep 1932; d Toronto, 4 Oct 1982), Canadian pianist. Studied at the Royal Cons. of Music in Toronto, graduating at the age of 12, the youngest ever to do so. Made his debut in Toronto, aged 14, and his European debut (under Karajan) in 1957. From 1964 confined himself to broadcasts and recordings.

Gould, Morton (b Richmond Hill, NY, 10 Dec 1913), American composer and conductor. He studied at NY Univ.; later worked as a pianist at Radio City Music Hall and presented music programmes on radio. His works are much indebted to popular idioms: BALLETS: *Interplay* (1945), *Fall River Legend*, on Lizzie Borden — America's most famous orphan (1947) and *Fiesta* (1957); FOR ORCH.: *Little Symphony* (1939), 4 symphs. (1942, 1944, 1947, 1952), 3 *American Symphonettes* (1922, 1935, 1937), pf. concerto (1937), vln. concerto (1938), *A Lincoln Legend* (1941), *Spirituals* (1941), vla. concerto (1943), *Concerto for Orch.* (1945), *Dance Variations* for 2 pfs. and orch. (1953), *Concerto for Tap Dancer* (1953), *Jekyll and Hyde Variations* (1957), *Festive Music* (1965), *Venice* for double orch. and brass bands (1966), *Vivaldi Gallery* (1967), *Symphony of Spirituals* (1976), *American Ballads* (1976), *Housewarming* (1982). Also music for Broadway shows, films and state occasions (Los Angeles Olympics, 1984).

Gounod, Charles (François) (b Paris, 18 Jun 1818; d Saint-Cloud, 18 Oct 1893), French composer. Son of a painter. His mother, a good pianist, taught him music from an early age and he was educ. at the Lycée Saint-Louis and in music at the Paris Cons., where his masters incl. Halévy, Paer and Lesueur. He gained the Prix de Rome in 1839 and spent the statutory 3 years in Rome, studying old It. church music. After a tour in Aust. and Ger. he returned to Paris and was app. organist at the church of the Missions Étrangères. Intending to become a priest, he did not prod. any important music until his opera *Sapho* appeared in 1851. In 1852–60 he cond. the united choral societies named Orphéon. In 1870–5 he lived in London, where he founded what became the Royal Choral Society.

Works incl. operas *Sapho* (1851), *La Nonne sanglante* (1854), *Le Médecin malgré lui* (on Molière, 1858), *Faust* (after Goethe, 1859), *Philémon et Baucis*, *La Reine de Saba*, *Mireille* (after Mistral), *La Colombe*, *Roméo et Juliette* (after Shakespeare, 1867), *Cinq-Mars* (after Alfred de Vigny), *Polyeucte* (after Corneille, 1878), *Le Tribut de Zamora*; incid. music for Ponsard's *Ulysse*, Legouvé's *Les Deux Reines* and Barbier's *Jeanne d'Arc*; oratorios *La Rédemption*, *Mors et Vita*, *Tobie*; 8 cantatas; 16 Masses, Requiem (1895), *Stabat Mater*, Te Deum, *De profundis*, *Ave verum corpus*, *Pater noster*, Magnificat and other sacred vocal pieces; 2 symphs. (1855–6); some pf. comps. incl. the *Funeral March for a Marionette*; *Méditation sur 1er Prélude de Bach* for soprano, vln. pf., and organ; some smaller choral works; many songs.

Gow, Scottish family of musicians:

1. Niel G. (b Strathbrand, Perthshire, 22 Mar 1727; d Inver nr. Dunkeld, 1 Mar 1807), violinist. Intended to become a weaver, he made his fame by playing Scot. dance tunes at balls in Scot. and pub. 3 collections of reels (1784–92).

2. Donald G. (b Inver nr. Dunkeld, c 1730), cellist, brother of prec.

3. William G. (b Inver, c 1760; d Edinburgh, 1791), violinist, son of 1. Leader of the Edinburgh Assembly orch. until his death.

4. Nathaniel G. (b Inver nr. Dunkeld, 28 May 1763; d Edinburgh, 19 Jan 1831), trumpeter, violinist and pub., brother of prec. At 16, when living at Edinburgh, he was app. royal trumpeter, learnt the vln. from Mackintosh, became leader of the Edinburgh Assembly orch. on the death of his brother and provided dance music by playing, comp. and after 1796 pub. it. He wrote songs, pieces descriptive of Edinburgh street cries (incl. 'Caller Herrin' ', at first an instrumental piece and not fitted with words by Lady Nairne until c 20 years later).

5. Neil G. (b Edinburgh, c 1795; d Edinburgh, 7 Nov 1823), composer, son of prec. He joined his father in the pub. business in 1818. Wrote songs, incl. 'Flora Macdonald's Lament', 'Cam' ye by Athol', etc.

Goyescas, opera by Granados (lib., in Span., by F. Periquet y Zuaznabar), prod. NY Met, 28 Jan 1916. Much of the material is taken from the pf. work below.

2 sets of pf. pieces by Granados inspired by etchings of Span. scenes by Goya, fp Paris, 4 Apr 1914: I. *Los requiebros* (*The Compliments*), *Coloquio en la reja* (*Colloquy at the Grilled Window*), *El fandango del candil* (*The F. of the Lantern*), *Quejas, ó La maja y el ruiseñor* (*Plaints, or The Maja and the Nightingale*); II. *El Amor y la Muerte* (*Love and Death*), *Epilogo: la serenata del espectro* (*Epilogue: the Spectre's Serenade*). (A *maja* is the fem. counterpart of *majo* = a fop, a dandy). Granados also wrote a separate *escena goyesca* for pf.: *El pelele* (a puppet or straw-man tossed in a blanket).

Gozzi, Carlo (1722–1806), Italian dramatist. See **Chagrin** (*Re cervo*), **Danzi** (*Turandot*), **Donna serpente** (Casella), **Einem** (*Turandot*), **Feen** (Wagner), **Hartmann** (J. P. E.) (*Ravnen*), **Himmel** (*Sylphen*), **Jensen**

(*Turandot*), **König Hirsch** (Henze), **Lach-ner (V.)** (*Turandot*), **Liuzzi** (*Augellin bel verde*), **Love for Three Oranges** (Prokofiev), **Sessions** (*Turandot*), **Stenhammar** (*Turandot*), **Turandot** (incid. music Weber; operas, Busoni and Puccini).

Graarud, Gunnar (b Holmestrand nr. Oslo, 1 Jun 1886; d Stuttgart, 6 Dec 1960), Norwegian tenor. He sang at Mannheim, Berlin and Hamburg, 1920–8, and made his Bayreuth debut in 1927, as Tristan; returned for Parsifal, Siegmund and Siegfried. Vienna Staatsoper 1928–37, and appeared as guest in London, Paris and Milan. At Salzburg he was heard in *Elektra* and *Der Corregidor*.

Grabmusik (*Funeral music*), cantata by Mozart for soloists, chorus and small orch.; comp. 1767 (when Mozart was ill), perf. Salzburg Cathedral, 7 Apr 1767.

Grabu (or **Grabut, Grebus**), **Louis** (*fl* 1665–94), French violinist and composer. App. comp. to Charles II in 1665 and Master of the King's Music from 1666–74.

Works incl. operas *Ariane, ou le mariage de Bacchus* (1674) and *Albion and Albanius* (lib. by Dryden), 1685.

Grace Notes or **Graces** = Ornaments.
Gradual (Lat. *gradus*, a step), the 2nd item of the Proper of the Mass. It is a responsorial chant following the reading of the epistle.

Gradus ad Parnassum (Lat. = steps to Parnassus). (I) a treatise on counterpoint by Fux, pub. in 1725; (II) a series of 100 instructive and progressive pf. pieces by Clementi, pub. in 1817. The 1st piece in Debussy's *Children's Corner* for pf. alludes to Clementi's collection.

Graener, Paul (b Berlin, 11 Jan 1872; d Salzburg, 13 Nov 1944), German composer. Was a choir-boy in Berlin Cathedral and at 16 entered the Veit Cons., but soon began to teach himself, leading a wandering life, cond. at var. theatres and comp. a number of immature works. In 1896–1908 he was in London as teacher at the RAM and cond. at the Haymarket Theatre, and was then app. director of the New Cons. in Vienna and in 1910 of the Mozarteum at Salzburg. After some years in Munich he succeeded Reger as prof. of comp. at the Leipzig Cons., but resigned in 1924. In 1930 he became dir. of the Stern Cons. in Berlin and under the Nazi régime vice-president of the Reichsmusikkammer, being succeeded by Egk in 1941.

Works incl. operas *Der vierjährige Posten* (Körner, 1918), *Das Narrengericht* (1913), *Don Juans letztes Abenteuer* (1914), *Theophano* (*Byzanz*, 1918), *Schirin und Gertraude, Hanneles Himmelfahrt* (after G.

Hauptmann, 1927), *Friedemann Bach, Der Prinz von Homburg* (after Kleist, 1935); choral works; symph. (*Schmied Schmerz*), *Romantic Fantasy, Variations on a Rus. folksong* and other orchestral works; 6 string 4tets, 3 pf. trios and other chamber music; sonata and suite for vln. and pf., suite for cello and pf.; pf. pieces; over 100 songs.

Graf (or **Graff**), **Friedrich Hartmann** (b Rudolstadt, 23 Aug 1727; d Augsburg, 19 Aug 1795), German flautist and composer. Travelled widely as a fl. virtuoso, and was app. music director in Augsburg in 1772. Later visited Vienna, and 1783–4 was cond. of the Professional Concerts in London.

Works incl. oratorios, cantatas, symphs., concertos, chamber music.

Graffman, Gary (b New York, 14 Oct 1928), American pianist. Studied at the Curtis Inst. and with Serkin and Horowitz. Debut Philadelphia 1947. His world-wide career was interrupted in 1979 by a hand injury.

Grainger, Percy (Aldridge) (b Melbourne, 8 Jul 1882; d White Plains, NY, 20 Feb 1961), Australian-American pianist and composer. Studied under his mother and Louis Pabst at Melbourne, later in Ger. with Kwast, Knorr and Busoni. He lived in London in 1900–14 and became interested in folk music, toured Scand. in 1909 and settled in USA in 1914, later becoming naturalized.

Works incl. comps. for chorus and orch. with and without solo voices: *Marching Song of Democracy* (1901–17), *The Bride's Tragedy* (Swinburne, 1908), *Father and Daughter* (Faroe folksong), *Sir Eglamore, We have fed our seas* (Kipling, 1900–4), *Tribute to Foster, Bridal Song*, etc.; partsongs *Brigg Fair, Morning Song of the Jungle* (Kipling), etc.; pieces for small orch.: *Molly on the Shore* (1907), *Colonial Song, Shepherd's Hey* (1913), *Mock Morris, Irish Tune from County Derry* (Londonderry Air), clog dance *Handel in the Strand*; suite *In a Nutshell* for 2 pfs.; 4 Ir. dances on themes by Stanford, *Walking Tune*, etc. for pf.; songs. He ed. and arr. hundreds of Brit. and Scand. folksongs.

Gramm, Donald (b Milwaukee, 26 Feb 1927; d New York, 2 Jan 1983), American bass-baritone. He sang Donizetti's Raimondo in Chicago in 1944. After study in Chicago and Santa Barbara sang Colline at the NY City Opera in 1952; other roles there were Leporello, Falstaff and Ochs. In 1963 he sang Dr. Schön at Santa Fe in the 1st US perf. of Berg's *Lulu* (2-act vers.) and at Boston in 1966 was Moses in the US première of

Moses und Aron; also heard in Schoenberg's oratorio *Die Jakobsleiter*. Glyndebourne 1975–6 as Nick Shadow and Falstaff, 1980 as Ochs.

Gramophone (formerly Phonograph), an instrument invented in its primitive form by Edison in 1877. The music is now recorded on magnetic tape, afterwards transferred to a disc of vinylite. The sound-waves of the music are reproduced thereon in a continuous groove. In perf. the disc revolves, a static needle is brought into contact with the groove, and the 'frozen' sound-waves are released and electronically amplified. From 1958 sounds were directed to the listener with greater realism by means of stereophonic recordings, followed in the 1970s by quadraphonic recordings. A more recent development is the compact disc on which the musical signal is digitally encoded so that it can be decoded by laser with absolutely no wear to the disc, with complete fidelity and with virtually no danger of destroying the disc through careless handling.

Gran Cassa (It., lit. great case, great box) = Bass Drum.

Gran Mass ('Graner Messe'), a Mass by Liszt for solo voices, chorus, orch. and org., comp. in 1855 for the inauguration of a church at Gran (Esztergom) in Hung. and perf. there 31 Aug 1856.

Granados, Enrique (b Lérida, 27 Jul 1867; d at sea, 24 Mar 1916), Spanish composer. Studied comp. with Pedrell at Barcelona and pf. in Paris. Returning to Spain in 1889, he became a well-known pianist and in 1900 he founded the Sociedad de Conciertos Clásicos in Madrid, which he cond. After a visit to NY for the prod. of *Goyescas* in the operatic version in Jan 1916, he went down in the *Sussex*, torpedoed by a Ger. submarine in the English Channel.

Works incl. operas and zarzuelas *Maria del Carmen* (1898), *Gaziel* (1906), *Goyescas* (based on the pf. work), *Petrarca, Picarol, Follet, Liliana*; symph. poem *La nit del mort*, 4 suites etc. for orch.; *Cant de las Estrelles* for chorus, org. and pf.; pf. trio, *Oriental* for ob. and strings; *Goyescas* (2 vols.), 10 Span. Dances, 6 pieces on Span. folksongs, *Escenas románticas, Escenas poéticas* (1926), *Libro de horas*, Impromptus, children's pieces for pf.; songs *Escritas en estilo antiguo* and a collection of *tonadillas*.

Grand Chœur (Fr., lit. great choir) = Full Org., a direction that the organ is to be used with all the registers.

Grand Duke, The, or The Statutory Duel, operetta by Sullivan (lib. by W.S. Gilbert), prod. London, Savoy Theatre, 7 Mar 1896. Gilbert's last lib. for Sullivan.

Grand Jeu (Fr., lit. great play) = Grand Chœur; also used for a harmonium stop that brings the whole instrument into play.

Grand Macabre, Le, opera by Ligeti (lib. by comp. and M. Meschke, after M. de Ghelderode), prod. Stockholm, 12 Apr 1978. London, Coliseum, 2 Dec 1982, with the original roles of Spermando and Clitoria 'translated' by G. Skelton as Amando and Miranda.

Grand Piano. *See* **Pianoforte.**

Grande-Duchesse de Gérolstein, La, operetta by Offenbach (lib. by H. Meilhac and L. Halévy), prod. Paris, Théâtre des Variétés, 12 Apr 1867.

Grande Messe des Morts (Requiem), work by Berlioz for tenor, chorus and orch. (comp. 1837; rev. 1852 and 1867. Fp Paris, 5 Dec 1837).

Grandi, Alessandro (b Ferrara, *c* 1575; d Bergamo, *c* 1630), Italian composer. Pupil of (?) G. Gabrieli at Venice, *maestro di cappella* of the church of the Santo Spirito at Ferrara, 1610–17, and then at St Mark's, Venice, until 1628, when he became choirmaster at the church of Santa Maria Maggiore at Bergamo. He died of the plague.

Works incl. 5 Masses, *c* 200 motets, psalms; madrigals; cantatas, arias for solo voice.

Grandi, Margherita (b Hobart, 4 Oct 1894), Australian soprano. She studied with Calvé in Paris and in 1922 created Massenet's Amadis, at Monte Carlo. She sang in Italy from 1932 and was admired as Aida and Monteverdi's Octavia. Glyndebourne 1939, as Lady Macbeth; in 1949 she sang Amelia with the co. at Edinburgh. London 1947–50, as Tosca, Donna Anna and the *Trovatore* Leonora.

Grant, Clifford (b Randwick, New South Wales, 11 Sep 1930), Australian bass. Stage debut Sydney 1952, as Donizetti's Raimondo. He studied with Otakar Kraus in London and was heard with SW/ENO from 1966 as Silva, Seneca, Sarastro and Hagen. US debut San Francisco 1967. Glyndebourne 1972, as Monteverdi's Neptune; CG 1974, Mozart's Bartolo. Other roles incl. Pogner, Trulove and Philip II.

Graphic Scores, scores by 20th-cent. composers which seek to convey musical ideas by means of non-traditional notation. Some scores are intended to symbolise particular sounds or textures, others allow the interpreter more latitude. Examples are by Feldman, Stockhausen, Cage, Ligeti, Bussotti and Cornelius Cardew. Graphic scores have been admired as much for their visual as their musical qualities; they have not been seen (or heard) in recent years.

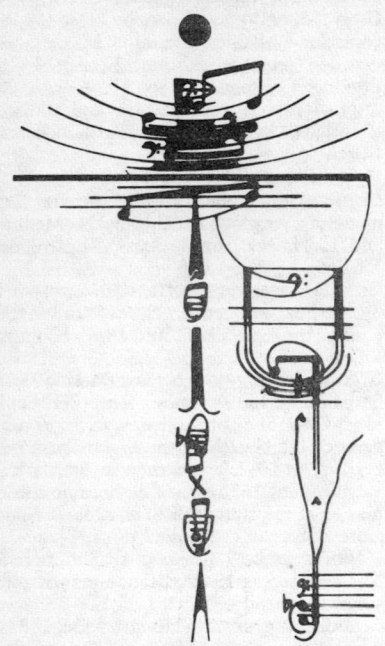

Detail from Cornelius Cardew, *Treatise*, 1963–7
Peters Edition Ltd.

GRAPHIC SCORE

Grassi, Cecilia (b Naples, c 1740; d after 1782), Italian soprano. Went to London in 1766, where she married J.C. Bach, c 1776; at the King's Theatre she had sung in his oratorio *Gioas* (1770) and serenata *Endimione* (1772). She was left destitute on the death of her husband.

Grassini, Josephina (b Varese, 18 Apr 1773; d Milan, 3 Jan 1850), Italian contralto. Studied singing at Milan and made her 1st appearances there in 1790 in operas by Guglielmi, Paisiello and Sarti. She 1st sang in Paris in 1800; continued an affair with Napoleon and received a generous salary. London 1804, in operas by Winter (Proserpine to Mrs Billington's Ceres), Nasolini and Fioravanti.

Graun, German family of musicians:

1. August Friedrich G. (b Wahrenbrück, Saxony, 1699; d Merseburg, 5 May 1765), cantor at Merseburg from 1729.

2. Johann Gottlieb G. (b Wahrenbrück, c 1703; d Berlin, 27 Oct 1771), violinist and composer, brother of prec. Pupil of Pisendel and, of Tartini; played in the Dresden court orch. until 1726, when he became orch. leader at Merseburg. In 1732 he went into the service of the Crown Prince of Prus. at Rheinsberg and followed him to Berlin when he became Frederick II, becoming cond. of the court orch.

Works incl. symphs.; concertos for vln., for harpsichord and for organ; trio sonatas with 2 fls.; vln. sonatas.

3. Carl Heinrich G. (b Wahrenbrück, 1703 or 1704; d Berlin, 8 Aug 1759), tenor and composer, brother of prec. Chorister at Dresden, went in 1725 to Brunswick, first as a singer, later as comp. and vice-*Kapellmeister* (1727). In 1735 he joined his brother (2) at Rheinsberg, and on the accession of Frederick II in 1740 was app. court *Kapellmeister*, with responsibility for the Berlin opera. His opera *Cleopatra e Cesare* opened the new opera house in 1742. His most famous work is the Passion oratorio to words by Ramler, *Der Tod Jesu* (1755), perhaps the most popular continental oratorio of the 18th cent.

Works incl. operas *Sancio und Sinilde* (1727), *Iphigenia in Aulis* (1731), *Polidorus, Scipio Africanus, Lo specchio della fedeltà* (1733), *Pharao Tubaetes, Rodelinda, regina de Langobardi* (1741), *Cleopatra e Cesare, Artaserse* (1743), *Demofoonte, Ifigenia in Aulide* (It.), *Silla* (1753), *Montezuma* (1755), *Merope*, etc.; several Passion cantatas incl. *Der Tod Jesu*, Te Deum; funeral music for the Duke of Brunswick and for Frederick William I of Prus.; secular cantatas, songs; harpsichord concertos; trio sonatas.

Graupner, Christoph (b Kirchberg, Saxony, 13 Jan 1683; d Darmstadt, 10 May 1760), German composer. Pupil of Schelle and Kuhnau at St Thomas's, Leipzig, he was harpsichordist at the Hamburg opera under Keiser 1707–9, and there prod. his 1st operas. In 1709 entered the service of the Landgrave Ernst Ludwig of Hesse-Darmstadt as vice-*Kapellmeister*, becoming *Kapellmeister* in 1712 on the death of Briegel. Elected cantor of St Thomas's, Leipzig, in 1722/3, he was unable to obtain his release from Darmstadt, so that the post fell to Bach.

Works incl. operas *Dido* (1707), *Antiochus und Stratonica* (1708), *La costanza vince l'inganno* (1715), etc.; over 1,400 church cantatas; 113 symphs.; 87 overtures; c 50 concertos; quantities of chamber music, keyboard music.

Grave (It. = heavy, serious), a direction indicating a slow tempo.

Gravicembalo (It.) = Clavicembalo (harpsichord), of which it is a perversion.

Gray, Cecil (b Edinburgh, 19 May 1895; d Worthing, 9 Sep 1951), Scottish writer on music and composer. Studied music privately. In 1920 he became joint ed. of the *Sackbut* with Philip Heseltine, with whom he also wrote a book on Gesualdo, and whose biog. as a comp. (Peter Warlock) he pub. Other books are a *History of Music*, essays *Predicaments* and *Contingencies*, and 2 works on Sibelius.

Works incl. operas *Deirdre*, *The Temptation of St Anthony* (after Flaubert) and *The Trojan Women* (after Euripides).

Gray, Linda Esther (b Greenock, 29 May 1948), Scottish soprano. She studied in Scot. and with Eva Turner in London. Debut as Mimi with Glyndebourne Touring co. 1972; debut at Glyndebourne as Mozart's Electra, 1974. Scottish Opera from 1975 as Donna Elvira, Eva, Ariadne and Amelia. ENO debut 1978 as Micaela, later Aida and Tosca. She sang Isolde with the WNO in 1979 and Sieglinde on her CG and US (Dallas, 1981) debuts.

Grazia, Con (It. = with grace) = *grazioso*.

Graziani, Francesco (b Fermo, 26 Apr 1828; d Fermo, 30 Jun 1901), Italian baritone. Debut Ascoli Piceno 1851, in *Gemma di Vergy*. At CG he was heard 1855–80 as the 1st local Luna, Germont, Rigoletto and Renato; also admired as Don Giovanni, Nelusko and Thomas' Hamlet. He was Macbeth in Dublin (1859) and on 22 Nov 1862 created Don Carlo in *La forza del destino*, at St Petersburg.

Grazioli, Giovanni Battista (b Bogliaco, Lake Garda, 6 Jul 1746; d Venice, c 1820), Italian organist and composer. Pupil of Bertoni, he was app. 2nd organist of St Mark's, Venice, in 1782, 1st organist 1785.

Works incl. 12 harpsichord sonatas, 6 sonatas for vln. and harpsichord, church music.

Grazioso (It. = graceful), an adj. sometimes used alone to indicate the character of a piece or passage and more often in combination with a tempo indication, e.g. *allegro grazioso, andantino grazioso,* etc.

Great Fugue (Beethoven). *See* **Grosse Fuge.**

Great Organ, the principal manual keyboard of the organ.

Great Staff, a theoretical construct to clarify the relationship of the traditional clefs. On an 11-line stave with, for example, the treble clef four lines from the top and the bass clef, four lines from the bottom, the middle line will represent middle C.

Greaves, Thomas (*fl.* 1604), English lutenist and composer. In the service of Sir Henry Pierpoint, whose wife was a cousin of Michael Cavendish. In 1604 he pub. a book of *Songs of Sundrie Kindes* containing 7 songs to the lute, 4 songs for voice and viols and 4 madrigals.

Greber, Jakob (d Mannheim, buried 5 Jul 1731), German composer. Went to London c 1702 with Margherita de l'Épine and stayed there until c 1706. In Innsbruck, then Vienna, in the service of the Emperor Charles VI, from c 1708, and in the Palatinate (Heidelberg, etc.) in 1717–23.

Works incl. opera *Gli amori d'Ergasto* (1705; *The Temple of Love* attrib. to him is by Saggione), shorter stage pieces, serenatas, etc.; cantatas for solo voice and var. instruments.

Greco, Gaetano (b Naples, c 1657; d Naples, c 1728), Italian composer. Possibly pupil of A. Scarlatti at Naples. Taught for many years at the Cons. dei Poveri di Gesù there. Wrote harpsichord music, *Salve Regina* (1681) etc.

Greef, Arthur de (b Louvain, 10 Oct 1862; d Brussels, 29 Aug 1940), Belgian pianist and composer. Pupil of Brassin at the Brussels Cons. and of Liszt at Weimar. He began his career about the age of 20 and became pf. prof. at the Brussels Cons. in 1887. He toured widely in Europe and frequently visited Eng.

Works incl. opera, *De Marketenster* (1879); symph., *4 Old Flemish Folksongs* for orch.; Ballad for string orch.; Concerto & Fantasy for pf. and orch., *Menuet varié* for pf. and strings; *Chants d'amour* for voice and orch.; sonata for 2 pfs.; pf. pieces; songs.

Greek Passion, The, opera by Martinů (lib. by comp. from the novel by N. Kazantzakis); comp. 1955–8 in Nice, New York, Pratteln and Rome, prod. Zurich, 9 Jun 1961, cond. Sacher.

Greenberg, Noah (b New York, 9 Apr 1919; d New York 9 Jan 1966), American conductor and music editor. Founded NY Pro Musica Antiqua 1952, for perf. of medieval and Renaissance music. Revived medieval dramas *The Play of Daniel* (1958) and *The Play of Herod* (1963). Toured Europe with ens. 1960 and 1963.

Greene, Maurice (b London, 12 Aug 1696; d London, 1 Dec 1755), English organist and composer. Son of a clergyman, he was a chorister at St Paul's Cathedral, studied the organ there under Richard Brind, and after holding church posts was app. organist of St Paul's in 1718. On Croft's death in 1727 he became organist and comp. of the Chapel Royal, and in 1730 succeeded Tudway as prof. at Cambridge Univ. App. Master of the King's Music in 1735. An inheritance in 1750 enabled him to devote time to a collection of Eng. church music, which after his death was completed by Boyce and pub. under the title *Cathedral Music*.

Works incl. over 100 anthems, the most notable pub. in *Forty Select Anthems* (1743), and other church music; oratorios *The Song of Deborah and Barak* (1732) and *Jephtha* (1737); pastorals *Florimel, or Love's Revenge* (1734), *The Judgment of Hercules* and *Phoebe* (1747); Odes for St Cecilia's Day and other occasions; misc. songs, catches, etc.; overtures; organ voluntaries; harpsichord music.

Grefinger, Wolfgang (b c 1475; d after 1525), German organist and composer. He was a pupil of Hofhaimer and was organist of St Stephen's Cathedral, Vienna, early in the 16th cent. Wrote Latin church music and secular Ger. songs and ed. a hymn book.

Greghesca. A type of *villanella*, pub. 1564, for 3 voices to words that are a mixture of Gk. and Venetian dialect, written by the Levantine Venetian Antonio Molino. The music was by var. Venetian comps.

Gregor, Bohumil (b Prague, 14 Jul 1926), Czech conductor. He studied in Prague and worked at the Ostrava Opera 1958–62, where he gave Janáček's *Katya Kabanová* and *Mr. Brouček*. Prague Nat. Theatre from 1962; brought *From the House of the Dead* to the Edinburgh Festival in 1964. He has given *The Cunning Little Vixen* all over Europe and cond. *Jenůfa* in San Francisco in 1969. In 1970 returned to Edinburgh with Prague co. to give the first prod. in Brit. of *The Excursions of Mr. Brouček*.

Gregorian Chant, the official repertory of plainsong traditionally assoc. with the name of Pope (St) Gregory (c 540–604), who is said to have been the first to supervise its organization.

Gregorian Tones, the chants of the Gregorian psalmody sung in groups corresponding to the 8 church modes (4 authentic and 4 plagal).

Greindl, Josef (b Munich, 23 Dec 1912), German bass. He studied with Bender and Bahr-Mildenburg in Munich. Debut, Krefeld 1936 and sang in Düsseldorf before moving to Berlin during the war. First sang at Bayreuth in 1943, as Pogner, and returned often up to 1969. His perfs. of Hagen in *Götterdämmerung* were memorable: the declamatory style which he developed was used also in Berlin 1959, when he gave Schoenberg's Moses at the Deutsche Oper. NY Met debut, 1952, as Heinrich in *Lohengrin*.

Greiter, Matthias (b Aichach, Bavaria, c 1495; d Strasbourg, 20 Dec 1550), German singer, poet and composer. He was a monk and a chorister in Strasbourg Cathedral, but became a Lutheran in 1524. In 1549 returned to the Catholic church. He wrote words and music of hymns and comp. Ger. songs for 4 and 5 voices.

Grenon, Nicolas (b c 1380; d Cambrai, 1456), French composer. First heard of in Paris in 1399; he later worked at Laon and Cambrai cathedrals, at the Burgundian court chapel under John the Fearless, at the papal chapel and finally again at Cambrai where he was for many years Dufay's neighbour and was probably an influence on the younger composer. Wrote sacred Latin music and *chansons*.

Gresham, Thomas (1519–79), founder of Gresham Coll. in London. Knighted 1559. The Coll. was provided for by his will and among the professorships was one for music, which has continued to the present day. The 1st prof. app. in 1596 was Bull.

Gresse, André (b Lyons, 23 Mar 1868; d Paris, 1937), French bass. Debut Paris, Opéra-Comique, 1896 as the Commendatore, in a perf. with Victor Maurel as Don Giovanni. He followed his father, Leon, as princ. bass at the Opéra in 1900; the 1st local Marke, Titurel and Fasolt, and sang in the 1909 fp of Massenet's *Bacchus*: the following year he created Massenet's Sancho Panza, at Monte Carlo. Retired c 1930.

Gretchaninov, Alexander Tikhonovich (b Moscow, 25 Oct 1864; d New York, 3 Jan 1956), Russian composer. Although the son of semi-literate, small shop-keepers, he managed to study the pf. at the Moscow Cons. under Safonov, but in 1890 he went to that of St Petersburg as a comp. pupil of Rimsky-Korsakov. He settled in Paris, c 1925, and later in USA.

Works incl. operas *Dobrinya Nikitich* and *Sister Beatrice* (after Maeterlinck's play, 1910), incid. music for plays; much music for the Rus. Church, incl.44 complete liturgies; Catholic church music, incl. Masses and motets; choral works; 5 symphs. (1894–1936), Elegy for orch.; concertos for cello, vln. and fl.; 4 string 4tets; *Music Pictures* for bass solo, chorus and orch.

Gretchen am Spinnrade (*Margaret at the Spinning-Wheel*), Schubert's setting of Gretchen's song in Goethe's *Faust*, Part I, comp. 1814 at the age of 17, pub. as op. 2 in 1821.

Grétry, André Ernest Modeste (b Liège, 8 Feb 1741; d Montmorency nr. Paris, 24 Sep 1813), Belgian composer. Chorister at St Denis's, Liège, received his initial training from his father (a violinist) and local church musicians. By 1759 he had already comp. some symphs. and church music, which won him a scholarship to study in Rome, where he remained till 1765, producing there in 1765 the intermezzo *La vendemmiatrice*. After a time in Geneva he went to Paris in 1767 to make his way as an opera comp. From 1768 he prod. a continuous stream of *opéras-comiques*, the most popular being *Richard Cœur-de-Lion* (1784), an early ex. of a 'rescue opera'. He was made an inspector of the Paris Cons. on its foundation in 1795, and the same year became one of the orig. members of the Institut de France. He pub. his memoirs in 3 vols. 1789–97, and wrote other lit. works.

Works incl. opéras-comiques: *La vendemmiatrice* (1765), *Isabelle et Gertrude*, *Le Huron* (1768), *Lucile, Le Tableau parlant* (1769), *Silvain, Les Deux Avares, L'Amitié à l'épreuve, Zémire et Azor* (1771), *L'Ami de la maison, Le Magnifique, La Rosière de Salency, La Fausse Magie* (1775), *Les Mariages samnites* (several versions), *Matroco* (1777), *Le Jugement de Midas, Les Fausses Apparences, ou L'Amant jaloux* (1778), *Les Événements imprévus, Aucassin et Nicolette* (1779), *Thalie au Nouveau Théâtre, Théodore et Paulin* (later *L'Épreuve villageoise*), *Richard Cœur-de-Lion* (1784), *Les Méprises par ressemblance, Le Comte d'Albert* (1786), *Le Prisonnier anglais* (later *Clarice et Belton*), *Le Rival confident, Raoul Barbebleue* (1789), *Pierre le Grand, Guillaume Tell* (1791), *Basile, Les Deux Couvents, Joseph Barra, Callias* (1794), *Lisbeth, Le Barbier du village, Elisca*.

Prod. at the Opéra: *Céphale et Procris* (1773), *Les Trois Âges de l'Opéra* (1778), *Andromaque, La Double Épreuve, ou Colinette à la cour, L'Embarras des richesses* (1782), *La Caravane du Caire, Panurge dans l'île des lanternes* (after Rabelais, 1785), *Amphitryon, Aspasie, Denys le Tyran, La*

Fête de la Raison, Anacréon chez Polycrate (1979), *Le Casque et les Colombes* (1801), *Delphis et Mopsa*, etc.

Grétry, Lucile (b Paris, 16 Jul 1772; d Paris, 25 Aug 1790), French composer, daughter of prec. At the age of 13 she comp. the opera *Le Mariage d'Antonio* which, scored by her father, was successfully prod. in 1786 at the Comédie Italienne, followed by *Toinette et Louis* a year later.

Grieg, Edvard (Hagerup) (b Bergen, 15 Jun 1843; d Bergen, 4 Sep 1907), Norwegian composer of Scottish descent (orig. Greig). Son of a merchant. He was taught the pf. by his mother from 1849. Ole Bull persuaded his parents to send him to Leipzig for study in 1858, and he entered the Cons. there. In 1863 he went to live in Copenhagen and studied with Gade. In 1864 he met Rikard Nordaak, who fired his enthusiasm for Nor. national music, and became engaged to his cousin Nina Hagerup, whom he married in 1867. Settled as teacher and cond. at Christiania in 1867. In 1874 Ibsen invited him to write incid. music for his *Peer Gynt*, which was prod. on 24 Feb 1876. In 1888–9 he and his wife appeared in London, Paris and Vienna, and in 1894 he was made hon. Mus.D. by Cambridge Univ. and hon. D.Mus. by Oxford Univ. in 1906.

Works incl. incid. music for Ibsen's *Peer Gynt* (1874–5) and Bjørnson's *Sigurd Jorsalfar* (1872); symph. in C min. (1864); concert overture *In Autumn*; *Holberg Suite* for string orch. (1884); pf. concerto in A min. (1868).

WORKS FOR SOLO VOICES, CHORUS AND ORCH.: *Before the Cloister Gate, Landsighting, Olaf Trygvason; Bergliot* (Bjørnson) for declamation and orch.; 4 Psalms for mixed voices unaccomp.; a set of part-songs for male voices; *Den bergtekne* (*The Solitary*) for baritone solo, strings and 2 horns (1878).

CHAMBER AND SOLO VOCAL: String 4tet in G min. (1878); 3 sonatas for vln. and pf.; sonata for cello and pf.; 24 op. nos. of pf. pieces, incl. 10 vols. of *Lyric Pieces*, sonata in E min., Ballad in variation form, arrs. of Nor. folk tunes; 4 for pf. duet; old Nor. melody with variations for 2 pfs.; 143 songs, incl. *Haugtussa* cycle (Garborg, 1895), settings of Ibsen, Bjørnson.

Grieg (*née* Hagerup), **Nina** (b Bergen, 24 Nov 1845; d Copenhagen, 9 Dec 1935), Norwegian singer, cousin and wife of Edvard Grieg, most of whose songs she was the 1st to sing both at home and on their tours abroad.

Griffes, Charles T(omlinson) (b Elmira, New York, 17 Sep 1884; d New York, 8 Apr 1920), American composer. Studied in Berlin and taught there for a time. Returned to USA in 1907, and became music teacher at a boys' school at Tarrytown, NY, until his early death, brought about by ill-health and overwork.

Works incl. Jap. mime play *Schojo* (1917); dance drama *The Kairn of Koridwen* (1916); *The Pleasure Dome of Kubla Khan* (after Coleridge) for orch. (1917); Poem for fl. and orch.; *These things shall be* (J. A. Symonds) for unison chorus; Sketches on Indian themes for string 4tet; pf. sonata and pieces; songs.

Griffiths, Paul (b Bridgend, Glam., 24 Nov 1947), English critic and writer on music. He studied at Oxford; critic for various journals from 1971. Chief music critic *The Times* from 1982. A specialist in 20th-cent. music, he had responsibility for this area in the *New Grove Dictionary of Music* (1980), and the *New Oxford Companion to Music* (1983). His own books incl. studies of Boulez, Davies, Ligeti, Bartók and Messiaen; also *A Concise History of Modern Music* (1978), *A Guide to Electronic Music* (1979), *Modern Music: the Avant Garde since 1945* (1981), *The String Quartet* (1983) and *An Encyclopedia of 20th-Century Music* (1986).

Grigny, Nicolas de (b Rheims, bap. 8 Sep 1672; d Rheims, 30 Nov 1703), French organist and composer. Son of Louis de G. (c 1646–1709), organist at Notre-Dame of Rheims. Studied under his father and in Paris, was organist of Saint-Denis Abbey, Paris, in 1693–5 and then of Rheims Cathedral. Wrote organ music (pub. 1699) which Bach knew and copied in his early years.

Grillparzer, Franz (1791–1872), Austrian poet and dramatist. Friend of Beethoven and Schubert. Wrote funeral oration for the former and sketched inscription for the latter's gravestone.

For works used by comps. *see* **Hummel (J. N.)** (*Ahnfrau*), **Kreutzer (C.)** (*Libussa* and *Melusine*), **Sappho** (Kaun), **Schöne Melusine** (Mendelssohn and C. Kreutzer), **Schubert** (*Ständchen* and *Mirjams Siegesgesang*), **Schulz-Beuthen** (*Meeres und der Liebe Wellen*), **Seyfried** (*Ahnfrau* and *König Ottokar*), **Straus (O.)** (*Traum ein Leben*).

Grisar, Albert (b Antwerp, 26 Dec 1808; d Asnières, 15 Jun 1869), Belgian composer. He was intended for a business career and sent to Liverpool, but ran away to Paris to study music in 1830; became a pupil of Reicha, but was driven to Antwerp by the Revolution; prod. *Le Mariage impossible* at Brussels in 1833, returned to Paris, where he made further operatic successes. Studied with Mercadante at Naples in 1840 and returned to Paris in 1844.

Works incl. operas *Sarah* (after Scott, 1836), *L'An 1000*, *Lady Melvill* (1838) and *L'Eau merveilleuse* (both with Flotow), *Le Naufrage de la Méduse* (with Flotow and Pilati), *Les Travestissements* (1839), *L'Opéra à la cour* (with Boïeldieu, jun.), *Gille Ravisseur* (1848), *Les Porcherons* (1850), *Bonsoir M. Pantalon*, *Le Carillonneur de Bruges* (1852), *Les Amours du diable*, *Le Chien du jardinier* (1855), *Voyage autour de ma chambre* (after Xavier de Maistre, 1859), *La Chatte merveilleuse* (1862), *Bégaiements d'amour*, *Douze innocentes* (1865).

Griselda, La, opera by A. Scarlatti (lib. after A. Zeno), prod. Rome, Teatro Capranica, Jan 1721. The last of Scarlatti's 69 operas, beginning with *Gli equivoci* (1679). Modern ed. by L. Salter.

Grisélidis, opera by Massenet (lib. by A. Silvestre and E. Morand), prod. Paris, Opéra-Comique, 20 Nov 1901. Revived Wexford Festival, 1983.

Grisi, Giuditta (b Milan, 28 Jul 1805; d Robecco nr. Cremona, 1 May 1840), Italian mezzo-soprano. Studied at the Milan Cons., and made her debut in Vienna in 1826 (Rossini's *Bianca e Falliero*). In 1830 she created Romeo in Bellini's *I Capuleti*; sang Isoletta in *La Straniera*, Venice, London and Paris, 1832.

Grisi, Giulia (b Milan, 22 May 1811; d Berlin, 29 Nov 1869), Italian soprano, sister of prec. Pupil of her sister, Boccabadati, Guglielmi and others. Made her debut in 1828 and was engaged for Milan in 1829; created Adalgisa in *Norma*, 1831. In 1832 she 1st sang in Paris, as Semiramide, and in 1834 in London, in operas by Rossini, Mozart and Bellini. Other roles incl. Elvira (*Puritani*), Susanna and Lucrezia Borgia.

Grist, Reri (b New York, 1932), American soprano. She appeared in *West Side Story* on Broadway and sang Blondchen at Santa Fe in 1959; European debut Cologne 1960, as Queen of Night. She sang Despina and Zerbinetta at Glyndebourne in 1962; CG from 1962 as Olympia, Gilda and Susanna. NY Met debut 1966, as Rosina. Other roles incl. Mozart's Aminta and Zerlina, Sophie and Adina.

Griswold, Putnam (b Minneapolis, 23 Dec 1875; d New York, 26 Feb 1914), American bass-baritone. Debut CG 1901 in the fp of Stanford's *Much ado about Nothing*. Toured US 1904–5 as Gurnemanz in an English vers. of *Parsifal* and sang in Berlin 1906–11; decorated by the Kaiser. NY Met debut 1911, as Hagen; returned until 1914 as Pogner, Marke and Daland.

Grobe, Donald (b Ottawa, Ill., 16 Dec 1929; d Berlin, 1 Mar 1986), American tenor. Debut Chicago 1952, in *Rigoletto*. Sang in NY 1953–6 and moved to Germany 1956; Deutsche Oper, Berlin, from 1960 (fps Henze's *Der junge Lord*, 1965, and Fortner's *Elisabeth Tudor*, 1972). With the Munich Opera he sang Ferrando at Edinburgh in 1965 and visited CG in 1972, as Strauss's Flamand and Henry Morosus. Highly regarded in modern opera, sang Alwa, Tom Rakewell and Aschenbach, and appeared in *Mathis der Maler* and Orff's *Trionfi*.

Grocheio, Johannes de, music theorist of uncertain nationality who worked in Paris *c* 1300. His *De musica* survives in two MSS. and is important for the light it throws on the secular music of his day and how it was perf.

Groot, Cor de (b Amsterdam, 7 Jul 1914), Dutch pianist and composer. Studied at the Amsterdam Cons. and in 1936 won the international pf. competition in Vienna. He has toured widely in Europe.

Works incl. ballet *Vernisage*; 2 pf. concertos, pf. concertino, concerto for 2 pfs., and a number of pf. pieces.

Grosse Caisse (Fr. lit. great case or chest) = Bass Drum.

Grosse Fuge (*Great Fugue*), a work for string 4tet by Beethoven, op. 133, in a fugal form 'tantôt libre, tantôt recherchée', written in 1825 as the finale of the B♭ maj. string 4tet, op. 130, and 1st perf. with it, Vienna, 21 Mar 1826. Beethoven was persuaded by his publisher that it was too long, difficult and abstruse for that purpose and subsequently wrote the new finale, now part of op. 130.

Also title for 1st version of Busoni's *Fantasia contrappuntistica* (1910).

Grossi, Carlo (b Vicenza, *c* 1634; d Venice, 14 May 1688), Italian singer and composer. Worked as singer and *maestro di cappella* successively at Reggio, Vicenza, Venice and Mantua.

Works incl. 4 operas, incl. *Artaxerse* (1669); Masses and other church music; sacred concertos; sonatas; cantatas, songs, etc.

Grossi, Giovanni Francesco. *See* **Siface**.

Grossin (Grossim), Estienne French composer, chaplain at St Merry, Paris, 1418, and *clerc de matines* at Notre Dame, 1421. Wrote church music and *chansons*, incl. a Mass (without *Agnus*) with a part labelled 'trombetta'.

Grossinquisitor, Der (*The Grand Inquisitor*), oratorio by Blacher (text by L. Borchard, from Dostoievsky's *The Brothers Karamazov*); comp. 1942, fp Berlin, 14 Oct 1947.

Grossvater-Tanz (Ger. = grandfather's dance). Believed at one time to be a 17th-cent. Ger. dance, with words referring to a grandfather's wooing, sung and danced at weddings and later used as the final dance at balls and therefore called 'Kehraus' (sweepout). Schumann used it both in *Papillons*, op. 2, and *Carnaval*, op. 9, in the latter to stand for the 'Philistines' in the finale. The dance was actually written by Karl Gottlieb Hering (1765–1853).

Grosz, Wilhelm (b Vienna, 11 Aug 1894; d New York, 10 Dec 1939), Austrian composer. Pupil of Adler for theory and Schreker for comp. Cond. at Mannheim Opera in 1921, but returned to Vienna in 1922 to make a living as pianist and comp.; worked with a gramophone company in Berlin from 1928, cond. the Kammerspiele in Vienna, 1933–4, when he became a refugee in London and NY.

Works incl. operas *Sganarell* (1925) and *Achtung, Aufnahme* (1930); play with music *St Peters Regenschirm*; ballets *Der arme Reinhold* (1928) and *Baby in der Bar*; incid. music to Werfel's *Spiegelmensch* and Hauptmann's *Die versunkene Glocke*; music for films and radio; Symph. Variations, serenade, suite, overture to an opera buffa, etc. for orch.; Symph. Dance for pf. and orch.; string 4tet; 2 vln. and pf. sonatas; 3 pf. sonatas.

Ground, a comp. built on a Ground Bass, or the Bass itself.

Ground Bass, a melodic figure used as a bass in a comp., constantly repeated without change, except sometimes by way of transposition, while the upper structure of the music is developed freely at the composer's will.

Grout, Donald J(ay) (b Rock Rapids, Iowa, 28 Sep 1902; d Skaneateles, NY, 9 Mar 1987), American musicologist. Studied at Syracuse and Harvard Univs. and in Strasbourg and Vienna. Taught at Harvard 1936–42; prof. of music Cornell Univ. 1945–70. Early opera, eg. A. Scarlatti, was at the centre of his research. His books incl. *A Short History of Opera* (1948, rev. 1965),

A History of Western Music (1960, rev. 1973, 1980 and, with C.V. Palisca, 1988), *Mozart in the History of Opera* (1972).

Grove, George (b London, 13 Aug 1820; d London, 28 May 1900), English civil engineer, biblical scholar and writer on music. Sec. to the Crystal Palace co., 1852–1873; 1st dir. of RCM 1883–94. Ed. of the 1st edition of the *Dictionary of Music and Musicians* (1879–89) and author of a book on Beethoven's symphs. Knighted in 1883.

Groves, (Sir) Charles (b London, 10 Mar 1915), English conductor. He studied at the RCM and was chorus master at the BBC 1938–42. BBC Northern Orch. 1944–51; Bournemouth SO 1951–61; Royal Liverpool PO 1963–77 (also brief spells as opera cond. with WNO, 1961–3, and ENO 1978–9). Noted for his solid performances of the standard repertory, and the choral works of Delius and Mahler. Knighted 1973.

Grove's Dictionary of Music and Musicians, 1st ed. compiled by George Grove and pub. in 4 vols. 1879–89; 2nd ed. J. A. Fuller Maitland, 1904–10; 3rd ed. H. C. Colles, 1927; 4th ed. H. C. Colles, 1940; 5th ed. Eric Blom, 1954; 6th as *The New Grove Dictionary of Music and Musicians* ed. Stanley Sadie, 1980.

Grovlez, Gabriel (Marie) (b Lille, 4 Apr 1879; d Paris, 20 Oct 1944), French conductor, pianist and composer. Studied at the Paris Cons., later taught pf. at the Schola Cantorum and in 1939 became prof. of chamber music at the Cons. Cond. at Lisbon, Chicago and Paris, from 1914 dir. at the Opéra.

Works incl. operas *Cœur de rubis* (1906) and *Psyche*; *conte lyrique*, *Le Marquis de Carabas*; 3 ballets incl. *Maïmouna* (1916); symph. poems *Dans le Jardin*, *Madrigal lyrique*, etc.; cello and pf. sonata; pieces for wind instruments; *Almanach aux images*, *Le Royaume puéril*, 2 Impressions, etc. for pf.; 3 *Ballades françaises* and other songs.

Gruber, H(einz) K(arl) (b Vienna, 3 Jan 1943), Austrian composer. Studied at the Vienna Hochschule and with von Einem. He has played the double bass in various Viennese orchs.; co-founded the avant-garde group MOB art and tone ART.

Works incl. the melodrama *Die Vertreibung aus dem Paradies* for speakers and 6 insts. (1966), the spectacle *Gomorrah* (1972), 'pandemonium' *Frankenstein!!* for bar. and orch. (1977); Concerto for orch. (1964), *Manhattan Broadcasts* for chamber orch., *Arien* for vln. and orch., *Demilitarized Zones* for brass band (1979), *Rough Music*, concerto for perc. and orch. (1983); Mass for chorus, 2 trumpets, horn, double bass and perc. (1960), *Reportage aus Gomorrah* for 5 singers and 8 players (1976).

Gruberová, Edita (b Bratislava, 23 Dec 1946), Czech soprano. Debut Bratislava 1968, as Rosina. She sang Queen of Night at the Vienna Staatsoper in 1970 and has returned as Lucia, Gilda and Violetta. Salzburg from 1974, often with Karajan. NY Met debut 1979, as Lucia. In 1984 sang Giulietta in a new prod. of Bellini's *I Capuleti e i Montecchi*, at CG. At Munich she has sung Massenet's Manon.

Gruenberg, Erich (b Vienna, 12 Oct 1924), British violinist of Austrian birth. After study in Vienna he made his solo debut in Jerusalem, 1938. Moved to London 1946; leader, LSO 1962–5, RPO from 1972. Well-known as a recitalist, he has partnered Edmund Rubbra, William Pleeth and William Glock; all Beethoven's vln. sonatas recorded with David Wilde. He led the London String Quartet and has been heard in works by Messiaen, Goldschmidt, Gerhard and Britten.

Gruenberg, Louis (b Brest-Litovsk, 3 Aug 1884; d Los Angeles, 10 Jun 1964), American pianist and composer of Russian descent. He was taken to USA at the age of 2. Studied in Berlin and Vienna, pf. pupil of Busoni; 1st appeared as pianist in Berlin in 1912 and then began to travel, but from 1919 remained in USA to devote himself wholly to comp.

Works incl. operas *The Bride of the Gods* (1913; lib. by Busoni), *The Dumb Wife, Jack and the Beanstalk, Emperor Jones* (after Eugene O'Neill, 1931), *Helena of Troy* (1936); children's opera *The Witch of Brocken*; radio opera *Green Mansions* (after W. H. Hudson); 5 symphs., *Hill of Dreams, Enchanted Isle*, Serenade for orch.; vln. concerto; *The Daniel Jazz* (V. Lindsey), *Animals and Insects* and *The Creation* for voice and chamber orch.; *4 Indiscretions* for string 4tet, 2 string 4tets, 2 sonatas for vln. and pf; pf. pieces

Grumiaux, Arthur (b Villers-Perwin, 21 Mar 1921; d Brussels, 16 Oct 1986), Belgian violinist. He studied in Brussels and with Enescu in Paris. British debut 1945, and perf. with great distinction world wide in classical rep.; formerly with Clara Haskil in sonatas by Mozart and Beethoven. Also played Berg and Bartók. Made a baron by King Baudouin in 1973.

Grümmer, Elisabeth (b Diedenhofen,

Alsace-Lorraine, 31 Mar 1911; d Berlin, 6
Nov 1986), German soprano. After 3 years
as an actress she made her singing debut in
1941 as Octavian, in Aachen. Sang in many
of the leading European opera houses, incl.
CG in 1951 as Eva. Bayreuth 1957–61: Eva,
Elsa, Gutrune. NY Met debut 1967, as Elsa.
She was esp. well known for her singing of
Mozart and R. Strauss. Her best roles were
Donna Elvira, Pamina, Ilia, the Countess in
Capriccio and *Figaro* and the Marschallin.

Grünbaum, Therese (b Vienna, 24 Aug
1791; d Berlin, 30 Jan 1876), Austrian soprano. Her father was the popular Viennese
theatre composer Wenzel Müller. At Prague
she sang in operas by Mozart, from 1807,
and was a leading member of the Kärntnertortheater, Vienna, from 1816; created Weber's Eglantine (1823) and often heard in
Rossini. Taught in Berlin from 1830.

Grünewald, Gottfried (b Eywau, Lusatia,
1675; d Darmstadt, 19 Dec 1739), German
singer and composer. Sang at Hamburg
1703–1704, where 2 of his operas *Germani-
cus* and *Der ungetreue Schäfer Cardillo* were
prod. App. vice-*Kapellmeister* in Weissenfels 1709, and settled in Darmstadt as vice-
Kapellmeister under Graupner *c* 1712.

Gruppen, work by Stockhausen for 3
orchs., placed in different parts of the hall
and playing different music; comp. 1955–7,
fp Cologne, 24 Mar 1959.

Gruppo, gruppetto (It.) = Trill, Turn.

Grützmacher, Friedrich (Wilhelm Ludwig)
(b Dessau, 1 Mar 1832; d Dresden, 23 Feb
1903), German cellist and composer. Studied at Leipzig, where he became 1st cellist
at the Gewandhaus in 1849 and later teacher
at the Cons. In 1860 he became chamber
virtuoso to the King of Saxony at Dresden.
Comp. mainly concertos and studies for cello, but also orchestral and chamber works,
songs. His ed. of the 'Boccherini cello concerto in B♭' is a pasticcio from several
works.

Guadagni, Gaetano (b Lodi or Vicenza, *c*
1725; d Padua, Nov 1792), Italian castrato
alto, later soprano. Made his 1st appearance
at Parma in 1747 and went to London in
1748, where he sang in *Messiah, Samson*
and *Theodora* (fp 1750). Later sang in Dublin, Paris, Lisbon, Italy and Vienna, where he
was the 1st Orpheus in Gluck's *Orfeo* in
1762.

Guadagnini, Italian family of vln. makers:
1. Lorenzo G. (b ? Piacenza, before 1695;
d Piacenza, *c* 1748), ? pupil of Stradivari,
worked at Piacenza.
2. Giovanni Battista (J.B.) G. (b ? Piacen-

za, 1711; d Turin, 18 Sep 1786), son of prec.
Worked at Piacenza, Milan, Cremona, Parma and Turin.
3. Giuseppe G. ('Il soldato') (b *c* 1736; d *c*
1805), son of prec. Worked at Como, Pavia
and Turin.

Guami, Francesco (b Lucca, *c* 1544; d Lucca, 30 Jan 1602), Italian composer and
organist. Sackbut player at the Munich
court, 1568–80; *maestro di cappella* at San
Marciliano, Venice, from 1593 and at Lucca
from 1598. Wrote madrigals, church music,
instrumental music.

Guami, Gioseffo (b Lucca, *c* 1535; d Lucca,
1611), Italian organist and composer,
brother of prec. Pupil of Willaert at St
Mark's, Venice. He was at Munich with
Francesco G., and organist of St Mark's,
Venice, from 1588 to 1591; later organist at
Lucca Cathedral. Wrote numerous madrigals, church music and instrumental music.
Bull wrote a fantasia for keyboard on a
theme from his instrumental canzona *La
Guamina.* Of his 8 sons Domenico (*c* 1580–
1631) and Valerio (1587–1649) are known
as comps. Vincenzo (d 1615) was for a short
time from 1613 organist at the chapel of the
Archduke Albert at Antwerp.

Guarducci, Tommaso (b Montefiascone, *c*
1720), Italian singer. Pupil of Bernacchi at
Bologna. Made his 1st appearance *c* 1745
and went to London in 1766.

Guarini, Giovanni Battista (1537–1612).
Italian poet. *See* **Pastor fido** (Handel), **Rossi (S.)** (*Idropica*), **Settle** (*Pastor fido*).

Guarneri, Italian family of vln. makers:
1. Andrea G. (b *c* 1626; d Cremona, 7 Dec
1698). Pupil of Amati.
2. Pietro Giovanni G. (b Cremona, 18 Feb
1655; d Mantua, 26 Mar 1720), son of prec.
Worked at Mantua.
3. Giuseppe Giovanni Battista G. (b Cremona, 25 Nov 1666; d Cremona, *c* 1740),
brother of prec.
4. Pietro G. (b Cremona, 14 Apr 1695; d
Venice, 7 Apr 1762), nephew of 2. Worked
at Venice.
5. Giuseppe G. (b Cremona, 21 Aug 1698;
d Cremona, 17 Oct 1744), son of 3. Worked
at Cremona and is known as Giuseppe G. del
Gesù; the most important vln. maker in the
family.

Guarneri Quartet, American string quartet
formed in Vermont 1964 with the members
Arnold Steinhardt and John Dalley (vlns.),
Michael Tree (vla.) and David Soyer (cello).
First visited Europe 1965 and gave the complete Beethoven 4tets in London 1970. Recordings of most classical rep. works (pf.

5 tets with Arthur Rubinstein) and also heard in Bartók.

Guarnieri, (Mozart) Camargo (b Tietê, 1 Feb 1907), Brazilian composer. Pupil of Koechlin in Paris; often visited the USA where many of his works were perf. Cond. of the Orquestra Sinfônica Municipal, São Paulo, and dir. of the Cons. from 1960.

Works incl. 4 symphs.; 5 pf. concertos (1936–70), 2 vln. concertos (1940, 1953); chamber music; cello and pf. sonata; pf. pieces; songs.

Gudehus, Heinrich (b Altenhagen nr. Celle, 30 Mar 1845; d Dresden, 9 Oct 1909), German tenor. Studied with Malwina Schnorr von Carolsfeld at Brunswick and Gustav Engel in Berlin; made his debut there in 1871 in Spohr's *Jessonda*; sang Parsifal at Bayreuth in 1882; also sang Walther and Tristan there. 1st went to London in 1884, when he sang Parsifal in the 1st (concert) perf. of the opera in Brit. NY Met debut 1890 as Tannhäuser. Retired 1896.

Gueden, Hilda (b Vienna, 15 Sep 1917), Austrian soprano. Studied at the Vienna Cons., making her debut in Zurich in 1939. In 1946 she joined the Vienna Staatsoper, becoming an Austrian *Kammersängerin* in 1950. Also sang at Salzburg, London and NY: roles incl. Zerbinetta, Susanna, Daphne and Anne Trulove.

Guédron, Pierre (b Châteaudun, c 1565; d ? Paris, c 1621), French singer and composer. He was a chorister in the chapel of the Cardinal de Guise and later of Henri IV. In 1601 he was app. comp. to the king in succession to Claude Le Jeune and held var. other posts at court, finishing as Surintendant de la Musique under Louis XIII in 1613. His daughter Jeanne married Boësset, with whom, as well as Bailly, Maudit and Bataille, he collaborated in the comp. of court ballets. He also pub. 6 books of airs with lute accomp. (*airs de cour*) and contrib. others to var. collections.

Guerre des Bouffons (Fr., lit. War of the Buffoons), the quarrel that broke out in Paris in 1752 between the adherents of Fr. music, esp. opera, and the imported art of the Its., who prod. or revived several exs. of *opera buffa* in the Fr. capital that year.

Guerrero, Francisco (b Seville, 4 Oct 1528; d Seville, 8 Nov 1599), Spanish composer. Pupil of his brother Pedro G. and of Fernández de Castilleja at Seville Cathedral, where he was a chorister; he also had some lessons from Morales as a child. App. to the cathedral of Jaén in 1546 and after the death of Morales to that of Málaga, though he never

resided there, filling posts at Seville Cathedral until he succeeded Castilleja as *maestro de capilla* on 9 Mar 1574. Visited Lisbon, Rome (twice), Venice and the Holy Land.

Works incl. 18 Masses, c 150 liturgical pieces, incl. motets, psalms, vespers, Magnificats, Te Deum; sacred and secular songs.

Gueymard, Louis (b Chapponay, 17 Aug 1822; d Paris, Jul 1880), French tenor. He sang at CG in 1854 and at the Paris Opéra 1848–68; created roles in *Les vêpres siciliennes* (1855), *Le Prophète* (1849) and Gounod's *La Reine de Saba* (1862); his wife **Pauline** (b 1834) appeared with him in Gounod's opera and also created Verdi's Eboli and Thomas' Gertrude (1867–8).

Guglielmi, Pietro Alessandro (b Massa Carrara, 9 Dec 1728; d Rome, 19 Nov 1804), Italian composer. Pupil of Durante in Naples, he prod. his first opera there in 1757, and thereafter had great success throughout It. and abroad. He was in Eng. intermittently 1767–72, and also visited Brunswick and Dresden. In 1793 he was app. *maestro di cappella* at St Peter's, Rome.

Works incl. c 100 operas, e.g. *Il ratto della sposa* (1765), *La sposa fedele* (1767), *La villanella ingentilita* (1779), *I finti amori*, *La virtuosa di Mergellina* (1785), *L'inganno amoroso*, *La pastorella nobile*, *La bella pescatrice* (1789); oratorios, e.g. *La morte d'Abele*, *La Betulia liberata*, etc.; church music, symphs.; chamber music, keyboard music.

Guglielmi, Pietro Carlo (b ? Naples, c 1763; d Naples, 21 Feb 1817), Italian composer, son of prec. Studied at the Cons. di Santa Maria di Loreto in Naples, prod. the first of many successful operas in 1794 in Madrid. Also visited London, Lisbon and Paris.

Works incl. almost 50 operas, e.g. *Amor tutto vince* (1805), *Guerra aperta* (1807); oratorio *La distruzione di Gerusalemme* (1803).

Guglielmo, Ebreo da Pesaro, (b ? Pesaro; c 1425; d ? after 1480), Jewish-Italian dancing-master and theorist. He served many Eur. courts. His book, *De pratica seu arte tripudii vulgare opusculum* (c 1460), incl. both tunes and choreography.

Guglielmo Ratcliff (*William R.*), opera by Mascagni (lib. by comp., based on Heine's tragedy), prod. Milan, La Scala, 16 Feb 1895. An earlier work than *Cavalleria rusticana*, although prod. later.

Gui, Vittorio (b Rome, 14 Sep 1885; d Florence, 16 Oct 1975), Italian conductor and composer. Student at the Liceo di Santa Cecilia in Rome. App. cond. at the Teatro

Adriano there and later cond. opera at Turin, Naples and Milan. In 1928 he founded the Orchestra Stabile (later Maggio Musicale) festival at Florence, and cond. operas by Spontini, Gluck and Cherubini there. Glyndebourne 1948–64, *Così fan tutte*, *Macbeth*, *Alceste*, *Figaro*, *Zauberflöte* and *Falstaff*.

Works incl. opera *La fata Malerba*; symph. poems; chamber music.

Guidetti, Giovanni (b Bologna, Dec 1530; d Rome, 30 Nov 1592), Italian priest. Pupil of Palestrina, whom he assisted in compiling the revised church services commissioned by Pope Gregory XIII, the *Directorium chori* (pub. 1582), in 1576–81.

Guido d'Arezzo (b Arezzo, *c* 990; d Pomposa, *c* 1050), Italian Benedictine monk and music theorist. Lived in Pomposa and Arezzo and visited Rome. He greatly advanced solmization and mutation by adapting the syllables Ut, Re, Mi, Fa, Sol, La to the hexachord and by demonstrating the hexachordal positions on the fingers by the use of the 'Guidonian hand'. He was once, rather doubtfully, credited with the invention of the music stave, the use of which he certainly encouraged. His chief theoret. work is entitled *Micrologus de musica* (*c* 1026).

Guignon, Jean-Pierre (Giovanni Pietro Ghignone) (b Turin, 10 Feb 1702; d Versailles, 30 Jan 1774), Italian-French violinist and composer, a champion of the It. style of playing in France. In 1733 app. at court, and received in 1741 the title of *Roi des violons et des ménétriers*, being the last to hold the position.

Works incl. sonatas, concertos, etc. for vln., trio sonatas.

Guildhall School of Music and Drama, a music school established in 1880 to serve the City of London; it was housed in a new building in 1887 and in another in 1977. Its principal from 1978 has been John Hosier.

Guilelmus Monachus, 15th-cent. theorist of uncertain nationality who lived in Italy but may possibly have been English. His treatise *De praeceptis artis musicae* contains references to the Eng. use of 'fauxbourdon' and 'gymel'.

Guillaume Tell (*William Tell*), opera by Grétry (lib. by J. M. Sedaine), prod. Paris, Comédie-Italienne, 9 Apr 1791.

Opera by Rossini (lib. by V. J. E. de Jouy and H. L. F. Bis, based on Schiller's drama), prod. Paris, Opéra, 3 Aug 1829. Rossini's last opera.

Guillemain, (Louis) Gabriel (b Paris, 15 Nov 1705; d Paris, 1 Oct 1770), French

violinist and composer. App. to the court in Versailles in 1737, comp. sonatas for vln. and chamber music.

Guilmant, (Félix) Alexandre (b Boulogne-sur-Mer, 12 Mar 1837; d Meudon, 29 Mar 1911), French organist and composer. Pupil of his father, an organist at Boulogne, where he afterwards held several church appts., studying briefly in Brussels with Lemmens in 1860 and moving to Paris in 1871, where he was organist at the Trinité Church until 1901. He toured widely with great success and was prof. of organ at the Schola Cantorum, which he had helped Bordes and d'Indy to found, and at the Cons.

Works incl. 2 symphs. for organ and orch.; 8 sonatas and 25 sets of pieces for organ, organ music for church use.

Guimbarde (Fr.) = Jew's Harp.

Guiraud, Ernest (b New Orleans, 23 Jun 1837; d Paris, 6 May 1892), French composer. Son of a musician. Studied at the Paris Cons. and gained the Prix de Rome in 1859. He became prof. at the Cons. in 1876, following Massé as the head of the advanced comp. class in 1880. Debussy was one of his pupils.

Works incl. operas *Sylvie* (1864), *En Prison* (1869), *Le Kobold* (1870), *Madame Turlupin*, *Piccolino* (1876), *Galante Aventure*, *Le Feu*, *Frédégonde* (unfinished, completed by Saint-Saëns); ballet *Gretna Green* (1873); overture *Arteveld*, *Chasse fantastique* (after Hugo's *Beau Pécopin*), and suite for orch.; Caprice for vln. and orch., etc. Recitatives for Bizet's *Carmen* and orch. of Offenbach's *Contes d'Hoffmann*.

Guirlande, La, ou Les fleurs enchantées, acte de ballet by Rameau (lib. by J.-F. Marmontel), prod. Paris, Opéra, 21 Sep 1751.

Guitar, a string instrument of great antiquity. Its back is flat, its belly has a waist, as though to allow for the playing with a bow, but the strings are plucked with the fingers or a plectrum. The sound-hole in the sound-board is often very decoratively carved. The modern classical guitar has 6 strings, tuned:

The finger-board is fretted.

Guitar Violoncello. See **Arpeggione**.

Gulbranson, Ellen (b Stockholm, 4 Mar 1863; d Oslo, 2 Jan 1947), Swedish soprano. Concert debut 1886; stage debut Stockholm 1889, as Amneris (mezzo role). She sang Brünnhilde at Bayreuth in 1896 and repeated in the role until 1914, gaining a reputation for reliability rather than brilliance; also sang Kundry. She sang in Berlin from 1895, Vienna from 1896. CG 1900 and 1907–8, as Brünnhilde under Richter.

Gulda, Friedrich (b Vienna, 16 May 1930), Austrian pianist. Studied with Bruno Seidlhofer, winning 1st prize in the Geneva International Pianists' Competition in 1946. Toured Europe in 1947–8, and made his Amer. debut in 1950. Outside the classical repertory he is also well known as a jazz pianist; from 1962 has given jazz and improvised music concerts.

Gumpeltzhaimer, Adam (b Trostberg, Bavaria, c 1559; d Augsburg, 3 Nov 1625), German composer. Studied at the monastery of St Ulric at Augsburg. From 1581 until his death he was cantor at the church of St Anna at Augsburg. He pub. a treatise, *Compendium musicae latinum-germanicum*, in 1591.

Works incl. psalms, hymns, sacred songs.

Gundry, Inglis (b London, 8 May 1905), English composer. Educ. at Oxford, where he read law, but turned to literature, writing poems and a novel, *The Countess's Penny*. Studied RCM under Vaughan Williams, Gordon Jacob and R. O. Morris. After war service in the navy became instructor Lieutenant and music adviser to the Admiralty educ. dept., for which he ed. a *Naval Song Book*.

Works incl. operas *Naaman: the Leprosy of War* (1937), *The Return of Odysseus* (after Homer, 1938), *The Sleeping Beauty* and *Partisans* (1946); ballet *Sleep*; Variations on an Indian theme and overture *Per mare, per terram* for orch.; Comedy Overture for small orch.; *Sostenuto and Vivace* for strings; Fantasy string 4tet; songs.

Gungl, Joseph (b Zsámbék, 1 Dec 1810; d Weimar, 31 Jan 1889), Austro-Hungarian bandmaster and composer. Entered the Aus. army and later made tours with a military band of his own. In 1849 he visited the USA, becoming music director to the King of Prus. on his return and in 1858 to the Aus. Emperor. In 1864 he went to live at Munich and in 1876 at Frankfurt. He wrote hundreds of marches and dances.

Günther von Schwarzburg, opera by Holzbauer (lib. by A. Klein), prod. Mannheim, at court, 5 Jan 1777.

Guntram, opera by R. Strauss (lib. by comp.), prod. Weimar, 10 May 1894. Strauss's 1st opera; rev. version prod. Weimar, 22 Oct 1940.

Gura, Eugen (b Pressern nr. Saatz, 8 Nov 1842; d Aufkirchen, Bavaria, 26 Aug 1906),

Bohemian-German baritone. After technical and art studies in Vienna, he studied singing at the Munich Cons. and made his 1st stage appearance there in 1865. In 1876 he appeared in the prod. of Wagner's *Ring* at Bayreuth as Donner and Gunther. Sang Sachs and Marke in the 1st Brit. prods. of *Meistersinger* and *Tristan* (Drury Lane, 1882, cond. Richter).

Guridi, Jesús (b Vitoria, 25 Sep 1886; d Madrid, 7 Apr 1961), Spanish composer of Basque descent. Studied at the Schola Cantorium in Paris, also at Liège and Cologne. His music is based on Basque themes.

Works incl. operas *Mirentxu* (1915) and *Amaya* (1920), zarzuela *El caserío* (1926); orch. and organ. music; church music; 4 string 4tets; settings of Basque folksongs.

Gurlitt, Manfred (b Berlin, 6 Sep 1890; d Tokyo, 29 Apr 1972), German conductor and composer. Studied comp. with Kaun and Humperdinck, cond. with Muck and pf. with Breithaupt in Berlin. After var. operatic appts. he was general music director at Bremen from 1914 and of the Berlin Staatsoper from 1924. Later he appeared as guest opera cond. in Germany and Spain. Lived in Japan from 1939.

Works incl. operas *Die Heilige, Wozzeck* (after Büchner, 1926), *Soldaten, Nana* (after Zola, 1933), *Seguidilla bolero, Feliza*; incid. music for 2 Sp. plays; music for films; *Goya* symph., *Shakespeare* symph.; cello concerto; chamber concertos for pf. and vln.; pf. 5tet in C min.; pf. sonata; songs with chamber orch.

Gurney, Ivor (Bertie) (b Gloucester, 28 Aug 1890; d Dartford, Kent, 26 Dec 1937), English composer and poet. He was a choir-boy at Gloucester Cathedral and later studied at the RCM in London with a scholarship. He suffered much from ill-health and during the 1914–18 war was badly wounded and shell-shocked. He struggled for a time against poverty, but in 1922 lost his reason; he died of tuberculosis.

Works incl. *The Apple Orchard* and *Scherzo* for vln. and pf.; 2 sets of pf. pieces; song cycles *Ludlow and Teme* (A. E. Housman) and *The Western Playland*, over 200 songs, some to his own poems. 2 vols. of poetry, *Severn and Somme* and *War's Embers*.

Gurrelieder (*Songs of Gurra*), work by Schoenberg for 5 soloists, speaker, 4 choruses and large orch., incl. iron chains (text a German trans. of the Danish poems by J. P. Jacobsen); comp. 1900–11, fp Vienna 23 Feb 1913, cond. Franz Schreker.

Gusla. *See* **Guzla.**

Gustave III, ou Le Bal masqué (*Gustavus III, or The Masked Ball*), opera by Auber (lib. by Scribe), prod. Paris, Opéra, 27 Feb 1833. *See also* **Ballo in maschera.**

Gutheil-Schoder, Marie (b Weimar, 16 Feb 1874; d Ilmenau, 4 Oct 1935), German soprano. She made her debut in Weimar, where she received coaching from Richard Strauss, and after engagements in Berlin and Leipzig was engaged by Mahler at the Hofoper, Vienna. Early roles, from 1900, were Nedda and Carmen; she was criticised for her small voice but the force of her dramatic characterisations made her a favourite until 1926; she was the first Viennese Elektra and sang Octavian at CG in 1913. She sang the soprano part in the fp of Schoenberg's 2nd string 4tet (Vienna, 1908) and was The Woman in the fp of *Erwartung* (Prague, 1924).

Gutiérrez, Antonio Garcia (1812–84), Spanish dramatist. *See* **Simon Boccanegra** (Verdi), **Trovatore** (do.).

Gutmann, Adolph (b Heidelberg, 12 Jan 1819; d Spezia, 27 Oct 1882), German pianist and composer. Pupil and friend of Chopin. Wrote numerous pf. works, incl. 10 *Études caractéristiques.*

Guy, Barry (b London, 22 Apr 1947), English composer and double bass player. His early interest was in jazz; later studied at the GSM with Buxton Orr and Patric Standford. After forming the Jazz Composers' Orchestra in 1971 his works have combined improvisatory with more controlled avant-garde techniques: *D* for 15 solo strings (1972); *Anna* for amplified db. and orch. (1974); *Statements III and IV* for jazz orch. (1972–5); string 4tet *III* (1973); *Songs from Tomorrow* for 13 insts. (1975); *Voyages of the Moon* for db. and orch. (1983); *Blitz*, 7tet (1984).

Guy-Ropartz (Joseph Guy Marie Ropartz) (b Guingamp, Côtes du Nord, 15 Jun 1864; d Lanloup, 22 Nov 1955), French composer. He 1st studied law, but went to the Paris Cons. as a pupil of Dubois, Massenet and Franck. In 1894 he became director of the Nancy Cons. and in 1919 of that of Strasbourg. Later he retired to Brittany, where he was born and to which he belonged by race.

Works incl. operas *Le Diable couturier*, *Marguerite d'Écosse*, *Le Miracle de Saint-Nicolas* (1905), *Le Pays* (1913); ballet *L'Indiscret*; incid. music for a stage version of Pierre Loti's *Pêcheur d'Islande* and for Sophocles' *Oedipus at Colonus*; *Messe de Sainte-Odile*, *Messe de Sainte-Anne*, Requiem (1939), Psalm cxxxvi, motets and

other church music.

INSTRUMENTAL: 5 symphs. (1895–1945), *Petite Symphonie*, *Paysage de Bretagne*, *Les Landes*, *Dimanche breton*, *La Cloche des morts*, *Concert in D maj.* and other orchestral works; *Rhapsodie* for vln. and orch.; 6 string 4tets (1893–1951), string trio, pf. trio; 3 vln. and pf. sonatas, 2 cello and pf. sonatas; songs; organ music.

Guyon, Jean (b *c* 1514; d after 1574), French composer, first a choir-boy (from 1523) and later canon (from 1545) of Chartres Cathedral. Wrote 2 Masses, a motet and several *chansons*.

Gwendoline, opera by Chabrier (lib. by C. Mendès), prod. Brussels, Théâtre de la Monnaie, 10 Apr 1886.

Gyffard Part-Books, a set of 4 books containing sacred Lat. works, written down *c* 1555 but incl. works written earlier, such as John Taverner's Mass *The Western Wind.* It once belonged to a Dr Philip Gyffard.

Gymel (from Lat. *gemellum* = a 'twin-song'), vocal music in 2 parts, both of the same range. A characteristic feature is the use of parallel 3rds. The term 1st occurs in the 15th cent., when it usually refers to a divided voice-part in a polyphonic composition, but examples are found as early as the 14th cent.

Gymnopédies, 3 pieces for pf. by Satie, comp. 1888. Nos. 1 and 3 (*Lent et triste*, *Lent et grave*) were orch. by Debussy and perf. Paris, 20 Feb 1897. *Gymnopédies* refers to Greek dances in honour of Apollo, perf. by naked men and boys; Debussy's music has become a popular ballet.

Gyrowetz (Jírovec), Adalbert (Vojcĕch), (b Budĕjovice, 20 Feb 1763; d Vienna, 19 Mar 1850), Bohemian composer. Learnt music from his father, a choirmaster; later studied law in Prague, but continued to work at music. As private secretary to Count Franz von Fünfkirchen, he was expected to take part in the domestic music. He then went to It. for study under Sala at Naples and later visited Paris, where symphs. of his had been perf. under the name of Haydn. In 1789 the Revolution drove him to London, where the score of his opera *Semiramis* was burnt in the fire of the Pantheon in 1792. He returned to Vienna soon after, and in 1804 was app. cond. at the court theatres, where he prod. many works until 1831.

Works incl. It. operas *Federica ed Adolfo* (1812) and *Il finto Stanislao* (1818), Ger. operas *Agnes Sorel* (1806), *Ida die Büssende* (1807), *Der Augenarzt*, *Robert, oder Die Prüfung* (1815), *Helene, Felix und Adele*,

Hans Sachs, Die Junggesellen-Wirtschaft, Der Sammtrock, Aladin (after Oehlenschläger), *Das Ständchen* (1823), etc.; ballet *Die Hochzeit der Thetis* (1816) and others; melodramas *Mirina* and others; comic cantata *Die Dorfschule*; over 60 symphs., serenades, overtures and other orchestral works; c 60 string 4tets, 5tets, numerous trios; c 40 vln. and pf. sonatas; instrumental pieces, dances; songs.

H

H, the German symbol for the note B♮.

HMS Pinafore, operetta by Sullivan (lib. by W.S. Gilbert), prod. London, Opéra Comique, 25 May 1878. The 1st work by Gilbert and Sullivan to be a world-wide success.

Haas, Joseph (b Maihingen, Bavaria, 19 Mar 1879; d Munich, 30 Mar 1960), German composer. Pupil of Reger at Munich and then at the Leipzig Cons. Teacher of comp. at Stuttgart from 1911 and Munich from 1921.
Works incl. operas *Tobias Wunderlich* (1937) and *Die Hochzeit des Jobs* (1944); choral works; serenade for orch.; 2 string 4tets, divertimento for string trio, trio for 2 cellos and pf. and other chamber music; sonata and sonatina for vln. and pf.; many pf. works; org. pieces; songs.

Haas, Monique (b Paris, 20 Oct 1906; d Paris, 6 Jun 1987), French pianist. She studied at the Paris Cons. and privately with Casadesus and Serkin. Debut 1927; many recitals and recordings of Schubert and Mozart, French music and modern classics. Was married to the composer Marcel Mihalovici who died 1985.

Haas, Robert (Maria) (b Prague, 15 Aug 1886; d Vienna, 4 Oct 1960), Austrian musicologist. Took his Ph.D. at Prague Univ. and became asst. to Adler. Later lecturer at Vienna Univ. and director of the music dept. of the State Library there. Part ed. of the orig. versions of Bruckner's works, etc., author of books on Baroque music, musical performance, Mozart, Bruckner.

Hába, Alois (b Vizovice, Moravia, 21 Jun 1893; d Prague, 18 Nov 1973), Czech composer. Gained a knowledge of folk music before he studied at the Prague Cons. under Novák; later a pupil of Schreker in Vienna and Berlin. App. prof. at the Prague Cons. in 1924. He became interested in the division of the scale into quarter-tones, on which much of his later work is based (from 2nd string 4tet, 1920). Later employed sixthtones (5th 4tet, 1923) and fifth-tones (16th 4tet, 1967).
Works incl. opera *Matka (Mother,* prod. Munich 1931), Overture and Symph. Music for orch.; Fantasy for pf. and orch.; vln. concerto; 16 string 4tets (1919–67) and other chamber music; pf. sonata and other

works (some for quarter-tone pf.); works for string instruments.

Hába, Karel (b Vizovice, 21 May 1898; d Prague, 21 Nov 1972), Czech violinist and composer, brother of prec. Studied vln. under Karel Hoffmann, comp. under Křička, Foerster and Novák, and 4ter-tone music with his brother. He played vla. in the Cz. PO in 1929–36 and in 1949 became head of the educ. section of the Czech Radio.
Works incl. opera *Jánošik* (1934); 2 symphs. (1947–54), vln. and cello concertos; 4 string 4tets (1922–69), 7tet; pf. music; songs.

Habanera, a dance, with words to be sung, intro. into Spain from Africa via Cuba. It is in a moderate 2–4 time and has a basic rhythm of 4 quavers, the 1st of which is dotted. Famous ex. is that in the 1st act of Bizet's *Carmen.*

Habeneck, François Antoine (b Mézières, 22 Jan 1781; d Paris, 8 Feb 1849), French violinist and conductor of German descent. Pupil of Baillot. Founder of the Société des Concerts du Cons. in Paris; cond. at the Opéra 1824–47; gave the fps of *Guillaume Tell, Les Huguenots, La Juive* and *Benvenuto Cellini.* The 1st cond. to cultivate Beethoven in France.

Habich, Eduard (b Kassel, 3 Sep 1880; d Berlin, 15 Mar 1960), German baritone. Debut Koblenz, 1904. Berlin Staatsoper 1910–30 as Falke and Faninal; Bayreuth 1911–31 as Alberich and Klingsor. From 1924 to 1938 he was heard at CG, London, as Telramund and Beckmesser.

Hacker, Alan (b Dorking, 30 Sep 1938), English clarinettist. He studied at the RAM; taught there since 1959. Member of the LSO 1959–66; founder member of the Pierrot Players, later Fires of London, giving fps of many works by Peter Maxwell Davies. Founded his own group, Matrix, in 1971 and has given fps of works by Boulez, Blake, Birtwistle and Goehr. He has been involved in 'authentic' perfs. of classical music, often with early versions of the clar.

Hacomblene (Hacomplaynt), Robert (b London, c 1456; d Cambridge, 8 Sep 1528), English composer. He was scholar of Eton, 1469–72, and of King's Coll., Cambridge, from 1473. He was a Fellow there, 1475–93, and Provost from 1509 until his death. A *Salve Regina* is in the Eton Choirbook.

Haddon Hall, operetta by Sullivan (lib. by Sydney Grundy), prod. London, Savoy Theatre, 24 Sep 1892.

Hadley, Henry (Kimball) (b Somerville, Mass., 20 Dec 1871; d New York, 6 Sep

1937), American conductor and composer. Studied with his father, with Chadwick at Boston and Mandyczewski in Vienna. Cond. opera in USA and Ger., and in 1909 became cond. of the symph. orch. at Seattle; San Francisco 1911–15. From 1920 lived in NY.

Works incl. operas *Safié* (1909), *Azora, Daughter of Montezuma* (1917), *Bianca, Cleopatra's Night* (1920) and *Mirtil in Arcadia*; *Music, The New Earth* and *Resurgam* for solo voices, chorus and orch.; 5 symphs., overtures *In Bohemia, Herod* and to Shakespeare's *Othello*, Symph. Fantasy, tone-poems *Salome, Lucifer* and *The Ocean*.

Hadley, Patrick (Arthur Sheldon) (b Cambridge, 5 Mar 1899; d King's Lynn, 17 Dec 1973), English composer. Educ. at Winchester Coll. and Cambridge Univ., and studied music at the RCM in London, where in 1925 he joined the teaching staff. Mus.D. Cambridge in 1938, app. lecturer at the univ. and Prof. of Music in succession to Dent from 1946 to 1962.

Works incl. incid. music to Sophocles' *Antigone*; symph. for baritone and chorus *The Trees so high* (1931), *La Belle Dame sans merci* (Keats) for tenor, chorus and orch., *My Beloved Spake* (Song of Solomon) for chorus and orch.; cantatas *The Hills* for soprano, tenor, bass, chorus and orch. (1944), and *Travellers*; *Ephemera* (Yeats) and *Mariana* (Tennyson, 1937) for voice and chamber orch.; string 4tet in C maj., fantasy for 2 vlns. and pf.; songs; part-songs.

Hadow, (W(illiam) H(enry) (b Ebrington, Glos., 27 Dec 1859; d London, 8 Apr 1937), English educationist and music scholar. Educ. at Malvern Coll. and Oxford, where later he lectured on music, having studied at Darmstadt and under C.H. Lloyd. Principal of Armstrong Coll., Newcastle-upon-Tyne, 1909–19, and Vice-Chancellor of Sheffield Univ., 1919–30. He ed. the *Oxford History of Music* and wrote vol. v, *The Viennese Period*; other pubs., incl. *Studies in Modern Music, English Music*, etc. He also comp. chamber music and songs. Knighted 1919.

Haebler, Ingrid (b Vienna, 20 Jun 1926), Austrian pianist. She studied in Salzburg and Vienna, and with Marguerite Long in Paris. Debut Salzburg, 1937. She has recorded all the concertos of Mozart and all Schubert's sonatas; has appeared world wide with these comps., Haydn, Schumann and early Beethoven. Frequent concerts with the London Mozart Players. Has taught at the Salzburg Mozarteum since 1969.

Haefliger, Ernst (b Davos, 6 Jul 1919), Swiss tenor. Studied in Zurich and later in Vienna with Patzak and in Prague with Carpi. He made his debut in Salzburg in 1949 and from 1953 sang in Berlin. He appeared in Glyndebourne in 1956 as Belmonte. He was esp. noted as a Mozart singer, Evangelist in the Bach Passions and also as a perf. of modern music; he created Tiresias in Orff's *Antigonae*, Salzburg, 1949.

Haendel, Ida (b Chelm, Poland, 15 Dec 1924), British violinist. She studied in Warsaw and with Flesch and Enescu. Brit. debut 1937 at a Promenade Concert, under Wood; gave further concerts in London throughout the war, and toured US 1946–7. Has lived in Canada since 1952. A popular performer of the standard repertory.

Haessler, Johann Wilhelm (b Erfurt, 29 Mar 1747; d Moscow 29 Mar 1822), German pianist, organist and composer. Pupil of the organist Kittel, a pupil of Bach. Travelled much, estab. concerts at Erfurt in 1780, visited London and St Petersburg in 1790–4, when he settled at Moscow.

Works incl. pf. sonatas, *Grande Gigue* in D Min. and many other works for pf., org. works; songs.

'Haffner' Serenade, Mozart's Serenade in D maj., K250, written at Salzburg in Jul 1776 for the marriage of Elisabeth Haffner, daughter of the late burgomaster Sigmund Haffner, celebrated on 22 Jul.

'Haffner' Symphony, Mozart's symph. in D maj. K385, comp. in Vienna in summer 1782 for the Haffner family, probably on the occasion of the ennoblement of Sigmund Haffner, jun., on 29 Jul 1782

Hafgren, Lily (b Stockholm, 7 Oct 1884; d Berlin, 27 Feb 1965), Swedish soprano. She began her career as a pianist but was advised to take up singing by Siegfried Wagner: Bayreuth 1908–24 as Freia, Elsa and Eva. She sang further in Mannheim and in Berlin, 1912–20, where she was the first local Empress in *Die Frau ohne Schatten*. She was active in Paris, Milan and Stockholm; retired Dresden 1934. Other roles incl. Ariadne, Isolde and Brünnhilde.

Hageman, Richard (b Leeuwarden, 9 Jul 1882; d Beverly Hills, Calif., 6 Mar 1966), Dutch-American conductor and composer. Studied at the Amsterdam Cons., of which his father was director, and later at the Brussels Cons. He was app. cond. of the Amsterdam Opera and in 1907 settled in USA, where he cond. opera and concerts in var. cities. From 1908 to 1922 he cond. at the Met Opera, NY.

Works incl. opera *Caponsacchi* (prod. Freiburg, 1932); many songs. incl. *At the Well*.

Hagegård, Håkan (b Karlstad, 25 Nov 1945), Swedish baritone. He studied in Stockholm and with Tito Gobbi and Gerald Moore. Debut Stockholm 1968, as Papageno; later sang role in Bergman's film version of *Die Zauberflöte*. He has appeared at Drottningholm since 1970 and Glyndebourne from 1973 (as the Count in *Figaro* and *Capriccio*, and Guglielmo); made concert tours of the USA in 1975 and 1977: Met debut in 1979, as Malatesta; CG debut, Wolfram, 1987. He is well known in operas by Mozart, Verdi and Rossini, and often appears in concert.

Hagith, opera in 1 act by Szymanowski (lib. by comp. after F. Dormann); comp. 1912–13, while S. was living in Vienna; prod. Warsaw, 13 May 1922.

Hahn, Reynaldo (b Caracas, Venezuela, 9 Aug 1874; d Paris, 28 Jan 1947), French composer and conductor. Was sent to the Paris Cons. at the age of 11, where he studied under var. masters, incl. Massenet. In 1934 he was app. music critic of *Le Figaro*, and in 1945 became music director of the Paris Opéra.

Works incl. operas *L'Ile du rêve* (1898), *La Carmélite* (1902), *La Colombe de Bouddha* (1921), *Nausicaa*, *Le Pauvre d'Assise*, *La Reine de Saba*, *Le Temps d'aimer*, *Brummel* (1931), *Le Marchand de Venise* (after Shakespeare, 1935), many operettas incl. *Ciboulette*; ballets *La Fête chez Thérèse* (1907) and *Le Dieu bleu* (1912); incid. music for Shakespeare's *Much Ado*, Rostand's *Le Bois sacré*, Sacha Guitry's *Mozart* (1925), etc.; ode *Prométhée* for solo voices, chorus and orch.; symph. poem *Nuit d'amour bergamasque*; string 4tet and other chamber music; pf. pieces; songs incl. cycles *Chansons grises*, *Chansons latines*, *Chansons espagnoles*.

Hairpins, the colloq. word for *crescendo* and *diminuendo* marks shown by the conventional signs < and >.

Haitink, Bernard (b Amsterdam, 4 Mar 1929), Dutch conductor. Initially an orchestral violinist, in 1955 he became cond. of the Radio Orch. in Amsterdam. He was guest cond. of the Concertgebouw Orch. on their Amer. tour of 1961, becoming their permanent cond. when they returned to Hol. and subsequently cond. of the LPO 1967–79. Glyndebourne debut 1972 (*Die Entführung*); music dir. from 1977. NY Met debut 1982. Music dir. CG, London, from 1987 (*Arabella* there 1986). He is well known for his solid, unspectacular performances of the standard classics. Honorary KBE 1977.

Haitzinger, Anton (b Wilfersdorf, Liechtenstein, 14 Mar 1796; d Karlsruhe, 31 Dec 1869), Austrian tenor. Made his 1st appearance at the Theater an der Wien in Vienna in 1821; created Adolar in *Euryanthe*, 1823. Sang later in Paris, London and St Petersburg. London, CG, 1833 as Tamino, Max and Florestan.

Hale, Adam de la . *See* **La Halle.**

Halévy (actually **Lévy**), **(Jacques François) Fromental (Elias)** (b Paris, 27 May 1799; d Nice, 17 Mar 1862), French composer. Studied at the Paris Cons. under Berton and Cherubini from 1809 and, after twice taking a 2nd prize, gained the Prix de Rome in 1819. He continued to study in It., and on his return to Paris tried to gain a foothold on the operatic stage, for which he had already written more than one work. He succeeded with *L'Artisan* in 1827, after which he wrote an enormous number of operas. He became prof. of harmony and accomp. at the Cons. in 1827, of counterpoint and fugue in 1833 and of comp. in 1840.

Works incl. *c* 40 operas, e.g. *La Dilettante d'Avignon*, *Ludovic* (begun by Hérold), *La Juive* (1835), *L'Éclair*, *Guido et Ginevra*, *Le Shérif*, *Le Guitarréro*, *La Reine de Chypre*, *Charles VI* (1843), *Les Mousquetaires de la reine* (1846), *Le Val d'Andorre*, *La Fée aux roses*, *La Tempestà* (in It., after Shakespeare, 1850), *La Dame de Pique* (after Mérimée), *Le Juif errant* (after Sue), *Jaguarita l'Indienne* (1855), *La Magicienne*, etc.; ballets *Yella*, *Manon Lescaut* (after Prévost); incid. music to *Prométhée enchaîné* (trans. from Aeschylus); cantatas *Les Derniers Moments du Tasse*, *La Mort d'Adonis* and *Herminie*; funeral march and *De profundis* on the death of the Duc de Berry.

Half-Close, an imperfect cadence, i.e. one in which the dominant chord is preceded by the tonic, e.g.:

Halffter, Cristóbal (b Madrid, 24 Mar 1930), Spanish composer. Nephew of Ernesto and Rodolfo H. Studied with Conrado del Campo and Alexandre Tansman. In 1962 he became prof. of comp. at Madrid Cons. His music tends toward total serialism.

Works incl. opera, *Don Quichotte* (prod. Düsseldorf, 1970), *Cantata in Expectatione Resurrectionis Domini* (1962); concertino for string orch.; *Sinfonia* for 3 instrumental groups (1904); *Cinco microformas* for orch.; *Dos movimientos* for timpani and string orch.; cello concerto (1974); *Espejos* for 4 percussionists and tape (1963); ballet *Saeta*; *Misa ducal*; *Tres piezas* for string 4tet.; *Formantes* for 2 pfs.; *Tres piezas* for solo fl.; sonata for solo vln.; *Antifona pascual* for soloists, chorus and orch.

Halffter, Ernesto (Esriche) (b Madrid, 16 Jan 1905), Spanish conductor and composer. Cond. of the Orquesta Bética de Cámera. After the Span. war he settled in Port. He completed Falla's cantata *Atlántida* (prod. Milan, 1962).

Works incl. *Dos retratos*, *Dos bocetos*, *Rapsodia portuguesa* for orch.; *Suite ancienne* for wind instruments; 2 string 4tets.

Halffter, Rodolfo (b Madrid, 20 Oct 1900; d Mexico City, 14 Oct 1987), Spanish composer, brother of prec. He was self-taught in comp. and began to write music in 1924. In 1939 he left Spain and settled in Mexico, having fled after the fall of the Republic and lost some of his works in an air-raid during his escape to Fr. on foot.

Works incl. ballets *Don Lindo de Almeria* (1935, prod. 1940) and *The Baker's Morning*; *Obertura concertante* for pf. and orch., vln. concerto (1940); pf. pieces.

Halíř, Karel (b Hohenelbe, Bohemia, 1 Feb 1859; d Berlin, 21 Dec 1909), Czech violinist. Studied at the Prague Cons., and under Joachim, of whose 4tet he became a member, besides leading one of his own.

Halka, opera by Moniuszko (lib., in Pol., by W. Wolski, basedon a story by K.W. Wójcicki), concert perf. Wilno, 11 Jan 1848; prod. Wilno, 28 Feb 1854; rev. version Warsaw, 1 Jan 1858. The chief Polish nat. opera. Wallek-Walewski's opera *Jontek's Revenge* is a sequel to it.

Hall, Henry (b New Windsor, c 1655; d Hereford, 30 Mar 1707), English organist and composer. He was a choir-boy in the Chapel Royal in London under Cooke. App. organist at Exeter Cathedral in 1674 and at Hereford Cathedral in 1688.

Works incl. Te Deum in Eb maj., Benedicite in C min., *Cantate Domino* and *Deus misereatur* in Bb maj., anthems and other church music; songs, duets, catches.

Hall, Marie (b Newcastle-on-Tyne, 8 Apr 1884; d Cheltenham, 11 Nov 1956), English violinist. Taught the harp by her father, she decided to take up the vln. and studied with Elgar, Wilhelmj, at the RAM in London and with Ševčik in Prague, where she 1st appeared in 1902; in Vienna and London in

1903. US debut 1905. In 1921 she gave the fp of Vaughan Williams's *The Lark Ascending*.

Hall, (Sir) Peter (b Bury St Edmunds, 22 Nov 1930), English producer. First opera prod. Gardner's *The Moon and Sixpence*, SW 1957. In 1965 he mounted with John Bury at CG, London, the first prod. in Brit. of Schoenberg's *Moses und Aron*. Tippett's *The Knot Garden* (1970) was another successful prod., but Hall did not find congenial the working conditions of an international opera house. From 1970 he has worked at Glyndebourne, mounting well-received prods. of Mozart's 3 Da Ponte operas and Raymond Leppard's eds. of operas by Cavalli and Monteverdi (*L'Incoronazione di Poppea*, 1984, with his wife, Maria Ewing, in the title role). *Simon Boccanegra* 1986. Productions of *Macbeth* at the NY Met (1982) and *The Ring* at Bayreuth (1983) have found less favour. Knighted 1977.

Hall, Richard (b York, 16 Sep 1903; d Horsham, 24 May 1982), English composer and teacher. Studied at Cambridge. After early church appts. was prof. of comp. RMCM 1938–56; taught Goehr, Maxwell Davies and Birtwistle. Dir. of music, Dartington Hall 1956–67. His works were influenced by Hindemith: 5 symphs. (1941–64), 2 string 4tets (1946, 1973).

Halle (or Hale), Adam de la. *See* **La Halle.**

Hallé, Charles (orig. Carl Halle) (b Hagen, Westphalia, 11 Apr 1819; d Manchester, 25 Oct 1895), German-English pianist and conductor. Studied 1st under his father, an organist, then at Darmstadt and Paris, where he had pf. lessons from Kalkbrenner. Settled in Eng. in 1848 and founded the Hallé concerts at Manchester; 1st concert 30 Jan 1858. He cond. many concerts and festivals elsewhere in the country as well and frequently appeared as pianist, usually in sonatas by Schubert and Beethoven. His 2nd wife was the violinist Wilma Neruda, whom he married in 1888. 1st Prin. RMCM, 1893. Knighted 1888.

Hallé, Lady. *See* **Neruda.**

Hallé Orchestra. Founded by Charles Hallé at Manchester in 1857. John Barbirolli was chief cond. 1943–70, James Loughran 1971–83. Stanislav Skrowaczewski from 1984.

Hallén, (Johan) Andreas (b Göteborg, 22 Dec 1846; d Stockholm, 11 Mar 1925), Swedish conductor, critic and composer. Studied at Leipzig, Munich and Dresden and later worked mainly at Göteborg and Stockholm.

Works incl. operas *Harold der Wiking* (in Ger. prod. Leipzig, 1881), *Hexfällan* (later revised as *Valborgsmässan* (Stockholm, 1902), and *Valdemarsskatten*; ballads for solo voices, chorus and orch.; symph. suite *Gustaf Vasas Saga*, symph. poems *The Island of the Dead* (after Böcklin's picture 1898; pre-dates work by Rakhmaninov of same title by 11 years), *Sounds of the Spheres, Autumn* and *A Summer Saga*, 2 rhapsodies for orch.; instrumental pieces; songs.

Halling, a Norwegian dance originating from the Hallingdal between Oslo and Bergen. It is usually in 2–4 time and goes at a moderately quick pace. In its early form, as distinct from that cultivated by Grieg and other comps., its music is played on the Hardanger Fiddle.

Hallström, Ivar (b Stockholm, 5 Jun 1826; d Stockholm, 11 Apr 1901), Swedish pianist and composer. Had private music lessons and studied law at Uppsala Univ. There he met Prince Gustaf, with whom he wrote an opera, which was prod. at Stockholm in 1847. After the prince's death he became librarian to Prince Oscar, later Oscar II, and in 1861 he was app. director of Lindblad's music school, where he had taught the pf.

Works incl. operas *Hvita frun på Drottningholm* (with Prince Gustaf, 1847), *Den bergtagna* (1874), *Hertig Magnus och sjöjungfrun, Vikingarne, Nero* (1882), *Liten Karin*; operettas *Den förtrollade katten* (*The enchanted cat*, 1869), *Mjölnarvargen, Per Svinaherde*; ballets *En dröm, Ett äventyr i Skottland*; cantatas; songs.

Haman and Mordecai (Handel). *See* **Esther.**

Hamari, Julia (b Budapest, 21 Nov 1942), Hungarian mezzo. She studied in Budapest and in 1966 sang in the *St Matthew Passion* (Vienna, under Richter) and the *Alto Rhapsody* (Rome, under Gui). She has appeared with Karajan, Solti and Böhm as a concert singer, in works by Bach, Mahler and Handel, and from 1973 in operas by Verdi, Gluck and Mascagni. In 1979 she sang Celia in *La fedeltà premiata*, at Glyndebourne.

Hambourg, Mark (b Boguchar, 31 May 1879; d Cambridge, 26 Aug 1960), English pianist of Russian origin. A pupil of Leschetizky, he 1st app. in Moscow in 1888. With his brothers Jan H. (1882–1947) and Boris H. (1884–1954) he formed a pf. trio, but in later years devoted himself entirely to solo perf. He lived in London for most of his life.

Hambraeus, Bengt (b Stockholm, 29 Jan 1928), Swedish composer and musicologist.

Studied musicology at the Univ. of Uppsala from 1947 to 1956, and from 1957 worked for Swed. Radio, at the same time teaching at Uppsala Univ. He participated in the Darmstadt courses, being chiefly influenced by the work of Webern, Stockhausen and Boulez. Works incl. *Rota* for 3 orchs., perc. and electronic tape (1964); *Constellation I* for org.; *Constellation II* for recorded tape; *Constellation III* derived from nos I and II; *Doppelrohr II*, an electronic piece; *Introduzione-Sequenze-Coda*; chamber opera *Experiment X* (1971), church opera *Se nännis kan* (1972).

Hamerik (orig. Hammerich), **Asger** (b Copenhagen, 8 Apr 1843; d Frederiksborg, 13 Jul 1923), Danish composer of German descent. Pupil of Gade at Copenhagen, later of Bülow in Berlin for pf. and of Berlioz in Paris for orch. In 1872–98 he was in USA as director of the Cons. of the Peabody Inst. at Baltimore.

Works incl. operas *Tovelille* (1865), *Hjalmar og Ingeborg, La vendetta* (1870) and *Den Rejsende*; Requiem, 2 choral trilogies; 8 symphs., the last for strings, 5 Northern Suites and other orchestral works.

Hamerik, Ebbe (b Copenhagen, 5 Sep 1898; d nr. Copenhagen, 11 Aug 1951), Danish conductor and composer, son of prec. Pupil of his father and Frank van der Stucken. Cond. of the royal theatre at Copenhagen, 1911–22, and of the Musikforeningen there, 1927–30. He then went to live in Austria, but returned home in 1934. He was drowned in the Kattegat.

Works incl. operas *Stepan* (1924), *Leonardo da Vinci* (1939), *Marie Grubbe* (after Jacobsen) and *Rejsekammeraten* (*The Travelling Companion*, after Andersen, 1946); 5 symphs. (1937–50), *Quasi Passacaglia e Fuga*, Variations on an old Dan. folk-tune; 2 string 4tets; suite for contralto and chamber orch.; pf. pieces; org. works; songs.

Hamilton, Iain (Ellis) (b Glasgow, 6 Jun 1922), Scottish pianist and composer. Studied at the RAM in London, where var. works of his were introd. and he won the Royal Phil. Society prize for his clar. concerto and the Koussevitsky Award for his 2nd symph. Professor, Duke Univ., N. Carolina, 1961–81.

Works incl. operas *Agamemnon* (1969), *The Royal Hunt of the Sun* (1967–9; prod. 1977), *The Catiline Conspiracy* (after Jonson, 1974), *Tamburlaine* (1977), *Anna Karenina* (1981), *Lancelot* (1984); ballet *Clerk Saunders*; 4 symphs. (1950–81), 2 vln. concertos (1952, 1971); 2 pf. concertos

(1949, 1967). Variations for strings; clar. 5tet, string 4tet, fl. 4tet; Variations for solo vln.; vla. and pf. sonata; pieces for wind instruments and pf.; pf. sonata; vln. concerto; 8tet for strings.

Hamlet. *See also* **Ambleto; Amleto; Shakespeare.**

Incid. music for Shakespeare's tragedy by Tchaikovsky, op. 67a, incl. 16 numbers and an abridged version of the *Hamlet* fantasy-overture, op. 67, fp St Petersburg, 17 Nov 1888; the play fp with Tchaikovsky's music, St Petersburg, 21 Feb 1891.

Opera by Aristide Hignard (1822–98) (lib. by P. de Garal, after Shakespeare), pub. 1868, but not then prod. on account of A. Thomas' rival opera; prod. Nantes, 21 Apr 1888.

Opera by Searle (text of Shakespeare's play), prod. (in German) Hamburg, 5 Mar 1968.

Opera by A. Thomas (lib. by J. Barbier and M. Carré, after Shakespeare), prod. Paris, Opéra, 9 Mar 1868.

Symph. poem by Liszt, comp. 1858 as a prelude to Shakespeare's tragedy; 1st concert perf. Sondershausen, 2 Jul 1876.

Hammerclavier, Ger. name (lit. 'hammer keyboard instrument') used to distinguish the piano from the (plucked) harpsichord. Beethoven designated his sonatas opp. 101 and 106 as 'für das H.', and the word is now used as a nickname for the latter sonata.

Hammerschmidt, Andreas (b Brüx, 1612; d Zittau, 29 Oct 1675), Bohemian composer. Taken to Freiberg, Saxony, in 1626. Became organist there, 1635, and at Zittau, 1639. Wrote much Lutheran church music.

Works incl. sacred concertos and madrigals for several voices, sacred dialogues for 2 voices, odes, motets and hymns, 17 short Lutheran Masses; thanksgiving for 8 voices for the Saxon victory at Liegnitz; dances for viols.

Hammond, (Dame) **Joan** (b Christchurch, 24 May 1912), New Zealand soprano. Opera debut Sydney 1929. Sang in Vienna 1938 and with the Carl Rosa Co., London, during the war as Violetta, Butterfly and Tosca. CG 1948–51, debut as the *Trovatore* Leonora. SW 1951 and 1959 as Elisabeth de Valois and Rusalka. She sang with NY City Opera in 1949 and toured Russia in 1957. Frequent recordings and concerts. Most often heard in Puccini but opera roles also incl. Tatyana, Desdemona and Aida. DBE 1974.

Hammond Organ, an electrophonic organ invented by Laurens Hammond of Chicago in 1934, prod. its notes by means of electromagnets and offering a choice of tone colours by the selection and combination of the appropriate harmonics.

Hammond-Stroud, Derek (b London, 10 Jan 1929), English baritone. After study with Gerhard Hüsch he made his London debut as Creon in a concert perf. of Haydn's *Orfeo* (1955); stage debut 1957, as Publio in *La Clemenza di Tito*. From 1962 he has sung with SW (later ENO) Opera as Bartolo, Melitone, Alberich and Beckmesser. CG from 1971, Glyndebourne from 1973. NY Met debut 1977, as Faninal.

Hampton, John, (b *c* 1455; d after 1522), English composer. Master of the choristers at Worcester Priory, 1484–1522. He is represented in the Eton Choirbook.

Hanboys, John, English Franciscan friar and music theorist of the 15th cent. His treatise *Summa . . . super musicam* is a commentary on Franco of Cologne.

Handbass! (Aus. & S. Ger. dialect = little hand bass), Leopold Mozart's name for the violoncello piccolo.

Handel, George Frideric (orig. Händel, Georg Friedrich) (b Halle, 23 Feb 1685; d London, 14 Apr 1759), German-English composer. After initial opposition from his father, a barber-surgeon, he studied music with Zachow in Halle, and in 1702 matriculated at the univ. there to read law, at the same time holding the probationary post of organist at the Domkirche. The next year he left for Hamburg, where he played vln., later harpsichord, at the opera under Keiser, and had the operas *Almira* and *Nero* prod. in 1705. Travelled in It. 1706–9, visiting the principal cities and meeting the leading comps. *Agrippina* was successfully prod. at Venice in 1709, and he also made a great reputation as a harpsichordist. Other works comp. in It. incl. the oratorios *La resurrezione* and *Il trionfo del tempo*, solo canatatas, chamber duets, etc. With the support of Steffani he was app. to succeed the latter as *Kapellmeister* to the Elector of Hanover in 1710, but left almost immediately on leave of absence for London, where *Rinaldo* was prod. with great success the next year. Again in London on leave in 1712, he settled there, never returning to his post in Hanover. Between 1712 and 1715 he prod. 4 operas, and in 1713 comp. a *Te Deum* and *Jubilate* to celebrate the Peace of Utrecht, receiving a life pension of £200 from Queen Anne. On her death in 1714 the Elector of Hanover succeeded to the throne as George I, but apparently took a lenient view of his former

Kapellmeister's truancy, for Handel's pension was soon doubled. As music director to the Earl of Carnavon (later Duke of Chandos) 1717–20, he wrote the *Chandos Anthems, Acis and Galatea* and the masque *Haman and Mordecai.*

With the founding of the RAM in 1720 began Handel's most prolific period as an opera comp., and over the next 20 years he wrote more than 30 works. Difficulties arose from the formation of partisan factions round himself and his rival Bononcini, and were aggravated by internal strife between his 2 leading ladies, Faustina and Cuzzoni. The popular success of *The Beggar's Opera* in 1728 made matters worse, and in that year the RAM went bankrupt. Handel continued to prod. operas, acting as his own impresario in partnership with Heidegger, but rival factions, now of a political nature, again undermined his success, and in the 1730s he increasingly turned to oratorio. *Esther* (a revision of the masque *Haman and Mordecai*), 1732, was followed by *Deborah, Saul* and *Israel in Egypt*. His last opera was prod. in 1741, after which he devoted his time chiefly to oratorio, *Messiah* being perf. in Dublin in 1742, followed by 12 more. He continued to appear in public as cond. and organist, playing concertos between the parts of his oratorios, but his health declined and he spent his last years in blindness.

Works incl. OPERAS: *Almira* (1705), *Nero, Rodrigo* (1707), *Agrippina, Rinaldo* (1711), *Il pastor fido, Teseo, Silla, Amadigi di Gaula* (1715), *Radamisto, Muzio Scevola, Floridante* (1721), *Ottone* (1723), *Flavio, Giulio Cesare* (1724), *Tamerlano, Rodelinda, Scipione, Alessandro, Admeto* (1727), *Riccardo Primo, Siroe* (1728), *Tolomeo, Lotario, Partenope* (1730), *Poro, Ezio, Sosarme* (1732), *Orlando, Arianna, Ariodante* (1735), *Alcina, Atlanta* (1736), *Arminio, Giustino, Berenice, Faramondo, Serse* (1735), *Imeneo, Deidamia* (1741); incid. music to Ben Jonson's *The Alchemist* and Smollett's *Alceste.*

ORATORIOS: *Brockes Passion* (1716) *La resurrezione, Esther, Deborah, Athalia* (1733), *Saul* (1739), *Israel in Egypt* (1739), *Messiah* (1742), *Samson* (1743), *Joseph and his Brethren* (1744), *Belshazzar* (1745), *Occasional Oratorio, Judas Maccabaeus* (1747), *Joshua, Alexander Balus, Susanna, Solomon* (1749), *Theodora, Jephtha* (1752), *The Triumph of Time and Truth.*

OTHER CHORAL WORKS: *Roman Vespers* (c 1709), *Acis and Galatea* (1718); *Alexander's Feast* (1736), *Ode for St Cecilia's Day*

(1739), *L'Allegro, il Penseroso ed il Moderato* (after Milton), *Semele* (1744), *Hercules* (1745), *The Choice of Hercules*; 11 'Chandos' Anthems, anthems for the coronation of George II, funeral anthem for Queen Caroline, Utrecht *Te Deum* and *Jubilate*, Dettingen *Te Deum* (1743), and other church music; numerous It. cantatas, chamber duets etc.

INSTRUMENTAL: sonatas for various instruments and continuo, trio sonatas, etc.; 12 *concerti grossi* for strings, 'oboe concertos', org. concertos, *Water Music* (1717), *Fireworks Music* (1749), etc.; keyboard music, incl. organ fugues and harpsichord suites.

Handford, Maurice (b Enfield, 11 Nov 1929; d Warminster, 16 Dec 1986), English conductor and horn player. Studied at the RAM. Prin. horn, Hallé Orch., 1949–61; cond. the orch. from 1966, notably in complex scores by Messiaen and Lutosławski, but resigned in 1971. Often heard with regional BBC orchs. and was prin. cond. of the Calgary PO 1971–5.

Handl, Jacob (Latinized Jacobus Gallus) (b Reifnitz, Carniola, ? 31 Jul 1550; d Prague, 18 Jul 1591), Austrian composer. *Kapellmeister* to the Bishop of Olomouc in 1579–1585 and later cantor in Prague. Wrote 16 Masses, motets, Te Deum and other church music, incl. cycle of music for the liturgical year.

Handley, Vernon (b Enfield, 11 Nov 1930), English conductor. He studied at Oxford and the GSM. Debut Bournemouth SO 1961; cond. and taught at the RCM, 1966–72. From 1970 he gave concerts with the LSO and LPO; frequent perfs. of Brit. music with the BBC; Ulster Orch. from 1985.

Handt, Herbert (b Philadelphia, 26 May 1926), American tenor, conductor and musicologist. He studied at Juilliard and in Vienna; debut there as singer, 1949. He sang in the 1958 Brussels fp of Menotti's *Maria Golovin* and later appeared in operas by Malipiero, Berg and Britten. Since his cond. debut (Rome 1960) he has led his own instrumental and vocal ensembles in perfs. of rare and early music. Among his operatic roles have been Don Ottavio, Haydn's Orfeo and Rossini's Otello.

Hann, Georg (b Vienna, 30 Jan 1897; d Munich, 9 Dec 1950), Austrian bassbaritone. After study in Vienna he joined the Munich Opera in 1927; created La Roche there in 1942. At Salzburg (1931–47) his roles were Pizarro, Sarastro and Leporello. London, CG, 1947 with Vienna co. Other roles incl. Kecal, Falstaff, Ochs and Amfortas.

Hannikainen, Ilmari (b Jävaskylä, 19 Oct 1892; d Helsinki, 25 Jul 1955), Finnish pianist and composer. Studied at the Helsinki Cons., also in Vienna, Leningrad, Berlin, Paris, Antwerp and London. With his brothers Arvo and Tauna, a violinist and a cellist, he founded a pf. trio and toured Europe widely with them.

Works incl. opera *Talkootanssit*; pf. concerto; pf. 4tet; pf. music, songs.

Hans Heiling, opera by Marschner (lib. by E. Devrient, orig. written for Mendelssohn), prod. Berlin, Opera, 24 May 1833.

Hans Sachs, opera by Lortzing (lib. by comp. and F. Reger, based on a play by J.L.F. Deinhardstein), prod. Leipzig, 23 Jun 1840. An earlier opera on the subject of Wagner's *Meistersinger*, which was also used before that by Gyrowetz.

Hänsel und Gretel, opera by Humperdinck (lib. by A. Wette, Humperdinck's sister, from a tale by the Brothers Grimm), prod. Weimar, 23 Dec 1893.

Hanslick, Eduard (b Prague, 11 Sep 1825; d Baden nr. Vienna, 6 Aug 1904), Austrian music critic. Wrote for the *Neue freie Presse* in Vienna and was lecturer on music hist. at the Univ. A fierce opponent of Wagner's later music and ardent partisan of Brahms. His books incl. *Vom Musikalisch-Schönen* (*Of the Beautiful in Music*). In Wagner's original draft for the lib. of *Die Meistersinger* the role of Beckmesser was given as Hans Lich.

Hanson, Howard (b Wahoo, Neb., 28 Oct 1896; d Rochester, NY, 26 Feb 1981), American composer of Swedish descent. Studied music in NY and at Evanston, Ill. Univ. After var. appts., he gained the American Prix de Rome, and after his stay in It. was director of the Eastman School of Music at Rochester, NY 1924–64.

Works incl. opera *Merry Mount* (after Hawthorne, 1934); choral work *The Lament for Beowulf*; 7 symphs. (1923–77), symph. poems *North and West, Lux aeterna* and *Pan and the Priest* for orch.; string 4tet (1923), pf. 5tet, concerto for pf. 5tet; pf. pieces; songs.

Harawi, chant d'Amour et de Mort, song cycle by Messiaen for sop. and pf. (text by comp.), perf. Brussels 1946. The first of a trilogy of works inspired by the Tristan legend: others are the *Turangalîla* symph. (1946–8) and *Cinq Rechants* for chorus *a cappella* (1949).

Harbison, John (b Orange, NJ, 20 Dec 1938), American composer. Studied at Harvard and with Sessions at Princeton. Taught at MIT 1969–82; comp.-in-residence Pittsburgh SO 1982–4.

Works incl. operas *The Winter's Tale* (1979) and *Full Moon in March* (after Yeats, 1979); ballets after Homer *Ulysses' Raft* and *Ulysses' Bow* (1983–4); vln. concerto (1980), symph. (1981).

Hardanger Fiddle (Norw. *Hardengerfelen*), a Norwegian vln. with 4 strings and 4 sympathetic strings used for playing folk dances.

Harding, James (b *c* 1560; buried Isleworth, 28 Jan 1626), English composer and instrumentalist. Wrote 2 keyboard fancies and instrumental dance music.

Hardy, Thomas (1840–1928), English novelist and poet. *See* **Egdon Heath** (Holst), **Harper, E.** (*Fanny Robin*), **Hoddinott** (*Trumpet Major*), **Muldowney** (*Lovemusic for Bathsheba and Gabriel Oak*), **Tess** (Erlanger); poems set as songs by among others, Bax, Britten, Finzi, Holst, Ireland.

Harewood, Earl of (George H.H.L.) (b London, 7 Feb 1923), British administrator, critic and writer. He studied at Cambridge and in 1950 founded *Opera* magazine, which he edited until 1953; held var. posts at CG 1951–72 and was managing director of SW (later ENO) Opera 1972–85; at the end of his tenure led the co. on a tour of the USA. Artistic adviser New Philharmonia Orch. 1966–76. He was editor of the 8th, 9th and 10th eds. of *Kobbé's Complete Opera Book* (1953, 1976, 1986).

Harington, Henry (b Kelston, Som., 29 Sep 1727; d Bath, 15 Jan 1816), English physician and amateur musician. Studied 1st theology and then medicine at Oxford and settled in practice at Bath. Comp. glees, catches, rounds, songs, etc. The popular setting of Ben Jonson's 'Drink to me only with thine eyes' is attrib. to him.

Hark, hark, the lark, song by Schubert from Shakespeare's *Cymbeline*, trans. by A.W. Schlegel as *Ständchen aus 'Cymbeline'* and comp., in Ger., in 1826.

Harmonic, a prefix denoting org. pipes, prod. harmonic notes from pipes of double, triple or quadruple speaking-length. *See also* **Harmonics.**

Harmonic Analysis, a method of describing the chords and progressions mainly in music of the 18th and 19th cents. The principles, apparently 1st estab. by Gottfried Weber in his *Versuch einer geordneten Theorie der Tonsetzkunst* (1817–21), rest on the identification of a chord by its root (*q.v.*) and by the position of the root within the scale.

Thus a root-position chord on the tonic is designated as I, its first inversion as 1b (or, using the parlance of thorough bass (*q.v.*), I⁶) and its second inversion as Ic (or I⁶₄); further elaborations of the system are all based on figured bass notation. Within diatonic music with straightforward harmonies, the main chords are I, IV and V; II and VI are also common, but III and VII are used more rarely. 1st inversions are important and used frequently except in structural cadences. 2nd inversions of triads are normally considered discords and can be used only in partic. circumstances.

A further refinement of this system is 'Functional Harmony', 1st devised by Heinrich Riemann in his *Vereinfachte Harmonielehre* (1893). Here every chord is described as part of a tonic (I), dominant (V) or subdominant (IV) function. This system, still little practised outside Ger., makes the entire chordal vocabulary of the classical and romantic eras more comprehensible as a logical system; but at the same time many details need to be glossed over and this leads to the use of 'reduction' graphs which describe certain chords as passing chords within a broader progression. Hierarchical reductions of this kind inevitably led to the analytical techniques of Heinrich Schenker and his followers.

Harmonic Bass, another name for the Acoustic Bass org. stop.

Harmonic Flute. *See under* **Flute, Harmonic.**

Harmonic Minor, the minor scale conforming to the key signature, with the exception of the leading-note (*see* illustration).

faster chord changes at that point help to clarify the end of the phrase. Another example might be the moment before the recapitulation in sonata-form movements (sometimes called the 'retransition'): here the harmonic rhythm often slows down to a standstill, normally on the dominant, thus not only increasing the tension but allowing for a sudden change in harmonic rhythm at the moment of recapitulation.

Harmonic Series, the composite series of notes that can be prod. by a vibrating substance or air column (*see* illustration).

Those marked x are not in tune with the normal scale. The members of the series have a proportional relation to each other. Thus if the lowest note vibrates at 64 cycles per second, the octave above it will be at 128 c.p.s., the G (no. 3) at 172 c.p.s., middle C at 256, and so on.

Harmonica, a modern term for the mouth organ. For the Glass Harmonica *see* **Armonica.**

Harmonics, a commonly used term for (upper) partial tones (overtones) in the notes of a musical inst. Also a technical term for notes prod. by touching a bowed string at suitable (nodal) points, or similarly by making a hole in an open org. pipe. In acoustics, compound elements of a periodic vibration. The corresponding elements in the vibration of a bell or a drum are 'inharmonic'. *See* **Harmonic Series.**

Harmonie der Welt, Die (*The Harmony of the World*), opera by Hindemith (lib. by the composer) in 5 acts, prod. Munich, 11 Aug 1957. Symph. from the opera 1951; fp Basle 24 Jan 1952. Based on the life of the astro-

HARMONIC MINOR

Harmonic Rhythm, the rhythm of chord change. For most tonal music, the variety of harmonic rhythm is of considerable importance to the musical effect. Thus it may be noted, for instance, that in many simple melodies of the classical era the harmonic rhythm speeds up towards the cadence: the

nomer Johannes Kepler (1571–1630), who maintained in *Harmonices mundi* that the planets emit musical sounds in their orbits round the sun.

Harmoniemesse, mass in B♭ by Haydn, comp. 1802 and perf. Eisenstadt, 8 Sep 1802. Title derives from prominent use of

1 2 3 4 5 6 7 8 9 10 11 12 13 14 15 16

HARMONIC SERIES

wind insts (Ger. 'Harmonie' = wind band). Haydn's last Mass.

Harmoniemusik (Ger.), music for a combination of woodwind and brass insts. with or without perc., i.e. for military band.

Harmonious Blacksmith, The, name given to the Air and Variations in Handel's E maj. harpsichord suite (Book I, no. 5, pub. 1720). Despite the traditional story that Handel comp. the piece after hearing a blacksmith singing at his work, the nickname is of 19th-cent. origin.

Harmonium, a keyboard instrument, the sound of which is prod. by reeds played by wind coming from bellows worked by the player's feet. It dates from the early 19th cent. The American Organ is similar to it, except that the wind is sucked into instead of driven out through the reeds.

Harmony, the musical effect derived from combining different pitches simultaneously. In general parlance this is contrasted with counterpoint (*q.v.*), the combination of musical lines, though the one is often difficult to separate from the other. Harmony and counterpoint are perhaps best seen as different aspects of the combination of musical sounds, or even merely as tendencies. The distinction between harmony and counterpoint first became important for Western musical theory in the use of a continuo (*q.v.*) section playing from thorough bass (*q.v.*) at a time when written music was otherwise largely imitative polyphony. Harmonic theory as it is understood today goes back to Rameau's recognition of the notion of the root (*q.v.*) of a chord; and this led to the principle of harmonic analysis (*q.v.*) in the early 19th cent. as a way of describing the vertical component of music in the 18th-and 19th-cent. traditions. Yet it is also possible to talk of 'modal harmony', 'atonal harmony' and 'melodic harmony' (i.e. the harmonies implied within a single line).

The main stages in the hist. of harmony in Western music may be summarised as follows. 12th–13th-cents.: open 5th and 8ves as the main consonances, with the open 4th gradually losing favour. 14th–16th-cent.: elimination of the open 4th as a consonance; increasing use of full triads, though most often in root position and only rarely as a concluding chord; increasingly systematic and sophisticated use of suspensions. 17th–18th-cent.: incorporation of dominant 7th chord, Neapolitan 6th (*q.v.*), diminished chords and certain secondary 7ths. Classical era: augmented 6th chords (*q.v.*). Later 19th-cent.: chromatically altered chords.

From around 1900: a wide variety of practices including whole-tone harmony, chords of superimposed 4ths, diatonic harmony within unusual scales, atonal and polytonal harmony.

Harnasie, ballet pantomime by Szymanowski (scenario by J. Iwaszkiewicz and J.M. Rytard); comp. 1923–31, prod. Prague, 11 May 1935.

Harnoncourt, Nikolaus (b Berlin, 6 Dec 1929), Austrian conductor, cellist and musicologist. He studied in Vienna and played with the Vienna SO 1952–69; formed the Vienna Concentus Musicus and from 1957 gave concerts of Baroque music using period insts.; attempted to re-create original performing practice. Recorded the Brandenburg concertos in 1962, gave *Messiah* in London 1966 and recorded Rameau's *Castor et Pollux* and Monteverdi's operas. Harnoncourt's own eds. of Monteverdi are a valuable alternative to the free realizations of Raymond Leppard, and his perfs. of the Bach solo cello suites are in contrast to the subjective approach of Casals and Rostropovich.

Harnoy, Ofra (b Hadera, 31 Jan 1965), Canadian cellist of Israeli birth. Began her studies in Tel-Aviv and moved to Toronto in 1972; debut with the Boyd Neel Orch., after further study at the Royal Cons. of Music. She has played in New York from 1982 and has given perfs. in the US of concertos by Bliss and Sullivan, with Sir Charles Mackerras. She gave the fp of a recently-discovered concerto by Offenbach and has recorded works by Haydn and Vivaldi.

Harold en Italie, a descriptive symph. by Berlioz, op. 16, for solo vla. and orch., based on Byron's *Childe Harold*, comp. in 1834, fp Paris, 23 Nov. It was suggested by Paganini, but not played by him.

Harp, an instrument dating from prehistoric times, so shaped that the strings stretched parallel across its frame are graded in length and thus prod. the different notes of a mus. scale. Old harps had comparatively few strings and their notes were fixed; the modern concert harp has a range of 6½ 8ves and the strings represent the diatonic scale of Cb maj.; but each note can be raised individually throughout all the octaves at once by a semitone and by a whole tone at will by means of a set of pedals at the base of the instrument. Thus the harp can be tuned in a moment to any diatonic scale. The chromatic scale is available only on the Chromatic Harp (*q.v.*).

Harp Lute, an instrument sometimes called

Dital Harp, invented early in the 19th cent. It was derived from insts. of the lute type, but had a larger number of strings held by pegs in the harp-shaped head, c half of them changeable in pitch by a finger-board, the others remaining open and thus capable of playing only a single fixed note.

'Harp' Quartet, the nickname given to Beethoven's string 4tet in E♭ maj., op. 74, comp. in 1809, because it contains, in the 1st movt., several arpeggios divided between the instruments.

Harper, Edward (b Taunton, 17 Mar 1941), English composer. He studied at Oxford and with Gordon Jacob and at the RCM; lecturer at Edinburgh Univ. from 1964.

Works incl. pf. concerto (1969); *Bartók Games* for orch. (1972); *Ricercari in memoriam Luigi Dallapiccola* for 11 insts. (1975), *Fanny Robin*, opera in 1 act from an episode in Hardy's *Far from the Madding Crowd*, 1975); *7 poems by e.e. cummings* for sop. and orch. (1977); *Chester Mass* for chorus and orch. (1979); clar. concerto (1982); *Intrada after Monteverdi* for chamber orch. (1982); *Hedda Gabler*, opera after Ibsen's play (1985).

Harper, Heather (Mary) (b Belfast, 8 May 1930), British soprano. Studied at TCM, London, and privately. First appeared in opera at Oxford 1954; Glyndebourne from 1957, CG from 1962. She has sung at Bayreuth (Elsa, 1967–8) and Buenos Aires, 1969–72. Other roles incl. Britten's Helena and Ellen Orford, Eva, Arabella and The Woman in *Erwartung* (1st London prod., 1960). Has also made a reputation as a concert singer; sang in the fps of Britten's *War Requiem* (1962) and Tippett's 3rd symph. (1972). Hon. D.Mus., Queen's Univ., Belfast, 1966.

Harpsicall ⎱ Old Eng. terms, corruptions
Harpsicon ⎰ of 'Harpsichord'.

Harpsichord, a keyboard instrument shaped usually in the wing form of a grand pf. and played by means of a similar keyboard, but prod. its notes by plucking the strings with plectra, not striking them with hammers. The square-shaped Virginal and the Spinet are instruments of the same type but smaller. Harpsichords often have 2 keyboards, each controlling a different set of quills, harder and softer, and there are frequently stops by which yet other ranges of quills can be set into action; but the tone cannot be controlled by the player's fingers.

Harrell, Lynn (b New York, 30 Jan 1944), American cellist. He studied at Juilliard with Leonard Rose; debut Carnegie Hall 1960.

Prin., Cleveland Orch. 1965–71, under Szell; soloist since 1971. British debut 1975, with LSO under Ashkenazy.

Harrhy, Eidwenn (b Trowbridge, 14 Apr 1949), Welsh soprano. She sang Despina at the RMCM, 1970, and appeared professionally from 1974 (Alcina with Handel Opera and in *The Ring* at CG). At the London Coliseum she has sung Adèle (1977) and with Kent Opera Pamina and the Taurian Iphigénie; she sang Diana in *La Fedeltà premiata* at the 1979 Glyndebourne Festival. Other roles incl. Donna Anna, Butterfly (Coliseum 1984) and Berg's Marie (WNO 1986).

Harris, Renatus, English 17th–18th-cent. organ builder. Worked in London. Built many famous organs and enlarged that made by his grandfather for Magdalen Coll., Oxford.

Harris, Roy (actually Leroy Harris) (b Lincoln Co., Okla, 12 Feb 1898; d Santa Monica, Calif., 1 Oct 1979), American composer. His father was a farmer who migrated to California during Harris's boyhood, and at 18 Harris had a farm of his own. In 1916 he enlisted in World War I, returning to USA in 1918 and becoming a music student at the Univ. of California, driving a dairy cart to earn a living. Next he studied under Arthur Farwell for 2 years and prod. an Andante for strings with the NY PO in 1926, when he went to Paris for a further 2 years' study with Nadia Boulanger. He returned to USA in 1929 and later held posts at the Westminster Choir school at Princeton, NJ, Cornell Univ., Colorado, Logan (Utah), Nashville and Pittsburgh.

Works incl. 13 symphs. (1934–76), *Farewell to Pioneers* (1936), *Three Symph. Essays, Memories of a Child's Sunday* and other works for orch.; *Chorale* and *Prelude and Fugue* for string orch.; concerto for vln. and orch., symph. for chorus and orch., *Whitman Suite* and *Second Suite* for women's chorus and 2 pfs., *Song for Occupation, Story of Noah* and *Symph. for Voices* for 8-pt. unaccomp. chorus.

CHAMBER AND INSTRUMENTAL: 3 string 4tets (1930–9), 6tet and 5tet for wind and pf., string 6tet, pf. 5tet, pf. trio, *Variations on a Theme* for string 4tet, *4 Minutes 20 Seconds* for fl. and string 4tet, concerto for pf. clar. and string 4tet; vln. and pf. sonata; pieces for vln. and vla. and pf.; pf. works, incl. sonatas and *Children's Suite*.

Harrison, Beatrice (b Roorkee, India, 9 Dec 1892; d Smallfield, Sussex, 10 Mar 1965), English cellist. She studied at the RCM and made her 1907 debut with Wood; in 1920 took part with him in the fp of Delius's Double Concerto. With Hamilton Harty she gave the 1918 fp of the Delius cello sonata and in 1923 the 1st Brit. perf. of the concerto, under Goossens. 1924 1st London perf. of Kodály's solo sonata op. 8; recorded the Elgar concerto with the composer.

Harrison, Frank Llewelyn (b Dublin, 29 Sep 1905), Irish musicologist and educationist. Studied at the RIAM and Trinity Coll., Dublin, and subsequently under Schrade and Hindemith at Yale Univ. He was music director at Queen's Univ., Kingston (Canada), from 1935 to 1946, and Prof. of Music at Colgate Univ., Hamilton (NY), from 1946 to 1947 and at Washington Univ., St Louis, from 1947 to 1952. From 1952 to 1970 he was a lecturer in music, subsequently reader, at Oxford Univ. Professor of Ethnomusicology at Amsterdam Univ., 1970–80. He specialized in the study of Eng. medieval music, and has ed. *The Eton Choirbook* (3 vols.) and pub. *Music in Medieval Britain* (1958). He was general ed. of the series *Early English Church Music*.

Harrison, Julius (b Stourport, Worcs., 26 Mar 1885; d Harpenden, 5 Apr 1963), English conductor and composer. Studied under Bantock at the Midland Inst., Birmingham. Cond. opera under Beecham's management and with the BNOC and from 1930 to 1940 was music dir. at Hastings.

Works incl. Mass for solo voices, chorus and orch.; Requiem Mass; suite *Worcestershire Pieces* for orch.; *Troubadour Suite* for strings, harp and 2 horns; string 4tet *Widdicombe Fair* and other chamber music; vla. and pf. sonata; pf. works, instrumental pieces; songs.

Harrison, Lou (b Portland, Oregon, 14 May 1917), American composer. Studied with Cowell and Schoenberg from 1937 to 1940. He then taught at Mills College and at the Univ. of California in 1942. From 1945 to 1948 he was a music critic for the *New York Herald-Tribune*. Harrison has experimented with new sonorities, incl. novel scales and methods of tuning.

Works incl. opera *Rapunzel* (1959); ballets *Solstice*, *The Perilous Chapel* (1949), *Almanac of the Seasons*, *Johnny Appleseed*, *Changing World* and others; Prelude and Saraband for orch., symph. in G maj., 3 suites; *Four Strict Songs* for 8 baritones and orch. in pure intonation (1955); *Recording Piece* for perc.; *Simfony I*; vln. concerto with perc. orch.; string trio; suite for cello and harp; pf. music.

Harsányi, Tibor (b Magyarkanizsa, 27 Jun 1898; d Paris, 19 Sep 1954), Hungarian composer. Studied at the Budapest Cons. under Kodály and later settled in Paris in 1923.

Works incl. operas *Illusion*, *Les Invités* (1928); ballets *The Last Dream* and *Shota Roustaveli* (1945) (with Honegger and A. Tcherepnin); Christmas Cantata for chorus and strings (1939); suite, *Suite hongroise*, *Ouverture symphonique*, *La Joie de vivre* for orch.; *Concertstück* for pf. and orch., Divertimento No. 1 for 2 vlns. and orch.; *Aria and Rondo* for cello and orch., Divertimento No. 2 for tpt. and strings; *The Story of the Little Tailor* for 7 instruments and perc.; 2 string 4tets (1918, 1935), pf. trio, concertino for pf. and string 4tet; sonatas for vln. and pf. and cello and pf.; pf. pieces; songs.

Harshaw, Margaret (b Narbeth, Penn., 12 May 1909), American mezzo, later soprano. She studied at Juilliard, NY, and made her debut at the Met in 1942; after Senta there in 1950 she sang in the soprano repertory; succeeded Helen Traubel as Isolde, Kundry and Brünnhilde. Glyndebourne 1955 (Donna Anna); CG, London, 1953–60, as Brünnhilde. She left the Met in 1963 and taught at Bloomington Univ. from 1962.

Hartmann, German-Danish family of musicians:

1. Johann Ernst H. (b Glogau, Silesia, 24, Dec 1726; d Copenhagen, 21 Oct 1793), German violinist, conductor and composer. Worked at Breslau and Rudolstadt before he settled in Copenhagen, where he became leader of the royal orch. in 1768.

Works incl. opera *The Fishermen*, prod. 1780, containing the song *Kong Christian* by D.L. Rogert, now the Danish nat. anthem.

2. August Wilhelm H. (b Copenhagen, 6 Nov 1775; d Copenhagen, 15 Nov 1850), organist, son of prec. Organist at the Garrison Church in Copenhagen from 1800.

3. Johann Peter Emilius H. (b Copenhagen, 14 May 1805; d Copenhagen, 10 Mar 1900), composer, son of prec. Succeeded his father as organist of the Garrison Church in Copenhagen in 1824, app. organist of the cathedral 1843. Prof. at Copenhagen Cons., he became one of its directors in 1867.

Works incl. operas *Ravnen* (1832), *Korsarerne* (1835), *Liden Kirsten* (after Andersen); melodrama *Guldhornene*; incid. music for plays; ballets; 2 symphs.; sonatas, etc., for pf.

4. Emil H. (b Copenhagen, 21 Feb 1836; d Copenhagen, 18 Jul 1898), organist and composer, son of prec. Pupil of his father and Gade, who was his brother-in-law. Organist at var. churches in 1861–73 and cond. of the Music Society from 1891 to 1892, succeeding Gade.

Works incl. operas *En Nat mellem Fjaeldene* (1863), *Elverpigen* (1867), *Korsikaneren* and *Ragnhild* (1896); ballet *Fjeldstuen*; cantata *Winter and Spring*; 7 symphs., *Northern Folk Dances* and overture *A Northern Campaign*; concertos for vln. and for cello; serenade for clar., cello and pf.- songs.

Hartmann, Karl Amadeus (b Munich, 2 Aug 1905; d Munich, 5 Dec 1963), German composer. Studied with Josef Haas at the Munich Acad. and later with Scherchen. Began comp. late in life, but destroyed his early works and turned to serialism under the influence of Webern. After World War II he organized the important 'Musica Viva' concerts in Munich to propagate new music. In 1952 he was elected to the German Acad. of Fine Arts and in 1953 became president of the German section of the ISCM.

Works incl. chamber opera *Des Simplicius Simplicissimus Jugend* (1934–5; prod. 1949), 8 symphs. (1936–62); concerto for pf., wind and perc.; *Musik der Trauer* for vln and strings (1939); concerto for vla., pf., strings and perc.; 2 string 4tets.

Hartmann, Rudolf (b Ingolstadt, 11 Oct 1900), German producer and administrator. He prod. opera at Nuremberg (1928–34) and the Berlin Staatsoper (1934–8) then became associated with Clemens Krauss and the operas of Strauss at Munich: fps of *Friedenstag* (1938) and *Capriccio* (1942). Prod. *The Ring* at CG (1954) and returned for *Arabella* (1965). His work was noted for its discretion and good taste. Wrote book on the prod. of Strauss's stage works (1980).

Harty, (Herbert) Hamilton (b Hillsborough, Ireland, 4 Dec 1879; d Hove, 19 Feb 1941), Irish conductor and composer. Studied pf., vla. and comp. under his father and became an organist at the age of 12. Later organist at Belfast and Dublin, where he studied further under Esposito. In 1900 he settled in London as accompanist and comp. and married the soprano Agnes Nicholls (*q.v.*). He then took to cond. and after much much experience in London was app. cond. to the Hallé Orch. at Manchester in 1920; gave the 1st Brit. perf. of Mahler's 9th symph. in 1930. Retired 1933. Knighted and Mus.D. Dublin, 1925.

Works incl. arrs. of Handel's *Water Music*

and *Fireworks Music*, Ir. Symph. (1924), *Comedy Overture*, symph. poem *With the Wild Geese* for orch. (1910); vln. concerto; cantata *The Mystic Trumpeter* (Whitman); *Ode to a Nightingale* (Keats) for soprano and orch. (1907); many songs.

Harvey, Jonathan (b Sutton Coldfield, 3 May 1939), English composer. He studied at Cambridge and Glasgow Univs.; prof. at Sussex Univ. from 1980. He has worked with Stockhausen and Babbitt.

Works incl. symph. (1966); *Persephone Dream* for orch. (1973), *Smiling Immortal* for chamber orch. and tape (1977), *Easter Orisons* for strings (1983); 10 Cantatas for soloists and various inst. combinations (1965–76), *Hymn* for chorus and orch. (comp. 1979 for the 900th anniversary of Winchester Cathedral), *Passion and Resurrection*, church opera, perf. Winchester 1981); chamber and inst. music incl. *Mortuos plango, vivos voco* for computer-processed concrete sounds, perf. Lille 1980: *Modernsky Music* of 1981, for 2 oboes, bassoon and harpsichord, derives its title from one of Schoenberg's 3 Satires op. 28, in which Stravinsky is mocked as 'Modernsky', for apparently following musical fashion. In 1986 Harvey's *Madonna of Winter and Spring*, for orch. and electronics, was premièred at the Promenade Concerts, London.

Harwood, Basil (b Woodhouse, Olveston, Glos., 11 Apr 1859; d London, 3 Apr 1949), English organist and composer. Educ. at Charterhouse and Oxford, studied music at Bristol, Oxford and the Leipzig Cons. Organist 1st in London, then at Ely Cathedral, 1887–92, and Christ Church, Oxford, 1892–1909, and choragus of the univ.

Works incl. psalms and motets with orch.; services, anthems and other church music; *Ode on a May Morning* (Milton) for chorus and orch. (1913), cantata *Love Incarnate*; org. concerto with orch.; 2 sonatas and other works for organ.

Harwood, Elizabeth (b Barton Seagrave, Northants., 27 May 1938), English soprano. She studied at the RMCM. SW, London, from 1961 as Gilda, Zerbinetta, Constanze and Rossini's Adèle. In 1967 she sang for the first time at CG, with Scottish Opera and at the Aix Festival: roles incl. Tippett's Bella, Fiordiligi (role of NY Met debut, 1975), and Strauss's Sophie. Salzburg from 1970, as Donna Elvira and Mozart's Countess. In 1980 she sang the Marschallin at Glyndebourne.

Háry János, ballad opera by Kodály (lib. by B. Paulini and Z. Harsányi, based on a poem by János Garay), prod. Budapest, 16 Oct 1926. It contains popular Hung. tunes and begins with an orchestral imitation of a sneeze. Orch. Suite perf. NY, 15 Dec 1927.

Haskil, Clara (b Bucharest, 7 Jan 1895; d Brussels, 7 Dec 1960), Rumanian pianist. Made her debut aged 7 in Vienna, then entered the Paris Cons., where she studied with Cortot and Fauré and won a prize at the age of 14. She later studied with Busoni on his invitation. She was esp. well known as a perf. of Mozart and Beethoven; vln. sonatas with Arthur Grumiaux.

Hassan, or The Golden Journey to Samarkand, incidental music by Delius for the play by James Elroy Flecker; 1920, prod. London, His Majesty's, 20 Sep 1923, with ballets arr. by Fokine. Orch. suite by Eric Fenby, with inst. incl. camel-bells, perf. on BBC, 1 Aug 1933.

Hasse, Faustina. *See* **Bordoni.**

Hasse, Johann Adolf (b Bergedorf nr. Hamburg, bap 25 Mar 1699; d Venice, 16 Dec 1783), German composer. Sang tenor at the Hamburg Opera under Keiser, 1718–19, then at Brunswick, 1719–22, where his first opera, *Antioco*, was prod. in 1721. Went to It. 1722, and studied with Porpora and A. Scarlatti. After many successful operas for Naples, became *maestro di cappella* at the Cons. degli Incurabili in Venice in 1727. Married the singer Faustina Bordoni (*q.v.*) in 1730, and in 1734 went to Dresden as *Kapellmeister* to the Saxon Court, a post he held for 30 years. But he was allowed generous leave of absence, and travelled widely, incl. a visit to London in 1734, becoming the most successful *opera seria* comp. of his generation. In 1764, after the death of the Saxon Elector, he moved to Vienna, then in 1733 to Venice, where he lived for the rest of his life.

Works incl. operas *Antioco* (1721), *Il Sesostrate* (1726), *Tigrane* (1729), *Artaserse, Cleofide, Cajo Fabricio* (1732), *Il Demetrio, Siroe, rè di Persia, Tito Vespasiano* (1735), *Lucio Papirio* (1742), *Didone abbandonata, Antigono, Semiramide riconosciuta* (1744), *Arminio, Leucippo, Demofoonte* (1748), *Attilio Regolo* (1750), *Il Ciro riconosciuto, Solimano, Ezio, Olimpiade, Alcide al Bivio, Il trionfo di Clelia* (1762), *Partenope, Piramo e Tisbe* (1768), *Ruggiero* (1771), and many others; oratorios *I Pellegrini al sepolcro, Sant' Elena al calvario* (1746), *La Conversione di Sant' Agostino* (1750); Masses and other church music; concertos for fl., vln., etc.; solo sonatas, trio sonatas, harpsichord pieces.

Hasselmans, Alphonse (Jean) (b Liège, 5 Mar 1845; d Paris, 19 May 1912), Belgian, naturalized French, harpist and composer. Settled early in Paris and became harp prof. at the Cons. in 1884. Appeared frequently as a virtuoso and comp. *c* 50 works for the harp, incl. *Patrouille* and *L'Orientale.*

Hassler, Hans Leo (b Nuremberg, 25 Oct 1564; d Frankfurt, 8 Jun 1612), German organist and composer. Pupil of his father, Isaac H. (*c* 1530–91) and, after an appt. at Nuremberg, was sent to Venice for further study under A. Gabrieli (the 1st Ger. to study in It.). Organist to Octavian Fugger at Augsburg, 1585–1600. Having returned to Nuremberg as organist of the church of Our Lady, he married and went to live at Ulm in 1604, but soon went into the service of the Emperor Rudolph in Prague. In 1608 he became organist to the Elector of Saxony at Dresden, but suffered from tuberculosis and died during a visit with the elector to Frankfurt.

Works incl. Masses, Magnificats, hymntunes, motets (incl. 2 collections *Sacrae cantiones* and *Sacri concentus*), fugal psalms and Christian songs; It. canzonets for 4 voices, It. and Ger. madrigals, *Lustgarten neuer teutscher Gesäng* (32 German songs for 4–8 voices, 1601);*ricercari,* toccatas, etc. for org.

Hassler, Jacob (b Nuremberg, bap. 18 Dec 1569; d ? 1622), German organist and composer, brother of prec. Studied under his father and at Venice, became organist to Christoph Fugger at Augsburg and then to Prince Eitel-Fritz of Hohenzollern at Hechingen, and in 1602–12 was in the service of the court in Prague.

Works incl. Masses and other church music. It. madrigals; organ works.

Hassler, Kaspar (b Nuremberg, bap. 17 Aug 1562; d Nuremberg, Aug 1618), German organist and composer, brother of prec. Studied under his father and (?) at Venice. Organist at the church of St Laurence at Nuremberg. Ed. collections of motets, incl. some by his brother Hans Leo H.

Hatton, John (Liptrott) (b Liverpool, 12 Oct 1808; d Margate, 20 Sep 1886), English composer. He was almost wholly self-taught in music. In 1832 he settled in London, in 1842 became attached to Drury Lane Theatre as comp. and in 1844 visited Vienna to prod. his opera *Pascal Bruno.* In 1848 he went to USA and later became music director of the Prince's Theatre in London, where he wrote much incid. music for Kean's prods.

Works incl. operas *Pascal Bruno* (1844) and *Rose, or Love's Ransom* (1864), operetta *The Queen of the Thames*; incid. music for Shakespeare's *Macbeth*, *Henry VIII*, *Richard II*, *King Lear*, *The Merchant of Venice* and *Much Ado About Nothing*, Sheridan's *Pizarro*, an adaptation of Goethe's *Faust* and other plays; Mass, 2 services, 8 anthems; oratorio *Hezekiah*; cantata *Robin Hood*; over 150 songs, incl. *To Anthea* (Herrick); many part-songs.

Haubenstock-Ramati, Roman (b Kraków, 27 Feb 1919), Polish, later Israeli, composer. Studied comp. in Kraków and Lwów from 1937 to 1940. From 1947 to 1950 he was music director of Radio Kraków and then emigrated to Israel, where he became director of the music library in Tel-Aviv. In 1957 he moved to Paris, living also in Vienna, where he worked for Universal Edition. His early works are conservative in idiom, but his mature music uses serial and experimental techniques.

Works incl. opera *Amerika* (after Kafka, 1966); *Ulysses*, ballet (1977), *La Symphonie des timbres* for orch.; *Vermutungen über ein dunkles Haus* for 3 orchs.; *Papageno's Pocket-size Concerto* for glockenspiel and orch. (1955); *Recitativo and Aria* for cembalo and orch.; *Sequences* for vln. and orch.; *Petite Musique de nuit*, mobile for orch. (1958); *Blessings* for voice and 9 players; *Mobile for Shakespeare* for voice and 6 players (1960); *Jeux* for 6 perc. groups; concerto for strings (1977); *Interpolation*, mobile for solo fl.; *Ricercari* for string trio.

Hauer, Josef (Matthias) (b Wiener-Neustadt, 19 Mar 1883; d Vienna, 22 Sep 1959), Austrian composer. Pub. a series of pamphlets on comp. according to a 12-note system of his own, different from that of Schoenberg, his material being based on groups of notes he called *Tropen*, derived from the combinations of the 12 notes of the chromatic scale allowed by the agreement of their overtones.

Works (all based on this system) incl. opera *Salammbô* (after Flaubert, 1929; perf. Vienna, 1983); play with music, *Die schwarze Spinne* (after Jeremias Gotthelf, 1932; perf. Vienna, 1966); Mass for chorus, org. and orch.; cantata *Wandlungen*; music for Aeschylus's *Prometheus Bound* and tragedies by Sophocles: *Vom Leben*, recitation with singing voices and chamber orch. for broadcasting.

Sinfonietta, 8 suites, 7 Dance Fantasies (1928), Concert Piece, *Apocalyptic Fantasy* (1913), *Kyrie*, etc. for orch.; symph. for

strings, harmonium and pf.; vln. concerto, pf. concerto; 6 string 4tets (1924–6), 5tet for clar., vln., vla., cello and pf.; many pf. pieces incl. 2 sets of Studies and pieces on Hölderlin titles; c 87 *Zwölftonspiele* for different instruments and instrumental combinations; 6 song-cycles to poems by Hölderlin and other songs.

Haug, Hans (b Basle, 27 Jul 1900; d Lausanne, 15 Sep 1967), Swiss conductor and composer. Studied at Basle and Munich and became orch. and chorus cond. of various Swiss towns and prof. at the Lausanne Cons.

Works incl. operas *Don Juan in der Fremde* (1930), *Madriso* (1934), *Tartuffe* (after Molière, 1937), *E liederlieg Kleeblatt* (in Swiss dialect), *Ariadne*; Te Deum; oratorio *Michelangelo* (1943); symph. and other orch. works; vln. concerto, pf. concerto; chamber music, incl. 3 string 4tets; part-songs, arrs. of Swiss folksongs, songs with pf.; film and radio music.

Haugland, Aage (b Copenhagen, 1 Feb 1944), Norwegian bass. He sang first at Oslo and Bremen; Stockholm from 1973. In 1975 he was heard as Hunding at CG and as Hagen at the ENO; other London roles have been Varlaam and Ochs. US debut St Louis 1979, as Boris; NY Met from 1979 as Klingsor, Gremin, Marke, Boris and Khovansky. In 1982 he sang Rocco at Salzburg and the following year Hagen at Bayreuth. A noted concert artist.

Hauk, Minnie (b New York, 16 Nov 1851; d Triebschen, Lucerne, 6 Feb 1929), American mezzo of German descent. Made her debut at Brooklyn in 1866 and her European debut at CG, London, 1868; 1st London Carmen, 1878.

Haunted Tower, The, opera by Storace (lib. by James Cobb), prod. London, Drury Lane Theatre, 24 Nov 1789.

Hauptmann, Moritz (b Dresden, 13 Oct 1792; d Leipzig, 3 Jan 1868), German theorist, writer on music and composer. Studied at Dresden and began to work there, lived in Rus. in 1815–10, played vln. in Spohr's orch. at Kassel from 1822 and was cantor at St Thomas's Church in Leipzig from 1842 to his death. Wrote on acoustics, harmony, fugue, etc.

Works incl. opera *Mathilde* (1826); 2 Masses, motets and psalms; choruses and part-songs; 3 sonatas for vln. and pf., vln. duets; songs.

Hausegger, Siegmund von (b Graz, 16 Aug 1872; d Munich, 10 Oct 1948), Austrian conductor and composer. Studied under his father, a Wagnerian critic, and others. After cond. at Graz, he shared the conductorship of the Kaim Orch. at Munich with Weingartner. Later in charge of concerts at Frankfurt, Glasgow and Edinburgh (Scot. Orch.) and Hamburg, and at Munich again in 1920–38. 0 Works incl. opera *Zinnober* (1898), *Barbarossa* and *Natursinfonie*, *Dionysische Phantasie*, *Wieland der Schmied* and *Aufklänge* for orch.; Mass and Requiem; choral works, part-songs.

Hauser, Franz (b Krasovice, nr. Prague, 12 Jan 1794; d Freiburg i/B., 14 Aug 1870), Bohemian-German baritone. Pupil of Tomášek and successful opera singer until 1837; sang under Spohr in Kassel and under Weber in Dresden. Roles incl. Figaro, William Tell and Spohr's Faust. From 1846 to 1864 he was dir. of the Munich Cons. He pub. a singing method in 1866.

Hausmann, Robert (b Rottleberode, Harz, 13 Aug 1852; d Vienna, 18 Jan 1909), German cellist. Studied at the Hochschule für Musik in Berlin and with Piatti in London and It. He joined the Joachim 4tet in 1879. In 1886 gave the fp of Brahms's F maj. cello sonata and in 1887 the fp of the Double concerto, with Joachim.

Haussman, Valentin (d *c* 1612), German 16th–17th-cent. organist and composer. He was organist and town councillor at Gerbstädt nr. Merseburg. Ed. vocal pieces by Marenzio, Vecchi, Gastoldi and Morley with Ger. words. Works incl. Ger. secular songs for 4–8 voices, instrumental dances, incl. *Venusgarten* containing 100 dances, mostly Polish.

Hautboy (from Fr. *hautbois* = lit. 'loud wood'), the old Eng. name for the ob., sometimes spelt 'hoboy').

Haute-contre (Fr.), alto or high tenor, whether voice or instrument. Hence one of the old names for the alto or tenor viol and the vla.

Hawes, William (b London, 21 Jun 1785; d London, 18 Feb 1846), English musician. He was master of choristers at St Paul's Cathedral and the Chapel Royal but neglected and brutalised his charges. From 1804 he made many adaptations for the stage of operas by Mozart and Weber.

Hawkins, John (b London, 29 Mar 1719; d London, 21 May 1789), English music historian. Devoted at first to architecture and then to law, he gradually became interested in lit. and music. Having married a wealthy wife in 1753, he was able to retire and to undertake, in addition to minor works, his *General History of the Science and Practice of Music*, pub. in 5 vols. in 1776, the same year as the 1st vol. of Burney's similar work. Knighted 1772.

Hawte, William (b Canterbury, *c* 1430; d 2 Jul 1497), English composer. Wrote 4 settings of the *Benedicamus Domino* (Cambridge, Magdalene Coll., Pepys MS. 1236) and a processional antiphon, *Stella caeli*.

Haydn, Franz Joseph (b Rohrau, Lower Austria, 31 Mar 1732; d Vienna, 31 May 1809), Austrian composer. Son of a wheelwright, he went at the age of 8 as a chorister to St Stephen's Cathedral in Vienna under Georg Reutter (jun.). On leaving the choirschool *c* 1749 he lived at first as a freelance, playing vln. and organ, teaching, etc. He was for a time pupil-manservant to Porpora, but in comp. he was largely self-taught, studying the works of C.P.E. Bach, Fux's *Gradus ad Parnassum*, etc. From these years date his earliest comps., esp. church music, incl. 2 Masses. His first string 4tets were written *c* 1755 for Baron Fürnberg, through whom he obtained the post of music director to Count Morzin in 1759. The next year he contracted what was to prove an unfortunate marriage, and in 1761 entered the service of the Esterházy family, in 1766 succeeding Franz Gregor Werner as *Kapellmeister*, a post he held for the rest of his life. At Eszterháza, the magnificent palace in the Hung. marshes completed in 1766, where the household now spent the greater part of the year, Haydn was responsible for all the musical entertainment, and there wrote the majority of his instrumental music and operas. Though he was isolated in Eszterháza his fame spread; his works were pub. abroad, and he received invitations to travel, which, however, his duties obliged him to refuse. In 1786 he was commissioned to comp. 6 symphs. for the Concert de la Loge Olympique in Paris.

On the death of Prince Nicolaus in 1790 the Esterházy musicians were disbanded and Haydn, though retaining his title and salary, was free to accept an invitation from the violinist and impresario J.P. Salomon to go to Eng. His first visit to London, 1791–2, for which he comp. an opera (not prod.) and 6 symphs., was a great success, and was followed by another in 1794–5, for which a further 6 symphs. were written. In 1792 he received the honorary degree of D.Mus. at Oxford. On the accession of Prince Nicolaus II in 1795 the Esterházy music estab. was in part revived, but Haydn's duties were light, chiefly involving the comp. of a Mass each year for the princess's name-day, and giving rise to the 6 great Masses of 1796–1802.

Inspired by the works of Handel he had heard in London, he comp. *The Creation* (1798) and *The Seasons* (1801). From 1803 he comp. little, living in retirement in Vienna.

Works (some still unpub.) incl.:

OPERAS: 20 works for the stage, of which 7 are lost (all fps at Eszterháza, unless otherwise stated): *Acide*, festa teatrale (Eisenstadt, 1763), *La cantarina*, intermezzo (Eisenstadt, 1766), *Lo speziale*, dramma giocosa (1768), *Le pescatrici*, dramma giocosa (1770), *L'infedeltà delusa*, burletta (1773), *L'incontro improvviso*, dramma giocosa (1775), *Il mondo della luna*, dramma giocosa (1777), *La vera costanza*, dramma giocosa (1779), *L'isola disabitata*, azione teatrale (1779), *La fedeltà premiata*, dramma pastorale giocosa (1781), *Orlando Paladino*, dramma eroicomico (1782), *Armida*, dramma eroico (1784), *L'anima del filosofo* (now known by its alternative title of *Orfeo ed Euridice*. Written for London in 1791 but not perf. First known prod. Florence, 10 Jun 1951, with Callas and Christoff.) Marionette operas *Philemon und Baucis* (1773), *Hexen-Schabbas* (1773; lost), *Dido* (1776; lost), *Die Feuerbrunst* (1776), *Die Bestrafte Rachbegierde* (1779).

14 MASSES: *Missa 'Rorate coeli desuper'* (1748), *Missa brevis* in F (1749), *Missa Cellensis*, *Cäcelienmesse*, in C (1766), *Missa in honorem BVM*, *Grosse Orgelmesse*, in Eb (1771), *Missa Sancti Nicolai*, in G (1772), *Missa brevis* in Bb, *Kleine Orgelmesse* (1778), *Missa Cellensis*, *Mariazeller Messe* (1782), *Missa Sancti Bernardi (Heiligmesse)* Bb (1796), *Missa in tempore belli*, *Paukenmesse*, in C, (Vienna, 26 Dec 1796); Mass in D minor, *Nelson Mass* (Eisenstadt, 23 Sep 1798); Mass in Bb, *Theresienmesse* (1799); Mass in Bb, *Schöpfungsmesse* (Eisenstadt, 13, Sep 1801); Mass in Bb, *Harmoniemesse* (Eisenstadt, 8, Sep 1802). A fragment of the lost Mass *Sunt bona mixta malis*, (c 1769) was discovered in Ireland in 1983.

CANTATAS AND ORATORIOS: *Stabat Mater* (1767), *Applausus* (Zwettl, 17 Apr 1768), *Il ritorno di Tobia* (Vienna, 2 Apr 1775), *Die Sieben letzten Worte unseres Erlösers am Kreuze*, *Seven Last Words* (Vienna, 26 Mar 1796), *Die Schöpfung (The Creation)*, (Vienna, 29 Apr 1798), *Die Jahreszeiten*, *The Seasons* (Vienna, 24 Apr 1801). Also Te Deum in C (1800)

104 SYMPHONIES: nos 1–5 (1758–60); nos 6–8, *Le Matin, Le Midi, Le Soir* (1761); nos 9–21 (c1762); no. 22 in Eb, *The Philosopher* (1764); nos 23–5 (1764); no. 26 in D min., *Lamentatione* (1770); nos 27–9 (1765); no. 30 in C, *Alleluja* (1765); no. 31 in D, *Hornsignal* (1765); nos 32–42 (c 1768) no. 43 in Eb, *Mercury* (1772); no. 44 in E min., *Trauersinfonie* (1772); no. 45 in F# min. *Farewell* (1772); no. 46 in B and no. 47 in G (1772); no. 48 in C, *Maria Theresia*, and no. 49 in F min., *La Passione* (c1768); nos 50–2 (1773); no. 53 in D, *The Imperial* (1778); nos 54–9 (1774); no. 60 in C, *Il Distratto* (1774); nos 61–72 (c 1779); no. 73 in D, *La Chasse* (1782); nos 74–81 (1781–4); nos 82–7 *Paris Symphonies*; no. 82 in C, *The Bear*, no. 83 in G min., *The Hen*, no. 84 in Eb, no. 85 in Bb, *La Reine*, no. 86 in D, no. 87 in A (1785–6); no. 88 in G, no. 89 in F, no. 90 in C, no. 91 in Eb (1787–8); no. 92 in G, *The Oxford* (1789); nos 93–104 *London Symphonies*: no. 93 in D, no. 94 in G, *The Surprise*, no. 95 in C min., no. 96 in D, *The Miracle*, no. 97 in C, no. 98 in Bb, no. 99 in Eb, no. 100 in G, *The Military*, no. 101 in D, *The Clock*, no. 102 in Bb, no. 103 in Eb, *The Drumroll*, no. 104 in D, *The London* (1791–1795).

CONCERTOS: 4 for vln., in C, D, A, and G (1769–71); 2 for cello in C and D (1761 and 1783); organ concerto in C (1756); concerto for vln. and harpsichord (1766); harpsichord concertos in F, G and D (1771–84); for trumpet in Eb (1796); Sinfonia concertante in Bb for oboe, vln., cello and bassoon (1792); 5 concertos for lire organizzate (c 1786); concertos for oboe, flute, horn and bassoon are either lost or spurious.

STRING QUARTETS: The usually given number of 83 is incorrect; from this must be subtracted the set of six op. 3, now known to be by Romanus Hoffstetter, and the arrangement of *The Seven Last Words*, hitherto counted as 7 separate quartets. Op. 1 nos 1–6 (c 1757); op. 2 nos 1, 2, 4 and 6 (c 1762); op. 9 nos. 1–6 (c 1771); op. 17 nos. 1–6 (c 1772), op. 20, nos 1–6, *Sun Quartets*: in Eb, C, G min., D, F min., A. (1772); op. 33 nos. 1–6, *Russian Quartets*: B min., Eb *(The Joke)*, C *(The Bird)*, Bb, G D (1781); op. 42 in D min. (1785); op. 50 nos 1–6: in Bb, C, Eb, F# min., F and D *(The Frog)* (1787); op. 54 nos 1–3: in G, C and E (1788); op. 55 nos 1–3: in A, F min. and Bb (1790); op. 64 nos 1–6: in C, B min., Bb, G, D *(The Lark)* and Eb (1791); op. 71 nos 1–3: in Bb, D and Eb (1795); op. 74 nos 1–3: in C, F and G min. *(The Rider)* (1796); op. 76 nos 1–6: in G, D min. *(The Fifths)*, C *(The Emperor)*, Bb *(The Sunrise)*, D, Eb (1797); op. 77 nos 1 and 2: in G and F (1802); op. 103 in D min. (1803).

OTHER INSTRUMENTAL: 32 piano trios, 126 baryton trios and other chamber music; 60 pf. sonatas (1760–94), 5 sets of variations, for pf. incl. F min. (1793); solo songs, partsongs, arrs. of Scot. and Welsh folksongs. 12 Canzonettas to English words for solo voice and pf. incl. *My mother bids me bind my hair, Sailor's Song* and *She never told her love* (1794–5); Solo cantatas *Arianna a Naxos* (1789) and *Berenice che fai* (1795).

Haydn, (Johann) Michael (b Rohrau, Lower Austria, 14 Sep 1737; d Salzburg, 10 Aug 1806), Austrian composer, brother of prec. Chorister at St Stephen's Cathedral in Vienna under Reutter from c 1745. App. *Kapellmeister* to the Archbishop of Grosswardein (Hung.) in 1757, and became *Konzertmeister* to the Archbishop of Salzburg in 1762, where he was cathedral organist from 1781. Apart from occasional visits to Vienna, he remained in Salzburg till his death, in 1801 refusing the post of vice-*Kapellmeister* (under his brother Joseph H.) to Prince Esterházy.

Works incl. 32 Masses incl. *Missa Hispanica* (1786), 2 Requiem Masses, incl. C min. Requiem, for Archbishop Sigismund, 1771; influenced Mozart's Requiem, 8 Ger. Masses, 6 *Te Deum* settings, 117 Graduals, 45 Offertories, 27 Holy Week Responsories, etc.; opera *Andromeda e Perseo* (1787), Ger. *Singspiele* and other music for the stage, oratorios; cantatas; 46 symphs. incl. one with a slow introd. by Mozart (K 444: M.'s '37th' symph.); 5 concertos; 6 string 5tets; 11 string 4tets; keyboard music.

'Haydn' Quartets, the familiar name of Mozart's 6 string 4tets ded. to Haydn: G maj., K387 (1782), D min., K421 (1783), E♭ maj., K428 (1783), B♭ maj., K458 (1784), A maj., K464 (1785), C maj., K465 (1785).

'Haydn' Variations, a set of variations by Brahms for orch., op. 56a, or for 2 pfs., op. 56b on a theme called the 'St Anthony Chorale' from a Divertimento for wind insts., attrib. formerly to Haydn, where it is also treated in variation form. Fp of the orchestral version, Vienna, 2 Nov 1873.

Hayes, Catherine (b Limerick, 25 Oct 1825; d London, 11 Aug 1861), Irish soprano. Studied under Antonio Sapio at Dublin, where she made her 1st appearance in 1840. Later she studied with Garcia in Paris and Ronconi at Milan, where she sang at La Scala in 1845 in *Linda di Chamounix*, after a debut at Marseilles as Bellini's Elvira. After many successes in It. and Vienna, she 1st

appeared in London in 1849, in operas by Ricci, Mercadante and Rossini.

Hayes, Philip (b Oxford, bap. 17 Apr 1738; d London, 19 Mar 1797), English organist and composer, son of the following. He succeeded his father as prof. and organist at Magdalen Coll.; ed. many works by earlier composers, partic. Purcell and Boyce, and supervised Haydn's visit to Oxford in 1791. His works show some familiarity with symphonic style and incl. the oratorios *Prophecy* (1778), *The Judgement of Hermes* (1783), 16 psalms, about 50 anthems, the masque *Telemachus* (1763), 17 Odes incl. *Ode for St Cecilia's Day* (1779); glees and catches; keyboard concertos and sonatas. His extreme corpulence was responsible for his nickname 'Fill Chaise'.

Hayes, William (b Gloucester, bap. 26 Jan 1708; d Oxford, 27 Jul 1777), English organist and composer, father of prec. He was organist at Worcester Cathedral from 1731 and organist and master of the choristers, Magdalen Coll., Oxford, from 1734; prof. 1742. He introduced many of Handel's works to Oxford, Bath and Winchester; his own works were indebted to Handel and incl. oratorios *The Fall of Jericho* and *David* (c 1776), 16 psalms, Te Deum in D, 20 anthems, masques *Circe* (1742), and *Peleus and Thetis*; Odes *When the fair consort* (1735), *Where shall the Muse* (1751), *O that some pensive Muse* (Ode to the memory of Handel, c 1760), *Ode on the Passions* (c 1760) and *Daughters of Beauty* (1773); 6 cantatas, concertos and trios.

Haym, Nicola Francesco (b Rome, 6 Jul 1678; d London, 11 Aug 1729), Italian cellist, librettist and composer of German descent. Went to London in 1702, and with Dieupart and Clayton was active in estab. Italian opera there. From 1713 wrote several libretti for Handel, incl. *Teseo*, *Radamisto*, *Giulio Cesare* and *Rodelinda*, also for Bononcini and Ariosti. His own works incl. a Latin oratorio and a serenata, anthem *The Lord is King*, 2 sets of trio sonatas.

Hayman, Richard (b Sandia, New Mexico, 29 Jul 1951), American composer. Studied at Columbia Univ., later learned from Cage and Boulez. Early employment incl. renovating church organ pipes; also sold earplugs in the subway. In 1975 wrote *Dali*, commissioned by the artist and enscribed on a toothpick. *It is not here* was realized in Morse Code at the Museum of Modern Art in NY in 1974. Later works incl. *sleep whistle* (1975), which the comp. performs while asleep in a store window, and *roll*, executed while lying down in the street and covered by Hindu bells. *Dreamsound* was perf. at Berkeley, Calif., in 1976.

Hayne van Ghizeghem (b c 1445; d between 1472 and 1497), Franco-Flemish composer whose life is documented only for his years at the court of Burgundy, 1457–72. His entire surviving output is of Fr. *chansons*, several of which were among the most successful of their age, incl. *'De tous biens plaine'*, *'Allez regretz'* and *'Amours, amours'*.

Hayward, Marjorie (Olive) (b Greenwich, 14 Aug 1885; d London, 10 Jan 1953), English violinist. Studied with Sauret at the RAM and with Ševčik in Prague (1903–6). In 1924 she became vln. prof. at the RAM. She led the Eng. String Quartet and the Virtuoso Quartet, also played in the Eng. Ensemble Pf. Quartet and the Kamaran Trio.

Head, Michael (Dewar) (b Eastbourne, 28 Jan 1900; d Cape Town, 24 Aug 1976), English singer, pianist and composer. Gave up the study of mechanical engineering for music, which he studied at the RAM in London, incl. comp. under Corder. In 1927 he became pf. prof. there. He gave many song recitals and broadcasts, playing his own accomps., and toured widely in the Commonwealth.

Works incl., Tone Poem and Scherzo for orch.; *Jabberwocky* (Lewis Carroll) for chorus; pf. concerto; c 60 songs incl. cycles *Songs of the Countryside* (W.H. Davies), *Over the Rim of the Moon*, part-songs.

Heart's Assurance, The, song cycle by Tippett for high voice and pf. (poems by Sidney Keyes and Alun Lewis); commissioned by Peter Pears and perf. by him and Britten in London on 7 May 1951.

Heath, John, English 16th-cent. composer. His morning and communion services were printed by John Day (1560), but had already been in use in Edwardian times (c 1548). There is also an anthem and a part-song, and a keyboard piece in the Mulliner Book (*q.v.*) is almost certainly his. He is not to be confused with his namesake of Rochester (d 1668), possibly his grandson, who wrote Eng. church music.

Hebenstreit, Pantaleon (b Eisleben, 1667; d Dresden, 15 Nov 1750), German dulcimer player. At 1st a violinist and dancing-master at Leipzig, he made his name as a virtuoso on the dulcimer towards the end of the 17th cent. and had such a success in Paris in 1705 that Louis XIV named his instrument after him, and it was long called 'Pantaleon'. In

1714 it was intro. into the court band at Dresden, with him as player.

'Hebrides' Overture (Mendelssohn). *See* **Fingal's Cave.**

Heckel, Johann Adam (b Adorf, 14 Jul 1812; d Biebrich, 13 Apr 1877), German instrument-maker and founder (1831) of the family firm at Biebrich. Became the foremost Ger. bassoon-maker, making many improvements to the inst.

Heckel, Wolff (b Munich, c 1515; d c 1562), German lutenist and composer. His lute-book (incl. some pieces for 2 lutes) was pub. in 1556 in Strasbourg.

Heckelclarina, the name of a special instrument created by the firm of Heckel at Biberich for the playing of the shepherd's pipe part in Act III of Wagner's *Tristan*.

Heckelphone, a double-reed instrument invented by the Ger. instrument maker Wilhelm Heckel (1856–1909) in 1905. The standard type has a compass an 8ve lower than the oboe. There are also smaller members of the family.

Hedley, Arthur (b Dudley, Northumberland, 12 Nov 1905; d Birmingham, 8 Nov 1969), English writer on music. Studied at Durham Univ.. In 1946 became correspondent of the Chopin Inst. at Warsaw. Author of a book on Chopin and many articles. His collection of Chopin MSS. and related material is in the Museo de Chopin, Majorca.

Hedmont, Charles (b Ontario, 24 Oct 1857; d London, 25 Apr 1940), Canadian tenor. Sang at Leipzig from 1882 as Max and in operas by Mozart. Sang with the Carl Rosa Co. from 1891 and at CG, in Wagner, from 1895; Loge in *The Ring*, with Clarence Whitehill as Wotan (1908).

Heger, Robert (b Strasbourg, 19 Aug 1886; d Munich, 14 Jan 1978), German conductor and composer. Studied at Zurich and Munich, Schillings being his chief master. He cond. opera in many Ger. cities, also in Vienna and London; cond. the fp of Strauss's *Capriccio* in Brit. at CG, 1953.

Works incl. operas *Ein Fest zu Haderslev, Der Bettler Namenlos* (from Homer's *Odyssey*, 1932), *Der verlorene Sohn* (1936), *Lady Hamilton* (1951); melodrama *Die Jüdin von Worms*; *Ein Friedenslied* for solo voices, chorus, orch. and org.; 3 symphs.

Heifetz, Jascha (b Vilna, 2 Feb 1901; d Los Angeles, 10 Dec 1987), Russian-American violinist. First played in public aged 5, having learned from his father, and at the age of 6 played the Mendelssohn concerto. In 1910 he entered the St Petersburg Cons., soon becoming a pupil of Auer. In 1912 he played in

Berlin with great success. After the Revolution of 1917 he went to Amer. His perfect technical mastery was not always allied with comparable interpretative insight.

Heiligmesse (*Holy Mass, Missa Sancti Bernardi von Offida*, in Bb); comp. 1796 by Haydn as a companion to the *Missa in tempore belli*: *Mass in time of war.*

Heiller, Anton (b Vienna, 15 Sep 1923; d Vienna, 25 Mar 1979), Austrian composer and organist. After studying org. and comp. privately, he entered the Vienna Cons. from 1941 to 1942. In 1945 he was app. prof. of organ at the Vienna Acad. of Music. In 1952 he won 1st prize at an international organ competition in Haarlem, Holland.

Works incl. *Symphonie Nordique*; *Psalmen-Kantate*; *Te Deum*; 5 Masses; *Tentatio Jesu* for soloists, chorus and 2 pfs. (1952); toccata for 2 pfs.; much organ music.

Heimchen am Herd, Das (*The Cricket on the Hearth*), opera by Goldmark (lib. by A.M. Willner, based on Dickens's story), prod. Vienna, Opera, 21 Mar 1896.

Heimkehr aus der Fremde, Die (*The Return from Abroad*, better known as *Son and Stranger*), operetta by Mendelssohn (lib. by K. Klingemann), prod. Leipzig, 10 Apr 1851.

Heine, Heinrich (1797–1856), German poet. *See* Brian (*Pilgrimage to Kevlaar*), Dichterliebe (Schumann), Fliegende Holländer (Wagner), Giselle (Adam), Guglielmo Ratcliff (Mascagni), Humperdinck (*Wallfahrt nach Kevlaar*), Liederkreis (Schumann), Schwanengesang (Schubert), William Ratcliff (Cui). 6 songs by Brahms, 6 by Schubert, 39 by Schumann.

Heinichen, Johann David (b Krössuln nr. Weissenfels, 17 Apr 1683; d Dresden, 16 Jul 1729), German composer and theorist. Pupil of Schelle and Kuhnau in Leipzig, first practised as a lawyer in Weissenfels, but in 1709 returned to Leipzig, as an opera comp. The following year he went to Italy to study, remaining there till 1716. In 1717 app. *Kapellmeister* to the Elector of Saxony in Dresden, where he lived till his death. Wrote 2 important treatises on figured bass.

Works incl. operas, numerous Masses, motets and other church works, cantatas, symphs., orchestral suites, solo and trio sonatas.

Heinlen, Paul (b Nuremberg, 11 Apr 1626; d Nuremberg, 6 Aug 1686), German organist, wind player and composer. Studied with a town musician at Nuremberg and in 1646–9 in Italy. App. to var. Nuremberg churches

in 1655–8, finishing as organist at St Sebald's Cathedral. Wrote church music and set many sacred poems by contemporary authors.

Heinrich von Müglin, German 14th-cent. song composer. He worked in Prague, Budapest and Vienna.

Heise, Peter Arnold (b Copenhagen, 11 Feb 1830; d Ny Taarback, 12 Sep 1879), Danish composer. Pupil of Berggreen at Copenhagen and Hauptmann at Leipzig.

Works incl. *Paschaens Datter* (1869) and *Drot og Marsk* (1878); incid. music for many plays, incl. Oehlenschläger's *Palnatoke* and Hauch's *Marsk Stig*; *Rusk Cantata* and cantata *Tornerose* (*Sleeping Beauty*); symph; 6 string 4tets; pf. music.

Heldenleben, Ein (*A Hero's Life*), symph. poem by R. Strauss, comp. Autumn 1898. Fp Frankfurt, 3 Mar 1899. The work is autobiographical.

Helffer, Claude (b Paris, 18 Jun 1922), French pianist. He studied with Casadesus and Leibowitz; debut Paris 1948. He has toured widely since the 1960s and given many perfs. of works by Amy, Boulez, Ravel and Barraqué. The complete pf. works of Schoenberg and the Boulez sonatas are among his recordings.

Heliogabalus Imperator, 'allegory for music' by Henze, after M. Enzensberger; comp. 1971–2, fp Chicago, 16 Nov 1972, cond. Solti.

Hellendaal, Pieter (b Rotterdam, bap. 1 Apr 1721; d Cambridge, 19 Apr 1799), Dutch violinist, composer and organist. After his family moved to Amsterdam during 1737 he studied with Tartini in It. He was active as a composer from 1744, and at Leiden between 1749 and 1751 attempted to establish himself as a musician. After moving to London in 1751 he obtained posts in Oxford and King's Lynn, finally moving to Cambridge in 1762; widely respected in East Anglia as musician and composer.

Works incl. sonatas for vln. and basso continuo, concertos for strings (pub. Amsterdam, London and Cambridge), glees, vocal canons and catches (pub. London and Cambridge) and the cantata *Strephon and Myrtilla* (c1785).

Heller, Stephen (b Pest, 15 May 1813 or 1814; d Paris, 14 Jan 1888), Hungarian pianist and composer. Studied with Anton Halm in Vienna and made his 1st public appearance at Pest in his teens and later went on tour in Ger. He lived at Augsburg in 1830–8 after a long illness, working quietly at comp., and settled in Paris in 1838. He visited Eng. in 1850 and 1862.

Works (nearly all for pf.) incl. 4 sonatas, a very large number of studies, variations and fantasies on operatic tunes, 5 Tarantellas, Caprice on Schubert's *Trout*, several sets entitled *Im Walde, Promenades d'un solitaire* (after Rousseau's letters on botany), *Blumen-, Frucht- und Dornenstücke* (after Jean Paul, 1853), *Dans le bois, Nuits blanches*, etc. With Ernst he wrote vln. and pf. pieces entitled *Pensées fugitives*.

Helletsgruber, Luise (b Vienna 30 May 1901; d Vienna, 5 Jan 1967), Austrian soprano. She made her debut in Vienna in 1922 and sang there until 1942, often in the operas of Mozart. Salzburg 1928–37 as Cherubino, Donna Elvira, Liù and Zdenka. Glyndebourne 1934–8 as Dorabella, Cherubino and Donna Elvira.

Hellmesberger, Austrian family of musicians:

1. Georg H. (b Vienna, 24 Apr 1800; d Neuwaldegg, 16 Aug 1873), violinist, conductor and composer. Studied in Vienna and became in 1821 asst. teacher and in 1833 prof. of the vln. at the Cons. In 1829 he was app. cond. of the court Opera. Wrote many works for his instrument.

2. Joseph H. (b Vienna, 23 Nov 1828; d Vienna, 24 Oct 1893), violinist and conductor, son of prec. Pupil of his father. Appeared as an infant prodigy and was app. vln. prof. at the Cons. in 1851, and cond. of the Gesellschaft concerts. He resigned the latter post to Herbeck in 1859, but retained that of director of the Cons. He also held posts at the Opera and the court concerts, and led a string 4tet from 1849 to 1887; gave fps of works by Schubert, Brahms and Bruckner.

3. Georg H. (b Vienna, 27 Jan 1830; d Hanover, 12 Nov 1852), violinist and composer, brother of prec. Studied with his father and toured with him and his brother Joseph in Ger. and Eng. In 1850 he was app. leader of the opera orch. at Hanover, where he wrote the operas *Die Bürgschaft* (after Schiller, prod. Hanover 1851) and *Die beiden Königinnen*.

4. Joseph H. (b Vienna, 9 Apr 1855; d Vienna, 26 Apr 1907), violinist and composer, son of 2. Pupil of his father, in whose 4tet he played 2nd vln. until 1887, when he succeeded him as leader. Solo violinist at the Opera and court chapel and vln. prof. at the Cons. from 1878. App. court *Kapellmeister* in 1890; succeeded Mahler as cond. of VPO in 1901.

Works incl. 22 operettas and 6 ballets.

Helmholtz, Hermann (Ludwig Ferdinand)

von (b Potsdam, 31 Aug 1821; d Berlin, 8 Sep 1894), German scientist. After holding 3 professorships in physiology he turned to physics, of which he became prof. at Berlin Univ. in 1871. He specialized in acoustics and in 1863 pub. his *Lehre von den Tonempfindungen als physiologische Grundlage für die Theorie der Musik*.

Hely-Hutchinson, (Christian) Victor (b Cape Town, 26 Dec 1901; d London, 11 Mar 1947), English pianist and composer. Educ. at Eton and Balliol Coll., Oxford, and became lecturer in music at Cape Town Univ. in 1922. In 1926 he returned to England and joined the staff of the BBC 1st in London and then as regional director of music at Birmingham, where he became prof. of music at the univ. in 1934. He resigned in 1944 to take up the app. of music director of the BBC.

Works incl. *A Carol Symph.* and variations for orch.; pf. 5tet, string 4tet; choral works; songs, incl. settings of Edward Lear; film music.

Heming, Percy (b Bristol, 6 Sep 1883; d London, 11 Jan 1956), English baritone. Studied at the RAM in London and early began to specialize in opera; joined the Beecham Opera Co. in 1915 and sang Amfortas, Scarpia and Ford. BNOC from 1922, SW from 1933. He sang a great variety of parts with great distinction.

Hemiolia (or Hemiola) (Gk. lit. the proportion 3 : 2), a change of rhythm effected by the substitution of 3 beats where 2 would be normal; e.g. by writing 3 minims instead of 2 dotted minims in a bar of 6–4, or over 2 bars of 3–4.

Hemmel, Sigmund (d 1564), German composer. He comp. the first complete polyphonic metrical psalter in Ger. (pub. Tübingen, 1569). He also wrote Ger. and Lat. sacred songs, and a Mass.

Hempel, Frieda (b Leipzig, 26 Jun 1885; d Berlin, 7 Oct 1955), German soprano. Studied at the Cons. of Leipzig and Berlin, and made her 1st appearance at the Berlin Royal Opera in 1905 as Nicolai's Frau Fluth. London, CG, 1907; Drury Lane 1914 as Queen of Night and the Marschallin. She won worldwide fame and made her 1st appearance in NY as Marguerite de Valois, 1912; other roles incl. Euryanthe, Eva and Violetta. She settled in USA and pursued a concert career.

Hemsley, Thomas (b Coalville, 12 Apr 1927), English baritone. Debut Purcell's Aeneas, London 1951. Glyndebourne 1953–61 as Masetto, the Speaker, Don

Fernando and Dr Reischmann in Henze's *Elegy for Young Lovers*. He sang with the EOG from 1955, creating Britten's Demetrius (1960) and appeared in Aachen, Düsseldorf and Zurich 1953–67. He has been heard in Bayreuth and London as Beckmesser and is a frequent recitalist.

Henderson, Roy (b Edinburgh, 4 Jul 1899), British baritone and teacher. He studied at the RAM and in 1925 was heard as Delius's Zarathustra. Stage debut CG 1928, as Donner. Glyndebourne 1934–9 as Figaro, Guglielmo, Papageno and Masetto. He continued to appear in concert and took part in the fps of Vaughan Williams's *Dona nobis pacem* (Huddersfield, 1936) and *Five Tudor Portraits* (Norwich, 1936). Kathleen Ferrier was among his pupils.

Henderson, W(illiam) J(ames) (b Newark, NJ, 4 Dec 1855; d New York, 5 Jun 1937), American music critic. After some general journalistic work he became music critic to the *NY Times* in 1887 and the *NY Sun* in 1902. In 1904 he was app. lecturer at the Inst. of Musical Art in NY. His books incl. studies of the hist. and practice of singing, aesthetics, the evolution of music, Wagner, early It. opera, etc. He was a savage opponent of much modern music; died by suicide.

Hendricks, Barbara (b Stephens, Arkansas, 20 Nov 1948), American soprano. She studied at Juilliard and made her debut in the NY fp of Virgil Thomson's *Lord Byron* (1972). She sang Calisto at Glyndebourne in 1974 and the title role in *The Cunning Little Vixen* at Santa Fe the following year. Further opera engagements in Boston, Berlin and at Orange. CG 1982, as Nannetta. Other roles incl. Susanna, Pamina and Amor.

Henkemans, Hans (b The Hague, 23 Dec 1913), Dutch composer and pianist. Studied pf. with Sigtenhorst-Meyer and comp. with Pijper. Made his debut, aged 19, in his own pf. concerto. He later studied medicine and for some time practised as a psychiatrist, before devoting himself entirely to music.

Works inc. symph.; 2 pf. concertos (1923, 1936); concertos for fl., vln., vla., harp; 3 string 4tets; sonatas for cello, vln., 2 pfs.

Henrici, Christian Friedrich (known as Picander) (b Stolpen, nr. Dresden, 14 Jan 1700; d Leipzig, 10 May 1764), German poet and cantata librettist. After study in Wittenberg he moved to Leipzig in 1720. He was well known as a playwright and pub. 5 vols. of poems, under the title *Ernst schertzhaffte und satyrische Gedichte*. From 1726 he was involved in a collaboration with Bach which resulted in the texts for the *St Mat-*

thew Passion, St Mark Passion and part of the *Christmas Oratorio*. He also furnished libretti for many of Bach's occasional vocal works and some of the church cantatas.

Henry, Pierre (b Paris, 9 Dec 1927), French composer. Studied with Messiaen and Nadia Boulanger. Worked with Pierre Schaeffer at the Groupe de Recherche de Musique Concrète 1950–8. Founded private electroacoustical effects: collaborations with Schaeffer *Symphonie pour un homme seul* (1950) and opera *Orphée* (1953); also ballets *Haut Voltage* (1956), *Le Voyage* (1962), *Messe pour le temps présent* (1967) and *Nijinsky, clown de Dieu* (1971); *Messe de Liverpool* (1967), *Gymkhana* (1970), *Ceremony* (1970), *Futuriste I* (1975).

Henry IV (b Bolinbroke Castle, 3 Apr 1367; d Westminster, 20 Mar 1413), King of England 1399–1413. He is a less likely candidate than his son Henry V as comp. of the pieces ascribed to 'Roy Henry' in the Old Hall MS. (*q.v.*).

Henry V (b Monmouth, Aug 1387; d Bois de Vincennes, 31 Aug 1422), King of England, 1413–22. *See* **Henry IV.**

Henry VIII (b Greenwich, 28 Jun 1491; d Windsor, 28 Jan 1547), King of England, 1509–47. He comp. or arr. several songs found in a MS. (Brit. Mus., Add. 31,922) dating from his reign, and a 3-part motet *Quam pulchra es.*

Henry VIII, opera by Saint-Saëns (lib. by L. Détroyat and P.A. Silvestre, prod. Paris, Opéra, 5 Mar 1883.

Henschel, (Isidor) Georg (later **George**) (b Breslau, 18 Feb 1850; d Aviemore, Inverness, 10 Sep 1934), German (naturalized Brit.) baritone, conductor, pianist and composer. Appeared as pianist in Berlin in 1862 and at Hirschberg as singer in 1866. After studying at the Leipzig and Berlin Cons. he appeared at the Lower Rhine Festival in 1874, sang Christus in *St Matthew Passion* under Brahms, 1875, and sang for the 1st time in Eng. in 1877. He remained there until 1881, when he married the Amer. soprano Lillian Bailey and became cond. of the new Boston SO. In 1884 he settled in London and organized var. orchestral and choral concerts, also cond., the Scot. Orch. in 1893–5. His wife died in 1901 and he married Amy Louis in 1907. He sang again, in Eng. and on the Continent, often accompanying himself, until he gave his last recital in London in 1914, when he was knighted.

Works incl. operas *Friedrich der Schöne* and *Nubia* (prod. Dresden, 1899); operetta *A Sea Change*; incid. music for

Shakespeare's *Hamlet*; Eng. Mass for 8 voices, Te Deum, Stabat Mater (1894), Requiem (1901), Psalm cxxx, anthems; Festival March for orch.; Ballade for vln. and orch.; string 4tet in B♭ maj.; many pf. works; numerous songs (some with orch.).

Hensel, Heinrich (b Neustadt, 29 Oct 1874; d Hamburg, 23 Feb 1935), German tenor. He studied in Vienna and Frankfurt and sang at Freiburg 1897–1900. In Karlsruhe he took part in the 1910 fp of Siegfried Wagner's *Banadietriech*; sang Loge under Wagner at Bayreuth 1911–12. Hamburg Opera 1912–29. New York and Chicago 1911–12 as Siegmund, Siegfried and Lohengrin. CG 1914, as the 1st stage Parsifal in Brit.

Henselt, Adolf von (b Schwabach, Bavaria, 9 May 1814; d Warmbrunn, Silesia, 10 Oct 1889), German pianist and composer. Pupil of Hummel at Weimar and Sechter in Vienna. He toured Ger. in 1836 and settled in St Petersburg in 1838. He was app. court pianist and teacher to the Tsar's children.

Works incl. pf. concerto in F min., pf. trio; much pf. solo music, comprising 2 sets of Studies (e.g. *Si oiseau j'étais*), *Frühlingslied*, *Wiegenlied*, impromptu in C min., *La Gondola*.

Henze, Hans Werner (b Gütersloh, 1 Jul 1926), German composer. Studied with Fortner at Heidelberg and Leibowitz in Paris. He is influenced by Schoenberg, though not strictly a 12-note comp., and has also done much to further the ballet in Ger.; in 1950–2 he was ballet adviser to the Wiesbaden Opera. He moved to Italy in 1953, and his music began to show a wider range of influences. From the late 1960s his works reflected current political trends; the opera *We Come to the River* (1976) and the ballet *Orpheus* (1980) were written in collaboration with Edward Bond. In recent years Henze has returned to the musical past: his reconstruction of Monteverdi's *Il Ritorno di Ulisse* was staged at Salzburg in 1985.

STAGE WORKS: *Das Wundertheater*, opera for actors (Heidelberg, 1949; rev. for singers and prod. Frankfurt 1965), *Jack Pudding*, ballet (Wiesbaden, 1951), *Die schlafende Prinzessin*, ballet after Tchaikovsky (Essen, 1954), *Ein Landarzt*, radio opera after Kafka (1951; rev. for stage 1965), *Boulevard Solitude*, opera after Prévost's novel *Manon Lescaut* (Hanover, 1952), *Der Idiot*, ballet after Dostoievsky (Berlin, 1952), *Das Ende einer Welt*, radio opera (1953; rev. for stage 1965), *König Hirsch*, opera after Gozzi (Berlin, 1956; rev. as *Il re Cervo* and prod.

Kassel, 1963), *Maratona*, ballet (Berlin, 1957), *Ondine*, ballet (London, 1958), *Der Prinz von Homburg*, opera after Kleist (Hamburg, 1960), *The Emperor's Nightingale*, pantomime after Andersen (Venice, 1959), *Elegy for Young Lovers*, chamber opera (Schwetzingen and Glyndebourne, 1961), *Der junge Lord*, comic opera (Berlin, 1965), *The Bassarids*, opera seria (Salzburg, 1966), *Moralities*, scenic cantatas after Aesop (Cincinnati, 1968), *La Cubana, oder ein Leben für die Kunst*, vaudeville (prod. Munich, 1975), *We Come to the River*, actions for music (London, 1976), *Don Chisciotte*, opera after Paisiello (Montepulciano, 1976), *Orpheus*, ballet by Edward Bond (Stuttgart, 1979), *Pollicino*, fairy-tale opera (Montepulciano, 1980), *The English Cat*, chamber opera (Schwetzingen, 1983), *Il Ritorno di Ulisse in Patria*, realization of Monteverdi (Salzburg, 1985).

VOCAL MUSIC: *Whispers from Heavenly Death*, cantata after Whitman (1948), *5 Neapolitan Songs* for bar. and orch. (1956), *Nocturnes and Arias* for sop. and orch. (1957), *Novae de Infinito Laudes*, cantata for soloists, chorus and orch., after Giordano Bruno, the early astronomer who was burned at the stake for his beliefs (1962), *Ariosi* for sop., vln. and orch. after Tasso (1963), *Being Beauteous*, cantata after Rimbaud (1963), *Muses of Sicily*, for chorus, 2 pfs., wind and perc. (1966), *Versuch über Schweine* (*Essay on Pigs*, 1969), *Das Floss der Medusa*, oratorio to the memory of Ché Guevara (1968), *El Cimarrón*, for bar. and ens. (1970), *Voices*, for mezzo, tenor and insts. (22 revolutionary texts; 1973), *Jephtha*, realization of Carissimi (1976), *The King of Harlem*, for mezzo and insts. after Lorca (1980), 3 Auden poems, for voice and pf. (1983).

FOR ORCH: 7 symphs. (1947–1984); 2 vln. concertos (1948, 1978), 2 pf. concertos (1950, 1967), *Ode to the West Wind* for cello and orch., after Shelley, *Sonata for Strings* (1958), 3 Dithyrambs for chamber orch. (1958), *Antifone* (1960), *Los Caprichos* (1963), *Doppio Concerto* for oboe, harp and strings (1966), *Telemanniana* (1967), *Heliogabalus Imperator* (1972), *Tristan* for pf., tape and orch. (1973), *Aria de la folia española* (1977), *Il Vitalino raddopiato* for vln. and chamber orch. (1977), *Barcarola* (1979), *Orpheus*, scenes from the ballet (1980), *I sentimenti di C.P.E. Bach* for fl., harp and strings (1982), *Le Miracle de la Rose* for clar. and 13 insts. (1982), guitar concerto (1986).

CHAMBER MUSIC incl. 5 string 4tets (1947–77), *Apollo et Hyazinthus* for mezzo and ens. (1949), Wind 5tet (1952), *Concerto per il Mariۍny* for pf. and 7 insts. (1956), *Royal Winter Music*, 2 sonatas for guitar on Shakesperean characters (1975–9), Sonata for vla. and pf. (1980), *Capriccio* for cello (1983).

Heptachord (from Gk.), a scale of 7 notes.

Herbeck, Johann (Franz) von (b Vienna, 25 Dec 1831; d Vienna, 28 Oct 1877), Austrian conductor and composer. Lived in Vienna; app. cond. of the Gesellschaft concerts in 1859 and director of the Court Opera in 1871.

Works incl. 7 Masses; 4 symphs., symph. variations and other orch. mus.; 3 string 4tets; songs, part-songs.

Herbert, Victor (b Dublin, 1 Feb 1859; d NY, 26 May 1924), Irish-American cellist, conductor and composer. Studied in Germany and toured Europe; settled in NY in 1886. Director of the Pittsburgh SO 1898–1904.

Works incl. operas *Natoma* (1911) and *Madeleine* (1914), operettas *The Wizard of the Nile* (1895), *Babes in Toyland* (1903) and over 30 others; cantata *The Captive*; symph. poem *Hero and Leander* and 3 suites for orch.; Serenade for strings; songs.

Herbig, Günther (b Ustí-nad-Labem, 30 Nov 1931), Czech-born German conductor. He studied in Weimar and was asst. to Scherchen and Karajan. Held posts in Erfurt, Weimar, Potsdam and East Berlin before becoming music dir. Dresden PO 1972. Chief cond. East Berlin SO from 1977; guest cond. Dallas SO 1979–81, and became music dir. Detroit SO in 1984. Guest cond. BBC Philharmonic from 1980. Well-known in Bruckner.

Herbst, Johann Andreas (b Nuremberg, 9 Jun 1588; d Frankfurt 24 Jan 1666), German composer. He was *Kapellmeister* at various places, incl. Darmstadt, Nuremberg and Frankfurt. Pub. 4 theoret. works.

Works incl. German and Latin madrigals; motets; settings of hymn-tunes etc.

Hercules, secular oratorio by Handel (lib. by T. Broughton), prod. London, King's Theatre, Haymarket, 5 Jan 1745.

Herder, Johann Gottfried von (1744–1803), German philosopher, philologist and author. *See* Bach **(J.C.F.)** (*Brutus*, oratorios and cantatas), Jensen (*Stimmen der Völker*), Prometheus (Liszt), Reichardt (*Morning Hymn*).

Herincx, Raimund (b London, 23 Aug 1927), English bass-baritone. Debut WNO 1950, as Mozart's Figaro. London, SW (later ENO) in almost 50 roles from 1953, incl. Nick Shadow, Germont and Wotan (1974–6). In 1968 he sang King Fisher in a new prod. of *The Midsummer Marriage*, at CG, and returned for the fps of *The Knot Garden* (1970) and *Taverner* (1972). US debut in Delius's *A Mass of Life* (NY 1966); US opera debut Boston, 1967. In the seasons 1973–4 he sang Pogner and Fafner at Salzburg, under Karajan.

Hermann, Roland (b Bochum, 17 Sep 1936), German baritone. Debut Trier, 1967, as Mozart's Figaro; member of Zurich opera from 1968 and guest appearances in Munich, Buenos Aires, Paris and Berlin. Among his best roles are Don Giovanni, Amfortas, Wolfram and Germont. He has a wide rep. and has recorded Busoni's *Doktor Faust*, Schumann's *Genoveva*, Marschner's *Vampyr*, Orff's *Prometheus* and Schoenberg's *Moses und Aron*.

Hermann von Salzburg, 14th-century Austrian monk and composer. He belonged to the tradition of the *Minnesinger* but also wrote a few polyphonic pieces and a love song addressed to a lady acquaintance of the Archbishop of Salzburg.

Hermannus Contractus (Hermann the Cripple) (b Sulgen, 18 Jul 1013; d Alleshausen nr. Biberach, 24 Sep 1054), German music scholar and composer. Studied in Switz. at the monastery of Reichenau and became a Benedictine monk. Wrote musical treatises and comp. hymns, sequences, etc.

Hermione, opera by Bruch (lib. by E. Hopffer, based on Shakespeare's *Winter's Tale*), prod. Berlin, Opera, 21 Mar 1872.

Hernried, Robert (b Vienna, 22 Sep 1883; d Detroit, 3 Sep 1951), American scholar and composer of Austrian birth. Studied in Vienna and after a career as opera cond. in 1908–14 he held var. teaching posts and professorships in Ger. and USA, to which he emigrated in 1934. In 1946 he was app. prof. at Detroit Univ. He wrote several books and over 300 articles.

Works incl. operas *Francesca da Rimini* (after Dante) and *The Peasant Woman*; Mass; over 60 choral works; concert overture for orch.; chamber music and songs.

Hero and Leander. *See* Ero e Leandro.

Hero's Life (R. Strauss). *See* Heldenleben.

Hérodiade (*Herodias*), opera by Massenet (lib. by P. Milliet and 'Henri Grémont' = Georges Hartmann, based on a story by Flaubert), prod. Brussels, Théâtre de la Monnaie, 19 Dec 1881.

Herodiade, Orchestral recitation by Hindemith, after Mallarmé; comp. 1944, fp Washington DC, 30 Oct 1944, with the Martha Graham dance group.

Hérold, (Louis Joseph) Ferdinand (b Paris, 28 Jan 1791; d Paris, 19 Jan 1833), French composer. Studied under his father, the pianist François Joseph H. (1755–1802), and later under Fétis, Louis Adam, Catel and Méhul, and took the Prix de Rome in 1812. In Rome and Naples, where he became pianist to Queen Caroline, he comp. several instrumental works, also a comic opera *La Jeunesse de Henri V.* Returning to Paris in 1816, he collaborated with Boieldieu in *Charles de France* and in 1817 began to prod. operas of his own. He was accompanist at the Théâtre Italien from 1820 to 1827, when he married Adèle Élise Rollet and became choirmaster at the Opéra. About this time he began to suffer seriously from tuberculosis, from which he died.

Works incl. operas *Les Rosières* (1817), *La Clochette* (1817), *Le Premier Venu*, *Les Troqueurs* (1819), *L'Amour platonique*, *L'Auteur mort et vivant* (1820), *Le Muletier* (1823), *Lasthénie, Le Lapin blanc, Vendôme en Espagne* (with Auber), *Le Roi René* (1824), *Marie, L'Illusion, Emmeline* (1829), *L'Auberge d'Auray* (with Carafa), *Zampa* (1831), *Le Pré aux Clercs* (1832), *Ludovic* (unfinished, completed by Halévy); ballets *Astolphe et Joconde* (1827), *Le Sonnambule* (1827), *Lydie, La Fille mal gardée, La Belle au bois dormant* (after Perrault); incid. music for Ozaneaux's *Dernier Jour de Missolonghi*; 2 symphs.; 4 pf. concertos; cantata *Mlle. de la Vallière, Hymne sur la Transfiguration*; 3 string 4tets; 2 sonatas, variations, rondos, etc. for pf.

Heroldt, Johannes (b Jena, *c* 1550; d Weimar, buried 8 Sep 1603), German composer. His works incl. a setting of the St Matthew Passion for 6 voices, pub. Graz, 1594.

Herrmann, Bernard (b New York, 29 Jan 1911; d Los Angeles, 24 Dec 1975), American composer and conductor. After winning a comp. prize at the age of 13, he began studying with Phillip James at NY Univ. and later at the Juilliard Graduate School of Music. He then became a radio cond. with CBS, later living in Hollywood where he comp. many film scores, in particular for Hitchcock.

Works incl. opera *Wuthering Heights* (1948–50; prod. Portland, Oreg., 1982), cantatas *Moby Dick, Johnny Appleseed*; symph. poem *City of Brass; Fiddle Concer-* to; symph.; string 4tet; film scores incl. *Citizen Kane, Psycho* and *The Birds*.

Herschel, Friedrich Wilhelm (b Hanover, 15 Nov 1738; d Slough, 25 Aug 1822), English astronomer and musician of German parentage. He played the oboe in the band of the Hanoverian Guards and in 1755 was posted to Durham. For the next 11 years he was active in Newcastle, Halifax and Leeds as an organist, violinist and composer of symphs. He moved to Bath in 1766 and dir. choral concerts. While earning his living as a musician he pursued a private interest in astronomy; his discovery of Uranus in 1781 led to his appointment as Astronomer Royal in 1782. He now cultivated music only as an amateur. After his knighthood in 1817 he became in 1821 the first President of the Royal Astronomical Society. Works incl. 24 symphs. (1760–4), concertos for oboe, organ and vln.; 6 fugues, 24 sonatas and 33 voluntaries for organ.

Hertz, Alfred (b Frankfurt, 15 Jul 1872; d San Francisco, 17 Apr 1942), American conductor of German birth. Conducted opera in Germany, then gave fp of *Parsifal* outside Bayreuth, NY Met 1903; also cond. early US perfs. of Strauss. San Francisco SO 1915–29. Hollywood Bowl from 1922.

Hertzka, Emil (b Budapest, 3 Aug 1869; d Vienna, 9 May 1932), Austrian music publisher of Hungarian birth. Studied chemistry at the Univ. of Vienna, and also music. In 1901 he joined Universal Ed., founded that year, becoming director in 1907 until his death. He did great service to modern music, pub. the work of such comps. as Bartók, Berg, Krenek, Schoenberg, Webern, Weill and others. He also encouraged many other young composers. *See also* **Kalmus.**

Hervé (real name Florimond Ronger) (b Houdain, Pas de Calais, 30 Jun 1825; d Paris, 3 Nov 1892), French composer. Studied music as a choir-boy, then with Elwart and Auber. Organist at var. Paris churches, incl. Saint-Eustache; later theatre manager, operetta singer, librettist, and cond.

Works incl. more than 80 operettas, e.g. *Don Quixote et Sancho Pança* (after Cervantes, 1848), *Le Hussard persécuté, La Fanfare de Saint-Cloud, Les Chevaliers de la Table Ronde* (1866), *L'Œil crevé, Chilpéric, Le Petit Faust, Les Turcs* (parody of Racine's *Bajazet*, 1869), *La Belle Poule, Le Nouvel Aladin, Frivoli* (1886); ballets *Dilara, Sport, La Rose d'Amour, Cléopâtre, Les Bagatelles*; symph. *The Ashanti War* for solo voices and orch. (1874); many light songs.

Herz, Das (*The Heart*), opera by Pfitzner

(lib. by H. Mahner-Mons); comp. 1930–1, prod. Berlin and Munich, 12 Nov 1931. Pfitzner's last opera.

Herz, Henri (Heinrich) (b Vienna, 6 Jan 1803; d Paris, 5 Jan 1888), Austrian pianist and composer. Pupil of his father and of Hünten, entered the Paris Cons. in 1816 and settled there, becoming a fashionable teacher. App. pf. prof. at the Cons, in 1842. Toured USA, Mex. and the W. Indies in 1845–51, making a fortune with which to begin a pf. manufacture, and built a concert hall.

Works incl. 8 pf. concertos and some 200 works for pf. solo: variations, studies, fantasies.

Herz, Joachim (b Dresden, 14 Jun 1924), German producer and administrator. He was assistant to Felsenstein at the Komische Oper, Berlin 1953–6; returned as dir. 1976. Leipzig Opera 1957–76, and has worked as guest in Moscow, Hamburg and London: *Salome* and *Fidelio* with ENO; *Butterfly* with WNO 1979. His work is marked by strong beliefs in politics and in music theatre; *Parsifal* at the London Coliseum (Mar 1986) had mixed reviews.

Herzgewäsche, work by Schoenberg for high sop., celesta, harmonium and harp, op. 20; comp. 1911: Schoenberg's last work before *Pierrot lunaire*. 1st Brit. perf. BBC concert, 1 Dec 1960.

Herzogenberg, Heinrich von (Baron H. Peccaduc) (b Graz, 10 Jun 1843; d Wiesbaden, 9 Oct 1900), Austrian composer and conductor. Studied at the Vienna Cons. and settled at Leipzig in 1872. Cond. the Bach society there in 1875–85 and then became prof. of comp. at the Berlin Hochschule für Musik. Husband of Elisabeth von H. (1842–92), a fine amateur pianist and pupil of Brahms.

Works incl. Mass (1895), Requiem (1891), psalms; oratorios *Die Geburt Christi* and *Die Passion*, cantata *Columbus*; 3 symphs., no. 1 entitled *Odysseus*; 5 string 4tets (1876–90), 2 pf. trios, 2 string trios; 2 vln. and pf. sonatas, cello and pf. sonata; 2 sets of variations for 2 pfs., many pf. pieces and duets; fantasies for organ; songs, vocal duets, part-songs.

Hesch, Wilhelm (b Týnec nad Labem, 3 Jul 1860; d Vienna, 4 Jan 1908), Czech bass. Debut Brno 1880, as Kecal; sang with Prague Nat. Theatre from 1882 and joined the Hamburg Opera in 1894. Vienna, Hofoper, 1896–1908; often sang under Mahler as Beckmesser, Papageno, Leporello and Rocco.

Heseltine, Philip. *See* **Warlock, Peter.**

Hess, Myra (b London, 25 Feb 1890; d London, 25 Nov 1965), English pianist. Studied at the RAM with Matthay, making her debut in 1907 under Beecham in London. Her success was immediate and she toured widely. In 1941 she received the DBE for her work in organizing the Nat. Gallery wartime concerts. She was especially noted for her playing of Mozart, Beethoven and Schumann, and her own Bach transcriptions.

Hess, Willy (b Mannheim, 14 Jul 1859; d Berlin, 17 Feb 1939), German violinist. Studied with his father, a pupil of Spohr, was taken to USA as a child, played in T. Thomas's orch. there and made his 1st appearance as a soloist in Hol. in 1872. Later studied with Joachim in Berlin, became prof. at Rotterdam, leader of the Hallé Orch. at Manchester, and worked by turns at Cologne, London, Boston and Berlin.

Hessenberg, Kurt (b Frankfurt, 17 Aug 1908), German composer. Studied with Günther Raphael at Leipzig and then taught comp. there. In 1933 he became prof. of comp. at the Hoch Cons. at Frankfurt.

Works incl. incid. music for Shakespeare's *Tempest*; cantata (Matthias Claudius) and other choral works; 3 symphs. (1935–54), *Concerto grosso*, etc. for orch.; harpsichord and pf. concertos; 5 string 4tets, pf. 4tet; 2 vln. sonatas, cello sonata; pf. music, songs, etc. His *Concerto Grosso* and 2nd symph. were premièred by Furtwängler.

Heterophony (from Gk. = other sound), the use of two parts to be simultaneously perf. in different versions, one more elaborate than the other.

Heuberger, Richard (Franz Josef) (b Graz, 18 Jun 1850; d Vienna, 28 Oct 1914), Austrian music critic and composer. Studied engineering at first, but at the age of 26 devoted himself to music, becoming a chor. cond. in 1878 and a critic in 1881.

Works incl. operas *Abenteuer einer Neujahrsnacht* (1896), *Manuel Venegas* (1889), *Miriam* (later *Das Maifest* 1894), *Barfüssele*; operettas *Der Opernball* (1898), *Ihre Excellenz*, *Der Sechsuhrzug*, *Das Baby*, *Der Fürst von Düsterstein*, *Don Quixotte* (after Cervantes); ballets *Die Lautenschlägerin* and *Struwwelpeter*.

Heugel, Johannes (Heigel, Hegel, etc.), (b Degendorf, before 1500; d Kassel, *c* 1585), German composer. He wrote numerous Latin motets.

Heure espagnole, L' (*The Spanish Hour*), opera by Ravel (lib. by Franc-Nohain, based on his own comedy), prod. Paris, Opéra-Comique, 19 May 1911.

Heward, Leslie (Hays) (b Liversedge, Yorks, 8 Dec 1897; d Birmingham, 3 May 1943), English conductor. In 1924 he went to Cape Town as music director to the S. African Broadcasting Corporation and cond. of the Cape Town Orch., but returned to Eng. in 1927 and rejoined the BNOC. In 1930 he succeeded Boult as cond. of the CBSO and gave frequent perfs. of Dvořák and Sibelius. He also comp.

Hexachord (from Gk. = six strings), a scale of 6 notes, which Guido d'Arezzo in the 11th cent. named Ut, Re, Mi, Fa, Sol, La. There were 3 hexachords, beginning respectively on G, C and F, and the same names were used for the notes of each. Since the hexachords overlapped, every note after the first three could have 2 or more names:

Hexachordum durum:

Hexachordum naturale:

Hexachordum molle:

The G hexachord was called hard (*durum*), the C natural (*naturale*) and the F soft (*molle*). (*Durum* and *molle* are the origins of the Ger. words for major and minor.) *See* **Solmization.**

Hexachord Fantasy, a type of comp. cultivated part. by 16th–17th-cent. Eng. comps., a piece based on the 1st 6 notes of the scale, ascending or descending. The pieces were often entitled 'Ut, re, mi, fa, sol, la'.

Hexameron, a collective pf. work, pub. in 1837, consisting of bravura variations on the march in Bellini's *Puritani* by Liszt, Thalberg, Pixis, Herz, Czerny and Chopin, with an intro., finale and connecting passages by Liszt.

Hey, an old country dance similar to the Reel and prob. to the Canarie.

Heyden, Sebald (b Bruck, near Erlangen, 8 Dec 1499; d Nuremberg, 9 Jul 1561), German theologian and music theorist. He is particularly valuable for his explanations of the musical notation of his time.

Heyns, Cornelius, Flemish 15th-century composer. He was succentor at St Donatian in Bruges in 1452–3 and 1462–5. His Mass

Pour quelque paine has also been attrib. to Ockeghem.

Heyse, Paul (Johann Ludwig) (1830–1914), German poet and novelist. *See* **Italienisches Liederbuch** (H. Wolf), **Jensen** (*Spanisches Liederbuch*). **Spanisches Liederbuch** (H. Wolf).

Heyther (Heather), William (b Harmondsworth, *c* 1563; d Jul 1627), English singer, from 1586 to 1615 at Westminster Abbey and from 1615 in the Chapel Royal. He founded the chair of music at Oxford Univ. in Feb 1627 and presented the Music School with instruments and music.

Heywood, John (b ? London, 1497; d ? Mechlin, 1587), English musician. He was 'player of the virginals' to Henry VIII, succentor of St Paul's Cathedral and a friend of Thomas Mulliner. He was also a playwright and may have collaborated with Redford in the prod. of music plays. After the death of Mary in 1558 he fled to Mechlin on account of his Catholicism.

Hiawatha, 3 cantatas for solo voices, chorus and orch. by Coleridge-Taylor, a setting of parts of Longfellow's poem: 1. *Hiawatha's Wedding Feast*, 2. *The Death of Minnehaha*, 3. *Hiawatha's Departure*, fp as a whole, London, 22 Mar 1900.

Hickox, Richard (b Stokenchurch, Bucks., 5 Mar 1948), English conductor. He was an organ scholar at Cambridge and studied at the RCM; founded the R.H. Singers, giving concerts with a wide range of rep. He has worked with the City of London Sinfonia and the Northern Sinfonia (Newcastle). In 1983 became asst. conductor of the San Diego SO and asst. to Abbado at the LSO.

Hidalgo, Elvira de (b Aragón, 27 Dec 1892; d Milan, 21 Jan 1980), Spanish soprano. Debut Naples 1908, NY Met 1910, as Rosina; sang Gilda there and at CG in 1924. Taught in Athens from 1932; Maria Callas was among her pupils.

Hidalgo, Juan (d Madrid, 30 Mar 1685), Spanish composer. Harpist in the royal chapel at Madrid. Said to have invented an instrument called the *claviharpa*.

Works incl. operas *Celos aun del aire matan* (lib. by Calderón, 1660), and *Los celos hacen estrellas* (lib. by Guevara); incid. music to var. plays by Calderón incl. *Ni Amor se libra de Amor.*

Hidden Fifths }
Hidden Octaves } the movement of 2 parts in the same direction to a 5th or an 8ve. In many contrapuntal styles this is to be avoided, especially when involving the top or bottom line. Textbooks in formal

counterpoint gave them this title as having an effect similar to that of consecutives (*q.v.*).

Highland Fling, a Scottish dance-step, rather than a dance itself, although that is often so called. The music is that of the Strathspey and the step is a kick of the leg backwards and forwards.

Hignard, (Jean Louis) Aristide (b Nantes, 20 May 1822; d Vernon, 20 Mar 1898), French composer. Pupil of Halévy at the Paris Cons., where he gained the 2nd Prix de Rome in 1850.

Works incl. operas *Hamlet* (after Shakespeare; comp. 1868 but not prod. until 1888, owing to success of Thomas' *Hamlet*), *Le Colin-Maillard*, *Les Compagnons de la Marjolaine* and *L'Auberge des Ardennes* (all on libs. by Jules Verne and Michael Carrol) and 8 others; choruses; *Valses concertantes* and *Valses romantiques* for pf. duet; songs.

Hildegard, Saint (b Böckelheim, 1098; d Rupertsberg, nr. Bingen, 17 Sep 1179), German abbess and musician. Educ. at the Benedictine nunnery of Disisbodenberg, where she became abbess in 1136. She wrote monophonic music for the church which shows some departures from traditional plainsong style.

Hill, Alfred (b Melbourne, 16 Nov 1870; d Sydney, 30 Oct 1960), Australian composer, conductor and teacher. His early career was in Leipzig; moved to New Zealand 1902 and became influenced by Maori music. Prof., NSW Cons 1915–35.

Works incl. 8 operas, e.g. *Tapu* (1903), *A Moorish Maid* (1905), *Giovanni, the Sculptor* (1914); 10 symphs. (1896–1958); 17 string 4tets, 6 sonatas for vln. and pf.

Hill, Joseph (b 1715; d London, 1784), English vln. maker. He worked in London. The house of his descendants W.E. Hill and Sons is now in Gt Missenden.

Hillebrecht, Hildegard (b Hanover, 26 Nov 1927), German soprano. Debut Freiburg 1951, as the *Trovatore* Leonora; she sang in Berlin from 1954 and in 1968 took part in the fp of Dallapiccola's *Ulisse* there. Munich from 1961 and Zurich from 1972, as the Marschallin, Ariadne and Leonore. CG 1967 as the Empress. Other roles incl. Tosca, Donna Anna and the Duchess of Parma in *Doktor Faust*.

Hillemacher, Paul (Joseph Wilhelm) (b Paris, 29 Nov 1852; d Versailles, 13 Aug 1933) and **Lucien (Joseph Édouard)** (b Paris, 10 Jun 1860; d Paris, 2 Jun 1909), French composers, brothers who wrote all their works in collaboration. Studied at the Paris Cons., where Paul gained the Prix de Rome in 1876 and Lucien in 1880.

Works incl. operas *Saint-Mégrin* (1886), *La Légende de Sainte Geneviève*, *Une Aventure d'Arlequin* (1888), *Le Régiment qui passe* (1894), *Le Drac*, *Orsola*, *Circé* (1907); mimed dramas *One for Two* and *Fra Angelico*; incid. music for Haraucourt's *Héro et Léandre* and for George Sand's *Claudie*; symph. legend *Loreley* and other orchestral works; chamber music, songs, part-songs.

Hiller, Ferdinand (b Frankfurt, 24 Oct 1811; d Cologne, 11 May 1885), German pianist, conductor and composer. Was taught music privately as a child and appeared as pianist at the age of 10. In 1825 he went to Weimar to study under Hummel. After a brief return to Frankfurt he lived in Paris from 1828 to 1835, where he taught and gave concerts. He prod. his 1st opera at Milan in 1839 and his 1st oratorio at Leipzig in 1840, then studied with Baini in Rome, lived at Frankfurt, Leipzig and Dresden, became cond. at Düsseldorf in 1847 and at Cologne in 1850, where he remained and founded the Cons.

Works incl. operas *Romilda* (1839), *Die Katakomben* (1862), *Der Deserteur* (1865); oratorios *Die Zerstörung Jerusalems* (1840) and *Saul*; cantatas *Nala und Damajanti*, *Prometheus*, *Rebecca* and others, incl. one from Byron's *Hebrew Melodies*; 4 symphs., 4 overtures (e.g. to Schiller's *Demetrius*) and other orchestral works; 2 pf. concertos (1835, 1861), vln. concerto (1875); 3 string 4tets, 3 pf. 4tets, 5 pf. trios; vln. and cello sonata; sonata, 24 studies, *Modern Suite* and many other works for pf.; songs, part-songs.

Hiller, Johann Adam (b Wendisch-Ossig nr. Görlitz, 25 Dec 1728; d Leipzig, 16 Jun 1804), German composer. Chorister under Homilius in Dresden, studied law at Leipzig Univ. After a short period in the service of Count Brühl, he returned to Leipzig, working as flautist, singer, conductor, etc. In 1763 he estab. subscription concerts on the model of the Paris Concert Spirituel, these becoming the Gewandhaus concerts in 1781. He also prod. a musical weekly (*Wöchentliche Nachrichten*, 1766–70) and was one of the originators of the Ger. *Singspiel*, of which he prod. many successful examples, 1766–82. Left Leipzig in 1785, but after some short-term posts returned to succeed Doles as municipal music dir. and Cantor of St Thomas's.

Works incl. *Singspiele: Der Teufel ist los* (after Coffey's *The Devil to Pay*, 1766), *Lisuart und Dariolette, Lottchen am Hofe* (1767), *Die Muse, Die Liebe auf dem Lande* (1768), *Die Jagd, Der Dorfbalbier* (1771), *Der Aerndtekranz, Der Krieg* (1772), *Die Jubelhochzeit, Das Grab des Mufti, Das gerettete Troja*; settings of Gellert's odes and other choral works; cantatas; 100th Psalm; instrumental music; also many theoret. and critical writings on music.

Hilton, John (d Cambridge, Mar 1608), English organist and composer. App. organist to Trinity Coll., Cambridge, in 1594. Comp. anthems, madrigals, etc.

Hilton, John (b ? Oxford, 1599; d Westminster, buried 21 Mar 1657), English organist and composer, (?) son of prec. Took the Mus.B. degree at Cambridge in 1626 and 2 years later became organist at St Margaret's Church, Westminster.

Works incl. services and anthems; madrigals, *Ayres, or Fa La's* for 3 voices (pub. 1627; the last Eng. madrigal publication); Elegy on the death of Wm. Lawes for 3 voices and bass; collection of catches, rounds and canons *Catch that catch can* (1652); songs, fantasies for viols, hymn 'Wilt Thou forgive that sin where I begun' from Donne's *Divine Poems*.

Himmel, Friedrich Heinrich (b Truenbrietzen, Brandenburg, 20 Nov 1765; d Berlin 8 Jun 1814), German harpsichordist, pianist and composer. Read theology at Halle Univ., but later under the patronage of Frederick William II of Prussia studied music at Dresden under Naumann and in Italy, where he prod. 2 operas. App. court *Kapellmeister* in Berlin in 1795, he was still able to travel and visited Rus., Scand., Paris, London and Vienna.

Works incl. operas *Il primo navigatore* (1794), *La morte di Semiramide* (1795), *Alessandro* (1799), *Vasco da Gama* (1801), *Frohsinn und Schwärmerei, Fauchon das Leyermädchen* (1804), *Die Sylphen, Der Kobold* (1813), oratorio *Isacco*; funeral cantata for the King of Prussia; Masses, Te Deum, motets, psalms and other church music; instrumental music, songs.

Hin und Zurück (*There and Back*) opera in 1 act by Hindemith (lib. by M. Schiffer after an Eng. revue sketch), prod. Baden-Baden, 17 Jul 1927. The plot, concerning a jealous husband, goes into reverse at half way. At the fp the part of the errant, palindromic wife was sung by Otto Klemperer's wife, Joanna.

Hindemith, Paul (b Hanau, 16 Nov 1895; d Frankfurt, 28 Dec 1963), German composer. He was taught the vln. as a child and entered the Hoch Cons. at Frankfurt, where he studied under Arnold Mendelssohn and Sekles. Later he played in the Frankfurt Opera orch. and was leader there in 1915–23; and in 1921 he founded a string 4tet with the Turkish violinist Licco Amar (Amar-Hindemith 4tet) in which he played vla. Works of his were heard at the Donaueschingen festival in 1921 and at the ISCM festival at Salzburg in 1922, and from that time he became known abroad. From 1927 he taught comp. at the Berlin Hochschule für Musik, and his music was conducted by Furtwängler and Klemperer, but the Nazis proscribed his works as degenerate art (see **Neues vom Tage**). His opera *Mathis der Maler* was therefore prod. in Switz., at Zurich, in 1938. For some years after 1933 he was at Ankara in an official capacity to reorganize Turkish music educ. In 1939 he emigrated to USA, where he taught at Yale Univ., but in 1946 he returned to Europe and was active for several years as a cond.

Works incl. OPERAS: *Mörder, Hoffnung der Frauen* (Kokoschka, 1921), *Das Nusch-Nuschi* (for Marionettes), *Sancta Susanna* (1922), *Cardillac* (after E.T.A. Hoffmann, 1926), *Hin und Zurück* (1927), *Neues vom Tage* (1929), *Mathis der Maler* (1938), *Harmonie der Welt* (1957), *The Long Christmas Dinner* (1961); ballets *Der Dämon* (1923), *Nobilissima Visione* (1938), *Cupid and Psyche, Hérodiade* (after Mallarmé, 1944); incid. music for Christmas play on Immermann's *Tuttifänchen* (1922); *Wir bauen eine Stadt* (Let's build a town), children's opera (1930); realization of Monteverdi's *Orfeo* (1943).

ORCH: *Lustige Sinfonietta* (1916), *Kammermusik* nos. 1–7 (1922–7; see separate entry), *Concerto for Orchestra* (1925), *Konzertmusik* nos. 1–3, with vla., with pf., brass and 2 harps, with brass and strings (1930), *Konzertstück* for trautonium and strings (1931), *Philharmonisches Konzert* (1932), *Mathis der Maler*, symph. from the opera (1934), *Der Schwanendreher*, concerto after folk songs, for vla. and small orch. (1935), *Trauermusik* for vla. and strings (1936), *Symphonische Tänze* (1937), *Nobilissima Visione*, suite from the ballet (1938), vln. concerto (1939), cello concerto (1940), Symphony in E♭ (1940), *Theme and Variations 'The Four Temperaments'* for pf. and strings (1940), *Cupid and Psyche*, ballet overture (1943), *Symphonic Metamorphosis on Themes of Carl Maria von Weber*

(1943), pf. concerto (1943), *Symphonia Serena* (1946), clar. concerto (1947), horn concerto (1949), Sinfonietta, in E (1950), Symphony in Bb for concert band (1951), *Die Harmonie der Welt*, symph. from the opera (1951), *Pittsburgh Symphony* (1958), organ concerto (1962).

CHAMBER AND KEYBOARD: 6 string 4tets; 2 string trios (1924, 1933); 16 sonatas for var. insts.; some pieces for solo insts. and pf.; 3 sonatas, *1922 Suite, Ludus tonalis*: 12 fugues with prelude and postlude, and some other works for pf.; 7 waltzes for pf. duet (unpub.); sonata for 2 pfs.; 3 organ sonatas. *See also* Gebrauchsmusik.

CHORAL AND SOLO VOCAL: *Die junge Magd*, 6 songs for mezzo, fl., clar. and string 4tet (texts by Trakl, 1922), *Das Marienleben*, 15 songs for sop. and pf. (texts by Rilke, 1922–3; rev. 1948; vers. with orch. 1938 and 1948), *Die Serenaden*, cantata for sop., oboe, vla. and cello (1924), *Lehrstück*, cantata to texts by Brecht for soloists, chorus and orch. (1929), *Das Unaufhörliche* (The Unending), oratorio for soloists, chorus and orch. (1931), Requiem, after Walt Whitman, *When Lilacs Last in the Dooryard Bloom'd* (1946), *Ite, angeli veloces* (Go, flights of angels), cantata to texts by Paul Claudel in 3 parts: *Triumphgesang Davids, Custos, quid de nocte* and *Cantique de l'esperance* (1953), *Mainzer Umzung* for soloists, chorus and orch. (1962), Mass for unaccompanied chorus (1963); many other works for chorus, incl. canons, chansons, motets and madrigals; Lieder and *Nine English Songs* (1942–4; texts by Moore, Thompson, Shelley, Blake, Whitman and Herrick).

Hines, Jerome (b Hollywood, 8 Nov 1921), American bass and composer. Debut 1941 San Francisco, in *Tannhäuser*. Méphistophélès in New Orleans 1944; Boris Godunov at the NY Met 1954 and sang the role at the Bolshoy, Moscow, 1962. Bayreuth 1958–60 as Gurnemanz, King Marke and the *Walküre* Wotan. Other roles incl. Sarastro, Don Giovanni, Nick Shadow (Edinburgh, 1953), and Rossini's Basilio. Pub. autobiog. 1968 and *Great Singers on Great Singing* 1983. His own opera, *I am the Way*, is based on the life of Christ.

Hingston, John (b ? York, *c* 1610; d London, buried 17 Dec 1688), English organist, violinist and composer. Pupil of O. Gibbons. Musician to Charles I and later to Cromwell, in whose household he was organist at Hampton Court and played on the organ removed from Magdalen Coll., Oxford. He

taught Cromwell's daughters. At the Restoration in 1660 he became violinist in the royal band and keeper of the organs at court, in which he was succeeded by Purcell.

Hippolyte et Aricie (*Hippolytus and Aricia*). *See also* **Ippolito ed Aricia.**
Opera by Rameau (lib. by S.J. de Pellegrin), prod. Paris, Opéra, 1 Oct 1733.

Hirt auf dem Felsen, Der (*The Shepherd on the Rock*), song by Schubert D965, for pf. and sop. with clar. obbligato (text by W. Muller and ? H. von Chezy); commissioned by Anna Milder-Hauptmann (1785–1838), the first Leonore in *Fidelio* (1805). With *Die Taubenpost*, Schubert's last work; comp. Oct 1828.

Hislop, Joseph (b Edinburgh, 5 Apr 1884; d Upper Largo, Fife, 6 May 1977), Scottish tenor. Debut Stockholm, 1916, as Faust; repeated the role at CG opposite Shalyapin, and sang there 1920–8 in operas by Verdi and Puccini. US debut Chicago, 1921; Milan, La Scala, 1923 as Edgardo. He sang in Stockholm until 1937 and was well-known as Roméo and Des Grieux. Birgit Nilsson and Jussi Björling were among his Stockholm pupils, and he taught in London from 1948 (GSM, SW and CG).

Histoire du soldat (*The Soldier's Tale*), action for a narrator, actors and dancers by Stravinsky (lib. by C.F. Ramuz), prod. Lausanne, 28 Sep 1918, cond. Ansermet.

Histoires Naturelles, song cycle by Ravel for voice and pf.; comp. 1906, fp Paris, 19 Mar 1907. The 5 animals depicted are *The Peacock, The Cricket, The Swan, The Kingfisher* and *The Guinea-fowl.*

Hoboken, Anthony van (b Rotterdam, 23 Mar 1887; d Zurich, 1 Nov 1983), Dutch musicologist. He studied in Frankfurt and Vienna and in 1927 founded a MS. archive in the Nat. Library in Vienna; an almost complete thematic catalogue of Haydn's works was pub. 1957, 1971. Haydn's works are commonly designated 'Hob.' with roman numeral denoting group classification (e.g. opera, symph. etc.) followed by Arabic numeral for work within group.

Hobrecht, Jacob. *See* **Obrecht.**

Hochzeit des Camacho, Die (*Camacho's Wedding*), opera by Mendelssohn (lib. by C.A.L. von Lichtenstein, based on Cervantes' *Don Quixote*), prod. Berlin, Schauspielhaus, 29 Apr 1827.

Hocket, a word similar to 'hiccup' and derived from the Fr. equiv. *hoquet*. It is used for a devise in medieval vocal and instrumental music, consisting of phrases when broken up by rests, in such a way that when one part is silent another fills the gap. Also a piece written in this style.

Hoddinott, Alun (b Bargoed, Glam., 11 Aug 1929), Welsh composer. He studied at the Univ. Coll. of S. Wales, Cardiff, where he was app. Prof. of Music in 1968.

Works incl. operas *The Beach of Falseá* (1974), *Murder, the Magician* (1976), *The Rajah's Diamond* (1979), *The Trumpet Major*, after Hardy (1981); 6 symphs. (1954–73), Sinfonietta, *Variants*, *Night Music* for orch., 2 clar. concertos (1954, 1986), ob. concerto, 3 pf. concertos, org. concerto; choral music; clar. 4tet. string 4tet (1966), string trio; 6 pf. sonatas.

Hoengen, Elisabeth (b Gevelsberg, 7 Dec 1906), German mezzo. Debut Wuppertal 1933; sang in Düsseldorf and Dresden and, from 1943, Vienna. Roles there incl. the Nurse in *Die Frau ohne Schatten*. London, CG, 1947 with Vienna Co. as Dorabella and Marcellina. Salzburg 1948–59 in operas by Strauss, Britten and Erbse. NY Met debut June 1952 as Herodias.

Hoesslin, Franz von (b Munich, 31 Dec 1885; d off Site, 28 Sep 1946), German conductor and composer. Pupil of Mottl for cond. and Reger for comp. After engagements at var. theatres in Ger. and Switz. he became cond. at the Volksoper in Berlin from 1922 to 1923, later cond. at Dessau and Breslau and for 6 years at Bayreuth (1927–40: *Parsifal* and *The Ring*). He was killed in a plane crash.

Works incl. orch. and choral music; chamber music; songs.

Høffding, (Nils) Finn (b Copenhagen, 10 Mar 1899), Danish composer. Pupil of Jeppesen in Copenhagen and J. Marx in Vienna. App. prof. at the Royal Dan. Cons. in 1931, where he started the Copenhagen Folk Music School with Jørgen Bentzon. Author of several theoret. books.

Works incl. operas *The Emperor's New Clothes* (after Andersen, 1928), etc.; 4 symphs. (1 with chorus); 2 string 4tets (1920, 1925), duet for ob. and clar.; pf. pieces; songs.

Höffer, Paul (b Barmen, 21 Dec 1895; d Berlin, 31 Aug 1949), German composer. He was trained as a pianist in the 1st place, at Cologne, and later studied comp. with Schreker in Berlin, where he became prof. of pf. at the Hochschule für Musik in 1923 and prof. of comp. in 1930. He was app. director in 1948, but died of a heart attack.

Works incl. operas *Borgia* (1931) and *Der falsche Waldemar* (1934), 3 children's operas; incid. music for Shakespeare's *Coriola-*

nus, Goethe's *Faust*, etc.; 4 oratorios incl. *Der reiche Tag* (1938) and *Von edlen Leben* (1941) and other choral works; symph., 2 serenades, etc. for orch.; various concertos; 3 string 4tets, clar. 5tet, wind 6tet.

Hoffman, Grace (b Cleveland, 14 Jan 1925), American mezzo. She studied in NY and Milan; small roles in US and Europe from 1951. Stuttgart and La Scala, Milan, from 1955. Bayreuth 1957–70 as Brangaene, Waltraute and Fricka. NY Met debut 1958. London, CG, 1959–71; debut as Eboli. Prof. of voice Stuttgart Hochschule from 1978.

Hoffmann, (E)rnst (T)heodor (A)madeus (orig. Wilhelm) (b Könisberg, 24 Jan 1776; d Berlin, 25 Jun 1822), German novelist, composer and writer on music. He changed his 3rd name to Amadeus in homage to Mozart. He is the hero of Offenbach's *Tales of Hoffmann*.

Comps incl. operas (mostly lost) *Der Renegat* (1803), *Faustine* (1804), *Die lustigen Musikanten* (Brentano, 1805), *Der Kanonikus von Mailand, Liebe und Eifersucht* (after Calderón, 1807), *Der Trank der Unsterblichkeit* (1808), *Das Gespenst* (1809), *Aurora, Undine* (after Fouqué, 1816; vocal score ed. by Pfitzner, 1907), *Julius Sabinus* (unfinished); ballet *Harlekin* (unfinished); incid. music to Goethe's *Scherz, List und Rache* and other plays; 2 Masses; symph.

For musical works based on his writings *see* **Braunfels** (*Prinzessin Brambilla*), **Brautwahl** (Busoni), **Cardillac** (Hindemith), **Contes d'Hoffmann** (Offenbach), **Delibes** (*Coppélia*), **Kreisleriana** (Schumann), **Malipiero, G.** (*Capricci di Callot*), **Nutcracker** (Tchaikovsky), **Offenbach** (*Goldsmith of Toledo*).

Hoffmann, Karel (b Smichov, Prague, 12 Dec 1872; d Prague, 30 Mar 1936), Czech violinist. Studied at the Prague Cons. and founded the Bohemian 4tet with Suk, Nedbal and Berger in 1892. App. vln. prof. at the Cons. in 1922.

Hoffmeister, Franz Anton (b Rothenburg am Neckar, 12 May 1754; d Vienna, 9 Feb 1812), Austrian publisher and composer. He started in Vienna as a law student but in 1783 est. his pub. firm; Beethoven and Mozart (see below) incl. in clients. With Kühnel in Leipzig he est. a bureau which became the pub. house C.F. Peters. The best known of his 9 operas was *Der Königssohn aus Ithaka* (Vienna, 1803); also wrote 66 symphs., about 60 concertos, incl. 25 for flute; 42 string 4tets and 18 string trios.

Whether by accident or design, many of his works were ascribed to Haydn.

Hoffmeister Quartet, string 4tet no. 20, in D maj., by Mozart (K499); comp. 1786 and pub. by F.A. Hoffmeister (see above).

Hofhaimer (Hoffheimer), Paul (b Radstadt, 25 Jan 1459; d Salzburg, 1537), Austrian organist and composer. In the service of the Emperor Maximilian at Innsbruck, 1480–1519, and was organist to the Archbishop of Salzburg from 1522 to his death. Works incl. setting of odes by Horace *Harmoniae poeticae* for 4 voices, Ger. songs for 3 and 4 voices, org. music.

Hofmann, Heinrich (Karl Johann) (b Berlin, 13 Jan 1842; d Gross-Tabarz, Thur., 16 Jul 1902), German pianist and composer. Was a chorister at the cathedral in Berlin and studied at Kullak's acad. He taught the pf. and played much in public. Works incl. operas *Cartouche* (1869), *Der Matador, Armin* (1872), *Aennchen von Tharau* (1878), *Wilhelm von Oranien* (1882), *Donna Diana* (Moreto, 1886), *Hungarian Suite, Fritdjof* symph. (after Tegnér), suite *Im Schlosshof*, scherzo *Irrlichter und Kobolde*, etc. for orch.; cantatas *Die schöne Melusine* (1876), *Aschenbrödel* (1881), *Editha, Prometheus* (1892), *Waldfräulein, Festgesang*; several works for voices and orch.; cello concerto; pf. 4tet, pf. trio, string 6tet, octet; pf. pieces; songs, duets.

Hofmann, Josof (Casimir) (b Kraków, 20 Jan 1876; d Los Angeles, 16 Feb 1957), Polish-American pianist and composer. Studied early with his elder sister and his father, the pianist and cond. Casimir H., and made his 1st public appearance at the age of 6. At 19 he toured Europe and in 1887 paid his 1st visit to USA where, after further study with Anton Rubinstein, and success in Europe, he settled in 1898 and became naturalized in 1926. His works appeared for a time under the pseud. of Michel Dvorsky. Works incl. symph. in E maj., symph. narrative *The Haunted Castle*; 5 pf. concertos and *Chromaticon*, for pf. and orch.; numerous pf. works.

Hofmann, Leopold (b Vienna, 14 Aug 1738; d Vienna, 17 Mar 1793), Austrian composer. *Kapellmeister* at St Stephen's Cathedral in Vienna from 1772. He belongs to the Viennese school of symphonists. Works incl. church music, symphs., concertos.

Hofmann, Ludwig (b Frankfurt, 14 Jan 1895; d Frankfurt, 28 Dec 1963), German bass-baritone. Debut Bamberg 1918. Bayreuth 1928–42 as Gurnemanz, Marke,

Hunding, Hagen and Daland. Berlin 1918–35; Vienna 1935–55. Salzburg Festival as Osmin, Mozart's Figaro and Marke. CG and NY Met 1923–9 in It. and Fr. rep.

Hofmann, Peter (b Marienbad, 12 Aug 1944), German tenor. He studied in Karlsruhe; debut Lübeck 1972 as Tamino. In 1976 sang Siegmund in Bayreuth and London, CG, prods. of *The Ring*. US debut San Francisco 1977, Siegmund; NY Met 1980, Lohengrin. Has sung Parsifal at CG and Salzburg. Other roles incl. Max, Tristan, Florestan and Bacchus.

Hofmannsthal, Hugo von (b Vienna, 1 Feb 1874; d Rodaun, 15 Jul 1929), Austrian poet and dramatist. See **Ägyptische Helena** (R. Strauss), **Alkestis** (Wellesz), **Arabella** (R. Strauss), **Ariadne auf Naxos** (do.), **Bourgeois gentilhomme** (do.), **Elektra** (do.), **Everyman** (Sibelius), **Frau ohne Schatten** (R. Strauss), **Josephslegende** (do.), **Martin (F.)** (*Jedermann*), **Oedipus und die Sphinx** (Varèse), **Reuss** (*Tor und der Tod*), **Rosenkavalier** (R. Strauss), **Tcherepnin (A.)** (*Hochzeit der Sobeide*), **Unger (H.)** (*Tor und der Tod*), **Wagner-Régeny** (*Bergwerk zu Falun*), **Wellesz** (*Alkestis, Lied der Welt* and *Leben, Traum und Tod*), **Zemlinsky** (*Das gläserne Herz*).

Hogwood, Christopher (b Nottingham, 10 Sep 1941), English harpsichordist, musicologist and conductor. He studied at Cambridge and in Prague. Co-founder 1967 with David Munrow of Early Music Consort. Played with Academy of St Martin-in-the-Fields and in 1973 founded Academy of Ancient Music; 'authentic' perfs. with original insts., incl. complete recording of Mozart's symphs. Toured US 1974; from 1979 prof.-in-residence Sydney Univ. Has ed. works by Purcell, J.C. Bach and Croft and pub. a book on Handel for the tercentenary year.

Hoiby, Lee (b Madison, Wis., 17 Feb 1926), American composer. He studied at the Curtis Inst. and in Rome and Salzburg. Best known for his operas, influenced by Menotti: *The Scarf* (after Chekhov, prod. Spoleto 1958), *Beatrice* (after Maeterlinck, 1959), *Natalia Petrovna* (after Turgenev, 1964), *Summer and Smoke* (after Tennessee Williams, 1971); also incid. music to Webster's *The Duchess of Malfi* (1957).

Holborne, Anthony (b ? London; d ? 29 Nov 1602), English musician and composer in the service of Queen Elizabeth I. He pub. a vol. of music for strings or wind in 1599 and in 1597 *The Cittharn Schoole*, which incl. 3-part songs by his brother William.

Holbrooke, Joseph (or Josef) (b Croydon, Surrey, 5 Jul 1878; d London, 5 Aug 1958), English composer. Studied at the RAM. After a hard struggle as pianist and cond. he came under the patronage of Lord Howard de Walden, who wrote the libs. for his dramatic trilogy. He engaged in much militant propaganda on behalf of some British composers.

Works incl. operas *Pierrot and Pierrette* (1909; rev. 1924 as *The Stranger*), *The Snob*, *The Wizard*, and the trilogy *The Cauldron of Annwen* (*The Children of Don*, *Dylan* and *Bronwen*); ballets *The Red Mask* (after Poe), *The Moth and the Flame*, *Coromanthe*, etc.; *Dramatic Choral Symph.* and *The Bells* for chorus and orch. (both after Poe, 1903); symph. poems *The Raven*, *Ulalume* and *The Masque of the Red Death* (all after Poe); vln. concerto (1917); 6 string 4tets (incl. *Pickwick Club* after Dickens), 3 trios, 4 4tets, 5 5tets, 4 6tets for various instruments, sinfonietta for chamber orch. and other chamber music; pf. pieces; songs.

Hölderlin, Johann Christian Friedrich (1770–1843), German poet. See **Apostel** (songs), **Britten** (*Hölderlin Fragmente*), **Schicksalslied** (Brahms), **Strauss (R.)** (3 hymns).

Hole, William (d 15 Sep 1624) and **Robert** English music engravers and publishers. William H. produced *Parthenia* for keyboard, the first music ever engraved on copper plates in England, in 1612 or 1613, and Robert H. produced its successor, *Parthenia In-violata*, in 1614.

Hollander, Benno (Benoit) (b Amsterdam, 8 Jun 1853; d London, 27 Dec 1942), Dutch (anglicized) violinist and composer. Studied at the Paris Cons. with Massart, later comp. with Saint-Saëns. After a tour in Europe he settled in London in 1876. He played vla. in Auer's 4tet and led several important orchs., later formed one of his own.

Works incl. opera *Mietje*; symph. *Roland*, symph. poem *Pompeii*, orchestral pieces *Drame* and *Comédie*; 2 concertos and *Pastoral Fantasy* for vln. and orch.; 2 string 4tets, 7tet for pf., strings and horns, pf. trio, string trio; 2 vln. and pf. sonatas; pf. sonata.

Hollander, Christian Janszon (b Dordrecht, c 1510; d Innsbruck, 1568 or 1569), Flemish singer and composer. App. choirmaster at St Walburg's Church at Oudenarde in 1549 and from 1559 was a singer in the Imp. Chapel in Vienna. Innsbruck from 1564.

Works incl. many motets, sacred songs for several voices, secular Ger. songs.

Holländer, Gustav (b Leobschütz, Silesia, 15 Feb 1855; d Berlin, 4 Dec 1915), German violinist, teacher and composer. Studied with David at Leipzig and Joachim in Berlin and became 4tet player, orch. leader and prof. of vln. at Cologne and Berlin. Director of the Stern Cons. in Berlin from 1895.

Works incl. 4 vln. concertos, 1 for students.

Höller, Karl (b Bamberg, 25 Jul 1907), German composer. Studied at Munich under Josef Haas. Taught at the Musikhochschule in Frankfurt in 1937–49, and became President of the Musikhochschule in Munich in 1954.

Works incl. orch. and solo concertos, symph. fantasy on a theme by Frescobaldi (1934), *Gregorianische Hymnen*; concertos for org., vlns. (2) and cello (2); 6 string 4tets, 8 vln. sonatas, cello sonatas, pf. and organ works.

Höller, York (b Leverkusen, 11 Jan 1944), German composer. He studied at the Cologne Musikhochschule, under Zimmermann and Alfons Kontarsky, and came under the influence of Boulez at Darmstadt; has worked at the electronic studio, Cologne.

Works incl. *Topic* for orch. (1967), cello sonata (1969), pf. concerto (1970), *Horizont*, electronic (1972), *Chroma* for orch. (1974), *Tangens*, electronic (1973), *Antiphon* for string 4tet (1977), *Arcos* for orch. (1978), *Moments musiceaux* for flute and pf. (1979), *Mythos* for orch. (1980).

Holliger, Heinz (b Langenthal, 21 May 1939), Swiss oboist and composer. Studied oboe and pf. in Berne and Paris, and comp. with Veress in Berne and Boulez in Paris. He has won several prizes for his ob. playing; Henze, Krenek, Berio, Penderecki and Stockhausen have written works for him.

Works incl. cantata *Himmel und Erde* for tenor and chamber group (1961); *Studie* for soprano, ob. and cello with harpsichord; *Improvisation* for ob., harp and 12 string insts. (1963); sonata for ob. and pf.; sonata for ob. solo.

Holloway, Robin (b Leamington Spa, 19 Oct 1943), English composer who studied at Cambridge. His music has been much influenced by Ger. Romanticism.

Works incl. *Scenes from Schumann*, 7 paraphrases for orch. (1970) and *Fantasy-Pieces*, on the Heine *Liederkreis* of Schumann, for 13 players (1971). Other works incl. the opera *Clarissa* (1975); 2 Concertos for Orchestra (1969, 1979); *Serenata Notturna* for 4 horns and orchestra (1982);

Clarissa Symphony, for sop., tenor and orch. (1981); *Serenade in G* (1986); *Inquietus* for chamber orch., in memory of Peter Pears (1986).

Hollreiser, Heinrich (b Munich, 24 Jun 1913), German conductor. He held posts in Darmstadt and Mannheim before Munich Staatsoper, 1942. Düsseldorf 1945–52; Vienna Staatsoper until 1961. Deutsche Oper Berlin 1961–4. Has given operas by Henze, Britten and Hindemith. Well known in Strauss and has cond. *Tannhäuser* and *Die Meistersinger* at Bayreuth (debut 1973). Guest cond. Cleveland Orch. from 1978.

Holm, Richard (b Stuttgart, 3 Aug 1912), German tenor. Made his debut in Kiel in 1936. In 1948 he joined the Munich Staatsoper and first sang at CG in 1953 as David; also role of NY Met debut, 1952. A fine Wagner singer, he also excelled in Mozart. Roles incl. Flamand in 1st GB *Capriccio* (1953), Belmonte, Tamino and Aschenbach.

Holmboe, Vagn (b Horsens, Jutland, 20 Dec 1909), Danish composer. Studied with Jeppesen and Høffding in Copenhagen and Toch in Berlin. With his wife, the Rumanian pianist Meta Graf, he explored Rum. for folk music.

Works incl. opera *Fanden og Borgmesteren* (1940); ballet *Den galsindede Tyrk*; 11 symphs. (1935–83); 13 chamber concertos (1939–56), 14 string 4tets (1948–75), 3 vln. sonatas.

Holmes, Alfred (b London, 9 Nov 1837; d Paris, 4 Mar 1876), English violinist and composer. With very little regular instruction he became a famous violinist, playing duets with his brother Henry (1839–1905) and later touring widely with him in Europe. He settled in Paris in 1864. He met Spohr in London and Kassel; dedicatee of Spohr's vln. duos.

Works incl. opera *Inez de Castro*: symphs. *Jeanne d'Arc, The Youth of Shakespeare, Robin Hood, The Siege of Paris, Charles XII* and *Romeo and Juliet* (after Shakespeare); overtures *The Cid* (after Corneille) and *The Muses*.

Holmès (orig. Holmes), **Augusta (Mary Anne)** (b Paris, 16 Dec 1847; d Paris, 28 Jan 1903), Irish naturalized French pianist and composer. Although her parents were against her taking up music, she played the pf. and sang as a child prodigy and began to comp. under the name of Hermann Zenta. Later studied with Franck.

Works incl. operas *Héro et Léandre, La Montagne noire* (1895), *Astarté, Lancelot du Lac*; choral works *Les Argonautes* (on

Homer's *Iliad,* 1881), psalm *In exitu,* ode *Ludus pro patria* and *Ode triomphale*; symphs. on Ariosto's *Orlando furioso, Lutèce* and *Pologne,* symph. poem *Irlande* (1882); song-cycle *Les Sept Ivresses.*

Holmes, Edward (b 1797; d London, 28 Aug 1859), English author and critic. He wrote *A Ramble among the Musicians of Germany* (1828) and the 1st Eng. biography of Mozart (1845).

Holmes, George (b Lincoln, 1721), English organist and composer. At 1st organist to Bishop of Durham, he was app. organist of Lincoln Cathedral in 1704. Wrote anthems, burial sentences for Lincoln Cathedral, Ode for St Cecilia's Day, catches.

Holmes, Ralph (b Penge, 1 Apr 1937; d Beckenham, 4 Sep 1984), English violinist. After study at the RAM and with Enescu in Paris he made his London debut in 1951, with the RPO. US debut Carnegie Hall 1966, under Barbirolli. He was heard in chamber works by Delius, Bartók and Prokofiev and in concertos by Berg, Shostakovich and Schoenberg, as well as the standard rep. Formed a pf. trio in 1972 with Anthony Goldstone and Moray Welsh.

Holst, Gustav (Theodore) (b Cheltenham, 21 Sep 1874; d London, 25 May 1934), English composer of Swedish descent. The family had been in Eng. since 1807. His father was a music teacher and his mother a pianist, and he was intended to follow their career; he also had early experience as organist and choral and orchestral cond. in a small way. In 1892 he was sent to the RCM in London, but disliked the keyboard instruments and studied comp. under Stanford. Suffering from neuritis, he took up the tromb. instead of the pf., and on leaving played in the orch. of the Carl Rosa Opera Co. and later in the Scottish Orch. In 1903 he became music master at a school in south London, in 1905 at St Paul's Girls' School, where he remained to his death, and in 1907 was app. music dir. at Morley Coll. for Working Men and Women. From 1919 he taught comp. at the RCM and in 1919–23 at Reading Coll.

Works incl. operas *The Idea* (1898), *The Wandering Scholar, Sāvitri* (1908; prod. 1916), *The Perfect Fool* (1923), *At the Boar's Head* (on Shakespeare's *Henry IV,* 1925); ballets *The Golden Goose* (1926) and *The Morning of the Year* with chorus and orch. (1926–7).

CHORAL: Choral hymns from the *Rig Veda* with orch. (1908–12), 2 psalms for chorus, strings and org., *The Hymn of Jesus* for chorus and orch. (1917), Festival Te Deum, *Ode to Death* (Whitman) for chorus and orch., choral symph. (Keats) for soprano, chorus and orch. (1925), choral fantasy (Bridges) for chorus, org., strings, brass and perc.; 2 motets for unaccomp. chorus, *Ave Maria* for fem. voices, part-songs and arrs. of folksongs for unaccomp. chorus.

ORCHESTRAL: *A Somerset Rhapsody* (1907), *Beni Mora* suite (1910), *The Planets* (1914–16), *Jap. Suite, Fugal Overture, Egdon Heath* (after Thomas Hardy) for orch. (1927); *St Paul's* suite for strings; *Fugal Concerto* for fl., ob. and strings, concerto for 2 vlns. and orch. (1929); 2 suites for military band: *A Moorside Suite* for brass band.

9 hymns from the *Rig Veda* for voice and pf. (1908), 12 songs (Humbert Wolfe) for voice and pf., 4 songs for voice and vln.; a few pf. pieces.

Holst, Imogen (b Richmond, Surrey, 12 Apr 1907; d Aldeburgh, 9 Mar 1984), English pianist and composer, daughter of prec. Studied with her father and at the RCM in London and became music mistress at several schools, did much work for the Eng. Folk Dance Society and wrote books on Holst, Purcell and Britten.

Works incl. overture for orch., pf. pieces, folksong arrs., string 5tet (1981).

Holstein, Franz (Friedrich) von (b Brunswick, 16 Feb 1826; d Leipzig, 22 May 1878), German composer. Although trained for the army, he studied music under Griepenkerl. When he had written 2 operas *Zwei nächte in Venedig* and *Waverley* (after Scott), Moritz Hauptmann persuaded him in 1852 to take entirely to music and gave him further instruction.

Works incl. operas *Der Haideschacht*, *Der Erbe von Morley*, *Die Hochländer* and *Marino Faliero* (after Byron); overtures *Loreley* and *Frau Aventiure*; vocal scene from Schiller's *Braut von Messina* and another, *Beatrice*.

Holz, Carl (b Vienna, 1798; d Vienna, 9 Nov 1858), Austrian violinist. Lived in Vienna, where he became a member of Schuppanzigh's 4tet in 1824 and took part in the fps of Beethoven's last string 4tets. A devoted friend of Beethoven.

Holzbauer, Ignaz (b Vienna, 17 Sep 1711; d Mannheim, 7 Apr 1783), Austrian composer. Originally intended for the law, he was largely self-taught in music, and visited It. to complete his studies. Director of the court opera in Vienna intermittently 1742–1750, he was app. *Kapellmeister* in Stuttgart in

1751, and 2 years later to the court of the Elector Palatine in Mannheim, where the orch. under Johann Stamitz was the most famous of the time. During visits to It. on leave of absence he prod. several operas, and in Mannheim prod. the Ger. opera *Günther von Schwarzburg*. As a comp. of symphs. he belongs to the Mannheim School.

Works incl. operas *Il figlio delle selve* (1753), *L'isola disabitata* (1754), *Nitetti* (1758), *Alessandro nell' Indie, Tancredi, Günther von Schwarzburg* (1777), etc.; oratorios *La Passione* (1754), *Isacco* (1757), *La Betulia liberata* (1760), etc.; Masses, motets and other church music; 65 symphs.; concertos, chamber music.

Holzbläser (Ger. lit. woodblowers) = woodwind instruments.

Holzblasinstrumente (Ger.) = wood-wind instruments.

Holztrompete (Ger. = wooden tpt.), an instrument designed for use in the 3rd act of Wagner's *Tristan*, actually a revival of the Cornett, but provided with a valve.

Homer, Greek poet. *See* **Bruch** (*Achilles* and *Odysseus*), **Gnecchi** (*Cassandra*), **Heger** (*Bettler Namenlos*), **Herzogenberg** (*Odysseus* symph.), **Holmès** (*Argonautes*), **Homerische Welt** (Bungert), **Ritorno di Ulisse** (Monteverdi, Henze), **Ulisse** (Dallapiccola).

Homer, Louise (b Pittsburgh, 30 Apr 1871; d Winter Park, Florida, 6 May 1947), American contralto. She studied in Boston and Paris and in 1898 at Vichy was heard as Leonora (*La favorite*). CG 1899–1900 as Lola and Ortrud. NY Met 1900–29 as Amneris and Azucena and in Wagner; she sang under Toscanini in Gluck's *Orfeo* and *Armide* and was the Witch in the 1910 fp of Humperdinck's *Königskinder*. Also sang in San Francisco and Chicago and was successful as Dalila.

Homerische Welt (*Homeric World*), operatic tetralogy by Bungert (lib. by comp., based on Homer's *Odyssey*)

I. *Kirke* (*Circe*), prod. Dresden, 29 Jan 1898.

II. *Nausikaa* (*Nausicaa*), prod. Dresden, 20 Mar 1901.

III. *Odysseus Heimkehr* (*The Return of Ulysses*), prod. Dresden, 12 Dec 1896.

IV. *Odysseus Tod* (*The death of Ulysses*), prod. Dresden, 30 Oct 1903.

Bungert's attempt to create a Wagnerian cycle, but based, like Berlioz's *Troyens* and Taneiev's *Oresteia*, on classical Greek subjects.

Homilius, Gottfried August (b Rosenthal,

Saxony, 2 Feb 1714; d Dresden, 2 Jun 1785), German composer and organist. Pupil of Bach at Leipzig, app. organist of the church of Our Lady, Dresden, 1742, and music dir. of the 3 principal churches there, 1755.

Works incl. many cantatas and motets, *Messiah* (*c* 1776), a Passion cantata, Christmas oratorio, several settings of the Passions, a book of 167 hymns; 6 Ger. arias; organ music.

Homme armé, L' (Fr. = the armed man), the name of an old Fr. secular song the tune of which was often used by comps. of the 15th and 16th cents. as *cantus firmus* for their Masses, which were then designated by that name.

Homme et son désir, L' (*Man and his Desire*), ballet by Milhaud (words, 'plastic poem', by Paul Claudel, choreog. by Jean Borlin), prod. Paris, Théâtre des Champs-Élysées, 6 Jun 1921.

Homophonic (from Gk., lit. alikesounding), applied to music in which the individual lines making up the harmony have no independent significance, that is to say, for most purposes chordal.

Honauer, Leontzi (b ? Strasbourg, *c* 1735; d *c* 1790), German composer. Settled in Paris *c* 1760 and pub. 3 sets of harpsichord sonatas, some movements of which were later arr. as concerto movements in Mozart's K37, 40 and 41.

Honegger, Arthur (b Le Havre, 10 Mar 1892; d Paris, 27 Nov 1955), Swiss composer. Was 1st taught by the organist R.C. Martin at his birthplace, then sent to the Zurich Cons., 1909–11, and, his parents still living at Le Havre, studied at the Paris Cons. 1911–13. After that he became a private pupil of Widor and d'Indy and in 1914 began to comp. Though always in touch with Switz., he belonged mainly to the Fr. school, and he joined the group which *c* 1920 became known as 'Les Six'. He married the comp. Andrée Vaurabourg, who was also attached to it, though not as a member.

Works incl. OPERAS: *Antigone* (after Sophocles, 1927), *L'Aiglon* (with Ibert, 1937) and *Charles le Téméraire* (1944); stage oratorios *Le Roi David* (1921), *Judith*, *Cris du monde*, *Jeanne d'Arc au bûcher* (Paul Claudel, 1938) and *Nicolas de Flue*; BALLETS: *Horace victorieux* (1920), *Sémiramis* (Paul Valéry, 1934), *Amphion* (Valéry, 1931), *Un oiseau bleu s'est envolé* (Sacha Guitry), *Shota Roustaveli* (with A. Tcherepnin and Harsányi, 1946).

INCID. MUSIC for *Le Dit des jeux du monde* (1918), *La Mort de Sainte Alméenne* (Max Jacob), *Saül* (André Gide, 1922), *Fantasio* (Musset), *Phœdre* (d'Annunzio, 1926), *Les Suppliantes* (Aeschylus), *La Mandragora* (Machiavelli), *Le Soulier de satin* (Claudel), *Sodôme et Gomorrhe* (Jean Giraudoux, 1943), *Hamlet* (Shakespeare, 1946), *Prométhée* (Aeschylus), *Oedipe-Roi* (Sophocles, 1948).

ORCH. AND VOCAL WITH ORCH.: radio and film music; *La Danse des morts* (Claudel) for solo voices, chorus and orch. (on Holbein), prelude to Maeterlinck's *Aglavaine et Sélysette*, *Chant de joie*, prelude to Shakespeare's *Tempest*, *Mouvements symphonique*: *Pacific 231*, *Rugby* and No. 3 (1923–33), 5 symphs. (1930–51), *Prélude, Arioso et Fugue* on B.A.C.H., suite *Jour de fête suisse*, *Suite archaïque* for orch., *Pastorale d'été* (1920) and *Sérénade à Angélique* for chamber orch.; concertino for pf. and orch., cello concerto; 5 Poems by Guillaume Apollinaire for voice and orch. (1910–17).

CHAMBER AND SOLO VOCAL: 3 string 4tets (1916–36) and other chamber music, 2 vln. and pf. sonatas, sonatas for vla. and pf., cello and pf., clar. and pf.; pf. and organ music; songs to poems by Apollinaire, Paul Fort, Jean Cocteau, Claudel, Giraudoux and others.

Hook, James (b Norwich, ? 3 Jun 1746; d Boulogne, 1827), English organist and composer. Studied under Garland, the Norwich Cathedral organist. He made a success in London in early manhood and in 1769 became organist and comp. to Marylebone Gardens, and acted in the same posts at Vauxhall in 1774–1820. He married Miss Madden *c* 1766 and wrote music for her play, *The Double Disguise*, in 1784. In 1795 and 1797 he did the same for 2 libretti by his son James (1772–1828), *Jack of Newbury* and *Diamond cut Diamond*, and from 1805 for several works by his 2nd son, Theodore Edward (1788–1841). Of his vast output of songs for Vauxhall, some are still remembered, e.g. 'The Lass of Richmond Hill'.

Works incl. musical plays *Love and Innocence* (1769), *Country Courtship* (1772), *The Lady of the Manor* (1778), *Too civil by half* (1782), *The Triumph of Beauty, The Peruvian, The Soldier's Return* (1805), *The Siege of St Quintin* (1808), Hannah Moore's *The Search after Happiness*, etc.; odes, cantatas, catches.

Hooper, Edmund (b Halberton, Devon, *c* 1553; d London, 14 Jul 1621), English organist and composer. After being (?) a chorister at Exeter Cathedral he went to

London and joined the Westminster Abbey choir, becoming a Gentleman of the Chapel Royal in 1604 and organist of the abbey in 1606. He contrib. harmonizations of hymn tunes to East's and Ravenscroft's Psalters, also 2 vocal pieces to Leighton's *Teares or Lamentacions* and 1 to Myriell's *Tristitiae remedium.*
Works incl. services and anthems; secular music for several voices; virginal music.
Hopak. *See* **Gopak.**
Hopf, Hans (b Nuremberg, 2 Aug 1916), German tenor. Debut 1936, as Pinkerton; sang in Augsburg and Dresden, and in Oslo during the Nazi occupation of Norway. Berlin from 1946; member of Munich Co. from 1949. Bayreuth from 1951 as Walther and Siegfried. London, CG, 1951–3 as Radames. NY Met debut 1952, Walther. La Scala, Milan, 1963 as Siegfried. Other roles incl. Strauss's Emperor and Max, Tristan and Otello.
Hopkins, Antony (orig. Reynolds) (b London, 21 Mar 1921), English educator, conductor, writer on music and composer. He studied at the RCM with Cyril Scott and Gordon Jacob; successful as writer of incidental music for films, radio and the theatre (music for 15 of Shakespeare's plays). For SW he wrote the opera *Lady Rohesia* (1948) and while music dir. of Intimate Opera, from 1952, several 1 act works. His series of radio broadcasts, *Talking About Music,* started in 1954. Books incl. *Understanding Music* (1979), *The Nine Symphonies of Beethoven* (1980) and *The Concertgoer's Companion* (2 vols. 1984, 1986).
Hopkins, Bill (b Prestbury, Cheshire, 5 Jun 1943; d Chopwell, nr. Newcastle, 10 Mar 1981), English composer and writer on music. Studied with Nono (at Dartington), Wellesz and Messiaen. His music was also influenced by Boulez and Barraqué: *Sousstructures,* for pf. (1964), *2 Pomes* for sop. and ens. (after Joyce, 1964), *Musique de l' indifférence,* ballet after Beckett (1965), *Études en série,* pf. pieces in 3 Books (1965–72), *En attendant,* for ens. (1977).
Hopkinson, Francis (b Philadelphia, 21 Sep 1737; d Philadelphia, 9 May 1791), American lawyer, politician and amateur musician, sometimes regarded as the first Amer. comp. Wrote a number of songs, incl. 'Beneath a weeping willow's shade', and the 'oratorical entertainment' *The Temple of Minerva.* Also developed some mechanical improvements for keyboard instruments.
Horenstein, Jascha (b Kiev, 6 May 1898; d

London, 2 Apr 1973), Russian-born conductor. Went with his family to Ger. as a child. Studied with Max Bode in Königsberg and with Adolph Busch in Vienna, also studying comp. with Schreker in Berlin. He was app. cond. of the Düsseldorf Opera in 1926 and settled in the USA in 1941; gave the 1st US perf. of Busoni's *Doktor Faust* there in 1964. Well known in Schubert, Bruckner and Mahler and cond. the fps of Berg's 3 Movts. for strings (Berlin, 1929) and *Altenberg Lieder* (Rome, 1953). Cond. *Parsifal* at CG a few weeks before his death.
Horizon Chimérique, L', song cycle by Fauré, op. 118 (texts by Jean de la Ville de Mirmont); comp. 1921, fp Paris, 13 May 1922, with Charles Pinzéra.
Horn, a brass wind instrument with its tube bent in a circular form. In its early stages it could prod. only the natural harmonics and was used mainly for hunting fanfares. When comps. began to write for it in the early 18th cent. they were still restricted to the natural harmonics; but by the invention of a series of crooks which could be inserted the length of the tube could be altered and the instrument played in a variety of keys. Some extra notes, of rather uncertain quality, could also be obtained by inserting the hand into the bell. It was only by the intro. of valves about the 1830s that the full chromatic scale could be played on a single instrument.

The modern horn is built in F and high B♭, with 4 valves, one of which transposes the instrument from the lower to the higher pitch. The normal compass is:

with one or two higher and lower notes possible.
Horn, Charles Edward (b London, 21 Jun 1786; d Boston, Mass., 21 Oct 1849), English tenor-baritone singer and composer of German descent. He studied under his father, Karl Friedrich H., and had singing lessons from Rauzzini at Bath in 1808, making his 1st stage appearance in London in 1809. He then began to write theatrical pieces, starting with *The Magic Bride* in 1810. In 1823 he visited Dublin and brought Balfe back with him as a pupil. Having been music dir. at the Olympic Theatre in 1831–2, he went to USA in 1833, became a music teacher and pub. at Boston, where after a brief return to Eng. he settled for good in 1847, becoming cond. of the Handel and Haydn Society.

Works incl. stage pieces *Lalla Rookh* (after Moore), *The Beehive* (1811), *Rich and Poor, Peveril of the Peak* (after Scott), *Honest Frauds* (1830), and many others, some with Blewitt, Braham, T. Cooke or Reeve; overture to Thomas Moore's *M.P., or The Blue Stocking*; songs in Shakespeare's *Merry Wives of Windsor* (with Webbe, jun. and Parry); oratorios *The Remission of Sin* (later *Satan*) and *Daniel's Prediction*; glees, canzonets and many songs, incl. 'Cherry ripe' (Herrick).

Horn, Karl Friedrich (b Nordhausen, Thuringia, 13 Apr 1762; d Windsor, 5 Aug 1830), German organist and composer, father of C.E.H. Pupil of C.G. Schröter, settled in Eng. 1782, where under the patronage of Count Bruhl he quickly rose to become music teacher to Queen Charlotte and her daughters. In 1810 he pub. with S. Wesley the first Eng. edn. of Bach's *Wohltemperirte Clavier*. He was app. organist of St George's Chapel, Windsor, in 1824.

Works incl. sonatas for pf. and fl. or vln., divertimenti for piano and vln., divertimenti for military band.

Horn Signal, Symphony with the, nickname of Haydn's symph. no. 31 in D maj., comp. 1765, so called because of the horn fanfares at the beginning and end.

Hornbostel, Erich (Moritz) von (b Vienna, 25 Feb 1877; d Cambridge, 29 Nov 1935), Austrian musicologist. Studied physics and philosophy at Vienna and Heidelberg, and in 1906 became head of the gramophone archives in Berlin for the recording of ethnic music, on which he wrote several learned works. In 1933 he went to NY and the following year to London and Cambridge. He is most famous for his part in the Sachs-H. classficiation of musical insts., still employed by most scholars and museums.

Horne, Marilyn (b Bradford, Pa., 16 Jan 1934), American mezzo. She studied in Calif.; stage debut Gelsenkirchen, 1957 as Giulietta. US debut, San Francisco, 1960 as Berg's Marie; London, CG, 1964 in same role. In 1962 began stage and concert assoc. with Joan Sutherland; many perfs. of operas by Rossini and Bellini. NY Met debut 1970, as Adalgisa; other roles there incl. Rosina, Carmen, Isabella and Fides. Has sung Rinaldo and Tancredi in Houston, and Malcolm in *La donna del lago* at CG (1985).

Horneman, Christian (Frederik Emil) (b Copenhagen, 17 Dec 1840; d Copenhagen, 8 Jun 1906), Danish composer. Studied with his father and at the Leipzig Cons. On his return to Copenhagen he founded a concert society and in 1880 a music school.

Works incl. opera *Aladdin* (Oehlenschläger, 1885); overture *A Hero's Life*; pf. pieces; songs.

Hornpipe, an English dance, so called because it was at first accomp. on a pipe of the same name, made from an animal's horn. It did not always have nautical associations and up to the time of Handel, who has such an ex. in one of his concerti grossi, it was in 3–2 time. The later form is in 2–4.

Horowitz, Vladimir (b Kiev, 1 Oct 1904), Russian, later American pianist. Studied in Kiev with Felix Blumenfeld and made his debut in Kharkov, aged 17. Later he went to Paris and in 1928 made his American debut under Beecham. In 1933 he married Toscanini's daughter Wanda. From 1938 to 1939 he lived in Switz. and in 1940 settled in America. He retired from concert life for 12 years, returning in 1965; retired again, but reappeared 1974 and played in Russia 1986. Horowitz ranked as one of the most technically gifted and musicianly pianists of his day.

Horsley, Charles Edward (b London, 16 Dec 1822; d New York, 28 Feb 1876), English pianist, organist and composer. Studied under his father, William H., and Moscheles, later with Hauptmann at Cassel and Mendelssohn at Leipzig. In 1845 he returned to London and became organist at St John's Church, Notting Hill, wrote several works for provincial festivals, etc. In 1862 he went to Australia and in the early 1870s to USA.

Works incl. oratorios *David* (1850), *Joseph* (1853) and *Gideon* (1860); setting of Milton's *Comus*; Ode *Euterpe* for the opening of Melbourne Town Hall; pf. trio.

Horsley, William (b London, 15 Nov 1774; d London, 12 Jun 1858), English organist and composer, father of prec. Studied music privately, but had some advice from Callcott. He became organist of Ely Chapel, Holborn, in 1794, asst. Callcott as organist at the Asylum for Female Orphans and succeeded him in 1802. Later he held several other appts. He was one of the founders of the Phil. Society in 1813. His family were close friends of Mendelssohn's.

Works incl. anthem *When Israel came out of Egypt*, hymn and psalm tunes; 3 symphs.; many glees.

Horsowski, Mieczyslaw (b Lwów, 23 Jun 1892), American pianist of Polish birth. Debut Warsaw; appeared all over Europe as soloist and settled in NY 1940 (US citizen 1948); gave many chamber concerts with Szigeti and Casals and solo recitals of

Mozart and Beethoven. He played at Aldeburgh in 1984.

Horwood, William (d 1484), English composer. He became master of the choristers at Lincoln Cathedral in 1477. His music, consisting of Latin antiphons and a Magnificat, is included in the Eton Choirbook (*q.v.*); a fragmentary *Kyrie* has also survived.

Hothby, John (b *c* 1410; d ? Nov 1487), English Carmelite, music scholar, composer and doctor of theology. Graduated at Oxford and lectured there in 1435. Travelled (?) in Spain, Fr. and Ger., settled *c* 1440 (?) at Florence and also (?) lived at Ferrara. He was called Giovanni Ottobi in It. and spent *c* 1468–86 at Lucca. He taught there, but was recalled to Eng. by Henry VII. Wrote a number of theoretical treatises. Some sacred and secular comps. were entered in the Faenza Codex (*q.v.*).

Hotter, Hans (b Offenbach-am-Main, 19 Jan 1909), German bass-baritone. Initially an organist and choirmaster, studying church music, he later turned to opera. After studying with Roemer, a pupil of De Reszke, he made his debut in 1929 at Troppau; later sang at Breslau, Prague and Hamburg. In 1940 he became a member of the Munich and Vienna operas. London, CG, 1947–67; Bayreuth from 1952. He created roles in Strauss's *Friedenstag* (1938), *Capriccio* (1942) and *Die Liebe der Danae* (1944). Produced the *Ring* at CG, 1962–4. He was one of the leading Wagner singers of his day and also an impressive actor. Both these qualities were seen at their best in his Wotan, which he sang for the last time in Paris, 1972. Other roles incl. Sachs, the Dutchman, Don Giovanni and Palestrina's Borromeo. Still heard at Munich (as Schigolch).

Hotteterre, French 17th and 18th cent. family of woodwind instrument makers, performers and composers; developments of the oboe from the shawm, the bassoon from the curtal and the transverse flute from the cylindrical flute are often credited to them. **Jacques H.** (b Paris, 29 Sep 1674; d Paris, 16 Jul 1763) is the best known of the family; called himself *Le Romain* after an early visit to Italy. From 1708 at the latest he was a bassoonist in the Grands Hautbois and was a flautist in the service of the king. His book *Principes de la flute traversière* (1707) was the first such treatise to be published; it was followed by *L'art de préluder sur la flute traversière* and *Methode pour la musette* (1737).

House of the Dead, From the (*Z Mrtvého Domu*), opera in 3 acts by Janáček (lib. by the comp. after Dostoievsky), prod. Brno, 12 Apr 1930.

Housman, A(lfred) E(dward) (1859–1936), English poet and Latin scholar. Poems from *A Shropshire Lad* and *Last Poems* set to music by many composers, incl. Barber, Butterworth, Gurney, Ireland, Moeran, C.W. Orr, Somervell and Vaughan Williams.

Houston Symphony Orchestra, US orch. founded 1913 with Julian Paul Blitz as cond.; reorganized 1930 and increased in size under Ernst Hoffmann (1936–47). Later conductors have been Efrem Kurtz (1948–54), Beecham (1954–5), Stokowski (1955–60), Barbirolli (1961–7), Previn (1967–9), Lawrence Foster (1971–8). Sergiu Comissiona from 1980.

Hove, Joachim van den (b Antwerp, 1567; d The Hague, 1620), Flemish lutenist and composer. Pub. a book of songs for 2 voices and lute, 1 of songs and dances arr. for lute and 1 of preludes for lute and viol.

Hovhaness, Alan (b Somerville, Mass., 8 Mar 1911), American composer of Armenian descent. Studied pf. with Heinrich Gebhard and comp. with Converse and Martinu. He is much influenced by Indian and other oriental music. He has comp. much, but destroyed a great deal of it in 1940.

Works incl. 61 symphs. (1939–86), *And God Created Whales* (1970) incl. taped part for humpbacked whale, 2 *Armen. Rhapsodies* for strings, 23 concertos (1936–80) incl. *Elibris* for fl. and strings; *Lousadzak* for pf. and strings; concerto for tpt. and strings; *Sosi* for vln. pf., perc. and strings; *Arekeval* for orch.; concerto for orch.; *Ad Lyram* for orch.; chamber music incl. 5 string 4tets (1936–76).

Howard, Ann (b Norwood, 22 Jul 1936), English mezzo. After 1961 debut at CG, London, she studied further in Paris. From 1964 she has sung widely in Britain and North Amer. as Carmen, Fricka and Azucena and in operettas by J. Strauss and Offenbach. Her Witch in *Hansel and Gretel* has been recorded.

Howard, Samuel (b 1710; d London, 13 Jul 1782), English organist and composer. Pupil of Croft at the Chapel Royal and later of Pepusch. App. organist at the churches of St Clement Danes and St Bride. Mus.D., Cambridge, in 1769. He asst. Boyce in compiling his *Cathedral Music*.

Works incl. anthems and other church music; pantomimes, *The Amorous Goddess*, or *Harlequin Married* and *Robin Goodfellow*; cantatas and songs.

Howarth, Elgar (b Cannock, Staff., 4 Nov 1935), English conductor, trumpeter and composer. He studied at the RMCM and played the trumpet in the Philip Jones brass ens. and the RPO (1963–8). He has been dir. of the London Sinfonietta since 1973 and has toured widely, often in modern music; cond. the 1978 Stockholm fp of Ligeti's opera *Le Grand Macabre* and in 1986 the London, Coliseum, fp of Birtwistle's *The Mask of Orpheus*. He has comp. and arr. works for brass band, e.g. Mussorgsky's *Pictures at an Exhibition*.

Howell, Gwynne (Gorseinon, 13 Jun 1938), Welsh bass. He studied at the RMCM and sang in operas by Wagner there. London, SW, from 1968; CG from 1970 in operas by Strauss, Puccini, Verdi and Mussorgsky, and in the 1972 fp of Maxwell Davies's *Taverner*. He is well known as a concert singer in Europe and N. Amer. (e.g. the *Missa solemnis*) and in Mar 1986 sang Gurnemanz in a new prod. of *Parsifal* at the London Coliseum.

Howells, Anne (b Southport, 12 Jan 1941), English mezzo. She studied at the RMCM and sang Helen there in the 1st Brit. prod. of Gluck's *Paride e Helena* (1963). London, CG, from 1967; roles have incl. Ophelia in Searle's *Hamlet*, Rosina, Cherubino and Siebel. Glyndebourne 1967, as Eribse in the Cavalli-Leppard *L'Ormindo*, and has returned in operas by Maw, Strauss and Monteverdi; in 1974 she was Diana in *Calisto*. NY Met debut 1975, Dorabella.

Howells, Herbert (Norman) (b Lydney, Glos., 17 Oct 1892; d Oxford, 24 Feb 1983), English composer. Pupil of Herbert Brewer at Gloucester Cathedral and later under Stanford at the RCM in London, where he became prof. of comp. Later, having been 1st sub-organist at Salisbury Cathedral, lived a retired life in 1917–20 owing to poor health. Music Dir. at St Paul's Girls' School from 1936, in succession to Holst. D.Mus., Oxford, 1937. He was Prof. of Music at London Univ. from 1952 to 1962 and was created CBE in 1953.

Works incl. ballet *Penguinski*; *Sine Nomine*, *A Kent Yeoman's Song* and *Hymnus Paradisi* for soli, chorus and orch. (1938); *Procession*, *Pastoral Rhapsody* (1923), *Paradise Rondel, Merry-Eye, Puck's Minuet, King's Herald* for orch.; *Lady Audrey's Suite* for string orch.; *Pageantry* for brass band; 2 pf. concertos (1913, 1924); song cycle *In Green Ways* with orch.

CHAMBER: fantasy string 4tet, string 4tet *In Gloucestershire* (1923), clar. 5tet; 3 vln. and pf. sonatas, 2 org. sonatas; ob. sonata, clar. sonata; *Lambert's Clavichord* and *Howells' Clavichord* for clavichord; pf. pieces; much church music; songs.

Howes, Frank (b Oxford, 2 Apr 1891; d Standlake, Oxon., 28 Sep 1974), English music critic. Educ. at St John's Coll., Oxford. He joined *The Times* as asst. music critic in 1925, became lecturer at the RCM in 1938 and was chief *Times* critic from 1943 to 1960. His books incl. a life of Byrd, studies of Vaughan Williams and Walton, of musical appreciation, psychology, opera, the orch. and others.

Hubay, Jenö (orig. Eugen Huber) (b Budapest, 15 Sep 1858; d Budapest, 12 Mar 1937), Hungarian violinist and composer. Pupil of his father Karl Huber, he appeared as a prodigy at the age of 11, but later went to study with Joachim in Berlin. He travelled much, ed. and completed some of Vieuxtemps' works and became vln. prof. at the Brussels Cons. in 1882 and at the Budapest Cons. in 1886, of which he was dir. from 1919 to 1934.

Works incl. operas *Alienor* (1891), *A Cremonai Hegedüs* (after Coppée's *Luther de Crémone*, 1894), *A Falu Rossza, Karenina Anna* (after Tolstoy, 1915), *Az álarc*, etc.; 4 symphs.; 4 vln. concertos; *Sonate romantique* for vln. and pf.; many vln. pieces, studies.

Huber, Hans (b Eppenburg, Solothurn, 28 Jun 1852; d Locarno, 25 Dec 1921), Swiss composer. After attending seminary at Solothurn, he studied music under Carl Munzinger there and later at the Leipzig Cons. After teaching in Alsace, he settled at Basle in 1877. In 1889 he became prof. at the Cons. there and succeeded Selmar Bagge as its dir. in 1896, retiring in 1918.

Works incl. operas *Weltfrühling* (1894), *Kudrun* (1896), *Simplicius* (1912), *Die schöne Bellinde, Frutta di mare* (1918); Masses, cantatas, etc.; 9 symphs. (No. 2 on pictures by Böcklin) and other orchestral works *Sommernächte, Serenade, Carneval* and *Römischer Carneval*; 4 pf. concertos, vln. concerto; much chamber music; pf. music; songs, incl. Hafiz cycle.

Huber, Klaus (b Berne, 30 Nov 1924), Swiss composer. Studied with Willy Burkhard at the Zurich Cons. and with Blacher in Berlin. From 1950 he taught vln. in Zurich and from 1960 music hist. at the Lucerne Cons.

Works incl. cantata for voices and 4 instruments *Des Engels Anredung an die Seele* (1957); oratorio *Mechthildis* for alto voice and chamber orch. (1957). *Auf die ruhige*

Nacht-Zeit for soprano and chamber group (1958); *Soliloquia* for soloists, chorus and orch.; *Sonata da chiesa* for vln. and organ, *Concerto per la Camerata* (1955), *Tempora*, vln. concerto (1970).

Huberman, Bronislaw (b Czestochowa, 19 Dec 1882; d Nant-sur-Corsier, Switzerland, 15 Jun 1947), Polish violinist. Studied at the Warsaw Cons., in Paris and Berlin, played in public at the age of 7 and later toured the world. With William Steinberg organized the Palestine SO (1936; Israel PO from 1948). Admired for the freedom of his interpretations.

Hucbald (b ? Tournai *c* 840; d Saint-Amand, 20 Jun 930), French monk and musician. Lived at the monastery of Saint-Amand. Wrote the treatise *De harmonica institutione* (*c* 880), one of the earliest known writings on Western music theory.

Hudson, George (b *c* 1615; d Greenwich, Dec 1672), English violinist and composer. Worked in London. Took part, with Coleman, sen., Cooke, H. Lawes and Locke, in providing music for Davenant's *Siege of Rhodes* (entertainment at Rutland House) in 1656; member of the King's Band from 1661 and comp. to the king.

Hüe, Georges (Adolphe) (b Versailles, 6 May 1858; d Paris 7 Jun 1948), French composer. Studied at the Paris Cons., where he obtained the Prix de Rome in 1879. Member of the Académie des Beaux-Arts in 1922 in succession to Saint-Saëns.

Works incl. operas *Les Pantins, Le Roi de Paris* (1901), *Le Miracle, Titania* (after Shakespeare, 1903), *Dans l'ombre de la cathédrale* (1921), *Riquet à la Houppe* (after Perrault); ballets *Siang Sin* and *Nimba*, pantomime *Coeur brisé*.; incid. music to Rostand's *Les Romanesques*, Kalidasa's *Sakuntala*, etc.; symph., symph. legend *Rübezahl*, and other orchestral works; songs.

Hugh the Drover, or Love in the Stocks, opera by Vaughan Williams (lib. by Harold Child), prod. London, RCM, 4 Jul 1924.

Hughes, Anselm (actually Humphrey Vaughan) (b London, 15 Apr 1889; d Nashdom, 8 Sep 1974), English music scholar and Angl. Benedictine, Prior of Nashdom Abbey. Part-ed. of the pub. of the Old Hall MS. He was a member of the Ed. Board of the *New Oxford History of Music*, ed. of Vol. II and joint ed. of Vol. III.

Hughes, Gervase (b Birmingham, 1 Sep 1905), English composer. He took the B.Mus. at Oxford in 1927 and in 1926 joined the music staff of the BNOC.; later cond. at various theatres. In 1933 he left the music profession, but after World War II took to comp. again. Wrote books on Sullivan (1960) and Dvořák (1967).

Works incl. opera *Imogen's Choice*, operettas *Castle Creevy* and *Venetian Fantasy*; symph. in F min., *Overture for a Musical Comedy* for orch.; pf. music, songs.

Hugo, Victor (1802–85), French poet, novelist and dramatist. *See* Armourer of Nantes (Balfe), Ce qu'on entend ... (Liszt), Cui (*Angelo*), Dargomizhsky (*Esmeralda* and *Notre-Dame de Paris*), Delibes (*Le Roi s'amuse*), Djinns (Franck), Ernani (Verdi), Esmeralda (Campana, Dargomizhsky), Fauré(songs), Gioconda (Ponchielli), Giuramento (Mercadante), Lucrezia Borgia (Donizetti), Maria Tudor (Gomes), Mazeppa (Liszt), Notre Dame (Schmidt, F.), Pedrotti (*Marion Delorme*), Ponchielli (do.), Rigoletto (Verdi), Ruy Blas (Glover, Marchetti and Mendelssohn), Wagner-Régeny (*Der Günstling*).

Huguenots, Les, opera by Meyerbeer (lib. by Scribe and Émile Deschamps), prod. Paris, Opéra, 29 Feb 1836.

Huizar, Candelario (b Jérez, 2 Feb 1888; d Mexico City, 3 May 1970),Mexican composer of Indian origin. Studied at the Cons. Nacional in Mexico, where he later taught.

Works incl. 4 symphs. on native tunes (1930–42); string 4tet.

Hulda, opera by C. Franck (lib. by C. Grandmougin, based on a play by Bjørnson), not perf. in Franck's lifetime; prod. Monte Carlo, 8 Mar 1894.

Hull, Arthur Eaglefield (b Market Harborough, 10 Mar 1876; d Huddersfield, 4 Nov 1928), English writer on music. He was ed. of the *Monthly Musical Record* from 1912; an early champion of Skriabin, and in 1924 pub. a *Dictionary of Modern Music and Musicians* (German trans., with many corrections, by Alfred Einstein, 1926). His *Music: Classical, Romantic and Modern* (1927) was exposed by Percy Scholes as consisting of unadorned borrowings from other writers. Such accusations were taken seriously in the 1920s, and Hull felt obliged to throw himself under a train at Huddersfield station. He ed. the complete organ works of Bach and Mendelssohn.

Hullah, John (Pyke) (b Worcester, 27 Jun 1812; d London, 21 Feb 1884), English conductor, teacher and composer. Had music lessons from Wm. Horsley in London and studied singing at the RAM. In 1836 he became known as the comp. of Dickens's opera, *The Village Coquettes*. After a stay in Paris he taught singing in London, esp. at a school opened at Exeter Hall in 1841 for the instruction of schoolmasters, In 1847 his friends opened St Martin's Hall for him, and he gave concerts there until 1860, when the hall was burnt down. Later he held a number of music appts. and wrote several books.

Hüllmandel, Nicolas Joseph (b Strasbourg, 23 May 1756; d London, 19 Dec 1823), Alsatian harpsichordist, pianist and composer. Pupil of C.P.E. Bach. He appeared in London in 1771 and settled there in 1790 after a visit to It. and residence in Paris. Wrote a treatise on pf. playing. Works incl. numerous sonatas for harpsichord and later for pf., many with vln. accomp.

Hume, Tobias (b c 1569; d London, 16 Apr 1645), English vla. da gamba player and composer. He was an army captain and towards the end of his life a pensioner in the Charterhouse. Wrote dances for vla. da gamba, songs to the lute, etc., pub. in *Musicall Humours* and *Poeticall Musicke* (1607).

Humfrey, Pelham (b ? London, 1647; d Windsor, 14 Jul 1674), English composer. Entered the re-estab. Chapel Royal in London in 1660 under Cooke, joined Blow and Turner in the comp. of the so-called 'club anthem' and was sent abroad for study by Charles II in 1664. Returned in 1667 from Fr. and It. and became a Gentleman of the Chapel Royal, where he succeeded Cooke as Master of the Children in 1672; he died aged only 26.

Works incl. music to Shakespeare's *Tempest* (1674), Dryden's *Conquest of Granada* and *The Indian Emperor*, Crowne's *History of Charles VIII* and Wycherley's *Love in a Wood*; anthems; odes, sacred songs, airs for 1 and 2 voices.

Hummel, Ferdinand (b Berlin, 6 Sep 1855; d Berlin, 24 Apr 1928), German pianist, harpist and composer. After playing pf. and harp in public as a child, he studied at Kullak's Cons. in Berlin and later had a success with realistic operas.

Works incl. operas *Mara* (1893), *Angla* (1894), *Ein treuer Schelm* (1894), *Assarpai*, *Sophie von Brabant* (1899), *Die Beichte* (1899), *Die Gefilde der Seligen*; incid. music for 14 plays by Wildenbruch and others; symph., overture; pf. concerto, fantasy for harp and orch.; choral works; chamber music; pf. pieces.

Hummel, Johan Nepomuka (Johann Nepomuk) (b Pozsony, 14 Nov 1778; d Weimar, 17 1837), Hungarian pianist and composer. Learnt music at first from his father, the cond. Joseph H., who went to

Vienna in 1785 as cond. of the Theater auf der Wieden. By that time he was already a brilliant pianist and Mozart took him as a pupil for 2 years. In 1787 he went to tour in Ger., Hol., Scot. and Eng. and had further lessons from Clementi in London, where he stayed until 1792. In 1793 he was back in Vienna, studying comp. with Albrechtsberger, Haydn and Salieri. In 1803 he visited Rus. and from 1804–11 he was music dir. to Prince Esterházy. In 1816–19 he held a similar post at the court of Württemberg at Stuttgart and in 1819–22 and 1833–7 at that of Weimar, undertaking extensive concert tours in between, spending much time in London. He married the singer Elisabeth Röckl (1793–1883).

Works incl. operas *Die Rückfahrt des Kaisers* (1814) and *Mathilde von Guise* (1810); ballets *Hélène et Paris* (1807), *Das belebte Gemälde*, *Sappho*; pantomime *Der Zauberring* (1811), incid. music to Grillparzer's *Die Ahnfrau*; Masses and other church music; 7 pf. concertos; trumpet concerto (1803), chamber music; sonatas for pf. with another instrument; pf. sonatas, rondos, variations.

Humoreske (Ger.) ⎱ a piece (or in Schu-
Humoresque (Fr.) ⎰ mann a series of movements) of capricious or fantastic rather than humorous character.

Humperdinck, Engelbert (b Siegburg, 1 Sep 1854; d Neustrelitz, 27 Sep 1921), German composer. Studied under F. Hiller at the Cologne Cons. and later with F. Lachner and Rheinberger at Munich. In 1879 he met Wagner in It. and acted as his asst. at Bayreuth in 1880–1. Later he travelled in France, It. and Spain and taught at the Barcelona Cons. in 1885–7. In 1890–6 he taught at the Hoch Cons. at Frankfurt and was for a time music critic of the *Frankfurter Zeitung*. In 1900 he became dir. of the Meisterschlule for comp. in Berlin.

Works incl. operas *Hänsel und Gretel* (1893), *Dornröschen* (1902), *Die Heirat wider Willen* (1905), *Königskinder* (1910), *Die Marketenderin*, *Gaudeamus*; play with music *Königskinder* (an earlier version of the opera); spectacular pantomime *The Miracle*; incid. music to Shakespeare's *Merchant of Venice* (1905), *Winter's Tale* (1906), *The Tempest* (1906) and *Twelfth Night*, Maeterlinck's *The Blue Bird* (1912), Aristophanes' *Lysistrata*; choral works *Das Glück von Edenhall* (Uhland), *Die Wallfahrt nach Kevlaar* (Heine); *Humoreske* and *Maurische Rhapsodie* for orch.; part-songs, songs.

Humphrey, Pelham. See **Humfrey.**

Humphries, John (b c 1707; d c 1740), English composer. Pub. 6 solos for vln. and bass and 2 sets of concertos. He is possibly identical with J.S. Humphries, who c 1733 pub. a set of sonatas for 2 vlns.

Hungarian Sketches, work for orch. by Bartók, arr. from pf. pieces incl. *4 Dirges* and *3 Burlesques,* 1931; fp Budapest, 26 Nov 1934. Movts. are titled *An evening in the village, Bear dance, Melody, Slightly tipsy, Swineherd's Dance.*

Hunnenschlacht (*Battle of the Huns*), symph. poem by Liszt inspired by Kaulbach's fresco, comp. 1857; fp Weimar, 29 Dec 1857.

Hunnis, William (d London, 6 Jun 1597), English composer. Gentleman of the Chapel Royal in the reigns of Edward VI, Mary I and Elizabeth, though dismissed as a Protestant in Mary's time. He became Master of the Children in 1566.
Works incl. metrical psalms and other portions of the Bible versified by himself.

Hunt, Arabella (b c 1645; d London, 26 Dec 1705), English singer and lutenist. Music teacher of Princess (later Queen) Anne and a favourite of Queen Mary. Blow and Purcell wrote many songs for her. Congreve wrote an ode on her and Kneller painted her portrait.

'Hunt' Quartet, the familiar nickname of Mozart's B♭ maj. string 4tet, K458, because the opening suggests hunting-horns.

Hunter, Rita (b Wallasey, 15 Aug 1933), English soprano. She studied in Liverpool and London. SW chorus from 1954 and Carl Rosa Co., solo roles with SW, from 1959, incl. Marcellina, Senta and Odabella in *Attila.* Sang Brünnhilde in *Die Walküre* at the London Coliseum 1970, also role of NY Met debut in 1972. Brünnhilde in *Ring* cycle at Coliseum 1973; other roles have been Norma, Santuzza and Leonora (*Trovatore*).

Hunyady László, opera by Erkel (lib. by B. Egressy), prod. Budapest, 27 Jan 1844. The chief Hung. nat. opera.

Huon de Bordeaux, medieval French romance. See **Oberon** (Weber and Wranitzky).

Hurdy-Gurdy (onomat.), the English name for the medieval *organistrum.* Its strings, usually 6, are set vibrating by a wheel turned with a handle. The tune is played on the top string by means of a keyboard, the lower strings remaining unchanged in pitch and thus acting as a drone.

Hurlebusch, Heinrich Lorenz (b Hanover, 8 Jul 1666; d Brunswick), German organist and composer. Wrote organ works.

Hurlebusch, Konrad Friedrich (b Bruns-

wick, 1696; d Amsterdam, 17 Dec 1765), German organist and composer, son of prec. Travelled much as a virtuoso, visiting Italy and Swed., holding brief offices at Brunswick and Hamburg, and finally settling at Amsterdam.
Works incl. operas, cantatas, hymns, overtures, harpsichord pieces, songs, etc.

Hurlstone, William (Yeates) (b London, 7 Jan 1876; d London, 30 May 1906), English pianist and composer. Studied at the RCM in London, having already pub. waltzes for pf. at the age of 9. Prof. of counterpoint at the RCM from 1905 to his early death.
Works incl. Fantasy-Variations on a Swed. Air and suite *The Magic Mirror* for orch. (1896); pf. concerto (1896); string 4tet in E min., pf. and wind 5tet, pf. 4tet, Fantasy string 4tet. (1906); sontats for vln. and pf., cello and pf., bassoon and pf., suite for clar. and pf.

Hurwitz, Emanuel (b London, 7 May 1919), English violinist. Leader of the Goldsborough (later English) Chamber Orch. 1948–68; Melos Ensemble 1956–72; Aeolian Quartet from 1970. Hurwitz Chamber Orch. 1968, from 1972 known as the Serenata of London. CBE 1978.

Husa, Karel (b Prague, 7 Aug 1921), American composer and conductor of Czech birth. Studied at Prague Cons. and with Boulanger and Honegger in Paris. Emigrated to US 1954; prof. Cornell Univ. from 1961. He has been influenced by Czech folk music, neoclassicism and serialism.
Works incl. ORCH: Sinfonietta (1947), *3 Fresques* (1949), Divertimento for strings (1949), Symphony (1954), *Fantasies* (1957), Mosaïques (1961), Concerto for brass 5tet and orch. (1970), trumpet concerto (1974), *Monodrama* (1976), *The Trojan Women,* ballet for orch. (1981); 3 string 4tets (1948–68); *12 Moravian Songs.*

Hüsch, Gerhard (b Hanover, 2 Feb 1901; d Munich, 21 Nov 1984), German baritone. Made his debut in Osnabrück in 1924 and then sang at the Cologne Opera from 1927 to 1930 and in Bayreuth 1930–1 (Wolfram), Berlin from 1930 to 1942, London, CG 1930–8 as Falke and Papageno. In addition to being a fine opera-singer he was also a distinguished Lieder-singer, partic. in Schubert.

Husitská, concert overture by Dvořák, op. 67, comp. 1883, fp Prague, reopening of the Nat. Theatre, 13 Nov 1883. Based on the 10th-cent. St Vaclav chorale and the 15th-cent. Hussite hymn.

Hutchings, Arthur (James Bramwell) (b

Sunbury-on-Thames, 14 Jul 1906), English writer on music and composer. Author of books on Schubert, Mozart's pf. concertos, Delius and the Baroque concerto. In 1947 he followed Bairstow as Prof. of Music at Durham Univ., becoming prof. at Exeter Univ. from 1968 to 1971. Pub. *Mozart: The Man, the Musician* (1976), *Purcell* (1982). Works incl. *O quanta qualia, or Heart's Desire* (Abélard) for double chorus, orch., brass band and org.; motets and other church music; works for string orch.

Hüttenbrenner, Anselm (b Graz, 13 Oct 1794; d Ober-Andritz, nr. Graz, 5 Jun 1868), Austrian composer. Pupil of Salieri and friend of Schubert, whose unfinished symph. he withheld from the world until 1865.

Works incl. operas *Die Französische Einquartierung* (1819), *Ödipus auf Kolonos* (Sophocles, 1836), *Armella* and *Lenore*; incid. music for several plays; 10 Masses, 4 Requiems and other church music; 8 symphs.; 2 string 4tets; songs incl. a setting of Goethe's *Erlkönig*.

Huygens, Constantin (b The Hague, 4 Sep 1596; d The Hague, 28 Mar 1687), Dutch official, physicist, poet, writer, linguist and musician. He was military secretary at The Hague from 1625 to his death. He was a lutenist and also played viol and the keyboard instruments, paying 3 visits to England and others to Ger., It. and Fr. He collected a library and wrote on the use of the organ in church and other musical subjects. Comp. nearly 900 pieces for lute, theorbo, guitar, etc. One of his sons, Christian H. (1629–95), was also a musician as well as a mathematician.

Hyde, Walter (b Birmingham, 6 Feb 1875; d London, 11 Nov 1951), English tenor. While still a student at the RCM he appeared in operas by Weber and Stanford. CG, London, 1908–23; sang Siegmund under Richter, 1908, and Sali in the 1st London perf. of *A Village Romeo and Juliet* (1910). NY Met debut Mar 1910, as Siegmund. Often sang Mozart with the Beecham Opera Company and the BNOC.

Hygons, Richard (b c 1435; d Wells, 1508), English composer. He was one of the organists at Wells Cathedral, 1461–2, and master of the choristers there, 1479–1508, when he was succeeded by John Clausy. His only complete surviving work, a 5-part *Salve regina*, is in the Eton Choirbook.

Hymn, a metrical song in praise of God. Many medieval hymns survive with plainsong melodies, which should properly be sung unacc. The Protestant churches in the 16th cent. adopted the practice of harmonizing hymn tunes. *See* **Choral.**

Hymn of Jesus, The, work by Holst for 3 choruses and orch., op. 37 (text Holst's trans. from the Apocryphal Acts of St John); comp. 1917 and ded. to Vaughan Williams; fp London, 25 Mar 1920.

Hymn of Praise (Lobgesang), Mendelssohn's symph. cantata, op. 52, in which three movements of a symph. precede the choral portion; prod. Leipzig, St Thomas's Church, 25 Jun 1840; in Eng., Birmingham Festival, 23 Sep 1840.

Hymn of the Nations (Verdi). *See* **Inno delle nazioni.**

Hymne au Saint Sacrement, work for orch. by Messiaen; comp. 1932, fp Paris, 23 Mar 1933. 1st US perf. NY, 13 Mar 1947, cond. Stokowski.

Hymnen (*Anthems*) work for electronic insts. by Stockhausen, which re-processes a selection of the world's national anthems; comp. 1966, fp Cologne, 30 Nov 1967. Also in versions with added soloists and, shorter, with orch.

Hymnus Amoris (*Hymn of Love*), work by Nielsen for soloists, adult and children's choruses and orch. (text in Danish by A. Olrik, in Latin by J.L. Heiberg); comp. 1896, fp Copenhagen, 27 Apr 1897, cond. Nielsen.

Hyperprism, work by Varèse for wind and perc.; fp NY, 4 Mar 1923.

I

IRCAM (abbr.) = Institut de recherche et de co-ordination acoustique musique. Electronic studios in Pompidou Centre, Paris. Established 1977 under Pierre Boulez, to explore modern comp. techniques. The tape for Harrison Birtwistle's opera *The Mask of Orpheus* (1986) was prepared there.

ISCM (abbr.) = International Society for Contemporary Music. Annual festival founded at Salzburg in 1922, under presidency of E.J. Dent. Held at different centre each year.

Iberia, 4 sets of pf. pieces by I. Albéniz, representing different parts of Spain, comp. at various times before 1909; I. *Evocación*, *El Puerto*, *Fête-Dieu à Séville*; II. *Triana*, *Almeria*, *Rondeña*; III. *El Albaicin*, *El Polo*, *Lavapiés*; IV. *Málaga*, *Jérez*, *Eritaña*.

Ibéria (Debussy). *See* Images pour Orchestre.

Ibert, Jacques (François Antoine) (b Paris, 15 Aug 1890; d Paris, 5 Feb 1962), French composer. Studied at the Paris Cons. and gained the Prix de Rome in 1919. He became director of the Fr. Acad. in Rome in 1937 and returned there after World War II. From 1955 to 1957 he was director of the Opéra-Comique in Paris.

Works incl. OPERAS: *Angélique* (1927), *Persée et Andromède* (1929), *On ne saurait penser à tout*, *Le Roi d'Yvetot* (1930), *Gonzague*, *L'Aiglon* (after Rostand, with Honegger, 1937), *Le Petit Cardinal* (with Honegger, 1938); radio opera *Barbe-bleue* (1943).

BALLETS: *Les Rencontres* (1925), *Diane de Poitiers* and contrib. to *L'Eventail de Jeanne*.

INCID. MUSIC to Labiche's *Le Chapeau de paille d'Italie* and other plays, also (with 6 others) for Rolland's *Le 14 Juillet*; film music incl. *Don Quichotte*; cantata *Le Poète et la Fée*.

ORCHESTRAL: Symph. poem *La Ballade de la geôle de Reading* (after Wilde, 1922); suites *Escales* and *Paris*, *Scherzo féerique*, *Nationale* (for Paris Exhib., 1937), *Jeux*, *Donogoo*, *Ouverture pour une fête*, all for orch.; *Divertissement* for chamber orch. (1930); concertos for pf., for saxophone and for cello and wind.

CHAMBER: String 4tet (1944).

PIANO: incl. *Pièces romantiques*, *Noël de Picardie*, *Le Vent dans les ruines*, *Matin sur l'eau*, *Le Petit Âne blanc*, etc.; 5 pieces for harp; pieces for pipes and pf.

Ice Break, The, opera by Tippett (lib. by comp.), prod. London, CG, 7 Jul 1977, cond. C. Davis.

Ideale, Die (*The Ideals*), symph. poem by Liszt, based on a poem by Schiller, comp. 1857, fp Weimar, 5 Sep 1857 at the unveiling of the Goethe-Schiller monument.

Idée fixe, Berlioz's term for a theme (e.g. in the *Fantastic Symph*.) which recurs in varying forms in the course of a comp. as an allusion to some definite idea.

Idiot, Der, ballet-pantomime by Henze (scenario by I. Bachmann after Dostoievsky), prod. Berlin, 1 Sep 1952.

Idoménée (*Idomeneus*), opera by Campra (lib. by A. Danchet), prod. Paris, Opéra, 12 Jan 1712.

Idomeneo, rè di Creta, ossia Ilia ed Idamante (*Idomeneus, King of Crete, or Ilia and Idamantes*), opera by Mozart (lib. by G.B. Varesco, based on the Fr. lib. by A. Danchet), prod. Munich, 29 Jan 1781.

Idyll, work for string orch. in 7 movts. by Janáček; 1878, fp Brno, 15 Dec 1878.

Idyll: Once I passed through a populous city, work by Delius for sop., bar. and orch. (text from Walt Whitman); comp. 1930–2, with re-workings from the then unperf. opera *Margot-la-Rouge*, 1901–2; fp London, 3 Oct 1933, cond. Wood. Delius's last work.

Ifigenia, L', opera by Jommelli (lib. by M. Verazi), prod. Rome, Teatro Argentina, 9 Feb 1751.

Ifigenia in Aulide (*Iphigenia in Aulis*), opera by Caldara (lib. by A. Zeno), prod. Vienna, 4 Nov 1718.

Opera by Cherubini (lib. by F. Moretti), prod. Turin, Teatro Regio, 12 Jan 1788.

Opera by Graun (lib. by L. de Villati, after Racine's *Iphigénie en Aulide*), prod. Berlin, Royal Opera, 13 Dec 1748. Frederick II of Prus. prob. collaborated.

Opera by Zingarelli (lib. by F. Moretti), prod. Milan, La Scala, 27 Jan 1787.

(All libs. based ultimately on Euripides.)

Ifigenia in Tauride (*Iphigenia in Tauris*), opera by Galuppi (lib. by M. Coltellini), prod. St Petersburg, at court, 2 May 1768.

Opera by Maio (lib. by M. Verazi), prod. Mannheim, at court, 4 Nov 1764.

Opera by Traetta (lib. by M. Coltellini), prod. Vienna, Schönbrunn Palace, at court, 4 Oct 1763.

(Libs. based on Euripides.)

See also Iphigénie.

Île de Merlin, L',ou Le Monde renversé (*Merlin's Island or the World Upside-down*), opera by Gluck (lib. by L. Anseaume), prod. Vienna, Schönbrunn Palace, at court, 3 Oct 1758.

Ileborgh, Adam, 15th-cent. German priest and musician. He compiled and owned a collection of keyboard music, now in the Curtis Inst. of Music, Philadelphia. It bears the date 1448 and contains early exs. of preludes for organ incl. pedals.

Illica, Luigi (b Piacenza, 9 May 1857; d Colombarone, 16 Dec 1919), Italian playwright and librettist. The first of his 88 libs. was for Smareglia's *Il vassallo di Szigeth* (prod. Vienna, 1889); also collaborated with Catalani, Giordano, Mascagni and D'Erlanger. Best known for libs. for Puccini's *Manon Lescaut*, *La Bohème* (with G. Giacosa), *Tosca* and *Madama Butterfly*.

Illuminations, Les, song cycle by Britten for high voice and strings (text 9 prose poems by A. Rimbaud, 1872–3); comp. 1938–9, fp London, 30 Jan 1940.

Ilosvay, Maria von (b Budapest, 8 May 1913), Hungarian mezzo. She toured N. Amer. with the Salzburg Opera Guild 1937–9, as Dorabella; joined Hamburg Opera 1940 and guest in Vienna, Munich and Stuttgart after the war. She took part in the 1949 fp of Orff's *Antigonae*, at Salzburg, and from 1951 was heard as Erda at Bayreuth. CG 1956. Berg's Countess Geschwitz is among her recorded roles.

Images, 2 sets of pf. pieces by Debussy: 1st series comp. 1905, *Reflets dans l'eau*, *Hommage à Rameau*, *Mouvement*, fp Paris, 3 Mar 1906; 2nd series, comp. 1907, *Cloches à travers les feuilles*, *Et la lune descend sur le temple qui fut*, *Poissons d'or*, fp Paris, 21 Feb 1908.

Images pour Orchestre, 3 symph. pieces by Debussy: *Gigues* (orig. *Gigues tristes*), comp. 1906–11; *Rondes de printemps*, comp. 1909; *Ibéria* (*Par les rues et par les chemins*, *Les Parfums de la nuit* and *Le Matin d'un jour de fête*), finished 1908. *Ibéria* fp Paris, 20 Feb 1910, cond. Pierné; fp 3 pieces Paris, 26 Jan 1913, cond. Pierné.

Imbrie, Andrew (Welsh) (b New York, 6 Apr 1921), American composer and pianist. He studied with Sessions and at Univ. of Calif., at Berkeley; prof. there from 1960. Writes in standard forms, with 12-note technique.

Works incl. 3 symphs. (1966–70), concertos for vln. (1954), cello (1972), pf. (1973, 1974) and flute (1977); 4 string 4tets (1942–69), cello sonata (1969); operas *Christmas*

in Peebles Town (1964) and *Angle of Repose* (1976).

Imeneo (*Hymeneus*), opera by Handel (lib. adapted from S. Stampiglia), comp. 1738, prod. Lincoln's Inn Fields, London, 22 Nov 1740. Handel's penultimate opera.

Imitation, a device in comp. whereby a musical figure is repeated after its 1st statement, either exactly or with some change, such as displacement to a higher or lower position, augmentation, diminution, rhythmic distortion, elaboration, simplification, etc. Such an imitation may either be deferred until the 1st statement has been completed or made to overlap with it.

Immortal Hour, The, opera by Boughton (lib. by comp. adapted from plays and poems by Fiona Macleod), prod. Glastonbury, 26 Aug 1914.

Imperfect Cadence. See **Half-Close**.

Impériale, L', nickname of Haydn's symph. no. 53 in D maj., comp, c 1775.

Impresario in angustie, L'(*The Impresario in Distress*), opera by Cimarosa (lib. by G.M. Diodati, similar to that of Mozart's *Schauspieldirektor*), prod. Naples, Teatro Nuovo, Oct 1786.

Impresario, The (Mozart). See **Schauspieldirektor**.

Impressionism, a term properly belonging to painting but transferred, more or less loosely, to comps. (esp. Fr.) contemporary with the school of impressionist painters. Debussy, although he disapproved, was designated as the leader of musical impressionism. One of the chief aims of impressionism is to interpret artistically a momentary glimpse of things rather than their permanent state.

Impromptu (from Lat. *in promptu* = in readiness), a piece of music suggesting, or intended to suggest, that it resembles an improvisation.

Improvisation, performance of music that is not written down or goes beyond the details of the written score. The term inevitably covers a wide range of musical phenomena, since it can involve merely slight deviation of rhythm and articulation from what had been rehearsed; the relatively carefully planned realization of a continuo line or embellishment along accepted lines; the addition of accompaniments or counterpoints in a received style; and many freer kinds of unplanned music. The apparently unfettered improvisation of the church organist or the jazz player is rarely entirely original but rather an assembly and juxtaposition of received formulas.

Improvisation sur Mallarmé, 2 works by Boulez after Stéphane Mallarmé: no. 1 for sop., harp, tubular bells, vib. and 4 perc.; comp. 1957, fp Hamburg, 13 Jan 1958, cond. Rosbaud. Also for sop. and orch., fp Donaueschingen, 20 Oct 1962, cond. Boulez. no. 2, same forces as 1.i, with pf.; comp. 1957, fp 13 Jan 1958.

In Nature's Realm (Dvořák). *See* **Amid Nature.**

In Nomine, an instrumental piece of the later 16th cent. for viols or keyboard, similar to the Fancy or Fantasia, but based on a plainsong melody used as a *cantus firmus*. The melody is that of 'Gloria tibi Trinitas', an antiphon for Trinity Sunday, which was used by Taverner as the *cantus firmus* of a Mass with the title *Gloria tibi Trinitas.* Part of the *Benedictus* of this Mass, beginning at the words 'In nomine Domini', was arranged as an instrumental piece, and this seems to have suggested to other comps. the idea of writing orig. instrumental pieces on the same *cantus firmus.* The last comp. to write In nomines was Purcell.

In questa tomba oscura, a collective work, of which only Beethoven's song remains known today. In 1808 comps. were invited to set this poem by Giuseppe Carpani, probably at the invitation of Countess Rzewuska in Vienna. Among the 63 comps. who responded were, apart from Beethoven, Asioli, Cherubini, Czerny, Paer, Reichardt, Righini, Salieri, Tomášek, Weigl and Zingarelli.

In the Mists (*V mlhách*), work by Janáček in 4 movts for pf.; comp. 1912.

In the South, Alassio, concert overture by Elgar, op. 50, comp. during a visit to It. in 1903 and pub. in 1904. Fp London, 16 Mar 1904, cond. Elgar.

Incalzando (It.) = persuading, urging forward, *i.e.* accelerating the pace.

Incidental Music, songs and instrumental music intro. into spoken drama, either in the form of preludes or interludes or as an essential part of the action, e.g. marches, dances.

Incledon, Charles (Benjamin) (b St Keverne, Cornwall, bap. 5 Feb 1763; d London, 18 Feb 1826), English tenor. Chorister at Exeter Cathedral, he joined the Navy at the age of 16, but on his return to Eng. in 1783 became a professional singer. Made his London debut at Vauxhall Gardens in 1790. In 1800 sang in 1st Brit. perf. *The Creation,* at CG.

Incognita, opera by Wellesz (lib. by E. Mackenzie, on Congreve's story), prod. Oxford, 5 Dec 1951.

Incontro improvviso, L' (*The Unforeseen*

Meeting), opera by Haydn (lib. by K. Friberth, trans. into It. from Dancourt's *La Rencontre imprévue,* comp. by Gluck), prod. Eszterháza, 29 Aug 1775.

Incoronazione di Poppea, L' (*The Coronation of Poppaea*), opera by Monteverdi (lib. by Busenello, based on Tacitus), prod. Venice, Teatro SS. Giovanni e Paolo, autumn 1642. Modern eds. by Westrup (1st Brit. prod., Oxford 1927), Krenek, d'Indy, Malipiero, Ghedini, Leppard, Norrington, Harnoncourt and Curtis.

Indes galantes, Les (*Love in the Indies*), opera-ballet by Rameau (lib. by L. Fuzelier), prod. Paris, Opéra, 23 Aug 1735. The 4 entrées are *Le turc généreux, Les Incas du Pérou, Les fleurs, Les sauvages.*

India, Sigismondo d' (b Palermo, *c* 1582; d ? Modena, before 1629), Italian composer and singer. Best known as composer of madrigals and regarded as the most important of Monteverdi's contemporaries: collections pub. in Milan and Venice 1609–23. During this time he was dir. of music to the Duke of Savoy in Turin. In 1625 his sacred drama *Sant' Eustachio* was prod. in Cardinal Maurizio's palace, Rome. The following year he moved to Modena.

Indian Queen, The, play by Dryden and Robert Howard, prod. 1664; adapted as a semi-opera with music by Henry and Daniel Purcell, prod. London, Drury Lane Theatre, 1695.

Indianische Fantasie, work by Busoni for pf. and orch. op. 44, based on Amer. Indian themes (Busoni was prof. at New England Cons. 1891–4); comp. 1913, fp Berlin, 12 Mar 1914.

Indigo und die vierzig Räuber (*I. and the Forty Robbers*), operetta by J. Strauss, jun. (lib. by M. Steiner), prod. Vienna, Theater an der Wien, 10 Feb 1871. Strauss's 1st operetta.

Indy, (Paul Marie Théodore) Vincent d' (b Paris, 27 Mar 1851; d Paris, 2 Dec 1931), French composer. Although born in Paris, he belonged to a noble family of the Ardèche district in the Vivarais. His mother died at his birth and he was brought up by his paternal grandmother, a good musician. At the age of 11 he was sent to Diémer for the pf. and Lavignac for theory, and later studied pf. under Marmontel. In 1870 he pub. his 1st works and served in the defence of Paris against the Prus. army. To please his family he studied law, but was determined to be a musician and went for advice to Franck, who offered to teach him. He also joined Colonne's orch. as timpanist to gain experience. Pasdeloup gave the fp of one of his works, the overture to Schiller's *Piccolomini*, afterwards part of his *Wallenstein* trilogy. Next to Franck he admired Liszt, with whom he spent 2 months at Weimar in 1873, and Wagner, whose 1st *Ring* cycle he attended at Bayreuth in 1876. In 1894 he joined Charles Bordes, together with Guilmant, in founding the Schola Cantorum; he taught there until his death and had many pupils of the highest distinction. From 1912 he also directed the orchestral class at the Cons.

Works incl. operas *Attendez-moi sous l'orme* (after Regnard, 1882), *Le Chant de la cloche* (1879–83), *Fervaal* (1897), *L'Étranger*, *La Légende de Saint Christophe* (1908–15), *La Rêve de Cinyras.*
INCID. MUSIC for Catulle Mendès's *Médée.*
ORCH: 2 symphs., *Jean Hunyade* and *De bello gallico*, symph. trilogy *Wallenstein* (after Schiller), symph. variations *Istar* (1896), *Jour d'été à la montagne* (1905); *Symphonie sur un chant montagnard français (Symph. cévenole)* for pf. and orch. (1886).
CHAMBER: 3 string 4tets (1890, 1897, 1929), string 6tet, pf. 4tet and pf. 5tet (1888, 1924), trios for pf., clar. and cello and pf., vln. and cello, suite for tpt., 2 fls. and string 4tet, and some other chamber works; sonatas for vln. and pf. and cello and pf.
PIANO AND SONGS: 18 op. nos. of pf. works, incl. *Poèmes des montagnes, Tableaux de voyage*, sonata in E maj., *Thème varié, Fugue et Chanson*; 3 organ works; 10 songs; 90 *Chansons populaires du Vivarais* arr.; 12 Fr. folksongs for unaccomp. chorus; var. vocal works with and without orch.
Inextinguishable, The (*Det Uudslukkelige*), title of Nielsen's 4th symph.; comp. 1915–16, fp Copenhagen, 1 Feb 1916, cond. Nielsen.
Inez de Castro, opera by Persiani (lib. by S. Cammarano), prod. Naples, Teatro San Carlo, 28 Jan 1835. It was written for Malibran.
Infantas, Fernando de las (b Córdoba, 1534; d after 1609), Spanish composer, descendant of the Fernández family of Córdoba, known by that name because one of his ancestors conveyed the infantas Constanza and Isabella to Bayonne, occupied by the Eng. in the 14th cent., before their marriage to John of Gaunt and Edmund Langley. His comps. attracted the attention of the Bishop of Córdoba, the Archduke Charles of Austria. He settled in Rome c 1559, but took holy orders in 1584 and went to Paris; returned to Spain by 1608.

Works incl. motets, some for special occasions, such as the death of the Emperor Charles V (1558) and the battle of Lepanto (1571), a setting of Psalm xcix, etc.
Infinite Canon, a canon contrived to make the end overlap with the beginning, so that it can be repeated to infinity.
Inganno felice, L' (*The Happy Deceit*), opera by Rossini (lib. by G.M. Foppa), prod. Venice, Teatro San Moise, 8 Jan 1812.
Ingegneri, Marc Antonio (b Verona, c 1545; d Cremona, 1 Jul 1592), Italian composer. Learnt music from V. Ruffo at Verona Cathedral and c 1570 became *maestro di cappella* at Cremona Cathedral. Monteverdi was his pupil there.
Works incl. 2 books of Masses, 3 books of motets, 1 of hymns and 8 of madrigals; also 27 responsories for Holy Week (long attrib. to Palestrina).
Ingenhoven, Jan (b Breda, 29 May 1876; d Hoenderloo, 20 May 1951), Dutch conductor and composer. He was a choral cond. before he had any systematic musical educ., but studied later with Brandts-Buys and with Mottl at Munich, where he cond. both orchestral and choral concerts, as he did later both in Hol. and abroad. He also sang tenor and played the pf. and clar.
Works incl. 3 symph. pieces for orch.; symph. fantasy on Nietzsche's *Zarathustras Nachtlied* (1906) and ballad *Klaus Tink* for voice and orch.; 3 string 4tets (1908–12); vln. and pf. sonata in C maj., cello and pf. sonata in G maj.; choruses and vocal 4tets; songs, etc.
Inghelbrecht, D(ésiré-) É(mile) (b Paris, 17 Sep 1880; d Paris, 14 Feb 1965), French conductor and composer. Cond. many concerts of modern music in Paris, also the Swed. Ballet in Paris and London.
Works incl. operas *La Nuit vénitienne* (after Musset, 1908), and *La Chêne et le tilleul* (1960); 2 operettas; ballets *El Greco* (1920) and *Le Diable dans le beffroi* (1921); Requiem; *Cantique des créatures de Saint François* for chorus and orch.; *Sinfonia breve* (1930); string 4tet; sonata for fl. and harp; 5tet for strings and harp; *Suite Petite-Russienne* and other pf. works; *La Nursery* for pf. duet (3 books); songs.
Inghilleri, Giovanni (b Porto Empedocle, 9 Mar 1894; d Milan, 10 Dec 1959), Italian baritone and composer. Debut Milan 1919, as Valentin. He sang at CG 1928–35 and Chicago 1929–30; sang in the fps of Casella's *La Donna Serpente* (Rome 1932) and Malipiero's *Giulio Cesare* (Genoa 1936).

Well known as Gérard, Scarpia, Amonasro and Amfortas. Taught at Pesaro from 1956. The opera *La burla* is among his compositions.

Innig (Ger. = inward, intimate, heartfelt), a term frequently used by Ger. romantic comps, esp. Schumann, where profound feeling is required in perf.

Inno delle nazioni (Hymn of the Nations), cantata by Verdi written for the International Exhibition in London, but prod. at Her Majesty's Theatre, 24 May 1862. It intro. nat. airs in contrapuntal combination.

Innocenza giustificata, L' (*Innocence Vindicated*), opera by Gluck (lib. by G. Durazzo, with words for the airs by Metastasio), prod. Vienna, Burgtheater, 8 Dec 1755.

Inori (*Adorations*), work for soloist(s) and orch. by Stockhausen, fp Donaueschingen, 20 Oct 1974.

Insanguine, Giacomo (b Monopoli, Bari, 22 Mar 1728; d Naples, 1 Feb 1795), Italian composer. Studied at the Cons. di Sant' Onofrio at Naples, where he taught from 1767, eventually becoming *maestro di cappella*. Between 1756 and 1782 he prod. 21 operas. Other works incl. Masses and other church music, cantatas, arias.

Institut de recherche et de co-ordination acoustique/musique. *See* **IRCAM.**

Instrumentation, the art of writing for instruments in a manner suited to their nature, also Orchestration.

Instruments, classification of. Among the many possible ways of classifying musical instruments, the one most commonly used by instrument museums is that devised by Curt Sachs and Erich von Hornbostel in 1914 which describes instruments in terms of the vibrating body: Idiophones (a solid body, as in a wood-block); Membranophones (a stretched skin, as in a drum); Chordophones (a string, as in a violin, guitar or piano); and Aerophones (a hollow body, as in wind instruments). To this more recent studies have inevitably added the Electrophones, accounting for a wide range of electronic instruments.

Intavolatura (It.), Tablature. In the 16th and 17th cents. the term was used for pubs. issued for keyboard instruments and written on 2 staves, as distinct from instrumental music printed in score or in separate parts.

Intégrales, work for small orch. and perc. by Varèse; comp. 1923, fp NY, 1 Mar 1925, cond. Stokowski.

Intendant (Ger.), the manager or director of an opera-house or other theatre in Ger., esp. one attached to a court in former times.

Interdominant, a useful term to describe temporary dominants in the keys in which episodes may appear in the course of a comp., other than the dominant of the prescribed key. The same as the Ger. *Zwischendominante.*

Interlude, a piece of music played or (more rarely) sung between 2 others or forming a bridge between 2 distinct sections of a large-scale comp.; also a musical piece perf. between parts of some other perf. or function, such as certain liturgical portions of a church service, acts or scenes of a play, dances at a ball or courses of a dinner, etc. Act-tunes (*entr'actes*) in a theatre are, properly speaking, interludes.

Intermède (Fr.) = Interlude, Intermezzo.

Intermedio. *See* **Intermezzo.**

Intermezzo (It. = interlude), in the 16th cent. (*intermedio*) a series of vocal and instrumental pieces interpolated in a festival play or other dramatic entertainment.

In the 18th cent. a comic operatic piece, usually in 2 scenes and for 2 or 3 characters, 1 of whom could be a 'mute', played as an interlude between the acts of a serious opera in It., esp. Naples. The most famous ex. is Pergolesi's *La serva padrona.*

In general any musical piece played between the parts of a larger work, musical or theatrical. Also a short concert piece, not necessarily designed for any purpose implied by the name, e.g. Brahms's Intermezzi for pf.

Intermezzo, opera by R. Strauss (lib. by comp.), prod. Dresden, 4 Nov 1924. The material of the lib. is autobiographical.

International Society for Contemporary Music. *See* **ISCM.**

Interval, the difference between two musical pitches. There are two main ways of measuring intervals: diatonically, that is in terms of the major or minor scale, for which purposes it is normal to include the first and last notes, thus the distance between C and D is called a major 2nd; and acoustically, particularly in terms of 'cents', divisions of the semitone into 100 equal parts and the octave into 1200 equal parts.

Intimate Letters (*Listy důverné*), sub-title of Janáček's 2nd string 4tet, comp. 1928 and inspired by his unrequited love for Kamilla Stoesslová, 38 years his junior, and to whom he wrote almost daily letters during the last 10 years of his life. Fp Brno, 11 Sep 1928; one month after Janáček's death.

Into the Labyrinth, cantata for tenor and orch. by Maxwell Davies (text by G. Mackay Brown), fp Kirkwall, Orkney, 22 Jun 1983.

Intonazione (It., lit. Intonation), a 16th-cent. term for a prelude, esp. one for organ used in church to precede a service.

Intoning, in plainsong, the singing of the opening phrase by a singer in authority to ensure that the right melody will be sung and at the proper pitch.

Intrada (It., now *entrada*; lit. entrance, entry) = Introduction, Prelude.

Introduction and Allegro, work for string 4tet and string orch. by Elgar; comp. 1904–5, fp London, 8 Mar 1905, cond. Elgar.

Title of Ravel's Septet for harp, string 4tet, flute and clar.; comp. 1906, fp Paris, 22 Feb 1907.

Introit (Lat. *introitus* = entrance), the 1st item of the Proper of the Mass, accompanying the entry of the ministers. Orig. a complete psalm with antiphon before and after each verse, it was reduced in the Middle Ages to its present form of antiphon, psalm-verse, *Gloria Patri* and repeat of antiphon. The antiphon is a freely-comp. melody, the psalm being sung to a slightly ornate psalm-tone.

Inventions, the title given to Bach's 2 sets of short keyboard pieces written strictly in 2 and 3 parts respectively, and prob. designed as technical studies. He called the 3-part set 'symphonies', but there is no essential difference in character between them and the 2-part inventions.

Inversion. (1) Of an interval. The inversion of a 5th is a 4th.

(2) Of a melody. Writing a melody upside-down, i.e. the intervals remain the same but go in the opposite direction.

(3) Of a chord. A 3-note chord has 2 possible inversions, e.g.:

'Root' position 1st inversion 2nd inversion

A 4-note chord has 3 possible inversions, and so on.

(4) Of counterpoint. *See* **Counterpoint.**

Invertible Counterpoint. *See* **Counterpoint.**

Invitation to the Dance (Weber). *See* **Aufforderung zum Tanz.**

Iolanta, opera by Tchaikovsky (lib. by Modest Tchaikovsky, T's brother, based on Hertz's play *King René's Daughter*), prod. St Petersburg, 18 Dec 1892.

Iolanthe, or The Peer and the Peri, operetta by Sullivan (lib. by W.S. Gilbert), prod. London, Savoy Theatre, 25 Nov 1882, and NY, Standard Theatre, same date.

Ione (old It. spelling *Jone*), opera by Petrella (lib. by G. Peruzzini, based on Bulwer-Lytton's novel *The Last Days of Pompeii*), prod. Milan, La Scala, 26 Jan 1858.

Ionian Mode, one of the 2 authentic modes recognized by Glareanus in the 16th cent., the other being the Aeolian Mode. Represented by the white keys of the pf. beginning from C, it corresponds exactly to the modern C maj. scale. *See* **Modes.**

Ionisation, work by Varèse for 13 perc., pf. and 2 sirens; 1931, fp NY 6 Mar 1933, cond. Slonimsky.

Ipermestra (*Hypermnestra*), opera by Gluck (lib. by Metastasio), prod. Venice, Teatro San Giovanni Cristostomo, 21 Nov 1744.

Iphigénie en Aulide (*Iphigenia in Aulis*), opera by Gluck (lib. by F.L.L. du Roullet, based on Racine and further back on Euripides), prod. Paris, Opéra, 19 Apr 1774. Gluck's 1st opera for the Paris stage, though not his 1st Fr. work.

Iphigénie en Tauride (*Iphigenia in Tauris*), opera by Desmarets and Campra (lib. by J.F. Duché and A. Danchet), prod. Paris, Opéra, 6 May 1704.

Opera by Gluck (lib. by N.F. Guillard), prod. Paris, Opéra, 18 May 1779.

Opera by Piccinni (lib. by A.C. Dubreuil), prod. Paris, Opéra, 23 Jan 1781.

(All libs. based on Euripides.)

See also **Ifigenia.**

Ippolito ed Aricia (*Hippolytus and Aricia*), opera by Traetta (lib. by C.I. Frugoni, trans. from S.J. de Pellegrin's lib. for Rameau's *Hippolyte et Aricie*, 1733); prod. Parma, 9 May 1759.

Ippolitov-Ivanov, Mikhail Mikhailovich (b Gatchina nr. St Petersburg, 19 Nov 1859; d Moscow, 28 Jan 1935), Russian composer. Studied under Rimsky-Korsakov at the St Petersburg Cons. In 1884 he was app. cond. of the Imp. opera at Tiflis, and in 1893 prof. at the Moscow Cons., of which he was director from 1906 to 1922.

Works incl. operas *Ruth* (1887), *Azra*, *Assia* (after Turgenev's story, 1900), *Treachery* (1910), *Ole from Norland* (1916), *The Last Barricade*, also completion of Mussorgsky's *Marriage* (1931); *Hymn to Labour* for chorus and orch. (1934), 2 symphs., *Caucasian Sketches* (1894), *Iberia*, *Armenian Rhapsody* (1895), *Mtsyri* (after Lermontov), *From Ossian*, *Episode from Schubert's Life*, *Turkish Fragments* (1930), *Mus. Scenes from Uzbekistan*, *The Year 1917*, *Catalonian Suite*, etc. for orch.

2 string 4tets; *An Evening in Georgia* for

harp and wind instruments; vln. and pf. sonata; pf. and other instrumental pieces; cantatas for chorus and pf.; 116 songs.

Ireland (real name Hutcheson), **Francis** (b Dublin, 13 Aug 1721; d Dublin, 1780), Irish physician and amateur composer. Wrote madrigal 'Return, return', glees, catches.

Ireland, John (b Bowdon, Ches., 13 Aug 1879; d Washington, Sussex, 12 Jun 1962), English composer. Studied at the RCM in London 1893–1901, his comp. master being Stanford. Apart from organist's appts., and his later comp. professorship at the RCM, he devoted himself entirely to creative work. In 1932 he received the hon. D.Mus. degree from Durham Univ.

Works incl. film music *The Overlanders* (1946–7); *Greater Love Hath no Man*, motet for chorus, orch. and organ (1912), Morning and Evening Services; *These Things shall be* (John Addington Symonds) for chorus and orch. (1936–7).

Prelude *The Forgotten Rite* (1913), symph. rhapsody *Mai-Dun* (1920–1), *A London Overture* (1936), *Epic March* and overture on Petronius's *Satyricon* for orch.; *Concertino pastorale* for string orch. (1939); concerto in Eb and *Legend* for pf. and orch.; *A Downland Suite* for brass band; *Maritime Overture* for military band (1944).

2 string 4tets (1895–7), 3 pf. trios; 2 vln. and pf. sonatas, cello and pf. sonata, fantasy-sonata for clar. and pf.; pf. sonata, sonatina; settings of poems by C. Rossetti, Housman and Masefield.

Iris, opera by Mascagni (lib. by L. Illica), prod. Rome, Teatro Costanzi, 22 Nov 1898.

Irische Legende, opera by Egk (lib. by comp. after Yeats's drama *The Countess Cathleen*, 1898), prod. Salzburg, 17 Aug 1955, cond. Szell; rev. 1970.

Irish Symphony, Stanford's 3rd symph., in F min, op. 28, comp. 1887, fp London, 27 Jun.

Irmelin, opera in 3 acts by Delius (lib. by comp.), prod. Oxford, 4 May 1953, cond. Beecham. Composed 1890–2.

Irrelohe, opera by Schreker (lib. by comp.); comp. 1919–23, prod. Cologne, 27 Mar 1924, cond. Klemperer.

Isaac, Henricus (Heinrich) (b Brabant or E. Flanders, c 1450; d Florence, 26 Mar 1517), Flemish composer. In c 1484, when he seems to have been at Innsbruck and in touch with Hofhaimer there, he went *via* Ferrara to Florence as musician to the Medici family. He became organist at the chapel of San Giovanni there, visited Rome in 1489 and married Bartolomea Bello, the daughter of a wealthy butcher. Lorenzo de' Medici having died in 1492 and his successor, Pietro, keeping a less lavish household, Isaac accepted an invitation from the Emperor Maximilian, who visited Pisa in 1496, to join the Imp. court, just then about to be transferred from Augsburg to Vienna; but he seems to have visited Innsbruck again to be formally app. and possibly Augsburg too. His duties were not arduous, so that he was able to live by turns in Vienna, Innsbruck, Constance (all connected with the court) and It. He also spent much time at the court of Ercole d'Este, Duke of Ferrara, and during his last years he remained at Florence.

Works incl. many Masses, c 50 motets, sequences, Lamentation *Oratio Jeremiae*, 58 4-part settings of the offices under the title *Choralis Constantinus*, the 1st polyphonic cycle of liturgical works for the ecclesiastical year: Webern wrote a dissertation on the CC in 1906; 4-part Monodia on the death of Lorenzo de' Medici (words by Poliziano); many Ger., It., Fr. and Lat. songs (incl. 'Innsbruck, ich muss dich lassen', which may not be his own tune), 58 instrumental pieces in 3–5 parts, 29 domestic pieces in 2–5 parts.

Isabeau, opera by Mascagni (lib. by L. Illica), prod. Buenos Aires, 2 Jun 1911, cond. Mascagni.

Isidor of Seville (b Carthage, c 560; d Seville, 4 Apr 636), philosopher and theologian. He was Archbishop of Seville from 599. His contrib. to music theory is contained in book III of his *Etymologiae* (largely a summary of Cassiodorus), and he deals with practical matters of church music in *De Ecclesiasticis Officiis*.

Isis, opera by Lully (lib. by Quinault), prod. Saint-Germain, 5 Jan 1677 and 1st perf. Paris, Apr 1677.

Isle of the Dead, The, symph. poem by Rakhmaninov, after a painting by A. Böcklin; comp. 1907, fp Moscow, 1 May 1909.

Isola disabitata, L' (*The Desert Island*), opera by Bonno (lib. by Metastasio), prod. Aranjuez, at the Spanish court, spring 1754, and Schlosshof nr. Vienna, before the Aus. court, 23 Sep 1754.

Opera by Haydn (lib. do.), prod. Eszterháza, 6 Dec 1779.

Opera by G. Scarlatti (lib. by Goldoni), prod. Venice, Teatro San Samuele, 20 Nov 1757.

Opera by Traetta (lib. by Metastasio), prod. Bologna, Teatro Comunale, ? 26 Apr 1768.

Isometric (from Gk. = equally metrical), a

manner of writing vocal music in several parts mainly in block chords, i.e. in the same rhythm.

Isorhythmic (from Gk. = equally rhythmic), a modern term for a method of construction used by comps. of polyphonic music in the 14th and 15th cents. One or more of the parts were arr. in a rhythmic pattern several bars long which was repeated throughout the piece, sometimes with changes of tempo (indicated by the use of smaller note-values, or different mensuration signs).

Isouard, Nicolò (also known as Nicolò di Malta, or just Nicolò) (b Mosta, Malta, 6 Dec 1775; d Paris, 23 Mar 1818), Maltese composer of French descent. Educ. at a military acad. in Paris, he had to leave Fr. at the Revolution, and after a time in Malta studied music in Palermo and in Naples under Sala and Guglielmi. Made his debut as an opera comp. in Florence with *L'avviso ai maritati* in 1794. The following year he was app. organist to the Order of St John of Malta in Valetta, and later became *maestro di cappella* there. Leaving Malta in 1799 he settled in Paris, where he prod. many operas and also appeared as a pianist.

Works incl. over 40 operas, e.g. *L'avviso ai maritati, Artaserse* ((1794), *Le Tonnelier* (1801), *Michel-Ange* (1802), *Cendrillon* (1810), *Le Billet de loterie* (1811), *Joconde, Jeannot et Colin, Aladin ou La Lampe merveilleuse* (1822), etc.; Masses, motets, cantatas and other vocal works.

Israel in Egypt, oratorio by Handel (words from the Bible and the Prayer Book version of the psalms), comp. 1738, perf. London, King's Theatre, Haymarket, 4 Apr 1739.

'Israel' Symphony, a symph. by Bloch, comp. 1912–16, fp NY, 3 May 1916.

Issé, opera by Destouches (lib. by A.H. de la Motte), prod. Fontainebleau, at court, 7 Oct 1679; 1st Paris perf., Opéra, 30 Dec 1697.

-issimo (It. superl. ending), e.g. *pianissimo* = softest; *fortissimo* = loudest, etc.

Istar, symph. variations by d'Indy, op. 42, fp Brussels, 10 Jan 1897. The work is based on the Babylonian legend of Ishtar's descent into limbo and illustrates her disrobing at the 7 stations of her progress by the devices of presenting the variations 1st, in diminishing complexity, and stating the theme only at the end, in bare 8ve unison.

Istel, Edgar (b Mainz, 23 Feb 1880; d Miami, Florida, 17 Dec 1948), German musicologist. Studied at Munich, comp. with Volbach and Thuille and musicology with Sandberger. He lived and taught there until 1913, when he went to Berlin as lec-

turer on music. In 1920 he was in Madrid and later went to the USA. His books incl. works on Wagner, Cornelius, Paganini and esp. on var. aspects of opera.

Istesso tempo, L' (It. from *Io stesso tempo* = the same pace), a direction given where a change is indicated in the time-signature, but the comp. wishes the music to continue at the same pace or beat in the new rhythm. The change is thus merely one of metre, not of movement.

Istomin, Eugene (b New York, 26 Nov 1925), American pianist. He studied at the Curtis Inst., Philadelphia, with Serkin. Debut with NY PO 1943. Chamber music at the Casals Prades Fest. from 1950; married Casals's widow in 1975. Trios with Isaac Stern and Leonard Rose.

Italian Concerto, a harpsichord work in 3 movements by Bach, pub. (together with the 'French Overture') in the second part of the *Clavierübung* in 1735. The 2 manuals of the harpsichord are used to reproduce the contrast between *concertino* and *ripieno* characteristic of the *concerto grosso*.

Italian Overture. *See* **Overture.**

Italian Sixth. *See* **Augmented Sixth Chords.**

'Italian' Symphony, Mendelssohn's 4th symph., op. 90, in A maj. and min., begun in It. in 1831 and finished in Berlin, 31 Mar 1833; London, 13 May 1833, cond. by the comp.

Italiana in Algeri, L' (*The Italian Girl in Algiers*), opera by Rossini (lib. by A. Anelli), prod. Venice, Teatro San Benedetto, 22 May 1813.

Italiana in Londra, L' (*The Italian Girl in London*), opera by Cimarosa (lib. by G. Petrosellini), prod. Rome, Teatro Valle. 28 Dec 1778.

Italienisches Liederbuch (*Italian Song Book*), H. Wolf's settings of It. poems in Ger. trans. by Paul Heyse, comp. (22 nos.) 1890–91 and (24 nos.) 1896.

Iturbi, José (b Valencia, 28 Nov 1895; d Hollywood, 28 Jun 1980), Spanish pianist and conductor. Studied as a child in Barcelona, and afterwards played in cafés to earn money. Later he studied in Paris at the Cons. and graduated in 1912. He began teaching at the Geneva Cons. in 1919 and in 1923 began his career as a concert pianist. Conducted Rochester PO 1936–44.

Ivan le Terrible, opera by Bizet (lib. by A. Leroy and H. Trianon, 1st offered to Gounod and abandoned by him), comp. in 1865 and accepted for prod. by the Théâtre Lyrique in Paris, but withdrawn by the

comp. The fp (concert) took place at Mühringen (Württemberg) in 1946. 1st stage perf. Bordeaux, 12 Oct 1951.
Ivan Susanin, opera by Cavos (lib. by Prince A.A. Shakhovskoy), prod. St Petersburg, 31 Oct 1815. The subject is that on which Glinka's *Life for the Tsar* was based in 1836. The title given to Glinka's *Life for the Tsar* in Soviet Russia.
Ivan the Terrible (Rimsky-Korsakov). See **Pskovitianka**.
Ivanhoe, opera by Sullivan (lib. by J.R. Sturgis, based on Scott's novel), prod. London, Royal Eng. Opera House (now Palace Theatre), 31 Jan 1891.
Ivanov, Mikhail Mikhailovich (b Moscow, 23 Sep 1849; d Rome, 20 Oct 1927), Russian composer and critic. Studied with Tchaikovsky and others at the Moscow Cons., lived mainly in Rome in 1870–6 and then became music critic to the *Novoie Vremya*.
Works incl. operas *Potemkin's Feast* (1902), *Zabava Putiatishna* (1899), *The Proud Woman* and *Woe to the Wise*; ballet *The Vestal Virgin* (1888); Requiem; symph., symph. prologue *Savonarola*, *Suite champêtre* for orch.; pf. pieces; songs.
Ivanov, Nikolay (b Poltava, 22 Oct 1810; d Bologna, 19 Jul 1880), Russian tenor. He visited Italy with Glinka in 1830 and made his debut at Naples in 1832, as Donizetti's Percy; repeated the role on his London debut, 1833, and returned until 1837. Often heard in Rossini's operas and in 1843 at Palermo was Riccardo in the fp of Pacini's *Maria Tudor*; Vienna 1844, as Roberto Devereux. Other roles incl. Ernani, Arnold and Gianetto.
Ive (or Ives), Simon (b Ware, 1600; d London, 1 Jul 1662), English singer, organist and composer. Vicar-choral at St Paul's Cathedral in London; singing-master during the Commonwealth, returned to St Paul's in 1661. In 1633 he took part with W. Lawes in the comp. of Shirley's masque *The Triumph of Peace*. Other works incl. elegy on the death of W. Lawes, catches and rounds; fancies and other instrumental works, etc.
Ives, Charles (Edward) (b Danbury, Conn., 20 Oct 1874; d New York, 19 May 1954), American composer. Pupil of H. Parker and D. Buck. Engaged in business, but wrote much music, some in a polytonal idiom employing intervals smaller than the semitone. In addition, he experimented with conflicting rhythms, dissonant harmony and counterpoint, chord clusters and the spatial presentation of music. He also made frequent use of hymn and folk tunes. Ives is now recognized as the real founder of Amer. music.

Works incl. ORCH.: 4 symphs.: no. 1 in D min. (1896–8), no. 2 (1897–1901, fp NY, 22 Feb 1951), no. 3 (1901–4, for chamber orch., *The Camp Meeting*; fp NY, 5 Apr 1946), no. 4 (1910–16, fp NY, 26 Apr 1965 cond. Stokowski); *New England Holidays* (*Washington's Birthday, Decoration Day, Fourth of July, Thanksgiving*; 1904–13); *Three Places in New England* (Orchestral Set no. 1: *The St Gaudens in Boston Common, Putnam's Camp, Redding, Connecticut* and *The Housatonic at Stockridge*; 1903–14, fp NY 1931 cond. Slonimsky); Orchestral Set no. 2: *An Elegy to our Forefathers, The Rockstrewn Hills Join in the People's Outdoor Meeting* and *From Hanover Square North at the end of a Tragic Day*; 1909–15); *Central Park in the Dark* (1898–1907, fp NY, 11 May 1947); *The Unanswered Question* (1908); Theater Orchestra Set: *In the Cage, In the Inn, In the Night* (1904–11); *Tone Roads*, 2 pieces for chamber orch. (1911, 1915); *Robert Browning Overture* (1908–12); Orchestral Set no. 3 (1919–27).

CHORAL: *The Circus Band* for bass, chorus and orch. (1894); *The Celestial Country*, cantata (1899); *General William Booth Enters into Heaven* for bass, chorus and orch. (1914); *Lincoln the Great Commoner* for chorus and orch. (1912); 8 Psalm settings (1897–1901); *3 Harvest Home Chorales* for chorus, brass, db. and organ (1898–1912).

CHAMBER: string 4tet no. 1 (*A Revival Service*, 1898; 1st public perf. NY, 1957), no. 2 (1907–13); pf. trio (1904–13); 4 sonatas for vln. and pf. (1902–15); *From the Steeples and the Mountains* for brass 5tet (1901); *Adagio Sostenuto* for horn, fl., strings and pf. (1910).

PIANO AND SONGS: Pf. sonata no. 1 (1909), no. 2 (*Concord, Mass., 1840–1860: Emerson, Hawthorne, The Alcots, Thoreau*; 1909–15, fp NY 1939); 22 Studies for pf.; organ music; 114 songs (1884–1921).

Ivogün, Maria (b Budapest, 18 Nov 1891; d Beatenberg, 2 Oct 1987), Hungarian soprano. She studied in Munich; debut there 1913, Mimi; created Ighino in Pfitzner's *Palestrina*, 1917. London, CG, 1924–7 as Zerbinetta, Gilda, Constanze. Left Munich 1925 and sang in Berlin until 1934. Other roles incl. Queen of Night and Norina. Married to Karl Erb 1921–32; and to Michael Raucheisen, her accompanist, from 1933.
Ivrea Codex, a large collection of 14th-cent.

music, and an important source of music by Philippe de Vitry and Machaut. It is housed in the cathedral of the city of Ivrea.

Ivrogne corrigé, L' (*The Reformed Drunkard*), opera by Gluck (lib. by L. Anseaume on a fable by La Fontaine), prod. Vienna, Burgtheater, Apr 1760.

Opera by Laruette (lib. do.), prod. Paris, Opéra-Comique, 24 Jul 1759.

J

Jaches de Wert. *See* **Wert.**

Jachet da Mantova (Jaquet ?) (b Vitré; d Mantua, 1559), Flemish singer and composer. Attached to San Pietro Cathedral at Mantua in 1527–58. Wrote Masses, Magnificats, motets, psalms, hymns, etc.

Jack, the mechanism in the virginal, harpsichord and similar instruments by which the strings are plucked.

Jackson, Francis (b Malton, Yorks., 2 Oct 1917), English organist and composer. He studied at Durham Univ. and with Edward Bairstow; succeeded him as organist at York Minster in 1946. He is well known as a recitalist, most often heard in Vierne and Franck. His own works incl. a *Te Deum* and *Jubilate* (1964), Symph. in D min. for orch., and *Sonata giocosa* for organ (1972).

Jackson, William (b Exeter, 29 May 1730; d Exeter, 5 Jul 1803), English organist and composer. Learnt music as a choir-boy in Exeter Cathedral, then studied in London, became music teacher at Exeter and from 1777 held var. appts. at the cathedral there.

Works incl. operas *The Lord of the Manor* (1780), and *The Metamorphosis* (1783); a stage piece *Lycidas* (based on Milton, 1767), Te Deum, services, anthems and other church music; setting of Pope's ode *The Dying Christian*; var. vocal pieces and songs; harpsichord sonatas.

Jacob, Gordon (Percival Septimus) (b London, 5 Jul 1895; d Saffron Walden, 8 Jun 1984), English composer and conductor. Studied under Stanford and C. Wood at the RCM, where later he became prof. of orchestration. D. Mus., London, 1935.

Works incl. ballets *The Jew in the Bush* and *Uncle Remus* (after J.C. Harris); music for films; sinfonietta (1942), variations on an air by Purcell and on an orig. theme for orch., *Passacaglia on a Well-known Theme* ('Oranges and Lemons') for orch. (1931); 2 symphs. (1929, 1944) and *Denbigh* suite for strings, Divertimento for small orch.; concertos for pf., vln., vla., ob., bassoon and horn; clar. concerto (1980); suite for military band; 4tets for ob. and strings and clar. and strings and other chamber music; instrumental pieces.

Jacobi, Frederick (b San Francisco, 4 May 1891; d New York, 24 Oct 1952), American conductor and composer. Pupil of Bloch and others in USA and of Juon in Berlin. Asst. cond. at Met. Opera in NY, 1913–17, later studied music of the Pueblo Indians in Mexico and Arizona. Prof. of comp. in NY from 1924. Taught at Juilliard, 1936–50.

Works incl. opera *The Prodigal Son* (1944); 2 symphs. (1924, 1948), *Indian Dances, The Eve of St Agnes* (after Keats), etc. for orch.; concertos for pf., vln. and cello; concerto for pf. and strings; Sabbath Evening Service (1931); *Two Assyrian Prayers* and *The Poet in the Desert* for voice and orch.; 3 string 4tets (1924–45), pf. 5tet *Hagiographia,* scherzo for wind instruments.

Jacobin, The, opera by Dvořák (lib. by M. Cervinková-Riegrová); comp. 1887–8, prod. Prague, 12 Feb 1889; rev. 1897.

Jacobs, Arthur (b Manchester, 14 Jun 1922), English critic, translator and editor. Music critic var. newspapers from 1947; 1960–71 deputy ed. *Opera* magazine. Lecturer at RAM from 1964, Huddersfield Poly. 1979–85. Has trans. 20 opera libs. and pub. *A New Dict. of Music* (4 eds. 1958–78), *Short History of Western Music* and two vols. on Sullivan (1951, 1984). His work is notable for its concision.

Jacobsen, Jens Peter (1847–85), Danish poet and novelist. *See* **Fennimore und Gerda** (Delius), **Gurrelieder** (Schoenberg), **Hamerik (E.)** (*Marie Grubbe*).

Jacques, Reginald (b Ashby de la Zouch, 13 Jan 1894; d Stowmarket, 2 Jun 1969), English organist and conductor. He studied at Oxford and held var. posts there before founding the Bach Choir, London, in 1931; cond. until 1960. Founded Jacques Orch. 1936 and gave many war-time concerts. Well-known for perfs. of the Bach Passions with traditional forces and style. CBE 1954.

Jacquet, Élizabeth. *See* **La Guerre.**

Jadin, Louis Emmanuel (b Versailles, 21 Sep 1768; d Paris, 11 Apr 1853), French composer, son of the violinist and comp. Jean J. Worked as accompanist at the Théâtre de Monsieur in Paris from 1789 and became pf. prof. at the Cons. in 1802.

Works incl. opera *Joconde* (1790) and *c* 40 others; vocal and instrumental works for the Revolution festivals; *La Bataille d'Austerlitz* for orch.; chamber music; works for 1 and 2 pfs.

Jadlowker, Hermann (b Riga, 5 Jul 1877; d Tel Aviv, 13 May 1953), Latvian tenor. Studied in Vienna and made his debut at Cologne in 1899, as Nicolai's Fenton. He sang in Berlin 1907–12. NY Met debut

1910, as Faust; sang in the fp of *Königskinder* the same year. In 1912 he created Bacchus, in *Ariadne auf Naxos* (Stuttgart). Retired 1929. Other roles incl. Parsifal, Tannhäuser, Florestan and Don Carlos.

Jagd, Die (*The Hunt*), opera by J.A. Hiller (lib. by C.F. Weisse, based on J.M. Sedaine's lib. for Monsigny's *Le Roi et le fermier*), prod. Weimar, 29 Jan 1770.

Jagel, Frederick (b Brooklyn, 10 Jun 1897; d San Francisco, 5 Jul 1982), American tenor. He studied in NY and Milan; debut Livorno 1924, as Rodolfo. After appearing widely in It. he sang at the NY Met from 1927 (debut as Radames). San Francisco from 1931, Buenos Aires 1939–41. He sang the title role in the 1st professional US perf. of *Peter Grimes*.

Jahn, Otto (b Kiel, 16 Jun 1813; d Göttingen, 9 Sep 1869), German philologist, archaeologist and writer on art and music. Studied at Kiel, Leipzig and Berlin, became prof. at Greifswald and later at Bonn. His numerous writings on music include the 1st large-scale work written on Mozart.

Jakobsleiter, Die (*Jacob's Ladder*), oratorio by Schoenberg; comp. 1917–22, unfinished. Scoring completed by Winfried Zillig, fp Vienna 16 Jun 1961, cond. Kubelik.

Jaleo, a Spanish dance in moderate 3–8 time, accomp. by castanets.

James, Philip (b Jersey City, NJ, 17 May 1890; d Southampton, Long Island, 1 Nov 1975), American conductor, organist, teacher and composer. Studied in NY and became prof. at Columbia and NY Univs.

Works incl. *Missa imaginum*, *Stabat Mater* and other choral works; 3 symphs., incl. *Sea Symph.* for bar. and orch. (1928), overtures on Fr. Noëls and *Bret Harte*, Welsh rhapsody *Gwallia*, *Station WGZBX*, for orch. (1932); suite for string orch.; pf. 4tet, woodwind 5tet, string 4tet (1924).

Janáček, Leoš (b Hukvaldy, Moravia, 3 Jul 1854; d Morava-Ostrava, 12 Aug 1928), Czech composer. Son of a poor schoolmaster; became choir-boy at the monastery of the Austin Friars at Brno; later earned his living as music teacher and went to the Org. School in Prague for study. Cond. var. choral societies, made some desultory studies at Leipzig and Vienna, and in 1881 returned to Brno to found an org. school there. His 1st mature work was the opera *Jenůfa*, started in 1894 and staged at Brno in 1904. Although a success, wider recognition did not come until the opera's prod. in Prague (1916), followed by prods. in Germany. The last 10 years of Janáček's life saw a great burst of creative activity. He made close studies of folksong and speech, which he applied to his vocal music.

Works incl. operas *The Beginning of a Novel* (1894), *Osud* (Fate, 1903–7; prod. 1958), *Jenůfa* (Her foster-daughter, 1904), *The Excursions of Mr. Brouček* (after Čech, 1920), *Káta Kabanová* (1921), *The Cunning Little Vixen* (1924), *Šárka* (1925), *The Makropoulos Case* (on a play by Čapek, 1926), *From the House of the Dead* (after Dostoievsky, 1930).

Amarus (1897–1906), *The Eternal Gospel* (1914) and *Glagolitic Mass* for solo voices, chorus and orch. (1926), *The Wandering Madman* (Tagore) for soprano and male-voice chorus, numerous choral works, many for male voices.

Šumařovo Dítě, rhapsody *Taras Bulba* (on Gogol, 1918), *The Ballad of Blaník*, Sinfonietta for orch. (1926); concertino for pf. and chamber orch. (1925), *Capriccio* for pf. left hand and ens. (1926).

2 string 4tets (1 on Tolstoy's *Kreutzer Sonata*, 1923, no. 2 *Intimate Letters*, 1928), wind 6tet *Mládí* (*Youth*), suite for 2 vlns., vla., cello and double bass; vln. and pf. sonata, *Fairy Tale* for cello and pf.; pf. sonata (1905), *By an Overgrown Path* (1901–8), variations, etc.; organ works; *The Diary of a Young Man who Disappeared* (1921) for voice and pf., Moravian folksongs for voice and pf.

Janiewicz, Felix (b Vilna, 1762; d Edinburgh, 21 May 1848), Polish violinist. Studied in Vienna, where he met Haydn and Mozart and in It. Appeared in Paris and London (Haydn's concerts, 1794), and settled 1st at Liverpool and then at Edinburgh, in 1815.

Janigro, Antonio (b Milan, 21 Jan 1918), Italian cellist and conductor. He studied in Milan and with Casals. Debut as cellist 1934, as cond. 1948; founded I Solisti di Zagreb 1954 and gave frequent perfs. with them in Baroque rep. until 1967. Formed trio with Jean Fournier and Paul Badura-Skoda. Prof. cello Düsseldorf Cons. 1964; cond. Saar Radio Orch. from 1968.

Janissaries, Turkish infantry forming a bodyguard for the sultan. Their music made use of special perc. instruments incl. the Turkish Crescent or Jingling Johnny, imitated by western comps., as in Haydn's 'Military' Symph. (no. 100) and Mozart's *Entführung*. Brahms playfully called the 3rd movement of his 4th symph. 'janissaries' music'.

Janků, Hana (b Brno, 25 Oct 1940), Czech

soprano. Debut Brno 1959; later sang at Prague. Wider recognition came in 1967, with Turandot at La Scala and Vienna. Deutsche Oper Berlin from 1970 as the *Trovatore* Leonora, Gioconda, Ariadne and Elisabeth. CG 1973, as Tosca. Other roles incl. Lady Macbeth and Smetana's Milada.

Jannacom, Giuseppe (b Rome, 1741; d Rome, 16 Mar 1816), Italian composer. Studied in Rome, where in 1811 he became *maestro di cappella* at St Peter's in succession to Zingarelli.

Works incl. 30 Masses, 42 psalms, motets and other church music, some for several antiphonal choirs.

Jannequin, Clément (b Châtellerault, *c* 1485; d Paris, 1558), French composer. Pupil (?) of Josquin des Prés. He may have become a Huguenot in the course of his long life.

Works incl. Masses on his own songs *La Bataille* and *l.'Aveugle Dieu*, motet *Congregati sunt*, *Proverbes de Salomon*, *Psaumes de David* (both to Fr. rhymed versions); 280 *chansons* for 4 voices, many of which contain imitative and descriptive passages, e.g. *Le chant des oiseaux*..

Janowitz, Gundula (b Berlin, 8 Feb 1937), German soprano. A protégée of Karajan, she sang Pamina, Mimi, and the Empress at Vienna in the early 1960s; Countess in *Figaro* and Fiordiligi at Salzburg and Sieglinde at the NY Met in 1967, when Karajan gave *Die Walküre* there. London, CG, 1976 (Donna Anna). Other roles incl. Agathe, Elisabeth, Eva and Arabella. Returned to CG 1987, Ariadne.

Janowski, Marek (b Warsaw, 18 Feb 1939), Polish conductor. He studied in Cologne and Vienna. Conducted opera in Hamburg Munich and Berlin before music dir. Freiburg, then Dortmund, 1973–9. London debut 1969, SW Theatre, Henze's *Der Junge Lord* with Cologne Opera; Royal Liverpool PO 1983–6. US from 1983 (San Francisco Opera). With Dresden forces made the first compact disc recording of Wagner's *Ring*.

Janssen, Herbert (b Cologne, 22 Sep 1892; d New York, 3 Jun 1965), German baritone. He studied in Berlin and made his debut in the 1st local prod. of Schreker's *Der Schatzgräber*; remained at the Staatsoper until 1938 in Wagner and Verdi rep. London, CG, 1926–39. Bayreuth 1930–7 as Wolfram, Amfortas, and Gunther. Met co. debut on tour in Philadelphia, 1939, as the Wanderer; also heard as Sachs in US.

Japanische Festmusik, work for orch. by Strauss, op. 84; comp. for the 2,600th anniversary of the Japanese Empire, fp Tokyo, 11 Dec 1940: less than a year before Pearl Harbor. See also *Sinfonia da Requiem.*

Japart, Johannes 15th–16th-cent. composer, many of whose *chansons* were printed by Petrucci in Venice. He was a singer at the Ferrara court.

Jaques-Dalcroze, Émile (b Vienna, 6 Jul 1865; d Geneva, 1 Jul 1950), Swiss teacher and composer. Studied with Delibes in Paris, with Bruckner and Fuchs in Vienna and at the Geneva Cons., where in 1892 he became prof. of harmony. There he invented a system of teaching music by co-ordination with bodily movement, known as Eurhythmics. In 1910 he founded an institute for this purpose at Hellerau nr. Dresden.

Works incl. operas *Le Violon maudit* (1893), *Janie* (1894), *Sancho Panza* (after Cervantes, 1897), *Le Bonhomme Jadis* (1906), *Les Jumeaux de Bergame*, *La Fille au vautour* (after W. von Hillern's *Die Geier-Wally*), festival play *La Fête de la jeunesse et de la joie* (1932); choral works *La Veillée*, *Festival vaudois*; suite for orch.; 2 vln. concertos (1902, 1911); 3 string 4tets; pf. pieces; many collections of popular and children's songs, *Chansons de route*, *Rondes enfantines*, *Chansons de gestes.*

Jarnach, Philipp (b Noisy, Fr., 26 Jul 1892; d Bornsen, nr. Bergedorf, 17 Dec 1982), Franco-Spanish composer. Studied pf. with Risler and comp. with Lavignac in Paris, went to Switz. in 1914 and taught counterpoint at the Zurich Cons. in 1918–1921, when he settled in Berlin and continued to study with Busoni, whose unfinished opera *Doktor Faust* he completed.

Works incl. prelude to *Prometheus*, suite *Winterbilder* (1915), *Prologue to a Tournament*, *Sinfonia brevis*, *Morgenklangspiel* (1925), Prelude No. 1, *Musik mit Mozart* for orch. (1935), string 4tet and 5tet (1916, 1920); vln. and pf. sonata, 2 sonatas for unaccomp. vln.; *Konzertstück* for org.; sonatina and other works for pf.; songs with orch. and with pf.

Järnefelt, Armas (b Viborg, 14 Aug 1869; d Stockholm, 23 Jun 1958), Finnish conductor and composer. Studied at Helsinki, Berlin and Paris, cond. at var. Ger. theatres and from 1898 to 1903 at Helsinki. App. cond. of the Opera there in 1903 and at Stockholm 1907–32. He often cond. Sibelius and gave the 1st Swedish perfs. of works by Mahler and Schoenberg.

Works incl. incid. music to *The Promised Land*; choral works; orchestral music incl.

Praeludium and *Berceuse* for small orch.; songs.

Järvi, Neeme (b Tallinn, 7 Jun 1937), Estonian conductor. Studied with Mravinsky at Leningrad Cons.; cond. widely in Estonia and Rus. Emigrated to US 1980 and was guest cond. with leading orchs. Principal guest cond. CBSO 1981–4. Music dir. Scottish National Orch. from 1984.

Jazz, American dance music of the early 20th cent. developed out of Ragtime and relying for its effects mainly on syncopations and rhythmic displacement of accents; and on a special combination of instruments, incl. plucked string instruments and saxophones, made to play abnormally for the most part, e.g. *pizzicato* double bass, muted brass, etc. Jazz has influenced certain comps., e.g. Stravinsky in *Ragtime* and *Ebony Concerto*, Milhaud in *La Création du monde* and *Le Bœuf sur le toit*, Krenek in *Jonny spielt auf*, Gershwin in the *Rhapsody in Blue*, Copland in the ballet *Billy the Kid*, Blitzstein in his operas, etc., Hindemith in *Kammermusik no. 1*, Lambert in *The Rio Grande*, Weill in *Mahagonny* and *Dreigroschenoper*.

Jean de Paris, opera by Boieldieu (lib. by C.G. de Saint-Just), prod. Paris, Opéra-Comique, 4 Apr 1812.

Jeanne d'Arc au bûcher (*Joan of Arc at the Stake*), dramatic oratorio by Honegger (lib. by Paul Claudel), prod. Basle, 12 May 1938.

Jeffreys, George (b c 1610; d Weldon, Northants, 1 Jul 1685), English composer. Steward to Lord Hatton of Kirby, Northants., member of the Chapel Royal, organist to Charles I at Oxford in 1643 during the Civil War.

Works incl. services, anthems, over 120 motets, sacred solos and duets, carols; music for masques and plays; secular songs, duets, etc.; fancies for strings and virginals.

Jeffries, Matthew, English 16th–17th-cent. composer. Vicar-choral at Wells Cathedral. Comp. services, anthems, etc.

Jélyotte, Pierre de (b Lasseube, Basses-Pyrénées, 13 Apr 1713; d Estos, Basses-Pyrénées, 11 Sep 1787), French tenor, guitarist and composer. Orig. intended for the priesthood, he made his operatic debut in Paris in 1733. He created roles in the revised vers. of Rameau's *Castor et Pollux* (1754) and in *Zaïs* (1748). He was also guitar-teacher to the king, and as a comp. prod. the opera-ballet *Zelisca* (1746).

Jemnitz, Alexander (b Budapest, 9 Aug 1890; d Balatonfüred, 8 Aug 1963), Hungarian composer and critic. Studied at the

Budapest Cons., then with Reger at Leipzig and lastly with Schoenberg in Berlin, where he also taught. Later he returned to Budapest.

Works incl. ballet *Divertimento* (1947); Prelude and Fugue, 7 *Miniatures* for orch. (1947); choral music; string 4tet, 2 string trios (1924, 1927), trios for var. other instruments, Partita for 2 vlns., 3 vln. and pf. sonatas, sonata for vla. and cello.

'Jena' Symphony, a symph. in C maj. discovered at Jena in 1910 and attrib. to Beethoven because it bears the inscription 'par L. van Beethoven' in an unidentifiable hand; it is now known to be by Friedrich Witt (1771–1837). Ed. by Fritz Stein and 1st perf. by him, Jena, 17 Jan 1910.

Jenkins, John (b Maidstone, 1592; d Kimberley, Norfolk, 27 Oct 1678), English composer, lutenist and string player. He lived under the patronage of the gentry and nobility, esp. Sir Hamon L'Estrange in Norfolk and Lord North, whose sons, incl. Roger, he taught music. His last patron was Sir Philip Wodehouse at Kimberley.

Works incl. fancies and consorts for viols and vlns. with organ anthems and psalms; Elegy on the death of W. Lawes, *Theophila,* or *Love's Sacrifice* (Benlowes), *A Divine Poem* for voices; rounds, songs.

Jensen, Adolph (b Königsberg, 12 Jan 1837; d Baden-Baden, 23 Jan 1879), German pianist and composer, grandson of the organist and composer Wilhelm J. (d 1842), prof. of music at Königsberg Univ. A.J. studied under various masters, visited Rus. and Copenhagen, where he made friends with Gade, was back at Königsberg in 1860–6, taught the pf. in Berlin for the next 2 years and then lived at Dresden, Graz and elsewhere for his health.

Works incl. opera *Die Erbin von Montfort* (adapted to a new lib. based on Gozzi's *Turandot* by Kienzl after his death, 1858–65); cantatas *Jephthas Tochter* (1864), *Der Gang der Jünger nach Emmaus* (1865), *Donald Caird* (Scott, 1875), and *Adonisfeier*; concert overture and *Geistliches Tonstück* for orch.; c 25 op. nos. of pf. music and settings of Heyse and Geibel (*Spanisches Liederbuch*) and Herder.

Jenůfa, opera by Janáček (lib. by comp. after G. Preissova; known in Cz. as *Její Pastorkyna – Her Foster-daughter*); comp. 1894–1903, prod. Brno, 21 Jan 1904. Revised 1906–16 and perf. Prague 26 May 1916 with some re-orch. by the cond., Karel Kovařovic (1862–1920).

Jephtas Gelübde (*Jephtha's Vow*), opera

by Meyerbeer (lib. by A. Schreiber); prod. Munich, 23 Dec 1812. Meyerbeer's 1st opera.

Jephte, oratorio by Carissimi; comp. by 1650 and pub. in several modern eds.; realized by Henze and perf. London, 14 Jul 1976.

Jephté (*Jephtha*), opera by Montéclair (lib. by S.J. de Pellegrin), prod. Paris, Opéra, 28 Feb 1732.

Jephtha, oratorio by Handel (lib. by T. Morell), prod. London, CG, 26 Feb 1752.

Jeremiáš, Jaroslav (b Písek, 14 Aug 1889; d Budějovice, 16 Jan 1919), Czech composer and pianist. Pupil of Novák and others at the Prague Cons.
Works incl. opera *The Old King* (1919), choral and chamber music.

Jerger, Alfred (b Brno, 9 Jun 1889; d Vienna, 18 Nov 1976), Austrian bass-baritone. He began his career as cond. and actor; began singing 1915 and after 2 years at Munich joined Vienna Staatsoper in 1920; remained until 1964 in 146 roles, incl. Don Giovanni, Sachs, Scarpia and Almaviva. In 1924 he created The Man in Schoenberg's *Die glückliche Hand*, at the Vienna Volksoper, and in 1933 was the 1st Mandryka in *Arabella* (Dresden), his role in London, CG, debut (1934). After the war he worked as producer and teacher in Vienna.

Jeritza (real name **Jedlitzka**), **Maria** (b Brno, 6 Oct 1882; d Orange, NJ, 10 Jul 1982), Czech soprano. Studied in Brno and first appeared in the chorus of the Brno Opera. She made her debut as a soloist at Olmütz in 1910 and was a member of the Vienna Staatsoper from 1913 to 1932; she created the title role in both versions of *Ariadne* and was the 1st Empress in *Die Frau ohne Schatten* (1919). She also sang at the NY Met from 1921 to 1932 as Jenůfa, Tosca, Turandot and Marietta in *Die tote Stadt*.

Jérusalem, the title of the Fr. version of Verdi's opera *I Lombardi alla prima crociata*.

Jerusalem, Siegfried (b Oberhausen, 17 Apr 1940), German tenor. His career began as a bassoonist; opera roles at Stuttgart from 1975. Bayreuth debut 1977 and in recent years has sung Lohengrin, Siegmund, Parsifal and Walther there. Berlin, Deutsche Oper, 1977–80; has sung widely in Europe and N. Amer. as Max, Florestan, Idomeneo and Lensky. In March 1986 he sang Parsifal at the London Coliseum and Erik at CG.

Jessonda, opera by Spohr (lib. by E. H. Gehe, based on Lemierre's tragedy *La Veuve de Malabar*), prod. Kassel, 28 Jul 1823.

Jesus and the Traders (*Jezus es a kufarok*), motet by Kodály for mixed voices a cappella, comp. 1934.

Jeté (Fr. = thrown), a style of bowing on string instruments. The upper part of the bow is made to fall lightly on the string so that it rebounds several times during the downward motion and repeats notes in a rapid *staccato*.

Jeu de Cartes (*Card Game*), ballet in 3 deals by Stravinsky; comp. 1936 in Paris, prod. NY Met 27 Apr 1937, with choreog. by Balanchine.

Jeune France, La, a group of young French composers formed in 1936 by Baudrier, Jolivet, Lesur and Messiaen.

Jeune Henri, Le (*The Young Henry*), opera by Méhul (lib. by J.N. Bouilly, orig. intended for Grétry and called *La Jeunesse de Henri IV*), prod. Paris, Opéra-Comique, 1 May 1797. The overture called *La Chasse du jeune Henri* was known as a concert piece long after the opera was forgotten.

Jeune Sage et le vieux fou, Le (*The Wise Youth and the Old Fool*), opera by Méhul (lib. by F.B. Hoffman), prod. Paris, Opéra-Comique, 28 Mar 1793.

Jeux, ballet by Debussy (choreog. by Nizhinsky), comp. in 1912 and prod. Paris, Théâtre du Châtelet, 13 May 1913.

Jeux d'enfants, suite for pf. duet by Bizet, op. 22, comp. 1871; *Petite Suite* for orch. arr. from 5 pieces of it, 1872, fp Paris, 2 Mar 1873.

Jewels of the Madonna (Wolf-Ferrari). *See* **Gioielli della Madonna.**

Jew's Harp, an ancient instrument consisting of a metal frame held between the player's teeth and a vibrating metal tongue set in motion by the fingers and emitting a note which can be varied by changes in the cavity of the mouth.

Jig, an old dance in binary form in some kind of animated duple time, usually 6–8 or 12–8; the It. *giga* and Fr. *gigue*. It was the 4th of the dances regularly found in the classical suite. The 2nd half was often built on an inversion of the theme of the 1st.

Jirák, Karel Boleslav (b Prague, 28 Jan 1891; d Chicago, 30 Jan 1972), Czech composer and conductor. Studied with Novák in Prague and was later influenced by J.B. Foerster. Prof. of comp. at Prague Cons. from 1920 and head of music at the Cz. Radio 1930–1945. Prof. at Roosevelt Coll., Chicago, from 1949.
Works incl. opera *Apollonius of Tyana* (later called *Woman and the God*, 1928); 6 symphs. (1915–68); pf. concerto; 7 string

4tets (1915–60), string 6tet; sonatas for vln. and pf., vla. and pf. and cello and pf.; song-cycles *Tragi-Comedy* (Heine), *Meditations, Brief Happiness, 3 Songs of Home, Evening and the Soul; Suite in the Old Style* for pf.

Joachim, Joseph (b Kittsee nr. Pozsony, 28 Jun 1831; d Berlin, 15 Aug 1907), Hungarian (Germanized) violinist, composer and conductor. Made his 1st appearance at the age of 7. Studied at the Vienna Cons. and in Leipzig, where he came under the influence of Mendelssohn. Leader of the orch. at Weimar, 1849–53, and at Hanover, 1853–1868. App. director of the Berlin Hochschule für Musik, 1868. Founded the Joachim 4tet, 1869. He visited England every year from 1862 and in 1877 cond. the 1st Brit. perf. of Brahms's 1st symph.; took part in the fp of the Double Concerto, 1887. Works incl. overtures for orch. to Shakespeare's *Hamlet* and *Henry IV*, in commemoration of Kleist and on 2 comedies by Gozzi; 3 vln. concertos (incl. 'Hung.'), variations for vln. and orch.

Joan of Arc. *See* **Giovanna d'Arco, Jeanne d'Arc au bûcher, Maid of Orleans.**

Job, masque for dancing by Vaughan Williams (choreog. by Ninette de Valois, settings by Gwendolen Raverat, based on Blake's illustrations to the Book of Job), prod. London, Cambridge Theatre, 5 Jul 1931.
    Oratorio by Parry (words from the Book of Job), prod. Gloucester Festival, 1892.

Jochum, Eugen (b Babenhausen, 1 Nov 1902; d Munich, 26 Mar 1987), German conductor. Studied pf. and organ at Augsburg Cons. (1914–22) and comp. at the Munich Acad. of Music (1922–4). After some time as a *répétiteur* in Munich and Kiel, he cond. at Mannheim and Duisburg, becoming music director of the Hamburg Staatsoper from 1934 to 1945. From 1949 he was cond. of the Munich Radio Orch. US debut, with Concertgebouw Orch., 1961. He cond. Bartók and Stravinsky during the war in Hamburg and was well-known in Bach and Bruckner.

Johannes de Grocheo. *See* **Grocheio.**

Johnny strikes up (Krenek). *See* **Jonny spielt auf.**

Johnson, Edward, English 16th–17th-cent. composer ? in the service of Lord Hertford at Elvetham, where (?) he contrib. music to an entertainment given to Queen Elizabeth in 1591. Mus.B., Cambridge, 1594. He contrib. to East's psalter and the *Triumphes of Oriana.*

Works incl. madrigals, viol music, virginal pieces.

Johnson, Edward (b Guelph, Ontario, 22 Aug 1878; d Toronto, 20 Apr 1959), Canadian tenor. He studied in NY and Florence. Debut Padua 1912, as Chénier. At La Scala he was the first It. Parsifal, in 1914, and the following year sang there in the fp of Pizzetti's *Fedra*; returned 1918 for the fp of Montemezzi's *La Nave.* CG 1923, as Faust. Chicago 1919–22; NY Met 1922–35, in the fps of works by Howard Hanson and Deems Taylor. Other roles incl. Siegfried, Tannhäuser and Pelléas. Manager, Met, 1935–50.

Johnson, John (b *c* 1540; d London, 1595), English lutenist and composer. Attached to Queen Elizabeth's court and (?) to the household of Sir Thomas Kitson at Hengrave Hall, Suffolk, and in London, 1572–4. Took part in Leicester's entertainments at Kenilworth Castle in 1575. Wrote lute solos and duets.

Johnson, Robert (b Duns, *c* 1500;d 1554), Scottish priest and composer. Fled to Eng. as a heretic and settled at Windsor where he may have been chaplain to Anne Boleyn. Wrote Latin motets, Eng. services and prayers, In Nomines for instruments, songs.

Johnson, Robert (b *c* 1583; d London, 1633), English lutenist and composer, son of John J. Was taught music at the expense of Sir George Carey, husband of Sir Thomas Kitson's granddaughter, in whose household he was brought up, and was app. lutenist to James I in 1604; taught Prince Henry and remained in his post under Charles I.
    Works incl. songs for several voices; songs to the lute; catches; pieces for viols; also songs in Shakespeare's *Tempest,* in Fletcher's *Valentinian* and *The Mad Lover.*

Johnson, Robert Sherlaw (b Sunderland, 21 May 1932), English composer and pianist. He studied at Durham Univ., the RAM and in Paris (authority on Messiaen). Has taught at Leeds and York Univs. and, from 1970, Oxford.
    Works incl. opera *The Lambton Worm* (prod. Oxford, 1978); *Carmen Vernalia* for sop. and chamber orch. (1972); *Where the Wild things Are* for sop. and tape; *Festival Mass of the Resurrection* for chorus and orch.; *Anglorum Feriae* for sop. tenor, chorus and orch. (1977); 3 pf. sonatas; 2 string 4tets (1966, 1969).

Joio, Norman dello. *See* **Dello Joio.**

Jolie Fille de Perth, La (*The Fair Maid of Perth*), opera by Bizet (lib. by J.H.V. de Saint-Georges and J. Adenis, based on

Scott's novel), prod. Paris, Théâtre Lyrique, 26 Dec 1867.

Jolivet, André (b Paris, 8 Aug 1905; d Paris, 20 Dec 1974), French composer. Pupil of Le Flem and Varèse. He formed the group of 'La Jeune France' with Baudrier, Lesur and Messiaen in 1936.

Works incl. opera *Dolorès* (1947); 2 ballets; oratorio *La Vérité de Jeanne* (1956); 3 symphs. (1953, 1959, 1964); concertos for tpt. (2), fl., pf., harp, bassoon and Ondes Martenot; string 4tet; sonata and suite *Mana* for pf., songs.

Jommelli, Niccolò (b Aversa nr. Naples, 10 Sep 1714; d Naples, 25 Aug 1774), Italian composer. Pupil of Durante, Feo and Leo in Naples, made his debut as an opera comp. there in 1737, and soon became famous throughout It. and in Vienna. *Kapellmeister* to the Duke of Württemberg at Stuttgart 1753–69, he then returned to Naples, but was unable to recapture his old success in It.

Works incl. over 50 extant operas, e.g. *Ricimero* (1740), *Ezio* (3 settings: 1741, 1748, 1758), *Semiramide* (1741), *Sofonisba* (1746), *Artaserse* (1749), *Ifigenia in Aulide* (1751), *Talestri, Attilio Regolo* (1753), *Fetonte, La clemenza di Tito* (2 settings: 1753, 1765), *Pelope, Il matrimonio per concorso, La schiava liberata, Armida* (1770), *Ifigenia in Tauride* (1771); oratorios *Isacco, Betulia liberata* (1743), *Santa Elena al Calvario*, etc.; Passion oratorio, *Miserere*, Masses and other church music; cantatas; symphs. and other instrumental music.

Joncières, Victorin de (actually Félix Ludger Rossignol) (b Paris, 12 Apr 1839; d Paris, 26 Oct 1903), French composer. Began by studying painting, but set a friend's adaptation of Molière's *Le Sicilien* as a comic opera with such success that he entered the Cons. He left again after a disagreement about Wagner, whom he admired, and studied privately. In 1871 he became music critic to *La Liberté*.

Works incl. operas *Sardanapale* (1867), *Le Dernier Jour de Pompéi* (after Bulwer-Lytton, 1869), *Dimitri, La Reine Berthe* (1878), *Le Chevalier Jean* (1885), *Lancelot*, incid. music to Shakespeare's *Hamlet*; *La Mer*, symph. ode for mezzo, chorus and orch. (1881); suite for orch. *Les Nubiennes, Sérénade hongroise*, overture, marches and other orchestral music; vln. concerto.

Jones, Daniel (b Pembroke, 7 Dec 1912), Welsh composer. Studied at Univ. Coll., Swansea, where he read Eng. and later at the RAM in London. He studied cond. with Sir Henry Wood and comp. with Harry Far-

jeon. He began comp. at a very early age and has since produced a large quantity of music. OBE 1968.

Works incl. operas *The Knife* (1963) and *Orestes* (1967); incid. music for *Under Milk Wood* (Dylan Thomas); 10 symphs.; symph. poems *Cystuddiau Branwen, Cloud Messenger*; concertino for pf. and orch.; 8 string 4tets, string 5tet, 5 string trios, vln. sonata, cello sonata, pf. sonata, sonata for kettledrums, wind septet, wind nonet.

Jones, Edward (b Llanderfel, Merioneth, bap. 29 Mar 1752; d London, 18 Apr 1824), Welsh harpist and song collector. Taught the harp by his father, he went to London in 1775 and was app. bard to the Prince of Wales in 1783. Pub. several collections of Welsh and other national airs.

Jones, Gwyneth (b Pontnewyndd, 7 Nov 1936), Welsh soprano. She studied at the RCM and in Siena. Debut Zurich, 1962, Gluck's Orpheus. Sang Lady Macbeth with WNO 1963; Fidelio and the *Trovatore* Leonora, CG, 1964. First Wagner role in London was Sieglinde, 1965, and following year she made her Bayreuth debut; Brünnhilde in the centenary *Ring* 1976. Vienna since 1966; NY Met 1972. In Nov 1985 she sang both the Empress and the Dyer's Wife in a perf. of *Die Frau ohne Schatten* at the Zurich Opera. In 1986 she returned to CG, as Salome. CBE 1976; DBE 1986.

Jones, John (b London, 1728; d London, 17 Feb 1796), English organist and composer. App. organist of the Middle Temple in 1749, of Charterhouse, succeeding Pepusch, in 1753 and of St Paul's Cathedral in 1755. Wrote chants, harpsichord lessons, etc.

Jones, Parry (b Blaina, Mon., 14 Feb 1891; d London, 26 Dec 1963), Welsh tenor. After a tour of the US he sang with the Carl Rosa co. 1919–22; CG debut with the co. 1921, as Turiddu. BNOC 1922–9. He was the Kardinal in the 1st Brit. perf. of *Mathis der Maler* (concert, 1939) and Mephistopheles in a concert perf. of Busoni's *Doktor Faust* (under Boult, 1937). He took part in the 1st concert and stage perfs. of *Wozzeck* in England (1934, 1952). Other roles incl. Walther, Parsifal and Lohengrin.

Jones, Robert (b c 1485; d c 1536), English composer. He was a Gentleman of the Chapel Royal from 1513. He composed a song, 'Who shall have my fair lady', a Mass, *Spes nostra*, and a Magnificat.

Jones, Robert (b c 1570; d c 1617), English lutenist and composer. He worked for several patrons and took the B.Mus. degree at Oxford in 1597. In 1610, with Rosseter and others, he obtained a patent to train children for the queen's revels, and in 1615 they were allowed to erect a theatre in Blackfriars, but its opening was subsequently prohibited.

Works incl. madrigals, 5 books of *Songs and Ayres* to the lute, anthems.

Jongen, Joseph (b Liège, 14 Dec 1873; d Sart-lez-Spa nr. Liège, 12 Jul 1953), Belgian composer. Studied at the Liège Cons. Gained a prize from the Académie Royale in 1893 and the Belg. Prix de Rome in 1897. After teaching for a short time at the Liège Cons., he went to Rome and later travelled in Ger. and Fr., taking up a professorship at Liège in 1903. In 1914–18 he was in England as a war refugee, but returned to Liège until 1920, when he became prof. at the Brussels Cons., of which he was later app. director.

Works incl. ballet *S'Arka*; symph. (1910), *Fantaisie sur deux Noëls wallons* (1902), symph. poem *Lalla Rookh* (after Thomas Moore, 1904), *Impressions d'Ardennes* (1913), *Tableaux pittoresques* (1917), *Passecaille et Gigue* for orch. (1930); *Pièce symphonique* for pf. and wind orch., vln. concerto, harp concerto (1944), suite for vla. and orch., *Symphonie concertante* for org. and orch. (1926), concerto for wind 5tet (1923); 3 string 4tets (1894, 1916, 1921), 2 serenades for string 4tet, pf. trio; 2 vln. and pf. sonatas, cello sonata; *Sonata eroica* for org.; songs.

Jongleur (Fr. = juggler), a medieval wandering minstrel, one of whose accomplishments was juggling, but who also sang and played.

Jongleur de Notre Dame, Le (*Our Lady's Juggler*), opera by Massenet (lib. by M. Léna on a story by Anatole France in *L'Étui de nacre*, based on a medieval miracle play), prod. Monte Carlo, 18 Feb 1902.

Jonny spielt auf (*Johnny strikes up*), opera by Krenek (lib. by comp.), prod. Leipzig, Munic. Opera, 10 Feb 1927.

Jonson, Ben(jamin) (1573–1637), English poet and dramatist. *See* **Alchemist** (Handel), **Angiolina** (Salieri), **Auric** (*Volpone*), **Ferrabosco (A. ii)** (masques), **Harington** ('Drink to me only'), **Lanier** (*Lovers made Men* and *Vision of Delight*), **Lothar** (*Lord Spleen*), **Pastoral** (Bliss), **Schweigsame Frau** (R. Strauss), **Spanish Lady** (Elgar), **Vaughan Williams** (*Pan's Anniversary*).

Jörn, Karl (b Riga, 5 Jan 1873; d Denver, 19 Dec 1947), American tenor of Latvian birth. Debut Freiburg 1896, as Lionel; sang at Hamburg 1899–1902 and Berlin from 1902: first local Parsifal, 1914. CG 1905–8. He sang at the NY Met 1908–14 and

attempted to retire in 1916. After a business disaster he toured with Johanna Gadski and the German Opera co. 1928–31; particularly successful as Parsifal. Other roles incl. Faust and Don José. Taught in NY from 1932.

Joseph, opera by Méhul (lib. by A. Duval), prod. Paris, Opéra-Comique, 17 Feb 1807. Weber wrote pf. variations, Op. 28, on a romance from it.

Joseph and his Brethren, oratorio by Handel (lib. by J. Miller), perf. London, CG, 2 Mar 1744.

Josephs, Wilfred (b Newcastle, 24 Jul 1927), English composer. He studied at the GSM and in Paris. His *Requiem* of 1963 won 1st prize in a La Scala competition.

Other works incl. opera *Rebecca* (after Hollywood rather than du Maurier; prod. Leeds 1983); dramatic works for children and for TV; 3 ballets; 9 symphs. (1955–80); 2 pf. concertos, vln. concerto, clar. concerto (1975), concerto for vla. and chamber orch. (1983); *Mortales* for soloists, chorus and orch. (texts by Blake, Shelley, Nashe and Luther; fp Cincinnati, 1970); 4 string 4tets (1954–81), octet (1964), 2 vln. sonatas, pf. trio (1974).

Josephslegende, ballet in 1 act by Strauss (scenario by H. Kessler and Hugo von Hofmannsthal); comp. 1912–14, prod. Paris, Opéra, 14 Feb 1914, Ballet Russe.

Joshua, oratorio by Handel (lib. by T. Morell), perf. London, CG, 23 Mar 1748.

Josquin Desprez (or des Pres) (b NE France, *c* 1440; d Condé, 27 Aug 1521), French composer. By 1459 he was a singer at Milan Cathedral, remaining there for nearly 20 years, also working at the court of René of Anjou and in the Papal Chapel (1486–94). In the years *c* 1500 he was briefly at the French royal court, then at Ferrara (1503–4) before becoming provost at Condé, where he seems to have spent the rest of his life.

His reputation throughout the 16th cent. as the purest and most accomplished comp. of his time is partly endorsed (though also confused) by the enormous number of spurious works ascribed to him in the MSS – exceeding double the number that are accepted as authentic by scholars today. His 18 authentic complete Mass cycles incl. exs. of the canonic, *cantus firmus*, paraphrase and so-called 'parody' types; the most famous in his own time was the Mass *De beata virgine*, whereas today the Mass *Pange lingua* is perhaps best known. His numerous motets and psalm-settings (63 seem certain to be his) are remarkable for their careful adherence to the spirit of the words: for example, in the inexpressible sadness of *Absalon fili mi* and the anguished passion of his extended *Miserere*. His shorter secular works (over 50) are mostly from the years after 1500 and many of them treat received semi-popular songs in the most elaborate polyphonic texture, though *Mille regretz* and his lament for Ockeghem, *Nymphes des bois*, make their impact through superficially simpler means.

Josten, Werner (b Elberfeld, 12 Jun 1885; d New York, 6 Feb 1963), German-American composer. Studied in Munich, Geneva (with Jaques-Dalcroze) and Paris. In 1918 he became asst. cond. at the Munich Opera, but in 1920 emigrated to USA. App. prof. at Smith Coll., Northampton, Mass., in 1923.

Works incl. ballets *Batouala* (1931), *Joseph and his Brethren* (1936), *Endymion* (1933); *Crucifixion* for bass solo and chorus, *Hymnus to the Quene of Paradys* for contralto solo, women's chorus, strings and org., *Ode for St Cecilia's Day* for solo voices, chorus and orch. (1925); symph. in F maj., serenade, symph. movement *Jungle* (on Henri Rousseau's picture 'Forêt exotique', 1929), etc. for orch.; symph. and 2 *Concerti sacri* for strings and pf.

Jota, Spanish dance, esp. of Aragon and Navarre. It dates from the 12th cent. and is said to derive its name from the Moor Aben Jot. It is in quick 3–4 time. The music is played on instruments of the guitar type and often accomp. by castanets and other perc.

Joubert, John (b Cape Town, 20 Mar 1927), S. African composer. Studied at Cape Town Univ. and the RAM in London. Lecturer at Hull Univ., 1950–62, at Birmingham Univ., 1962–86.

Works incl. operas *Antigone* (1954), *In the drought* (1956), *Silas Marner* (1961), *Under Western Eyes* (1968); cantatas *The Leaves of Life* and *Urbs beata*; 3 motets; symph. prelude, 2 symphs. (1956, 1971), *In Memoriam, 1820* for orch.; vln. concerto (1954), pf. concerto; 2 string 4tets (1950, 1977) and other chamber music; choral works; songs.

Jour de Fête, a collective work for string 4tet: 1. *Les Chanteurs de Noël* (Glazunov); 2. *Glorification* (Liadov); 3. *Chœur dansé russe* (Rimsky-Korsakov).

Journet, Marcel (b Grasse, 25 Jul 1867; d Vittel, 5 Sep 1933), French bass. Studied at the Paris Cons. and made his 1st appearance at Béziers in 1891 in *La favorite*. He sang in Brussels 1894–1900 and at CG, London, 1897–1928. Paris, Opéra, 1908–31 as

Dosifey, Sachs, Wotan and Gurnemanz. NY Met debut 1900, as Ramfis.

Joyce Book, a collection of settings of poems by James Joyce by George Antheil, Arnold Bax, Arthur Bliss, Edgardo Carducci, Bernard van Dieren, Eugene Goossens, Herbert Howells, Herbert Hughes, John Ireland, E.J. Moeran, C.W. Orr, Albert Roussel and Roger Sessions, ed. by Herbert Hughes, pub. in 1932.

Jubel-Ouvertüre (*Jubilee Overture*), a concert overture by Weber, op. 59, comp. in 1818 as a companion-piece to the *Jubel-Cantate* for the 50th anniv. of the accession of the King of Saxony, Frederick Augustus, and perf. Dresden, 20 Sep. It concludes with the tune of 'God save the King'.

Juch, Emma (b Vienna, 4 Jul 1863; d New York, 6 Mar 1939), American soprano. Stage debut London 1881, in *Mignon*; sang in US with Mapelson's co. from 1881. Toured with American Opera co. 1884–9 and formed her own co. which toured widely in Central and N. America until 1894. Well known as Senta and the Queen of Night.

Judas Maccabaeus, oratorio by Handel (lib. by T. Morell), comp. 9 Jul–11 Aug 1746, prod. London, CG, 1 Apr 1747.

Judenkünig, Hans (d ? Vienna, 4 Mar 1526), German or Austrian lutenist. Lived in Vienna and wrote and arr. pieces for his instrument.

Judgment of Paris, The, masque by Congreve, for the comp. of which a prize was advertised in the *London Gazette* in 1700, the 1st 4 prizes being won by Weldon, Eccles, D. Purcell and Finger in 1701. Eccles's setting prod. London, Dorset Gardens Theatre, 21 Mar and Finger's 27 Mar 1701. The lib. was later set by G. Sammartini, prod. Cliveden, Bucks. 1 Aug 1740, and by Arne, prod. Drury Lane, London, 12 Mar 1742.

Judith, opera by Natanael Berg (1879–1957), (lib., in Swed., by comp., based on Hebbel's drama), prod. Stockholm, 22 Feb 1936.

Opera by Goossens (lib. by Arnold Bennett), prod. London, CG, 25 Jun 1929.

Opera by Serov (lib., in Rus., by comp. and A.N. Maikov, based on P. Giacometti's drama *Giuditta*), prod. St Petersburg, 28 May 1863.

Oratorio by Arne (lib. by I. Bickerstaffe), perf. London, Drury Lane Theatre, 27 Feb 1761.

Oratorio by Parry (lib. from the Bible), perf. Birmingham Festival, 1888.

Play with music by Honegger (lib. by R.

Morax), prod. Mézières, open air Théâtre du Jorat, 13 Jun 1925; operatic version, Monte Carlo, 13 Feb 1926.

Juditha triumphans devicta Holofernes barbarie, oratorio by Vivaldi (text by J. Cassetti), perf. Venice 1716. Sometimes given in modern revivals as a stage work, e.g. Camden Festival, London, 1984.

Juif polonais, Le (*The Polish Jew*), opera by C. Erlanger (lib. by H. Cain and P.B. Gheusi, based on Erckmann-Chatrian's novel), prod. Paris, Opéra-Comique, 11 Apr 1900. The subject is that of the play *The Bells*, in which Irving made his greatest popular success.

Juilliard Quartet, American string quartet founded 1946 by William Schuman, then president of the J. School, NY, with Robert Mann as leader. Other members are Earl Carlyss, Samuel Rhodes and Joel Krosnick. Many tours in US and Europe with 4tets by Mozart and Beethoven; fps of Carter's 4tets nos. 2 and 3, and works by Sessions and Piston. Made the first recording of the 4tets of Schoenberg. In residence, Library of Congress, Washington DC, since 1962.

Juive, La (*The Jewess*), opera by Halévy (lib. by Scribe), prod. Paris, Opéra, 23 Feb 1835.

Julie, opera by Dezède (lib. by J.M.B. de Monvel), prod. Paris, Comédie-Italienne, 28 Sep 1772. Mozart wrote pf. variations K264) on the air 'Lison dormait' in 1778.

Julien, ou La Vie du poète (*Julian, or The Poet's Life*), opera by G. Charpentier, sequel to *Louise* (lib. by comp.), prod. Paris, Opéra-Comique, 4 Jun 1913.

Juliette, or The Key to Dreams, lyric opera by Martinů (lib. by comp. after the play by G. Neveux); comp. 1936–7, prod. Prague, National Theatre, 16 Mar 1938.

Julius Caesar (Handel and Malipiero). See Giulio Cesare.

Jullien, (Jean Lucien) Adolphe (b Paris, 1 Jun 1845; d Chaintreauville, 30 Aug 1932), French critic. Studied law at first, and music with a retired prof. of the Cons. He began to write for the music papers and to champion Berlioz, Wagner, Schumann and modern music. App. music critic to *Le Français* in 1872 and the *Journal des Débats* in 1873. His books incl. studies of 18th-cent. opera, Berlioz, Wagner, Goethe and music, etc.

Jullien (orig. Julien), **Louis Antoine** (b Sisteron, 23 Apr 1812; d Paris, 14 Mar 1860), French conductor. Son of a bandmaster, he studied unsuccessfully at the Paris Cons., became a cond. of dance music and compiler of quadrilles on popular operas.

June, Ava (b London, 23 Jul 1931), English soprano. She sang with SW/ENO from 1957 as Mozart's Countess and Donna Anna, the Marschallin and Sieglinde. CG from 1958. US debut San Francisco 1974, as Ellen Orford. Other roles incl. Leonore, Katya Kabanova and Donizetti's Elizabeth I.

Jung, Manfred (b Oberhausen, 9 Jul 1945), German tenor. He studied in Essen and was a member of Bayreuth chorus before Dortmund debut, 1974. Sang the *Götterdämmerung* Siegfried at Bayreuth, 1977, and in the TV version of the Chéreau-Boulez *Ring* cycle; same role in Solti-Hall Bayreuth *Ring*, 1983. NY Met debut 1981; Tristan and Parsifal at Salzburg Easter Fest. 1980.

Junge Lord, Der (*The Young Lord*), opera by Henze (lib. by Ingeborg Bachmann, after Wilhelm Hauff), prod. Berlin, Deutsche Oper, 7 Apr 1965.

Junge Magd, Die (*The Young Girl*), 6 songs for alto, flute, clar. and string 4tet by Hindemith (texts by George Trakl); fp Donaueschingen, 31 Jul 1922.

Jungfernquartette (Ger. = Maiden 4tets), another nickname for Haydn's 6 string 4tets, op. 33, also known as 'Russian 4tets' and more generally as 'Gli Scherzi'.

Jungfrun i Tornet (*The Maiden in the Tower*), opera in 1 act by Sibelius (lib. by Hertzberg); comp. 1896 for Robert Kajanus's Helsinki Orch. and orch. school, fp 7 Nov 1896.

Jungwirth, Manfred (b St Polten, 4 Jun 1919), Austrian bass. Debut Bucharest 1942, as Méphistophélès. From 1948 he sang widely in Aus. and Ger.; member Frankfurt Opera from 1960. His best role is Ochs; Glyndebourne 1965, later recorded under Solti. Has also been heard in operas by Wagner and Lortzing.

Juon, Paul (b Moscow, 6 Mar 1872; d Vevey, Switz, 21 Aug 1940), Russian composer. Studied with Taneiev and Arensky in Moscow and with Bargiel in Berlin, where he settled and was later app. prof. at the Hochschule für Musik by Joachim.

Works incl. ballet *Psyche*; symph. in A, serenade and other works for orch.; 3 vln. concertos (1909, 1913, 1931), *Épisodes concertantes* for vln., cello and pf. and orch.; chamber symph., 5 pieces for string orch.; 3 string 4tets (1898, 1904, 1920), 6tet for pf. and strings, 2 pf. 5tets (1906, 1909), 2 pf. 4tets (1908, 1912), pf. trios (1901, 1915), Divertimento for wind and pf., do. for clar. and 2 vlas.; instrumental pieces; *Satyrs and Nymphs*, *Preludes* and *Capriccios*, etc. for pf.

'Jupiter' Symphony, nickname (not the

comp.'s own) given to Mozart's last symph., K551 in C maj., finished 10 Aug 1788.

Jurinac, Sena (b Travnik, 24 Oct 1921), Yugoslav soprano. Studied singing in Zagreb, making her debut there in 1942. From 1944 she was a member of the Vienna Staatsoper. She also sang at Glyndebourne (from 1949) and CG (debut 1947), and was esp. noted for her singing of Mozart and R. Strauss, e.g. Cherubino, Donna Anna, Donna Elvira, Octavian and the Marschallin.

Just Intonation, singing or instrumental playing in what is said to be the pure natural scale, not that artificially fixed on keyboard instruments by Equal Temperament.

Justiniana, a type of 16th-cent. *villanella* for 3 voices the words of which satirized the Venetian patricians. There is no connection between the J. and the *villanella* set to poetry of the type originated by L. Giustinian (*q.v.*).

K

K. (abbr.) = **Köchel,** the thematic catalogue of Mozart's works ed. by Ludwig von Köchel. Mozart's works are identified by the letter K followed by catalogue numbers instead of by op. numbers.

K. Anh. (abbr.) = Köchel Anhang, Köchel's appendix to his catalogue in which works are given the suffix KAnh. followed by the number.

Kk (abbr.). *See* **Kirkpatrick, Ralph.**

Kabaivanska, Raina (b Burgas, 15 Dec 1934), Bulgarian soprano, well known in Italian opera. Appeared in Bellini's *Beatrice di Tenda* at La Scala in 1961 and in the following year sang for the first time at CG, London, and the NY Met. In 1973 she sang Hélène in Maria Callas's production of *Les Vêpres siciliennes* in Turin. Other roles incl. Nedda, Imogene, Desdemona, Elisabeth de Valois, Lisa, Liù, Tosca and Madama Butterfly.

Kabale und Liebe, opera by Einem (lib. by comp. after Schiller's tragedy, 1784), fp Vienna, Staatsoper, 17 Dec 1976. *See also* **Luisa Miller.**

Kabalevsky, Dmitri Borisovich (b St Petersburg, 30 Dec 1904; d Moscow, 16 Feb 1987), Russian composer. Entered the Skriabin School of Music at Moscow when the family settled there in 1918, studying pf. and becoming a comp. pupil of Vassilenko and Catoire, afterwards of Miaskovsky. Later became prof. of comp. there.

Works incl. operas *The Golden Spikes, The Craftsman of Clamecy* (after Romain Rolland's novel *Colas Breugnon* 1938), *Before Moscow* (1943), and *Nikita Vershinin* (1955); incid. music for Shakespeare's *Measure for Measure,* Sheridan's *School for Scandal* and an adaptation of Flaubert's *Madame Bovary*; film music *Poem of Struggle, Our Great Fatherland* and *People's Avengers* for chorus and orch.; 4 symphs. (no. 3 *Requiem for Lenin*); 3 pf. concertos (1931–53), vln. concerto, 2 cello concertos; 2 string 4tets (1928, 1945); 3 sonatas, 2 sonatinas and other pf. music; Requiem; songs.

Kabeláč, Miloslav (b Prague, 1 Aug 1908; d Prague, 17 Sep 1979), Czech composer. Studied comp. at the Prague Cons. with K.B. Jirák from 1928 to 1931 and later also the pf. at the Master School. In 1932 he joined

the staff of Czech Radio.

Works incl. 8 symphs. (1941–70); cantatas *Mystery of Time, Do not retreat*; 2 overtures; wind 6tet; suite for saxophone and pf.; vln. and pf. pieces; choral music.

Kabós, Ilona (b Budapest, 7 Dec 1893; d London, 28 May 1973), British pianist of Hungarian birth. She studied with Leo Weiner and Kodály and began her career during the First War. She was a champion of contemporary music and gave fps of works by Dallapiccola and Chávez. With husband, Louis Kentner, gave fp of Bartók's concerto for 2 pf. and orchestra (London, 1942). Highly regarded as a teacher, among her pupils were Peter Frankl and John Ogdon. In the last ten years of her life she taught at the Juilliard School, NY, and the Dartington Summer School.

Kadosa, Pál (b Leva, now Levice, Cz., 6 Sep 1903; d Budapest, 30 Mar 1983), Hungarian composer and pianist. He studied with Kodály at the Budapest Academy and taught pf. at Fodor Cons. 1927–43. Prof., Budapest Acad., from 1945. Influenced by Bartók.

Works incl. opera *The Adventure of Huszt* (1951); 5 cantatas (1939–50); 8 symphs. (1941–68); 4 pf. concertos (1931–66); 2 vln. concertos (1931, 1941); concerto for string 4tet and chamber orch. (1936); 3 string 4tets (1934–57); 2 string trios (1930, 1955); 4 pf. sonatas (1926–60).

Kagel, Mauricio (b Buenos Aires, 24 Dec 1931), Argentine composer of advanced tendencies. Studied in Buenos Aires, settling in Cologne in 1957. He has evolved a very complex style employing serial and aleatory techniques, permutations of different languages, light effects and aural distortions.

Works incl. *Anagrama* for 4 soloists, speaking chorus and chamber ensemble (1958); *Sur scène,* theatrical piece in 1 act for speaker, mime, singer and 3 instruments (1962); *The Women,* dramatic scene for 3 female voices, 3 actresses, a dancer, chorus of women, and electronic tapes; *Match* for 3 players; *Diaphony* for chorus, orch. and 2 projectors (1964); *Transición I* for electronic sounds; *Transición II* for pf., perc. and 2 tapes; *Hetrophonie* for an orch. of solo instruments; string 6tet. *Ludwig Van,* film score (1970); *Staatstheater,* 'ballet for nondancers', with inst. incl. chamber pot (1971); opera, *Die Erschöpfung der Welt* (prod. Stuttgart, 8 Feb 1980), *Sankt - Bach - Passion* (1985).

Kaiser Quartett (Haydn). *See* **Emperor Quartet.**

Kajanus, Robert (b Helsinki, 2 Dec 1856; d

Helsinki, 6 Jul 1933), Finnish conductor and composer. Studied at the Helsinki and Leipzig Conss., also comp. with Svendsen in Paris. Founded the orch. of the Helsinki Phil. Society in 1882, with which later he paid several important visits to foreign countries, giving many early perfs. of Sibelius. Director of music at Helsinki Univ., 1897–1926.
Works incl. symph. *Aino* (on an incident from the *Kalevala*), etc.

Kalafaty, Vassily Pavlovich (b Eupatoria, Crimea, 10 Feb 1869; d Leningrad, 30 Jan 1942), Russian composer. Pupil of Rimsky-Korsakov. In 1900 he was app. prof. of comp. at the St Petersburg Cons., where he had Stravinsky and Prokofiev among his pupils. Died during Nazi siege of Leningrad (*see* **Kamensky**).
Works incl. symph. and other orchestral works; chamber music, pf. pieces; songs.

Kalbeck, Max (b Breslau, 4 Jan 1850; d Vienna, 4 May 1921), German critic and writer of music. Worked in Vienna. Trans. opera libs. and wrote the 1st full Brahms biog.

Kalcher, Johann Nepomuk (b Freising, Bavar., 15 May 1764; d Munich, 2 Dec 1827), German organist and composer. Studied at Munich, where he became court organist in 1798. Weber was one of his pupils. Wrote Masses, symphs., organ music, songs.

Kalenberg, Josef (b Cologne, 7 Jan 1886; d Vienna, 8 Nov 1962), German tenor. Debut Cologne 1911, as Turiddu. He sang at Krefeld, Barmen and Düsseldorf 1912–25 and returned to Cologne 1925. In 1927 he sang Parsifal at the Vienna Staatsoper and returned there until 1942. Salzburg 1928–36; Tristan 1935. Retired 1949.

Kalevala, The, Finish national epic. *See* **Dallapiccola** (2 lyrics), **Kajanus** (*Aino*), **Kullervo** (Sibelius), **Lemminkainen's Return** and 3 other Legends (do.), **Merikanto (A.)** (*Abduction of Kylliki*), **Pohjola's Daughter** (Sibelius), **Swan of Tuonela** (do.), **Tapiola** (do.).

Kalichstein, Joseph (b Tel Aviv, 15 Jan 1946), Israeli pianist. He studied at the Juilliard School and in 1967 won the Leventritt Competition. Has appeared all over the US; among his recordings are the Mendelssohn concertos, with Previn. Also noted as interpreter of Brahms, Prokofiev, Chopin and Bartók.

Kalinnikov, Vassily Sergeyevich (b Voina, 13 Jan 1866; d Yalta, 11 Jan 1901), Russian composer. He was educ. at a seminary, where he cond. the choir. In 1884 went to

Moscow and, in spite of great poverty, obtained a music educ. at the Phil. Society Music School. After cond. It. opera for the 1893–4 season, he was found to suffer from consumption and lived mainly in the Crimea, devoted to comp.
Works incl. incid. music to Alexey Tolstoy's *Tsar Boris* (1899); cantatas *St John Chrysostom* and *Russalka*; 2 symphs., suite, 2 Intermezzi and 2 sketches for orch.; string 4tets; pf. pieces; songs.

Kalisch, Alfred (b London, 13 Mar 1863; d London, 17 May 1933), English critic of German descent. Educ. at Oxford for law, but became a music journalist in 1894. Translator of R. Strauss's operas.

Kalisch, Paul (b Berlin, 6 Nov 1855; d St Lorenz am Modensee, 27 Jan 1946), German tenor. His early career was in Italy, and after a year in Munich he sang with the Berlin Opera from 1884 to 1887. In 1888 he married the soprano Lilli Lehmann and from the following year appeared with her in many productions at the Metropolitan. He was well-known as Pollione, Florestan, Don Ottavio and Manrico and he was successful in such lighter Wagnerian roles as Tannhäuser and Siegmund.

Kalkbrenner, Friedrich (Wilhelm Michael) (b on a journey between Kassel and Berlin, Nov 1785; d Enghien-les-Bains, 10 Jun 1849), German pianist, teacher and composer. Studied under his father, Christian K. (1755–1806) and at the Paris Cons. Made his 1st public appearance in Vienna in 1803, returning to Paris in 1806. Lived in London as teacher and perf. in 1814–23 and then settled in Paris as a member of the pf. firm of Pleyel, but continued to teach and perf.
Works incl. 4 pf. concertos (1823–35), concerto for 2 pfs.; pf. 7tet, 6tet and 5tet; pf. school with studies appended, sonatas, variations and numerous other works for pf.

Kalliwoda, Johan Vaclav (b Prague, 21 Feb 1801; d Karlsruhe, 3 Dec 1866), Bohemian violinist and composer. Studied at the Prague Cons. in 1811–17 and played in the orch. in 1817–22. He then became music director to Prince Fürstenberg at Donaueschingen until his retirement in 1866.
Works incl. opera *Blanka*; 7 symphs. (1826–43); concertinos for vln., for clar. and other instruments; 3 string 4tets; vln. duets, vln. pieces.

Kálmán, Emmerich (b Siófok, 24 Oct 1882; d Paris, 30 Oct 1953), Hungarian composer. He studied in Budapest. In 1908 he had great success with the operetta *Tatárjárás* (given in NY and elsewhere as *The Gay Hussar*);

lived in Vienna until 1938 and among other works produced *Der gute Kamerad* (1911), *Der Zigeunerprimas* (1912), *Die Csárdásfürstin* (1915), *Die Faschingsfee* (1917), *Gräfin Mariza* (1924), *Die Zirkusprinzessin* (1924) and *Der Teufelsreiter*. He moved to Paris in 1939, then to NY and Hollywood.

Kálmán, Oszkár (b Kis-Szent-Péter, 18 Jun 1887; d Budapest, 18 Sep 1971), Hungarian bass. He sang at the Budapest Opera from 1913 and in 1918 sang Bluebeard in the fp of Bartók's opera. He joined Otto Klemperer at the Kroll Opera, Berlin, in 1927 and took part in the 1st Ger. perf. of Stravinsky's *Oedipus Rex*. In 1929 he sang in the fp of Hindemith's *Lehrstück* (Baden-Baden). He was successful all over Europe until 1939 and was noted in Hungary as an interpreter of Kodály's songs.

Kalmus, Alfred (b Vienna, 16 May 1889; d London, 25 Sep 1972), English music publisher of Austrian birth. He studied with Guido Adler and joined Universal Edition in 1909; helped further the careers of Bartók, Janáček and comps. of the Second Viennese School. He moved to London in 1936 and founded the local branch of Universal; continued his services for modern music after the war and pub. leading continental composers, e.g. Stockhausen and Boulez, and such home-grown talent as Birtwistle and David Bedford.

Kalomiris, Manolis (b Smyrna, 26 Dec 1883; d Athens, 3 Apr 1962), Greek composer. Studied in Athens, Constantinople and Vienna. He taught at Kharkov in 1906–10 and then settled in Athens as prof. at the Cons. From 1919 he was director of the Hellenic Cons. there but in 1926 he founded the National Cons. and became its director.

Works incl. operas *The Master Builder* (after N. Kazantzakis, 1915), *The Mother's Ring* (after J. Kambyssis, 1917), *Anatoli* and *The Haunted Waters* (after Yeats, 1950–2); incid. music; 2 symphs., symph. poems, etc., for orch.; chamber music; pf. works; songs.

Kalter, Sabine (b Jaroslaw, 28 Mar 1889; d London, 1 Sep 1957), Hungarian mezzo. Debut Vienna 1911 and sang in Hamburg 1915–35; admired for her interpretations of roles by Wagner, Meyerbeer, Verdi and Gluck. She was obliged to leave Ger. in 1935 and until the war was successful at CG, as Ortrud, Brangaene and Fricka. At the Kroll Opera, Berlin, she took part in the 1929 fp of Hindemith's *Neues vom Tage*, under Klemperer. Other roles incl. Herodias and Lady Macbeth.

Kamarinskaya, fantasy for orch. on 2 Rus-

sian themes by Glinka, comp. 1848 and known only in an ed. revised by Rimsky-Korsakov and Glazunov.

Kamensky, Alexander (b Geneva, 12 Dec 1900; d Leningrad, 7 Nov 1952), Russian pianist. He graduated from the Petrograd Conservatory in 1923 and became widely known in Russia before the war. During the two-year siege of Leningrad by the Germans he gave nearly 500 recitals, often in conditions of extreme danger and hardship; featured works by Schoenberg and Stravinsky as well as Soviet comps.

Kamieński, Maciej (b Sopron, 13 Oct 1734; d Warsaw, 25 Jan 1821), Hungarian-Polish composer. Studied in Vienna and settled at Warsaw in *c* 1760. He prod. the 1st Pol. opera there on 11 May 1778.

Works incl. opera *Happiness in Unhappiness* and 5 others in Pol. and 2 in Ger.; church music, cantata for the unveiling of the Sobjeski monument.

Kamionsky, Oscar (b Kiev, 1869; d Yalta, 15 Aug 1917), Russian baritone. He studied at St Petersburg and made his debut in Naples, 1891. From 1893 until his retirement in 1915 his career was in Russia; many appearances at Kharkov, Kiev, Tiflis, St Petersburg and the Zimin theatre, Moscow, as Onegin, Mazeppa, Renato and the Figaro of Mozart and Rossini. Recorded from 1901 in Fr. and It. rep.

Kammel, Antonin (b Běleč, bap. 21 Apr 1730; d ? London by 1787), Czech-born violinist and composer. He studied at Prague University and in Italy, and by 1764 he was established in London; mentioned by Leopold Mozart in his travel notes. He appeared in the Bach-Abel concerts and was probably a royal chamber musician. He was successful as a composer and nearly all his works feature the violin.

Kammermusik (*Chamber Music*), 7 works by Hindemith comp. 1921–7; no. 1 for small orch., fp Donaueschingen, 31 Jul 1922, cond. Scherchen; no. 2 for pf. and 12 insts., fp Frankfurt 31 Oct 1924, cond. Clemens Krauss; no. 3 for cello and 10 insts., fp Bochum, 30 Apr 1925, cond. Hindemith; no. 4 for vln. and chamber orch., fp Dessau, 25 Sep 1925; no. 5 for viola and chamber orch., fp Berlin, 3 Nov 1927, cond. Klemperer; no. 6 for viola d'amore and chamber orch., fp Cologne, 29 Mar 1928; no. 7 for organ and chamber orch., fp Frankfurt, 8 Jan 1928. *See* also **Neo-classicism.**

Kammerton (Ger., lit. chamber-pitch), the pitch to which orch. instruments in Germany were tuned in the 17th–18th cent. It was lower, by a whole tone or more, than the *Chorton* (choir-pitch) used for church organs, and it was for this reason that Bach, in his Leipzig cantatas, transposed the org. parts down a tone in order to make them agree with the orch. The transposition applied only to the organ parts: the orchestral parts could be used as they stood.

Kamu, Okko (b Helsinki, 7 Mar 1946), Finnish conductor and violinist. Debut as a violinist before his teens and was leader of Finnish Nat. Opera Orch. 1966–9; won first Karajan International Competition 1969. London debut 1970; chief cond. Helsinki PO from 1979. In 1987 at CG he cond. the Brit. fp of Sallinen's *The King goes forth to France.*

Kapell, William (b New York, 20 Sep 1922; d King's Mount., Calif., 29 Oct 1953), American pianist. He studied at Philadelphia and at the Juilliard school; debut 1941, widely known as champion of the Khachaturian concerto and therefore had a reputation for virtuosity rather than musicianship. Killed in Californian aircrash on returning from tour of Australia.

Kapelle (Ger. = chapel), orig. the music estab. of a king's or prince's chapel; later by transfer. an orch.

Kapellmeister (Ger.), orig. choirmaster later also cond.

Kapellmeistermusik (Ger. = conductor's music), a contemptuous term for a musical work which betrays creative weakness and has no merit but that of a knowledge of rules and glib craftsmanship.

Kapp, Julius (b Steinbach, Baden, 1 Oct 1883; d Hinang bei Alstädten-im-Allgau, 18 Mar 1962), German writer on music. Studied chemistry and then became a literary ed. In 1921 he ed. the paper of the Berlin Staatsoper and in 1923 he became dramatic director there and adapted a number of works for its stage. He ed. Wagner's letters and his books incl. studies of Liszt, Wagner, Berlioz, Weber, Meyerbeer, and R. Strauss. His book *Wagner und die Frauen* (1912) was reprinted 15 times by 1929.

Kappel, Gertrude (b Halle, 1 Sep 1884; d Munich, 3 Apr 1971), German soprano. She sang at Hanover 1903–24 and between 1912 and 1926 appeared in major roles by Wagner and Strauss at CG. A member of the NY Met 1928 to 1936, roles incl. Brünnhilde, Isolde and Elektra; retired shortly before the war.

Kapsberger, Johann Hieronymus (b Venice, *c* 1575; d Rome, *c* 1651), German lutenist and composer. Lived in Venice and pub. 3 books of music for chitarrone in tablature. He also wrote vocal *villanelle* with that instrument, motets, an epithalamium and an apotheosis of Ignatius Loyola.

Karajan, Herbert von (orig. Heribert Karajannis) (b Salzburg, 5 Apr 1908), Austrian conductor and producer. Studied at Salzburg Mozarteum and in Vienna. Made his debut at Ulm in 1928, remaining there until 1933. He continued to work under the Nazi régime and was a member of the party. From 1934 to 1938 he was at Aachen, and at the Berlin Staatsoper 1938–42. After Furtwängler's death in 1954 he took over the Berlin PO and in 1956 became director of the Vienna Staatsoper, resigning in 1964. Cond., and recorded with, the Philharmonia Orch., London, 1948–60. Founded Salzburg Easter Fest. 1967 and took its prod. of *Die Walküre* to the NY Met in 1967. One of the best-known conds. of the day, Karajan is esp. noted for his perfs. of Mozart, Wagner, Bruckner and R. Strauss. In recent years he has added Mahler and the Second Viennese School to his repertory. At Salzburg he has produced operas by Wagner, Mussorgsky and Verdi. Karajan's performances are renowned for their technical perfection.

Karel, Rudolf (b Pizeň [Pilsen], 9 Nov 1880; d Terezín, 6 Mar 1945), Czech composer. Studied comp. under Dvořák at the Prague Cons. In 1914, on holiday in Rus. he was interned as an Aus. subject, then taught at Taganrog and Rostov-on-Don, fled to Siberia and eventually escaped to Cz., where he became prof. at the Prague Cons. He died tragically in a concentration camp.

Works incl. operas *Ilsa's Heart* (1909) and *Godmother's Death* (1932); incid. music to Knud Hamsun's *The Game of Life; Awakening*, symph. for solo voices, chorus and orch.; 2 symphs., *Renaissance* and *Spring*, symph. poems *The Ideals* and *Demon*, suite, fantasy, Slavonic dances, etc. for orch.; vln concerto, 3 string 4tets (1902–36).

Karelia, incid. music in 9 movements by Sibelius; comp. 1893, fp Viipuri, 13 Nov 1893. Suite for orch. in 3 movements op. 11, 1893.

Karg-Elert (real name **Karg**), **Sigfrid** (b Oberndorf-am-Neckar, 21 Nov 1877; d Leipzig, 9 Apr 1933), German organist, pianist and composer. Studied at the Leipzig Cons. and became prof. at those of Magdeburg and Leipzig; was a brilliant pianist, but was persuaded by Grieg to devote himself to comp.

Works incl. a symph., 2 pf. concertos

(1901, 1913); string 4tet; vln. and pf. sonatas; sonata and other works for pf.; over 100 songs; pieces for harmonium and many organ works, incl. 66 chorale improvisations (1908–10), 24 preludes and postludes, Sonatina, passacaglia, fantasy and fugue in D maj., *Chaconne, Fugue-Trilogy and Chorale*, 10 characteristic pieces, 3 symph. chorales, 7 *Pastels from Lake Constance* (1919), 6 *Cathedral Windows* (1923), 54 variation-studies *Homage to Handel.*

Karl V, opera by Krenek (lib. by comp.), prod. Prague, German Opera, 15 Jun 1938; revised vers., Vienna, 1984.

Karlowicz, Miecyslaw (b Wisziezwo, 11 Dec 1876; d Zakopane, 8 Feb 1909), Polish composer. The son of a noble family, he travelled much as a child and learnt the vln. in Prague, Dresden and Heidelberg, and soon played chamber music with his parents, a cellist and a pianist. Later studied at Warsaw, where his comp. teacher was Noskowski, and afterwards with Urban in Berlin; also cond. with Nikisch at Leipzig. Settled at Zakopane in the Tatra mountains in 1908 and was killed by an avalanche there.

Works incl. incid. music to *Biala Golabka*; symph. in E min., symph. poems *Returning Waves* (1907), *The Sad Story* (*Preludes to Eternity*), *Stanislas and Anna Oswiecim* (1912), *An Episode of the Masquerade*, serenade (1897), *Lithuanian Rhapsody* for orch.; vln. concerto (1902); songs.

Karr, Gary (b Los Angeles, 20 Nov 1941), American double-bass player. His career began in 1962 with appearances with the NY PO and as a solo recitalist; he toured Europe in 1964 and in 1967 was the soloist in the fp of Henze's Concerto for double bass and orch., a work which he also commissioned.

Kars, Jean-Rodolphe (b Calcutta, 15 Mar 1947), Austrian pianist. He studied at the Paris Conservatoire and in 1968 won the Messiaen Competition at Royan; has since become renowned for his interpretations of the French composer's works, in particular the massive *Vingt regards sur l'enfant Jésus.* Also noted for his Debussy and Ravel.

Kaschmann, Giuseppe (b Lussimpiccolo, Istria, 14 Jul 1847; d Rome, 7 Feb 1925), Italian baritone. He studied at Padua and Udine and sang in the perf. of Zajc's *Mislav* which opened the Zagreb Opera, 1870. Turin 1876, as Donizetti's Alphonse; La Scala from 1878. He sang Enrico (*Lucia*) in the inaugural season at the NY Met and returned 1896 for Telramund. Bayreuth 1892–4, as Wolfram and Amfortas. Towards the end of his career sang *buffo* roles

in operas by Rossini, Donizetti and Cimarosa.

Kashperov, Vladimir Nikitich (b Simbirsk, 6 Sep 1826; d Romantsevo, 8 Jul 1894), Russian composer. Studied with Henselt in St Petersburg and later in Berlin and Italy. Prof. of singing at the Moscow Cons. from 1866 to 1872.

Works incl. operas *The Gypsies, Mary Tudor* (after Hugo, Milan, 1859), *Rienzi* (after Bulwer-Lytton, Florence, 1863), *Consuelo* (after George Sand, Venice, 1865), *The Storm* (after Ostrovsky, Moscow, 1867), *Taras Bulba* (after Gogol, Moscow, 1893).

Kashtchey the Immortal (*K. Bessmertny*), opera by Rimsky-Korsakov (lib. by comp.), prod. Moscow, 25 Dec 1902. Kashtchey is the wizard of Rus. fairy lore who appears also in Stravinsky's *Firebird* ballet.

Kastner, Jean Georges (Johann Georg) (b Strasbourg, 9 Mar 1810; d Paris, 19 Dec 1867), Alsatian composer and theorist. Studied theology at home, but prod. an opera *Die Königin der Sarmaten* and was sent by the Strasbourg town council to study with Berton and Reicha at the Paris Cons. He wrote a treatise on orchestration, a manual on military music, and methods for var. instruments.

Works incl. operas, cantatas and songs.

Kastorsky, Vladimir (Bolshiye Soly, 14 Mar 1871; d Leningrad, 2 Jul 1948), Russian bass. He started his career as a chorister. Debut Maryinsky Theatre St Petersburg, in Serov's *Rodneda*; remained until 1930 as Gremin, Dargomyzhky's Miller, Hagen, Wotan and Marke. Visited Paris 1908 and sang Pimen in the prod. of *Boris Godunov* mounted by Diaghilev.

Káta Kabanová, opera by Janáček (lib. by V. Červinka, based on Ostrovsky's play *Groza*), prod. Brno, 23 Nov 1921.

Katchen, Julius (b Long Branch, NJ, 15 Aug 1926; d Paris, 29 Apr 1969), American pianist. Studied in New York with David Saperton, making his debut in 1937. He toured widely; well-known in Beethoven, Brahms and Schumann.

Katerina Izmailova (Shostakovich). *See* **Lady Macbeth of the Mtsensk District.**

Katims, Milton (b New York, 24 Jun 1909), American violist and conductor. He worked for a NY radio station, after studying at Columbia Univ., and in 1943 joined the NBC SO, under Toscanini. He remained there until 1954, when he became cond. of the Seattle SO; was well known as a performer of chamber music, in partic. as additional violist with the Budapest quartet.

Katin, Peter (b London, 14 Nov 1930), British pianist. He studied at the RAM and made his debut in 1948; has toured world wide, specializing in Romantic repertory. Noted interpreter of Chopin, on whom he has written a book. Now a Canadian citizen.

Katz, Mindru (b Bucharest, 3 Apr 1925; d Istanbul, 30 Jan 1978), Israeli pianist of Rumanian birth. From 1947 to 1957 his career was restricted to eastern Europe, then toured in the west making his British debut in 1958. The following year he became an Israeli citizen and in 1962 joined the music staff at Tel Aviv Univ. Died during a recital.

Kauer, Ferdinand (b Dyjákovičky, Moravia, 18 Jan 1751; d Vienna, 13 Apr 1831), Austrian composer. Studied at Znaim and Vienna, where he was app. leader and 2nd cond. at the Leopoldstadt Theatre, for which he wrote music for c 100 pantomimes, farces, etc. as well as operettas and operas.

Works incl. operas *Das Donauweibchen* (1798), *Das Waldweibchen*; oratorio *Die Sündflut*; trio *Nelsons grosse See-Schlacht*.

Kaun, Hugo (b Berlin, 21 Mar 1863; d Berlin, 2 Apr 1932), German composer. He had written over 150 works before he was 16 and studied with Kiel at the Berlin Acad. of Arts. In 1884 he went to USA as pianist, but had to give up that career owing to an injury; in 1887 settled in Milwaukee, but returned to Berlin in 1901, teaching comp. 1st at the Acad. and from 1922 at the Klindworth-Scharwenka Cons.

Works incl. operas *Der Pietist*, *Sappho* (1917), *Der Fremde* (1920) and *Menandra* (1925); several choral works; 3 symphs., *Minnehaha und Hiawatha* (after Longfellow), symph. prologue *Marie Magdalene*, humoresque *Falstaff* (after Shakespeare) and other orchestral works; 4 string 4tets, pf. 5tet, 2 pf. trios, 8tet; vln. and pf. sonata.

Kay, Ulysses Simpson (b Tuscon, 7 Jan 1917), black American composer. He studied with Howard Hanson at the Eastman School and with Hindemith at Tanglewood. Prof., Lehman College, NY, from 1968.

Works incl. operas *The Boor* (after Chekhov; comp. 1955, prod. 1968), *The Juggler of our Lady* (comp. 1956, prod. 1962), *The Capitoline Venus* (1971), *Jubilee* (1976); Suite for Strings (1949), *Song of Jeremiah*, cantata (1954), Serenade for Orch. (1954), Fantasy Variations for orch. (1963), *Scherzi musicali* for chamber orch. (1971); 2 string 4tets (1953, 1956), pf. 5tet (1949); choral pieces and songs.

Kee, Piet (b Zaandam, 30 Aug 1927), Dutch organist and composer. He has

toured widely, with a largely Dutch and German repertory, and has also recorded extensively; well known for his improvisations, and as a teacher.

Keeble, John (b Chichester, c 1711; d London, 24 Dec 1786), English organist and composer. He studied at Chichester Cathedral and in London, under Pepusch. In 1737 he became organist at St George's, Hanover Square, and was later organist at Ranelagh Gardens. Works incl. sets of voluntaries and psalm interludes.

Keene, Christopher (b Berkeley, Calif., 21 Dec 1946), American conductor. He conducted operas by Britten and Henze while at the Univ. of California and later assisted Kurt Adler in San Francisco and Menotti at Spoleto; princ. cond. NY City Opera 1970–86 (Met from 1971); gave the 1971 première of Menotti's opera *The Most Important Man*.

Keilberth, Joseph (b Karlsruhe, 19 Apr 1908; d Munich, 21 Jul 1968), German conductor. From 1935 to 1940 he cond. at the Karlsruhe Staatsoper and from 1940 to 1945 was cond. of the Berlin PO. He cond. at Dresden from 1945 to 1951 and at Bayreuth from 1952 to 1956 (*The Ring*, *Fliegende Holländer* and *Lohengrin*). He was best known as a cond. of R. Strauss's operas (*Rosenkavalier* at Edinburgh, 1952). He died while conducting *Tristan und Isolde*. Among his recordings are operas by Hindemith and Pfitzner.

Keiser, Reinhard (b Teuchern, nr. Weissenfels, Saxony, bap. 12 Jan 1674; d Hamburg, 12 Sep 1739), German composer. A pupil of Schelle at St Thomas's School, Leipzig, worked at Brunswick from 1692 under Kusser, whom he succeeded as chief comp. to the Hamburg Opera in 1695. There he comp. over 100 operas, making Hamburg the most distinguished operatic centre in Ger. App. *Kapellmeister* to the Dan. Court in Copenhagen in 1723, returned to Hamburg as Cantor of the cathedral, 1728.

Works incl. operas *Basilius*, *Circe* (1702), *Penelope* (1702), *Der geliebte Adonis*, *Augustus*, *Orpheus* (1702), *La forza della virtù*. *Stoertebecker und Joedge Michaels*, *Die verdammt Statt-Sucht* (1703), *Nebucadnezar* (1704), *Octavia*, *Masagniello furioso* (1706), *Desiderius* (1709), *Croesus* (1710), *Fredegunda* (1715), *Die grossmüthige Tomyris* (1717), *Ulysses*, *Der lächerliche Printz Jodelet* (1726), etc.; Passion oratorios *Der für die Sünde der Welt gemartete und sterbende Heiland Jesus* (text by Brockes, 1712), *Der blutige und sterbende Jesus*

(Hunold, 1704); cantatas; motets; instrumental music.

Kelemen, Milko (b Podravska, Slatina, 30 Mar 1924), Croatian composer. Studied at the Zagreb Cons. with Sulek. His mature style employes serial and aleatory techniques.

Works incl. operas *König Ubu* (1965), *State of Siege* (after Camus' *The Plague*, 1970); *Koncertantne Improvizacije* for strings (1955); *Concerto giocoso* for chamber orch.; concertos for vln. and bassoon; concertino for double bass and strings; *Symphonic Music 57*; *Abecedarium* for strings (1973); *Games* song cycle; pf. sonata.

Kelemen, Zoltán (b Budapest, 12 Mar 1926; d Zurich, 9 May 1979), Hungarian bass. After study in Budapest and Rome his early career was in West Ger. opera houses; sang Alberich in the *Ring* at Bayreuth in 1964 and later repeated the role under Karajan at the Salzburg Easter Festival and at CG (1970) and the NY Met. Well known as Klingsor, also admired in such *buffo* roles as Falstaff, Leporello, Osmin and Ochs.

Kell, Reginald (b York, 8 Jun 1906; d Frankfort, Ky., 5 Aug 1981), English clarinettist. After study at the RAM he was princ. clarinettist under Beecham with the LPO at CG, joined the Philharmonia on its foundation in 1945, and from 1948 his career was largely in the United States. He pub. a clarinet method in 1968.

Keller, Gottfried (1819–90), Swiss poet and novelist. *See* **Kleider machen Leute** (Zemlinsky), **Romeo und Julia auf dem Dorfe** (Delius), **Schoeck** (*Gesangfest im Frühling, Lebendig begraben, Gaselen, Unter Sternen, Sommernacht* and songs), **Vrieslander** (songs). 6 of his poems set by Hugo Wolf.

Keller, Hans (b Vienna, 11 Mar 1919; d London, 6 Nov 1985), British journalist and critic of Austrian birth. After studying in Vienna he fled to England in 1938; played the violin and viola in var. enss. and in 1959 joined the BBC. He had much influence on broadcasting policy, and in his programmes of functional analysis sought to elucidate structure and ideas by musical example, rather than verbal explanation. A mastery of his adopted language led to a prolific career as a journalist; natives were sometimes bemused by a certain subjectivity and love of paradox. He wrote the libretto for Benjamin Frankel's opera *Marching Song* (BBC 1983). Author of *The Great Haydn Quartets* (1986).

Kelley, Edgar Stillman (b Sparta, Wis., 14 Apr 1857; d New York, 12 Nov 1944),

American composer and writer on music. Studied at Chicago and Stuttgart, and on his return to USA became organist and critic in Calif., where he also made a study of Chinese music. He then taught at Yale Univ., in Berlin and, from 1910, at the Cincinnati Cons.

Works incl. operetta *Puritania* (1892); incid. music for Shakespeare's *Macbeth*; orchestral suite on Chin. themes, *Aladdin*, *Gulliver* symph. (after Swift), *New England Symph.*, suite *Alice in Wonderland* (after Lewis Carroll, 1913); cantata *Pilgrim's Progress* (after Bunyan, 1918), *Wedding Ode* for tenor, male chorus and orch.; *My Captain* (Whitman) and *The Sleeper* (Poe) for chorus; variations for string 4tet, string 4tet, pf. 5tet; pf. pieces; songs.

Kellner, Johann Peter (b Gräfenroda, Thuringia, 28 Sep 1705; d Gräfenroda, 17 Apr 1772), German organist and composer. App. Cantor at Frankenhain in 1725, he returned in a similar capacity to his home town in 1728, a post which he held till his death. He knew Bach and Handel personally.

Works incl. cantatas, an oratorio, organ and harpsichord music.

Kellogg, Clara Louise (b Sumterville, SC, 9 Jul 1842; d New Hartford, Conn., 13 May 1916), American soprano. Studied in NY and made her debut there in 1861, as Gilda; sang Marguerite in NY and London (debut 1867).

Kelly, Bryan (b Oxford, 3 Jan 1934), English composer who studied with Gordon Jacob and Herbert Howells; has written extensively for brass band and for educational use.

Works include *The Tempest* Suite, for strings (1967); *Edinburgh Dances* and Concertante Music, for brass band (1973); *Stabat Mater*, for soloists and orchestra (1970); *Latin Magnificat*, for chorus and wind instruments (1979); *The Spider Monkey Uncle King*, opera pantomime (1971); *Herod, do your worst*, nativity opera (1968).

Kelly, Michael (b Dublin, 25 Dec 1762; d Margate, 9 Oct 1826), Irish tenor, actor and composer. Pupil of M. Arne and others, went to Naples in 1779 to study with Fenaroli and Aprile, and there made his operatic debut in 1781. At the Court Opera in Vienna, 1784–7, he was the first Basilio and Curzio in Mozart's *Figaro* (1786). Returned to London in 1787, and 2 years later prod. the first of over 60 theatrical comps. His entertaining *Reminiscences* (pub. 1826), though not fully reliable, contain valuable information on his contemporaries, esp. Mozart.

Works incl. dramatic works *A Friend in Need* (1797), *The Castle Spectre*, *Blue Beard* (1798), *Pizarro* (Sheridan, 1799), *The Gipsy Prince* (1801), *Love laughs at Locksmiths* (1803), *Cinderella*, *Polly* (1813).

Kellyk, Hugh, English 15th-cent. composer. Nothing is known of his life. An antiphon, *Gaude flore virginali*, and a Magnificat are in the Eton Choirbook.

Kelterborn, Rudolf (b Basle, 3 Sep 1931), Swiss composer. Studied with J. Handschin and Willy Burkhard, Blacher and Fortner. In 1960 he became an instructor at the Detmold Music Acad. In his music he tends toward total serialism.

Works incl. operas *Die Erretung Thebens* (1963), *Kaiser Jovian* (1967), *Ein Engel kommt nach Babylon* (1977); *Der Kirschgarten* (after Chekhov, 1984). *Metamorphosen* for orch. (1960); concertino for vln. and chamber orch.; concertino for pf. and chamber orch.; suite for woodwind, perc. and strings; sonata for 16 solo strings (1955).

Cantata Profana for baritone, chorus and 13 instruments (1960); cantata *Ewige Wiederkehr* for mezzo, fl. and string trio (1960); cello concerto (1962); chamber music for var. instrumental groups incl. 4 string 4tets (1954–70), *5 Fantasien* for fl., cello and harpsichord; *7 Bagatellen* for wind 5tet; *Metamorphosen* for pf.; *Meditation* for 6 wind insts.

Kelway, Joseph (b ? Chichester, c 1702; d London, May 1782), English organist and harpsichordist. Pupil of Geminiani, he was organist of St Michael's Cornhill, London, 1730–6, then of St Martin-in-the-Fields. Made a great reputation as a player, was teacher to Queen Charlotte, and often deputized for Handel at the organ. Wrote harpsichord music.

Kelway, Thomas (b Chichester, c 1695; d Chichester, 21 May 1744), English organist and composer, elder brother of prec. Chorister at Chichester Cathedral under John Reading, whom he succeeded as organist in 1733. Comp. church music.

Kemble, Adelaide (b London, 1814; d Warsash House, Hants., 4 Aug 1879), English soprano, daughter of the actor Charles Kemble. She 1st appeared in London and at the York Festival in 1835, then went to Ger. and It. for further study, last with Pasta. In 1839 she appeared as Norma in Venice, toured widely in It. and returned to London for an appearance in the same part in 1841. Also

sang in operas by Mozart, Rossini and Cimarosa.

Kemp, Barbara (b Kochem, 12 Dec 1881; d Berlin, 17 Apr 1959), German soprano and producer. She sang in Berlin 1913–32 and assumed Wagnerian roles at the NY Met and at Bayreuth (1914–27); married the comp. Max von Schillings in 1923 and later the same year sang the title part of the 1st Met perf. of his *Mona Lisa*; also sang Elsa, Isolde and Kundry there. She prod. *Mona Lisa* in Berlin shortly before the war.

Kempe, Rudolf (b Nieder-Poyritz, nr. Dresden, 14 Jun 1910; d Zurich 12 May 1976), German conductor. Studied ob., becoming 1st ob. in the Leipzig Gewandhaus Orch. in 1929. Began cond. in 1936 and from 1949 to 1952 was music director of the Dresden Staatsoper and from 1952 to 1954 of the Munich Staatsoper. From 1954 to 1956 he cond. at the NY Met. He cond. at many of the great opera houses of the world, including many opera appearances at CG (1953–74), and was music director of the RPO 1961–75. Well known in Strauss and Wagner.

Kempen, Paul van (b Zoeterwoude, 16 May 1893; d Hilversum, 8 Dec 1955), Dutch conductor and violinist whose career began in 1910 as a violinist in the Concertgebouw Orch., under Mengelberg; he became chief conductor of the Dresden PO in 1934 and remained in Germany during the war years, a fact which did not endear him to his Dutch colleagues. He was nevertheless chief cond. of Hilversum Radio from 1949.

Kempff, Wilhelm (b Jüterborg, 25 Nov 1895), German pianist and composer. Studied pf. with H. Barth and comp. with R. Kahn. After winning both the Mendelssohn Prizes in 1917, he took up the career of a concert pianist. From 1924 to 1929 he was head of the Hochschule für Musik in Stuttgart. He was best known as one of the finest and most thoughtful interpreters of the classical pf. repertory, esp. the music of Beethoven.

His comps. incl. the operas *König Midas* (1930) and *Die Familie Gozzi* (1934); symphs. and ballets; concertos for pf. and vln.; string 4tets; and many pieces for solo pf. and organ.

Kendale, Richard (d 1431), English grammarian and music theorist. A short musical treatise by him is incl. in the MS written down by John Wylde, precentor of Waltham Holy Cross Abbey, c 1460 (Brit. Mus., Lans. 763).

Kennedy, Michael (b Manchester, 19 Feb 1926), English critic and writer on music. He joined the northern edition of *Daily Telegraph* in 1941; editor 1960–86. Active as music critic since 1950. His books incl. histories of the Hallé Orch. (1960 and 1983) and studies of Vaughan Williams (1964), Elgar (1968), Barbirolli (1971), Mahler (1974), Strauss (1976), Britten (1981) and Boult (1987). Ed. *Concise Oxford Dict. of Music* (1980; rev. as *Oxford Dict. of Music*, 1985).

Kennedy, Nigel (b Brighton, 28 Dec 1956), English violinist. He studied at the Yehudi Menuhin school and in NY; debut 1977. In the first rank of his generation of violinists, and has become particularly associated with the Elgar and the Mendelssohn concertos. He has joined Stephan Grappelli in jazz concerts; appeared with the Berlin PO in 1980 and toured the US 1985; returned 1987, with BBC SO.

Kenny, Yvonne (b Sydney, 25 Nov 1950), Australian soprano. Debut London 1975, as Donizetti's Rosamunda d'Inghilterra (concert perf.). CG debut 1976, in the fp of Henze's *We Come to the River*; other London roles have been Ilia, Oscar, Pamina and Micaela. ENO 1977, Sophie. Victoria State Opera, Melbourne, since 1978 as Mélisande, Adèle and Gilda. She sang Ilia at Glyndebourne in 1985. Many concert engagements in Europe.

Kentner, Louis (b Karwin, Silesia, 19 Jul 1905; d London, 22 Sep 1987), Hungarian-born pianist, British citizen since 1946. He studied in Budapest and made his debut in 1920; closely identified with the music of Bartók, giving the fp in Hungary of the 2nd pf. concerto and taking part in the world première of the concerto for two pfs. and orch. (London, 1942). With Yehudi Menuhin, his brother-in-law, gave the fp of Walton's violin sonata.

Kepler, Johannes. *See* **Harmonie der Welt.**

Kerl (or **Kerll**), **Johann Caspar** (b Adorf, Saxony, 9 Apr 1627; d Munich, 13 Feb 1693), German organist and composer. Settled early in Vienna as a pupil of Valentini; then studied in Rome under Carissimi and prob. the org. under Frescobaldi. In the service of the Elector of Bavaria in Munich, 1656–74. Again went to Vienna, as private teacher, and was app. court organist there in 1677, but returned to Munich in 1684.

Works incl. operas *Oronte*, *Erinto*, *Le pretensioni del sole* (1667), *I colori geniali*; Masses, motets and other church music; sonatas for 2 vlns. and bass; toccatas, *ricercari* and other works for organ.

Kerle, Jacob van (b Ypres, *c* 1531; d Pra-

gue, 7 Jan 1591), Flemish composer. He spent some time in It., partly in Rome in the service of Otto von Truchsess, Cardinal-Archbishop of Augsburg, in whose service he was in 1562–75, with whom he was also at Augsburg at times, and with whom he (?) attended the Council of Trent in 1562–3. Later he became canon of Cambrai, but was often in Vienna and Prague attending on the Emperor Rudolf.

Works incl. *Preces*, commissioned by the Cardinal of Augsburg in 1562, Masses, motets, Te Deums, Magnificats, hymns, *Sacrae cantiones*.

Kerman, Joseph (Wilfred) (b London, 3 Apr 1924), American music scholar and critic. Studied London, NY and Princeton. Professor at Univ. of California from 1960; Oxford 1971–4. He is an authority on William Byrd. Books incl. *Opera as Drama* (1956) and *The Beethoven Quartets* (1967).

Kern, Adele (b Munich, 25 Nov 1901; d Munich, 6 May 1980), German soprano. Debut in Munich and appeared there for almost 20 years, as well as Vienna and Salzburg and at CG, London (1931–4); sang regularly under Clemens Krauss and was admired in Strauss (Sophie and Zerbinetta) and Mozart (Susanna and Despina).

Kern, Jerome (David) (b New York, 27 Jan 1885; d New York, 11 Nov 1945), American composer. Pupil of Paolo Gallico and Alexander Lambert in NY. He turned to the comp. of musical comedy and other light music.

Works incl. musical comedies *Sunny* (1925), *Show Boat* (1927), *Music in the Air* and others; film music.

Kern, Patricia (b Swansea, 4 Jul 1927), Welsh mezzo who first sang with the WNO; joined SW, London, in 1959. She has been much admired in operas by Rossini and Mozart; in 1966 took part in the premiere of *The Violins of St Jacques*, by Malcolm Williamson. She has sung widely in North America.

Kerns, Robert (b Detroit, *c* 1933), American baritone. He appeared with the NY City Opera in 1959 but since then his career has been in Europe; has sung in Berlin and Vienna and at the Aix-en-Provence and Salzburg Festivals. At CG (debut 1964) he has performed Mozart's Guglielmo many times and has also been heard as Billy Budd, Count Almaviva and Rossini's Figaro.

Kertész, István (b Budapest, 28 Dec 1929; d Kfar Saba, Israel, 16 Apr 1973), Hungarian conductor. Kodály was among his teachers and after experience at the Budapest Opera he left Hungary at the 1956 uprising. He was musical dir. of the Cologne Opera from 1964 until his death and brought the company to London in 1969. His British debut was with the Royal Liverpool PO in 1960, prin. cond. LSO 1965–8. Noted for his interpretations of Mozart and Dvořák; also heard in Britten, Prokofiev, Bartók, Stravinsky and Henze. He drowned while swimming near Tel-Aviv.

Ketting, Piet (b Haarlem, 29 Nov 1905; d Rotterdam, 25 May 1984), Dutch pianist and composer. Studied with Pijper and later became prof. at the Rotterdam Cons.

Works incl. 2 symphs (1929, 1970); choral music, 3 string 4tets (1927–8), trio for fl., clar. and bassoon and other chamber music, sonatas for fl., bass clar. and pf. and fl., ob. and pf., partita for 2 fls.; 4 sonatinas, fugue, etc., for pf.; songs, incl. Shakespeare sonnets.

Kettledrums, drums with a single head of skin stretched over a cauldron-shaped receptacle. They produce notes of definite pitch which can be altered by the turning of screws at the rim of the 'kettle', thus tightening or relaxing the skin. A mechanical device now widely used enables the player to increase or relax the tension by means of a pedal. The modern orch. has at least 3 kettledrums of different sizes, and more may be demanded by the comp., in which case 1 player may not be sufficient. A variety of sticks covered with different materials can be used to prod. a harder or softer impact. *See also* **Nackers.**

Keuchenthal, Johannes (b Ellrich am Harz, *c* 1522; d St Andreasberg, 1583), German clergyman and musician. Pub. *Kirchengesang, lateinisch und deutsch*, a collection of music for the Lutheran Church, incl. a setting of the Passion, at Wittenberg in 1573.

Key. (1) The levers by means of which notes are prod. on keyboard instruments by being pressed down or struck. Also those on wind instruments stopping the note-holes which cannot be reached directly by the fingers.

(2) The tonality of a piece of music which is based on a particular maj. or min. scale and accepts harmonic relationships deriving from the notes of those scales. The 1st note of the scale (or Tonic) gives its name to the key, e.g. key of D maj., key of Eb min.

Key Bugle (also **Kent Bugle**), an instrument invented in the early 19th cent.; a bugle with side-holes covered with keys similar to those used on woodwind instruments.

Key Relationships. Those may be close or remote, e.g. in the key of C maj. the relation of the tonic chord (C) with the dominant (G) is close:

The relation of C min. with Eb maj. (its relative major) is also close:

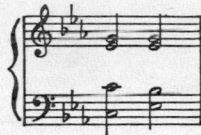

whereas the relation of C maj. with Eb maj. is less close:

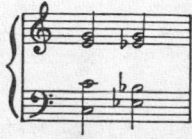

Transference from one key to another may be abrupt or may be effected by Modulation.

Key Signature, the sharps and flats which occur in the key of a given comp., written at the beginning of each stave. The signatures are shown overleaf.

Keys with 5 to 7 sharps or flats overlap enharmonically; in the tempered scale of the pf. they are identical as follows: B maj. and G# min. = Cb maj. and Ab min.; F# maj. and D# min. = Gb maj. and Eb min.; C# maj. and A# min. = Db maj. and Bb min.

Keyboard, the array of levers on instruments of the pf. type and on the organ, also on such instruments as the Hurdy-gurdy and the Accordion, by means of which the fingers, and on the organ also the feet, control the sound.

Keynote, the Tonic: the note on which the scale begins and ends, which determines the key of a piece of music in maj. or min. and after which that key is named.

Khachaturian, Aram Ilich (b Tbilisi, 6 Jun 1903; d Moscow 1 May 1978), Russian composer. His father, a poor workman, was able to send him to Moscow only after the Revolution; he entered the Gnessin School

Maj. Min.

KEY SIGNATURE

of Music there and studied under that master in 1923; in 1929 he went to the Moscow Cons. as a pupil of Vassilenko and afterwards of Miaskovsky. Studied the folksongs of Russian Armenia and other southern regions, which influenced his compositions.

Works incl. ballets *Happiness* (1939) and *Gayaneh* (1942), incid. music for Shakespeare's *Macbeth*, Lope de Vega's *Widow of Valencia*, Pogodin's *Kremlin Chimes*, Kron's *Deep Drilling*, Lermontov's *Masquerade*, etc.; film music *Song of Stalin* for chorus and orch.; 3 symphs (1932–47), *Dance Suite* and *Solemn Overture*, 'To the End of the War' for orch.; marches and pieces on Uzbek and Armen. themes for wind band; concertos for pf., vln., cello and vln. and cello.; string 4tet (1932), trio for clar., vln. and pf.; sonata and pieces for vln. and pf.; pf. music, part-songs; songs for the Rus. army.

Khaikin, Boris Emmanuilovich (b Minsk, 26 Oct 1904; d Moscow, 10 May 1978), Russian conductor. Graduated from the Moscow Cons. in 1928 and conducted opera at the Stanislavsky theatre; moved to Leningrad in 1936 and gave the fps of Prokofiev's *The Duenna* (1946) and *The Story of a Real Man* (1948). He made guest appearances cond. opera in Florence and Leipzig and in 1966 took the Leningrad PO to Italy. Kiril Kondrashin was among his pupils.

Khamma, battle-pantomime in 2 scenes by Debussy (scenario W.L. Courtney and M. Allan), comp. in short score 1911–2, orch. by Koechlin 1912–3; fp (concert) Paris, 15 Nov 1924, cond. Pierné. 1st stage perf. Paris, Opéra-Comique, 26 Mar 1947.

Khoklov, Pavel (b Spassky, Tambov, 2 Aug 1854; d Moscow, 20 Sep 1919), Russian baritone. He studied in Moscow and made his debut there in 1879; two years later he sang the title part in the first professional perf. of Tchaikovsky's *Eugene Onegin*. He was closely identified with this role, as well as Rubinstein's Demon, and also appeared in operas by Verdi, Wagner and Meyerbeer; noted Boris Godunov and Prince Igor.

Khorovod (Rus.), a type of ancient Russian folksong sung in chorus of 2 or more parts in a primitive kind of counterpoint. It was sung mainly at religious and family festivals and on seasonal occasions.

Khovanshchina, unfinished opera by Mussorgsky (lib. by comp. and V.V. Stassov), prod., as completed and scored by Rimsky-Korsakov after Mussorgsky's death, St Petersburg, 21 Feb 1886.

Khrennikov, Tikhon Nikolaievich (b Elets, 10 Jun 1913), Russian composer. He was taught music at home, but entered the Gnessin School of Music at Moscow in 1929 and the Cons. in 1932 as a pupil of Shebalin. Secretary, Union of Sov. Composers, from 1948; Hero of Socialist Labour 1973. He played a prominent part in the Stalinist-inspired denunciations of Prokofiev and Shostakovich.

Works incl. operas *The Brothers (In the Storm*, 1939); *Mother* (after Gogol, 1957); incid. music for Shakespeare's *Much Ado about Nothing*, an adaptation of Cervantes's *Don Quixote*, etc., film music for *The Pigs and the Shepherd*; 3 symphs. (1955–73); 3 pf. concertos (1933–82); pf. pieces; songs to words by Pushkin and Burns; war songs.

Kielflügel (Ger., lit. quill-wing) = Harpsichord, so named from the quills that pluck the strings and the wing shape of the instrument's body.

Kienlen, Johann Christoph (b Ulm, bap. 14 Dec 1783; d Dessau, 7 Dec 1829), German composer. He appeared as singer and pianist at the age of 7 and was later sent to Paris to study with Cherubini. After being music director at Ulm he went to Vienna in 1811, where he taught, and in 1823 he became singing-master to the Berlin opera.

Works incl. operas, e.g. *Claudine von Villa Bella* (Goethe, 1810); a symph.; additions to E.T.A. Hoffmann's incid. music for Goethe's *Scherz, List und Rache*; 2 pf. sonatas; many songs.

Kienzl, Wilhelm (b Waizenkirchen, Styria, 17 Jan 1857; d Vienna, 19 Oct 1941), Austrian composer. His father, a lawyer, became mayor of Graz in 1861 and the family settled there. He studied there under W. Mayer, who also taught Weingartner and Busoni, later went to Prague and Vienna for further study. Jensen and Liszt encouraged him to comp. and he came into close touch with Wagner at Bayreuth for a time. He was an opera cond. at Amsterdam, Krefeld, Hamburg and Munich (till 1893).

Works incl. operas *Urvasi* (1886), *Heilmar der Narr* (1892), *Der Evangelimann* (1895), *Don Quixote, In Knecht Rupprechts Werkstatt* (1907), *Der Kuhreigen* (1911), *Das Testament* (1916), *Hassan der Schwärmer* (1925), *Sanctissimum*; orch., choral and chamber works; *Dichterreise* and many other pf. works; *Tanzbilder* for pf. duet; over 100 songs; etc. He adapted Jensen's opera *Die Erbin von Montfort* to a new lib. based on Gozzi's *Turandot*.

Kiepura, Jan (b Sosnowiec, 16 May 1902; d Harrison, NY, 15 Aug 1966), Polish tenor. He studied in Warsaw and Milan and came to wider notice in Vienna (1926, Cavaradossi); he appeared there until the war and sang major roles in operas by Bizet, Massenet and Puccini in Europe and the US. Sang at the Met 1938–42, debut as Rodolfo, but after his marriage to the Hungarian sop. and film star Martha Eggerth turned increasingly to films as the focus of his endeavours.

Kilpinen, Yrjö (b Helsinki, 4 Feb 1892; d Helsinki, 2 Mar 1959), Finnish composer. Had a few lessons in theory at the Helsinki Cons. and in Berlin and Vienna, but was otherwise self-taught. In receipt of a small government grant, he devoted himself entirely to comp.

Works incl. cello sonata, vla. da gamba sonata; pf. sonatas; over 500 songs on Fin. Swed. and Ger. poems.

Kindermann, Johann Erasmus (b Nuremberg, 29 Mar 1616; d Nuremberg, 14 Apr 1655), German composer and organist. He studied with J. Staden and in common with other German composers of his time probably visited Venice, where he would have met Frescobaldi and Cavalli. Organist, Egidienkirche Nuremberg, from 1640.

Vocal works incl. *Cantiones Jesu Christi* (1639), *Friedens Clag* (1640), *Concentus Salomonis* (1642), *Opitianischer Orpheus* (1642), *Musica catechetica* (1643), *Gottliche Liebesflamme* (1651) and 9 cantatas. Instrumental works incl. *Harmonia organica* (1645), 27 Canzoni, 9 sonatas and 30 suite movements.

Kinderscenen (*Scenes from childhood*), 13 pf. pieces by Schumann, op. 15; comp. 1838.

Kindertotenlieder (*Songs of Dead Children*), cycle of 5 songs by Mahler, with orch. or pf., to poems by Rückert; comp. 1902, fp Vienna, 29 Jan 1905, cond. Mahler.

King and Collier (or **Charcoal-Burner**) (*Král a Uhlíř*, opera by Dvořák (lib. by B. Guldener), prod. Prague, Czech Theatre, 24 Nov 1874. Dvořák's 1st opera to be produced.

King Arthur, or The British Worthy, semi-opera by Purcell (lib. by Dryden), prod. London, Dorset Gardens Theatre, 1691.

King Charles II, opera by Macfarren (lib. by M.D. Ryan, based on a play by J.H. Payne), prod. London, Princess's Theatre, 27 Oct 1849.

King, Charles (b Bury St Edmunds, 1687; d London, 17 Mar 1748), English singer, organist and composer. Chorister under Blow at St Paul's Cathedral, where he succeeded his father-in-law Clarke as Almoner and Master of the Children in 1708. Wrote church music.

King Christian II, incidental music by Sibelius for a play by A. Paul; comp. 1898, fp Helsinki, 28 Feb 1898, cond. Sibelius. Suite for orch. in 6 movts., 1898. 1st Brit. perf. London, 26 Oct 1901, cond. Wood.

King, James (b Dodge City, 22 May 1925), American tenor, formerly baritone. He was engaged in Berlin from 1962 and in that year appeared at the Salzburg Festival in Gluck's *Iphigénie en Aulide*; Bayreuth Festival from 1965 and NY Met from 1966 (debut as Florestan), specialising in Strauss and Wagner, e.g. the Emperor and Siegmund; sang Bacchus at CG in 1985, Florestan 1986.

King Lear. *See also* **Re Lear.** Verdi worked at the Shakespearian subject for many years, but never brought the opera anywhere near completion, and his sketches were destroyed after his death, by his own wish.

Incid. music for Shakespeare's tragedy by J. André, prod. Berlin, 30 Nov 1778.

Incid. music by Balakirev, prod. St Petersburg, 1861.

Incid. music by Stegmann, prod. Hamburg, 17 Jul 1778.

Overture by Berlioz, op. 4, comp. in Italy, 1831, fp Paris, 9 Nov 1834.

Opera by Frazzi (1922–8, prod. Florence, 1939).

For opera by Reimann see **Lear.**

King, Matthew (Peter) (b London, 1773; d London, Jan 1823), English composer. Studied under C.F. Horn.

Works incl. many stage pieces (some with Braham, Kelly and others); oratorio *The Intercession*; 4 sets of pf. sonatas; solo cantatas, glees, songs.

'King of Prussia' Quartets (Mozart). *See* **'Prussian' Quartets.**

King Olaf, cantata for solo voices, chorus and orch. by Elgar, op. 30, set to words by Longfellow altered by H.A. Acworth, prod. at the N. Staffs. Festival, Hanley, 30 Oct 1896.

King Priam, opera in 3 acts by Tippett (lib. by comp.), prod. Coventry, 29 May 1962.

King, Robert, English 17th–18th-cent. composer. He joined the royal band in 1680 on the death of Banister, received a licence to give concerts in 1689 and took the Mus.B. at Cambridge in 1696.

Works incl. incid. music for Crowne's *Sir Courtly Nice* and many other plays; Shadwell's Ode on St Cecilia's Day, Motteux's Ode for John Cecil, Earl of Exeter; many songs for one and more voices.

King Roger, opera by Szymanowski (lib. by comp. and J. Iwaszkiewicz), prod. Warsaw, 19 Jun 1926.

King Stephen (Beethoven). *See* **König Stephan.**

King, Thea (b Hitchin, 16 Dec 1925), English clarinettist. She studied at the RCM and from 1956–64 was princ. clarinettist of the London Mozart Players; moved to the ECO in 1964 and until 1968 was a member of the all-female Portia ens. She has given the fps of works by Howells, Ireland, Searle and Rawsthorne and has been associated with the modern revival of interest in the music of the 19th-cent. Finnish clarinettist and composer Bernhard Crusell.

King, William (b Winchester, 1624; d Oxford, 17 Nov 1680), English organist and composer, son of George K., organist of Winchester Cathedral (d 1665). He went to Oxford as a clerk of Magdalen Coll. in 1648, took the BA there in 1649, became a chaplain at the coll. in 1652, went to All Souls' Coll. as probationer-fellow in 1654 and became organist of New Coll. in 1664.

Works incl. a service, a litany, anthems; songs to a thorough-bass for theorbo, harpsichord or bass viol to poems by Cowley, etc.

Kingdom, The, oratorio by Elgar, op. 51 (lib. compiled from the Bible by the comp.), Part II of a trilogy of which I is *The Apostles* and III was never completed. Fp Birmingham Festival, 3 Oct 1906.

Kinkeldey, Otto (b New York, 27 Nov 1878; d Orange, NJ, 19 Sep 1966), American musicologist. After a general academic educ. in NY and Berlin, he studied music with MacDowell in 1900–2 while he was a schoolmaster and chapel organist. After further studies at the univ. and acad. for church music in Berlin, he became organ teacher at a similar institution at Breslau, and later lecturer and prof. of musicology. Returning to USA in 1914 he was alternately chief of the music division of the NY Public Library and prof. at Cornell Univ. He wrote a dissertation on 16th-cent. keyboard music and many valuable contribs. to periodicals, old music, etc.

Kinsky, Georg (b Marienwerder, Prus., 29 Sep 1882; d Berlin, 7 Apr 1951), German music scholar and ed. Self-taught in music he worked at first at the Prus. State Library in Berlin and then became curator until 1927 of the Heyer Museum of musical instruments, of which he compiled a valuable catalogue. From 1921 he was also active at the Cologne Cons., from which he retired in 1932. His books incl. a *History of Music in Pictures*, works on instruments and a catalogue of Beethoven's works.

Kipnis, Alexander (b Zhitomir, 13 Feb 1891; d Westport, Conn., 14 May 1978), Russian bass. Studied cond. at the Warsaw Cons, and later singing in Berlin, making his debut in 1915. From 1918 to 1925 he sang in Berlin, in Chicago from 1923 to 1932 and at the NY Met from 1940 to 1946; heard there as Gurnemanz, Pogner, Marke, Boris, Ochs and Philip II. In 1931 became an Amer. citizen. One of the finest singers of his time.

Kipnis, Igor (b Berlin, 27 Sep 1930), American harpsichordist, son of the prec. After an early career as a critic and as dir. of a NY radio station he made his public debut as a harpsichordist in 1962; appeared with the NY PO in 1975 and has toured all over the world. His large repertory includes contemporary American works and he has taught Baroque performing practice.

Kirbye, George (b ? Suffolk, c 1565; d Bury St Edmunds, buried 6 Oct 1634), English composer. He 1st appeared as the most copious contributor, except Farmer, to East's Psalter. In 1598 he married Anne Saxye, and he seems to have lived at that time at Rushbrooke nr. Bury St Edmunds as domestic musician at the residence of Sir Robert Jermyn, to whose daughters he ded. his book of 24 madrigals in 1597. In 1601 he contrib. a madrigal to *The Triumphes of Oriana*.

Works incl. motets, a hymn; madrigals; pavan for viols.

Kircher, Athanasius (b Geisa nr. Fulda, 2 May 1601; d Rome, 27 Nov 1680), German mathematician, philosopher and music scholar. He was prof. at the Jesuit Coll. of Würzburg, but was driven from Ger. by the 30 Years War in 1633, going to Avignon, Vienna and in 1637 to Rome, where he settled for the rest of his life. His chief musical-literary work is *Musurgia universalis* (1650).

Kirchgassner, Marianne (b Bruchsal, 5 Jun 1769; d Schaffhausen, 9 Dec 1808), German glass harmonica player, blind from infancy. On her first concert tour she was heard by Mozart, then only months before his death, and he composed three works for her instrument. She continued performing until her death, which is alleged to have been caused by the unique vibrations set up by the glass harmonica.

Kirchner, Leon (b Brooklyn, 24 Jan 1919), American composer, pianist and conductor. He studied with Ernest Bloch in San Francisco and Roger Sessions in NY. Prof. Harvard Univ. from 1961. Early influences were Bartók and Stravinsky; then followed Schoenberg, but in a non-doctrinaire way.

Works incl. opera *Lily* (after Bellow's *Henderson, the Rain King*, 1977); *Toccata* for strings, wind and perc. (1956), 2 pf. concertos (1956, 1963), *Music for Orchestra* (1969); 3 string 4tets (no. 3 with electronics, 1948, 1958, 1967), pf. trio (1954), *Lily* for chamber ens. and voice (from the opera, 1973); *The Times are Nightfall* for sop. and pf. (1943), *Dawn* for chorus and organ (1946), *Of Obedience and the Runner* for sop. and pf. (after Whitman, 1950), *Words from Wordsworth* for chorus (1966).

Kirchoff, Walter (b Berlin, 17 Mar 1879; d Wiesbaden, 26 Mar 1951), German tenor. He studied at Berlin; debut there 1906, as Faust. He remained at the Hofoper until 1920, often in Wagner. Bayreuth 1911–14, as Walther, Siegfried and Parsifal. CG 1913, 1924. NY Met 1926–31; 1929 as Max in the US fp of Krenek's *Jonny spielt auf*. Guest at Paris, Rio and Buenos Aires.

Kirkby, Emma (b Camberley, 26 Feb 1949), English soprano. Studied Classics at Oxford before her London debut in 1974; with her pure, vibrato-free voice she has become a specialist in early music, appearing with the Academy of Ancient Music, the Consort of Musicke and similar ensembles. Her US debut was in 1978; 3 tours of the Middle East with the lutenist Anthony Rooley. Formerly married to Andrew Parrott (*q.v.*).

Kirkby-Lunn, Louise (b Manchester, 8 Nov 1873; d London, 17 Feb 1930), English mezzo-soprano. After study in Manchester and at the RCM she made her debut at the College in the 1st Brit. perf. of Schumann's only opera, *Genoveva*. She had several seasons at CG, London, on either side of the First War, and sang at the NY Met 1902–8; was well known in operas by Wagner and Verdi; in 1910 appeared in NY in one of the last concerts conducted by Mahler (Elgar's *Sea Pictures*).

Kirkman, English family of harpsichord and later pf. makers:

1. Jacob K. (orig. Kirchmann) (b Bischweiler, 4 Mar 1710; d Greenwich, buried 9 Jun 1792), was a Ger. by birth, settled in London early in the 18th cent., working for Tabel, a Flemish maker, whose widow he married.

2. Abraham K. (b Bischweiler, 1737; d Hammersmith, buried 16 April 1794), nephew of prec.

3. Joseph K (d London), son of prec.

4. Joseph K. (b 1790; d London, 1877), son of prec.

5. Henry K. (b London; d London), son of prec.

Kirkpatrick, John (b New York, 18 Mar 1905), American pianist and scholar. He studied at Princeton and with Nadia Boulanger in Paris; has perf many modern American composers, in particular Charles Ives. In 1939 he gave the fp in NY of the Concord Sonata, vital in the wider recognition of the music of Ives; his work as a scholar has also contributed here.

Kirkpatrick, Ralph (b Leominster, Mass., 10 Jun 1911; d Guilford, Conn., 13 Apr 1984), American harpsichordist and musicologist. Studied pf. at home and theory at Harvard, later with Nadia Boulanger in Paris. In Paris he took harpsichord lessons with Landowska, also working with Arnold Dolmetsch in Haslemere. He received a Guggenheim Fellowship in 1937 and toured Europe studying old MSS., etc. In 1940 he was app. to Yale Univ. He pub. a number of scholarly eds. incl. Bach's *Goldberg Variations* and an important book on D. Scarlatti (1953) which gives definitive listings for all the sonatas, given 'Kk' nos.

Kirnberger, Johann Philipp (b Saalfeld, Thuringia, 24 Apr 1721; d Berlin, 27 Jul 1783), German theorist and composer. Pupil of Bach in Leipzig, 1739–41, after var. posts he entered the service of Frederick the Great as a violinist in 1751. App. *Kapellmeister* and teacher of composition to Princess Amalia of Prussia in 1758, he increasingly abandoned perf. and composition to devote his time to theoretical writings. Among many treatises the most important is *Die Kunst des reinen Satzes*.

Comps. incl. cantatas, motets and instrumental music.

Kirshbaum, Ralph (b Denton, Texas, 4 Mar 1946), American cellist and conductor. Debut as soloist with the Dallas SO aged 13. He won the 1970 International Tchaikovsky Competition in Moscow and in the following year settled in London; has appeared all over the world as a soloist and plays in a pf. trio with György Pauk and Peter Frankl.

Kirsten, Dorothy (b Montclair, NJ, 6 Jul 1915), American soprano. After appearances in Chicago and San Francisco she sang Mimi at the NY Met in 1945; remained there on a regular basis until 1956 and gave a farewell perf. there in 1975. She was admired in operas by Puccini, Gounod and Charpentier; sang in the first US perfs. of Walton's *Troilus and Cressida* (1955) and Poulenc's *Carmélites* (1957) – both in San Francisco.

Kiss, The (*Hubička*), opera by Smetana (lib. by E. Krásnohorská, based on a story by K. Svetlá), prod. Prague, 7 Nov 1876.

Kit, a diminutive vln., formerly used by dancing-masters, who on account of its small size and narrow shape were able to carry it in the long pockets of their tail-coats. Its Fr. name is therefore *pochette* and its Ger. *Taschengeige*.

Kitezh (Rimsky-Korsakov). *See* **Legend of the Invisible City of Kitezh.**

Kithara, a plucked string instrument of ancient Greece. *See* **Lyre.**

Kittel, Hermine (b Vienna, 2 Dec 1879; d Vienna, 7 Apr 1948), Austrian contralto. Debut Lwów 1897; studied further with Materna and sang in Vienna 1901–36, at first under Mahler (later appeared often as soloist in *Das Lied von der Erde*). Bayreuth 1908, Erda. Salzburg 1922–5 as Mozart's Marcellina.

Kittel, Kaspar (b Lauenstein, 1603; d Dresden, 9 Oct 1639), German lutenist, organist and composer. Studied under Schütz and in 1624–8 in It. at the expense of the Elector of Saxony. He taught theorbo at Dresden from 1630 and 2 years later became inspector of instruments. He wrote arias and cantatas in the style of Caccini.

Kittl, Johann Friedrich (b Vorlík, Boh., 8 May 1806; d Lissa, Pol., 20 Jul 1868), Bohemian composer. Pupil of Tomášek in Prague, where he gave a 1st concert in 1836. In 1843 he succeeded Dionys Weber as director of the Prague Cons.

Works incl. operas *Bianca und Giuseppe, oder Die Franzosen vor Nizza* (lib. by Wagner, orig. written for himself, 1848), *Die Waldblume* (1852), and *Die Bilderstürmer* (1854); *Jagdsymphonie* for orch.

Kiurina, Berta (b Linz, 18 Feb 1882; d Vienna, 3 May 1933), Austrian soprano. Debut Linz 1904; Vienna Hofoper 1905–27, as Liù, Desdemona, Nedda, Eva and Pfitzner's Ighino. Salzburg 1906 as Cherubino, under Mahler. Guest in Brno, Budapest and Buenos Aires and was admired in Schoenberg's *Gurrelieder*.

Kjerulf, Halfdan (b Christiania, 17 Sep 1815; d Grefsen, nr. Christiania, 11 Aug 1868), Norwegian composer. At his father's desire he studied law at Christiania Univ., but on the death of his father in 1840 he decided to devote himself to music. He taught, and pub. some songs, even before he had done much in the way of theoretical study. About 1850 he received a government grant to study at Leipzig for a year, and on his return he tried to estab. classical subscription concerts, with little success. He became a friend of Bjørnson, who wrote many poems esp. for him to set.

Works incl. choruses and 4tets for male voices; pf. pieces; over 100 songs.

Klafsky, Katharina (b Szt. János, 19 Sep 1855; d Hamburg, 22 Sep 1896), Hungarian mezzo, later soprano. Appeared in Leipzig, as Venus and Brangaene, and after perfs. with Angelo Neumann's touring co. was engaged at Hamburg; added roles in operas by Weber and Mozart to her repertory and in 1892 visited London with the Hamburg Co., under the direction of Mahler, sang Leonore, Agathe and Isolde at Drury Lane in 1894. She had a brief career in the US.

Klagende Lied, Das (*The Song of Lamentation*), cantata by Mahler (text by comp.) for soloists chorus and orch. 1st. vers. 1880 in 3 parts: *Waldmärchen, Der Spielmann, Hochzeitstück*. Revised 1888 with part 1 omitted, fp Vienna, 17 Feb 1901, cond. Mahler; fp original vers. Vienna, 8 Apr 1935, cond. Arnold Rosé.

Klaviatur (Ger.) = Keyboard.

Klavier (Ger.) = Pianoforte (but *see also* **Clavier**).

Klavierübung (J.S. Bach) *See* **Clavierübung**.

Klebe, Giselher (b Mannheim, 28 Jun 1925), German composer. Studied at the Berlin Cons. with Kurt von Wohlfurt and later with Josef Rufer and Blacher. From 1946 to 1949 he worked for Berlin Radio. His music follows the traditions of Schoenberg and Webern.

Works incl. operas *Die Räuben* (after Schiller, 1957), *Die tödlichen Wünsche* (1959), *Alkmene* (1961), *Figaro lässt sich scheiden* (1963), *Jacobowsky und der Oberst* (1965), *Ein wahrer Held* (after Synge, 1975), *Des Mädchen aus Domrémy* (1976), *Des Rendez-vous* (1977); *Con moto* for orch, 4 symphs. (1951–71), *Divertissement joyeux* for chamber orch., *Zwitschermaschine* for orch. (after Paul Klee); concerto for vln., cello and orch.; ballet *Pas de trois*; *Geschichte der lustigen Musikanten* for tenor, chorus and 5 instruments; wind 5tet, 2 sonatas for solo vln., vla. sonata, 2 string 4tets.

Kleber, Leonhard (b ? Göppingen, *c* 1495; d Pforzheim, 4 Mar 1556), German composer and organist. He compiled a tablature, dated 1524, containing music by himself and others and arrs. by himself of vocal music.

Kleiber, Carlos (b Berlin, 3 Jul 1930), Argentine conductor of German birth, the son of Erich Kleiber. He studied in Argentina

and was advised against a career in music by his father; after early experience in Munich, Berlin and Zurich he was engaged at Stuttgart in 1966. Wider recognition came in 1974, when he conducted *Der Rosenkavalier* at CG, London, and *Tristan und Isolde* at Bayreuth. US debut San Francisco, 1977, *Otello*. He became an Austrian citizen in 1980.

Kleiber, Erich (b Vienna, 5 Aug 1890; d Zurich, 27 Jan 1956), Austrian conductor. He became music dir. of the Staatsoper Berlin, 1923, after apprentice years in Darmstadt and Düsseldorf. He gave several important premières, in particular that of *Wozzeck* (1925), of which he also cond. the first British stage perf. (1952). Differences with the Nazis over artistic policy obliged him to resign his Berlin post, and from 1937 to 1949 he was active in Buenos Aires, becoming an Argentine citizen in 1938. He returned to Europe in 1948, conducting the LPO, and in Florence, 1951, gave the first known perf. of Haydn's last opera, *Orfeo ed Euridice*, with Maria Callas.

Kleider Machen Leute, opera by Zemlinsky (lib. by L. Feld after G. Keller), prod. Vienna, Volksoper, 2 Dec 1910).

Klein, Peter (b Zündorf, 25 Jan 1907), German tenor. His early career was in Düsseldorf and Zurich, and from 1934 he was much admired in Hamburg and Vienna in such character roles as Mozart's Basilio, Monostatos and Pedrillo and Wagner's Mime; appeared as Mime at CG, London, until 1960. He sang the baritone role of Beckmesser at the Vienna Staatsoper in 1965.

Kleine Nachtmusik, Eine (Ger. = *Little Serenade*), Mozart's own title for his serenade in G maj. for strings, K525 finished 10 Aug 1787.

Kleinknecht, German family of musicians;

1. Johannes K. (b Ulm, bap. 7 Dec 1676; d Ulm, buried 4 Jun 1751), violinist and organist. Studied in Venice, 2nd organist of Ulm Cathedral from 1712.

2. Johann Wolfgang K. (b Ulm 17 Apr 1715; d Ansbach, 20 Feb 1786), violinist and composer, son of prec. Entered the service of the court at Stuttgart in 1733, from 1738 to his death *Konzertmeister* at Bayreuth.

3. Jakob Friedrich K. (b Ulm, bap. 8 Jun 1722; d Ansbach, 11 Aug 1794), flautist, violinist and composer, brother of prec. Entered the service of the court at Bayreuth in 1743, and rose to *Kapellmeister*.

Works incl. *Sinfonia concertata*, fl. sonatas, trio sonatas.

4. Johann Stephan K. (b Ülm, 17 Sep 1731; d Ansbach, after 1791), flautist, brother of prec. Toured as a fl. virtuoso, entered the service of the court at Bayreuth in 1754.

Kleist, (Bernd) Heinrich (Wilhelm) von (1777–1811), German poet, novelist and dramatist. *See* **Draeseke** (*Penthesilea* overture), **Goldmark (C.)** (do.), **Graener** (*Prinz von Homburg*), **Joachim** (commemoration overture), **Klenau** (*Michael Kohlhaas*), **Marschner** (*Prinz von H.*), **Penthesilea** (Schoeck), **Pfitzner** (*Käthchen von Heilbronn*), **Prinz von Homburg** (Henze), **Reinthaler** (do.), **Unger (H.)** (*Penthesilea*), **Vesque von Püttlingen** (*Käthchen von H.*), **Wagenaar (J.)** (*Amphitryon*), **Wagner-Régeny** (*Zerbrochene Krug*), **Wolf (H.)** (*Penthesilea*).

Klemperer, Otto (b Breslau, 14 May 1885; d Zurich, 6 Jul 1973), German conductor. He studied in Frankfurt, with James Kwast and Ivan Knorr, and in Berlin with Pfitzner. Debut Berlin 1906, *Orpheus in the Underworld*. On Mahler's recommendation was appointed to the German Theatre, Prague, in 1907; moved to Hamburg 1910 but was obliged to leave in 1912, following a scandalous liaison with the recently-married Elisabeth Schumann. After appointments in Barmen and Strasbourg, where he was Pfitzner's deputy, he became music dir. of the Cologne Opera in 1917; gave there the 1st German perf. of *Káťa Kabanová* and the fps of Zemlinsky's *Der Zwerg* and Schreker's *Irrelohe*. In 1927 was appointed dir. of the Kroll Opera, Berlin, with a brief to perform new works, and repertory pieces in an enlightened manner. Few major premières were given by K. in Berlin, but he led the 1st German perf. of *Oedipus Rex*; *Erwartung* and *From the House of the Dead* were given by his deputies, Zemlinsky and Fritz Zweig.

After the 1931 closure of the Kroll K. moved to the State Opera, Berlin, and emigrated to the USA in 1933. His debut there had been in 1926, and until the war he led orchs. of Philadelphia and NY; with the Los Angeles PO gave the 1938 fp of Schoenberg's arr. of the Brahms G min. pf. 4tet. Illness restricted his wartime activity, but he worked at the Budapest Opera 1947–50. He conducted the Philharmonia, London, the following year; cond. for life 1964, when Walter Legge attempted to disband the orch. A manic-depressive all his life, Klemperer's earlier conducting style had been aggressive and hard-driven; in his London years he won renown for his massive, monumental perfs.

of Mahler and the Viennese classics. In the early 1960s he led new prods. of *Fidelio, Die Zauberflöte* and *Lohengrin* at CG. Retired to Switzerland in 1972. Among his comps. are 6 symphs (from 1960) and 9 string 4tets.

Klenau, Paul von (b Copenhagen, 11 Feb 1883; d Copenhagen, 31 Aug 1946), Danish conductor and composer of German descent. Studied vln. and comp., the latter with Malling, at Copenhagen, and after 1902 with Bruch in Berlin and Thuille in Munich. When app. operatic cond. at Stuttgart in 1908 he studied further with Schillings. In 1914 he returned home and estab. the Phil. Society, at which he introduced many modern orchestral works; he also cond. orchestral and choral concerts in Vienna.

Works incl. operas *Sulamith* (1913), *Kjartan and Gudrun* (revised as *Gudrun in Iceland*, 1918), *The School for Scandal* (after Sheridan, 1927), *Michael Kohlhaas* (after Kleist), *Rembrandt van Rijn* (1937); ballet *Lille Ida's blomster* (after Andersen); 7 symphs (1908–41), 3 orchestral fantasies on Dante's *Inferno, Bank-Holiday Souvenir of Hampstead Heath* for orch.; oratorio *Job, The Song of the Love and Death of Cornet Christof Rilke* for baritone solo, chorus and orch. (1915); *Dialogues with Death* for contralto and orch., *Ebbe Skammalsen* for baritone and orch.; string 4tet in E min.; pf. pieces.

Klengel, August (Alexander) (b Dresden, 29 Jun 1783; d Dresden, 22 Nov 1852), German organist and composer. Pupil of Clementi, with whom he travelled from 1803 onwards. He visited Rus., Paris and London, and in 1816 was app. court organist at Dresden.

Works incl. 2 pf. concertos; pf. 5tet; much pf. music incl. esp. canons and fugues, etc.

Klengel, Julius (b Leipzig, 24 Sep 1859; d Leipzig, 27 Oct 1933), German cellist and composer. Studied cello with Emil Hegar and comp. with Jadassohn, joined the Leipzig Gewandhaus orch. at the age of 15, began to travel as virtuoso in 1875 and in 1881 became leading cellist in the orch. and prof. of cello at the Cons.

Works incl. 4 cello concertos, double concertos for vln. and cello and 2 cellos, *Hymnus* for 12 cellos; *Caprice in form of a Chaconne* for cello solo, many cello pieces and studies.

Klenovsky, Nikolai Semenovich (b Odessa, 1853; d Petrograd, 6 Jul 1915), Russian composer and conductor. Studied at the Moscow Cons., Tchaikovsky being among his masters, cond. the fp of the latter's

Eugène Onegin; later cond. of the univ. orch. and asst. cond. at the Imp. Opera. Collected and ed. folksongs with Melgunov. App. dir. of the school of music at Tiflis, 1893, and asst. dir. of the Imp. Chapel at St Petersburg, 1902. Works incl. several ballets; incid. music to Shakespeare's *Antony and Cleopatra* and other plays; *Georgian Liturgy* for unaccomp. chorus; cantatas.

Klenovsky, Paul, a name invented by Sir Henry Wood to shoulder his orchestral arr. of Bach's D min. Toccata and Fugue.

Kletzki, Paul (b Łódź, 21 Mar 1900; d Liverpool, 5 Mar 1973), Polish conductor. Studied the vln. and played in the Łódź PO. Later (1921–33) he studied and cond. in Berlin. From 1935 to 1938 he taught comp. in Milan, while continuing as a cond. Between 1958 and 1961 he was cond. of the Dallas SO. Suisse Romande Orch. 1967–9.

Klien, Walter (b Graz, 27 Nov 1928), Austrian pianist who has been appearing in public since 1951; American debut 1969. He has recorded most of the piano music of Brahms, Schubert and Mozart and appears as an accompanist to instrumentalists and singers.

Klimov, Valery (b Kiev, 16 Oct 1931), Russian violinist. He was a pupil of David Oistrakh at the Moscow Cons. and won the 1958 Tchaikovsky Competition; this was followed by an international career. His British debut was in 1967, at the Festival Hall.

Klindworth, Karl (b Hanover, 25 Sep 1830; d Stolpe, 27 Jul 1916), German pianist and conductor. Pupil of Liszt; arranger of music for his instrument, incl. vocal scores of Wagner's works. He lived in London as pianist, cond. and teacher in 1854–68, then became pf. prof. at the Moscow Cons., but returned to Germany in 1884 and opened a school of music in Berlin, 1893. His adopted daughter Winifred Williams(1897–1980) married Siegfried Wagner.

Klingsor, Tristan (Léon Leclère) (1874–1966), French poet. See **Shéhérazade** (Ravel).

Klopstock, Friedrich (1724–1803), German poet. See **Bach (C.P.E.)** (*Morgengesang am Schöpfungstage*), **Gluck** (odes), **Lesueur** (*Mort d'Adam*), **Meyerbeer** (sacred cantatas), **Resurrection Symphony** (Mahler), **Schröter (C.)** (songs), **Schwenke** (odes), **Spohr** (*Vater unser*), **Stadler** (*Frühlingsfeier*), **Wolfram** (*Grosse Hallelujah*). 13 songs by Schubert.

Klose, Margarete (b Berlin, 6 Aug 1902; d

Berlin, 14 Dec 1968), German mezzo. Stage debut Ulm, 1927. Berlin 1929–56. Bayreuth 1936–42 as Fricka, Waltraute, Ortrud and Brangaene. London, CG, 1935–7. Other roles incl. Carmen, Adriano, the Kostelnička and Orpheus.

Klotz, German 17th–18th-cent family of vln. makers in Mittenwald, incl.:
  1. Matthias K. (b 11 Jun 1653; d 16 Aug 1743). He worked for a time at Florence and Cremona, but returned to Mittenwald *c* 1683.
  2. Georg K. (b 31 Mar 1687; d 31 Aug 1737), son of prec.
  3. Sebastian K. (b 18 Jan 1696; d 20 Jan 1775), brother of prec.
  4. Johann Carl K. (b 29 Jan 1709; d 25 May 1769), brother of prec.
  At least 18 members of succeeding generations are known.

Kluge, Die (*The Clever Girl*), opera by Orff (lib. by comp. after Grimm), prod. Frankfurt, 20 Feb 1943.

Knaben Wunderhorn, Des (*The Youth's Magic Horn*), Ger. anthology of old folk poetry. See **Mahler** (songs, 9 with pf., 13 with orch.), **Vrieslander** (songs). The 13 *Knaben Wunderhorn* songs which Mahler scored for voice and orch., in 1900, are 1) *Der Schildwache Nachtlied*; 2) *Verlor'ne Muh*; 3) *Trost im Unglück*; 4) *Wer hat dies Liedlein erdacht?*; 5) *Das irdische Leben*; 6) *Des Antonius von Padua Fischpredigt*; 7) *Rheinlegendchen*; 8) *Lied des Verfolgten in Turm*; 9) *Wo die schönen Trompeten blasen*; 10) *Lob des hohen Verstandes*; 11) *Es sungen drei Engel*; 12) *Urlicht*; 13) *Das himmlische Leben*.

Knappertsbusch, Hans (b Elberfeld, 12 Mar 1888; d Munich, 26 Oct 1965), German conductor. Studied at the Cologne Cons. with Steinbach and Lohse (1909–12) and then took var. positions as an opera cond. In 1922 he became cond. at the Munich Staatsoper, where he remained until 1938, in which year he became director of the Vienna Staatsoper; guest cond. VPO 1947–64. He was best known for his perfs. of Wagner, esp. *Parsifal*, which he cond. at Bayreuth from 1951.

Knecht, Justin Heinrich (b Biberach, 30 Sep 1752; d Biberach, 1 Dec 1817), German organist and composer. Worked as organist and cond. in Biberach from 1771, and was vice-*Kapellmeister* in Stuttgart, 1806–8.
  Works incl. a symph. entitled *Le Portrait musical de la nature* (*c* 1784) which has a programme similar to that of Beethoven's 'Pastoral' Symph.

Kniegeige (Ger. = knee fiddle) = Viola da gamba.

Knight, Robert, English 16th-cent composer. A 5-part motet *Propterea maestum* is possibly his.

Knight, Thomas, English 16th-cent composer. Organist and vicar-choral of Salisbury Cathedral for 5 or 10 years from 1535. Works incl. Magnificat and (?) Mass, motets, evening canticles, some of which may be by Robert K.

Kniplová Naděžda (b Ostrava, 18 Apr 1932), Czech soprano. After study in Prague she sang in Brno; roles there incl. Libuše, the Kostelnička, Emilia Marty, Renata and Katerina Izmaylova. From 1965 she has sung in Prague and in W. Europe and the US. Other roles incl. Aida, Tosca, Senta; Brünnhilde in a complete recording of Wagner's *Ring.*

Knöfel, Johann (b Lauban, Silesia, *c* 1530; d ? Prague, after 1592), German composer. He wrote church music and a collection, *Newe Teutsche Liedlein,* 1581.

Knorr, Iwan (b Mewe, W. Prus., 3 Jan 1853; d Frankfurt, 22 Jan 1916), German composer and teacher. Studied at the Leipzig Cons. after having lived in small Rus. towns in 1857–68. He returned to Rus. and became prof. at Kharkov in 1874, but settled at Frankfurt in 1883, where he became director of the Hoch Cons. in 1908. He had a number of Eng. pupils, incl. C. Scott and H. Balfour Gardiner.

Works incl. operas *Dunja* (1904), *Die Hochzeit* (1907) and *Durchs Fenster* (1908); symph. fantasy for orch.; pf. 4tets, variations on a theme by Schumann for pf. trio; *Ukrainian Love-Songs* for vocal 4tet and pf.; pf. works for 2 and 4 hands; songs.

Knot, the ornamental fretwork sound-hole of many flat-bellied string instruments and keyboard instruments, more generally called Rose.

Knot Garden, The, opera by Tippett (lib. by comp.) prod. London, CG, 2 Dec 1970, cond. C. Davis.

Knote, Heinrich (b Munich, 26 Nov 1870; d Garmisch, 15 Jan 1953), German tenor. Debut Munich 1892 in Lortzing's *Waffenschmied;* Lohengrin there in 1900. London, CG, 1901–13 as Siegfried, Walther and Tristan. NY Met 1904–8 in Wagner rep. and as Manrico. Other roles incl. Rienzi and Goldmark's Assad.

Knüpfer, Paul (b Halle, 21 Jun 1866; d Berlin, 4 Nov 1920), German bass. Studied at the Cons. of Sondershausen and made his 1st stage appearance there in 1885. He sang

at Bayreuth 1901–12 as Gurnemanz, Daland, Marke and Pogner, London from 1909 (1st Brit. Ochs), and was leading bass at the Berlin Opera, 1898–1920.

Knussen, Oliver (b Glasgow, 12 Jun 1952), English composer and conductor. He studied in US with Gunter Schuller. An eclectic and prolific composer, his works incl. the operas *Where the Wild Things Are* and *Higglety Pigglety Pop* (1979–84; produced at Glyndebourne); 3 symphs (1966–79); Concerto for Orch (1970); *Coursing* for chamber orch. (1979); *Chiara* for orch. (1986); *Hums and Songs of Winnie-the-Pooh* for sop. and ens. (1970–83), *Trumpets,* for sop. and 3 clars. (1975); *Sonya's Lullaby,* pf.(1978).

Knyvett, English family of musicians:
1. Charles K. (b ? London, 22 Feb 1752; d London, 19 Jan 1822), alto and organist. App. Gentleman of the Chapel Royal, 1786, and one of the organists, 1796. Estab. the Vocal Concerts with Samuel Harrison in 1791.

2. Charles K. (b London, 1773; d London, 2 Nov 1859), organist, teacher and composer, son of prec. Pupil of Samuel Webbe. App. organist of St George's, Hanover Square, 1802, and pub. a *Selection of Psalm Tunes,* 1823.

3. William K. (b London, 21 Apr 1779; d Ryde, 17 Nov 1856), alto and composer, brother of prec. App. Gentleman of the Chapel Royal, 1797, and comp. to it in succession to Arnold, 1802. He sang and cond. much at concerts and festivals, and comp. anthems, glees, songs.

4. Deborah K., *née* Travis (b Shaw nr Oldham; d London, 10 Feb 1876), singer, wife of prec. Studied under Greatorex and made her 1st appearance in 1815.

Koanga, opera by Delius (lib. by C.F. Keary, based on G.W. Cable's novel *The Grandissimes*), prod. Elberfeld, in Ger., 30 Mar 1904.

Kobbé, Gustav (b New York, 4 Mar 1857; d Long Island, 27 Jul 1918), American writer on music. He studied at Wiesbaden and NY; visited 1882 Bayreuth Festival and pub. a 2-vol. biography of Wagner (1890). Also wrote *Loves of the Great Composers* (1905) and *Wagner and his Isolde* (1906). His *Complete Opera Book,* containing detailed synopses, was pub. 1919. Many reprints; 9th ed. Lord Harewood, 1976, 10th ed. 1986. Kobbé was killed in his yacht by a navy seaplane.

Koch, Erland von (b Stockholm, 26 Apr 1910), Swedish composer. Studied at the

Stockholm Cons. and later in London, Paris and Dresden.
Works incl. 4 symphs. (1938–53); symph. poem *A Tale from the Wilderness*, *Symph. Episode*, *Symph. Dance*; 3 pf. concertos (1936–72); vln. concerto; suite for chamber orch.; 6 string 4tets (1934–63), string trio; vln. and pf. sonata; pf. works; songs.

Köchel, Ludwig (Alois Friedrich) von, Ritter (b Stein, nr. Krems, 14 Jan 1800; d Vienna, 3 Jun 1877), Austrian naturalist and music bibliog. He lived at Salzburg in 1850–63 for the purpose of compiling his thematic catalogue of Mozart's works, pub. in 1862 (6th ed. 1964).

Koczwara. See **Kotzwara.**

Kodály, Zoltán (b Kecskemét, 16 Dec 1882; d Budapest, 6 Mar 1967), Hungarian composer. Learnt the vln. in his childhood, sang in a cathedral choir and tried to comp. without systematic instruction. In 1900, after living in small provincial towns, he entered the Univ. of Budapest for science, but also became a pupil at the Cons. Studied Hung. folksong and in 1906 wrote his univ. thesis on it, afterwards collecting songs in collaboration with Bartók. App. prof. at the Cons. that year and deputy director in 1919. He was often from the first (1923) repres. at the ISCM festivals. In 1945 he became president of the newly founded Hung. Arts Council, and in 1967 was awarded the Gold Medal of the Royal Phil. Society. Hon. D. Mus., Oxford, 1960.

Works incl. plays with music *Háry János* (1926) and *Székely Fonó* (1932); ORCH: *Summer Evening* (1906), *Ballet Music* and *Suite,* for *Háry János* (1925–7), *Theatre Overture, Dances of Galánta* (1933), *Marosszék Dances* (1930), *Variations on a Hungarian Folksong, The Peacock* (1939), Concerto for orch. (1940), Symphony in C (1930s–61).

CHAMBER AND VOCAL: 2 string 4tets (1909, 1918); duo for vln. and cello (1914); serenade for 2 vlns. and vla.; sonatas for cello solo (1915) and for cello and pf. (1909); *Meditation on a motif by Debussy, Valsette,* 9 pieces (op. 3), 7 pieces (op. 11) for pf.; 21 songs, *Énekszó* (16 songs on folk words); 57 folksong arrs.; 21 works for chorus with and without orch., incl. *Psalmus Hungaricus, Jesus and the Traders, Budavari Te Deum* (1936), *Bicinia Hungarica* (60 children's songs), *Missa brevis.*

Koechlin, Charles (b Paris, 27 Nov 1867; d Canadel, Var, 31 Dec 1950), French composer. Studied at the Paris Cons., finally under Fauré. He never appeared as an execu-

tive musician or held any official appt., but devoted himself wholly to comp. and the writing of some theoret. books as well as studies of Debussy and Fauré.

Works incl. ballet *La Divine Vesprée* (1918); incid. music to Rolland's *14 Juillet* (with 6 others, 1936); 2 symphs., orchestral cycles *La Forêt* and *Les Saisons, Seven Stars Symph.* (on film stars incl. Garbo, Dietrich and Chaplin)), *Les Bandar-Log* (after Kipling, 1939–40), and other orchestral works: *En Mer la nuit, Études antiques, Nuit de Walpurgis classique* (after Goethe), *Rapsodie sur des chansons françaises, Les Heures persanes, La Course de printemps* (after Kipling's *Jungle Book,* 1925–7); 3 *Chorals* for org. and orch., *Ballade* for pf. and orch.

CHAMBER MUSIC: 3 string 4tets, pf. 5tet, trio for fl., clar. and bassoon, pieces for pf., vln. and horn, suite for pf., vla. and fl.; sonatas for vln., vla., cello, fl., ob., clar., bassoon and horn, all with pf., sonata for 2 fls.; sonatinas, *Esquisses, Pastorales, Petites Pièces,* etc. for pf., suites and *Sonatines françaises* for pf. duet and 2 pfs.; choruses, songs.

Koffler, Józef (b Stryj, 28 Nov 1896; d Wieliczka, near Kraków, during a round up of Jews, 1943), Polish composer. Studied comp. with Grädener and musicology with Adler in Vienna, where he came under the influence of Schoenberg and began to cultivate the 12-note system; was the 1st Polish composer to do so. Later he became prof. at the Lwów State Cons.

Works incl. ballet *Alles durch M.O.W.*; 3 symphs. (no. 3 perf. London, 1938) and *Pol. Suite* for orch., 15 variations for string orch.; string 4tet, string trio (perf. Oxford, 1931), cantata *Die Liebe* for voices, vla., cello and clar.; pf. music, 40 *Pol. Folksongs, Musique de ballet, Musique quasi una sonata,* sonatina, etc.; 4 poems for voice and pf.

Kogan, Leonid (b Dniepropetrovsk, 14 Nov 1924; d Mytishcha, 17 Dec 1982), Russian violinist. Studied first with his father and later with Abram Yampolsky at the Moscow Cons., graduating in 1948 and becoming a teacher there. In 1951 he won 1st prize at the international competition in Brussels. He was married to the sister of Emil Gilels, Elisabeth.

Kokkonen, Joonas (b Iisalmi, 13 Nov 1921), Finnish composer. He studied with Palmgren and Hannikainen at the Sibelius Acad., Helsinki; prof. of comp. there 1959–63. His early work was neo-classical in spirit; later influences have been Bach, Sibelius and Bartók.

Works incl. opera *Viimeiset Kiusauset*
(The Last Temptations, prod. Helsinki
1975, London 1979); 5 symphs. (1960–82),
Music for Strings (1957), cello concerto
(1969); *Missa a capella* (1963), Requiem
(1983); pf. trio (1948), 3 string 4tets (1959,
1966, 1976), *Sinfonia da camera* for 12
strings (1962), . . . *durch einen spiegel* for 12
strings and harpsichord (1977), *Improvvisa-
zione* for vln. and pf. (1982).

Kokoschka, Oskar (1886–1980), German
poet, playwright and painter. *See* **Mörder,
Hoffnung der Frauen** (Hindemith),
Orpheus und Eurydike (Krenek).

Kol Nidre (*All Vows*), work for cello and
orch. by Bruch. comp. 1881. Also vers. for
cello and pf.

Work by Schoenberg for speaker (rabbi),
chorus and orch., op. 39; comp. autumn
1938, fp Los Angeles, 4 Oct 1938, cond.
Schoenberg.

Kolb, Carlmann (b Kösslarn, Lower Bavar.,
bap. 29 Jan 1703; d Munich, 15 Jan 1765),
German priest, organist and composer. In
1729 was ordained priest and became
organist of Ansbach Abbey, but later spent
much of his time as music tutor to a noble
household in Munich. Comp. organ music
for liturgical use.

Kolenda (Pol.), a type of Polish folksong
(carol) sung at Christmas, some specimens
dating back to the 13th cent.

Köler, David (b Zwickau, *c* 1532; d Zwickau, 25 Jul 1565), German composer. After
working at Altenburg and Güstrow in
Mecklenburg, he was recalled to Zwickau to
become cantor at St Mary's Church.

Works incl. 10 psalms for 4–6 voices,
Mass on a motet by Josquin des Prés, sacred
songs.

Kolisch, Rudolf (b Klamm, Austria, 20 Jul
1896; d Watertown, Mass., 1 Aug 1978), Austrian violinist. Studied at the Music Acad.
and the Univ. in Vienna, graduating in 1913.
He also studied the vln. with Ševcik and
comp. with Schoenberg, who was his
brother-in-law from 1924. In 1922 he
founded the Kolisch 4tet, who were esp. well
known for their perfs. of modern music;
gave the fps of Berg's *Lyric Suite* (1927) and
the last 2 string 4tets of Schoenberg and
Bartók. Disbanded 1941. In 1944 Kolisch
became leader of the Pro Arte 4tet. He
taught at Univ. of Wisconsin until 1967.

Kollmann, August Friedrich Christoph (b
Engelbostel, Hanover, 21 Mar 1756; d London, 19 Apr 1829), German organist, theorist and composer. Held a post at Lüne, nr.
Lüneburg, but in 1782 went to London,

where he was app. sacristan and cantor of
the Ger. Chapel, St James's. Wrote many
theoretical works, and also comp. a pf. concerto, chamber music.

Kollo, René (b Berlin, 20 Nov 1937), German tenor. Studied in Berlin, opera debut
Brunswick, 1965. Bayreuth since 1969 as
Lohengrin, Walther and Parsifal; Siegfried
in the cent. *Ring*, 1976. London, CG, 1976
as Siegmund. He sang Walther at Salzburg in
1974 and Lohengrin on his NY Met debut in
1976.

Kolo, a Siberian dance in quick 2–4 time.
The 15th of Dvorák's *Slavonic Dances* for
pf. duet is a Kolo.

Kondracki, Michal (b Poltava, 4 Oct 1902),
Polish composer. Studied with Szymanowski at Warsaw and with Dukas and Nadia
Boulanger in Paris, returning to Poland in
1931.

Works incl. opera *Popieliny* (1934); ballet
Legend of Kraków (1937); *Cantata ecclesiastica* and humorous cantata *Krasula*;
orchestral works *Little Mountain Symph.*,
symph. action *Metropolis* (1929), toccata
and fugue, symph. picture *Soldiers march
past, Match*, partita for small orch., nocturne for chamber orch.; pf. concerto.

Kondrashin, Kiril (b Moscow, 6 Mar 1914;
d Amsterdam, 7 Mar 1981), Russian conductor. He conducted opera in Leningrad
and Moscow 1936–56 and was prin. cond.
Moscow PO 1960–75; asst. cond. Concertgebouw Orch. from 1975. He recorded the
Shostakovich symphs. and gave the fps of
no. 13 (1962) and the 2nd vln. concerto
(1967). Cond. at Hollywood Bowl one
month before his death.

Konetzni, Anny (b Ungarisch-Weisskirchen,
12 Feb 1902; d Vienna, 6 Sep 1969), Austrian soprano. She studied in Berlin and
sang Adriano in Vienna in 1927. Berlin
1931–4; Hélène in the German fp of *Les
vêpres Siciliennes*. She appeared at CG and
at the NY Met in the 1930s, and in 1935
sang Isolde at Salzburg. Other roles incl.
Ortrud, Elektra, the Marschallin and Brünnhilde (CG 1951).

Konetzni, Hilde (b Vienna, 21 Mar 1905; d
Vienna, 20 Apr 1980), Austrian soprano,
sister of the prec. She studied in Prague and
Vienna and sang in both centres in the
1930s. She sang Mařenka, Donna Elvira and
Elisabeth at CG in 1938–9, and after the war
Leonore, Sieglinde and Gutrune. Sang at
Salzburg from 1936 and in the US 1937–9.
Taught in Vienna from 1954.

König Hirsch (*The Stag King*), opera by
Henze (lib. by H. von Cramer after Gozzi's

Re Cervo, 1762), prod. Berlin, 23 Sep 1956. Revised as *Il Re Cervo* 1962 and prod. Kassel, 10 Mar 1963.

König Stephan, incid. music by Beethoven, op. 117, for Kotzebue's play written for the opening of the new theatre at Pest and perf. there 9 Feb 1812.

Königin von Saba, Die (*The Queen of Sheba*), opera by C. Goldmark (lib. by S.H. Mosenthal), prod. Vienna, Opera, 10 Mar 1875.

Königskinder (*King's Children*), opera by Humperdinck (lib. by E. Rosmer), prod. as a play with accompanying music, Munich, 23 Jan 1897; the operatic version prod. NY Met 28 Dec 1910.

Königsperger, Marianus (b Roding, Bavaria, 4 Dec 1708; d Prüfening, nr. Regensburg, 9 Oct 1769), German priest, organist and composer. He was educ. and took his vows at the Benedictine abbey of Prüfening, where he was organist and choirmaster all his life. Works incl. Masses, offertories, Litanies, etc.; symph. and sonatas for var. instruments with organ preludes, fugues and other works for organ.

Kontakte, work by Stockhausen for pf, perc. and 4-track tape (1959–60, fp Cologne, 11 Jun 1960).

Kontarsky, Aloys (b Iserlohn, 14 May 1931), German pianist. He studied at Cologne and Hamburg. Formed duo with his brother **Alfons** (b Iserlohn, 9 Oct 1932) in 1955 and gave many perfs. of modern works, incl. fps of duos by Berio, Bussotti, Kagel and B. Zimmermann. In 1966 he gave the fp of Stockhausen's *Klavierstücke I– XI*. Has taught at Darmstadt from 1960.

Kontrapunkte, work by Stockhausen for six wind insts., pf., harp, vln. and cello (1952–3, fp Cologne, 26 May 1953).

Konwitschny, Franz (b Fulnek, 14 Aug 1901; d Belgrade, 28 Jul 1962), German conductor. Studied in Leipzig and Brünn, playing vln. and vla. in various orchs. His cond. career began at Stuttgart in 1926. He later cond. in many of the leading Ger. opera houses and in 1959 cond. *The Ring* at Covent Garden. Chief cond. Leipzig Gewandhaus Orch. from 1949.

Konya, Sandor (b Sarkad, 23 Sep 1923), Hungarian tenor. Debut Bielefeld, 1951, as Turiddu. Berlin Stadttheater, from 1955; created Leandro in Henze's *König Hirsch*, 1956. Bayreuth from 1958 as Lohengrin and Walther. San Francisco 1960–5; NY Met 1961–74 (debut as Lohengrin). London, CG, from 1963. Other roles incl. Radames, Rodolfo and Pinkerton.

Konzertmeister (Ger. = concert master), the leader of an orch.

Konzertstück. See **Concertstück.**

Koopman, Ton (b Zwolle, 2 Oct 1944), Dutch harpsichordist, organist and conductor. Studied in Amsterdam with Leonhardt. He has cond. Musica Antiqua and formed the Amsterdam Baroque Orch. 1977.

Korchmaryov, Klementy Arkadievich (b Verkhni Udinsk, 3 Jul 1899; d Moscow, 7 Apr 1958), Russian composer. Pupil of Malishevsky at the Odessa Cons. Works incl. operas *Ivan the Soldier* and *Ten Days that Shook the World;* ballet *The Serf Ballerina* (1927); incid. music for plays; vocal symph. on his 2nd opera; 2 pf. sonatas.

Kord, Kazimierz (b Pogorze, 18 Nov 1930), Polish conductor. He studied at Leningrad and Kraków; Kraków Opera from 1962, Polish Radio Orch. 1968–73. NY Met 1972, and has conducted opera in San Francisco and London; guest cond. with the Chicago SO and Cleveland Orch., and from 1977 artistic dir. National PO, Warsaw. Princ. guest cond. Cincinnati SO 1980–2.

Korngold, Erich (Wolfgang) (b Brno, 29 May 1897; d Hollywood, 29 Nov 1957), Austrian composer. Son of Julius K. (1860–1945), music critic of the *Neue Freie Presse* in Vienna, thanks to whose influence he had his pantomime *Der Schneemann* (orch. Zemlinsky) prod. at the Court Opera at the age of 13. He studied with Fuchs, Grädener and Zemlinsky. App. cond. at the Hamburg Opera, 1919, and prof. at the Vienna State Acad., 1927. After the *Anschluss* he emigrated to USA. Collaborated with Max Reinhardt at his Theatre School at Hollywood; successful as a writer of film music, without really altering his earlier style.

Works incl. operas *Der Ring des Polycrates, Violanta* (1916), *Die tote Stadt* (1920), *Das Wunder der Heliane* (1927), *Die Katrin* (1939); ballet-pantomime *Der Schneemann* (1910); incid. music to Shakespeare's *Much Ado about Nothing* (1919); film music *Sea Hawk, The Adventures of Robin Hood,* etc.

Symphonietta, symph.-overture, overture to a play; pf. concerto for the left hand (1923); vln. concerto (1946); string 4tet, pf. trio, pf. 5tet, 6tet; vln. and pf. sonata; 3 pf. sonatas and pieces; songs.

Kossuth, symph. poem in 10 tableaux by Bartók; comp. 1903, fp Budapest, 13 Jan 1904.

Kostelanetz, André (b St Petersburg, 22 Dec 1901; d Port-au-Prince, Haiti, 13 Jan 1980), American conductor of Russian birth. After study in Petrograd he emigrated to the USA; worked for CBS from 1930 as cond. and arranger. His versions of the popular classics, in the manner of film music, found favour in his adopted homeland; more serious work was commissioned from Schuman, Walton and Copland (Lincoln Portrait). He married Lily Pons in 1938.

Kotter, Johannes (b Strasbourg, c 1480; d Berne, 1541), German organist and composer, a pupil of Hofhaimer. He compiled a tablature in the form of an instruction book in organ playing and comp. He worked in Fribourg (Switzerland) but was tortured and then dismissed because he was a Protestant.

Kotzebue, August (Friedrich Ferdinand) von (1761–1819), German playwright. *See* **Busby** (*Johanna von Montfaucon*), **Generali** (*Misantropia e pentimento*), **König Stephan** (Beethoven), **Lortzing** (*Wildschütz*), **Reichardt** (*Kreuzfahrer*), **Ritter (P.)** (*Eremit auf Formentara*), **Ruins of Athens** (Beethoven), **Salieri** (*Hussiten vor Naumburg*), **Süssmayr** (*Wildfang*), **Teufels Lustschloss** (Schubert), **Walter (I.)** (*Spiegelritter*), **Wessely (C.B.)** (*Sonnenjungfrau*), **Wildschütz** (Lortzing), **Wolf (E.W.)** (*Eremit auf Formentara*), **Wranitzky** (music for plays).

Kotzwara (Kočžwara), Franz (František) (b Prague, 1730; d London, 2 Sep 1791), Bohemian composer. Settled in London in the 1780s, visited Ireland in 1788 and played in the King's Theatre Orch. in London, 1790. He accidentally hanged himself while entertaining a prostitute.
Works incl. *The Battle of Prague* for pf. with vln., cello and drums ad lib.

Koukourgi (Cherubini). *See* **Ali Baba**.

Koussevitzky, Sergey (b Tver, 26 Jul 1874; d Boston, Mass., 4 Jun 1951), Russian conductor (US citizen from 1941). Studied in Moscow and became a double bass player in the Imp. Orch., later specialized as a soloist on the instrument and toured Europe. He then formed an orch. of his own and took to cond. In 1924 he was app. cond. of the Boston SO; in 1931 he commissioned Stravinsky's *Symphony of Psalms* and in 1943 Bartók's Concerto for orch. The K. Music Foundation, set up as a memorial to his wife, commissioned *Peter Grimes* (1945).

Kovařovic, Karel (b Prague, 9 Dec 1862; d Prague, 6 Dec 1920), Czech conductor and composer. Studied clar. and harp at the Prague Cons., became an orchestral harpist in 1885 and then studied comp. with Fibich. He toured as accompanist with the violinist Ondříček. Cond. at Brno and Plzeň, 1885–8,

in 1895 cond. at the Ethnographic Exhibition in Prague, and from 1900 to 1920 chief cond. at the Nat. Opera there. In 1916 he cond. Janáček's *Jenůfa*, with his own revisions.
Works incl. operas *The Peasants' Charter*, *At the Old Bleaching-House* (1901), comic operas *The Bridegrooms* (1884), *The Way through the Window* (1886), *The Night of Simon and Jude* (1892); ballets *Hashish* (1884) and *A Tale of Luck Found*; incid. music to Tyl's *Wood Nymph*, Čech's *The Excursions of Mr. Brouček* and other plays; symph. poem *The Rape of Persephone*, dramatic overture in C min.; pf. concerto in F min.; 3 string 4tets; choral pieces, songs.

Koven, (Henry Louis) Reginald de (b Middletown, Conn., 3 Apr 1859; d Chicago, 16 Jan 1920), American composer. Graduated at Oxford in 1879 and then studied music on the Continent. He was music critic for several Amer. papers.
Works incl. operas *The Begum*, *Robin Hood* (*Maid Marian*) and *Rob Roy* (both after Scott), *The Canterbury Pilgrims* (after Chaucer), *Rip van Winkle* (after Washington Irving), many operettas and ballets; orchestral works; pf. sonata and pieces; c 400 songs, etc.

Kozeluch (Kotzeluch, Koželuh), Leopold (b Welwarn 26 Jun 1747; d Vienna, 7 May 1818), Bohemian composer. Pupil of his cousin Johann Anton K. (1738–1814), studied law at Prague Univ., but devoted himself entirely to comp. from 1771. Went to Vienna in 1778 and succeeded Mozart as Imp. comp. in 1792.
Works incl. operas *Didone abbandonata*, *Judith*, *Deborah*, etc.; oratorio *Moisé in Egitto* (1787); 24 ballets and 3 pantomimes; 11 symphs.; 22 pf. concertos and several for other instruments; 6 string 4tets, 63 trios,; pf. sonatas, folksong arrs.

Kozub, Ernst (b Duisburg 1925; d Frankfurt, 27 Dec 1971), German tenor. Debut Berlin, Komische Oper, 1950, in *Czar und Zimmermann*. Frankfurt 1954–62. Hamburg from 1962; sang Hoffmann, Radames and Don José and was the Emperor in the 1st London perf. of *Die Frau ohne Schatten* (SW, 1966). Milan 1963, as Siegmund and Siegfried.

Kraft, Anton (b Rokitzan, nr. Plzeň, 30 Dec 1749; d Vienna, 28 Aug 1820), Bohemian cellist and composer. Originally intended for the law, he was engaged by Prince Esterházy as principal cellist in 1778, remaining till 1790 and receiving tuition in comp. from Haydn. Subsequently in the service of Prince

Grassalkovich and (from 1795) Prince Lobkowitz. Beethoven's Triple Concerto was comp. for him, and he played in the fp of the 7th symph. (1813).

Works incl. concertos, sonatas, etc. for cello, duets for 2 cellos, etc. Haydn's D maj. cello concerto was once ascribed to Kraft.

Kraft, Nicolaus (b Eszterháza, 14 Dec 1778; d Stuttgart, 18 May 1853), Bohemian cellist and comp., son of prec. Pupil of his father, with whom he travelled. Settled in Vienna, 1790, and became chamber musician to Prince Lobkowitz in 1796; played in the Schuppanzigh Quartet from the same time. In 1801 he had further lessons with Duport in Berlin. In 1809 he became a member of the Vienna Court Orch., and in 1814 went to Stuttgart as a member 1st of the Court Opera and then of the Court Chapel.

Works incl. 4 cello concertos, *Scène pastorale* for cello and orch.; fantasy for cello and string 4tet; duets and divertissements for 2 cellos.

Krakowiak, a Polish dance from the region of Kraków, sometimes intro. into ballets and ballrooms in the 19th cent. under the name of *Cracovienne.* In its orig. form it was danced by all the assembled couples and sometimes words were sung to it. It is in quick 2–4 time.

Krämerspiegel (*The Shopkeeper's Mirror*), cycle of 12 songs for voice and pf. by Strauss (texts by A. Kerr); comp. 1918 and incl. ironic references to Ger. publishers: no. 2 *Einst kam der Bock als Bote*, refers to Berlin pub. firm, Bote und Bock. Fp Berlin, 1 Nov 1926.

Krasner, Louis (b Cherkassy, 21 Jun 1903), American violinist. As a small child he was taken to the USA, studying at the New Eng. Cons. and graduating in 1923. He then studied abroad, where his teachers incl. Flesch, Lucien Capet and Ševčik. After a period as leader of the Minneapolis SO, he became prof. at Syracuse Univ. He commissioned Berg's vln. concerto, giving its fp (Barcelona, 1936) and also gave the fp of Schoenberg's vln. concerto (Philadelphia, 1940).

Krásová, Marta (b Protivin, 16 Mar 1901; d Vráž, 20 Feb 1970), Czech mezzo. Debut Bratislava 1924, as Julia in Dvořák's *Jacobin*; joined the Prague Opera 1927 and sang there until 1966 as the Kostelnička, Eboli, Amneris and Carmen. She appeared as guest in Germany and France; sang Wagner in N. America 1937–9. Edinburgh 1964, with Prague Co.

Kraus, Alfredo (b Las Palmas, 24 Sep 1927), Spanish tenor. Debut Cairo, 1956, Duke of Mantua. La Scala, Milan, and CG from 1959. US debut Chicago 1962; NY Met from 1966. Roles incl. Faust, Nemorino, Werther, Arturo and Don Ottavio.

Kraus, Ernst (b Erlangen, 8 Jun 1863; d Waldstadt, 6 Sep 1941), German tenor. Debut Mannheim 1893, as Tamino. He sang at Bayreuth 1899–1909 as Siegfried, Walther and Erik. NY Met debut 1903, as Siegmund. In 1910 he was the first London Herod (*Salome*), under Beecham.

Kraus, Felix von (b Vienna, 3 Oct 1870; d Munich, 30 Oct 1937), Austrian bass. His early career was in concert. In 1899 he sang Hagen at Bayreuth; appeared there until 1909 as Gurnemanz, the Landgrave and Marke. London, CG, 1907. Taught in Munich 1908–25.

Kraus, Joseph Martin (b Miltenberg, nr. Mainz, 20 Jun 1756; d Stockholm, 15 Dec 1792), German Swedish composer. Studied law and philosophy at Mainz, Erfurt and Göttingen, also comp. with Vogler. He accomp. a Swed. friend to Stockholm and remained there as theatre cond., becoming music director in 1781. In 1782–7 he travelled widely with a grant from the King of Swed. In 1788 he succeeded Uttini as *Kapellmeister.*

Works incl. operas *Soliman II, Aeneas at Carthage* (prod. 1799), *Proserpina* (1781), church music; *Funeral Cantata for Gustavas III* (1792); symphs. and overtures; string 4tets.

Kraus, Lili (b Budapest, 4 Mar 1903; d Asheville, NC, 6 Nov 1986), Hungarian pianist. Studied at the Budapest Academy under Kodály and Bartók. She taught in Vienna during the 1920s, after study with Schnabel, then toured widely in the classical rep.; continued her career in 1948 after wartime internment by the Japanese. She taught at Austin Univ., Texas, from 1967 and retired in 1983. Also heard in recital with the violinist Szymon Goldberg.

Kraus, Otakar (b Prague, 10 Dec 1909; d London, 28 Jul 1980), Czech, later English baritone. Studied in Prague and later in Milan with Fernando Carpi, making his debut in Brno in 1935. He came to England in World War II, joining the EOG in 1946. He sang in the fps of Britten's *Rape of Lucretia*, Walton's *Troilus and Cressida* and Tippett's *Midsummer Marriage*, and also created the role of Nick Shadow in Stravinsky's *Rake's Progress* in 1951. A fine Wagner singer, he was esp. noted for his Alberich.

Krause, Tom (b Helsinki, 5 Jul 1934), Finnish baritone. Debut Berlin 1958 as

Escamillo. Hamburg from 1962; in 1964 created Jason in Krenek's *Der goldene Bock* and in 1968 the title role in Searle's *Hamlet*. He sang the Count in *Capricco* on his Glyndebourne debut, in 1963, and Almaviva at the NY Met in 1967. The following year sang Don Giovanni at Salzburg. Other roles incl. Malatesta, Germont and Guglielmo.

Krauss, Clemens (b Vienna, 31 Mar 1893; d Mexico City, 16 May 1954), Austrian conductor. Studied with Grädener and Heuberger at the Vienna Cons. and from 1912 cond. at var. provincial opera-houses in Ger. and Aus. In 1922 he became cond. at the Vienna Staatsoper and in 1924 Opera intendant and cond. of the Museum concerts at Frankfurt. In 1929–34 he was dir. of the Vienna and in 1934–6 of the Berlin Staatsoper after which he directed the Opera at Munich. He was closely assoc. with Richard Strauss as cond. and in the case of *Capriccio*, as joint librettist; conducted the fps of *Arabella*, *Friedenstag* and *Die Liebe der Danae*. He married the singer Viorica Ursuleac (1894–1985).

Krauss, (Marie) Gabrielle (b Vienna, 24 Mar 1842; d Paris, 6 Jan 1906), Austrian soprano. Studied at the Vienna Cons. and with Mathilde Marchesi; after singing at concerts she made her stage debut at the Vienna Opera in 1859 as Rossini's Mathilde, and in Paris, at the Théâtre des Italiens, in 1867; in 1875–88 she was a member of the Opéra almost continuously. Other roles incl. Norma, Lucia, Gilda, Elsa and Donna Anna.

Krebs, Helmut (b Dortmund, 8 Oct 1913), German tenor. His career began as a concert singer; stage debut Berlin (1938): from 1947 engaged at the Städtische Oper there. In 1953 he sang Belmonte and Idamante at Glyndebourne and the following year was Aron in the fp (concert) of Schoenberg's *Moses und Aron*, at Hamburg. Made guest appearances in Milan, London, Vienna and Munich and was well known in the passions and oratorios of Bach. He recorded Stravinsky's *Oedipus* and Monteverdi's *Orfeo*.

Krebs, Johann Ludwig (b Buttelstedt, Thuringia, 10 Oct 1713; d Altenburg, 1 Jan 1780), German organist, harpsichordist and comp. Pupil of Bach at Leipzig from 1726, organist at Zwickau, Zeitz and Altenburg.

Works incl. Magnificat, settings of the Sanctus; trios; sonatas, suites, fugues, choruses, with variations, etc., for clavier; fl. sonatas, organ music.

Krebs, Johann Tobias (b Heichelheim, 7 Jul 1690; d Buttstädt, 11 Feb 1762), German

organist and composer, father of prec. Pupil of Walther, later of Bach, app. organist at Buttstädt in 1721. Comp. organ music.

Krehbiel, Henry (Edward) (b Ann Arbor, Mich., 10 Mar 1854; d New York, 20 Mar 1923), American music critic and author. After studying law at Cincinnati, he became music critic to the *Cincinnati Gazette*, 1874, and to the *NY Tribune*, 1880. He ed. Thayer's life of Beethoven, collected and wrote on Negro folksongs and wrote many books incl. studies of opera, of Wagner and of Amer. musical life.

Kreidekreis, Der (*The Chalk Circle*), opera by Zemlinsky (lib. by comp. after Klabund); 1932, prod. Zurich, 14 Oct 1933. Zemlinsky's last completed opera.

Kreisler, Fritz (b Vienna, 2 Feb 1875; d New York, 29 Jan 1962), Austrian, later American, violinist and composer. Appeared as an infant prodigy at the age of 7. Studied at the Vienna Cons. under Hellmesberger and J. Auber, and at the Paris Cons. under Massart and Delibes, winning the gold medal at the age of 12. After touring in USA in 1889 he returned to Aus. to study medicine. After his military service and a period of intense study he reappeared as a soloist in Berlin in 1899 and again toured in USA. After 3 months' service in the Aus. army in 1914 he was discharged on account of wounds and returned to USA, where he eventually made his home. He made frequent tours in Europe and gave the fp of Elgar's vln. concerto (10 Nov 1910). His comps. incl. a string 4tet and an operetta (*Apple Blossoms*, 1919), and a number of vln. solos, some of which were orig. pub. as the work of 18th-cent. composers.

Kreisleriana, a cycle of pf. pieces by Schumann, op. 16, comp. in 1838 and ded. to Chopin. The title is borrowed from the musician Kreisler in E.T.A. Hoffmann's stories *Fantasiestücke in Callots Manier*.

Kreissle von Hellborn, Heinrich (b Vienna, 19 Jan 1822; d Vienna, 6 Apr 1869), Austrian lawyer and state official, 1st biog. of Schubert, on whom he pub. *F. Schubert: eine biographische Skizze*, 1861, and *Franz Schubert*, 1865.

Krejči, Iša (b Prague, 10 Jul 1904; d Prague, 6 Mar 1968), Czech composer. Pupil of Novák and Jirák. After working for some time at Bratislava he returned to Prague and joined the radio service.

Works incl. opera *Confusion at Ephesus* (on Shakespeare's *Comedy of Errors*, 1946), operatic scene *Antigone* (after Sophocles, 1934), sinfonietta for orch.; *Little Ballet* for chamber orch.; string 4tet in D maj., nonet, trios for ob., clar and bassoon and clar., double bass and pf.; sonatina for clar. and pf.; songs.

Kremer, Gidon (b Riga, Latvia, 27 Feb 1947), Russian violinist. He studied with D. Oistrakh at the Moscow Cons. and won the 1970 Tchaikovsky Competition: international career in standard concertos and modern works. Often heard in works by Schnittke. At London in May 1986 he was heard in Bernstein's *Serenade*, before the Queen.

Kremer, Martin (b Geisenheim, 23 Mar 1898; d Prien, 19 Feb 1971), German tenor. He studied with Giuseppe Borgatti in Milan; Kassel 1924–7. At the Dresden Staatsoper he created 3 roles by Richard Strauss: Matteo (*Arabella*, 1933), Henry (*Die schweigsame Frau*, 1935) and Leukippos (*Daphne*, 1938). Visited London with the Dresden co. 1936 and sang in Oslo during the German occupation. Well known as David.

Krenek, Ernst (b Vienna, 23 Aug 1900), Austrian, later American composer. Pupil of Schreker in Vienna and Berlin. In the 1920s he appeared at several of the smaller festivals in Ger. and in 1925–7 he was cond. at the operas of Kassel, Wiesbaden and other smaller towns in order to gain experience in operatic stage-craft. His 1st wife was Anna Mahler, the composer's daughter. After the prod. of *Jonny spielt auf* at Leipzig in 1927 his success was assured, but he later worked in 12-note music as a disciple of Schoenberg. In 1933, when the Nazi régime gained the upper hand, he settled in Vienna and worked on behalf of progressive Aus. comps., but was interfered with by the Fascist party; left Aus. for USA in 1937, where he later became Dean of the School of Fine Arts and director of the Music Dept. at Hamline Univ., St Paul, 1942–7; has lived in California from 1948. His book, *Über neue Musik*, is a defence of the 12-note system.

Works incl. OPERAS *Zwingburg* (1924) *Der Sprung über den Schatten* (1924), *Orpheus und Eurydike* (1926), *Jonny spielt auf* (1927), *Leben des Orest* (1930), *Karl V* (1938), *Tarquin* (1941), *Ausgerechnet und Verspielt* (1962), *Der goldene Bock* (1964), *Sardakai* (1970), also 3 1-act operas: *Der Diktator, Das geheime Königreich* and *Schwergewicht* (1928); BALLETS *Mammon*, *Der vertauschte Cupido* (after Rameau, 1925); incid. music to Shakespeare's *Midsummer Night's Dream*, Goethe's *Triumph der Empfindsamkeit* and Calderón's *La vida es sueño*.

CHORAL MUSIC: choruses on poems by John Donne, *Cantata for Wartime* (Herman Melville), Lat. choral works; *The Seasons* for unaccomp. chorus.

ORCHESTRAL: 5 symphs. (1921–50) and *Little Symph.*, 2 *Concerti grossi*, variations on *I wonder where I wander* for orch.; *Symph. Elegy* for strings, on the death of Webern (1946); 4 pf. concertos (1923–50), 2 vln. concertos (1924, 1954), cello concerto; theme and 13 variations for orch. (1931), concerto for organ and strings (1979).

CHAMBER AND SOLO VOCAL: 8 string 4tets (1921–52); vln. and pf. sonata, sonata for solo vla.; 6 pf. sonatas; 25 songs, song cycles *Reisebuch aus den österreichischen Alpen*, *Fiedellieder, Gesänge des späten Jahres*.

Krenn, Fritz (b Vienna, 11 Dec 1887; d Vienna, 17 Jul 1964), Austrian bassbaritone. He sang at the Vienna Volksoper in 1917 and at the Staatsoper 1919–50, with intervals. At the Kroll Opera, Berlin he sang in the fp of Hindemith's *Neues vom Tage* (under Klemperer, 1929). At Salzburg he was heard as Ochs (1936) and repeated the role on his 1951 NY Met debut.

Krenn, Werner (b Vienna, 21 Sep 1942), Austrian tenor. After an early career as a bassoonist he sang in *The Fairy Queen*, at Berlin in 1966. The following year he was heard in the Missa Solemnis at Salzburg, the first of many concerts under Karajan. Aix 1969, Ottavio. He has recorded roles in operas by Berg and Shostakovich but is best known in Mozart: as Titus and in *Il rè Pastore, Ascanio in Alba* and *Idomeneo*.

Krenz, Jan (b Wioclawek, 14 Jul 1926), Polish conductor and composer. He studied in Łódź and worked at Poznań in orch. and opera rep. from 1948. Chief cond. Polish Radio Orch. from 1953; world-wide tours. Artistic dir. Warsaw Opera 1967–73. Music dir., Bonn Opera 1979–83. Has cond. in Eng. since 1961 (BBC SO). Works incl. *Nocturnes* for orch., *Capriccio* for 24 insts., *Antisymphony* (1962).

Kreusser, Georg Anton (b Heidingsfeld, 27 Oct 1746; d Aschaffenburg, 1 Nov 1810), German violinist and composer. Studied in Fr. and It. entered the service of the court at Mainz in 1773, app. *Konzertmeister* 1774.

Works incl. Passion oratorio *Der Tod Jesu* (Ramler, 1783); symphs.; chamber music.

Kreutzer, Conradin (b Messkirch, Baden, 22 Nov 1780; d Riga, 14 Dec 1849), German conductor and composer. He 1st learnt music as a choir-boy, went to Freiburg i/B. to study law, but gave it up for music, travelled in Switzerland as pianist and singer and in 1804 went to Vienna to study comp. with

Kreutzer

Albrechtsberger. After cond. at the court of Stuttgart and Donaueschingen, he returned to Vienna and became cond. at the Kärntnertortheater for 3 periods between 1822 and 1840 and of the Josefstadt-theater in 1833–40. Later he worked at Cologne and Paris, and again in Vienna.
Works incl. operas *Conradin von Schwaben* (1812), *Die Alpenhütte* (1815), *Libussa* (lib. by Grillparzer, 1822), *Melusine* (lib. do., 1833), *Das Nachtlager von Granada* (1834), *Cordelia* and *c* 25 others; incid. music to plays incl. Raimund's *Der Verschwender*; oratorio *Sending Moses* (1814); church music; chamber music; pf. works; male-voice part-songs and songs.

Kreutzer, Rodolphe (b Versailles, 16 Nov 1766; d Geneva, 6 Jan 1831), French violinist and composer. He was taught mainly by his father and at the age of 16 was app. by Marie Antoinette 1st vln. in the royal chapel, where he learnt much from hearing Mestrino and Viotti. Later he became leader at the Théâtre Italien, where he began to prod. operas of his own. He toured much and became vln. prof. at the Paris Cons. in 1795. In 1798 he went to Vienna in the suite of Bernadotte and made friends with Beethoven. He often played vln. duets with Rode, on whose departure to Russia in 1801 Kreutzer became leader at the Opéra, and later he held court appts. under both Napoleon I and Louis XVIII. He compiled a *Méthode de violon* with Baillot.
Works incl. operas *Jeanne d'Arc à Orléans* (1790), *Paul et Virginie* (after Saint-Pierre), *Lodoïska* (1791), *Imogène, ou La Gageure indiscrète* (after Boccaccio, 1796), *Astyanax*, *Aristippe* (1808), *La Mort d'Abel* (1810), *Mathilde* and many others; ballets *Paul et Virginie*, *Le Carnaval de Venise*, *Clari* and others; 19 vln. concertos (1783–1810), 4 *Symphonies concertantes*; 15 string 4tets; 15 trios; sonatas, caprices, studies, airs with variations for vln.

'Kreutzer' Sonata, the nickname of Beethoven's A maj. vln. and pf. sonata, op. 47, comp. in 1803 and ded. to R. Kreutzer. The work is the subject of Tolstoy's novel *The Kreutzer Sonata*, in which it has a disastrous effect on the morals of the characters. Beethoven and George Bridgetower (*q.v.*) gave the fp on 17 May 1803.
Sub-title of Janáček's 1st string 4tet, comp. 1923–4, based on lost pf. trio of 1908–9. Fp Prague, 17 Sep 1924.

Křička, Jaroslav (b Kelc, Morav., 27 Aug 1882; d Prague, 23 Jan 1969), Czech composer. Studied at the Prague Cons., 1902–5,

and came under the influence of Novák, enlarged his experience in Berlin, and then went to Rus., teaching at the music school of Ekaterinoslav. On his return to Prague in 1909 he became cond. of the Glagol choral society. Director of the Prague Cons., 1942–5.
Works incl. operas *Hypolita* (after one of Maurice Hewlett's *Little Novels of Italy*, 1916) and *The Gentleman in White* (after Wilde's *Canterville Ghost*, 1929); several operas for children; choral works *The Temptation in the Wilderness* (1922) and many others with and without orch.; symph. in D min., symph. poems *Faith*, overture to Maeterlinck's *Blue Bird* (1911), *Polonaise* and *Elegy on the Death of Rimsky-Korsakov*, *Children's Suite* for small orch. (1907), *Nostalgia* for string orch.; 3 string 4tets (1907–39), vln. and pf. sonata; pf. music and songs.

Krieger, Adam (b Driesen, Prus., 7 Jan 1634; d Dresden, 30 Jun 1666), German organist, composer and poet. Pupil of Scheidt, organist of St Nicholas's Church at Leipzig and afterwards court organist at Dresden.
Works incl. cantatas and funeral songs, arias for voice and bass, songs for 1–5 voices and instruments, etc.

Krieger, Johann (b Nuremberg, 28 Dec 1651; d Zittau, 18 Jul 1735), German organist and composer. Pupil of his brother; court organist at Bayreuth, 1671–7, and later organist and town music director at Zittau.
Works incl. plays with music; sacred and secular songs for several voices with insts.; org. works; 6 partitas, preludes & fugues, for clavier.

Krieger, (Johann) Philipp (b Nuremberg, 25 Feb 1649; d Weissenfels, 6 Feb 1725), German organist and composer, brother of prec. Travelled in It. and studied under Rosenmüller at Venice; entered the service of the Duke of Saxe-Weissenfels, was chamber musician and organist at Halle from 1677 and music director at Weissenfels from 1712.
Works incl. opera *Der grossmütige Scipio* (1690) and others; plays with music; church music; arias for 1–4 voices with instruments; sonatas for vln. and vla. da gamba, *Partien* for wind instruments.

Krips, Josef (b Vienna, 8 Apr 1902; d Geneva, 13 Oct 1974), Austrian conductor. Studied in Vienna with Mandyczewski and Weingartner and became a violinist in the Volksoper there. In 1924 he began his career as a cond. and from 1926 to 1933 was general music director at Karlsruhe. In 1933 he became a cond. at the Vienna Staatsoper and in 1935 prof. at the Vienna Acad. of Music. During World War II he lost these positions, but rejoined the Vienna Staatsoper in 1945. From 1950 to 1954 he was cond. at the LSO; San Fransicso SO 1963–70, NY Met from 1966. He cond. *Don Giovanni* at Salzburg in 1946 and at CG in 1963.

Krombholc, Jaroslav (b Prague, 30 Jan 1918; d Prague, 16 Jul 1983), Czech conductor. Debut 1940, Prague Nat. Theatre; chief cond. there 1968–75. 1973–8 cond. Prague Radio SO. Gave Czech opera widely in Europe.

Krommer, Franz (orig. Kramář, František Vincenc) (b Kamenice, 27 Nov 1759; d Vienna, 8 Jan 1831), Moravian violinist, organist and composer. Having been an organist from 1776 to 1784, he went to Hun, and later became music director to Prince Grassalkovich in Vienna. In 1818 he succeeded Kozeluch as court music director.

Works incl. 2 Masses; music for wind band; symphs.; 69 string 4tets and 5tets.

Krull, Annie (b Rostock, 12 Jan 1876; d Schwerin, 14 Jun 1947), German soprano. She sang at Dresden 1901–10 and created Strauss's Diemut (*Feuersnot*), 1901, and Elektra (1909); Elektra under Beecham at CG, 1910. Later sang at Mannheim and Weimar as Elisabeth and Sieglinde.

Krummhorn. *See* **Crumhorn.**

Krumpholz, Johann Baptist (b Zlonice nr. Prague, 3 May 1742; d Paris, 19 Feb 1790), Bohemian-French harpist and composer. He grew up in Paris, travelled as a virtuoso, and was in the service of Prince Esterházy, 1773–6, receiving tuition in comp. from Haydn. After further travels he settled in Paris, and was responsible for some notable improvements to his instrument. On the desertion of his wife with J.L. Dussek (*q.v.*) he drowned himself in the Seine.

Works incl. 8 concertos, 32 sonatas for harp; 2 symphs. for harp and small orch.; harp ducts.

Krumpholz, Wenzel (b *c* 1750; d Vienna, 2 May 1817), Bohemian-French violinist, mandolin player and composer, brother of prec. He was a member of Prince Esterházy's orch. under Haydn, and in 1796 entered the service of the court in Vienna. He was friendly with Beethoven, who wrote a mandolin sonata for him. Wrote vln. music.

Kruszelnicka, Salomea (b Bilavyntsy, 23 Sep 1873; d Lwów, 16 Nov 1952), Russian soprano. Debut Lwów 1892; sang the *Forza*

Leonora at Trieste in 1897 and Butterfly at Brescia in 1904. La Scala from 1907 as Isolde, Salome and Elektra and in the fps of Cilea's *Gloria* and Pizzetti's *Fedra* (1915). Buenos Aires 1906–13, Palermo 1911, as the *Götterdämmerung* Brünnhilde. Last stage appearance Naples 1920; concert tour USA 1927, for Ukranian emigrés.

Kubelík, Jan (b Michle, nr. Prague, 5 Jul 1880; d Prague, 5 Dec 1940), Czech violinist. He was taught by his father, a gardener and good music amateur, and made his 1st public appearance in Prague in 1888. In 1892 he entered the Cons. as a pupil of Ševčik and began his real career with a concert in Vienna, 1898. London debut 1900; US from 1902. Retired 1940. Among his comps. are 6 vln. concertos.

Kubelík, Rafael (b Býchory, nr. Kolín, 29 Jun 1914), Czech conductor and composer, son of prec. Studied at the Prague Cons., making his debut with the Cz. SO in 1934. From 1939 to 1941 he was cond. of the National Theatre in Brno and from 1942 to 1948 of the Cz. PO. Between 1948 and 1950 he was much in Eng. and in 1950 was app. prin. cond. of the Chicago SO. He returned to Europe in 1953 and became music dir. at CG, London (1955–8); cond. the 1st Brit. *Jenůfa* there in 1956 and the 1st complete *Troyens* (1957). In 1961 he became cond. of the Bavarian Radio SO and in Vienna gave the fp of Schoenberg's oratorio *Die Jakobsleiter*. He has also comp.; his works incl. the operas *Veronika* (1947) and *Cornelia Faroli* (on the life of Titian, 1972), a choral symph., concertos for vln. and cello, a Requiem and some chamber music.

Kubik, Gail (b Coffeyville, Okla., 5 Sep 1914; d Covina, Calif., 20 Jul 1984), American violinist and composer. Studied at the Eastman School of Music, Rochester, NY, and gained several comp. prizes.

Works incl. ballet *Frankie and Johnnie* for dance band and folk singer (1946); *In Praise of Johnny Appleseed* (Vachel Lindsay) for baritone, chorus and orch.; 3 symphs. (1949–57); suite for orch.; 2 vln. concertos, *American Caprice* for pf. and 32 instruments; 2 *Sketches* for string 4tet, pf. trio, wind 5tet, *Trivialities* for fl., horn and string 4tet.

Kugelmann, Hans (b ? Augsburg, *c* 1495; d Königsberg, summer 1542), German trumpeter and composer. He was trumpeter in the service of the Emperor Maximilian at Innsbruck in 1519 and afterwards at the ducal court of Königsberg, where he became music dir. In 1540 he pub. a Lutheran service book, containing a Mass, a Magnificat and hymns, some comp. by himself.

Kuhlau, (Daniel) Frederik (Rudolph) (b Ülzen, Hanover, 11 Sep 1786; d Copenhagen, 12 Mar 1832), Danish composer of German origin. A child of poor parents, he picked up musical knowledge at Brunswick and Hamburg. During the Fr. occupation he went to Den. to escape conscription and became flautist in the court orch. at Copenhagen. In 1825 he visited Vienna and met Beethoven, who comp. a punning canon on his name.

Works incl. operas *Røverborgen* (1814), *Trylleharpen* (1817); *Lulu* (1824) and several others; incid. music for Heiberg's *Elverhøj* (1828); pf. works; fl. pieces.

Kuhlmann, Kathleen (b San Francisco, 7 Dec 1950), American mezzo. She studied in Chicago and first sang at the Lyric Opera there in 1979. In 1980 she sang Meg Page at La Scala, Milan, and in 1982 Charlotte and Rosina in Cologne and Ino and Juno in *Semele* at CG. The following year sang Cenerentola at Glyndebourne and in 1985 Penelope in the fp of Henze's reconstruction of Monteverdi's *Il Ritorno di Ulisse*, at Salzburg. Returned to CG in 1986 as Rosina.

Kuhnau, Johann (b Geising, Saxony, 6 Apr 1660; d Leipzig, 5 Jun 1722), German organist, harpsichordist, composer and writer on music. Cantor at Zittau, went to Leipzig in 1682; became organist at St Thomas's Church in 1684, music director of the univ. and the churches of St Nicholas and St Thomas in 1700, and cantor of St Thomas's in 1701, in which post he preceded Bach. His biblical sonatas for harpsichord are early exs. of programme music.

Other works incl. motets on hymn-tunes and other church music; partitas and other pieces for harpsichord, incl. 7 sonatas entitled *Frische Clavier-Früchte*, and the 6 sonatas *Biblische Historien* (1700).

Kühnel, August (b Delmenhorst, 3 Aug 1645; d c 1700) German vla. da gamba player and composer. He was in the court chapel of Zeitz, 1661–81, visited Fr. in 1665 to study the players there, played at var. Ger. courts on his return, visited London in 1685 and was subsequently *Kapellmeister* at the court of Kassel. He wrote sonatas for his instrument.

Kuijken, Sigiswald (b Dilbeck, nr. Brussels, 16 Feb 1944), Belgian conductor and violinist. He studied at the Brussels Cons.; has taught Baroque violin at Hague Cons. since 1971. Co-founder of La Petite Bande, 1971; perfs. of Handel, Rameau, Haydn and Bach.

His ens. The Age of Enlightenment gave its 1st London concert in 1986. His brothers are **Wieland K.** (b 1938), a cellist and viola da gamba player, and **Barthold K.** (b 1949) a flautist and recorder player.

Kulenkampff, Georg (b Bremen, 23 Jul 1898; d Schaffhausen, 4 Oct 1948), German violinist. He studied in Berlin and taught there from 1923. Leader Bremen PO 1916, followed by distinguished career as soloist. He recorded the Beethoven concerto, and partnered Georg Solti in recordings of the sonatas. His memoirs were pub. posthumously.

Kullak, Theodor (b Krotoschin, Posen, 12 Sep 1818; d Berlin, 1 Mar 1882), German pianist and composer. He was intended for the law and at some time studied medicine, but in 1842 decided definitely in favour of music and went to Vienna to finish his pf. studies with Czerny. In 1846 he became court pianist to the King of Prus. and settled in Berlin, founding a Cons. with Stern and Marx there, 1850, and one of his own in 1855.

Works incl. pf. concerto in C min.; pf. trio; duets for pf. and vln.; a vast number of pf. pieces, studies.

Kullervo, symph. poem by Sibelius for soloists, chorus and orch., based on legends from the *Kalevala*. Withdrawn after its fp in Helsinki on 28 Apr 1892 and not heard again until after S.'s death in 1957.

Kullman, Charles (b New Haven, Conn., 13 Jan 1903; d New Haven, 8 Feb 1983), American tenor. He studied in NY and in 1931 sang Pinkerton under Klemperer at the Kroll Opera, Berlin; Staatsoper 1932–5. London, CG, 1934–8. Salzburg 1934–6 as Ferrando, Belmonte and Walther. NY Met 1935–60 as Faust, Fenton, Tamino, Tannhäuser and Parsifal. Took part in Walter's 1936 recording of *Das Lied von der Erde*.

Kunst der Fuge, Die (*The Art of Fugue*), Bach's last work, left unfinished at his death in 1750. A series of exs. of the art of fugal and canonic writing, all based on the same theme. *See* **Per Arsin et Thesin.**

Kunz, Erich (b Vienna, 20 May 1909), Austrian bass baritone. Studied in Vienna and made his debut in 1933 in Breslau. He sang in the Glyndebourne chorus in 1935, returned 1948 as Guglielmo. Vienna from 1940; sang Beckmesser at Bayreuth in 1943. He was one of the finest *buffo* baritones of the day, Mozart's Figaro and Papageno being among his most famous roles.

Kunzen, Friedrich Ludwig Aemilius (b Lübeck, 24 Sep 1761; d Copenhagen, 28 Jan

1817), German conductor and composer. Pupil of his father, Adolph Karl K. (1720–81). Having given up legal studies, he went to the Copenhagen Opera, where he prod. his 1st work. After a period in Berlin, where he ed. a music journal with Reichardt, he went as cond. to Frankfurt, 1792, and Prague, 1794, prod. his only Ger. opera at the former city. He returned to Copenhagen 1795 as dir. of the Opera.

Works incl. operas *Holger Danske* (1789), *Ossians Harfe, Hemmeligheden* (1796), *Dragedukken* (1797), *Erik Ejegod* (1798), *Min Bedstemoder, Kærlighed paa Landet, Stormen* (on Shakespeare's *Tempest*).

Kupper, Annelies (b Glatz, 21 Aug 1906), German soprano. Debut Breslau 1935. Hamburg 1940–6. Bayreuth 1944, Eva. Munich 1946–61. Sang in *The Rape of Lucretia* at Salzburg in 1950 and in 1952 the title role in the 1st official prod. of Strauss's *Die Liebe der Danae*. Other roles incl. Elsa, Senta and Chrysothemis (CG 1953).

Kurt, Melanie (b Vienna, 8 Jan 1880; d New York, 11 Mar 1941), Austrian soprano. Debut Lübeck, 1902, Leonore. Sang in Brunswick and Berlin 1905–14. CG 1910–14 as Brünnhilde, and Kundry in the 1st London stage perf. of *Parsifal*. NY Met 1915–17 as Isolde, Pamina and Gluck's Taurean Iphigénie.

Kurtág, György (b Lugoj, Rumania, 19 Feb 1926), Hungarian composer. He studied in Budapest and Paris; early influences were Bartók and Kodály, later employed serial technique.

Works incl. string 4tet (1959); 8 Duets for violin and cimbalom (1961); *In Memory of a Winter Sunset*, for sop., vln. and cimbalom (1969), string 5tet (1971); *Splinters*, for solo cimbalom (1975); *Homage to Luigi Nono*, for chamber ens. (1980).

Kurz, Selma (b Bielitz, Silesia, 15 Oct 1874; d Vienna, 10 May 1933), Austrian coloratura soprano. Studied with Pless, making her debut at the Frankfurt opera. In 1899 Mahler engaged her at the Vienna Hofoper and she remained with that co. until 1926; her roles incl. Tosca, Eva, Sieglinde, Oscar and Violetta. She 1st sang in London in 1904 as Gilda. In 1916 she sang Zerbinetta in the revision of *Ariadne auf Naxos*.

Kurzwellen (*Shortwaves*), work by Stockhausen for electronics and 4 short wave radios; fp Bremen, 5 May 1968. Developed as *Beethausen, opus 1970, von Stockhoven*.

Kusche, Benno (b Freiburg, 30 Jan 1916), German bass-baritone. Debut Koblenz, 1938, as Renato. Sang in Augsburg during war, Munich from 1946; London, CG, 1953 as La Roche in the 1st Brit. perf. of *Capriccio*. He sang Beckmesser at Bayreuth, and on his NY Met debut, in 1971.

Kusnetzova, Maria (b Odessa, 1880; d Paris, 26 Apr 1966), Russian soprano and dancer. St Petersburg, Maryinsky Theatre, 1905–13 as Tatyana, Oxana, Juliette; created Rimsky-Korsakov's Fevronia (*Kitezh*, 1907). London, CG, 1909–10 as Mimi and Marguerite. Danced Potiphar's Wife in the fp of Strauss's ballet *Josephslegende*, Paris 1914.

Kusser (or **Cousser**), **Johann Sigismund** (b Pressburg = Pozsony, 13 Feb 1660; d Dublin, Nov 1727), German conductor and composer. Pupil of Lully in Paris, where he lived from 1674 to 1682. He was one of the dirs. of the Hamburg Opera from 1694 to 1696, and *Kapellmeister* at Stuttgart from 1700 to 1704. He went to London in 1705, and later to Dublin, where he became director of music to the viceroy.

Works incl. operas *Erindo* (1694), *Porus, Pyramus and Thisbe* (1694), *Scipio Africanus, Jason* and *Ariadne* (1692); serenade for the king's birthday; ode on the death of Arabella Hunt; suites (with overtures) for strings; collection of opera overtures and airs.

Kutchka (Rus. = handful; short for *mogutchaya kutchka* = the mighty handful), the group of 5 Rus. comps. who under the leadership of Balakirev began a conscious campaign in favour of nationalist music based on folk music. The other members of the group were Borodin, Cui, Mussorgsky and Rimsky-Korsakov.

Kvapil, Jaroslav (b Fryšták, Morav., 21 Apr 1892; d Brno, 18 Feb 1958), Czech composer. Studied with Janáček at Brno and was later app. prof. of org. and counterpoint at the Org. School there. In 1911–13 he continued studying at the Leipzig Cons., and on his return to Brno became prof. of pf. and comp. at the Cons. and cond. of the Phil Society.

Works incl. 4 symphs., variations and fugue for orch.; cantata for baritone solo, chorus and orch.; 6 string 4tets, pf. 5tet, pf. trio; 2 vln. and pf. sonatas, cello and pf. sonata; pf. sonata and pieces; songs, etc.

Kwella, Patrizia (b Mansfield, 26 Apr 1953), British soprano of Polish–Italian parentage. She studied at the RCM and appeared with John Eliot Gardiner at the 1979 Promenade concerts; later sang with Richard Hickox, Christopher Hogwood and

Kynaston

Trevor Pinnock. Much valued for her Handel (as Esther and in *Alcina*, *L'Allegro* and *La Resurrezione*), Bach (B minor Mass) and Monteverdi (*Orfeo*). US debut San Diego 1983. At the 1985 Aldeburgh Festival she sang in the fp of *Night's Mask*, by Colin Matthews.

Kynaston, Nicolas (b Morebath, Devon, 10 Dec 1941), English organist. He studied with Fernando Germani and Ralph Downes; Westminster Cathedral 1960–71. Solo debut London 1966; toured US 1974. Well known in Franck, Messiaen and Reger.

Kyrie (Gk., *Kyrie eleison* = 'Lord, have mercy'). The 1st item of the Ordinary of the Mass. Orig. it was not part of the Mass but of var. Litanies, at the head of which it still stands. In the Mass it has a 9-fold structure, and the simplest melodic form consisted of 8 repetitions of a simple melody followed by a quite different melody for the 9th clause (*see* illustration).

1.2.3. Ky - ri - e - le - i - son.   9.Ky - ri - e   •   le - i - son.
4.5.6.Chri-ste - e - le - i - son.
7.8.   Ky - ri - e - le - i - son.

KYRIE

This melody closely resembles that still used for the Litany Kyries for Rogationtide and Holy Saturday. Other musical forms in common use were: *aaa bbb aaa'*; *aaa bbb ccc'*; and *aba cdc efe'* (a stroke represents an extended form of the phrase concerned).

L

l, the submediant note in any key in Tonic Sol-fa notation, pronounced Lah.

La, the old name for the note A (*see* **Solmization**), still used in Lat. countries, and in Tonic Sol-fa notation the submediant note in any key, repres. by the symbol l, pronounced Lah.

La Borde, Jean Benjamin de (b Paris, 5 Sep 1734; d Paris, 22 Jul 1794), French author and composer. Pupil of Rameau for comp., chamberlain to Louis XV. He died on the scaffold during the Revolution.

Works incl. 32 operas, e.g. *Le Chat perdu et retrouvé* (1769), songs with vln. and bass, songs with pf. He wrote books incl. an *Essai sur la musique ancienne et moderne.*

La Grotte, Nicolas de (b *c* 1530; d *c* 1600), French composer and keyboard-player. He pub. settings of Ronsard in 1569 and examples of *musique mesurée à l'antique*. In 1583 he pub. with Le Jeune pieces for the *Balet comique de la Royne.*

La Guerre (*née* **Jacquet**), **Elisabeth Claude de** (b Paris, ? 1664; d Paris, 27 Jun 1729), French harpsichordist and composer. A pupil of her father, she showed early promise and attracted the patronage of Louis XIV and later Mme. de Montespan. She married the comp. Marin La Guerre in 1687.

Works incl. opera *Céphale et Procris* (1694); cantatas; *Te Deum* and other church music; vln. sonatas, trio sonatas, harpsichord music.

La Guerre, Michel de (b Paris, *c* 1605; d Paris, buried 13 Nov 1679), French organist and composer, father-in-law of prec. Organist of the Sainte-Chapelle in Paris, 1633–79. His 2 sons, Jérôme (*c* 1654–?) and Marin (1658–1704) were both organists and composers; the latter married Elisabeth Jacquet.

Works incl. opera *Le Triomphe de l'Amour sur des bergers et bergères; airs de cour.*

La Halle (or **La Hale**), **Adam de** (b ? Arras, *c* 1230; d Naples, before 1288), French poet and composer. Educ. for the priesthood, but fell in love and married a young girl, whom he left to retire to Douai in 1263 (?) to rejoin the Church. In 1282 he went to Naples with the Comte d'Artois.

Works incl. stage pieces *Le Jeu d'Adam, ou de la feuillée* and *Le Jeu de Robin et de Marion* (1285); motets; *chansons.*

La Hèle (or **Helle**), **Georges de** (b Antwerp, 1547; d Madrid, 27 Aug 1586), Flemish composer. Chorister at the royal chapel in Madrid in his youth. Choirmaster at Tournai Cathedral in 1578, but prob. back in Spain by 1580. He obtained 2 prizes at the Puy de Musique at Évreux in 1576.

Works (some destroyed in a fire at Madrid in 1734) incl. Masses, motets; *chansons.*

La Pouplinière (or **Poupelinière**), **Alexandre Jean Joseph le Riche de** (b Chinon, 26 Jul 1693; d Paris, 5 Dec 1762), French music patron. He was farmer-general of taxes and amassed a huge fortune. He kept a private orch., had Rameau living in his house for several years and studied under him, and patronized a number of other comps. and perfs, incl. Mondonville.

La Rue, Jan (b Kisaran, Sumatra, 31 Jul 1918), American musicologist of Indonesian birth. He studied at Harvard and Princeton; NY Univ. from 1957. He has written partic. about style analysis and 18th-cent. music, with a special emphasis on objectively verifiable conclusions.

La Rue, Pierre de (b ? Tournai, *c* 1460; d Courtrai, 20 Nov 1518), Flemish composer. Pupil of Ockeghem, in the service by turns of the court of Burgundy, Charles V and Margaret of Aus. when governor of the Netherlands. He was app. prebendary of Courtrai and later of Namur.

Works incl. 31 Masses, Requiem, 38 motets; *chansons.*

La Scala. *See* **Scala.**

Labbette, Dora (b Purley, 4 Mar 1898; d Purley, 3 Sep 1984), English soprano. She studied at the GSM and from 1917 her career was in oratorios and song recitals. Opera debut Oxford, 1934, as Telaire in Rameau's *Castor et Pollux.* Mimi was the role of her 1st and last appearances in London (CG, 1935, and SW, 1943). She sang Mimi, Desdemona and Mignon in Ger. and Fr. in the late 1930s. Other roles incl. Marguerite, Mélisande and Delius's Vreli. She was persuaded by Beecham to adopt the stage name Lisa Perli (Purley = Perli).

Labèque, Katia and **Marielle** (b Hendaye, 3 Mar 1950 and 6 Mar 1952 respectively), French piano duo. Studied at the Paris Cons. Well known in standard repertory and in works by Boulez, Lutosławski and Messiaen.

Labia, Maria (b Verona, 14 Feb 1880; d Malcesine del Garda, 11 Feb 1953), Italian soprano. She sang in Milan and Stockholm before joining the Komische Oper Berlin in 1906; debut as Tosca and distinguished as

Mimi, Thaïs, and Carmen. Manhattan Opera 1908–10. She sang Salome at La Scala in 1913 and was the 1st European Giorgetta (Rome, 1919). Retired 1936; taught in Warsaw and It. from 1930. Her sister **Fausta** (1870–1935) was heard in Italy and Spain 1892–1912 as Eva, Sieglinde and Brünnhilde.

Labinsky, Andrey (b Kharkov, 26 Jul 1871; d Moscow, 8 Aug 1941), Russian tenor. He sang at the Maryinsky Theatre St Petersburg 1897–1911; created Vsevold in Rimsky-Korsakov's *Kitezh* (1907) and was admired as Lohengrin, Sinodal in *The Demon* and Don José. Bolshoy 1912–24; taught in Moscow from 1920.

Lablache, Luigi (b Naples, 6 Dec 1794; d Naples, 23 Jan 1858), Italian bass, of French descent. Made his debut at the Teatro San Carlo, Naples in 1812; sang Dandini at La Scala in 1817. Paris from 1830 and created there Lord Walton in *I Puritani* (1835) and Don Pasquale (1843). London 1830–55 as Leporello, Pollione and Bartolo. At Vienna in 1827 he sang in Mozart's Requiem, for Beethoven's funeral service.

Labroca, Mario (b Rome, 22 Nov 1896; d Rome, 1 Jul 1973), Italian critic and composer. Pupil of Respighi and Malipiero. Critic of *Il Lavoro fascista* and *L'Idea nazionale*, superintendent of the Teatro Vittorio Emanuele at Florence and organizer of the *Maggio musicale*.

Works incl. *Stabat Mater* (1935), *Il lamento dei mariti e delle mogli* for 6 voices and small orch; symph. for pf. and small orch.; 3 string 4tets, pf. trio; sonata for vln. and pf., suite for vln. and pf.; pieces; songs.

Labuński, Feliks Roderyk (b Ksawerynówo, 27 Dec 1892; d Cincinnati, 28 Apr 1979), Polish, later American, composer. Studied at Warsaw and with Dukas and Nadia Boulanger in Paris. He founded a society of Pol. musicians there and later went to live in USA.

Works incl. symph. and *Pastoral Triptych* for orch. (1931); concertino for pf. and orch.; string 4tet; divertimento for fl. and pf.; *Olympic Hymn* for chorus and orch.; *The Birds* for voice and orch. (1934), Polish Cantata, for solo voices and chorus (1932); pf. pieces; songs.

Lac des cygnes (Tchaikovsky). *See* **Swan Lake.**

Lächerliche Prinz Jodelet, Der (*The Ridiculous Prince J.*), opera by Keiser (lib. by J.P. Praetorius, based on P. Scarron's comedy, *Jodelet, ou Le Maître valet*), prod. Hamburg, Theater beim Gänsemarkt, 1726.

Lachner, German family of musicians:
1. Theodor L. (b Rain, Bavaria, 1788; d Munich, 23 May 1877), organist and conductor. He was the eldest son and pupil of an organist at Rain o/Lech and became organist at Munich, also chorus-master at the court theatre.
2. Thekla L. (b Rain, *c* 1800; d ? Augsburg), organist, sister of prec. Pupil of her father, became organist at Augsburg.
3. Franz L. (b Rain, 2 Apr 1803; d Munich, 20 Jan 1890), conductor and composer, brother of prec. Pupil of his father and later of Stadler and Sechter in Vienna, where he became a friend of Schubert. App. asst. cond. at the Kärntnertortheater there, 1826, and succeeded Weigl as chief cond. 1827. In 1834 he went to Mannheim as opera cond. and in 1836 to Munich as court music director.

Works incl. operas *Die Bürgschaft* (on Schiller's poem, 1828), *Alidia* (1839), *Catarina Cornaro* (1841) and *Benvenuto Cellini* (1849); oratorios *Moses* and *Die vier Menshcenalter* (1829); Requiem, 3 Masses; cantatas and other choral works; 8 symphs.; harp and bassoon concertos; 6 string 4tets, nonet for wind insts., trios and other chamber music, pf. pieces; songs.

4. Christiane L. (b Rain, 1805; d Rain), organist, sister of prec. She studied under her father and succeeded him as organist at Rain o/Lech.
5. Ignaz L. (b Rain, 11 Sep 1807; d Hanover, 24 Feb 1895), conductor and composer, brother of prec. Studied under his father and at Augsburg, joined his brother Franz in Vienna, 1824, became asst. cond. at the Kärntnertortheater there, 1825, app. court music director at Stuttgart, 1831, and at Munich, 1842, jointly with Franz. Later he filled var. posts at Hamburg, Stockholm and Frankfurt.

Works incl. operas *Der Geisterturm* (1837), *Die Regenbrüder* (1839) and *Loreley* (1846); ballets and melodramas; Masses; symph.; string 4tets; pf. music; songs.
6. Vincenz L. (b Rain, 19 Jul 1811; d Karlsruhe, 22 Jan 1893), conductor and composer, brother of prec. Studied with his father and at Augsburg. He became organist in Vienna, 1834, and was court music director at Mannheim, 1836–73. He retired to Karlsruhe, where he taught at the Cons.

Works incl. incid. music to Schiller's adaptation of Gozzi's *Turandot*; part-songs, songs.

Lachrimae, John Downland's collection of

21 dances for five bowed insts. with lute (London, 1604). Its opening pavan, *Lachrimae antiquae*, is a version of his song *Flow my teares* (1st pub. 1600), though in its orig. form it was probably a pavan for solo lute. In the early 17th cent. the piece appeared in many other arrs. for different ensembles and by different hands, usually with the title *Lachrimae*.

Lachrymae, work for vla. and pf. by Britten, 'Reflections on a song of John Dowland'; comp. 1950, fp Aldeburgh, 20 Jun 1950. Arr. for vla. and string orch. 1976, fp Recklinghausen, 3 May 1977.

Lacy, John (d Devonshire, c 1865), English bass. Pupil of Rauzzini at Bath. He sang in London with success at an early age and went to It., settling in London afterwards, except for a period spent at Calcutta, 1818–26, with his wife.

Lacy, Michael Rophino (b Bilbao, 19 Jul 1795; d London, 20 Sep 1867), Irish violinist. Learnt music as a child in Spain, was sent to school at Bordeaux, 1802, and in 1803 went to Paris to finish his training with R. Kreutzer. He 1st appeared in Paris, 1804, and London, 1805. He played with success for many years there as well as at Liverpool, Edinburgh, Glasgow, Dublin, etc., and made a number of tasteless adaptations of operas and oratorios by var. comps. He was an early Handel scholar and collab. with Schoelcher.

Lady Macbeth of the Mtsensk District (*L.M. Mtsenskago Uyezda*), opera by Shostakovich (lib. by A. Preis and comp., based on a novel by N.S. Leskov), prod. Moscow, 22 Jan 1934. Very successful at first, but afterwards discountenanced as decadent by the Soviet Government. Revised as *Katerina Izmailova* and prod. 1963.

Lady of the Lake, The, songs by Schubert set to Ger. transs. from Scott's poem by P.A. Storck in 1825 and pub. in 1826 as op. 52. 1. Ellen's 1st song, 'Soldier, rest!'; 2. Ellen's 2nd song, 'Huntsman, rest!'; 3. Ellen's 3rd song, 'Ave Maria'; 4. Norman's song, 'The heath this night'; 5. Lay of the Imprisoned Huntsman, 'My hawk is tired'. Op. 52 contains 2 more poems from Scott's work, *Boating Song* for male chorus and *Coronach* for female chorus.

Laffitte, Léon (b Saint-Genies, 28 Jan 1875; d Paris, Sep 1938), French tenor. Debut Paris, Opéra, 1898 as David; sang Mime there in the 1st French perf. of *Siegfried*, 1908. Brussels 1899–1914; was heard there and at CG in 1906 as Jean in *Le Jongleur de Notre Dame*. Buenos Aires 1916; returned

Paris 1923, as Samson and the Berlioz Faust.

Lafont, Charles Philippe (b Paris, 1 Dec 1781; d nr. Tarbes, 23 Aug 1839), French violinist, singer and composer. He was at 1st taught by his mother, a sister of the violinist Berthaume, and he travelled to Ger. with his uncle as a child, playing there with success. Later he studied with R. Kreutzer in Paris, appeared as a ballad singer at the Théâtre Feydeau, completed his vln. studies with Rode and went on tour in 1801–8. In 1808–15 he was solo violinist to the Tsar in St Petersburg, and then received a similar appt. from Louis XVIII. In 1831–9 he made long tours with Herz, cut short by a carriage accident that caused his death.

Works incl. 2 operas; 7 vln. concertos; duets for vln. and pf. written with Kalkbrenner, Herz and others; more than 200 songs.

Lah, the name for the submediant note in any key in Tonic Sol-fa, so pronounced, but in notation represented by the symbol l.

Lai (Fr., later Eng. *lay*), a medieval lyrical poem in pairs of stanzas in different metrical forms; also the music set to such poems.

Laidlaw, Robena Anna (b Bretton, Yorks., 30 Apr 1819; d London, 29 May 1901), English pianist. Pupil of Herz and L. Berger. Played with much success on the Continent. App. court pianist to the Queen of Hanover, 1840. Schumann ded. his *Fantasiestücke*, op. 12, to her.

Lajtha, László (b Budapest, 30 Jun 1892; d Budapest, 16 Feb 1963), Hungarian folksong expert and composer. Studied at the Music High School at Budapest, specialized in folk music and joined the folklore dept. of the Nat. Museum in 1913. Prof. at the Budapest Cons., 1919–49.

Works incl. 3 ballets incl. *Lysistrata* (1933) and *Capriccio* (1944); 2 Masses and other choral works; 10 symphs. (1936–61); vln. concerto; 10 string 4tets and other chamber music; sonatas for vln., cello and pf., etc.

Lakmé, opera by Delibes (lib. by E. Gondinet and P. Gille), prod. Paris, Opéra-Comique, 14 Apr 1883.

Lalande, Henriette-Clémentine. See **Méric-Lalande.**

Lalande, Michel (Richard) de (b Paris, 15 Dec 1657; d Versailles, 18 Jun 1726), French organist and composer. He learnt music as a chorister at the church of Saint-Germainl'Auxerrois in Paris and taught himself the vln., bass viol and harpsichord. On being refused admission to Lully's orch., he took to the organ and secured organist's appts. at

3 churches. He failed to obtain the post of court organist, but was given charge of the princesses' musical educ. and in 1683 was app. one of the superintendents of the royal chapel. He became master of the royal chapel in 1704. In 1684 he married the court singer Anne Rebel, who died in 1722, and in 1723 he married again, Mlle. de Cury, daughter of one of the court surgeons.

Works incl. ballets and opera-ballets *Ballet de la jeunesse* (1686), *Le Palais de Flore* (1689), *Adonis* (1696), *Myrtil et Mélicerte* (1698), *Les Fées* (1699), *L'Amour fléchi par la Constance*, *L'Hymen champêtre* (1700), *Ballet de la Paix*, *Les Folies de Cardenio* (from Cervantes's *Don Quixote*, 1720), *Ballet de l'inconnu*, *Les Éléments* (with Destouches, 1725), *L'Amour berger*, *Églogue, ou Pastorale en musique*, *Les Fontaines de Versailles*; 42 motets with orchestral accomp.; cantata *Le Concert d'Esculape*; 3 Leçons des Ténèbres, Miserere for solo voice; music for the royal table.

Lalla-Roukh, opera by F. David (lib. by H. Lucas and M. Carré, based on Moore's *Lalla Rookh*), prod. Paris, Opéra-Comique, 12 May 1862.

Lallouette, Jean François (b Paris, 1651; d Paris, 31 Aug 1728), French violinist and composer. He studied vln. with Guy Leclerc and comp. with Lully. From 1668 to 1677 he was violinist and cond. at the Opéra, but Lully dismissed him for claiming collaboration in his *Isis*, which may have been true, for he was said to have often assisted Lully. In 1693 he became *maître de chapelle* at Rouen Cathedral, in 1695 at Notre-Dame at Versailles, and in 1700 at Notre Dame in Paris.

Works incl. dramatic interludes and ballets; Masses, motets, Misereres.

Lalo, (Victor Antoine) Édouard (b Lille, 27 Jan 1823; d Paris, 22 Apr 1892), French composer of Spanish descent. He 1st studied vln. and cello at the Lille Cons. and then vln. at that of Paris, taking comp. lessons privately at the same time. In 1855 he became vla. in the Armingaud-Jacquard 4tet. He wrote little until 1865, the year of his marriage to Mlle. Bernier de Maligny, who sang his songs in public. Gradually his success grew both in the opera-house and the concert-room.

Works incl. operas *Fiesque* (after Schiller, comp. 1866–7), *Le Roi d'Ys* (1888), *La Jacquerie* (unfinished, completed by Coquard, perf. 1895); pantomime with choruses *Néron*; ballet *Namouna* (1882); symph. in G min. (1886), *Divertissement*, *Rhapsodie norvégienne* and scherzo for

orch., 2 aubades for small orch., concerto, *Symphonie espagnole* (1874), *Fantaisie norvégienne* (1878), *Romance-Sérénade* (1879) and *Concerto russe* (1879) for vln. and orch., concertos for pf. and for cello.

String 4tet (later revised as No. 2), 3 pf. trios; vln. and pf. sonata and a number of pieces, cello and pf. sonata and pieces; *La Mère et l'enfant* for pf. duet; over 30 songs and 2 vocal duets; church music.

Lambe, Walter (b Salisbury, *c* 1452; d ? *c* 1500), English composer. He was King's Scholar at Eton in 1467 (aged 15), and clerk at St George's, Windsor, from 1479 to 1499 or later, acting as master of the choristers (at first jointly with William Edmunds), 1480–4. His known music was all incl. in the Eton Choirbook: it consists of a Magnificat and 5 votive antiphons (a 6th can be completed from another MS.; another is partially lost and 4 more completely so.)

Lambert, Constant (b London, 23 Aug 1905; d London, 21 Aug 1951), English composer, conductor and critic. Son of the painter George Washington L. Studied at the RCM in London. Diaghilev commissioned a ballet from him when he was still a student and prod. it at Monte Carlo in 1926. He began to make his mark as a cond. of ballet with the Camargo Society and was later engaged to cond. ballet at SW Theatre, with which he appeared in Paris in 1937, having already cond. at the ISCM Festival at Amsterdam, 1933. He also became a concert cond., was for a time music critic to the *Referee* and pub. a book of criticism, *Music Ho!*

Works incl. ballets *Romeo and Juliet* (Monte Carlo, 1926), *Pomona* (Buenos Aires, 1927), *Horoscope* (London, 1938); incid. music for Shakespeare's *Hamlet*; music for films *Merchant Seamen* and *Anna Karenina* (after Tolstoy); *Summer's Last Will and Testament* (Nash), masque for baritone solo, chorus and orch. (1932–5); *The Rio Grande* for pf., orch. and chorus (1927); dirge in Shakespeare's *Cymbeline* for voices and orch.; *Music for Orch.*, *Aubade héroïque* for small orch.; concerto for pf. and chamber orch.; pf. sonata; 4 poems by Li-Po for voice and pf.

Lambert, Michel (b Champigny-sur-Veude, *c* 1610; d Paris, 29 Jun 1696), French lutenist, singer and composer. He was master of the royal chamber music and in 1663 became master of the children in the royal chapel. Lully married his daughter Madeleine. He wrote songs to the lute.

Lambertini, Giovanni Tomaso (b Bologna,

Italian 16th-17th cent. priest and composer. Singer at San Petronio at Bologna, 1548–73. From 1573 active in Rome.

Works incl. penitential psalms and other church music; madrigals, *villotte*.

Lamentatione, name (apparently authentic) given to Haydn's symph. no. 26 in D min., comp. *c* 1768, on account of the use it makes of a chant associated with the Lamentations of Jeremiah.

Lamentations, the L.s of Jeremiah used in the Roman Catholic service at matins in Holy Week; orig. sung in plainsong and still surviving in that form, but from the early 16th cent. also used in polyphonic settings.

Lamento (It. = lament), a plaintive aria in early 17th-cent. Italian opera conventionally placed before the tragic culmination of the plot. The best known ex. is the *Lamento d'Arianna*, the only surviving fragment from Monteverdi's *Arianna*.

Lammers, Gerda (b Berlin, 25 Sep 1915), German soprano. After study in Berlin sang until 1955 in Lieder and concert; her stage debut, at Bayreuth, was followed by an engagement at Kassel (1955–70); debut as Marie, other roles incl. Senta, Alceste, Isolde and Brünnhilde. London, CG, 1957, as Elektra; Kundry 1959. NY Met debut Mar 1962, as Elektra. She also sang Medea and Purcell's Dido and recorded Hindemith's song cycle *Das Marienleben*.

Lamond, Frederic (b Glasgow, 28 Jan 1868; d Stirling, 21 Feb 1948), Scottish pianist. Studied pf., organ and vln. at home and after becoming a church organist went to the Raff Cons. at Frankfurt in 1882. Although he wished to become a comp. he studied pf. further with Bülow and Liszt, making his debut in Berlin in 1885. In Brit. he first played in 1886, at Glasgow and London. He toured widely, but mainly in Ger., and from 1904, when he married the actress Irene Triesch, he had his home in Berlin. It was not until the 1939–45 war that he settled in London.

Lamoureux, Charles (b Bordeaux, 28 Sep 1834; d Paris, 21 Dec 1899), French violinist and conductor. Studied vln. and theory at the Paris Cons., joined a theatre orch., then played at the Opéra, in 1860 helped to found a chamber music society for the intro. of new works, cond. choral works by Bach, Handel and others in the 1870s, became cond. at the Opéra and in 1881 founded the Concerts Lamoureux, at which he made a great deal of orchestral music, incl. Wagner, known to a wide public. Toured Russia 1893; regular concerts in London from 1896.

Lampe, Johann Friedrich (John Frederick) (b Saxony, 1703; d Edinburgh, 25 Jul 1751), German bassoonist and composer. Went to England from Brunswick about 1725 and settled in London, but went to Dublin in 1748 and to Edinburgh in 1750. Married Isabella Young, sister of T.A. Arne's wife.

Works incl. burlesque operas *The Dragon of Wantley*(1757) and *Margery, or A Worse Plague than the Dragon* (1738; libs. by Carey), mock opera *Pyramus and Thisbe* (from Shakespeare's *Midsummer Night's Dream*, 1745), masque *The Sham Conjurer* (1741); music for Carey's *Amelia; c* 10 other stage works; cantata to celebrate the suppression of the Stuart rebellion; songs.

Lamperti, Francesco (b Savona, 11 Mar 1813; d Como, 1 May 1892), Italian teacher of singing. Master of many eminent singers and author of vocal studies and a treatise on singing.

Lampugnani, Giovanni Battista (b Milan, 1706; d Milan, 1786), Italian composer. Studied in Naples, and made his debut as an opera comp. there in 1732. Successful throughout It., he went to London in 1743 to take over from Galuppi the opera at the King's Theatre, but later returned to Milan. From 1779 he was *maestro al cembalo* at the Teatro alla Scala.

Works incl. *c* 30 operas, e.g. *Semiramide* (1741), *Rossane, Tigrane* (1747), *Artaserse, Siroe* (1755), *L'amor contadino* (1760), etc.; also trio sonatas, church music.

Lancelot and Elaine, symph. poem no. 2 by MacDowell, op. 25, based on the Arthurian legend, comp. 1888.

Landarzt, Ein (*A Country Doctor*), radio opera by Henze after the story by Kafka; broadcast Hamburg, 29 Nov 1951; rev. for Dietrich Fischer-Dieskau as a monodrama, 1964; fp Berlin, 12 Oct 1965. Radio opera rev. for stage 1964, fp Frankfurt, 30 Nov 1965.

Landi, Stefano (b Rome, *c* 1586; d Rome, 28 Oct 1639), Italian singer and composer. He was *maestro di cappella* at Padua about 1620 and in Rome from 1624, and sang alto in the Papal Chapel from 1630.

Works incl. operas *La morte d'Orfeo* (1619) and *Il Sant' Alessio* (1631); Masses and psalms; madrigals and cantatas; arias for 1 voice.

Landini (or **Landino**), **Francesco** (b ? Fiesole, *c* 1325; d Florence, 2 Sep 1397), Italian organist, lutenist, composer and poet. Although blind from early childhood, he perfected himself on var. instruments, in particular the portative organ, and became organist of the church of San Lorenzo at Florence (1369–96). He is one of the chief exponents of the It. Ars nova.

Works incl. madrigals, *ballate*, etc.

Landini Sixth, a cadence in music of the 14th and 15th cents. named after the prec., of whose vocal works it is a feature, e.g.:

The idiom is not confined to Italian music nor is there any evidence to suggest that Landini invented it.

Ländler, an Austrian country dance having the character of a slow waltz. Mozart, Beethoven and Schubert left many exs.

Landon, H(oward) C(handler) Robbins (b Boston, Mass., 6 Mar 1926), American musicologist. He studied at Swarthmore Coll. and Boston Univ. Since 1947 he has lived in Europe. He has devoted himself particularly to the study of late 18th-cent. music and has pub. a number of articles and books, incl. *The Symphonies of Joseph Haydn* (1955), *The Collected Correspondence and London Notebooks of Joseph Haydn* and *Haydn: Chronicle and Works*, 5 vols. (1976–80), as well as eds. of numerous works by Haydn, incl. several operas and the complete symphs. He has pub. books on Beethoven (1970) and Mozart as a Mason (1983), and also in 1983 edited recently discovered material for Handel's Roman Vespers.

Landowska, Wanda (b Warsaw, 5 Jul 1877; d Lakeville, Conn., 16 Aug 1959), Polish harpsichordist, pianist and music research scholar. She toured widely and settled in Fr., where in 1927 she opened a school for the study of early music at Saint-Leu-la-Forêt, nr. Paris. From 1941 she lived in the USA. She wrote books and articles on aspects of old music. Falla's harpsichord concerto (1923–6) and Poulenc's *Concert Champêtre* (1927–8) were comp. for her.

Lane, Gloria (b Trenton, 6 Jun 1930), American mezzo. Debut Philadelphia 1950, in the fp of Menotti's *The Consul*; 1954 on Broadway in the fp of *The Saint of Bleecker Street*. Glyndebourne 1958–63 as Baba the Turk and Dorabella; returned 1972 for Ariadne and Lady Macbeth. CG 1960, Carmen. Guest at Vienna, Paris and Florence; Santuzza at NY City Opera, 1971.

Lang, Paul Henry, (b Budapest, 28 Aug 1901), American musicologist of Hungarian

birth. In 1924 he went to the Univ. of Paris and 4 years later, with a scholarship, to USA. He became prof. of musicology at Columbia Univ. in NY in 1939. In 1945 he became ed. of the *Musical Quarterly*. Among his writings are *Music in Western Civilization* (1941) and *George Frideric Handel* (1966).

Langdon, Michael (b Wolverhampton, 12 Nov 1920), British bass. He studied in Geneva and London. From 1951 leading roles at CG and took part in the fps of *Billy Budd* (1951), *Gloriana* (1953), *The Midsummer Marriage* (1955), and Henze's *We Come to the River* (1976). Retired 1977 and became dir. Nat. Opera Studio 1978–86. Best known as Ochs; other roles incl. Hagen, Hunding, Rocco, Varlaam and Don Pasquale.

Langlais, Jean (b La Fontenelle, Ille-et-Vilaine, 15 Feb 1907), French organist and composer. He was educ. at an inst. for the blind and studied organ under André Marchal, also blind, later with Dupré at the Paris Cons., where he also studied comp. with Dukas. He held several organist's appts. at Paris churches, lastly at Sainte-Clotilde, and taught organ and comp. at the Inst. des Jeunes Aveugles. His best-known works are for organ, but he has written many others.

Langridge, Philip (b Hawkhurst, Kent, 16 Dec 1939), English tenor. He studied at the RAM and began his career as a violinist. An unusually wide repertory, and has been heard in operas by Handel, Rameau and Monteverdi as well as in perfs. of contemporary music; recorded Schoenberg's Aron, with Solti, and in 1986 co-created the title role in Birtwistle's opera *The Mask of Orpheus*, at the London Coliseum. He is married to the mezzo Ann Murray.

Lanier (or Laniere), Nicholas (b London, bap. 10 Sep 1588; d London, buried 24 Feb 1666), English painter, flautist, singer and composer of French descent (? Lanière). He was prob. a pupil of his father, John Lanier (or Lanyer), a sackbut player. In 1613, with Coperario and others, he comp. a masque for the marriage of the Earl of Somerset and in 1617 he not only set Ben Jonson's *Lovers made Men*, but sang in it and painted the scenery. In 1625 he was sent to It. to collect pictures for the royal collection. App. Master of the King's Music in 1626. Lived in the Netherlands during the Commonwealth, but resumed his post at the Restoration. Several other members of the family were musicians in the royal service.

Works incl. masques, e.g. *Lovers made*

Men (1617) and *The Vision of Delight* (Jonson, 1617); cantata *Hero and Leander*, New Year's songs; vocal dialogues, songs.

Lanner, Joseph (Franz Karl) (b Vienna, 12 Apr 1801; d Oberdöbling, nr. Vienna, 14 Apr 1843), Austrian violinist and composer. Son of a glove-maker, he taught himself the vln. Anxious to cond. an orch. he began by getting together a string 4tet, in which J. Strauss, sen., played vla. They played at var. taverns selections from favourite operas arr. by him. He soon turned to the comp. of country dances and waltzes, in which he was to be Strauss's greatest rival. He was engaged to cond. the orch. at dances, visited provincial cities with his own band and finally cond. the court balls in turn with Strauss.

Works incl. over 200 waltzes, country dances, quadrilles, polkas, galops, marches.

Lantins, Arnold de, early 15th-cent. Flemish composer from the diocese of Liège. He was in Venice in 1428 and was incl. (with Dufay) in a list of papal singers in 1431. He comp. *chansons*, motets and a Mass, *Verbum incarnatum*.

Lantins, Hugo de, Flemish composer, possibly brother of prec. Like Arnold he visited It., and in 1420 wrote an epithalamium for Cleofe Malatesta di Pesaro. Two of his 5 motets connect him with Venice (1423) and Bari respectively. He also wrote numerous *chansons*.

Laparra, Raoul (b Bordeaux, 13 May 1876; d Suresnes, 4 Apr 1943), French composer. Studied at the Paris Cons.

Works incl. operas *Peau d'âne* (1899), *La Habanera* (1908), *La Jota* (1899), *Le Joueur de viole*, *Las Toreras* (1929), *L'Illustre Fregona*; *Un Dimanche busque* for pf. and orch.; string 4tet; songs.

Lapicida, Erasmus (b 1445–50; d Vienna, 19 Nov 1547), German composer. Towards the end of his life he is found in the Imp. court, described as being 'in extreme old age'. He wrote church music, a *frottola* (the latter and much of the former pub. by Petrucci) and Ger. songs.

Lappas, Ulysses (b Athens, 1881; d Athens, 26 Jul 1971), Greek tenor. After his 1913 debut in Athens he studied further in Italy; La Scala 1917 in de Sabata's *Il Macigno*. CG 1919–33 as Loris and Don Carlos. He appeared at Monte Carlo and Chicago in the 1920s; returned to Milan 1934, for Lattuada's *Don Giovanni*.

Lara (actually Cohen), **Isidore de** (b London, 9 Aug 1858; d Paris, 2 Aug 1935), English composer. Studied comp. with Maz-

zucato and singing with Lamperti at the Milan Cons., later went to Lalo in Paris. He returned to London and became well known in wealthy drawing-rooms as a song comp. and perf. Later he came under the patronage of the Princess of Monaco, which enabled him to have his operas staged in the grand manner.

Works incl. operas *The Light of Asia* (1892), *Amy Robsart* (after Scott's *Kenilworth*, 1893), *Moïna* (1897), *Messaline* (1899), *Soléa, Sanga, Naïl, Les Trois Masques* (1912), *The Three Musketeers* (after Dumas, 1921), and others; cantata *The Light of Asia* (1st version of the opera); many songs.

Largamente (It. = broadly, spaciously), an indication that a movement or phrase is to be played in a broad manner.

Large, the largest note-value in the medieval system of measured notation. It was known in Lat. as *duplex longa* or *maxima*, and was divisible into 2 Longs.

Larghetto (It. lit. little *largo*), a tempo indication for a slow movement, less slow than a Largo.

Largo (It. = large, broad, wide, spacious), a tempo indication for a slow movement denoting a broad style as much as a slow pace. *See also* **Larghetto**.

'Largo', the popular name for the aria 'Ombra mai fù' ('Shade never was') from Handel's opera *Serse* (*Xerxes*), more generally known as an instrumental piece pub. in all kinds of arrs. The familiar title is not even the original tempo indication, which is *Larghetto*.

Lark Ascending, The, romance for vln. and orch. by Vaughan Williams, comp. 1914, fp London, Queen's Hall, 14 Jun 1921, cond. Boult.

'Lark' Quartet, a nickname sometimes given to Haydn's string 4tet in D, op. 64 No. 5 on account of the exposed high 1st-vln. passage at the opening.

Larrivée, Henri (b Lyons, 9 Jan 1737; d Paris, 7 Aug 1802), French baritone. He sang at the Paris Opéra from 1755, at 1st in operas by Rameau; became closely assoc. with Gluck and took part in the fps of the two *Iphigénie* operas as well as *Armide* and the revised *Alceste*. Was also heard in operas by Philidor, Gossec (*Sabinus*, 1773), Piccinni and Grétry (*Andromaque*, 1780). In 1784 he created Danaus in Salieri's *Les Danaïdes*.

Larrocha, Alicia de (b Barcelona, 23 May 1923), Spanish pianist. Concert debut with Madrid SO in 1935. London debut 1953; US debut, with San Francisco SO, 1955.

Formed duo with cellist Gaspar Cassado in 1956. Well known in Falla, Granados and Albeniz; also heard in Mozart and the Romantics.

Larsen, Jens Peter (b Copenhagen, 14 Jun 1902), Danish musicologist. Studied at Copenhagen Univ. and taught there from 1928, becoming prof. in 1945. Organist at Vangede Church, 1930–45. Ed. of several works by Haydn and other comps., and author of *Die Haydn-Überlieferung*, *Drei Haydn Kataloge* and *Handel's 'Messiah'*. Wrote entry for Haydn in the *New Grove Dictionary* (1980).

Larsen-Todsen, Nanny (b Hagby, 2 Aug 1884; d Stockholm, 26 May 1982), Swedish soprano. Debut Stockholm 1906, as Agathe; regular in Sweden until 1923, when she sang Isolde at La Scala, Milan. NY Met debut 1925 as the *Götterdämmerung* Brünnhilde; also sang Kundry, Leonore, Rachel and Gioconda. Bayreuth 1927–31. Other roles incl. Donna Anna, Tosca, Reiza and Aida.

Larsson, Lars-Erik (b Åkarp nr. Lund, 15 May 1908; d Helsingborg, 27 Dec 1986), Swedish conductor and composer. Studied at the RAM at Stockholm, and later in Leipzig and Vienna, where he was a pupil of Berg. Cond. for Swed. radio 1937–54; prof. of comp., Stockholm Cons., 1947–59; dir. of music, Uppsala Univ., 1961–6.

Works incl. opera *The Princess of Cyprus* (1937); incid. music to Shakespeare's *Winter's Tale*; 3 symphs. (1927–45), 2 concert overtures, lyric suite for orch.; sinfonietta for strings (1932), divertimento for chamber orch.; saxophone concerto.

Laruette, Jean Louis (b Toulouse, 27 Mar 1731; d Toulouse, 10 Jan 1792), French actor, singer and composer. He appeared at the Opéra-Comique and the Comédie-Italienne in Paris.

Works incl. operas *Cendrillon* (1759), *L'Ivrogne corrigé* (after La Fontaine) and 8 others, operettas.

Las Huelgas Codex, an important MS., *c* 1325, containing monophonic and polyphonic music, the latter incl. *conductus*, motets and settings of the Mass Ordinary. It is housed in the monastery of Las Huelgas nr. Burgos in N. Spain.

LaSalle Quartet, American string quartet founded 1949 at the Juilliard School, NY; members are Walter Levine and Henry Meyer (vlns.), Peter Kamnitzer (vla.), Lee Fiser (cello). European debut 1954. Much valued for perfs. and recordings of works by Second Viennese School and 4tets by Apos-

tel, Ligeti, Lutosławski, Penderecki and Kagel.

Laserna, Blas (b Corella, Navarre, bap. 4 Feb 1751; d Madrid, 8 Aug 1816), Spanish composer. He became official comp. to several Madrid theatres in 1779.

Works incl. numerous *tonadillas*, comic opera *La gitanilla por amor* (1791); incid. music for plays by Calderón, Lope de Vega, Moreto, Ramón de la Cruz's *El café de Barcelona* (1788) and others, lyric scene *Idomeneo* (1792), etc.

Lassalle, Jean Louis (b Lyons, 14 Dec 1847; d Paris, 7 Sep 1909), French baritone. He was intended to follow his father in the business of a silk merchant, but went to Paris, 1st to study painting and then singing at the Cons. and privately. He made his debut at Liège in 1868 in *Les Huguenots*, Paris, Opéra, from 1872 as William Tell and in operas by Reyer and Saint-Saëns. London, CG, 1879–93 as Sachs, the Dutchman and Telramund. NY Met from 1892 (debut as Nelusko).

Lassen, Eduard (b Copenhagen, 13 Apr 1830; d Weimar, 15 Jan 1904), Danish-born conductor and composer. Was taken to Brussels at the age of 2 and studied at the Cons. there, and took the Belg. Prix de Rome in 1851. Unable to get his 1st opera staged at Brussels, he took it to Liszt at Weimar, who prod. it in 1857. He was music dir. there from 1858 and cond. of the opera from 1860. He cond. the fp of Saint-Saëns's *Samson et Dalila* (1877).

Works incl. operas *Landgraf Ludwigs Brautfahrt* (1857), *Frauenlob* (1860), *Le Captif*; incid. music to Sophocles' *Oedipus*, Goethe's *Faust* and *Pandora*, Calderón's *Circe*, Hebbel's *Nibelungen* (1876; the year of the 1st prod. of *The Ring*, at Bayreuth); festival cantata, Te Deum; *Biblische Bilder* for voices and orch.; 2 symphs., *Beethoven* and *Festival* overtures.

Lasso, Orlando di. *See* **Lassus**.

Lassus, Orlande de (Orlando di Lasso) (b Mons, prob. 1532; d Munich, 14 Jun 1594), Flemish composer. He seems to have gone to It. as a boy, and he travelled there and served in var. noble households, in Sicily, Naples and Milan. In 1553–4 he was choirmaster at St John Lateran in Rome, after which he returned home and settled for 2 years at Antwerp, where in 1555–6 he began to pub. his 1st works. In 1556 he went to Munich and entered the service of the Duke of Bavaria. There he married Regina Weckinger in 1558, and in 1563 became chief *Kapellmeister* in succession to Daser. Visit to Venice,

1567, to find musicians for Munich, and to Ferrara. In 1570 he was ennobled by the Emperor Maximilian. After a visit to Paris in 1571 Charles IX offered him a post as chamber musician, but he returned to Munich after the king's death in 1574. That year he went to Rome to present Pope Gregory XIII with a vol. of Masses and received the order of the Golden Spur. In spite of an offer from Dresden, he remained attached to the Bavarian court to the end. His Latin motets were collected and pub. in 1604 by his sons Ferdinand and Rudolph under the title *Magnum opus musicum*.

Works incl. some 1,250 comps.: about 60 Masses, 4 Passions, 101 Magnificats, Requiem, about 500 motets, *Sacrae cantiones*, psalms (incl. 7 penitential psalms); madrigals, It. *canzoni*, Fr. *chansons*, Ger. songs for several voices.

Last Judgment, The, the Eng. title of Spohr's oratorio *Die letzten Dinge*, prod. Kassel, 25 Mar 1826.

László, Magda (b Marosvásárehely, *c* 1920), Hungarian soprano. She studied in Budapest and sang there during the war as Elisabeth and Maria Boccanegra. Created The Mother in the 1st prod. of Dallapiccola's *Il Prigionero* (Florence, 1950). She sang Alceste at Glyndebourne in 1953; returned in 1954 for Dorabella and 1962 as Poppea in the fp of the Leppard version of Monteverdi's opera. Other roles incl. Marie, Senta, Norma. Created Walton's Cressida (CG 1954).

Latilla, Gaetano (b Bari, 12 Jan 1711; d Naples, 15 Jan 1788), Italian composer. Chorister at Bari Cathedral, he studied with Prota and Feo at the Cons. di Sant'Onofrio in Naples, where his first opera was prod. in 1732. App. vice-*maestro di cappella* at Santa Maria Maggiore, Rome, in 1738, he returned to Naples in 1741 for health reasons. Later choirmaster at the Cons. della Pietà in Venice (1756) and vice-*maestro di cappella* at St Mark's (1762). Retired to Naples 1772.

Works incl. *c* 50 operas, e.g. *Li marite a forza* (1732), *Gismondo* (1737), *Madame Ciana, Romolo* (1739), *Siroe* (1740), etc.; oratorio *Omnipotenza e misericordia divina*; church music; instrumental music.

Latrobe, Christian Ignatius (b Fulneck, Leeds, 12 Feb 1757; d Fairfield, nr. Liverpool, 6 May 1836), English clergyman and composer. Studied at the coll. of the Morav. Brethren at Niesky in Upper Lusatia and in 1795 became secretary of the Eng. branch. Ded. 3 sonatas to Haydn, with whom he made friends during the latter's visits to Eng.

Ed. Moravian hymn-tunes and 6 vols. of Ger. and It. church music.

Works incl. *Dies irae* (1823), Te Deum, Miserere (1814), anthems and other church music; instrumental sonatas; airs to poems by Cowper and Hannah More, etc.

Laubenthal, Horst (b Eisfeld, Thuringia, 8 Mar 1939), German tenor. Born Neumann, he adopted the name of his teacher, Rudolf L. Debut Würzburg 1967, as Ottavio. Stuttgart Staatsoper from 1968; Deutsche Oper Berlin from 1973. He sang Belmonte at Glyndebourne in 1972. Guest at Aix, Salzburg and Munich as Lensky, Tamino, Palestrina and Florestan. Well-known in sacred music by Bach.

Laubenthal, Rudolf (b Düsseldorf, 18 Mar 1886; d Pöcking, Starnbergsee, 2 Oct 1971), German tenor. He studied in Berlin, debut there in 1913; remained until 1923, when he sang Walther at the NY Met. Appeared until 1933 in Wagner roles and was the 1st US Steva (1924), Menelaos (1928) and Babinski (1931). London, CG, 1926–30. Guest in Chicago and Vienna.

Lauda Sion, a sequence sung at Mass on the Feast of Corpus Christi in the Rom. Church, words by St Thomas Aquinas, *c* 1264.

Cantata by Mendelssohn written for a festival at Liège and perf. there on 11 Jun 1846.

Laudi spirituali, Italian sacred songs of the 13th cent. and later, with words in the vernacular, at first for single voice and later in parts. Their centre of origin was Florence.

Laudon Symphony, nickname of Haydn's symph. no. 69 in C, comp. *c* 1778 and ded. to Field-Marshal Baron Gideon Ernst von Loudon.

Lauri-Volpi, Giacomo (b Rome, 11 Dec 1892; d Valencia, 17 Mar 1979), Italian tenor. He studied in Rome. Debut Viterbo 1919, as Arturo. NY Met debut 1923 as Duke of Mantua; sang until 1934 in Italian rep., incl. the 1st US Calaf (1926). London, CG, 1925 and 1936 as Chénier, Radames and Cavaradossi. Other roles incl. Nerone, Arnold, Des Grieux, Raoul and Manrico.

Lavallée, Calixa (b Verchères, Quebec, 28 Dec 1842; d Boston, Mass., 21 Jan 1891), Canadian pianist and composer. Studied at the Paris Cons. and later toured as pianist in N. America.

Works incl. opera *The Widow* (1882); symphs.; 2 string 4tets; nat. air 'O Canada'.

Lavignac, (Alexandre Jean) Albert (b Paris, 21 Jan 1846; d Paris, 28 May 1916), French musicologist. Studied at the Paris Cons., where he became prof. in 1882. Founder and

1st ed. of the *Encyclopédie de la musique* (1913–16); also wrote many technical treatises, a study of Wagner.

Lavolta, or (It.) *Volta* or (Fr.) *Volte,* an old dance in 3–2 time, prob. of It. orig., since the jump that was a feature of it retained the It. word *volta.*

Lavotta, János (b Pusztafödémes, 5 Jul 1764; d Tállya, 11 Aug 1820), Hungarian violinist and composer. He was of noble birth, but left home on his father's remarriage and became a professional musician, at the same time following a legal career. He became very fashionable in Vienna and Pest, cond. at var. theatres, but took to drink and ended in decay. As a comp. he was one of the outstanding exponents of *verbunkos* music.

Lawes, Henry (b Dinton, Wilts., 5 Jan 1596; d London, 21 Oct 1662), English composer. Pupil of Coperario, app. gentleman of the Chapel Royal in 1626. Having supplied music for Thomas Carew's masque *Coelum Britannicum,* prod. at court, 18 Feb 1634, he was commissioned by the Earl of Bridgewater to set Milton's *Comus* for perf. at Ludlow Castle, 29 Sep 1634. He was the subject of a sonnet by Milton, 1646. He was re-app. to the court service on the Restoration in 1660 and wrote a coronation anthem for Charles II.

Works incl. opera *The Siege of Rhodes* (with Locke, Cooke, Colman and Hudson); masques (as above); coronation anthem *Zadok the Priest,* anthems, psalm-tunes; elegy on the death of his brother William; songs in plays by William Cartwright, Christmas songs in Herrick's *Hesperides;* airs, dialogues and songs for 1 and more voices.

Lawes, William (b Salisbury, bap. 1 May 1602; d Chester, 24 Sep 1645), English composer, brother of prec. Studied with Coperario and became a musician at Charles I's court. He joined the Royalist army during the Civil War and was killed by a shot during the siege of Chester.

Works incl. music for Shirley's masque *The Triumph of Peace* (with Ive, 1634) and Davenant's *The Triumph of the Prince d'Amour* and *The Unfortunate Lovers* (1638); anthems and psalms; music for consorts of viols; airs for vln. and bass; catches and canons; airs and dialogues for 1 and more voices.

Lawrence, Marjorie (b Dean's Marsh, Victoria, 17 Feb 1907; d Little Rock, Ark., 13 Jan 1979), Australian soprano. She studied in Paris. Debut Monte Carlo 1932, as Eli-

sabeth. Paris, Opéra, 1933–6 as Ortrud, Brünnhilde, Massenet's Salomé, Reyer's Brunehild, Donna Anna and Brangaene. NY Met debut 18 Dec 1935 as the *Walküre* Brünnhilde; also sang Salome, Thaïs and Tosca. Stricken by polio in 1941 but sang in opera until 1943, with limited stage movement. Retired 1953. Autobiog., *Interrupted Melody,* 1949.

Layolle, François de (Francesco dell' Aiolle) (b Florence, 4 Mar 1492; d Lyons, *c* 1540), French organist and composer. He was Benvenuto Cellini's music teacher; worked at church of SS Annunziate, Florence, until 1518. His son Aleman L. afterwards taught Cellini's daughter and became organist at Lyons by 1521.

Works incl. Masses, motets; *canzoni,* madrigals.

Lays (or **Lay, Lai** or **Lais**), **François** (b La Barthe-de-Nesthes, Gascony, 14 Feb 1758; d Ingrande, nr. Angers, 30 Mar 1831), French singer. He learnt music at the monastery of Guaraison, but left to become a public singer and made his 1st appearance at the Paris Opéra in 1780 in Candeille's *Laure et Pétraque.* He also sang at court, at the Concert Spirituel, etc., and on the foundation of the Cons. in 1795 became prof. of singing there.

Lazaro, Hippolito (b Barcelona, 13 Aug 1887; d Madrid, 14 May 1974), Spanish tenor. Debut Barcelona 1909; sang in the fp of Mascagni's *Parisina* (Milan, 1913), and at Rome in 1921 created the title role in *Piccolo Marat.* NY Met debut 1918, as the Duke of Mantua; also successful as Arturo. Returned to La Scala 1924 (fp Giordano's *La cena della beffe).*

Lazzari, Sylvio (b Bozen, 30 Dec 1857; d Paris, 18 Jun 1944), Austro-Italian composer, later belonging to the French school and naturalized French. Studied at Innsbruck, Munich and the Paris Cons., where Franck was one of his masters.

Works incl. operas *Amor* (Prague, 1898), *La Lépreuse* (Paris, 1912), *Le Sautériot* (Chicago, 1918), *Melaenis, La Tour de feu* (Paris, 1928); incid. music for Goethe's *Faust;* symph. in E♭ maj., orchestral suite in F maj., symph. tableau *Effet de nuit* (after Verlaine), *4 Tableaux maritimes, Rapsodie* (after Shakespeare), *Rapsodie espagnole, Impressions d'Adriatique,* etc.; *Concertstück* for pf. and orch., *Rapsodie* for vln. and orch.; string 4tet, pf. trio, octet for wind insts.

Lazzari, Virgilio (b Assisi, 20 Apr 1887; d Castel Gandolfo, 4 Oct 1953), Italian, later

American, bass. Opera debut Rome 1914. US debut St Louis 1916, as Ramfis; Chicago 1918–36 and NY Met 1933–50 (debut as Pedro, in *L'Africaine*). He sang Pistol and Leporello at Salzburg 1934–9. CG 1939. Sang Montemezzi's Archibaldo at Genoa in the year of his death.

Le Brun, Jean, French priest and composer of the 2nd half of the 15th cent. He wrote motets and *chansons*.

Le Couppey, Félix (b Paris, 14 Apr 1811; d Paris, 5 Jul 1887), French pianist and teacher. Studied at the Paris Cons., where later he was pf. prof. He wrote many studies for his instrument and several books on its perf.

Le Flem, Paul (b Lézardrieux, Côtes-du-Nord, 18 Mar 1881; d Trégastel, Côtes-du-Nord, 31 Jul 1984), French composer and critic. Pupil of d'Indy and Roussel, among others, later prof. at the Schola Cantorum, chor. master at the Opéra-Comique, cond. of the Chanteurs de Saint-Gervais and critic for *Comoedia*.

Works incl. operas *Le Rossignol de Saint-Malo* (1942) and *Dahut*; choreographic drama on Shakespeare's *Macbeth*; cantata *Aucassin et Nicolette*; 4 symphs. (1908–78), *Triptyque symphonique* for orch.; fantasy for pf. and orch.; chamber music; vln. and pf. sonata; pf. works; choral music.

Le Franc, Guillaume (b Rouen; d Lausanne, Jun 1570), French composer. Fled to Switz. as a Protestant, settled at Geneva in 1541 and estab. a school of music, becoming master of the children and singer at the cathedral the next year, and ed. Calvin's Genevan Psalter, in which Bourgeois and Marot also had a hand; but in 1545 he left for the cathedral of Lausanne. In 1565 he issued a new Psalter there with some tunes of his own.

Le Jeune, Claude (or **Claudin**) (b Valenciennes, *c* 1530; d Paris, buried 26 Sep 1600), Franco-Flemish composer. Worked most of his life in Paris. Having turned Huguenot, he tried to escape from Paris during the siege of 1588, and his MSS. were saved from seizure by the Catholic soldiers by his colleague Mauduit, himself a Catholic. Later Le Jeune became chamber musician to the king. Like Baïf and Mauduit, he was an exponent of *musique mesurée*.

Works incl. motets, psalms set to rhymed versions in measured music and also to tunes in the Genevan Psalter set for 3 voices; *chansons*, madrigals; instrumental fantasies, etc.

Le Maistre, Matthieu (b Roclenge-sur-Geer, nr. Liège, *c* 1505; d Dresden, 1577), Flemish composer. He succeeded Walther as *Kapellmeister* to the Saxon court at Dresden in 1554, a post from which he retired with a pension in 1568.

Works incl. Masses, motets; Latin and German sacred songs, setting of the Lutheran catechism in Latin; German secular songs, etc.

Le Roy, Adrien (b Montreuil-sur-mer, *c* 1520; d Paris, 1598), French singer, lutenist, publisher and composer. He worked in Paris and assoc. himself with Ballard (1) in 1552, having married his sister the prec. year. Lassus visited him in 1571 and he pub. some works of his. He pub. an instruction book for the lute and another for the cittern.

Le Sure, François (b Paris, 23 May 1923), French musicologist and librarian. He worked at the Bibliothèque Nationale, Paris, from 1950 to 1987 and taught at the École des Hautes-Études. His interests incl. bibliography, the sociology of music and 16th-cent. Fr. music.

Leader, the usual English name for the principal 1st violin in an orch. or of a string 4tet or other chamber music team. In Amer. esp. in journalism, the cond. is often called 'leader', the usual term for the leading 1st orchestral vln. there being Concertmaster, from Ger. *Konzertmeister*.

Leading Motif. *See* **Leitmotiv.**

Leading-Note, the seventh note of a maj. or ascending min. scale 'leading' to the tonic by a semitonal step.

Lear, opera by Reimann (lib. by C. Henneberg after Shakespeare), prod. Munich 9 Jul 1978.

Lear, Evelyn (b Brooklyn, 8 Jan 1926), American soprano. She studied at Juilliard and in Berlin; debut there as the Composer, 1958. Created Klebe's Alkmene, Berlin 1961, and in 1962 sang the 1st of many perfs. of Berg's Lulu (London, SW, 1966; also recorded, under Böhm). She created Lavinia in Levy's *Mourning Becomes Elektra*, on her NY Met debut (1967) and has sung there since in operas by Mozart, Puccini and Verdi; often with her husband Thomas Stewart, whom she married in 1955. Sang the Marschallin at NY Met Oct 1985.

Lebel, Firmin (b Noyon; d Rome, 18 Nov 1573), French cleric and musician. Worked in the diocese of Noyon, but in 1540 succeeded Mallapert as *maestro di cappella* at Santa Maria Maggiore in Rome and later occupied a similar post at San Luigi dei Francesi, eventually becoming, in 1561, a singer in the Papal choir.

Leben des Orest 408

Leben des Orest (*The Life of Orestes*), opera by Krenek (lib. by comp.), prod. Leipzig, 19 Jan 1930.

Lebrun (*née* **Danzi**), **Franziska** (b Mannheim, bap. 24 Mar 1756; d Berlin, 14 May 1791), German soprano and composer of Italian descent, daughter of a cellist at the court of Mannheim, sister of Franz D. and wife of Ludwig L. She made her 1st appearance in 1772 in Sacchini's *La contadina in corte*, was engaged by the court opera Mannheim, where she sang in the fp of Holzbauer's *Gunther von Schwarzburg*. Comp. sonatas. Sang in the 1st prod. at La Scala, (Salieri's *Europa riconsciuta*, 1778), and in Eng. She was an exact contemporary of Mozart.

Lebrun, Jean (b Lyons, 6 Apr 1759; d Paris, 1809), French horn player. Pupil of Punto in Paris. Played in the Paris Opéra orch., 1786–92, and later worked in London and Berlin. He is said to have invented the mute for the horn.

Lebrun, Louis (Sébastien) (b Paris, 10 Dec 1764; d Paris, 27 Jun 1829), French tenor and composer. He sang at the Paris Opéra and Opéra-Comique and was Napoleon's *maître de chapelle*.

Works incl. operas *Marcelin* (1800), *Le Rossignol* (1816) and many others; a Te Deum, etc.

Lebrun, Ludwig (August) (b Mannheim, bap. 2 May 1752; d Berlin, 16 Dec 1790), German oboist and composer of French descent. He was oboist at the Mannheim court, which he followed to Munich in 1778, and toured all over Europe with his wife, Francesca L.

Works incl. 7 ob. concertos; 12 trios with ob. parts.

Lechner, Leonhard (b Etsch valley, c 1553; d Stuttgart, 9 Sep 1606), Austrian composer. Pupil of Lassus in the court chapel at Munich, became a schoolmaster at Nuremberg in 1570 and in 1579 began to pub. a revised ed. of Lassus's works. In 1584–5 he was music director to Count Eitel Friedrich of Hohenzollern at Hechingen and in 1595 was app. to a similar post at the court of Württemberg at Stuttgart.

Works incl. Masses, motets, Magnificat, psalms, introits, wedding motet for the Elector Johann Georg I of Saxony; sacred and 160 secular Ger. songs for 2–5 voices in 7 pub. books; St John Passion (1594).

Leclair, Jean-Marie (b Lyons, 10 May 1697; d Paris, 22 Oct 1764), French composer and violinist. Began his career as a dancer, and in 1722 was ballet master in Turin, but while there turned to the vln., studying with Somis. In 1728 he settled in Paris, having great success as a player and comp. Member of the royal orch. 1734–6, he then went to Hol., returning to Paris after various travels in 1743. For a time in the service of Don Philip of Spain at Chambéry, he joined the orch. of the Duke of Gramont in 1748. He met his death at the hand of an unknown murderer.

Works incl. opera *Scylla et Glaucus* (1746; concert perf. London, 1979); ballets and 'divertissements'; 12 vln. concertos; 48 vln. sonatas; vln. duets; trio sonatas.

Lecocq, (Alexandre) Charles (b Paris, 3 Jun 1832; d Paris, 24 Oct 1918), French composer. Studied at the Paris Cons., 1849–54, and prod. his 1st operetta, *Le Docteur Miracle*, in 1857, having tied with Bizet in a competition organized by Offenbach. He did not make a great success until he prod. *Fleur de thé* in 1868 and until then supplemented his income by teaching and org. playing. After that he made a fortune with his many operettas.

Works incl. opera *Plutus* (1886); operettas *Les Cent Vierges*, *La Fille de Madame Angot* (1872), *Giroflé-Girofla* (1874), *La Petite Mariée* (1875), *Le Petit Duc* (1878), *Camargo* (1878), *Ninette*, *Barbe-bleue* and about 40 others; orchestral works; vln. and pf. sonata; sacred songs for women's voices *La Chapelle au couvent*; instrumental pieces; pf. works; songs.

Leçons des Ténèbres (Fr.), settings of the Lamentations of Jeremiah for perf. at matins on the last 3 days of Holy Week. *See* **Lamentations**.

Ledger, Philip (b Bexhill, 12 Dec 1937), English conductor, keyboard player and editor. He studied at Cambridge and has held posts there and at the Univ. of E. Anglia. Active at Aldeburgh Fests. since 1968 and has been accompanist to leading singers. As cond. has given Purcell's *King Arthur* with the EOG in GB and abroad. Recordings of Bach and Handel with a sure sense of period style. Prin. Royal Scot. Acad. of Music and Drama since 1982.

Leduc, Simon (b Paris, c 1748; d Paris, Jan 1777), French composer and publisher. A pupil of Gaviniès, he was joint director (with the latter and Gossec) of the Concert Spirituel from 1773. As a pub. he issued 1767 works by himself and other comps.

Comps. incl. 3 vln. concertos; 3 symphs. and 2 *symphonies concertantes*; vln. sonatas and duets; trio sonatas.

Lee, Nathaniel (? 1653–92), English playwright. *See* **Finger** (*Rival Queens*, with D. Purcell), **Purcell** (*Oedipus, Massacre of Paris, Sophonisba* and *Theodosius*), **Staggins** (*Gloriana*).

Leeds Musical Festival, a triennial music festival estab. at Leeds, on the opening of the new town hall, in 1858. Many perfs. of choral music incl. fps of works by Elgar, Vaughan Williams, Holst and Walton. John Warrack (*q.v.*) director 1977–83.

Lees, Benjamin (b Harbin, Manchuria, 8 Jan 1924), American composer of Russian parentage, brought to the USA as a child. He studied pf. in San Francisco and Los Angeles. After serving in the US Army from 1942 to 1945, he studied at the Univ. of S. California, Los Angeles, theory, harmony and comp. with Halsey Stevens, Ingolf Dahl and Ernst Kanitz, also taking private lessons from George Antheil. In 1955 he won a Guggenheim Fellowship and in 1956 a Fulbright Fellowship.

Works incl. operas *The Oracle* (1955) and *The Gilded Cage* (1971); 3 symphs. (1953–69; no. 3 for string 4tet and orch.); concertos for vln., ob. and pf. (2); *Profile* for orch., concerto for orch., *Declamations* for string orch. and pf.; *Visions of Poets*, a dramatic cantata (1961); concerto for brass, chorus and orch. (1983); string 4tet, vln. sonata; pf. music.

Leeuw, Ton de (b Rotterdam, 16 Nov 1926), Dutch composer. Studied comp. in Paris with Messiaen and Thomas de Hartmann. He became interested in musical folklore and in 1961 toured India to collect material. His chief interest is in experimental music.

Works incl. opera *De Droom* (*The Dream*, 1965): oratorio *Job* (1956); 2 symphs., *Ombres* for orch. and perc., concertos for pf. and string orch.; 2 string 4tets (1958, 1964).

LeFanu, Nicola (b Wickham Bishops, Essex, 28 Apr 1947), English composer, daughter of Elizabeth Maconchy. She studied at Oxford and with Wellesz and Petrassi. Lecturer, Morley Coll. 1970–5, King's Coll., London, from 1977.

Works incl. opera *Dawnpath* (1977), ballet *The Last Laugh* for sop. tape and chamber orch. (1972); *Preludio* for strings (1967; rev. 1976), *The Hidden Landscape* for orch. (1973), *Columbia Fall* for perc. harp and strings (1975), *Farne* for orch. (1979); *The Valleys shall Sing* for chorus and wind (1973), *For we are the Stars* for 16 voices (1978), *Like a Wave of the Sea* for chorus and ens. of early insts. (1981), *Stranded on my Heart* for tenor, chorus and strings (1984); Clar. 5tet (1971), *Collana* for 6 insts. (1976), *Deva* for cello and 7 insts. (1979).

Leffler-Burckhard, Martha (b Berlin, 16 Jun 1865; d Wiesbaden, 14 May 1954), German soprano. She studied with Viardot in Paris. Debut Strasbourg 1888; sang in Breslau, Cologne and Bremen 1889–97, Wiesbaden 1900–12 and at the Hofoper Berlin 1913–18. Bayreuth 1906–8 as Kundry, Sieglinde and Ortrud. CG 1903 and 1907 as Brünnhilde, Leonore and Isolde. NY Met 1908.

Legato (It. = bound, tied). In music the word is used to designate a sustained manner of singing or playing, one note leading smoothly to the next.

Legend of Joseph, The, (Strauss)). *See* **Josephslegende.**

Legend of the Invisible City of Kitezh and the Maiden Fevronia (*Skazhanie o nevidimom gradie Kitezh i dieve Fevronie*), opera by Rimsky-Korsakov (lib. by V.I. Bielsky), prod. St Petersburg, 20 Feb 1907.

Legend of Tsar Saltan, The (*Skazka o Tsarie Saltanie*), opera by Rimsky-Korsakov (lib. by V.I. Bielsky after Pushkin), prod. Moscow, 3 Nov 1900.

Légende de Saint Christophe, La, opera by d'Indy (lib. by comp.), prod. Paris, Opéra, 6 Jun 1920.

Legende von der heiligen Elizabeth, Die (*The Legend of St Elizabeth of Hungary*), oratorio by Liszt (words by Otto Roquette), fp in Hung., Budapest, 15 Aug 1865; 1st prod. as an opera, Weimar, 23 Oct 1881.

Leger Lines, the short strokes drawn through or between those notes which go above or below the stave in musical notation.

Legge, Walter (b London, 1 Jun 1906; d St Jean, Cap Ferrat, 22 Mar 1979), English administrator and writer. Engaged 1927 by HMV record co. as a writer and formed subscription socs. for recording of then neglected music such as Haydn's 4tets and Wolf's Lieder. After a war spent in troop entertainment he was not reluctant to engage artists who had been tainted with Nazism: many major recordings incl. opera sets cond. by Karajan, Knappertsbusch and Furtwängler and a *Rosenkavalier* with his wife, Elisabeth Schwarzkopf. Founded Philharmonia Orch., London, 1945 and helped set new standards in orch. perf. He attempted to disband the orch. in 1964 but it was immediately reformed as the NPO with Otto Klemperer as cond. for life.

Leggenda di Sakuntala, La, opera by Alfano (lib. by comp., based on Kalldasa's play), prod. Bologna, Teatro Comunale, 10 Dec 1921. The MS. was destroyed during the war. Alfano reconstructed the opera for prod. in 1952, as *Sakuntala.*

Legrant, Guillaume Franco-Flemish composer. Between 1419 and 1421 he was a member of the papal chapel. He wrote 3 *chansons*, a florid org. piece without title, and a very chromatic *Gloria-Credo* pair.

Legrenzi, Giovanni (b Clusone nr. Bergamo, bap. 12 Aug 1626; d Venice, 27 May 1690), Italian composer. Organist at his birthplace, then *maestro di cappella* at Ferrara. In 1672 he became director of the Cons. dei Mendicanti at Venice and in 1685 *maestro di cappella* of St Mark's there. Works incl. operas *Achille in Sciro* (1663), *Eteocle e Polinice* (1675), *La divisione del mondo, Germanico sul Reno* (1676), *Totila, I due Cesari* (1683), *Il Giustino, Pertinace* (1684), and *c* 10 others; Masses, motets, psalms and other church music; orchestral works; church sonatas.

Legros, Joseph (b Monampteuil, nr. Laon, 7 Sep 1739; d La Rochelle, 20 Dec 1793), French tenor and concert manager. Made his operatic debut in 1764 in Paris and sang in Rameau's *Castor et Pollux, Zoroastre, Hippolyte et Aricie* and *Dardanus.* Later became Gluck's principal tenor; he was the 1st tenor Orphée and created roles in *Alceste* and both *Iphigénie* operas. True to his name, he was forced by corpulence to abandon the stage in 1783, and turned to concert management.

Lehár, Ferencz (Franz) (b Komárom, 30 Apr 1870; d Ischl, 24 Oct 1948), Hungarian composer. Studied at the Prague Cons. and became a military bandmaster. Later he devoted himself entirely to the successful comp. of operettas. During his last years he lived in retirement at Ischl. Works incl. opera *Kukuška* (later called *Tajana*, 1896), operettas *The Merry Widow* (1905), *The Count of Luxembourg* (1909), *Gypsy Love* (1910), *The Three Graces, Pompadour, Springtime, Frasquita* (1922), *Clo Clo, The Blue Mazurka, Frederica* (1928), *The Land of Smiles* (1929) and many others; symph. poem *Fieber*, 3 comedy scenes for orch.

Lehmann, Lilli (b Würzburg, 24 Nov 1848; d Berlin, 17 May 1929), German soprano. Studied under her mother, the singer and harpist Marie Loew, appeared at Prague in 1865 in *Die Zauberflöte.* At an early age, was engaged at Danzig in 1868, at Leipzig in 1869, and made her 1st appearance in Berlin in 1870. In 1876 she sang minor roles in the 1st prod. of the *Ring*, at Bayreuth, and in 1880 1st visited London, returned 1884, CG, as Isolde and Elisabeth. NY Met 1885–99 as Carmen, Brünnhilde, Venus and Marguerite. She was successful in more than 150 roles.

Lehmann, Liza (Elizabetta Nina Mary Frederika) (b London, 11 Jul 1862; d Pinner, Middlesex, 19 Sep 1918), English singer and composer. Studied 1st with her mother, Amelia Chambers, an accomplished amateur comp. and later at Rome, Wiesbaden and at home with MacCunn, also singing with Randegger. In 1885 she made her 1st appearance as a singer at St James's Hall, where she sang for the last time in 1894, when she married Herbert Bedford. The composer David Bedford (*q.v.*) is her grandson. Works incl. light opera *The Vicar of Wakefield* (after Goldsmith, 1906), musical comedy *Sergeant Brue* (L. Housman); incid. music for *Everyman* and other plays; ballads for voice and orch.; song cycles *In a Persian Garden* (Omar Khayyám), *In Memoriam* (Tennyson).

Lehmann, Lotte (b Perleberg, 27 Feb 1888; d Santa Barbara, 26 Aug 1976), German soprano. Studied in Berlin with Erna Tiedke, Eva Reinhold and Mathilde Mallinger, making her debut in Hamburg in a small role. She soon estab. herself and in 1914 was engaged at the Vienna Staatsoper, where R. Strauss selected her to sing the Composer in *Ariadne auf Naxos* and Octavian in *Der Rosenkavalier.* Later she also sang the Marschallin in the latter opera, one of her greatest roles; she created the Dyer's Wife in *Die Frau ohne Schatten* (1919) and Christine in *Intermezzo* (1924). She was a great Wagner singer and made her Amer. debut in the role of Sieglinde in *Die Walküre.* London, CG, 1924–38 as Donna Elvira, Leonore, Elsa, Eva and Desdemona; much valued for the warmth of personality revealed in her interpretations. In 1938 she settled in the USA, living mostly in California. She pub. a novel, an autobiog. and other writings on music.

Lehrstück (Ger. = didactic piece, educational play), a small form of music drama cultivated in Ger. in the 1920s–1930s by Eisler, Hindemith, Weill and other comps., the chief literary exponent being Bert Brecht. It was cultivated mainly by the working classes in Ger. at first, though later the influence spread to other European countries and to USA. The Lehrstück makes use of hist.

material and dialectical discussion for the purpose of enlightening the masses, and it was for a time a counteragent to the Nazi movement until its exponents were forced to emigrate.

The fp of Hindemith's *Lehrstück*, for soloists, chorus and orch. (texts by Brecht) was at Baden-Baden, 28 Jul 1929.

Leibowitz, René (b Warsaw, 17 Feb 1913; d Paris, 29 Aug 1972), French–Polish composer. Settled in Paris in 1926 and in 1930–3 studied in Ger. and Aus. with Schoenberg and Webern. He destroyed all his works written up to 1937, incl. 6 string 4tets and devoted himself entirely to 12-note music. He cond. works of that school in USA in 1947–8. He was known as a leading teacher of 12-note comp. and pub. *Schoenberg et son école* and *Introduction à la musique de douze sons.*

Works incl. music drama *La Nuit close* (1949); 4 unaccomp. choruses; symph. and variations for orch.; chamber symph. for 12 insts., chamber concerto for vln., pf. and 17 insts., *Tourist Death* for soprano and chamber orch. (1943), *L'Explication des métaphores* for speaker, 2 pfs., harp and perc.; string 4tet, 10 canons for ob., clar. and bassoon, wind 5tet; vln. and pf. sonata; sontata and pieces for pf.; songs.

Leicester, ou Le Château de Kenilworth, opera by Auber (lib. by Scribe and A.H. Mélesville, based on Scott's *Kenilworth*), prod. Paris, Opéra-Comique, 25 Jan 1823.

Leich (Ger., = lay), a medieval type of Ger. song similar to the Fr. Lai.

Leichtentritt, Hugo (b Pleszow, Posen, 1 Jan 1874; d Cambridge, Mass., 13 Nov 1951), German musicologist. Studied with Paine at Harvard Univ. and later at the Hochschule für Musik in Berlin, where he became prof. at the Klindworth-Scharwenka Cons. In 1933 he left Ger. as a refugee from the Nazi régime and returned to USA to join the staff of Harvard Univ. His books incl. studies of Keiser, Handel, Chopin, Busoni and the motet.

Leider, Frida (b Berlin, 18 Apr 1888; d Berlin, 4 Jun 1975), German soprano. Debut Halle 1915, as Elisabeth. Berlin, Staatsoper, 1923–40 as Dido in *Les Troyens*, Donna Anna and Leonore. London, CG, 1924–38 as the Marschallin, Armide, Senta, Venus and the *Trovatore* Leonora. Bayreuth 1928–38 as Brünnhilde, Kundry and Isolde; NY Met 1933–4, same roles. Also sang in Chicago (debut 1928), Buenos Aires, Paris and Milan.

Leigh, Walter (b London, 22 Jun 1905; d nr. Tobruk, Libya, 12 Jun 1942), English composer. Studied at Cambridge and with Hindemith in Berlin. In 1932 a work of his was perf. at the ISCM festival in Vienna. He joined up during World War II and was killed in action.

Works incl. comic operas *The Pride of the Regiment, Jolly Roger* (1933); pantomime *Aladdin* (1931); revues *Nine Sharp* and *Little Revue, 1939*; incid. music to Aristophanes' *Frogs*, Shakespeare's *Midsummer Night's Dream*; overture *Agincourt, Music for String Orch., 3 Pieces for Amateur Orch.*; concertino for harpsichord and strings; 3 movements for string 4tet (1929), trio for fl., ob. and pf. and sonatina for vla. and pf.; songs.

Leighton, Kenneth (b Wakefield, 2 Oct 1929), English composer. Studied at Queen's Coll., Oxford and, after winning the Mendelssohn Scholarship in 1951, with Petrassi in Rome. He has won several prizes for comp. Lecturer at Edinburgh Univ. 1956–68, and at Oxford Univ., 1968–70. Prof. at Edinburgh Univ. from 1970.

Works incl. opera *Columba* (1980); concerto for strings; 2 symphs (1964, 1974); 3 pf. concertos (1951–69), vln. concerto, cello concerto; string 4tet, 2 vln. sonatas; 3 pf. sonatas; Fantasy-Octet, 'Homage to Percy Grainger' (1982); choral works.

Leighton, William (b ? Plash, Shropshire, c 1565; d London, buried 31 Jul 1622), gentleman pensioner under Elizabeth and James I. He pub. in 1614 a collection of airs for voices and instruments entitled *The Teares or Lamentacions of a Sorrowfull Soule* with contributions by Bull, Byrd, Coperario, Dowland, A. Ferrabosco (jun.), Ford, O. Gibbons, Giles, Hooper, Robert Johnson, Robert Jones, Kindersley, Leighton, T. Lupo, John Milton (sen.), Peerson, Pilkington, John Ward, Weelkes and Wilbye.

Leinsdorf, Erich (b Vienna, 4 Feb 1912), Austrian, later American, conductor. Studied with Paul Emerich and Hedwig Kammer-Rosenthal at the Vienna Gymnasium. In 1934 he became asst. to Bruno Walter and Toscanini at the Salzburg Festival and later appeared as a cond. in It., Fr. and Belg. In 1938 he was engaged as an asst. cond. at the NY Met, debut with *Die Walküre*, becoming chief cond. from 1939 to 1943. He served in the US Army from 1944 and returned to the Met 1958–62. Music dir. Boston SO 1962–9. 1977–80 princ. cond. West Berlin Radio SO.

Leipzig Gewandhaus Orchestra. *See* **Gewandhaus.**

Leitmotiv (Ger. lit. leading motif, plur. *Leitmotive*), a short theme assoc. with a personage, object or idea in an opera or other work, quoted at appropriate moments or worked up symphonically. Its chief exponent is Wagner, but it was not his invention, for it occurs in earlier comps.

Leitner, Ferdinand (b Berlin, 4 Mar 1912), German conductor. He studied in Berlin with Schreker, Schnabel and Muck; cond. in Berlin, Hamburg and Munich before moving to Stuttgart. He was music dir. until 1969 and led many prods. of Wieland Wagner; also gave fps of Orff's *Oedipus der Tyrann* (1959) and *Prometheus* (1968). He was at Zurich Opera 1969–84 and was prin. cond. of the Hague PO 1976–80. Well known in Bruckner and Mozart and has given operas by Berg and Busoni (the only recording of *Doktor Faust*).

Lekeu, Guillaume (b Heusy, nr. Verviers, 20 Jan 1870; d Angers, 21 Jan 1894), Belgian composer. Studied with Franck and d'Indy in Paris. In 1891 he obtained the 2nd Belg. Prix de Rome with the lyric scene *Andromède*.
Works incl. symph. study on Shakespeare's *Hamlet* (1887), *Fantasie sur deux airs populaires angevins* for orch.; Adagio for string 4tet and orch.; Intro. and Adagio for brass; *Chant lyrique* for chorus and orch.; pf. 4tet (completed by d'Indy); trio; vln. and pf. sonata (1891), cello and pf. sonata (completed by D'Indy); 3 pf. pieces; *3 Poèmes* for voice and pf.

Lélio, or Le Retour à la Vie (*L., or The Return to Life*), 'lyric monodrama' by Berlioz for an actor, solo voices, chorus, pf. and orch., op. 14bis, comp. in 1831 as a sequel to the *Symphonie fantastique* and 1st perf. with the latter, Paris Cons., 9 Dec 1832.

Lemare, Edwin (Henry) (b Ventnor, Isle of Wight, 9 Sep 1865; d Los Angeles, 24 Sep 1934), English organist and composer. Studied at the RAM in London and after var. church apps. became organist of St Margaret's, Westminster. In 1900 he toured in USA having by that time become a very successful concert organist. He was attached to the Carnegie Inst. at Pittsburg from 1902–15, was municipal organist at San Francisco, 1917–21, and at Portland, Maine, from 1921.
Works incl. 2 symphs. for organ and a vast amount of other concert music for his instrument.

Lemeshev, Sergey (b Knyazevo, 10 Jul 1902; d Moscow, 26 Jun 1977), Russian tenor. He studied with Stanislavsky; debut

Sverdlovsk 1926. Bolshoy, Moscow, from 1931 as Lensky, Faust, Roméo and Alamaviva and in operas by Glinka, Rimsky-Korsakov and Nápravník. Retired 1961. Made some films, and dir. opera from 1951.

Lemmens, Jaak Nikolaas (b Zoerle-Parwijs, Westerloo, 3 Jan 1823; d Linterpoort, nr. Malines, 30 Jan 1881), Belgian organist, pianist and composer. Studied at the Brussels Cons. and with Hesse at Breslau. In 1849 he became organ prof. at the Brussels Cons., but after 1857, when he married Hellen Sherrington, he lived much in England.
Works incl. sonata, offertories and other concert music for organ, a treatise for accomp. of plainsong, etc.

Lemmens-Sherrington (*née Sherrington*), **Hellen** (b Preston, 4 Oct 1834; d Brussels, 9 May 1906), English soprano, wife of prec. Studied with Verhulst at Rotterdam and at the Brussels Cons., and made her debut in London in 1856.

Lemminkainen's Return, symph. legend by Sibelius, op. 22, one of 4 on subjects from the *Kalevala*, comp. in 1893–5, fp Helsinki, 13 Apr 1896. The other three are *The Swan of Tuonela, L. and the Maidens of Saari, L. in Tuonela.*

Lemnitz, Tiana (b Metz, 26 Oct 1897), German soprano. Studied in Metz and then at the Hoch Cons. in Frankfurt. She made her debut in 1921 and from 1922 to 1929 sang at Aachen. From 1929 to 1933 she was the leading soprano at Hanover and from 1934 to 1957 at the Berlin Staatsoper; roles there incl. Mimi, Aida, Desdemona, Sieglinde and Jenůfa. She sang at CG in 1936 and 1938, as Eva, Octavian and Pamina.

Lemoyne, Jean Baptiste (b Eymet, Périgord, 3 Apr 1751; d Paris, 30 Dec 1796), French composer and conductor. Having cond. in the provinces, he went to Berlin to study with Graun, Kirnberger and Schulz, and was there app. 2nd *Kapellmeister* by Frederick the Great. But after visiting Warsaw he returned to France and prod. in 1782 the opera *Électre* in the style of Gluck, whose pupil he claimed to be. When Gluck denied this, he joined the partisans of Piccinni.
Works incl. operas *Electre* (after Sophocles, 1782), *Phèdre* (after Racine, 1786), *Les Prétendus* (1789), *Nephté*, etc.; ballets.

Lenér Quartet, Hungarian ensemble founded 1918 with Janö Lenér and Joseph Smilovits (vlns.), Sandor Roth (vla.), Imre Hartmann (cello). Many concerts in London 1922–39; most often heard in 4tets of Beethoven, which they recorded complete. NY from 1929. Largely avoided modern repertory. **'Leningrad' Symphony**, Shostakovich's 7th symph., op. 60, awarded the Stalin prize in 1942 and 1st perf. Kuibishev, by the evacuated Bolshoy Theatre Orch. of Moscow, 5 Mar 1942. The Nazi march in the 1st movt. is parodied by Bartók in his Concerto for Orchestra (1944).

Lento (It.). = slow.

Lenton, John (b 1656; d London, c 1719), English violinist and composer. He was a musician at court under Charles II, William and Mary and Anne, pub. an instruction book for the vln. containing airs of his own, revised the tunes for Durfey's *Wit and Mirth* and contrib. songs for var. collections.
Works incl. incid. music for Shakespeare's *Othello* (1697), Otway's *Venice Preserved* (1707), Rowe's *Tamerlane* and *The Fair Penitent* and other plays.

Lenz, Wilhelm von (b Riga, 1 Jun 1809; d St Petersburg, 31 Jan 1883), Latvian statesman and writer on music. Councillor at St Petersburg. Pub. 2 books on Beethoven, *Beethoven et ses trois styles* and *Beethoven: eine Kunststudie*, as well as studies of contemporary pf. virtuosi.

Leo, Leonardo (Lionardo Oronzo Salvatore de) (b San Vito degli Schiavi, nr. Brindisi, 5 Aug 1694; d Naples, 31 Oct 1744), Italian composer. Pupil of Provenzale and Fago in Naples at the Cons. della Pietà dei Turchini, 1709–13, where his first oratorio was perf. in 1712. App. supernumerary organist to the court in 1713, he rose to become royal *maestro di cappella* just before his death. As a teacher at the Cons. della Pietà (from 1715, *maestro* 1741) and the Cons. S. Onofrio (from 1725, *maestro* 1739) he incl. among his pupils Piccinni and Jommelli.
Works incl. operas *Sofonisba* (1718), *Lucio Papirio*, *Caio Gracco* (1720), *La 'mpeca scoperta* (in Neapol. dialect, 1723), *Timocrate*, *Il trionfo di Camilla*, *La semmeglianza di chi l'ha fatta*, *Il Cid*, *Catone in Utica* (1729), *La clemenza di Tito* (1835), *Demofoonte*, *Farnace* (1736), *Siface*, *Ciro riconosciuto*, *L'amico traditore*, *La simpatia del sangue*, *L'Olimpiade* (1737), *Vologeso*, *Amor vuol sofferenza* (*La finta Frascatana*, 1739), *Achille in Sciro* (1740), *Scipione nelle Spagne* (1740), *Il fantastico* (*Il nuovo Don Chisciotte*, after Cervantes, 1743) and c 40 others; oratorios *Il trionfo della castità di S. Alessio* (1713), *Dalla morte alla vita* (1722), *La morte di Abele*, *S. Elena al Calvario* (1734), *S. Francesco di Paolo nel deserto* and

others; Masses, motets, psalms and other church music; concerto for 4 vlns., 6 cello concertos; harpsichord pieces.

Leoncavallo, Ruggiero (b Naples, 23 Apr 1857; d Montecatini, nr. Florence, 9 Aug 1919), Italian composer. Studied pf. privately at first and then entered the Naples Cons., which he left in 1876 with a master diploma. He went to Bologna to attend Carducci's lectures in lit. There he was on the point of prod. his 1st opera, *Chatterton*, but was swindled and found himself penniless. He made a precarious living by lessons and playing the pf. at cafés, but later managed to travel widely as café pianist. He then began a trilogy on the It. Renaissance, *Crepusculum*, with *I Medici*, but never prod. the 2 following works, *Savonarola* and *Cesare Borgia*. In the meantime he made an enormous success with *Pagliacci* at Milan in 1892 and soon all over It. *La Bohème* at Venice in 1897 suffered from the appearance of Puccini's work on the same subject, and in spite of a commission for a Ger. opera for Berlin, *Der Roland von Berlin*, in 1904, he never repeated his *Pagliacci* success. He wrote all his own libs. and some for other comps.
Works incl. operas *Chatterton* (after Alfred de Vigny, comp. 1876, prod. 1896), *I Medici*, *Pagliacci* (1892), *La Bohème* (after Murger, 1897), *Zaza*, *Der Roland von Berlin* (after Willibald Alexis, 1904), *Maia* (1910), *Gli zingari*, *Goffredo Mameli*, *Edipo rè* (after Sophocles, 1920), *Tormenta* (unfinished); operettas *A chi la giarettiera* (1919), *Il primo bacio*, *Malbruk* (1910), *La reginetta delle rose*, *Are you there?* (1913), *La candidata* and *Prestami tua moglie*; ballet *La vita d'una marionetta*; symph. poem *Serafita* (after Balzac's novel).

Leonhardt, Gustav (b 's Graveland, 30 May 1928), Dutch harpsichordist and conductor. He studied in Basle; debut Vienna 1950 in a solo perf. of *The Art of Fugue*. Frequent tours of Europe and USA in wide range of early keyboard music; has cond. Baroque opera and choral music. He has ed. most of Sweelinck's keyboard works and two perfs. of the *Goldberg Variations* by Bach are among his recordings.

Leoni, Leone (b Verona, c 1560; d Vicenza, 24 Jun 1627), Italian composer. *Maestro di cappella* of Vicenza Cathedral from 1588.
Works incl. Masses, motets (some in many parts with instruments), *Sacrae cantiones*, psalms, Magnificats and other church music, sacred and secular madrigals.

Leoninus (**Leonius**, now sometimes called Léonin) (d Paris, c 1201), French poet, theologian and composer. 1st documented in 1179, he was active mainly at Notre-Dame, Paris, for which he is said to have comp. the *Magnus liber organi* containing at least 42 settings of music for the Mass and Office in 2 voices. This formed the basis of the great Notre-Dame repertory later elaborated by Perotinus and others.

Leonora, ossia L'amore conjugale (*Leonora, or Wedded Love*), opera by Paer (lib. by ? G. Cinti, based on Bouilly's lib. for Gaveaux), prod. Dresden, 3 Oct 1804.

Leonora Overtures (Beethoven). *See Fidelio.*

Léonore, ou L'Amour conjugal (*Leonora, or Wedded Love*), opera by Gaveaux (lib. by J.N. Bouilly, based on a real event), prod. Paris, Théâtre Feydeau, 19 Feb 1798. A forerunner and model of Beethoven's *Fidelio.*

Leonova, Daria (Mikhailovna) (b Vyshny-Volotchok, 21 Mar 1829; d St Petersburg, 6 Feb 1896), Russian contralto. Pupil of Glinka; made her 1st appearance at St Petersburg in his *Life for the Tsar* in 1852. She created roles in Dargomizhsky's *Rusalka* and *Boris Godunov*; helped Mussorgsky towards the end of his life by engaging him as pianist on a tour in S. Rus. and at her singing-school at St Petersburg.

Leopold I (b Vienna, 9 Jun 1640; d Vienna, 5 May 1705), Holy Roman Emperor. Composed an opera, *Apollo deluso*, to a lib. by his court musician Antonio Draghi, 1669, and contrib. to numerous other operas by the same comp. His oratorios incl. *Il sagrifizio d'Abramo* (1660), *Il figliuol prodigo* (1663), *Il lutto dell' universo* (1668).

Leopolita, Martinus (Marcin Lwowczyk) (b Lwów, c 1540; d Lwów, 1589), Polish composer. Member of the Coll. of Roratists and court comp. at Kraków from 1560.

Works incl. Masses (e.g. *Missa Paschalis*), motets; secular songs for several voices, etc.

Lepetit, Nono (Ninot) (d Rome, 1502), French composer. His sacred and secular music appears in the pubs. of Petrucci as well as in MSS. He wrote *chansons* and motets.

L'Épine, (Francesca) Margherita de (b c 1683; d London, 8 Aug 1746), French soprano. She settled in Eng. in 1692, and married Pepusch in 1718; sang in many masques and cantatas by him.

Leppard, Raymond (b London, 11 Aug 1927), English conductor, harpsichordist and editor. He studied at Cambridge. Debut as cond. London, 1952; regular cond. ECO since 1960, BBC Northern SO 1973–80. He gave *Solomon* at CG in 1959 and in 1962

Monteverdi's *L'incoronazione di Poppea* at Glyndebourne. This was the first of several realizations of Venetian opera, all of which have attracted scholarly comment for making too many transpositions, having too much music from other sources and inst. parts realized in too lavish a manner. However, Leppard's versions of Monteverdi, and Cavalli's *L'Ormindo, La Calisto, L'Egisto* and *Orione*, have been popular with the public. He has been based in the US since 1980: prin. guest cond. St Louis SO from 1984; Indianapolis SO from 1986. CBE 1983.

Leroux, Xavier (Henri Napoléon) (b Velletri, It., 11 Oct 1863; d Paris, 2 Feb 1919), French composer. Studied at the Paris Cons., among his masters being Massenet, and gained the Prix de Rome in 1885. He became harmony prof. there in 1896 and ed. the periodical *Musica.*

Works incl. operas *Évangeline* (1885), *Astarté, La Reine Fiammette* (after Catulle Mendès, 1903), *William Ratcliff* (after Heine, 1906), *Théodora, Le Chemineau* (1907), *Le Carillonneur* (1913), *La Fille de Figaro* (1914), *Les Cadeaux de Noël, 1814, Nausithoé, La Plus Forte, L'Ingénu*; incid. music to Sardou and Moreau's *Cléopâtre* (1890), Aeschylus's *The Persians* and Richepin's *Xantho chez les courtisanes*; cantatas *Endymion* (1885) and *Vénus et Adonis* (1897); overture *Harald*; Mass with orch.; motets; numerous songs.

Leschetizky, Theodor (b Lańcut, Pol., 22 Jun 1830; d Dresden, 14 Nov 1915), Polish–Austrian pianist, teacher and composer. Pupil of Czerny and Sechter in Vienna. He was pf. prof. at St Petersburg Cons., 1852–78, and then settled in Vienna as an independent teacher of many famous pupils, incl. Paderewski.

Works incl. opera *Die erste Falte* (prod. Prague 1867); many pf. pieces.

L'Escurel, Jehannot de (d prob. 1303), French composer. His 34 secular works, all but one of which are monophonic, are incl. in the same MS. as the *Roman de Fauvel* (*see* **Fauvel**).

Lessel, Franz (Franciszek) (b Puławy, c 1780; d Piotrków, 26 Dec 1838), Polish–Austrian composer. Studied medicine in Vienna, but became a pupil of Haydn, whom he looked after until his death. He then returned to Poland and lived with Prince Czartoryski's family until they were driven away by the Revolution. The rest of his life was unsettled.

Works incl. 3 Masses, Requiem and other

church music; 5 symphs.; pf. concerto; chamber music; pf. sonatas and fantasies, etc.

Lesson, a 17th–18th-cent. term for a keyboard piece, generally of an instructive character.

Lesueur, Jean François (b Drucat-Plessiel, nr. Abbeville, 15 Feb 1760; d Paris, 6 Oct 1837), French composer. He 1st learnt music as a choir-boy at Abbeville, then held church appts. at Amiens and Paris. After 1781 he became *maître de chapelle* successively at Dijon Cathedral, Le Mans, Tours, SS. Innocents, Paris, 1784, and Notre-Dame, Paris, 1786. He was allowed to use a full orch. at Mass and to open the proceedings with an overture. This aroused a controversy which led to his resignation, and he spent 1788–92 in the country, devoted to the comp. of operas. In 1793 he was app. prof. at the school of the Nat. Guard and in 1795 one of the inspectors at the newly opened Cons. In 1804 he succeeded Paisiello as *maître de chapelle* to Napoleon, after whose fall he was app. superintendent and comp. to the chapel of Louis XVIII. In 1818 he became prof. of comp. at the Cons., where his pupils incl. Berlioz and Gounod.

Works incl. operas *Télémaque* (1796), *La Caverne* (1793), *Paulin et Virginie* (after Saint-Pierre, 1794), *Ossian, ou Les Bardes* (1804), *Le Triomphe de Trajan* (with Persuis, 1807), *La Mort d'Adam* (after Klopstock, 1809), and some others; Mass and Te Deum for Napoleon's coronation, 3 Solemn Masses, *Stabat Mater*, motets, psalms and other church music; oratorios *Messe de Noël, Debora, Rachel, Ruth et Noémi, Ruth et Boaz*; cantatas.

Lesur, Daniel (b Paris, 19 Nov 1908), French organist and composer. Pupil of Tournemire, Caussade and others. In 1938 he became prof. of counterpoint at the Schola Cantorum in Paris. He was also app. organist at the Benedictine abbey, and with Baudrier, Jolivet and Messiaen formed the group known as 'La Jeune France'.

Works incl. opera *Andrea del Sarto* (1969); *Suite française* for orch. (1935); *Passacaille* for pf. and orch. (1937); suite for string trio and pf.; 3 Heine songs for voice and string 4tet; *Noëls* and suite *Le Carillon* for pf.; *La Vie intérieure* for org.; songs.

Letters, Music based on. Composers have sometimes amused themselves by turning names or other words into notes representing in musical nomenclature the letters of which they are formed, or as many as can be thus used. In Eng. the letters A to G can be thus represented; in Ger. H (= B♮) and S (Es

= E♭) can be added, and in Fr. and It. the syllables Do, Re, Mi, Fa, Sol, La, Si may be used. In Fr. a system was devised for the works on the names of Fauré and Haydn listed below, whereby the notes A to G were followed by further 8ves named from H onwards. Here are some exs.:

Abegg (supposed friends of Schumann's): Schumann, *Variations on the Name of A.* for pf., op. 1.

Asch (the birthplace of Ernestine von Fricken): Schumann, *Carnaval* for pf. op. 9.

Bach. *See* **B.A.C.H.**, *also* Faber *below*.

Bamberg (the maiden name of Cui's wife): Cui, scherzo for pf. duet (on B.A.B.E.G. and C.C. = César Cui).

Belaiev: Borodin, Glazunov, Liadov and Rimsky-Korsakov, string 4tet on 'B-la-F.'

Faber: canon in 7 parts by Bach, dated 1 Mar 1749, sung over a Ground or *Pes* on the notes F. A. B(♭). E. and marked 'F A B E Repetatur,' thus forming the name Faber, which may be a Latin form of some Ger. surname derived from some kind of manual labour. The canon also bears an inscription in Latin containing the following acrostics on the names of Faber and Bach: 'Fidelis Amici Beatum Esse Recordari' and 'Bonae Artis Cultorem Habeas.' *See also* **B.A.C.H.**

Fauré: pieces by Aubert, Enescu, Koechlin, Ladmirault, Ravel, Roger-Ducasse and Schmitt contrib. to a Fauré number of the *Revue musicale* in 1924.

Gade: Schumann's pf. piece so entitled in *Album für die Jugend*. Rheinberger, fughetta for org.

Gedge: Elgar, allegretto for vln. and pf. on G.E.D.G.E., ded. to the Misses Gedge.

Haydn: Ravel, *Menuet sur le nom d'Haydn* for pf.

Sacha: Glazunov, *Suite sur le thème du nom diminutif russe* for pf., op. 2.

Schumann (letters S.C.H.A. only): *Carnaval* (inversion of the letters Λ.S.C.H.).

Leutgeb (or **Leitgeb**), **Ignaz** (b ? Salzburg, c 1745; d Vienna, 27 Feb 1811), Austrian horn-player. He was 1st horn in the orch. of the Archbishop of Salzburg, then settled in Vienna as a cheese merchant. Mozart wrote his 4 horn concertos and the horn 5tet for him.

Levasseur, Nicolas (Prosper) b Bresles, Oise, 9 Mar 1791; d Paris, 6 Dec 1871), French bass. Studied at the Paris Cons. and made his 1st stage appearance in 1813 in Grétry's *La caravane du Caire*; created roles in Rossini's *Moïse*, Meyerbeer's *Margherita d'Anjou, Robert le diable, Les Huguenots* and *Le Prophète* and Donizetti's *La favorite*.

Levasseur, Rosalie (Marie Claude Josephe) (b Valenciennes, 8 Oct 1749; d Neuwied-on-Rhine, 6 May 1826), French soprano. Sang at the Paris Opéra from 1766 (debut in Campra's *L'Europe galante*), and in the 1770s had great success in Gluck's Paris operas; created the title roles in *Armide, Alceste, Iphigénie en Tauride*.

Leveridge, Richard (b London, c 1670; d London, 22 Mar 1758), English bass and composer. He appeared as a singer mainly in pantomimes etc., but also in It. opera, his career extending from 1695 to 1751. As a comp. he is remembered for his songs.

Works incl. incid. music for Shakespeare's *Macbeth* (1702), Farquhar's *The Recruiting Officer, Love and a Bottle* and (with D. Purcell) *The Constant Couple*, Vanbrugh's *Aesop* and other plays; masque *Pyramus and Thisbe* (after Shakespeare, 1716); songs, e.g. 'The Roast Beef of Old England'.

Levi, Hermann (b Giessen, 7 Nov 1839; d Munich, 13 May 1900), German conductor. Studied with V. Lachner at Munich and at the Leipzig Cons. After var. appts. he became dir. of the Munich court theatre, 1872–96 (gave his own eds. of Mozart's operas). Cond. the fp of Wagner's *Parsifal* at Bayreuth, continued at Bayreuth until 1894.

Levine, James (b Cincinnati, 23 Jun 1943), American conductor. He studied at the Juilliard School and was asst. cond. to George Szell in Cleveland 1964–70. Brit. debut with WNO 1970, with *Aida*, and in 1971 cond. *Tosca* at the NY Met; music dir. from 1975. Salzburg Fest. from 1976, and in 1982 gave *Parsifal* at Bayreuth. Often heard in Mahler's symphs.

Levy, Marvin David (b Passaic, NJ, 2 Aug 1932), American composer. He studied at NY and Columbia Univs.; worked as music critic in 1950s.

Works incl. operas *Sobota Komachi* (1957), *The Tower* (1957), *Escorial* (1958), *Mourning Becomes Elektra* (prod. NY Met 1967), *The Balcony* (1978); string 4tet (1955); Christmas Oratorio, *For the Time Being* (1959); Symph. (1960); *Sacred Service* (1964); pf. concerto (1970).

Lewenthal, Raymond (b San Antonio, 29 Aug 1926), American pianist and editor. He studied at Juilliard and with Cortot. Well known in Thalberg, Henselt and Liszt and has ed. a collection of pf. works by Alkan.

Lewis, Anthony (Carey) (b Bermuda, 2 Mar 1915; d Haslemere, 5 Jun 1983), English musicologist, conductor and composer. Educ. at Wellington Coll. and Cambridge, he studied music at the latter, at the RCM in London and with Nadia Boulanger in Paris. He was on the music staff of the BBC in 1935–47 (except during his war service in 1939–45), organizing various series of music incl. finally the music on the 3rd Programme. From 1947 to 1968 was Prof. of Music at Birmingham Univ. and in 1968 was app. prin. of the RAM in London; remained until 1982. He edited and cond. operas by Purcell, Rameau and Handel. Knighted 1972.

Works incl. *Choral Overture* for unaccomp. voices; *Elegy and Capriccio* for tpt. and orch.; horn concerto.

Lewis, Richard (b Manchester, 10 May 1914), English tenor. Studied privately with T.W. Evans at the RMCM and later at the RAM with Norman Allin. He made his debut in the Glyndebourne chorus in 1947. In the same year he also sang at CG, London, as Peter Grimes; created Walton's Troilus and Tippett's Mark there, and sang Aron in the 1st GB perf. of Schoenberg's *Moses und Aron* (1965). Also heard in concert (Elgar and Mahler) and sang in the fp of Stravinsky's *Canticum Sacrum* (Venice 1956).

Ley, Henry G(eorge) (b Chagford, Devon, 30 Dec 1887; d nr. Ottery St Mary, 24 Aug 1962), English organist and conductor. Studied at Keble Coll., Oxford, and was app. organist at Christ Church Cathedral there in 1909. Later taught organ at the RCM in London. Dir. of music at Eton Coll. from 1926 to 1945.

Works incl. church music; variations on a theme by Handel for orch.; chamber music; organ music; songs.

Lhérie, Paul (b Paris, 8 Oct 1844; d Paris, 17 Oct 1937), French tenor, later baritone. He sang at the Paris Opéra-Comique from 1866 and in 1875 created Don José there. By 1884 he had changed to a baritone and sang Posa at La Scala, in Verdi's revision of *Don Carlos*. CG 1887, as Rigoletto and Luna. Retired 1894.

L'Héritier, Jean (b c 1480; d after 1552), French composer. Pupil of Josquin Desprez. Wrote Masses, motets, etc. He was in Rome in the 1520s and was music dir. to the Cardinal de Vermont at Avignon 1540–1.

Lhévinne, Josef (b Orel, 13 Dec 1874; d New York, 2 Dec 1944), Russian pianist. After some study at home he entered the Moscow Cons. and studied with Safonov, playing Beethoven's 5th piano concerto at the age of 15. He graduated in 1891 and in 1895 won the Rubinstein Prize. From 1900 to 1902 he taught at the Tiflis Cons. and in 1902–6 at the Cons. in Moscow. He made many tours and from 1907 to 1919 lived mostly in Berlin. He went to the USA in 1919 and taught at the Juilliard Graduate School. He had an impeccable technique and a profound understanding of music. His wife **Rosina** (1880–1976), gave pf. recitals until the mid-1960s and taught at Juilliard from 1922.

L'Homme armé. See **Homme armé.**

Liadov, Anatol (Constantinovich) (b St Petersburg, 10 May 1855; d Novgorod, 28 Aug 1914), Russian composer. Studied under his father and later with Rimsky-Korsakov at the St Petersburg Cons., where he became a teacher in 1878. The Imp. Geographical Society commissioned him, with Balakirev and Liapunov, to collect folksongs in var. parts of the country.

Works incl. symph. poems *Baba Yaga* (1904), *The Enchanted Lake* (1909), *Kikimora* (1909), 2 orch. scherzos, *The Inn-Muzurka, Polonaise in Memory of Pushkin for orch.; choral settings from Schiller's* Bride of Messina and Maeterlinck's *Sœur Béatrice*, 3 choral works for female voices; *c* 40 op. nos. of pf. pieces, incl. *Birulki (Spillikins)*, ballads *From Days of Old, Marionettes, Musical Snuff-Box*, variations on a theme by Glinka and on a Pol. song, *From the Book of Revelation*, studies, preludes, marurkas, etc.; songs, folksong settings (1903).

Liapunov, Sergey Mikhailovich (b Yaroslav, 30 Nov 1859; d Paris, 8 Nov 1924), Russian pianist and composer. Studied at Nizhny-Novgorod and at the Moscow Cons. In 1893 the Imp. Geographical Society commissioned him, with Balakirev and Liadov, to collect folksongs. From 1891 to 1902 he was ass. dir. of the Imp. Chapel, and from 1910 prof. at the St Petersburg Cons. He took refuge in Paris from the Revolution.

Works incl. 2 symphs. (1887, 1910–17), *Ballad, Solemn Overture,* Polonaise and symph. poem *Hashish* for orch.; 2 pf. concertos (1890, 1909), rhapsody on Ukrainian themes for pf. and orch. (1908); numerous pf. pieces, incl. suite *Christmas Songs*, etc.; folksong settings.

Liberati, Antimo (b Foligno, 3 Apr 1617; d Rome, 24 Feb 1692), Italian singer, organist and composer. Pupil of Allegri and Benevoli in Rome, where in 1661 he became a singer in the Papal Chapel (and later *maestro di cappella*) and organist at 2 churches. He wrote a letter giving particulars for Palestrina's biog. and another defending a passage in Corelli.

Works incl. oratorios, madrigals, arias.

Liberté, '14 tableaux inspirés par l'histoire

du peuple de France,' music by Delannoy, Honegger, Ibert, Lazarus, Milhaud, Roland-Manuel, Rosenthal, Tailleferre and others, prod. Paris, Théâtre des Champs-Élysées, May 1937.

Libretto (It. = booklet), the text of an opera or other vocal work in dramatic form.

Libuše, opera by Smetana (lib., in Ger., by J. Wenzig, Czech trans. by E. Spindler), prod. Prague, Cz. Theatre, 11 Jun 1881.

Licenza (It., plur. *licenze*) = licence, freedom, liberty, e.g. the direction *con alcune licenze* = 'with some freedom' (in form, style or perf.); up to the 18th cent., a cadenza or ornament inserted at the performer's discretion and not written down by the comp.; also, in 17th-cent. opera, esp. in Vienna, a musical epilogue to a stage perf. with special reference to the occasion (royal birthday, wedding, etc.).

Licette, Miriam (b Chester, 9 Sep 1892; d Twyford, 11 Aug 1969), English soprano. She studied in Milan and Paris. Debut Rome 1911, Butterfly. Joined Beecham's co. 1915 and sang at CG 1919–29. Other roles incl. Eva, Eurydice (with Clara Butt), Juliette, Pamina, Gutrune and Desdemona.

Lichnovsky, (Prince) Karl (b Vienna, 21 Jun 1761; d Vienna, 15 Mar 1814). Polish aristocrat, resident in Vienna. After early patronage of Mozart he was introduced to Beethoven by Haydn. Beethoven's early chamber works were played at his house before publication, notably the string 4tets op. 18, with the Schuppanzigh quartet.

Licht (Light), cycle of 7 projected operas by Stockhausen, 1 for each day of the week. See **Donnerstag aus Licht, Samstag aus Licht.**

Lickl, Johann Georg (b Korneuburg, 11 Apr 1769; d Pécs, 12 May 1843), Austrian composer. He wrote several musical plays for Schikaneder's theatre.

Works incl. plays with music; Masses, motets; chamber music, etc.

Lidarti, Christian Joseph (b Vienna, 23 Feb 1730; d Pisa, after 1793), Austro-Italian composer. Pupil of his uncle, Bonno, in Vienna and later of Jommelli in It. In the service of the Cavalieri di S. Stefano in Pisa, 1757–1784.

Works incl. trio sonatas, catches and glees.

Lidholm, Ingvar (b Jönköping, 24 Feb 1921), Swedish composer. Studied at the Stockholm Cons. with, among others, Hilding Rosenberg and Tor Mann. Later he studied in It. and Fr., and also with Seiber. From 1947 to 1956 he was cond. of the Örebro SO.

Works incl. opera *The Dutchman* (after Strindberg, 1967), concerto for string orch., *Toccata e canto* for chamber orch. (1944), *Ritornell* for orch. (1956); concertino for fl., cor anglais, ob. and bassoon; *Cantata* for baritone and orch.; string 4tet, 4 pieces for cello and pf., sonata for solo fl.

Lidl, Andreas (b Vienna, *c* 1740; d London, *c* 1789), Austrian baryton virtuoso and composer. He increased the strings on his instrument, travelled much on the Continent and 1st appeared in London in 1778.

Works incl. chamber music; pieces for the baryton.

Lie, Sigurd (b Drammen, 23 May 1871; d Vestre Aker, 30 Sep 1904), Norwegian conductor, violinist and composer. Studied at the Leipzig Cons. and in 1894 became choral and theatre cond. at Bergen. After further study in Berlin he became choral cond. at Christiania.

Works incl. symph. in A min. (1903), *Orientalisk Suite* (1899), *Marche symphonique* for orch.; cantatas and other choral works; pf. 5tet; songs.

Liebe der Danae, Die (*Danae's Love*), opera by R. Strauss (lib. by Josef Gregor), intended for prod. at the Salzburg Festival and given public dress rehearsal on 16 Aug 1944. Prod. postponed owing to war; prod. there 14 Aug 1952. The title was orig. *Der Kuss der Danae* (*D.'s Kiss*).

Liebe im Narrenhaus, Die (*Love in the Madhouse*), opera by Dittersdorf (lib. by G. Stephanie, jun.), prod. Vienna, Kärntnertortheater, 12 Apr 1787.

Liebermann, Rolf (b Zurich, 14 Sep 1910), Swiss composer and administrator. Studied cond. with Scherchen and comp. with Vladimir Vogel at Zurich, and was later app. to the staff of Radio-Zurich. Dir. Hamburg Opera, 1959–73. Intendant, Paris Opéra 1973–80. Some of his work is based on the 12-note system. In 1987 his 1st opera for 30 years was prod. in Geneva.

Works incl. operas *Leonore 40/45* (1952), *Penelope* (1954), *School for Wives* (after Molière 1957), *La forêt* (1987); incid. music; film music; cantata *Streitlied zwischen Leben und Tod*; polyphonic studies and folksong suite for orch.; concerto for jazz band and orch.; solo cantatas *Une des fins du monde* (Giraudoux), *Chinesische Liebeslieder* (Klabund) and *Chinesisches Lied* (do.), pf. sonata.

Liebert, Reginaldus, early 15th-cent French composer. He prob. succeeded Grenon at Cambrai in 1424. His main work is a complete Mass (Ordinary and Proper) of the Blessed Virgin Mary for 3 voices. A Gautier Liebert, composer of 3 *rondeaux*, was a papal singer in 1428.

Liebeslieder (*Love Songs*), a set of waltzes by Brahms for pf. duet with solo vocal quartet *ad lib.*, op. 52, comp. in 1869. There is a 2nd set of *Neue Liebeslieder*, op. 65, written in 1874.

Liebesverbot, Das, oder Die Novize von Palermo (*The Love-Ban, or The Novice of P.*), opera by Wagner (lib. by comp., based on Shakespeare's *Measure for Measure*), prod. Magdeburg, 29 Mar 1836.

Lied (Ger.) = Song.

Lied von der Erde, Das (*The Song of the Earth*), symph. for mezzo, tenor and orch. by Mahler (so called by the comp., but not numbered among his other symphs.). The words are from Hans Bethge's anthology of Ger. transs. of Chinese poetry, *Die chinesische Flöte*: 1. (Li-Tai-Po). *Das Trinklied vom Jammer der Erde* (*The Drinking-Song of Earth's Misery*); 2. (Tchang-Tsi) *Der Einsame im Herbst* (*The Lonely One in Autumn*); 3. (Li-Tai-Po) *Von der Jugend* (*Of Youth*); 4. (do.) *Von der Schönheit* (*Of Beauty*); 5. (do.) *Der Trunkene im Frühling* (*The Drunkard in Spring*); 6. (Mong-Kao-Yen and Wang-We) *Der Abschied* (*The Farewell*). Comp. in 1908; fp Munich, 20 Nov 1911, after Mahler's death.

Lieder eines fahrenden Gesellen (Songs of a wayfaring man), song-cycle by Mahler for low voice and pf. (texts by M.); comp. 1884, orch. *c* 1895 and perf. in this vers. Berlin, 16 Mar 1896, cond. Mahler. Titles of songs are 1. *Wenn mein Schatz Hochzeit macht* (*When my sweetheart gets married*), 2. *Ging heut' Morgen übers Feld* (*I walked this morning through the fields*: thematically related to the 1st. movt of the contemp. 1st. symph.); 3. *Ich hab ein glühend Messer in der Brust* (*I have a burning knife in my breast*; 4. *Die zwei blauen Augen* (*The two blue eyes*). Also heard in vers. with chamber ens. by Schoenberg.

Lieder ohne Worte, 36 pf. pieces by Mendelssohn in the form and character of songs exploiting the principle of accomp. melody rather than polyphonic textures. Vol. I, op. 19, nos. 1–6 (1830–2); II, op. 30, 7–12 (1833–7); III, op. 38, 13–18 (1836–7); IV, op. 53, 19–24 (1841); V. op. 62, 25–30 (1842–3); VI, op. 67, 31–6 (1843–5). The only titles which are Mendelssohn's own are those of the 3 *Venezianische Gondellieder* (*Venetian Barcarolles*), nos. 6, 12, and 29, the *Duetto*, no. 18, and the *Volkslied*, no. 23.

Liederkreis (Ger.). Title used for 2 sets of

songs by Schumann: 9 Heine settings op. 24 and 12 Eichendorff settings op. 39 (both 1840). *See also* **Song Cycle.**

Liederspiel (Ger. lit. 'song-play'), a play with songs similar to the *Singspiel.* The term was 1st used by Reichardt in 1800. It may also mean 'song cycle', e.g. Schumann's *Spanisches Liederspiel.*

Liedertafel (Ger. lit. 'song-table' or 'singing-table'), a male-voice choral assoc. doubtless deriving its name from early gatherings seated round a table drinking and singing.

Lieutenant Kijé, symphonic suite by Prokofiev, arr. in 1934 from film music comp. 1933. 5 movts. are *Birth of K., Romance, Wedding, Troika, Burial*; fp Paris, 20 Feb 1937, cond. Prokofiev.

Life for the Tsar, A (*Zhizn za Tsaria*; now *Ivan Susanin*), opera by Glinka (lib. by C.F. Rosen), prod. St Petersburg, 9 Dec 1836.

Ligabue, Ilva (b Reggio Emilia, 23 May 1932), Italian soprano. She studied in Milan; debut at La Scala in Wolf-Ferrari's *I quattro Rusteghi.* Glyndebourne 1958–61 as Alice Ford, Fiordiligi and Donna Elvira. In 1961 she sang Bellini's Beatrice at La Scala, Milan, and Margherita in Boito's *Mefistofele* at the Lyric Theatre, Chicago; NY debut (in concert) 1963. She has appeared as guest in Vienna, Dallas and Buenos Aires.

Ligature(s), a group of 2 or more notes in medieval and Renaissance music. Also the var. signs, originating in plainsong notation, by which such groups are indicated, e.g.:

Modern equivalent

Ligendza, Catarina (b Stockholm, 18 Oct 1937), Swedish soprano. Debut Linz, 1963, as Mozart's Countess. After singing in Germany she was heard as Arabella at La Scala, Milan, in 1970; sang Leonore at the NY Met the following year, also Brünnhilde at Bayreuth; Isolde there 1974–7. Salzburg Easter Fest. from 1969.

Ligeti, György (b Dicsöszentmarton, Transylvania, 28 May 1923), Hungarian composer. Studied comp. with Sándor Veress and Ferenc Farkas at the Budapest Music Acad. (1945–9), becoming an instructor there from 1950 to 1956. In 1956 he went to the Studio for Electronic Music at Cologne, and in 1959 was app. instructor at the International Courses for New Music at Darmstadt. In 1961 he was visiting prof. of comp. at the Stockholm Music Acad., and eventually settled in Vienna. His mature music is experimental in nature.

Works incl. opera *Le Grand Macabre* (prod. Stockholm 1978); *Artikulation* for electronic sounds (1958); *Apparitions* for orch. (1959); *Atmosphères* for large orch. (1961); *Poème symphonique* for 100 metronomes; *Aventures* for soprano, alto and baritone with 7 insts. (1962); *Nouvelles Aventures* for soprano and 7 instruments; Requiem for soloists, chorus and orch. (1965; Kyrie used in film *2001*); *Lux aeterna* for 16 solo voices; cello concerto (1967); *Ramifications* for string orch. (1969); Chamber Concerto for 13 insts. (1970); *San Francisco Polyphony* for orch. (1974); Trio for vln., horn and pf. (1982), *3 Phantasien* and *Hungarian Studies*, both for 16 voices (1983).

Light of Life, The (*Lux Christi*), oratorio by Elgar for soloists, chorus and orch., op. 29 (text by E. Capel-Dure from the Scriptures); comp. 1896, fp Worcester, 10 Sep 1896, cond. Elgar.

Lighthouse, The, chamber opera in 1 act by Peter Maxwell Davies (text by comp., based on 1900 disappearance of 3 Outer Hebridean lighthouse keepers); comp. 1979, fp Edinburgh, 2 Sep 1980.

Lill, John (b London, 17 Mar 1944), English pianist. He studied at the RCM and with Wilhelm Kempff. London debut (Festival Hall) 1963. In 1970 won the Tchaikovsky Comp., Moscow. NY (Carnegie Hall) from 1969. OBE 1978. A powerful performer in 19th-cent. music, esp. Beethoven.

Lilliburlero, a satirical song sung in Ireland after the appt. of General Talbot to the lord-lieutenancy in 1687. It is not likely that the earlier attribution of the tune to Purcell is justified: it was prob. a popular melody merely arr. by him, much as *The Prince of Denmark's March* was arr. by J. Clarke.

Lima, Jeronymo Francisco de (b Lisbon, 30 Sep 1743; d Lisbon, 19 Feb 1822), Portuguese composer and organist. He was elected to the Brotherhood of St Cecilia, visited Italy and in 1798 became cond. of the Royal Opera at Lisbon.

Works incl. opera *Le nozze d'Ercole e d'Ebe* (1785) and 5 others (all It.); church music; cantatas.

Lima, Luis (b Cordoba, 12 Sep 1948), Argentine tenor. Debut Lisbon 1974 as Turiddu. He sang Edgardo at La Scala in 1977 and at the Vienna Staatsoper in 1981. In 1978 he was heard as Pinkerton at Verona and as Alfredo at the NY Met. At CG he has been admired as Nemorino and Don Carlos, both in 1985.

Limburgia, Johannes de, late 14th- and early 15th-cent. composer from N. France. He worked at churches in Liège, 1408–19, and in Italy from c 1430. His 50 or so comps. (all church music) incl. a complete Mass (3 and 4 voices) and 16 motets.

Lincke, Josef (b Trachenberg, Prus. Silesia, 8 Jun 1783; d Vienna, 26 Mar 1837), German cellist and composer. He settled in Vienna in 1808, becoming a member of Rasumovsky's quartet and later 1st cellist at the Vienna opera. Beethoven wrote the 2 sonatas op. 102 for him. He wrote concertos, variations, etc. for the cello.

Lincoln Portrait, A, work by Copland for orch. and a speaker, who declaims portions of Lincoln's speeches, fp by Cincinnati SO, 14 May 1942.

Lind, Jenny (b Stockholm, 6 Oct 1820; d Wynd's Point, Malvern Wells, 2 Nov 1887), Swedish soprano. 1st appeared at Stockholm, 1838, when she sang Agathe, Pamina and Euryanthe; studied with Garcia in Paris; sang much in Ger.; went to Eng. in 1847 and settled in London permanently; her roles there incl. Alice in *Robert le diable*, Amina, Marie, Susanna and Amalia in the fp of Verdi's *I Masnadieri* (1847). Distinguished in opera in her early years, but afterwards mainly as a concert singer. She made many extensive tours. Married Otto Goldschmidt in 1852. She was called 'The Swedish Nightingale'.

Linda di Chamounix, opera by Donizetti (lib. by G. Rossi, after a vaudeville, *La Grâce de Dieu*), prod. Vienna, Kärntnertortheater, 19 May 1842.

Lindberg, Oskar Fredrik (b Gagnef, 23 Feb 1887; d Stockholm, 10 Apr 1955), Swedish

organist and composer. Studied at the Stockholm Cons. and at Sonderhausen. In 1906 he was app. organist at a Stockholm church and in 1919 prof. at the Cons.

Works incl. Requiem (1922) and cantata for solo voices, chorus and orch.; symph. in F maj. (1912); *3 Pictures from Dalarne*, 3 overtures. poems *Wilderness, Flor and Blancheflor* and *From the Great Forests*, suite *Travel Memories* for orch.; pf. pieces; songs with orch. and with pf.

Lindblad, Adolf Fredrik (b Skänninge nr. Stockholm, 1 Feb 1801; d Linköping, 23 Aug 1878), Swedish composer and singing-teacher. Studied with Zelter in Berlin and in 1827 settled at Stockholm as teacher of singing. Jenny Lind was among his pupils.

Works incl. opera *Frondörerna* (1835); 2 symphs.; 7 string 4tets; duo for vln. and pf.; vocal duets, trios and 4tets; numerous songs.

Lindblad, Otto Jonas (b Karlstorp, 31 Mar 1809; d Ny Mellby, 24 Jan 1864), Swedish composer. Learnt the organ while studying theology, which he afterwards abandoned in order to study music, mainly by himself, though he had a few lessons at Copenhagen. Having learnt the vln. he joined a touring opera company, took part in a music festival at Hamburg in 1841 and founded a students' choral society at Lund.

Works incl. numerous choruses, vocal 4tets, trios and duets, songs.

Lindelheim, Johanna Maria (*fl.* 1703–17), German singer, sometimes wrongly identified with Maria Margherita Gallia. Made her London debut in 1703 and later seems to have appeared under the name of 'the Baroness', in operas by Bononcini and A. Scarlatti.

Lindholm, Berit (b Stockholm, 18 Oct 1934), Swedish soprano. Debut Stockholm, 1963, as Mozart's Countess. She sang Chrysothemis at CG in 1966; later heard there as Isolde and Brünnhilde. Bayreuth from 1967 (debut as Venus). US debut San Francisco, 1972; NY Met 1975, as the *Walküre* Brünnhilde. Other roles incl. Elisabeth, Tosca, Leonore and Cassandre in the Colin Davis recording of *Les Troyens*.

Lindley, Robert (b Rotherham, 4 Mar 1776; d London, 13 Jun 1855), English cellist and composer. Learnt vln. and cello from his father, then studied the latter under Cervetto, played at the Brighton theatre, and in 1794–1851 was princ. cellist at the Opera in London. He wrote concertos and other works for cello.

Lindner, Friedrich (b Liegnitz, Silesia, c 1540; d Nuremberg, buried 15 Sep 1597),

German composer and editor. He was choirboy in the electoral chapel at Dresden and later studied at Leipzig Univ., became musician to the Margrave of Brandenburg and in 1574 cantor at St Giles's Church at Nuremberg. He ed. several books of Italian church music and madrigals, and comp. 2 Passions.

Lindpaintner, Peter Joseph von (b Koblenz, 9 Dec 1791; d Nonnenhorn, Lake Constance, 21 Aug 1856), German composer and conductor. Studied at Augsburg and (?) with Winter at Munich, where in 1812 he became cond. at a minor theatre. In 1819 he went to Stuttgart as court *Kapellmeister*. In 1853–4 he visited London to cond. the New Phil. concerts.

Works incl. operas *Der Bergkönig* (1825), *Der Vampyr* (1828), *Die Genueserin* (1839), *Lichtenstein* (1846) and 24 others; ballet *Joko* and 2 others; incid. music to Goethe's *Faust*; *Stabat Mater*, 6 Masses; oratorios *Ahraham* and others; cantatas *The Widow of Nain*, Schiller's *Lied von der Glocke*; symphs. and overtures; concertos; chamber music; over 50 songs.

Lindsay String Quartet, British ensemble founded in 1966. Members are Peter Cropper and Ronald Birks (vlns.), Robin Ireland (who replaced Roger Bigley in 1985, vla.) and Bernard Gregor-Smith (cello). Their many recordings incl. complete cycles of 4tets by Bartók and Beethoven. In 1979 they gave the fp of Tippett's 4th 4tet at the Bath Festival. Haydn series in Sheffield and at the Wigmore Hall, London, 1987. 4tet in residence at the Univ. of Manchester.

Linear Counterpoint, a term for a kind of counterpoint in 20th-cent. music which regards the individuality of melodic lines as more important than the harmony they prod. in combination.

Linley, English family of musicians:
1. Thomas L. (b Badminton, 17 Jan 1733; d London, 19 Nov 1795), singing-master and composer. Studied with Thomas Chilcot, organist of Bath Abbey, and with Paradisi in London; settled at Bath as singing teacher and concert promoter. From 1774 he managed the oratorios at Drury Lane Theatre in London jointly with Stanley and from 1786 with Arnold. Sheridan having become his son-in-law in 1773, he and his son Thomas (3) wrote music for Sheridan's play *The Duenna* in 1775. In 1776 he moved to London and bought Garrick's share in Drury Lane Theatre, where he managed the music and wrote music for var. pieces.

Works incl. opera *The Royal Merchant* (1767); music for Sheridan's *Duenna* (1781)

and *School for Scandal* (the song 'Here's to the maiden'), *The Carnival of Venice* (1781), *The Gentle Shepherd, Robinson Crusoe* (pantomime by Sheridan, after Defoe), *The Triumph of Mirth, The Spanish Rivals* (1784), *The Strangers at Home* (1785), *Love in the East* (1788), and other plays; adaptations from Grétry: *Zelmire and Azor* and *Richard Cœur de Lion*; accomps. for *The Beggar's Opera*; music for Sheridan's monody on the death of Garrick; 6 elegies for 3 voices; 12 ballads; cantatas, madrigals.

2. Elizabeth Ann L. (b Bath, 5 Sep 1754; d Bristol, 28 Jun 1792), soprano, daughter of prec. Pupil of her father, she 1st sang in his concerts in Bath. Made her London debut in 1770 but after her marriage to Sheridan in 1773 retired from singing. Her portrait was painted by Gainsborough and Reynolds.

3. Thomas L. jun. (b Bath, 5 May 1756; d Grimsthorpe, Lincs., 5 Aug 1778), violinist and composer, brother of prec. Pupil of his father and of Boyce, later of Nardini in Florence, where he struck up a friendship with the young Mozart in 1770. On his return to Eng. he played in his father's concerts, and collaborated with him in the comp. of *The Duenna* in 1775. He was drowned in a boating accident.

Works incl. opera *The Cadi of Bagdad* (1778); music for Shakespeare's *The Tempest* (1777) and Sheridan's *The Duenna* (with his father); oratorio *The Song of Moses* (1777); *Ode on the Witches and Fairies of Shakespeare*; anthem 'Let God arise'; vln. concerto, several elegies.

4. Mary L. (b Bath, 4 Jan 1758; d Clifton, Bristol, 27 Jul 1787), singer, sister of prec. Pupil of her father, sang at festivals, oratorios, etc., but retired on her marriage to Richard Rickell, commissioner of stamps and dramatist (wrote *The Carnival of Venice* for his father-in-law and altered Ramsay's *Gentle Shepherd* for him).

5. Maria L. (b Bath, autumn 1763; d Bath, 5 Sep 1784), singer, sister of prec. Pupil of her father, sang at concerts and oratorios, but died young, of tuberculosis.

6. Ozias Thurston L. (b Bath, Aug 1765; d London, 6 Mar 1831), clergyman and organist, brother of prec. Pupil of his father, entered the church, but resigned his living on becoming fellow and organist at Dulwich Coll. in 1816.

7. William L. (b Bath, Feb 1771; d London, 6 May 1835), government official and composer, brother of prec. Pupil of his father and Abel, he held official posts in India, but in between he was Sheridan's partner in the

management of the Drury Lane Theatre, for which he comp. some unsuccessful works. Settled in London in 1806 as writer and comp.

Works incl. pantomimes, etc. *Harlequin Captive, The Honey Moon, The Pavilion*; songs to Shakespeare's plays; glees.

'Linz' Symphony, Mozart's symph. in C maj., K425, comp. at the house of Count Thun at Linz, where Mozart and his wife stayed on their return from Salzburg to Vienna, and perf. there 4 Nov 1783.

Lioncourt, Guy de (b Caen, 1 Dec 1885; d Paris, 24 Dec 1961), French musicologist and composer. Studied under d'Indy at the Schola Cantorum in Paris and later taught there. In 1918 he gained a prize with a musical fairy-tale, *La Belle au bois dormant* (after Perrault).

Other works incl. opera *Jean de la lune*, liturgical drama *Le Mystère d'Emmanuel* (1924); church music; cantata *Hyalis le petit faune* (Samain, 1909–11) and sacred cantatas; chamber music, etc.

Lionel and Clarissa, opera by Dibdin (lib. by I. Bickerstaffe), prod. London, CG 25 Feb 1768.

Lipatti, Dinu (b Bucharest, 19 Mar 1917; d Geneva, 2 Dec 1950), Rumanian pianist and composer. Studied at the Bucharest Cons. and with Cortot, Dukas and Nadia Boulanger in Paris. He had a very brilliant career which was cut short by illness. Much admired in Bach, Chopin and Mozart.

Works incl. symph. suite *Satrarii*; concertino for pf. and orch.; *Symphonie concertante* for 2 pfs. and strings; 3 nocturnes and sonatina for pf., left-hand; 3 Rum. dances for 2 pfs.

Lipinski, Karol Józef (b Radzyń, 30 Oct 1790; d Urlow, nr. Lwów, 16 Dec 1861), Polish violinist and composer. Travelled widely and became leader of the court orch. at Dresden, 1839. Ed. a collection of Pol. and Ruthenian folksongs with the poet Zalewski. Schumann's *Carnaval* was ded. to him.

Works incl. opera *The Siren of the Dnieper* (1814); *Polonaise guerrière* for orch.; 4 vln. concertos; string trio; vln. pieces, etc.

Lipkin, Malcolm (b Liverpool, 2 May 1932), English composer and pianist. Studied at the RCM and with Seiber. Lecturer, Kent Univ. from 1975. Works incl. 3 symphs. (1958–82), pf. concerto (1957), concerto for flute and strings (1974); string 4tet, 4 pf. sonatas.

Lipp, Maria Magdalena (d 1827), Austrian singer. Married Michael Haydn at Salzburg in 1768.

Lira (It.), a generic name given to var. old bowed string instruments, such as the Rebec and Crwth in earlier times.

Lira da braccio (It., lit. 'arm lyre'), a bowed string instrument current in the 16th and early 17th cents. It had 7 strings, 2 or more of which served as drones. As the name implies, it was played on the arm.

Lira da gamba (It., lit. 'leg lyre'), a larger version of the *lira da braccio*, played between the legs. The number of strings, incl. drones, varied from 11 to 15.

Lira organizzata. *See* **Vielle organisée.**

Lisley, John, English 16th–17th-cent. composer. One of the contribs. to the madrigal coll. *The Triumphes of Oriana* of 1601, of whom nothing is otherwise known.

Lissenko, Nikolai Vitalievich (b Grilky, Government of Poltava, 22 Mar 1842; d Kiev, 6 Nov 1912), Russian composer. Studied natural science, but while making researches in ethnography he became interested in Ukrainian folksong, specimens of which he began to collect. He then studied at the Leipzig Cons. and later with Rimsky-Korsakov at St Petersburg. He settled at Kiev.

Works incl. operas *Taras Bulba* (after Gogol, prod. 1903), *Sappho, The Aeneid* (after Virgil) and others; operettas; cantatas and other choral works; *Ukrainian Rhapsody* for vln. and pf.; pf. pieces; songs, settings of Ukrainian folksongs.

List, Emmanuel (b Vienna, 22 Mar 1888; d Vienna, 21 Jun 1967), Austrian bass. He sang as a chorister and in vaudeville before Vienna Volksoper debut, 1922, as Gounod's Méphistophélès, Berlin Staatsoper 1923–33. CG from 1925 as Pogner, Marke and Ochs. NY Met debut 1933 as the Landgrave; sang Gurnemanz, Hunding and Hagen at Bayreuth same year. Salzburg 1931–5 as Osmin, the Commendatore and Rocco. Lived in Vienna from 1952.

List, Eugene (b Philadelphia, 6 Jul 1918; d New York, 28 Feb 1985), American pianist. Studied in Philadelphia, debut there 1934. Toured widely as sergeant in US army. Eastman School 1964–75. Often heard in Gottschalk (*q.v.*).

Liszt, Ferencz (more commonly **Franz**) (b Raiding, Hung., 22 Oct 1811; d Bayreuth, 31 Jul 1886), Hungarian pianist and composer. His father, a steward of the Esterházy family's property, was Hung., his mother Aus. At the age of 9 he gave a concert at Sopron and in 1823 he had advanced so amazingly that his father took him to Vienna and Paris, where he had an immense success.

In Vienna he studied briefly with Salieri and Czerny. In 1824–5 he paid 2 visits to Eng. and another in 1827. At 14 he attracted attention as a comp. as well, prod. his opera *Don Sanche* in Paris. His father died in 1827 and he was taken to Paris by his paternal grandmother, who looked after his educ. there. He remained there and after a period of religious mysticism under the influence of Lamennais and great success as a pianist, he began a love affair with the Comtesse d'Agoult in 1833. They went to live at Geneva in 1835, where a daughter, Blandine, was born, followed by another, Cosima (later Wagner's 2nd wife) at Como in 1837. A son, Daniel, was born in Rome, 1839.

He travelled widely as pianist and made much money. In 1840 he collected funds for the Beethoven memorial at Bonn, and he often played for charitable purposes organized on a large scale. In 1840–1 he paid further vists to Eng., playing before Queen Victoria, and in 1842–4 he toured in Rus., Turkey, Den. etc. After a break with the countess in the latter year, he went to Spain and Port. in 1845; 2 years later, at Kiev, he met Princess Caroline Sayn-Wittgenstein, the wife of a wealthy Rus. landowner, who fell violently in love with him and in 1848 left with him for Weimar, where he was engaged as cond. and music director to the grand-ducal court for certain periods of the year. He prod. many new operas there, incl. Wagner's *Lohengrin* and Berlioz's *Béatrice et Bénédict*, and settled down to write var. works, some on a very large scale, having previously confined himself almost exclusively to pf. music.

He retired to Rome in 1861, and in 1865 took minor orders. He continued, however, to visit Weimar and also Budapest as a teacher.

Works incl. a vast number of pf. comps. incl. 3 vols. of *Années de pèlerinage* (1866–77), 12 *Études d'exécution transcendante* (1851), 2 *Légendes* (*Saint François d'Assise prédicant aux oiseaux* and *Saint François de Paule marchant sur les flots*), *Liebsträume* (3 nocturnes, orig. songs), sonata in B min. (1853), 20 Hung. Rhapsodies; innumerable transcriptions for pf. incl. 50 operatic pieces and fantasies of themes from operas by Bellini, Meyerbeer, Verdi and Wagner, *c* 40 works by var. comps. (Beethoven's symphs., Berlioz's *Symph. fantastique*, 6 caprices by Paganini, 9 waltzes by Schubert [*Soirées de Vienne*], etc., *c* 150 songs incl. many by Schubert).

Faust and *Dante* symphs. (1854–7 and 1856); 13 symph. poems for orch.; *Ce qu'on entend sur la montagne* (1849, orch. Raff, rev. 1850–4); *Tasso: lamento e trionfo* (1849, orch. Conradi, rev. 1850–4); *Les Préludes* (1848); *Orpheus* (1854); *Prometheus* (1850, orch. Raff, rev. 1855); *Mazeppa* (1851, orch. with Raff); *Festklänge* (1853); *Héroïde funèbre* (1850, orch. Raff. rev. 1854); *Hungaria* (1854); *Hamlet* (1858); *Hunnenschlacht* (1857); *Die Ideale* (1857); *Von der Wiege bis zum Grabe* (1882). Other orchestral works incl. 2 Episodes from Lenau's *Faust*; 2 pf. concertos in E♭ (1849, rev. 1853, 1856) and A (1839, rev. 1849–61), Hung. fantasy, *Malédiction*, *Totentanz* and fantasy on Beethoven's *Ruins of Athens* for pf. and orch.

Oratorios *St Elizabeth* (1857–62) and *Christus* (1862–7); *Gran Mass* for solo voices, chorus and orch., Hung. Coronation Mass (1867), and 2 other Masses, 3 psalms and a number of other choral works; 55 songs; 6 recitations with pf.; fugue on B.A.C.H., fantasy (1885) and fugue on *Ad nos, ad salutarem undam* and a few other org. works.

Litaniae Lauretanae (Lat. = Litanies of Loreto), a litany sung in honour of the Virgin Mary in the Roman church, dating prob. from the 13th cent. It has its own plainsong melody, but has also been set by comps., incl. Palestrina, Lassus and Mozart.

Litany, a supplicatory chant consisting of a series of petitions with an infrequently changing response to each. The best known litanies in the Roman Church are the Litany of the Saints, sung on Holy Saturday and during Rogationtide, and the 13th-cent. *Litaniae Lauretanae* (*see above*). The reformed churches have also adopted the litany, excluding refs. to the saints, as in Cranmer's litany still used in the Anglican Church.

Literes, Antonio (b Artá, Majorca, ?18 Jun 1673; d Madrid, 18 Jan 1747), Spanish bass viol player and composer (often confused with his son, also called Antonio, who was a well-known organist). Member of the royal band in Madrid from 1693.

Works incl. operas *Júpiter y Danae*, *Los Elementos*, *Dido y Eneas*; zarzuela *Coronis*; 14 psalm settings; 8 Magnificat settings.

Litolff, Henry (Charles) (b London, 7 Aug 1818; d Bois-les-Combes, nr. Paris, 5 Aug 1891), Anglo-Alsatian composer, pianist and publisher. His father was Alsatian, his mother Eng. As a boy of 13 he became a pupil of Moscheles for pf., made his 1st appearance in 1832 and at 17 left for Fr., having married against his parents' wish. He travelled widely as concert pianist until 1851, when he acquired a music pub. business at Brunswick, marrying as his 2nd wife the widow of the former owner. But he soon left his adopted son Theodor L. in charge and settled in Paris, where later he married again, a Comtesse de la Rochefoucauld. He prod. his best opera at Brussels in 1886. Works incl. operas *Les Templiers* (1886) and *Héloïse et Abelard* (1872); oratorios *Ruth and Boaz*; 5 pf. concertos, vln. concerto; overture *Robespierre* and others; chamber music; pf. works.

'Little Russian' Symphony, Tchaikovsky's 2nd symph. in C min., op. 17, also called 'Ukrainian' symph., comp. 1872, perf. Moscow, 18 Feb 1873.

Little Slave Girl, The (*Den lilla slavinnan*), opera by Crusell (lib. by comp.), prod. Stockholm, 18 Feb 1824.

Little, Vera (b Memphis, 10 Dec 1928), American mezzo. Debut NY City Opera 1950, as Preziosilla. She sang in Europe from 1951 and was heard in Berlin in 1958 as Carmen; sang at the Deutsche Oper from 1959 and in 1965 created Begonia in Henze's *Der junge Lord*; the following year she created Beroe in *The Bassarids*, at Salzburg. Guest in Milan and Genoa and was heard in concert music by Bach and Mozart. Recorded Gaea in Strauss's *Daphne*.

Liturgical Drama, a medieval church representation of Bible and other stories. It originated, prob. in Fr., in a 10th-cent. trope to the Introit for Easter Day, which takes the form of a dialogue for the Angel and the Marys at the sepulchre. In the second half of the cent. it was transferred to Matins. The music was originally an extension of plainsong but in course of time came to consist of original comps. Later subjects treated include the Walk to Emmaus, the Nativity, Epiphany, the Massacre of the Innocents, Old Testament stories and the lives of the saints. The texts were generally in Latin but sometimes also in the vernacular.

Lituus (Lat.), the Rom. cavalry tpt. In the 18th-cent. the word was occasionally used to mean 'horn'.

Litvinne (actually Litvinova), **Félia** (b St Petersburg, 1861; d Paris, 12 Oct 1936), Russian soprano. Studied with Maurel and others in Paris and made her 1st appearance there in 1880. She was partic. successful in Wagnerian roles; sang Isolde and Brünnhilde in Paris, London, Brussels. Other roles incl. Aida, Donna Anna, Alceste and Selika.

Liuzzi, Fernando (b Senigallia, 19 Dec

1884; d Florence, 6 Oct 1940), Italian musicologist and composer. Studied with Fano and later with Reger and Mottl at Munich. He became prof. of harmony at the Conss. of Parma and of Florence successively, and prof. of music hist. at Rome Univ. in 1927–8. He ed. old It. *laudi*, arr. perfs. of Vecchi's *Amfiparnaso* (Florence, 1938) and of Sophocles' *Oedipus Rex* with A. Gabrieli's music (Rome, 1937). Wrote books on the *laudi*, on It. musicians in Fr. and a vol. of critical studies *Estetica della musica*, also numerous learned articles.

Works incl. puppet opera *L'augellin bel verde* (after Gozzi, 1917); incid. music to Pirandello's *Scamandro*; oratorios *La Passione* (1935), *Laudi Francescane* and *Le vergini savie e le vergini folli*; Neapol. impression *Giaola e Marecchiaro* for orch.; vln. and pf. sonata and 2 pieces; organ music; 5 sets of songs, incl. It., Gk. and Serbian folksongs.

Livietta e Tracollo, intermezzo by Pergolesi (lib. by T. Mariani), prod. Naples, Teatro San Bartolommeo, between the acts of Pergolesi's serious opera *Adriano in Siria*, 25 Oct 1734.

Livre pour quatuor, work in 6 movts. for string quartet by Boulez; comp. 1948–9, perf. Donaueschingen and Darmstadt 1955–62. Revised as *Livre pour cordes*, for string orch. and perf. Brighton, 8 Dec 1969, cond. Boulez.

Ljunberg, Göta (b Sundsvall, 4 Oct 1893; d Lidingo, nr. Stockholm, 30 Jun 1955), Swedish soprano. Debut Stockholm 1918, as Gutrune; sang Elsa the same season. She returned to Stockholm until 1937. CG 1924–9; created the title role in Goossens' *Judith* (1929) and also sang Sieglinde. Salzburg 1928–33. NY Met 1931–5, as Isolde and Brünnhilde and in the fp of Hanson's *Merry Mount* (1933). Particularly convincing as Salome.

Lloyd, Charles Harford (b Thornbury, Glos., 16 Oct 1849; d Slough, 16 Oct 1919), English organist and composer. Educ. at Oxford; D.Mus. there in 1892. App. organist at Gloucester Cathedral, 1876, and Christ Church, Oxford, 1882; precentor at Eton Coll., 1892–1914, then organist at Chapel Royal, London.

Works incl. services and anthems; motet *The Souls of the Righteous* (1901); cantatas *Hero and Leander* (1884), *Song of Balder*, *Andromeda*, *The Longbeards' Saga* (1887), *A Song of Judgment* (1891), *Sir Ogie and Lady Elsie* (1894); incid. music to Euripides' *Alcestis* (1887); sonata, concerto, and other works for organ; madrigals and part-songs.

Lloyd, Edward (b London, 7 Mar 1845; d Worthing, 31 Mar 1927), English tenor. Choir-boy at Westminster Abbey in London until 1860 and one of the Gentlemen of the Chapel Royal from 1869. 1st important public appearance at Gloucester Festival, 1871, when he sang in Bach's *St Matthew Passion*; sang in fp of Elgar's *King Olaf*, 1896, and was the 1st Gerontius, 1900.

Lloyd, George (b St Ives, Cornwall, 28 Jun 1913), English composer. Studied vln. with Albert Sammons and comp. with Harry Farjeon. His father wrote the libs. for his 3 operas, the 1st of which was prod. at Penzance in 1934 and the 2nd at CG in 1938. He was severely wounded in the 1939–45 war. OBE 1970.

Works incl. operas *Iernin* (1934), *The Serf* (1938) and *John Socman* (1951); 11 symphs. (1932–83); 4 pf. concertos; 2 vln. concertos.

Lloyd (also **Floyd**), **John** (b c 1475; d London, 3 Apr 1523), English composer. He sang at the funeral of Prince Henry in 1511 and was present at the Field of the Cloth of Gold in 1520. He comp. a Mass *O quam suavis*, preceded by an antiphon, *Ave regina*, bearing the inscription 'Hoc fecit iohannes maris' (*mare* = sea = flood = Floyd or Lloyd).

Lloyd, Jonathan (b London, 30 Sep 1948), English composer. Studied with Roxburgh 1965–9 at the RCM and worked with Tristram Cary at the electronic studio there. Later study with Pousseur and Ligeti. Has worked as street musician and was composer-in-residence at Dartington College 1978–9.

Works incl. *Cantique* for small orch. (1968), *Everything Returns* for sop. and orch. (1978), *Toward the Whitening Dawn* for chorus and chamber orch. (1980), *Fantasy* for vln. and orch. (1980), *If I Could Turn You On* for sop. and chamber orch. (1981), *Rhapsody* for cello and orch (1982), vla. concerto (1980), 2 symphs. (1983–4); *Three Dances*, *Waiting for Gozo* and *Won't it Ever be Morning*, for ens. (1980–2); *John's Journal* for saxophone and pf. (1980), 2 string 5tets (1982), *Almeida Dances* for clar., pf. and string 4tet (1986); Mass for 6 voices (1983).

Lloyd-Jones, David (b London, 19 Nov 1934), English conductor and editor. He studied at Oxford and with Iain Hamilton. Guest cond. with the BBC Welsh SO from 1963. Opera cond. from 1967 and has given the 1st Brit. stage perfs of Haydn's *La fedeltà premiata* and Prokofiev's *War and Peace*;

has made an ed. of *Boris Godunov* which returns to Mussorgsky's full score, and given the opera with Scottish Opera and ENO and at CG. Music dir. ENO North, Leeds, from 1977; in 1983 cond. the fp of Josephs's *Rebecca*.

Lloyd, Robert (b Southend, 2 Mar 1940), English bass. Debut London 1969, in the 1st vers. of *Fidelio*. SW 1969–72; CG from 1972 as Banquo, Sarastro, Fiesco, Boris and Philip II in the French vers. of *Don Carlos*. Has sung as guest in Aix, Paris, Boston, San Francisco and Milan. Also heard in Lieder (esp. *Winterreise*) and oratorio. Appeared as Gurnemanz in the Syberberg film version of *Parsifal*. Sang this role at CG in 1988.

Lloyd Webber, Andrew (b London, 22 Mar 1948), English composer. He studied at Oxford and in 1965 formed a partnership with Tim Rice as librettist. Their first musical success was *Joseph and the Amazing Technicolor Dreamcoat* (staged 1972). This was followed by *Jesus Christ Superstar* and *Evita* (1976). *Cats* (after T.S. Eliot, 1981), *Song and Dance* (1983) and *Starlight Express* (1984) were all popular successes. More lofty ambition was shown with *The Phantom of the Opera* (1986). A *Requiem* (1984) is not regarded as making a significant contribution to the liturgical music of the 20th century.

Lloyd Webber, Julian (b London, 14 Apr 1951), English cellist, brother of prec. He studied at the RCM and with Pierre Fournier. London debut, QE Hall, 1971; soloist with leading orchs. NY debut 1980. In 1981 he gave the fp of a concerto written for him by Rodrigo. Prof. at GSM since 1978.

Lobe, Johann Christian (b Weimar, 30 May 1797; d Leipzig, 27 Jul 1881), German flautist, composer and writer on music. Studied at the expense of the Grand Duchess of Weimar, Maria Pavlovna, appeared as fl. soloist at Leipzig in 1811, and then joined the court orch. at Weimar, where his 5 operas were prod. He left in 1842 and 4 years later became ed. of the *Allgemeine Musik-Zeitung* at Leipzig; he also pub. several books on music.

Works incl. operas *Wittekind* (1819), *Die Flibustier* (1829), *Die Fürstin von Granada* (1833), *Der rote Domino* (1835) and *König und Pächter* (1844); 2 symphs., overtures; pf. 4tets.

Lobgesang. *See* **Hymn of Praise**.

Lobkowitz (Prince) **Joseph Franz Maximilian** (b Roudnice nad Labem, 7 Dec 1772; d Třeboň, 15 Dec 1816), Bohemian aristocrat and patron of music, resident in Vienna; he had sole direction of the Viennese theatres from 1807. Commissioned Haydn's string 4tets op. 77 and was a co-sponsor of *The Creation* and *The Seasons*. The Eroica Symph. was 1st perf. in his house and Beethoven ded. the 4tets op. 18 and 5th and 6th symphs. the Triple Concerto, the string 4tet op. 74 and *An die ferne Geliebte* to him.

Lobo, Alonso (b Osuna, *c* 1555; d Seville, 5 Apr 1617), Spanish composer. He was a choirboy at Seville Cathedral and asst. to the *maestro di capilla* from 1591; princ. post there from 1604. Palestrina, Victoria and Guerrero were among his models.
Works incl. *Liber primus missarum* (1602), containing 6 Masses and 7 motets; Credo romano, 3 passions, Lamentations, psalms, hymns.

Lobo (also called **Lopez** or **Lupus**), **Duarte** (b Alcáçovas, bap. 19 Sep 1565; d Lisbon, 24 Sep 1646), Portuguese composer. Studied under Mendes at Evora and later became choirmaster there. Afterwards he went to Lisbon with an appt. to the Royal Hospital and became *maestro di cappella* at the cathedral *c* 1590. Widely known as a polyphonist.
Works incl. Masses, offices for the dead, canticles, motets and much other church music.

Locatelli, Pietro (b Bergamo, 3 Sep 1695; d Amsterdam, 30 Mar 1764), Italian violinist and composer. Pupil of Corelli in Rome. Travelled widely as a virtuoso and settled down at Amsterdam, where he estab. public concerts.
Works incl. a set of 12 concerti grossi, op. 1, and solo concertos; sonatas; studies, caprices, etc. for vln.

Lochamer (also **Locheimer**) **Liederbuch**, a German 15th-cent songbook, now in Berlin. It contains 44 Ger. and 3 Lat. songs, mostly monophonic and all anon. It dates *c* 1455–65. Also bound with the book is a copy of Paumann's *Fundamentum Organisandi*.

Locke (or **Lock**), **Matthew** (b Exeter, *c* 1622; d London, Aug 1677), English composer. He was a choir-boy at Exeter Cathedral under Edward Gibbons. He visited the Netherlands in 1648, and having returned to London collaborated in Shirley's masque *Cupid and Death* perf. before the Port. ambassador in 1653. In 1656 he wrote the *Little Consort* for viols in 3 parts for William Wake's pupils and the same year he was one of the comps. who took part in the setting of Davenant's *Siege of Rhodes*. He was Comp. in Ordinary to the King and for Charles II's coronation in 1661 he wrote instrumental

music for the procession. In 1663, having turned Roman Catholic, he became organist to Queen Catherine. He was a vigorous and acrimonious defender of 'modern music', writing in 1666 a pamphlet defending his church music and in 1672 opening a controversy with Thomas Salmon. Purcell wrote an elegy on his death.
Works incl. operas, Davenant's *The Siege of Rhodes* (with Coleman, Cooke, Hudson and H. Lawes, 1656), *Psyche* (with G.B. Draghi); masque, Shirley's *Cupid and Death* (with C. Gibbons, 1653); incid. music to Stapylton's *The Stepmother*, (?) Shakespeare's *Macbeth* altered by Davenant and containing material from Middleton's *The Witch*, and for Shadwell's version of Shakespeare's *Tempest* (1674), song in Durfey's *The Fool turned Critic*; Kyrie, Credo, anthems, Lat. hymns; consorts for viols in 3 and 4 parts; songs in 3 parts, duets; songs for 1 voice with accomp.

Lockey, Charles (b Thatcham, nr. Newbury, 23 Mar 1820; d Hastings, 3 Dec 1901), English tenor. Made his 1st important appearance in the prod. of Mendelssohn's *Elijah* at Birmingham Festival, 1846.

Lockhart, James (b Edinburgh, 16 Oct 1930), Scottish conductor and pianist. He worked as an organist in Edinburgh and London, then asst. cond. in German opera houses at CG, London; regular cond. there 1962–8 and in 1967 gave the fp at Aldeburgh of Walton's *The Bear*. Music dir. WNO 1968–73 (Berg's *Lulu*, 1971). Director, Kassel Opera 1972–80; Koblenz Opera from 1981. He often perfs. in partnership with the soprano Margaret Price.

Lockspeiser, Edward (b London, 21 May 1905; d London, 3 Feb 1973), English critic. Studied with Nadia Boulanger in Paris and at the RCM in London. Author of *Debussy: His Life and Mind* (2 vols., 1962–5) and many other books.

Loco (It. = place, sometimes *al loco* = to the place), a direction indicating that a passage is to be played in the normal position indicated by the written notes, often given for greater safety after a passage shown to be played an 8ve higher or lower.

Loder, Edward (James) (b Bath, 1813; d London, 5 Apr 1865), English composer. He 1st learnt music from his father, John David L. (1788–1846), a violinist and music pub., and in 1826–8 studied with F. Ries at Frankfurt. After a 2nd period of study there he settled in London and was induced by Arnold to set an opera, *Nourjahad*, for the

New Eng. Opera House, under which name the Lyceum Theatre opened with it in 1834. He was theatre cond. in London and later in Manchester. About 1856 began to suffer from a disease of the brain.

Works incl. operas and plays with music, *Nourjahad* (1834), *The Dice of Death* (1835), *Francis I* (a concoction from his songs), *The Foresters* (1838), *The Deerstalkers* (1841), *The Night Dancers* (1846), *Robin Goodfellow* (1848), *The Sultana*, *The Young Guard, Raymond and Agnes*, etc.; masque *The Island of Calypso* (1852); string 4tets; numerous songs, incl. *12 Sacred Songs*, and *The Brooklet* (a trans. of Wilhelm Müller's *Wohin* set by Schubert in *Die schöne Müllerin*).

Loder, Kate (Fanny) (b Bath, 21 Aug 1825; d Headley, Surrey, 30 Aug 1904), English pianist and composer, cousin of the prec. Studied at the RAM in London, where she later became prof. of harmony; made her 1st appearance in 1844, when she played Mendelssohn's G min. concerto. The fp in Eng. of Brahms's Requiem took place at her house on 7 Jul 1871, the accomp. being played on the piano by herself and C. Potter.

Works incl. opera *L'elisir d'amore*, etc.

Lodoïska, opera by Cherubini (lib. by C.F. Fillette-Loraux), prod. Paris, Théâtre Feydau, 18 Jul 1791.

Opera by R. Kreutzer (lib. by J.C.B. Dejaure), prod. Paris, Comédie-Italienne, 1 Aug 1791.

Lodoiska, opera by Mayr (lib. by F. Gonella), prod. Venice, Teatro Le Fenice, 26 Jan 1796.

Lodoletta, opera by Mascagni (lib. by G. Forzano, after Ouida), prod. Rome, Teatro Costanzi, 30 Apr 1917.

Loeffler, Charles Martin (Tornow) (b Mulhouse, 30 Jan 1861; d Medfield, Mass., 19 May 1935), Alsatian-American composer. Before Alsace was lost to France in the 1870–1 war, Loeffler, whose father was an agricultural chemist and an author who wrote under the name of 'Tornow', was taken to Smela, nr. Kiev, and it was there that he was 1st given vln. lessons. The family later moved to Debreczin in Hung. and about 1873 to Switz. There he decided to become a violinist and went to Berlin to study with Rappoldi, Kiel, Bargiel and lastly Joachim. Later he had a period of study with Massart and Guiraud in Paris, joined the Pasdeloup Orch. and that of a wealthy amateur, where he remained until 1881. That year he went to USA, played in Damrosch's orch., in 4tets and with touring com-

panies. In 1882 he joined the Boston SO, where he remained, sharing the 1st desk with the leader, until 1903. In 1887 he became a naturalized American.

Works incl. psalm *By the waters of Babylon* for women's voices and insts., *Beat! Beat! Beat! Drums!* (from Whitman's *Drum Taps*, 1917) for male voices and orch., *Evocation* for women's voices and orch., *For one who fell in battle* for unaccomp. chorus; dramatic poem for orch. and vla. d'amore *La Mort de Tintagiles* (after Maeterlinck), fantasy for orch. and org. (1900) *La Villanelle du Diable* (1901), *A Pagan Poem* (after Virgil) for orch. with pf., Eng. horn and 3 tpts. (1906), *Poem* and *Memories of my Childhood* for orch.; *Canticum Fratris Solis* (St Francis) for voice and orch.; chamber music.

Lœillet, Jean-Baptiste (b Ghent, bap. 18 Nov 1680; d London, 19 Jul 1730), Flemish flautist, oboist and composer. He made an early success as a perf., went to Paris in 1702 and to London in 1705, where he joined the orch. of the King's Theatre in the Haymarket. He retired in 1710 and made a living by teaching and giving concerts in his house in Hart Street (now Floral Street), Covent Garden.

Works incl. sonatas for 1, 2 and 3 fls., for ob. or vln.

Loeschhorn, Albert (b Berlin, 27 Jun 1819; d Berlin, 4 Jun 1905), German pianist, teacher and composer. Studied in Berlin, where he taught from 1851 and became prof. in 1858.

Works incl. 4tets; sonatas and esp. studies and other instructive works for pf., etc.

Loewe. *See also* **Löwe.**

Loewe, (Johann) Carl (Gottfried) (b Löbejün, nr. Halle, 30 Nov 1796; d Kiel, 20 Apr 1869), German composer. He was a choirboy at Cöthen, and in 1809 went to the grammar-school at Halle. Encouraged by Jérôme Bonaparte, then king of Westphalia, he devoted himself to comp., to further studies, to the learning of Fr. and It. and later, at Halle Univ., the study of theology. The flight of Jérôme in 1813 deprived him of his income, but he managed to make a living and in 1820 became prof. and cantor at Stettin, and in 1821 music dir. and organist. He visited Vienna in 1844, London in 1847, Swed. and Norw. in 1851 and Fr. in 1857. In 1864 he suffered from a 6 weeks' coma and was asked to resign in 1866, when he went to live at Kiel. He died there after a similar attack.

Works incl. operas *Die Alpenhütte*

(1816), *Rudolf der Deutsche* (1825), *Malekadhel* (after Scott's *The Talisman*, 1832), *Neckerein* (1833), *Die drei Wünsche* (1834), *Emmy* (after Scott's *Kenilworth*, 1842); oratorios *Die Zerstörung Jerusalems* (1829), *Palestrina* (1841), *Hiob*, *Die Auferweckung des Lazarus* (1863) and 12 others; symphs.; concertos; pf. solos and duets; numerous songs and ballads, incl. Goethe's *Erlkönig*, Fontane's Ger. versions of *Archibald Douglas*, *Tom the Rhymer*.

Loewe, Sophie (b Oldenburg, 24 Mar 1815; d Budapest, 28 Nov 1866), German soprano. She sang in Vienna from 1832 and at La Scala in 1841 created Donizetti's Maria Padilla; sang in London the same year. At the Teatro Fenice, Venice, she created Verdi's Elvira (1844) and Odabella (1846).

Loewenberg, Alfred (b Berlin, 14 May 1902; d London, 29 Dec 1949), English music bibliographer of German origin. Studied at Jena Univ. and graduated there in 1925. The Nazi régime drove him from Ger. in 1934, and he settled in London, where he compiled *Annals of Opera 1597—1940*, containing details of *c* 4,000 operas in chronological order (pub. 1943; 3rd ed. 1978, ed Harold Rosenthal).

Loewenstern, Matthaeus (Apelles) von (b Neustadt, Silesia, 20 Apr 1594; d Bernstadt, nr. Breslau, 16 Apr 1648), German poet and composer. Studied (?) at the Univ. of Frankfurt o/O. Having been schoolmaster and cantor at Leobschütz, he entered the service of the Duke of Oels-Bernstadt.
Works incl. shoruses for Opitz's tragedy *Judith*; Lat. and Ger. motets; sacred concertos; book of 30 sacred songs to words of his own entitled *Frühlings-Mayen*.

Logier, Johann Bernhard (b Kassel, 9 Feb 1777; d Dublin, 27 Jul 1846), German musician of French descent. Pupil of his father. He settled in Eng. as a boy after his parents' death and soon went to Ir., settling finally at Dublin in 1809 as bandmaster and music dealer. He invented the Chiroplast, an appliance used in learning the pf., spent 3 years in Berlin, returned to Dublin, and comp. and arr. pf. music. In 1809 he prod. an ode on the 50th year of George III's reign.

Logroscino, Nicola (b Bitonto, bap. 22 Oct 1698; d ? Palermo, after 1765), Italian composer. Pupil at the Cons. di Santa Maria de Loreto, 1714–27, he held an organ post in Conza, 1728–31. He was chiefly a comp. of *opera buffa*, though his first known opera was not written till 1738. From 1747 taught counterpoint at the Cons. in Palermo.

Works incl. operas *Inganno per inganno* (1738), *L'Inganno felice* (1739), *Ciommetella correvata* (1744), *Il Governadore* (1747), *Giunio Bruto* (1748), *Leandro*, *Li zite*, *Don Paduano*, *La Griselda* (1752), *Le finte magie* (1756) and many others; oratorio *La spedizione di Giosué* (1763); 2 settings of the *Stabat Mater*; church music.

Lohengrin, opera by Wagner (lib. by comp.), prod. Weimar, Court Theatre, by Liszt, 28 Aug 1850.

Lohet, Simon (b Liège, *c* 1550; d Stuttgart, Jul 1611), German organist and composer. App. organist to the court of Württemberg at Stuttgart in 1571.
Works incl. pieces in fugal style, *canzoni* and hymn-tune fantasies for organ, etc.

Lolli, Antonio (b Bergamo, *c* 1725; d Palermo, 10 Aug 1802), Italian violinist and composer. In the service of the court of Württemberg at Stuttgart, 1758–74, and of Catherine II of Rus. in St Petersburg, 1774–83, he nevertheless spent most of his time as a touring virtuoso. Of his many works for vln. (concertos, sonatas, etc.), prob. only the solo parts are by Lolli.

Lombardi alla prima crociata, I (*The Lombards at the First Crusade*), opera by Verdi (lib. by T. Solera, founded on a romance by T. Grossi), prod. Milan, La Scala, 11 Feb 1843.

London (real name Burnstein), **George** (b Montreal, 5 May 1919; d Armonk, NY, 24 Mar 1985), Canadian bass-baritone and opera producer. Studied in Los Angeles with Richard Lert and made his debut in 1941, in Coates's *Gainsborough's Duchess*. Later he studied in NY and toured the USA. He was engaged to sing at the Vienna Staatsoper in 1949 as Amonasro and in 1951 sang at the NY Met. Appeared there until 1966 as Boris, Mandryka, Don Giovanni, Almaviva and Escamillo. Bayreuth 1951–64 as Amfortas and the Dutchman. Prod. *The Ring* in Seatle, 1973–5.

London College of Music. Founded 1887, mainly for part-time students. Now caters for *c* 300 full-time students. Dir. is John McCabe (*q.v.*). Michael Berkeley composer-in-residence 1987–8.

London Philharmonic Orchestra. Founded in 1932 by Sir Thomas Beecham and assoc. with the Royal Phil. Society for its concerts in London, also with the Covent Garden Opera. During World War II it became a self-governing co. Prin. conds. have been Adrian Boult (1951–7), William Steinberg (1958–62), John Pritchard (1962–71), Bernard Haitink (1967–79), Georg Solti (1979–

83), Klaus Tennstedt 1983–7. Glyndebourne Opera orch. since 1964.

London Sinfonietta, English chamber orch. founded 1968, with David Atherton as music dir. Later conds. have incl. Elgar Howarth, Simon Rattle and Lothar Zagrosek. Berio, Birtwistle, Boulez, Henze and Ligeti have led the orch. in perfs. of their own music. Joined forces in 1984 with Opera Factory; works by Tippett, Cavalli and Nigel Osborne have been given.

London Symphony, (Haydn's symph. no. 104, in D maj. (no. 12 of the 'Salomon' symphs.), written for perf. in London in 1795.

London Symphony, A., the 2nd symph. by Vaughan Williams, comp. 1912, fp London, 27 Mar 1914; revised vers. London, Queen's Hall, 4 May 1920.

London Symphony Orchestra, founded in 1904 from the bulk of players of the 1st Queen's Hall Orch., who left Henry J. Wood, since he insisted on abolishing the system of sending deputies to rehearsals and concerts. Recent conds. have been Josef Krips (1950–4), Pierre Monteux (1961–4), Istvan Kertesz (1965–8), André Previn (1968–79); Claudio Abbado 1979–87; Michael Tilson Thomas from 1988.

Long, the name of a note-value in old mensural notation, half the value of the Large and equal to either 2 or 3 Breves.

Long, Marguerite (b Nîmes, 13 Nov 1874; d Paris, 13 Feb 1966), French pianist and teacher. She studied at the Paris Cons. and taught there 1906–40. Formed own school in 1920 and in 1920 began a partnership with the violinist Jacques Thibaud; a competition was est. in their name. A champion of French music, Long gave the fps of Ravel's pf. concerto (1932) and Le Tombeau de Couperin (1919).

Long Christmas Dinner, The (Der Lange Weihnachtsmal), opera in 1 act by Hindemith (lib. by Thornton Wilder), prod. Mannheim, 17 Dec 1961; 1st prod. in English, Juilliard School, NY, 1963.

Longo, Alessandro (b Amantea, 30 Dec 1864; d Naples, 3 Nov 1945), Italian pianist and editor. He became prof. of pf. at the Naples Cons., but later moved to Bologna, where he founded the Cercolo Scarlatti and the Società del Quartetto. He ed. the journal L'arte pianistica and brought out eds. of old It. keyboard music incl. the sonatas of D. Scarlatti in 11 vols. His system of numbering the sonatas was in use until superseded by that of Ralph Kirkpatrick.

Longueval, Antoine de, N. French 15th-

cent. composer about whom very little is known. He wrote 3 motets, a chanson, and a Passion, formerly attrib. to Obrecht, based on all four gospels.

Loosemore, George (b Cambridge; d ? Cambridge, c 1682), English organist and composer. Studied under his father, Henry L., as a chorister at King's Coll. Chapel, Cambridge, and in 1660 became organist of Trinity Coll. there.

Works incl. anthems, etc.

Loosemore, Henry (b Devon; d Cambridge, 1670), English organist and composer, father of prec. He learnt music as a choir-boy at Cambridge and became organist of King's Coll. Chapel there in 1627.

Works incl. Service in D min., anthems, 2 Latin litanies; a piece for 3 viols and organ, etc.

Lopatnikov, Nikolai Lvovich (b Reval, 16 Mar 1903; d Pittsburgh, 7 Oct 1976), American pianist and composer of Estonian birth. Studied at the St Petersburg Cons., left for Fin. during the 1917 Revolution and in 1920 settled in Germany, studying pf. with Willi Rehberg and comp. with Toch in Berlin. In 1933 he returned to Fin. and sought the advice of Sibelius. Settled in USA in 1939 and became an Amer. citizen in 1944. App. prof. of composition at Carnegie Inst. of Technology, Pittsburgh, 1945.

Works incl. opera Danton (after Rolland's play, 1930–2); 4 symphs. (1928–71), variations, concertino and Intro. and Scherzo for orch.; 2 pf. concertos (1921, 1930), concerto for 2 pfs., vln. concerto; 3 string 4tets (1920, 1924, 1955); vln. and pf. sonata (with side-drum ad lib.), 3 pieces for vln. and pf.; cello sonata.

López de Velasco, Sebastián (b Segovia; d ? Madrid, c 1650), Spanish composer. He may have been a pupil of Victoria, whose post as maestro de capilla he was given later by the Infanta Juana at the convent of the Descalzas Reales in Madrid.

Works incl. Masses, motets, psalms, Magnificats and other church music.

Loqueville, Richard de (d Cambrai, 1418), French composer. He was in the service of Duke Robert of Barvaria in 1410 and maître de chant at Cambrai Cathedral from 1413 until his death. He wrote church music and chansons in the Burgundian style of his day. He probably taught Dufay.

Loreley. See also **Lurline**

Opera by Bruch (lib. by E. Geibel, orig. written for Mendelssohn), prod. Mannheim, 14 Jun 1863.

Unfinished opera by Mendelssohn (lib. by

E. Geibel). Only the 1st-act finale, an *Ave Maria* and a chorus of vintners exist.

Lorengar, Pilar (b Saragossa, 12 Oct 1921), Spanish soprano. After early perfs. in concert her career in opera started in 1955: Cherubino at Aix and Violetta at CG. Glyndebourne 1956–60 as Pamina and Mozart's Countess. NY Met debut 1966, as Donna Elvira. Other roles incl. Donna Anna, Fiordiligi, Eurydice, Eva, Mélisande and Regina in *Mathis der Maler*.

Lorenz, Alfred (Ottokar) (b Vienna, 11 Jul 1868; d Munich, 20 Nov 1939), Austrian conductor and writer on music. After var. other appts. he became cond. at Coburg-Gotha in 1898; but he retired, took a degree in 1922, became lecturer at Munich Univ., 1923, and prof. 1926. He ed. Wagner's literary works and Weber's early operas, and wrote several books on the form of Wagner's music dramas, on the hist. of western music and on A. Scarlatti's early operas.

Lorenz, Max (b Düsseldorf, 10 May 1901; d Vienna, 12 Jan 1975), German tenor. He studied in Berlin and sang at the Staatsoper 1929–44. Vienna 1929–54 in Wagner rep. and as Otello and Bacchus. NY Met debut 1931, as Walther; sang there until 1950. Bayreuth 1933–54 as Siegfried, Parsifal, Lohengrin and Tristan. At Salzburg he sang in the fps of von Einem's *Der Prozess* (1953) and Liebermann's *Penelope* (1954).

Lorenzani, Paolo (b Rome 1640; d Rome, 28 Nov 1713), Italian composer. Pupil of Benevoli in Rome. In 1675 he went to Sicily and became *maestro di cappella* at the cathedral of Messina. In 1678 the French viceroy, Marshal de Vivonne, induced him to go to Paris. From 1679 to 1683 he was one of the superintendents of the queen's music. After her death he became *maître de chapelle* at the Theatine monastery, where he wrote motets. His opera *Orontée* was prod. at Chantilly in 1688 by order of the Prince de Condé. He returned to Rome as *maestro di cappella* of the Papal chapel in 1694.

Works incl. operas *Nicandro e Fileno* (1681) and *Orontée* (1688); motets and Magnificats; cantatas; Italian and French airs.

Loriod, Yvonne (b Houilles, Seine-et-Oise, 20 Jan 1924), French pianist. She studied with Messiaen and later became his second wife; closely associated with his music since the fp of *Visions de l'Amen* in 1943. US debut Boston 1949, in the fp of the *Turangalîla* symph, under Bernstein. Has also played Boulez, Schoenberg, Bartók and Barraqué.

Loris, Heinrich. *See* **Glareanus.**

Lortzing, (Gustav) Albert (b Berlin, 23 Oct 1801; d Berlin, 21 Jan 1851), German composer, singer, conductor and librettist. He had some lessons with Rungenhagen in Berlin as a child, but his parents being wandering actors, he had to obtain his general and music educ. as best he could. He learnt the pf., vln. and cello and studied such theoret. works as he could pick up. He married in 1823 and found it very difficult to make a living in a travelling opera co. His 1st stage work, *Ali Pascha von Janina*, was prod. at Münster in 1828 and repeated at Cologne, Detmold and Osnabrück. In 1833–4 he was able to lead a more settled life, being engaged as tenor and actor at the Leipzig municipal theatre. The 1st 2 comic operas he wrote there were very successful, and so was his adaptation from Kotzebue, *Der Wildschütz*, in 1842, when he gave up acting. 2 short terms as cond. at Leipzig and Vienna were unsuccessful. He had a large family by this time and fell upon more and more difficult times. The conductorship at a suburban theatre in Berlin in 1850 merely humiliated him without doing much to relieve the situation.

Works incl. operas *Die beiden Schützen* (1837), *Zar und Zimmermann* (1837), *Hans Sachs* (1840), *Casanova*, *Der Wildschütz* (after Kotzebue, 1842), *Undine* (after de La Motte Fouqué, 1845), *Der Waffenschmied* (1846), *Zum Grossadmiral*, *Rolandsknappen* (1849), *Regina* and others; operettas *Ali Pascha von Janina* (1824), *Die Opernprobe oder Die vornehmen Dilettanten* (1851); oratorio *Die Himmelfahrt Christi* (1828); incid. music for plays incl. Goethe's *Faust*, Grabbe's *Don Juan und Faust* (1829), Scribe's *Yelva*; plays with music *Der Pole und sein Kind* (1832), *Der Weihnachtsabend* (1832), *Szenen aus Mozarts Leben* (with music adapted from Mozart, 1832); part-songs, songs.

Los Angeles, Victoria de (real name Victoria Gomez Cima), (b Barcelona, 1 Nov 1923), Spanish soprano. She made her debut in Madrid in 1944 and in 1947 won an international contest at Geneva. In 1949 she toured Europe and S. Amer. and appeared at the Salzburg Festival in 1950. London, CG, 1950–61 as Mimi, Eva, Elsa, Santuzza, Butterfly and Manon. NY Met 1951–61 as Marguerite and Desdemona. La Scala 1950–6 as Ariadne, Donna Anna, Agathe and Rosina. In 1979 she sang Carmen at the NY City Opera.

Lotario, opera by Handel (lib. by ?, based on

Antonio Salvi's *Adelaide*, not, as Burney says, on Matteo Noris's *Berengario*), prod. London, King's Theatre, Haymarket, 2 Dec 1729.

Lothar, Mark (b Berlin, 23 May 1902; d Munich, 7 Apr 1985), German composer. He studied at the Berlin Musikhochschule with Schreker (comp.), Juon (harmony) and Krasselt (cond.). Later he had lessons with Wolf-Ferrari and others. After appts. as dir. of music at 2 Berlin theatres, he was in charge of the music at the Bavarian Staatstheater in Munich from 1945 to 1955. Works incl. operas *Tyll* (1928), *Lord Spleen* (after Ben Jonson's *Epicoene*, 1930), *Münchhausen* (1933) and *Schneider Wibbol* (Berlin, 1938), *Rappelkopf* (Munich, 1958), *Der Widerspenstige Heilige* (Munich, 1968); incid. music for Eichendorff's *Die Freier* and other plays; *Narrenmesse* for male chorus; *Orchesterstücke* and suite for orch.; serenade for chamber orch.; music for film and radio; pf. trio; pf. pieces; songs.

Lott, Felicity (b Cheltenham, 8 Apr 1947), English soprano. She studied at the RAM and in 1975 sang Pamina with ENO. Anne Trulove at Glyndebourne in 1977, and has sung Christine in *Intermezzo* and Arabella there. In 1984 she sang with the Chicago SO. Other roles incl. Octavian and the Countess in *Capriccio*. She has often been heard in concert with the Songmakers' Almanac, a group which incls. readings in its recitals. She sang at the Royal Wedding of 1986.

Lottchen am Hofe (*Lottie at Court*), opera by J.A. Hiller (lib. by C.F. Weisse after Goldoni and C.S. Favart), prod. Leipzig, 24 Apr 1767.

Lotti, Antonio (b ? Venice, *c* 1667; d Venice, 5 Jan 1740), Italian composer. Pupil of his father and of Legrenzi in Venice. App. singer at St Mark's 1687, and rose to become 2nd organist (1692), 1st organist (1704), finally *maestro di cappella* (1736). Prod. his first opera, *Il trionfo dell' innocenza* in Venice in 1692 (*Giustino*, 1683, commonly ascribed to him, is by Legrenzi). Visited Dresden 1717–19 as an opera comp., but after his return to It. devoted himself entirely to church music.

Works incl. operas *Porsenna* (1713), *Irene Augusta* (1713), *Polidoro* (1714), *Alessandro Severo*, *Constantino* (for Vienna, 1716, with Fux and Caldara), *Giove in Argo* (1717), *Ascanio, Teofane* (1719), etc.; oratorios *Il voto crudele* (1712), *L'umiltà coronata in Esther* (1714), *Gioa, Giuditta*; Masses, Requiems, Misereres, motets and other church music.

Loughran, James (b Glasgow, 30 Jun 1931), Scottish conductor. He was an assistant cond. at opera houses in Bonn, Amsterdam and Milan before he became associate of the Bournemouth SO in 1962. Prin. cond. BBC Scottish SO 1965–71, Hallé Orch. 1971–83. Bamberg SO 1978–83.

Louis Ferdinand of Prussia, Prince (b Friedrichsfelde, nr. Berlin, 18 Nov 1772; d Saalfeld 13 Oct 1806), German amateur composer and pianist. Beethoven praised his playing and ded. to him the C min. pf. concerto. From 1804 Dussek was in his service as his companion and teacher. He fell in the battle of Saalfeld. Wrote pf. trios, pf. 4tets and 5tets and other chamber music; pf. pieces.

Louise, opera by G. Charpentier (lib. by comp.), prod. Paris, Opéra-Comique, 2 Feb 1900.

Loure (Fr.), orig. a special type of bagpipe, found esp. in Normandy; later the name of a dance in fairly slow 6–4 time.

Lourié, Arthur (Vincent) (b St Petersburg, 14 May 1892; d Princeton, 13 Oct 1966), Russian-born composer of French descent. Studied for a short time at the St Petersburg Cons., but was self-taught later. App. dir. of the music section of the Ministry of Public Instruction in 1918, but left in 1921. He settled in Fr. and in 1941 in the USA, where he became an Amer. citizen.

Works incl. operas *A Feast in Time of Plague* (after Pushkin, 1935), and *The Blackamoor of Peter the Great* (1961); ballet *Le Masque de neige* and others; 2 symphs.; *Sonate liturgique* for orch., pf. and chorus; *Ave Maria, Salve Regina* and other church music; *Regina coeli* for contralto, ob. and tpt. (1915), *Improperium* for baritone, 4 vlns. and double bass (1923); *Canzona di Dante* for chorus and strings; Jap. Suite for voice and orch.; 3 string 4tets; sonata for vln. and double bass; 3 pf. sonatinas; song-cycles *Elysium* (Pushkin, 1918) and *Alphabet* (A. Tolstoy).

Love for Three Oranges, The (*Liubov k trem Apelsinam*), opera by Prokofiev (lib. by comp., based on Gozzi's comedy *Fiaba dell' amore delle tre melarancie*), prod., in Fr. trans., Chicago, Auditorium, 30 Dec 1921. The March from it has become popular.

Love in a Village, opera by Arne (lib. by I. Bickerstaffe), prod. London, CG, 8 Dec 1762. Partly a ballad opera and pasticcio, Arne having intro. popular songs and airs by Handel, Galuppi, Geminiani and others.

Love of the Three Kings (Montemezzi). *See* **Amore dei tre re**.

Lowe, Edward (b Salisbury, *c* 1610; d Oxford, 11 Jul 1682), English organist and composer. Chorister at Salisbury Cathedral; became organist of Christ Church, Oxford, about 1630. App. one of the organists at the Chapel Royal in London, 1660. Wrote on the perf. of cathedral music and comp. anthems.

Löwe, Ferdinand (b Vienna, 19 Feb 1865; d Vienna, 6 Jan 1925), Austrian conductor. Studied at the Vienna Cons. and taught there, 1884–97. From 1896 to 1898 he cond. the Wiener Singakademie, and from 1900 to 1904 the Gesellschaft concerts. He held further posts in Munich, Budapest and Berlin and was director of the Vienna Acad. of Music from 1919 to 1922. He championed the symphs. of Bruckner, in spurious eds.

Löwe, Johann Jakob (b Vienna, bap. 31 Jul 1629; d Lüneburg, Sep 1703), German organist and composer. Pupil of Schutz at Dresden; held appts. at Wolfenbüttel from 1655 and Zeitz from 1663, app. organist of St Nicholas's Church, Lüneburg in 1682.

Works incl. operas *Amelinde*, *Andromeda* and *Orpheus aus Thracien*; ballets; symphs.

Lowe, Thomas (d London, 1 Mar 1783), English tenor. Made his 1st stage appearance at Drury Lane Theatre, London, in 1740. He sang in many Handel oratorios, incl. the fps of *Samson*, *Joshua*, *Alexander Balus*, *Susanna*, *Solomon* and *Theodora*.

Lowinsky, Edward (E)lias (b Stuttgart, 12 Jan 1908; d Chicago, 12 Oct 1985), American musicologist of German birth. He studied in Stuttgart and Heidelberg. US citizen from 1947. Taught at Queens College, NY (1947–56), Berkeley (1956–61) and at Univ. of Chicago. He was ed. of the series Monuments of Renaissance Music (1964–77). Josquin, Lassus, Willaert and Gombert featured in his research.

Lübeck, Vincenz (b Padingbüttel, Hanover, Sep 1654; d Hamburg, 9 Feb 1740), German organist and composer. Organist at Stade until 1702, when he was app. organist at St Nicholas's Church at Hamburg.

Works incl. cantatas, chorale-preludes and other organ music.

Lubin, Germaine (b Paris, 1 Feb 1890; d Paris, 27 Oct 1979), French soprano. She studied at the Paris Cons. and with Lilli Lehmann. Paris, Opéra, 1914–44 in Wagner rep. and as Octavian, Elektra, Donna Anna, Thaïs and in the fps of works by d'Indy, Sauguet and Milhaud. London, CG, 1937 as Alceste and Dukas' Ariane. Bayreuth 1938–9 as Kundry and Isolde.

Lubotsky, Mark Davidovich (b Leningrad, 18 May 1931), Russian violinist. Studied at Moscow Cons. and with D. Oistrakh. He has toured widely from the early 1960s; GB debut 1970 with Britten's concerto, at the Promenade Concerts.

Lucas, Leighton (b London, 5 Jan 1903; d London, 1 Nov 1982), English composer and conductor. He studied music by himself while engaged in the career of a dancer and at 19 became a theatre cond. He served in the RAF during the 1939–45 war.

Works incl. ballets *Orpheus* and *The Horses* (1946), masques (tragic) *The Wolf's Bride* and (Japanese) *Kanawa, the Incantation*; film music for *Target for To-night*; *Missa pro defunctis* for solo voices, chorus and orch. (1934); *Masque of the Sea* for chorus and orch.; passacaglia, chaconne and Litany for orch.; sonnets for pf. and orch.; *La Goya*, 2 dance impressions for chamber orch.; partita for pf. and chamber orch., *Eurhythmy* for vln. and strings., 4 divertissements for vln. and chamber orch., pf. trio in F maj.; songs.

Lucca, Pauline (b Vienna, 25 Apr 1841; d Vienna, 28 Feb 1908), Austrian soprano of Italian origin. Studied in Vienna, joined the Opera chorus and made her 1st stage appearance at Olomouc in 1859 as Elvira in *Ernani*. In 1863 she 1st visited London; appeared until 1882 as Valentine, Marguerite, Selika, Cherubino, Elisabeth de Valois and Carmen. She was a member of the Vienna Opera from 1874 to 1889; sang La Gioconda and Boito's Margherita.

Lucia di Lammermoor, opera by Donizetti (lib. by S. Cammarano, based on Scott's *Bride of Lammermoor*), prod. Naples, Teatro San Carlo, 26 Sep 1835.

Lucia, Fernando de. *See* De Lucia

Lucio Papiro, opera by Caldara (lib. by A. Zeno), prod. Vienna, 4 Nov 1719.

Opera by Hasse (lib. do.), prod. Dresden, at court, 18 Jan 1742.

Lucio Silla, opera by J.C. Bach (lib. by G. de Gamerra, with alterations by Metastasio), prod. Mannheim, at court, 4 Nov 1774.

Opera by Mozart (lib. do.), prod. Milan, Teatro Regio Ducal, 26 Dec 1772.

Lucio Vero, opera by Pollarolo (lib. by A. Zeno), prod. Venice, Teatro San Giovanni Crisostomo, 1700.

Opera by Sacchini (lib. do.), prod. Naples, Teatro San Carlo, 4 Nov 1764.

Lucrezia Borgia, opera by Donizetti (lib. by F. Romani, based on Victor Hugo's tragedy), prod. Milan, La Scala, 26 Dec 1833.

Ludford, Nicholas (b c 1485; d London, c 1557), English composer. He was for long active at the Royal Chapel of St Stephen, Westminster. He wrote 7 festal Masses, motets, a Magnificat, and a set of 7 Masses for the daily Mass of Our Lady which is unique. A John L., comp. of a Mass *Dame sans per*, belonged to the previous generation; nothing is known of his life.

Ludikar, Pavel (b Prague, 3 Mar 1882; d Vienna, 19 Feb 1970), Czech bass-baritone. Debut Prague 1904, as Sarastro; sang in Vienna and Dresden and at Rome in 1911 was the 1st Italian Ochs. Boston 1913–14 and appeared frequently at Buenos Aires. NY Met 1926–32, in *La Rondine* and *Luisa Miller* and as Rossini's Figaro. Dir., Prague Opera, from 1935 and in 1938 created there the title role in Krenek's *Karl V*, under Karl Rankl.

Ludovic, opera by Hérold, left unfinished and completed by Halévy (lib. by J.H.V. de Saint-Georges), prod. Paris, Opéra-Comique, 16 May 1833. Chopin wrote pf. variations on an air from it, op. 12.

Ludwig, Christa (b Berlin, 16 Mar 1924), German mezzo. Studied with her mother and with Felice Hüni-Mihaček, making her debut in 1946. After appearing in a number of Ger. opera houses she sang at the Salzburg Festival in 1954 as Cherubino, and was engaged by the Vienna Staatsoper in 1955. She was married to the baritone Walter Berry 1957–70. NY Met since 1959 as the Dyer's Wife, Dido in *Les Troyens* and Leonore. London, CG, 1968 and 1976 as Amneris and Carmen. Other roles incl. Eboli, Lady Macbeth, Dorabella and Brangaene. Much admired in Mahler and for the vocal warmth and dramatic strength of her stage performances.

Ludwig, Friedrich (b Potsdam, 8 May 1872; d Göttingen, 3 Oct 1930), German musicologist. Studied at Marburg and Strasbourg Univs. He became a lecturer at Strasbourg in 1905 and prof. at Göttingen in 1911, where he was later app. Rector. His comprehensive studies of 13th- and 14th-cent. music remain indispensable.

Ludwig, Leopold (b Ustrava-Witkowitz, 12 Jan 1908; d Lüneburg, 24 Apr 1979), Austrian conductor. After appts. in Cz. and Ger. he worked in Vienna and Berlin 1939–50. Hamburg 1951–70; led the fps of Krenek's *Pallas Athene weint* (1955) and Henze's *Der Prinz von Homburg* (1960). In 1952 he took the Hamburg Co. to Edinburgh for the Brit. première of *Mathis der Maler*, and in 1962 to London for the 1st

Lulu in Britain. He cond. *Der Rosenkavalier* at Glyndebourne in 1959 and *Parsifal* at the NY Met in 1970.

Ludwig, Walther (b Bad Oeynhausen, 17 Mar 1902; d Lahr, 15 May 1981), German tenor. He studied medicine and started his stage career in 1928. Schwerin 1929–32, and in 1931 created there the title role in Graener's *Wilhelm Friedemann Bach*. Städtische Oper, Berlin, 1932–45, in the lyric repertory. Glyndebourne 1935, as Belmonte and Tamino; also highly praised at Salzburg as a Mozart singer. Many concert tours in Europe and S. Amer. Retired 1962 and resumed his medical career.

Luening, Otto (b Milwaukee, 15 Jun 1900), American composer, conductor, flautist and educator. Studied at Munich and cond. opera there and in Zurich 1917–20; also cond. opera in the US (Chicago and Eastman School) and gave the fps of Menotti's *The Medium* and Thomson's *The Mother of us All* (NY, 1946–7). A pioneer of electronic music; co-dir. Columbia-Princeton Elec. Music Center from 1959. Works incl. opera *Evangeline* (1928–33, prod. NY 1948); fl. concertino (1923), *Kentucky Concerto* (1951), *Wisconsin Symphony* (1975); 3 string 4tets (1919–28); electronic music, incl. *Rhapsodic Variations*, with Ussachevsky (1954).

Lugg (or **Lugge**), **John** (b c 1587; d Exeter, after 1647), English organist and composer. He was vicar-choral and organist at Exeter.

Works incl. services, anthems, motets; organ voluntaries; canons; jig for harpsichord, etc.

Lugg (or **Lugge**), **Robert** (b Exeter, 6 Nov 1620), English organist and composer, son of prec. B.Mus. Oxford, 1638, and organist at St John's Coll. He became a Roman Catholic and went abroad.

Works incl. services, anthems.

Luigini, Alexandre (Clément Léon Joseph) (b Lyons, 9 Mar 1850; d Paris 29 Jul 1906), French violinist, conductor and composer. Studied at the Paris Cons., became leader at the Grand Théâtre of Lyons in 1869 and cond. in 1877. In 1897 he became cond. of the Opéra-Comique in Paris.

Works incl. operas *Faublas* (after Louvet de Couvray, prod. 1881) and *Les Caprices de Margot* (prod. 1877); ballets; cantata *Gloria victis*; *Ballet égyptien* (1875), *Ballet russe*, *Carnaval turc* and other light works for orch.

Luisa Miller, opera by Verdi (lib. by S. Cammarano, based on Schiller's drama *Kabale*

und Liebe), prod. Naples, Teatro San Carlo, 8 Dec 1849.

Lukomska, Halina (b Suchedniów, 29 May 1929), Polish soprano. From 1960 has been heard most often in technically demanding music: Webern, Lutosławski, Serocki and *Pli selon pli* by Boulez.

Lully, Jean Baptiste (orig. Giovanni Battista Lulli) (b Florence, 28 Nov 1632; d Paris, 22 Mar 1687), Italian-French composer. Son of a miller, he had little educ. and learnt guitar and vln. without much guidance. At first joined strolling players, but in 1646 was discovered by the Chevalier de Guise and taken to Fr., where he entered the household of Mlle. de Montpensier, the king's cousin, as a scullion; but when she found that he was musical she made him a personal servant and leader of her string band. In 1652 he passed into the service of Louis XIV, who was then 14. Lully became ballet dancer, violinist in the king's '24 vlns.' and comp. In 1658 he began to comp. ballets of his own, having contrib. to some since 1653, in which the king himself danced. In 1661 he became a naturalized Frenchman and Comp. to the King's Chamber Music and in 1662 Music Master to the Royal Family; continued to enjoy royal protection, in spite of his open activity as a pederast — at that time punishable by death.

His 1st opera, *Cadmus et Hermione*, appeared in 1673, when he obtained a royal patent granting him the monopoly of operatic prod. and annulling a previous patent given to Perrin and Cambert. The Académie Royale de Musique, as the Opéra was 1st called, was opened in 1672 with a pasticcio from earlier works of his, *Les Festes de l'Amour et de Bacchus*. Most of his operas were written in collaboration with Philippe Quinault, and most of the ballets with Molière. His last complete opera was *Acis et Galatée* in 1686. In 1687 he injured his foot with the stick with which he cond. a Te Deum to celebrate the king's recovery and died of blood poisoning. The opera *Achille et Polyxène* left unfinished by him, was completed by Colasse.

Works incl. OPERAS: *Cadmus et Hermoine* (1673), *Alceste* (1674), *Thésée* (1675), *Atys, Isis* (1677), *Psyché* (1678), *Bellérophon* (1679), *Proserpine, Persée, Phaéton* (1683), *Amadis de Gaule* (1684), *Roland, Armide et Renaud* (1686), *Acis et Galatée* (1686), *Achille et Polyxène* (Act I only by Lully; prod. 1687); COMEDY-BALLETS (all with Molière): *Les Fâcheux, La Mariage forcé, L'Amour médicin* (1665), *La*

Princesse d'Elide (1664), *Le Sicilien, Georges Dandin, Monsieur de Pourceaugnac* (1669), *Les Amants magnifiques* (1670), *Le Bourgeois Gentilhomme* (1670); PASTORALS AND DIVERTISSEMENTS: *Les Plaisirs de l'île enchantée* (1664), *La Pastorale comique* (1667), *L'Églogue de Versailles* (or *La Grotte de Versailles*, words by Quinault, 1668), *L'Idylle sur la paix* (or *Idylle des Sceaux*, words by Racine, 1685).

BALLETS: (some poss. by Boësset and others) *Ballet d'Alcidiane* (1658), *B. de la raillerie* (1659), *B de Xerxès* (for Cavalli's opera, 1660), *B. de l'impatience* (1661), *B. des saisons, B. de l'Ercole amante* (1662), *B. des arts* (1663), *B. des noces de village, B. des amours déguisés* (1664), *La Naissance de Vénus* (1665), *B. des gardes, Le Triomphe de Bacchus dans les Indes* (1666), *B. des Muses* (1666), *Le Carnaval ou Mascarade de Versailles, B. de Flore* (1669), *B. des ballets* (1671), *Le Triomphe de l'Amour* (1681), *Le Temple de la paix* (1685).

Incid. music to Corneille's *Œdipe*; church music, *Miserere, Plaude laetare*, Te Deum, *De profundis, Dies irae* and Benedictus, 5 Grands Motets, 12 Petits Motets, motets for double chorus; dances for var. instruments. *Suites de trompettes, Suites de symphonies et trios.*

Lulu, unfinished opera by Berg. (lib. by comp., based on Frank Wedekind's plays *Erdgeist* and *Die Büchse der Pandora*), Acts 1 and 2 and a fragment of 3 prod. Zurich, 2 Jun 1937. 3rd act realized by Friedrich Cerha; 1st complete perf. Paris, 24 Feb 1979, cond. Boulez.

Lumbye, Danish family of musicians:

1. **Hans Christian L.** (b Copenhagen, 2 May 1810; d Copenhagen, 20 Mar 1874), conductor and composer. Cond. a light orch. at the Tivoli in Copenhagen from 1848 and wrote much dance and other light music for it.

2. **Carl Christian L.** (b Copenhagen, 9 Jul 1841; d Copenhagen, 10 Aug 1911), conductor and composer, son of prec. He succeeded his father in 1865 and also wrote dances, marches, etc.

3. **Georg August L.** (b Copenhagen, 26 Aug 1843; d Oringe, 29 Oct 1922), conductor and composer., brother of prec. Wrote chiefly for the stage, incl. the opera *The Witch's Flute.*

Lumsdaine, David (b Sydney, 31 Oct 1931), British composer of Australian birth. Educated in Sydney, moved to London in 1952 and studied with Seiber at the RAM. Lecturer at Durham Univ. from 1970;

founded electronic studio there.
Works incl. *Episodes* (1969) and *Shoalhaven* (1982) for orch., *Mandala* II and III for chamber orch.; *Easter Fresco* for sop. and ens. (1966); *Mandala* IV for string 4tet (1983).

Lunn, Louise Kirkby. *See* **Kirkby-Lunn.**

Lupi, Johannes (Jean Leleu) (b Cambrai, *c* 1506; d Cambrai, 20 Dec 1539), French composer. He was assoc. with Cambrai Cathedral from 1526, first as singer then as choirmaster. He wrote church music and *chansons*. A different Johannes Lupi was organist at Nivelles in 1502, possibly the comp. of a lament on the death of Ockeghem (1495); the name is also found in the records of Antwerp Cathedral in 1548. It is often impossible to be certain to which of these comps. to assign var. works. Lupus Hellinck (*c* 1496–1541) is again a distinct comp., as is the slightly younger Didier Lupi of Lyons.

Lupo, Thomas (d London, Jan 1628), English composer and player of stringed instruments. His father Joseph (b ? Milan; d London, 1616), his uncle Ambrose (b? Milan, d London, 10 Feb 1591) and his son Theophilus (*fl.* 1628–42) are also known as comps. But Thomas is distinguished by his pavans and fantasies for viol consort, partic. in 5 and 6 voices.

Luprano, Filippo de (b ? Cremona, *c* 1475; d after 1520), Italian composer.
Works incl. *frottole*, etc.

Lupu, Radu (b Galati, 30 Nov 1945), Rumanian pianist. He studied at the Moscow Cons.; won the Van Cliburn Competition in 1966 and the Leeds International in 1969. London debut 1969; US 1972, with the Cleveland SO. He has played in the 19th-cent. rep. with all the leading orchs., and with the violinist Szymon Goldberg has given the Mozart sonatas.

Luria, Juan (b Warsaw, 20 Dec 1862; d Auschwitz, 1942), Polish baritone. Debut Stuttgart 1885; sang widely in Ger., often in Wagner. NY Met 1890–1. At La Scala he was the 1st local Wotan (1893) and at Elberfeld he took part in the fp of Pfitzner's *Die Rose vom Liebesgarten* (1901). He taught in Berlin from 1914 and with the rise of the Nazis fled, as a Jew, to Holland. Although in his 80th year he was arrested and transported to Auschwitz.

Lurline, opera by V. Wallace (lib. by E. Fitzball), prod. London, CG, 23 Feb 1860. The subject is that of the German legend of the Loreley.

Luscinius (real name Nachtgall or Nachtigall), **Othmar,** (b Strasbourg, *c* 1478; d

Freiburg i/B. 5 Sep 1537), German organist and composer. Pupil of Hofhaimer. He was organist at Strasbourg, but left for Freiburg in 1523, owing to the Reformation, and settled at a Carthusian monastery. He wrote musical treatises and comp. organ music.

Lusingando or **Lusinghiero** (It. = wheedling, coaxing), a direction to perf. a piece or passage in a charming, alluring manner.

Lusitano, Vicente (b ? Olivença, d after 1553), Portuguese theorist and composer. He was known as Vicente de Olivença in Port., but was called L. ('the Port.') in Rome, where he settled about 1550. In 1551 he had a learned dispute with Vicentino, which was settled in his favour, with Danckerts and Escobedo as judges. He pub. a treatise on *cantus firmus* in 1553.
Works incl. motets *Epigrammata*, etc.

Lussan, Zélie de (b Brooklyn, NY, 21 Dec 1861; d London, 18 Dec 1949), American mezzo of French origin. After some parental opposition, she was trained by her mother and made her stage debut at Boston in 1886. In 1888 she went to London and sang Carmen at CG, which became her great part. She also sang soprano parts and commanded Fr., It. and Eng. with equal ease; other roles incl. Mignon, Zerlina and Cherubino. She appeared all over the world, but on her marriage in 1907 retired and settled in London.

Lustige Witwe, Die (*The Merry Widow*), operetta by Lehár (lib. by V. Léon and L. Stein), prod. Vienna, Theater an der Wien, 30 Dec 1905.

Lustigen Weiber von Windsor, Die (*The Merry Wives of W.*), comic opera by Nicolai (lib. by S.H. Mosenthal, after Shakespeare), prod. Berlin, Opera, 9 Mar 1849.

Lute, a plucked string instrument with a pear-shaped body. Its origin is eastern. It gained currency in Europe in medieval times and was still very popular in the 17th cent., but declined in the 18th. In the 16th cent. there were 5 pairs of strings, 2 to each note, and one single string. The tuning was:

Other tunings were adopted in the 17th cent. Music for the lute is played from a tablature of letters or figures.

Lute-Harpsichord, an instrument made for Bach in 1740, called *Lautenclavicymbel*, with gut strings and a keyboard.

Lutenist, a lute-player, also a singer to the lute and often a comp. for the instrument.

Luther, Martin (b Eisleben, 10 Nov 1483; d Eisleben, 18 Feb 1546), German reformer and amateur musician. The musically relevant facts of his biog. are that his reforms of the church service, begun in 1522, incl. the much greater scope given to singing by the congregation and the consequent necessity to sing in the vernacular, instead of in Lat. He arranged a Ger. Mass in 1524 and he had the assistance of Walter and of Conrad Rupff, music director to the Elector of Saxony, in compiling a Ger. hymn-book, with tones selected by him, some adapted from Lat. and earlier Ger. hymns and some possibly invented by himself.

For literary works set by other comps. see **Burkhard** (*Musikalische Uebung*), **Otto (S.)** (hymn 'Ein' feste Burg'), **Walther (J.)** (sacred songs).

Luthier (Fr.), orig. a lute-maker, later, by transference, a maker of string instruments in general.

Lutosławski, Witold (b Warsaw, 25 Jan 1913), Polish composer. Studied at the Warsaw Cons. with Maliszewski (theory and comp.) and Lefeld (pf.), graduating in 1937. At the same time he studied mathematics at Warsaw Univ. His earlier music is influenced by Bartók and Stravinsky, and also by Polish folk music, but during recent years he has adopted a more advanced, aleatory technique.

Works incl. 3 symphs. (1941–83), *Symph. Variations* (1938), *Concerto for Orch.*, *Venetian Games* for small orch. (1961), *Musique funèbre* for strings (in memory of Bartók), *5 Dance Preludes* for clar., strings, harp and perc.; cello concerto (1970), *Preludes and fugues* for 13 strings (1971), *Mi Parti* for orch. (1976), Concerto for oboe, harp and chamber orch. (1982), *Chain I* for chamber orch. (1983), *Chain II* for voilin and orch. (1984); *Trois Poèmes d'Henri Michaux* for wind instruments, 2 pfs., perc. and 20-part chorus; *Silesian Tryptich* for soprano and orchestra (1951), *Paroles tissées* for voice and orch. (1965), *Les espaces du sommeil* for bar. and orch. (1975), string 4tet (1964); *Variations* on a theme of Paganini for 2 pfs.

Lutyens, Elisabeth (b London, 9 Jul 1906; d Hampstead, 14 Apr 1983), English composer. Daughter of the architect Sir Edwin Lutyens. Studied vla. and comp. at the RCM in London, the latter with Harold Darke, and later with Caussade in Paris. She married the BBC cond. Edward Clark. Her later work was generally, though not invariably, written in 12-note technique.

Works incl. operas *Infidelio* (1956, prod. 1973) and *Time Off? Not a Ghost of a Chance* (prod. 1972); ballet *The Birthday of the Infanta* (after Oscar Wilde, 1932); chamber cantata *Winter the Huntsman* (Osbert Sitwell), *Bienfaits de la lune* (Baudelaire) and other choral works; 3 symph. preludes, *Petite Suite*, *Divertissement* and other orchestral works; vla. concerto, *Lyric Piece* for vln. and orch.; 6 chamber concertos (1939–48).

6 string 4tets (1938–82), string trio, *Suite gauloise* for wind octet; *Aptote* for solo vln., sonata for solo vla.; pf. music, suite for org.; *O saisons, o châteaux* (Rimbaud, 1946), and other works for voice and chamber music; songs.

Luxon, Benjamin (b Redruth, 24 Mar 1937), English baritone. He studied at the GSM and in 1971 created Britten's Owen Wingrave on TV. Glyndebourne from 1972 as Ulisse, Almaviva, Janáček's Forester and Don Giovanni. At CG his roles have incl. the Jester and Death in the fp of *Taverner* (1972), Eugene Onegin, and Diomed in the revised vers. of *Troilus and Cressida*. Other roles incl. Posa, Papageno, Eisenstein and Wolfram. Often heard in Lieder.

Luyton, Karel (b Antwerp, c 1556; d Prague, Aug 1620), Flemish organist and composer. He was in the service of the Emperor Maximilian II at Prague in 1576, when that monarch died, and was app. to the Emperor Rudolf II in the same capacity. He was court composer in succession to Monte from 1603.

Works incl. Masses, motets, Lamentations, *Sacrae cantiones*; It. madrigals; *Fuga suavissima* and *Ricercare* for organ.

Luzzaschi, Luzzasco (b Ferrara ? 1545; d Ferrara, 10 Sep 1607), Italian organist and composer. Pupil of Rore at Ferrara and by 1576 organist and *maestro di cappella* to Duke Alfonso II. Among his organ pupils was Frescobaldi.

Works incl. motets, *Sacrae cantiones*; madrigals; organ music, etc. His *Madrigali per cantare et sonare* (1601) are for 3 voices and have keyboard accompaniments.

Lvov, Alexis Feodorovich (b Reval, 5 Jun 1798; d Romanovo, nr. Kovno, 28 Dec 1870), Russian composer. Studied with his father, Feodor L., an authority on church music and folksong, who succeeded Bortniansky as dir. of the Imp. Chapel in 1825. His son, who rose to high rank in the army and became adjutant to Nicholas I, succeeded him there from 1837 to 1861. He was a good violinist and founded a string 4tet at

St Petersburg. He became deaf and retired in 1867.

Works incl. operas *Bianca e Gualtiero* (1844), *Undine* (after Fouqué, 1847) and *The Bailiff* (1854), much church music; vln. concerto; fantasy *The Duel* for vln. and cello; Russian Imperial hymn 'God save the Tsar'.

Lyadov, Anatol. *See* **Liadov.**

Lydian Mode, one of the old ecclesiastical modes with semitones between the 4th and 5th and 7th and 8th notes of the scale, represented by the scale beginning on F on the white notes of the pf. keyboard.

Lympany, Moura (b Saltash, 18 Aug 1916), English pianist. Studied at the RCM; debut 1928, Harrogate. Often heard in Russian music and has toured widely with concertos by Delius, Rawsthorne and Ireland. CBE 1979.

Lyra (l) = **Lira** (*q.v.*)

(2), a percussion instrument with tuned steel bars or plates which are played with hammers, similar to the Stahlspiel, used in Eng. military bands and made for them in the shape of a lyre.

Lyra viol, a small bass viol, tuned in various ways and played from a tablature. It was is use in Eng. *c* 1650–1700; also variously called 'Lero Viol', 'Leero Viol' or 'Viol Lyra Way'.

Lyre, the most important instrument of ancient Greece, of eastern origin. The number of strings varied. They were stretched on a framework with a hollow sound-box at the bottom and plucked, like those of a harp, with both hands, but only the left used the finger-tips, while the right played with a plectrum. The large instrument of the type was called Kithara, a name from which the modern word 'guitar' derives.

Lyre-Guitar, or Apollo Lyre, a string instrument prod. in France near the end of the 18th cent., built to suggest the shape of the ancient Gk. lyre, but with a fretted fingerboard. It had 6 strings.

Lyric Suite, work for string 4tet in 6 movts. by Berg; comp. 1925–6, fp Vienna 8 Jan 1927. Movts. 2, 3 and 4 were arr. for string orch. and perf. Berlin, 31 Jan 1929, cond. Horenstein. Berg quotes from *Tristan* and Zemlinsky's *Lyric Symph.* and bases the work's note-row on the name of Hanna Robettin-Fuchs, with whom he had an affair. An alternative vocal finale, with text a trans. by Stefan George of Baudelaire, was perf. NY, 1 Nov 1979.

Lyrische Symphonie (*Lyric Symphony*), work by Zemlinsky in 7 movts. for sop., bar. and orch. (texts a German trans. by the comp. of Tagore); comp. 1922–3, fp Prague, 4 Jun 1924, cond. Zemlinsky (two days later Z. cond. the fp of Schoenberg's *Erwartung*). The format of the Lyric Symph. is modelled on *Das Lied von der Erde,* although the content is Zemlinsky's own.

Lyzarden or **Lyzardyne,** the old English name for the bass Cornett or Corno torto, the predecessor of the Serpent, which latter came into use in the 17th cent. Also sometimes called Lizard or Lysard.

M

M'. For names with this prefix see **Mac. . .**

m. The Mediant note in any key in Tonic Sol-fa notation, pronounced Me.

Ma Mère l'Oye (*Mother Goose*), suite by Ravel, written for pf. duet in 1908 and pub. in 1910, scored for orch. and prod. as a ballet, Paris, Opéra, 11 Mar 1915, scenario by Louis Laloy, choreography by L. Staats. The movements are based on tales by Perrault: 1. *Pavan of the Sleeping Beauty*; 2. *Hop-o'-my-Thumb*; 3. *Little Ugly, Empress of the Pagodas*; 4. *Colloquy between the Beauty and the Beast*; 5. *The Fairy Garden*.

Ma, Yo Yo (b Paris, 7 Oct 1955), Chinese cellist. He studied at Juilliard with Leonard Rose. Many appearances with leading orchs. and plays in trio with Emanuel Ax and Young Uck Kim.

Má Vlast (*My Country*), cycle of 6 symph. poems by Smetana, comp. 1874–9 and containing programme works on var. aspects of Cz. hist. and geography: 1. *Vyšehrad* (the citadel of Prague); 2. *Vltava* (the river); 3. *Šárka* (the Cz. Amazon); 4. *From Bohemia's Woods and Fields*; 5. *Tabor* (the city); 6. *Blaník* (the mountain).

Maag, Peter (b St Gallen, 10 May 1919), Swiss conductor. Studied pf. and theory with Marek and cond. with Franz von Hoesslins and Ansermet. After a number of lesser posts became 1st cond. of Düsseldorf Opera, 1952–4, and then music dir. of Bonn Opera, specializing in the perf. of lesser-known works. US debut 1959, Cincinnati SO; NY Met 1972 (*Don Giovanni*).

Maas, Joseph (b Dartford, 30 Jan 1847; d London, 16 Jan 1886), English tenor. He was a choir-boy at Rochester Cathedral, and after working as a clerk in Chatham dockyard he went to Milan in 1869 to study singing under San Giovanni. He 1st appeared at a concert in London, taking Sims Reeves's place, in 1871, and on the stage in 1872. His roles incl. Rienzi, Radames, Des Grieux and Lohengrin.

Maazel, Lorin (b Neuilly, France, 6 Mar 1930), American conductor and violinist. Brought to USA as a child, and soon displayed great musical ability, cond. NY PO aged 9. At 15 formed his own string 4tet and also appeared as vln. soloist. He became a member of the Pittsburgh SO and its cond. in 1949. He has since appeared with all the great European orchs., incl. the Vienna PO., and also at Salzburg, Bayreuth (*Lohengrin* and the *Ring*; 1960, 1968) and La Scala, Milan. He was music dir. of the Deutsche Oper Berlin and chief cond. of the Berlin Radio SO 1965–71 and from 1971 assoc. cond. of the New Philharmonia Orchestra; prin. guest cond. from 1976. Music dir. Cleveland Orch. 1972–82. Dir. Vienna Opera 1982–4; CG 1978, *Luisa Miller*. Music dir. Pittsburgh SO from 1986.

Mabellini, Teodulo (b Pistoia, 2 Apr 1817; d Florence, 10 Mar 1897), Italian conductor and composer. Studied at the Istituto Reale Musicale at Florence and prod. his 1st opera there at the age of 19. After further study with Mercadante at Novara, he settled at Florence, became cond. of the Società Filarmonica in 1843 and of the Teatro della Pergola in 1848. In 1860–87 he was prof. at the Istituto.

Works incl. operas *Matilda a Toledo* (1836), *Rolla* (1840), *Ginevra degli Almieri* (1841), *Il conte di Lavagna*, *I Veneziani a Constantinopoli* (1844), *Maria di Francia* (1846), *Il venturiero*, *Baldassare* (1852), and *Fiammetta* (1857); oratorios *Eudossio e Paolo* (1845) and *L'ultimo giorno di Gerusalemme* (1857); cantatas *La caccia* (1839), *Il ritorno* (1846), *Elegiaca*, *Rafaelle Sanzio* and *Lo spirito di Dante* (perf. 1865); much church music.

Macbeth, incid. music by (?) Locke for Davenant's version of Shakespeare's play, prod. London, Dorset Gardens Theatre, summer 1674. There were later prods. with music by D. Purcell, Eccles, Leveridge, etc.

Opera by Bloch (lib. by E. Fleg, after Shakespeare), prod. Paris, Opéra-Comique, 30 Nov 1910.

Opera by Chelard (lib. by R. de Lisle, after Shakespeare), prod. Paris, Opéra, 29 Jun 1827.

Opera by Collingwood (lib. by comp., chosen from Shakespeare), prod. London, SW, 12 Apr 1934.

Opera by Taubert (lib. by F. Eggers, after Shakespeare), prod. Berlin, Royal Opera, 16 Nov 1857.

Opera by Verdi (lib. by F.M. Piave and A. Maffei, after Shakespeare), prod. Florence, Teatro della Pergola, 14 Mar 1847; revised version (Fr. lib. by C. Nuitter and A. Beaumont) prod. Paris, Th. Lyrique, 21 Apr 1865.

Overture by Spohr, op. 75.

Symph. poem by R. Strauss, op. 23, comp. 1886–7, revised 1890, fp Weimar, 13 Sep 1890.

McBride, Robert (b Tucson, Arizona, 20 Feb 1911), American composer. Studied and took the Mus.B. at Arizona Univ. and obtained the Guggenheim Fellowship in 1937. Later he joined the faculty of Bennington Coll.

Works incl. ballet *Show Piece*; *Mexican Rhapsody* (1934) and *Prelude to a Tragedy* for orch.; fugato for 25 instruments, *Workout* for 15 instruments (1936); prelude and fugue for string 4tet; sonata *Depression* for vln. and pf., *Workout* for ob. and pf., *Swing Music* for clar. and pf. (1938); dance suite for pf., *Lament for the Parking Problem* for trumpet, horn and trombone (1968).

McCabe, John (b Huyton, 21 Apr 1939), English composer and pianist. He studied at the RMCM and in Munich. Often heard as pianist in the sonatas of Haydn.

Works incl. operas *The Play of Mother Courage* (1974) and *The Lion, the Witch and the Wardrobe* (1969); ballets *Mary, Queen of Scots* (1976) and *Don Juan* (1973); 3 symphs. (1965, 1971, 1978), *Variations on a theme of Hartmann* (1964), *The Chagall Windows* (1974), *The Shadow of Light* (1979); Concerto for Orchestra (1982), 3 pf. concertos (1966, 1970, 1976), 2 vln. concertos (1959, 1980); *Notturni ed Alba* for sop. and orch. (1970), *Stabat Mater* for sop., chorus and orch. (1976); 3 string 4tets (1960, 1972, 1979); pf. and organ music, songs.

McCormack, John, Count (b Athlone, 14 Jun 1884; d Dublin, 16 Sep 1945), Irish tenor. Began as chorister in Dublin Roman Catholic Cathedral. Without previous training won the gold medal at the Irish Festival, Dublin, 1902. In 1905 went to Italy to study with Sabbatini at Milan. Made his 1st concert appearance in London in 1907 and was engaged for opera by CG in the autumn as Turiddu, Ottavio and the Duke of Mantua. Later roles (until 1914) incl. Faust, Gounod's Roméo, Gerald and Pinkerton. He soon sang in It., USA, etc. and made a great reputation, but in later years made popularity rather than serious musical interest his chief concern. His title was a papal one.

McCracken, James (b Gary, Indiana, 16 Dec 1926), American tenor. Appeared as light entertainer before making his debut at the NY Met in 1953; he sang only small roles and left for Europe in 1957. He has frequently sung in Europe and is best known for his Otello which he sang first in Washington, 1960. Other roles incl. Florestan, Don José, Bacchus and Samson.

MacCunn, Hamish (b Greenock, 22 Mar 1868; d London, 2 Aug 1916), Scottish composer and conductor. Studied with Parry and Stanford at the RCM in London and had an overture *Cior Mhor* perf. at the Crystal Palace at the age of 17. He married a daughter of the painter John Pettie in 1889 and soon afterwards cond. the Carl Rosa Opera Co. for some time, also German's light operas at the Savoy Theatre.

Works incl. operas *Jeanie Deans* (after Scott, 1894), *Diarmid* (1897) and *Breast of Light* (unfinished), light operas *The Golden Girl* (1905) and *Prue*; music for *The Masque of War and Peace* and *Pageant of Darkness and Light*; cantatas *The Moss Rose* (1885), *Lord Ullin's Daughter* (Thomas Campbell, 1888), *The Lay of the Last Minstrel* (after Scott), *Bonny Kilmeny* (James Hogg), *The Cameronian's Dream* (James Hyslop, 1890), *Queen Hynde of Caledon* (Hogg), *The Death of Parcy Reed*, *The Wreck of the Hesperus* (Longfellow, 1905), and others; Psalm viii for chorus and organ; overture *The Land of the Mountain and the Flood*; ballads *The Ship o' the Fiend* and *The Dowie Dens o' Yarrow*, 3 descriptive pieces *Highland Memories* for orch.; 3 Romantic pieces for cello and pf. (1914).

McDonald, Harl (b nr. Boulder, Colorado, 27 Jul 1899; d Princeton, NJ, 30 Mar 1955), American pianist, scientist and composer. Studied at home, at California Univ., and the Leipzig Cons. He toured as a pianist in Europe and USA, settled in Philadelphia as teacher and cond. and in 1930–3 studied physics in relation to acoustic problems with a Rockefeller grant and wrote a book on *New Methods of Measuring Sound*.

Works incl. 84th Psalm and *Missa ad Patrem* for chorus and orch.; 4 symphs. (1934–8: no. 1 *The Santa Fé Trail*, no. 2 *Rhumba*), 2 suites and 3 Poems on Aramaic Themes for orch.; 2 pf. concertos; string 4tet on Negro themes (1932), pf. trio; pf. works; songs.

MacDowell, Edward (Alexander) (b New York, 18 Dec 1860; d New York, 23 Jan 1908), American composer and pianist. Learnt the pf. at home at first, was taken to the Paris Cons. in 1876, where he studied pf. under Marmontel and theory under Savard; afterwards worked with Louis Ehlert at Wiesbaden, 1878, and entered the Frankfurt Cons. in 1879, where Raff taught him comp. In 1881 he became pf. prof. at the Darmstadt Cons. and the next year played his 1st pf. concerto at Zurich at Liszt's invitation. Returned to USA in 1884 and married Marian

Mace   440

Nevins, who had been his pupil at Frankfurt, 21 Jul. After another period at Frankfurt and Wiesbaden, he went home for good and settled at Boston in 1888, making his 1st public appearance in USA there, 19 Nov. In 1896 he was app. head of the new music dept. at Columbia Univ. in NY and became hon. Mus.D. at Princeton Univ. Resigned in 1904, but continued to teach and comp. In 1904 he began to suffer from mental illness which afflicted him until his death.

Works incl. symph. poems *Hamlet and Ophelia* (after Shakespeare, 1885), *Lancelot and Elaine*, *Lamia* (after Keats, 1889); 2 suites (no. 2 *Indian*) for orch.; 2 pf. concertos (1882, 1889); 6 orchestral works; 26 op. nos. of pf. solos, incl. 4 sonatas, 2 *Modern Suites*, 24 studies, *Woodland Sketches*, *Sea Pieces*, *Fireside Tales*, *New England Idylls*, also 2 books of technical exercises; 2 sets of pieces for pf. duet; 42 songs; 26 part-songs.

Mace, Thomas (b Cambridge *c* 1613; d ? Cambridge, *c* 1709), English writer on music. Clerk of Trinity Coll., Cambridge; pub. *Musick's Monument* in 1676. He invented a 'table org.' for use with a consort of viols and in 1672 a lute with 50 strings which he called the 'Dyphone', designed to serve him when he was becoming deaf. His comps. incl. an anthem 'I heard a voice'.

Macfarren, George (Alexander) (b London, 2 Mar 1813; d London, 31 Oct 1887), English composer and educationist. Pupil of C. Lucas from 1827, entered the RAM in 1829, of which he became a prof. in 1834 and principal in 1876. In 1845 he married the Ger. contralto and translator Natalia Andrae (1828–1916). He ed. works by Purcell and Handel. In the 1870s his eyesight began to fail and he eventually became blind, but he continued to work at comp. and to teach. Knighted 1883.

Works incl. operas *The Devil's Opera* (1838), *The Adventures of Don Quixote* (after Cervantes, 1846), *King Charles II* (1849), *Robin Hood* (1860), *Jessy Lea* (1863), *She Stoops to Conquer* (after Goldsmith, 1864), *The Soldier's Legaey*, *Helvellyn*; masque *Freya's Gift*; oratorios *St John the Baptist* (1873), *The Resurrection* (1876), *Joseph* (1877), *King David*; cantatas *Emblematical Tribute on the Queen's Marriage* (1840), *The Sleeper Awakened*, *Lenora*, *May Day*, *Christmas*, *The Lady of the Lake* (after Scott, 1876); much church music; symph. in F min. and 7 others (1831–74), overtures, to Shakespeare's *Hamlet*, *Romeo and Juliet* and *The Merchant of Venice*,

Schiller's *Don Carlos* (1842), overture *Chevy Chase* and other orchestral works; vln. concerto; 5 string 4tets and other chamber music; sonatas for var. instruments.

M'Gibbon, William (b Edinburgh, *c* 1690; d Edinburgh, 3 Oct 1756), Scottish violinist and composer. Pupil of his father, the oboist Matthew M'G., and of Corbett in London, on his return to Edinburgh he became leader of the orch. in the Gentlemen's Concerts. Comp. overtures, vln. concertos, vln. sonatas etc., and pub. 3 vols. of Scot. tunes.

M'Guckin, Barton (b Dublin, 28 Jul 1852; d Stoke Poges, Bucks., 17 Apr 1913), Irish tenor. Choir-boy at Armagh Cathedral, became a singer at St Patrick's Cathedral, Dublin, and made his 1st concert appearance there in 1874. The next year he sang in London, then studied briefly at Milan, and afterwards took to opera. In 1887–8 he appeared in USA. Sang with Carl Rosa Co. 1878–96. His roles incl. Des Grieux, Don José and Wilhelm Meister.

Machaut (or Machault), Guillaume de (b at or nr. Rheims, ? 13 Apr 1300; d Rheims, 1377), French composer and poet. He became secretary, *c* 1323, to John of Luxemburg, King of Bohemia, and went with him to Pol. Lithuania and It. On the king's death in 1346 Machaut went into the service of his daughter, the Duchess of Normandy, and on her death in 1349 into that of Charles, King of Navarre; later into that of the dauphin (afterwards Charles V) and his brother Jean, Duc de Berry. He became canon of Rheims Cathedral in 1333. An exponent of the *Ars nova* in France.

Works incl. Mass for 4 voices, *La Messe de Nostre Dame*; the earliest complete polyphonic mass setting by a single composer. Motets, vocal ballades and *rondeaux*, *chansons balladées*, *lais*, etc.

McIntyre, Donald (b Auckland, NZ, 22 Oct 1934), English bass-baritone. He studied at the GSM and sang Zaccaria with the WNO in 1959. SW, London, 1960–6 as Attila and the Dutchman. CG debut 1967, as Pizarro; other roles there incl. Orestes, Kurwenal, Klingsor and Barak in the 1st prod. of *Die Frau ohne Schatten* by a Brit. company. In 1967 he sang Telramund at Bayreuth and returned as Wotan in 1973 (1976 in the Boulez-Chéreau cent. production of the *Ring*), Also sang Wotan at CG and the NY Met in 1974.

Macintyre, Margaret (b India, *c* 1865; d London, April 1943), English soprano. London, CG, 1888–97 as Donna Elvira, the Countess and Elisabeth. She created Rebecca in Sullivan's *Ivanhoe* (1891) and sang Sieglinde at La Scala.

Mackenzie, Alexander (Campbell) (b Edinburgh, 22 Aug 1847; d London, 28 Apr 1935), Scottish composer. Studied in Ger. and at the RAM in London, of which, after 14 years as violinist and teacher at Edinburgh and some years at Florence, he became principal in 1888. Knighted 1895. Works incl. operas *Colomba* (1883), *The Troubadour* (1886), *The Cricket on the Hearth* (after Dickens, 1914) and *The Eve of St John* (1924); incid. music. for *Marmion* and *Ravenswood* (plays based on Scott), Shakespeare's *Coriolanus*, Byron's *Manfred* and Barrie's *The Little Minister*.

Oratorios *The Rose of Sharon* (1884), *Bethlehem* (1894), *The Temptation* (after Milton, 1914); cantatas *The Bride, Jason, The Story of Sayid, The Witch's Daughter, The Sun-God's Return*; *The Cottar's Saturday Night* (Burns) for chorus and orch. (1888). Suite, Scot. Rhapsody, Canadian Rhapsody, ballad *La Belle Dame sans merci* (after Keats, 1883), *Tam o' Shanter* (after Burns), overtures *Cervantes* (1877), *Twelfth Night* (Shakespeare), *Britannia* and *Youth, Sport and Loyalty* for orch.; concerto, Scot. Concerto (1897), suite and *Pibroch* suite for vln. and orch.; string 4tet (1875); pf. 4tet, pf. trio; vln. and pf. pieces; organ and pf. music; songs; part-songs.

Mackerras, (Sir) Charles (b Schenactady, NY, 17 Nov 1925), Australian conductor and editor. Taken to Sydney aged 2. Studied at Sydney Cons. and then became 1st oboe of Sydney SO and began his career as a cond. Came to Eng. in 1946 and from 1947 to 1948 studied with V. Talich in Prague. On his return to Eng. he was engaged by SW Opera and has since cond. throughout the world with considerable success. Principal cond. of SW Opera, 1970–80; Sydney SO from 1982. Best known for his perfs. of Janáček's operas, and has given works by Gluck, Sullivan, Handel, Mozart and J.C. Bach. Knighted 1979. Music dir., WNO, from 1986.

Mackintosh, Robert (b Tullymet, Perthshire, 1745; d London, Feb 1807), Scottish violinist and composer. Settled at Edinburgh as vln. teacher and concert organizer, but went to live in London in 1803. He wrote and arr. reels, strathspeys, minuets, gavottes, etc.

MacMillan, Ernest (b Mimico, Ont., 18 Aug 1893; d Toronto, 6 May 1973), Canadian conductor, organist and composer. Organist from 1903; cond. Toronto SO 1931–56.

MacNeil, Cornell (b Minneapolis, 24 Sep 1922), American baritone. Became well known after appearing in Menotti's *The Consul* (1950) and joined NY City Opera Co. Has also sung in Europe, appearing at La Scala, Milan, in 1959, as Carlo in *Ernani*, NY Met debut 1959, as Rigoletto.

Maçon, Le (*The Mason*), opera by Auber (lib. by Scribe and G. Delavigne), prod. Paris, Opéra-Comique, 3 May 1825.

Maconchy, (Dame) Elizabeth (b Broxbourne, Herts., 19 Mar 1907), English composer of Irish descent. Studied comp. under Vaughan Williams and pf. under Arthur Alexander at the RCM in London; later in Prague. Several of her works were perf. at the ISCM festivals abroad and were successful in Belgium and E. Europe. She married Wm. LeFanu, who trans. poems by Anacreon for her. Their daughter is the composer Nicola LeFanu (*q.v.*). CBE 1977, DBE 1987. Works incl. operas *The Sofa* (1957), *The Departure* (1961) and *The Three Strangers* (1967): perf. as trilogy Middlesbrough 1977. Ballets *Great Agrippa* (from Hofmann's *Shock-headed Peter*) and *The Little Red Shoes* (after Andersen); 2 motets for double chorus (Donne); *The Leaden Echo and the Golden Echo* (Gerard Manley Hopkins) for chorus and chamber orch. (1978). Symph. and suites for orch. *The Land* (on a poem by V. Sackville-West) and *Puck*; pf. concerto (1930), vln. concerto (1963), concertino for clar.; *Samson at the Gates of Gaza* for voice and orch.; Sinfonietta (1976), *Little Symphony* (1981), *Music for Strings* (1983); 13 string 4tets (1933–85), string trio, *Prelude Interlude* and *Fugue* for 2 vlns.; song-cycle *The Garland* (Anacreon).

McPhee, Colin (b Montreal, 15 Mar 1901; d Los Angeles, 7 Jan 1964), Canadian-American composer. Studied at Peabody Cons., Baltimore, with Strube and graduated in 1921. Studied pf. with Friedheim at the Canadian Acad. of Music, where he played a pf. concerto of his own in 1924. Then studied comp. in Paris with Paul le Flem and pf. with I. Philipp. Meetings with Varèse from 1926 much influenced his own music. From 1934 to 1939 he spent much time in Bali and Mexico.

Works incl. 3 symphs. (1955, 1957, 1962); concerto for pf. and 8 wind insts. (1928), *Tabuh-Tabuhan* for 2 pfs. and orch. (1936); *Balinese Ceremonial Music* for 2 pfs. (1942), and other pf. music; *4 Iroquois Dances* for orch. Also a number of books on Bali and its music.

Macque, Giovanni de (b Valenciennes, *c*

1551; d Naples, Sep 1614), Flemish composer. Pupil of Philippe de Monte. He went to It. living in Rome, 1576–82, and at Naples from 1586, where he was choirmaster of the royal chapel from 1594. Wrote 14 vols. of madrigals and *madrigaletti*. Other works incl. motets, and keyboard music.

Madama Butterfly, opera by Puccini (lib. by Giacosa and L. Illica, based on David Belasco's dramatic version of a story by John Luther Long), prod. Milan, La Scala, 17 Feb 1904.

Madame Sans-Gêne, opera by Giordano (lib. by R. Simoni after the play by Sardou and Moreau), prod. NY Met 25 Jan 1915, cond. Toscanini.

Maddalena, opera in 1 act by Prokofiev (lib. by comp. after M. Lieven); 1911–13, fp BBC, 25 Mar 1979: orch. by E. Downes and cond. by him.

Madeira, Jean (b Centralia, Ill., 14 Nov 1918; d Providence, 10 Jul 1972), American mezzo. Studied at the Juilliard School and sang small roles at the NY Met from 1948. Carmen in Vienna in 1955 and appeared at Bayreuth and CG as Erda. The following year she sang Clytemnestra at Salzburg and returned to the Met, as Carmen. In 1968 she created Circe in Dallapiccola's *Ulisse* at the Deutsche Oper, Berlin.

Mademoiselle Fifi, opera by Cui (lib. in Rus., based on Maupassant's story), prod. Moscow, 15 Dec 1903.

Maderna, Bruno (b Venice, 21 Apr 1920; d Darmstadt, 13 Nov 1973), Italian composer and conductor. Studied vln. and pf., and comp. with Bustini at Acad. of St Cecilia in Rome, and then took comp. and cond. lessons with Malipiero and Scherchen. He then cond. throughout Europe, specializing in modern music.

Works incl. *Hyperion*, composite theatre work (perf. Venice 1964); concertos for pf., 2 pfs., fl., ob.; *Introduzione e Passacaglia* for orch. (1947); *Musica su due Dimensioni* for fl., perc. and electronic tape (1952–8); instrumental works incl. *Composizione in tre tempi, Improvisizione I, II, Serenata I, II* for 11 and 13 insts. (1946–57); *Studi per il Processo di Fr. Kafka* for speaker, soprano and chamber orch. (1949); electronic music incl. *Notturno, Syntaxis, Continuo, Dimensioni*.

Madetoja, Leevi (Antti) (b Uleaaborg, 17 Feb 1887; d Helsinki, 6 Oct 1947), Finnish conductor, critic and composer. Studied at the Cons. of his native town and later with Järnefelt and Sibelius at Helsinki; after-

wards with d'Indy in Paris and Fuchs in Vienna. In 1912–14 he cond. the Helsinki orch., afterwards that of Viborg; became music critic at Helsinki in 1916 and teacher at the Cons., and in 1926 at the univ.

Works incl. operas *Pohjalaisia* (1924) and *Juha* (1935); ballets; 3 symphs. (1916, 1918, 1926), symph. poems and overtures; *Stabat Mater*; 8 cantatas; pf. trio; vln. and pf. sonata; *Lyric Suite* for cello and pf.; pf. pieces; songs.

Madonna of Winter and Spring, work for orch. and electronics by Jonathan Harvey; fp London, 27 Aug 1986, cond. Peter Eötvös.

Madrigal, a comp. for several voices cultivated in the 16th cent. and continuing until the early 17th. Among its special features were a richly polyphonic style and its association with poetry of high value. The texts were secular, except where they were otherwise designated (e.g. *madrigali spirituali*), and the music showed a tendency to keep a definite melody in the top part; indeed madrigals were often sung by a single voice, the lower parts being played by instruments; and sometimes the whole perf. was instrumental. The madrigal was cultivated partic. by Flem., It. and Eng. composers. In the 14th cent. the word was used for a poetic form and its music.

Madrigal Comedy (*see also* **Amfiparnaso**), a sequence of madrigals in a quasi-dramatic form. The most famous but not the earliest ex. is Orazio Vecchi's *L'Amfiparnaso*, and similar works of his are *La selva di varie ricreazioni* (*The Forest of Multifarious Delights*), *Il convito musicale* (*The Musical Banquet*) and *Le veglie di Siena* (*The Vigils of Siena*). A similar work, Simone Balsamino's *Novellette*, based on Tasso's *Aminta*, appeared the same year as *L'Amfiparnaso* (1594), but there were earlier ones, notably Striggio's *Il cicalamento delle donne al bucato* (*The Cackling of Women at the Wash*), and later Vecchi was imitated by Banchieri and others.

Maessins, Pieter (b Ghent, *c* 1505; d Vienna, prob. Oct 1563), Flemish composer. Chief *Kapellmeister* in Vienna, 1546–60. Composed Lat. motets.

Maestoso (It. lit. 'majestic') = stately, dignified.

Maestro (It.) = master, a title given by Italians to a distinguished musician, whether comp., perf. or teacher.

Maestro al cembalo (It. lit. 'master at the harpsichord'), in the late 17th and 18th cents. the harpsichord player who not only played continuo in the orch. but also acted as asst. to the cond. and helped to coach singers.

Maestro de capilla (Span.) = Maestro di cappella.

Maestro di cappella (It.), director of music in a cathedral, a royal or princely chapel, or any similar musical establishment.

Magalhães, Filippe de (b Azeitão nr. Lisbon, *c* 1571; d Lisbon, 17 Dec 1652), Portuguese composer. Pupil of Mendes at Evora. *Maestro de capilla* of the Misericordia at Lisbon and from 1614 of the royal chapel there under the Span. king, Philip III.

Works incl. Masses, canticles to the Blessed Virgin, chants.

Magaloff, Nikita (b St Petersburg, 8 Feb 1912), Swiss pianist of Russian birth. Studied pf. with I. Philipp at the Paris Cons., and comp. with Prokofiev. Began his career as accompanist to Szigeti, later turning to solo concert perfs. In 1949 he succeed Lipatti as prof. of pf. at the Geneva Cons. Well known in Ravel, Prokofiev and Stravinsky.

Magelone Romances, a cycle of 15 songs by Brahms, settings of poems from Ludwig Tieck's *Die schöne Magelone* (*Story of the Fair Magelone*), Op. 33, comp. in 1861–6.

Maggiore (It.) = major. The word is sometimes explicitly stated at a point in a comp. where the maj. key returns after a prolonged section in min., esp. in variations, to prevent the perf. from overlooking the change of key.

Magic Flute (Mozart). *See* **Zauberflöte.**

Magic Fountain, The, opera by Delius (lib. by comp. and J. Bell); comp. 1894–5, fp BBC broadcast, 20 Nov 1977, cond. Del Mar.

Magic Opal, The, opera by Albéniz (lib. by A. Law), prod. London, Lyric Theatre, 19 Jan 1893.

Magic Opera, a species of opera not unlike the Eng. pantomime, popular partic. on the Viennese stage at the end of the 18th and opening of the 19th cent., where it was called *Zauberoper*. It consisted of dialogue and musical numbers, had a fairy-tale subject with incidents of low comedy, and contained numerous scenic effects. The outstanding ex. is Mozart's *Zauberflöte*; others are Müller's *Zauberzither*, Wranitzky's *Oberon*, Süssmayr's *Spiegel von Arkadien*, Schubert's *Zauberharfe*; the Eng. work nearest to it in character is Weber's *Oberon*.

Magini-Coletti, Antonio (b Iesi, nr. Ancona, 1855; d Rome, 7 Jul 1912), Italian baritone. He sang in Italy from 1880; at La Scala he took part in the fps of Puccini's *Edgar* (1889) and Mascagni's *Le Maschere* (1901). NY

Met from 1891 as Nevers and Amonasro, with the De Reszkes, Nordica and Lilli Lehmann. He appeared as guest at CG and Monte Carlo.

Magnard, (Lucien Denis Gabriel) Albéric (b Paris, 9 Jun 1865; d Baron, Oise, 3 Sep 1914), French composer. Studied at the Paris Cons. and in 1888 became a private pupil of d'Indy. As the son of Francis M., ed. of *Le Figaro*, he was comfortably off and never held any official posts. He retired to Baron to devote himself to comp., pub. his works himself and never took any trouble to have them perf., though some were brought out by enthusiastic friends. During the very first days of the 1914–18 war he fired on the Germans from his window, was killed as a sniper, and his house, incl. several of his MSS., was burnt down.

Works incl. operas *Yolande*, 1891, (destroyed), *Guercœur* (partly destroyed 1900; perf 1931) and *Bérénice*; 4 symphs., (1890, 1893, 1896, 1913), *Suite dans le style ancien*, *Chant funèbre*, overture *Hymne à la Justice* and *Hymne à Vénus* for orch. (1904); string 4tet (1903), pf. trio, pf. and wind 5tet; vln. and pf. sonata, cello and pf. sonata; pf. pieces; songs.

Magnetton (Ger. = magnet tone), an electrophonic instrument invented by Stelzhammer of Vienna in 1933, prod. its notes by means of electro-magnets and capable of imitating var. instruments.

Magnificat, the song of the Blessed Virgin, regularly sung as a Vesper canticle in the Roman Catholic Church and as part of the evening service in the Anglican Church; also, more rarely, in a form better suited to concert perf., e.g. Bach, Vaughan Williams, etc.

Mahillon, Victor (b Brussels, 10 Mar 1841; d Saint-Jean, Cap Ferrat, 17 Jun 1924), Belgian music scholar. Son of the instrument maker Charles M. (1813–87). Studied at the Brussels Cons., where he became curator of the museum of musical instruments. He wrote on acoustics and instruments.

Mahler, Fritz (b Vienna, 16 Jul 1901; d Winston-Salem, N.C., 17 Jun 1973), Austrian conductor and composer. Second cousin of Gustav M., he studied comp. with Berg and Schoenberg and musicology with Guido Adler (1920–4) at Vienna Univ. After cond. at the Vienna Volksoper he was in charge of the Radio Orch. in Copenhagen from 1930 to 1935, emigrating to the USA in 1936. He taught at the Juilliard Summer School from 1947 to 1953, when he became cond. of the Hartford SO.

Mahler, Gustav (b Kalište, Boh., 7 Jul 1860; d Vienna, 18 May 1911), Austrian composer and conductor. Son of a Jewish shopkeeper. He showed great talent as a pianist in his childhood, and in 1875 his family, who had removed to Jihlava (Iglau) soon after his birth, succeeded in entering him at the Vienna Cons. His pf. prof., Julius Epstein, seeing his real gifts, advised him to study comp. and cond. After leaving the Cons. in 1878 he wrote the 1st vers. of his cantata *Das Klagende Lied*. His cond. career began in the summer of 1880 in Hall, Upper Austria. Posts followed at theatres in Ljubljana (1881) and Olmütz (1882). While in Kassel (1883–5) he wrote the *Lieder eines fahrenden Gesellen* and began the thematically related 1st symph. In 1885 he was cond. at the Prague Opera, where he gave perfs. of the operas by Mozart and Wagner which were to form the basis of his repertory; his cond. was already noted for its precision of ensemble, pronounced rubato and individuality in choice of tempi. At Leipzig (1886–8) he was 2nd cond. to Nikisch; his completion of Weber's sketches for *Die Drei Pintos* was premièred in 1888. While at Budapest (1888–9) he led the unsuccessful fp of his 1st symph.

From 1891–7 he was chief cond. of·the Hamburg Opera, where he furthered his reputation for inspiring high standards of theatrical, as well as musical, perf. In Dec 1895 he led the Berlin fp of his *Resurrection* symph., achieving his 1st success as a comp. In 1897 Mahler's timely baptism into the Catholic church led to his app. as dir. of the Vienna Court Opera. In the next ten years he estab. a magnificent co. of singing actors and, most notably with the help of the stage designer Alfred Roller, mounted influential prods. which sought to harmonise all aspects of stage and musical experience. He succeeded Richter as cond. of the Vienna PO in 1898 but largely as a result of his autocratic methods he departed in 1901. Various intrigues at the Opera led to his resignation in 1907. During his years in Vienna Mahler wrote his symphs. nos. 4–8 near a villa on the Wörthersee in Carinthia. In 1902 he had married Alma Schindler; through her teacher, Alexander Zemlinsky, he met Schoenberg. Their friendship is reflected in the complex polyphony and extreme chromaticism of Mahler's later music. On 1 Jan 1908 he made his debut as prin. cond. of the NY Met; due to artistic and personal differences his tenure there and with the NY Philharmonic Soc. was brief. In 1910 he led the triumphant Munich fp of his 8th symph.,

and the following year returned to Europe for the last time, mortally ill with a bacterial infection of the blood. Mahler's music took many years to gain acceptance – four of the symphs. were not heard in Brit. until after 1945 – but he is now estab. as a founder of 20th cent. music.

Works incl. 10 SYMPHONIES; all except last two premièred by Mahler: no. 1 in D (1883–8, fp Budapest, 20 Nov 1889); no. 2 in C min. with sop., mezzo and chorus in finale, *Resurrection* (text by comp. and Klopstock; 1887–94, fp Berlin, 13 Dec 1895); no. 3 in D min. with alto, women and boys' voices (texts from Nietzsche and *Des Knaben Wunderhorn*; 1893–6, fp Krefeld, 9 Jun 1902); no. 4 in G with sop. in the finale (1899–1901, fp Munich, 25 Nov 1901); no. 5 in C♯ min. (1901–2, fp Cologne, 18 Oct 1904); no. 6 in A min. (1903–6, fp Essen, 27 Apr 1906); no. 7 in E min. (1904–6, fp Prague, 19 Sep 1908); no. 8 in E♭ '*Symphony of a Thousand*', with soloists, adult and boys' choruses (text 9th. cent. hymn *Veni creator spiritus* in 1st movt. and from Goethe's *Faust* part II in 2nd; 1906, fp Munich, 12 Sep 1910); no. 9 in D (1908–9, fp Vienna, 26 Jun 1912, cond. Walter); no. 10 in F♯ min. was incomplete at Mahler's death: a performing version by Deryck Cooke was given in London on 13 Aug 1964.

Cantata *Das klagende Lied* (1878–80); song-cycles *Lieder eines fahrenden Gesellen* (1884), *Kindertotenlieder* (1901–4), 3 books of early songs, 5 songs to words by Rückert, many other songs, incl. settings from *Des Knaben Wunderhorn*, *Das Lied von der Erde*, symph. for mezzo and tenor solo and orch. (1907–9). (*See also* separate entries for vocal works.)

Maichelbeck, Franz Anton (b Reichenau nr. Constance, 6 Jul 1702; d Freiburg i/B., 14 Jun 1750), German organist and composer. Studied music in Rome, 1725–7, and on his return to Freiburg became organist at the Minster (1728) and prof. of It. at the univ. (1730). Wrote chiefly keyboard music.

Maid of Orleans, The (*Orleanskaya Dieva*), opera by Tchaikovsky (lib. by comp., based on V.A. Zhukovsky's trans. of Schiller's drama), prod. St Petersburg, 25 Feb 1881.

Maikl, Georg (b Zell, 4 Apr 1872; d Vienna, 1951), Austrian tenor. He was discovered by Pollini; debut Mannheim 1899, as Tamino. He was a leading member of the Vienna Opera 1904–44, in operas by Mozart and Wagner, and in the 1916 fp of the revised vers. of *Ariadne auf Naxos*. Salzburg 1906 and 1910, as Ottavio; 1937 as Aegisthus and in *Die Meistersinger.*

Mainardi, Enrico (b Milan, 19 May 1897; d Munich, 10 Apr 1976), Italian cellist. Studied cello and comp. at Milan Cons. until 1920 and then cello with H. Becker in Berlin. In 1933 he was appointed prof. of cello at the Acad. of St Cecilia in Rome. Recorded *Don Quixote* under Strauss.

Works incl. 4 cello concertos, suite for cello and pf. and some chamber music.

Maine, Basil (b Norwich, 4 Mar 1894; d Sheringham, Norfolk, 13 Oct 1972), English critic, novelist and biographer. Studied at Cambridge, and after school-mastering and acting became music critic to the *Daily Telegraph* in London, 1921, and the *Morning Post*, 1926. In 1939 he took orders in the Church of Eng. His music books incl. a large biog. of Elgar (1933).

Mainzer Umzug, work by Hindemith for soloists, chorus and orch.; comp. 1962, fp Mainz, 23 Jun 1962, cond. Hindemith.

Maison, René (b Frameries, 24 Nov 1895; d Mont d'Or, 11 Jul 1962), Belgian tenor. Debut Geneva 1920, as Rodolfo. He sang in Paris from 1925 and made his US debut at Chicago, in 1928; NY Met 1935–43, debut as Walther. At Buenos Aires, 1934–7, he was heard in the It. and Fr. repertory. He taught in NY and Boston after his retirement; Ramon Vinay was among his pupils.

Maison à vendre (*House for Sale*), opera by Dalayrac (lib. by A. Duval), prod. Paris, Opéra-Comique, 23 Oct 1800.

Maître de chapelle (Fr.) = Maestro di cappella (*q.v.*).

Maîtrise (Fr.) = mastership, the former French name for the whole estab. of the choir at cathedrals and collegiate churches, incl. not only all that appertained to their perf. in church, but also to their accommodation and maintenance. The maîtrises were actually schools of music.

Majo, Gian Grancesco di (b Naples, 24 Mar 1732; d Naples, 17 Nov 1770), Italian composer. Pupil of his father, Giuseppe di M. (1697–1771), *maestro di cappella* at the court at Naples, and later of Padre Martini in Bologna. App. 2nd organist at court in 1750, but lived chiefly as an opera comp.

Works incl. 20 operas, e.g. *Ricimero, rè dei Goti* (1758), *Astrea Placata* (1760), *Cajo Fabricio, Ifigenia in Tauride* (1764), *Eumene* (unfinished at his death, completed by Errichelli and Insanguine), etc.; 8 oratorios incl. *La passione di Gesù Cristo* (1780); 5 Masses and other church music; cantatas.

Major, one of the 2 predominant scales (the other being Minor) of the tonal system. *See* **Scale.** A major key is one based on the major scale. *See also* **Major Interval.**

Major Interval. 2nds, 3rds, 6ths and 7ths can be major intervals. If the upper note of the major interval is flattened (or the lower note is sharpened) it becomes a min. interval. If the upper note of a major interval is sharpened (or the lower note is flattened it becomes an augmented interval, e.g.:

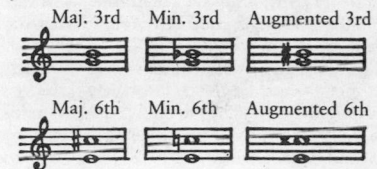

Makropoulos, Case, The (*Věc Makropulos*), opera by Janáček (lib. based on Karel Čapek's play), prod. Brno, 18 Dec 1926.

Maksymiuk, Jerzy (b Grodno, 9 Apr 1936), Polish conductor and composer. He studied at the Warsaw Cons. and after working with the Polish Radio orch. founded the Polish Chamber Orch., 1972. Prin. cond. BBC Scot. Orch. from 1983. A ballet, *Capriccio,* and a string trio are among his comps.

Malagueña, a Span. (Andalusian) song whose place of origin is Málaga. It also appears often as an instrumental piece. It begins and ends on the dominant of its key. The 2nd movt. of Ravel's *Rapsodie espagnole* (1907) is titled Malagueña.

Malanotte, Adelaide (b Verona, 1785; d Salo, 31 Dec 1832), Italian contralto. Debut Verona 1806. In 1813, at the Teatro Fenice, Venice, she created Rossini's Tancredi. Said by Hérold to share Susanna's secret.

Malbecque, Guillermus (b c 1400; d Soignies 29 Aug 1465), French composer, member of the papal chapel, 1431–8, and a canon of Soignies from 1440 until his death. Comp. 3-part *chansons.*

Malcolm, George (b London, 28 Feb 1917), English pianist, harpsichordist and conductor. He studied at the RCM; 1947–59 master of music Westminster Cathedral. Has cond. most major orchs. in Brit. Artistic dir. Philomusica, London, 1962–6, and has been heard as a pianist in chamber ensembles. CBE 1965.

Malcuzyński, Witold (b Warsaw, 10 Aug 1914; d Palma, 17 Jul 1977), Polish pianist. Studied at Warsaw Cons. with Turczyski, and then with Paderewski in Switz. In 1939 he married the pianist Colette Gaveau and moved to Paris. He played in all parts of the world and was esp. well known as an interpreter of Chopin and Liszt.

Maldere, Pierre van (b Brussels, 16 Oct 1729; d Brussels, 1 Nov 1768), Belgian violinist and composer. Travelled as a virtuoso, 1752–8, visiting Dublin, Paris and Vienna, and on his return to Brussels entered the service of the Duke of Lorraine. Dir. of the Brussels Opera, 1763–6.

Works incl. operas *Le Déguisement pastoral* (1756), *Les Précautions inutiles* (1760), *La Bagarre* (1763), etc.; symphs.; concertos; sonatas.

Male Alto, an artificial extension of the highest male-voice register, prod. by falsetto, used in Anglican church choirs and in male-voice 4tets and choral societies, partic. in glees and part-songs.

Maler, Wilhelm (b Heidelberg, 21 Jun 1902; d Hamburg, 29 Apr 1976), German composer. Studied with var. masters, incl. Jarnach, and was influenced by Hindemith. He was app. prof. of comp. at Cologne Cons. in 1925 and later also taught at Bonn Univ.

Works incl. oratorio *Der ewige Strom* (1934) and cantata on poems by Stefan George.

Malfitano, Catherine (b New York, 18 Apr 1948), American soprano. She studied in NY and made her debut in 1972. After appearances at Sante Fe, Houston and NY she sang with success in Europe: 1984 Mimi and Manon in Florence and Paris, 1985 Fiorilla in Geneva and Lulu in a new prod. of Berg's opera by John Pierre Ponnelle at Munich. Also sings Juliette and Poppea.

Malgoire, Jean-Claude (b Avignon, 25 Nov 1940), French conductor, oboist and musicologist. He studied at the Paris Cons. and in 1966 founded the ens. La Grande Ecurie et La Chambre du Roy, for perfs. of Baroque music with an empirical approach towards instrumentation and performing practice: best known for perfs. of operas by M.-A. Charpentier, Lully and Rameau. Many tours in Europe and US with this ens. and Florilegium Musicum de Paris (medieval and Renaissance music). In 1986 he cond. a revival of Campra's *Tancrède*, at Aix-en-Provence.

Malheurs d'Orphée, Les (*The Miseries of Orpheus*), opera by Milhaud (lib. by A. Lunel), prod. Brussels, Théâtre de la Monnaie, 7 May 1926.

Malibran (*née* Garcia), **Maria (Felicità)** (b Paris, 24 Mar 1808; d Manchester, 23 Sep 1836), Spanish soprano. Studied under her father, Manuel Garcia. After much travell-

ing in It., etc., and appearing in a child's part in Paer's *Agnese* at Naples in 1814, she made her 1st concert appearance in Paris in 1824, and on the stage in London in 1825 as Rosina, and Felicia in Meyerbeer's *Il Crociato in Egitto*. NY Park Theatre, 1825–6 in Rossini's *Tancredi, Otello* and *Il Turco in Italia*; Paris 1828 in *Semiramide*. She created the title roles in Balfe's *The Maid of Artois* and Donizetti's *Maria Stuarda*. In 1826 she married Malibran, an elderly Frenchman, but left him when he went bankrupt in 1827, and in 1830 she formed an attachment with Bériot, whom she married shortly before her sudden death, after a riding accident.

Malipiero, (Gian) Francesco (b Venice, 18 Mar 1882; d Treviso, 1 Aug 1973), Italian composer. In 1898 he began studying vln. at the Vienna Cons., but on failing an examination turned to comp., returning to Venice in 1899. Graduated from Bologna Liceo Musicale in 1904. In 1913 he went to Paris. From 1921 to 1923 he was prof. of comp. at Parma Univ. and from 1939 to 1953 was director of the Liceo Musicale Benedetto Marcello in Venice. He was the ed. of the complete edition of Monteverdi's works.

Works incl. operatic trilogy *L'Orfeide* (*La morte delle maschere, Sette canzoni, Orfeo* (1st complete perf. 1925), operas *Tre commedie goldoniane* (Goldoni's plays *La bottega da caffè, Sior Todero Brontolon, Le baruffe chiozzotte* (1926), *Filomela e l'infatuato* (1928), *Merlino mastro d'organi, Il mistero di Venezia* (*Le aquile Aquileia, Il finto Arlecchino, I corvi di San Marco*, 1932), *Torneo notturno* (1931), *La favola del figlio cambiato* (lib. by Pirandello, 1934), *Giulio Cesare* and *Antonio e Cleopatra* (both after Shakespeare, 1936, 1938), *Ecuba, I capricci di Callot* (after E.T.A. Hoffmann, 1941), *La vita è sogno* (1943), *L'allegra brigata* (1950), *Il figliuol prodigo* (1957), *Donna Urraca* (1954), *Il capitan spavento* (1963), *Don Giovanni* (1963), *Don Tartufo* (1970), *Uno dei dieci* (1971); ballets *La mascherata della principesse prigioniere* (1924), *Pantea.*

CHORAL AND ORCHESTRAL: *Virgilli Aeneis* for solo voices, chorus and orch. (1944; prod. 1958), *Li sette peccati mortali* (7 sonnets by Fazio degli Uberti) for chorus and orch. (1946); for orch.: *Sinfonia del mare* (1906), *Sinfonia del silenzio e della morte* (1908), *Ditirambo tragico, Impressioni dal vero* (3 sets, 1913), *Per una favola cavaleresca, Pause del silenzio* (1917–26), *Concerti, Inni, Invenzioni, Sinfonia in quattro tempi come le quattro stagioni* (1933), *Sin-*

fonia elegiaca, Sinfonie delle campane and 8 others (1946–69); 6 pf. concertos (1934–58), *Variazioni senza tema* for pf. and orch., 2 vln. concertos, cello concerto.

CHAMBER AND SOLO VOCAL: *Il commiato* (Leopardi) for baritone and orch.; oratorios *San Francesco d'Assisi, La cena, La passione* (1935), *Missa pro mortuis* (1938); 8 string 4tets (1920–64); incl. *Rispetti e strambotti, Stornelli e ballate* and *Canzoni alla madrigalesca*; *Sonata a tre* for vln., cello and pf., *Sonata a cinque* for fl., harp, vln. vla. and cello, *Ricercari* and *Ritrovari* for 11 instruments, *Le sette allegrezze d'amore* for voice and 14 insts. (1945) and other chamber music; many pf. works: *Preludi autunnali, Poemi asolani, Barlumi, Maschere che passano*, etc.; songs *Tre poesi di Angelo Poliziano, Quattro sonetti del Burchiello, Due sonetti del Berni, Le stagioni italiche*.

Malipiero, Riccardo (b Milan, 24 Jul 1914), Italian composer, nephew of prec. Studied at Milan and Turin and with his uncle in Venice. Early comps. are neo-classical in spirit; turned to scrialism in 1945.

Works incl. operas *Minnie la Candida* (1942), *La Donna è mobile* (1957) and *Battano alla Porta* (1962); 3 pf. concertos (1937–61), 2 cello concertos (1938, 1957); 3 symphs. (1949–59), *Cadencias* for orch. (1964), *Mirages* for orch. (1966); Requiem (1975); 3 string 4tets (1941, 1954, 1960), pf. 5tet (1957), *Cassazione* for string 6tet (1967); pf. music.

Maliponte, Adriana (b Brescia, 26 Dec 1938), Italian soprano. She studied at Mulhouse; debut Milan 1958, as Mimi. Paris, Opéra, 1962, as Micaela. US debut Philadelphia 1963; NY Met from 1971 as Pamina, Juliette, Luisa Miller and Eurydice. La Scala 1970, Manon; CG 1976, Nedda. In 1985 she sang Alice Ford at the Met.

Maliszewski, Witold (b Mohylev, Podolia, 20 Jul 1873; d Warsaw, 18 Jul 1939), Polish violinist, pianist and composer. Pupil of Rimsky-Korsakov at St Petersburg Cons. and in 1908–21 was director of the Odessa school of music. He then left for Warsaw, where he taught at the Cons. and the Chopin School of Music. In 1933 he founded the Chopin Inst. in Warsaw.

Malko, Nikolai (Andreievich) (b Brailov, 4 May 1883; d Roseville, Sydney, 23 Jun 1961), Russian conductor. He studied at St Petersburg with Rimsky-Korsakov, Glazunov and N. Tcherepnin, and at Karlsruhe with Mottl. After teaching in Moscow and Leningrad he became cond. of the Leningrad PO in 1926 and gave the fps of Shostako-

vich's 1st & 2nd symphs. but left Russia in 1928 for Denmark and USA. He was cond. of the Yorkshire SO from 1954 to 1956 and was app. cond. of the Sydney SO in 1957.

Mallarmé, Stéphane (1842–98), French poet. See **Boulez** (*Pli selon pli*), **Debussy** (3 poems), **Herodiade** (Hindemith), **Improvisations sur S.M.** (Boulez), **Prélude à l'Après-midi d'un faune** (Debussy), **Ravel** (3 poems).

Mallinger (*née* **Lichtenegger**), **Mathilde** (b Zagreb, 17 Feb 1847; d Berlin, 19 Apr 1920), German-Croatian soprano. Studied 1st with her father, then at the Prague Cons. and in Vienna; made her 1st stage appearance at Munich in 1866 as Norma and created the part of Eva in Wagner's *Meistersinger* in 1868. Berlin 1869–82, debut as Elsa. Other roles incl. Leonore, Agathe, Pamina, Donna Anna and Sieglinde. Lotte Lehmann was among her pupils.

Malten (actually **Müller**), **Therese** (b Insterburg, 21 Jun 1855; d Neu-Zschieren nr. Dresden, 2 Jan 1930), German soprano. Studied with Gustav Engel in Berlin and made her debut at Dresden in 1873, as Pamina, remaining attached to the Court Opera there. She sang Kundry at Bayreuth in 1882. Other roles incl. Leonore (London, 1882), Isolde, Brünnhilde, Eva and Armide. Sang in *Ring* cycles presented by Angelo Neumann in Russia in 1889.

Malvezzi, Cristoforo (b Lucca, 28 Jun 1547; d Florence, 22 Jan 1599), Italian composer. Wrote music for the Florentine stage performances of 1589 and 1591.

Mälzel, Johann Nepomuk (b Regensburg, 15 Aug 1772; d at sea, 21 Jul 1838), German inventor. Settled in Vienna in 1792 and invented var. mechanical instruments, incl., in 1815, the Metronome. Later he lived in Paris and from 1826 in USA. Beethoven's *Battle of Victoria* was orig. written for Mälzel's 'Panharmonicon' and the 2nd movt. of the 8th symph. imitates the ticking of the metronome.

Mamelles de Tirésias, Les (*The Breasts of Tiresias*), *opéra bouffe* in 2 acts by Poulenc. (lib. by G. Apollinaire), prod. Paris, Opéra-Comique, 3 Jun 1947.

Manara, Francesco, Italian 16th-cent. composer. In 1555 he was in the service of Alfonso II of Ferrata. Wrote madrigals and some church music.

Manchicourt, Pierre de (b Béthune, c 1510; d Madrid, 5 Oct 1564), Flemish composer. He worked at Tournai, 1539–45, Arras, c 1555 and Antwerp from 1557. In 1561 he took charge of the Flemish choir of Philip II in Madrid.

Works incl. Masses, motets; *chansons*.

Mancinelli, Luigi (b Orvieto, 5 Feb 1848; d Rome, 2 Feb 1921), Italian conductor and composer. Studied at Florence, incl. the cello, and joined the orch. at the Teatro della Pergola there. In 1874 he went to the Teatro Apollo in Rome, where he deputized for a cond. so successfully that he made operatic cond. his future career. In 1876 he appeared as comp. of incid. music and in 1884 prod. his 1st opera. From 1881 to 1886 he was dir. of the Liceo Musicale at Bologna, as well as *maestro di cappella* at San Petronio and cond. of the Teatro Comunale there, and he organized orchestral and chamber music. Later he appeared as a cond. in London, Madrid and NY. From 1906 to 1912 he was prin. cond. at the Teatro Colón in Buénos Aires.

Works incl. operas *Isora di Provenza* (1884), *Ero e Leandro* (1896), *Paolo e Francesca* (after Dante, 1907), *Tizianello, Sogno di una notte d'estate* (after Shakespeare, 1915–17); incid. music to Pietro Cossa's *Messalina* and *Cleopatra*; oratorio *Isaias* (1887), cantata *St Agnes* (1905); 2 Masses.

Mancini, Francesco (b Naples, 16 Jan 1672; d Naples, 22 Sep 1737), Italian composer. Pupil of Provenzale and Ursino at the Cons. della Pietà dei Turchini in Naples, entered the service of the court and rose to become *maestro di cappella* (1707) and from 1725 till his death. Dir. of the Cons. S. Maria di Loreto from 1720.

Works incl. operas *L'Idaspe fedele* (orig. title *Gli Amanti generosi*, 1705), *Trajano* (1723) and 19 others; 6 oratorios; cantatas; vln. sonatas; keyboard music.

Mancinus (real name Mencken), **Thomas,** (b Schwerin, 1550; d Schwerin, *c* 1612), German composer. Cantor at the cathedral school of Schwerin, 1572–6, tenor at court in Berlin, 1579–81, and then in the service of the Duke of Brunswick at Wolfenbüttel.

Works incl. Passions according to St Matthew and St John, Lat. and Ger. motets and madrigals, secular Ger. songs for several voices.

Mandolin(e), a string instument related to the lute, but with a more rounded back and metal strings, which are played with a plectrum. The fingerboard is fretted to facilitate fingering and intonation.

Mandore, a small string instrument of the lute family.

Mandragola, La (*The Mandrake*), opera by Castelnuovo-Tedesco (lib. based on

Machiavelli's comedy), prod. Venice, Teatro La Fenice, 4 May 1926.

Mandyczewski, Eusebius (b Czernowitz [Cernauti], 18 Aug 1857; d Vienna, 13 Jul 1929), Rumanian born musicologist. Studied at the Vienna Cons. In 1887 he became keeper of the archives of the Vienna Phil. Society and in 1897 prof. at the Cons. Co-ed. of the complete Schubert and Brahms eds. and of that of Haydn's works (later abandoned).

Manelli, Francesco (b Tivoli, *c* 1595; d Parma, Jul 1667), Italian bass and composer. Singer at Tivoli Cathedral, 1605–24, and *maestro di cappella* there, 1627–9. He then went to Rome, married a singer, and about 1636 settled at Venice, where his wife ed. his collected non-operatic works. From about 1645 he was in the service of the Duke of Parma, Ranuccio II. The S. Cassiano theatre (the 1st public theatre in Venice) opened with his 1st opera.

Works incl. operas *L'Andromeda* (1637), *La maga fulminata* (1638), *L'Alcate* (1642), *La Licaste* (1664) and others; cantatas, *canzonets, chaconnes.*

Manfred, incid. music for Byron's drama by Schumann, op. 115, comp. 1849; 1st concert perf. of the overture, Leipzig, Gewandhaus, Mar 1852. The whole prod. with Byron's play, Weimar, 13 Jun 1852.

Symph. by Tchaikovsky, op. 58, based on the same play 1885, fp Moscow 6 Apr 1886.

Manfredini, Francesco Onofrio (b Pistoia, bap. 22 Jun 1684; d Pistoia, 6 Oct 1762), Italian composer. He studied with Torelli and Perti in Bologna and held appts. in Ferrara and Monaco before returning to Pistoia by 1727, as *maestro di cappella* at St Philip's Cathedral. His 43 pub. instrumental works incl. a set of 12 'Concertini', chamber sonatas (1704), 12 *Sinfonie da chiesa* (1709) and 6 sonatas pub. in London 1764. 4 oratorios date from his return to Pistoia.

Manfredini, Vincenzo (b Pistoia, 22 Oct 1737; d St Petersburg, 16 Aug 1799), Italian theorist and composer, son of prec. After study with his father he went to Moscow in 1758. He became *maestro* at the court of St Petersburg's Italian opera co. in 1762; until he was superceded by Galuppi wrote operas for Catherine II. After his return to It. in 1769 he became a teacher and writer on music, notably *Regole armoniche, o sieno Precetti ragionati* (1775). His comps. incl. settings of Metastasio's *Sermiramide* (1760), *Olimpiade* (1762) and *Artaserse* (1772); 6 symphs. and 6 string 4tets.

Mangold, German family of musicians:
1. (Johann) August Daniel M. (b Darmstadt, 25 Jul 1775; d Darmstadt, 1842), cellist 1st at the Frankfurt theatre and from 1814 in the Grand-Ducal orch. at Darmstadt.
2. (Johann) Wilhelm M. (b Darmstadt, 19 Nov 1796; d Darmstadt, 23 May 1875), violinist and composer, nephew of prec. Studied with Vogler and under Méhul and Cherubini at the Paris Cons. In court service at Darmstadt from 1819. Comp. operas, overtures, chamber music.
3. Karl Ludwig Amand M. (b Darmstadt, 8 Oct 1813; d Oberstdorf, Allgäu, 4 Aug 1889), conductor and composer, brother of prec. Studied with his father and brother, and later at the Paris Cons. Court music director at Darmstadt from 1848.
Works incl. opera *Tanhauser* (1846) and others; cantatas; orchestral pieces: male voice choruses.

Mann, William (Somervell) (b Madras, 14 Feb 1924), English critic and writer on music, educ. at Winchester and Cambridge. As a member of a large musical family he had much opportunity to play chamber music in his youth; later he studied comp. with Seiber and pf. with Ilona Kabós, and in 1948 joined the music staff of *The Times*; retired as chief music critic 1980. He pub. a short introduction to Bach (1950), contrib. to the Britten symposium (1952) and to the 5th and 6th eds. of Grove's *Dictionary* (1954, 1980). He has also written books on R. Strauss's and Mozart's operas and a trans. of Wagner's *Ring*.

Männergesangverein (Ger. lit. 'men's singing-association'), a male-voice choral society.

Manners, Charles (actually Southcote Mansergh) (b London, 27 Dec 1857; d Dundrum, Co. Dublin, 3 May 1935), Irish singer and impresario. Studied in Dublin and the RAM in London; later in It. After joining an opera chorus he made his 1st solo stage appearance in 1882, creating Private Willis in *Iolanthe*. Having married Fanny Moody in 1890 he estab. the Moody-Manners Opera Co. in 1897 and encouraged the perf. of British operas.

Mannheim School, a group of composers associated with the Electoral court at Mannheim in the mid-18th cent. Under the leadership of Johann Stamitz (1717–57) the court orch. became the most famous of the time, estab. a completely modern style of playing, and placing part. emphasis on dynamic contrasts, *crescendo* and *diminuendo*, etc.

The Mannheim comps, e.g. (in addition to Stamitz) F.X. Richter, Holzbauer, Beck and Cannabich, made notable contributions to the early development of the symph.

Manning, Jane (b Norwich, 20 Sep 1938), English soprano. She studied at the RAM and in Switzerland. Many perfs. of works by Cage, Schoenberg and Dallapiccola; fps of music by Davies, Birtwistle and Wood. She is married to the composer Anthony Payne (*q.v.*)

Manns, August (Friedrich) (b Stolzenberg nr. Stettin, 12 Mar 1825; d London, 1 Mar 1907), German-born conductor. At first cellist and violinist in var. bands and orchs. in Ger.; later bandmaster. Went to London as sub-cond. at Crystal Palace, 1854, becoming full cond. in 1855, when he enlarged the orch. Began popular Saturday concerts in 1856, giving early London perfs. of music by Schubert, Schumann, Wagner and Berlioz, and cond. the Handel Festival, 1883–1900. Knighted 1903.

Manon, opera by Massenet (lib. by H. Meilhac and P. Gille, based on Prévost's novel *Manon Lescaut*), prod. Paris, Opéra-Comique, 19 Jan 1884.

Manon Lescaut, ballet by Halévy (scenario by Scribe, based on Prévost's novel, choreography by Jean-Pierre Aumer), prod. Paris, Opéra, 3 May 1830.
Opera by Auber (lib. by Scribe, based on Prévost's novel), prod. Paris, Opéra-Comique, 23 Feb 1856.
Opera by Puccini (lib., in It., by M. Praga, D. Oliva and L. Illica, based on Prévost's novel), prod. Turin, Teatro Regio, 1 Feb 1893.

Manowarda, Josef von (b Kraków, 3 Jul 1890; d Berlin, 24 Dec 1942), Austrian bass of Polish birth. Vienna Staatsoper 1919–42; Salzburg from 1922, as Alfonso and Barak. Bayreuth 1931–42 as Gurnemanz, Marke, Hagen, Pogner and Daland. Berlin Staatsoper 1934–42; roles there incl. Osmin and Philip II.

Manru, opera by Paderewski (lib. by A. Nossig after J.I. Kraszewski's novel *The Cabin behind the Wood,* 1843; comp. 1892–1901, prod. Dresden, 29 May 1901.

Mantelli, Eugenia (b *c* 1860; d Lisbon, 3 Mar 1926), Italian mezzo. Debut Lisbon, 1883, as Urbain. She toured with Julián Gayarre and appeared with Tamagno in Moscow. CG 1896, as Brünnhilde. At the NY Met she was heard 1894–1903 as Dalila, Amneris and Ortrud. Retired 1910 and taught in Lisbon.

Mantra, work by Stockhausen for 2 amplified pfs; comp. 1969–70, fp Donaueschingen, 18 Oct 1970. Pianists also play woodblock and bells, while they contemplate Indian word 'Mantra', or mystical repetition.

Manual (from Lat. *manus* = hand), a keyboard played by the hand, esp. the keyboards of the organ as distinct from the pedals.

Manuel Venegas, unfinished opera by H. Wolf (lib. by M. Hoernes, based on Alarcón's *El niño de la bola*), begun 1897. Fragments perf. Munich, 1 Mar 1903.

Manzoni Requiem, the name sometimes given to Verdi's Requiem, comp. in 1873 for the anniversary of the death of Alessandro Manzoni, on which it was 1st perf. at Milan, church of San Marco, 22 May 1874; repeated at La Scala on 25 May. The 'Libera me' is adapted from that contrib. by Verdi to the collective Requiem he suggested should be written by var. It. comps. on the death of Rossini in 1868, a plan which did not materialize. That the 'Libera me' was not merely taken over as it stood is proved by the fact that it contains allusions to material occurring earlier in the Manzoni Requiem. The 'Lachrymosa' is derived from the prison scene in the 1st vers. of *Don Carlos* (1867).

Manzuoli, Giovanni (b Florence, *c* 1720; d Florence, *c* 1780), Italian castrato soprano. Made his It. debut in Florence (1731). Later visited Madrid, London and Vienna. In 1763 he sang in the fp of Gluck's *Trionfo di Clelia* (Bologna) and in 1765 was in London, to create the title role in J.C. Bach's *Adriano in Siria*. He retired in 1771, after creating Ascanio in Mozart's serenata *Ascanio in Alba*.

Maometto Secondo (*Mahomet II*), opera by Rossini (lib. by C. della Valle, Duke of Ventignano), prod. Naples, Teatro San Carlo, 3 Dec 1820. A Fr. version entitled *Le Siège de Corinthe*, prod. Paris, 9 Oct 1826.

Mara (née Schmeling), Gertrud Elisabeth (b Kassel, 23 Feb 1749; d Reval, 20 Jan 1833), German soprano. Taken on tour by her father, a poor musician, as a child prodigy violinist. Her talent as a singer was discovered in 1759 in London, where she had lessons from Paradisi. Sang under Hiller in Leipzig, and made her operatic debut in Dresden in 1767. She married the cellist Mara in 1771 and entered the service of Frederick the Great in Berlin, but left in 1780 and appeared with great success in Vienna and Paris; London 1784–1802, as Handel's Cleopatra and Nasolini's Andromaca.

Maraca, a perc. instrument used mainly in jazz and swing bands, a rattle made of the dried gourd containing beads, dried seeds or shot.

Marais, Marin (b Paris, 31 May 1656; d Paris, 15 Aug 1728), French bass violist and composer. Pupil of Chaperon at the Sainte-Chapelle and of viol masters; later member of the royal band and the orch. at the Opéra, where he studied comp. under Lully. In 1725 he retired to devote himself to gardening, but continued to teach. He added a 7th string to the bass viol.

Works incl. operas *Idylle dramatique, Alcide* (1693) and *Pantomime des pages* (both with Lully's son Louis), *Ariane et Bacchus* (1696), *Alcyone* (1706), *Séméle* (1709); Te Deum; concertos for vln. and bass; trios for fl., vln. and bass; pieces for 1 and 2 viols; *La Gamme* pieces for vln., viol and harpsichord.

Marais, Roland (b *c* 1680; d *c* 1750), French vla. da gamba player and composer, son of prec. Succeeded his father as solo gamba in the royal band, pub. a *Nouvelle méthode de musique* (1711) and 2 books of pieces for viol.

Mařák, Otakar (b Ostrihom, Hungary, 5 Jan 1872; d Prague, 2 Jul 1939), Czech tenor. Debut Brno 1899, Faust. He sang in Prague from 1900 and was engaged by Mahler for the Vienna Hofoper in 1903. At Berlin in 1911 he created Gennaro in Wolf-Ferrari's *I Gioielli della Madonna*; sang in London from 1908 as Canio, Don José and Turiddu, and in 1913 was the 1st local Bacchus, under Beecham. At Chicago he was heard as Parsifal (1914) and sang in Prague until 1934. Highly regarded as a lyric tenor.

Maratona, ballet by Henze (scenario by Luchino Visconti); comp. 1956, prod. Berlin, 24 Sep 1957.

Marazzoli (or Marazzuoli), Marco (b Parma, *c* 1605; d Rome, 26 Jan 1662), Italian singer, harpist and composer. Sang in the Papal Chapel in Rome in the 1630s and was in the service of Christina of Swed. there.

Works incl. operas *Chi soffre speri* (with V. Mazzocchi, 1637), *Dal male il bene* (with Abbatini, 1653), *La vita umana* (1656) and others; oratorios, cantatas; songs.

Marbeck (or Merbecke), John (b ? Windsor, *c* 1505; d Windsor, *c* 1585), English singer, organist and composer. He was layclerk and organist at St George's Chapel, Windsor, from 1541. In 1543 he was arrested and in 1544 tried and condemned for heresy, as a Calvinist, but he was pardoned and allowed to retain his office.

Works incl. Mass and 2 motets (prob.

early); carol *A Virgine and Mother*; *The Booke of Common Praier noted*, 1550 (i.e. set to notes), being the 1st musical setting of Anglican prayer book (1st version authorized by Edward VI).

Marcabru, the earliest troubadour of importance (early 12th cent.). The most famous of his 4 surviving songs with tunes is the semi-religious 'Pax in nomine Domini'.

Marcato (It. = marked, accentuated), a direction indicating that a piece or movement is to be played in a decided, energetic manner, to that a part is to be brought out strongly above the accomp. or surrounding parts in a passage.

Marcel, Lucille (b New York, 1877; d Vienna, 22 Jun 1921), American soprano. She studied in Paris with Jean de Reszke; sang Elektra at Vienna in 1909. She married the dir. of the Hofoper, Felix Weingartner, in 1911 and with him appeared at Boston in 1913 as Bizet's Djamileh. Also sang in Paris, Hamburg and Darmstadt as Tosca, Aida, Desdemona and Eva.

Marcello, Benedetto (b Venice, 2 Aug 1686; d Brescia, 25 Jul 1739), Italian violinist, composer and author. A pupil of Gasparini and Lotti, he combined his musical interests with a career in law and the civil service. As well as comp. he wrote the lib. for Ruggeri's opera *Arato in Sparta*, and in 1720 pub. the important satire on contemporary opera *Il teatro alla moda*.

Works incl. operas and serenatas *La fede riconosciuta*, *Arianna*, etc.; oratorios *Il pianto e il riso delle quattro stagioni* (1731), *Giuditta*, *Gioaz* (1726), *Il trionfo della poesia e della musica*(1733); Masses, Misereres and other church music; *Estro poetico-armonico*, settings of 50 psalm-paraphrases by G.A. Giustiniani; concertos, sonatas, for var. instruments. His brother **Alessandro** (b Venice, 24 Aug 1669; d Padua, 19 Jun 1747), wrote cantatas and concertos.

March, a piece of music in strongly emphasized regular metre, usually in 4–4 or 2–4 time, but sometimes in 6–8, primarily intended for use at military parades to keep marching soldiers in step, but also the music most often used for processions of var. kinds, incl. those occurring on the stage in operas and other theatre pieces. Funeral marches also have primarily a processional purpose, and they are considerably slower in pace. Marches of all kinds, however, may occur in sonatas, symphs. or suites and are often labelled *alla marcia* or *alla marcia funebre*.

Marchal, André (b Paris, 6 Feb 1894; d St Jean-de-Luz, 27 Aug 1980), French organist, blind from birth. Studied at the Paris Cons. and from 1915 to 1945 was organist in Paris at St Germain-des Prés and from 1945 at St Eustache. He was esp. well known for his improvisations at the organ.

Marchand de Venise, Le (*The Merchant of Venice*), opera by Hahn (lib. by M. Zamaçoïs, after Shakespeare), prod. Paris, Opéra, 25 Mar 1935.

Marchand, Louis (b Lyons, 2 Feb 1669; d Paris, 17 Feb 1732), French harpsichordist, organist and composer. A child prodigy, he was organist of Nevers Cathedral at the age of 14 and later of Auxerre Cathedral, before settling in Paris, *c* 1689. Organist of various churches there and of the Royal Chapel, 1708–14, he then toured Ger. visiting Dresden in 1717 and there declining to compete with Bach at the organ. On his return to Paris he lived mainly by teaching.

Works incl. organ music, 2 books of harpsichord pieces.

Marchesi (de Castrone), Italian family of singers:

1. Salvatore M. (b Palermo, 15 Jan 1822; d Paris, 20 Feb 1908), baritone and teacher. He came of a noble family, succeeding later to the title of Marchese della Raiata. Studying law and philosophy at Palermo, he took singing and comp. lessons from Raimondi and later studied at Milan under Lamperti and others. Having fled to Amer. as a political refugee from the 1848 revolutions, he made his 1st stage appearance in NY as Carlo in *Ernani*. On his return to Europe he settled in London for a time and appeared there as Leporello and Méphistophélès. He married Mathilde Graumann in 1852. Wrote books on singing, vocal exercises, a number of songs and made It. translations of var. opera libretti, incl. several by Wagner.

2. Mathilde M. (*née* Graumann) (b Frankfurt, 24 Mar 1821; d London, 17 Nov 1913), mezzo and teacher, wife of prec. Began to study singing when her father, a wealthy merchant, lost his fortune in 1843. In 1845 she went to Paris to continue her studies with García, whose pupils she took over when he was incapacitated by an accident. Settled in London in 1849, she sang much at concerts. Soon after her marriage to Marchesi she became prof. of singing at the Vienna Cons., 1854–61; later taught mainly in Paris. Her only stage role was Rosina.

3. Blanche M. (b Paris, 4 Apr 1863; d London, 15 Dec 1940), soprano and

teacher, daughter of prec. Studying the vln. at first, she took to singing in 1881, appeared in Berlin and Brussels in 1895, in London in 1896, and settled there as teacher and concert singer. She sang Brünnhilde in Prague in 1900; CG 1902 as Elisabeth, Elsa and Isolde.

Marchesi, Luigi (Lodovico) (b Milan, 8 Aug 1754; d Inzago, 14 Jul 1829). Italian castrato soprano. Pupil of Fioroni in the choir of Milan Cathedral, made his operatic debut in Rome in 1773 in Anfossi's *L'incognita perseguitata*. Later travelled widely, visiting London, 1788–1790 Also sang in operas by Bianchi, Sarti and Mayr.

Marchettus (b Padua), Italian 13th-14th cent. theorist. Lived at Cesena and Verona at some time and was in the service of Rainier, Prince of Monaco. He wrote a treatise on the division of the scale and 2 more on notation, which aroused much opposition.

Marcia (It.) = march.

Marching Song, opera by Benjamin Frankel (lib. by H. Keller, after John Whiting's play); comp. 1972–3 and left in short score at Frankel's death. Fp, in ed. by Buxton Orr, BBC 3 Oct 1983.

Marcolini, Marietta (b Florence, *c* 1780), Italian mezzo. She sang in Venice from 1800 and later appeared in Naples, Rome and Milan. She attracted the attention of Rossini and created leading roles in *Ciro in Babilonia*, *La Pietra del Paragone* and *L'italiana in Algeri*. Retired 1820.

Maréchal, Adolphe (b Liège, 26 Sep 1867; d Brussels, 1 Feb 1935), Belgian tenor. Debut Dijon, 1891. At the Paris Opéra-Comique he created Julien in *Louise* (1900) and Alain in Massenet's *Grisélidis*; Jean in *Le jongleur de Notre Dame*, Monte Carlo (1902). At CG in 1902 he was heard as Faust, Don José and Des Grieux. Guest in Brussels, Nice and Moscow.

Marenzio, Luca (b Coccaglio nr. Brescia, *c* 1553; d Rome, 22 Aug 1599), Italian singer and composer. Studied with Giovanni Contini, organist at Brescia Cathedral, pub. his 1st work in 1581, went to Rome soon afterwards where he became *maestro di cappella* to Cardinal d'Este, leaving in 1586. In 1588 he entered the service of Ferdinando de' Medici and in 1589 contributed 2 *intermedi* for wedding festivities in Florence. He was in Warsaw 1596–8, at the court of Sigismondo III of Poland. His madrigals were introduced into England through Yonge's *Musica transalpina* in 1588 and he was in correspondence with Dowland in 1595.

Works incl. Mass, motets, *Sacri concenti*;

500 madrigals (9 vols.), *Villanelle ed arie alla napolitana* (5 vols.)

Margherita d'Anjou, opera by Meyerbeer (lib. in It., by F. Romani, based on a play by R.C.G. de Pixérécourt), prod. Milan, La Scala, 14 Nov 1820.

Margot-la-Rouge, opera in 1 act by Delius (lib. by B. Gaston-Danville); comp. 1901–2, vocal score by Ravel 1902. Unperf. in Delius's lifetime but part of score was used in the *Idyll* of 1930. Given in orch. by Eric Fenby, BBC 21 Feb 1982; the Delius orch. was then discovered and given at stage fp, St Louis 17 Jun 1983.

Maria Antonia Walpurga (or Walpurgis) (b Munich, 18 Jul 1724; d Dresden, 23 Apr 1780), German composer. Daughter of the Elector of Bavaria, afterwards Emperor Charles VII. Pupil of Giovanni Ferrandini, Porpora and Hasse; married Frederick Christian, electoral prince of Saxony. She was a member of the Arcadian Acad. in Rome under the name of Ermelinda Talèa Pastorella Arcada (pseud. E.T.P.A.).

Works incl. operas *Il trionfo della fedeltà* (with add. music by Hasse, 1754) and *Talestri, regina della Amazoni* (1760).

Maria di Rohan, opera by Donizetti (lib. by S. Cammarano), prod. Vienna, Kärntnertortheater, 5 Jun 1843.

Maria di Rudenz, opera by Donizetti (lib. by S. Cammarano), prod. Venice, Teatro La Fenice, 30 Jan 1838.

Maria Theresa Symphony, name given to Haydn's symph. no. 48 in C maj., supposedly comp. for a visit of the Empress Maria Theresa to Eszterháza in 1773.

Maria Tudor, opera by Gomes (lib. by M. Praga, based on Victor Hugo's tragedy), prod. Milan, La Scala, 27 Mar 1879.

Mariages samnites, Les, opera by Grétry (lib. by B.F. de Rozoy, based on a story by Marmontel), prod. Paris, Comédie-Italienne, 12 Jun 1776.

Mariani, Angelo (b Ravenna, 11 Oct 1821; d Genoa, 13 Jun 1873), Italian conductor and composer. Studied at home at Rimini and under Rossini at the Liceo Filarmonico of Bologna; debut as violinist-cond. at Messina in 1844 and was cond. of the court theatre at Copenhagen, 1847–8. After fighting in the revolutionary army in 1848, he went to the sultan's court at Constantinople, 1849–52, and then became cond. at the Teatro Carlo Felice at Genoa. He appeared in many places in It. and abroad as guest cond. and gave the 1st Italian perfs. of Wagner's *Lohengrin* and *Tannhäuser* at Bologna in 1871 and 1872. Also cond. operas by

Verdi and Meyerbeer.

Works incl. Requiem; hymn for the Sultan of Turkey, cantatas *La fidanzata del guerriero* and *Gli esuli*; orchestral music; songs.

Mariani, Luciano (b Cremona, 1801; d Piacenza, 10 Jun 1859), Italian bass. He created Rodolfo in *Sonnambula* (1831) and Alfonso in *Lucrezia Borgia* (1833). With his sister **Rosa** (b Cremona, 1799) as Arsace he sang Oroe in the fp of *Semiramide* (1823).

Mariazell Mass, the familiar name of Haydn's C maj. Mass orig. entitled *Missa Cellensis.* Comp. in 1782 for Anton Liebe von Kreutzner, who on his ennoblement wished to make a votive offering at the Marian shrine at Mariazell.

Marie, opera by Hérold (lib. by F.A.E. de Planard), prod. Paris, Opéra-Comique, 12 Aug 1826.

Marienleben, Das (*The Life of Mary*), cycle of 15 songs for sop. and pf. by Hindemith (texts by R.M. Rilke); comp. 1922–3, fp Frankfurt, 15 Oct 1923. Revised 1936–48 and perf. Hanover, 3 Nov 1948. Six of the songs were arr. for sop. and orch., 1938–48.

Mariés de la Tour Eiffel, Les (*The Wedded Pair of the Eiffel Tower*), ballet by 5 of 'Les Six': Auric, Honegger, Milhaud, Poulenc and Tailleferre (scenario by Jean Cocteau), prod. Paris, Théâtre des Champs-Élysées, 18 Jun 1921.

Mariette, Auguste Edouard (Mariette Bey) (1821–81), French Egyptologist. Founder of the museum at Cairo. He outlined the lib. for Verdi's *Aida*, drafted in Fr. by C. du Locle and written in It. by Ghislanzoni.

Marimba, a Mexican perc. instrument of African origin, made of wood, similar to the Xylophone, but larger and with resonance-boxes to each note.

Marimba Gongs, a perc. instrument similar to the Marimba, but with metal plates instead of wooden strips to prod. the notes.

Marin, José (b ? Madrid, 1619; d Madrid, Mar 1699), Spanish tenor and composer. He sang in the Encarnación convent at Madrid in his younger years, became a highwayman and a priest, fled to Rome after committing murder, was imprisoned, but at the end of his life had a great reputation as a musician.

Works incl. songs with continuo, songs with guitar accomp.

Marin, (Marie-Martin) Marcel de, Viscount (b Saint-Jean-de-Luz, 8 Sep 1769; d Toulouse, after 1861), French harpist, violinist and composer (?) of Italian descent. In 1783 he became a member of the Arcadian Acad. in Rome and during the French Revolution settled in London; later in Toulouse.

Works incl. chamber music, harp sonatas and pieces, vln. sonatas.

Marini, Biagio (b Brescia, *c* 1587; d Venice, 1663), Italian composer and violinist. He was employed successively as violinist at Venice, as music dir. at the church of Sant' Eufemia at Brescia, at the courts of Parma and Munich, at Düsseldorf, Ferrara and Milan.

Works incl. psalms, vespers and other church music; symphs.; sonatas, dances, etc., for string inst.; vocal and inst. chamber music, madrigals, *canzonets*, etc., for several voices; sacred songs for several voices.

Marini, Ignazio (Bergamo, 28 Nov 1811; d Milan, 29 Apr 1873), Italian bass. He sang at La Scala from 1832 and in London and NY 1850–2; appeared in the fps of *Attila* and *Oberto* and was heard at St Petersburg 1856–63. Other roles incl. Silva, Mosè and Oroveso.

Marino Faliero, opera by Donizetti (lib. by E. Bidera, based on Byron's drama), prod. Paris, Théâtre Italien, 12 Mar 1835.

Marinuzzi, Gino (b Palermo, 24 Mar 1882; d Milan, 17 Aug 1945), Italian composer and conductor. Studied at the Palermo Cons. 1st appeared as cond. at Catania, later worked at Palermo, Madrid, Trieste, Buenos Aires and Chicago. On his return to It. he cond. opera in all the large cities and he was dir. of the Liceo Musicale at Bologna, 1915–19. He gave the fp of Puccini's *Rondine* (Monte Carlo, 1917), and 1st European perf. of *Il Trittico* (Rome 1919).

Works incl. operas *Barberina* (1918), *Jacquerie Palla de' Mozzi* (1932); suites *Siciliana* and *Romana*, symph. poem *Sicania*, *Elegia*, *Rito nuziale* for orch.; *Andantino all' antica* for fl., strings and harp.

Mario (Giovanni Matteo), Cavaliere di Candia (b Cagliari, 17 Oct 1810; d Rome, 11 Dec 1883), Italian tenor. 1st appearance, Paris, 1838 as Robert le Diable; 1st visit to London the following year as Gennaro in *Lucrezia Borgia*. He was Ernesto in the fp of *Don Pasquale* (Paris, 1843). Other roles incl. Duke of Mantua, Roméo, and Rossini's Otello, Lindoro and Ramiro. Companion to Giulia Grisi.

Mariotte, Antoine (b Avignon, 22 Dec 1875; d Izieux, Loire, 30 Nov 1944), French composer. A naval officer at first, he left the Navy in 1897 and became a student at the Schola Cantorum in Paris as a pupil of d'Indy. He cond. at Saint-Étienne and then at Lyons, and became dir. of the Orléans Cons. in 1920. In 1935–9 he was dir. of the Opéra-Comique in Paris. He was accused of having plagiarized R. Strauss in his *Salomé*, but the work was written before Strauss's was prod.

Works incl. operas *Salomé* (Oscar Wilde, 1908), *Le Vieux Roi* (1911), *Esther: Princesse d'Israël (1925), Léontine Sœurs, Nele Dooryn, Gargantua* (after Rabelais); *Avril, Pâques françaises* and *Toujours* for unaccomp. chorus; *Impressions urbaines* and *Kakemonos* for pf. and orch.; *En montagne* for 3 wind or string instruments with string 5tet or pf.; pf. music and songs.

Maritana, opera by V. Wallace (lib. by E. Fitzball, based on the play *Don César de Bazan* by A.P. d'Ennery and P.F. Dumanoir), prod. London, Drury Lane Theatre, 15 Nov 1845.

Markevich, Igor (b Kiev, 27 Jul 1912; d Antibes, 7 Mar 1983), Russian-born conductor and composer. His parents emigrated and lived in Switzerland, but he went to Paris at the age of 15 as a pupil of Nadia Boulanger. Became an Italian citizen during war years. He was cond. of the Lamoureux Orch., Paris, 1958–61. Monte Carlo Orch. from 1967.

Works incl. ballets *Rébus* (1931) and *L'Envoi d'Icare* (1932); cantata on Milton's *Paradise Lost* (perf. London, 1935) and others, *Cantique d'Amour, Nouvel Age,* cantata for soprano and male-voice chorus (Jean Cocteau); *Hymnes*, concerto grosso and sinfonietta for orch.; concerto and partita for pf. and orch.; *Galop* for small orch.; psalm for soprano and orch.; serenade for vln., clar. and bassoon.

Marmontel, Jean François (b Bort, Limousin, 11 Jul 1723; d Abloville, Eure, 31 Dec 1799), French author. Librettist for Rameau, Grétry, Piccinni, Cherubini and others; defender of Piccinni against Gluck and author of an *Essai sur les révolutions de la musique en France* (1777).

See also **Acante et Céphise** (Rameau), **Amitié a l'épreuve** (Grétry), **Antigone** (Zingarelli), **Atys** (Piccinni), **Céphale et Procris** (Grétry), **Clari** (Bishop, from *Laurette*), **Démophoon** (Cherubini), **Didon** (Piccinni), **Guirlande** (Rameau), **Mariages samnites** (Grétry), **Rameau** (*Lysis et Délie, Les Sybarites*), **Zémire et Azor** (Grétry), **Zemire und Azor** (Spohr).

Mârouf, savetier du Caire (*M., the Cobbler of Cairo*), opera by Rabaud (lib. by L. Népoty, based on a story in the *Arabian Nights*), prod. Paris, Opéra-Comique, 15 May 1914.

Marpurg, Friedrich Wilhelm (b Sechof nr. Seehausen, Brandenburg, 21 Nov 1718; d Berlin, 22 May 1795), German theorist and writer on music. In Paris as secretary to Gen.

Bodenburg (?) in 1746 he met, among others, Voltaire and Rameau, and was influenced by the latter's theories. From 1749 he lived mainly in Berlin, where he began a music weekly, *Der critische Musicus an der Spree*. This was followed by numerous other critical and theoret. writings, incl. a notable preface to the 2nd ed. of Bach's *Kunst der Fuge*, treatises on fugue, thorough-bass, keyboard playing, etc. He also comp. some songs and keyboard music.

Marquise de Brinvilliers, La, comic opera by Auber, Batton, Berton, Blangini, Boieldieu, Carafa, Cherubini, Hérold and Paer (lib. by Scribe and Castil-Blaze), prod. Paris, Opéra-Comique, 31 Oct, 1831.

Marriage of Figaro (Mozart). *See* **Nozze di Figaro.**

Marriage, The (*Zhenitba*), unfinished opera by Mussorgsky (lib. taken from Gogol's comedy), comp. 1864; never perf. in Mussorgsky's lifetime; prod. with pf. accomp., St Petersburg, 1 Apr 1909; with orch., Petrograd, 26 Oct 1917, with Mussorgsky's *Sorotchintsy Fair.*

Comic opera by Martinů (lib. by comp. after Gogol); comp. 1952, fp NBC TV, NY, 7 Feb 1953.

Marriner, (Sir) Neville (b Lincoln, 15 Apr 1924), English conductor and violinist. He studied at the RCM and the Paris Cons. His early experience was in the perf. of Baroque music; from 1952–68 played the violin in the Philharmonia, then the LSO. Founded Academy of St Martin-in-the-Fields 1958; dir. until 1978. Minnesota Orch. 1979–86. CBE 1979. Knighted 1985.

Marschner, Heinrich (August) (b Zittau, 16 Aug 1795; d Hanover, 14 Dec 1861), German composer. As a boy he played the pf., sang soprano and comp. tentatively without much instruction. In 1813 he was sent to Leipzig to study law, but met Rochlitz, who induced him to take music. In 1816 he went to Vienna and Pressburg with a Hung., Count de Varkony, and settled in the latter place, comp. several operas, until 1823, when he became asst. cond. to Weber and Morlacchi at Dresden. In 1827 he became cond. of the Leipzig theatre and from 1831 to 1859 court cond. at Hanover. He married 4 times.

Works incl. operas *Saidar, Heinrich IV und Aubigné* (1820),*Der Kyffhäuserberg* (1822), *Der Holzdieb* (1825), *Lucretia, Der Vampyr* (1828), *Der Templer und die Jüdin* (after Scott's *Ivanhoe*, 1829), *Des Falkners Braut* (1832), *Hans Heiling* (1833), *Der Bäbu* (1838), *Das Schloss am Aetna, Kaiser*

Adolf von Nassau (1845), *Austin, Sangeskönig Hiarne* (1863); incid. music to Kleist's *Prinz Friedrich von Homburg* and other plays; overture on 'God Save the King' and other orchestral works; male-voice choruses; sonatas; songs.

Marsh, John (b Dorking, 1752; d Chichester, 1828), English amateur composer. Practised as a lawyer until 1783, when a legacy enabled him to retire and devote his time to music, in which he was largely self-taught. Cond. concerts in Chichester and elsewhere, and comp. some notable symphs., also concertos, chamber music, keyboard music.

Marshall, Margaret (b Stirling, 4 Jan 1949), Scottish soprano. She studied in Glasgow and with Hans Hotter; won the Munich International Comp. in 1974. London debut 1975. Florence 1979 as Eurydice; she returned in 1979 for Mozart's Countess and sang the same role at CG in 1980. US debut 1980, with Boston SO; later NY PO. Fiordiligi at La Scala and Salzburg in 1982.

Marson, George (b Worcester, *c* 1573; d Canterbury, 3 Feb 1632), English organist and composer. He became organist and choirmaster at Canterbury Cathedral *c* 1598.

Works incl. services, anthem, psalms and other church music; madrigal contrib. to *The Triumphes of Oriana.*

Marteau sans maître, Le (*The hammer without a master*), work by Boulez for mezzo, flute, guitar, vibraphone, xylorimba, vla. and perc.; comp. 1952–4, rev. 1957, fp Baden-Baden, 18 Jun 1955, cond. Rosbaud.

Martelé (Fr.)   } lit. 'hammered', detached, strongly accentuated playing or singing, used esp. for a stroke of the bow prod. such an effect on string instruments.
Martellato (It.)

Martelli, Henri (b Bastia, Corsica, 25 Feb. 1895; d Paris, 15 Jul 1980), French composer. Studied at the Paris Con., Widor being among his masters.

Works incl. opera *La Chanson de Roland* (1921–3; perf. 1967) incid. music; 3 symphs. (1953–7), symph. poem *Sur la vie de Jeanne d'Arc, Bas-reliefs assyriens* and concerto for orch.; pf. concerto; 2 string 4tets; string 5tet; pf. pieces; songs.

Martenot, Maurice (b Paris, 14 Oct 1898; d Paris, 10 Oct 1980), French scientist and musician. Studied pf. and cello at the Paris Cons. and comp. with Gédalge. After var. appts. as cond. and teacher he opened the École d'Art Martenot at Neuilly. Inventor of the radio-electrical instrument Ondes Musicales, a development of Theremin's, which

he prod. in 1928 and is generally known as the Ondes Martenot. In Fr. a number of comps. Honegger, Milhaud, Koechlin and esp. Messiaen (whose sister-in-law Jeanne Loriod is the instrument's foremost living exponent), have written for it.

Martha, oder Der Markt von Richmond (*M., or The Market at R.*), comic opera by Flotow (lib. by F.W. Riese, pseud. 'W. Friedrich', based on a ballet-pantomime, *Lady Henriette, ou La Servante de Greenwich*, by J.H.V. de Saint-Georges, prod. Paris, 21 Feb 1844, with music by F. Burgmüller and Deldevez), prod. Vienna, Kärntnertortheater, 25 Nov 1847.

Martin. The French name of a type of baritone voice of exceptional range, derived from Jean Blaise Martin (1768–1837); he specialized in comic roles in operas by Dalayrac, Boieldieu and Méhul.

Martin, Frank (b Geneva, 15 Sep 1890; d Naarden, Holland, 21 Nov 1974), Swiss composer and pianist. Studied with Joseph Lauber at Geneva and in 1928 became prof. at the Institut Jaques-Dalcroze there. Wrote in generally conservative idiom.

Works incl. operas *The Tempest* (Shakespeare, 1956), *Monsieur Pourceaugnac* (1963); *Six Monologues from 'Jedermann'* (after Hofmannsthal, 1943), ballet *Die blaue Blume*; incid. music for Sophocles' *Oedipus Coloneus* and *Oedipus Rex* and Shakespeare's *Romeo and Juliet.*

Mass for double chorus, oratorios *In terra pax* (1945), *Golgotha* (1948); *Le Mystère de la Nativité* (1957–9); symph., suite *Rhythmes, Esquisse,* symph. for orch.; *Petite Symphonie concertante* for harp, harpsichord, pf. and strings (1945); pf. concerto, vln. concerto. (1951), cello concerto (1966); *Cornet* (Rilke) for contralto and orch.

Pf. 5tet, rhapsody for string 5tet, string 4tet, string trio, pf. trio on Ir. tunes; *Le Vin herbé* for 12 voices, strings and pf. (on the subject of Tristram and Yseult, from Joseph Bédier, 1938–41); 2 vln. and pf. sontatas.

Martin, Janis (b Sacramento, 16 Aug 1939), American soprano, originally mezzo. Debut San Francisco 1960; sang at the NY Met from 1962 and in Europe from 1965. Her first soprano role was Donna Elvira, in 1970, and at Bayreuth she sang Eva, Sieglinde and Kundry. In London, Milan, Berlin and Vienna she has been admired as Brangaene, Tosca, Marina, Elektra and Octavian.

Martín y Soler, Vicente (b Valencia, 2 May 1754; d St Petersburg, 11 Feb 1806), Spanish composer. Chorister at Valencia, made his debut as an opera comp. in Madrid in 1776, then went to It., where he prob. studied with Padre Martini, and prod. operas successfully in Naples, Turin, Venice, etc. In Vienna, 1785–8, he comp. 3 operas on libs. by da Ponte, the most successful of which, *Una cosa rara* (1786), for a time eclipsed Mozart's *Figaro*; Mozart quotes from it in the supper scene in *Don Giovanni*. Apart from a visit to London, 1794–5, he lived from 1788 in St Petersburg, in the service of the Rus. court.

Works incl. operas *Ifigenia in Aulide* (1779), *Ipermestra, Andromaca* (1780), *Astartea, Partenope, L'amor geloso* (1782), *In amor si vuol destrezza (L'accorta cameriera,* 1782), *Vologeso, Le burle per amore* (1784), *La vedova spiritosa, Il burbero di buon cuore* (1786), *Una cosa rara, o Bellezza ed onestà* (1786), *L'arbore di Diana* (1787), *Gore Bogatyr Kosometovich* (1789), *Melomania* (Rus.), *Fedul and his Children* (Rus. libs. of these 3 by Catherine II), *Il castello d'Atlante* (1791), *La scuola de' maritati* (1795), *L'isola del piacere* (1795), *Le nozze de contadini spagnuoli, La festa del villaggio* (1798); prologue *La Dora festeggiante* for *Vologeso*; several ballets; church music; cantatas *La deità benefica* and *Il sogno; canzonets; canons.*

Martinelli, Giovanni (b Montagnana, 22 Oct 1885; d New York, 2 Feb 1969), Italian tenor. After he played the clar. in an army band his voice was discovered and he studied singing in Milan, making his debut in 1910 as Ernani. He sang at CG 1912–14, 1919 and 1937, as Cavaradossi, Otello and Calaf. The greater part of his career was spent at the NY Met, from 1913 to 1946, as Manrico, Radames, Don Carlos, Faust and Don José. He became one of the most famous tenors of the cent.

Martinez, Marianne (b Vienna, 4 May 1744; d Vienna, 13 Dec 1812), Austrian composer and clavier player of Spanish descent. Daughter of the master of ceremonies to the Pope's nuncio in Vienna; pupil of Metastasio, Porpora and Haydn.

Works incl. oratorios *Isacco* (1782) and *Santa Elena al Calvario,* psalms trans. by Metastasio, Mass, motets, cantatas; symphs.; overtures; concertos; sonatas.

Martini, Giovanni Battista (or **Giambattista,** known as **Padre Martini**) (b Bologna, 24 Apr 1706; d Bologna, 3 Aug 1784), Italian priest, theorist, teacher and composer. Received a thorough educ. from his father and others in vln. harpsichord, singing and comp. Entered the Franciscan Order in 1721

(priest 1729), and was app. *maestro di cappella* of San Francesco in Bologna in 1725, after which he rarely left his home town. As the most famous teacher and theorist of his time he attracted many distinguished pupils, incl. Mozart, and corresponded with musicians throughout Europe. His most important works are the unfinished hist. of music (3 vols., 1757–81) and a treatise on counterpoint (1773–5).

Comps. incl. *c* 1500 works, with *c* 1000 canons; oratorios *L'assunzione di Salomone* (1734), *San Pietro, Il sacrificio d'Abramo; c* 32 Masses, motets, psalm settings and other church music; stage works; keyboard works.

Martini, Jean Paul Egide (real name Johann Paul Aegidius Schwartzendorf) (b Freistadt, Upper Palatinate, 31 Aug 1741; d Paris, 10 Feb 1816), German organist and composer, adopted the name of M. on settling in Nancy as a music teacher in 1760. In the service of the Duke of Lorraine (the former King Stanislaus of Pol.) at Lunéville, 1761–4, he then went to Paris, where he wrote military music and prod. his 1st opera in 1771. After 3 years absence during the Revolution, he returned to Paris in 1794 to become one of the inspectors of the Cons. (1795) and prof. of comp. (1800). At the Restoration in 1814 he was app. superintendent of the court music.

Works incl. operas *L'Amoureux de quinze ans* (1771), *Le Fermier cru sourd* (1772), *Le Rendezvous nocturne* (1773), *Henry IV* (1774), *Le Droit du Seigneur, L'Amant sylphe* (1783), *Sapho, Annette et Lubin* (1789), *Ziméo* and others; 2 Masses, 2 Requiems, Te Deum, psalm settings and other church music, cantata for the marriage of Napoleon and Marie-Louise; chamber music; marches, etc., for military band; songs incl. 'Plaisir d'amour'.

Martino, Donald (b Plainfield, NJ, 16 May 1931), American composer. Studied with Bacon, Babbitt and Sessions in US, with Dallapiccola in Florence. Prof. of comp. New England cons. of Music 1970–80; Harvard from 1983. Works often feature his own inst., the clarinet: 4tet for clar. and strings (1957); concerto for wind 5tet (1964); B,A,B,B,I,T,T for clar. (1966); cello concerto (1972); *Paradiso Choruses,* oratorio after Dante (1974); Triple Concerto for 3 clars. and orch (1977); string 4tet (1983).

Martinon, Jean (b Lyons, 10 Jan 1910; d Paris, 1 Mar 1976), French conductor and composer. Studied vln. at the Lyons Cons. and comp. under Roussel at the Paris Cons. He began to produce works shortly before

World War II, during which he was imprisoned in Ger., where he wrote several works. After the war he appeared with success as cond. in Europe and Amer. (Chicago SO 1963–9); often heard in Roussel, Bartók and Prokofiev.

Works incl. opera *Hécube* (lib. by S. Moreaux after Euripides, 1949–54); Psalm cxxxvi for solo voices, reciter, chorus and orch., *Absolve Domine* for men's chorus and orch.; 4 symphs (1936–65), *Symphoniette*.

Martinů, Bohuslav (b Policka, 8 Dec 1890; d Liestal, Switz., 28 Aug 1959), Czech composer. Studied vln. at the Prague Cons. from 1906 to 1913 while playing in the Prague Phil. Orch. In 1922 he took comp. lessons with Suk at Prague Cons. and from 1923 to 1924 studied with Roussel in Paris, where he lived for a greater part of the time until he fled to USA in 1941. He remained in Amer. until 1946, when he became prof. of comp. at Prague Cons., returning to USA in 1948, where he taught at Princeton and the Berkshire Music Center. From 1957 he lived in Switz. His music is often neo-classical in style, with an emphasis on rhythm and counterpoint.

Works incl. OPERAS: *The Soldier and the Dancer* (after Plautus, 1928), *Les Larmes du couteau* (1928; prod. 1968), *Les Vicissitudes de la vie* (1929; prod. 1971), *Journée de bonté*, *The Miracles of Our Lady* (1935), *The Suburban Theatre* (1936), *Alexandre bis*, *Julietta* (1938); *Mirandolina*, *Ariadne* (1961), *The Greek Passion* (1961); radio operas *The Voice of the Forest* (1935), *Comedy on a Bridge*; television opera *The Marriage* (1953); ballets *Istar* (1924), *Who is the Most Powerful in the World?* (1925), *Revolt* (1928), *On tourne*, *La Revue de cuisine*, *Échec au roi*, *The Butterfly that Stamped* (1926), *Špalíček*, *Le Jugement de Paris*.

CHORAL: Cz. *Rhapsody*, *Bouquet of Flowers*, *Field Mass* for solo voices, chorus and orch.; madrigals for 6 voices, *The Epic of Gilgamesh*, oratorio (1955).

FOR ORCH: 6 symphs. (1942–63); sinfonia for 2 orchs., symph. poem *Vanishing Midnight*, tone-poem *The Frescoes of Piero della Francesca* (1955), pieces *Half-time*, *La Bagarre*, *La Rapsodie*, overture for the Sokol Festival, *Memorial to Lidice* (1943), Inventions for grand orch., concerto grosso, *Tre Ricercari*, *Les Sérénades* and *Les Rondes* for chamber orch., partita for string orch.; 5 pf. concertos (1934–57) and concertino, concerto for 2 pfs.; vln. concerto, 2 cello concertos, harpsichord concerto and var. other works for instruments and orch.

CHAMBER: String 4tet and pf. trio with orch.; 7 string 4tets (1918–47), string 5tet, wind 5tet, pf. 4tet, 2 pf. 5tets (1933, 1944) and other chamber music, 3 vln. and pf. sonatas, 3 cello and pf. sonatas; var. instrumental pieces; *Film en miniature*, *3 Danses tchèques*, *Préludes*, *Esquisses de danse*, *Ritournelles*, *Train-Fantôme*, etc. for pf.; 2 preludes for harpsichord.

Marton, Eva (b Budapest, 18 Jun 1943), Hungarian soprano. She studied at the Liszt Academy, Budapest, and made her debut in 1968 as The Queen of Shemaka, in *Le Coq d'Or*. She has since sung with Frankfurt Opera, 1972–7, and in Hamburg; also heard in Salzburg, San Francisco, New York and at Bayreuth. Chicago 1980, as Giordano's Maddalena. Other roles incl. Tosca, Desdemona, Donna Anna, Eva, Elsa, Elisabeth de Valois and Korngold's Violanta. CG debut 1987, Turandot.

Martucci, Giuseppe (b Capua, 6 Jan 1856; d Naples, 1 Jun 1909), Italian pianist, conductor and composer. Was 1st taught by his father, a bandmaster, and appeared as pianist in his childhood. He then studied at the Naples Cons., 1867–72, and became prof. there in 1874. He travelled widely as pianist, founded the Quartetto Napoletano for the cultivation of chamber music and became an orch. cond. In 1886 he was app. director of the Liceo Musicale at Bologna and there prod. the 1st It. perf. of Wagner's *Tristan* in 1888. In 1902 he returned to Naples as director of the Cons.

Works incl. oratorio *Samuele*; 2 symphs., *4 piccoli pezzi* for orch.; pf. concertos in D min., B♭ min. (1878, 1885); pf. 5tet, 2 pf. trios; cello and pf. sonata; var. instrumental pieces; variations and fantasy for 2 pfs.; songs, *Pagine sparse*, *Due sogni* and others.

Martyrdom of St Magnus, The, chamber opera in 9 scenes by Peter Maxwell Davies (lib. by comp. from 'Magnus' by George Mackay Brown), prod. Kirkwall, Orkney, 18 Jun 1977.

Martyre de Saint Sébastien, Le (*The Martyrdom of St Sebastian*), incid. music by Debussy for the mystery play, written in Fr., by G. d'Annunzio, comp. for solo voices, chorus and orch. in 1911, fp Paris, Théâtre du Châtelet, 22 May 1911, in 5 acts, and Opéra, 17 Jun 1922, in 4 acts.

Martyrs, Les, opera by Donizetti (lib. by Scribe, based on Corneille's *Polyeucte*), prod. Paris, Opéra, 10 Apr 1840.

Martzy, Johanna (b Temesvár, 26 Oct 1924), Hungarian violinist. Studied at Budapest Acad. from 1932 to 1942, winning the Reményi Prize at 16, and 1st prize at the Concours International d'Exécution in Geneva in 1947, in which year she began her true concert career. Brit. debut 1953, US 1957. Well known in Schubert and Bartók.

Marx, Adolph Bernard (b Halle, 28 Nov 1795; d Berlin, 17 May 1866), German musicologist and composer. Studied law, but gave it up for music, to which he devoted himself in Berlin, where in 1824 he founded the *Berliner allgemeine musikalische Zeitung*. In 1830 he became prof. of music and in 1850 founded a music school with Kullak and Stern (later Stern Cons.). He wrote books on the hist. of music, teaching, on Gluck, Handel, Beethoven, comp., tonepainting, etc.

Works incl. opera *Jery und Bätely* (Goethe, 1824); melodrama *Die Rache wartet*; oratorios *Johannes der Täufer, Moses* (1841), *Nahid und Omar*; instrumental works.

Marx, Joseph (b Graz, 11 May 1882; d Graz, 3 Sep 1964), Austrian composer. Studied in Vienna and in 1922 became director of the Acad. of Music there in succession to Ferdinand Löwe. From 1947 he was prof. at Graz Univ.

Works incl. *Autumn Symph.* (1921); *Symph. Night Music, Spring Music* for orch.; romantic concerto for pf. and orch.; several choral pieces; 3 string 4tets, pf. 4tet, fantasy for pf. trio; vln. and pf. sonata, cello and pf. sonata; *c* 120 songs.

Marx, Karl (b Munich, 12 Nov 1897; d Stuttgart, 8 May 1985), German composer. Studied natural science at first, but met Carl Orff during the 1914–18 war and later studied music with him. App. prof. of the Munich Acad. in 1924 and cond. of the Bach Society there in 1928. From 1939 to 1945 he taught at Graz Cons., becoming prof. in 1944, and in 1946 he became prof. at the Hochschule für Musik in Stuttgart. He was much occupied with school music.

Works incl. passacaglia for orch. (1932); concertos for pf., vln., 2 vlns., vla. and fl.; var. choral works, some to words by Rilke; divertimento for wind insts. (1934), string 4tet and other chamber music; songs, some to words by Rilke.

Marziale (It.) = martial, warlike.

Masagniello furioso, oder Die neapolitanische Fischer-Empörung (*M. enraged, or The Neapolitan Fisherman's Revolt*), opera by Keiser (lib. by Barthold Feind), prod. Hamburg, Theater beim Gänsemarkt, Jun 1706.

Masaniello (Auber). *See* **Muette de Portici.**

Masaniello, ou Le Pêcheur napolitain (*M., or The Neapolitan Fisherman*), opera by Carafa (lib. by C. Moreau and A.M. Lafortelle), prod. Paris, Opera-Comique, 27 Dec 1827. Auber's *Muette de Portici* was prod. at the Opéra 2 months later.

Mascagni, Pietro (b Livorno, 7 Dec 1863; d Rome, 2 Aug 1945), Italian composer. His father, a baker, wished him to study law, but he managed to take lessons in secret at the Istituto Cherubini. On being discovered, he was adopted by an uncle, and soon reconciled with his father by having 2 works perf. at the Instituto. Later Count Florestano de Larderel paid for his further musical educ. at the Milan Cons., where Ponchielli was among his masters. But he deserted, not wishing to apply himself to solid study, and joined a travelling opera co. After many wanderings and a marriage that forced him to settle at Cerignola nr. Foggia to make a precarious living by teaching, he won the 1st prize in an operatic competition with *Cavalleria rusticana* in 1889, and after its prod. in Rome, 17 May 1890, he began to accumulate a great fortune, though his many later operas never repeated its success.

Works incl. operas *Cavalleria rusticana* (1890), *L'amico Fritz* (1891), *I Rantzau* (both based on Erckmann-Chatrian), *Guglielmo Ratcliff* (after Heine, 1895), *Silvano, Zanetto* (1896), *Iris, Le maschere, Amica* (1905), *Isabeau* (1911), *Parisina* (d'Annunzio), *Lodoletta* (1917), *Il piccolo Marat* (1921), *Pinotta, Nerone* (1935); operetta *Sì*; incid. music for Hall Caine's *The Eternal City; Kyrie,* Requiem in memory of King Humbert; cantata for Leopardi centenary (1898), setting of It. trans. of Schiller's *Ode to Joy* for chorus and orch., cantata *In Filanda*; symph. in C min., symph. poem for a film *Rapsodia satanica* (1917).

Maschera, Fiorenzo (b ? Brescia, *c* 1540; d Brescia, *c* 1584), Italian composer. Succeeded Merulo as organist at Brescia Cathedral in 1557. Wrote instrumental *canzone*.

Mascherata (It. = masquerade), a type of 16th-cent. *villanella* to be sung at masked balls or during fancy-dress processions.

Maschere, Le, opera by Mascagni (lib. by L. Illica), prod. Genoa, Milan, Rome, Turin, Venice and Verona, 17 Jan 1901.

Mascheroni, Edoardo (b Milan, 4 Sep 1859; d Ghirla, 4 Mar 1941), Italian conductor and composer. He began to study music as an adult under Boucheron at Milan. In 1883 he secured an engagement at the Teatro Goldini at Livorno. Not long after he moved to the Teatro Apollo in Rome, and in 1893 he was chosen by Verdi to cond. the prod. of his *Falstaff* at Milan. Also conducted Puccini, Wagner and Catalani (fp *La Wally*, 1892).

Works incl. operas *Lorenza* (1901) and *La Perugina* (1909); 2 Requiems, for solo voices, chorus and orch. and for voices alone (both on the death of Victor Emmanuel I); chamber music; album of pf. pieces.

Masculine Cadence, a cadence, or full close, the final note or chord of which falls on a strong accented beat of a bar.

Maschinist Hopkins, opera by Max Brand (lib. by comp.), prod. Duisburg, 13 Apr 1929. The opera pre-figures several dramatic themes in Berg's *Lulu* and was widely perf. in Europe before the rise of the Nazis. 1st complete post-war perf. BBC, London, 9 Feb 1986.

Masini, Angelo (b Terra del Sole nr. Forlì 28 Nov, 1844; d Forlì 28 Sep 1926), Italian tenor. His early studies were retarded by poverty. He appeared in opera for the 1st time in 1867, at Modena, as Pollione, and thereafter acquired a wide reputation, particularly in Verdi's operas, as Radames, Don Alvaro and in the Requiem. Also sang in Cairo, Paris and Russia; roles incl. Faust, Lohengrin and Vasco da Gama.

Masini, Galliano (b Livorno, 1896; d Livorno, 15 Feb 1986), Italian tenor. Debut Livorno 1923, Cavaradossi. He sang in Rome 1930–50 (debut as Pinkerton) and at La Scala was heard as Turiddu and Falla's Paco. In Chicago he sang Edgardo, Rodolfo and Enzo, 1937–8; NY Met 1939, as Radames. Guest in Vienna and Buenos Aires; retired 1957.

Mask. *See* **Masque.**

Mask of Orpheus, The, opera by Birtwistle (lib. by P. Zinovieff), comp. 1973–84, prod. London, Coliseum, 21 May 1986.

Mask of Time, The, oratorio by Tippett in 2 parts for soloists, chorus and orch.; comp. 1981–3, fp Boston, 5 Apr 1984, cond. C. Davis.

Maskarade, opera by Nielsen (lib. by V. Andersen after a play by Holberg); comp. 1904–6, fp Copenhagen, 11 Nov 1906.

Masnadieri, I (*The Brigands*), opera by Verdi (lib. by A. Maffei, based on Schiller's drama *Die Räuber*), prod. London, Her Majesty's Theatre, 22 Jul 1847. The only opera commissioned by London from Verdi. Jenny Lind and Lablache appeared in it.

Mason, Colin (b Northampton, 26 Jan 1924; d London, 6 Feb 1971), English critic. Studied at the TCM in London, 1944–5, and in Budapest 1947–9, where he learnt Hung. He was music critic to the *Manchester Guardian* from 1951 to 1959 and later ed. of *Tempo*.

Mason, Daniel Gregory (b Brookline, Mass., 20 Nov 1873; d Greenwich, Conn., 4 Dec 1953), American composer and writer on music, grandson of Lowell Mason and son of a member of the firm of pf. makers Mason & Hamlin. Graduated from Harvard and studied music in NY, later with d'Indy in Fr. He wrote a number of books on music.

Works incl. 3 symphs. (1916, 1930, 1937); prelude and fugue for pf. and orch.; chamber music and songs.

Mason, Lowell (b Medfield, Mass., 8 Jan 1792; d Orange, NJ, 11 Aug 1872), American hymnologist, grandfather of prec. Self-taught in music and a bank clerk at Savannah from 1812. He practised any instrument he could lay hands on and with F.L. Abel adapted Gardiner's *Sacred Melodies*, mainly themes from the classics, to the psalms, with the result that in 1827 he was called to Boston to supervise church music here. A more important service was his intro. of music teaching into schools.

Masque, a stage entertainment cultivated in England in the 17th cent. and laying great stress on spectacular presentation, but also incl. songs and dances. It closely resembled the Fr. *ballet de cour*, except that it retained spoken dialogue, which was replaced by recitative in Fr. The subjects, mainly based on It. models, were mythological, heroic or allegorical.

Masques et bergamasques, music by Fauré, op. 112, for an entertainment by René Fauchois prod. Monte Carlo, 10 Apr 1919; Paris, Opéra-Comique, 4 Mar 1920, with a Watteau setting. It incl. an overture and 3 dances, newly comp., as well as the Pavane, op. 50, of 1887 and an orchestral version of the Verlaine song *Clair de Lune*, op. 46 no. 2, of the same year, in which the words 'masques et bergamasques' occur.

Mass, the chief ritual of the Rom. Catholic church service, i.e. the celebration of the Eucharist. Only High Mass is concerned with music, Low Mass being spoken, not sung. The Mass is still sung to plainsong melodies, but from the 14th cent. onwards it has also been treated as a form of musical comp., as a rule primarily for the purpose of religious service, but sometimes more elaborately for concert use. Masses orig. written, esp. in the 18th and 19th cents., for church use with orchestral accomp. can now generally be perf. only in the concert hall,

Pius X's *Motu proprio* of 1903 having forbidden orchs. in church.

The Ordinary of the Mass falls into 5 main sections: Kyrie, Gloria, Credo, Sanctus with Hosanna and Benedictus, and Agnus Dei with Dona nobis pacem; these remain invariable throughout the year and are usually all that is set to music by comps. The Proper of the Mass consists of additional matter (Introit, Gradual, Alleluia or Tract, Offertory and Communion), and these are far more rarely found as parts of a Mass comp.

The medieval practice of writing the movements of a Mass on plainsong melodies, sung by the tenor, was soon extended to the employment of secular tunes. *L'Homme armé* on the Continent and *The Western Wind* in Eng., for ex., were esp. favoured for this purpose. In the course of the 16th cent., however, more and more composers wrote wholly original Masses, though the practice of borrowing material from motets or *chansons* was also common. Even in later times the treatment of the Mass remained essentially polyphonic, though not necessarily throughout. Certain portions, e.g. 'Et vitam venturi saeculi' at the end of the Credo, were almost invariably set as fugues. *See also* **Requiem.**

Mass in B minor (Bach). *See* **B minor Mass.**

Mass of Life, A, setting of words from Nietzsche's *Also sprach Zarathustra* for solo voices, chorus and orch. by Delius, comp. 1904–5, prod. (2nd part only in Ger.) Munich Music Festival, 1908; 1st complete perf. (in Eng.), London, 7 June 1909, cond. Beecham.

Massaini, Tiburtio (b Cremona, before 1550; d prob. Lodi or Piacenza, after 1609), Italian composer. He served as *maestro di cappella* in Salò, Prague, Salzburg, Cremona (from 1595), Piacenza and Lodi successively. Comp. church music and 8 books of madrigals, 9 of motets, 4 of Masses and 2 of psalms.

Massart, Joseph (Lambert) (b Liège, 19 Jul 1811; d Paris, 13 Feb 1892), Belgian violinist and teacher. Studied under Auguste Kreutzer (1778–1832) in Paris and in 1843 became vln. prof. at the Cons. there.

Massé, Victor (actually Félix Marie) (b Lorient, 7 Mar 1822; d Paris, 5 Jul 1884), French composer. Studied at the Paris Cons. where Halévy was his comp. master, and gained the Prix de Rome in 1844. He travelled in It. and Ger. after his stay in Rome; in 1860 became chorus-master at the Paris Opéra and in 1866 prof. of comp. at the Cons.

Works incl. operas and operettas *La Chambre gothique* (1849), *La Chanteuse violée* (1850), *Galathée* (1852), *Les Noces de Jeannette* (1853), *La Reine Topaze* (1856), *Le Cousin de Marivaux* (1857), *La Fiancée du Diable, Miss Fauvette, Les Saisons, La Fée Carabosse, Mariette la promise* (1862), *La Mule de Pedro* (1863), *Fior d'Aliza* (after Lamartine, 1866), *Le Fils du brigadier* (1867), *Paul et Virginie* (after Saint-Pierre), *La favorita e la schiava, Les Chaises à porteurs, Le Prix de famille, Une Loi somptuaire, Les Enfants de Perrette, La Petite Sœur d'Achille, La Trouvaille* (comp. 1873), *Une Nuit de Cléopâtre* (1885); *Messe solennelle*; cantata *Le Rénégat*; songs.

Massenet, Jules (Émile Frédéric) (b Montaud nr. Saint-Étienne, 12 May 1842; d Paris, 13 Aug 1912), French composer. Entered the Paris Cons. at the age of 11, studying comp. with A. Thomas and gaining the Prix de Rome in 1863. On his return from Rome in 1866 he married a pf. pupil and his his 1st opera, *La Grand'tante*, prod. at the Opéra-Comique the next year. The 1st really successful opera, *Hérodiade*, was prod. at Brussels in 1881 and *Manon* at the Opéra-Comique in 1884. Prof. of comp. at the Cons., 1878–96.

Works incl. operas *Don César de Bazan* (1872), *Le Roi de Lahore* (1877), *Hérodiade* (1881), *Manon* (after Prévost, 1884), *Le Cid* (after Corneille, 1885), *Esclarmonde* (1889), *Le Mage, Werther* (after Goethe, 1892), *Le Portrait de Manon, La Navarraise* (1894), *Sapho* (after Daudet), *Cendrillon* (1899), *Grisélidis* (1901), *Le Jongleur de Notre-Dame* (1902), *Thaïs* (1894), (both after A. France), *Chérubin* (1905), *Ariane* (1906), *Thérèse* (1907), *Bacchus, Don Quichotte* (after Cervantes, 1910), *Roma, Panurge* (after Rabelais), *Cléopâtre* (1914), *Amadis* (comp. 1895; prod. 1922); ballets *Le Carillon, La Cigale, Espada*; incid. music to Leconte de Lisle's *Les Erynnies*, Racine's *Phèdre* and other plays.

Oratorios *Marie-Magdeleine* (1873), *Ève* (1875), *La Vierge, La Terre promise* (1900); cantatas *David Rizzio, Narcisse, Biblis.*

13 orchestral works incl. *Scènes pittoresques* (1874), *Scènes napolitaines* (1876), and 3 other similar suites, symph. poem *Visions*; pf. concerto, fantasy for cello and orch.; c 200 songs; duets; choruses.

Mässig (Ger.) = moderate.

Massimilla Doni, opera by Schoeck (lib. by A. Rüeger, based on Balzac's novel), prod. Dresden, 2 Mar 1937.

Massol, Jean-Etienne August (b Lodève,

23 Aug 1802; d Paris, 30 Oct 1887), French baritone. Debut Paris, Opéra, 1825, in *La Vestale*. He sang as a tenor in the fps of *Guillaume Tell*, Cherubini's *Ali Baba* and *Les Huguenots*; 1840 as baritone in the fp of Donizetti's *Les Martyrs*, 1843 in *Dom Sébastien*. He sang in London 1846–51 in operas by Auber, Meyerbeer and Donizetti (*La favorite*); returned to Paris until 1858.

Masson, Diego (b Tossa, Spain, 21 Jun 1935), French conductor. Studied at the Paris Cons. with Leibowitz, Maderna and Boulez; worked with Domaine Musical (*q.v.*) and founded ens. *Musique Vivante* 1966; early perfs. of works by Stockhausen, Boulez (*Domaines*), Globokar and Berio. He has dir. opera and ballet at Marseilles and Angers from 1968.

Master Peter's Puppet Show (Falla). See **Retablo de Maese Pedro**.

Master-Singers. See **Meistersinger.**

Mastersingers of Nuremberg, The (Wagner). See **Meistersinger von Nürnberg.**

Masterson, Valerie (b Birkenhead, 3 Jun 1937), English soprano. She sang with D'Oyly Carte 1966–70. London, Coliseum, from 1971 as Constanze, Adèle, Oscar, Manon and Sophie; CG from 1974. At the Aix Festival she has sung Rossini's Elisabetta, Fiordiligi and Mozart's Countess. US debut San Francisco, 1980, as Violetta. Her Handel roles have incl. Morgana (*Alcina*), Cleopatra, Semele (CG 1982) and Romilda in *Xerxes* (ENO 1985).

Mastilovič, Danica (b Negotin, 7 Nov 1933), Yugoslav soprano. She sang in Belgrade 1955–9; Frankfurt from 1959, debut as Tosca. At Hamburg she was heard as Turandot (1964) and during the 1970s sang in Europe and N. Amer. as Abigaille, Kundry, Brünnhilde and the Dyer's Wife. CG and NY Met debuts as Elektra (1973, 1975). Zurich 1973, as Ortrud.

Masur, Kurt (b Brieg, Silesia, 18 Jul 1927), German conductor. He studied in Breslau and Leipzig. After minor engagements at Erfurt and Leipzig cond. Dresden PO 1955–8 (returned 1964–7). Music dir. Komische Oper, Berlin, 1960–4; Leipzig Gewandhaus Orch. from 1970. London debut 1973, with the New Philharmonia. Widely admired in Bruckner and Beethoven. US debut 1974, Cleveland Orch.

Matačič, Lovro von (b Sušak, 14 Feb 1899; d Zagreb, 4 Jan 1985), Yugoslav conductor, producer and composer. As a boy he sang with the Wiener Sängerknaben, later studying org. and pf. with Dietrich, theory with Walker and comp. and cond. with Herbst

and O. Nebdal, making his debut as cond. in Cologne in 1919. After appts. in Ljubljana and Zagreb he became dir. of the Belgrade Opera in 1938. From 1956 to 1958 he was music dir. of the Dresden Opera and in 1961 succeeded Solti at Frankfurt; worked there until 1966. Monte Carlo from 1974. He also wrote a quantity of orchestral and incid. music.

Materna, Amalie (b St Georgen, Styria, 10 Jul 1844; d Vienna, 18 Jan 1918), Austrian soprano. 1st appeared on the stage at Graz in 1865, then married the Ger. actor Karl Friedrich, with whom she was engaged at one of the minor theatres in Vienna. In 1869 she 1st sang at the Imp. Opera as Selika; remained until 1894 as Amneris, Elisabeth and Goldmark's Queen of Sheba. She was Wagner's 1st Brünnhilde and Kundry at Bayreuth in 1876 and 1882. NY Met, 1885, as Rachel, Valentine and Brünnhilde.

Matheus de Sancto Johanne (Mayhuet de Joan), French 14th–15th-cent. composer. He served in the chapel of the antipopes at Avignon, 1382–6, and is almost certainly the 'Mayshuet' of the Old Hall MS. Wrote *chansons* and motets.

Mathias, William (b Whitland, Carmarthenshire, 1 Nov 1934), Welsh composer and pianist. He studied at the RAM with Lennox Berkeley and Peter Katin. Lecturer, Univ. College N. Wales, 1959–68; prof. from 1970.

Works incl. opera *The Servants* (1980); *Divertimento* for strings (1958), Concerto for Orch. (1966), 2 symphs. (1966, 1983), *Dance Variations* for orch. (1977); concertos for pf. (1955, 1961, 1968), harp (1970), clar. (1975), horn (1982); *This Worldes Joie* for soloists, chorus and orch. (1974); *Lux Eterna* for soloists, chorus, organ and orch. (1982), *Let us now praise famous men* for chorus and orch. (1984); 2 vln. sonatas, wind quintet, 2 pf sonatas (1964, 1979), 2 string 4tets (1968, 1982).

Mathis der Maler (*Matthew the Painter*), opera by Hindemith (lib. by comp.), prod. Zurich, 28 May 1938. The painter is Matthias Grünewald (15th–16th cent.). Symph. in 3 movts. perf. Berlin, 12 Mar 1934, cond. Furtwängler: *Engelkonzert* (*Concert of Angels*), *Grablegung* (*Entombment*), *Versuchung des heiligen Antonius* (*The Temptation of St Anthony*).

Mathis, Edith (b Lucerne, 11 Feb 1938), Swiss soprano. After her Lucerne debut (1959) she sang at Cologne until 1963; Berlin, Deutsche Oper from 1963. From 1960 she has been heard at Salzburg as Nannetta and Sophie. Glyndebourne 1962–3, as Cherubino. NY Met and CG debuts 1970, as Pamina and Susanna. She took part in the fp of Henze's *Der junge Lord* (Berlin 1965).

Matilde di Shabran, ossia Bellezza e cuor di ferro (. . ., *or Beauty and Heart of Iron*), opera by Rossini (lib. by J. Ferretti), prod. Rome, Teatro Apollo, 24 Feb 1821.

Matin, Le, Le Midi, Le Soir et la Tempête (*Morning, Noon, Evening and Storm*), the orig. titles of Haydn's symphs. Nos. 6 in D maj., 7 in C maj. and 8 in G maj., comp. 1761.

Matinsky, Mikhail (b nr. Moscow, 1750; d St Petersburg, *c* 1825), Russian librettist and composer. A liberated serf, he was educ. in Moscow and in It. Wrote lib. and music of *The St Petersburg Bazaar* (1779).

Matrimonio segreto, Il (*The Clandestine Marriage*), opera by Cimarosa (lib. by G. Bertati, based on G. Colman and D. Garrick's play of that name), prod. Vienna, Burgtheater, 7 Feb 1792.

Mattei, Filippo, called Pippo, the supposed composer of the 1st act of the opera *Muzio Scevola* (often attrib. to Ariosti), the others being by Bononcini and Handel, is prob. no other than Filippo Amadei.

Mattei, Stanislao (b Bologna, 10 Feb 1750; d Bologna, 12 May 1825), Italian priest, theorist and composer. Pupil of Padre Martini, whom he succeeded as *maestro di cappella* at the church of San Francesco in Bologna, and later at San Petronio. From 1804 prof. at the newly founded Liceo Filarmonico, his pupils incl. Rossini and Donizetti. He wrote a treatise on playing from figured bass.

Works incl. 8 Masses and other church music; a Passion; intermezzo *La bottega del libraio*, etc.

Matteis, Nicola (b Naples; d London, *c* 1710), Italian violinist. Went to Eng. about 1672; pub. 3 collections of vln. music, 1 of songs and a treatise, *The False Consonances of Musick*.

Matthay, Tobias (b London, 19 Feb 1858; d Haslemere, Surrey, 15 Dec 1945), English pianist, teacher and composer. Studied at the RAM in London, where he became sub-prof. in 1876 and full prof. of pf. in 1880, remaining until 1925, although he had opened his own school of pf. playing in 1900. He wrote several books on his own method of pf. playing and comp. much pf. music, mainly of educational value.

Mattheson, Johann (b Hamburg, 28 Sep 1681; d Hamburg, 17 Apr 1764), German writer on music, organist and composer. From the age of 9 sang at the Hamburg Opera, and there prod. his 1st opera in 1699. Became friendly with Handel in 1703 and went with him to Lübeck as a candidate to succeed Buxtehude; but both declined on learning that marriage to Buxtehude's daughter was a condition of the post. After some years as tutor, then secretary to the Eng. Legation, he was app. minor canon and music dir. at Hamburg Cathedral in 1715, but had to resign in 1728 because of deafness. Among his many writings on music the most important are *Der vollkommene Capellmeister* (1739), *Grundlage einer Ehrenpforte* (1740) and a treatise on thorough-bass.

Works incl. operas *Die Pleiades* (1699); *Die unglückselige Cleopatra* (1704), *Henrico IV, Boris Goudenow* (1710) and *Nero* (1723); 24 oratorios and cantatas; trio sonatas; etc.; keyboard music.

Matthews, Colin (b London, 13 Feb 1946), English composer. He studied at Nottingham Univ. and taught at Sussex Univ. 1972–7. Worked with Deryck Cooke on the performing vers. of Mahler's 10th symph. and was asst. to Britten 1974–6.

Works incl. 2 *Sonatas* for Orch. (1975, 1980), cello concerto (1984), *Night's Mask* for sop. and chamber orch. (1984); *Ceres* for 9 players (1972), *Rainbow Studies* for pf. and 4 wind (1978), 2 string 4tets (1979, 1982), oboe 4tet (1981); *Five Sonnets: to Orpheus* (texts by Rilke) for tenor and harp (1976), *Shadows in the Water* for tenor and pf. (1978).

Matthews, David (b London, 9 Mar 1943), English composer, brother of prec. Collaborated with prec. and Deryck Cooke on performing vers. of Mahler's 10th symph. Graduated in Classics from Nottingham Univ. Worked as an assistant to Britten 1966–9. Pub. biog. of Tippett 1980.

Works incl. 3 symphs. (1975–85); 3 songs for sop. and orch. (1971); 5 string 4tets (1970–84); *Songs & Dances of Mourning* for cello (1976); *September Music* for small orch. (1979); *Serenade* for chamber orch. (1982); vln. concerto (1982); clar. 4tet (1984); *In The Dark Time* for orch. (1985); Variations for Strings (1986).

Matthews, Denis (b Coventry, 27 Feb 1919), English pianist and writer on music. Studied with Harold Craxton and William Alwyn at the RAM, making his debut in 1939. He has travelled widely and is esp. noted for his playing of Mozart. Prof. of Music, Newcastle upon Tyne, 1971–84. Pub *Beethoven* in Master Musicians series, 1985. CBE 1975.

Matthisson, Friedrich von (1761–1831), German poet. Remembered chiefly by Beethoven's setting of his 'Adelaide'; Schubert set 26 of his poems. *See also* **Schröter (C.)** (songs).

Matzenauer, Margarete (b Temesvar, 1 Jun 1881; d Van Nuys, Calif., 19 May 1963), Hungarian mezzo and soprano. She made her debut in Strasbourg and sang in Munich 1904–11. NY Met 1911–30, debut as Amneris. A versatile artist, she also sang Azucena, Eboli, Aida, Kundry and Brünnhilde, and was the first US Kostelnička, in *Jenůfa* (Met, 1924). Carnegie Hall 1938.

Mauduit, Jacques (b Paris, 16 Sep 1557; d Paris, 21 Aug 1627), French lutenist and composer. He was, like his father before him, registrar to the courts of justice in Paris, but became famous as a musician. In 1581 he gained the 1st prize at the annual Puy de Musique at Évreux, and he was assoc. with Baïf in his experiments with *musique mesurée*, though after Baïf's death in 1590 he relaxed the rigid subordination of music to verbal rhythm in his settings of verse. In 1588 he saved the MSS. of the Huguenot Le Jeune from destruction by the Catholic soldiers, though he was himself a Catholic.

Works incl. Requiem on the death of Ronsard (1585), motets, *chansons, Chansonnettes mesurées* for 4 voices, etc.

Maugars, André (b *c* 1580; d *c* 1645), French violist, politician and translator. He lived in Eng. for 4 years *c* 1620, on his return entered the service of Cardinal Richelieu, became interpreter of Eng. to Louis XIII and trans. Bacon's *Advancement of Learning*. In 1639 he visited Rome and wrote a pamphlet on It. music. He wrote viol music (lost).

Maunder, John Henry (b London, 21 Feb 1858; d Brighton, 25 Jan 1920), English composer and organist. He studied at the RAM and later played the organ in var. London churches. He 1st wrote operettas, incl. *The Superior Sex*, and *Daisy Dingle* (1885) but then turned to sacred music. His oratorio *The Martyrs* was perf. in Oxford in 1894 and his church cantata *From Olivet to Calvary* (1904) was popular for many years.

Maurel, Victor (b Marseilles, 17 Jun 1848; d New York, 22 Oct 1923), French baritone. Went to the school of music at Marseilles, after studying architecture, and later to the Paris Cons. Made his 1st appearances in 1868, at the Paris Opéra, as Luna, Nelusko and Alfonso XI, in *La Favorite*, but was later devoted more to It. opera. He was the 1st Iago in Verdi's *Otello* and the 1st Falstaff; he also sang Boccanegra in the fp of the revised

vers. (1881). London, CG, 1873–1904 as Telramund, Wolfram and the Dutchman. NY Met debut 1894, as Iago.

Mavra, opera in 1 act by Stravinsky (lib., in Rus., by B. Koshno, based on Pushkin's *The Little House at Kolomna*), prod. in Fr. trans. by J. Larmanjat, Paris, Opéra, 3 Jun 1922.

Maw, Nicholas (b Grantham, 5 Nov 1935), English composer. Studied with L. Berkeley at the RAM from 1955 to 1958 and with Nadia Boulanger in Paris from 1958 to 1959. Has taught at Cambridge (1966–70) and Yale. Music is largely traditional in character.

Works incl. Requiem for soprano and contralto soloists, women's chorus, string trio and string orch.; comic operas *One Man Show* (1964) and *The Rising of the Moon* (1970); *Nocturne* for mezzo-soprano and orch. (1958); *Scenes and Arias* for solo voices and orch. (1962); Sonata for strings and 2 horns (1967); *La Vita Nuova* for sop. and chamber ens. (1979); *Morning Music* for orch. (1982); *Spring Music* for orch. (1983); *Sonata Notturno* for cello and strings (1985); *Odyssey* for orch. (1972–85); *Life Studies* for 15 solo strings (1973–6); Chamber Music for fl., clar., horn, bassoon and pf. (1962); 2 string 4tets (1965, 1982).

Maximilien, opera by Milhaud (lib. by A. Lunel, trans. from a Ger. lib. by R.S. Hoffmann, based on Franz Werfel's play, *Juarez und Maximilian*), prod. Paris, Opéra, 4 Jan 1932.

Maxwell Davies, (Sir) **Peter.** *See* **Davies, P.M.**

May Night (*Maïskaya Notch*), opera by Rimsky-Korsakov (lib. by comp., based on a story by Gogol), prod. St Petersburg, 21 Jan 1880.

Mayer, Robert(b Mannheim, 5 Jun 1879; d London, 9 Jan 1985), German–English patron of music, a business man resident in London from 1896. His importance in Brit. musical life was as the founder of the RM Concerts for children and Youth and Music, and other ways of encouraging youthful love of music. Knighted 1939.

Maynard, John (b St Julians, nr St Albans, bap. 5 Jan 1577; d after 1614), English lutenist and composer. He was connected with the school of St Julian in Herts., and at some time in the service of Lady Joan Thynne at Cause Castle in Salop.

Works incl. pavans and galliards for the lute; an organ piece; lessons for lute and bass viol and for lyra-viol; 12 songs *The XII*

Wonders of the World, describing var. characters, for voice, lute and vla. da gamba.

Mayone, Ascanio (b Naples, *c* 1565; d Naples, 9 Mar 1627), Italian composer. Pupil of Jean de Macque in Naples; was organist at SS. Annunziata from 1593, *maestro di cappella* from 1621.

Works incl. madrigals, and solo and chamber instrumental music. His 2 vols. of keyboard music, *Capricci per sonar* (1603, 1609) contain canzonas and toccatas in an advanced idiom.

Mayr, Johann Simon (b Mendorf, Bavaria, 14 Jun 1763; d Bergamo, 2 Dec 1845), German–Italian composer. Educ. at the Jesuit Seminary at Ingolstadt, he later studied with Lenzi in Bergamo and Bertoni in Venice where he settled, at first writing oratorios and church music until 1794, when on the success of his opera *Saffo* he turned to the stage. From 1802 to his death he was *maestro di cappella* at Santa Maria Maggiore, and from 1805 taught at the newly founded Inst. of Music there, Donizetti being among his pupils.

Works incl. over 60 operas, e.g. *Lodoiska* (1796), *Che originali* (1798), *Adelaide di Guesclino* (1799), *Il carretto del venditore d'aceto* (1800), *Ginevra di Scozia* (1801), *I misteri eleusini* (1802), *Alonso e Cora, Elisa* (1801), *L'amor coniugale* (1805), *Adelasia e Aleramo, La rosa rossa e la rosa bianca, Medea in Corinto* (1813); oratorios *Jacob a Labano fugiens, Sisara, Tobiae matrimonium, Davide* (1795), *Il sacrifizio di Jefte* and others; Passion; Masses, motets and other church music.

Mayr, Richard (b Henndorf, nr. Salzburg, 18 Nov 1877; d Vienna, 1 Dec 1935), Austrian bass-baritone. Studied medicine at Vienna Univ., but left it for the Cons. and made his debut at Bayreuth in 1902, as Hagen; sang there until 1924 as Pogner and Gurnemanz. Vienna 1902–35 as Wotan, Sarastro, Figaro and Barak in the fp of *Die Frau ohne Schatten* (1919). London, CG, 1924–31; debut as Ochs, NY Met 1927–30. Salzburg, 1921–34. In 1910 he sang in the fp of Mahler's 8th symph. (Munich).

Mayrhofer, Johann (1787–1836), Austrian poet. *See* **Freunde von Salamanka** (Schubert).

47 of his poems were set by Schubert.

Mayseder, Joseph (b Vienna, 26 Oct 1789; d Vienna, 21 Nov 1863), Austrian violinist and composer. 1st appeared in Vienna, 1800, and later held several important appts., incl. that of chamber musician to the emperor.

Works incl. Mass; 3 vln. concertos; 8 string 4tets; 5 string 5tets; pf. trios and other chamber music, vln. duets; pf. pieces and studies for vln.

Mazas, Jacques (Féréol) (b Béziers, 23 Sep 1782; d Bordeaux, 26 Aug 1849), French violinist and composer. Studied under Baillot at the Paris Cons., appeared with a vln. concerto written for him by Auber, travelled widely, lived in Paris 1829–37 and was dir. of the music school at Cambrai, 1837–41.

Works incl. opera *Le Kiosque* (1842); 2 vln. concertos; string 4tets; vln. duets; many vln. pieces.

Mazeppa, opera by Tchaikovsky (lib. by comp. and V.P. Burenin, based on Pushkin's *Poltava*), prod. Moscow, Bolshoy Theatre, 15 Feb 1884.

Symph. poem by Liszt, comp. in 1854 on Victor Hugo's poem and on the basis of one of the *Grandes Études pour le piano* of *c* 1838 and their new version, the *Etudes d'exécution transcendante* of 1851, fp Weimar, 16 Apr 1854.

Mazura, Franz (b Salzburg, 21 Apr 1924), Austrian bass-baritone. Debut Kassel 1949. He sang in Mainz and Mannheim and became a member of the Deutsche Oper Berlin in 1963; successful as Pizarro, Scarpia and Schoenberg's Moses. From 1974 he has appeared at Bayreuth; at first as Alberich and Klingsor, then Gunther in the Solti–Hall *Ring*. In 1985 he sang Berg's Doctor at the NY Met.

Mazurka, a Polish national dance dating at least as far back as the 16th cent. and originating in Mazowsze (Mazovia). It was at first accomp. with vocal music. The dance-figures are complicated and subject to much variation, not excluding improvisation. The music is in moderate 3–4 time orig. in 2 sections of 8 bars each, both repeated; there is a tendency to accentuate the 2nd or the 3rd beat. Its treatment by comps. (e.g. Chopin) often extends and develops it.

Mazurok, Yuri (b Krasnik, Poland, 18 Jul 1931), Russian baritone. He studied in Lwów and Moscow; debut 1964 at the Bolshoy as Eugene Onegin. He later sang Andrei in *War and Peace* in Moscow. CG, 1975, as Renato. US debut 1977, San Francisco. In 1979 he sang Escamillo at the Vienna Staatsoper. Other roles incl. Rossini's Figaro and Verdi's Posa and Germont.

Mazzaferrata, Giovanni Battista (b Como or Pavia; d Ferrara, 26 Feb 1691), Italian composer. *Maestro di cappella* at the Accademia della Morte at Ferrara, 1670–1680. His oratorio was perf. at Siena in 1684.

Works incl. oratorio *Il David* and cantatas; *Salmi concertati* for 3–4 voices; madrigals and canzonets; cantatas for solo voices; 12 sonatas for 2 vlns. and bass.

Mazzinghi, Joseph (b London, 25 Dec 1765; d Downside nr. Bath, 15 Jan 1844), English pianist, of Italian descent. Pupil of J.C. Bach. At the age of 10 he succeeded his father as organist of the Port. Chapel in London. He then studied further with Bertoni, Sacchini and Anfossi during their stays in Eng. and in 1784 became cond. and comp. to the King's Theatre. He taught much and was music master to the Princess of Wales (later Queen Caroline).

Works incl. operas *La bella Arsena* (1795) and *Il tesoro* (1796); plays with music *A Day in Turkey* (1791), *Paul and Virginia* (with Reeve, after Saint-Pierre, 1800), *The Wife of Two Husbands, The Exile, The Free Knights* and others; several ballets; Mass for 3 voices; 6 hymns; many keyboard sonatas; glees, arias, songs.

Mazzocchi, Domenico (b Veia nr. Civita Castellana, bap. 8 Nov 1592; d Rome, 21 Jan 1665), Italian composer. Was in the service of the Aldobrandini Borghese family for 20 years. His music has some of the earliest printed dynamics, e.g. 'crescendo' and 'diminuendo'.

Works incl. opera *La catena d'Adone* (1626); oratorios *Querimonia di S. Maria Maddalena, Il martirio dei SS. Abbundia ed Abbundanzio* (1641); *Musiche sacre*; madrigals, *Dialoghi e sonetti*.

Mazzocchi, Virgilio (b Veia, 22 Jul 1597; d Veia, 3 Oct 1646), Italian composer, brother of prec. *Maestro di cappella* at St John Lateran in Rome, 1628–9, and then at St Peter's until his death.

Works incl. operas *Chi soffre speri* (with Marazzoli, 1637) and *L'innocenza difesa* (1641); psalms for double chorus; *Sacri flores* for 2–4 voices.

Mazzoleni, Ester (b Sebenico, 12 Mar 1883; d Palermo, 17 May 1982), Italian soprano. Debut Rome 1906, as the *Trovatore* Leonora; La Scala 1908–17, as Giulia in *La Vestale* and Médée. In 1913 she sang Aida at Verona, opposite Zenatello. Appeared as guest in Lisbon, Barcelona and Cairo and sang widely in Italy as Norma, Lucrezia Borgia, Elisabeth de Valois and Meyerbeer's Valentine.

Mc (for names with this prefix *see* **Mac. . .**).

Me, the name of the Mediant note in any key in Tonic Sol-fa, so pronounced, but in notation represented by the symbol m.

Meale, Richard (b Sydney, 24 Aug 1932),

Australian composer. Studied as pianist at NSW Cons. Later music has been influenced by Boulez, Messiaen and Indonesian music.

Works incl. opera *Juliet's Memoirs* (1975); *Images* for orch. (1966), *Clouds Now and Then* for orch. (1969); *Viridian* for strings (1979); fl. sonata (1960), wind 5tet (1970), 2 string 4tets (1974, 1980).

Meantone. In tuning the meantone system was used for keyboard instruments before Equal Temperament came into general use. It provided for the pure intonation of the key of C maj. and those lying near it at the expense of the more extreme sharp and flat keys; which is the reason why remote keys were rarely used in keyboard works, before the adoption of Equal Temperament. There was, for ex., a pure F♯ and B♭, but these notes were out of tune when used as G♭ or A♯.

Meares, Richard (d London, c 1722), English instrument maker. Made lutes, viols, etc. in London in the 2nd half of the 17th cent.

Meares, Richard (b London; d London, c 1743), English instrument maker and music publisher, son of prec. He succeeded to his father's business, but enlarged it by selling not only instruments, but music books and cutlery, and he began to pub. music c 1714, incl. several operas by Handel, e.g. *Radamisto* (1720).

Measure (Amer.) = Bar. In Eng. (poet.) a 'measure' is a regularly rhythmic piece of music, esp. a dance.

Medea, play with music (melodrama) by G. Benda (text by F.W. Gotter), prod. Leipzig, 1 May 1775.

Medea in Corinto, opera (*melodramma tragico*) by Mayr (lib. by F. Romani); prod. Naples, Teatro San Carlo, 28 Nov 1813.

Médecin malgré lui, Le (*Doctor against his Will*), opera by Gounod (lib. a small alteration of Molière's comedy by comp., J. Barbier and M. Carré), prod. Paris, Théâtre Lyrique, 15 Jan 1858.

Médée, opera by Marc-Antoine Charpentier (lib. by T. Corneille), prod. Paris, Opéra, 4 Dec 1693.

Opera by Cherubini (lib. by F.B. Hoffmann), prod. Paris, Théâtre Feydeau, 13 Mar 1797.

Opera by Milhaud (lib. by Madeleine Milhaud, the comp.'s wife), prod. in Flem. trans., Antwerp, 7 Oct 1939.

Meder, Johann Valentin (b Wasungen o/ Werra, bap. 3 May 1649; d Riga, Jul 1719), German singer and composer. After var. appts. he became cantor at Reval in 1674 and at Danzig in 1687, later music dir. at Königsberg and Riga Cathedral.

Works incl. operas *Nero* (1695, indebted to Strungk) and others: oratorio, motets; trios; organ music.

Mederitsch, Johann Georg Anton Gallus (also known as Johann Gallus) (b Vienna, 26 Dec 1752; d Lwów, 18 Dec 1835), Bohemian composer and conductor. He was a theatre cond. at Olomouc and Pest, and later for many years a private music teacher in Vienna, Grillparzer being among his pupils. Works incl. operas *Babylons Pyramiden* (with Winter, 1797), *Orkatastor und Illiane* (1779), *Der reditche Verwalter* (1779) and others; incid. music for Shakespeare's *Macbeth*; Masses; chamber music.

Medesimo tempo (It. = 'same time'), a direction indicating that a change of metre does not imply a change of pace. The more usual term is *l'istesso tempo* (formerly *lo stesso tempo*).

Mediant, the 3rd degree of the maj. or min. scale, so called because it stands half way between Tonic and Dominant. The names of the degrees of the whole scale are Tonic, Supertonic, Mediant, Subdominant, Dominant, Submediant and Leading-note.

Medium, The, opera in 2 acts by Menotti (lib. by the comp.), prod. Columbia Univ., NY, 8 May 1946.

Medtner, Nikolai Karlovich (b Moscow, 5 Jan 1880; d London, 13 Nov 1951), Russian composer. Studied pf. under Safonov at the Moscow Cons., gained the Rubinstein Prize there and toured Europe as pianist in 1901–2, becoming prof. at the Cons. for a year on his return, but then retiring to devote himself to comp. After the Revolution he taught at a school in Moscow and in 1921 went on another tour in the west, but found himself unable to return. He settled in Paris for a time and later in London, which he left temporarily for Warwickshire in 1940.

Works incl. 3 pf. concertos (1914–43); pf. 5tet; 3 sonatas and 3 nocturnes for vln. and pf.; 12 pf. sonatas and a great number of pieces for pf. incl. *Fairy Tales* op. 8, 9, 14, 20, 26, 34, 35, 42, 48, 51, *Forgotten Melodies* op. 38–40, *Dithyrambs, Novels, Lyric Fragments, Improvisations, Hymns in Praise of Toil*, etc.; *Rus. Dance* and *Knight-Errant* for 2 pfs.; sonata-vocalise for voice and pf.; 17 op. nos. of songs to words by Pushkin, Tiutchev, Goethe, Heine, Nietzsche and others.

Meeresstille und Glückliche Fahrt (*Calm Sea and Prosperous Voyage*) two poems by Goethe, set by Beethoven as a cantata for chorus and orch. in 1815, op. 112, and ded. to the poet; and used by Mendelssohn as the subject for a concert overture, op. 27, in 1828. Elgar quotes from the latter in the romance of the 'Enigma' Variations.

Mefistofele, opera by Boito (lib. by comp., based on Goethe's *Faust*), prod. Milan, La Scala, 5 Mar 1868.

Mehta, Zubin (b Bombay, 29 Apr 1936), Indian conductor, son of the violinist Mehli M. Received 1st training from his father and in 1954 went to Vienna, where he studied cond. with Swarowsky. In 1958 he won the competition for young conds. in Liverpool and in 1959 was guest cond. with the Vienna PO. He has since cond. throughout Europe, and in 1962 became dir. of the Los Angeles PO; left in 1977 to become music dir. NY PO. Israel PO and CG, London, from 1977. Guest cond. Vienna PO.

Méhul, Étienne Nicolas (b Givet nr. Mézières, Ardennes, 22 Jun 1763; d Paris, 18 Oct 1817), French composer. Organist in his home town at the age of 10, he went to Paris in 1778, where Gluck's operas and the encouragement of the comp. himself gave him the ambition to write for the stage. He took piano lessons from Edelmann, and supported himself by teaching until *Euphrosine* (1790) estab. him as an opera comp., after which he became one of the most notable comps. of the Revolution, his greatest success being *Joseph* (1807). On the foundation of the Cons. in 1795 he became one of its inspectors.

Works incl. operas *Euphrosine et Coradin, ou Le Tyran corrigé* (1790), *Cora, Stratonice* (1792), *Le Jeune Sage et le vieux fou* (1793), *Horatius Coclès, Mélidore et Phrosine* (1794), *La Caverne, Doria, Le Jeune Henri* (1797), *Le Pont de Lodi* (1797), *Adrien, Ariodant* (1799), *Épicure* (with Cherubini), *Bion, L'irato, ou L'Emporté* (1801), *Une Folie, Le Trésor supposé* (1802), *Joanna, Héléna* (1803), *Le Baiser et la quittance* (with Kreutzer, Boieldieu and Isouard, 1803), *L'Heureux malgré lui, Les Deux Aveugles de Tolède* (1806), *Uthal* (without vlns.), *Gabrielle d'Estrés, Joseph* (1807), *Les Amazones, Le Prince Troubadour* (1813), *L'Oriflamme* (with Paer, Berton and Kreutzer, 1814), *La Journée aux aventures* (1816), *Valentine de Milan* (unfinished, completed by his nephew Louis Joseph Daussoigne-M., 1790–1875).

Ballets: *Le Jugement de Paris* (with adds. from Haydn and Pleyel), *La Dansomanie* (1800), *Daphnis et Pandrose* (1803), *Persée et Andromède* (1810); incid. music to Joseph

Chénier's *Timoléon*; Mass for the coronation of Napoleon I (not perf.); cantatas *Chanson de Roland*, *Chant lyrique* (for the unveiling of Napoleon's statue at the Institut); patriotic songs *Chant national du 14 juillet*, *Chant du départ*, *Chant de retour*; symphs.; 2 pf. sonatas.

Mei, Girolamo (b Florence, 27 May 1519; d Florence, Jul 1594), Italian theorist. His 4 surviving works incl. the *Discorso sopra la musica antica e moderna*, pub. Venice, 1602.

Meiland, Jacob (b Senftenberg, Saxony, 1542; d Hechingen, 31 Dec 1577), German composer. He learnt music as a choir-boy in the Saxon court chapel at Dresden, studied at Leipzig Univ., travelled, and was app. *Kapellmeister* to the Margrave of Ansbach, whose chapel was dissolved in 1574. Meiland was *Kapellmeister* to the Hohenzollem court at Heichingen from 1577.

Works incl. Lat. and Ger. motets; *Cantiones sacrae* for 5–6 voices; Ger. songs for 4–5 voices.

Meistersinger (Ger. = Master-Singers), 14th–16th-cent. guilds of poets and musicians who cultivated poetry and singing in var. Ger. towns, prob. founded at Mainz in 1311 by Heinrich von Meissen (Frauenlob). The members passed through var. stages from apprenticeship to mastery, and they were middle-class burghers, merchants, tradesmen and artisans, not nobles like the Minnesinger.

Meistersinger von Nürnberg, Die (*The Mastersingers of Nuremberg*), music drama by Wagner (lib. by comp.), prod. Munich, Court Theatre, 21 Jun 1868.

Mel, Rinaldo del (b Malines, c 1554; d c 1598), Flemish composer. He went to Rome in 1580 after serving at the Port. court, entered the service of Cardinal Gabriele Paleotto and (?) studied under Palestrina. 1587–91 he was at Liège in the household of Ernst, Duke of Bavaria, but he rejoined Paleotto at Bologna, who app. him *maestro di cappella* to Magliano Cathedral.

Works incl. motets, *Sacrae cantiones*, a Litany; 12 vols of *madrigaletti* and spiritual madrigals.

Melani, Jacopo (b Pistoia, 6 Jul 1623; d Pistoia, 19 Aug 1676), Italian composer. His father was a sexton at Pistoia and had 7 other musical sons. He was *maestro di cappella* of Pistoia Cathedral, 1657–67, and wrote a number of comic operas for Florence.

Works incl. operas *Il potestà di Colognole* (1657), *Il girello*, *Il pazzo per forza* (1658),

Il vecchio burlato (1659), *Enea in Italia*, *Ercole in Tebe* (1661), *Il ritorno d'Ulisse* (1669).

His brothers were: Atto M. (1626–1714), castrato; Francesco Maria M. (1628–c 1703), castrato and later a monk; Bartolomeo M. (1634–1703), singer; Alessandro M. (1639–1703), *maestro di cappella* at Bologna, Pistoia and Rome, comp. of 5 operas, motets, oratorios, cantatas, etc.; Antonio M., comp. of instrumental music; Domenico M. (1629–1693), castrato; Nicola M. (b c 1632), castrato.

Melartin, Erkki (b Käkisalmi, 7 Feb 1875; d Pukinmäki, 14 Feb 1937), Finnish composer. Studied at the Helsinki Cons., Wegelius being his comp. master; later in Germany. He became prof. of comp. at the Cons. in 1901, and cond. at Viipuri in 1908–10. He was dir. of the Cons. in 1911–22.

Works incl. opera *Aino* (1907); ballet *Sininen helmi*; 8 symphs. (1902–24), 5 orchestral suites, symph. poems; vln. concerto; 4 string 4tets; vln. and pf. sonatas; pf. sonata and c 400 pieces; c 300 songs.

Melba, Nellie (actually Helen Mitchell) (b Burnley, nr. Melbourne, 19 May 1861; d Sydney, 23 Feb 1931), Australian soprano. Studied singing at an early age, but was not allowed to take it up professionally until her marriage to Captain Charles Armstrong in 1882 enabled her to do so. She appeared in London in 1886, went to Paris for further study with Mathilde Marchesi and made her debut at the Théâtre de la Monnaie in Brussels, 1887, as Gilda; CG, London, in 1888 as Lucia. She 1st visited Paris in 1889, when she sang Juliette, Rus. in 1891, It. in 1892 and N. Amer. in 1893; Met until 1911. London until 1924 as Rosina, Violetta, Mimi, Desdemona, Aida and Elsa. She was highly regarded as a coloratura soprano, particularly successful in roles requiring ornamentation. DBE 1918.

Melchior, Lauritz (b Copenhagen, 20 Mar 1890; d Santa Monica, 18 Mar 1973), Danish-American tenor. Studied in Copenhagen, making his debut as a baritone in 1913. In 1918, after further studies, he made a second debut as a tenor, singing at CG and Bayreuth in 1924; Bayreuth until 1931 as Siegmund, Parsifal, Siegfried and Tristan. NY Met 1926–1950; debut as Tannhäuser. He was one of the finest Wagner singers of his time.

Melis, Carmen (b Cagliari, 16 Aug 1885; d Longone al Segrino, nr. Como, 19 Dec 1967), Italian soprano. She studied with Jean de Reszke in Paris. Debut Novara 1905, as Thaïs; Naples 1906, as Mascagni's Iris. Manhattan Opera House 1909, as Tosca; she sang Leoncavallo's Zazà at Chicago in 1916. Paris Opéra 1913, as Minnie, with Caruso and Tita Ruffo. CG 1913 and 1929 as Tosca, Nedda and Musetta. Other roles incl. Manon Lescaut, Fedora and the Marschallin.

Melkus, Eduard (b Baden-bei-Wien, 1 Sep 1928), Austrian violinist. He studied in Vienna and has taught at the Hochschule there from 1958. He played in several Swiss orchs. and in 1965 founded the Vienna Capella Academica; many perfs. and recordings of 17th and 18th cent. instrumental music.

Melisma (from Gk. = song, plur. *melismata*), an ornament: in plainsong a group of notes sung to a single syllable; in modern music any short passage of a decorative nature.

Mell, Davis (b Wilton nr. Salisbury, 15 Nov 1604; d London, 4 Apr 1662), English violinist and composer. Became a member of the King's Band at the Restoration (1660) and joint master. Wrote viol music, etc.

Mellers, Wilfrid (Howard) (b Leamington, 26 Apr 1914), English critic and composer. Studied at Cambridge and began to write criticism in the review *Scrutiny*, of which he became music asst. ed. Prof. of music at York Univ. 1964–81. OBE 1982. He has written books on Couperin, American music, Bach and Beethoven.

Works incl. opera *Christopher Marlowe* (1950–2), *Ricercare* for orch., do. (no. 2) for chamber orch., do. (no. 3) for string orch.; *Concerto grosso* for chamber orch.; string 4tet, pf. 4tet, *Eclogue* for string trio trio (1945); choral music; songs.

Melodic Minor Scale, a minor scale in which the 6th and 7th are sharpened when ascending and flattened when descending (*see* illustration).

Humperdinck's *Königskinder* and works by Fibich are later ones; familiar exs. of the latter occur in Beethoven's *Fidelio* and Weber's *Freischütz*.

Melodramma (It. = music drama), a term for 'opera' current in It. from the end of the 18th cent. onwards. *See also* **Melodrama.**

Melody, an intelligible succession of notes defined by pitch and rhythm. In western music it is unusual to find melodies which do not at least imply harmony.

Melos Ensemble, English chamber music group formed 1950 by Cecil Aronowitz (vla.), Gervase de Peyer (clar.), Richard Adeney (flute) and Terence Weil (cello). Further players, up to a total of 12, have been added to give frequent perfs. and recordings of major chamber works. Also active in modern music, incl. fp Britten's *War Requiem*, 1962.

Melos Quartet of Stuttgart. German string quartet founded 1965; many concert appearances since winning competitions in Geneva and Rio de Janiero. Members are Wilhelm Melcher (b Hamburg, 1940), Gerhard Ernst (b Burscheid, 1939), Hermann Voss (b Brünen, 1934) and Peter Buck (b Stuttgart, 1937).

Melusine, overture (Mendelssohn). *See* **Schöne Melusine.**

Mendelssohn, Arnold (Ludwig) (b Ratibor, 26 Dec 1855; d Darmstadt, 19 Feb 1933), German composer, son of a cousin of Felix M.-Bartholdy. Studied law at Tübingen and music in Berlin, and held teaching and cond. appts. at Bonn, Bielefeld, Cologne, Darmstadt and Frankfurt, where Hindemith was his pupil.

Works incl. operas *Elsi, die seltsame Magd* (after Jeremias Gotthelf, 1896), *Der Bärenhäuter* (1900) and *Die Minneburg*; cantatas; madrigals to words from Goethe's *Werther*; much church music, symph. in E♭ maj.; vln. concerto; 2 string 4tets; sonatas

MELODIC MINOR SCALE

Mélodie (Fr.) lit. a melody or tune, now generally current in Fr. as an exact equivalent of the Eng. 'Song' or the Ger. 'Lied'.

Melodrama, a spoken play or spoken passages in an opera accomp. by a musical background. Rousseau's *Pygmalion* and Benda's *Ariadne* and *Medea* are early instances of the former, and the 1st version of

for vln. and pf., cello and pf. and pf.; songs, part-songs.

Mendelssohn (-Bartholdy, Jakob Ludwig) Felix (b Hamburg, 3 Feb 1809; d Leipzig, 4 Nov 1847), German composer. Son of the banker Abraham M. and grandson of the Jewish philosopher Moses M. Mendelssohn's branch of the family embraced

Christianity and moved to Berlin in 1812. At 6 he had pf. lessons from his mother and at 7 from Marie Bigot in Paris. In 1817, back in Berlin, he learnt comp. form Zelter, whose friend Goethe he visited at Weimar in 1821. Before that, in 1818, aged 9, he appeared at a public chamber concert, and before he was 13 he had written many works, incl. the pf. 4tet op. 1. His father was wealthy enough to enable him to cond. a private orch. and he wrote his 1st symph. at 15, after writing 13 symphonies for strings. By 1825 he had ready the short opera *Camacho's Wedding*, prod. at the family's expense in 1827, and at 17 he had written the overture to Shakespeare's *Midsummer Night's Dream* (the rest of the incid. music followed in 1842). In 1829 he cond. Bach's forgotten St Matthew Passion at the Vocal Acad. and paid the 1st of his 10 visits to England, cond. the Phil. Society in London and taking a holiday in Scotland, where he gathered impressions for the *Hebrides* overture and the 'Scottish' symph., at which he worked in It. in 1830–1. The 'Italian' symph. he finished in 1833, the year he cond. the Lower Rhine Festival at Düsseldorf, where he was engaged to stay as general music dir. He left, however, for Leipzig, where he was app. cond. of the Gewandhaus concerts in 1835.

During a visit to Frankfurt he met Cécile Jeanrenaud, descendent of a Fr. Huguenot family, whom he married on 28 Mar 1837. In Sep of the same year he cond. *St Paul* at the Birmingham Festival. In 1841 he left for Berlin, having been app. dir. of the music section of the Acad. of Arts, and there furnished incid. music for several classical plays, Gk., Eng. and Fr. He returned to Leipzig late in 1842 and founded the Cons. there in Nov. opening it in Apr 1843. He was still living in Berlin, however, but resumed his conductorship at Leipzig in Sep 1845 and taught pf. and comp. at the Cons. But he was in poor health, and his visit to Eng. to conduct *Elijah* at the Birmingham Festival on 26 Aug 1846 was his last but one. After the last, in the spring of 1847, the death of his sister Fanny Hensel greatly depressed him, and he went to Switz. too ill to do any work, returning to Leipzig in Sep completely exhausted.

Works incl. OPERAS: *Die Hochzeit des Camacho* (1827), *Die Heimkehr aus der Fremde* (*Son and Stranger*, 1829) and *Loreley* (unfinished); incid. music to Sophocles' *Antigone* and *Oedipus at Colonos*, Shakespeare's *Midsummer Night's Dream* (1843), Racine's *Athalie*.

ORATORIOS: *St Paul* (1836) and *Elijah*

(1846); many choral settings of psalms and other sacred vocal works, *Lobgesang* (*Hymn of Praise*: the 2nd symph. followed by a short cantata), cantata *Lauda Sion*, Goethe's *Erste Walpurgisnacht* for solo voices, chorus and orch.

ORCH: 13 symphs. for strings (1821–3), 5 symphs., in C min (1824), B♭ (1840)', A min. (1842), A (1833), D (1832); 4 concert overtures, *A Midsummer Night's Dream* (1826), *Fingal's Cave* (1830), *The Fair Melusine* (1833), *Ruy Blas* (1839), and some miscellaneous orchestral works; 2 concertos and 3 shorter works for pf. and orch.; vln. concerto in E min.

CHAMBER MUSIC: incl. 6 string 4tets, op. 12 in E♭, op. 13 in A min, op. 44 nos 1–3, in D, E min and E♭, op. 80 in F min, 3 pf. 4tets, 2 string 5tets, 2 pf. trios in D min, op. 49, in C min, op. 66, string octet in E♭ op. 20 (1830), 6tet, 4 pieces for string 4tet, etc.; vln. and pf. sonata, 2 cello and pf. sonatas.

KEYBOARD AND SONGS: A large amount of pf. music incl. 48 *Lieder ohne Worte* (Songs without words) 3 sonatas, fantasies, characteristic pieces, capriccios, variations, preludes and fugues, studies, etc.; 6 sonatas, 3 preludes and fugues and other pieces for organ, over 80 songs; 12 sets of vocal duets and part-songs.

Mendès, Catulle (1841–1909), French writer, poet and dramatist. He wrote libs. for several composers, incl. Chabrier, Messager, Pierné, Pessard, Massenet and Debussy. Debussy's work, *Rodrigue et Chimène*, was never finished. Married Judith Gautier (1850–1917), with whom he visited Wagner at Triebschen in Switz., 1869; she had an affair with Wagner 7 years later at Bayreuth, during the 1st prod. of the *Ring. See also* **Bruneau** (*Chansons à danser* and *Lieds de France*), **Gwendoline** (Chabrier), **d'Indy** (*Médée*), **Leroux** (*Reine Fiammette*).

Ménestrandise (Fr.), in 17th- and 18th-cent. Paris a corporation of *Ménestriers* protected by an official privilege against the encroachment of other musicians on their exclusive right to play for dancing. Couperin wrote a satirical harpsichord suite on it entitled *Les Fastes de la Grande Mxnxs-trxndxsx*.

Mengelberg, Willem (b Utrecht, 28 Mar 1871; d Zuort, Switz., 22 Mar 1951), Dutch conductor. Studied at Cologne, became cond. at Lucerne in 1891 and in 1895 was app. cond. of the Concertgebouw Orch. in Amsterdam. He made this one of the finest orchs. in Europe, giving early perfs. of works by Strauss and Mahler, but fell under a cloud when he openly declared his sympathy with the Nazi rule during World War II, and went into exile in Switz. In 1933 he had been made Prof. of Music at Utrecht Univ.

Menges, Isolde (b Hove, 16 May 1893; d Richmond, Surrey, 13 Jan 1976), British violinist of German parentage, sister of the cond. Herbert Menges (1902–72).Studied Leipzig and St Petersburg. London debut 1913, US tour 1916. Recorded Beethoven Concerto 1922. Founded Menges Quartet 1931.

Mengozzi, Bernardo (b Florence, 1758; d Paris, Mar 1800), Italian tenor and composer. Studied at Florence and Venice, visited London in 1786 and settled in Paris soon after, becoming prof. of singing on the estab. of the Cons. in 1795. Wrote opera *Pourceaugnac* (after Molière) and *c* 15 others, operettas.

Mennin, Peter (b Erie, Pa., 17 May 1923; d New York, 17 Jun 1983), American composer. He studied at the Eastman School and taught comp. at Juilliard 1947–58; president there from 1962.

Works incl. 9 symphs. (1942–81), *Sinfonia* for chamber orch. (1947), *Fantasia* for strings (1948), vln. concerto (1950), Concertato, *Moby Dick* (1952), cello concerto (fp NY, 1956, with Leonard Rose), pf. concerto (1958), *Cantata de Virtute*, based on *The Pied Piper* of Hamelin (1969), Symphonic Movements (1971) *Reflections of Emily*, to texts by E. Dickinson (1979), flute concerto (1982); 2 string 4tets (1941, 1951), pf. sonata (1963).

Meno mosso (It. = less moved), a direction indicating that a slower pace is to be adopted.

Menotti, Gian Carlo (b Cadegliano, 7 Jul 1911), American composer. Studied comp. with Scalero at the Curtis Inst., Philadelphia. Has written libs. of his own operas and of Barber's *Vanessa*. He founded Festival of Two Worlds at Spoleto, Italy, in 1958.

Works incl. operas *Amelia goes to the Ball* (1937), *The Telephone, The Medium* (1946), *The Consul* (1950), *Amahl and the Night Visitors* (1951), *The Saint of Bleecker Street* (1954), *Maria Golovin* (1958), *Le dernier Sauvage* (1963), *Martin's Lie* (1964), *Help, Help the Globoniks!* (1968), *The Hero* (1976), *The Most Important Man* (1971), *Tamu-Tamu* (1973), *La loca* (1979), *A Bride from Pluto* (1982), *Goya* (1986); radio opera *The Old Maid and the Thief* (1939).

Symph. poem *Apocalypse* (1951); *Pastorale* for pf. and string orch., 2 pf. concertos,

vln. concerto (1952); 4 pieces for string 4tet, *Trio for a House-warming Party* for fl., cello and pf.; *Poemetti*, pf. pieces for children; pieces for carillon, etc; symphony *The Halcyon* (1976).

Mensurable Music, measured or measurable music which can be grouped according to regular successions of beats, as distinct from plainsong, which has no measured rhythmic pulse.

Mensural Notation, the musical notation which, as distinct from Modal notation, came into use during the 13th cent. and for the 1st time began to indicate the exact value of notes and rests by its symbols.

Menter, Joseph (b Deutenkofen, Bavaria, 19 Jan 1808; d Munich, 18 Apr 1856), German cellist. Played in the orch. of the Royal Opera at Munich most of his life.

Menter, Sophie (b Munich, 29 Jul 1848; d Stockdorf nr. Munich, 23 Feb 1918), German pianist and teacher, daughter of prec. Studied at the Munich Cons., toured 1st at the age of 15, resumed studies with Tausig and Liszt, married Popper in 1872 and became pf. prof. at St Petersburg, 1883. Work for pf. and orch., *Hungarische Zigeunerweisen*, was orchestrated by Tchaikovsky and cond. by him at its fp in 1893. This has recently been advertised as Liszt's '3rd pf. concerto', although the former attribution was to Menter herself.

Menuet (Fr.) = Minuet. The word is diminutive of *menu* = small.

Menuetto (Ger.-It). The German classics often labelled their minuets thus under the impression that they were using an It. term. The correct It. is *minuetto*, the Ger. *Menuett*.

Menuhin, Hephzibah (b San Francisco, 20 May 1920; d London, 1 Jan 1981), American pianist. She studied in San Francisco and made her debut there in 1928. Frequent recitals with her brother Yehudi and was often heard in the Mozart concertos.

Menuhin, (Sir) Yehudi (b New York, 22 Apr 1916), British violinist and conductor of American birth. Began studying the vln. aged 4, first with S. Anker and then with L. Persinger. Aged 7 he played the Mendelssohn vln. concerto publicly in San Francisco, then went to Europe for further study with A. Busch and Enescu. He made his London debut in 1929 with the Brahms concerto and in 1932 rec. the Elgar concerto with the comp. By 1934 he had completed the first of many world tours; often perf. with his sister, Hephzibah. He quickly became recognized as one of the world's outstanding musicians and virtuosi and in 1944 gave the fp of Bartók's sonata for solo vln. Recently he has devoted less time to solo perfs., and concentrated more on cond. (e.g. at the Bath Festival, 1959–69), in which sphere he has also attained eminence. Founded Menuhin School of Music, 1963. He now lives in London. Honorary KBE 1965; British citizen 1985. OM 1987.

Mer, La (*The Sea*), 3 symph. sketches by Debussy, *De l'aube à midi sur la mer, Jeux de vagues* and *Dialogue du vent et de la mer*, comp. in 1903–5, fp Paris, 15 Oct 1905.

Merbecke, John. *See* Marbeck.

Mercadante, (Giuseppe) Saverio (Raffaele) (b Altamura nr. Bari, bap. 17 Sep 1795; d Naples, 17 Dec 1870), Italian composer. Studied at the Collegio di San Sebastiano at Naples and, having learnt the fl. and vln., became leader of the orch. there. On being dismissed he began to earn his living as a stage composer. After several successes in Italy he won favour in Vienna, visited Spain in 1827–9, and in 1833 became *maestro di cappella* at Novara Cathedral in succession to Generali and in 1840 dir. of the Naples Cons. While at Novara he lost an eye and in 1862 he became totally blind.

Works incl. *c* 60 operas, e.g. *Violenza e costanza* (1820), *Elisa e Claudio* (1821), *Caritea, regina di Spagna* (1826), *Gabriella di Vergy* (1828), *I Normanni a Parigi, I briganti, Il giuramento* (1837), *I due illustri rivali* (1838), *Elena da Feltre, Il bravo* (1839), *La Vestale* (1840), *Leonora, Gli Orazi ed i Curiazi* (1846), *Virginia*; 20 Masses, motets, psalms, etc.; cantata *L'apoteosi d'Ercole* and others; instrumental pieces; songs.

Mercury, nickname of Haydn's symph. no. 43, in E♭ maj., comp. *c* 1771.

Méreaux, Nicolas Jean (Le Froid de) (b Paris, 1745; d Paris, 1797), French organist and composer. Organist at the Paris churches of Saint-Sauveur and Petits Augustins and of the royal chapel.

Works incl. operas *Le Retour de tendresse, Le Duel comique, Laurette, Alexandre aux Indes, Oedipe à Thèbes*, etc.; oratorio *Samson*; motets.

Méric-Lalande, Henriette-Clémentine (b Dunkirk, 4 Nov 1799; d Chantilly, 7 Sep 1867), French soprano. As the daughter of a provincial opera manager she acquired enough experience to appear on the stage at Naples in 1814, but after a good deal of success she decided in 1822 to take lessons from García and appeared in 1823 at the Opéra-Comique in Paris, marrying the horn player Méric there. She studied further in It., sang there and 1st appeared in London in 1830, as Bellini's Imogene; she took part in the fp of Meyerbeer's *Il crociato in Egitto* (Venice, 1824) and created roles in Bellini's *Bianca e Gernando, Il Pirata* and *La Straniera*. In 1833 she created Donizetti's Lucrezia Borgia.

Merikanto, Aare (b Helsinki, 29 Jun 1893; d Helsinki, 29 Sep 1958), Finnish composer. Studied with Reger and others at Leipzig and with Vassilenko at Moscow. Later became prof. at the Helsinki Cons.

Works incl. opera *Juha* (1922); ballet *The Abduction of Kylliki* (on a subject from the *Kalevala*); 3 symphs. (1916, 1918, 1953), variations and fugue and several suites for orch.; 4 vln. concertos (1916–54), 3 pf. concertos, 2 cello concertos, concerto for vln., clar., horn and strings; partita for woodwind and harp; choral works; folksong arrs.

Merkel, Gustav (Adolf) (b Oberoderwitz, Saxony, 12 Nov 1827; d Dresden, 30 Oct 1885), German organist and composer. Studied at Dresden and became organist at the orphanage church there in 1858, the Kreuzkirche in 1860 and court organist in 1864. He also cond. the Vocal Acad. and was prof. at the Cons.

Works incl. 9 sonatas, preludes and fugues, fantasies, studies, etc., for organ; instrumental pieces with organ; pf. works; songs.

Merker (Ger. lit. marker = judge, adjudicator, umpire), one of the masters among the German Meistersinger, who was elected to judge the competitions for mastership and prizes. Beckmesser is the Merker in Wagner's *Meistersinger*.

Merli, Francesco (b Milan, 27 Jan 1887; d Milan, 12 Dec 1976), Italian tenor. Debut Milan 1914, in *Mosè*. Alvaro in Spontini's *Fernando Cortez* at La Scala 1916; sang there until 1946, often under Toscanini. In London and Rome he was the 1st local Calaf; created Respighi's Belfagor, Rome 1923. Other roles incl. Otello, Walther, Don José and Samson.

Merlo, Alessandro (called Alessandro Romano or A. della Viola) (b Rome, *c* 1530; d ? Rome, after 1594), Italian tenor-bass, violist and composer. Pupil of Willaert and Rore. Singer in the Papal Chapel in Rome.

Works incl. motets; madrigals, *Canzoni alla Napolitana, villanelle*.

Merope, opera by Gasparini (lib. by A. Zeno), prod. Venice, Teatro San Cassiano, 26 Dec 1711.

Opera by Graun (lib., in Fr., by Frederick

II of Prus.), prod. Berlin, Opera, 27 Mar 1756.

Opera by Jommelli (lib. by Zeno), prod. Venice, Teatro San Giovanni Grisostomo, 26 Dec 1741.

Opera by Terradellas (lib. do.), prod. Rome, Teatro della Dame, Carnival 1743.

Merrem-Nikisch, Grete (b Duren, 7 Jul 1887; d Kiel, 12 Mar 1970), German soprano. Debut Leipzig, 1910. She sang at the Berlin Hofoper 1913–30, in lyric roles and as Sophie and Eva, and at the Dresden Staatsoper took part in the fps of *Die toten Augen* (1916), *Intermezzo* (1924) and *Cardillac* (1926). She married Arthur Nikisch's eldest son in 1914 and from 1918 was successful in Lieder recitals.

Merrick, Frank (b Clifton, Bristol, 30 Apr 1886; d London, 19 Feb 1981), English pianist and composer. Studied 1st with his parents and then with Leschetizky in Vienna, making his London debut in 1903. In 1910 he won a Rubinstein Prize in St Petersburg and from 1911 to 1929 taught at the RMCM, after which he became prof. at the RCM. In 1928 he won a prize offered by the Columbia Graphophone Co., for completing Schubert's 'Unfinished' symph.

Merrill, Robert (b Brooklyn, 4 Jun 1917), American baritone. Studied 1st with his mother and then with S. Margolis in NY, making his debut in 1944 and joining the NY Met in 1945, as Germont. Other roles incl. Posa, Amonasro and Renato. London, CG, 1967.

Merriman, Nan (b Pittsburgh, 28 Apr 1920), American mezzo. Studied in Los Angeles with Alexia Bassian, making her debut in Cincinnati in 1942 as La Cieca, but her real career began with Toscanini's patronage, and recorded roles in *Falstaff, Rigoletto* and *Otello* with him. Sang Baba the Turk in *The Rake's Progress* at Edinburgh, 1953.

Merry Widow (Lehár). *See* Lustige Witwe.

Merry Wives of Windsor. *See* Falstaff, Lustigen Weiber, Sir John in Love.

Mersenne, Marin (b La Soultière, Maine, France, 8 Sep 1588; d Paris, 1 Sep 1648), French monk, mathematician, philosopher and music theorist. Educ. at Le Mans and La Flèche, he became a Minorite friar, being ordained in 1612. He taught philosophy at Nevers and then studied mathematics and music in Paris, Descartes and the elder Pascal being among his colleagues. He corresponded with scholars in Eng., Hol. and It., the last of which he visited 3 times. His treatises incl. *Harmonie universelle*, 2 vols., pub. Paris, 1636–7, with a section on instru-

ments, *Questions harmoniques, De la nature des sons.*

Merula, Tarquinio (b Cremona, c 1594; d Cremona, 10 Dec 1665), Italian composer and organist. Held appts. alternately at Bergamo and Cremona, and was court and church organist at Warsaw in 1624. From 1628 to 1639 he was at Cremona as *maestro di cappella* at the cathedral, and returned to this post in 1652 after an interval at Bergamo.

Works incl. Masses, motets, psalms, *Concerti spirituali* and other church music; madrigals, *canzoni* for voices and/or instruments; church sonatas.

Merulo, Claudio (also called Claudio da Correggio; real name Merlotti), b Correggio, 8 Apr 1533; d Parma, 5 May 1604), Italian organist, teacher and composer. App. organist at Brescia in 1556 and 2nd organist at St Mark's, Venice, in 1557, advancing to 1st organist in 1564. In 1584 he left Venice, visited the court of Mantua and became organist to the ducal chapel at Parma. Best known for his keyboard music.

Works incl. intermezzi for Dolce's *Le Troiane* (1566) and Cornelio Frangipani's *La tragedia* (1574); Masses, motets, *Sacrae cantiones*, Litanies; madrigals; toccatas and *ricercari* for organ.

Messa di voce (It. setting or placing of the voice), sustained singing of notes or phrase; but *messa* may also mean a *crescendo* followed by a *diminuendo* on a single breath.

Messager, André (Charles Prosper) (b Montluçon, 30 Dec 1853; d Paris, 24 Feb 1929), French composer and conductor. Studied at Niedermeyer's school in Paris and later under Saint-Saëns. In 1876 he won prizes for a symph. and a cantata and in 1883 he prod. a completion of an operetta *François les Bas-bleus* left unfinished by Firmin Bernicat. He became cond. of the Opéra-Comique and in 1898 its general dir.; from 1901 to 1906 he was artistic dir. at CG, London, and from 1901 to 1913 joint dir. of the Opéra. He was also a concert cond. His wife was the Ir. comp. Hope Temple (Dotie Davies, 1859–1938), who had been a pupil of his. He cond. the fp of Debussy's *Pelléas et Mélisande* in 1902.

Works incl. operas and operettas *La Fauvette du Temple* (1885), *La Béarnaise, Le Bourgeois de Calais* (1887), *Isoline* (1888), *Le Mari de la reine* (1889), *La Basoche* (1890), *Madame Chrysanthème* (after Pierre Loti's novel, 1893), *Miss Dollar, Mirette, Le Chevalier d'Harmental* (1896), *Les P'tites Michu* (1897), *Véronique*

(1898), *Les Dragons de l'impératrice* (1905), *Fortunio, Béatrice* (1914), *Monsieur Beaucaire*, (in Eng., 1919), *La Petite Fonctionnaire* (1921), *L'Amour masqué, Passionnement* (1926), *Coup de roulis*; ballets *Les Deux Pigeons* (1886), *Scaramouche* (1891), *Le Chevalier aux fleurs* (1897), *Une Aventure de la Guimard* (1900) and others; instrumental pieces; pf. duets; songs.

Messchaert, Johannes (Martinus) (b Hoorn, 22 Aug 1857; d Zurich, 9 Sep 1922), Dutch bass-baritone. Studied with J. Stockhausen. He sang much in Hol., Ger. and elsewhere and toured as interpreter of songs with Julius Röntgen as pianist.

Messe (Fr. and Ger.) = Mass.

Messe solennelle. *See* **Missa solemnis.**

Messiaen, Olivier (Eugène Prosper Charles) (b Avignon, 10 Dec 1908), French composer and organist, son of the poet Cécile Sauvage. Studied organ under Marcel Dupré, theory under Maurice Emmanuel and comp. under Dukas at the Paris Cons. App. organist of the Trinité in Paris, 1931, and prof. at the École Normale de Musique and the Schola Cantorum. With Baudrier, Jolivet and Lesur he formed the group 'La Jeune France'. In 1940 he was taken prisoner by the Germans but repatriated later and app. prof. of harmony at the Cons. in 1942 and prof. of music and rhythmic analysis in 1947. He married (1) Claire Delbos, (2) Yvonne Loriod. His music makes use of bird-song, Eastern rhythms and exotic sonorities. His influence as a teacher has been considerable.

Works incl. opera *St François d'Assise* (1983); *O sacrum convivium* (1937) and *Cinq rechants* (1949) for chorus; *Trois petites liturgies de la Présence Divine* for women's chorus, celesta, vibraphone, Ondes Martenot, pf., perc. and strings (1944), *La Transfiguration* for tenor, bar., chorus and orch. (1969).

ORCH.: *Les Offrandes oubliées* (1930), *Hymne au Saint Sacrement, Turangalîla-Symphonie* (1946–8), *Chronochromie* for orch. (1960) *Couleurs de la cité céleste* (1963); *Et expecto resurrectionem mortuorum* for woodwind, brass and perc. (1964), *Réveil des oiseaux* for pf. and orch. (1953), *Oiseaux exotiques* for pf. and wind instruments, *Sept Haikai* for pf. and wind instruments (1963), *Des canyons aux étoiles* for pf., horn and orch (1970–4).

INSTRUMENTAL AND SOLO VOCAL: *Quatuor pour la fin du temps* for clar., vln., cello and pf. (1940); theme and variations for vln. and pf.; ORGAN: *Diptyque, Le Ban-*

quet céleste, L'Ascension (1934), *La Nativité du Seigneur* (1935), *Apparition de l'église éternelle, Les Corps glorieux* (1939), *Messe de la Pentecôte* (1950), *Le Livre d'orgue, Livre du Saint-Sacrement*, in 18 movts. (1985); *Fantaisie burlesque, Vingt regards sur l'Enfant Jésus, Île de feu, Catalogue des oiseaux* (1956–8), *Cantéyodajayâ* for pf.; *Visions de l'amen* for 2 pfs. (1943); *Poèmes pour Mi* (1936) and *La mort du nombre* for voice and orch.; *Chants de terre et de ciel* and *Harawi* (1945) for voice and pf.

Messiah (not *The Messiah*), oratorio by Handel (words selected from the Bible by Charles Jennens), perf. Dublin, Music Hall in Fishamble Street, 13 Apr 1742; 1st perf. in Eng. CG, London, 23 Mar 1743.

Messidor, opera by Bruneau (lib. by E. Zola), prod. Paris, Opéra, 19 Feb 1897. Bruneau had already written operas on subjects from Zola's works (*L'Attaque du moulin* and *Le Rêve*), but this was the 1st for which Zola himself wrote the lib.

Messner, Joseph (b Schwaz, Tyrol, 27 Feb 1893; d Salzburg, 23 Feb 1969), Austrian organist, conductor and composer. Studied in Munich and was app. organist to Salzburg Cathedral in 1922. He also cond. there, incl. the music in the cathedral during the Salzburg Festival.

Works incl. operas *Hadassa* (1925), *Das letzte Recht* (1932), *Ines, Agnes Bernauer* (1935); 11 Masses, Te Deum and other church music; oratorios *Das Leben* and *Die vier letzten Dinge*; 3 symphs., *Symphonische Festmusik* for orch.; *Sinfonietta* for pf. and orch.

Mesto (It.) = sad, gloomy.

Metamorphosen, study in C min. for 23 solo strings by Strauss; comp. 1945, in response to the wartime devastation of Europe, in partic. the destruction of the opera houses, in which his works were performed throughout the war. Dedicated to Paul Sacher and the Collegium Musicum; fp Zurich, 25 Jan 1946.

Metamorphoses after Ovid, Six, (*Pan, Phaeton, Niobe, Bacchus, Narcissus, Arethusa*), work for solo oboe by Britten; comp. 1951, fp Thorpeness, 14 Jun 1951.

Metamorphosis, the transformation of theme or motif, esp. rhythmically while the same notes are retained, as for ex. the *idée fixe* of Berlioz, the themes in Liszt's symph. poems, etc. and the *Leitmotive* in Wagner's operas.

Metaphor Aria. *See* **Parable Aria.**

Metastasio (real name Trapassi), **Pietro** (b Rome, 3 Jan 1698; d Vienna, 12 Apr

1782), Italian poet and librettist. His 1st original lib., *Didone*, was prod. in 1724 (music by Sarro). The rigid musical and dramatic conventions imposed by his verse dominated opera until Gluck's reforms of 1762. Operas on his libs. *see* **Achille in Sciro, Adriano in Siria, Alessandro nell' Indie, Antigono, Artaserse, Catone in Utica, Cinesi, Clemenza di Tito, Cleofide, Contesa dei numi, Demetrio, Demofoonte, Démophoön, Didone abbandonata, Eroe cinese, Ezio, Galatea, Innocenza giustificata, Ipermestra, Isola disabitata, Lucio Silla, Olimpiade, Partenope, Rè pastore, Ruggiero, Semiramide riconosciuta, Siface, Siroe, Sogno di Scipione, Tito Vespasiano, Trionfo di Clelia.** *See also* **Hasse, Jommelli** and **Paisiello.**

Metre, the rhythmic patterns prod. in music by notes of varying length combined with strong and weak beats (*arsis* and *thesis*), similar to the different 'feet' (spondees, dactyls, anapaests, trochees, iambics, etc.) in poetry.

Metronome, an instrument invented by Mälzel in 1815 and designed to determine and prescribe the pace of any musical comp. by the beats of a pendulum. The tempo is indicated by the comp., who prescribes how many time-units of a certain note-value are to occupy 1 minute: e.g. ♩ = 60 shows that there are to be 60 crotchets to the minute.

Metropolitan Opera House, America's leading opera house, founded 1883 in New York. From earliest days main emphasis has been on quality of singing, rather than total musical/production values. Early managers incl. Anton Seidl, Walter Damrosch, Heinrich Conried and Giulio Gatti-Casazza (1908–35). Singers before World War I incl. C. Nilsson, Sembrich, Caruso, the De Reszkes, Melba and Destinn. Edward Johnson became manager in 1935; famous singers of the inter-war years were Flagstad, Gigli, Leider, Melchior and Tibbett. Under Rudolf Bing's management (1950–72) some attempt was made to improve theatrical standards. In 1966 the co. moved to the Lincoln Center for the Performing Arts, NY. Recent managers incl. Anthony Bliss (1975–85); Bruce Crawford from 1986. James Levine music dir. from 1975.

Metternich, Josef (b Hermuhlheim, nr. Cologne, 2 Jun 1915), German baritone. Debut Berlin, Städtische Oper, 1945, as Tonio. Sang at the NY Met and was guest in London, Milan and Vienna, as Jochanaan, the Dutchman, Scarpia and Don Carlo. He joined the Munich Opera in 1954 and was

Johannes Kepler in the 1957 fp of Hindemith's *Die Harmonie der Welt.*

Metzger-Lattermann, Ottilie (b Frankfurt, 15 Jul 1878; d Auschwitz, Feb 1943), German contralto. She sang at Halle and Cologne 1899–1903 and was engaged at Hamburg 1903–15; guest in Berlin, Vienna and St Petersburg. In Dec 1910 she was Herodias in the 1st London perf. of *Salome*, at CG, under Beecham. Bayreuth 1901–12, as Erda and Waltraute. She sang in Dresden 1915–21 and in 1923 was Magdalena in the 1st US perf. of *Der Evangelimann*, at Chicago. Arrested by the Nazis and died in Auschwitz.

Mewton-Wood, Noel (b Melbourne, 20 Nov 1922; d London, 5 Dec 1953), Australian pianist, studied at the Melbourne Cons., the RAM in London and under Schnabel. He 1st appeared in London in 1940 and made a great impression. His interest in modern comps. and in chamber music gave him many special opportunities. He died after taking prussic acid.

Meyer, Ernst Hermann (b Berlin, 8 Dec 1905), German musicologist and composer. Studied in Berlin and Heidelberg. Lived in London from 1933 to 1948, when he was app. prof. of music sociology at the Humbolt Univ., Berlin. His books incl. studies of 17th-cent. instrumental music and Eng. chamber music from the Middle Ages to Purcell.

Works incl. opera *Reiter der Nacht* (1973); film and chamber music, etc.

Meyer, Gregor (d Basle, Nov 1576), Swiss organist and composer. He was organist at Solothurn Cathedral and supplied Glareanus with comps. exemplifying the correct use of modes. Works incl. Motets, Kyries, Antiphons.

Meyer, Kerstin (Stockholm, 3 Apr 1928), Swedish mezzo. Debut Stockholm, 1952 as Azucena. NY Met debut 1960, Carmen. Glyndebourne since 1961; roles there incl. Monteverdi's Ottavia and Debussy's Geneviève. Also sang in the 1st Brit. perfs. of *Elegy for Young Lovers* and *The Visit of the Old Lady* (von Einem). London, CG, from 1960 as Berlioz's Dido, Octavian and Clytemnestra. Bayreuth 1962–4, as Brangaene. She has sung in the fps of works by Goehr and Searle in Hamburg, and in 1966 created Agave in Henze's *The Bassarids* (Salzburg). Has often returned to Stockholm, and in 1978 created Spermando in Ligeti's *Le Grand Macabre*.

Meyer, Leonard B(unce) (b New York, 12 Jan 1918), American theorist and aesthetician. Studied at Columbia Univ. and the Univ. of Chicago; taught at the Univ. of

Chicago (1961) and the Univ. of Pennsylvania (1975). His books incl. *Emotion and Meaning in Music* (1956) and (with Grosvenor Cooper) *The Rhythmic Structure of Music* (1960).

Meyer von Schauensee, Franz (Joseph Leonti) b Lucerne, 10 Aug 1720; d Lucerne, 2 Jan 1789), Swiss organist and composer. Studied in Lucerne and Milan, and after a period of military service, 1742–4, returned to Lucerne as a civil servant and musician. Ordained priest in 1752, he became organist of the collegiate church, and in 1762 choirmaster. He founded the Lucerne coll. of music in 1760.

Works incl. *Singspiele Hans Hüttenstock* and others; Masses and other church music; arias; instrumental music.

Meyerbeer, Giacomo (actually Jakob Liebmann Beer) (b Berlin, 5 Sep 1791; d Paris, 2 May 1864), German composer. His father Herz Beer, a Jewish banker, gave him every facility to develop his precocious gifts. He was at first trained as a pianist and had some lessons from Clementi during the latter's stay in Berlin. He played in public at the age of 7, but afterwards studied theory and comp. under Zelter, B.A. Weber and Vogler, to whose house at Darmstadt he moved in 1810, being a fellow-student with C.M. von Weber there. His 1st opera was prod. at Munich in 1812 and the 2nd at Stuttgart in 1813. He then went to Vienna and, hearing Hummel play, he retired for further pf. studies, after which he appeared again as a virtuoso.

On Salieri's advice he went to It. to study vocal writing in 1815, and prod. his 1st It. opera at Padua in 1817. In 1823 he tried his luck in Berlin, but without much success, and having prod. *Il crociato* at Venice in 1824, went to Paris for its fp there in 1826. He settled and spent much time there for the rest of his life. He wrote no new work between 1824 and 1831, among the reasons being his father's death, his marriage and the loss of 2 children. In 1831 *Robert le Diable* made him sensationally fashionable in Paris. In 1842 the King of Prus. app. him General Music Dir. in Berlin. He visited Vienna and London in 1847 and the latter again in 1862, when he represented Ger. music at the Internat. Exhibition. His health began to fail about 1850.

Works incl. operas *Jephthas Gelübde* (1812), *Alimelek, oder Die beiden Kalifen*, *Romilda e Costanza* (1817), *Semiramide riconosciuta* (1819), *Emma di Resburgo* (1819), *Margherita d'Anjou* (1820), *L'esule*

di Granata, Das Brandenburger Tor, Il crociato in Egitto (1824), *Robert le Diable* (1831), *Les Huguenots* (1836), *Ein Feldlager in Schlesin* (1844); *Le Prophète* (1849), *L'Étoile du Nord* (1854), *Le Pardon de Ploërmel* (*Dinorah*), *L'Africaine* (1865), *Judith* (unfinished).

Monodrama *Thevelindens Liebe*; incid. music to Michael Beer's (his brother's) drama *Struensee*, Blaze de Bury's *Jeunesse de Goethe* and Aeschylus' *Eumenides*; masque *Das Hoffest von Ferrara*; ballet *Der Fischer und das Milchmädchen* (1810); oratorio *Gott und die Natur* (1811); *Stabat Mater*, Te Deum, psalms and other church music; several cantatas, incl. 2 for the Schiller centenary, 1859, 7 sacred cantatas (Klopstock) for unaccomp. chorus; March for do., 3 Torch Dances, Coronation March, *Overture in the Form of a March* for the London Exhibition; pf. works; songs.

Meyerowitz, Jan (b Breslau, 23 Apr 1913), American composer of German birth. Studied in Berlin with Zemlinsky and Rome with Respighi. Moved to US 1946, citizen from 1951.

Works incl. operas *The Barrier* (1950), *Eastward in Eden* (1951), *Esther* (1957), *Godfather Death* (1961), *Winterballade* (1967); *Silesian Symphony* (1957), oboe concerto (1963), 6 pieces for orch. (1967); Cantatas on texts by E. Dickinson, Cummings and Herrick; chamber music.

Meyrowitz, Selmar (b Bartenstein, E. Prus., 18 Apr 1875; d Toulouse, 24 Mar 1941), German conductor. Studied at the Leipzig Cons. and with Bruch in Berlin. His appts. as opera cond. incl. Karlsruhe, NY, Prague and Berlin, and later he was a concert cond. in Berlin, Hamburg, Vienna, Rome, etc. In 1933 he emigrated to Paris.

Mezza (It. fem.) = *half*, as in *mezza voce* = half-voice, a special way of prod. the voice as if under the breath, resulting not only in a soft tone, but in a quality different from that of the full voice.

Mezzo (It. masc.) = half, as in *mezzo-soprano*, a voice half-way between soprano and contralto in range.

mf (abbr.) = *mezzo forte* (half-loud).

Mi, the old name for the note E (*see* **Solmization**), still used in Lat. countries, and in Tonic Sol-fa the Mediant note in any key, represented by the symbol m, pronounced Me.

Mi contra Fa, a medieval designation of the Tritone (the forbidden interval of the augmented 4th), the Mi being the mediant of the hard hexachord beginning on G.

Miaskovsky, Nikolai Yakovlevich (b Novogeorgievsk nr. Warsaw, 20 Apr 1881; d Moscow, 9 Aug 1950), Russian composer. Son of a Rus. military engineer stationed in Poland, whence the family moved successively to Orenburg, Kazan and Nizhny-Novgorod, where Maiskovsky joined the cadet corps. Intended to follow his father's career, he did not finally take to music until 1907, when he resigned his commission, though he had comp. many pf. preludes, studied with Glière and Krizhanovsky and entered the St Petersburg Cons. in 1906, where he studied with Rimsky-Korsakov, Liadov and Wihtol. In 1914–17 he fought on the Aus. front and was badly wounded; in 1921 he became comp. prof. at the Moscow Cons.

Works incl. oratorio *Kirov is with us*; 27 symphs. (1908–50), 2 sinfoniettas, symph. poems *Silence* (after Poe) and *Alastor* (after Shelley), serenade and *Lyric Concertino* for small orch.; vln. concerto (1938); *Salutatory Overture* on Stalin's 60th birthday (1939); 13 string 4tets; 2 cello and pf. sonatas; 9 pf. sonatas and other pf. pieces; 13 op. nos. of songs.

Miča, František Václav (b Třebič, Morav., 5 Sep 1694; d Jaroměřice, 15 Feb 1744), Moravian tenor and composer. Probably studied in Vienna, and in 1711 entered the service of Count Questenberg in Jaroměřice, becoming *Kapellmeister* in 1722 and there producing 5 operas of his own and many by other comps. 2 symphs. sometimes attrib. to him, though clearly too modern in style, are the work of his nephew, Jan Adam František M. (1746–1811)

Works incl. operas; cantatas; Passion oratorios.

Michael, Roger (Rogier) (b Mons, c 1550; d Dresden, c 1619), Flemish tenor and composer. Studied under his father, Simon M., a musician to the Emperor Ferdinand I. He became a tenor in the electoral chapel at Dresden in 1575 and *Kapellmeister* in 1587, being succeeded in the latter post by Schütz in 1619.

Works incl. introits in the motet style, settings of hymn-tunes in 4 parts and other sacred music. incl. *Christmas Story*.

Michael, Tobias (b Dresden, 13 Jun 1592; d Leipzig, 26 Jun 1657), German composer, son of prec. Studied as a boy chorister under his father in the Dresden court chapel and became music dir. at Sondershausen in 1619. In 1631 he succeeded Schein as cantor of St Thomas's Church at Leipzig.

Works incl. *Musikalische Seelenlust* con-taining sacred madrigals for voices and sacred concertos for voices and instruments (1634–7), other church music.

Micheau, Janine (b Toulouse, 17 Apr 1914; d Paris, 18 Oct 1976), French sopra-no. Debut Paris, Opéra-Comique, 1933, as Cherubino; sang there until 1956 as Mireil-le, Olympia and the 1st local Zerbinetta and Anne Trulove. At the Opéra she took part in the fp of Milhaud's *Bolivar* (1950) and was well known as Sophie, Gilda and Pamina. CG 1937, Micaela. US debut 1938 San Fran-cisco, as Mélisande. At Aix she was heard in Rameau's *Platée* (1955).

Michelangeli, Arturo Benedetti (b Brescia, 5 Jun 1920), Italian pianist. Studied at the Instituto Musicale Venturi in Brescia and at Milan Cons. In 1939 he won the internation-al pf. competition in Geneva. Though he is among the foremost pianists of his day, his concert appearances have been infrequent and much of his time is taken up with teaching. London debut 1946, US 1948.

Micheletti, Gaston (b Tavaco, Corsica, 5 Jan 1892; d Ajaccio, 21 May 1959), French tenor. Debut Rheims 1922, as Faust. He joined the Paris Opéra-Comique in 1925 and was successful there for 20 years as Werther, Don José and Des Grieux. He appeared as guest in Brussels and Monte Carlo.

Micheli, Romano (b Rome, c 1575; d Rome, c 1660), Italian composer. Studied under Soriano, travelled widely in It., became a priest, held appts. at Modena and Aquileia, and returned to Rome in 1625 as *maestro di cappella* of the church of San Luigi de' Fran-cesi.

Works incl. Masses, motets, psalms; mad-rigals, canons.

Microphone, the receiver which transmits and amplifies the sounds of a broadcast perf. It can also be used for other than radio or television purposes, e.g. in theatres and pub-lic halls for the relaying of speech, song and taped sound to amplifiers placed at var. points of the building.

Microtones, the small fractional notes into which the musical scale was divided by the Mex. comp. Julián Carrillo, who invented special instruments for the purpose; earlier, though unsystematic, use of microtones was made by Ives and Bartók. Alois Hába em-ployed quarter-tones from 1920; later fifth and sixth-tones. With the advent of electro-nic music and the growing interest in revi-ving earlier scale temperaments, virtually all pitches have become part of the composer's potential vocabulary.

Middle C, the note C in the centre of the keyboard, variously represented in notation according to the clef used, e.g.:

Midgley, Walter (b Bramley, 1914; d Ramstead, Surrey, 18 Sep 1980), English tenor. He sang with the Carl Rosa chorus before the war and from 1945 was heard at SW as Rodolfo, Turiddu and Almaviva. In 1947 he had much success at CG as Calaf; remained until 1953 as Alfredo, Manrico and Cavaradossi. Edinburgh 1947, as Macduff, with the Glyndebourne Co.

Midsummer Marriage, The, opera by Tippett (lib. by the composer), prod. London, CG, 27 Jan 1955.

Midsummer Night's Dream, A. *See also* **Songe d'une nuit d'été.**

Incid. music by Mendelssohn to Shakespeare's play. Overture comp. summer 1826 fp Stettin in Feb 1827; the rest of the music comp. in 1842 and used for a stage prod. at Potsdam on 14 Oct 1843.

Opera by Britten (lib. from Shakespeare), prod. Aldeburgh, Jubilee Hall, 11 Jun 1960.

Mighty Handful, The. *See* **Kutchka.**

Mignon, opera by A. Thomas (lib. by J. Barbier and M. Carré, based on Goethe's *Wilhelm Meister*), prod. Paris, Opéra-Comique, 17 Nov 1866.

Mignone, Francisco (b São Paulo, 3 Sep 1897; d Rio de Janiero, 18 Feb 1986), Brazilian composer. Studied at São Paulo Cons. and later in Milan, in 1929 becoming prof. at the Nat. Cons. in Rio de Janeiro. Works incl. operas *O contratador dos diamantes* (1924), *El jayon* (= *L'innocente*, 1927); ballet *Maracatú de Chico-Rei* (1933); clar. and bassoon concertos; orchestral music; and songs, etc.

Migot, Georges (Elbert) (b Paris, 27 Feb 1891; d Levallois, nr. Paris, 5 Jan 1976), French composer. Studied with var. masters, incl. Widor, and made a speciality of medieval music. In 1917 he made himself known in Paris by giving a concert of his own, and, holding no official post, he relied on his own efforts to keep before the public. Works incl. opera *Le Rossignol en amour* (1926); ballets *La Fête de la bergère* (1924), *Le Paravent de laque*, *Les Aveux et les promesses*; Psalm xix for chorus and orch., *The Sermon on the Mount* for solo voices, chorus, org. and strings; 13 symphs (1919–67), *Les Agrestides*, *3 Guirlandes sonores* for strings; *La Jungle* for organ and orch.; *Le Livre des danseries* for vln., fl. and pf. and other chamber music; songs.

Mihalovich, Odön (Péter Jozsef de) (b Fericsancze, 13 Sep 1842; d Budapest, 22 Apr 1929), Hungarian composer. Studied with Mosonyi at Budapest, Hauptmann at Leipzig, Cornelius and Bülow in Munich. In 1887 he succeeded Liszt as director of the Music Acad. at Budapest, and remained there until 1919.

Works incl. operas *Hagbarth und Signe* (1882) and *Wieland der Schmied* (Wagner's lib.) (both in Ger.), *Toldi Szerelme* (*Toldi's Love*) and *Eliána* (after Tennyson's *Idylls of the King*, prod. 1908), (both in Hung.); 4 symphs. (1879–1902), *Faust* overture (after Goethe), 4 Ballads for orch.

Mihalovici, Marcel (b Bucharest, 22 Oct 1898; d Paris, 12 Aug 1985), Rumanian composer. Studied with d'Indy in Paris and joined a group of advanced Fr. and Rus. comps. there after the 1914–18 war. He was married to the pianist Monique Haas.

Works incl. opera *L'Intransigeant Pluton* (1928); ballets *Karagueuz* (1926), *Divertissement* and others; *Cortège des divinités infernales* (from the opera), *Introduction au mouvement*, *Notturno* and fantasy for orch.; 3 string 4tets (1923, 1931, 1946); string trio; vln. and pf. sonata, sonatina for ob. and pf.

Mikado, The, or The Town of Titipu, operetta by Sullivan (lib. by W.S. Gilbert), prod. London, Savoy Theatre, 14 Mar 1885.

Mikhailova, Maria (b Kharkov, 3 Jun 1866; d Leningrad, 4 Nov 1921), Russian soprano. Debut St Petersburg 1892, as Marguerite de Valois; in 1895 she was Electra there, in the fp of Taneiev's *Oresteia* trilogy, and until 1912 she was heard as Lakmé, Juliette, Ludmila and Amina. She made many early recordings and was guest in Prague, Moscow and Tokyo.

Mikrokosmos (*Microcosm*), a set of 153 small pf. pieces by Bartók, arr. in progressive order and pub. in 6 vols., setting the player var. problems of modern technique, each piece being written on a partic. principle or system (special rhythms, time-signatures, chords, intervals, atonal or bitonal combs., etc.), comp. 1926–37, pub. 1940.

Milán, Luis (b Valencia, c 1500; d Valencia, after 1561), Spanish vihuelist and composer. He was the son of a nobleman, Don Luis de M., played the vihuela, visited It. and Port. One of the first composers to write tempo indications.

Works, all pub. in *El Maestro* (1536), the

earliest surviving vihuela collection, incl. fantasies and pavans for vihuela, Span. and Port. *villancicos*, Spanish ballads and It. sonnets for voice and vihuela.

Milanese Chant. *See* **Ambrosian Chant.**

Milano, Francesco da (b Monza, ? 18 Aug 1497; d 15 Apr 1543), Italian lutenist. He served successively at the Gonzaga Court (Mantua), with Cardinal Ippolito de' Medici and at the Papal court of Paul II. Well known as lute virtuoso and wrote 3 vols. of pieces for his instrument.

Milanov (orig. Kunc), **Zinka** (b Zagreb, 17 May 1906), Yugoslav soprano. Studied first in Zagreb and then with Ternina, and Carpi in Prague, making her debut in Ljublana in 1927 as the *Trovatore* Leonora. From 1928 to 1935 she sang in Zagreb and from 1937 her career centred on the NY Met; roles there until 1966 incl. Norma, Donna Anna, Tosca and Gioconda. She was esp. known for her Verdi singing.

Milder-Hauptmann, (Pauline) Anna (b Constantinople, 13 Dec 1785; d Berlin, 29 Aug 1838), Austrian soprano. The daughter of a courier in the Aus. diplomatic service, she was brought to Vienna as a child and on the recommendation of Schikaneder studied singing under Tomaselli and Salieri, making her 1st stage appearance in 1803. Beethoven wrote the part of Leonore in *Fidelio* for her and she early became interested in Schubert's songs; she sang in the fp of S.'s last work, *Der Hirt auf dem Felsen*. In 1810 she married the jeweller Hauptmann. She sang in Mendelssohn's revival of Bach's *St Matthew Passion* in 1829. Famous in Gluck's *Iphigénie en Tauride* and also sang in operas by Süssmayr, Weigl and Cherubini.

Mildmay, Audrey (b Hurstmonceaux, 19 Dec 1900; d London, 31 May 1953), English soprano. Orig. a member of the Carl Rosa Opera Co., she married John Christie in 1931 and with him founded the Glyndebourne Festival, which opened on 28 May 1934. She sang at the Fest. 1934–9 as Susanna, Zerlina and Norina. In 1947 she and Rudolf Bing began the Edinburgh Festival.

Milford, Robin (Humphrey) (b Oxford, 22 Jan 1903; d Lyme Regis, 29 Dec 1959), English composer. Educ. at Rugby and studied music at the RCM, where his masters were Holst, Vaughan Williams and R.O. Morris.

Works incl. oratorio *A Prophet in the Land*; cantata *Wind, Rain and Sunshine*, *Bemerton Cantatas*, *5 Songs of Escape* for unaccomp. chorus; symph., concerto gros-

so, double fugue for orch.; vln. concerto, *The Dark Thrush* (on Hardy's poem) for vln. and small orch.; 2 *Easter Meditations* for org.; pf. works; songs; part-songs.

Milhaud, Darius (b Aix-en-Provence, 4 Sep 1892; d Geneva, 22 Jun 1974), French composer. Studied vln. and comp. at the Paris Cons. from 1909, under Gédalge, Widor and d'Indy. His teachers also incl. Dukas. In 1917–19 he was attaché to the Fr. Legation at Rio de Janeiro, where he met Paul Claudel, who collaborated frequently with him as librettist. About 1920 he became a member of 'Les Six', and in 1922 he was repres. for the 1st time at the festival of the ISCM. He emigrated to USA in 1940, but returned to Paris in 1947, where he taught at the Cons.

Works incl. STAGE: operas *La Brebis égarée* (1923), *Les Malheurs d'Orphée* (1926), *Esther de Carpentras* (1938), *Le Pauvre Matelot* (1927), *Christophe Colomb* (1930), *Maximilien, Bolivar* (1950), minute-operas *L'Enlèvement d' Europe* (1927), *L'Abandon d'Ariane, La Délivrance de Thésée* (1928), *La Mère Coupable* (1966); ballets *L'Homme et son désir* (1918), *Le Bœuf sur le toit* (1919), *Les Mariés de la Tour Eiffel* (with others, 1921), *La Création du monde* (1923), *Salade, Le Train bleu* (1924), *La Bien-aimée* (after Schubert and Liszt, 1928), *Jeux de printemps* (1944); incid. music for works by Claudel: *Protée, L'Annonce faite à Marie* and *Oreste* trans. from Aeschylus (*Agamemnon, Les Choëphores* and *Les Euménides*, 1917–22), and for Rolland's *14 Juillet* (with 6 others).

ORCH.: works incl. 12 symphs. for large orch. (1940–62), 2 symph. suites, *Suite provençale* (1937), *Sérénade, Suite française, Jeux de printemps, Saudades do Brazil*; 6 symphs. for small orch. (1917–22); 5 études, *Ballade, Le Carnaval d'Aix* (1926) and 5 concertos for pf. and orch.; concerto and *Concertino de printemps* for vln. and orch. (1934), vla, cello and clar. concertos and concerto for perc. and small orch.

CHAMBER: 18 string 4tets (1912–62); wind 5tet *La Cheminée du Roi René* (1939); 2 vln and pf. sonatas, 2 sonatas for vla. and pf., sonata for 2 vlns. and pf.; sonata for pf., fl., ob. and clar.; sonatinas for fl. and pf. and clar. and pf.; some smaller instrumental pieces; sonatina for org.; 6 pf. works incl. suite, sonata, *Printemps* (2 vols.), *Saudades do Brazil* (2 vols, 1920–1), *3 Rag Caprices*; suite *Scaramouche* (1939) and *Bal martiniquais* for 2 pfs.

SOLO VOCAL AND CHORAL: 14 books of

songs incl. *Poèmes de Léo Latil, Poèmes de Paul Claudel, Poèmes juifs, Poèmes de Cocteau, Les Soirées de Pétrograde; Machines agricoles* for voice and 7 instruments, *Catalogue des fleurs* for voice and chamber orch. (1920); 2 psalms for baritone and orch.; Psalm cxxi for male voices; cantata *Cain and Abel*; 4 *Poèmes* for voice and vln., *Pacem in Terris* for chorus & orch. (1963).

Military Band, a wind band attached to military regiments and used by them for their ceremonial occasions, but also often engaged to play for the entertainment of the general public in parks, at the seaside, etc. It incl. woodwind, brass and perc.

'Military' Symphony, Haydn's symph. no. 100 in G maj. (no. 8 of the 'Salomon' symphs.), comp. for London in 1794; so called because of the tpt. call and perc. effects found in the 2nd movement.

Mill, Arnold van (b Schiedam, 26 Mar 1921), Dutch bass. Debut Brussels, 1946. He sang in a revival of Spontini's *Agnes von Hohenstaufen* at Florence, in 1953, and in the same year joined the Hamburg Opera. Bayreuth 1951–60, as Hunding, Daland and Fafner; recorded Marke under Solti. He appeared as guest at Berlin, Edinburgh and Rio, as Zaccaria, Osmin and Abul Hassan in Cornelius's *Barbier von Bagdad.*

Miller, Jonathan (b London, 21 Jul 1934), English producer. He studied at Cambridge and qualified as doctor of medicine. Prod. plays for Old Vic and National Theatre Cos. 1st opera prod. Goehr's *Arden Must Die,* for New Opera Co. at SW, 1974. In 1975 he prod. *The Cunning Little Vixen* at Glyndebourne and *Così fan tutte* for Kent Opera. ENO since 1978: *Figaro, Arabella, Otello* and *Don Giovanni* (1985). His Mafia-style *Rigoletto* (1982) provoked some local opposition when the ENO visited NY in 1984. By modern standards, Miller's work is faithful to the composers' intentions; his *Mikado* (ENO, 1986) made a successful transition from Japan to 1920s England.

Millico, Giuseppe (b Terlizzi nr. Modena, 19 Jan 1737; d Naples, 2 Oct 1802), Italian castrato soprano and composer. He was discovered by Gluck, in whose *Le feste d'Apollo* he sang at Parma in 1769. Engaged by the imp. opera in Vienna, he sang the following year in the fp. of Gluck's *Paride ed Elena.* Later visited London, Paris and Berlin, and from 1780 lived in Naples.

Works incl. operas *La pietà d'amore* (pub. 1782), *La Zelinda, Ipermestra, Le Cinesi* (1780); cantata *Angelica e Medoro* (with Cimarosa).

Millo, Aprile (b New York, 14 Apr 1958), American soprano. After study in Hollywood she sang Aida at Utah in 1980. Her Giselda in a NY concert perf. of *I Lombardi* was much applauded, and she made her Met debut in 1985, as Amelia Boccanegra. At La Scala she has appeared as Elvira (*Ernani*). One of the most promising Verdi sopranos of her generation.

Millöcker, Karl (b Vienna, 29 Apr 1842; d Baden nr. Vienna, 31 Dec 1899), Austrian composer and conductor. Studied at the Vienna Cons. and became cond. at Graz in 1864 and at the Harmonietheater in Vienna, 1866. In 1869 he was app. cond. at the Theater an der Wien there and prod. operettas for it.

Works incl. operettas *Der tote Gast* (1865), *Die beiden Binder, Diana* (1867), *Die Fraueninsel, Ein Abenteuer in Wien* (1873), *Das verwunschene Schloss* (1878), *Gräfin Dubarry* (1879), *Apajune der Wassermann, Der Bettelstudent* (1882), *Der Feldprediger* (1884), *Der Vice-Admiral, Die sieben Schwaben* (1887), *Der arme Jonathan* (1890), *Das Sonntagskind* (1892), *Gasparone* and many others; numerous pf. pieces.

Mills, Charles (b Asheville, NC, 8 Jan 1914; d New York, 7 Mar 1982), American composer. Studied with a 6 years' scholarship under Copland, Sessions and Roy Harris, 2 years with each, and later devoted himself entirely to comp.

Works incl. music for solo dance *John Brown;* 5 symphs. (1940–80), slow movement for string orch.; concertino for fl. and orch., prelude for fl. and strings; Festival Overture for chorus and orch.; *Ars poetica* for unaccomp. chorus (1940); chamber symph. for 11 insts. (1939), chamber concerto for 10 insts, chamber concertino for woodwind 5tet, 5 string 4tets (1939–59), pf. trio in D min., sonatas for cello, vln. and pf.

Milner, Anthony (b Bristol, 13 May 1925), English composer. Studied pf. with H. Fryer and comp. with R.O. Morris and later with Seiber (1944–7). From 1947 to 1962 he taught at Morley Coll., when he was app. to the RCM and then lecturer at King's College, London Univ., in 1965.

Works incl. 2 symphs. (1972, 1978), *Sinfonia Pasquale* for string orch., *April Prologue* for orch.; *The Song of Akhenaten* for sop. and chamber orch. (1954); cantatas *Salutatio Angelica* (1948), *The City of Desolation* (1955), *St Francis, The Water and the Fire* (1961), *Emmanuel Cantata* (1975);

Mass for *a cappella* chorus (1951); string 4tet (1975), ob. 4tet, wind 5tet; songs.

Milnes, Sherrill (b Downers Grove, Ill., 10 Jan 1935), American baritone. He joined Boris Goldovsky's touring co. in 1960, and studied with Ponselle in Baltimore. In 1964 he sang Rossini's Figaro at Milan and made his NY, City Opera, debut as Valentin; repeated the role the next year at the Met. London, CG, from 1971 as Renato, Luna, Macbeth and Boccanegra. In 1977 he sang Don Giovanni at Salzburg. Other roles incl. Scarpia, Iago, Don Carlo, Thomas' Hamlet and Scindia in Massenet's *Le Roi de Lahore*.

Milstein, Nathan (b Odessa, 31 Dec 1904), American violinist of Russian birth. Studied 1st at Odessa School of Music and then in St Petersburg with Auer at the Cons. At 1st he appeared publicly with the pianist Horowitz, then moved to Europe in 1925 where he built up his reputation. US debut 1929, with Philadelphia Orch. One of the most musicianly among contemporary virtuosi.

Milton, opera by Spontini (lib. by V.J.E. de Jouy and M. Dieulafoy), prod. Paris, Opéra-Comique, 27 Nov 1804. A 2nd Milton was planned by Spontini in 1838, when he visited Eng. in the summer to study the environment. It was to be entitled *Miltons Tod und Busse für den Königsmord* (*Milton's Death and Expiation for the King's Murder*) (lib. by E. Raupach), but turned into *Das verlorene Paradies* (*Paradise Lost*); it remained unfinished.

Milton, John (b Stanton St John nr. Oxford, *c* 1563; d London, buried 15 Mar 1647), English composer, father of John M., the poet. Educ. at Christ Church, Oxford. He is said to have received a gold medal from a Pol. prince for an In Nomine in 40 parts, was cast out by his father as a Protestant, went to London and in 1600 became a member of the Scriveners' Co., marrying Sarah Jeffrey about that time. Having made a fair fortune as a scribe, he retired to Horton (Bucks.) in 1632, but after his wife's death moved to Reading, *c* 1640 and back to London in 1643, where he lived with his son John.

Works incl. var. sacred pieces for several voices; madrigal contrib. to *The Triumphes of Oriana*, 4 vocal pieces contrib. to Leighton's *Teares or Lamentacions*; 2 tunes for Ravenscroft's Psalter; 5 fancies for viols.

Mines of Sulphur, The, opera by R.R. Bennett (lib. by Beverley Cross), prod. London, SW, 24 Feb 1965, cond. C. Davis.

Minghetti, Angelo (b Bologna, 6 Dec 1889; d Milan, 10 Feb 1957), Italian tenor. He sang in Italy from 1911 and had an interna-

tional career from 1921; appearances at Rio, Chicago and Buenos Aires. La Scala debut 1923 as Rodolfo; returned until 1932. At CG he was successful 1926–34. At Rome he created Donello in the fp of Respighi's *La Fiamma* (1934).

Mingotti (*née* **Valentini**), **Regina** (b Naples, 16 Feb 1722; d Neuburg o/Danube, 1 Oct 1808), Austro-Italian soprano, who became an orphan as a child, was sent to a convent by an uncle at Graz, but had to leave on his death and married the It. musician Pietro M. (attached to the Dresden Opera), who had her taught singing by Porpora. She made her debut at Hamburg in 1743. She appeared in It., Spain, Eng. and Fr. in operas by Porpora, Hasse and Jommelli. Her brothers Pietro and Angelo were opera impresarios, active in Dresden, Graz, Prague and Hamburg.

Minim, in modern notation the white note with a tail on it, with the value of half a semibreve or 2 crotchets:♩; orig. the shortest note-value (Lat. *minima*).

Minimalism, a musical style initiated in the 1960s and represented chiefly by the work of comps. such as Terry Riley, Steve Reich and Philip Glass. (See also separate entries for these comps.) The simplest possible material is repeated many times, occasionally with small changes intro. gradually or with the addition of other comparably simple repetitive material that eventually changes in its synchronisation. The style is admirably suited to an age dominated by machines, and has been termed by the Belgian writer Wim Merten as Repetitive Music.

Minnesinger or **Minnesänger** (Ger. plur.), the singers in 12th- and 13th-cent. Ger. who cultivated minstrelsy on the lines of that of the Troubadours in Fr., and preceded the Meistersinger, but unlike them were aristocrats, not middle-class merchants and artisans.

Minor, 1 of the 2 predominant scales (the other being Maj.) of the tonal system. There are 2 forms of the minor scale: the harmonic and the melodic. *See* **Harmonic Minor, Melodic Minor.**

Minor Intervals, 2nds, 3rds, 6ths and 7ths which are a semitone smaller than the corresponding Major intervals, e.g.:

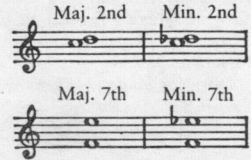

Minore (It.) = Minor. In older music the word is often used as a warning in the course of a comp. which is predominantly in a maj. key.

Minotaur, The, ballet in 1 act by Elliott Carter; comp. 1947, prod. NY, 26 Mar 1947.

Minstrel, orig. the English equivalent of the French *Jongleur* and the German *fahrender Sänger,* but in a wider sense any travelling musician.

Minton, Yvonne (b Sydney, 4 Dec 1938), Australian mezzo. She studied in Sydney and moved to Europe in 1960. London, CG, from 1965 as Marina, Dorabella, Brangaene, Waltraute, Orpheus, Sextus and Thea in the 1970 fp of Tippett's *The Knot Garden.* She sang Octavian at Chicago in 1970 and at the NY Met in 1973. She appeared at Bayreuth in the 1976 centenary prod. of the *Ring* (as Fricka and Waltraute). In 1979, at the Paris Opéra, she was Countess Geschwitz, in the fp of completed 3-act version of Berg's *Lulu.* Retired from stage in 1983, but continued to appear in concert. CBE 1980.

Minuet, a dance of French origin (*menuet,* from *menu* – small) 1st appearing in artistic music about the time of Lully. It is in moderately animated 3–4 time and in its later developments always has a contrasting trio section, after which the 1st section is repeated. It was not a regular feature of the suite, but appeared in many of its examples; on the other hand it was the only dance form normally retained in sonatas, 4tets, symphs., etc.

Minuetto (It.). This, not 'Menuetto', is the correct It. name for the Minuet.

'Minute Waltz', the nickname sometimes given to Chopin's Waltz in Db maj., op. 64 no.1.

Miracle in the Gorbals, ballet by Bliss (scenario by M. Benthall, choreog. by Robert Helpmann), prod. London, Prince's Theatre, 26 Oct 1944.

Miracle, The, nickname of Haydn's symph. no. 96, in D maj. (no. 4 of the 'Salomon' symphs.), written for London in 1791. The name is due to the story that a chandelier fell from the ceiling at the fp, when the audience miraculously escaped injury; but in fact the accident occurred at the fp of symph. no. 102 in Bb maj. (1794–5).

Miracles of our Lady, cycle of 4 1-act operas by Martinů: *The Wise and Foolish Virgins* (lib. by V. Nezval after 12th-cent. Fr. text); *Little Mariken of Nijmegen* (lib. by H. Gheon after 15th-cent. Flem. legend); *The*

Nativity (lib. by comp. after Moravian folk texts); *The Legend of Sister Pasqualina* (lib. by comp. after poem by J. Zeyer and folk texts). Composed 1933–4, fp Brno, 23 Feb 1935.

Miraculous Mandarin, The (*A csodálatos mandarin*), pantomime in 1 act by Bartók (scenario by M. Lengyel); 1918–19, prod. Cologne, 27 Nov 1926. Orch. Suite perf. Budapest, 15 Oct 1928, cond. Ernö Dohnányi. The Mandarin of the title is mugged by a prostitute and her gang, but he cannot die until he is sexually united with the woman who has attempted to murder him.

Mireille, opera by Gounod (lib. by M. Carré, based on the poem *Mirèio* by F. Mistral), prod. Paris, Théâtre Lyrique, 19 Mar 1864.

Mirliton (Fr.), a toy instrument similar to the Eunuch fl. (*q.v.*). Was also known as Kazoo in Eng.

Miroirs, set of 5 pf. pieces by Ravel; comp. 1905, fp Paris, 6 Jan 1906: *Noctuelles, Oiseaux tristes, Une barque sur l'océan* (orch. vers., fp Paris, 3 Feb 1907), *Alborada del gracioso* (orch. vers. fp Paris, 17 May 1919), *La Vallée des Cloches.*

Mirror Canon ⎱
Mirror Fugue ⎰ a Canon or Fugue in which 2 or more voices are so inverted that the intervals appear simultaneously upside down as well as right side up, looking on paper like a reflection in water.

Miserly Knight, The (*Skupoy ritsar*), opera in 3 scenes by Rakhmaninov (lib. by comp. after Pushkin); 1903–5, prod. Moscow, Bolshoy, 24 Jan 1906.

Misón, Luis (b Barcelona, ?; d Madrid, 13 Feb 1766), Spanish woodwind player and composer. He entered the royal orch. at Madrid in 1748 as flautist and oboist, became cond. there in 1756 and prod. his 1st *tonadilla* in 1757.

Works incl. numerous *tonadillas,* 3 operas *La festa cinese, El tutor enamorado* and *El amor a todos vence;* 6 sonatas for fl. and bass.

Miss Julie, opera by Ned Rorem (lib. by K. Elmslie after Strindberg), prod NY, 5 Nov 1965.

Opera by William Alwyn (lib. by comp. after Strindberg); comp. 1961–76, fp BBC 16 Jul 1977.

Missa (Lat.) = Mass.

Missa parodia (Lat., lit. 'parody Mass'), a term arising from a mistaken conjunction of the words *Missa* and *parodia* which occur separately on the title-page of a Mass by the 16th-cent. comp. Jacques Paix. His Mass is described as 'Parodia mottetae Domine da nobis auxilium', i.e. it is based on material from the motet cited. Neither in this work nor in any other are the words *Missa* and *Parodia* joined together. Many 15th- and 16th-cent. Mass cycles were based on material from a motet or polyphonic song, usually named in the title.

Missa pro defunctis (Lat.) = Mass for the dead. *See* **Requiem.**

Missa solemnis (or **solennis**) (Lat.) = Solemn Mass, a title sometimes used by comps. for a Mass of a particularly festive or elaborate kind, e.g. Beethoven's op. 123. Schubert also used it, and it occurs in Fr. as *Messe solennelle* (e.g. Gounod). The title is now used partic. for Beethoven's work, comp. in 1818–23; fp St Petersburg, 7 Apr 1824. 3 sections were given in Vienna on 7 May 1824, in the concert with the fp of the Choral Symph.

Misura (It.) = measure, time; thus *senza m.* = without time, not strictly in time. Also the It. term for 'bar'.

Mitchell, Donald (Charles Peter) (b London, 6 Feb 1925), English music critic, publisher and author. Largely self-taught in music, though he studied for a year at Durham Univ. (1949–50). He has specialized in late 19th- and 20th-cent. music, esp. Mahler (3 vols. of a projected 4 pub. 1958–84), Reger and Britten. Chairman, Faber Music, from 1977.

Mitchell, Leona (b Enid, Okla., 13 Oct 1948), American soprano. Debut San Francisco 1973, Micaela; NY Met debut 1975, same role, and has since sung Pamina, Musetta and the *Forza* Leonora. At Sydney in 1985 she sang her first *Trovatore* Leonora. Other roles incl. Elvira (*Ernani*), Amelia and Butterfly.

Mitridate Eupatore, Il (*Mithridates Eupator*), opera by A. Scarlatti (lib. by G.F. Roberti), prod. Venice, Teatro San Giovanni Grisostomo, Carnival 1707.

Mitridate, Rè di Ponto (*Mithridates, King of Pontus*), opera by Mozart (lib. by V.A. Cigna-Santi, based on a tragedy by Racine), prod. Milan, Teatro Regio Ducal, 26 Dec 1770.

Mitropoulos, Dimitri (b Athens, 1 Mar 1896; d Milan, 2 Nov 1960), Greek conductor, pianist and composer. He studied pf. and comp. at the Athens Cons. and subsequently with Gilson in Brussels and Busoni in Berlin. He cond. the Athens Cons. Orch. from 1929 to 1937, Minneapolis SO from 1937 to 1949, New York PO from 1950 to 1958; gave early perfs. in the US of works by Berg, Krenek and Schoenberg and the fp of

Barber's *Vanessa* (NY Met, 1958).

Works incl. opera *Sœur Béatrice*; concerto grosso for orch.; string 4tet, vln. sonata; pf. music; songs, etc.

Mixolydian Mode, the scale beginning on G on the white notes of the pf. keyboard.

Mixtures, org. stops controlling a range of pipes with more than 1 note to each key, sounding not only the fundamental note but some of its harmonics.

Mizler (von Kolof), Lorenz Christoph (b Heidenheim, Württemberg, 25 Jul 1711; d Warsaw, Mar 1778), German music writer and editor. One of Bach's pupils at St Thomas's School, Leipzig; founded the Assoc. for Musical Science there in 1738 and ed. a periodical, *Neu eröffnete musikalische Bibliothek*, 1736–54.

Mlada, opera-ballet commissioned from Borodin, Cui, Mussorgsky and Rimsky-Korsakov by the Russ. Imp. Theatres in 1872, but never completed (lib. by V.A. Krilov).

Opera by Rimsky-Korsakov (lib. as above), prod. St Petersburg, 1 Nov 1892.

Mládí (*Youth*), suite for wind sextet in 4 movts. by Janáček, fp Brno, 21 Oct 1924, by professors of the Brno Cons.

Mlynarski, Emil (b Kibarty, 18 Jul 1870; d Warsaw, 5 Apr 1935), Polish violinist, conductor and composer. Studied at St Petersburg. Cond. of the Warsaw PO from 1901 to 1905 and dir. of the Cons. there from 1904 to 1909. Cond. of the Scot. Orch., 1910–15. Resumed his posts in Warsaw in 1919. From 1929 to 1931 taught at the Curtis Inst., Philadelphia.

Works incl. opera *A Summer Night* (1914); *Polonia* symph. (1910); vln. concerto in D min. (1897).

Mock Trumpet, an early English name for the clarinet.

Modal Notation, a form of notation in use for vocal music in the 12th and early 13th cents., where the rhythm was determined not by the shapes of individual notes but by the various types of ligature in which they were combined according to one or other of the rhythmic modes.

Moderato (It. = moderate), a direction used either singly or in comb. with words meaning fast or slow.

Moderne, Jacques (b *c* 1495 Pinguente, Istria; d Lyons, *c* 1562), French 16th-cent. musician and pub., (?) of It. stock. He became *maître de chapelle* at the church of Notre-Dame du Confort at Lyons and about 1530 estab. a printing-press there, pub. books of Masses, motets and *chansons* between 1532 and 1567, with contribs. by var. comp., incl. himself.

Modes, the scales which became estab. in the Middle Ages and were still accepted, at least in theory, in the 16th cent. They are easily identified by reference to the white notes of the pf. keyboard. They were orig. known by the Gk. words for 1st, 2nd, 3rd and 4th as follows:

1. *Protus:* D-D
2. *Deuterus:* E-E
3. *Tritus:* F-F
4. *Tetrardus:* G-G

A distinction was made between the Authentic modes, with the compass given above, and the four Plagal modes which had the same final notes but a different range:

1. A-A (with final D)
2. B-B (with final E)
3. C-C (with final F)
4. D-D (with final G)

The whole series was later renumbered and Gk. names were attached, in the belief that the modes corresponded to ancient Gk. modes. In each mode a 'reciting note' (now often called 'dominant') was estab. In the Authentic modes this note is normally a 5th above the final, and in the Plagal modes a 3rd below the note in the Authentic mode; but where it would logically be B, the note C is substituted. The complete scheme is as follows (*F.* = Final, *D.* = Dominant):

No.	Name	Range	F.	D.
I	Dorian	D-D	D	A
II	Hypodorian	A-A	D	F
III	Phrygian	E-E	E	C
IV	Hypophrygian	B-B	E	A
V	Lydian	F-F	F	C
VI	Hypolydian	C-C	F	A
VII	Mixolydian	G-G	G	D
VIII	Hypomixolydian	D-D	G	C

The frequent intro. of Bb in medieval music tended to change the character of some of the modes. Thus mode I with Bb was simply a transposed form of a mode with a final on A, and mode V with Bb was identical with a scale of C major transposed to F. Hence Glareanus in the 16th cent. proposed that 2 further modes with their plagal forms, should be recognized, as follows:

No.	Name	Range	F.	D.
IX	Æolian	A-A	A	E
X	Hypoæolian	E-E	A	C
XI	Ionian	C-C	C	G
XII	Hypoionian	G-G	C	E

Modes, Rhythmic, the rhythms of medieval music were classified in 6 patterns (corresponding to poetic rhythms), units of which, in modern notation, were as below; (see illustration)

Mödl, Martha (b Nuremberg, 22 Mar 1912), German soprano. Studied in Nuremberg and made her debut in 1942. Sang at Bayreuth 1951–1967 as Kundry, Gutrune, Sieglinde, Isolde and Brünnhilde and has specialized in dramatic roles, esp. Wagner. Hamburg from 1949, London 1950–72. Other roles incl. Leonore, Carmen and Clytemnestra.

Modulation, the art of changing from one key to another in the course of a comp. by means of logical harmonic progressions.

Moeran, E(rnest) J(ohn) (b Heston, Middlesex, 31 Dec 1894; d Kenmare, Co. Kerry,

RHYTHMIC MODES

Ir., 1 Dec 1950), English composer of Irish descent. He lived in Norfolk in his childhood, his father, a clergyman, holding a living there. Educ. at Uppingham School and later studied music at the RCM in London. After serving in the 1914–18 war, he continued his studies with Ireland. In 1923 he came before the public with a concert of his works given in London, but after some years spent there he retired to Herefordshire.

Works incl. Magnificat and Nunc Dimittis, Te Deum and Jubilate, 2 anthems; *Nocturne* for baritone, chorus and orch. (1934), *Songs of Springtime* and suite *Phyllida and Corydon* for unaccomp. chorus (1934), *Blue-eyed Spring* for baritone and chorus, madrigals, part-songs and folk-song arrs.

Sinfonietta, 2 rhapsodies, symph. impression *In the Mountain Country* for orch. (1921), 2 pieces for small orch. *Whythorne's Shadow* (1931) and *Lonely Waters* (1932), symph. in G min. (1934–7); concertos for pf., vln. and cello (1942–5); string 4tet in A min., string trio in G maj., pf. trio in D maj., sonata for 2 vlns., vln. and pf. sonata in E min.; song cycle *Ludlow Town* (texts by Housman) for bar. and pf. (1920); *7 Poems of James Joyce* for bar. and pf. (1929), etc.

Moeschinger, Albert (b Basle, 10 Jan 1897; d Thun, 25 Sep 1985), Swiss composer. Studied at Berne, Leipzig and Munich, in the latter place under Courvoisier. In 1927 he settled at Berne as prof., but in 1943 he retired to Saas Fee, Ct Valais, and later to Ascona.

Works incl. motet *Gottes Pfad*, cantata *Angelus Silesius*, *Das Posthorn* for male chorus and orch., cantata *Tag unseres Volks*, Mass for chorus and organ (1943), part-songs and other choral works; 5 symphs. incl. *Symphonie à la gloire de ...* and suite for orch., variations on a theme by Purcell for strings and perc., divertimento for strings, *Fantasia 1944* for chamber orch.; 5 pf. concertos, vln. concerto; 6 string 4tets, pf. 5tet, 6 wind trios, etc.

Moffat, Alfred (b Edinburgh, 4 Dec 1866; d London, 9 Jun 1950), Scottish composer and editor. Studied in Berlin and worked there for a time. Settled in London in the 1890s and ed. a large collection of old string music, incl. many English and French works, also several vols. of Scottish, Welsh and Irish folksongs.

Moffo, Anna (b Wayne, Penn., 27 Jun 1932), American soprano. Studied at Curtis Institute, Philadelphia, in NY and in Rome, making her debut on Italian television in 1956 as Butterfly. NY Met from 1959 as Violetta, Pamina, Gilda, Manon, Mélisande and Marguerite.

Mohaupt, Richard (b Breslau, 14 Sep 1904; d Reichenau, Austria, 3 Jul 1957), German conductor and composer. Studied at Breslau Univ. He cond. opera at several German towns and later toured as cond. in Rus. His ballet was prod. in Berlin in 1936, but soon afterwards his works were forbidden by the Nazi régime because he did not subscribe to its ideology and refused to divorce his Jewish wife. In USA, 1939–1955.

Works incl. operas *Die Wirtin von Pinsk* (1937) and *Boleslav der Schamhafte*, comic opera for children; ballets *Die Gaunerstreiche der Courasche* (after Grimmelshausen, 1936) and *Lysistrata* (after Aristophanes, 1941), ballet for children; symph., concerto, *Drei Episoden* and *Stadtpfeifermusik* (on Dürer's mural *Nürnberger Stadtpfeifer*, for orch. (1939); pf. concerto, 1938), vln. concerto (1945).

Moïse (*Moses*), opera by Rossini, Fr. version of *Mosè in Egitto* (lib. by G.L. Balochi and V.J.E. de Jouy), prod. Paris, Opéra, 26 Mar 1827.

Moiseiwitsch, Benno (b Odessa, 22 Mar 1890; d London, 9 Apr 1963), English pianist of Russian birth. He studied at the Imp. Music Acad., Odessa, winning the Rubinstein Prize at the age of 9, and from 1904 to 1908 with Leschetizky in Vienna. He first appeared as a soloist in 1908 in London, where he subsequently settled, becoming a British subject in 1937. After World War I he embarked on a series of tours which took him to every continent in the world. US debut NY, 1919. Best known in Russian music.

Moissonneurs, Les (*The Reapers*), opera by Duni (lib. by C.S. Favart, based on an incident in Thomson's *Seasons*), prod. Paris, Comédie-Italienne, 27 Jan 1768.

Moke (or **Mocke** or **Mooke**), **Marie** (**Félicité Denise**) (b Paris, 4 Jul 1811; d Saint-Josse-ten-Noode nr. Brussels, 30 Mar 1875), French pianist. Studied under Herz, Moscheles and Kalkbrenner, and toured very successfully. Berlioz fell in love with her before he went to Rome in 1830 and she became engaged to him, but married Camille Pleyel, as whose wife she made an international reputation. Pf. prof. at the Brussels Cons., for 24 years until 1872.

Moldenhauer, Hans (b Mainz, 13 Dec 1906; d Spokane, Wash., 19 Oct 1987), American musicologist. Studied with Rosbaud in Mainz and was active as a *répétiteur* and cond. in different European cities. In 1939 he went to the USA, where after further studies he became director and then president of the Spokane (Washington) Cons. and lecturer at the Univ. of Washington. Moldenhauer's most important contrib. to scholarship was his recovery of a large number of Webern MSS. and documents, including some previously unknown works, and their pub. Books on Webern incl. *The Death of Anton W.*, *A Drama in Documents* (1961), *Anton W: Chronicle of his Life and Work* (1978). Became blind in 1980.

Moldoveanu, Vasile (b Consantine, 6 Oct 1935), Rumanian tenor. Debut Bucharest 1966; guest in Brussels, Dresden and Barcelona. Member of Stuttgart Opera from 1973. NY Met debut 1977, Rodolfo; CG 1979, Don Carlos. At Munich and Vienna he has been heard as Alfredo, the Duke of Mantua and Edgardo. Also sings Ottavio, Tamino and Pedrillo.

Molière (Jean-Baptiste Poquelin) (1622–1673), French dramatist. *See* **Ariadne auf Naxos** (*Bourgeois Gentilhomme*, R. Strauss), **Auric** (*Les Fâcheux*), **Bourgeois Gentilhomme** (R. Strauss), **Charpentier** (**M.-A.**) (*Comtesse d'Escarbagnas* and *Malade imaginaire*), **Festes de l'Amour** (Lully), **Galuppi** (*Vertuouse ridicole*), **Grétry** (*Amphitryon*), **Grosz** (*Sganarell*), **Haug** (*Tartuffe*), **Joncières** (*Sicilien*), **Liebermann** (*School for Wives*), **Lully** (*Mariage forcé*, *Amour médicin*, *Princesse d'Elide*, *Sicilien*, *George Dandin*, *M. de Pourceaugnac*, *Amants magnifiques* and *Bourgeois G.*), **Médecin malgré lui** (Gounod), **Mengozzi** (*Pourceaugnac*), **Mortari** (*Scuola delle mogli*), **Ollone** (*George Dandin*), **Purcell** (*Female Virtuosos*), **Quinault** (**J.B.**) (*Bourgeois G.* and *Princesse d'Elide*), **Roger-Ducasse** (*Madrigal*), **Sauguet** (*Sicilien*), **Schulhoff** (**E.**) (*Bourgeois G.*,), **Schweitzer** (do.), **Shaporin** (*Tartuffe*), **Signor di Pourceaugnac** (Franchetti), **Szymanowski** (*Bourgeois G.*,), **Veretti** (*Medico volante*), **Wagner-Régeny** (*Sganarelle*), **Wolf-Ferrari** (*Amor medico*), **Zich** (*Précieuses ridicules*).

Molinari-Pradelli, Francesco (b Bologna, 4 Jul 1911), Italian conductor. Studied in Bologna and Rome, making his debut in 1938, rapidly becoming known as one of the leading conds. of It. opera; London, CG, 1955 and 1960 (*Tosca* and *Macbeth*), San Francisco 1957–66, NY Met 1966–73. Several recordings with Tebaldi.

Molinaro, Simone (b Genoa, c 1565; d Genoa, c 1615), Italian lutenist, editor and composer. Pupil of Gostena, his uncle, whom he succeeded as *maestro di cappella* of Genoa Cathedral in 1599. In 1613 he ed. the madrigals of Gesualdo.

Works incl. Masses, motets, Magnificats, sacred concertos; madrigals, canzonets; lute pieces.

Molique, (Wilhelm) Bernhard (b Nuremberg, 7 Oct 1802; d Cannstadt nr. Stuttgart, 10 May 1869), German violinist and composer. Pupil of Spohr and of Rovelli at Munich, succeeding him in 1820 as leader of the orch.; after some time in the orch. of the Theater an der Wien in Vienna, he toured widely, became leader in the royal orch. at Stuttgart in 1826, settled in London in 1849 and returned to Ger. in 1866.

Works incl. 2 Masses; oratorio *Abraham* (1861); symph.; 6 vln. concertos (1827–46); 8 string 4tets (1841–53), 2 pf trios, duets for vlns. and fl. and vln.; vln. studies and pieces.

Moll (Ger., from Lat. *mollis* = soft), the German word for Minor.

Moll, Kurt (b Buir, nr. Cologne, 11 Apr 1938), German bass. Debut Aachen 1961. He has sung Marke and Pogner at Bayreuth since 1968; joined the Hamburg Opera in 1970. In 1972 he sang Osmin at La Scala and Gurnemanz at the Paris Opéra. Salzburg from 1973. CG debut 1977, as Kaspar; NY Met 1978, as the Landgrave. Also heard in sacred music by Bach and Beethoven.

Molteni, Benedetta Emilia (b Modena, 1722; d Berlin, 1780), Italian soprano. App. to the court of Frederick II of Prussia in Berlin, 1742–74, where she married J.F. Agricola in 1751. She sang in the fp of Graun's *Tod Jesu* (1755).

Molter, Johann Melchoir (b Tiefenort, nr. Eisenach, 10 Feb 1696; d Karlsruhe, 12 Jan 1765), German composer. He was *Kapellmeister* at the court of Baden, where he was responsible for opera prods., 1722–33. Dir. of church music at Eisenach and returned to Baden in 1743. He made several visits to Italy and is known today for having written 170 symphs. (strictly, sinfonias). Also wrote 66 concertos, incl. 6 for clar., and a Passion.

Molto (It.) = much, very.

Mombelli, Ester (b Naples, c 1794), Italian contralto. She sang throughout Italy and was successful in operas by Rossini and Donizetti: created leading roles in Donizetti's *Zoraida di Granata* (Rome 1822) and *L'aio nell'imbarazzo* (Rome, 1824). Her father **Domenico** (1751–1835) was a tenor and composer who sang in Rossini's early operas.

Moments musicals, the title, which in correct Fr. should be *Moments musicaux,* of Schubert's 6 pf. pieces op. 94, written between 1823 and 1828.

Mompou, Federico (b Barcelona, 16 Apr 1893; d Barcelona, 30 Jun 1987), Spanish pianist and composer. Studied at the Barcelona Cons. and later in Paris, where I. Philipp was his pf. master and Samuel Rousseau taught him comp. He lived at Barcelona again in 1914–21, then settled in Paris. returning to Barcelona in 1941.

Works incl. pf. pieces 6 *Impresiones intimas* (1911–14), *Scènes d'enfants* (1915–18), *Suburqis, 3 Pessebres* (1914–17), *Canço i dansa, Cants magics, Fêtes lointaines,* 6 *Charmes* (1920–1), *Dialogues, 3 Variations* (1921), *10 Préludes* (1927–51); songs *L'hora grisa, Cançoneta incerta, 4 Mélodies, Le Nuage, 3 Comptines.*

Mond, Der (*The Moon*), opera by Orff (lib. by comp. after Grimm), prod. Munich, 5 Feb 1939.

Mondo alla roversa, Il, o sla Le donne che comandano (*The World Upside Down, or Women in Command*), opera by Galuppi (lib. by Goldoni), prod. Venice, Teatro San Cassiano, 14 Nov 1750.

Mondo della luna, Il (*The World of the Moon*), opera by Galuppi (lib. by Goldoni), prod. Venice, Teatro San Moisè, 29 Jan 1750.

Opera by Haydn (lib. do.), prod. Eszterháza, 3 Aug 1777.

Mondonville, Jean Joseph (Cassanea) de (b Narbonne, bap. 25 Dec 1711; d Belleville nr. Paris, 8 Oct 1772), French violinist and composer. His parents were aristocrats in reduced circumstances, but he succeeded in studying the vln. He settled in Paris in 1733, made his name as a violinist and comp. and appeared at the Concert Spirituel in 1737, for which he wrote motets until 1770. In 1744 he became superintendent of the royal chapel and in 1755–62 he was director of the Concert Spirituel. During the *guerre des bouffons* in 1752 he was chosen as the representative of the Fr. Nat. school opposing the Its. under the patronage of Mme. de Pompadour.

Works incl. operas and opera-ballets *Isbé* (1742), *Le Carnaval du Parnasse* (1749), *Titon et l'Aurore* (1753), *Daphnis et Alcimaduro* (in Provençal, 1754), *Les Fêtes de Paphos* (1758), *Thésée, Psyché* (1762), *Érigone, Vénus et Adonis, Les Projets de l'Amour;* oratorios *Les Israélites au Mont Oreb* (1758), *Les Fureurs de Saül* (1758), *Les Titans;* the *Privilège du Roi* set as a

cantata; trio sonatas for 2 vlns. or fls. and bass; sonatas incl. *Les Sons harmoniques* for vln. and bass; sonatas and pieces for harpsichord with vln. or voice; harpsichord works incl. *Pièces de clavecin en sonates;* organ pieces.

Moniuszko, Stanisław (b Ubiel, Lithuania, 5 May 1819; d Warsaw, 4 Jun 1872), Polish composer. After studying at home, he went to Berlin as a pupil of Rungenhagen, 1837–9, and on his return settled down at Wilno as music teacher and organist, prod. the opera *Halka* there in 1848 (revised version prod. in 1858). In 1858 he became cond. at the Opera in Warsaw and later prof. at the Cons.

Works incl. opera *Halka* (perf. 1848, rev. 1857), *Flis, Hrabina* (*The Countess,* 1860), *Verbum nobile* (1860), *Straszny Dwór* (*The Haunted Mansion,* 1865), *Paria, Beata* (1872); incid. music for Shakespeare's *Hamlet* and *Merry Wives of Windsor* and other plays; cantatas *Spectres, Crimean Sonnets,* etc.; 7 Masses (1850–74), Litanies and other church music; overture *Bajka* (*Fairy Tale*); 270 songs, incl. ballads by Adam Mickiewicz.

Monn, Matthias Georg (b Vienna, 9 Apr 1717; d Vienna, 3 Oct 1750), Austrian composer and organist. Chorister at Klosterneuburg nr. Vienna, he was from *c* 1738 organist of the Karlskirche in Vienna. His symph. in D maj. of 1740 is the earliest dated symph. to have 4 movements with minuet in 3rd place.

Works incl. 21 symphs.; 10 partitas for string orch.; 6 string 4tets; 7 harpsichord concertos, incl. one arr. by Schoenberg for cello and orch. (1933); keyboard music; church music.

Monna Vanna, opera by Février (lib. Maeterlinck's play with alterations), prod. Paris, Opéra, 13 Jan 1909.

Opera by Rakhmaninov (lib. ditto); comp. (1 act) 1907, fp (concert) Saratoga, NY, 11 Aug 1984.

Monochord, an early instrument, not for playing, but for measuring the vibration of strings. It has a single string (hence its name) stretched over a long, narrow box. it is at least as old as the 6th cent. B.C., when it was used by Pythagoras, and it is mentioned by Euclid *c* 300 B.C., but it still occupied scientists in the Middle Ages. It was found that if the string was stopped exactly in the centre, it gave out the higher 8ve on each side, and other intervals were found to sound at proportional points.

Monocorde (Fr.) }
Monocordo (It.) } = single string, a

direction used in vln. music where the comp. wishes a passage to be played on 1 string.

Monodrama, a musical stage work for a single singer, an opera with a cast of 1, as for ex. Meyerbeer's *Tevelindens Liebe*, Gomis's *Sensibilidad y prudencia* or Schoenberg's *Erwartung. See also* **Lélio** (Berlioz).

Monody (from Gk. for 'single song'), a term used to describe music making its effect with a single melodic part, accomp. or not, instead of a collaboration of var. parts as in Polyphony.

Monophonic, music in a single melodic part, without harmony, as distinct from Homophonic, which is melodic music accomp. by harmony, or Polyphonic, which is music in a number of melodic parts moving simultaneously.

Monothematic, an adj. used for a work based throughout, esp. in the course of more than one movement, on a single dominating theme. Haydn more than once wrote monothematic movements, e.g. the finale of symph. no. 103 in E♭ maj. and the first movement of symph. no. 104 in D maj.

Monro (or Monroe), George (d London, ? 1731), English organist and composer. He was organist at St Peter's Cornhill, in London and played harpsichord at the theatre in Goodman's Fields.

Works incl. incid. music to Fielding's *The Temple Beau*; a great number of songs, incl. 'My lovely Celia'.

Monsigny, Pierre Alexandre (b Fauquembergue nr. St Omer, 17 Oct 1729; d Paris, 14 Jan 1817), French composer. He studied the vln. in his youth, but after the death of his father took an official position in Paris in order to support his family. A perf. of *La serva padrona* in 1754 re-awakened his musical interests, and he took comp. lessons from the double-bass player Gianotti. His first opera was prod. in 1759, and his assoc. with Sedaine as librettist soon consolidated his success. After *Félix* (1777), at the height of his fame, he wrote no more. He lost his fortune during the Revolution, but was given an annuity by the Opéra-Comique.

Works incl. operas *Les Aveux indiscrets* (1759), *Le Maître en droit* (1760), *Le Cadi dupé* (1761), *On ne s'avise jamais de tout*, *Le Roi et le fermier* (1762), *Rose et Colas* (1764), *Aline, reine de Golconde* (1766), *L'Isle sonnante* (after Rabelais), *Le Déserteur* (1769), *Le Faucon* (1771), *La Belle Arsène* (1775), *Félix, ou L'Enfant trouvé* (1777), etc.

Montagnana, Antonio (b Venice, *c* 1700), Italian bass. Sang in several of Handel's operas in London, 1731–8, incl. the fps of *Ezio, Sosarme* and *Orlando*. Also sang in operas by Porpora and Hasse.

Montagnana, Domenico (b ? *c* 1690; d Venice, 7 Mar 1750), Italian violin-maker. Possibly a pupil of Antonio Stradivari, he worked first at Cremona, and set up a workshop in Venice in 1721.

Montarsolo, Paolo (b Portici, nr. Naples, 16 Mar 1925), Italian bass. From 1954 he sang at La Scala in operas by Rossini, Donizetti and Mozart. Glyndebourne 1957, Mustafa; 1967–71, as Leporello, Osmin, Alfonso and Rossini's Selim. He has sung at the NY Met and in Paris and Moscow.

Monte, Philippe de (b Malines, 1521; d Prague, 4 Jul 1603), Flemish composer. He lived in Naples, 1542–54, and then in the Netherlands. He was in England (1554–5) as a member of the choir of Philip II of Spain, when he met the Byrd family. In 1558 or before he returned to It. In 1568 he went to Vienna as *Kapellmeister* to the Emperor Maximilian II, after whose death in 1576 he followed the next emperor, Rudolph II, to Prague. He was made a canon of Cambrai Cathedral, but did not reside there. Among the most important of late Renaissance polyphonists.

Works incl. 38 Masses, motets; over 30 books of madrigals, incl. 1,073 secular and 144 spiritual works. His motet *Super flumina Babylonis* was sent to Byrd in 1583, to which the latter responded with *Quomodo cantabimus* in 1584.

Montéclair, Michel (Pinolet) de (b Andelot, Haute-Marne, 4 Dec 1667; d Saint-Denis, 22 Sep 1737), French composer, theorist and teacher. Studied music as a chorister at Langres Cathedral, later sang in other churches and went to It. in the service of the Prince de Vaudémont. After 1702 he settled in Paris and he was double-bass player at the Opéra from 1707–37.

Works incl. operas and opera-ballets, e.g. *Les Festes de l'été* (1716) and *Jephté* (1732), ballet music for C.F. Pollaroli's opera *Ascanio*; chamber music.

Montemezzi, Italo (b Vigasio, 4 Aug 1875; d Vigasio, 15 May 1952), Italian composer. Learnt the pf. as a child, then went to Milan to be trained for engineering, but wished to take up music. He entered the Cons. with some difficulty, but obtained a diploma there in 1900. After the prod. of his 1st opera in 1905 he was able to give all his time to comp. From 1939 to 1949 he was in the USA, after which he returned to It.

Works incl. operas *Giovanni Gallurese*

(1905), *Hellera* (1909), *L'amore dei tre re* (1913), *La Nave* (d'Annunzio, 1918), *La notte di Zoraima* (1931), *La principessa lontana* (after Rostand's *Princesse lointaine*, 1931); *The Song of Songs* for chorus or orch.; symph. poem *Paolo e Virginia* (after Saint-Pierre); elegy for cello and pf.

Monteux, Pierre (b Paris, 4 Apr 1875; d Hancock, Maine, 1 Jul 1964), French conductor. Studied vln. and comp. at Paris Cons., winning first prize for vln. in 1896. Then played vla. in Colonne Orch. and in 1911 began cond. for Diaghilev, giving fps of, among other works, Stravinsky's *Petrushka*, *The Rite of Spring*, *The Nightingale*, Ravel's *Daphnis et Chloé*, Debussy's *Jeux*. He was cond. of the Boston SO 1919–24, San Francisco SO 1936–52, LSO 1961–64. Monteux conducted all over the world and was recognized as equally fine in both the Fr. and Ger. repertories.

Monteverdi, Claudio (Zuan Antonio) (b Cremona, 15 May 1567; d Venice, 29 Nov 1643), Italian composer. Son of a doctor; was a choir-boy at Cremona Cathedral and a pupil of Ingegneri; became an organist and violist and at 16 pub. sacred madrigals, 1583. Entered the service of the Duke of Mantua, Vincenzo Gonzaga, as violist and singer, and there married the harpist Claudia Cataneo. He was in Gonzaga's retinue in the war against the Turks on the Danube and again in Flanders in 1599. He prob. heard Peri's *Euridice* at Florence in 1600, and in 1602 was made music master to the court of Mantua. His wife died after a long illness on 10 Sep 1607, the year Monteverdi finished his 1st opera, *Orfeo*; this remains the earliest opera to be regularly performed today. The next opera, *Arianna*, made him widely famous. When Francesco Gonzaga succeeded his brother to the dukedom in 1612 he quarrelled with Monteverdi, who left for his native Cremona to wait for a new appt., which came from Venice in 1613, where he was made master of music to the republic and worked at St Mark's. He had by this time written much church music and numerous madrigals. In 1630 he took holy orders after escaping the plague at Venice. In 1639 the 2nd public opera theatre in Venice, the Teatro dei SS. Giovanni e Paolo, was opened with Monteverdi's *Adone*, and *Arianna* was revived the same year when the Teatro di San Moisè was inaugurated. His last opera was *L'Incoronazione di Poppea*, widely performed today in an increasing variety of editions.

Works incl. operas *Orfeo* (1607), *Arianna*

(lost except the *Lament*, 1608), *Il combattimento di Tancredi e Clorinda* (after Tasso, 1624), *Il ritorno d'Ulisse in patria* (1640), *L'incoronazione di Poppea* (1642), and about a dozen lost stage works; ballets *Ballo delle ingrate* (1608) and *Tirsi e Clori* (1619); Masses, Magnificats and psalms; *Vespers* (1610), *Sancta Maria* for voice and 8 instruments; 40 sacred madrigals; 21 *canzonette* for 3 voices; 9 books of secular madrigals cont. 250, incl. book VIII, *Madrigali guerrieri e amorosi* (Madrigals of love and war); 26 madrigals published in var. collections; 25 *Scherzi musicali* for 1–3 voices (1607).

Montezuma, opera by Roger Sessions (lib. by G.A. Borgese); comp. 1941–63, prod. W. Berlin, 19 Apr 1964.

Monti, Laura (b ? Rome, after 1704; d Naples, 1760), Italian soprano. From 1726 to 1735 she sang in comic opera in Rome and in 1733 created Serpina in Pergolesi's intermezzo *La serva padrona*. She sang in the fp of Auletta's *La locandiera* (Naples, 1738) and created a demand for further perfs. of comic operas in Naples. Also sang in operas by Hasse and Leo. Her cousin **Marianna** (b Naples 1730; d Naples 1814) was popular in Naples for 20 years in operas by Jommelli, Traetta, Paisiello, Cimarosa and Sacchini. Retired 1780.

Monticelli, Angelo Maria (b Milan, *c* 1710; d Dresden, 1764), Italian castrato soprano. Made his debut in Rome in 1730, sang in London, 1741–6 (in Gluck's 2 operas for London, *La caduta dei giganti* and *Artamene*), later in Naples, Vienna and, from 1756, in Dresden under Hasse.

Montpellier Manuscript, a large MS. (400 folios) in 8 gatherings, representing about 100 years of music history (1200–1300). It is the largest source of 13th-cent. motets and was written down between *c* 1280 and *c* 1310. It is in the library of the Faculté de Médecine, Montpellier, MS. 196.

Montsalvatge (Bassols), Xavier (b Gerona, 11 Mar 1912), Catalan composer. Studied with Morera and Pahissa at Barcelona Cons., winning the Pedrell Prize in 1936.

Works incl. opera *El gato con botas* (1947); 4 ballets; *Sinfonia mediterranea* (1949); *Concerto breve* for pf. and orch. (1956), *Poema concertante* for vln. and orch.; orchestral suite *Calidoscopo*; string 4tet (1952); songs.

Monumentum pro Gesualdo di Venosa ad CD annum, 3 madrigals recomposed in 1960 by Stravinsky for 12 wind insts. and strings to celebrate the 400th anniversary of Gesualdo's birth. Fp Venice, 27 Sep 1960.

The madrigals are *Asciugate i belli occhi, Ma tu, cagion di quella, Belta poi che t'assenti*.

Mood (Lat. *modus*), the relationship between the Long (⊓) and the Breve (∎) in mensural notation.

Moodie, Alma (b Brisbane, 12 Sep 1900; d Frankfurt, 7 Mar 1943), Australian violinist. Studied with César Thomson at Brussels and travelled widely, making her reputation esp. in Ger., where she married a lawyer at Cologne. Pfitzner wrote his vln. concerto for her.

Moody, Fanny (b Redruth, Cornwall, 23 Nov 1866; d Dundrum, Co. Dublin, 21 Jul 1945), English soprano. Studied with Charlotte Sainton-Dolby and made her 1st stage appearance at Liverpool in 1887. In 1890 she married Charles Manners and in 1897 became his partner in the Moody-Manners Opera Co. She sang Tatyana in the 1st London perf. of *Eugene Onegin* (1892).

Moog, Robert. *See* **Synthesizer.**

Moonlight Sonata, the nickname of Beethoven's pf. sonata in C♯ min., op. 27 no. 2, prob. due to a description of the 1st movement by Rellstab.

Moór, Emanuel (b Kecskemét, 19 Feb 1863; d Chardonne, 20 Oct 1931), Hungarian pianist, composer and inventor. Studied at Budapest and Vienna, and toured in Europe and Amer. as pianist and cond. Inventor of the Duplex-Coupler pf. Married the Eng. pianist Winifred Christie.

Works incl. operas *La Pompadour* (after Musset, 1902), *Andreas Hofer* (1902), *Hochzeitsglocken* (1908); 8 symphs. (1893–1910); 4 vln. concertos (1905–7); chamber music; pf. works.

Moore, Douglas (Stuart) (b Cutchogue, NY, 10 Aug 1893; d Greenport, Long Island, 25 Jul 1969), American composer. Studied at Yale Univ. and with Horatio Parker, Bloch, d'Indy, Tournemire and Nadia Boulanger. He served in the US Navy in the 1914–18 war, was organist and lecturer at Cleveland, 1921–5, and became assoc. prof. of music at Columbia Univ. in NY in 1926 and later professor.

Works incl. operas *The Devil and Daniel Webster* (1939), *The Ballad of Baby Doe* (1956) and *Carrie Nation* (1966), operetta *The Headless Horseman* (1936), chamber opera *White Wings* (1935); motet *Dedication* for 6 voices, *Simon Legree* for male chorus, *Perhaps to dream* for female chorus; *A Symph. of Autumn*, Overture on an Amer. Tune, *Pageant of P.T. Barnum* (1924), *Moby Dick* (after Herman Melville), *In Memoriam*, symph. in A for orch. (1945); string 4tet; sonata and *Down East*

suite for vln. and pf.; wind 5tet, clar. 5tet.

Moore, Gerald (b Watford, 30 Jul 1899; d Penn, Bucks., 13 Mar 1987), English pianist. Studied in Canada and after a short career as a concert performer became an accompanist, in which profession he quickly rose to fame as the most distinguished of his time, playing for most of the great instrumentalists and singers and raising his art to a level with that of his partner. Among the singers he worked with were Gerhardt, Schumann, Hotter, Fischer-Dieskau and Schwarzkopf. He wrote some valuable books, incl. *The Unashamed Accompanist, Singer and Accompanist* and *Am I too Loud?*

Moore, Grace (b Nough, Tenn., 5 Dec 1898; d Copenhagen, 26 Jan 1947), American soprano. She appeared in musical comedy 1921–6 and after study in France sang Mimi at the NY Met in 1928; continued there until 1946 as Manon, Lauretta, Tosca and Louise. London, CG, 1935, as Mimi. Also popular in concerts and films. She was killed in an air crash.

Moore, Thomas (1779–1852), Irish poet. From about 1802 he began to pub. songs with words and occasionally music by himself, and between 1807 and 1834 he prod. collections of Ir. tunes with new words of his own. He also prod., in 1811, an opera *M.P., or The Blue Stocking* with music by himself and C.E. Horn. He wrote the tune as well as the words of 'The Last Rose of Summer', used by Flotow in *Martha*. For works used by comps. *see* **Bennet (W.S.)** (*Paradise and the Peri*), **Bishop** (nat. melodies), **Clay** (*Lalla Rookh*), **David (Fél.)** (do.), **Feramors** (A. Rubinstein), **Horn (C.E.)** (*Lalla R.* and *M.P., or The Blue Stocking*), **Jongen** (*Lalla R.*), **Kelly** (*Gypsy Prince*), **Lalla-Roukh** (F. David), **Paradise and the Peri** (Schumann), **Spontini** (*Nurmahal* and *Lalla R.,*), **Stevenson (J.)** (Ir. songs ed.), **Veiled Prophet** (Stanford).

Moorehead, John (b Ir., *c* 1760; d nr. Deal, Mar 1804), Irish violinist and composer. Studied in Ir., went to Eng. as a youth and played at var. provincial theatres, vla. at Sadler's Wells Theatre in London from 1796, and vln. at CG from 1798. He had already prod. his 1st stage work in 1796 and wrote several more for CG. In 1802 he became insane and was confined, entered the Navy on being released, but hanged himself in a fit of madness.

Works incl. stage pieces *Birds of a Feather* (1796), *Harlequin's Tour* (with Attwood), *Perouse* (with Davy), *The Cabinet* (with Braham, Davy and others), *Family Quarrels* (with Braham and Reeve, 1802), *The Naval Pillar* (1799), Morton's *Speed the Plough* and others; pantomimes.

Morales, Cristóbal (b Seville, *c* 1500; d ? Marchena, Autumn 1553), Spanish composer. Studied at Seville under the cathedral *maestro de capilla* Fernández de Castilleja. Was *maestro de capilla* at Avila, 1526–30, and some time later went to Rome, where he was ordained a priest and became cantor in the Pontifical Chapel, 1535. In 1545 he was given leave to visit Spain, but did not return, living at Toledo, Málaga and Marchena, app. *maestro de capilla* at the former 2 places and serving in the household of the Duke of Arcos at the last. Palestrina based a mass on his motet *O sacrum convivium*.

Works incl. 21 Masses, 16 Magnificats, 91 motets, Lamentations and other church music; cantatas for the peace conference at Nice (1538) and for Ippolito d'Este; madrigals.

Moralt, Rudolf (b Munich, 26 Feb 1902; d Vienna, 16 Dec 1958), German conductor. Studied at the Munich Music Acad. with W. Courvoisier and Schmid-Lindner, and in 1919 became a *répétiteur* at the Munich Staatsoper. After a number of posts in var. German opera houses he became 1st cond. at the Vienna Staatsoper in 1940. Well known in Mozart and Strauss.

Moravia, Hieronymus de, 13th-cent. theorist, prob. a Dominican friar living in Paris. His *Tractatus de Musica* is a comprehensive compilation dealing mainly with plainsong, with an extensive tonary attached.

Mordent, an ornament over a note, indicated by the sign: ♫. The interpretation, depending on the speed of the music and the length of the note, is approximately:

The double mordent ♫ repeats the same process. *See also* **Pralltriller.**

Mörder, Hoffnung der Frauen (*Murder, the Hope of Women*), opera in 1 act by Hindemith (lib. by Oskar Kokoschka); comp. 1919, fp Stuttgart, 4 Jun 1921, cond. Fritz Busch.

Moreau, Jean-Baptiste (b Angers, 1656; d Paris, 24 Aug 1733), French composer. He learnt music as a boy chorister at Angers Cathedral and comp. motets as a youth.

App. choirmaster at the cathedral of Langres, where he married, and later that of Dijon, and went to Paris during the 1680s. He found his way into the court, for which he began to write stage pieces, and in 1688 he was commissioned to write music for Racine's *Esther* for perf. at the young ladies' acad. of Saint-Cyr. This earned him a pension for life and an appt. at Saint-Cyre jointly with the organist Nivers and later with Clérambault. He remained under the patronage of the king and Mme. de Maintenon. He taught both singing and comp., among his pupils for the former being his daughter Claude-Marie M. and for the latter Clérambault, Dandrieu and Montéclair.

Works incl. Requiem, motet *In exitu Israel* (1691), *Cantiques spirituels* (Racine), Te Deum for the king's recovery (1687) and other church music; stage divertissements incl. *Les Bergers de Marly*; chorus for Racine's *Athalie* (1691); *Idylle sur la naissance de Notre Seigneur*; drinking-songs.

Morena, Berta (b Mannheim, 27 Jan 1878; d Rottach-Egern, 7 Oct 1952), German soprano. Debut Munich 1898, as Agathe; remained until 1924 as Elsa, Eva and Isolde. NY Met debut 1908, as Sieglinde; sang there until 1912 and returned 1925 for Brünnhilde. CG 1914. Retired 1927.

Morendo (It.) = dying, a direction used where a phrase is intended to die away. It may mean a decrease not only in tone but in pace as well.

Moresca, a Moorish dance of remote antiquity, 1st intro. by the Moors into Spain and popular all over Europe by the 15th–16th cent. Allied to the Eng. Morris Dance, 'morys' being an Eng. variant of 'Moorish'; at any rate one of the latter's features — bells or jingles tied to the legs — belonged to the moresca also.

Morhange, Charles Henri Valentin. *See* **Alkan.**

Mori, Nicholas (b London, 24 Jan 1796 or 1797; d London, 14 Jun 1839), English violinist and publisher of Italian descent. Pupil of Barthélemon, at whose concerts he played at the age of 8, and later of Viotti. He appeared as soloist at the Phil. Society's concerts and became leader of its orch. In 1819 he married the widow of the music pub. Lavenu and became a partner with her son.

Moriani, Napoleone (b Florence, 10 Mar 1808; d Florence, 4 Mar 1878), Italian tenor. Made his 1st appearance at Pavia in 1833; in Pacini's *Gli Arabi nelle Gallie*, and sang in many Eur. cities during the next 14 years. Much admired in operas by Donizetti, Vaccai, Mercadante and Federico Ricci.

Mörike, Eduard (Friedrich) (1804–75), German poet. *See* **Schoeck** (songs), **Sutermeister** (*Jorinde*), **Trapp** (*Letzte König von Orplid*).

2 songs by Brahms, 3 by Schumann, 57 (incl. 4 early) by H. Wolf.

Morison, Elsie (b Ballarat, Victoria, 15 Aug 1924), Australian soprano. After study in Melbourne she moved to Eng. in 1946. London, SW, 1948–54. She was the first Brit. Anne Trulove, Edinburgh 1953, and in the same year made her CG debut; remained until 1962 as Mimi, Susanna, Pamina, Micaela and Blanche in *The Carmelites*. Glyndebourne 1954–59 as Anne Trulove, Zerlina and Marzelline.

Morlacchi, Francesco (b Perugia, 14 Jun 1784; d Innsbruck, 28 Oct 1841), Italian composer and conductor. Studied with her father, then at Perugia Cathedral, later with Zingarelli at Loreto and finally with Mattei at Bologna. In 1810 he was app. music dir. of the It. opera at Dresden, where he remained to the end of his life.

Works incl. operas *Il ritratto* (1807), *Enone e Paride* (1808), *Oreste, Le Daniadi* (1810), *Raoul de Créqui* (1811), *La capricciosa pentita, Il barbiere di Siviglia* (after Beaumarchais, 1816), *Boadicea, Gianni di Parigi* (1818), *Il Simoncino, Donna Aurora, Tebaldo ed Isolina* (1820), *La gioventù di Enrico V* (1823), *Il Colombo, Francesca da Rimini* (after Dante, unfinished, 1836), and *c* 10 others.

13 Masses, Requiem for the King of Saxony (1827), Miserere for 16 voices, unaccomp. Mass for the Gk. service and other church music; oratorios *Gli angeli al sepolcro* (1803), *La morte di Abele* (1821) and *Il sacrifizio d'Abramo*, Passion oratorio (words by Metastasio, 1811); cantatas for the coronation of Napoleon as king of Italy (1805) and for the taking of Paris (1814); Narration of Ugolino from Dante's *Inferno* for baritone and pf.

Morlaye, Guillaume (b ? Paris, *c* 1515; d after 1560), French amateur composer and lutenist, a merchant by profession. He is said to have been in the slave trade and was definitely a publisher; pub. several books of music for lute and for guitar.

Morley, Thomas (b Norwich 1557 or 1558; d London, Oct 1602), English composer. Although a Roman Catholic he was *magister puerorum* at Norwich Cathedral, 1583–7. A pupil of Byrd, he took his B.Mus. degree at Oxford in 1588 and about that time became organist of St Giles's Church, Cripplegate, in London. Soon afterwards he was organist of St Paul's Cathedral and in 1592 became a Gentleman of the Chapel Royal. In 1598 both Morley and Shakespeare, who were prob. acquainted, appealed against the assessment for taxes, and in 1599 Morley contrib. the setting of 'It was a lover and his lass', if not more music, to the prod. of *As You Like It*. Morley obtained a patent for the printing of music and music paper in 1598, but he had already pub. his treatise, *A Plaine and Easie Introduction to Practicall Musick*, in 1597. He resigned from the Chapel Royal in 1602, (?) owing to ill health.

Works incl. services, anthems and responses, 10 Latin motets; madrigals (incl. 2 in *The Triumphes of Oriana*), *canzonets* and ballets for voices; 4 tunes contrib. to *The Whole Booke of Psalmes*; fancies for viols; virginal pieces.

Morning Heroes, symph. for orator, chorus and orch. by Bliss (words by Homer, Li-Tai-Po, Whitman, Robert Nichols and Wilfred Owen), fp Norwich Festival, 6 Oct 1930.

Moross, Jerome (b Brooklyn, 1 Aug 1913; d Miami, 25 Jul 1983), American composer. Studied at Juilliard and worked in Hollywood from 1940. Best known for ballets and ballet-operas: *Paul Bunyan* (1934), *American Patterns* (1937), *Susannah and the Elders* (1940), *The Eccentricities of Davy Crockett* (1946), *The Golden Apple* (1952), *Sorry, Wrong Number* (comp. 1983).

Morris Dance, an old Eng. folk dance, deriving its name from the Moorish *Moresca* (old Eng. 'morys' = 'Moorish'), intro. into Eng. about the 15th cent. It partook of a pageant in character and was danced in var. kinds of fancy dress, with jingles tied to the dancers' legs. In some districts elements of the Sword Dance were intro. into it. The music, a great variety of tunes, was played by a pipe and tabor, or more rarely by a bagpipe or vln.

Morris, James (b Baltimore, 10 Jan 1947), American bass-baritone. He studied with Rosa Ponselle. Debut Baltimore 1967, as Crespel; NY Met 1972, Ramfis. Glyndebourne 1972, as Banquo. He sang the Dutchman at Houston (1984) and in 1985 was Wotan at San Francisco. Salzburg 1985, as Guglielmo. Other roles incl. Méphistophélès, Claggart and Donizetti's Henry VIII.

Morris, R(eginald) O(wen) (b York, 3 Mar 1886; d London, 14 Dec 1948), English teacher and composer. Educ. at Harrow, New Coll., Oxford, and the RCM in London, where later he became prof. of counter-

point and comp. In 1926 he was app. to a similar post at the Curtis Inst. at Philadelphia, but soon returned to Eng. His books incl. *Contrapuntal Technique in the 16th Century, Foundations of Practical Harmony and Counterpoint, The Structure of Music.*
Works incl. symph. in D maj.; vln. concerto in G min., *Concerto piccolo* for 2 vlns. and strings; fantasy for string 4tet, Motets for string 4tet; songs with 4tet accomp.

Mors et Vita (*Death and [New] Life*), oratorio by Gounod, a sequel to *The Redemption*, prod. Birmingham Festival, 26 Aug 1885.

Mortari, Virgilio (b Passirana di Lainate nr. Milan, 6 Dec 1902), Italian composer. Pupil of Pizzetti. Prof. of comp. at the S. Cecilia Cons. in Rome from 1940. Dir. of the Teatro La Fenice, Venice, from 1955 to 1959.
Works incl. operas *Seechi e sberlecchi* (1927), *La scuola delle mogli* (after Molière, 1930); rhapsody for orch.; concerto for 4tet and orch., pf. concerto; chamber music; partita for vln.; songs.

Morton (Mourton in Fr.), **Robert** (b c 1430; d c 1476), English singer and composer. He was employed at the court of Burgundy from 1457–76 under Philip the Good and Charles the Bold. He comp. Fr. *chansons*, of which 2 were among the most popular of their day.

Moscheles, Ignaz (b Prague, 23 May 1794; d Leipzig, 10 Mar 1870), Bohemian pianist and composer. Studied under Dionys Weber at the Prague Cons., played a concerto in public at the age of 14, was sent to Vienna and there took lessons in counterpoint from Albrechtsberger and comp. from Salieri. He made Beethoven's acquaintance when he arr. the vocal score of *Fidelio* in 1814. He then began to travel widely, and in 1821 appeared in Hol., Paris and London. In 1824 he taught Mendelssohn in Berlin; in 1826 he married Charlotte Embden at Hamburg and settled permanently in London. In 1832 he cond. the fp there of Beethoven's *Missa solemnis*. In 1846 he went to Leipzig at Mendelssohn's invitation to become 1st pf. prof. at the new Cons.
Works incl. symph. in C (1829); 8 pf. concertos (1819–38), e.g. G min. and *Concerto pathétique*; a great number of pf. works incl. *Sonate mélancolique, Characteristic Studies, Allegro di bravura* and numerous sonatas, variations, fantasies, studies, etc.; *Hommage à Händel* for 2 pfs.

Moscona, Nicola (b Athens, 23 Sep 1907; d Phildelphia, 17 Sep 1975), Greek bass. Debut Athens 1929. He sang in Florence and

Milan during the 1930s. NY Met debut 1937, as Ramfis; remained until 1962 as leading bass. He recorded the Verdi Requiem, under Toscanini, and roles in *Bohème, Mefistofele* and *Rigoletto*.

Mosè in Egitto (*Moses in Egypt*). See also **Moïse.**
Opera by Rossini (lib. by A.L. Tottola), prod. Naples, Teatro San Carlo, 5 Mar 1818.

Moser, Edda (b Berlin, 27 Oct 1938), German soprano. Debut Berlin 1962, in *Butterfly*. She sang under Henze in London (1967) and appeared with Karajan in the *Ring* at the 1968 Salzburg Easter Festival. NY Met 1970, the Queen of Night. Salzburg 1971 as Aspasia in Mozart's *Mitridate*. Other roles incl. Constanze, Leonore and Lucia. She sang Donna Anna in the Lorin Maazel–Joseph Losey film version of *Don Giovanni.* In Jan 1971 she took part in the fp of Henze's *The Raft of the Medusa*, at Vienna.

Moser, Hans Joachim (b Berlin, 25 May 1889; d Berlin, 14 Aug 1967), German singer, musicologist and composer. Studied with his father – Andreas M. (1859–1925) violinist and writer on music, biog. of Joachim – and later at Berlin, Marburg and Leipzig. Became prof. of musicology at Halle, Heidelberg and later Berlin. His lit. works incl. a hist. of Ger. music, studies of medieval string music, Luther's songs, Ger. song, etc., biogs. of Hofhaimer, Schütz and Bach, etc.

Moses und Aron (*Moses and Aaron*), opera in 2 acts by Schoenberg (projected 3rd act never composed; lib. by comp.), fp (concert), Hamburg, 12 Mar 1954; prod. Zurich, 6 Jun 1957. (The music was comp. 1930–2).

Mosonyi, Mihály (orig. Michael Brand), (b Frauenkirchen, Wieselburg, 4 Sep 1815; d Pest, 31 Oct 1870), Hungarian composer. Studied at Pozsony (Pressburg) and was music master in a noble family in 1835–1842, when he settled at Budapest. He changed his Ger. name of Brand in 1859, when he began to aim at writing Hung. nat. music.
Works incl. operas *Kaiser Max auf der Martinswand* (comp. 1857), *The Fair Ilonka* (1861) and *Almos*, 1862; both in Hung.; 3 Masses; symphs., symph. poems *Mourning for Széchényi* and *Festival Music* and other orchestral works; 20 pf. pieces in the Hung. manner; 25 Hung. folksong arrs.

Mosso (It.) = moving, in motion, animated.

Mossolov, Alexander Vassilievich (b Kiev, 10 Aug 1900; d Moscow, 12 Jul 1973), Russian pianist and composer. His family, which cultivated var. branches of art, moved to Moscow in 1904 and in 1921 he entered the Cons. there, studying under Glière until 1925. He travelled much as pianist and to study folk music in central Asia.

Works incl. operas *The Dam*, *The Hero* (1928), *The Signal* (1941); cantatas *Sphinx* (Oscar Wilde) and *Kirghiz Rhapsody*; 6 symphs. (1929–50), symph. poem *The Iron Foundry (Music of Machines)*, *Turcomanian Suite* and *Uzbek Dance* for orch.; 2 pf. concertos (1927, 1935), vln. concerto, harp concerto, 2 cello concertos; string 4tet, *Dance Suite* for pf. trio; vla. and pf. sonata; songs to words by Pushkin, Lermontov and Blok; massed choruses, battle songs.

Mosto, Giovanni Battista (b Udine, before 1550; d after 1590), Italian 16th-cent. composer. Pupil of Merulo, *maestro di cappella* of Padua Cathedral, 1580–9, and then in the service of Prince Bathori of Transylvania.

Works incl. church music; madrigals.

Moszkowski, Moritz (b Breslau, 23 Aug 1854; d Paris, 4 Mar 1925), Polish-German pianist and composer. Studied at Dresden and Berlin, where he became prof. at Kullak's acad. later on. After a successful career as pianist and comp. he retired to Paris in 1897. He died in poverty.

Works incl. opera *Boabdil* (1892); ballet *Laurin* (1896); symph. *Jeanne d'Arc*, 2 suites, *Phantastischer Zug* and other pieces for orch.; pf. concerto in E maj., 2 concert pieces for pf. and orch., vln. concerto; chamber music; pf. pieces.

Motet (Lat. *motetus*, a dim. of Fr. *mot* = word), a form of sacred vocal comp. for several voices arising out of the rhythmical *clausulae* of Organum in the 13th cent. It was at first an elaboration of a given plainsong melody by the contrapuntal addition of other melodies with different words (in Latin, Fr. or both). The earliest motets were most frequently for 3 voices, *triplum, motetus* – hence the name of the species – and *tenor* – which was the lowest part. In the 15th cent. it became more independent, and gradually developed into an elaborate form of polyphonic sacred comp. set to any Latin words not incl. in the Mass. In the 16th cent. it was not uncommon to use the musical material of a motet as the basis for the comp. of a Mass.

Mother Goose (Ravel). *See* **Ma Mère l'Oye**.

Mother of Us All, The, opera by Virgil Thomson (lib. by G. Stein), prod. NY Brander Matthews Theatre, Columbia Univ., 7 May 1947.

Motion, the succession of notes of different pitch. The word is used only with some adjectival qualification or other:

Conjunct Motion: a single part moving by steps of adjoining notes.

Contrary Motion: 2 or more parts moving together in different directions.

Disjunct Motion: a single part moving by larger than stepwise intervals.

Oblique Motion: one part moving when another stands still.

Similar Motion: 2 or more parts moving together in the same direction.

Motiv (Ger.) } a brief melodic or
Motive (Eng.) } rhythmic figure, too short to be called a theme, sometimes used as a purely abstract subject, sometimes in programme music or opera in assoc. with a character, object or idea, in which case it becomes a Leading Motive like the *idée fixe* of Berlioz or the *Leitmotiv* of Wagner.

Moto perpetuo (It. = perpetual motion), a piece exploiting rapid figuration of a uniform and uninterrupted pattern; also called by the Lat. name of *perpetuum mobile*.

Mottl, Felix (Josef) (b Unter-St-Veit nr. Vienna, 24 Aug 1856; d Munich, 2 Jul 1911), Austrian conductor and composer. Studied at a choir-school and at the Cons. in Vienna, became cond. of the Wagner Society there and in 1876 was engaged by Wagner to cond. the music on the stage in the prod. of the *Ring*; gave *Tristan* and *Parsifal* at Bayreuth in 1886. In 1881–1903 he was cond. at the ducal court of Karlsruhe, where he dir. the symph. concerts and the opera, prod. many unfamiliar works incl. the fp of all 5 acts of *Les Troyens* (1890). From 1903 he was cond. in Munich. He collapsed while conducting *Tristan* and died shortly after.

Works incl. operas *Agnes Bernauer* (after Hebbel), *Rama* and *Fürst und Sänger*; festival play *Eberstein*; music for O.J. Bierbaum's play *Pan im Busch*; string 4tet (1904); songs.

Motto, in music a short and well-defined theme usually occurring at the opening of a comp. and used again during its course, in its 1st form or altered, in the manner of a quotation or an allusion to some definite idea. The opening themes in Tchaikovsky's 4th and 5th symphs. are familiar exs.

Motu proprio (Lat. lit. of one's own motion), a decree issued by the Pope personally, esp. that issued by Pius X in 1903 setting down the principles of, and intro. reforms into, the singing of Roman Catholic church music.

Moulu, Pierre (b ? Flanders, *c* 1485; d *c* 1550), Franco-Flemish 16th-cent. composer.

Pupil of Josquin Desprez. Wrote Masses, motets and *chansons*.

Mount-Edgcumbe, Earl of (Richard Edgcumbe) (b Plymouth, 13 Sep 1764; d Richmond, Surrey, 26 Sep 1839), English music amateur and composer. Known chiefly by his *Musical Reminiscences*, pub. privately in 1823, mainly of operatic singing in London between 1773–1823.

Works incl. opera *Zenobia*.

Mount of Olives, The (Beethoven). *See* Christus am Oelberge.

Mouret, Jean Joseph (b Avignon, 11 Apr 1682; d Charenton, 22 Dec 1738), French composer. He entered the service of the Duchess of Maine in Paris about 1707 and in 1714 began to write for the stage. He was dir. of the Concert Spirituel 1728–34, also for a time cond. of the Comédie-Italienne. In 1736 he became insane and was taken to the lunatic asylum of Charenton.

Works incl. operas and opera-ballets *Les Festes de Thalie, Ragonde, Ariane* (1717), *Les Amours des dieux* (1727), *Le Triomphe des sens* (1732), etc.; Mass, 2 books of motets; cantatas *Cantatilles*; 2 *Suites de Symphonies*, 47 divertissements for orch.; 2 books of *Concerts de chambre*; fanfares.

Mourning Symphony (Haydn). *See* Trauer-Sinfonie.

Moussorgsky. *See* Mussorgsky.

Mouton, Charles (b 1626; d after 1700), French lutenist and composer. Lived in Turin in the 1670s, twice visited Paris, and eventually settled there. Wrote lute pieces, etc.

Mouton, Jean (b Haut-Wignes, c 1459; d St Quentin, 30 Oct 1522), French composer. Pupil of Josquin des Prés. He was in the service of Louis XII and François I, became canon of Thérouanne, which he left prob. on its being taken by the Eng. in 1513, and afterwards of the collegiate church of Saint-Quentin.

Works incl. 14 Masses, 110 motets, psalms, *Alleluia* and *In illo tempore* for Easter, *Noe, noe, psallite* for Christmas, etc.

Mouvement (Fr.) = tempo, pace; also a movement of a sonata, symph.

Mouvements de cœur, 7 songs for bass and pf. in memory of Chopin (poems by Louise de Vilmorin): 1. *Prélude*; Henri Sauguet; 2. *Mazurka*: Francis Poulenc; 3. *Valse*: Georges Auric; 4. *Scherzo Impromptu*: Jean Françaix; 5. *Étude*: Léo Preger; 6. *Ballade* (*Nocturne*): Darius Milhaud; 7. *Postlude*: *Polonaise*: Sauguet.

Movable Doh, the Tonic or Keynote in the Tonic Sol-fa system which shifts the tonal centre at each modulation into another Key instead of prescribing Accidentals.

Movement, an independent section of a large-scale work such as a symph. or sonata. The term is used even when there is a link with the section that follows, e.g., in Mendelssohn's 'Scottish' symph.

Movements, work for pf. and orch. by Stravinsky; comp. 1958–9, fp NY, 10 Jan 1960, with Margit Weber, who commissioned the score.

Mozarabic Chant, one of the important branches of early Latin chant, also called Visigothic, and used in central and S. Spain during the Middle Ages. Liturgically it is associated with the Gallican and Ambrosian rites, pre-dating that of Rome and showing similarities with Eastern liturgies. Its music is found in MSS. of the 8th–11th cent., but mostly in undecipherable neumes. Only a few melodies survive in readable form. Roman chant and rite were imposed everywhere by 1076 except in Toledo, and in spite of the attempted revival under Cardinal Francisco de Cisneros (c 1500), little of the musical tradition has been preserved.

Mozart and Salieri, opera by Rimsky-Korsakov (lib. Pushkin's dramatic poem, set as it stands), prod. Moscow, 7 Dec 1898.

Mozart, Franz Xaver. *See* Mozart (Franz Xaver) Wolfgang Amadeus.

Mozart, (Johann Georg) Leopold (b Augsburg, 14 Nov 1719; d Salzburg, 28 May 1787), violinist and composer. Educ. at the Jesuit coll. in Augsburg and at Salzburg Univ., he turned entirely to music in 1739, and first held a post with Count Thurn-Valsassina und Taxis. In 1743 he entered the service of the Archbishop of Salzburg, later rising to become court comp. (1757) and vice-*Kapellmeister* (1763). Married in 1747 Anna Maria Pertl; of their 7 children the only 2 to survive were Maria Anna and Wolfgang Amadeus. His important vln. tutor, *Versuch einer gründlichen Violinschule*, was pub. in 1756.

Works incl. church music; symphs.; divertimenti and descriptive pieces for orch. (incl. 'Musical sleigh-ride', 'Toy Symphony', etc.); concertos for var. insts.; chamber music, sonatas for vln.

Mozart, Maria Anna (Nannerl) (b Salzburg, 30 Jul 1751; d Salzburg, 29 Oct 1829), Austrian pianist and teacher, daughter of prec. Like her brother Wolfgang Amadeus she developed very early as a clavier player, though not as a comp., and was taken on tour with him by Leopold. Later she taught at Salzburg, in 1784 married Baron von

Berchtold zu Sonnenberg, a court councillor at Salzburg and warden of St Gilgen, where she lived. She returned to Salzburg as teacher on his death in 1810 and in 1820 became blind.

Mozart, Wolfgang Amadeus (Johannes Chrysostomus Wolfgangus Theophilus) (b Salzburg, 27 Jan 1756; d Vienna, 5 Dec 1791), Austrian composer, brother of prec. He showed early signs of talent, learnt the harpsichord from the age of 3 or 4, and began to comp. under his father's supervision when he was 5. With his sister (then 11) he was taken to Munich in 1762, then to Vienna, where they played at court. Encouraged by their success, Leopold Mozart set out with the children the following year on a longer tour, which took them first through S. Ger. to Brussels and Paris (arrival 18 Nov 1763). They appeared at court at Versailles, and 4 sonatas for vln. and harpsichord by Mozart were pub. in Paris. Moving on to London in Apr 1764, they played before the royal family and made a sensation in public concerts. In London Mozart was befriended by J.C. Bach, 3 of whose sonatas he arranged as pf. concertos, and who also influenced the symphs., etc., he wrote at the time. They left for Hol. on 24 Jul 1765, and after several stops on the journey through Fr. and Switz. returned to Salzburg in Nov 1766. The next months were spent in study and comp., but on 11 Sep 1767 the whole family went to Vienna. There Mozart comp. his first Mass (C min., K139) and prod. the *Singspiel, Bastien und Bastienne*, though intrigues thwarted the perf. of the opera *La finta simplice*. Returning to Salzburg on 5 Jan 1769, Mozart had barely a year at home before setting out with his father on an extended tour of It.; in Rome he wrote down Allegri's *Miserere* from memory, in Bologna took lessons from Padre Martini and gained election to the Phil. Society with a contrapuntal exercise, in Milan prod. the opera *Mitridate* with great success on 26 Dec 1770. Two further visits to It. followed, both to Milan, for the perfs. of the serenata *Ascanio in Alba* (17 Oct 1771) and the opera *Lucio Silla* (26 Dec 1772). Apart from short visits to Vienna (1773) and Munich (for the prod. of *La finta giardiniera*, 1775), most of the next 5 years was spent in Salzburg, his longest period at home since infancy. In Sep 1777, in company with his mother, he embarked on a lengthy journey which took them *via* Mannheim to Paris, where his mother died on 3 Jul 1778. The main object of this trip was to find suitable employment,

but being unsuccessful Mozart returned in Jan 1779 to the uncongenial post of court organist at Salzburg.

His opera seria *Idomeneo* was prod. in Munich on 29 Jan 1781, but later the same year, on a visit to Vienna with the household of the Archbishop of Salzburg, he gave up his post to settle in Vienna as a freelance, living by teaching and playing in concerts. His Ger. opera *Die Entführung aus dem Serail* was prod. on 15 Jul 1782, and the next month he married Constanze Weber, whose sister Aloysia, a notable singer, he had courted unsuccessfully in Mannheim 4 years before. At the height of his fame as a pianist, 1782–6, he comp. many concertos for his own use, but thereafter was increasingly plagued by financial worries, which his appt. in 1787 as court comp. on the death of Gluck did little to ease. The first of 3 operas on libs. by da Ponte, *Le nozze di Figaro*, was prod. in 1786, followed by *Don Giovanni* (for Prague, 1787) and *Così fan tutte* (1790). A visit to Berlin with Prince Lichnowsky in 1789 took him through Leipzig, where he discussed Bach's music with Doles, Bach's successor, and in 1790 he made a fruitless journey to Frankfurt, hoping to earn money as a pianist. After several lean years 1791 was one of overwork, which must have contrib. to his early death; in addition to the last pf. concerto (K595), the clar. concerto (K622) and several smaller works, he comp. the operas *La clemenza di Tito* (for the coronation of the Emp. Leopold II, prod. Prague 6 Sep) and *Die Zauberflöte* (prod. Vienna, 30 Sep). The Requiem, commissioned anonymously by a mysterious stranger who was the steward of a nobleman wishing to pass the work off as his own, remained unfinished at Mozart's death, and was completed later by his pupil Süssmayr.

Works incl. OPERAS: *Apollo et Hyacinthus* (1767), *Bastien und Bastienne* (1768), *La finta semplice* (1769), *Mitridate, Rè di Ponto* (1770), *Ascanio in Alba* (1771), *Il sogno di Scipione* (1772), *Lucio Silla* (1772), *La finta giardiniera* (1775), *Il Rè Pastore* (1775), *Zaide* (1780), *Idomeneo, Rè di Creta* (1781), *Die Entführung aus dem Serail* (1782), *L'Oca del Cairo* (1783), *Lo Sposo deluso* (1783), *Der Schauspieldirektor* (1786), *Le nozze di Figaro* (1786), *Don Giovanni* (1787), *Così fan tutte* (1790), *Die Zauberflöte* (1791), *La Clemenza di Tito* (1791). Ballet *Les petits riens* (1778).

CHURCH MUSIC: incl. Motet, *Exsultate, jubilate* for sop., organ and orch., (K165, 1773), *Litaniae Laurentenae*, K195, 1774),

Litaniae de venerabili altaris Sacramento (K243, 1776), *Vesperae de Domenica* (K321, 1779), *Kyrie* in D min. (K341, 1781), Mass in C, *Coronation* (K317, 1779), Mass in C, *Missa Solemnis* (K337, 1780), *Vesperae solennes de confessore* (K339, 1780), Mass in C min., unfinished (K427, 1783), Motet, *Ave verum corpus* (K618, 1791), Requiem Mass in D min., unfinished (K626, 1791).

CHORUS AND ORCH: *Die Schuldigkeit des ersten Gebotes*, 1st part of sacred drama written for Salzburg in 1767; *Grabmusik*, Passion cantata (K42, 1767); *La Betulia Liberata*, oratorio (K118, 1771); *Davidde Penitente*, cantata based on C min. Mass (K469, 1785); concert arias for insertion in Mozart's own operas and operas by Anfossi and Paisiello.

SYMPHONIES: (41; nos. 1–24 comp. 1764–73), no. 25 in G min. (K183, 1773), no.26 in Eb (K184, 1773), no. 27 in G (K199, 1773), no. 28 in C (K200, 1773), no. 29 in A (K201, 1774), no. 30 in D (K202, 1774), no. 31 in D, *Paris* (K297, 1778), no. 32 in G (K318, 1779), no. 33 in Bb (K319, 1779), no. 34 in C (K338, 1780), no. 35 in D, *Haffner* (K385, 1782), no. 36 in C, *Linz* (K425, 1783), no. 37 in G is a slow introd. to a symph. by M. Haydn (K444, 1783 or 4), no. 38 in D, *Prague* (K504, 1786), no. 39 in Eb (K543, 1788), no. 40 in G min. (K550, 1788), no. 41 in C, *Jupiter* (K551, 1788). Other music for orch. includes sets of Country Dances and German Dances, also Cassation in Bb (K99, 1769); Divertimenti in Eb (K113, 1771), in D (K131, 1772), in D (K136, 1772), in Bb (K137, 1772), in F (K138, 1772), in D (K205, 1773), in F (K247, 1776), in D (K251, 1776), in Bb (K287, 1777), in D (K334, 1779–80); Serenades in D (K203, 1774), in D (K204, 1775), in D (K239, 1776, *Serenata Notturna*), in D (K250, 1776, *Haffner*), in D, for 4 orchs. (K286, 1777), in D (K320, 1779, *Posthorn*), in Bb for 13 wind insts. (K361, 1781), in Eb for 8 wind insts. (K375, 1781), in C min. for 8 wind insts. (K388, 1782 or 3), in G for strings (K525, 1787, *Eine kleine Nachtmusik*); *Maurerische Trauermusik* (Masonic Funeral Music, K477, 1785).

CONCERTOS: 27 for piano. Nos. 1–4 arr. in 1767 from sonata movts. by Raupach, Honauer, and Schobert. No. 5 in D (K175, 1773), no. 6 in Bb (K238, 1776), no. 7 in F for 3 pianos (K242, 1776), no. 8 in C (K246, 1776), no. 9 in Eb (K271, 1771), no. 10 in Eb for 2 pianos (K365, 1770), no. 11 in F (K413, 1783), no. 12 in A (K414, 1782), no.

13 in C (K415, 1783), no. 14 in Eb (K449, 1784), no. 15 in Bb (K450, 1784), no. 16 in D (K451, 1784), no. 17 in G (K453, 1784), no. 18 in Bb (K456, 1784), no. 19 in F (K459, 1784), no. 20 in D min. (K466, 1785), no. 21 in C (K467, 1785), no. 22 in Eb (K482, 1785), no. 23 in A (K488, 1786), no. 24 in C min. (K491, 1786), no. 25 in C (K503, 1786), no. 26 in D, *Coronation* (K537, 1788), no. 27 in Bb (K595, 1791); 5 for violin: no. 1 in Bb (K207, 1775), no. 2 in D (K211, 1775), no. 3 in G (K216, 1775), no. 4 in D (K218, 1775), no. 5 in A (K219, 1775); Concertone in C for 2 violins (K190, 1774); Sinfonia Concertante for vln., vla. and orch. (K364, 1779); for bassoon in Bb (K191, 1774); for flute, in G (K313, 1778), for oboe in C (K314, 1778); for flute and harp in C (K299, 1778); for clar. in A (K622, 1791), Sinfonia Concertante in Eb for oboe, clar., horn and bassoon (K297b, 1778, judged as spurious by some scholars); 4 for horn: no. 1 in D (K412, 1782), no. 2 in Eb (K417, 1783), no. 3 in Eb (K447, ?1784–7), no. 4 in Eb (K495, 1786).

CHAMBER MUSIC: 23 string 4tets, nos. 1–13 (1770–3), nos. 14–19 ded. to Haydn (1782–5): in G (K387), in D min. (K421), in Eb (K428), in Bb (K458, *The Hunt*), in A (K464), in C (K465, *Dissonance*), no. 20 in D (K499, 1786, *Hoffmeister*), nos. 21–3 ded. to King of Prussia (1789–90): in D (K575), in Bb (K589), in F (K590); 6 string 5tets: no. 1 in Bb (K174, 1773), no. 2 in C min. (K406, 1788; arr. of serenade K388), no. 3 in C (K515, 1787), no. 4 in G min. (K516, 1787), no. 5 in D (K593, 1790), no. 6 in Eb (K614, 1791); string trio in Eb, Divertimento (K563, 1788); 5 piano trios: in Bb (K254, 1776), in G (K496, 1786), in Bb (K502, 1786), in E (K542, 1788), in C (K548, 1788); 2 piano 4tets: in G min. (K478, 1785), in Eb (K493, 1786); oboe 4tet (K370, 1781); horn 5tet (K407, 1782); 5tet for pf. and wind (K452, 1784); clar. 5tet (K581, 1789); clar. trio in Eb (K498, 1786). 17 pf sonatas, incl no. 8 in A min. (K310, 1778), no. 9 in D (K311, 1777), nos. 10–13 in C, A and F (K330–3, 1781–4), no. 14 in C min. (K457, 1784), no. 15 in C (K545, 1788), no. 16 in Bb (K570, 1789), no. 17 in D (K576, 1789); sonata in D for 2 pfs. (K448, 1781); 35 sonatas for vln. and pf.: nos. 1–16 comp. 1762–6, no. 17 in C (K296, 1778), nos. 18–23, in G, Eb, C, E min., A and D (K301–306, 1778), no. 24 in F (K376, 1778), no. 25 in F (K377, 1781), no. 26 in Bb (K378, 1779 or 81), no. 27 in G (K379, 1781), no. 28 in Eb (K380, 1781), no. 29 in A (K402, 1782), no. 30 in C (K403, 1782), no. 31 in C (K404, 1782 or 88), no. 32 in Bb (K454, 1784), no. 33 in Eb (K481, 1785), no. 34 in A (K526, 1787), no. 35 in F (K547, 1788). Variations for pf., Fantasia in D min. (K397, 1782 or 1786–7), Fantasia in C min. (K475, 1785), Rondo in A min. (K511, 1787), Adagio in B min. (K540, 1788), Gigue in G (K574, 1789).

SOLO SONGS AND LIEDER inc. *Die Zufriedenheit* (K349), *Oiseaux, si tous les ans* (K307), *Der Zauberer* (K472), *Das Veilchen* (K476), *Als Luise* (K520), *Abendempfindung* (K523), *Das Traumbild* (K530), *Sehnsucht nach dem Frühlinge* (Longing for Spring, K596; theme also used in finale of the last pf. concerto).

Mozart, (Franz Xaver) Wolfgang Amadeus (b Vienna, 26 Jul 1791; d Karlsbad, 29 Jul 1844), Austrian pianist and composer, son of prec. Pupil of Hummel, Salieri and Vogler. He settled as music master at Lwów in 1808, but toured in Aus. and Ger. in 1819–22. He settled in Vienna in 1838. Works incl. orchestral and chamber music.

Mozartiana, Tchaikovsky's 4th suite for orch., op. 61, comp. in 1887. It consists of 4 works by Mozart scored for orch. by Tchaikovsky: jig and minuet for pf., K475 and 355; motet *Ave, verum corpus*, K618 and variations on a theme from *La rencontre imprévue* by Gluck for pf., K455. Fp Moscow, 26 Nov 1887.

mp (abbr.) = *mezzo piano* (half soft).

Mravina, Evgeniya (b St Petersburg, 16 Feb 1864; d Yalta, 25 Oct 1914), Russian soprano. She was as highly regarded for her dramatic as for her vocal ability; St Petersburg 1886–97 as Antonida, Tatyana, Elsa and Marguerite de Valois.

Mravinsky, Evgeny (b St Petersburg, 4 Jun 1903; d Leningrad, 20 Jan 1988), Russian conductor. He studied at the Leningrad Cons. and was cond. of the Leningrad PO from 1938. Active on behalf of Soviet music, he gave fps of Shostakovich's symphs. nos. 5, 6, 8, 9 and 10. Cond. the fp of Prokofiev's 6th symph., Leningrad, 1947. Often heard in the stage works of Tchaikovsky, and cond. orch. music by Bartók and Stravinsky.

Much Ado about Nothing. *See also* **Béatrice et Bénédict.**

Opera by Stanford (lib. by J.R. Sturgis, after Shakespeare), prod. London, CG, 30 May 1901.

Muck, Carl (b Darmstadt, 22 Oct 1859; d Stuttgart, 3 Mar 1940), German conductor. Studied at Heidelberg Univ. and at the Leip-zig Univ. and Cons. In 1880 he began a pianist's career, but became cond. at Salzburg, Brno and Graz in succession, at Prague in 1886, and finally in Berlin, at the Royal Opera, in 1892. He gave the 1st Russian perfs. of the *Ring* (1889); cond. Wagner in London and from 1901 at Bayreuth (*Parsifal* until 1930), also the Phil. concerts in Vienna. From 1906 to 1918, with an interruption, he cond. the Boston SO. He was arrested as an enemy alien in 1918. He returned to Europe after the war and cond. in Hamburg from 1922 to 1933. He was well known in the symphs. of Bruckner.

Mudarra, Alonso de (b Palencia diocese *c* 1508; d Seville, 1 Apr 1580), Spanish vihuelist and composer. He became a canon of Seville Cathedral in 1546, and in the same year pub. a book of vihuela pieces and songs with vihuela incl. variations and dances.

Mudd, John (b London, 1555; d Peterborough, buried 16 Dec 1631), English organist and composer. Organist at Peterborough Cathedral from 1583 to 1631. Wrote services, anthems, etc.

Mudd, Thomas (b London, *c* 1560; d after 1619), English composer. He went to St Paul's School in London and in 1578 to Cambridge as a sizar for the sons of London mercers.

Works incl. services, anthems; dances for 3 viols.

Muette de Portici, La (*The Dumb Girl of Portici*), opera by Auber (lib. by Scribe and Delavigne), prod. Paris, Opéra, 29 Feb 1828. Carafa's *Masaniello*, on the same subject, had been prod. at the Opéra-Comique 2 months earlier. Auber's work is often called *Masaniello.*

Muffat, Georg (b Mégève, Savoy, bap. 1 Jun 1653; d Passau, 23 Feb 1704), Austrian organist and composer. Studied in Paris, with Lully or members of his school. In 1678 he was app. organist to the Archbishop of Salzburg, and after visiting Vienna and Rome went to Passau to become organist to the bishop in 1690.

Works incl. chamber sonatas *Armonico tributo* (1682), *Auserlesene mit Ernst und Lust gemengte Instrumental-Musik*, *Apparatus musico-organisticus* for org. (12 toccatas, chaconne and passacaglia, 1690), *Suaviores harmoniae* (1695), 2 vols. for harpsichord.

Muffat, Gottlieb (Theophil) (b Passau, bap. 25 Apr 1690; d Vienna, 9 Dec 1770), German organist and composer, son of prec. Pupil of Fux in Vienna from 1704, he entered the service of the court in 1717 and became 1st organist in 1741. Among his pupils were Wagenseil and the Empress Maria Theresa.

Works incl. 72 fugues and 12 toccatas for org., *Componimenti musicali* for harpsichord.

Mugnone, Leopoldo (b Naples, 29 Sep 1858; d Naples, 22 Dec 1941), Italian conductor and composer, studied at Naples and at the age of 12 wrote a comic opera; a 2nd was prod. in public in 1875. He also began to cond. very young, at 16, but afterwards gained more experience as chorus master and accompanist. In 1890 he was engaged to cond. the prod. of *Cavalleria rusticana* in Rome, and after that he made a brilliant career as operatic and concert cond.; active on behalf of Giordano, Wagner and Charpentier in Europe and S. America. He wrote several more comic operas.

Mühlfeld, Richard (b Salzungen, 28 Feb 1856; d Meiningen, 1 Jun 1907), German clarinettist. In the grand-ducal orch. at Meiningen from 1873. 1st clarinettist at Bayreuth, 1884–96. Brahms wrote the 4 late chamber works with clar. parts, opp. 114, 115, 120 (i and ii) for him.

Muldowney, Dominic (b Southampton, 19 Jul 1952), English composer. He studied with Jonathan Harvey at Southampton and with Birtwistle in London. Composer in residence, National Theatre, London, since 1976.

Works incl. *An Heavyweight Dirge* for soloists and chamber ens. (1971); *Driftwood to the Flow* for 18 strings (1972); *Klavier-Hammer* for one or more pfs. (1973); *Music at Chartres* for 16 insts. (1973); 2 string 4tets (1973 and 1980), *Lovemusic for Bathsheba Evergreen and Gabriel Oak* for chamber ens. (1974); *Double Helix* for 8 players (1977), *Macbeth*, ballet music (1979); *5 Theatre Poems*, after Brecht (1981); *The Duration of Exile* for mezzo and chamber ens. (1982); a realization of *The Beggar's Opera* (1982); pf. concerto (1983), saxophone concerto (1984).

Mulè Giuseppe (b Termini, Sicily, 28 Jun 1855; d Rome, 10 Sep 1951), Italian cellist and composer. Studied at the Palermo Cons., of which he was dir. from 1922 to 1925, when he became dir. of the Santa Cecilia Cons. in Rome. He also became secretary to the Fascist syndicate of musicians. He studied Sicilian folksong and found that its roots went back to Gk. music; wrote much incid. music for the perfs. of Gk. plays at Syracuse.

Works incl. operas *La Baronessa di Carini*

(1912), *Al lupo*, *La monacella della fontana* (1923), *Dafni* (1928), *Liolà* (on Pirandello's play, 1935), *Taormina*; music for Gk. plays; Aeschylus' *Choephori*, *Seven against Thebes*, Euripides' *Bacchae*, *Medea*, *The Cyclops*, *Hippolytus*, *Iphigenia in Aulis*, *Iphigenia in Taruis*, Sophocles' *Antigone*; incid. mus. for Corradini's *Giulio Cesare*; oratorio *Il cieco di Gerico* (1910); symph. poems *Sicilia canora* and *Vendemmia*; *Tre canti siciliani* for voice and orch.; string 4tet; vln. and cello pieces.

Müller, August Eberhard (b Northeim, Hanover, 13 Dec 1767; d Weimar, 3 Dec 1817), German organist and composer. Held appts. at Magdeburg and Leipzig, where he became cantor of St Thomas's Church in 1804. App. court *Kapellmeister* at Weimar in 1810.

Works incl. Singspiel *Der Polterabend* (1813), 2 operettas; 3 cantatas; 2 pf. concertos, 11 fl. concertos; pf. trio; 2 vln. and pf. sonatas; pf. sonatas, variations, etc.; sonata, suites, chorale variations, etc., for organ; fl. duets and pieces.

Müller-Hartmann, Robert (b Hamburg, 11 Oct 1884; d Dorking, Surrey, 15 Dec 1950), German critic and composer. He was lecturer in music theory at Hamburg Univ. in 1923–33 and settled in London in 1937.

Works incl. incid. music to Büchner's *Leonce und Lena* and other plays; variations on a Pastoral Theme and other works for orch.; chamber music; songs, etc.

Müller, Maria (b Teresienstadt, 29 Jan 1898; d Bayreuth, 13 Mar 1958), Austrian soprano. Debut Linz 1919, as Elsa. NY Met 1925–35, debut as Sieglinde; in 1932 she was the 1st US Maria Boccanegra. Bayreuth 1930–44 as Elisabeth, Eva, Gutrune, Elsa and Senta. Berlin 1926–52. London, CG, 1934 and 1937. Other roles incl. Jenůfa, Strauss's Helen and Donna Elvira.

Müller, Wenzel (b Trnava, Morav., 26 Sep 1767; d Baden nr. Vienna, 3 Aug 1835), Austrian composer and conductor. Pupil of Dittersdorf, became cond. at the Brno theatre in 1783, aged 16 and in 1786 at the Leopoldstadt Theatre in Vienna, where he settled until 1808, and again in 1813, being dir. at the Prague Opera during those years, when his daughter Therese was engaged there. (*See* **Grünbaum, Therese**). On his return to Vienna he became again cond. of the Leopoldstadt Theatre.

Works incl. nearly 200 operas and musical plays, e.g. *Das Sonnenfest der Braminen* (1790), *Die Zauberzither, oder Kaspar der Fagottist* (1791), *Das Neusonntagskind*

(1793), *Die Schwestern von Prag* (1794), *Die Teufelsmühle auf dem Wienerberge* (1799), *Die travestierte Zauberflöte* (a parody of Mozart's *Magic Flute*, 1818); Masses; symph.

Müller, Wilhelm (1794–1827), German poet. *See* **Schöne Müllerin** (Schubert), **Winterreise** (do.).

Mulliner Book, The, a large MS. collection of English keyboard music dating from *c* 1550 to 1575, apparently copied by Thomas Mulliner. It contains both organ and virginal pieces, incl. transcriptions of viol and vocal music with the names of Blitheman, Shepherd, Redford and Tallis predominating. There are 123 pieces, and 11 more for cittern.

Mullings, Frank (b Walsall, 10 May 1881; d Manchester, 19 May 1953), English tenor, studied at the Birmingham and Midland School of Music, appeared at Coventry in *Faust* in 1907 and at a concert in London in 1911. He then specialized in heroic tenor parts in opera, joined the Denhof Co. in 1913 and was engaged by Beecham in 1919, singing Wagnerian parts with great intensity and being esp. impressive as Verdi's Otello. Other roles incl. Parsifal, Siegfried, Tristan and Radames.

Mullova, Viktoria (b Moscow, 27 Nov 1959), Russian violinist. She made her debut aged 12 and studied with Kogan at the Moscow Cons. After winning the 1982 Tchaikovsky Competition, she left Russia to pursue a career in the West; concerts with the Boston SO, Pittsburgh SO, Philadelphia Orchestra, LSO and the Berlin PO. Her virtuosity has been admired in the concertos of Sibelius, Shostakovich, Tchaikovsky and Paganini.

Mumma, Gordon (b Framingham, Mass., 30 Mar 1935), American composer. In 1957 co-founded Space Theatre, giving perf. with computerised electronics. Worked at elec. studio, Ann Arbour, from 1958; Merce Cunningham Dance Co. from 1968. Works involve use of computer techniques, called sybersonics; *Sinfonia* for 12 insts. (1960), *Le Corbusier* (1965), *Mesa* (1966), *Ambivex* (1972). .

Munch, Charles (b Strasbourg, 26 Sep 1891; d Richmond, Penn., 6 Nov 1968). French conductor. Studied at Strasbourg Cons. and then went to Paris for further vln. studies with Capet and Berlin with Flesch. From 1919 to 1925 he taught the vln. at Strasbourg Cons. and led the city orch., becoming leader of the Leipzig Gewandhaus Orch. in 1926. He made his debut as cond. in 1932 in Paris and after var. teaching and cond. posts he was cond. of the Boston SO 1949–1962 and in 1951 dir. of the Berkshire Music Center in Tanglewood. Helped found L'Orchestre de Paris, in 1967.

Münchinger, Karl (b Stuttgart, 29 May 1915), German conductor. Studied in Leipzig with H.Abendroth and in 1945 founded the Stuttgart Chamber Orch., which soon became known as one of the finest ensembles of its kind. Frequent perfs. of Bach in world tours.

Mundy, John (b *c* 1555; d Windsor, 29 Jun 1630), English organist and composer. Studied under his father, William M., became a Gentleman of the Chapel Royal in London and succeeded Marbeck as one of the organists of St George's Chapel, Windsor, about 1585.

Works incl. anthems, *Songs and Psalmes* for 3–5 voices; madrigals (one in *The Triumphes of Oriana*); virginal pieces incl. the 'Weather' fantasia.

Mundy, William (b *c* 1529; d London, *c* 1591), English singer and composer, father of prec. He was a vicar-choral at St Paul's Cathedral in London and became a Gentleman of the Chapel Royal in 1564.

Works incl. services, anthems, Lat. motets, etc.

Munrow, David (b Birmingham, 12 Aug 1942; d Chesham Bois, 15 May 1976), English early music specialist and performer of wind insts. He founded the Early Music Consort in 1967 and taught at Leicester Univ. and the RAM. Often heard in medieval and Renaissance music and a frequent broadcaster. Died by suicide.

Muratore, Lucien (b Marseilles, 29 Aug, 1876; d Paris, 16 Jul 1954), French tenor. Debut Paris, Opéra-Comique, in the 1902 fp of Hahn's *La Carmélite*. At the Opéra he sang in the fps of Massenet's *Ariane* (1906) and *Bacchus* (1909). At Monte Carlo he was Ulysses in the fp of Fauré's *Pénélope* (1913). At Chicago and Buenos Aires he was Prinzivalle in the local fps of Février's *Monna Vanna*. Other roles incl. Faust and Reyer's Sigurd.

Murino, Aegidius de, 14th-cent. theorist and composer of uncertain nationality. He may possibly be the 'Egidius Anglicus' of the MS. Chantilly 1047. His treatise *Tractatus de diversis figuris* is about note-forms and motet comp. 2 motets and 1 *chanson* also survive.

Muris, Johannes de (b Lisieux, *c* 1300; d *c* 1350), French mathematician, astronomer and music theorist. He lived for some time in

Paris and worked there as mathematician and astronomer. The chief among the music treatises attrib. to him is the *Ars novae musicae*, 1319.

Murky Bass, an 18th-cent. term of unknown origin for a bass played in broken octaves on keyboard instruments.

Murray, Ann (b Dublin, 27 Aug 1949), Irishborn mezzo. She studied at the RMCM. Opera debut as Alceste, with Scottish Opera; CG since 1976 as Cherubino, Dorabella and the Composer. She sang Nicklausse at the 1981 Salzburg Festival and returned in 1985 for Minerva in the Henze realization of Monteverdi's *Ulisse*: she had sung the same role in the Leppard version of the work at Glyndebourne in 1979. ENO 1985, Xerxes. NY Met 1984–5 as Sextus, Annius and Dorabella. Highly regarded as a concert singer.

Murrill, Herbert (Henry John) (b London, 11 May 1909; d London, 25 Jul 1952), English composer. Studied at the RAM in London and at Worcester Coll., Oxford. After holding var. organist's posts from 1926, he became prof. of comp. at the RAM in 1933, joined the music staff of the BBC in 1936 and became Head of Music in 1950.

Works incl. opera *Man in Cage* (1930); 3 hornpipes for orch.; 2 concertos and 3 pieces for cello and orch.; string 4tet and other chamber music.

Murschhauser, Franz Xaver Anton (b Zabern, bap. 1 Jul 1663; d Munich, 6 Jan 1738), Alsatian composer. Pupil of Kerl at Munich, where he became *Kapellmeister* at the church of Our Lady. In 1721, by a remark made in his treatise on comp., *Academia musico-poetica*, he came into conflict with Mattheson.

Works incl. *Vespertinus latriae* for 4 voices and strings (1700); org. books *Octitonium novum organum, Prototypon longobreve organicum, Opus organicum tripartitum* (1696).

Murska, Ilma di. *See* **Di Murska.**

Muset, Colin, French 12th-cent. trouvère and jongleur. The poems of 15 and the music of 8 of his songs are extant.

Musette (Fr.). (1) A form of bagpipe popular in France in the 17th and 18th cents.

(2) A piece on a drone bass imitating more or less faithfully the music of a bagpipe. It often took the place of a trio section alternating with a Gavotte in classical suites.

Musgrave, Thea (b Barnton, Midlothian, 27 May 1928), Scottish composer and pianist. Studied at Edinburgh Univ. and with N. Boulanger in Paris. Lectured at London

Univ. 1959–65; Univ. of California from 1970. Her music has employed serial and improvisatory techniques.

Works incl. operas *The Abbot of Drimock* (1955), *The Decision* (1967), *The Voice of Ariadne* (1974), *Mary, Queen of Scots* (1977), *A Christmas Carol* (1979), *An Occurrence at Owl Creek Bridge* (1981); *Scot. Dance Suite* for orch., *Divertimento* for string orch., *Perspectives* for small orch.; 3 chamber concertos for var. insts., Concerto for Orch (1967), *Peripateia* for orch (1981); *Triptych* for tenor and orch.; *The Five Ages of Man* for chorus and orch.; string 4tet (1958); 2 pf. sonatas; songs.

Music Drama, an alternative term for 'opera' used by comps., notably Wagner, who felt that the older term implies methods and forms for which they had no use.

Music Makers, The, ode for contralto solo, chorus and orch. by Elgar, op. 69 (poem by Arthur O'Shaughnessy), fp Birmingham Festival, 1 Oct 1912. The work contains a number of quotations from earlier works by Elgar.

Musica ficta (Lat. = false music), in common parlance, unwritten accidentals added to editions of medieval and Renaissance music because they would have been incorporated automatically by musicians of the time. Most often they are added to correct augmented or diminished intervals (whether vertical or horizontal) as well as to raise the leading note (or lower the 2nd degree) at a cadence. They are normally placed above the stave or in small print to distinguish them from MS accidentals. But originally the term meant any note that is not on the gamut (see *musica recta*) and therefore incl. written accidentals as well as unwritten ones. The modern meaning dates perhaps from the 15th cent. though it seems to have been normal to operate *musica recta* before *musica ficta*.

Musica figurata (Lat. and It. = figured or decorated music), the ornamenting of Plainsong by auxiliary notes or the addition of a Descant sung against a fundamental melody.

Musica recta (Lat. = orthodox music), a term used in the 14th and 15th cents. to mean the notes of the gamut as projected by the three kinds of hexachord, that is, the white-note scale from G to e'' but including B♭ as well as B♮ (or, with a key-signature of one flat, including E♭ as well as E♮, and so on). Since this was the normal scale, the note B could be sung either flat or natural without special indications. This concept is important for editorial accidentals and *musica fic-*

ta: where there is an alternative, *musica recta* should be operated before *musica ficta*.

Musica reservata (Lat. = reserved music), a 16th-cent. term applied to music intended for connoisseurs and private occasions, partic. vocal music which faithfully interpreted the words.

Musica Transalpina, the title of a collection of It. (transalpine) madrigals with Eng. words pub. in London by Nicholas Yonge in 1588, containing 75 pieces, incl. 2 by Byrd, *La verginella*, set to a trans. of 2 stanzas from Ariosto. The Italian contributors incl. Palestrina and Marenzio, and there are also Italian madrigals by Flemish comps. incl. Lassus, de Vert and Verdonck. A 2nd vol. followed in 1597, containing 24 works, this time all by Italian comps.

Musical Box, a toy instrument made in var. shapes of fancy boxes and containing a cylinder with pins which, turning round by clockwork, twangs the teeth of a metal comb prod. the notes of a musical scale. The pins are so arranged as to make the pattern of a piece of music, and several sets of pins can be set in the barrel, only one touching the teeth at a time, a choice of more than one piece being thus producible by the simple device of shifting the barrel slightly sideways. The musical box industry is centred mainly in Switzerland.

Musical Comedy (now generally abbr. to 'Musical'), a light 20th-cent. musical entertainment similar to operetta. As a nonspecific term it appears as early as 1765 in a title of a Covent Garden pasticcio, *The Summer's Tale*.

Musical Offering (Bach). *See* **Musikalische Opfer**.

Musical Snuffbox, a kind of musical box made esp. in the 18th cent., with a double bottom concealing a mechanical music apparatus beneath its normal contents.

Musicology, the scientific and scholarly study of any aspect of music; hence musicologist, one who pursues such a study.

Musikalische Opfer, Das (*The Musical Offering*), a late work by Bach (BWV 1079) containing 2 *ricercari*, a fugue in canon, 9 canons and a sonata for fl., vln. and continuo, all based on a theme given to Bach by Frederick II of Prus. during the comp.'s visit to Potsdam in 1747.

Musikalischer Spass, Ein (Ger. = *A Musical Joke*), a work in 4 movements for 2 horns and strings by Mozart, K522 (comp. Jun 1787), sometimes also known by such names as 'The Village Band'. But the joke is not at the expense of rustic performers; the

work is a parody of a symph. by an incompetent composer.

Musique concrète, music composed by recording live sounds and subjecting them to electronic modification or modification on tape. The term was invented by Pierre Schaeffer in the late 1940s. See also **Henry, Pierre,**

Musique mesurée (Fr. = measured music), a special method of setting words to music cultivated in 16th-cent. Fr. by Baïf, Le Jeune, Mauduit and others. The metrical rhythm of the words was based on classical scansion and the musical rhythm followed this exactly, long syllables being set to long notes, and short syllables to short notes.

Mussorgsky, Modest Petrovich (b Karevo, Gvt. of Pskov, 21 Mar 1839; d St Petersburg, 28 Mar 1881), Russian composer. The son of well-to-do landowners, he was sent to St Petersburg at the age of 10 to prepare for a military school, which he entered in 1852. He joined a regiment in 1856 and he did not seriously think of a music career until he met Dargomizhsky and Balakirev in 1857 and began to study under the latter. He resigned his commission in 1858, but never studied systematically. His family's fortune waned after the liberation of the serfs in 1861, but he was in sympathy with that movement and content to live on the small pay he obtained for a government employment. His interest in the common people led him to write realistic songs following the inflections of their speech, and he endeavoured to do the same with his operatic characters. He finished *Boris Godunov* in its 1st form in 1869, but it was rejected by the Imp. Opera and he recast it in 1871–2, this 2nd version being prod. in 1874. He sank more and more into poverty and ruined his health with drink. He died in hospital from a spinal disease.

Works incl. operas *Salammbô* (after Flaubert, unfinished, 1863–6), *The Marriage* (Gogol, unfinished, 1868, prod. 1909), *Boris Godunov* (after Pushkin, 1869 rev. 1872), *Khovanshchina* (1886), *Sorochintsy Fair* (after Gogol, unfinished, 1874–80); an act for a collective opera, *Mlada* (with Borodin, Cui and Rimsky-Korsakov, afterwards used for other works); incid. music for Ozerov's *Oedipus Rex*; *The Destruction of Sennacherib* (after Byron, 1867), and *Jesus Navin* for chorus and orch.

4 Rus. folksongs for male chorus; *Night on the Bare Mountain* for orch. (later used in *Mlada* [with chorus] and further revised) and 3 small orchestral pieces; suite *Pictures*

at an Exhibition (1874) and 12 small pieces for pf.; over 60 songs incl. cycles *The Nursery* (1870), *Sunless* and *Songs and Dances of Death* (1875–7).

Mustafà, Domenico (b Sterpara nr. Foligno, 14 Apr 1829; d Montefalco nr. Perugia, 18 Mar 1912), Italian castrato and composer. He was the last male soprano of the Sistine Chapel, which he entered in 1848. He was later *maestro di cappella* there until 1902, when he was succeeded by Lorenzo Perosi.
Works incl. Miserere, *Tu es Petrus, Dies irae* for 7 voices, *Laudate* and other church music.

Mustel Organ, an instrument invented by Victor Mustel (1815–90) of Paris. It is of the Harmonium type, but contains some improvements, incl. a device by which the top and bottom halves of the keyboard can be separately controlled for dynamic expression.

Muta (It. imper. = change), a direction used in scores where a change is to be made between instruments (e.g. A and Bb clar. or different horn crooks) or in tunings (e.g. kettledrums, strings of instruments of the vln. family temporarily tuned to abnormal notes), etc. The plural is *mutano*.

Mutation Stops, a range of organ stops sounding notes a 12th, 17th, 19th or flat 21st above those of the key pressed down. They are not played alone, but only with other stops which sound their own proper notes, and they fulfil, together with those normal keys, the function of Mixture Stops.

Mute, the name of various devices of different kinds but all serving to damp the tone of an instrument. The 'soft pedal' of the pf. is a mute, but is rarely so called. Mutes of string instruments are a kind of fork whose prongs are made to grip the bridge and lessen its vibration, and with it the vibration of the strings. Brass wind instruments have cone-shaped mutes inserted into the bell. Drums can be muted without any special mechanical device, merely by a cloth spread over the head.

Müthel, Johann Gottfried (b Mölln, Lauenburg, 17 Jan 1728; d Bienenhof nr. Riga, 14 Jul 1788), German organist, harpsichordist and composer. Pupil of Kunzen in Lübeck, app. court organist to the Duke of Mecklenburg-Schwerin in 1747. On leave of absence to study in 1750 he visited Bach in Leipzig just before Bach's death, also Altnikol in Naumburg, C.P.E. Bach in Berlin and Telemann in Hamburg. From 1755 organist in Riga.

Works incl. concertos, sonatas and miscellaneous pieces for harpsichord.

Muti, Riccardo (b Naples, 28 Jul 1941), Italian conductor. He studied in Naples and won the 1967 Cantelli International Comp. Princ. cond. Florence Maggio Musicale from 1969; has led *Guillaume Tell, L'Africaine* and operas by Spontini and Verdi there. US debut 1972, Philadelphia Orch.; princ. cond. from 1981. Chief cond. Philharmonia Orch., London, 1973–82; CG debut 1977, *Aida*. From 1971 has often been heard in Salzburg and Vienna. Musical dir., La Scala, from 1986.

Mutter, Anne-Sophie (b Rheinfeldin, 29 Jun 1963), German violinist. She attracted the attention of Karajan at the 1976 Lucerne Festival and appeared with him at Salzburg the following year. Brit. debut 1977, with the LSO under Barenboim; later appeared in London with Rostropovich and at the 1985 Aldeburgh Festival. US debut Washington 1980, Moscow Mar 1985. Her youthful virtuosity is admired in the standard concertos, and in Jan 1986 she gave the fp of Lutosławski's *Chain 2* for vln. and orch.

Muzen Siciliens, Die (*The Muses of Sicily*), concerto by Henze for chorus, 2 pfs., wind and perc. (text from Virgil's *Eclogues*), fp Berlin, 20 Sep 1966.

Muzio, Claudia (b Pavia, 7 Feb 1889; d Rome, 24 May 1936), Italian soprano. Studied pf. and harp at first, but her teachers discovered great vocal gifts, and she made her 1st stage appearance at Arezzo in 1910 as Manon. Soon afterwards she 1st visited London and sang Desdemona, Tosca and Mimi. NY Met 1916–34; roles incl. Giorgetta, Tatyana and Catalani's Loreley.

Muzio Scevola, Il (*Mucius Scaevola*), opera by Filippo Mattei (or Amadei), Giovanni Bononcini and Handel (lib. by P.A. Rolli), prod. London King's Theatre, Haymarket, 15 Apr 1721.

My Country (Smetana). *See* **Má Vlast.**

Myaskovsky, Nikolay. *See* **Miakovsky.**

Myers, Rollo H(ugh) (b Chislehurst, 23 Jan 1892; d Chichester, 1 Jan 1985), English critic and writer on music. Educ. privately and at Oxford, and had a year at the RCM in London. Music correspondent to *The Times* and *Daily Telegraph* in Paris 1919–34 and on BBC staff in London, 1935–44, Music Officer for British Council in Paris, 1945–6. Ed. *Chesterian* from 1947 and *Music To-day* from 1949. Pub. books *Modern Music, Music in the Modern World, Erik Satie, Debussy*; comp. songs.

Mysliveček, Josef (b nr. Prague, 9 Mar

1737; d Rome, 4 Feb 1781), Bohemian composer. Studied organ and comp. in Prague, and pub. there in 1760 a set of symphs. named after the first 6 months of the year. Went to study with Pescetti in Venice in 1763, and a year later prod. his first opera in Parma. Between 1767 and 1780 followed *c* 30 further operas, most to texts by Metastasio, for the principal theatres in It. He also visited Munich, where Mozart, who had already met him in 1772, saw him in 1777.

Works incl. operas *Medea* (1764), *Il Bellerofonte* (1767), *Farnace*, *Demofoonte* (1769), *Ezio*, *Il Demetrio* (1773), etc.; oratorio *Abramo ed Isacco* (1776) and 3 others; symphs.; concertos; chamber music; church music.

Mystic Trumpeter, The, scena for soprano and orch. by Holst (text by Whitman); 1904, fp London, 29 Jun 1905. Revised 1912 and perf. London, 25 Jan 1913.

N

Nabokov, Nikolai (b Lubtcha, 17 Apr 1903; d New York, 6 Apr 1978), Russian composer. Studied in Berlín and Stuttgart. He became attached to Diaghilev's Rus. Ballet in the 1920s, and later he settled in USA. Works incl. operas *The Holy Devil* (1958) and *Love's Labour Lost* (1973); ballets *Ode on seeing the Aurora Borealis* (1928), *Union Pacific* (1934) and *Don Quixote* (1965); incid. music to a dramatic version of Milton's *Samson Agonistes*; symph., *Sinfonia biblica* for orch.; pf. concerto (1932); 3 symphs (1930–68); cantata *Collectionneur d'échos* for soprano, bass, chorus and perc.

Nabucco. See below.

Nabucodonosor (*Nebuchadnezzar*: colloquially *Nabucco*), opera by Verdi (lib. by T. Solera), prod. Milan, La Scala, 9 Mar 1842.

Nachbaur, Franz (b Giessen, nr. Friedrichshafen, 25 Mar 1835; d Munich, 21 Mar 1902), German tenor. Studied with Lamperti at Milan and others, sang at var. Ger. opera houses and became attached to the Munich Court opera in 1866, creating the part of Walther in Wagner's *Meistersinger* there in 1868; also created Froh in *Das Rheingold* (1869). London, Drury Lane, 1882 as Adolar. Other roles incl. Faust, Rienzi, Radames and Roméo.

Nacht in Venedig, Eine (*A Night in Venice*), operetta by J. Strauss, jun. (lib. by F. Zell and R. Genée), prod. Berlin, Städtisches Theater, 3 Oct 1883. Written for the opening of that theatre, 1st Vienna perf. Theater an der Wien, 9 Oct 1883.

Nachtanz (Ger. lit. after-dance), a quicker dance following a slower one, often with the same music in different rhythm in the 15th–16th cents., esp. the Galliard following the Pavan.

Nachtlager von Granada, Das (*The Night-Camp at Granada*), opera by C. Kreutzer (lib. by K.J.B. von Braunthal, based on a play by Friedrich Kind), prod. Vienna, Josefstadt Theatre, 13 Jan 1834.

Nachtmusik (Ger., lit. night piece) = Nocturne.

Nachtstücke und Arien (*Nocturnes and Arias*), work by Henze for sop. and orch. (text by I. Bachmann), fp Donaueschingen, 20 Oct 1957, cond. Rosbaud.

Naderman, François Joseph (b Paris, 1781; d Paris, 3 Apr 1835), French harpist and composer. Son of a harp maker, he became harpist at the Paris Opéra and in the royal chapel, also harp prof. at the Cons. from 1825.
Works incl. 2 harp concertos; chamber music with harp parts; harp solos; also with Duport, nocturnes for cello and harp.

Nägeli, Hans Georg (b Wetzikon, nr. Zurich, 26 May 1773; d Zurich, 26 Dec 1836), Swiss composer, teacher, author and publisher. Studied at Zurich and Berne and began to pub. music at Zurich in 1792. In 1803 he began a series entitled *Répertoire des clavecinistes* and incl. in it Beethoven's sonatas op. 31 Nos. 1 and 2, adding 4 bars to the former, much to the comp.'s annoyance. He estab. the *Schweizerbund* choral society which soon formed branches, and reformed music teaching in schools on the lines of Pestalozzi's educ. system. He also wrote on music educ. and lectured on music in Switz. and Ger.
Works incl. church and school music; toccatas and other pf. pieces; 15 books of popular songs, inc. 'Freut euch des Lebens' and 'Lied vom Rhein'.

Naich, Hubert (b ? Liège, c 1513, d ? Liège after 1546), Flemish composer. Lived in Rome, where he was a member of the Accademia degli Amici and pub. a book of madrigals there c 1540.

Nail Violin, an 18th-cent instrument also called Nail Fiddle or Nail Harmonica, invented by a Ger. violinist Johann Wilde, living at St Petersburg. It was a semi-circular sound-board studded with nails along the rounded edge, which were scraped with a bow.

Naïs, pastoral-héroïque by Rameau (lib. by L. de Cahusac); comp. for the peace of Aix-la-Chapelle, prod. Paris, Opéra, 22 Apr 1749.

Naissance de la Lyre, La (*The Birth of the Lyre*), lyric opera in 1 act by Roussel (lib. by T. Reinach, after Sophocles), prod. Paris, Opéra, 1 Jul 1925, with choreography by Nijinska. Symphonic fragments in 6 movts. perf. Paris, 13 Nov 1927, cond. Paray.

Nakers (from Arabic through old French *nacaires*), an old English name for the Kettledrums, which were then much smaller and therefore higher in pitch, and could not have their tuning altered. In cavalry regiments they were played on horseback, hung on each side of the horse's neck.

Naldi, Giuseppe (b Bologna, 2 Feb 1770; d Paris, 14 Dec 1820), Italian baritone. Studied law at Bologna and Pavia Univs., but turned to music and made his 1st stage appearance at Milan at an early age. He sang in London each year in 1806–19 in operas by Guglielmi, Mayr, Paer, Paisiello and Piccinni. He was the 1st London Don Alfonso (1811), Papageno (1811), Figaro (1812) and Leporello (1817). He was killed by an exploding kettle.

Namensfeier (*Name*[*-Day*] *Celebration*), concert overture by Beethoven, op. 115, in C maj., comp. 1814, Vienna, Redoutensaal, 25 Dec 1815, cond. by the comp. The name-day was that of the Aus. emperor, which happened to coincide with the completion of the work; it was not comp. specially for that occasion.

Namouna, ballet by Lalo (scenario by Charles Nuitter; choreog. by Marius Petipa), prod. Paris, Opéra, 6 Mar 1882.

Nanino, Giovanni Bernardino (b Vallerano, *c* 1560; d Rome, 1623), Italian composer. Studied under his brother, went to Rome, and from 1591 to 1608 was *maestro di cappella* at the church of San Luigi de' Francesi there, later at that of San Lorenzo in Damaso. He made early use of the basso continuo.

Works incl. motets, psalms and other church music some with organ accomp.; 5-part madrigals.

Nanino, Giovanni Maria (b Tivoli, *c* 1545; d Rome, 11 Mar 1607), Italian tenor and composer, brother of prec. After learning music as a choir-boy at Vallerano, he went to Rome as a pupil of Mel, became a singer at the church of Santa Maria Maggiore, *maestro di cappella* at the church of San Luigi de' Francesi in 1575, singer in the Papal Chapel, 1577, and *maestro di cappella* at Santa Maria Maggiore, 1579. He opened a music school in 1580 with the assistance of his brother and Palestrina, supplied music to the Sistine Chapel and became *maestro di cappella* there in 1604.

Works incl. motets (e.g. 2 for Christmas, *Hodie nobis caelorum rex* and *Hodie Christus natus est*), psalms and other church music; madrigals, canzonets, etc.

Nantier-Didiée, Constance (Betsy Rosabella) (b Saint-Denis, Île de Bourbon [Réunion], 16 Nov 1831; d Madrid, 4 Dec 1867), French mezzo. Studied with Duprez at the Paris Cons. and made her 1st stage appearance at Turin, in Mercadante's *La Vestale* (1850), and sang in Paris in 1851. Married a singer named Didiée and 1st visited London in 1853; returned until 1864 as Ascanio, Siebel and Ulrica. She created Preziosilla in St Petersburg on 22 Nov 1862.

Napolitana, a light song for several voices, allied to the *villanella* and cultivated at Naples esp. in the 16th and 17th cents.

Nápravník, Eduard Franzevich (b Byšt, nr. Hradec-Králove, 24 Aug 1839; d Petrograd, 23 Nov 1916), Czech (naturalized Russian) composer and conductor. Studied music precariously as a child, being the son of a poor teacher, and was left an orphan and destitute in 1853, but succeeded in entering the Organ School in Prague, where he studied with Kittel and others, and became an asst. teacher. In 1861 he went to St Petersburg as cond. of Prince Yussipov's private orch., became organist and asst. cond. at the Imp. theatres in 1863, 2nd cond. in 1867 and chief cond., succeeding Liadov, in 1869, holding the post until his death; he gave the fps of *Boris Godunov*, 5 operas by Tchaikovsky and 3 by Rimsky-Korsakov. He also cond. concerts of the Rus. Music Society.

Works incl. operas *The Nizhni-Novgorodians* (1868), *Harold* (1886), *Dubrovsky* (1895) and *Francesca da Rimini* (on Stephen Phillips's play, 1902); incid. music for Alexei Tolstoy's *Don Juan* (1892); ballads for voices and orch. *The Voyevode*, *The Cossack* and *Tamara* (after Lermontov); 4 symphs (1860–79), no. 3 *The Demon* (after Lermontov), suite, *Solemn Overture*, marches and nat. dances for orch.; concerto and fantasy on Rus. themes for pf. and orch., fantasy and suite for vln. and orch.; 3 string 4tets (1873–8), string 5tet (1897), 2 pf. trios, pf. 4tet; vln. and pf. sonata, 2 suites for cello and pf.; string instrument and pf. pieces.

Narciso (*Narcissus*), opera by D. Scarlatti (lib. by C.S. Capece), prod. Rome, private theatre of Queen Maria Casimira of Pol., 20 Jan 1714, under the title of *Amor d'un' ombra*. Perf. in London, 31 May 1720, with add. music by T. Roseingrave, under the new title.

Nardini, Pietro (b Livorno, 12 Apr 1722; d Florence, 7 May 1793), Italian violinist and composer. Studied at Livorno and later with Tartini at Padua. Solo violinist at the ducal court of Württemberg at Stuttgart, 1762–5, then settled at Livorno and in 1769 at Florence as music dir. to the ducal court of Tuscany.

Works incl. 6 vln. concertos (pub. in Amsterdam *c* 1765 as op. 1); 6 string 4tets; sonatas for vln., 2 vlns., solo and duets for vlns.; trios for fl., vln., and bass.

Nares, James (b Stanwell, Mdx., bap. 19 Apr 1715; d London, 10 Feb 1783), English organist and composer. Studied with Gates, Croft and Pepusch as a chorister at the

Chapel Royal in London, became deputy organist at St George's Chapel, Windsor, and in 1734 was app. organist of York Minster. Mus.D., Cambridge, 1756, in which year he returned to the Chapel Royal as organist and comp., becoming Master of the Children in succession to Gates, 1757. He pub. treatises on singing and on harpsichord and organ playing.

Works incl. services and anthems; dramatic ode *The Royal Pastoral* (*c* 1769); catches, glees and canons; harpsichord lessons; org. fugues.

Narváez, Luis de (b Granada, *c* 1500; d after 1550), Spanish vihuelist and composer. His collection of Vihuela music *Los seys libros* (1538), contains early exs. of variation writing.

Nasco, Jean (b *c* 1510; d Treviso, 1561), Flemish composer. He was a master of a music acad. at Verona in the 1540s and *maestro di cappella* at Treviso Cathedral from 1559. Comp. 2 Passions, Lamentations, madrigals, *canzoni*, etc.

Nash, Heddle (b London, 14 Jun 1896; d London, 14 Aug 1961), English tenor. He studied in London and after the 1914–1918 war in Milan, where he appeared in Rossini's *Il barbiere di Siviglia*. He appeared in Eng. for the 1st time at the Old Vic in 1925. He subsequently sang with the BNOC and at Glyndebourne (1934–8 as Ferrando, Don Basilio and Pedrillo). Other roles incl. Don Ottavio, David and Des Grieux. Sang in oratorio at the Three Choirs Festival and elsewhere. His last appearance in opera was Benjamin's *A Tale of Two Cities* in 1957.

Nasolini, Sebastiano (b Piacenza, *c* 1768; d Venice, 1798, or Naples, 1816), Italian composer. Pupil of Bertoni in Venice, in 1787 app. *maestro al cembalo* at the opera in Trieste, and 1788–90 *maestro di cappella* of the cathedral there. From 1790 he devoted himself to opera comp.

Works incl. operas *Nitteti* (1788), *Andromaca* (1790), *La morte di Cleopatra* (1791), *Eugenia* (1792), *Le feste d'Iside* (1794), *Merope*, *La morte di Mitridate* (1796), *Il medico di Lucca* (1797), *Gli umori contrari* (1798), *Il ritorno di Serse* (1816).

Nathan, Isaac (b Canterbury, 1792; d Sydney, 15 Jan 1864), English singer and composer. Studied Hebrew, etc., at Cambridge, being intended for a Jewish religious career, but turned to music, studying with D. Corri in London and appearing as a singer at CG. In 1841 he went to Australia settling in Sydney as a singing-master. Sir Charles Mackerras (*q.v.*) is a descendant.

Works incl. stage pieces with music, *Sweethearts and Wives* (1823), *The Alcaid* (1824), *The Illustrious Stranger* (1827), *Merry Freaks in Troublous Times* (comp. 1843), *Hebrew Melodies* and other songs to words by Byron.

Nationalism. In music nationalism manifests itself through the endeavour of individual comps. or schools to find some sort of musical idiom that may be said to express their countries' characteristics, either idiomatically or spiritually. Idiomatic expression of this kind is most usually and easily attained through the adoption, imitation or adaptation of folksong and nat. dances, which however may become more or less strongly coloured by each comp.'s individuality and will certainly be much elaborated in the process of sustained comp. (e.g. Smetana in Cz., Grieg in Norw., Balakirev in Rus., Falla in Spain, Bartók in Hung., etc.). The reflection of a country's spirit in music is less definite, more subtle and not so easily perceptible, but there is no doubt that certain comps. have achieved this without consciously resorting to folk music, and those who sometimes do so may remain just as strongly nat. when they happen to refrain (e.g. Tchaikovsky and Mussorgsky in Rus. [in different ways], Elgar in Eng., Fauré and Ravel in Fr., Sibelius in Fin., etc.).

Nattiez, Jean-Jacques (b Amiens, 30 Dec 1945), Canadian musicologist. As dir. of the Groupe de Recherches en Semiologie Musicale at the University of Montreal (1974) he is important for developing the use of semiotics in musical analysis, as first expounded in his book *Fondements d'une sémiologie musicale* (1975).

Natural, the sign ♮, which restores to its normal position a note previously raised by a ♯ or lowered by a ♭.

Naturale (It. = natural), a direction indicating that a voice or instrument, after perf. a passage in some unusual way (*mezza voce*, muted, etc.), is to return to its normal manner.

Naudin, Emilio (b Parma, 23 Mar 1823; d Bologna, 5 May 1890), French tenor of Italian birth. Debut Cremona, 1843. He sang in London from 1858, and at CG in 1867 was the 1st local Don Carlos. Created Meyerbeer's Vasco da Gama at the Paris Opéra (1865) and was successful as Tannhäuser, Lohengrin and Masaniello.

Naumann, Johann Gottlieb (b Blasewitz, nr. Dresden, 17 Apr 1741; d Dresden, 23 Oct 1801), German composer. At the age of 16 accomp. the Swed. violinist Wesström to

Hamburg, then to It. where he studied with Tartini, Hasse and Padre Martini. Prod. his 1st opera in Venice in 1763, and the following year was app. to the court at Dresden as 2nd comp. of church music. Revisited Italy to prod. operas 1765–8 and 1772–4, and in 1776 became *Kapellmeister* in Dresden, where, apart from visits to Stockholm, Copenhagen and Berlin, he remained till his death.

Works incl. operas *Achille in Sciro* (1767), *La clemenza di Tito* (1769), *Solimano*, *Armida* (1773), *Ipermestra*, *Amphion* (1778), *Cora och Alonzo* (1782), *Gustaf Vasa*, 1786; all 3 in Swed.), *Orpheus og Euridice* (in Dan., 1786), *Protesilao* (with Reichardt), *La dama soldato* (1790), *Aci e Galatea* (1801) and others; 21 Masses and other church music, 13 oratorios.

Navarini, Francesco (b Cittadella, nr. Rome, 1853; d Milan, 23 Feb 1923), Italian bass. Debut Ferrara 1876, in *Lucrezia Borgia*. La Scala 1883–1900; created Lodovico in *Otello*, 1887. He appeared widely in Rus. and Europe and toured the USA 1902 with Mascagni's co. Highly regarded as Verdi's Silva and Grand Inquisitor; Wagner's Pogner, Hunding and Hagen.

Navarra, André (b Biarritz, 13 Oct 1911), French cellist. Studied at Toulouse and Paris Cons. and in 1949 became prof. at the Paris Cons. He gave the fps of concertos by Jolivet (1962) and Tomasi (1970).

Navarraise, La (*The Girl of Navarre*), opera by Massenet (lib. by J. Claretie and H. Cain, based on the former's story *La Cigarette*), prod. London, CG, 20 Jun 1894.

Navarro, Juan (b Seville, c 1530; d Palencia, 25 Sep 1580), Spanish composer. After the death of Morales in 1553 he competed unsuccessfully for the post of *maestro de capilla* at Málaga Cathedral, but he later obtained a similar post in Salamanca. He (?) visited Rome in 1590, where his nephew Fernando Navarro Salazar arr. for the pub. of some of his church music. After his death Passions and Lamentations in plainsong were pub. in Mex. by his brother, but he probably never lived there himself. He was highly regarded as a polyphonist.

Works incl. psalms, hymns, Magnificats and other church music, madrigals, etc.

Nave, La (*The Ship*), incid. music by Pizzetti for Gabriele d'Annunzio's tragedy, prod. Rome, 11 Jan 1908.

Opera by Montemezzi (lib. by T. Ricordi, based on d'Annunzio), prod. Milan, La Scala, 1 Nov 1918.

Naylor, Bernard (b Cambridge, 22 Nov 1907; d London, 19 May 1986), English composer, conductor and organist. He studied at the RCM with Vaughan Williams and Holst; cond. in Winnipeg and Montreal from 1932, settled in Canada 1959.

Works incl. 12 motets in 2 sets (1949, 1952), *The Annunciation according to St Luke* for soloists, chorus and orch. (1949); *Variations* for orch. (1960); string trio (1960); *Stabat Mater* (1961); *The Nymph and the Faun* for mezzo and ens. (text by Marvell, 1965); *3 Sacred Pieces* for chorus and orch. (1971).

Naylor, Edward (Woodall) (b Scarborough, 9 Feb 1867; d Cambridge, 7 May 1934), English organist, musicologist and composer. Studied at Cambridge and the RCM in London, and after 2 organist's appts. there he returned to Cambridge in 1897 to become organist at Emmanuel Coll., taking the Mus.D. degree at the univ. He lectured and wrote on music, pub. a book on *Shakespeare and Music*.

Works incl. opera *The Angelus* (prod. CG 1909); cantata *Arthur the King* (1902); part-songs; pf. trio in D maj.

Neapolitan Sixth, a chord consisting of a min. 3rd and a min. 6th on the subdominant of the key, which came into vogue in the 17th cent. It occurs most often in a cadential progression in a min. key, e.g.:

which may further be abbr. as follows:

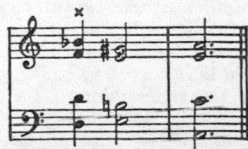

Neapolitan Songs, Five (*Fünf neapolitanische Lieder*) work by Henze for bar. and orch. (anon. 17th-cent. text), fp Frankfurt, 26 May 1956, with Fischer-Dieskau.

Neate, Charles (b London, 28 Mar 1784; d Brighton, 30 Mar 1877), English pianist and cellist. He became a pupil of Field, who learnt the cello with him under Wm. Sharp, and made his debut at CG in 1800. He also studied comp. with Woelfl. In 1815 he spent 8 months in Vienna and made friends with

Beethoven, and then 5 at Munich for counterpoint lessons with Winter. He taught and perf. for many years in London with much success and wrote music mainly for pf.

Nebra, José de (b Calatayud, bap. 6 Jan 1702; d Madrid, 11 Jul 1768), Spanish organist and composer. He became organist at the Convent of the Descalzas Reales in Madrid and 2nd organist at the royal chapel in 1724. After the destruction of the library there in the fire of 24 Dec 1734, he and Literes were commissioned to replace the lost church music and to restore what had survived. In 1751 he was made vice-*maestro de capilla* under Corselli, who neglected his duties for the comp. of It. operas, and by 1757 he had completely reorganized the court music. In 1758 he comp. a Requiem for 8 voices, fl. and strings for the funeral of Queen Barbara of Braganza, who had been D. Scarlatti's patroness.

Works incl. *c* 20 operas: Requiem, Miserere, psalms and other church music; *villancico* for 4 voices.

Nedbal, Oskar (b Tábor, 26 Mar 1874; d Zagreb, 24 Dec 1930), Czech conductor, vla. player and composer. Pupil of Dvořák, member of the Bohemian String 4tet and from 1896 cond. of the Cz. Phil. Society in Prague. From 1906 he cond. concerts and opera mainly in Vienna. He comp. light opera *Polenblut* (1913) and others; ballets *Pohádka o Honzovi* (1902), *Princezna Hyacinta* (1911), *Des Teufels Grossmutter* (1912).

Neefe, Christian Gottlob (b Chemnitz, 5 Feb 1748; d Dessau, 26 Jan 1798), German conductor and composer. Studied in Leipzig under Hiller, whom he succeeded as cond. of a touring opera co. in 1776. He settled in Bonn in 1779, where he was app. court organist 3 years later. Beethoven was his pupil from the age of 11. The Fr. occupation of Bonn in 1794 cost him his post, and from 1796 he was music dir. of the Bossann theatre co. in Dessau.

Works incl. operas *Die Apotheke* (1771), *Adelheid von Veltheim, Amors Guckkasten* (1772), *Die Einsprüche* (1772), *Heinrich und Lyda* (1776), *Sophonisbe, Zemire und Azor* (1776) and others; incid. music for Shakespeare's *Macbeth*; church music; chamber music.

Neel, Boyd (b Blackheath, 19 Jul 1905; d Toronto, 30 Sep 1981), English conductor. Founded B.N. String Orch. 1933 (fp Britten's *Vars. on theme of Frank Bridge*, Salzburg 1937); Orch. renamed Philomusica of London, 1957. Dean, Toronto Cons. 1953–70.

Neidhart von Reuental (b Bavaria, *c* 1180; d *c* 1240), German Minnesinger. Went on a crusade in 1217–19 and settled in Aus. on his return. Several songs of his are preserved; many others are attrib. to him. A younger contemporary of Walther von der Vogelweide, his music survived in print during the Renaissance.

Neidlinger, Gustav (b Mainz, 21 Mar 1912), German bass-baritone. He made his debut in Mainz and was in Hamburg 1936–50. Stuttgart from 1950; visited Edinburgh 1958 with co., as Lysiart and Kurwenal. His best role was Wagner's Alberich, which he sang at Bayreuth 1952–75, CG from 1963 and in the first studio recording of the *Ring*. Other roles incl. Pizarro, Klingsor, Sachs and Telramund.

Nelson Mass, the name given to Haydn's Mass in D min., comp. in 1798. It is sometimes said that the fanfares in the Benedictus commemorate Nelson's victory in the battle of the Nile; in fact Haydn cannot have heard the news of the battle until after the Mass was finished. His own title was *Missa in angustiis*. Perf. Eisenstadt, 23 Sep 1798.

Nelsova, Zara (b Winnipeg, 23 Dec 1918), Canadian cellist. She studied in London and made her debut there in 1931 with the LSO. Prin. cellist with Toronto SO 1940–3. NY debut 1942 and studied further with Casals and Piatigorsky; US citizen 1953. Has taught at Juilliard from 1962. In 1969 she gave the fp of Hugh Wood's concerto.

Németh, Mária (b Körmend, 13 Mar 1897; d Vienna, 28 Dec 1967), Hungarian soprano. She studied in Budapest and made her debut there in 1923. Vienna 1925–46 as Tosca, Santuzza, Aida, Queen of Night and Constanze. London, CG, 1931, as Turandot. Also heard at Salzburg and La Scala, Milan.

Nenna, Pomponio (b Bari, nr. Naples, *c* 1550; d Rome before 1613), Italian composer. Lived mainly at Naples and was the teacher of Gesualdo, Prince of Venosa, 1594–9; and moved to Rome in about 1608.

Works incl. 2 books of Responsories and 9 books of Madrigals.

Neo-Bechstein Piano, an electrophonic pf. invented by Vierling of Berlin in 1928–33 and further developed by Franco and Nernst, prod. its notes by the conversion of electrical waves into audible sounds.

Neo-Classicism. Term used to designate modern music which rejected Romantic expressiveness as exemplified by the music of Wagner, and attempted to re-create the forms and content of 18th-cent. music. The movement was foreshadowed by Busoni (*Fantasia contrappuntistica*, after The Art of Fugue (1910–12) and 6 Sonatinas for pf., 1910–20). Prokofiev's *Classical Symph.* of 1916 was comp. in emulation of Haydn, and Stravinsky's *Pulcinella* ballet (after Pergolesi, 1920) rejects the huge orch. and extended forms of *The Firebird*. Hindemith's *Kammermusik* series of 7 chamber works (*q.v.*, 1921–7) emulates the inst. style of Bach, while his 1 act opera *Das Nusch-Nuschi* contains satirical allusions to Wagner's *Tristan* which shocked contemporary audiences. Later neo-classical works were Stravinsky's opera-oratorio *Oedipus Rex* (after Sophocles, 1927) and the ballet *Apollo* (1928). Schoenberg satirised Neo-Classicism in the last of his 3 pieces for chorus, op. 28 (1925): *Der neue Klassizismus* contains a reference to 'Modernsky' – i.e. Stravinsky. However, Schoenberg himself employed classical forms for his twelve-tone works; the Suite for pf. op. 25 (1921–3) is a series of Baroque dance movts. and the 3rd string 4tet (1927) is a dodecaphonic re-creation of classical 4-movt. form.

Neo-Modal, modern music using new derivations from the modes, harmonized, transposed or otherwise altered.

Neri, Filippo (St Philip Neri) (b Florence, 21 Jul 1515; d Rome, 26 May 1595), Italian saint. Of importance to music for his foundation of the Society of Oratorians in 1564, which cultivated music at the oratory of San Girolamo in Rome, for which among others Animuccia and Palestrina worked in his lifetime and which in 1600 prod. Cavalieri's *Rappresentazione di anima e di corpo.* It was from this society that the Oratorio received its name as a musical form.

Neri, Giulio (b Turrite di Siena, 21 May 1909; d Rome, 21 Apr 1958), Italian bass. He sang in Rome from 1928 and was a leading bass there from 1938; also appeared at Milan, Florence and Venice. CG 1953, as Oroveso and Ramfis. Later sang at Barcelona and Buenos Aires; Verona 1951–7. Well known as Mefistofele, Alvise and the Grand Inquisitor.

Nero. *See also* **Nerone.**

Opera by Rubinstein (lib., in Fr. [*Néron*], by J. Barbier), prod., in Ger., Hamburg, Municipal Theatre, 1 Nov 1879.

Nerone (*Nero*), opera by Boito (lib. by comp.), begun 1879, but left unfinished at Boito's death in 1918. Prod., ed. by Tommasini and A. Toscanini, Milan, La Scala, 1 May 1924.

Neruda, Wilma (Wilhelmina) (Norman-

Neruda; Lady Hallé) (b Brno, 21 Mar 1839; d Berlin, 15 Apr 1911), Moravian violinist. Studied under her father, Josef N. (1807–75) and with Jansa, and made her 1st appearance in Vienna with her sister Amalie, a pianist, in 1846. She then went on tour in Ger. and appeared in London in 1849. Afterwards she appeared all over Eur., often with her brother, the cellist Franz N. (1843–1915). In 1864 she played in Paris and married the Swed. comp. Ludvig Norman. In 1888 she became the 2nd wife of Charles Hallé and settled at Manchester. Given title Violinist to the Queen by Queen Alexandra, in 1901.

Nesbet(t), J. (d ? 1468), English composer. Wrote a 5-part Magnificat (Carver and Eton choirbooks, incomplete in the latter) and a 3-part *Benedicamus* (Pepys MS., Magdalene Coll., Cambridge).

Nessler, Viktor (Ernst) (b Baldenheim, Alsace, 28 Jan 1841; d Strasbourg, 28 May 1890), German composer. Studied theology at Strasbourg, but took to music and prod. a Fr. opera there in 1864. He went to Leipzig, became choral and afterwards operatic cond.

Works incl. operas *Fleurette* (1864), *Die Hochzeitreise*, *Dornröschens Brautfahrt* (1867), *Nachtwächter und Student*, *Am Alexandertag*, *Irmingard* (1876), *Der Rattenfänger von Hameln* (1879), *Der wilde Jäger* (1881), *Der Trompeter von Säckingen* (after Scheffel's poem, 1884), *Otto der Schütz* (1886), *Die Rose von Strassburg* (1890); part-songs.

Nesterenko, Evgeny (b Moscow, 8 Jan 1938), Russian bass. Debut Leningrad, 1963, as Gremin. Moscow, Bolshoy, from 1971; sang Boris with the Co. in Milan 1973 and at the NY Met in 1975. He returned to La Scala in 1978 for Verdi's Philip II and also sang the role on his CG debut the same year. Other roles incl. Ruslan, Méphistophélès and Don Basilio. Often heard in Shostakovich's 14th symph.

Neues vom Tage (*News of the Day*), opera by Hindemith (lib. by M. Schiffer), prod. Berlin, Kroll Opera, 8 Jun 1929, cond. Klemperer. The opera was condemned by Goebbels in 1934: 'in their eagerness to make a sensation atonal musicians exhibit naked women in the bathtub on stage in the most obscene situations'. (Exactly 50 years later Peter Hall's wife, Maria Ewing, took a nude bath in the Glyndebourne prod. of *Poppea*).

Neukomm, Sigismund von (b Salzburg, 10 Jul 1778; d Paris, 3 Apr 1858), Austrian composer. As a chorister at Salzburg Cathedral he was a pupil of M. Haydn, who in 1798 sent him to J. Haydn in Vienna. In 1806 he went to Swed. and Rus., becoming cond. at the Tsar's Ger. theatre in St Petersburg. He returned to Vienna in 1809 and went to live in Paris soon after, succeeding Dussek in 1812 as pianist to Talleyrand. From 1816 to 1821 he was *maestro de capilla* to Pedro I of Brazil, with whom he returned to Lisbon, after the revolution, afterwards travelling with Talleyrand. In 1829 he visited London, meeting Mendelssohn, and lived there and alternately in Paris for the rest of his life.

Works incl. opera *Alexander in Indien* (1804), *Niobé* (1809) and others; 48 Masses and Requiem for Louis XVI; oratorios *Mount Sinai*, *David* and 6 others; incid. music for Schiller's *Braut von Messina* (1805); songs.

Neumann, Angelo (b Vienna, 18 Aug 1838; d Prague, 20 Dec 1910), Austrian tenor and opera impresario. He made his debut in Berlin, 1859, and sang in Vienna 1862–76. He then worked in Leipzig as an opera manager until 1882 and formed a touring company which gave perfs. of Wagner's operas all over Europe; the royalties were important to the survival of the Bayreuth Festival. From 1882 he worked in Bremen, then Prague; pub. a vol. of reminiscences of Wagner in 1907.

Neumann, František (b Přerov, Moravia, 16 Jun 1874; d Brno, 25 Feb 1929), Czech composer and conductor. Started in commercial and military career but went to study music at the Leipzig Cons. After filling var. chorus-master's and cond.'s posts at Ger. and Cz. theatres, he went to Brno as chief cond. at the Nat. Theatre. He cond. the fps of Janáček's *Katya Kabanova*, *The Cunning Little Vixen*, *Šárka* and *The Makropoulos Case*.

Works incl. operas *Idalka*, *Die Brautwerbung* (1901), *Liebelei* (on Schnitzler's play, 1910), *Herbststurm* (1919), *Beatrice Caracci* (1922); melodrama *Pan*; ballets *In Pleasant Pastures*, *The Peri*, *Pierrot*; Masses and motets; symph. poem *Infernal Dance*, suite *The Sunken Bell*, *Morav. Rhapsody*, overtures, etc. for orch.; octet, pf. trio; choruses, songs.

Neumann, Václav (b Prague, 29 Oct 1920), Czech conductor. He studied at the Prague Cons. and was a violist with the Czech PO; deputy cond. 1948, prin. cond. from 1968. He worked at the Komische Oper, Berlin, 1956–64 and cond. there the Felsenstein

prod. of *The Cunning Little Vixen*. He gave the fp of Cikker's *Play of Love and Death* (Munich, 1969) and was music dir. of Stuttgart Opera 1969–72.

Neumark, Georg (b Langensalza 7 Mar 1621; d Weimar, 8 Jul 1681), German poet and musician. He pub. a collection of sacred and secular songs, *Musikalische-poetischer Lustwald* in 1657, some set to music by himself, incl. the hymn 'Wer nur den lieben Gott lässt walten'.

Neumes, the signs in Eastern chant and Western plainsong (and in some medieval song-books) indicating the single notes or groups of notes to which each syllable was to be sung. Orig. not set on staves, but merely marked above the words and showing neither precise length nor exact pitch, they served as reminders of tunes already known to the singers.

Neusidler, Hans (b Poszony [Pressburg], *c* 1509; d Nuremberg, 2 Feb 1563), Hungarian lutenist. Settled at Nuremberg, where he pub. books of pieces arr. for lute in tablature in 1536, 1540 and 1544.

Neusidler, Konrad (b Nuremberg, bap. 13 Feb 1541; d Augsburg, prob. after 1604), German lutenist, son of prec. He lived in Augsburg from 1562.

Neusidler, Melchior (b Nuremberg, 1531; d Augsburg, 1590), German lutenist, brother of prec. He settled in Augsburg in 1552. He visited It. and pub. 2 books of lute music at Venice in 1566. In 1574 he pub. at Strasbourg a book of music (*Teutsch Lautenbuch*) by Josquin, Lassus, Arcadelt, Rore and others arr. for the lute. Pub. lute arrangements of 6 motets by Josquin in 1584.

Nevada (actually Wixom), **Emma** (b Alpha nr. Nevada City, Calif., 7 Feb 1859; d Liverpool, 20 Jun 1940), American soprano. Studied with Mathilde Marchesi in Vienna and made her debut in London in 1880 as Amina, later singing in Italy, Paris, the Eng. festivals, etc. Sang at CG, London, until 1922 as Ophelia, Olympia, Desdemona and Zerlina.

Neveu, Ginette (b Paris, 11 Aug 1919; d San Miguel, Azores, 28 Oct 1949), French violinist. Appeared with the Colonne Orch. at the age of 7. Studied at the Paris Cons. and with Flesch, and won the highest reputation for virtuosity and passionate musicality. She was killed in an air accident.

New England Holidays, unnumbered symph. by Ives, comp. 1904–13: 1. *Washington's birthday* 2. *Decoration Day* 3. *The Fourth of July* 4. *Thanksgiving*.

'New World' Symphony, Dvořák's 9th symph. in E min., op. 95, with the subtitle *From the New World*, because it was written in USA. Comp. 1893, fp NY Phil. Society, 16 Dec 1893.
New York Philharmonic Orchestra, US orch. founded 1842. Early conds. incl. Theodore Thomas, Anton Seidl and the Damrosch brothers; Mahler 1909–11; Mengelberg 1921–9; Toscanini 1928–36; Barbirolli 1936–42; Rodzinski 1943–7; Walter 1941–9; Mitropoulos 1949–58; Bernstein, 1958–69; Boulez 1971–7; Mehta from 1978. Merged with NY SO 1928.
Newark, William (b ? Newark-on-Trent, c 1450; d Greenwich, 11 Nov 1509), English composer. Became a Gentleman of the Chapel Royal in London, 1477 and, after var. other apps., Master of the Children there in 1493. Comp. part-songs.
Newlin, Dika (b Portland, Oregon, 22 Nov 1923), American musicologist and composer. Studied privately with Sessions and Schoenberg and then taught at Western Maryland Coll. and Syracuse Univ. In 1952 she estab. a music dept. at Drew Univ., NJ. Her writings incl. studies of Bruckner, Mahler and Schoenberg, translations, partic. of Schoenberg's writings. She has also comp. for various media, esp. chamber music.
Newman, Ernest (actually William Roberts) (b Liverpool, 30 Nov 1868; d Tadworth, 7 Jul 1959), English critic and writer on music. Educ. at Liverpool. Became critic of the *Manchester Guardian*, 1905, the *Birmingham Post*, 1906, the *Observer*, 1919, and the *Sunday Times*, 1920. Books incl. *Gluck and the Opera, Hugo Wolf, A Musical Critic's Holiday* and several works on Wagner, incl. the largest modern biog. (1933–47).
Newman, John Henry (1801–90), English cardinal and poet. See Dream of Gerontius (Elgar).
Newmarch (*née* Jeaffreson), Rosa (Harriet), (b Leamington, 18 Dec 1857; d Worthing, 9 Apr 1940), English writer on music. Wrote programme notes for London Queen's Hall concerts, 1908–27. Her books incl. *The Russian Opera* and *The Music of Czechoslovakia*; she brought Janáček to London in 1926 and he ded. his *Sinfonietta* to her.
Newton, Ivor (b London, 15 Dec 1892; d Bromley, 21 Apr 1981), English pianist and accompanist. Studied in London, Amsterdam and Berlin and then concentrated mainly on accomp., playing for many great artists.

Ney, Elly (b Düsseldorf, 27 Sep 1882; d Tutzing, 31 Mar 1968), German pianist. Studied with Böttcher and Seiss at Cologne Cons. and then with Leschetitsky and Sauer in Vienna. After winning the Mendelssohn and Ibach Prizes she taught at the Cologne Cons. in 1906 and began a very successful concert career, becoming esp. well known as a Beethoven interpreter; recorded the C min sonata op. 111 in 1936 and 1958.
Nezhdanova, Antonina (b Krivaya Balka, nr. Odessa, 16 Jun 1873; d Moscow, 26 Jun 1950), Russian soprano. She studied in Moscow and sang at the Bolshoy 1902–36 as Ludmilla, Antonida, Tatyana, the Snow Maiden and Lakmé. She was a regular guest in the Russian provinces and sang Gilda in Paris in 1912. Taught in Moscow from 1936.
Nibelung Saga (*Nibelungenlied*), ancient Teutonic epic in the Middle High German dialect. See Dorn (*Nibelungen*), Draeseke (*Gudrun*), Ring des Nibelungen (Wagner), Sigurd (Reyer).
Nibelung's Ring, The (Wagner). See Ring des Nibelungen.
Niccolini, Giuseppe (b Piacenza, 29 Jan 1762; d Piacenza, 18 Dec 1842), Italian composer. Studied at the Cons. di Sant' Onofrio, Naples, under Insanguine. Was at first very successful in opera, but was eventually driven from the stage by Rossini. *Maestro di cappella* at Piacenza Cathedral from 1819.
Works incl. operas *I baccanti di Roma* (1801), *Traiano in Dacia* (1807), *Coriolano* (1808) and *c* 40 others; Masses and other church music, etc.
Nichelmann, Christoph (b Treuenbrietzen, Brandenburg, 13 Aug 1717; d Berlin, 20 Jul 1762), German harpsichordist and composer. Pupil of Bach at St Thomas's School, Leipzig; lived at Hamburg and Berlin, being app. 2nd harpsichordist to Frederick the Great in 1744.
Works incl. opera (serenata) *Il sogno di Scipione*; harpsichord concertos; harpsichord sonatas.
Nicholls, Agnes (b Cheltenham, 14 Jul 1877; d London, 21 Sep 1959), English soprano. Studied RCM; debut London 1895, as Purcell's Dido. CG 1901–10, as Sieglinde and the *Siegfried* Brünnhilde, under Richter, and as Elsa. She married Hamilton Harty in 1904 and toured with him in N. America. Often heard in concert and as guest with Beecham, BNOC and Carl Rosa Co. Other roles incl. Nannetta and Donna Elvira.
Nicholson, George (b Durham, 24 Sep

1949), English composer who studied with Bernard Rands and David Blake. His music is largely for chamber groups. Overture, 7 winds (1976), *Recycle*, 11 insts. (1976), *The Arrival of the Poet in the City*, melodrama for actor and 7 instruments (1983), Chamber concerto (1980), Brass 5tet (1977), *Aubade* for sop. and 5 insts. (1981), *Movements* for 7 insts. (1983).

Nicholson, Richard (d Oxford, 1639), English organist and composer. Became choirmaster and organist at Magdalen Coll., Oxford, in 1595, took the B.Mus. there, 1596, and became the 1st Prof. of Music there in 1627.

Works incl. anthems, madrigals (1 in *The Triumphes of Oriana*), music for viols, 'dialogue' (or song-cycle) for 3 voices 'Joane, quoth John'.

Nicholson, Sydney H(ugo) (b London, 9 Feb 1875; d Ashford, Kent, 30 May 1947), English organist and church educationist. Studied at the RCM in London and under Knorr at Frankfurt. Organist of Manchester Cathedral, 1908–18, and Westminster Abbey, 1918–27, when he founded the School of English Church Music at Chislehurst, later transferred to Addington. Knighted 1938. His works incl. church music, a comic opera, *The Mermaid* (lib. by George Birmingham, 1928) and an opera for boys' voices, *The Children of the Chapel* (1934).

Nicodé, Jean Louis (b Jerczig, nr. Poznan, 12 Aug 1853; d Langebrück, nr. Dresden, 5 Oct 1919), German–Polish conductor and composer. The family having moved to Berlin in 1856, Nicodé studied there, 1st under his father and from 1869 at the Neue Akademie der Tonkunst. Afterwards he taught there and arr. concerts at which he appeared as pianist, toured in the Balkans with Désirée Artot and in 1878 became prof. at the Dresden Cons. From 1885 he devoted himself to cond. and comp.

Works incl. symph. ode *Das Meer* for solo voices, male chorus, orch. and org. (1889); symph. poems *Maria Stuart* (after Schiller, 1880), *Die Jagd nach dem Glück, Gloria,* symph. variations, etc., for orch.; romance for vln. and orch.; cello and pf. sonata; sonata and numerous pieces for pf.; songs, incl. cycle *Dem Andenken an Amarantha* (1886); male-voice choruses.

Nicolai, Elena (b Sofia, 26 Sep 1912), Bulgarian mezzo. Debut (as E. Stoianka) in Malta as Verdi's Maddalena. She sang at Naples from 1938 and at Verona was successful from 1946 as Amneris, Laura and Ortrud; sang in the fp of Pizzetti's *La Figlia di Jorio* (1954) and as guest in Paris, Buenos Aires and Cairo. At Florence she was heard as Handel's Cornelia and as Satire in Spontini's *Olympie*.

Nicolai, (Carl) Otto (Ehrenfried) (b Königsberg, 9 Jun 1810; d Berlin, 11 May 1849), German composer and conductor. Studied the pf. as a child, but was so unhappy at home that in 1826 he ran away and was sent to Berlin by a patron the following year for study under Zelter and Klein. In 1833 another patron sent him to Rome as organist in the Prus. Embassy chapel, and there he studied under Baini. He returned there after a year at the Kärntnertortheater in Vienna, 1837–8. He became court *Kapellmeister* in Vienna in 1841 and founded the Phil. concerts there in 1842. In 1847 he became dir. of the cathedral choir and the Court Opera in Berlin, where he died of a stroke, 2 months after the prod. of his *Merry Wives of Windsor*.

Works incl. operas *Enrico II* (later *Rosmonda d'Inghilterra*, 1839), *Il templario* (1840), *Odoardo e Gildippe, Il proscritto* (later *Die Heimkehr des Verbannten*, 1841), *Die lustigen Weiber von Windsor* (after Shakespeare, 1849); Mass for Frederick William IV of Prus., Requiem, Te Deum; Symph. Festival Overture on 'Ein' feste Burg' for the jubilee of Königsberg Univ.

Nicolai, Philipp (b Mengeringhausen, 10 Aug 1556; d Hamburg, 26 Oct 1608), German pastor, poet and amateur musician. In 1599 he pub. a hymnbook, *Freudenspiegel des ewigen Lebens*, containing the tunes of 'Wachet auf' and 'Wie schön leuchtet der Morgenstern'.

Nicolaus de Cracovia 16th-cent. Polish organist and composer in the service of the royal court. Organ music by him is incl. in two MSS.: that of Jan of Lublin (1537–48) and the Kraków Tablature (1548).

Nicolini, Ernest (b St Malo, 23 Feb 1834; d Pau, 19 Jan 1898), French tenor. Debut Paris, Opéra-Comique, 1857, in Halévy's *Les mousquetaires*. He sang at La Scala from 1859, as Alfredo and Rossini's Rodrigo, and at CG and Drury Lane from 1866; the 1st London Lohengrin and Radames (1875, 1876). Also successful as Edgardo, Faust and Roméo. He first sang with Patti in 1866; married her 1886, after tours with her in Europe and USA.

Nicolini (Nicola Grimaldi) (b Naples, bap. 5 Apr 1673; d Naples, 1 Jan 1732), Italian castrato. 1st appearance in Rome, about 1694; sang in Naples 1697–1724, often in operas by A. Scarlatti. 1st went to Eng. in 1708 and sang the title role in Handel's *Rinaldo* in 1711; created Amadigi in 1715. He returned to It. in 1718.

Niedermeyer, (Abraham) Louis (b Nyon, Vaud, 27 Apr 1802; d Paris, 14 Mar 1861), Swiss composer and educationist. Studied in Vienna, Rome and Naples, settled as music teacher at Geneva and went to Paris in 1823, settling there after a brief teaching period at Brussels. In Paris he took over Choron's school of music and called it École de Musique Religieuse Classique.

Works incl. operas *Il reo per amore* (1820), *La casa nel bosco* (1828), *Stradella* (1837), *Marie Stuart* (after Schiller, 1844), *La Fronde* (1853); numerous Masses, motets and anthems; songs to words by Lamartine (e.g. *Le Lac*), Hugo and Deschamps.

Nielsen, Alice (b Nashville, 7 Jun 1876; d New York, 8 Mar 1943), American soprano. Sang in operetta at St Paul and San Francisco from 1893; Shaftesbury Theatre, London, from 1901. Opera debut Naples 1903, as Marguerite. CG 1904, Zerlina. She sang Norina in NY, 1905, and was popular in Boston and at the NY Met 1909–13 (debut as Mimi). Reverted to operetta 1917.

Nielsen, Carl (August) (b Nørre-Lyndelse, nr. Odense, 9 Jun 1865; d Copenhagen, 3 Oct 1931), Danish composer and conductor. Being poor as a youth, he joined a military band at the age of 14, but at 18 succeeded in entering the Copenhagen Cons. as a pupil of Gade. In 1891 he entered the royal orch. and was its cond. in 1908–14. He also became cond. of the Music Society and dir. of the Cons. One of the most remarkable late Romantic symphonists, combining traditional forms with a new and orig. approach to tonality.

Works incl. operas *Saul og David* (1902), *Maskarade* (after Holberg, 1906); incid. music for Oehlenschläger's *Aladdin* and many other plays; *Hymnus Amoris* for chorus and orch. (1897); 3 motets for unaccomp. chorus.

6 symphs. 1., in G min. (1892), 2. *The Four Temperaments* (1902), 3. *Espansiva* (1911), 4. *The Inextinguishable* (1916), 5. (1922), 6 *Sinfonia semplice* (1925), *Saga-Dream*, symph. rhapsody for orch.; vln. concerto (1911), fl. concerto (1926), clar. concerto (1928).

4 string 4tets (1887–1919), 2 string 5tets, wind 5tet (1922) and other chamber music; 2 vln and pf. sonatas; *Commotio* for org. (1931); suites and other pf. works; songs.

Nielsen, Hans (b ? Roskilde, c 1580; d ? Copenhagen, c 1626), Danish lutenist and composer. After learning music as choir-boy in the royal chapel at Copenhagen, he studied with G. Gabrieli at Venice between 1599 and 1606, and in 1606–8 with the Eng. lutenist Richard Howett at Wolfenbüttel. After that he was lutenist at the Dan. court until 1611, when he was dismissed and went to Heidelberg Univ. In 1623 he was app. vice-director of the royal chapel in succession to Pedersøn.

Nielsen, Ludolf (b Nørre Tvede, 29 Jan 1876; d Copenhagen, 16 Oct, 1939), Danish conductor and composer. Studied at the Copenhagen Cons., became cond. at the Tivoli and the Palace until 1909.

Works incl. operas, Isabella (1915), *The Clock*, *Lola* (after Victor Hugo, 1920); ballet *Lakschmi*; 3 symphs. (1903–13), 3 symph. poems, 2 suites and concert overture for orch.; 3 string 4tets; pf. pieces; songs.

Nielsen, Riccardo (b Bologna, 3 Mar 1908), Italian composer of Scandinavian descent. Studied at the Liceo Musicale of Bologna and at Salzburg, and was influenced by Casella.

Works incl. monodrama *L'Incubo* (1948), radio opera *La via di Colombo* (1953); incid. music for *Maria ed il Nazzareno*; Psalms for male voices and orch. (1941); concerto for orch. (1936), 2 symphs. (1933, 1935); capriccio and *Sinfonia concertante* for pf. and orch., vln. concerto (1932); divertimento for bassoon, tpt., vln., vla. and cello, trio for ob., bassoon and horn (1934), Adagio and Allegro for cello and 11 instruments; sonatas for vln. and pf. and cello and pf.; *Musica* for 2 pfs. (1939), sonata and *ricercare*, chorale and toccata on BACH for pf.; *Laude di Jacopone da Todi* and *Tre satire di Giusti* for voice and pf.

Niemann, Albert (b Erxleben, Magdeburg, 15 Jan 1831; d Berlin, 13 Jan 1917), German tenor. After a precarious beginning on the stage at Dessau, he was discovered by F. Schneider, the court music dir., and given some lessons, and was also taught by a singer. He gradually obtained better engagements and was sent to Paris by the King of Hanover to study under Duprez. In 1866–88 he was court opera singer in Berlin and in 1876 Wagner chose him to create the part of Siegmund in the *Ring* at Bayreuth; he had sung the title role in the Paris prod. of *Tannhäuser*, 1861. NY Met 1886–8, as the first US Siegfried and Tristan.

Niente (It. = nothing). The word is generally used in connection with *quasi* (so to speak, almost) when extreme softness of tone is required.

Nietzsche, Friedrich (1844–1900), German philosopher and author. He met Wagner in 1868 and celebrated the ideals of Wagnerian music-drama in *Das Geburt des Tragödie aus dem Geiste der Musik* (1871). Later turned to Bizet. Suffered nervous collapse in last years. *See* Also sprach Zarathustra (R. Strauss), Ingenhoven (do.), Mass of Life (Delius), Mahler (3rd symph.), Medtner (songs), Reznicek (*Ruhm und Ewigkeit*), Rihm (3rd symph).

Nigg, Serge (b Paris, 6 Jun 1924), French composer. Studied under Messiaen at the Paris Cons., but in 1946 adopted the 12-note technique under the influence of Leibowitz, with which he in turn came to disagree 2 years later.

Works incl. melodrama *Perséphone* (1942); symph. movement for orch. *Timour* (1944), *La Mort d'Arthus* for voice and orch.; pf. concerto, *Concertino* for pf., wind and perc.; *Jérôme Bosch-Symphonie* (1960); variations for pf., and 10 instruments; 2 pf. concertos (1954, 1971); sonata and *Fantaisie* for pf., etc.

Night on the Bare Mountain, a work in var. forms by Mussorgsky, more properly called *St John's Night on the B.M.*, based on the incident of the witches' sabbath in Gogol's story *St John's Eve*; comp. as a symph. poem for orch. in 1866–7; later used in a version for chor. and orch. and called *Night on Mount Triglav* in 1872 as part of the opera *Mlada* commissioned from Mussorgsky, Borodin, Cui and Rimsky-Korsakov, but never completed; revised version of this used as intro. to Act III of the unfinished opera *Sorotchintsy Fair*, began in 1875; this last version revised and arranged as an orchestral piece by Rimsky-Korsakov after Mussorgsky's death.

Nightingale, The, (*Soloveg*) opera by Stravinsky (lib. by comp. and S.N. Mitusov, from Hans Andersen's fairy-tale), prod. Paris, Opéra, 26 May 1914; revived in form of a ballet (choreography by Leonid Massin), Paris, Opéra, 2 Feb 1920.

Nights in the Gardens of Spain (Falla). *See* Noches en los jardines de España.

Nikisch, Arthur (b Lébényi Szant Miklos, 12 Oct 1855; d Leipzig, 23 Jan 1922), Hungarian–German conductor. Studied in Vienna and played the vln. in the court orch. from 1874–7. He was cond. at the Leipzig Opera 1878–89. Subsequent posts incl. the Boston SO, 1889–93, Budapest Opera, 1893–5, Leipzig Gewandhaus, from 1895,

and the Berlin PO. He cond. the fp of Bruckner's 7th symph. (1884) and in 1913 gave Wagner's *Ring* at CG, London.

Nikisch, Mitja (b Leipzig, 21 May 1899; d Venice, 5 Aug 1936), Hungarian–German pianist, son of prec. Studied at the Leipzig Cons. and made his 1st appearance there in 1912.

Nilsson, Birgit (b Karup, 17 May 1918), Swedish soprano. Studied in Stockholm, making her debut in 1946 and becoming a member of the Swed. Royal Opera in 1947. Sang in operas by Wagner, Strauss and Verdi, Brit. debut Glyndebourne, 1951, as Electra in *Idomeneo*; CG from 1957 as Brünnhilde, Isolde, Turandot and Elektra. Bayreuth 1954–70. NY Met debut 1959, as Isolde. Other roles incl. Amelia, Aida, Salome and the Dyer's Wife. Last stage app. 1982. The leading post-war Wagnerian soprano.

Nilsson, Bo (b Skelleftea, 1 May 1937), Swedish composer. Largely self-taught, he belongs to the younger generation of avant-garde composers.

Works incl. *Songs on the Death of Children* for soprano and small orch.; *Moments of Time* for 10 wind instruments; *Frequencies* for chamber ensemble; *A Prodigal Son* for contralto, alto fl. and chamber ensemble; *Reactions* for perc. 4tet (1960); *Audiograms* for electronic generators; *Quantities* for pf. *Attraktionen* for string 4tet (1968), *Madonna* for mezzo and ens. (1977).

Nilsson, Kristina (Christine) (b Sjöabol, nr. Vexiö, 20 Aug 1843; d Stockholm, 22 Nov 1921), Swedish soprano. Studied at Stockholm and Paris, and after several appearances in Sweden she made her debut in Paris in 1864 as Violetta, and 1st went to London the same year where she married Auguste Rouzeaud in 1872. In 1877 she married Count Casa Miranda. She created Thomas' Ophelia (1868) and sang Marguerite at the opening of the NY Met (1883). Other roles incl. Lucia (CG 1869), Mignon and Laura.

Nilsson, Sven (b Gavle, 11 May 1898; d Stockholm, 1 Mar 1970), Swedish bass. Studied with Ivar Andrésen and sang at the Dresden Staatsoper 1930–44; created Peneios in Strauss's *Daphne* (1938) and was a distinguished Ochs, Sarastro and Osmin. He sang Pogner and other Wagner roles at Zoppot, 1934–42. CG 1936–7. NY Met debut 1950, as Daland. At the Royal Opera, Stockholm, from 1946 until his death, just after a perf. of *Les Contes d'Hoffmann*.

Nimsgern, Siegmund (b St Wendel, 14 Jan 1940), German bass-baritone. Studied at

Saarbrucken and was a member of the Staatstheater there 1971–4; Deutsche Oper, Düsseldorf, from 1975. He was Mephistopheles in a concert perf. of the Berlioz *Faust*, London 1972, and sang Amfortas at CG in 1973; returned as Dapertutto in a new prod. of *Les Contes d'Hoffmann*. He has sung in N. America from 1973; NY Met debut 1978, Pizarro. Well known in the sacred music of Bach, Haydn, Pergolesi and Telemann. His Wotan in the 1983 Solti-Hall *Ring*, at Bayreuth, was much discussed.

Nin (y Castellanos), Joaquín (b Havana, 29 Sep 1878; d Havana, 24 Oct 1949), Spanish pianist, musicologist and composer. Studied at Barcelona and in Paris, where in 1906 he became pf. prof. at the Schola Cantorum. After short periods in Berlin and Cuba, he settled in Brussels and later in Paris again. He ed. much old Spanish music and wrote 3 books.

Works incl. mimodrama *L'Autre*, ballet *L'Écharpe bleue*; vln. pieces; pf. works; songs.

Nina, o sia La pazza per amore (*Nina, or the Lunatic from Love*), opera by Paisiello (lib. by G. Carpani, with additions by G.B. Lorenzi, based on the Fr. lib. by B.J. Marsollier), prod. Naples, Caserta Palace, for the visit of Queen Maria Carolina of Sicily, 25 Jun 1789; 1st public perf. Naples, Teatro Fiorentino, 1790.

Nina, ou La Folle par amour (do.), ballet by Persuis, partly based on Dalayrac's music (choreography by Louis Milon), prod. Paris, Opéra, 23 Nov 1813.

Opera by Dalayrac (lib. by Marsollier), prod. Paris, Comédie-Italienne, 15 May 1786.

Ninth, the interval a whole tone larger than an 8ve. (maj. ninth) or a semitone larger (min. ninth), e.g.:

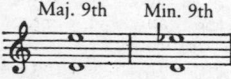

Maj. 9th   Min. 9th

Ninth Symphony (Beethoven). *See* **'Choral' Symphony.**

Nissen, Georg Nikolaus (b Haderslev, 22 Jan 1761; d Salzburg, 24 Mar 1826), Danish diplomat and author, married Mozart's widow in 1809. His important biog. of Mozart, incorporating many of Mozart's letters, was pub. posthumously in 1828.

Nissen, Hans Hermann (b Zippnow, nr. Danzig, 20 May 1893; d Munich, 28 Mar 1980), German bass-baritone. Debut Berlin 1924, as the Caliph in *Der Barbier von*

Bagdad. Munich 1925–67 as Almaviva, Renato, Barak and Iago. London, CG, 1928 and 1934 as Sachs and Wotan. NY Met debut 1938, as Wotan. He sang Sachs under Toscanini at Salzburg in 1936 and recorded Act III of *Die Meistersinger* under Böhm the following year.

Nivers, Guillaume (Gabriel) (b Melun, *c* 1631; d Paris, 30 Dec 1714), French organist, harpsichordist, theorist and composer. Pupil of Chambonnières in Paris and organist of the church of Saint-Sulpice in 1654, also app. organist to the king in 1678 and music master to the queen. He wrote a treatise on singing, and others.

Works incl. motets and other church music.

Nobilissima Visione, dance legend (ballet) in 6 scenes by Hindemith (choreography by comp. and Massine on story of St Francis), prod. CG, London, 21 Jul 1938. Orch-Suite in 3 movts. perf. Venice, 13 Sep 1938.

Noble, Dennis (b Bristol, 23 Sep 1899; d Jávea, Spain, 14 Mar 1966), English baritone. Educated as a chorister at Bristol Cathedral, he became a member of Covent Garden Opera in 1938. He sang the solo at the fp of Walton's *Belshazzar's Feast* (Leeds, 1931). Often heard in Verdi, Puccini and Bizet.

Noble, (Thomas) Tertius (b Bath, 5 May 1867; d Rockport, Mass., 4 May 1953), English organist and composer. In 1881 he went to Colchester, where he received his educ. from the rector of All Saints Church, who also made him organist there. In 1886 he entered the RCM in London, studying under Parratt, Bridge and Stanford, and later he joined the staff. After 2 smaller appts. he became organist at Ely Cathedral in 1892 and at York Minster in 1898, but went to NY in 1912 as organist and cond.

Works incl. incid. music for Aristophanes' *Wasps*; services and other church music, *The Sound of War*, *Gloria Domini* and other choral works; orchestral works; chamber music.

Noces, Les (Stravinsky). *See* **Wedding.**

Noches en los jardines de España (*Nights in the Gardens of Spain*), symph. impressions for pf. and orch. by Falla, begun in 1909, finished in 1915. Fp Madrid, 9 Apr 1916. There are 3 movements: 1. *En el Generalife*; 2 *Danza lejana* (*Dance in the distance*); 3. *En los jardines de la Sierra de Córdoba*.

Nocturne (Fr.), a 'night piece' or instrumental serenade, generally of a quiet, lyrical character, but sometimes (as in Chopin) with a more agitated middle section. As a pf. piece it originated with Field, but it existed already as the It. Notturno in the 18th cent., when, however, it was similar to the Serenade or Divertimento in several movements. The nocturne in the modern sense is not necessarily slow, soft and sentimental. *Fêtes* in Debussy's work below is a very animated piece; in Vaughan Williams's *London Symph.* the scherzo is a nocturne, i.e. a piece suggesting London's life by night.

Nocturne, song cycle for tenor, 7 obbligato insts. and strings by Britten (texts, all about night, by Shelley, Tennyson, Coleridge, Middleton, Wordsworth, Owen, Keats and Shakespeare), fp Leeds, 16 Oct 1958, with Pears.

Nocturnes, 3 orchestral pieces by Debussy, *Nuages*, *Fêtes* and *Sirènes*, the last with female chorus, comp. in 1893–9, fp Paris, 9 Dec 1900 (nos. 1 and 2); 27 Oct 1901 (complete).

Node (from Lat. *nodus* = knot), the point in a vibrating string at which the vibration becomes cut into segments.

Nola, Domenico da (Joan Domenico del Giovane) (b Nola, Naples, *c* 1510; d Naples, 5 May 1592), Italian composer. *Maestro di cappella* of the church of the Annunciation at Naples, 1563–88. Comp. motets, madrigals, *villanelle*, etc.

Non nobis Domine, a canon for voices, ? by Byrd, often sung in Eng. for 'grace' after public dinners. It is a Riddle Canon capable of being sung with the entries in var. positions, also in Inversion.

Nonet, a comp. for 9 instruments, usually in several movements.

Nono, Luigi (b Venice, 29 Jan 1924), Italian composer, whose work was initially perf. principally in Ger. He studied with Scherchen, who cond. his *Polifonia-monodia-ritmica* at Darmstadt in 1951. He married a daughter of Schoenberg, whose music has had a strong influence on him.

Works incl. opera-oratorio *Intolleranza* (1961); *Variazioni canoniche* on a theme of Schoenberg's (from *Ode to Napoleon*), *Due espressioni* and *Diario polacco '58* for orch.; *Canti* for 13 insts., *Incontri* for 24 insts., *Il canto sospeso* (1956) and other choral works incl. *La Victoire de Guernica*, *Epitaph I for F. Garcia Lorca*, *Cori di Didone* (1958).

Cantata *Sul ponte di Hiroshima* for soprano and tenor and orch. (1962); *La Fabbrica illuminata* for mezzo and electronic tape; *Epitaphs II & III for F. Garcia Lorca* (II for fl., strings and perc., III for speaker, speaking chorus and orch.); opera *Al gran sole carico d'amore* (1974), electronic music incl. *Omaggio a Emilio Vedova*, (1960), *Sofferte onde serene* (1976); *Quando stanno morendo* for voices and ens. (1982).

Noonday Witch, The (Cz. *Polednice*), symphonic poem by Dvořák, op. 108; comp. 1896, fp London, 21 Nov 1896.

Noordt, Anthony van (d Amsterdam, buried 23 Mar 1675), Dutch organist and composer. Organist of the Nieuwe Kerk at Amsterdam in 1659, when he pub. a book of organ works in tablature, incl. variations on Fr. psalm tunes and fugal fantasies.

Norcome, Daniel (b Windsor, 1576; d Windsor, before 1626), English singer and composer. He went to the Danish court in his early 20s, but fled from Copenhagen to Ger., Hung. and Venice *c* 1600. Later he became a lay-clerk at St George's Chapel, Windsor, but lost that post on turning Roman Catholic and went to Brussels as an instrumental player to the viceregal chapel.

Works incl. viol pieces; madrigal contrib. to *The Triumphes of Oriana*.

Nordica, Lilian (actually Lillian Norton), (b Farmington, Me., 12 May 1857; d Batavia, Java, 10 May 1914), American soprano. Studied at Boston and, after successful concert appearances in USA and Eng. made her 1st stage appearance at Milan in 1879 as Donna Elvira. US debut Boston 1885; NY Met debut 1895 as Valentine. London, CG and Drury Lane, 1887–1902 as Lucia, Aida, Donna Anna, Isolde and Brünnhilde.

Norena, Eidé (b Horten, nr. Oslo, 26 Apr 1884; d Lausanne, 19 Nov 1968), Norwegian soprano. She studied with Gulbranson and made her stage debut in Oslo as Amor (1907); sang in Stockholm until 1924, then gave Gilda at La Scala, under Toscanini. CG 1924–37, as Desdemona, Violetta and Olympia. At Chicago in 1926 she sang in the fp of Cadman's *A Witch of Salem*. NY Met 1933–8, debut as Mimi. At the Paris Opéra, 1925–37, she was successful in operas by Meyerbeer, Rimsky-Korsakov and Rossini.

Norgård, Per (b Gentofte, 13 Jul 1932), Danish composer. Studied with Holmboe and Boulanger; has taught at Aarhus from 1965. An early influence was Sibelius, later turned to 'infinite' serialism, pointillism and graphic notation. Works incl. operas *The Labyrinth* (1967), *Gilgamesh* (1973), *Siddharta* (1983), *The Divine Tivoli* (1983); 4 symphs. (1954–81), *Illuminationi* for orch. (1984), cello concerto (1985); 3 string 4tets (1958–69).

Norma, opera by Bellini (lib. by F. Romani,

based on L.A. Soumet's tragedy), prod. Milan, La Scala, 26 Dec 1831.

Norman, Jessye (b Augusta, 15 Sep 1945), American soprano. She studied at the Univ. of Michigan and made her stage debut in Berlin in 1969 as Elisabeth. She sang Aida at La Scala in 1972 and Cassandre in *Les Troyens* at CG the same year, the latter being also role of her NY Met debut in 1983. She returned to CG in 1985, as Ariadne. Well known in Lieder and in concerts, she has sung Berg's aria *Der Wein* and the Berlioz song cycle *Les Nuits d'été*.

Norman, John English 15th–16th-cent. organist and composer. He was master of the choristers, St David's Cathedral, 1509–22; he was at Eton, 1534–45.

Works incl. Masses, e.g. Mass in 5 parts, on an Easter plainsong, motets, etc.

Norman, (Fredrik Vilhelm) Ludvig (b Stockholm, 28 Aug 1831; d Stockholm, 28 Mar 1885), Swedish pianist, conductor and composer. Pub. a book of songs at the age of 11, was left a poor orphan, but enabled by patrons, incl. Jenny Lind, to study at the Leipzig Cons. In 1851 his 1st pf. work was pub. at Schumann's instigation. Returning to Stockholm in 1861, he became cond. of the royal opera, which he cond. until 1879, and was cond. of the symph. concerts to his death. In 1864 he married the violinist Wilma Neruda.

Works incl. incid. music to Shakespeare's *Antony and Cleopatra*; 3 symphs. (1858, 1874, 1885), 4 overtures; chamber music, incl. 6 string 4tets; instrumental sonatas; pf. works; songs.

Norman-Neruda, Wilma. *See* **Neruda.**

Norrington, Roger (b Oxford, 16 Mar 1934), English conductor. He studied at the RCM with Boult and perf. as a tenor 1962–70. Founded the Schütz Choir 1962, succeeded by the Schütz Choir of London. Music dir. Kent Opera 1968–84; has given Monteverdi's 3 principal operas in his own eds. US debut Oakland 1974. In 1985 he cond. at the RCM the 1st stage perf. in Brit. of Rameau's tragédie-lyrique *Les Boréades*.

Norris, William (b *c* 1669; d ? Lincoln, Jul 1710), English singer and composer. Choirboy in the Chapel Royal in London, later a singer there and choirmaster at Lincoln Cathedral from 1690.

Works incl. services and anthems; Ode for St Cecilia's Day.

North, Roger (Hon.) (b Tostock, Suffolk, 3 Sep 1653; d Rougham, 1 Mar 1734), English lawyer and amateur musician, brother of Francis N., Lord Guilford (1637–85), who was also a musician and pub. *A Philosophical Essay on Musick* in 1677. Roger North wrote *Memoires of Musick* incl. the treatise *The Musicall Gramarian.*

North Country Sketches, work for orch. in 4 movts. by Delius; comp. 1913–14, fp London, 10 May 1915, cond. Beecham.

Norwich Festival, a triennial music festival estab. at Norwich in 1824, but preceded by festivals held at irregular intervals between 1770 and 1817.

Nose, The, opera by Shostakovich (lib. by A. Preis, A. Zamyatin, G. Yonin and comp., after Gogol); 1927–8, fp Leningrad, Maly Theatre, 12 Jan 1930. Story concerns disappearance of nose belonging to government official; described by contemporary Rus. critics as an example of bourgeois decadence.

Nota cambiata (It. = changed note), a term used in two senses in the analysis of 16th-cent. polyphony: (1) a dissonant passing-note on the beat (in Palestrina only on the weak beats); (2) a curling figure (also called 'changing note group') in which a dissonant passing-note (not on the beat) leads to a note a 3rd lower, which then rises one step, e.g.:

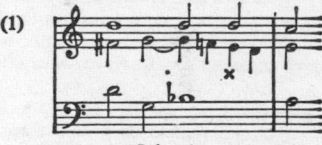

Palestrina, *Missa brevis*

Palestrina, *Veni sponsa Christi*

Notation, the act of writing down music by means of special symbols, as by specially devised letters in Gk. music, by neumes in the early Middle Ages, in tablature for old lute and organ music, in notes according to the present system, or in the special syllable form of the Tonic Sol-fa system. Standard musical notation today follows a binary system that was more or less established in the 16th cent., though at that time the note-values used were normally longer than those now preferred (which is why modern editions of such music often have their note-values halved or quartered), and as late as the 17th cent. there are occasional examples of the earlier ternary-based notational systems which operated according to a complicated set of rules. Many details and ambiguities in current musical notation can be understood only in the light of its historical development; and even the notation of standard 19th-cent. works involves many ambiguities and conventions that are rarely observed today.

Noté, Jean (b Tournai, 6 May 1859; d Brussels, 1 Apr 1922), Belgian baritone. Debut Ghent 1883; sang in Brussels, Lyons and Marseilles before his debut at the Paris Opéra in 1893. He remained until his death, as Rigoletto, Thomas' Hamlet, Nelusko, Wolfram and Beckmesser. NY Met debut 1908, as Escamillo.

Note-Row, *See* Serialism and **Twelve Note Music.**

Notker Balbulus (= 'The Stammerer') (b St Gall, *c* 840; d St Gall, 6 Apr 912), Swiss monk and musician at the monastery of St Gall. He wrote on musical notation, the organ and the perf. of plainsong, and as a comp. contrib. to the development of the Sequence.

Notker Labeo (b 950; d St Gall, 29 Jun 1022), also known as Teutonicus, German monk at St Gall. He wrote on music and other subjects, including a short treatise in Old High Ger. on the measurement of organ pipes.

Notot, Joseph (b Arras, 12 Feb 1751; d Paris, 24 Aug 1840), French organist and composer. Was sent to Paris as a child for his educ., but was discovered as a wonderful extempore player on the organ by Leclerc, the organist of the church of Saint-Germain-des-Prés, who undertook to teach him. Later he became organist at Arras, but the Revolution drove him to Eng. and he gave up music.

Works incl. 4 symphs.; 3 pf. concertos; pf. sonatas.

Notre Dame, opera by Franz Schmidt (lib. by comp. and L. Wilk, after Hugo) comp. 1902–4, prod. Vienna, 1 Apr 1914. The well-known *Intermezzo* was perf. Vienna, 6 Dec 1903.

Nottebohm, (Martin) Gustav (b Lüdenscheid, Westphalia, 12 Nov 1817; d Graz, 29 Oct 1882), German writer on music. Friend of Mendelssohn and Schumann at Leipzig; settled in Vienna, 1846. He compiled thematic catalogues of Beethoven's and Schubert's works; wrote a book on the former's sketches.

Notturno (It. = night piece), the 18th-cent. forerunner of the Nocturne, not then a single lyrical instrumental piece, but a comp. in

several movements similar to the Serenade or Divertimento. In the 19th cent. it became simply the It. equivalent of the Nocturne, as for ex. in Mendelssohn's *Midsummer Night's Dream* music.

Nouguès, Jean (b Bordeaux, 25 Apr 1875; d Auteuil, 28 Aug 1932), French composer. Worked and prod. operas at Bordeaux at 1st, later in Paris.

Works incl. operas *Le Roy du Papagey* (1890), *Thamyris* (1904), *La Mort de Tintagiles* (after Maeterlinck, 1905), *Chiquito, Quo vadis?* (after Sienkiewicz, 1909), *L'Auberge rouge* (from Balzac's *Nouveaux Contes philosophiques*), *La Vendetta* (1911), *L'Aiglon* (1912), *L'Éclaircie, Dante, Jeanne de France, Le Scarabée bleu* (1931), *Une Aventure de Villon*; ballets *La Danseuse de Pompéi* and *Narcisse*; incid. music for Rostand's *Cyrano de Bergerac*; film music, etc.

Nourrit, Adolphe (b Montpellier, 3 Mar 1802; d Naples, 8 Mar 1839), French tenor. Made his 1st appearance at the Paris Opéra 1821, remaining attached to that theatre for 16 years. He created roles there in Rossini's *Le siège de Corinthe* (1826), Moïse (1827), *Comte Ory* (1828) and *Guillaume Tell* (1829) and in Meyerbeer's *Robert le diable* and *Les Huguenots.*

Nováček, Ottokar (b Fehertemplom, 13 May 1866; d New York, 3 Feb 1900), Hungarian violinist and composer. Studied with his father, later in Vienna and Leipzig. In the latter city he joined the string 4tet of his teacher, Brodsky, as 2nd vln. and then as vla. In 1892 he went to NY and became vla. leader in Damrosch's orch. In 1899 he retired for reasons of health and took to composition.

Works incl. pf. concerto, *Perpetuum mobile* for vln. and orch.; 3 string 4tets; 8 caprices and other works for vln. and pf.; pf. music; 6 songs to words by Tolstoy.

Novae de Infinito Laudes (New Praises of the Infinite), cantata by Henze for soloists, chorus and orch. (text by Giordano Bruno, 1548–1600, Italian astronomer burnt at the stake by the Inquisition); comp. 1962, fp Venice, 24 Apr 1963, with Söderström, Meyer, Pears and Fischer-Dieskau.

Novák, Vítězslav (b Kamenice, 5 Dec 1870; d Skuteč, 18 Jul 1949), Czech composer. He was the son of a doctor, but lost his father early and had to support the family by teaching. While studying law at Prague Univ. he attended the Cons., studying pf. with Jiránek and comp. with Dvořák, who persuaded him to devote himself wholly to music. His first works were pub. with the help of Brahms. He soon made a career as a distinguished teacher of comp. and in 1909 was app. prof. at the Cons. After the 1914–18 war, which restored his country's independence, he became prof. of the 'Master School' and was its dir. in 1919–22.

Works incl. operas *The Imp of Zvíkov* (1915), *A Night at Karlstein* (1916), *The Lantern* (1923), *The Grandfather's Will* (1926), *The Wood Nymph*; ballets *Signorina Gioventù* and *Nikotina*; cantatas *The Storm*, *The Spectre's Bride* and choral ballads; symph. (1945), ded. to Stalin after the liberation of Prague, symph. poems *In the Tatra*, *Eternal Longing*, *Toman and the Wood Nymph*, *De profundis* (1941), overtures *The Corsair* (after Bryon), *Maryša*, *Lady Godiva*, serenade for small orch.; pf. concerto (1895).

2 string 4tets, 2 pf. trios, pf. 4tct, pf. 5tet; *Sonata eroica*, *Manfred* (ballad after Byron), *Songs of Winter Nights*, *Pan*, *Exoticon*, 6 sonatinas, *Youth* (children's pieces), etc., for pf.; song cycles *Gypsy Songs*, *Melancholy*, *In the Valley of a New Kingdom*, *Melancholy Songs of Love*, *Nocturnes*, *Eroticon*, and other songs; part-songs.

Novelletten (Ger. lit. 'short stories'), a category title used by Schumann for his 8 pf. pieces op. 21, comp. in 1838, also for no. 9 of the *Bunte Blätter* for pf., op. 99.

Novello, Clara (Anastasia) (b London, 10 Jun 1818; d Rome, 12 Mar 1908), English soprano. Studied at the Paris Cons. and 1st appeared at Worcester in 1833. Lived in London but had many successes abroad, esp. in It. and Ger. She sang in the 1st London perf. of Beethoven's *Missa Solemnis*, 1832, and sang Semiramide in Bologna (1841). Married Count Gigliucci in 1843.

Novello, Vincent (b London, 6 Sep 1781; d Nice, 9 Aug 1861), English composer, organist, editor and publisher, father of prec. Founder of the music pub. firm of Novello & Co. in London, 1811. Ed. valuable collections of music incl. Masses by Haydn and Mozart, and comp. church music, cantatas, etc.

November Woods, a symph. poem by Bax, comp. 1917, fp Manchester, Hallé Orch., 18 Nov 1920.

Novotná, Jarmila (b Prague, 23 Sep 1907), Czech soprano. She studied with Emmy Destinn and made her debut in Prague in 1926 as Violetta. She joined the Berlin Staatsoper in 1928 and sang in Vienna 1933–8; created Lehár's *Giuditta* there in 1934. Salzburg 1935–7 as Octavian, Eurydice and Pamina.

NY Met debut 1939, as Mimi; remained until 1940 as Elvira, Butterfly and Mélisande.

Novotný, Jaroslav (b Jičin, 28 Mar 1886; d Miass, Ural, 1 Jun 1918), Czech composer. Studied in Prague, joined the Austrian army during World War I, was a prisoner in Rus., where he wrote much in camp, and was released and killed near the end of the war fighting on the other side with the Czech legion.

Works incl. string 4tet; choruses; pf. sonata; song cycles *The Eternal Wedding* and *Ballads of the Soul*.

Nowowiejski, Feliks (b Wartenburg, E. Prussia, 7 Feb 1877; d Poznań, 23 Jan 1946), Polish composer and conductor. Studied in Berlin and church music at Regensburg, afterwards in France, Belgium and Italy. In 1909 he returned to Poland, cond. the Kraków Music Society until 1914 and in 1919 became prof. of org. at the Poznań Cons. and cond. orchestral concerts there.

Works incl. operas *Baltic Legend* (1924), *The Mountain Goblin*; opera-ballet *Leluja*; ballets *Tatra*, *Polish Wedding*; Masses, motets and psalms; oratorios *Quo vadis?* (1907), *Beatum scelus*, *Missa pro pace*, etc.; cantata *Upper Silesian Folk Scene*; symph. poems *Beatrix*, *Nina*, overture *Polish Wooing*, *The Prodigal Son*, *Jerusalem*; 9 symphs.

Noyes Fludde, opera in 1 act by Britten (text from the Chester Miracle Play), prod. Orford, 18 Jun 1958. Story based on Noah; setting makes much use of children's voices.

Nozzari, Andrea (b Vertova, nr. Bergamo, 1775; d Naples, 12 Dec 1832), Italian tenor. He studied in Bergamo and sang in Rome, Milan and Paris before joining the San Carlo Theatre, Naples; took part in the fps of nine Rossini operas, incl. *Elisabetta*, *Otello*, *Armida*, *La donna del lago*, *Maometto II* and *Zelmira*.

Nozze d'Ercole e d'Ebe, Le (*The Nuptials of Hercules and Hebe*), opera by Gluck, prod. Pillnitz, nr. Dresden, at the double wedding of Max Joseph, Elector of Bavaria, and Maria Anna, Princess of Saxony, and Frederick Christian, Prince of Saxony, and Maria Antonia Walpurgis, Princess of Bavaria, 29 Jun 1747.

Opera by Porpora (lib. as above), prod. Venice, 18 Feb 1744.

Nozze di Figaro, Le (*The Marriage of Figaro*), opera by Mozart (lib. by L. da Ponte, based on Beaumarchais's comedy, *La Folle Journée, ou Le Mariage de Figaro*), prod. Vienna, Burgtheater, 1 May 1786.

Nozze di Teti e di Peleo, Le (*The Nuptials of Thetis and Peleus*), opera by Cavalli (lib. by O. Persiani), prod. Venice, Teatro San Cassiano, prob. 24 Jan 1639.

Nucius (or Nux or Nucis), Joannes (b Görlitz, *c* 1556; d Himmelwitz, Silesia, 25 Mar 1620), German monk and composer. Entered the Cistercian abbey of Rauden, Upper Silesia, and in 1591 became abbot of its offshoot at Himmelwitz. Comp. Masses, motets, etc.

Nuits d'été, Les (Summer Nights), 6 songs by Berlioz (poems by T. Gautier), comp. 1840–1 for mezzo or tenor and pf.; revised for voice and orch. 1843 (no. 4) and 1856. 1. *Villanelle*, 2. *Le spectre de la rose*, 3. *Sur les lagunes*, 4. *Absence*, 5. *Au cimetière*, 6. *L'île inconnue*.

Nuitter (actually Truinet), **Charles (Louis Étienne)** (b Paris, 24 Apr 1828; d Paris, 24 Feb 1899), French librettist and writer on music. A lawyer at first, he later devoted himself to the writing and trans. of libs. and of books on opera. In 1865 he became archivist of the Paris Opéra.

Nunc dimittis (Lat. = 'Now lettest thou [thy servant] depart [in peace]'). Part of the Evening Service of the Anglican Church and of Compline in the R.C. Church. Often set by comps. as a 2nd part following the Magnificat.

Nursery, The, song cycle by Mussorgsky (words by comp.), comp. 1868–72: 1. *With Nurse*; 2 *In the Corner*; 3. *The Cockchafer*; 4. *With the Doll*; 5. *Going to sleep*; 6 *On the Hobby-Horse*; 7. *The Cat 'Sailor'*.

Nusch-Nuschi, Das, opera in 1 act for Burmese marionettes by Hindemith (lib. by F. Blei); comp. 1920, prod. Stuttgart, 4 Jun 1921; cond. by Fritz Busch, who claimed to be shocked by satirical references to Wagner's *Tristan*. (The castration of an Oriental philanderer is accompanied by a quotation from King Marke's music: '*Mir-dies?*'; 'This – to me?').

Nut, the contrivance at the heel of a vln. or other bow at which the hairs are attached and can be stretched by the turn of a screw; also the strip, usually of ebony, at the end of the fingerboard of a string instrument near the pegs, serving to raise the strings clear of the board.

Nutcracker (*Casse-Noisette*), ballet by Tchaikovsky (choreography by Lev Ivanovich Ivanov, based on a tale by E.T.A. Hoffmann), prod. St Petersburg, Maryinsky Theatre, 18 Dec 1892.

Nystroem, Gösta (b Österhaninge, nr. Stockholm, 13 Oct 1890; d Göteborg, 10 Aug 1966), Swedish composer and painter. Son of a headmaster who taught him music and painting, which he afterwards studied at Stockholm, Copenhagen and Paris, where he lived for 12 years and where d'Indy and Sabaneiev were among his masters for comp. and he came under the influence of Picasso, Braque, Chirico and other modern painters. After some further studies in Italy and Spain he settled at Göteborg and in 1933 became music critic of the *Göteborgs Handelstidning*.

Works incl. ballet-pantomime *Maskerade*; incid. music to var. plays incl. Shakespeare's *Merchant of Venice* and *The Tempest*; 4 symphs. (*Sinfonia breve, S. espressiva, S. del mare, S. Shakespeariana*), symph. poems *The Arctic Sea, The Tower of Babel*, Lyric Suite and Festival Overture for orch., *Concerto grosso* for string orch.; vln. concerto, vla., concerto, *Sinfonia concertante* for cello and orch.; pf. suites and pieces; songs.

O

Oakeley, Herbert (Stanley) (b London, 22 Jul 1830; d Eastbourne, 26 Oct 1903), English organist, educationist and composer. Educ. at Rugby and Oxford, studied music in London, Dresden and Leipzig. He became Prof. of Music at Edinburgh Univ. in 1865 and Mus.D. (Cantuar.) in 1871. Knighted 1876.

Works incl. services and anthems; Jubilee Cantata (1887) and other choral works, part-songs; Festal and Funeral Marches for orch.; organ and pf. music; songs.

Obbligato (It. = obligatory, compulsory), instrumental part in a work that is 'essential' in the sense that it performs an important soloistic function.

Oberlin, Russell (b Akron, Ohio, 11 Oct 1925), American counter-tenor. He studied at Juilliard and was a co-founder with Noah Greenberg of the NY Pro Musica Antiqua; many perfs. of medieval and Renaissance music. He sang Oberon in *A Midsummer Night's Dream* at CG, in 1961. Well known as a concert singer, he has also recorded *Messiah*.

Oberon, König der Elfen (*Oberon, King of the Fairies*), opera by Wranitzky (lib. by K.L. Gieseke, based on Wieland's poem and F.S. Seyler's lib. *Hüon und Amande*), prod. Vienna, Theater auf der Wieden, 7 Nov 1789.

Oberon, or The Elf King's Oath, opera by Weber (lib. by J.R. Planché, based on Wieland's poem and further back on the medieval Fr. romance *Huon de Bordeaux*), prod. London, CG, 12 Apr 1826.

Obertas, a Polish dance perf. in figures by couples following a leader. The music is in 3–4 time, not unlike that of the Mazurka, but wilder in character.

Oberthür, Charles (b Munich, 4 Mar 1819; d London, 8 Nov 1895), German harpist and composer. After var. orchestral engagements in Ger. and Switz. he settled in London in 1844 as perf. and teacher.

Works incl. opera *Floris von Namur* (1840); Mass *St Philip Neri*; cantatas *The Pilgrim Queen*, *The Red Cross Knight*, *Lady Jane Grey* (1881–6); overture *Rübezahl*, overture for Shakespeare's *Macbeth* (1852) and others; *Loreley* and concertino for harp and orch.; trios for harp, vln. and cello, 4tets for harps; many harp solos.

Oberto, Conte di San Bonifacio, opera by Verdi (lib. by A. Piazza, altered by B. Merelli and T. Solera), prod. Milan, La Scala, 17 Nov 1839, Verdi's 1st opera.

Oboe, a woodwind instrument formerly called hautboy, held vertically and played with a double reed. It descended from the Shawm and was in full use by the 17th cent., though it was not properly developed until the 18th and not wholly perfected until the 19th. 2 oboes together with 2 horns, were the most constant instruments in the orch., apart from the strings, in the 18th cent. The oboe has a compass of about 2½ 8ves:

Oboe d'amore (It. = love ob.), an oboe tuned a min. 3rd lower and transposing a min. 3rd down.

Oboe da caccia (It. = hunting ob.), an oboe tuned a 5th lower and transposing a 5th down. Its parts in old music are now generally played on the Eng. horn, whose pitch is the same.

Oborin, Lev (Nikolayevich) (b Moscow, 11 Sep 1907; d Moscow, 5 Jan 1974), Russian pianist. Studied at Moscow Cons. with Igumnov, graduating in 1926. Taught at the Moscow Cons. from 1928, becoming prof. in 1935. Although he had much success as a concert performer, he devoted much of his time to teaching. Formed a trio with D. Oistrakh and Knushevitsky.

Obraztsova, Elena (b Leningrad, 7 July 1937), Russian mezzo. She studied in Leningrad and made her debut at the Bolshoy, Moscow, as Marina in 1963; sang same role at NY Met in 1975. Debut with Met Co. 1976, in *Adriana Lecouvreur*. She has appeared widely in Europe as Carmen, Dalila, Amneris, Eboli and Helen in *War and Peace*. Her Azucena at CG in 1985 had a mixed response.

Obrecht (or Hobrecht), Jacob (or Jacobus Obertus) (b ? Bergen-op-Zoom, 22 Nov c 1450; d Ferrara, 1505), Netherlands composer. In 1479 became choirmaster at Bergen-op-Zoom. Dir. of the singing-school at Cambrai, 1484–5, and teacher at Bruges, 1491–6, though he must have resided at Antwerp, where he was app. *maître de chapelle* at the cathedral in 1491. Towards the end of his life he went to Italy and was for a time at the court of Lorenzo de' Medici at Florence.

Works incl. 27 Masses, e.g. *Fortuna*

desperata, Maria zart and *Sub tuum praesidium*; motets, *chansons*.

Obukhov, Nikolai (b Kursk, 22 Apr 1892; d Paris, 13 Jun 1954), Russian composer. pupil of N. Tcherepnin and Steinberg at the St Petersburg Cons. He settled in Paris in 1918 and made further studies with Ravel and others. He experimented with a 12-note system.
Works incl. mystery *Le Livre de la vie*, *Poèmes liturgiques*.

Oca del Cairo, L' (*The Goose of Cairo*), unfinished opera by Mozart (lib. by G.B. Varesco). Prod. in a version completed with other Mozartian fragments (lib. by V. Wilder), Paris, Fantaisies-Parisiennes, 6 Jun 1867; new version by Virgilio Mortari (lib. by L. Cavicchioli), Salzburg, 22 Aug 1936; another by Hans Redlich, London, SW, 30 May 1940.

Ocarina, an early instrument of the flute type with finger-holes, approx. pearshaped, with a mouthpiece protruding like a fish's fin, and usually made of terracotta.

Occasional Oratorio, oratorio by Handel (lib. from Milton's Psalms completed by ? Morell), comp. to celebrate the suppression of the Jacobite rebellion, prod. London, CG, 14 Feb 1746.

Occasione fa il ladro, L' (*Opportunity makes a Thief*), opera by Rossini (lib. by L. Prividali), prod. Venice, Teatro San Moisè, 24 Nov 1812.

Oceanides, The (*Aollottaret*), symphonic poem by Sibelius, op. 73; comp. 1914, fp Norfolk, Conn., 4 Jun 1914, cond. Sibelius.

Ochs, Siegfried (b Frankfurt, 19 Apr 1858; d Berlin, 5 Feb 1929), German conductor and composer. After a general educ. at Darmstadt and at Heidelberg Univ., he studied music in Berlin and founded a choral society in 1882, which in assoc. with the Phil. Orch. became the Philharmonische Chor in 1888. In the 1920s he became prof. at the Hochschule für Musik and cond. the oratorios and other choral concerts there. Gave frequent perfs. of Bach and Schütz.
Works incl. opera *Im Namen des Gesetzes*; songs, etc.

Ochsenkuhn, Sebastian (b Nuremberg, 6 Feb 1521; d Heidelberg, 20 Aug 1574), German lutenist. In the service of Otto Heinrich, Elector Palatine of the Rhine, and his successors, 1534–71. He pub. in 1558 a book of arrs. of motets and Fr. and Ger. songs in lute tablature.

Ockeghem, Johannes (or Ockenheim, Okeghem, Hoquegan) (b *c* 1420, d Tours, 6 Feb 1497), Flemish composer. Pupil (?) of Binchois, chorister at Antwerp Cathedral until 1444, in the service of Charles, Duke of Bourbon, at Moulins in 1446–8, and in the service of the Fr. court from *c* 1452, where he became 1st *maître de chapelle*. Louis XI app. him treasurer of Saint-Martin at Tours, where he lived during the latter part of his life, though he visited Spain in 1469.
Works incl. 10 Masses, e.g. *Ecce ancilla Domini, L'homme armé* and *Mi-mi*; motets; Fr. *chansons*.

Octandre, work by Varèse for small orch.; comp. 1923, fp NY, 13 Jan 1924.

Octave, an interval embracing 8 notes of a diatonic scale. The upper note having exactly twice the number of vibrations of the lower, the phenomenon results that the 2 appear to be the same, although different in pitch.

Octet, a comp. for 8 instruments, usually in several movements. Mendelssohn's Octet for strings, op. 20 and Schubert's for wind and strings, op. 166, are familiar examples.

Octo Basse (Fr.), **Octobass** (Eng.), a 3-stringed double bass of huge size invented in 1849 by J.B. Vuillaume in Paris, which never became current. It was capable of playing extremely low notes, the strings being tuned:

8ve lower —|

It was very unwieldly and its strings were so thick and heavy that they had to be stopped by means of levers and pedals.

Ode, a comp. in several movements, with alternating solos and choruses, often of a dedicatory or congratulatory character.
Work for orch. by Stravinsky; comp. 1943, fp. Boston, 8 Oct 1943, cond. Koussevitzky.

Ode for St Cecilia's Day, setting by Handel of Dryden's poem, prod. London, Theatre in Lincoln's Inn Fields, 22 Nov 1739.

Odes for St Cecilia's Day by Purcell; 1. *Laudate Ceciliam* (1683); 2. *Welcome to all the pleasures* (Fishburn; 1683); 3. *Hail, bright Cecilia* (Brady; 1692); 4. *Raise, raise the voice.*

Ode to Napoleon Buonaparte, work by Schoenberg for string 4tet, pf. and reciter (text by Byron); comp. 1942. Vers. with string orch. perf. NY, 24 Nov 1944, cond. Rodzinski.

Ode to the West Wind, work for cello and orch. after Shelley by Henze; comp. 1953, fp Bielefeld, 30 Apr 1954.

Odington, Walter de (or W. of Evesham) (b

? Oddington, Glos.; d ? Evesham), English 13th-cent. monk, musician and astronomer. He entered the Benedictine monastery at Evesham and wrote a treatise *De speculatione musicae*.

Odnoposoff, Ricardo (b Buenos Aires, 24 Feb 1914), Argentine violinist. A child prodigy, he first appeared in public aged 5. Studied first in Buenos Aires and then in Berlin with Flesch, winning prizes in Vienna and Brussels (1932 and 1937). Brustad, Berger and Francisco Mignone wrote works for him.

Odo (b 879; d Tours, 18 Nov 942), French monk and musician. Educ. at the court of Guillaume, Duke of Aquitaine, took holy orders, joined the monastery of Saint-Martin at Tours, and after studying dialectics and music in Paris, returned there, then entered the Benedictine monastery of Beaume, nr. Besançon, became abbot of that of Cluny, nr. Macon, 927–42, but returned to Tours to die. He comp. hymns and antiphons and wrote treatises on music.

Odzmek, a Slovak dance in quick 2–4 time with a more moderately paced middle section. The 9th of Dvořák's *Slavonic Dances* for pf. duet is an Odzmek.

Œdipe à Colone (*Oedipus Coloneus*), opera by Sacchini (lib. by Nicolas François Guillard, after Sophocles), prod. Versailles, at court, 4 Jan 1786; 1st Paris perf. Opéra, 1 Feb 1787.

Oedipus auf Kolonos, incid. music by Mendelssohn for Sophocles' tragedy, op. 93, for male chorus and orch., prod. Potsdam, 1 Nov 1845.

Oedipus der Tyrann musical play after Sophocles by Orff, prod. Stuttgart, 11 Dec 1959.

Oedipus Rex, stage oratorio by Stravinsky (lib., in Lat., by J. Daniélou, trans. from Fr. by Jean Cocteau, after Sophocles), prod. Paris, Théâtre Sarah Bernhardt, 30 May 1927. The parts are sung in costume but without action, and the words are in Latin in order not to distract the ordinary listener by verbal associations. 1st stage perf. Vienna, Staatsoper, 23 Feb 1928.

Oedipus Tyrannus, incid. music by Mendelssohn for Sophocles' tragedy, never perf. and now lost.

Incid. music for do. by Stanford, prod. Cambridge, 22–6 Nov 1887.

Oedipus und die Sphinx, unfinished opera by Varèse (text by Hofmannsthal); comp. 1909–13. The MS. is lost.

Oestvig, Karl (b Christiana 17 May 1889; d Oslo, 21 Jul 1968), Norwegian tenor. He studied in Cologne and sang in Stuttgart 1914–19. Vienna 1919–27; created the Emperor in *Die Frau ohne Schatten*, 1919. Berlin 1927–30 as Bacchus, Don José, Lohengrin, Walther and Parsifal. Retired to Oslo in 1932 and prod. opera there during the Nazi occupation.

Offenbach, Jacques (actually **Jakob Levy Eberst**) (b Cologne, 20 Jun 1819; d Paris, 5 Oct 1880), German-French composer. His father was cantor at the synagogue of Cologne, but he was sent to Paris early in his youth, studying at the Cons. in 1833–7, perfecting himself in cello playing and then playing in the orch. of the Opéra-Comique even before he left the Cons. In 1850 he became cond. at the Théâtre Français. In 1853 he prod. his 1st operettas and during a quarter of a century he turned out nearly 100 light stage pieces. In 1855 he took over the management of the Théâtre Comte and renamed it the Bouffes-Parisiens. This lasted until 1861, after which he had no theatre of his own until 1873, when he managed the Théâtre de la Gaîté until 1875. In 1876–7 he was in USA, but returned to Paris, where alone he found that his success was permanent. His only large-scale opera, *Les Contes d'Hoffmann*, occupied him for many years, but he left it not quite finished at his death, and it was revised and partly scored by Guiraud.

Works incl. opera *Les Contes d'Hoffmann* (1881), 89 operettas incl. *Barbebleue* (1866), *Ba-ta-clan* (1855), *La Belle Hélène* (1864), *Chanson de Fortunio, Le Docteur Ox* (after Jules Verne), *La Fille du tambour-major* (1879), *La Foire de Saint-Laurent, Geneviève de Brabant* (1859), *La Grande-Duchesse de Gérolstein* (1867), *L'Île de Tulipatan, La Jolie Parfumeuse, Madame Favart, Orphée aux enfers* (1858), *La Périchole* (1874), *Princesse de Trébizonde, Robinson Crusoe* (after Defoe, 1867), *Vert-Vert, La Vie Parisienne* (1866), *Voyage dans la lune* (after Verne), *Whittington and his Cat* (1874); ballet *Le Papillon*; incid. music for Barrière's *Le Gascon* and Sardou's *La Haine*; cello concerto. A 2nd opera, *The Goldsmith of Toledo* (after a tale by E.T.A. Hoffmann) is a pasticcio from var. operettas, esp. *Le Corsaire noir*, prod. Mannheim, 1919.

Offertory (Lat. *Offertorium*), the 3rd or 4th item of the Proper of the Roman Mass, following the gospel or the *Credo*. It was orig. an antiphonal chant, sung with a complete psalm and accomp. the offering of bread and wine. In the 10th cent. it became an elaborate responsorial chant provided with complex verses sung by soloists. The verses were later dropped, but the style of what remains is still closer to the Gradual than to the Introit or Communion. In the Anglican church it survived as a spoken biblical sentence, occasionally set to music. The offertory was frequently set by 16th-cent. comps., and with instrumental accomp. by Michael Haydn, Mozart, Schubert, and others.

Offrandes, work by Varèse for sop. and chamber ens. (texts by V. Huidobro and J.J. Tablada); comp. 1921, fp NY, 23 Apr 1922.

Offrandes oubliées, Les (*The Forgotten Offerings*), work for orch. in 3 parts by Messiaen; comp. 1930, fp Paris, 19 Feb 1931.

Ogdon, John (Andrew Howard) (b Manchester, 27 Jan 1937), English pianist and composer. Studied at Royal Manchester Coll. of Music; London debut 1958, in the Busoni concerto. In 1962 won the Tchaikovsky Competition in Moscow. He is equally at home in both the classical and modern repertory, and has also pub. a number of compositions, incl. a pf. concerto. For some years he was afflicted with mental illness, and left hospital to perform. He has now recovered.

Ogiński, Polish noble family of amateur musicians:

1. Prince Michał Kazimierz O. (b Warsaw, 1728; d Warsaw, 31 May 1800). Studied the vln. with Viotti and also played the harp. He kept a small opera co. and orch. on his estate.

Works incl. a comic opera, incid. music for 2 plays, and polonaises for vln. and pf.

2. Prince Michał Kleofas O. (b Gozuw, nr. Warsaw, 25 Sep 1765; d Florence, 15 Oct 1833), nephew of prec. Was taught the pf. by Kozlowski and vln. by Viotti and others. After the 3rd partition of Poland he emigrated, 1st to Turkey, then to Hamburg, Paris (1823) and finally Florence. Works incl. opera *Zélis et Valeur, ou Bonapart au Caire* (1799); military marches; polonaises and mazurkas for pf.

Öglin, Erhard (b Reutlingen), German 15th-16th-cent. music publisher. He worked in Augsburg, where he pub. an important collection of 4-part songs in 1512.

Ohana, Maurice (b Casablanca, 12 Jun 1914), English composer of Moroccan descent. Studied in Barcelona, Rome and at the Schola Cantorum in Paris. His music belongs to the *avant-garde* school of his time.

Works incl. opera *Chanson de Toile*

(1969), opera for marionettes *Autodafé* (1972); ballets *Prométhée* (1956) and *Paso*; *Les Représentations de Tanit* and *Suite pour un Mimodrame* for small orch.; guitar concerto; concertino for tpt.; *Études, Choréographiques* for perc.; pf. music; choral music, film music.

Ohms, Elisabeth (b Arnhem, 17 May 1888; d Marquartstein, 16 Oct 1974), Dutch soprano. Debut Mainz 1921; Munich from 1923 as Brünnhilde, Isolde, Turandot and Strauss's Helen. She sang Fidelio and Kundry under Toscanini at Milan, 1927–8. London, CG, 1928–35 as Venus, Ortrud and the Marschallin. NY Met debut 1930, as Brünnhilde.

Oiseau de feu, L'. *See* **Firebird.**

Oiseaux exotiques (*Exotic birds*), work for orch., by Messiaen for 2 clar., xylophone, glockenspiel, perc. and wind; comp. 1955–6, fp Paris, 10 Mar 1956.

Oistrakh, David (Fedorovich) (b Odessa, 30 Sep 1908; d Amsterdam, 24 Oct 1974), Russian violinist. Began his studies aged 5, entered the Odessa Cons. and graduated in 1926, winning a number of prizes, incl. the Brussels Competition in 1937, which gave him international fame. From 1934 he taught at the Moscow Cons., and also appeared widely as a soloist. He gave the fps of vln. concertos by Miaskovsky, Khachaturian and Shostakovich; collaborated with Prokofiev in an arr. of the flute sonata for violin and pf.

Oistrakh, Igor (b Odessa, 27 Apr 1931), Russian violinist, son of prec. Studied with his father at the Moscow Cons., graduating in 1955 after winning prizes in Budapest (1949) and Poznań (1952). Has taught at Moscow Cons. from 1958.

Okeland, Robert, 16th-cent. English composer. He was a member of Eton Coll., 1532–4, and of the Chapel Royal, 1547–8. Music of his is preserved in the 'Gyffard' part-books, *c* 1555.

Olav Trygvason, unfinished opera by Grieg (lib. by Bjørnson), 3 scenes only, perf. in concert form, Christiania, 19 Oct 1889; never staged in Grieg's lifetime, but prod. Christiania, 8 Oct 1908.

Olczewska, Maria (b Ludwigsschwaige, nr. Donauwörth, 12 Aug 1892; d Klagenfurt, 17 May 1969), German mezzo. She studied in Munich and was engaged in Hamburg, Vienna and Munich 1917–25 as Fricka, Ortrud, Carmen and Amneris. London, CG, 1924–33 as Octavian and Orlofsky. NY Met debut 1933, as Brangaene. Taught in Vienna from 1947.

Old Hall Manuscript, a collection of English church music, copied c 1420–30 and named after the college in Ware which housed it until it was purchased by the British Library in 1973.

Oldham, Arthur (William) (b London, 6 Sep 1926), English composer. Studied comp. with Howells and pf. with Kathleen Long at the RCM in London, also privately with Britten. He was for a time music dir. at the Mercury Theatre and to the Ballet Rambert, but later devoted himself wholly to comp. Works incl. 4 ballets incl. *Bonne-Bouche* (1952), incid. music for Ronald Duncan's *This Way to the Tomb*; 6 anthems; orchestral music, incl. Sinfonietta for wind band (1974); vln. and pf. sonata; songs.

Olimpia vendicata (*Olympia revenged*), opera by A. Scarlatti (lib. by A. Aureli), prod. Naples, Palazzo Reale, 23 Dec 1685.

Olimpiade, L' (*The Olympiad*). *see also* **Olympie.** Lib. by Metastasio

Opera by Caldara, prod. Vienna, 28 Aug 1733.

Opera by Cimarosa, prod. Vicenza, 10 Jul 1784.

Opera by Ignazio Fiorillo (1715–87), prod. Venice, Teatro San Samuele, May 1745.

Opera by Galuppi, prod. Milan, Teatro Regio Ducal, 26 Dec 1747.

Opera by Hasse, prod. Dresden, at court, 16 Feb 1756.

Opera by Jommelli, prod. Stuttgart, at court, 11 Feb 1761.

Opera by Leo, prod. Naples, Teatro San Carlo, 19 Dec 1737.

Opera by Mysliveček, prod. Naples, Teatro San Carlo, 4 Nov 1778.

Opera by Pergolesi, prod. Rome, Teatro Tordinona, 8 Jan 1735.

Opera by Sacchini, prod. Padua, Jun 1763.

Opera by Traetta, prod. Verona, autumn 1758.

Opera by Vivaldi, prod. Venice, Teatro Sant' Angelo, Carnival 1734. (There are at least 30 other settings of this lib. *Olimpiade* is prob. the most frequently comp. work by Metastasio or by any other librettist).

Oliphant (from old Eng. 'olifaunt' = elephant), a bugle-like horn made of an elephant's tusk, used for signalling and hunting in old times, often beautifully carved.

Oliver, Stephen (b Liverpool, 10 Mar 1950), English composer. He studied at Oxford; electronic music with Robert Sherlaw Johnson. The best known of his many operas and theatre pieces is *Tom Jones*, after Field-

ing, prod. Snape, Newcastle and London 1976. Other pieces incl. *Perseverance* (1974), *Bad Times* (1975), *The Great McPorridge Disaster* (1976), *The Duchess of Malfi* (1971–7), *The Dreaming of the Bones* (1979), *Nicholas Nickelby* (1980), *Blondel* (1983), and *Brittania Preserv'd* (1984). Popular as a teacher and broadcaster.

Olivero, Magda (b Saluzzo, nr. Turin, 25 Mar 1912), Italian soprano. Debut Turin 1933, as Lauretta. Sang in Italy until 1941 as Manon, Elsa, Lucia and Adriana Lecouvreur. Retired on marriage 1941 but returned 1951 as Minnie, Fedora and Iris. London debut 1952 as Mimi. US debut Dallas 1967, as Medea; NY Met 1975, Tosca.

Olivieri-Sangiacomo, Elsa. *See* **Respighi.**

Ollone, Max (properly Maximilien-Paul-Marie-Félix) **d'** (b Besançon, 13 Jun 1875; d Paris, 15 May 1959), French conductor and composer. Studied under Massenet and Lenepveu at the Paris Cons. and gained the Prix de Rome in 1897. After cond. at Angers, Geneva and Paris (Opéra-Comique, concerts, etc.), and touring as cond. he became prof. at the Cons. in 1939.

Works incl. operas *Le Retour*, *Les Amants de Rimini* (after Dante, 1912), *Les Uns et les autres* (on a comedy by Verlaine, 1922), *L'Arlequin, Georges Dandin* (after Molière, 1930), and *La Samaritaine* (after Rostand, 1937); ballet *Le Peuple abandonné*; pantomime *Bacchus et Silène*; oratorio *François d'Assise*, cantatas *Frédégonde* (1897), *Jeanne d'Arc à Domrémy*; fantasy for pf. and orch., *Le Ménétrier* for vln. and orch., string 4tet, pf. trio; songs.

Olsen, Ole (b Hammerfest, 4 Jul 1850; d Oslo, 9 Nov 1927), Norwegian organist, conductor and composer. Studied engineering at Trondhjem, but took to music, taking any appt. as organist and travelling theatre cond. he could secure. In 1870–4 he consolidated his studies at the Leipzig Cons. and then settled at Christiania where he taught cond. and wrote criticism.

Works incl. operas *Stig Hvide* (1876), *Lajla, Klippeøerne* (1910), and *Stallo*; incid. music to Nordahl Rolfsen's *Svein Urœd* (1890); oratorio *Nidaros*, cantatas *Ludwig Holberg* (1884), *Griffenfelt* (1897), *Broderbud, Tourist Cantata*; symph. in G maj., symph. poems *Aasgaardsreien, Elfdans*.

Olthoff, Statius (b Osnabrück, 1555; d Rostock, 28 Feb 1629), German composer. Became cantor at St Mary's Church at Rostock in 1579 and there comp. 4-part settings of

George Buchanan's Latin verse paraphrase of the psalms.

Olympians, The, opera by Bliss (lib. by J.B. Priestley), prod. London, CG, 29 Sep 1949.

Olympie, opera by Spontini (lib. by M. Dieulafoy and C. Brifaut, based on Voltaire's tragedy), prod. Paris, Opéra, 22 Dec 1819.

Olyver, early 15th-cent. English composer. Repres. in the Old Hall MS.

O'Mara, Joseph (b Limerick, 16 Jul 1861; d Dublin, 5 Aug 1927), Irish tenor. Studied at Milan and made his 1st appearance in London, 1891, as Sullivan's Ivanhoe. He sang with the Moody-Manners Co. 1902–8 and formed his own Grand Opera Co. in 1912.

Ombra di Don Giovanni, L' (*Don Juan's Shade*), opera by Alfano (lib. by E. Moschino), prod. Milan, La Scala, 2 Apr 1914; revised as *Don Giovanni de Mañara*, Florence, 28 May 1941.

Omphale, opera by Destouches (lib. by A.H. de la Motte), prod. Paris, Opéra, 10 Nov 1700.

On Hearing the First Cuckoo in Spring, 1 of 2 pieces for small orch. by Delius (the other being *Summer Night on the River*), comp. 1912 and 1911 respectively; fp Leipzig Gewandhaus, 2 Oct 1913. The cuckoo call is heard unobtrusively on the clar. and the main theme is a Norw. folksong, *In Ole Dale*, previously used by Grieg, arr. for pf. in *Norske Folkeviser*, op. 66 (no. 14).

On Wenlock Edge, song cycle for tenor, pf. and string 4tet by Vaughan Williams (text by A.E. Housman), fp London, 15 Nov 1909. Version with string orch. perf. London, 24 Jan 1924.

Oncina, Juan (b Barcelona, 15 Apr 1925), Spanish tenor. Debut Barcelona 1946, as Massenet's Des Grieux; later that year sang Almaviva, opposite Tito Gobbi, at Bologna. Glyndebourne 1952–61, as Don Ramiro, Ferrando, Comte Ory, Busoni's Scaramuccio, Fenton, Don Ottavio and Lindoro. At Florence he was heard in operas by Cherubini and Lully. Attempted Verdi and Puccini roles from 1963.

Ondes, Martenot, an electrophonic instrument invented by Maurice Martenot of Paris in 1929, prod. notes from the air graded according to the chromatic scale by a special device, not indeterminate in pitch like those of the Aetherophone or Theremin. Often used by Messiaen (e.g. *Turangalîla Symph.*)

Ondříček, František (b Prague, 29 Apr 1857; d Milan, 12 Apr 1922), Czech violinist. Pupil of his father and at the Prague and Paris Conss. 1st appeared in London in 1882 and then went on tour; gave the fp of Dvořák's Concerto (Prague 1883) and formed a 4tet which took part in the Haydn centenary celebrations (Vienna, 1809). Director of the New Vienna Cons., 1912–19, and then at that of Prague.

Onegin (*née* Hoffmann), **Sigrid** (b Stockholm, 1 Jun 1889; d Magliaso, Switz., 16 Jun 1943), Swedish contralto of German/French parentage. Studied in Swed. and Ger. and appeared frequently in both countries, also in Eng; debut Stuttgart 1912, as Carmen. Munich 1919–22, Berlin 1926–31. Roles incl. Amneris, Eboli, Fides and Orpheus. Bayreuth 1933–4 as Fricka, Erda and Waltraute. Her 1st husband was a great-nephew of Lvov.

O'Neill, Norman (b London, 14 Mar 1875; d London, 3 Mar 1934), Anglo-Irish composer and conductor. Great-grandson of Callcott. Studied with Somervell in London and with Knorr at the Hoch Cons. at Frankfurt. In 1899 he married the Fr. pianist Adine Rückert and in 1908 became cond. at the Haymarket Theatre, for which he wrote much incid. music. In 1919 he became treasurer of the Royal Phil. Society and in 1924 prof. at the RAM.

Works incl. incid. music for Shakespeare's *Hamlet* (1904), *Henry V, Julius Caesar* (1920), *King Lear* (1909), *Macbeth, Measure for Measure* and *The Merchant of Venice* (1922), Maeterlinck's *Blue Bird*, Barrie's *Mary Rose* and *A Kiss for Cinderella*, Ibsen's *Pretenders* (1913), Stephen Phillips's *The Lost Heir*: dramatic adaptations of Dicken's *Pickwick* and Scott's *Bride of Lammermoor*, etc.; *Swinburne Ballet* and *Punch and Judy* ballet; concert overtures, variations, *Miniatures* and other works for orch.; choral works; pf. 5tet, 2 pf. trios (1895, 1900); Variations and Fugue on an Ir. Air for 2 pfs.; pf. pieces; many songs.

Onslow, (André) George (or **Georges**) **(Louis)** (b Clermont-Ferrand, 27 Jul 1784; d Clermont-Ferrand, 3 Oct 1853), French composer of English descent. Grandson of the 1st Lord Onslow. He studied pf. with Hüllmandel, Dussek and Cramer while living in London for some years as a young man, but settled at Clermont-Ferrand as a country squire, held regular chamber music practices there, studied the cello and went for 2 years to Vienna to study comp. In the 1820s, wishing to write operas, he made further studies with Reicha in Paris, where he lived alternatively.

Works incl. operas *L'alcade de la Vega*

(1824), *Le Colporteur* (1827) and *Le Duc de Guise* (1837); 4 symphs.; 3 string 4tets, 34 string 5tets, 2 pf. 6tets, pf. 7tet, nonet for strings and wind, 6 pf. trios; vln. and pf. and cello and pf. sonatas; sonatas for pf. duet; pf. pieces.

Op. (abbr.) = Opus (Lat. = work), a prefix used for the enumeration of a comp.'s works. It was at first a publisher's rather than a composer's device and in the early 18th cent. (e.g. Handel) was used only for instrumental comps. Later in that cent. it began to become more general, being used for Haydn but not for Mozart, and from Beethoven onward it began to be used regularly, though the number of an opus is not necessarily a guide to the date of its comp.

Open, organ pipes of which the upper end is left open and which, unlike the Stopped pipes, prod. notes corresponding to their full length.

Open Notes, on wind instruments the notes prod. naturally as harmonics as distinct from Stopped Notes prod. by valves, keys or other mechanical means, or by the hand in horn playing.

Open Strings, the strings of string instruments as played without being stopped by the left hand on the fingerboard.

Opera (It. = work: the same as the Lat. *opus* and orig. used in the same sense), a musical work for the stage of varying types, originating in the last years of the 16th cent. in It. The dramatic foundation of it is a Libretto, which is set to music in var. ways that may be divided into 3 main types: (1) recitative carrying on the action and set musical numbers such as arias, concerted pieces for several voices, choruses, etc., forming musical climaxes; (2) similar musical numbers, but with the action carried on in spoken dialogue instead of recitative; (3) the text set continuously throughout, but often with traces of separate musical numbers still apparent. The instrumental share in an opera is almost always orchestral.

See also **Action musicale; Azione teatrale; Ballad Opera; Burlesque; Burletta; Comédie lyrique; Commedia per musica; Dramma giocoso; Dramma per musica; Extravaganza; Favola per musica; Festa teatrale; Intermezzo; Melodrama; Melodramma; Music Drama; Musical Comedy; Opera-Ballet; Opéra bouffe; O. buffa; Opéra comique; O. seria; Operetta; Pastorale; Singspiel; Tragédie lyrique; Vaudeville.**

Opera-Ballet, a combination of opera and ballet orig. in 17-cent. Fr. and there called *opéra-ballet* from the beginning.

Opéra bouffe (Fr. = comic opera, derived from It. *opera buffa*), a type of Fr. comic opera, or rather operetta, lighter in tone and flimsier in mus. workmanship than an *opéra comique*

Opera buffa (It. = comic opera), a light type of opera with a comedy lib., partic. of the 18th cent. in It., with dialogue in recitative (accomp. by the harpsichord) and musical numbers: arias, duets, etc., and (more rarely) choruses.

Opéra comique (Fr. lit. comic opera), an exclusively Fr. type of opera, not always comic and often by no means light, but orig. always with spoken dialogue.

Opera seria (It. = serious opera), a type of 18th-cent. opera, esp. that cultivated by the librettists Zeno and Metastasio, treating mythological or heroic-historical subjects. The musical treatment is mainly by recitative and arias, more rarely duets and other concerted numbers or choruses.

Operetta (It. = little opera), a light opera or musical comedy, normally with spoken dialogue.

Opernball, Der (*The Opera Ball*), operetta by Heuberger (lib. by V. Léon and H. von Waldberg), prod. Vienna, Theater an der Wien, 5 Jan 1898.

Ophicleide (lit. 'keyed snake' from Gk. *ophis*, a snake, and *kleis*, a key), a bass brass instrument similar to the Key Bugle, played with a cup-shaped mouthpiece and having holes covered with keys in the side. It was patented by Halary (i.e. Jean-Hilaire Asté) in Paris in 1821. It had a compass of about 3 8ves. It was gradually superseded by the bass tuba.

Opieński, Henryk (b Kraków, 13 Jan 1870; d Morges, nr. Lausanne, 21 Jan 1942), Polish musicologist, composer and conductor. Studied pf. with Paderewski, comp. with d'Indy at the Schola Cantorum in Paris and cond. and musicology with Nikisch and Riemann at Leipzig. He formed a vocal society at Lausanne in 1918 and lived in Switz. until his death, except when he was dir. of the Poznań Cons. in 1920–6. He ed. Chopin's letters and wrote on him, Paderewski, and Pol. music in general.

Works incl. operas *Maria* (Malczewski, 1904), and *Jacob the Lutenist* (1918); incid. music for Calderón's *El principe constante*; oratorio *The Prodigal Son*; cantata *Mickiewicz*; symph. poems *Zymunt August i Barbara* and *Lilla Weneda*; string 4tet; instrumental pieces; songs.

Opitiis, Benedictus de, 16th-cent Franco-Flemish composer. He wrote 2 motets for the entry of the future emperor Charles V into Antwerp in 1515; he was the organist at the church of Our Lady in Antwerp, c 1514–16, and stayed in England, 1516–18 at Henry VIII's court. He disappears from records after 1522.

Opus (Lat. = work). Its abbr., op., is used as a prefix to enumerations of a comp.'s works. *See* **Op.**

Oratorio, a vocal work, usually for solo voices and chorus with some kind of instrumental accomp. and generally set to sacred works, often direct from the Bible or paraphrased from it, and at any rate nearly always treating a subject of a sacred character (such notable exceptions as Handel's *Hercules* and Haydn's *Seasons* are not strictly speaking oratorios). It originated in the congregation of the Oratorians founded by St Philip Neri in the 16th cent., where scenes from Scripture were enacted with music. In the 17th cent. the oratorio developed side by side with Opera and was indistinguishable from it in some of its features, except that greater prominence was nearly always given to the chorus. Settings of one of the Evangelists' narratives of the Passion developed a special type of oratorio, esp. in Ger. The form was developed by Mendelssohn, Dvořák and Elgar. Modern examples incl. Schoenberg's *Die Jakobsleiter* (1917–22), Stravinsky's *Oedipus Rex* (1927) and Tippett's *A Child of our Time* (1939–41).

Orazi ed i Curiazi, Gli (*The Horatii and the Curiatii*), opera by Cimarosa (lib. by A.S. Sografi), prod. Venice, Teatro La Fenice, 26 Dec 1796.

Opera by Mercadante (lib. by S. Cammarano), prod. Naples, Teatro San Carlo, 10 Nov 1846.

Orchestra (Gk. = dancing-place), orig. the space in the Gk. theatre equivalent to that now occupied by the orchestra in an opera-house; now the name for the assembly of instrumental players itself. The modern orchestra originated in the ballets and operas of the early 17th cent. At that time various groups, e.g. strings, brass, were used separately and it was only gradually that they were combined. In the course of the 17th cent. tpts. and timpani, originally ceremonial and military instruments, were intro. into the orch. for festal or heroic music. By the early 18th cent. fls., obs. and bassoons were normal members of the orchestra, though recorders often appeared as alternatives to the fls., and horns came to be used

for music of a jovial character. Throughout this time keyboard instruments were used to support and enrich the ensemble. In the course of the 18th cent. clars. were added, though they only gradually became a normal part of the orch., and the keyboard continuo disappeared, except in church music. Up to this time trombs. were used only in church music and in solemn operatic scenes; Beethoven incorporated them in ordinary orchestral music. The 19th cent. saw the gradual establishment of the piccolo, Eng. horn, bass clar., double bassoon, tuba and harp as normal members of the orchestra and the replacement of the older horns and tpts. by valve instruments. Until the end of the 18th cent., and sometimes later, the cond. sat at the harpsichord or played 1st vln.

Orchestration (or Scoring), the art of setting out a comp. for the instruments of an orch. Methods of orchestration have changed considerably. Monteverdi in *Orfeo* (1607) used his instruments mainly in groups; Bach chose a particular combination of instruments and retained it throughout a movement or even throughout a work; Haydn, Mozart and Beethoven developed a new art of combining, doubling and contrasting instruments. Modern orchestration developed mainly from the works of Berlioz, Wagner, Strauss and Debussy, all of whom exploited the characteristic colours of the instruments and their combinations.

Ordonez, Carlo d' (or Ordoñez) (b Vienna, 19 Apr 1734; d Vienna, 6 Sep 1786), Austrian composer and violinist, a major influence in the developing instrumental style of the years 1750–75. He was for most of his life a government administrator in Vienna.

Works incl. 2 operas, over 70 symphs., over 30 string 4tets and other chamber music.

Ordoñez, Pedro (b Plasencia c 1510; d Palencia 5 May 1585), Spanish singer and composer. In 1539 he went to Rome as a singer in the Pontifical chapel and remained there to his death, attending the Council of Trent in 1545 and again in 1547, when it had moved to Bologna.

Ordre (Fr.), the old Fr. name for the Suite.

Orefice, Giacomo (b Vicenza, 27 Aug 1865; d Milan, 22 Dec 1922), Italian composer. Studied at the Bologna Liceo Musicale, Mancinelli being among his masters. In 1909 became prof. of comp. at Milan Cons.

Works incl. operas *Consuelo* (after George Sand, 1895), *Chopin* (on music by Chopin, 1901), *Cecilia* (1902), *Mosè*

(1905), *Pane altrui, Radda, Il castello del sogno* and others; symph. in D min., *Sinfonia del bosco, Anacreontiche* for orch. (1917); suite for cello and orch.; *Riflessioni ed ombre* for 5tet, pf. trio; 2 vln. and pf. sonatas, cello and pf. sonata; *Preludi del mare, Quadri di Böcklin, Crepuscoli, Miraggi,* etc. for pf.

Orel, Alfred (b Vienna, 3 Jul 1889; d Vienna, 11 Apr 1967), Austrian musicologist. A lawyer and civil servant at first, he studied music with Adler when nearly 30. Later app. prof. at Vienna Univ. and head of the music dept. of the municipal library. Author of works on Bruckner and co-ed. with Robert Haas of the ed. of the orig. versions of Bruckner's works.

Oresteia, trilogy of short operas by Taneiev (lib. by A.A. Venkstern, after Aeschylus), prod. St Petersburg, 29 Oct 1895.

Orestes. *See also* **Leben des Orest.**

   Opera by Weingartner (lib. by comp., after Aeschylus), prod. Leipzig, 15 Feb 1902.

Orfeide, L', cycle of operas by Malipiero (lib. by comp.), prod. complete, in Ger. trans., Düsseldorf, 30 Oct 1925.

   I. La morte delle maschere (*The Death of the Masks*).

   II. Sette canzoni (*Seven Songs*), prod. in Fr. trans., Paris, Opéra, 10 Jul 1920.

   III. L'Orfeo, ossia l'ottava canzone (*Orpheus, or the Eighth Song*).

Orfeo (Monteverdi). *See* **Favola d'Orfeo.**

Orfeo ed Euridice (*Orpheus and Eurydice*), opera by Bertoni (lib. by R. da Calzabigi, written for Gluck), prod. Venice, Teatro San Benedetto, 3 Jan 1776.

   Opera by Gluck (lib. do.), prod. Vienna, Burgtheater, 5 Oct 1762. (For Fr. version *see* **Orphée et Euridice**).

Orfeo, L' (*Orpheus*), opera by Luigi Rossi (lib. by F. Buti), prod. Paris, Palais Royal, 2 Mar 1647.

Orff, Carl (b Munich, 10 Jul 1895; d Munich, 29 Mar 1982), German composer and teacher. Studied at Munich and became prof. of comp. at the Günther School there. He was also a cond. and ed. of old music.

   Works incl. mainly 11 operas and musical plays, incl. *Carmina Burana* (settings of medieval poetry, 1937), *Die Kluge* (1943), *Catulli Carmina, Antigonae* and *Oedipus der Tyrann* (both Hölderlin, after Sophocles, 1949, 1959), *Trionfo di Afrodite* (1953), *Prometheus* (1966), *De temporum fine comoedia* (1973), cantata *Des Turmes Auferstehung* (Franz Werfel); ballet *Der Feuerfarbene; Schulwerk* for combinations of popular instruments and similar comps. intended for use by amateurs. Incid. music for Shakespeare's *Midsummer Night's Dream,* 1939–62; first vers. comp. to replace Mendelssohn's music, banned by the Nazis.

Organ, the most elaborate instrument playable by a single perf. Its origin lies in remote antiquity, e.g. the syrinx or pan-pipe. Later the wind was no longer supplied by the player's breath, but by bellows; the pipes were opened and closed by an action of keys, and a keyboard of pedals, played by the feet, was added to control the largest bass pipes. The number of pipes, ranging from 32 ft. down to a fraction of an inch. was enormously increased, and they were made in a growing variety of shapes from different materials, and with different speaking-mechanisms, each range being controlled by stops which could bring it into action or shut it off at the player's will. The number of manuals (hand keyboards) increased to 3 or more, which meant that a greater number of stops drawn before the perf. could be controlled and varied. From the late 19th cent. the bellows, formerly blown by hand, were operated mechanically and devices by which whole ranges of stops could be brought into action in var. combinations were invented, still further increasing the resources already enlarged by the couplers, but which the registration controlled by 2 manuals or by a manual and the pedals could be mechanically united. Expression was added by swell pedals prod. *crescendo* and *diminuendo,* but beyond that the player's hands and feet have no power to vary the tone either in strength or in quality.

Organ-Point (from Ger. *Orgelpunkt*), another term, used mainly in Amer. for Pedal-Point.

Organ Stops. *See* **Diapason, Dulciana, Gedackt, Principal, Quint, Sesquialtera, Tremulant, Tromba, Voix celeste.**

Organo pieno (It.) or [Pro] **Organo pleno** (Lat.) = full organ, a direction indicating that an organ passage is to be played with the use of the full extent of the instrument's power, or in earlier music with a substantial body of tone.

Organum (Lat., lit. 'instrument', also 'organ'), a term (orig. a nickname) for early medieval music in parts, either moving wholly or mainly in parallel lines (9th cent.) or independently (11th cent.) or with florid melodies above a slow-moving plainsong (12th cent.).

Orgeni (actually Görger St Jörgen) (**Anna Maria**) **Aglaia** (b Rima Szombat, 17 Dec 1841; d Vienna, 15 Mar 1926), Austrian soprano. Pupil of Pauline Viardot-Garcia. Made her debut in Berlin, 1865, as Amina. London, CG, 1866 as Lucia and Violetta. Vienna and Munich from 1872 as Agathe, Marguerite, the *Trovatore* Leonora and Valentine. Taught at Dresden Cons. 1886–1914.

Orione, o sia Diana vendicata (*Orion, or Diana Avenged*), opera by J.C. Bach (lib. by G.G. Bottarelli), prod. London, King's Theatre, 19 Feb 1763. J.C. Bach's 1st opera for London.

Orlandi, Santi (b Florence, ?; d Mantua, Jul 1619), Italian composer. He was *maestro di cappella* to Ferdinando Gonzaga at Florence and succeeded Monteverdi as *maestro di cappella* to the Gonzaga family at Mantua in 1612.

Works incl. opera *Gli amori di Aci e Galatea* (perf. Mantua, Mar 1617); 5 books of madrigals, etc.

Orlandini, Giuseppe Maria (b Florence, 19 Mar 1675; d Florence, 24 Oct 1760), Italian composer. *Maestro di cappella* to the Duke of Tuscany at Florence, and app. to the same post at the cathedral there in 1732.

Works incl. *c* 50 operas, e.g. *Amore e maestà* (1715), *Antigona* (1718), *Il marito giocatore*, *Nerone* (1720), etc.; oratorios; cantatas.

Orlando (*Roland*), opera by Handel (lib. by G. Braccioli, based on Ariosto's *Orlando furioso*), prod. London, King's Theatre, Haymarket, 27 Jan 1733.

Orlando Furioso, opera by Vivaldi (lib. by G.B. Braccioli), prod. Venice, Teatro Sant' Angelo, autumn 1727.

Orlando Paladino, opera (dramma eroico-mico) by Haydn (lib. by C.F. Badini and N. Porta), prod. Eszterháza, 6 Dec 1779.

Ormandy (actually Blau), **Eugene** (b Budapest, 18 Nov 1899; d Philadelphia, 12 Mar 1985), American conductor of Hungarian origin. Studied vln. 1st with his father and then entered the Budapest RAM for further studies with Hubay. He graduated in 1917, becoming leader of the Blüthner Orch. in Berlin. In 1921 he went to the USA, taking various posts both as perf. and cond.; US citizen 1927. In 1931 he was app. permanent cond. of the Minneapolis SO, and in 1938 of the Philadelphia SO; gave the fps of Rakhmaninov's Symphonic Dances (1941) and Bartók's 3rd pf. concerto (1946). He was awarded the Fr. *Légion d'honneur* in 1952. Was often heard in Shostakovich and Mahler.

Ormindo, opera by Cavalli (lib. by G. Faustini), prod. Venice, Teatro San Cassiano,

1644. Revived in new version by Raymond Leppard, Glyndebourne, 16 Jun 1967.

Ornaments. Throughout musical history until at least the early 19th cent. there are many repertories in which it was expected that the performer would add ornamental details, ranging from the smallest trills, appoggiaturas and portamentos through to elaborate cadential embellishments. Shorthand signs to denote the simpler ornaments are found at least from the ealy 16th cent. (though there are traces of them much earlier in the chant repertory); but they began to be codified in elaborate systems described in detailed tables of ornaments from the 17th cent. and had their heyday in the first half of the 18th cent. See **Acciaccatura, Appoggiatura, Arpeggio, Cadenza, Mordent, Plica, Shake, Turn, Tremolo, Vibrato.**

Ornithoparcus (actually Vogelgesang or Vogelsang), **Andreas** (b Meiningen, *c* 1490), German music scholar. Studied ? at Tübingen Univ., travelled in many countries and held some posts at Wittenberg Univ. Author of the Lat. treatise *Musicae activae micrologus* (1517), which was trans. into Eng. by J. Dowland (1609).

Ornstein, Leo (b Krementchug, 11 Dec 1892), Russian pianist and composer, naturalized in USA. Studied at the St Petersburg Cons., where he appeared as a child prodigy, settled in NY in 1907, studying further at the Inst. of Musical Art, and made his 1st concert appearance there in 1911. Taught in Philadelphia and retired 1953.

Works incl. pantomime *Lima Beans*, pantomime ballet; incid. music to Aristophanes' *Lysistrata* (1930); symph., 2 Nocturnes, *Nocturne and Dance of the Fates*, symph. poem *The Fog* for orch. (1915); pf. concerto (1923), 3 string 4tets, pf. 5tet; 2 vln. and pf. sonatas, sonata for cello and pf.; choral works; pf. music incl. 20 Waltzes (1955–68) and *Biography in Sonata Form* (1974).

Orologio, Alessandro (b Italy, *c* 1550; d ? Vienna, 1633), Italian composer and instrumentalist. His career took him to Prague, Kassel, Dresden and Wolfenbüttel; became choirmaster at the Austrian monastery of Garsten at the end of his career. He pub. several books of madrigals and canzonets, and a collection of Intradas 'for all kinds of instruments'.

Orontea, opera by Cesti (lib. by G.A. Ciognini), prod. Venice, Teatro dei Apostoli, 1649. Cesti's 1st opera; successfully revived in modern eds.

Orozco, Rafael (b Cordoba, 24 Jan 1946), Spanish pianist. He studied at the Madrid

Cons. and in 1966 won the Leeds International Comp. Often heard in Europe and the US in the Romantic repertory.

Orpharion, an early instrument of the Cittern type. It had 6 or 7 pairs of strings played with a plectrum.

Orphée aux enfers (*Orpheus in the Underworld*), operetta by Offenbach (lib. by H. Crémieux and L. Halévy), prod. Paris, Bouffes-Parisiens, 21 Oct 1858.

Orphée et Euridice, opera by Gluck (lib. by P.L. Moline, trans from Calzabigi's *Orfeo ed Euridice*, of Gluck's 1st setting of which it is a revised version), prod. Paris, 3 Aug 1774.

Orphéon (Fr.), a French male-voice choral society similar to the Ger. *Liedertafel*.

Orpheus. *See also* **Favloa d'Orfeo; Malheurs d'Orphée; Orfeide; Orfeo; Orfeo ed Euridice; Orphée; Orphée aux enfers; Orpheus; Orpheus og Euridice; Orpheus und Eurydike.**

Ballet by Stravinsky (choreog. by George Balanchine) prod. NY, 29 Apr 1948.

Opera by Keiser (lib. by F.C. Bressand), prod. Brunswick (Part I: *Die sterbende Eurydice*) 1699. Hamburg (Part II: *Die verwandelte Leyer des Orpheus*), 1709.

Symph. poem by Liszt, comp. 1853–4, fp as an intro. to Gluck's *Orfeo*, Weimar, 16 Feb 1854, with closing music on the same themes after the opera.

Orpheus, ballet in 2 acts by Henze (scenario by Edward Bond), prod. Stuttgart 17 Mar 1979; Suite for ballet, *Apollo triofante*, perf. Gelsenkirchen, 1 Sep 1980; *Arias of Orpheus* for guitar, harp, harpsichord and strings perf. Chicago, 25 Nov 1981; *Dramatic Scenes from O.* for large orch. perf. in 2 parts: no. 2 Zurich, 6 Jan 1981, no. 1 Frankfurt, 12 Sep 1982; Concert version of the ballet perf. Cologne, 4 Mar 1983.

Orpheus Britannicus, a collection of vocal music by Purcell begun soon after Purcell's death by Henry Playford, who pub. a 1st vol. in 1698 and a 2nd in 1702; also a collection of Purcell's songs pub. by John Walsh in 1735.

Orpheus og Euridice, opera by Naumann (lib. by C.D. Biehl, based on Calzabigi), prod. Copenhagen, 21 Jan 1786. The 1st grand opera on a Dan. lib.

Orpheus und Eurydike, opera by Krenek (lib. by Oskar Kokoschka), prod. Kassel, 27 Nov 1926.

Orr, C(harles) W(ilfred) (b Cheltenham, 31 Jul 1893; d Stroud, 24 Feb 1976), English composer. Educ. at Cheltenham Coll. He suffered much from ill-health in his youth and did not begin to study music at the GSM

in London until 1917. He lived most of his life quietly at Painswick, Glos., and never held any official musical posts; but he did warwork in London during World War II.

Works incl. *A Cotswold Hill Tune* for string orch.; numerous songs, esp. settings of A.E. Housman, also D.G. Rossetti, James Joyce, etc.

Orr, Robin (b Brechin, 2 Jun 1909), Scottish composer. Studied at the RCM in London and with E.J. Dent at Cambridge, also with Casella at Siena and Nadia Boulanger in Paris. From 1938 to 1956 he was organist and dir. of studies at St John's Coll., Cambridge. Prof. of music at Glasgow Univ. 1956–64, and at Cambridge 1964–76.

Works incl. opera *Full Circle* (1968); 2 symphs., divertimento for chamber orch.; 3 Lat. psalms for voice and string 4tet; string 5tet (1971); sonatina for vln. and pf., vln. sonata, vla. sonata; pf. pieces; songs, etc.

Ortiz, Diego (b Toledo, *c* 1510; d Naples, *c* 1570), Spanish composer. He went to Naples in 1555 to become *maestro de capilla* to the viceroy, the Duke of Alva, where he worked with many other Spanish musicians, incl. Salinas. He wrote an important treatise on ornamentation in viol music, the *Trattado de Glosas*, pub. in 2 eds. (Span. and It.) in Rome, 1553.

Works incl. motets; variations for bass viol.

Orto, Marbriano de (b *c* 1460; d Nivelles, Feb 1529), Flemish singer and composer. His name may have been Dujardin, the It. form being taken when he went to Rome, where he was a singer in the Papal chapel in 1484–94, with Josquin Desprez. Early in the 16th cent. he became chaplain and singer at the court of Philip the Fair of Burgundy.

Works incl. Masses, motets and other church music; *chansons*.

Osborne, George Alexander (b Limerick, 24 Sep 1806; d London, 16 Nov 1893), Irish pianist. Studied in Belg. and afterwards taught pf. in Brussels. In 1826 he went to Paris, making further studies with Pixis and Kalkbrenner and becoming a friend of Chopin, Berlioz and Rossini. He settled in London in 1843, where he taught and championed Chopin's work.

Osborne, Nigel (b Manchester, 23 Jun 1948), English composer. He studied at Oxford with Wellesz and Leighton and in Poland with Witold Rodziński. Lecturer at Nottingham Univ. from 1978.

Works incl. *Byzantine Epigrams* for chorus (1969); 7 *Words*, cantata (1971); *Charivari* for orch. (1973); *Chansonnier* for chamber ens. (1975); *I am Goya* for bar. and insts. (1977); *Concert Piece* for cello and orch. (1977); *In Camera* for 13 insts. (1979); *Gnostic Passion* for 36 voices (1980); Flute concerto (1980); *The Cage* for tenor and ens. (1981); *Sinfonia* for orch. (1982); *Alba* for mezzo, insts. and tape (1984); *Zansa* for ensemble (1985); *Pornography* for mezzo and ens. (1985), *The Electrification of the Soviet Union*, opera, (1986).

Osiander, Lucas (b Nuremberg, 16 Dec 1534; d Stuttgart, 17 Sep 1604), German theologian and composer, son of the reformer Andreas O. He comp. sacred songs and psalms in 4 parts with Ger. words.

Ossia (It. from *o sia* = or be it, or else), a word shown with an alternative passage, usually easier and sometimes more difficult which may be perf. at will instead of that orig. written down by the comp. Such passages are usually shown in smaller notes above or below the stave. The word may also be used for alternatives where a comp. clearly wrote a passage of pf. music for a short keyboard and where it is clear that he would have written it otherwise for a modern pf. It also occurs, like the older *ovvero*, in 2nd alternative titles of operas (e.g. 'Così fan tutte, ossia La scuola degli amanti,' etc.).

Ossian, semi-mythical Gaelic bard whose works, allegedly translated by James Macpherson (1736–96), influenced the early Romantic movement. Ossian's works were in fact by Macpherson, drawing on ancient sources. Schubert set 9 Ossian songs (1815–17).

Osten, Eva von der (b Insel, Heligoland, 19 Aug 1881; d Dresden, 5 May 1936), German soprano. She studied in Dresden and made her debut there in 1902; remained until 1927, creating Octavian and heard also as Ariadne, the Dyer's Wife, Kundry, Tatyana and Brünnhilde. London 1913–14 in Wagner and Strauss roles. Other roles incl. Louise, Tosca and Zazà.

Ostinato (It. = obstinate), a persistently repeated figure in a comp. If it is in the bass, it is called *basso ostinato*. A rhythm also can be called ostinato, and so can some instrumental device, like Tchaikovsky's *pizzicato ostinato* in the 4th symph.

Ostrčil, Otakar (b Smichov, nr. Prague, 25 Feb 1879; d Prague, 20 Aug 1935), Czech conductor and composer. Studied at Prague Univ. and became prof. of modern languages at the Commercial Acad. there. He had already studied music esp. with Fibich, and in 1909 he became cond. of an amateur orch.

and in 1914 at the Vinohrady Theatre. He succeeded Kovařovic as cond. of the Nat. Theatre in 1920, when he gave the fp of Janáček's *The Excursions of Mr Brouček*. Works incl. operas *The Death of Vlasta*, *Kunala's Eyes* (1908), *The Bud*, *Legend of Erin* (1921), and *John's Kingdom* (1934); incid. music for Jaroslav Kvapil's play *The Orphan*; *The Legend of St. Zita* for tenor, chorus, orch. and organ (1913) and other choral works; symph. in A maj., sinfonietta (1921), 2 suites, symph. poem *The Tale of Semik*, *Rustic Festival* and *Impromptu* for orch.; *Ballad of the Dead Cobbler* and *Cz. Ballad* for declamation and orch.; string 4tet in B maj. (1899), sonatina for vln., vla. and pf.; songs.

Ostrovsky, Alexander Nikolaievich (1823–86), Russian dramatist. *See* **Arensky** (*Dream on the Volga*), **Dzerzhinsky** (*Storm*), **Kashperov** (do.), **Káťa Kabanová** (Janáček), **Serov** (*Power of Evil*), **Snow Maiden** (Rimsky-Korsakov), **Tchaikovsky** (*Snegurotchka*), **Tcherepnin (N.)** (*Poverty no Crime*), **Voyevoda** (Tchaikovsky).

Osud (*Fate*), opera in 3 scenes by Janáček (lib. by comp. and F. Bartosova); comp. 1903–4, fp Brno Radio 18 Sept 1934; prod. Brno, 25 Oct 1958. Prod. London, Coliseum, 8 Sep 1984.

O'Sullivan, Denis (b San Francisco, 25 Apr 1868; d Columbus, Ohio, 1 Feb 1908), American baritone of Irish descent. Studied in Florence, London and Paris. Made his 1st concert appearance in London and his 1st on the stage in Dublin in 1895, in *Trovatore*; also sang Wagner's Dutchman on tour. His best known role was Stanford's Shamus O'Brien (London 1896 and on tour).

Oswald von Wolkenstein. See **Wolkenstein.**

Otello, opera by Verdi (lib. by Boito, after Shakespeare), prod. Milan, La Scala, 5 Feb 1887.

Otello, ossia Il Moro di Venezia (*Othello, or The Moor of Venice*), opera by Rossini, lib. by F.B. Salsa, after Shakespeare, prod. Naples, Teatro Fondo, 4 Dec 1816.

Othello. *See also* **Otello.**

Concert overture by Dvořák, op. 93, ref. to Shakespeare's tragedy, comp. 1892 and forming, with *Amid Nature* and *Carnival*, a cycle with thematic connections orig. called *Nature, Life and Love*.

Othmayr, Kaspar (b Amberg, 12 Mar 1515; d Nuremberg, 4 Feb 1553), German clergyman and musician. Studied at Heidelberg Univ. and was a pupil of Lemlin for music there. He held church appts. at Heilsbronn and Ansbach, but *c* 1550 retired to Nuremberg on account of religious controversies, himself being a Lutheran. He took part in the development of Ger. polyphonic song.

Works incl. Latin motets, German hymns and other sacred music; an Epitaph on Luther's death; 26 secular songs contrib. to George Foster's collection, etc.

Ott, Hans (b Rain am Lech, nr. Donauwörth, *c* 1500; d Nuremberg, 1546), German music editor. His collections, all pub. at Nuremberg, incl. 121 songs (1534) and an important collection of 13 Masses (1539).

Ottavino (It. from *ottava* = 8ve), the current It. name of the 8ve fl. elsewhere called Piccolo (from *flauto piccolo* = little fl.).

Otter, Anne Sophie von (b Stockholm, 9 May 1955), Swedish mezzo. Studied at the GSM and has sung in London from 1982. Her US debut was in 1985, with the Chicago SO, and she has appeared widely in Europe. Roles incl. Orpheus, Octavian, Bellini's Romeo and Mozart's Sextus, Cherubino and Dorabella.

Otterloo, (Jan) Willem van (b Winterswijk, 27 Dec 1907; d Melbourne, 28 Jul 1978), Dutch conductor and composer. Studied at the Amsterdam Cons. under Dresden and others. App. 2nd cond. of the Utrecht Munic. Orch. in 1933 and 1st in 1937; until 1973, when he became music dir. at Düsseldorf.

Works incl. symph., 3 suites and passacaglia for orch.; chamber music, pf. and organ works.

Otto, Lisa (b Dresden, 14 Nov 1919), German soprano. Studied pf. and singing at the Dresden Hochschule für Musik from 1938 to 1940, making her debut as a singer in 1941, as Sophie. From 1945 to 1950 she sang at the Dresden Opera and in 1952 became a member of the Berlin Staatsoper. She was best known in lighter soubrette roles, e.g. Blonde, Despina and Marzelline.

Otto, Stephan (b Freiberg, Saxony, bap. 28 Mar 1603; d Schandau, 2 Oct 1656), German composer. Studied at Freiberg under Christoph Demantius, and after an appt. at Augsburg he became cantor at his home town in 1632 and at Schandau in 1639. Hammerschmidt was among his pupils.

Works incl. *Kronen-Krönlein*, a collection of sacred vocal pieces in a mixed motet and madrigal style, for 3–8 voices, setting of Luther's hymn 'Ein' feste Burg' for 19 voices.

Ottone, rè di Germania (*Otho, King of Germany*), opera by Handel (lib. by N.F.

Haym), prod. London, King's Theatre, Haymarket, 12 Jan 1723.

Oudin, Eugène (Espérance) (b New York, 24 Feb 1858; d London, 4 Nov 1894), American baritone of French descent. Studied law at Yale Univ. and practised it for a time, but during a holiday in London in 1886 decided to turn to music. He made his debut in NY that year, with Louise Parker, who became his wife on 4 Dec. In 1891 he 1st appeared in opera in London as the Templar in Sullivan's *Ivanhoe*; he was first Eugene Onegin in London (1892); St Petersburg 1893–4 as Wolfram and Telramund.

Our Hunting Fathers, song cycle for high voice and orch. by Britten (text by W.H. Auden), fp Norwich, 25 Sep 1936, cond. Britten.

Ours, L' (*The Bear*), nickname of Haydn's symph. no. 82 in C maj., comp. for Paris in 1786.

Ouseley, Frederick (Arthur) Gore (b London, 12 Aug 1825; d Hereford, 6 Apr 1889), English organist, composer and clergyman. Studied at Oxford, where he took the D.Mus. in 1854 and was app. Prof. of Music in 1855. Founder of St Michael's Coll., Tenbury. He succeeded to his father's baronetcy in 1844. He ed. old music and wrote books on technique.

Works incl. 11 services, *c* 70 anthems; oratorios, *The Martyrdom of St Polycarp* and *Hagar*; over 30 preludes and fugues, 2 sonatas and other works for org.; 2 string 4tets; part-songs, glees; songs.

Ousset, Cécile (b Tarbes, 3 Mar 1936), French pianist. Studied at Paris Cons., graduated 1950. Many appearances with leading orchs. British debut Edinburgh Fest. 1980.

Overblowing, the playing of wind instruments in such a way that the upper harmonics are prod. instead of the fundamental notes. Brass instruments prod. a greater number of harmonics than woodwind. Overblowing may occur by accident in organ pipes by too great a pressure of wind, but safety-valve devices have been invented to prevent this.

Overspun, the lower strings of instruments of the vln. family and also those of the pf. are overspun, i.e. spun round with wire.

Overstrung, strings in pfs. which are made in 2 ranges crossing each other diagonally to save space and to secure greater length in the strings.

Overtones. *See* **Harmonics** *and* **Partials.**

Overture (from Fr. *ouverture* = opening),

an instrumental introductory comp. preceding some other large work, esp. an opera or oratorio; also sometimes an independent comp. for concert use, e.g. Mendelssohn's *Hebrides* and Brahms's *Tragic* Overtures. From the time of Lully to that of Handel the overture in its Fr. form had a slow intro. and a fugal *allegro*, often followed by a return to the slow section or by a new slow portion, and in some cases by one or more independent pieces in dance form, in which case it resembled the Suite; hence Bach's overtures are in fact suites with 1st movements in Fr. overture form. The It. overture form differed from the Fr. in the late 17th and 18th cents. by being in several movements approximating more to the early symph., to which in fact it gave birth.

In opera the music for the overture had no special relevance to the work itself up to the time of Rameau, and sometimes not afterwards (e.g. Rossini, except his overture to *Guillaume Tell*). Gluck's mature overtures foreshadow the character and atmosphere of the operas to which they belong, and from his time on the actual musical material of the overture was more often than not drawn from the opera itself to a greater or smaller extent.

Ovvero (It. = or rather, or else, lit. from *o vero*, or truly), an earlier word for *ossia*; also found in front of 2nd, alternative titles of musical works.

Owen Wingrave, opera in 2 acts by Britten (lib. by M. Piper after Henry James), fp BBC TV 16 May 1971; prod. CG, London, 10 May 1973.

Ox Minuet. *Die Ochsenmenuette* is the title of a *Singspiel* by Seyfried, prod. in Vienna in 1823, with music arr. from comps. by Haydn. It was based on 2 earlier Fr. works, *Le Menuet de bœuf, ou Une Leçon de Haydn* (1805) and *Haydn, ou le Menuet du bœuf* (1812). The title is sometimes mistakenly thought to be the nickname of one of Haydn's minuets.

Oxford Elegy, An, work by Vaughan Williams for speaker, small chorus and orch. (text from Matthew Arnold, *The Scholar Gipsy* and *Thyrsis*), fp (private) Dorking, 20 Nov 1949; 1st public perf. Queen's College, Oxford, 19 June 1952.

Oxford Symphony, the name given to Haydn's symph. no. 92 in G maj., comp. 1788. It was not written for Oxford, but received its title after it was perf. there in Jul 1791 when Haydn was given the hon. degree of D.Mus.

Ozawa, Seiji (b Hoten, Manchuria, 1 Sep 1935), Japanese conductor. He studied in Tokyo and with Karajan in Berlin. Asst. to Bernstein at the NY PO 1961–5 (debut with orch. Carnegie Hall 1961). London debut 1965, with LSO. Toronto SO 1965–9; He has cond. *Così fan tutte* at Salzburg and in 1983 led the fp of Messiaen's *St François d'Assise*, at the Paris Opéra. Boston SO from 1973; world-wide tours, and has cond. Mahler's 8th symph. and Schoenberg's *Gurrelieder* (also recorded).

P

p (abbr.). Used in music for *piano* = soft, in this form: *p*; sometimes also for the pedal in pf. music in this: *P*. In the latter case, however, it is more often *Ped*.

Pabst. German family of musicians:
1. August P. (b Elberfeld, 30 May 1811; d Riga, 21 Jul 1885), organist and comp. He became organist at Königsberg and later dir. of the Music School at Riga. Wrote operas, etc.
2. Louis P. (b Königsberg, 18 Jul 1846; d Moscow, after 1903), pianist and composer, son of prec. Studied under his father, made his 1st appearance as pianist in 1862, lived at Liverpool, Riga, Melbourne, founding music schools in the latter 2 places, and finally held a professorship in Moscow. Wrote melodramas, pf. works, songs.
3. Paul P. (b Königsberg, 27 May 1854; d Moscow 9 Jun 1897), pianist and composer, brother of prec. Studied under his father and brother, later under Liszt. Settled in Moscow as prof. at the Cons. Wrote pf. music, operatic paraphrases, etc.

Pacchiarotti, Gasparo (b Fabriano nr. Ancona, bap. 21 May 1740; d Padua, 28 Oct 1821), Italian castrato soprano. Chorister at Forli Cathedral, then at St Mark's Venice, under Bertoni, he made his operatic debut in 1766 and became *primo musico* at the Teatro San Benedetto in Venice. Later sang in Palermo, London, Naples, etc., and retired to Padua in 1792. He was admired in Bertoni's *Olimpiade*, *Artaserse*, *Quinto Fabio* and *Armida*.

Pacchioni, Antonio (Maria) (b Modena, bap. 5 Jul 1654; d Modena, 15 Jul 1738), Italian priest and composer. Studied at Modena Cathedral, where he became chaplain at the ducal court and later asst. choirmaster. In 1733 he and Pitoni settled a dispute between Marhini and Redi about the solution of a canon by Animuccia.

Works incl. Masses and other church music, oratorios.

Pace (also called Pacius), **Pietro** (b Loreto, 1559; d Loreto, 15 Apr 1622), Italian composer. Was organist at Pesaro in 1597 and of the Santa Casa at Loreto, 1591–2, and again, 1611–22.

Works incl. music for Ignazio Bracci's *L'ilarocosmo, ovvero Il mondo lieto* (perf. Urbino, 29 Apr 1621); Magnificats, motets

(with accomp.) and other church music; *Arie spirituali* and madrigals with and without accompaniment.

Pacelli, Asprilio (b Vasciano nr. Narni, Umbria, 1570; d Warsaw, 4 May 1623), Italian composer. Choirmaster of the Ger. Coll. (1592–1602), and later at the Vatican basilica in Rome until 1602, when he went to the court of Sigismund III of Poland at Warsaw, succeeding Marenzio.

Works incl. motets, psalms, *Sacrae cantiones*; madrigals.

Pachelbel, Johann (b Nuremberg, bap. 1 Sep 1653; d Nuremberg, buried 3 Mar 1706), German organist and composer. Studied under Heinrich Schwemmer at home and after holding brief appts. at Altdorf and Regensburg, went to Vienna, *c* 1671–2. Between 1677 and 1695 he was organist successively at Eisenach, Erfurt, Stuttgart and Gotha, and in 1695 was app. organist at St Sebaldus's Church at Nuremberg.

Works incl. vocal music, arias, motets, sacred concertos (i.e. cantatas) and 11 Magnificat settings. 94 organ fugues on the Magnificat, organ variations and preludes on chorales; suites for 2 vlns. *Musikalisches Ergötzen*; 6 sets of variations for harpsichord *Hexachordum Apollinis* (1699).

Pachelbel, Wilhelm Hieronymus (b Erfurt, bap. 29 Aug 1686; d Nuremberg, 1764), German organist and composer, son of prec. Pupil of his father. Organist at St Sebaldus's Church, Nuremberg, from 1719. Wrote organ and harpsichord music.

Pachmann, Vladimir de (b Odessa, 27 Jul 1848; d Rome, 7 Jan 1933), Russian pianist of Austrian descent. Studied 1st under his father, a univ. prof., and later in Vienna, and made his 1st concert appearance in Rus. in 1869. In 1882 he 1st visited London. He became a famous but somewhat eccentric exponent of Chopin.

Pacific 231, symph. movement by Honegger, named after a railway engine and depicting its start and progress, not merely realistically, but, the comp. claims, 'lyrically'. Fp Paris, at a Koussevitsky concert, 8 May 1924.

Pacini, Giovanni (b Catania, 17 Feb 1796; d Pescia, 6 Dec 1867), Italian composer. Studied 1st under his father, a famous tenor, and later at Bologna and Venice. At the age of 17 he prod. his 1st opera at Venice. He became *maestro di cappella* to Napoleon's widow, the Empress Marie Louise, and in 1834 settled at Viareggio, where he opened a music school, later transferred to Lucca. For this he wrote some theoretical treatises.

Works incl. operas *Annetta e Lucindo* (1813), *La sacerdotessa d'Irminsul* (1820), *La schiava in Bagdad* (1820), *La gioventù di Enrico V* (after Shakespeare's *Henry IV*, 1820), *L'ultimo giorno di Pompei* (not based on Bulwer-Lytton, 1825), *Gli Arabi nelle Gallie* (1827), *Saffo* (1840), *Medea* (1843), *Lorenzino de' Medici* (1845), *La regina di Cipro*, *Il saltimbanco*, *Ivanhoe* (after Scott, 1832) and over 60 others; incid. music for Sophocles' *Oedipus Rex*; Masses, oratorios, cantata for Dante anniversary and others; 6 string 4tets (*c* 1860).

Paciotti, Pietro Paulo (b Tivoli, *c* 1550; d ? Rome, after 1614), Italian composer. Choirmaster of the Seminario Romano in Rome, 1591. Wrote Masses, motets, madrigals.

Pacius, Fredrik (b Hamburg, 19 Mar 1809; d Helsinki, 9 Jan 1891), German violinist and composer, naturalized Finn. Pupil of Spohr and Hauptmann at Kassel, violinist in the court orch. at Stockholm, 1828–34, when he became music teacher at Helsinki Univ. He remained in the Fin. capital, estab. orchestral concerts there in 1845 and became prof. of music at the univ. in 1860.

Works incl. operas *Kung Karls Jakt* (1852) and *Loreley* (1887); incid. music for Topelius's *Princess of Cyprus* (1860); vln. concerto; cantatas; songs incl. *Suomis Saang* and *Vaart Land*, both adapted as Finnish nat. anthems.

Packe, Thomas, English 15th–16th-cent. composer. He was a knight and prob. held no official musical post.

Works incl. Masses, *Rex summe* and *Gaudete in Domino*, motets and a Te Deum.

Paderewski, Ignacy (Jan) (b Kurylówka, Podolia, 18 Nov 1860; d New York, 29 Jun 1941), Polish pianist, composer and statesman. Studied at the Warsaw Cons. and went on his 1st concert tour in 1877. After teaching in 1878–81 at the Cons. he went to Berlin for further study, finishing with Leschetizky in Vienna, reappearing there and in Paris in 1887. In 1890 he paid his 1st visit to England and in 1891 to USA. During World War I he collected large sums for the Polish relief fund and in 1919 became the 1st president of the Polish Republic.

Works incl. opera *Manru* (1901); symph. in B min. (1903–9); concerto in A min (1888) and Pol. Fantasy for pf. and orch.; vln. and pf. sonata; sonata in E♭ min. and many other pf. works; songs.

Padilla y Ramos, Mariano (b Murcia, 1842; d Auteuil nr. Paris, 23 Nov 1906), Spanish baritone. Studied in It. and toured Europe extensively. Married Désirée Artôt in 1869.

Padlock, The, opera by Dibdin (lib. by I. Bickerstaffe, based on a story by Cervantes, *El celoso extremeño*), prod. London, Drury Lane Theatre, 3 Oct 1768.

Padmâvatî opera-ballet by Roussel (lib., in Fr., by L. Laloy), prod. Paris, Opéra, 1 Jun 1923.

Padua, Bartolino da, Italian 14th–15th-cent. composer. Wrote madrigals and *ballate* in the It. *Ars nova* style.

Paer, Ferdinando (b Parma, 1 Jun 1771; d Paris, 3 May 1839), Italian composer. Studied with Gasparo Ghiretti at Parma, and at the age of 20 became a cond. at Venice. Having married the singer Riccardi, he was invited to Vienna in 1798, where she was engaged at the court opera, and prod. *Camilla* there. In 1803 he went to Dresden, remaining as opera cond. until 1806, and there prod. *Leonora*, a setting of an It. version of Gaveaux's opera on which Beethoven's *Fidelio* was also based later. In 1807, after accomp. Napoleon to Warsaw and Posen, he was app. his *maître de chapelle* and settled in Paris.

Works incl. *Circe* (1792), *Il tempo fa giustizia a tutti* (1792), *Il nuovo Figaro* (after Beaumarchais' *Mariage de Figaro*, 1794), *Il matrimonio improvviso*, *Idomeneo* (1794), *Eroe e Leandro* (1794), *L'intrigo amoroso*, *Il principe di Taranto*, *Camilla*, *o Il sotterraneo* (1799), *La sonnambula* (1800), *Achille*, *Leonora*, *o L'amore conjugale* (1804), *Sofonisba*, *Numa Pompilio* (1808), *Agnese di Fitz-Henry* (1809), *Didone abbandonata* (1810), *Le Maître de chapelle* (1821), *La Marquise de Brinvilliers* (with Auber, Batton, Berton, Blangini, Boieldieu, Carafa, Cherubini and Hérold, 1831) and over 20 others; oratorios *Il santo sepolcro* and *La passione*, Masses and motets; *c* 12 cantatas (It., Fr. and Ger.); Bacchanalian symph. for orch., Bridal March for the wedding of Napoleon and Joséphine.

Paganini, Niccolò (b Genoa, 27 Oct 1782; d Nice, 27 May 1840), Italian violinist and composer. Learnt guitar and vln. from his father, afterwards with the theatre violinist Servetto and the cathedral *maestro di cappella* Giacomo Costa. At the age of 11 he made his 1st appearance as a violinist. As a comp. he profited by the advice of Gnecco, and in 1795 his father sent him to the violinist Alessandro Rolla at Parma. While there he also studied comp. with Gasparo Ghiretti, and in 1797 made his 1st professional tour. After that he became increasing-

ly famous, travelled widely, beginning with Vienna and Paris in 1828–1831, and in the latter year went to Eng. for the 1st time. In 1834 he invited Berlioz in Paris to write a concert work for vla. *Harold en Italie* was the result, but he never played it.
Works incl. 6 vln. concertos (1815–30; op. 7 with the *Rondo alla campanella*), variations (e.g. on 'God save the King') and concert pieces for vln. and orch., 3 string 4tets with a guitar part; 12 sonatas for vln. and guitar; 24 *Capricci* (studies) for vln. solo.

Paganini Rhapsody, a work by Rakhmaninov for pf. and orch. entitled *Rhapsody on a Theme by Paganini*, but actually a set of variations, without opus number, comp. in 1934, fp Baltimore, 7 Nov 1934. The theme, in A min., from Paganini's *Capricci* for unaccomp. vln., is the same as that used by Brahms for the variations below.

Paganini Studies, a set of 6 studies for pf. by Liszt, transcribed from Paganini's vln. *Capricci* (except no. 3 which is another version of *La Campanella*), ded. to Clara Schumann. There is an orig. version, *Études d'exécution transcendante d'après Paganini*, written in 1838, and a revised one, *Grandes Études de Paganini*, written in 1851.
2 sets of studies for pf. (6 each) by Schumann on themes from Paganini's vln. *Capricci*: op. 3, written in 1832, and op. 10, written in 1833.

Paganini Variations, 2 sets of studies for pf. in variation form by Brahms, op. 35, comp. in 1866, on a theme in A min. from Paganini's vln. *Capricci*.

Pagliacci (*Clowns*), opera by Leoncavallo (lib. by comp.), prod. Milan, Teatro dal Verme, 21 May 1892.

Pagliardi, Giovanni Maria (b Genoa, 1637; d Florence, 3 Dec 1702), Italian composer. *Maestro di cappella* to the Duke of Tuscany at Florence and in the 1660s at 2 churches in Rome.
Works incl. operas *Caligula delirante* (1672), *Lisimaco* (1673), *Numa Pompilio* (1674), *Attilio Regolo*, *Il pazzo per forza* (1687) and *Il tiranno di Colco*; motets, sacred songs; vocal duets, etc.

Pagliughi, Lina (b Brooklyn, 27 May 1907; d Rubicone, 2 Oct 1980), American soprano of Italian parentage. Debut Milan 1927, Gilda; La Scala from 1930, sang Rossini's Sinaida there 1937 and Lucia 1947. CG 1938, as Gilda. Sang widely in Italy and on Italian radio as the Queen of Night, Amina, Rosina and Stravinsky's Nightingale.

Pahissa, Jaime (b Barcelona, 7 Oct 1880; d

Buenos Aires, 27 Oct 1969), Spanish composer. Pupil of Morera.
Works incl. operas *La presó de Lleida* (1906), *Canigó, Gala Placidia* (1913), *La Morisca, Marianela, La Princesa Margarida* (1928); orchestral works; pf. pieces.

Paine, John Knowles (b Portland, Me., 9 Jan 1839; d Cambridge, Mass., 25 Apr 1906), American organist, composer and teacher. Studied at home and at the Hochschule für Musik in Berlin, gave organ recitals in Ger. and returned to USA in 1861. He became instructor of music at Harvard Univ. in 1862, asst. prof. in 1872 and full prof. in 1875. Hon. D.Music of Yale, 1890.
Works incl. opera *Azara* (prod. Leipzig, 1901); incid. music for Sophocles' *Oedipus Tyrannus* and Aristophanes' *Birds*; Mass in D (1867); oratorio *St Peter* (1872); cantatas *A Song of Promise* (1888), *Phoebus arise* (Wm. Drummond), *The Realm of Fancy* (Keats, 1882), *The Nativity* (Milton); symphs. in C min. (1875) and A maj. (*Spring*, 1880), symph. poems *An Island Fantasy* and *The Tempest* (after Shakespeare), overture for Shakespeare's *As You Like It*; string 4tet, pf. trio; vln. and pf. sonata; instrumental pieces.

Paintings, Drawings, etc. Music associated with artists includes:

DAVIES, P. MAXWELL, *Vesalii Icones* for dancer, cello and ens. (Vesalius)

DEBUSSY, *L'Île Joyeuse* for pf. (Watteau).

GRANADOS, *Goyescas* for pf., and opera (Goya).

FELDMAN, *De Kooning* for pf., cello, vln., horn and perc.

——, *The Rothko Chapel* for vla., chorus and perc.

FERNEYHOUGH, *Carceri d'Invenzione* (etchings by Piranesi).

HENZE, *Los Caprichos* for orch. (Goya).

——, *Das Floss der Medusa*, oratorio (Géricault).

HINDEMITH, *Mathis der Maler,* opera (Grünewald)

HONEGGER, *Danse des morts* (Holbein).

LISZT, *Hunnenschlact* (The Battle of the Huns), symph. poem (Kaulbach).

——, *Il sposalizio* (Ralphael) in *Années de pèlerinage* for pf.

——, *Totentanz* for pf. and orch. (Orcagna).

MCCABE, *The Chagall Windows* for orch.

MARTINŮ, *The Frescoes of Piero della Francesca* for orch.

MENOTTI, *Goya,* opera.

MUSSORGSKY, *Pictures at an Exhibition* for pf. (Victor Hartmann).

POTTER, *The Enigma* (variations in the style

of 5 painters).

RAKHMANINOV, *The Isle of the Dead*, symph. poem (Böcklin).

REGER, Böcklin suite for orch. (4 pictures).

RESPIGHI, *Trittico Botticelliano* for orch.

SCHILLINGS, *Mona Lisa*, opera

SCHUBERT song *Liebeslauschen* (Schlechta's poem on a picture by Schnorr).

SCHULLER, *Seven Studies on Themes of Paul Klee* for orch.

STRAUSS, R., *Friedenstag*, opera (Velásquez).

STRAVINSKY, *The Rake's Progress*, opera (Hogarth).

VAUGHAN WILLIAMS, *Job*, masque for dancing (based on Blake's illustrations for the Book of Job); settings by Gwendolen Raverat.

WALTON, *Portsmouth Point* and *Dr. Syntax* overtures (Rowlandson).

Paisible (or Peasable), James (b ? Fr., c 1650; d London, Aug 1721), English musician, ? of French extraction. Member of the King's Band in London.

Works incl. incid. music for Shakespeare's *Henry IV* (*The Humours of Sir John Falstaff*, 1699), Southerne's adaptation of Aphra Behn's *Oroonoko* (1695), Bancroft's *King Edward III* (1690), Cibber's *She wou'd and she wou'd not* and *Love's Last Shift* (1695) and Mme. La Roche Guilhen's *Rare en tout*; duets, sonatas and pieces for fl.

Paisiello, Giovanni (b Taranto, 9 May 1740; d Naples, 5 Jun 1816), Italian composer. Pupil of Durante, later of Cotumacci and Abos at the Cons. Sant' Onofrio in Naples 1754–63, where he first wrote some oratorios and church music. But with *Il ciarlone* (Bologna, 1764) he began his successful career as a comp. of *opera buffa*, and over the next 20 years prod. many works in Modena, Naples, Venice, etc. In the service of the Rus. court at St Petersburg 1776–84, he there wrote, among others, his most famous opera, *Il barbiere di Siviglia* (after Beaumarchais' *Le Barbier de Séville*, 1782), which held the stage until Rossini's setting of the same story (1816). Back in Naples, he was app. *maestro di cappella* and court comp. to Ferdinand IV. Summoned to Paris as music dir. of Napoleon's household in 1802, he remained only a year, and returned to his old post in Naples.

Works incl. c 100 operas, e.g. *Il ciarlone* (after Goldoni's *La pupilla*, 1764), *I Francesi brillanti*, *Demetrio* (1765), *Le finte Contesse* (1760), *L'idolo cinese*, *Socrate immaginario* (1775), *La serva padrona*, *Il barbiere di Siviglia* (after Beaumarchais, 1782), *Il mondo della luna* (1782), *Il Rè Teodoro in* *Venezia* (1784), *L'Antigono* (1785), *Nina, ossia La pazza per amore*, *La molinara* (1789), *Proserpine* (1803), etc.; oratorios *La Passione di Gesù Cristo*, *Christus* (1783), etc.; cantatas; Masses, 2 Requiems, *Miserere* and other church music; symphs.; concertos, etc.; 6 string 4tets, 12 pf. 4tets; keyboard music.

Paix, Jakob (b Augsburg, 1556; d ? Ailtpolstein, after 1623), German composer, organist at Lauingen in Swabia 1576–1601; 1601–17 court organist at Neuburg an der Donau. He wrote Ger. songs and Lat. church music, but his chief work was his collection of keyboard music (pub. 1583), incl. orig. comps. as well as highly ornamented arrangements of songs and motets.

Paladilhe, Émile (b Montpellier, 3 Jun 1844; d Paris, 8 Jan 1926), French composer. Studied at the Paris Cons. and gained the Prix de Rome in 1860.

Works incl. operas *Le Passant* (lib. by F. Coppée, 1872), *L'Amour africain* (1875), *Suzanne* (1878), *Diana, Patrie* (after Sardou, 1886); oratorio *Saintes Maries de la mer*; 2 Masses; symph. and *Fragments symphoniques* for orch.; songs.

Palazol, Berenguier de (b Palol, Catalonia, ?), Catalan troubadour of the 2nd half of the 12th cent. 8 melodies survive.

Palester, Roman (b Sniatyn, 28 Dec 1907), Polish composer. Studied at Lwów and under Kasimierz Sikorski in Warsaw. For some years he lived in Paris, later settled in Warsaw. During the 1939–45 war he was imprisoned by the Germans.

Works incl. opera *The Living Stones* (1941); ballets *Song of the Earth* (1937) and *The End of the World*; incid. and film music; Requiem (1948) and Psalm v for solo voices, chorus and orch.; 5 symphs. (1935–72), symph. suite, *Symph. Music* (1931), *Wedding Celebration*, *Musique polonaise*, variations (overture) and other orchestral works, *Concertino* for saxophone, pf. concerto; *Divertimento* for 6 instruments, 3 string 4tets (1932–43), sonatinas for 3 clars. and for vln. and cello, sonata for 2 vlns. and pf.; organ toccata; pf. pieces; songs.

Palestrina, Giovanni Pierluigi da (b Palestrina, 9 May 1525; d Rome, 2 Feb 1594), Italian composer. Son of Sante Pierluigi, a well-to-do citizen. Became a choir-boy at the cathedral of St Agapit in his native town. When the Bishop of Palestrina went to the church of Santa Maria Maggiore in Rome in 1534, he took Palestrina with him, and he remained there until he was 14, when his voice broke. After a stay at home he returned to Rome in 1540 and (?) became a pupil of Firmin Le Bel. At 19 he was app. organist and singing-master at St Agapit's at his home. On 12 Jun 1547 he married Lucrezia Gori, who inherited money and property from her father.

Palestrina was app. *maestro di cappella* of the Julian choir in Rome, 1551, and pub. a madrigal and a 1st book of Masses in 1554. Pope Julius III made him a member of the Pontifical Choir in 1555, in spite of the resentment of members of his having been elected without examination. Pope Marcellus II, who succeeded that year, to whom Palestrina ded. the *Missa Papae Marcelli*, intended to reform the church music with Palestrina's help, but died, and under his successor, Paul IV, Palestrina retired from the choir with a pension, becoming *maestro di cappella* at the church of San Giovanni, in the Lateran. When under Pius IV in 1560 that church wished to make economies, Palestrina resigned and was app. the next year *maestro di cappella* at Santa Maria Maggiore.

Before the accession of Pius V in 1566, Palestrina was made director of the new Roman seminary in 1565. The Council of Trent having already laid down some reforms in church music in 1563, the new pope, Gregory XIII, in 1577 directed Palestrina and Zoilo to revise the Gradual. Palestrina's wife having died in Jul 1580, he applied for admission to the priesthood, but having been made a canon, he renounced his vows and was married again on 28 Mar 1581 to Virginia Dormuli, the widow of a prosperous furrier, in whose business he now took a considerable interest. After the accession of the next pope, Sixtus V, there was a scheme to app. Palestrina *maestro di cappella* of the Pontifical Choir, but it was defeated, 1585. Much of Palestrina's music was pub., partic. in the last 10 years of his life, incl. 4 vols. of motets and 6 of Masses; the 7th of the latter was sent to press in Jan 1594 when Palestrina was seized with the illness from which he died.

Works: 104 Masses, 41 for 4 voices, 37 for 5 voices, 22 for 6 voices, 4 for 8 voices, 1 Mass movt. for 12 voices; 373 motets, etc., 1 for 3 voices, 127 for 4 voices, 128 for 5 voices, 40 for 6 voices, 2 for 7 voices, 62 for 8 voices, 2 for 9 voices, 11 for 12 voices; Lamentations, 5 sets; 11 Litanies; 35 Magnificats; 68 Offertories for 5 voices; 94 secular madrigals; 49 sacred madrigals for 5 voices.

Palestrina, opera by Pfitzner (lib. by comp.), prod. Munich, 12 Jun 1917.

Paliashvili, Zakharia Petrovich (b Kutais, 16 Aug 1871; d Tiflis, 6 Oct 1933), Russian (Georgian) composer. Studied at the Moscow Cons. under Taneiev, later taught at Tiflis, cond. the orch. and made excursions into eastern Georgia to study its folk music on which his work is based.

Works incl. operas *Abessalom and Eteri* (1919), *Twilight* (1923) and *Latavra*; choral works; folksong arrs.

Palindrome, lit. a word or poem reading the same backwards as forwards. In music a piece constructed in the same way, more or less loosely, as e.g. the prelude and postlude in Hindemith's *Ludus tonalis*, his 1-act opera *Hin und zurück* (q.v.), Act III of Berg's *Lulu* or Bartók's 5th string quartet. The procedure is that of *Recte et retro* or *Rovescio* on a larger scale.

Pallavicini, Carlo (b Salò, c 1630; d Dresden, 29 Jan 1688), Italian composer. Lived at Salò, married Giulia Rossi at Padua and settled there, prod. operas between 1666 and 1687 at Venice, where he also lived for a time. In 1667–73 he was at the Saxon court at Dresden; 1st as asst. and later as 1st music dir. In 1674 he was back at Venice, but was recalled to Dresden in 1685 to reorganize the It. opera.

Works incl. *Demetrio* (1666), *Diocletiano* (1674), *Enea in Italia* (1675), *Vespasiano* (1678), *Nerone, Le amazoni nell' isole fortunate* (1779), *Messalina* (1679), *Bassiano, overro Il maggior impossibile* (1682), *Penelope la casta* (1685), *Massimo Puppieno, Didone delirante* (1686), *L'amazone corsara, La Gerusalemme liberata* (after Tasso, 1687), *Antiope* (finished by Strungk, 1689), and 9 others; a Mass and an oratorio; arias and *canzoni* with instruments; string fantasies.

Pallavicini, Vincenzo (b Brescia; d after 1756), Italian composer. *Maestro di cappella* at the Cons. degl' Incurabili at Venice.

Works incl. opera *Lo speziale* (with Fischietti, lib. by Goldoni, 1754).

Pallavicino, Benedetto (b Cremona, 1551; d Mantua, 26 Nov 1601), Italian composer. He was in the service of the Duke of Mantua from 1582, succeeded de Wert as *maestro di cappella* there in 1596, but was in turn succeeded in 1601, when he retired to the monastery of Camaldoli in Tuscany.

Works incl. Masses, psalms and other church music; 10 vols. of madrigals.

Palm, Siegfried (b Wuppertal, 25 Apr 1927), German cellist. He studied with his father and with Enrico Mainardi; played in var. N. German orchs. and with the Hamann

4tet, 1950–62. From 1962 he has been soloist with leading orchs. and a prof. at the Cologne Hochschule für Musik. Intendant, Deutsche Oper, Berlin, 1977–81. A pioneer in *avant-garde* techniques, he has given the fps of works by Penderecki (*Capriccio per S.P.*), Blacher, Feldman, Ligeti, Xenakis, B.A. Zimmermann and Fortner.

Palma, Silvestro (b Ischia, 15 Mar 1754; d Naples, 8 Aug 1834), Italian composer. Studied at Naples and was a pupil of Paisiello.

Works incl. operas *La pietra simpatica* (1795), *I vampiri* (1812), and c 15 others; church music.

Palmer, Felicity (b Cheltenham, 6 Apr 1944), English soprano. She studied at the GSM and in Munich. Appeared in various choirs, concert debut 1970. Opera debut 1971, Dido with Kent Opera; then sang Pamina and Elvira with ENO. US debut 1973, as Mozart's Countess in Dallas. Successful in a wide repertory, she has sung Gluck's Armide and works by Messiaen and Shostakovich in concert.

Palmer, Robert (b Syracuse, New York, 2 Jun 1915), American composer. Studied at the Eastman School of Music at Rochester, NY, where he took degrees in 1938–9, also privately with Roy Harris. In 1943 he became asst. prof. of music at Cornell Univ., Ithaca, NY; retired 1980.

Works incl. ballet *Irish Legend* with chamber orch.; symph., elegy *K. 19* (1945) and concerto for orch.; concerto for chamber orch. (1940), pf. concerto (1970); *Abraham Lincoln Walks at Midnight* (V. Lindsay) for chorus and orch. (1948); 4 string 4tets (1939–60), 2 pf. 4tets (1947, 1974), 2 string trios; concerto for fl., vln., clar., Eng. horn and bassoon; vla. and pf. sonata; sonata for 2 pfs.; sonata and 3 preludes for pf.

Palmgren, Selim (b Björneborg, 16 Feb 1878; d Helsinki, 13 Dec 1951), Finnish pianist, composer and conductor. Studied at the Helsinki Cons., where Wegelius was among his masters, and later with Ansorge in Ger. and Busoni in It. On his return he became cond. of the Fin. Students' Choral Society and later of the Music Society at Turku. He also frequently appeared as pianist. Married the singer Maikki Järnefelt, toured Europe and USA with her and from 1923 to 1926 was prof. of comp. at the Eastman School of Music at Rochester, NY.

Works incl. operas *Daniel Hjort* (1910) and *Peter Schlemihl* (after Chamisso); incid. music to Kyösti's *Tukhimo* (*Cinderella*); choral works; 5 pf. concertos (II. *The River*;

III. *Metamorphoses*; IV. *April*); numerous pf. pieces.

Palotta, Matteo (b Palermo, c 1688; d Vienna, 28 Mar 1758), Italian composer, priest and music scholar. Studied at Naples, returned to Sicily after being ordained, but was app. one of the court comps. in Vienna in 1733. He wrote treatises on solmization and the modes and comp. Masses, motets and other church music.

Paminger, Leonhard (b Aschau, Upper Aus., 25 Mar 1495; d Passau, 3 May 1567), Austrian composer. Educ. at the monastery of St Nicholas at Passau, studied in Vienna afterwards, but returned to Passau in 1513 to become a teacher and later secretary at the monastery. He became a Lutheran and pub. religious pamphlets and a series of motets for the Lutheran year.

Works incl. Lat. motets, Ger. hymns, psalms, etc.

Pammelia, the 1st part of a collection of canons, rounds and catches pub. by Ravenscroft in 1609, the 2nd being *Deuteromelia*.

Pan (or Pandean) Pipe, an early wind instrument, also called Syrinx, consisting of a bundle of reeds of graded lengths made into pipes giving out a scale of different notes.

Pan Tvardovsky, opera by Verstovsky (lib. by K.S. Aksakov), prod. Moscow, 5 Jun 1828.

Pan Voyevoda, opera by Rimsky-Korsakov (lib. by I.F. Tiumenev), prod. St Petersburg, 16 Oct 1904.

Pandolfini, Angelica (b Spoleto, 21 Aug 1871; d Lenno, 15 Jul 1959), Italian soprano. She studied in Paris and made her debut in Modena, 1894, as Marguerite. The following season she was in Malta but returned to Italy and sang in Milan 1897–1908: in 1902 created Adriana Lecouvreur and in 1906 sang in the fp of Franchetti's *La Figlia di Jorio*.

Pandoura (from Gk.; also from Arabic *tanbur*, Tamboura), a string instrument of the lute type with a long neck and a small body, surviving in var. forms only in the Balkans, Turkey, Egypt and the East.

Pane, Domenico del (b Rome, d Rome, 10 Dec 1694), Italian singer and composer. Pupil of Abbatini in Rome, went to Vienna in 1650 as a singer in the Imp. chapel, but returned to Rome to join the Papal Chapel in 1654 and became choirmaster there in 1669.

Works incl. Masses on motets by Palestrina, motets of his own; sacred concertos; madrigals.

Panerai, Rolando (b Campi Bizenzio, nr. Florence, 17 Oct 1924), Italian baritone. He studied in Florence and Milan. Debut Naples 1947 as Faraone in *Mosè*. La Scala from 1951 and Salzburg from 1957 as Luna, Germont, Ford, Guglielmo and Rossini's Figaro. At Venice in 1955 he took part in the stage fp of Prokofiev's *The Fiery Angel*. CG debut 1960; returned 1985, as Dulcamara.

Panizza, Ettore (b Buenos Aires, 12 Aug 1875; d Milan, 27 Nov 1967), Argentine conductor and composer of Italian descent. Studied at the Milan Cons. and 1st appeared as cond. in Rome, 1899, 1st visiting London (CG) in 1907; he gave there operas by Erlanger, Zandonai and Massenet. La Scala, Milan, 1916–48. NY Met 1934–42.

Works incl. operas *Il fidanzato del mare* (1897), *Medio evo latino, Aurora* (1908), *Bisanzio*, etc.

Panny, Joseph (b Kolmitzberg, 23 Oct 1794; d Mainz, 7 Sep 1838), Austrian violinist and composer. Studied at home and with Eybler in Vienna, made friends with Paganini during his visits there, appeared in Ger., Norway, Paris and London, founded a school of music at Weisserling in Alsace and another at Mainz.

Works incl. 3 Masses, Requiem; 3 string 4tets; pf. trios; *Scène dramatique* for the vln. G string (for Paganini) and other solos; choruses; songs.

Panofka, Heinrich (b Breslau, 3 Oct 1807; d Florence, 18 Nov 1887), German violinist, singing-teacher and composer. Studied at home and with Mayseder in Vienna, where he 1st appeared in public in 1827. After living in Munich and Berlin, he settled by turns in Paris, London and Florence, teaching singing and pub. treatises on the subject. Wrote works for vln. with pf. and with orch.

Panseron, Auguste (Matthieu) (b Paris, 26 Apr 1795; d Paris, 29 Jul 1859), French composer and singing-teacher. Studied at the Paris Cons. and took the Prix de Rome in 1813, making further studies in It. under Mattei. As accompanist at the Opéra-Comique in Paris, he gained much experience in singing and he became prof. at the Cons. in 1826, writing treatises on solfège and singing.

Works incl. operas *La Grille du parc* (1820), *Le Mariage difficile* (1823) and *L'École de Rome* (1826); 2 Masses for treble voices, motets and canticles *Mois de Marie*; numerous songs.

Pantaleon, an instrument of the Dulcimer type invented by Pantaleon Hebenstreit in the 18th cent. and called Pantaleon after him by Louis XIV.

Pantaleoni, Romilda (b Udine, 1847; d Milan, 20 May 1917), Italian soprano. She studied in Milan and made her debut there in 1868. Among the roles she created were Desdemona (1887), Tigrana in Puccini's *Edgar* (1889) and Ponchielli's Marion Delorme (1885). Also heard as Boito's Margherita and as Santuzza.

Pantomime (from Gk. = 'all-imitating'), properly a play in dumbshow, but in Eng. since the 18th cent. a popular stage entertainment with music, deriving from the It. *commedia dell'arte*. It is still based, even if remotely, on fairy-tales, but it has lost the Harlequinade which used to be an indispensable supplement and has become a spectacular extravaganza, often intro. songs popular at the time. Also term used in 20th cent. for mimed episode in ballet (Ravel, *Daphnis et Chloé*), or ballet as a whole (Bartók, *Miraculous Mandarin*).

Pantonality, a term used by R. Réti (*q.v.*) to describe development in tonality in late 19th and early 20th cents. whereby music shifts from one key centre to another, without becoming atonal. Such music is heard first in Wagner (*Tristan*) and is found later in Debussy, Bartók and Hindemith.

Panufnik, Andrzej (b Warsaw, 24 Sep 1914), Polish composer. Studied with Sikorski at the Warsaw Cons. and received a diploma in 1936. Some of his music was destroyed in the bombardment of Warsaw. He settled in Eng. in 1954 and from 1957 to 1959 was cond. of the Birmingham SO.

Works incl. ballet, *Miss Julie* (prod. Stuttgart, 1970), film music; Psalm cxlv for chorus and orch., 9 symphs. e.g. *Rustica* (1948), *Elegaica* (1957), *Sacra* (1963), *Sfere* (1975), *Mistica* (1977), *Votiva* (1981), no. 9, *Sinfonia di Speranza* (1986), symph. variations, symph. studies, Tragic Overture, Heroic Overture; tpt. concerto, pf. concerto (1962–72).

Pf. trio and other chamber music, 5 Pol. folksongs for treble voices, 2 fls., 2 clars. and bass clar.; preludes, mazurkas and other works for pf., 2 string 4tets (1976, 1980).

Panzéra, Charles (b Geneva, 16 Feb 1896; d Paris, 6 Jun 1976), Swiss baritone. He studied at the Paris Cons. and sang Massenet's Albert at the Opéra-Comique in 1919. He was well known as Pelléas, but his career was largely as a concert singer. He gave the fp of Fauré's *L'horizon chimérique* in 1922 and was heard in Europe and the US in songs by Debussy, Ravel and Duparc. He taught at the Juilliard School, NY, and from 1949 was prof. at the Paris Cons.

Paolo e Francesca, opera by Mancinelli (lib. by A. Colautti, after Dante), prod. Bologna, Teatro Comunale, 11 Nov 1907.

Paolo e Virginia, opera by P.C. Guglielmi (lib. by G.M. Diodati, based on Bernardin de Saint-Pierre's novel), prod. Naples, Teatro Fiorentino, 2 Jan 1817.

Papandopulo, Boris (b Honnef o/Rhine, 25 Feb 1906), Yugoslav composer and conductor. Studied at Zagreb and Vienna, and became choral and orchestral cond. at Zagreb, returning there after teaching at the Music School of Split in 1935–8. Later active as an opera cond.
Works incl. operas *The Sun Flower* (1942), *Amphitryon* (1940) and *Rona*; ballet *Gold* (1930); oratorio for unaccomp. chorus *The Torments of Our Lord Jesus Christ* (1935), *Laudamus* for solo voices, chorus and orch., *Croatian Mass* for soloists and chorus; 2 symphs. (1933, 1945), symph. picture *The Overflowing*; 2 pf. concertos; 5 string 4tets (1927–70), and other chamber music, pf. mus.; songs, etc.

Papillons(*Butterflies*), a set of short pf. pieces by Schumann, op. 2, with a finale suggesting the end of a ball in the early morning, with a clock striking 6 and a quotation of the *Grossvatertanz* or *Kehraus*, which also appears in *Carnaval*, for which this smaller work might almost be a kind of preliminary sketch. There is a further connection between the 2, the opening of *Papillons* being quoted in the *Florestan* piece in *Carnaval*. The 1st part of op. 2 was comp. (before op. 1) in 1829, the end in 1831.

Parable Aria (esp. Ger. *Gleichnisarie*) or Metaphor Aria, a type of mainly operatic aria cultivated in the early 18th cent., esp. by Zeno and Metastasio in their libs., where certain abstract conceptions are illustrated by concrete ideas resembling them, e.g. fidelity by a rock in a stormy sea, love by cooing turtle-doves, etc. 'As when the dove' in Handel's *Acis and Galatea* is a parable aria and 'Come scoglio' ('Like a rock') in Mozart's *Così fan tutte* is both verbally and musically a parody of the type. The music of a parable aria was usually illustrative of the image chosen by the librettist.

Parabosco, Girolamo (b Piacenza, 1520 or 1524; d Venice, 21 Apr 1557), Italian composer and organist. He became a pupil of Willaert in Venice, and pub. 2 pieces in the miscellaneous collection of instrumental music *Musica Nova* (1540). He succeeded J. Buus as 1st organist at St Mark's, Venice in 1551, a post which he held until his death. Well known for improvisations on the organ.

Parade, ballet in 1 act by Satie (scenario by Cocteau), prod. Paris, Théâtre de Châtelet, 18 May 1917, with Diaghilev's Ballets Russes: curtain, décor and costumes by Picasso, cond. Ansermet. Suite for pf. four hands in 6 movts. from ballet pub. 1917.

Paradies, Domenico. *See* Paradisi.

Paradis, Maria Theresia von (b Vienna, 15 May 1759; d Vienna, 1 Feb 1824), Austrian pianist, organist, singer and composer. She was blind from childhood, but had a great success, which she extended to Paris and London. Mozart wrote the pf. concerto in Bb maj. (K456) for her.
Works incl. operas *Der Schulcandidat* (1792), *Rinaldo und Alcina* (1797); melodrama *Ariadne und Bacchus* (1791); cantata *Deutsches Monument* (on the death of Louis XVI); pf. trios; sonatas and variations for pf.; songs incl. a setting of Burger's *Lenore*.

Paradise and the Peri (*Das Paradies und die Peri*), a setting for solo voices, chorus and orch. of one of the poems in Thomas Moore's *Lalla Rookh*, trans. into Ger. with alterations, by Schumann, op. 50; comp. 1st contemplated in 1841, begun Feb 1843; fp Leipzig, 4 Dec 1843.

Paradise Lost, opera, '*sacra rappresentazione*', by Penderecki (lib. by C. Fry after Milton), prod. Chicago, Lyric Opera, 29 Nov 1978.

Paradisi (or Paradies), (Pietro) Domenico (b Naples, 1707; d Venice, 25 Aug 1791), Italian harpsichordist and composer. Pupil of Porpora, lived for many years in London as a teacher.
Works incl. operas *Alessandro in Persia*, (1738), *Il decreto del fato*, *Fetonte* (1747), *La forza d'amore* (1751); cantata *Le Muse in gara*; harpsichord sonatas, toccatas.

Parallel Motion, 2 or more parts in counterpoint moving up or down in unchanging intervals.

Paray, Paul (Charles) (b Tréport, 24 May 1886; d Monte Carlo, 10 Oct 1979), French conductor and composer. Studied with Leroux and others at the Paris Cons. and took the Prix de Rome in 1911. Returning to Paris from imprisonment during the 1914–18 war he became asst. and later successor to Chevillard, whose concerts he continued to cond. until 1933, when he succeeded Pierné as cond. of the Colonne Orch. In 1952 he became cond. of the Detroit SO, remained until 1963.
Works incl. oratorio *Jeanne d'Arc* (1931); ballet *Artémis troublée* (1922); Mass for the 500th anniversary of the death of Joan of Arc (rev. of oratorio, 1956); symph. in C

maj.; fantasy for pf. and orch.; string 4tet; vln. and pf. sonata.

Pardon de Ploërmel, Le, opera by Meyerbeer (lib. by J. Barbier and M. Carré), prod. Paris, Opéra-Comique, 4 Apr 1859. The work is also known as *Dinorah*.

Parepa-Rosa, Euphrosyne (b Edinburgh, 7 May 1836; d London, 21 Jan 1874), Scottish soprano of Wallachian descent. She was taught by her mother, the singer Elizabeth Seguin, and by several famous masters, and made her debut at Malta at the age of 16, as Amina, and in London in 1857, as Elvira in *I Puritani*. Married Carl Rosa in 1867 and was the leading soprano of his opera company. US tours 1863–72. Other roles incl. Donna Anna, Norma and Elsa.

Paride ed Elena (*Paris and Helen*), opera by Gluck (lib. by R. Calzabigi), prod. Vienna, Burgtheater, 3 Nov 1770.

Parikian, Manoug (b Mersin, Turkey, 15 Sep 1920; d London, 24 Dec 1987), British violinist. He studied at the TCL and was leader of the Liverpool PO (1947–8) and the Philharmonia Orch. (1949–57). Solo career from 1957, and gave the fps of concertos by Crosse, Goehr and Wood; also works by Seiber, Skalkottas and Musgrave. He taught at the RCM 1954–6, RAM from 1959. Dir. of the Manchester Camerata 1980–4.

Paris Opéra. See **Académie de Musique.**

Paris Symphonies, a set of 6 symphs. by Haydn commissioned by the Concert de la Loge Olympique in Paris: no. 82 in C maj. (*L'Ours*), comp. 1786; no. 83 in G min (*La Poule*), 1785; no. 84 in E♭ maj., 1786; no. 85 in B♭ maj. (*La Reine*), 1785–6; no. 86 in D maj., 1786; no. 87 in A maj., 1785.

'Paris' Symphony, Mozart's symph. in D man., K297, written in Paris for perf. at the Concert Spirituel in 1778. After the fp Mozart replaced the slow movement by another.

Paris: The Song of a Great City, nocturne for orch. by Delius; comp. 1898 and ded. to Hans Haym, who gave the fp, Elberfeld 1902. Given by Busoni in Berlin on 15 Nov 1902; 1st Brit. perf. Liverpool, 11 Jan 1908, cond. Beecham.

Parisina, opera by Donizetti (lib. by F. Romani, based on Byron's poem) prod. Florence, Teatro della Pergola, 17 Mar 1833.

Opera by Mascagni (lib. by G. d'Annunzio), prod. Milan, La Scala, 15 Dec 1913.

Parker, Horatio (William) (b Auburndale, Mass., 15 Sep 1863; d Cedarhurst, New York, 18 Dec 1919), American organist and composer. Studied at Boston and Munich, where he was a pupil of Rheinberger. In 1884 he returned to NY and became an organist and choirmaster, and taught at the Nat. Cons. directed by Dvořák. Later he became organist at Trinity Church, Boston, and in 1894 prof. of music at Yale Univ. He visited Eng. several times for perfs. of his works at the festivals and to receive the Mus.D. from Cambridge in 1902.

Works incl. operas *Mona* (1912) and *Fairyland* (1915); oratorios *Hora novissima* (1893), *The Legend of St. Christopher* (1897), *Morven and the Grail* (1915); *The Holy Child* (1893), *The Dream of Mary* (1918) and other cantatas, choral ballads and songs; church services; symph. in C maj (1885), overtures and other orchestral works; org. concerto; string 4tet in F maj. (1885); organ sonata; pf. pieces; songs.

Parlando or **Parlante** (It. = speaking), a direction indicating, in instrumental music, that a passage is to be perf. in a 'speaking' manner, expressively but not sustained or 'sung'; in vocal music, that the tone is to be reduced to something approximating to speech.

Parody Mass *See* **Missa parodia.**

Paroles tissées (*Woven Words*), work for tenor, strings, harp, pf. and perc. by Lutoslawski (text by J.F. Chabrun); commissioned by Peter Pears, who gave the fp at the Aldeburgh Fest. on 20 Jun 1965.

Parmeggiani, Ettore (b Rimini, 15 Aug 1895; d Milan, 28 Jan 1960), Italian tenor. Debut Milan 1922, Cavaradossi; La Scala 1927–37, debut as Max. Sang Siegmund, Lohengrin and Parsifal and appeared in the fps of Mascagni's *Nerone* (1935) and Respighi's *Lucrezia* (1937). At Genoa in 1936 he took part in the fp of Malipiero's *Giulio Cesare*. After his retirement he taught in Milan, then led the claque at La Scala.

Parrott, Andrew (b Walsall, 10 Mar 1947), English conductor. He studied at Oxford and researched early perf. practice. Founded the Taverner Choir 1973, later the Taverner Consort and Players; he has since been guest cond. with the ECO and the London Bach Orch. In 1977 he cond. Monteverdi *Vespers* at the Promenade Concerts and in later seasons gave Bach's B minor Mass and the *St Matthew Passion* in eds. with authentic insts. and small choruses.

Parrott, Ian (b London, 5 Mar 1916), English composer and writer on music. Studied at the RCM and with B. Dale. After var. appts. he was Prof. of Music at Univ. Coll. of Wales, Aberystwyth, 1950–83.

Works incl. operas *The Sergeant-Major's Daughter* (1943), *The Black Ram* (1957), ballet *Maid in Birmingham* (1951); inst. music and songs.

Parry, (Charles) Hubert (Hastings) (b Bournemouth, 27 Feb 1848; d Rustington, 7 Oct 1918), English composer and writer on music. Studied at Oxford and with Macfarren and Sterndale Bennett. He did not make his mark in public until his pf. concerto was played by Dannreuther at the Crystal Palace in 1880 and his choral scenes from Shelley's *Prometheus Unbound* appeared at the Gloucester Festival the same year. Hon. Mus.D., Cambridge 1883, D.Mus., Oxford 1884 and Dublin 1891. After examining for London Univ. and teaching at the RCM, he was app. dir. of the latter in succession to Grove in 1894, remaining until his death. Knighted in 1898 and app. Prof. of Music at Oxford in 1900, a post he resigned in 1908. He wrote several books on music, incl. a study of Bach and a volume of the *Oxford History of Music*.

Works incl. STAGE: opera *Guinevere* (1885–6); incid. music to Aristophanes' *The Birds*, *The Frogs* (1891), *The Clouds* (1905), and *The Acharnians* (1914), Aeschylus' *Agamemnon* (1900), Ogilvy's *Hypatia*, P.M.T. Craigie's *A Repentance* and Keats's *Proserpine*.

VOCAL: Oratorios *Judith*, *Job*, *King Saul*; 6 motets, 4 *Songs of Farewell* and 2 other motets for chorus; scenes from Shelley's *Prometheus Unbound* (1880), ode *The Glories of our Blood and State* (Shirley, 1883), ode *Blest Pair of Sirens* (Milton, 1887), *Ode on St Cecilia's Day* (Pope), *L'Allegro ed il penseroso* (Milton), ode *Eton* (Swinburne, 1891), choric song from Tennyson's *Lotus Eaters* (1892), *Jerusalem* (Blake) for chorus.

ORCHESTRAL: 5 symphs. (1878–1912), 3 concert overtures, symph. poem *From Death to Life* and *Suite Moderne* for orch., *Lady Radnor's Suite* (1894) and *An English Suite* for string orch. (1921); pf. concerto in F♯ min. (1879).

CHAMBER AND SONGS: String 5tet, 3 string 4tets (1867–80), pf. 4tet, nonet for wind instruments, 4 pf. trios; sonatas for vln. and pf. and cello and pf., 2 suites and many smaller pieces for vln. and pf.; organ and pf. music; over 100 songs incl. 74 in 12 books of *English Lyrics* (1885–1920).

Parry, John (b Bryn Cynan *c* 1710; d Ruabon, 7 Oct 1782), Welsh harpist. Appeared at Dublin in 1736 and in London and Cambridge in 1746. Handel admired him and Gray wrote his poem *The Bard* on him. He pub. collections of Welsh and other Brit. national melodies.

Parry, John (b Denbigh, 18 Feb 1776; d London, 8 Apr 1851), Welsh clarinettist, bandmaster and composer. Settled in London in 1807 and in 1809 was engaged to write songs for Vauxhall Gardens. Later he became a theatre comp. and music critic to the *Morning Post* in 1834–48. In the 1820s he cond. Welsh festivals at Wrexham and Brecon.

Works incl. stage pieces *Harlequin Hoax* (lib. by T. Dibdin, 1814), *Oberon's Oath* (1816), *Ivanhoe* (1820), *The Sham Prince* (1836), etc.; songs and ballads; arrs. of Welsh songs.

Parry, John Orlando (b London, 3 Jan 1810; d East Molesey, 20 Feb 1879), Welsh harpist, pianist, singer and composer, son of prec. Studied with his father and later in It. under Lablache. In 1836 he began a career in London as stage singer, music entertainer and mimic of singers. He wrote and arr. comic songs, glees.

Parsifal, music drama (*Bühnenweihfestspiel*, Sacred festival drama) by Wagner (lib. by comp.), prod. Bayreuth, Wagner Festival Theatre, 26 Jul 1882.

Parsley, Osbert (b 1511; d Norwich, 1585), English singer and composer. Attached to Norwich Cathedral for 50 years. Comp. services, motets, Latin psalm settings, a set of Lamentations and *Persli's Clock*.

Parsons, John (b *c* 1575; d London, buried 3 Aug 1623), English composer. Became parish clerk and organist at St Margaret's Church, Westminster, in 1616, and in 1621 organist and choirmaster of Westminster Abbey. He wrote a Burial Service, which Purcell used in 1685 for the funeral of Charles II.

Parsons, Robert (b Exeter, *c* 1530; d Newark-on-Trent, 25 Jan 1570), English composer, (?) father of prec. He became a Gentleman of the Chapel Royal in London, 1563. He was drowned in the Trent.

Works incl. services, anthems, motets; madrigals; In Nomines for viols or virginal; song *Pandolpho* for a stage play.

Part, the musical perf. by any single singer or player in a work for a number of performers; a single strand of melody in a polyphonic or other comp. in a number of voices, whether perf. by several people or by a single player on a keyboard instrument; also the copy of the music from which a single singer or player perfs. in a work for a number of people.

Pärt, Arvo (b Paide, 11 Sep 1935), Estonian

composer. He graduated from the Tallinn Cons. in 1963 and settled in West Berlin 1982. He adopted serial techniques early in his career, later shifted to aleatorism. His *Nekrolog* for orch. of 1960 was ded. to the victims of the Holocaust.

Other works incl. *Stride of the World*, oratorio (1960); 3 symphs. (1964, 1966, 1971); *Pro et Contra* for cello and orch. (1964); *Cantus in Memory of Britten* for strings and glockenspiel (1977); *Arbos* for 7 insts. (1977); *Wenn Bach Bienen gezüchtet hätte* (If Bach had been a bee-keeper), 2 versions for harpsichord and ens. (1978, 1980); *St John Passion* (1981); cello concerto (1981); concerto for vln., cello and chamber orch. (perf. London 1981); Te Deum (1985).

Part du diable, La (*The Devil's Share*), opera by Auber (lib. by Scribe), prod. Paris, Opéra-Comique, 16 Jan 1843. The work is sometimes called *Carlo Broschi*, the real name of Farinelli, who is the chief character, sung by a soprano.

Part-Writing, in comp. the way of managing the satisfactory progress of each single part or voice in texture of any number of parts.

Partbooks, books containing printed or MS music to be sung or played by 1 or 2 perfs. in a work written for a larger number.

Partch, Harry (b Oakland, Calif., 24 Jun 1901; d San Diego, 3 Sep 1974), American composer. Largely self-taught, he experimented with microtonal scales and new instrumental designs.

Works incl. *8 Hitch-hiker Inscriptions from a California Highway Railing* and *U.S. Highball, a Musical Account of a Transcontinental Hobo Trip* for chorus and insts. (1944); *The Letter, a Depression Message from a Hobo Friend*, for voices and insts. (1944); *Oedipus*, music drama (1952); *The Bewitched*, a dance satire (1957); *Revelation in the Courthouse Park*, a music tragedy; *Water, Water*, an Amer. ritual (1962).

Partenope, opera by Handel (lib. by S. Stampiglia), prod. London, King's Theatre, Haymarket, 24 Feb 1730.

Opera by Hasse (lib. by Metastasio), prod. Vienna, Burgtheater, 9 Sep 1767.

Parthenia, the title of the 1st collection of virginal music to be printed in Eng., pub. in 1612–13 and containing 21 pieces by Byrd, Bull and O. Gibbons.

Parthenia inviolata, a companion vol. to the prec. containing 20 pieces for virginals and bass viol.

Parthia, a variant spelling of the German *Partie*, used by Haydn and Beethoven among others. *See* **Partita**.

Partials. *See* **Harmonics**.

Partita (It., lit. = set [as in tennis]), in the 17th and early 18th cent. a variation used in the plural (*partite diverse*) to mean a set of Variations, e.g. by Bach in some of his org. works based on chorales. It also acquired the meaning Suite (Ger. *Partie*) and was so used also by Bach, e.g. in his 6 partitas for harpsichord and his 3 partitas for solo vln. The term has been revived by 20th-cent. comps., e.g. Casella, Dallapiccola, Vaughan Williams and Walton. *See also* **Suite**.

Partos, Ödön (b Budapest, 1 Oct 1907; d Tel Aviv, 6 Jul 1977), Hungarian-Israeli composer. Studied vln. with Hubay and comp. with Kodály. Led various orchs. in Lucerne, Berlin and Budapest between 1925 and 1936, and from 1938 played vla. with the Israel PO.

Works incl. *Yis Kor* (*In Memoriam*) for vla. and string orch. (1947); *Song of Praise* for vla. and orch. (1949); symph. fantasy *En Gev* (1952); *Phantasy on Yemeni Themes* for chorus and orch.; *Images* for orch. (1960); *Fuses* for vla. and chamber orch. (1970); *Arabesque* for oboe and chamber orch. (1975); 2 string 4tets (1932, 1960).

Part-song, a comp. for several voices (mixed, female or male) usually less polyphonic than a madrigal.

Pasatieri, Thomas (b New York, 20 Oct 1945), American composer. He studied at Juilliard and with Milhaud in Aspen. True to his Italian ancestry, Pasatieri has avoided the *avant-garde* and remained faithful to bel canto.

Among his operas are *The Widow* (Aspen, 1965); *La Divina* (NY, 1966); *Padrevia* (Brooklyn, 1967); *Calvary* (Seattle, 1971); *The Trial of Mary Lincoln* (Boston, 1972); *Black Widow* (Seattle, 1972); *The Seagull* (Houston, 1974); *Signor Deluso* (Greenway, Va., 1974); *The Penitentes* (Aspen, 1974); *Ines de Castro* (Baltimore, 1976); *Washington Square* (Detroit, 1976); *Maria Elena* (Tuscon, 1983); *Three Sisters* (Columbus, Ohio, 1986).

Pasdeloup, Jules (Étienne) (b Paris, 15 Sept 1819; d Fontainebleau, 13 Aug 1887), French conductor. Studied at the Paris Cons. Founder of the Société des Jeunes Artistes du Cons., 1851, and the Concerts Pasdeloup, 1861, at which he prod. many works previously unknown in France, incl. music by Wagner and Schumann. Founded Société des Oratories in 1868; joined Théâtre Lyrique the same year.

Pasero, Tancredi (b Turin, 11 Jan 1893; d Milan, 17 Feb 1983), Italian bass. He studied in Turin and sang in the It. provinces from 1918. In 1926 he sang Philip II under Toscanini at La Scala, Milan; remained until 1951. NY Met 1928–33 (debut as Alvise). He sang at the Florence Festival 1933–48 and created roles in operas by Mascagni, Pizzetti and Ghedini. Other roles incl. Wotan, Gurnemanz, Boris and Sarastro.

Pashchenko, Andrey Filipovich (b Rostov-on-Don, 15 Aug 1883; d Moscow, 16 Nov 1972), Russian composer. Entered the St Petersburg Cons. in 1914, after receiving private musical instruction, and studied comp. under Steinberg and Wihtol. He was active as teacher and music organizer, but devoted most of his time to comp. During World War II he remained at Leningrad all through the siege.

Works incl. operas *The Revolt of the Eagles* (1925), *Emperor Maximilian* (1927), *The Black Cliff* (1931), *The Pompadours* (after Saltikov-Shtchedrin's story, 1939), *The Stubborn Bride* (1956), *Radda and Loyko* (after Gorki's story *Makar Tchudra*, 1957); film music; oratorios *The Liberation of Prometheus* and *Lenin*, Requiem in memory of the heroes of the great war; 15 symphs. (1915–70), *Solemn Polonaise* and *Festive Overture*, symph. poems *The Giants* and *The Bacchantes*, scherzo *Harlequin and Columbine*, Suite in the Classical Style, *Legend* for orch.; 3 pieces for a band of folk insts.; 9 string 4tets; songs.

Pashkevich, Vassily Alexeievich (b *c* 1742; d St Petersburg, 9 Mar 1797), Russian violinist and composer. Entered the service of Catherine II in 1763 and became cond. and court comp.

Works incl. operas *The Carriage Accident* (1779), *Fevey*, *The Miser*, *Fedul and his Children* (with Martín y Soler), 1791), *The Early Reign of Oleg* (with Sarti and Canobbio, 1790), *The Pasha of Tunis*.

Pasino (called Ghizzolo Stefano) (b Brescia; d ? Salò), Italian 17th-cent composer. Became town organist at Lonato 1635 and *maestro di cappella* at Salò in 1651.

Works incl. Masses and motets; sonatas for 2–4 instruments, instrumental *ricercari*.

Paskalis, Kostas (b Livadia, 1 Sep 1929), Greek baritone. He studied in Athens and made his debut there in 1951 as Rigoletto. Wider recognition came with his Renato at the Vienna Staatsoper in 1958 and in 1964 he sang Macbeth at Glyndebourne; London, CG, 1969–72, as Iago and Scarpia. NY Met debut 1965, as the *Forza* Carlos, and the

following year he created Pentheus in *The Bassarids*, at Salzburg.

Pasquali, Francesco (b Cosenza; d Rome, in or after 1635), Italian 16th–17th-cent composer. Studied and worked in Rome.

Works incl. sacred and secular songs, madrigals.

Pasquali, Niccolò (b *c* 1718; d Edinburgh, 13 Oct 1757), Italian violinist and composer. Settled at Edinburgh *c* 1740, lived at Dublin in 1748–51, but returned to Edinburgh, visiting London in 1752. Wrote treatises on thorough-bass and harpsichord playing.

Works incl. opera *The Enraged Musician* (1753), Masque *The Triumph of Hibernia*; dirge in Shakespeare's *Romeo and Juliet*; oratorios *Noah* and *David*; 12 overtures for (or with) horns; sonatas for vln. or 2 vlns. and bass; songs contrib. to var. collections.

Pasquini, Bernardo (b Massa Valdinievole, Tuscany, 7 Dec 1637; d Rome, 21 Nov 1710), Italian harpsichordist, organist and composer. Studied with Loreto Vittori and Cesti. As a young man he settled in Rome and became organist of the church of Santa Maria Maggiore. His *Accademia per musica* was perf. at the Roman palace of Queen Christina of Swed. in 1687 to celebrate the accession of James II, Corelli leading a string orch. of 150 players.

Works incl. operas *La donna ancora è fedele* (1676), *Dov' è amore e pietà* (1679), *La forza d'amore* and 11 others; 13 sonatas and other works for harpsichord.

Passacaglia (prob. from Span. *pasar calle* = to walk the street), orig. an It. or Span. dance, but now an instrumental comp. based on a Ground, i.e. a tune continuing throughout, usually but not necessarily in the bass. The best-known ex. is Bach's for organ. The finale of Brahms's 4th symph., although not so entitled, is also in this form. A modern ex. is the Passacaglia by Webern, op. 1 (1908).

Passage, any melodic or decorative feature in a comp., esp. if it is conspicuous or calls for brilliant perf.

Passaggio (It.), as above, but used in more specialized senses for Modulations (i.e. passing from key to key) and for florid vocal or instrumental decorations.

Passamezzo (It., prob. a corruption of *passo e mezzo* = pace and a half), a brisk dance of the late 16th and early 17th cents., popular not only in It. but throughout Europe. Its name is prob. due to the fact that it was a more lively form of the Pavane. It consisted basically of variations on a ground bass. The *passamezzo antico* (Shakespeare's 'passy measures pavyn') was in the min. key, the *passamezzo moderno* in the maj. *See also* **Romanesca.**

Passepied (Fr. lit., pass-foot), a French (prob. Breton) dance at least as old as the 16th cent. The music is in 3–4 or 3–8 time taken at a moderately running pace. It sometimes occurs in suites, but is not an obligatory part of them.

Passereau (*fl.* 1533–55), French 16th-cent composer. His *chansons*, some humorous, some obscene, were pub. by Attaingnant and others at var. times between 1529 and 1572. The best known of them, 'Il est bel et bon', was arr. for organ by Girolamo Cavazzoni.

Passing Notes, incidental notes in one or more parts of a comp. which create a temporary dissonance with the prevailing harmony (*see* illustration).

Anna Bolena. Also sang in operas by Mayr, Pacini, Mercadante and Paer.

Pasterwiz, Georg (b Bierhütten nr. Passau, 7 Jun 1730; d Kremsmünster, 26 Jan 1803), Austrian monk, organist and composer. Studied at Kremsmünster Abbey, where he was ordained priest in 1755, and with Eberlin at Salzburg. In 1767–82 he was choirmaster at the abbey, but later lived chiefly in Vienna.

Works incl. opera *Samson* (1775); 14 Masses, Requiem; numerous fugues and other pieces for keyboard instruments.

Pasticcio (It. lit. pie or pasty), a stage entertainment with music drawn from existing works by one or more comps. and words written to fit the music. It was part. popular in the 18th cent.

Pastor fido, Il (*The Faithful Shepherd*),

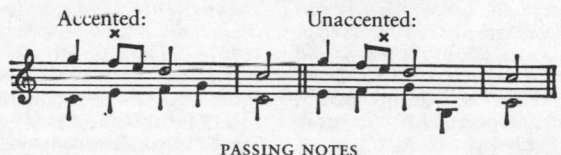

Accented: Unaccented:

PASSING NOTES

Passion Music. The medieval recitation of the gospel story of Christ's Passion was sung, as it still is, by three singers with different vocal ranges. The singer representing the Evangelist had a medium range, Christus a low range, and the singer responsible for the other characters and the crowd (*turba*) a high range. By the 15th cent. the *turba* began to be entrusted to a vocal ensemble, and in the course of the 16th cent. the whole text was sung in a polyphonic setting. In the 17th cent. Lutheran comps. intro. recitative, chorales and instrumental accomp. In the early 18th cent. the incl. of arias set to non-Biblical words turned the Lutheran Passion into an oratorio, indistinguishable in style from opera. Bach's 2 surviving Passions belong to this new category.

Passione, La (*The Passion*), name given to Haydn's symph. no. 49 in F min., comp. 1768.

Pasta (*née* Negri) **Giuditta** (b Saronno nr. Milan, 28 Oct 1797; d Blavio nr. Como, 1 Apr 1865), Italian soprano. Studied at home, at the Milan Cons. and in Paris, made her 1st appearance in 1815 and went to London in 1817, as Telemachus in Cimarosa's *Penelope*. In Paris she was 1st heard at the Théâtre Italien in 1821 as Rossini's Desdemona. She created Bellini's Norma, Amina and Beatrice di Tenda and Donizetti's

opera by Handel (lib. by G. Rossi after Guarini's pastoral play), prod. London, Queen's Theatre, Haymarket, 22 Nov 1712.

Pastoral, a light-hearted Eng. madrigal with words of a pastoral character. *See also* **Pastorale.**

Pastoral, an anthology by Bliss for mezzo, chorus, fl., drums and strings (words by Theocritus, Poliziano, Ben Jonson, John Fletcher and Robert Nichols), fp London, 8 May 1929.

'Pastoral' Sonata, Beethoven's pf. sonata in D maj., op. 28, comp. in 1801 and ded. to Joseph, Edler von Sonnenfels. The nickname was not Beethoven's own, but was invented later by the Hamburg pub. Cranz. It suits only the finale.

'Pastoral' Symphony, Beethoven's 6th symph., in F maj., op. 68, comp. in 1807–8, fp Vienna, 22 Dec 1808. The title-page bears Beethoven's own heading of *Symphonie pastorale,* and on the 1st vln. part is the inscription, 'Pastoral-Sinfonie oder Erinnerung an das Landleben (mehr Ausdruck der Empfindung als Mahlerey).' (Pastoral Symphony or Recollection of Country Life [Expression of Emotion rather than Painting].)

Pastoral Symphony, A, the 3rd symph. by Vaughan Williams, for orch. with a soprano voice (without words), comp. 1920, fp London, Queen's Hall, 26 Jan 1922, cond. Boult.

Pastorale (Fr. and It.), a type of 17th-cent. opera, or opera-ballet, with recitatives, airs and choruses, often prod. on special festive occasions and treating pastoral subjects in a courtly and artificial manner, often allegorically. Its origin was the pastoral drama of the 16th cent. In later times pastorale has been often used as a title for all kinds of comps. of a pastoral character.

Pastorale, La (called *La Pastorale d'Issy*), opera by Cambert (lib. by Pierre Perrin), prod. at Issy nr. Paris, Apr 1659. Long regarded as the 1st Fr. opera (but *see* **Triomphe de l'Amour**).

Pastorella nobile, La (*The Noble Shepherdess*), opera by P. Guglielmi (lib. by S. Zini), prod. Naples, Teatro Nuovo, 19 Apr 1788.

Pastourelle (Fr.), a medieval pastoral song.

Patanè, Giuseppe (b Naples, 1 Jan 1932), Italian conductor. Studied at Naples and cond. *La traviata* there in 1951. Worked at the Deutsche Oper, Berlin, 1962–8 and cond. *Rigoletto* at La Scala, 1969. CG debut 1973, *La forza del destino*. Widely known as orch. cond. in Europe and US (American Symph., NY, 1982–4).

Pathétique Sonata (Grande sonate pathétique), Beethoven's pf. sonata in C min., op. 13, comp. *c* 1798 and ded. to Prince Carl von Lichnowsky. The title (in Fr.) is, exceptionally, Beethoven's own.

Pathétique Symphony, Tchaikovsky's 6th symph., in B min., op. 74, comp. 1893 and 1st perf. under the comp., St Petersburg, 28 Oct 1893. The title 'Tragic' Symph. was suggested by the comp.'s brother Modest, but rejected by Tchaikovsky, who afterwards agreed to the adj. 'Pathétique'.

Patience, or Bunthorne's Bride, operetta by Sullivan (lib. by W.S. Gilbert), prod. London, Opéra-Comique, 25 Apr 1881.

Patiño, Carlos (b Galicia, ?; d Madrid, 5 Sep 1675), Spanish composer. Was in the service of John IV of Port. early in the cent. and in 1633 became choirmaster in the royal chapel at Madrid.

Works incl. Masses, Benedictus for the funeral of Philip II (1599) and other church music; incid. music for plays; *villancicos*, etc.

Paton, Mary Ann (b Edinburgh, Oct 1802; d Chapelthorpe, Yorks., 21 Jul 1864), Scottish soprano. Appeared as a child playing the harp, pf. and vln. and made her 1st stage appearance in London in 1822 as Susanna. Married Lord William Pitt Lennox in 1824, but they separated later. She was the 1st Reiza in Weber's *Oberon* in 1826. Other roles incl. Agathe, Meyerbeer's Alice and Mandane in Arne's *Artaxerxes*.

Patrie, overture by Bizet (not for Sardou's play of that name), comp. 1873, fp Paris, 15 Feb 1874.

Patter Song, a type of song, usually comic, the effect of which depends on a rapid, syllabic delivery of the words to quick music. Many familiar exs. occur in Sullivan's operettas.

Patterson, Paul (b Chesterfield, 15 Jun 1947), English composer. He studied with R.R. Bennett and at the RAM: dir. of electronic studies since 1975.

Works incl. wind 5tet (1967); trumpet concerto (1969); Concertante (1969); *Piccola Sinfonia* (1971); horn concerto (1971); *Fiesta Sinfonica* (1972); Requiem for chorus and orch. (1975); concerto for clar. and strings (1976); *Cracovian Counterpoints* for 14 insts. (1977); Concerto for Orch. (1981); *Canterbury Psalms* for chorus and orch. (1981); *Sinfonia* for strings (1982); *Mass of the Sea* for soloists, chorus and orch. (1984).

Patti, Adelina (Adela Juana Maria) (b Madrid, 19 Feb 1843; d Craig-y-Nos, Wales, 27 Sep 1919), Italian soprano. Made her 1st appearance in NY at the age of 7, and after a brief period of study reappeared there in 1859, as Lucia. She went to London in 1861 and sang at CG, as Amina, and in Paris in 1862; appeared at CG until 1894 as Aida, Violetta, Rosina, Juliette and Zerlina. She sang for the last time in 1914.

Patti, Carlotta (b Florence, 30 Oct 1835; d Paris, 27 Jun 1889), Italian soprano, sister of prec. Studied pf. with Herz in Paris, but turned to singing and made her 1st appearance in NY in 1861.

Pattiera, Tino (b Cavtat, nr. Ragusa, 27 Jun 1890; d Cavtat, 24 Apr 1966), Italian tenor. He studied in Vienna and sang at Dresden 1915–41; took part in the Verdi renaissance and was successful as Andrea Chénier, Tannhäuser, Hermann and Bacchus. Berlin Staatsoper 1924–9; Chicago 1922–3.

Patzak, Julius (b Vienna, 9 Apr 1898; d Rottach-Egern, 26 Jan 1974), Austrian tenor. Studied at Vienna Univ. and School of Music, making his debut in Liberec in 1926, as Radames. Brno 1927–8; Munich 1928–45; Vienna 1945–60. His fine lyrical voice and great musical intelligence made him one of the great singers of the century. Well known as Florestan, Palestrina, Tamino and Lohengrin and often heard in concert (*Das Lied von der Erde* and Schmidt's *Das Buch mit sieben Siegeln*).

Pauk, György (b Budapest, 26 Oct 1936),

British violinist of Hungarian birth. Studied at the Liszt Academy, Budapest, and after winning important competitions in Genoa, Munich and Paris settled in London in 1961. Often plays Bartók; pf. trio with Peter Frankl (*q.v.*) and Ralph Kirshbaum (*q.v.*).

Pauke (Ger.; plur. *Pauken*) = Kettledrum.

Paukenmesse (Ger., 'Kettledrum Mass'), the name given to Haydn's Mass in C maj., comp. in 1796; perf. Vienna, 26 Dec 1796. The reason for the unusually prominent timpani, esp. in the *Agnus Dei*, is suggested by Haydn's own title, *Missa in tempore belli* ('Mass in time of war').

Paukenschlag, Sinfonie mit dem (Haydn). *See* **Surprise Symphony.**

Paukenwirbel, Sinfonie mit dem (Haydn). *See* **Drum-Roll Symphony.**

Paul Bunyan, choral operetta by Britten (lib. by W.H. Auden), prod. Columbia Univ., NY, 5 May 1941; revised 1974 and given on BBC 1 Feb 1976: this vers. prod. Aldeburgh, 4 Jun 1976.

Paul et Virginie. *See also* **Paolo e Virginia.**
Opera by R. Kreutzer (lib. by E.G.F. de Favières, based on Bernardin de Saint-Pierre's novel), prod. Paris, Comédie-Italienne, 15 Jan 1791.

Opera by Massé (lib. by J. Barbier and M. Carré, after Saint-Pierre), prod. Paris, Opéra National Lyrique, 15 Nov 1876.

Paulin et Virginie, opera by Lesueur (lib. by A.C. Dubreuil, after Saint-Pierre), prod. Paris, Théâtre Feydeau, 13 Jan 1794.

Paulli, Holger (Simon) (b Copenhagen, 22 Feb 1810; d Copenhagen, 23 Dec 1891), Danish conductor and composer. Made the vln. his prin. study, became violinist in the royal orch., leader in 1849 and cond. in 1864, also cond. orchestral and choral societies. In 1866, with Gade and J.P.E. Hartmann, he became one of the directors of the Cons.

Works incl. opera *Lodsen* (*The Pilot*, 1850); 13 ballets; overture and other orchestral works; vln. pieces; songs.

Paulus, the Ger. title of Mendelssohn's oratorio *St Paul.*

Pauly, Rosa (b Eperjes, 15 Mar 1894; d Tel Aviv, 14 Dec 1975), Hungarian soprano. She studied in Vienna and made her debut in Hamburg as Aida, 1918. In 1922 she joined Otto Klemperer at Cologne and sang there Rachel, Salome and the 1st Katya Kabanova in Germany. She moved with Klemperer to the Kroll Opera, Berlin, and sang Leonore, Donna Anna and Carmen, and in Krenek's *Der Diktator.* Vienna 1922–38; London, CG, and NY Met 1938–40 as Elektra, Venus and Ortrud. Banned by the Nazis in Europe, she sang in N. and S. America during the war. Other roles incl. Gutrune and Strauss's Helen and Dyer's Wife.

Paumann, Conrad (b Nuremberg, *c* 1410; d Munich, 24 Jan 1473), German organist, lutenist and composer. Although blind from birth, he was educ. by the Grundherr family of Nuremberg, learnt the organ and comp. and became organist at St Sebald's Church in 1440. In 1451 he was app. organist to Duke Albrecht III at Munich. He travelled as organist and also played other instruments.

Works incl. a *Fundamentum organisandi* (1452), or 'Principles of Comp.', laid out in keyboard tablature, which exists in several versions; organ arr. of monophonic and polyphonic pieces; and a Ger. song, 'Wiplich figur'.

Paumgartner, Bernhard (b Vienna, 14 Nov 1887; d Salzburg, 27 Jul 1971), Austrian musicologist and composer. Studied 1st with his parents, the critic Hans P. and the singer Rosa P., *née* Papier, and afterwards with Bruno Walter. He was dir. of the Mozarteum at Salzburg, 1917–38, and was one of the organizers of the Salzburg festivals; his eds. of *Idomeneo* and Cavalieri's *Rappresentazione* were prod. there in 1956 and 1968. He wrote mainly on Mozart.

Works incl. operas *Das heisse Eisen* (after Hans Sachs), *Die Höhle von Salamanca* (after Cervantes, 1923), *Rossini in Neapel* (1935), *Aus dem Leben eines Taugenichts* (after Eichendorff's novel); ballet *Pagoden*; incid. music to Shakespeare's *King Lear* and *Twelfth Night* (on old Eng. tunes), Goethe's *Faust*, Gozzi's *Turandot*, music for chorus and for orch.; songs.

Pause, the prolongation of a note, chord or rest beyond its normal value, indicated by the sign ⌢. In the 18th-cent. concerto it is regularly placed over the ⁶/₄ chord which precedes the cadenza. In a *da capo* it marks the point at which the piece ends after repetition of the first section. In the Ger. chorale or in works based on it, it marks the end of each line and is to be ignored in perf.

Pause (Ger.) = Rest.

Pause del silenzio (*Pauses of Silence*), 7 symph. expressions by Malipiero, prod. Rome, Augusteo, 27 Jan 1918.

Pauvre Matelot, Le (*The Poor Sailor*), opera by Milhaud (lib. by Cocteau), prod. Paris, Opéra-Comique, 16 Dec 1927.

Pavan (Eng.)
Pavane (Fr.) } an old dance, prob. of Italian origin, since one of its It. names is Padovana (i.e. 'from Padua'), dating back to at least the

16th cent. But the name may also come from Latin *pavo* (peacock), and the real orig. of the dance may be Span. It was normally in common time and moved at a stately pace (*see* illustration).

Works incl. incid. music for Ibsen's *Julian the Emperor*; *Canto de Navidad*, *Movimiento sinfónico*, Polytonal Variations, chamber and inst. music.

Peacock Variations, Vars. on a Hungarian

PAVANE

Byrd

The pavane was often followed by a Galliard based on the same thematic material.

Pavane pour une infante défunte (*Pavan for a dead Infanta*). A pf. piece by Ravel (1899); fp Paris, 5 Apr 1902. Orch. vers. 1910, fp Paris, 25 Dec 1910, cond. Casella.

Pavarotti, Luciano (b Modena, 12 Oct 1935), Italian tenor. After his debut in Reggio Emilia, 1961, he sang Rodolfo at CG in 1963; has returned for Elvino, Alfredo, Cavaradossi, Riccardo and Tonio. La Scala, Milan, from 1965. NY Met debut 1968, Rodolfo. Other roles incl. Edgardo, Nemorino, Enzo, Idamante (Glyndebourne), Idomeneo (Met, 1982) and Arturo. The outstanding lyric tenor of his generation.

Pavesi, Stefano (b Vaprio nr. Crema, 22 Jan 1779; d Crema, 28 Jul 1850), Italian composer. Studied at the Cons. dei Turchini, Naples, 1795–9, and became very popular as an opera comp. e.g. *La festa della rosa* (1808), *Fenella* (1831), *Ser Marcantonio*.

Payne, Anthony (b London, 2 Aug 1936), English composer and critic. He studied at Durham Univ. 1958–61; critic with *Daily Telegraph* from 1965. He has written on Schoenberg and British comps.

Works incl. *Phoenix Mass* for chorus and brass (1965–72); *Sonatas and Ricercars* for wind 5tet (1971); Concerto for Orch. (1975); *First Sight of her and After*, song cycle for 16 voices (texts by Hardy, 1975); *The World's Winter* for sop. and 8 insts. (text by Tennyson, 1976); string 4tet (1978); *Spring's Shining Wake* for chamber orch. (1981); *Songs and Dances* for strings (1984).

Paz, Juan Carlos (b Buenos Aires, 5 Aug 1901; d Buenos Aires, 25 Aug 1972), Argentinian composer. Studied in Buenos Aires and was one of the founders of the Group Renovación of progressive comps. in 1929, also founded a society for the perf. of new music.

Folk-Song, by Kodály; comp. 1938–9 to celebrate the 50th anniversary of the Concertgebouw Orch., fp Amsterdam, 23 Nov 1939, cond. Mengelberg.

Pears, Peter (b Farnham, 22 June 1910; d Orford, 3 Apr 1986), English tenor. Studied at RCM in London and later with Elena Gerhardt. He sang with the BBC and Glyndebourne choruses (1938) and made his stage debut in London in 1942. From 1943 to 1946 he was a member of SW, but much of his artistic career was assoc. with Britten's music; he created Peter Grimes (1945) and Albert Herring (1947), and was the first Captain Vere (*Billy Budd*), Essex (*Gloriana*), Quint (*The Turn of the Screw*), Flute (*A Midsummer Night's Dream*), Sir Philip Wingrave, and Aschenbach in *Death in Venice*. He also created roles in the fps of all three church parables. Other composers were not neglected and he created Pandarus in Walton's *Troilus and Cressida* (1954), and sang in the fps of Henze's *Novae de Infinito Laudes* (1963) and Lutosławski's *Paroles tissées* (1965). His intelligence and musicianship made him one of the great Lieder-singers of his day. Knighted 1978.

Pearsall, Robert (Lucas) (b Clifton, Bristol, 14 Mar 1795; d Wartensee, 5 Aug 1856), English composer. Studied law and was called to the Bar in 1821, but had already comp. In 1825 he settled at Mainz and studied with Panny there, devoting himself entirely to music. Another year in Eng., 1829–30, was his last, except for visits; he settled in Ger. for good, although he inherited a property at Willsbridge, Glos., in 1836. He sold this and bought Wartensee Castle on Lake Constance.

Works incl. church music (Angl. and Rom.), Requiem (1853–6); overture and chorus for Shakespeare's *Macbeth*; madrigals, part-songs.

Peasant a Rogue, The (*Selma Sedlák*),

comic opera by Dvořák (lib. by J.O. Veselý), prod. Prague, Cz. Theatre, 27 Jan 1878.

Peasant Cantata (*Mer hahn en neue Oberkeet = We have a new magistracy*), a secular cantata by Bach for solo voices, chorus and orch., comp. in 1742, to words in Saxon dialect. The music is noticeably rustic and comes as near to the manner of folksong as anything Bach ever wrote.

Pêcheurs, Les (*The Fishermen*), opera by Gossec (lib. by A.N. de La Salle d'Offémont), prod. Paris, Comédie-Italienne, 7 Jun 1766.

Pêcheurs de perles, Les (*The Pearl Fishers*), opera by Bizet (lib. by E. Cormon and M. Carré), prod. Paris, Théâtre Lyrique, 30 Sep 1863.

Ped., an abbr. used in the notation of pf. music to indicate the use of the sustaining pedal. (The use of the damping pedal is indicated by the words *una corda* [one string], or sometimes its abbr. *u.c.*) The abbr. also occurs in organ music written on 2 staves, to indicate which notes or passages are to be played on the pedals.

Pedal. (1) A sustained note in a polyphonic comp., generally but not invariably in the bass. It often occurs at the climax of a fugue.

(2) *See* **Pedals.**

Pedal Board, the keyboard of pedals.

Pedal Harp, the ordinary harp in current use, as distinct from the chromatic harp.

Pedal Notes, the fundamental notes of tromb. and other brass wind instruments, the normal compass of which consists of the upper harmonics.

Pedal Piano, a pf. specially constructed with a keyboard of pedals and used mainly for org. practice at home. Very little music was written expressly for it except by Schumann.

Pedal-Point, another name for the Pedal as applied to comp.

Pedalflügel (Ger.), the German name for the Pedal (grand) pf., *See* **Pedal Piano.**

Pedals, mechanical devices in certain instruments which require manipulation by the feet. Pedals may actually produce notes, as in the organ; they may be means of obtaining certain effects of tone, as in the sustaining and damping pf. pedals; or they may be used to alter the length, and thus the tuning, of strings, as in the harp.

Pedersøn, Mogens (b *c* 1585; d Copenhagen, *c* 1623), Danish singer and composer. Pupil of Melchior Borgrevinck in the royal chapel of Christian IV. After a visit to Venice, 1599–1600, he became a singer in the chapel. In 1605–9 he was at Venice again

studying with G . Gabrieli. In 1611–14 he was in Eng., but returned to Den. and became vice-director of the chapel in 1618.

Works incl. 31 madrigals for 5 voices, *Pratum spirituale* for voices; a book of Masses and motets, etc.

Pedrell, Carlos (b Minas, 16 Oct 1878; d Montrouge nr. Paris, 9 Mar 1941), Uruguayan composer of Spanish descent. Studied at Montevideo, with his uncle Felipe P. at Barcelona in 1898–1900 and then with d'Indy and Bréville at the Schola Cantorum in Paris. In 1906 he went to Buenos Aires, where he held var. official music posts and founded the Sociedad Nacional de Música in 1915. In 1921 he settled in Paris.

Works incl. operas *Ardid de amor* (1917) and *Cuento de abril*; ballet *Alleluia* (1936); *Une Nuit de Schéhérazade* (1908), *Danza y canción de Aixa* (1910), *En el estrado de Beatriz, Fantasia Argentina* and *Ouverture catalane* for orch.; choruses; songs with orch. and with pf.

Pedrell, Felipe (b Tortosa, 19 Feb 1841; d Barcelona, 19 Aug 1922), Spanish composer and musicologist, uncle of prec. He began to pub. works in 1871 and prod. his 1st opera in 1874, at Barcelona. From that time he taught music history and aesthetics at the Madrid Cons., but he settled at Barcelona in 1894, where he worked for the revival of old and the spread of new Span. music, ed. the complete works of Victoria and a collection of old Span. church music, also old stage and organ music, etc.

Works incl. operas *El último Abencerraje* (after Chateaubriand, 1868), *Quasimodo* (on Victor Hugo's *Notre-Dame de Paris*, 1875), *Cleopatra* (1881), *Los Pirineos* (1902), *La Celestina, El Conde Arnau* (1904), *Visión de Randa* and 4 early light operas; incid. music for Shakespeare's *King Lear*; Mass, Requiem and Te Deum; Symph. poems; string 4tet; pf. music; songs.

Pedrollo, Arrigo (b Montebello Vicentino, 5 Dec 1878; d Vicenza, 23 Dec 1964), Italian conductor and composer. Studied under his father and at the Milan Cons.

Works incl. operas *Juana* (1914), *La veglia* (after Synge's *The Shadow of the Glen*, 1920), *L'uomo che ride* (after Victor Hugo, 1920), *Delitto e castigo* (after Dostoievsky's *Crime and Punishment*, 1926), *L'amante in trappola* (1936) and 5 others, 3 mimodramas; 2 *Poemetti* for chorus and orch.; symph. in D min. (1900); chamber music.

Pedrotti, Carlo (b Verona, 12 Nov 1817; d Verona, 16 Oct 1893), Italian composer and conductor. Studied under Domenico Foroni at Verona and prod. his 1st opera there in 1840. From that time until 1845 he was cond. at the It. Opera of Amsterdam, and in 1845–68 he dir. the Nuovo and Filarmonico theatres at Verona. In the latter year he settled at Turin, where he became dir. of the Liceo Musicale, cond. at the Teatro Regio where he gave *Carmen* and *Lohengrin*, and operas by Massenet, Gounod and Goldmark. Founded popular orchestral concerts for classical music. He committed suicide.

Works incl. operas *Lina* (1840), *Matilde, La figlia dell' arciere* (1844), *Romea di Montfort* (1846), *Fiorina* (1851), *Il parrucchiere della reggenza* (1852), *Gelmina, Genoveffa del Brabante* (1854), *Tutti in maschera* (1856), *Isabella d'Aragona, Mazeppa* (1861), *Guerra in quattro, Marion Delorme* (after Hugo, 1865), *Il favorito, Olema la schiava* (1872).

Peer Gynt, incid. music for Ibsen's drama by Grieg, prod. Christiania, 24 Feb 1876. Grieg afterwards arr. 2 orch. suites from it, opp. 46 and 55.

Opera by Egk (lib. by comp.), prod. Berlin 24 Nov 1938; admired by Hitler.

Peerce, Jan (actually Jacob Pincus Perelmuth) (b New York, 3 Jun 1904; d New York, 17 Dec 1984), American tenor. After beginning his career as a dance-band violinist and singer he was engaged by Radio City Music Hall in 1933 and made his operatic debut in Phildelphia in 1938 as the Duke of Mantua. Sang largely at the NY Met (1941–66), as Cavaradossi, Rodolfo and, Faust; sang Florestan, Riccardo and Alfredo under Toscanini. The 1st US singer to appear with the Bolshoi co., Moscow (Alfredo, 1956).

Peerson, Martin (b March nr. Ely, *c* 1572; d London, buried 15 Jan 1651), English organist and composer. He took the B.Mus. at Oxford in 1613 and was soon afterwards app. organist and choirmaster at St Paul's Cathedral in London.

Works incl. church music, airs and dialogues for voices, *Mottects or Grave Chamber Musique* for voices and instruments on sonnets from Fulke Greville's *Caelica* (1630), fancies and almains for viols, virginal pieces, *Private Musick* (1620), and contributed to Leighton's *Teares* and Ravenscroft's psalter.

Peeters, Flor (b Tielen, 4 Jul 1903; d Antwerp, 4 Jul 1986), Belgian organist and composer. He studied at Mechlin and at Paris (under Dupré and Tournemire). In 1925 he was app. organist of Mechlin Cathedral. He held teaching posts at the Lemmens Institute, Mechlin, Ghent Cons.,

Tilburg Cons. (Hol.) and Antwerp Cons., of which he was app. dir. in 1952; remained until 1968. Made a baron by King Baudouin in 1971. He also toured widely as a recitalist and ed. several collections of early organ music.

Works incl. 8 Masses, Te Deum; organ concerto, pf. concerto, concerto for organ and pf.; about 200 organ works; chamber music, pf. works; songs.

Péghuilan, Aimeric de (b Toulouse), French troubadour of the 12th–13th cent. 54 poems and 6 melodies have survived.

Peinemann, Edith (b Mainz, 3 Mar 1937), German violinist. Has toured widely from 1956 in broad repertory. US debut 1962. Duos with Jörg Demus.

Peintre amoureux de son modèle, Le (*The Painter in Love with his Model*), opera by Duni (lib. by L. Anseaume), prod. Paris, Opéra-Comique, 26 Jul 1757.

Pélissier, Marie (b 1707; d Paris, 21 Mar 1749), French singer. She made her debut at the Paris Opéra in 1722 and in the next 10 years had much success there and at the Académie Royale. In 1733 she created Rameau's Aricia but the following year was obliged to leave Paris after a public scandal. She returned in 1735 and created leading roles in Rameau's *Indes Galantes, Castor et Pollux, Les fêtes d'Hébé* and *Dardanus*.

Pèlerins de le Mecque (Gluck). See **Rencontre imprévue.**

Pelléas et Mélisande, incid. music for Maurice Maeterlinck's play by Fauré, prod. London, Prince of Wales Theatre, 21 Jun 1898.

Opera by Debussy (lib. Maeterlinck's play, slightly altered), prod. Paris, Opéra-Comique, 30 Apr 1902.

Symph. poem on do. by Schoenberg, op. 5, comp. 1902, fp. Vienna, 26 Jan 1905.

Incid. music, orch suite in 9 movts., for do. by Sibelius, op. 46, comp. 1905, prod. Helsinki, 17 Mar 1905.

Pellegrini, Valeriano. See **Valeriano.**

Pellegrini, Vincenzo (b Pesáro; d Milan, 23 Aug 1640), Italian 16th–17th-cent. cleric and composer. He was a canon at Pesaro from 1594 and *maestro di cappella* at Milan Cathedral in 1611–31.

Works incl. Masses and other church music; org. canzonets; instrumental pieces in 3–4 parts; secular canzonets for voices.

Peñalosa, Francisco (b Talavera de la Reina, *c* 1470; d Seville, 1 Apr 1528), Spanish composer. He was choirmaster to Ferdinand the Catholic 1512–16 and singer in the

Julian Chapel in Rome under Leo X, 1517–21.

Works incl. 7 masses and other church music; secular songs for several voices.

Penderecki, Krzysztof (b Debica, 23 Nov 1933), Polish composer. Studied comp. with Malawaki and Wiechowicz in Kraków, graduating in 1958. His music has made frequent use of aleatory techniques and microtonal clusters, belonging to the present-day *avant-garde*; recent works have shown an awareness of traditional values and techniques.

Works incl. operas, *The Devils of Loudun* (1969), *Paradise Lost* (1978) and *Die schwarze Maske* (1986); *St Luke Passion* for speaker, 2 soloists, chorus and orch. (1963–6); *Stabat Mater* and *Psalms of David* for chorus and orch. (1963, 1958); *Emanations* for 2 string orchs. (1958); *Anaclasis* for strings and perc. (1960); *Threnody for the Victims of Hiroshima* for 52 strings (1960); *Fluorescences* for chamber ensemble (1961), *De natura sonoris* for orch. (1966); *Dies Irae*, for soloists, chorus and orch. (1967); *Utrenja* for soloists, chorus and orch. (1969–71); 2 cello concertos (1972, 1982); 2 symphs. (1973, 1980); *Canticum canticorum* (1972); Magnificat (1974), vln. concerto (1977); Te Deum (1979); Vla. concerto (1983); *Polish Requiem* (1983); 2 string 4tets (1960, 1968).

Penelope. See *Circe* for Keiser's opera.

Opera by Galuppi (lib. by P.A. Rolli), prod. London, King's Theatre, Haymarket, 12 Dec 1741.

Pénélope, opera by Fauré (lib. by R. Fauchois), prod. Monte Carlo, 4 Mar 1913; 1st Paris perf., Théâtre des Champs-Élysées, 10 May 1913. Other operas on Penelope myth by Monteverdi (*Il ritorno di Ulisse*, 1641), A. Scarlatti (1696), Piccinni (1785), Cimarosa (1795) and Liebermann (1954).

Penillion, an old form of Welsh song to the harp which was improvised (often the words as well as the music) as a counterpoint or descant to the harp part. It is still cultivated, but now tends to rely on tradition rather than improvisation.

Penna, Lorenzo (b Bologna, 1613; d Bologna 31 Oct 1693), Italian monk and composer. Entered the Carmelite order at Bologna (1630) and in 1672 became *maestro di cappella* at the Carmelite church of Parma, also a prof. of theology. He wrote treatises on counterpoint and figured bass, incl. *Primi albori musicali*, in 3 vols. (1672).

Works incl. Masses and other church music; *correnti francesi* for 4 instruments.

Penny for a Song, opera by Richard Rodney Bennett (lib. by C. Graham from John Whiting's play), prod. London, SW, 31 Oct 1967).

Penny Whistle, a small and rudimentary pipe of the Fife or Recorder type, also known as 'tin whistle', played vertically and having a small range of treble notes controlled by 6 finger-holes.

Pentatone (from Gr. = 5 notes), another name for the Pentatonic Scale.

Pentatonic, Scale, a scale of 5 notes; actually any 'gapped' scale that omits 2 of the normal 7 notes of the ordinary diatonic scales, but more partic. that represented by the black notes of the pf.

Penthesilea, opera by Schoeck (lib. by comp., based on Kleist's drama), prod. Dresden, 8 Jan 1927.

Symph. poem on do. by H. Wolf, comp. 1883–5.

Pepita Jiménez, opera by I. Albéniz (lib., in Eng., by F.B. Money-Coutts, based on a story by Juan Valera), prod. in Span., Barcelona, Liceo, 5 Jan 1896.

Pepping, Ernst (b Duisburg, 12 Sep 1901; d Berlin, 1 Feb 1981), German composer. Studied at the Hochschule für Musik in Berlin and devoted himself chiefly to the cultivation of Protestant church music being app. prof. at the Kirchenmusikschule at Spandau in 1947.

Works incl. setting of the 90th Psalm, unaccomp. motets, Te Deum, *Spandauer Chorbuch* containing vocal pieces for 2–6 voices for the whole eccles. year in 20 vols., 1934–8; 3 symphs. (1939–44), pf. concerto (1951), 2 org. concertos; 4 pf. sonatas; chamber music; songs.

Pepusch, Johann Christoph (John Christopher) (b Berlin, 1667; d London, 20 Jul 1752), German composer and theorist. App. to the Prus. court at the age of 14; emigrated 1st to Hol. and went to Eng. about 1700, where he settled in London for the rest of his life. Married Margherita de l'Épine in 1718. He arranged the music of *The Beggar's Opera* for John Gay in 1728.

Works incl. recitatives and songs for a pasticcio opera *Thomyris* (1707) and prob. others; incid. music for Colley Cibber's *Myrtillo* (1715); music for masques *Apollo and Daphne* (1716), *The Death of Dido* (1716), *The Union of the Sister Arts, Venus and Adonis* (1715); dramatic ode for the Peace of Utrecht; overture for *The Beggar's Opera* and arrs. for it and its sequel, *Polly,* and another ballad opera, *The Wedding* (1729); services, anthems and Lat. motets; cantatas to words by John Hughes (incl. *Alexis*) and others; odes, concertos, sonatas.

Pepys, Samuel (b London, 23 Feb 1633; d London, 26 May 1703), English official, diarist and amateur musician. Educ. at Huntingdon, St Paul's School in London and Cambridge Univ. He held several government posts and was last secretary to the Admiralty. He kept his diary from Jan 1660 to May 1669. It testifies to his interest in musical perfs. of all kinds and to his cultivation of music in his home. In 1665 he made a setting of the song 'Beauty retire' from Davenant's *Siege of Rhodes*, prod. in 1656 with music by H. Lawes, Locke and others.

Per arsin et thesin (Lat. = by rise and fall), imitation by contrary motion. One part goes up where the other goes down (see illustration).

burgh Festival. Frequently conducts from the keyboard and has recorded all the Mozart concertos.

Percussion, a term used in harmony for the actual incident of a discord, after its Preparation and before its Resolution.

Percussion Instruments. All instruments played by being struck are called perc. instruments, incl. all varieties of drums, bells, cymbals, triangles, gongs, etc., also some in which the perc. is prod. by the intermediary of a keyboard, such as the Celesta. These last instruments, as also bells, xylophone and kettledrums, prod. notes of definite pitch; others prod. sound without pitch. The piano is classed as a perc. instrument, particularly when used in the orchestra (e.g. by Stravinsky).

Perdendosi (It. = losing itself), a direction

Bach, *The Art of Fugue*

PER ARSIN ET THESIN

Perabo, Ernst (b Wiesbaden, 14 Nov 1845; d Boston, Mass., 29 Nov 1920), German pianist and composer. A very gifted pianist as a child, he was taken to NY in 1852, studied there and from 1848 in Ger., finishing at the Leipzig Cons. He returned to USA in 1865 and soon afterwards settled in Boston.

Works incl. studies and pieces for pf., e.g. *Pensées* containing an impression of the soliloquies in *Hamlet*, 10 transcriptions from Sullivan's *Iolanthe*, concert fantasies on Beethoven's *Fidelio*, etc.

Perahia, Murray (b New York, 19 Apr 1947), American pianist and conductor. He studied at Mannes College and with Horszowski and Balsam. Carnegie Hall debut 1968. He won the Leeds International Comp. in 1972; London debut 1973. From 1982 he has been co-artistic dir. of the Alde-

indicating that the sound of a note or passage is to become gradually weaker until it fades away.

Perez, Davide (b Naples, 1711; d Lisbon, 30 Oct 1778), Spanish composer. Studied at the Cons. di Santa Maria di Loreto at Naples and prod. his 1st opera, *La nemica amante*, in 1735. He became *maestro di cappella* to Prince Naselli at Palermo and in 1752 went to Lisbon, where he became attached to the royal chapel and the new Opera opened in 1755.

Works incl. operas *Siroe* (1740), *I travestimenti amorosi* (1740), *L'eroismo di Scipione* (1741), *Astartea* (1743), *Medea* (1744), *L'isola incantata*, *La clemenza di Tito* (1749), *Semiramide* (1750), *Alessandro nell' Indie* (1755), *Demetrio* (1766), *Demofoonte*, *Soimano* (1757), *Il ritorno d'Ulisse in Itaca* (1774) and others, many to libs. by Metastasio; *Mattutino de' morti*, Masses and other church music; oratorio *Il martirio di San Bartolomeo*, etc.

Perfall, Karl von (b Munich, 29 Jan 1824; d Munich, 14 Jan 1907), German composer and administrator. Studied at Leipzig with Moritz Hauptmann, returned to Munich in 1850 and founded an oratorio society in 1854. Became Intendant of the court music in 1864 and also of the court theatres in 1867, and had personal differences with Wagner but mounted 700 perfs. of the operas in 25 years.

Works incl. operas *Sakuntala* (after Kalidasa, 1853), *Das Konterfei* (1863), *Raimondin (Melusine,* 1881) and *Junker Heinz* (1886); incid. music for Shakespeare's *Pericles*; fairy tales for solo voices, chorus and orch; *Dornröschen, Undine* (after Fouqué) and *Rübezahl*; choruses, songs.

Perfect Cadence, a cadence which conclusively leads to the common chord of the tonic, either by a step from the Dominant to the Tonic in the bass (Authentic cadence) or from the Sub-dominant to the Tonic (Plagal cadence). In Eng. the term is generally confined to the former. *See* **Cadence.**

Perfect Fool, The, opera by Holst (lib. by comp.), prod. London, CG, 14 May 1923.

Perfect Intervals, those intervals which do not possess alternative major and minor forms, but become Augmented or Diminished by being enlarged or reduced by a semitone, viz. 4ths, 5ths and 8ves, also their repetitions beyond the 8ve, i.e. 11ths, etc.

Performing Practice, the study of how music is or was performed, normally with the emphasis on how a particular notation is to be realized in sound taking account of the history of instruments and how they were played, the available ensembles, notational practice, improvisation, articulation, temperament and tempo. While this most obviously concerns music of the Baroque era and earlier, it also takes account of considerable changes in, for example, orchestral sound over the past few decades.

Pergolesi, Giovanni Battista (b Jesi nr. Ancona, 4 Jan 1710; d Pozzuoli nr. Naples, 16 Mar 1736), Italian composer. Studied in Jesi and from 1725 under Greco, Vinci and Durante at the Cons. dei Poveri di Gesù Cristo in Naples. His earliest works were sacred pieces, but he made his debut as a comp. for the stage in 1731, and 2 years later prod. the comic intermezzo *La serva padrona* (perf. between the acts of his serious opera *Il prigionier superbo*), which was to be decisive in the history of *opera buffa. Maes-*

tro di cappella to the Prince of Stigliano from 1732, he entered the service of the Duke of Maddaloni *c* 1734, but returned to Naples the next year, becoming organist to the court. In Feb 1736 he retired on grounds of ill health to the Capuchin monastery in Pozzuoli, where he completed his last work, the *Stabat Mater*, just before his death.

Works incl. operas *Salustia* (1732), *Il prigionier superbo* (1733), *Adriano in Siria* (1734), *L'Olimpiade, Lo frate 'nnamorato Flaminio* (1735); intermezzi *La serva padrona, Livietta e Tracollo* (1737); oratorios *La morte di S. Giuseppe* (1731), *La Conversione di S. Guglielmo d'Acquitania* (1731), *La morte d'Abel*, etc.; Masses, *Stabat Mater* for soprano and alto soloists and strings (1736), settings of *Salve Regina* (1736), and other church music; chamber music; keyboard music etc. There are also many other works attrib. to Pergolesi which are of doubtful authenticity.

Peri, Jacopo (b Rome, 20 Aug 1561; d Florence, 12 Aug 1633), Italian singer and composer. Pupil of Cristoforo Malvezzi, a canon at the church of San Lorenzo at Florence and *maestro di cappella* to the Medici family. Peri himself became attached to their court from about 1588, later as *maestro di cappella* and chamberlain. He became a member of the progressive artists grouped round Count Giovanni Bardi with Caccini, Corsi, V. Galilei and the poet Ottavio Rinuccini. In their endeavour to revive Gk. drama with the kind of music they imagined to be genuine Gk. they stumbled on the invention of opera. His *Dafne*, begun 1595, is considered to be the earliest opera.

Works incl. operas *Dafne* (1598), *Euridice* (1600), *Tetide* (comp. 1608), *Adone* (comp. 1611), tournament with music *La precedenza delle dame* (1625); parts of operas (with others) *La guerra d'amore* and *Flora* (with Gagliano); several ballets; *Lamento d'Iole* for soprano and insts., madrigals, sonnets and arias in *Songbook* of 1609.

Péri, La, (ballet (*poème dansé*) by Dukas; prod. Paris, Théâtre du Châtelet, 22 Apr 1912.

Périchole, La, operetta by Offenbach (lib. by H. Meilhac and L. Halévy, based on Mérimée's *Le Carrosse du Saint-Sacrement*), prod. Paris, Théâtre des Variétés, 6 Oct 1868.

Périgourdine, a French country dance from the region of Périgord, known to musicians from at least the 18th cent. Its music is in 6–8 time.

Perkowski, Piotr (b Oweczacze, 17 Mar

1901), Polish composer. Studied with Statkowski and Szymanowski at the Warsaw Cons. and later with Roussel in Paris, where in 1927 he founded a society of young Pol. comps. with Czapski, Labuński and Wiechowicz.. He returned to Pol. and in 1935 became director of the Torum Cons. Works incl. ballets *Swantewid, Klementyna*; 2 symphs. (1925, 1963), sinfonietta for small orch.; pf. concerto, 2 vln. concertos (1938, 1960); string 4tet; instrumental pieces; choral works; songs.

Perle, George (b Bayonne, NJ, 6 May 1915), American composer and theorist. Krenek was among his teachers; taught at Queens College, NY, from 1961; retired 1984. His studies have centred on the Second Viennese School; books incl. *Twelve-tone tonality* (1977).

Works incl. *3 Movements* for orch. (1960), cello concerto (1966), *A Short Symphony* (fp 1980); 3 wind 5tets (1956–67), 7 string 4tets (1938–73).

Perle du Brésil, La (*The Pearl of Brazil*), opera by Fél. David (lib. by J.J. Gabriel and S. Saint-Étienne), prod. Paris, Théâtre Lyrique, 22 Nov 1851.

Perlea, Jonel (b Orgrada, 13 Dec 1900; d New York, 29 Jul 1970), Rumanian conductor. Studied in Munich and Leipzig, making his debut in 1923. From 1934 to 1944 he was music dir. of the Bucharest Opera and cond. in leading opera houses both in Europe and Amer.; in 1949–50 he cond. *Tristan, Carmen* and *Rigoletto* at the NY Met.

Perlemuter, Vlado (b Kaunas, Lithuania, 26 May 1904), French pianist of Polish parentage. He studied at the Paris Cons. with Cortot; prof. of comp. there from 1950. He studied Ravel's pf. music with the comp. in the 1920s; has also specialized in Chopin.

Perlman, Itzhak (b Tel Aviv, 31 Aug 1945), Israeli violinist. Afflicted with polio from infancy but studied at the Tel Aviv Cons. and moved to NY (Juilliard School) in 1958. Carnegie Hall debut 1963; winner, Leventritt Competition 1964. London debut 1968. Has appeared with all leading orchs. and in chamber music with Barenboim and Zukerman. Brooklyn College, NY, from 1975.

Pernerstorfer, Alois (b Vienna, 3 Jun 1912; d Vienna, 12 May 1978), Austrian bassbaritone. Debut Graz 1936, as Biterolf. He appeared at the Vienna Volksoper during the war and at the Staatsoper from 1945. Salzburg from 1948, Zurich 1947–51. Glyndebourne 1951, as Leporello and Mozart's Figaro. At La Scala he sang Alberich under Furtwängler (also recorded).

Other roles incl. Pogner, Marke and Ochs.

Perosi, Lorenzo (b Tortona, 20 Dec 1872; d Rome, 12 Dec 1956), Italian priest and composer. Studied at Milan and Ratisbon, and among other appts. became choirmaster at St Mark's, Venice, 1894, and music dir. of the Sistine Chapel in Rome, 1898. In 1905 he was nominated perpetual master of the Pontifical Chapel.

Works incl. 33 Masses, 4 Requiems, *Stabat Mater*, a Te Deum and much other church music; oratorios *The Transfiguration* (1898), *The Raising of Lazarus* (1898), *The Resurrection, Moses, Leo the Great, The Last Judgment* (1904) and *Il sogno interpretato; Florence, Rome, Venice* and *Bologna* from 10 planned symphs. on the names of It. cities; organ works.

Perotinus Magnus (now sometimes called Pérotin) (b c 1160; d c 1205), French composer and scholar. *Maître de chapelle* of the church of the Blessed Virgin Mary (later Notre-Dame Cathedral). He is said to have revised the *liber organi de graduali* of Leoninus, and comp. *Organa* in as many as 4 parts. His best known *organa* are on the Christmas and St Stephen's Day Graduals, (1198, 1199).

Perotti, Giovanni Agostino (b Vercelli, 12 Apr 1769; d Venice, 28 Jun 1855), Italian composer. Studied under his brother G.D.P. and Mattei, visited Vienna in 1795 and London in 1798, settled in Venice c 1800, became 2nd *maestro di cappella* at St Mark's, 1812, and 1st in succession to Furlanetto, 1817.

Works incl. operas, e.g. *La contadina nobile* (1795), ballets; church music, oratorios, e.g. Metastasio's *Abele* (1794); pf. sonatas.

Perotti, Giovanni Domenico (b Vercelli, 20 Jan 1761; d Vercelli, 24 Mar 1825), Italian composer, brother of prec. Pupil of G.B. Martini and *maestro di cappella* of Vercelli Cathedral from 1779. Comp. operas, e.g. *Agesilao re di Sparta* (1789) and *Zemira e Gandarte* (1787).

Perpetual Canon, a canon in which each part begins again as soon as it is finished, the other parts being at that moment at other stages of their progress. Since even a perpetual canon must finish sooner or later, however, it is broken off at a point agreed to by the perf.

Perpetuum mobile (Lat. = perpetually in motion). *See* **Moto perpetuo**.

Perrin, Pierre (b Lyons, c 1620; d Paris, buried 26 Apr 1675), French author, who in 1669–72 prec. Lully in holding the patent for the management of the Académie de Musique (Opéra) in Paris. Librettist for Cambert and others. *See also* **Boësset (J.-B.)** (*Mort d'Adonis*), **Pomone** (Cambert).

Perron, Karl (b Frankenthal, 3 Jun 1858; d Dresden, 15 Jul 1928), German bass-baritone. He studied in Berlin and made his debut in Leipzig, as Wolfram. During his career at Dresden (1892–1924) he created Strauss's Jochanaan, Orestes and Ochs. At Bayreuth (1889–1904) he sang Amfortas, Wotan and Gunther.

Perry, George Frederick (b Norwich, 1793; d London, 4 Mar 1862), English violinist, organist, conductor and composer. Learnt music as a choir-boy at Norwich Cathedral and later became violinist at the theatre there. Settled in London as cond. of the Haymarket Theatre, 1822, was organist at Quebec Chapel and became leader and later cond. of the Sacred Harmonic Society.

Persée (*Perseus*), opera by Lully (lib. by Quinault), prod. Paris, Opéra, 18 Apr 1682.

Perséphone, melodrama for the stage or concert-room by Stravinsky (lib. by André Gide), prod. Paris, Opéra, 30 Apr 1934.

Persiani (*née* **Tacchinardi**), **Fanny** (b Rome, 4 Oct 1812; d Neuilly nr. Paris, 3 May 1867), Italian soprano. Studied under her father, Niccolò Tacchinardi, and appeared at his private pupils' theatre near Florence at the age of 11. Married the comp. Giuseppe P. in 1830 and made her debut at Leghorn in 1832; created Donizetti's Lucia in 1835. She 1st went to Paris in 1837 and to London in 1838, debut as Amina; returned until 1849. Vienna 1837–44 in operas by Donizetti and Verdi.

Persiani, Giuseppe (b Recanati, 11 Nov 1799; d Paris, 14 Aug 1869), Italian composer, husband of prec. He settled as singing-master in Paris.

Works incl. operas *Inez di Castro* (1835, a vehicle for Malibran), *Eufemio di Messina*, *Il fantasma* (1843), *L'orfana savoiarda* (1846).

Persichetti, Vincent (b Philadelphia, 6 Jun 1915; d Philadelphia, 14 Aug 1987), American composer. Studied pf. with A. Jonás and O. Samaroff, comp. with P. Nordoff and Roy Harris, cond. with Fritz Reiner. From 1942 to 1948 he taught comp. at the Philadelphia Cons., and then at Juilliard, NY. His *Lincoln Address* of 1973 was scheduled for fp at Nixon's inauguration in Washington; the perf. was postponed owing to an allusion to the Vietnam War.

Works incl. operas *Parable XX* (1976) and *Sibyl* (1984); 9 symphs. (1942–71); ballet *King Lear*; 14 serenades for different instrumental groups; *The Hollow Men* for tpt. and string orch.; pf. concerto; 2 pf. 5tets, 4 string 4tets (1939–72); 12 pf. sonatas, 6 pf. sonatinas; vocal music.

Persuis, Louis (Luc Loiseau) de (b Metz, 4 Jul 1769; d Paris, 20 Dec 1819), French violinist and composer. Studied under his father, member of the music staff at Metz Cathedral, became a violinist in the theatre orch. and went to Avignon following an actress with whom he had fallen in love. There he studied further, went to Paris, appeared at the Concert Spirituel in 1787, again became a theatre violinist, in 1793 at the Opéra. In 1795–1802 he was vln. prof. at the Cons., in 1810–15 court cond. to Napoleon, inspector of music in 1814 and manager of the Opéra in 1817.

Works incl. operas *La Nuit espagnole* (1791), *Estelle* (1794), *Phanor et Angéla* (1798), *Fanny Morna*, *Le Triomphe de Trajan* (with Lesueur, 1807), *Jérusalem délivrée* (after Tasso), *Les Dieux rivaux* (with Berton, R. Kreutzer and Spontini, 1816), and others; ballets *Nina, ou La Folle par amour* (1813) and 5 others (some with R. Kreutzer); church music; cantatas *Chant de victoire*, *Chant français* and others.

Persymfans (abbr. of Pervyi Symfonitchesky Ansamble = Rus. for 1st symph. ensemble), a conductorless orch. organized in Moscow and making its 1st appearance there on 13 Feb 1922. It was later discontinued, not from any lack of success, but because it was found that its principle involved an enormous amount of discussion and rehearsing.

Perti, Giacomo (Antonio) (b nr. Bologna, 6 Jun 1661; d Bologna, 10 Apr 1756), Italian composer. Studied with his uncle Lorenzo P., a priest at San Petronio at Bologna, and later with Petronio Franceschini. After visits to Venice and Modena in the 1680s, he became *maestro di cappella* at San Pietro at Bologna in 1690 and of San Petronio in 1696.

Works incl. operas *Oreste* (1685), *Marzio Coriolano*, *L'incoronazione di Dario* (1686), *Teodora*, *Il furio Camillo* (1692), *Pompeo*, *Nerone fatto Cesare* (1710), *Penelope la casta* (1696), *Fausta*, *Rodelinda* (1710), *Lucio Vero* (1717) and 17 others; *Missa solemnis* for solo voices, chorus and orch., other Masses, motets, etc.; oratorio *Abramo* (1683), 4 Passion oratorios and several others.

Pertile, Aureliano (b Montagnana nr. Padua, 9 Nov 1885; d Milan, 11 Jan 1952), Italian tenor. Studied with Orefice, making his debut in Vincenza in 1911. After further study he sang at the NY Met from 1921 to 1922, at La Scala, Milan, from 1921 to 1937 as Lohengrin, Chénier, Radames, Riccardo and Manrico; he took part in the fps of *Nerone* by Boito (1924) and Mascagni (1935). CG, London, from 1927 to 1931. On his retirement he taught at the Milan Cons.

Pes (Lat. = foot), in medieval English music the lowest part of a vocal comp. in several parts, partic. one that consists of a recurrent figure, as in 'Sumer is icumen in'.

Pesante (It. = heavy, weighty), a direction indicating that a passage is to be played very firmly.

Pescatrici, Le (*The Fisher Girls*), opera by Bertoni (lib. by Goldoni), prod. Venice, Teatro San Samuele, 26 Dec 1751.

Opera by Haydn (lib. ditto), prod. Eszterháza, Sep 1770.

Pescetti, Giovanni Battista (b Venice, *c* 1704; d Venice, 20 Mar 1766), Italian composer. A pupil of Lotti, he prod. his first opera, *Nerone detronato*, in Venice in 1725. From 1737 to 1745 he lived in London, and was for a time music dir. of the CG and King's theatres. App. 2nd organist at St Mark's, Venice, in 1762.

Works incl. operas *Gli odi delusi del sangue* (1728), *Dorinda* (1729, both with Galuppi), *Demetrio* (1732), *Diana ed Endimione* (1739), *La conquista del vello d'oro*, *Tamerlano* (with Cocchi, 1754) and *c* 20 others; oratorio *Gionata*; church music; harpsichord sonatas.

Pesenti, Michele (b Verona, *c* 1475; d after 1524), Italian priest and composer. Wrote *frottole*, canzonettas, madrigals, etc.

Peter and the Wolf, symphonic tale for narrator and orch. by Prokofiev (text by comp.), op.67; comp. 1936, fp Moscow, 2 May 1936.

Peter Grimes, opera by Britten (lib. by M. Slater, based on part of Crabbe's poem *The Borough*), prod. London, SW, 7 Jun 1945.

Peter Ibbetson, opera by Deems Taylor (lib. by comp. and C. Collier, based on George du Maurier's novel), prod. NY Met, 7 Feb 1931.

Peter Schmoll und seine Nachbarn (*P.S. and his Neighbours*), opera by Weber (lib. by J. Turk, based on a novel by Carl Gottlob Cramer), prod. Augsburg, Mar 1803.

Peters, C.F., a music pub. firm founded at Leipzig in 1814 by Carl Friedrich P. (1779–1827), who bought the Bureau de Musique founded by F.A. Hoffmeister and A. Kühnel in 1800. London branch estab. 1938; NY branch 1948. In 1950 the firm was re-estab. in Frankfurt.

Peters, Roberta (b New York, 4 May 1930), American soprano. Studied in NY with W. Hermann, making her debut at the NY Met in 1950 as Zerlina. She remained as one of America's leading coloratura singers for almost 30 years; other roles incl. Gilda Queen of Night, Violetta, Manon and Lucia.

Petite messe solennelle (*Little Solemn Mass*), Mass setting by Rossini for soloists, chorus, 2 pf. and harmonium; comp. 1863, fp Paris 14 Mar 1864. Arranged with full orch., 1867, fp Paris, 24 Feb 1869.

Petite Symphonie Concertante, work by Frank Martin for harp, harpsichord, pf. and double string orch.; comp. 1944–5, fp Zurich, 17 May 1946. Version with full orch. in place of solo insts., Symphonie Concertante, 1946.

Petites Liturgies de la Presence Divine, Trois. *See* Trois Petites Liturgies.

Petits Riens, Les (*The Little Nothings*), ballet by Mozart, K299b (choreog. by Jean Noverre), written in Paris and prod. there, Opéra, 11 Jun 1778.

Petrarch (Francesco Petrarca) (1304–1374), Italian poet. There are 3 sonnets set as songs by Schubert in trans. by A.W. Schlegel and 3 *Sonetti di Petrarca* in Liszt's *Années de Pèlerinage* for pf., arr. in 1846 from earlier settings of the poems for voice and pf. Many settings by It. 16th–17th cent. madrigalists.

Petrassi, Goffredo (b Zagarolo nr. Palestrina 16 Jul 1904), Italiian composer. Learnt music as a child in the singing-school of the church of San Salvatore in Lauro at Rome, but did not study systematically until the age of 21, when he entered the Cons. di Santa Cecilia, gaining comp. and org. prizes there. He also had advice from Casella, and in 1933 he made his comp. debut with a perf. of his orchestral Partita at the Augusteo, which was later given at the ISCM festival in Amsterdam. His music makes individual use of 12-note methods.

Works incl. operas *Il Cordovano* (1949) and *La morte dell' aria* (1950); ballet *Il ritratto di Don Chisciotte* (after Cervantes, 1947); incid. music for A. Aniante's play *Carmen*; Psalm ix for chorus and orch.; *Il coro dei morti* and *Noche oscura* for chorus (1940); Magnificat for voice and orch. (1940).

Partita, Passacaglia, concertos and concert overture for orch. (1933–72); *Tre Cori* for chamber orch.; pf. concerto; *Lamento d'Arianna* (Rinuccini) for voice and chamber orch. (1936), *Introduzione ed Allegro* for vln. and 11 insts. (1933).

Sinfonia, Siciliana e Fuga for string 4tet; *Preludio, Aria e Finale* for cello and pf.; toccata for pf., *Siciliana e Marcetta* for pf. duet; song cycle *Colori del tempo* and other songs.

Petrella, Enrico (b Palermo, 10 Dec 1813; d Genoa, 7 Apr 1877), Italian composer. Studied at Naples with Zingarelli and others and prod. his 1st opera, *Il diavolo color di rosa*, there in 1829.

Works incl. operas *Le precauzioni* (1851), *Elena di Tolosa* (1852), *La contessa d'Amalfi* (on Feuillet's *Dalila*), *Ione* (1858), *Marco Visconti, Giovanna II di Napoli* (1869), *I promessi sposi* (after Manzoni, 1869), *Bianca Orsini* (1874) and many others.

Petri, Egon (b Hanover, 23 Mar 1881; d Berkeley, Calif., 27 May 1962), American pianist of Dutch origin, son of the violinist Henri Wilhelm Petri (1856–1914). He studied both the vln. and the pf. (the latter with Busoni). From 1899 to 1901 he was a violinist in the Dresden Opera orch. He first appeared as a solo pianist in 1902. He taught at the RMCM, 1905–11, and subsequently in Berlin, Poland and Basle. He lived in Poland from 1926 to 1939. In 1939 he settled in the USA, teaching at Cornell Univ., from 1940 to 1947 and at Mills Coll., Oakland, from 1947 to 1957. He excelled as an interpreter of pf. music of Liszt and Busoni.

Petrić, Ivo (b Ljubljana, 16 Jan 1931), Slovenian composer. Studied at Ljubljana Academy. Early music was neo-classical in inspiration, later employed aleatory techniques and tone clusters.

Works incl. 3 symphs. (1954, 1957, 1960), Concerto Grosso (1955), Concertante music (1962), *Dialogues Concertantes* for cello and orch. (1972), *3 Images* for vln. and orch. (1973), *Fresque Symphonique* (1973); 3 wind 5tets, chamber concerto (1966), *Quatuor 69* for string 4tet.

Petridis, Petro (b Nigdé, Asia Minor, 23 Jul 1892; d Athens, 17 Aug 1977), Greek composer. Studied at Constantinople and in Paris.

Works incl. opera *Zemfyra* (1923–5); ballet; 5 symphs. (1928–51), dramatic symph. *Digenis Afrikas*, Gk. and Ionian Suites, Elegiac Overture, *Prelude, Aria and Fugue* for orch.; 2 pf. concertos, cello concerto, concerto grosso for wind insts., vln. concerto (1977); pf. trio; 2 *Modal Suites* for pf.; songs.

Petrov, Ossip Afanassievich (b Eli-

savetgrad, 15 Nov 1806; d St Petersburg, 11 Mar 1878), Russian bass. Discovered singing in the market at Kursk in 1830, he was brought to St Petersburg and made his 1st stage appearance there that year, as Sarastro. In 1836 he created the part of Ivan Sussanin in Glinka's *Life for the Tsar*, also created Ruslan (1842) and Varlaam in *Boris Godunov* (1874).

Petrucci, Ottaviano dei (b Fossombrone nr. Ancona, 18 Jun 1466; d Venice, 7 May 1539), Italian music printer. He estab. himself at Venice *c* 1491 and held a patent for the pub. of music in tablature and notes in 1498–1511, when he returned to Fossombrone to continue business there. He issued many famous collections of Masses, motets, *frottole*, etc.

Petrus de Cruce (b ? Amiens, *c* 1250), 13th-cent. composer, possibly from Amiens. His mensural theory is expounded in the works of Robert de Handlo and J. Hanboys. 2 motets from the Montpellier MS. can be assigned to him on the authority of the *Speculum Musicum* by Jacobus of Liège.

Petrushka, ballet by Stravinsky (scenario by comp. and A. Benois; choreography by Fokin), prod. Paris, Théâtre du Châtelet, 13 Jun 1911. New vers. in 4 parts with 15 movts. written 1946; 3 dances for pf. 1921, ded. Arthur Rubinstein; *Russian Dance, In P.'s Cell, The Shrove-tide Fair.*

Petrželka, Vilém (b Královo Pole, 10 Sep 1889; d Brno, 10 Jan 1967), Czech composer. He studied with Novák in Prague and Janáček at Brno, became a cond. at Pardubice and in 1919 went to Brno as prof. at the Cons.

Works incl. symph. drama *Sailor Nicholas* (19?.?); *Hymn to the Sun* for chorus and orch.; Symph. (1956), *Eternal Return*, 2 suites, Dramatic Overture for orch.; 5 string 4tets (1909–15), fantasy and suite for string 4tet; sonata and *Intimate Hours* for vln. and pf.; pf. pieces; songs; part-songs, etc.

Pettersson, Gustaf Allan (b Västra Ryd, 19 Sep 1911; d Stockholm, 20 Jun 1980), Swedish composer. Studied at Stockholm Academy and after playing vla. in local orch. 1940–51 studied further, in Paris, with Honegger and Leibowitz. Best known for 16 symphs. (1950–80), influenced by Mahler. Also wrote 3 concertos for string orch. (1949–57), vln. concerto (1977); *Vox humana*, 18 songs for vocal soloists, chorus and strings (texts by American Indians, 1974); 7 sonatas for 2 vlns. (1952).

Petto (It.), Chest. Hence *voce di petto,* Chest Voice.

Petyrek, Felix (b Brno, 14 May 1892; d Vienna, 1 Dec 1951), Czech pianist and composer. Studied with his father, an organist and cond. and with Adler in Vienna for theory, with Godowsky and Sauer for pf. and with Schreker for comp. Later he taught at Salzburg, Berlin, Athens and Stuttgart.

Works incl. operas *Die arme Mutter und der Tod* (1923), *Der Garten des Paradieses* (1942); pantomime *Comedy*; incid. music for Hans Reinhart's *Der Schatten*; *Das heilige Abendmahl*, *Litanei* and other cantatas, 3 sacred madrigals; 6tet (1922); *Kammerlieder* for voice and chamber music; vln. and pf. sonata; studies, rhapsodies and folksongs for pf.

Pevernage, André (b Harlebeke nr. Courtrai, 1543; d Antwerp, 30 Jul 1591), Flemish composer. After holding an appt. at Courtrai, 1565–85, he moved to Antwerp *c* 1587 and became choirmaster at the cathedral, holding the post until his early death. Apart from cultivating church music he held weekly concerts at his house.

Works incl. *Cantiones sacrae* and other church music; madrigals and 5 vols. of *chansons*; ode to St Cecilia.

Peyro, José, Spanish composer of early 18th cent.

Works incl. incid. music to Calderón's *El jardin de Falerina* and Lope de Vega's *Selva sin amor*.

Pezzo (It., plur. *pezzi*). A piece of music.

Pfeifertag, Der (*The Piper's Day*), opera by Schillings (lib. by F. von Sporck), prod. Schwerin, 26 Nov 1899.

Pfitzner, Hans (b Moscow, 5 May 1869; d Salzburg, 22 May 1949), German composer and conductor. The family moved to Frankfurt, where Pfitzner's father, a violinist, became music director of the municipal theatre. He studied pf. with Kwast and comp. with Knorr at the Cons. there. In 1893 he gave a 1st concert of his own works in Berlin, and after some teaching and cond. appts. he became prof. at the Stern Cons. there in 1897, 1st cond. at the Theater des Westens in 1903. He also cond. the Kaim orch. at Munich and the Opera at Strasbourg. After the success of his *Palestrina* in 1917 he devoted himself mainly to comp., but wrote many essays and pamphlets attacking modern music, esp. Busoni, and defending Romantic and Germanic ideals. He was also a political conservative and wrote *Krakauer Begrüssung* in honour of Hans Frank, Nazi governor of Poland.

Works incl. operas *Der arme Heinrich* (1895), *Die Rose vom Liebesgarten* (1901);

Christelflein (1906), *Palestrina*, *Das Herz* (1931); incid. music to Ibsen's *Feast at Solhaug* (1890) and Kleist's *Käthchen von Heilbronn* (1905); cantatas *Von deutscher Seele* (Eichendorff, 1922), *Das dunkle Reich* (1930) and others.

3 symphs., scherzo for orch.; pf. concerto (1921), vln. concerto (1923), 2 cello concertos; ballads and songs for voice, and orch.; 4 string 4tets (1886–1942), pf. 5tet, pf. trio; vln. and pf. sonata, cello and pf. sonata; 106 Lieder (1884–1931).

Phaedra, dramatic cantata for mezzo and orch. by Britten (text by R. Lowell, after Racine's *Phèdre*); comp. 1975, fp Aldeburgh, 16 Jun 1976, with Janet Baker.

Phaëton, opera by Lully (lib. by Quinault), prod. Versailles, 9 Jan and 1st perf. Paris, 27 Apr 1683.

Symph. poem by Saint-Saëns, fp Paris, 7 Dec 1873.

Phagotus (= It. *fagotto* = faggot, bundle), an early instrument developed from the Serbian bagpipe by Afranio Albonese of Pavia early in the 16th cent. It consisted of 2 pipes like those of an organ, supplied with wind from hand bellows, but their pitch was variable by their being fingered on holes.

Phalèse, Flemish family of music printers:

1. Pierre P. (b Louvain, *c* 1510; d Louvain, 1573 or 4), began to pub. music at Louvain, in 1545.

2. Corneille (or Cornelius) P. (b Louvain, ?), son of prec., who gave up his share in the business to his brother (3) at an early date.

3. Pierre P. (b Louvain, *c* 1550; d Antwerp, 13 Mar 1629), brother of prec., who moved to Antwerp to join his father's partner, Jean Bellère, there. Pub many madrigal books, incl. works by Frescobaldi, Croce, Monteverdi, Marenzio and Vecchi.

4. Madeleine P. (b Antwerp, bap. 25 Jul 1586; d Antwerp, 30 May 1652), daughter of prec., who continued her father's business in partnership with her sister (5).

5. Marie P. (b Antwerp, 1589; d Antwerp, *c* 1674), sister of prec., with whom she continued in partnership and after her death ran the business under her married name of de Meyer.

Phantasy. *See* **Fantasy.**

Philadelphia Orchestra, American orch. founded 1900 by Fritz Scheel. Stokowski was prin. cond. 1912–38; Eugene Ormandy 1938–80. Riccardo Muti from 1981.

Philémon et Baucis, opera by Gounod (lib. by J. Barbier and M. Carré, after Ovid), prod. Paris, Théâtre Lyrique, 18 Feb 1860.

Philemon und Baucis, oder Jupiters Reise

auf der Erde (*P. and B., or Jupiter's journey to earth*), marionette opera by Haydn (lib. by G.K. Pfeffel), prod Eszterháza, 2 Sep 1773.

Philharmonia Orchestra, London-based orch. founded 1945 by Walter Legge (*q.v.*). Many important concerts and recordings with Toscanini, Furtwängler, Karajan and Giulini. Otto Klemperer gave his 1st concert with orch. in 1951 and became prin. cond. in 1959. Legge attempted to disband the orch. in 1964 but it immediately re-formed under the title New Philharmonia, with Klemperer as cond. for life. Prin. conds since Klemperer's death in 1973 have been Riccardo Muti (until 1982) and Giuseppe Sinopoli (from 1984). Orig. title, Philharmonia, re-adopted in 1977.

Philharmonic Society, London, *see* Royal Philharmonic Society; **Vienna,** *see* Gesellschaft der Musikfreunde.

Philidor, French family of musicians:

1. Jean P. (b *c* 1620; d Paris, 8 Sep 1679), fifer, oboist, crumhorn and tromba marina player, brother of Michel Danican, which was the orig. family name (for reasons of the change of name *see* **Danican**). He entered the service of Louis XIII about the time of his brother's death, *c* 1659. Wrote dance music.

2. André P. (b Versailles, *c* 1647; d Dreux, 11 Aug 1730), bassoonist, oboist, etc., and composer, son of prec. Entered the royal service as a boy, played all sorts of instruments there, competed with Lully in writing fanfares, marches, etc., and was soon commissioned to provide dances and stage diversions. In 1684 he became librarian of the king's music library and made a huge MS. collection of court and church music. Works incl. divertissements *Le Carnaval de Versailles* (1687), *Le Mariage de la Couture avec la grosse Cathos, La Princesse de Crète* (1688), *La Mascarade du vaisseau marchand* (1700), *Le Jeu d'échecs.*

3. Jacques P. (b Paris, 5 May 1657; d Versailles, 27 May 1708), oboist, bassoonist, etc., and composer, brother of prec. Entered court service in 1668, the royal chapel in 1683 and the chamber music as bassoonist in 1690. Comp. marches, airs for oboe, dance music.

4. Alexandre P. (b Paris, *c* 1660), cromorne and tromba marina player, brother of prec. He too was in service at court.

5. Anne Danican P. (b Paris, 11 Apr 1681; d Paris, 8 Oct 1728), oboist and composer, son of 2 by his 1st wife, Marguerite Monginot. Entered court service as oboist in the chamber music and the royal chapel, found-ed the Concert Spirituel in Paris, 1725, and later in life superintended the Duchesse de Maine's and the Prince de Conti's private concerts.
Works incl. pastorals *L'Amour vainqueur* (1697), *Diane et Endymion* (1698), *Danaé,* (1701) etc.

6. Michel P. (b Versailles, 2 Sept 1683), drummer, brother of prec. In service at court.

7. François P. (b Versailles, 17 Mar 1689; d ? Versailles, 1717–18), oboe, cromorne, tromba marina and bass viol player and composer, brother of prec. In court service, comp. fl. pieces, etc.

8. François André (Danican) P. (b Dreux, 7 Sep 1726; d London, 31 Aug 1795), composer and chess-player, half-brother of prec., being the son of 2 by his 2nd wife. As a page at court he studied music under Campra, and also showed a remarkable precocity for chess, which took him on a tour of Holl., Ger. and Eng. in 1745. Further travels followed, and in 1749 he pub. in London his *Analyse du jeu des échecs.* He returned to Paris in 1754, and there prof. his first *opéra comique* in 1759, the beginning of a long series of spectacular successes. He continued to visit Eng. as a chess-player, and in 1792 took refuge from the Fr. Revolution in London, where he remained till his death.
Works incl. operas *Blaise le savetier* (1759), *L'Huître et les plaideurs, Le Quiproquo* (1760), *Le Soldat magicien, Le Jardinier et son seigneur* (after La Fontaine, 1760), *Le Maréchal ferrant, Sancho Pança dans son île* (after Cervantes, 1762), *Le Bûcheron* (1763), *Les Fêtes de la paix, Le Sorcier, Tom Jones* (after Fielding, 1765), *Le Jardinier de Sidon* (1768), *L'Amant déguisé* (1769), *La Nouvelle école des femmes* (1770), *Mélide, ou Le Navigateur, Le Bon Fils* (1773), *Les Femmes vengées* (1775), *Ernelinde, Persée* (after Lully's old lib, 1780), *Thémistocle* (1785), *L'Amitié au village, La Belle Esclave, ou Valcour et Zeila* (1787), *Bélisaire* (1796) and others; Requiem for Rameau (1764), motet *Lauda Jerusalem* (1754) and others; settings of Horace's *Carmen saeculare* and Congreve's *Ode on St Cecilia's Day* (1754).

9. Pierre P. (b Paris, 22 Aug 1681; d ? Paris, 1 Sep 1731), flautist, violist and composer, son of 3. Was in the royal band, comp. fl. suites, etc.

10. Jacques P. (b ? Paris, 7 Sep 1686; d Pamplona, 25 Jun 1726), oboist and drummer, brother of prec. Succeeded his father in the royal service.

11. François P. (b Paris, 21 Jan 1695; d
Paris, 27 Oct 1728), oboist, brother of prec.
Member of the royal chamber music.

12. Nicholas P. (b Versailles, 3 Nov 1699;
d ? Paris, 1769), oboist and violist, brother
of prec. In service at court.

Philipottus da Caserta. *See* **Caserta.**

Philips, Peter (b ? London, 1561; d Brussels, 1628), English organist and composer.
He left Eng. in 1582, prob. because he was a
Roman Catholic, visited It. and Spain, settled at Antwerp in 1590 and became a canon
at the collegiate church of Soignies and in
1611 was app. organist at the royal chapel in
Brussels. In 1621 he became chaplain of the
church of Saint-Germain at Tirlemont and *c*
1623 canon of Béthune, but may not have
resided at either place. He was famous as an
organist throughout the Netherlands.

Works incl. Masses, 106 motets pub. in
Paradisus sacris cantionibus (Antwerp,
1628), hymns, *Sacrae cantiones*; madrigals;
fantasies, pavans and galliards for var. instruments; org. and virginal pieces, etc.

Phillipps, Adelaide (b Stratford-on-Avon,
26 Oct 1833; d Carlsbad, 3 Oct 1882),
English contralto. The family settled in USA
in 1840, where she 1st appeared as a dancer.
On the recommendation of Jenny Lind she
turned to music and studied singing with
Garcia in London. In 1854 made her debut
at Milan, as Rosina. Later she sang chiefly in
USA; debut NY, 1856, as Azucena.

Phillips, Henry (b Bristol, 13 Aug 1801; d
London, 8 Nov 1876), English baritone.
Appeared on the stage as a boy, sang in the
chorus at Drury Lane Theatre in London
and gradually worked his way up as a concert singer. He also sang in opera, e.g. as
Weber's Kaspar, and prod. table entertainments from 1843. Gave farewell concert
1863, then taught in Birmingham.

Philosopher, The, nickname of Haydn's
symph. no. 22 in Eb maj., comp. 1764 and
containing, exceptionally, parts for 2 cors
anglais.

Philtre, Le (*The Love Potion*), opera by
Auber (lib. by Scribe), prod. Paris, Opéra, 20
Apr 1831. *See also* **Elisir d'amore, L'.**

Phinot (or **Finot**), **Dominique** (b *c* 1510; d *c*
1555), French composer. He was assoc. with
the courts of Urbino and Pesaro and wrote
many motets and *chansons*.

Phoebus and Pan (Bach). *See* **Streit zwischen Phöbus und Pan.**

Phrase, a small group of notes forming a
definite melodic or thematic feature in a
comp.

Phrygian Cadence, a Cadence which owes
its name to the fact that in the Phrygian
Mode (E–E) the 6th degree of the scale (D)
was not sharpened by *musica ficta*, since this
would have resulted in an augmented 6th
with the note F, and altering F to F♯ would
have destroyed the character of the mode.
Hence the normal practice was to harmonize
the Cadence as follows:

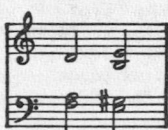

This Cadence was so firmly estab. that it
survived the disappearance of the modes and
acquired the flavour of a kind of imperfect
Cadence on the dominant of A min. Transposed into any key that was required it was
widely used in the late 17th and early 18th
cent., partic. to mark a transition from one
movement to another. This transition was
not always harmonically obvious; it was
common practice to use it at the end of a
slow middle movement in a min. key in order
to lead into a final movement in a maj. key.
In Bach's 3rd Brandenburg Concerto it is
used by itself without any middle movement
at all.

Phrygian Mode, the 3rd ecclesiastical
mode, represented on the pf. by the scale
beginning with the note E played on the
white notes.

Physharmonica, a small reed organ invented by Anton Hackel of Vienna in 1818;
a forerunner of the Harmonium.

Pia de' Tolomei, opera by Donizetti (lib. by
S. Cammarano), prod. Venice, Teatro Apollo, 18 Feb 1837.

Piacere (It. = pleasure). *See* **A Piacere.**

Piacevole (It.), pleasantly, agreeably.

Piangendo (It.), weeping, wailing, plan-
gent.

Pianissimo (It., superlative = very soft), a
direction rarely written out in full, but indicated by the sign *pp* or a multiplication
thereof.

Piano (It. adj. = soft). This too is as a rule
represented by a symbol: *p*. The comparable
'softer' for a dynamic direction between *p*
and *pp*, etc., has no symbol, but is expressed
by the words *più piano* (or *più p*).

Piano (noun), the current abbr. name of the
Pianoforte.

Piano-Organ (or Handle-Piano), a mechanical instrument similar to the Barrel Organ
in the shape of an upright pf., prod. its notes
in the same way by a studded cylinder, but

from strings struck by hammers instead of pipes. It was widely used by street musicians in the larger Eng. cities in the late 19th and early 20th cent., esp. in London, of which it was long part of the atmosphere. It was often wrongly called 'barrel organ' and even more incorrectly 'hurdy-gurdy'.

Piano Quartet, 4tet for pf., vln., vla. and cello.

Piano Quintet, a 5tet for pf. and string 4tet.

Piano Trio, a trio for pf., vln. and cello.

Pianoforte (It. lit. soft-loud), a keyboard instrument orig. similar to the harpsichord in appearance, but prod. its sound by striking the strings with hammers (a principle derived from the medieval Dulcimer) instead of plucking them with quills or leather tongues. Its beginnings go back to It. at the end of the 16th cent., but the 1st inventor who prob. consolidated it in its present form was Bartolomeo Cristofori of Padua, who settled in Florence about the 1st decade of the 18th cent. The table-shaped square pf. came later in the cent. and the upright pf. followed last in the 19th cent. The hammer action was improved by very gradual processes, and Eng. makers contrib. the invention of the iron frame, which was capable of supporting a much greater tension of strings, resulting in more powerful tone.

Pianola, a mechanical device attached to an ordinary pf. whereby the hammers are made to touch the strings not by action of the hand on the keyboard but by air-pressure. This is regulated by a roll of perforated paper running over a series of slits corresponding with the musical scale and releasing the air only where the holes momentarily pass over the slits. The mechanism is set in motion by pedals like those of a harmonium. Dynamics were at first controlled by action of the player's hands, more or less roughly, according to his skill, but they were later repro. mechanically exactly as played by the recording artist. This, however, left the manipulator with nothing of any interest to do, and no doubt for that reason the pianola, after enjoying a great vogue in the early 20th cent., later fell into neglect. In 1986 the Viennese firm Bösendorfer produced an inst. which, it is claimed, can reproduce every nuance of a performance. Optical sensors scan the keys, hammers and pedals 800 times a second and the registered information is fed into a computer. It is stored on tape or floppy disc and can be relayed back to the piano for 'performance'.

Piatigorsky, Gregor (b Ekaterinoslav, 17 Apr 1903; d Los Angeles, 6 Aug 1976),

Russian-born cellist. First studied the vln. with his father and then the cello with von Glehn, subsequently playing with various Moscow orchs. He left Rus. in 1921 and went to Berlin, where he studied with J. Klengel and became 1st cello with the Berlin PO. US debut, with NY PO, 1929. Later became known as one of the leading solo performers of his day. In 1930 formed a trio with Horowitz and Milstein; 1949 with Heifetz and Rubinstein. He gave the fps of the concertos by Hindemith (1941) and Walton (1957).

Piatti, Alfredo (Carlo) (b Bergamo, 8 Jan 1822; d Crocetta di Mozzo, 18 Jul 1901), Italian cellist. Studied music under his father, a violinist, and cello under his great-uncle Zanetti. He soon entered a theatre orch., came under the notice of Mayr and was sent to study at the Milan Cons., making his 1st public appearance in 1837. He travelled widely later and lived much of his life in London, where he became assoc. with Joachim and played frequently at the Popular Concerts at St James's Hall. He made his London debut in 1844 and in 1866 gave the fp of Sullivan's Concerto. He wrote 2 concertos and a number of pieces and studies for cello.

Piave, Francesco Maria (b Murano, 18 May 1810; d Milan, 5 Mar 1876), Italian librettist. He studied briefly for the priesthood and for a time earned subsistence from a publisher. A collaboration with Verdi began in 1844 with *Ernani*. Others libs. for Verdi were *I due Foscari, Macbeth, Il corsaro, Stiffelio, Rigoletto, La Traviata, Simon Boccanegra, Aroldo* and *La Forza del Destino*. An abandoned project, *Allan Cameron*, was taken up with Pacini and prod. in Venice, 1848. In the same year Piave's lib. for Mercadante (*La schiava Saracena*: The Saracen Slave-Girl) was prod. in Milan. Piave did not write libs. for Ponchielli, as has been stated elsewhere.

Picander. *See* **Henrici.**

Piccaver, Alfred (b Long Sutton, Lincs., 25 Feb 1884; d Vienna, 23 Sep 1958), English tenor. He worked as an electrical engineer in NY, where he was brought up, and also sang in student perfs. at the Met Opera School. On a visit to Europe in 1907 he applied for an audition and made his debut at the Prague Opera in the same year, as Roméo. After a period of further study he joined the Vienna Opera in 1910 and remained there until 1937. Among his roles were Radames, Lohengrin, Walther, Faust and Florestan. Retired 1937 and settled in London. He returned to Vienna in 1955 and was active as a teacher.

Picchi, Mirto (b S Mauro, Florence, 15 Mar 1915; d Florence, 25 Sep 1980), Italian tenor. Debut Milan 1946, as Radames. At the Cambridge Theatre, London, he sang Rodolfo, Cavaradossi and the Duke of Mantua (1947–8) and visited Edinburgh, with the Glyndebourne co., as Verdi's Riccardo, in 1949. At Florence he appeared in Rossini's *L'Assedio di Corinto* (1949) and in 1957 was heard in *Lucrezia Borgia*, at La Scala. Britten's Billy Budd and Peter Grimes were among his modern roles. Retired 1975.

Piccinni, Niccolò (b Bari, 16 Jan 1728; d Passy nr. Paris, 7 May 1800), Italian composer. Studied at the Cons. di Sant' Onofrio at Naples, Leo and Durante being among his masters. He prod. his 1st opera at Naples in 1754. In spite of Logroscino's exclusive success, it was well received and soon followed by other operas, both comic and serious. In 1756 he married the singer Vincenza Sibilia, his pupil. In 1760 he made an enormous success in Rome with *La buona figliuola*. After some years of success there he was ousted by Anfossi and returned to Naples in 1773. In 1776 he was invited to Paris, where he was at first in great difficulties, but was helped by Marmontel, who taught him Fr. and wrote the lib. of his 1st Fr. opera, *Roland*, for him, which was prod. in Jan 1778. By this time he had been artifically made into an opponent to Gluck by those who were determined to organize a partisan feud, though neither he nor Gluck had any desire to take a share in this and liked and respected each other. The quarrel of their adherents was heightened by their being both given an *Iphigénie en Tauride* to set to music. At the Revolution he left for It., visited Venice and then returned home to Naples, where, however, he was placed under close surveillance and lived in great poverty. In 1798 he at last succeeded in returning to Paris. After a period of comparative affluence, he again fell into poverty, was relieved by a gift from Bonaparte and an inspector's post at the Cons. ,but became paralysed and finally died in distress. His son Luigi (1766–1827) and his natural grandson Louis-Alexandre (1779–1850) were both comps. The former wrote operas for Paris and Stockholm, the latter ballets, melodramas, etc., for the Paris theatres.

Works incl. c 120 operas, e.g. *Le donne dispettose* (1754), *Le Gelosie, Zenobia* (1756), *Alessandro nell' Indie* (2 versions), *Madama Arrighetta* (1758), *La buona fig-*

liuola, La buona figliuola maritata (both after Richardson's *Pamela*, 1760, 1761), *Il cavaliere per amore* (1762), *Le contadine bizarre, Gli stravaganti* (1764), *L'Olimpiade (1761), I viaggiatori* (1775), *La pescatrice* (1766), *Le finte gemelle, Vittorina* (Goldoni), *Roland, Atys, Iphigénie en Tauride,* (1781), *Didon* (1783), *Le Faux Lord* (1783), *Pénélope, Endymion* (1784); oratorio *Jonathan* and 3 others; Mass, psalms and other church music.

Picco Pipe, a woodwind instrument of the recorder or flageolet type which became fashionable in Eng. on being introd. to London in 1856 by a Sardinian player named Picco.

Piccola musica notturna (*Little night Music*), work for orch. by Dallapiccola, fp Hanover, 7 Jun 1954; arr. for 8 insts., 1961.

Piccolo (It., abbr. for *flauto piccolo* = little flute), the small 8ve fl., more usually called *ottavino* in It., similar in shape and technique to the ordinary fl., but smaller in size and standing an 8ve higher in pitch. Its music is written an 8ve below the actual sound.

Piccolo Marat, Il, opera by Mascagni (lib. by G. Forzano and G. Targioni-Tozzetti), prod. Rome, Teatro Costanzi, 2 May 1921. Story deals with the aftermath of the assassination of Marat, when Paris was scourged by revolutionary fanatics: at the end of the World War II Mascagni was in disgrace for having supported Mussolini.

Pichl, Wenzel (b Bechyně nr. Tábor, 25 Sep 1741; d Vienna, 23 Jan 1805), Bohemian violinist and composer. Studied in Prague and in 1765 became violinist and vice-dir. of music (under Dittersdorf) to the Bishop of Grosswardein. In 1769 he moved to Vienna and thence to Milan in the service of the Archduke Ferdinand, remaining in It. until his return to Vienna in 1796. He was admired by Cherubini and Gyrowetz; his 4tets were perf. at Eszterháza by Haydn.

According to Pichl's own catalogue, works incl. 12 operas, e.g. 4 Latin operas (1765–76), 4 opere buffe, *Der Krieg* (1776) and It. arrangements of French operas; over 30 Masses; 89 symphs.; c 30 concertos; 172 4tets, 21 5tets, etc.; 148 pieces for baryton, etc.

Pick-Mangiagalli, Riccardo (b Strakonice, 10 Jul 1882; d Milan, 8 Jul 1949), Czech-Italian composer. Studied in Prague, Vienna and Milan. In 1936 he succeeded Pizzetti as director of the Milan Cons.

Works incl. operas *Basi e Bote* (1927), *L'ospite inatteso* and *Notturno romantico* (1936); ballets *Salice d'oro, Il carillon magi-*

co, *Casanova a Venezia* (1929), *La Berceuse* and *Variazioni coreografiche*; mime dramas *Sumitra* (1917) and *Mahit* (1923); *Sortileggi* for pf. and orch.; string 4tet; vln. and pf. sonata; pf. works, etc.

Pictures at an Exhibition, a suite of pf. pieces by Mussorgsky, comp. in 1874 in memory of the painter and architect Victor Alexandrovich Hartmann (d 1873) and illustrating pictures and designs by him shown at a memorial exhibition, organized by V.V. Stassov. Orchestral versions of the work have been made by Henry J. Wood, Ravel, Stokowski, and Walter Goehr; brass band arr. by Elgar Howarth. Fp of Ravel orch., Paris, Opéra, 19 Oct 1922, cond Koussevitzky.

Pieno (It. = full), a direction used esp. in org. music in combination, *organo pieno*, meaning either that a figured bass is to be filled with ample harmony or that the instrument is to be played with full registration.

Pierné, (Henri Constant) Gabriel (b Metz, 16 Aug 1863; d Ploujean, Côtes du Nord, 17 Jul 1937), French conductor and composer. Studied at the Paris Cons. and gained the Prix de Rome in 1882. In 1890 he succeeded Franck as organist of the church of Sainte-Clotilde, became 2nd cond. of Colonne's orch. in 1903 and at Colonne's death in 1910 succeeded him as chief cond. He gave many important fps, incl. Debussy's *Khamma* (1924) and *La Boîte à joujoux* (1923).

Works incl. operas *Les Elfes, Pandore, La Coupe enchantée* (after La Fontaine, 1905), *La Nuit de Noël, Vendée, La Fille de Tabarin, On ne badine pas avec l'amour* (after Musset, 1910), *Fragonard, Sophie Arnould* (1927); ballets, pantomimes and incidental music; oratorios, suites for orch.; pf. 5tet, pf. trio; songs.

Pierrot lunaire, Schoenberg's song-cycle with chamber ens., op. 21, consisting of 21 poems by Albert Giraud trans. into Ger. by Otto Erich Hartleben; comp. 1912, fp Berlin, 16 Oct 1912. The treatment of the voice-part is one of the outstanding exs. of the use of Speechsong (*Sprechgesang*). The 21 poems are arranged in 3 sections: 1: *Mondestrunken, Colombine, Der Dandy, Eine blasse Wäscherin, Valse de Chopin, Madonna, Der Kranke Mond.* 2: *Die Nacht, Gebet an Pierrot, Raub, Rote Messe, Galgenlied, Enthauptung, Die Kreuze.* 3: *Heimweh, Gemeinheit, Parodie, Der Mondfleck, Serenade, Heimfahrt, O alter Duft.* The work was commissioned by Albertine Zehme (*q.v.*); it was soon admired by comps. as different as Puccini and Stravinsky

but wider public success did not come until a perf. in Berlin on 5 Jan 1924, with Marie Gutheil-Schoder (*q.v.*) and Gregor Piatigorsky (cello), Artur Schnabel (pf.) and Fritz Stiedry (cond.).

Pierson (orig. **Pearson**), **Henry Hugh** (or **Heinrich Hugo**) (b Oxford, 12 Apr 1815; d Leipzig, 28 Jan 1873), English composer. Educ. at Harrow and Cambridge, studied music with Attwood and Corfe, and interrupted a medical course to continue music studies at Leipzig, where he met Mendelssohn, Schumann and others. He became Reid Prof. of Music at Edinburgh in 1844 in succession to Bishop, but soon resigned and returned to Ger., where he remained, married Caroline Leonhardt and changed the spelling of his name.

Works incl. operas *Der Elfensieg* (1845), *Leila* (1848) and *Conturini* (comp. 1853, prod. 1872), *Fenice* (1883); incid. music to Goethe's *Faust* (Part II); oratorio *Jerusalem* (1852); *Macbeth* symph. (1859), overtures to Shakespeare's *Twelfth Night, Julius Caesar* and *Romeo and Juliet* (1874), funeral march for *Hamlet* (1859); numerous songs; part-songs, etc.

Piéton, Loyset (b Bernay, Normandy; d after 1545), French composer, often confused with Compère, both being usually called only by their Christian names. Wrote Masses, motets, psalms and *chansons*. His work was pub. in Lyons and Venice.

Pietoso (It. from *pietà* = pity), pityingly, compassionately.

Pietra del paragone, La (*The Touchstone*), opera by Rossini (lib. by I. Romanelli), prod. Milan, La Scala, 26 Sep 1812.

Piffaro (It. = fife), a small fl.-like pipe, also a shepherd's pipe akin to the ob. or bagpipe. It was often played in Italian cities, esp. Rome and Naples, at Christmas time, by pipers from the hills, who seem to have played tunes of the Siciliana type akin to that of the *Pastoral Symph.* in Handel's *Messiah*, which bears the word 'Pifa' in the MS., evidently in reference to the piffaro.

Pigheaded Peasants, The (*Tvrdé Palice*), opera by Dvořák (lib. J. Stolba), prod. Prague, Cz. Theatre, 2 Oct 1881.

Pijper, Willem (b Zeist, 8 Sep 1894; d Leidschendam, 18 Mar 1947), Dutch composer. Studied with Wagenaar and was app. prof. of comp. at the Amsterdam Cons. in 1925; dir. of the Rotterdam Cons. in 1930.

Works incl. opera *Halewijn* (1933); incid. music for Euripides' *The Cyclops* and *The Bacchantes* (1924), Sophocles' *Antigone* and Shakespeare's *Tempest* (1930); 3

symphs., 6 symph. Epigrams for orch., pf.
concerto (1927), vln. concerto, cello concerto; 5 string 4tets (1914–46), 2 pf. trios, 6tet
for wind and pf.; vln. and pf. sonatas; pf.
music; choruses; songs.

Pilarczyk, Helga (b Schöningen, 12 Mar
1925), German soprano. Studied in Brunswick and Hamburg, making her debut at the
Brunswick State Theatre in 1951. From
1954 she was a member of the Hamburg
State Opera. She was best known for her
singing of modern music; Schoenberg's
Erwartung and *Pierrot lunaire*. The 1st Lulu
in Brit. (SW theatre, London, 1962) and
sang Berg's Marie on her NY Met debut in
1965.

Pilgrim's Progress, The, opera by Vaughan
Williams (lib. by the comp. after Bunyan),
prod. London, CG, 26 Apr 1951. It incorporates most of the comp.'s 1-act opera *The
Shepherds of the Delectable Mountains*
(prod. London, RCM, 11 Jul 1922).

Pilgrims to Mecca, The (Gluck). *See* Rencontre imprévue.

Pilkington, Francis (b c 1570; d Chester,
1638), English composer. Took the B.Mus.
at Oxford in 1595 and was soon after app. as
singer at Chester Cathedral where he remained to his death, becoming a minor
canon in 1612.

Works incl. anthems (1 in Leighton's
Teares or Lamentacions); madrigals and
pastorals for 3–6 voices; lute pieces; songs to
the lute.

Pimmaglione (*Pygmalion*), opera by Cimadoro (lib. by A.S. Sografi, based on Rousseau's *Pygmalion*), prod. Venice, Teatro San
Samuele, 26 Jan 1790.

Pimmalione (*Pygmalion*), opera by Cherubini (lib. by S. Vestris), prod. Paris, Tuileries, at Napoleon's private theatre, for which
it was written, 30 Nov 1809.

Pimpinone, intermezzo by Albinoni (lib. by
P. Pariati), prod. with the opera *Astarto*
Venice, 1708. As with Pergolesi's *La serva
padrona*, the intermezzo is now better
known than the *opera seria* for which it was
intended to provide light relief.

Intermezzo by Telemann, prod. Hamburg, 1725.

Pincherle, Marc (b Constantine, Algeria, 13
Jun 1888; d Paris, 20 Jun 1974), French
musicologist. Prof. at the École Normale de
Musique in Paris and ed. successively of *Le
Monde musical* and *Musique*. His works
incl. studies of Corelli, Vivaldi, the vln. and
vln. music.

Pinelli, Ettore (b Rome, 18 Oct 1843; d
Rome, 17 Sep 1915), Italian violinist and
conductor. Studied in Rome and with
Joachim at Hanover, organized chamber
concerts in Rome and with Sgambati founded the Liceo Musicale there, became vln.
prof. and cond. orchestral and choral concerts. Comp. an overture, a string 4tet, etc.

Pinello di Gherardi, Giovanni Battista (b
Genoa, *c* 1544; d Prague, 15 Jun 1587),
Italian composer. After an appt. at Vicenza
Cathedral he went to Innsbruck in the 1570s
as musician to the archduke, to the Imp.
chapel in Prague soon afterwards and to the
Saxon court at Dresden in 1580 in succession to Scandello, but was dismissed because
of differences with other musicians, and returned to Prague.

Works incl. motets, Ger. Magnificats and
other church music; madrigals and *canzone
napoletane*; part-songs.

Pini-Corsi, Antonio (b Zara, Jun 1858; d
Milan, 22 Apr 1918), Italian baritone. Made
his 1st appearance at the age of 20 at Cremona, as Dandini and became one of the leading interpreters of comic parts, Verdi choosing him for Ford in his *Falstaff* in 1893. CG
debut 1894, as Puccini's Lescaut; NY Met
1899, as Masetto. Other roles incl.
Schaunard (creation, 1896), Pasquale and
Leporello.

Pinnock, Trevor (b Canterbury, 16 Dec
1946), English harpsichordist and conductor. Studied RCM; solo debut London 1971.
He played with the Galliard Harpsichord
Trio 1966–72 and often appeared with the
Academy of St Martin-in-the-Fields. Founded the English Concert 1973; 'authentic'
perfs. of early music. He has cond. from
1980; gave Handel's *Solomon* at the 1986
Promenade Concerts, London.

Pinsuti, Ciro (b Sinalunga, Siena, 9 May
1829; d Florence, 10 Mar 1888), Italian
pianist, singing-teacher and composer. Studied with his father and played the pf. in
public as a child, was taken to Eng. studying
comp. with Potter, returning to It. in 1845
and becoming a pupil of Rossini at Bologna.
From 1848 he was in Eng. again, teaching
singing for many years in London and
Newcastle-on-Tyne and becoming prof. at
the RAM in 1856.

Works incl. operas *Il mercante di Venezia*
(after Shakespeare, 1873), *Mattia Corvino*
(1877) and *Margherita* (1882); Te Deum for
the annexation of Tuscany to It. (1859);
hymn for the International Exhibition in
London (1871); 30 pf. pieces; 230 songs;
many vocal duets and trios; part-songs.

Pinto, George Frederic (b London, 25 Sep
1786; d London, 23 Mar 1806), English

violinist and composer. His real name was
Sanders, but he adopted that of his maternal
grandfather. Studied with Salomon and
others and appeared at Salomon's concerts
from 1796. He then toured in Eng. and Scot.
and visited Paris. His early death was
allegedly the result of dissipation.

Works incl. vln. and pf. sonatas, vln.
duets, pf. sonatas, canzonets.

Pinto, Thomas (b England 1714; d ?Edin-
burgh 1783), English violinist of Italian descent, grandfather of prec. through his 1st
wife. In 1766 he married the singer Charlotte Brent as his 2nd wife. He played in London at an early age, later at the Three Choirs
Festival, etc., failed in a speculation with
Arnold to run Marylebone Gardens and last
lived in Scot. and Ir.

Pinza, Ezio (Fortunato), (b Rome, 18 May
1892; d Stamford, Conn., 9 May 1957),
Italian bass. He studied at the Bologna Cons.
and 1st appeared at Soncino (nr. Milan) in
Norma, 1914. After the 1914–18 war he
sang in Rome and other It. cities as Marke,
Pogner and Colline. He joined the Met
Opera, NY, in 1926 and sang Fiesco, Figaro,
Don Giovanni and Boris. London, CG,
1930–9. Salzburg, 1934–7, under Walter. In
1948 he left the Met to devote himself to
operetta, films and television.

Piozzi, Gabriel(e) (Mario) (b Brescia, 8 Jun
1740; d Dymerchion, Denbighshire, 26 Mar
1809), Italian, later English, music teacher
and composer. Settled in Eng. *c* 1776, and
won a good reputatation as a singing-
teacher and pianist. In 1784 he married Mrs.
Hester Thrale, to the displeasure of her
friend Dr. Johnson.

Works incl. string 4tets, pf. 4tets, vln.
sonatas, canzonets.

Pipe and Tabor, a combination of 2 early
instruments, a small pipe of the recorder
type, but held with one hand only while the
other beats the tabor, a small drum without
snares hung round the player's shoulder or
strapped to his waist. The instruments have
been revived for folk-dancing.

Pipelare, Matthaeus, Flemish 15th–16th-
cent. composer. In 1498 he became master
of the choristers at 's-Hertogenbosch. He
wrote Masses, motets, and secular works to
Fr. and Dutch texts. His motet *Memorare
mater Christi* commemorates the 7 sorrows
of the Virgin.

Pique-Dame, the Ger. title of Tchaikovsky's opera *The Queen of Spades (Pikovaya
Dama)*.

Pirame et Thisbé (*Pyramus and Thisbe*),
opera by Rebel and Francœur (lib. by J.L.I.

de La Serre), prod. Paris, Opéra, 17 Oct
1726.

Pirata, Il (*The Pirate*), opera by Bellini (lib.
by F. Romani), prod. Milan, La Scala, 27
Oct 1827.

**Pirates of Penzance, The, or The Slave of
Duty,** operetta by Sullivan (lib. by W.S. Gil-
bert), prod. Paignton, Bijou Theatre, 30 Dec
1879); pirated perf., NY, Fifth Avenue
Theatre, 31 Dec 1879; 1st London perf.,
Opéra-Comique, 3 Apr 1880.

Pirro, André (b Saint-Dizier, 12 Feb 1869; d
Paris, 11 Nov 1943), French musicologist.
Studied law and literature in Paris and at the
same time picked up as much music educ. as
he could, attending the organ classes of
Franck and Widor. In 1896 he became prof.
and a director of the newly opened Schola
Cantorum. In 1904 he began to lecture at the
École des Hautes Études Sociales and in
1912 succeeded Rolland as prof. of music
hist. at the Sorbonne. His books incl. studies
of Schütz, Buxtehude, Bach (general and
organ works), the Fr. clavecinists, Descartes
and music, old Ger. church and secular
music, etc.

Pirro e Demetrio (*Pyrrhus and Demetrius*),
opera by A. Scarlatti (lib. by A. Morselli),
prod. Naples, Teatro San Bartolommeo,
prob. 28 Jan 1694.

Pirrotta, Nino (b Palermo, 13 Jun 1908),
Italian musicologist. He studied at the
Conss. of Palermo and Florence; librarian of
the S. Cecilia Cons., Rome, 1948–56. Prof.
at Harvard (1956–72) and at Rome (1972–
83). His major studies have been of 14th
cent. It. music, incl. the Ars Nova, and
17th-cent. Italian opera.

Pisador, Diego (b Salamanca, *c* 1508; d
after 1557), Spanish vihuelist. Son of a notary attached to the household of the
Archbishop of Santiago. He took holy
orders but did not enter the church. In 1552
he pub. a book of transcriptions of old Span.
songs, portions of Masses by Josquin Desprez, motets by Morales and others, etc. for
vihuela.

Pisari, Pasquale (b Rome *c* 1725; d Rome,
27 Mar 1778), Italian singer and composer,
pupil of Gasparini and Biordi. From 1752 he
was a singer in the Papal Chapel in Rome,
and wrote church music in the old *a cappella*
style.

Works incl. Masses, motets, etc. His
elaborate church music was admired by
Martini and Burney.

Pisaroni, Benedetta (Rosamunda) (b
Piacenza, 16 May 1793; d Piacenza, 6 Aug
1872), Italian contralto. Studied under

Marchesi and others and made her 1st appearance at Bergamo in 1811, as a soprano, but changed to contralto on Rossini's advice in 1813. She sang in the fps of Rossini's *Ricciardo e Zoriade* (1818), *Erminio* (1819) and *La donna del lago* (1819). Paris from 1827 as Arsace, Tancredi and Isabella.

Pischek (or Pišek), Johann Baptist (b Melnik, 13 Oct 1814; d Stuttgart, 16 Feb 1873), Czech baritone. Made his 1st stage appearance at the age of 21 and in 1844 was app. court singer to the King of Württemberg. Paid his 1st visit to Eng. in 1845, returned until 1853 in oratorio and in operas by Mozart, Gluck, Spohr and Kreutzer.

Pisendel, Johann Georg (b Cadolzburg, Bavaria, 26 Dec 1687; d Dresden, 25 Nov 1755), German violinist and composer. Studied the vln. under Torelli while he was a choir-boy at the chapel of the Margrave of Ansbach and theory under Pistocchi. After studying at Leipzig Univ. He went to Dresden to enter the service of the king of Poland there in 1712, travelled widely with the king, became concert master in 1728 on the death of Volumier and led the opera orch. under Hasse. Wrote concertos and pieces for the vln.

Pisk, Paul A(madeus) (b Vienna, 16 May 1893), Austrian musicologist and composer. Studied under Adler at Vienna Univ. and comp. with Schreker and Schoenberg. After cond. at var. Ger. theatres, he returned to Vienna, cond. and broadcasting, and became dir. of the music dept. of the Volkshochschule, but left for USA in 1936 and became prof. of musicology at the Univ. of Texas. In 1963 he joined the staff of Washington Univ., St Louis; retired 1973 and moved to Los Angeles. He has ed. old music incl. masses by Jacobus Gallus, and written on modern music and the Second Viennese School.

Works incl. monodrama *Schattenseite* (1931); ballet *Der grosse Regenmacher (1927); cantata Die neue Stadt* (1926); Requiem for baritone and orch.; Partita for orch., suite for small orch., *Bucolic Suite* for strings and other orchestral works; string 4tet and other chamber music; pf. music; songs with organ.

Pistocchi, Francesco (Antonio Mamiliano) (b Palermo, 1659; d Bologna, 13 May 1726), Italian singer and composer. The family moved to Bologna in 1661, where he began to comp. at a very early age, entered San Petronio as a choir-boy in 1670 and in 1675 began to appear in opera. In 1679 his 1st opera, for puppets, *Il Leandro (Gli amori*

fatali), was prod. at Venice. In 1687–94 he was a singer at the ducal court of Parma, and he then became music director to the Margrave of Ansbach, returning to Bologna in 1701, founding a singing-school there.

Works incl. operas *Il girello, Narciso* (1697), *Le pazzie d'amore* (1699), *Le risa di Democrito* (1700), and *Il Leandro* (1692); oratorios *Il martirio di Sant' Adriano* (1698), *Maria Vergine addolorata* (1698), *La fuga di Santa Teresa*; church music; vocal duets and trios; airs *Scherzi musicali,* etc.

Piston, Walter (b Rockland, Me., 20 Jan 1894; d Belmont, Mass., 12 Nov 1976), American composer. Studied at the École Normale de Musique in Paris and at Harvard Univ., also with Nadia Boulanger and others. App. asst. prof. at Harvard in 1926 and prof. from 1944 to 1960.

Works incl. ballet *The Incredible Flutist* (1938); 8 symphs. (1937–65), suite, concerto, Symph. Piece, Prelude and Fugue for orch.; concertino for pf. and chamber orch. (1937), clar. concertino, 2 vln. concertos (1939, 1960); *Carnival Song* for male chorus and brass instruments; 5 string 4tets (1933–62), pf. trio, 3 pieces for fl., clar. and bassoon; vln. and pf. sonata, fl. and pf. sonata, suite for ob. and pf., partita for vln., vla. and organ.

Pistor, Gotthelf (b Berlin, 17 Oct 1887; d Cologne, 4 Apr 1947), German tenor. After his 1923 Nuremberg debut he sang in Wurzburg, Darmstadt and Magdeburg; Cologne from 1929. Widely known in Wagner, he appeared at Bayreuth 1925–31, as Froh, Siegmund, Siegfried and Parsifal. Zoppot 1930–8.

Pitch, the exact height (or depth) of any musical sound according to the number of vibrations that prod. it; also the standard by which notes, with the A above middle C as a starting-point, are to be tuned, a standard which determines at how many vibrations to the second that A is to be taken, as well as every other note in relation to it. Pitch varied at different times and in different countries. Early in the 19th cent. it was gradually raised, esp. by makers of wind instruments to secure more brilliant effect, but with results dangerous to singers, and in Eng. 2 pitches were in use, the higher for orch. perf. and the lower Classical or Fr. pitch for church and purely vocal music. The pitch with A at 440 cycles per second is now in general use, even by military bands, which until 1927 used the old Philharmonic pitch, which was slightly higher. *See* **A.**

Pitoni, Giuseppe Ottavio (b Rieti, 18 Mar

1657; d Rome, 1 Feb 1743), Italian composer. Studied with Pompeo Natale from an early age, and became a chorister at the churches of S. Giovanni dei Fiorentini and SS. Apostoli in Rome, where he was a pupil of Foggia. After church posts in Monterotondo and Assisi he became *maestro di cappella* at Rieti in 1676, and from the next year to his death at the Collegio San Marco in Rome, later also at the Lateran and St Peter's.

Works incl. over 250 Masses, 780 psalm settings (incl. a 16-part *Dixit Dominus* still sung at St Peter's in Holy Week), Magnificats, motets, Litanies, 2 Passions.

Pitt, Percy (b London, 4 Jan 1869; d London, 23 Nov 1932), English conductor and composer. Educ. in Fr. and studied music there and at Leipzig with Reinecke and Jadassohn, and at Munich with Rheinberger. In 1896 he became organist at Queen's Hall in London and in 1902 adviser and cond. at CG; he gave *Ivanhoe*, *Khovanshchina* and *Pelléas* during Beecham's seasons. Later dir. of the Grand Opera Syndicate at CG, of the BNOC and in 1922 music dir. of the BBC. In Jan 1923 he cond. *Hänsel und Gretel* at CG; the broadcast was claimed as the 1st in the world of an opera.

Pittore e Duca (*Painter and Duke*), opera by Balfe (lib. by F.M. Piave), prod. Trieste, 21 Nov 1854.

Pittore parigino, Il (*The Parisian Painter*), opera by Cimarosa (lib. by G. Petrosellini), prod. Rome, Teatro Valle, 4 Jan 1781.

Pittsburgh Symphony Orchestra, US orch. founded 1895. Elgar and Strauss were early guest conds. but the orch. was disbanded in 1910; re-formed 1926 and cond. by Antonio Modarelli (1930–7). Prin. conds. since 1938: Fritz Reiner (until 1948), William Steinberg (1952–76), André Previn (1976–86); Lorin Maazel from 1986. Resident in Heinz Hall for Performing Arts from 1971.

Più (It. = more), used for var. musical directions in combinations such as *più allegro* (faster), *più lento* (slower), *più mosso* (more animated), *un poco più* (a little more [of whatever has been happening before]), etc.

Piuttosto (It. = somewhat, rather), a word used with directions where the comp. wishes to make sure that an indication of tempo or expression is obeyed in moderation.

Pixérécourt, René Charles Guilbert de (1773–1844), French dramatist and librettist, biog. of Dalayrac, author of melodramas with music. *See* **Margherita d'Anjou** (Meyerbeer).

Pixis, Johann Peter (b Mannheim, 10 Feb 1788; d Baden-Baden, 22 Dec 1874), German pianist and composer. Studied with his father, Friedrich Wilhelm P. (*c* 1760–*c*1810), and began to appear as pianist with his brother Friedrich Wilhelm P. (1786–1842), a violinist. Settled in Munich in 1809 and in Paris in 1825, where he became a noted pf. teacher. In 1845 he bought a villa at Baden-Baden and continued to train pupils there. He adopted and trained the singer Franzilla Göhringer (1816–?); she created Pacini's Saffo in 1840.

Works incl. operas *Almazinde* (1820), *Bibiana* (1829) and *Die Sprache des Herzens* (1836); pf. concertos; sonatas and pieces for pf., etc.

Pizzetti, Ildebrando (b Parma, 20 Sep 1880; d Rome, 13 Feb 1968), Italian composer. Son of a pf. teacher. Studied at Parma Cons. 1895–1901. In 1908 he was app. prof. of harmony and counterpoint at the Istituto Musicale at Florence, of which he became dir. in 1917. Appt. dir. of the Cons. Giuseppe Verdi, Milan, 1924 and in 1936 he succeeded Respighi as prof. of advanced comp. at the Accademia di Santa Cecilia in Rome.

Works incl. STAGE: operas *Fedra* (1915), *Debora e Jaele* (1922), *Lo straniero*, *Fra Gherardo* (1928), *Orséolo* (1935), *L'oro*, *Cagliostro* (1952), *La figlia d'Jorio*, *Assassinio nella cattedrale* (after T.S. Eliot, 1958), *Clitennestra* (1965); incid. music for *La Nave* and *La Pisanella* (both by d'Annunzio), Feo Belcari's *Sacra rappresentazione di Abraam ed Isacco* (1917), Sophocles' *Trachiniae* (1933); Corrado d'Errico's *Rappresentazione di Santa Uliva* (1933), *Le feste delle Panatence*, Shakespeare's *As You Like It*.

ORCHESTRAL WORKS: symph. in A maj. (1940); dances for Tasso's *Aminta*, 3 symph. preludes for Sophocles' *Oedipus Rex* and *Coloneus* (1903), *Ouverture per una farsa tragica* (1911), *Concerto dell' estate* (1928), *Rondo veneziano* (1929); pf. concerto (1930); cello concerto (1934); vln. concerto (1944), harp concerto (1960).

CHORAL AND ORCHESTRAL WORKS: *L'ultima caccia di Sant' Uberto* (1930), intro. to Aeschylus's *Agamemnon* and *Epithalamium* (1931); film music; *Sinfonia del fuoco* (1914) for d'Annunzio's *Cabirio* and orchestral and choral music for *Scipione l'Africano*; *Missa di Requiem* (1922) and *De profundis* for unaccomp. chorus (1937), also some smaller sacred and secular works.

CHAMBER: 2 string 4tets (1906, 1933), pf. trio; sonatas for vln. and pf. and for cello and pf.; sonata, *Foglio d'album* and suite *Da un autunno già lontano* for pf.; 2 songs for baritone and pf. 4tet, 3 with string 4tet and 21 with pf.

Pizzicato (It. = pinched), a direction indicating that the strings on instruments of the vln. family are to be played, not with the bow, but by being plucked with a finger of the right hand, or occasionally with fingers of the left hand between bowed notes.

Pizzicato tremolando (It. = pinched and trembling), an effect 1st used by Elgar in the accomp. cadenza of his vln. concerto, where the orch. strings play chords by thrumming the strings both ways across with the fingers of the right hand.

Plaichinger, Thila (b Vienna, 13 Mar 1868; d Vienna, 19 Mar 1939), Austrian soprano. Debut Hamburg 1893; Strasbourg 1894–1901. She sang Isolde at the Berlin Hofoper in 1901 and remained until 1914 as Elektra and Brünnhilde. CG 1904 as Ortrud, Isolde and Venus. Guest in Vienna, Munich and Dresden.

Plainchant or **Plainsong** } The medieval church music still surviving in some services of the Roman Catholic Church, properly sung in unison, without harmony and with no definitely measured rhythms. Its groupings of notes have, however, a strongly rhythmic character, but it resembles the free rhythm of prose, whereas that of measured music is comparable to the rhythm of verse. The old notation on a stave of 4 lines, with square or diamond-shaped notes and Ligatures, is still used for plainsong.

Plainte (Fr. = complaint), a lament or memorial piece, whether vocal or instrumental.

Plamenac, Dragan (b Zagreb, 8 Feb 1895; d Ede, Holland, 15 Mar 1983), American musicologist of Croatian origin. Studied law at the Univ. of Zagreb, then comp. with Schreker, musicology with Adler in Vienna and with Pirro in Paris, taking his doctorate in 1925. In 1939 he went to the USA, becoming Prof. of Musicology at the Univ. of Illinois in 1955. He pub. a number of studies of pre-classical music and ed. the works of Ockeghem.

Planché, James Robinson (b London, 27 Feb 1796; d London, 30 May 1880), English dramatist, librettist and critic of French descent. Lived in London and wrote a number of libs. incl. *Maid Marian* for Bishop, *Oberon* for Weber and *The Surrender of Calais*, intended for Mendelssohn and later offered to H. Smart, who left it unfinished.

Plançon, Pol (Henri) (b Fumay, Ardennes, 12 Jun 1851; d Paris, 11 Aug 1914), French bass. Studied with Duprez and Sbriglia in Paris, made his debut at Lyons in 1877, as St Bris in *Les Huguenots*. Méphistophélès, NY Met, 1893–1908; debut as Jupiter in Gounod's *Philémon et Baucis*. He sang in Paris from 1880 (fps of Massenet's *Le Cid* and Saint-Saëns' *Ascanio*) and 1st visited London in 1891.

Planets, The, suite by Holst for orch. with org. and (in final section) female chorus. 1. *Mars, the Bringer of War*; 2. *Venus, the Bringer of Peace*; 3. *Mercury, the Winged Messenger*; 4. *Jupiter, the Bringer of Jollity*; 5. *Saturn, the Bringer of Old Age*; 6. *Uranus, the Magician*; 7. *Neptune, the Mystic*. 1st (private) perf. London, Queen's Hall, 29 Sep 1918; 1st public perf., London, 15 Nov 1920. The idea of writing music on the planets was not new: Buxtehude wrote a harpsichord suite on them; but Holst dealt with them from the astrological aspect.

Planquette, (Jean) Robert (b Paris, 31 Jul 1848; d Paris, 28 Jan 1903), French composer. Studied briefly at the Paris Cons. and then wrote songs perf. at café-concerts. From this he passed on to operettas, the 4th of which, *Les Cloches de Corneville*, was immensely successful in 1877.

Works incl. operettas *Valet de cœur*, *Le Serment de Mme. Grégoire*, *Paille d'avoine* (1874), *Les Cloches de Corneville* (1877), *Le Chevalier Gaston* (1879), *Les Voltigeurs de la 32me* (*The Old Guard*), *La Cantinière*, *Rip van Winkle* (after Washington Irving, 1882), *Nell Gwynne* (1884), *La Cremaillère, Surcouf* (*Paul Jones*), *Capitaine Thérèse, La Cocarce tricolore, Le Talisman, Panurge* (after Rabelais, 1895), *Mam'zelle Quat' Sous* (1897), *Le Paradis de Mahomed* (prod. 1906).

Plantade, Charles Henri (b Pontoise, 14 Oct 1764; d Paris, 18 Dec 1839), French pianist, harpist, cellist and composer. Learnt singing and cello as one of the royal pages and later studied comp. with Langlé, pf. with Hüllmandel and harp with Petrini. Having set up as a teacher of singing and harp, he began to write duets and they gained him access to the stage. He taught singing to Queen Hortense, became *maître de chapelle* at court and prof. at the Cons., and held other posts and distinctions.

Works incl. operas *Palma, ou Le Voyage en Grèce* (1797), *Zoé, ou La Pauvre Petite* (1800), *Le Mari de circonstance* (1813) and many others; Masses, Requiem, Te Deum, motets, etc.; romances and nocturnes for 2 voices.

Plaschke, Friedrich (b Jaroměr, 7 Jan 1875; d Prague, 4 Feb 1952), Czech bass-baritone. Debut Dresden, 1900; remained until 1937 and sang in the fps of Strauss's *Feuersnot, Salome, Ägyptische Helena, Arabella* and *Die schweigsame Frau*. London, CG, 1914 as Amfortas in the Brit. première of *Parsifal*. Other roles incl. Barak, Pogner, Sachs and Gérard.

Platée (*Plataea*), comédie-ballet by Rameau (lib. by J. Autreau and A.J.V. d'Orville), prod. Versailles, at court, 31 Mar 1745; 1st Paris perf., Opéra, 4 Feb 1749.

Platel, Nicolas Joseph (b Versailles, 1777; d Brussels, 25 Aug 1835), French cellist. As the son of a royal chamber musician he was educ. as a page at court, learning the cello from Duport. After some orchestral appts. in Paris and Lyons, he toured in Belgium and England, settled at Antwerp and then at Brussels, where he became prof. at the Cons. in 1831. Wrote 5 cello concertos; duets for vln. and cello.

Plato (*c* 428–*c*348 B.C.), Greek philosopher. He outlined a system of 'harmony', as understood by the Greeks, in *Timaeus* and discussed the nature of the modes, from their supposed moral aspect, in *The Republic. See also* **Socrate** (Satie).

Platti, Giovanni (b Padua, 9 Jul 1697; d Würzburg, 11 Jan 1763), Italian harpsichordist and composer. Little is known of his life, but he was from 1722 in the service of the archepiscopal court in Würzburg. He made important contribs. towards the development of a modern style of keyboard music.

Works incl. 6 Masses and other church music; oratorios, cantatas, etc.; sonatas for fl., cello, etc.; concertos and sonatas for harpsichord and other keyboard music.

Playford, Henry (b London, 5 May 1657; d London, *c* 1709), English bookseller and publisher. Succeeded to his father's business in 1684; estab. regular concerts, held 3 times a week at a London coffee-house from 1699, and another series at Oxford in 1701.

Playford, John (b Norwich, 1623; d London, ? Dec 1686), English bookseller and publisher, father of prec. Estab. in London about 1648. His 1st music pub., *The English Dancing Master*, appeared in 1650, dated 1651.

Playford, John (b Stanmore Magna, *c* 1655; d London, 20 Apr 1685), English printer, nephew of prec. Was apprenticed to the printer William Godbid in London and in 1679 went into partnership with his widow,

Anne Godbid. He printed the musical works issued by his cousin Henry.

Plectrum (Lat.), a hard spike of quill or metal with which the strings of certain instruments are made to sound. In the virginals, spinet and harpsichord, the plectrum is attached to the jack, and when used for instruments of the lute type, such as the cittern and the mandoline, it projects from a metal ring placed on the thumb.

Pleeth, William (b London, 12 Jan 1916), English cellist. He studied with Julius Klengel in Leipzig and made his debut there in 1932. London debut 1933. Many appearances as soloist but best known as chamber music player: Blech quartet 1936–41, Allegri quartet 1952–67; often heard in Schubert's string 5tet, with the Amadeus quartet. Professor, GSM, from 1948.

Plein jeu (Fr. = full play), the French equivalent of *Organo pleno* (or *Pieno*).

Pleyel, Camille (b Strasbourg, 18 Dec 1788; d Montmorency nr. Paris, 4 May 1855), French pf. maker, publisher and pianist, husband of Marie Moke. He succeeded to his father's business in 1824 and associated himself with Kalkbrenner. Studied music with his father and Dussek and pub. some pf. pieces.

Pleyel, Ignaz Joseph (b Ruppertsthal, Lower Aus., 18 Jun 1757; d Paris, 14 Nov 1831), Austrian pianist, pf. maker and composer, father of prec. Pupil of Wanhal and Haydn, in 1777 became *Kapellmeister* to Count Erdödy, who gave him leave for further study in Rome. In 1783 he moved to Strasbourg as vice-*Kapellmeister*, succeeding Richter as *Kapellmeister* in 1789. Three years later he visited London as cond. of a rival series of concerts to those given by Salomon and Haydn. Settled in Paris in 1795, and in 1807 founded his pf. factory.

Works incl. 2 operas, *Die Fee Urgele* (prod. Eszterháza, 1776) and *Ifigenia en Aulide* (prod. Naples, 1785); 29 symphs. and 5 *sinfonie concertanti*; concertos; 45 string 4tets and much other chamber music.

Pli selon pli, 'Portrait de Mallarmé' for sop. and orch. in 5 parts by Boulez. Fp Donaueschingen, 20 Oct 1962.

Plica (Lat., for *plicare*, to fold), an ornamental passing note indicated in medieval notation by a vertical stroke at the side of the note. Its length was determined by the length of the stroke, its pitch by the context (*see* illustration overleaf).

According to theorists it should be sung with a kind of quavering in the throat, but its convenience as an abbr. led to its frequent employment as a substitute for a written note.

Modern equivalent

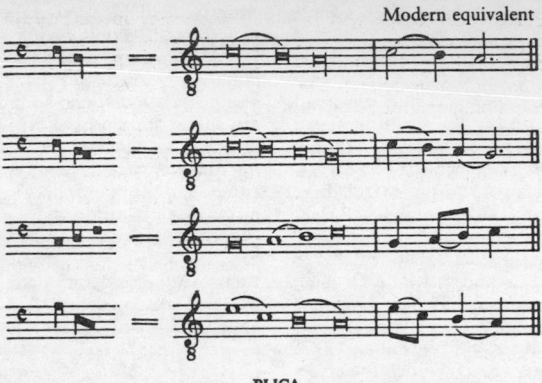

PLICA

Plishka, Paul (b Old Forge, Penn., 28 Aug 1941), American bass. He studied in New Jersey and Baltimore. NY Met since 1967 as Leporello, Marke, Procida, Varlaam and Banquo (in the Peter Hall prod. of *Macbeth*). At San Francisco in 1984 he was admired as Verdi's Silva. Other roles incl. Henry VIII, Méphistophélès and Orovesco.

Plowright, Rosalind (b Worksop, 21 May 1949), English soprano. She studied at the RMCM; debut there, 1968, in J.C. Bach's *Temistocle*. She sang Donna Elvira with the Glyndebourne Touring co. in 1977. ENO, London, debut 1979, as Britten's Miss Jessel; later sang Desdemona, Donizetti's Elisabeth and Verdi's Elena there. US opera debut 1982, in *Il Corsaro*. Her first major role at CG was Donna Anna (1983); returned for Aida in 1984. She has appeared in Paris, Milan, Berne and Munich as Strauss's Ariadne and Danae, Amelia, Suor Angelica and Alceste. Returned to CG in 1986 for Senta, and the *Trovatore* Leonora.

Plummer, John (b *c* 1410; d Windsor, *c* 1484), English composer. He was a clerk of the Chapel Royal by 1441 and in 1444 became the first official master of its children. In *c* 1458 he became verger at St George's Chapel, Windsor, while continuing as a member of the Chapel Royal; the Windsor post he held until 1484. His surviving works consist of 4 antiphons for 2 and 4 voices, a Mass, *Omnipotens Pater*, and a Mass fragment.

Pneuma (Gk. = breath), a vocal ornament in Plainsong inserting long cadential phrases on the syllables of certain words, notably 'Alleluia'. The pneuma were also called by the Latin name of Jubili, and they developed later into Tropes and Sequences. Sometimes written *neuma*, by confusion with the word for a Neume.

Pocahontas, ballet by Elliott Carter; comp. 1936–9, prod. NY, 24 May 1939. Pocahontas was an American Indian princess (1595–1617) who befriended the early settlers in America.

Poco (It. = little), often used as a qualifying direction where any indication of tempo or expression is to be applied in moderation; e.g. *poco più mosso*, a little faster; *poco rallentando*, slowing down a little; *poco forte*, fairly loud.

Poème de l'amour et de la mer (*Poem of love and of the sea*), work for mezzo and orch. by Chausson (text by M. Bouchor), comp. 1882–90, rev. 1893. The work's 3 sections are *La fleur des eaux*, *Interlude* and *La mort de l'amour* (closing section *Le temps de lilas*).

Poèmes pour Mi (*Poems for Mi*), cycle of 9 songs for sop. and pf. by Messiaen (texts by comp.), fp Paris, 28 Apr 1937; orch. vers. 1937, perfs. Paris 1946, cond. Désormière. (Mi was comp.'s name for his 1st wife.)

Poem of Ecstasy (*Poema ekstasa*), work for orch. by Scriabin; comp. 1905–8, fp NY, 10 Dec 1908; 1st Russian perf. St Petersburg, 1 Feb 1909.

Poet's Echo, The, cycle of 6 songs for high voice and pf. by Britten (texts by Pushkin), fp Moscow, 2 Dec 1965, with Vishnevskaya and Rostropovich.

Poglietti, Alessandro (b ? Tuscany; d Vienna, Jul 1683), Austrian organist and composer. His early career is unknown; he became organist of the Imp. chapel in Vienna, 161, and was killed during the Turkish siege of the Aus. capital.

Works incl. opera, *Endimione festeg-*

giante (1677); sacred vocal comps. with instrumental accomp.; *ricercari*, toccatas and other works for organ; harpsichord suites incl. *Rossignolo, Sopra la ribellione di Ungheria*, another containing a capriccio on the cries of cocks and hens.

Pogorelich, Ivo (b Belgrade, 20 Oct 1958), Yugoslav pianist. At the Moscow Cons. he studied with Aliza Kezeradze (b *c* 1935); they were married in 1980. He won 1st prize in Montreal Int. Competition 1980, but when he was eliminated before the final rounds of Chopin Internat. the same year, one of the jury members, Martha Argerich resigned; his success thereafter was assured. Noted for the brilliance, rather than the profundity, of his interpretations.

Pohjola's Daughter, symph. poem by Sibelius, op. 49, comp. 1906 and based on an incident in the *Kalevala*; fp St Petersburg, Siloti concerts (cond. by comp.), 29 Dec 1906.

Pohl, Carl Ferdinand (b Darmstadt, 6 Sep 1819; d Vienna, 28 Apr 1887), German organist, bibliographer and writer on music. Studied with Sechter in Vienna, was organist at the Protestant church in the Gumpendorf suburb, 1849–55, lived in London, 1863–6, and in the latter year became librarian to the Phil. Society in Vienna. He wrote on this, on Haydn and Mozart in London and the standard biog. of Haydn (finished by Botstiber).

Pohl, Richard (b Leipzig, 12 Sep 1826; d Baden-Baden, 17 Dec 1896), German critic and author. Studied at Göttingen and Leipzig, and was for a time ed. of the *Neue Zeitschrift für Musik*. Wrote mainly on Wagner, also on Berlioz, Liszt, etc., and comp. songs. He claimed that the chromaticism in *Tristan* was derived from Liszt.

Pohlenz, (Christian) August (b Sallgast, Lusatia, 3 Jul 1790; d Leipzig, 10 Mar 1843), German organist, teacher and conductor. Studied at Leipzig, where he became organist at St Thomas's Church and cond. of the Gewandhaus concerts before Mendelssohn.

Poi (It. = then), used in directions where some music section is to follow another in a way not made immediately obvious by the notation: e.g. after a repeat of an earlier section, *poi la coda* or *e poi la coda*.

Pointing, the distribution of the syllables of the Psalms in Anglican chant according to the verbal rhythm.

Poise, (Jean Alexandre) Ferdinand (b Nîmes, 3 Jun 1828; d Paris, 13 May 1892), French composer. Studied with Adam and others at the Paris Cons. and in 1853 prod. his 1st opera.

Works incl. operas *Bonsoir Voisin* (1853), *Les Charmeurs* (1855); *Polichinelle* (1856), *Le Roi Don Pèdre, Le Jardinier galant* (1861), *Les Absents, Corricolo* (1868), *Les Trois Souhaits* (1861), *La Surprise de l'amour* (after Marivaux), *L'Amour médecin (after Molière, 1880), Les Deux Billets, Joli Gilles, Carmosine* (after Musset, prod. 1928); oratorio *Cécile* (1888).

Poisoned Kiss, The, or The Empress and the Necromancer, opera by Vaughan Williams (lib. by Evelyn Sharp), prod. Cambridge Arts Theatre, 12 May 1936. Much of the score is a satire on var. musical styles.

Poissl, Johann Nepomuk von (b Haukenzell, Bavaria, 15 Feb 1783; d Munich, 17 Aug 1865), German composer. Studied with Danzi at Munich and became Intendant of the royal orch. and director of the royal opera there.

Works incl. operas *Athalia* (after Racine, 1814), *Der Wettkampf zu Olympia* and *Nittetis* (trans. of Metastasio's *Olimpiade* and *Nitteti*, 1815 and 1817), *Zayde* (1843) and *c* 10 others; Mass, *Stabat Mater*, Psalm xcv; oratorio *Der Erntetag* (1835).

Polacca (It. = Polonaise). Although Polacca is the exact It. equivalent of the Polonaise, the word is often more loosely used for pieces in polonaise rhythm, but not necessarily in polonaise form, in which case they are actually, as indeed they are often designated, *alla polacca*.

Polaroli, another form of the surname of Antonio and Carlo Francesco Pollarolo.

Poldini, Ede (b Budapest, 13 Jun 1869; d Vevey, 28 Jun 1957), Hungarian composer. Studied at Budapest and with Mandyczewski in Vienna.

Works incl. operas *The Vagabond and the Princess* (1903), *Wedding in Carnival-Time* (*Love Adrift*, 1924), *Himfy* (1938); ballet *Night's Magic*; *Marionettes* for orch. (orig. pf.); numerous pf. suites and pieces incl. *Arlequinades, Morceaux pittoresques, Épisodes à la Cour, Images, Moments musicaux, Poupée valsante.*

Polidori, John William (1795–1821), English novelist, Byron's secretary and physician. *See* **Vampyr** (Lindpaintner and Marschner).

Polifemo, opera by Giovanni Bononcini (lib. by A. Ariosti), prod. Berlin, Lietzenburg Palace, summer 1702.

Poliphant, a string instrument, also called Polyphone, of the lute or cittern type but with anything from 25 to 40 strings, invented *c* 1600 by Daniel Farrant and played by Queen Elizabeth.

'Polish' Symphony, Tchaikovsky's 3rd symph., in D maj., op. 29, finished Aug 1875 and prod. Moscow, 19 Nov 1875. The finale is in polonaise rhythm.

Poliuto (later *Martyrs* and *I martiri*), opera by Donizetti (lib. devised by A. Nourrit and written by S. Cammarano, based on Corneille's tragedy *Polyeucte*), finished 1838 for prod. at Naples, but forbidden by censor; prod. in Fr. (trans. by Scribe), Paris, Opéra, 1 Apr 1840.

Poliziano (real name Angelo Ambrogini) (1454–94), Italian poet. *See* **Favola d'Orfeo** (Casella), **Isaac** (Monody on Lorenzo de' Medici), **Malipiero** (3 songs), **Pastoral** (Bliss).

Polka, a dance dating from *c* 1830 and prob. originating in Bohemia, though the story of its being invented there by a servant-girl, the tune being written down by a musician named Neruda, is not authenticated. It is danced in couples and the music is in 2–4 time and divided into regular 2-bar patterns grouped into periods of 8 bars.

Pollak, Egon (b Prague, 3 May 1879; d Prague, 14 Jun, 1933), Austrian conductor. He studied at the Prague Cons. and worked at opera houses in Bremen, Leipzig and Frankfurt. He cond. Wagner in Paris (1914) and gave *Ring* cycles at the Chicago Lyric Opera 1915–17; returned 1929–32. Hamburg 1917–31. He took the Vienna Staatsoper Co. to Egypt in 1933 and in the same year collapsed and died during a perf. of *Fidelio* in Prague. His daughter **Anna** (b Manchester, 1 May 1912), sang with the SW co. 1945–61 and appeared at Glyndebourne 1952–3 as Dorabella.

Pollarolo, Antonio (b Brescia, bap. 12 Nov 1676 d Venice, 30 May 1746), Italian composer. Pupil of his father, became asst. *maestro di cappella* at St Mark's in Venice, 1723, and *maestro di cappella* in 1740.

Works incl. operas *Aristeo*, *Leucippo e Teonoe*, *Cosroe*, *I tre voti* and 10 others; church music.

Pollarolo, Carlo Francesco (b Brescia, 1653; d Venice, 7 Feb 1723), Italian organist and composer, father of prec. Pupil of Legrenzi at Venice, became a singer at St Mark's there in 1665, 2nd organist in 1690 and asst. *maestro di cappella* in 1692. Later taught music at the Cons. degli Incurabili.

Works incl. operas *Roderico* (1686), *La forza della virtù* (1693), *Ottone* (1694), *Faramondo*, *Semiramide* (1713), *Marsia deluso*, *Ariodante* (1716), *Le pazzie degli amanti*, *Gl'inganni felici*, *Santa Genuinda* (with Violone and A. Scarlatti, 1694) and *c*

65 others, most lost; 12 oratorios; organ music.

Polledro, Giovanni Battista (b Piovà nr. Turin, 10 Jun 1781; d Piovà, 15 Aug 1853), Italian violinist and composer. Pupil of Pugnani. Made his 1st appearance at Turin in 1797 and, after touring widely, was leader of the orchestra at Dresden, 1814–24, and court *maestro di cappella* at Turin from 1824 to 1844.

Works incl. 2 vln. concertos, chamber music, symph., Mass.

Pollini, Francesco (Giuseppe) (b Ljubljana, 25 Mar 1762; d Milan, 17 Sep 1846), Italian pianist and composer. Pupil of Mozart in Vienna and later of Zingarelli at Milan, where he was app. pf. prof. at the Cons. in 1809.

Works incl. *Stabat Mater*; music for the stage; many pf. studies and pieces.

Pollini, Maurizio (b Milan, 5 Jan 1942), Italian pianist and conductor. He studied at the Milan Cons. and in 1960 won the Chopin Internat. Competition, Warsaw. Many appearances in recital and as soloist in Europe and the US (debut, Carnegie Hall, NY, 1968). He plays Boulez, Nono and Schoenberg, in addition to the standard repertory, and has cond. from the keyboard. In 1981 he cond. Rossini's *La donna del lago* at Pesaro.

Polly, ballad opera, sequel to *The Beggar's Opera* (words by John Gay), pub. 1729, but not allowed to be perf. Prod. London, with the music arr. by Arnold, Little Haymarket Theatre, 19 Jun 1777. Modern version by F. Austin, prod. London, Kingsway Theatre, 30 Dec 1922.

Polonaise, a Polish dance of a stately, processional character, dating back to at least the 16th cent. The music is in 3–4 time and is characterized by feminine cadences at the end of each section, also often by dotted rhythms. The more primitive exs. were in binary form: 2 sections, each repeated; but later (e.g. Chopin) a trio section developed, after which the main section is repeated.

Polonia, symph. prelude for orch. by Elgar, op. 76, written for a concert given for the Pol. Relief Fund, London, 6 July 1915, and ded. to Paderewski, a quotation from whose *Polish Fantasy* it contains as well as one from Chopin and the Pol. Nat. Anthem.

Polyeucte. *See also* **Poliuto.**

Opera by Gounod (lib. by J. Barbier and M. Carré, based on Corneille's drama), prod. Paris, Opéra, 7 Oct 1878.

Polyphone. *See* **Poliphant.**

Polyphony, music which combines 2 or more independent melodic lines.

Polyrhythm, the combination of different rhythmic formations.

Polytonality, the simultaneous combination of 2 or more different keys.

Pomo d'oro, Il (*The Golden Apple*), opera by Cesti (lib. by F. Sbarra), prod. Vienna, Carnival 1667, for the wedding of the Emperor Leopold I and the Infanta Margherita of Spain (reputed to be the most expensive opera prod. ever mounted). The subject is the judgment of Paris.

Pomone, opera by Cambert (lib. by P. Perrin), prod. Paris, Opéra, 3 Mar 1671.

Pomp and Circumstance, 5 military marches by Elgar, orig. intended as a set of 6, op. 39. 1–4 comp. 1901–7, 5 in 1930. 1 contains, as a trio, the tune afterwards used in the *Coronation Ode* to the words 'Land of hope and glory'. The title of the set comes from *Othello* , III. iii: 'pride, pomp and circumstance of glorious war'. nos. 1 & 2 fp Liverpool, 19 Oct 1901; no. 3 fp London, 8 Mar 1905; no. 4 fp London, 24 Aug 1907; no. 5 fp London, 20 Sep 1930.

Pomposo (It. = pompous, stately), a direction used for music of a sumptuous character.

Ponce, Manuel (b Fresnillo, 8 Dec 1882; d Mexico City, 24 Apr 1948), Mexican composer. Learnt music from his sister at first, became cathedral organist at Aguas Calientes and at 14 comp. a gavotte which was later made famous by the dancer Argentina. He entered the Nat. Cons. at Mexico City and in 1905 went to Europe for further study with Bossi at Bologna and Martin Krause in Berlin. In 1906 he returned home and became prof. at the Nat. Cons. In 1915–18 he lived at Havana and at the age of 43 went to Paris to take a comp. course with Dukas.

Works incl. symph. triptych *Chapultepec* (1929), *Canto y danza de los antiguos Mexicanos* (1933), *Poema elegiaco, Ferial* for orch. (1940); pf. concerto, vln. concerto (1943), concerto for guitar and chamber orch. (1941); 3 Tagore songs with orch.; *Sonata en duo* for vln. and vla.; 2 Mexican Rhapsodies and many other pf. works; numerous songs.

Ponchielli, Amilcare (b Paderno Fasolaro nr. Cremona, 31 Aug 1834; d Milan, 17 Jan 1886), Italian composer. Studied at the Milan Cons. and prod. his 1st opera, on Manzoni's *Promessi sposi*, at Cremona in 1856. In 1881 he was app. *maestro di cappella* at Bergamo Cathedral.

Works incl. operas *I promessi sposi* (1856); *La Savoiarda* (1861), *Roderico* (1863), *Bertrand de Born, Il parlatore eterno* (1873), *I Lituani* (*Aldona*), *Gioconda* (after Hugo's *Angelo*, 1876), *Il figliuol prodigo* (1880), *Marion Delorme* (on Hugo's play, 1885), *I Mori di Valenza*, unfinished; prod. Monte Carlo, 1914; ballets *Le due gemelle* and *Clarina*; cantatas for the reception of the remains of Donizetti and Mayr at Bergamo and in memory of Garibaldi.

Poniatowski, Józef Michal Xawery Franciszek Jan, Prince of Monte Rotondo (b Rome, 20 Feb 1816; d Chislehurst, 3 Jul 1873), Polish composer and tenor. Studied at the Liceo musicale at Florence and under Ceccherini. He sang at the Teatro della Pergola there and prod. his 1st opera there in 1839, singing the title-part. After the 1848 Revolution he settled in Paris, but after the Franco-Prussian war he followed Napoleon III to England, 1871.

Works incl. operas *Giovanni da Procida* (1838), *Don Desiderio* (1840), *Ruy Blas* (after Hugo), *Bonifazio de' Geremei* (*I Lambertazzi*, 1843), *Malek Adel* (1846), *Esmeralda* (after Hugo's *Notre-Dame de Paris*, 1847), *La sposa d'Abido* (after Byron's *Bride of Abydos*), *Pierre de Médicis* (1860), *Gelmina* (1872) and others; Mass in F maj.; songs incl. *The Yeoman's Wedding Song*.

Ponnelle, Jean-Pierre (b Paris, 19 Feb 1932), French opera designer and producer. He designed the première prods. of Henze's *Boulevard Solitude* (1952), and *König Hirsch* (1956). His first opera prod. was *Tristan* in Düsseldorf, 1962, and he has since prod. and designed operas by Mozart in Salzburg and Cologne and a Monteverdi cycle in Zurich. His *Don Pasquale* has been seen at CG, London, and his *Cenerentola* at the NY Met. Noted for his stylish prods. and his attention to detail.

Pons, José (b Gerona, Catalonia, 1768; d Valencia, 2 Aug 1818), Spanish composer. Studied at Córdoba, became *maestro de capilla* at Gerona and later at Valencia.

Works incl. Misereres and other church music; *villancicos* for Christmas with orch. or organ.

Pons, Lily (Alice Joséphine Pons) (b Draguignan, 16 Apr 1898; d Dallas, 13 Jan 1976), American coloratura soprano of French birth. Studied pf., aged 13, at the Paris Cons., and then singing with A. de Gorostiaga, making her debut at Mulhouse in 1928 as Lakmé. From 1931 to 1959 she sang at the NY Met as Lucia, Amina, Gilda and Olympia.

Ponselle (actually Ponzillo), **Rosa** (b Meridan, Conn., 22 Jan 1897; d Green Spring Valley, Md., 25 May 1981), American soprano of Italian parentage. Studied in NY with W. Thorner and Romani, making her debut at the Met Opera in 1918, as the *Forza* Leonora. She sang there from 1918 to 1937 as Reiza, Laura, Mathilde, Donna Anna, Santuzza and Elisabeth de Valois. At CG 1929–31 as Norma and Violetta. One of the great singers of the century, she retired at the height of her powers to teach.

Pont-neuf (Fr. lit. new bridge), a satirical song of the 18th cent. similar to the Vaudeville, sung in public mainly on the pont-neuf in Paris.

Ponte, Lorenzo da (actually Emmanuele Conegliano) (b Ceneda nr. Venice, 10 Mar 1749; d New York, 17 Aug 1838), Italian poet and librettist. Of Jewish parentage, he took the name da Ponte at his baptism. Educ. at the theological seminary in Portogruaro, he was ordained in 1773, but led the life of an adventurer, being banished from Venice because of scandal in 1779. App. poet to the Court Opera in Vienna in 1784, he moved to London in 1792, and thence, to escape his creditors, to NY in 1804. He pub. his memoirs in 1823–7. Wrote the libs. of *Le nozze di Figaro, Don Giovanni* and *Così fan tutte* for Mozart, others for Bianchi, Martín y Soler, Winter, etc. *See also* **Burbero di buon cuore** (Martín y Soler), **Ratto di Proserpina** (Winter), **Scuola de' maritati** (Martín y Soler), **Tarare** (Salieri), **Una cosa rara** (Martín y Soler).

Ponticello (It. = little bridge), the bridge of string instruments over which the strings are stretched to keep clear of the body of the instrument. The direction sul ponticello (on the bridge) indicates that the bow is to be drawn close to the bridge, which results in a peculiar nasal tone.

Poole, Elizabeth (b London, 5 Apr 1820; d Langley, Bucks., 14 Jan 1906), English soprano and actress. Appeared as a child actress at the Olympic Theatre and made her 1st appearance in opera at Drury Lane in 1834.

Poot, Marcel (b Vilvoorde nr. Brussels, 7 May 1901), Belgian composer. Studied at the Brussels Cons. and with Mortelmans at that of Antwerp. He early became interested in film, radio and jazz music. In 1935 he founded the group known as Les Synthétistes and in 1930 gained the Rubens Prize and went to Paris to study with Dukas. On his return he held several teaching posts, incl. at the Brussels Cons., of which he became dir. in 1949.

Works incl. operas *Het Ingebeeld Eiland* (1925), *Het Vrouwtje van Stavoren* (1928), and *Moretus* (1944); ballets *Paris in verlegenheid* (1925), and *Pygmalion* (1951); oratorios *Le Dit du routier* and *Icaros*; 6 symphs. (1929–78) and other orchestral works; chamber music, etc.

Pope, Alexander (1688–1744), English poet. *See* **Acis and Galatea, Jephtha, Semele.**

Popov, Gavryil Nikolaievich (b Novotcherkass, 25 Sep 1904; d Repino, 17 Feb 1972), Russian composer. Studied at the School of Music at Rostov-on-Don and from 1922 at the St Petersburg Cons., where Steinberg and Shtcherbatchev were his comp. masters.

Works incl. operas *The Slow Horseman* (after Pushkin) and *Alexander Nevsky*; film music; *Heroic Intermezzo* for solo voice, chorus and orch., based on the 2nd opera; 6 symphs., 2 suites for orch.; vln. concerto; 7tet for fl., clar., bassoon, tpt., vln., vla. and double bass (1927); suite and pieces for pf.

Popp, Lucia (b Uhorska Ves, 12 Nov 1939), Austrian soprano of Czech birth . She studied in Bratislava; appeared at the Vienna Staatsoper and at Salzburg in 1963. CG, London, debut 1966, as Oscar; has returned for Gilda, Despina, Sophie, Eva and Arabella (1986). NY Met debut, 1967, as Queen of Night, a role which she recorded with Klemperer. Other roles incl. Pamina, Ilia and Zerlina. Much admired for her charming stage presence, she is also in demand as a concert singer, e.g. in Orff and Mahler.

Popper, David (b Prague, 16 Jun 1843; d Baden nr. Vienna, 7 Aug 1913), German-Czech cellist and composer. Studied music in general at the Prague Cons. and the cello under Goltermann at Frankfurt, and made his 1st concert tour in Ger. in 1863. In 1868 he became 1st cellist at the Court Opera in Vienna, in 1872 he married Sophie Menter (*q.v.*), but the marriage was dissolved in 1886. In 1896 he became cello prof. at the Budapest Cons.

Works incl. 4 cello concertos, *Requiem* for 3 cellos (perf. London, 1891), numerous pieces for cello, etc.

Poradowski, Stefan Boleslaw (b Wloclawek, 16 Aug 1902; d Posnań, 9 Jul 1967), Polish composer. Studied at the Cons. and Univ. of Poznań and in 1930 became prof. at the former and music critic.

Works incl. cantatas *Triumph, The Song of Spring* (1926), *The Horse of Swiatowid* (1931); 8 symphs. (1928–67), sinfonietta on folk themes, *Lyrical Overture* and other orchestral works; *Antique Suite* for strings; double bass concerto (1929), *Concerto antico* for vla. d'amore and string orch. (1925); 3 string 4tets and *Metamorphoses* for string 4tet, 3 string trios, duets for 2 vlns.; Prelude and Pol. Dance for pf.; songs, part-songs.

Porgy and Bess, opera in 3 acts by Gershwin (lib. by D.B. Heyward and I. Gershwin, after the play *Porgy* by D. B. and D. Heyward), prod. Boston, 30 Sep 1935. Not produced by British co. until 1986 (Glyndebourne).

Poro, rè dell' Indie (*Porus, King of the Indies*), opera by Handel (lib. by ?, altered from Metastasio's *Alessandro nell' Indie*), prod. London, King's Theatre, Haymarket, 2 Feb 1731.

Porpora, Nicola Antonio (b Naples, 17 Aug 1686; d Naples, 3 Mar 1768), Italian composer and singing teacher. Pupil of Greco and Campanile at the Cons. dei Poveri in Naples, where his first opera, *Agrippina*, was prod. in 1708. At first *maestro di cappella* to the Imp. Commandant in Naples, Prince Philip of Hesse-Darmstadt, he was app. singing teacher at the Cons. di S. Onofrio there in 1715, and 10 years later became *maestro* at the Cons. degli Incurabili in Venice. Among his pupils were Farinelli and Caffarelli, and, briefly, Hasse. Travelling as an opera cond., he rivalled Handel in London (1733–6) and Hasse in Dresden (1748–52). In Vienna Haydn was his pupil-valet. Porpora finally settled in Naples in 1760, remaining there till his death.

Works incl. operas *Basilio* (1713), *Berenice* (1718), *Flavio Anicio Olibrio*, *Faramondo* (1719), *Eumene*, *Amare per regnare* (1723), *Semiramide* (1724), *Semiramide riconosciuta*, *L'Imeneo* (1726), *Adelaide*, *Siface*, *Mitridate* (1730), *Annibale* (1731), *Il trionfo di Camilla*, *Arianna* (1733), *Temistocle* (1743), *Filandro* and *c* 20 others; oratorios *Il martirio di Santa Eugenia* (1721) and 8 others; Masses, motets, duets on the Passion and other church music; cantatas; vln. sonatas; keyboard music.

Porrino, Ennio (b Cagliari, Sardinia, 20 Jan 1910; d Rome, 25 Sep 1959), Italian composer. Studied in Rome with Respighi and others and won a competition at the Accademia di Santa Cecilia.

Works incl. operas *Gli Orazi* (1941), *L'organo di Bambû* (1955), and *I Shardana* (1959); ballets; choral comps.; symph. poem *Sardegna*, overture *Tartarin de Tarascon* (after Daudet, 1932), concertos.

Porsile, Giuseppe (b Naples, 5 May 1680;
d Vienna, 29 May 1750), Italian composer. He was vice-*maestro de capilla* to the Spanish court in Barcelona from 1695 (*maestro* 1697), and from 1720 court *Kapellmeister* in Vienna.

Works incl. *c* 12 operas, e.g. *Il ritorno di Ulisse* (1707), *Alceste* (1718), *Meride e Selinunte* (1721), *Spartaco* (1726); 12 oratorios; serenades, cantatas, canzonets.

Porta, Costanzo (b Cremona, *c* 1529; d Padua, 19 May 1601), Italian monk and composer. Pupil of Willaert at Venice. He took orders and became choirmaster at Osimo nr. Ancona, 1552–64, when he went to Padua to take up a similar post at the Cappella Antoniana, the church of the Minorite order to which he belonged, which he left for a time to work at Ravenna (1567–74), then Loreto (1574–80). Returned to Ravenna 1580–9.

Works incl. Masses, motets, psalms, hymns, introits and other church music, madrigals.

Porta, Ercole (b Bologna, 10 Sep 1585; d Carpi, 30 Apr 1630), Italian organist and composer. Organist at the coll. of San Giovanni in Persiceto in 1609. His *Sacro Convito* of 1620 includes a Mass with trombones in the orch. accompaniment.

Works incl. sacred vocal concertos; secular works; vocal music.

Porta, Francesco della (b Monza, *c* 1600; d Milan, Jan 1666), Italian organist and composer. Studied with the organist Ripalta at Monza and became organist and *maestro di cappella* of 3 churches at Milan.

Works incl. motets, psalms; instrumental *ricercari*; *villunelle* for 1–3 voices with instruments, etc.

Porta, Giovanni (b Venice, *c* 1690; d Munich, 21 Jun 1755), Italian composer. Worked in Rome 1706–16 in the service of Cardinal Ottoboni, then at the Cons. della pietà in Venice, and also visited London, where his opera *Numitore* was prod. in 1720. From 1736 to his death he was *Kapellmeister* to the court in Munich.

Works incl. over 30 operas, e.g. *Arianna* (1723), *Antigono* (1724), *Ulisse* (1725) and *Semiramide* (1733); oratorios; cantatas; 19 Masses and other church music, etc.

Portamento. Moving from one note to another with some element of slide or glide, particularly on the voice or stringed instruments. In many musical repertories, stylish performance involves considerable use of portamento with a special emphasis on variety of approaches.

Portative Organ, a small organ with a single

keyboard and 1 range of pipes, which could be carried, placed on a table or suspended from the shoulder by a strap. Representations are frequent in medieval and Renaissance paintings.

Portato (It.), a manner of delivering a musical phrase somewhere between *legato* and *staccato*.

Porter, Andrew (b Cape Town, 26 Aug 1928), English music critic and scholar. He studied at Oxford Univ. and worked for various newspapers and journals from 1949 (ed. *Musical Times* 1960–7). He is noted for his research on Verdi and has prepared for perf. much material for *Don Carlos* which Verdi discarded at the 1st prod. in 1867; several transs. of Verdi libretti. His translation of the *Ring* was heard at the Coliseum, London, in 1973 and his vers. of the *Parsifal* lib. was given there in 1986. Critic, *New Yorker*, from 1972; 2 vols. of criticism were pub. 1974 and 1978.

Porter, Cole (b Peru, Indiana, 9 Jun 1893; d Santa Monica, Calif., 15 Oct 1964), American composer. Studied at Yale and at Harvard Law School and School of Music. While still a student he became well known for his football songs. In 1916 he joined the Foreign Legion and after the war studied at the Schola Cantorum in Paris. His output consists entirely of musicals, of which the best known are *Kiss me, Kate*, *Can-Can* and *Silk Stockings*.

Porter, (William) Quincy (b New Haven, Conn., 7 Feb 1897; d Bethany, Conn., 12 Nov 1966), American composer. Studied at Yale Univ. and School of Music with H. Parker and D.S. Smith, later with Bloch and with d'Indy in Paris. He taught at the Cleveland Inst. of Music for 2 periods during 1922–32, at Vassar Coll., Poughkeepsie, 1932–8, and at the New Eng. Cons. at Boston from 1938. He also played vla. in var. string 4tets.

Works incl. incid. music for Shakespeare's *Antony and Cleopatra* (1934) and T.S. Eliot's *Sweeney Agonistes* (1933); symph., *Poem and Dance* for orch.; *Ukrainian Suite* for strings (1925); *Dance in Three Time* for chamber orch. (1937); vla. concerto, harpsichord concerto (1959), concerto for 2 pfs.; 3 Gk. Mimes for voices, string 4tet and perc.; 9 string 4tets (1923–58); 2 vln. and pf. sonatas, suite for vla. solo.

Porter, Walter (b c 1588; d London, buried 30 Nov 1659), English composer. He became a Gentleman of the Chapel Royal in London in 1617. At some time, prob. earlier, he was a pupil of Monteverdi. In 1639 he became choirmaster at Westminster Abbey and when the choral service was suppressed in 1644 came under the patronage of Sir Edward Spencer.

Works incl. motets for 2 voices and insts., psalms (George Sandys's paraphrases) for 2 voices and org.; madrigals and airs for voices and insts. (pub. 1632).

Portinaro, Francesco (b Padua, c 1520; d ? Padua, after 1578), Italian composer. He was assoc. with the *Accademia degli Elevati* in Padua (1557), and later with the d'Este family at Ferrara and Tivoli. His 3 books of motets and 6 of madrigals were pub. at Venice.

Portman, Richard (d ? London, c 1655), English organist and composer. Pupil of O. Gibbons, succeeded Thomas Day as organist of Westminster Abbey in London, 1633. Like W. Porter, who was choirmaster, he lost this post in 1644 and became a music teacher.

Works incl. services, anthems; *Dialogue of the Prodigal Son* for 2 voices and chorus, meditation; *The Soules Life, exercising itself in the sweet fields of divine meditation*; harpsichord music, etc.

Portogallo. *See* **Portugal.**

Portsmouth Point, concert overture by Walton, inspired by Rowlandson's drawing, fp ISCM Festival, Zurich, 22 Jun 1926.

Portugal, Marcus Antonio da Fonseca (called Portogallo in It.) (b Lisbon, 24 Mar 1762; d Rio de Janeiro, 7 Feb 1830), Portuguese composer. Educ. at the Patriarchal Seminary at Lisbon, where later he became cantor and organist, and learnt music from João de Sousa Carvalho. He was also a theatre cond. and in 1785 prod. his 1st stage work. In 1792 he went to Naples and began to write It. operas in great numbers. In 1800 he returned to Lisbon to become dir. of the San Carlos Theatre, where he continued to prod. It. operas. In 1807 the Fr. invasion drove the court to Brazil, and he followed it in 1810, but was unable to return with it in 1821, being incapacitated by a stroke.

Works incl. *Licença pastoril*, *A Castanheira* and 20 other Port. operas; *La confusione nata della somiglianza* (1793), *Demofoonte* (1794), *Lo spazzacamino principe*, *La donna di genio volubile* (1796), *Fernando nel Messico* (1799), *Alceste*, *La morte di Semiramide* (1801), *Non irritare le donne*, *L'oro non compra amore* (1804), *Il trionfo di Clelia* (1802), *Il diavolo a quattro*, *La pazza giornata* (on Beaumarchais' *La Folle Journée* [*Figaro*, 1799]) and c 25 other It. operas; church music; cantata *La speranza*; songs.

Posaune (Ger.) = Trombone.
Positif (Fr.) = Choir Organ.
Positions. (1) The points at which the left hand is placed in order to stop the strings on a string instrument. Since only 4 fingers are available, the hand has to change from one position to another in order to reach higher notes e.g. on the vln. (*see* illustration).

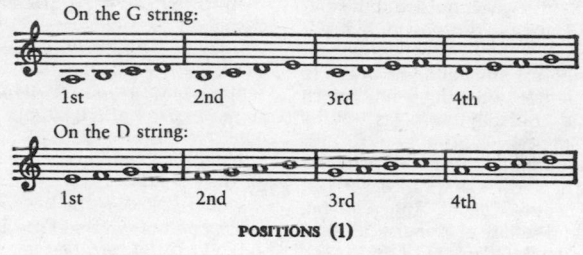

POSITIONS (1)

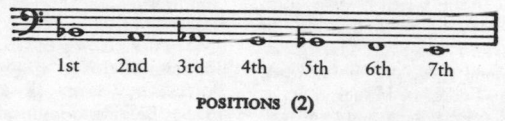

POSITIONS (2)

(2) The points at which the slide of the tromb. is arrested, e.g. on the Bb tenor tromb. (*see* illustration).
Each position offers a complete series of harmonics and hence provides the instrument with a chromatic compass. *See* **Trombone.**
Positive Organ. A small chamber organ.
Posthorn, brass instrument akin to the bugle rather than the horn, used by postillions in the 18th and early 19th cent. It had no valves and could therefore prod. only the natural harmonics, which were coarse and penetrating in tone. It was hardly ever used in serious music, but Bach imitated it in his Capriccio on his brother's departure for harpsichord and Mozart scored parts for 2 in his German Dances, K605 and in his Posthorn Serenade, K320.
Postillon de Lonjumeau, Le, opera by Adam (lib. by A. de Leuven and L. L. Brunswick), prod. Paris, Opéra-Comique, 13 Oct 1836.
Postlude
or } the opposite of Prelude or
Postludium
Praeludium: a final piece, esp. an organ piece played after service.
Postnikova, Viktoria (b Moscow, 12 Jan 1944), Russian pianist. She studied at the Moscow Cons. and in 1966 was second to

Rafael Orozco at the Leeds International Comp.; London debut, 1967. Many concerts with leading conds., also with her husband, Gennady Rozhdestvensky.
Poston, Elizabeth (b Highfield, Herts., 24 Oct 1905; d Stevenage, 18 Mar 1987), English composer. Studied at the RCM in London and pf. with Harold Samuel. In 1925 she pub. 7 songs and in 1927 a prize-work, a vln. and pf. sonata was broadcast. From 1940 to 1945 she was dir. of music in the foreign service of the BBC.
Works incl. music for radio prods.; choral music, songs.
Pot-Pourri (Fr. lit. rotten pot), a medley of preserves, identical with the Span. *olla podrida*, the name of which is applied to selections of themes from var. musical works, esp. operas or operettas.
Potter (Philip) Cipriani (Hambley) (b London, 3 Oct 1792; d London, 26 Sep 1871), English pianist and composer. Studied under Attwood, Callcott and Crotch, and had finishing pf. lessons from Woelfl from 1805–10. He became an assoc. of the Phil. Society on its foundation in 1813 and a member when he reached majority, and in 1816 wrote an overture for it, also playing the pf. there that year in a 6tet of his own. In 1817 he went to Vienna, studied with Aloys Förster and met Beethoven. After visiting Ger. and It. he returned to London in 1821, became prof. of pf. at the RAM the next year and prin. in succession to Crotch in 1832, but resigned in 1859. In 1855 Wagner cond. one of his symphs. with the Phil Society.
Works incl. cantata *Medora e Corrado*, Ode to Harmony; 9 symphs. (1819–34), 4 overtures for orch.; 3 pf. concertos (1832–

5), Concertante for cello and orch.; 3 pf trios, 6tet for pf. and strings; horn and pf. sonata, duo for vln. and pf.; 2 sonatas, *The Enigma* ('Variations in the style of 5 eminent artists', 1825) and other music for pf.; songs.

Pougin, (François Auguste) Arthur (Eugène Paroisse-) (b Châteauroux, 6 Aug 1834; d Paris, 8 Aug 1921), French musicologist. He had little general educ., but studied vln. with Alard and theory with Réber at the Paris Cons. After working at var. theatres as violinist and cond., he began to write biog. articles on 18th-cent. French musicians and gradually made his way by writing for papers, contributing to dictionaries and writing music criticism. He wrote biogs. of Verdi, Campra, Meyerbeer, V. Wallace, Bellini, Rossini, Auber, Adam, Méhul, etc., and studies of Fr. music history.

Pouishnov, Lev (b Odessa, 11 Oct 1891; d London, 28 May 1959), Russian pianist. He 1st appeared in public when 5 years old. From 1907 to 1910 he studied at the St Petersburg Cons. and then toured Europe as a soloist, subsequently playing also in USA, Australia and the Far East. He left Rus. in 1920 and settled in Eng., becoming naturalized in 1931.

Poule, La (*The Hen*), the nickname of a symph. by Haydn, no. 83, in G min., (no. 2 of the 'Paris' symphs.), comp. in 1786.

Poulenc, Francis (b Paris, 7 Jan 1899; d Paris, 30 Jan 1963), French composer. Received a classical educ., but was able to take pf. lessons from Ricardo Viñes and to pick up technical knowledge in var. ways. When he was called up for war service in 1918 he had already written 1 or 2 works under the influence of Satie, and on being demobilized he joined the group of 'Les Six' with Auric, Durey, Honegger, Milhaud and Tailleferre, and thus came for a time under the influence of Jean Cocteau.

Works incl. STAGE: opera *Dialogues des Carmélites* (1957); comic opera *Les Mamelles de Tirésias* (lib. by G. Apollinaire, 1947), monodrama *La voix humaine* (1959); ballets *Les Biches* (*The House-Party*, 1942), and *Les Animaux modèles* (after La Fontaine, 1942).

CHORAL: Mass in G min (1937) and cantata *Figure humaine* (P. Éluard), *Sécheresses* for chorus and orch.; choruses (unaccomp.), 7 *Chansons* (Éluard and Apollinaire, 1945), *Poésie et Vérité*.

ORCH: 2 *Marches et un Intermède* for orch.; *Concert champêtre* for harpsichord and orch. (1928), *Marches militaires* for pf. and orch., concerto in D min. for 2 pfs. and

orch. (1932), organ concerto (1938); *Aubade* for pf. and 18 insts. (1929).

CHAMBER: *Rapsodie nègre* for fl., clar. and string 4tet, trio for ob., horn and pf. (1926); sonatas for 2 clars., for clar. and bassoon (1922) and for horn, tpt. and tromb. (1922); vln. and pf. and cello and pf. sonatas (1943, 1948).

SONG CYCLES WITH CHAMBER INSTS.: *Le Bestiare* (G. Apollinaire, 1919), *Bal Masqué* (M. Jacob, 1932) and *Cocardes* (Cocteau, 1919).

PIANO: *Mouvements perpétuels* (1918), *Suite, Impromptus* (1920), *Feuillets d'album, Nocturnes* (1929–38), *Suite française* (1935), *Villageoises*, etc. for pf.; sonata for pf. duet (1918).

SONGS: 5 *Poèmes de Ronsard* (1924–5), 8 *Chansons polonaises* (1934). *Tel jour, telle nuit* (1937), *Fiançailles pour rire* (1939), *Chansons villageoises* (1942, also with chamber orch.) and other songs.

Poussé (Fr. = pushed), the upstroke of the bow in the playing of string instruments, the opposite of *tiré* (= drawn).

Pousseur, Henri (b Malmédy, 23 Jun 1929), Belgian composer. Studied at Brussels Cons. and took private comp. lessons from André Souris and Pierre Boulez. In 1958 he founded a studio for electronic music in Brussels; works investigate computer and aleatory techniques, influenced by Berio and Stockhausen. Has lectured at Darmstadt (1957–67), Cologne and State Univ. of NY, Buffalo (1966–9). Prof. of comp., Liège cons. from 1971.

Works incl. operas *Votre Faust* (1969), *Die Erprobung des Petrus Hebraïcus* (1974); 3 *Chants sacrés* for soprano and string trio; *Symphonies* for 15 solo instruments; *Modes* for string 4tet; 5tet to the memory of Webern (1955); *Seismographs* for magnetic tape; *Scambi* for tape (1957); *Rimes pour différentes sources sonores* for orch. and tape (1959); *Répons* for 7 musicians (1960); *Mobile* for 2 pfs., *Portrait de Votre Faust* for soloists, insts. and tape (1966); *Couleurs croisées* for orch. (1967); *L'effacement du Prince Igor* for orch. (1971); *Système des paraboles*, 7 tape studies (1972); *Schoenbergs Gegenwart* for actors, singers and insts. (1974); *Chronique illustrée* for bar. and orch. (1976); *Agonie* for voices and electronics (1981).

Powell, Mel (b New York, 12 Feb 1923), American composer. Played pf. in dance bands, later studied with Wagenaar, Toch and Hindemith. Founded electronic music studio at Yale, 1960. Dean of Music, Calif.

Inst. of Arts, 1969–75.

Works incl. *Stanzas* for orch. (1957); *Filigree Setting* for string 4tet (1959); *Setting* for cello and orch.; *Immobiles* 1–5 for tape and orch. (1967–9); string 4tet (1982).

Power, Leonel (b *c* 1375; d Canterbury, 5 Jun 1445), English composer and theorist. He wrote a treatise on the singing of descant and comp. Masses, incl. *Alma redemptoris*, motets and other church music.

pp (abbr.) = *pianissimo* (It. = softest). Although the sign indicates a superlative, it can be further multiplied to demand even greater softness of tone.

Praeger, Ferdinand (Christian Wilhelm) (b Leipzig, 22 Jan 1815; d London, 2 Sep 1891), German pianist and composer. Studied under his father and settled in London in 1834; wrote an unreliable book *Wagner as I knew him* in 1885 and comp. a symph. prelude to Byron's *Manfred*, an overture *Abellino*, a pf. trio, pf. pieces, etc.

Praeludium. *See* Prelude.

Praetorius (real name Schulz, Schulze, Schultz or Schultze), German 16th–17th-cent. musicians not of the same family, except 3 and 5:

1. Godescalcus P. (b Salzwedel, 28 Mar 1524; d Wittenburg, 8 Jul 1573), scholar. Prof. of philosophy at Wittenburg Univ. Pub. in 1557 a vol. *Melodiae scholasticae* in which he was asst. by M. Agricola.

2. Bartholomeaus P. (b Marienburg, *c* 1590; d Stockholm, buried 3 Aug 1623), composer. Pub. pavans and galliards in 5 parts in 1616.

3. Hieronymus P. (b Hamburg, 10 Aug 1560; d Hamburg, 27 Jan 1629), organist and composer. Pupil of his father, Jacob P. (or Schultz), organist at St James's Church, Hamburg, whom he succeeded in 1582. He wrote in the Venetian antiphonal choral style. His collected church music, *Opus Musicum* (1616–22), contains more than 100 motets.

Works incl. Masses, motets, Magnificats, *Cantiones sacrae*, hymn-tunes; Lat. and Ger. songs in 5–20 parts.

4. Michael P. (b Kreuzberg, Thuringia, 15 Feb 1571; d Wolfenbüttel, 15 Feb 1621), organist, composer and author. He was music director at Lüneburg until 1603, when he was app. organist to the Duke of Brunswick, who later made him his music director. He wrote the voluminous treatise on music and instruments entitled *Syntagma musicum* (1619) and comp. a number of vols. of Lat. and Ger. sacred and secular songs for several voices. His 9-vol. *Musae Sioniae* contains 1,244 chorale settings.

5. Jacob P. (b Hamburg, 8 Feb 1586; d Hamburg, 21 Oct 1651), organist and composer, son of 3. Pupil of Sweelinck at Amsterdam; app. organist of St Peter's Church, Hamburg, in 1603. Wrote motets, etc.

'Prague' Symphony, Mozart's symph. in D maj., K504, comp. in Vienna, Dec 1786 and perf. in Prague, 19 Jan 1787, during a visit for the prod. there of *Le nozze di Figaro*.

Pralltriller (Ger.), the rapid repetition of a note, with a note a degree higher in between, indicated by the sign ∿:

Pratella, Francesco (Balilla) (b Lugo, Romagna, 1 Feb 1880; d Ravenna, 17 May 1955), Italian composer. Studied at the Liceo Musicale of Pesaro, where Mascagni was among his masters. He settled at Milan, where in 1910 he began to make propaganda for futurist music, on which he lectured and wrote in the more progressive periodicals.

Works incl. operas *Il regno lontano* (1905), *La Sing d'Vargöun* (1909), *L'aviatore Dro* (1920), *Il dona primaverile, Fabiano* (1923), children's opera *La ninna nanna della bambola* (1923); incid. music to plays; symph. poems on Carducci's ode *La chiesa di Polenta*, 5 symph. poems *(Romagna,* 1903–4), *Inno alla vita* (musica futuristica, 1912), 3 dances *La guerra,* etc. for orch.; pf. trio; vln., organ and pf. pieces; songs.

Prati, Alessio (b Ferrara, 19 Jul 1750; d Ferrara, 17 Jan 1788), Italian composer. Pupil of Piccinni at the Cons. di Loreto in Naples, went to Paris in 1779, then to St Petersburg (1781) and Warsaw (1782). Travelling by way of Vienna (1783) he returned to Ferrara in 1784.

Works incl. *c* 12 operas, e.g. *L'École de la jeunesse* (1779), *Ifigenia in Aulide* (1784) *Olimpia* (1786), *Demofoonte* (1786), etc.; Masses and other church music, arias and miscellaneous other vocal pieces; symph. and *sinfonia concertante;* concertos; vln. sonatas.

Prausnitz, Frederik (b Cologne, 26 Aug 1920), American conductor of German birth. Studied at Juilliard and taught there 1947–61. Music dir. Syracuse SO (NY)

1971–4 Peabody Cons., Baltimore, from 1976. Often heard in Europe and US in music by Carter, Varèse, Stockhausen, Schoenberg and Sessions.

Pré aux clercs, Le (*The Scholars' Meadow*), opera by Hérold (lib. by F.A.E. de Planard), prod. Paris, Opéra-Comique, 15 Dec 1832.

Precentor, a dignitary in an Anglican cathedral, orig. the leading singer in the choir, but also in charge of the vocal church music and superior to the organist. His seat is opposite that of the dean (who takes the Decani side) on the Cantoris side of the chancel.

Preciosa, play with music by Weber (lib. by P.A. Wolff, based on Cervantes's story *La Gitanella*), prod. Berlin, Opera House, 15 Mar 1821.

Precipitando (It. = precipitately), a direction indicating that an *accelerando* is to be made to increase in pace very rapidly.

Predieri, Luc' Antonio (b Bologna, 13 Sep 1688; d Bologna, 1767), Italian composer. *Maestro di cappella* of the cathedral at Bologna; went to the court chapel in Vienna, 1738, and became chief *Kapellmeister* there in 1746; but returned to It. in 1751.

Works incl. operas *Il sogno di Scipione* (1735), *Perseo* (1738), *Armida* (1750) and others, serenades and festival plays for the stage oratorios.

Preindl, Joseph (b Marbach, Lower Aus., 30 Jan 1756; d Vienna, 26 Oct 1823), Austrian church musician and composer, pupil of Albrechtsberger. App. *Kapellmeister* at St Peter's, Vienna in 1793, he held the same post at St Stephen's from 1809. Pub. treatises on singing and on comp.

Works incl. at least 13 Masses, 2 Requiems, Offertories, motets and other church music; keyboard music.

Prelude (from Lat. *praeludium*), an intro. piece played, for ex., before a church service or a music perf., or forming the 1st movement of a suite or other sectional work; also one paired with a fugue, to which it forms an intro.; from the 19th cent. onwards sometimes a separate concert work, esp. for pf. (Chopin, etc.) or orch.; and from Wagner onwards the orchestral intro. to an opera where it does not take the form of a detached overture and leads straight into the 1st act.

Prélude à l'Après-midi d'un faune (*Prelude to 'The Afternoon of a Faun'*). An orchestral piece by Debussy intended as a musical intro. to Stéphane Mallarmé's poem of that name, comp. in 1892–4 and 1st perf. Paris, Société Nationale, 23 Dec 1894.

Ballet on this work (choreog. by Vaslav Nizhinsky), prod. Paris, Théâtre du Châtelet, 29 May 1912.

Préludes, 2 sets of pf. pieces, 12 in each, by Debussy, comp. in 1910–13. Their contents are: I. 1. *Danseuses de Delphes* (*Dancing Women of Delphi*); 2 *Voiles* (*Sails*); 3. *Le Vent dans la plaine* (*The wind in the plain*); 4. *Les Sons et les parfums tournent dans l'air du soir* (*Sounds and scents whirl in the evening air*: a quotation from Baudelaire); 5. *Les Collines d'Anacapri* (*The hills of Anacapri*); 6. *Des Pas sur la neige* (*Footprints in the snow*); 7 *Ce qu'a vu le vent d'Ouest* (*What the West Wind saw*); 8. *La Fille aux cheveux de lin* (*The Flaxen-haired Girl*: based on a Scot. song by Leconte de Lisle); 9. *La Sérénade interrompue* (*The interrupted serenade*); 10. *La Cathédrale engloutie* (*The Submerged Cathedral*: on the old Breton tale of the sunken city of Ys); 11. *La Danse de Puck* (*Puck's dance*, after Shakespeare's *Midsummer Night's Dream*); 12. *Minstrels* (music-hall artists, not troubadours). II. 1. *Brouillards* (*Mists*); 2. *Feuilles mortes* (*Dead Leaves*); 3. *La Puerta del Vino* (a gate at Granada); 4. *Les Fées sont d'exquises danseuses* (*The Fairies are exquisite Dancers*); 5. *Bruyères* (*Heather*); 6. *General Lavine-eccentric* (a music-hall character); 7. *La Terrasse des audiences du clair de lune* (*The Terrace of the Moonlight Audiences*; a reference to an account of George V's Durbar in 1912; the piece contains a quotation of the folksong 'Au clair de la lune'); 8. *Ondine* (Water-spirit maiden of 19th-cent story); 9. *Hommage à S. Pickwick, Esq., P.P.M.P.C.* (after Dickens; the piece quotes 'God save the King' in the bass); 10. *Canope* (a Canopic jar holding the ashes of a dead lover); 11. *Les Tierces alternées* (*Alternating Thirds*); 12. *Feux d'artifice* (*Fireworks*; quoting a few notes of the *Marseillaise* at the end).

Préludes, Les, symph. poem by Liszt, comp. 1848, revised early 1850s, fp Weimar, 28 Feb 1854. The title is taken from a poem by Lamartine, with which in fact the music has no connection.

Preparation, a term used in harmony for a chord, one note of which will create a dissonance in the chord that follows, e.g.:

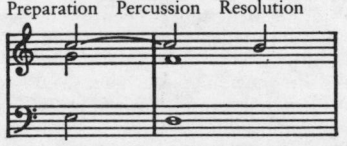

Preparation Percussion Resolution

Prestissimo (It.) = extremely fast.

Presto (It.) = quick, fast, the direction most commonly used to indicate the fastest speeds in music. *Presto* is quicker than *allegro*.

Preston, Simon (b Bournemouth, 4 Aug 1938), English organist, harpsichordist and conductor. He studied at the RAM and Cambridge; debut London 1962, as organist. Sub-organist Westminster Abbey 1962–7; organist from 1981. Christ Church, Oxford, 1970–81. He has been heard in Europe and the US in the organ works of Handel, Liszt and Messiaen and has recorded Masses by Haydn with the Christ Church choir.

Preston, Thomas (d ? Windsor, c 1563), English composer. He was (?) organist and master of the choristers, Magdalen Coll., Oxford, and is recorded as having played at Windsor Chapel in 1558 and 1559. He wrote a large amount of organ music for the Latin rite, incl. the Proper of the Mass for Easter Day (incomplete).

Prêtre, Georges (b Waziers, 14 Aug 1924), French conductor. Studied at Douai and in Paris, making his debut in 1946 at the Paris Opéra-Comique; music dir. there 1956–9. London debut 1961, NY Met 1964. Frequent perfs. and recordings with Callas. In 1959 cond. the fp of Poulenc's *La voix humaine*.

Preussisches Marchen (*Prussian Tales*), ballet-opera by Blacher (lib. by H. von Cramer); comp. 1949, prod. Berlin, 23 Sep 1952.

Previn, André (born Andreas Ludwig Priwin, Berlin, 6 Apr 1929), American conductor, pianist and composer. He studied in Berlin and Paris and worked in Hollywood from 1940 (US citizen 1943). He studied further, with Ernst Toch and Pierre Monteux, and was active as a concert pianist before debut as cond. with St Louis SO in 1962; Houston SO 1967–9, Pittsburgh SO 1976–86. He was chief cond. of the LSO 1968–79 and gave many perfs. of English music, notably Walton and Vaughan Williams. Music dir., RPO from 1985, Los Angeles PO from 1986.

Previtali, Fernando (b Adria, 16 Feb 1907; d Rome, 1 Aug 1985), Italian conductor and composer. Studied comp., org., pf. and cello at Turin Cons. From 1928 to 1936 he cond. in Florence (Maggio Musicale Fiorentino), from 1936 to 1953 with the Rome Radio Orch., and in 1953 became cond. of the Santa Cecilia Orch. US debut Cleveland orch., 1955; opera debut Dallas, 1975, *Anna Bolena*. Prin. cond. San Carlo, Naples, from 1972.

Works incl. ballet *Alluzinazione* (1945);

cantata for chorus and orch.; string 4tet, string trio; songs.

Prévost (d'Exiles), Antoine François (1697–1763), French novelist. For works based on *Manon Lescaut see* **Henze** (*Boulevard Solitude*), **Manon** (opera, Massenet), **Manon Lescaut** (ballet, Halévy; operas, Auber and Puccini).

Prévost, Eugène (Prosper) (b Paris, 23 Apr 1809; d New Orleans, 19 Aug 1872), French composer and singing-teacher. Studied at the Paris Cons. with Lesueur and others and gained the Prix de Rome in 1831. After prod. works in Paris, he became cond. at the theatre of Le Havre for a time, but left for New Orleans in 1838, where he cond. at the Fr. theatre and taught singing. In 1862 he returned to Paris, but went again to New Orleans in 1867.

Works incl. operas *L'Hôtel des Princes* (1831), *Le Grenadier de Wagram* (1831), *Cosimo* (1835), *Le Bon Garçon, Esmeralda* (after Hugo's *Notre-Dame de Paris*), *L'Illustre Gaspard* (1863); Mass with orch.; cantata *Bianca Capello*, etc.

Prey, Hermann b Berlin, 11 Jul 1929), German baritone. Studied at the Berlin Hochschule für Musik with Jaro Prohaska. From 1952 to 1953 he sang at Wiesbaden and then became a member of the Hamburg Staatsoper where he created Meton in Krenek's *Pallas Athene weint* (1955). Has sung frequently in Berlin at the Städtische Oper and at the Vienna Staatsoper. NY Met debut 1960, as Wolfram; London, CG, 1973, as Rossini's Figaro. Other roles incl. Papageno, Guglielmo and Storch in the 1st Brit. perf. of Strauss's *Intermezzo* (Edinburgh, 1965). He is also well known as a Lieder singer. Pub. autobiography 1986.

Pribyl, Vilem (b Nachod, 10 Apr 1925), Czech tenor. He sang as an amateur during the 1950s; professional debut Ustí nad Labem 1961, as Lukas in Smetana's *The Kiss*. He joined the Janáček Opera, Brno, the same year and was heard as Smetana's Dalibor and Janáček's Laca, in operas by Prokofiev and Shostakovich and as Radames, Otello and Lohengrin; often appeared with the Prague National Opera and sang Dalibor with the co. when it visited Edinburgh in 1964 (Brit. première of the opera). Florestan at CG.

Price, Leontyne (b Laurel, Miss., 10 Feb 1927), American soprano. Studied at Central State Coll., Ohio, and at Juilliard in NY (1949–1952), achieving her first success in *Porgy and Bess*; also sang Bess on her London debut, in 1952; CG debut 1958, as

Aida. From 1958 to 1959 she sang with the San Francisco Opera Co., and in 1959 became a lyric soprano with the Chicago Opera. She made her debut at the NY Met in 1961 as the *Trovatore* Leonora and sang at La Scala, Milan, in 1962, as Aida. In 1966 she created Cleopatra in Barber's *Antony and C.*, at the opening of the new Met house.

Price, Margaret (b Blackwood, Mon., 13 Apr 1941), Welsh soprano. She sang Cherubino with WNO in 1962 and at CG in 1963; later London roles have been Pamina, Fiordiligi and Donna Anna. Glyndebourne 1968, as Constanze. Pamina in San Francisco in 1969 and sang with the Paris Opéra on its 1976 tour of the USA. She has been successful in Germany, notably Cologne and Munich, and has given many recitals with James Lockhart. Has avoided Wagner on stage but recorded Isolde in 1983. CBE 1982.

Prick-Song. From the 15th to the 18th cent. 'to prick' was used to mean 'to write notes'. Hence prick-song meant written, as opposed to improvised, music.

Prigione di Edimburgo, La (*Edinburgh Gaol*), opera by F. Ricci (lib. by G Rossi, based on Scribe and Planard's *Prison d'Édimbourg* and further back on Scott's *Heart of Midlothian*), prod. Trieste, 13 Mar 1838.

Prigioniero, Il (*The Prisoner*), opera (prologue and 1 act) by Dallapiccola (lib. by comp. after V. de L'Isle Adam and C. de Coster); comp. 1944–8, fp Turin Radio, 4 Dec 1949. Prod. Florence, 20 May 1950.

Prima donna (It. = 1st lady), the singer of the leading soprano part in a partic. opera or the leading soprano in an opera co.

Prima volta (It. = 1st time), a direction sometimes given where a repeated portion of a comp. takes a new turn after the repetition. The join leading to the repeat is then called *prima volta*, while the different one taking the music on to its continuation is marked *Seconda volta*. The figures 1 and 2 are commonly used as abbrs. for these terms.

Primavera, Giovanni Leonardo (b Barletta, Naples, *c* 1540; d after 1585), Italian composer. *Maestro di cappella* to the Span. governor of Milan in 1573. Palestrina used his madrigal 'Nasce la gioia mia' as a *cantus firmus* for a Mass, called by that name.

Works incl. madrigals *Canzoni napoletane* for 3 voices, *villotte* for 3 voices, etc.; most works pub. Venice, 1565–84.

Primo (It. = first). *Primo* is often written over the top part in pf. duets, the bottom one being *Secondo*; the word also appears in orchestral scores where the comp. wishes to

make sure that a passage is played by only the 1st of a pair or groups of similar instruments.

Primo uomo (It. = 1st man), the singer of the leading male soprano part in an opera or the leading male soprano in an opera company in the 18th cent.

Primrose, William (b Glasgow, 23 Aug 1903; d Provo, Utah, 1 May 1982), Scottish vla. player. After studying in Glasgow and at the GSM in London, he studied with Ysaÿe in Belgium from 1925 to 1927, and on his advice took up the vla. From 1930 to 1935 he played with the London String Quartet, and in 1937 was selected by Toscanni to become 1st vla. of the NBC SO, with which he remained until 1942. In 1939 he founded his own string quartet. He also commissioned a vla. concerto from Bartók, of which he gave the fp in 1949. He taught in Tokyo from 1972.

Prince Igor (*Kniaz Igor*), opera by Borodin (lib. by comp. based on a sketch by Stassov), comp. between 1871 and 1887 and left unfinished at Borodin's death in the latter year. Completed and scored by Rimsky-Korsakov and Glazunov. Prod. St Petersburg, 4 Nov 1890.

Prince of the Pagodas, The, ballet by Britten (choreography by John Cranko), prod. London, CG, Jan 1 1957.

Princess Ida, or Castle Adamant, operetta by Sullivan (lib. by W.S. Gilbert, a parody of Tennyson's *Princess*), prod. London, Savoy Theatre, 5 Jan 1884.

Princesse de Navarre, La, comédie-ballet by Rameau (lib. by Voltaire), prod. Versailles, 23 Feb 1745, to celebrate the wedding of the Dauphin with Maria Teresa of Spain.

Princesse jaune, La (*The Yellow Princess*), opera by Saint-Saëns (lib. by L. Gallet), prod. Paris, Opéra-Comique, 12 Jun 1872.

Principal, an open Diapason organ stop which sounds an 8ve higher, 4 ft. in the manuals and 8ft. in the pedals. Also, in old music, the lowest tpt. part, in which high and florid notes were not demanded. In modern terminology a principal is the leading player of any group of orchestral instruments.

Pring, Katherine (b Brighton, 4 Jun 1940), English mezzo. She studied at the RCM; SW/ENO from 1968 as Eboli, Azucena, Waltraute and Agave in the Brit. stage première of *The Bassarids* (1974). Other roles incl. Poppea, Dorabella, Fricka, Tippett's Thea and Stravinsky's Jocasta.

Printemps, symphonic suite for chorus and orch. by Debussy; comp. 1887, pub. 1904 in a reduction for pf. four hands. Re-orch. by

Henri Busser and perf. Paris, Salle Gaveau, 18 Apr 1913.

Prinz von Homburg, Der, opera by Henze (lib. by I. Bachmann, after Kleist), prod. Hamburg, Staatsoper, 22 May 1960.

Prioris, Johannes, Franco-Netherlands 15th–16th-cent. organist and composer. Organist at St Peter's in Rome in 1490 and *maître de chapelle* to Lousi XII in 1507. Wrote Masses, motets, Magnificats, Requiem, *chansons* etc.

Prise de Troie, La (Berlioz). *See* **Troyens.**

Prison d'Édimbourg, La (*Edinburgh Gaol*), opera by Carafa (lib. by Scribe and F.A.E. de Planard, based on Scott's *Heart of Midlothian*), prod. Paris, Opéra-Comique, 20 Jul 1833.

Prisoner in the Caucasus, The (*Kavkasky Plennik*), opera by Cui (lib. by V.A. Krilov, based on Pushkin's poem), prod. St Petersburg, 16 Feb 1883.

Pritchard, (Sir) **John** (b London, 5 Feb 1921), English conductor. He studied in Italy and went to Glyndebourne in 1947; gave 3 Mozart operas there in 1951: music dir. 1969–77. He cond. the fps of Britten's *Gloriana* and Tippett's *Midsummer Marriage* at CG; *King Priam* with the co. at Coventry, 1962. US debut 1953, Pittsburgh SO; NY Met 1971. Music dir. LPO 1962–6; BBC SO from 1981. Prin. cond. Cologne Opera from 1978. Knighted 1983.

Priuli, Giovanni (b Venice, *c* 1575; d Vienna, 1629), Italian composer. *Kapellmeister* to the Archduke Ferdinand of Austria at Graz early in the 17th cent.; remained in his service when he became the Emperor Ferdinand II. He studied with G. Gabrieli; his inst. canzonas contain echo effects.

Works incl. motets, psalms and other church music; madrigals, *Musiche concertate*, *Delicie musicali* for several voices, etc.

Prix de Rome (Fr. = Prize of Rome; officially Grand Prix de Rome), a prize instituted in 1803 and offered annually in Paris by the Académie des Beaux-Arts, a branch of the Institut de France, to var. artists. The prize for music comp. was given to the successful competitor at the Cons. and entitled the holder to 3 years' study at the French Acad. housed in the Villa Medici in Rome. The work required was formerly a dramatic cantata, but was later a 1-act opera. Among winners were Berlioz (after 3 attempts), Gounod, Bizet, Massenet and Debussy. The competition ceased in 1968.

Pro Arte Quartet, Belgian string quartet, founded 1912 with members Alphonse Onnou and Laurent Halleux (vlns), Germain Prévost (vla.) and Robert Maas (cello). Many perf. of modern works (Salzburg, 1923, US tour 1926). First visit to Brit. 1925; recorded many Haydn 4tets 1931–8 (reissued 1985). Moved to US in 1940; Rudolf Kolisch leader from 1944. Title adopted by 4tet of Univ. of Wisconsin at Madison. In 1973 an Austrian string 4tet with the same name was founded.

Prodaná Nevěstá (Smetana). *See* **Bartered Bride.**

Prod'homme, J(acques) G(abriel) (b Paris, 28 Nov 1871; d Paris, 18 Jun 1956), French musicologist. Studied in Ger. and lived at Munich from 1897–1900, where he founded a periodical. After his return to Paris he founded the Fr. section of the SIM, became its secretary and performed various other music administrative functions, succeeding Bouvet in 1931 as librarian and archivist at the Opéra, and Expert in 1934 as Cons. librarian. He wrote several works both on Beethoven and on Berlioz, also on Mozart, Schubert, Wagner, etc.

Prodigal Son, The, church parable by Britten (lib. by W. Plomer), prod. Orford, 10 Jun 1968, cond. Britten.

Ballet by Prokofiev (*L'Enfant prodigue*); comp. 1928, fp Paris, 21 May 1929 (Ballets Russes; scenario by B. Kokno, choreography Balanchine, décor Georges Roualt; cond. Prokofiev).

See also **Enfant prodigue** (Debussy).

Programme Music, any kind of instrumental music, esp. orchestral, based on a literary, pictorial, historical, autobiographical, descriptive or other extra-musical subject and not intended to appeal only as music pure and simple.

Programme Notes, analyses printed in concert programmes, esp. in Britain, describing the music performed. Early exs. in Eng. were those written by Grove for the Crystal Palace concerts.

Progression, the logical movement of 2 or more chords in succession, either harmonically with all the notes moving simultaneously or polyphonically with each one being part of a continuously moving horizontal melodic line.

Prohaska, Carl (b Mödling, nr. Vienna, 25 Apr 1869; d Vienna, 28 Mar 1927), Austrian composer. Studied pf. with d'Albert and comp. with Mandyczewski and Herzogenberg, being also befriended by Brahms. He taught at the Strasbourg Cons. in 1894–5 and cond. the Warsaw PO in 1901–5. In 1908 he became prof. at the Cons. of the Vienna Phil. Society.

Works incl. opera *Madeleine Guimara* (1930); oratorio *Frühlingsfeier* (1913), motet *Aus dem Buch Hiob, Lebensmesse, Der Feind, Infanterie* and other choral works; variations on a theme from Rousseau's *Devin du village*, symph. prelude to Anzengruber's *Das vierte Gebot*, symph. fantasy, serenade, passacaglia and fugue for orch.; string 4tet, string 5tet, pf. trio; sonata and *Allegro con spirito* for vln. and pf.; songs, duets.

Prohaska, Jaro (b Vienna, 24 Jan 1891; d Munich, 28 Sep 1965), Austrian bassbaritone. He was a choirboy and organist before his stage debut in 1922 at Lübeck. He was soon engaged at Nuremberg and sang at Bayreuth 1933–44 as Wotan, Sachs, Amfortas, Telramund and the Dutchman. He sang in the 1935 fp of Graener's *Prinz von Homburg*, in Berlin, and taught there from 1949; Hermann Prey was among his pupils.

Prokofiev, Sergey Sergeyevich (b Sontsovka, Ekaterinoslav, 27 Apr 1891; d Moscow, 5 Mar 1953), Russian composer. Began to comp. almost before he could write and tried his hand at an opera at the age of 9. He was sent to Glière for lessons, wrote 12 pf. pieces in 1902 as well as a symph. for pf. duet, and at 12 set Pushkin's play *A Feast in Time of Plague* as an opera. At the St Petersburg Cons., which he left in 1914, he studied pf. with Anna Essipova, comp. with Rimsky-Korsakov and Liadov, and cond. with N. Tcherepnin. By that time he had written many works, incl. the 1st pf. concerto, and he then set to work on the *Scythian Suite* for orch. During the war of 1914–18 he lived in London for a time and at its close he went to the USA by way of Japan. The opera *The Love for Three Oranges* was prod. at Chicago in 1921, and the next year he went to live in Paris and became connected with Diaghilev's Russ. Ballet, which prod. several of his works. In 1933 he settled in Moscow and was induced by the Soviet government to simplify and popularize his style, a tendency which is very noticeable in such works as *Peter and the Wolf* and the quantities of film music he wrote there.

Works incl. OPERAS: *Maddalena* (1911–13, fp 1979), *The Gambler* (after Dostoievsky, 1929), *The Love for Three Oranges* (after Gozzi, 1921), *The Fiery Angel* (1919–27, prod. 1955), *War and Peace* (after Tolstoy, 1941–52, prod. 1953), *Betrothal in a Monastery* (after Sheridan's *Duenna*, 1940–1), *Semyon Kotko* (1940).

BALLETS: *The Buffoon* (1921), *Le Pas d'acier* (1927), *L'Enfant prodigue, Sur le*

Borysthène (1932), *Romeo and Juliet* (after Shakespeare, 1938), *Cinderella* (1945).

ORCH.: incl. *Classical symphony* (1921) and 6 other symphs. (1924–52), *Sinfonietta, Scythian Suite* (1914), *Symphonic Song*, Rus. Overture *Toast to Stalin* and *Ode to the End of the War*; incid. music for *Egyptian Nights* (after Pushkin, Shakespeare and Shaw, 1934), *Boris Godunov* and *Eugene Onegin* (both Pushkin); film music for *Lieutenant Kijé* (1934), *The Queen of Spades* (after Pushkin), *Ivan the Terrible*, etc.; 5 pf. concertos (1911–32), 2 vln. concertos (1917, 1935), 2 cello concertos.

CHAMBER: *Overture on Hebrew Themes* for clar., string 4tet and pf. (1919); 2 string 4tets (1930, 1941), 5tet for wind and pf., sonata for 2 vlns. sonata in D maj. and F min. for vln. and pf. (1944, 1946), Ballade for cello and pf.

PIANO AND SONGS: 9 pf. sonatas, c 25 other op. nos. of pf. pieces, incl. 3 studies, toccata, *Sarcasms, Visions fugitives, Contes de la vieille grand'mere* and 2 sonatinas; 8 sets of songs (1 without words, 1 to words by Pushkin).

CHORAL: *Seven, they are Seven*, for tenor, chorus and orch. (1918), *Alexander Nevsky* (1939), and some other choral works; cantata for the 30th anniversary of the Oct. Revolution (words by Stalin, Lenin and Marx) for orch., military band, accordion band, percussion and double chorus (1947).

Prolation, the division of the Semibreve into Minims in old notation, where according to the time-signature a semibreve could be equal to 2 minims (min.P) or to 3 (maj.P).

Promenade Concerts, a type of popular orchestral concert, cultivated espec. at the London Queen's Hall from 1895 until its destruction in 1941, under the direction of Sir Henry Wood, and continued at the Albert Hall. Malcolm Sargent was chief cond. at the London Proms 1948–67. The programmes gradually improved, until they contained most of the best orchestral music and modern novelties. A special feature is that the floor of the hall is left bare for people to stand, not to walk about, for which they have neither room nor inclination. In recent years operas and chamber music have been included in the programmes; William Glock, from 1959, then Robert Ponsonby, further improved the content of the programmes; John Drummond responsible from 1987. Promenade concerts were not new to London in 1895; they were started by Musard at Drury Lane in 1840 and by Jullien at CG about the same time.

Promessi sposi, I (*The Betrothed*).

Opera by Petrella (lib. by A. Ghislanzoni, based on Manzoni's novel), prod. Lecco, 2 Oct 1869; prod. Milan, Oct 1872. The prod. at Lecco was given there because it is the scene of Manzoni's book.

Opera by Ponchielli (lib. by E. Praga based on Manzoni's novel), prod. Cremona, 30 Aug 1856.

Prométhée (*Prometheus*), open-air spectacle by Fauré (lib. by J. Lorrain and A.F. Hérold, based on Aeschylus), prod. Béziers, Arènes, 27 Aug 1900; 1st Paris perf., Hippodrome, 5 Dec 1907.

Prometheus (Beethoven). *See* **Geschöpfe des Prometheus.**

Symph. poem by Liszt, comp. 1850 as an overture to the choruses from Herder's *Prometheus*, perf. Weimar, 28 Aug 1850; revised 1855, fp Brunswick, 18 Oct 1855.

Opera by Orff (lib. by comp. after Aeschylus) prod. Stuttgart, 24 Mar 1968.

Prometheus, the Poem of Fire, symph. work for pf. and orch. by Skriabin, fp Moscow, 15 Mar 1911. The score contains a part for an instrument projecting coloured lights, called *Tastiera per luce*, which was however never perfected.

Prometheus Unbound, setting of Shelley's poem for solo voices, chorus and orch. by Parry, perf. Gloucester Festival, 1880.

Prometheus Variations (Beethoven). *See* 'Eroica' Variations.

Prophète, Le, opera by Meyerbeer (lib. by Scribe), prod. Paris, Opéra, 16 Apr 1849.

Prophetess, The, or The History of Dioclesian, music by Purcell for the play adapted from Beaumont and Fletcher by Thomas Betterton, prod. London, Dorset Gardens Theatre, spring 1690. Pepusch wrote new music for its revival, London, Lincoln's Inn Fields Theatre, 28 Nov 1724.

Proportion, the mathematical relationship between the numbers of vibrations of different notes, which are exactly in tune with each other when the ratios between these vibrations are mathematically correct, e.g. a perfect 5th stands in the relation of 2:3 in the number of vibrations of its 2 notes. The term proportion was also used in old music to designate the rhythmic relationships between one time-signature and another.

Proscritto, Il (*The Outlaw*), opera by Nicolai (lib., orig. written for Verdi, by G. Rossi), prod. Milan, La Scala, 13 Mar 1841.

Prose, another name, chiefly French, for the sequence (in the medieval sense of an ornamental interpolation into the music of the Mass). After the 9th cent. words began to be added to the sequences, and this is the reason for their being called proses, since the texts were not orig. in verse.

Proserpine, opera by Lully (lib. by Quinault), prod. Saint-Germain, 3 Feb 1680; 1st Paris perf., 15 Nov 1680.

Opera by Paisiello (lib. by Quinault, revised by N.F. Guillard), prod. Paris, Opéra, 29 Mar 1803. Paisiello's only French opera.

Proske, Karl (b Gröbnig, Silesia, 11 Feb 1794; d Regensburg, 20 Dec 1861), German priest and editor. Studied medicine and practised for a time, but was ordained priest in 1826 and became attached in a musical capacity to Regensburg Cathedral. There and in Italy he made his great collection of church music entitled *Musica Divina*, 4 vols. pub. 1853–64.

Prout, Ebenezer (b Oundle, 1 Mar 1835; d London, 5 Dec 1909), English theorist and composer. Studied pf. and organ and began to make a career as organist, pf. teacher, music ed. and critic. In 1876 he became prof. at the Nat. Training-School for Music in London and 3 years later at the RAM. He wrote a number of books on harmony, counterpoint, form, orchestration, etc. and comp. cantatas, symphs., org. concertos, chamber music.

Provenzale, Francesco (b Naples, ? 1627; d Naples, 6 Sep 1704), Italian composer. Studied (?) at Naples and in 1663–74 taught at the Cons. Santa Maria di Loreto there. He was also *maestro di cappella* at the church of San Gennaro and in the royal chapel.

Works incl. operas *Il Ciro* (1653), *Xerse* (1655), *Artemisa* (1657), *Il Theseo* (1658), *Lo schiavo di sua moglie* (1671), *Difendere l'offensore* (1674); church music; 9 cantatas, etc.

Prozess, Der (*The Trial*), opera by Einem (lib. by Blacher and H. von Cramer, after Kafka), prod. Salzburg, 17 Aug 1953.

Prudent, Émile (Racine Gauthier) (b Angoulême, 3 Feb 1817; d Paris, 14 May 1863), French pianist and composer. Having no parents, he was adopted by a pf. tuner, entered the Paris Cons. at the age of 10 and afterwards had a hard struggle to make a living, but eventually made his way successfully.

Works incl. concerto-symph. *Les Trois Rêves* and concerto in Bb maj. for pf. and orch.; pf. trio; *Étude de genre* and many pieces, fantasies and transcriptions for pf.

Prunières, Henry (b Paris, 24 May 1886; d Nanterre, 11 Apr 1942), French musicologist and editor. Studied with Rolland at the Sorbonne, founded the *Revue musicale* in

1920 and was app. ed. of the complete ed. of Lully's works. He wrote books on that comp., on Monteverdi, Cavalli, Fr. and It. opera and ballet, etc., also a history of music (unfinished).

'Prussian' Quartets, a set of 3 string 4tets by Mozart, comp. in 1789–90 and ded. to the cello-playing King Frederick William II of Prussia. The 4tets K575 in D, K589 in Bb, K590 in F) are the first 3 of an intended set of 6. All have prominent cello parts.

Psalms. The psalms form part of the offices of the Roman Catholic Church and of the Anglican morning and evening services; in the former they are chanted in Plainsong, in the latter to Chants. Psalms have also been set by comps. as motets and also as concert works for solo voices, chorus and orch.

Psalmus Hungaricus, work by Kodály for tenor, chorus and orch., based on the 55th psalm, fp Budapest, 19 Nov 1923.

Psaltery, an instrument of the Dulcimer type, triangular in shape and with strings stretched across its frame harp-wise, which were played with the bare fingers or with a plectrum. It became extinct during the 17th cent.

Pskovitianka (*The Maid of Pskov,* also known as *Ivan the Terrible*), opera by Rimsky-Korsakov (lib. by comp. based on a play by L.A. Mey), prod. St Petersburg, 13 Jan 1873. Revived with a new prologue-opera, *Boyarina Vera Sheloga,* Moscow, 27 Dec 1898.

Psyche, opera by Locke (lib. by Shadwell), prod. London, Dorset Gardens Theatre, 27 Feb 1675.

Psyché, opera by Lully (lib. by T. Corneille and B de Fontenelle), prod. Paris, Opéra, 19 Apr 1678.

Suite by Franck for orch. with choral interpolations, comp. 1887–8, fp Paris, Société Nat., 10 Mar 1888.

Puccini. Italian family of musicians and opera composers of Lucca:

1. Giacomo P. (1712–81).
2. Antonio P. (1747–1832), son of prec.
3. Domenico P. (1771–1815), son of prec.
4. Michele P. (1813–64), son of prec.

Puccini, Giacomo (Antonio Domenico Michele Secondo Maria) (b Lucca, 23 Dec 1858; d Brussels, 29 Nov 1924), Italian composer, son of prec. Although his father died early, he was given a musical education and at the age of 19 was organist and choirmaster at the church of San Martino and had written a motet. In 1880 his mother managed with the aid of a grant from the queen to send him to the Milan Cons., where he studied comp. 1st under Bazzini and later under Ponchielli. Here he wrote a *Capriccio sinfonico* for orch. Ponchielli urged him to take part in a competition for a 1-act opera advertised by the music pub. Sonzogno, and he wrote *Le Villi;* but the prize was won by Mascagni's *Cavalleria rusticana. Le Villi,* however, was prod. at Milan in 1884, as a result of which Ricordi commissioned him to write a 2nd opera, *Edgar,* prod. in 1889. It failed but Puccini had his 1st great success with *Manon Lescaut* at Turin in 1893. The same city brought out *La Bohème* in 1896. His successes now made him immensely wealthy and he bought an estate at Torre del Lago near Lucca, where he lived with Elvira Bonturi, who had left her husband for him, but whom he was unable to marry until much later, when she became a widow. In the last years of his life he suffered from cancer of the throat and died after an operation undergone at Brussels.

Works incl. operas *Le Villi* (1884), *Edgar* (1889), *Manon Lescaut* (1893), *La Bohème* (1896), *Tosca* (1900), *Madama Butterfly* (1904), *La fanciulla del West* (1910), *La rondine* (1917), *Trittico; Il tabarro, Suor Angelica* and *Gianni Schicchi* (1918), *Turandot* (unfinished, completed by Alfano, 1926), *Scherzo sinfonico* for orch. (later used in *La Bohème*); cantata *Juno;* 2 minuets for strings; a Mass and a motet: *Inno a Roma* for chorus.

Pugnani, Gaetano (b Turin, 27 Nov 1731; d Turin, 15 Jul 1798), Italian violinist and composer. Pupil of Somis and possibly, later, Tartini, worked for most of his life at the Turin court, and became leader of the orch. in 1770. But he also travelled widely, visiting Paris (1754) and London (1767–70), where his first opera, *Nanetta e Lubino,* was prod. in 1769. His pupils incl. Viotti, Bruni and Conforti.

Works incl. operas *Nanetta e Lubino* (1769), *Issea* (1771), *Tamas Kouli-Kan nell' India* (1772), *Aurora, Adone e Venere* (1784), *Achille in Scior, Demofoonte* (1787), *Demetrio a Rodi* (1789), etc.; oratorio *La Betulia liberata;* orchestral suite on Goethe's *Werther;* concertos, sonatas, etc. for vln. and other instrumental music.

Pugno, (Stéphanie) Raoul (b Paris, 23 Jun 1852; d Moscow, 3 Jan 1914), French pianist and composer. Studied at the Paris Cons. where after some organist's and choirmaster's posts he became prof. of harmony 1892 and of pf. in 1896. He 1st appeared in London in 1894.

Works incl. operas *Ninetta* (1883), *La*

Sosie (1887), *La Valet de cœur* ((1888), *Le Retour d'Ulysse* (1889), *La Vocation de Marius* (1890), *La Petite Poucette* (1891), etc.; ballets *Les Papillons* (1884), *Viviane*, *Le Chevalier aux fleurs* (with Messager, 1897); fairy-plays, pantomimes and mimo-drama; incid. music for d'Annunzio's *Città morte* (with Nadia Boulanger); oratorio *La Resurrection de Lazare* (1879); sonata and *Les Nuits* for pf.; songs.

Puits d'amour, Le (*The Well of Love*), opera by Balfe (lib. by Scribe and A. de Leuven), prod. Paris, Opéra-Comique, 20 Apr 1843. Balfe's 1st Fr. opera.

Pujol, Juan (b Barcelona, *c* 1573; d Barcelona, May 1626), Spanish priest and compo-ser. He was *maestro de capilla* at Tarragona, 1593–5, Saragossa Cathedral, 1595–1612, and Barcelona, 1612–26.

Works incl. 13 Masses, 74 psalms, 9 motets, 9 Passions and other church music; secular songs, etc.

Pulcinella, ballet by Stravinsky with music adapted from Pergolesi and others (choreography by Massin), prod. Paris, Opéra, 15 May 1920. The settings were designed by Picasso. (Orch. Suite perf. Bos-ton, 22 Dec 1922).

Pullois, Jean (b ? Antwerp, *c* 1420; d 23 Aug 1478), Flemish composer. Choirmaster at Antwerp, 1444–7; failed an audition to join the Burgundian court chapel, 1446; sin-ger at the papal chapel, 1447–68. He is important as one of the few named compos-ers active during Dufay's middle years. Comp. mainly songs but some sacred music. His single Mass cycle may really be the work of an English comp.

Punch and Judy, opera in 1 act by Birtwis-tle (lib. by S. Pruslin), prod. Aldeburgh, 8 Jun 1968, cond. Atherton. Revised vers. prod. London, 3 Mar 1970.

Punto. *See* **Stich.**

Puppo, Giuseppe (b Lucca, 12 Jun 1749; d Florence, 19 Apr 1827), Italian violinist. Studied at the Naples Cons. and made a great success as a youth; visited Paris in 1775, then Spain and Eng. Wrote vln. con-certos, studies, duets, etc.

Purcell, Daniel (b ? London, *c* 1663; d London, buried 26 Nov 1717), English organist and composer, brother of the fol-lowing. He was a choir-boy in the Chapel Royal and was organist at Magdalen Coll., Oxford, 1688–95, when he came to London and added music to his dead brother Henry's *Indian Queen*. After a busy career writing music for plays, he became organist of St Andrew's Church, Holborn, in 1713.

Works incl. music for *Brutus of Alba* (1696), Cibber's *Love's Last Shift* and *Love makes a Man* (1700), Durfey's *Cynthia and Endymion* (1696), Lacy's *Sawny the Scot* (based on Shakespeare's *Taming of the Shrew*, 1698), Steele's *Funeral and Tender Husband* (1705), Farquhar's *The Beaux' Stratagem* (1707), *The Inconstant* and (with Leveridge) *The Constant Couple* (1699), Vanbrugh's *The Relapse* and (with Finger) *The Pilgrim* (1701), an adaptation of Shakespeare's *Macbeth* (1704), and many others; odes for St Cecilia's Day; music for Congreve's *Judgment of Paris* (3rd prize in competition with Eccles, Finger and Wel-don, 1700); odes; church music; sonatas for vln. and bass, and for fl. and bass; sonatas for tpt. and strings; cantatas for 1 voice.

Purcell, Henry (b London, 1659; d London, 21 Nov 1695), English composer, brother of prec. Probably son of Thomas P., musician attached to the court after the Restoration of 1660. He showed genius in early childhood and became a choir-boy at the Chapel Royal (?) in 1669 under Cooke, from 1672 under Humfrey. Left in 1673 and became asst. to the keeper of the king's instruments and the following year, on Humfrey's death, pupil of Blow; tuned the organ and copied parts for Westminster Abbey; app. Composer in Ordinary for the Violins, Sep 1677. Songs of his were pub. from the age of 16. In 1679 he succeeded Blow as organist of Westminster Abbey; the next year he wrote string fanta-sies in the old polyphonic style and his 1st theatre music for Lee's *Theodosius*. Married in (?) 1681 and became a very successful church and theatre comp.; also in 1683, pub. his 1st instrumental sonatas. Made a special-ity of welcome-songs for royalty and odes for official occasions. Wrote a coronation anthem for James II, 1685, and played at that of William and Mary, 1689. Prod. the operas *Dido and Aeneas* at a girls' school in Chelsea, 1689, and collaborated with Dryden in *King Arthur*, prod. 1690. Ed. the 12th ed. of Playford's *Introduction to the Skill of Music* (with substantial additions), 1694. Anthem for the funeral service of Queen Mary comp. 1695, the year of his own death.

Works incl. OPERAS AND QUASI-OPERAS: *Dido and Aeneas* (1689), *The Fairy Queen* (adapted from Shakespeare's *Midsummer Night's Dream*, 1692), *King Arthur* (1691), *The Prophetess. See also* **Tempest** (Wel-don), formerly attrib. to Purcell.

INCID. MUSIC AND SONGS FOR PLAYS: Ban-croft) *Henry II* (1692), Beaumont and

Fletcher, *Bonduca, The Double Marriage* (*c* 1684), Behn, *Abdelazer* (1695), Congreve, *The Double Dealer* (1693), *The Old Bachelor* (1693), Crowne, *The Married Beau, Regulus*, Chas. Davenant, *Circe* (1690), Dryden, *Amphitryon* (1690), *Aureng-Zebe, Cleomenes* (1692), *Love Triumphant, The Spanish Friar, Tyrannic Love* (1694), Dryden and Howard, *The Indian Queen* (1695), Dryden and Lee, *Oedipus* (1692), Durfey, *Don Quixote* (1695), *A Fool's Preferment* (adapt. from Fletcher), *The Marriage-Hater Matched* (1692), *The Richmond Heiress* (1693), *Sir Barnaby Whigg, The Virtuous Wife* (1694), Fletcher, *Rule a Wife and Have a Wife* (1693), Gould, *The Rival Sisters*, Lee, *The Massacre of Paris* (1690), *Sophonisba* (1685), *Theodosius*, Molière (adapted Wright), *The Female Virtuosos* (*Les Femmes savantes*), Norton, *Pausanias*, Ravenscroft, *The Canterbury Guests* (1694), Thomas Scott, *The Mock Marriage*, Settle, *Distressed Innocence*, Shadwell, *Epsom Wells* (1693), *The Libertine* (1692), Shakespeare (adapted Tate), *King Richard II*, (adapted Shadwell), *Timon of Athens* (1694), Southerne, *The Fatal Marriage* (1694), *The Maid's Last Prayer, Oroonoko* (adapted from Behn, 1695), *Sir Anthony Love, The Wives' Excuse* (1691), *The Gordian Knot Untied*.

CHORAL AND SONGS: 15 odes for voices and orch. incl *Ode for St. Cecilia's Day* (1692) and *Come, ye sons of art away*, for birthday of Mary II (1694); 9 welcomesongs for voices and orch.; *Yorkshire Feast Song* for voices and orch.; 9 secular cantatas; 66 anthems; 3 services; 26 hymns, psalms, chants and sacred canons; 22 sacred songs; 53 catches; 4 3-part songs; 42 vocal duets; over 100 songs (not counting *c* 150 in the plays).

INSTRUMENTAL: 13 fantasies and 4 other works for strings; 22 sonatas for 2 vlns. and bass and some other miscellaneous chamber works; 8 suites (lessons) and *c* 30 other pieces for harpsichord; 3 or 4 voluntaries for organ.

Puritani di Scozia, I (*The Puritans of Scotland*), opera by Bellini (lib. by C. Pepoli), based on a play by J. Ancelot and X.B. Saintine, *Têtes rondes et cavaliers*, and farther back on Scott's *Old Mortality*), prod. Paris, Théâtre Italien, 25 Jan 1835.

Puschmann, Adam Zacharias (b Görlitz, 1532; d Breslau, 4 Apr 1600), German master-singer. Pupil of Hans Sachs at Nuremberg. He pub. in 1574 a treatise on master-singing, containing songs of his own as well as by Sachs, Behaim and others.

Pushkin, Alexander (1790–1837), Russian poet, dramatist and novelist. *See* **Aleko** (Rakhmaninov), **Assafiev** (*Feast in Time of Plague, Bronze Horseman* and *Fountain of Bakhchissarai*), **Boris Godunov** (Mussorgsky), **Cui** (*Captive in the Caucasus, Feast in Time of Plague* and songs), **Dargomizhsky** (*Bacchus' Feast*), **Eugene Onegin** (Tchaikovsky), **Francesca da Rimini** (Rakhmaninov), **Gaigerova** (songs), **Golden Cockerel** (Rimsky-Korsakov), **Khrennikov** (songs), **Legend of Tsar Saltan** (Rimsky-Korsakov), **Leoncavallo** (*Zingari*), **Lourié** (*Feast in Time of Plague* and songs), **Mavra** (Stravinsky), **Mazeppa** (Tchaikovsky), **Medtner** (songs), **Mossolov** (songs), **Mozart and Salieri** (Rimsky-Korsakov, **Poet's Echo** (Britten), **Popov** (*Slow Horseman*), **Prisoner in the Caucasus** (Cui), **Prokofiev** (*Feast in Time of Plague, Boris Godunov, Eugene Onegin, Egyptian Nights, Queen of Spades* and songs), **Queen of Spades** (Tchaikovsky), **Russalka** (Dargomizhsky), **Ruslan and Ludmila** (Glinka), **Shaporin** (*Boris Godunov* and songs), **Shebalin** (*Mozart and Salieri, Stone Guest* and songs), **Shostakovich** (songs), **Stone Guest** (Dargomizhsky), **Tcherepnin (N.)** (*Golden Fish*), **Vasilenko** (*Gypsies*), **Verstovsky** (*Black Shawl*).

Putnam, Ashley (b New York, 10 Aug 1952), American soprano. Debut Norfolk, Va., 1976, as Lucia; returned 1977 as Mary in Musgrave's *Mary Queen of Scots*. NY City Opera from 1978 as Violetta, Maria Stuarda, Ophelia and Bellini's Elvira. Glyndebourne 1978, Musetta; Arabella 1984. In 1986 her Fiordiligi was seen on BBC TV, and she sang Jenůfa at CG. Other roles incl. Gilda, Donna Anna and Strauss's Danae.

Puy (Fr.), a competitive festival held in France in the Middle Ages by literary and music guilds, incl. the Troubadours of the 12th cent. Puys continued to the 16th cent. and the most famous was that of Évreux, held annually on St Cecilia's Day (22 Nov), 1570–1614. Prizes were given and the laureate was called *roy de puy*

Puyana, Rafael (b Bogotà, 14 Oct 1931), Colombian harpsichordist. Studied at New England Cons., Boston, and with Wanda Landowska. NY debut 1957; London 1966. He performs in a wide range of Baroque music and is often heard in modern works.

Pyamour, John (d before 4 Jul 1431), English composer. He was a member of the Chapel Royal, 1420–1, and of the chapel of the Duke of Bedford in 1427. Wrote church music.

Pycard, French composer, represented in the Old Hall MS. His music is remarkable for its extensive use of canon. He served in John of Gaunt's household, in the 1390s.

Pygmalion, acte de ballet by Rameau (lib. by B. de Savot, after A.H. de La Motte), prod. Paris, Opéra, 27 Aug 1748.

Pygott, Richard (b *c* 1485; d ? Greenwich, 1552), English composer. He was in Wolsey's private chapel in 1517 as master of the children and in 1533 became a Gentleman of the Chapel Royal. Later he was given a corrody at Coggeshall monastery in Essex and a canonry at Tamworth, but lost some of the benefits at the dissolution of the monasteries; Henry VIII, however, and after him Edward VI, retained his services.

Works incl. Masses, motets, *Salve Regina*; carols, etc.

Pythagoras, Greek 6th-cent (B.C.) philosopher. He contributed to the science of music by working out by mathematics the intervals of the scale according to the number of vibrations to each note and by helping to systematize the Tetrachords.

Q

Quadrille, a dance originating from the figured displays of mounted squadrons at tournaments, intro. into the ballet in the 18th cent., where dancers perf. similar figures, and in the 19th cent. passing into the ballroom for the perf. of country dances, 5 in number and each calling for different figures and different music. Its music, like that of the Lancers, which evidently had a military origin, soon ceased to use the orig. country-dance tunes and was made up of arrs. of popular songs or more esp. fashionable operatic tunes.

Quadruple Counterpoint, counterpoint in which 4 parts are reversible. *See also* **Triple Counterpoint.**

Quadruplets, groups of 4 notes occurring abnormally in music written in a time in which the regular units are divisible by 3.

Quagliati, Paolo (b Chioggia, *c* 1555; d Rome, 16 Nov 1628), Italian composer. He was organist at the church of Santa Maria Maggiore in Rome from 1601. For the wedding of Gesualdo's daughter, Isabella, in 1623 he wrote a collection of inst. pieces, *La sfera armoniosa*.

Works incl. dramatic cantata *Carro di fedeltà d'amore* (1806); motets; spiritual and secular madrigals and canzonets; organ and harpsichord works.

Quail, a toy instrument. *See* **Toy Symphony.**

Quantz, Johann Joachim (b Oberscheden nr. Göttingen, 30 Jan 1697; d Potsdam, 12 Jul 1773), German flautist and composer. As a boy he learned several instruments, and studied comp. with Zelenka in Vienna in 1717. The following year he was app. oboist to the court of August II in Dresden and Warsaw, but later turned to the fl., studying under Buffardin. After travels in It., Fr. and Eng. he returned to Dresden, becoming 1st flautist to the court, until in 1741 he entered the service of Frederick II of Prussia. He was the king's fl. teacher and wrote for him over 500 works for fl. His important treatise, *Versuch einer Anweisung die Flöte traversiere zu spielen*, was pub. in 1752.

Works incl. *c* 300 concertos and *c* 200 other works for fl.; hymns on poems by Gellert.

Quartal Harmony, a harmonic theory, expounded by Yasser and others, which bases the harmonic system on the intervals of the 4th, instead of the 3rd which decisively determines maj. or min. tonalities.

Quarter Note (Amer.), crotchet.

Quarter-tones, intervals half-way between a semitone. They were known to the Greeks and were apparently used in early plainsong but soon came to be abandoned and were not revived in western music until the 20th cent. The chief exponent of quarter-tone music is Alois Hába; others, e.g. Bartók and Bloch, have used the device, but not systematically.

Quartet, any work or musical number in a work written for 4 vocal or instrumental parts; more partic. a chamber work for 2 vlns., vla. and cello (string 4tet) or vln., vla., cello and pf. (pf. 4tet). The use of the word quartet without further specification usually suggests a string 4tet. *See also* **String Quartet.**

Quartetto Italiano, Italian string quartet active 1945–86. Members were Paolo Borciani and Elisa Pegreffi (vlns.), Piero Farulli (vla.) and Franco Rossi (cello). Played wide repertory from memory.

Quartettsatz (Ger. = quartet movement), the name given to the 1st movement of Schubert's unfinished string 4tet in C min., comp. in Dec 1820 (D703) and not perf. until 1 Mar 1867, in Vienna. The work was clearly intended to be completed, for Schubert wrote 41 bars of a slow movement in A♭ maj.

Quasi (It. = as it were, so to speak), a qualifying word used in directions suggesting an approximate manner of perf. (e.g. *quasi allegro*) or an apparent contradiction of a time signature by the music's actual effect (e.g. *andante quasi allegro*, meaning that although the beats are moderately slow, the figuration is rapid and will give an effect of quickness). Quasi is also used for titles of compositions approximating to some partic. style, e.g. 'Quasi Scherzo', Beethoven's sonatas 'quasi una fantasia' (op. 27), etc.

Quatorze Juillet, Le (*The Fourteenth of July*), play by Romain Rolland, forming part of the trilogy *Le Théâtre de la Révolution* with *Danton* and *Les Loups*, pub. and perf. *c* 1900–2, collectively pub. 1909. It was prod. in the open air, Paris, Arènes de Lutèce, 14 Jul 1936, with music by Auric, Honegger, Ibert, Koechlin, Lazarus, Milhaud and Roussel.

Quattro pezzi sacri (*Four Sacred Pieces*), 4 works for chorus and orch. by Verdi: Ave Maria, Lauda alla Vergine Maria, Te Deum and Stabat Mater, comp. 1888–97. The last

3 pieces were perf. Paris, 7 Apr 1898.

Quattro rusteghi, I., (*The Four Boors*), opera by Wolf-Ferrari (lib. by G. Pizzolato, based on Goldoni's comedy), prod., in Ger., Munich, 19 Mar 1906; in Eng. as *The School for Fathers*, London, SW, 7 Jun 1946.

Quatuor (Fr.), quartet.

Quatuor pour la fin du temps (*Quartet for the end of time*), work by Messiaen for pf., clar., vln. and cello; comp. 1940 in a Silesian prisoner-of-war camp. Fp 15 Jan 1941.

Quaver, the black note (♪) of half the time-value of a crochet or an eighth of a semibreve, symbolized by the figure 8 in time-signatures, e.g. 3–8 indicates bar-lengths of 3 quavers.

Queen Mary's Funeral Music, music by Purcell for the Westminster Abbey funeral in 1695 of Mary, wife of William III; sequence incl. music written 3 years earlier for Shadwell's play *The Libertine*. Other sections were given at Purcell's own funeral in Nov 1695.

Queen of Cornwall, The, opera by Boughton (lib. Thomas Hardy's play, with alterations), prod. Glastonbury, 21 Aug 1924. The subject is Tristram and Iseult.

Queen of Golconda, The (*Drottningen av G.*), opera by Berwald (lib. by comp. after J.B.C. Vial and E.G.F. de Favieres); comp. 1864, fp Stockholm, 3 Apr 1968.

Queen of Sheba. *See* **Königin von Saba; Reine de Saba.**

Queen of Spades, The (*Pikovaya Dama*), opera by Tchaikovsky (lib. by M.I. Tchaikovsky, Tchaikovsky's brother, based on Pushkin's story), prod. St Petersburg, 19 Dec 1890.

Queler, Eve (b New York, 1 Jan 1936), American conductor. She studied at Mannes College and with Walter Susskind. Debut NY, 1967, with *Cavalleria Rusticana*. She was asst. to Julius Rudel at the NY City Opera for five years and from 1971 gave concert perfs. in NY of rarely heard operas, e.g. Respighi's *Belfagor*, Zandonai's *Francesca da Rimini* and Donizetti's *Parisina d'Este*. In 1977 she cond. the 1st US perf. of Puccini's *Edgar*. Concerts with the Philadelphia Orch. and the Montreal SO. Recorded Strauss's *Guntram*, 1985.

Quentin Durward, opera by Gevaert (lib. by F. Cormon and M. Carré, based on Scott's novel), prod. Paris, Opéra-Comique, 25 Mar 1858.

Querflöte (Ger.), Transverse Flute.

Quest, The, ballet by Walton (choreogra-phy by Frederick Ashton, based on Spenser's *Faery Queen*), prod. London, Sadler's Wells Ballet, 1943.

Quilico, Louis (b Montreal, 14 Jan 1929), Canadian baritone. Studied in Rome and NY; debut City Opera, 1953. Met. 1972. European debut Spoleto, 1959, in Donizetti's *Il Duca d'Alba*; CG 1961, as Rigoletto. In 1966 he sang in the fp of Milhaud's *La mère coupable*, at Geneva.

Quilter, Roger (b Brighton, 1 Nov 1877; d London, 21 Sep 1953), English composer. Educ. at Eton and studied music with Knorr at Frankfurt.

Works incl. opera *Julia* (prod. CG, 1936), radio opera *The Blue Boar*; incid. music for Shakespeare's *As You Like It* (1922) and the children's fairy-play *Where the Rainbow ends* (1911); *Children's Overture* on nursery tunes, serenade, *3 Eng. Dances*, for orch. (1910); song-cycle *To Julia* (Herrick, 1906), songs to words by Shakespeare, Tennyson and others, etc.

Quinault, Jean-Baptiste (Maurice) (b Verdun, 9 Sep 1687; d Gien, 30 Aug 1745), French singer, actor and composer. Sang at the Théâtre Français in Paris 1712–18, and worked as an actor there from 1718. His comps. were almost all written for the Comédie Française. In 1733 he retired to Gien.

Works incl. ballet *Les Amours des déesses* (1729) and others; stage divertissements; incid. music for Molière's *Bourgeois Gentilhomme* (1716) and *La Princesse d'Élide* (1722), etc.

Quinault, Philippe (b Paris, bap. 5 Jun 1635; d Paris, 26 Nov 1688), French poet and librettist. *See* **Alceste** (Lully), **Amadis** (Lully), **Amadis de Gaule** (J.C. Bach), **Armida** (Mysliveček), **Armide** (Gluck and Lully), **Atys** (Lully and Piccinni), **Cadmus et Hermoine** (Lully), **Festes de l'Amour** (Lully), **Floquet** (*Nouvelle Omphale* and *Alceste*), **Isis** (Lully), **Lully** (*Églogue de Versailles*), **Persée** (Lully), **Phaéton** (Lully), **Proserpine** (Lully and Paisiello), **Roland** (Lully and Piccinni), **Thésée** (Lully).

Quinet, Fernand (b Charleroi, 29 Jan 1898; d Liège, 24 Oct 1971), Belgian cellist, conductor and composer. Studied at the Brussels Cons., where he was awarded the Belg. Prix de Rome in 1921. Later became dir. of the Charleroi Cons., and of the Liège Cons. in 1938.

Works incl. *Esquisses symphoniques, Mouvements symphoniques* (1931) for orch.; suite *L'École buissonière* and fantasy for string 4tet, *Charade* for pf. trio, suite for 2 clars. and bass clar. (1930); *Moralités non légendaires* for voice and 18 insts. (1930); vla. and pf. sonata; song-cycle *La Bonne Aventure* and other songs.

Quint, 5⅓ ft. org. stop transposing a 5th upwards; also called Great Quint.

Quinta falsa (Lat. = false 5th), another name for the Tritone when it appears as a diminished 5th, not an augmented 4th.

Quinte (Fr.). The word is now used for the interval of the 5th, but was formerly also the name of a string instrument of the viol family, the tenor viol with 5 strings; also later of the vla., another Fr. name of which was Taille.

Quintet, any work or musical number in a work written in 5 vocal or instrumental parts; more partic. a chamber work of 5 instruments, e.g. pf. and string 4tet (pf. 5tet) or 5 string instruments. *See also* **String Quintet.**

Quinton (Fr.), a 19th-cent. name for a hybrid string instrument, half viol and half vln.

Quintuple Time. Music with 5 beats to the bar, the time-signature of which is 5–4, 5–8, etc., is said to be in quintuple time.

Quintuplets, groups of 5 notes occupying a beat or the space of a note of normal duration.

Quintus (Lat. = the fifth), the 5th part in a comp. for 5 or more voices in old music. It was so called because its range was always equal to that of one of the other parts, so that it could not be described as *cantus, altus, tenor* or *bassus.*

Quire, the old Eng. spelling of Choir.

Quiterne (Fr. and old Eng.) = Cittern.

Quo vadis?, opera by Nouguès (lib. by H. Cain, based on Sienkiewicz's novel), prod. Nice, 9 Feb 1909.

Quodlibet (Lat. *quod libet* = as it pleases), a comp. made up of a medley of tunes, usually familiar songs, in polyphonic combinations. Obrecht's *Missa diversorum tenorum* is an elaborate quodlibet, introducing the melodies of *chansons* by 15th-cent. comps. A more familiar ex. is the quodlibet at the end of Bach's Goldberg Variations. The Span. term for a quodlibet was *ensalada.*

Quotations, short passages in musical works taken from other music (*a*) by the same composer (*b*) by another, e.g.,

(*a*) Brahms, *Regenlied* in finale of G maj. vln. sonata;

Elgar, a number of themes from earlier works in *The Music Makers*; demons' chorus from *The Dream of Gerontius* in *The Fourth of August* (as a theme for the enemy);

Mozart, 'Non più andrai' from *Figaro* in 2nd-act finale of *Don Giovanni*;

Prokofiev, March from *The Love for Three Oranges* in ballet *Cinderella*;

Puccinni, 'Mimi' theme from *La Bohème* in *Il tabarro*;

Rimsky-Korsakov, theme from *Pskovitianka (Ivan the Terrible)* in *The Tsar's Bride* (ref. to Ivan);

Saint-Saëns, theme from *Danse macabre* in *Fossils* section of *Le Carnaval des animaux*;

Schumann, opening of *Papillons*, op. 1, in *Florestan* piece in *Carnaval*, op. 9;

Shostakovich, themes from 10th symph. and 1st cello concerto in 8th string 4tet (1960);

Smetana, theme assoc. with the Vyšehrad citadel of Prague in the 1st symph. poem of *Má Vlast* and ref. to in the later one entitled *Vltava*;

Strauss, theme from *Guntram* in 'Childhood' section of *Tod und Verklärung*; a number of themes from earlier works in the 'Hero's Works' section of *Heldenleben* and in the dinner music in the *Bourgeois Gentilhomme* incid. music; *Ariadne auf Naxos* in *Capriccio*; transfiguration theme from *Tod und Verklärung* in *Im Abendrot* ('Last Songs');

Vaughan Williams, theme from *Hugh the Drover* in vln. concerto;

Wagner, 2 themes from *Tristan* in *Meistersinger*, III. i; swan motive from *Lohengrin* in *Parsifal*, I; themes from *Siegfried* in *Siegfried Idyll* (some going back to a projected string 4tet);

Wolf, song, 'In dem Schatten meiner Locken' from *Span. Song-Book* in opera *Der Corregidor*, I.

(*b*) Bartók, Nazi march theme from Shostakovich's 7th symph. in Concerto for Orchestra; Beethoven's 'Song of Thanksgiving' in the 3rd piano concerto (both composers had just recovered from illness);

Bax, theme from Wagner's *Tristan* in symph. poem *Tintagel*; passage from Elgar's vln. concerto, in G maj. string 4tet ded. to Elgar;

Beethoven, 'Notte e giorno faticar' from Mozart's *Don Giovanni* in Vars. on a theme by Diabelli, op. 120;

Berg, themes from Wagner's *Tristan* and Zemlinsky's *Lyric Symphony* in Lyric Suite for string 4tet; Bach chorale *Es ist genug* in vln. concerto;

Berio, scherzo from Mahler's 2nd symph. in *Sinfonia* (1968);

Brahms, 'Batti, batti' from Mozart's *Don Giovanni* in song *Liebe und Frühling*, op. 3 no. 2;

Bréville, 'Tarnhelm' motive from Wagner's *Ring* in *Portraits de Maîtres* for pf., indicating a transformation between the pieces imitating various composer;

Britten, theme from Wagner's *Tristan* in *Albert Herring*;

Chabrier, Serenade from Mozart's *Don Giovanni* in song *Ballade des gros dindons*;

Charpentier, theme from Wagner's *Ring* in *Louise*, II;

Chopin, air from Rossini's *Gazza ladra* in Polonaise in B min. ded. to Kolberg (1826);

Debussy, theme from Wagner's *Tristan* in *Golliwogg's Cake-Walk (Children's Corner)*; Elgar, theme from Mendelssohn's overture *Calm Sea and Prosperous Voyage* in 'Enigma' Variations (*Romance*); Chopin's G min. nocturne and Paderewski's *Polish Fantasy* for pf. and orch. in symph. prelude *Polonia*;

Falla, opening motive from Beethoven's 5th symph. ('Fate knocking at the door') in ballet *The Three-cornered Hat*;

Fibich, var. themes from Mozart's *Don Giovanni* in opera *Hedy* (based on Byron's *Don Juan*);

Krenek, Mendelssohn's *Spring Song* in incid. music for Goethe's *Triumph der Empfindsamkeit*;

Mahler, theme from Charpentier's *Louise* and Hunding's motive from Wagner's *Ring* in the 1st movement of the 9th symphony; prelude to scene 3 of *Boris Godunov* in *Der Einsame im Herbst* (*Das Lied von der Erde*);

Mozart, tunes from Martín y Soler's *Una cosa rara* and Sarti's *Fra due litiganti* in 2nd act finale of *Don Giovanni*;

Mussorgsky, Handel's 'See the conquering hero' and themes by Famitsin and from Serov's opera *Rogenda* in satirical song *The Peep-Show*; sea motive from Rimsky-Korsakov's *Sadko* in song *The Classicist*;

Offenbach, 'Notte e giorno faticar' from Mozart's *Don Giovanni* in *Tales of Hoffmann*, prologue: 'Che farò' from Gluck's *Orfeo* in *Orphée aux enfers*;

Rimsky-Korsakov, themes from Mozart's *Requiem* in opera *Mozart and Salieri*;

Saint-Saëns, themes from overture to

Offenbach's *Orphée aux enfers* in Tortoises section of *Le Carnaval des animaux* (because Orpheus's lute was made of tortoiseshell), also Berlioz's *Danse des Sylphes* in *Elephants* and a phrase from Rossini's *Barber of Seville* in *Fossils* in the same work;

Schumann, theme from Beethoven's *An die ferne Geliebte* in *Carnaval*, op. 9 (written while S. was separated from Clara Wieck); aria from Marschner's *Der Templer und die Jüdin* in finale of *Études symphoniques*, op. 13;

Shostakovich, overture from Rossini's *William Tell* and the fate motif from Wagner's *Ring*, in the 15th symphony;

Strauss, Denza's song *Funiculi, funiculà* in symph. *Aus Italien* (under the impression that it was an It. folksong); giants' motive in Wagner's *Ring* in *Feuersnot*; Wagner's Rhinemaidens' theme in dinner music (salmon) of Strauss's *Bourgeois gentilhomme* (*Ariadne*, 1st version); themes by Bull, Legrenzi, Monteverdi and Peerson in *Die schweigsame Frau*; fragment from funeral march in Beethoven's 'Eroica' symph. in *Metamorphosen* for strings;

Stravinsky, waltz by Lanner (played on a barrel-organ) in ballet *Petrushka*; themes from Tchaikovsky's pf. music and songs in ballet *The Fairy's Kiss* (*Le Baiser de la fée*);

Tchaikovsky, song from Grétry's *Richard, Cœur de Lion* in *The Queen of Spades*;

Vaughan Williams, opening theme from Debussy's *L'Après-midi d'un faune* in incid. music for Aristophanes' *Wasps*;

Wagner, *Di tanti palpiti*, from Rossini's *Tancredi*, parodied in the tailor's episode in *Meistersinger*, III.

Walton, 2 themes from Rossini's *William Tell* overture in *Façade* (*Swiss Yodelling Song*); theme from Rossini's *Tancredi* overture in *Scapino* overture;

Also numerous exs. of quotations from earlier works in the music of contemporary composers, e.g. Kagel, Holloway and Stockhausen (*Beethausen, opus 1970, von Stockhoven*).

R

r, the Supertonic note in any key in Tonic Sol-fa notation, pronounced Ray.

RAM (abbr.) = Royal Academy of Music (London).

RCM (abbr.) = Royal College of Music (London).

RIAM (abbr.) = Royal Irish Academy of Music.

RMCM (abbr.) = Royal Manchester College of Music.

RNCM (abbr.) = Royal Northern College of Music, Manchester.

RV. In catalogues of Vivaldi's works refers to Ryom (*q.v.*).

Raaff, Anton (b Gelsdorf nr. Bonn, bap. 6 May 1714; d Munich, 28 May 1797), German tenor. Studied in Munich in Bologna, sang much in Italy as well as in Ger. and Aus. From 1770 in the service of the Elector Palatine. The first Idomeneo in Mozart's opera of that name.

Rabaud, Henri (Benjamin) (b Paris, 10 Nov 1873; d Paris, 11 Sep 1949), French composer. Studied under his father, the cellist Hippolyte R. (1839–1900), and with Gédalge and Massenet at the Paris Cons., where he gained the Prix de Rome in 1894. After his stay in Rome he visited Vienna and travelled elsewhere, and after his return to Paris he became harmony prof. at the Cons. and cond. at the Opéra. In 1920 he succeeded Fauré as dir. of the Cons., and was in turn succeeded in that post by Delvincourt in 1941.

Works incl. operas *La Fille de Roland* (1904), *Le Premier Glaive* (1907), *Mârouf, savetier du Caire* (1914), *L'Appel de la mer* (after Synge's *Riders to the Sea*, 1924), *Rolande et les mauvais garçons* (1934); incid. music for Shakespeare's *Merchant of Venice* and *Antony and Cleopatra* (1917); music for films *Joueurs d'échecs* and *Le Miracle des loups*; Psalm iv for chorus; 2 symphs., symph. poem *Andromède, La Procession nocturne* (after Lenau's *Faust* (1899), *Le Sacrifice d'Isaac, La Flûte de Pan, Divertissement grec, Divertissement sur des airs russes, Poème sur le livre de Job*, etc., for orch.; string 4tet; songs.

Rachmaninoff. *See* **Rakhmaninov.**

Racine, Jean (1639–99), French poet and dramatist. *See* **Andromaque** (Grétry), **Athalie** (Mendelssohn and others), **Boieldieu**

(*Athalie*), **Esther** (Handel), **Fauré** (*Cantique*), **Hervé** (*Nouvel Aladin*), **Ifigenia in Aulide** (Graun), **Iphigénie en Aulide** (Gluck), **Lemoyne** (*Phèdre*), **Lully** (*Idylle sur la paix*), **Massenet** (*Phèdre*, incid. music) **Mitridate** (Mozart), **Moreau** (*Cantiques spiritueles, Esther* and *Athalie*), **Poissl** (*Athalia*), **Roseingrave (2)** (*Phaedra and Hippolytus*), **Rossini** (*Ermione*), **Saint-Saëns** (*Andromaque*), **Schulz** (*Athalie*), **Thompson (V.)** (*Air de Phèdre*), **Vogler** (*Athalie*).

Rackett, a double-reed instrument, also called Racket, Ranket or Sausage Bassoon. Its long tube was folded many times, so that the actual size of the instrument seemed small.

Radamisto, opera by Handel (lib. by N.F. Haym, after Tacitus), prod. London, King's Theatre, Haymarket, 27 Apr. 1720.

Radcliffe, Philip (FitzHugh) (b Godalming, 27 Apr 1905, d nr. Dunkirk, 2 Sep 1986), English scholar, author and composer. Educ. at Charterhouse and King's Coll., Cambridge. Univ. lecturer in music at Cambridge, 1947–72. His comps. incl. chamber music, part-songs and songs. Also wrote a book on Mendelssohn, and contrib. chapters on the Scarlattis, Corelli and Vivaldi to *The Heritage of Music.*

Radford, Robert (b Nottingham, 13 May 1874; d London, 3 Mar 1933), English bass. Studied at the RAM in London and 1st appeared at the Norwich Festival in 1899 and in opera at CG in 1904, as the Commendatore. He sang in the *Ring* under Richter (1908) and was the 1st Brit. Boris.

Radicati, Felice Alessandro (b Turin, 1775; d Bologna, 19 Mar 1820), Italian violinist and composer. Pupil of Pugnani, he toured as a vln. virtuoso in It., Fr. and Eng. then settled in Bologna in 1815 as leader of the munic. orch., *maestro di cappella* at San Petronio and vln. prof. at the Liceo Filarmonico.

Works incl. operas *Riccardo Cuor di Leone, Fedra, Coriolano, Castore, e Polluce* and some others; vln. concertos; vln. pieces; aria.

Radino, Giovanni Maria, Italian 16th-cent. organist and composer. He was organist at the church of San Giovanni di Verdara at Padua, 1592–8.

Works incl. madrigals for 4 voices; dances for harpsichord or lute.

Radnai, Miklós (b Budapest, 1 Jan 1892; d Budapest, 4 Nov 1935), Hungarian composer. Studied at Budapest and Munich, became a prof. at the Budapest Cons., 1919–25, and then dir. of the Opera there.

Works incl. opera *The Former Lovers*; ballet *The Infanta's Birthday* (after Wilde, 1918); Hung. Symph., *Mosaic* suite, 5 poems, *Fairy Tale, Orcan the Hero*, for orch.; pf. trio; instrumental sonatas; pf. works; songs.

Raff, (Joseph) Joachim (b Lachen, Ct. Zurich, 27 May 1822; d Frankfurt, 24 Jun 1882), Swiss composer. Studied to become a schoolmaster, but took to music and in 1843 had some works pub. on Mendelssohn's recommendation. He met Liszt, and at Cologne in 1846 Mendelssohn, who invited him to become his pupil at Leipzig but died before this was done. He then wrote criticism at Cologne, studied further at Stuttgart and in 1850 settled at Weimar to be near Liszt. In 1856 he went to Wiesbaden, where he wrote incid. music for a drama by Wilhelm Genast and married his daughter Doris, an actress. In 1877 he became dir. of the Hoch Cons. at Frankfurt.

Works incl. operas *König Alfred* (1851), *Dame Kobold* (on Calderón's *Dama duende*, 1870) and others; incid. music for Genast's *Bernhard von Weimar* and other plays; oratorio *Weltende* and other choral works; 11 symphs., incl. programme symphs. *An das Vaterland, Im Walde, Lenore* (on Bürger's ballad), *Gelebt, gestrebt ...*, *In den Alpen, Frühlingsklange, Im Sommer, Zur Herbstzeit, Der Winter* (unfinished), 2 suites, 3 overtures for orch.; sinfonietta for wind instruments; concerto, suite and *Ode au printemps* for pf. and orch., 2 vln. concertos, cello concerto; 8 string 4tets, string 6tet, string 8tet, 4 pf. trios, 2 pf. 4tets, pf. 5tet; 5 vln. and pf. sonatas; numerous pf. works; vln. pieces.

Ragtime, an American form of syncopated dance music of Negro orig. and coming into fashion *c* 1910, the forerunner of Jazz and Swing. Also title of work by Stravinsky for 11 insts.; comp. 1918, fp London, 27 Apr 1920, cond. Bliss.

Raimann, Rezsö (b Veszprém, 7 May 1861; d Vienna, 26 Sep 1913), Hungarian composer, music. dir. to Prince Esterházy at Totis Castle.

Works incl. operas *Enoch Arden* (after Tennyson, 1894), *Imre Kiraly* and others, operettas; incid. music to plays; pf. pieces; songs.

Raimondi, Gianni (b Bologna, 13 Apr 1923), Italian tenor. He sang Ernesto at Bologna in 1948 and in 1953 Alfredo at the Stoll Theatre, London; returned in 1958 for Lord Percy in *Anna Bolena*. US debut, San Francisco, 1957; NY Met, 1965, as Edgar-

do. La Scala, Milan, from 1955. Other roles incl. Pollione, Gabriele Adorno and Pinkerton.

Raimondi, Ignazio (b Naples, *c* 1737; d London, 14 Jan 1813), Italian violinist and composer. After playing vln. in the San Carlo opera orch. in Naples he went to Amsterdam, where he was dir. of the subscription concerts *c* 1762–80, after which he settled in London. Works incl. opera *La Muette* (prod. Paris); programme symphs. *The Adventures of Telemachus* (1777) and *The Battle* (1785); *sinfonie concertanti*; string 4tets and other chamber music.

Raimondi, Pietro (b Rome, 20 Dec 1786; d Rome, 30 Oct 1853), Italian composer. Studied at the Cons. di Pietà de' Turchini at Naples and wandered all over It. in great poverty until he succeeded in prod. an opera at Genoa in 1807. Prod. operas at Rome, Milan, Naples and in Sicily until 1824, became dir. of the royal theatres there until 1832, when he became prof. of comp. at the Palermo Cons. In 1852 he was app. *maestro di cappella* at St Peter's in Rome in succession to Basili.

Works incl. operas *Le bizzarrie d'amore* (1807), *Il ventaglio* and 60 others incl. a serious and a comic one which could be perf. together; 21 ballets; 8 oratorios incl. trilogy *Giuseppe* (incl. *Putifar, Farao* and *Giacobbe* performable separately or simultaneously), Masses, Requiems, psalms and other church music, much of it in very numerous parts; vocal fugues, one in 64 parts and incl. others in 4 parts, 4 of which could be sung together in 16 parts.

Raimondi, Ruggero (b Bologna, 3 Oct 1941), Italian bass. He studied in Rome and made his debut at Spoleto in 1964 as Colline; sang Procida in Rome the same year and in 1965 appeared as Méphistophélès in Venice. In 1969 he sang Don Giovanni at Glyndebourne, and has become identified with this role; cinema version of the opera under Lorin Maazel. NY Met debut 1970, as Silva. CG from 1972 (debut as Fiesco). Other roles incl. Attila, Boris Godunov, Mosè and Philip II.

Raindrop Prelude, Chopin's pf. prelude in Db maj., op. 28 no. 15, written at Valdemosa, Majorca, in 1838 and said to have been suggested by the dripping of raindrops from the roof; hence the continuously repeated Ab = G#, which is the dominant both of the main key and of the C# min. middle section.

Rainforth, Elizabeth (b ? 23 Nov 1814; d Bristol, 22 Sep 1877), English soprano. Studied under George Perry and T. Cooke

Rainier

and made her 1st stage appearance in London in 1836, in Arne's *Artaxerxes*, and in oratorio the following year. She appeared at CG until 1843 as Susanna, the Countess and Cherubini's Lodoïska.

Rainier, Priaulx (b Howick, Natal, 3 Feb 1903; d Besse-en-Chandesse, Auvergne, 10 Oct 1986), S. African composer. She studied at Cape Town and after 1920 at the RAM in London; lastly with Nadia Boulanger in Paris. In 1942 she was app. prof. at the RAM.

Works incl. *Archaic Songs* for chorus; ballet suite for orch. (1950), *Sinfonia da camera* for strings (1947); *Incantation* for clar. and orch.; cello concerto (1964); *Aequora Lunae* for orch. (1967); *Ploërmel* for winds and perc. (1973); vln. concerto (1977), Concertante for ob., clar. and orch. (1981); string 4tet (1939); vla. and pf. sonata; pf. works; songs.

Raisa, Rosa (b Bialystok, 23 May 1893; d Los Angeles, 28 Sep 1963), Polish soprano. She studied in Naples and made her debut in Parma in 1913, as Leonora in *Oberto*. Chicago, 1913–36, in operas by Mascagni and Respighi. She was admired by Toscanini, and under him at La Scala, Milan, sang Asteria in the fp of Boito's *Nerone* (1924) and the title role in the fp of *Turandot* (1926). London, CG, 1914 and 1933. Other roles incl. Mimi, Norma, Tosca and Wolf-Ferrari's Maliella. Opened a singing school in Chicago, 1937.

Raison, André (b before 1650; d Paris, 1719), French organist. Held posts at the Sainte-Geneviève and Jacobin churches in Paris. Comp. organ music.

Raitio, Väinö (b Sortavala, 15 Apr 1891; d Helsinki, 10 Sep 1945), Finnish composer. Studied the pf. with his mother, later comp. with Melartin and Furuhjelm and in 1916–17 with Ilyinsky in Moscow. Taught comp. at Viipuri in 1932–8, but settled at Helsinki and devoted himself entirely to comp.

Works incl. operas *Jephtha's Daughter* (1931), *Princess Cecilia* (1936) and 3 others; ballet *Waterspout* (1929); symph., 10 symph. poems; pf. concerto, concerto for vln. and cello (1936), Poem for cello and orch. (1915); string 4tet, pf. 5tet; vln. and pf. sonata; songs.

Rakastava (*The Lover*), 3 songs for male chorus a capella by Sibelius, op. 14; comp. 1893, fp Helsinki, 28 Apr 1894. Version for male chorus and strings, 1894. Rewritten for strings, triangle and timp., 1911: *The Lover*, *The Path of the Beloved*, *Good night*.

Rake's Progress, The, opera by Stravinsky

(lib. by W.H. Auden and C. Kallman, based on Hogarth), prod. Venice, 11 Sep 1951. *See also* **Whitaker**.

Rakhmaninov, Sergey Vassilievich (b Oneg, Novgorod, 1 Apr 1873; d Beverly Hills, Calif., 28 Mar 1943), Russian pianist and composer. Son of a captain in the Imp. Guards and descendant of a wealthy and noble family. The family fortune was gravely impaired during his childhood and his parents separated in 1882, Rakhmaninov living with his mother in St Petersburg. There he continued music lessons in a desultory way until Siloti, who was his cousin, advised his mother to send him to Moscow to study under Nikolai Sverev. He went to the Moscow Cons. and lived in Sverev's house for 4 years. Later he went to live with his aunt, whose daughter, Natalia Satin, was later to become his wife. He wrote the 1-act opera *Aleko* while still a student, and the pf. pieces op. 3, containing the popular C♯ min. prelude, at the age of 19. In 1895 he wrote his 1st symph. and in 1898 he was invited by the Phil. Society in London to appear as pianist and to cond. his orchestral fantasy *The Rock*. In 1905–6 he became cond. of the Imp. Grand Opera at Moscow and in 1909 he visited the USA for the 1st time, writing the 3rd pf. concerto for the occasion and playing it himself. He had by this time developed into one of the finest pianists of the time and he remained pre-eminent in that respect throughout his life.

He lived in Moscow again from 1910 to 1917 and cond. the Phil. concerts there, 1911–13. During the war of 1914–18 he played much for charity, and at the death of Skriabin, who had been his fellow-pupil under Arensky, he decided to make a tour playing that composer's works only. It was from that time on that he became a much-travelled pianist, and finding himself out of sympathy with the Revolution in Russia, he took the opportunity of a concert journey to Scandinavia in 1917 to leave his country for ever. He lived in Paris for a time and then spent most of the rest of his life in Amer. touring there each year from Jan to Apr and visiting Europe as pianist in Oct and Nov, spending some of the summer months at a small property he had acquired in Switz. on the lake of Lucerne.

Works incl. operas *Aleko* (1893), *The Miserly Knight* (1906), *Francesca da Rimini* (1906) and *Monna Vanna* (1907; perf. Philadelphia, 1985); choral symph., *The Bells* (Poe), for solo voices, chorus and orch. (1913); cantata *The Spring*; *Liturgy of St.*

John Chrysostom (1910) and Vesper Mass; 3 Rus. folksongs and chorus.

4 pf. concertos (1890–1926) and *Rhapsody on a Theme by Paganini* for pf. and orch. (1934); 3 symphs. (1895, 1907, 1936), fantasy *The Rock*, *Caprice bohémien* and symph. poem *The Isle of the Dead* (after Böcklin's picture) for orch. (1909); *Symphonic Dances* (1940).

Elegiac Trio for vln., cello and pf. (1893), string 5tet and pf. trio (unpub); cello and pf. sonata, 2 pieces for vln. and pf. and 2 for cello and pf.; a dozen works for pf. solo, incl. 2 sonatas, variations on themes by Chopin (1903) and Corelli (1931) and 57 smaller pieces (preludes, *Études-Tableaux*, etc.); 4 works for 2 pfs.; 77 songs.

Rakoczy March, a Hungarian national tune named after Prince Ferencz Rákócki, the leader of the revolt against Aus. in 1703–11. The orig. of the tune is unknown. The Hung. March in Berlioz's *Damnation of Faust* is an orchestral arr. of it and Liszt's 15th Hung. Rhapsody for pf. is based on it. Liszt also made a symph. arr. for orch. and himself transcribed this for pf. duet.

Ralf, Torsten (b Malmö, 2 Jan 1901; d Stockholm, 27 Apr 1954), Swedish tenor. He studied in Berlin and made his debut in Stettin as Cavaradossi, 1930. Dresden, 1933–44; he created Apollo in Strauss's *Daphne* (1938) and sang in the 1942 fp of Sutermeister's *Die Zauberinsel* (after *The Tempest*). London, CG, 1935–9, 1948, as Lohengrin, Parsifal, Walther, Bacchus and Radames. NY Met, 1945–7. Lived in Sweden from 1948 and retired in 1952.

Rallentando (It. = slowing down). The same direction is also expressed by *ritenuto* (held back) or *ritardando* (retarding).

Rameau, Jean Philippe (b Dijon, bap. 25 Sep 1683; d Paris, 12 Sep 1764), French composer and theorist. A pupil of his father, who sent him to study in Italy in 1701, he worked first as an organist in Avignon (1702), Clermont-Ferrand (1702–5), Paris (1705–8), Dijon (succeeding his father as cathedral organist in 1709), Lyons (1714) and from 1715 again in Clermont-Ferrand, where he wrote his important treatise, *Traité de l'Harmonie* (pub. 1722). In the latter year he settled in Paris, where he received support from the wealthy patron La Pouplinière. He had previously pub. some harpsichord pieces, but with *Hippolyte et Aricie* (1733) he began at the age of 50 a second career as an opera comp. Though at first opposed by the adherents of Lully's operas, he quickly estab. himself as the leading Fr. comp. for the stage, and during the Guerre des Bouffons was the champion of Fr. music against the It. party.

Works incl. operas and opera-ballets *Hippolyte et Aricie* (1733), *Les Indes galantes* (1735), *Castor et Pollux* (1737, rev. 1754), *Les Fêtes d'Hébé* (1739), *Dardanus* (1739), *Les Fêtes de Polyhymnie* (1745), *Le Temple de la gloire, Zaïs* (1748), *Pygmalion*, *Les Fêtes de l'Hymen et de l'Amour* (1747), *Platée* (1751), *Naïs, Zoroastre* (1749), *Acante et Céphise* (1751), *Les Surprises de l'amour, Les Paladins, Abaris, ou Les Boréades* (comp. 1764, perf. London, 1975), *Lysis et Délie* (lost), *Daphnis et Églé, Les Sybarites, La Naissance d'Osiris* (1754), *Anacréon, La Princesse de Navarre* (lib. by Voltaire, 1745), *La Guirlande* and others; incid. music for *L'Endriague* and 4 other plays by Prion; cantatas incl. *Thétis* (1718), *Aquilon et Orinthie* (1719), *Orphée* (1721), *Le Berger Fidèle* (1728); *Pièces en concert* for vln. or fl. and harpsichord; 3 vols. of harpsichord pieces, some adapted from the operas.

Ramey, Samuel (b Colby, Kansas, 28 Mar 1942), American bass-baritone. Debut 1973, Zuniga with NY City Opera; other roles there have been Méphistophélès, Don Giovanni, Leporello, Donizetti's Henry VIII and Attila. Glyndebourne from 1976, as Mozart's Figaro and Nick Shadow. He has taken part in the revival of interest in Rossini's serious operas: Mosè at the Paris Opéra (1983) and Assur in a 1986 concert perf. of *Semiramide* at CG. He recorded the title role in *Maometto II*. NY Met 1984, *Rinaldo*.

Ramis de Pareja, Bartolome (b Baeza, *c* 1440; d ? Rome, after 1491), Spanish theorist and composer. He lectured at Salamanca, went to It., living at Bologna in 1480–2 and later in Rome. He wrote a theoretical work in which he devised a way of tuning the monochord and wrote church music.

Ramler, Karl Wilhelm (1725–98), German poet. See **Bach (J.C.F.)** (*Tod Jesu*), **Graun (K.H.)** (do.), **Kreusser** (do.), **Telemann** (*Tod Jesu* and *Auferstehung Christi*), **Veichtner** (*Cephalus und Procris*), **Vogler** (*Ino*).

Ramondon, Lewis (d. ? London, *c* 1720), English singer and composer. He sang in opera in London until *c* 1711 and then made a success as a comp. of songs, some pub. in *Pills to Purge Melancholy* (1714). Also contrib. to var. plays.

Rampal, Jean-Pierre (b Marseilles, 7 Jan 1922), French flautist. He studied in Marseilles and Paris. He founded the French

Wind Quintet in 1945 and the Paris Baroque ens. in 1953. Many concert tours as soloist from 1947. He has specialized in 18th-cent. music. In 1958 he pub. *Ancient Music for the Flute*.

Ramsey, Robert (*fl*. Cambridge, *c* 1612–44), English organist and composer. He took the Mus.B. at Cambridge in 1616 and became organist and master of the children at Trinity Coll. there, 1628–44.

Works incl. services, anthems, motets; madrigals, canons; dialogue between Saul and the Witch of Endor; songs, etc.

Randall, John (b 26 Feb 1717; d Cambridge, 18 Mar 1799), English organist, scholar and composer. He was a choir-boy under Gates at the Chapel Royal in London; organist of King's Coll., Cambridge, from 1743 and prof. of music there in succession to Greene from 1755, taking the Mus.D. the same year; also organist of Trinity Coll. later.

Works incl. church music, hymn tunes, setting of Gray's ode for the installation of the Duke of Grafton as Chancellor of the Univ.

Randegger, Alberto (b Trieste, 13 Apr 1832; d London, 18 Dec 1911), Italian-born conductor, singing-master and composer. Studied at Trieste with L. Ricci, became known locally as a comp. for the church and stage, and in the 1850s settled in London, where he became prof. of singing at the RAM in 1868. He also cond. opera, orchestral and choral concerts and in 1881–1905 the triennial Norwich Festival.

Works incl. operas *Il lazzarone* (1852), *Bianca Capello* (1854), *The Rival Beauties* (1864); Masses and other church music; cantata *Fridolin* (1873), 150th Psalm, Funeral Anthem for the Prince Consort and other choral works; scena for tenor *The Prayer of Nature*; songs with orch. and with pf.

Randhartinger, Benedikt (b Ruprechtshofen, Lower Austria, 27 Jul 1802; d Vienna, 22 Dec 1893), Austrian tenor, conductor and composer. Fellow-pupil of Schubert's at the Seminary in Vienna; sang in the court chapel from 1832 and in 1862 became 2nd cond. there.

Works incl. opera *König Enzio*; *c* 20 Masses, *c* 600 motets; choruses; chamber music; *c* 400 songs.

Randová, Eva (b Kolin, 1936), Czech mezzo. She made her debut at Ostrava (1962) and joined the National Theatre, Prague, in 1968. Stuttgart from 1971, as Amneris, Eboli, Santuzza and Azucena. CG debut 1977, as

Ortrud; returned for Marina and Venus. Bayreuth from 1973, as Fricka in the Chéreau *Ring*, and Kundry. Salzburg debut 1975, as Eboli under Karajan. NY Met 1981, Fricka. Janáček's Kostelnička is one of her best roles (CG, 1986).

Rands, Bernard (b Sheffield, 2 Mar 1935), English composer. Studied at Univ. Coll., Bangor, and then in It. with Roman Vlad and Dallapiccola. He was a lecturer at Bangor (1961–70), and at York Univ., (1970–6). Since 1976 he has worked in the USA (Univs. of Calif. and Boston). Experienced in electronic techniques.

Works incl. *Refractions* for 24 performers; *Actions for 6* for fl., vla., cello, harp and 2 perc. players (1963), *Quartet Music* for pf. 4tet; *4 Compositions* for vln. and pf.; *Espressione IV* for 2 pfs.; *3 Aspects* for pf.; *Formants* for harp (1965); *Agenda* for orch. (1970); *As All Get Out* for chamber ens. (1972); *Canti del Sole* for tenor and orch. (won 1984 Pulitzer Prize).

Rangström, Türe (b Stockholm, 30 Nov 1884; d Stockholm, 11 May 1947), Swedish conductor, critic and composer. Studied with Lindegren at Stockholm and Pfitzner at Munich, also in Berlin. He settled in Stockholm as critic in 1907 and in 1922–5 cond. the Göteborg SO.

Works incl. *Kronbruden* (after Strindberg) and *Medeltida* (after Drachman, 1918); incid. music to Ibsen's *Brand* and Strindberg's *Till Damaskus*; 4 symphs. (1914–36), *August Strindberg in memoriam, Mitt land, Sång under stjärnorna*, symph. poems *Dityramb, Ett midsommarnattstycke*, symph. poems *Dityramb, Ett midsommarnattstycke, En höstsång, Havet sjunger*; chamber music; songs; etc.

Rankl, Karl (b Gaaden, 1 Oct 1898; d St Gilgen, 6 Sep 1968), Austrian conductor and composer. He studied comp. privately with Schoenberg and Webern. He was an opera conductor at Reichenberg (1925–27), Königsberg (1927–28), at the Berlin Staatsoper (1928–31), Wiesbaden (1931–33), Graz (1933–37), at the German Theatre, Prague, (1937–38), where he cond. the fp of Krenek's *Karl V*), and at CG, London, (1946–51). He did much to re-establish opera in London after the war. From 1952 to 1957 he was cond. of the Scot. Nat. Orch., and in 1957 was app. cond. of the Elizabethan Trust Opera Co. in Australia.

Works incl. opera *Deirdre of the Sorrows* (based on Synge's play, 1951); 8 symphs.; string 4tet; choruses; songs.

Ranz des Vaches, a Swiss cowherds' song

or Alphorn signal by which the cattle is called in June from the valleys to the mountain pastures. There are many different tunes, varying according to the cantons or even districts. They are metrically very irregular and use only the natural notes of the alphorn. Versions are heard in the *William Tell* ov., the *Pastoral* symph. (link between last 2 movts.), and the *Scène aux champs* in the *Symphonie Fantastique*.

Rape of Lucretia, The, opera by Britten lib. by R. Duncan, based on Livy, Shakespeare and Obey's *Viol de Lucrèce*), prod. Glyndebourne, 12 Jul 1946.

Raphael, Günther (b Berlin, 30 Apr 1903; d Herford, 19 Oct 1960), German composer. Studied under his father, a church organist, and later with Trapp, R. Kahn and others at the Berlin Hochschule für Musik. In his early 20s he succeeded in having works pub., played by the Busch 4tet, cond. by Wilhelm Furtwänglei and others. Prof. at the Leipzig Cons. (1926–34), at Duisburg Cons. (1949–53), and from 1957 at the Cologne Musikhochschule.

Works incl. Requiem (1928), Te Deum (1930), cantata *Vater unser* (1945); 16 motets, Psalm civ and other unaccomp. sacred choral works; 5 symphs. (1926–53), sinfonietta, *Theme, Variations and Rondo*, divertimento, *Smetana Suite* for orch.; 2 vln. concertos (1921, 1960), org. concerto (1936); chamber concerto for cello with wind and strings, much other chamber music; organ and pf. works.

Rapimento di Cefalo, Il (*The Abduction of Cephalus*), opera by Caccini (lib. by G. Chiabrera), prod. Florence, Palazzo Vecchio, 9 Oct 1600.

Rappresentazione di anima e di corpo (*Representation of Soul and Body*), a dramatic allegory, words by Manni, music by Emilio de' Cavalieri, prod. Rome, oratory of St Philip Neri, Feb 1600.

Rapsodie espagnole (*Spanish Rhapsody*), an orchestral work by Ravel in a Span. manner as cultivated by a typically Fr. comp. with a strong taste for and leanings towards Span. music; comp. 1907, fp Paris, 15 Mar 1908.

Raselius (orig. **Rasel**), **Andreas** (b Hahnbach nr. Amberg, Upper Palatinate, *c* 1563; d Heidelberg, 6 Jan 1602), German clergyman, theorist and composer. Studied at the Lutheran Univ. of Heidelberg, became cantor at Regensburg, 1584–1600, and then music dir. to the Elector Palatine at Heidelberg. Wrote a treatise on the hexachord, set hymn and psalm tunes in 5 parts and comp. Ger. motets.

Rasi, Francesco (b Arezzo, 4 May 1574; d after 1620), Italian singer, poet and composer. He came of a noble family and was a pupil of Caccini at Florence. Musician at the court of Mantua, 1598–1620. He sang in the fps of Peri's *Euridice* and Caccini's *Il rapimento di Cefalo* and is believed to have created Monteverdi's Orfeo.

Works incl. *Musica di camera e di chiesa*; madrigals, (*Dialoghi*, 1620) and opera *Ati e Cefale* (Mantua, 1617).

Raskin, Judith (b New York, 21 Jun 1928; d New York, 21 Dec 1984), American soprano. Studied in NY and in 1956 created the title role in Douglas Moore's *The Ballad of Baby Doe* (Central City, Colorado). Appeared with NBC TV in operas by Poulenc and Mozart and in 1959 sang Despina at the NY City Opera; Met debut 1962, as Susanna. She sang Pamina at Glyndebourne in 1963 and in the same year appeared in the fp of Menotti's *The Labyrinth*. Well known as a recitalist and was heard in music by Monteverdi, Rameau, Purcell and Pergolesi.

Rasumovsky Quartets, Beethoven's 3 string 4tets, op. 59 in F maj., E min. and C maj., comp. in 1806 and ded. to the Rus. ambassador to Vienna, Count (later Prince) Andrey Kyrillovich Rasumovsky (1752–1836), by whose domestic 4tet, led by Schuppanzigh, they were 1st perf. The 1st two 4tets contain Rus. themes.

Rataplan (Fr. onomat. = Eng. rub-a-dub), a word imitating the sound of the side-drum and used for music pieces, esp. in opera, of a military-march character.

Ratcliff, opera by Andreae (lib. taken from Heine's tragedy *William R.*), prod. Duisburg, 25 May 1914.

Rathaus, Karol (b Tarnopol, Galacia, 16 Sep 1895; d New York, 21 Nov 1954), Polish-born composer. Studied with Schreker in Vienna and followed him to Berlin when Schreker became dir. of the Hochschule für Musik, where Rathaus taught in 1925–33. In 1934 he took refuge from the Nazi regime in London and later settled in USA, becoming a US citizen in 1946.

Works incl. opera *Strange Soil* (1930); ballets *The Last Pierrot* (1927), and *Lion amoureux* (1937); incid. music to Shakespeare's *Merchant of Venice*, Gutzkow's *Uriel Acosta*, Hebbel's *Herodes und Mariamne*, etc.; choral works; 3 symphs. (1921–43), overture, serenade, suites, *4 Dance Pieces, Kontrapunktisches Triptychon* (1934), *Jacob's Dream, Polonaise symphonique* for orch.; concertino for pf.

and orch., suite for vln. and orch., *Little Prelude* for tpt. and strings; 5 string 4tets, 2 trios for vln., clar. and pf.; film music, incl. *The Brothers Karamazov* (1931) and *The Dictator* (1934).

Ratswahlkantate, cantata by Bach (BWV 71), *Gott ist mein König*, written for the election of the town council of Mühlhausen on 4 Feb 1708, and perf. on that day in St Mary's Church. Bach was at the time organist of St Blasius's.

Rattle, a noise-prod. toy, a ratchet, occasionally used as a perc. instrument in the modern orch.

Rattle, Simon (b Liverpool, 19 Jan 1955), English conductor. He studied at the RAM and held various posts in Liverpool before asst. cond. with Bournemouth SO and Sinfonietta in 1975. London debut 1975, and in the following year made his US debut, with the LSO. In 1977 he cond. *The Cunning Little Vixen* at Glyndebourne (*Porgy and Bess,* 1986) and in 1983 gave the first public perf. of Janáček's *Osud* in Brit.; *Kátya Kabanová* at the London Coliseum, 1985. He worked with the BBC Scottish SO and RLPO 1977–80 and in 1980 became prin. cond. CBSO; has given adventurous programmes which he would be denied in London. Prin. guest cond. Los Angeles PO from 1981. He is blessed with a telegenic personality; CBE 1987.

Ratto di Proserpina, Il (*The Rape of Proserpine*), opera by Winter (lib. by L. da Ponte), prod. London, King's Theatre, Haymarket, 3 May 1804.

Rauchfangkehrer, Der (*The Chimney-Sweep*), Singspiel by Salieri (lib. by L. von Auenbrugger), prod. Vienna, Burgtheater, 30 Apr 1781.

Raupach, Christoph (b Tondern, Slesvig, 5 Jul 1686; d Stralsund, 1744), German organist and writer on music. Lived at Hamburg for a time and in 1703 became organist at Stralsund.

Raupach, Hermann Friedrich (b Stralsund, 21 Dec 1728; d St Petersburg, Dec 1788), German harpsichordist and composer, son of prec. Pupil of his father, he was in the service of the Rus. court at St Petersburg from 1755. In Paris in 1766 he met Mozart, who arr. some movements from sonatas by Raupach for piano and string orch.

Works incl. operas *Alceste* (1758) and *Good Soldiers* (perf. 1780) and *Siroe* (It.); *c* 15 ballets; vln. sonatas.

Rauzzini, Matteo (b Camerino, 1754; d Dublin, 1791), Italian composer and singing-master. Brought out his 1st opera at

Munich in 1772, went to Eng. and then to Ir., settling in Dublin as singing-master.

Works incl. operas *I finti gemelli, L'opera nuova, Il rè pastore.*

Rauzzini, Venanzio (b Camerino, bap. 19 Dec 1746; d Bath, 8 Apr 1810), Italian castrato soprano, brother of prec. Made his operatic debut in Rome in 1765, and two years later entered the service of the court in Munich. In 1772 sang the leading role in Mozart's *Lucio Silla* in Milan, where Mozart also wrote for him the motet *Exsultate, jubilate.* In 1774 he settled in Eng., appearing both as a singer and opera comp. From 1778 he lived increasingly in Bath, where he taught singing and was director of the Assembly Room concerts. Among his pupils were Nancy Storace, John Braham, Mara and Michael Kelly.

Works incl. operas *Piramo e Tisbe* (1769), *L'ali d'amore* (1776), *L'Eroe Cinese* (1771), *Astarto, Creusa in Delfo* (1783), *La Regina di Golconda* (1784), *La Vestale* (1787); Requiem (1801); cantatas; It. arias, duets, etc.; 12 string 4tets and other chamber music; harpsichord sonatas.

Raval, Sebastián (b Diocese of Cartagena, Murcia, *c* 1550; d Palermo, 25 Oct 1604), Spanish composer. He went to It. early in his career and served var. patrons at (?) Naples, Urbino, Rome and Palermo. In Rome in 1593 he was challenged through his boastfulness to a contest with Nanini and Soriano, and defeated by them. His last post was that of *maestro de capilla* to the Span. Duke of Maqueda at Palermo.

Works incl. motets, Lamentations; madrigals, canzonets for 4 voices.

Ravel, (Joseph) Maurice (b Ciboure, Basses-Pyrénées, 7 Mar 1875; d Paris, 28 Dec 1937), French composer. His father was of Swiss and his mother of Basque descent. They moved to Paris the year of his birth and after some preliminary teaching he entered the Cons. in 1889, studying pf. with Anthiome and later with Bériot, also theory under Pessard from 1891. He comp. a good deal and in 1897 passed to Fauré's class for comp. and to that of Gédalge for counterpoint. In 1899 he had an overture *Schéhérazade* (unconnected with the later song-cycle) and the *Pavane pour une infante défunte* in the orig. pf. version perf. by the Société Nationale. During the next 10 years he wrote some of his best works, but his 1st great public success came in 1911, when the Opéra-Comique brought out *L'Heure espagnole,* and the second in 1912, when Diaghilev's Rus. Ballet prod. *Daphnis et*

Chloé. During the war of 1914–18 he served in an ambulance corps at the front, but was demobilized owing to ill-health in 1917. In the 1920s he visited London more than once with great success and in 1928 he was made an Hon. D. Mus. of Oxford Univ. In 1933, after a car accident, he began to suffer from a kind of mental paralysis, and he died after an operation on his brain.

Works incl. opera *L'Heure espagnole* (1911); opera-ballet *L'Enfant et les sortilèges* (1925), ballet *Daphnis et Chloé* (1912) and 2 others arr. from pf. works: *Ma Mère l'Oye* (1912) and *Adélaïde, ou Le Langage des fleurs = Valses nobles et sentimentales* (1912), also *La Valse* (comp. 1919–20; fp as ballet, 1928) and 2 from orchestral works: *Boléro, Rapsodie espagnole* for orch. (1908); concerto for pf. and orch. (1929–31); pf. concerto for the left hand with orch. (1930).

CHAMBER: String 4tet (1903) *Introduction et Allegro* for harp, fl., clar. and string 4tet, (1905), pf. trio in A min. (1914); sonata for vln. and cello (1922), sonata and *Tzigane* for vln. and pf.

PIANO: 15 pf. works incl. *Menuet antique, Pavane pour une infante défunte* (1899), *Jeux d'eau* (1901), *5 Miroirs* (1905), *Sonatine, (1905), Gaspard de la nuit* (3 pieces after Louis Bertrand's prose poems, 1908), suite *Le Tombeau de Couperin* (1917); suite *Ma Mère l'Oye* for pf. duet.

SONGS: 29 songs incl. cycles *Shéhérazade* (1903), *Cinq Mélodies populaires grecques* (1906), *Histoires naturelles* (1906); *3 Poèmes de Mallarmé* for voice, 2 fls., 2 clars., string 4tet and pf. (1913); *Chansons madécasses* for voice, fl., cello and pf. (1926); *Don Quichotte à Dulcinée* (after Cervantes) for baritone and small orch. (1933); 3 part-songs.

Ravenscroft, Thomas (b *c* 1582; d ? London, *c* 1633), English composer. He was a chorister at St Paul's Cathedral under Edward Pearce, took the Mus.B. at Cambridge in 1607 and in 1618–22 was music master at Christ's Hospital.

Works incl. anthems, 48 hymn-tune settings in his Psalter containing 100; madrigals, some of the 4-part songs *The Pleasures of 5 usuall Recreations* in his treatise on notation *A Briefe Discourse* (1614) are by himself; some of the rounds and catches in the collections *Pammelia* (1609), *Deuteromelia* (1609) and *Melismata* (1611) are prob. of his own composition.

Rawsthorne, Alan (b Haslingden, Lancs., 2 May 1905; d Cambridge, 24 Jul 1971), Eng-

lish composer. He studied dentistry at first but turned to music at the age of 20 and in 1926–9 studied at the RMCM. In 1932–4 he taught at Dartington Hall, Totnes; but settled in London in 1935 and married the violinist Jessie Hinchliffe. In 1938–9 he had works perf. at the ISCM festivals in London and Warsaw.

Works incl. ORCHESTRAL: ballet *Mme. Chrysanthème* (after Loti, 1955); incid. music for Shakespeare's *King Lear*; film music for *Burma Victory, The Captive Heart* and Army films; 3 symphs. (1950, 1959, 1964), *Symph. Studies*, overture *Street Corner* and fantasy-overture *Cortèges* for orch.; 2 pf. concertos, 2 vln. concertos (1948, 1956), concerto for clar. and strings, cello concerto (1965).

CHAMBER AND VOCAL: 2 string 4tets (1954, 1964), Theme and Variations for string 4tet (1939), pf. 5tet; vla. and pf. sonata, Theme and Variations for 2 vlns.; 4 Bagatelles for pf.; *The Creel* suite for pf. duet based on Izaak Walton's *Compleat Angler*; songs *The Enemy Speaks* (C. Day Lewis), *Away Delights* and *God Lyaeus* (John Fletcher), *3 Fr. Nursery Songs*.

Ray, the name for the Supertonic note in any key in Tonic Sol-fa, so pronounced, but in notation represented by the symbol r.

Raymond, ou Le Secret de la Reine (*R., or The Queen's Secret*), opera by A. Thomas (Lib. by A. de Leuven and J.B. Rosier), prod. Paris, Opéra-Comique, 5 Jun 1851.

Raymonda, ballet by Glazunov (choreography by Marius Petipa), prod. St Petersburg, Maryinsky Theatre, 19 Jan 1898.

'Razor' Quartet (*Rasiermesser*), nickname of Haydn's string 4tet in F min., op. 55, no. 2, comp. 1788, so called because Haydn is said to have offered the pub. Bland his best 4tet in return for a good razor.

Re, the old name for the note D in Solmization, still used in Latin countries, and in Tonic Sol-fa notation the Supertonic in any key, represented by the symbol r, pronounced Ray.

Re Cervo, Il (*The Stag King*), revision made in 1962 by Henze of his 1955 opera *König Hirsch*; fp Kassel, 10 Mar 1963.

Re in ascolto, Un (*A King in waiting*), opera by Berio (lib. by I. Calvin prod. Salzburg, 7 Aug 1984, cond. Maazel; prod. Götz Friedrich, with Theo Adam.

Re Lear (*King Lear*), opera by Alberto Ghislanzoni, (lib. by comp., based on Shakespeare), prod. Rome, Teatro Reale, 24 Jun 1937.

For Verdi *see* **King Lear.**

Re pastore, !l (*The Shepherd King*), opera by Bonno (lib. by Metastasio), prod. Vienna, Schönbrunn Palace, 13 May 1751.
Opera by Gluck (lib. do.), prod. Vienna, Burgtheater, 8 Dec 1756.
Opera by Mozart (lib. do.), prod. Salzburg, 23 Apr 1775.

Re Teodoro in Venezia, !l (*King Theodore at Venice*), opera by Paisiello (lib. by G.B. Casti), prod. Vienna, Burgtheater, 23 Aug 1784.

Realism. (1) Strictly realistic representation in music is not easily attainable. Exs. are the anvils in Wagner's *Rheingold*, the sheep and wind machine in R. Strauss's *Don Quixote* and the nightingale (gramophone record of the bird's song) in Respighi's *Pini di Roma*. Imitations of bells, birds, etc. are very frequent, but usually the more musical they are the less they approach realism.

(2) More generally, a realistic style of Italian opera is known as *Verismo*.

Realization, the writing out or playing at sight of the harmony from a Thorough-bass (*q.v.*). Also involves preparation for performance of uncompleted or sparsely written score, e.g. Friedrich Cerha's vers. of Act 3 of Berg's *Lulu*, or Raymond Leppard's popular and imaginative versions of Venetian opera.

In the music of the 18th cent. and earlier continuo lines were written in a shorthand that needs realization, often taking account of extremely refined skills cultivated in the Baroque era. Up to the end of the 18th cent. many works were written in the expectation that the soloists would improvise and embellish, often quite elaborately. Before about 1700 comps. often do not specify the ensembles to be used, and it can be a complex business devising an ens. appropriate to the style and techniques of the music. Beyond that, there could be a good argument for believing that an historically accurate reconstruction would be insufficient for present-day audiences; and there is a considerable history – going back to the early 19th cent. – of recasting earlier works to make them more acceptable to later conditions.

Rebab
or } an early string instrument of
Rebec(k)
vln. type of Arab origin, the ancestor of the vln. family, though its shape was more like that of the mandoline, which is prob. one of its descendants. It had 3 gut strings and was played with a bow. In Fr. it survived until the 18th cent., but only as a street instrument.

Rebel, French family of musicians:

1. Jean R. (d ? Versailles, 1692), singer. Was in the service of the court from 1661.
2. Jean-Féry R. (b Paris, bap. 18 Apr 1666; d Paris, 2 Jan 1747), violinist and composer, son of prec. Pupil of Lully, entered the Opéra orch. as a violinist *c* 1700 and prod. his 1st opera there in 1703. It failed, but a vln. solo, *Le Caprice*, was so successful that it was long afterwards used as a test piece for ballet dancers. He then wrote similar pieces for a number of ballets, became one of the 24 vlns. at court in 1717 and chamber musician to the king in 1720.
Works incl. opera *Ulysse* (1703); ballet pieces for vln.; vln. sonatas.
3. Anne-Renée R. (b Paris, bap. 6 Dec 1663; d Versailles, 5 May 1722), singer, sister of prec. Appeared in stage pieces at court from the age of 11, became one of the best singers there and married Lalande in 1684.
4. François R. (b Paris, 19 Jun 1701; d Paris, 7 Nov 1775), violinist and composer, son of 2. A pupil of his father, he entered the Opéra orch. at the age of 13, where he met Francœur, with whom he was to collaborate extensively. Three years later he became a member of the 24 Violons du Roi. In 1723 he went with Francœur to Prague for the coronation of Charles VI. They were joint leaders of the Opéra 1733–43, and directors 1757–67, when they were succeeded by Berton and Trial.
Works incl. *Pyrame et Thisbé* (1726), *Tarsis et Zélie*, *Scanderbeg* (1755), *Les Augustales* (1744), *Le Retour du roi*, *Zélindor* (1745), *Le Trophée*, *Ismène* (1747), *Les Génies tutélaires*, *Le Prince de Noisy* (1749), *Ballet de la Paix* (all with Francœur), *Pastorale héroïque* (1730); Te Deum, De Profundis, cantatas.

Rebelo (Rebello), **João Soares** (or **João Lourenço**) (b Caminha, 1609; d S. Amaro nr. Lisbon, 16 Nov 1661), Portuguese composer. A fellow-student of King John IV, who promoted him on his accession.
Works incl. psalms, Magnificat, Lamentations, Miserere, St Matthew Passion, Requiem etc.

Reber, Napoléon-Henri (b Mulhouse, 21 Oct 1807; d Paris, 24 Nov 1880), French composer. Studied at the Paris Cons. with Lesueur and others. He was app. prof. of harmony there in 1851 and of comp. in 1862 in succession to Halévy.
Works incl. operas *La Nuit de Noël* (1848), *Le Père Gaillard* (1852), *Les Papillotes de M. Benoît* (1853), *Les Dames capitaines* (1857); 2nd act of ballet *Le Diable*

amoureux; cantata *Roland* (1887); 4 symphs. (1858), overtures to unpub. operas *Le Ménétrier à la cour* and *Naïm*; 3 string 4tets, string 5tet, pf. 4tet, 7 pf. trios; duets for vln. and pf.; pf. pieces and duets.

Rebhuhn, Paul (b Waidhofen, *c* 1500; d Ölsnitz, after 10 May 1546), German poet and composer. Wrote dramas, *Susanna* (1536) and others, for which he wrote his own incid. music.

Rebikov, Vladimir Ivanovich (b Krasnoiarsk, 31 May 1866; d Yalta, 4 Aug 1920), Russian composer. Studied at Moscow and Berlin and later settled in the south of Rus. and founded music societies at Odessa and Kishinev.

Works incl. operas and dramatic scenes *The Storm* (1894), *The Christmas Tree* (1903), *Thea, The Woman with the Dagger* (based on Schnitzler's play, 1911), *Alpha and Omega* (1911), *The Abyss* (after Andreiev), *Narcissus* (after Ovid's *Metamorphoses*, 1913), *Fables* (after Krilov); ballet *Snow-White*; suites for orch. and string orch.; numerous sets of pf. pieces incl. *Rêveries d'automne* (1897), *Mélomimiques*, *Aspirer et attendre*, *Chansons blanches* (on the white keys).

Recapitulation. *See* **Sonata.**

Recherché (Fr. = searched out), the Fr. equivalent of *ricercato*, from which the Ricercare is derived, Beethoven still used this old term, as meaning strict fugal writing, in his *Great Fugue* for string 4tet, op. 133, which he called a fugue 'tantôt libre, tantôt recherchée.'

Récit (Fr.), in the 17th cent. a term for an accomp. solo, such as a vocal aria, an organ piece with a solo stop, etc. Also = Swell Organ.

Recital, a musical performance, usually with a miscellaneous programme, given by a single perf. or by one singing or playing an instrument with a pf. accompanist.

Recitative, declamation in singing, with fixed notes but without definite metre or time, except where this is imposed by an orchestral accomp. Although the time is free, recitative is generally written by convention in 4–4 time, with bar-lines. There are, broadly speaking, 2 kinds of recitative, as follows:

Recitativo accompagnato (or *stromentato*), a type of recitative accomp. by the orch. *Recitativo accompagnato* served to modulate to or near the key of the set musical number, usually an aria, that followed it, and also to give the singer an opportunity for dramatic declamation, aided and abetted by the orch.

Recitativo secco, a 19th-cent. term for a type of recitative accomp. by a keyboard instrument, played from figured bass. Its chief function was to advance the action and to facilitate dialogue. It also served to modulate from the key of one set musical number to the next.

Recitativo stromentato (It. = instrumented recitative), another term for *Recitativo accompagnato*, though a distinction was sometimes made between *Recitativo accompagnato*, with a plain orch. accomp., and recitativo stromentato with a more independent instrumental participation.

Recorder, a woodwind instrument, also known formerly as the English flute. Unlike the flute it is held vertically and blown into through a mouthpiece in which the air is diverted by an obstructive block called the 'fipple' and prod. a milder tone than that of the fl. Recorders were made in 5 different sizes from high treble (sopranino) to bass. In modern times the recorder has been revived, mainly for amateur perf., esp. in Eng. and Ger. (*Blockflöte*); but it has also engaged the attention of professionals, and modern works have been written for it. In the early 18th cent. *flauto* by itself always means recorder.

Recte et retro (Lat. = right way and backwards), a form of canon, also called, in It., *al rovescio*, in which a 2nd entry brings in the tune sung or played backwards. Recte et retro is similar to Cancrizans.

Redemption, The, English oratorio by Gounod (words compiled by the comp.), prod. Birmingham Festival, 1882.

Redford, John (d London, Nov 1547), English organist, composer and playwright. He was a vicar-choral at St Paul's Cathedral in 1534, when he signed an acknowledgement of Henry VIII's supremacy, and prob. succeeded Thomas Hickman as Almoner and Master of the Choristers there in the same year. His duties certainly included the playing of the organ, although the post of organist was not officially recognized at that date. He also supervised the prod. of choir-boy plays with music.

He wrote a large amount of organ music for the liturgy, a few Lat. vocal works, and a play, *Wyt and Science.*

Redi, Tommaso (b Siena, *c* 1675; d Montelupone nr. Loreto, 20 Jul 1738), Italian composer. App. *maestro di cappella* of the church of the Santa Casa at Loreto in 1731. In 1733 he had a dispute with Martini of Bologna about the solution of a canon by

Animuccia, which was settled by Pacchioni and Pitoni in Martini's favour.

Works incl. Requiem (1713), Masses and other church music.

Redlich, Hans (Ferdinand) (b Vienna, 11 Feb 1903; d Manchester, 27 Nov 1968), British musicologist of Austrian birth. Studied at the Univs. of Vienna, Munich and Frankfurt. In 1925–9 he was opera cond. at Mainz, but in 1939 he took refuge in Eng. From 1955 to 1962 he was lecturer at Edinburgh Univ. and in 1962 was app. prof. at Manchester Univ. He specialized in Monteverdi, several of whose works he ed., incl. the *Vespers* of 1610 and *L'Incoronazione di Poppea*, and on whom he wrote 2 books (1932 and 1949, Eng. 1952). He also wrote on modern music incl. a book on Alban Berg. Also composed.

Redoute (Fr., used also in Ger., and derived from It. *ridotto*), a kind of public ball, partic. in the 18th cent.; but carried on into the 19th in Aus. and Ger. where dancers gathered haphazardly from all classes of society, usually at assembly halls called *Redoutensäle* in Ger. Comps. of note, esp. in Vienna, often wrote dances for redoutes.

Réduction (Fr.), an arr., esp. from a complex to a simpler score, e.g. an opera 'reduced' to a vocal score or an orchestral work arr. for pf.

Reed, W(illiam) H(enry) (b Frome, Somerset, 29 Jul 1876; d Dumfries, 2 Jul 1942), English violinist and composer. Studied vln. with Sauret and comp. with F. Corder and Prout at the RAM in London. He joined the LSO on its foundation in 1904 and became its leader in 1912; also vln. prof. at the RCM. He took part in the fps of Elgar's vln. sonata, string 4tet and pf 5tet and wrote 2 books on Elgar.

Works incl. symph. poems *The Lincoln Imp* and *Aesop's Fables*, 2 *Somerset Idylls* for small orch., symph. and variations for string orch.; concerto in A min. and rhapsody for vln. and orch.; chamber music.

Reeds, the vibration tongues prod. the tone of certain woodwind instruments and of organ pipes (in the latter case made of brass). These instruments use so-called 'beating reeds', single for clars., saxophones and organ pipes and double for oboes, bassoons and bagpipes. There are also 'free reeds', used in harmoniums and instruments of the concertina and mouth-organ type.

Reel, a Scot., Ir. and Scand. dance, either of Celtic or Scand. origin. It is perf. with the dancers standing face to face and the music is in quick 2–4 or 4–4, occasionally 6–8, time and divided into regular 8-bar phrases. A musical characteristic of many reels is a drop into the triad of the subdominant unprepared by modulation.

Reese, Gustave (b New York, 29 Nov 1899; d Berkeley, Calif. 7 Sep 1977), American musicologist. Studied at NY Univ. and became lecturer in music there in 1927 and prof. in 1955. He was assoc. ed. of *The Music Quarterly* and its ed. on the death of Carl Engel in 1944, but resigned in 1945. His work incl. books on *Music in the Middle Ages* and *Music in the Renaissance*.

Reeve, William (b London, 1757; d London, 22 Jun 1815), English composer. Studied with Richardson, the organist at St James's Church, Westminster, and was organist at Totnes, Devon, 1781–3. After var. engagements at London theatres, he joined the Covent Garden chorus, and there was asked to complete the ballet-pantomime *Oscar and Malvina* (after Ossian) left unfinished by Shield in 1791 on account of differences with the management. He then became comp. to that theatre and in 1802 part-owner of Sadler's Wells Theatre.

Works incl. pieces for the stage, *The Apparition* (1794), *Merry Sherwood* (1795), *Harlequin and Oberon* (1796), *Harlequin and Quixote* (after Cervantes), *Joan of Arc* (1798), *Paul and Virginia* (with Mazzinghi, based on Saint-Pierre, 1800), *Rokeby Castle* (1813) and many others (some with Braham, Davy, Mazzinghi or Moorehead); music for Sadler's Wells pantomimes.

Reeves, (John) Sims (b Woolwich, 26 Sep 1818; d Worthing, 25 Oct 1900), English tenor. Learnt music from his father, a musician in the Royal Artillery, studied singing and made his 1st stage appearance at Newcastle-on-Tyne, as a baritone. After further study, incl. Paris and Milan, he made his debut there as Edgardo and 1st London appearance, 1847. He sang Faust in the oratorio by Berlioz and in the opera by Gounod. Well known in *Messiah* and *St Matthew Passion*.

Refice, Licinio (b Patrica, Rome, 12 Feb 1883; d Rio de Janeiro, 11 Sep 1954), Italian composer. He became prof. of church music at the Scuola Pontifica in Rome in 1910 and in 1911 cond. at the church of Santa Maria Maggiore.

Works incl. operas *Cecilia* (1934) and *Margherita da Cortona* (1938); 40 Masses, motets, Requiem, *Stabat Mater* and other church music, 2 oratorios, 3 sacred cantatas, 3 choral symph. poems.

'Reformation' Symphony, Mendelssohn's

5th symph., op. 107, in D min., comp. in 1830 for the tercentenary of the Augsburg Conference. It was not perf. there owing to Roman Catholic opposition, but prod. Berlin, Nov 1832.

Refrain (from Fr.), a recurrent strain in a song, returning with the same words at the beginning, middle or end of each verse with music which may or may not be derived from the 1st strain.

Regal, a small portable reed organ said to have been invented about 1460 by Heinrich Traxdorff of Nuremberg.

Reger, Max (Johann Baptist Joseph Maximilian) (b Brand, Bavar., 19 Mar 1873; d Leipzig, 11 May 1916), German composer. 1st learnt music from his mother and was so precocious that at the age of 13 he became organist at the Catholic church of Weiden in Bavaria, where his parents had moved in 1874. After 3 years there Reimann was consulted about his gifts and invited him to become his pupil at Sondershausen. Reger went there in 1890 and the next year followed his master to Wiesbaden, where he soon became a teacher at the Cons. A period divided between hard work and dissipation led to a serious breakdown, and he lived with his parents at Weiden again 1899–1901, writing vast quantities of music. In the latter year he went to Munich in the hope of making his way as a comp., but posing as a progressive and being in reality a conservative, he made enemies all round and had some success only with his pf. playing. But he began to tour Ger. and also visited Prague and Vienna, and gradually he made his work known; he also made a reputation as a remarkable comp. teacher. In 1907 he settled at Leipzig as music dir. to the Univ. and prof. at the Cons., soon resigning the former post as uncongenial, but retaining the latter for the rest of his life. In 1911 he became cond. of the ducal orch. at Meiningen, with which he went on tour, but this came to an end in 1914, when he went to live at Jena, travelling to Leipzig each week to carry out his duties at the Cons.

Works incl. CHORAL AND ORCH: *Gesang der Verklärten* (1903) and Psalm C (1909) for chorus and orch.; sinfonietta (1905), serenade (1906), variations on themes by J.A. Hiller (1907) and by Mozart (1914), Symph. Prologue to a Tragedy (1908), Comedy Overture, Concerto in the Old Style (1912), Romantic Suite (1912), 4 tone-poems on pictures by Böcklin for orch. (1913); pf. concerto (1910), vln. concerto (1908), 2 romances for vln. and orch.

CHAMBER: 5 string 4tets (1900–11), string 6tet (1910), clar. 5tet, 2 pf. 4tets, string trio, 2 pf. trios, pf. 5tet; 7 vln. and pf. sonatas, 4 cello and pf. sonatas, 3 clar. and pf. sonatas.

ORGAN: 2 sonatas, 2 suites, Fantasy and Fugue on B.A.C.H., Variations and Fugue on orig. theme, chorale preludes, preludes and fugues, Introduction, Passacaglia and Fugue, Symph. Fantasy and Fugue, etc. for organ.

PIANO AND SONGS: Introduction, Passacaglia and Fugue for 2 pfs. (1906); 2 sonatas, Variations and Fugue on theme by Bach (1904) and numerous smaller works for pf., pf. duets; many songs incl. *Schlichte Weisen*; part-songs.

Reggio, Pietro (b Genoa, bap. ? 6 Jul 1632; d London, 23 Jul 1685), Italian singer, composer and lutenist. In the service of Queen Christina of Swed. in Rome; later settled at Oxford, where he pub. *A Treatise to sing well any Song whatsoever,* 1677. Wrote motets, song for Shadwell's adaptation of Shakespeare's *Tempest* (1674), songs, duets.

Regino of Prüm (b ? Altrip nr. Ludwigshafen, *c* 842; d Trier, 915), Benedictine monk and music theorist. He was abbot of Prüm, 892–9. He was (?) the 1st to arrange antiphons and responsories according to their mode in a *tonarius*.

Regis, Jean (b *c* 1430; d Soignies, *c* 1495), Flemish composer. He was choirmaster at Antwerp Cathedral and was Dufay's secretary at Cambrai in the 1440s. He went *c* 1451 to Soignies where he remained.

Wrote 2 Masses, incl. one on *L'Homme armé,* songs in parts, 8 motets, etc.

Register, a certain set of pipes brought into action in organ playing to prod. a particular kind of tone and dynamics; also the different parts of the range of the human voice according to the manner, or supposed manner, of its prod. as 'head register' or 'chest register'.

Registration, the use of the organ stops by means of which the qualities and power of the instrument, over which the manuals and pedals have no dynamic control, can be altered according to the composer's prescription or the perf.'s skill and taste.

Regnart, François (b Douai, *c* 1540; d *c* 1600), Flemish composer. Learnt music at Tournai Cathedral and studied at Douai Univ.

Works incl. motets; *chansons*; *Poésies de Ronsard et autres* for 4–5 voices.

Regnart, Jacques (b Douai, *c* 1539; d Prague, 16 Oct 1599), Flemish composer, brother of prec. Went to Vienna and Prague as a pupil to the Imp. chapel at an early age, became a tenor there in the 1560s, and in the 1570s choirmaster and vice-*Kapellmeister*. In 1585–96 he was in the service of the Archduke Ferdinand at Innsbruck, but lived in Prague for the last 5 years of his life. Works incl. 37 Masses, 195 motets; *canzone italiane* and Ger. songs for 5 voices, etc.

There were 2 other brothers, Charles and Paschasius, who contrib. motets to a collection in which François and Jacques also appeared, ed. by a 5th brother, Augustin, a canon at Lille.

Rehfuss, Heinz (Julius) (b Frankfurt, 25 May 1917), Swiss bass-baritone. Studied with his father and from 1940 to 1952 sang at the Zurich Opera. From 1952 he was heard widely as Don Giovanni, Boris, Golaud and Dr. Schön. He took part in the Venice 1961 fp of Nono's *Intolleranza 60*.

Reich, Günter (b Liegnitz, Silesia, 22 Nov 1921), German baritone. His stage debut was in 1961 at Gelsenkirchen, as Iago. Later sang at the Deutsche Oper, Berlin, Munich and Salzburg. Best known in modern music; sang in the fps of Zimmermann's *Die Soldaten* (1965) and Penderecki's *Die schwarze Maske* (1986) and recorded Schoenberg's Moses with Boulez and Gielen.

Reich, Steve (b New York, 3 Oct 1936), American composer. He studied at Juilliard and with Berio and Milhaud. In 1966 founded ens. Steve Reich and Musicians, and began study of African, Balinese and Hebrew music; became associated with minimalist school of comps., in whose music the same simple phrases are endlessly repeated, without development or argument: orthodox notions of harmony and counterpoint are abandoned in favour of 'timeless' repetitions.

His works have had much success in Europe and the US: *Pitch Charts* for inst. ens. (1963); *Music for Piano and Tapes* (1964); *It's Gonna Rain* for tape (1965); *My Name Is*, with audience participation (1967); *Pulse Music* (1969); *Drumming* for 8 small tuned drums, 3 marimbas, 3 glockenspiels, 2 female voices and piccolo (1971); *Clapping Music* (1972); *Music for Pieces of Wood* (1973); *Music for 18 Musicians* (1975); *Octet* (1979); *Tehillim*, Hebrew psalms (1981); *Vermont Counterpoint* for 11 flutes (1982).

Reich, Willi (b Vienna, 27 May 1898; d Zurich, 1 May 1980), Austrian music author and editor. Studied at Vienna Univ. and music with Berg and Webern. He founded and ed. the review 23 in 1932, but in 1938

went to Switz., settling at Basle. He pub. a study of Berg's *Wozzeck* and worked with Krenek and Theodor Wiesengrund-Adorno on a biog. of the same comp., and later prod. independent works on Schoenberg and Berg.

Reicha, Antonín (b Prague, 26 Feb 1770; d Paris, 28 May 1836), Bohemian theorist, teacher and composer, naturalized French. Studied at Wallerstein, Bavaria, under his uncle Joseph R. (1746–95), from whose wife he learnt Fr. In 1785 he went to Bonn with his uncle, who became music dir. there and worked at the electoral court, where he made friends with Beethoven. From 1794 to 1799 he was a music teacher in Hamburg. In 1799–1802 he had some success as a comp. in Paris, but went to Vienna, where he remained until 1808 and was patronized by the empress. He then settled in Paris for the rest of his life and became prof. at the Cons. in 1818.

Works incl. operas *Godefroid de Montfort* (1796), *Ouboualdi, ou Les Français en Égypte* (1798), *Cagliostro* (with Dourlen, 1810), *Natalie* (1816), *Sapho*; 16 symphs., *Scènes italiennes* for orch.; 20 string 4tets, 6 string 5tets, Diecetto and Octet for strings and wind, 24 wind 5tets, 6 string trios, duets for vlns. and for fls.; 12 vln. and pf. sonatas; pf. sonatas and pieces.

Reichardt, Johann Friedrich (b Königsberg, 25 Nov 1752; d Giebichenstein nr. Halle, 27 Jun 1814), German composer. Studied at Königsberg Univ. and picked up a rather haphazard music educ. He travelled widely in 1771–4 and pub. his experiences in *Vertraute Breife*. After working as a civil servant at Königsberg, he obtained the post of music dir. at the Prussian court in 1776, lived at Berlin and Potsdam, prod. operas and in 1783 founded a Concert spirituel. He also pub. collections of music and wrote criticism. After the death of Frederick II he made himself disliked more and more and in 1793 he was dismissed, ostensibly for his sympathy with the Fr. Revolution. He retired to Giebichenstein in 1794, only briefly holding a post at the court of Jérôme Bonaparte at Kassel in 1808. He wrote several books on music, was a forerunner of Schubert in song comp., married Juliane Benda (1752–83), a singer, pianist and comp., daughter of F. Benda, and had a daughter, Louise (1780–1826), who became a singer and also wrote songs.

Works incl. operas and plays with music *Hänschen und Gretchen* (1772), *Amors Guekkasten* (1773), *Cephalus und Procris* (1777), *Le feste galanti, Claudine von Villa*

Bella (Goethe, 1789), *Erwin und Elmire* (Goethe, 1793), *L'Olimpiade* (Metastasio, 1791), *Tamerlan* (in Fr.), *Jery und Bätely* (Goethe), *Der Taucher* (after Schiller's ballad, 1811), *Brenno, Die Geisterinsel* (after Shakespeare's *Tempest*, 1798) and *c* 12 others; incid. music to Shakespeare's *Macbeth* (1795), several plays by Goethe and Kotzebue's *Die Kreuzfahrer*; cantatas *Ariadne auf Naxos, Ino* (1779), *Morning Hymn* (Milton, trans. Herder) and others; instrumental works; about 1500 songs.

Reichenau, Berno of (d 1048), German Benedictine monk and music theorist. He was 1st a monk at Prüm, and abbot of Reichenau from 1008. He compiled a *tonale*, dealing with the organization of the church chants into modes.

Reicher-Kindermann, Hedwig (b Munich, 15 Jul 1853; d Trieste, 2 Jun 1883), German mezzo-soprano, daughter of the baritone August Kindermann (1817–91). Studied with her father, and made var. small stage appearances in her youth, 1st appeared as a concert singer at Leipzig in 1871 and on the stage in Berlin in 1874 as Pamina and Agathe. She appeared at Bayreuth in 1876 and from 1880 sang with Angelo Neumann's Co. as Fricka, Brünnhilde, Ortrud and Isolde.

Reichmann, Theodor (b Rostock, 15 Mar 1849; d Marbach, Lake of Constance, 22 May 1903), German bass. Studied in Ger. and with Lamperti at Milan and made his 1st appearance at Magdeburg in 1869. He created Amfortas in *Parsifal* (1882) and also sang Sachs and Wolfram at Bayreuth. In 1892 he sang Wotan under Mahler at CG.

Reigen (Ger.) = Roundelay.

Reimann, Aribert (b Berlin, 4 Mar 1936), German composer and pianist. Studied with Blacher in Berlin; his early music uses serial technique. He is best known for his opera *Lear* (1978), after Shakespeare's *King Lear*.

Other works incl. operas *Traumspiel* (after Strindberg's *Dream Play*, 1965), *Melusine* (1971), *Gespenstersonate* (after Strindberg's *Ghost Sonata*, 1984) and *Troades* (1986); the ballet *Stoffreste*, (1957, rev. as *Die Vogelscheuchen*, The Scarecrows, 1970); 2 pf. concertos (1961, 1972), cello concerto (1959); *Totentanze* for bar. and orch. (1960), *Hölderlin-Fragmente* for sop. and orch. (1963); *Inane*, monologue for sop. and orch. (1969), *Lines* for sop. and 14 insts. after Shelley (1973), *Wolkenloses Christfest* (Cloudless Christmas), Requiem for bar., cello and orch. (1974), *Lear*, symph. for bar.

and orch. (1980). Frequent recitals and recordings with Dietrich Fischer-Dieskau.

Reina Codex, an important source of It. and Fr. 14th–15th-cent. music now in the Bibl. Nat. at Paris (n.a. fr. 6771). It also includes 2 keyboard arrs., one of them incomplete, of vocal works by Landini.

Reinach, Théodore (b Saint-Germain-en-Laye, 3 Jul 1860; d Paris, 30 Oct 1928), French archaeologist and historian. Author of several works on Gk. music and of the libs. of Maurice Emmanuel's *Salamine* (after Aeschylus' *Persae*) and Roussel's *La Naissance de la lyre*.

Reine de Chypre, La (*The Queen of Cyprus*), opera by Halévy (lib. by J.H.V. de Saint-Georges), prod. Paris, Opéra, 22 Dec 1841.

Reine (de France), La (*The Queen of France*), nickname of Haydn's symph. No. 85 in Bb maj., comp. for Paris in 1785–6.

Reine de Saba, La (*The Queen of Sheba*), opera by Gounod (lib. by J. Barbier and M. Carré), prod. Paris, Opéra, 28 Feb 1862.

Reinecke, Carl (Heinrich Carsten) (b Altona, 23 Jun 1824; d Leipzig, 10 Mar 1910), German pianist, composer and conductor. Settled in Leipzig from 1843. App. pianist to the Dan. court, 1846–8 and several times visited Copenhagen. Cond. of the Gewandhaus concerts and prof. of comp. at the Leipzig Cons. from 1860.

Works incl. STAGE AND CHORAL: operas *König Manfred* (after Byron, 1867), *Der vierjährige Posten* (after Körner, 1855), *Ein Abenteuer Händels* (1874), *Auf hohen Befehl* (1886), *Der Gouverneur von Tours* (1891); incid. music for Schiller's *Wilhelm Tell*; oratorio *Belsazar* (1865), 2 Masses; cantatas *Haakon Jarl, Die Flucht nach Aegypten*, fairy-tale cantatas for female voices *Schneewittchen, Dornröschen, Aschenbrödel* and others.

ORCHESTRAL AND INSTRUMENTAL: 3 symphs 1870–95), overtures *Dame Kobold* (Calderón's *Dama duende*), *Aladdin, Friedensfeier, Zenobia* and other orchestral works; 4 pf. concertos (1879–1900), concertos for vln. and for cello; 5 string 4tets, wind 8tet, 7 pf. trios and other chamber music; 3 pf. sonatas and many pieces; songs.

Reiner, Fritz (b Budapest, 19 Dec 1888; d New York, 15 Nov 1963), American conductor of Hungarian birth. He studied in Budapest and at Jura Univ. He held a number of cond. posts in Europe, incl. Budapest and Dresden, where he gave *Parsifal* and *Die Frau ohne Schatten*, before succeeding Ysaÿe as cond. of the Cincinnati SO in 1922.

From 1938 to 1948 he was cond. of the Pittsburgh SO, from 1948 at the Met and from 1953 cond. of the Chicago SO. He returned to Europe from time to time as a guest cond. and in 1936 cond. *Tristan* at CG; 1955 *Die Meistersinger* for the reopening of the Vienna Opera.

Reiner, Jacob (b Altdorf, Württemberg, *c* 1560; d Weingarten, 12 Aug 1606), German singer and composer. Learnt music at the monastery of Weingarten and from 1574–5 studied with Lassus at Munich. He returned to Weingarten about 1585 and remained there as singer and choirmaster to his death.

Works incl. masses, motets, Magnificats, 3 Passions; German songs for 3–5 voices.

Reinhardt, Delia (b Elberfeld, 27 Apr 1892; d Arlesheim, 3 Oct 1974), German soprano. She made her debut in Breslau and from 1916 to 1923 sang in Munich, often with Bruno Walter as cond. Berlin Staatsoper 1923–38, in operas by Strauss, Schreker and Wagner. London, CG, 1924–29 as Octavian, Cherubino and Mimi. NY Met debut 1923, as Sieglinde. Other roles incl. Christine, the Empress, Desdemona, Elsa and Eva.

Reinhold, Henry Theodore (d London, 14 May 1751), English bass of German birth. He sang small roles in a wide variety of theatre pieces in London during the 1730s. Took part in the fps of Handel's last two operas, *Imeneo* and *Deidamia*, and many parts in the oratorios were written for him: *Samson, Semele, Belshazzar, Judas Maccabeus* and *Saul*.

Reining, Maria (b Vienna, 7 Aug 1903), Austrian soprano. She sang at the Vienna Staatsoper in the early 1930s as a soubrette and returned in 1937 as a dramatic sop.; sang there until 1956. In 1937 she also sang Eva at Salzburg, under Toscanini, and returned as Arabella and the Marschallin; she repeated the latter role at the NY City Opera in 1949. Prof. of singing at the Mozarteum, Salzburg, from 1962.

Reinken (or Reincken), Johann Adam (Jan Adams) (b Wilshausen, Alsace, 27 Apr 1623; d Hamburg, 24 Nov 1722), German organist and composer. Pupil of Heinrich Scheidemann. App. organist of the church of St Catherine at Hamburg, 1663, where he remained to his death. Bach walked from Lüneburg as a youth and later came from Cöthen to hear him play.

Works incl. chorale preludes, toccatas, fugues, etc. for organ; *Hortus musicus* for 2 vlns., vla. da gamba and bass (pub. Hamburg, 1687); keyboard pieces.

Reinmar, Hans (b Vienna, 11 Apr 1895; d

Berlin, 7 Feb 1961), Austrian baritone. He studied in Vienna and Milan. After a 1919 debut in Olomouc he sang in Nuremberg, Zurich and Hamburg. Sang in various Berlin houses, 1928 to 1961; in the 1930s took part in the German revival of Verdi's operas (his roles incl. Macbeth, Boccanegra and Posa). During the war appeared at Bayreuth and Salzburg as Gunther, Amfortas and Mandryka. Munich, 1945–57. Other roles incl. Boris and Iago.

Reinthaler, Karl (Martin) (b Erfurt, 13 Oct 1822; d Bremen, 13 Feb 1896), German composer and conductor. After some early music training he went to Berlin to study theology, but turned to music, studying under A.B. Marx. With a grant from Frederick William IV he then studied further in Paris and Italy; in 1825 he joined the staff of the Cologne Cons. and in 1858 became cathedral organist and choral cond. at Bremen. He cond. the fp of Brahms's German Requiem, in 1868.

Works incl. operas *Edda* (1875), *Das Käthchen von Heilbronn* (after Kleist, 1881); oratorio *Jephtha* (1856), cantata *In der Wüste*; hymns and other church music; symph.; part-songs.

Reissiger, Karl (Gottlieb) (b Belzig nr. Wittenberg, 31 Jan 1798; d Dresden, 7 Nov 1859), German composer and conductor. Studied under his father, the cantor and comp. Christian Gottlieb R., and with Schicht at St Thomas's School, Leipzig. Later he studied in Vienna and with Winter at Munich, toured in Hol., Fr. and It. in 1824, and in 1826 succeeded Weber as cond. of the Dresden opera.

Works incl. operas *Dido* (1824), *Libella* (1829), *Turandot* (after Gozzi, 1835), *Die Felsenmühle zu Estalières* (1831) and others; melodrama *Yelva*; oratorio *David*; 9 Masses, motets and other church music; pf. concerto; pf. trios and other chamber music; pf. pieces incl. *Danses brillantes* (with that known as *Webers letzter Gedanke*).

Reiter, Josef (b Braunau, Upper Aus., 19 Jan 1862; d Vienna, 2 Jun 1939), Austrian composer. Studied with his father, an organist. Taught and cond. in Vienna, 1886–1907, was dir of the Mozarteum at Salzburg, 1908–11, and cond. at the Hofburgtheater in Vienna, 1917–18. He ded. his *Goethe Symph.* to Hitler in 1931 and wrote a cantata to celebrate the Anschluss.

Works incl. operas *Klopstock in Zurich* (1894), *Der Bundschuh* (1894), *Totentanz* (1908) and *Der Tell*; incid. music for Raimund's *Bauer als Millionär*; Masses and

Requiem; choral works; 6 string 4tets, 2 string 5tets and other chamber music; part-songs; *c* 120 songs.

Reizen, Mark (b Zaytsevo nr. Lugansk, 3 Jul 1895), Russian bass. He studied in Kharkov and made his debut there in 1921 as Pimen. He sang in Leningrad, 1925–30 and at the Bolshoy, Moscow, 1930–54; returned in 1985 to celebrate his 90th birthday, as Gremin in *Eugene Onegin*. Other roles incl. Boris, Dosifey, Don Basilio, Ivan Susanin and Philip II.

Reizenstein, Franz (b Nuremberg, 7 Jun 1911; d London, 15 Oct 1968), English pianist and composer of German birth. He was very precocious and studied at the State Acad. for Music in Berlin in 1930–4, Hindemith being among his masters. The Nazi régime drove him to England in 1934 and he studied with Vaughan Williams at the RCM in London, also pf. with Solomon. From 1958 he taught the pf. at the RAM.

Works incl. radio opera *Anna Kraus* (1952); film music; oratorio *Genesis* (1958), cantata *Voices of Night* (1957); orchestral music, cello, pf. (2) and vln. concertos; chamber music; pf. works.

Réjouissance (Fr. = enjoyment), a sprightly movement sometimes found as one of the accessory pieces in old suites.

Relative, the connection between maj. and min. keys with the same key-signature is said to be relative. Thus Eb maj. is the relative maj. of C min. (3b s), B min. the relative min. of D maj. (2 ♯ s), etc.

Reliquie (Ger. from Lat. = the relic), a nickname sometimes given to Schubert's unfinished C maj. pf. sonata begun in 1825, of which only the 1st and slow movements were completed. The fragmentary minuet and finale have been completed by Ludwig Stark, by Ernst Krenek and by Willi Rehberg.

Rellstab, (Heinrich Friedrich) Ludwig (b Berlin, 13 Apr 1799; d Berlin, 27 Nov 1860), German critic, novelist and poet, son of the pub. and critic Johann Karl Friedrich R. (1759–1813). He studied with Ludwig Berger and Bernhard Klein, and followed his father as music critic of the *Vossische Zeitung* and ed. the periodical *Iris im Gebiete der Tonkunst* in 1830–1842. He was imprisoned for satirizing Henriette Sontag's devotion to Rossini's operas and attacking Spontini. His books incl. various musical studies and several novels on musical themes. Schubert set 10 of his poems to music incl. *Ständchen. See* **Schwanengesang.**

Remedios Alberto (b Liverpool, 27 Feb 1935), English tenor. He studied at the RCM. SW, London, from 1957; first major role Alfredo, 1960. CG debut 1965, as Dmitri; other roles have been Mark, Bacchus and Siegfried; he sang Siegfried in the Coliseum *Ring* of 1973 and other Wagner roles have been Lohengrin, Walther and Siegmund. Has also sung Otello and Berlioz's Faust and Aeneas. US debut San Francisco, 1973; NY Met 1976, as Bacchus.

Reményi (actually Hoffmann), **Eduard** (b Miskolc, 17 Jan 1828; d San Francisco, 15 May 1898), Hungarian violinist. Studied at the Vienna Cons. with Joseph Böhm and others. He took part in the 1848 Revolution, toured with Brahms in 1852–3 and intro. Hung. gypsy music to him, made friends with Liszt at Weimar and afterwards toured widely in Europe and USA.

Remigius of Auxerre (b *c* 841; d *c* 908), Benedictine monk and music theorist. He was at the monastery of St Germain in Auxerre from 861. His music theory takes the form of a commentary on Martianus Capella.

Remoortel, Edouard van, (b Brussels, 30 May 1926; d Paris, 16 May 1977), Belgian conductor. Studied at Brussels Cons., and then privately with Joseph Krips. In 1951 he became chief cond. of the Belg. Nat. Orch., and in 1958 permanent cond. of the St Louis SO in the USA. He left in 1962 and worked in Monte Carlo from 1964.

Renard, burlesque by Stravinsky; comp. 1915–16, fp Paris, 18 May 1922.

Renaud, Maurice (Arnold) (b Bordeaux, 24 Jul 1861; d Paris, 16 Oct 1933), French baritone. Studied at the Conss. of Paris and Brussels, and in 1883 made his 1st stage appearance at the Théâtre de la Monnaie there; he sang in the fps of Reyer's *Sigurd* and *Salammbô*. In 1890 he 1st sang in opera in Paris and in 1897 in London, returned until 1904 as Don Giovanni, Escamillo and Rigoletto. US debut 1893, New Orleans; NY Met 1910–12.

Rencontre imprévue, La (*The Unforeseen Meeting*), later known as *Les Pèlerins de le Mecque* (*The Pilgrims to Mecca*), opera by Gluck (lib. by L.H. Dancourt, based on a vaudeville by Lesage and d'Orneval), prod. Vienna, Burgtheater, 7 Jan 1764.

Rendano, Alfonso (b Carolei nr. Cosenza, 5 Apr 1853; d Rome, 10 Sep 1931), Italian pianist and composer. Studied at Naples and Leipzig, also with Thalberg. Appeared at the Leipzig Gewandhaus in 1872, then in Paris and London, where he remained some time, afterwards becoming pf. prof. at the Naples Cons.

Works incl. opera *Consuelo* (after George Sand, 1902); pf. concerto; pf. music, etc.

Rennert, Günther (b Essen, 1 Apr 1911; d Salzburg, 31 Jul 1978), German producer and Intendant. He studied in Germany and Argentina; before the war worked in Wuppertal, Frankfurt and Mainz. He worked in Hamburg 1946–56 and staged operas by Britten, Berg and Hindemith. Head of prod. Glyndebourne 1960–7 (Monteverdi's *Poppea* 1962). NY Met from 1960; Munich 1967–76. With his meticulous standards, and respect for the composer's intentions, he set a standard which many of his younger colleagues have unfortunately not chosen to emulate.

Renvoysy, Richard de (b Nancy, c 1520; d Dijon, 6 Mar 1586), French cleric, lutenist and composer. Canon and choirmaster at the Sainte Chapelle of Dijon. He was condemned to death by fire for committing sodomy with his choir-boys.

Works incl. psalms; Anacreontic odes for 4 voices, etc.

Reomensis, Aurelianus (Aurelian of Réomé) French 9th-cent. Benedictine monk and musician. His theoretical works describe the modal significance of melodic formulae and the correspondence between the rhythm of text and melody.

Repeat, the restatement of a section of a composition, not written out a 2nd time, but indicated by the signs:

In classical music the expositions of movements in sonata form are nearly always marked for repetition, and more rarely the working-out and recapitulation also, with or without the coda.

Répétiteur (Fr. = coach), the musician at an opera-house whose function it is to teach the singers their parts before they gather for rehearsal with the conductor.

Répons, work by Boulez for chamber orch. and 6 solo insts. and computer; comp. 1981, fp Donaueschingen, 18 Oct 1981. Revised London, 18 Jun 1982.

Reprise (Fr. lit. re-taking = Repetition). Although the Fr. meaning is simply that of Repeat, in Eng. the word is sometimes used in a special sense, indicating the reappearance of the 1st subject in a sonata-form movement at the point where the recapitulation begins.

Requiem, the Mass for the Dead in the Roman Catholic church service, used generally on All Souls' Day (2 Nov) and specifically at funeral services at any time. It may be sung to plainsong or in more or less elaborate musical settings. Some of the greatest settings, although orig. written to order (Mozart) or intended for a special religious occasion (Berlioz, Verdi), are now fit mainly or solely for concert use, and some were actually written for that purpose (e.g. Dvořák). Britten's *War Requiem* combines the liturgical text with settings of poems by Wilfrid Owen.

Requiem (Brahms). *See* **German Requiem.**

Requiem (Verdi). *See* **Manzoni Requiem.**

Requiem Canticles, work by Stravinsky for mezzo, bass, chorus and orch.; comp. 1965–6, fp Princeton, 8 Oct 1966. Stravinsky's last major work.

Requiem for Rossini, a Mass for the Dead planned by Verdi for perf. in memory of Rossini's death in 1868, his suggestion being that each portion should be written by a different It. comp. of eminence. He himself comp. the 'Libera me' in 1869, and the other contrib. were Bazzini, Cagnoni, Coccia, Mabellini, Pedrotti, Petrella and Ricci. Mercadante was also invited, but was unable to comply on account of blindness and infirmity. The work was never perf. and the comps. all withdrew their contribs. Verdi's was later used, with some alterations, for the Manzoni Requiem of 1873–4.

Rescue Opera, a type of French opera the lib. of which is based on plots, often taken from true happenings (the words *fait historique* sometimes appear in the subtitle), in which the hero or heroine are saved after fearful trials and tribulations. The taste for such works arose during the Revolution. The most familiar exs. are Cherubini's *Les Deux Journées* and Beethoven's *Fidelio*, both with libs. by Bouilly, the latter a Ger. trans. of *Léonore* written for Gaveaux.

Resnik, Regina (b New York, 30 Aug 1922), American mezzo, originally soprano. Studied in New York, making her debut in Brooklyn in 1942. In 1943 she sang in Mexico, and at the NY Met in 1944 as the *Trovatore* Leonora; other roles there have been Ellen Orford, Leonore, Donna Anna and Elvira. She has also sung in Eur. (Bayreuth in 1953). London, CG, from 1957 as Carmen, Marina and Clytemnestra.

Resolution, a term used in harmony for the process by which a discord is made to pass into a concord. *See* **Preparation.**

Reson, Johannes, early 15th-cent French

composer. He wrote *chansons* and a few sacred works, incl. a Mass cycle.

Respighi (*née* **Olivieri-Sangiacomo), Elsa** (b Rome, 24 Mar 1894), Italian singer and composer. Pupil of Ottorino R. at the Accademia di Santa Cecilia in Rome and later (1919) his wife. She finished the orch. of his opera *Lucrezia* and wrote 3 of her own, also choral works, a symph. poem, a dance suite for orch., songs from the *Rubáiyát* of Omar Khayyám and many others.

Respighi, Ottorino (b Bologna, 9 Jul 1879; d Rome, 18 Apr 1936), Italian composer, husband of prec. He entered the Liceo Musicale of Bologna as a vln. student in 1891 and in 1898 he began to study comp. under Luigi Torchi and later under Martucci. In 1900 he became 1st vla. in the Opera orch. at St Petersburg and the next year studied comp. and orch. with Rimsky-Korsakov. In 1902 he took an additional comp. course with Bruch in Berlin, but returned home in 1903 to join the Mugellini 5tet, of which he remained a member until 1908, when Bologna prod. his 1st opera. In 1913 he was app. prof. of comp. at the Accademia di Santa Cecilia in Rome and toured It. as cond. of his own works. In 1919 he married his pupil Elsa Olivieri-Sangiacomo, a comp. and singer, and from about that time he began to take a keen interest in old It. music and the church modes. App. dir. of the Accademia in 1923, but resigned in 1925, though retaining the comp. professorship.

Works incl. STAGE: operas *Re Enzo* (1905), *Semirama* (1910), *Belfagor, Marie Victoire, La campana sommersa* (after Gerhart Hauptmann, 1927), *La bella addormentata nel bosco* (marionette vers. 1922, child mime vers. 1934), *Maria Egiziaca,* (1932), *La fiamma* (1934), *Lucrezia* (orch. finished by his wife), also a transcription of Monteverdi's *Orfeo* (1935); ballets *Scherzo veneziano, La Boutique fantasque* (music adapted from Rossini, 1919), *Belkis, regina di Saba, Il ponticello dei sospiri* and *Gli uccelli* (adapted from the orchestral suite to form a triology with *Maria E.* and *Lucrezia*).

ORCH: incl. the suites *Fontane di Roma* (1916), *Pini di Roma, Vetrate di chiesa, Trittico Botticelliano* (1927), *Gli uccelli* (bird pieces by old masters, 1927), *Feste romane* (1928) and *Sinfonia drammatica*, 2 sets of old lute airs and dances arr., concerto

in the Mixolydian mode, also 3 works by Bach arr.; fantasy and toccata for pf. and orch., concerto in the old style and *Concerto gregoriano* for vln. and orch., Adagio with variations for cello and orch. (1920), concerto for ob., tpt., vln., double bass, pf. and strings (1933).

CHAMBER AND VOCAL: 2 string 4tets (2nd in the Dorian mode), pf. 5tet; sonata in B min. and 5 pieces for vln. and pf.; 3 Preludes on a Gregorian melody for pf.; *Aretusa* for mezzo and orch. (1910); *La primavera,* for solo voices, chorus and orch. (1919); eds. of Monteverdi's *Lamento d'Arianna* and Marcello's *Didone* for voice and orch.; *Il tramonto* (1914) and *La sensitiva* (1914) for voice and string 4tet; 52 songs.

Respond. *See* **Responsory.**

Responses, in Anglican church music the choral and congregational cadences answering the versicles read or chanted in monotone by the priest, e.g. the 'Amens' or 'Have mercy upon us . . .' in the Litany.

Responsorial Psalmody, an ancient method of singing the psalms (borrowed from the Jews), in which a soloist is answered by a chorus.

Responsory (Lat. *responsorium*), a chant involving the response by a choir to a verse sung by soloists, also called Respond. Originally this would have taken the form of a response by the congregation to the leader or *cantor*. In the 9th cent. it became an elaborate musical form demanding trained soloists and choir. The Gradual, Alleluia and (for a time) the Offertory of the Mass were responsorial chants. In the Offices the most important were the *responsoria prolixa*, sung at Mattins. Like those of the Mass, they became a vehicle for polyphonic settings, the polyphony being reserved for the soloists' portions of the chant. When from the mid-15th cent. choral polyphony became the norm the procedure was frequently, though not invariably, reversed. Late 16th-cent. settings, such as those by Victoria for Holy Week, assign the entire text to the polyphonic choir.

Rest. All organized music consists not only of notes, but also of rests which, like the notes, take part of the measured scheme of a composition and thus have definite time-values in the same way as the notes. The symbols are:

Breve	Semibreve	Minim	Crotchet	Quaver	Semiquaver	Demisemiquaver

Dots can be added to rests as they are to notes.

Resta, Natale (b Milan), Italian 18th-cent. composer.

Works incl. opera *Gli tre cicisbei ridicoli*, 1748 (containing the song 'Tre giorni son che Nina', formerly ascribed to Pergolesi and later said to be by Ciampi, under whose direction Resta's opera was prod. in London, 1749, but more probably a popular Neapol. air).

Resurrection (Alfano). *See* **Risurrezione**.

Resurrection Symphony, Mahler's 2nd symph. in C min. for sop., mezzo, chorus and orch.; comp. 1888–94, revised 1910. The finale is a setting of Klopstock's chorale *Aufersteh'n* (Resurrection). Fp Berlin, 13 Dec 1895, cond. Mahler.

Reszke, Edouard de. *See* **De Reszke, E.**

Reszke, Jean de. *See* **De Reszke, J.**

Retablo de Maese Pedro, El (*Master Peter's Puppet Show*), marionette opera by Falla (lib. by comp., based on a chapter from Cervantes's *Don Quixote*), prod. Seville, 23 Mar 1923, in concert form; 1st stage perf. Paris, 25 Jun 1923.

Retardation, a term sometimes used for a Suspension which resolves upwards, e.g.:

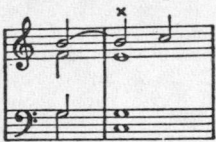

Rethberg, Elisabeth (b Schwarzenberg, 22 Sep 1894; d Yorktown Heights, NY, 6 Jun 1976), German soprano. She studied in Dresden and sang there 1915–22 as Octavian, Sophie, Constanze and Mimi. NY Met 1922–42, as Aida, Amelia Boccanegra, Elsa, Eva and in operas by Mozart, Respighi and Meyerbeer. She was a regular visitor to Salzburg, where she sang Leonore, Donna Anna and the Marschallin, and in 1928 returned to Dresden to create the title role in Strauss's *Die Ägyptische Helena.*

Réti, Rudolf (b Užice, Serbia, 27 Nov 1885; d Montclair, NJ, 7 Feb 1957), Austrian composer, pianist, critic and musical analyst. Studied at Vienna Cons. A champion of new music from the first, he gave the fp of Schoenberg's op. 11 pf. pieces and was one of the founders of the ISCM in 1922. In 1938 he emigrated to the USA. Books incl. *The Thematic Process in Music* and *Tonality, Atonality and Pantonality.*

Works incl. opera *Ivan and the Drum* (after Tolstoy), opera-ballet *David and Goliath*; *The Dead Mourn the Living, Three Allegories* for orch. (1953); 2 pf concertos; *The Greatest of All* for chorus and orch.; string 4tet; pf. pieces; songs.

Retrograde Motion. *See* **Cancrizans** and **Recte et retro.**

Reubke, Julius (b Hausneindorf nr. Quedlinburg, 23 Mar 1834; d Pillnitz, 3 Jun 1858), German composer and pianist. Son of the organ builder Adolf R. (1805–75). Pupil of Liszt at Weimar. His early death cut short a very promising career.

Works incl. organ sonata *The 94th Psalm* (1857); sonata (1857) and pieces for pf.; songs, etc.

Reusner, Esajas, German 17th-cent. lutenist. Pub. a book of sacred songs arr. for the lute in 1645.

Reusner, Esajas (b Löwenberg, Silesia, 29 Apr 1636; d Berlin, 1 May 1679), German lutenist and composer, son of prec. Studied with a French lutenist at the court of the Pol. Princess Radziwill, became lutenist at the court of Leignitz-Brieg in 1655 and at that of Brandenburg in 1674.

Works incl. 4 books of lute suites, lute arrs. of 100 sacred tunes.

Reuss, August (b Liliendorf nr. Znaim, Moravia, 6 Mar 1871; d Munich, 18 Jun 1935), German-Moravian composer. Pupil of Thuille at Munich, where he became prof. at the Acad. of Music in 1929.

Works incl. opera *Herzog Philipps Brautfahrt* (1909); 2 pantomimes; orchestral prologue to Hofmannsthal's *Der Tor und der Tod* (1901); *Johannisnacht* (1903), *Judith, Sommer Idylle* (1920), ballet suite for orch.; pf. concerto, serenade for vln. and orch.; 2 string 4tets, pf. 5tet, string trio; instrumental sonatas; choruses; songs and duets.

Reutter, Georg (sen.) (b Vienna, bap. 3 Nov 1656; d Vienna, 29 Aug 1738), Austrian organist and composer. In the service of the Viennese court as theorbo player (1697–1703) and organist (from 1700). App. organist at St Stephen's Cathedral in 1686, he rose to succeed Fux as 2nd *Kapellmeister,* 1712, and became 1st *Kapellmeister* in 1715. Wrote principally church music.

Reutter, (Johann Adam Karl) Georg (jun.) (b Vienna, bap. 6 Apr 1708; d Vienna, 11 Mar 1772), Austrian organist and composer, son of prec. Pupil of his father and of Caldara, was app. court comp. in Vienna in 1731, and in 1738 succeeded his father as 1st *Kapellmeister* of St Stephen's Cathedral, where Haydn was his pupil as a chorister. 2nd court *Kapellmeister* 1747, 1st 1751, he held these posts, in plurality with that at St Stephen's to the detriment of both estabs. He was ennobled in 1740.

Works incl. *c* 40 operas, e.g. *Archidamia* (1727), *La forza dell' amicizia* (with Caldara, 1728), *Alessandro il Grande* (1732), *Dafne* (1734) and *Il sacrifizio in Aulide* (1735); oratorios *Abel, La Betulia liberata* (1734), *Gioas* etc.; 81 Masses; 6 Requiems; 126 motets, and much other church music; symphs.; serenades; chamber music; keyboard music.

Reutter, Hermann (b Stuttgart, 17 Jun 1900; d Heidenheim an der Brenz, 1 Jan 1985), German composer. Studied under Courvoisier and others at Munich. In 1932 he became prof. at the Musikhochschule of Stuttgart and later became dir. of the State Hochschule at Frankfurt. In 1956 he became dir. of the Stuttgart State Cons.

Works incl. operas *Saul* (1928), *Der verlorene Sohn* (Gide, trans. by Rilke, 1929), *Doktor Johannes Faust* (on the old Ger. puppet play, 1936), *Odysseus, Die Witwe von Ephesus* (1954), *Die Brücke von San Luis Rey* (1954), *Hamlet* (1980); ballets *Die Kirmes von Delft* (1937), and *Topsy* (1950); oratorios *Volks-Seele* and *Der grosse Kalender*, cantata *Gesang des Deutschen*; 4 pf. concertos (1925–44), vln. concerto; chamber music, pf. works; song cycle *Weise von Liebe und Tod* (Rilke).

Rêve, Le (*The Dream*), opera by Bruneau (lib. by L. Gallet, based on Zola's novel, prod. Paris, Opéra-Comique, 18 Jun 1891.

Reveil des oiseaux (*Awakening of the birds*), work by Messiaen for pf. and orch., fp Donaueschingen, 11 Oct 1953, cond. Rosbaud.

Revelation and Fall, work for sop. and 16 insts. by Maxwell Davies (text by Georg Trakl; comp. 1965, fp London, 26 Feb 1968, cond. Davies.

Revisor, Der, opera in 5 acts by Egk (lib. by comp. after Gogol's story *The Government Inspector*), prod. Schwetzingen, 9 May 1957.

Revolutionary Study, the nickname of Chopin's study in C min., op. 10 No. 12, for pf., written at Stuttgart in Sep 1831, where, on his way to Paris, he heard of the taking of Warsaw by the Russians.

Revueltas, Silvestre (b Santiago Papasquiaro, 31 Dec 1899; d Mexico City, 5 Oct 1940), Mexican violinist and composer. Studied at Mex. City and at St Edward's Coll., Austin, Texas, also comp. with Felix Borowski at Chicago. App. at Mex. as violinist in 1920, but continued to study the

instrument in 1922 under Kochansky and Ševčik. Later he gave recitals of modern music with Chávez as pianist, whom after some theatre appts. he went to assist. in cond. the Orquesta Sinfónica at Mex. City where he also became prof. at the Cons.

Works incl. music for numerous films: *Cuauhnahuac, Esquinas* (1930), *Ventanas, Alcancías* (1932), *Colorines, Planos* (1934), *Caminos, Janitzio, homenaje á García Lorca, El renacuajo paseador, Sensemayá,* etc. for orch.; toccata for vln. and small orch.; 2 string 4tets (1930, 1931), *Feria* for string 4tet; pieces for vln. and pf.; *Siete canciones* and other songs.

Rey, Jean-Baptiste (b Lauzerte, 18 Dec 1734; d Paris, 15 Jul 1810), French conductor and composer. A chorister at the Abbey of St Sernin, he was app. at the age of 17 *maître de chapelle* at the cathedral in Auch, but left to become opera cond. in Toulouse. Later cond. at var. provincial theatres until 1776, when he settled in Paris, becoming chief cond. at the Opéra in 1781; he gave there operas by Gluck and Piccinni. He was a prof. at the Cons. 1799–1802.

Works incl. operas, Masses, motets, *solfèges.*

Reyer, Ernest (actually Louis Étienne Rey) (b Marseilles, 1 Dec 1823; d Le Lavandou, Hyères, 15 Jan 1909), French composer. Learnt music at the Free School of Music at Marseilles, but showed no exceptional promise. At the age of 16 he was sent to live with an uncle at Algiers and there began to comp. songs, etc., and in 1847 succeeded in having a Mass perf. at the cathedral. In 1848 he went to Paris and studied with his aunt, the comp. Louise Farrenc. He met Flaubert, Gautier and others, with whom he had an interest in oriental subjects in common, and they provided him with subjects for his works. He became a critic in the 1850s and in 1871 succeeded d'Ortigue as music critic to the *Journal des Débats,* becoming a champion of Wagner and the new Fr. school.

Works incl. operas *Maître Wolfram* (1854), *La Statue* (1861), *Érostrate, Sigurd* (on the Nibelung Saga, 1884), *Salammbô* (after Flaubert, 1890); ballet-pantomime *Sacountala* (after Malidasa, 1858); symph. ode *Le Sélam* (words by Gautier), dramatic cantata *Victoire; L'Hymne du Rhin* for soprano, chorus and orch. (1865), hymn *L'Union des Arts; Ave Maria, Salve Regina* and *O Salutaris; La Madeleine au désert* for baritone and orch. (1874); male-voice choruses; pf. pieces; songs.

Reynolds, Anna (b Canterbury, 4 Oct

1928), English mezzo. Her early operatic career, from 1958, was confined largely to Italy; she sang Tancredi, Donizetti's Elizabeth I and Charlotte in Rome, Venice and Milan. She was successful in Wagner roles and sang at Bayreuth 1970–6 and in Karajan's *Ring* cycles at Salzburg and the NY Met as Fricka and Waltraute. As a concert singer she appeared with Giulini, Barbirolli and Abbado; many recordings of Bach's cantatas. Now a teacher of singing.

Rezniček, E(mil) N(ikolaus) von (b Vienna, 4 May 1860; d Berlin, 2 Aug 1945), Austrian composer and conductor. Studied law at Graz, but at 22, when he was already married to Milka Thurn, a kinswoman of Weingartner's, he went to the Leipzig Cons. to study with Reinecke and Jadassohn. He gained stage experience as theatre cond. in var. towns and finally became military cond. at Prague. From 1896 to 1899 he was successively court cond. at Weimar and Mannheim. In 1906 he was app. prof. at the Klindworth-Scharwenka Cons. in Berlin, where he founded a chamber orch., and later he cond. the Warsaw Opera (1907–8) and the Komische Oper in Berlin (1908–11). He taught at the Hochschule für Musik in Berlin from 1920 to 1926.

Works incl. operas *Die Jungfrau von Orleans* (after Schiller, 1887), *Satanella*, *Emmerich Fortunat* (1889), *Donna Diana* (after Moreto, 1894), *Till Eulenspiegel* (1902), *Ritter Blaubart*, *Holofernes* (after Hebbel's *Judith*, 1923), *Satuala*, *Spiel oder Ernst* (1930), *Der Gondoliere des Dogen* (1931); incid. music for Strindberg's *Dream Play*; Mass in F maj., Requiem in D min., *Vater unser* for chorus (1919); 4 symphs. (incl. *Schlemihl* [after Chamisso], 'Tragic' and 'Ironic'), 2 symph. suites, Comedy and Idyllic Overtures, fugue in C♯ min. for orch.; serenata for strings; vln. concerto (1925), Intro. and Valse-Caprice for vln. and orch.; *Ruhm und Ewigkeit* (Nietzsche) for tenor and orch.; 3 string 4tets (1921–32).

rfz, an abbr. used in musical notation for *Rinforzando*.

Rhapsodie (so-called 'Alto Rhapsody'), a setting of a fragment from Goethe's *Harzreise im Winter* for contralto solo, male chorus and orch by Brahms, op. 53, comp. 1869, fp Jena, 3 Mar 1870.

Rhapsody (from Gk. *rhapsōidia* = an epic poem, lit. 'songs stitched together'; in Fr. *rapsodie*), in the 18th cent. a poem set to music of an improvisatory character. Hence an instrumental piece showing similar freedom. In the 19th cent. and later the term was applied to large-scale comps. in which different elements, sometimes derived from folksong, were strung together, e.g. Liszt's *Hungarian Rhapsodies*. Brahms's rhapsodies for pf., on the other hand, are self-contained pieces which might equally well be called Capriccio or Intermezzo.

Rhau (or **Rhaw**), **Georg**, (b Eisfeld, Franconia, 1488; d Wittenberg, 6 Aug 1548), German composer and publisher. Cantor at St Thomas's School, Leipzig, until 1520, then schoolmaster at Eisleben and printer at Wittenberg, where he pub. var. Lutheran music collections incl. works of his own. Wrote vocal works incl. hymn-tunes.

Rheinberger, Joseph (Gabriel) (b Vaduz, Liechtenstein, 17 Mar 1839; d Munich, 25 Nov 1901), German organist, teacher and composer. He was so precociously gifted that he was app. organist at the parish church of his native place at the age of 7. After some lessons at Feldkirch, he went to the Munich Cons. in 1850, continued to study with F. Lachner on leaving in 1854, supported himself by teaching and in 1859 became pf. prof. at the Cons. He also worked for a time at the Court Opera, and became a church organist and choral cond. When the Cons. was reorganized by Bülow in 1867 he was app. organ and comp. prof. In 1877 he became dir. of the court church music in succession to Wüllner.

Works incl. operas *Die sieben Raben* (1869), *Der Türmers Töchterlein* (1873) and *Das Zauberwort*; incid. music for Calderón's *Mágico prodigioso*; numerous Masses, 3 Requiems, *Stabat Mater*, motets; cantatas and choral ballads; symphs. *Wallenstein* (after Schiller) and 'Florentine', overtures to Shakespeare's *Taming of the Shrew* and Schiller's *Demetrius*, *Academic (fugal) Overture* for orch.; 2 organ concertos, pf. concerto.

3 string 4tets, 2 pf. trios, pf. 5tet, pf. 4tet, string 5tet; sonatas for vln. and pf., cello and pf., horn and pf.; 20 organ sonatas and many other organ works; numerous pf. works; songs, part-songs.

Rheingold, Das (*The Rhinegold*, Wagner). *See* **Ring des Nibelungen**.

'Rhenish' Symphony, the name of Schumann's 3rd symph., in E♭ maj., op. 97, begun after a Rhine excursion in Sep 1850. The 4th of the 5 movements is an impression of Cologne Cathedral. Fp Düsseldorf, 6 Feb 1851.

Rhys, Philip ap, 16th-cent. English or Welsh organist and composer. He was organist at St Mary-at-Hill, London, until

1547, when he took over Redford's duties as organist at St Paul's. He was still organist there in 1559, although Sebastian Westcott had become almoner (Redford's official post) in 1551. He wrote organ music for the liturgy, incl. a setting of the Ordinary of the Mass (without the Credo).

Rhythm. In its largest sense the word means all that is concerned in music with matters dependent on time, such as the metre, the proper division of the music into bars, the distribution and balance of phrases, etc. Rhythm, however, is not synonymous with metre and may be independent of bar-lines. It also implies the proper perf. of music in a natural, living and breathing way, as distinct from a merely mechanical accuracy. What is often called rhythm in modern dance music which is rigidly accurate in time, is therefore not rhythm but merely a strict application of Time. See also **Harmonic Rhythm.**

Riadis (actually Khu), **Emilios** (b Salonika, 1 May 1886; d Salonika, 17 Jul 1935), Greek composer. Studied with Mottl and others at Munich and with Ravel in Paris. Asst. director of the Solonika Cons. from 1918.

Works incl. operas Le Chant sur le fleuve, Galatea (1913) and La Route verte (1914); incid. music for Euripides' Hecuba (1927) and Wilde's Salome (1922); Byzantine Mass; Sunset on Salonika and other orchestral works; chamber music; pf. pieces, etc.

Riccardo I, rè d'Inghilterra (Richard I, King of England), opera by Handel (lib. by P.A. Rolli), prod. London, King's Theatre, Haymarket, 11 Nov 1727.

Ricci, Federico (b Naples, 22 Oct 1809; d Conegliano, 10 Dec 1877), Italian composer. Studied with Bellini and Zingarelli at the Naples Cons. In 1835 he prod. his 1st opera with his brother Luigi R. at Naples and the 1st of his own at Venice and from 1853 to 1869, after several stage successes, he was music dir. at the Imp. theatres in St Petersburg.

Works incl. operas Monsieur de Chalumeaux (1835), La prigione d'Edimburgo (on Scott's Heart of Midlothian, 1838), Un duello sotto Richelieu (1839), Luigi Rolla e Michelangelo (1841), Corrado d'Altamura, Vallombra, Isabella de' Medici (1845), Estella di Murcia (1846), Griselda, I due ritratti, Il marito e l'amante (1852), Il paniere d'amore, Una Folie à Rome, Le Docteur rose and 4 others in collaboration with Luigi Ricci; 2 Masses; cantata for the marriage of Victor Emmanuel; songs.

Ricci, Luigi (b Naples, 8 Jul 1805; d Prague,

31 Dec 1859), Italian composer, brother of prec. Studied under Zingarelli at the Naples Cons., where he and Bellini became subprofs. in 1819. His 1st opera was prod. there in 1823. In 1835, after a number of successful prods., he became cond. of the Opera and music dir. of the cathedral at Trieste. In 1844 he married Lidia Stoltz of Prague, where he was confined in an asylum in 1859, having become hopelessly insane.

Works incl. opera L'impresario in angustie (1823), Il diavolo condannato (1826), Il Colombo, L'orfanella di Ginevra (1829), Chiara di Rosemberg, Il nuovo Figaro (1832), Un avventura di Scaramuccia (1834), Gli esposti (Eran due ed or son tre), Chi dura vince, Chiara di Montalbano (1835), La serva e l'ussaro, Le nozze di Figaro (after Beaumarchais, 1838), Il birraio di Preston (1847), La festa di Piedigrotta, Il diavolo a quattro (1859), and 14 others incl. 4 in collaboration with Federico Ricci; church music, song-books Mes Loisirs and Les Inspirations du thé, etc.

Operas written jointly by the 2 brothers: Il colonello (1835), Il disertore per amore (1836), L'amante di richiamo (1846) and Crispino e la comare (1850).

Ricci, Ruggiero (b San Francisco, 24 Jul 1918), American violinist. Studied with Persinger, making his 1st public appearance aged 8. In 1932–4 he undertook his 1st European tour and in 1957 a world tour. He gave the fps of the concertos by Ginastera (1963) and von Einem (1970). Often heard in Paganini.

Ricciardo e Zoraide, opera by Rossini (lib. by M.F.B. di Salsa), prod. Naples, Teatro San Carlo, 3 Dec 1818.

Ricciarelli, Katia (b Rovigo, 16 Jan 1946), Italian soprano. She studied in Venice and made her debut in Venice as Mimi, in 1969. US debut Chicago, 1972, as Lucrezia in I due Foscari; NY Met, 1975, as Mimi. At CG she has sung Amelia (Ballo in Maschera), Aida and Giulietta. Other roles incl. Elisabeth de Valois, Lucrezia Borgia, Imogene and Giovanna d'Arco. She sang Desdemona in Zeffirelli's 1986 film version of Otello.

Riccio, (Antonio) Teodoro (b Brescia, c 1540; d Ansbach, after 1599), Italian composer. Choirmaster at a church at Brescia, app. music dir. by the Margrave of Brandenburg-Ansbach, settled there and followed the margrave to Königsberg in 1579, having become a Lutheran, and returned to Ansbach with his patron in 1586. Eccard served under him there from 1581 and succeeded him at his death.

Works incl. motets and other church music; madrigals, *Canzoni alla napoletana*; some of his canzonas are based on themes by Gabrieli.

Ricercare (It. = to search out), a fugal comp., also called *ricercar* or *ricercata*, the instrumental counterpart of the motet or madrigal in the 17th cent., played on keyboard instruments or by a consort of string or wind instruments.

Richafort, Jean (b Hainault, *c* 1480; d ? Bruges, *c* 1547), Flemish composer. Pupil of Josquin Desprez. He was choirmaster at the church of Saint-Gilles at Bruges in the 1540s. Wrote Masses, motets, *chansons*, etc. Palestrina wrote a parody Mass on his 4-part motet *Quem dicunt homines*.

Richard I (Cœur de Lion) (b Oxford, Sep 1157; d Limoges, 11 Apr 1199), King of Eng. and French trouvère. He was the son of Henry II and his mother was Eleanor of Aquitaine. She intro. the art of the Troubadours to the north of France and this estab. the school of the Trouvères to which Richard belonged both as poet and as musician.

According to legend another trouvère, Blondel de Nesle, discovered his place of imprisonment in Aus. in 1192, when he is said to have sung outside the castle of Dürenstein and to have been answered by Richard in song from within, a fanciful story which furnished the plot for the following opera: **Richard Cœur-de-Lion**, opera by Grétry (lib. by J.M. Sedaine), prod. Paris, Comédie-Italienne, 21 Oct 1784. Beethoven wrote pf. variations on the song 'Une fièvre brûlante' from it (WoO 72, 1795).

Richards, (Henry) Brinley (b Carmarthen, 13 Nov 1817; d London, 2 May 1885), Welsh pianist and composer. Studied at the RAM in London and with Chopin in Paris. Settled in London, where he taught the pf. and lectured on Welsh music.

Works incl. overture in F min.; additional songs for Auber's *Diamants de la couronne*; pf. pieces; songs, incl. 'God bless the Prince of Wales'; part-songs.

Richardson, Ferdinand(o) (real surname Heybourne) (b *c* 1558; d Tottenham, 4 Jun 1618), English composer. Pupil of Tallis. Groom of the Privy Chamber, 1587–1611. Comp. virginal pieces, etc.

Richardson, Vaughan (b London, *c* 1670; d London, Jun 1729), English organist and composer. Chorister in the Chapel Royal. App. organist of Winchester Cathedral in 1692.

Works incl. services, anthems *O Lord*

God of my salvation, O how amiable and others; *Song in Praise of St Cecilia* (1700); *Entertainment for the Peace of Ryswick* (1697); songs for 1–3 voices with instruments.

Richter, Ferdinand (Tobias) (b Würzburg, 22 Jul 1651; d Vienna, 3 Nov 1711), German organist and composer. App. court organist in Vienna, succeeding Poglietti, 1683, and music teacher to the Imp. children.

Works incl. serenatas *L'istro ossequioso* (1694) and *Le promesse degli dei* (1697); sacred dramas for the Jesuit Coll.; sonata for 7 instruments and others in 8 parts, *balletti* in 4 and 5 parts; organ toccatas and other works; suites for harpsichord.

Richter, Franz Xaver (b Holešov, Morav., 1 Dec 1709; d Strasbourg, 12 Sep 1789), Moravian bass, violinist and composer. App. vice *Kapellmeister* at the Abbey of Kempten in 1740, he entered the service of the Mannheim court *c* 1747, first as a singer and violinist, later becoming court comp. From 1769 he was music dir. of Strasbourg Cathedral. His work at Mannheim made him a prominent member of that school of symphonists.

Works incl. 39 Masses; 2 Requiems; 2 Passions; numerous motets, and other church music; almost 70 symphs.; concertos; string 4tet and other chamber music.

Richter-Haaser, Hans (b Dresden, 6 Jan 1912; d Brunswick, 16 Dec 1980), German pianist. He studied in Dresden and made his debut there in 1928. International recognition did not come until 1953 and he was then heard widely in Europe and N. and S. America, often in Schumann and Beethoven. He played in the US, 1959–74. Also active as a cond. and comp.

Richter, Hans (b Györ, Hungary, 4 Apr 1843; d Bayreuth, 5 Dec 1916), Austro-Hungarian conductor. Studied in Vienna, where he played horn at the Kärntnertortheater, 1862–6. Asst. to Wagner, opera cond. at Budapest and Vienna; 1st to cond. Wagner's *Ring* at Bayreuth, 1876; cond. much in London between 1877 and 1910; at Drury Lane gave the 1st Brit perfs. of *Tristan* and *Meistersinger* (1882). Cond. of the Hallé Orch., Manchester, 1900–11. He gave the fps of Bruckner's 1st, 3rd, 4th and 8th symphs. and Elgar's *Enigma Vars.* and 1st symph.

Richter, Karl (b Plauen, 15 Oct 1926; d Munich, 15 Feb 1981), German organist and conductor. He studied in Dresden and Leipzig; organist Thomaskirche, Leipzig,

619   **Ries**

from 1947. He moved to Munich in 1951 and founded the Munich Bach Orch. and Choir. Many recordings and tours in the Baroque rep.; US debut Carnegie Hall, NY, 1965. He recorded Bach's B minor Mass and *St Matthew Passion* and was often heard in the keyboard music of Bach.

Richter, Sviatoslav (Teofilovich) (b Zhitomir, 20 Mar 1915), Russian pianist. Entered Moscow Cons. in 1937, where he studied with H. Neuhaus, graduating in 1942. He won a national competition in 1945 and was awarded the Stalin Prize in 1949. A magnificent technique and fine musicianship place him in the front rank of modern pianists; US debut 1960, London 1961. He gave the fps of Prokofiev's 6th, 7th and 9th pf. sonatas.

Richochet (Fr. = rebound), a special kind of *staccato* in vln. music, prod. by letting the bow bounce on the strings, whereas in ord. *staccato* it remains on the string and is moved in rapid jerks.

Ricordi, Giovanni (b Milan, 1785; d Milan, 15 Mar 1853), Italian publisher. Founded the pub. house at Milan *c* 1808.

Ricordi, Giulio (b Milan, 19 Dec 1840; d Milan, 6 Jun 1912), Italian publisher, grandson of prec. Became head of the Milan firm on his father's death in 1888. He was also a comp. under his own name and that of J. Burgmein.

Ricordi, Tito (b Milan, 29 Oct 1811; d Milan, 7 Sep 1888), Italian publisher, father of prec. Succeeded his father, Giovanni R., in 1853. Published many operas by Verdi.

Ridderbusch, Karl (b Recklinghausen, 29 May 1932), German bass. He studied in Essen and from 1961 sang in Munster, Essen and Düsseldorf. Wider opportunities came in 1967, when he made his Bayreuth and NY Met debuts. He first appeared at the Vienna Staatsoper in 1968 and in 1971 made his London, CG, debut as Hunding and Hagen. He has sung Sachs under Karajan at Salzburg and is often heard in sacred music by Bach, Schubert and Bruckner.

Riddle Canon, a form of canon written in a single part with no indication where the subsequent entries of the parts are to occur, the perfs. being left to guess how the music fits by solving a riddle.

Riders to the Sea, opera by Vaughan Williams (lib. Synge's play), prod. London, RCM, 1 Dec 1937; 1st public perf. Cambridge, Arts Theatre, 22 Feb 1938.

Riedel, Carl (b Kronenberg nr. Elberfeld, 6 Oct 1827; d Leipzig, 3 Jun 1888), German choral conductor. Studied at the Leipzig Cons. after starting life in commerce and

founded a choral society there. He gave perfs. of then-neglected works by Schütz. Studied at the Leipzig Cons. after starting life in commerce and founded a choral society there. He gave perfs. of then-neglected works by Schütz.

Rieder, Ambrosius (b Döbling nr. Vienna, 10 Oct 1771; d Perchtoldsdorf nr. Vienna, 19 Nov 1855; Austrian composer. Pupil of Albrechtsberger in Vienna, where he became a choirmaster later on.
Works incl. Masses and other church music; chamber music; organ works.

Riegger, Wallingford (b Albany, Ga., 29 Apr 1885; d New York, 2 Apr 1961), American composer. Studied in NY and Berlin, with Goetschius, Stillman-Kelley and others. After cond. in Ger., he returned to USA, where he held var. teaching appts.
Works incl. *American Polonaise–Triple Jazz* (1922), Rhapsody, Fantasy and Fugue (1955), Lyric Suite, 2 Dance Suites, Canon and Fugue, etc. for orch., var. works for dancers; *La Belle Dame sans merci* (Keats) for 4 voices and chamber orch. (1924); 4 symphs. (1943–57); *Dichotomy* and *Scherzo* for chamber orch.; *Study in Sonority* for 10 vlns.; 2 string 4tets (1939, 1948), pf. trio, *Divertissement* for harp, fl., and cello, 3 Canons for woodwind and other chamber music; Suite for solo fl.

Riemann, (Karl Wilhelm Julius) Hugo (b Grossmehlra nr. Sondershausen, 18 Jul 1849; d Leipzig, 10 Jul 1919), German musicologist. Studied law at Berlin and Tübingen, music at the Leipzig Cons. and later became lecturer at the univ. there, 1878–80, and again, after var. appts. elsewhere, in 1895–1901, when he became prof. Among his many publications are a *Musiklexikon* (1882), *Handbuch der Musikgeschichte* (1904), *Opernhandbuch* (1887), works on notation, harmony, phrasing, history, etc. He ed. many standard works and also comp., mainly teaching pieces for pf.

Rienzi, der Letzte der Tribunen (*Rienzi, the Last of the Tribunes*: first called *Cola Rienzi*, . . .), opera by Wagner (lib. by comp., based on Bulwer-Lytton's novel and, further back, on Mary Russell Mitford's play), prod. Dresden, 20 Oct 1842.

Ries, German family of musicians:
1. Johann R. (b Benzheim o/Rhine, 1723; d Cologne, 1784), violinist and trumpeter. Worked at the court of the Elector of Cologne at Bonn.
2. Franz Anton R. (b Bonn, 10 Nov 1755; d Godesberg, 1 Nov 1846), violinist, son of prec. Pupil of Salomon, he entered the ser-

vice of the court at Bonn in 1774, becoming 1st vln. after a visit to Vienna in 1779, and music dir. in 1791. Beethoven was his pupil.

3. Ferdinand R. (b Godesberg, bap. 28 Nov 1784; d Frankfurt, 13 Jan 1838), pianist, violinist and composer, son of prec. Pupil of his father for pf. and vln. and of B. Romberg for cello. After a short course in comp. with Winter at Munich in 1801, he went to Vienna that year, studying pf. with Beethoven and comp. with Albrechtsberger and becoming pianist to Counts Browne and Lichnowsky. Later he lived by turns in Paris, Vienna, Kassel, Stockholm and St Petersburg. In 1813–24 he lived in London, where he married an Englishwoman and played, taught and comp. He bought a property at Godesberg nr. Bonn, but in 1826 went to live at Frankfurt, where he returned again after 2 years as cond. at Aachen, 1834–6. He cond. several of the Lower Rhine Festivals.

Works incl. operas *Die Räuberbraut* (1828), *Liska* (*The Sorceress*, 1831) and *Eine Nacht auf dem Libanon* (1834); oratorios *Der Sieg des Glaubens* and *Die Könige Israels*; 8 symphs., 4 overtures; 8 pf. concertos; 26 string 4tets; 8 string 5tets, 3 pf. 4tets, 5 pf. trios, octet, 7tet and other chamber mus.; 20 duets for vln. and pf.; 10 sonatas and many other works for pf.

4. Peter Joseph R. (b Bonn, 6 Apr 1791; d London, 6 Apr 1882), pianist, brother of prec. He lived in London, was a friend of Charles Lamb and worked for a time in Broadwood's pf. manufacture, also taught the pf.

5. Hubert R. (b Bonn, 1 Apr 1802; d Berlin, 14 Sep 1886), violinist, brother of prec. Pupil of his father and Spohr. Held var. appts. in Berlin from 1824.

6. Louis R. (b Berlin, 30 Jan 1830; d London, 3 Oct 1913), violinist, son of prec. Studied under his father and Vieuxtemps, and lived in London from 1853.

7. Adolph R. (b Berlin, 20 Dec 1837; d Apr 1899), pianist and composer, brother of prec. Studied pf. with Kullak and comp. with Boehmer. Settled in London as pf. teacher. Comp. pf. works and songs.

8. Franz R. (b Berlin, 7 Apr 1846; d Naumburg, 20 Jan 1932), violinist and editor, brother of prec. Pupil of his father and of Massart and Vieuxtemps in Paris. Appeared in London in 1870, but later gave up playing and took to music pub. and ed.

Rieti, Vittorio (b Alexandria, 28 Jan 1898), Italian composer. Studied with Frugatta at Milan and Respighi in Rome, but destroyed all his works written up to 1920. In 1939 he

became an Amer. citizen.

Works incl. opera *Teresa nel bosco* (1934); ballets *Noah's Art* (1922), *Barabau* (1925), *Waltz Academy, The Sleep-walker, Robinson and Friday* (after Defoe, 1924) and *David's Triumph* (1937); incid. music for Pierre Corneille's *L'Illusion comique* and Giraudoux's *Électre*; 7 symphs. (1929–77); *Notturno* for strings; concerto for wind instruments and orch., vln. concerto, harpsichord concerto, 3 pf. concertos (1926, 1937, 1955), 2 cello concertos; *Madrigal* for 12 insts. (1927), partita for fl., ob., string 4tet and harpsichord; sonata for fl., ob., bassoon and pf.; *Second Avenue Waltzes* for 2 pfs., pf. pieces.

Rietz, Eduard (b Berlin, 17 Oct 1802; d Berlin, 22 Jan 1832), German violinist. Pupil of his father and of Rode. He joined the royal orch. in Berlin and founded an orch. of his own, but suffered from tuberculosis and had to give up work.

Rietz, Julius (b Berlin, 28 Dec 1812; d Dresden, 12 Sep 1877), German composer and conductor, brother of prec. Studied under his father, cello under B. Romberg and others and comp. under Zelter. In 1835 he succeeded Mendelssohn as cond. of the opera at Düsseldorf, and the next year became town music dir. and cond. the orchestral and choral concerts. In 1847–60 he was cond. of the Vocal Acad. and the Gewandhaus orch. at Leipzig and taught comp. at the Cons. In 1860 he was app. cond. of the Royal Opera, dir. of the church chapel and of the Cons. at Dresden. He ed. works by Bach, Beethoven, Mendelssohn and Mozart.

Works incl. operas *Der Corsär, Das Mädchen aus der Fremde* and *Georg Neumark*, operetta *Jery und Bätely* (Goethe); incid. music for Shakespeare's *Hamlet* and *As You Like It*, Holtei's *Lorbeerbaum und Bettelstab* and plays by Goethe, Calderón, Immermann, etc.; 2 symphs. and 3 overtures; *Dithyrambe* for male chorus and orch.

Rifkin, Joshua (b New York, 22 Apr 1944), American musicologist, conductor and pianist. He studied at Juilliard and Princeton and with Stockhausen at Darmstadt. He has researched Renaissance and Baroque music; authentic perfs., incl. a recording of the B minor Mass without chorus.

Rigadoon (Eng.)
Rigaudon (Fr.) } a Fr. dance, prob. from the south (Provence or Languedoc), dating back to the 17th cent. at the latest. It is in lively common or 2–4 time and consists of 3 or 4 parts, each repeated, the 3rd being the shortest.

Righetti-Giorgi, Geltrude (not Maria Brighenti). *See* **Giorgi-Righetti.**

Righini, Vincenzo (b Bologna, 22 Jan 1756; d Bologna, 19 Aug 1812), Italian composer and singer. A chorister at San Petronio in Bologna and pupil of Padre Martini, he made his stage debut in Parma and went as a singer to Prague, where his *Don Giovanni* was prod. in 1776, 11 years before Mozart's opera on the same subject. App. director of the *opera buffa* in Vienna in 1780, he was in the service of the court at Mainz 1787–92, and from 1793 court *Kapellmeister* in Berlin.

Works incl. operas *Il convitato di pietra* (*Don Giovanni*), *La vedova scaltra* (1778), *Demogorgone* (1786), *Alcide al bivio* (1790), *Enea nel Lazio, Il trionfo d'Arianna* (1793), *Ariadne, Tigrane* (1800), *La selva incantata* and *Gerusalemme liberata* (both after Tasso, 1803, 1799) and others; oratorio *Der Tod Jesu*; cantatas, etc.; *Missa solemnis,* Requiem, Te Deum and other church music; chamber music; keyboard music; songs.

Rignold, Hugo (Henry) (b Kingston-on-Thames, 15 May 1905), English conductor. Taken to Canada as a child, studied vln. in Winnipeg, but returned to study at the RAM, vln. with H. Wessely, ob. with L. Goossens and vla. with L. Tertis. After some years as a freelance violinist in London he became cond. of the Palestine SO, 1944, and in 1945–7, of the Cairo SO. After a year at Covent Garden, where later he gave the fp in Britain of Stravinsky's *Agon*, he became cond. of the Liverpool PO (1948 to 1954), music dir. of the Royal Ballet, 1957–60, and from 1960 to 1969 cond. of the CBSO.

Rigoletto, opera by Verdi (lib. by F.M. Piave, based on Victor Hugo's play *Le Roi s'amuse*), prod. Venice, Teatro la Fenice, 11 Mar 1851.

Rihm, Wolfgang (b Karlsruhe, 13 Mar 1952), German composer. He studied in Karlsruhe and with Stockhausen and Fortner.

Works incl. operas *Faust and Yorick* (1976), *Harlekin* (1977) and *Jacob Lenz* (1979); 3 symphs. (1966–77, no. 3 to texts by Nietzsche and Rimbaud); *Ein Imaginäres Requiem* for soloists, chorus and orch. (1976); *Dis-kontur* and *Sub-kontur* for orch. (1974–5); *Konzertarie* for sop. and orch. based on telegram sent by Ludwig II to Wagner (1976); *Cuts and Dissolves,* concerto for 29 players (1976); *Abgesangsszene* nos. 1–5 for voice and orch. (1979–81);

Lenz-Fragmente and 5 songs for sop. and orch. (1980); *Tutuguri,* series of 7 works for var. inst. combinations inspired by Paul Claudel (1981); *Monodram* for cello and orch. (1983); 5 string 4tets (1968–81); *Deploration* for flute, cello and perc. (1973); *Erscheinung,* sketch after Schubert for 9 strings (1978), *Nature Morte* for 13 strings (1980); *Fremde Szene* for pf. trio (1983); solo songs and music for pf. and for organ.

Riisager, Knudåge (b Port Kunda, Estonia, 6 Mar 1897; d Copenhagen, 26 Dec 1974), Danish composer. Studied political economy at Copenhagen Univ., but later turned to music studying comp. with Peder Gram and Otto Malling, later with Roussel and Le Flem in Paris and finally with Hermann Grabner at Leipzig.

Works incl. opera *Susanne* (1950); ballets *Benzin* (1930), *Cocktail Party* and *Slaraffenland* (*Land of Cockaigne,* 1942); incid. music to Johannes Jensen's fairy play *Darduse;* chorus works; 5 symphs. (1925–50), variations *Poème mécanique, Jabiru T— DOXC* and overture to Holberg's *Erasmus Montanus* for orch.; concerto for tpt. and strings; 6 string 4tets (1918–43), sonata for fl., clar., vln. and cello, serenade for fl., vln. and cello; vln. and pf. sonata; sonata and var. pieces for pf.; songs.

Riley, Terry (b Colfax, Calif., 24 Jun 1935), American composer and saxophonist. He studied at Berkeley and since 1970 has been influenced by Indian music; works involve repeated patterns and series, and contain freedom for improvisation. Belongs to the Minimalist school of comps.

Spectra for 6 insts. (1959); String trio (1965); *Keyboard Studies* (1965); *Poppy Nogood and the Phantom Band* for saxophone, tape and electronics (1968); *Rainbow in Curved Air* (1970); *Genesis '70,* ballet; *Sunrise of the Planetary Dream Collector* and *The Medicine Wheel,* both for string 4tet (1981, 1983), works which reflect his interest in astrology.

Rilke, Rainer Maria (1875–1926), German poet. *See* **Beck** (*Lyric Cantata*), **Burkhard** (*song cycle*), **Foss (L.)** (*Parable of Death*), **Klenau, Martin (F.)** (*Cornet*), **Marienleben** (Hindemith), **Marx (K.)** (choruses and songs), **Reutter (H.)** (*Weise von Liebe und Tod* and opera trans. from Gide), **Webern** (songs), **Weill** (songs with orch.)

Rimbault, Edward F(rancis) (b London, 13 Jun 1816; d London, 26 Sep 1876), English music historian and antiquarian. Wrote books on early English music and pub. editions.

Rimonte

Rimonte (Ruimonte), Pedro (b Saragossa, *c* 1570; d after 1618), Spanish composer. The Infanta Isabella took him to the Netherlands on her marriage to the Archduke Albert, governor of the Netherlands, at whose court at Brussels he became chamber musician in 1603. He returned to Spain in 1614, but was in Brussels again 4 years later.

Works incl. Masses and *Cantiones sacrae*; madrigals and *villancicos*, etc.

Rimsky-Korsakov, Andrey Nikolaievich (b St Petersburg, 17 Oct 1878; d Leningrad, 23 May 1940), Russian critic and music historian. Studied at the Univs. of St Petersburg, Strasbourg and Heidelberg, and did not turn to music until 1913, after his father's death. In 1915 he founded the monthly journal *Muzikalny Sovremennik* (*The Musical Contemporary*) and in 1922 he became ed. of *Muzikalnayu Lietopis* (*Musical Chronicle*). He ed. his father's and Glinka's memoirs, Mussorgsky's letters and documents, Cui's critical writings, his father's correspondence with Tchaikovsky; wrote on Mussorgsky's *Boris Godunov*, the music MSS. in the Leningrad Public Library, of which he was curator, etc. He married the comp. Julia Lazarevna Weissberg (1878–1942).

Rimsky-Korsakov, Nikolay Andreievich (b Tikhvin, Gvt. Novgorod, 18 Mar 1844; d St Petersburg, 21 Jun 1908), Russian composer, father of prec. He came of a naval family and his ambition was to become a sailor, though he showed great interest in the Russ. folksongs and church music he heard in his childhood, as well as in the operas he knew from pf. selections. In 1856 he was sent to the Naval Coll. at St Petersburg, where he remained until 1862. He had more pf. lessons during that time and learnt a little theory, but was not taught anything systematic even when in 1861 he met Balakirev and his circle, and came under their influence. He began a symph. in Eb min., but in 1862 was ordered on a 3-years' cruise. He wrote the slow movement of the symph. off Gravesend and heard opera in London and NY, but did not take up music again until his return to St Petersburg in 1865, when he worked more seriously under Balakirev, who cond. the symph. The 1st important works were the symph. poem *Sadko* (1867) and the programme symph. *Antar* (1868). In 1868 he also began his 1st opera, *The Maid of Pskov*, finished in 1872. Meanwhile he had been app. prof. of comp. at the Cons., though in theoret. knowledge he was always little more than 1 lesson ahead of his pupils, and in 1872 he married the pianist Nadezh-

da Purgold.

App. inspector of naval bands in 1873 and dir. of the Free School of Music in 1874, in succession to Balakirev, until 1881, when he became the latter's asst. in the direction of the Imp. Chapel. He became rather pedantically scholastic during those years, in reaction against his earlier amateurism, but this tendency was counteracted by his interest in Rus. folk music and by the influence of Wagner. In 1892–3 he had a serious nervous breakdown and temporarily took a dislike to music, but his interest revived. In 1905, when he had sided with the 'wrong' party during political disturbances, he was dismissed from the Cons., but there was such a storm of protest that he was reinstated later. His last opera, based on Pushkin's *Golden Cockerel* (comp. 1906–7), was a satire on official stupidity and its perf. was forbidden. He cond. a festival of Rus. music in Paris at Diaghilev's invitation in 1907. In 1908 he suffered from angina and died 4 days after the marriage of his daughter Nadia to his pupil M. Steinberg. Stravinsky was his most important pupil.

Works incl. OPERAS: *The Maid of Pskov* (*Ivan the Terrible*, 1873), *May Night* (1880), *The Snow Maiden* (*Snegurotchka*, 1882), *Mlada* (based on the collective opera commissioned earlier from him, Borodin, Cui and Mussorgsky, comp. 1872), *Christmas Eve* (1895), *Sadko* (1898), *Mozart and Salieri* (1898), *Boyarina Vera Sheloga* (prologue to *The Maid of Pskov*, 1898), *The Tsar's Bride* (1899), *The Legend of Tsar Saltan* (1900), *Servilia* (1902), *Kashtchey the Immortal* (1902), *Pan Voievoda*, *The Legend of the Invisible City of Kitezh* (1907), *The Golden Cockerel* (1909).

ORCHESTRAL: 3 symphs. (2nd *Antar*); symph. poem *Sadko* (1867), concert overtures on Rus. themes and *Russian Easter*, fantasy on Serbian themes, sinfonietta on Rus. themes (1884), symph. suite *Sheherazade* (1888), *Spanish Capriccio*, *Fairy-Tale*, *On the Tomb* (Belaiev's) and *Dubinushka* for orch.; pf. concerto and fantasy for vln. and orch. (both on Rus. themes).

CHAMBER AND SONGS: 2 string 4tets (1875, 1897) and 3 movements for string 4tet contrib. to collective sets by var. comps., string 6tet, 5tet for pf. and wind insts. (1876); 4 cantatas; pf. pieces; many partsongs, songs, vocal duets, 2 collections of Rus. folksongs.

Rinaldo, cantata for tenor solo, male chorus and orch. by Brahms, op. 50, on a ballad by Goethe, perf. Vienna, 28 Feb 1869.

Opera by Handel (lib. by G. Rossi, from a sketch based on Tasso by Aaron Hill), prod. London, Queen's Theatre, Haymarket, 24 Feb 1711. Handel's 1st London opera.

Rinaldo di Capua (b Capua or Naples, *c* 1705; d Rome, *c* 1780), Italian composer, according to Burney the illegitimate son of a Neapolitan nobleman. Of more than 30 operas most were prod. in Rome, the first in 1737. But some appeared in Florence and Venice, and in 1752–3 the *Bouffons* in Paris perf. his *La donna superba* and *La zingara*. His last *opera seria* was written in 1758, after which he devoted himself to comic opera. Burney found him living in poor circumstances in Rome in 1770, after which nothing is known. Only fragments of his music survive.

Works incl. operas *Ciro riconosciuto* (1737), *Vologeso, rè de' Parti* (1739), *Mario in Numidia* (1749), *Adriano in Siria* (1758), etc.; intermezzi, etc. *Il bravo burlato, La donna superba* (1738), *La zingara, Le donne ridicole* (1759), *I finti pazzi per amore* (1770), etc.; *Cantata per la natività della Beata Vergine* (1755), etc.

Rinck, (Johann) Christian Heinrich (b Elgersburg, Saxe-Gotha, 18 Feb 1770; d Darmstadt, 7 Aug 1846), German organist, composer and teacher. Studied at Erfurt under the Bach pupil Kittel. In 1805 he settled at Darmstadt, where he became prof., court organist and ducal chamber musician.

Works incl. *Practical Organ School* and many other works for organ; motets and *Pater noster* for voices and organ; sonatas for pf., vln. and pf., cello and pf.; pf. duets.

Rinforzando (It. = reinforcing), a sudden *crescendo* made on a short phrase, similar to the *sforzando*, which is made on a single note or chord.

Ring des Nibelungen, Der (*The Nibelung's Ring*), trilogy of music dramas, with a prologue, by Wagner (lib. by comp. based on the Nibelung Saga).

Das Rheingold (*The Rhinegold*), prod. Munich, Court Opera, 22 Sep 1869.

Die Walküre (*The Valkyrie*), prod. Munich, Court Opera, 26 Jun 1870.

Siegfried, prod. Bayreuth, Wagner Festival Theatre, 16 Jun 1876.

Götterdämmerung (*The Twilight of the Gods*), prod. Bayreuth, Wagner Festival Theatre, 17 Aug 1876.

The whole cycle prod. Bayreuth, Wagner Festival Theatre, 13–17 Aug 1876.

Rinuccini, Ottavio (b Florence, 20 Jan 1562; d Florence, 28 Mar 1621), Italian poet and librettist. *See* **Arianna** (Monteverdi),

Bonini (*Lamento d'Arianna*), **Dafne** (Gagliano, Peri and Schütz), **Euridice** (Caccini and Peri), **Petrassi** (*Lamento d'Arianna*).

Rios, Alvaro de los (b *c* 1580; d Madrid, 1623), Spanish composer. App. chamber musician to the queen, Margaret of Austria, in 1607.

Works incl. incid. music to Tirso de Molina's play *El vergonzoso en palacio*, etc.

Riotte, Philipp Jacob (b St Wendel, Saar, 16 Aug 1776; d Vienna, 20 Aug 1856), German composer and conductor. Studied with André at Offenbach, became theatre cond. at Gotha and in 1809 went to Vienna, where he settled, being app. cond. at the Theater an der Wien in 1818.

Works incl. operas and operettas *Mozarts Zauberflöte, Nureddin, Der Sturm* (on Shakespeare's *Tempest*) and many others; ballets; incid. music; cantata *Der Kreuzzug*; symph.; 3 clar. concertos; 6 vln. and pf. sonatas; 9 pf. sonatas, pf. piece *The Battle of Leipzig*.

Ripieno (It. adj. = full, noun = filling, stuffing), an instrument subordinate to a soloist or the leader of a section. In the 18th-cent. *concerto grosso* the string players other than the soloists are *ripieni*. Similarly in the brass band a ripieno cornet is one that comes 2nd to the solo cornet.

Rippe, Albert de (b Mantua, *c* 1500; d Paris, 1551), Italian composer, lutenist at the French court from 1529, after service with the Cardinal of Mantua. Most of his lute music was pub. in Paris after his death.

Ripresa (It. = re-taking, repetition), a refrain, esp. in the 14th-cent. It. *ballata*.

Riquier, Guiraut (b Narbonne, *c* 1230; d *c* 1300), French troubadour. He was the last great exponent of this art. 48 tunes of his songs are extant.

Rising of the Moon, The, opera by Maw (lib. by B. Cross and comp.), prod. Glyndebourne, 19 Jul 1970.

Rispetto, a type of old Italian improvised folk poem of 6–10 (usually 8) interrhyming lines, sung to popular tunes.

Rist, Johann (b Ottensen nr. Hamburg, 8 Mar 1607; d Wedel on Elbe, 31 Aug 1667), German clergyman, poet and musician. He founded a song school at Hamburg and wrote words for a great number of songs and hymns, some of which he comp. himself.

Ristori, Giovanni Alberto (b ? Bologna, 1692; d Dresden, 7 Feb 1753), Italian composer. His 1st opera was prod. in Venice in 1713, but 2 years later he moved to Dresden with his father, director of an It. theatrical co. whose music dir. he became in 1717.

App. dir. of the Polish chapel in Dresden in 1718, he became vice-*Kapellmeister* to the court, under Hasse, in 1750.

Works incl. *c* 20 operas, e.g. *Calandro* (1726), *Don Chisciotte* (1727), *Le fate* (1736), *Didone* (prod. CG, 1737), *Temistocle* (1738), *I lamenti di Orfeo* (1749), etc.; 3 oratorios; 15 cantatas; 15 Masses, 3 Requiems, motets and other church music.

Risurrezione (*Resurrection*), opera by Alfano (lib. by C. Hanau, based on Tolstoy's novel), prod. Turin, Teatro Vittorio Emanuele, 30 Nov 1914.

Rita, opera in 1 act by Donizetti (lib. by G. Vaez); comp. 1841, fp (posthumous) Paris, Opéra-Comique, 7 May 1860.

Ritardando (It. = retarding). The same direction is also expressed by *rallentando* (slowing down) or *ritenuto* (held back).

Rite of Spring, The, ballet by Stravinsky (scenario by comp. and Nikolay Roerich, choreog. by Nizhinsky), prod. as *Le Sacre du printemps*, Paris, Théâtre des Champs-Élysées, 29 May 1913. There was a riot between partisans and opponents on the first night.

Ritenuto (It. = held back). The same direction is also expressed by *rallentando* (slowing down) or *ritardando* (retarding).

Ritmo di . . . battute (It. = rhythm of . . . beats), an indication that the metrical scheme of a piece or movement is to be accented in groups of as many bars as may be shown in this direction between the 2nd and 3rd word, e.g. in the scherzo of Beethoven's 9th symph., where the metre changes between *ritmo di tre battute* and *ritmo di quattro battute*.

Ritornello (It. lit. 'little return'), orig. a refrain and thence, in the early 17th cent., a recurrent instrumental piece played in the course of a musical stage work; later the instrumental passages between vocal portions of an anthem or aria, from which in turn is derived the meaning of the word ritornello as applied to the orchestral *tutti* in concertos, esp. in rondos where the same theme returns several times.

Ritorno d'Ulisse in patria, Il (*Ulysses' Return to his Country*), opera by Monteverdi (lib. by G. Badoaro), prod. Venice, Teatro San Cassiano, Feb 1641. Realizations by d'Indy (prod. 1925), Dallapiccola (1942), Krenek (1959), Leppard (1972), Harnoncourt and Henze (1985).

Ritter, Alexander (b Narva, Russia, 7 Jun 1833; d Munich, 12 Apr 1896), German violinist, conductor and composer. Studied vln. with Franz Schubert of Dresden and later went to the Leipzig Cons. Married Wagner's niece, Franziska Wagner, in 1854, became an ardent Wagnerian, cond. at Stettin in 1856, settled at Würzburg in 1863, ran a music shop there in 1875–82 and then joined the ducal orch. at Meiningen under Bülow, whose retirement caused him to move to Munich in 1886. He was a close friend of Richard Strauss.

Works incl. operas *Der faule Hans* (1885), and *Wem die Krone?* (1890); symph. poems, etc.

Ritter Blaubart (*Knight Bluebeard*), opera by Rezniček (lib. by H. Eulenberg), prod. Darmstadt, 29 Jan 1920.

Ritter, Christian (b *c* 1650; d after 1717), German organist and composer. Worked at Halle, Dresden, Stockholm and Hamburg.

Works incl. 22 motets, Te Deum for double chorus; cantatas incl. *O amantissime sponse Jesu* for soprano and strings; instrumental works.

Ritter, Peter (b Mannheim, 2 Jul 1763; d Mannheim, 1 Aug 1846), German cellist and composer. Studied cello with Danzi, comp. with Vogler, succeeded Danzi in the Mannheim orch. in 1784 and became cond. in 1803.

Works incl. operas *Der Eremit auf Formentara* (Kotzebue, 1788), *Die lustigen Weiber* (after Shakespeare's *Merry Wives*, 1794), and *c* 20 others; plays with music; church music, oratorio *Das verlorene Paradies* (after Milton, 1819); cello concertos; chamber music; cello and pf. sonatas.

Ritual Dances, 4 dances for chorus and orch. in Tippett's opera *The Midsummer Marriage: The Earth in Autumn, The Waters in Winter, The Air in Spring, Fire in Summer*. Often heard as concert work; fp Basle, 13 Feb 1953 – two years before 1st prod. of opera, at CG.

Rituel in memoriam Bruno Maderna, work for orch. by Boulez, fp London, 2 Apr 1975, cond. Boulez.

Rizzio, Davidde (b *c* 1525; d Edinburgh, 9 Mar 1566), Italian bass and diplomat. In service at the court of Savoy, he visited Scot. in 1561 in the ambassador's suite and remained in the service of Queen Mary with his brother Giuseppe. He arr. masques at court and became her foreign secretary in 1564, but her favour aroused jealousies and he was stabbed to death in Holyrood Palace. Erroneously alleged to have written several tunes now regarded as traditional Scot.

Roberday, François (b Paris, bap. 21 Mar 1624; d Auffargis, 13 Oct 1680), French organist and composer. He held appts. as a goldsmith under the Queens Anne of Aus. and Marie-Thérèse, and was one of Lully's teachers.

Works incl. *Fugues et Caprices* for org.

Robert le Diable (*Robert the Devil*), opera by Meyerbeer (lib. by Scribe), prod. Paris, Opéra, 21 Nov 1831.

Roberto Devereux, Conte d'Essex, opera by Donizetti (lib. by S. Cammarano, based on Jacques Ancelot's tragedy *Élisabeth d'Angleterre*), prod. Naples, Teatro San Carlo, 2 Oct 1837.

Opera by Mercadante (lib. by F. Romani, based on Corneille's *Comte d'Essex*), prod. Milan, La Scala, 10 Mar 1833.

Robertsbridge Manuscript, the earliest known source of keyboard music consisting of 2 leaves bound in with an old Robertsbridge Abbey register (British Museum Additional 28,550). It contains 3 *estampies* (the 1st incomplete) showing It. influence, and 3 Latin motets (the 3rd incomplete), of which the first 2 are arrs. of motets incl. in the Fr. *Roman de Fauvel*. No convincing arguments have been put forward against an Eng. origin for the MS. The date is *c* 1325.

Robertson, Alec (b Southsea, 3 Jun 1892; d Midhurst, 18 Jan 1982), English musicologist. Studied at the RAM in London and became an organist and choirmaster in 1913. After serving in the 1914–18 war he lectured at LCC evening institutes and in 1920 became lecturer and later head of the Gramophone co.'s educ. dept. Lived in Rome for 4 years to study plainsong and in 1940 joined the BBC in charge of the music talks in the Home Service. His books incl. *The Interpretation of Plainchant, Art and Religion, Dvořák* and *Requiem: Music of Mourning and Consolation.*

Robeson, Paul (b Princeton, NJ, 9 Apr 1898; d Philadelphia, 23 Jan 1976), American bass. After studying law at Rutgers and Columbia Univs. he began a career as an actor, becoming esp. well known as Othello. In 1925 he first appeared as a singer, with a recital of negro spirituals, and soon attained world fame, but his career was impeded by his Communist sympathies. In 1952 he was awarded the Stalin Peace Prize.

Robin et Marion, Le Jeu de (*The Play of Robin and Marion*), a pastoral play with monophonic music by Adam de la Halle, written in Naples between 1283 and his death in 1286 or 1287.

Robin Hood, opera by Macfarren (lib. by J. Oxenford), prod. London, Her Majesty's Theatre, 11 Oct 1860.

Robin Hood, or Sherwood Forest, opera

by Shield (lib. by L. MacNally), prod. London, CG, 17 Apr 1784.

Robinson, Anastasia (b Italy, *c* 1692; d Southampton, Apr 1755), English soprano. A pupil of Croft, she made her stage debut in 1714 and during the next 10 years sang in many of Handel's operas, creating roles in *Amadigi, Radamisto, Ottone, Flavio* and *Giulio Cesare.* Having married the Earl of Peterborough, she retired in 1724.

Robinson Crusoé, operetta by Offenbach (lib. by E. Cormon and H. Crémieux, based distantly on Defoe's novel), prod. Paris, Opéra-Comique, 23 Nov 1867.

Robinson, Forbes (b Macclesfield, 21 May 1926; d London, 13 May 1987), English bass. After study at La Scala, he sang at CG from 1954; created the title role in *King Priam* (Coventry, 1962) and was Moses in the Brit. fp of *Moses und Aron* (1965). Also sang Boris, Claggart and Don Giovanni, and in oratorios by Handel and Walton.

Robinson, John (b ? London, 1682; d London, 30 Apr 1762), English organist and composer. Chorister in the Chapel Royal, became organist of St Lawrence, Jewry, and St Magnus, London Bridge, and in 1727 succeeded Croft as organist of Westminster Abbey. In 1716 he married Wm. Turner's daughter Ann (d London, 5 Jan 1741), a singer at the It. Opera.

Works incl. Double Chant in Eb maj.

Robinson, Stanford (b Leeds, 5 Jul 1904; d Brighton, 25 Oct 1984), English conductor. He studied at the RAM and worked with the BBC, 1924–66, as chorus master and orch. conductor; many studio perfs. of operas. He was at CG, London, in the Coronation season of 1937. Appeared widely in Europe after the war.

Robledo, Melchior (b *c* 1520; d Saragossa, 1587), Spanish composer. Spent some time in Rome, but returned to Spain in 1569 and became *maestro de capilla* at the old cathedral of Saragossa, where, as at the new one, his work alone was sung with that of Morales, Victoria and Palestrina.

Works incl. Masses, motets.

Robles, Marisa (b Madrid, 4 May 1937), Spanish harpist. She studied at the Madrid Cons. and made her debut in 1954. Settled in England 1959, teaching at RCM from 1971. Well known in concert and recital.

Rocca, Lodovico (b Turin, 29 Nov 1895; d Turin, 25 Jun 1986), Italian composer. Pupil of Orefice. App. director of the Turin Cons. in 1940.

Works incl. operas *La morte di Frine, La corona del rè Gaulo, Il Dibuk* (1934), *In* terra di leggenda (1933), Monte Ivnor (1939) and L'uragano (1952); symph. poems Contrasti, Aurora di morte, L'alba del malato (1922), and La foresta delle Samodive (1921), also La cella azzurra, Chiaroscuri and Interludio epico for orch.; chamber music.

Rochberg, George (b Paterson, NJ, 5 Jul 1918), American composer. Studied composition with Szell and L. Mannes (1939–41) in NY, and then at the Curtis Inst., Philadelphia, with Scalero and Menotti. In 1950 he was awarded a Fulbright Fellowship and in 1956 a Guggenheim Fellowship. From 1948 to 1954 he taught at the Curtis Inst.

Works incl. opera The Confidence Man (after Melville, 1982), symph. poem Night Music, 4 symphs. (1958–76), Time-Span (1960), Waltz Serenade, Sinfonia Fantasia for orch.; Cantio Sacra for chamber orch.; 6 string 4tets (1952–76); clar. sonata; fantasia for vln. and pf.; 2 pf. sonatas.

Rochlitz, Johann Friedrich (b Leipzig, 12 Feb 1769; d Leipzig, 16 Dec 1842), German music critic and poet. Studied under Doles at the St Thomas School, Leipzig, later theology at the univ. In 1798 he founded the Allgemeine musikalische Zeitung, which he ed. until 1818. He also comp., wrote libs. and poems, 3 of which were set by Schubert; others were set by Weber and Spohr.

Rode, (Jacques) Pierre (Joseph) (b Bordeaux, 16 Feb 1774; d Château de Bourbon nr. Damazon, 25 Nov 1830), French violinist and composer. After making great progress as a child, he was sent to Paris in 1787 and became a pupil of Viotti, making his 1st public appearance in 1790; subsequently gave many perfs. of Viotti's concertos. He joined the orch. at the Théâtre Feydeau and in 1794 began to tour abroad, visiting Hol., Ger. and Eng. On his return to Paris he became prof. at the new Cons. and leader at the Opéra. In 1799 he visited Spain, where he met Boccherini. In 1800 he became violinist to Napoleon and in 1803 went to St Petersburg with Boieldieu, remaining until 1808. In 1811–13 he travelled in Ger. again, going to Vienna in the latter year, where Beethoven finished the sonata op. 96 for him. In 1814 he settled in Berlin, where he married, but soon afterwards went to live in retirement near Bordeaux.

Works incl. 13 vln. concertos; many string 4tets; vln. duets; 24 caprices, variations, etc., for vln.

Rodelinda, opera by Handel (lib. by A. Salvi, adapted by N.F. Haym), prod. London, King's Theatre, Haymarket, 13 Feb 1725.

Rodelinda, regina de' Longobardi, opera by Graun (lib. by G.G. Bottarelli, altered from A. Salvi), prod. Berlin, at court, 13 Dec 1741.

Rodgers, Richard (b New York 28 Jun 1902; d New York, 30 Dec 1979), American composer. Studied at Columbia Univ (1919–21) and at the Inst. of Musical Art, NY (1921–3). For 18 years he worked with the librettist Hart, producing very successful musical comedies, incl. The Girl Friend and The Boys from Syracuse. After Hart's death he worked with Oscar Hammerstein II, producing Oklahoma (1943), which was awarded a Pulitzer Prize in 1944; also Carousel, South Pacific (1948, Pulitzer Prize 1950), The King and I (1951), The Flower Drum Song and many others.

Rodio, Rocco (b Bari, c 1535; d Naples, shortly after 1615), Italian composer. He wrote church music (incl. 10 Masses), madrigals and instrumental music and a treatise, Regole di Musica, pub. Naples, 1600, but known only from its 2nd and 3rd eds. (1609, 1626), ed. by his pupil Olifante.

Rodolphe, Jean Joseph (orig. Johann Joseph Rudolph) (b Strasbourg, 14 Oct 1730; d Paris, 18 Aug 1812), French horn and vln. player and composer. Studied horn and vln. with his father, and from 1746 vln. with Leclair in Paris. In 1754 he went to Parma, in 1761 to Stuttgart and in 1767 back to Paris. He studied comp. under Traetta and Jommelli. In later years he taught, from 1798 at the Cons.

Works incl. operas Le Mariage par capitulation (1764), L'Aveugle de Palmyre (1767) and Isménor (1773); ballets; horn concertos; vln. duets; horn pieces.

Rodrigo, Joaquín (b Sagunto, Prov. Valencia, 22 Nov 1901), Spanish composer and critic. He was blind from the age of 3, but contrived to study music and in 1927 he went to Paris as a pupil of Dukas. He returned to Spain in 1933 and again, after travels in Europe, in 1936, settling in Madrid in 1939.

Works incl. Ausencias de Dulcinea for bass, 4 sopranos and orch.; Heroic concerto and other works for orch.; 'Arunjuez' concerto for guitar (1939), 'Summer' concerto for vln. (1944), cello concerto; songs.

Rodríguez de Hita, Antonio (b c 1724; d Madrid, 21 Feb 1787), Spanish composer. He was maestro de capilla of Palencia Cathedral, and from 1757 of the Convent of the Incarnation in Madrid. In collaboration with the poet Ramón de la Cruz he made important contribs. to Span. opera.

Works incl. operas *Briseida* (1768), *Las segadoras de Vallecas* (1768), *Las labradoras de Murcia* (1769); hymns for 4 and 8 voices.

Rodzinski, Artur (b Spalato, Dalmatia, 1 Jan 1892; d Boston, 27 Nov 1958), Yugoslav, later American conductor. Studied law at the Univ. of Vienna, and then music at the Vienna Acad., with E. Sauer, F. Schalk and Schreker. He made his debut as a cond. in Lwów in 1920, then took up posts in Warsaw. In 1926 he became asst. to Stokowski and in 1929 permanent cond. of the Los Angeles PO and of the Cleveland Orch. in 1933. In 1937 he organized the NBC SO for Toscanini and cond. many of its concerts. From 1942 to 1947 he was permanent cond. of the NY PO and from 1948 of the Chicago SO. In 1953 in Florence he cond. the fp (stage) of Prokofiev's *War and Peace*.

Rogé, Pascal (b Paris, 6 Apr 1951), French pianist. Studied at Paris Cons. London and Paris debuts, 1969. Won Long-Thibaud Competition, 1971. Often heard in Ravel and Liszt.

Rogel, José (b Orihuela, Alicante, 24 Dec 1829; d Cartagena, 25 Feb 1901), Spanish composer and conductor. Studied under the cathedral organist at Alicante, but was sent to Valencia to study law. There he pursued further studies under Pascual Pérez, and after taking his degree in law, became a theatre cond. He wrote or collaborated in over 80 stage works, some with Barbieri.

Works incl. operas and *zarzuelas: Loa a la libertad* (1854), *El joven Telémaco, Revista de un muerte* (1865), *Un viaje de mil demonios, El General Bumbum*, etc.

Roger-Ducasse (Jean Jules Aimable Roger Ducasse) (b Bordeaux, 18 Apr 1873; d Taillan nr. Bordeaux, 20 Jul 1954), French composer. Studied at the Paris Cons., where he was a comp. pupil of Fauré. App. inspector of singing in the Paris city schools in 1909, and in 1935 succeeded Dukas as comp. prof. at the Cons.

Works incl. opera *Cantegril* (1931), mimed drama *Orphée* (1914); *Au Jardin de Marguerite* (1905) and *Ulysse et les Sirènes* for voices and orch.; motets and secular vocal works incl. *Sur quelques vers de Virgile, Madrigal sur des vers de Molière; Suite française* (1909), *Le Joli Jeu de furet, Prélude d'un ballet, Nocturne de printemps* (1920), *Épithalame, Poème symphonique sur le nom de Fauré* for orch.; *Variations plaisantes* for harp and orch.; pf. works; instrumental pieces; songs.

Rogers, Benjamin (b Windsor, May 1614; d Oxford, Jun 1698), English organist and composer. Learnt music from his father, Peter R., a lay-clerk at St George's Chapel, Windsor, and from the organist, Giles. He became himself a lay-clerk, but in 1639 went to Dublin as organist of Christ Church Cathedral. He returned to Windsor in 1641, but in 1644 the choir was disbanded and he taught music privately. Mus.B., Cambridge, 1658, and in 1669 D.Mus., Oxford, where he had become organist and choirmaster at Magdalen Coll., in 1664, being dismissed for musical and other irregularities in 1685, but given a pension.

Works incl. services and anthems, *Hymnus Eucharisticus* (sung at Magdalen tower at 5 a.m. on 1 May each year); instrumental pieces; organ works.

Rogers, Bernard (b New York, 4 Feb 1893; d Rochester, New York, 24 May 1968), American composer. Studied at the NY Inst. of Musical Art and with Bloch at Cleveland. He gained several prizes and distinctions and for a time did music journalism. In 1938 he became prof. of comp. at the Eastman School of Music at Rochester, NY.

Works incl. operas *The Marriage of Aude* (1931), *The Warrior* (1947), *The Veil* and *The Nightingale* (1940); cantatas *The Raising of Lazarus* and *The Exodus, Passion* with org. accomp.; 5 symphs. (1926–59), overture *The Faithful, 3 Eastern Dances, 2 Amer, Frescoes, 4 Fairy Tales, The Supper at Emmaeus* (1937), *The Colours of War, The Dance of Salome* (1940), *The Song of the Nightingale, The Plains, The Sailors of Toulon, Invasion* and *Characters from Hans Andersen* for orch.; soliloquies for fl. and strings and bassoon and strings, fantasy for fl., vla. and orch.; *Pastorale* for 11 insts., string 4tet; *Music for an Industrial Film* for 2 pfs. songs.

Rogers, Nigel (b Wellington, 21 Mar 1935), English tenor. He studied at Cambridge and with Gerhard Hüsch in Munich. Has been heard in Lieder and in modern music, e.g. Goehr's *Arden must Die* (London, 1974), but is best known in Baroque opera: frequent perfs. of Monteverdi under Nikolaus Harnoncourt and Gustav Leonhardt.

Rogg, Lionel (b Geneva, 21 Apr 1936), Swiss organist and harpsichordist. He studied in Geneva and made his debut there in 1961. Has recorded all the organ works of J.S. Bach and is partic. admired in *The Art of Fugue*. Also gifted as an improvisor.

Rogier, Philippe (b Namur *c* 1560; d Madrid, 29 Feb 1596), French composer. He must have been sent to Spain as a child, being a choir-boy at Madrid in 1572; member of the royal chapel from 1586, *maestro de capilla* from 1588, working for Philip II. Works incl. Masses, motets, etc.

Rogneda, opera by Serov (lib., in Rus., by D.V. Averkiev), prod. St Petersburg, 8 Nov 1865.

Rogowski, Ludomir (Michal) (b Lublin, 3 Oct 1881; d Dubrovnik, 14 Mar 1954), Polish composer. Studied at the Warsaw Cons. and with Riemann and Nikisch at Leipzig. On his return to Poland he founded a symph. orch. at Wilno, lived in Paris in 1914–21 and withdrew to a monastery in Yugoslavia in 1926.

Works incl. opera *Tamara* (after Lermontov, 1918) and *Prince Marco* (1930); film opera *Un Grand Chagrin de la Petite Ondine* (1920), ballets *St John's Eve* and *Fairy Tale* (1923); 7 symphs (1926–51), suites *Pictures of my Daughter, The Seasons, Les Sourires, Villafranca, Phantasmagoria* (1920), *Sporting Scene, Fantasy Pictures* for orch.; 4tet for 4 cellos, suites for 6 and 9 insts. and other chamber music; instrumental pieces; pf. works; choral songs with and without accomp.

Roi Arthus, Le (*King Arthur*), opera by Chausson (lib. by comp) written 1886–95, under the influence of Wagner's *Tristan*, prod. Brussels, Théâtre de la Monnaie, 30 Nov 1903.

Roi David, Le, dramatic Psalm by Honegger (lib. by R. Morax), prod. Mézières, Switz., open-air Théâtre du Jorat, 11 Jun 1921.

Roi de Lahore, Le (*The King of L.*), opera by Massenet (lib. by L. Gallet), prod. Paris, Opéra, 27 Apr 1877.

Roi des Violons (Fr. = King of the Violins), the title of the head of the guild of vln. players, the Ménétriers, founded in Paris in 1321. It was not abolished until 1773.

Roi d'Ys, Le, opera by Lalo (lib. by E. Blau), prod. Paris, Opéra-Comique, 7 May 1888. Ys is the submerged city of Debussy's pf. prelude *La Cathédrale engloutie*.

Roi et le fermier, Le (*King and Farmer*), opera by Monsigny (lib. by J. M. Sedaine), prod. Paris, Comédie-Italienne, 22 Nov 1762.

Roi l'a dit, Le (*The King has said it*), opera by Delibes (lib. by E. Gondinet), prod. Paris, Opéra-Comique, 24 May 1873.

Roi malgré lui, Le (*King against his Will*), opera by Chabrier (lib. by E. de Najac and P. Burani, based on a comedy by Ancelot), prod. Paris, Opéra-Comique, 18 May 1887.

Roland. See also **Orlando.**

Opera by Lully (lib. by Quinault), prod. Versailles, at court, 8 Jan 1685; 1st Paris perf., 8 Mar 1685.

Roland-Manuel (actually Lévy), **Alexis** (b Paris, 22 Mar 1891; d Paris, 2 Nov 1966), French composer and critic. Pupil of Roussel at the Schola Cantorum in Paris and of Ravel. In 1947 he became a prof. at the Paris Cons. He wrote much criticism and books on Ravel and Falla.

Works incl. operas *Isabelle et Pantalon* (1920), *Le Diable amoureux* (1932); ballets *Le Tournoi singulier, L'Écran des jeunes filles, Elvire* (on music by D. Scarlatti) (1936); film music *L'Ami Fritz* (after Erckmann-Chatrian) *La Bandéra* and others; oratorio *Jeanne d'Arc*; symph. poems *Le Harem du vice-roi, Tempo di ballo* (1924), suite *Pena de Francia* for orch.; suite in the Spanish style for harpsichord, ob., bassoon and tpt., string trio; part-songs; songs.

Rolfe Johnson, Anthony (b Tackley, Oxon., 5 Nov 1940), English tenor. Debut 1973, with EOG, in *Iolanthe*. Glyndebourne 1974–6, as Storch, Lensky and Fenton. From 1977 he has toured widely in Europe as opera and concert singer. Other roles incl. Ottavio, Ferrando and Handel's Acis. He has recorded operas by Haydn and oratorios by Handel (*Jephtha, Alexander's Feast*).

Roll, a very rapid succession of notes on drums prod. by quick alternating strokes of the 2 sticks.

Rolla, Alessandro (b Pavia, 6 Apr 1757; d Milan, 15 Sep 1841), Italian violinist (later esp. vla. player) and composer. Studied with Renzi and Conti, was in the service of the court at Parma 1782–1802, where Paganini was his pupil in 1795. In 1803 he was app. orch. director at the Scala in Milan, in 1805 prof. at the Cons. there.

Works incl. ballets; 2 symphs.; vln. and vla. concertos; string 5tets, 6 4tets, and other chamber music; vln. duets, studies.

Rolland, Romain (b Clamency, Nièvre, 29 Jan 1866; d Vézelay, Yvonne, 30 Dec 1944), French musicologist and author. He had a 1st-rate general educ., but devoted himself to music and other artistic studies. In 1901 he became president of the music section of the École des Hautes Études Sociales and lectured on music 1st at the École Normale Supérieure and from 1903 at the Sorbonne. He also contrib. essays on music to var. periodicals and wrote plays and other lit. works. From 1913 he lived in Switz., having retired owing to bad health. He returned to Fr. in 1938 in order not to evade the war, was interned in a concentration camp by the Germans and released only when he was mortally ill. His works incl. books on Handel and Beethoven, on early opera, *Musiciens d'autrefois*, *Musiciens d'aujourd'hui*, *Voyage musical au pays du passé*, the novel *Jean-Christophe* (10 vols.) with a musician as hero, etc.

Rolle, Johann Heinrich (b Quedlinburg, 23 Dec 1716; d Magdeburg, 29 Dec 1785). German organist and composer. Pupil of his father, Christian Friedrich R. (1681–1751) he was app. organist of St Peter's, Magdeburg, at the age of 17. After legal studies in Leipzig he entered the service of Frederick II of Prus. in 1741, but returned to Magdeburg in 1746 as organist of St John's, and became municipal music dir. in 1752, succeeding his father.

Works incl. over 20 dramatic oratorios, e.g. *David und Jonathan* (1766), *Der Tod Abels Saul* (1770), etc.; Passion oratorios; cantatas and numerous other church works; instrumental music; songs.

Roller, Alfred (b Vienna, 2 Oct 1864; d Vienna, 12 June 1935) Austrian stage designer and painter. In the 1890s he was assoc. with Klimt and Egon Schiele in Vienna. From 1903 he worked with Mahler at the Vienna Hofoper, and with his designs for *Tristan*, *Fidelio*, *Don Giovanni* and *Die Walküre* helped to provide settings in which colour and light were integral parts of the dramatic conception. He provided the sets for the first prods. of Strauss's *Elektra* and *Rosenkavalier*, in Dresden, and returned to Vienna for *Die Frau ohne Schatten* (1919). Continued to work in Vienna and in Salzburg until 1934.

Rolón, José (b Ciudad Guzmán, Jalisco, 22 Jun 1883; d Mexico City, 3 Feb 1945), Mexican composer. Studied with his father and later with Moszkowski in Paris, where however he came under the influence of the modern school. He returned to Mex. in 1907 and founded a music school at Guadalajara, but at the age of 44 he returned to Paris to study with Dukas and Nadia Boulanger.

Works incl. symph., ballet, *El festin de los enanos* (1925), *Scherzo sinfónico*, *Baile Michoacana*, *Zapotlán*, *Cuauhtémoc* for orch.; pf. concerto (1935).

Roma, orchestral suite by Bizet, comp. 1866–8, fp Paris, 1869.

Roman, Johan Helmich (b Stockholm, 26 Oct 1694; d Haraldsmåla nr. Kalmar, 20 Nov 1758), Swedish composer. Pupil of his father, leader of the court orch. in Stockholm, he entered the royal service in 1611. In Eng. from 1714, he studied with Ariosti and Pepusch and was in the service of the Duke of Newcastle. Returning to Stockholm he became vice-*Kapellmeister* (1721), then *Kapellmeister* (1729). Toured Eng., Fr. and It. 1735–7, became a member of the Swed. Acad. in 1740 and retired in 1745.

Works incl. Mass, motets, psalms, festival cantatas; 21 symphs., 6 overtures; concertos; over 20 vln. sonatas, 12 sonatas for fl., vla. da gamba and harpsichord, *Assaggio* for solo vln., etc.

Romance (Eng. and Fr.), a piece or song of a 'romantic' nature, usually moderate in tempo and emotional in style. There is no prescribed form, but it is as a rule fairly short and in the character of a song.

Romance (Fr.), as above, but more often and more specifically a song. In France single-voice songs were called *romances* from about the end of the 18th cent. onward until recently, and the term is still in use, though the more general one now is *mélodie*.

Romanesca, originally the melody of a 16th-cent. Span. song with a simple bass, used as a theme for variations. The bass, of which the simplest form is:

came to be used independently as a ground, as in the *passamezzo*.

Romani, Felice (b Genoa, 31 Jan 1788; d Moneglia, 28 Jan 1865), Italian librettist and poet. His first libretti were for Simone Mayr, (*Medea in Corinto*, 1813). He soon began a collaboration with Rossini and wrote *Aureliano in Palmira* and *Il Turco in Italia*. For Donizetti he wrote *L'Elisir d'amore* (1832) and *Anna Bolena* (1835). His most important work was for Bellini: *Il Pirata* (1827), *I Capuleti* (1830), *La Sonnambula* and *Norma* (1831) and *Beatrice di Tenda* (1833). His only libretto for Verdi was *Un Giorno di Regno* (1840).

Romantic Symphony, Bruckner's 4th symph., in E♭. First version comp. 1874, fp Linz, 20 Sep 1875; vers. with new scherzo and revised finale perf. Vienna, 20 Feb 1881, cond. Richter.

Romanticism, a term subject to as vague an application as are Classicism and Modernism. Applied to a period it defines with fair accuracy the greater part of music of the 19th cent., from Schubert to Brahms, as well as a good deal of the music of the early 20th cent. As a definition of mood and outlook it may be said to describe music which is consciously an expression of the composer's state of mind, a mood of place, season or time of day, the feeling or content of some other work of art (e.g. a poem or a picture), etc.

Romanze (Ger.) = Romance, in the 1st sense defined above.

Romberg, Andreas (Jakob) (b Vechta nr. Münster, 27 Apr 1767; d Gotha, 10 Nov 1821), German violinist and composer. Pupil of his father, Gerhard Heinrich R. (1745–1819). He appeared in string duets with his cousin Bernhard R. at the age of 7 and at 17 played at the Concert Spirituel in Paris. In 1790 he joined the electoral orch. at Bonn and in 1793–6 he was in It., Spain and Port. with Bernhard, whom he joined again in Paris in 1800 after visits to Vienna and Hamburg. He returned to the latter place, married and remained for 15 years, after which he became court music dir. at Gotha.

Works incl. operas *Don Mendoce, ou Le Tuteur portugais* (with Bernhard R.), *Das blaue Ungeheuer* (comp. 1793), *Der Rabe* (1794), *Die Ruinen zu Paluzzi* (1811), *Die Grossmut des Scipio* (1816) and others; Te Deum, Magnificat, psalms and other church music; setting of Schiller's *Lied von der Glocke* for solo voices, chorus and orch., and other cantatas *The Transient and the Eternal, The Harmony of the Spheres, The Power of Song*, etc.; 6 symphs. and Toy Symph.; string 4tets and 5tets.

Romberg, Bernhard (b Dinklage, Oldenburg, 12 Nov 1767; d Hamburg, 13 Aug 1841), German cellist and composer, cousin of prec. Pupil of his father Anton R., appeared at the age of 7 with his cousin and in Paris at 14. In 1790–3 he was in the electoral orch. at Bonn, together with Andreas, also Beethoven, Reicha and F.A. Ries; then, until 1796, he was in It., Spain and Port. with Andreas. After visits to Vienna and Hamburg he taught the cello at the Paris Cons., 1801–3, and in 1804–6 he was cellist in the royal orch. in Berlin, where he was court music dir. in 1815–19, after a tour in Rus., retiring to Hamburg in 1819. In the meantime he had visited London, Paris, Vienna, St Petersburg and Moscow.

Works incl. operas *Don Mendoce, ou le tuteur portugais* (with Andreas R.), *Die wiedergefundene Statue* (after Gozzi, comp. 1792, *Der Schiffbruch, Alma, Ulysses und Circe* (1807), *Rittertreue*; 10 cello concertos, concerto for 2 cellos; funeral symph. for Queen Louise of Prus.; 11 string 4tets, pf. 4tets and other chamber music, cello pieces.

Romberg, Siegmund (b Szeged, 29 Jul 1887; d New York, 9 Nov 1951), American composer of Hungarian origin. Studied at Univ. of Bucharest and then in Vienna with Heuberger. In 1909 he went to the USA as an engineer, but later began comp. with great success.

Works incl. operettas *Blossom Time* (after music by Schubert, 1921), *The Rose of Stamboul, The Student Prince* (1924), *The Desert Song* (1926).

Romeo and Juliet. See also **Giulietta e Romeo, Capuleti e Montecchi.**

Fantasy overture by Tchaikovsky, based on Shakespeare's tragedy; fp Moscow, 16 Mar, 1870; revised Oct 1870.

Ballet by Prokofiev, fp Brno 30 Dec 1938.

Roméo et Juliette, opera by Gounod (lib. by J. Barbier and M. Carré, after Shakespeare), prod. Paris, Théâtre Lyrique, 27 Apr 1867.

Opera by Steibelt (lib. by J.A.P. de Ségur, after Shakespeare), prod. Paris, Théâtre Feydeau, 10 Sep 1793.

Symph. by Berlioz, op. 17, for solo voices, chorus and orch., based on Shakespeare's tragedy, comp. in 1839, fp Paris Cons., 24 Nov 1839.

Romeo und Julia, opera by Sutermeister (lib. by comp., after Shakespeare), prod. Dresden, 13 Apr 1940.

Opera by Blacher (lib. ditto); comp. 1943, prod. Salzburg, 9 Aug 1950.

Romeo und Julia auf dem Dorfe (*A Village Romeo and Juliet*), opera by Delius (lib. by comp., in Ger., based on a story by Gottfried Keller), prod. Berlin, 21 Feb 1907. Fp in Eng., London, CG, 22 Feb 1910.

Romeo und Julie, opera by G. Benda (lib. by F.W. Gotter), prod. Gotha, at court, 25 Sep 1776. The 1st opera to be based on Shakespeare's tragedy.

Romero, Mateo (known as Maestro Capitán) (b Liège, c 1575; d Madrid, 10 May 1647), Spanish singer, composer and priest. He joined the royal chapel at Madrid in 1594. He was a pupil of Rogier and belonged to the Flemish section of the choir. In 1598 he succeeded Rogier as *maestro de capilla*. He was ordained priest in 1609 and retired with a pension in 1633, but was sent on a musical mission to Portugal in 1638.

Works incl. motets and other church music; secular song for 3 and 4 voices, incl. settings of poems by Lope de Vega, etc.

Romilda e Costanza, opera by Meyerbeer (lib. by G. Rossi), prod. Padua, 19 Jul 1817.

Ronald, Landon (b London, 7 Jun 1873; d London, 14 Aug 1938), English conductor, pianist and composer, illegitimate son of

Henry Russell. Studied at the RCM, made his 1st public appearance as pianist in Wormser's *L'Enfant prodigue* and gained experience as asst. cond. to Mancinelli at Covent Garden and accompanist to Melba. Later he cond. symph. concerts and visited Ger., Aus. and It. as cond. In 1910 he was app. principal of the GSM in London. Knighted 1922; Recorded Beethoven's violin concerto with Isolde Menges the same year.

Works incl. incid. music to dramatic version of Robert Hichens's *Garden of Allah*; *Birthday Overture* for orch.; *Adonais* (Shelley) for voice and orch.; pf. pieces; songs.

Ronconi. Italian family of singers:

1. Domenico R. (b Lendinara nr. Rovigo, 11 Jul 1772; d Milan, 13 Apr 1839), made his 1st appearance, at the Teatro La Fenice in Venice, in 1797, later worked at St Petersburg, Vienna, Paris and Munich. He founded a school of singing at Milan in 1829.

2. Giorgio R. (b Milan, 6 Aug 1810; d Madrid, 8 Jan 1890), baritone, son of prec. Pupil of his father, made his 1st appearance at Pavia in 1831 in *La Straniera*. He sang in the fps of Donizetti's *Torquato Tasso*, *Il campanello di notte*, *Pia de 'Tolomei*, *Maria Padilla* and *Maria di Rohan*. Travelled all over It. and 1st visited London in 1842. Married the singer Elguerra Giannoni and visited many European countries as well as the USA. In 1874 he became prof. of singing at the Madrid Cons.

3. Felice R. (b Venice, 1811; d St Petersburg, 10 Sep 1875), brother of prec. Pupil of his father, taught at Würzburg, Frankfurt, Milan, London and St Petersburg.

4. Sebastiano R. (b Venice, May 1814; d Milan, 6 Feb 1900), baritone, brother of prec. Pupil of his father and made his 1st appearance at Lucca in 1836, and in London later that year. He travelled widely and in 1849 settled at Milan as singing-master.

Rondeau (Fr.), a medieval song with a refrain. Also, by analogy, in the 17th and 18th cents. and instrumental piece in which one section recurs. *See also* **Rondo.**

Rondeña, a Spanish folksong type of Andalusia, resembling the Fandango, with words in stanzas of 4 lines of 8 syllables.

Rondine, La (*The Swallow*), operetta by Puccini (lib. by G. Adami, trans. from the Ger. of A.M. Willner and H. Reichert), prod. Monte Carlo, 27 Mar 1917. Orig. intended to be set to the Ger. words for the Carl Theater in Vienna, but It. being at war with Aus., this fell through.

Rondo, an instrumental piece or movement in which a theme heard at the beginning recurs between contrasting episodes and at the end. In the late 18th and early 19th cents. the form was combined with sonata form, i.e. the 1st episode, in a related key, was repeated in the tonic key before the last appearance of the rondo theme. Thus a simple rondo might be in the following form: *ABACADA*, and a sonata rondo: *ABACAB'A*, where *C* has the character of a development. Variants of the latter scheme are not uncommon. The final movements of sonatas, symphs., etc. in the period mentioned are often rondos.

Röntgen, Engelbert (b Deventer, 30 Sep 1829; d Leipzig, 12 Dec 1897), Dutch violinist. Studied at the Leipzig Cons. and became a member of the opera and Gewandhaus orchs. there, and in 1869 vln. prof. at the Cons. In 1873 he succeeded David as leader at the Gewandhaus. He married a daugher of a former leader, Moritz Klengel.

Röntgen, Julius (b Leipzig, 9 May 1855; d Utrecht, 13 Sep 1932), German pianist, composer and conductor of Dutch descent, son of prec. Studied at the Leipzig Cons., but reverted to Hol. living at Amsterdam in 1878–1924 as teacher and cond., becoming dir. of the Cons. in 1914. He was a great friend of Grieg, of whom he wrote a biog.

Works incl. operas *Agnete*, *The Laughing Cavalier* (on Frans Hals's painting), *Samûm* (on Strindberg's play); film music; 21 symphs.; 7 pf. concertos; chamber music; arrs. of old Dutch songs and dances.

Ronzi de Begnis, Giuseppina (b Milan, 11 Jan 1800; d Florence, 7 Jun 1853), Italian soprano. She made her debut in Bologna, 1816, and much of her early career, in Italy, London and Paris was devoted to Rossini: well known as Ninetta and Rosina and in *Il Turco in Italia*, *La donna del lago* and *Matilde di Shabran*. From 1831 she sang in the fps of 5 operas by Donizetti, incl. *Fausta*, *Maria Stuarda*, *Gemma di Vergy* and *Roberto Devereux*. Her husband Giuseppe (1793–1849) was the first Dandini, in *Cenerentola*.

Root, according to 19th-cent. theory the lowest note of a maj. or min. triad, or of chords in which one or more 3rds are superimposed on such triads (7ths, 9ths, 11ths, 13ths). Thus the following chord:

Root position

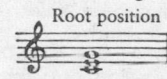

is said to be in root position. Rearrangements of the notes of the chord:

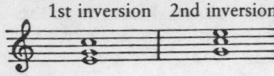

1st inversion 2nd inversion

are described as Inversions. According to this theory, which takes no account of the different functions of chords, a 4-note chord has 3 possible inversions, and so on.

Rootham, C(yril) B(radley) (b Bristol, 5 Oct 1875; d Cambridge, 18 Mar 1938), English organist, educationist and composer. Studied under his father, the singer, organist and cond. Daniel R. (1837–1922), later at St John's Coll., Cambridge, and the RCM in London. In 1901 he went back to Cambridge as organist and music dir. at St John's Coll. and took the Mus. D. in 1910.

Works incl. opera *The Two Sisters* (1922); choral and orchestral works *Andromeda Coronach, For the Fallen* (Binyon), *Brown Earth, Ode on the Morning of Christ's Nativity* (Milton), *City in the West*, Psalm ciii: 2 symphs. (2nd with choral finale); inst. music and songs.

Rooy, Anton(ius Maria Josephus) van (b Rotterdam, 1 Jan 1870; d Munich, 28 Nov 1932), Dutch bass-baritone. Originally engaged in commerce, he went to Frankfurt to study singing with Stockhausen, sang at concerts in Germany and obtained his 1st stage engagement at Bayreuth in 1897; sang there until 1902 as Wotan, Sachs and the Dutchman: banned after 1903 for singing Amfortas in the 'pirate' NY perf. of *Parsifal*. He visited London as a Wagner singer at Covent Garden 1898–1913.

Rore, Cipriano de (Cyprien de) (b Mechelen, *c* 1516; d Parma, Sep 1565), Flemish composer. Studied under his fellow-countryman Willaert at Venice, where he was a singer at St Mark's, and began to pub. madrigals in 1542. He left Venice *c* 1550 to enter the service of Ercole II, Duke of Ferrara. In 1558 he visited his parents at Antwerp and the court of Margaret of Aus. in the Netherlands, into the service of whose husband, Ottavio Farnese, Duke of Parma, he passed. He succeeded Willaert as *maestro di cappella* of St Mark's, Venice, in 1563, but returned to Parma in Jul 1564.

Works incl. 5 Masses, 65 motets, 1 Passion and other church music; 125 madrigals; instrumental fantasies and *ricercari*, etc.

Rorem, Ned (b Richmond, Ind., 23 Oct 1923), American composer. He studied at the Curtis Institute and Juilliard. Has held academic posts at Univs. of Buffalo and Utah, and the Curtis Inst. (from 1980).

Works incl. operas *A Childhood Miracle* (1955), *The Robbers* (1958), *Miss Julie* (1965), and *Hearing* (1976); 3 symphs. (1950–7), 3 pf. concertos (1950–70); *The Poet's Requiem* for sop., chorus and orch. (1957); *Eagles* for orch. (1958); Double concerto for vln., cello and orch. (1979); *Sunday Morning*, symph. suite (1981); song cycles *Flight for Heaven, King Midas, Poems of Love and the Rain, War Scenes, Women's Voices* and *After Long Silence*.

Rosa (orig. Rose), **Carl (August Nikolaus)** (b Hamburg, 22 Mar 1842; d Paris, 30 Apr 1889), German violinist and conductor. Studied at the Leipzig and Paris Conss., became orch. leader at Hamburg and visited Eng. in 1866 and afterwards the USA, where he met and in 1867 married Euphrosyne Parape (1836–74), with whom he formed an opera co., which incl. Santley and G. Ronconi. This he took to Eng. and carried on as the C.R. Opera Company; many perfs. of Eng. operas, and foreign works in trans.

Rosalia, the usual name for the Real Sequence repeating a phrase higher or lower, not within the scale of the same key, as in the Tonal Sequence, but by so changing the key that its steps retain exactly the same succession of whole tones and semitones e.g.:

ROSALIA

The name derives from an Italian popular song, 'Rosalia, mia cara', in which this device occurs. *See also* **Schusterfleck**.

Rosamond, opera by Arne (lib. by J. Addison), prod. London, Theatre in Lincoln's Inn Fields, 7 Mar 1733.

Opera by Clayton (lib. do.), prod. London, Drury Lane Theatre, 4 Mar 1707.

Rosamunde, incid. music by Schubert for a play by Helmina von Chézy, *Rosamunde, Prinzessin von Cypern*, prod. Vienna, Theater an der Wien, 20 Dec 1823. The music consists of 3 entr'actes, 2 ballet tunes, a romance for contralto, a chorus of spirits, a shepherd's melody and shepherds' chorus and a hunting-chorus. No overture was specially written for the piece. At the fp, that to the opera *Alfonso und Estrella* was used; later that to the melodrama *Die Zauberharfe* was pub. as *Rosamunde* overture and is still so played.

Rosbaud, Hans (b Graz, 22 Jul 1895; d Lugano, 29 Dec 1962), Austrian conductor. He studied at the Frankfurt Cons. and began his career as a cond. at Mainz in 1921. His numerous other appts. incl. the Radio Orch. at Baden-Baden, from 1948, the Zurich Opera, 1950–8, and the festivals at Aix-en-Provence and Donaueschingen. He had a unique reputation as an interpreter of contemporary music; gave the concert and stage fps of Schoenberg's *Moses und Aron* (1954, 1957). His Boulez fps incl. *Le marteau sans maître* and *Improvisation sur Mallarmé*.

Rose, the ornamental fretwork soundhole of many flat-bellied string instruments of the lute and guitar type, also of dulcimers, harpsichords, etc., sometimes serving as the makers' trade-mark. Another name for it is Knot.

Rosé, Arnold (Josef) (b Jassy, Rumania, 24 Oct 1863; d London, 25 Aug 1946), Austro-Hungarian violinist. He was leader of the opera orch. in Vienna from 1881 to 1938 and founded the Rosé 4tet in 1882; gave the fps of Schoenberg's 1st two 4tets (1907, 1908), also *Verklärte Nacht* (1902). He married a sister of Mahler.

Rose et Colas, opera by Monsigny (lib. by J.M. Sedaine), prod. Paris, Comédie-Italienne, 8 Mar 1764.

Rose, Leonard (b Washington, DC, 27 Jun 1918; d White Plains, NY, 16 Nov 1984), American cellist. Studied at Curtis Inst., Philadelphia, with F. Salmond and then played in the NBC Orch. under Toscanini and later as 1st cello in the NY PO. From 1951 he taught at the Juilliard and the Curtis Inst., and also pursued a distinguished career as a soloist.

Rose of Castille (*sic*), **The,** opera by Balfe (lib. by A.G. Harris and E. Falconer, based on a Fr. lib., *Le Muletier de Tolède*, by A.P. d'Ennery and Clairville, set by A. Adam and prod. 1854), prod. London, Lyceum Theatre, 29 Oct 1857.

Rose of Persia, The, or The Story-Teller and the Slave, operetta by Sullivan (lib. by B. Hood), prod. London, Savoy Theatre, 29 Nov 1899.

Rose vom Liebesgarten, Die, opera by Pfitzner (lib. by J. Grun); comp. 1897–1900, prod. Elberfeld, 9 Nov 1901.

Roseingrave, (English) family of musicians:
1. **Daniel R.** (*c* 1650; d Dublin, May 1727), organist and composer. Educ. in music as a chorister in the Chapel Royal in London. From 1679–98 he was successively organist of Gloucester, Winchester and

Salisbury Cathedrals, and was then app. to St Patrick's and Christ Church Cathedrals, Dublin.
Works incl. services, anthems, etc.

2. **Thomas R.** (b Winchester, 1688; d Dunleary nr. Dublin, 23 Jun 1766), English organist and composer, son of prec. Pupil of his father at Dublin, where he was educ. at Trinity Coll. In 1710 he went to It. where he met A. and D. Scarlatti, making great friends with the latter and travelling with him. He went to London before 1720, when he prod. D. Scarlatti's opera *Narcisco* with interpolations of his own. In 1725 he was app. organist of St. George's church, Hanover Square. He retired in 1741 and moved to Dublin, living prob. with his nephew William R.
Works incl. opera *Phaedra and Hippolytus* (on Edmund Smith's play based on Racine, 1753); services and anthems; org. voluntaries and fugues; suites for harpsichord and an intro. piece for his ed. of Scarlatti's sonatas; 12 solos for fl. and harpsichord; 12 It. cantatas (1735).

3. **Ralph R.** (b Salisbury, *c* 1695; d Dublin, 1747), English organist and composer, brother of prec. Studied with his father, who petitioned for him to succeed him as organist of St Patrick's Cathedral, Dublin, in 1719; but he was app. vicar-choral and not organist till 1726. He also became organist of Christ Church Cathedral on his father's death.
Works incl. services, anthems, etc.

Rosen, Charles (b New York, 5 May 1927), American pianist and musicologist. He studied at Princeton (M.A. 1949). Debut as pianist, NY, 1951; well known for his thoughtful interpretations of Bach, Beethoven and modern music. He has taught in NY and at Berkeley, Calif. Books incl. *The Classical Style* (1971), *Schoenberg* (1975) and *Sonata Forms* (1980).

Rosenberg, Hilding (Constantin) (b Bosjökloster, 21 Jun 1892; d Stockholm, 19 May 1985), Swedish composer and conductor. Studied at the Stockholm Cons., and at Dresden, Berlin, Vienna and Paris. On his return to Swed. he was cond. of the Stockholm Opera from 1932 to 1934.
Works incl. operas *Journey to America* (incl. *Railway Fugue*), *The Marionettes* (on Benavente's *Los intereses creados*, 1939), *The Isle of Felicity* (1945) and *The Two Princesses* (1940); choreographic pantomime *The Last Judgment*; ballet *Orpheus in the City* (1938), incid. music for Sophocles' *Oedipus Tyrannus*, Euripides' *Medea* and plays by Calderón, Goethe, Musset, O'Neill,

Masefield, and Obey; film music.

8 symphs. (1917–75) incl. no. 2 *Sinfonia grave*, no. 3 *The 4 Ages of Man*, no. 4 *The Revelation of St John*), 2 *Sinfonie da chiesa*, *Adagio non troppo*, 3 *Fantasy Pieces* for orch.; chamber symph., concerto and suite on Swed. folk tunes for strings, vln. concerto, 2 cello concertos.

12 string 4tets (1920–57), trios for fl., vln. and vla. and for ob., clar. and bassoon; sonata and suite for vln. and pf., sonatina for fl. and pf., sonata for unaccomp. vln.; pf. suite.

Rosenhain, Jacob (b Mannheim, 2 Dec 1813; d Baden-Baden, 21 Mar 1894), German pianist and composer. Studied with Kalliwoda, Schnyder von Wartensee and others, and made his 1st appearance as a pianist at Frankfurt in 1832. He visited London in 1837 and then settled in Paris, where he played and taught.

Works incl. operas *Der Besuch im Irrenhause*, *Liswenna (Le Démon de la Nuit* 1851), *Volage et jaloux*; 3 symphs.; pf. concerto; 3 string 4tets, 4 pf. trios; 2 cello and pf. sonatas; sonata, studies and pieces for pf.; songs.

Rosenkavalier, Der (*The Rose Cavalier*), opera by R. Strauss (lib. by Hugo von Hofmannsthal), prod. Dresden, Royal Opera, 26 Jan 1911.

Rosenmüller, Johann (b Ölsnitz, Saxony, *c* 1619; d Wolfenbüttel, buried 12 Sep 1684), German composer. Studied at Leipzig Univ. and in 1642 became asst. master at St Thomas's School there, studying music with the cantor, Tobias Michael, and acting as his deputy when he became infirm. He was marked out for the succession and in 1651 became organist of St Nicholas's Church; but in 1655 he was imprisoned for homosexual offences with his choir-boys, escaping to Hamburg and later fleeing to Venice, where he settled and was influenced as a comp. by the local style. There J.P. Krieger became his pupil. In 1674 he was recalled to Ger. by an appt. to the court of Duke Anton Ulrich of Brunswick, at Wolfenbüttel.

Works incl. Masses, motets, vesper psalms and Lamentations, Lat. and Ger. motets *Kernsprüche* for 3–7 voices and insts., Ger. motets and cantatas, hymns, hymn by Albinus 'Straf mich nicht'; *Sonata da camera* for 5 insts., sonatas for 2–5 insts., suites of instrumental dances.

Rosenstock, Joseph (b Kraków, 27 Jan 1895; d New York, 17 Oct 1985), American conductor of Polish birth. Studied at Kraków Cons. and with Schreker in Vienna.

Held opera appts. at Darmstadt, Wiesbaden and Mannheim (1922–33). NY Met debut 1929 (*Meistersinger*). Tokyo 1936–41. Music dir. NY City Opera 1948–55; Cologne Opera 1958–61; returned to cond. in US 1961.

Rosenthal, Harold (b London, 30 Sep 1917; d London, 19 Mar 1987), English critic and writer on opera. He was archivist at CG, London, 1950–6 and in 1953 became editor of *Opera Magazine* (retired 1986). He broadcast and lectured in USA and Brit. Books incl. *Two Centuries of Opera at Covent Garden* (1958), *Concise Oxford Dictionary of Opera* (co-ed. with John Warrack, 1964, rev. 1979), autobiog. *My Mad World of Opera* (1983). Contrib. many entries on singers to the *New Grove Dictionary* and revised the Loewenberg *Annals of Opera*, 1978.

Rosenthal, Manuel (orig. **Emmanuel**) (b Paris, 18 Jun 1904), French composer and conductor. Studied at the Paris Cons., with Ravel and others. He became leader of var. orchs. From 1935 to 1939 and from 1944 to 1946 he cond. the Fr. Nat. Radio Orch. and from 1949 to 1951 the Seattle SO.

Works incl. operas *Rayon des soieries* (1928) and *Hop Signor!* (1961); operettas *Les Bootleggers* and *La Poule noire*; ballet *Un Baiser pour rien*; oratorio *Saint François d'Assise* (1944); suite *Jeanne d'Arc*, *Fête du vin*, *Les Petits Métiers*, serenade for orch.; sonatina for 2 vlns. and pf.; pf. pieces; songs.

Rosenthal, Moriz (b Lwów, 18 Dec 1862; d New York, 3 Sep 1946), Polish pianist, son of a prof. at the Academy of Lwów. He began to learn the pf. at the age of 8 and in 1872 entered the Lwów Cons., where he studied under the director Carl Mikuli. In 1875 the family moved to Vienna, where he continued his studies under Joseffy. He gave his 1st recital there in 1876 and then began to tour, finishing his studies with Liszt and also qualifying in philosophy. In 1895 he 1st appeared in Eng.

Rosetti, Francesco Antonio. *See* **Rösler.**

Rosin (also called Resin), a preparation made of gum of turpentine applied to the hair of the bows of string instruments to prod. the required friction on the strings.

Rosina, ballad opera by Shield (lib. by F. Brooke, based on an episode in Thomson's *Seasons* and Favart's *Les Moissonneurs* with Duni's music, prod. London, CG, 31 Dec 1782.

Rosinda, opera by Cavalli (lib. by G. Faustini), prod. Venice, Teatro San Apollinaire, 1651.

Roslavets, Nikolai Andreievich (b Surai, Gvt. of Tchernigov, 5 Jan 1881; d Moscow, 23 Aug 1944), Russian composer. He came of peasant stock, but studied music at the Moscow Cons. and attracted attention by his advanced tendencies.

Works incl. cantata *Heaven and Earth* (after Byron, 1912); symph., 2 symph. poems; 5 string 4tets (no. 3 12-tone), 5tet for ob., 2 vlns., cello and harp, 2 pf. trios; 5 vln. and pf. sonatas, 2 cello and pf. sonatas; many pf. pieces; songs.

Rösler, Franz Anton (b Litoměřice, c 1750; d Ludwigslust, Mecklenburg-Schwerin, 30 Jun 1792), Bohemian composer. Destined for the priesthood, he attended the Jesuit Coll. of Olomouc, but in 1773 entered the service of the Prince of Ottingen as double bass player and later became cond. He left for Ludwigslust in 1789 and was court music dir. there to his death. He wrote under the name of Francesco Antonio Rosetti.

Works incl. opera *Das Winterfest der Hirten* (1789); oratorios *Der sterbende Jesus* (1786) and *Jesus in Gethsemane*; Requiem for Mozart (1791); 34 symphs.; concertos for pf., vln., fl., ob., clar. and horn; chamber music, vln. sonatas.

Rosmene, La, ovvero L'Infedeltà fedele (*R., or Faithful Faithlessness*), opera by A. Scarlatti (lib. by G.D. de Totis), prod. Naples, Palazzo Reale, Carnival 1688.

Rosselini, Renzo (b Rome, 2 Feb 1908; d Monte Carlo, 14 May 1982), Italian composer. Pupil of Sallustio, Setacioli and Molinari.

Works incl. operas *Alcassino e Nicoletta* (1930), *La guerra* (1956), *Uno squàrdo dal ponte* (after A. Miller, 1961) and *La Reine Morte* (1973); ballet *La danza di Dassine* (1935), (music adapted from *Hoggar* suite); 2 oratorios; film music, rhapsodic suite *Hoggar*, *Preludio all' Aminta del Tasso*, *Canti di marzo* and *Ditirambo a Dioniso* for orch.; pf. trio.

Rosseter, Philip (b c 1568; d London, 5 May 1623), English lutenist and composer. Worked in London and was assoc. with R. Jones, Kingham and Reeve in the training of the children for the queen's revels; from 1610 he was licensed with Jones to mount plays at the Whitefriars theatre. With Campion pub. a book of songs to the lute, some if not all of the words by Campion and half of the music by Rosseter.

Works incl. *A Booke of Ayres* with lute, orpheoreon and bass viol; *Lessons for the Consort* for 6 insts. by various composers.

Rossetto, Stefano (b Nice), Italian 16th-cent. organist and composer. He lived at Florence in the 1560s as musician to Cardinal de' Medici, was court organist at Munich in 1579–80 and later (?) organist at Novara.

Works incl. motets in 5–6 parts for voice and insts. in different combinations; madrigal cycle *Il lamento di Olimpia* (1566), other madrigals for 4–6 voices.

Rossi, Giovanni Gaetano (b Borgo San Donnino nr. Parma, 5 Aug 1828; d Genoa 31 Mar 1886), Italian composer and conductor. Studied at the Milan Cons. App. leader of the theatre orch. and organist at the court chapel of Parma; dir. of the Cons. there in 1864–73; cond. of the Teatro Carlo Felice at Genoa, 1873–9.

Works incl. operas *Elena di Taranto* (1852), *Giovanni Giscala* (1855), *Nicolò de' Lapi* (1865), *La Contessa d'Altemberg*; 3 Masses, Requiem; oratorio; symph *Saul*.

Rossi, Lauro (b Macerata, 19 Feb 1810; d Cremona, 5 May 1885), Italian composer. Studied at Naples with Zingarelli and others, and began to prod. operas at the age of 18. He had much success in It. cities until 1835, when he left for Mex. in disgust after a failure. Thence he went as far as India, but returned to Europe in 1843 and again prod. many operas. In 1870 he succeeded Mercadante as dir. of the Naples Cons.

Works incl. operas *La contesse villane* (1829), *Il casino di campagna*, *Costanza ed Oringaldo*, *La casa disabitata* (1834), *Amelia*, *Leocadia*, *Cellini a Parigi* (1845), *Azema di Granata* (1846), *Il borgomastro di Schiedam*, *Il domino nero* (1849), *Bianca Contarini*, *La Contessa di Mons* (1874), *La figlia di Figaro* (1846), *Biorn* (after Shakespeare's *Macbeth*) and 15 others; oratorio *Saul*; Mass; 6 fugues for strings; elegies on the deaths of Bellini and Mercadante.

Rossi, Luigi (b Torremaggiore c 1598; d Rome, 20 Feb 1653), Italian singer and composer. He was in the service of Cardinal Barberini in Rome 1641–6. In 1646 he was called to Paris at the instigation of Mazarin and prod. his *Orfeo* in 1647 as one of the 1st It. operas to be given there.

Works incl. operas *Il palagio d'Atlante* (or *Il palazzo incantato*), *L'Orfeo* (1647); oratorio *Giuseppe, figlio di Giacobbe*, cantatas, etc.

Rossi, Michel Angelo (b Genoa c 1600; d Rome, buried 7 Jul 1656), Italian organist and composer, pupil of Frescobaldi. His opera *Erminia sul Giordano*, to a lib. by Giulio Rospigliosi, later Pope Clement IX, was given in Rome in 1633.

Works incl. operas *Erminia sul Giordano*

(after Tasso) and *Andromeda* (1638); toccatas and *correnti* for org. or harpsichord.

Rossi, Salomone (b ?Mantua, 19 Aug 1570; d ?, Mantua, *c* 1630), Italian composer. He worked at the court of Mantua (1587–1628) and enjoyed the privilege of dispensing with the wearing of the yellow badge that stigmatized the Jews in Italy.

Works incl. music for Guarini's *Idropica* and oratorio *Maddalena* (both with Monteverdi and others, 1608, 1617); 28 Hebrew psalms for 4–8 voices; madrigals and canzonets; instrumental works *Sinfonie e gagliarde* and *Sonate*.

Rossignol, Le (Stravinsky). *See* **Nightingale.**

Rossini, Gioachino (Antonio) (b Pesaro, 29 Feb 1792; d Passy nr. Paris, 13 Nov 1868), Italian composer. His father was a horn and tpt. player, his mother a singer in a small way. He learnt pf., singing and harmony early and sang in churches and in theatres; at 13 he was employed as an accompanist at the theatre; at 14, when he had already tried his hand at an opera and other works, he entered the Bologna Liceo Musicale, studying counterpoint and cello. In 1808 he won a prize with a cantata and in 1810 had his 1st comic opera, *La cambiale di matrimonio*, prod. at Venice. From that time he went from success to success, the 1st great one being *Tancredi* at Venice in 1813, but *Il barbiere di Siviglia* was at first a failure in Rome in 1816. His 1st great foreign success came during a visit to Vienna in 1822, soon after his marriage to the Span. soprano Isabella Colbran, 16 Mar. *Semiramide*, prod. at Venice in 1823, was his last opera written for the It. stage: he and his wife went to Paris and to London that year, remaining in Eng. until Jul 1824, being well received at court. He wrote a lament on the death of Byron for 8 voices.

On returning to Paris he was app. dir. of the Théâtre Italien, where he prod. a new and 2 revised works, followed by a Fr. comic opera, *Le Comte Ory*, and finally *Guillaume Tell* (1829) at the Opéra. After that, although only 37, he gave up opera and lived alternately at Bologna and Paris. In the early 1830s he met Olympe Pélissier, a *demi-mondaine*, and entered into a liaison with her; his separation from Isabella was legalized in 1837, she died in 1845, and he married Olympe on 21 Aug 1846. Serious illness afflicted him at this time, but he completed the *Stabat Mater* (1832–42). In 1839 he was commissioned to reform the Liceo Musicale at Bologna, where he had

once been a pupil, and he worked there at intervals until 1848, when he left for Florence, to remain until 1855, leaving It. for the last time for Paris that year. In his retirement he wrote many small pieces for the entertainment of his friends and in 1863 the *Petite Messe solennelle*; his musical soirées were much sought after by fashionable society and contemporary musicians.

Works incl. OPERAS: *La cambiale di matrimonio* (1810), *L'equivoco stravagante* (1811), *L'inganno felice* (1812), *Ciro in Babilonia* (1812), *La scala di seta* (1812), *La pietra del paragone* (1812), *L'occasione fa il ladro* (1812), *Il signor Bruschino* (1813), *Tancredi* (1813), *L'Italiana in Algeri* (1813), *Aureliano in Palmira* (1813), *Il Turco in Italia* (1814), *Sigismondo* (1814), *Elisabetta, regina d'Inghilterra* (1815), *Torvaldo e Dorliska* (1815), *Il barbiere di Siviglia* (after Beaumarchais, 1816), *La gazzetta* (1816), *Otello* (last act after Shakespeare, 1816), *La Cenerentola* (1817), *La gazza ladra* (1817), *Armida* (1818), *Adelaide di Borgogna* (1817), *Mosè in Egitto* (1818), *Adina* (1818), *Ricciardo e Zoraide* (1818), *Ermione* (on Racine's *Andromaque*, 1819), *Eduardo e Cristina* (1819), *La donna del lago* (after Scott, 1819) *Bianca e Falliero* (1819), *Maometto secondo* (1820), *Matilde di Shabran* (1821), *Zelmira* (1822), *Semiramide* (1823), *Il viaggio a Reims* (1825), *Le Siège de Corinthe* (Fr. revised version of *Maometto secondo*, 1826), *Moïse* (Fr. revised version of *Mosè in Egitto*, 1827), *Le Comte Ory* (1828), *Guillaume Tell* (after Schiller, 1829).

Messa di Gloria (1820), *Stabat Mater* (1842), *La Foi, l'Espérance, la Charité*, *Petite Messe solennelle* and some shorter sacred pieces; *Soirées musicales* (songs and duets); *Péchés de vieillesse* (small pf. pieces, songs, etc.); a number of works written in his youth incl. the opera *Demetrio e Polibio* (1812), a Mass for male voices, duets for horns, 4 overtures and 6 string 4tets. Pasticcios with music from his works were prod. in his lifetime, and a modern one is the ballet *La Boutique fantasque* arr. by Respighi from *Péchés de vieillesse*.

Rössler, Franz Anton. *See* **Rösler.**

Rostal, Max (b Teschen, 7 Aug 1905), Austrian violinist of British nationality. Studied with Rosé and Flesch, and in 1927 became leader of the Oslo PO. From 1930 to 1933 was prof. at the Berlin Hochschule für Musik. Since 1934 he has lived in Eng. and from 1944 to 1958 was prof. at the GSM. Among his many pupils have been members of the Amadeus Quartet. Although much of his time was spent teaching, his technical excellence and musicianship made him one of the leading violinists of his day. CBE 1977.

Rostropovich, Mstislav (Leopoldovich) (b Baku, 27 Mar 1927), Russian cellist, pianist and conductor. Studied at the Moscow Cons., where he became a prof. in 1957. He rapidly acquired a world-wide reputation as a soloist. He is also an accomplished pianist; often accompanies his wife, Galina Vishnevskaya; they were obliged to leave Russia in 1974. Debut as cond. Moscow, Bolshoy, 1968; London 1974. Prokofiev and Shostakovich wrote concertos for him, Britten the 3 suites for solo cello and cello symphony. Hon. KBE 1987.

Roswaenge, Helge (b Copenhagen, 29 Aug 1897; d Munich, 19 Jun 1972), Danish tenor. Debut Neustrelitz 1921, as Don José. He sang at the Berlin Staatsoper 1929–49 and in Vienna 1936–1960, as the Duke of Mantua, Calaf and Manrico. Bayreuth 1934–6, as Parsifal. He was admired by Toscanini and sang at Salzburg as Huon, Tamino and Florestan.

Rota, Andrea (b Bologna, c 1553; d Bologna, Jun 1597), Italian composer. He became choirmaster at San Petronio at Bologna in 1583.

Works incl. Masses, motets, *Agnus Dei* (with double canon), *Dixit Dominus* for 8 voices and other church music; madrigals.

Rota, Nino (b Milan, 3 Dec 1911; d Rome, 10 Apr 1979), Italian composer. Studied with Pizzetti, Casella and in USA. On his return to Milan he obtained a degree with a treatise on Zarlino and It. Renaissance music. App. director of the Bari Cons. in 1950.

Works incl. operas *Il principe porcaro* (after Hans Anderson, comp 1925), *Ariodante* (1942), *Il capello di paglia di Firenze* (The Italian straw hat, 1955); oratorio *L'infanzia di San Giovanni Battista*; 2 Masses; 3 symphs. (1936–9), serenade and concerto for orch.; *Invenzioni* for string 4tet, 5tet for fl., ob., vla., cello and harp., *Il presepio* for voice, string 4tet and pf.; sonatas for vln. and pf., vla. and pf. and fl. and harp; songs *Liriche di Tagore*, *Tre liriche infantili*; film music.

Rote, an instrument of the lyre type, also called Rota or Rotte, and similar to the Crwth. It was in use up to medieval times.

Rothenberger, Anneliese (b Mannheim, 19 Jun 1924), German soprano. Studied at Mannheim Musikhochschule and made her debut in Koblenz in 1943. She sang in Hamburg 1946–74, as Lulu, Sophie, Cherubino and Hindemith's Regina (role of Brit. debut, Edinburgh, 1952). In 1956 she became a member of the Deutsche Oper am Rhein, and in 1958 of the Vienna Staatsoper. She was equally at home in the classical and modern repertory and was one of the most successful singers on the German stage. NY Met debut 1960, as Zdenka.

Rothmüller, Marko (b Trnjani, 31 Dec 1908), Yugoslav baritone. He sang Rigoletto on his Hamburg debut, in 1932, and from 1935 to 1947 appeared at Zurich. In 1947 he sang Jochanaan at CG and returned until 1955 as Scarpia, and Wozzeck in the 1952 Brit. 1st stage perf. of Berg's opera. Glyndebourne 1949–55, as Guglielmo, the Count, Don Carlo, Macbeth and Nick Shadow. NY Met debut 1959, as Kothner; returned until 1964.

Rouget de Lisle, Claude Joseph (b Lons-le-Saulnier, 10 May 1760; d Choisy-le-Roi, 26–7 Jun 1836), French soldier, author and musician. Having embarked on a military career, he was stationed at Strasbourg in 1791 and made a name as poet, violinist and singer. He wrote the *Hymne à la liberté*, set by I. Pleyel, that year and words and music of the *Marseillaise* in 1792. Similar later pieces of the kind were *Hymne dithyrambique*, *Le Chant des vengeances*, *Le Chant des combats*, *Hymne à la Raison*, *Hymne du 9 Thermidor* and *Les Héros du Vengeur*. He also wrote libs., incl. *Bayard dans Bresse* for Champein and *Macbeth* (based on Shakespeare) for Chelard.

Round, a kind of Canon best defined by saying that its successive entries consist of complete melodies rather than mere phrases. The entries are thus apt to lie farther apart. Unlike canons, rounds are always sung with the theme in its orig. position or in the octave, never at other intervals. An older name for the round was Rota: *Sumer is icumen in*, known as the 'Reading Rota', is a typical early round. A familiar later ex. is in the 2nd-act finale of Mozart's *Così fan tutte*.

Rounds, round dances, i.e. dances perf. in circles, and hence tunes intended for such dances.

Rousseau, Jean-Jacques (b Geneva, 28 Jun 1712; d Ermenonville nr. Paris, 2 Jul 1778), Swiss-French, philosopher, author and composer. He was a chorister at Annecy Cathedral but had little formal training in music. Went to Paris in 1741, where he presented a paper to the Académie des Sciences advocating a new system of notation (pub. in 1743 as *Dissertation sur la musique moderne*) and later contrib. music articles to Diderot's *Encyclopédie* which were severely criticized by Rameau for their inaccuracy. As secretary to the Fr. ambassador in Venice 1743–4 he became acquainted with It. music, and during the Guerre des Bouffons sided with the It. party, decrying Fr. music in his controversial essay, *Lettre sur la musique française* (1753). His most important comp., the one-act *intermède Le Devin du village*, though in Fr., was supposedly written in tuneful It. style. In 1767 he pub. his valuable *Dictionnaire de musique*. The 'monodrama' *Pygmalion* (1770), only 2 pieces of which were by Rousseau, attempted to found a new form, and in its combination of spoken words and music was the ancestor of the later melodrama. Among his other writings are 2 essays in support of Gluck.

Comps. incl. operas *Iphis et Anaxerète* (1740), *La Découverte du nouveau monde* (1741), *Le Devin du village* (1752), *Daphnis et Chloé* (unfinished); opera-ballet *Les Muses galantes* (1745); monodrama *Pygmalion* (1770). *c* 100 songs, etc., pub. as *Consolations des misères de ma vie*.

Roussel, Albert (b Tourcoing, 5 Apr 1869; d Royan, 23 Aug 1937), French composer. Educ. in Paris for the Navy, but took pf. lessons at the same time. Wrote his 1st comps. while engaged in naval service and voyaging to the East, but he resigned in 1893 to devote himself to music, studying with Gigout and d'Indy. In 1902 he became prof. at the Schola Cantorum, where he had studied. In the 1914–18 war he served with the Red Cross and later with the transport service, in 1918 retired, broken in health, to Perros-Guirec in Brittany and in 1920 to a villa nr. Varengeville.

Works incl. STAGE: opera *Padmâvatî* (1923); operetta *Le Testament de Tante Caroline* (1936); ballets *Le Festin de l'araignée* (1913), *Bacchus et Ariane* (1931), *Énée*, *Les Enchantements d'Alcine* (after Ariosto) and contrib. to *L'Éventail de Jeanne*; incid. music to Jean-Aubry's *Le Marchand de sable qui passe* (1908), *La naissance de la Lyre* (1925), prelude to Act II of Roland's *14 Juillet* (with 6 others).

VOCAL AND ORCHESTRAL: Psalm lxxx for tenor, chorus and orch. (in Eng.); 4 symphs, 1908–34; (no. 1 *Le Poème de la forêt*), 3 *Évocations* (3rd with chorus), *Pour une fête de printemps*, *Suite en Fa* (1927), *Concert*, *Petite Suite* (1929), *Rapsodie flamande* for orch. (1936); sinfonietta for strings; *A Glorious Day* for military band; pf. concerto

(1927), concertino for cello and orch. (1936).

CHAMBER AND SONGS: string 4tet (1932), *Divertissement* for wind and pf. (1906), serenade for fl., vln., vla., cello and harp (1925), string trio, trios for vln. clar. and pf. and fl., vln. and clar.; 2 vln. and pf. sonatas, *Joueurs de flûte* for fl. and pf.; Impromptu for harp; *Segovia* for guitar; suite *Des heures passent*, *Rustiques*, suite, sonatina, prelude and fugue (*Hommage à Bach*), etc., for pf.; songs 6 *Odes anacréontiques* (1926), 2 *Poèmes chinois* (1927), 8 poems by Henri de Régnier, 2 poems by Ronsard, *A Flower given to my Daughter* (James Joyce).

Rousselière, Charles (St Nazir, 17 Jan 1875; d Joue-les-tours, 11 May 1950), French tenor. He studied in Paris and made his debut there in 1900 as Samson. He sang in operas by Mascagni and Saint-Saëns in Monte Carlo. In 1913 he created Charpentier's Julien and took part in the fp of Fauré's *Pénélope*. Met debut 1906, as Gounod's Roméo. Other roles incl. Siegmund, Parsifal, Loge, Max and Manrico.

Rovescio. *See* **Al Rovescio.**

Rovetta, Giovanni (b Venice, *c* 1595; d Venice, 23 Oct 1668), Italian priest and composer. Learnt music as a choir-boy at St Mark's in Venice and in 1623 was app. a bass there. He was ordained priest, became vice-*maestro di cappella* at St Mark's in 1627 and 1st *maestro di cappella* in succession to Monteverdi in 1644.

Works incl. Masses, motets, psalms, operas, *Ercole in Lidia* (1645) and *Argiope* (1649); madrigals.

Rowe, Walter (d Berlin, 1647), English 16th–17th-cent. violinist and composer. He was at Hamburg before 1614, when he was app. violist at the court chapel in Berlin. His son (d Berlin, Apr 1671) had the same name and occupation.

Works incl. music for vla. da gamba.

Rowicki, Witold (b Taganrog, 26 Feb 1914), Polish conductor of Russian birth. Studied at Kraków Cons. Music dir. Katowice Radio SO 1945–50, Warsaw PO 1958–77. Dir. Warsaw Theatre Opera Centre 1965–70. Often heard in Penderecki and Lutosławski.

Roxburgh, Edwin (b Liverpool, 6 Nov 1937), English composer, teacher and conductor. Studied at RCM and with Nono and Dallapiccola. Prof. of comp. at RCM from 1967. Active as oboist and cond. on behalf of modern music.

Works incl. Vars. for orch. (1963), *The Tower*, ballet (1964), *A Mosaic for Cum-*

mings for 2 narrators and orch. (1973), wind 5tet (1974), *The Rock*, oratorio (1979).

Roxelane, La, authentic name of Haydn's symph. no. 63 in C maj., comp. *c* 1777–80, so called apparently after an old Fr. melody used for variations in the slow movement.

Roy, Bartolomeo (b Burgundy, *c* 1530; d Naples, 2 Feb 1599), composer of French origin who lived for a time in Rome, and from 1583 until his death as *maestro di cappella* at the royal palace at Naples. Comp. madrigals and church music.

Royal Academy of Music, founded in London in 1822 and opened in Mar 1823 with Crotch as principal, who was followed by Potter (1832), Charles Lucas (1859), Sterndale Bennett (1866), Macfarren (1875), Mackenzie (1888), McEwen (1924), Stanley Marchant (1936), Reginald Thatcher (1949), Thomas Armstrong (1955), Anthony Lewis (1968), David Lumsden (1982).

Royal College of Music, founded in London in 1882 and opened on 7 May 1883 with Grove as director, who was followed by Parry (1894), Hugh Allen (1918), George Dyson (1937), Ernest Bullock (1953), Keith Falkner (1960), David Willcocks (1974), M. Gough Matthews (1985).

Royal Liverpool Philharmonic Orchestra, British orchestra founded 1840 with John Russell as cond. Julius Benedict was cond. 1867–79, Max Bruch 1880–3 and Charles Hallé 1883–95. Recent conds. have been Malcolm Sargent (1942–8), Hugo Rignold (1948–54), John Pritchard (1955–63), Charles Groves (1963–77) and Walter Weller (1977–80). David Atherton was chief cond. 1980–3, succeeded by Marek Janowski (1983–6). Libor Pesek from 1987.

Royal Manchester College of Music, founded in 1893. 1st prin. was Sir Charles Hallé, followed by A. Brodsky (1895), J.R. Forbes (1929), F.R. Cox (1953) and J. Wray (1970–2). In 1972 the RMCM merged with the Northern School of Music to form the Royal Northern College of Music (prin. J. Manduell).

Royal Musical Association, a society formed to promote the investigation of all aspects of music. It was founded in London in 1874 as The Musical Association and became 'Royal' in 1944. Apart from regular meetings and conferences, the Association publishes the *Proceedings of the RMA* (from 1987, *Journal of the RMA*), *RMA Research Chronicle* (founded 1961), *RMA Monographs* (founded 1985) and initiated *Musica Britannica* (1951).

Royal Northern College of Music. *See* **Royal Manchester College of Music.**

Royal Opera House. *See* **Covent Garden.**

Royal Philharmonic Orchestra. London-based orch. founded in 1946 by Beecham; he remained prin. cond. until his death in 1961. Rudolf Kempe was chief cond. 1961–3, cond. for life from 1970. Later conds. have been Antal Dorati (1975–8), Walter Weller (1980–5) and André Previn (1985–6). Vladimir Ashkenazy became musical dir. in 1987. The RPO was house orch. at the Glyndebourne Fest. 1947–63.

Royal Philharmonic Society, a society formed in London for the cultivation of good orchestral music in 1813 by J. B. Cramer, P. A. Corri and W. Dance. The 1st concert was given at the Argyll Rooms, 8 Mar 1813, cond. by Clementi (at the pf.) and led by J. P. Salomon. Among the 1st members were Attwood, Ayrton, Bishop, Horsley, Knyvett, V. Novello, Potter, Shield, G. Smart, Viotti and Webbe, jun. It has continued uninterruptedly until the present day. Among later conds. were Weber, Mendelssohn, Spohr, Wagner, Sullivan, Mackenzie, H. J. Wood, Nikisch, Chevillard, Elgar, Safonov, Bruno Walter, Beecham, Mengelberg, Stanford, Hamilton Harty, Furtwängler, Weingartner and Monteux. Beethoven figured in the programmes from the first and when he was on his deathbed the Society sent him the sum of £100.

Royal Winter Music, 2 sonatas on Shakespearean characters for guitar by Henze: no. 1 1975–6, fp Berlin, 20 Sep 1976, with Julian Bream; no. 2 1979, fp Brussels, 25 Nov 1980.

Rozhdestvensky, Gennady (b Moscow, 4 May 1931), Russian conductor. He studied at the Moscow Cons. and worked at the Bolshoy 1951–70, giving operas by Prokofiev and Britten as well as the usual ballets. His London debut was in 1956 and in 1970 he cond. *Boris Godunov* at CG. Chief cond. BBC SO 1978–81, Vienna SO from 1981. He is experienced in a much wider range of modern works than suggested by his limited programmes in London.

Rozkošný, Josef Richard (b Prague, 21 Sep 1833; d Prague, 3 Jun 1913), Czech pianist and composer. Studied in Prague and toured widely as pianist. Later had a great success as a popular opera comp.

Works incl. operas *Nicholas* (1870), *The Rapids of St John* (1871), *Cinderella* (1885), *Stoja, Zavis of Falkenstein* (1877), *Krakonos* (1889), *The Poacher, Satanella, The Black Lake* (1906); pf. pieces; songs.

Rózsa, Miklós (b Budapest, 18 Apr 1907), American composer of Hungarian birth. Studied pf. and comp. in Leipzig, and in 1932 settled in Paris, achieving success as a comp. In 1935 he moved to London, where he worked in the film industry and in 1939 settled in Hollywood.

Works incl. *Ballet Hungarica*; symph. (1930), *Scherzo, Theme, Variations and Finale* for orch. (1933); concert overture, serenade for chamber orch.; concerto for string orch.; 2 vln concertos, vla. concerto (1984); string 4tet; pf. 5tet, trio for vln., vla. and clar.; film music etc.

Rózycki, Ludomir (b Warsaw, 6 Nov 1883; d Katowice, 1 Jan 1953), Polish conductor and composer. Studied with Noskowski at the Warsaw Cons. and with Humperdinck in Berlin. In 1912 he became cond. at Lwów, and later lived by turns in Warsaw and Berlin.

Works incl. operas *Bolesław the Bold* (1908), *Medusa* (1911), *Eros and Psyche* (1916), *Casanova, Beatrice Cenci* (1926), *The Devil's Mill* (1930); ballet *Pan Twardowski*; symph. poems *Bolesław the Bold, Anhelli* and others, prelude *Mona Lisa Giaconda* and ballad for orch.; pf. concerto in G min.; string 4tet (1916), pf. 5tet (1913), pf. music, songs.

Rubato (Italian lit. 'robbed'), a manner of perf. music without adhering strictly to time. Var. rules have been estab. at different times, e.g. that what is taken away by hurrying from the time properly occupied by a comp. as written, must be given back elsewhere by slackening, or that in pf. music the right hand only may play rubato while the left keeps strict time; but rubato should be subject, not to rules, but to feeling, and it cannot be taught to those who have either no musical sense or an exaggerated notion of it.

Rubbra, Edmund (b Northampton, 23 May 1901; d Gerrards Cross, 14 Feb 1986), English composer. Studied at Reading Univ. and the RCM in London, Holst, Vaughan Williams and R.O. Morris being among his masters. Lecturer at Oxford Univ. from 1947 to 1968.

Works incl. STAGE AND CHORAL: *Bee-Bee-Bei* (1933), incid. music for Shakespeare's *Macbeth*; Canterbury Mass, (1945), *Missa in honorem Sancti Dominici* (1948), Festival Te Deum; *La Belle Dame sans merci* (Keats) and *The Morning Watch* (Henry Vaughan) for chorus and orch.; Masses, motets, madrigals and other choral works.

ORCH: 11 symphs. (1935–79), Double and Triple Fugues, *Improvisations on Virginal*

Pieces by Farnaby (1939) and Festival Overture for orch.; *Sinfonia concertante* for pf. and orch., rhapsody for vln. and orch., vla. concerto (1953), pf. concerto (1956), *Soliloquy* for cello and small orch.; works for voice and orch.

CHAMBER: 4 string 4tets (1934–77), trio for vln., cello and pf. and other chamber music; 5 sonnets by Spenser for voice and string 4tet (1935); 3 sonatas and sonatina for vln. and pf., cello and pf. sonata; pf. and organ music; songs.

Rubinelli, Giovanni Battista (b Brescia, 1753; d Brescia, 1829), Italian castrato alto. Made his debut in 1771 in Stuttgart, where he was in the service of the Duke of Württemberg, but from 1774 sang in the leading It. opera houses. Visited London in 1786, singing in revivals of operas by Handel. He retired in 1800.

Rubini, Giovanni Battista (b Romano nr. Bergamo, 7 Apr 1794; d Romano, 3 Mar 1854), Italian tenor. He began with small engagements, but made his way to Venice, Naples and Rome, where his successes in opera increased steadily. In 1819 he married the Fr. singer Chomel at Naples, visited Paris for the 1st time in 1825 and sang in Rossini's *Cenerentola, Otello* and *Donna del lago*. He created leading roles in Bellini's *Bianca e Gernando, Il pirata, La sonnambula* and *I Puritani*. London, 1831–43. In 1843 he toured Hol. and Ger. with Liszt, and went on alone to St Petersburg.

Rubinstein, Anton Grigorievich (b Vykhvatinets, Volhynia, 28 Nov 1829; d Peterhof, 20 Nov 1894), Russian pianist and composer of German–Polish descent. Learnt the pf. from his mother and from a teacher named Villoing at Moscow. He appeared in public at the age of 9 and in 1840 went on tour with his teacher, who took him to Paris and placed him under Liszt for further instruction. He afterwards toured in Europe and from 1844 to 1846 studied comp. with Dehn in Berlin. After teaching in Vienna and Pressburg he returned to Russia in 1848, becoming chamber virtuoso to the Grand Duchess Helena Pavlovna. From 1854 onward he again travelled widely as a pianist and in 1858 he was app. imperial music dir. at St Petersburg, founding the Cons. in 1862.

Works incl. OPERAS AND STAGE ORATORIOS: *Dimitry Donskoy* (1852), *The Siberian Hunters* (1854), *Children of the Heath* (1858), *Feramors* (from Moore's *Lalla Rookh*, 1863), *The Tower of Babel* (1870), *The Demon* (after Lermontov, 1875), *The Maccabees* (after Otto Ludwig, 1875) *Para-*

dise Lost (after Milton, 1875), *Nero* (1879), *The Merchant of Moscow* (1880), *The Shulamite, Moses* (1892), *Christus* and others.

VOCAL AND ORCHESTRAL: Songs and Requiem for Mignon from Goethe's *Wilhelm Meister* for solo voices, chorus and pf.; 6 symphs., 1850–86: (2. *Ocean*, 4. *Dramatic*), 4 concert overtures (1 on Shakespeare's *Antony and Cleopatra*), musical portraits *Faust* (after Goethe), *Ivan the Terrible, Don Quixote* (after Cervantes), suite in E♭ maj. for orch. (1894); 5 concertos and *Conzertstück* for pf. and orch. (1850–89); vln. concerto, 2 cello concertos.

CHAMBER: 10 string 4tets (1855–81), string 5tet and 6tet, octet for pf., strings and wind, 5 pf. trios, pf. and wind 5tet, pf. 5tet and 4tet; 3 vln. and pf. sonatas; instrumental pieces; 4 sonatas, Theme and Variations and many other works for piano; songs.

Rubinstein, Arthur (b Łódź, 28 Jan 1886; d Geneva, 20 Dec 1982), American pianist of Polish birth. After early studies in Poland he was sent to Berlin, studying pf. with H. Barth and R.M. Breithaupt, comp. with R. Kahn and with Bruch. He made his debut aged 12 in a concert cond. by Joachim. He then studied with Paderewski in Switz., and toured the USA in 1906. In 1946 he became an American citizen. He was best known for his playing of Chopin, to which he brought great virtuosity combined with elegance and poetry.

Rubinstein, Nikolai Grigorievich (b Moscow, 14 Jun 1835; d Paris, 23 Mar 1881), Russian pianist and composer of German–Polish descent, brother of Anton. Studied under Kullak and Dehn in Berlin and after his return to Rus. settled at Moscow, where he founded the Rus. Music Society in 1859 and the Cons. in 1864, to which he invited Tchaikovsky as prof.

Rubsamen, Walter H(oward) (b New York, 21 Jul 1911; d Los Angeles, 19 Jun 1973), American musicologist. Studied at Columbia Coll., NY, and at Munich Univ., later joined the music dept. of his coll. and in 1938 became lecturer and in 1955 prof. at the Univ. of California at Los Angeles. His works incl. studies of Pierre de La Rue, old It. secular music, etc.

Ruckers. Flemish family of harpsichord makers:

1. Hans R. (b Mechlin, *c* 1550; d Antwerp, 1598).

2. Joannes R. (b Antwerp, bap. 15 Jan 1578; d Antwerp, 24 Apr 1642), son of prec.

3. Andries R. (b Antwerp, bap. 15 Aug 1579; d Antwerp, *c* 1645), brother of prec.

4. Andries R. (b Antwerp, bap. 31 Mar 1607; d Antwerp, before 1667), son of prec.

Rückert, Friedrich (1788–1866), German poet. See **Kindertotenlieder** (Mahler), also 5 other songs by Mahler for voice and orch. (*Ich atmet' einen linden Duft, Liebst du um Schönheit, Blicke mir nicht in die Lieder, Ich bin der Welt abhanden gekommen, Um Mitternacht*, 1901–3), 5 songs by Schubert, 18 by Schumann, 2 by Brahms.

Rückpositiv (Ger. = back positive), small organ at organist's back, to the front of the gallery. From 15th–17th cents. the second main manual of most organs, providing colouristic and contrasting functions.

Ruddigore, or The Witch's Curse, operetta by Sullivan (lib. by W.S. Gilbert), prod. London, Savoy Theatre, 22 Jan 1887.

Rudersdorff, Hermine (b Ivanovsky, Ukraine, 12 Dec 1822; d Boston, 26 Feb 1882), German soprano. Learnt music from her father, the violinist Joseph R., and singing in Paris, Milan and London. She made her 1st appearance in Ger. at the age of 18, sang in the prod. of Mendelssohn's *Hymn of Praise* at Leipzig in 1840 and then appeared in opera at Karlsruhe and Frankfurt. In 1854 she 1st visited London, where she remained for a number of years, but settled in Boston in the 1870s.

Rudhyar, Dane (actually Daniel Chennevière) (b Paris, 23 Mar 1895; d San Francisco, 13 Sep 1985), French-American composer. Studied in Paris and settled in USA in 1916, receiving a comp. prize in 1920.

Works incl. ballet *Dance Poem*; symph. poem *Surge of Fire* (1920), 6 'syntonies' for orch. (1920–59), *Cosmic Cycle* for orch. (1981); pf. music and songs.

Rudolph (Johann Joseph Rainer) of Habsburg, Archduke (b Florence, 8 Jan 1788; d Baden nr. Vienna, 24 Jul 1831), Austrian amateur musician. Pupil of Anton Teyber (music instructor of the Imperial children), and later of Beethoven, who wrote the *Missa solemnis* for his installation as Archbishop of Olomouc (1820), though he finished it 2 years too late. Beethoven also dedicated the 4th and 5th pf. concertos, Archduke trio and 'Hammerklavier' sonata to him.

Works incl. sonata for clar. and pf.; variations for pf. on themes by Beethoven and Rossini.

Rudorff, Ernst (Friedrich Karl) (b Berlin, 18 Jan 1840; d Berlin, 31 Dec 1916), German pianist, teacher and composer. Pupil of Bargiel, Clara Schumann and others, later studied at the Leipzig Univ. and Cons. In 1865 he became prof. at the Cologne Cons. and in 1869–1910 at the Hochschule für Musik in Berlin. He also cond. Stern's Vocal Acad. in 1880–90.

Works incl. *Der Aufzug der Romanze* (Tieck) for solo voices, chorus and orch., *Gesang an die Sterne* (Rückert) for chorus and orch.; 3 symphs., 2 sets of variations, ballad, serenade, 3 overtures for orch.; romance for cello and orch.; string 6tet; variatïons for 2 pfs.; pieces for pf. solo and duet; songs, part-songs.

Rue, Pierre de la. *See* **La Rue.**

Rufer, Josef (b Vienna, 18 Dec 1893; d Berlin, 7 Nov 1985), Austrian writer on music. Studied with Zemlinsky and Schoenberg, becoming Schoenberg's asst. in Berlin from 1925 to 1933. In 1945, with H.H. Stuckenschmidt, he founded the periodical *Stimmen*, and from 1956 taught at the Free Univ. in Berlin. His books on music incl. *Composition with 12 notes related only to one another* (a study of Schoenberg's methods) and the valuable catalogue *The Works of Arnold Schoenberg* (1959).

Ruffo, Titta (b Pisa, 9 Jun 1877; d Florence, 6 Jul 1953), Italian baritone. He studied in Rome and made his debut there in 1898. Wider recognition came in 1903, with appearances in London and Milan, and until 1931 he was heard in Europe and N. and S. America as Hamlet, Luna, Renato, Nelusko and Barnaba. US debut Philadelphia 1912, as Rigoletto; NY Met 1922–8 (debut as Rossini's Figaro).

Ruffo, Vincenzo (b Verona, *c* 1510; d Sacile nr. Udine, 9 Feb 1587), Italian male soprano and composer. App. *maestro di cappella* at Verona Cathedral in 1554 and from 1563 to 1572 at that of Milan. He occupied a similar post at Pistoia in 1574–9, but then returned to Milan. His sacred music shows the influence of Tridentine reforms, which insisted on verbal clarity.

Works incl. Masses, motets, Magnificat, psalms and other church music; madrigals.

Rugby, Honegger's 2nd symph. movement for orch., following *Pacific 231* and succeeded by *Mouvement symphonique No. 3.* It is an impression of a game of rugby football. Fp Paris, Orchestre Symphonique, 19 Oct 1928.

Ruggiero, a simple bass line, 1st found in the 16th cent., which was widely used for variations. A typical form is illustrated below. It may have orig. have been a dance, though it is found also in vocal settings. *See also* **Romanesca.**

Ruggiero, o vero L'eroica gratitudine(*Ruggiero, or Heroic Gratitude*), opera by Hasse (lib. by Metastasio), prod. Milan, Teatro Regio Ducal, 16 Oct 1771. Hasse's last opera.

Ruggles, Carl (b Marion, Mass., 11 Mar 1876; d Bennington, Vermont, 24 Oct 1971), American composer and painter. Studied at Harvard Univ., with Walter Spalding and others. Afterwards he cond. the Symph. Orch. at Winona, Minnesota, for a time.

Works incl. opera *The Sunken Bell* (comp. 1912–23), *Men and Angels* (1920), *Men and Mountains, Portals, Sun Treader* (1932), *Evocations* for orch. (1971); concertino for pf. and orch.; *Vox clamans in deserto* for voice and chamber orch.; *Polyphonic Comps.* for 3 pfs., *Evocations* and other works for pf.

Ruins of Athens, The, incid. music by Beethoven, op. 113, for a play by Kotzebue written for the opening of the Ger. theatre at Pest, 9 Feb 1812. It comprises an overture and 8 numbers, incl. the *Turkish March*, already comp. by Beethoven for his pf. variations, op. 76, in 1809.

Rule, Britannia, a patriotic song by Arne, now almost a 2nd Brit. nat. anthem, orig. part of the masque *Alfred*, prod. 1 Aug 1740, at Cliefden (now Cliveden) House nr. Maidenhead, the residence of Frederick, Prince of Wales.

Rule of the Octave, an 18th-cent. procedure in the treatment of Thorough-bass, esp. in It. (*regola dell' ottava*), providing a series of simple chords of the tonic, dominant and subdominant for the elementary harmonization of a bass formed by a rising diatonic scale.

Rung, Frederick (b Copenhagen, 14 Jun 1854; d Copenhagen, 22 Jan 1914), Danish composer and conductor. Pupil of his father

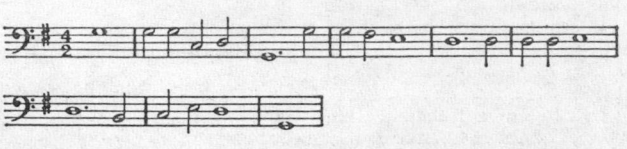

Henrik R. (1807–71), of Gade and others. He went to the Royal Opera, as coach, became asst. cond. in 1884 and succeeded Svendsen as 1st cond. in 1911; gave early Danish perfs of Wagner and Puccini. He also taught at the Cons. and Horneman's music school and cond. choral societies, incl. a madrigal choir founded by him.

Works incl. 2 operas, 2 ballets, symph. in D min, 2 string 4tets.

Rungenhagen, Carl Friedrich (b Berlin, 27 Sep 1778; d Berlin, 21 Dec 1851), German composer and conductor. Worked in Berlin, where he became asst. cond. to Zelter of the Vocal Acad. in 1815 and succeeded to the post of 1st cond. in 1833.

Works incl. 4 operas, 3 oratorios; Mass, *Stabat Mater* for female voices and other church music; orchestral works; chamber music; songs.

Ruslan and Ludmila, opera by Glinka (lib. by V.A. Shirkov and C.A. Bakhturin, based on Pushkin's poem), prod. St Petersburg, 9 Dec 1842.

Russalka (*The Water-Sprite*), opera by Dargomizhsky (lib. by comp., from Pushkin's dramatic poem), prod. St Petersburg, 16 May 1856.

Opera by Dvořák (lib. by J. Kvapil), prod. Prague, Cz. Theatre, 31 Mar 1901.

Russell, Henry (b Sheerness, 24 Dec 1812; d London, 8 Dec 1900), English singer, organist and composer. Studied at Bologna and with Rossini at Naples, appeared as singer in London in 1828, lived in Canada and USA (organist at Rochester, NY) in 1833–41 and then gave entertainments in London with Charles Mackay for which he wrote many popular songs. Landon Ronald (*q.v.*) was his illegitimate son.

Works incl. songs 'Cheer, boys, cheer', 'There's a good time coming', 'A life on the ocean wave' (march of the Royal Marines), etc.

Russian Bassoon, a Serpent made in the shape of a bassoon.

'Russian' Quartets, one of the nicknames of Haydn's 6 string 4tets, op. 33, comp. in 1781 and ded. to the Grand Duke of Russia. Also known as *Gli scherzi* or *Jungfernquartette*.

Russolo, Luigi (b Portogruaro, 30 Apr 1885; d Cerro, 6 Feb 1947), Italian composer. In 1909 he joined the Futurist movement of Marinetti and formulated a music based on noise, about which he pub. a book in 1916, *L'arte dei rumori*. His Futurist manifesto of 1913 expanded the orch. to include explosions, clashes, shrieks, screams and

groans. He also invented the Russolophone, which could produce 7 different noises in 12 different gradations.

Works incl. *Meeting of the Automobiles and the Aeroplanes, Awakening of a City*.

Rust, Friedrich Wilhelm (b Wörlitz nr. Dessau, 6 Jul 1739; d Dessau, 28 Feb 1796), German violinist and composer. Pupil of W.F. Bach in Halle, where he studied law, then of F. Benda and C.P.E. Bach in Berlin, later of G. Benda, Pugnani and Tartini in It. 1765–6. He returned to Dessau in 1766, taught at Basedow's *Philanthropin* from its foundation in 1774, and a year later became municipal music director.

Works incl. monodramas and duodramas *Inkle und Yariko* (1777), *Colma* (1780), etc.; cantatas; odes and songs; pf. sonatas and other keyboard music.

Rust, Wilhelm (b Dessau, 15 Aug 1822; d Leipzig, 2 May 1892), German pianist, violinist and composer, grandson of prec. Studied with his uncle W.K.R. and F. Schneider and settled in Berlin as pianist organist and teacher. In 1870 he became prof. at the Stern Cons. there and in 1878 organist and 2 years later cantor at St Thomas's Church, Leipzig. He ed. his grandfather's pf. sonatas, much modernizing them, on the strength of which ed. d'Indy declared F.W.R. to be a prophetic forerunner of Beethoven.

Works incl. pf. and vocal music.

Rust, Wilhelm Karl (b Dessau, 29 Apr 1787; d Dessau, 18 Apr 1855), German pianist and teacher, uncle of prec. and son of F.W.R. Pupil of his father and of Türk at Halle. In 1807 he went to Vienna, where he met Beethoven, and remained there as teacher until 1827, when he returned to Dessau.

Rustic Wedding (*Ländliche Hochzeit*), symphonic poem by Goldmark, fp Vienna, 5 Mar 1876. Usually described today as a symphony.

Rutini, Fernando (b Modena, 1767; d Terracina, 13 Nov 1827), Italian composer, son and pupil of Giovanni Maria R., later *maestro di cappella* at Macerata and Terracina.

Works incl. 36 operas; cantatas; sonatas.

Rutini, Giovanni Maria (also called G. Marco and G. Placido) (b Florence, 25 Apr 1723; d Florence, 22 Dec 1797), Italian composer, father of prec. Pupil of Leo and Fago at the Cons. della Pietà dei Turchini in Naples, he went to Prague in 1748, where his first opera was prod. in 1753. Visited Dresden and Berlin, and went to St Petersburg in 1758. Returning to It. in 1762, he was *maestro di cappella* to the Crown Prince of Modena

1765–70, and lived mostly in Florence.

Works incl. *c* 20 operas, e.g. *Semiramide* (1753), *Il matrimonio in maschera* (1763), *L'Olandese in Italia* (1765), etc.; cantatas; vln. sonatas; numerous harpsichord sonatas.

Ruy Blas, opera by William Howard Glover (1819–75) (lib. by comp., based on Victor Hugo's drama), prod. London, Covent Garden Theatre, 24 Oct 1861.

Opera by Marchetti (lib., in It., by Carlo d'Ormeville, based on Hugo), prod. Milan, La Scala, 3 Apr 1869.

Overture and chorus for Hugo's drama by Mendelssohn, op. 95 and op. 77 no. 3, comp. for a prod. at Leipzig, 9 Mar 1839.

Ruyneman, Daniel (b Amsterdam, 8 Aug 1886; d Amsterdam, 25 Jul 1963), Dutch composer. He was trained for commerce and self-taught in music. He made many experiments with comp. and instruments and invented cup-bells with a rich and long-sustained sonority, which he used in several of his works.

Works incl. opera *The Brothers Karamazov* (1928), psycho-symbolic play with vocal and instrumental orch. *The Clown* (1915); scena for tenor and orch. from Kafka's *Der Prozess*; 2 symphs, partita for strings, *Hieroglyphs* for chamber orch.; string 4tet (1946); sonata in G maj. and *Klaaglied van een Slaaf* for vln. and pf.; 9 sonatas, 3 *Pathemologies* and sonatina for pf.; 2 Sacred Songs (Tagore) and several other sets.

Ryelandt, Joseph (b Bruges, 7 Apr 1870; d Bruges, 29 Jun 1965), Belgian composer. Pupil of Tinel.

Works incl. opera *Sainte Cécile*; oratorios *La Parabole des vierges* (1894), *Purgatorium* (1904), *De Komst des Heeren* (1907), *Maria, Agnus Dei* and *Christus Rex* (1922), cantatas *Le Bon Pasteur* and *L'Idylle mystique*; 5 symphs. (1897–1934), symph. poem *Gethsémani*, 2 overtures for orch.; chamber music; 11 pf. sonatas; numerous songs.

Ryom, Peter (b Copenhagen, 31 May 1937), Danish musicologist. He catalogued Vivaldi's works in *Verzeichnis der Werke Antonio Vivaldis* (Leipzig, 1974; 2nd ed. 1979).

Rysanek, Leonie (b Vienna, 12 Nov 1926), Austrian soprano. Studied in Vienna with Jerger, and later with R. Grossmann, whom she married. She made her debut in Innsbruck in 1949 as Agathe, Bayreuth from 1951 as Sieglinde, Elsa, Senta and Elisabeth. From 1950 to 1952 she sang at the Saarbrucken Opera as Tosca and Arabella, and in 1954 became a member of the Vienna Opera. Admired in Strauss.

Rytel, Piotr (b Wilno, 20 Sep 1884; d Warsaw, 2 Jan 1970), Polish composer. Studied at the Warsaw Cons., and taught there from 1911 to 1952. He was rector of the Zoppot Cons. from 1952 to 1962. For many years he was active as a critic.

Works incl. opera *Ijola* (1828); ballet *Faun and Psyche* (1931); 4 symphs, symph. poems *The Corsair* (Byron), 1911, *Grazyna* (Mickiewicz), *Dante's Dream, The Holy Grove, The Legend of St George* (1918), *An Intro. to a Drama*; pf. concerto, vln. concerto (1950); chamber music; pf. works; songs.

S

s, the Dominant note in any key in Tonic Sol-fa notation, pronounced Soh.

Sabaneiev, Leonid Leonidovich (b Moscow, 1 Oct 1881; d Antibes, 3 May 1968), Russian critic and composer. Studied with Taneiev at the Moscow Cons. and at the univ. there. He left Rus. in 1929 and settled eventually in France. He wrote on Skriabin, Debussy and Taneiev; also wrote an attack on Prokofiev's *Scythian Suite* at a concert that did not take place.

Works incl. ballet *L'Aviatrice*; symph. poem *Flots d'azur*; chamber music; songs; pf. music.

Sabata, Victor de. *See* De Sabata.

Sabatier, Caroline. *See* Unger.

Sabbatini, Galeazzo (b ? Pesaro, 1597; d Pesaro, 6 Dec 1662), Italian composer. He was *maestro di cappella* at Pesaro in the 1620s and dir. of chamber music to the Duke of Mirandola in the 1630s. He was also at Bergamo some time. In 1628 he pub. a treatise on thorough-bass.

Works incl. Masses, motets, 2 books of *Sacrae faudes* (1637, 1641) and other church music; madrigals.

Sabbatini, Luigi Antonio (b Albano Laziale nr. Rome, 24 Oct 1732; d Padua, 29 Jan 1809), Italian composer. A pupil of Padre Martini and Vallotti, he was *maestro di cappella* of Marione Cathedral 1766, at the Church of the Holy Apostles in Rome 1772, finally from 1786 at S Antonio in Padua. He pub. a number of treatises on counterpoint, fugue, etc. Comp. chiefly church music.

Works incl. Masses, motets, psalms.

Sabbatini, Pietro Paolo (b Rome, *c* 1600; d ? Rome, after 1657), Italian composer. He was *maestro di cappella* in Rome, from 1630 of the church of San Luigi de' Francesci, and prof. of music from 1650, when he pub. a treatise on thorough-bass.

Works incl. psalms, spiritual songs; *villanelle* and *canzonette* for 1–3 voices, etc.

Sabino, Ippolito (b Lanciano, Chieto, 1550; d Lanciano, 25 Aug 1593), Italian composer. In 1587 he was employed as a musician in the cathedral of his native town. He pub. many collections of church music and madrigals; two of the latter contain madrigals by his brother (?) Giovanni Francesco.

Sacchini, Antonio Maria Gaspare (b Florence, 14 Jun 1730; d Paris, 6 Oct 1786), Italian composer. Pupil of Durante at the Cons. Santa Maria di Loreto at Naples, where his intermezzo *Fra Donato* was prod. in 1756. He worked first at the Cons., but prod. his 1st serious opera, *Andromaca*, in 1761, and 3 years later gave up his teaching to devote himself to comp. After a time in Rome he went to Venice in 1769, where he became dir. of the Ospedaletto. Visited Ger., and in 1772 went to London, remaining there 10 years and prod. many operas. Settling in Paris in 1782, he had the support of Marie Antoinette, and there wrote 2 operas which show the influence of Gluck. But (like Gluck before him) he became unwillingly involved in rivalry with Piccinni and had little success.

Works incl. *c* 60 operas, e.g. *Alessandro nell' Indie* (1763), *Semiramide* (1764), *Isola d'amore*, *Il Cidde* (after Corneille), *Armida* (1772), *Tamerlano*, *Perseo* (1774), *Nitetti*, *Montezuma* (1775), *Rosina*, *Dardanus*, *Oedipe à Colone* (1786), etc.; Masses, motets and other church music; 2 symphs.; string 4tets, trio sonatas and other chamber music; vln. sonatas.

Sacher, Paul (b Basle, 28 Apr 1906), Swiss conductor. Studied with Nef and Weingartner, and in 1926 founded the Basle Chamber Orch., for which he commissioned works from many distinguished comps. incl. Bartók (Divertimento), Fortner, Henze, Hindemith, Honegger, Ibert, Krenek, Martin, Martinů, Malipiero, Roussel, Strauss, Stravinsky and Tippett; composers of the Second Viennese School were not favoured. In 1933 he also founded the distinguished chamber ensemble Schola Cantorum Basiliensis.

Sachs, Curt (b Berlin, 29 Jun 1881; d New York, 5 Feb 1959), German musicologist. First studied history of art at Berlin Univ., graduating in 1904. After some years as an art critic he studied music with Kretzschmar and J. Wolf, specializing in the history of musical insts. In 1919 he became dir. of the Berlin Museum of Musical Instruments, and also prof. at Berlin Univ. From 1933 to 1937 he lived in Paris, then moved to NY, where he became prof. at the univ. From 1953 he was also prof. at Columbia Univ., in NY. His many writings extend not only over the field of musical insts. but also over many others.

Sachs, Hans (1494–1576), German cobbler, master-singer and poet. He wrote more than 4,000 poems and features in Wagner's *Die Meistersinger* (the longest role in all opera).

Sack, Erna (b Berlin, 6 Feb 1898; d Wiesbaden, 2 Mar 1972), German soprano. She sang in Berlin from 1925 and joined the Dresden Opera 1935; created Isotta in *Die schweigsame Frau*. She visited CG with the Dresden co. in 1936, as Zerbinetta, and Chicago in 1937, as Rosina and Lucia. World wide concert tours either side of the war. Her unusually wide vocal range earned her the nickname 'the German nightingale'.

Sackbut, early version of the trombone. 4 sizes were listed by Praetorius, from alto to great bass.

Sadie, Stanley (John) (b Wembley, 30 Oct 1930), English critic, writer and editor. He studied at Cambridge with Thurston Dart and Charles Cudworth; MA 1957, PhD 1958. Music critic with *The Times* 1964–81, ed. *The Musical Times* 1967–87. He has written books on Handel, Mozart and Beethoven, and in 1970 became ed. of *The New Grove Dictionary of Music and Musicians*; 10 years and 2,326 contributors later the 20 vols. were pub. Many offshoots have since appeared under Sadie's direction, e.g. the *NG Dictionary of Musical Insts.* (1984) and, with H. Wiley Hitchcock, the *NG Dictionary of American Music* (1986). General ed. of *Master Musicians* series since 1976. CBE 1982.

Sadko, opera by Rimsky-Korsakov (lib. by comp. and V.I. Bielsky), prod. Moscow, 7 Jan 1898. The music is partly based on Rimsky-Korsakov's symph. poem of the same name, op. 5, comp. 1867, prod. St Petersburg, 21 Dec 1867; revised 1869 and 1892.

Sadler's Wells Opera. The Sadler's Wells theatre was built in the 18th cent., when Islington was a village outside London and Sadler's Wells a watering-place and pleasure garden dating back to the end of the 17th cent. It was used for plays and pantomime into the 19th cent., then became a music hall and later fell into disuse, but was acquired as a northern branch of the Old Vic Theatre for the alternate prod. of classical drama and opera, rebuilt and opened on 6 Jan 1931. From 1935 plays were confined exclusively to the Old Vic and opera to Sadler's Wells, which became the only permanent repertory opera-house in Brit. for the prod. of opera in Eng. In 1968 the operas were transferred to the Coliseum: co. became English National Opera in 1974 and continued with an adventurous repertory despite straitened circumstances (Busoni's *Dr. Faust* and Birtwistle's *The Mask of Orpheus*, 1986). Lord Harewood (*q.v.*) was manager 1972–85, then Peter Jonas.

Saedén, Erik (b Vänersborg, Stockholm, 3 Sep 1924), Swedish bass-baritone. Debut Stockholm 1952; well known there as Figaro, Pogner, Wozzeck and Wolfram, and took part in the fps of Blomdahl's *Aniara* (1959), Berwald's *Queen of Golconda* (1968) and Ligeti's *Le Grand Macabre* (1978). Bayreuth 1958, Kurwenal; visited Edinburgh in 1959 and 1974. In 1968 he created Dallapiccola's Ulisse, at the Deutsche Oper, Berlin.

Saeta (Span.), an unaccomp. Andalusian folksong sung during a halt in a religious procession.

Sæverud, Harald (b Bergen, 17 Apr 1897), Norwegian composer and conductor. Studied at Bergen and Berlin, cond. under Clemens Krauss. He returned to Bergen as cond. and received a state pension for comp. in 1933.

Works incl. *Minnesota Symph.*; 9 symphs. (1916–66); concertos for ob., cello, vln. and pf.; incid. music for Shakespeare's *Rape of Lucretia* (1935) and Ibsen's *Peer Gynt*; 50 variations for chamber orch.; pf. pieces, etc.

Saffo (*Sappho*), opera by Pacini (lib. by S. Cammarano), prod. Naples, Teatro San Carlo, 29 Nov 1840.

Safonov, Vassily Ilich (b Itsiursk, Terek, 6 Feb 1852; d Kislovodsk, Caucasus, 27 Feb 1918), Russian conductor and pianist. Studied at St Petersburg; prof. at the Cons. there, 1881, and at Moscow, 1885. Became dir. of Moscow Cons., 1889. Estab. popular concerts there and was cond. of the Moscow branch of the Russian Musical Society, 1890–1905. Appeared frequently in London and NY; guest cond. NY PO from 1904.

Saga, En, symph. poem by Sibelius, op. 9, comp. in 1891, fp Helsinki, 16 Feb 1893, revised in 1901. It depicts no partic. incident, but has a distinctly narrative, ballad-like tone.

Sagittarius, the Latin form of the name of Schütz, sometimes used on his title-pages. Like his Ger. name it = archer.

'St Anne' Fugue, the fugue in E♭ maj. at the end of Pt. III of Bach's *Clavierübung*, so named in Eng. because its subject is identical with the opening of Croft's (?) hymn-tune *St Anne*.

'St Anthony' Variations (Brahms). *See* **'Haydn' Variations.**

St Elizabeth (Liszt). *See* **Legende von der heiligen Elisabeth.**

Saint-Foix, (Marie Olivier) Georges (du Parc Poullain) de, Count (b Paris, 2 Mar 1874; d Aix-en-Provence, 26 May 1954), French musicologist. Studied law, and music at the Schola Cantorum in Paris. He wrote

on var. subjects, incl. Beethoven and Boccherini, but mainly on the classification and
analysis of Mozart's works in a large 5-vol.
work, the 1st 2 vols. in collaboration with
Théodore de Wyzewa.

Saint François d'Assise, opera in 8 tableaux by Messiaen (lib. by comp.; 1975–83.
fp Paris, Opéra, 28 Nov 1983).

St Gall, Swiss monastery famous for its
MSS. of Gregorian chant, the earliest of
which date back to the 10th cent.

Saint-Huberty (actually Clavel), **Antoinette
(Cécile)** (b Strasbourg, 15 Dec 1756; d London, 21 Jul 1812), French soprano. Studied
with the cond. Lemoyne at Warsaw and
made her 1st appearance there, then sang in
Berlin and Strasbourg, and 1st appeared in
Paris in 1777 as Melissa in the fp of Gluck's
Armide; later took part in the fps of Piccinni's *Didon*, Salieri's *Les Danaïdes* and Sacchini's *Chimène*. In 1790 she married the
Comte d'Entraigues, a royalist, with whom
she escaped to Lausanne. In 1797 she rescued her husband from prison at Milan.
They went 1st to St Petersburg and then to
London, where they settled and were murdered by a servant.

St James's Hall, a concert hall in London,
between Regent Street and Piccadilly (the
site of the present Piccadilly Hotel), opening
on 25 Mar 1858 and sold for demolition in
1905, when the last concert took place on 11
Feb. It was large enough for an orch., but
used also for chamber music, partic. the
Monday Popular Concerts ('Monday
Pops'), at which artists of internat. fame
appeared.

St John Passion, Bach's setting of the Passion narrative as told in St John's Gospel,
with interpolated texts after Brockes and
chorales, for soloists, chorus and orch.,
1st perf. in St Nicholas's, Leipzig, on
7 Apr 1724; a 2nd version was given
in St Thomas's, Leipzig, on 30 Mar
1725.

Saint-Lambert, (? Michel) de, French
17th–18th-cent. harpsichord player, teacher
and author. He lived and taught in Paris, and
wrote 2 books, *Les Principes du clavecin*
(1702) and *Nouveau Traité de l'accom-
pagnement* (1707).

St Ludmilla, oratorio by Dvořák, op. 71
(Cz. words by J. Vrchlický), comp. 1886 and
perf. on 15 Oct at the Leeds Festival, in an
Eng. translation.

St Luke Passion, work by Penderecki for
narrator, soloists, choruses and orch.; fp
Münster, 30 Mar 1966, cond. Czyz.

St Martial, the Benedictine abbey at
Limoges. The important MSS. of 12th-cent.
tropes, sequences, *versus* and early
polyphony known as the St-Martial repertory are now known to come from many
parts of Aquitaine and the repertory is better
described as Aquitanian. Concentrated
mainly in the early 12th cent., it is the main
coherent repertory before that of Notre-
Dame.

St Matthew Passion, Bach's setting of the
Passion narrative as told in St Matthew's
Gospel, with interpolated texts by Picander
and chorales, for soloists, chorus and orch.,
and perf. in St Thomas's, Leipzig, probably
on 11 Apr 1727 and certainly on 15 Apr
1729.

St Paul, oratorio by Mendelssohn, op. 36,
perf. Düsseldorf, Lower Rhine Festival, 22
May 1836; in Eng., Liverpool, 7 Oct 1836.

St Paul's Suite, work for string orch. in 4
movts. by Holst. Composed for St Paul's
Girls' school and perf. there 1913.

Saint-Saëns, (Charles) Camille (b Paris, 9
Oct 1835; d Algiers, 16 Dec 1921), French
composer. He began to compose at the age
of 5 and played the pf. well at that age. Gave
a public recital in 1846 and entered the
Cons. as an organ scholar in 1848, gaining a
1st prize in 1851, when he entered Halévy's
class for comp. App. organist at the church
of Saint-Merry in Paris, 1853, the
Madeleine, 1857, and pf. prof. at the École
Niedermeyer in 1861. His 1st 2 symphs.
were perf. in 1853 and 1859, he played his
2nd pf. concerto in 1868 and founded the
Société Nationale de Musique with Romain
Bussine in 1871. He played in Eng. several
times from 1871 and toured Spain and Port.
in 1880. The biblical opera *Samson et Dalila*, begun in 1868 and prohibited on the Fr.
stage on account of its subject, was prod. by
him at Weimar in 1877; it was allowed in
Paris from 1892, the year he received the
hon. Mus. D. at Cambridge. In 1906 he
visited the USA, and again in 1916, together
with S. Amer.

Works incl. STAGE: *La Princesse jaune*
(1872), *Le Timbre d'argent* (1877), *Étienne
Marcel* (1879), *Samson et Dalila* (1877),
Henri VIII (1883), *Proserpine, Ascanio*
(1890), *Phryné, Les Barbares,* Hélène
(1904), *L'Ancêtre, Déjanire* (1911); ballet
Javotte; incid. music for Sophocles' *Antigone,* Racine's *Andromaque* and 6 other
plays.

ORCH: 3 symphs. (1853, 1859, 1886, the
3rd with org. and pf. duet), symph. poems
Le Rouet d'Omphale (1872), *Phaëton,
Danse macabre* (orig. a song), *La Jeunesse*

d'Hercule (1877), suite and *Suite algérienne* for orch., other orchestral pieces incl. *Une Nuit à Lisbonne*, *Jota aragonesa* (1880), *Ouverture de fête*; 5 pf. concertos (1858–96), *Allegro appassionato*, *Rapsodie d'Auvergne* and *Africa* for pf. and orch., 3 vln. concertos (1858, 1859, 1890) and *Intro. et Rondo capriccioso*, Romance, *Morceau de concert* and *Caprice andalou* for vln. and orch., 2 cello concertos (1872, 1902), var. pieces for wind instruments and orch.

CHAMBER: *Le Carnaval des animaux* for chamber ens. (1886); 2 string 4tets (1899, 1918), pf. 5tet and 4tet, 2 pf. trios, 7tet for pf., strings and tpt.; 2 vln. and pf. sonatas, 2 cello and pf. sonatas, suite for cello and pf., sonatas for ob., clar. and bassoon and pf.; fantasies for harp and for vln. and harp; many smaller instrumental pieces with pf.

PIANO AND VOCAL: 24 op. nos. of pf. music, 6 op. nos. for pf. duet, 5 op. nos. for 2 pfs. incl. variations on a theme by Beethoven (1874); 7 org. works; Mass (1855), Requiem (1878), 2 Psalms and other church music for chorus and orch. (some with solo voices); *Ode à Sainte Cécile* and *La Fiancée du timbalier* for voice and orch.; oratorio *Le Déluge*; several cantatas; many songs.

St Victor, Adam of (d 1177 or 1192), French monk. In *c* 1130 he joined the abbey of St Victor near Paris. He wrote sequences comp. in pairs of metrically regular 3-line stanzas, and was the first important exponent of this type. He apparently comp. the melodies of his sequences.

Sainton-Dolby (*née* **Dolby**), **Charlotte (Helen)** (b London, 17 May 1821; d London, 18 Feb 1885), English contralto and composer. Studied at the RAM in London and made her 1st appearance at a Phil. concert there in 1842. In 1845 Mendelssohn invited her to sing with Jenny Lind at Leipzig, and later she had success in Fr. and Hol. In 1860 she married Prosper Sainton.

Works incl. cantatas *The Legend of St Dorothea* and *The Story of a Faithful Soul*, cantata for female voices *Florimel*.

Sainton, Prosper (Philippe Cathérine) (b Toulouse, 5 Jun 1813; d London,17 Oct 1890), French violinist and composer, husband of prec. Studied vln. under Habeneck at the Paris Cons., played at the Société des Concerts and the Opéra there, then travelled widely in Europe and in 1840 became prof. at the Toulouse Cons. In 1844 he visited London and played under Mendelssohn, returning in 1845 to settle down as member of the Beethoven 4tet Society, orch. leader and teacher.

Works incl. 2 vln. concertos and other solos with orch.; variations, romances, operatic fantasies, etc. for vln. and pf., etc.

Saite(n) (Ger.) = string(s).

Saiteninstrumente (Ger.) = string instruments.

Sakuntala. *See also* **Leggenda di Sakuntala.**

Opera by Weingartner (lib. by comp., based on Kalidasa's drama), prod. Weimar, 23 Mar 1884.

Sala, Nicola (b Tocco-Caudio nr. Benevento, 7 Apr 1713; d Naples, 31 Aug 1801), Italian composer and theorist. Studied with Fago and Leo at the Cons. de'Turchini at Naples and later became a master there, principal in 1787, succeeding Cafaro. In 1794 he pub. *Regole del contrappunto prattico* in 3 vols.

Works incl. operas *Vologeso* (1737), *Zenobia* (1761), *Merope* (1769) and *Demetrio* (1762); oratorio *Giuditta*; Mass, Litany and other church music; Prologues for the birth of kings of Naples.

Salammbô, opera by Reyer (lib. by C. duLocle, based on Flaubert's novel), prod. Brussels, Théâtre de la Monnaie, 10 Feb 1890.

Unfinished opera by Mussorgsky (lib. by comp., based on Flaubert), partly comp. in the 1860s.

Salazar, Adolfo (b Madrid, 6 Mar 1890; d Mexico City, 27 Sep 1958), Spanish musicologist and composer. Pupil of Pérez Casas and Falla. He ed. the *Revista Musical Hispano-Americano* in 1914–18 and from 1918 to 1936 was music critic to *El Sol* in Madrid. He emigrated to Buenos Aires after the Spanish Civil War and lived in Mexico after 1939. His books incl. studies of modern music, Span. music, symph. and ballet, etc.

Works incl. symph. poem *Don Juan en los infiernos*, *Paisajes* and *Tres preludios* for orch.; string 4tet, *Arabia* for pf. 5tet; vln. and pf. sonata; pf. pieces; *Romancilla* for guitar.

Salazar, Manuel (b San José, 3 Jan 1887; d San José, 6 Aug 1950), Costa-Rican tenor. Studied in Italy and NY. After his 1913 debut in Vicenza, as Edgardo, he had a wide success in Italy; sang with Titta Ruffo in Havana, 1917. NY Met 1921–3, as Alvaro, Canio, Radames and Andrea Chénier.

Sales, Pietro Pompeo (b Brescia, *c* 1729; d Hanau, 21 Nov 1797), Italian composer App. *Kapellmeister* to the Prince-Bishop of Augsburg in 1756, he served the Electoral Court in Koblenz in the same capacity from

1770. Also travelled in It. and Eng. (1776), appearing as a virtuoso gamba-player.

Works incl. operas *Le nozze di Amore e di Norizia* (1765), *L'Antigono* (1769), *Achille in Sciro*, *Il rè pastore*, etc.; oratorios *Giefte* (1762), *Giuseppe ricognosciuto*, *La Betulia liberata*, etc.; church music; 2 symphs.; concertos; arias.

Saléza, Albert (b Bruges, Basses-Pyrénées, 28 Oct 1867; d Paris, 26 Nov 1916), French tenor. Debut Paris 1888, in *Le Roi d'Ys*; the same year he was the 1st local Otello, at the Opéra. Sang in Monte Carlo and Nice and in the 1898 1st London perf. of Mancinelli's *Ero e Leandro*. NY Met 1899–1905; debut as Faust and also successful as Rodolfo and Don José.

Salieri, Antonio (b Legnago nr. Verona, 18 Aug 1750; d Vienna, 7 May 1825), Italian composer, conductor and teacher. Studied with his brother Francesco S., a pupil of Tartini. Orphaned at 15; his educ. at the school of San Marco in Venice was cared for by the Mocenigo family. There he met Gassmann, who in 1766 took him to Vienna, saw to his further educ. and intro. him at court. On Gassmann's death in 1774 he became court comp. and cond. of the It. opera. Visited It. 1778–80, where his opera *Europa riconosciuta* was prod. at the opening of La Scala, Milan, and Paris (1774 and 1786–7), but from 1788, when he succeeded Bonno as court *Kapellmeister*, lived mostly in Vienna. His intrigues against Mozart were exaggerated into the story that he had poisoned Mozart. He was cond. of the Tonkünstler Society until 1818, and played the continuo in the fp of Haydn's *Creation* in 1798. Among his pupils were Beethoven, Schubert, Hummel and Liszt.

Works incl. *c* 40 operas, e.g. *Armida* (1771), *La fiera di Venezia* (1772), *La locandiera* (1773), *Europa riconosciuta* (1778), *La scuola de gelosi* (1778), *La dama pastorella*, *Der Rauchfangkehrer* (1781), *Les Danaïdes* (1784), *Tarare*, *Les Horaces* (the last 3 for Paris), *La grotta di Trofonio* (1785), *Il talismano*, *Palmira, regina di Persia* (1795), *Falstaff* (after Shakespeare, 1799), *Cesare in Farmacusa*, *Angiolina* (1800).

Incid. music to Kotzebue's *Die Hussiten vor Naumburg*; Passion oratorio and others; 7 Masses, Requiem, Litanies and other church music; cantatas incl. *La riconoscenza* for the 25th anniversary of the Tonkünstler-Societät (1796); 3 symphs. and *sinfonia concertante*; concertos; serenades, etc.; arias, duets, canons and miscellaneous other small vocal pieces.

Salignac, Thomas (b Generac, nr. Nimes, 19 Mar 1867; d Paris, 1945), French tenor. He sang at the Paris Opéra-Comique from 1893 and made his NY Met debut in 1896, as Don José. CG 1897–1904. In Paris he sang in the fps of operas by Widor, Leroux, Laparra and Milhaud (*La Brebis égarée*, 1923; 1st-private-perf. Falla's *El retablo de Maese Pedro*, the same year). He later worked as opera dir., teacher and administrator.

Salimbeni, Felice (b Milan, *c* 1712; d Ljubljana, Aug 1751), Italian male soprano. Pupil of Porpora, made his 1st appearance in Rome in 1731 and afterwards sang in Italy, Vienna, Berlin and Dresden, and was one of Hasse's chief interpreters.

Salinas, Francisco de (b Burgos, 1 Mar 1513; d Salamanca, 13 Jan 1590), Spanish organist, theorist and folksong investigator. He was the son of an official in the treasury of Charles V and became blind at the age of 10, whereupon his parents decided to let him study music. He was taken to Rome in 1538, where he met the lutenist Francesco da Milano and became a great admirer of Lassus. In 1558 he became organist to the Duke of Alba, viceroy of Naples, under Ortiz. In 1561 he returned to Spain, became organist at León in 1563 and prof. of music at Salamanca Univ., 1567. There he made friends with the poet Luis de León, who wrote a poem on his organ playing. In his treatise *De musica libri septem* (1579) he quotes the tunes of many Span. folksongs.

Sallinen, Aulis (b Salmi, 9 Apr 1935), Finnish composer. He studied at the Sibelius Academy, Helsinki, and taught there 1963–76. Manager Finnish Radio SO 1960–70.

Works incl. operas *The Horseman* (1975), *The Red Line* (1978), *The King goes forth to France* (1984); ballet *Variations sur Mallarmé* (1968); 4 symphs. (1971–9), *Mauermusik*, for a German killed at Berlin Wall (1962), *Metamorphoses* for pf. and chamber orch. (1964), vln. concerto (1968), cello concerto (1978); *Chorali* for wind, perc., harp and celesta (1970), *Dies Irae* for sop., bass, male chorus and orch. (1978); 5 string 4tets (1958–82).

Salmhofer, Franz (b Vienna, 22 Jan 1900; d Vienna, 22 Sep 1975), Austrian composer and conductor. Having learnt music as a choir-boy, he studied at the Vienna Acad. under Schreker and others, later taught at Horak's music school and in 1929–39 was cond. at the Burgtheater, for which he wrote incid. music to over 300 plays. From 1955 he was dir. of the Vienna Volksoper.

Works incl. operas *Dame im Traum*

(1935), *Iwan Sergejewitsch Tarassenko* (1938), *Das Werbekleid* (1946) and several others; ballets *Das lockende Phantom* (1927), *Der Taugenichts in Wien, Weihnachtsmärchen* (1933), *Österreichische Bauernhochzeit*; incid. music for Shakespeare's *The Tempest, King Lear, Romeo and Juliet, Othello, The Merry Wives of Windsor*, Goethe's *Faust* (pts. I and II), etc.; overture to Maeterlinck's *L'Intruse* and others, *Der geheimnisvolle Trompeter, Fairy-Tale* for orch.; suite for chamber orch.; concertos for cello, vln. and cello and tpt.; 6 string 4tets, pf. 4tet in F min., serenade for string trio, etc.

Salmo (It., plur. *salmi*) = psalm.

Salmon (*née* **Munday**), **Eliza** (b Oxford 1787; d London, 5 Jun 1849), English soprano. Studied with John Ashley and made her 1st appearance at a Lenten concert at CG in 1803. She married James Salmon in 1806 and they settled at Liverpool, but she continued to sing in London and at the festivals until she lost her voice in 1825. She died in poverty, after earning £5,000 in 1823.

Salmon, Jacques (b Picardy), 16th-cent French composer. He was in the royal service from 1575 and contrib. to the *Ballet comique de la Royne* (1581). A few *chansons* have also survived.

Salmon, Thomas (b London, 24 Jun 1648; d Mepsal, Beds., buried 16 Aug 1706), English clergyman and writer on music. Wrote on notation and temperament. His *Essay on the Advancement of Musick* in 1672 involved him in a controversy with Locke.

Salmond, Felix (b London, 19 Nov 1888; d New York, 19 Feb 1952), English cellist. Studied at the RAM in London, later in Brussels, and made his debut in London in 1909. In 1919 he played in the fps of Elgar's string 4tet, pf. 5tet and cello concerto. He settled in USA in 1922 and in 1942 became cello prof. at the Juilliard School in NY. He toured extensively.

Salò, Francesco da (b Brescia, 1565), Italian violin maker. Succeeded his father, whose business, however, he sold after his death, and he seems to have left Brescia in 1614.

Salò, Gasparo da (real name G. di Bertoletti) (b Salò, May 1540; d Brescia, 14 Apr 1609), Italian violin maker, father of prec. He began working at Brescia in the 1560s.

Salomé, opera by Mariotte (lib. Oscar Wilde's orig. in Fr.), prod. Lyons, 30 Oct 1908. Comp. earlier than R. Strauss's opera, although prod. later.

Salome, opera by R. Strauss (lib. H. Lach-

mann's Ger. trans. of Oscar Wilde's play, written in Fr.), prod. Dresden, Royal Opera, 9 Dec 1905.

Ballet in 2 acts by Peter Maxwell Davies (choreog. by Flemming Flindt), prod. Stockholm, 10 Nov 1978. Concert suite perf. London, 6 Mar 1979.

See also **Tragédie de Salome**.

Salomon, Johann Peter (b Bonn, bap. 20 Feb 1745; d London, 28 Nov 1815), German violinist, conductor, manager and composer. Studied at Bonn and joined the electoral orch. in 1758. After a tour in 1765 he became court musician at Rheinsberg to Prince Henry of Prus., who, however, dissolved his orch. *c*1780, when Salomon went to Paris and thence to London, 1781, where he settled as concert violinist, 4tet player and cond. He gave subscription concerts at the Hanover Square Rooms and invited Haydn to London in 1790 and again in 1794. He wrote 4 Fr. operas and an Eng. one, *Windsor Castle*, for the marriage of the Prince of Wales in 1795, an oratorio *Hiskias*, vln. sonatas.

Salomon Symphonies, the 12 symphs. written by Haydn in 1791–5 for the concerts given by Johann Peter Salomon in London during Haydn's 2 visits to Eng. in 1791–2 and 1794–5. They are nos. 93–104.

Saltando (It. = springing, bounding), a special way of playing the vln. and other string instruments in such a manner that the bow is made to rebound from the strings.

Saltarello, an Italian dance, obviously incl. jumps (*salti*) and in the 16th cent. a kind of after-dance in common time, also called by the Latin name of *proportio* and the Ger. one of *Proporz*, the name being due to its using the same music as the 1st dance (Passamezzo), but with the 'proportions' (i.e. time) altered; later a Roman dance in animated 3–4 or 6–8 time, not unlike the Neapolitan Tarantella, but using jerky instead of even musical figuration. In perf. by dancers it gradually increased its pace towards the end. The best known Saltarello is the finale of Mendelssohn's Italian symph.

Salter, Lionel (b London, 8 Sep 1914), English harpsichordist, pianist, conductor and writer. He studied at Cambridge and with Constant Lambert and Arthur Benjamin at the RCM. He started work at the BBC before the war in music on TV and held var. administrative posts until 1974; head of TV opera 1963, asst. Controller of Music 1967–74. He is well known as a critic and writer and has trans. operas; several eds. of Scarlatti, Cavalli and Lully.

Saltzmann-Stevens, Minnie (b Bloomington, 17 Mar 1874; d Milan, 25 Jan 1950) American soprano. She studied with Jean de Reszke in Paris and sang Brünnhilde and Isolde at CG 1909–13. Bayreuth 1911–13, as Sieglinde and Kundry. Chicago 1914–16. After illness sang only in concert.

Salve Regina (Lat. *Hail, queen*), one of four antiphons to the Virgin Mary. Earliest MS. source is from 11th cent., probably by Adhemar of Pui. Many settings by 15th-cent. Eng. comps.; also set by La Rue, Josquin, Obrecht and Ockeghem. 6 settings by Schubert (1812–24).

Salvini-Donatelli, Fanny (b Florence, *c* 1815; d Milan, Jun 1891), Italian soprano. Debut Venice 1839, as Rosina. She sang Abigaille at Vienna in 1842; other Verdi roles were Lady Macbeth, Elvira and Gulnara. She created Violetta (Venice, 1853) but as a supposed consumptive did not create a convincing impression, owing to her corpulence. London, Drury Lane, 1858.

Salzburg Festivals, summer festivals of music and drama begun at Salzburg in 1921, mainly at the instigation of the poet Hugo von Hofmannsthal, the producer Max Reinhardt, the cond. Franz Schalk and the composer Richard Strauss (8 Mozart festivals had been held, 1877–1910). The music perfs. incl. opera, church music, orchestral concerts, chamber music and serenades, a festival opera-house being built in 1926. As Mozart's birthplace, Salzburg gave prominence to his works, but cultivated a wide range of music. The Festivals were interrupted in 1944, but resumed in 1946. The fps of operas by Strauss, Orff, Henze, Cerha, Berio and Penderecki have been given there. Herbert von Karajan artistic dir. from 1964; Easter Festival from 1967.

Salzedo, Carlos (b Arcachon, Gironde, 6 Apr 1885; d Waterville, Me., 17 Aug 1961), French-American harpist and composer. Studied pf. and harp at the Paris Cons. and went to NY at Toscanini's invitation to become 1st harp at the Met Opera. Much interested in modern music, he founded the Internat. Composers' Guild with Varèse, ed. *Eolus* and cond. many concerts. Prof. of harp at the Juilliard School in NY and the Curtis Inst. at Philadelphia.

Works incl. *The Enchanted Isle* for harp and orch., concerto for harp and 7 wind instruments, *Préambule et Jeux* for harp and chamber orch.; sonata for harp and pf., many pieces and arrs. for harp.

Salzman, Eric (b New York, 8 Sep 1933), American composer and musicologist. Studied with Beeson and Babbitt. Music critic in NY, founded Quog Music Theater 1970. Ed. *Music Quarterly* from 1984.

Works incl. *Larynx Music* (1968), *Civilization and its Discontents*, opera (1977).

Samara, Spiro (b Corfu, 29 Nov 1863; d Athens, 7 Apr 1917), Greek composer. Studied at Athens, later with Delibes and others at the Paris Cons. The It. pub. Sonzogno procured him his 1st operatic prod. at Milan. He subsequently prod. other works at Rome, Naples, Florence, Milan and Genoa, with no more than ephemeral success, and the last came out at Athens in 1914.

Works incl. operas *Flora mirabilis* (1886), *Medgé, Lionella* (1891), *La martire, La furia domata* (after Shakespeare's *Taming of the Shrew*, 1895), *Storia d'amore* (1903), *Mademoiselle de Bella-Isle, Rhea, La guerra in tempo di guerra, The Princess of Saxony* (in Gk.); suite for pf. duet, pf. pieces; songs.

Samazeuilh, Gustave (Marie Victor Fernand) (b Bordeaux, 2 Jun 1877; d Paris 4 Aug 1967), French composer and critic. Pupil of Chausson and after his master's death of d'Indy and Dukas at the Schola Cantorum. His writings incl. studies of Rameau and Dukas, transs. of Wagner's *Tristan* and Schumann's *Genoveva*, songs by Wagner and Liszt, etc. He also made pf. arrs. of modern Fr. music.

Works incl. *Étude symphonique pour 'La Nef'* (Élemire Bourges), *Nuit, Naïades au soir, Le Sommeil de Canope* for orch.; the last also for voice and orch.; string 4tet; etc.

Saminsky, Lazare (b nr. Odessa, 8 Nov 1882; d Port Chester, NY, 30 Jun 1959), Russian-American composer, conductor and writer on music. Pupil of Liadov and Rimsky-Korsakov at St Petersburg Cons. Cond. at Tiflis in 1915–18 and then dir. of the People's Cons. there. After a period in London, he went to the USA, where he became naturalized. He was one of the founders of the League of Comps. in 1924, became music dir. of the Jewish Temple of Emanu-El, and did much cond. in Amer. and Eur. Author of *Music of Our Day* and *Music of the Ghetto.*

Works. incl. opera-ballets *The Vision of Ariel, Lament of Rachel* (1913) and *The Daughter of Jephtha* (1929), chamber opera *Gagliarda of the Merry Plague*; Requiem; 5 symphs. (1917–30), 3 symph. poems.

Sammarco, Mario (b Palermo, 13 Dec 1868; d Milan, 24 Jan 1930), Italian baritone. Pupil of Antonio Cantelli; made his 1st appearance at Milan as Hamlet and 1st visited London in 1904, when he sang Scarpia;

appeared in London until 1914 and the USA 1907–13. He created Gérard in *Andrea Chénier* (1896) and sang in operas by Leoncavallo, Donizetti and Wolf-Ferrari. He was a dir. of La Scala, Milan, from 1918.

Sammartini (or San Martini), Giovanni Battista (b Milan, *c* 1700; d Milan, 15 Jan 1775), Italian composer. He spent his whole life in Milan as a church musician, from 1730 *maestro di cappella* at the convent of Santa Maria Maddelena. Gluck was his pupil 1737–41 and borrowed material from S.'s symphs. for 2 of his operas. He was the most important It. symphonist of his time, and contrib. much towards the founding of a modern style of instrumental music.

Works incl. 2 operas incl. *L'Agrippina, moglie di Tiberio* (1743); 2 oratorios; 3 Masses and other church music; over 80 symphs.; *c* 15 concertos; 6 *concerti grossi*; 6 string 5tets, *c* 20 4tets, almost 200 trios, and other chamber music.

Sammartini (or San Martini), Giuseppe (b Milan, 6 Jan 1695; d London, Nov 1750), Italian oboist and composer, brother of prec. Settled in Eng. *c* 1727, became oboist at the opera, and 1732–44 was dir. of the Hickford's Room concerts with Arrigoni, then was app. dir. of chamber music to the Prince of Wales.

Works incl. setting of Congreve's masque *The Judgment of Paris* (1740); *Concerti grossi*; concertos for harpsichord and for vln.; sonatas for 2 fls., 2 vlns., etc. with bass, fl. solos (? all fl. works intended also for ob.).

Sammons, Albert (b London, 23 Feb 1886; d Southdean, Sussex, 24 Aug 1957), English violinist. Taught by his father, an amateur, John Saunders and F. Weist-Hill, he 1st played at a London hotel, where Beecham heard him in 1908 and engaged him as leader of his orch. Sammons later led the London String 4tet and gradually emerged as a splendid soloist; he gave the fp of the Delius Concerto (1919) and made the 1st recording of the Elgar (1929). He excelled both in virtuosity and in musicianship.

Samori, opera by Vogler (lib. by F.X. Huber), prod. Vienna, Theater an der Wien, 17 May 1804. Weber wrote a set of pf. variations, op. 6, on a theme from it.

Samson, oratorio by Handel (lib. by N. Hamilton, based on Milton's *Samson Agonistes, Hymn on the Nativity* and *At a Solemn Musick*), prod. London, CG, 18 Feb 1743.

Samson et Dalila, opera (orig. oratorio) by Saint-Saëns (lib. by F. Lemaire), prod. Weimar, in Ger., 2 Dec 1877; not perf. in Paris until 31 Oct 1890, and at the Opéra, 23 Nov 1892, having been at first forbidden on account of its biblical subject.

Samstag aus Licht (*Saturday from Light*), opera by Stockhausen, 2nd of his cycle *Licht.* The 4 scenes are Lucifer's Dream, Kathinka's Song, Lucifer's Dance and Lucifer's Farewell. Fp Milan, 25 May 1984.

Samuel, Harold (b London, 23 May 1879; d London, 15 Jan 1937), English pianist. Studied under Dannreuther and Stanford at the RCM in London, where he became pf. prof. later. He made a speciality of Bach's keyboard works, but he also excelled as a chamber music player.

San Carlo, Naples, Teatro di, Italian opera house opened 1737. Works by Pergolesi, Piccinni, Cimarosa and Rossini (*Elisabetta*) prod. there until house destroyed by fire in 1816; rebuilt same year. Later Rossini fps incl. *Armida* (1817), *Mosè* (1818) and *La donna del Lago* (1819). Donizetti's *Lucia di Lammermoor* (1835) and Verdi's *Luisa Miller* (1849) also 1st perf. there.

San Francisco Symphony Orchestra, American orch. founded 1911. Pierre Monteaux was cond. 1935–52. Recent conds. have been Seiji Ozawa (1970–6) and Edo de Waart (from 1977).

Sances, Giovanni Felice (b Rome, *c* 1600; d Vienna, buried 12 Nov 1679), Italian tenor and composer. He went to Vienna as a singer in the Imp. Chapel in 1637, became vice-music dir. in 1649 and 1st music dir. in 1669.

Works incl. operas *Apollo deluso* (with the Emperor Leopold I), *Aristomene Messenio* and others; oratorios; cantatas for solo voice, *Capricci poetici, Trattenimenti musicali per camera*.

Sánchez de Fuentes y Peláez, Eduardo (b Havana, 3 Apr 1874; d Havana, 7 Sep 1944), Cuban composer and music historian. He wrote several books on the history of Cuban folk music.

Works incl. operas *Dolorosa* (1910), *Doreya* (1918) and 3 others, operettas and zarzuelas; oratorio *Novidad*; suite *Bocetos cubanos*, symph. prelude *Temas del Patio* for orch.; vocal *habañera Tú espera*.

Sancho Pança dans son île (*Sancho Panza on his Island*), opera by Philidor (lib. by A.A.H. Poinsinet, based on Cervantes's *Don Quixote*), prod. Paris, Comédie-Italienne, 8 Jul 1762.

Sancho Panza, opera by Jaques-Dalcroze (lib. by R.Yve-Plessis, based on Cervantes's *Don Quixote*), prod. Geneva, 13 Dec 1897.

Sancio Panza, governatore dell' isola

Barattaria (*Sancho P., Governor of the Isle of Barataria*), opera by Caldara (lib. by G.C. Pasquini, based on Cervantes's *Don Quixote*), prod. Vienna, Burgtheater, 27 Jan 1733.

Sancta Civitas (*The Holy City*), oratorio by Vaughan Williams (words from the Bible, etc.) for solo voices, chorus and orch., fp Oxford, 7 May 1926.

Sancta Susanna, opera in 1 act by Hindemith (lib. by A. Stramm); comp. 1921, prod. Frankfurt, 26 Mar 1922. Story concerns a sex-obsessed nun.

Sanctus, the fourth chant of the Ordinary of the Roman Mass. Its text is founded on Isaiah vi. 3 and Matthew xxi. 9, and it was incorporated into the Lat. liturgy at least as early as the 6th cent. in Gaul. The earliest known melody is that of Mass XVIII (Vatican edition). It is basically syllabic; it forms a natural continuation from the music of the Preface which precedes it; it is psalmodic in structure; and its last phrase echoes the *Per omnia saecula saeculorum* formula which occurs 3 times during the Preface and Canon of the Mass. Later settings are more complex: a total of 231 melodies were catalogued in 1962. The Sanctus was set in polyphony from the 13th cent., and became an integral part of all settings of the Ordinary of the Mass.

Sandberger, Adolf (b Würzburg, 19 Dec 1864; d Munich, 14 Jan 1943), German musicologist and composer. Studied in a number of European centres and in 1894 became lecturer in music at Munich Univ. and was prof. in 1900–29, being at the same time curator of the music dept. of the State Library. He was chief ed. of the incomplete ed. of Lassus and the *Denkmäler der Tonkunst in Bayern*, and his books incl. studies of the Bavarian court chapel under Lassus, of Cornelius, etc.

Works incl. operas *Ludwig der Springer* and *Der Tod des Kaisers*; symph. poem *Viola* (on Shakespeare's *Twelfth Night*), symph. prologue *Riccio*; chamber music; pf. works; songs.

Sanderling, Kurt (Arys, 9 Sep 1912), German conductor. He worked at the Berlin Staatsoper from 1931 but left Ger. at the rise of the Nazis. He became cond. of the Moscow Radio SO in 1937 and joined the Leningrad PO in 1941. Returned to Berlin 1960 and was cond. East Berlin SO until 1964; then worked in Dresden with the Staatskapelle and at the opera house. London debut 1970, with Leipzig Gewandhaus Orch. Well known in late Romantic music.

Sanderson (or **Saunderson**), **James** (b Washington, Durham, Apr 1769; d London, c 1841), English violinist and composer. He was self-taught and in 1783 obtained an engagement as violinist at the Sunderland theatre. Later he taught at Shields, became leader at the Newcastle-on-Tyne theatre, 1787, and at Astley's Amphitheatre in London, 1788. He began to write stage pieces and in 1793 went as music dir. and comp. to the Royal Circus (Surrey Theatre).

Works incl. stage pieces and pantomimes *Harlequin in Ireland, Blackbeard, Cora, Sir Francis Drake, The Magic Pipe, Hallowe'en* and many others; instrumental interludes for Collins's *Ode to the Passions*; vln. pieces; many popular songs.

Sanderson, Sibyl (b Sacramento, Calif., 7 Dec, 1865; d Paris, 15 May 1903), American soprano. Studied at the Paris Cons. and made her debut at The Hague in 1888, in Massenet's *Manon*. She was later Massenet's mistress, and created the title roles in *Esclarmonde* and *Thaïs*.

Sándor, György (b Budapest, 21 Sep 1912), Hungarian pianist. Studied Budapest with Bartók and Kodály. Moved to US 1939 and in 1946 gave the fp of Bartók's 3rd concerto, at Philadelphia.

Sandrin (Pierre Regnault) (d after 1561), French composer. He was a member of the royal chapel, 1543–60, during which time he also travelled to It. He comp. only *chansons*, of which the majority were pub. by Attaingnant. Lassus based a Mass on the *chanson* 'Doulce memoire'.

Sanguine Fan, The, ballet by Elgar, op. 81 (scenario by Ina Lowther); comp. 1917, prod. Chelsea, 20 Mar 1917, cond. Elgar; not heard again complete until recording of 1973.

Santa Cruz (Wilson), Domingo (b La Cruz, 5 Jul, 1899; d Santiago, 7 Jan 1987), Chilean composer, teacher and critic. Studied at Santiago de Chile and Madrid. In 1918 he founded a Bach Society at Santiago and in 1932 became dean of the Fine Arts Dept. at the Univ. of Chile and rector of the univ. from 1948 to 1951.

Works incl. 4 symphs. (1948–69); *5 Piezas brevas* for string orch.; 3 string 4tets; 3 vln. and pf. pieces; pf. works; songs.

Santa Maria, Tomás de (b Madrid c 1515; d Valladolid, 1570), Spanish monk and organist. He joined a Dominican monastery and in 1565 pub. a treatise on playing polyphonic fantasies on keyboard instruments and lutes.

Santini, Fortunato (b Rome, 5 Jan 1778; d

Rome, 14 Sep 1861), Italian priest, music scholar and composer. He studied music with Jannaconi and after being ordained in 1801 began to make an immense collection of old music, scoring it from parts in various music libraries. He made friends with Mendelssohn and through him intro. many works by Bach into Italy, as well as other Ger. sacred music.

Works incl. Requiem for 8 voices, Masses and other church music.

Santley, Charles (b Liverpool, 28 Feb 1834; d London, 22 Sep 1922), English bass-baritone. Learnt music as a choir-boy and at first appeared as an amateur singer, but went to Milan in 1855 to study with Gaetano Nava, made a stage appearance at Pavia and in 1857 returned to Eng. continuing his studies with Manuel García in London, where he 1st appeared on 16 Nov, as Adam in *Die Schöpfung*. He soon sang in opera, oratorio and at the great festivals with enormous success, notably in operas by Balfe, Wallace and Benedict; sang Valentine in the 1st Brit. perf. of *Faust* (1865) and was the 1st London Daland (1870). He toured the USA in 1871 and Australia in 1890. In 1907 he celebrated his 50th anniversary as a singer and was knighted.

Santoliquido, Francesco (b San Giorgio a Cremano, Naples, 6 Aug 1883; d Anacapri, 26 Aug 1971), Italian composer. Studied at the Liceo di Santa Cecilia in Rome, cond. his student work, *Crepuscolo sul mare*, at Nuremberg in 1909 and prod. his 1st opera at Milan in 1910. He then went to live in Tunisia, in the small Arab village in Hammamek, where he became interested in the study of native music.

Works incl. operas *La favola di Helga*

(1910), *Ferhuda* (1918), *L'ignota* and *La porta verde* (1953), mimed drama *La baiadera della maschera gialla* (1917); symph. in F maj.

Sanzogno, Nino (b Venice, 13 Apr 1911; d Milan, 4 May 1983), Italian conductor and composer. Studied with Malipiero and Scherchen, and then played vln. in the Guarnieri 4tet, later becoming cond. at La Fenice opera house in Venice and at La Scala, Milan. He cond. the 1st prods. of Prokofiev's *The Fiery Angel* (1955) and Poulenc's *Carmélites*; also gave operas by Berg, Shostakovich and Britten.

Works incl. symph. poems *The 4 Horsemen of the Apocalypse*, *Vanitas*; concertos for vla., cello; songs.

Sapho, opera by Gounod (lib. by Émile Augier), prod. Paris, Opéra, 16 Apr 1851. Gounod's 1st opera.

Opera by Massenet (lib. by H. Cain and A. Bernède, based on Daudet's novel), prod. Paris, Opéra-Comique, 27 Nov 1897. The heroine is not the Gk. poet Sappho.

Sappho. *See also* **Saffo, Sapho.**

Opera by Hugo Kaun (1863–1932) (lib. by comp. based on Grillparzer's play), prod. Leipzig, 27 Oct 1917.

Saraband (Eng.)
Sarabande (Fr.) } a dance, possibly originating in Spain in the 16th cent. Its name was formerly supposed to be derived from a dancer called Zarabanda, but it is very likely of more remote eastern origin. It was intro. to the Fr. court in 1588 and in 17th-cent. Eng. became a country dance. The music is in slow 3–2 time with, as a rule, a peculiar rhythm of a minim, dotted minim and crotchet in the 1st bar (see illustration). The Sarabande was one of the 4 regular

Bach, *English Suite*, No.6

SARABANDE

movements in the 17th and 18th-cent. Suite, together with the Allemande, Courante and Gigue (Jig).

Sarabande and Cortège, 2 studies for orch. by Busoni for his opera *Doktor Faust*; comp. 1918–19, fp Zurich, 31 Mar 1919.

Sarasate (y Navascuéz), Pablo (Martín Melitón) (b Pamplona, 10 Mar 1844; d Biarritz, 20 Sep 1908), Spanish violinist and composer. Pupil of Alard at the Paris Cons. He soon began to make a remarkable career as a virtuoso, at first in Fr. and Spain, later all over Europe and Amer. He 1st appeared in London in 1861. Bruch, Saint-Saëns, Lalo and Wieniawski dedicated concertos to him.

Works incl. romances, fantasies, 4 books of Span. Dances, etc. for vln.

Sardana, a Spanish dance of Catalonia revived in the middle of the 19th cent. and perf. to pipe and drum.

Sarema, opera by Zemlinsky (lib. by A. von Zemlinsky, the composer's father) comp. 1895, prod. Munich, Hofoper, 10 Oct 1897. Zemlinsky's 1st opera.

Sargent (Harold) Malcolm (Watts) (b Stamford, Lincs., 29 Apr 1895; d London, 3 Oct 1967), English conductor. Studied at the Royal Coll. of Organists, winning the Sawyer Prize in 1910. From 1911 to 1914 he was asst. organist at Peterborough Cathedral; served in World War I and in 1919 took his D. Mus. at Durham. He made his debut as a cond. at a Promenade Concert in a work of his own in 1921. Later he taught at the RCM and cond. in many parts of the world, incl. a period with the Diaghilev ballet co. from 1927 to 1930. In 1928 he became chief cond. of the Royal Choral Society and from 1950 to 1957 chief cond. of the BBC SO, and of the Promenade Concerts until his death. He gave the fps of *Belshazzar's Feast* (1931), *Troilus and Cressida* (1954) and Vaughan Williams's 9th Symph. (1958). Knighted 1947.

Šárka (Smetana). *See* **Má Vlast.**

Opera by Fibich (lib. by A. Schulzová), prod. Prague, Cz. Theatre, 28 Dec 1897.

Opera by Janáček (lib. by J. Zeyer; comp. 1887–8, revised 1918 and 1925, scoring completed by O. Chlubna, prod. Brno, 11 Nov 1925.

Sarro (or Sarri), Domenico (b Trani, Naples, 24 Dec 1679; d Naples, 25 Jan 1744), Italian composer. Pupil of Durante at the Cons. S. Onofrio in Naples, he became vice-*maestro di cappella* to the court in 1703. He lost his post in 1707 but returned in 1725, succeeding Mancini as *maestro di cappella* in 1737.

Works incl. *c* 50 operas, e.g. *Didone*

abbandonata (the first setting by any comp. of a lib. by Metastasio, prod. Naples, 1724); 4 oratorios; cantatas, etc.; much church music; instrumental music.

Sarrusophone, a brass wind instrument with a double-reed mouthpiece invented in 1856 by Sarrus, a bandmaster in the Fr. army, intended to be made in var. sizes to cover a whole range of tone replacing oboes and bassoons in military bands. In the orch. only the contrabass has been used, mainly in Fr. comps.

Sarti, Giuseppe (b Faenza, bap. 1 Dec 1729; d Berlin, 28 Jul 1802), Italian composer and conductor. Pupil of Vallotti in Padua and of Padre Martini in Bologna, he was organist of Faenza Cathedral 1748–51, then music dir. of the theatre there in 1752 and prod. his 1st opera the same year. In 1753 he went to Copenhagen as cond. of the Mingotti opera co., and 2 years later was app. *Kapellmeister* to the Dan. court, staying there, except for 3 years in It. 1765–8, until 1775. Director of the Ospedaletto Cons. in Venice 1775–9, he was then *maestro di cappella* of Milan Cathedral, where Cherubini was his pupil. App. music dir. to the Rus. court in 1784, he travelled to St Petersburg *via* Vienna, there meeting Mozart, who quoted the aria 'Come un agnello' from his opera *Fra due litiganti* in the supper scene in *Don Giovanni.* He prod. a number of operas in Rus., incl. *Oleg* on a lib. by the empress, and stayed there until 1802, founding a music school in the Ukraine and becoming dir. of the Cons. in St Petersburg in 1793. He then intended retiring to It., but died in Berlin on the way.

Works incl. operas (libs. in It., Dan., Fr. and Rus.), e.g. *Pompeo in Armenia* (1752), *Il rè pastore* (1753), *La giardiniera brillante* (1768), *Farnace, Le gelosie villane, Fra due litiganti* (1782), *Medonte* (1777), *Giulio Sabino, I finti eredi, Armida e Rinaldo* (1786), *Oleg* (Rus., with Pashkevich and Canobbio), etc.; 2 Rus. oratorios; Requiem for Louis XVI (1793); Masses, Te Deum and other church music; keyboard music.

Sartorio, Antonio (b Venice, *c* 1630; d Venice, 30 Dec 1680), Italian composer. He was music dir. at the Court of Brunswick from 1666 to 1675 and then vice-*maestro di cappella* at St Mark's, Venice, preceding Legrenzi.

Works incl. operas *Seleuco* (1666), *La prosperità di Elio Seiano* (1667), *La caduta di Elio Seiano, Adelaide, Orfeo* (1672) and 10 others; psalms and motets; cantatas for chorus and for solo voices; canzonets.

Sartorius (= Schneider), **Paul** (b Nuremberg, 16 Nov 1569; d Innsbruck, 28 Feb 1609), German organist and composer. He was organist to the Archduke Maximilian of Aus. in 1599 and lived at Nuremberg.

Works incl. Masses, *Sonetti spirituali* for 6 voices (1601), motets, madrigals, *Neue teutsche Liedlein*.

Sarum Use, the liturgy in use at Salisbury before the Reformation, differing in some respects from that of Rome and widely spread through medieval Eng. until it was abolished in 1547, though revived from 1553–9.

Sás Orchassal, André (b Paris, 6 Apr 1900; d Lima, 25 Jul 1967), Peruvian composer, of French-Belgian parentage. Studied in Brussels and went to Peru in 1924 as vln. teacher at the Nat. Acad. of Music at Lima. He married the Peruvian pianist Lily Rosay and with her founded a private music school in 1929. He made extensive research into Peruvian folklore and frequently used folk-tunes in his works.

Works incl. *Himno al sol, Himno y danza* and *Poema Indio* for orch.; *Rapsodia peruana* for vln. and orch; *Quenas* for voice, fl. and harp; *Sonatina india* for fl. and pf.; works for vln. and pf.; pf. pieces; songs.

Sass (Saxe), Marie (Constance) (b Ghent, 26 Jan 1838; d Auteuil nr. Paris, 8 Nov 1907), Belgian soprano. Pupil of Delphine Ugalde, had her debut in Paris in 1859 and went to the Opéra in 1860, where the following year she sang Elisabeth in the Fr. version of Wagner's *Tannhäuser*; created Sélika (1865) and Elisabeth de Valois (1867). Died impoverished.

Sass, Sylvia (b Budapest, 12 Jul 1951), Hungarian soprano. She studied in Budapest and made her debut there in 1971. She sang Desdemona with Scottish Opera in 1975 and in 1976 was Giselda in the 1st CG prod. of Verdi's *I Lombardi*. Sang Violetta at Aix in the same year and Tosca on her NY Met debut in 1977. She has been heard in Vienna, Hamburg and Paris as Donna Anna, Fiordiligi and Bartók's Judith.

Satie, Erik (Alfred Leslie) (b Honfleur, 17 May 1866; d Paris, 1 Jul 1925), French composer. He was brought up in a musical home, his father being a comp. and music pub. in Paris and his mother, of Scot. origin, a minor comp. of pf. pieces under the name of Eugénie Satie-Barnetsche. He spent only a year at the Paris Cons. and later made a precarious living by playing at cafés, writing music for the Montmartre song-writer Hypsa and the music-hall singer Paulette Darty.

Through his friendship with Debussy, *c* 1890, he came into contact with intellectual circles. He also studied at the Schola Cantorum under d'Indy and Roussel at the age of 40. He continued to pub. small pf. works under eccentric titles. In later years he came into touch with Jean Cocteau and estab. a school at Arcueil where he exercised some influence on younger comps.

Works incl. STAGE AND CHORAL: symph. drama *Socrate* (1920); incid. music for Péladan's *Le Fils des étoiles*; ballets *Parade* (1917), *Relâche* (1924) and *Mercure*, 1924; operettas *Geneviève de Brabant* (for marionettes, 1899), *Pousse-l'Amour* and *Le Piège de Méduse*; pantomime *Jack in the Box* (orch. by Milhaud); *Messe des pauvres* for voices and org. (1895).

PIANO: Pf. pieces *Ogives*, *3 Sarabandes*, *3 Gymnopédies* (1888), *3 Gnossiennes* (1890), *Danses gothiques* (1893), *Sonneries de la Rose-Croix*, *Pièces froides* (1897), *Prélude en tapisserie*, *3 Véritables Préludes flasques* (*pour un chien*), *3 Descriptions automatiques* (1913), *3 Embryons desséchés* (1913), *3 Croquis et agaceries d'un gros bonhomme en bois* (1913), *3 Chapitres tournés en tous sens* (1913), *3 Vieux Sequins et vieilles cuirasses* (1913), *Heures séculaires et instantanées* (1914), *3 Valses du précieux dégoûté*, *Avant-dernières pensées*, etc.; *3 Morceaux en forme de poire* (1903), *Aperçus désagréables* and *En habit de cheval* for pf. duet; 4 sets of songs.

Satyagraha, opera by Philip Glass (lib. by C. DeJong), based on the life of Gandhi, prod. Rotterdam, 5 Sep 1980. Title is based on Gandhi's slogan, the 2 Hindu words *saty* ('truth') and *agraha* ('firmness'). The opera is sung in Sanskrit.

Sauer, Emil (George Konrad) (b Hamburg, 8 Oct 1862; d Vienna, 27 Apr 1942), German pianist and composer. Studied with N. Rubinstein at the Moscow Cons. and later with Liszt. Began to tour Europe in 1882 and 1st visited Eng. in 1894. From 1901, with certain intervals, he directed a master class at the Vienna Cons.

Works incl. 2 pf. concertos; 2 sonatas, 24 concert studies, *Suite moderne* and many pieces for pf.

Sauguet, Henri (actually Jean Pierre Poupard) (b Bordeaux, 18 May 1901), French composer and critic. Studied pf. and organ at Bordeaux, then became a pupil of J. Canteloube at Montauban and in 1922 of Koechlin in Paris. Intro. by Milhaud to Satie, he joined the latter's school at Arcueil. In 1936 he succeeded Milhaud as music critic to *Le Jour-Écho de Paris.*

Works incl. operas *La Chartreuse de Parme* (after Stendhal, 1939) and *La Gageure imprévue* (Sedaine, 1944), operettas *Le Plumet du colonel* (1924) and *La Contrebasse* (1932); ballets *La Charte*, *David*, *La Nuit*, *Fastes* and *Les Forains*; incid. music for Molierè's *Le Sicilien*, Roger Ferdinand's *Irma*, Pierre Emmanuel's *Les Lépreux* and other plays.

4 symphs. incl. *Symphonie expiatoire* (in memory of war victims); 3 pf. concertos; *La Voyante* for soprano and chamber orch.; 2 string 4tets (1926, 1948); sonatina for fl. and pf.; sonata in D maj. and other works for pf.; songs to poems by Tagore; film music.

Saul, oratorio by Handel (lib. by C. Jennens), prod. London, King's Theatre, 16 Jan 1739.

Saul og David, opera in 4 acts by Nielsen (lib. by E. Christiansen); comp. 1898–1901, prod. Copenhagen, Royal Theatre, 28 Nov 1902, cond. Nielsen.

Saunders, Arlene (b Cleveland, 5 Oct 1935), American soprano. Debut NY 1958, as Rosalinde. She sang in Italy from 1960 and was a member of the Hamburg Opera from 1963; sang in the 1965 fp of Klebe's *Jacobowsky und der Oberst* and well known as Agathe, Arabella, the Marschallin and Mozart's Countess. Glyndebourne 1966, Pamina. At Washington in 1971 she was heard in the fp of Ginastera's *Beatrix Cenci*. NY Met debut 1976, as Eva.

Sauret, Émile (b Dun-le-Roi, 22 May 1852; d London, 12 Feb 1920), French violinist and composer. Pupil of Bériot. He began to travel at an early age, 1st visited London in 1862, played much at the Fr. court in the last years of the 2nd Empire, visited the USA twice in 1872–6, studied comp. with Jadassohn at Leipzig and appeared with Liszt. In 1872 he married Teresa Carreño, but they were divorced before long. In 1891 he succeeded Sainton as vln. prof. at the RAM in London and in 1903 he took up a similar post at Chicago.

Works incl. 2 concertos, *Ballade*, *Légende*; serenade for vln. and orch.; many vln. pieces, studies and arrs.

Sausage Bassoon. *See* **Racket.**

Sautillé (Fr. = springing, bounding), a special way of playing the vln. and other string instruments in such a manner that the bow is made to rebound from the strings.

Sauzay, Charles Eugène (b Paris, 14 Jul 1809; d Paris, 24 Jan 1901), French violinist and composer. Studied at the Paris Cons.,

Baillot and Reicha being among his masters. He joined Baillot's 4tet and married his daughter, became court violinist in 1840 and prof. at the Cons. in 1860.

Works incl. incid. music for Molière's *George Dandin* and *Le Sicilien*; string trio; pf. trio; vln. and pf. pieces; *Études harmoniques* for solo vln.; songs, etc.

Savile, Jeremy, English 17th-cent. composer. Contrib. songs to *Select Musicall Ayres and Dialogues* in 1653. Comps. incl. partsong *The Waits*, song 'Here's a health unto His Majesty'.

Sāvitri, opera by Holst (lib. by comp., based on an episode in the *Mahabharata*), prod. London, Wellington Hall, 5 Dec 1916; 1st public perf. London, Lyric Theatre, Hammersmith, 23 Jun 1921.

Savonarola, opera by Stanford (lib. by G.A. à Beckett), prod., in Ger. (trans. by Ernst Frank), Hamburg, 18 Apr 1884.

Sawallisch, Wolfgang (b Munich, 26 Aug 1923), German conductor and pianist. Studied at the Munich Hochschule für Musik with J. Haas, making his debut in Augsburg in 1947, where he remained until 1953, when he became music dir. at the opera in Aachen. From 1957 to 1959 he cond. at the Wiesbaden opera and from 1959 to 1963 in Cologne. Bayreuth 1951–62 (*Tristan*, *Holländer* and *Tannhäuser*). Music dir. Bavarian Opera, Munich 1971–86. Suisse Romande Orch. 1970–80. Well known as pf. accompanist to leading singers.

Sax. Belgian family of instrument makers:

1. Charles Joseph S. (b Dinant, 1 Feb 1791; d Paris, 26 Apr 1865). He set up in business at Brussels, made wind instruments and prod. several inventions, esp. in connection with horns and other brass instruments.

2. Adolphe (actually Antoine Joseph) S. (b Dinant, 6 Nov 1814; d Paris, 4 Feb 1894), son of prec. Studied fl. and clar. at the Brussels Cons. and worked with his father, made several improvements in wind instruments and estab. himself in Paris in 1842. His chief inventions are the Saxhorn and the Saxophone.

3. Alphonse S. (b Brussels, 9 May 1822; d Paris, 26 Jun 1874), brother of prec. He made some inventions in connection with the valves of brass instruments and estab. himself independently in Paris but did not succeed.

Saxe, Marie. *See* **Sass.**

Saxhorn, a brass wind instrument allied to the Bugle, but with valves, invented by Adolphe Sax and patented by him in 1845. It is played with a cup mouthpiece and made in 7 different pitches, covering between them a range of some 5 8ves: soprano in Eb, alto in Bb (both also called Flügelhorns), tenor in Eb, baritone in Bb (both also called Althorns), bass in Bb (Euphonium), bass tuba in Eb (Bombardon) and contrabass in Bb. They are rarely used in the orch., but are regular constituents of military and brass bands.

Saxophone, a wind instrument made of brass, but with woodwind characteristics, invented by Adolphe Sax c 1840 and patented by him in 1846. It is played through a mouthpiece with a single reed of the clar. type and the notes are controlled by keys. It

Vilna. He wrote some theoretical tracts.

Works incl. operas *Il ratto di Helena*, *Narciso transformato*, *Armida abbandonata*, *Enea*, *Le nozze d'Amore e di Psiche* and *Circe delusa*; Masses; oratorio *S. Cecilia*; madrigals.

Scala di seta, La (*The Silken Ladder*), opera by Rossini (lib. by G. Rossi, based on Planard's lib. *L'Échelle de soie* set by Gaveaux), prod. Venice, Teatro San Moisè, 9 May 1812.

Scala enigmatica (It. = enigmatic scale; also *enimmatica*), Verdi's term for the curious scale on which he constructed his *Ave Maria* for 4 voices comp. c 1889:

SCALA ENIGMATICA

is made in 5 or 6 pitches: sopranino in Eb (rare), soprano in Bb, alto in Eb, tenor in Bb (these 2 the most common), baritone in Eb and bass in Bb.

Saxton, Robert (b London, 8 Oct 1953), English composer. He studied with Elisabeth Lutyens, Robin Holloway, Robert Sherlaw Johnson and Berio.

Works incl. *La Promenade d'Automne* for sop. and ens. (1972), *What does the song hope for?* for sop. and ens. (1974), *Reflections on Narziss and Goldmund* for two chamber groups, harp and pf. (1975), *Canzona* for chamber ens. (1978), *Choruses to Apollo* for orch. (1980), *Traumstadt* for orch. (1980), *Processions and Dances* for 11 insts. (1981), *Piccola Musica per Luigi Dallapiccola* for chamber ens. (1981), *Eloge* for sop. and ens. (1981), *Ring of Eternity* for orch. (1983), Concerto for Orchestra (1984), *Circles of Light* for chamber orch. (1985), vla. concerto (1986).

Sayão, Bidú (Balduina de Oliveira Sayão) (b Niteroi, Rio de Janiero, 11 May 1902), Brazilian soprano. After study with Jean de Reszke she sang Rosina in Rome (1926). Appeared widely in Italy and S. Amer. and gave Lakmé at Washington in 1936. NY Met debut 1937, as Manon. Other NY roles were Juliette, Mélisande, Norina, Zerlina and Susanna. Sang in concert from 1952; retired 1957.

Scacchi, Marco (b Rome, c 1602; d Gallese nr. Rome, c 1685), Italian composer and writer on music, pupil of G.F. Anerio. In 1628 he was app. dir. of music to the court at Warsaw, whence he returned to It. in 1648. He intro. It. opera to Warsaw, Danzig and

Scala Theatre (Teatro alla Scala), the great opera-house at Milan, built, after the destruction by fire of the Teatro Regio Ducal in 1776, on the site of the church of Santa Maria alla Scala, and opened 3 Aug 1778 with Salieri's *Europa riconosciuta*. Operas by Rossini, Donizetti, Bellini (*Norma*), Verdi (*Falstaff* and *Otello*) and Puccini (*Madama Butterfly*) later received their premières there. Toscanini was cond. at var. times between 1899 and 1929, giving many perfs. of Wagner and fps of Italian works. Victor De Sabata was dir. 1931–57, Claudio Abbado 1968–86; Riccardo Muti from 1986.

Scalabrini, Paolo (b ? Bologna or Lucca, c 1713; d Lucca, 28 Feb 1806), Italian composer. Went to Copenhagen in 1747 as cond. of the Mingotti opera co., and stayed there as music dir. to the Dan. court 1748–53 and again 1775–81, when he retired to It. He was among the 1st to write an opera to Dan. words.

Works incl. Dan. operas *Love rewarded, or The Faithful Lovers* (1756), *The Oracle* (1776), *Love without Stockings*, and c 20 It. operas; oratorio *Giuseppe riconosciuto*; symphs.

Scalchi, Sofia (b Turin, 29 Nov 1850; d Rome, 22 Aug 1922), Italian contralto. Studied with Boccabadati and made her debut at Mantua in 1866, as Ulrica. She 1st visited Eng. in 1868 and sang regularly in London until 1890; roles there incl. Amneris, Fides, Ortrud and Leonore in *La Favorite*. Also travelled widely in Europe and 1st went to USA in 1882, when she sang Arsaces; Siebel on the opening night of the Met (1883).

Scale (from Lat. and It. *scala* = ladder), succession of adjoining notes whether proceeding in ascent or descent. For possible varieties see illustration below. *See also* **Scala enigmatica.**

Blasewitz nr. Dresden, 22 Jul 1886), Austrian bass. Studied at the Vienna Cons. and made his 1st stage appearance at Budapest in 1860 as St Bris in *Les Huguenots.* In 1862 he visited London to study under Manuel Gar-

SCALE

Scandello (or Scandellus), Antonio (b Bergamo, 17 Jan 1517; d Dresden, 18 Jan 1580), Italian composer. He is 1st heard of as a cornettist in Bergamo (1541) and was a member of the Saxon court chapel at Dresden in 1553, but he often returned to Brescia for visits, as in 1567, when he and his family took refuge there during the plague at Dresden. Among the court musicians was his brother Angelo S., and also employed at the court was the It. painter Benedetto Tola, whose daughter Agnese became Scandello's 2nd wife in 1568. In the same year he was app. *Kapellmeister* in place of Matthieu Le Maistre, whose asst. *Kapellmeister* he had been for 2 years. He became involved in quarrels with the Ger. court musicians and the Flem. singers because the Italians received higher pay.

Works incl. Masses, motets, setting for voices of the Passion and Resurrection narrative according to St John (1561), hymn tunes for several voices and other church music; madrigals, epithalamia, *canzoni napoletane* for 4 voices, sacred and secular Ger. songs for several voices and instruments; lute music.

Scapino, comedy-overture by Walton; fp Chicago, 3 Apr 1941, cond. Stock.

Scaria, Emil (b Graz, 18 Sep 1838; d

cía and sang at the Crystal Palace. In 1882 he sang Gurnemanz in the fp of Wagner's *Parsifal* at Bayreuth. He sang Wotan with Angelo Neumann's touring co. (Berlin 1881, London 1882).

Scarlatti. Italian family of musicians:

1. (Pietro) Alessandro (Gaspare) S. (b Palermo, 2 May 1660; d Naples, 22 Oct 1725), composer. At the age of 12 he moved with his parents to Rome, where the success of his first opera, *Gli equivoci nel sembiante* (1679), won him the appt. of *maestro di cappella* to Queen Christina of Sweden (1680–3). He also held a similar post at the church of San Gerolamo della Carità before moving to Naples as cond. of the San Bartolomeo opera house (1683–4) and *maestro di cappella* to the court (1684), remaining there for almost 20 years. In Florence 1702–3 he found a patron in Ferdinand (III) de' Medici, for whom he continued to write operas later, but 1703–8 lived mostly in Rome, working first as asst. (1703) then as chief *maestro di cappella* (1707) at the church of Santa Maria Maggiore, and receiving support from Cardinal Ottoboni, who made him his private *maestro di cappella.* In Rome he was restricted by eccles. opposition to opera, but, in addition to operas for Florence, comp. numerous oratorios, serenatas, cantatas, etc.

After a brief visit to Venice in 1707 he was recalled to his old post in Naples at the end of the following year, and was knighted in 1715. He again lived chiefly in Rome 1717–22, but then returned finally to Naples. Among his pupils were his son Domenico S. (5. below), Geminiani and Hasse.

Works incl. 115 operas, incl. *Gli equivoci nel sembiante* (1679), *L'honestà negli amori*, *Il Pompeo* (1683), *Olimpia vendicata*, *La Rosmene* (1686), *La Statira* (1690), *Gli equivoci in amore*, *Pirro e Demetrio* (1694), *La caduta de' decemviri* (1697), *Il prigioniero fortunato* (1698), *L'Eraclea*, *Il Mitridate Eupatore* (1707), *Il Tigrane* (1715), *Il trionfo dell' onore*, *Marco Attilio Regolo* (1719), *La Griselda* (1721), etc.; oratorios *La Maddalena pentita*, *Giuditta*, *San Filippo Neri*; Passion; 16 extant Masses, incl. 5 with orch.; *Salve Regina*, *Stabat Mater*, motets and other church music; over 600 cantatas; 12 *Sinfonie da concerto grosso*; concertos; chamber music; keyboard music.

2. Francesco S. (b Palermo, 5 Dec 1666; d ? Dublin, c 1741), violinist and composer, brother of prec. He became violinist to the court at Naples on Alessandro Scarlatti's appt. as *maestro di cappella* in 1684, and later worked in Palermo. In Vienna in 1715 Fux unsuccessfully recommended him for appt. at court. He was in London 1619–24, and later prob. went to Dublin.

Works incl. operas; church music; cantatas, arias.

3. Tommaso S (b Palermo, c 1671; d Naples, 1 Aug 1760), tenor, brother of prec. Lived in Naples, where he studied at the Cons. di S. Onofrio and sang in the operas of his brother Alessandro S.

4. Pietro Filippo S. (b Rome, 5 Jan 1679; d Naples, 22 Feb 1750), organist, nephew of prec., son of 1. Pupil of his father, he was *maestro di cappella* of Urbino Cathedral 1705–8, then moved to Naples, where he became supernumerary, in 1712 chief, organist of the court chapel. Of his works only 6 toccatas survive.

5. (Giuseppe) Domenico S. (b Naples, 26 Oct 1685; d Madrid, 23 Jul 1757), harpsichordist and composer, brother of prec. Pupil of his father, in 1701 he was app. organist and comp. to the court at Naples, where his operas *L'Ottavia restituita al trono* and *Il Giustino* were prod. in 1703. Sent by his father to Venice in 1705, he travelled by way to Florence, where he presented himself to Alessandro's patron, Ferdinando de' Medici. In Venice he met Gasparini, and prob. studied with him. Moving to Rome, he is said to have engaged with Handel in a contest in harpsichord and organ playing, arranged by Cardinal Ottoboni. He was *maestro di cappella* to Queen Maria Casimira of Pol. in Rome 1709–14, and of the Cappella Giulia 1714–19, but the next year went to the Port. court in Lisbon. Back in It 1724–9, he then went to Seville (later Madrid) in the service of the Span. court, where he remained until his death.

Works incl. operas *La silvia* (1710), *Tolomeo ed Alessandro* (1711), *L'Orlando* (1711), *Tetide in Sciro*, *Ifigenia in Aulide* (1713), *Ifigenia in Tauride* (1713), *Amor d'un' ombra*, *Ambleto*, etc.; oratorios; church music; cantatas, etc.; c 600 harpsichord pieces (30 of them pub. in his lifetime under the title *Essercizi*), now commonly called sonatas.

6. Giuseppe S. (b Naples, c 1718; d Vienna, 17 Aug 1777), composer, cousin (?) of prec. Wrote operas for the It. stage, possibly spent some time in Spain, and settled in Vienna in 1757.

Works incl. operas *Merope* (1740), *Dario* (1741), *I portentosi effetti della Madre Natura* (lib. by Goldoni, 1752), *L'isola disabitata* (1757), *L'amor geloso*, etc.; arias; cantatas; keyboard music.

Scena (It. = stage, or scene, i.e. the subdivision of an act in a dramatic piece), a technical term for operatic solo numbers on a large scale, usually a recitative followed by one or more aria-like sections; also similar pieces designed for concert perf.

Scenario (It.), the sketch or rough draft for the plot of an opera lib. or for the story of a ballet, etc.

Scenes from Goethe's 'Faust' (Schumann). *See* Szenen aus Goethe's 'Faust'.

Scènes Historiques, 2 suites for orch. by Sibelius: no. 1 in 3 movts., 1899, rev. 1911; no. 2 in 3 movts., 1912.

Schachbrett (Schachtbrett), prob. an early form of harpsichord. It is mentioned in Cersne von Minden's *Minneregeln* of 1404. The name does not, apparently, mean 'chessboard' but derives from an old Germanic word *Schacht*, meaning spring or quill (*cf.* Eng. 'jack').

Schack (orig. Žák), **Benedict** (b Mirotice, 7 Feb 1758; d Munich, 10 Dec 1826), Bohemian tenor and composer. A member of Schikaneder's opera co., he was the 1st Tamino in Mozart's *Magic Flute*. Mozart wrote pf. variations on a song prob. by him, 'Ein Weib ist das herrlichste Ding' (K613).

Works incl. *Singspiele* (some with Gerl and others), *Der dumme Gärtner* (1789),

Der Stein der Weisen (1790), *Der Fall ist noch weit seltner* (sequel to Martín y Soler's *Una cosa rara*, 1790), etc.; also church music.

Schadaeus, Abraham (b Senftenberg, 1566; d Finsterwalde, 10 Oct 1626), German composer. He became *Rektor* of the *Lateinschule* in Speyer in 1603. His *Promptuarium musicum*, a collection of motets, was pub. in Strasbourg in 3 parts, in 1611, 1612 and 1613. A *bassus generalis* was added to his friend Caspar Vincentius. (A 4th part, 1617, was entirely by Vincentius.)

Schaeffer, Pierre (b Nancy, 14 Aug 1910), French composer, acoustician and novelist. Worked in Paris radio studio from 1942 and in 1948 broadcast a programme of pieces assembled from random noises, made into montage with the use of tape; coined the term 'musique concrète' to define such activity.

Works incl. (some in collaboration with Pierre Henry), *Étude aux chemins de fer*, *Concerts de bruits* (1948), *Symphonie pour un homme seul* (1950) and *Orphée* (1953). Later turned to writing novels.

Schaeffner, André (b Paris, 7 Feb 1895; d Paris, 11 Aug 1980), French musicologist. Studied at the Schola Cantorum in Paris and after 1920 became music critic to var. periodicals. His books incl. studies of Stravinsky and of the origin of musical instruments. In 1929 he became dir. of the ethnomusicological section of the Musée de l'Homme in Paris.

Schafer, R. Murray (b Sarnia, Ont., 18 Jul 1933), Canadian composer and teacher. He studied in Toronto and Vienna and worked in England as a journalist. Works employ electronics and involve transformation and motivic distortion: opera *Loving/Toi* (staged Toronto, 1978), *Minnelieder* for mezzo and wind 5tet (1956), *St Jean de Brebeuf* for bar. and orch. (1961), *Requiems for the Party Girl* for sop. and 9 insts. (1966), *From the Tibetan Book of the Dead* for sop., chorus and ens. (1968), *The Son of Heldenleben* (after a work by Strauss, 1968), *Sappho* for mezzo and ens. (1970), string 4tet (1970), *In Search of Zoroaster* for male voice, chorus and perc. (1971), *Adieu, Robert Schumann* for mezzo and orch. (after Clara Schumann's diaries detailing her husband's madness, 1976), *Apocolypsis* for soloist, chorus and orch. (after St John the Divine, 1980).

Schäffer, Boguslaw (b Lwów, 6 Jun 1929), Polish composer. Studied in Kraków with A. Malawski and musicology in Warsaw with

Jachimecki. For some of his works he has evolved graphic notation.

Works incl. *Scultura* for orch.; *Monosonata* for 24 string instrs.; *Topofonica* for 40 insts.; *Equivalenze sonore* for perc. insts.; concerto for harpsichord, perc. and orch.; *4 Movements* for pf. and orch.; *Tertium datum* for clavichord and chamber orch; 10 symphs. (1960–79); 2 pf. concertos (1957, 1967); 2 harpsichord concertos (1958, 1961); violin concerto (1963); *Kesukaan* for strings (1978); 6 string 4tets (1954–73).

Schaffrath, Christoph (b Hohenstein nr. Dresden, 1709; d Berlin, 17 Feb 1763), German harpsichordist, organist and composer. In 1733, when in the service of a Pol. prince, he competed unsuccessfully with W.F. Bach for the post of organist at St Sophia's Church at Dresden, but in 1736 he became chamber musician to the crown prince of Prus. and remained with him when he acceded as Frederick II.

Works incl. 13 symphs. and overtures for orch.; harpsichord and vln. concertos; chamber music.

Schale, Christian Friedrich (b Brandenburg, 10 Mar 1713; d Berlin, 2 Mar 1800), German organist and composer. Pupil of C.F. Rolle in Magdeburg, he entered the service of Frederick II of Prussia in 1741 and became organist of Berlin Cathedral in 1763. Comp. mostly keyboard music.

Schalk, Franz (b Vienna, 27 May 1863; d Edlach, 2 Sep 1931), Austrian conductor. Pupil of Bruckner and, after var. engagements, chief cond. at the Vienna Court Opera in succession to Ferdinand Löwe, and dir. (partly with R. Strauss) from 1918 to 1929. He 1st visited Eng. in 1898. He was responsible for a spurious revision of Bruckner's symphs. He cond. Wagner in NY and London (1898–1911) and gave the fp of *Die Frau ohne Schatten* (Vienna, 1919).

Scharwenka, (Ludwig) Philipp (b Szamotuły, Poznań, 16 Feb 1847; d Bad Nauheim, 16 Jul 1917), German-Polish composer and teacher. On the family's removal to Berlin he studied music at Kullak's school there and remained as teacher until 1881, when he joined his brother's newly opened Cons., which he directed in 1891 on the latter's departure for Amer., together with Hugo Goldschmidt. In 1880 he married the violinist Marianne Stresow (1856–1918).

Works incl. 2 symphs., serenade, Festival Overture, *Liebesnacht, Arcadian Suite*, symph. poems *Frühlingswogen* and *Traum und Wirklichkeit*; vln. concerto (1895); *Herbstfeier* and *Sakuntala* (after Kalidasa)

for solo voices, chorus and orch.; pf. trio in C♯ min.; 3 concert pieces for vln. and pf., vln. and cello studies; *Album polonais*, 3 sonatas and many other works for pf.

Scharwenka, (Franz) Xaver (b Szamotuly, Poznań, 6 Jan 1850; d Berlin, 8 Dec 1924), German-Polish pianist, composer and teacher, brother of prec. Studied at Kullak's school of music in Berlin, where the family had settled in 1865, and made his 1st appearance as a pianist there in 1869. Later he travelled widely, paying his 1st visit to Eng. in 1879. In 1881 he opened a Cons. of his own in Berlin, which in 1893 became amalgamated with Klindworth's. In 1891–8 he lived mainly in NY, where he had opened a branch of his school.

Works incl. opera *Mataswintha* (on Felix Dahn's novel *Ein Kampf um Rom*, 1896); symph. in C min.; 4 pf. concertos (pub. 1876–1908); pf. 4tet, 2 pf. trios; 2 cello and pf. sonatas; Theme and Variations, Pol. dances and numerous other works for pf.

Schat, Peter (b Utrecht, 5 Jun 1935), Dutch composer. Studied in Utrecht and The Hague, and then with Seiber and Boulez. Became well known as an experimental comp.

Works incl. *Mosaics* for orch.; *Cryptogamen* for bar. and orch. *Signalement* for 6 perc. insts. and 3 dbs.; *Improvisations and Symphonies* for wind 5tet; *Labyrinth*, work for 'musical theatre' with 'happenings' (prod. Amsterdam, 1966); *Houdini*, circus opera (1976).

Schauspieldirektor, Der (*The Impresario*), play with music by Mozart (lib. by G. Stephanie, jun.), prod. Vienna, Schönbrunn Palace, at court, 7 Feb 1786; 1st Vienna perf., Kärntnertortheater, 18 Feb 1786.

Schechner, Anna (Nanette) (b Munich, 1806; d 29 Apr 1860), German soprano. Pupil of Weber and studied in It. 1st appeared in Munich and in 1826 in Vienna; sang there until 1835 as Leonore, Donna Anna, Euryanthe, and in operas by Gluck and Spontini. She married the painter Karl Waagen in 1832.

Scheff, Fritzi (b Vienna, 30 Aug 1879; d New York, 8 Apr 1954), Austrian soprano. Debut Munich 1897, as Donizetti's Marie. CG 1897–1900, as Nedda, Zerlina and Martha. NY Met 1900–4; debut as Marzelline and also heard as Elsa, Cherubino and Juliette, and in the 1902 local fp of Paderewski's *Manru*. Operetta from 1904.

Scheherazade (Ravel and Rimsky-Korsakov). *See* **Shéhérazade** and **Shahrazad**.

Scheibe, Johann Adolph (b Leipzig, 5 May 1708; d Copenhagen, 22 Apr 1776), German writer on music, critic and composer. Studied law at Leipzig Univ. and in 1736 settled in Hamburg, where he ed. the periodical *Der critische Musikus* (1737–40), in which he attacked Bach. He was *Kapellmeister* to the Margrave of Brandenburg-Culmbach 1739–44, and cond. of the court opera in Copenhagen 1744–8.

Works incl. one opera (*Thusnelde*, 1749); cantatas; Masses and other church music; instrumental music; songs.

Scheidemann. German family of organists and composers.

1. David S. (b Hamburg; d Hamburg), organist in Wöhrden and subsequently at St Catherine's Church, Hamburg. Pub. a hymn-book with H. and J. Praetorius and Joachim Decker in 1604, with the tunes in the soprano part, not, as earlier, in the tenor.

2. Heinrich S. (b Wöhrden, *c* 1596; d Hamburg, 1663), son of prec. Pupil of his father and later of Sweelinck at Amsterdam. In 1625 he succeeded his father as organist at St Catherine's Church, Hamburg, where on his death he was himself succeeded by Reinken, who was his pupil, as were Fabricius and Weckmann. He contrib. to Part V of Rist's hymn-book *Neue himmlische Lieder* (1651).

Works incl. church music and organ pieces.

Scheidemantel, Karl (b Weimar, 21 Jan 1859; d Weimar, 26 Jun 1923), German baritone. Studied with Bodo Borchers and made his 1st stage appearance at Weimar in 1878. After further study with Stockhausen he became famous, mainly as a Wagner singer. He 1st visited London in 1884, when he sang Pizarro, Telramund and Kurwenal, and was 1st engaged at the Bayreuth Wagner theatre in 1886; sang there until 1892 as Klingsor, Sachs, Amfortas and Wolfram. From 1920 to 1922 he was director of the Dresden Landesoper. He wrote 2 books on singing.

Scheidl, Theodor (b Vienna, 3 Aug 1880; d Tübingen, 22 Apr 1959), Austrian baritone. Debut Vienna 1910, in *Lohengrin*; Stuttgart 1913–21. Bayreuth 1914–30, as Klingsor, Amfortas and Kurwenal. Also admired as Wagner singer at the Berlin Staatsoper, 1921–32, and at Prague from 1932.

Scheidt, Robert vom (b Bremen, 16 Apr 1879; d Frankfurt, 10 Apr 1964), German baritone. He sang at Cologne 1897–1903 and Hamburg 1903–12. Frankfurt 1912–40, in the fps of Schreker's *Die Gezeichneten*

(1918) and *Der Schatzgräber* (1920), and Egk's *Die Zaubergeige* (1935). Bayreuth 1904, as Donner and Klingsor.

Scheidt, Samuel (b Halle, bap. 3 Nov 1587; d Halle, 24 Mar 1654), German organist and composer. Organist at St Maurice's Church, Halle, 1603. Pupil of Sweelinck at Amsterdam. He returned to Halle in 1609, and became court organist to the Margrave of Brandenburg, in his capacity as Protestant administrator of the archbishopric of Magdeburg, and *Kapellmeister* in 1619. He lost his appt. in 1625 as a result of the 30 Years War. His *Tabulatura nova* for the organ (1624) was printed in score, not in the old Ger. tablature.

Works incl. *Cantiones sacrae* for 8 voices; sacred concertos for 2–12 voices with instruments; pavans and galliards for 4–5 voices; *Liebliche Krafft-Blümlein* for 2 voices and instruments; organ accomps. for or transcriptions of 100 hymns and psalms; *Tabulatura nova* containing a great variety of organ pieces in 3 vols.

Schein, Johann Hermann (b Grünhain, Saxony, 20 Jan 1586; d Leipzig, 19 Nov 1630), German composer. After the death of his father, a Lutheran pastor, he went to Dresden as a choir-boy in the court chapel in 1599, to the grammar-school at Schulpforta in 1603 and to Leipzig Univ. in 1607. In 1615 he was app. *Kapellmeister* at the court of Weimar and in 1616 became cantor at St Thomas's School, Leipzig, on the death of Calvisius, remaining there until his death. His music is influenced by Lutheran chorales and by the latest expressive techniques of the early Italian madrigalists.

Works incl. *Cantiones sacrae* for 5–12 voices; 2 vols. of sacred concertos for 3–5 voices with insts.; *Fontana d'Israel* containing biblical words set for 4–5 voices and insts.; *Cantional* hymn-book with c 80 tunes of his own; songs for 5 voices, *Venus-Kränzlein, Studenten-Schmaus* and *Diletti pastorali;* instrumental dances *Banchetto musicale;* songs with insts. *Musica boscareccia;* wedding and funeral cantatas.

Schelble, Johann Nepomuk (b Hüfingen, Black Forest, 16 May 1789; d Frankfurt, 7 Aug 1837), German singer, teacher and conductor. Studied with Vogler and others, lived and sang in Vienna in 1813–16 and then settled at Frankfurt, where he taught and founded the Caecilian Society in 1818.

Schelle, Johann (b Geissing nr. Meissen, 6 Sep 1648; d Leipzig, 10 Mar 1710), German organist and composer. He was a choirboy at Dresden, Wolfenbüttel and Leipzig. Stud-ied at Leipzig, became cantor at Eilenburg and in 1677 cantor at St Thomas's Church, Leipzig.

Works incl. cantatas, songs.

Schelling, Ernest Henry (b Belvidere, NJ, 26 July 1876; d New York, 8 Dec 1939), American pianist and composer. After his debut as a child prodigy at Philadelphia at the age of 4, he studied at the Paris Cons., also in Vienna with Leschetizky for pf. and Bruckner for comp., as well as elsewhere with Paderewski, Moszkowski and others. He toured widely, joined the American army in 1918 and later lectured on the orch. to children.

Works incl. symph. in C min., *Symph. Legend* (1904), fantasy *A Victory Ball* and *Morocco* for orch.; *Fantastic Suite* and *Impressions from an Artist's Life* for pf. and orch.

Schelomo, Hebrew rhapsody for cello and orch. by Bloch, based on Book of Ecclesiastes; comp. 1916, fp NY 3 May 1917, cond. Bloch.

Schemelli, Georg Christian (b Herzberg, c 1678; d Zeitz, 5 Mar 1762), German musician and music ed. Pupil at St Thomas's school, Leipzig; cantor at the palace of Zeitz. His *Musicalisches Gesang-Buch,* ed. by Bach, was pub. in 1736. On some of the hymns in it Bach wrote chorale preludes.

Schenck, Johan(n) (b Amsterdam, bap. 3 Jun 1660; d c 1712), German or Dutch vla. da gamba player and composer. He worked at the electoral court at Düsseldorf and in Amsterdam.

Works incl. opera *Ceres en Bacchus;* chamber sonatas for 2 vlns., vla. da gamba and bass, vla. da gamba sonatas and suites.

Schenk, Johann Baptist (b Wiener Neustadt, 30 Nov 1753; d Vienna, 29 Dec 1836), Austrian composer. Pupil of Wagenseil 1774–7, he made his public debut as an opera comp. in 1785. Beethoven was his pupil in 1793, and he was also a friend of Mozart and Schubert.

Works incl. *Singspiele: Die Weinlese* (1785), *Die Weihnacht auf dem Lande* (1786), *Achmet und Almanzine, Der Dorfbarbier* (1796), *Die Jagd, Der Fassbinder* (1802), etc.; Masses and other church music; cantatas *Die Huldigung* and *Der Mai;* 10 symphs.; 4 harp concertos; 5 string 4tets and trios; songs.

Schenk, Otto (b Vienna, 12 Jun 1930), Austrian producer. Prod. *Die Zauberflöte* at Salzburg (Landestheater) 1957. *Lulu* (1962) and *Jenůfa* (1964) at Vienna Staatsoper. *Fidelio* at NY Met 1970; began *Ring* prod.

with *Die Walküre* in 1986. Prod. an austere *Ballo in Maschera* at CG in 1975.

Schenker, Heinrich (b Wisniowczyki, 19 Jun 1868; d Vienna, 13 Jan 1935), Polish-Austrian theorist. Studied with Bruckner at the Vienna Cons. and on Brahms's recommendation pub. some early compositions. He taught a number of pupils privately and in his literary works, incl. *Neue musikalische Theorien und Phantasien* and *Das Meisterwerk in der Musik*, laid down his detailed analytical methods.

Scherchen, Hermann (b Berlin, 21 Jun 1891; d Florence, 12 Jun 1966), German conductor. Self-taught in music, he played the vla. in the Blüthner Orch. from 1907 to 1910, also playing with the Berlin PO. He made his debut as a cond. in 1912 with Schoenberg's *Pierrot lunaire,* and in 1914 became cond. of the Riga SO, being interned in Russia during World War I. After the war he founded the Neue Musikgesellschaft and edited the periodical *Melos* (1920–1). From 1928 to 1933 he was cond. of the Königsberg Radio Orch. He was esp. well known as a conductor of new music, the cause of which he championed throughout his life; he gave the fps of Dallapiccola's *Il prigioniero* (1950) and Henze's *König Hirsch* (1956) and the 1st German prod. of *Moses und Aron* (Berlin, 1959).

Scherer, Sebastian Anton (b Ulm, Oct 1631; d Ulm, 26 Aug 1712), German organist and composer. He rose through var. posts to that of organist of Ulm Cathedral in 1671.

Works incl. Masses, motets and psalms; sonatas for 2 vlns. and bass; organ pieces; suites for lute.

Schering, Arnold (b Breslau, 2 Apr 1877; d Berlin, 7 Mar 1941), German musicologist. Studied at Leipzig Univ., where in 1907 he became lecturer and later prof. of music. From 1909 he also lectured at the Cons. In 1920 he became prof. at Halle Univ. and in 1928 at Berlin Univ. His books incl. studies of the early vln. concerto, the development of the oratorio and sonata, the perf. of old music, early organ and chamber music and a series of attempts to prove that Beethoven's sonatas and 4tets are based on Shakespeare's plays and other dramatic works.

Scherz, List und Rache (*Jest, Cunning and Revenge*), operetta by Bruch (lib. by Goethe, altered by L. Bischoff), prod. Cologne, 14 Jan 1858.

For other settings *see* **Goethe.**

Scherzando (It. = playful, humorous, skittish), a direction written by comps. over passages intended to be perf. in that manner.

It may also be used as an adj. in tempo directions, e.g. *allegretto scherzando.*

Scherzi, Gli (*The Jokes*), one of the nicknames of Haydn's 6 string 4tets, op. 33, comp. 1781. Also known as the *Russian* 4tets or *Jungfernquartette.*

Scherzo, one of the 2 middle movements, more usually the 3rd, of a 4-movement symph., sonata or other sonata-form work, where it displaced the Minuet. It does not occur regularly before the early 19th cent., being estab. mainly by Beethoven and Schubert; but the term scherzo dates back to the 17th cent., when It. canzonets were often called 'scherzi musicali' and instrumental pieces were also sometimes pub. under that title. (For an early use of the name *see* Haydn's work above.) The scherzo, having arisen from the minuet, is normally in fast triple time, generally 3–4 with one beat in a bar, and it has as a rule a contrasting trio section. But exs. in duple or quadruple time occur, e.g. in Beethoven's E♭ maj. pf. sonata, op. 31 no. 3, in Mendelssohn and in Schumann. Sometimes the trio occurs twice, e.g. in Beethoven's 7th symph., or there may be, esp. in Schumann, 2 different trios. A coda, often based on the trio, is neither normal nor unusual. There are very successful scherzos which do not conform to the classical pattern, e.g. Chopin's.

Schiavetto, Giulio, Italian composer, active in Dalmatia during the 2nd half of the 16th cent. His madrigals and motets, pub. in Venice in 1563 and 1565 respectively, were dedicated to Gerolamo Savorgnano, bishop of Šibenik.

Schibler, Armin (b Kreuzlingen, Lake Constance, 20 Nov 1920; d Zurich, 7 Sep 1986), Swiss composer. Studied music while at school at Aarau and then at the Zurich Cons. In 1942 he became a pupil of Burkhard.

Works incl. oratorio *Media in vita;* operas *Der spanische Rosenstock* (1950), *The Devil in the Winter Palace* (1953), *The Feet in the Fire*; 3 chamber ballets; cantatas *Marignano, Vision des Mittelalters, Die Hochzeit* (Gotthelf) and *Cantata domestica*; 3 symphs. (1946–57), symph. variations, toccata and fugue for string orch.; vln. concerto, pf. concerto, horn concerto (1956), trombone concerto (1957), perc. concerto, fantasy for vln. and orch; concerto for vln., cello and strings; toccata, interlude and fugue for wind instruments; pf. 4tet; 4 string 4tets (1945–60), vln. and pf. sonata; toccata for org.; *Circulus Fugae* for pf.; songs.

Schicht, Johann Gottfried (b Reichenau nr.

Zittau, 29 Sep 1753; d Leipzig, 16 Feb 1823), German harpsichordist and composer. Studied law at Leipzig Univ. but turned to music and was engaged as harpsichordist by J.A. Hiller for his concerts, later succeeding him as their cond. In 1810 he was app. cantor at St Thomas's Church. Works incl. 3 oratorios, church music, chamber works.

Schick, Ernst (b The Hague, Oct 1756; d Berlin, 10 Feb 1815), Dutch violinist. Married the singer Margarete Luise Hamel in 1791 and was engaged for the Berlin Court Opera in 1793. He estab. chamber concerts there with Bohrer.

Schick (*née* **Hamel**), **Margarete Luise** (b Mainz, 26 Apr 1773; d Berlin, 29 Apr 1809), German soprano. Studied at Würzburg and with Righini at Mainz, where she made her debut in 1788. In 1791 she married Ernst Schick and in 1793 they were both engaged by Frederick William II of Prussia and went to Berlin.

Schicksalslied (*Song of Destiny*), a setting by Brahms for chorus and orch. of a poem in Hölderlin's *Hyperion*, op. 54, comp. in 1871; fp Karlsruhe, 18 Oct 1871.

Schiedermair, Ludwig (b Regensburg, 7 Dec 1876; d Bensberg nr. Cologne, 30 Apr 1957), German music scholar. Studied with Sandberger and Beer-Walbrunn at Munich, where he took a degree in 1901. After further studies with Riemann and Kretzschmar in Berlin he became lecturer at Marburg and in 1914 prof. of music at Bonn Univ. There he became dir. of the Beethoven Archives, and among his books are bibliog. works on Beethoven and an ed. of Mozart's letters with an iconographical volume.

Schiff, Andras (b Budapest, 21 Dec 1953), Hungarian pianist. He studied at the Liszt Academy, Budapest and with George Malcolm in London. He made his debut in Budapest and won prizes at the Tchaikovsky Comp., Moscow, in 1974 and the Leeds International in 1975. He has a wide repertory but is best known for his interpretations of Bach.

Schiff, Heinrich (b Gmunden, 18 Nov 1951), Austrian cellist. He studied in Vienna and with André Navarra in Detmold. He has won prizes in competitions in Warsaw, Geneva and Vienna, and has appeared as soloist with orchestras in Vienna, London, Stockholm and Tokyo. Also plays in recital.

Schikaneder, (Johann Josef) Emanuel (b Straubing, 1 Sep 1751; d Vienna, 21 Sep 1812), German actor, singer, playwright and theatre manager. Settled in Vienna in

1784. Author (or ? part-author with Ludwig Gieseke) of the lib. of Mozart's *Magic Flute*, which he prod. with himself as Papageno. He also wrote libs. for Schack, Gerl, Süssmayr, Woelfl, Seyfried, Winter and others.

Schiller, (Johann Christoph) Friedrich von (1759–1805), German poet and dramatist. *See* **Bride of Messina** (Fibich), **Briganti** (Mercadante), **Bruch** (*Lied von der Glocke* and *Macht des Gesanges*), **'Choral' Symphony** (Beethoven), **Costa** (*Don Carlos*), **Don Carlos** (Verdi), **Giovanna d'Arco** (Verdi), **Guillaume Tell** (Rossini), **Ideale** (Liszt), **Luisa Miller** (Verdi), **Maid of Orleans** (Tchaikovsky), **Mascagni** (*Ode to Joy*), **Masnadieri** (Verdi), **Seyfried** (*Räuber* and *Jungfrau von O.*), **Smetana** (*Wallenstein's Camp*), **Turandot** (Weber), **Vaccai** (*Giovanna d'Arco* and *Sposa di Messina*), **Zumsteeg** (*Räuber, Wallensteins Lager* and *Ritter Toggenburg*).
42 songs by Schubert.

Schillinger, Joseph (b Kharkov, 31 Aug 1895; d New York, 23 Mar 1943), Russian, later American, composer and theoretician. Studied at St Petersburg Cons. with Tcherepnin, among others, and then taught at Kharkov Music Acad. from 1918 to 1922, and from 1926 to 1928 in Leningrad. In 1929 he settled in the USA, teaching a mathematical method of his own; among his many pupils was Gershwin. He pub. his system in a number of books, and also some comps. incl. *March of the Orient; First Airphonic Suite* for theremin, orch. and pf.; pf. pieces.

Schillings, Max von (b Düren, Rhineland, 19 Apr 1868; d Berlin, 24 Jul 1933), German conductor and composer. Studied at Bonn and Munich, where he settled, taking part in the Wagner perfs. at Bayreuth. In 1908 he went to Stuttgart, where he gradually rose to the post of general music dir. of the Court Opera. In 1919 he went to Berlin as dir. of the Staatsoper.
Works incl. operas *Ingwelde* (1894), *Der Pfeifertag* (1899), *Moloch* (after Hebbel, 1906) and *Mona Lisa* (1915); incid. music for Aeschylus's *Orestes* and Goethe's *Faust*; symph. fantasies *Meergruss* and *Seemorgen,* symph. prologue, *Oedipus* (after Sophocles) for orch.; recitations with orch. incl. Wildenbruch's *Hexenlied*; vln. concerto (1910), *Zweigespräch* for vln., cello and small orch. (1896); *Hochzeitslied* for solo voices, chorus and orch. (1910); *Dem Verklärten* (Schiller) and *Glockenlieder* for solo voice and orch.; string 4tet in E min., string 5tet in E♭ maj.; improvisation for vln. and pf.

Schindler, Anton (b Meedl nr. Neustadt, Moravia, 13 Jun 1795; d Bockenheim nr. Frankfurt, 16 Jan 1864), Austrian violinist and writer on music. Studied in Vienna, met Beethoven in 1814, played at his concerts and later became his factotum and early biog. He was successively leader of the orch. at the Josephstadt Theatre and the Kärntnertortheater, and later music director at Münster and Aachen.

Schiøtz, Aksel (b Roskilde, 1 Sep 1906; d Copenhagen, 19 Apr 1975), Danish tenor. He studied in Copenhagen and made his debut there in 1939, as Ferrando. He gave his first Lieder recital in 1942 and was later widely admired in Schubert and Schumann. In 1946 he sang the Male Chorus in the first prod. of Britten's *Rape of Lucretia*, at Glyndebourne. After a brain tumour operation in 1950 he was heard occasionally as a baritone, and taught in Canada and the USA. Returned to Denmark in 1968.

Schipa, Tito (actually Raffaele Attilio Amadeo) (b Lecce, 2 Jan 1889; d New York, 16 Dec 1965), Italian tenor. First studied comp., producing some songs and pf. pieces. Then studied singing, making his debut in Vercelli in 1910 as Alfredo. From 1919 to 1932 he was a member of the Chicago Civic Opera and from 1932 to 1935 sang at the NY Met as Don Ottavio and in operas by Thomas, Mascagni and Massenet. He lived in the USA until 1941, when he returned to It. and sang there until 1952; concert tour of Russia 1957.

Works incl. operetta *La Principessa Liana*; a Mass; a Hosanna.

Schippers, Thomas (b Kalamazoo, 9 Mar 1930; d New York, 16 Dec 1977), American conductor. First appeared in public aged 6, at the pf., and became a church organist aged 14. From 1944 to 1945 he studied at the Curtis Inst. in Philadelphia and from 1946 to 1947 privately with O. Samaroff. He also studied at Yale Univ. and the Juilliard; made his debut as a cond. with the Lemonade Opera Co. in 1948; started an association with the operas of Menotti in 1950. After appearances with the NY City Opera Co. and the NY PO, he appeared at the NY Met; led the prod. of Barber's *Antony and Cleopatra* which opened the new house at Lincoln Center. Bayreuth 1963, *Die Meistersinger*; London, CG, 1968, *Elektra*.

Schira, Francesco (b Malta, 21 Aug 1809; d London, 15 Oct 1883). Italian composer and conductor. Studied at the Cons. of Milan and prod. his 1st opera there in 1832, on the strength of which he was engaged as cond. and comp. for the Opera at Lisbon, where he also taught at the Cons. In 1842 he left for Paris in the hope of obtaining a Fr. lib., but met the manager of the Princess's Theatre in London, who engaged him as cond. In 1844 he went to Drury Lane as Benedict's successor and in 1848 to CG. He remained in London to his death. In 1873 the Birmingham Festival commissioned a cantata from him.

Works incl. operas *Elena e Malvina* (1832), *I cavalieri di Valenza* (1837), *Il fanatico per la musica*, *Kenilworth* (in Eng., after Scott), *Mina* (1849), *Theresa, the Orphan of Geneva* (1850), *Niccolo de' Lapi*, *Selvaggia* (1875), *Lia*, operetta *The Ear-Ring*; cantata *The Lord of Burleigh* (after Tennyson); vocal trios and duets; songs.

Schirmer, G., Inc., firm of US music publishers founded jointly in NY (1861) by Gustav Schirmer and Bernard Beer; Schirmer in full control from 1866. Comps. published by firm incl. Schoenberg, Harris, Barber, Schuman and Menotti.

Schläger (Ger. lit. beaters), sometimes used in scores, etc. as an abbr. for the following. Also in the singular a popular song.

Schlaginstrumente (Ger. lit. beaten instruments) = Percussion instruments.

Schlagobers (*Whipped Cream* in Viennese dialect), ballet by R. Strauss (choreography by H. Kröller), prod. Vienna, Opera, 9 May 1924.

Schlagzither (Ger. lit. striking-zither), a zither the strings of which are struck with hammers, i.e. a dulcimer rather than a zither.

Schlegel, August Wilhelm von (1767–1845), German poet, critic and translator. *See* **Fierrabras** (Schubert).

7 poems by S. set as songs by Schubert.

Schleppen (Ger. = to drag), sometimes used by German composers as a negative imperative, *nicht schleppen* = 'do not drag'.

Schlick, Arnolt (b Heidelberg, before 1460; d Heidelberg, after 1521), German organist, composer and theorist. His early life was spent in Heidelberg, but he subsequently travelled widely: to Frankfurt in 1486, where he played the organ during the festivities for the coronation of Maximilian I; to Hol. in 1490; to Strasbourg (many times); to Worms in 1495, where he met Sebastian Virdung; and subsequently to Speyer, Hagenau and elsewhere. During these journeys he gained an enormous reputation for testing new organs. He was blind, probably from infancy.

In 1511 he pub. his *Spiegel der Orgelmacher und Organisten*, a treatise on organ building and playing. The *Tabulaturen etlicher lobgesang und lidlein* (Mainz, 1512) followed; it was the first printed book of keyboard music to appear in Germany, and contained liturgical organ music, lute pieces and songs with lute. He also wrote music for the coronation of Charles V in Aachen, 1520.

Schlick, Johann Konrad (b ? Münster, 1748; d Gotha, 12 Jul 1818), German cellist and composer. He worked in the episcopal chapel at Münster, and in 1777 entered the service of the court in Gotha. He married the violinist Regina Strinasacchi in 1785.

Works incl. concertos; string 5tets and 4tets; pf. trios; cello sonatas; guitar pieces.

Schlosser, Karl (b Amberg, 17 Oct 1835; d Utting am Ammersee, 2 Sep 1916), German tenor. His early career was in Switzerland; sang at Munich 1868–1904 and created David in *Die Meistersinger*. Created Mime in *Siegfried* (Bayreuth 1876) and sang the role with Neumann's co. in London 1882. Other roles incl. Max, Almaviva and Beckmesser.

Schlusnus, Heinrich (b Braubach, 6 Aug 1888; d Frankfurt, 19 Jun 1952), German baritone. Studied with Bachner in Berlin and made his debut in Frankfurt in 1912 as a concert singer, and as an opera singer in Hamburg in 1915. From 1915 to 1917 he was a member of the Nuremberg Opera, and from 1917 to 1945 of the Berlin Staatsoper. His last role was Rigoletto (Frankfurt 1948). He took part in the pre-war Verdi revival and sang Amfortas at Bayreuth in 1933.

Schlüssel (Ger. lit. key) = Clef.

Schlüter, Erna (b Oldenburg, 5 Feb 1904; d Hamburg, 1 Dec 1969), German soprano. Debut Oldenburg 1922; Mannheim from 1925, Düsseldorf 1930–40. She appeared at Hamburg 1940–56 and was the 1st Ellen Orford there (1947). NY Met 1946–7, as Brünnhilde and Isolde. Salzburg 1948, Leonore. Sang as guest at CG, Vienna and Brussels. Well known as Elektra.

Schmedes, Erik (b Gjentofte nr. Copenhagen, 27 Aug 1866; d Vienna, 23 Mar 1931), Danish tenor. Studied in Ger. and Aus. and with Padilla in Paris; made his 1st stage appearance at Wiesbaden in 1891. From 1898 to 1924 he sang at the Vienna Court Opera, at first under Mahler, and in 1899 he was 1st engaged for the Wagner theatre at Bayreuth; sang there until 1906 as Siegfried and Parsifal. Other roles incl. Cavaradossi, Palestrina and Florestan.

Schmeltzl, Wolfgang (b Kemnat, Upper Palatinate, c 1500; d c 1560), German composer. He became cantor at Amberg and married there, but later became a Catholic priest and left his family. He was a schoolmaster in Vienna in 1540.

Works incl. a book of songs, quodlibets and folksong settings for 4–5 voices.

Schmelzer (von Ehrenruff), Andreas (Anton) (b Vienna, 26 Nov 1653; d Vienna, 13 Oct 1701), Austrian violinist and composer. He was in the service of the Aus. court in 1671–1700.

Works incl. ballet music for more than 30 of Draghi's operas.

Schmelzer, (Johann) Heinrich (b Scheibs, Lower Austria, c 1623; d Prague, Mar 1680), Austrian composer, father of prec. He was chamber musician at the Aus. court in Vienna from 1649, asst. cond. from 1671 and 1st cond. from 1679.

Works incl. ballet music for c 40 operas by Draghi and others; *Missa nuptialis* and other church music; instrumental sonatas; tpt. fanfares.

Schmetternd (Ger. = brassy, brazen, clanging). The term is prescribed, like the Fr. *cuivré*, when that kind of tone is required of brass instruments, esp. horns.

Schmid(t), Bernhard the Elder (b ? Strasbourg, 1535; d Strasbourg, 1592), German composer and poet. He pub. a collection of music arr. for organ in 2 parts: the 1st contained motets, the 2nd secular songs and dances (Strasbourg, 1577).

Schmid(t), Bernhard the Younger (b Strasbourg, bap. 1 Apr 1567; d Strasbourg, 1625), German composer, son of prec. His own collection of organ arrs., highly ornamented, was pub. at Strasbourg in 1607.

Schmidt, Bernhard. *See* **Smith, Bernard.**

Schmidt, Franz (b Pressburg, 22 Dec 1874; d Perchtoldsdorf, 11 Feb 1939), Austrian cellist, pianist and composer. Studied at the Vienna Cons. and in 1896 became cellist in the Hofoper orch., under Mahler from 1897. He left in 1910 to become pf. prof. at the Vienna Music Acad., of which he became dir. in 1925. He also appeared as concert pianist.

Works incl. operas *Notre-Dame* (after Hugo, 1914) and *Fredigundis* (1922); oratorio *Das Buch mit sieben Siegeln* (1938); 4 symphs. (1899, 1913, 1928, 1933) chaconne and *Variations on a Hussar's Song* for orch.; variations on a theme by Beethoven for pf. and orch.; string 4tet (1925), pf. 5tet, 2 clar. 5tets (1932, 1938); 7 org. works.

Schmidt, Gustav (b Weimar, 1 Sep 1816; d Darmstadt, 11 Sep 1882), German composer and conductor. Studied with Hummel and others at Weimar and with Mendelssohn at Leipzig. He began as opera cond. at Brno and then served in the same capacity in several Ger. towns, last at Darmstadt.

Works incl. operas *Prinz Eugen der edle Ritter, Weibertreue, La Réole, Alibi*; incid. music for a play based on Dickens's *Christmas Carol*; male-voice choruses; songs.

Schmidt, Isserstedt, Hans (b Berlin, 5 May 1900; d Hamburg, 28 May 1973), German conductor. Studied with Schreker and also at the Univ. of Cologne, graduating in 1923. He began his career at the Wuppertal opera and then from 1928 to 1931 cond. at Rostock, from 1931 to 1933 at Darmstadt, and from 1935 to 1942 was principal cond. at the Hamburg Staatsoper. He was dir. of the Deutsche Oper in Berlin from 1942 to 1945 and then chief cond. of the North Ger. Radio SO. He gave *Figaro* at Glyndebourne in 1958 and *Tristan* at CG, London, in 1962.

Schmidt, Johann Christoph, sen. and jun. *See* **Smith, John Christopher.**

Schmidt, Joseph (b Davidende, 4 Mar 1904; d Girenbad, 16 Nov 1942), German tenor of Rumanian birth. He sang in the synagogue at Czernowitz and studied at Vienna. In 1928 he was heard on Berlin radio in *Idomeneo*. His diminutive stature prevented a stage career but he gained a huge following through records, concerts and films: the 1932 film *Ein Lied geht um die Welt* further increased his popularity. With the rise of the Nazis he was obliged to tour Europe and America. He escaped to Switzerland but died in an internment camp, near Zurich.

Schmidt, Trudelise (b Saarbrücken, 7 Nov 1943), German mezzo. Debut Saarbrücken; sang at Düsseldorf from 1969, Hamburg and Munich from 1971. Bayreuth debut 1975, in *The Ring*. Glyndebourne 1976, Dorabella. Guest appearances at Salzburg and Milan. Among her best roles are Strauss's Composer and Octavian, Mozart's Cherubino and Idamante, and Janáček's Vixen. *Iphigénie en Tauride* and *Mathis der Maler* are among her recordings.

Schmidt, (Georg) Aloys (b Hanover, 2 Feb 1827; d Dresden, 15 Oct 1902), German conductor, pianist and composer. Pupil of his father, the pianist and comp. Aloys S. (1788–1866). He toured widely in Europe as pianist and after var. cond.'s posts settled at Dresden in 1893 as dir. of the Mozart Society. He married the singer Cornelia Czany (1851–1906) and completed and ed. Mozart's unfinished C min. Mass.

Works incl. opera *Trilby* (adapted from Nodier by Scribe), *Das Wunderwasser* and *Maienzauber*; incid. music for plays; overtures and other orchestral works; concert piece for ob. and orch.; string 4tets, pf. trios; pf. pieces; songs.

Schmitt, Florent (b Blamont, 28 Sep 1870; d Neuilly-sur-Seine, 17 Aug 1958), French composer. Studied music at Nancy from 1887 and in 1889 was sent to the Paris Cons., where he was 1st a pupil of Dubois and Lavignac and afterwards of Massenet and Fauré for comp. Won the Prix de Rome in 1900 and wrote his 1st mature works during his 3 years in Rome. Director, Lyons Cons. 1922–4.

Works incl. ballets *La Tragédie de Salomé* (1907), *Le Petit Elfe Ferme-l'œil* (1924), *Reflets, Ourvasi* and *Oriane et le Prince d'Amour* (1938), incid. music for Shakespeare's *Antony and Cleopatra* (trans. by Gide); film music for an adaptation of Flaubert's *Salammbô* (1925); Psalm xlvi for soprano solo, chorus, org. and orch.

Symph. study *Le Palais hanté* (after Poe), symph. (1958), *3 Rapsodies, Ronde burlesque, Çancunik, Kermesse-Valse, Symphonie concertante* and *Suite sans esprit de suite* for orch.; *Légende* for saxophone and orch. (1918), *Final* for cello and orch.; pf. 5tet, *Lied et Scherzo* for double wind 5tet, *Andante et Scherzo for chromatic harp and string 4tet, Suite en Rocaille* for strings, fl. and harp, *Sonatine en trio* for fl., clar. and harpsichord (or pf.), string 4tet (1949), string trio; *Sonate libre* for vln. and pf.; pf. pieces.

Schmittbauer, Joseph, Aloys (b Bamberg, 8 Nov 1718; d Karlsruhe, 24 Oct 1809), German composer. Pupil of Jommelli, he was *Kapellmeister* of Cologne Cathedral 1775–7, and at the court at Karlsruhe from 1777 to his retirement in 1804.

Works incl. operas *L'isola disabitata* (1762), *Lindor und Ismene* (1771), *Herkules auf dem Oeta* (1772), *Betrug aus Liebe*, etc.; much church music; cantatas; symphs.; concertos; chamber music.

Schmitt-Walter, Karl (b Gernesheim am Rhein, 29 Dec 1900; d Kreuth, Oberbayern, 14 Jan 1985), German baritone. Studied in Nuremberg and made his debut there in 1921. After singing in Wiesbaden 1929–34 he was engaged in Berlin until 1950. Munich 1950–61; appeared at CG, London, 1953 with the Co. as the Count in the Brit. première of *Capriccio*. He sang Papageno at Salzburg and from 1956–61 was Beckmesser at Bayreuth.

Schnabel, Artur (b Lipnik, Aus., 17 Apr 1882; d Axenstein, Switz., 15 Aug 1951), Austrian pianist and composer. Studied pf. with Essipova and Leschetizky, music in general with Mandyczewski in Vienna. He married the singer Therese Behr in 1905, travelled extensively and made a great reputation for himself as a thoughtful interpreter, partic. of Beethoven, Schubert and Brahms. He taught in Berlin, but was forced by the Nazi rule to leave in 1933; settled in USA in 1939, but later returned to Europe. Frequent recitals with his wife and in various ensembles with Casals, Hindemith, Fournier and Szigeti.

Works incl. symph. and other orchestral music; pf. concerto; string 4tet and other chamber music; pf. pieces.

Schnabelflöte (Ger. lit. beak fl., from Fr. *flûte à bec*) = Recorder.

Schnadahüpfeln (Aus. dialect), folk dances, often sung with words, of the *Ländler* or slow waltz type as a rule, belonging to the Tyrol or other Aus. mountain regions.

Schnebel, Dieter (b Lahr, Baden, 14 Mar 1930), German composer and theologian. Has taught religious studies from 1953. Influenced by Kagel and Stockhausen, has prod. such 'non-music' items as music for reading (*mo-no*, 1969), and for cond. only (*Nostalgie*, 1969).

Schnéevoigt, Georg (Lennart) (b Viipuri, 8 Nov 1872; d Malmö, 28 Nov 1947), Finnish conductor. Studied in Helsinki, Leipzig, Dresden and Vienna, became cellist in the Helsinki orch. and in 1901 decided to make cond. his whole career. He held several appts. abroad and toured extensively. From 1930 to 1947 he cond. the Malmö SO, and from 1932 to 1941 was permanent cond. of the Finnish Nat. Orch. in succession to Kajanus.

Schneider, Alexander (b Vilna, 21 Oct 1908), American violinist and conductor of Russian birth. He studied in Frankfurt and worked in Germany before joining the Budapest Quartet as 2nd vln. (1932–44, 1955–64). Emigrated to US 1939 and became active in chamber music and as teacher. Co-founded Prades Festival 1950, with Casals.

Schneider, (Johann Christian) Friedrich (b Alt-Waltersdorf nr. Zittau, 3 Jan 1786; d Dessau, 23 Nov 1853), German composer, teacher and conductor. Studied at Zittau and at Leipzig while a student at the Univ. He advanced through several posts there to that of organist at St Thomas's Church and cond. at the municipal theatre. In 1821 he

moved to Dessau, where he was app. *Kapellmeister* to the ducal court. There he founded a vocal academy and a music school.

Works incl. 7 operas; oratorios *Die Höllenfahrt des Messias, Das Weltgericht, Die Sündflut, Das verlorene Paradies* (after Milton), *Das befreite Jerusalem, Gethsemane und Golgotha* and several others; 14 Masses and other church music; 25 cantatas; 23 symphs., overture on 'God save the King'; 6 concertos; 60 sonatas; 400 male-voice part-songs; 200 songs.

Schneider, Johann Gottlob (b Alt-Gersdorf, 28 Oct 1789; d Dresden, 13 Apr 1864), German organist and composer, brother of prec. Studied at Leipzig and became organist to the Univ. there, remaining until 1825, when he became court organist at Dresden. His fame was enormous and he had many distinguished pupils, incl. Mendelssohn, Schumann and Liszt.

Works incl. fantasy and fugue in D min., and others for organ.

Schneider-Siemssen, Günther (b Augsburg, 7 Jun 1926), German designer. He studied in Munich and worked in Bremen 1954–62. He designed the Peter Brook prod. of *Erwartung* at CG, 1961 and returned 1962–4 for *The Ring*. He has worked at Salzburg since 1965, both summer and Easter Festivals; notable collaborations with Karajan incl. *Boris Godunov, The Ring, Tristan* and *Die Frau ohne Schatten*. Also designed première prod. of Berio's *Un Re in Ascolto*, Salzburg 1984. Noted for subtle use of colour and light; influenced by ideas of Alfred Roller (*q.v.*)

Schneiderhan, Wolfgang (Eduard) (b Vienna, 28 May 1915), Austrian violinist. Studied with Ševčík in Písek, in Prague and with Winkler in Vienna. In 1932 he became leader of the Vienna SO and in 1936 joined the Vienna Staatsoper Orch., becoming prof. at the State Acad. and leader of the Vienna PO. From 1938 to 1951 he led his string 4tet, and from 1949 to 1960 a pf. trio; from the 1970s he has also conducted. In 1948 he married the soprano Irmgard Seefried; gave with her the fp of Henze's *Ariosi* (1963).

Schnittke (Schnitke, Shnitke), **Alfred** (b Engels, 24 Nov 1934), Russian composer. He studied in Vienna and at the Moscow Cons.; taught there 1961–72. He has been influenced by serialism and the advanced techniques of Ligeti and Stockhausen, but has more recently accepted the social-realist principles of Shostakovich.

Works incl. 4 symphs. (1972–84), 4 vln.

concertos (1957–82), pf. concerto (1960), concerto for pf. and strings, 2 concerti grossi (1972, 1980); 2 oratorios, *Nagasaki* (1958) and *Songs of War and Peace* (1959); *Der gelbe Klang* for 9 insts., tape, chorus and light projection, after Kandinsky; *Requiem* (1975), *Minnesang* (Lovesong) for 48 voices a cappella (1981), *Seid nüchtern und wachet ...* based on the Faust legend of 1587, for chorus (1983); 2 vln. sonatas (1963, 1968), 3 string 4tets (1966, 1981, 1984), pf. 5tet (1976; also with orch.), cello sonata (1978), *Moz-art* for 2 vlns.

Schnorr von Carolsfeld, Ludwig (b Munich, 2 Jul 1836; d Dresden, 21 Jul 1865), German tenor. Studied at Dresden, Leipzig and Karlsruhe, where he sang at the Opera and married the soprano Malwina Garrigues (1825–1904). In 1860 they were engaged by the Dresden Court Opera and sang in operas by Wagner and Meyerbeer. He was Wagner's 1st Tristan at the Munich prod. in 1865, but died 6 weeks later.

Schnorr von Carolsfeld, Malwina. *See* **Garrigues.**

Schoberlechner, Franz (b Vienna, 21 Jul 1797; d Berlin, 7 Jan 1843), Austrian pianist and composer. He played a pf. concerto by Hummel, comp. for him, at the age of 10 and was sent to Vienna by Prince Esterházy to study with Förster. In 1814 he went to It. and in 1823 to Rus., marrying the singer Sophie dall' Occa there in 1824. After 4 years in St Petersburg they retired to a villa near Florence in 1831.

Works incl. operas *I virtuosi teatrali* (1817), *Il Barone di Dolzheim* (1827) and *Rossane* (1839); 2 pf. concertos; chamber music; sonatas and other works for pf.

Schoberlechner (née dall' Occa), Sophie (b St Petersburg, 1807; d St Petersburg, Jan 1864), Russian singer of Italian descent, daughter of a singing-master, with whom she studied. She married Schoberlechner in 1824, sang at concerts at first, but in 1827 was engaged by the Imp. Opera in St Petersburg. She retired with her husband in 1831, but returned to Rus. later to teach singing.

Schobert, Johann (Jean) (b ? Silesia or Nuremberg, *c* 1720; d Paris, 28 Aug 1767), German harpsichordist and composer. He lived in Paris, in the service of the Prince of Conti from *c* 1720, but died young, with his wife and child, as a result of fungus poisoning. Mozart arr. one of his sonata movements as the 2nd movement of the concerto K39.

Works incl. *opéra comique Le Garde-Chasse et le braconnier;* 6 harpsichord con-

certos; 6 *Sinfonies* for harpsichord, vln. and 2 horns; pf 4tets (with 2 vlns); pf. trios; sonatas for pf. and vln.; sonatas for harpsichord.

Schock, Rudolf (b Duisburg, 4 Sep 1915; d Gürzenich, 14 Nov 1986), German tenor. Debut Brunswick 1937; sang in Berlin after the war, Hamburg 1947–56 (visited Edinburgh with the co. 1952. Salzburg from 1948, as Idomeneo and in the 1954 fp of Liebermann's *Penelope*). He sang Walther at Bayreuth in 1959 and recorded the role with Kempe. Other roles incl. Florestan, Tamino and Bacchus; also popular in operetta.

Schoeck, Othmar (b Brunnen, 1 Sep 1886; d Zurich, 8 Mar 1957), Swiss composer. He was at first undecided whether to follow his father's calling of a painter, but at 17 went to the Zurich Cons. to study with Niggli and others, finishing with Reger at the Leipzig Cons. In 1907–17 he cond. choral societies at Zurich and remained there when app. cond. of the St Gall symph. concerts that year. The univ. conferred an hon. doctor's degree on him in 1928. His music is lyrical in character and was successfully performed in Germany during the Nazi era.

Works incl. OPERAS *Don Ranudo* (after Holberg, 1919), *Venus* (after Mérimée, 1922), *Penthesilea* (after Kleist, 1927), *Vom Fischer und syner Fru* (after Grimm, 1930), *Massimilla Doni* (after Balzac, 1937), *Das Schloss Dürande* (after Eichendorff, 1943), operetta *Erwin und Elmire* (Goethe), *scena* and pantomime *Das Wandbild.*

CHORAL: *Der Postillon* (Lenau) for tenor solo, chorus and orch. (1909), *Dithyrambe* (Goethe) for double chorus and orch. (1911); *Trommelschläge* (Whitman's *Drum Taps*) for chorus and orch., *Für ein Gesangfest im Frühling* (Keller) for male voices and orch. (1942).

ORCHESTRAL: Serenade for small orch., praeludium for orch., pastoral intermezzo *Sommernacht* (after Keller) for strings (1945), suite for strings; *Lebendig begraben* (Keller), song-cycle for baritone and orch.; vln. concerto, cello concerto (1947), horn concerto (1951).

CHAMBER AND SOLO VOCAL: 2 string 4tets (1913, 1923); 2 vln. and pf. sonatas, sonata for bass clar. and pf.; song-cycles *Elegie* with chamber orch. (1923), *Gaselen* (Keller) with 6 insts., *Wandersprüche* (Eichendorff) with 4 insts., *Notturno* with string 4tet (1933); pf. pieces; song-cycles *Wandsbecker Liederbuch* (Matthias Claudius), *Unter Sternen* (Keller), *Das stille Leuchten* (C.F. Meyer) and numerous sets of songs to words by

Eichendorff, Goethe, Hafiz, Hebbel, Heine, Keller, Lenau, Mörike and Uhland.

Schoeffler, Paul (b Dresden, 15 Sep 1897; d Amersham, Bucks., 21 Nov 1977), German, later Austrian, baritone. Studied in Dresden, Berlin and Milan, making his debut in Dresden in 1925, where he remained until 1937, when he was engaged by the Vienna Staatsoper. He also sang at CG, 1934–9 and 1949–53, as Scarpia, Gunther, Figaro, Don Giovanni and Wotan. NY Met 1949–56. He was esp. well known in the role of Hans Sachs, which he sang at Bayreuth during the war. He created Von Einem's Danton (1947) and Strauss's Jupiter (1952), both at Salzburg.

Schoelcher, Victor (b Paris, 21 Jul 1804; d Houilles, 24 Dec 1893), French politician and writer on music. He lived in exile in London during the reign of Napoleon III and worked on Handel research, part of the result of which he published in an English biography in 1857. He also made a collection of music which he presented to the Paris Cons.

Schoenberg, Arnold (b Vienna, 13 Sep 1874; d Los Angeles, 13 Jul 1951), Austrian composer. He played vln. as a boy and cello as a youth, and at 16 decided to become a musician, studying counterpoint with Zemlinsky, but being otherwise self-taught. About the turn of the century he earned his living by scoring operettas, but his own works of that period were the string 6tet *Verklärte Nacht* and the *Gurrelieder*. He married Mathilde von Zemlinsky, his teacher-friend's sister, and in 1901 became cond. of the *Überbrettl* cabaret in Berlin and a little later teacher at the Stern Cons. there. Back in Vienna in 1903, he gradually changed his style, and his *Chamber Symph.* op. 9 created a riot in 1906, but Mahler defended him. The 2nd string 4tet, with sop. solo, is the 1st work in which he moved away from tonality; its fp in 1908 was the occasion of further disturbances. By 1911 he had returned to Berlin and had taken to painting in an expressionist manner. The highly influential *Pierrot lunaire* was given in Berlin in 1912; the *5 Orch. Pieces* were perf. in London the same year.

After the war of 1914–18, during which he did garrison duty, Schoenberg settled at Mödling, nr. Vienna, but in 1920 taught at Amsterdam, where he had begun to attract attention. In 1921 he wrote his 1st work wholly in the 12-note method, the *Suite* op. 25 for pf. Further renewed creative vigour resulted in the *Serenade,* the wind 5tet, 3rd

string 4tet and the comic opera *Von Heute auf Morgen,* in all of which dodecaphony was further explored. His wife died in 1923 and in 1926 he was recalled to Berlin, to teach at the Prussian Acad. of Arts; Zemlinsky had given the première of his monodrama *Erwartung* at Prague (1924) and in 1928 Furtwängler cond. the Berlin fp of the *Variations for Orch.* op. 28. He remained at Berlin until 1933 and married a sister of the violinist Rudolf Kolisch. His masterpiece, the opera *Moses und Aron,* was comp. 1930–2 but not perf. until 3 years after his death.

The Nazi regime drove Schoenberg from Ger. and he settled in the USA, teaching in Boston and NY, 1933–4, and later in Los Angeles, where he was app. prof. at the Univ. of California in 1936, retiring in 1944. In 1947 he was elected a member of the American Acad. of Arts and Letters; a trans. of his *Harmonielehre* (1911) was pub. the same year. Through this and other writings Schoenberg's influence as a teacher remained considerable; Berg and Webern were the best-known pupils of his pre-war years.

Works incl. OPERAS: *Erwartung,* monodrama, op. 17 (1909, prod. Prague, 1924; cond. Zemlinsky), *Die glückliche Hand,* 1-act drama, (1910–13, prod. Vienna, 1924; cond. Stiedry), *Von Heute auf Morgen,* 1-act comedy (1929, prod. Frankfurt, 1930, cond. Steinberg), *Moses und Aron* (1930–2, fp Hamburg, concert, 1954; stage, Zurich, 1957, cond. Rosbaud).

ORCH. *Frühlingstod,* symph. poem (1899; fp Berlin, 1983, cond. R. Chailly), *Pelleas und Melisande,* symph. poem after Maeterlinck (1902–3), Chamber Symph. no. 1 for 15 insts. op. 9 (1906; arr. for orch. 1922), *5 Orch. Pieces* (1909; fp London, 1912, cond. Wood), *3 Little Pieces* for chamber orch. (1911; fp Berlin, 1957), *Variations* op. 31 (1926–8; fp Berlin, 1928, cond. Furtwängler), *Begleitungsmusik zu einer Lichtspielszene,* op. 34 (1929–30; fp Berlin, 1930, cond. Klemperer), Suite in G for strings (1934; fp Los Angeles, 1935, cond. Klemperer), vln. concerto, op. 36 (1934–6; fp Philadelphia, 1940, with Krasner, cond. Stokowski), Chamber Symph. no. 2 (1906–16, rev. 1939; fp NY, 1940, cond. Stiedry), pf. concerto op. 42 (1942; fp NY, 1944, with Steuermann, cond. Stokowski), theme and vars. for wind op. 43a, arr. for orch. op. 43b. Also: string 6tet *Verklärte Nacht* arr. for strings (1917), cello concerto after Georg Monn (1933), concerto for string quartet and orch. after Handel (1933) and vers. for orch. of Brahms G min. pf. 4tet op. 25

(1937; fp Los Angeles, 1938, cond. Klemperer).

VOCAL AND CHORAL: *Friede auf Erden* for unaccomp. chorus (1907), *Gurrelieder* for soloists, chorus and orch. (1900–11), 6 *Songs with Orch.* (1904), *Das Buch der hängenden Gärten* (S. George) for sop. and pf. (1909), *Herzgewächse* for sop., celesta, harmonium and harp (1911), *Pierrot lunaire* for speaker and chamber ens. op. 21 (1912), *4 Songs* with orch. (1916), *Die Jakobsleiter*, oratorio (1917–22), *3 Satires* for chorus (1925), *Kol Nidre* for rabbi, chorus and orch. (1938), *Ode to Napoleon Buonaparte* for reciter, string 4tet and pf. (1942), *A Survivor from Warsaw* for speaker, male chorus and orch. (1947), *Modern Psalms* for chorus, speaker and orch. (1950)

CHAMBER: 5 string 4tets (1897, 1905, 1908, 1927, 1936), *Verklärte Nacht* for string 6tet, op. 4 (1899), Serenade op. 24 for 7 insts. with bar. in 4th movt. (1923), wind 5tet op. 26 (1924), *Suite* for 3 clars. and pf 5tet op. 29 (1926), string trio op. 45 (1946), *Phantasy* for vln. and pf. (1947)

PIANO: *3 Pieces* op. 11 (1909), *6 Little Pieces* (1911), *5 Pieces* op. 23 (1923), Suite op. 25 (1921), *2 Pieces* op. 33 (1931).

Arrangements for orch. of Bach organ music and Johann Strauss; Theme and variations for wind band op. 43 (1943); cabaret pieces; 7 sets of Lieder comp. 1897–1903, 3 Lieder op. 48 (1933) and songs for Ernst von Wolzogen's *Überbrettl.*

Scholes, Percy A(lfred) (b Leeds, 24 Jul 1877; d Vevey, Switzerland, 31 Jul 1958), English critic, music author and editor. He became music critic to the *Evening Standard* and the *Observer* in London, founded and ed. the *Music Student* and *Music and Youth*, in 1923 became music critic to the BBC, but later settled in Switz., where he lived until the outbreak of the 1939–45 war and twice after it. He was a D. Litt. of Lausanne and Oxford Univs. and an hon. D.Mus. of Oxford. He wrote many books to further the popularity and appreciation of music and compiled the dictionaries *The Oxford Companion to Music* (1938) and *The Concise Oxford Dictionary of Music* (1952).

Schöne, Lotte (b Vienna, 15 Dec 1891; d Paris, 22 Dec 1977), Austrian soprano. She studied in Vienna and made her debut there in 1915. She sang in Vienna until 1926 and then appeared at the Städtische Oper Berlin until 1933; her roles incl. Cherubino, Susanna, Zerlina, Norina and Zerbinetta. Also much admired in operas by Puccini, and sang Liù at CG in 1927. Salzburg 1922–35.

She was obliged by the Nazis to leave Ger. but returned to Berlin in 1948 and sang there until her retirement in 1953.

Schöne Melusine, Die (*The Fair Melusina*), concert overture by Mendelssohn, op. 32, comp. in 1833 after a perf. in Berlin of K. Kreutzer's opera *Melusina*, with a lib. by Grillparzer orig. written for Beethoven.

Schöne Müllerin, Die (*The Fair Maid of the Mill*), song cycle by Schubert (poems by Wilhelm Müller), comp. 1823, D795. The 17 songs are 1. *Das Wandern* 2. *Wohin ?* 3. *Halt; Danksagung an den Bach* 4. *Am Feierabend* 5. *Der Neugierige* 6. *Ungeduld* 7. *Morgengrüss* 8. *Des Müllers Blumen* 9. *Tränenregen* 10. *Pause; Mit dem grünen Lautenbande* 11. *Der Jäger* 12. *Eifersucht und Stolz* 13. *Die liebe Farbe* 14. *Die böse Farbe* 15. *Trockne Blumen* 16. *Der Müller und der Bach* 17. *Des Baches Wiegenlied.*

School for Fathers, The (Wolf-Ferrari). *See* **Quattro rusteghi.**

Schoolmaster, The, nickname of Haydn's symph. no. 55 in E♭ maj., comp. in 1774.

Schöpfungsmesse (Creation Mass), the nickname of Haydn's Mass in B♭ maj. of 1801, where a theme from *The Creation* is used in the 'Qui tollis'.

Schorr, Friedrich (b Nagyvárad, 2 Sep 1888; d Farmington, Conn., 14 Aug 1953), Austro-Hungarian baritone. Studied in Vienna and made his debut at Graz in 1910, as Wotan, a part he made peculiarly his own. Sang in Cologne 1918–23, under Klemperer; Berlin, Staatsoper, 1923–30 as Barak, Nelusko and Doktor Faust. The outstanding Wagnerian baritone of his time. He 1st appeared in London and NY in 1924 and from 1925 until 1931 was the Wotan in the Bayreuth Wagner perfs.

Schott, Anton (b Castle Staufeneck, Swabia, 24 Jun 1846; d Stuttgart, 6 Jan 1913), German tenor. Pupil of Pischek and Agnes Schebest, made his debut at Frankfurt in 1870; sang with Angelo Neumann's touring co. from 1882 (Rienzi, Lohengrin, Tannhäuser) and in US from 1884 (1st Met Siegmund).

Schott, B., and Sons, German music publishers. The company was founded by Bernhard Schott in 1780 at Mainz and continued by his sons from 1817. The London branch was opened in 1835, and others were established in Paris, Leipzig, Rotterdam and New York. The firm published late works of Beethoven and among other comps. pub. are Haydn, Hindemith, Henze, Tippett, Davies and Goehr. Owner of Eulenberg Ed. since 1957.

Schottisch (Ger. = Scottish), a ballroom dance fashionable in the 19th cent. intro. to Eng. in 1848, not identical with the *Écossaise*. In Eng. it is usually called by its plural, *Schottische*. The music is in 2–4 time, much like that of the Polka, but played rather slower.

Schrade, Leo (b Allenstein, 13 Dec 1903; d Spéracédès, 21 Sep 1964), German musicologist. He studied at several Ger. univs. and taught at Königsberg Univ. from 1929 to 1932 and at Bonn Univ. from 1932 to 1937, when he left Ger. and settled in USA. He taught at Yale Univ. from 1938 to 1958, becoming prof. in 1948. From 1958 he was prof. at Basle Univ. His studies ranged widely over medieval, Renaissance and Baroque music and incl. a book on Monteverdi and eds. of the works of Philippe de Vitry, Machaut, Landini and other 14th-cent. composers.

Schramm, Hermann (b Berlin, 7 Feb 1871; d Frankfurt, 14 Dec 1951), German tenor. Debut Breslau 1895, in Kreutzer's *Die Nachtlager von Granada*. Cologne 1896–1900, Frankfurt 1900–33; sang in the 1920 fp of Schreker's *Der Schatzgräber* and was the best-known Mime and David of his time. CG 1899, also guest in Paris and Brussels. His son **Friedrich** (b 1900) prod. *Fidelio* and operas by Wagner at CG 1947–51.

Schreier, Peter (b Meissen, 29 Jul 1935), German tenor and conductor. He sang as a choirboy in Dresden during the war and made his adult debut there in 1959. He has sung at the Berlin Staatsoper since 1963 and in 1966 made his London debut, as Ferrando. In 1967 he made his first appearances at the NY Met, Salzburg and the Vienna Opera; among his roles have been Tamino, Sextus, Loge, Don Ottavio and Belmonte. He has been widely admired in Lieder and in the Bach Passions. Active as a cond. since 1969.

Schreker, Franz (b Monaco, 23 Mar 1878; d Berlin, 21 Mar 1934), Austrian composer, conductor and teacher. Studied under Fuchs in Vienna, founded the Phil. Choir there in 1911 and cond. the fp of Schoenberg's *Gurrelieder* in 1913. Taught at the Imp. Acad. of Music until his appt. as dir. of the Acad. of Music in Berlin in 1920; forced by the Nazis to resign in 1933. His operas were late Romantic in expression and popular in the 1920s; fps were conducted by Otto Klemperer (Cologne) and Bruno Walter (Munich).

Works include OPERAS: *Flammen* (1902), *Der ferne Klang* (1912), *Das Spielwerk und die Prinzessin* (1913; revised as a mystery play, *Das Spielwerk*, 1920), *Die Gezeichneten* (1918), *Der Schatzgräber* (1920), *Irrelohe* (1924), *Der singende Teufel* (1928), *Christophorus* (1924–9; prod. 1978), *Der Schmied von Gent* (1932); pantomime *Der Geburtstag der Infantin*, after Wilde, 1908; reworked as *Spanisches Fest*, 1927).

ORCH.: symph. (1899), *Intermezzo* for strings (1900), *Romantic Suite* (1902), Chamber symph. for 23 solo insts. (1917; also in vers. for full orch., as Sinfonietta), *Kleine Suite* for small orch. (1931).

VOCAL: Psalm 116 for female chorus and orch. (1900), *Schwanengesang* for chorus and orch. (1902), *Zwei lyrische Gesänge* for voice and orch. to poems by Whitman, 1929); 43 Lieder to texts by Heyse, Tolstoy, and Scherenberg (1895–1916).

Schröder-Devrient, Willhelmine (b Hamburg, 6 Dec 1804; d Coburg, 26 Jan 1860), German soprano. She learnt much from her parents, the baritone Friedrich S. (1744–1816) and the actress Antoinette Sophie Bürger, and when still in her teens appeared as a classical actress at the Burgtheater in Vienna, where she made her 1st operatic appearance in 1821 as Pamina. In 1822 she greatly pleased Beethoven as Leonore in the revival of *Fidelio*. In 1823 she was engaged by the Dresden Court Opera and soon afterwards married the actor Karl Devrient, from whom she separated in 1828; her roles incl. Donna Anna, Norma, Euryanthe and Reiza. In 1830 she 1st sang in Paris and in 1832 in London. She worked long enough to create Wagner's Adriano (1842), Senta (1843) and Venus (1845).

Schröder-Feinen, Ursula (b Gelsenkirchen, 21 Jan 1936), German soprano. She sang in Gelsenkirchen during the 1960s as Aida, Alceste, Oscar, Turandot and Salome. NY Met debut 1970 as Chrysothemis. She has sung Brünnhilde at Bayreuth (debut 1971) and in Paris and NY. In London she has been heard as Ortrud and Kundry and at the 1975 Edinburgh Festival she sang Salome.

Schroeter, Christoph Gottlieb (b Hohnstein, Saxony, 10 Aug 1699; d Nordhausen, 20 May 1782), German musician. He was educ. in theology as well as music and in 1721 invented a hammer action to apply to the harpsichord, but was anticipated in the actual invention of the pf. by Cristofori.

Schroeter, Leonhard (b Torgau, c 1540; d Magdeburg, c 1595), German composer. Succeeded Gallus Dressler as cantor of Magdeburg Cathedral in 1564.

Works incl. Ger. Te Deum for double choir (1584), *Hymni sacri* for 4–5 voices, *Weihnachts-Liedlein* for several voices (1587).

Schröter, Corona (Elisabeth Willhelmine) (b Guben, 14 Jan 1751; d Ilmenau, 23 Aug 1802), German singer, actress and composer. She learnt music from her father, the oboist Johann Friedrich S., lived in Warsaw and Leipzig as a child, appeared in the latter town at the age of 14. Between 1772 and 1774 she was in London with her family, but Goethe invited her to the court of Weimar in 1776, where she appeared in his plays and wrote the music for his play *Die Fischerin*, which incl. a setting of *Erlkönig* by her. She retired in 1786 to teach, paint and compose.

Works incl. play with music *Die Fischerin*; songs, i..cl. settings of Goethe's *Der neue Amadis* and *Erlkönig*, Schiller's *Der Taucher* and *Würde der Frauen*, poems by Herder, Klopstock, Matthisson.

Schröter, Johann Samuel (b Warsaw, c 1752; d London, 2 Nov 1788), German pianist and composer. Pupil of his father, he made his debut as a pianist in Leipzig in 1767, and in 1772 went on tour with his father and sister to Hol. and Eng., where he appeared at one of the Bach–Abel concerts. Settling in Eng., he succeeded J.C. Bach as music master to the queen in 1782. It was his widow with whom Haydn had an autumnal affair during his 1st visit to London; Haydn made copies of her letters to him.

Works incl. keyboard concertos, sonatas, etc.; pf. 5tets and trios.

Schubart, Christian Friedrich Daniel (b Obersontheim, Swabia, 24 Mar 1739; d Stuttgart, 10 Oct 1791), German author, ed. and musician. Lived as organist and teacher in Geislingen and Ludwigsburg, later in Augsburg, where he ed. the *Deutsche Chronik* (from 1774), and Ulm (1777–87), held as a political prisoner at Hohenasperg. From 1787 was poet to the court and theatre in Stuttgart. He was the author of *Die Forelle*, *An den Tod* and *Grablied auf einen Soldaten*, all set to music by Schubert. His autobiog. was pub. in 1791–3. Also wrote keyboard music and songs.

Schubaur, Johann Lukas (b Lechfeld, Swabia, bap. 23 Dec 1749; d Munich, 15 Nov 1815), German composer. Had a distinguished career as a doctor, but was also a successful *Singspiel* comp. (from 1783).

Works incl. *Singspiele Die Dorfdeputierten*, *Das Lustlager*, *Die treuen Köhler*.

Schubert, Franz (Peter) (b Vienna, 31 Jan 1797; d Vienna, 19 Nov 1828), Austrian composer. Son of a schoolmaster who cultivated music in his household. Began to learn pf. and vln. early and received lessons from Michael Holzer at the age of 9, learning also organ and counterpoint. Admitted to the Seminary for choristers in the Imp. Chapel in 1808, played vln. in the orch. there and sometimes cond. as deputy. At 13 he wrote a fantasy for pf. duet and sketched other works, and in 1811 comp. his 1st song. Played vla. in the string 4tet at home. His mother died in 1812 and his father married again in 1813, when Schubert wrote the 1st symph. and left the Seminary, continuing studies under Salieri. At 17 he became asst. teacher in his father's school, but disliked teaching; comp. the G maj. Mass, the 2nd and 3rd symphs. and several dramatic pieces. In 1816 he left the school and joined his friend Schober in rooms, gathering a circle of literary and artistic rather than musical friends round him and in 1817 meeting the singer Michael Vogl, who took a great interest in his songs and succeeded in getting his play with music *Die Zwillingsbrüder* (*The Twin Brothers*) prod. in Jun 1820. His reputation grew beyond his own circle, but pubs. failed to recognize him until his friends had 20 songs pub. at their own expense in 1821. (Most of his large-scale works were unpublished during his lifetime, however.)

He lived in Vienna all his life, except for some summer excursions and 2 visits to Hung. as domestic musician to the Esterházy family on their country estate at Zséliz, 1818 and 1824. He never held an official appt. and failed to stabilize his financial position, but earned enough casually to lead a modest if improvident and Bohemian existence. His industry was phenomenal. His death was due to typhoid, his condition having been weakened by syphilis.

OPERAS AND SINGSPIELE (some incomplete): *Der Spiegelritter* (1811–12, fp Swiss Radio 1949), *Des Teufels Lustschloss* (1813–15; fp Vienna, 1879), *Adrast* (1817–19, fp Vienna, 1868), *Der vierjährige Posten* (1815, fp Dresden, 1896), *Fernando* (1815, fp Vienna, 1905), *Claudine von Villa Bella* (1815, fp Vienna, 1913), *Die Freunde von Salamanka* (1815, fp Halle, 1928), *Die Burgschaft* (1816, fp Vienna, 1908), *Die Zwillingsbrüder* (1819, fp Vienna, 1820), *Alfonso und Estrella* (1821–2, fp Weimar, 1854), *Die Verschworenen* (1823, fp Vienna, 1861), *Fierrabras* (1823, fp Karlsruhe, 1897); also melodrama *Die Zauberharfe* (1820, fp Vienna, 1820) and incidental music *Rosamunde, Fürstin von Zypern* (1823, fp Vienna, 1823).

VOCAL WITH ORCH.: church music incl. 5 Masses, in F, G, C, A♭ and E♭ (1814–28),

Deutsche Messe (1827), *Lazarus,* unfinished oratorio (1820), 6 settings of the *Salve regina* (1812–24). Works for voices, with and without acc., incl. *Frühlingsgesang* (1822), *Gesang der Geister über den Wassern* (1817; 2nd vers. with orch. 1821), *Gondelfahrer* (1824), *Miriams Siegesgesang* (1828) and *Ständchen* (1827).

ORCH.: 9 symphs.: no. 1 in D (1813), no. 2 in B♭ (1815), no. 3 in D (1815), no. 4 in C min. (1816), no. 5 in B♭ (1816), no. 6 in C (1818), no. 7 in E (1821; sketches, unscored), no. 8 in B min. ('Unfinished', 1822), no. 9 in C ('Great', 1825); 2 overtures in the Italian style (1817, 1819), 5 German Dances (1813; also in scoring by Webern), Rondo in A for vln. and orch. (1816).

CHAMBER: 15 string 4tets, nos. 1–7 comp. 1812–14, no. 8 in B♭ (1814, D112), no. 9 in G min. (1815, D173), no. 10 in E♭ (1813, D87), no. 11 in E (1816, D353), no. 12 in C min. (*Quartettsatz*, 1820, D703), no. 13 in A min. (1824, D804), no. 14 in D min. (*Der Tod und das Mädchen*, 1824, D810), no. 15 in G (1826, D887); Octet in F for string 4tet, double bass, clar., bsn. and horn (1824, D803), string 5tet in C (1828, D956), pf. 5tet in A (*Die Forelle*, 1819, D667), pf. trios in B♭ (1827, D898) and E♭ (1827, D929); for pf. and vln.: sonata in A (1817, D574), 3 sonatinas, in D, A min. and G min. (1816, D384, D385 and D408), *Rondo brillant* in B min. (1826, D895), Fantasia in C, based on song *Sei mir gegrüsst* (1827, D934).

WORKS FOR PIANO incl. *Divertissement à la hongroise* (D818), Fantasia in F min. (D940), sonata in B♭ (D617) and sonata in C, Grand Duo (D813), all for four hands; 21 pf. sonatas: nos. 1–12 comp. 1815–19, some unfinished, no. 13 in A (D664), no. 14 in A min. (D784), no. 15 in C (D840), no. 16 in A min. (D845), no. 17 in D (D850), no. 18 in G (D894), no. 19 in C min. (D958), no. 20 in A (D959), no. 21 in B♭ (D960); Fantasia in C, based on the song *Der Wanderer* (D760), 8 impromptus in 2 sets: in C min, E♭, G♭ and A♭ (D899), in F min, A♭, B♭, F min. (D935), 3 Klavierstücke, in E♭ min., E♭ and C (D946), 6 *Moments Musicaux,* in C, A♭, F min., C♯ min., F min. and A♭ (1823–8, D780); 2 sets of waltzes, D145 and D365.

SONGS: 3 cycles, *Die schöne Müllerin* (1823), *Winterreise* (1827) and *Schwanengesang* (1828). Some of the best known of more than 600 Lieder are *Abendstern* (Mayrhofer, 1824), *Die Allmacht* (Pyrker, 1825), *Am Bach im Frühling* (Schober, 1816, *An den Mond* (Goethe, 1815), *An die*

Entfernte (Goethe, 1822), *An die Musik* (Schober, 1817), *An Schwager Kronos* (Goethe, 1816), *An Sylvia* (Shakespeare, 1826), *Auf dem Wasser zu singen* (Stolberg, 1823), *Auf der Donau* (Mayrhofer, 1817), *Auflösung* (Mayrhofer, 1824), *Ave Maria* (Scott, trans. Storck, 1825), *Bei dir allein* (Seidl, 1826), *Delphine* (Schütz, 1825), *Du bist die Ruh* (Rückert, 1823), *Der Einsame* (Lappe, 1825), *Erlkönig* (Goethe, 1815), *Der Fischer* (Goethe, 1815), *Fischerweise* (Schlechta, 1826), *Die Forelle* (Schubart, 1817), *Frühlingsglaube* (Uhland, 1820), *Ganymed* (Goethe, 1817), *Die Götter Griechenlands* (Schiller, 1819), *Gretchen am Spinnrade* (Goethe, 1814), *Gruppe aus dem Tartarus* (1817), *3 Harfenspieler Lieder* (Goethe, 1816), *Heidenröslein* (Goethe, 1815), *Der Hirt auf dem Felsen*, with clar. obbligato (Müller, 1828), *Horch, horch die Lerch* (Shakespeare, 1826), *Im Frühling* (Schulze, 1826), *Die junge Nonne* (Craigher, 1825), *Lachen und Weinen* (Rückert, 1823, *Liebhaber in aller Gestalten* (Goethe, 1817), *Der Musensohn* (Goethe, 1822), *Nacht und Träume* (Collin, 1822), *Nur wer die Sehnsucht kennt* (Goethe, 5 versions), *Prometheus* (Goethe, 1819), *Sei mir gegrüsst* (Rückert, 1822), *Die Sterne* (Leitner, 1828), *Der Tod und das Mädchen* (Claudius, 1817), *Dem Unendlichen* (Klopstock, 1815), *Der Wanderer* (Lübeck, 1816), *Wanderers Nachtlied* (Goethe, 1822), *Der Zwerg* (Collin, 1822).

Schubert, Richard (b Dessau, 15 Dec 1885; d Oberstaufen, Allgau, 12 Oct 1959), German tenor. Debut Strasbourg 1909, as baritone. Studied further in Milan and Dresden, sang as tenor at Nuremberg 1911–13 and Wiesbaden 1913–17. Hamburg 1917–35, in Wagner and as Paul in the 1920 fp of Korngold's *Die tote Stadt.* Vienna 1920–9. Chicago 1921–2, as Tristan and Tannhäuser.

Schuch, Ernst von (b Graz, 23 Nov 1846; d Dresden, 10 May 1914), Austrian conductor. Studied at Graz and Vienna, had his 1st cond. engagement at Breslau, and after several others went to Dresden in 1872 and was made court music dir. the next year; while in Dresden he gave the fps of Strauss's *Feuersnot, Elektra, Salome* and *Rosenkavalier.* He also cond. the symph. concerts of the Royal (later State) Orch.

Schuch-Proska, Clementine (b Vienna, 12 Feb 1850; d Kötzschenbroda nr. Dresden, 8 Jun 1932), Austrian soprano, wife of prec. Pupil of Mathilde Marchesi at the Vienna Cons., was engaged by the Dresden Court

Opera in 1873 and married Schuch there in 1875; she sang in Dresden until 1904.

Schuh, Willi (b Basle, 12 Nov 1900; d Zurich, 4 Oct 1986), Swiss musicologist. Studied under Courvoisier and Sandberger at Munich and Ernst Kurth at Berne, where he took a doctor's degree in 1927. He became a critic at Zurich. From 1930 to 1944 he taught at the Zurich Cons. His works incl. studies of Schütz, Swiss folk and early music, Schoeck, etc. In 1976 he pub. the 1st vol. in the authorized biography of Richard Strauss.

Schuhplattler (Ger.), a Bavarian country dance with music in moderate 3–4 time similar to that of the Ländler. The dancers are men only and they strike their palms on their knees and soles.

Schulhoff, Erwin (b Prague, 8 Jun 1894; d Wülzburg, Ger., 18 Aug 1942), Czech pianist and composer. Studied at the Prague, Vienna, Leipzig and Cologne Conss. As a communist in Nazi-ruled Cz., he sought refuge in Soviet citizenship; after the 1941 invasion of Russia he was arrested. He died in a concentration camp.

Works incl. operas *Don Juan's Destination* and *Flames*; ballets *Ogelala* and *Moonstruck*; incid. music to Molière's *Bourgeois gentilhomme*; 2 symphs.; pf. concerto; chamber music; pf. works.

Schulhoff, Julius (b Prague, 2 Aug 1825; d Berlin, 13 Mar 1898), Czech pianist and composer, great-greatuncle of prec. Settled in Paris from 1842 until the 1848 Revolution, then toured, and finally lived at Dresden and Berlin. Comp. drawing-room music for his instrument, also a sonata in F min. and 12 studies.

Schuller, Gunther (b New York, 22 Nov 1925), American composer and horn player. After playing horn in the Cincinnati SO he joined the NY Met Orch. (1945–59). Prof. of comp. at the New Eng. Cons., Boston, Mass. 1966–77.

Works incl. operas *The Visitation,* after Kafka (1966) and *The Fisherman and his Wife* (1970); *Seven Studies on Themes of Paul Klee* (1959), *Three Studies in Texture* for orch.; ballet *Variants*; symph.; concertos for cello, horn, pf.; violin concerto (1976), double-bassoon concerto (1978), saxophone concerto (1983); *Fantasia concertante* for 3 trombs. and pf.; 4tet for 4 double basses; 5 pieces for 5 horns.

Schuloper (Ger. = school opera), a Ger. work of a special type of the 20th cent. with a didactic purpose; the same as a *Lehrstück,* but invariably intended for the stage.

Schultheiss, Benedict (b Nuremberg, 20 Sep 1653; d Nuremberg, 1 Mar 1693), German organist and composer. Pupil of his father, Hieronymus S. (1600–69). He was app. organist of the church of St Giles at Nuremberg.

Works incl. hymn tunes; harpsichord pieces.

Schultz (or **Schulz**), prob. the German form of the name of the musicians calling themselves Praetorius.

Schulz-Beuthen, Heinrich (b Beuthen, Silesia, 19 Jun 1838; d Dresden, 12 Mar 1915), German composer. Studied at the Leipzig Cons., taught at Zurich in 1866–80, at Dresden in 1880–93, in Vienna in 1893–5, and at the Dresden Cons. from 1895.

Works incl. operas *Aschenbrödel* (1879; text by Mathilde Wesendonk), *Die Verschollene* and 3 others; Christmas play *Die Blume Wunderhold*; Requiem, 6 Psalms and other choral works; 8 symphs. (no. 6 on Shakespeare's *King Lear*), symph. poems on Schiller's *Wilhelm Tell*, on Böcklin's picture 'The Isle of the Dead', on Grillparzer's *Des Meeres und der Liebe Wellen* and others, 2 suites, 2 scenes from Goethe's *Faust*, serenade and other works for orch.; pf. concerto; wind octet, string 5tet and trio; 2 sonatas and pieces for pf.; numerous songs.

Schulz, Johann Abraham Peter (b Lüneburg, 31 Mar 1747; d Schwedt, 10 Jun 1800), German composer, conductor and musicologist. A pupil of Kirnberger, he travelled in Aus., It. and Fr. in 1768, and after holding a post in Pol. returned in 1773 to Berlin, where he collaborated in Kirnberger and Sulzer's encyclopaedia. Cond. at the Fr. theatre in Berlin 1776–8, he was court comp. to Prince Heinrich of Prus. at Rheinsberg 1780–7, then at the Dan. court in Copenhagen until his return to Ger. in 1795. Wrote a number of theoretical works, incl. (with Kirnberger) a treatise on harmony.

Works incl. operas (Fr.) *Clarisse, La Fée Urgèle* (after Voltaire, 1782), *Le Barbier de Séville* (after Beaumarchais, 1786) and *Aline, reine de Golconde* (Dan. 1787), *The Harvest Home* (1790), *The Entry* (1793) and *Peter's Wedding*; Ger. melodrama *Minona*; incid. music for Racine's *Athalie* and other plays; *Christi Tod, Maria und Johannes* and other sacred works; chamber music, *Lieder im Volkston* and many other songs.

Schuman, William H(oward) (b New York, 4 Aug 1910), American composer. Studied at Columbia Univ. and at the Mozarteum,

Salzburg. In 1936 he was app. teacher at the Columbia Univ. summer school and in 1938 at the Sarah Lawrence Coll. in NY. In 1945 he succeeded Carl Engel as director of music pubs. in the house of Schirmer in NY and Ernest Hutcheson as president of the Juilliard School of Music. Dir. of the Lincoln Center, NY 1961–9.

Works incl. baseball opera *The Mighty Casey* (1953); ballets *Choreographic Poem, Undertone, Night Journey*; incid. music for Shakespeare's *Henry VIII*; film music for *Steeltown*; 2 secular cantatas for chorus and orch.; 10 symphs. (1936–76), *Amer. Festival* and *William Billings* overtures, *Prayer in Time of War* (1943) and *Side-Show* for orch.; symph. for string orch. (1943); *Judith* (choreographic poem); *Newsreel* for military band; pf. concerto, vln. concerto (1947); 4 *Canonic Choruses, Pioneers, Requiescat* (without words), etc., for unaccomp. chorus; 4 string 4tets (1936–50), canon and fugue for pf. trio; quartettino for 4 bassoons; *Three-Score Set* for pf.

Schumann (*née* Wieck), **Clara (Josephine)** (b Leipzig, 13 Sep 1819; d Frankfurt, 20 May 1896), German pianist and composer. Pupil of her father, Friedrich Wieck, made her 1st public appearance at the age of 9 in 1828 and gave her own 1st concert at the Leipzig Gewandhaus on 8 Nov 1830. In 1837 she was in Vienna for some time. Her engagement to Schumann was violently opposed by her father, but they married after many difficulties on 12 Sep 1840. She appeared less frequently during her married life, but after Schumann's death in 1856 she was obliged to do so continuously and to teach. She went to live in Berlin with her mother, who had married Bargiel, but in 1863 she settled at Baden-Baden and in 1878 became chief pf. prof. at the Hoch Cons. at Frankfurt.

Works incl. pf. concerto in A min.; pf. trio in G min.; variations on a theme by Robert S. and *c* 12 other op. nos. for pf.; several sets of songs.

Schumann, Elisabeth (b Merseburg, 13 Jun 1888; d New York, 23 Apr 1952), German soprano. Studied at Dresden, Berlin and Hamburg; at the last she made her stage debut in 1909 and remained attached to the Opera until she joined the Vienna Opera in 1919; NY met debut 1914, as Sophie. She toured the USA in 1921 with Strauss and 1st appeared at CG in 1924; sang there until 1931 in Strauss and Mozart. Her Susanna, Zerlina and Sophie set new standards in lyrical singing. In 1938 she settled in USA

and taught at the Curtis Inst. in Philadelphia, becoming an Amer. citizen in 1944.

Schumann-Heink (*née* Rössler), **Ernestine** (b Lieben nr. Prague, 15 Jun 1861; d Hollywood, Calif., 16 Nov 1936), German, later American, contralto. Studied with Marietta Leclair at Graz and made her 1st stage appearance at Dresden in 1878; in 1909 she created Clytemnestra there. In 1892 she paid her 1st visit to London and sang under Mahler in the 1st CG perfs. of *The Ring*. In 1896 made her 1st appearance at the Wagner theatre at Bayreuth, where she remained until 1906. She settled in USA after 1898, though continuing to appear in Europe, and was naturalized in 1908.

Schumann, Robert (Alexander) (b Zwickau, Saxony, 8 Jun 1810; d Endenich nr. Bonn, 29 Jul 1856), German composer. Son of a bookseller and pub. Began to learn the pf. from a schoolmaster and organist at the age of 8 and played well by the time he was 11, besides studying all the music found at his father's shop, where he also developed a literary taste. He played at school concerts and private houses and made such progress in improvisation and comp. that in 1825 Weber was approached to teach him, but could not, being busy preparing *Oberon* for London and expecting to go there. Schumann's father died in 1826, and in 1828 he was sent to Leipzig Univ. to study law. There he met Wieck, from whom he took pf. lessons, neglecting his legal studies, as he did again when in 1829 he moved to Heidelberg Univ., where he came under the influence of Thibaut. Back at Leipzig in 1830, he lodged at Wieck's house, wrote his 1st pub. works (op. 1 and 7) and the next year went to the St Thomas cantor, Weinlig, for instruction, but left him for the younger Dorn. In 1832 he permanently injured his hand with a mechanical contrivance he had invented for finger-development and thus had to give up a pianist's career for that of a comp.

With a circle of young intellectuals he founded the *Neue Zeitschrift für Musik* in 1833, and the circle calling itself the 'Davidsbündler'. He fell in love with Ernestine von Fricken in 1834, but the engagement was broken off next year. In 1836 Wieck's daughter Clara, already a remarkable pianist, was 17 and she and Schumann fell seriously in love. The father violently opposed a match and in 1839 they took legal proceedings against him; he failed to yield, but they married on 12 Sep 1840, the day before she came of age. In 1843 Schumann suffered a crisis of mental exhaustion and he had a more serious breakdown after a tour in Rus. with Clara in 1844, at the end of which year they settled at Dresden.

Although his nervous complaint grew more marked after periods of recovery, he accepted the conductorship at Düsseldorf, incl. subscription concerts, choral practices and church music, in 1850, a post for which he proved quite unfit. The committee tactfully suggested his resignation in 1852, but with Clara's injudicious support he obstinately refused to withdraw. Signs of a mental collapse grew more and more alarming and his creative work progressively less convincing, and in Feb 1854 he threw himself into the Rhine. On being rescued he was sent at his own request to a private asylum at Endenich, where he died more than 2 years later.

Works incl. opera *Genoveva* (1850); incid. music to Byron's *Manfred* (1852); 15 works for chorus and orch. with or without solo voices, incl. *Das Paradies und die Peri* (1843), *Vom Pagen und der Königstochter* (Geibel); *Das Glück von Edenhall* (Uhland); *Requiem für Mignon* and scenes from Goethe's *Faust* (1844–53).

ORCH.: 4 symphs. (1841, 1846, 1850, 1841; rev. 1851); *Overture, Scherzo and Finale*; 5 concert overtures; concertos for pf., vln. and cello (1841–5, 1853, 1850), 2 short works for pf. and orch., fantasy for vln. and orch. and *Concertstück* for 4 horns and orch. (1849).

CHAMBER: 3 string 4tets, op. 41 nos. 1–3 (1842), 3 pf. trios, pf. 4tet (1842), pf. 5tet, *Fantasiestücke* and *Märchenerzählungen* for pf. trio (the latter with clar. and vla.); 2 vln. and pf. sonatas; sets of pieces for horn, clar., ob., vla. and cello with pf.

PIANO: 36 op. nos. of pf. music incl. *Papillons* (1831), 6 *Intermezzi, Davidsbündlertänze* (1837), *Carnaval* (1835), 3 sonatas, *Fantasiestücke* (2 sets), *Études symphoniques* (1837), *Kinderscenen* (1838), *Kreisleriana* (1838), *Humoreske, Nachtstücke, Faschingsschwank aus Wien* (1840), 3 romances, *Album für die Jugend, Waldscenen, Bunte Blätter, Albumblätter*; 4 works for pf. duet (33 pieces); *Andante and Variations* for 2 pfs.; Studies and Sketches for pedal pf.; 6 org. fugues.

SONGS: 35 op. nos. of songs (some containing numerous pieces), incl. *Kerner Lieder* op. 35 and the cycles *Frauenliebe und -leben* (1840) and *Dichterliebe* (1840), also *Liederkreise* (Heine and Eichendorff, 1840) and *Myrthen*; 3 pieces for declamation and pf; 4 op. nos. of vocal duets, 1 of vocal

trios, 4 of vocal 4tets; 14 op. nos. of partsongs.

Schuppanzigh, Ignaz (b Vienna, 20 Nov 1776; d Vienna, 2 Mar 1830), Austrian violinist. Worked in Vienna; dir. of the Augarten concerts, founder of a 4tet of his own and that of Prince Rasumovsky. He was the 1st to lead 4tets by Beethoven and Schubert.

Schuricht, Carl (b Danzig, 3 Jul 1880; d Corseaux-sur-Vevey, 7 Jan 1967), German conductor. He studied with Humperdinck and Reger. Wiesbaden 1911–44; many early perfs. of Debussy, Schoenberg and Stravinsky. From 1944 he was guest cond. with leading orchs. and in London was heard in the standard repertory with the LSO. Toured the USA with the Vienna PO in 1956 and in 1957 appeared with the Chicago SO and the Boston SO.

Schürmann, Georg Caspar (b Idensen, Hanover, *c* 1672; d Wolfenbüttel, 25 Feb 1751), German singer and composer. He was 1st engaged at the Hamburg opera in 1693–7, then at Wolfenbüttel, entered the service of the Duke of Brunswick, who sent him to It. for further study and gave him leave in 1702–7 to enter the service of the Duke of Meiningen, after which he remained at Wolfenbüttel to his death.

Works incl. operas *Télémaque* (after Fénelon), *Heinrich der Vogler* (in 2 parts, 1718 and 1721), *Die getreue Alceste* (after Euripides, 1719), *Ludovicus Pius* (1726) and *c* 16 others; New Year cantata.

Schurmann, Gerard (b Kertosono, Indonesia, 19 Jan 1928), British composer of Dutch parentage. He came to England in 1941 and studied at the RCM; largely self-taught.

Works incl. Wind 5tet (1963, rev. 1976), 2 string 4tets, fl. sonatina (1968), *Variants* for orch. (1970), 6 *Studies of Francis Bacon* for orch. (1968), pf. concerto (1973), *Contrasts* for pf. (1973), *The Double Heart*, cantata (1976), vln. concerto (1978), *Piers Plowman* for soloists, chorus and orch. (1980), pf. quartet (fp Cheltenham, 1986).

Schusterfleck (Ger. cobbler's patch), a playful German description of a technical device, esp. the Rosalia, used as an easy subterfuge in comp. Beethoven called Diabelli's waltz, on which he wrote the variations op. 120, a Schusterfleck.

Schütz, Hans (b Vienna, 16 Dec 1862; d Wiesbaden, 12 Jan 1917), Austrian baritone. Debut Linz 1891. After engagements in Zurich and Düsseldorf sang at Leipzig 1898–1908, often in Wagner. Bayreuth 1899–1902, as Amfortas, Klingsor and Donner. CG 1902–4. Wiesbaden from 1908.

Schütz, Heinrich (b Köstritz, Saxony, bap. 9 Oct 1585; d Dresden, 6 Nov 1672), German composer. Learnt music as a choir-boy in the chapel of the Landgrave of Hesse-Kassel, studied law at Marburg Univ. and music under G. Gabrieli at Venice, 1609–12. He returned to Kassel as court organist, but left for Dresden in 1614, with an appt. as music dir. to the Elector Johann Georg of Saxony. He did much there to estab. the fashion for It. music and musicians, but although he had written It. madrigals at Venice, he set his own words to Ger. or Lat. words. In 1627 he wrote the 1st Ger. opera, *Dafne*, on a translation of Rinuccini's lib. by Martin Opitz, for the marriage of the elector's daughter to the Landgrave of Hesse-Darmstadt. After the death of his wife in 1628, he again went to It. in 1629. In 1633, the 30 Years War having disorganized the Dresden court chapel, he obtained leave to go to Copenhagen, and he spent the years until 1641 there and at other courts. Returning to Dresden, he did not succeed in reorganizing the court music satisfactorily until the later 1640s. In the 1650s he became much dissatisfied with the new tendencies among the It. court musicians and had many quarrels with Bontempi, but did not succeed in obtaining his release, and after some improvements later on he remained at the Saxon court for the rest of his life.

Works incl. operas *Dafne* (1627, lost) and *Orpheus und Euridice* (1638, lost); motets, *Cantiones sacrae*, psalms, sacred symphs. and concertos for voices and insts. and other church music; Christmas (1664), Passion and Resurrection oratorios, *The 7 Words of Christ*; It. madrigals; *Exequien* (funeral pieces) for 6–8 voices, Elegy on the death of the electress of Saxony.

Schützendorf, Gustav (b Cologne, 1883; d Berlin, 27 Apr 1937), German baritone. He studied in Milan; debut Düsseldorf 1905, as Don Giovanni. NY Met 1922–35, in operas by Strauss, Janáček, Stravinsky and Weinberger.

Schützendorf, Leo (b Cologne, 7 May 1886; d Berlin, 18 Dec 1931), German baritone, brother of prec. After singing in Düsseldorf, Vienna and Wiesbaden he joined the Berlin Staatsoper in 1920, where he created the role of Wozzeck in 1925; sang in Berlin until 1929 as Ochs, Boris and Beckmesser. His brothers Guido and Alfons were also successful singers.

Schuyt, Cornelis (b Leyden, 1557; d Leyden, buried 12 Jun 1616), Flemish composer. He travelled to Italy to study music,

returning in 1581. He held a succession of organ appts. in the Netherlands. He pub. several books of madrigals and a book of instrumental pieces.

Schwanda (Švanda) the Bagpiper. *See* **Švanda Dudák.**

Schwanenberg **(Schwanenberger), Johann Gottfried** (b Wolfenbüttel, 28 Dec 1740; d Brunswick, 5 Apr 1804), German composer. Pupil of Hasse. He was app. court cond. at Brunswick in 1762.

Works incl. operas *Romeo e Giulia* (1776), (after Shakespeare), *Adriano in Siria* (1762), *Solimano* (1762), *Zenobia* and *c* 10 others; symphs.; pf. concertos; pf. sonatas.

Schwanendreher, Der (*The Swan-Turner*), concerto after German folksongs for vla. and small orch. by Hindemith; comp. 1935, fp Amsterdam, 14 Nov 1935 cond. Mengelberg. The title alludes to the cooking of swans by turning them on a spit.

Schwanengesang (*Swan Song*), song cycle by Schubert, containing the last songs written by him in 1828, incl. 7 settings of Rellstab, 6 of Heine (his only settings of that poet) and Seidl's *Pigeon Post (Die Taubenpost)*. The idea of a cycle was not Schubert's, but that of the pub., as was the title, which was invented as an allusion to Schubert's death; the inclusion of Seidl's song was also the publisher's afterthought. The songs are *Liebesbotschaft, Kriegers Ahnung, Frühlingssehnsucht, Ständchen, Aufenthalt, In der Ferne, Abschied, Der Atlas, Ihr Bild, Das Fischermädchen, Die Stadt, Am Meer, Der Doppelgänger* and *Die Taubenpost*.

Schwarz, Boris (b St Petersburg, 26 Mar 1906; d New York, 31 Dec 1983), American musicologist, violinist and conductor. He studied with Flesch and Thibaud in Berlin and Paris; after a 1920 debut he perf. widely in Europe, settling in the USA in 1936. He held various academic posts in NY from 1941 and made a special study of Soviet music.

Schwarz, Hanna (b Hamburg, 15 Aug 1943), German mezzo. Studied Hamburg and Essen; debut Hanover 1970. From 1973 she has been a member of the Hamburg Opera; many guest appearances in Europe and N. America. Sang under Boulez in the 1976 Bayreuth *Ring* (Erda) and in the 1979 Paris fp of the complete *Lulu*. Other roles incl. Fricka, Jocasta and Brangaene.

Schwarz, Joseph (b Riga, 10 Oct 1880; d Berlin, 10 Nov 1926), German baritone. He was a member of the Vienna Volksoper and later of the Berlin Court (afterwards State)

Opera; also sang in London and NY; he sang Rigoletto at CG in 1924.

Schwarz, Paul (b Vienna, 30 Jun 1887; d Hamburg, 24 Dec 1980), Austrian tenor. He sang at Bielitz and Vienna 1909–12; appeared in many roles at Hamburg, 1912–33: Manrico, Turiddu, David and Pedrillo. Glyndebourne 1936, Monostatos. Lived in USA during the war. Retired 1949.

Schwarz, Rudolf (b Vienna, 29 Apr 1905), Austrian, later English, conductor. Studied pf. and vln., playing vla. in the Vienna PO. In 1923 he became an asst. cond. at the Düsseldorf Opera and from 1927 to 1933 cond. at the Karlsruhe Opera, after which he became music dir. of the Jewish Cultural Union in Berlin until 1941, when he was sent to Belsen concentration camp. He survived and went to Swed. in 1945 and then Eng., where he became cond. of Bournemouth SO (1947–51), CBSO (1951–7), and BBC SO (1957–62) and Northern Sinfonia Orch. (1964–73).

Schwarz, Vera (b Agram, 10 Jul 1888; d Vienna, 4 Dec 1964), Yugoslav soprano. She sang in Vienna from 1912, Hamburg from 1914. In Berlin she was popular in the operettas of Lehár, and sang in the 1927 fp of *Der Zarewitsch*, opposite Tauber. Salzburg 1929, Octavian; Glyndebourne 1938, Lady Macbeth, in the 1st Eng. prod. of *Macbeth*. Appeared widely in USA during the war.

Schwarze Maske, Die (*The Black Mask*), opera by Penderecki (lib. by comp. after G. Hauptmann), prod. Salzburg, 15 Aug 1986.

Schwarzkopf, Elisabeth (b Jarotschin, nr. Poznań, 9 Dec 1915), German soprano. Studied in Berlin with M. Ivogün, making her debut at the Berlin Staatsoper in 1938. In 1943 she joined the Vienna Staatsoper. Salzburg and CG, London, debuts, 1947; La Scala, 1948. She was esp. well known for her singing of Mozart and R. Strauss, and also created the role of Anne Trulove in Stravinsky's *The Rake's Progress* (Venice, 1951); other roles incl. the Marschallin (CG 1959, Met 1964), Elvira, the Countess, Alice Ford and Leonore. She was equally famous as a Lieder-singer.

Schweigsame Frau, Die (*The Silent Woman*), opera by R. Strauss (lib. by Stefan Zweig, based on Ben Jonson's *Epicoene*), prod. Dresden, 24 Jun 1935.

Schweitzer, Albert (b Kaysersberg, Upper Alsace, 14 Jan 1875; d Lambaréné, 4 Sep 1965), Alsatian theologian, medical missionary, organist and music scholar. Studied org. at Strasbourg and with Widor in Paris.

He was lecturer in theology at Strasbourg Univ. in 1902–12 and later undertook medical missions in Central Africa, where he spent most of his life, visiting Europe periodically and giving organ recitals of Bach's works. Author of a work on Bach pub. in Fr. in 1905 and in an enlarged Ger. ed. in 1908. He was awarded the Nobel Peace Prize in 1952.

Schweitzer, Anton (b Coburg, bap. 6 Jun 1735; d Gotha, 23 Nov 1787), German composer and conductor. Studied with Kleinknecht in Bayreuth and in It. 1764–6, and was app. to the court in Hildburghausen in 1766. Cond. of the Seyler opera troupe 1769, he was at Weimar 1772–4 and Gotha from 1774 to his death, succeeding G. Benda as court cond. there in 1780.

Works incl. *Singspiele* and operas *Walmir und Gertraud* (1769), *Die Dorfgala* (1772), *Alceste* (lib. by Wieland, 1773), *Rosamunde* (do.), etc.; monodramas *Pygmalion* (after Rousseau, 1772), *Polyxena;* dramatic prologues *Elysium, Apollo unter den Hirten,* etc.; incid. music to Goethe's *Clavigo* (1776), Molière's *Le Bourgeois Gentilhomme* (1771), etc.; ballets; cantatas; symphs.

Schweizerfamilie, Die (*The Swiss Family*), opera by Weigl (lib. by I.F. Castelli), prod. Vienna, Kärntnertortheater, 14 Mar 1809.

Schwemmer, Heinrich (b Gumbertshausen, Franconia, 28 Mar 1621; d Nuremberg, 26 May 1696), German composer. Studied with Kindermann at Nuremberg, where he became a master at a school in 1650 and in 1656 choirmaster at the church of Our Lady. Among his pupils were J. Krieger and Pachelbel.

Works incl. wedding and funeral anthems, motets, hymn tunes and other church music.

Schwenke, Christian Friedrich Gottlieb (b Wachenhausen, Harz, 30 Aug 1767; d Hamburg, 27 Oct 1822), German organist, composer, conductor and editor. Pupil of his father, Johann Gottlieb S. (1744–1823) and of Kirnberger and Marpurg in Berlin, he succeeded C.P.E. Bach as municipal music dir. in Hamburg in 1789. His sons Johann Friedrich S. (1792–1852) and Karl S. (1789–after 1870), as well as the former's son, Friedrich Gottlieb S. (1823–96), were also musicians.

Works incl. music for the stage; 2 oratorios; cantatas; church music settings of odes by Klopstock; ob. concerto; 6 organ fugues; pf. sonatas, etc. Also ed. Bach's '48', Mozart's Requiem, and works by Hasse, Handel and Spohr.

Schwindel, Friedrich (b Amsterdam, 3 May 1737; d Karlsruhe, 7 Aug 1786), Dutch or German violinist, flautist, harpsichordist and composer. He was at The Hague when Burney stayed there in 1770, later at Geneva and Mulhouse, and finally at Karlsruhe as music dir. to the Margrave of Baden. As a symphonist he belonged to the Mannheim school.

Works incl. operas *Das Liebesgrab* and *Die drei Pächter*; Mass in Eb ; 28 symphs.; 4tets, trios.

Schytte, Ludvig Theodor (b Aarhus, Jutland, 28 Apr 1848; d Berlin, 10 Nov 1909), Danish pianist and composer. He was in business as a chemist, but took to music in 1870, studying with Gade and others in Copenhagen and later with Taubert in Berlin and Liszt at Weimar. In 1887 he settled in Vienna as concert pianist and teacher.

Works incl. monodrama *Hero,* operettas *Der Mameluk* and *Der Student von Salamanca;* pf. concerto; piano music.

Scio, Julie-Angélique (b Lille, 1768; d Paris, 14 Jul 1807), French soprano. Sang in the provinces from 1786, Paris from 1792. She created Cherubini's Médée, Théâtre Feydeau 1797, and sang there in the 1800 fp of *Les Deux Journées.* Also appeared in works by Berton and Dalayrac.

Scipione (*Scipio*), opera by Handel (lib. by P.A. Rolli, based on Zeno's *Scipione nelle Spagne*), prod. London, King's Theatre, Haymarket, 12 Mar 1726.

Scipione Affricano, opera by Cavalli (lib. by Minato), prod. Venice, Teatro SS Giovanni e Paolo, 9 Feb 1664.

Sciutti, Graziella (b Turin, 17 Apr 1927), Italian soprano. Studied in Rome, making her debut at Aix-en-Provence in 1951; roles there have been Despina, Susanna and Zerlina. She was esp. well known in soubrette roles. Glyndebourne debut 1954 (Rosina); CG from 1956 as Oscar, Nannetta and Despina. In recent years she has turned to operatic production (*La Voix Humaine,* Glyndebourne, *L'elisir d'amore* at CG).

Scola de' maritati, La (*The School for the Married*), opera by Martín y Soler (lib. by Lorenzo da Ponte), prod. London King's Theatre, Haymarket, 27 Jan 1795.

Scontrino, Antonio (b Trapani, Sicily, 17 May 1850; d Florence, 7 Jan 1922), Italian double bass player and composer. Although the son of a poor carpenter, he was brought up in a musical atmosphere, his father running a primitive but enthusiastic amateur orch. in which he played double bass parts on an adapted cello. In 1861 he went to the Palermo Cons. and in 1870 began to tour as a double bass virtuoso. In 1876 he prod. his 1st opera, having studied for another 2 years at Munich. In 1891 he became prof. at the Palermo Cons. and in 1892 at the Reale Istituto Musicale at Florence.

Works incl. operas *Matelda* (1879), *Il progettista* (1882), *Il sortilegio* (1882), *Gringoire* (after Banville's play) and *La cortigiana* (1896); incid. music for d'Annunzio's *Francesca da Rimini;* motet *Tota pulchra, O Salutaris, Salve Regina* and other church music; *Sinfonia marinesca* and *Sinfonia romantica* for orch.; 3 string 4tets and prelude and fugue for string 4tet; songs.

Scordatura (It. = mistuning), tuning of the vln. or other string instruments temporarily to other intervals than the normal perfect 5ths, etc., for the purpose of facilitating the playing of chords with certain intervals or altering the instrument's tone-quality. The music is still written as for the normal tuning (and fingering), so that the instrument becomes to that extent a transposing instrument.

Score, the copy of any music written in several parts on separate staves, with the coincident notes appearing vertically over each other. Complete orchestral or choral scores showing all the parts are given the name of Full Score; arrs. of operas, oratorios, etc., for voices and pf. are Vocal Scores; arrs. for pf. only are Piano Scores; comps.' sketches reduced to a few staves, to be elaborated and fully written out later, are known as Short Scores. The usual lay-out of orchestral scores is in groups of var. types of instruments, with the treble instruments of each group at the top and the bass instruments at the bottom. The order is as a rule woodwind at the top, brass in the middle and strings at the bottom. Harps, perc. and any other extras are placed between brass and strings.

Scoring. *See* **Orchestration.**

Scotch Snap, the technical name for rhythmic figures inverting the order of dotted notes, the short note coming 1st instead of last (see illustration overleaf).

Its name in Eng., which is also Scots Catch, is no doubt due to the fact that the Scotch Snap is a feature in the Scot. Strathspey. It was popular in It. in the 17th and 18th cents. and was called by Ger. writers the 'Lombardy rhythm'.

Scott, Cyril (Meir) (b Oxton, Cheshire, 27 Sep 1879; d Eastbourne, 31 Dec 1970), English composer and poet. He played the pf. and began to comp. as a child. Studied in Frankfurt as a child and from 1895 to 1398.

Handel, *Alcina*

SCOTCH SNAP

In 1898 he settled at Liverpool as pianist and gave some lessons, and soon after the turn of the cent. he began to become known as a comp. in London, having some works perf. and a number of songs and pf. pieces pub. In 1913 Alma Mahler, the composer's widow, invited him to Vienna, where he gave some perfs. During the 1914–18 war some works were prod. in Eng. and in 1925 the opera *The Alchemist* was given, in Ger., at Essen.

Works incl. opera *The Alchemist* (1917); ballet *The Incompetent Apothecary* (1923); *La Belle Dame sans merci* (Keats), *Nativity Hymn* (Milton), *Let us now praise famous men* for chorus and orch. (1935); 2 symphs., pf. concerto, vln. concerto; 3 string 4tets; piano music, songs.

Scott, Marion M(argaret) (b London, 16 Jul 1877; d London, 24 Dec 1953), English musicologist. Studied at the RCM in London, 1896–1904, with which she afterwards remained assoc. as sec. of the RCM Union and ed. of the *RCM Magazine*. She wrote criticism for var. periodicals and many articles, notably on Haydn, in whose work she specialized and on whom she was engaged in writing a large work. She also contributed a vol. on Beethoven to the Master Musicians Series (1934).

Scott, Walter (1771–1832), Scottish poet and novelist.

Among operas based on his novels are: THE BRIDE OF LAMMERMOOR: **Adam** (*Le Caleb de Walter Scott*, 1827), **Carafa** (*Le nozze di Lammermoor*, 1829), **Donizetti** (*Lucia di Lammermoor*, 1835). THE FAIR MAID OF PERTH: **Bizet** (*La Jolie Fille de Perth*, 1867). THE HEART OF MIDLOTHIAN: **Bishop** (1819), **Carafa** (*La Prison d'Edimbourg*, 1833), **F. Ricci** (*La prigione d'Edimburgo*, 1838). IVANHOE: **Marschner** (*Der Templer und die Jüdin*, 1829), **Nicolai** (*Il Templario*, 1840), **Pacini** (1832), **Sullivan** (1891). KENILWORTH: **Auber** (*Leicester*, 1823), **Donizetti** (*Elizabetta al castello di Kenilworth*, 1829). THE LADY OF THE LAKE: **Bishop** (*The Knight of Snowdoun*, 1811), **Rossini** (*La donna del lago*, 1819). ROB

ROY: **Flotow** (1836). THE TALISMAN: **Adam** (*Richard en Palestine*, 1844), **Balfe** (1874), **Bishop** (1826), **Pacini** (*Il Talismano, ovvero La terza crociata in Palestina*, 1829). Also: overtures by **Berlioz**, *Rob Roy* (1832) and *Waverley* (1828), and 8 songs by **Schubert** in Ger. trans.

Scotti, Antonio (b Naples, 25 Jan 1866; d Naples, 26 Feb 1936), Italian baritone. Pupil of Ester Trifani-Paganini. Made his 1st appearance at Malta in 1889 and 1st visited London, after successful tours in It., Spain and S. Amer., in 1899, as Don Giovanni. NY Met 1899–1933 as Scarpia, Rigoletto and Falstaff.

Scottish Fantasy, work for vln. and orch. in 4 movts. by Bruch, based on Scottish folk songs. Comp. 1879–80 and ded. to Sarasate, who gave the fp in Hamburg, 1880.

Scottish National Orchestra, symph. orch. founded 1891 as Scottish Orch., with George Henschel as cond. (until 1894). Prin. conds. since 1933–6 (Barbirolli) have been George Szell (1936–9), Warwick Braithwaite (1940–6), Walter Susskind (1946–52), Karl Rankl (1952–7), Hans Swarowsky (1957–9) and Alexander Gibson (1959–84); Neeme Järvi from 1984. Present title adopted 1950.

Scottish Opera, opera co. founded 1962 by Alexander Gibson. Based in Glasgow but tours widely and has visited London (*Pelléas* and *Tristan*, 1973). *Les Troyens* was mounted in 1969 and *The Ring* 1966–71. An enterprising approach to modern opera (Janáček series with WNO) and some interesting new prods. (*Orlando* and *Oberon*, 1985). John Mauceri music dir. from 1987.

'Scottish' Symphony, Mendelssohn's 3rd symph., op. 56, in A min. and maj., begun in Italy in 1831 and finished in Berlin, 20 Jan 1842; fp Leipzig, Gewandhaus, 3 Mar 1842.

Scotto, Renata (b Savona, 24 Feb 1933), Italian soprano. Studied in Milan, making her debut at the Milan Nat. Theatre in 1953. In 1957 she sang Violetta and Donna Elvira in London, and replaced Callas as Amina in *La sonnambula* at the Edinburgh Fest. CG from 1962, Met from 1965. Other roles incl. Adina, Lucia, Norma and Lady Macbeth.

Scriabin. *See* **Skriabin.**

Scribe, Eugène (b Paris, 25 Dec 1791; d Paris, 21 Feb 1861), French playwright and librettist. *See* **Adriana Lecouvreur** (Cilea), **Africaine** (Meyerbeer), **Alexandrov (A.N.)** (*Adrienne Lecouvreur*), **Ali Baba** (Cherubini), **Ballo in maschera** (Verdi), **Châlet** (*Adam*), **Cheval de bronze** (Auber), **Comte Ory** (Rossini), **Dame blanche** (Boieldieu), **Diamants de la Couronne** (Auber), **Domino noir** (Auber), **Dom Sébastien** (Donizetti), **Elisir d'amore** (do.), **Étoile du Nord** (Meyerbeer), **Favorite** (Donizetti), **Fra Diavolo** (Auber), **Gustave III** (do.), **Huguenots** (Meyerbeer), **Juive** (Halévy), **Leicester** (Auber), **Lortzing** (*Yelva*), **Maçon** (Auber), **Manon Lescaut** (Auber), **Marquise de Brinvilliers** (8 comps.), **Martyrs** (Donizetti), **Muette de Portici** (Auber), **Part du diable** (Auber), **Philtre** (Auber), **Prophète** (Meyerbeer), **Puits d'Amour** (Balfe), **Robert le Diable** (Meyerbeer), **Schmitt (A.)** (*Trilby*), **Setaccioli** (*Adrienne Lecouvreur*), **Shebalin** (*Glass of Water*), **Vêpres siciliennes** (Verdi).

Sculthorpe, Peter (Launceston, Tasmania, 29 Apr 1929), Australian composer. Studied at Melbourne Univ. Cons. and Oxford. Lecturer at Sydney Univ.

Works incl. opera *Rites of Passage* (1971–3), *Sun Music* (1968); *Sun Music I* for orch.; *Irkanda IV* for strings and perc.; *Sun Music II* for chorus and perc. (1969); *Mangrove* for orch. (1979); pf. concerto (1983); 10 string 4tets (1947–82), string trio, pf. trio; sonata for vla. and perc.; pf. sonatina.

Scylla et Glaucus, opera by Leclair (lib. by d'Albaret), prod. Paris, Opéra, 4 Oct 1746; revived London (concert) 1979.

Sea Drift, setting of a poem by Walt Whitman for baritone solo, chorus and orch. by Delius, comp. 1903; in Ger., Essen Music Festival, 24 May 1906; in Eng., Sheffield Festival, 7 Oct 1908.

Sea Interludes (Britten). *See* **Four Sea Interludes.**

Sea Pictures, song cycle for contralto and orch. by Elgar, op. 37: 1. *Sea Slumber Song* (Roden Noel); 2. *In Haven* (Alice Elgar); 3. *Sabbath Morning at Sea* (Elizabeth Barrett Browning); 4. *Where Corals lie* (Richard Garnett); 5. *The Swimmer* (A.L. Gordon); fp Norwich Festival, 5 Oct 1899, with Clara Butt.

Sea Symphony, A, the 1st symph. by Vaughan Williams, for solo voices, chorus and orch. (words by Walt Whitman), perf. Leeds Festival, 12 Oct 1910.

Seal Woman, The, opera by Bantock (lib. by Marjorie Kennedy Fraser), prod. Birmingham, Repertory Theatre, 27 Sep 1924. A Celtic folk opera containing many traditional Hebridean tunes.

Searle, Humphrey (b Oxford, 26 Aug 1915; d London, 12 May 1982), English composer and writer on music. Educ. at Winchester Coll. and Oxford, he studied music with Ireland at the RCM in London and in Vienna under Webern. In 1938 he joined the BBC and in 1947 became Hon. Sec. to the ISCM. He served in the army in 1940–6. Prof., RCM 1965–77.

Works incl. operas *The Diary of a Madman* (after Gogol, 1958), *The Photo of the Colonel* (after Ionesco, 1964), *Hamlet* (Shakespeare, 1968); ballets *The Great Peacock, Dualities; Gold Coast Customs* and *The Shadow of Cain* (Edith Sitwell) and *The Riverrun* (James Joyce) for speakers, chorus and orch. *Jerusalem* for speaker, ten., chorus and orch. (1970).

5 symphs. (1953–64), 2 suites and *Highland Reel* for orch.; 2 nocturnes and 2 suites for chamber orch.; pf. concerto; *Intermezzo* for chamber ensemble, 5tet for horn and strings; 4tet for vln., vla., clar. and bassoon; sonata, *Vigil* and *Ballad* for pf.; 2 Housman songs.

Seasons, The, ballet by Glazunov (choreography by Petipa), prod. St Petersburg, Maryinsky Theatre, 20 Feb 1900.

Oratorio (*Die Jahreszeiten*) by Haydn (Ger. words by Gottfried van Swieten, based on Thomson's poem), comp. 1798–1801; prod. Vienna, Schwarzenberg Palace, 24 Apr 1801.

Sébastian, Georges (b Budapest, 17 Aug 1903), French conductor of Hungarian birth. He studied with Bartók and Kodály at the Budapest Academy; worked as opera coach in Munich and NY, cond. Leipzig Gewandhaus orch. and Berlin Städtische Oper 1927–31. Cond. Moscow PO in the 1930s and worked in N. and S. Amer. during the war. From 1946 he has been heard at the Paris Opéra, and with the Orchestre National in Brahms, Strauss and Verdi.

Sebastiani, Claudius (*fl.* 1557–65), German music theorist. Organist at Fribourg and Metz, but famous partic. for his treatise *Bellum Musicale* (Strasbourg, 1563).

Sebastiani, Johann (b Weimar, 30 Sep 1622; d Königsberg, spring 1683), German composer. Studied prob. in It. Went to Königsberg *c* 1650, where he became cantor in 1661 and music dir. at the electoral church in 1663, retiring in 1679.

Works incl. a Passion for voices and strings; sacred concertos for voices and instruments and other church music; wedding and funeral cantatas; sacred and secular songs *Parnass-Blumen*.

Sec (Fr. = dry), a term used by some French composers, esp. Debussy, where a note or chord is to be struck and released again abruptly without any richness of tone.

Secco (It. = dry). *See* **Recitativo secco**, for which it sometimes serves as an abbr.

Sechter, Simon (b Friedberg, Boh., 11 Oct 1788; d Vienna, 10 Sep 1867), Bohemian-Austrian theorist, organist and composer. Settled in Vienna in 1804 and continued studies there, wrote pf. accomps. for Dragonetti's double bass concertos in 1809, while the It. player took refuge in Vienna, and in 1812 became teacher of pf. and singing at the Institute for the Blind. In 1825 he succeeded Voříšek as court organist. In 1850 he became prof. at the Cons. He wrote several theoretical works.

Works incl. opera *Ali Hitsch-Hatsch* (1844); Masses, Requiem and other church music; oratorios and cantatas; choruses from Schiller's *Braut von Messina*; chorale preludes, fugues, etc. for organ; variations, fugues and other works for pf.

Second, the interval between 2 adjacent notes on the stave, e.g.:

Maj.   Min.   Augmented

Second Subject. *See* **Sonata**.

Secondo (It. = second), the part of the 2nd player in a pf. duet, that of the 1st being called Primo. Also as an adj., applied to the 2nd player of a pair or a group, e.g. *clarinetto secondo*.

Secret, The (*Tajemstvi*), opera by Smetana (lib. by E. Krásnohorská), prod. Prague, Czech Theatre, 18 Sep 1878.

Sedaine, Michel Jean (b Paris, 4 Jul 1719; d Paris, 17 May 1797), French playwright and librettist. *See* **Aline, Reine de Golconde** (Berton and Monsigny), **Aucassin et Nicolette** (Grétry), **Blaise le savetier** (Philidor), **Déserteur** (Monsigny), **Diable à quatre** (Philidor), **Félix** (Monsigny), Grétry (*Raoul Barbe-bleue*), **Guillaume Tell** (Grétry), **Jagd** (J.A. Hiller), **Richard Cœur de Lion** (Grétry), **Roi et le fermier** (Monsigny), **Rose et Colas** (do.).

Sedie, Enrico delle. *See* **Delle Sedie**.

Seefried, Irmgard (b Königfried, Bavaria, 9 Oct 1919), German soprano. Studied singing at the Augsburg Cons. and after her first engagement at Aachen (1939–43) joined the Vienna Staatsoper; sang with the co. at CG in 1947 as Fiordiligi and Susanna. Other roles incl. Eva, Ariadne, Judith and Marie. She was esp. well known as a Mozart singer, and also in Lieder. In 1948 she married the violinist Wolfgang Schneiderhan. Last stage appearance Vienna, 1977.

Seeger, Charles (Louis) (b Mexico City, 14 Dec 1886; d Bridgewater, Conn., 7 Feb 1979), American conductor, teacher and composer. Studied at Harvard Univ. After cond. at the Cologne Opera in 1910, he was Prof. of Music at California Univ., 1912–19, where from 1958 he was engaged in research. Author of books on theory and ethnomusicology.

Works incl. masques *Derdra* and *The Queen's Masque*; overture *Shadowy Waters* for orch.; chamber music; vln. and pf. sonata; numerous songs.

Seegr, Joseph (Ferdinand Norbert) (b Repin, nr. Mělník, 21 Mar 1716; d Prague, 22 Apr 1782), Bohemian organist and composer. Studied in Prague and became singer, violinist and organist at several churches there. On hearing him play, Joseph II offered him a court appt. in Vienna, but he died before he could take it up.

Works incl. Masses, psalms, litanies and other church music; toccatas and fugues for organ.

Segal, Uri (b Jerusalem, 7 Mar 1944), Israeli conductor. Studied in Jerusalem and at the GSM. He won the 1969 Mitropoulos Comp. and in the same year made his debut, in Copenhagen. He was asst. to Bernstein with the NY PO 1969–70 and in 1972 made his US debut, with the Chicago SO. He has lived in London since 1970 and was prin. cond. Bournemouth SO 1980–2.

Segerstam, Leif (b Vasa, 2 Mar 1944), Finnish conductor and composer. Studied at the Sibelius Academy, Helsinki, and the Juilliard School, NY. He was cond. of the Finnish National Opera, then Stockholm Royal Opera, 1965–72, and the Deutsche Oper, Berlin, 1971–3. Prin. cond. Austrian Radio Orch. 1975–82.

Works incl. Divertimento for strings (1963), *Concerto Serioso* for vln. and orch. (1967), 2 pf. concertos (1978, 1981), 5 symphs. (1977–83), many works for orch. under title *Orchestral Diary Sheets; Song of Experience* after Blake and Auden for sop. and orch. (1971); 25 string 4tets (1962–82),

2 pf. trios (1976–7), 3 string trios (1977–8), 22 Episodes for various inst. combinations (1978–81).

Segni, Giulio (Giulio da Modena) (b Modena, 1498; d Rome, 24 Jul 1561), Italian composer. After a short period as organist of St Mark's, Venice (1530–3), he entered the service of Pope Clement VII. Comp. 3 *ricercari à 4* (pub. in *Musica Nova*, 1540) and other instrumental works.

Segovia, Andrés (b Linares, 17 Feb 1893; d Madrid, 3 Jun 1987), Spanish guitarist. Self-taught, he 1st appeared in public aged 14. From his 1st concert in Paris in 1924 he was regarded as foremost among modern guitarists, and Falla, Ponce, Rodrigo, Turina and Villa-Lobos wrote works esp. for him. Last London concert Jun 1986.

Segreto di Susanna, Il (*Susanna's Secret*), opera by Wolf-Ferrari (lib. by E. Golisciani), prod. Munich, Court Opera, in Ger. trans. by Max Kalbeck, 4 Dec 1909. (Susanna is a secret smoker.)

Segue (It. = follows), an indication, like *attacca*, that a piece, number or section is to be played or sung immediately after another one. In MSS. the word is sometimes used instead of *V.S. (volti subito)* where a blank space is left at the bottom of a page to avoid turning over during the perf. of what follows on the next.

Seguidilla, a Spanish dance dating back to at least the 16th cent. and 1st heard of in La Mancha, though possibly of earlier Moorish origin. The orig. form was the Seguidilla Manchega, but when the dance spread over Spain others developed: the Seguidilla Bolero—slow and stately; the Seguidilla Gitana—slow and sentimental. The seguidilla is usually played on guitars, often with castanet accomp. and sometimes with vln. or fl. Frequently popular verses are sung to the seguidilla consisting of *coplas* (couplets) of 4 lines followed by *estribillos* (refrains) of 3 lines.

Seguin, Arthur (Edward Shelden) (b London, 7 Apr 1809; d New York, 9 Dec 1852), English bass. Studied at the RAM in London and made his 1st appearance at the Exeter Festival in 1829 and at CG and Drury Lane, London, in 1833 in operas by Handel and Cimarosa. Visited USA in 1838, settling later in NY. He married the soprano Ann Childe (1814–88).

Seiber, Mátyás (b Budapest, 4 May 1905; d Kruger National Park, SA, 24 Sep 1960), Hungarian composer, conductor and cellist. Studied with Kodály at the Budapest Acad. of Music. Travelled abroad, incl. N. and S. Amer.; from 1928 to 33 taught in the newly estab. jazz class at the Hoch Cons. in Frankfurt, also cellist in a string 4tet there and cond. at a theatre and of a workers' chorus. In 1935 he settled in London, as choral cond. and film comp., and joined the teaching staff at Morley Coll.

Works incl. opera *Eva plays with Dolls* (1934); 2 operettas; incid. music for plays; film and radio music; *Missa brevis* for unaccomp. chorus; cantata *Ulysses* (chapter from James Joyce, 1947); 2 Besardo Suites (from 16th-cent. lute tablatures), *Transylvanian Rhapsody* for orch.; *Pastorale* and *concertante* for vln. and strings (1944), *Notturno* for horn and strings; concertino for clar. and strings; 4 Gk. songs for voice and strings.

3 string 4tets (1924, 1935, 1951), wind 6tet, 5tet for clar. and strings, duo for vln. and cello; fantasy for cello and pf., vln. pieces; pf. works; songs, choruses, folksong arrs.

Seidl, Anton (b Pest, 7 May 1850; d New York, 28 Mar 1898), German conductor of Hungarian birth. Studied at the Leipzig Cons. from 1870 and 2 years later went to Bayreuth as Wagner's asst. Cond. at the Leipzig Opera, 1879–82, afterwards toured and cond. German opera at the Met Opera House in NY from 1885 to his death; cond. the 1st US perfs. of *Tristan, Meistersinger* and *The Ring* and the fp of Dvořák's 'New World' symph. (1893).

Seidl-Kraus, Auguste (b Vienna, 28 Aug 1853; d Kingston, NY, 17 Jul 1939), Austrian soprano, wife of prec. She sang in Vienna from 1877; married Anton S. 1884 and they made their NY Met debuts together, the following year, in *Lohengrin*. She was the 1st US Eva (1886) and Gutrune (1888) and the 1st Met Sieglinde.

Seinemeyer, Meta (b Berlin, 5 Sep 1895; d Dresden, 19 Aug 1929), German soprano. Debut Berlin 1918, as Eurydice; also sang Elisabeth and Agathe. Dresden from 1925, as Marguerite, the *Forza* Leonora and Manon Lescaut. At CG in 1929 she sang Sieglinde, Elsa and Eva, shortly before her early death.

Seixas, (José Antonio) Carlos de (b Coimbra, 11 Jun 1704; d Lisbon, 25 Aug 1742), Portuguese organist and composer. Pupil of his father, whom he succeeded as organist at Coimbra Cathedral in 1718, he was from 1720 to his death organist to the court in Lisbon, at first serving under D. Scarlatti.

Works incl. church music; symph. and overture; toccatas, sonatas, etc. for organ and harpsichord.

Séjan, Nicolas (b Paris, 19 Mar 1745; d Paris, 16 Mar 1819), French organist and composer. Pupil of his uncle N.-G. Forqueray, he was organist of various Paris churches from 1760, succeeding Daquin at Notre Dame in 1772 and Armand-Louis Couperin at the chapel royal in 1789. At the Revolution he lost his post, but returned to it in 1814, having been meanwhile prof. at the Cons. and organist at the Invalides.

Works incl. 3 pf. trios; 6 vln. and pf. sonatas; keyboard music.

Sekles, Bernhard (b Frankfurt, 20 Mar 1872; d Frankfurt, 15 Dec 1934), German composer. Studied at the Hoch Cons. at Frankfurt, under Knorr and others, cond. for a time at Heidelberg and Mainz and then joined the teaching staff at his former school.

Works incl. operas *Schahrazade* (after the *Arabian Nights*, 1917), and *Die zehn Küsse* (1926), burlesque *Die Hochzeit des Faun*, dance play *Der Zwerg und die Infantin* (after Wilde); symph. poem *Aus den Gärten der Semiramis, Kleine Suite, Die Temperamente* for orch.; passacaglia and fugue for organ and orch.; serenade for 11 instruments; passacaglia and fugue for string 4tet; cello and pf. sonata; pf. pieces; songs.

Selle, Thomas (b Zörbig, Saxony, 23 Mar 1599; d Hamburg, 2 Jul 1663), German composer. Was rector and cantor at var. places, finally at the Johanneum in Hamburg from 1641.

Works incl. Passion music incl. St John Passion (1641), the 1st Passion to incl. instrumental interludes, motets, sacred concertos; madrigals; sacred and secular songs.

Selneccer, Nikolaus (b Hersbruck nr. Nuremberg, 6 Dec 1528; d Leipzig, 12 May 1592), German theologian and organist. Court preacher at Dresden, 1557–61, later held var. posts at Jena, Leipzig and Wolfenbüttel. Wrote words and music of many chorales, of which he pub. an important book, containing the work of others and his own, in 1587.

Sembach, Johannes (b Berlin, 9 Mar 1881; d Bremerhaven, 20 Jun 1944), German tenor. He studied in Vienna, and with Jean de Reszke. Dresden 1905–13; created Aegisthus in *Elektra* (1909) and was admired as Lensky and in Wagner. NY Met 1914–22, as Siegmund and Siegfried. Guest appearances in London and Paris.

Sembrich, Marcella (actually Praxede Marcelline Kochanska) (b Wisniewczyk, Galicia, 15 Feb 1858; d New York, 11 Jan 1935), Polish soprano. Pupil of her father, Kasimir Kochanski (S. being her mother's name), and

appeared at the age of 12 as pianist and violinist. In 1875 she began to study singing with Rokitansky in Vienna and then with Lamperti at Milan and Richard Lewy in Ger. In 1877 she made her debut at Athens as Elvira (*I Puritani*). In 1880 she 1st visited London (CG, Lucia). Later sang mainly at the Met; until 1917 as Lucia, Rosina, Queen of Night, Elsa, Eva and Mimi.

Semele, opera-oratorio by Handel (lib. by Congreve with anonymous alterations), perf. London, CG, 10 Feb 1744. Congreve's lib. was originally intended for an opera. Revived CG 1982.

Semi-Chorus, a group of singers detached from a chorus for the purpose of obtaining antiphonal effects or changes of tone-colour. It does not often lit. consist of half the voices, but is more usually a much smaller contingent.

Semibreve, the largest note-value now in current use, called 'whole note' in America. It is half the value of the old Breve, and is represented by the symbol 𝄾.

Semicroma (It.) = Semiquaver.

Semiquaver, the note-value of half a Quaver, and one 16th of a Semibreve, represented by the symbol 𝅘𝅥𝅯.

Semiramide (*Semiramis*), opera by Rossini (lib. by Giacomo Rossi, based on Voltaire's tragedy), prod. Venice, Teatro La Fenice, 3 Feb 1823.

Semiramide riconosciuta (*Semiramis Recognized*), opera by Gluck (lib. by Metastasio), prod. Vienna, Burgtheater, 14 May 1748.

Opera by Hasse (lib. do.), prod. Venice, Teatro San Giovanni Grisostomo, 26 Dec 1744.

Opera by Vinci (lib. do.), prod. Rome, Teatro delle Dame, 6 Feb 1729.

Sémiramis, opera by Catel (lib. by Philippe Desriaux, after Voltaire), prod. Paris, 4 May 1802.

Semiseria (It. fem. = half-serious), the term for a hybrid between *opera seria* and *opera buffa*.

Semitone, the smallest interval normally used in Western music. Except for adjustments of leading-notes (*see* **Musica ficta**) only 2 semitone intervals occur in any of the Modes and in the Diatonic Scales, the others being whole tones; in the chromatic scales all the intervals are semitones. *See* Scale.

Semkow, Jerzy (b Radomsko, 12 Oct 1928), Polish conductor. He studied in Kraków and in 1950 was asst. to Mravinsky at the Leningrad PO. He worked at the Bolshoy Theatre and had further study with Kleiber,

Walter and Serafin. Prin. cond. Warsaw Opera 1959–62, Copenhagen 1966–76. US debut 1968, with the Boston SO, and has returned with all the leading orchs. there. His London debut was in 1968, and in 1970 he cond. *Don Giovanni* at CG. Well known in Romantic and modern repertory.

Semplice (It. = simple), a direction indicating that a passage or whole work is to be perf. in an unaffected or not over-expressive manner.

Senallié (Senaillé), **Jean Baptiste** (b Paris, 23 Nov 1687; d Paris, 8 or 15 Oct 1730), French violinist and composer. Studied under his father, Jean S., a member of the royal orch., and with the latter's colleague there, Queversin; later with Corelli's pupil Anet and with Vitali at Modena, where he was app. to the ducal court. He returned to Paris in 1720 and received an appt. at court under the regent, the Duke of Orleans, later confirmed under Louis XV.

Works incl. sonatas for unaccomp. vln.; vln. sonatas with bass; pieces for vln. and harpsichord.

Sénéchal, Michel (b Tavery, 11 Feb 1927), French tenor. He studied at the Paris Cons. and in 1952 won the Geneva Internat. Competition. He sang at Salzburg in 1953 and in 1956 was heard as Rameau's Platée at Aix. In 1966 he sang Ravel's Gonzalve at Glyndebourne. Much admired in Europe in operas by Britten, Massenet and Mozart. From 1980 dir. opera school at the Paris Opéra.

Senesino (actually Francesco Bernardi) (b Siena, *c* 1680; d Siena, *c* 1758), Italian male soprano. Studied with Bernacchi at Bologna. Attached to the court opera at Dresden in 1717 and there invited by Handel to London, where he 1st appeared in 1720; sang in the fps of *Floridante, Ottone, Giulio Cesare, Admeto, Sosarme* and *Orlando*.

Senfl, Ludwig (b Basle, *c* 1490; d Munich, *c* 1543), Swiss composer. Pupil of Isaac in Vienna and his successor as *Kapellmeister* to Maximilian I, which post he held until the emperor's death in 1519. In 1520 he went to Augsburg and in 1523 to Munich, where he settled, as 1st musician at the ducal court. In 1530 he was in correspondence with Luther.

Works incl. 7 Masses, Magnificats, motets and other church music; odes by Horace for voices; *c* 250 German songs.

Senilov, Vladimir Alexeievich (b Viatka, 8 Aug 1875; d Petrograd, 18 Sep 1918), Russian composer. Studied law at first, but went to Leipzig for musical studies under Riemann and later worked under Glazunov and Rimsky-Korsakov at the St Petersburg Cons.

Works incl. operas *Vassily Buslaiev* and *Hippolytus* (after Euripides), music action *George the Bold*; symph. in D maj., overture *In Autumn*, symph. poems *The Wild Geese* (after Maupassant), *The Mtsyrs* (after Lermontov), *Pan, The Scythians* and *Variations on a Chant of the Old Believers* for orch.; *Chloe forsaken* for voice and orch.; cantata *John of Damascus*; 3 string 4tets; poems for cello and pf., scherzo for fl. and pf.

Sennet, a word found in stage-directions of English plays of the Elizabethan period where the author asks for music to be played on or off the stage. It is prob. either a variant of 'signet' = 'sign' or a corruption of *sonata*.

Sensible (Fr. noun, or *note sensible*) = Leading-note.

Senza (It.) = without.

Sept Haï-kaï work by Messiaen for pf., 13 wind insts., xylophone, marimba, 4 perc. insts. and 8 vlns.; comp. 1962, fp Paris, 30 Oct 1963.

Septet, any work, or part of a work, written in 7 parts for voices or instruments.

Septimole ⎫
or ⎬ a group of 7 notes to be fitted
Septuplet ⎭
into a beat or other time-unit in which its number is irregular.

Sequence. (1) A development of the long vocalizations at the end of the Alleluia in the Mass. In the late 9th or early 10th cent. words were fitted to these melodies on the principle of one syllable to a note. Since the melodies were in no regular rhythm the texts were not in verse and were in fact known in Fr. as *prosae*. The sequence was so called because it followed (Lat. *sequor* = I follow) the Alleluia, which in turn followed the Gradual. In the course of time new melodies were written and rhyming verse came to be adopted for the texts. At the Council of Trent in the 16th cent. all but 4 sequences were abolished: *Victimae paschali* (Easter), *Veni, sancte spiritus* (Whitsun), *Lauda Sion* (Corpus Christi) and *Dies irae* (Requiem Mass). *Stabat mater* (Seven Dolours) (13th cent.), not orig. liturgical, was admitted as a sequence in the 18th cent.

(2) The repetition of a melodic figure at a higher or lower degree of the scale (see illustration overleaf).

Serafin, Tullio (b Rottanova di Cavarzere nr. Venice, 8 Dec 1878; d Rome, 2 Feb 1968), Italian conductor. Studied at the Milan Cons., making his debut in 1900 in Ferrara, in 1909 becoming cond. at La Scala, Milan. From 1924 he was one of the chief

conds. at the NY Met and gave there the fps of operas by Deems Taylor, Louis Gruenberg and Howard Hanson. Returned to Italy in 1935, where he cond. mostly in Milan and Rome; gave there operas by Pizzetti, Alfano, Berg and Britten. He also appeared in London and Paris (CG 1959, *Lucia*).

Serafino, Giorgio, Italian 18th-cent. vln. maker, who worked at Venice.

Serafino, Santo, Italian 17th–18th-cent. vln. maker, uncle of prec. He worked at Udine, *c* 1678–98, and then at Venice until *c* 1735.

Serebrier, José (b Montevideo, 3 Dec 1938), Uruguayan conductor and composer. He moved to the USA in 1956; studied at the Curtis Institute and with Copland at Tanglewood. Early experience as cond. with Monteux and Dorati (Minneapolis SO, 1958–60). Music dir. Cleveland PO, 1968–71; guest cond. in Europe and Australia. His comps. use mixed-media devices and incl. *Colores Mágicos* for orch. (1971) in which sounds are converted by 'synchorama' into visual patterns. He is married to the sop. Carole Farley (b 1946) who is widely known as Berg's Lulu (NY Met, 1977, in Germany and with WNO).

Serenade, evening song or evening music, whether for one or more voices or for instruments. In the 18th cent. it often took the form of a suite.

Serenade, work for vln., perc. and strings by Bernstein, after Plato's *Symposium*, fp Venice, 12 Sep 1954, with Isaac Stern.

Serenade for Tenor, Horn and Strings, song cycle by Britten (texts by Cotton, Tennyson, Blake, Jonson and Keats, all on the theme of night), fp London, 15 Oct 1943, with Dennis Brain and Peter Pears.

Serenade to Music, work by Vaughan Williams for 16 solo voices and orch. (text from *The Merchant of Venice*); comp. 1938 for the jubilee of Henry Wood and cond. by him London, 5 Oct 1938. Version for orch. perf. London 10 Feb 1940, cond. Wood.

Serenaden, Die, cantata by Hindemith for sop., oboe, vla. and cello (texts by A. Licht, J.L.W. Gleim, L. Tieck, J. von Eichendorff, J.W. Meinhold and S.A. Mahlmann), fp Winterthur, 15 Apr 1925.

Serenata (It.), actually the It. word for Serenade, but used in Eng. with a specific mean-

ing for 18th-cent. works, often of an occasional or congratulatory type, either prod. on the stage as small topical and allegorical operas or at concerts (and even then sometimes in costume) in the manner of a secular cantata.

Sereni, Mario (b Perugia, 25 Mar 1928), Italian baritone. Debut Florence 1953. He sang Wolfram at Palermo in 1955; Buenos Aires 1956. NY Met debut 1957, Gérard. La Scala from 1963, Vienna from 1965. Other roles incl. Germont, Rigoletto and Posa.

Seria (It. fem. = serious). *See* **Opera seria.**

Serialism, composition that uses as a prime structural basis a fixed sequence of musical elements. Most commonly this sequence is a series of twelve pitches embracing the entire chromatic octave, *see* **Twelve-Note Music;** but shorter and longer sets are also encountered. This series can characteristically be presented in any transposition as well as inverted or retrograde, or any combination of those. In the years after World War II certain comps. expanded this system to incl. the serialization of note-lengths, of tempo, of dynamics and even of tone-colour.

Series. *See* **Tone-Row.**

Serkin, Peter (b New York, 24 Jul 1947), American pianist. He studied with his father and at the Curtis Inst. Regular chamber and orch. concerts since 1959. He has a wide repertory and favours Bach, Schoenberg and Messiaen; formed the chamber group Taschi in 1973 and has been heard as an improviser and in jazz music.

Serkin, Rudolf (b Eger, Bohemia, 28 Mar 1903), American pianist of Russian parentage, father of prec. He studied in Vienna, pf. with R. Robert and comp. with J. Marx and Schoenberg. Although making his debut aged 12, it was not until 1920 that he began his true concert career. He appeared frequently with the violinist A. Busch and married Busch's daughter. US solo debut 1936, with the NY PO; from 1939 he taught at the Curtis Inst. in Philadelphia; dir., 1968–76. He excelled in the Viennese classics.

Sermisy, Claudin de (b *c* 1490; d Paris, 13 Oct 1562), French composer (usually known as **Claudin**). In 1508–14 he was attached to the Sainte-Chapelle in Paris and in 1515 became a singer in Louis XII's royal chapel, just before that king's death, and later he succeeded Antoine de Longueval as master of the choir-boys. In 1533 he was made a canon of the Sainte-Chapelle, with a living and a substantial salary attached to it; but his duties there were light and he remained in the royal chapel, with which, under François I, he visited Bologna, where his choir competed with the Papal choir before Leo X, in 1515. In 1520, with the same king, he met Henry VIII at the Field of the Cloth of Gold, a similar meeting following in 1532 at Boulogne; and on both occasions the Fr. and Eng. choirs sang together.

Works incl. 11 Masses, motets; over 200 *chansons* for several voices.

Serocki, Kazimierz (b Toruń, 3 Mar 1922; d Warsaw, 9 Jan 1981), Polish composer. Studied at Łódź and later with N. Boulanger (1947–8). From 1950 to 1952 he appeared in Europe as a pianist, but later devoted himself to comp. in a modernist idiom.

Works incl. 2 symphs. (1952, 1953; 2nd for sop., bar., chorus and orch.), *Triptych* for orch.; pf. concerto, tromb. concerto; choral music; *Episodes* for strings and 3 perc. groups, *Segmenti* for chamber ensemble and perc. (1960); *Symphonic Frescoes* (1963); *Dramatic Story* for orch. (1971); *Ad ·Libitum*, 5 pieces for orch. (1976); *Pianophonie* for pf. and electronics (1978); chamber music.

Serov, Alexander Nikolaievich (b St Petersburg, 23 Jan 1820; d St Petersburg, 1 Feb 1871), Russian composer and critic. Studied law, but found time to cultivate music, which eventually, after a career as a civil servant, he took up professionally. He studied cello and theory from *c* 1840 and began an opera on Shakespeare's *Merry Wives* in 1843, but was reduced to a taking correspondence course of musical instruction when transferred to Simferopol. He became a music critic and in 1858, when he returned from a visit to Ger. as an ardent admirer of Wagner, he began to attack the Rus. nat. school of comps., but found a powerful opponent in Stassov. He was over 40 when he began his 1st opera. He married the comp. Valentina Semionovna Bergman (1846–1927), who wrote some operas of her own, incl. *Uriel Acosta* (based on Gutzkow's play). When he died from heart disease, he had just begun a 4th opera on Gogol's *Christmas Eve Revels*.

Works incl. operas *Judith* (1863), *Rogneda* (1865), *The Power of Evil* (after Ostrovsky's play; orch. finished by Soloviev, 1871); incid. music to Nikolai Pavlovich Zhandr's tragedy *Nero; Stabat Mater* and *Ave Maria;*

Gopak, Dance of the Zaporogue Cossacks and other orchestral works.

Serpent, early wind instrument, formerly the bass of the Cornett family, with a long winding wooden tube covered with leather and played with a cup-shaped mouthpiece. It prob. originated in Fr. late in the 16th cent. and was used both in bands and in churches, but fell out of use in the 19th cent.

Serra, Luciana (b Genoa, 1942), Italian soprano. Debut Budapest 1966, in Cimarosa's *Il convito*. Teheran Opera 1969–76. From 1974 she has sung widely in Italy as Gilda, Rosina, Ophelia, and Bellini's Elvira and Giulietta. CG debut 1980, as Olympia; her coloratura has been admired as Norina, Amina and the Queen of Night. Chicago, Lyric Opera, 1983.

Serrano y Ruiz, Emilio (b Victoria, Alava, 15 Mar 1850; d Madrid, 9 Apr 1939), Spanish pianist and composer. He became court pianist to the Infanta Isabella, director of the Royal Opera in Madrid and prof. at the Cons.

Works incl. operas *Mitridate* (1882), *Giovanna la pazza, Irene de Otranto* (1891), *Gonzalo de Córdoba* (1898) and *La maja de Rumba* (1910); symph. poem *La primera salide de Don Quijote* (after Cervantes).

Serrao, Paolo (b Filadelfia, Catanzaro, 1830; d Naples, 17 Mar 1907), Italian composer. Studied at the Naples Cons. and became a prof. there in 1863.

Works incl. operas *Pergolesi* (1857), *La duchessa di Guisa* (1865), *Il figliuol prodigo* (1868), *L'impostore, Leonora de' Bardi;* oratorio *Gli Ortonesi in Scio* (1869), Passion *Le tre ore d'agonia;* Mass, Requiem and other church music; funeral symph. for Mercadante (1871); overture for orch.; pf. pieces.

Serse (*Xerxes*) (*see also* **Xerse**), opera by Handel (lib. by N. Minato, altered), prod. London, King's Theatre, Haymarket, 15 Apr 1738. It contains the famous so-called *Largo*, 'Ombra mai fù'. The original lib. was that for Cavalli's *Xerse* (1654).

Serva padrona, La (*The Maid as Mistress*), intermezzo by Paisiello (lib. by G.A. Federico), prod. St Petersburg, Hermitage, at court, 10 Sep 1781.

Intermezzo by Pergolesi (lib. do.), prod. Naples, Teatro San Bartolommeo, between the acts of Pergolesi's serious opera *Il prigionier superbo*, 28 Aug 1733.

Servais, (Adrien) François (b Hal nr. Brussels, 6 Jun 1807; d Hal, 26 Nov 1866), Belgian cellist and composer. Studied with Platel at the Brussels Cons., visited Paris and

London, later toured all over Europe and in 1848 became prof. at the Cons.

Works incl. 3 cello concertos and 16 fantasies for cello and orch.; duets for vln. and cello; many cello studies and pieces.

Servais, Joseph (b Hal nr. Brussels, 28 Nov 1850; d Brussels, 29 Aug 1885), Belgian cellist, son of prec. Pupil of his father, with whom he travelled afterwards. In 1868–70 he was at the court of Weimar, in 1875 made his 1st appearance in Paris, and eventually settled at Brussels.

Service. As a musical term the word implies the setting of those parts of the services of the Anglican Church which lend themselves to musical treatment, i.e. Morning Prayer, Evening Prayer (Magnificat and Nunc dimittis) and Communion.

Servilia, opera by Rimsky-Korsakov (lib. by comp., based on a play by L.A. Mey), prod. St Petersburg, 14 Oct 1902.

Sosquialtera (Lat., short for *pars sesqualtera* = a quantity 1½ times as much). In mensural notation the proportion 3:2. *See* **Proportion.**

Sessions, Roger (b Brooklyn, NY, 28 Dec 1896; d Princeton, NJ, 16 Mar 1985), American composer. Studied at Harvard Univ. and later at Yale Univ. with H. Parker, also with Bloch in NY and Cleveland. In 1917–21 he taught at Smith Coll., Northampton, Mass. and in 1921–5 was head of the theoret. dept. of the Cleveland Inst. of Music. He lived in It. and Ger. 1925–33, then taught for 2 years at Boston Univ. and afterwards at var. places. He was prof. at Princeton Univ.

Works incl. operas *Lancelot and Elaine* (after Tennyson), *The Trial of Lucullus* (1947) and *Montezuma* (1964); incid. music for Andreiev's *The Black Maskers* (1923) and Gozzi's *Turandot* (trans. by Vollmöller); *Turn O Libertad* (Whitman) for chorus and pf. duet.

ORCH. AND CHAMBER: 9 symphs. (1927–80), 3 dirges for orch.; music for 4 trombs. and tuba; vln. concerto (1940), pf. concerto, Concerto for Orch. (1981); 2 string 4tets (1935, 1951), pf. trio, duo for vln. and pf.; sonata and 3 chorale preludes for org.; 2 sonatas and pieces for pf.; songs to words by James Joyce and others.

Set, an old English name for the suite. Also a series, normally of pitches but also of rhythms or other musical parameters, used in the composition of a piece. *See* **Serialism** and **Twelve-Note music.**

Setaccioli, Giacomo (b Corneto Tarquinia, 8 Dec 1868; d Siena, 5 Dec 1925), Italian composer. Studied at the Accademia di Santa Cecilia in Rome and became a prof. there in 1922, but moved to Florence in 1925 on being app. dir. of the Cherubini Cons. there.

Works incl. operas *La sorella di Mark* (1896), *L'ultimo degli Abenceragi* (after Chateaubriand, 1893), *Il mantellaccio* (prod. 1954) and *Adrienne Lecouvreur* (after Scribe); Requiem for Humbert I, *Cantica* for solo voices, chorus and orch., motets, *Quadro sinfonico* for chorus, org. and orch.; symph. in A maj., symph. poems, chamber music, songs.

Sette canzoni (*Seven Songs*), opera by Malipiero (lib. by comp.), prod., in Fr. version by Henry Prunières, Paris, Opéra, 10 Jul 1920. Part II of the operatic cycle *L'Orfeide.*

Settle, Elkanah (1648–1724), English poet and dramatist. *See* **Clarke (J.)** (*World in the Moon*, with D. Purcell), **Fairy Queen** (Purcell), **Finger** (*Virgin Prophetess*), **Purcell** (*Distressed Innocence*), **Turner** (*Pastor fido,* from Guarini).

Sevčík, Otakar (b Horaždovice, 22 Mar 1852; d Písek, 18 Jan 1934), Czech violinist and teacher. Studied at the Prague Cons. and became leader at the Mozarteum at Salzburg and gave concerts in Prague. In 1873 he settled in Vienna, was prof. at the Music School at Kiev in 1875–92 and then became chief vln. prof. at the Prague Cons. He wrote a vln. method in 4 vols. and in 1903 formed a string 4tet.

Seven, They are Seven, Akkadian Incantation for tenor, chorus and orch. by Prokofiev, op. 30 (text by K. Balmont), comp. 1917–18, fp Paris, 29 May 1924, cond. Koussevitzky.

Seven Words of the Saviour on the Cross, The (or *The Seven Last Words*). 1. Orchestral work by Haydn consisting of 7 slow movements, commissioned by Cádiz Cathedral in 1785 as musical meditations for a 3-hour service on Good Friday. Later arr. by Haydn for string 4tet (op. 51, 1787) and as a choral work (1796).

2. Oratorio by Schütz (*The 7 Words of Christ*) (words from the 4 Gospels plus 2 verses of a chorale), comp. 1645.

Seventh, the interval between 2 notes lying 6 degrees of a diatonic scale apart, e.g.:

Maj.   Min.   Diminished

Séverac, (Joseph Marie) Déodat de (b Saint-Félix de Caraman, Lauragais, 20 Jul 1873; d Céret, Pyrénées Orientales, 24 Mar

1921), French composer. Studied at the Toulouse Cons. and the Schola Cantorum in Paris, with Magnard and d'Indy. He returned to the S. of Fr. and devoted himself entirely to comp., neither his health nor his taste permitting him to hold any official position.

Works incl. opera *Le Cœur du moulin* (1909); ballet *La Fête des vendanges*; incid. music for Sicard's *Héliogabale* and for Verhaeren's *Hélène de Sparte; Ave, verum corpus* and other church music; *Chant de vacances* for chorus; string 5tet; 19 songs to poems by Ronsard, Verlaine, Maeterlinck and Poe.

Sevillana (Span.), an Andalusian folksong type similar to the Seguidilla and orig. confined to Seville.

Sextet, any work, or part of a work, written in 6 parts for voices or instruments. *See also* **String Sextet.**

Sextolet, a group of 6 notes, or double Triplet, when used in a comp. or movement whose time-unit is normally divisible into 2, 4 or 8 note-values.

Sextus, in old vocal music the 6th part in a comp. for 6 or more voices, always equal in compass to one of the voices in a 4-part comp.: soprano, alto, tenor or bass.

Seyfried, Ignaz Xaver von (b Vienna, 15 Aug 1776; d Vienna, 27 Aug 1841), Austrian composer, teacher and conductor. Orig. intended for a legal career, he turned to music, and was a pupil of Mozart and Kozeluch for pf., Albrechtsberger and Winter for comp. From 1797 to 1828 he was cond. and comp. to Schikaneder's theatre (from 1801 known as the Theater an der Wien; in 1806 he cond. the 1st revival of *Fidelio*). After his retirement he comp. almost exclusively church music.

Works incl. over 100 operas, *Singspiele*, e.g. *Der Löwenbrunnen, Der Wundermann am Rheinfall* (1799), *Die Ochsenmenuette* (pasticcio arr. from Haydn's works, 1823), *Ahasverus* (arr. from piano works of Mozart); biblical dramas; incid. music to Schiller's *Die Räuber* and *Die Jungfrau von Orleans*, etc.; about 20 Masses, Requiem, motets and other church music; *Libera me* for Beethoven's funeral, etc. Also ed. Albrechtsberger's theoretical works and pub. an account of Beethoven's studies in figured bass, counterpoint and comp. (1832).

Sf. (abbr.) = *Sforzando.*

Sfogato (It. = airy), sometimes used as a direction by comps., e.g. Chopin, to indicate a delicate and ethereal perf. of certain passages; also as an adj., esp. 'soprano sfogato' = light soprano.

Sforzando
or   } (It. = forced, reinforced) a
Sforzato
direction indicating that a note or chord is to be strongly emphasized by an accent.

Sfz. (abbr.) = *Sforzando.*

Sgambati, Giovanni (b Rome, 28 May 1841; d Rome, 14 Dec 1914), Italian pianist and composer. Studied at Trevi in Umbria and in Rome and was a pupil of Liszt; later estab. important orch. and chamber concerts for the cultivation of serious music in the It. capital; conducted Liszt's *Dante Symphony* and *Christus*. In 1869 he visited Ger. and 1st heard works by Wagner, whom he met in Rome in 1876 and who induced his pub., Schott, to bring out some of Sgambati's works. In 1882 he 1st revisited Eng.

Works incl. Requiem; symphs. in D and Eb maj., *Epitalamio sinfonico*, overture *Cola di Rienzi* and Festival Overture for orch.; pf. concerto in G min.; string 4tet, 2 pf. 5tets; pf. music.

Shacklock, Constance (b Sherwood, 16 Apr 1913), English mezzo. Studied at the RAM. CG 1947–56, debut as Mercédès and often heard as Octavian, Carmen and Amneris. She sang Brangaene in Amsterdam and Berlin, under Kleiber. Well known in *Messiah* and *The Dream of Gerontius*.

Shahrazad (*Sheherazade*), symph. suite by Rimsky-Korsakov on the subject of the story-teller in the *Arabian Nights* and of some of the tales, op. 35, finished summer 1888 and prod. St Petersburg, 3 Nov 1888. Ballet based on it (choreog. by Mikhail Fokin, settings by Leon Bakst), prod. Paris, Opéra, 4 Jun 1910. *See also* **Shéhérazade.**

Shake, a musical ornament consisting of the rapid alternation of the note written down with that a whole tone or semitone above, according to the key in which the piece is written, or according to the comp.'s notation (see illustration overleaf).

Shakespeare, William (1564–1616), English poet and dramatist. Among works based on his plays are:

ANTONY AND CLEOPATRA: **Barber** (opera, 1966), **R. Kreutzer** (ballet, *Amours d'Antoine et de Cléopâtre*, 1808), **Malipiero** (opera, 1938), **Prokofiev** (Symph. Suite, *Egyptian Nights*, 1934).

AS YOU LIKE IT: **Veracini** (opera, *Rosalinda*, 1744).

COMEDY OF ERRORS, THE: **Storace** (opera, *Gli equivoci*, 1786).

CORIOLANUS: **Cikker** (opera, 1974).

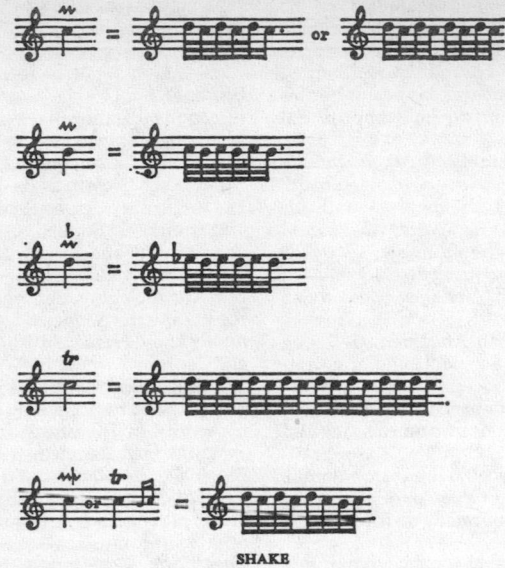

SHAKE

CYMBELINE: **Schubert** (*Hark, hark, the lark*, 1826), **Zemlinsky** (incidental music, 1914).

HAMLET: **Berlioz** (*La Mort d'Ophélie* and *Marche funèbre* from *Tristia*, 1848), **Blacher** (ballet, 1950), **Bridge** (*There is a willow* for orch., 1928), **Faccio** (opera, 1865), **Liszt** (symphonic poem, 1858), **Mercadante** (opera, 1822), **Searle** (opera, 1967), **Shostakovich** (incidental music, 1931, and suite, 1932), **Szokolay** (opera, 1969), **Tchaikovsky** (Fantasy overture, 1888), **Thomas, A.** (opera, 1868), **Walton** (film music, 1947).

HENRY IV, parts 1 and 2: **Elgar** (*Falstaff*, symphonic study, 1913), **Holst** (opera, *At the Boar's Head*, 1925), **Mercadante** (opera, *La gioventù di Enrico V*, 1834), **Pacini** (opera, ditto, 1820).

HENRY V: **Vaughan Williams** (*Thanksgiving for Victory*, 1945), **Walton** (film music, 1944).

JULIUS CAESAR: **Klebe** (opera, *Die Ermordrung Cäsars*, 1959), **Malipiero** (opera, 1936), **Schumann** (overture, 1851).

KING LEAR: **Berlioz** (overture, 1831), **Frazzi** (opera, *Re Lear*, 1939), **Ghislanzoni** (opera, ditto, 1937), **Reimann** (opera, *Lear*, 1978), **Shostakovich** (incidental music, 1940).

LOVE'S LABOUR LOST: **Nabokov** (opera, 1973).

MACBETH: **Bloch** (opera, 1910), **Colling**wood (opera, 1934), **Strauss** (tone poem, 1890), **Verdi** (opera, 1847).

MEASURE FOR MEASURE: **Wagner** (opera, *Das Liebesverbot*, 1836).

MERCHANT OF VENICE, THE: **Castelnuovo-Tedesco** (opera, *Il mercante di Venezia*, 1961), **J.B. Foerster** (opera, *Jessika*, 1905), **Vaughan Williams** (*Serenade to Music*, 1938).

MERRY WIVES OF WINDSOR, THE: **A. Adam** (opera, *Falstaff*, 1856), **Balfe** (opera, ditto, 1838), **Dittersdorf** (opera, *Die lustigen Weiber von Windsor und der dicke Hans*, 1796), **Nicolai** (opera, *Die lustigen Weiber von Windsor*, 1849), **Salieri** (opera, *Falstaff osia le tre burle*, 1799), **Vaughan Williams** (opera, *Sir John in Love*, 1929), **Verdi** (opera, *Falstaff*, 1893).

MIDSUMMER NIGHT'S DREAM, A: **Britten** (opera, 1960), **Mendelssohn** (incidental music, 1842; overture written 1826), **Orff** (incidental music, 1939; commissioned under the Nazi régime to replace Mendelssohn's music), **Purcell** (*The Fairy Queen*, 1692), **Siegmeister** (opera, *Night of the Moonspell*, 1976).

MUCH ADO ABOUT NOTHING: **Berlioz** (opera, *Béatrice et Bénédict*, 1862), **Stanford** (opera, 1901).

OTHELLO: **Blacher** (ballet, *Der Mohr von Venedig*, 1955), **Dvořák** (overture, 1892), **Rossini** (opera – last act only after

Shakespeare – 1816), **Verdi** (opera, 1887). RICHARD III: **Smetana** (symphonic poem, 1856), **Walton** (film music, 1954). ROMEO AND JULIET: **Bellini** (opera, *I Capuleti e i Montecchi*, based on S.'s sources, 1830), **Berlioz** (dramatic symphony, 1839), **Blacher** (scenic oratorio, 1947; revised as opera, 1950), **Gounod** (opera, 1867), **Malipiero** (opera, 1950), **Prokofiev** (ballet, 1938), **Sutermeister** (opera, 1940), **Tchaikovsky** (Fantasy overture, 1869, rev. 1870 and 1880), **Vaccai** (opera, 1825), **Zandonai** (opera, 1922), **Zingarelli** (opera, 1796).

TAMING OF THE SHREW, THE: **Goetz** (opera, *Der Widerspänstigen Zähmung*, 1874), **Wolf-Ferrari** (opera, *Sly*, 1927).

TEMPEST, THE: **Arne** (incid. music, 1740), **Halévy** (opera, *La Tempestà*, 1850), **Martin** (opera, *Der Sturm*, 1956), **Sibelius** (incidental music, 1924), **Sutermeister** (opera, *Die Zauberinsel*, 1942, **Tchaikovsky** (Symphonic fantasy, 1873), **John Weldon** (incidental music, 1712; formerly attributed to Purcell), **Winter** (opera, *Der Sturm*, 1798), **Zumsteeg** (opera, *Die Geisterinsel*, 1798).

TIMON OF ATHENS: **Antonio Draghi** (1634–1700) (opera, *Timone misantropo*, 1696).

TROILUS AND CRESSIDA: **Zillig** (opera, 1951).

TWELFTH NIGHT: **Smetana** (opera, *Viola*, 1874–84, unfinished; prod. 1924).

TWO GENTLEMEN OF VERONA, THE: **Schubert** (*An Sylvia*, 1826).

WINTER'S TALE, THE: **Bruch** (opera, *Hermione*, 1872), **Goldmark** (opera, *Ein Wintermärchen*, 1908).

Shakespeare, William (b Croydon, 16 Jun 1849; d London, 1 Nov 1931), English tenor, teacher and composer. Studied under Molique in London and later at the RAM with Sterndale Bennett, afterwards with Reinecke at the Leipzig Cons., where he prod. his symph. Later he studied singing with Lamperti at Milan. In 1875 he returned to London and made his name as a concert singer, and in 1878 became prof. of singing at the RAM; Perceval Allen (*q.v.*) was among his pupils. He wrote several books on singing.

Works incl. symph. in C min., 2 overtures for orch.; concerto and *Capriccio* for pf. and orch.; 2 string 4tets, pf. trio; pf. pieces; songs, etc.

Shalyapin, Feodor Ivanovich (b Kazan, 13 Feb 1873; d Paris, 12 Apr 1938), Russian bass-baritone. After a childhood spent in poverty, he joined a provincial opera co. and in 1892 studied singing at Tiflis. In 1894 he made his 1st appearance at St Petersburg and

began to become famous when he was engaged for Mamontov's Private Opera at Moscow in 1896; Bolshoy 1899–1914. He sang at Milan 1901–33 as Mefistofele, Don Basilio, Ivan the Terrible and Boris and was engaged for Paris and London by Diaghilev in 1913. He left Rus. in 1920 and from 1921 to 1925 sang at the Met; appeared at Drury Lane, London, 1913–14 as Dosifey and Konchak. Monte Carlo 1905–37 as the Demon, Philip II and Don Quichotte.

Shaporin, Yuri Alexandrovich (b Glukhov, 8 Nov 1887; d Moscow, 9 Dec 1966), Russian composer. Educ. at St Petersburg, where he graduated in law at the univ. In 1913 he entered the Cons. there, studying under Sokolov, Steinberg and N. Tcherepnin. On leaving he became interested in stage music and founded the Great Dramatic Theatre with Gorky and Blok. In 1937 he moved to Moscow.

Works incl. opera *The Decembrists* (lib. by A.N. Tolstoy, 1953); incid. music for Shakespeare's *King Lear* and *Comedy of Errors*, Schiller's *Robbers*, Molière's *Tartuffe*, Pushkin's *Boris Godunov*, Beaumarchais's *Marriage of Figaro*, Turgenev's *The Nest of Gentlefolk (Liza)*, Labiche's *The Italian Straw Hat*, etc.; film music incl. *General Suvarov*; symph. cantata *On the Kulikov Field* (1939); symph. in E min., suite *The Flea* for orch., 2 suites for pf.; song cycles to words by Pushkin and Tiutchev, and other songs.

Sharp, the sign ♯, which raises a note by a semitone; also an adj. describing out-of-tune intonation on the sharp side.

Sharp, Cecil (James) (b London, 22 Nov 1859; d London, 28 Jun 1924), English folksong collector. Educ. at Uppingham and Clare Coll., Cambridge. After living in Australia in 1889–92, he returned to London and in 1896 became principal of the Hampstead Cons. In 1899 he began to collect folksongs and dances, later he joined the Folksong Society and in 1911 founded the Eng. Folk-Dance Society. In 1916–18 he visited the USA to collect songs in the Appalachian mountains, where many Eng. songs were still preserved in the early form by descendants of the 17th-cent. emigrants.

Shaw, George Bernard (b Dublin, 26 Jul 1856; d Ayot St Lawrence, Herts., 2 Nov 1950), Irish critic, dramatist, novelist and political author. Settled in London early in his career and wrote music criticism for the *Star* and the *World*, 1890–4. *See also* **Corno di Bassetto**.

Shaw (*née* **Postans**), **Mary** (called Mrs.

Alfred Shaw) (b Lea, Kent, 1814; d Hadleigh Hall, Suffolk, 9 Sep 1876), English contralto. Student at the RAM in London and then pupil of G. Smart. She made her 1st appearance in 1834 and the following year married the painter Alfred S. In 1838 she sang at the Gewandhaus, Leipzig, under Mendelssohn, and the next year at La Scala, Milan, as Cuniza in the fp of *Oberto*. London from 1842, in Rossini's *Semiramide* and *La donna del lago*.

Shaw, Robert (b Red Bluff, Calif., 30 Apr 1916), American conductor. He founded the Collegiate Chorale, NY, in 1941 and with them gave the 1946 fp of Hindemith's Walt Whitman *Requiem*; debut as orch. conductor the same year, with the NBC SO. He worked at Juilliard and Tanglewood and in 1948 founded the R.S. Chorale; many perfs. in the US and abroad in works by Bartók, Britten and Copland, in addition to the standard rep. He worked with George Szell and the Cleveland Orch. 1956–67; Atlanta SO from 1967.

Shawe-Taylor, Desmond (b Dublin, 29 May 1907), Irish critic. He was educated at Shrewsbury and Oxford, became a literary critic at first, but in 1945 became music critic to the *New Statesman and Nation* and in 1959 to the *Sunday Times*, in succession to Ernest Newman; retired as regular critic in 1983. He is esp. interested in singing and the gramophone. His books are *Covent Garden* ('World of Music' series, 1948) and, with Edward Sackville-West, *The Record Guide* (1951) and *The Record Year* (1952).

Shawm (or **Shalm**), an early woodwind instrument, the forerunner of the oboe, with a double-reed mouthpiece and a wide bell. The largest types had bent tubes to their mouthpieces and thus approximated more to the bassoon.

Shchedrin, Rodion (b Moscow, 16 Dec 1932), Russian composer. Studied at Moscow Cons. with Shaporin, graduating in 1955.

Works incl. opera *Not for Love Alone* (1961); ballet *The Little Hump-backed Horse* (1955); 2 symphs (1958, 1964); Musical Offering for organ and ens. (1982); 3 pf. concertos; pf. 5tet, 2 string 4tets; songs.

Shcherbachev, Andrey Vladimirovich (b Manuilovo, Gvt. of Poltava, 20 Jan 1869; d Kiev, 14 Feb 1916), Russian composer. Studied under Blumenfeld, Liadov and Rimsky-Korsakov at the St Petersburg Cons.

Works incl. march for orch.; pf. sonata and pieces; songs.

Shcherbachev, Vladimir Vassilievich (b

Warsaw, 24 Jan 1889; d Leningrad, 5 Mar 1952), Russian composer. Studied with Steinberg, Liadov and Wintol at the St Petersburg Cons., and later became prof. at the Leningrad Cons.

Works incl. opera *Anna Kolossova* (1939); film music. *The Tempest*; 5 symphs. (no. 4 choral), suite and other orchestral works; nonet for voice and insts. and other chamber music; 2 pf. sonatas and other pf. works.

Shebalin, Vissarion Yakovlevich (b Omsk, 11 Jun 1902; d Moscow, 28 May 1963), Russian composer. Son of a teacher; received his 1st musical training at the Omsk School of Music, entered the Moscow Cons. as a pupil of Miaskovsky in 1923 and stayed there as a prof. in 1928, as well as teaching at the Gnessin School of Music. Director of the Moscow Cons. 1942–8.

Works incl. operas *The Taming of the Shrew* (1957), *Sun over the Steppes* (1958), comic opera *The Embassy Bridegroom* (1942); incid. music for Schiller's *Robbers* and *Mary Stuart*, Pushkin's *Mozart and Salieri* and *The Stone Guest* (Don Juan), Lermontov's *Masquerade*, Scribe's *A Glass of Water*, etc.; film music; symph. cantata *Lenin* for solo voices, chorus and orch.; 5 symphs. (1925–62), 2 suites and 2 overtures for orch.; vln. concerto, concertinos for vln. and strings and for harp and small orch.; 9 string 4tets (1923–63), string trio; sonatina for vln. and vla., suite for solo vln.; 2 pf. sonatas and 3 sonatinas; songs (Pushkin, Heine, etc.), popular choruses and war songs.

Sheherazade (Rimsky-Korsakov). *See* **Shahrazad.**

Shéhérazade, song-cycle with orch. by Ravel (poems by Tristan Klingsor), comp. 1903 on the basis of an unpub. overture of the same name of 1898. There are 3 songs: *Asie, La Flûte enchantée* and *L'indifférent.* Fp Paris, 17 May 1904.

Shekhter, Boris Semionovich (b Odessa, 20 Jan 1900; d Moscow, 16 Dec 1961), Russian composer. Pupil of Miaskovsky at the Moscow Cons. Later he made a close study of Turcomanian folk music, and based some of his works on it.

Works incl. operas *The Year 1905* (with Davidenko, 1935) and *The Son of the People*; suite *Turkmenia* for orch., 5 symphs. (1929–51, incl. symph. Dithyramb for the celebrations of the 20th anniversary of the Rus. Revolution); pf. concerto; song cycles.

Shelbye, William, English composer and organist. He was organist at Canterbury

Cathedral, 1547–53. A *Felix namque* and *Miserere* are in the Mulliner Book (*q.v.*).

Shenshin, Alexander Alexeievich (b Moscow, 18 Nov 1890; d Moscow, 18 Feb 1944), Russian composer. Studied philology in Moscow and became a teacher of history and Latin. Only then did he begin to study music with Gretchaninov and Glière, and in 1912 he pub. his 1st work.

Works incl. opera *O'Tao* (1925) and other works for the stage; song cycles *From Jap. Anthologies* and other songs.

Shepherd, Arthur (b Paris, Idaho, 19 Feb 1880; d Cleveland, 12 Jan 1958), American composer and conductor. After a period of teaching at Salt Lake City he was prof. at the New Eng. Cons., Boston, from 1908 to 1917, when he joined the army. From 1920 to 1926 he was asst. cond. of the Cleveland SO, and from 1927 to 1950 at Western Reserve Univ.

Works incl. 2 symphs. incl. *Horizons, Choreographic Suite* for orch. (1927); fantasy for pf. and orch.; vln. concerto; 3 string 4tets (1935, 1936, 1944); *Triptych* (from Tagore's *Gitanjali*) for voice and string 4tet; vln. and pf. sonata; 2 pf. sonatas and pieces; songs.

Shepherd's Pipe. A rustic wind instrument akin to the ob., the Fr. Musette, played with a double reed, like the chanter of a bagpipe, but usually used separately.

Shepherds of the Delectable Mountains, The, opera by Vaughan Williams (lib. by comp., based on Bunyan's *Pilgrim's Progress*), prod. London, RCM, 11 Jul 1922. *See also* **Pilgrim's Progress**.

Sheppard, John (b ? London, c 1515; d c 1563), English composer. Learnt music as a choir-boy at St Paul's Cathedral in London under Thomas Mulliner. In 1542 he became organist and choirmaster at Magdalen Coll., Oxford, and later was in Queen Mary's Chapel Royal.

Works incl. Masses *The Western Wynde, The French Masse, Be not afraide* and *Playn Song Mass for a Mene*, 21 Office responds, 18 hymns, motets, 2 Te Deums, 2 Magnificats, anthems, etc.

Sherrington, Hellen. *See* **Lemmens-Sherrington**.

Shield, William (b Swalwell, Co. Durham, 5 Mar 1748; d London, 25 Jan 1829), English violinist and composer. Orphaned at the age of 9, he was apprenticed to a shipbuilder, but studied music with Avison in Newcastle, where he also appeared as a solo violinist and led the subscription concerts from 1763. After engagements in Scarborough and Stockton-on-Tees he went to London as 2nd vln. of the Opera orch. in 1772, becoming principal vla. the following year. After the success of his first opera, *The Flitch of Bacon* (1778), he was app. comp. to Covent Garden Theatre (1778–91 and again 1792–1807). In 1791 he met Haydn in London, and visited Fr. and It. Two treatises, on harmony and thorough-bass, were pub. in 1800 and 1817, in which year he was app. Master of the King's Music.

Works incl. over 50 works for the stage, e.g. *The Flitch of Bacon* (1778), *Rosina* (1782), *Robin Hood* (1784), *Richard Cœur de Lion* (1786), *The Marriage of Figaro* (after Beaumarchais, 1797), *Aladdin, The Woodman* (1791), *The Travellers in Switzerland* (1794), *Netley Abbey, The Italian Villagers*, etc.; string 4tets and trios; vln. duets; songs.

Shifrin, Seymour J. (b Brooklyn, 28 Feb 1926; d Boston, 26 Sep 1979), American composer. Studied with Otto Luening and William Schuman. Taught at Brandeis Univ., Mass., from 1966. Music is known for chromatic intensity: Chamber Symphony (1953), 3 pieces for orch. (1958), *5 Last Songs* (1979); 5 string 4tets (1949–72), pf. trio (1974), *A Renaissance Garland* (1975), *The Nick of Time* for ens. (1978).

Shirley, George (b Indianapolis, 18 Apr 1934), American tenor. After private study he sang Rodolfo in Milan in 1960. NY Met debut 1961, as Ferrando. Glyndebourne 1966–74, as Tamino, Lord Percy and Idomeneo; CG since 1967 as Don Ottavio, Pelléas, Loge and David. He has been heard in the US in the first local perfs. of operas by Berg, Henze, Busoni and Rameau.

Shirley-Quirk, John (b Liverpool, 28 Aug 1931), English bass-baritone. Studied with Roy Henderson. Early in his career he was identified with Britten's operas: created roles in the church parables, *Death in Venice* and *Owen Wingrave* (CG 1973). With Scottish Opera he has been heard as Golaud, Almaviva and Henze's Mittenhofer; returned to CG in 1977 to create Lev in Tippett's *The Ice Break*. Widely admired as a concert singer, in Lieder, and in oratorios by Bach, Elgar, Berlioz and Tippett.

Shnitke, Alfred. *See* **Schnittke**.

Shore. English family of musicians:

1. **Mathias S.** (d London, 1700), trumpeter. In the service of the court of James II and William and Mary in the post of Sergeant Trumpeter.

2. **William S.** (b London, c 1665; d London, Dec 1707), trumpeter, son of prec.

Succeeded his father in his post.

3. Catherine S. (b London, c 1668; d London, c 1730), singer and harpsichordist, sister of prec. Pupil of Purcell; married Colley Cibber in 1693.

4. John S. (b London, c 1662; d London, 20 Nov 1752), trumpeter and lutenist, brother of prec. Succeeded in his brother's post in 1707. Often heard in works by Purcell, e.g. the Ode Come, ye Sons of Art (1694).

Short Octave. On old keyboard instruments the notes governed by the extreme bottom keys were sometimes not tuned to the ordinary scale, but to a selection of lower notes more likely to be frequently required, e.g.:

The bottom octave so tuned was called the short octave.

Short Score. See Score.

Shostakovich, Dmitri (b St Petersburg, 25 Sep 1906; d Moscow, 9 Aug 1975), Russian composer. Entered the Petrograd Cons. in 1919 and studied with Nikolaiev, Steinberg and Glazunov. He left in 1925, having already written a great many works. The 1st symph., which dates from that year, was perf. in 1926. He quickly made his mark, but came into conflict with Soviet authority in 1930, when his opera, The Nose, based on a story by Gogol, was denounced as bourgeois and decadent. The next, Lady Macbeth of Mtsensk, prod. in 1934, was even more violently attacked in 1936 and had to be withdrawn; his 4th symph. was also withdrawn. Thereafter, however, he suited his manner to the government's requirements, which in turn became somewhat modified, and estab. himself as the leading comp. of the day, gaining the Stalin Prize with his pf. 5tet in 1941. His son Maxim (conductor, b Leningrad, 10 May 1938) and grandson Dmitri (pianist, b Moscow, 9 Aug 1961) are active on behalf of his music.

Works incl. operas The Nose and Lady Macbeth of Mtsensk; ballets The Golden Age, The Bolt, The Limpid Stream and The Golden Key; incid. music to several plays incl. Shakespeare's Hamlet, King Lear and Othello, Piotrovsky's Rule, Britannia and an adaptation from Balzac's Human Comedy; cantata The Execution of Stefan Razin; music to c 14 films.

ORCH.: 15 symphs, no. 1 in F min. (1925), no. 2 in B (October, with chorus, 1927), no. 3 in Eb (First of May, with chorus, 1929), no. 4 in C min. (1936; not perf. until 1961), no. 5 in D min. (1937; sub-title, A Soviet Artist's Practical Creative Reply to Just Criticism, was given by a party hack, not by S. himself), no. 6 in B min. (1939), no. 7 in C (Leningrad, 1941), no. 8 in C min. (1943), no. 9 in Eb (1945), no. 10 in E min. (1953), no. 11 in G min. (The Year 1905, 1957), no. 12 in D min. (1917, 1961), no. 13 in Bb min. (Babi Yar, with bass, bass chorus and orch., 1962), no. 14 for sop., bass, strings and perc. (1969; 11 poems on the theme of death by Lorca, Apollinaire, Küchelbecker and Rilke), no. 15 in A (1971); 2 pf. concertos (1933, 1957), 2 vln. concertos (1948, 1967), 2 cello concertos (1959, 1966).

CHAMBER: 15 string 4tets, no. 1 in C (1938), no. 2 in A (1944), no. 3 in F (1946), no. 4 in D (1949), no. 5 in Bb (1953), no. 6 in G (1956), no. 7 in F# min. (1960), no. 8 in C min. (1960), no. 9 in Eb (1964), no. 10 in Ab (1964), no. 11 in F min. (1966), no. 12 in Db (1968), no. 13 in Bb min. (1970), no. 14 in F# maj. (1973), no. 15 in Eb min. (1974); 2 pf. trios (1923, 1944), pf. 5tet (1940), sonata for cello and pf. (1934), sonata for vln. and pf. (1968), sonata for vla. and pf. (1975).

VOCAL AND PIANO: Songs to texts by Pushkin, Shakespeare, Lermontov, Blok, Michelangelo and Dostoievsky; 2 pf. sonatas (1926, 1942), 24 Preludes for pf. (1933), 24 Preludes and Fugues for pf. (1951).

Orchestrations of Mussorgsky's Boris Godunov (1940, perf. 1959) and Khovanshchina (1959), re-orch. of Schumann's cello concerto, for Rostropovich (1963).

Shuard, Amy (b London, 19 Jul 1924; d London, 18 Apr 1975), English soprano. Studied at the TCM in London, making her debut in Johannesburg in 1949. Appeared in London, SW, 1949–55 as Katya Kabanová, Carmen, Eboli and Tosca. She was well known as a dramatic singer, esp. in Wagner. From 1954 she sang at CG; roles there incl. Aida, Turandot, Brünnhilde, Kundry, Elektra and Jenůfa. She sang Isolde at Geneva in 1972 and appeared in N. and S. Amer.

Shudi, Burkat (Burkhardt Tschudi) (b Schwanden, Glarus, 13 Mar 1702; d London, 19 Aug 1773), Swiss (anglicized) harpsichord maker. He settled in London as a cabinet maker in 1718, joined the harpsichord maker Tabel and set up on his own account in the 1730s. See also Broadwood.

Shumsky, Oscar (b Philadelphia, 23 Mar 1917), American violinist and conductor.

Debut 1925 with Philadelphia Orch., under Stokowski; studied with Auer and Zimbalist and joined the NBC orch., under Toscanini, in 1938. After a brief career as a soloist he played with and cond. var. chamber groups in Canada and the USA; Juilliard School from 1953. His career as a virtuoso was resumed in the 1980s, to wide acclaim.

Sibelius, Jean (Johan Julius Christian) (b Tavastehus, 8 Dec 1865; d Järvenpää nr. Helsinki, 20 Sep 1957), Finnish composer. Son of a surgeon. Having been given a classical educ., he was intended for the law, entering Helsinki Univ. He learned pf. and vln. as a child and tried comp. long before he had any instruction. While studying law he managed to take a special course under Wegelius at the Cons. and in 1885 went there altogether, giving up the univ. He left in 1889 and had a string 4tet and a suite for string orch. perf. in public. With a government grant he went to study counterpoint with A. Becker in Berlin and later orch. with Fuchs in Vienna, where he also consulted Goldmark. When he returned home he became a passionate nationalist, studying the *Kalevala* and other Fin. literature for subjects for his works, the 1st being *Kullervo*, prod. at Helsinki on 28 Apr 1892, the year in which he married Aino Järnefelt, sister of the comp. of that name, and was asked by Kajanus to write an orchestral work for perf. at the Cons., a request to which he responded with *En Saga*. His only opera, *The Maiden in the Tower*, had a single perf. in 1896, but like *Kullervo* remained unpub.

An annual grant was voted to Sibelius by the government in 1897 and increased in 1926, and he was thus enabled to devote himself entirely to comp. without having to fill any official or administrative post. He gradually made his way abroad, but not in every country. Much of his work was pub. in Ger., but not widely perf. there; in Eng. he became much better known after the perf. of the 4th symph. at the Birmingham Festival in 1912, and in Amer. after his visit in 1914, when Yale Univ. conferred a doctor's degree on him. During the Rus. Revolution after the 1914–18 war there was much unrest in Fin., and Sibelius's country home at Järvenpää was invaded; but he spent most of his life there quietly, devoted wholly to composition.

Works incl. opera, *The Maiden in the Tower (Jungfrun i Tornet); incid. music to Adolf Paul's King Christian* (1898), Arvid Järnefelt's *Kuolema* (incl. *Valse triste*, 1903), Maeterlinck's *Pelléas et Mélisande*

(1905), Hjalmar Procopé's *Belshazzar's Feast* (1906), Strindberg's *Svanevit*, Paul Knudsen's *Scaramouche*, Hofmannsthal's version of *Everyman*, Shakespeare's *Tempest.*

ORCH.: 7 symphs., no. 1 in E min. (1899), no. 2 in D (1902), no. 3 in C (1904–7), no. 4 in A min. (1911), no. 5 in E♭ (1915), no. 6 in D min. (1923), no. 7 in C (1924); *Kullervo,* with solo voices and chorus (1892), symph. poem *En Saga, Karelia* overture and suite (1893), *Rakastava* for strings and timpani, *Spring Song,* 4 Legends (*Lemminkäinen and the Maidens of Saari, The Swan of Tuonela, Lemminkäinen in Tuonela, Lemminkäinen's Return* (1895), 2 suites of *Scènes historiques* (1899), tone-poem *Finlandia* (1899), 2 pieces *The Dryads* and *Dance Intermezzo,* vln. concerto (1903). symph. fantasy *Pohjola's Daughter* (1906), dance intermezzo *Pan and Echo,* tone-poem *Night-Ride and Sunrise,* funeral march *In Memoriam,* tone-poems *The Bard* (1913); symph. poems *The Oceanides* (1914) and *Tapiola* (1926), a number of smaller orchestral pieces;

CHAMBER: String 4tet *Voces intimae* (1909), sonatina and many smaller pieces for vln. and pf.; *Malinconia* (1901) and 2 *Serious Pieces* for cello and pf.; 18 op. nos. of pf. works incl. sonata in F maj., *Pensées lyriques* (1914), *Kyllikki,* 3 sonatinas; 2 organ pieces.

VOCAL: Choral works with orch. (with or without solo voices): *Impromptu* (female chorus), *The Origin of Fire, The Ferryman's Bride, The Captive Queen; Luonnotar* for sop. and orch. (1910–13); a number of part-songs; 85 songs; Rydberg's *Skogsrået* and Runeberg's *Nights of Jealousy* for recitation and instrumental accomp.

Siberia, opera by Giordano (lib., by L. Illica), prod. Milan, La Scala, 19 Dec 1903; rev. 1921, prod. Milan, 5 Dec 1927.

Siboni, Erik (Anton Valdemar) (b Copenhagen, 26 Aug 1828; d Frederiksberg, 11 Feb 1892), Danish pianist, organist and composer of Italian origin. Studied at Copenhagen, J.P.E. Hartmann being among his masters, and with Moscheles and Hauptmann at Leipzig. He fought on the Dan. side in the war of Slesvig-Holstein in 1848. In 1851–3 he continued his studies with Sechter in Vienna. After his return to Copenhagen he settled as a music teacher, among his pupils being Princess Alexandra. In 1864–83 he was prof. of the Royal Acad. at Sorø.

Works incl. operas *Loreley* (1859) and

Carl den Andens Flugt (1861); Psalm cxi, *Stabat Mater*, cantatas *The Battle of Murten* and *The Assault of Copenhagen* for solo voices, chorus and orch.; 2 symphs. and other orchestral works; pf. concerto (1864); string 4tets, pf. 4tet, pf. trio; vln. and pf. and cello, and pf. sonatas; duet for 2 pfs.; pf. pieces; songs.

Siboni, Giuseppe (b Forlì 27 Jan 1780; d Copenhagen, 29 Mar 1839), Italian tenor, father of prec. He made his 1st appearance at Florence in 1797, and having appeared elsewhere in It., went to Prague, London (from 1806), Vienna and St Petersburg, settling at Copenhagen in 1819, where he became director of the Royal Opera and the Cons. He was well known in operas by Paer, Portugal, Paisiello and Nasolini.

Sicher, Fridolin (b Bischofszell, Switzerland, 6 Mar 1490; d Bischofszell, 13 Jun 1546), Swiss organist, priest and arranger. He compiled a MS. (St Gall, MS. 530) incl. works by himself and arrs. of vocal works by others.

Sicilian Vespers (Verdi). *See* **Vêpres siciliennes.**

Siciliana or **Siciliano** } (It.), a piece or song in dotted 6–8 rhythm derived from a Sicilian dance. It is rather slow, and indeed may form the slow movement of a sonata or suite. Arias in siciliano rhythm were common in the 18th cent.

Sicilienne (Fr.) = Siciliana, Siciliano.

Side Drum, the military drum, which is the smallest drum used in the orch., covered with a skin at either end and having a snare of catgut string stretched over the lower one, to produce a rattling sound when the upper one is struck by a pair of hard wooden drumsticks. Single strokes on the side drum are ineffective: it is usually made to prod. small patterns of repeated notes or more or less prolonged rolls. Its tone is bright and hard, without definite pitch. It can be muted by relaxing the tension of the snare.

Sieben Todsünden der Kleinbürger, Die (*The Seven Deadly Sins of the Petit-Bourgeois*), ballet with songs by Weill (lib. by Brecht), prod. Paris, 7 Jun 1933; choreog. by Balanchine.

Siefert, Paul (b Danzig, 28 Jun 1586; d Danzig, 6 May 1666), German organist and composer. Pupil of Sweelinck at Amsterdam. After serving in the royal chapel of Sigismund III at Warsaw, he became organist at St Mary's Church, Danzig, c 1620.

Works incl. Te Deum, psalms for 4–8 voices and other church music; organ pieces.

Siège de Corinthe (Rossini). *See* **Maometto II.**

Siege of Belgrade, The, opera by Storace (lib. by J. Cobb), prod. London, Drury Lane Theatre, 1 Jan 1791.

Siege of Rhodes, The, opera by Locke, H. Lawes, H. Cooke, Coleman and Hudson (lib. by W. Davenant), prod. London, Rutland House, Sep 1656. The 1st English opera.

Siege of Rochelle, The, opera by Balfe (lib. by E. Fitzball, based on the Comtesse de Genlis's novel), prod. London, Drury Lane Theatre, 29 Oct 1835.

Siegfried (Wagner). *See* **Ring des Nibelungen.**

Siegfried Idyll, a symph. piece for small orch. by Wagner, comp. at Triebschen on the Lake of Lucerne in Nov 1870 and perf. on Cosima Wagner's birthday, 25 Dec, on the staircase of the villa. It was therefore at first entitled *Triebschener Idyll* and called 'Treppenmusik' in the family circle. The thematic material is taken from *Siegfried*, except the Ger. cradle song 'Schlaf, Kindlein, schlaf', but some of it, even though incl. in *Siegfried*, dates back to a string 4tet of 1864.

Siegl, Otto (b Graz, 6 Oct 1896; d Vienna, 9 Nov 1978), Austrian composer, conductor and violinist. Studied vln. with E. Kornauth and comp. with Mojsisovics in Vienna. Joined the Vienna SO as a violinist, worked at the Graz Opera and then went to Ger., becoming music dir. at Paderborn, at the same time cond. and teaching at Bielefeld and Essen. In 1933 he became comp. prof. at the Cologne Cons., returning to Vienna in 1948.

Works incl. fairy opera *Der Wassermann*; music for 2 puppet plays; oratorios *Das Grosse Halleluja* (Claudius), *Eines Menschen Lied* (1931), *Klingendes Jahr* (1933), *Trostkantate, Mutter Deutschland; Missa Mysterium Magnum; Verliebte alle Reime* for chorus; 3 symphs., sinfonietta, *Lyrische Tanzmusik, Festliche Ouvertüre, Pastoralouvertüre* (1939), *Concerto grosso antico* (1936), *Galante Ahendmusik, Festmusik und Trauermusik* for orch.; pf. concerto (1963), vln. concerto, concerto for string 4tet and string orch.; 5 string 4tets; songs.

Siegmeister, Elie (b New York, 15 Jan 1909), American composer. Studied Columbia Univ., Paris and Juilliard. Organized ensemble American Ballad Singers, 1939.

Works incl. operas *Dublin Song* (1963) and *Night of the Moonspell* (1976); 6 symphs. (1947–85), pf. concerto (1976, rev. 1982); choral and chamber music.

Siehr, Gustav (b Arnsberg, 17 Sep 1837; d Munich, 18 May 1896), German bass. Debut Neustrelitz 1863. He sang in Prague, Wiesbaden and Munich, 1865–96; created Hagen at Bayreuth (1876) and from 1882 to 1889 was successful there as Gurnemanz and Marke.

Siems, Margarethe (b Breslau, 30 Dec 1879; d Dresden, 13 Apr 1952), German soprano. Debut Prague 1902, as Marguerite de Valois. Her career was centred in Dresden, where she appeared 1908–25; created there Strauss's Chrysothemis (1909) and the Marschallin (1911). She also created Zerbinetta (Stuttgart, 1912) and was heard in a wide repertory, incl. Norma, Lucia, Aida, Venus and Isolde.

Siepi, Cesare (b Milan, 10 Feb 1923), Italian bass. Studied at Milan Cons., making his debut in 1941. From 1946 he sang at La Scala, Milan, and from 1950 was a leading member of the NY Met; roles there incl. Philip II, Boris, Gurnemanz and Figaro. He sang Don Giovanni at Salzburg under Furtwängler in 1953 (also filmed) and at CG in 1962.

Siface (Giovanni Francesco Grossi) (b Uzzanese Chiesina nr. Pescia, 12 Feb 1653; d nr. Ferrara, 29 May 1697), Italian male soprano. Became singer at the Papal Chapel in Rome, 1675, and went to Eng. about 1679. Sang at the court of James II, but soon returned to It. Purcell wrote a harpsichord piece, *Sefauchi's Farewell*, on his departure. He was murdered on the orders of a jealous rival.

Siface (*Syphax*), opera by Feo (lib. by Metastasio), prod. Naples, Teatro San Bartolommeo, 13 May 1723.

Opera by Porpora (lib. do.), prod. Milan, Teatro Regio Ducal, 26 Dec 1725.

Signature. *See* **Key Signature; Time Signature.**

Signor Bruschino, Il, ossia Il figlio per azzardo (*Mr. B., or The Son by Accident*), opera by Rossini (lib. by G.M. Foppa), prod. Venice, Teatro San Moisè, Jan 1813.

Signor di Pourceaugnac, Il, opera by Franchetti (lib. by F. Fontana, based on Molière's comedy, *Monsieur de P.*), prod. Milan, La Scala, 10 Apr 1897.

Sigtenhorst Meyer, Bernhard van den (b Amsterdam, 17 Jun 1888; d The Hague, 17 Jul 1953), Dutch musicologist and composer. Studied with Zweers, D. de Lange and others and later in Paris, afterwards travelling to Java and the Far East. He returned to Amsterdam, but moved to The Hague, where he lived for many years. Ed. of works by Sweelinck and author of books on him.

Works incl. incid. music to Tagore's play *The King's Letter*; oratorio *The Temptation of Buddha, Stabat Mater, Hymn to the Sun* (St Francis of Assisi); 2 string 4tets; songs.

Sigurd, opera by Reyer (lib. by C. du Locle and A. Blau, based on the Nibelung Saga), prod. Brussels, Théâtre de la Monnaie, 7 Jan 1884.

Siklós, Albert (b Budapest, 26 Jun 1878; d Budapest, 3 Apr 1942), Hungarian cellist, musicologist and composer. Studied at the Hung. Music School in Budapest and appeared as cellist in 1891, as lecturer in 1895 and began to comp. seriously in 1896, when he finished a cello concerto, a symph. and an opera. He held distinguished teaching-posts in Budapest and was app. prof. in 1913.

Works incl. 3 operas, 2 ballets, choral and a vast number of orchestral works, concertos, chamber and much pf. music, etc., also 10 books of songs.

Sikorski, Kazimierz (b Zurich, 28 Jun 1895; d Warsaw, 5 Jul 1985), Polish composer. Studied at the Chopin High School in Warsaw and later in Paris. In 1927 he became prof. at the Warsaw Cons. In 1936 he was one of the founders of the Society for the Pub. of Polish Music.

Works incl. Psalm vii for chorus and orch.; 4 symphs. (1918–71) and symph. poem for orch.; 3 string 4tets, string 6tet; songs; part-songs. His son **Tomasz** (b Warsaw, 19 May 1939) is a pianist and composer who has written instrumental music in var. advanced idioms; noted as an early Polish minimalist.

Silbermann. German family of organ builders and harpsichord makers.

1. Andreas S. (b Kleinbobritzsch nr. Frauenstein, Saxony, 16 May 1678; d Strasbourg, 16 Mar 1734), son of the carpenter Michael S. Worked with Casparini in Görlitz 1797–c 99. Settled in Strasbourg in 1721 and built the cathedral organ there in 1713–16.

2. Gottfried S. (b Kleinbobritzsch, 14 Jan 1683; d Dresden, 4 Aug 1753), brother of prec. At first apprenticed to a bookbinder, he joined his brother Andreas in Strasbourg in 1702, staying there till 1710. He then settled in Freiberg, where he built the cathedral organ (1711–14), and died while at work on a new organ for the Dresden court. He also built harpsichords and clavichords (one of them commemorated by a piece by C.P.E. Bach entitled 'Farewell to my Silbermann

Clavichord'), and was the first Ger. to make pfs.

3. Johann Andreas S. (b Strasbourg, 26 May 1712; d Strasbourg, 11 Feb 1783), son of 1. He built 54 organs.

4. Johann Daniel S. (b Strasbourg, 31 Mar 1717; d Leipzig, 9 May 1766), brother of prec. Worked with his uncle, 2, whose organ at Dresden he finished.

5. Johann Heinrich S. (b Strasbourg, 24 Sep 1727; d Strasbourg, 15 Jan 1799), brother of prec. He made harpsichords and pfs., some with pedal boards.

Silbersee, Der, opera by Weill (lib. by G. Kaiser), prod. Leipzig, Erfurt and Magdeburg, 18 Feb 1933.

Silcher, Friedrich (b Schnaith nr. Schorndorf, Württemberg, 27 Jun 1789; d Tübingen, 26 Aug 1860), German composer and conductor. Pupil of his father and others. He became a schoolmaster, but in 1815 went to Stuttgart as cond. and in 1817 to the Univ. of Tübingen in the same capacity. Some of his songs have become what in Ger. are called folksongs.

Works incl. 2 hymn-books (3 and 4 voices), collections of songs, some arr., some comp. by himself, incl. *Aennchen von Tharau, Loreley* (Heine), *Morgen muss ich fort, Zu Strassburg auf der Schanz.*

Silent Woman (R. Strauss). *See* **Schweigsame Frau.**

Silja, Anja (b Berlin, 17 Apr 1940), German soprano. She sang Rosina at Brunswick aged 15; formed a close personal and artistic relationship with Wieland Wagner and sang many times at Bayreuth and Stuttgart until his death in 1966. In London she has been heard since 1963 as Leonore, Marie, and Cassandre. US debut Chicago 1968, as Senta; NY Met 1972, Leonore. Other roles incl. Lulu, Salome, Isolde and The Woman in *Erwartung.* With her husband Christoph von Dohnányi she is often heard in concert. Highly regarded as an actress.

Silk, Dorothy (b Alvechurch, Worcs., 4 May 1884; d Alvechurch, 30 Jul 1942), English soprano. Studied at Birmingham and in Vienna, giving her 1st recital in London in 1920. She specialized in Bach and earlier comps., but also studied modern works; she sang in Boughton's *Bethlehem* and in the fp of Holst's *Sāvitri* (1921).

Sills, Beverly (b Brooklyn, NY, 25 May 1929), American soprano. She performed on radio from the age of 3 and soon acquired the nickname Bubbles. Opera debut Philadelphia, 1947; NY City Opera from 1955 (debut as Rosalinde). Wider fame came with her Cleopatra, in a 1966 adaptation of Handel's *Giulio Cesare*; also successful as Manon and Violetta and in Donizetti's 3 Tudor operas. She sang Lucia at CG in 1970, and Pamira in Rossini's *Le siège de Corinthe* was the role of her belated NY Met debut. In 1979 she became dir. of the NY City Opera.

Siloti, Alexander (Ilyich) (b nr. Kharkov, 9 Oct 1863; d New York, 8 Dec 1945), Russian pianist and conductor. Studied at the Moscow Cons. under Tchaikovsky, N. Rubinstein and others, later with Liszt. He 1st appeared at Moscow in 1880 and later travelled widely. He left Rus. in 1919 and lived in USA at the end of his life. From 1925 to 1942 he taught at the Juilliard School in NY.

Silva, Andreas de (Silvanus or Sylvanus), Spanish 15th–16th-cent. singer and composer. Sang in the Papal Chapel in Rome early in the 16th cent. and was in the service of the Duke of Mantua from 1522. 1 of his motets was used as the basis of a Mass by Palestrina.

Works incl. Masses, motets; madrigals.

Silva Leite, António Joaquim da (b Oporto, 23 May 1759; d Oporto, 10 Jan 1833), Portuguese composer. Pupil of the It. Girolamo Sartori (?), he was *mestre de capela* at Oporto Cathedral from 1814.

Works incl. It. operas *Puntigli per equivoco* and *Le astuzie delle donne; Tantum ergo* with orch.; sonatas and studies for guitar. A projected anthology of organ music was never finished.

Silvana, opera by Weber (lib. by F.K. Hiemer, altered from Steinsberg's *Waldmädchen*), prod. Frankfurt, 16 Sep 1810. Weber's 2nd version of *Das Waldmädchen* of 1800.

Silvani, Giuseppe Antonio (b Bologna, 21 Jan 1672; d Bologna, before 1727), Italian composer and publisher. *Maestro di cappella* at the church of San Stefano at Bologna, 1702–25. He inherited Marino S., his father's music pub. business.

Works incl. Masses, motets, Lamentations, *Stabat Mater,* Litanies, sacred cantatas and other church music for voices with string or organ accompaniment.

Silveri, Paolo (b Ofena nr. Aquila, 28 Dec 1913), Italian baritone. Made his debut in Rome in 1944 as Germont and sang at Covent Garden from 1947 to 1949, as Rigoletto, Escamillo and Boris, and at the NY Met from 1950 to 1953. After a brief period as a tenor in 1959 (Otello in Dublin) he reverted to baritone in 1960. Other roles incl. Marcello, Don Giovanni and Renato.

Silverstein, Joseph (b Detroit, 21 Mar

1932), American violinist and conductor. Studied with Zimbalist at the Curtis Inst. Played in various orchs. before joining Boston SO in 1955; leader 1962, asst. cond. 1971–83. Guest cond. with most major American orchs. Music dir. Utah SO from 1983. Has taught at Yale and Boston Univs. A leading interpreter of modern music.

Silvestri, Constantin (b Bucharest, 13 May 1913; d London, 23 Feb 1969), Rumanian conductor, composer and pianist. Studied at the Bucharest Cons., making his debut as a pianist in 1924 and as a cond. in 1930. He became cond. at the Bucharest Opera in 1935 and of the Bucharest PO in 1945. British debut 1957 (LPO); from 1961 he cond. the Bournemouth SO. CG debut 1963 (*Khovanshchina*).

Works incl. *Music for Strings, Three Pieces for String Orchestra*; 2 string 4tets; 2 sonatas for vln. and pf.; sonatas for harp, fl., clar., bassoon.

Simile (It. = like), an abbr. often used to indicate that certain passages are to be perf. in the same way as similar passages occurring before.

Simionato, Giulietta (b Forlì 15 Dec 1910), Italian mezzo. Studied in Florence, winning a prize at a competition there in 1933. Her early roles incl. Rosina, Cherubino and Mignon. La Scala 1946–66 as Charlotte, Carmen and Cinderella. CG 1953 as Adalgisa and Amneris. NY Met debut 1959, Azucena. Retired 1966.

Simmes (or **Simes** or **Sims**), **William**, English 16th–17th-cent. composer.

Works incl. anthems; fantasies for viols.

Simon, Antoine (Antony Yulievich) (b Paris, 5 Aug 1850; d St Petersburg, 1 Feb 1916), French composer and conductor. Studied at the Paris Cons. and in 1871 settled at Moscow, where he became cond. of the Théâtre-Bouffe. In the 1890s he became pf. prof. at the Phil. Music School and superintendent of the orch. of the Imp. theatres.

Works incl. operas *Rolla* (1892), *The Song of Love Triumphant* (after Turgenev, 1897), *The Fishers* (after Hugo, 1899); mimed drama *Esmeralda* (after Hugo's *Notre-Dame*, 1902); ballets *The Stars* and *Living Flowers*; incid. music for Shakespeare's *Merchant of Venice*; Mass; concertos for pf. and for clar.; string 4tets; songs.

Simon Boccanegra, opera by Verdi (lib. by F.M. Piave, based on a Span. drama by A.G. Gutiérrez), prod. Venice, Teatro La Fenice, 12 Mar 1857; revised version, with the lib. altered by Boito, prod. Milan, La Scala, 24 Mar 1881.

Simon, Simon (b Vaux-de-Cernay nr. Rambouillet, *c* 1730; d ? Versailles, after 1780), French harpsichordist and composer. Pupil of Dauvergne. He was app. harpsichord master to the queen and the royal children at Versailles.

Works incl. 3 books of harpsichord pieces, pieces and sonatas for harpsichord with vln.

Simoneau, Léopold (b Quebec, 3 May 1918), Canadian tenor. He studied in NY and made his debut in Montreal in 1941. He moved to Europe in 1949 and was heard at the Paris Opéra-Comique in operas by Gounod and Stravinsky. Glyndebourne 1951–4 as Don Ottavio and Idamante. He was heard in Aix, London, Vienna and Chicago during the 1950s. NY Met debut 1963, as Ottavio. He taught singing in San Francisco from 1973.

Simonetti, Achille (b Turin, 12 Jun 1857; d London, 19 Nov 1928), Italian violinist and composer. Pupil of Pedrotti for comp. and later of Sivori at Genoa for vln. Having appeared as a concert artist, he went to Paris for further study with Dancla and Massenet. Later he settled in London as perf., teacher and member of the London Trio. Toured throughout Europe as a soloist; well known in the Brahms concerto.

Works incl. 2 string 4tets; 2 vln. and pf. sonatas, vln. pieces.

Simonov, Yuri (b Saratov, 4 Mar 1941), Russian conductor. Studied at Leningrad Cons.; cond. Kislovodsk PO 1967–9. Bolshoy Theatre, Moscow, from 1970.

Simple Intervals, any Intervals not larger than an 8ve, those exceeding that width being called Compound Interval.

Simple Time, any musical metre in which the beats can be subdivided into two, e.g. 2–4, 3–4, 4–4. *Cf.* **Compound Time.**

Simpson, Christopher (b Yorkshire, *c* 1605; d London, summer 1669), English viola da gamba player, theorist and composer. He joined the royalist army under the Duke of Newcastle in 1643 and endured much hardship, but later came under the patronage of Sir Robert Bolles, at whose residences at Scampton and in London he lived in comfort, teaching the children of the family and taking charge of the domestic music-making. He wrote an instruction book for the vla. da gamba, *The Division Violist*. He bought a house and farm at Pickering, Yorks., but died at one of Sir John Bolles's houses. He wrote another treatise, *The Principles of Practicle Musick* and annotations to Campion's *Art of Descant*.

Works incl. *Months and Seasons* for a treble and 2 bass viols, fancies and consorts for viols, suite in 3 parts for viols, divisions (variations) and pieces for vla. da gamba.

Simpson, Robert (Wilfred Levick) (b Leamington, 2 Mar 1921), English composer and music critic. Studied privately with Howells and took D. Mus. at Durham in 1952. He was active in the BBC and is a writer on music, esp. that of Bruckner, Nielsen and Sibelius.

Works incl. 9 symphs. (1951–85), *Nielsen Vars.* (1986), overture for orch.; fantasia for strings; 11 string 4tets (1952–84); pf. music.

Simpson, Thomas (b Milton nr. Sittingbourne, bap. 1 Apr 1582; d after 1630), English violist and composer. Settled in Ger. early in the 17th cent., was in the service of the Elector Palatine in 1610, in that of the Prince of Holstein-Schaumburg in 1617–21, and afterwards at the Dan. court in Copenhagen (1622–5).

Works incl. pavans, galliards and other dances for viols; songs with instruments.

Sinclair, John (b nr. Edinburgh, 9 Dec 1791; d Margate, 23 Sep 1857), Scottish tenor. Studied at Aberdeen and 1st appeared in London in 1810; at CG he was heard in operas by Linley and Bishop. In 1819 he visited Paris, studied in It. and sang there with success until 1823. He often sang in operas by Rossini and appeared in the fp of *Semiramide* (Venice 1823).

Sinclair, Monica (b Evercreech, Somerset, 1925), English mezzo. Studied RAM and RCM. She sang Suzuki with the Carl Rosa co. in 1948; CG from 1949, appeared in the fp of *Pilgrim's Progress*, 1951. Glyndebourne 1954–60, in operas by Mozart, Strauss and Rossini. At Bordeaux in 1955 she sang Lully's Armide. Married a CG horn player and had six children by him.

Sinding, Christian (b Kongsberg, 11 Jan 1856; d Oslo, 3 Dec 1941), Norwegian pianist and composer. Studied at Leipzig, Berlin and Munich. He settled at Oslo as pianist and comp.

Works incl. opera *The Holy Mountain* (1912); 4 symphs. and *Rondo infinito* for orch., pf. concerto in Db maj, 3 vln. concertos (1898, 1901, 1917); string 4tet (1904), pf. 5tet, pf. trio; sonatas and suite for vln. and pf.; variations for 2 pfs.; suite, studies and numerous pieces for pf.; songs.

Sinfonia (It.) = Symphony. In the early 18th cent. the sinfonia was simply an instrumental piece in an opera or other vocal work, esp. the Overture; it is in fact out of the latter that the symph. developed.

Title of work by Berio (1968) which uses collage techniques: scherzo of Mahler's 2nd symph. is quoted.

Sinfonia Antartica, symphony by Vaughan Williams (his 7th) for sop., women's chorus and orch.; comp. 1949–52 and based on his music for the film *Scott of the Antarctic*, 1947–8; fp Manchester, 14 Jan 1953, cond. Barbirolli.

Sinfonia concertante, a work in symph. form with 1 or more solo instruments, similar to a concerto. Familiar exs. are Mozart's K364 for vln., vla. and orch. of 1779 and K App. 9 (K297b) for ob., clar., horn and bassoon with orch. of 1778.

Sinfonia da Requiem, work for orch. in 3 movts. by Britten; commissioned to celebrate the 2,600th anniversary of the Imperial Japanese dynasty. The work was rejected for its allusions to the Catholic liturgy and the fp was in NY on 29 Mar 1941, cond. Barbirolli; 8 months before Pearl Harbor.

Sinfonia domestica (R. Strauss). *See* **Symphonia domestica.**

Sinfonia Espansiva, symph. no. 3 (with wordless sop. and bar. voices) by Nielsen, op. 27; comp. 1910–11, fp Copenhagen, 30 Apr 1912, cond. Nielsen. Not perf. in public in Brit. until London, 7 May 1962, cond. B. Fairfax.

Sinfonia Semplice, sub-title of Nielsen's 6th and last symph.; comp. 1924–5, fp Copenhagen, 11 Dec 1925, cond. Nielsen.

Sinfonietta (It. = little symph.), a work in symph. form, but of smaller dimensions and usually lightly scored. Exs. are by Janáček, Prokofiev, Poulenc, Britten and Roussel.

Singakademie (Ger. lit. singing-academy = vocal academy), the special name of certain choral societies in Ger. and Aus.

Singspiel (Ger. = song play), orig. a trans. of the It. *dramma per musica*, i.e. opera. In the course of the 18th cent. the term was restricted to comic opera with spoken dialogue, e.g. Mozart's *Die Entführung*.

Sinigaglia, Leone (b Turin, 14 Aug 1868; d Turin, 16 May 1944), Italian composer. Studied at the Turin Cons. and with Mandyczewski in Vienna. After his return home he settled down to comp. and folksong collecting.

Works incl. suite *Piemonte*, overture to Goldoni's *Le baruffe chiozzote*, *Danze piemontesi* for orch. (1903); concerto, *Rapsodia piemontese* and romance for vln. and orch.; string 4tet in D maj. concert study and variations on a theme by Brahms for string 4tet; sonatas for cello and vln., folksongs.

Sino (It. = till, until, or abbr. *sin'* when

followed by a vowel), a word used in such directions as that indicating a repeat *sin' al fine* (until the end) or *sin' al segno* . . . (to the sign . . .), etc.

Sinopoli, Giuseppe (b Venice, 2 Nov 1946), Italian conductor and composer. He studied medicine in Padua, then conducting in Vienna, with Swarowsky. Founded the Bruno Maderna ens. in 1975, for perfs. of modern music, and appeared with the Berlin PO from 1979. In 1983 he made his US debut with the NY PO, and led *Manon Lescaut* at CG, London. Bayreuth debut *Tannhäuser*, 1985. Prin. cond. Philharmonia orch. from 1984.

Works incl. opera *Lou Salomé* (1981), *Sunyata* for string 5tet (1970), *Opus daleth* for orch. (1971), *Symphonie imaginaire* for solo voices and chorus (1973), pf. concerto (1974), *Requiem Hashshirim* for unaccomp. chorus (1976), string 4tet (1977).

Sir John in Love, opera by Vaughan Williams (lib. selected by comp. from Shakespeare's *Merry Wives of Windsor*), prod. London, RCM, 21 Mar 1929.

Sirius, work by Stockhausen for sop., bar. and ensemble, ded. to American pioneers and astronauts. Fp Washington, DC, 18 Jul 1976.

Sirmen (*née* Lombardini), Maddalena (b Venice, ? 1735; d after 1785), Italian violinist, singer and composer. Studied at the Cons. dei Mendicanti at Venice and vln. with Tartini at Padua. In 1760 she began to tour in It. and at Bergamo she met Ludovico Sirmen, a violinist and cond. at the church of Santa Maria Maddalena there, and married him. They visited Paris in 1768 and in 1771 she 1st appeared in London, where she also played the harpsichord.

Works incl. 6 vln. concertos; 6 string 4tets, 6 trios for 2 vlns. and cello; 6 duets and 6 sonatas for 2 vlns.

Siroe, rè di Persia (*Siroes, King of Persia*), lib. by Metastasio.

Opera by Handel, prod. London, King's Theatre, Haymarket, 17 Feb 1728.

Opera by Hasse, prod. Bologna, Teatro Malvezzi, 2 May 1733.

Opera by Pérez, prod. Naples, Teatro San Carlo, 4 Nov 1740.

Opera by Vinci, prod. Venice, Teatro San Giovanni Grisostomo, Jan 1726.

Širola, Božidar (b Žakanj, 20 Dec 1889; d Zagreb, 10 Apr 1956), Yugoslav composer. Studied at Zagreb and in Vienna, where he took a doctor's degree. Later dir. of the Music Acad. at Zagreb.

Works incl. operas *Stanac* (1915), *The Wandering Scholar* and 4 others; ballet *Shadows*; incid. music to plays; 3 oratorios; symph., suite and overtures for orch.; 13 string 4tets (1920–55), 3 pf. trios; songs.

Sistrum, an ancient instrument, prob. orig. in Egypt, played like a rattle. It had a metal frame fitted to a handle and metal bars or loops were loosely hung on the frame and made to strike against it by shaking the instrument.

Sitt, Hans (b Prague, 21 Sep 1850; d Leipzig, 10 Mar 1922), Czech-German violinist, teacher and editor. Studied at the Prague Cons., became leader at Breslau, 1867, and cond. at Breslau and Prague, 1870–3, Chemnitz, 1873–80, and Nice. He returned to Leipzig, where he joined Brodsky's 4tet as violist. He was prof. of vln. at the Leipzig Cons., 1883–1921. He edited much vln. music.

Works incl. 3 vln. concertos, vla. concerto, 2 cello concertos, chamber music, vln. studies and pieces, songs.

Sivori, (Ernesto) Camillo (b Genoa, 25 Oct 1815; d Genoa, 19 Feb 1894), Italian violinist and composer. Pupil of Paganini, who wrote his works for 4tet with guitar for him and, going on tour, sent him to another master, Giacomo Costa, and later to Dellepiane, with whom he went on tour, making his 1st appearance at Turin in 1827. They went on to Fr. and London, but in 1829 Sivori returned to Genoa to study comp. with Giovanni Serra. He then travelled widely in Europe and N. and S. Amer. until 1870.

Works incl. 2 concertos, *Tarantelle napolitaine*, etc. for vln. and orch.; duet for vln. and double bass (with Bottesini); 2 *Duos concertants* for vln. and pf.; *Andante spianato* and numerous other pieces and fantasies on operatic airs for vln. and pf.; vln. studies.

Six, Les, a group of French composers who in their youth gathered together, under the leadership of Satie and Jean Cocteau, for the furtherance of their interests and to some extent those of modern music in general. It was formed in Paris in 1917 and its active comp. members were Auric, Durey, Honegger, Milhaud, Poulenc and Tailleferre; the chief perfs. were the singer Jane Bathori and the pianist Andrée Vaurabourg, the latter becoming Honegger's wife. The group gradually lost its solidarity during the 1920s.

Sixth, the interval between 2 notes lying 5 degrees of a diatonic scale apart, e.g.:

The so-called 'chord of the 6th' — or 6–3 chord — (maj. or min.) consists of a 3rd with a 4th above it, e.g.:

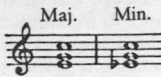

The '6–4' chord (the 2nd inversion of a chord) consists of a 4th with a 3rd above it, e.g.

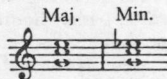

Chords of the augmented 6th are known in 3 forms, French Sixth, German Sixth and Italian Sixth. See **Augmented Sixth Chords.**

Sjögren (Johan Gustaf) Emil (b Stockholm, 16 Jun 1853; d Stockholm, 1 Mar 1918), Swedish composer. Studied at the Stockholm Cons. and later in Berlin, also came under the influence of Lange-Müller during a stay of 6 months at Meran. In 1891 he became organist at St John's Church, Stockholm, but devoted most of his time to teaching and comp.

Works incl. 5 vln. and pf. sonatas; organ works; 2 pf. sonatas, *Erotikon, Novellettes* and numerous other works for pf.; songs.

Skalkottas, Nicos (b Chalkis, Euboea, 21 Mar 1904; d Athens, 19 Sep 1949), Greek composer. Studied at the Athens Cons. and with Economidis, later in Germany with Schoenberg, Weill and Jarnach, living there for 12 years. From 1933 he lived in Athens. Much of his music was not perf. until after his death, notably in Hamburg and London.

Works incl. 2 ballets, 36 Gk. Dances (1931–6), *Sinfonietta*, overture *The Return of Ulysses* and 2 suites for orch.; concerto and symph. for wind insts., 3 pf. concertos (1931, 1938, 1939), vln. concerto, cello concerto, concerto for vln. and vla., concerto for 2 vlns.; 4 string 4tets (1928–40), Octet for woodwind 4tet and string 4tet (1931), 4 sonatinas for vln. and pf. (1929–35).

Škerjanc, Lucijan Marija (b Graz, 17 Dec 1900; d Ljubljana, 27 Feb 1973), Yugoslav pianist, composer and conductor. Studied in Prague, Vienna (J. Marx), Basle and Paris (d'Indy), taught and cond. at Ljubljana, but later retired to devote himself to comp.

Works incl. cantatas, 5 symphs. (1931–43) and other orchestral works, vln. and pf. concertos, 5 string 4tets (1917–45).

Skilton, Charles Sanford (b Northampton, Mass., 16 Aug 1868; d Lawrence, Kans., 12 Mar 1941), American composer. Studied at Yale Univ. and in Ger. In 1903 he was app. Prof. of Music at Kansas Univ. and there made a study of Indian tribal tunes.

Works incl. operas *Kalopin* (comp. 1927), *The Sun Bride* (1930), *The Day of Gayomair* (comp. 1936); incid. music for Sophocles' *Electra* and Barrie's *Mary Rose*; oratorio *The Guardian Angel* and cantatas; *Primeval Suite* and other suites and overtures for orch.; 2 *Indian Dances* for string 4tet; vln. and pf. sonata; organ and pf. works.

Skočná, a Czech dance in quick 2–4 time in which 3-bar phrases are a feature. The 5th, 7th and 11th of Dvořák's *Slavonic Dances* for pf. duet are *Skočnás*.

Skram, Knut (b Saebo, 18 Dec 1937), Norwegian baritone. Debut Oslo 1964, as Amonasro. Well known in concerts and Lieder recitals. Glyndebourne 1969–76, as Guglielmo, Papageno and Mozart's Figaro.

Skriabin, Alexander Nikolaievich (b Moscow, 6 Jan 1872; d Moscow, 27 Apr 1915), Russian composer and pianist. Giving up a military career, he studied pf. with Safonov and comp. with Taneiev at the Moscow Cons., where he became prof. of pf. in 1898 after touring successfully in western Europe. He gave up that post in 1904 to devote himself entirely to comp. and occasional appearances as pianist. He visited Eng. on several occasions, notably in 1913 and 1914.

Works incl. 3 symphs. (1899–1904; no. 3 *The Divine Poem*), *Rêverie* and *Poem of Ecstasy* for orch.; pf. concerto in F♯ min. (1896), *Prometheus: a Poem of Fire* for orch., pf. and organ (and a projected colour org., 1910); 10 pf. sonatas (1892–1913) and 58 op. nos. of other pf. works, incl. preludes, impromptus, studies, mazurkas, nocturnes, *Tragic Poem, Satanic Poem, Vers la flamme*, prelude and nocturne for the left hand.

Škroup, František Jan (b Osice nr. Pardubice, 3 Jun 1801; d Rotterdam, 7 Feb 1862), Bohemian composer. Studied law, but was from 1827 2nd and in 1837–57 1st cond. at the Nat. Theatre in Prague; from 1860 cond. at the Opera of Rotterdam. Comp. the 1st Czech opera and the national anthem.

Works incl. operas *Drátenik (The Tinker,* 1826), *The Marriage of Libuša* (1835), *Oldřich and Božena* (1828), *Drahomira* (1848) and some other Cz. and Ger. operas; incid. music to Tyl's *Fidlovačka;* 3 string 4tets and other chamber music; songs.

Skrowaczewski, Stanislaw (b Lwów, 3 Oct 1923), American conductor of Polish birth. He studied in Poland, and with Boulanger in Paris. After an early career as a pianist he held var. cond. posts in Poland, 1946–59. US debut Cleveland, 1958; music dir. Minneapolis SO 1960–79. Prin. cond. Hallé Orch. from 1984. Also composes.

Skuherský, František Zdeněk (b Opočno, 31 Jul 1830; d Budejovice, 19 Aug 1892), Bohemian composer and teacher. He gave up medical studies for music, which he studied under Kittl and Pitsch, the directors of the Prague Cons. and Organ School respectively. In 1854–65 he was cond. at Innsbruck, but returned to Prague as dir. of the Organ School in the latter year. He was also active as pianist and as lecturer at the Czech Univ., and he took part in the reform of church music after studying it in Rome and Regensburg. He wrote several theoretical treatises.

Works incl. operas *Samo* (comp. 1854), *Vladimir: God's Chosen* (1863), *Lora* (1861), *Rector and General* (1873) and *The Love Ring*; symph. poem *May* and 3 fugues for orch.; string 4tet (1871), pf. 5tet, pf. trio.

Skyscrapers, ballet by Carpenter (choreography by Heinrich Kröller), prod. Monte Carlo, Rus. Ballet, 1925; 1st US perf. NY Met 19 Feb 1926.

Slatkin, Leonard (b Los Angeles, 1 Sep 1944), American conductor. He studied with Castelnuovo-Tedesco in Los Angeles and at the Juilliard School. He has been guest cond. with most leading orchs. in the USA and with the LSO and Concertgebouw Orch. Prin. cond. St Louis SO from 1979. Many perfs. of contemporary music.

Sleeping Beauty, The (*Spyashchaya krasavitsa*), ballet by Tchaikovsky (choreography by Petipa), prod. St Petersburg, Maryinsky Theatre, 15 Jan 1890; new version, with addit. orchs. by Stravinsky and addits. to the choreography by Bronislava Nizhinska, London, Alhambra Theatre, 2 Nov 1921.

Slentando (It.) = Gradually decreasing in pace.

Slezak, Leo (b Šumperk, 18 Aug 1873; d Egern, Bavaria, 1 Jun 1946), Moravian tenor. He studied engineering, but had his voice trained at the same time and in 1896 made his debut at Brno as Lohengrin. He was a member of the Vienna Staatsoper from 1901 to 1926 as Tannhäuser, Lohengrin and Radames. NY Met 1908–13 as Otello, Walther and Manrico. After retiring from the stage he made a successful career as a film actor. He pub. several autobiog. works.

Slide, the device of passing from one note to another on string instruments by moving the finger along the string instead of lifting it to make way for another finger; also the mov-

able part of the tube of the tromb. by which the positions, and therefore the notes, are altered, as well as mechanisms on other wind instruments by which the pitch can be adjusted by a change in the length of the tube.

Slobodskaya, Oda (b Vilna, 10 Dec 1888; d London, 29 Jul 1970), Russian soprano. Debut St Petersburg, 1919, as Lisa; much admired in operas by Rimsky-Korsakov and Glinka and as Sieglinde and Elisabeth de Valois. She created Parasha in Stravinsky's *Mavra*, Paris 1922, and at CG in 1935 she was Palmyra in the 1st Brit. perf. of Delius's *Koanga*, under Beecham. In Milan and Buenos Aires she was heard in operas by Tchaikovsky and Mussorgsky. She settled in London and taught at the GSM.

Slonimsky, Nicolas (orig. Nikolai) (b St Petersburg, 27 Apr 1894), Russian musical author, conductor and composer. Studied at the St Petersburg Cons. and in 1923 settled in USA, becoming a naturalized Amer. in 1931. He compiled a survey, *Music since 1900* (1937, rev. 1971; supplement 1986); ed. *Baker's Biographical Dictionary of Musicians*, editions 5, 6 and 7 (1958, 1978, 1985). As a cond. he gave early perfs. of works by Varèse, Ruggles, Cowell and Ives.

Works incl. *Fragment from Orestes* (Euripides) for orch. (in quarter-tones); *Studies in Black and White* for pf. The opera *Mary Stuart* by his nephew **Sergei** (b 1932) was prod. at the 1986 Edinburgh Fest.

Slur, an arching stroke in musical notation drawn over a group of notes and indicating that they are to be played *legato*. It is also used in vocal music where 2 or more notes are to be sung to the same syllable.

Sly (i.e. Christopher Sly), opera by Wolf-Ferrari (lib. by G. Forzano, based on the prologue of Shakespeare's *Taming of the Shrew*), prod. Milan, La Scala, 29 Dec 1927.

Smallens, Alexander (b St Petersburg, 1 Jan 1889; d Tucson 24 Nov 1972), American conductor of Russian birth. He studied in NY and at the Paris Cons.; became a US citizen in 1919 and cond. the Chicago Opera 1919–23 (fp Prokofiev *The Love for Three Oranges*). He worked in Philadelphia 1924–36 and gave there the 1st US perfs. of Strauss's *Feuersnot* and *Ariadne auf Naxos*, Rimsky-Korsakov's *Invisible City of Kitezh* and Gluck's *Iphigénie en Aulide*. He cond. the fp of *Porgy and Bess*, Boston 1935, and gave its Brit. première in London in 1952. Retired 1958.

Smalley, Roger (b Swinton, Manchester, 26 Jul 1943), English composer and pianist. He studied at the RCM with Fricker; study with

Stockhausen in Cologne was a formative influence. From 1969 to 1976 active with group Intermodulation; electronic and aleatory effects also present in his music.

Works incl. 7tet for sop. and ens. (text by cummings, 1963), *Gloria tibi Trinitas* for orch. (1965), *Missa Parodia* for ens. (1967), *The Song of the Highest Tower* for sop., bar., chorus and orch. (texts by Blake and Rimbaud, 1968), *Pulses* for 5 × 4 players (1969), *Beat Music* for 4 elec. insts. and orch. (1971), *Zeitebenen* for 4 players and tape (1973), *William Derrincourt* for bar., chorus and ens. (1977), string 4tet (1979), *Konzertstück* for vln. and orch. (1980), Symphony in 1 movt. (1981).

Smareglia, Antonio (b Pola, Istria, 5 May 1854; d Grado nr. Trieste, 15 Apr 1929), Italian composer. He was sent to Vienna to study engineering, but on hearing works by the great masters there he left for Milan in 1872 and studied comp. under Faccio at the Cons. He prod. his 1st opera there in 1879, but he never had any real success, in spite of the good quality of his work, and in 1900 he went blind.

Works incl. operas *Preziosa* (1879), *Bianca da Cervia* (1882), *Rè Nala* (1887), *Der Vasall von Szigeth* (1889), *Cornelius Schutt* (1893), *Nozze istriane*, *La Falena* (1897), *Oceàna* (1903), *L'Abisso*; symph. poem *Leonore*, songs.

Smart, George (Thomas) (b London, 10 May 1776; d London, 23 Feb 1867), English organist, composer and conductor. He was sent by his father, George S., a music pub., to become a choir-boy at the Chapel Royal under Ayrton, and later became a comp. pupil of Arnold. He became an organist, teacher and cond., was one of the orig. members of the Phil. Society in 1813 and succeeded Charles Knyvett as organist of the Chapel Royal in 1822. In 1825 he gave the fp in Britain of Beethoven's 9th symph. and went to Dresden with Charles Kemble to engage Weber to write *Oberon* for Covent Garden. It was at his house that Weber stayed during the prod. in 1826 and died in the night of 4–5 Jun. Smart was knighted in 1811, and became a favourite festival cond.

Works incl. anthems, chants and other church music; canons and glees.

Smart, Henry (Thomas) (b London, 26 Oct 1813; d London, 6 Jul 1879), English organist and composer, nephew of prec. Learnt music from his father, the violinist Henry S. (1778–1823), and later under W.H. Kearns, but was largely self-taught. After an organist's appt. at Blackburn in 1831–6 he re-

turned to London and was successively organist at several churches until he became blind in 1864.

Works incl. operas *Berta, or The Gnome of the Hartzberg* (1855), *Undine* and *The Surrender of Calais* (last 2 unfinished); cantatas *The Bride of Dunkerron, King René's Daughter* (after Herz, 1871), *The Fishermaidens* (1871) and *Jacob* (1873); festival anthems *Sing to the Lord* and *Lord, thou hast been our refuge*; organ works; part-songs.

Smert, Richard (b ? Devon) English 15th-cent. composer. Carols of his for 2 voices and 3-part chorus, some written with John Truelove, are preserved. He was a vicar-choral of Exeter Cathedral, 1428–*c* 1465 and rector at Plymtree, Devon, 1435–77.

Smetáček, Václav (b Brno, 30 Sep 1906; d Prague, 18 Feb 1986), Czech conductor and oboist. He studied at the Prague Cons.; played in Prague Wind Quintet 1928–55. Cond. Prague Radio orch. 1934–43 and was often heard with the Czech PO. British debut 1938. On record and in tours of Europe and S. Amer. he cond. operas by Smetana, Janáček, Mussorgsky and Shostakovich.

Smetana, Bedřich (b Litomyšl, Boh., 2 Mar 1824; d Prague, 12 May 1884), Czech composer. Son of a brewer. He played pf. and vln. at a very early age and was soon able to play in the domestic string 4tet. He was educ. in Ger. and all his life, in spite of his musical nationalism, spoke and wrote Cz. like a foreigner. He was sent to school 1st in Prague and then at Pilsen. His father opposed a musical career, but he was in the end allowed to study music in Prague, though with a very small allowance. In 1844 he obtained the post of music master in Count Thun's family, which helped to support him until 1847. In 1848 he took part in the revolution against Aus., married the pianist Kateřina Kolařová, estab. a school of music for which Liszt supplied funds, and was recommended by the latter to the Leipzig pub. Kistner.

In 1856 he went to Göteborg in Swed., where at first he taught but later became cond. of the new Phil. Society and gave pf. and chamber music recitals. He returned to Prague in 1859 because the northern climate did not suit his wife, who died at Dresden on the way back, 19 Apr. He married Bettina Ferdinandová in Jul 1860 and returned to Swed. in the autumn, but finally returned to Prague in the spring of 1861. After a long tour in Ger., Hol. and Swed. to collect funds, he settled in the Cz. capital in 1863 and opened another school of music, this time with dinstinctly national tendencies, and became cond. of the choral society Hlahol. His work too was now becoming thoroughly Cz. in character, and he began to prod. Cz. operas in the national theatre estab. in 1864, of which he became cond. in Sep 1866. In 1874 he suddenly became totally deaf, as the result of a syphilitic infection, but still comp. operas as well as the string 4tet *From my Life* and the cycle of symph. poems *My Country*. In 1883 he became insane and in May 1884 he had to be taken to an asylum, where he died.

Works incl. OPERAS *The Brandenburgers in Bohemia* (1866), *The Bartered Bride* (1866), *Dalibor* (1868), *Libuše* (1881), *Two Widows* (1874), *The Kiss*, *The Secret* (1878), *The Devil's Wall* (1882), *Viola* (based on Shakespeare's *Twelfth Night*, unfinished).

ORCHESTRAL: 3 concert overtures; symph. poems *Richard III* (after Shakespeare, 1858), *Wallenstein's Camp* (after Schiller), *Haakon Jarl* (1861); cycle of symph. poems *My Country* containing *Vyšehrad, Vltava, Šárka, In the Bohemian Woods and Fields, Tábor, Blanik* (1872–94); Festival March.

CHAMBER AND PIANO: Pf. trio in G min. (1855), 2 string 4tets (1876, 1883; 1st *From my Life*); 8 op. nos. of pf. works and many miscellaneous pf. pieces incl. *Wedding Scenes, Scenes from Macbeth*, Cz. dances, etc.; a cantata and a number of part-songs; 3 books of songs.

Smirnov, Dmitry (b Moscow, 7 Nov 1881; d Riga, 27 Apr 1944), Russian tenor. Sang at Bolshoy 1904–10, St Petersburg until 1917. Appeared in the Diaghilev seasons, Paris. NY Met debut 1910, Duke of Mantua. Sang in Rimsky-Korsakov's *May Night* at Drury Lane, London, 1914. Other roles incl. Lensky, Luigi and Lohengrin.

Smith, Bernard (Bernhard Schmidt) (b Germany, 1629; d London, Feb 1708), German organ builder. Settled in Eng. from 1660. His 1st Eng. organ was at the Chapel Royal in London. App. organist at St Margaret's Church, Westminster, after building the organ there. He also built organs at Durham Cathedral and St Paul's Cathedral, London. Known as Father Smith.

Smith, Carleton Sprague (b New York, 8 Aug 1905), American critic, musicologist and flautist. Studied at Harvard Univ. and in Vienna. After a year as critic to the *Boston Transcript*, he became chief librarian of the music section of the NY Public Library and lecturer in history of music at Columbia

Univ. In 1938 he was president of the Amer. Musicological Society.

Smith, Cyril (James) (b Middlesbrough, 11 Aug 1909; d London, 2 Aug 1974), English pianist. Studied at RCM; debut Birmingham. Well known in Brahms and Rakhmaninov. Married Phyllis Sellick and formed pf. duet with her from 1941. Suffered stroke 1956, paralysing left arm; thereafter played music for 3 hands with his wife. OBE 1971.

Smith, David Stanley (b Toledo, Ohio, 6 Jul 1877; d New Haven, Conn., 17 Dec 1949), American composer, conductor and teacher. Studied with H. Parker at Yale Univ. and later in London, Munich and Paris. In 1903 he became instructor and later prof. of music at Yale.

Works incl. *The Fallen Star* for chorus and orch. (1904), *Rhapsody of St Bernard* for solo voices, chorus and orch. (1915), *The Vision of Isaiah* for chorus (1926); anthems; part-songs; 4 symphs. (1905–37); 10 string 4tets; songs.

Smith, John Christopher (b Ansbach, 1712; d Bath, 3 Oct 1795), German (anglicized) organist and composer, son of Johann Christoph Schmidt of Ansbach, who went to London as Handel's treasurer and copyist. Smith became a pupil of Handel, and later of Pepusch and T. Roseingrave. In 1746–8 he travelled on the Continent and in 1754 became organist of the Foundling Hospital. He acted as Handel's amanuensis during the composer's blindness.

Works incl. operas *Teraminta, Ulysses* (1733), *Issipile* (1743), *Ciro riconosciuto* (1745), *Dario* (1746), *The Fairies* (from Shakespeare's *Midsummer Night's Dream*, 1755), *The Tempest* (after Shakespeare, 1756); *Rosalinda* (1740), *The Enchanter, or Love and Magic* (Garrick, 1760); oratorios *David's Lamentation over Saul and Jonathan* (1738), *Paradise Lost* (after Milton, 1758), *Rebecca, Judith* (1758), *Jehoshaphat* (1764), *The Redemption* (1774); Burial Service; instrumental works.

Smith, John Stafford (b Gloucester, 30 Mar 1750; d London, 21 Sep 1836), English organist, tenor and composer. Pupil of his father, Martin S., organist at Gloucester Cathedral, and later of Boyce and Nares in London, where he was a chorister in the Chapel Royal. He became a Gentleman of the Chapel Royal in 1784, organist of Gloucester Cathedral in 1790 and in 1802 of the Chapel Royal in succession to Arnold, succeeding Ayrton as Master of the Children in 1805. He assisted Hawkins in his *History of Music*.

Works incl. anthems, glees, catches, canons, madrigals, part-songs; songs incl. *Anacreon in Heaven* (now *The Star-spangled Banner*).

Smith, Robert (b *c* 1648; d ? London, 22 Nov 1675), English composer. Chorister at the Chapel Royal in London under Cooke; became Musician in Ordinary to the King on the death of Humfrey in 1674. Works incl. incid. music for numerous plays (some with Staggins and others); music for strings; harpsichord pieces; songs, duets.

Smith, Ronald (b London, 3 Jan 1922), English pianist and writer on music. He studied at the RCM and made his debut in London at a 1942 Promenade concert; he has given many perfs. of the huge pf. works of Alkan: his books on the comp. incl. *Alkan, The Man and His Music* (1975), *A. The Enigma* (1976) and *A. in Miniature* (1978).

Smith Brindle, Reginald (b Bamber Bridge, 5 Jan 1917), English composer, teacher and writer on music. He studied in Italy with Pizzetti and Dallapiccola and worked for RAI, Italian radio, 1956–61. Professor, Univ. of Surrey, from 1970. His music is influenced by Berio and Stockhausen, and employs electronic techniques.

Works incl. chamber opera *Antigone* (1969), Symph. (1954), *Vars. on theme of Dallapiccola* for orch. (1955), *Extremum carmen* for voices and orch. (1956), *String 4tet Music* (1958), *Creation Epic* for orch. (1964), *Worlds without End* for speaker, voices, orch. and tapes (1973), *The Walls of Jericho* for tuba and tape (1974), *Guitar Cosmos* (1976). His books incl. *Serial Composition* (1966) and *The New Music* (1975).

Smorzando (It. = toning down), a direction indicating that a passage is to be perf. with an effect of calming down or fading away.

Smyth, Ethel (Mary) (b London, 22 Apr 1858; d Woking, 9 May 1944), English composer. Studied at the Leipzig Cons. and then privately there with Herzogenberg. She had some works perf. there and after her return to Eng. one or two appeared in London, incl. the Mass in 1893. Her earlier operas were prod. in Ger. She lived much abroad, but in 1910 received the hon. D. Mus. degree from Durham Univ. and about that time joined actively in the movement for women's suffrage. In her later years she lived at Woking in Surrey and, regarding herself as neglected on account of her sex, comp. less and less, but wrote a number of autobiog. books. She received the honour of a DBE in 1922. Dur-

ing her last years she suffered much from deafness and distorted hearing.

Works incl. operas *Fantasio*, after Musset (Weimar, 1898), *The Forest* (Berlin, 1902), *The Wreckers* (Leipzig, 1906), *The Boatswain's Mate* (after W.W. Jacobs, 1916), *Fête galante* (1923), *Entente cordiale* (1925); Mass in D maj.; *The Prison*, for solo voices, chorus and orch.; overture to Shakespeare's *Antony and Cleopatra*, serenade for orch. (1890); concerto for vln., horn and orch.; 3 Anacreontic Odes for voice and orch.; string 5tet, string 4tet; sonatas, songs.

Smythe, William (b *c* 1550; d Durham, *c* 1600), English composer. He was a minor canon and later master of the choristers (1594–98) at Durham Cathedral. He wrote a number of works for the Anglican church, not to be confused with those by his later namesake, 'William Smith of Durham'.

Snares, gut strings stretched over one of the heads of some types of drum, esp. the Side-drum, adding brilliance to their tone by vibrating against the skin as the drum is struck. If that effect is not required, the snares can be temporarily slackened.

Snow Maiden, The (*Snegurotchka*), opera by Rimsky-Korsakov (lib. by comp. based on a play by A.N. Ostrovsky), prod. St Petersburg, 10 Feb 1882.

Snow, Valentine (b ? London; d London, Dec 1770), English trumpeter. Son of (?) Moses S., a Gentleman of the Chapel Royal in London and lay-vicar at Westminster Abbey. In 1753 he succeeded John Shore as Sergeant Trumpeter to the King. Handel wrote the tpt. obbligato parts in his oratorios for him.

Sobinov, Leonid (b Yaroslavl, 7 Jun 1872; d Riga, 14 Oct 1934), Russian tenor. He sang minor roles in Moscow from 1893; Bolshoy from 1897. In Russia and at La Scala, Monte Carlo and Berlin he was successful as Roméo, Lohengrin and Werther, and in such native roles as Lensky, Dubrovsky and Vladimir in *Prince Igor*. Noted for his elegance of manner and voice.

Sobolewski, (Friedrich) Eduard (b Königsberg, 1 Oct 1808; d St Louis, 17 May 1872), German-Polish composer and conductor. He was cond. at the Königsberg Theatre in succession to Dorn, 1830–6. Later he lived at Weimar and in 1859 he emigrated to USA, where he became cond. to the St Louis Phil. Society.

Works incl. operas *Komala* (after Ossian, prod. by Liszt at Weimar, 1858), *Imogene* (after Shakespeare's *Cymbeline*, 1833), *Velleda* (1836), *Salvator Rosa* and *Mohega*

(1859); oratorio *The Saviour*; symphs., symph. poems.

Socrate (*Socrates*), symph. drama by Satie (lib. taken from Victor Cousin's Fr. trans. of Plato's *Dialogues*), prod. Paris, 14 Feb 1920, and perf. Prague, festival of the ISCM, May 1925.

Söderman, (Johan) August (b Stockholm, 17 Jul 1832; d Stockholm, 10 Feb 1876), Swedish composer. Learnt music from his father, a theatre cond., at 18 went to Fin. as dir. of music to a Swed. company of musicians, and in 1856 prod. his 1st operetta at Helsinki. After a period of study at Leipzig he was app. chorus master at the Royal Opera at Stockholm in 1860 and 2nd cond. in 1862.

Works incl. operetta *The Devil's First Lesson* (1856) and others; incid. music to Schiller's *Maid of Orleans*, Topelius's *Regina* and other plays; Mass for solo voices, chorus and orch.; *Swedish Wedding* for female voices, cantatas and part-songs; vocal settings of Bellman's rhapsodies; *Circassian Dance* and concert overture for orch.; sacred songs and hymns with organ; ballads and songs for voice and pf.

Söderström, Elisabeth (b Stockholm, 7 May 1927), Swedish soprano. Studied in Stockholm, making her debut there in 1947 as Bastienne. Glyndebourne since 1957 as the Composer, Octavian, Christine and Leonore. London, CG, since 1960 as the Countess, Fiordiligi and Mélisande. NY Met 1959–64 (debut as Susanna). Janáček roles incl. Jenůfa and Emilia Marty. Noted for her warmth of voice and appealing stage presence.

Sofonisba, La, opera by Caldara (lib. by Francesco Silvani), prod. Venice, Teatro S. Giovanni Crisostomo, Dec 1708.

Opera by Gluck (lib. do., with airs from different libs. by Metastasio), prod. Milan, Teatro Regio Ducal, 18 Jan 1744.

Soft Pedal, the popular name for the Damping Pedal of the pf.

Soggetto (It.) = Subject, in the musical sense, esp. the subject of a fugue.

Soggetto cavato (It. = extracted subject), in the 15th cent. and thereabouts a vocal theme sung to a melody formed from the vowels of a sentence converted by the composer into musical notes of the hexachord: a = fa or la, e = re, i = mi, o = do, u = ut.

Sogno di Scipione, Il (*Scipio's Dream*), dramatic serenade by Mozart (lib. by Metastasio), prod. Salzburg, at the installation of the new archbishop, Hieronymus von Colloredo, 1 May 1772.

Dramatic serenade by Predieri (lib. do.), prod. Laxenburg, nr. Vienna, 1 Oct 1735.

Soh, the name for the Dominant note in any key in Tonic Sol-fa, so pronounced, but in notation represented by the letter **s**.

Sohier, Mathieu (b Noyon; d *c* 1560), French composer. He was master of the choristers at Notre-Dame, Paris, from 1533, and later canon of St-Denis-du-Pas. Comp. Masses, motets and *chansons*.

Sol, the old name for the note G (*see* **Solmization**), still used in Latin countries, and in Tonic Sol-fa notation the Dominant note in any key represented by the symbol **s** pronounced Soh.

Sol-fa. *See* **Solmization** and **Tonic Sol-fa**.

Solage, late 14th-cent. French composer. Wrote several *chansons*, found in the Chantilly MS.

Soldaten, Die (*The Soldiers*), opera in 4 acts by Bernd Alois Zimmermann (lib. by comp. after the play by Jakob Lenz, 1776); comp. 1958–60, rev. 1963–4, fp Cologne, 15 Feb 1965, cond. Gielen. Vocal Symphony for 5 soloists and orch. derived from the opera in 1958; use is made of ballet, mime, *sprechstimme*, electronics and film. The composer committed suicide in 1970, two years before the 1st Brit. perf., in Edinburgh.

Soleil des eaux, Le (*The Sun of the Waters*), music by Boulez for radio play by René Char, 1948; rev. as cantata for sop., tenor, bar. and chamber orch.; fp Paris, 18 Jul 1950; rev. with addition of chorus and perf. Darmstadt, 9 Sep 1958; further revision perf. London, Jan 25 1988.

Soler, Antonio (b Olot, Catalonia, bap. 3 Dec 1729; d El Escorial, 20 Dec 1783), Spanish friar, organist and composer. A chorister at Montserrat, he was *maestro de capilla* at Lérida Cathedral and entered the Escorial monastery in 1752, becoming organist and choirmaster there the following year. He was prob. a pupil of D. Scarlatti 1752–7. His treatise *Llave de la Modulación* was pub. in 1762.

Works incl. incid. music for plays by Calderón and others; 9 Masses, motets and other church music; 132 *villancicos*; 5tets for org. and strings; organ concertos; 120 harpsichord sonatas.

Solerti, Angelo (b Savona, 20 Sep 1865; d Massa Carrara, 10 Feb 1907), Italian musicologist. He wrote several works on the origins of dramatic music in the early 17th century.

Solfège (Fr.)
Solfeggio (It.)   } an elementary method of teaching sight-reading and of ear-training,

practised mainly in Fr. and It. The names of the notes ('Do, re, mi', etc.) are pronounced while the notes are sung unaccomp. and the intervals have thus to be learnt by ear.

Soli (It. plur. of **Solo**). The word designates a group of solo perfs. as distinct from the whole vocal or orchestral body employed in a work.

Solié (orig. Soulier), **Jean-Pierre** (b Nîmes, 1755; d Paris, 6 Aug 1812), French singer, cellist and composer. A chorister at Nîmes Cathedral, he learnt the cello from his father and played in local theatres. He made his debut as a singer in 1778 and from 1787 was at the Opéra-Comique in Paris, rising to become leading baritone. Many of Méhul's roles were written for him. From *c* 1790 he also had success as an opera composer.

Works incl. 33 *opéras-comiques*, e.g. *Jean et Geneviève* (1792), *Le Jockey* (1796), *Le Secret*, *Le Chapitre second* (1799), *Mademoiselle de Guise*, *Le Diable à quatre* (1809), *Les Ménestrels* (1811).

Solmization (from Lat. *solmisatio*), the designation of the musical scales by means of syllables, at the same time indicating Mutation according to the Gamut. The notes of the Greek Tetrachords were already designated by syllables, but Guido d'Arezzo in the 11th cent. replaced them by the Hexachords and used the Lat. syllables Ut, Re, Mi, Fa, Sol, La for their 6 notes, Si being added later for the 7th and Ut being replaced by Do in It. and elsewhere, though still largely retained

lines of the plainsong of which began on the successive notes of the hexachord:

UT queant laxis
REsonare fibris
MIra gestorum
FAmuli tuorum
SOLve polluti
LAbii reatum
Sancte Ioannes.

The 7th syllable, Si, was derived from the initial letters of the last line.

Solo (It. = alone), as a noun, a piece or part of a comp. sung or played by a single perf., with or without accomp. The word is also used adjectivally in directions given in It., e.g. *violino solo* (to be played by one vln. alone), *voce sola* (voice unaccomp.), etc.

Solomon, oratorio by Handel (lib. ? by Newburgh Hamilton), perf. London, CG, 17 Mar 1749.

Solomon (actually Solomon Cutner) (b London, 9 Aug 1902), English pianist. Made his first public appearance at Queen's Hall aged 8, in Tchaikovsky's 1st pf. concerto, and then studied in Paris, beginning his true career in 1923. His brilliant technique and musicianship made him outstanding among modern pianists; widely admired in Mozart, Chopin and Brahms. Paralysed from 1965.

Soloviev, Nikolai Feopemptovich (b Petrozavodsk, 9 May 1846; d Petrograd, 27 Dec 1916), Russian composer. Began by studying medicine, but turned to music and en-

SOLMIZATION

in Fr. These syllables, as in modern Tonic Sol-fa with movable Doh, were not immutably fixed to C, D, E, F, G, A, but could be transferred by Mutation to other degrees of the scale, so long as the semitone always occurred between Mi and Fa. The so-called 'natural hexachord' beginning on C could thus be changed to the 'hard hexachord' beginning on G, in which case Mi–Fa corresponded with B–C, or to the 'soft hexachord' beginning on F (*see* **Hexachord**). The syllables were derived from a hymn of the year 770 for the festival of St John the Baptist, the

tered the St Petersburg Cons., Zaremba being among his masters. He became prof. there in 1874. In 1871 Serov, when dying, charged him with the orch. of his opera *The Power of Evil*. He was also a critic and collector of folksongs.

Works incl. operas *Cordelia* (after Sardou's *La Haine*, 1885), *Vakula the Smith* (on Gogol's *Christmas Eve*, 1875) and *The Cottage of Kolomua*; cantata for the bicentenary of Peter the Great; symph. poem *Russians and Mongols* and Fantasy on a Folksong for orch.; pf. pieces; songs.

Solti, Sir **Georg** (b Budapest, 21 Oct 1912), Hungarian conductor and pianist. Studied at the Budapest Cons., pf. with Dohnányi and comp. with Kodály and Bartók. From 1930 to 1939 he cond. at the Budapest Opera and then went to Switz., where he was active both as pianist and cond., winning first prize for pf. at the Concours International at Geneva in 1942. In 1946 he became cond. at the Munich Staatsoper and in 1952–61 dir. of the Frankfurt Opera. US debut San Francisco 1953 (*Elektra*). In 1959 he made his debut at Covent Garden in *Der Rosenkavalier* and was dir. from 1961 to 1971; his decade was noted for prods. of *The Ring, Arabella, Moses und Aron* and *Die Frau ohne Schatten*. Chicago SO from 1969, LPO 1979–83. In spite of an international career he has not neglected British music: often heard in Tippett and Elgar. Noted for the brilliance of his style. Re-appeared as concert soloist 1986 (Mozart's D min. concerto). He has also made many highly successful recordings, among them the complete *Ring* (1958–64), and is the 1st cond. to record all of Wagner's major operas. Honorary knighthood 1971; Brit citizen from 1972.

Sołtys, Adam (b Lwów, 4 Jul 1890; d Lwów, 6 Jul 1968), Polish composer and conductor. Studied at Lwów Cons., the Berlin Hochschule für Musik and the Kunstakademie, and Berlin Univ. Prof. at Lwów Cons. from 1921 (director, 1930–9) and cond. of the symph. orch.
Works incl. 2 symphs., symph. poem *Slowianie (The Slavs)*; chamber music; variations for pf.; songs.

Sołtys, Mieczysław (b Lwów, 7 Feb 1863; d Lwów, 12 Nov 1929), Polish composer and conductor, father of prec. Studied in Vienna and Paris, where he was a pupil of Saint-Saëns. He returned to Lwów in 1891 and became director of the Cons. and cond. of the Music Assoc.
Works incl. operas *The Republic of Babin* (1905), *Maria* (on Antoni Malczewski's poem), *Panie Kochanku* (1924) and others; oratorios; symph., symph. poem *The Fugitive*.

Sombrero de tres picos, El (*The Three-cornered Hat*), ballet by Falla (scenario by Martínez Sierra, based on Alarcón's story; choreog. by Massin), prod. London, Alhambra Theatre, 22 Jul 1919. The setting and dresses were designed by Picasso.

Somervell, Arthur (b Windermere, 5 Jun 1863; d London, 2 May 1937), English composer and educationist. Educ. at Uppingham School and King's Coll., Cambridge, where

he studied comp. with Stanford, going later to Kiel in Berlin, to the RCM in London in 1885 and to Parry as a private pupil in 1887. In 1894 he became prof. at the RCM. Knighted 1929.
Works incl. Masses in C min. (1891) and D min. (the latter for male voices, 1907), anthem *Let all the world*, oratorio *The Passion of Christ*, cantatas *A Song of Praise, The Power of Sound, The Forsaken Merman* (Matthew Arnold), *Ode to the Sea* and others; symph. in D min., *Thalassa* (1912), concerto in G min. and *Concertstück* for vln. and orch.; clar. 5tet; vln. and pf. sonata; Variations on an Original Theme for 2 pfs.; vln. pieces; pf. pieces; song cycles *Maud* (Tennyson), *A Shropshire Lad* (A.E. Housman, 1904).

Somigli, Franca (b Chicago, 1901; d Trieste, 14 May 1974), American soprano (orig. Marion Bruce Clark). Debut Rovigo 1926, as Mimi; Pavia 1927, as the *Trovatore* Leonora. Rome and La Scala 1933–44; 1935 in the fp of Pizzetti's *Orséleo*, and as Arabella, the Marschallin, Kundry and Sieglinde. At Salzburg she sang Alice Ford, under Toscanini. NY Met 1937, Butterfly. At the Berlin Staatsoper in 1944 she was Salome, under De Sabata.

Somis, Giovanni Battista (b Turin, 25 Dec 1686; d Turin, 14 Aug 1763), Italian violinist and composer. Pupil of Corelli in Rome and (?) Vivaldi at Venice. Returning to Turin, he was app. violinist to the King of Piedmont and leader of the royal orch. About 1733 he lived in Paris for a time. He taught many famous pupils, incl. Leclair, Giardini and Pugnani.
Works incl. vln. concertos; sonatas.

Somis, Lorenzo (b Turin, 11 Nov 1688; d Turin, 29 Nov 1775), Italian violinist and composer, brother of prec. Lived in Turin as violinist in the royal orch. Comp. vln. sonatas, etc.

Sommeils (Fr., plur. of *sommeil* = sleep), quiet airs in old French operas supposed to induce sleep.

Sommer, Hans (actually Hans Friedrich August Zincken, sometimes anag. 'Neckniz') (b Brunswick, 20 Jul 1837; d Brunswick, 28 Apr 1922), German composer. Studied at Göttingen Univ. and became prof. of physics there. In 1875 he became dir. of the Technical High School at Brunswick, settled in Berlin in 1885, at Weimar in 1888, and in 1898 returned to Brunswick. He had been comp. as an amateur since before 1865, when he prod. his 1st opera.
Works incl. operas *Der Nachtwächter*

(1865), *Loreley* (1891), *Saint-Foix, Der Meermann, Augustin, Münchhausen, Rübezahl* (1904), *Riquet mit dem Schopf* (1907) and *Der Waldschratt* (1912); song cycles from Julius Wolff's *Der wilde Jäger (Mädchenlieder), Hunold Singuf* and *Tannhäuser*, from Carmen Sylva's *Sappho* and many other songs.

Son and Stranger (Mendelssohn). *See* **Heimkehr aus der Fremde**.

Sonata (It. and Eng.), a term designating both a type of composition and a musical form. The classical sonata is normally a comp. in 3 or 4 movements, the 1st of which is with few exceptions in sonata form, and often the last, though that is at least as frequently a Rondo. The word is derived from *suonare* or *sonare* = 'to sound': a sonata is thus orig. simply 'a thing sounded', i.e. played, as distinct from a Cantata (from *cantare*), 'a thing sung'. But in the 17th cent. the sonata developed into the two types described hereunder, the sonata da camera and the sonata da chiesa. In the 18th cent. the 1-movement sonatas of D. Scarlatti began to approximate to the modern 1st-movement form, while other works of the kind, esp. in Ger., still approximated to the Suite, from which indeed the mature sonata borrowed the minuet (later developed into the Scherzo), but often dropped it in favour of a 3-movement comp.: 1st movement in sonata form, slow movement, and finale in sonata or rondo form.

The modern 1st-movement form, developed through C.P.E. Bach and some of his contemporaries, reached full maturity in the hands of Haydn, Mozart and others, and was greatly strained by the innovations of Beethoven, e.g. in his type of sonata quasi una fantasia and late works, which admitted fugal developments and variations. After Beethoven the sonata became often so much modified as to lose its classical shape, e.g. in the hands of Schumann and Chopin, to whom it was uncongenial, or in those of Liszt, who intro. his principle of thematic transformation (as distinct from development) into it.

The sonata form in its fully matured but not sophisticated manifestations shows the following main outlines: a single movement in 2 principal sections, the 1st called the Exposition, ending in another key than that of the tonic. Two main thematic groups make up its material, with room for subsidiary themes and connecting bridge passages. These groups are traditionally described as First and Second Subjects. The 1st is in the

tonic key, the 2nd in a related key (e.g. the dominant in a movement in a maj. key and the relative maj. in one in a min. key). The 2nd section begins with a Development, which, as its name suggests, develops some of the foregoing material in new ways, but may also partly or even exclusively intro. new matter (e.g. as in Mozart). This Development leads to the Recapitulation, where the opening of the movement, i.e. the 1st subject, returns as before, though possibly with varied treatment; the 2nd subject also appears in the tonic key, maj. or min., and in the latter case it is often in min. even if in the 1st section it appeared in maj. All this necessitates a new modulatory transition between 1st and 2nd subjects. The movement may end in the tonic exactly as the 1st section ended in another key; but there may be a Coda added, either a very brief tail-piece of a merely ceremonial nature or a more developed section which may further work upon the foregoing material, as often in the case of Beethoven. Not only works so called are sonatas, but also chamber music of the normal classical type and symphs.

Sonata da camera (It. = chamber sonata), an instrumental work of the late 17th and early 18th cent. of the Suite or Partita type in several movements, mainly in dance forms, but always for more than 1 instrument, most usually 2 vlns. with continuo for bass viol or cello with a keyboard instrument, generally harpsichord. Unlike the sonata da chiesa, the sonata da camera usually had a quick 1st movement.

Sonata da chiesa (It. = church sonata), an instrumental work of the late 17th and early 18th cent., frequently, though not invariably, in 4 movements (slow intro., fugal *allegro*, slow *cantabile* movement and quick finale), written for more than 1 instrument, most usually 2 vlns. with continuo for bass viol or cello with a keyboard instrument, which if played in church must have been generally the organ.

Sonata quasi una fantasia (It. = sonata, as it were a fantasy), a term invented by Beethoven for some of his sonatas in which he began to modify the form freely, the 2 works of op. 27 for pf. being the 1st of the kind.

Sonatina (It. dim. of sonata = little sonata), a work of the sonata type in a condensed form or easy to play. The 1st movement of a sonatina usually contains the normal 1st and 2nd subjects, though as a rule they are less extended, but it may have only a rudimentary working-out section and coda or none at all. The key-scheme for the reappearance of the 2 subjects in the 2nd section, however, will be similar to that in a sonata. Sonatinas have often been written for teaching purposes, esp. for the pf.

Song, strictly speaking any poem set to music for a single voice, with or without an accomp., is a song, but the species is distinct from other forms of vocal comp. such as the aria, the ballad, the couplet, etc. A song may either be set to a repetition of the same tune ('strophic'), or be set continuously ('through-composed'), the music developing throughout in a manner calculated to illustrate the progress of the words.

Song Cycle, a series of songs set as a rule to a number of poems with a connected narrative or some other unifying feature. Schubert's *Die schöne Müllerin* and *Winterreise*, for cx., are thus song cycles properly speaking, while his *Schwanengesang* is not. An earlier example is Beethoven's *An die ferne Geliebte*: later ones are Schumann's *Dichterliebe* and *Frauenliebe und -leben*, Fauré's *La Bonne Chanson*, Debussy's *Chansons de Bilitis* and Vaughan Williams's *On Wenlock Edge.*

Song of Destiny (Brahms). *See* **Schicksalslied.**

Song of the Earth (Mahler). *See* **Lied von der Erde.**

Song of the High Hills, The, work by Delius for wordless chorus and orch.; comp. 1911, fp London, 26 Feb 1920, cond. Albert Coates.

Song of Triumph (Brahms). *See* **Triumphlied.**

Songe d'une nuit d'été, Le (*The Dream of a Midsummer Night*), opera by A. Thomas (lib. by J.B. Rosier and A. de Leuven, not based on Shakespeare's play), prod. Paris, Opéra-Comique, 20 Apr 1850. Shakespeare, Queen Elizabeth and Falstaff appear in it as characters.

Songs and Dances of Death, song cycle by Mussorgsky (poems by A.A. Golenishtchev-Kutuzov), comp. 1875–7: 1. *The Peasant's Lullaby*; 2. *Serenade*; 3. *Trepak*; 4. *The Field Marshal.* Orch. by Shostakovich, 1962.

Songs of Farewell, work by Delius for chorus and orch. (text by Walt Whitman); comp. 1930, fp London, 21 Mar 1932, cond. Sargent.

Songs of Sunset, work by Delius for mezzo, bar., chorus and orch. (text by Ernest Dowson); comp. 1906–8, fp London, 16 Jun 1911, cond. Beecham.

Songs of Travel, 9 songs for voice and pf. by Vaughan Williams (texts by Robert Louis Stevenson), fp of nos. 1–8 London, 2 Dec

1904, with Hamilton Harty at the pf.; 1st complete perf. BBC, 21 May 1960.

Songs without Words (Mendelssohn). *See* **Lieder ohne Worte.**

Sonnambula, La (*The Sleepwalker*), opera by Bellini (lib. by F. Romani), prod. Milan, Teatro Carcano, 6 Mar 1831.

Sonore (Fr. = sonorous), an indication that a passage is to be played or sung with full tone. The It. term is *sonoro.*

Sons, Maurice (b Amsterdam, 13 Sep 1857; d London, 28 Sep 1942), Dutch violinist. Studied at the Brussels Cons. with Wieniawski and others, and with Rappoldi at Dresden. After an appt. in Switz. he settled in Scot. as leader of the Scot. Orch. and in 1904 became leader of the Queen's Hall Orch. in London, where he remained until 1927. He was vln. prof. at the RCM 1903–37.

Sontag, Henriette (Gertrud Walpurgis) (b Koblenz, 3 Jan 1806; d Mexico City, 17 Jun 1854), German soprano. The daughter of actors, she appeared on the stage as a child, but in 1815 entered the Prague Cons. as a singing-student, and in 1821 made a very successful stage appearance as an understudy in Boieldieu's *Jean de Paris.* She was then taken to Vienna for further study and at once appeared there in It. and Ger. opera, Weber choosing her to sing the title-part in *Euryanthe* in 1823. The following year in Vienna she took part in the fp of the Choral Symph. She 1st visited Paris in 1826 and London in 1828 (both debuts as Rosina). She married Count Rossi, a diplomat of the Sardinian court, and retired, living with him at var. courts in Hol., Ger. and Rus., but after the 1848 revolutions she reappeared on the stage, esp. in Eng. and USA. Other roles, incl. Donna Anna, Semiramide and Carolina in *Il matrimonio segreto.*

Soomer, Walter (b Liegnitz, Silesia, 12 Mar 1878; d Leipzig, Aug 1955), German bassbaritone. He studied in Berlin. Debut Kolmar, 1902. Leipzig 1906–27, Dresden 1911–15. He had an important career at Bayreuth: 1906–25 as Kurwenal, Wotan, Amfortas, Sachs, Hagen and Gurnemanz. NY Met 1908–11.

Soot, Fritz (b Neunkirchen, 20 Aug 1878; d Berlin, 9 Jun 1965), German tenor. Stage debut Dresden 1908, as Tonio; remained until 1918 and created the Italian Singer in *Der Rosenkavalier.* Stuttgart 1918–22. At the Berlin Staatsoper he created the Drum Major in *Wozzeck* (1925) and was the 1st local Laca and Mephistopheles (Busoni); also sang in the fps of Schreker's *Der singende Teufel* (1928) and Pfitzner's *Das Herz*

(1931). At Zoppot and CG (1924–5) he was heard as Siegfried, Tristan and Walther. He was well known as Waldemar, in Schoenberg's *Gurrelieder*.

Sophocles (497 or 495–405 BC), Greek dramatist. *See* **Antigonae** (Orff), **Antigone** (incid. music, Mendelssohn; operas, Honegger, Zingarelli), **Bantock** (*Electra*), **Elektra** (R. Strauss), **Enescu** (*Œdipe*), **Hüttenbrenner (A.)** (*Ödipus auf Kolonos*), **Oedipus auf Kolonos** (Mendelssohn), **Oedipus Rex** (Stravinsky), **Oedipus der Tyrann** (Orff), **Oedipus und die Sphinx** (Varèse), **Pizzetti** (*Trachiniae, Oedipus Rex* and *Coloneus*), **Saint-Saëns** (*Antigone*), **Zingarelli** (*Edipo a Colono*).

Sopra (It. = above). The word is used in pf. music to indicate in passages for crossed hands whether the right is to go above the left or *vice versa*. *See also* **Come sopra.**

Sopranino, as an adj. indicates the highest member of a family of wind instruments, e.g. sopranino recorder, sopranino saxophone.

Soprano, the highest female voice, with approx. the following compass:

but often extended further in florid operatic arias requiring dexterity. Up to the end of the 18th cent. there were also artificial male sopranos, prod. by castration. Boy sopranos are more often described as Trebles. Some instruments made in var. ranges use the word soprano as a prefix for those types which roughly equal the compass of the soprano voice (e.g. soprano saxophone).

Soprano Clef, the C clef so used as to indicate that middle C stands on the bottom line of the stave:

Sor (or Sors), Fernando (b Barcelona, 13 Feb 1778; d Paris, 10 Jul 1839), Spanish guitarist and composer. Educ. at the Escolanía at Montserrat, prod. his first opera at the age of 19, went to Paris and *c* 1815 to London, where he played and taught the guitar, returning to Paris in 1823.

Works incl. operas *Telemaco nell' isola di Calipso* (1797); 6 ballets incl. *Cendrillon* (1822), successful in London, Paris and Moscow; guitar pieces and studies. His guitar tutor was pub. in 1830.

Sorabji, Kaikhosru Shapurji (orig. Leon Dudley) (b Chingford, Essex, 14 Aug 1892),

Parsee pianist and composer. Lived in Eng. all his life and has European blood in him through his Spanish mother. Except for the pf., he was mainly self-taught, but was fortunate to be able to give all his time to musical studies. He appeared as pianist in his own works in London, Paris and Vienna, and also wrote criticism, incl. a book, *Around Music.*

Works incl. 2 symphs. for orch., pf., organ and chorus (1922, 1951); *Chaleur and Opusculum* for orch.; 8 pf. concertos (1915–22), symph. variations for pf. and orch.; 2 symphs. for organ; 2 pf. 5tets (1920, 1953); 5 sonatas, *Opus clavicembalisticum, Fantasia Hispanica*, 3 toccatas, symph., variations on *Dies irae* for pf.; *3 Poèmes* (Verlaine and Baudelaire), *Fêtes galantes* (Verlaine) for voice and pf.

Sorcerer, The, operetta by Sullivan (lib. by W.S. Gilbert), prod. London, Opera Comique, 17 Nov 1877.

Sorcerer's Apprentice, The (Dukas). *See* **Apprenti sorcier.**

Soriano, Francesco (b Soriano sul Cimino, *c* 1549; d Rome, 19 Jul 1621), Italian composer. Became a choir-boy at St John Lateran in Rome and studied with var. masters incl. G.B. Nanini and Palestrina. After a 1st appt. he went to the court of Mantua, 1583–6, and then became *maestro di cappella* in Rome, by turns at Santa Maria Maggiore, St John Lateran and in 1603 St Peter's.

Works incl. Masses, an arrangement of Palestrina's *Missa Papae Marcelli* for 8 voices, motets, psalms, Magnificat, a Passion and other church music; madrigals.

Sorochintsy Fair (*Sorochinskaya Yarmarka*), unfinished opera by Mussorgsky (lib. by comp., based on Gogol's *Evenings on a Farm near Dakanka*), comp. begun 1875; revised by Liadov for concert perf., 1904; perf. in orig. form, St Petersburg, Comedia Theatre, 30 Dec 1911; a version by Sakhnovsky prod. Moscow, Free Theatre, 3 Nov 1913; version by Cui with music of his own added prod. St Petersburg, Musical Drama Theatre, 26 Oct 1917; version by N. Tcherepnin prod. Monte Carlo, 17 Mar 1923 (in Fr.); another version made by Shebalin in 1931 was prod. Leningrad, Little Opera Theatre, 21 Dec 1931.

Sortita (It. from *sortire* = to come out), the aria sung by a principal character in an 18th-cent. opera at his 1st entry on the stage.

Sosarme, rè di Media (*Sosarmes, King of the Medes*), opera by Handel (lib. based on Matteo Noris's *Alfonso primo*), prod. London, King's Theatre, Haymarket, 15 Feb 1732.

Sostenuto (It. = sustained), a direction which may mean either that a note or notes are to be held to their full value (as with *tenuto*) or that a passage is to be played broadly, though not exactly slowed down (as with *ritenuto*).

Sotin, Hans (b Dortmund, 10 Sep 1939), German bass. He made his Hamburg debut in 1964 and sang there in the 1966 fp of Blacher's *Incidents at a Forced Landing* and the 1969 fp of Penderecki's *The Devils of Loudun*. Sarastro was the role of his Glyndebourne (1970) and NY Met (1972) debuts. Bayreuth since 1972 as the Landgrave, Marke, Pogner and Gurnemanz. He sang Hunding at CG (1974) and returned 1977, in a new prod. of *Der Freischütz*.

Soto de Langa, Francisco (b Langa nr. Osma, 1534; d Rome, 25 Sep 1619), Spanish priest, male soprano and arranger. He entered the Papal choir in Rome in 1562, joined the Oratory of St Philip Neri and continued to sing to the end of his long life. He adapted 5 books of *laudi spirituali* for 3 and 4 voices (pub. Rome, 1577–88), using It. folksongs and various It. and Span. comps.

Sotto voce (It. = under the voice), a direction indicating that a passage is to be perf. in an undertone. As the term indicates, it was orig. applied to vocal music, but it became current for instrumental music also.

Soubrette (Fr. from Prov. *soubret* = coy), a stock figure in opera given to a singer with a light soprano voice and impersonating characters of the type of servants, young confidantes, girls usually connected with the sub-plot, etc. (e.g. Despina in Mozart's *Così fan tutte*, Aennchen in Weber's *Freischütz*). Occasionally the soubrette may assume a principal part (e.g. Serpina in Pergolesi's *Serva padrona*, Susanna in Mozart's *Figaro*, etc.).

Souez, Ina (b Windsor, Col., 3 Jun 1908), American soprano. She studied in Denver and Florence and in 1929 sang Liù at CG. After marrying an Englishman she settled in Eng. and sang every season at Glyndebourne 1934–9 as Fiordiligi and Donna Anna in the 1st prods. there of *Così fan tutte* and *Don Giovanni*. She returned to the US in 1939 and after the war sang in a jazz band.

Souliotis, Elena (b Athens, 28 May 1943), Greek soprano. She studied in Milan; debut Naples, 1964, as Santuzza. Wider fame in 1966, with Abigaille at La Scala and Boito's Elena at the Lyric Opera, Chicago. NY Met

and CG debuts 1969, as Lady Macbeth. An apparent attempt to model herself on Callas led to an early vocal decline.

Sound-Board, a resonant wooden part of var. instruments, incl. organ, pf., dulcimer, cimbalom, etc. which adds to the volume of tone by vibrating with the notes.

Sound-Holes, the holes in the tables of string instruments, also in the sound-boards of harpsichords, etc. In instruments of the vln. family they take the shape of *f* holes or something approximating to them; in keyboard instruments as well as lutes, guitars, etc., usually the shape of a 'Rose'.

Sound-Post, the piece of pine wood standing upright between the table and the back of string instruments, inserted partly to support the pressure of the strings on the bridge, but mainly to act as the chief distributor of the vibrations.

Sourdine (Fr. from *sourd* = deaf), an instrument of the bassoon type, which derived its name from the fact that its tone was muffled. It was known as *Sordun* in Ger. and *sordone* in It.

Šourek, Otakar (b Prague, 10 Oct 1883; d Prague, 15 Feb 1956), Czech music critic. Although an engineer by profession, he became critic to 2 Prague newspapers and pub. important works, mainly on Dvořák, incl. a thematic catalogue and a large 2-vol. life and study of the works. Also showed interest in Janáček.

Souris, André (b Marchienne-au-Pont, 10 Jul 1899; d Paris, 12 Feb 1970), Belgian composer. He worked under the influence of Fr. impressionism at first, but from 1926 endeavoured to prod. in music some equivalent to the surrealist painters.

Works incl. incid. music for *Le Dessous des cartes; Musique* for orch. (1928); fanfare *Hommage à Babeuf* (1934); *Petite Suite* for 4 brass instruments; *Quelques airs de Clarisse Juranville* for contralto and pf.

Sousa, John Philip (b Washington, 6 Nov 1854; d Reading, Penn., 6 Mar 1932), American bandmaster and composer. After some years' experience as an orch. violinist he became master of the US Marine Corps band in 1880 and in 1892 formed a band of his own.

Works incl. operetta *El Capitán* (1896) and others; military marches, dances, incl. *The Washington Post*, etc.

Sousaphone, a brass instrument of the Tuba type made for Sousa's band in 1899 with a bell opening towards the audience.

Sousedská, a Bohemian country dance in slow triple time. The 3rd, 4th and 16th of

Dvořák's *Slavonic Dances* for pf. duet are sousedskás.

Souster, Tim(othy) Andrew James (b Bletchley, Bucks., 29 Jan 1943), English composer. He studied at Oxford and Darmstadt and was asst. to Stockhausen in Cologne, 1971–3. Co-founder with Roger Smalley of group Intermodulation, to explore electronic and aleatory techniques. Has worked at King's College, Cambridge, and Keele Univ.

Works incl. *Songs of the Seasons* for sop. and vla. (1965), *Poem in Depression* for sop. and ens. (1965), *Metropolitan Games* for pf. duet (1967), *Titus Groan Music* for wind 5tet, tape and electronics (1969), *Chinese Whispers* for perc. and synthesizers (1970), *Waste Land Music*, for sax., pf. and organ (1970), *Triple Music* for 3 orchs. (1970), *Song of an Average City* for small orch. and tape (1974), *Afghan Amplitudes* for keyboards and synthesizers (1976).

Souter Liedekens (Dutch = little psalter songs), metrical psalms sung in Hol. to popular tunes, trans. and provided with appropriate melodies by (prob.) Willem van Zuylen van Nyevelt. The 1st complete collection, printed by Symon Cock at Antwerp in 1540, contained 159 texts: Psalm cxix was in 4 sections, and the Te Deum and 5 canticles were incl. Clemens non Papa later arr. the whole collection for 3 voices, pub. in Antwerp as the 4th–7th of Susato's *Musyck Boexken* (little music books) in 1556–7. 10 settings are by Susato himself, perhaps because of Clemens's premature death. The 8th–11th books contained another complete setting, the work of Gerhard Mes.

Souzay, Gérard (Marcel) (b Angers, 8 Dec 1918), French baritone. Studied with Pierre Bernac. Paris debut 1945, NY 1950. Well known in Lieder and French song; took part in 1956 fp of Stravinsky's *Canticum Sacrum*. NY Met and Glyndebourne, 1965, as Mozart's Count.

Sowerby, Leo (b Grand Rapids, Mich., 1 May 1895; d Fort Clinton, Ohio, 7 Jul 1968), American composer and pianist. Studied at the Amer. Cons. of Chicago, where he taught later. He served as bandmaster in Europe during the 1914–18 war and in 1922 won the Amer. Prix de Rome. He appeared as pianist in USA, Eng., It. and Aus. He was organist of St James's Episcopal Cathedral in Chicago from 1927 to 1962.

Works incl. oratorio *Christ Reborn*, cantata *Great is the Lord* and Te Deum for mixed chorus and organ; 5 symphs. (1921, 1928, 1940, 1947, 1964), suite *From the Northland*, overture *Comes Autumn Time*, *Irish Washerwoman*, *Money Musk*, *Set of Four*, symph. poem *Prairie*, *Theme in Yellow* for orch.; sinfonietta for strings; rhapsody for chamber orch.; *Sinconata* for jazz orch.; 2 pf. concertos (1912, 1932), organ concerto, 2 cello concertos (1917, 1934), vln. concerto, ballad *King Estmere* for 2 pfs. and orch., *Medieval Poem* for organ and orch.

2 string 4tets (1924, 1935), wind 5tet, serenade for string 4tet; sonata and suite for vln. and pf.; symph., sonata and suite for organ; *Florida Suite* and other pf. works; songs.

Soyer, Roger (b Paris, 1 Sep 1939), French bass. He studied at the Paris Cons. and has appeared at the Opéra since 1962 as Arkel, Procida and Méphistophélès. Aix Festival since 1965 in operas by Monteverdi, Mozart and Rossini. He is particularly identified with the role of Don Giovanni and sang it on his NY Met (1972) and Edinburgh (1973) debuts.

Spagna, La, a 15th-cent. *basse danse* tune originating in Castile.

Spagnoletti, Paolo (real surname ? Diana) (b Cremona, 1768; d London, 23 Sep 1834), Italian violinist. Studied at Naples and settled in London in 1802 as orch. leader, teacher and soloist and worked mainly as leader of the orch. of the Philharmonic Society. He wrote some vln. pieces and songs.

Spalding, Albert (b Chicago, 15 Aug 1888; d New York, 26 May 1953), American violinist and composer. Studied at Bologna and Paris and made his 1st appearance at the latter in 1905. After touring widely in Europe he 1st appeared in NY in 1908. Wrote a fanciful biog. of Tartini, *A Fiddle, a Sword and a Lady* (1953).

Works incl. suite for orch.; 2 vln. concertos; string 4tet in E min.; sonata and suite for vln. and pf., *Etchings* and other works for vln. and pf.; pf. pieces; songs.

Spanisches Liederbuch (*Span. Song Book*), H. Wolf's settings of Span. poems in Ger. trans. by Emanuel Geibel and Paul Heyse, comp. Oct 1889–Apr 1890. There are 10 sacred and 34 secular poems in his set.

Spanish Lady, The, unfinished opera by Elgar (lib. by B. Jackson, based on Ben Jonson's play *The Devil is an Ass*). Begun 1932–3; only a number of sketches are left; arrangements by Percy Young pub. 1955–6.

Špasírka, a Czech dance in alternating slow and quick 4–8 time. The 13th of Dvořák's *Slavonic Dances* for pf. duet is a Špasírka.

Spataro, Giovanni (b Bologna, ? 1458; d

Bologna, 17 Jan 1541), Italian composer and theorist. He was a pupil of Ramos de Pareia and corresponded with Pietro Aron; *maestro di cappella* at San Petronio, Bologna, from 1512. He was involved in a protracted controversy with Gafurius, against whom 2 of his printed treatises are directed. He comp. a number of sacred works; 6 motets and one *laude* are extant.

Speaker Keys, extra keys fitted to reed wind instruments to facilitate the prod. of harmonic notes: e.g. 2 on the ob. prod. octaves (also known as Octave Keys) and 1 on the clar. prod. 12ths.

Speaking-Length, that portion of an organ pipe in which the air vibrates to prod. the note.

Specht, Richard (b Vienna, 7 Dec 1870; d Vienna, 18 Mar 1932), Austrian writer on music. Studied architecture, but encouraged by Brahms and others took up music criticism, joined the staff of *Die Zeit* and in 1909 founded *Der Merker* with Bittner and Richard Batka. His books incl. studies of Brahms, J. Strauss, R. Strauss, Mahler (1913), Puccini, Bittner, Beethoven, Furtwängler (1922), the Vienna Opera, etc.

Species, the var. types of Counterpoint taught in academic contrapuntal instruction.

Specification, the detailed list of the pipes, stops, keyboards and mechanisms of an organ given to the builder or used to describe the instrument.

Spectre's Bride, The (actually *The Wedding-Shift*), dramatic cantata by Dvořák, op. 69 (Cz. words by K J. Erben), comp. 1884, perf. in Eng., Birmingham Festival, Aug 1885.

Speech-Song. *See* **Sprechgesang.**

Spelman, Timothy Mather (b Brooklyn, NY, 21 Jan 1891; d Florence, 21 Aug 1970), American composer. Studied in NY, at Harvard Univ. and with Courvoisier at the Munich Cons.

Works incl. operas *La Magnifica* (1920), *The Sea Rovers* (1928), *Babakan* and *The Sunken City* (1930); pantomimes *The Romance of the Rose* and *Snowdrop; Litany of the Middle Ages* for soprano, women's chorus and orch. (1928), *Pervigilium Veneris* for soprano, baritone, chorus and orch. (1929); symph. in G min., symph. poem *Christ and the Blind Man* (1918); instrumental music.

Speyer, Wilhelm (b Offenbach, 21 Jun 1790; d Offenbach, 5 Apr 1878), German violinist and composer. Studied at Offenbach with Thieriot and André and with Baillot in Paris. He became a merchant at Frank-

furt, but continued to comp.

Works incl. string 4tets and 5tets; vln. duets; numerous songs.

Speziale, Lo (*The Apothecary*), opera by Haydn (lib. by Goldoni), prod. Eszterháza, autumn 1768.

Spianato (It.) = smoothed, level.

Spiccato (It. = articulated), a direction indicating a special kind of bowing on instruments of the vln. family, possible only in rapid passages of notes of equal duration, which are played with the middle of the bow and a loose wrist, allowing the bow to rebound off the strings after each note.

Spiegel von Arkadien, Der (*The Mirror of Arcadia*), opera by Süssmayr (lib. by Schikaneder), prod. Vienna, Theater auf der Wieden, 14 Nov 1794. See also **Magic Opera.**

Spieloper (Ger. = play-opera), a type of light German opera of the 19th cent. the subject of which is a comedy and the musical numbers of which are interspersed with dialogue.

Spielwerk und die Prinzessin, Das (*The Musical Box and the Princess*), opera by Schreker (lib. by comp.); 1909–12, prod. Frankfurt and Vienna, 15 Mar 1913; rev. in 1 act as a mystery play, *Das Spielwerk*, and prod. Munich, 30 Oct 1920, cond. Walter.

Spies, Claudio (b Santiago, 26 Mar 1925), American composer of Chilean birth. Moved to USA 1942 and studied at New England Cons. and with Fine and Piston at Harvard. Appt. Prof. of Music, Princeton, 1970. Has written extensively on Stravinsky and cond. the ſp of an early version of *The Wedding*.

Works incl. *Music for a Ballet* for orch. (1955), *Il Cantico del frate Sole* for bar. and orch. (1958), *Tempi* for 14 insts. (1962), 7 *Enzensberglieder* for bar. and ens. (1972).

Spies, Hermine (b Löhneberger Hütte nr. Weilburg, Nassau, 25 Feb 1857; d Wiesbaden, 26 Feb 1893), German contralto. Studied at the Wiesbaden Cons., in Berlin and with Stockhausen at Frankfurt. She sang while a student at the Mannheim Festival in 1880, made her 1st professional appearance at Wiesbaden in 1882, later travelled widely and visited London in 1889. She married a lawyer at Wiesbaden in 1892. Brahms was one of her warmest admirers; often heard in his Lieder.

Spiess, Ludovic (b Cluj, 13 May 1938), Rumanian tenor. He studied in Bucharest and Milan and sang in operetta before singing Dmitri in *Boris Godunov* at the 1967 Salzburg Fest., under Karajan; the following year he was heard as Radames in Zurich and as Dalibor in Vienna. NY Met debut 1971; CG 1973. In Europe and S. Amer. he has sung Calaf, Don José, Florestan and Lohengrin.

Spinaccino, Francesco (b Fossombrone; d Venice, after 1507), Italian 15th–16th-cent. lutenist. Pub. 2 books of arrs. of songs, *ricercari* and dances in lute tablature (pub. 1507).

Spinelli, Nicola (b Turin, 29 Jul 1865; d Rome, 17 Oct 1909), Italian pianist, conductor and composer. Studied at Florence, Rome and Naples, pupil of Mancinelli and Sgambati. His 2nd opera, *Labilia*, came 2nd to Mascagni's *Cavalleria rusticana* in the competition for the Sonzogno Prize in 1889. He suffered from a mental complaint during his last years.

Works incl. operas *Labilia* (1890), *A basso porto* (1894), etc.

Spinet, a small harpsichord, pentagonal in shape and with a single manual. Its name may derive from the It. *spina* = thorn, ref. to the plectra with which the strings were plucked.

Spinner, Leopold (b Lwów, 26 Apr 1906; d London, 12 Aug 1980), Austrian composer of Polish birth. Settled in Eng. 1938.

Works are influenced by Webern, with whom he studied 1935–8: symph. (1934), Passacaglia for chamber orch. (1936), Concerto for Orch. (1957); 2 string 4tets (1941, 1952), pf. trio (1950), sonatina for cello and pf. (1973).

Spirit of England, The, 3 cantatas for soprano solo, chorus and orch. by Elgar, op. 80, *The Fourth of August, To Women* and *For the Fallen* (poems by Laurence Binyon); comp. 1916–17; nos. 1 and 2 perf. London, 7 May 1916; complete perf. London, 24 Nov 1917.

Spiritoso (It. = spirited), a direction indicating that a comp., movement or passage is to be perf. briskly and energetically.

Spiritual, a negro song of the southern states of USA, with religious words and folksong tunes. One of the chief influences from which jazz and swing have sprung. It has influenced many serious Amer. comps. as well as some European ones; Tippett's oratorio *A Child of our Time* (1939–41) uses spirituals.

Spitta, (Julius August) Philipp (b Wechold, Hanover, 27 Dec 1841; d Berlin, 13 Apr 1894), German musicologist. Studied at Göttingen Univ. and in 1875 became prof. of music hist. at Berlin Univ. He also taught the subject at the Hochschule für Musik, of

which he became director in 1882. He was joint ed. with Adler and Chrysander of the *Vierteljahrsschrift für Musikwissenschaft*, and ed. the complete works of Schütz and the organ works of Buxtehude. His chief lit. work is his book on Bach in 2 vols. (1873–80).

Spivakovsky, Tossy (b Odessa, 4 Feb 1907), American violinist of Russian birth. Studied in Berlin and made debut there aged 10. Toured Europe and Australia between the wars, then settled in USA. Has displayed novel bowing techniques in the solo works of Bach.

Spofforth, Reginald (b Southwell, 1768 or 1770; d London, 8 Sep 1827), English composer. Pupil of his uncle Thomas S., organist of Southwell Minster, and of B. Cooke in London, where he settled. He gained several of the Glee Club's prizes.

Works incl. farce with music *The Witch of the Wood, or The Nutting Girls* (1796), adds. to Salomon's *Windsor Castle* (1795); many glees, incl. 'Hail, smiling morn'.

Spohr, Louis (b Brunswick, 5 Apr 1784; d Kassel, 22 Oct 1859), German composer and violinist. He 1st learnt music from his parents, who were both musical, although his father was a physician. They lived at Seesen in his childhood, and he was afterwards taught by 2 amateurs, but sent to school and for further studies to Brunswick. He played a vln. concerto of his own at a school concert and at 14 went to Hamburg trying to gain a hearing. He failed and on his return petitioned the duke for assistance and was sent to Franz Eck for lessons, the duke paying half the expenses for his accompanying that violinist on his travels. They went to Russia in 1802, where he met Clementi and Field. He practised and comp. much at that time, returned to Brunswick in 1803, heard Rode there and entered the ducal orch. In 1804 he visited Berlin and played there with Meyerbeer, aged 13. In 1805 he became leader in the Duke of Gotha's orch. and married the harpist Dorette Scheidler, with whom he toured widely. After prod. his 3rd opera at Hamburg in 1811, he visited Vienna in 1812, becoming leader at the Theater an der Wien and staying until 1815. After prod. *Faust* in Prague, he travelled in It. 1816–17 and then became cond. at the Frankfurt opera 1817–19. In 1820 he 1st visited London and Paris, meeting Cherubini, R. Kreutzer, Viotti and others.

After a visit to Dresden he became court music director at Kassel on 1 Jan 1822, having accepted the post declined by Weber, who had recommended him in his place. He remained there for the rest of his life, but continued to travel. In 1831 he finished his *Vln. School*, in 1834 his wife died, and in 1836 he married the pianist Marianne Pfeiffer. In 1839 he revisited Eng. for the perf. of *Calvary* at the Norwich Festival, and was commissioned to write an Eng. oratorio, *The Fall of Babylon*, for the next festival of 1842, in which year he prod. Wagner's *Flying Dutchman* at Kassel. He was not allowed leave to go to Eng. for the oratorio, but went during his summer vacation in 1843, when he appeared before Queen Victoria and Prince Albert and toured Eng. and Wales. During the 1848 revolutions he showed liberal leanings and so annoyed the elector that he was refused leave of absence, and having taken his vacation without leave, he became involved in a long law-suit, which he lost after 4 years. In 1852 he adapted *Faust* without recitatives for a prod. in It. in London and in 1863 he prod. Wagner's *Tannhäuser* at Kassel. He was pensioned off against his will in 1857.

Works incl. operas *Die Prüfung* (1806), *Alruna* (1808), *Der Zweikampf mit der Geliebten* (1811), *Faust* (1816, rev. 1852), *Zemire und Azor* (1819), *Jessonda* (1823), *Der Berggeist* (1825), *Pietro von Albano* (1827), *Der Alchymist* (1830), *Die Kreuzfahrer* (1845); oratorios *Das jüngste Gericht*, *Die letzten Dinge* (both *The Last Judgment*), *Des Heilands letzte Stunden* (*Calvary*, 1835), *The Fall of Babylon* (1842); Mass, psalms, hymn *St Cecilia*, cantata *Vater unser* (Klopstock).

ORCH.: 9 symphs. (4. *Die Weihe der Töne*, 1832, 6. Hist. Symph., 1839, 9. *The Seasons*, 1850), 5 overtures (incl. one on Shakespeare's *Macbeth*); 15 vln. concertos (8. *In modo d'una scena cantante*, 1816) and concertinos, concert pieces for vln. and orch.; 4 clar. concertos (1812–28).

CHAMBER: 33 string 4tets (1807–57), 4 double string 4tets, 8 string 5tets, 2 string 6tets, 7tet for pf., strings and wind, octet for strings and wind (1814), nonet for do. (1813), 5 pf. trios; pieces, variations, potpourris, etc. for vln.; vln. duets; sonatas for vln. and harp; harp pieces; songs; partsongs.

Spontini, Gaspare (Luigi Pacifico) (b Maiolati nr. Jesi, 14 Nov 1774; d Maiolati, 24 Jan 1851), Italian composer and conductor. His parents, who were poor peasants, and an uncle destined him for the priesthood, but he ran away to Monte San Vito, where another uncle allowed him to study

music, and when he had advanced sufficiently, he returned home and was allowed to study at the Cons. de' Turchini at Naples from 1791, Sala and Tritto being among his masters. In 1795 he became a pupil-teacher. In 1796 he prod. his 1st opera in Rome, having run away from the Cons., but he was readmitted at the intercession of Piccinni, from whom he learnt much. He now prod. one opera after another, and in 1798 went to Palermo with the Neapolitan court, which took refuge there and app. him music dir. in the place of Cimarosa, who refused to leave Naples. In 1803 he left for Paris, where he taught singing and tried his hand at Fr. comic opera, but made his 1st real success with the serious opera *La Vestale* in 1807. He was app. comp. to the Empress Joséphine and in 1810 became dir. of the It. opera at the Théâtre de l'Impératrice. In 1812 he was dismissed, but the Bourbon restoration in 1814 reinstated him. He soon sold his post to Angelica Catalani, however.

In 1820 he was summoned to the court of Frederick William III in Berlin as general music director to the Prus. court. He was not on good terms with the intendant, Count Brühl, though he succeeded in intro. excellent reforms at the court opera; but his success was obscured in 1821 by that of Weber's *Freischütz*, which aroused an appetite for Ger. opera, as distinct from foreign opera set to Ger. words. In 1822–3 he visited Dresden, where he met Weber, also Vienna and Paris. In 1838 he spent the summer in Eng. to study Eng. hist. and local colour for a new opera on the subject of Milton, differing from his early one, which however was never finished; neither was an earlier work, *Les Athéniennes*. On the king's death in 1840 his position became more and more difficult, partly through his own fault, for he quarrelled with the new intendant, Count Redern, and became involved in a law-suit, and after much trouble and threatened imprisonment he left Berlin in Jul 1842. He went to live in Paris, visited Dresden in 1844 to cond. a perf. of *La Vestale* rehearsed for him by Wagner, became deaf in 1848 and returned to his birthplace, founding a music school at Jesi.

Works incl. operas *I puntigli delle donne* (1796), *Adelina Senese* (1798), *L'eroismo ridicolo*, *Il finto pittore*, *La finta filosofa*, *La fuga in maschera* and 8 other It. operas, *La Petite Maison* (1804), *Julie, ou Le Pot de fleurs* (1805), *Milton* (in Fr.), *La Vestale* (1807), *Fernand Cortez* (1809), *Olympie* (Fr., revised in Ger. as *Olympia*, 1819), *Pélage, ou Le Roi de la paix* (1814), *Nurmahal* (Ger., after Moore's *Lalla Rookh*, 1821), *Alcidor, Agnes von Hohenstaufen* (1829), *Les Dieux rivaux* (with Berton, R. Kreutzer and Persuis); festival play with music on Moore's *Lalla Rookh* (orig. version of the opera); ballet for Salieri's *Les Danaïdes; Domine salvum fac* and other church music; cantata *L'eccelsa gara* for the victory of Austerlitz, coronation cantata for Nicholas I of Rus.; vocal duets and trios; songs with pf. or harp; *Sensations douces.*

Spontone, Bartolommeo (b Bologna, bap. 22 Aug 1530; d Treviso, 1592), Italian composer. Pupil of Nicola Mantovano and Morales, singer and in 1577–83 *maestro di cappella* at San Petronio at Bologna, and in 1584–6 at Santa Maria Maggiore, Bergamo. Comp. Masses, madrigals.

Sporer, Thomas (b c 1490; d Strasbourg, 1534), German composer. Wrote songs with accomp., then rare, but cultivated by Isaac, Hofhaimer, Senfl and others beside Sporer.

Sprechgesang (Speech-song), a term for a kind of singing that approximates to speech and touches the notes, indicated by special signs, without intoning them clearly at the proper pitch. It is used esp. by Schoenberg (e.g. in *Pierrot lunaire*) and his disciples (e.g. Berg in *Wozzeck* and *Lulu*).

'Spring' Sonata, the familiar nickname given to Beethoven's vln. and pf. sonata in F maj., op. 24, comp. 1801.

'Spring' Symphony, Schumann's orig. name for his 1st symph., in Bb maj., op. 38, finished Feb 1841 and 1st perf. at Leipzig by Mendelssohn, 31 Mar 1841. Also the title of a choral work by Britten, fp Amsterdam, 9 Jul 1949.

Sprung Rhythm, a term invented by Gerard Manley Hopkins for displacements of metrical stresses in poetry, not new to his verse, but exploited by him consciously and with great persistence and variety; and transferred to musical terminology by Michael Tippett in the prefatory notes to his 2nd string 4tet, where sprung rhythm is used with a deliberation similar to Hopkins's in the finale. It is no new thing to music, where it may be said to incl. such devices as syncopation, transference of stresses to weak beats or by tying notes over bar-lines or beats, the omission of rhythmic units by rests or the addition of them by triplets, etc.

Squarcialupi, Antonio (b Florence, 27 Mar 1416; d Florence, 6 Jul 1480), Italian composer and organist. He was organist at Florence Cathedral from 1432 until his death, and was a friend of Dufay. No compositions

have survived. He was the owner of a MS. now in the Laurentian Library at Florence (Med. Pal. 87), containing a large repertory of It. 14th- and 15th-cent. music. It has been ed. by Johannes Wolf (Lippstadt, 1955).

Squire, W(illiam) Barclay (b London, 16 Oct 1855; d London, 13 Jan 1927), English musicologist. Educ. at Frankfurt and Pembroke Coll., Cambridge. In 1885 he took charge of the dept. of printed music in the British Museum. He was also a critic and the author of the lib. of Stanford's opera *The Veiled Prophet*, hon. sec. of the Purcell Society and one of the hon. secs. of the IMS. He pub. catalogues for the British Museum and the RCM, ed. Purcell's harpsichord music and other works, and with Fuller-Maitland the *Fitzwilliam Virginal Book.*

St. *See* **Saint** for names combined with it.

Stabat Mater, a medieval Latin sacred poem, prob. by Jacopone da Todi, not orig. liturgical, but increasingly used for devotional purposes until it was admitted as a Sequence to the Roman missal in 1727.

Stabile, Annibale (b Naples, c 1535; d Rome, Apr 1595), Italian composer. Pupil of Palestrina in Rome, where he became *maestro di cappella* at the Lateran. From 1579 to 1590 he held a similar post at the Collegio Germanico there, in 1591 at the church of Santa Maria Maggiore.

Works incl. motets, Litanies and other church music; madrigals.

Stabile, Mariano (b Palermo, 12 May 1888; d Milan, 11 Jan 1968), Italian baritone. Studied in Rome and made his 1st appearance on the stage at Palermo in 1909, as Amonasro. His internat. reputation dated from his perf. in the title role of Verdi's *Falstaff* at La Scala, Milan, in Dec 1921. He appeared several times in opera at Covent Garden (1926–31), Glyndebourne (1936–9, as Figaro, Malatesta and Alfonso) and Salzburg (1935–9). Other roles incl. Don Giovanni, Hamlet, Iago and Scarpia.

Staccato (It. = detached), a special manner of perf. musical phrases without slurring the notes together, articulating each separately. The staccato actually shortens the value of each note as written by the insertion of a minute pause, so that for ex. crotchets marked staccato become something like dotted quavers followed by a semiquaver rest. The notation of staccato is a dot placed over each note or chord to be so perf.

Stade, Frederica von (b Somerville, NJ, 1 Jun 1945), American mezzo. She studied in NY and made her Met debut in 1970; rep. there has incl. Zerlina, Adalgisa, Idamante and Octavian. She sang Cherubino on her Glyndebourne (1973) and Salzburg (1974) debuts, and returned to Glyndebourne in 1979 for Monteverdi's Penelope. CG, 1965, as Rosina; 1985 as Elena in *La Donna del Lago*. Other roles incl. Cenerentola, Sextus, Dorabella and Nina in Pasatieri's *The Seagull* (fp, Houston, 1974).

Staden, Johann (b Nuremberg, bap. 2 Jul 1581; d Nuremberg, buried 15 Nov 1634), German organist and composer. He was in the service of the Margrave of Kulmbach and Bayreuth in 1603–16, after which he became organist of St Lorenz's Church at Nuremberg and soon afterwards of St Sebald's Church.

Works incl. motets for voices alone, motets with instrumental thorough-bass, sacred concertos for voices and instruments; *Hausmusik* for voices and instruments with Ger. words (1628); sacred and secular songs with continuo for organ or lute; secular songs for 4–5 voices; instrumental pavans, galliards, *canzoni*.

Staden, Sigmund Gottlieb (or Theophilus) (b Kulmbach, bap. 6 Nov 1607; d Nuremberg, 30 Jul 1655), German organist, violist and composer, son of prec. Pupil of his father, then of Jacob Baumann at Augsburg, 1620, and for *viola bastarda* of Walter Rowe in Berlin, 1626. In 1627 he became town musician at Nuremberg and in 1634 organist of St Lorenz's Church, whose organist, Valentin Dretzel, succeeded his father at St Sebald's. In 1636 he pub. a book on singing.

Works incl. opera *Seelewig* (1644); hymn-tunes for 4 voices; *Seelenmusik* containing hymn-tunes for 4 voices with thorough-bass for domestic use (1644–8); songs with figured bass.

Stader, Maria (b Budapest, 5 Nov 1911), Swiss soprano. Studied at Karlsruhe with H. Keller, I. Darigo at Zurich and Lombardi in Milan, in 1939 winning 1st prize at an internat. singing competition in Geneva. She was well known as an opera and concert singer, esp. of Mozart and Bach, and taught at the Zurich Acad. of Music. Retired 1969.

Stadler, Anton (b Bruck an der Leitha, 28 Jun 1753; d Vienna, 15 Jun 1812), Austrian clarinettist. Lived in Vienna and there became acquainted with Mozart, who wrote for him, e.g. the 5tet K452, trio (K498), 5tet (K581) and concerto (K622). He also played the basset-horn and took part in the fp of *La Clemenza di Tito*.

Stadler, Maximilian (b Melk, 4 Aug 1748; d Vienna, 8 Nov 1833), Austrian priest, organist and composer. Pupil of Albrechts-

berger, he entered the Benedictine monastery of Melk in 1766 (priest 1772), became prior there in 1784, abbot of Lilienfeld (1786) and of Kremsmünster (1789). In 1796 he settled in Vienna, and after working as a parish priest 1803–15 returned there to devote himself entirely to music. A friend of Mozart, he completed some of the latter's unfinished works, and wrote in defence of the authenticity of the Requiem (pub. Vienna, 1825).

Works incl. Masses, 2 Requiems, Te Deum, 3 Magnificat settings and other church music; oratorio *Die Befreyung von Jerusalem* (1811); music for Collin's tragedy *Polyxena* (1811); cantatas *Frühlingsfeyer* (Klopstock, 1813), etc.; organ sonatas and fugues; pf. music.

Stadlmayr, Johann (b ? Freising, Bavaria, c 1575; d Innsbruck, 12 Jul 1648), German composer. He was in the service of the Archbishop of Salzburg from 1603, and *Kapellmeister* of the Archdukes Maximilian and Leopold in 1610 and 1625 and of the Archduchess Claudia in 1636, at Innsbruck.

Works incl. Masses, Magnificats, Marian canticles, introits, hymns, psalms and other sacred music, some with instruments.

Staempfli, Edward (b Berne, 1 Feb 1908), Swiss composer. Studied medicine at first but gave it up for music, which he studied with Jarnach at Cologne and with Dukas in Paris.

Works incl. ballets *Das Märchen von den zwei Flöten* and *Le Pendu* (1942); cantata *Filles de Sion* for solo voices, chorus and orch.; 3 symphs. (1938, 1942, 1945), 4 *Sinfonie concertanti* and other orchestral works; 4 pf. concertos (1932–63), 2 vln. concertos, concerto for 2 pfs. and strings; music for 11 insts., concerto for pf. and 8 insts., 6 string 4tets (1926–62), 5tet for wind, 4tet for fl. and strings, pf. trio, string trio and other chamber music; pf. pieces; songs.

Staff Notation, the ordinary musical notation, so called to distinguish it from the notation used for Tonic Sol-fa.

Staggins, Nicholas (b ? London, 1645; d Windsor, 13 Jun 1700), English composer. Pupil of his father, Isaac S. (d 1684). Charles II app. him Master of the King's Band in 1674. He took the Mus.D. degree at Cambridge in 1682, becoming prof. of music there in 1684. He advanced to the post of Master of the King's Music, but was succeeded in it by Eccles in 1698.

Works incl. masque *Calisto, or The Chaste Nimph* (Crowne); incid. music for

Etheredge's *The Man of Mode*, Lee's *Gloriana*, Dryden's *Conquest of Granada* and *Marriage à la Mode* and Shadwell's *Epsom Wells* (last 2 with Robert Smith); odes for the birthday of William III; songs.

Stagione (It. = season). The term is used esp. for an opera season.

Stahlspiel (Ger. lit. steel-play), a perc. instrument with tuned steel plates or bars which are played with hammers. It is known in Eng. military bands as Lyra, being made for them in the shape of a lyre. The modern Glockenspiel, being also made of steel bars, and no longer of actual bells, is now to all intents and purposes the same instrument.

Stainer, Jacob (b Absam nr. Hall, 14 Jul 1621; d Absam, 1683), Austrian vln. maker. He learnt his craft at Innsbruck and (?) with one of the Amati family at Cremona or (?) with Vimercati at Venice. He began to work on his own account at Absam *c* 1640. He died insane, after being accused of Lutheran tendencies.

Stainer, John (b London, 6 Jun 1840; d Verona, 31 Mar 1901), English organist and composer. He became a choir-boy at St Paul's Cathedral at the age of 7 and before long was able to deputize at the organ. After working under var. masters and receiving an organist's appt. in the City of London, he was app. by Ouseley organist of St Michael's Coll., Tenbury, in 1856. In 1860 he went to Oxford as an undergraduate at St Edmund Hall and organist to Magdalen Coll., then became organist to the Univ. in succession to Elvey and in 1865 took the D.Mus. degree. In 1872 he returned to London as organist at St Paul's Cathedral. In 1888, having resigned from St Paul's through failing eyesight, he was knighted and in 1889 became Prof. of Music at Oxford. He wrote on music in the Bible, and ed. *Early Bodleian Music, Dufay and his Contemporaries*, etc.

Works incl. oratorios *Gideon* (1865) and *The Crucifixion* (1887); *Sevenfold Amen*, services and anthems; cantatas *The Daughter of Jairus* (1878) and *St Mary Magdalen* (1887).

Stamitz. Bohemian family of musicians:

1. Johann Wenzel Anton S. (b Německý Brod, 19 Jun 1717; d Mannheim, 27 Mar 1757), violinist and composer. He entered the service of the Electoral court at Mannheim in 1741, became principal violinist in 1743 and later music director. Under him the orch. became the most famous in Europe, called by Burney 'an army of generals'. He was the founder and most important member of the Mannheim school of symphonists.

Works incl. 74 symphs. (58 extant); concertos for vln., harpsichord, fl., ob., clar.; trio sonatas and other chamber music, vln. sonatas.

2. Carl S. (b Mannheim, bap. 8 May 1745; d Jena, 9 Nov 1801), violinist and composer, son of prec. Pupil of his father, entered the Mannheim orch. as 2nd vln. in 1762, then went to Strasbourg (1770), Paris and London, appearing as a virtuoso on the vln. and vla. d'amore. He continued to travel widely, visiting Prague in 1787 and Rus. in 1790, until in 1794 he settled in Jena as music director to the univ.

Works incl. operas *Der verliebte Vormund* (1787) and *Dardanus* (1800); *c* 80 symphs. and *sinfonies concertantes*; concertos; chamber music.

3. Johann Anton S. (b Německý Brod, 27 Nov 1750; d Paris, before 1809), violinist and composer, brother of prec. Pupil of his father and of Cannabich, in 1770 he went with his brother Carl S. to Paris, where he settled as violinist in the court orch. Kreutzer was his pupil.

Works incl. 12 symphs.; concertos for vln., vla., fl., ob., etc.; chamber music.

Standage, Simon (b High Wycombe, 8 Nov 1941), English violinist. He studied at Cambridge and in NY; joined the LSO 1969 and became sub-leader of the ECO. From 1973 he has led the English Concert, under Trevor Pinnock, and the City of London Sinfonia, under Richard Hickox. Founded the Salomon String Quartet 1981; performs with authentic instruments. Teacher of baroque violin at the RAM since 1983.

Ständchen (Ger.) = Serenade.

Standford, Patric (actually John Patric Standford Gledhill) (b Barnsley, 5 Feb 1939), English composer and teacher. Studied with Rubbra at GSM and Lutosławski at Dartington.

Works incl. opera *Villon* (1972–84); 5 symphs.: no. 1 for orch. (1972), no. 2 *Christus-Requiem* for soloists, chorus and orch. (1972), no. 3 *Towards Paradise* for chorus and orch. (1973), no. 4 *Taikyoku* for 2 pfs. and 6 perc. (1976), no. 5 for orch. (1984); cello concerto (1974), vln. concerto (1975), pf. concerto (1979); Mass for brass and chorus (1980); 2 string 4tets (1964, 1973).

Standfuss, J.C. (d ? Hamburg, *c* 1759), German violinist and composer. At one time a member of Koch's opera troupe in Leipzig, he was the 1st to prod. a Ger. *Singspiel*, in adapting Coffey's *The Devil to Pay* as *Der*

Teufel ist los (1752). Coffey's sequel *The Merry Cobbler* was similarly arr. as *Der lustige Schuster* in 1759. His 3rd *Singspiel* was *Der stolze Bauer Jochem Tröbs* (1759).

Stanford, Charles Villiers (b Dublin, 30 Sep 1852; d London, 29 Mar 1924), Irish composer. In 1870 he became choral scholar at Queens' Coll., Cambridge, and in 1873 organist of Trinity Coll., where he took classical honours the next year; also cond. of the Cambridge Univ. Musical Society. In 1874-6 he studied with Reinecke at Leipzig and with Kiel in Berlin, and in the latter year Tennyson suggested him as comp. of incid. music for his *Queen Mary*. D.Mus. at Oxford 1883 and Mus.D. at Cambridge 1888, where he had succeeded Macfarren as Prof. of Music in 1887. He was also cond. of the Bach Choir in London and prof. of comp. at the RCM, where he cond. the orchestral and opera classes. Knighted 1901.

Works incl. operas *The Veiled Prophet of Khorassan* (1881), *Savonarola* (1884), *The Canterbury Pilgrims* (after Chaucer, 1884), *Shamus O'Brien* (after Le Fanu), *Much Ado About Nothing* (on Shakespeare, 1901), *The Critic* (on Sheridan, 1916), *The Travelling Companion* (prod. 1926); incid. music for Tennyson's *Queen Mary* and *Becket*, Aeschylus' *Eumenides*, Sophocles' *Oedipus Tyrannus*, Binyon's *Attila* and Louis N. Parker's *Drake*.

ORCH.: 7 symphs. (1876–1911); 5 Ir. rhapsodies (1901–14), 3 concert overtures, serenade and Ir. dances for orch.; 3 pf. concertos (1896–1919), 2 vln. concertos, cello concerto (1919), clar. concerto, suite for vln. and orch., Variations on an Eng. Theme for pf. and orch.

CHAMBER: 8 string 4tets (1891–1919), 2 string 5tets, 2 pf. trios, 2 pf. 4tets, pf. 5tet, serenade for 9 instruments; 2 sonatas for vln. and pf., 2 sonatas for cello and pf., clar. and pf. sonata, some smaller instrumental pieces with pf.; pf. works incl. suite, toccata, sonata, 3 *Dante Rhapsodies*; 11 organ works incl. 5 sonatas; oratorios *The Three Holy Children*, *Eden* (1891); Mass (1892), Requiem, Te Deum, *Stabat Mater*, Magnificat; 2 psalms, 6 services, 3 anthems; choral ballads and 20 op. nos. of songs.

Stanley, John (b London, 17 Jan 1712; d London, 19 May 1786), English composer and organist. He was blind from the age of 2, but became a pupil of Greene and showed var. organist's appts. in London later. In 1759 he joined John Christopher Smith to continue Handel's oratorio concerts, and when Smith retired in 1774, he continued with T. Linley.

In 1779 he succeeded Boyce as Master of the King's Music.

Works incl. opera *Teraminta*; dramatic cantata *The Choice of Hercules*; music for Lloyd's *Arcadia, or The Shepherd's Wedding* (1761) and *Tears and Triumphs of Parnassus* and Southerne's *Oroonoko* (1759); oratorios *Jephtha* (1752), *Zimri* (1760) and *The Fall of Egypt* (1774); 12 cantatas to words by John Hawkins; 6 concertos for strings; solos for fl. or vln.; cantatas and songs for voice and instruments.

Stappen, Crispinus van (b *c* 1470; d Cambrai, 10 Mar 1532), Flemish composer. He became a singer at the Ste Chapelle, Paris, in 1492, and shortly afterwards, until 1507, at the Papal Chapel in Rome. In 1524–5 he was *maestro di cappella* at the Casa Santa, Loreto. He held a canonry at Cambrai from 1504. He wrote sacred and secular works, incl. a *strambotto* in praise of Padua.

Starer, Robert (b Vienna, 8 Jan 1924), American composer of Austrian birth. Studied in Vienna, then moved to Jerusalem at the Anschluss. Moved to USA 1947, studying at Juilliard; has taught at Brooklyn College from 1963.

Works incl. operas *The Intruder* (1956), *Pantagleize* (1973), *The Last Lover* (1975) and *Apollonia* (1979); ballets *The Dybbuk* (1960), *Samson Agonistes* (1961), *Phaedra* (1962), *The Lady of the House of Sleep* (1968), *Holy Jungle* (1974); 3 symphs. (1950–69); 3 pf. concertos (1947, 1953, 1972), concertos for viola (1959), vln. and cello (1968) and vln. (1981); string 4tet (1947), 2 pf. sonatas; cantatas on biblical subjects.

Starker, János (b Budapest, 5 Jul 1924). American cellist of Hungarian birth. Studied at Budapest Acad. of Music, becoming 1st cello in the Budapest Opera orch. In 1946 he settled in the USA, playing with the Dallas SO, the orch. of the NY Met (1949–53) and the Chicago SO (1953–8). In 1958 he became prof. at Indiana Univ., Bloomington. As a soloist he has toured widely in both Europe and America; well known in the solo suites of Bach.

Starlight Express, The, incidental music by Elgar for a play by V. Pearn, after Algernon Blackwood's *A Prisoner from Fairyland*; comp. 1915. Suite in 9 movts., with sop. and bass soloists, perf. Kingsway Theatre, London, 29 Dec 1915; very popular as escapist entertainment during the worst days of the First War, but forgotten until recent recording.

Staryk, Steven (b Toronto, 28 Apr 1932),

Canadian violinist and teacher. Studied at the Royal Cons., Toronto, and in 1956 became leader of the RPO, under Beecham. Led the Concertgebouw Orch. 1960 and the Chicago SO 1963–7. Has been heard as soloist and has taught at Amsterdam Cons., in the USA, Toronto and Ottawa.

Starzer, Josef (b Vienna, 1726; d Vienna, 22 Apr 1787), Austrian composer and violinist. Violinist at the French theatre in Vienna from 1752, he was court comp. and leader of the orch. in St Petersburg 1758–70. Back in Vienna he wrote music for Noverre's ballets, and was active in the Tonkünstler-Soc., for whose concerts he re-orch. Handel's *Judas Maccabeus* in 1779. From 1783 increasing corpulence enforced his retirement.

Works incl. *Singspiele Die drei Pächter* and *Die Wildschützen*; ballets *Roger et Bradamante* (1771), *Adèle de Ponthieu* (1773), *Gli Orazi ed i Curiazi* (all with Noverre) and many others; oratorio *La Passione di Gesù Cristo*; symphs., divertimenti, etc. for orch.; vln. concerto; chamber music.

Stassov, Vladimir Vassilievich (b St Petersburg, 14 Jan 1824; d St Petersburg, 23 Oct 1906), Russian scholar and art critic. Educ. at the School of Jurisprudence and joined the Imp. Public Library in 1845. He studied in It. from 1851 to 1854, after which he returned to the Library and in 1872 became dir. of the dept. of fine arts there. He was the 1st champion of the Rus. nationalist school of composers.

Statkowski, Roman (b Szczypiórno nr. Kalisz, 5 Jan 1860; d Warsaw, 12 Nov 1925), Polish composer. Studied with Zeleński at Warsaw and with Soloviev at St Petersburg. On the death of Noskowski in 1909 he was app. prof. of comp. at the Warsaw Cons.

Works incl. operas *Philaenis* (1904) and *Maria* (after Malczewski, 1906); fantasy, polonaise and other works for orch.; 5 string 4tets (1896–1929); vln. and pf. pieces; *Krakowiak* and other works for pf.; songs.

Staudigl, Joseph (b Wöllersdorf, 14 Apr 1807; d Döbling nr. Vienna, 28 Mar 1861), Austrian bass. Learnt music as a novice at the monastery of Melk, but ran away to Vienna in 1827 and entered the chorus of the Kärntnertortheater, where he soon rose through small parts to a position of eminence. He 1st visited Eng. in 1841, when he sang Sarastro and Lysiart at Drury Lane; later sang at CG and Her Majesty's in *Les Huguenots*, *Norma* and *Robert le diable*. In 1846 he created the title part in Mendelssohn's *Elijah* at the Birmingham Festival. He died insane.

Staudigl, Joseph (b Vienna, 18 Mar 1850; d Karlsruhe, Apr 1916), Austrian baritone, son of prec. He studied at the Vienna Cons. and sang in Karlsruhe 1875–83. He appeared at the NY Met 1884–6 and was Pogner in the 1st US perf. of *Die Meistersinger*. In 1886 he also sang Don Giovanni at Salzburg under Richter. His wife **Gisela** (born Koppmayer) sang in Vienna, Hamburg and Karlsruhe from 1879. She sang Adriano and the Queen of Sheba with the Met Co. on tour, in 1886, and Brangaene and Magdalene at Bayreuth, 1886–92.

Steber, Eleanor (b Wheeling, W.Va., 17 Jul 1916), American soprano. Studied at the New Eng. Cons. and with P. Althouse in NY. After winning a NY Met radio competition in 1940, she made her debut there in the same year as Sophie; sang there until 1966 as Donna Anna, Pamina, the Countess, Desdemona, Tosca, Eva, Elsa and Marie. She created the title role in Barber's *Vanessa* (1958).

Stefan, Paul (b Brno, 25 Nov 1879; d New York, 12 Nov 1943), Austrian writer on music. Studied at Brno, at Vienna Univ. and with Graedener and Schoenberg. Settled in Vienna as music critic and correspondent and in 1921 founded the *Musikblätter des Anbruch*. In 1938 he left Aus. owing to the Nazi régime and went to Switz., later to USA. He wrote books on music in Vienna, on Schubert, Dvořák, Mahler, Schoenberg, Toscanini, Bruno Walter, etc.

Steffani, Agostino (b Castelfranco, 25 Jul 1654; d Frankfurt, 12 Feb 1728), Italian diplomat and composer. Learnt music as a choirboy at Padua and was taken to Munich, where he studied music under Kerl at the expense of the Elector Ferdinand Maria. After further studies in Rome, 1673–4, he returned to Munich and became court organist in 1675; having also studied mathematics, philosophy and theology he was ordained priest in 1680. He was made dir. of the court chamber music, but in 1688 the younger Bernabei was app. general music dir. on the death of his father, and Steffani, disappointed of the post, left Munich. After a visit to Venice he went to the court of Hanover, where the post of music dir. was offered him, and there he also filled other posts, incl. diplomatic ones. The philosopher Leibniz, who was also at the court, sent him on a diplomatic mission to var. Ger. courts in 1696; in 1698 he was ambassador to Brussels, and on the death of the Elector Ernest Augustus transferred his services to the Elector Palatine at Düsseldorf. In 1706 he was made a nominal bishop. In 1708–9 he was on a diplomatic mission in It., where he met Handel, who went into service at the Hanoverian court at his suggestion. In 1722–5 he lived at Padua and in 1727 he was elected hon. president of the London Acad. of Vocal Music. In 1727 he went to It. for the last time. He died at Frankfurt during a diplomatic visit.

Works incl. operas *Marco Aurelio* (1680), *Solone* (1685), *Servio Tullio, Alarico il Baltha* (1687), *Niobe* (1688), *Enrico Leone, La lotta d'Hercole con Achelao* (1689), *La superbia d'Alessandro* (1690), *Orlando generoso* (1691), *Le rivali concordi, La libertà contenta* (1693), *I trionfi del fato* (1695), *Baccanali, Briseide, Arminio, Enea* and *Tassilone* (1709); music for a tournament *Audacia e rispetto*; motets, vesper psalms for 8 voices, *Stabat Mater* for 6 voices, strings and organ (1727), *Confitebor* for 3 voices and strings and other church music; madrigals; vocal chamber duets with bass; chamber sonatas for 2 vlns., vla. and bass.

Steffkins. Family of lutenists and violists of German origin settled in London in the 17th cent.:

1. Dietrich (or Theodore) S. (d *c* 1674), teacher of the lute and vla. da gamba and member of Charles I's band. He lived in Hamburg during the Commonwealth, returning in 1660 to serve under Charles II. He was much admired by John Jenkins.

2. Frederick William S. (b London; d ? London), son of prec. Violist in the royal service after the Restoration.

3. Christian S. (b London; d London), brother of prec. Violist in the royal service.

Stehle-Garbin, Adelina (b Graz, 1860; d Milan, 24 Dec 1945), Austrian soprano. After her 1881 debut in Broni, as Amina, she sang widely in Italy; created Nedda (1892) and Nannetta (1893) and sang in the fps of operas by Gomez, Catalani and Mascagni. She appeared elsewhere in Europe with her husband, Edoardo Garbin, as Mimi, Manon, Adriana Lecouvreur and Fedora.

Stehle, Sophie (b Hohenzollern-Sigmaringen, 15 May 1838; d Schloss Harterode nr. Hanover, 4 Oct 1921), German soprano. Debut Munich 1860, in Weigl's *Die Schweizerfamilie*; created Fricka in *Das Rheingold* (1869) and Brünnhilde in *Die Walküre* (1870). Other roles incl. Elisabeth, Elsa, Eva, Senta and Marguerite.

Steibelt, Daniel (b Berlin, 22 Oct 1765; d St Petersburg, 2 Oct 1823), German composer and pianist. He learnt much about keyboard instruments in his childhood, being the son of a harpsichord and pf. maker, and studied music with Kirnberger. After serving in the army, he made his 1st appearance as pianist and comp. in Paris during the late 1780s. At the end of 1796 he visited London, where he remained until 1799 and married an Englishwoman. He visited Hamburg, Dresden, Prague, Berlin and Vienna, where he had an encounter with Beethoven at the pf., and in Aug 1800 again settled in Paris, but spent as much of his time in London. In 1808 he left for the court at St Petersburg, where he became dir. of the Fr. Opera on the departure of Boieldieu in 1810.

Works incl. operas *Roméo et Juliette* (after Shakespeare, 1793), *La Princesse de Babylone, Cendrillon* (1810), *Sargines* and *Le Jugement de Midas* (unfinished); ballets *Le Retour de Zéphyr* (1802), *Le Jugement du berger Paris* (1804), *La Belle Laitière, La Fête de l'empereur* (1809); intermezzo *La Fête de Mars* for the victory at Austerlitz; incid. music; 8 pf. concertos (1796–1820); 50 studies and numerous pieces and transcriptions for pf.

Steigleder, Hans Ulrich (b Schwäbisch-Hall, 22 Mar 1593; d Stuttgart, 10 Oct 1635), German organist and composer. After an appt. as organist at Lindau on Lake Constance, he became organist at a monastery at Stuttgart in 1617 and musician to the court of Württemberg.

Works. incl. *ricercari* and variations on a Lord's Prayer hymn-tune for organ.

Stein. German family of pf. makers:

1. Johann Andreas S. (b Heidelsheim, 6 May 1728; d Augsburg, 29 Feb 1792), organ builder and pf. maker. Learnt his craft from his father, Johann Georg S. (1697–1754), worked with J.A. Silbermann in Strasbourg and settled in Augsburg in 1751. Mozart preferred his pfs. above all others.

2. Maria Anna (Nanette) S. (b Augsburg, 2 Jan 1769; Vienna, 16 Jan 1833), pianist and pf. maker, daughter of prec. She played to Mozart as a child during his visit to Augsburg in 1777, and on her father's death in 1792 carried on the business with her brother, 3, but married Andreas Streicher in 1794 and moved with him to Vienna, where they estab. a new firm, jointly with 3. Later she and her husband became friends of Beethoven.

3. Matthäus Andreas S (b Augsburg, 12 Dec 1776; d Vienna, 6 May 1842), pf. maker, brother of prec. He accomp. his sister and her husband to Vienna in 1793 and joined their firm, but estab. himself independently in 1802.

4. **Andreas Friedrich S.** (b Augsburg, 26 May 1784; d Vienna, 5 May 1809), pianist and composer, brother of prec. Went to Vienna as a child with his sister and brother, and studied pf. playing, also comp. with Albrechtsberger. He appeared in public frequently, esp. with Mozart's concertos.

Works incl. 3 operettas; pantomime *Die Fee Radiante*; vln. concerto; pf. trio; pf. sonata; songs.

5. **Karl Andreas S.** (b Vienna, 4 Sep 1797; d Vienna, 28 Aug 1863), composer and pf. maker, nephew of prec., son of 3. Pupil of Förster. He 1st devoted himself to comp., but later mainly to his father's factory, to which he succeeded.

Works incl. comic opera *Die goldene Gans*; 2 overtures; 2 pf. concertos, etc.

Stein, Erwin (b Vienna, 7 Nov 1885; d London, 19 Jul 1958), Austrian musicologist. Pupil of Schoenberg. After cond. at var. places, he joined the Universal Ed. in Vienna, but settled in London after the Anschluss. He wrote much on Schoenberg.

Stein, Horst (b Elberfeld, 2 May 1928), German conductor. He studied in Cologne; from 1951 he has held major posts at opera houses in Hamburg, Berlin (Staatsoper, 1955–61), Mannheim (1963–70) and Vienna (Staatsoper) from 1970. He is a sound, if unspectacular, cond. of Mozart, Bruckner, Schoenberg and Wagner (*Parsifal* and *The Ring* at Bayreuth from 1969.)

Steinbach, Emil (b Lengenrieden, Baden, 14 Nov 1849; d Mainz, 6 Dec 1919), German conductor and composer. Studied at the Leipzig Cons. and became cond. and theatre dir. at Mainz. Comp. orchestral works, chamber music, songs, etc. He gave the 1st public perf. of the *Siegfried Idyll* (1877) and cond. *Tristan* and *Siegfried* at CG in 1893.

Steinbach, Fritz (b Grünsfeld, Baden, 17 Jun 1855; d Munich, 13 Aug 1916), German conductor and composer, brother of prec. Studied with his brother and at the Leipzig Cons. After working as 2nd cond. at Mainz in 1880–6, he went to the court of Meiningen, with whose orch. he visited London in 1902, when he succeeded Wüllner as municipal cond. and dir. of the Cons. at Cologne. His works incl. a 7tet and a cello sonata.

Steinberg, Maximilian Osseievich (b Wilno, 4 Jul 1883; d Leningrad, 6 Dec 1946), Russian composer. Studied at St Petersburg Univ. and Cons. Pupil (and later son-in-law) of Rimsky-Korsakov, also of Liadov and Glazunov. He became prof. at the Leningrad Cons. Stravinsky's *Fireworks* was given its fp at his wedding (1908).

Works incl. ballets *Midas* (after Ovid) and *Till Eulenspiegel*; incid. music; oratorio *Heaven and Earth* (after Byron); 4 symphs. (1907, 1909, 1929, 1933), dramatic fantasy on Ibsen's *Brand*, overture to Maeterlinck's *La Princesse Maleine* and other orchestral works; vln. concerto (1946); 2 string 4tets; songs incl. 2 Tagore cycles, folksong arrs.

Steinberg, William (b Cologne, 1 Aug 1899; d New York, 16 May 1978), American conductor of German birth. After an early start in comp. he studied at Cologne Cons., graduating in 1920 and becoming asst. to Klemperer at the Cologne Opera and in 1924 its prin. cond. In 1925 he went to the Ger. Theatre in Prague and in 1929 became music director of the Frankfurt Opera; gave there an early perf. of *Wozzeck* and the fp of Schoenberg's *Von Heute auf Morgen* (1930). In 1933 he was removed from this post by the Nazis and became connected with the Jewish Cultural Society; from 1936 to 1938 cond. the Palestine SO and in 1938 the NBC SO in America. From 1945 he cond. the Buffalo PO and from 1952 the Pittsburgh SO (retired 1976). He worked with the LPO 1958–60.

Steinitz, (Charles) Paul (Joseph) (b Chichester, 25 Aug 1909), English organist and conductor. He studied at the RCM and was church organist in Ashford 1933–42. Founded South London Bach Society 1947 (later known as London Bach Society). With the Steinitz Bach Players (founded 1969) he has given annual perfs. in London of the *St Matthew Passion*. Prof., RAM, from 1945.

Steinway (orig. Steinweg), a firm of pf. makers in NY, founded in 1849 by Heinrich Engelhard Steinweg (1797–1871) at Brunswick, who emigrated with 5 sons and estab. himself in 1853. Branches of the firm were later set up in London, Hamburg and Berlin.

Stella, Antonietta (b Perugia, 15 Mar 1929), Italian soprano. Debut Spoleto 1950, as the *Trovatore* Leonora. She sang in Ger. from 1951; La Scala 1953–63, as Tosca. Violetta and Elisabeth de Valois. CG and Verona 1955, as Aida and the *Forza* Leonora. NY Met 1956–60. Also successful as Amelia Boccanegra, Mimi and Linda di Chamounix.

Stem, the stroke attached to the heads of all notes of smaller value than a semibreve.

Stendhal (actually **Henri Beyle**) (1783–1842), French critic and novelist. Wrote biog. of Rossini, letters on Haydn (partly plagiarized from Carpani), etc. *See* **Chartreuse de Parme** (Sauguet).

Stenhammar, (Karl) Wilhelm (Eugen) (b

Stockholm, 7 Feb 1871; d Stockholm, 20 Nov 1927), Swedish composer, conductor and pianist. Pupil of his father, the comp. Per Ulrik S. (1829–75), and later of Sjögren and others; also studied in Berlin. He became cond. of the royal orch. at Stockholm and also cond. at Göteborg.

Works incl. operas *The Feast of Solhaug* (based on Ibsen, 1899), and *Tirfing* (1898); incid. music to Shakespeare's *Twelfth Night*, *Hamlet* and *Romeo and Juliet*, Strindberg's *Ett drömspel*, Gozzi's *Turandot*, Tagore's *Chitra* and other plays; cantatas *The Princess and the Page*, *Snöfrid* (1891), *Hem-marschen* and *Sången*.

ORCH. AND CHAMBER: 2 symphs. (1903, 1915), symph. overture *Excelsior*, *Prelude and Bourrée*, serenade in F maj. for orch.; 2 pf. concertos (1893–1907), 2 *Sentimental Romances* for vln. and orch.; 6 string 4tets (1894–1909), pf. 4tet; vln. and pf. sonata; 4 sonatas and fantasy for pf.; part-songs incl. *Sverige*; songs.

Stenka Razin, symph. poem by Glazunov, op. 13, comp. 1884, fp St Petersburg, 1885. It contains the tune of the Volga boatmen's song *Ey ukhnem*.

Stentando (It. = toiling, labouring), a direction indicating a dragging delivery of a passage.

Štěpán, Vaclav (b Pečky, 12 Dec 1889; d Prague, 24 Nov 1944), Czech pianist, critic and composer. Studied with Novák and others and became prof. of musical aesthetics at the Prague Cons. His literary works incl. a study of *Musical Symbolism of Programme Music* and his comps. a poem *Life's Halcyon Days* for cello and pf.

Stepanian, Aro (b Elisabetopol, 24 Apr 1897; d Erevan, 9 Jan 1966), Russian composer. He began to teach music in the Armenian school of his native town and later of Alexandropol before he was 20; then studied at the Moscow School of Music under Glière and Gnessin and at the Leningrad Cons. under Shcherbatchev. Settled as prof. of music at Erevan in Rus. Armenia, the folksongs of which he studied.

Works incl. operas *Nazar the Brave* (1935), *David Sassunsky* (1937) and *The Dawn* (1938); 3 symphs. (1944–53); symph. poem *To the Memory of Twenty-six Commissars*; chamber music, instrumental pieces; songs.

Stephan, Rudi (b Worms, 29 Jul 1887; d Gorlice, Galicia, 29 Sep 1915), German composer. Studied at Worms, with Sekles at Frankfurt and at Munich. He fell in battle near Gorlice.

Works incl. opera *Die ersten Menschen* (prod. 1920); ballad *Liebeszauber* (Hebbel) for baritone and orch.; *Music for Orch.* (1912); *Music for Fiddle and Orch.*; *Music for 7 Stringed Instruments* (incl. pf. and harp, 1912), pf. pieces; songs.

Stephens, Catherine (b London, 18 Sep 1794; d London, 22 Feb 1882), English soprano. 1st appeared in It. opera in 1812 in London, and at CG in 1813, as Mandane in Arne's *Artaxerxes*; later sang Polly in *The Beggar's Opera* and Susanna and Zerlina in the 1st Eng. versions of *Figaro* and *Don Giovanni*. Weber wrote his last composition for her (1826).

Sterkel, Johann Franz Xaver (b Würzburg, 3 Dec 1750; d Würzburg, 12 Oct 1817), German composer and pianist. Educ. at Würzburg Univ., he was ordained priest in 1774, and in 1778 became chaplain and musician at the court in Mainz. After a visit to It. in 1782, where he met Padre Martini, he returned to Mainz, becoming music dir. to the court in 1793. Lived in Regensburg 1802–10, then in Aschaffenburg, and finally retired to Würzburg in 1815.

Works incl. opera *Farnace* (1782); 24 symphs., 2 overtures for orch.; 6 pf. concertos; string 5tet, pf. 4tet, 6 string trios; sonatas for pf. solo and duet, pf. pieces, variations, etc.; Ger. songs, It. canzonets; vocal duets.

Sterling, Antoinette (b Sterlingville, NY, 23 Jan 1850; d London, 9 Jan 1904), American contralto. Studied in NY and made her 1st appearance in Eng. in 1868. After a visit to Ger. and further studies with Pauline Viardot-García and Manuel García, she sang in USA and London, where she settled and married John MacKinlay. Often heard in Sullivan. Mother of the folksong singer Jean Sterling MacKinlay and the baritone Sterling MacKinlay.

Stern, Isaac (b Kemenetz, 21 Jul 1920), American violinist of Russian origin. Brought to San Francisco as a child, he received his first musical training at home, later studying the vln. with N. Blinder and L. Persinger and making his debut in San Francisco, aged 11. He has toured widely and is one of the most musical and successful of modern virtuosi; formed a trio with Leonard Rose and Eugene Istomin in 1961. He has given the fps of concertos by Schuman, Bernstein and Peter Maxwell Davies (1986).

Stern, Julius (b Breslau, 8 Aug 1820; d Berlin, 27 Feb 1883), German conductor and educationist. Studied in Berlin, Dresden and Paris, and after a career as choral cond.

opened a Cons. in Berlin with Kullak and Marx, who later withdrew from it.

Stern, Leo(pold Lawrence) (b Brighton, 5 Apr 1862; d London, 10 Sep 1904), English cellist. After beginning a career as chemist, he studied at the RAM in London and with J. Klengel and Davidov at Leipzig, making his 1st appearance in London in 1886. Toured USA 1897–8.

Sterndale Bennett. *See* **Bennett, William Sterndale.**

Sternklang (*Starsound*), 'park music' for 5 electronic groups by Stockhausen. Fp Berlin, 5 Jun 1971.

Stesso tempo, Lo (It., more frequently *l'istesso tempo* = the same pace), a direction given where a change is indicated in the time-signature, but the comp. wishes the music to continue at the same pace or beat.

Steuermann, Eduard (b Sambor nr. Lwów, 18 Jun 1892; d New York 11 Nov 1964), Polish, later American, pianist. Studied pf. with Busoni and comp. with Schoenberg (1911–14). Later taught at the Paderewski School in Lwów and from 1932 to 1936 at the Jewish Cons. in Kraków. In 1937 he settled in the USA. He ded. himself to the cause of modern music, esp. that of Schoenberg, from whose operas and orchestral works he made pf. scores; he took part in the fps of *Pierrot lunaire* (1912), Schoenberg's Suite op. 29 (1927) and the pf. concerto (1944).

Stevens, Bernard (b London, 2 Mar 1916; d Gt Maplestead, Essex, 2 Jan 1983), English composer. Studied at Cambridge with E.J. Dent and Rootham and at the RCM in London with R.O. Morris. He gained the Leverhulme Scholarship and Parry Prize for comp. In 1940–6 he served in the army. App. prof. of comp. at the RCM, 1948.

Works incl. film music; cantata *The Harvest of Peace* (1952) and other choral works; symph., *Symph. of Liberation* (1946) and Fugal Overture for orch., *Ricercar* and *Sinfonietta* for strings, overture *East and West* for wind band; vln. concerto (1946), cello concerto (1952); string 4tet, pf. trio, theme and variations for string 4tet (1949), *Fantasia* for 2 vlns. and pf.; vln. and pf. sonata; pf. music; songs.

Stevens, Denis (William) (b High Wycombe, 2 Mar 1922), English musicologist and conductor. He studied at Oxford in 1940–2 and 1946–49, and after playing in orchs. was a member of the BBC music dept. in London 1950–4. He has ed. the Mulliner Book in *Musica Britannica* and Monteverdi's *Vespers* and *Orfeo*; has pub. books

on Tomkins and Tudor church music. Prof. at Columbia Univ., NY, 1964–74. He was co-founder of the Ambrosian Singers. CBE 1984.

Stevens, John (Edgar) (b London, 8 Oct 1921), English literary historian and musicologist. Lecturer in Eng. at Cambridge Univ., 1952; Prof. of Medieval and Renaissance Eng. there 1978. In addition to his important eds. of early Eng. music he is partic. influential for his books *Music and Poetry in the Early Tudor Court* (1961) and *Words and Music in the Middle Ages* (1986). CBE 1980.

Stevens, Richard (John Samuel) (b London, 27 Mar 1757; d London, 23 Sep 1837), English organist and composer. Learnt music as a choir-boy at St Paul's Cathedral and became organist of the Temple Church in 1786, also at the Charterhouse in 1796, and was app. Gresham Prof. of Music in 1801.

Works incl. harpsichord sonatas; glees; songs.

Stevens, Risë (b New York, 11 Jun 1913), American mezzo. Studied in NY at Juilliard and with Gutheil-Schoder in Vienna, making her debut in Prague in 1936; sang Orpheus and Octavian there. She sang at the NY Met (1938–61) and also in Europe; Glyndebourne 1939 and 1955, as Cherubino and Dorabella. Among her most distinguished roles was that of Carmen. Taught at Juilliard School from 1975.

Stevenson, John (Andrew) (b Dublin, Nov 1761; d Kells, Co. Meath, 14 Sep 1833), Irish organist and composer. Learnt music as a chorister at Christ Church and St Patrick's Cathedrals at Dublin and later became vicar-choral at both. In 1814 he was app. organist and music dir. at the Castle Chapel. Knighted in 1803.

Works incl. operas *The Contract* (with Cogan, 1782) and *Love in a Blaze* (1799); music for O'Keeffe's farces *The Son-in-Law*, *The Dead Alive* (1781) and *The Agreeable Surprise* (1782), music for other stage pieces; oratorio *Thanksgiving*; services and anthems; glees, canzonets and duets; songs; accomps. for Ir. songs ed. with words by Thomas Moore.

Stevenson, Robert M(urrell) (b Melrose, New Mexico, 3 Jul 1916), American musicologist. Studied at Juilliard, Yale, Harvard and Oxford (with Westrup). Professor at Univ. of California (LA) from 1949. His chief areas of study have been Latin American colonial music and Spanish music. Many articles for *The New Grove Dictionary* (1980).

Stevenson, Ronald (b Blackburn, 6 Mar 1928), English composer, pianist and writer on music. He studied at the RMCM and in Italy, and has taught at Edinburgh Univ. Has made a special study of Busoni: 1st pf. concerto (*Triptych*) is based on themes from *Doktor Faust*. Other works incl. *Passacaglia on DSCH*, an 80-minute work for pf. (fp Cape Town, 1963), and *Peter Grimes Fantasia* for pf. (1971).

Stewart, Thomas (b San Saba, Texas, 29 Aug 1926), American baritone. He sang La Roche while still a student in NY, and in 1957 appeared as Ashton opposite the Lucia of Callas, in Chicago. He soon moved to Europe and from 1960–78 was heard at CG as Gunther, Don Giovanni and Golaud. Bayreuth 1960–72 as Wotan, Amfortas and the Dutchman. Met debut 1966, as Ford; sang in San Francisco from 1971 and in 1981 was heard there in the title role of Reimann's *Lear*; frequent performances with his wife, Evelyn Lear. Other roles incl. Onegin, Sachs, Luna, Iago and Escamillo.

Stiastný, Jan (b Prague, 1764; d Mannheim, after 1826), Czech composer and cellist. Studied at Prague, together with his brother, Bernard Wenzel S. (1760–1835), also a cellist, later lived by turns at Frankfurt, Nuremberg and Mannheim, and became known both in London and in Paris.

Works incl. concertino and Andante for cello with fl. and strings; trio for cello with vla. and 2nd cello; duets for 2 cellos; cello pieces and studies.

Sticcado-Pastrole, a glass dulcimer popular in Eng. in the 18th cent.

Stich, Johann Wenzel (called Punto) (b Žehušice nr. Časlav, 28 Oct 1746; d Prague, 16 Feb 1803), Bohemian horn player and composer. Studied in Prague, Munich and Dresden, held posts in var. court orchs., and made a great reputation as a travelling virtuoso under the name of Punto. Beethoven's horn sonata, op. 17, was written for him.

Stich-Randall, Teresa (b W. Hartford, Conn., 24 Dec 1927), American soprano. Studied at Hartford School of Music, making her debut aged 15 as Aida; sang in *Falstaff* and *Aida* under Toscanini. In 1951 she won a singing competition at Lausanne and in 1952 joined the Vienna Staatsoper. NY Met debut 1961, as Fiordiligi. She was esp. well known as a Mozart singer.

Stiedry, Fritz (b Vienna, 11 Oct 1883; d Zurich, 8 Aug 1968), American conductor of Austrian birth. Studied law at Vienna Univ. and music theory at the Vienna Cons. From 1907 to 1908 he was asst. to E. von Schuch in Dresden and from 1914 to 1923 was principal cond. at the Berlin Staatsoper. From 1923 to 1925 he cond. in Vienna at the Volksoper, where he gave the 1924 fp of Schoenberg's *Die glückliche Hand*, and from 1928 to 1933 at the Berlin Städtische Oper; associated with the Verdi revival and gave *Macbeth* and *Boccanegra* there. Forced to leave Germany by the Nazis, he cond. in Leningrad from 1933 to 1937 and in 1938 settled in the USA. From 1946 to 1958 cond. at the NY Met. He was esp. distinguished as a Wagner cond., and also in modern music. CG, 1953–4 (*The Ring* and *Fidelio*).

Stiehl, Heinrich (Franz Daniel) (b Lübeck, 5 Aug 1829; d Reval, 1 May 1886), German organist, composer and conductor. Studied with his father, Johann Dietrich S. (1800–72), organist at Lübeck, and at Weimar and Leipzig. He lived by turns in Rus., Aus., It., Eng., Ir., and Eng. and Rus. again, working as organist, cond. and teacher. His brother Karl Johann Christian S. (1826–1911) was an organist and cond.

Works incl. operas *Der Schatzgräber* and *Jery und Bätely* (Goethe); *The Vision* and other orchestral pieces; string 4tets, 3 pf. trios; cello and pf. sonata; *Sonata quasi fantasia* and other pf. works.

Stierhorn (Ger. = bull horn), a primitive wind instrument, made of a bull or cow horn, sounding a single note of rough quality. Wagner used it for the watchman in *The Mastersingers*.

Stiffelio, opera by Verdi (lib. by F.M. Piave), prod. Trieste, 16 Nov 1850. Revised as *Aroldo* (1856–7).

Stignani, Ebe (b Naples, 10 Jul 1904; d Imola, 5 Oct 1974), Italian mezzo. She studied in Naples and made her debut there in 1925, as Amneris. A favourite of Toscanini, she appeared at La Scala, Milan, from 1926 as Eboli, Azucena, Ortrud, Brangaene and Orpheus. London, CG, 1937–57 as Adalgisa and Amneris. She appeared in San Francisco before and after World War II.

Stile rappresentativo (It. = representative style), a term used by Italian musicians of the new monodic school in the early years of the 17th cent. to describe the new vocal style of declamatory, recitative-like dramatic music which tried to imitate human speech as closely as possible and thus endeavoured to 'represent' dramatic action in a naturalistic way.

Still, William Grant (b Woodville, Miss., 11 May 1895; d Los Angeles, 3 Dec 1978), American negro composer. Educ. at Wilberforce Univ. and studied music at Oberlin

Cons., later with Chadwick at Boston and with Varèse.

Works incl. opera *Blue Steel* (1935); ballets *La Guiablesse* (1927) and *Sahdji* (1930), *Lenox Avenue* for radio announcer, chorus and orch. (1937); 4 symphs., incl. *Afro.-Amer. Symph.* (no. 1, 1930), *Africa, Poem, Phantom Chapel* for strings and other orchestral works; *Kaintuck* for pf. and orch. (1935); *From the Black Belt* and *Log Cabin Ballads* for chamber orch.

Stilwell, Richard (b St Louis, 6 May 1942), American baritone. Debut NY City Opera 1970, as Pelléas; also role of CG debut, 1974. Glyndebourne from 1973 as Ulisse, Olivier, Onegin and Ford. At Houston in Mar 1974 he sang in the fp of Pasatieri's *The Seagull*; Baltimore 1976 in the same composer's *Ines de Castro*. NY Met debut 1975, as Guglielmo.

Stimme (Ger. = voice and part), not only the human voice, but also any part, vocal or instrumental, in a comp., esp. a polyphonic one; also the copy of an orchestral, vocal or chamber music part used for perf.

Stimmführung (Ger.) = part-writing.

Stimmung (Mood), work by Stockhausen for 6 amplified voices. Fp Paris, 9 Dec 1968.

Sting, an old term describing the effect of Vibrato in lute playing.

Stivori, Francesco (b Venice, *c* 1550; d Graz, 1605), Italian organist and composer. Pupil of Merulo. He became town organist at Montagnana in 1579 and was later in the service of the Archduke Ferdinand of Aus. until 1605.

Works incl. Masses, Magnificat, *Sacrae cantiones* (1595); madrigals; instrumental *ricercari*.

Stobaeus, Johann (b Graudenz, W. Prussia, 6 Jul 1580; d Königsberg, 11 Sep 1646), German composer and bass. While attending the Univ. at Königsberg, he studied music with Eccard, and after holding various minor appts. there became *Kapellmeister* to the Elector of Brandenburg in 1626.

Works incl. *Cantiones sacrae* for 5–10 voices (pub. 1624), Magnificats for 5–6 voices, 5-part settings of hymn-tunes; Prus. Festival Songs for 5–8 voices (with Eccard; 2 vols., pub. 1624 and 1644); sacred and secular occasional comps.

Stock-and-Horn, an early Scottish instrument, similar to the Pibgorn, made of wood or bone fitted with a cow horn. It was played like the chanter of a bagpipe, with a single reed. A different instrument from the Stockhorn, which was a forester's horn.

Stock, Frederick (Friedrich August) (b Jülich, 11 Nov 1872; d Chicago, 20 Oct 1942), German, later American, violinist and conductor. Studied with his father, a bandmaster, and at the Cologne Cons., later with Humperdinck, Jensen and Wüllner. He joined the Cologne orch. as a violinist in 1890, but settled at Chicago in 1895 in the same capacity, becoming asst. cond. to Theodore Thomas and succeeding him in 1905, as cond. of the orch. to become the Chicago SO; remained until his death and gave early perfs. of works by Mahler, Schoenberg, Hindemith and Prokofiev. Also composed.

Stockhausen, Julius (b Paris, 22 Jul 1826; d Frankfurt, 22 Sep 1906), German baritone. Pupil of his mother and later of Manuel García in Paris for singing and Hallé and Stamaty for pf. He made his 1st important concert appearance at Basle in 1848, visited Eng. the next year and then divided his attention between Fr. opera and Ger. song. In May 1856 he gave the 1st public perf. of Schubert's *Die schöne Müllerin* (Vienna). From 1862–9 he was dir. of the Phil. Concerts in Hamburg. In 1869 he became chamber singer to the King of Württemberg, but left Stuttgart in 1874, teaching by turns at Berlin and Frankfurt. Well known in the Lieder of Brahms; the *Magelone Lieder* were written for him.

Stockhausen, Karlheinz (b Mödrath nr. Cologne, 22 Aug 1928), German composer. He studied at the Cologne Musikhochschule and in Paris with Messiaen and Milhaud. Since 1953 he has worked intensively at the studio for electronic music of the W. Ger. Radio at Cologne. He is one of the most enterprising of the comps. creating electronic music but has also written music for traditional media. He has lectured in the USA and Britain, building up a specialist audience for his music. Professor of comp. at Hochschule für Musik, Cologne, from 1971. Members of his family take part in perfs.of his works.

Works incl. *Kreuzspiel*, for oboe, clar., pf. and 3 perc. (1951), *Formel* for 29 insts. (1951), *Punkte* for orch. (1952), *Kontra-Punkte* for ens. (1952), *Klavierstücke I–XI* (1952–6), *Zeitmasze* for wind 5tet (1956), *Gruppen* for 3 orchs. (1957), *Gesang der Jünglinge* for voice and tapes (1956), *Zyklus* for perc. (1959), *Carré* for 4 choruses and 4 orchs. (1960), *Refrain* for ens. (1959), *Kontakte* for pf., perc. and 4-track tape (1960), *Momente* for sop., 4 choruses and ens. (1961–4), *Mikrophonie* I and II for electronics (1964–5), *Mixtur* for 5 orchs., sine-wave generators and 4 ring modulators (1964–7), *Stop* for inst. ens. (1969–73), *Telemusik* for 4-track tape (1966), *Hymnen* for 4-track tape (1967), *Stimmung* for voices and ens. (1968), *Kurzwellen (Short Waves)* for electronics and 4 short-wave radios (1968).

Aus den sieben Tagen, 15 pieces for various inst. groups (1968), *Spiral* for soloist and short-wave receiver (1969), *Mantra* for 2 pfs., woodblock and 2 ring modulators (1970), *Sternklang*, park music for 5 groups (1971), *Trans* for orch. and tape (1971), *'Am Himmel wandre ich . . .'* for sop. and bar. (1972), *Intervall* for pf. duo (1972), *Inori* for 1/2 soloists and orch. (1974), *Atmen gibt das Leben* for chorus (1974), *Herbstmusik* for 4 players (1974), *Musik im Bauch (Music in the Belly*, for 6 perc., 1975), *Sirius* for sop., bar. and ensemble (1977), *Jubiläum* for orch. (1977).

Operas *Donnerstag aus Licht* (1981) and *Samstag aus Licht* (1984); scenes from *Licht* have been given as concert pieces: no. 1 *Der Jahreslauf* for dancers and orch. (1977), no. 2 *Michaels Reise um die Erde* for trumpet and ens. (1978), no. 3 *Michaels Jugend* for sop., tenor, brass insts., pf., dancers and tape (1979), no. 4 *Michaels Heimkehr* for soloists, chorus and orch. (1979); also *Lucifer's Dream* from *Samstag* (1983).

Beethausen, opus 1970, von Stockhoven was compiled for the Beethoven bicentenary and includes fragments of music in quotation and a reading of the Heiligenstadt Testament (developed from *Kurzwellen*).

Stockhausen (*née* Schmuck), Margarete (b Gebweiler, 1803; d Colmar, 6 Oct 1877), German soprano, mother of Julius S. and wife of the harpist and composer Franz S. (1792–1868). Studied with Catrufo in Paris and 1st toured with her husband in 1825.

Stodart, a firm of English 18th–19th-cent. harpsichord and pf. makers, founded c 1776 by Robert S., carried on by his son William S., whose workman William Allen invented the metal frame for the pf., and later by his grandson Malcolm S.

Stoessel, Albert (Frederic) (b St Louis, 11 Oct 1894; d New York, 12 May 1943), American violinist, composer and conductor. Studied at home and later at the Hochschule für Musik in Berlin. On his return to America he appeared as solo violinist, served as a bandmaster during the 1914–18 war and in 1922 succeeded W. Damrosch as cond. of the Oratorio Society of NY and director of music at the Chautauqua Institution. In 1930 he became director of the opera

and orch. at the Juilliard Graduate School there.

Works incl. opera *Garrick* (1937); suites *Hispania* (1921) and *Early Americana* (1935), *Suite antique*, symph. portrait *Cyrano de Bergerac* (after Rostand), Concerto grosso, etc. for orch.; *Suite antique* arr. for 2 vlns. and pf. (1922), vln. and pf. sonata and pieces.

Stojowski, Zygmunt (Denis Antoni) (b Strzelce, 14 May 1869; d New York, 6 Nov 1946), Polish composer and pianist. Studied with Żeleński at Kraków, then with Diémer, Dubois, Delibes and Massenet in Paris, and finally, on his return, with Gorski and Paderewski. After touring Europe as a pianist he settled in NY in 1905 and became head of the pf. dept. at the Inst. of Musical Art in 1911.

Works incl. *A Prayer for Poland* for chorus, org. and orch. (1915), cantata; symph. in D min.; 2 pf. concertos, *Symph. Rhapsody* for pf. and orch., Concerto and Romanza for vln. and orch., cello concerto; chamber music; instrumental sonatas; pf. pieces; songs.

Stokem, Johannes (also Stokhem, etc.) (b c 1440; d c 1500), Flemish composer. He was prob. born and spent his early life nr. Liège. He was in the service of Beatrice of Hung. in the early 1480s and a singer in the Papal Choir, 1487–9. He was a friend of Tinctoris, who sent him portions of his 12th treatise (all that survives) with a letter. A few sacred and secular works survive, incl. 4 *chansons* printed in Petrucci's *Odhecaton A* (1501).

Stoker, Richard (b Castleford, Yorks., 8 Nov 1938), English composer. He studied in Huddersfield and at the RAM with Lennox Berkeley; prof. since 1963.

Works incl. operas *Johnson Preserv'd* (1967) and *Thérèse Raquin* (after Zola, 1975), *Petite Suite* (1962) and *Little Symph.* (1969) for orch.; 3 string 4tets (1960–9), Wind 5tet (1963), vln. sonata (1964), Sextet (1965), pf. trio (1965), Oboe 4tet (1970).

Stokowski, Leopold (Antonin Stanisław Bolesławowicz) (b London, 18 Apr 1882; d Nether Wallop, Hants., 13 Sep 1977), American conductor, the son of a Polish father and an Irish mother. Studied at the RCM and took the B.Mus. at Oxford. In 1900 he became organist at St James's Church, Piccadilly, and later studied in Paris and Munich. From 1905 to 1908 he was organist in NY, and in 1908 cond. in London, in 1909 becoming cond. of the Cincinnati SO and of the Philadelphia SO in 1912, where he intro. much modern music; he gave the 1926 fp of *Amériques*, by Varèse, and in 1931 cond. the Amer. première of Berg's *Wozzeck*; also gave 1st US perfs. of Mahler's 8th symph., *The Rite of Spring* and the *Gurrelieder*. From 1942 to 1944 cond. the NBC SO with Toscanini; he cond. with the orch. the 1944 fp of Schoenberg's pf. concerto: NBC terminated his contract after the concert. In 1945 he became music director of the Hollywood Bowl and in 1949–50 of the NY PO, taking over the Houston SO in 1955. In 1962 he formed the American SO, in NY, and gave the 1965 fp of Ives's 4th symph. with the orch. He was thrice married, acted in films, made many arrs. of music and was one of the most colourful and gifted executants of the century.

Stollen (Ger. = props). The songs of the Ger. Minnesinger and Meistersinger usually had stanzas divided into 3 sections: 2 stollen of equal length often sung to the same and always to very similar music (called *Aufgesang*, fore-song) followed by an *Abgesang* (after-song) forming a concluding section of unspecified length and with different music. The whole song was called a *Bar*.

Stoltz, Rosine (actually Victorine Noël) (b Paris, 13 Feb 1815; d Paris, 28 Jul 1903), French mezzo. Studied at Choron's school, became a chorus singer after the 1830 Revolution, made a 1st appearance as a soloist at Brussels in 1832 and from 1837 to 1847 sang at the Paris Opéra. She created Ascanio in *Benvenuto Cellini* (1838) and sang in the fps of operas by Donizetti and Halévy. Her success was as much due to her amatory as to her musical talent; she became the mistress of the Emperor of Brazil and made several highly rewarded tours.

Stoltzer, Thomas (b Schweidnitz, Silesia, *c* 1486; d Ofen, 1526), German composer. Became *Kapellmeister* to King Louis of Boh. and Hung. at Buda, but left after the battle of Mohács in 1526 and took up a post in the service of Duke Albert of Prus. at Königsberg. He drowned in the river Taja.

Works incl. Latin motets and psalms, Latin hymns for 4–5 voices, Psalm xxxvii in Luther's German trans. for 3–7 voices in motet form and 4 others; German sacred and secular songs.

Stolz, Robert (Elisabeth) (b Graz, 25 Aug 1880; d Berlin, 27 Jun 1975), Austrian composer and conductor. Early career was as pianist; cond. at the Theater an der Wien from 1907. 1st of about 60 operettas and musicals was *Die lustigen Weiber von Wien* (prod. Munich, 1909). Worked in Berlin in 1920s, writing for early film musicals.

Moved to Hollywood 1940 and after returning to Vienna in 1946 wrote music for ice revues. Cond. while in his 90s.

Works incl. *Der Favorit* (1916), *Der Tans ins Glück* (1921), *Mädi* (1923), *Wenn die kleinen Veilchen blühen* (1932), *Venus in Seide* (1932), *Der verlorene Walzer* (1933), *Frühling in Prater* (1949), *Trauminsel* (1962); *c* 100 film scores, many individual songs, waltzes, and a funeral march for Hitler, written in anticipation of his death.

Stolz (orig. Stolzová), **Teres(in)a** (b Kostelec nad Labem, 2 Jun 1834; d Milan, 22–3 Aug 1902), Bohemian-Italian soprano. Studied under Lamperti at Milan and made her 1st stage appearance in 1860. She was Verdi's 1st Aida at Milan and the soprano in the fp of his Requiem. Other roles incl. Elisabeth de Valois and Leonora (*Forza*). Her elder twin sisters, **Francesca** and **Ludmilla** (b Kostelec, 13 Feb 1826), were also singers.

Stolze, Gerhard (b Dessau, 1 Oct 1926; d Garmisch-Partenkirchen, 11 Mar 1979), German tenor. Studied in Dresden and made his debut there in 1949. From 1951 he sang at Bayreuth and from 1957 at the Vienna Staatsoper; London, CG, 1960–3 as Mime. He was a highly dramatic character singer, specializing in more modern roles. He created Orff's Oedipus (Stuttgart 1959).

Stölzel, Gottfried Heinrich (b Grünstädtel, Saxony, 13 Jan 1690; d Gotha, 27 Nov 1749), German composer. Studied at Leipzig Univ., taught in Breslau 1710–12, and visited It. 1713–14, meeting Gasparini, Vivaldi and others. Lived in Prague, Bayreuth and Gera, and from 1719 was *Kapellmeister* to the court at Gotha.

Works incl. 22 operas, e.g. *Narcissus* (1711), *Orion* (1712), *Venus und Adonis* (1714), etc.; 14 oratorios; Masses, motets, etc.; Passions; *concerti grossi*; trio sonatas.

Stonard, William (d Oxford, 1630), English organist and composer. In 1608 he took a degree at Oxford and became organist of Christ Church Cathedral there, retaining the post until his death.

Works incl. services, anthems; catch 'Ding dong bell'.

Stone Flower, The (*Kamenny Tsvetok*), ballet in 3 acts by Prokofiev (scenario by L. Lavrovsky and M. Mendelson-Prokofieva after a story by P. Bazhov); comp. 1948–53, prod. Moscow, Bolshoy, 12 Feb 1954.

Stone Guest, The (*Kamenny Gost*), opera by Dargomizhsky (lib. Pushkin's drama, set unaltered), not perf. in the comp.'s lifetime; prod. St Petersburg, 28 Feb 1872.

Stone, Robert (b Alphington, Devon, 1516; d London, 2 Jul 1613), English composer. He learnt music as a chorister at Exeter Cathedral, but c 1543 went to London to enter the Chapel Royal, of which he became a Gentleman. Wrote a setting of the Lord's Prayer, part of his Morning Service.

Stone to Thorn, From, work by Peter Maxwell Davies for mezzo and ens., fp Oxford, 30 Jun 1971, cond. Davies.

Stonings (Stoninge), **Henry,** English composer of the 2nd half of the 16th cent. Wrote (?) a Latin Magnificat; also *In nomines* and other works for strings. His first name is known only from a statement by Hawkins, and it is possible that the Magnificat, at least, may be by Oliver Stonyng (*q.v.*).

Stonyng, Oliver, English 16th-cent. composer. He was a fellow of Eton Coll., 1530–47, and precentor, 1533–5. He comp. (?) a Latin Magnificat (Brit. Mus. Add. MSS. 17802–5).

Stopped Notes, on wind instruments the notes not prod. naturally as harmonics, but by valves, keys or other mechanical means, or sometimes by the hand in horn playing. On string instruments any notes not prod. on open strings.

Stopping, the placing of the left-hand fingers on the strings of string instruments to change the pitch of the notes of the open strings. The playing of 2 notes in this way simultaneously is called double stopping, but the term is also used loosely for the playing of chords with more than 2 notes. Stopping is also a device in horn playing: the placing of the hand in the bell to prod. a special quality of sound and formerly, before the invention of the valves, to change the pitch of some notes.

Stops, the devices by which the registration of the organ can be regulated and altered. The larger kinds of harpsichords also have stops, producing different qualities of tone and different pitches.

Storace, (Ann Selina), Nancy (b London, 27 Oct 1765; d London, 24 Aug 1817), English soprano. Pupil of Rauzzini in London and of Sacchini in It., sang leading roles in Florence, Milan and Venice. In 1784 was engaged as *prima donna* at the Vienna opera, where she was the first Susanna in Mozart's *Nozze di Figaro* (1786). She returned to London in 1787. Retired 1808.

Storace, Stephen (b London, 4 Apr 1762; d London, 19 Mar 1796), English composer, brother of prec. Studied at the Cons. di Sant' Onofrio in Naples, in c 1784 went to Vienna, where he prod. 2 operas and became friendly with Mozart, and returned to London with his sister in 1787, becoming comp. to Sheridan's co. at the Drury Lane Theatre.

Works incl. operas *Gli sposi malcontenti* (1785), *Gli equivoci* (after Shakespeare's *Comedy of Errors*, 1786), *La cameriera astuta* (1788), *The Haunted Tower, No Song, No Supper* (1790), *The Siege of Belgrade* (1791), *The Pirates, Dido: Queen of Carthage* (1792), *The Cherokee* (1794), *The Iron Chest* (Colman), *Mahmoud, or The Prince of Persia* (unfinished, completed by Kelly and Ann S., prod. 1796) and others; ballet *Venus and Adonis.*

Storchio, Rosina (b Venice, 19 May 1876; d Milan, 24 Jul 1945), Italian soprano. Debut Milan 1892, as Micaela; La Scala from 1895; created Madama Butterfly, 1904. Other creations were Leoncavallo's Musetta (1897) and Zazà (1900), Giordano's Stefana (*Siberia*, 1903) and Mascagni's Lodoletta (1917). At Buenos Aires (1904–14) and in NY she was admired as Norina, Violetta, Manon and Linda di Chamounix.

Story of a Real Man, The (*Povest' o nastoyashchem cheloveke*), opera in 4 acts by Prokofiev (lib. by comp. and M. Mendelson-Prokofieva); comp. 1947–8. Prokofiev sought to gain official favour with story of heroic Soviet aviator, but after private perf. in Leningrad, 3 Dec 1948, it was not staged until 8 Oct 1960, at the Bolshoy, Moscow.

Strada, Anna Maria (also known by her married name of S. del Pò), Italian soprano. Brought to London by Handel in 1729, she sang in several of his operas, remaining in England till 1738. She created leading roles in *Partenope, Ezio, Sosarme, Orlando, Ariodante, Alcina* and *Berenice.*

Stradella (Flotow). *See* **Alessandro Stradella.**

Stradella, Alessandro (b Rome, 1 Oct 1644; d Genoa, 25 Feb 1682), Italian composer, singer and violinist. Of noble birth, he never held any official posts, and most of what is known of his career seems to be based on legend rather than fact. He wrote operas and oratorios for Rome, Modena and Genoa. He (?) entered the service of the Duchess of Savoy and regent of Piedmont, Marie de Nemours, at Turin. He had numerous love affairs, the last of which led to his assassination.

Works incl. operas *La forza dell' amor paterno* (1678), *Doriclea, Il trespolo tutore balordo* (1679), *Il Floridoro*) motets and other church music; oratorio *San Giovanni Battista* (1675) and others; sacred and secular cantatas; serenade *Qual prodigio che io miri* and others; madrigals; concerto for strings.

Stradivari (Latinized Stradivarius), Italian family of vln. makers:

1. Antonio S. (b Cremona, 1644; d Cremona, 18 Dec 1737), founder of the workshop at Cremona in the 1660s, after serving an apprenticeship to Nicolo Amati.

2. Francesco S. (b Cremona, 1 Feb 1671; d Cremona, 11 May 1743), son of prec. He carried on his father's craft with

3. Omobono S. (b Cremona, 14 Nov 1679; d Cremona, 8 Jun 1742), brother of prec.

Straeten, Edmond van der (b Oudenarde, 3 Dec 1826; d Oudenarde, 25 Nov 1895), Belgian musicologist. Studied law at Alost and Ghent, but on returning home cultivated music history. He became sec. to Fétis for the purpose of studying with him and contrib. to his Dictionary. He also acted as critic and wrote books on Flemish music, incl. *La Musique aux Pays-bas* in 8 vols. He also comp. incid. music and a Te Deum.

Strambotto (It.), a form of verse used by the comps. of *frottole* in the 15th–16th cents. It had 8 lines (*ottava rima*), the 1st 6 rhyming alternately and the last 2 consecutively. In the *strambotto siciliano* all 8 lines rhyme alternately.

Strangways, A.H. Fox. *See* **Fox Strangways.**

Straniera, La (*The Stranger*), opera by Bellini (lib. by F. Romani), prod. Milan, La Scala, 14 Feb 1829.

Stransky, Josef (b Humpolec, 9 Sep 1872; d New York, 6 Mar 1936), Czech conductor and composer. Studied medicine at 1st, but turned to music, studying under Fibich and Dvořák in Prague and Fuchs and Bruckner in Vienna. He became cond. of the German Opera in Prague, then of the Hamburg Opera, 1909, and in 1911–22 cond. the NY Phil. Society, following Mahler. In 1922 gave the fp of Schoenberg's transcriptions of Bach chorale preludes. Figures in Strauss's *Intermezzo* as Stroh.

Works incl. opera *Beatrice and Benedick* (after Shakespeare's *Much Ado*), operetta *The General* (prod. Hamburg); symphs.; chamber music; songs.

Strascinando (It.), dragging, slurring.

Stratas, Teresa (b Toronto, 26 May 1938), Canadian soprano. She studied in Toronto and made her debut there in 1958 as Mimi. NY Met from 1959 as Lisa, Nedda, Zerlina and Cherubino. In 1962 she took part in the posthumous fp of Falla's *Atlántida*. She has sung Susanna at CG, London, and Salzburg.

In 1979 she sang the title role in the 1st complete perf. of Berg's *Lulu* (Paris, under Boulez). Other roles incl. Micaela, Giovanna d'Arco, Mélisande and Violetta.

Strathspey, a Scottish folk dance in quick common time, similar to the Reel, but with dotted rhythms. The name derives from the strath (valley) of Spey and is 1st heard of in 1780, though dances of the kind are much older.

Straube, (Montgomery Rufus) Karl (Siegfried) (b Berlin, 6 Jan 1873; d Leipzig, 27 Apr 1950), German organist and conductor, son of a German father and an English mother. Studied with his father, an organist and harmonium maker, and with Heinrich Reimann among others. He was app. organist of Wesel Cathedral in 1897 and of St Thomas's, Leipzig, in 1902. There he became cond. of the Bach Society in 1903, prof. of organ at the Cons. in 1907, and cantor of St Thomas's in 1918. He travelled all over Europe with the choir of St Thomas's. He pub. many eds. of organ and choral music of the past. He was made an hon. Ph.D. of Leipzig Univ. in 1923.

Straus, Ludwig (b Pressburg, 28 Mar 1835; d Cambridge, 23 Oct 1899), Austrian violinist. Studied at the Vienna Cons. and made his debut there in 1850. In 1855 he made a tour incl. It. and in 1857 another in Ger. and Swed., with Piatti. In 1860 he 1st visited Eng. and in 1864 settled in Manchester as leader of the Hallé Orch., and in 1888 in London.

Straus, Oscar (b Vienna, 6 Mar 1870; d Ischl, 11 Jan 1954), Austrian composer and conductor. Studied with Graedener and Bruch in Berlin and became theatre cond. at var. towns. He then settled in Berlin and in 1927 in Vienna and subsequently in Paris. In 1940 he emigrated to the USA, returning to Europe in 1948.

Works incl. operas *Die Waise von Cordova* and *Das Tal der Liebe* (1909), operettas *Ein Walzertraum (A Waltz Dream,* 1907), *Der tapfere Soldat (The Chocolate Soldier,* after Shaw's *Arms and the Man,* 1908), *Love and Laughter* (1913), *The Last Waltz, Riquette* and others; overture to Grillparzer's *Der Traum ein Leben,* serenade for string orch.

Strauss. Austrian family of musicians:

1. Johann (Baptist) S. (b Vienna, 14 Mar 1804; d Vienna, 25 Sep 1849), composer, conductor and violinist. His parents were innkeepers and apprenticed him to a bookbinder, but he learnt the vln. and vla. and was eventually allowed to study with Sey-

fried. He played vla. in private string 4tets, at 15 managed to join Pamer's orch. at the Sperl, a place of entertainment, music and dancing, then Lanner's band, in which he became deputy cond. In 1825 he and Lanner parted and he began a rival band, for which he wrote dances, esp. waltzes, which had by that time become fashionable. He was invited to return to the Sperl, which had enlarged the orch., and in 1833 began travelling abroad with a visit to Pest. By 1837 he had been to Ger., Hol., Belg., Fr. and Brit. He added the quadrille to the music of the Viennese ballrooms, having picked it up in Paris, and made a great hit with the *Radetzky Marsch*. He toured again and was then made cond. of the court balls.

Works incl. 150 waltzes (*Täuberl, Kettenbrücken, Donaulieder Walzer*, etc.), 35 quadrilles, 28 galops, 19 marches, 14 polkas.

2. Johann S. (b Vienna, 25 Oct 1825; d Vienna, 3 Jun 1899), composer, conductor and violinist, son of prec. He was not allowed to follow his father's profession, but learnt the vln. and studied secretly with Drechsler and others. In 1844 he appeared as cond. at Dommayer's hall in the Heitzing suburb, and his father capitulated. After the latter's death he amalgamated his orch. with his own, toured in Aus., Pol. and Ger. and in 1855–65 visited St Petersburg in the summer. In 1863 he became cond. of the court balls.

Works incl. operettas *Indigo und die vierzig Räuber* (1871), *Der Karneval in Rom* (1873), *Die Fledermaus* (1874), *Cagliostro in Wien* (1875), *Prinz Methusalem, Blindekuh, Das Spitzentuch der Königin* (1880), *Der lustige Krieg* (1881), *Eine Nacht in Venedig, Der Zigeunerbaron* (1885), *Simplizius* (1887), *Ritter Pázmán, Fürstin Ninetta* (1893), *Jabuka, Waldmeister* (1895), *Die Göttin der Vernunft* (1897); ballet *Aschenbrödel; Traumbilder* for orch.; a large number of waltzes (*An der schönen blauen Donau* (1867), *Tausend und eine Nacht, Wiener Blut* (1870), *Künstlerleben, Man lebt nur einmal, Morgenblätter, Geschichten aus dem Wiener Wald* (1868, etc.), polkas, galops and other dances.

3. Josef S. (b Vienna, 22 Aug 1827; d Vienna, 21 Jul 1870), composer and conductor, brother of prec. He became an architect at his father's wish, but secretly studied music and during an illness of Johann S. cond. his band with success. He then formed his own band and wrote 283 dances for it. He died after a visit to Warsaw, where he injured his hand in a fall on the platform at his last concert.

4. Eduard S. (b Vienna, 15 Mar 1835; d Vienna, 28 Dec 1916), composer and conductor, brother of prec. Studied harp and comp. and appeared as cond. in 1862. After 1865 he took Johann S.'s place at the summer concerts in St Petersburg and in 1870 became cond. of the court balls. He toured much, appearing at the Inventions Exhibition in London in 1885. His works incl. over 300 dances.

Strauss, Christoph (b Vienna, c 1580; d Vienna, Jun 1631), Austrian organist and composer. He entered the service of the court in 1594 and in 1601 became organist at the church of St Michael. In 1617–19 he was court cond. and afterwards *Kapellmeister* at St Stephen's Cathedral.

Works incl. Masses, Requiems, motets for voices and instruments.

Strauss, Richard (Georg) (b Munich, 11 Jun 1864; d Garmisch-Partenkirchen, 8 Sep 1949), German composer and conductor. His father, Franz S. (1822–1905), was horn player at the Court Opera in Munich, but had married into the wealthy brewers' family of Pschorr. Strauss began to comp. at the age of 6 and at 10 wrote his 1st two pub. works, the *Festival March* and the serenade for wind instruments. In 1880 he finished a symph. in D min. and the next year his A maj. string 4tet was perf. in public. He entered Munich Univ. in 1882, but left it in 1883, went to Berlin for a short period of study, but became asst. cond. to Bülow at Meiningen very soon after. A member of the orch., Alexander Ritter, turned his classical leanings into admiration for Berlioz, Wagner and Liszt. In 1885 Bülow resigned and Strauss became 1st cond. at Meiningen. In spring 1886 he visited It. and afterwards wrote the symph. *Aus Italien*, prod. at Munich in spring 1887, when he became sub-cond. at the Opera there. *Macbeth*, his 1st symph. poem, was comp. that year. In 1889 he became asst. cond. to Lassen at the Weimar Court Opera and in 1891 Cosima Wagner invited him to cond. *Tannhäuser* at Bayreuth.

Under Wagner's influence he wrote his 1st opera, *Guntram*, most of it during a tour in the Mediterranean undertaken to counteract threatening lung trouble. It was prod. at Weimar on 10 May 1894. The heroine was sung by Pauline de Ahna (*q.v.*), whom he married in June, and he was that year app. cond. of the Berlin PO in succession to Bülow. After the prod. of *Salome* at Dresden in 1905 Strauss began his series of operas written with Hugo von Hofmannsthal as librettist with *Elektra*, prod. there in 1909, and about that time he bought a country house at Garmisch in the Bavarian highlands, where all his later works were written. After Hofmannsthal's death in 1929 Strauss, who had already written a lib. of his own for *Intermezzo*, prod. at Dresden, 1924, worked with Stefan Zweig on *Die schweigsame Frau* (based on Ben Jonson's *Epicoene*), which was prod. at Dresden in 1935 but quickly withdrawn on a trumped-up excuse because Zweig, as a Jew, had to be boycotted by the Nazi party. Strauss thereupon resigned his appt. as president of the Reichs-Musikkammer and was himself under a cloud for a time, but had long been too important a figure in Ger. musical life to be ignored. He wrote music for the 1936 Berlin Olympic Games and comp. 4 further operas during the Nazi regime.

Works incl. OPERAS *Guntram, Feuersnot* (1901), *Salome* (1905), *Elektra, Der Rosenkavalier* (1911), *Ariadne auf Naxos* (1912), *Die Frau ohne Schatten* (1919), *Intermezzo, Die ägyptische Helena* (1928), *Arabella* (1933), *Die schweigsame Frau* (1935), *Friedenstag* (1938), *Daphne* (1938), *Die Liebe der Danae* (prod. 1944), *Capriccio* (1942); ballets *Josephs-Legende, Schlagobers*; incid. music to Molière's *Le Bourgeois Gentilhomme* (orig. connected with *Ariadne auf Naxos*, 1912).

ORCH.: 2 symphs.: F min. and *Aus Italien* (1884, 1887); symph. poems *Macbeth, Don Juan* (1889), *Tod und Verklärung* (1890), *Till Eulenspiegels lustige Streiche* (1895), *Also sprach Zarathustra* (1896), *Don Quixote* (1898), *Ein Heldenleben* (1899), *Symphonia domestica* (1904), *Eine Alpensinfonie* (1915); other orch. works: *Festival March*, 2 serenades for wind instruments (1881–4), 2 military marches, *Festliches Praeludium*; vln. concerto (1883), 2 horn concertos (1885, 1942), *Burleske* for pf. and orch. (1886), *Parergon zur Symphonia domestica* for pf. left hand and orch. (1925), *Japanische Festmusik* (1940), Divertimento on pieces by Couperin (1942), ob. concerto (1945); 2 sonatinas for wind insts. (1943, 1945), *Metamorphosen* for 23 solo string insts. (1946).

CHAMBER: string 4tet in A maj. (1880), pf. 4tet in C min.; sonatas for vln. and pf. and cello and pf. (1883, 1887).

VOCAL: 11 songs with orch. incl. 3 Hymns by Hölderlin, *Vier letzte Lieder* (1948); 26 op. nos. of songs (*c* 150) incl. cycles *Schlichte*

Weisen (Felix Dahn), *Mädchenblumen, Krämerspiegel* and 6 songs by Shakespeare and Goethe; pf. sonata, 9 pf. pieces; Tennyson's *Enoch Arden* (1890) and Uhland's *Das Schloss am Meer* for recitation and pf. (1899).

Stravaganza (It. = extravagance), a word sometimes used for a comp. of a freakish nature.

Stravinsky, Igor (Fyodorovich) b Oranienbaum nr. St. Petersburg, 17 Jun 1882; d New York, 6 Apr 1971), Russian composer. His father was a bass at the Imp. Opera. In 1903 Stravinsky met Rimsky-Korsakov at Heidelberg and played him his early comps., but did not become his pupil until 1907, by which time he had finished a pf. sonata, begun a symph. and married his 2nd cousin, Nadezhda Sulima, 11 Jan 1906. In 1908 he had the symph. perf. and wrote *Fireworks* for orch. for the marriage of Nadia Rimsky-Korsakov and M. Steinberg, and a *Funeral Chant* on Rimsky-Korsakov's death. The perf. of the *Fantastic Scherzo* in 1909 drew Diaghilev's attention to Stravinsky, who was commissioned to write *The Firebird* for the Rus. Ballet. It was prod. in Paris in 1910, and Stravinsky began to become known in western Europe. *Petrushka* followed in 1911 and *The Rite of Spring* in 1913, both prod. in Paris, where the latter provoked a riot of protest and fanatical partisanship. In 1914 he settled in Switz., on the Lake of Geneva. From 1914 he became as well known in London as in Paris, and in 1925 he 1st made a tour in USA. In the inter-war years many of his works were written in the spirit of neoclassicism (*q.v.*). In 1934 he became a Fr. citizen, but from 1939 he lived in Amer., becoming an Amer. citizen in 1945. He came under the influence of Robert Craft (*q.v.*) and from the early 1950s adopted serial technique. In 1962 he revisited Rus. for the 1st time since 1914.

Works incl. STAGE: *The Firebird* (ballet, 1910), *Petrushka* (ballet, 1911), *The Rite of Spring* (ballet, 1913), *The Nightingale* (opera after Andersen, 1914), *Renard* (*The Fox*, burlesque, chamber opera; comp. 1916, fp 1922), *The Soldier's Tale* (dance scene, 1918), *Pulcinella* (ballet with song, 1920), *Mavra* (opera buffa, 1922), *Les Noces* (*The Wedding*, Russian choreographic scenes; comp. 1914–17 and 1921–3, fp 1923), *Oedipus Rex* (opera-oratorio, 1927), *Apollon Musagète* (ballet, 1928), *The Fairy's Kiss* (ballet after Tchaikovsky, 1928), *Perséphone* (melodrama, 1934), *Jeu de Cartes* (*The Card Game*, ballet, 1937),

Scènes de ballet (1944), *Orpheus* (ballet, 1948), *The Rake's Progress* (opera, 1951), *Agon* (ballet, 1957), *The Flood* (musical play, 1962).

CHORAL: *The King of the Stars* (cantata, 1912), *Symphony of Psalms* (1930), *Babel* (cantata, 1944), *Mass*, with double wind 5tet (1944–8),*Cantata* (1952), *Canticum Sacrum* (1955), *Threni* (1958), *A Sermon, A Narrative and A Prayer* (cantata, 1961), *Anthem, The Dove Descending* (text by T.S. Eliot, 1962), *Requiem Canticles* (1966).

ORCH.: Symph. in Eb (1907), *Scherzo fantastique* (1908), *Fireworks* (1908), Suite from *The Firebird* (1911; rev. 1919 and 1945), *Rag-time* for 11 insts. (1918), *Symphonies of wind instruments* (1920), *The Song of the Nightingale*, symph. poem from *The Nightingale* (1917; staged 1920), Suite from *Pulcinella* (1922), Concerto for pf. and wind (1924), *Capriccio* for pf. and orch. (1929), Vln. concerto in D (1931), Divertimento from *The Fairy's Kiss* (1934), Concerto, *Dumbarton Oaks* (1938), *Symphony in C* (1940), *Danses concertantes* (1942), *Ode, elegiacal chant* (1943), *Symphony in 3 movts.* (1945), *Ebony concerto* for clar. and jazz band (1945), Concerto in D for strings (1946), *Movements* for pf. and orch. (1959), *Variations* (1964).

CHAMBER AND INSTRUMENTAL: 3 Pieces for string 4tet (1914), Suite from *The Soldier's Tale* (1918), Concertino for string 4tet (1920), Octet (1923), Suite from *Pulcinella* for vln. and pf. (1925); *Suite Italienne* for cello and pf. (1934), *Duo Concertante* for vln. and pf. (1932), Septet (1952). For pf.: 2 sonatas (1904 and 1924), 3 Movements from *Petrushka* (1921), Serenade in A (1925), Concerto for 2 pf. (1935), Sonata for 2 pf. (1944).

SOLO VOCAL incl. *Faun and Shepherdess* for mezzo and orch. (1906), *2 Poems of Paul Verlaine* (1910), *2 Poems of Balmont* (1911), *3 Japanese Lyrics* for sop. and ens. (1913), *Pribaoutki* for male voice and ens. (1914), *4 Russian Songs* (1919), *3 Songs from Shakespeare* for mezzo, fl., clar. and vla. (1953), *In memoriam Dylan Thomas* for tenor, string 4tet and 4 trombones (1954), *Abraham and Isaac*, sacred ballad for bar. and chamber orch. (1963), *Elegy for J.F.K.* for bar. and 3 clar. (1964).

Streich, Rita (b Barnaul, Siberia, 18 Dec 1920; d Munich, 20 Mar 1987), German soprano. Studied 1st in Augsburg and then with Maria Ivogün and Erna Berger in Berlin and later with Domgraf-Fassbänder, making her debut in 1943. From 1946 to 1950 she sang at the Berlin Staatsoper and from 1950 at the Berlin Städtische Oper. In 1953 she joined the Vienna Staatsoper and made her debut in London in 1954. US debut San Francisco, 1957, as Sophie. Glyndebourne 1958, Zerbinetta. She was best known for her singing of Mozart and R. Strauss and coloratura roles, e.g. Queen of Night, Constanze and Olympia.

Streicher (Ger. plur.), strings, as in English, for string instruments.

Streicher. German family of pf. makers:

1. Johann Andreas S. (b Stuttgart, 13 Dec 1761; d Vienna, 25 May 1833), music teacher in Vienna and founder there of a pf. manufacture after 1794, when he married

2. Maria Anna (Nanette) S. (*née* Stein) (b Augsburg, 2 Jan 1769; d Vienna, 16 Jan 1833). *See* **Stein**, family, 2.

3. Johann Baptist S. (b Vienna, 3 Jan 1796; d Vienna, 28 Mar 1871), son of above. He succeeded his parents in business, and from him it descended to his son Emil.

Streicher, Theodor (b Vienna, 7 Jun 1874; d Wetzelsdorf nr. Graz, 28 May 1940), Austrian composer, great-grandson of J.A. and M.A.S. Studied in Vienna, Dresden and Bayreuth.

Works incl. *Mignons Exequien* (after Goethe's *Wilhelm Meister*) for chorus, children's chorus and orch. (1907), *Die Schlacht bei Murten* for chorus and orch.; *Kleiner Vogel Kolibri* for chamber orch.; *Um Inez weinten* for soprano and orch.; *Die Monologe des Faust* (after Goethe) for string 6tet (1912); many songs, incl. 36 settings from *Des Knaben Wunderhorn*.

Streichinstrumente (Ger.), string instruments.

Streichzither (Ger. lit. stroke-zither), a variety of Zither played with a vln. bow instead of being plucked with the fingers or with a plectrum.

Streit zwischen Phöbus und Pan, Der (*The Dispute between Phoebus and Pan*), secular cantata by Bach, written in 1731 and satirizing Johann Adolf Scheibe, ed. of *Der critische Musikus*, in the part of Midas.

Strepitoso (It. = noisy), a direction suggesting a forceful and spirited perf., but more often used in the sense of a climax growing in force and speed.

Strepponi, Giuseppina (b Lodi, 8 Sep 1815; d Busseto, 14 Nov 1897), Italian soprano, daughter of the comp. Feliciano S. (1797–1832). Studied at the Milan Cons. and made her 1st appearance in 1835, at Trieste in Rossini's *Mathilde di Shabran*.

Verdi's 2nd wife, previously his mistress; she created Abigaille in *Nabucco* (Milan 1842).

Stretta (It. lit. pressure, tightening, squeezing), a passage, usually at the end of a comp., esp. an operatic finale, in which the tempo is accelerated either gradually or by sections and so makes a climax.

Stretto (It. lit. narrow, tightened, squeezed), a device in fugal writing whereby the entries of the subject are drawn more closely together in time. Instead of following each other voice by voice, each waiting until the last has been fully stated, in stretto they are made to overlap, the 2nd coming in before the end of the 1st, and so on.

Stretto maestrale (It. lit. masterly stretto), a stretto in which the fugal subject not only appears in close, overlapping entries, but is carried through from beginning to end at each entry.

Strict Counterpoint, the traditional name for counterpoint written according to the rules of the Species.

Striggio, Alessandro (b Mantua, *c* 1535; d Mantua, 29 Feb 1592), Italian composer, organist, lutenist and violist. He was in the service of Cosimo de' Medici at Florence, 1560–74, contributing to the local *intermedi*, and subsequently visited several European courts. He returned to Mantua, to the court of Duke Guglielmo Gonzaga.

Works incl. Masses, motet in 40 parts for voices and insts.; madrigal comedy *Il cicalamento delle donne al bucato* (1567); intermezzi for perf. between the acts of plays; madrigals; var. works for voices and insts. in many parts.

Striggio, Alessandro (b Mantua, 1573; d Venice, 6 Jun 1630), Italian librettist, son of prec. He was secretary to the Duke of Mantua and string player at court until 1628. Author of the text of Monteverdi's *Orfeo* and *Tirsi e Clori.*

Strinasacchi, Regina (b Ostiglia nr. Mantua, 1764; d Dresden, 1839), Italian violinist and guitar player. Studied at the Cons. della Pietà in Venice, toured It. 1780–3, and in 1784 visited Vienna, where Mozart wrote for her the vln. sonata in B♭ maj., K454. She married the cellist J.C. Schlick in 1785.

String Quartet, a chamber combination consisting of 2 vlns., vla. and cello. The form was devised early in the 18th cent. and developed by Haydn and Mozart. Some of the most profound music of Beethoven and Schubert employs the medium; later 19th-cent. comps. wrote important 4tets, e.g. Mendelssohn, Schumann, Brahms, Smetana and Dvořák. In the 20th cent. the most

highly regarded string 4tets are by Bartók (6), Schoenberg (4) and Janáček (2). Other comps. incl. Shostakovich (15), Britten (4) and Elliott Carter (4).

String Quintet. Boccherini wrote many works for 2 vlns., vla. and 2 cellos. The same form was adopted by Schubert for the greatest of his chamber works (1828). 2 vlns., 2 vlas. and cello were favoured by Mozart- in 4 of his finest instrumental pieces – and by Beethoven, Brahms and Nielsen. Dvořák's string 5tet op. 77 uses a db. instead of 2nd vla.

String Sextet. The combination of 2 vlns., 2 vlas. and 2 cellos, e.g. Dvořák's op. 48, Brahms's op. 18 and op. 36 and Schoenberg's *Verklärte Nacht* (Transfigured Night, 1899). The prologue to Strauss's *Capriccio* (1940–1) is a string sextet.

String Trio. After humble beginnings with Haydn and Boccherini the combination of vln., vla. and cello is found in one of Mozart's finest works, the Divertimento K563. Beethoven emulated Mozart's example in his trio op. 3 and further developed the form's potential in his set of 3 trios op. 9. After comparative neglect during the Romantic period, notable trios of the 20th cent. incl. those of Roussel, Hindemith, Dohnányi and Webern. Schoenberg's string trio of 1945 depicts the comp.'s feelings as he lay ill after an operation.

Strings, the cords, usually of gut (vln. family, harps, etc.) or wire (lute, vln. and guitar families, pfs., etc.), by means of which the notes are prod. on such instruments. The term strings is also used to designate string instruments collectively, esp. those of the vln. family in the orch.

Strogers, E. (properly E. Strowger), early 16th-cent. English composer. Wrote a *Miserere* for organ (Brit. Mus. Add. MS. 29996).

Strogers, Nicholas, English 16th–17th-cent. organist and composer, (?) son of prec.

Works incl. motets, services and other church music; madrigals; *In nomines* for strings; organ, lute and virginal pieces.

Strohfiedel (Ger. lit. straw fiddle), a 16th-cent. perc. instrument similar to the xylophone.

Stromentato (It. = instrumented, orchestrated, scored). The word is assoc. mainly with recitative (*recitativo stromentato*), where it implies a more or less independent orchestral accomp.

Strong, G(eorge) Templeton (b New York, 26 May 1856; d Geneva, 27 Jun 1948), American composer. Studied at the Leipzig Cons., became a member of the Liszt circle, was in close touch with MacDowell while living at Wiesbaden in 1886–9, and after teaching at Boston in 1891–2 settled in Switz. on the Lake of Geneva, living 1st at Vevey and later in Geneva.

Works incl. *Knights and Dryads* for solo voices, chorus and orch.; 2 cantatas for solo voices, male chorus and orch.; 3 symphs.: *Sintram* (after Fouqué, 1888), *In the Mountains* (1886) and *By the Sea*, symph. poem *Undine* (after Fouqué); *2 Amer. Sketches* for vln. and orch.; trio for 2 vlns. and vla. *A Village Music-Director* and other chamber music.

Strong, Susan (b Brooklyn, 3 Aug 1870; d London, 11 Mar 1946), American soprano. Studied RCM; debut London 1895, with Hedmont co., as Sieglinde. CG 1895–1902, as Brünnhilde, Donna Anna and Venus. Mapelson co. in NY 1896, as Elsa and Marguerite. Vienna Hofoper 1901, under Mahler.

Strophic Bass, an instrumental bass part used without change throughout a series of verses of a song or chorus the upper parts of which vary at each occurrence; or a similar device in instrumental music.

Strophic Song, the simplest form of song, structurally considered, in which each verse of a poem is set to the same music.

Strozzi, Barbara (b Venice, 6 Aug 1619; d (?) Venice, c 1664), Italian singer and composer. Adopted daughter of the poet Giulio S. Comp. madrigals, cantatas, sacred songs with continuo, duets, ariettas, etc.

Strozzi, Gregorio (b San Severino, c 1615; d Naples, c 1690), Italian priest, organist and composer. Studied with Sabino in Naples, and succeeded him as organist of the Church of the Madonna there.

Works incl. responsories, Lamentations, psalms, motets, etc.; *Capricci da sonare Cembali et Organi.*

Strungk (or Strunck), Delphin (b c 1601; d Brunswick, buried 12 Oct 1694), German organist and composer. He was, after 1630, successively organist at Wolfenbüttel, Celle and Brunswick.

Works incl. music for the Duke of Brunswick in 5 vocal and 8 instrumental parts; var. vocal works with instruments; chorale preludes and other works for organ.

Strungk, Nikolaus Adam (b Brunswick, bap. 15 Nov 1640; d Dresden, 23 Sep 1700), German composer, violinist and organist, son of prec. Pupil of his father, for whom he deputized at the organ at Brunswick from the age of 12. While at Helmstedt Univ. he learnt the vln. at Lübeck during vacations. In 1660 he joined the court orch. at Wolfenbüttel, then at Celle, and in 1665 went to the court of Hanover. After a period at Hamburg from 1678, two visits to Vienna and one to It., he returned to Hanover, 1682–6, but in 1688 he went to Dresden as chamber organist and 2nd *Kapellmeister* to the Saxon court in succession to Ritter, and succeeded Bernhard as 1st *Kapellmeister* in 1692. In 1693 he opened an opera-house at Leipzig, where he prod. his later opera stage works and where his daughters Philippine and Elisabeth sang.

Works incl. operas *Der glückselig-steigende Sejanus, Der unglücklichfallende Sejanus* (1678), *Esther, Doris* (1680), *Semiramis, Nero, Agrippina* (1699) and others, completion of Pallavicini's *L'Antiope*; oratorio *Die Auferstehung Jesu* (1688); *ricercare* on the death of his mother; sonatas and chaconnes for vln. or vla. da gamba; sonatas for 2 vlns. and vla. and for 6 strings; airs and dances for recorders.

Strunk (William) Oliver (b Ithaca, NY, 22 Mar 1901; d Grottaferrata, nr. Rome, 24 Feb. 1980), American musicologist. He studied at Cornell Univ. and in Berlin; worked at the Library of Congress from 1928 and taught at Princeton 1937–66. His *Source Readings in Music History* remains a classic. He was among the most influential musicological teachers of his generation, but his most important pubs. concerned Byzantine chant.

Strunz, Jacob (b Pappenheim, 1783; d Munich, 23 May 1852), German composer. Pupil of Winter at Munich. He travelled all over Europe in 1798–1845 and also visited Egypt; then settled at Munich for the rest of his life. He was a friend of Meyerbeer, Berlioz and Balzac, who ded. his story *Massimilla Doni* to him.

Works incl. operas *Le Maître de chapelle* and *Les Courses de Newmarket*; several ballets; incid. music (the 1st) for Hugo's *Ruy Blas*; 3 string 4tets; songs.

Stuck, Jean Baptiste (usually called Batistin) (b Florence, c 1680; d Paris, 8 Dec 1755), French cellist and composer of German origin. He went to Fr. at an early age and was the 1st cellist in the Paris Opéra orch., also court musician to the Duke of Orleans.

Works incl. operas *Rodrigo in Algieri* (with Albinoni), *Méléagre* (1709), *Mantho la fée* (1711) and *Polidore* (1720); many court ballets; cantatas, airs.

Stucken, Frank (Valentin) van der (b Fredericksburg, Texas, 15 Oct 1858; d

Hamburg, 16 Aug 1929), American conductor and composer. Studied in Europe with Benoît, Reinecke, Grieg and others. In 1884–95 he cond. a male-voice choir in NY, where he also cond. orchestral concerts. In 1895–1903 he was dir. of the Cincinnati Coll. of Music and from the same year to 1907 he cond. the Symph. Orch. there. After 1908 he lived much in Europe.

Works incl. opera *Vlasda*; incid. music to Shakespeare's *Tempest*; choral works; songs.

Stuckenschmidt, Hans Heinz (b Strasbourg, 1 Nov 1901), German musicologist. Studied pf., vln. and comp. in Berlin, and also analysis with Schoenberg. He has held many posts as music critic and from 1948 taught at the Technical Univ. in Berlin; Prof. Emeritus 1967. He is esp. well known as a writer on 20th-cent. music, incl. Schoenberg and the Viennese School; pub. biographies of Schoenberg in 1951 and 1978.

Stückgold, Grethe (b London, 6 Jul 1895; d Falls Village, Conn., 15 Sep 1977), German soprano. After singing in concert made her stage debut, Nuremberg 1917. Berlin from 1922; sang in the 1929 fp of Hindemith's *Neues vom Tage*, under Klemperer, at the Kroll Opera. NY Met 1927–40; debut as Eva. Also sang in San Francisco, Philadelphia and Chicago.

Study, an instrumental piece, usually for a single instrument, written mainly for the purpose of technical exercise and display, but not necessarily devoid of expression and high artistic quality. The Fr. word *étude* is more often used for it.

Stump, a string instrument of the Cittern type invented *c* 1600 by Daniel Farrant. The MS. of the only surviving piece written for it, 'To the Stump by F.P.', is in Christ Church, Oxford. (MUS.532) From it have been inferred var. details such as length of strings, no. of courses and compass.

Stumpf, Carl (b Wiesentheid, 21 Apr 1848; d Berlin, 25 Dec 1936), German music scientist and psychologist. Studied at Göttingen Univ. and held professorships at Würzburg, Prague, Halle, Munich and, from 1893, in Berlin. He collaborated with Hornbostel in ed. the *Beiträge zur Akustik und Musikwissenschaft* and wrote much on the psychological aspects of acoustical phenomena.

Stuntz, Joseph (Hartmann) (b Arlesheim nr. Basle, ? 23 Jul 1793; d Munich, 18 Jun 1859), Swiss composer and conductor. Studied with Winter at Munich and Salieri in Vienna. He spent 3 years in It. and in 1825 succeeded Winter as 1st cond. of the Royal Opera at Munich.

Works incl. operas *La rappresaglia* (1820), *Costantino, Argene e Dalmiro, Elvira e Lucindo, Heinrich IV. zu Givry* (after Voltaire's *Charlot*, 1820) and *Maria Rosa*; ballets; church music; cantatas and part-songs, symph. in D min. and concert overtures; songs.

Sturgeon, Nicholas (b *c* 1390; d London, 31 May 1454), English composer. He was a scholar of Winchester Coll., 1399, aged 8–12. He may have visited France with Henry V in 1416. In 1442, after serving as a clerk of the Chapel Royal, he became a canon of Windsor and precentor of St Paul's Cathedral. He contrib. to the Old Hall MS. during the second phase of its existence, when it was in use at the Chapel Royal. 5 known works by him survive.

Sturm, Der (*The Tempest*), operas based on Shakespeare's play with this title by Peter Winter (Munich, 1798) and Frank Martin (Vienna, 17 Jun 1956): work for chorus and orch. by Haydn (not based on Shakespeare) comp. 1798 and perf. at his concerts in London.

Sturton, Edmund, English 15th–16th-cent. composer. He was (?) clerk and instructor of the choristers at Magdalen Coll., Oxford, 1509–10. He wrote an *Ave Maria* and *Gaude virgo mater*, the latter in the Eton Choirbook.

Sturzenegger, Richard (b Zurich, 18 Dec 1905; d Berne, 24 Oct 1976), Swiss composer and cellist. He studied at the Zurich Cons. and with Alexanian, Casals and Nadia Boulanger in Paris. Later he joined the Dresden Opera orch. and studied further with Feuermann for cello and Toch for comp. He settled as cello prof. in Berne.

Works incl. cantatas and other choral works; theatre music; 4 cello concertos (1933–72); chamber music.

Subdiapente (*see also* **Diapente**; from Lat. and Gk.), a 5th lower. The term is used esp. for canons at the 5th.

Subdiatessaron (from Lat. and Gk.), a 4th lower.

Subdominant, the 4th degree of the maj. or min. scale. For the subdominant chord see **Cadence.**

Subject, a theme used as a principal feature in a composition, esp. in a Fugue, where it is brought in a number of times, voice by voice, or in a Rondo, where it is a recurrent main theme returning after a series of episodes. In sonata form 1st and 2nd subjects are the main structural features, but there they are thematic groups more often than single themes.

Submediant, the 6th degree of the maj. or min. scale, so called because it is the opposite of the Mediant, i.e. it is a 3rd below instead of above the Tonic. The submediant of a maj. scale is the tonic of its relative min.

Subotnick, Morton (b Los Angeles, 14 Apr 1933), American composer. Studied at Mills College with Milhaud. Dir. of electronic music at Calif. Inst. of Arts, LA, from 1969.

Works incl. *Concert,* for wind 5tet and electronics; *Music for 12 Elevators; Before the Butterfly* for orch. (1975); *The Double Life of Amphibians,* music drama; *Angels* for string 4tet and electronics (fp 1984); incid. music for plays by Brecht and Beckett.

Subsemitonium (Lat. = under-semitone), the old name for the Leading-note, esp. when used in the Modes by sharpening the 7th of the scale.

Subtonium (Lat. = under-[whole] tone), the old name for the 7th degree of the Modes, except the Lydian (and later the Ionian), so called because it was a whole tone below the final, though it was often sharpened in perf. according to the principle of Musica ficta.

Sucher, Josef (b Döbör, Hungary, 23 Nov 1843; d Berlin, 4 Apr 1908), Austro-Hungarian conductor and composer. Learnt music as choir-boy of the Aus. court chapel at the Löwenburg seminary in Vienna and later studied with Sechter. After var. cond. appointments at Viennese theatres, incl. the Court Opera, he went to Leipzig as cond. of the municipal theatre in 1876; in 1878 he gave the 1st local *Ring* cycle. In 1877 he married the singer Rosa Hasselbeck. He was cond. of the court opera in Berlin from 1888 to 1899; gave there a complete cycle of Wagner's operas, from *Rienzi.*

Works incl. opera *Ilse;* Masses and cantatas, overtures for orch.; song cycle *Ruheort.*

Sucher (née Hasselbeck), Rosa (b Velburg, Bavaria, 23 Feb 1849; d Eschweiler nr. Aachen, 16 Apr 1927), German soprano, wife of prec. She made her 1st appearance at Trier and advanced rapidly to more important opera houses, going with her husband to Hamburg in 1879, where he became cond. of the Opera. They visited Eng. in 1882 and at Drury Lane, under Richter, she was the 1st London Isolde and Eva; CG 1892 as Brünnhilde and Isolde, under Mahler. In 1886 she sang Isolde at Bayreuth; remained until 1894. NY Met debut 1895, as Isolde.

Suchon, Eugen (b Pezinok, 25 Sep 1908), Slovak composer. Studied at Bratislava Cons. (1927–31), and then in Prague with Novák (1931–3). From 1933 to 1941 he taught at the Bratislava Acad. of Music and was prof. at the State Cons (1941–7). From 1947 to 1953 he was prof. at the Slovak Univ. and from 1953 at the Pedagogic High School in Bratislava.

Works incl. opera *The Whirlpool* (1949); serenades for strings, for wind 5tet (1932–3); choral music; pf. 4tet, pf. pieces.

Suggia, Guilhermina (b Oporto, 27 Jun 1888; d Oporto, 31 Jul 1950), Portuguese cellist. She played in the Oporto orch. and a string 4tet before she was 13, in 1904 was sent to Leipzig to study with Klengel, appeared there under Nikisch and lastly studied with Casals, with whom she lived from 1906 to 1912, in Spain. She lived in London for many years, but returned to Portugal some years before her death. Her portrait was painted by Augustus John in 1923.

Suite, a form of instrumental music consisting of a number of movements, orig. dances, but now any pieces the comp. desires, incl. chosen numbers from operas, ballets, etc. In the late 17th cent. a tradition was estab. of incl. 4 regular dance movements: Allemande, Courante, Sarabande and Gigue (to give the Fr. names as the most frequently used). These were almost invariably in the same key, prob. because suites were often written for lutes, which had to be newly tuned for each key. Other dances could be added at will, such as the Gavotte, Minuet, Bourrée, Rigaudon, Hornpipe, etc., and the whole could be preceded by a Prelude (e.g. Purcell, Bach's English Suites, etc.). There could also be fancy pieces with a var. of titles, as in Bach's Partitas (*partita* being another name for suite) and more esp. in the suites by Fr. comps., e.g. those by Couperin. The chief features inherited from the suite by the sonata were the binary form of the dances, which became the exposition, working-out and recapitulation of the sonata form, and the minuet, which was retained partic. in symphs. and in the 19th cent. turned into the scherzo. The form was revived in the 20th cent. by Schoenberg (Suite for pf. op. 25, 1921, and Suite op. 29 for 3 clars. and pf. 5tet, 1924–6).

Suitner, Otmar (b Innsbruck, 16 May 1922), Austrian conductor. Studied with Clemens Krauss. In 1960 became chief cond. of the Dresden Staatsoper and Staatskapelle. Music dir. Deutsche Staatsoper, Berlin, 1964; gave there the fps of Dessau's *Puntila* (1966) and *Einstein* (1974). He has cond. at the San Francisco Opera from 1969.

Suivez (Fr. imper. = follow), a direction used in two senses: (1) to indicate that one movement of a comp. is to follow the preceding one immediately (equivalent to It. *attacca*); (2) to indicate that accompanying parts are to follow a vocal or other solo part moving independently of the prescribed rhythm or tempo (equivalent to It. *colla parte*).

Suk, Josef (b Křečovice, 4 Jan 1874; d Benešov nr. Prague, 29 May 1935), Czech composer, violinist and violist. Studied with Dvořák in Prague and in 1898 became his son-in-law. In 1892 he formed the Bohemian String 4tet with Karel Hofmann, Oscar Nedbal and Otto Berger, playing 2nd vln. He began to comp. early and in 1922 became prof. of comp. at the Prague Cons., of which he was dir. in 1924–6. Much of his music was influenced by personal experiences, esp. the death of his wife in 1905, e.g. the pf. pieces *About Mother* written for his infant son, and by that of Dvořák, e.g. the *Asrael* symph., which refers to those 2 deaths.

Works incl. Mass in Bb maj.; incid. music for Julius Zeyer's *Radúz and Mahulena* (1898); *Epilogue* for baritone solo, women's chorus and orch.; symphs. in E maj. (1899) and *Asrael* (1906), symph. poems *Prague, A Summer Tale* and *Maturity*, Dramatic Overture and overture to Shakespeare's *Winter's Tale* (1894), *A Tale* and *Under the Appletrees* for orch.; serenade (1892) and meditation on a chorale for string orch.; fantasy for vln. and orch. (1902); 2 string 4tets (1896, 1911), pf. 4tet, pf. trio, elegy for vln. and cello with string 4tet, harmonium and harp; *Ballade and Serenade* for cello and pf.; sets of pf. pieces; part songs.

Suk, Joseph (b Prague, 8 Aug 1929), Czech violinist. Grandson of prec. and great-grandson of Dvořák. Studied at Prague Cons. with J. Kocian, graduating in 1950. Founded Suk Trio 1952. US debut 1964, with Cleveland Orch. Named National Artist of Czechoslovakia in 1977.

Suk, Váša (b Kladno, 1 Nov 1861; d Moscow, 12 Jan 1933), Czech violinist, conductor and composer. Studied at the Prague Cons. and became violinist and cond. successively at Warsaw, Kiev and Moscow.

Works incl. opera *The Forest King*; symph. poem *Jan Hus*; serenade for string orch., etc.

Sul ponticello (It.) = on the bridge, a direction in music for bowed string instruments to play a passage very near (not actually on) the bridge to prod. a peculiar nasal and rustling sound.

Sul tasto (It.), a direction indicating that a passage of string music is to be played with the bow over the finger-board.

Sullivan, Arthur (Seymour) (b London, 13 May 1842; d London, 22 Nov 1900), English composer. Son of a bandmaster and prof. at the Royal Military School of Music, entered the Chapel Royal in 1854 and was taught by Helmore. In 1856 he gained the Mendelssohn scholarship at the RAM, where he studied under Sterndale Bennett, Goss and O'Leary. The scholarship entitled him to a course of study at the Leipzig Cons., where he studied comp., cond. and pf., returning in 1861 to London, where he became organist at St Michael's Church, Chester Square. He 1st made his mark as comp. with incid. music to Shakespeare's *Tempest*. His 1st operetta, *The Sapphire Necklace*, was prod. in 1864 and the 1st for which Gilbert wrote the lib. in 1871. After that he and Gilbert repeated their joint triumphs until 1889, when they reached their climax in *The Gondoliers*. Sullivan taught and conducted intermittently; he had been app. prof. of comp. at the RAM in 1866. The following year he and Grove went to Vienna and discovered a pile of forgotten MSS. of Schubert's works. Knighted 1883.

Works incl. opera *Ivanhoe*; operettas (with Gilbert as librettist) *Thespis, or The Gods Grown Old, Trial by Jury* (1875), *The Sorcerer, H.M.S. Pinafore* (1878), *The Pirates of Penzance* (1879), *Patience* (1881), *Iolanthe* (1882), *Princess Ida, The Mikado* (1885), *Ruddigore* (1886), *The Yeomen of the Guard* (1888), *The Gondoliers* (1886), *Utopia Limited, The Grand Duke*; other operettas: *The Sapphire Necklace, Cox and Box* (1867), *The Contrabandista, The Zoo* (1875), *Haddon Hall, The Chieftain* (adapted from *The Contrabandista*, 1894), *The Beauty Stone* (1898), *The Rose of Persia, The Emerald Isle* (unfinished, completed by German, 1901); ballets *L'Île enchantée* and *Victoria and Merrie England*; incid. music to Shakespeare's *Tempest, Merchant of Venice, Merry Wives of Windsor, Henry VIII* and *Macbeth*, Tennyson's *The Foresters* and Comyns Carr's *King Arthur*.

CHORAL: *Kenilworth* (after Scott), *The Prodigal Son, On Shore and Sea, The Light of the World* (1873), *The Martyr of Antioch, The Golden Legend* (1886; revived in perf. cond. by Charles Mackerras, Leeds, 15 Mar 1986).

ORCH.: symph. in E maj.; overtures *In Memoriam, Di ballo*, to Shakespeare's *Timon of Athens* and *Marmion* (after Scott);

Procession March, Princess of Wales March, Imperial March; cello concerto (1866; score was destroyed but reconstructed by Charles Mackerras and perf. 1985).

CHAMBER: romance for string 4tet; var. pf. pieces; song cycle *The Window* (Tennyson), a number of songs incl. 'Orpheus with his lute', *The Lost Chord* and Kipling's *The Absent-minded Beggar*.

Sulzer, Salomon (b Hohenems, Vorarlberg, 30 Mar 1804; d Vienna, 17 Jan 1890), Austrian baritone, Jewish cantor and editor. He was placed in charge of the music at the new Vienna synagogue in 1825 and studied with Seyfried. He ed. a collection of Jewish hymns and commissioned var. comps. to contribute to it. Schubert's setting of Psalm xcii in Moses Mendelssohn's trans. for baritone and male chorus originated in this way. In 1844–7 Sulzer was prof. of singing at the Vienna Cons.

Sumer is icumen in (Summer has come), an English song in parts, dating from *c* 1270 and known as the Reading Rota (round). It is a canon for 4 voices and there are 2 additional bass voices adding a Pes or Ground-bass, also in canon. In the MS. the tune is also provided with Lat. words, beginning *Perspice, Christicola*, but the accompanying voices (or Pes) merely have 'Sing cuccu nu' in both versions, though the music they sing is actually part of an Easter antiphon.

'Sun' Quartets, the nickname of the 6 string 4tets op. 20 by Haydn, comp. in 1772.

Sunderland (*née* **Sykes**), **Susan** (b Brighouse, Yorks., 30 Apr 1819; d Brighouse, 6 May 1905), English soprano. The daughter of a gardener, she was discovered by accident, induced to join the Halifax Choral Society and, after a 1st appearance at Bradford in 1838, given a few months' training in London. She at first sang in Yorkshire only, but in 1849 sang in London in *Messiah*; continued there until 1856 and retired 1864.

Sunless, song cycle by Mussorgsky (words by A.A. Golenishchev-Kutuzov), comp. 1874: 1. *Between four walls*; 2. *Thou didst not know me in the crowd*; 3. *The idle, noisy day is ended*; 4. *Boredom*; 5. *Elegy*; 6. *On the River*.

Suor Angelica (Puccini). *See* **Trittico**.

Supertonic, the 2nd degree of the maj. or min. scale, so called because it stands above the Tonic.

Supervia, Conchita (b Barcelona, 9 Dec 1899; d London, 30 Mar 1936), Spanish mezzo. She made her debut in Buenos Aires (1910) and the following year sang Octavian in Rome. She 1st appeared in London in the 1920s as a concert singer, excelling in Spanish songs as well as in arias from the parts written by Rossini for his wife, Isabella Colbran; later she appeared in some of these parts, as well as in *Carmen*, at Covent Garden, 1934–5. Other roles incl. Isabella, Rosina and Cenerentola. She became Eng. by marriage.

Suppé, Franz von (actually Francesco Ezechiele Ermenegildo Suppe Demelli) (b Spalato [Split], 18 Apr 1819; d Vienna, 21 May 1895), Austrian composer and conductor of Belgian descent. He showed a talent for comp. early, prod. a Mass and a comic opera *Der Apfel* at Zara in 1834; but he was sent to Padua Univ. by his father to study medicine. On his father's death, however, he settled in Vienna with his mother, studied with Seyfried and cond. at var. Viennese and provincial theatres, incl. the Josephstadt, Wieden and Leopoldstadt Theatres in Vienna from 1841 to his death.

Works incl. operettas *Das Mädchen vom Lande* (1847), *Das Pensionat* (1860), *Paragraph 3, Zehn Mädchen und kein Mann* (1862), *Flotte Bursche* (with an overture on students' songs, 1863), *Die schöne Galatee* (1865), *Leichte Kavallerie (Light Cavalry), Fatinitza, Boccaccio* (1879), *Donna Juanita* (1880), *Die Afrikareise* and several others; farces; ballets; incid. music to Elmar's *Dichter und Bauer* (*Poet and Peasant, 1846*), Shakespeare's *Midsummer Night's Dream*, Schiller's *Wallensteins Lager* and others (more than 200 stage works); Mass, Requiem (*L'estremo giudizia, 1855*; 1st Brit. perf. 1984, BBC).

Surinach, Carlos (b Barcelona, 4 Mar 1915), American composer of Spanish birth. After study in Ger. cond. Barcelona PO from 1944. Settled in US 1951, citizen 1959.

Works incl. ballets *Monte Carlo* (1945) and *David and Bathsheba* (1960); 3 symphs. (1945–57), *Sinfonietta flamenca* (1954), *Melorhythmic Dramas* for orch. (1966); chamber music, songs.

'Surprise' Symphony, Haydn's symph. no. 94 in G maj., comp. for London in 1791, so called after the sudden loud interruption after 16 quiet bars at the beginning of the slow movement. Known in Ger. as 'Symphonie mit dem Paukenschlag' (Symph. with the Drum-beat).

Survivor from Warsaw, A, work by Schoenberg for narrator, men's chorus and orch., op. 46 (text. by comp.), fp Albuquerque, 4 Nov 1948.

Surzyński, Józef (b Szrem nr. Poznań, 15 Mar 1851; d Kościan, 5 Mar 1919), Polish priest and composer. Studied at Regensburg and Leipzig, later taking holy orders in Rome. In 1882 he became dir. of the cathedral choir at Poznań and in 1894 provost at Kościan. He ed. the *Monumenta Musices Sacrae in Polonia* and *Musica Ecclesiastica*.

Works incl. numerous Masses, hymns and other church music, *Polish Songs of the Catholic Church*.

Susanna, oratorio by Handel (lib. anon.), perf. London, CG, 10 Feb 1749.

Susanna's Secret (Wolf-Ferrari). See **Segreto di Susanna**.

Susato, Tielman (b Cologne, *c* 1500; d ? Antwerp, between 1561 and 1564), Flemish composer, publisher and editor. He worked in Antwerp from 1529 and was the outstanding Dutch music pub. of his time; estab. his business 1543, and in 1547 built his own premises 'At the Sign of the Crumhorn'. His 11 *Musyck Boexken* (little music books, 1551) contained Dutch songs, dance music and the *Souter Liedekens* of Clemens non Papa and Gerhard Mes. He also pub. vols. of Masses, motets and *chansons* by the leading comps. of his day. Many of these incl. works by himself.

Suspension (Eng.), the sustaining of a note which forms part of a consonant chord so that it creates a dissonance with one or more of the notes of the next chord: the dissonant note then descends ('resolves' is the technical term) to the next note below so as to turn the dissonance into a consonance, e.g.:

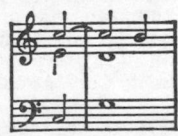

In normal 16th-cent. practice the suspended note is first heard on a weak beat, the dissonance occurs on a strong beat, and the resolution follows on a weak beat: this practice was largely followed by later comps., who extended the idea by resolving the dissonant note upwards (also known as retardation) as well as downwards. Suspensions can occur simultaneously in more than one part, and the effect is the same if the note which is to create the dissonance is repeated instead of being tied over.

Susskind, Walter (b Prague, 1 May 1913; d Berkeley, Calif., 25 Mar 1980), English conductor and pianist of Czech origin. Studied comp. with J. Suk and A. Hába, cond. with Szell, making his debut at the German Opera House in Prague in 1932. From 1942 to

1945 he cond. with the Carl Rosa Opera Co. and then at SW in 1946. From 1946 to 1952 he was also cond. of the Scot. Nat. Orch., and from 1954 to 1956 he cond. in Australia, becoming cond. of the Toronto SO from 1956 to 1965. In 1968 he took over the St Louis SO and cond. it until 1975, when he became prin. guest cond. Cincinnati SO. In England he was heard as a piano soloist, and in 1977 gave the fp in Brit. of Zemlinsky's *Lyric Symphony*.

Süssmayr, Franz (Xaver) (b Schwanenstadt, Upper Aus., 1766; d Vienna, 17 Sep 1803), Austrian composer. Educ. at the monastery of Kremsmünster and pupil of Salieri and Mozart in Vienna. He asst. Mozart with *La clemenza di Tito* (prob. the recitatives) and completed his unfinished Requiem. In 1792 he became cond. of the Kärntnertortheater.

Works incl. operas *Moses* (1792), *L'incanto superato* (1793), *Der Spiegel von Arkadien* (1794), *Il Turco in Italia, Idris und Zenide* (1795), *Die edle Rache, Die Freiwilligen, Der Wildfang* (after Kotzebue), *Der Marktschreier* (1799), *Soliman II* (after Favart, 1799), *Gulnare* (1800), *Phasma* and others; 2 ballets; Masses and other church music; cantatas *Der Retter in Gefahr* (1796), and *Der Kampf für den Frieden* (1800); clar. concerto; serenades for fl., vla. and horn and for vln., guitar and Eng. horn; instrumental pieces.

Sustaining Pedal, the so-called 'loud' pedal of the pf., not used to prod. greater volume of tone, but to sustain any notes struck after it has been depressed, even after the fingers have left the keys, until it is released again.

Sutermeister, Heinrich (b Feuerthalen, Ct. Schaffhausen, 12 Aug 1910), Swiss composer. Studied philology at Paris and Basle, where he entered the Cons., later studying with Courvoisier, Pfitzner and others at Munich. In 1934 he settled at Berne, at 1st as operatic coach at the municipal theatre. In 1963 app. prof. of comp. at the Hochschule für Musik in Hanover.

Works incl. operas *Romeo und Julia* (1940) and *Die Zauberinsel* (*The Tempest*, 1942) (both based on Shakespeare), *Niobe, Raskolnikov* (on Dostoievsky's *Crime and Punishment*, 1948), *Madame Bovary* (after Flaubert, 1967), radio opera *Die schwarze Spinne* (after Jeremias Gotthelf, 1936; prod. 1949); ballet *Das Dorf unter dem Gletscher*; Christmas radio play *Die drei Geister* (after Dickens); incid., film and radio music; chamber oratorio *Jorinde und Jorindel* (after Mörike); *Baroque Songs* for tenor, women's chorus and instruments, songs for chorus; *Cantata 1944* for contralto, small chorus and pf.; Requiem (1952) and 7 other cantatas; *7 Liebesbriefe* for tenor and orch.; divertimento for string orch.; 3 pf. concertos (1943, 1953, 1962), 2 cello concertos; 3 string 4tets, string trio and other chamber music; pf. and organ pieces; songs.

Suthaus, Ludwig (b Cologne, 12 Dec 1906; d Berlin, 7 Sep 1971), German tenor. He made his debut in Aachen (Walther, 1928) and sang in Berlin 1941–65. Bayreuth 1943–57 as Loge, Siegmund and Walther. After the war he sang in N. and S. America as Tristan, Steva and the Emperor. At the Vienna Staatsoper, 1948–70, he was heard as Florestan, Otello and Bacchus. He was a favourite of Furtwängler and recorded Tristan and Siegmund with him. Other roles incl. Rienzi, Samson and Sadko.

Sutherland, (Dame) Joan (b Sydney, 7 Nov 1926), Australian soprano. Studied 1st in Australia and then at the RCM in London with C. Carey. She made her London debut at CG in 1952 and in 1959 obtained internat. acclaim in *Lucia di Lammermoor* at that opera house. She has since estab. herself as one of the leading coloratura sopranos of the day. Her early rep. incl. Jenifer in the fp of Tippett's *The Midsummer Marriage* (CG 1955) and roles in operas by Poulenc, Mozart and Handel. Wider fame has come in the operas of Massenet, Donizetti, Bellini and Rossini, under the guidance of her husband, the cond. Richard Bonynge (b Sydney, 1930). NY Met debut 1961, as Lucia. Since 1964 has re-visited her native Australia. DBE 1978.

Sutor, Wilhelm (b Edelstetten, Bavaria, *c* 1774; d Linden nr. Hanover, 7 Sep 1828), German composer and tenor. Studied singing with Valesi and others, settled at Stuttgart in 1800 and from 1818 was music dir. at the court of Hanover.

Works incl. opera *Apollos Wettgesang* and 4 others; incid. music to Shakespeare's *Macbeth*; oratorio and cantatas; part-songs; songs.

Sutton, John, English 15th-cent. composer. He was a fellow of Magdalen Coll., Oxford, 1476, and of Eton, 1477–*c* 1479. He (?) obtained the Mus.B. at Cambridge, 1489. A *Salve regina* for 7 voices is in the Eton Choirbook.

Švanda Dudák (*Shvanda the Bagpiper*), Opera by Weinberger (lib. by Miloš Kareš), prod. Prague, Cz. Theatre, 27 Apr 1927.

Svanholm, Set (b Västerås, 2 Sep 1904; d Saltsvoe-Duvnaes, 4 Oct 1964), Swedish tenor. Studied at Stockholm Cons. with Forsell, making his debut in Stockholm in 1930 as a baritone. After further study he developed a tenor voice, making a second debut in 1936. In 1942 he first sang at Bayreuth and from 1946 to 1956 at the NY Met; debut as Siegfried, last perf. as Parsifal. London, CG, 1948–57, often with Flagstad. Other roles incl. Tristan, Radames, Otello and Siegmund. After retiring became intendant of the Stockholm Opera House until 1963. He was best known as a heroic tenor, esp. in the works of Wagner.

Svendsen, Johan (Severin) (b Christiania, 30 Sep 1840; d Copenhagen, 14 Jun 1911), Norwegian composer. Learnt music from his father, a bandmaster, and at first adopted that profession himself. But, playing several instruments, he joined the orch. at the Christiania theatre, began extensive travels in Swed. and Ger. in 1861 and studied at the Leipzig Cons. from 1863 to 1867. After travelling in Scandinavia and Scotland in 1867, he settled in Paris in 1868. In 1870–1 he was in Ger. again, mainly at Leipzig and Weimar, and in 1872–7 he taught and cond. at Christiania. After visits to Munich, Rome, London, and Paris, he became court cond. at Copenhagen, 1883–1908.

Works incl. incid. music to Coppée's *Le Passant* (1869), 2 symphs., overture to Bjørnson's *Sigurd Slembe*, *Carnaval à Paris*, *Carnaval des artistes norvégiens*, 4 Norw. Rhapsodies, legend *Zorahayda*, overture to Shakespeare's *Romeo and Juliet*, etc. for orch.; vln. concerto (1870) and romance, cello concerto (1870); string 4tet (1865), string 5tet, string 8tet; Marriage Cantata; songs.

Svetlanov, Evgeny (b Moscow, 6 Sep 1928), Russian conductor and composer. He studied at the Moscow Cons. and was cond. with the Bolshoy theatre 1954–65; took the co. to La Scala, Milan, in 1964. Prin. cond. USSR State SO from 1965: many perfs. of Soviet works and tours to Europe, Japan and the USA. Prin. guest cond. LSO from 1979.

Works incl. pf. concerto (1951), *Siberian Fantasy* for orch. (1953), Symph. (1956), chamber music.

Svoboda, Josef (b Časlav, 10 May 1920), Czech stage designer. He worked in Prague from 1945; influenced by Appia and Roller, he developed a style which used novel lighting techniques, incl. film projections and laser beams, in order to create an integrated stage picture. His designs for *Les vêpres siciliennes* were first seen in Hamburg

(1969) and did the rounds of the major houses before appearing at the London Coliseum in 1984. Also on view in London, at CG, have been *Die Frau ohne Schatten* (1967), *Pelléas et Mélisande* (1969), *Nabucco* (1972) and *The Ring* (1974–6).

Swain, Freda (b Portsmouth, 31 Oct 1902; d Chinnor, Oxon., 29 Jan 1985), English composer and pianist. Studied at the Tobias Matthay Pf. School in London and at the RCM, comp. with Stanford and pf. with Arthur Alexander, to whom she was married in 1921. In 1924 she became prof. at the RCM.

Works incl. *Pastoral Fantasy* for orch.; pf. concerto (*Airmail*), *The Harp of Aengus* (after Yeats) for vln. and orch.; string 4tet *Norfolk*; vln. and pf. sonatas in C min. and *The River*, cello and pf. sonata, duets for 2 vlns.; songs to texts by Burns, Bridges and Housman.

Swan Lake (*Lebedinoye ozero*), ballet by Tchaikovsky (choreography by Marius Petipa and L.I. Ivanov), prod. Moscow, Bolshoy Theatre, 4 Mar 1877.

Swan of Tuonela, The, symph. legend by Sibelius, op. 22, one of 4 on subjects from the *Kalevala*; comp. 1893–5, fp Helsinki, 1895.

Swan Song (Schubert). *See* **Schwanengesang.**

Swarowsky, Hans (b Budapest, 16 Sep 1899; d Salzburg, 10 Sep 1975), Austrian conductor and teacher. Studied with Schoenberg, Webern and R. Strauss, and then devoted himself mainly to cond., being active at opera houses in Stuttgart, Hamburg, Berlin and Zurich. From 1944 to 1945 he cond. the Kraków PO, the Vienna SO from 1947 to 1950, and was director of the Graz Opera from 1947 to 1950. Worked at the Vienna Opera from 1965. Often gave perfs. of the Mahler and the Second Viennese School. An influential teacher; among his pupils were Zubin Mehta and Claudio Abbado.

Swarthout, Gladys (b Deepwater, Missouri, 25 Dec 1900; d Florence, 7 Jul 1969), American contralto. Debut Ravinia, nr. Chicago, 1925, as Carmen. NY Met 1929–45; debut as La Cieca and popular as Mignon, Siebel, Adalgisa and Carmen. She sang in the 1934 fp of Hanson's *Merry Mount*. From 1940 widely known as concert singer; retired 1954.

Swayne, Giles (b Stevenage, 30 Jun 1946), English composer. He studied at Cambridge and the RAM, and with Messiaen from 1976. Has worked as an opera répétiteur

and at Bryanston School.

Works incl. 2 string 4tets (1971, 1977), *The Good Morrow,* for mezzo and pf., to texts by Donne (1971), *Synthesis* for 2 pf. (1974), *Orlando's Music* for orch. (1974), *Pentecost-Music* for orch. (1977), *Cry* for 28 amplified solo voices, in which the creation of the world is depicted (1979), *A World Within,* ballet with tape, on the life of the Brontës (1978), *Count-Down* for 16-part chorus and 2 perc. (1981), *Song for Hadi* for drums and insts. (1983), opera *Le Nozze di Cherubino* (1984), *Missa Tiburtina* (1985).

Sweelinck, Jan Pieterszoon (b Deventer, May 1562; d Amsterdam, 16 Oct 1621), Dutch composer, organist and harpsichordist. Studied under his father, Pieter S., who became organist at the Old Church at Amsterdam in 1566, and others. His father died in 1573 and he succeeded to his post between 1577 and 1580, holding it to his death. He had many famous pupils, some from foreign countries, and his organ playing was celebrated; he was also a highly skilled harpsichordist. His music was influenced by the English virginalists and the Venetian organists. The poet Vondel wrote an epitaph on his death.

Works incl. 4 books of psalms for 4–8 voices, incl. 3 books of *Psalms of David* (1604–14), *Cantiones sacrae* for several voices; org. fantasias, toccatas and chorale variations; harpsichord pieces; *chansons* for 5 voices, *Rimes françoises et italiennes.*

Swell, a device on the harpsichord and the organ for the artificial prod. of *crescendo* and *diminuendo,* which these instruments are incapable of prod. by touch. It took var. forms, the most successful being a contrivance in the form of a slatted blind (hence the name Venetian swell), which, opening and shutting by means of a pedal, increased or reduced the volume of tone.

Swieten, Gottfried (Bernhard) van (b Leyden, 29 Oct 1733; d Vienna, 29 Mar 1803), Austrian diplomat and amateur musician of Dutch descent. Came to Vienna with his family in 1745 and in 1755 entered the diplomatic service. He held posts in Brussels, Paris and Warsaw, and visited Eng. in 1769, but spent much of his time on music and wrote 2 *opéras comiques* and some symphs. As ambassador in Berlin 1770–7 he became acquainted with the works of the Bach family and of Handel, and on his return to Vienna did much to promote interest in their music. He commissioned 6 symphs. from C.P.E. Bach, and Mozart's arrs. of Handel oratorios were made for the concerts he organized; in 1791 he made the preparations for Mozart's hasty funeral. He was librettist of Haydn's *Creation* and *Seasons*, and a patron of the young Beethoven, who ded. his 1st symph. to him.

Syberg, Franz (Adolf) (b Kerteminde nr. Odense, 5 Jul 1904; d Kerteminde, 11 Dec 1955), Danish composer and organist. His father, the painter Fritz S., sent him to study at the Leipzig Cons., and later he became a private pupil of Karg-Elert. In 1930 he returned to Den. to study organ with Peder Thomsen in Copenhagen, and in 1933 he became organist at Kerteminde.

Works incl. incid. music to Büchner's *Leonce and Lena* (1931) and the marionette comedy *Uffe hin Spage* (1929); symph.; concertino for ob. and strings; string 4tet (1931), string trio, 5tet for fl., clar., vln., vla. and cello; suite for org.

Sygar, John, English 15th-cent. composer. He was a singer and chaplain at King's College, Cambridge, in 1499–1501 and 1508–15, and contrib. a Magnificat (now incomplete) to the Eton Choirbook.

Sylphides, Les, ballet with music adapted from Chopin (choreography by Fokin), prod. Paris, Théâtre du Châtelet, 2 Jun 1909.

Sylvia, ou La Nymphe de Diane, ballet by Delibes (scenario by Jules Barbier and Baron de Reinach, choreography by Louis Mérante), prod. Paris, Opéra, 14 Jun 1876.

Sympathetic Resonance, an acoustical phenomenon observed in resonant bodies, such as a string, a glass, a tuning-fork, etc., which will vibrate and give forth a faint sound without being touched, if their fundamental note is sung or played on an instrument near them.

Sympathetic Strings, a set of strings in certain types of bowed instruments vibrating in accord with those actually touched by the bow.

Symphonia (Lat.), lit. = symphony, esp. in the earlier sense of any piece of music in which instruments play together in consort; also an early instrument, possibly a kind of Bagpipe and, in a later sense, a Clavichord. *See also* **Sinfonia** (the It. term).

Symphonia domestica (*Domestic Symph.*), a symph. by R. Strauss, op. 53, comp. 1903, fp NY, 31 Mar 1904. Like *Heldenleben* the work is autobiog., but describes the comp.'s private life, incl. lovemaking and bathing the baby, while the earlier work showed him as a public figure.

Symphonic Metamorphosis on Themes by Carl Maria von Weber, work for orch. by Hindemith; comp. 1940–3, fp NY, 20 Jan 1944 cond. Rodzinski. The 4 movts. use material from Weber's pf. music and the incidental music for a Stuttgart prod. of Gozzi's *Turandot* in Schiller's trans., 1809.

Symphonic Poem, a type of orch. work coming under the category of Programme Music, i.e. descriptive of lit. subjects, actual events in history or contemporary life, landscapes and natural phenomena, paintings, etc. The term symphonic poem was the invention of Liszt, who wrote 13 works of the kind.

Symphonic Study, a term invented by Elgar for his *Falstaff*, prob. because it is intended to be as much an outline of Falstaff's character as a description of the events surrounding him.

Symphonie concertante (Fr.). *See* **Sinfonia concertante.**

Symphonie fantastique, symph. by Berlioz, op. 14, comp. in 1830, revised in Italy and 1st perf. Paris, 5 Dec 1830, and with its sequel, *Lélio*, Paris, 9 Dec 1832. Berlioz gave it a programme arising out of his disappointed love for Harriet Smithson and representing the crazy dreams of a poet crossed in love who has taken poison. The 5 movts. are 1 *Rêveries-passions.* 2 *Un bal.* 3 *Scène aux champs.* 4 *Marche au supplice.* 5 *Songe d'une nuit de Sabbat.*

Symphonie funèbre et triomphale, symph. by Berlioz, op. 15, for military band, strings and chorus, comp. in 1840 by order of the Fr. government and perf. at the 10th anniversary of the 1830 Revolution, Paris, 28 Jul 1840.

Symphonie liturgique, Honegger's 3rd symph., comp. 1945–6 and ded. to Charles Munch, who gave the fp in Zurich on 17 Aug 1946.

Symphonies of Wind Instruments, work by Stravinsky, ded. to the memory of Debussy; comp. 1920, rev. 1945–7, fp London, 10 Jun 1921, cond. Koussevitzky.

Symphony, orig. a piece of music for several perfs., e.g. Schütz's *Symphoniae sacrae* (1629–50), which are for voices and instruments. In 17th-cent. It. a symphony (*sinfonia*) was an instrumental movement, partic. the overture, in an opera or similar work. The term was still used in this sense in the early part of the 18th cent., e.g. in Bach's cantatas. The development of the opera overture into a work in 3 movements in the time of A. Scarlatti led to the comp. of similar works independent of the theatre. Symphonies of this kind were written in the 18th cent. not only in Italy but also in Vienna and partic. in Mannheim. The German and Austrian symphony came to incorporate elements of the Suite (Minuet) and the Divertimento. The originality of Haydn's symphonies owed much to his isolation from the world at Eszterháza. Mozart, more cosmopolitan, was influenced as a boy by the elegance of J.C. Bach's symphonies but rapidly developed a style of his own. Dramatic elements are to be found in the symphonies of

Symphony of Psalms, work by Stravinsky for mixed chorus and orch.; written 1930, to celebrate the 50th anniversary of the Boston SO, but the fp was in Brussels on 13 Dec 1930, cond. Ansermet.

Syncopation, a displacement of the musical accent to weak beats or off-beats in the bar, where they are normally expected to lie on the 1st beat and, less pronounced, on the other main divisions of the bar, e.g.:

SYNCOPATION

Handel, *Water Music*

C.P.E. Bach, Haydn and Beethoven, and programmatic features in those of Spohr, Berlioz and Liszt. The problem of integrating symph. structure and Romantic expression was solved most successfully by Brahms. The Scherzo came to replace the Minuet in the symphonies of Beethoven, whose use of voices in his 9th symphony was followed by Mendelssohn (*Lobgesang*), Mahler and others. The linking of movements into a continuous whole, practised by Schumann and Mendelssohn, was followed by a number of later composors, e.g. Sibelius. Thematic relationships between movements occur in the symphonies of Franck, Tchaikovsky and Elgar among others. A symphony is not necessarily a heavily serious or weighty comp.: Prokofiev's *Classical Symphony* and Shostakovich's 9th symphony are both lighthearted works.

Symphony in 3 Movements, work for orch. by Stravinsky; comp. 1942–5, fp NY, 24 Jan 1946. The outer movts. were inspired by Stravinsky's experiences of the war, as viewed from the US. The central slow movt. derives from music for a planned film on St Bernadette.

Symphony of a Thousand, name sometimes given to Mahler's 8th symph., in E♭, comp. 1906–7. Forces required incl. 8 vocal soloists, double chorus, boys' chorus, and orch. with 20 woodwind, 17 brass insts., celesta, pf., harmonium and mandolin. The first movt. is a setting on the hymn *Veni creator spiritus* and the 2nd the closing scene from Goethe's *Faust*. The fp, in Munich on 12 Sep 1910, was cond. by Mahler and was the greatest public success of his career. 1st US perf. Philadelphia, 2 Mar 1916, cond. Stokowski. Not perf. in Brit. until 15 Apr 1930 (London, cond. Wood).

The effect is that of a syncope (i.e. missing a heart-beat): hence the name.

Synthesizer. An electronic machine, invented by Robert Moog in 1965, used for the generation and modification of sounds, often connected to a computer and employed in the composition of electronic music.

Syrian Chant, the earliest of the independent branches of Christian chant. Its language was the E. Aramaic dialect, also called Syriac. In addition to the cantillation of the lessons and the singing of psalms, common to all liturgies, a repertory of hymns emerged, anticipating in some cases the forms of Byzantine chant (*q.v.*). The *memrâ* was a poetical homily, sung to a recitative formula. The *madráshâ* was a strophic hymn sung by a soloist, with a refrain sung by the choir (*cf.* Byzantine *kontakion*). The *sogîthâ* was a poem of dramatic character. Lesser forms, inserted between the verses of psalms, are comparable to the *troparion* and *sticheron* of the Byzantine liturgy. The outstanding poet was St Ephraem (306–73). Apart from some indecipherable cantillation formulae the music of the early Syrian church has not survived; and it is impossible to say how closely what is sung today resembles it.

Syrinx. *See* **Pan Pipe.**

System. In England a system is a number of music staves required for the scoring of a comp., e.g. 2 for a pf. work, 1 + 2 for a song, 4 for a 4tet, etc., up to any number needed for an orchestral full score. Such a system is connected on the left-hand side of the page by var. kinds of braces or brackets; an open space between these shows that the next system begins lower down on the same page.

Szabelski, Boleslaw (b Radoryż, 3 Dec 1896; d Katowice, 27 Aug 1979), Polish composer. Studied with Szymanowski and Statkowski at the Warsaw Cons., and from 1945 taught comp. and organ at the Katowice Cons.

Works incl. 5 symphs. (1926–68), sinfonietta, *Concerto grosso* for orch.; concertino and concerto for pf. and orch.; 2 string 4tets; Magnificat for soprano, chorus and orch.; pf. and organ music.

Szábo, Ferenc (b Budapest, 27 Dec 1902; d Budapest, 4 Nov 1969), Hungarian composer. Pupil of Bartók and Kodály at the Budapest Cons. Settled in Rus. in 1932, returning to Hungary after the war and becoming dir. of the Budapest High School for Music in 1957.

Works incl. opera *Be Faithful unto Death* (posth. prod. Budapest 1975); *Song Symph.*, symph. poems *Class Struggle* and *November 7th*, suite *The Collective Farm*; 2 string 4tets, 3 pf. trios; mass songs incl. *A Song of Voroshilov*; songs.

Szałowski, Antoni (b Warsaw, 21 Apr 1907; d Paris, 21 Mar 1973), Polish composer. Studied with his father, a vln. prof. at the Warsaw Cons., also pf. with 2 masters and comp. with Sikorski; later with Nadia Boulanger in Paris, where he settled.

Works incl. symph., symph. variations; capriccio and overture for string orch.; pf. concerto (1930); 3 songs with orch.; 4 string 4tets (1928–56); trio for ob., clar. and bassoon; suite for vln. and pf., sonatina for clar. and pf.; vln. and pf. pieces; partita for solo cello; sonata, 2 sonatinas and other works for pf.

Szamotulczyk, Wacław (Wacław of Szamotuly) (b Szamotuly nr. Poznań, c 1525; d ? Pińczów on the Nida, 1560), Polish composer. He studied at Poznań and at Kraków Univ., and in 1547 became comp. to the king; from 1555 *Kapellmeister* to Prince Michael Radziwiłł. He wrote much church music, some of it pub. by Berg and Neuber of Nuremberg.

Szántó, Tivadar (or Theodor) (b Vienna, 3 Jun 1877; d Budapest, 7 Jan 1934), Hungarian composer and pianist. Studied in Vienna and Budapest, and with Busoni in Berlin. Lived in Paris in 1905–14, in Switz. in 1914–21 and then settled at Budapest. He revised Delius's C min. pf. concerto, which is ded. to him.

Works incl. opera *Typhoon* (after Lengyel's play, 1924); symph. *Land and Sea, Japan Suite* (1926) and other suites, symph. rhapsody for orch.; vln. and pf. sonata; Variations on a Hung. Folksong, *Essays in Japanese Harmony* and other works for pf.

Székely, Mihály (b Jászberény, 8 May 1901; d Budapest, 6 Mar 1963), Hungarian bass. Debut Budapest 1920, as Ferrando in *Trovatore*; soon graduated to Marke and Méphistophélès. NY Met 1946–50 (debut as Hunding). Glyndebourne 1957–61, as Sarastro, Osmin, Mozart's Bartolo and Rocco. At Paris and the Holland Festival he was admired as Bartók's Bluebeard.

Székely, Zoltán (b Kocs, 8 Dec 1903), Hungarian violinist and composer. Studied vln. with Hubay and comp. with Kodály at Budapest. After touring as soloist he formed the Hungarian String 4tet in 1935. In 1939 he gave the fp of Bartók's 2nd concerto (Amsterdam).

Works incl. string 4tet; sonata for unaccomp. vln., duet for vln. and cello, etc.

Szeligowski, Tadeusz (b Lwów, 13 Sep 1896; d Poznan, 10 Feb 1963), Polish composer. Studied at Lwów and Kraków, later with Nadia Boulanger in Paris. He taught at Poznań, Lublin, Wilno and Warsaw. He made special studies of folksong and old church music.

Works incl. incid. music for plays, e.g. Maeterlinck's *Blue Bird*; 2 psalms for solo voices, chorus and orch.; concerto, *Phantaisie rapsodique*, suite *St Casimir Fair* for orch.; clar. concerto, pf. concerto; 2 string 4tets (1929, 1934); *Lithuanian Song* for vln. and pf.; *Children's Album* for pf.; *Green Songs, Flower Allegories* and other songs.

Szell, Georg (b Budapest, 7 Jun 1897; d Cleveland, 29 Jul 1970), Hungarian-born conductor and pianist. A child prodigy, he studied with R. Robert in Vienna, playing a work of his own with the Vienna SO aged 11. He studied comp. with J.B. Foerster, Mandyczewski and Reger, and then, through the influence of R. Strauss, he obtained a cond. post in Strasbourg, which he held from 1917 to 1918, having already made his debut in Berlin in 1914. After further posts in Prague, Darmstadt and Düsseldorf he became 1st cond. at the Berlin Staatsoper from 1924 to 1930, also teaching at the Berlin Hochschule für Musik from 1927 to 1930. From 1930 to 1936 he again cond. in Prague, taking over the Scot. Nat. Orch. from 1937 to 1939, when he went to the USA. There he was guest cond. with the NBC SO from 1941 to 1942, cond. at the NY Met; much admired in Wagner. From 1942 to 1945, and from 1943 to 1956, frequent guest cond. with the NY PO. In 1946 he became permanent cond. of the Cleveland PO. Bartók and Janáček were among the few modern composers in his programmes.

Szenen aus Goethes 'Faust', a setting of a number of scenes from Goethe's drama for solo voices, chorus and orch. by Schumann; comp. begun with a setting of the final chorus, Aug 1844, resumed 1849, completed without the overture, 1850, overture added 1853.

Szeryng, Henryk (b Warsaw, 22 Nov 1918), Polish, now Mexican, violinist. Studied with W. Hess and with Flesch in Berlin, emigrating to the USA in 1933. From 1948 he taught as prof. in Mexico City. Toured Europe and US in 1983, to mark the 50th anniversary of his career.

Szigeti, Joseph (b Budapest, 5 Sep 1892; d Lucerne, 19 Feb 1973). Hungarian, later American, violinist. Studied in Budapest with Hubay, and received advice from Joachim and Busoni, making his debut in 1905. From 1917 to 1925 he was prof. at the Geneva Cons., settling in the USA in 1926. He gave the fps of vln. concertos by Busoni and Bloch, and did much for the cause of modern music; often played works by Bartók and Prokofiev.

Szokolay, Sándor (b Kúnágota, 30 Mar 1931), Hungarian composer. He studied at the Budapest Academy; teacher there since 1966. He has been influenced by Hungarian national music and by Stravinsky and Orff.

Works incl. vln. concerto (1957), *Urban and the Devil*, ballet (1958), pf. concerto (1958), *Fiery March*, oratorio (1958), *The Ballad of Horror*, ballet (1960), *Ishtar's Descent into Hell*, oratorio (1960), *Blood Wedding*, opera after Lorca (1964), *Déploration*, Requiem for Poulenc for pf., chorus and chamber orch. (1964), tpt. concerto (1968), *Hamlet*, opera (1968), *Apocalypse*, oratorio after Dürer (1971), *Samson*, opera (1974), *Deluded Peter*, radio opera (1978).

Szulc, Józef (Zygmunt) (b Warsaw, 4 Apr 1875; d Paris, 10 Apr 1956), Polish composer and pianist. Studied with Noskowski at the Warsaw Cons. and later with Mosz-kowski in Paris. On the advice of Paderewski he began a career as concert pianist, but later devoted himself to comp. He settled in Paris.

Works incl. French operettas *Une Nuit d'Ispahan, Flup!* (1913), *Divin Mensonge, Flossie, Le Garçon de chez Prunier, Le Coffre-fort vivant* and others; overture for orch.; vln. and pf. sonata; songs.

Szymanowski, Karol (Maciej) (b Timashovka, Ukraine, 6 Oct 1882; d Lausanne, 29 Mar 1937), Polish composer. Learnt music privately as a child and comp. a set of pf. preludes, op. 1, in 1900. In 1903 he entered the Warsaw Cons., studying with Noskowski, and at the Lwów Chopin Festival won a 1st prize with a C min. pf. sonata in 1905. Lived in Berlin for a time from 1906 and worked on behalf of Polish music; also influenced by Debussy and Strauss. As an aristocrat he lost his property in the 1914–18 war and was imprisoned in Rus., but escaped to Warsaw, where in 1922 he became prof. of comp. and director of the State Cons. His last years were marred by tuberculosis and he had to go to a sanatorium in Switz., where he died.

Works incl. operas *Hagith* (1922) and *King Roger* (1926); ballets *Mandragora* (also incid. music to Molière's *Le Bourgeois Gentilhomme*) and *Harnasie* (1935); incid. music to Miciński's *Prince Potemkin*.

ORCH.: 4 symphs. incl. *Sinfonia concertante* for pf. and orch. (1932); 2 vln. concertos (1916, 1933); *Penthesilea* (Wyspiański) for soprano and orch.; *Hafiz Love Songs* for voice and orch.; *Stabat Mater* (1926), *Veni Creator* (1929) and *Litany* for solo voices, chorus and orch.

CHAMBER: 2 string 4tets (1917, 1927); pf. trio; numerous vln. and pf. pieces; 3 sonatas and many other works for pf.; many songs incl. cycles *Songs of the Infatuated Muezzin* (J. Iwaszkiewicz), *Słopiewnie* (Julian Tuwim), *Children's Rhymes* (J. Iłłakowicz) and settings of poems by Kasprowicz, Miciński, James Joyce, Tagore and others.

T

t, the leading-note in Tonic Sol-fa notation, pronounced **Te**.

Tabarro, Il (Puccini). *See* **Trittico**.

Tablature, various old systems of writing down music, esp. for organ (for the left hand only or for both hands) and for lute, without notes, but by means of letters or numbers. The only modern instruments for which a tablature notation is now normally in use are the Ukelele and similar guitar types. (For the old Ger. Mastersingers' tablature *see* **Tabulatur**.)

Table (Fr.). (1) The belly of a string instrument. (2) The sounding-board of the harp. *Près de la table* is an instruction to play near the sounding-board, prod. a metallic sound. (3) *Musique de table*. *See* **Tafel-Musik**.

Table Entertainment, an 18th-cent. English entertainment, only partly musical in character, given by a single perf. sitting at a table and telling stories and jokes, giving displays of mimicry, singing songs, etc. The 1st table entertainments on record are those of George Alexander Steevens at Dublin in 1752. Dibdin began a series in London in 1789 and continued for 20 years, introducing most of his songs in this way.

Tableau parlant, Le (*The Speaking Picture*), opera by Grétry (lib. by L. Anseaume), prod. Paris, Comédie-Italienne, 20 Sep 1769.

Tabor, a small drum with a high, narrow body and small drum-heads made of animal skin, sounding an indefinite pitch and struck with drum-sticks. It was rarely used alone, but accomp. a pipe of a Fife or Recorder type, similar to the modern Tin Whistle. It is occasionally used in the modern orch. to prod. a dry, dull, percussive sound, and has been revived for folk-dancing.

Tabor (Smetana). *See* **Má Vlast**.

Tabulatur (Ger. = Tablature). In one sense the Ger. word differs from the Eng., meaning the table of rules for the instruction and guidance of the Mastersingers.

Tacchinardi, Nicola (b Livorno, 3 Sep 1772; d Florence, 14 Mar 1859), Italian tenor. He studied literature and art at first, but learnt the vln., joined the orch. at the Florence Opera in 1789, and in 1794 began to appear as a singer. He soon sang in the principal theatres of It., in operas by Paer, Morlacchi and Zingarelli, and in 1811–14 visited Paris, where he sang Don Giovanni (transposed) and in operas by Paisiello, Pucitta and Cimarosa. He then settled at Florence in the service of the Grand Duke of Tuscany. Later in his career he often appeared in operas by Rossini.

Tacet (Lat. = is silent), an indication in old vocal part-books and later in orchestral parts to show that a voice or instrument has finished its part in a work, although the work itself is still continuing. In that case wording is usually *tacet al fine* (tacet to the end). But the word tacet alone may also stand below a certain number or section of a work to show that the voice or instrument in question does not perform during that portion of the music, though it will come in again later.

Tacitus, Cornelius (*c* 55–120), Roman historian. *See* **Incoronazione di Poppea** (Monteverdi), **Radamisto** (Handel).

Taddei, Giuseppe (b Genoa, 26 Jun 1916), Italian baritone. Made his debut in Rome in 1936, as the Herald in *Lohengrin*. He was esp. well known as a dramatic Verdi singer, and also in *buffo* roles: Scarpia, Falstaff, Dulcamara. Also sang Pizarro, Rigoletto, Sachs and the Dutchman. CG, London, from 1960.

Tadolini, Giovanni (b Bologna, 18 Oct ?1789; d Bologna, 29 Nov 1872), Italian singer and composer. Studied comp. with Mattei and singing with Babini, and in 1811 was engaged by Spontini as accompanist and chorus master at the Théâtre des Italiens in Paris, leaving in 1814, but going there again in 1830–39, after living in It. and comp. operas in between. He married the soprano, Eugenia Savonari (1809–after 1848); she created Donizetti's Linda di Chamounix (1842) and Maria di Rohan (1843) and Verdi's Alzira (1845).

Works incl. operas *Le bestie in uomini* (1815), *La principessa di Navarra* (1816), *Il credulo deluso* (*Il finto molinaro*) (1817), *Tamerlano* (1818), *Moctar, Mitridate* (1826), *Almanzor* (1827); canzonets, incl. *Eco di Scozia* with horn obbligato, etc.

Tafel-Musik (Ger. = table music), music perf. at or after dinner (Fr. *musique de table*).

Tag, Christian Gotthilf (b Beierfeld, Saxony, 2 Apr 1735; d Niederzwönitz nr. Zwönitz, 19 Jul 1811), German composer. Pupil of Homilius at Dresden. In 1755 he became cantor at Hohenstein-Ernstthal, Saxony.

Works incl. 11 Masses, motets; 103 cantatas; symphs. for organ and orch., songs.

Tag des Gerichts, Der (*The Day of Judgement*), oratorio by Telemann (text by C.W. Alers), comp. 1762.

Tageszeiten, Die (*The times of the day*), song cycle for male chorus and orch. by R. Strauss (text by Eichendorff); comp. 1927, fp Vienna, 21 Jul 1928. The movts. are 'Der Morgen', 'Mittagsruh', 'Der Abend' and 'Die Nacht'.

Cantata by Telemann.

Tageweisen (Ger. = day tunes), songs formerly used in Germany to announce the break of day from church towers or by night-watchmen in the streets. They were often folksongs and some have passed into currency as hymns for the Lutheran church.

Taglia, Pietro, Italian 16th-cent. composer, active at Milan. Wrote 3 books of madrigals (1555, 1557, 1564).

Tagliapietra, Gino (b Ljubljana, 30 May 1887; d Venice, 8 Aug 1954), Italian composer and pianist. Studied with Julius Epstein in Vienna and with Busoni in Berlin. In 1906 he was app. prof. of pf. at the Liceo Musicale at Venice. He pub. an anthology of keyboard music in 18 vols.

Works incl. ballet *La bella addormentata nel bosco* (1926); Requiem and other choral works; pf. concerto; pf. pieces and studies.

Tagliapietra, Giovanni (b Venice, 24 Dec 1846; d New York, 11 Apr 1921), Italian baritone. Studied architecture at Venice and Padua, but later took to singing, toured in It. and S. Amer. and in 1874 settled in NY.

Tagliavini, Ferrucio (b Reggio Emilia, 14 Aug 1913), Italian tenor. Studied at Parma Cons. and won 1st prize in a singing competition in Florence in 1938, which enabled him to study in that city with A. Bassi, where he made his debut in 1938 as Rodolfo. He soon estab. himself as a leading *bel canto* singer, appearing at the NY Met 1947–54 and CG 1950–56. Other roles incl. Edgardo, Werther, Cavaradossi and Mascagni's Fritz.

Täglichsbeck, Thomas (b Ansbach, 31 Dec 1799; d Baden-Baden, 5 Oct 1867), German violinist and composer. Studied in Munich and became deputy cond. to Lindpaintner there in 1820. From 1827 he was music director to the Prince of Hohenzollern-Hechingen until the 1848 Revolution. He toured frequently during this period as soloist and as cond.

Works incl. operas *Webers Bild* (1823), *König Enzio* (1843); Mass; 2 symphs.; 2 vln. concertinos; pf. trio; part-songs.

Taglietti, Giulio (b Brescia, *c* 1660; d Brescia, 1718), Italian composer. *Maestro di cappella* of the Jesuit Collegio dei Nobili at Brescia. Comp. numerous works for 2 vlns. and bass with org. or harpsichord, vln. sonatas with bass, etc.

Tailer, John (also Taylor, etc.) (d ? London, after 1569), English composer. From 1561 to 1569 he was master of the choristers at Westminster Abbey. A *Christus resurgens* (Christ Church, Oxford, MSS. 948–8) may be by him, or by Thomas Taylor, who obtained the B.Mus. at Oxford, 1531.

Taille (Fr. = cut, edge), the tenor part in a vocal and instrumental ensemble, applied partic. in the 17th and 18th cents. to the vla. and the *oboe da caccia*.

Tailleferre, Germaine (b Parc Saint-Maur nr. Paris, 19 Apr 1892; d Paris, 7 Nov 1983), French composer. Studied in Paris and joined the group of 'Les Six', 1st appearing as a comp. in public in 1920. She lived in the USA from 1942 to 1946.

Works incl. opera *Il était un petit navire* (1951); ballet *Le Marchand d'oiseaux* (1923); *Pastorale* for small orch.; pf. concerto (1919) and ballade for pf. and orch.; string 4tet (1918); 2 vln. and pf. sonatas (1921, 1951); *Jeux de plein air* for 2 pfs. (1918); songs.

Tajo, Italo (b Pinerolo, Piedmont, 25 Apr 1915), Italian bass. Debut Turin, 1935, as Fafner in *Das Rheingold*. Sang Figaro and Banquo at the 1947 Edinburgh Festival with the Glyndebourne co. In London he was heard as Donizetti's Don Pasquale and Dulcamara (1947–50). In the USA he sang at Chicago, San Francisco and the NY Met during the 1940s; taught at the Cincinnati Cons. from 1966. Other roles incl. Leporello, Don Magnifico and Berg's Doctor.

Takemitsu, Tōru (b Tokyo, 8 Oct 1930), Japanese composer. He studied privately and in 1951 co-founded an experimental laboratory in Tokyo, to examine oriental music and the best in Western techniques; uses tape and has been influenced by serialism, Messiaen and *musique concrète*.

Works incl. *Requiem* for strings (1957), *Music of Trees* for orch. (1961), *Textures* for pf. and orch. (1964), *The Dorian Horizon* for 17 strings (1966), *November Steps* for biwa, shakuhachi and orch. (1967), *Asterism* for pf. and orch. (1968), *Corona* for 22 strings (1971), *Cassiopea* for perc. and orch. (1971), *Gemeaux* for ob., tromb. and 2 orchs. (1972), *Bouquet of Songs* for marimba and orch. (1975), *A Flock Descends into the Pentagonal Garden* for orch. (1977), *Dream Time* for orch. (1981; ballet vers. 1983), *Rain Coming* for chamber orch. (1982), *To the Edge of Dream* for guitar and orch. (1983), *Star Isle* for orch. (1984); chamber music incl. string 4tet *A Way Alone*

(1981), series of works for insts. with title *Stanza*, works for tape alone, etc.

Tal, Josef (b Pinne nr. Poznań, 18 Sep 1910), Israeli composer. Studied in Berlin with Tiessen and Trapp, settling in Palestine in 1934. In 1937 he became prof. of comp. and pf. at the Jerusalem Cons. and in 1950 lecturer at the Hebrew Univ. there, also being director of the Cons. from 1948 to 1955.

Works incl. operas *Saul at Ein Dor* (1957), *Amnon and Tamar* (1961), *Ashmedai* (1971), *Massada 967* (1973), *Die Versuchung* (1976); *The Death of Moses*, requiem oratorio for soloists, chorus and tape (1967); 2 symphs.; *Exodus*, choreog. poem for orch.; *Visions* for string orch.; 6 pf. concertos (1944–70), vla. concerto; symph. cantata *A Mother Rejoices*; sonatas for vln., ob.; pf. pieces; songs; electronic music.

Talea (Lat. = a cutting), the name given to the repeated rhythmic pattern used in isorhythmic motets. *See* **Isorhythmic.**

Tales of Hoffmann (Offenbach). *See* **Contes d'Hoffmann.**

Talich, Václav (b Kroměříž, 28 May 1883; d Beroun nr. Prague, 16 Mar 1961), Czech conductor. He studied with his father and was a pupil of Ševčík for the vln. at the Prague Cons. He held various posts as violinist, cond. and teacher from 1904 to 1919, when he was app. cond. of the Czech PO. He retained this post till 1941 and was also director of the National Opera at Prague from 1935 to 1945. Post-war conditions made his position in Prague impossible and he moved to Bratislava. His merits were finally recognized by the government in the last years of his life. Well known in works by Smetana, Dvořák and Janáček.

Talismano, Il, unfinished opera by Balfe, completed by Macfarren (lib. *The Knight of the Leopard*, based on Scott's *Talisman*, by A. Matthison; It. trans. by G. Zaffira), prod. London, Her Majesty's Theatre, 11 Jun 1874.

Tallis, Thomas (b c 1505; d Greenwich, 23 Nov 1585), English composer and organist. He was organist at the Benedictine Priory, Dover, in 1532, and held a post at Waltham Abbey before its dissolution in 1540. He became a Gentleman of the Chapel Royal c 1543. In 1557 Queen Mary granted him, jointly with Richard Bowyer, Master of the Children in the Chapel Royal, a lease of the manor of Minster, Thanet, and at her death he passed into the service of Elizabeth, who in 1575 granted him, jointly with Byrd, a patent for the sole right to print music and

music paper in Eng.; but 2 years later, not finding this immediately profitable, they petitioned for an annual grant, which was sanctioned. The 2 masters were then joint organists at the Chapel Royal. In his last years he and his wife Joan, whom he had married c 1552, lived at their own house at Greenwich.

Works incl. 3 Masses, incl. *Puer natus est nobis* (1554), 2 Lat. Magnificats, 2 sets of Lamentations for 5 voices, c 40 Latin motets etc., incl. *Spem in alium* in 40 parts; services, psalms, Litanies, c 30 anthems and other Eng. church music; secular vocal pieces; 2 In Nomines for strings; organ and virginal pieces.

Talon (Fr.), the heel (or nut) of the bow of a string instrument.

Talvela, Martti (Olavi) (b Hiitola, Karelia, 4 Feb 1935), Finnish bass. Debut Stockholm, 1961, Commendatore. Bayreuth, 1962–70, as Hunding, Hagen, Daland and Marke. NY Met debut 1968, as the Grand Inquisitor; returned in 1974 as Boris Godunov, in the original vers. of Mussorgsky's opera. At CG he was admired in the early 1970s as Hagen, Dosifey and Gurnemanz. Since 1972 he has been artistic dir. of the summer Savonlinna Festival, Finland, and has taken part in the fps of works by Kokkonen and Sallinen there. Other roles incl. Sarastro and King Henry.

Tam-Tam (onomat.) = Gong (*q.v.*).

Tamagno, Francesco (b Turin, 28 Dec 1850; d Varese, 31 Aug 1905), Italian tenor. At first a baker's apprentice and locksmith, he studied at the Turin Cons., sang in the opera chorus there, studied further with Pedrotti at Palermo and made his 1st appearance there in 1873. He sang at La Scala 1877–87, the NY Met 1891–5 and CG 1895 and 1901. Among his best roles were Ernani, Don Carlos, Manrico, Radames, Faust and Samson. Verdi's 1st Otello (1887). Retired 1904.

Tamara, symph. poem by Balakirev, based on a poem by Lermontov (sometimes called *Thamar* in Eng.), begun 1866, finished 1882; fp St Petersburg, Free School of Music, 1882. Ballet on this work (choreog. by M. Fokine, setting by L. Bakst), prod. Paris, Théâtre du Châtelet, 20 May 1912.

Tamberlik, Enrico (b Rome, 16 Mar 1820; d Paris, 13 Mar 1889), Italian tenor. At first intended for a lawyer, he made his debut at Naples in 1841 as Tybalt in Bellini's *I Capuleti*; sang in Port. and Spain. In 1850 1st appeared in London, as Auber's Masaniello; sang there until 1877 as Manrico,

Cellini and Rossini's Otello. At St Petersburg in 1862 he created Alvaro in *La forza del destino*.

Tambourin (Fr.) = Tabor. The tambourin du Béarn was a zither with strings sounding only tonic and dominant and struck by a stick. Hence tambourin was used to mean a dance with a drone bass.

Tambourine, a small, shallow drum with a single skin stretched over the edge of one side of its rim, into which jingles are loosely set to add their noise when the skin is struck or rubbed by the hand or to resound separately when the instrument is shaken.

Tamburini, Antonio (b Faenza, 28 Mar 1800; d Nice, 8 Nov 1876), Italian baritone. Was at first taught the horn, but appeared in opera at the age of 18 at Bologna, in Generali's *La Contessa*. He 1st sang in London in 1832, his roles over the next 20 years there incl. Donizetti's Alfonso, Earl of Nottingham and Enrico. At the Paris Théâtre-Italien he created Riccardo in *I Puritani* (1835) and Malatesta in *Don Pasquale* (1843). Sang in Russia for 10 years.

Tamburo (It. = drum). The term is used in scores, with various adjectival qualifications, for any kind of drum except the Kettledrums, which are called *timpani* in It.

Tamerlano (*Tamburlane*), opera by Handel (lib. by A. Piovene, adapted by N.F. Haym), prod. London, King's Theatre, Haymarket, 31 Oct 1724.

Taming of the Shrew, The. *See* Sly; Widerspänstigen Zähmung.

Tampur, a Caucasian instrument of the lute type, but played with a bow. It has 3 strings.

Tancrède, tragédie-lyrique by Campra (lib. by A. Danchet after Tasso), prod. Paris, Opéra, 7 Nov 1702. Rev. Aix-en-Provence, 1986.

Tancredi (*Tancred*), opera by Rossini (lib. by G. Rossi, based on Tasso's *Gerusalemme liberata* and Voltaire's tragedy *Tancrède*), prod. Venice, Teatro La Fenice, 6 Feb 1813. Rossini's 1st serious opera. Rev. Wexford, 1986.

Taneiev, Alexander Sergeievich (b St Petersburg, 17 Jan 1850; d Petrograd, 7 Feb 1918), Russian composer. Entered state service after studies at St Petersburg Univ., but also studied music there and at Dresden, and came under the influence of the Balakirev circle.

Works incl. operas *Cupid's Revenge* (1899) and *The Snowstorm*; 3 symphs. (1890, 1903, 1908), symph. poem *Alesha Popovich*, overture to Shakespeare's *Hamlet*, 2 suites for orch.; 3 string 4tets; pieces

for vln. and pf. and for pf.; songs, partsongs.

Taneiev, Sergey Ivanovich (b Gvt. of Vladimir, 25 Nov 1856; d Djudkowa, 19 Jun 1915), Russian composer. Studied at the Moscow Cons., intending at 1st to become a pianist, but also studying comp. with Tchaikovsky. In 1876 he toured Rus., in 1877–8 visited Paris, and after playing in the Baltic Provinces became prof. of orch. at the Moscow Cons., in 1881 chief prof. of pf. on N. Rubinstein's death and in 1885 director, succeeding Hubert. He was followed by Safonov in 1889 and concentrated on teaching counterpoint and fugue.

Works incl. operatic trilogy *Oresteia* (based on Aeschylus, 1895); cantata *John of Damascus* for solo voices, chotus and orch. (1884); 4 symphs., Overture on Rus. Themes for orch.; concert suite for vln. and orch.; 9 string 4tets, 2 string trios, pf. trio; prelude and fugue for 2 pfs.; *c* 40 songs to words by Tiutchev and others; part-songs.

Tañer (Span. – to touch), a 16th-cent. lute prelude with which the strings were 'touched', or tried; equivalent to a Toccata.

Tangents, the screwdriver-shaped pins striking the wire strings in the Clavichord. The strings continue to sound while the tangents touch them, and their tone can thus be made to vibrate like a vln. *vibrato* by shaking the finger on the key.

Tango, a Latin American dance whose origins, sometimes said to be African, are obscure. Clearly related to the Cuban habanera etc., it was indigenous to Arg. in the 19th cent. before becoming popular with dancers and jazz bands in Eur. in the first 15 years of the 20th. It is in 2–4 time, like the habanera, but faster in pace, and is accomp. with a rhythm of 4 quavers, the 1st of which is dotted.

Tango, Egisto (b Rome, 13 Nov 1873; d Copenhagen, 5 Oct 1951), Italian conductor. Debut Venice, 1893; La Scala from 1895. Rome 1911, in the 1st It. perf. of *Rosenkavalier*. At Budapest he gave the fps of Bartók's *Wooden Prince* (1917) and *Bluebeard's Castle* (1918). Copenhagen from 1927.

Tannhäuser und der Sängerkrieg auf der Wartburg (*Tannhäuser and the Singers' Contest at the Wartburg*), opera by Wagner (lib. by comp.), prod. Dresden, 19 Oct 1845; rev. for Paris, with bacchanale in 1st act, and prod. at the Opéra, 13 Mar 1861.

Tansman, Alexandre (b Łódź, 12 Jun 1897; d Paris, 15 Nov 1986), Polish-born French composer. Studied at home and then at Warsaw, and in 1919 took 2 prizes for comp. He settled in Paris, but travelled extensively as pianist and cond. Married the Fr. pianist Colette Cras.

Works incl. operas *La Nuit Kurde* (1927), *La Toison d'or, Le Serment* (1955) and *Sabbataï Lévi, le faux Messie* (1961); ballets *Sextuor* (1924) and *La Grande Ville* (1932); 7 symphs. (1925–44), *Sinfonietta* (1925), symph. overture, *Toccata, Sonatine transatlantique, 4 Danses polonaises, Triptyque, Partita, 2 Pièces, Etudes symphoniques*, serenade, *Rapsodie polonaise* and suites for orch.; variations on a theme by Frescobaldi for· strings; 2 concertos (1925–6) and concertino for pf. and orch.

CHAMBER: 8 string 4tets (1917–56), mazurka for 9 insts., *Divertimento* for ob., clar., tpt., cello and pf., *Danse de la sorcière* fr 5 wind insts. and pf.; *Sonata quasi una fantasia* for vln. and pf.; 5 sonatas and other pf. works; songs.

Tapiola, symph. poem by Sibelius, op. 112, comp. in 1926 for the Symph. Society in NY. The title is the old mythological name of Fin., derived from the forest god Tapio, who appears in the *Kalevala*. Fp NY, 26 Dec 1926.

Tapissier, Johannes (Jean de Noyers) (b *c* 1370; d before Aug 1410), French composer. Though at the Burgundian court from 1391 to the end of his life, he seems to have been active mainly in Paris. Two Mass movements and an isorhythmic motet survive, though records indicate that he was a prominent and prolific comp.

Tappert, Wilhelm (b Ober-Thomaswaldau, Silesia, 19 Feb 1830; d Berlin, 27 Oct 1907), German music scholar. Studied with Dehn and Kullak in Berlin and after 8 years as teacher and critic at Glogau settled in Berlin in 1866, where he taught at Tausig's pf. school and wrote numerous musico-lit. works, incl. a *Wagner-Lexikon* (a collection of anti-Wagner reviews) and other works on Wagner, studies of notation, old lute music, the settings of Goethe's *Erlkönig* (54), etc. He also wrote pf. pieces, incl. 50 studies for the left hand, songs, etc.

Tarantella, an Italian dance deriving its name from Taranto, formerly sometimes sung, but now purely instrumental. It is in quick 6–8 time, increasing its speed progressively towards the end, and consists of alternating maj. and min. sections. It was danced by a couple, or in couples, who often accompanied the music with timbrels. 2 superstitions were connected with it: (1) that the bite of the tarantula caused a kind of madness

which made people dance it; (2) that the dance was a remedy against such madness. **Tarare**, opera by Salieri (lib. by Beaumarchais), prod. Paris, Opéra, 8 Jun 1787. It became known later under the title of *Axur, re d'Ormus* (It. version by Da Ponte, prod. Vienna, Burgtheater, 8 Jan 1788).

Taras Bulba, rhapsody for orch. by Janáček, after Gogol; comp. 1915–18, fp Brno, 9 Oct 1924, cond. F. Neumann (*q.v.*). The 3 movts. are 'Death of Andrea', 'Death of Ostap' and 'Capture and Death of Taras Bulba'.

Tarchi, Angelo (b Naples, *c* 1760; d Paris, 19 Aug 1814), Italian composer. Studied at the Pietà dei Turchini Cons. at Naples with Fago and Sala. For La Scala, Milan, he wrote *Ademira* (1783), *Ariarte* (1786), *Il Conte di Saldagna* (1787), *Adrasto* (1792) and *Le Danaidi* (1794). He attempted to re-write the last 2 acts of Mozart's *Marriage of Figaro*. He visited London in 1789 and wrote the operas *Il disertore* and *La generosità d'Alessandro* for the King's Theatre. Later he lived in Paris.

Works incl. over 40 It. and 7 Fr. operas.

Tardando (It. = delaying), a direction indicating that a passage is to be played in a lingering manner.

Tarditi, Orazio (b Rome, 1602; d Forlì, 18 Jan 1677), Italian composer, monk and organist. He was organist at var. It. towns and from 1647 to 1670 *maestro di cappella* at Faenza Cathedral.

Works incl. Masses, motets, madrigals, canzonets.

Tarr, Edward H(ankins) (b Norwich, Conn., 15 Jun 1936), American trumpeter and musicologist. Studied in Boston, Chicago and Basle (with Schrade). Founded E.T. Brass Ensemble (1967) for perf. of Renaissance and Baroque music; edited complete trumpet works of Torelli. Also plays works by Kagel, Berio and Stockhausen (e.g. *Michaels Reise um die Erde*).

Tartaglino, Hippolito (b ? Modena, ? 1539; d Naples, 1582), Italian composer. He was successively *maestro di cappella* at Santa Maria Maggiore in Rome and organist at the Church of the Annunciation, Naples.

Works said to incl. Masses and motets for 3 and 4 choruses (now lost).

Tartini, Giuseppe (b Pirano, Istria, 8 Apr 1692; d Padua, 26 Feb 1770), Italian composer and violinist. Intended for the Church, he went to Padua Univ., but was forced to flee after his runaway marriage with Elisabetta Premazore in 1710, and supported himself as an orchestral violinist. Taking refuge at the Franciscan Monastery at Assisi, he was a vln. pupil of Černohorský, but a meeting with Veracini in Venice in 1716 convinced him of his technical inadequacy, and he went to Ancona for further study. In 1721 he was app. principal violinist at the Basilica of Sant' Antonio, where apart from a period in the service of Count Kinsky in Prague (1723–6) and occasional travels elsewhere, he remained till his death. In 1728 he estab. a school of vln. playing in Padua, where his pupils included Nardini and Pugnani. He claimed to have discovered combination tones (*q.v.*) and he commended their use to his pupils as a guide to true intonation. From 1750 he increasingly withdrew from comp. to devote himself to theoret. study, and pub. a number of treatises, incl. *Trattato di musica* (1754).

Works incl. *Miserere* (said to have been comp. for Pope Clement XII) and other church music; over 100 vln. concertos; 100 vln. sonatas, including *Il Trillo del diavolo* (*q.v.*: *The Devil's Trill*), trio sonatas.

Taskin, Émile Alexandre (b Paris, 18 Mar 1853; d Paris, 5 Oct 1897), French baritone. Studied at the Paris Cons. and was a member of the Opéra-Comique in 1879–94; saved many lives with his calm demeanour when the opera house caught fire in May 1887 during a perf. of Thomas' *Mignon*. Grandson of the organist and comp. Henri Joseph T. (1779–1852), great-grandson of Pascal Joseph T. (1750–1829), keeper of the royal instruments, and great-great-grandson of the instrument maker Pascale T. (1723–93).

Tasso, lamento e trionfo (*Tasso's Lament and Triumph*), symph. poem by Liszt, based on a poem by Byron; comp. 1849. Fp Weimar, 28 Aug 1849, as an overture to Goethe's drama *Torquato Tasso*; rev. 1850–51 with a new middle section and perf. Weimar, 19 Apr 1854.

Tasso, Torquato (1544–95), Italian poet. *See* **Armida** and **Armide** (11 operas on *Gerusalemme liberata*), **Belli (D.)** (*Aminta*), **Caccini (F.)**, (*Rinaldo innamorato*), **Combattimento di Tancredi e Clorinda** (Monteverdi), **Lenepveu** (*Renaud dans les jardins d'Armide*), **Madrigal Comedy** (*Aminta*), **Pallavacini (C.)** (*Gerus. lib.*), **Persuis** (*Jérusalem délivrée*), **Pizzetti** (*Aminta*), **Righini** (*Gerus. lib.*), **Rossellini** (*Aminta*), **Rossi (M.A.)** (*Erminia sul Giordano*), **Tancrède** (Campra), **Tancredi** (Rossini), **Torquato Tasso** (Donizetti).

Tastar (It., from *tastare* = to touch), a 16th-cent. lute prelude with which the strings

were 'touched', or tried; equivalent to a Toccata.

Tastiera per luce (It. = keyboard for light), an instrument appearing in the score of Skriabin's *Prometheus*, designed to throw differently coloured lights. It was never perfected for practical use.

Tasto (It.), key (of keyboard instruments); also fingerboard (of string instruments).

Tasto solo (It. = key alone), a direction indicating that in a comp. with a thoroughbass the bass notes are for the moment to be played alone on the keyboard instrument used, without any harmony above them.

Tate, Jeffrey (b Salisbury, 28 Apr 1943), English conductor. Overcoming the handicap of spina bifida, he was to become répétiteur at CG, 1971–7; asst. to Boulez at Bayreuth and Paris, 1976–80. Opera debut Göteborg, 1978, *Carmen*. At the NY Met he gave the 3-act version of *Lulu* (1980) and has returned for *Rosenkavalier, Wozzeck* and *Lohengrin*. CG debut 1982, *La Clemenza di Tito*; *Ariadne auf Naxos*, 1985. At the 1985 Salzburg Festival he cond. the fp of Henze's realization of Monteverdi's *Ulisse*. Regular concerts with ECO from 1982. Prin. cond. CG from 1986.

Tate, Phyllis (Margaret) (b Gerrards Cross, 6 Apr 1911; d London, 27 May 1986), English composer. Studied comp. with Harry Farjeon at the RAM in London, 1928–32. Several of her works were perf. when she was still a student, and in 1933 her cello concerto was her 1st work heard at a public concert.

Works incl. operas *The Lodger* (1960), *Dark Pilgrimage* (1963) and *Twice in a Blue Moon* (1968); operetta *The Policeman's Serenade* (A.P. Herbert); *Secular Requiem* for chorus and orch. (1967), *Serenade to Christmas* for mezzo, chorus and orch. (1972), *All the World's a Stage* for chorus and orch. (1977); symph. and suite for orch., *Valse lointaine* and prelude, interlude and postlude for chamber orch. (1941); cello and saxophone concertos (1933, 1944), *Panorama* for string orch. (1977).

Divertimento for string 4tet, sonata for clar. and cello (1947), *Nocturne* (S. Keyes) for 4 voices, string 5tet, celesta and bass clar.; *London Waits* for 2 pfs.; *Songs of Sundry Natures* on Elizabethan poems for voice and pf., songs to words by Blake, W.H. Davies, Hardy, Hood, Tennyson and others, *The Phoenix and the Turtle* for tenor and inst. ens.

Tattermuschová, Helena (b Prague, 28 Jun 1933), Czech soprano. She sang Musetta at

Ostrava in 1955 and joined the Prague National Theatre in 1959; many tours with the co., incl. Edinburgh 1970, in the 1st Brit. perf. of Janáček's *The Excursions of Mr. Brouček*. Sings Smetana, Mozart and Strauss; best known as Janáček's Vixen.

Tauber, Richard (b Linz, 16 May 1892; d London, 8 Jan 1948), Austrian, later British, tenor. Studied at Freiburg and made his debut at Chemnitz in 1913 as Tamino. Dresden 1913–26, after which he took largely to operetta; Vienna 1926–38. In 1931 he had 1st appeared in Eng., where he later settled in 1940. Sang in the USA 1931–47. Other roles. incl. Ottavio, Calaf, Rodolfo and parts in the operettas of Lehár.

Taubert, (Karl Gottfried) Wilhelm (b Berlin, 23 Mar 1811; d Berlin, 7 Jan 1891), German composer, conductor and pianist. Pupil of Ludwig Berger for pf. and of Klein for comp., and student at Berlin Univ. He became Prus. court pianist, in 1841 cond. of the Royal Opera and in 1845 court music director.

Works incl. operas *Die Kirmess* (1832), *Der Zigeuner* (1834), *Marquis und Dieb* (1842), *Joggeli, Macbeth* (after Shakespeare) and *Cesario* (on Shakespeare's *Twelfth Night*, 1874); incid. music to *Medea* (Euripides), *The Tempest* (Shakespeare) and other plays; 3 Psalms and other church music; 4 cantatas; 4 symphs.; 3 string 4tets; *c* 300 songs incl. *Kinderlieder*; duets, part-songs.

Taucher, Curt (b Nuremberg, 25 Oct 1885; d Munich, 7 Aug 1954), German tenor. Debut Augsburg, 1908, as Faust. After engagements in Chemnitz and Hanover he sang at the Dresden Staatsoper, 1920–34; created there Menelaos in *Ägyptische Helena* (1928) and the title role in Weill's *Der Protagonist* (1926). NY Met 1923–7, as Siegmund and Siegfried. London, CG, 1932, and sang in Barcelona, Berlin and Munich. Retired 1935. Well known in Wagner roles and as Strauss's Emperor.

Tausch, Julius (b Dessau, 15 Apr 1827; d Bonn, 11 Nov 1895), German composer and conductor. Pupil of Schneider at Dessau and at the Leipzig Cons. He became cond. of the Künstlerliedertafel at Düsseldorf in 1847, and succeeded Schumann as cond. of the Music Society in 1855.

Works incl. incid. music to Shakespeare's *Twelfth Night* (1863); Festival Overture for orch.; pf. pieces; songs.

Tausig, Carl (b Warsaw, 4 Nov 1841; d Lepizig, 17 Jul 1871), Polish pianist and composer of Bohemian origin. Pupil of his father, the pianist Aloys T. (1820–85), and of Liszt at Weimar. In 1858 he made his debut, at a concert cond. by Bülow in Berlin, then toured, settled at Dresden and in 1862 in Vienna, where he gave concerts with programmes of modern music. In 1865 he married, settled in Berlin and opened a school of advanced pf. playing.

Works incl. symph. poems; pf. concerto; concert studies, exercises, bravura pieces and numerous transcriptions for pf.

Tavener, John (Kenneth) (b London, 28 Jan 1944), English composer. He studied at the RAM with Lennox Berkeley and David Lumsdaine. His music shows a wide range of influences, and he is often drawn towards religious subjects (he is a member of the Gk. Orthodox Church).

Works incl. *3 Holy Sonnets* for bar. and orch. (texts by Donne, 1962), pf. concerto (1963), *The Cappemakers*, dramatic cantata (1965), *Cain and Abel*, dramatic cantata (1965), *Little Concerto* (1965), *The Whale*, cantata (1966), *Grandma's Footsteps* for ens. (1968), *Introit for the Feast of St John Damascene* for soloists, chorus and orch. (1968), *Concerto for Orch.* (1968), *In alium* for sop., orch. and tape (1968), *Celtic Requiem* (1969), *Ultimos Ritos* for soloists, speakers, chorus and orch. (1969–72), *Coplas* for soloist, chorus and tape (1970), *Ma fin est mon commencement* for tenor, chorus, brass and perc. (1972), *Little Requiem for Father Malachy Lynch* (1972), *Requiem for Father Malachy* (1973).

Thérèse, opera (1973–6; prod. 1979), *Kyklike kinesis* for sop., chorus, cello and orch. (1977), *Palintropos* for pf. and orch. (1977), *Liturgy of St John Chrysostom* for unaccomp. chorus (1978), *The Immurement of Antigone*, monodrama (1978), *Akhmatova: rekviem* (1980), *Sappho: Lyrical Fragments* for 2 sop. and strings (1980), *Risen!* for chorus, pf., organ and orch. (1980), *Funeral Ikos* for chorus (1981), *Trisagion* for brass 5tet (1981), *Ikon of Light* for chorus and string trio (1984), *Eis Thanaton*, dramatic cantata (1987).

Taverner, opera by Maxwell Davies (lib. by comp.); comp. 1962–70, prod. London, CG, 12 Jul 1972. Plot is based on now discredited story that John Taverner was an agent of Thomas Cromwell dedicated to the persecution of the Catholic church.

Taverner, John (b south Lincs., *c* 1490; d Boston, Lincs., 18 Oct 1545), English composer and organist. In 1526 he was app. master of the choristers at Wolsey's new coll. (Cardinal Coll., later Christ Church) at

Oxford and organist at St Frideswide's Church (later Cathedral) attached to it. In 1528 he was involved in heresy at the coll., and in 1530, following Wolsey's eclipse, he left, probably to return to his native Lincs. There is no foundation in the allegations that he gave up music to devote himself to the persecution of Catholics as an agent of Thomas Cromwell. In 1537 he was elected a member of the Gild of Corpus Christi in Boston. The inst. In Nomine tradition orig. from a passage at those words in his Mass *Gloria tibi Trinitas.*

Works incl. 8 Masses (incl. *The Western Wind, Gloria tibi Trinitas*), 25 Lat. motets, 3 Magnificats and other church music.

Taylor, (Joseph) Deems (b New York, 22 Dec 1885; d New York, 3 Jul 1966), American composer and critic. Studied at the Ethical Culture School and the Univ. in NY, received pf. lessons, but was self-taught in other musical subjects. He became music critic to the *NY World* in 1921, but from 1925 devoted himself to comp.

Works incl. operas *The King's Henchman* (1927), *Peter Ibbetson* (after G. du Maurier, 1931), and *Ramuntcho* (after Loti, 1942); incid. music for T. Wilder's *Lucrece* and for other plays; symph. poems *The Siren Song* and *Jurgen* (after J. B. Cabell), suites *Through the Looking-Glass* (after L. Carroll) and *Circus Day* (1925), *Lucrece* suite for string 4tet; choral works.

Tchaikovsky, Pyotr Il'yich (b Kamsko Votkinsk, 7 May 1840; d St Petersburg, 6 Nov 1893), Russian composer. His father, an inspector of mines, allowed him to have music lessons from the age of 4, and at 6 he played well. The family moved to St Petersburg in 1848; he received more systematic teaching there and in 1850 was sent to the School of Jurisprudence, which he left in 1859 to become a clerk in the Ministry of Justice. He approached music as an amateur, but in 1862 entered the newly opened Cons., having already studied with Zaremba, and had lessons in orch. from A. Rubinstein. N. Rubinstein, having opened a similar Cons. at Moscow, engaged him as prof. of harmony in 1865, and there he began to comp. seriously and professionally. In 1868 he met Balakirev and his circle of nationalist comps. in St Petersburg, but remained aloof.

The 2nd symph., a distinctly nationalist work, was prod. in 1873, and the B♭ min. pf. concerto, though at first rejected by N. Rubinstein, was done abroad by Bülow in 1875 and given its 1st Moscow perf. later that year by Taneiev. In 1876 began a corres-

pondence with Nadezhda von Meck, the widow of a wealthy engineer, who greatly admired his work and made him an allowance to free him from financial anxiety, but never met him face to face. In 1877 he married Antonina Milyukova; but he was an undeclared homosexual and left her less than a month after the wedding, on the verge of mental collapse. After some months in Switz. and It., he resigned the post at the Moscow Cons. and lived in the country, wholly devoted to comp. In 1888 he made a 1st international tour as cond. of his own works, which became known in many countries, and the following year he completed the finest of his 3 ballets, *The Sleeping Beauty*. In 1890 he had a misunderstanding with Mme von Meck which brought their friendship by correspondence to an end; but he was by that time quite able to earn his own living.

He visited the USA in 1892 and London in the summer of 1893, when the Mus.D. degree was conferred on him by Cambridge Univ. On his return to Rus., he completed the 6th symph. ('Pathétique'), which was fp at St Petersburg on 28 Oct. 9 days later Tchaikovsky was dead; the cause of death is usually given as cholera, although it has recently been suggested that he took poison at the decree of a secret court of honour instituted to avert a scandal following allegations of a liaison between him and an aristocrat's nephew.

Works incl. operas *The Opritchnik* (1874), *Vakula the Smith* (afterwards *Tcherevichki* or *Oxana's Caprices*, 1876), *Eugene Onegin* (1879), *Maid of Orleans* (1881), *Mazeppa* (1884), *The Sorceress, The Queen of Spades* (1890), *Iolanta* (1892) and 3 partly lost early works; incid. music to Ostrovsky's *Snegurochka* and Shakespeare's *Hamlet*; ballets *Swan Lake* (1877), *The Sleeping Beauty* (1890) and *The Nutcracker* (1892).

ORCH.: 7 symphs., no. 1 in G min. (*Winter Daydreams*, 1866, rev. 1874), no. 2 in C min. (*Little Russian*, 1872, rev. 1880), no. 3 in D (*Polish*, 1875), no. 4 in F min. (1878), no. 5 in E min. (1888), no. 6 in B min. (*Pathétique*, 1893), no. 7 in E♭ (unfinished, 1892); 4 suites: no. 1 in D (1879), no. 2 in C (1883), no. 3 in G (1884), no. 4 (*Mozartiana*, 1887); *Manfred* symph., after Byron (1885); fantasy-overture *Romeo and Juliet* (1869), symph. fantasies *The Tempest* (1873) and *Francesca da Rimini* (1876), *Capriccio italien,* Serenade for string orch. (1880), overture *The Year 1812* (1880), fantasy-overture *Hamlet* (1888), symph.

ballad *The Voyevoda* (1891); 3 pf. concertos, no. 1 in B♭ min. (1875), no. 2 in G (1880), no. 3 in E♭ (unfinished, 1893), vln. concerto (1878), *Variations on a Rococo Theme* for cello and orch. (1876) and some smaller pieces for solo insts. and orch.

CHAMBER: string 6tet *Souvenir de Florence* (1887), 3 string 4tets (1871, 1874, 1876), pf. trio (1882); 17 op. nos. of pf. comps. incl. 6 pieces on 1 theme, sonata in G maj., *The Seasons*; 50 Rus. folksongs for vocal duet; 13 op. nos. of songs (nearly 100); 6 vocal duets; 3 cantatas; some church music; part-songs.

Tchaikowsky, André (b Warsaw, 1 Nov 1935; d Oxford, 26 Jun 1982), British pianist and composer of Polish birth. He escaped from the Warsaw ghetto and was brought up in Paris. Returning to Poland, he studied with Stefan Askenase (*q.v.*). Lived in London from 1957 and was well known as a concert pianist; he was by no means reluctant to embellish Mozart's pf. concertos. He bequeathed his skull to the Royal Shakespeare Co., for use in its perfs. of *Hamlet*. The skull was duly placed in a stock cupboard, with two others, and appeared on stage in 1984.

Works incl. clar. sonata (1959), 2 string 4tets, (1967, 1970), pf. concerto (1971), *Trio notturno* (1973). An opera *The Merchant of Venice*, was almost complete at his death.

Tcherepnin, Alexander (Nikolaievich) (b St Petersburg, 21 Jan 1899; d Paris, 29 Sep 1977), Russian composer. Studied under his father, Nikolai T., Sokolov and others, learning the pf. from Anna Essipova. He appeared as a boy pianist and began to pub. his works, but in 1921 settled in Paris with his father, studying comp. with Gédalge and pf. with Philipp at the Cons. From 1925 and 1938 he taught in Paris, and from 1949 at De Paul Univ. in Chicago.

Works incl. operas 01–01 (after Andreiev, 1928) and *Die Hochzeit der Sobeide* (after Hofmannsthal, 1933); ballets incl. *The Frescoes of Ajanta* (1923) and (with Honegger and Harsányi) *Shota Roustaveli*; incid. music for Wilde's *Salome*, Rolland's *L'Esprit triomphant* and Hauptmann's *Hannele*; cantata *Le Jeu de la Nativité*.

4 symphs. (1927–58), 3 pieces for chamber orch., 6 pf. concertos (1923–72), *Rapsodie géorgienne* for cello and pf., *Concerto da camera* for fl., vln. and small orch.; 2 string 4tets (1922, 1926), pf. trio; vln. and pf. sonata, 3 cello and pf. sonatas; sonata, studies and pieces for pf.

Tcherepnin, Nikolai (Nikolaievich) (b St Petersburg, 15 May 1873; d Issy-les-Moulineaux nr. Paris, 26 Jun 1945), Russian composer and conductor, father of prec. He gave up a legal career at the age of 22 and studied at the St Petersburg Cons. with Rimsky-Korsakov and others. Having appeared as pianist, he became cond. of the Belaiev concerts in 1901, and then became cond. of opera at the Maryinsky Theatre. In 1908 he joined Diaghilev and cond. Rus. opera and ballet in Paris and elsewhere, remaining with the company until 1914, when he returned to Petrograd, to become director of the Cons. at Tiflis in 1918. In 1921 he settled in Paris.

Works incl. operas *Vanka the Chancellor* (after Sologub, 1935), and *Poverty no Crime* (after Ostrovsky); ballets *Armida's Pavilion* (1907), *Narcissus* (1911), *A Russian Fairy-Tale, The Romance of a Mummy* (after Gautier), *The Masque of the Red Death* (after Poe, 1916), *The Tale of the Princess Ulyba, Dionysius.*

Symph., sinfonietta, symph. poems *Narcissus and Echo* and *The Enchanted Kingdom,* witches' scene from *Macbeth,* suite *The Enchanted Garden* (1904), overture to Rostand's *La Princesse lointaine* (1903), 6 pieces on Pushkin's *The Golden Fish* for orch.; pf. concerto in C♯ min. (1907), lyric poem for vln. and orch.; string 4tet in A min.; pf. pieces on Benois' picture-book *The Russian Alphabet* and other pf. works; songs.

Te, the name for the leading-note in any key in Tonic Sol-fa, so pronounced, but in notation represented by the symbol **t.**

Te Deum laudamus (*We praise thee, O God*), Latin hymn or psalm in 'rhythmical prose', poss. by Nicetas of Remesiana (*c* 400). It is in 3 sections: a hymn to the Trinity, a hymn to Christ, and a series of prayers. The 1st part is set to a psalmodic formula ending on G, and the 2nd to a similar formula ending on E, but concluding with a more extended melody in the same mode to the words 'Aeterna fac'. The 3rd part makes further use of these last 2 melodies.

The Te Deum was set in polyphony during the Middle Ages, esp. in England, for voices or org. in altenation with the plainsong. It became a normal part of the Angl. 'Morning Service' and it has also been set in Eng. for occasions of rejoicing (e.g. by Handel, Walton). The Lat. text has often been set with orch. accomp., e.g. by Haydn (2), Berlioz, Bruckner and Kodály.

Te Kanawa, Dame Kiri (b Gisborne, Auckland, 6 Mar 1944), New Zealand-born British soprano. She sang Elena in Rossini's *La donna del lago* at the 1969 Camden Festival, London. Came to wider attention with Mozart's Countess at CG, in 1970, and since then has sung Amelia Boccanegra, Marguerite, Micaela, Fiordiligi, Arabella and the Marschallin in London. US debut 1972, San Francisco, as the Countess; NY Met 1974, Desdemona. In recent years she has broadened her appeal, and has sung at weddings and on television. DBE 1982.

Tear, Robert (b Barry, 8 Mar 1939), Welsh tenor. He studied at Cambridge and sang with the EOG 1963–71; created roles in Britten's church parables *The Burning Fiery Furnace* and *The Prodigal Son*. He created Dov in *The Knot Garden* at CG in 1970; other London roles have been Grimes, Lensky and Paris in *King Priam*. Loge was the role of his Paris, Opéra, debut (1976) and he returned in 1979 to sing the Painter in the 1st complete perf. of Berg's *Lulu*. Well known in oratorio and recitals.

Teares and Lamentacions of a Sorrowfull Soul, The. *See* **Leighton.**

Tebaldi, Renata (b Pesaro, 1 Feb 1922), Italian soprano. Studied at Parma Cons., and then with Carmen Melis from 1939 to 1942, making her debut in Rovigo in 1944 as Boito's Elena. She sang at the re-opening of La Scala, Milan, in 1946 under Toscanini and at CG in 1950, with the Scala co. US debut San Francisco, 1950, as Aida; NY Met debut 1955, as Desdemona. Returned to NY until 1973 and toured Rus., 1976. Other roles incl. Violetta, Tosca, Mimi, Adriana Lecouvreur and Eva. She was known as one of the best Verdi and Puccini singers of her day.

Tedesca (fem.)
Tedesco (masc.) } (It.) = German. The term *alla tedesca* means 'in the Ger. manner', but more partic. indicates a piece or movement in rather slow waltz time, in the character of the *Deutscher* or *Ländler*.

Telemaco, Il, ossia L'isola di Circe (*Telemachus, or Circe's Island*), opera by Gluck (lib. by M. Coltellini), prod. Vienna, Burgtheater, 30 Jan 1765.

Telemann, Georg Philipp (b Magdeburg, 14 Mar 1681; d Hamburg, 25 Jun 1767), German composer. Educ. at Magdeburg and Hildesheim, and at Leipzig Univ., where he read law, he seems to have been largely self-taught in music. In Leipzig he founded a student *Collegium musicum* and was app. organist of the New Church (St Matthew's)

in 1704, but the same year moved to Sorau as *Kapellmeister* to Count Promnitz. In the service of the court at Eisenach 1708–12 (*Kapellmeister* from 1709) he made the acquaintance of Bach in nearby Weimar, then worked in Frankfurt until his appt. in 1721 as Cantor of the Johanneum and municipal music director in Hamburg, where he stayed for the rest of his life. In 1722 he declined the post of Cantor of St Thomas's, Leipzig, and Bach was app. He travelled a good deal, several times visiting Berlin, and in 1737 made a successful visit to Paris.

Works incl. *c* 45 operas (few survive complete), e.g. *Der geduldige Socrates* (1721), *Der neumodische Liebhaber Damon* (1724), *Miriways* (1728), *Pimpinone* (1725), *Emma und Eginhard* (1728); oratorios *Die Tageszeiten*, *Die Auferstehung und Himmelfahrt Christi* (1760), *Der Tag des Gerichts* (1762), etc.; Passion oratorios (Brockes and Ramler); 46 liturgical Passions; 12 sets of cantatas for the church's year; motets, psalms, etc.; large quantities of inst. music, incl. collection called *Musique de table* (Hamburg, 1733); concertos, orch. suites, trio sonatas and other chamber music, keyboard music.

Temistocle (*Themistocles*), opera by Porpora (lib. by A. Zeno), prod. Vienna, 1 Oct 1718;

Opera by J.C. Bach (lib. M. Verazi, after Metastasio) prod. Mannheim, Hoftheater, 5 Nov 1772.

Temperament (*see also* **Equal Temperament**), a term used to designate the tuning of the musical scale in such a way as to prod. satisfying intonation in some way not according to the natural harmonics.

Tempest, The, incid. music by Sibelius, op. 109, comp. for prod. of Shakespeare's play at the Theatre Royal, Copenhagen, 1926.

Opera by Fibich (lib. by J. Vrchlický, based on Shakespeare), prod. Prague, Cz. Theatre, 1 Mar 1895.

Symph. fantasy by Tchaikovsky, after Shakespeare, suggested by Stassov, begun Aug 1873, fp Moscow, 19 Dec 1873.

Tempest, The, or The Enchanted Island, opera adapted from Shakespeare by T. Shadwell, with music by (?) Locke, Humfrey, Reggio, James Hart, G.B. Draghi and Banister, prod. London, Dorset Gardens Theatre, 30 Apr 1674.

Opera adapted from Shakespeare by Shadwell, with music by Weldon, formerly attrib. to H. Purcell, comp. *c* 1712.

Tempestà, La, opera by Halévy (lib. by Scribe, orig. written in Fr. for Mendelssohn, based on Shakespeare's *Tempest* and trans. into It.), prod. London, Her Majesty's Theatre, 8 Jun 1850.

Templario, Il (*The Templar*), opera by Nicolai (lib. by G. M. Marini, based on Scott's *Ivanhoe*), prod. Turin, Teatro Regio, 11 Feb 1840.

Templer und die Jüdin, Der (*The Templar and the Jewess*), opera by Marschner (lib. by W.A. Wohlbrück, based on Scott's *Ivanhoe*), prod. Leipzig, 22 Dec 1829.

Templeton, John (b Riccarton, Kilmarnock, 30 Jul 1802; d New Hampton, 2 Jul 1886), Scottish tenor. Appeared as a child singer at Edinburgh, studied there and in London, and made his debut at Worthing in 1828. In 1831 he became known in London and in 1833 Malibran engaged him as her partner. He was well known as Ottavio and Tamino and sang in operas by Auber, Hérold and Rossini.

Tempo (It. lit. time) = Pace, the speed of any musical comp., determined, not by the notevalues, which are relative, but by the directions set above the stave at the opening of a piece or section (e.g. *allegro, andante, adagio,* etc.). The exact pace can be estab. only by means of Metronome marks (e.g. ♩ = 96, i.e. 96 crotchets to the minute, etc.). In It. tempo also means a movement of a sonata, symph., etc.

Tempo giusto (It.) = Strict time, also the right speed.

Tempo ordinario (It. = common time, ordinary pace), either (1) moderate speed or (2) 4 beats in a bar (C), as opposed to *Alla breve* (₵), where there are 2 beats in a bar.

Tempo primo (It. lit. 1st time = 1st tempo), after a change of tempo the direction *tempo primo* means that the pace 1st indicated is to be resumed.

Tenaglia, Antonio Francesco (b Florence, *c* 1610–20; d Rome, after 1661), Italian composer. Studied and lived in Rome, where he was organist for a time at St John Lateran.

Works incl. 2 operas (lost); many cantatas for sop. and *continuo.*

Tender Land, The, opera by Copland (lib. by H. Everett), prod. NY, 1 Apr 1954, cond. Schippers. Orch. suite 1956.

Tenducci, Giusto Ferdinando (b Siena, *c* 1735; d Genoa, 1790), Italian castrato soprano and composer. Made his debut in Naples, then went to London in 1758, remaining there, apart from visits to Ir. (1765–8) and Scot. (1768–9), until 1791, when he returned to It. Popular in England as a singer of Handel, he was also heard in his own adaptation of Gluck's *Orfeo.* He pub. a

treatise on singing, comp. songs, harpsichord sonatas, etc., and compiled song collections, etc. He was thrice married: his nickname 'Triorchis' (triple-testicled) indicates that his condition as a castrato did not hinder his off-stage activities.

Tennstedt, Klaus (b Merseburg, 6 Jun 1926), German conductor. He studied at the Leipzig Cons. and worked in Halle until 1958. After posts at the Dresden Opera and with the Schwerin State Orch., 1958–61, he worked in Göteborg and Stockholm. Music dir. Kiel Opera, then US debut, with Boston SO, in 1974; NY Met debut 1983, with *Fidelio.* 1979–83 prin. guest cond. Minnesota Orch. and N. German Radio SO, Hamburg. LPO 1983–7, notably in symphs. of Bruckner and Mahler.

Tenor, the highest male voice prod. naturally, i.e. not in falsetto, like the male alto. It is so called (from Lat. *teneo* = 'I hold') because it 'held' the plainsong theme in early polyphonic comps. using a *Cantus firmus.* The compass is approx.:

The word tenor was formerly also used for the vla.

Tenor Clef, the C clef is used as to indicate that middle C stands on the 4th line of the stave:

It was formerly used for the tenor voice but is now used only for the tenor tromb. and the higher reaches of the bassoon, cello and double bass.

Tenor Cor, a military-band brass instrument invented *c* 1860 to provide a better substitute for the horn than had been found in the Saxhorn. It is in the circular form of a horn, though half the length, and has valves. It is made in F, with an extra slide to change it to E♭.

Tenor Drum, a drum with 2 skins stretched over either end, similar in shape to the side drum and bass drum, but of intermediate size. It prod. a duller sound than that of the side drum, having no snares, but gives out clearer notes, though of indefinite pitch, than the bass drum.

Tenor Horn, a brass valve wind instrument of the Saxhorn type, made in var. tunings and compasses.

Tenor Tuba, another name for the Euphonium.

Tenor Violin, early name for the viola. A small cello, tuned a 5th or a 4th above the normal cello, was sometimes known as a tenor violin.

Tenore robusto (It. = robust tenor), one of the categories of operatic voices: a tenor capable of sustaining parts of a heroic type; equivalent to the Ger. *Heldentenor*.

Tenoroon, an early instrument of the bassoon type, smaller and tuned higher than the bassoon.

Tenson, a Troubadour, Trouvère or Minnesinger song the words of which took the form of a dispute.

Tenuto (It. = held), a direction usually marked *ten.*, indicating that the note or notes to which it applies are to be sustained to their full value, or even an almost imperceptible fraction beyond, but not so much so as to give the different effect of *ritenuto*: the meaning is 'held', not 'held back'.

Ternary. A vocal or instrumental piece in 3 distinct sections, the 3rd of which is a repetition of the 1st, is said to be in ternary form. The middle section is usually a contrast, sometimes based on similar but more often on different thematic material, but always relevant in style if not in mood. In vocal music *da capo* arias and in inst. music minuets or scherzos with trios are outstanding exs. of ternary form.

Ternina, Milka (b Doljnji, Moslavina, 19 Dec 1863; d Zagreb, 18 May 1941), Croatian soprano. Studied at home from the age of 12 and in 1880–82 in Vienna. She appeared as Amelia at Zagreb when still a student, then sang light parts at Leipzig, rising gradually through greater parts at Graz and Bremen to the Court Opera at Munich, to which she was attached in 1890–99. In 1895 she 1st sang in London, making her 1st appearance at CG in 1898 as Isolde, and the next year, having become one of the great Wagner singers, she was engaged for Bayreuth. She sang there until 1903, when she was banned for having sung Kundry in the 'pirate' NY Met perf. of *Parsifal*. US debut Boston, 1896, as Elsa. Retired 1916.

Terpander (*fl. c* 675 BC), Greek poet and musician. He won a prize at the music festival in Sparta between 676 and 672 BC. His contribs. to music are uncertain, but are said to have incl. the comp. of drinking-songs, the increasing of the lyre strings from 4 to 7 and the intro. of new metres into poetry and consequently into music.

Terradellas, Domingo Miguel Bernabe (b Barcelona, bap. 13 Feb 1713; d Rome, 20 May 1751), Spanish composer. Pupil of Durante at the Cons. dei Poveri di Gesù at Naples 1732–8, he there comp. 2 oratorios. Prod. his 1st opera in 1739 in Rome, where he was *maestro di cappella* at the Span. church 1743–5. He visited London (1746–7) and Paris, then returned to Rome.

Works incl. operas *Astarto* (1739), *Gli intrighi delle cantarine, Cerere, Merope,* (1743), *Artaserse, Semiramide riconosciuta, Mitridate* (1746), *Bellerofonte* (1747), *Imeneo in Atene, Didone, Sesostri, rè d'Egitto*; oratorios, *Giuseppe riconosciuto* (1736) and *Ermenegildo martire*; Masses, motets and other church music.

Terrasse, Claude (Antoine) (b Grand-Lemps nr. Grenoble, 27 Jan 1867; d Paris, 30 Jun 1923), French composer and organist. He studied at the Lyons Cons. and then at Niedermeyer's school in Paris, afterwards privately with Gigout. After living obscurely as an organist at Auteuil and a pf. teacher at Arcachon, he began to comp. and settled in Paris in 1895 as organist of the Trinité.

Works incl. opera *Pantagruel* (after Rabelais), operettas *La Fiancée du scaphandrier, Choncette, Le Sire de Vergy* (1903), *Monsieur de la Palisse* (1904), *L'Ingénu libertin, Le Coq d'Inde, Le Mariage de Télémaque* (1910), *Les Transatlantiques* (1911), *La Petite Femme de Loth* (T. Bernard), *Les Travaux d'Hercule* (1901), *Cartouche* (1912), *Le Cochon qui sommeille, Faust en ménage, Le Manoir enchanté* and several others; incid. music for var. comedies; music for T. Gautier's and T. de Banville's *Matinées poétiques; Trio bouffe* for strings, *Sérénade bouffe* for pf. and strings; songs.

Terry, Charles Sanford (b Newport Pagnell, Bucks., 24 Oct 1864; d Westerton of Pitfodels nr. Aberdeen, 5 Nov 1936), English music historian. He was app. prof. of hist. at Aberdeen Univ. in 1903. He also did invaluable work for music by writing an authoritative biog. of J.S. Bach (1928) as well as numerous detailed studies of var. aspects of his work, and a biog. of J.C. Bach (1929, rev. 1967 by H.C.R. Landon).

Tertis, Lionel (b W. Hartlepool, 29 Dec 1876; d London, 22 Feb 1975), English viola player. First studied vln. at Leipzig Cons. and the RAM, and then took up the vla. at the suggestion of Alexander Mackenzie, playing with various string 4tets. This, and his appearances as a soloist, made him one of the most famous violists of his time. In 1925 he was soloist in the fp of Vaughan Williams's *Flos campi*. He also intro. a new, large vla. called the 'Tertis Model'. He retired from the concert platform in 1936, but re-emerged during the 1939–45 war. CBE 1950.

Terzet (Eng.) } a comp. for 3 voices or
Terzetto (It.) } for instruments in 3 parts.

Teschemacher, Margarete (b Cologne, 3 Mar 1903; d Bad Wiessee, 19 May 1959), German soprano. After her 1922 Cologne debut she sang widely in Germany; Dresden 1934–45, where she created Strauss's Daphne (1938) and Sutermeister's Miranda in his opera based on *The Tempest (Die Zauberinsel*, 1942). London, CG, 1931 and 1936 as Pamina, Elsa and Elvira. In Buenos Aires she was the first local Arabella. Other roles incl. Senta, Jenůfa, Minnie and Francesca da Rimini.

Teseo (*Theseus*), opera by Handel (lib. by N.F. Haym), prod. London, Queen's Theatre, Haymarket, 10 Jan 1713.

Tesi (Tramontini), Vittoria (b Florence, 13 Feb 1700; d Vienna, 9 May 1775), Italian contralto. Made her 1st appearance at a very early age. In 1719 she was at Dresden, from 1749 in Vienna. It is one of the well-known and purely fictitious Handel stories that he fell in love with her at Florence when his *Rodrigo* was prod. there in 1707: the date of her birth refutes it effectively. From 1716 she was successful in Italy, Dresden and Vienna in operas by Lotti, Gluck and Jommelli.

Tess, opera by F. d'Erlanger (lib., in It., by L. Illica, based on Hardy's *Tess of the D'Urbervilles*), prod. Naples, Teatro San Carlo, 10 Apr 1906.

Tessarini, Carlo (b Rimini, *c* 1690; d Amsterdam, after 15 Dec 1766), Italian composer and violinist. He worked as a violinist in Venice at St Mark's (from 1720) and SS. Giovanni e Paolo, obtained a post at Urbino Cathedral in 1733 but left the same year to enter the service of Cardinal Schrattenbach in Brno, returning to Urbino in 1738. He visited Hol. in 1747 and 1762, and prob. also Paris.

Works incl. *Concerti grossi*; vln. concertos; *sinfonie*; vln. sonatas and duets; trio sonatas, etc. Also wrote a treatise on vln. playing (1741).

Tessier, Charles (*fl. c* 1600), French lutenist and composer. He was a *musicien de la chambre du roy* to Henri IV and visited Eng. for some time in the 1590s, dedicating a book of *chansons* to Lady Penelope Rich (Sidney's Stella).

Works incl. *chansons* for 4–5 voices (1597), *Airs et villanelles* for 3–5 voices (1604), setting of the 8th song in Sidney's *Astrophel and Stella*.

Tessitura (It. lit. texture), the prevailing range of a voice part in a composition. It may be high, low or normal for the voice required.

Testament de la Tante Caroline, Le, opéra-bouffe by Roussel (lib. by Nino), prod. Olomouc, 14 Nov 1936.

Testudo (Lat. = tortoise), a Latin name for the Greek lyre, which was often made of tortoiseshell; transferred to the lute in 16th-cent. Lat.

Tetrachord (from Gk. = having 4 strings), a scale of 4 notes embracing the interval of a perfect 4th; a basis for melodic construction in ancient Gk. music theory.

Tetrazzini, Luisa (b Florence, 29 Jun 1871; d Milan, 28 Apr 1940), Italian soprano. Studied with Ceccherini at the Florence Liceo Musicale and with her sister Eva (1862–1938), the wife of the cond. Cleofante Campanini. She made her 1st appearance at Florence in 1890, as Meyerbeer's Ines, then toured, 1st in It. and later in Eur., Mex. and S. Amer. In 1907 she 1st appeared in London; returned (1908–12) as Violetta and Lucia. She sang the same roles in NY (1908–11) but soon retired from the stage. Active as concert singer until 1934.

Teufel ist los, Der, oder Die verwandelten Weiber (*The Devil to Pay, or The Women Metamorphosed*), *Singspiel* by J.C. Standfuss (lib. by C.F. Weisse, based on Coffey's *Devil to Pay*), prod. Leipzig, 6 Oct 1752. *See also* **Verwandelten Weiber** (J.A. Hiller).

Teufels Lustschloss, Das (*The Devil's Pleasure Palace*), opera by Schubert (lib. by A. von Kotzebue), comp. in 1814 but not perf. until 1879.

Teutsche (Ger.). *See* **Deutsche Tänze**.

Texture, the vertical density of a musical composition. While the nature of the texture is often one of the main distinguishing features of a work, particularly in 20th-cent. music, variety of texture is an important component of a work's progression and life in virtually all music.

Teyber, Anton (b Vienna, bap. 8 Sep 1754; d Vienna, 18 Nov 1822), Austrian composer. App. court comp. to the Imp. Chapel in 1793 and music teacher to the royal family.

Works incl. melodrama *Zermes und Mirabella* (1779); oratorio *Joas* (1786); Passion, Masses and other church music; symphs.; chamber music.

Teyber, Franz (b Vienna, bap. 25 Aug 1758; d Vienna, 21 or 22 Oct 1810), Austrian composer, conductor and organist, brother of prec. Cond. of Schikaneder's company and late in his life app. court organist.

Works incl. operas, e.g. *Laura Rosetti* (1785), *Adelheid von Veltheim* (1788), *Die Schlaftrunk* (1801) *Die Dorfdeputierten* (1785), *Alexander* (1801); oratorio; church music; songs.

Teyte (orig. Tate), **Maggie** (b Wolverhampton, 17 Apr 1888; d London, 26 May 1976), English soprano. Studied at the RCM and then in Paris with Jean de Reszke (1903–7), making her début in Monte Carlo in 1907. She appeared with Debussy in song recitals and was selected by him to succeed Mary Garden as Mélisande (1908). London, CG, 1910–38; in 1923 she created the Princess in Holst's *The Perfect Fool* there. Chicago 1911–14, Boston 1915–17. Other roles incl. Butterfly, Cherubino and Purcell's Belinda (London, 1951). DBE 1958.

Thaïs, opera by Massenet (lib. by L. Gallet, based on the novel by A. France), prod. Paris, Opéra, 16 Mar 1894. It contains the popular *Méditation* as an orch. interlude.

Thalben-Ball, George (Thomas) (b Sydney, 18 Jun 1896; d London, 18 Jan 1987), British organist of Australian birth. Studied at RCM and worked in London and Birmingham before and after the Second World War; associated with BBC 1939–70. Famed for a subjective approach to interpretation. Knighted 1982.

Thalberg, Sigismond (Fortuné François) (b Geneva, 8 Jan 1812; d Posillipo nr. Naples, 27 Apr 1871), Austrian pianist and composer. Said to be illegitimate son of Count Moritz Dietrichstein and Baroness von Wetzlar. When he was 10 his father sent him to school in Vienna, where he later studied pf. with Hummel and theory with Sechter. He soon played at private parties, appeared at Prince Metternich's house in 1826 and in 1830 made his 1st tour, in Germany, having by this time begun to pub. comps. In 1835 he made further studies with Pixis and Kalkbrenner in Paris, and in 1836 1st appeared in London.

Works incl. operas *Florinda* (1851) and *Cristina di Suezia* (1855); pf. concerto; pf. sonata, studies, nocturnes, romances and numerous other pieces for pf., operatic fantasies on works by Rossini, Weber and Verdi, and other transcriptions for pf.; over 50 Ger. songs.

Thamos, König in Aegypten (*Thamos, King of Egypt*), incid. music by Mozart (K345) to T.P. von Gebler's play, comp. 1779 (2 choruses already 1773), not prod. in Mozart's lifetime except in an adaptation to another play, Plümicke's *Lanassa*.

Thayer, Alexander Wheelock (b S. Natick, Mass., 22 Oct 1817; d Trieste, 15 Jul 1897), American biographer. Studied law at Harvard Univ. and in 1849 went to Ger., living at Bonn and Berlin, also to Prague and Vienna, collecting material for a Beethoven biog. After some journalistic activities in NY and Boston, he again went to Eur. in 1854–6 and for a 3rd time in 1858, eventually becoming US consul at Trieste. The 4th vol. of his biog., left unfinished, was completed by Hermann Deiters in a Ger. ed. of the work. An Eng. ed. was pub. in 1921 by Krehbiel and a rev. of this by Elliot Forbes in 1964.

Thebom, Blanche (b Monessen, Penn., 19 Sep 1918), American mezzo of Swedish parentage. She sang at the NY Met 1944–67 as Fricka, Carmen, Azucena and Ortrud. Glyndebourne 1950, as Dorabella; CG 1957 as Dido in the fp of *Les Troyens* in a single evening. She recorded Brangaene with Furtwängler and was well known as Baba the Turk, Amneris and Laura. Taught at San Francisco State Univ. from 1980.

Theile, Johann (b Naumburg, 29 Jul 1646; d Naumburg, buried 24 Jun 1724), German composer. Learnt music as a youth at Magdeburg and Halle, and later studied at Leipzig Univ., where he took part in the students' perfs. as singer and vla. da gamba player. He then became a pupil of Schütz at Weissenfels and taught music at Stettin and Lübeck. In 1673–5 he was *Kapellmeister* to the Duke of Holstein at Gottorp, but fled to Hamburg during the Dan. invasion. In 1676 he competed unsuccessfully for the post of cantor at St Thomas's Church, Leipzig. He was the 1st comp. to contrib. to the repertory of the newly opened opera at Hamburg in 1678. In 1685 he succeeded Rosenmüller as music director at Wolfenbüttel and in 1689 he was app. to a similar post at Merseburg. In his last years he lived in retirement at his birthplace.

Works incl. operas *Adam und Eva* (1678; lost) and *Orontes* (1678; 7 arias extant); 10 Masses, 7 Psalms; Passion according to St Matthew, church cantatas.

Theinred of Dover, 12th-cent. English music theorist and monk of Dover Priory. His treatise, a study of intervals and proportions, is known only from an early 15th-cent. copy (Oxford, Bodleian Library, MS. Bodley 842). It includes a diagram of the different forms of alphabetical notation, and a section on the measurement of organ pipes.

Theme, a musical idea, generally melodic,

sufficiently striking to be memorable and capable of being developed or varied in the course of a comp. A theme is generally complete in itself, whereas a motive is a figure which contrib. something to a larger conception; but a precise distinction between the two is impossible in practice.

Theodora, oratorio by Handel (lib. by T. Morell), prod. London, CG, 16 Mar 1750.

Theorbo, a bass lute of large size with a double neck on which only the upper strings are stretched over a fingerboard, the bass strings being at the side of it and capable only of prod. single notes, except by retuning. The number of strings varied from 14 to 17. It was used mainly to accomp. singers.

Theremin (*see also* **Aetherophone),** an electrophonic instrument invented by Lev Theremin (b 1896) of Leningrad in 1920. It was incapable of detaching notes, so that all intervals were linked together by a wailing *portamento,* like that of a siren; but later on Theremin invented another inst. shaped like a cello on which notes could be prod. detached from each other by means of a cello fingerboard.

Thérèse, opera by Massenet (lib. by J. Claretie), prod. Monte Carlo, 7 Feb 1907.

Opera by John Tavener (lib. by G. McLarnon); comp. 1973–6, prod. CG, 1 Oct 1979, cond. Downes.

Theresienmesse (*Theresa Mass*), Haydn's Mass in Bb no. 12, comp. in 1799. Despite its name, it seems to have no connection with Maria Theresa, wife of the Emperor Franz II.

Thésée (*Theseus*), opera by Lully (lib. by Quinault), prod. at Saint-Germain, 12 Jan 1675; 1st Paris perf., Apr 1675.

Thespis, or The Gods Grown Old, operetta by Sullivan (lib. by W.S. Gilbert), prod. London, Gaiety Theatre, 26 Dec 1871. Sullivan's 1st work written in assoc. with Gilbert.

Thétis et Pélée (*Thetis and Peleus*), opera by Colasse (lib. by B. de Fontenelle), prod. Paris, Opéra, 11 Jan 1689.

Thibaud, Jacques (b Bordeaux, 27 Sep 1880; d Mont Cemet nr. Barcelonette, 1 Sep 1953), French violinist. Studied at the Paris Cons. and took a 1st prize in 1896, but was at 1st obliged to play in a café. Colonne heard him and engaged him for his orch. and by 1898–9 he was estab. as a concert artist. He travelled widely, excelled in Mozart and gave much time to chamber music, forming a trio with Casals and Cortot. He was killed in a plane crash.

Thibaut IV (b Troyes, 30 May 1201; d Pamplona, 7 Jul 1253), King of Navarre and a trouvère, more than 45 of whose songs are still extant.

Thill, Georges (b Paris, 14 Dec 1897; d Paris, 17 Oct 1984), French tenor. He studied in Paris and sang with the Opéra 1924–40 and with the Opéra-Comique until 1953; appeared in the fps of works by Canteloube and Rabaud and was successful as Calaf, Julien, Don José, Tannhäuser and Parsifal. NY Met 1930–32 as Roméo, Faust and Radames. He sang in a Wagner concert as late as 1956 and made several films, incl. *Louise,* with Grace Moore.

Thillon (*née* **Hunt), Sophie Anne** (b Calcutta or London, 1819; d Torquay, 5 May 1903), English soprano. She was taken to Fr. for study at the age of 14 and married one of her masters, the Havre cond. Claude Thomas T. After appearing in the provinces she came out in opera in Paris, 1838, studied with Auber and sang with great success in his and other comps.' operas: she created roles in Auber's *La Neige* and *Les Diamants de la Couronne.* In 1844 she made her stage debut in London and sang much there during the next 10 years in operas by Balfe; also at Brussels and in USA.

Third, the interval between 2 notes lying 2 degrees of a scale apart, e.g.:

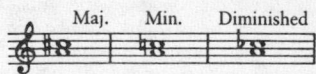

Thomas, (Charles Louis) Ambroise (b Metz, 5 Aug 1811; d Paris, 12 Feb 1896), French composer. Learnt music from his father as a child and in 1828 entered the Paris Cons., where he gained the Prix de Rome in 1832. He also privately studied pf. with Kalkbrenner and comp. with Lesueur. Soon after his return from Rome he began to win operatic successes in Paris. In 1852 he became prof. at the Cons. and in 1871 director in succession to Auber.

Works incl. operas *La Double Échelle* (1837), *Le Perruquier de la Régence* (1838), *Le Panier fleuri* (1839), *Carline* (1840), *Le Comte de Carmagnola, Le Guerillero* (1842), *Angélique et Médor* (1843), *Mina, Le Caïd, Le Songe d'une nuit d'été* (not Shakespeare, 1850), *Raymond* (1851), *La Tonelli, La Cour de Célimène* (1855), *Psyché* (1857), *Le Carnaval de Venise, Le Roman d'Elvire* (1860), *Mignon* (after Goethe's *Wilhelm Meister,* 1866), *Gille et Gillotin, Hamlet* (after Shakespeare, 1868), *Françoise de Rimini* (after Dante, 1882); ballets *La Gipsy* (1839), *Betty* and *La Tempête* (1889); *Messe solennelle* (1857), *Messe de Requiem,* motets; cantata *Hermann et Ketty,* cantatas for the unveiling of a Lesueur statue and for the Boieldieu centenary; fantasy for pf. and orch.; string 4tet, string 5tet, pf. trio; pf. pieces; 6 It. songs; part-songs, etc.

Thomas and Sally, or The Sailor's Return, opera by Arne (lib. by I. Bickerstaffe), prod. London, CG, 28 Nov 1760.

Thomas, Jess (Floyd) (b Hot Springs, S. Dakota, 4 Aug 1927), American tenor. He studied at Stanford Univ. and appeared in Eur. from 1958 (debut Karlsruhe, as Lohengrin); sang Bacchus at Munich in 1960 and returned in 1963 for the Emperor. Bayreuth 1961–9 as Parsifal and Siegfried. NY Met debut 1962, as Walther; created Caesar in the 1966 prod. of Barber's *Antony and Cleopatra,* which opened the Met's house at Lincoln Center. CG 1969–71 as Walther and Tristan. Other roles incl. Radames, Lensky and Tannhäuser.

Thomas, Michael Tilson (b Hollywood, 21 Dec 1944), American conductor. After study in Calif. he conducted at the Ojai Festival, initially as asst. to Boulez, and at Tanglewood. Music dir. Buffalo PO from 1971, prin. guest cond. Boston SO from 1972. London debut 1970, with LSO. LA PO from 1981. He conducts many works outside the standard rep. In 1979 at Santa Fe he cond. the 1st US perf. of the 3-act version of Berg's *Lulu.* He has recorded Stravinsky as cond. and pianist. Prin. cond. LSO from 1988.

Thomas, Theodore (Christian Friedrich (b Esens, E. Friesland, 11 Oct 1835; d Chicago, 4 Jan 1905), German, later American, conductor. He was taken to the USA in 1845 and became a professional violinist; appeared in NY, with an orch. formed by himself, in 1862; organized the Cincinnati Music Festival in 1873 and became cond. of the NY Phil. Society in 1877 and of the Chicago SO in 1891.

Thomé, Francis (actually Joseph François Luc) (b Port Louis, Mauritius, 18 Oct 1850; d Paris, 16 Nov 1909), French composer. Studied at the Paris Cons. He afterwards settled down as a private teacher of music.

Works incl. operas *Martin et Frontin* (1877), *Le Caprice de la reine* (1892), operettas *Vieil Air, jeune chanson* (1894), *Le Château de Koenigsberg* (1896), *Le Chaperon rouge* (1900); ballets incl. *Endymion et Phœbé, La Bulle d'amour* (1898), *La Folie parisienne* (1900); incid. music to plays, incl. Shakespeare's *Romeo and Juliet,* and mystery *l'Enfant Jésus; Hymne à la nuit*

for chorus; *Simple Aveu* for pf. with many arrs.

Thompson, Oscar (b Crawfordsville, Ind., 10 Oct 1887; d New York, 3 Jul 1945), American music critic. In 1937 he succeeded W.J. Henderson as music critic of the *NY Sun.* He was the author of several books on music and the ed. of the *International Cyclopedia of Music and Musicians* (1939).

Thompson, Randall (b New York, 21 Apr 1899; d Boston, 9 Jul 1984), American composer. He studied at Harvard Univ. and among his teachers was Bloch. He lived in Rome in 1922–5, was asst. prof. of music at Wellesley Coll. and was later app. to study musical conditions at the Amer. colls. Prof. of music at U. of California in 1937, director of the Curtis Inst. at Philadelphia in 1939, prof. at Harvard Univ. from 1948.

Works incl. opera *Solomon and Balkis* (after Kipling's *Just So Stories,* 1942); incid. music for Labiche's *The Italian Straw Hat;* 3 symphs. (1930–49), *Pierrot and Cothurnus* (1923) and *The Piper at the Gates of Dawn* (1924), for orch.; *Jazz Poem* for pf. and orch. (1928); *Passion according to St Luke,* cantata *The Testament of Freedom, Odes of Horace* for unaccomp. chorus, *Rosemary* for women's chorus, *Americana* for mixed chorus and pf.; 2 string 4tets (1941, 1967), *The Wind in the Willows* for string 4tet; sonata and suite for pf.; songs.

Thomson, César (b Liège, 17 or 18 Mar 1857; d Bissone nr. Lugano, 21 Aug 1931), Belgian violinist. Studied at the Liège Cons. from the age of 7, and in 1882 he became vln. prof. there, after a career as virtuoso that took him to It., Ger., etc. In 1897 succeeded Ysaÿe at the Brussels Cons. He taught in NY from 1924 to 1927, when he returned to Europe.

Thomson, George (b Limekilns, Fife, 4 Mar 1757; d Leith, 18 Feb 1851), Scottish official and music collector. Pub. collections of nat. Scot., Welsh and Ir. airs arr. by Haydn, Beethoven, Koželuch, Weber, Bishop and others.

Thomson, Virgil (b Kansas City, 25 Nov 1896), American composer. Studied at Harvard Univ. and comp. with Rosario Scalero and Nadia Boulanger. He was asst. music instructor at Harvard in 1920–25 and organist at King's Chapel in Boston from 1923 to 1924, then lived in Paris until 1932, when he became critic to several papers and periodicals in the USA.

Works incl. operas *Four Saints in Three Acts* (1934), *The Mother of us all* (1947) (libs. by G. Stein), *Byron* (1972); ballet *The*

Filling-Station; incid. music for Euripides' *Medea*, Shakespeare's *Hamlet* and other plays; film music; 2 symphs., suite *The Plough that Broke the Plains* (1936), *2 Sentimental Tangoes*, *Portraits*, *Symph. on a Hymn-Tune* (1948), *Sonata da Chiesa* for orch.

Oraison funèbre (Bossuet) for tenor and orch.; *2 Missae breves*, 3 Psalms for women's voices, *Capital Capitals* (G. Stein) for men's chorus and pf.; 2 string 4tets (1922, 1932), *5 Portraits* for 4 clars.; *Stabat Mater* for sop. and string 4tet, *5 Phrases from the Song of Solomon* for sop. and perc.; *50 Portraits* for vln. and pf., sonata for vln. and pf.; piano music, songs.

Thomyris, Queen of Scythia, pasticcio arranged by Pepusch from music by A. Scarlatti, G. Bononcini, Steffani, Gasparini and Albinoni (lib. by P.A. Motteux), prod. London, Drury Lane Theatre, 1 Apr 1707.

Thorborg, Kerstin (b Venjan, 19 May 1896; d Dalarna, 12 Apr 1970), Swedish mezzo. She studied in Stockholm and sang there 1924–30 as Ortrud and Amneris. Salzburg and Vienna from 1935. CG 1936–9 as Kundry, Brangaene and Fricka. NY Met 1936–50 as Orpheus, Marina, Dalila and Clytemnestra. She recorded *Das Lied von der Erde* with Walter (Vienna, 1936). Considered to be the foremost Wagnerian mezzo of her day.

Thorne, John (d York, 7 Dec 1573), English organist, composer and poet. He was app. organist of York Minster in 1542, and worked there in var. capacities until 2 years before his death. A motet, *Stella coeli*, was copied by John Baldwin, and another, *Exsultabant sancti*, is extant, in organ score. A 4-part In Nomine also survives, and there are 3 poems by him in the same MS. as Redford's *Play of Wit and Science* (Brit. Lib. Add. MS. 15233) and in the *Paradyse of Daintie Devices* (1576).

Thorough-Bass, a system of shorthand notation for keyboard instruments that came into use during the early part of the 17th cent. and persisted until *c* the middle of the 18th (and in church music later still). Comps., instead of writing out the full harmony they required for an accomp., provided only a single bass-line, under or over which they wrote figures or accidentals indicating what the harmony above that bass was to be, but not how it was to be spaced or distributed. The illustration overleaf shows (*a*) the use of figures and accidentals and (*b*) the implied harmony. Thoroughbasses were not always completely

figured, and sometimes not at all. The It. term is *basso continuo. See also* **Continuo.**

Thrane, Waldemar (b Christiania (now Oslo), 8 Oct 1790; d Christiania, 30 Dec 1828), Norwegian composer. Learnt music at home, his parents being keen amateurs at whose house many musicians met. Although intended for commerce, he continually exercised himself in music and in 1825 wrote the 1st Norw. opera, which however was not staged until 1850. He also studied Norw. folk music.

Works incl. opera *Fjeldeventyret (The Mountain Adventure*, 1825); overtures for orch.; choral works, etc.

Three Choirs Festival, a music festival, founded *c* 1715, centred on the combined cathedral choirs of Gloucester, Worcester and Hereford, and held annually at each town in turn in late summer. The programmes are predominantly choral, but orch. and chamber music concerts are also given. New works by Eng. comps., eg. Vaughan Williams, Holst and Bliss, have been a traditional feature of the festival.

Three-Cornered Hat. *See* **Sombrero de tres picos;** *also* **Corregidor.**

Three Places in New England, work for orch. by Ives, also known as *Orchestral Set no. 1*; comp. 1903–14, fp NY, 10 Jan 1931, cond. Slonimsky. The 3 movts. are: 1. 'The "St Gaudens" in Boston Common: Colonel Shaw and his Colored Regiment'; 2. 'Putnam's Camp, Redding, Connecticut'; 3. 'The Housatonic at Stockbridge'.

Threni (id est Lamentationes Jeremiae Prophetae), work by Stravinsky for sop., mezzo, 2 tenors, 2 basses, chorus and orch.; comp. 1957–8, fp Venice, 23 Sep 1958, cond. Stravinsky. *See* **Lamentations.**

Threnody for the Victims of Hiroshima, work by Penderecki for 52 solo strings; comp. 1959–60; fp Warsaw, 31 May 1961.

Thuille, Ludwig (b Bozen, 30 Nov 1861; d Munich, 5 Feb 1907), Austrian composer. Learnt music from his father, an amateur, on whose death he was sent as a choir-boy to the monastery of Kremsmünster. At the age of 15 he began to study with Joseph Pembaur in Innsbruck, and in 1879 he went to the Music School at Munich, where Rheinberger was among his masters. In 1883 he became prof. at the Munich school, and there was influenced by R. Strauss and Alexander Ritter, who wrote the lib. for his 1st opera, the 2 later ones being by Otto Julius Bierbaum. Apart from teaching and comp., he also cond. the male-voice choir Liederhort.

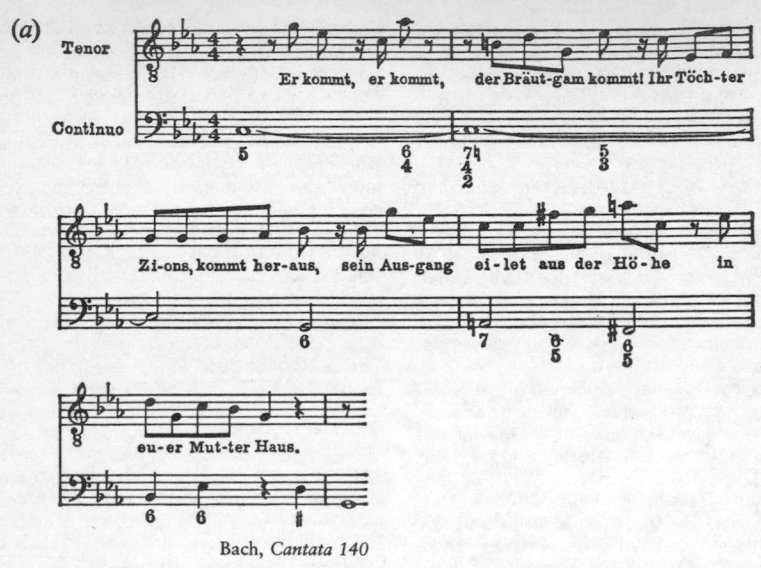

Bach, *Cantata 140*

THOROUGH-BASS

Works incl. operas *Theuerdank* (1897), *Lobetanz* (1898) and *Gugeline* (1901); *Romantic Overture* (orig. for *Theuerdank*) for orch.; *Weihnaht im Walde* for male chorus, *Traumsommernacht* and *Rosenlied* for female chorus; pf. 5tet, 6tet for wind and pf.; cello and pf. sonata; pf. pieces; songs.

Thump (old Eng.) = plucking of strings (*pizzicato*); also a piece employing *pizz*.

Thursfield (*née* **Reman**), **Anne** (b New York, 28 Mar 1885; d London, 5 Jun 1945), English mezzo. Educ. in music mainly in Berlin, but sang other languages as brilliantly as Eng. and Ger., partic. excelling in Fr. She specialized in song recitals chosen with enterprise and taste, and perf. with keenly intelligent interpretation.

Thus spake Zarathustra (R. Struass). *See* **Also sprach Zarathustra.**

Tibbett, Lawrence (b Bakersfield, Calif., 16 Nov 1896; d New York, 15 Jul 1960), American baritone. He studied singing after serving in the Navy in the 1914–18 war and 1st appeared at the NY Met in 1923; sang

until 1950 as Boccanegra, Wolfram, Telramund, Scarpia, Iago and Rigoletto. He took part in the fps of Taylor's *The King's Henchman* (1927) and *Peter Ibbetson* (1931) and Gruenberg's *Emperor Jones* (1933). In addition to a successful career in opera he became popular as a film actor.

Tiburtino, Giuliano (b *c* 1510; d Rome, 16 Dec 1569), Italian composer and violinist. In 1545 he was in the service of Pope Paul III. 12 *ricercari* and one fantasia for instrumental ensemble were incl. in a pub. of 1549 which also incl. works by Willaert and Rore.

Tichatschek (Tichá─ek), Joseph (Aloys) (b Ober-Weckelsdorf, Boh., 11 Jul 1807; d Blasewitz nr. Dresden, 18 Jan 1886), Bohemian tenor. Studied medicine at first, but learnt singing and in 1830 joined the chorus at the Kärntnertortheater in Vienna, then sang small parts, and made his 1st stage appearance at Graz. He was a member of the Dresden opera from 1838 until he retired in 1870, and was Wagner's 1st Rienzi and

Tannhäuser. London, 1841, in operas by Weber and Meyerbeer.

Tie, an arching stroke used to connect 2 notes of the same pitch (or a group of such notes in chords), indicating that the notes are to be sounded as one note having the duration of their combined value.

Tiefland (*The Lowland*), opera by d'Albert (lib. by R. Lothar based on a Catalan play, *Terra baixa*, by A. Guimerá), prod. Prague, Ger. Theatre, 15 Nov 1903.

Tiento (Span.), a 16th-cent. type of organ piece similar to the Ricercare.

Tierce, an early term for the interval of the 3rd, maj. or min. It survives, however, as the technical term for one of the tones of a church bell, a min. 3rd above the note of the bell.

Tierce de Picardie (Fr. = Picardy 3rd), the maj. 3rd intro. into the final chord of a comp. in a min. key. The maj. 3rd corresponds to a natural harmonic, the Tierce (*see above*), but the min. 3rd does not: it was therefore for a long time considered, if not an actual dissonance, at any rate not a finally satisfactory ingredient in a concluding chord, for which reason the tierce de Picardie was often substituted. The origin of the name is not known.

Tietjen, Heinz (b Tangier, 24 Jun 1881; d Baden-Baden, 30 Nov 1967), German conductor and producer. After working in Trier, Saarbrücken and Breslau he was engaged at the Berlin Städtische Oper 1925–30 and again 1948–54. He was Generalintendant of all Prussian State theatres 1930–45 and came into conflict with Otto Klemperer over the closing of the Kroll Opera, Berlin, in 1931. He was artistic dir. at Bayreuth 1931–44 and conducted there *The Ring, Meistersinger* and *Lohengrin*. He produced operas by Wagner at CG in 1950 and 1951 and worked in Hamburg 1954–9; returned to Bayreuth 1959 (*Lohengrin*).

Tietjens, Therese (Carolina Johanna Alexandra) (b Hamburg, 17 Jul 1831; d London, 3 Oct 1877), Hungarian soprano of Belgian descent. Made her 1st appearance at Hamburg in 1849; paid her 1st visit to Eng. in 1858, remaining there for good except for her appearances abroad. Her London roles incl. Verdi's Hélène, Amelia and Leonora (*Forza*), Marguerite, Norma, Donna Anna and Lucrezia Borgia.

Tigers, The, opera by Havergal Brian (lib. by comp.); 1916–19, orch. 1928–9. The score was lost, but rediscovered in 1977 and given by the BBC on 3 May 1983.

Tigrane, Il (*Tigranes*), opera by Gluck (lib.

by F. Silvani, altered by Goldoni), prod. Crema, 26 Sep 1743.

Opera by Hasse (lib. by F. Silvani), prod. Naples, Teatro San Bartolommeo, 4 Nov 1729.

Opera by A. Scarlatti (lib. by D. Lalli), prod. Naples, Teatro San Bartolommeo, 16 Feb 1715.

Tigrini, Orazio (b ? Arezzo, *c* 1535; d Arezzo, 15 Oct 1591), Italian composer. He appears to have spent his entire mature life in Arezzo, and was *maestro di canto* 1st at Santa Maria della Pieve and then at the cathedral where, after a period at Orvieto, he was *maestro di canto* and *di cappella* till his death. He pub. 2 books of madrigals and a treatise, *Il Compendio della Musica* (1588).

Till Eulenspiegels lustige Streiche (*Till Eulenspiegel's Merry Pranks*), symph. poem by R. Strauss, op. 28, based on the old Low Ger. folk-tale, comp. 1894–5, fp Cologne, 5 Nov 1895.

Tilney, Colin (b London, 31 Oct 1932), English harpsichordist. He studied at Cambridge and with Gustav Leonhardt. Widely heard since 1964 as recitalist and soloist with leading ensembles; plays on historical instruments and replicas. Often heard in Bach, Purcell and the English virginalists. US debut 1971.

Timbre (Fr. lit. Chime-bell). In music the word is used, in Eng. as well as Fr., for Tone-colour.

Time. The physical conditions in which all the arts have their existence, so far as they become communicable to the human senses, are either space (painting, sculpture, etc.) or time, or both (drama and in a sense all literature). Music exists in time, and has therefore to be written down in symbols representing certain divisions of time in which it is to be made audible. Time must not be confused with Tempo or pace, which determines the speed at which a comp. should go; the time of a comp. is its division into units of notes or rests, and their subdivisions. A piece in 3–4 time, for ex., has 3 crotchets to a Bar and normally a metrical stress on the 1st Beat after the bar-line; and it makes no difference to this fundamental time whether 2 crotchets are replaced by a Minim, or whether one is displaced by a rest or divided into smaller fractions in any pattern of notes. The time of a piece or movement remains fixed until the comp. changes the Time Signature. Time is called 'simple' when the beats are divisible by 2, e.g. 2–4, 3–4, 4–4, 'compound' when they are divisible by 3, e.g. 6–8, 9–8, 12–8. Where there are 5 beats in the bar the listener, and often the comp., tends to regard them as 2 + 3 or 3 + 2: bars with 7, 11 or 13 beats will divide in a similar way.

Time Signature, the sign at the beginning of a comp. indicating the time-divisions governing the metre of the piece. The time signature is shown in the shape of a fraction, but does not represent a mathematical fraction: it is a symbol showing in the lower figure the unit of the note-values into which each bar is divided and in the upper the number of such note-values contained in a bar: e.g. ¾ means that there are 3 crotchets to the bar, with either 3 beats or (in fast time) 1 beat to the bar; ⅜ is 6 quavers to the bar, with 2 basic beats; ²⁄₂ is 2 minims to the bar, etc. There are also 2 conventional abbrs., which are signs surviving from the old notation, where the time signatures were a full circle for Perfect Time (*tempus perfectum*) and a broken circle resembling letter C for Imperfect Time (*tempus imperfectum*). The broken circle has survived as indicating ⁴⁄₄ time and as ℂ indicating *alla breve* time, i.e. ⁴⁄₄ taken at double speed and beaten in 2s.

Timpan (or Timpe, from Lat. *tympanum*), a kind of Psaltery used in the Brit. Isles in medieval times. It had wire strings stretched on a frame and they were plucked by the fingers or a plectrum, later struck with a rod.

Timpani (It.) = Kettle-drums.

Tin Whistle, a small and rudimentary pipe of the Fife or Recorder type, also called 'penny whistle', played vertically and having a small range of high notes controlled by 6 finger-holes.

Tinctoris, Johannes (b Braine l'Alleud nr. Nivelles, *c* 1435; d ? 1511), Flemish theorist and composer. Studied both law and theology, was ordained priest and became a canon of Poperinghe. He went to It. and in 1476 was in the service of the King of Naples, Ferdinand of Aragon. He founded a school of music and between 1484 and 1500 was in the Papal Chapel in Rome. He wrote a number of important theoret. works and comp. Masses, motets and *chansons*. His dictionary of musical terms, *Terminorum musicae diffinitorium* (1495) was the 1st of its kind.

Tinsley, Pauline (b Wigan, 27 Mar 1928), English soprano. She studied in London and Manchester; sang professionally from 1951. WNO from 1962 as Lady Macbeth, Elsa, Susanna and Aida. Since 1963 she has appeared with SW, later ENO, in London as Mozart's Countess and Fiordiligi, Queen Elizabeth in *Maria Stuarda* and Verdi's

Elvira. US debut Santa Fe, 1969, as Anna Bolena; has since appeared in Houston, New Orleans and at the NY City Opera. Other roles incl. Elektra, Turandot and the Kostelnička.

Tippett, Sir **Michael (Kemp)** (b London, 2 Jan 1905), English composer. Studied with C. Wood and R.O. Morris at the RCM in London. He became cond. of educational organizations under the London County Council and music director at Morley Coll., a post formerly held by Holst. During the war he was imprisoned as a conscientious objector. His oratorio *A Child of our Time* was written in response to the persecution of the Jews. Hon. D.Mus. Oxford, 1967. Knighted 1966. OM 1985. With Britten, the foremost English composer of his generation.

Works incl. OPERAS: *The Midsummer Marriage* (1955), *King Priam* (1962), *The Knot Garden* (1970) and *The Ice Break* (1977).

CHORAL: oratorios *A Child of our Time* for soloists, chorus and orch. (1939–41), *The Vision of St Augustine* for baritone, chorus and orch. (1963–5) and *The Mask of Time* for soloists, chorus and orch. (1981–4); *A Song of Liberty* (from Blake's *Marriage of Heaven and Hell*) for chorus and orch.; anthem *Plebs angelica* for double chorus, motet *The Weeping Babe* (E. Sitwell) for soprano and chorus.

ORCH.: 4 symphs. (1944, 1957, 1972, 1976), concerto for double string orch. (1939), concerto for orch., *Fantasia concertante* on a theme by Corelli (1953); fantasy on a theme by Handel for pf. and orch. (1941), pf. concerto (1953–5), concerto for string trio and orch. (1979).

CHAMBER AND SOLO VOCAL: 4 string 4tets (1935, 1943, 1946, 1979); 4 pf. sonatas (1938, 1962, 1973, 1979); cantata *Boyhood's End* for tenor and pf. (from W.H. Hudson's *Far Away and Long Ago*, 1943); part-songs *The Source* and *The Windhover* (Hopkins).

Tirade (Fr. = pulling or dragging), an ornamental scale passage between 2 notes of a melody or 2 chords.

Tirana, a Spanish dance of Andalusia in 6–8 time, usually danced to guitar music and accomp. by words in 4-lined *coplas*.

Tiré (Fr. = drawn), the downstroke of the bow in the playing of string instruments, the opposite of *poussé* (= pushed).

Titelouze, Jean (b Saint-Omer, *c* 1563; d Rouen, 24 Oct 1633), French composer, priest and organist. He became a canon at

Rouen Cathedral in the 1580s; often visited Paris to inaugurate new organs, incl. that at Notre-Dame in 1610.

Works incl. 3 Masses; Magnificats and hymns for organ.

Tito Manlio, opera by Vivaldi (lib. by M. Noris), prod. Mantua, Teatro Arciducale, carnival 1720.

Tito Vespasiano, ovvero La clemenza di Tito (*Titus Vespasian, or The Clemency of Titus*), opera by Caldara (lib. by Metastasio, partly based on Corneille's *Cinna*), prod. Vienna, 1734.

Opera by Hasse (lib. do.), prod. Pesaro, Teatro Pubblico, 24 Sep 1735.

Titov. Russian family of musicians:

1. Alexey Nikolaievich T. (b St Petersburg, 24 Jun 1769; d St Petersburg, 20 Nov 1827), managed the Imp. Opera for some time before the death of Catherine the Great in 1796 and became a major-general in the cavalry guards. Wrote *c* 20 operas, vaudevilles, melodramas and other stage works. He is sometimes confused with his brother,

2. Sergey Nikolaievich T. (b 1770; d 1825), who wrote incid. music for 2 or 3 plays.

3. Nikolai Alexeievich T. (b St Petersburg, 10 May 1800; d St Petersburg, 22 Dec 1875), son of 1. Like his father, he was in the cavalry guard and rose to the rank of lieut.-general. He came under the influence of Glinka and Dargomizhsky. Wrote popular marches, pf. music and *c* 60 songs.

'To the memory of an Angel' (*Dem Andenken eines Engels*), Berg's ded. for his vln. concerto, comp. 1935 in memory of Manon Gropius, the daughter of Walter G. and Mahler's widow, Alma. The work begins with a musical portrait of Manon and ends with an adagio based on the Bach chorale *Es ist genug*. Fp Barcelona, 19 Apr 1936, with Louis Krasner, cond. Scherchen. 1st London perf. 1 May 1936, cond. Webern.

Toccata (from It. *toccare* = lit. to touch, fig. to play), orig., in the 17th cent., simply 'a thing to play', as distinct from *cantata*, 'a thing to sing'. But it soon acquired a sense of touching an instrument for the purpose of trying or testing it, which meant that it usually contained scales, trills and other brilliant figuration, often interspersed with slow chordal passages. 19th- and 20th-cent. toccatas usually lay stress on brilliance and rapid execution alone, and are often more or less uniform in figuration throughout.

Toch, Ernst (b Vienna, 7 Dec 1887; d Los Angeles, 1 Oct 1964), Austrian, later American, composer and pianist. Studied medi-

cine and philosophy at first and was self-taught in music, but in 1909 was awarded the Frankfurt Mozart prize and studied there under Willy Rehberg, being app. pf. prof. at the Mannheim Hochschule für Musik in 1913. He served in the 1914–18 war, settled in Berlin in 1929, but emigrated in 1932, visiting the USA, then London for a time, to settle permanently in the USA in 1934, 1st teaching in NY for 2 years and then moving to Hollywood as film composer and teacher.

Works incl. operas *Wegwende* (1925), *Die Prinzessin auf der Erbse* (1927), *Egon und Emilie* (1928), *Der Fächer* (1930); incid. music for Euripides' *Bacchantes*, Shakespeare's *As You Like It*, Zweig's *Die Heilige aus U.S.A.* and other plays; music for radio play *The Garden of Jade* and others; film music for *Catherine the Great, The Private Life of Don Juan*, etc.

Passover Service (1938); cantata *Das Wasser* (1930); *Der Tierkreis* for unaccomp. chorus; 7 symphs. (1949–64), *Bunte Suite, Kleine Theater Suite, Big Ben, Pinocchio* overture (after Collodi's story) for orch.; *Spiel* for wind band; concerto (1926) and symph. for pf. and orch.; *Poems to Martha* for bar. and strings; 13 string 4tets (1902–53), pf. 5tet, string trio, divertimento for vln. and vla.; 2 vln. and pf. sonatas; sonata, 50 studies and *c* 12 op. nos. of pf. pieces.

Tod und das Mädchen, Der (*Death and the Maiden*), song, D531, by Schubert on words by M. Claudius, comp. in 1817. The latter part was adapted as a theme for variations in the 2nd movt. of his D minor 4tet (1824, D810), which is for that reason commonly known by the same name.

Tod und Verklärung (*Death and Transfiguration*), symph. poem by R. Strauss, op. 24, comp. 1888–9, fp Eisenach, 21 Jun 1890.

Todi (*née* d'Aguiar), **Luiza Rosa** (b Setubal, 9 Jan 1753; d Lisbon, 1 Oct 1833), Portuguese mezzo. A pupil of Perez, she made her debut as an actress in 1768 and as a singer 2 years later in Scolari's *Il viaggiatore ridicolo*. Was at the It. opera in London in 1777, then went to Madrid, where she had her 1st big success in Paisiello's *Olimpiade* in 1777. She visited Paris, Berlin and Turin, sang at the opera in St Petersburg 1784–7, at the court of Catherine the Great in operas by Sarti, and subsequently in Prague and in several It. cities. She retired to Lisbon in 1803.

Toeschi, Carl Joseph (b Ludwigsburg, bap. 11 Nov 1731; d Munich, 12 Apr 1788), Italian composer and violinist. Attached to the Mannheim school of early symphonists, and its only It. member. He became violinist in the court orch. there in 1752 and leader in 1759; later he followed the court to Munich.

Works incl. ballet music for var. operas by other comps.; symphs.; chamber music.

Tofts, Catherine (b c 1685; d Venice, 1756), English soprano. She was one of the first Eng. singers to appear in It. opera in London in 1704; her maid threw oranges at her great rival L'Epine on stage at Drury Lane. She went mad in 1709; at least temporarily recovered, she married Joseph Smith, and accomp. him on his appt. as Eng. consul in Venice.

Togni, Camillo (b Gussago, Brescia, 18 Oct 1922), Italian composer and pianist. Studied comp. with Casella in Rome from 1939 to 1943 and pf. with Michelangeli. He also graduated in philosophy from Pavia Univ. in 1948.

Works incl. Variations for pf. and orch. (1946); *Psalmus cxxvii* for voices, vln., vla. and cello (1950); *Choruses after T.S. Eliot* for chorus and orch.; *Fantasia concertante* for fl. and string orch. (1958); *Tre Studi per 'Morts sans sépulture' di J.P. Sartre* and *Helian di Trakl* for sop. and pf.; *Ricerca* for bar. and 5 insts. (1953); fl. sonata.

Toinon et Toinette, opera by Gossec (lib. by J.A.J. des Boulmiers), prod. Paris, Comédie-Italienne, 20 Jun 1767.

Tolomeo, Rè di Egitto (*Ptolemy, King of Egypt*), opera by Handel (lib. by N.F. Haym), prod. London, King's Theatre, Haymarket, 30 Apr 1728.

Tom Jones, opera by Philidor (lib. by A.A.H. Poinsinet, based on Fielding's novel), prod. Paris, Comédie-Italienne, 27 Feb 1765.

Tomášek (Tomaschek), Václav Jan Křtitel (Wenzel Johann) (b Skuteč, 17 Apr 1774; d Prague, 3 Apr 1850), Bohemian composer, organist and pianist. His father having been reduced to poverty, he was educ. at the expense of 2 elder brothers. He became a choir-boy at the monastery of Jihlava, which he left in 1790 to study law and philosophy in Prague. He also studied the great theoret. treatises on music assiduously, as well as any music he could lay hands on, and estab. a reputation as teacher and comp. before the end of the cent. Count Bucquoi von Longueval offered him a well-paid post in his household, to which he remained attached even after his marriage to Wilhelmine Ebert in 1823. He often visited Vienna, and met Beethoven in 1814, and he played his settings of Goethe's poems to the poet at Eger.

He pub. his autobiog. in instalments during 1845–50.

Works incl. opera *Seraphine* (1811) and 2 not prod.; 3 Masses, incl. Coronation Mass (1836), 2 Requiems and other church music; vocal scenes from Goethe's *Faust* and Schiller's *Wallenstein, Maria Stuart* and *Die Braut von Messina*; 3 symphs. (1801, 1805, 1807), 2 pf. concertos (1805–6); 3 string 4tets (1792–3), pf. trio; 5 pf. sonatas, *Elegie auf eine Rose* (after Hölty), 7 sets of *Eclogues* and 2 of *Dithyrambs* and many other works for pf.; numerous songs to words by Goethe, Schiller and others.

Tomasi, Henri (b Marseilles, 17 Aug 1901; d Avignon, 13 Jan 1971), French composer and conductor. Studied at the Paris Cons. and in 1927 gained the Prix de Rome. On his return from Rome in 1930 became cond. of the nat. Radio-Paris. Cond. Monte Carlo Opera, 1946–50.

Works incl. operas *Don Juan de Mañara* (1956) and *Sampiero Corso* (1956); ballets *La Grisi* (1935), *La Rosière du village* (1936) and *Les Santons* (1938); symph., *Scènes municipales* (1933), *Chants laotiens* (1934), *Petite Suite médiévale, Deux Danses cambodgiennes, Danses brésiliennes* for orch.; capriccio for vln. and orch.; fl. concerto (1947), tpt. concerto (1949), vla. concerto, saxophone concerto (1951), horn concerto (1955); *Ajax* and *Chants de Cyrnos* for chorus and orch.

Tomasini. Italian and Austrian family of musicians:

1. Luigi T. (b Pesaro, 22 Jun 1741; d Eisenstadt, 25 Apr 1808), violinist and comp. Member of the orch. at Eisenstadt, from 1757, and later at Eszterháza, where he became leader in 1761; Haydn's vln. concertos were written for him. Wrote vln. concertos, string 4tets, divertimenti for baryton, vln. and cello, etc.

2. Anton (Edmund) T. (b Eisenstadt, 17 Feb 1775; d Eisenstadt, 12 Jun 1824), violist, son of prec. He played in Esterházy's orch. as an amateur from 1791 and became a regular member in 1796.

3. Alois (Basil Nikolaus) T. (b Eszterháza, 10 Jul 1779; d Neustrelitz, 19 Feb 1858), violinist, brother of prec. Travelled as a virtuoso, became a member of the Esterházy orch. in 1796, and in 1808 entered the service of the court of Neustrelitz, becoming *Konzertmeister* in 1725.

Tombeau (Fr. = tomb[stone]), a commemorative comp., esp. in 17th-cent. French music.

Tombeau de Couperin, Le (*Couperin's*

Tomb), a suite for pf. by Ravel in the form of a suite such as Couperin might have written, but resembling his music in spirit rather than in style, Ravel's idiom being as modern here as in any of his works. It was written in 1914–17 and consists of 6 movements: *Prélude, Fugue, Forlane, Menuet, Rigaudon* and *Toccata*. Ravel orch. it in 1919, without the fugue and toccata; fp of that version, Paris, 8 Nov 1920.

Tomkins. English family of musicians:

1. Thomas T. (b St Davids, Pembrokeshire, 1572; d Martin Hussingtree nr. Worcester, buried 9 Jun 1656), organist and composer. Pupil of Byrd, app. organist of Worcester Cathedral 1596. He married a widow Alice Patrick (*née* Hassard) and in 1607 took the B.Mus. at Oxford. Although remaining at Worcester until the 2nd siege of 1646, he became one of the organists in the Chapel Royal in 1621 and in 1625 wrote music for Charles I's coronation. His last 10 years were spent at Martin Hussingtree, where the manor house was the property of the wife of his son Nathaniel (5). The last English virginalist and writer of madrigals; most of his church music was pub. after his death (*Musica Deo sacra*, 1668).

Works incl. 7 services, *c* 100 anthems; madrigals and balletts for 3–6 voices; music for viols; pieces for virginals.

2. John T. (b St Davids, *c* 1586; d London, 27 Sep 1638), organist and composer, half-brother of prec. Educ. at King's Coll., Cambridge, where he became organist in 1606. In 1619 he went to London as organist of St Paul's Cathedral, and in 1625 he became a Gentleman Extraordinary of the Chapel Royal, with a reversion of the next vacant organist's post.

Works incl. 8 anthems; variations on *John come kiss me now* for virginals.

3. Giles T. (b St Davids, after 1587; d Salisbury, before 30 Nov 1668), organist and virginalist, brother of prec. In 1624 he succeeded Matthew Barton in his brother's former post as organist of King's Chapel, Cambridge, but in 1629 went to Salisbury Cathedral as organist and choirmaster, and in 1630, though remaining at Salisbury, he succeeded Dering as Musician for the Virginals to Charles I.

4. Robert T., composer, brother of prec. He became a musician to Charles I in 1633 and remained in the royal household until 1641 or later. Wrote anthems and other church music.

5. Nathaniel T. (b Worcester, 1599; d Martin Hussingtree, 20 Oct 1681), amateur

musician, son of 1. He joined the choir of Worcester Cathedral in 1629 and saw his father's *Musica Deo sacra* through the press in 1668.

Tommasini, Vincenzo (b Rome, 17 Sep 1878; d Rome, 23 Dec 1950), Italian composer. Studied at the Liceo di Santa Cecilia in Rome and became an associate of the Accademia di Santa Cecilia. He travelled much before 1910 and then settled down to comp.

Works incl. operas *Medea* (1906) and *Uguale Fortuna* (1913); ballet *The Good-humoured Ladies* (on music by D. Scarlatti, 1917); *Il Carnevale di Venezia* for orch. (1929); vln. concerto (1932); choral works on Dante, Petrarch and others; overture to Calderón's *Life is a Dream, Poema erotico*, prelude to Baudelaire's *Hymne à la beauté*, suite, *Chiari di luna, Il beato regno, Paesaggi toscani* for orch.; 3 string 4tets; vln. and pf. sonata.

Tomowa-Sintow, Anna (b Stara Zagora, 22 Sep 1941), Bulgarian soprano. Debut Stara Zagora, 1965, as Tatyana. Leipzig from 1967; Butterfly at the Berlin Staatsoper, 1969. She was 'discovered' by Karajan and in 1973 sang in the fp of Orff's *De temporum fine comedia*, at Salzburg; has returned there as Elsa, Mozart's Countess and the Marschallin. CG debut 1975; NY Met debut 1978, as Donna Anna. Paris Opéra 1984, as Wagner's Elisabeth.

Ton (Ger. lit. tone, sound). In its early sense the word was used by the Ger. Minnesinger for the words and melody of their songs, and by the Meistersinger for the melody alone. The latter used all kinds of adjectives, sometimes of extreme oddity, to differentiate the numerous tunes. (Specimens of such names appear in Wagner's *Meistersinger*, where a *Ton* is also called a *Weis* (= *Weise* = tune).)

Tonada (Span.), a type of Castilian ballad at least as old as the 16th cent.

Tonadilla (Span., der. from above), a stage interlude for a few singers intro. in the 18th cent.

Tonale *or* **Tonarium** (Lat.). Medieval theoret. work dealing with the arr. of chants according to their mode, and esp. of the antiphons and the choice of psalm-tone to go with them. The earliest known is by Regino of Prüm (*c* 900).

Tonality, synonymous with Key, but also meaning, more specifically, the feeling of a definite key suggested by a comp. or passage. In modern musical terminology 2 antithetical derivatives of the word have appeared. *See* **Atonality** and **Polytonality.**

Tondichtung (Ger.) = Tone-poem, symph. poem.

Tone. (1) In Eng. the term is used for pure musical notes not charged with harmonics, each harmonic being itself a tone; also for the quality of a musical sound, esp. with ref. to perf. In Amer. tone is synonymous with 'note', and 'note' is normally reserved for the written symbol.

(2) The interval between the 1st and 2nd degrees of the maj. scale, also between the 2nd and 3rd, 4th and 5th, 5th and 6th, and 6th and 7th.

(3) A melodic formula to which a psalm is sung in plainsong.

Tone-Colour, or timbre, is a convenient term for the sound of an inst. or voice as regards the peculiar quality prod. by it; also for combinations of such sounds.

Tone-Poem. *See* **Symphonic Poem.**

Tone-Row, a trans. of the Ger. *Tonreihe,* to designate the 'rows' of 12 notes on which comps. in Twelve-note music are based. Also known in Eng. as 'series'.

Tonelli (actually De' Pietri), **Antonio** (b Carpi, 19 Aug 1686; d Carpi, 25 Dec 1765), Italian composer and cellist. Learnt music from his parents, who were both good amateurs, then studied with the choirmaster of Carpi Cathedral and at Bologna and Parma, where the duke became his patron. He spent 3 years at the Dan. court, returned to his home town and became choirmaster at the cathedral in 1730, but resigned in the 1740s and spent some of his time in other towns and on tour, returning to his post in 1757.

Works incl. operas *L'enigma disciolto* and *Lucio Vero*; intermezzi *Canoppo e Lisetta*; oratorio *Il trionfo dell' umiltà di S. Filippo Neri* and others; church music; cantatas; a *Canzonieri* against nuns.

Tonic, the Keynote: the note on which the scale begins and ends which determines the key of a piece of music in maj. or min. or defines the mode. F, for ex., is the tonic of a piece in the Lydian mode or in F maj. or min. A Lydian piece, whether harmonized or not, will end on the note F, which is therefore also called the Final; one in F maj. or min. will usually end on the maj. or min. common chord of its tonic, F.

Tonic Sol-fa, a system of musical notation without staves and notes, invented by John Curwen in the middle of the 19th cent. on a basis of the principles of Solmization and Solfeggio, and once widely used in Brit. and the dominions by choral singers, for whom it simplifies the sight-reading of music.

Tonic sol-fa notation is based on the old syllabic system of Do (Ut), Re, Mi, etc. and takes the following form: **d, r,m, f, s, l, t,** the names of the notes being Doh, Ray, Me, Fah, Soh, Lah, Te. The substitution of 'Te' for the old 'Si' was made to avoid the duplication of the letter 's' in the abbrs. The range of voices being limited, upper and lower 8ves can be sufficiently indicated by a simple stroke placed behind the letters in a higher or lower position, thus: **d'** and **d'**. Accidentals are indicated by the addition of a letter 'a' (ra, ma, etc., or exceptionally 'u' for du) for flats and 'e' (de, re, etc., or exceptionally 'y' for my) for sharps. But accidentals appear comparatively rarely now that the system of the 'movable Doh' has been adopted. This is a system of transposition according to which everything is except, for some very short incidental modulations, sung from a notation that looks as though the music were always in C maj. or A min.

The actual key is indicated at the beginning of a piece, so that singers know at once, for ex., if the comp. is in A maj., that their **d** is to be read as A, their **r** as B, etc. If the piece modulates to another key, a change is indicated, so that temporarily **d** may become any other note of the scale, etc.; but in maj. keys it will always remain the tonic, in whatever key the music moves, **s** always the dominant, **f** always the sub-dominant, etc., while in min. keys **l** will be the tonic, **m** the dominant, **r** the sub-dominant, etc. (A special syllable, 'ba', is used for the sharp 6th in the melodic min. scale.) The time divisions are indicated by short barlines, and there are subdivisions between these. The way in which the notes fill these spaces determines their time-values, though there are special signs for dotted notes, triplets, etc. A blank space means a rest, dashes after a note mean that it is to be held beyond the space it occupies over one or more of the following time-divisions.

The merits of tonic sol-fa have always been subject to controversy, no doubt because there is much to be said on either side. Its great defect is that it is insufficient for any general study of music as an art and that it is apt to keep choral singers from expanding their musical experience. Its advantages to instrumental players, even where it might be applicable, as in the case of non-harmonic instruments, are very slight, since it is not so much easier to learn than staff notation, nor so flexible in picturing the comp.'s intentions. For choral singers it has not only the merit of simplicity, but the greater one of teaching them a sense of Relative Pitch as well as removing all difficulties connected with Transposition.

Tonkünstler-Societät ('Musicians' Society'), a musicians' benevolent society in Vienna, founded in 1771, which gave charity perfs. twice yearly, in Lent and Advent. These were the first truly public concerts in Vienna. Haydn's oratorio *Il ritorno di Tobia* and Mozart's cantata *Davidde Penitente* (adapted from the C min. Mass) were written for the society, though both comps. were refused membership.

Tonos (Span. plur.), short vocal pieces for several voices sung at the opening of plays in 17th-cent. Spain.

Tonreihe. *See* **Tone-Row.**

Tonus lascivus (Lat. = playful, frolicsome, wanton tone), the medieval name for what later became the Ionian mode and the maj. scale, not recognized as a church mode at the time, but often used for secular songs by minstrels and not unknown in plainsong melodies.

Tonus peregrinus (Lat. = foreign tone), a plainsong chant which, unlike the 8 regular psalm tones, had 2 reciting notes, one in the 1st half of the chant and another in the 2nd (*see* illustration). For this reason it was described as 'foreign' and was reserved for the psalm 'In exitu Israel' ('When Israel came out of Egypt'). So far as its tonality is concerned it is in Mode I with flattened B. The melody was also sung in the Lutheran church: Bach uses it in his Magnificat and also in the cantata *Meine Seel' erhebt den Herren* (a setting of the Ger. Magnificat).

Törne, Bengt (Axel) (b Helsinki, 22 Nov 1891; d Turku, 4 May 1967), Finnish composer. Studied with Furuhjelm at the Helsinki Cons. and later privately with Sibelius, on whom he wrote a book. Kajanus allowed him to try out his orch. works with the Fin. State Orch.

Works incl. 6 symphs. (1935–66), 3 sinfoniettas; 6 symph. poems; vln. concerto, pf. concerto; chamber music; pf. pieces.

Torquato Tasso, opera by Donizetti (lib. by J. Ferretti), prod. Rome, Teatro Valle, 9 Sep 1833.

Torri, Pietro (b Peschiera, Lake Garda, *c* 1650; d Munich, 6 Jul 1737), Italian composer. Pupil of Steffani. He became court organist at Bayreuth in 1667 and at Munich in 1689, visiting *Kapellmeister* at Hanover in 1696, and returned to Munich in 1703 as director of the chamber music, becoming music director in 1715. Like Abaco, he followed the Elector Max Emanuel into exile at Brussels.

Works incl. operas *Merope, Lucio Vero* (1720), *Griselda* (1723) and *c* 20 others; oratorio *Les Vanités du monde*; chamber concerto; chamber duets.

Tortelier, Paul (b Paris, 21 Mar 1914), French cellist and composer. He studied at the Paris Cons. and made his solo debut in 1931; played in the Monte Carlo and the Boston SOs before the war. In 1947 he was the soloist in Strauss's *Don Quixote*, under Beecham, in London; US debut 1955, with the Boston SO. He has composed cello music and an *Israel Symphony* (1956). His daugh-

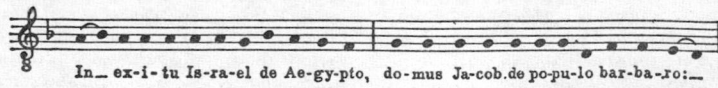

In— ex-i-tu Is-ra-el de Ae-gy-pto, do-mus Ja-cob.de po-pu-lo bar-ba-ro:—

TONUS PEREGRINUS

Tooley, (Sir) **John.** *See* **Covent Garden.**

Torelli, Giuseppe (b Verona, 22 Apr 1658; d Bologna, 8 Feb 1709), Italian composer and violinist. Prob. a pupil of Perti in Bologna, he played in the orch. of San Petronio there 1686–96, then went to Vienna, and was *Konzertmeister* at the court of the Margrave of Brandenburg 1697–9. He returned to Bologna in 1701. With Corelli he was one of the most important comps. in the hist. of the early concerto.

Works incl. *Concerti grossi* (op. 8, 1709); vln. concertos; *sinfonie* (concertos) for tpt. and orch.

Tornada (Span.), the refrain which is a feature of many old Catalan songs.

ter Maria de la Pau is a pianist and his son, Jan Pascal T., a conductor and violinist.

Torvaldo e Dorliska, opera by Rossini (lib. by C. Sterbini), prod. Rome, Teatro Valle, 26 Dec 1815.

Tosca, La, opera by Puccini (lib. by G. Giacosa and L. Illica, based on Sardou's drama), prod. Rome, Teatro Costanzi, 14 Jan 1900.

Toscanini, Arturo (b Parma, 25 Mar 1867; d New York, 16 Jan 1957), Italian conductor. Studied at the Conss. of Parma and Milan and began his career as a cellist. At a perf. of *Aida* in Rio de Janeiro, when the cond. was taken ill, he cond. the work from memory at a moment's notice. Engagements followed in It. where he cond. the fps of *Pagliacci* (1892) and *La Bohème* (1896). Such was his success that he was app. chief cond. in 1898 at La Scala and in 1907 at the NY Met; remained until 1915, giving the 1910 fp of *La fanciulla del West* and early US perfs. of operas by Mussorgsky, Giordano, Dukas and Gluck. He returned to La Scala 1921–9 and in 1930–31 gave *Tristan* and *Parsifal* at Bayreuth, but in 1933 he refused to cond. there on account of his anti-fascist convictions. At Salzburg (1934–7) he was heard in *Falstaff, Fidelio* and *Meistersinger*. He gave his first NY concert in 1913 and from 1940 cond. the NBC SO; recorded several Verdi operas and cond. works by Strauss, Ravel, Prokofiev and Debussy, in addition to the standard rep.

Toscanini had a reputation for fidelity to the printed score, but some of his later recordings leave an impression of relentlessly hard-driven perfs.

Tosi, Giuseppe Felice (b Bologna; *fl.* 1677–93), Italian composer. Organist at San Petronio at Bologna, and later *maestro di cappella* at San Giovanni in Monte and the cathedral of Monte di Ferrara.

Works incl. operas; *salmi concertati* and other church music; chamber cantatas.

Tosi, Pier Francesco (b Cesena, *c* 1653; d Faenza, 1732), Italian castrato, teacher and composer, son of prec. He learnt music from his father and travelled much until 1682, when he settled as singing-master in London. From 1705 to 1711 he was comp. at the Imp. court in Vienna. After a further visit to London he finally returned to It. and was ordained in 1730. He pub. a book on florid singing (1723), and wrote an oratorio, and cantatas for voice and harpsichord.

Tost Quartets, 12 string 4tets written by Haydn 1788–90 for the Viennese merchant and violinist Johannes Tost: op. 54 nos. 1–3, op. 55 nos. 1–3, op. 64 nos. 1–6. Tost also commissioned works from Mozart, incl. the D maj. string 5tet K593.

Tosti, (Francesco) Paolo (b Ortona sul Mare, Abruzzi, 9 Apr 1846; d Rome, 2 Dec 1916), Italian singing-master and composer. Studied at Naples under Mercadante and others from 1858 and was app. a student-teacher, remaining until 1869. During a long illness at home he wrote his 1st songs. He then went to Rome, where Sgambati helped him to give a concert and Princess Margherita of Savoy (afterwards queen of It.) app. him her singing-master. In 1875 he 1st visited London, returning each year until 1880, where he remained as singing-master

to the royal family. Knighted 1908.

Works incl. It., Eng. and Fr. songs, e.g. *Non m'ama più, Lamento d'amore, Aprile, Vorrei morire, Forever, Good-bye, Mother, At Vespers, That Day, Mattinata, Serenata; Canti popolari abruzzesi* for vocal duet, etc.

Tote Stadt, Die (*The Dead City*), opera by Korngold (lib. by P. Schott, based on G. Rodenbach's play *Bruges-la-morte*), prod. Hamburg and Cologne, 4 Dec 1920.

Toten Augen, Die (*The Dead Eyes*), opera by d'Albert (lib. orig. Fr. by M. Henry, Ger. trans. by H.H. Ewers), prod. Dresden, 5 Mar 1916.

Touch (modern), the way of approaching the keys in pf. playing to prod. the tone required. Scientists deny the possibility of varying the quality of tone by anything but weight, since it is obviously impossible to transmit to the hammers and strings anything but degrees of strength by the intermediary of the action, which (unlike the clavichord's) is not susceptible to any but a mechanical response to the player's hand. This is quite true so long as it is said of single notes only, but not of combinations of notes, which are capable of varying enormously in quality in countless different ways by the slightest inequalities in the strength of the constituent notes or by the minutest inaccuracies of synchronization. It is these infinitesimal inequalities and inaccuracies which account for subtleties of touch, and although they too are in the last resort mechanical, they do express the player's interpretative intentions and translate themselves into aesthetic values.

Touch (old). As a verb the word, up to *c* the early 17th cent., meant simply to 'sound' an instrument, exactly as *toccare* does in It.; as a noun ('a touch' or 'touche') it was equivalent to Toccata. *See* **Tucket.**

Tourel (actually Davidovich), **Jennie** (b Vitebsk, 22 Jun 1900; d New York, 23 Nov 1973), French-Canadian mezzo of Russian birth. Studied in Paris with Anna El-Tour, whose name she adopted in anagram form. Debut at the Paris Opéra-Comique in 1933 as Carmen; NY Met debut 1937, as Mignon. Other roles incl. Cherubino, Adalgisa, Rosina and Charlotte. Often heard in concert, in particular with Leonard Bernstein. She created the role of Baba the Turk in Stravinsky's *Rake's Progress* (Venice, 1951).

Tournai Mass, an early 14th-cent. polyphonic setting of the Ordinary of the Mass, incl. *Ite missa est*. It is not the work of a single comp., nor is it necessarily from Tournai, where the MS. now is, but may have been written at least in part in the S. of Fr.

Tournemire, Charles (Arnould) (b Bordeaux, 22 Jan 1870; d Arcachon, 4 Nov 1939), French composer and organist. Studied at the Paris Cons. and later with d'Indy. In 1898 he was app. to Franck's former organist's post at the church of Sainte-Clotilde. Later he became prof. of chamber music at the Cons. and travelled much as organ recitalist on the Continent.

Works incl. operas *Les Dieux sont morts* (1924) and *Nittetis* (1905–7); *Le Sang de la Sirène* for solo voices, chorus and orch.; 8 symphs.; pf. 4tet, pf. trio and other chamber music; *Pièces symphoniques, Triple Choral, l'Orgue mystique, Petites Fleurs musicales* and other organ works; pf. pieces; songs.

Tourte, François (b Paris, 1747; d Paris, 26 Apr 1835), French bowmaker. He learnt his craft from his father and set up in business with his elder brother Xavier, but they quarrelled and set up each for himself. He made great improvements in the vln. bow, esp. after 1775.

Tovey, Donald (Francis) (b Eton, 17 Jul 1875; d Edinburgh, 10 Jul 1940), English music scholar, pianist and composer. He was privately educ. and learnt the pf. early, playing it astonishingly as a child and memorizing Bach and other classics. At 13 he was a pupil of Parry. He went to Balliol Coll., Oxford, in 1894, after giving a concert with Joachim at Windsor, and there he distinguished himself by brilliant scholarship and by taking a leading part in the univ.'s musical life. In 1900–01 he gave pf. recitals at St James's Hall in London, and in 1901–2 in Berlin and Vienna. In 1914 he was app. Reid Prof. of Music at Edinburgh Univ., a post he held to his death, and also cond. the Reid orch. concerts there. He wrote several books, incl. 6 vols. of *Essays in Musical Analysis*. Knighted 1935.

Works incl. opera *The Bride of Dionysus* (1929); incid. music for Maeterlinck's *Aglavaine et Sélysette*; symph. in D maj.; suite for wind band; pf. concerto (1903), cello concerto (1935); 2 string 4tets; conjectural completion of Bach's *Art of Fugue* (1931).

Toy Symphony, piece by Leopold Mozart (formerly attrib. to Haydn) with parts for toy instruments (cuckoo, quail, nightingale, etc.). Similar works have been written by Mendelssohn, A. Romberg and others, most recently Malcolm Arnold.

Tozzi, Giorgio (b Chicago, 8 Jan 1923), American bass. He studied in Milan and appeared on Broadway in 1948 (Britten's

Rape of Lucretia). He sang widely in Europe 1950–54 as Philip II, Don Giovanni and Pogner. NY Met debut 1955, as Alvise; later roles were Figaro, Marke, Sachs and Boris. Also appeared in musicals and films.

Trabaci, Giovanni Maria (b Monte Pelusio [now Irsina], c 1575; d Naples, 31 Dec 1647), Italian composer and organist. He was app. organist in the royal chapel at Naples in 1603 and *maestro di cappella* in 1614.

Works incl. Masses, 4 Passions, motets, psalms; madrigals; toccatas, *ricercari* and other organ pieces.

Traci Amanti, I (*The Amorous Turks*), opera by Cimarosa (lib. by G. Palomba), prod. Naples, Teatro Nuovo, 19 Jun 1793.

Tract, a chant with penitential words, sung after the Gradual in the Mass in Lent (in place of the Alleluia). Tracts are the only surviving examples in the regular chants of the Mass of 'direct psalmody', sung without antiphon or respond. They occur only in modes 2 and 8, and it is possible that those of mode 2 were orig. Graduals. Their structure is that of a highly elaborated psalm-tone. The number of verses ranges from 2 to 14.

Traetta, Tommaso (Michele Francesco Saverio) (b Bitonto nr. Bari, 30 Mar 1727; d Venice, 6 Apr 1779), Italian composer. Pupil of Porpora and Durante at the Cons. di Santa Maria di Loreto in Naples 1738–48, he 1st worked as a comp. of church music, but after the success of *Farnace* (1751) soon estab. himself as an opera comp. *Maestro di cappella* and singing teacher at the court of the Infante Felipe of Spain in Parma 1758–65, he was director of the Cons. dell' Ospedaletto in Venice 1765–8, then went to St Petersburg as music director at the court of Catherine II of Rus. He returned to It. in 1775, visited London in 1777, and finally lived in Venice.

Works incl. over 40 operas, e.g. *Farnace* (1751), *Didone abbandonata* (1757), *Ippolito ed Aricia* (1759), *I Tindaridi* (1760), *Le serve rivali* (1766), *Amore in trappola, Antigona* (1772), *Merope, Germondo* (1776), *Il cavaliere errante*, etc.; oratorio *Rex Salomone*; Passion; *Stabat Mater* and other church music; divertimenti for 4 orchs. *Le Quattro stagioni e il dodici mesi dell'anno; sinfonie, etc.*

Tragédie de Salomé, La, ballet by Florent Schmitt (choreography by Guerra), prod. Paris, Théâtre des Arts, 9 Nov 1907.

Tragédie lyrique (Fr.), a 17th–18th-cent. term for French opera of a serious character, e.g. Rameau's *Les Boréades* (1764).

Tragic Overture (*Tragische Ouvertüre*), an overture by Brahms, op. 81, comp. in 1880 as a companion-piece to the *Academic Festival Overture*, written as an acknowledgment of the hon. degree of doctor of philosophy conferred on him by Breslau Univ. in 1879. Fp Vienna, 26 Dec 1880.

'Tragic' Symphony, Schubert's 4th symph., in C min., comp. 1816, 1st public perf. Leipzig, 19 Nov 1849. The title was added to the score by the composer.

Tragoedia, work for wind 5tet, harp and string 4tet by Birtwistle, comp. 1965.

Trampler, Walter (b Munich, 25 Aug 1915), German-born American violist and teacher. Played in German Radio SO then emigrated to US in 1939 (naturalized 1944). Played in New Music String Quartet 1947–55; extra viola for Budapest and Juilliard Quartets. Taught at Juilliard from 1962, Boston Univ. from 1972. Gave fp of the concerto by Simon Bainbridge (1978).

Tranquillo (It.) – Quiet, calm, tranquil. The adverb, more rarely used as a direction, is *tranquillamente*.

Trans, work by Stockhausen for string orch., wind, and perc. with tape and light projection. Fp Donaueschingen, 16 Oct 1971.

Transcription, an arr. of a composition for some other medium than that intended by the comp. Strictly speaking, a transcription differs from an arr. by not merely reproducing the orig. as closely as possible, but by intro. more or less imaginative changes which may be supposed to conform to the comp.'s own procedure if he had written for the different medium.

Transfiguration de Notre Seigneur Jésus-Christ, La, work in 14 movts. for soloists, chorus and orch. by Messiaen (texts from the Bible, the Missal and St Thomas Aquinas); comp. 1965–9, fp Lisbon, 7 Jun 1969, cond. Baudo.

Transitions, passages in a composition between 2 salient thematic features, more often than not modulating from one key to another. In a movement in sonata form the crux of the comp. often lies in the transition between 1st and 2nd subjects and in the different turn it takes in the Exposition and Recapitulation.

Tranposing Instruments. Many wind instruments are built in fundamental tunings in which the maj. scale without key signature, written as C maj., actually sounds higher or lower. A clar. in B♭, for ex., will automatically play the scale of that key when the music is written in C maj.; or, conversely stated, if it is to play a piece in F maj., the music must be written in G maj., and so on. A horn in F will transpose a 5th down, a tpt. in F a 4th up, and both will play, for ex., in E♭ if their music is written in B♭, but the former an octave lower than the latter. Among the most common orch. instruments Eng. horns, clars., horns and tpts. are transposing instruments; fls., obs., bassoons and trombs. are not. In brass bands all the instruments except the bass tromb. are transposing instruments.

Transposing Keyboards, contrivances of various sorts to shift the manuals of keyboard instruments so that the music played becomes automatically higher or lower, saving the players from acquiring the art of transposing at sight. Such keyboards appeared on some organs as early as the 16th cent. and later on Ruckers harpsichords. Several inventions of the kind were made for the pf. late in the 18th and throughout the 19th cents.

Transposition, the process, in either comp. or perf., of turning a piece or passage from one key into another in such a way that the music remains exactly the same except for the change in pitch. It follows that all Accidentals arising incidentally in the course of the music (i.e. not contained in the key signature) still remain accidentals, e.g. see illustration opposite. In a piece transposed from E maj. up to F maj., for ex., an incidental A♯ will become B♭, incidental F♮ will become G♭, and so on. Accompanists are often required to transpose at sight when a song is too high or low for a singer's voice, and occasionally the inst. parts of a whole orch. have to be transposed in the same way for similar reasons. Horn players, using today an F-B♭ horn, have to transpose at sight older horn parts written for horns in C, D, E♭, etc.

Transverse Flute, the modern fl. held hoizontally, as distinct from the fls. of the Recorder type, which are held vertically.

Trapp, Max (b Berlin, 1 Nov 1887; d Berlin, 29 May 1971), German composer. Studied comp. with Juon and pf. with Dohnányi at the Berlin Hochschule für Musik, became pf. prof. there in 1920 and prof. of advanced comp. in 1924. He also taught at Dortmund. The fp of his 2nd *Concerto for Orch.* (1935) was cond. by Furtwängler.

Works incl. marionette play *Der letzte König von Orplid* (after Mörike); incid. music to Shakespeare's *Timon of Athens*; 7 symphs., 2 concertos, 2 divertimenti, symph. suite, *Notturno* for orch.; pf. concerto, vln.

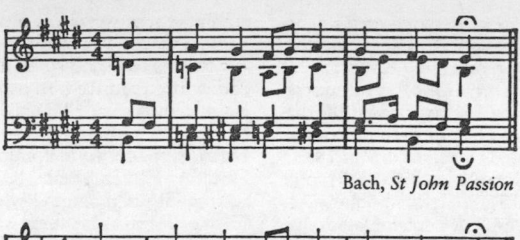

Bach, *St John Passion*

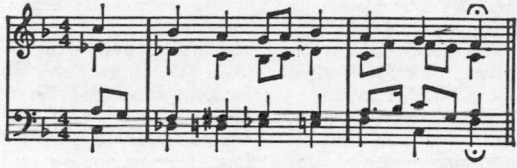

TRANSPOSITION

concerto (1926), cello concerto (1937); 2 string 4tets, pf. 5tet, 3 pf. 4tets; variations for 2 pfs.; sonatina for pf.

Traquenard (Fr. lit. trap, snare; also racking-pace[of horses]), a 17th-cent. dance the dotted rhythm of which refers to the 2nd sense of the word.

Traubel, Helen (b St Louis, 20 Jun 1899; d Santa Monica, 28 Jul 1972), American soprano. Studied in St Louis and made her debut there in 1925. In 1937 she began a long career at the NY Met, which lasted until 1953; roles incl. Elisabeth, Brünnhilde, Isolde, Kundry and the Marschallin. She also appeared in night clubs, which led to her resignation from the Met after a frank exchange of views with Rudolf Bing (*q.v.*). She pub. some successful detective novels, incl. *The Metropolitan Opera Murders*.

Trauer-Ode (*Funeral Ode*), Bach's cantata no. 198, written on the death of the Electress Christiane Eberhardine of Saxony and perf. at the memorial ceremony at Leipzig, 17 Oct 1727.

Trauer-Sinfonie (*Mourning Symph.*), the nickname of a symph. by Haydn, no. 44, in E min., comp. *c* 1771.

Trauermarsch (Ger.) = Funeral March.

Trauermusik, work for vla. and strings in 4 movts. by Hindemith; comp. 21 Jan 1936 in response to the death of George V and perf. the next day in London with Hindemith as soloist, cond. Boult.

Trauerwalzer (*Mourning Waltz*), the title given by the pub. to Schubert's waltz for pf., op. 9 no. 2, in 1821, a piece later wrongly attrib. to Beethoven. Schubert, who wrote it in 1816, disapproved of the title. The attrib. to Beethoven occurred in 1826, when Schott of Mainz brought out a *Sehnsuchtswalzer*

(also called *Le Désir*) under his name, althought it was a compound of Schubert's piece and Himmel's *Favoritwalzer*.

Traumgörge, Der (*Dreaming George*), opera by Zemlinsky (lib. by L. Feld); comp. 1904–6 and accepted for prod. at the Vienna Hofoper by Mahler. Not perf. until 11 Oct 1980, at Nuremberg.

Trautonium, an electrophonic instrument invented by Friedrich Trautwein of Berlin in 1930, prod. notes from the air graded according to the chromatic scale by means of a special device, not indeterminate in pitch like those of the Aetherophone or Theremin. Hindemith wrote a Konzertstück for trautonium and strings.

Travelling Companion, The, opera by Stanford (lib. by H. Newbolt, based on a story by Hans Andersen), pub. 1919, but not perf. in Stanford's lifetime: prod. Liverpool, 30 Apr 1925.

Travers, John (b *c* 1703; d London, Jun 1758), English organist and composer. Learnt music as a choir-boy at St George's Chapel, Windsor, and later studied with Greene and Pepusch in London, where in his early 20s he became organist at St Paul's Church, Covent Garden, and later at Fulham church. In 1737 he succeeded Jonathan Martin as organist in the Chapel Royal.

Works incl. services, anthems, Te Deum; *The Whole Book of Psalms* for 1–5 voices with continuo; 18 canzonets for 2–3 voices to words by M. Prior and others; organ voluntaries; harpsichord pieces.

Traversa (It. fem. = transverse), an abbr. sometimes used in old scores for the *flauto traverso*, the modern fl. played sideways, as distinct from fls. of the Recorder type, which are held vertically.

Traversière (Fr. fem. = transverse). The *flûte traversière* was the Fr. name for the *flauto traverso*, or Transverse fl.

Traviata, La (*The Lady Gone Astray*), opera by Verdi (lib. by F.M. Piave, based on the younger Dumas' *La Dame aux camélias*), prod. Venice, Teatro La Fenice, 6 Mar 1853.

Traxel, Josef (b Mainz, 29 Sep 1916; d Stuttgart, 8 Oct 1975), German tenor. Debut Mainz, 1942, as Don Ottavio; later sang at Nuremberg, then Stuttgart. In 1952 created Mercury in Strauss's *Die Liebe der Danaë* at Salzburg. Bayreuth 1953, Walther. Also sang Evangelist in Bach's Passions.

Tre corde (It. = 3 strings), a direction in pf. music indicating that after the use of the left pedal (*una corda*) normal playing is to be resumed.

Trebelli (real name Gillebert), **Zélia** (b Paris; 1838; d Etretat, 18 Aug 1892), French mezzo. She began serious music studies, incl. pf., at the age of 6, and at 16 was allowed to take a course in singing. She made her 1st stage appearances at Madrid in 1859, as Rosina, Azucena and Arsaces. Travelled in Ger. in 1860–61 with Merelli's It. co. and 1st visited London in 1862; returned until 1888 as Siebel, Preziosilla, and Cherubino. NY Met from 1883 as Boito's Elena and as Carmen.

Treble, the highest voice in a vocal comp. in several parts, derived from the Lat. *triplum*, which was the top part of the earliest 3-part Motets. It is the normal term for a boy's voice.

Treble Clef, the G clef (being a modification of that letter and indicating the position of the note G on the stave), the higher of the 2 clefs used for pf. music, also replacing the former different C clefs used for soprano, alto and tenor voices: it is now generally represented by:

If used for the tenor, it is understood that the voice sounds an 8ve lower:

Treble Viol, the smallest of the normal members of the viol family, tuned:

Trecento (It., literally '300' but normally a shorthand reference to 'the 1300s'). The It. musical rep. of the 14th cent., or more specifically, in terms of what survives, the years *c* 1340 to 1420. The music is notated with the techniques first described by Marchettus of Padua and tends to be extremely florid. The main comps. were Jacopo da Bologna and Francesco Landini.

Tree, Ann Maria (b London, Aug 1801; d London, 17 Feb 1862), English mezzo and actress. Studied singing with Lanza and T. Cooke, joined the chorus at Drury Lane Theatre and made her 1st important stage appearances at Bath in 1818 and in London in 1819. Later she became a good Shakespearian actress as well as a stage singer.

Tregian, Francis (b 1574; d London, 1619), English amateur musician. He was the eldest of a large, highly cultivated Cornish Roman Catholic family, and travelled extensively abroad, returning finally in 1605. He was imprisoned for recusancy in 1609 in the Fleet, where he died. He copied (prob. for the most part in prison) 2 collections of vocal works (the Sambrooke MS. in New York, and Brit. Lib., Egerton MS. 3665) and the Fitzwilliam Virginal Book. The 2 latter contain a few of his own comps.

Treigle, Norman (b New Orleans, 6 Mar 1927; d New Orleans, 16 Feb 1975), American bass. He studied in Louisiana and sang at the NY City Opera for almost 20 years from 1953; among his roles were Handel's Caesar, Boris, Don Giovanni and the villains in *Les Contes d'Hoffmann*. In NY and New Orleans he took part in the fps of operas by Carlisle Floyd. He sang Gounod's Méphistophélès at CG in 1974 and committed suicide the following year.

Tremolando (It. = trembling), a direction sometimes used instead of the conventional notation for string Tremolo, or for a passage to be sung in a tremulous voice.

Tremolo (It. noun = quivering). (1) The rapid repetition of a single note. In 17th-cent. It. the vocal tremolo was called *trillo*. On bowed string insts. this type of tremolo is prod. by a rapid movement of the bow, notated thus:

(2) The rapid alternation of 2 or more notes, prod. on wind instruments, the organ, the pf. and bowed string insts. by the fingers, notated thus:

Tremulant, a mechanical device on the organ, operated by a draw stop, for prod. *vibrato.*

Trenchmore, an English country dance 'longways for as many as will', known in the 16th and 17th cents. and intro. into the court and noble houses as a kind of democratic

1740 into the service of Count Schaffgotsch at Hirschberg.

Works incl. operas *Astarto* (1725), *Ulisse* (1726), *Don Chisciotte* (1727) and others; cantatas; orch. music.

Triad, a chord composed of 2 superimposed thirds, e.g.:

TRIAD

dance in which masters and servants could take part together and strict class distinctions were temporarily relaxed.

Trent Codices, 7 MSS. (Trent, 87–93) of 15th-cent. music, compiled 1440–80 and incl. works by Power, Dufay, Dunstable, Ockeghem and Binchois. The 1st 6 were bought by the Aus. Government in 1891, and a selection appeared in 6 vols. of the series *Denkmäler der Tonkunst in Österreich.* They became the property of Italy after World War I, and in 1920 the 7th MS. was found.

Trento, Vittorio (b Venice, 1761; d ? Lisbon, 1833), Italian composer. Pupil of Bertoni. In the last decade of the 18th cent. he visited London as cond. at the King's Theatre and in 1806 became impresario at Amsterdam, going to Lisbon in the same capacity soon after. After a further visit to London he returned to Venice before his death.

Works incl. operas *La finta ammalata, Quanti casi in un giorno* (1801), *Teresa vedova, Ifigenia in Aulide, Climene* (1812) and *c* 35 others; ballet *Mastino della Scala* and more than 50 others; oratorios *The Deluge, The Maccabees* and others.

Trepak, a Russian dance of Cossack origin in animated 2–4 time.

Treptow, Günther (Otto Walther) (b Berlin, 22 Oct 1907; d Berlin, 28 Mar 1981), German tenor. He studied in Berlin (debut 1936) and sang there until 1942, when he moved to Munich; roles incl. Adolar, Parsifal, Otello and Florestan. NY Met debut 1951, as Siegmund. CG 1953, as Siegfried. He sang in Vienna 1947–55; app. Kammersänger 1971.

Treu, Daniel Gottlob (b Stuttgart, 1695; d Breslau, Aug 1749), German violinist and composer. Pupil of Cousser and from 1716 of Vivaldi in Venice, where he was called, by lit. trans. of his name, Fedele. In 1725 he went to Breslau as cond. of an It. opera co., in 1727 to Prague as music director and in

Trial, a French term for a special type of operatic tenor voice of a high, thin, rather nasal quality suited to comic parts, derived from Antoine T. below.

Trial. French family of musicians:

1. Jean-Claude T. (b Avignon, 13 Dec 1732; d Paris, 23 Jun 1771), composer. Studied vln. with Garnier at Montpellier, settled in Paris, where he became a friend of Rameau, was app. cond. at the Opéra and later of the private orch. of the Prince de Conti, whose influence procured him the joint directorship of the Opéra with Berton.

Works incl. operas *Ésope à Cythère* (with Vachon, 1766), *La Fête de Flore* (1770), *Silvie* (with Berton), *Théonis* (do.) and *Renaud d'Ast* (with Vachon, 1765); cantatas; overture and divertissements for orch.

2. Antoine T. (b Avignon, 1737; d Paris, 5 Feb 1795), tenor and actor, brother of prec. He was educ. as a church singer, but went on the stage, toured in the provinces and in 1764 appeared for the 1st time in Paris. He took part in the Revolution, lost his reason and poisoned himself.

3. Marie-Jeanne T. (*née* Milon) (b Paris, 1 Aug 1746; d Paris, 13 Feb 1818), soprano and actress, wife of prec. Made her 1st stage appearance in 1766.

4. Armand-Emmanuel T. (b Paris, 1 Mar 1771; d Paris, 9 Sep 1803), pianist and composer, son of 2 and 3. He began to comp. at an early age, married Jeanne Méon, an actress at the Théâtre Favart, and died from the effects of a wild life.

Works incl. operas *Julien et Colette* (1788), *Adélaïde et Mirval* (1791), *Les Deux Petits Aveugles* (1792); revolutionary pieces *La Cause et les effets, Le Congrès des rois* (with other comps.) and *Le Siège de Lille.*

Trial by Jury, one-act opera by Sullivan (lib. by W.S. Gilbert), prod. London, Royalty Theatre, 25 Mar 1875.

Triangle, a perc. instrument consisting of a simple steel bar in 3-cornered form with an open end, hooked so that it can be suspended to hang freely. It is struck with a short steel rod and prod. a bright tinkling sound of no definite pitch.

Tridentine Council. *See* **Council of Trent.**

Trihoris, an old French dance of Lower Brittany, also called Trihory, Triori or Triory, allied to the Branle.

Trillo del diavolo, Il (*The Devil's Trill*), Tartini's vln. sonata written at Assisi *c* 1745 and said to have been inspired by a dream in which he bargained with the devil for his soul in return for musical inspiration, the devil playing the vln. to him. He related that on waking he immediately wrote down what he had heard, but that the music as written fell far short of the dream devil's perf. The work is in 4 movts., written for vln. and continuo; the famous trill is in the finale. An opera on the story of the sonata was written by Falchi.

Trinity College of Music, a school of music in London incorporated in 1875.

Trio. (1) A composition or movement for 3 vocal or instrumental parts: more partic. a chamber work for 3 instruments, esp. vln., cello and pf. (pf. trio) or vln., vla. and cello (string trio).

(2) The alternative section in a minuet, scherzo, march or similar movement, so called because such sections were orig. written for 2 obs. and bassoon.

Trio Sonata, the medium predominantly used for chamber music with a keyboard Continuo part in the later 17th and early 18th cent. Trio sonatas were most usually written for 2 vlns. and bass viol. or cello, with background supplied by a harpsichord or other keyboard inst. played from the figured bass part.

Triomphe de l'Amour sur des bergers et bergères, Le (*The Triumph of Love over Shepherds and Shepherdesses*), opera by La Guerre (lib. by C. de Beys), prod. Paris, Louvre, 22 Jan 1655. The 1st Fr. opera.

Trionfi del fato, I, ovvero Le glorie d'Enea (*The Triumphs of Fate, or The Glories of Aeneas*), opera by Steffani (lib. by O. Mauro), prod. Hanover, Court Opera, Dec 1695.

Trionfo dell' onore, Il (*The Triumph of Honour*), opera by A. Scarlatti (lib. by F.A. Tullio), prod. Naples, Teatro dei Fiorentini, autumn 1718.

Trionfo di Afrodite (*Aphrodite's Triumph*) concerto scenico by Orff, 2nd of 3 works called collectively *Trionfi* (text by comp. after Catullus, Sappho and Euripides), prod. Milan, La Scala, 14 Feb 1953, cond. Karajan.

Trionfo di Camilla, Il (*Camilla's Triumph*), opera by M.A. Bononcini (lib. by S. Stampiglia), prod. Naples, Teatro San Bartolommeo, ? Dec 1696.

Opera by Leo (lib. do.), prod. Rome, Teatro Capranica, 8 Jan 1726.

Trionfo di Clelia, Il (*Clelia's Triumph*), opera by Gluck (lib. by Metastasio), prod. Bologna, Teatro Comunale, 14 May 1763.

Opera by Hasse (lib. do.), prod. Vienna, Burgtheater, 27 Apr 1762.

Opera by Jommelli (lib. do.), prod. Lisbon, Teatro d'Ajuda, 6 Jun 1774.

Trionfo di Dori, Il (*The Triumph of Doris*), collection of Italian madrigals pub. by Gardano of Venice in 1592. It contains 29 6-part madrigals on var. poems all ending with the line 'Viva la bella Dori', which suggested the similar uniform final line in the Eng. collection modelled on this, *The Triumphes of Oriana*. The comps., all represented by 1 piece each, incl. Anerio, Asola, Baccusi, Croce, G. Gabrieli, Gastoldi, Marenzio, Palestrina, Striggio and Vecchi.

Tripla, an old term for triple time in old Mensurable music, but also the figure 3 shown in the time-signature and later, when the device of the Triplet came into use, the figure 3 set over a group of notes. Also a dance in quick triple time.

Triple Concerto, a concerto with 3 solo parts, e.g. Bach's 2 concertos for 2 harpsichords and strings, Beethoven's concerto for vln., cello and pf. and orch., or Tippett's concerto for string trio and orch.

Triple Counterpoint, counterpoint in which 3 parts are reversible, each being capable of appearing at the top, in the middle or at the bottom.

Triple Time, 3 beats in a bar, e.g. 3–4.

Triplet, a group of 3 notes perf. in the time of 2 and indicated by the figure 3, e.g.:

Rests instead of notes may form part of triplets.

Triplum (Lat. = the third), the highest of the orig. 3 voices in the Motet, and thus the origin of the English word Treble.

Tristan, work by Henze for pf., tape and orch.; comp. 1973, fp London, 20 Oct 1974, cond. C. Davis.

Tristan Chord. *See* **Augmented Sixth Chords.**

Tristan und Isolde, music-drama by Wagner (lib. by comp., based on the Tristram and

Iseult legend), prod. Munich, Court Opera, 10 Jun 1865.

Tristitiae remedium (*The Remedy for Sadness*), a MS. collection of motets, anthems and madrigals by English and Italian composers (Byrd, Croce, Milton, Peerson, Tallis, Tye, etc.) made by the clergyman Thomas Myriell of Barnet in 1616.

Tritone, the interval of the augmented 4th (e.g. F–B, progressing upwards). *See* **Diabolus in Musica.**

Tritonius, Petrus (actually Peter Treybenreif) (b Bozen (now Bolzano), *c* 1465; d ? Hall, Tyrol, ? 1525), Austrian composer and scholar. Studied at Vienna and Ingolstadt Univs. and later became teacher of Lat. and music at the cathedral school of Brixen. After study at Padua Univ., he was invited to settle in Vienna by Conradus Celtis, a prof. there whom he had met in It., and joined the lit. and humanist society founded by that scholar, making his setting of Horatian odes for it. Senfl later took the tenor parts of these as *cantus firmi* for his own settings, and Hofhaimer imitated Tritonius's settings. On the death of Celtis in 1508 Tritonius returned to the Tyrol and became director of the Lat. school at Bozen; in 1513 he was in Hall, and in 1521 he retired to Schwaz am Inn.

Works incl. hymns in 4 parts; odes by Horace and other Lat. poems set in 4 parts, etc.

Trittico (*Triptych*), cycle of 3 1-act operas by Puccini, prod. NY Met, 14 Dec 1918:

I. **Il Tabarro** (*The Cloak*) (lib. by G. Adami, based on D. Gold's *Houppelande*).

II. **Suor Angelica** (*Sister A.*) (lib. by G. Forzano).

III. **Gianni Schicchi** (lib. by do., based on the story of a rogue who is mentioned in Dante's *Divina commedia*).

Tritto, Giacomo (b Altamura nr. Bari, 2 Apr 1733; d Naples, 16 or 17 Sep 1824), Italian composer. Pupil of Cafaro at the Cons. dei Turchini in Naples, he later taught there and in 1806 became co-director (with Paisiello and Fenarolo). From *c* 1760 he wrote over 50 operas. He also wrote treatises on thorough-bass and counterpoint.

Works incl. operas *La fedeltà in amore* (1764), *Il convitato di pietra* (on the Don Giovanni story), *Arminio, La canterina, Gli Americani* (1802), *Marco Albinio* (1810), etc.; Masses and other church music.

Triumph of Neptune, The, ballet by Lord Berners (scenario by S. Sitwell, choreog. by Balanchine), prod. London, Lyceum Theatre, 3 Dec 1926. The settings were based on B. Pollock's 'penny plain, twopence coloured' toy theatre designs.

Triumph of Peace, The, masque by James Shirley with music by W. Lawes and Simon Ive, prod. at the Banqueting House in Whitehall, 3 Feb (Candlemas) 1634.

Triumphes of Oriana, The, an English collection of madrigals written in honour of Queen Elizabeth, ed. by Morley and pub. in 1601. It was modelled on the It. collection of *Il Trionfo di Dori* of 1592 and contains a similar series of different poems all ending with the same line, 'Long live fair Oriana'. There are 25 pieces by 23 Eng. comps.: Bennet, Carlton, Cavendish, Cobbold, Este, Farmer, E. Gibbons (2), Hilton, Holmes, Hunt, E. Johnson, R. Jones, Kirby, Lisley, Marson, Milton, Morley (2), Mundy, Nicolson, Norcome, T. Tomkins, Weelkes, Wilbye. A madrigal by Bateson intended for the collection arrived too late and was incl. in his own *First Set of English Madrigals* (1604).

Triumphlied (*Song of Triumph*), a setting by Brahms of words from the Revelation of St John for 8-part chorus, orch. and org. *ad lib.*, op. 55, comp. in spring 1871 to celebrate the Ger. victory in the Franco-Prus. war; fp Karlsruhe, 5 Jun 1872.

Troades, opera by Reimann (lib. based on Werfel's version of Euripides' *The Trojan Women*), prod. Munich, 7 Jul 1986.

Troilus and Cressida, opera in 3 acts by Walton (lib. by C. Hassall, after Chaucer), prod. Covent Garden, 3 Dec 1954. Rev. with Cressida's role altered to mezzo, London, CG, 12 Nov 1976.

Trois Fermiers, Les (*The Three Farmers*), opera by Dezède (lib. by J.M.B. de Monvel), prod. Paris, Comédie-Italienne, 24 May 1777.

Trois Petites Liturgies de la Présence Divine (*3 Little Liturgies of the Divine Presence*), work by Messiaen for 18 sopranos, pf., ondes Martenot, celesta, vibraphone, 3 perc. and strings (text by comp.), fp Paris, 21 Apr 1945, cond. Désormière.

Tromba (It.) = Trumpet, also one of the names for the Trumpet organ stop (8 ft.). *See also* **Clarino.**

Tromba da tirarsi (It. lit. tpt. to draw itself [out] = tpt. to be drawn), the Slide tpt., an instrument of the tpt. type. It was used in Ger. in the 18th cent. and had the advantage before the invention of valves of being capable of prod. more notes than the fundamental harmonics by the temporary changes in the length of the tube, as in the tromb. It never attained a wide currency.

Trombetti, Ascanio (b Bologna, bap. 27

Nov 1544; d Bologna, 20 or 21 Sep 1590), Italian composer. In the service of the Signoria of Bologna.

Works incl. motets in 5–12 parts for voices and instruments; madrigals for 4–5 voices, *napolitane* for 3 voices.

Tromboncino, Bartolomeo (b ? Verona, *c* 1470; d ? Venice, after 1534), Italian composer. At the ducal court of Mantua, 1487–95, then at Venice, Vicenza, Casale, at Mantua again in 1501–13, and then at Ferrara.

Works incl. Lamentations, 1 motet and 17 *laude*; over 170 *frottole* for 4 voices.

Trombone, a brass wind instrument, developed from the Sackbut, made in 4 basic sizes: alto, tenor, bass and contrabass, the 1st of which is now rarely used, parts written for it being played on the tenor trombone, while the last hardly ever appears in the orch., except in Wagner's *Ring*. The inst.'s most characteristic feature is the slide, by means of which the tube can be adjusted to different lengths in 7 positions, so that all the notes of the chromatic scale can be prod. as natural harmonics. The trombone was thus a chromatic inst. long before the horn and tpt. became so by the invention of the valves. The intonation, as in string insts., is not fixed, but depends entirely on the player's ear and skill. Many notes are, of course, available in more than one position (as different harmonics), so that the player often has the choice between an easier and a more difficult way of passing from note to note. A strict *legato* between notes in different positions is not possible, as the breath has to be interrupted during the change of the slide to avoid an unpleasant scoop; but this scoop, which is usually designated by the term *glissando*, can be used as a special effect.

The compass of the alto trombone in E♭ is:

of the tenor in B♭ :

of the bass in F:

The compass of the contrabass lies an 8ve below the tenor's. The tenor-bass, a combined inst. in B♭ with a switch lowering the pitch a 4th to F, is widely used at the present day. The length of the slide makes it impossible to play the lowest note (B♮) of the bass trombone on this inst.: the compass therefore starts from C and goes as high in the tenor range as the player can manage:

All trombones except the contrabass can play 2 or 3 'pedal' notes an 8ve below the normal bass notes, e.g. on the tenor trombone:

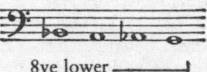

8ve lower ⌐⎯⎯⎯⎯⎯⎯⎯⎯⎯⏌

In the 19th cent. valve trombones were invented and gained favour in military and brass bands as being easier to play, though their tone is inferior. The valve trombone never gained a firm footing in the orch.

Trommelbass (Ger. lit. drum bass), a technical term for the notes of a bass part divided up into groups of repeated even quavers, a device used esp. in the 18th cent. to give a kind of artificial animation to music.

Trompeter von Säckingen, Der (*The Trumpeter of S.*), opera by Nessler (lib. by R. Bunge, based on Scheffel's poem), prod. Leipzig, 4 May 1884. Very popular in its day and often cond. by Mahler.

Tronco (It. = truncated, cut off, interrupted), a direction indicating that a note or chord is to cease abruptly.

Trope. The verb 'to trope' meant to insert Tropes into eccles. chanting. The process was also called 'farcing' (i.e. larding). *See* **Tropes.**

Tropen (Ger. = tropes). The term, which does not refer to the old Tropes, was used by Josef Hauer for his own version of the system of Twelve-Note Music. He divided the possible combinations of the 12 notes of the chromatic scale, which run into hundreds of millions, into 44 main groups, and these are what he called *Tropen*, and he further divided each row of 12 notes into 2 halves of 6, which form 2 fundamental chords, whatever the order in which each 6 may appear. The *Tropen* for him were equivalent to keys in the diatonic system, and a change from one *Trope* to another is equivalent to modulation.

Troper, a book or collection containing Tropes, e.g. the 11th-cent. Winchester Tropers, which contain tropes used at Winchester Cathedral.

Tropes, interpolations into liturgical chants

dating from the 8th or 9th cent. and prob. of Byzantine orig. They were at first vocalized as purely musical ornamentations or sung on syllables of certain words, esp. 'Alleluia', but later they became so important that special words were newly written for them. Sometimes new words came 1st and demanded new music; thus the Sequence, which began merely as a special kind of trope, developed into a poetical form with musical setting.

Troppo (It. = too much). The word is often used in the negative in musical directions; *non troppo* = not too much, or *ma non troppo* = but not too much.

Troubadour (Fr., from Prov. *trobador* [? from Lat. *tropus*]), a poet-musician of southern France in the 11th–13th cents. Troubadours always wrote their own poems and probably the tunes as well: some 280 melodies are still extant. The poems were usually *poésies courtoises* (mainly love-songs, but also incl. satires, etc.), while story-telling *chansons à personnages*, though also cultivated by them, belonged chiefly to the northern Trouvères. Only the melodies were written down, in a notation which showed the pitch but not, as a rule, the rhythm of the notes, the latter being either committed to memory or else determined by the poetic metre, a question that has never been solved beyond controversy. Neither is it known how the songs were accomp.: prob. on instruments of the harp or lute type, either by the troubadours themselves or by attendants, for the troubadours were not poor wandering musicians but gentlemen whose audiences were at courts and noble houses.

'Trout' Quintet, a 5tet in A maj. for vln., vla., cello, double bass and pf., D667, by Schubert, comp. summer 1819 during an excursion to Upper Aus.; so called because the 4th of the 5 movements is a set of variations on his song *The Trout (Die Forelle,* D550, 1817).

Trouvère (Fr., from old Fr. *trovere* or *troveur*), a poet-musician of northern France in the 12th and 13th cents. The trouvères cultivated an art similar to that of the Troubadours in southern Fr. The art was encouraged in the N. by Eleanor of Aquitaine, who married Louis VII in 1137: *c* 1,700 melodies have been preserved. The poems include *chansons à personnages* (narrative songs), *poésies courtoises* (courtly poems, mainly love-songs) and crusaders' songs. The notation and manner of perf. of the songs was similar to that of the Troubadours.

Trovatore, Il (*The Troubadour* or *The Min-*

strel), opera by Verdi (lib. by S. Cammarano, based on a Span. play, *El trovador*, by A.G. Gutiérrez), prod. Rome, Teatro Apollo, 19 Feb 1853.

Troyanos, Tatiana (b New York, 12 Sep 1938), American mezzo. She studied at the Juilliard and sang Britten's Hippolyta at the NY City Opera in 1963. She has sung in Europe since 1965 and in 1969 created Jeanne in the Hamburg fp of Penderecki's *The Devils of Loudun*. CG from 1969 as Octavian, Carmen and the Composer. NY Met debut 1976, as Octavian; she returned there in 1984 for Brangaene, and Dido in *Les Troyens*. On 11 Aug 1984 she sang the title role in the fp (concert) of Rakhmaninov's opera *Monna Vanna* (Saratoga, NY).

Troyens, Les (*The Trojans*), opera by Berlioz in 2 parts (lib. by comp., after Virgil): **I. La Prise de Troie** (*The Taking of Troy*), prod. Karlsruhe (in Ger.), 6 Dec 1890; **II. Les Troyens à Carthage,** prod. Paris, Théâtre-Lyrique, 4 Nov 1863, and later at Karlsruhe (in Ger.), 7 Dec 1890 (the fp of the complete work). The fp of the complete work in Fr. was at Brussels, 26 and 27 Dec 1906; fp in Fr. complete on one night, CG, 17 Sep 1969, cond. C. Davis.

Truelove (Trouluffe), John (*fl. c* 1470), English composer. He was a canon of St Probus, attached to Exeter Cathedral, 1465–78. He appears to have been assoc. with Richard Smert (*q.v.*) in the comp. of 4 carols in the Ritson MS.

Trumpet, a brass wind instrument of ancient origin. Until the invention of the valves in the 19th cent. the trumpet was capable of prod. only the natural harmonic notes, for which reason, combined with that of its incisive and carrying tone, it was found useful for fanfares, and for military purposes was often combined with timpani; this practice is clearly reflected in the scores of classical orch. works up to the early 19th cent. In order to make it possible to play in different keys, crooks were used, as with the horn. The valves made the trumpet a chromatic inst. The trumpets in modern use are usually in Bb or C, the written compass being:

sounding on the Bb trumpet:

A trumpet in D is used for 17th- and 18th-cent. works and has been employed also by modern comps.: its sounding compass is:

A still smaller trumpet in F (with a compass a min. 3rd higher than that of the D trumpet) has been made for the perf. of Bach's 2nd Brandenburg concerto, and there is also one in high Bb (with a compass an 8ve higher than that of the normal Bb trumpet). *See also* **Bach Trumpet, Bass Trumpet, Clarino, Principal** and **Tromba da tirarsi**.

Trumpet Marine, an early string instrument with a single string and thus allied to the Monochord, played with a bow. It was used mainly for popular music-making, esp. in Ger., but also in convents, as the Ger. name *Nonnengeige* (nun's fiddle) indicates. It was also called *Trummscheit* (trumpet [*tromba*] wood) or *Brummscheit* (humming wood), and the It. and Eng. names connecting it with a tpt. were doubtless due to its penetrating tone. The provenance of the adj. 'marine' is unknown. The instrument prod. harmonics very easily and, like the old tpt., often restricted itself to them, its normally prod. notes being very poor and coarse in quality.

Trumpet Voluntary, in the late 17th cent. a piece, not for tpt., but an organ voluntary the tune of which was played on the tpt. stop. The ex. still familiar is that by J. Clarke, long wrongly attrib. to Purcell, popularized by Henry Wood's orch. arr. This is in fact *The Prince of Denmark's March*, which Clarke pub. in 1700 as a harpsichord piece, but which also occurs in a suite for wind insts. by Clarke.

Tsar and Carpenter (Lortzing). *See* **Zar und Zimmermann**.

Tsar Saltan (Rimsky-Korsakov). *See* **Legend of Tsar Saltan**.

Tsar's Bride, The (*Tsarskaya Nevesta*), opera by Rimsky-Korsakov (lib. by I.F. Tumenev, based on a play by L.A. Mey), prod. Moscow, Imp. Opera, 3 Nov 1899.

Ts'ong, Fou. *See* **Fou Ts'ong**.

Tuba. (1) An ancient Rom. military tpt.

(2) The bass instrument of the saxhorn family, used in the orch. as the bass of the brass instruments. The orchestral inst. is normally in F (non-transposing) with 4 valves and the following compass;

8ve lower ⏌

Military and brass bands also use tubas in Eb and low Bb. *See also* **Bombardon, Euphonium** and **Wagner Tubas**.

Tubin, Eduard (b Kallaste, 18 Jun 1905; d Stockholm, 17 Nov 1982), Swedish composer of Estonian birth. Cond. in Estonia 1931–44, before settling in Sweden.

Works incl. operas *Barbara of Tisenhusen* (1969) and *The Priest from Reigi* (1971); 10 symphs. (1934–73), 2 vln. concertos (1942, 1945), balalaika concerto (1964); *Requiem for Fallen Soldiers* (1979); 2 vln. sonatas (1936, 1949).

Tubular Bells, metal tubes tuned to the musical scale and used for bell effects in the orch., real bells being cumbersome and difficult to play with precision.

Tucci, Gabriella (b Rome, 4 Aug 1929), Italian soprano. She sang in Milan, London and San Francisco from 1959; NY Met 1960 as Butterfly. Other roles incl. Marguerite, Mimi and Violetta.

Tuček, Vincenc (Tuczek, Vinzenz) (b Prague, 2 Feb 1773; d Pest, in or after 1821), Bohemian tenor, conductor and composer. After working as singer and cond. at theatres in Prague and Vienna, he was *Kapellmeister* to the Duke of Courland in Sagan 1797–9, then music director at the Silesian nat. theatre in Breslau (1799) and at the Leopold-städtertheater in Vienna (1806–9). Later he also worked in Budapest.

Works incl. operas and *Singspiele Dämona, Lanassa, Der Zauberkuss*, etc.; Masses and other church music; cantatas.

Tucker, Richard (b New York, 28 Apr 1914; d Kalamazoo, Mich., 8 Jan 1975), American tenor. Studied in NY with P. Althouse, making his debut at the NY Met in 1945, and remaining as its leading tenor; sang more than 600 perfs. in Fr. and It. rep. up to 1975. Eur. debut Verona, 1947, as Enzo; CG 1958 as Cavaradossi. He began his career in synagogues, and in 1973 sang Eléazar in *La Juive* (New Orleans).

Tucker, William (d London, 28 Feb 1679), English composer. Gentleman of the Chapel Royal in London, and minor canon and precentor of Westminster Abbey from 1660.

Works: services and anthems.

Tucket, a word found in stage directions of English plays of the Elizabethan period where the author asks for a fanfare to be played on or off the stage ('tucket within'). Another form is 'tuck'. A derivation from It. toccata seems unlikely since tuck and its variants are found in old Fr. and Middle Eng. before the early 17th-cent. It. tradition of tpt. fanfares called toccatas.

Tuckwell, Barry (Emmanuel) (b Melbourne, 5 Mar 1931), British horn player of Australian birth. He played with the Sydney SO before leaving for Britain in 1950. Prin., LSO, 1955; left in 1968 to pursue career as soloist and chamber music player. He formed his own quintet and has perf. with the London Sinfonietta; highly regarded in the standard rep. Thea Musgrave, Iain Hamilton and Don Banks are among comps. who have written works for him.

Tuczek-Ehrenburg, Leopoldine (b Vienna, 11 Nov 1821; d Baden nr. Vienna, 20 Oct 1883), Bohemian soprano. Pupil of Josephine Fröhlich at the Vienna Cons. and of It. masters. She appeared on the stage as a child and made her 1st important operatic appearance c 1840. In 1841–61 she was at the Berlin Court Opera.

Tuder, John (*fl.* 1466–96), English composer. Responsories, Lamentations and the hymn *Gloria, laus* are incl. in the Pepys MS. of c 1465 (Magdalene Coll., Cambridge), and there is a carol by him in the Fayrfax Book of c 1500.

Tudor, David (b Philadelphia, 20 Jan 1926), American pianist and composer. Studied pf. and comp. with S. Wolpe. Best known for his close assoc. with John Cage, much of whose music he perfs. or helps to realize. Gave the 1st US perf. of Boulez's 2nd pf. sonata (NY, 1950) and has been heard in works by Kagel and Bussotti.

Works (for var. electronics) incl. *Fluorescent Sound* (1964), *Bandoneon! Reunion, Rainforest* and *Fontana Mix* (in collaboration with Cage).

Tudway, Thomas (b ? Windsor, c 1650; d Cambridge, 23 Nov 1726), English composer and organist. Became chorister in the Chapel Royal in London soon after the Restoration (1660) and lay vicar at Windsor in 1664; app. organist at King's Coll., Cambridge, 1670, and prof. of music in the univ. there, 1705, in succession to Staggins. In 1714–20 he compiled a large collection of Eng. cathedral music in 6 vols.

Works incl. services, anthems.

Tulou, Jean-Louis (b Paris, 12 Sep 1786; d Nantes, 23 Jul 1865), French flautist and composer. 1st learnt music from his father, Jean Pierre T. (1749–99), a bassoonist, and studied at the Paris Cons. He played successively in the orchs. of the Théâtre Italien and the Opéra and in 1829 became fl. prof. at the Cons., leaving in 1856 to take up fl. manufacture.

Works incl. fl. concertos, fl. duets and trios, variations, fantasies and other pieces

for fl. and pf., test pieces for fl.

Tůma, František Ignác Antonín (b Kostelec nad Orlicí, 2 Oct 1704; d Vienna, 30 Jan 1774), Bohemian vla. da gamba player and composer. Came to Vienna by 1729, studied with Fux, was in the service of Count Kinsky 1731 (or earlier) to 1741, and *Kapellmeister* to the Dowager Empress Elisabeth Christina 1741–50. He retired to a monastery in 1768.

Works incl. numerous Masses, motets and other church music; inst. pieces.

Tunder, Franz (b Bannesdorf nr. Burg, Fehmarn, 1614; d Lübeck, 5 Nov 1667), German composer and organist. In 1632 he was app. court organist at Gottorf and in 1641 organist of St Mary's Church at Lübeck, where he prec. Buxtehude, who had to marry his daughter in order to secure the post. He greatly improved the church music and also instituted the 'Evening Music' (*Abendmusiken*) which soon became famous beyond the town.

Works incl. church cantatas, sacred arias with strings and organ; chorale variations for organ.

Tune, another word for Melody, more colloquial and therefore often considered vulgar. 'In tune' denotes accurate intonation, 'out of tune' the opposite. 'To tune' is to adjust the intonation of an instrument.

Tuning-Fork, a small and simple instrument in the form of a metal fork with 2 long prongs, invented by the trumpeter John Shore in 1711. It not only retains pitch accurately, but gives out a pure sound free from harmonic upper partials.

Tuotilo (or **Tutilo**) (d St Gall, 27 Apr 915), ? Swiss monk and musician at the monastery of St Gall. He comp. tropes, incl. (?) the Christmas trope *Hodie cantandus est nobis puer.*

Turanda, opera by Bazzini (lib. by A. Gazzoletti, based on Gozzi's play *Turandot*), prod. Milan, La Scala, 13 Jan 1867.

Turandot. *See also* Turanda.

Incid. music for Schiller's Ger. version of Gozzi's play by Weber, op. 37, comp. in 1809 and incl. the *Overtura cinese (Chin. Overture),* comp. on a Chin. theme in 1805.

Opera by Busoni (Ger. lib. by comp. based on Gozzi's play), prod. Zurich, 11 May 1917, together with another short opera *Arlecchino.* The music of *Turandot* was elaborated from incid. music for M. Reinhardt's prod. of K. Vollmöller's version of Gozzi's play, prod. Berlin, Deutsches Theater, 27 Oct 1911.

Opera by Puccini (It. lib. by G. Adami and R. Simoni, based on Gozzi's play), left unfinished by Puccini and completed by Alfano; prod. Milan, La Scala, 25 May 1926.

Turangalîla-symphonie, work for orch. in 10 movts. by Messiaen, with prominent parts for pf. solo and the ondes Martenot. Commissioned by Koussevitzky and comp. 1946–8; fp Boston, 2 Dec 1949, cond. Bernstein. The middle of a triptych of works inspired by the Tristan legend; the others are *Harawi* for sop. and pf. (1945) and *Cinq Rechants* for unaccomp. chorus. ('Turangalîla' is a compound Sanskrit word: *turanga* = time, rhythm, *lîla* = divine action.)

Turca (It. fem. = Turkish). The word is used in the combination *alla turca* (in the Turkish manner) by Mozart for the finale of the A maj. pf. sonata, K331, and by Beethoven for the *Marcia a.t.* in *The Ruins of Athens*, which is the theme of the pf. variations, op. 76.

Turco in Italia, Il (*The Turk in Italy*), opera by Rossini (lib. by F. Romani), prod. Milan, La Scala, 14 Aug 1814.

Tureck, Rosalyn (b Chicago, 14 Dec 1914), American pianist. Made her debut aged 11 with the Chicago SO and then studied with O. Samaroff at Juilliard, graduating in 1936. From 1943 she taught at the school, also becoming well known for her playing of Bach. Prof. at Juilliard from 1972.

Turges, Edmund (b *c* 1450), English composer. In 1469 he was admitted to a guild of parish clerks in London.

Works incl. a Magnificat (in the Eton Choirbook), *Gaude flore virginali* (2 settings); carols.

Turina, Joaquín (b Seville, 9 Dec 1882; d Madrid, 14 Jan 1949), Spanish composer. Studied at Seville and Madrid, later with d'Indy at the Schola Cantorum in Paris. He devoted much time to teaching as well as comp. and wrote a small treatise, *Enciclopedia abreviada de música*.

Works incl. operas *Margot* (1914) and *Jardin de oriente* (1923) (libs. by G. Martínez Sierra); incid. music for Moreto's *La adúltera penitente* (1917), Martínez Sierra's *Navidad* (1916) and other plays; *La procesión del Rocio* (1913), *Danzas fantásticas*, *Sinfonía sevillana* (1920), *Ritmos* and other works for orch.; string 4tet (1911), pf. 5tet (1907), *Escena andaluza* for vla., pf. and string 4tet; *Poema de una Sanluquena* for vln. and pf.; suites *Rincones sevillanos* and *Sevilla* and other works for pf.; songs.

Turini, Francesco (b Prague, *c* 1589; d Brescia, 1656), Italian composer. His father Gregorio T. was cornett player and comp. to the Emperor Rudolph II in Prague, but died early, whereupon the emperor sent Turini to Venice and Rome to study music and later made him his chamber organist. He left Prague in 1624 to become cathedral organist at Brescia.

Works incl. Masses and motets; madrigals, canons.

Türk, Daniel Gottlob (b Claussnitz nr. Chemnitz, 10 Aug 1750; d Halle, 26 Aug 1813), German theorist and composer. Studied under his father and under Homilius at Dresden. Later he went to Leipzig Univ., where he became a pupil and friend of J.A. Hiller, who procured him appts. as violinist at the Opera and the orch. concerts. In 1776 he became organist at St Ulrich's Church at Halle, in 1779 music director of the univ. and in 1787 organist at the church of Our Lady. He wrote treatises on organ, and clavier playing, thorough-bass and temperament.

Works incl. opera *Pyramus und Thisbe* (1784); cantata *Die Hirten bei der Krippe zu Bethlehem* (1782); pf. sonatas and pieces.

Turn. An ornament indicated by the sign ∾ and interpreted as follows:

TURN

Turn of the Screw, The, opera in a prologue and 2 acts by Britten (lib. by M. Piper, after Henry James), prod. Venice, 14 Sep 1954, and in London, 6 Oct 1954).

Turner, (Dame) **Eva** (b Oldham, 10 Mar. 1892), English soprano. Studied at the RAM and joined the Carl Rosa Opera chorus in 1916 and then appeared with them until 1924, singing Aida, Tosca and Butterfly. She then sang at La Scala, Milan, with Toscanini; roles incl. Freia and the *Trovatore* Leonora. She was well known as a dramatic singer in Verdi and Wagner; London, CG, 1920–48 as Sieglinde, Brünnhilde, Isolde and Amelia. One of her most famous roles was that of Puccini's Turandot. DBE 1962.

Turner, W(alter) J(ames) (Redfern) (b Shanghai, 13 Oct 1889; d London, 18 Nov 1946), English poet, novelist and music critic. Studied music with his father, became organist at Melbourne and later studied at Dresden, Munich and Vienna. He pub. books of misc. musical essays, works on Mozart, Beethoven, Berlioz and Wagner, *Eng. Music* for the *Britain in Pictures* series, ed. by him.

Turner, William (b Oxford, 1651; d London, 13 Jan 1740), English tenor and composer. Chorister at Christ Church, Oxford, and later in the Chapel Royal in London, where he joined Blow and Humfrey in comp. the so-called 'club anthem'. Later became singer successively at Lincoln Cathedral, St Paul's Cathedral and Westminster Abbey. Mus.D., Cambridge, 1696. The singer Ann T. (d 1741), wife of John Robinson, was his youngest daughter.

Works incl. services, anthems (1 for Queen Anne's coronation); masque *Presumptuous Love*; songs for Durfey's *A Fond Husband* (1677) and *Madam Fickle* (1676), Shadwell's *The Libertine* (1675), Settle's *Pastor fido* (1676) and other plays; catches, songs.

Turnhout, Gérard de (b Turnhout, *c* 1520; d Madrid, 15 Sep 1580), Flemish singer and composer. He became a church singer at Antwerp in 1545 and *maître de chapelle* of the cathedral in 1562. In 1571 he was called into the service of Philip II at Madrid.

Works incl. Masses and motets; *chansons*.

Turnhout, Jan-Jacob van (or Jean-Jacques de) (b ? Brussels, *c* 1545; d ? Brussels, after 1618), Flemish composer, brother or nephew of prec. He became *maître de chant* at St Rombaut, Malines, in 1577, and later at the viceregal court at Brussels. He pub. madrigals and sacred Lat. works.

Tusch (Ger.) = Fanfare. The word is prob. derived from French *touche* and is thus related to the English Tucket or tuck.

Tut, a device in lute-playing: the damping of a note by a finger not used for stopping.

Tutti (It. = all), a term used, in the 1st place, to designate the singing and playing together of all the forces engaged in a musical perf.; but it is also used for the purely orch. passages in a concerto, where the solo inst. is silent, whether the whole orch. happens to be playing or only part of it. Used as a noun, the word means any passage in an orch. work in which the whole force is employed, esp. when playing at full strength.

Tveitt (or Tveit), (Nils) Geirr (b Hardanger, 19 Oct 1908; d Oslo, 1 Feb 1981), Norwegian composer and pianist. After study in Vienna and Paris toured Eur. as pianist.

Works incl. operas *Dragaredokko, Roald Amundsen* and *Jeppe* (1964); 3 ballets; 6 pf. concertos (1930–60), concerto for string 4tet and orch. (1933), vln. concerto (1939), 2 harp concertos, 2 concertos for hardanger fiddle (*q.v.*), 4 symphs.; 2 string 4tets; 29 pf. sonatas.

Twelve-Note Music, the system of composition on which the later works of Schoenberg and the music of some of his disciples (e.g. Berg, Krenek, Pisk, Webern) are based, as well as that of many composers in var. countries. It abolishes keys and with them the predominance of certain notes in a scale (tonic, dominant, subdominant and mediant), using instead the 12 notes of the chromatic scale, each of which has exactly the same importance as any other. This rules out, in principle, any feeling of tonality, though in more recent twelve-note music tonal implications are often evident, and also discards the resource of modulation, so important to musical structure in the classical sense.

In order to make sure that no note assumes an even temporary predominance, the rule has been estab. that a 'series' must consist of all the 12 notes of the chromatic scale, and that each note must appear only once in its course (transposition into any 8ve being allowed); but this does not mean that all melodic patterns of twelve-note music are necessarily of the same length, for they may be given any rhythmic shape the comp. desires, and these shapes may be varied throughout a work, though the order of the notes, once determined at his desire, may not. Notes may, however, appear simultaneously as well as successively. Moreover, 3 ways of achieving melodic as distinct from

(Reproduced by permission of Edition Wilhelm Hansen AS, Copenhagen.)

Schoenberg, 'Waltz' from *5 Piano Pieces*, op. 23 (1923).

TWELVE-NOTE MUSIC

rhythmic or harmonic variety are open to the comp.: he may restate his theme (1) inverted (i.e. turned upside down), (2) in reverse or *cancrizans* (i.e. turned backwards) or (3) inverted and reversed at the same time.

In the years since 1945 the '12-note system' has found wide acceptance among comps. of the younger generation, and among already estab. figures Stravinsky was an oustanding convert, his later music being indebted to Webern. Although the techniques of Schoenberg and Webern have to a greater or lesser extent been superseded, their basic concepts are still recognized as one of the most practical and satisfying ways of organizing totally chromatic music. In addition, the sound world intro. by the Viennese comps., free from tonal ties, has resulted in a completely new attitude toward aural experience. The work of Schoenberg and his pupils has proved one of the great liberating forces in the history of music.

Among the comps. who have made use of the '12-note system' are Berio, Blacher, Boulez, Britten, Cage, Castiglioni, Dallapiccola, Davies (P.M.), Fortner, Goehr (A.), Hartmann, Haubenstock-Ramati, Henze, Kagel, Leibowitz, Ligeti, Lutosławski, Lutyens, Maderna, Martin, Messiaen, Nigg, Nono, Pousseur, Searle, Seiber, Stockhausen, Stravinsky, Xenakis.

Twilight of the Gods, The (Wagner). *See* **Ring des Nibelungen.**

Two Widows (*Dvě Vdovy*), opera by Smetana (lib. by E. Züngel, based on a Fr. comedy by P.J.F. Mallefille), prod. Prague, Cz. Theatre, 27 Mar 1874.

Tye, Christopher (b *c* 1505; d ? 1572), English composer and poet. He became a lay-clerk at King's Coll., Cambridge, in 1537. In 1543 he was app. choir-master at Ely Cathedral and in 1545 he took the Mus.D. at Cambridge. He may have been music master to Edward VI in 1544–50, and he was made a Gentleman of the Chapel Royal. In 1561 he resigned his post at Ely and was succeeded by R. White. Having been ordained, he accepted the living at Doddington-cum-Marche in the Isle of Ely, and for some time later held 2 other livings in the neighbourhood; but he had to resign them, on account of carelessness in the matter of payments due. He wrote a good deal of verse in his later years.

Works incl. Masses (e.g. *Euge bone* and *Western Wind*), motets, services, anthems, *The Actes of the Apostles* in Eng. metrical versions set for 4 voices (1533, ded. to Edward VI); In Nomines for instruments.

Tyes, J. (*fl. c* 1400), English composer. 2 pieces are preserved in the Old Hall MS.

Typp(e), William (*fl. c* 1410), English composer. He was precentor of Fotheringhay Coll., Northants., in 1438. 7 pieces are in the Old Hall MS., incl. an isorhythmic Credo.

Tyrolienne (Fr. fem. = Tyrolese), a country dance similar to the *Ländler* or slow waltz, supposed to be native of the mountain regions of the Tyrol, but really an artificial growth intro. into ballets and operas and loosely based on melodic figurations imitating var. forms of Yodel. Tyroliennes also became fashionable in the form of pf. pieces and songs, etc.

Tyrwhitt, Gerald. *See* **Berners, Lord.**

Tzigane (Fr., or *tsigane*), a gypsy or musician of the bohemian world of Paris. The title of a rhapsody for vln. and pf. by Ravel comp. in 1924; fp London, 26 Apr 1924, with Jelly d'Aranyi (*q.v.*).

U

U. C. An abbr. occasionally used for *una corda* (one string), indicating the use of the damping Pedal in pf. music.

Überbrettl, Das. *See* **Wolzogen, E.**

Uberti, Antonio (b Verona, 1697; d Berlin, 20 Jan 1783), Italian castrato of German origin. Pupil of Porpora and known as Porporino. He sang in It. opera in Ger. and became chamber singer to Frederick II of Prus. Among his pupils was Mara.

Uccellatori, Gli (*The Birdcatchers*), opera by Gassmann (lib. by Goldoni), prod. Venice, Teatro San Moisè, Carnival 1759.

Uccellini, Marco (b *c* 1603; d Forlimpopoli, 10 Sep 1680), Italian composer and violinist. Master of inst. music at the ducal court of Modena from 1641 to 1662 and *maestro di cappella* at Modena Cathedral from 1647 to 1665, after which he held that post at the Farnese Court at Parma.

Works incl. opera *Gli eventi di Filandro ed Edessa* (1675); ballets *La nave d'Enea* (1673) and *Giove di Elide fulminato* (1677); psalms and litanies for voices and insts.; *Composizioni armoniche* and *Sinfonici concerti* for vln. and other insts., *Sinfonie boscareocie* and sonatas for vln. and bass.

Uchida, Mitsuko (b Tokyo, 20 Dec 1948), Japanese pianist. She studied in Tokyo and in Vienna, where she won the Beethoven Competition in 1968. Prize-winner in Chopin International, Warsaw, 1969. In 1982 she gave a cycle of the complete Mozart sonatas in London and Tokyo; much success 1985–6 with the ECO in London as director–soloist in the complete Mozart concertos. Has appeared with the Berlin PO, Boston SO and Chicago SO. Esteemed in Bartók.

Ugarte, Floro M(anuel) (b Buenos Aires, 15 Sep 1884; d Buenos Aires, 11 Jun 1975), Argentine composer. Studied with Fourdrain in Paris and became a private music teacher on his return in 1913 and prof. at the Nat. Cons. at Buenos Aires in 1924. He also became music director of the Teatro Colón, resigning in 1943.

Works incl. opera *Saika* (1918) and others; symph. poems and suites for orch.; inst. pieces.

Ugolini, Vincenzo (b Perugia, *c* 1580; d Rome, 6 May 1638), Italian composer. Pupil of Bernardino Nassini. *Maestro di cappella*

at the church of Santa Maria Maggiore in Rome, 1603–9. He then retired after a severe illness, but in 1610 became *maestro di cappella* at Benevento Cathedral and returned in 1616 to Rome, where after some other appts. he became Soriano's successor in the Julian Chapel in 1620 and *maestro di cappella* of San Luigi dei Francesi in 1631, a post he had held 1616–20.

Works incl. Masses, motets, psalms and other church music, madrigals.

Ugolino of Orvieto (b ? Orvieto, *c* 1380; d Ferrara, 1457), Italian composer and theorist. His *Declaratio musicae disciplinae* (1435) is mainly a practical handbook for the perf. musician of his day.

Uhde, Hermann (b Bremen, 20 Jul 1914; d Copenhagen, 10 Oct 1965), German bassbaritone. He sang in Bremen and Freiburg before the war and in The Hague and Munich 1940–44. Prisoner-of-war 1944–7, after which he sang in Hamburg, Vienna and again Munich (1951–60). Bayreuth 1951–7 as Gunther, Klingsor, the Dutchman and Wotan. London, CG, 1953, as Mandryka, and 1954–60 in operas by Wagner and Offenbach. NY Met 1955–64 (debut as Telramund). He collapsed and died during a perf. of Niels Bentzon's *Faust III*. Other roles incl. Wozzeck and Creon in *Antigonae* (fp Salzburg, 1949).

Uhl, Fritz (b Vienna-Matzleinsdorf, 2 Apr 1928), Austrian tenor. He sang first in operetta; opera debut Graz, 1950. Sang widely on the Continent and was a member of the Munich opera from 1957. Bayreuth 1957–64 as Siegmund, Erik and Loge. He sang the title role in Solti's recording of *Tristan* (1960) and Walther at CG in 1962.

Uhland, Johann Ludwig (1787–1862), German poet. *See* **Black Knight** (Elgar), **Humperdinck** (*Glück von Edenhall*), **Schoeck** (songs), **Schumann** (*Glück von E.*), **Strauss (R.)** (*Schloss am Meer*).

Uhlig, Theodor (b Wurzen nr. Leipzig, 15 Feb 1822; d Dresden, 3 Jan 1853), German violinist, author and composer of theoretical works. Pupil of Schneider at Dessau. He entered the royal orch. at Dresden in 1841 and became an intimate friend of Wagner there; published articles in Wagner's praise and had an extensive correspondence with him.

Ukelele (lit. 'the jumping flea'), a small Hawaiian guitar, introduced to the Sandwich Islands by the Portuguese in 1877 and more recently into Europe as a popular instrument. It has 4 gut strings and can be played from a notation resembling lute tablature.

'Ukrainian' Symphony (Tchaikovsky). *See* 'Little Russian' Symphony.

Ulfung, Ragnar (Sigurd) (b Oslo, 28 Feb 1927), Norwegian tenor. Stage debut Oslo, 1951, in Menotti's *The Consul*. Royal Opera, Stockholm, from 1958; sang in the fp of Blomdahl's *Aniara* and visited CG with the co. in 1960. He created the title role in Maxwell Davies's *Taverner* (1972) and returned to CG as Mime in Friedrich's prod. of *The Ring*. US debut San Francisco, 1967; NY Met 1972, as Mime. Other roles incl. Tom Rakewell, Don Carlos, Alfredo and Cavaradossi. Also active in concert and oratorio.

Ulïbïshev, Alexander Dimitrievich (b Dresden, 13 Jan 1794; d Lukino nr. Nizhny-Novgorod, 8 Feb 1858), Russian writer on music and amateur musician. As the son of a nobleman he served in the army and then lived in retirement on his estate. He was a good violinist and 4tet player. He made a special study of Mozart and pub. a work in 3 vols. on him (Moscow, 1843), but disliked the late works of Beethoven and attacked Lenz's book on that composer.

Ulisse, opera by Dallapiccola (lib. by comp., after Homer); comp. 1959–68, prod. Berlin, Deutsche Oper, 29 Sep 1968, cond. Maazel. BBC, studio perf., 20 Sep 1969.

Ullmann, Viktor (b Prague, 1 Jan 1898; d ? Auschwitz, ? 1944), Sudeten-German composer. Pupil of Schoenberg in Vienna, later theatre cond. at Aussig and music teacher in Prague. In Theresienstadt concentration camp he wrote a one-act opera, *Der Kaiser von Atlantis*, about a tyrannical monarch who outlaws death (fp Amsterdam, 16 Dec 1975). He was transferred to Auschwitz on 16 Oct 1944.

Works incl. operas *Peer Gynt* (after Ibsen), *Der Sturz des Antichrist* and *Der Kaiser von Atlantis* (1943); variations and double fugue on a theme by Schoenberg for orch.; 8tet, 2 string 4tets.

Ultimo giorno di Pompei, L' (*The Last Day of Pompeii*), opera by Pacini (lib. by Tottola, not founded on Bulwer-Lytton's novel, which was not then pub.), prod. Naples, Teatro San Carlo, 19 Nov 1825.

Ultimos Ritos (*Last Rites*), oratorio by Tavener for soloists, 5 speakers, chorus and orch.; comp. 1972, fp Haarlem, 22 Jun 1974.

Ulysses (*see also* Circe and Penelope), opera by Keiser (lib. by F.M. Lersner), prod. (in Ger.) Copenhagen, at court, Nov 1722.

Cantata by Seiber for tenor, chorus and orch. (text by comp., after Joyce); 1946–7, fp London, 27 May 1949.

Umbreit, Karl Gottlieb (b Rehstadt nr. Gotha, 9 Jan 1763; d Rehstadt, 28 Apr 1829), German organist and composer. Pupil of Kittel. He was app. organist at Sonneborn, Coburg, and became a famous org. teacher.

Works incl. chorales, chorale preludes, preludes and fugues, etc. for org.

Umlauf(f), Ignaz (b Vienna, 1746; d Vienna, 8 Jun 1796), Austrian composer. He became a vla. player in the orch. of the court opera in 1772, and on the foundation of the nat. *Singspiel* theatre by Joseph II in 1778 became its director, the inaugural work being his *Die Bergknappen*. From 1789 he was Salieri's deputy as *Kapellmeister* of the court chapel. He also took part with Mozart in the perfs. of Handel's oratorios organized by Gottfried van Swieten.

Works incl. *Singspiele Die Insel der Liebe* (1722), *Die Bergknappen* (1778), *Die Apotheke, Die schöne Schusterin oder die pucegefarbenen Schuhe* (1779), *Das Irrlicht* (1782), *Welches ist die beste Nation?*, *Die glücklichen Jäger* (1786), *Die Ringe der Liebe* (sequel to Grétry's *Zémire et Azor*); incid. music for *Der Oberamtmann und die Soldaten* (after Calderón); church music.

Umlauf(f), Michael (b Vienna, 9 Aug 1781; d Baden nr. Vienna, 20 Jun 1842), Austrian composer and conductor, son of prec. Pupil of his father, became a violinist at the Opera and was cond. of the 2 court theatres in 1810–25 and again from 1840. On and after the revival of *Fidelio* in 1814 he asst. Beethoven, who was then too deaf to hear the orch., to conduct some of his major works.

Works incl. opera *Das Wirtshaus in Granada* (1812), play with music *Der Grenadier* (1812); 12 ballets; church music; pf. sonatas.

Un ballo in maschera (Verdi). *See* **Ballo in maschera**, *also* **Gustave III** (Auber).

Un giorno di regno (Verdi). *See* **Giorno di regno**.

Un poco (It. = a little), a qualifying direction used where any indication of tempo or expression is to be applied in moderation. Often used in the abbr. form *poco*.

Una corda (It. = one string), a direction used by Beethoven and others in pf. music to indicate the use of the Damping Pedal, which so shifts the hammers that they touch only a single string for each note, instead of 2 or 3.

Una cosa rara, o sia Bellezza ed onestà (*A Rare Thing, or Beauty and Honesty*), opera by Martín y Soler (lib. by L. da Ponte, based on a story by L.V. de Guevara), prod. Vienna, Burgtheater, 17 Nov 1786. Mozart quotes an air from it in the finale óf the 2nd act of *Don Giovanni*.

Undina, opera by Lvov (lib., in Rus., by Count V.A. Sollogub based on a Fr. lib. *La Marquise*, by J.H.V. de Saint-Georges), prod. St Petersburg, 20 Sep 1848.

Undine, opera by Karl Friedrich Girschner (1794–1860) (lib by F. de la Motte Fouqué, based on his own story of that name), prod. Danzig, 20 Apr 1837.

Opera by E.T.A. Hoffmann (lib. do.), prod. Berlin, Schauspielhaus, 3 Aug 1816.

Opera by Lortzing (lib. by comp., based on Fouqué), prod. Magdeburg, 21 Apr 1845.

Ballet in 3 acts by Henze (choreog. by Ashton); comp. 1956–7, prod. London, CG, 27 Oct 1958, cond. Henze, with Fonteyn. *Wedding Music* from the ballet arr. for wind orch. 1957; 2 orch. suites 1958; *Undine, Trois pas des Tritons* for orch. perf. Rome, 10 Jan 1959, cond. Celibidache.

Unequal Temperament, a system of tuning, esp. on old keyboard instruments, in which some of the accidentals were treated as sharps according to Just Intonation and some as flats (e.g. F♯, not G♭; B♭, not A♯). An attempt was thus made to make some of the more frequently used keys come nearer to just intonation than is possible in the tempered scale of the modern pf., but the result was also that the more extreme sharp and flat keys were out of tune. This is one of the reasons why these keys were rarely used by early comps.

Unequal Voices. A comp. for several voices which do not lie within the same compass is said to be for unequal voices.

Unfinished Symphony. Schubert's 'Unfinished' Symphony, in B minor, written Oct/Nov 1822, was planned as a 4-movt. work, though only the 1st 2 movts., and a sketch of the Scherzo, survive. Some authorities, however, believe that the Finale was used a year later as the basis of the B minor Entr'acte in *Rosamunde*. After the Styrian Music Society, through Josef and Anselm Hüttenbrenner, had awarded Schubert their Diploma of Honour in 1823, he promised to send in return 'one of my symphonies at the earliest opportunity'. Later he handed to Josef the score of the two completed movts. Anselm Hüttenbrenner made an arr. of the work for pf. duet in 1853, but made no attempt to get it perf. Johann Herbeck, who gave the fp in Vienna in Dec 1865, coaxed the score out of Anselm with a promise to perf. one of the latter's own works. Schubert was the 1st comp. to associate a tragic tone

and intense personal feeling with B minor in a substantial symphonic work; in this the 'Unfinished' looks forward to late Romantic works such as Tchaikovsky's 'Pathetic' Symph. and Dvořák's Cello Concerto. In the original *Gesamtausgabe* it is called no. 8, but is more often referred to simply as the 'Unfinished'.

Unger, Caroline (b Székesfehérvár, Hung., 28 Oct 1803; d nr. Florence, 23 Mar 1877), Austrian contralto. Pupil of Aloysia Lange, Mozart's sister-in-law, and Vogl in Vienna, where she made her debut in 1824. She sang the contralto part, with Sontag as soprano, in the fp of Beethoven's *Choral* symph. (1824); at the end of the perf. she turned the comp. towards the audience to see the applause he could not hear. Later she sang in It. and Paris; Donizetti wrote *Parisina* and *Maria di Rudenz* for her. She created the title role in Bellini's *La Straniera* (1829). In 1840 she married François Sabatier. She retired in 1843.

Unger, Georg (b Leipzig, 6 Mar 1837; d Leipzig, 2 Feb 1887), German tenor. Studied theol. at first, but took to singing and made his 1st stage appearance at Leipzig in 1867. He was Wagner's 1st Siegfried in the prod. of *The Ring* at Bayreuth in 1876.

Unger, Gerhard (b Bad Salzungen, Thuringia, 26 Nov 1916), German tenor. From 1947 he sang in Weimar and Dresden as Tamino, Alfredo and Pinkerton. Appeared at the Berlin Deutsche Oper from 1952, moved to Stuttgart in 1961; Hamburg 1962–73. He was best known as Pedrillo (recorded under Beecham) and David, which he sang in Kempe's recording of *Meistersinger*. Well known at Bayreuth, Salzburg, Vienna and in N. America; much admired as Mime, and at the end of his career in operas by Berg, Britten and Janáček.

Unger, (Gustav) Hermann (b Kamenz, Saxony, 26 Oct 1886; d Cologne, 31 Dec 1958), German composer. Studied in Munich and later with Reger at Meiningen. Taught for more than 30 years in Cologne. He wrote books on Reger and Bruckner and a treatise on harmony (1946).

Works incl. opera *Richmondis* (1928) and *Der Zauberhandschuh*; incid. music for Shakespeare's *Tempest*, Kleist's *Penthesilea*, Hofmannsthal's *Der Tor und der Tod*, Hauptmann's *Hannele*, Unruh's *Heinrich aus Andernach* and many other plays; *Der Gott und die Bajadere* (Goethe) and *Old Ger. Songs* for chorus and orch.; 2 symphs.; chamber music; songs.

Universal Edition. Publishing house

founded in Vienna, 1901. *See* **Hertzka** and **Kalmus.**

Unterbrochene Opferfest, Das (*The Interrupted Sacrificial Feast*), opera by Winter (lib. by F.X. Huber), prod. Vienna, Kärntnertortheater, 14 Jun 1796.

Up Bow, the motion of the bow in the playing of string instruments in the direction from the point to the heel.

Upbeat, an unstressed note or group of notes beginning a comp., or phrase, and standing before the 1st bar-line, which indicates the 1st main accent. The word derives from the act of beating time in cond., where opening notes before the bar-line are indicated by an upward motion.

Uppman, Theodore (b Pao Alto, Calif., 12 Jan 1920), American baritone. Studied at Curtis Inst. and sang Papageno at Stanford Univ. 1946. He created Billy Budd (CG 1951) and sang Pelléas at the NY Met in 1953. Also sang in fps of operas by Floyd, Villa-Lobos and Pasatieri.

Urbani, Peter (b Milan, 1749; d Dublin, Dec 1816), Italian singer, publisher and composer. After a period in London he went to Glasgow in 1780 and to Edinburgh in 1784, singing Scot. songs and later pub. them with his own accomps., with words by Burns, with whom he made friends, and others. Towards the end of the cent. he became a music-seller and pub., but *c* 1810 he failed and went to Dublin, where he died in poverty.

Works incl. operas *Il Farnace* (1784), *Il trionfo di Clelia* (1785) and others; Scot. songs with accomps.

Urbani, Valentino. *See* **Valentini.**

Urhan, Chrétien (b Montjoie nr. Aix-la-Chapelle, 16 Feb 1790; d Belleville nr. Paris, 2 Nov 1845), Belgian violinist, violist and composer. Learnt the vln. from his father, was heard by the Empress Joséphine and sent by her to Paris with a recommendation to Lesueur. He joined the Opéra orch. in 1814, becoming leader in 1823 and solo vln. in 1836. He played much in public, incl. the vla. and vla. d'amore, also in chamber music. He gave early Fr. perfs. of Bach, Schubert and Beethoven.

Works incl. 2 string 5tets, 2 5tets for 3 vlas., cello and double bass (with drums *ad lib.*) and other chamber music; vln. and pf. pieces; pf. works, incl. duets; songs and duets.

Uribe Holguín, Guillermo (b Bogotá, 17 Mar 1880; d Bogotá, 26 Jun 1971), Colombian composer. Studied at home and with d'Indy at the Schola Cantorum in Paris. In 1910 he became director of the Nat. Cons. at Bogotá, where he founded and cond. symph. concerts.

Works incl. Requiem; 11 symphs. (1916–59), 3 *Danzas*, *Carnavelesca*, *Marche funèbre*, *Marche de fête*, *Suite tipica*, all for orch.; concert and *Villanesca* for pf. and orch., 2 vln. concertos; 10 string 4tets, pf. 4tet, 2pf. 5tets; 5 vln. and pf. sonatas, 2 cello and pf. sonatas; pf. pieces, incl. 300 folk dances; songs.

Urio, Francesco Antonio (b Milan, *c* 1632; d Milan, 1719 or later), Italian priest and composer. A Franciscan monk, he was *maestro di cappella* at SS. Apostoli in Rome in 1690, seven years later at the Frari church in Venice, and finally from 1715 at S. Francesco in Milan.

Works incl. Te Deum (once attrib. to Handel, who borrowed from it for his *Dettingen Te Deum*, *Saul*, *Israel in Egypt* and *L'Allegro*); oratorios; motets and psalms for voices and insts.

Urlus, Jacques (b Hergenrath, 9 Jan 1867; d Noordwijk-aan-Zee, 6 Jun 1935), Dutch tenor. Studied at the Amsterdam Cons. and made his debut at Utrecht in 1887. He then studied opera and made his stage debut there in 1894. Becoming a Wagnerian singer, he was soon invited to Bayreuth (1911–12, Siegmund). In 1910 he 1st visited London (Tristan, under Beecham). Well known as a concert singer, especially in Mahler. He pub. his autobiog. in 1930.

Ursuleac, Viorica (b Czernowitz, 26 Mar 1894; d Ehrwald, Tyrol, 22 Oct 1985), Rumanian soprano. She studied in Berlin with Lilli Lehmann; debut Zagreb, 1922, as Charlotte. She sang in Frankfurt 1926–30, under her husband Clemens Krauss. In 1928 she took part in the Wiesbaden fp of Krenek's opera *Der Diktator*. Best known in Strauss, she created Arabella (Dresden, 1933), Maria in *Friedenstag* (Munich, 1938) and the Countess in *Capriccio* (Munich, 1942). In the 1930s she sang at the State Opera houses of Vienna and Berlin; Munich during the war. London, CG, 1934 as Desdemona. Other roles incl. Ariadne, the Empress, Sieglinde and Tosca.

Usiglio, Emilio (b Parma, 8 Jan 1841; d Milan, 7 or 8 Jul 1910), Italian composer and conductor. He cond. operas by Boito, Thomas and Bizet, but in 1874 had to abandon a perf. of *Aida* when he became too drunk to continue.

Works incl. operas *Le educande di Sorrento* (1868), *Le donne curiose* (after Goldoni, 1879) and 6 others; many ballets; chamber music.

Usper, Francesco (real name Spongia, Sponga or Sponza) (b Parenzo, before 1570; d Venice, 1641), Italian priest, organist and composer. In 1614 he became organist at the church of San Salvatore at Venice, in 1621 he deputized for Grillo as organist at St Mark's and in 1627 he became principal of the school of St John the Evangelist.

Works incl. Masses, motets, psalms, for voices with insts., vesper psalms for 4–8 voices and bass, some for double choir; *La battaglia* for voices and insts., madrigals; *ricercari* and *arie francesi* in 4 parts.

Ussachevsky, Vladimir (Alexis) (b Hailar, Manchuria, 3 Nov 1911), American composer of Russian parentage. Moved to US in 1930 and studied with Hanson at the Eastman School. Prof., Columbia Univ., NY, 1964–80. Collaborated with Luening in pioneering elec. music activities.

Works incl. (some with Luening) *Sonic Contours* for tape (1952), *Incantation* for tape (1953), *Rhapsodic Variations* for orch. and tape (1954), *Creation Prologue* for 4 chorus and tape (1961), *Missa brevis* for sop., chorus and brass (1972), *Celebration* for string orch. and electronic valve insts. (1980).

Ut, the old name for the note C, still used in France, but elsewhere replaced by Do. For its origin *see* **Solmization.**

Utendal, Alexander (b *c* 1535; d Innsbruck, 7 May 1581), Flemish composer. Learnt music as a choir-boy in the Archduke Ferdinand's chapel in Prague, and in 1566 became a singer in his chapel at Innsbruck. In *c* 1572 he became 2nd *Kapellmeister*. On the death of Scandello at Dresden in 1580 he was offered the post of *Kapellmeister* to the Saxon court, but declined it.

Works incl. 3 Masses, motets, *Sacrae cantiones*; secular Fr. and Ger. songs.

Uthal, opera by Méhul (lib. by J.M.B.B. de Saint-Victor, based on Ossian), prod. Paris, Opéra-Comique, 17 May 1806. The work is scored without vlns.

Utopia (Limited), or The Flowers of Progress, operetta by Sullivan (lib. by W.S. Gilbert), prod. London, Savoy Theatre, 7 Oct 1893.

Utrecht Te Deum and Jubilate, work by Handel, comp. for the celebration of the Peace of Utrecht and perf. London, St Paul's Cathedral, 7 Jul 1713.

Utrenja (*Morning Service*), work in 2 parts by Penderecki, for soloists, choruses and orch.: 1. *The Entombment of Christ* (fp Altenberg Cathedral, 8 Apr 1970); 2. *Resurrection of Christ* (fp Munster Cathedral, 28 May 1971).

Uttini, Francesco Antoni Baldassare (b Bologna, 1723; d Stockholm, 25 Oct 1795), Italian singer and composer. Pupil of Perti and Padre Martini in Bologna, he was elected a member of the Phil. Acad. there in 1743 and became president in 1751. As cond. of the Mingotti opera troupe he travelled to (?) Madrid and Copenhagen (1753–4), and in 1755 settled in Stockholm, becoming musical director to the court in 1767. He visited London the following year.

Works incl. 13 It. (texts by Metastasio) and 5 Fr. operas, Swed. operas *Thetis och Pelée* (1773) and *Aline* (1776) (all mostly lost); trio sonatas; harpsichord sonatas.

V

V.S. (abbr.) = *volti subito* (It. = turn at once). This is often written at the foot of a right-hand page in MS. music as an indication that a quick turn is necessary in order to be ready for what follows on the next page.

Vaccai, Nicola (b Tolentino, 15 Mar 1790; d Pesaro, 5 or 6 Aug 1848), Italian composer. He went to school at Pesaro, then studied law in Rome, but at the age of 17 or 18 gave it up for music and studied counterpoint with Jannaconi. In 1811 he studied with Paisiello at Naples and in 1815 prod. his 1st opera there. He then lived at Venice for 7 years, prod. 2 operas there, afterwards taught singing at Trieste and Vienna, in 1824 prod. 2 operas at Parma and Turin and in 1825 had his greatest success, at Milan, with a work on Shakespeare's *Romeo and Juliet*. In 1829–31 he lived in Paris and afterwards briefly in London, which he visited again in 1833–4. In 1838 he succeeded Basili as director of the Milan Cons., retiring to Pesaro in 1844.

Works incl. operas *I solitari di Scozia* (1815), *Pietro il grande* (1824), *La pastorella feudataria*, *Giulietta e Romeo* (1825), *Marco Visconti* (1838), *Giovanna Grey* (1836), *Virginia*, *Giovanna d'Arco* (1827), *La sposa di Messina* (both after Schiller) and others; church music; cantata on the death of Malibran and others; *Ariette per camera* for voice and pf.

Vaccari, Francesco (b Modena, 1773; d Lisbon, after 1823), Italian violinist. Pupil of Nardini at Florence. He soon began to play with great success all over It., then went to Spain, and later appeared in Paris, Ger., London, Spain and Port. Wrote vln. music, incl. vars. on 'God save the King'.

Vachon, Pierre (b Arles, June 1731; d Berlin 7 Oct 1803), French violinist and composer. Studied in Paris, where he appeared at the Concert Spirituel from 1756. Principal violinist in the orch. of the Prince of Conti 1761, he visited Eng. in 1772 and *c* 1775, and later settled in Berlin, where he was app. *Konzertmeister* to the court in 1786.

Works incl. operas *Les Femmes et le secret* (1767), *Sara, ou La Fermière écossaise* (1773), *Hippomène et Atalante* (1769), *Ésope à Cythère* (1766), *Renaud d'Ast* (both with J.C. Trial); vln. concertos; chamber music; sonatas for vln. and bass.

Vacqueras. *See* **Vaqueras.**

Vaet, Jacobus (b Courtrai or Harelbeke, 1529; d Vienna, 8 Jan 1567), Flemish composer. He was choirmaster to Maximilian, King of Boh., in the 1560s and in 1564 became chief music director in Vienna, a post formerly held by Jachet Buus, when his patron became the Emperor Maximilian II.

Works incl. Masses, motets, Magnificats, Te Deum for 8 voices and other church music; *chansons*.

Vagans (Lat. = wandering, vagrant), the name sometimes given in 5-part 15th- and 16th-cent. polyphonic music to the fifth part, which duplicates in range one of the basic 4 voices: treble, alto, tenor and bass. The voice required within one quintus partbook, though usually a second tenor, may vary from piece to piece; whence 'vagans'.

Vagrant Chord, a term coined by Schoenberg (as *vagierender Akkord*) to describe chromatic chords which confuse or lead away from any definite key-centre.

Vaisseau-fantôme, Le (*The Phantom Vessel*), opera by Dietsch (lib. by B.H. Révoil and P.H. Foucher, founded on Wagner's scenario for *The Flying Dutchman*, intended for an opera of his own to be prod. at the Opéra, which however accepted the lib. only and had it set by Dietsch), prod. Paris, Opéra, 9 Nov 1842.

Vakula the Smith (*Vakula Kuznets*), opera by Tchaikovsky (lib. by Y.P. Polonsky, based on Gogol's *Christmas Eve*), prod. St Petersburg, 6 Dec 1876; rev. version entitled *Tcherevitchki (The Little Shoes)*, prod. Moscow, 31 Jan 1887. It is also known as *Oxana's Caprices*.

Valdengo, Giuseppe (b Turin, 24 May 1914), Italian baritone. Studied in Turin, making his debut in Parma in 1936. He is best known for his recorded perfs. of Verdi's Iago (1947) and Falstaff (1950) under Toscanini; also recorded Amonasro (1949). Glyndebourne 1955, Don Giovanni and Raimbaud.

Valen, (Olav) Fartein (b Stavanger, 25 Aug 1887; d Haugesund, 14 Dec 1952), Norwegian composer. Studied languages at Oslo Univ., but later entered the Cons., finishing his studies with Reger at the Hochschule für Musik in Berlin. In 1925–35 he was in the music dept. of the library of Oslo Univ., but was then made the recipient of a government grant for comp.

Works incl. 3 sets of motets and other choral works; 5 symphs. (1937–51), *Sonetto di Michelangelo*, To Hope (after Keats), *Pastorale*, *Epithalamion*, *Le Cimetière marin* (after P. Valéry), *La isla en las calmas*, Ode *to Solitude* for orch.; pf. concerto, vln. concerto (1940); 6 works for soprano and orch.; 2 string 4tets (1928–31), pf. trio, serenade for 5 wind insts.; vln. and pf. sonata; 2 sonatas, vars. and other works for pf.; org. music; songs.

Valente, Antonio (*fl.* 1565–80), Italian composer, active in Naples. Blind from his youth, he was organist of S. Angelo a Nilo from 1565 to 1580. He pub. 2 collections of keyboard music (1576 and 1580).

Valentini (Valentino Urbani) (*fl.* 1690–1719), Italian alto castrato. 1st went to London in 1707. He sang in pasticcios and in the fps of Handel's *Rinaldo, Il pastor fido* and *Teseo.*

Valentini, Giovanni (b Venice, *c* 1583; d Vienna, 29 or 30 Apr 1649), Italian organist and composer. In 1614 he was organist to the Archduke Ferdinand at Graz, and on his patron's succession to the title of Emperor Ferdinand II in 1619 remained in his service, becoming *Kapellmeister* in 1629 and continuing in this employment under Ferdinand III. His church music is highly ornate for its time.

Works incl. Masses, motets and other church music; madrigals, *Musiche a 2 voci.*

Valentini, Giuseppe (b Florence, *c* 1680; d ? Paris, after 1759), Italian composer. In the service of the Grand Duke of Tuscany at Florence from *c* 1735.

Works incl. opera *La costanza in amore* (1715); oratorios *Absalone* (1705) and *S. Alessio* (1733); Concerti grossi; symphs., *Bizarrie*, 12 fantasies, *Idee per camera* and 12 sonatas for 3 string insts. and bass; chamber sonatas and *Alletamenti* for vln., cello and bass.

Valentini, Pier Francesco (b Rome, *c* 1570; d Rome, 1654), Italian composer. Pupil of G.M. Nanini in Rome.

Works incl. operas (*favole*) *La mitra* (1620) and *La transformazione di Dafne* (1623); motets, litanies and other church music; *Canzonetti spirituali* and *Musiche spirituali* for the Nativity; madrigals and canons; *canzoni* and arias for 1–2 voices.

Valentini–Terrani, Lucia (b Padua, 28 Aug 1948), Italian mezzo. Debut Brescia, 1969, as Cenerentola. NY Met debut 1974, as Rossini's Isabella. Guest appearances in Milan, Paris and Vienna. In 1987 she sang Rosina at CG.

Valenzuela, Pedro (*fl.* 1569–79), Spanish composer. He lived in It., was cantor at St Mark's, Venice, and cond. to the Phil. Acad. at Verona.

Works incl. madrigals.

Valeriano (Valeriano Pellegrini), Italian countertenor. He sang in Düsseldorf 1705–16, and took part in the fp of Steffani's *Tassilone* there. Sang in the fp of Handel's *Agrippina* (Rome, 1709). He was in Eng. 1712–13 and sang in the fps of Handel's *Il pastor fido* and *Teseo.*

Valesi, Giovanni (real name Johann Evangelist Walleshauser) (b Unterhattenhofen, Bavaria, 28 Apr 1735; d Munich, 10 Jan 1816), German tenor. Chamber singer to the Elector of Bavaria from 1756, later studied in It. and sang there with success. At Munich he sang in the fps of Mozart's *La finta giardiniera* (1775) and *Idomeneo* (1781). Weber was his pupil for a short time in 1798.

Valkyrie, The (*Die Walküre*, Wagner). *See* **Ring des Nibelungen.**

Valledor y la Calle, Jacinto (b Madrid, 1744; d Madrid, *c* 1809), Spanish composer. Settled in Madrid and wrote *tonadillas* and other works for the stage, incl. *La decantada vida y muerte del General Mambrú* (1785).

Valletti, Cesare (b Rome, 18 Dec 1922), Italian tenor. He made his debut at Bari in 1947, as Alfredo; wider recognition came in 1950: *Il Turco in Italia* in Rome and Fenton at CG. At La Scala he was heard as Lindoro, Nemorino and Almaviva. US debut San Francisco, 1953, as Werther. NY Met 1953–62 as Ottavio, Ferrando and Ernesto. Retired 1968.

Vallin, Ninon (b Montalieu-Vercieu, 8 Sep 1886; d Lyons, 22 Nov 1961), French soprano. Studied at Lyons Cons. Sang in fp of Debussy's *Le Martyre de Saint Sébastien* (1911). Opéra Comique 1912–16; Buenos Aires 1916–36, as Manon, Thaïs, Mélisande and Alceste. After the war sang in Paris as Mozart's Countess. Also heard in operas by Falla and Respighi and in the songs of Fauré and Chausson.

Vallotti, Francesco Antonio (b Vercelli, 11 Jun 1697; d Padua, 10 Jan 1780), Italian composer and theorist. He became 3rd organist at the basilica of Sant' Antonio at Padua in 1722 and *maestro* in 1730. He wrote a learned treatise, *Della scienza teorica e pratica della moderna musica.*

Works incl. motets, Requiem for Tartini and other church music.

Valls, Francisco (b Barcelona, 1665; d Barcelona, 2 Feb 1747), Spanish composer. After posts at Mataró and Gerona he moved to Barcelona in 1696; *maestro di capilla* at the cathedral there from 1709. Retired in 1740 to write a treatise called *Mapa armónico*, in which he defended the use of dissonance in church music as employed by Spanish composers against the more orthodox views of Alessandro Scarlatti. Valls is best known today for his Mass *Scala aretina*.

Works: Masses *Scala aretina* for 11 voices and orch. (1702), *Regalis* (for the King of Port., 1740), 10 others; 22 responsories, 16 Magnificats, 12 psalms, 2 Misereres, *c* 35 motets, *c* 120 *villancicos*.

Valse, La, choreographic poem for orch. by Ravel, finished 1920; fp Paris, 12 Dec 1920. It imitates or parodies the style of J. Strauss's waltzes and has several times served for ballets, as its description shows that it was intended to do.

Valses nobles et sentimentales, a set of waltzes by Ravel, comp. in 1911 and afterwards scored for orch. The title is derived from Schubert, who pub. 2 sets: *Valses nobles*, D969, and *Valses sentimentales*, D779. Ravel's work was turned into a ballet, *Adélaïde, ou Le Langage des fleurs*, prod. Paris, 22 Apr 1912.

Valverde, Joaquín (b Badajoz, 27 Feb 1846; d Madrid, 17 Mar 1910), Spanish flautist, composer and conductor. He played the fl. in theatre orchs., became theatre cond. at Madrid in 1871 and fl. prof. at the Cons. in 1879.

Works incl. several operettas (with Chueca), e.g. *La gran vía*.

Valves, the keys added to brass wind instruments, invented early in the 19th cent. to make it possible for horns, tpts., cornets, etc. to prod. the complete chromatic scale instead of only the natural harmonics. Valves are fitted to all members of the Saxhorn family and have also been used for the tromb. as a substitute for the slide.

Vampyr, Der (*The Vampire*), opera by Lindpaintner (lib. by C.M. Heigel, based on J.W. Polidori's story, pub. in 1819 and thought to be by Byron, and more directly on a Fr. melodrama by C. Nodier, P.F.A. Carmouche and A. de Jouffroy), prod. Stuttgart, 21 Sep 1828.

Opera by Marschner (lib. by W.A. Wohlbrück, based on the sources above), prod. Leipzig, 29 Mar 1828.

Van Allan, Richard (b Nottingham, 28 May 1935), English bass. He studied with David Franklin and appeared at Glyndebourne from 1966: sang in fp of Maw's *The Rising of the Moon*, 1970. ENO, London, since 1969; CG from 1971. He has sung with WNO and at Wexford, the Paris Opéra and in Boston and San Diego. Among his best roles are Leporello, Don Giovanni,

Philip II, Boris and Ochs (San Diego, 1976). Dir. National Opera Studio from 1986.

Van Beinum, Eduard. *See* **Beinum.**

Van Dam, José (b Brussels, 25 Aug 1940), Belgian bass. He studied in Brussels and sang in Paris 1961–5. Deutsche Oper, Berlin, from 1967 as Mozart's Figaro and Leporello, Attila and Prince Igor. He is well known at Salzburg and Aix and has often appeared in concert with Karajan. Much admired as Escamillo (CG, 1973). In 1983 he sang the title role in the fp of Messiaen's *St François d'Assise*.

Van Rooy, Anton(ius Maria Josephus) *see* **Rooy, Anton Van.**

Vaness, Carol (b San Diego, 27 Jul 1952), American soprano. Debut San Francisco, 1977, as Vitellia; later sang Cleopatra and Donna Anna. NY City Opera from 1979, as Antonia, Violetta and Alcina; Met 1984 as Armida in *Rinaldo*. Glyndebourne from 1982, as Donna Anna, Mozart's Electra and Fiordiligi and Amelia Boccanegra (1986). CG from 1982, as Mimi, Vitellia and Dalila in Handel's *Samson*.

Vanessa, opera by Barber (lib. by Menotti), prod. NY Met, 15 Jan 1958.

Vanhal, Johann Baptist (b Nové Nechanice, 12 May 1739; d Vienna, 20 Aug 1813), Bohemian composer. Came to Vienna in 1760 and studied there with Dittersdorf, travelled in It. 1769–71, and lived on the estate of Count Erdödy in Hung. 1772–80. Back in Vienna, he supported himself as a freelance comp.

Works incl. 2 operas (*Demofoonte* and *Il trionfo di Clelia*, both lost); over 50 Masses and much other church music; *c* 70 symphs.; *c* 100 string 4tets; many caprices and programmatic works for keyboard.

Vanni–Marcoux (b Turin, 12 Jun 1877; d Paris, 22 Oct 1962), French bass and baritone. Debut Turin, 1894. CG 1905–14, as Rossini's Don Basilio and Arkel. Sang in Paris from 1908, notably as Massenet's Don Quichotte. US debut Chicago, 1913, as Scarpia. Other roles incl. Don Giovanni, Boris Godunov and Golaud (CG, 1937).

Vaqueras, Bertrandus (b *c* 1450; d ? Rome, *c* 1507), Spanish singer and composer. He was in the Papal Chapel 1483–1507. Wrote church music and *chansons*.

Varady, Julia (b Oradea, 1 Sep 1941), Rumanian soprano. She studied in Cluj and sang there 1960–70 as Liù, Judith and Santuzza. After 2 years at Frankfurt sang in Munich from 1972; roles there have incl. Donna Elvira, Fiordiligi, Elisabeth de

Valois, Butterfly and Arabella. British debut Edinburgh, 1974, as Alceste. She is married to Dietrich Fischer-Dieskau.

Varèse, Edgard (Victor Achille Charles) (b Paris, 22 Dec 1883; d New York, 6 Nov 1965), American composer of French birth. Pupil of d'Indy and Roussel at the Schola Cantorum in Paris and of Widor at the Cons. He cond. choral and orch. music in Paris, Berlin and Prague until 1914, when he joined the Fr. army to take part in the 1st World War; but he was discharged for reasons of health in 1915 and settled in the USA in 1916. He did much to advance the cultivation of modern music in NY and joined Salzedo in 1921 to found the Internat. Comps.' Guild. Varèse is an important figure in the field of 20th-cent. experimental music, dispensing with thematic development and instead working with different types of 'noise', either purely instrumental (*Arcana*, 1927) or combined with tape-recorded sounds (*Déserts*, 1954), or derived from perc. (*Ionisation*, 1931). His influence on modern European and Amer. music has been considerable.

Works incl. *Amériques* for orch. (1918–21, rev. 1927), *Offrandes* for sop. and small orch. (1921), *Hyperprism* for 9 wind, 6 perc. (1922–3), *Octandre* for wind and db. (1923), *Intégrales* for 11 wind and 4 perc. (1923), *Arcana* for orch. (1925–7), *Ionisation* for 13 perc. (1929–31), *Ecuatorial* for 8 brass, pf., org., 2 ondes Martenot, 6 perc. and bass soloist (1932–4), *Density 21.5* for solo fl. (1936), *Études pour Espace* for chorus, 2 pfs. and perc. (1947), *Déserts* for 14 wind, pf., 5 perc. and 2-track tape (1950–54), *Poème electronique* for 3-track tape (1957–8), *Nocturnal* for sop., chorus and small orch. (1961, unfinished); opera, *Oedipus und die Sphinx* (1909–13, text by Hofmannsthal; lost).

Varesi, Felice (b Calais, 1813; d Milan, 13 Mar 1889), Italian baritone. Studied at Milan. He sang at the Kärntnertortheater, Vienna, 1842–7, in operas by Donizetti. He was Verdi's 1st Macbeth in 1847, 1st Rigoletto in 1851 and 1st Germont, père, in 1853. He visited London in 1864, when he sang Rigoletto.

Varga, Tibor (b Györ, 4 Jul 1921), Hungarian, later British, violinist. Studied at Budapest Music Acad. with Hubay and later with Flesch. From 1939 to 1943 he studied philosophy at Budapest Univ., and since 1949 he has been prof. of vln. at the Detmold Music Acad. He is best known for his playing of modern music, e.g. the concertos by Bartók and Schoenberg. Founded his own chamber orch., 1954.

Variations, varied treatments of a theme, sometimes with a restatement of the theme in its 1st form at the end (e.g. Bach's 'Goldberg' Vars.), sometimes with a more elaborate final section, such as a fugue (e.g. Beethoven's 'Eroica' Vars. for pf. or Brahms's Handel Vars. for pf.), or a passacaglia (e.g. Brahms's Haydn Vars. for 2 pfs. or orch.). There is at least one instance (d'Indy's *Istar*) where the theme does not appear in its primitive form until the end. Historically the var. principle goes back as far as inst. music, but sets of vars. 1st emerge in the course of the 16th cent., esp. in Eng. and Spain. The Eng. virginal comps. wrote sets on popular tunes for their instrument and another favoured medium for vars. was the lute. In 17th-cent. Engl vars. were called Divisions, because they split up the theme into smaller rhythmic patterns, and they could be based on a Ground, i.e. an unchanging bass.

The later hist. of the form continues to show the 2 different tendencies of (1) varying the tune and (2) maintaining the foundation of the same bass, with greater or lesser incidental changes while the superstructure can be handled very freely and need not keep to the melodic line of the theme at all. Mozart's vars., for ex., are predominantly melodic, and so are Beethoven's earlier sets, but the latter reverts to the 'ground' type by keeping chiefly to the harmonic framework in such a work as the 'Diabelli' Vars. and in the 32 Vars. for pf. he keeps so close to the bass that the work is more like a Passacaglia, which is true also of the finale of Brahms's 4th symph. In Elgar's 'Enigma' Vars. for orch., each of which represents a portrait of one of the comp.'s friends, and in R. Strauss's *Don Quixote*, the form is complicated by an element of Programme Music.

Variations on a Theme by Haydn (Brahms). *See* **Haydn Variations.**

Variations on a Theme of Frank Bridge, work for string orch. by Britten, comp. 1937 for the Boyd Neel Orch., perf. Salzburg, 27 Aug 1937. The theme is from Bridge's Idyll no. 2 for string 4tet.

Varnay, Astrid (Ibolyka Maria) (b Stockholm, 25 Apr 1918), American soprano of Austro-Hungarian parentage. Both her parents were singers. She studied 1st with her mother and then with H. Weigert, whom she married in 1944. She made her debut at the NY Met in 1941, as Sieglinde, and remained there as a leading Wagner and Strauss singer until 1956. CG, 1948–68; Bayreuth, 1951–67, as Brünnhilde, Isolde and Kundry. Other roles incl. Tosca, Lady Macbeth and Orff's Jocasta (1959).

Varviso, Silvio (b Zurich, 26 Feb 1924), Swiss conductor. He studied in Zurich and Vienna. Worked at the Basle Opera, 1950–62 (music director from 1956). At San Francisco in 1960 he cond. the US fp of *A Midsummer Night's Dream*; NY Met from 1961 (debut in *Lucia*). In 1962 he gave *Figaro* at Glyndebourne and *Rosenkavalier* at CG; has returned to London for operas by Mozart and Puccini. Music director, Stockholm Opera, 1965–72. Stuttgart from 1972; Bayreuth from 1969 (*Fliegende Holländer*, *Meistersinger* and *Lohengrin*). Paris, Opéra, 1981–5.

Varvoglis, Mario (b Brussels, 10 Dec 1885; d Athens, 31 Jul 1967), Greek composer. Studied painting at first, then music in Paris with Leroux and Caussade from 1904 and d'Indy from 1913, having his 1st successes there. He returned to Greece in 1922, became prof. at the Athens Cons. and in 1924 at the Hellenic Cons., of which he became director with Evangelatos in 1947.

Works incl. 1-act opera *The Afternoon of Love* (1935, prod. 1944); classical Gk. plays; *Pastoral Suite* (1912), *Meditation* and incid. music to prelude, chorale and fugue on B.A.C.H. for strings; chamber music; pf. works; songs.

Vásáry, Tamás (b Debrecen, 11 Aug 1933), Swiss pianist and conductor of Hungarian birth. He studied in Budapest and worked as an accompanist from 1948; encouraged by Kodály. He left Hungary in 1956; Swiss citizen from 1971. London debut 1961, NY 1962. Often heard in Chopin, Liszt, Bach and Mozart. Debut as cond. Menton, 1971; joint cond. Northern Sinfonia, 1979–82. He has also cond. widely in the USA.

Vasilenko, Sergey Nikiforovich (b Moscow, 30 Mar 1872; d Moscow, 11 Mar 1956), Russian composer, conductor and teacher. After receiving private lessons from Gretchaninov and Konius, and studying law, he entered the Moscow Cons. in 1895, studying comp. with Taneiev and Ippolitov-Ivanov. In 1905 he taught there and was soon app. full prof. He organized and cond. hist. concerts.

Works incl. operas *The Legend of the Holy City of Kitezh* (1902), *The Son of the Sun* (1929), *Christopher Columbus* (1933), *Suvarov* (1941); ballets *Joseph the Beautiful* (1925), *The Gypsies* (after Pushkin), etc.; 5 symphs. (1904–47), *Epic Poem*, symph.

poem on O. Wilde's *The Garden of Death* and others and suite *In the Sun* and others, *Three Bloody Battles* (after Tolstoy) and other orch. works; vln. concerto (1913); cantata for the 20th anniversary of the Oct Revolution; 4 string 4tets, woodwind 4tet, pf. trio and other chamber music; vla and pf. sonata; songs, folksong arrs.

Vasquez, Juan. *See* **Vázquez.**

Vaterländischer Künstlerverein (Ger. = *Patriotic Artists' Association*), the title of Part II of the variations commissioned by Cappi and Diabelli of Vienna to be written by Beethoven and others on a waltz by Diabelli. Beethoven eventually wrote 33 variations instead of 1, and they were pub. separately as Part I in 1824, Part II following with contribs. by Czerny, Hummel, Kalkbrenner, C. Kreutzer, Liszt (aged 11), Moscheles, Franz Xaver Mozart, the Archduke Rudolph, Schubert, Sechter and *c* 40 others.

Vaudeville (Fr.), a term with various meanings and of uncertain origin. Le Roy, in his *Airs de Cour* of 1571, says that such songs were formerly called 'voix de ville' (town voices); but the form 'vau de Vire' is also known, and may have referred to the valley of Vire in Normandy, the home of Olivier Basselin (*c* 1400–50), a comp. of such songs. In 18th-cent. Fr., vaudevilles were at first satirical songs, then songs with words set to popular tunes used in comedies with music (*comédies mélées de vaudevilles*), as in the Eng. ballad opera (songs specially comp. being called *ariettes*). In time vaudevilles in Fr. became songs sung at the end of spoken stage pieces, taken up verse by verse by all the characters and sometimes by the chorus, and this device was sometimes intro. into opera, in Fr. and elsewhere, as for ex. at the end of Rousseau's *Devin du village* and Mozart's *Entführung aus dem Serail*. The next step from this was to call a whole light music stage entertainment a vaudeville.

Vaughan, Elizabeth (b Llanfyllin, Montgomeryshire, 12 Mar 1936), Welsh soprano. She studied at the RAM and sang Abigaille with WNO in 1960. CG from 1961 as Mimi, Tytania, Teresa, Gilda, Amelia and Butterfly. NY Met debut 1972, as Donna Elvira.

Vaughan Williams, Ralph (b Down Ampney, Glos., 12 Oct 1872; d London, 26 Aug 1958), English composer. Son of a clergyman, he was educ. at Charterhouse School, 1887–90, and Trinity Coll., Cambridge, 1892–5, the intervening years being devoted to study at the RCM in London, where he returned for another year after Cambridge. He learnt pf. and org. for the sake of usefulness, but was from the 1st determined to be a comp. On leaving the RCM in 1896 he became organist at S. Lambeth Church in London and saved enough money to gain further experience by study abroad, 1st at the Akademie der Künste in Berlin, under Bruch, and in 1909 with Ravel, who was younger than him, in Paris. In 1901 he took the Mus.D. at Cambridge. In 1904 he joined the Folk-Song Society and began to take an active share in the recovery and study of old country tunes, collecting some in Norfolk; in 1906 he ed. *The Eng. Hymnal*. His 1st great public success he made with *Toward the Unknown Region* at the Leeds Festival in 1907. In the 1914—18 war he first served as a private in Macedonia and Fr., but later rose to officer's rank, and after the declaration of peace he was app. prof. of comp. at the RCM. His music was often perf. at the festivals of the ISCM.

Works incl. OPERAS: *Hugh the Drover* (1910—14, prod. 1924), *Sir John in Love* (on Shakespeare's *Merry Wives*, 1929), *The Poisoned Kiss* (1929, prod. 1936), *Riders to the Sea* (Synge, 1937) and *The Pilgrim's Progress* (after Bunyan, 1951); ballets *Old King Cole* (1923) and *On Christmas Night* (after Dickens, 1926), masque *Job* (on Blake's illustrations, 1931); incid. music for Aristophanes' *Wasps* (1909), film music incl. *49th Parallel* (1941) and *Scott of the Antarctic* (1948).

CHORAL: 3 motets, Mass in G min., Te Deum in G maj., Angl. services, Festival Te Deum, hymn tunes; (with orch.) *Toward the Unknown Region* (Whitman), *Willow Wood* (D.G. Rossetti), *A Sea Symph.* (no. 1) (Whitman, 1903—9), *5 Mystical Songs* (Herbert, 1911), *Fantasia on Christmas Carols*, *Flos Campi* (Song of Solomon, 1925), *Sancta Civitas* (1925), *Benedicite*, Magnificat, *Dona nobis pacem*, *Five Tudor Portraits* (Skelton, 1935), *The Sons of Light* (U. Wood), *Serenade to Music* for 16 solo voices and orch. (from Shakespeare's *Merchant of Venice*, 1938), *Oxford Elegy* (M. Arnold, 1949).

ORCH.: *Norfolk Rhapsodies*, nos. 1—3 (1905—6), *In the Fen Country*, *Fantasia on a Theme by Thomas Tallis* (strings, 1910), *A London Symph.* (no. 2, 1912—13), *A Pastoral Symph.* (no. 3, 1921), symphs. nos. 4—9 (1937, 1943, 1947, 1952, 1955, 1957), *5 Variants of 'Dives and Lazarus'* (strings and harps, 1939), *2 Hymn-tune Preludes* (small orch.), *Concerto grosso* (strings, 1950), *Eng. Folk Song Suite* (military band); *The Lark Ascending* (after Meredith) for vln. and

orch. (1914), *Concerto accademico* for vln. and strings (1925), pf. concerto (later version for 2 pfs., 1926—31), suite for vla. and orch. (1934), concerto for ob. and strings (1944), *Romance* for mouth org. and orch., tuba concerto (1954).

CHAMBER AND SONGS: 2 string 4tets (1909, 1944), Phantasy 5tet for strings, *On Wenlock Edge* (Housman) for tenor, string 4tet and pf. (1909); suite for pf., intro. and fugue for 2 pfs.; 3 preludes on Welsh hymn-tunes and prelude and fugue for org.; many songs incl. cycle *The House of Life* (D.G. Rossetti [incl. *Silent Noon*]), *Songs of Travel* (Stevenson, 1901—4), *Along the Field* (Housman), for low voice and vln. (1927); numerous part-songs; folksong arrs.

Vautor, Thomas (*fl.* 1600—20), English composer. Educ. at Lincoln Coll., Oxford, where he took the B.Mus. in 1616. He was for many years in the service of Sir George Villiers, father of the later Duke of Buckingham, at Brooksby, and later of his widow at Goadby. Pub. one book of madrigals (1619—20).

Vavrinecz, Mauritius (b Czegléd, 18 Jul 1858; d Budapest, 5 Aug 1913), Hungarian composer. Studied at the Budapest Cons. and with Volkmann and in 1886 became music dir. of Budapest Cathedral.

Works incl. operas *Ratcliff* (after Heine) and *Rosamunde*; 5 Masses, Requiem, *Stabat Mater*; oratorio *Christus*; symph, overture to Byron's *Bride of Abydos*, Dithyramb for orch.

Vázquez, Juan (b Badajoz, *c* 1510; d ? Seville, *c* 1560), Spanish composer. *Maestro de capilla* at Badajoz Cathedral, 1545—50, and was later in the service of Don Antonio de Zuñiga. He was an important exponent of the *villancico* (*q.v.*), and also wrote church music.

Veasey, Josephine (b Peckham, 10 Jul 1930), English mezzo. She studied in London and sang at CG from 1955; roles there incl. Carmen, Waltraute, Dorabella, Eboli, Dido and Octavian. Often sang under Solti. She sang Cherubino at Glyndebourne in 1958 and returned in 1969 for Charlotte. NY Met debut 1968, as Fricka, under Karajan. Paris, Opéra, 1973, Kundry. Often heard in concert. Retired from opera 1982 and is now vocal coach at the ENO, London.

Vecchi, Lorenzo (b Bologna, before 1564; d Bologna, 3 Mar 1628), Italian composer. He was a pupil at San Petronio at Bologna, where he became *maestro di cappella* in 1605. Wrote Masses, Requiem and other church music.

Vecchi, Orazio (Tiberio) (b Modena, bap. 6
Dec 1550; d Modena, 19 Feb 1605), Italian
composer and priest. *Maestro di cappella*
Salò Cathedral (1581), Modena (1584) and
Reggio Emilia (1586), canon (1586) and
archdeacon (1591) at Correggio. He returned to Modena as *maestro di cappella* in
1596, and then became *maestro* at the d'Este
court in 1598. He became famous, being
summoned to the court of the Emperor
Rudolph II at one time and invited to comp.
music for the king of Pol. In 1604 his pupil
Geminiano Capi-Lupi intrigued successfully against him and supplanted him in his
post.

Works incl. madrigal comedy *L'Amfiparnaso* (fp 1594); Masses, motets, Lamentations and other church music; madrigals,
canzonets.

Vecchi, Orfeo (b ? Milan, *c* 1550; d Milan,
before April 1604), Italian composer. *Maestro di cappella* of the church of Santa Maria
della Scala at Milan from *c* 1590.

Works incl. Masses, motets, psalms, Magnificats, *Cantiones sacrae* and other church
music; madrigals.

Veichtner, Franz Adam (b Regensburg, 10
Feb 1741; d Klievenhof, Courland, 3 Mar
1822), German violinist and composer.
Pupil of F. Benda for vln. and of Riepel for
comp., he was in the service of Count
Kaiserling at Königsberg 1763–4, *Konzertmeister* to the Duke of Courland in Mitau
1765–95, then in St Petersburg as chamber
musician to the Rus. court until his retirement in 1820.

Works incl. *Singspiele*, e.g. *Cephalus und
Prokris* (1779) and *Cyrus und Cassandana*
(1784); 5 symphs.; vln. concerto; 3 string
4tets (1802); 24 fantasias on Rus. songs for
vln. and bass; 24 vln. sonatas.

Veilchen, Das (*The Violet*) song by Mozart,
K476: his only setting of a poem by Goethe,
comp. 8 Jun 1785.

Veiled Prophet of Khorassan, The, opera
by Stanford (lib. by W.B. Squire based on
Moore's *Lalla Rookh*), prod., in Ger.,
Hanover, Court Theatre, 6 Feb 1881; 1st
London perf., in It., CG, 26 Jul 1893.

Vejvanovský, Pavel Josef (b Hukvaldy or
Hlučín, *c* 1655; d Kroměříž, buried 24 Sep
1693), Moravian composer and trumpeter.
He studied at Opava and from 1661 worked
at Kroměříž, composing and playing the
trumpet at the court there; many of his
Masses, offertories and motets feature technically fluent parts for trumpets, trombones
and cornets. Much of his music shows the
influence of J.H. Schmelzer (*q.v.*) and other

comps. at the court of Emperor Leopold I in
Vienna.

Velluti, Giovanni Battista (b Montolmo
[now Corridonia] nr. Ancona, 28 Jan 1780;
d Sambruson di Dolo, 22 Jan 1861), Italian
soprano castrato (one of the last). Made his
1st stage appearance at Forlì in 1800, and
then appeared in Naples, Milan and Venice
in operas by Guglielmi, Cimarosa and Mayr.
In 1812 he visited Vienna. He created Arsace
in Rossini's *Aureliano in Palmira* (Milan,
1813) and Armando in Meyerbeer's *Il crociato in Egitto* (Venice, 1824), and sang the
latter role on his 1st visit to London (1825).

Veloce (It. = quick, swift, rapid, fluent).
The direction does not so much indicate
increased speed, though it may include that
meaning, as smoothness of rapid figuration.

Vendemmia, La (*The Vintage*), opera by
Gazzaniga (lib by G. Bertati, partly based on
an earlier lib. of the same name by Goldoni),
prod. Florence, Teatro della Pergola, 15
May 1778.

Vendredis, Les, a set of pieces for string 4tet
by Artsibushev, Blumenfeld, Borodin, Glazunov, Kopylov, Liadov, M. d'Osten-
Sacken, Rimsky-Korsakov, Sokolov and
Wihtol, written for Friday chamber-music
reunions in St Peterburg.

Venegas de Henestrosa, Luis (b *c* 1510; d
c 1557 or later), Spanish vihuelist and composer. He pub. a book of variations and
transcriptions in a special tablature suitable
for keyboard insts., harp, vihuela or guitar
(1557). The notation was later used by
Cabezóni and Arauxo.

Ventadorn, Bernart de (d 1195), French
troubadour. 45 of his poems and 19 of his
melodies have been preserved.

Vento, Ivo de (b *c* 1544; d Munich, 1575), ?
Flemish composer. In 1564 he was app.
Kapellmeister to Duke William of Bavaria at
Landshut and in 1569 he became organist in
the ducal chapel at Munich under Lassus.

Works incl. motets; Ger. sacred and secular songs for several voices.

Vento, Mattia (b Naples, 1735; d London,
22 Nov 1776), Italian composer. Prod. operas in Rome and Venice, and settled in London in 1763.

Works incl. operas *La finta semplice*
(1759), *La Egiziana* (1763), *Leucippo*
(1764), *Demofoonte, Sofonisba* (1766), *La
conquista del vello d'orco* (1767), *Artaserse*
(1771), *Il bacio* (1776), *La Vestale*; cantata
Threnodia augustilia (Goldsmith) on the
death of George III's mother; trio sonatas;
vln. sonatas; keyboard music; songs.

Venturi del Nibbio, Stefano (*fl.* 1592–

1600), Italian composer. Wrote 2 choruses in Caccini's *Rapimento di Cefalo* (lost), 5 books of madrigals, 3 motets.

Venturini, Francesco (b ? Brussels, *c* 1675; d Hanover, 18 Apr 1745), German composer and violinist. Pupil of J.B. Farinelli at Hanover, where he joined the electoral chapel in 1698 and succeeded his master as head of the inst. music in 1713, later becoming court *Kapellmeister*. He pub. a set of chamber concertos (Amsterdam, *c* 1714).

Venus, opera by Schoeck (lib. by A. Rüeger, on Mérimée's story *La Vénus d'Ille*), prod. Zurich, 10 May 1922.

Venus and Adonis, masque by Blow (lib. unknown), prod. London, at court, *c* 1684.

Vénus et Adonis, opera by Desmarets (lib. by J.B. Rousseau), prod. Paris, Opéra, 17 Mar 1697.

Vêpres siciliennes, Les (*The Sicilian Vespers*), opera by Verdi (lib. by Scribe and C. Duveyrier), prod. Paris, Opéra, 13 Jun 1855. Verdi's 1st Fr. opera, the only other set to Fr. words being *Don Carlos*. Prod. in It., as *Giovanna di Guzman*, Milan, La Scala, 4 Feb 1856, but later called *I vespri siciliani* there.

Veprik, Alexander Moiseievich (b Balta, 23 Jun 1899; d Moscow, 13 Oct 1958), Russian composer. Studied with Reger at Leipzig, with Kalafati and Zhitomirsky at St Petersburg and with Miaskovsky at Moscow. He also had some lessons from Janáček.

Works incl. *5 Episodes* for chorus and orch.; *Songs and Dances of the Ghetto* (1927), *A Song of Mourning* (1932), *A Song of Joy* for orch. (1935); *Songs of Death* for vla. and pf.; 2 pf. sonatas.

Vera costanza, La (*True Constancy*), opera by Anfossi (lib. by F. Puttini), prod. Rome, Teatro delle Dame, 2 Jan 1776.

Opera by Haydn (lib. do., altered by P. Travaglia), prod. Eszterháza, 25 Apr 1779.

Vera Sheloga (Rimsky-Korsakov). *See* **Pskovitianka.**

Veracini, Antonio (b Florence, 17 Jan 1659; d Florence 26 Oct 1733), Italian violinist and composer. Was in the service of the Grand Duchess Vittoria of Tuscany at Florence.

Works incl. 4 oratorios (music lost); 3 volumes of sonatas for 1 and 2 vlns.

Veracini, Francesco Maria (b Florence, 1 Feb 1690; d Florence, 31 Oct 1768), Italian composer and violinist, nephew of prec. Pupil of his uncle and later of Casini and Gasparini in Rome, poss. also of Corelli, he began touring as a virtuoso in 1711, and visited Eng. in 1714. Returning *via* Germany to It., he demonstrated his superiority over Tartini (2 years his junior) in a contest in Venice in 1716. The following year he entered the service of the Elector of Saxony in Dresden (where he is said to have attempted suicide in 1722), but left for Prague in 1723, then returned to It. In 1735 he went again to London, where he prod. his first opera, *Adriano in Siria,* followed by several others (1735–44), but as a violinist was overshadowed by Geminiani. He prob. lived in Pisa *c* 1750–55, then retired to Florence.

Works incl. operas *Adriano in Siria* (1753), *La clemenza di Tito* (1737), *Partenio* (1738), *Rosalinda* (after Shakespeare's *As You Like It,* 1744), 8 oratorios (music lost); cantatas incl. *Nice e Tirsi* (1741) and *Parla al ritratto della amata*; vln. sonatas; concertos; treatise *Il Erionfo della pratica musicale.*

Verbonnet, Johannes. *See* **Ghiselin.**

Verbunkos, an 18th-cent. Hung. recruiting dance for soldiers, who perf. it in full uniform with swords and spurs. Like the later Csárdás, to which it is related, it contained a slow (*lassú*) and quick (*friss*) section. Liszt's Hungarian Rhapsodies make use of the dance.

Verdelot, Philippe (b Verdelot, Les Loges, Seine-et-Marné; d before 1552), French composer and singer. He went to It., prob. at an early age, and was *maestro di cappella* at Florence Cathedral in 1523–7.

Works incl. 2 Masses, *c* 50 motets; *c* 100 madrigals, 3 chansons.

Verdi, Giuseppe (Fortunino Francesco) (b Roncole nr. Busseto, 9 or 10 Oct 1813; d Milan, 27 Jan 1901), Italian composer. Son of an innkeeper and grocer. From the age of only 3 he was taught by the local organist, in whose place he was app. at 9. At 11 he was sent to Busseto and went to school there, walking home twice a week to carry on the organist's duties. Barezzi, a friend of Verdi's father at Busseto, took him into his house in 1826, and he learnt much from the cathedral organist Provesi. He had an overture for Rossini's *Il barbiere di Siviglia* perf. in 1828, and the next year he wrote a symph. and deputized for Provesi. In 1831 he was sent to Milan with a scholarship and some financial help from Barezzi, but rejected by the Cons. as over entrance age. He studied with Lavigna, the *maestro al cembalo* at La Scala. When Provesi died in 1833 he tried for the post of cathedral organist, and when it was given to an inferior musician the Phil. Society made him an allowance. In 1836 he married Barezzi's daughter, Margherita, by whom he had 2 children, but both mother and children died between 1837 and 1840. Meanwhile he had comp. his 1st opera, *Oberto*, prod. at La Scala, 17 Nov 1839.

A 2nd (comic) opera, *Un giorno di regno*, was a failure, having been comp. at the time of his bereavement; but *Nabucco*, prod. La Scala in 1842, had a great success. In the cast was Giuseppina Strepponi, who lived with Verdi from 1848 and in 1859 became his 2nd wife. He now went from strength to strength as an operatic comp. and his fame spread beyond Milan: *Ernani* was prod. at Venice in 1844, *I due Foscari* in Rome, 1844, *Alzira* at Naples, 1845 and *Macbeth* at Florence, 1847. Meanwhile *Ernani* had gone to Paris in 1846 and London commissioned *I masnadieri*, prod. there on 22 Jul 1847. Operas growing in mastery followed almost annually until 1871 and in his old age, after a long interval, he prod. his 2 great Shakespearian masterpieces with Boito as his librettist. Apart from these prods. and frequent travels to var. Eur. countries Verdi's life was spent mostly at his estate of Sant' Agata nr. Busseto, which he bought in 1848.

An opera on Shakespeare's *King Lear*, at which he worked intermittently, was never completed; otherwise all his plans materialized once they had taken definite shape. Fr., Rus. and Egypt offered him special commissions and his fame spread all over the world. He represented It. at the Internat. Exhibition in London in 1862 and wrote a *Hymn of the Nations*; in the same year *La forza del destino* was prod. at St Petersburg on 22 Nov. In 1868 he suggested a Requiem for Rossini, to be written by var. It. comps., but the plan came to nothing. He used his contrib. in 1873 for a Requiem of his own commemorating the death of Manzoni. *Otello* was prod. at La Scala on 5 Feb 1887. After a break from comp. of 6 years, *Falstaff* was given at the same theatre on 9 Feb 1893, when Verdi was in his 80th year. Giuseppina died in 1897 and he was himself growing very weak, but still wrote some sacred pieces for chorus and orch. in 1895–7.

Works incl. operas *Oberto, Conte di San Bonifacio* (1839), *Un giorno di regno* (1840), *Nabucodonosor (Nabucco)* (1842), *I Lombardi alla prima crociata* (1843), *Ernani* (1844), *I due Foscari* (1844), *Giovanna d'Arco* (1845), *Alzira* (1845), *Attila* (1845–6), *Macbeth* (1847), *I masnadieri* (1846–7), *Jérusalem* (Fr. rev. version of *I Lombardi*, 1847), *Il corsaro* (1848), *La battaglia di Legnano* (1849), *Luisa Miller* (1849), *Stiffelio* (1850), *Rigoletto* (1851), *Il trovatore*

(1853), *Là traviata* (1853), *Les Vêpres siciliennes* (1855), *Simon Boccanegra* (1857, rev. 1881), *Aroldo* (revision of *Stiffelio*) (1857), *Un ballo in maschera* (1859), *La forza del destino* (1862), *Don Carlos* (1867, rev. 1884), *Aida* (1871), *Otello* (1887), *Falstaff* (1893); choral works *Inno delle nazioni*, Requiem (1874), *Pater noster, Ave Maria, Stabat Mater, Lauda alla Vergine Maria*, Te Deum (1896); *Ave Maria* for soprano and strings; 16 songs; 1 part-song; string 4tet (1871).

Verdi, Giuseppina. *See* **Strepponi.**

Verdonck, Cornelis (b Turnhout, 1563; d Antwerp, 5 Jul 1625), Flemish singer and composer. In the service of Cornelius Pruenen, treasurer and later sheriff of Antwerp until 1598, when on the death of his patron he served 2 of his nephews. He was singer at the royal chapel in Madrid 1584–98.

Works incl. Magnificat, *Ave gratia plena*, 4 motets; 21 *chansons*, 42 madrigals.

Veress, Sándor (b Kolozsvár, Transylvania, 1 Feb 1907), Hungarian pianist and composer. Learnt the pf. from his mother and later entered the Budapest Cons. He also studied with Bartók and Kodály. In 1929 he studied at the Ethnological Museum and began collecting folksongs. He settled at Budapest as teacher of pf. and comp. and asst. to Bartók at the Scientific Acad. of Folk Music.

Works incl. ballet *The Magic Flute* (1937, prod. Rome 1941); 2 symphs. (1940, 1953) and divertimento for orch.; vln. concerto; cantata and folksong arrs. for unaccomp. chorus; 2 string 4tets (1931, 1937), string trio, trio for ob., clar. and bassoon; vln. and pf. sonata, cello and pf. sonata; 2 pf. sonatas.

Veretti, Antonio (b Verona, 20 Feb 1900; d Rome 13 Jul 1978), Italian composer. Studied at Bologna and took a diploma, also a newspaper prize in 1927 for the opera *Il medico volante* (after Molière). In 1943 he became director of the Cons. della GIL in Rome and in 1950 of the Pesaro Cons.

Works incl. opera *Il favorito del re* (1932); ballets *Il galante tiratore* and *Una favola di Andersen* (1934); film music; oratorio *Il figliuol prodigo* (1942), *Sinfonia sacra* for men's chorus and orch.; *Sinfonia italiana* (1929), *Sinfonia epica* (1938) and *Ouverture della Campanella* for orch.

Vergnet, Edmond (b Montpellier, 4 Jul 1850; d Nice, 25 Feb 1904), French tenor. Debut Paris, Opéra, 1874; also sang there 1875–93. In 1881 sang Radames and Faust at CG and appeared in the fp of Massenet's *Hérodiade*, at Brussels. Other roles incl. Samson, Florestan and Lohengrin.

Verheyen, Pierre Emmanuel (b Ghent, *c* 1750; d Ghent, 11 Jan 1819), Belgian composer and tenor. Pupil of the organist of St Bavon in Ghent, he abandoned his univ. career to become a singer in the choir there, and in 1779 was app. principal tenor at Bruges Cathedral, but soon after joined a travelling opera co. Later he returned to Ghent, where he became comp. to the archbishop and (from 1790) music director at the church of St Pharaïlde.

Works incl. operas *Les Chevaliers, ou Le Prix de l'arc* (1779) and *De Jachparty van Hendrik IV* (1794), *Arlequin magicien* (1795); Masses, psalms, Requiem for Haydn, Te Deum and other church music; cantata *La Bataille de Waterloo* (1816).

Verhulst, Johannes (Josephus Hermanus) (b The Hague, 19 Mar 1816; d The Hague, 17 Jan 1891), Dutch composer and conductor. Studied at The Hague Royal School of Music and after some work as violinist at the Opera at Cologne went to Leipzig in 1838 and became cond. of the Euterpe concerts at Mendelssohn's invitation; was a friend of Schumann and became a member of the *Davidsbund*. In 1842 He returned to The Hague as court music director and also cond. important music societies at Amsterdam and Rotterdam.

Works incl. Requiem for male voices and other church music; symphs., overtures, intermezzo *Greetings from Afar* for orch.; string 4tets; songs; part-songs.

Verismo (It. = realism), a term used to classify Italian opera of a supposedly 'realistic' order, incl. the works of Puccini, Mascagni, Leoncavallo, Giordano, Zandonai, etc.

Verklärte Nacht (*Transfigured Night*), string 6tet by Schoenberg, op. 4, comp. Sep 1899, fp Vienna, 18 Mar 1902. Arr. for string orch. *c* 1917, rev. 1942; given as ballet, *The Pillar of Fire*, at the NY Met on 8 Apr 1942. It was inspired by a poem in R. Dehmel's *Weib und die Welt*.

Vermeulen, Matthijs (b Helmond, 8 Feb 1888; d Laren, 26 Jul 1967), Dutch composer and critic. Studied with Diepenbrock and from 1908 to 1921 was a music critic, when he settled in Paris, where he remained until 1946, after which he returned to Amsterdam.

Works incl. 7 symphs. (1914–56); chamber music; songs.

Vermont, Pierre (d Paris, 1532), French

16th-cent. singer and composer. He sang in the Papal chapel in Rome from 1528 to 1530, then in the royal chapel in Paris. Wrote motets, *chansons* for several voices, etc. His (?) brother Pernot V. (d 1558) also sang, and wrote a few *chansons*.

Vernizzi, Ottavio (b Bologna, 27 Nov 1569; d Bologna, 28 Sep 1649), Italian organist and composer. Organist at San Petronio at Bologna from 1596 until his death.

Works incl. motets, *Concerti spirituali*; music (all lost) for *intermedii*.

Vernon, Joseph (b *c* 1739; d London, 19 Mar 1782), English actor, tenor and composer. He was a choir-boy at St Paul's Cathedral in London and 1st appeared on the stage as a boy soprano in 1751, and as a tenor in 1754. Later he became famous chiefly as a singing actor in Shakespeare and in Sheridan's *Duenna* and *School for Scandal*, where Linley's song was written for him.

Works incl. pantomime *The Witches*; songs for Shakespeare's *Two Gentlemen of Verona* and *Twelfth Night* and for Garrick's *The Irish Widow* and *Linco's Travels* (1767); ballads.

Véronique, operetta by Messager (lib. by A. Vanloo and G. Duval), prod. Paris, Bouffes-Parisiens, 10 Dec 1898.

Verrett, Shirley (b New Orleans, 31 May 1931), American mezzo, later soprano. She studied in Los Angeles and at Juilliard, NY. Opera debut NY City Opera, 1958; sang in Eur. from 1959, and in 1962 was heard at Spoleto as Carmen. She later sang the role on her Bolshoy, La Scala and NY Met (1968) debuts. In 1966 she sang Ulrica at CG; she returned for Eboli, Amneris, Orpheus and Selika in *L'Africaine*. In Oct 1973 she sang both Cassandre and Didon in *Les Troyens* at the Met. Other roles incl. Judith, Tosca, Azucena and Lady Macbeth.

Verschworenen, Die, oder Der häusliche Krieg (*The Conspirators, or Domestic Warfare*), operetta by Schubert (lib. by I.F. Casteli, based on Aristophanes' *Lysistrata*), never perf. in Schubert's lifetime; prod. Frankfurt, 29 Aug 1861.

Verse Anthem. *See* **Anthem.**

Verset (Fr.)
Versetto (It.) } a short organ piece, often but not necessarily fugal and frequently incorporating or containing some reference to a given plainsong tune. The name is derived from the former practice in the Roman Catholic service of replacing every other sung verse of psalms, etc. by interludes on the organ to relieve the supposed monotony of plainsong.

Verstovsky, Alexey Nicolaievich (b Seliverstavo, Gvt. of Tambov, 1 Mar 1799; d Moscow, 17 Nov 1862), Russian composer. Studied civil engineering at St Petersburg, but picked up musical training at the same time, studying theory, singing, vln. and pf., the last with Field and Steibelt. As a rich man's son he remained an amateur, but prod. his 1st operetta at the age of 19. In 1824 he was app. inspector of the Imp. Opera at Moscow, where in 1828 he prod. his 1st opera, which was influenced by Weber's *Freischütz*. In 1842 he married the famous actress Nadezhda Repina.

Works incl. *Pan Twardowski* (1828), *Vadim* (1832), *Askold's Tomb* (1835), *Homesickness* (1839), *The Valley of Tchurov* (1841) and *Gromoboy* (after Zhukovsky); 22 operettas; cantatas, melodramas and dramatic scenas; 29 songs, incl. Pushkin's *The Black Shawl*.

Versunkene Glocke, Die. *See* **Campana Sommersa.**

Opera by Zöllner (lib. by comp., based on G. Hauptmann's play), prod. Berlin, Theater des Westens, 8 Jul 1899.

Vertical, an adjective applied to the combination of simultaneous sounds, as seen on the page, in contrast to the horizontal appearance of notes in succession.

Verwandelten Weiber, Die, oder Der Teufel ist los, *Singspiel* by J.A. Hiller (lib. by C.F. Weisse, based on Coffey's *The Devil to Pay*), prod. Leipzig, 28 May 1766.

Vesalii Icones (*Images of Vesalius*), theatre piece by Maxwell Davies for dancer, solo cello and inst. ens.; comp. 1969, fp London, 9 Dec 1969. The 14 movts. are based on anatomical drawings in a treatise (1543) by the physician Andreas Vesalius depicting Christ's Passion and Resurrection.

Vespers (from Lat. *vespera*, evening), the service preceding Compline in the Office of the Roman Church. It incl. psalms with their antiphons, a hymn and the Magnificat. A number of comps. have made elaborate settings for voices and insts. of all or part of the texts, notably Monteverdi and Mozart.

Vespri siciliani, I (Verdi). *See* **Vêpres siciliennes.**

Vesque von Püttlingen, Johann (pseud. J. Hoven) (b Opole, Poland, 23 Jul 1803; d Vienna, 30 Oct 1883), Austrian composer of Belgian descent. He was born at the residence of Prince Alexander Lubomirsky. The family moved to Vienna in 1815 and he studied music there with Leidesdorf, Moscheles and Vořišek. In 1822 he entered Vienna Univ. and in 1827 the civil service. In

1829 he exercised himself in opera by setting the lib. of Rossini's *Donna del lago* (based on Scott) and in 1833 he studied counterpoint with Sechter.

Works incl. opera *Turandot* (after Gozzi, 1838), *Jeanne d'Arc* (1840), *Liebeszauber* (after Kleist's *Käthchen von Heilbronn*, 1845), *Ein Abenteuer Carl des Zweiten* (1850), *Der lustige Rath* (1852) and 2 unfinished; 2 Masses.

Vestale, La, opera by Mercadante (lib., in It., by S. Cammarano), prod. Naples, Teatro San Carlo, 10 Mar 1840.

Opera by Spontini (lib., in Fr., by V.J.E. de Jouy, ? based on Winckelmann's *Monumenti antichi inediti*), prod. Paris, Opéra, 16 Jan 1807.

Vestris (*née* **Bartolozzi**), **Lucia Elizabeth** (or **Eliza Lucy**) (b London, 3 Jan or 2 Mar 1797; d London, 8 Aug 1856), English actress and contralto of Italian descent, daughter of Gaetano B. and granddaughter of the engraver Francesco B. Studied singing with Domenico Corri, married the dancer Auguste-Armande V. (1788–1825) in 1813 and in 1815 made her debut in London; sang in the local fps of Rossini's *La gazza ladra*, *La donna del lago*, *Mathilde di Shabran*, *Zelmira* and *Semiramide*. She was Fatima in the fp of Weber's *Oberon* in 1826.

Viadana (real name Grossi da Viadana), **Lodovico** (b Viadana nr. Parma, *c* 1560; d Gualtieri nr. Parma, 2 May 1627), Italian composer. Pupil of Porta and before 1590 app. *maestro di cappella* at Mantua Cathedral. In 1596 he joined the Franciscan order, in 1609 became *maestro di cappella* at Concordia, in 1612 at Fano Cathedral; in 1615 went to live at Piacenza, whence he retired to the Franciscan monastery at Gualtieri.

Works incl. Masses, psalms and other church music; 100 *Concerti ecclesiastici* for 1–4 voices with organ continuo; madrigals, canzonets.

Viaggiatori felici, I (*The Happy Travellers*), opera by Anfossi (lib. by F. Livigni), prod. Venice, Teatro San Samuele, Oct 1780.

Viaggio a Reims, Il, ossia L'albergo del giglio d'oro (*The Journey to Rheims, or the Golden Lily Inn*), opera by Rossini (lib. by G.L. Balochi), prod. Paris, Théâtre-Italien, 19 Jun 1825. The opera failed but the music was largely re-used in *Le Comte Ory* (1828).

Vianna da Motta, José (b São Tomé, 22 Apr 1868; d Lisbon, 31 May 1948), Portuguese pianist and composer. Studied at the Lisbon Cons. and with the Scharwenka brothers in Berlin, later with Liszt at Weimar and Bülow at Frankfurt. He began to tour

Eur. and S. Amer. in 1902, was app. Prus. court pianist and taught at Geneva in 1915–17. He was director of the Lisbon Cons. from 1919 to 1938.

Works incl. *Lusiads* (Camões) for chorus and orch.; symph.; string 4tet; *Port. Scenes, Port. Rhapsodies*, etc. for pf.: songs.

Viardot-García, (Michelle Ferdinande) Pauline (b Paris, 18 Jul 1821; d Paris, 17 or 18 May 1910), French mezzo and composer of Spanish descent, daughter of Manuel García and sister of Maria Malibran. Pupil of her father, also studied pf. Made her 1st appearance as a singer at Brussels in 1837 and 1st visited London in 1839, as Rossini's Desdemona; in Paris she sang Fides, and Orpheus in an arr. of Gluck's opera by Berlioz. In 1840 she married the opera manager and critic Louis V. (1800–83). After retiring from stage, sang in the fps of Massenet's *Marie-Magdeleine* and Brahms's Alto Rhapsody (1870). She wrote operettas *Le Dernier Sorcier, L'Ogre* and *Trop de femmes*, to libs. by Turgenev, and songs.

Vibraphone, an electrophonic instrument the resonators of which are kept vibrating by an electric current, so that the notes struck give out an oscillating sound.

Vibrato (It. = vibrating, oscillating), a special musical effect prod. on a single note by means of fluctuation of pitch (or occasionally intensity). Until the 19th cent. it was often regarded as an expressive ornament. On the Clavichord a vibrato effect is possible by shaking the finger on the key without releasing it (*Bebung*). On string insts., a warmer and more vibrant tone is prod. by shaking the fingers of the left hand on the fingerboard while pressing down the string. On the org. a similar effect is made possible by the use of the tremulant. Vibrato on wind insts. is controlled by the breath.

Vicentino, Nicola (b Vicenza, 1511; d Milan, *c* 1576), Italian composer and theorist. Pupil of Willaert at Venice. He entered the service of Ippolito d'Este, cardinal of Ferrara, with whom he went to live in Rome. He sought to revive the Gk. modes in his madrigals, invented an inst. he called the archicembalo which could play var. microtones. His treatise *L'antica musica ridotta alla moderna prattica* (1555) involved him in a controversy with Lusitano in which he was defeated. He returned to Ferrara with his patron and became his *maestro di cappella*. He wrote madrigals and motets.

Vickers, Jon(athan Stewart) (b Prince Albert, Saskatchewan, 29 Oct 1926), Canadian tenor. Studied at the Toronto Cons. and made his debut at the Stratford Festival, 1956, as Don José. 1st appeared at CG, 1957, as Riccardo; has returned as Aeneas (Berlioz), Radames, Don Carlos, Samson (Saint-Saëns and Handel), Florestan and Tristan. Bayreuth, 1958 and 1964 (Siegmund and Parsifal). NY Met 1960, as Canio; later Grimes. He is notable for his Wagner, Verdi and Beethoven.

Victoria, Tomás Luis de (b Avila, 1548; d Madrid, 20 Aug 1611), Spanish composer. He knew Palestrina and poss. studied with him. He may have been in touch with St Teresa, also a native of Avila. In 1565 he received a grant from Philip II and went to Rome, where he became a priest and singer at the Ger. Coll. He was choirmaster there 1573 to *c* 1577. From 1578 to 1585 he was a chaplain at San Girolamo della Carità. From 1587 to 1603 he was chaplain to the dowager empress María, Philip II's sister, at the convent of the Descalzas Reales in Madrid, where the empress lived and her daughter, the Infanta Margaret, became a nun. On the death of the empress in 1603 he wrote an *Officium defunctorum* (Requiem Mass) for 6 voices.

Works: 20 Masses (incl. 2 Requiems), 18 Magnificats, 1 Nunc dimittis, 9 Lamentations, 25 responsories, 13 antiphons, 8 polychoral psalms, 52 motets, 36 hymns, 1 Litany, 2 Passions, 3 Sequences.

Victorinus, Georg, German 16th–17th-cent. monk and composer. He became music prefect at the Jesuit monastery of St Michael, where a sacred play with music by him was perf. in 1597. Other works incl. 3 Magnificats, 3 Litanies, *c* 20 sacred pieces.

Victory, opera by R.R. Bennett (lib. by B. Cross, after Conrad), prod. CG, 13 Apr 1970.

Vida breve, La (*Life is Short*), opera by Falla (lib., in Span., by C.F. Shaw), prod. Nice, in Fr., trans. by P. Milliet, 1 Apr 1913.

Vidal, Peire (*fl. c* 1175–*c* 1210), French troubadour, *c* 50 of whose poems are preserved, 12 with music.

Vie parisienne, La (*Life in Paris*), operetta by Offenbach (lib. by H. Meilhac and L. Halévy), prod. Paris, Théâtre du Palais-Royal, 31 Oct 1866.

Vielle organisée (Fr. = 'organed' [not 'organized'] hurdy-gurdy; It. *lira organizata*), a hurdy-gurdy (*vielle*) into which are incorporated one or two sets (stops) or organ pipes. These can be made to sound separately or together, or shut off at will. Haydn wrote 5 concertos for 2 of these insts.

Vienna Philharmonic Orchestra, Austrian orchestra founded 1842 with Otto Nicolai as cond. Richter was prin. cond. 1875–98; succeeded by Mahler (1898–1901), Weingartner (1907–27), Furtwängler (1927–8, 1933–54). Böhm and Karajan were regular post-war conds.; Abbado from 1971. Orch. is unsurpassed in a limited and conservative rep. Also plays at Vienna Staatsoper.

Vienna State Opera. Operas were staged at the Viennese court from the 1630s and for many years opera continued as a court entertainment. The Burgtheater was opened in 1748 and 10 operas by Gluck, incl. *Orpheus* (1762), were premièred there. Later in the cent. Mozart's *Figaro, Così fan tutte* and *Don Giovanni* were staged there, although operas by Salieri and Cimarosa were more popular successes.

A new house, the Oper am Ring, was opened in 1869. Mahler was dir. at this Court Opera (Hofoper) 1897–1907, achieving new standards in dramatic and musical integration. Later dirs. incl. Felix Weingartner (1907–11), Franz Schalk (1919–24) and Clemens Krauss (1929–34). In 1918 the Court Opera was re-named the State Opera (Staatsoper) and in 1919 Richard Strauss became joint dir.; among singers who took part in the fps of *Ariadne auf Naxos* (rev. vers., 1916) and *Die Frau ohne Schatten* (1919) were Maria Jeritza, Selma Kurz, Lotte Lehmann, Lucy Weidt, Richard Mayr and Karl Oestvig.

The opera house was heavily damaged by bombs in 1945 but, after rebuilding according to the original plans, was re-opened in 1955. Post-war dirs. have incl. Karl Böhm (1955–6), Herbert von Karajan (1957–64), Lorin Maazel (1982–4) and Claudio Abbado (from 1986).

Vier ernste Gesänge (*Four Serious Songs*), settings by Brahms for bar. and pf. of words from the Bible, op. 121, comp. May 1896. The corresponding passages in Eng. are 'One thing befalleth', 'So I returned', 'O death, how bitter is thy sting', 'Though I speak with the tongues of men and of angels'.

Vier letzte Lieder (Strauss). *See* **Four Last Songs.**

Vierdanck, Johann (b *c* 1605; d Stralsund, Mar 1646), German organist and composer. Learnt music as a choir-boy in the court chapel at Dresden, where he subsequently served as an instrumentalist. From 1635 until his death he was organist at St Mary's Church, Stralsund.

Works incl. sacred concertos for 2–9 voices; dances for 2 vlns., viol and continuo,

capriccios, canzonets and sonatas for 2–5 insts. with and without continuo.

Vierjährige Posten, Der (*The Four Years' Sentry*), comic opera by Schubert (lib. by T. Körner), comp. 1815, but never perf. in Schubert's lifetime. Prod. Dresden, Opera, 23 Sep 1896.

Vierling, Georg (b Frankenthal, Bavaria, 5 Sep 1820; d Wiesbaden, 1 May 1901), German organist and conductor. Studied under his father, Jacob V. (1796–1867), a schoolmaster and organist, later as Darmstadt and Berlin. In 1847 he became organist and choral cond. at Frankfurt an der Oder. Later he went to Mainz for a short time and then settled in Berlin, where he became royal music dir. in 1859 and prof. of the Acad. in 1882.

Works incl. cantatas for chorus and orch. *Hero and Leander, The Rape of the Sabines, Alaric's Death* and *Constantine*; symph., overtures to Shakespeare's *Tempest*, Schiller's *Maria Stuart* and others; pf. trio; *O Roma nobilis* for unaccomp. chorus; partsongs; pf. pieces; songs.

Vierling, Johann Gottfried (b Metzels nr. Meiningen, 25 Jan 1750; d Schmalkalden, 22 Nov 1813), German organist and composer. Studied at Schmalkalden with the organist J.N. Tischer (whom he succeeded as church organist there in 1773). In 1770 he studied with Kirnberger in Berlin. He wrote treatises on thorough-bass and on preluding to hymns.

Works incl. *Singspiel, Empfindung und Empfindelei*; *c* 160 cantatas, other church music; many chorales and chorale preludes for org.; 2 symphs.; pf. 4tet; 8 pf. sonatas.

Vierne, Louis (b Poitiers, 8 Oct 1870; d Paris, 2 Jun 1937), French organist and composer. Pupil of Franck and Widor at the Paris Cons. Although blind, he became asst. organist to Widor at the church of Saint-Sulpice and later organist at Notre-Dame, where he died at the console.

Works incl. *Messe solennelle* for chorus and 2 orgs.; symph.; string 4tets; sonatas for vln. and pf. and cello and pf.; 6 symphs (1899–1930) 24 *Pièces en style libre*, 24 *Pièces de fantaisie* and other works for org.

Vieuxtemps, Henry (b Verviers, 17 Feb 1820; d Mustapha, Algeria, 6 Jun 1881), Belgian violinist and composer. Learnt the vln. at home and at the age of 6 was able to play a concerto by Rode. At 7 he was taken on tour by his father and heard by Bériot, who offered to teach him at Brussels. In 1828 his master took him to Paris and prod. him there. In 1833 he went on tour in Ger.

and Aus., remaining in Vienna to study counterpoint with Sechter. In 1834 he 1st visited London, where he met Paganini, and the following year he studied comp. with Reicha in Paris. He afterwards travelled long and extensively in Eur. and in 1844 went to the USA. In 1845 he married the Viennese pianist Josephine Eder. In 1846–52 he was vln. prof. at the St Petersburg Cons. In 1871–3 he taught at the Brussels Cons.; he suffered a stroke in 1873, and finally resigned in 1879.

Works incl. 7 vln. concertos, *Fantaisie-Caprice* and *Ballade* and *Polonaise*, etc. for vln. and orch.; vln. and pf. sonata; cadenzas for Beethoven's vln. concerto.

Vihuela, a Spanish plucked instrument, approx. guitar-shaped but strung like a lute with 6 paired courses and normally ten frets. Its repertory appears mainly in 7 printed anthologies of the 16th cent., starting with Luis Milan's *El maestro* (1536), Luis de Narváez's *Delphin de música* (1538) and Alonso Mudarra's *Tres libros* (1546). Some pieces in these vols. appear also in Fr. lute collections, and there is little technical difference between lute and vihuela music except that the vihuela, with its small body and long neck, was able to be played in higher positions than the lute, as exploited partic. in the collections of Valderrábano (1547) and Fuenllana (1554). The name, used for any stringed instr. with a flat back, appears in the 13th cent., and as early as the 14th cent. there is a distinction between the *vihuela de arco* (bowed vihuela) and the *vihuela de peñola* (plectrum vihuela) which, with the development of finger-plucking, became the *vihuela de mano*. It seems likely that the *vihuela de arco* evolved into the viol at the end of the 15th cent.

Vila, Pedro Alberto (or Alberch Vila, Pere) (b Vich nr. Barcelona, 1517; d Barcelona, 16 Nov 1582), Spanish organist and composer, organist of Barcelona Cathedral from 1538.

Works incl. madrigals and org. music.

Vilar, José Teodor (b Barcelona, 10 Aug 1836; d Barcelona, 21 Oct 1905), Spanish composer and conductor. Studied with the cathedral organist Ramón Vilanova (1801–70) at Barcelona and in 1859 went to Paris to study pf. with Herz and comp. with Bazin and Halévy. Returning home in 1863, he became cond. at one of the minor theatres and later at the princ. theatre. He also did much teaching.

Works incl. *zarzuelas La romería de Recaseéns* (1867), *L'ultim rey de Magnolia* (1868), *Los pescadores de San Pol* (1869),

Una prometensa (1870), *La rambla de las flores* (1870), *Pot més que pinta* (1870), *La lluna en un cove*, *L'esca del pecat* (1871), *La torre del amore* (1871).

Vilback, (Alphonse Charles) Renaud de (b Montpellier, 3 Jun 1829; d Brussels, 19 Mar 1884), French organist, pianist and composer. Studied at the Paris Cons., Halévy being among his masters, and gained the Prix de Rome in 1844. He was organist of Ste Eugène, Paris, from 1856 to 1871. After an early success he was unfortunate, made a precarious living by arrs. and other editorial hack-work for unscrupulous publishers, became blind and died in poverty.

Works incl. operas *Au Clair de la lune* (1857) and *Don Almanzor* (1858); *Messe solennelle*; cantata *Le Renégat de Tanger* (1842); *Pompadour Gavotte*, *Chant cypriote*, *Marche serbe* for orch.; pf. pieces.

Villa-Lobos, Heitor (b Rio de Janeiro, 5 Mar 1887; d Rio de Janeiro, 17 Nov 1959), Brazilian composer. He studied the cello at 1st, but became a pianist and for some time toured as a concert artist. In 1912 he began to explore his country's folk music and in 1915 gave the 1st concert devoted to his own works at Rio de Janeiro. A government grant enabled him to live in Paris for a few years from 1923, but on his return he did much useful work as cond. and music educationist, being app. director of music educ. for the schools in the capital in 1930. In 1929 he pub. a book on Brazilian folk music, *Alma de Brasil.*

Works incl. operas *Izath* (1914, concert perf. 1940), *Yerma* (1956, prod. 1971); musical comedy *Magdalena* (1948); ballet *Uirapuru*; oratorio *Vidapura*; 14 works entitled *Chôros* cast in a new form and consisting of 4 for orch., 1 for pf. and orch., 1 for 2 pfs. and orch., 2 for chorus and orch. and 6 for var. combinations and solo insts. (1920–28); orch. works incl. symph. poem *Amazonas*, *Bachianas Brasileiras* (9 suites in the spirit of Bach, 1930–44), 12 symphs. (1916–57); 5 pf. concertos, 2 cello concertos, harp concerto; nonet for wind, harp, perc. and chorus, 5tet for wind insts. (1923); 17 string 4tets (1915–58), 3 pf. trios (1911–18); 4 sonata-fantasies for vln. and pf. (1912–23); a very large number of pf. works; songs.

Village Romeo and Juliet (Delius). *See* **Romeo und Julia auf dem Dorfe.**

Villancico (Span.), a type of verse with a refrain and a complex rhyme-scheme; also the music to which such poems were set, at first tunes without harmony, later pieces similar to madrigals; sometimes a comp. for solo voices, strings and org. to sacred words, esp. connected with the Nativity.

Villanella (It. lit. country girl), an Italian part-song of the middle 16th to the earlier 17th cent., set to rustic words and light in character.

Villanella rapita, La (*The Ravished Country Girl*) opera by Bianchi (lib. by G. Bertati, based on J.M. Favart's *Le Caprice amoureux*), prod. Venice, Teatro San Moisè, autumn 1783. Mozart wrote an addit. 4tet and a trio for the Vienna perf., 25 Nov 1785.

Villanelle (Fr.). In French music a *Villanelle* is not the equivalent of the It. *Villanella* and the Span. *Villancico*, but a vocal setting of a poem in *Villanelle* form, which consists of stanzas of 3 lines, the 1st and 3rd lines of the opening stanza being repeated alternately as the 3rd line of the succeeding stanzas. Best known ex. is 1st song of Berlioz's cycle *Les Nuits d'été*.

Villi, Le (*The Witches*), opera by Puccini (lib. by F. Fontana), prod. Milan, Teatro dal Verme, 31 May 1884.

Vinaccesi, Benedetto (b Brescia, ? 1670; d Venice, ? 1719), Italian composer. *Maestro di cappella* to Prince Ferdinand Gonzaga di Castiglione in 1687, he was app. 2nd organist at St Mark's, Venice, in 1704.

Works incl. 2 operas (lost); 4 oratorios (only *Susanna* (1694) extant); motets and other church music; 6 *Suonate da camera* and 12 *Sonate da chiesa* for 2 vlns. and continuo.

Vinay, Ramón (b Chillán, 31 Aug 1912), Chilean baritone, later tenor and baritone. Debut 1931, Mexico City, as Donizetti's Alfonso. Bar. roles until 1943, then sang Don José in Mexico. He was best known as Otello and recorded the role under Toscanini; also sang part at La Scala, CG and Salzburg. NY Met 1946–61. Bayreuth 1952–7 as Tristan, Tannhäuser, Siegmund and Parsifal; sang Telramund there in 1962. Other bar. roles were Iago, Scarpia and Falstaff.

Vincent, Thomas (b London, c 1720; d London, ? 10 May 1783), English oboist and composer. Pupil of Sammartini. He entered the king's band as oboist in 1735.

Works incl. solos for ob., fl. or vln. with harpsichord continuo; harpsichord lessons.

Vincentius, Caspar (b St Omer, c 1580; d Würzburg, 1624), Flemish composer and organist. He was a choir-boy at the Imp. chapel in Vienna 1595–7, and town organist at Speyer c 1602–4, where he met Schadaeus. He later held appts. at Worms and, from 1618 until his death, Würzburg. He provided a *bassus generalis* to the 3 vols. of

Schadaeus's *Promptuarium musicum*, and later added a 4th vol. of his own (1617). He also wrote a continuo part for Lassus's *Magnum opus musicum*.

Vinci, Leonardo (b Strongoli, Calabria, c 1690; d Naples, 27 or 28 May 1730), Italian composer. Pupil of Greco at the Cons. dei Poveri di Gesù Cristo in Naples, estab. himself 1st as a comp. of Neapolitan dialect *commedie musicali* (from 1719) and prod. his 1st *opera seria* in 1722. App. as an acting *maestro di cappella* at court in 1725, he was from 1728 also *maestro* at his old Cons., where Pergolesi was among his pupils.

Works incl. *commedie musicali: Lo cecato fauzo* (1719, lost), *Le zite 'n galera* (1722); *opere serie: Silla dittatore* (1723), *L'Astianatte* (1725), *Siroe* (1726), *La caduta dei Decemviri* (1727), *Artaserse* (1730) and 19 others; 6 cantatas; chamber music.

Vinci, Leonardo da (b Vinci nr. Empoli, 1452; d Amboise nr. Paris, 2 May 1519), Italian painter, scientist, inventor and musician. In this last capacity he excelled as a player of the *lira da braccio*. He investigated acoustics and designed many improved and new insts.

Vinci, Pietro (b Nicosia, Sicily, c 1535; d Nicosia or Piazza Armerina, c 1584), Italian composer. He was *maestro di cappella* at the Basilica of Santa Maria Maggiore at Bergamo in 1568–80 and in 1581 took on a similar post at his birth-place.

Works incl. Masses, motets; madrigals; ricercares.

Viñes, Ricardo (b Lérida, 5 Feb 1875; d Barcelona, 29 Apr 1943), Spanish pianist. Studied and lived in Paris, where he did much useful work for modern Fr. and Span. music. He gave early perfs. of music by Falla, Ravel and Debussy, incl. the fps of *Miroirs*, *Gaspard de la Nuit* and *Images I*.

Vingt-quatre Violons du Roy (Fr. = The King's 24 Vlns.), the French court string band of the 17th cent., used for ballets, court balls, dinners, etc., and incl. all the insts. of the vln. family. A similar string orch. was founded, on the Fr. model, by Charles II in London after his restoration in 1660.

Vingt regards sur l'Enfant Jésus, work for pf. in 20 sections by Messiaen; comp. 1944, fp Paris, 26 Mar 1945, by Yvonne Loriod.

Viol, the generic name of a family of bowed string instruments. The It. name was *viola da gamba* (leg viol). Viols 1st appeared in the 15th cent. and were in vogue until near the end of the 17th, disappearing completely, apart from the bass viol. in the 18th. The main representatives were the treble, the tenor and the bass, all of which were tuned on the same plan, i.e.:

Treble

Tenor

Bass

VIOL

The double bass of the family was called *violone*.

See also **Treble Viol, Viola da gamba** and **Violone**.

Viola, unfinished opera by Smetana (lib. by E. Krasnohorská, on Shakespeare's *Twelfth Night*), begun 1883.

Viola, the tenor instrument of the vln. family. It has 4 strings tuned as follows:

It is the regular middle part in the string section of the orch. and in the string 4tet, etc.

Viola, Alfonso dalla (b Ferrara, *c* 1508; d Ferrara, *c* 1573), Italian composer and instrumentalist. *Maestro di cappella* at Ferrara Cathedral and in charge of the *musica da camera segreta* at the court of Ercole d'Este (II), Duke of Ferrara, where he wrote music (now lost) for plays. He remained in the service of the next duke, Alfonso II. Like his relative Francesco dalla V. (d 1568), who also served at the cathedral and the court, he wrote madrigals.

Viola alta (It. = high vla.), an exceptionally large vla. designed by Hermann Ritter and made by Hörlein of Würzburg in the 1870s for use in the orch. at the Wagner festivals at Bayreuth. In 1898 a 5th string was added, tuned to the E of the highest vln. string.

Viola bastarda (It. lit. bastard viol), the It. name for the Lyra Viol, called *bastarda* because it was midway in size between the Tenor Viol and the Bass Viol.

Viola da braccio (It. = arm viol), in the 16th and early 17th cent. the generic name for members of the vln. family, since the smaller insts. were played on the arm and not, as was the case with the *viola da gamba* family, on

or between the legs. Since the cello was the bass of the family it was known, illogically, as *bassa viola da braccio*. The treble inst. came to be known exclusively by the diminutive *violino*, and *viola da braccio* was reserved for the alto or tenor, shortened to *viola* in It. and corrupted into *Bratsche* in Ger.

Viola da gamba (It. = leg viol), the generic name for the members of the viol family, all of which, small or large, are played on or between the legs. Unlike the vln. family they have flat backs, sloping shoulders, 6 strings and frets. The smaller insts. of the family gradually went out of use in the course of the 17th cent., but the bass was retained as a solo inst. and for continuo playing. Hence in the 18th cent. *viola da gamba* normally means the bass viol. Exs. of its use are Bach's 3 sonatas with harpsichord and the obbligatos in the *St Matthew Passion*. All the members of the family have been successfully revived in modern times. For their tuning *see* **Viol.**

Viola da spalla (It. = shoulder vla.), a portable cello used mainly by wandering musicians in the 17th and 18th cents., held by a shoulder strap. Also an alternative name for the cello.

Viola d'amore (It. lit. love viol), (1) In the 17th cent. a vln. with wire strings. (2) A bowed string inst. of the viol type with 7 strings and from 7 to 14 sympathetic strings not touched by the bow but vibrating with those actually played. There was no standard tuning.

Viola di bordone (It. = drone viol), an alternative name for the Baryton.

Viola pomposa, a special type of bowed string instrument of the vln. family, very rarely used. It seems to have had 5 strings, the lower 4 tuned as on the vla. and the 5th tuned to the E of the vln.

Violet, the Eng. name sometimes given to the Viola d'amore.

Violetta marina (It. lit. little marine viol), a special type of Viol, allied to the Viola d'amore, like which it has sympathetic strings.

Violetta piccola (It. small little viol), an early name for the treble viol and the vln.

Violin, the principal modern bowed string instrument, to whose family belong also the

Viola and Violoncello. The violin has 4 strings tuned:

It began to displace the Viol in the 17th cent. and completely superseded it in the 18th. *See also* **Basse-contre, Cellone, Dessus, Double Bass, Fiddle, Hardanger Fiddle, Haute-contre, Kit, Quinton, Taille, Tenor Violin, Viola, Viola alta, Viola da braccio, Viola da spalla, Viola pomposa, Violino piccolo, Violon d'amour, Violoncello, Violoncello piccolo, Violotta.**

Violino piccolo (It. = littl vln.), a small string instrument of the vln. family with 4 strings tuned either:

or

and thus standing a 4th or a min. 3rd above the vln. in pitch.

Violins of St Jacques, The, opera by Williamson (lib. by W. Chappell), prod. London, SW, 29 Nov 1966.

Violon d'amour (Fr. lit. love vln.), the member of the modern string family corresponding to the Viola d'amore of the Viol family, used in the 18th cent., but now obs. It had 5 strings, tuned:

and 6 sympathetic strings, not touched by the bow but vibrating with those actually played.

Violoncello, the bass instrument of the vln. family. It has 4 strings tuned:

Its upward range is considerable. In the 17th and 18th cents. it was also made with 5 strings, i.e. with an E string a 5th above the A.

Violoncello piccolo, a small cello on which the playing of high passages was easier than on the normal cello. A familiar example of its use is the obbligato in Bach's aria 'Mein gläubiges Herze' ('My heart ever faithful') in

the cantata no. 68, *Also hat Gott die Welt geliebt* (*God so loved the world*).

Violone, the double bass of the Viol family, similar to the Bass Viol but larger, with 6 strings similarly tuned an 8ve lower. The name was also applied to the double bass of the vln. family.

Violotta, a modern string instrument of the vln. family invented by Alfred Stelzner (d 1906) of Dresden. It has 4 strings tuned so as to stand in pitch between the vla. and the cello:

Viotti, Giovanni Battista (b Fontanetto da Po, Piedmont, 12 May 1755; d London, 3 Mar 1824), Italian violinist and composer. Pupil of Pugnani, joined the court orch. at Turin in 1775, but obtained leave of absence in 1780 to go on tour with Pugnani. (A supposed meeting with Voltaire, who died in 1778, is apparently apocryphal.) Visited Switz., Dresden, Berlin, Warsaw, St Petersburg and in 1782 arrived in Paris, where he stayed 10 years. He played at the Concert spirituel, was solo violinist to Marie Antoinette 1784–6, cond. some concerts of the Loge Olympique (for which Haydn wrote his 'Paris' symphs.), and from 1788 was involved in the foundation of a new opera co. at the Théâtre de Monsieur. In 1792 he went to London, where he played in Salomon's concerts and became acting manager and leader of the orch. at the King's Theatre opera, but was forced to leave Eng. for political reasons in 1798, and lived nr. Hamburg, writing an autobiog. sketch. Returning to London in 1801, he withdrew almost completely from music and entered the wine trade, but twice visited Paris (1802 and 1814) and in 1819 became director of the Opera there, finally returning to London in 1823.

Works incl. 29 vln. concertos (1782–c 1805); 2 *Symphonies concertantes* for 2 vlns. and orch.; 15 string 4tets (c 1783–1817); 21 string trios for 2 vlns. and cello; vln. duos, sonatas etc.; 6 pf. sonatas.

Virdung, Sebastian (b Amberg, Upper Palatinate, c 1465; d c 1511), German cleric and writer on music. Studied at Heidelberg Univ. He sang and then was *Kapellmeister* at the Palatine court chapel in Heidelberg, and in 1507 became succentor at Konstanz Cathedral. In 1511 he pub. at Basle his book on musical instruments, *Musica getutscht und auszgezogen*, ded. to the Bishop of Strasbourg.

Virelai (Fr., from *virer*, to turn, and *lai*, a song), a type of medieval French song with a refrain before and after each verse.

Virginal, a stringed keyboard instrument of the 16th and 17th cents., often called 'virginals' or 'a pair of virginals' in Eng. where the term was applied to any quilled keyboard inst. well into the 17th cent. The virginal is rectangular or polygonal in shape and is distinguished from the harpsichord and spinet by its strings being set at right angles to the keys, rather than parallel with them. The most likely explanation of the name is that the inst. was often played by girls. There are several MS. collections of virginal music by Eng. comps., incl. The Fitzwilliam Virginal Book, My Ladye Nevells Booke, Will Forster's Book, Benjamin Cosyn's Book and Elizabeth Rogers's Book.

Virginia, opera by Mercadante (lib. by S. Cammarano, based on Alfieri's tragedy), prod. Naples, Teatro San Carlo, 7 Apr 1866.

Visconti (di Modrone), Count **Luchino** (b Milan, 2 Nov 1906; d Rome, 17 Mar 1976), Italian producer. His first prod. was at La Scala in 1954 (*La vestale*, with Callas); later Milan prods. with Callas incl. *La sonnambula*, *Anna Bolena* and *Iphigénie en Tauride*. His 1st prod. at CG was *Don Carlos* (1958) and he returned for *Il trovatore*, *Traviata*, and *Der Rosenkavalier*. His work on *Macbeth* and *Manon Lescaut* (1972) at Spoleto was admired; his prods. were notable for taste, discretion and fidelity to the comps.' intentions. As an alleged Marxist, he was notable in not allowing his views to colour his work.

Visée Robert de (b *c* 1660; d *c* 1725), French lutenist, guitarist and composer. He was guitar and theorbo player to the dauphin and chamber musician to the king from near the end of the 17th cent. to 1720.

Works incl. 2 books of guitar pieces, and 1 of pieces for lute and theorbo.

Vishnevskaya, Galina (Pavlovna) (b Leningrad, 25 Oct 1926), Russian soprano. Opera debut Leningrad, 1950; Bolshoy, Moscow, from 1952. Her roles included Tatyana, Lisa, Tosca, Cherubino and Natasha. Aida was the role of her NY Met (1961) and CG (1962) debuts. She has been associated with Britten (*The Poet's Echo*, *War Requiem*) and Shostakovich (sang in fp of the 14th symph., Leningrad, 1969). She married Mstislav Rostropovich in 1955; they were obliged to leave Russia in 1975 and 3 years later they were stripped of their citizenship. Autobiog. (*Galina*), 1985.

Vision of St Augustine, The, work by Tippett for bar., chorus and orch. (text in Latin); comp. 1963–5, fp London, 19 Jan 1966, with Fischer-Dieskau.

Visions de l'Amen, suite by Messiaen in 7 movts. for 2 pf.; comp. 1943, fp Paris, 10 May 1943, by Loriod and Messiaen.

Visions Fugitives, 20 pieces for pf. by Prokofiev; comp. 1915–17, fp Petrograd, 15 Apr 1918, by comp. Orch. vers. by Rudolf Barschai.

Vitali, Filippo (b Florence, *c* 1590; d ? Florence, 1653), Italian priest, tenor and composer. He worked at Florence until 1631, when he was called to Rome as singer in the Papal chapel. While there he became attached to the household of Cardinal Francesco Barberini; but in 1642 he returned to Florence to become *maestro di cappella* to the Duke of Tuscany at San Lorenzo. In 1653 he became a canon there.

Works incl. opera *L'Aretusa* (1620); *intermedii* for J. Cicognini's comedy *La finta Mora* (1623); psalms for 5 voices, hymns, *Sacrae cantiones* (1625) and other church music; madrigals; var. works for voices and insts. in several parts.

Vitali, Giovanni Battista (b Bologna, 18 Feb 1632; d Bologna, 12 Oct 1692), Italian violist and composer. Pupil of Maurizio Cazzati, *maestro di cappella* of San Petronio at Bologna, where Vitali himself was a string player and singer from 1658. In 1673 he became *maestro di cappella* of the Santissimo Rosario, and in 1674 he went to Modena as *vice-maestro* of the ducal chapel. His oratorio on Monmouth was prod. there in 1686, the year after Monmouth's execution.

Works incl. psalms for 2–5 voices and insts.; oratorios *Il Giono* and *L'ambitione debellata overo La Caduta di Monmouth*; 10 cantatas; numerous dances for several insts.; sonatas for 2 vlns. and continuo and others for var. inst. combinations.

Vitali, Tomaso (Antonio) (b Bologna, 7 Mar 1663; d Modena, 9 May 1745), Italian violinist and composer, son of prec. Pupil of his father, later member of the court chapel at Modena under him. He taught the vln. to distinguished pupils, incl. Dall' Abaco and Senallié.

Works incl. sonatas for 2 vlns. and continuo.

Vitry, Philippe de (b Paris, 31 Oct 1291; d Paris, 9 Jun 1361), French diplomat, priest, music theorist, poet and composer. He was secretary to Charles IV and Philip VI of France, in 1350 arr. a meeting between the king and the pope at Avignon and was created Bishop of Meaux the following year.

His poetry, like his music, was much esteemed, Petrarch writing him a letter of appreciation. He wrote a treatise, *Ars nova*, in which he codified a new mensural notation that incl. the minim and imperfect mensuration. 12 motets by him survive.

Vittadini, Franco (b Pavia, 9 Apr 1884; d Pavia, 30 Nov 1948), Italian composer and conductor. Studied at the Milan Cons., became cond. at Varese and later settled at Pavia, where he became director of the Istituto Musicale.

Works incl. operas *Il mare di Tiberiade* (comp. 1914), *Anima allegra* (after the Quintero brothers, 1921), *Nazareth* (after Lagerlöf, 1925), *La Sagredo* (1930) and *Caracciolo* (1938); ballets *Vecchia Milano*, *Le dame galanti* and *Fiordisole*; 10 Masses and motets; oratorio *Il natale di Gesù* (1931), *Le sette parole di Cristo* for chorus (1933); symph. poem *Armonie della notte*; org. works.

Vittori, Loreto (b Spoleto, bap. 5 Sep 1600; d Rome, 23 Apr 1670), Italian soprano castrato and composer. Studied with Soto, Nanini and Soriano in Rome and lived for a time at the court of Cosimo II de' Medici at Florence, but returned to Rome and entered the Papal Chapel in 1622. Among his pupils were Queen Christina of Sweden, during her residence in Rome, and Pasquini.

Works incl. opera *La Galatea* (1639); plays with music *La fiera di Palestrina* and *Le zitelle canterine* (music of both lost); 3 sacred dramas (music lost); arias.

Vittoria, Tommaso Lodovico da. *See* **Victoria, Tomás Luis de.**

Vitzthumb, Ignaz (b Baden nr. Vienna, 20 Jul 1720; d Brussels, 23 Mar 1816), South Netherlands composer and conductor of Austrian birth. Studied in Vienna and settled in Brussels in the service of Prince Charles of Lorraine. He cond. at Ghent, Amsterdam and at the Théâtre de la Monnaie in Brussels, but lost his posts and pension during the Revolution and died in poverty.

Works incl. comic operas *Le Soldat par amour* (1766), *La Foire de village* (1786), etc., Masses, motets and other church music; 4 symphs.

Vivace (It.) = lively, animated.

Vivaldi, Antonio (Lucio) (b Venice, 4 Mar 1678; d Vienna, 28 Jul 1741), Italian composer and violinist. Pupil of his father Giovanni Battista V., a violinist at St Mark's, Venice, and possibly also of Legrenzi, he entered the church in 1693 and was ordained priest in 1703 (being commonly known as 'il prete rosso' – 'the red [-haired]

priest'), but soon afterwards was given dispensations from priestly duties; he nevertheless came into conflict with the church authorities for keeping a mistress. He was assoc. with the Cons. dell' Ospedale della Pietà in Venice 1703–40 (*maestro di violino*, 1711), for which he wrote oratorios and inst. music, but was frequently absent. His 1st opera was prod. in Vicenza in 1713, followed by many others in Venice, Florence, Munich, Parma, Milan, etc. He was in Mantua as *maestro di cappella da camera* to the Margrave Philip of Hesse-Darmstadt 1720–23, and toured Europe 1729–33, but of his extensive travels throughout his career little is known. He returned to Venice in 1739, but his popularity was falling, and 2 years later he died in poverty in Vienna. One of the most prolific comps. of his day, he was partic. influential through his concertos, several of which were transcribed by Bach.

Works incl. OPERAS: *c* 21 extant, incl. *Ottone in Villa* (1713), *Arsilda* (1716), *Tito Manlio* (1720), *Ercole* (1723), *Giustino* (1724), *Orlando furioso* (1727), *La fida ninfa* (1732), *L'Olimpiade* (1734), *Griselda* (1735); Latin oratorio *Juditha* and others.

SECULAR VOCAL: serenatas *Gloria e Himeneo* (*c* 1725), *La Sena festeggiante* (1729), *Mio cor povero cor*; 9 solo cantatas, with insts., 30 with continuo.

SACRED VOCAL: incl. Gloria (2 settings), *Dixit Dominus* (2), *Laudate pueri* (3), *Nisi Dominus*, *Magnificat* (2), *Salve regina* (3), *Stabat mater*.

INST.: over 230 vln. concertos (incl. 'The Four Seasons', nos. 1–4 of *Il cimento dell'armonia e dell'inventione*, op. 8), *c* 120 solo concertos (for bassoon, cello, ob., fl., ob. d'amore, recorder and mandolin), over 40 double concertos (*c* 24 for vlns., 3 for 2 obs.), over 30 ens. concertos (insts. incl. clars., horns, theorbos and timpani), nearly 60 string orch. concertos (without soloists) and over 20 concertos for solo ens. (without string ripieno); *c* 90 solo and trio sonatas.

Vivo (It.) = Lively, animated, the same as *vivace*, but more rarely used.

Vlad, Roman (b Cernauţi, 29 Dec 1919), Italian composer of Rumanian birth. Studied at the Cernauţi Cons. but in 1938 settled in Rome, where he finished studies under Casella. He is the author of books on Dallapiccola and Stravinsky.

Works incl. radio opera *Il dottore di vetro* (1959), ballets *La strada sul caffè* (1945) and *La dama delle camelie* (after Dumas); film music; *De profundis* for sop., chorus and orch.; *Divertimento* for 11 insts.; *Studi dodecafonici* for pf.

Vladigerov, Pancho (b Zurich, 13 Mar 1899; d Sofia, 8 Sep 1978), Bulgarian composer. Studied with Juon and Georg Schumann in Berlin and at the Sofia Cons.

Works incl. opera *Tsar Kaloyan* (1936); incid. music for Strindberg's *A Dream Play*; Bulg. Rhapsody *Vardar*; 2 vln. concertos (1921, 1968); pf. concerto; pf. trio; vln. and pf. sonata; pf. pieces; songs.

Vltava (Smetana). *See* **Má Vlast.**

Vocalise (Fr.) ⎱ any kind of vocal exercise
Vocalizzo (It.) ⎰ any kind of vocal exercise
without words, also sometimes in recent years a comp. for voice without words for concert perf. (the most ambitious being Medtner's *Sonata-Vocalise*); also used as a synonym for Solfège and Solfeggio.

Vogel, Charles (Louis Adolphe) (b Lille, 17 May 1808; d Paris, 11 Sep 1892), Franco–Belgian composer of German descent. Studied at the Paris Cons.

Works incl. operas *Le Podestat* (1831), *Le Siège de Leyde* (1847), *La Moissonneuse* (1853), *Rompons!* (1857), *Le Nid de cigognes* (1858), *Gredin et Pigoche* (1866), *La Filleule du roi*; oratorio *Le Jugement dernier*; symphs.; string 4tets, string 5tets; songs incl. *Les Trois Couleurs*.

Vögel, Die (*The Birds*), opera by Braunfels (lib. by comp., based on the comedy by Aristophanes), prod. Munich, 4 Dec 1920.

Vogel, (Johannes) Emil (Eduard Bernhard) (b Wriezen an der Oder, 21 Jan 1859; d Nikolassee nr. Berlin, 18 Jun 1908), German music scholar. Studied at Berlin Univ. and privately. In 1883 he went to It. as asst. to F.X. Haberl in his Palestrina ed. From 1893 to 1901 he was librarian of the Musikbibliothek Peters and ed. of the Peters *Jahrbuch*.

Vogel, Johann Christoph (b Nuremberg, bap. 18 Mar 1756; d Paris, 28 Jun 1788), German composer. Pupil of Riepel at Regensburg, went to Paris in 1776 and there became an enthusiastic supporter of Gluck, to whom he ded. his first opera, *La Toison d'or* and *Démophon* (1789); symphs.; *symphonies concertantes* for wind insts. and orch.

Vogel, Wladimir (Rudolfovich) (b Moscow, 29 Feb 1896; d Zurich, 19 Jun 1984), Swiss composer of German and Russian descent. Studied in Rus., later with Tiessen and Busoni in Berlin; settled in Switz. 1933.

Works incl. cantatas *Wagadu's Untergang* for solo voices, chorus, speaking chorus and 5 saxophones (1930); *Thyl Claes* (after *Till Eulenspiegel*, 1938–45); *Sinfonia*

fugata, 4 studies, *Devise*, *Tripartita* for orch.; vln. concerto (1937), cello concerto (1955); *Komposition* and *Étude Toccata* for pf.

Vogelhändler, Der (*The Bird Dealer*), operetta by Zeller (lib. by M. West and L. Held), prod. Vienna, Theater an der Wien, 10 Jan 1891.

Vogelweide, Walther von der (b *c* 1170; d ? Würzburg, *c* 1230), German poet, minnesinger and composer. Pupil of Reinmar von Hagenau in Aus. He was in service at the court of Duke Leopold V in Vienna, then led a wandering life in Ger. and after 1220 prob. lived at an estate given to him at Würzburg. Only a few of his tunes have been preserved.

Vogl, Heinrich (b Au nr. Munich, 15 Jan 1845; d Munich, 21 Apr 1900), German tenor and composer. Began his career as a schoolmaster, but learnt singing from F. Lachner at Munich and also studied acting. He made his debut there in 1865 as Max. He married the soprano Therese Thoma (1845–1921) in 1868. He appeared in the 1st 2 parts of Wagner's *Ring* at Munich in 1869–70, as Loge and Siegmund, and in the prod. of the whole work at Bayreuth in 1876, as Loge. He sang in the 1st London *Ring* cycle (1882) and at the NY Met from 1890 (Lohengrin, Tannhäuser and Tristan).

Works incl. opera *Der Fremdling* and songs.

Vogl, Johann Michael (b Ennsdorf nr. Steyr, 10 Aug 1768; d Vienna, 19 Nov 1840), Austrian baritone. Educ. at the monastery of Kremsmünster and Vienna Univ., he was engaged by Süssmayr in 1794 and made his debut as a court opera singer in 1795; well known as Pizarro, Gluck's Orestes and Mozart's Count. He met Schubert in 1816 and was the 1st important artist to sing his songs in public. He retired from the stage with a pension in 1821 and devoted himself to song; gave *Erlkönig* in public and many other Schubert songs in private.

Vogl (*née* Thoma), **Therese** (b Tutzing, 12 Nov 1845; d Munich, 29 Sep 1921), German soprano. Studied at the Munich Cons. and made her 1st stage appearance at Karlsruhe in 1865; she created Sieglinde (Munich, 1870) and also sang Ortrud, Isolde and Medea. In 1868 she married Heinrich Vogl.

Vogler, Carl (b Oberrohrdorf, Aargau, 26 Feb 1874; d Zurich, 17 Jun 1951), Swiss composer. Studied at Lucerne, with Hegar and others at Zurich and with Rheinberger and others at Munich. In 1915 he became prof. at the Zurich Cons. and in 1919 joint director with V. Andreae.

Works incl. operas *Rübezahl* (1917) and *Fiedelhänschen* (1924), play with music *Mutter Sybille* (1906); org. works; songs and part-songs.

Vogler, Georg Joseph (known as Abbé Vogler) (b Pleichach nr. Würzburg, 15 Jun 1749; d Darmstadt, 6 May 1814), German composer, teacher and theorist. Son of an inst. maker and violinist, he studied theology at Würzburg and Bamberg Univs., went to Mannheim in 1771, becoming court chaplain the following year, and in 1773 received a scholarship from the Elector to go to It. Studied with Padre Martini in Bologna and Palotti in Padua, and in 1775 returned to Mannheim as *vice-Kapellmeister*. Mozart met him there in 1778 and disliked him. When the electoral court moved to Munich in 1778 Vogler at first remained in Mannheim, but later followed, becoming *Kapellmeister* in 1784. He was *Kapellmeister* to the Swed. court in Stockholm 1786–99, but was able to travel extensively, going as far afield as N. Africa and Greece. After leaving Stockholm he lived successively in Copenhagen, Berlin, Prague, Vienna and Munich, until in 1807 he was app. *Kapellmeister* to the Grand Duke of Hesse-Darmstadt. He was a notable teacher: his pupils incl. Weber, Meyerbeer and Crusell, and he wrote a number of theoret. works.

Works incl. *Singspiele: Albert III von Bayern* (1781), *Erwin und Elmire* (1781, Goethe); operas *La Kermesse* (1783), *Castore e Polluce* (1787), *Gustav Adolph och Ebba Brahe* (1788), *Samori* (1804) and others; operetta *Der Kaufmann von Smyrna* (1771); ballet *Jäger-Ballet* (1772); incid. music to Shakespeare's *Hamlet* (1779); choruses for Racine's *Athalie* and Skjöldebrand's *Hermann von Unna*; Masses, 7 Requiems, motets, psalms and other church music; cantata *Ino* (Ramler); symphs.; several pf. variations for pf. and orch.; pf. trios and much other chamber music; pf. and vln. sonatas; pf. sonatas and vars.; 6 sonatas for 2 pfs.

Voice of Ariadne, The, opera by Thea Musgrave (lib. by A. Elguera, after Henry James's *The Last of the Valerii*); comp. 1972–3, fp Aldeburgh, 11 Jun 1974.

Voices, work by Henze for mezzo, tenor and inst. ens. (22 settings based on texts by Ho Chi Minh (*Prison Song*) E. Fried, Brecht, M. Enzensberger and others); comp. 1973, fp London, 4 Jan 1974.

Voices, the parts in a polyphonic comp., even those for instruments.

Voicing, the prod. of particular qualities of tone by mechanical means in org. construction, and more partic. the control of the tone of a whole range of pipes governed by a single stop in such a way that the tone-colour is exactly the same throughout.

Voix céleste (Fr. = heavenly voice), an 8-ft. organ stop with 2 pipes to each note, one tuned slightly sharper than the other, so that they prod. a quivering effect.

Voix Humaine, La (*The Human Voice*), tragédie lyrique (monodrama) by Poulenc (lib. by Cocteau), prod. Paris, Opéra-Comique, 6 Feb 1959.

Volbach, Fritz (b Wippelfürth, Rhineland, 17 Dec 1861; d Wiesbaden, 30 Nov 1940), German composer and conductor. Studied at the Cologne Cons. He joined the staff of the Royal Institute of Church Music in Berlin, 1886, became music director at Mainz in 1892 and prof. of music at Tübingen Univ. in 1907, moving to Münster Univ. in 1919.

Works incl. opera *Die Kunst zu lieben* (1910); ballads for male voices and orch. *Der Troubadour, Am Siegfrieds-Brunnen, König Laurins Rosengarten* (1913); *Raffael* for chorus, orch. and org.; *Hymne an Maria* (Dante) for chorus, solo insts. and org. (1922); symph. in B min., symph. poems *Es waren zwei Königskinder* and *Alt Heidelberg; Ostern* for org. and orch.; pf. 5tet for wind and pf.; song cycle *Vom Pagen und der Königstochter* (Geibel).

Völker, Franz (b Neu-Isenburg, 31 Mar 1899; d Darmstadt, 4 Dec 1965), German tenor. Debut Frankfurt, 1926, as Florestan. He sang at the Vienna Staatsoper 1931–50 and in Berlin from 1935. Salzburg 1931–9, as Ferrando, Max and the Emperor. Bayreuth 1933–42 as Siegmund, Lohengrin, Parsifal and Erik. CG 1934 and 1937 as Florestan and Siegmund. Retired 1952.

Volkert, Franz (Joseph) (b Vienna, 12 Feb 1778; d Vienna, 22 Mar 1845), Austrian organist, composer and conductor. Settled in Vienna as organist by 1801 and was deputy *Kapellmeister* at the Leopoldstadt Theatre *c* 1814–24.

Works incl. *c* 150 music pieces for the stage (farces, melodramas, pantomimes, etc.); Masses; org. and pf. pieces; songs.

Volkmann, (Friedrich) Robert (b Lommatzsch nr. Dresden, 6 Apr 1815; d Budapest, 29 Oct 1883), German composer. Pupil of his father, a schoolmaster and cantor, and of another local musician for string insts. In 1836 he went to Leipzig for further study, was a private music tutor in Prague,

1839–41, lived and taught at Budapest in 1841–54 and in Vienna in 1854–78, when he became prof. of comp. at the Nat. Music Acad. in Budapest.

Works incl. incid. music for Shakespeare's *Richard III*; 2 Masses for male voices; 2 symphs., 3 serenades, Festival Overture for orch.; *Concertstück* for pf. and orch.; cello concerto, 6 string 4tets, 2 pf. trios and other chamber music; 2 sonatinas for vln. and pf., vln. and pf. pieces, cello and pf. pieces; sonata and *c* 20 other op. nos. for pf.; several pf. duet works; 9 op. nos. of songs.

Volkonsky, Andrey Mikhaylovich (b Geneva, 14 Feb 1933), Russian composer. Studied pf. with Lipatti and comp. with N. Boulanger in Paris, and in 1948 went to Moscow to study with Shaporin. He is a modernist among Rus. comps., using a form of the 12-note system. Discouraged from composing by the Soviet authorities, he emigrated to Israel in 1973.

Works incl. cantata *The Image of the World* (1953); *The Laments of Shchaza* for sop. and chamber orch.; concerto for orch (1954); pf. 5tet (1954); vla. sonata.

Volkslied (Ger. = folksong). Although Germany possesses a treasury of old folksongs, many of which became hymns for the Lutheran church, the term *Volkslied* no longer exclusively or even principally designates them: what Gers. now mean by *Volkslied* is a type of popular song, such as Silcher's *Loreley*, the comps. of which are known (which is not the case with genuine folksongs), and which have passed into general currency.

Volkstümlich (Ger. adj. from *Volkstum* = folk matters, folklore), a word used in Germany to describe popular music that has become or is likely to become part of the nation's musical heritage, without actually belonging to folk music.

Volo di Notte (*Night Flight*), opera in 1 act by Dallapiccola (lib. by the comp., after St-Exupéry), prod. Florence, 18 May 1940.

Volta (It. = time, turn, jump). The word is used in such musical directions as *prima volta* (first time), *seconda volta* (second time), *ancora una volta* (once again). It is also the name of an old dance incl. a characteristic jump. *See* **Lavolta.**

Volumier, Jean Baptiste (b ? Spain, *c* 1670; d Dresden, 7 Oct 1728), Flemish violinist, dulcimer player and composer. Educ. at the Fr. court and in 1692 transferred to that of Prus. in Berlin, where he became leader of the orch. and director of the dance music. In 1709 he went to Dresden as music director

to the Saxon court; he was acquainted with J.S. Bach.

Works incl. ballets, divertissements, dances (all lost).

Voluntary, an organ piece intended for use in church, but not part of the service. In modern practice it is used only at the beginning and (esp.) at the end of a service, in the latter case often serving to play the congregation out.

Vom Fischer und syner Fru (*The Fisherman and his Wife*), dramatic cantata by Schoeck (lib. by comp. after P.O. Runge, after Grimm); comp. 1928–30, prod. Dresden, Staatsoper, 3 Oct 1930, cond. Busch.

Von deutscher Seele, romantic cantata by Pfitzner for soloists, chorus and orch. (text after Eichendorff); comp. 1921, fp Berlin, 27 Jan 1922.

Von Heute auf Morgen (*From Today until Tomorrow*), opera in 1 act by Schoenberg (lib. by 'Max Blonda' = the comp.'s wife Gertrud), prod. Frankfurt, 1 Feb 1930.

Von Stade, Frederica. *See* **Stade.**

Vonk, Hans (b Amsterdam, 18 Jun 1942), Dutch conductor. He studied in Amsterdam and with Scherchen. Associate cond. Concertgebouw Orch. 1969–72; Netherlands Opera from 1971. Dutch Radio Orch. from 1972, Residentie Orch. from 1980. He made his British debut with the RPO in 1974; associate cond. from 1977. US debut San Francisco SO, 1974. Often heard in Bruckner.

Vopelius, Gottfried (b Herwigsdorf nr. Zittau, 28 Jan 1645; d Leipzig, 3 Feb 1715), German composer. App. cantor of St Nicholas's Church, Leipzig, 1677. Compiled a book of chorales (1682) and harmonized many, besides writing tunes for some.

Voříšek (Worzischek), Jan Václav (Johann Hugo) (b Vamberk, 11 May 1791; d Vienna, 19 Nov 1825), Bohemian composer and organist. Pupil of his father, a schoolmaster, and later of Tomášek. He went to Vienna in 1813 and when Hummel left he recommended Voříšek as pf. teacher to all his pupils. He became pianist and cond. to the Phil. Society and in 1823 court organist.

Works incl. church music, incl. Mass (1824); symph.; duet for cello and pf.; divertissement for 2 pfs.; pf. works.

Voyevoda, opera by Tchaikovsky (lib. by comp. and A.N. Ostrovsky, based on a play by the latter), prod. Moscow, 11 Feb 1869.

Voz (or Vos), Laurent de (b Antwerp, 1533; d Cambrai, Jan 1580), Flemish composer. Brother of the painter Martin de Vos. Worked at Antwerp Cathedral and was app. music director and choirmaster at Cambrai Cathedral by the archbishop Louis de Berlaymont. When the latter's place was usurped by Inchy, Voz comp. a motet compiled from words from the Psalms in such a way as to attack Inchy, who had Voz hanged without trial.

Works incl. motets, *chansons*.

Vrchlický, Jaroslav (1853–1912), Czech poet and playwright. Works based on his writings incl.: Dvořák, opera *Armida*, oratorio *St Ludmilla*; Fibich, operatic trilogy *Hippodamia* and melodramas *Haakon* and *Queen Emma*; Foerster (J. B.), melodramas *The Three Riders* and *The Legend of St Julia*; Janáček, choral work *Amarus*; Novák, opera *A Night at Karlstein*.

Vrieslander, Otto (b Münster, 18 Jul 1880; d Tegna, 16 Dec 1950), German musicologist and composer. Studied at the Cologne Cons. Settled at Munich in 1906 and went to live at Locarno in Switz. in 1920. As a musicologist he was a pupil of Schenker, whose unfinished *Harmonielehre* he completed. He also wrote on C.P.E. Bach and ed. some of his works.

Works incl. songs from *Des Knaben Wunderhorn*, on Giraud's *Pierrot lunaire* (1904) and to words by Goethe, Keller, Theodor Storm.

Vučković, Vojislav (b Pirot, Serbia, 18 Oct 1910; d Belgrade, 25 Dec 1942), Yugoslav composer, musicologist and conductor. Studied in Prague and became prof. and cond. at Belgrade. He was murdered by the Nazi police.

Works inc. several choral comps.; 2 symphs., 3 symph. poems; string 4tet; 2 songs for sop. and wind insts.

Vuillaume, Jean-Baptiste (b Mirecourt, Vosges, 7 Oct 1798; d Paris, 19 Mar 1875), French vln. and cello maker. Estab. independently in Paris, 1828.

Vulpius, Melchior (b Wasungen nr. Meiningen, *c* 1570; d Weimar, buried 7 Aug 1615), German composer and writer on music. He became cantor at Weimar in 1602 and remained there to his death. He harmonized many hymn tunes not his own and wrote a treatise, *Musicae compendium* (1608).

Works incl. *Sacrae cantiones* for 5–8 voices, canticles, hymns for 4–5 voices and other sacred music; *St Matthew Passion* (1613).

Vuota (It. fem. adj. = void, empty), a direction to string players to play a note or notes on an open string. Also the equivalent of G.P. = general pause.

Vycpálek, Ladislav (b Vrsovice nr. Prague, 23 Feb 1882; d Prague, 9 Jan 1969), Czech composer. Studied philosophy at Prague Univ., took a doctorate in it, and became secretary to the Univ. library. He also studied comp. with Novák at the Cons.

Works incl. cantata *The Last Things of Man*; song-cycles *Quiet Reconcilement* (1909), *Visions*, *In God's Hands*, Morav ballads and folksongs; pf. pieces; chamber music; choruses for mixed and male voices.

Vyšehrad (Smetana). *See* **Má Vlast.**

Vyvyan, Jennifer (Brigit) (b Broadstairs, 13 Mar 1925; d London, 5 Apr 1974), English soprano. Studied at the RAM and then with F. Carpi in Switz., making her debut with the EOG in 1947. She created the roles of Penelope Rich in *Gloriana* (1953), the Governess in *The Turn of the Screw* (1954) and Tytania in *A Midsummer Night's Dream* (1960) all by Britten. Other roles incl. Mozart's Electra (Glyndebourne, 1953), Donna Anna and Constanze (SW, 1952). She was well known in Bach, Britten, Monteverdi and Handel.

Waart, Edo de (b Amsterdam, 1 Jun 1941), Dutch conductor. He was prin. oboe of the Concertgebouw Orch. in 1963, and after winning the Mitropoulos cond. competition in 1964 became asst. cond. in 1966; US tour 1967. He founded the Netherlands Wind Ens. and from 1967 was guest cond. with the Rotterdam PO; chief cond. 1973–9. Santa Fe Opera Festival 1971; CG 1976 (*Ariadne*). He appeared with the San Francisco SO in 1975; music director from 1977.

Wachtel, Theodor (b Hamburg, 10 Mar 1823; d Frankfurt am Main, 14 Nov 1893), German tenor. Debut Hamburg, 1849. CG debut 1862, as Edgardo; London debut 1865, as Vasco da Gama. He sang at Berlin 1862–79 and returned to London until 1877. Among his best roles were Arnold, Manrico, Raoul and Adam's Chapelou. An attempt to sing Wagner (Lohengrin, 1876) was a failure.

Wächterlieder (Ger. = watchmen's songs), songs formerly used in Germany by night watchmen in the streets to announce the hours and by fire-watchers on church towers to proclaim festival days, etc. They were often folksongs and some have passed into currency as hymns for the Lutheran church.

Waechter, Eberhard (b Vienna, 9 Jul 1929), Austrian baritone. Studied in Vienna, making his debut there in 1953 as Silvio and a year later became a member of the Vienna Staatsoper. CG 1956–9, as Almaviva, Amfortas and Renato. Bayreuth 1957–63. NY Met debut 1961, as Wolfram. He sang the title role in Giulini's recording of *Don Giovanni*. Also sings Lieder.

Waffenschmied (von Worms), Der (*The Armourer* [*of Worms*]), opera by Lortzing (lib. by comp., based on F.J.W. Ziegler's comedy *Liebhaber und Nebenbuhler in einer Person*), prod. Vienna, Theater an der Wien, 31 May 1846. Weigl's opera *Il rivale di se stesso* (*His own Rival*), prod. Milan 1808, was based on the same play.

Wagenaar, Bernard (b Arnhem, 18 Jul 1894; d York, Maine, 18 May 1971), American composer of Dutch birth. Studied with his father, Johan W., and at the Utrecht Cons. and learnt the vln. and keyboard insts. In 1921 he settled in NY and joined the NY PO and from 1927 taught at the Juilliard Graduate School there.

Works incl. chamber opera *Pieces of Eight* (1944); 4 symphs. (1926–46), sinfonietta, divertimento, *Feuilleton*, etc. for orch.; vln. concerto, triple concerto for fl., harp and cello (1935); 3 string 4tets (1932–60), concertino for 8 insts.; vln. and pf. sonata, sonatina for cello; 3 Chin. songs for voice, fl., harp and pf.; pf. sonata; Eclogue for org.; incl. settings of E. St Vincent Millay.

Wagenaar, Johan (b Utrecht, 1 Nov 1862; d The Hague, 17 Jun 1941), Dutch composer, father of prec. Studied with Richard Hol and with Herzogenberg in Berlin. App. organist at Utrecht Cathedral in 1888 and director of the Cons. there in 1904, also cond. of a choral society. In 1919 he became director of the Royal Cons. at The Hague, retiring in 1937 in favour of S. Dresden.

Works incl. operas *The Doge of Venice* (1901), *El Cid* (after Corneille, 1916) and *Jupiter amans* (1925); overtures to Shakespeare's *Taming of the Shrew*, Goldoni's *Philosophical Princess*, Kleist's *Amphitryon*, and Rostand's *Cyrano de Bergerac* (1905), overture *Saul and David* (1906), funeral march and waltz suite for orch.; fantasy on Dutch folksongs for male chorus and orch., female choruses with pf.; vln. and pf. pieces; pf. pieces; songs.

Wagenseil, Georg Christoph (b Vienna, 29 Jan 1715; d Vienna, 1 Mar 1777), Austrian composer. Studied in Vienna with Fux and others and in 1735, on recommendation, received a court scholarship, becoming court comp. in 1739. In 1741–50 he was also organist to the dowager empress and he was app. music master to the Empress Maria Theresa and her daughters. Mozart at the age of 6 played at court a concerto by Wagenseil, who turned pages for him.

Works incl. operas *Ariodante* (1745), *Le cacciatrici amanti* (1755) and *c* 10 others (6 on libs. by Metastasio); oratorios *La rendenzione* and *Gioas, rè di Giuda* (both 1735); nearly 20 Masses, Requiem, motets and other church music; symphs.; keyboard concertos; divertimenti for solo keyboard.

Wagenseil, Johann Christoph (b Nuremberg, 26 Nov 1633; d Altdorf, 9 Oct 1708), German historian and librarian. Wrote a treatise on the art of the Meistersinger, pub. in 1697, which served Wagner as a source for *Die Meistersinger*.

Waghalter, Ignaz (b Warsaw, 15 Mar 1882; d New York, 7 Apr 1949), Polish-German composer and conductor. Pupil of Gernsheim. He cond. opera in Berlin and Essen, 1907–23, and in 1925 cond. the State SO in NY, returning to Berlin later and going

to Prague in 1933. He settled in NY in 1938.
Works incl. operas *Der Teufelsweg*
(1911), *Mandragola* (after Machiavelli,
1914), *Jugend, Der späte Gast* (1922) and
Sataniel (1923), operettas; vln. concerto;
string 4tet; vln. and pf. sonata.

Wagner, Johanna (b Seelze nr. Hanover, 13
Oct 1826; d Würzburg, 16 Oct 1894), Ger-
man soprano, adopted daughter of Albert
W. (1799–1874), brother of Richard W.,
who engaged her for the Royal Opera at
Dresden, where she was the 1st Elisabeth in
his *Tannhäuser* in 1845. In 1847 she went to
Paris to study with García; sang at the Court
Opera, Berlin 1850–61 (Elisabeth, Ortrud).
London, Her Majesty's, 1856 as Tancredi,
Lucrecia Borgia and Bellini's Romeo. In
1859 she married an official named Jach-
mann. Lost her voice in the 1860s but sang in
1872 celebratory perf. of the *Choral* symph.
at Bayreuth.

Wagner-Régeny, Rudolf (b Szász-Régen,
28 Aug 1903; d East Berlin, 18 Sep 1969),
German composer of Rumanian descent.
Studied at Leipzig and Berlin.
Works incl. operas *Moschopulos* (1928),
Sganarelle (after Molière, 1929), *Der nackte
König* (1930), *Esau und Jakob* (1930), *La
Sainte Courtisane* (1930), *Günstling* (1935),
Die Bürger von Calais (after Froissart, 1939)
and *Das Bergwerk zu Falun* (after Hoff-
mannsthal, 1961); ballet *Der zerbrochene
Krug* (after Kleist's comedy, 1937); vocal
and insts. pieces.

Wagner, (Wilhelm) Richard (b Leipzig, 22
May 1813; d Venice, 13 Feb 1883), German
composer and author. Son of a clerk to the
city police, who died 6 months after Wagner's birth. His mother removed to Dresden
and married the actor and painter Ludwig
Geyer in 1815, who in turn died in 1821.
Wagner learnt the pf. but tried to read vocal
scores of operas instead of practising and
also acquired knowledge of opera from 2
elder sisters who were both stage singers. He
wrote poems and a tragedy at the age of
about 13 and at 14 went to school at Leipzig,
where the family had ·returned. There he
heard Beethoven's works and tried to imitate
them in comps. of his own. In 1830 Dorn
cond. an overture of his (*Columbus*, lost) in
the theatre, but it was received with scorn as
a very crude work. He then studied harmony
and counterpoint with Weinlig at St Thomas's School and entered the univ. in 1831.
At 19 he began an opera, *Die Hochzeit*, but
on the advice of his sister abandoned it for
Die Feen. The libs., as always later on, he
wrote himself.

He became chorus master at the theatre of
Würzburg in 1833 and cond. of a summer
theatre at Lauchstädt, the co. of which was
at Magdeburg in winter, where he went with
it. Minna Planer (1809–66) was there as an
actress, and he married her on 24 Nov 1836,
at Königsberg, where she had a new engagement. The Magdeburg company had been
dissolved soon after a disastrous prod. of
Wagner's 3rd opera, *Das Liebesverbot*, on
29 Mar 1836. The Königsberg theatre also
went into liquidation just after Wagner had
been app. cond. but in the summer of 1837
he became cond. at Riga. In Jan 1839 his
post was given to Dorn and he decided to go
to Paris by sea. A very stormy voyage took
them as far as the coast of Norw. and then to
Eng., they did not reach Paris until September. They spent nearly all the time there until
Apr 1842 in wretched poverty, but Wagner,
in such time as he could spare from hack-
work, had managed to finish both *Rienzi*
and *Der fliegende Holländer*, the former of
which had been accepted by Dresden and
was prod. there on 20 Oct 1842. The latter
work followed on 2 Jan 1843, and Wagner
was app. 2nd cond. at the court opera a
month later. *Tannhäuser* was finished in Apr
1845 and prod. on 19 Oct.

When the Fr. Revolution of 1848 spread
its influence across Eur., Wagner showed
sympathy with liberal ideas, and after the
revolt at Dresden failed in May 1849 he had
to fly and a warrant for his arrest was issued,
should he be found in Saxony. Not deeming
the rest of Ger. safe, he went to Switz. There,
at Zurich, he worked on the lib. and music
for the *Ring des Nibelungen* cycle, which
was interrupted by *Tristan und Isolde*, written under the influence of Mathilde Wesendonck, the wife of a friend and benefactor
with whom he was more and more deeply in
love. In 1858 Minna created a scene and
Mathilde decided to stay with her husband,
Wagner going to Venice and later to
Lucerne, where *Tristan* was finished in Aug
1859. In 1860 a revised version of *Tannhäuser*, with a ballet, was commissioned by
the Paris Opéra, and Wagner complied so far
as his artistic conscience would let him,
which was not enough for the patrons, who
saw to it that after the prod. on 13 Mar 1861
the work should fail disastrously. Wagner
next went to Vienna, where he heard *Lohengrin* for the 1st time, though it had been
prod. by Liszt at Weimar in 1850.

In 1862 he settled at Biebrich on the Rhine
to work on *Die Meistersinger*, but he was in
Vienna again by the end of the year, and

stayed there until Mar 1864, when he was pursued by his creditors and threatened with imprisonment. At the critical moment he was invited by Ludwig II of Bavaria to join his court at Munich as friend and artistic adviser, and he ensured that Hans von Bülow was app. cond. Bülow's wife, Cosima (1837–1930), was Liszt's daughter; she and Wagner soon fell deeply in love. This created a scandal which was fully exploited by his enemies, the courtiers and officials who feared his influence on the youthful and idealistic king, and soon after the prod. of *Tristan* (10 Jun 1865), Wagner was obliged to go into exile once more. He chose Tribschen on the lake of Lucerne in Switz., where Cosima joined him in Mar 1866. Bülow divorced her in 1870 and on 25 Aug she married Wagner, whose 1st wife had died on 25 Jan 1866.

After the prod. of *Die Meistersinger* on 21 Jun 1868 at Munich, Wagner quietly continued work on the *Ring* cycle, dropped so many years before, and planned a festival theatre to be erected by subscription at Bayreuth in Bavaria. The family took a house there in 1874; rehearsals began the following year, and the four works were prod. on 13–17 Aug 1876. *Parsifal* followed, after a slow process of comp. much interrupted by illness and by holidays in It. for his health, on 26 July 1882. Wagner left for Venice in Sep greatly exhausted and subject to frequent heart attacks, from one of which he died.

Works incl. operas *Die Hochzeit* (unfinished), *Die Feen* (comp. 1833; prod. 1888), *Das Liebesverbot* (1836), *Rienzi* (1842), *Der fliegende Holländer* (1843), *Tannhäuser* (1845), *Lohengrin* (1850), *Tristan und Isolde* (1865), *Die Meistersinger von Nürnberg* (1868), *Der Ring des Nibelungen* (comprising *Das Rheingold* (1869), *Die Walküre* (1870), *Siegfried* (1876) and *Götterdämmerung* (1876), *Parsifal* (1882).

Symph., 9 concert overtures (2 unpub.), incl. *Eine Faust Ouvertüre* (after Goethe), 3 marches for orch., *Siegfried Idyll* for small orch. (1870); several choral works; a number of songs, incl. 7 from Goethe's *Faust*, 5 poems by Mathilde Wesendonck (1857–8) and 6 settings of Fr. poems; a sonata and some smaller pf. works; string 4tet (lost).

Wagner, Siegfried (Helferich Richard) (b Tribschen, 6 Jun 1869; d Bayreuth, 4 Aug 1930), German composer and conductor, son of prec. Although intended for an architect, he studied music with Humperdinck and Kneise, and gained much experi- ence by assisting at the Wagner festival perfs. at Bayreuth, some of which he cond. after 1896. When his mother, Cosima, became too old to manage the affairs of the theatre, he took its direction in hand in 1909.

Works incl. operas *Der Bärenhäuter* (1899), *Herzog Wildfang* (1901), *Der Kobold* (1904), *Bruder Lustig* (1905), *Sternengebot* (1908), *Banadietrich* (1910), *An allem ist Hütchen schuld* (1917), *Schwarzschwanenreich* (1918), *Sonnenflammen* (1918), *Der Schmied von Marienburg* (1923), *Der Friedensengel* (1926), *Der Heidenkönig* (1933) and 2 others not perf. or pub.; symph. poem *Sehnsucht*; vln. concerto, fl. concerto.

Wagner, Wieland (Adolf Gottfried) (b Bayreuth, 5 Jan 1917; d Munich, 17 Oct 1966), German producer, son of prec. Studied painting in Munich, also music and stage prod. He designed sets for *Parsifal* at Bayreuth in 1937. His first prods. were at Nuremberg in 1942–4 (*Walküre* and *Siegfried*). From the reopening of the Bayreuth theatre in 1951 till his death he was in charge of prod. He was also invited to prod. operas in other Eur. cities, notably at Stuttgart (incl. *Fidelio*, *Salome*, *Wozzeck* and *Lulu*).

Wagner, Wolfgang (Manfred Martin) (b Bayreuth, 30 Aug 1919), German producer, brother of prec. Studied prod. at the Berlin Staatsoper, where he prod. one of his father's operas in 1944. He was assoc. with his brother at Bayreuth from 1951 and himself prod. operas there from 1953 (artistic dir. from 1966). He invited Patrice Chéreau (1976) and Peter Hall (1983) to produce *The Ring* there.

Wagner Tubas, brass wind instruments devised by Wagner for his *Ring des Nibelungen*, which requires 5, but only 3 different kinds: 2 tenor tubas not unlike the Euphonium, but with funnel-shaped mouthpieces, with the following compass:

2 bass tubas:

and a double-bass tuba an 8ve lower still.

Waisenhaus, Das (*The Orphanage*), opera by Weigl (lib. by G.F. Treitschke), prod. Vienna, Kärntnertortheater, 4 Oct 1808.

Wait, an instrument of the oboe type, similar to the Shawm, used in Eng. by the Christmas

Waits and, in the 13th cent., by the keepers of the City of London gates and other town gates for the purpose of signalling 'All's well', etc.

Waits, orig. the keepers of town gates, in the 15th–16th cents. salaried bands employed to play at var. functions, afterwards amateur singers and players perf. outside the houses of the more substantial citizens for rewards in money and refreshment at Christmas.

Wakefield, (Augusta) Mary (b Sedgwick nr. Kendal, 19 Aug 1853; d Grange-over-Sands, Lancs., 16 Sep 1910), English amateur contralto, pianist and composer. In 1885 she started the 1st competitive festival at her home at Sedgwick, which was later transferred to Kendal and became the Westmorland Music Festival.

Walcha, Helmut (b Leipzig, 27 Oct 1907), German organist. He studied at the Leipzig Inst. but became blind a year before his debut in 1924. He was asst. organist at the Thomaskirche, Leipzig, from 1926 and from 1929 perf. and taught in Frankfurt; retired 1972. He was best known in the org. music of Bach, all of which he recorded; he pub. a version of *Die Kunst der Fuge* for org. Also performed Reger, on whom he wrote a book.

Waldhorn (Ger. = forest horn), the German name for the horn without valves, prod. only the natural harmonics (It. *corno da caccia*).

Waldmädchen, Das (*The Woodland Maid*), opera by Weber (lib. by C.F. von Steinsberg), prod. Freiberg, Saxony, 23 Nov 1800. Early version of *Silvana*

Waldmann, Maria (b Vienna, 1844; d Ferrara, 6 Nov 1920), Austrian mezzo. The 1st Amneris in the Milan prod. of Verdi's *Aida* and the mezzo in the fp of his Requiem. Sang in Ger., Hol. and Moscow as Aennchen, Preziosilla and Zerlina. She married Duke Galeazzo Massari of Ferrara and retired from the stage.

Waldstein, Ferdinand (Ernst Joseph Gabriel), Count (b Duchov, 24 Mar 1762; d Vienna, 29 Aug 1823), Bohemian music amateur. Patron of Beethoven, whom he met in the early days at Bonn and knew later in Vienna.

'Waldstein' Sonata, Beethoven's pf. sonata in C maj., op. 53, comp. in 1804, so called (not by Beethoven) because it is ded. to the above.

Waldteufel (actually Lévy), **(Charles) Émile** (b Strasbourg, 9 Dec 1837; d Paris, 12 Feb 1915), French composer and pianist. Studied at the Paris Cons. He joined a pf. factory and was later app. pianist to the Empress Eugénie. He had a great success as a comp. of waltzes.

Works incl. many hundreds of waltzes and other dances, incl. a waltz on Chabrier's *España*.

Walker, Edyth (b Hopewell, NY, 27 Mar 1867; d New York, 19 Feb 1950), American mezzo. She studied in Dresden and Berlin; debut Berlin 1894, as Fides. Sang at the Vienna Hofoper 1895–1903, often under Mahler, but was eventually dismissed by him. CG 1900, as Ortrud, Fricka and Waltraute; returned in 1908 and 1910 for Isolde and Elektra. NY Met 1903–6 (debut as Amneris). At the 1908 Bayreuth Festival she sang Ortrud and Kundry. Hamburg 1903–12, Munich 1912–17. She taught singing in Fontainebleau and New York during the 1930s.

Walker, Frank (b Gosport, Hants., 10 Jun 1907; d Tring, *c* 25 Feb 1962), English writer on music. Educ. at Portsmouth Grammar School, engaged in an electro-technical career and during World War II was attached to the Royal Corps of Signals in It. His researches there resulted in his 2nd book, *The Man Verdi*, the 1st being a biog. of Hugo Wolf. He committed suicide.

Walker, Sarah (b Cheltenham, 11 Mar 1943), English mezzo. She studied vln. at the RCM. In 1970 she sang Monteverdi's Ottavia with Kent Opera and Cavalli's Diana at Glyndebourne. From 1972 she has sung Dorabella, Fricka and Mary Stuart with ENO; and Gloriana in London (1984) and with the co. at the NY Met. CG debut 1979, as Charlotte; Handel's Micah in 1985. Many recitals in Eur. and N. America with the pianist Roger Vignoles. In 1976 she sang in the London fp of Henze's *Jephte* (realization of Carissimi).

Walküre, Die (*The Valkyrie*, **Wagner**). *See* Ring des Nibelungen.

Wallace, (William) Vincent (b Waterford, 11 Mar 1812; d Château de Haget nr. Vieuzos, Hautes-Pyrénées, 12 Oct 1865), Irish composer. Pupil of his father, a bandmaster and bassoon player, who moved to Dublin, where Wallace played the org. and vln. in public as a boy. In 1831 he married Isabella Kelly, but they separated in 1835 (in 1850 he 'married' in NY the pianist Hélène Stoepel, by whom he had 2 sons). In 1834 he appeared at Dublin with a vln. concerto of his own. Between 1835 and 1845 he was in Austral. and elsewhere abroad, but he went to London in the latter year and was induced to comp. *Maritana* After a successful operatic career, incl. a visit to S. Amer. in 1849 and

14 years in Ger., a commission from the Paris Opéra (which he was unable to finish owing to failing eyesight) and another visit to S. and N. Amer. in 1850–53, his health broke down and he was ordered to the Pyrenees.

Works incl. operas *Maritana* (1845), *Matilda of Hungary* (1847), *Lurline* (1860), *The Maid of Zurich* (unpub.), *The Ambler Witch* (1861), *Love's Triumph* (1862), *The Desert Flower* (1863), *Estrella* (unfinished), operettas *Gulnare* and *Olga*; cantata *Maypole*; vln. concerto; pf. music.

Wallace, William (b Greenock, 3 Jul 1860; d Malmesbury, Wilts., 16 Dec 1940), Scottish ophthalmic surgeon, music author and composer. Educ. at Edinburgh and Glasgow Univs. and in Vienna as an eye specialist, began to practise in 1888, but gave up his profession for music except during the 1914–18 war. In 1889 he entered the RAM in London for a brief course in comp. and later he became successively secretary and trustee of the Phil. Society. His books incl. *The Threshold of Music* (1908), *The Musical Faculty* (1914), *Richard Wagner as he lived* (1925) and *Liszt, Wagner and the Princess* (1927).

Works incl. opera *Brassolis*; symph. *Koheleth* for chorus and orch.; symph. *The Creation*, symph. poems *The Passing of Beatrice* (after Dante's *Paradiso*, 1892), *Anvil or Hammer* (after Goethe's *Koptisches Lied*), *Sister Helen* (after D.G. Rossetti), *To the New Country*, *Wallace, A.D. 1305–1905*, *Villon*, suite *The Lady from the Sea* (after Ibsen), symph. prelude to Aeschylus's *Eumenides*; cantatas, chamber music and songs.

Wallek-Walewski, Bolesław (b Lwów, 23 Jan 1885; d Kraków, 9 Apr 1944), Polish composer and conductor. Studied at his home town, at Kraków with Żeleński and Szopski, and with Riemann at Leipzig. On returning to Lwów he became choral and operatic cond. and director of the Cons.

Works incl. operas *Destiny* and *Jontek's Revenge* (1926; a sequel to Moniuszko's *Halka*); oratorio *Apocalypse*; Masses, Requiem, motets, psalms and other church music; scherzo *Bawel and Gawel* for orch.; male-voice choruses; folksong arrs.

Wallenstein, 3 symph. poems by d'Indy, op. 12, after Schiller's dramatic trilogy, comp. 1873–9: 1. *Le Camp de W.*; 2. *Max et Thécla* (1st called *Piccolomini*); 3. *La Mort de W.* 1st complete perf. Paris, 26 Feb 1888.

Wallenstein, Alfred (b Chicago, 7 Oct 1898; d New York, 8 Feb 1983), American

conductor and cellist of German parentage. He studied medicine at Leipzig Univ., and also the cello with J. Klengel (1920–21). Returned to the USA and was 1st cello with the Chicago SO (1922–9) and then with the NY PO until 1936. He made his debut as a cond. in 1931 and from 1943 to 1956 was cond. of the Los Angeles PO, in 1952 also becoming music director of the Hollywood Bowl.

Walliser, Christoph Thomas (b Strasbourg, 17 Apr 1568; d Strasbourg, 26 Apr 1648), German composer. Pupil of Vulpius and others. In 1599 he became a teacher at the Acad. and later music director of 2 churches at Strasbourg.

Works incl. incid. music for Aristophanes' *The Clouds* and other plays; *Ecclesiodae* containing psalms for 4–6 voices (1614), *Ecclesiodae novae* incl. Te Deum, litany, etc., for 4–7 voices (1625), Ger. psalms for 5 voices and other church music.

Wally, La, opera by Catalani (lib. by L. Illica, based on W. von Hillern's novel *Die Geyer-Wally*), prod. Milan, La Scala, 20 Jan 1892.

Walmisley, Thomas Attwood (b London, 21 Jan 1814; d Hastings, 17 Jan 1856), English organist and composer. Learnt music from his father, the glee comp. and teacher, Thomas Forbes W. (1783–1866), and studied with his godfather, Attwood. After 3 years as organist at Croydon, he became organist of Trinity and St John's Colls., Cambridge, in 1833, where he also devoted himself to the study of mathematics and wrote poetry. In 1836 he became prof. of music, though he did not take the Mus.D. degree until 1848.

Works incl. services and anthems; 3 odes for the installation of univ. chancellors; madrigal *Sweete Flowers*; duets for ob. and pf.; org. works; songs.

Walsh, John (b 1665 or 1666; d London, 13 Mar, 1736), English music publisher and instrument maker. Founded his pub. house in London c 1690 and in 1692 became inst. maker to the King. Pub. much of Handel's music.

Walsh, John (b London, 23 Dec 1709; d London, 15 Jan 1766), son of prec. succeeded his father as music publisher.

Walter, Bruno (actually Bruno Walter Schlesinger) (b Berlin, 15 Sep 1876; d Beverly Hills, Calif., 17 Feb 1962), German conductor and pianist. He studied at Stern Cons. in Berlin and made his 1st appearance as a cond. at Cologne in 1894. After appts. as an opera cond. at Hamburg (under Mahler), Breslau, Pressburg, Riga, Berlin and Vienna

(1901–12) he was director of the Munich Opera from 1913 to 1922; cond. the fps of Pfitzner's *Palestrina* (1917) and Schreker's *Das Spielwerk* (1920). From 1925 to 1933 he was director of the Städtische Oper, Berlin, and from 1929 to 1933 of the Gewandhaus concerts in Leipzig, in succession to Furtwängler. He 1st appeared in England in 1909 and was the regular cond. of the German seasons at CG from 1924 to 1931 (prods. incl. *Figaro* and *Rosenkavalier*). He was also active during this period as cond. at the Salzburg festival. He was compelled to leave Ger. in 1933 and was artistic director of the Vienna Opera from 1936 to 1938. After the *Anschluss* he emigrated to Fr. in 1938 and to the USA in 1939, where he lived till his death. From 1941 he cond. frequently at the NY Met (debut with *Fidelio*; also *Don Giovanni* in 1st season). From 1946 returned to Eur. as guest cond., he appeared at the 1947 Edinburgh Festival.

He excelled in the works of Mozart and of Romantic comps., especially Mahler, of whose *Lied von der Erde* and 9th symph. he gave the fps (1911, 1912). As a pianist he accomp. many of the famous singers of his time, incl. Lotte Lehmann and Kathleen Ferrier, and also appeared as soloist in Mozart's concertos. He pub. a study of Mahler, an autobiog. (*Theme and Variations*) and 3 vols. of essays.

Walter, Gustav (b Bilin, 11 Feb 1834; d Vienna, 30 Jan 1910), Bohemian-Austrian tenor. Studied at the Prague Cons., appeared there and at Brno, and in 1856 made his 1st appearance in Vienna, where he settled.

Walter, (Johann) Ignaz (b Radonice, Bohemia, 31 Aug 1755; d Regensburg, 22 Feb 1822), Bohemian tenor and composer. A pupil of Starzer in Vienna, he made his debut as a singer there in 1780; later became music director of the Grossman opera co. and (1804) of the opera in Regensburg.

Works incl. *Singspiele: Doktor Faust* (after Goethe, 1797), *Der Spiegelritter* and others; *Cantata sacra* for the coronation of Emperor Leopold II; memorial music for Schiller.

Walter, Johann (b Kahla, Thuringia, 1496; d Torgau, 25 Mar 1570), German composer and bass. He sang in the service of the Elector of Saxony and in 1548 organized and directed the singers of the court chapel at Dresden. In 1554 he retired to Torgau with a pension. He was a friend of Luther and in 1524 went to Wittenberg to assist him in framing the Ger. Protestant Mass.

Works incl. Magnificat, Ger. hymns for 4 voices, sacred songs, some with words by Luther; inst. pieces.

Walter of Evesham. *See* **Odington.**

Waltershausen, Hermann Wolfgang (Sartorius) Freiherr von (b Göttingen, 12 Oct 1882; d Munich, 13 Aug 1954), German composer and music author. Studied at Strasbourg, lost his right arm and foot in an accident but learnt to play the pf. and cond, with the left hand. He further studied at Munich from 1901 and attended Sandberger's lectures at the univ., founded a music school in 1917 and in 1920 became prof. at the Munich State Acad. of Music, being app. director in 1922. His books incl. works on musical style, opera and R. Strauss.

Works incl. operas *Else Klapperzehen* (1909), *Oberst Chabert* (after Balzac, 1912), *Richardis* (1915), *Die Rauensteiner Hochzeit* (1919), *Die Gräfin von Tolosa* (comp. 1938); *Apocalyptic Symph.*, *Hero und Leander*, Partita on 3 Hymn-tunes, comedy overture, *Passions – und Auferstehungsmusik* for orch.; *Krippenmusik* for harpsichord and chamber orch.; pf. works; songs.

Walther, Johann Gottfried (b Erfurt, 18 Sep 1684; d Weimar, 23 Mar 1748), German composer organist and lexicographer. Pupil of J.B. Bach (*see* Bach, no. 20) at Erfurt, where in 1702 he became organist at St Thomas's Church. In 1707 he was app. town organist at Weimar, where he was in close touch with J.S. Bach, to whom he was related. He pub. a *Musicalisches Lexicon* in 1732.

Works incl. much org. music, incl. preludes and fugues and chorale vars.; concertos by other comps. arr. for solo harpsichord.

Walther, Johann Jakob (b Witterda nr. Erfurt, *c* 1650; d Mainz, 2 Nov 1717), German violinist and composer. In the service of the Elector of Saxony and later that of Mainz. Comp. *Scherzi* for vln. and continuo and *Hortulus chelicus* for solo vln. and strings containing pictorial effects.

Walther von der Vogelweide. *See* **Vogelweide.**

Walton, William (Turner) (b Oldham, Lancs., 29 Mar 1902; d Ischia, 8 Mar 1983), English composer. Showed great precocity of talent at home and was sent to Christ Church Cathedral, Oxford, as a choir-boy, later becoming an undergraduate at Christ Church. He had some comp. lessons from Hugh Allen, but after the age of 16 was self-taught, though he later received some advice from Busoni and others. In 1923 he appeared for the 1st time at the ISCM festival, at Salzburg, where his 1st string 4tet was perf. He settled in London and was in close touch with the literary family Edith, Osbert and Sacheverell Sitwell. In 1934 his symph. in Bb min. was perf. in London before it was completed (the finale was added the next year). In 1938 he went to the USA to confer with Jascha Heifetz about the solo part of the vln. concerto, which is ded. to him. During the 1939–45 war he wrote music for official films. A cello concerto for Piatigorsky followed in 1956 and a 2nd symph. in 1960. Knighted 1951. OM 1968.

Works incl. DRAMATIC: operas *Troilus and Cressida* (after Chaucer, 1954, rev. 1976) and *The Bear* (after Chekhov, 1967); ballets *The Wise Virgins* (arr. of Bach, 1940) and *The Quest* (after Spenser, 1943); incid. music for Shakespeare's *Macbeth*; film music for *As You Like It, Henry V* and *Hamlet* (Shakespeare), *Major Barbara* (Shaw), *The First of the Few* (incl. *Spitfire* prelude and fugue); radio music for *Christopher Columbus* (L. MacNeice).

VOCAL: *Façade* for reciter and inst. ens; (E. Sitwell, 1922). Cantatas *Belshazzar's Feast* (Bible, arr. by O. Sitwell, 1931) and *In Honour of the City of London* (Dunbar), Coronation Te Deum (1953), Gloria, all with orch.; *Where does the uttered music go?* (Masefield) for unaccomp. chorus; *A Song for the Lord Mayor's Table* for sop. and orch. or pf. (1962);

ORCH.: overtures *Portsmouth Point* (on Rowlandson's drawing) and *Scapino, Siesta* for small orch., 2 symphs. (1931–5 and 1960, Coronation Marches *Crown Imperial* and *Orb and Sceptre* (1937 and 1953), *Johannesburg Festival Overture, Partita*; *Sinfonia concertante* for pf. and orch. (1927), vla. concerto (1929), vln. concerto (1939), cello concerto (1956).

INST.: 2 string 4tets (1922 and 1947), pf. 4tet (1918–9, rev 1976); sonata for vln. and pf. (1949); pf. duets for children.

Waltz (*see also* **Valse à deux temps**), a ballroom dance coming into fashion in the earlier 19th cent. and developing from the Ger. dances (*Deutsche*) and the Aus. *Ländler*, Beethoven, Weber and Schubert being among the 1st comps. to cultivate it seriously, and the elder J. Strauss and Lanner among the 1st ballroom comps. to develop its vogue in Vienna, whence it rapidly spread all over Eur. It is in 3–4 time, varying in pace at different periods and in different countries, but usually rather leisurely, and its most typical feature is a bass note on the 1st

beat followed by 2 repeated chords of the upper harmony of that bass on the 2nd and 3rd.

Waltz Dream (Straus). *See* **Walzertraum**.

Waltz, Gustavus (*fl*. 1732–59), German bass. He is said, on scanty evidence, to have been for a time Handel's cook in London. In 1732 he appeared as Polyphemus in Handel's *Acis and Galatea* and then, until 1751, in many operas and oratorios. He sang in the fps of *Arianna, Ariodante, Alcina* and *Atalanta*.

Walzer (Ger.) = Waltz.

Walzertraum, Ein (*A Waltz Dream*), operetta by Straus (lib. by F. Dörmann and L. Jacobson), prod. Vienna, Karl Theatre, 2 Mar 1907.

Wand, Günter (b Elberfeld, 7 Jan 1912), German conductor and composer. After study in Cologne he held posts at Wuppertal and Detmold. He cond. at the Cologne Opera 1939–44 and was musical dir. there 1945–8. He was responsible for the Gürzenich concerts, Cologne, 1946–74, giving frequent perfs. of Ligeti, Varèse and Schoenberg. London debut 1951 (with the LSO at CG). He cond. the Berne SO from 1974 and has been prin. cond. of the NDR SO (Hamburg) from 1982. Also heard in operas by Mozart and Verdi.

Wand of Youth, The, 2 orchestral suites by Elgar, opp. 1a and b, which are based on music he wrote for a play in his childhood, 1869. Rev. and scored in the present form in 1907; fp London, 14 Dec 1907, cond. Wood.

'Wanderer' Fantasy, Schubert's fantasy in C maj. for pf., D760, comp. Nov 1822. It is so called because it contains material from his song *The Wanderer*, written in 1816.

Wannenmacher, Johannes (b ? Neuenburg am Rhein *c* 1485; d Berne, 1551), Swiss priest and composer. He was app. cantor of the collegiate foundation of St Vincent at Berne in 1510, but left in 1514 after a dispute and went to Ger. as canon and cantor at Freiburg, Baden. After a brief return to Switz., in 1519, when he went to Sion (Valais), he went back to Freiburg, but having come under the influence of the Swiss reformer Zwingli, he embraced Protestantism in 1530, was tortured and banished, returned to Berne and, finding no employment there, became town clerk at Interlaken.

Works incl. Psalm cxxxvii for 3–6 voices, motets; Ger. sacred and secular songs.

War and Peace (*Voyna i mir*), opera by Prokofiev (lib. by M. Mendelson, based on Tolstoy's novel), perf. in concert, Moscow,

17 Oct 1944; prod. Leningrad, 12 Jun 1946 (1st 8 of 13 scenes only). Rev. 1941–52, in 11 scenes, and prod. Florence, 26 May 1953, cond. Rodzinski.

War Requiem, choral work by Britten, op. 66 (text of the Requiem Mass, together with poems by W. Owen), fp Coventry Cathedral, 30 May 1962.

Ward, David (b Dumbarton, 3 Jul 1922; d Dunedin, NZ, 16 Jul 1983), Scottish bass. Studied at the RCM with C. Carey and then with H. Hotter. After singing with the chorus (1952) he made his debut as soloist in 1953. London, CG, from 1960 as Pogner, Wotan, Arkel, Rocco and Morosus in the 1st Brit. perf. of *Die Schweigsame Frau* (1961). He appeared in minor roles at Bayreuth and as Wotan in Buenos Aires (1967).

Ward, John (b Canterbury, bap. 8 Sep 1571; d before 31 Aug 1638), English composer. He was in the service of Sir Henry Fanshawe, Remembrancer of the Exchequer, at Ware Park, Herts., and in London.

Works incl. services and 22 verse anthems; madrigals; fantasies for viols.

Warlich, Reinhold von (b St Petersburg, 24 May 1879; d New York, 10 Nov 1939), German baritone. Studied music at the Hamburg Cons. and singing at Florence and Cologne. Made his 1st appearance at Florence in 1899.

Warlock, Peter (real name Philip (Arnold) Heseltine) (b London, 30 Oct 1894; d London, 17 Dec 1930), English composer (as Warlock) and musicologist and writer on music (as Heseltine). Educ. at Eton, where he studied music in partic. and later influenced by Delius and van Dieren. Founded the *Sackbut*, a combative music paper, wrote numerous articles, ed. old Eng. music, esp. of the lutenist school, and pub. books on the Eng. ayre, Delius and (with Cecil Gray) Gesualdo.

Works incl. *3 Dirges by Webster* (1925) and other choral works; *An Old Song* and *Serenade* for string orch.; *The Curlew* for tenor, fl., Eng. horn and string 4tet (1921), *Corpus Christi* and *Sorrow's Lullaby* (Beddoes) for sop., bar. and string 4tet; *Capriol* suite for full or string orch. on dances from Arbeau's *Orchésographie* (1926); over 100 songs, many on Elizabethan and Jacobean poems.

Warrack, Guy (Douglas Hamilton) (b Edinburgh, 8 Feb 1900; d Englefield Green, 12 Feb 1986), Scottish conductor and composer. He studied at Oxford and with Boult and Vaughan Williams at the RCM; taught there 1925–35. Debut as cond. London,

1925; BBC Scottish Orch. 1936–45, SW Ballet 1948–51. He wrote music for various documentary films, incl. the official film of the 1953 coronation.

Warrack, John (Hamilton) (b London, 9 Feb 1928), English writer on music and administrator, son of prec. After studying ob. at the RCM he was asst. music critic of the *Daily Telegraph* from 1954; *Sunday Telegraph* 1961–72. He has been a member of *Opera* magazine's editorial board from 1953 and a critic for *Gramophone* from 1958. The author of well-received books on Tchaikovsky and Weber, he co-ed. with Harold Rosenthal the *Concise Oxford Dictionary of Opera* (1964, rev. 1979). Artistic dir., Leeds Festival, 1977–83. Lecturer, Oxford Univ. from 1983.

Warren (actually Warenoff), **Leonard** (b New York, 21 Apr 1911; d New York, 4 Mar 1960), American baritone. Studied in NY and Milan, making his debut at the NY Met in 1939 as Verdi's Paolo. Sang at La Scala, 1953, as Rigoletto and Iago. Other roles incl. Tonio, Boccanegra and Scarpia. He was esp. well known as a Verdi singer; his death occurred during a perf. of *La forza del destino* at the Met.

Wasps, The, incid. music for Aristophanes' comedy by Vaughan Williams, fp Cambridge, in Gk., by undergraduates, 26 Nov 1909; orch. suite perf. London, 23 Jul 1912.

Watanabe, Akeo (b Tokyo, 5 Jun 1919), Japanese conductor. He studied with Joseph Rosenstock at the Tokyo Acad. and at the Juilliard School from 1950. Cond. Tokyo PO, 1948–54, Nippon PO 1956–68. Music dir. Kyoto SO from 1970. Frequent guest appearances with Eur. and US orchs.

Water Music, a set of instrumental pieces by Handel, fp London, 1715, on a boat following the royal barge on the Thames. The music is said to have reconciled George I to Handel after the latter's desertion from the court of Hanover, but the story is doubtful.

Watkinson, Carolyn (b Preston, 19 Mar 1949), English mezzo. She studied at the RMCM. Many appearances with the Concertgebouw Orch. and recordings of Handel (*Rinaldo*, *Serse*, *Messiah*) and Bach (B minor Mass and *St Matthew Passion*). At Brussels and Spoleto she has sung Poppea, at Salzburg Mozart's Idamantes, and at La Scala Ariodante. Glyndebourne from 1984 as Cherubino and Cenerentola. Sang with the Boston SO at Tanglewood, 1985.

Watson (*née* **McLamore**), **Claire** (b New York, 3 Feb 1927; d Utting, 16 Jul 1986), American soprano. She studied with Elisabeth Schumann in NY; debut Graz, 1951, as Desdemona. In 1955 she was engaged by Solti for the Frankfurt Opera and sang Pamina, Elisabeth and Aida. She was well known in operas by Strauss and made her CG (1958) and Glyndebourne (1960) debuts as the Marschallin; other Strauss roles incl. Arabella, the Countess and Ariadne. Munich from 1958 (Eva in the 1963 prod. of *Die Meistersinger,* which opened the rebuilt National Theatre). She appeared in the USA from 1969 and retired in 1976.

Watson, Thomas (b London, *c* 1557; d London, buried 26 Sep 1592), English scholar and amateur musician. He pub. in 1590 *The First Sett of Italian Madrigalls Englished,* the successor of N. Yonge's *Musica Transalpina* (1588) and with it the foundation of the native Eng. school of madrigalists.

Watts, André (b Nuremberg, 20 Jun 1946), American pianist, of Hungarian and black American parentage. He studied in Philadelphia and made his debut there aged 9, in Haydn's D maj. concerto. Wide success came with his 1963 perf. of the Liszt's E♭ concerto with the NY PO under Bernstein. Eur. debut 1966, with the LSO; returned to Nuremberg for a solo recital in 1970. Often performs Brahms and Chopin.

Watts, Helen (Josephine) (b Milford Haven, 7 Dec 1927), Welsh contralto. She studied at the RAM and made her concert debut in 1955; sang with the Handel Opera Society from 1958 in *Theodora* and as Ino and Rinaldo. She toured Rus. with the EOG in 1964 and made her US debut 3 years later. She has been heard in operas by Verdi, Tippett and Wagner but is best known in Lieder and oratorio; much admired in Mahler, Elgar and Berlioz.

Waverley, overture by Berlioz, op. 1b, inspired by Walter Scott, fp Paris, 26 May 1828.

We Come to the River, opera ('actions for music') by Henze (lib. by E. Bond); comp. 1974–6, prod. London, CG, 12 Jul 1976.

Webbe, Samuel (b 1740; d London, 25 May 1816), English composer and organist. From 1776 he held posts at var. foreign embassies in London. He was awarded a prize by the Catch Club in 1766 and became its secretary in 1794. He was also librarian of the Glee Club from 1787. Wrote principally glees, catches, etc., also church music.
Webbe, Samuel (b London, *c* 1770; d Liverpool, 25 Nov 1843), English pianist, organist and composer, son of prec. Pupil of his father. He obtained the Catch Club prize

in 1794 and others later. He settled at Liverpool in 1798, returning briefly to London in 1817 to teach jointly with Logier and became organist of the Span, embassy chapel, but he returned to Liverpool, where he held several church organist posts.

Works incl. operatic farce *The Speechless Wife;* motets, glees, songs.
Weber, Aloysia (Louise Antonia) (b Zell or Mannheim, between 1759 and 1761; d Salzburg, 8 Jun 1839), German soprano, 2nd daughter of Fridolin W. Mozart, who eventually married her sister Constanze, fell in love with her in Mannheim in 1778 and later wrote for her the part of Constanze in *Die Entführung;* he also wrote arias for her. She sang Donna Anna in the 1st Viennese prod. of *Don Giovanni* (1788). She married the actor Joseph Lange in 1780.
Weber, Ben (b St Louis, 23 Jul 1916; d New York, 9 May 1979), American composer and teacher. He studied at the Univ. of Chicago but was largely self-taught as a composer; adopted the 12-note system in 1938 and was encouraged by Schoenberg. His music retained tonal associations, however. Moved to NY in 1945.

Works incl. *Symph. on Poems of William Blake* for bar. and orch. (1952), vln. concerto (1954), *Prelude and Passacaglia* for orch. (1955), *Chamber Fantasy* for small orch. (1959), pf. concerto (1961); 2 string 4tets (1942, 1952), 2 string trios (1943, 1946), serenade for string 5tet (1955); *Sinfonia Clarion* for orch. (1974).
Weber, Bernhard Anselm (b Mannheim, 18 Apr 1764; d Berlin, 23 Mar 1821), German composer, conductor and pianist. Pupil of Vogler, he was music director of the Grossmann opera troupe in Hanover 1787–90, then toured Scand. with his old teacher, and cond. at the court opera in Berlin from 1792 (*Kapellmeister* 1804).

Works incl. operas and *Singspiele,* e.g. *Mudarra* (1800) and *Die Jungfrau von Orleans* and *Wallenstein* and other plays; 2 melodramas; songs.
Weber, Bernhard Christian (b Wolferschwenda, Thuringia, 1 Dec 1712; d Tennstedt nr. Erfurt, 5 Feb 1758), German organist and composer. App. organist at Tennstedt in 1732. It was long claimed that he anticipated Bach by writing a set of preludes and fugues for keyboard in all the keys, entitled *Das wohltemperierte Clavier,* but he actually was an imitator, the work, wrongly dated 1689 (23 years before his birth), being in fact written in 1743.
Weber, Carl Maria (Friedrich Ernst) von (b

Eutin nr. Lübeck, ? 18 Nov 1786; d London, 5 Jun 1826), German composer, conductor, pianist and critic, nephew of Fridolin W. He was taken about the country in his childhood and received a desultory educ., but his father, anxious to make a prodigy of him, taught him all the music he knew. When at last they settled down at Salzburg, the boy, aged 10, became a pupil of Michael Haydn. After his mother's death in Mar 1798 he was taken to Vienna and Munich. There he studied under Valesi (Wallishauser) and Kalcher, and at 13 was a good enough pianist to appear at concerts. By 1800 he had written a good deal of juvenile music and learned lithography with Senefelder; but the wandering life was resumed and he was reduced to continuing his studies with the aid of theoret. books.

At Augsburg in 1803 he succeeded in having his opera *Peter Schmoll und seine Nachbarn* prod. In Vienna again in 1803–4, he became Vogler's pupil for a time, and his master recommended him for a conductorship at Breslau, where he went in the autumn of 1804. In 1806 he became domestic musician to Duke Eugen of Württemberg, who, on being obliged to dismiss his musicians, recommended Weber as private secretary to his younger brother Ludwig. He settled at Stuttgart in July 1807, where he led a rather dissolute life and incurred the displeasure of the king, his patron's elder brother. In 1810 he was banished from the kingdom on a trumped-up charge and went to Mannheim and later to Darmstadt, where he resumed his studies with Vogler more seriously.

After much travelling he secured the conductorship at the Ger. theatre in Prague in 1813. In Dec 1816 he was app. cond. of the Dresden court opera, where he did much to estab. Ger. opera in the face of the strong opposition of Morlacchi and other Italians. On 4 Nov 1817 he married the opera singer Caroline Brandt, who was still at Prague, and he took her to Dresden after a concert tour. On 4 May 1821 his most famous opera, *Der Freischütz*, was prod. in Berlin; *Euryanthe* followed in Vienna on 25 Oct 1823. In 1824 CG commissioned an Eng. opera from him, and he took Eng. lessons to make a success of *Oberon*. He suffered badly from a severe disease of the throat and felt unfit to visit London, but in order to keep his family from want he took the risk in Feb 1826, visiting Paris on the way. He arrived in London on 5 Mar, cond. works of his own at a Phil. concert and prod. *Oberon* on 12 Apr.

Although he felt increasingly ill, he still cond. the succeeding perfs. and appeared at several concerts. Utterly worn out early in June he made preparations for a hasty return home but died during the night at the house of his host, George Smart.

Works incl. STAGE: operas *Die Macht der Liebe und des Weins* (lost), *Das Waldmädchen* (fragment; early version of *Silvana*, 1800), *Peter Schmoll und seine Nachbarn* (1803), *Rübezahl* (fragments only), *Silvana* (1810), *Abu Hassan* (1811), *Der Freischütz* (1821), *Die drei Pintos* (fragment; later finished by Mahler, prod. 1888), *Euryanthe* (1823), *Oberon* (1826); 32 other works incl. incid. music to Schiller's trans. of Gozzi's *Turandot* and P.A. Wolff's *Preciosa* and extra songs, arias and other interpolations for plays.

ORCH.: 2 symphs. (1807); 22 works for solo insts. and orch., incl. 2 pf. concertos (1810–12), *Concertstück* for pf. and orch. (1821), concertino for clar. and orch. (1811), 2 clar. and 1 bassoon concertos (all 1811); 3 overtures.

INST.: 5tet for clar., 2 vlns., vla. and cello (1815), trio for fl., cello and pf. (1819); 27 pf. works incl. 8 sets of variations, 4 sonatas (1812–22), *Momento capriccioso*, *Rondo brillante*, *Aufforderung zum Tanz (Invitation to the Dance)*.

VOCAL: 6 cantatas, 3 Masses, 2 offertories (all with orch.); accomp. and unaccomp. part-songs, over 80 songs.

Weber, Constanze. *See* **Mozart.**

Weber, (Friedrich) Dionys(us) (b Velichov, 9 Oct 1766; d Prague, 25 Dec 1842), Bohemian teacher and composer. Pupil of Vogler. He was one of the founders and the 1st director of the Prague Cons. and wrote several theoret. treatises. He cond. the 1st perf. of Wagner's C maj. symph. in 1832.

Works incl. operas and military band music.

Weber, Fridolin (b Zell, Baden, 1733; d Vienna, 23 Oct 1779), German singer and violinist, father of Aloysia, Constanze (Mozart) and Josepha W. and uncle of Carl Maria von W. In the service of the electoral court at Mannheim, later lived in Vienna.

Weber, (Jacob) Gottfried (b Freinsheim nr. Mannheim, 1 Mar 1779; d Kreuznach, 21 Sep 1839), German composer and theorist. He pursued a lawyer's profession at Mannheim (1804), Mainz (1812) and Darmstadt (1818). In 1810 his family provided refuge for their namesakes, C.M. von Weber and his father, after the former's banishment from Stuttgart, and they formed a music and cultural society. Weber wrote a number of theoret. books.

Works incl. 3 Masses and other church music; inst. sonatas and pieces; songs with pf. and guitar.

Weber, (Maria) Josepha (b Zell, 1758 or 1759; d Vienna, 29 Dec 1819), German soprano, eldest daughter of Fridolin W. Pupil of Righini, she joined Schikaneder's opera co. in Vienna, and was the 1st Queen of Night in Mozart's *Die Zauberflöte* (1791). Her husband Sebastian Mayer (1773–1835), created Beethoven's Pizarro (1805).

Weber, Ludwig (b Vienna, 29 Jul 1899; d Vienna, 9 Dec 1974), Austrian bass. Debut Vienna, Volksoper, 1920. He sang in Düsseldorf and Cologne and was engaged at the Staatsoper, Munich, 1933–45. CG 1936 as Pogner, Gurnemanz and Hagen; returned with Vienna co. in 1947 and sang Boris in 1950. His Gurnemanz at the 1951 Bayreuth Festival, under Knappertsbusch, set a standard (it was recorded); continued at Bayreuth until 1961 as Daland, Marke and Hagen. Other roles incl. Ochs, Sarastro, Osmin, Rocco and Wozzeck. Sang in fp of Strauss's *Friedenstag* (1938).

Webern, Anton (Friedrich Wilhelm von) (b Vienna, 3 Dec 1883; d Mittersill, 15 Sep 1945), Austrian composer and conductor. Studied musicology with Adler and took the Ph.D. degree at Vienna Univ. in 1906. He became a pupil of Schoenberg for comp. He cond. for a time at Ger. provincial theatres and in Prague. After the 1914–18 war he settled at Mödling nr. Vienna and devoted himself to teaching and comp., though he still cond. esp. the modern perfs. of the Verein für Musikalische Privataufführungen and the workers' symph. concerts. He also cond. in London and Barcelona, and in all the Ger. speaking countries. His death was the result of a tragic misunderstanding (he was shot by an Amer. soldier). Although almost entirely unrecognized during his lifetime, Webern's music has proved very influential in the years since 1945: it introd. new concepts of sound, rhythm and quasimathematical organization. It is almost as much through his work as through Schoenberg's that the '12-tone system' came to find so wide an acceptance.

Works incl. ORCH.: *Im Sommerwind*, idyll (1904; fp Seattle, 1962, cond. Ormandy), Passacaglia op. 1 (1908), 6 Pieces op. 6 (1909, fp 1913, cond. Schoenberg; rev. 1928), 5 Pieces op. 10 (1911–13, fp 1926), 5 Movements arr. for string orch. from 5

Movements for string 4tet (1928–9), symph. op. 21 (1928), Vars. op. 30 (1940).

VOCAL: *Entflieht auf leichten Kähnen* for unaccomp. chorus op. 2 (1908, fp 1927), 2 songs for chorus and ens. op. 19 (texts by Goethe, 1926), *Das Augenlicht* for chorus and orch. op. 26 (1935), Cantata no. 1 for sop., chorus and orch. (1938–9), Cantata no. 2 for sop., bass, chorus and orch. (1941–3, fp 1950); 2 sets of 5 songs for voice and pf. opp. 3 and 4 (texts by George, 1909), 2 songs for voice and ens. op. 8 (texts by Rilke, 1910), 4 songs for voice and pf. op. 12 (1915–17), 4 songs for voice and orch. op. 13 (1914–18), 6 songs for voice and insts. (texts by Trakl, 1919–21), 5 *Sacred Songs* for voice and insts. op. 15 (1917–22), 5 canons on Latin texts for voice, clar. and bass clar. op. 16 (1923–24, fp NY, 1951), 3 *Traditional Rhymes* for voice and insts. op. 17 (1925, fp NY, 1952), 3 songs for voice, clar. and guitar op. 18 (1925, fp LA, 1954), 3 songs for voice and pf. op. 23 (1934), 3 songs for voice and pf. op. 25 (1934).

INST.: string 4tet in 1 movt. (1905, fp Seattle, 1962), pf. 5tet in 1 movt. (1909), 5 Movements for string 4tet op. 5 (1909), 4 pieces for vln. and pf. op. 7 (1910), 6 Bagatelles for string 4tet op. 9 (1911–13), 3 *Little Pieces* for cello and pf. op. 11 (1914), string trio op. 20 (1927), 4tet for vln., clar., tenor saxophone and pf. op. 22 (1930), concerto for 9 insts. op. 24 (1934), string 4tet op. 28 (1938), vars. for pf. op. 27 (1936).

ARRS.: Incl. Schoenberg's 1st chamber symph. (inst. ens., 1923), Schubert's *Deutsche Tänze* (orch., 1931) and the 6-part ricercare from Bach's *Musical Offering* (orch.; fp London, 1935, cond. Webern).

Webster, David (Lumsden) (b Dundee, 3 Jul 1903; d London, 11 May 1971), British administrator. He assisted in several opera prods. while at Liverpool Univ. He was general administrator at CG 1945–70 and helped to estab. the Royal Opera House as a leading centre of opera and ballet. He encouraged many Brit. artists in internat. careers. Knighted 1961.

Wecker, Georg Caspar (b Nuremberg, bap. 2 Apr 1632; d Nuremberg, 20 Apr 1695), German organist and composer. Pupil of his father, an inst. perf., and Erasmus Kindermann. He was organist at var. Nuremberg churches from the age of 19 and in 1686 was app. to the principal one, St Sebald's. J. Krieger and Pachelbel were among his pupils.

Works incl. 18 sacred concertos (church cantatas) for voices and instruments; organ music.

Weckerlin, Jean-Baptiste (Théodore) (b Guebwiller, Alsace, 9 Nov 1821; d Trottberg nr. Guebwiller, 20 May 1910), French

Zerlina. Also sang in Vienna (1904), Berlin and Stockholm.

'Wedge' Fugue, (Bach's E min. organ fugue, BWV 548.ii, so called because of the progressively widening intervals of its subject:

'WEDGE' FUGUE

composer and editor. Studied at the Paris Cons. Although unsuccessful, he was determined to make his way as a musician, collected much old Fr. music and in 1863 became archivist of the Société des Compositeurs de Musique, whose library he estab. In 1869 Auber invited him to the Cons. library, of which he became head in 1876. He ed. many collections of old Fr. songs and other music.

Works incl. opera *L'Organiste dans l'embarras* (1953) and 5 others (some in Alsat. dialect); *Roland* for solo voices, chorus and orch.; Mass and motets; symph. and suite for orch.; chamber music; songs.

Weckmann, Matthias (b Niederdorla, Thuringia, *c* 1619; d Hamburg, 24 Feb 1674), German organist and composer. He became a pupil of Schütz as a choirboy in the electoral chapel at Dresden and in 1637 was sent at the elector's expense to study further with J. Praetorius at Hamburg. In 1641 he became court organist at Dresden, where he remained until 1655, except for a visit to Nykøbing in the service of the crown prince of Den., some time before 1647. He then became organist at St James's Church, Hamburg. He organized a concert society (*Collegium musicum* with Scheidemann, Selle, Schop and other Hamburg musicians and during a visit to Dresden competed as an organist with Froberger.

Works incl. sacred concertos for voices and insts.; org. music.

Wedding, The, ballet by Stravinsky (choreog. by B. Nizhinska), prod. Paris, Théâtre Gaîté-Lyrique, 13 Jun 1923. The work is scored for chorus (Rus. words), 4 pfs. and perc. It is more generally known as *Les Noces*.

Wedekind, Frank (1864–1918), German dramatist. *See* Ettinger (*Frühlingserwachen*), Lulu (Berg).

His sister **Erika** (1868–1944) sang at Dresden 1894–1909 as Eva, Mimi and Butterfly; Salzburg 1901–4 as Blondchen and

Weelkes, Thomas (b *c* 1576; d London, buried 1 Dec 1623), English composer. He was in the service of George Phillpot at Compton nr. Winchester in his early years and then that of Edward Darcye, Groom of the Privy Chamber. In 1598 he was app. organist at Winchester Coll. and in 1602 he took the B.Mus. at Oxford. In 1601 or 1602 he became organist and choirmaster at Chichester Cathedral, but increasing drunkenness led to his dismissal in 1617. He died during a visit to London.

Works incl. services and numerous anthems; 3 books of madrigals, *Ayeres or Phantasticke Spirites* for 3 voices (1608), 2 vocal pieces contrib. to Leighton's *Teares or Lamentacions*; 3 In Nomines for 4–5 viols and other pieces for 5 viols.

Weerbeke, Gaspar van (b Oudenaarde, *c* 1445; d after 1517), Flemish composer, singer and priest. Pupil of the *maîtrise* at Oudenaarde and of Ockeghem. He took holy orders at Tournai and went to It. in the 1470s, becoming *maestro di cappella* at Milan Cathedral and a singer at the ducal court. He was in Rome as a singer at the Papal Chapel in 1481–9, but in 1488 prod. music for allegorical plays given at the marriage of Galeazzo Sforza, Duke of Milan, to Isabella of Aragon. He visited his home town in 1490 and was received with honours.

Works incl. 8 Masses, 28 motets, *Stabat Mater* and other church music.

Weideman(n), Carl Friedrich (Charles Frederick) (d London, 1782), German flautist and composer. Settled in London *c* 1726. He was concerned with Festing in the foundation of the Royal Society of Musicians in 1739 and in 1778 became cond. of the royal orch. He wrote concertos, solos, duets, trios and 4tets for fl.

Weidemann, Friedrich (b Ratzeburg, 1 Jan 1871; d Vienna, 30 Jan 1919), German baritone. After study at Hamburg and Berlin he sang at Essen, Hamburg and Riga. In 1903 he moved to the Hopfoper, Vienna; he was admired there, until his death, in operas by Mozart and Wagner, at first under Mahler. He was the first Viennese Orestes, Golaud and Faninal, and in London sang Jochanaan and Kurwenal (1910). At the 1906 Salzburg Festival he was heard as Mozart's Count, again under Mahler.

Weidt, Lucie (b Troppau, Silesia, c 1876; d Vienna, 28 Jul 1940), Austrian soprano. She made her debut in Leipzig, 1900, and in 1902 was engaged by Mahler for the Vienna Hofoper; her debut role was Elisabeth and later she was the 1st Viennese Lisa, Kundry and Marschallin. In 1919 she created the Nurse in *Die Frau ohne Schatten*. She sang as guest in Paris and Buenos Aires and in 1910 was Brünnhilde at the NY Met.

Weigl, Joseph (Franz) (b Bavaria, 19 May 1740; d Vienna, 25 Jan 1820), German cellist. He joined Prince Esterházy's orch. at Eisenstadt under Haydn in 1761, but left in 1769 for the Vienna Court Opera and joined the Imp. Chapel there in 1792.

Weigl, Joseph (b Eisenstadt, 28 Mar 1766; d Vienna, 3 Feb 1846), Austrian composer, son of prec. and godson of Haydn. Pupil of Albrechtsberger and Salieri, he was the latter's deputy at the court opera in Vienna from 1790 and succeeded him as cond. and comp. in 1792. He visited It. to prod. operas 1807–8 and again in 1815, but shortly afterwards withdrew from opera comp. and wrote mainly church music. He became vice-*Kapellmeister* at court in 1827.

Works incl. over 30 operas, e.g. *Die betrogene Arglist* (1783), *Das Waisenhaus* (1808), *Der Bergsturz* (1813); 18 ballets; incid. music; 11 Masses and other church music; cantatas, arias, songs.

Weigl, Karl (b Vienna, 6 Feb 1881; d New York, 11 Aug 1949), Austrian composer. Studied musicology at Vienna Univ., worked as asst. cond. under Mahler at the Vienna Opera, became a teacher at the New Vienna Cons. in 1918 and later lecturer at the univ. He settled in the USA in 1938, becoming an Amer. citizen in 1943 and teaching successively at Hartford, Brooklyn and Boston.

Works incl. cantata *Weltfeier* for solo voices, chorus, orch. and org.; 6 symphs. (1908–47); var. concertos; 8 string 4tets (1903–49); cello and pf. sonata; songs with pf. and with chamber accomp.

Weigl, Thaddäus (b Vienna, 1776; d Vienna, 10 Feb 1844), Austrian composer and publisher, son of J. Weigl I. Pupil of his father, was for a time cond. at the court theatres, but in 1801 became a music publisher.

Works incl. opera *Der Jahrmarkt zu Grünewald* and others; ballet *Cyrus und Thomyris* and others.

Weihe des Hauses, Die (*The Consecration of the House*), overture by Beethoven, op. 124, written in 1822 for the opening of the Josefstadt Theatre in Vienna, and perf. there on 3 Oct under the comp.

Weikl, Bernd (b Vienna, 29 Jul 1942), Austrian baritone. He studied in Hanover and sang there 1968–70. After an engagement at Düsseldorf he sang in Hamburg from 1973. Salzburg from 1971 and Bayreuth from 1973. CG debut 1975, as Rossini's Figaro; NY Met 1977, Wolfram. Other roles incl. Mandryka and Don Giovanni.

Weil, Hermann (b Muhlburg nr. Karlsruhe, 29 May 1876; d Blue Mountain Lake, NY, 6 Jul 1949), German baritone. After study in Freiburg he made his 1901 debut there, as Wolfram. Stuttgart 1904–33. In 1911 he sang Kurwenal at the NY Met under Toscanini; he remained with the co. until 1917. Bayreuth 1911–25, as Sachs, Amfortas and Gunther. Vienna 1920–3. He emigrated to NY after the rise of the Nazis.

Weill, Kurt (Julian) (b Dessau, 2 Mar 1900; d New York, 3 Apr 1950), German composer. Studied locally at first, later with Humperdinck and Busoni in Berlin. He had his 1st stage success at the age of 26. His modern version of Gay's *Beggar's Opera (Die Dreigroschenoper)* made an enormous hit in 1928, but the Nazi regime condemned his works in 1933 as both Jewish and decadent, and he left Ger. He visited London in 1935 for the prod. of *A Kingdom for a Cow*, an Eng. version of an earlier operetta, but went the same year to settle in USA (naturalized 1943).

Works incl. operas and operettas (several on libs. by Brecht) *Der Protagonist* (1926), *Der Silbersee* (1933), *Der Zar lässt sich photographieren* (lib. by G. Kaiser), *Royal Palace* (1927), *Die Dreigroschen Oper* (1928), *Happy End* (1929), *Aufstieg und Fall der Stadt Mahagonny* (1930), *Der Jasager* (1930), *Die Bürgschaft, A Kingdom for a Cow* (1935), *Johnny Johnson* (1936), *Knickerbocker Holiday* (1938), *The Firebrand* (1945).

Biblical music drama *The Eternal Road;* ballet *Die sieben Todsünden* (*Anna Anna*, 1933); cantatas *Der neue Orpheus* and *Der Lindberghflug* (1929); 2 symphs. (1921, 1933), *Fantasia, Passacaglia und Hymnus, Divertimento* and *Quodlibet* for orch.; concerto for vln. and wind band (1924); 2 string 4tets (1919, 1923); works for voices and chamber orch., songs (Rilke) with orch.

Wein, Der (*The Wine*), concert aria by Berg. (text by Baudelaire, in Ger. trans. by S. George); comp. 1929, fp Königsberg, 4 Jun 1930, cond. Scherchen.

Weinberger, Jaromír (b Prague, 8 Jan 1896; d St Petersburg, Fla., 8 Aug 1967), Czech composer. Studied with Hoffmeister and Kricka in Prague and with Reger in Ger. Prof. of comp. at the Cons. of Ithaca, NY, 1922–6; returned to Eur. to cond. and teach. Settled in USA in 1938; committed suicide.

Works incl. operas *Shvanda the Bagpiper* (1927), *The Beloved Voice* (1931), *The Outcasts of Poker Flat* (after Bret Harte, 1932) and *Wallenstein* (after Schiller); pantomime *The Abduction of Eveline*; incid. music for Shakespeare's and other plays; var. on the Eng. song, *Under the Spreading Chestnut Tree* for pf. and orch. (1939), *Lincoln Symph.*, *Czech Rhapsody* for orch.; works for org., pf., vln.

Weiner, Leó (b Budapest, 16 Apr 1885; d Budapest, 13 Sep 1960), Hungarian composer. Studied at the Nat. Acad. of Music in Budapest, where he became a prof. in 1908.

Works incl. ballet on and incid. music for Vörösmarty's *Csongor and Tünde* (1916); 3 divertimentos (1934–49), scherzo, serenade and humoresque *Carnival* for orch.; *Pastoral, Fantasy and Fugue* for strings; 2 vln. concertos; 3 string 4tets (1906–38), string trio; 2 vln. and pf. sonatas; pf. works.

Weingartner, (Paul) Felix (b Zara, Dalmatia, 2 Jun 1863; d Winterthur, Switz., 7 May 1942), Austrian conductor and composer. Studied at Graz, at the Leipzig Cons. and under Liszt at Weimar, where he prod. his 1st opera in 1884. He became cond. at Königsberg, Danzig, Hamburg and Mannheim before 1891, when he was app. cond. of the Court Opera in Berlin and cond. of the symph. concerts. In 1898 he left for Munich to become cond. of the Kaim orch. and in 1908 he succeeded Mahler as chief cond. at the Vienna Hofoper; resigned 1911 but cond. Vienna PO concerts until 1927. After 1911 he frequently changed his sphere of activity, cond. much abroad, esp. in Fr., Eng. and the USA; at CG he gave *Tannhäuser* and *Parsifal* in 1939. The last years of his life he spent, still actively, in Switz., esp. at Basle. He was 5 times married. He wrote books on cond., on Beethoven's symphs., etc.

Works incl. operas *Sakuntala* (after Kalidasa, 1884), *Malawika* (1886), *Genesius*, *Orestes* trilogy (after Aeschylus, 1902), *Kain und Abel* (1914), *Dame Kobold* (after Calderón), *Die Dorfschule*, *Meister Andrea*, *Der Apostat*; incid. music for Shakespeare's

Tempest and Goethe's *Faust*; 7 symphs. (1899–1937), symph. poem *King Lear* (after Shakespeare); 3 string 4tets; songs.

Weinlig, Christian Theodor (b Dresden, 25 Jul 1780; d Leipzig, 7 Mar 1842), German theorist and composer. Pupil of his uncle, Christian Ehregott W. (1743–1813), cantor of the Kreuzschule at Dresden. He succeeded Schicht as cantor of St Thomas's School at Leipzig in 1823. Clara Schumann and Wagner were his pupils for a short time. He wrote a treatise on fugue. His comps. incl. an oratorio, 2 Ger. Magnificats and church cantatas.

Weir, Gillian (Constance) (b Martinborough, New Zealand, 17 Jan 1941), New Zealand organist. Studied at the RCM and with Anton Heiller and Marie-Claire Alain. From 1965 has been heard widely in Poulenc, Messiaen, Couperin and Bach. Also harpsichordist.

Weir, Judith (b Aberdeen, 11 May 1954), Scottish composer. She studied with John Tavener and worked with computer music, MIT (1973). Later studied with Robin Holloway at Cambridge.

Works incl. opera *A Night at The Chinese Opera* (1987) and orch. pieces *Wunderhorn* (1979) and *The Ride Over Lake Constance* (1984).

Weis, Flemming (b Copenhagen, 15 Apr 1898; d Copenhagen, 30 Sep 1981), Danish composer. A member of a musical family, he began to comp. as a child. In 1916 he entered the Copenhagen Cons. and in 1920 finished studies at Leipzig. Active on behalf of contemporary music and also as a music critic.

Works incl. *The Promised Land* for chorus and orch.; 2 symphs. (1942, 1948), symph. overture and *In temporis vernalis* for orch.; *Introduction grave* for pf. and strings, 4 string 4tets (1922–77) and other chamber music; sonatas for var. insts., suite and sonatina for pf.; songs.

Weis, Karel (b Prague, 13 Feb 1862; d Prague, 4 Apr 1944), Czech composer and conductor. Studied at the Prague Cons. and with Skuherský and Fibich at the Org. School. After var. posts as organist, teacher and orch. player (vln. and horn), he became cond. at the National Theatre at Brno in 1886, but from 1888 devoted himself to comp.

Works incl. operas *Viola* (after Shakespeare's *Twelfth Night*, 1892; rev. as *The Twins*, 1917), *The Polish Jew* (after Erckmann-Chatrian), *The Attack on the Mill* (after Zola, 1912), *The Blacksmith of Lesetin* (1920), operettas *The Village Musi-*

cians and *The Revisor* (after Gogol's comedy); choral scene *Triumfator*; symph. poem *Helios and Selene*; string 4tet; vln. and pf. sonata; pf. pieces; folksong arrs.

Weisgall, Hugo (David) (b Ivaniçice, Czechoslovakia, 13 Oct 1912), American composer of Czech origin. His family settled in the USA in 1920. He studied at the Peabody Cons., Baltimore, and later with Sessions in NY and R. Scalero at the Curtis Inst. in Philadelphia. He taught at the Juilliard School 1957–68.

Works incl. operas *Night* (1932), *Lillith* (1934), *The Tenor* (1952), *6 Characters in Search of an Author* (after Pirandello, 1959), *Athaliah* (1964), *9 Rivers from Jordan* (1968), *The 100 Nights* (1976), *The Gardens of Adonis* (1980); ballets *Quest, One Thing is Certain, Outpost*; overture in F maj. for orch.; choral music; songs.

Weismann, Julius (b Freiburg, 26 Dec 1879; d Singen, Bodensee, 22 Dec 1950), German composer. Studied at Munich with Herzogenberg in Berlin and again at Munich with Thuille.

Works incl. operas *Schwanenweiss* (1923), *Traumspiel* (1925), *Gespenstersonate* (all after Strindberg), *Leonce und Lena* (G. Büchner, 1924), *Landsknechte, Regina del Lago* (1928), *Die pfiffige Magd* (after Holberg, 1939); 3 symphs., 3 pieces for orch., 3 sinfoniettas; 4 vln. concertos, 3 pf. concertos, cello concerto; 11 string 4tets (1905–47), 3 pf. trios (1908–21); sonata for vln. solo, 5 vln. sonatas, 2 cello sonatas, var. for ob. and pf.; choral works; vars. for 2 pfs.; 7 op. nos. of pf. pieces; 15 op. nos. of songs.

Weiss, Adolph (b Baltimore, 12 Sep 1891; d Van Nuys, Calif., 21 Feb 1971), American composer of German parentage. Studied pf., vln. and bassoon, and at the age of 16 played 1st bassoon with the Rus. Symph. Orch. of NY and then in the NY PO under Mahler. He then studied comp. at Columbia Univ. with C. Rybner and later with Schoenberg in Vienna. Later worked with various Calif. orchs.

Works incl. *I Segreti* (1923) and *American Life* (1928) for orch.; *The Libation Bearers*, choreog. cantata for soloists, chorus and orch.; theme and vars. for orch.; tpt. concerto; 3 string 4tets (1925–32); music for wind insts.; songs; pf. music.

Weiss (actually Schneeweiss) **Amalie** (b Marburg, Styria, 10 May 1839; d Berlin, 3 Feb 1898), Austrian contralto. Made her 1st stage appearance at Troppau in 1853, was later engaged in Vienna and Hanover, and at the latter place married Joachim in 1863. She then appeared only as a concert singer. They separated in 1884.

Weiss, Franz (b Glatz, Silesia, 18 Jan 1778; d Vienna, 25 Jan 1830), Austrian violist and composer. Settled in Vienna and became the vla. player in Prince Rasumovsky's 4tet, founded in 1808.

Works incl. symph. for fl., bassoon and tpt. with orch., vars. for vln. and orch.; string 4tet; duets for vlns. and for fls; pf. sonatas.

Weiss, Sylvius Leopold (b Breslau, 12 Oct 1686; d Dresden, 16 Oct 1750), German lutenist and composer. He was in the service of the Pol. Prince Alexander Sobieski, with whom he went to Rome *c* 1708, later at the courts of Hesse-Kassel, Düsseldorf, and from 1718 Dresden, where he worked with Lotti, Hasse, Porpora, Hebenstreit, Pisendel and others; he was sent to Vienna with a visiting Saxon orch. that year. In 1723 he played in Prague with Quantz and H. Graun in Fux's coronation opera *Costanza e fortezza*. Wrote lute music, incl. over 70 partitas.

Weissenberg, Alexis (Sigismond) (b Sofia, 26 Jul 1929), French pianist of Bulgarian birth. Studied at the Juilliard School from 1946, won Leventritt Comp. 1948. Retired 1956–66 for study. London debut 1974.

Weissenburg, Hainz. *See* **Albicastro.**

Weissensee, Friedrich (b Schwerstedt, Thuringia, *c* 1560; d Altenweddingen, 1622), German clergyman and composer. Became rector of the grammar school at Gebesee, *c* 1590, and cantor of the town school of Magdeburg in *c* 1596. About 1602 he became rector at Altenweddingen. His works incl. motets in the Venetian style.

Weisshan (or **Winsheim**), **Abraham** 16th–17th-cent. lutenist and composer. In 1568 he went into service at the Saxon court at Dresden, where he still was in 1611.

Works incl. a collection of lute preludes, fantasies and dances *Silvae musicalis libri VII*.

Welcome-Odes
or   } cantatas by Purcell
Welcome-Songs
for the return to London of Charles II and James II on var. occasions. One, of 1682, is addressed to James as Duke of York, before his accession.

Weldon, George (b Chichester, 5 Jun 1906; d Cape Town, 16 Aug 1963), English conductor. Studied at the RCM with Sargent, and cond. various provincial orchs., in 1943 becoming cond. of the CBSO, which post he held until 1951; later asst. cond. of the Hallé Orch. under Barbirolli.

Weldon, John (b Chichester, 19 Jan 1676; d London, 7 May 1736), English organist and composer. Educ. at Eton, where he studied music under the coll. organist John Walton, he later became a pupil of Purcell in London. In 1694 he was app. organist of New Coll., Oxford, and in 1700 gained the 1st prize for the setting of Congreve's masque *The Judgement of Paris* against Eccles, Finger and D. Purcell. In 1701 he became a Gentleman of the Chapel Royal and in 1708 organist there on the death of Blow; he also became organist of St Bride's and (1726) St Martin-in-the-Fields churches.

Works incl. masque *The Judgment of Paris* (1701); music for *The Tempest* (*c* 1712), songs for Cibber's *She would and she would not* and other plays; anthems; songs.

Welitsch (actually Velickova), **Ljuba** (b Borissovo, 10 Jul 1913), Austrian soprano of Bulgarian birth. Played the vln. as a child, studied philosophy at Sofia Univ., and then studied singing in Vienna with Lierhammer, making her debut in Sofia in 1936. Sang at Graz, Hamburg and Munich, then visited CG with Vienna co. as Salome, her most famous role. She returned to CG for Musetta, Aida and Tosca. Met 1948–52.

Weller, Walter (b Vienna, 30 Nov 1939), Austrian conductor and violinist. He joined the Vienna PO in 1956 and founded the Weller Quartet in 1958; toured with the ens. in Eur. and the USA, and recorded works by Berg and Beethoven. After study with Krips and Szell became a cond. from 1966; Brit. debut 1973, with LSO. Prin. cond. RLPO 1977–80, RPO 1980–5. He has given concerts in Japan and Israel and cond. at Salzburg and Florence. Well known in late Romantic rep.

Well-tempered Clavier. *See* **Wohltemperierte Clavier, Das.**

Wellesz, Egon (b Vienna, 21 Oct 1885; d Oxford, 9 Nov 1974), Austrian musicologist and composer. Studied with Schoenberg, Bruno Walter and others in Vienna, also musicology with Adler at the univ., where he graduated Ph.D. in 1908. In 1913 he became lecturer in music hist. there and prof. from 1930 to 1938. He specialized in Byzantine and modern music, ed. and wrote on the former and pub. works on Schoenberg, Cavalli and the Venetian opera, modern orch., etc. In 1932 he received the hon. D.Mus. from Oxford Univ. and in 1938 he settled there, becoming lecturer in 1943 and

Reader from 1948 to 1956. He was a member of the ed. board of the *New Oxford History of Music* and ed. of vol. I and one of the eds. of *Monumenta Musicae Byzantinae*. His books include *A History of Byzantine Music* and *Eastern Elements in Western Chant*. CBE 1957.

Works incl. operas *Die Prinzessin Girnara* (J. Wassermann, 1921), *Alkestis* (Hofmannsthal, 1924) and *Die Bacchantinnen* (after Euripides, 1931), *Operfung des Gefangenen* (1926), *Scherz, List und Rache* (Goethe's lib., 1928), *Incognita* (on Congreve's story, 1951); ballets *Das Wunder der Diana* (1924), *Persian ballet* (1920), *Archilles auf Skyros* (1921) and *Die Nächtlichen* (1923).

VOCAL AND ORCH.: unaccomp. choruses to old Eng. poems: *Gebete der Mädchen zu Maria* for sop., chorus and orch.; 9 symphs. (1945–71), symph. poem *Vorfrühling*, symph. suite *Prosperos Beschwörungen* (after Shakespeare's *Tempest*, 1938), *Festival March* for orch.; *Amor timido* (Metastasio) and *Lied der Welt* (Hofmannsthal) for sop. and orch., *Leben, Traum und Tod* (Hofmannsthal) for contralto and orch. (1935); dance suite for vln. and chamber orch.; pf. concerto, vln. concerto; 3 Masses, motets, cantata *Mitte des Lebens*.

CHAMBER AND INST.: *The Leaden Echo and the Golden Echo* (G.M. Hopkins) for sop., clar., vla., cello and pf. (1944); 9 string 4tets (1911–66), string 5tet; clar. 5tet; octet; solo sonatas for vln., cello, ob., clar., etc.; pf. pieces; songs.

Welsh National Opera, opera co. founded 1946. Based in Cardiff and tours widely in Wales and the Eng. provinces. An adventurous rep. incl. early Verdi (1st Brit. perf. of *La battaglia di Legnano*, 1960) and a well-received cycle, with Scottish Opera, of Janáček's operas. The WNO prod. of *The Ring* was brought to London, CG, in 1986. Music directors from 1963 have been Bryan Balkwill (until 1967) James Lockhart (1968–73) and Richard Armstrong (1973–86); Charles Mackerras from 1986. Singers who have appeared with the co. incl. Gwyneth Jones, Geraint Evans and Margaret Price.

Wendling (*née* Spurni), **Dorothea** (b Stuttgart, 21 Mar 1736; d Munich, 20 Aug 1811), German soprano. Worked at the court of Mannheim and Munich; wife of Johann Baptist W. She created Ilia in *Idomeneo* (1781).

Wendling (*née* Sarselli), **Elisabeth Augusta** (b Mannheim, 20 Feb 1746; d Munich, 10 Jan 1786), German soprano, sister-in-law of prec. Attached to the courts of Mannheim and Munich; married the violinist Franz W. in 1764.

Wendling, Johann Baptist (b Rappoltsweiler, Alsace, 17 Jun 1723; d Munich, 27 Nov 1797), German flautist, brother-in-law of prec. In the service of the court at Mannheim from c 1751 to 1752, also travelled widely. He married the singer Dorothea Spurni in 1752.

Wenzinger, August (b Basle, 14 Nov 1905), Swiss conductor, cellist and gamba-player. Studied 1st at the Basle Cons., until 1927, and then with P. Jarnach in Cologne until 1929. Then played cello with various orchs., and taught at the Schola Cantorum Basiliensis 1934–70. He was esp. well known as a cond. of Baroque (and earlier) music, using period instruments.

Werba, Erik (b Baden nr. Vienna, 23 May 1918), Austrian composer, piano accompanist and writer on music. Studied with J. Marx, Wellesz and Schenk, graduating in 1940. In 1948 he became prof. at the Vienna State Acad. He is frequently heard in recital, with Christa Ludwig, Peter Schreier and Nicolai Gedda.

Werckmeister, Andreas (b Benneckenstein, 30 Nov 1645; d Halberstadt, 26 Oct 1706), German organist and theorist. Organist at Hasselfelde, Quedlinburg and Halberstadt in succession. Wrote theoret. works, esp. on keyboard tuning.

Werfel, Franz (b Prague, 10 Sep 1890; d Beverly Hills, Calif., 26 Aug 1945), Austrian novelist and playwright. Studied at Prague and Leipzig Univ. His works incl. a novel on Verdi and transs. of many of Verdi's operas e.g. *Forza del destino*(1925), *Simon Boccanegra* (1929) and *Don Carlos*; *See* **Grosz** *(Spiegelmensch)*, **Maximilien** (Milhaud), **Orff** *(Turmes Auferstehung,)*, **Troades** (Reimann), **Zwingburg** (Krenek).

Werner, Gregor Joseph (b Ybbs an der Donau, 28 Jan 1693; d Eisenstadt, Burgenland, 3 Mar 1766), Austrian composer. App. music director to the Esterházy family in 1728; predecessor of Haydn there and his superior for 5 years from 1761. Shortly before his death Werner reported to Prince Nikolaus von Esterházy on Haydn's alleged laziness and ineptitude.

Works incl. over 20 Masses, 3 Requiems and other church music; 18 oratorios; symphs.; string 4tet, 6 intros. and fugues for string 4tet (pub. by Haydn); sonatas, etc., for 2 vlns. and bass.

Werrecore (or **Verecore**), **Matthias Hermann** (died after 1574), ? Flemish 16th-cent.

composer. In 1522 he became *maestro di cappella* of Milan Cathedral in succession to Gafori.

Works incl. motets for 5 voices, 4-part song on the battles of Bicocca and Pavia, in which Francesco Sforza gained the mastery of Milan.

Wert, Giaches (or **Jaches**) **de** (b ? Weert, 1535; d Mantua, 6 May 1596), Flemish composer. Was sent to It. as a choir-boy when a small child and at 9 became a member of the choir of the Novellara at Reggio. He began to pub. madrigals towards the end of the 1550s and c 1560 went into service at the ducal court of Mantua under Guglielmo Gonzaga. He was also attached to the church of Santa Barbara, where he succeeded Giovanni Contina as *maestro di cappella* in 1565. In 1566 he accomp. the duke to Augsburg and there declined an offer from the Emperor Maximilian II. In 1567 he visited Venice with the court and later Ferrara under Alfonso (II) d'Este. About that time he suffered much from the intrigues of the It. musicians, who disliked him as a foreigner, and in 1570 one of them, Agostino Bonvicino, was dismissed for a love-affair with Wert's wife. In 1580 he and his family were given the freedom of the city of Mantua in perpetuity.

Works incl. motets, 11 books of madrigals for 5 voices (1558–95), 1 for 4 voices, canzonets, *villanelle*.

Werther, opera by Massenet (lib. by E. Blau, P. Milliet and G. Hartmann, based on Goethe's novel), prod., in Ger., Vienna, Opera, 16 Feb 1892 cond. Richter; 1st Paris perf., Opéra-Comique, 16 Jan 1893.

Wesendonck Lieder, 5 songs for voice and pf. by Wagner (texts by the comp.'s mistress, Mathilde Wesendonck (1828–1902)); comp. Zurich, 1857–8. Usually heard in orch. arr. by Felix Mottl. Titles are 1. *Der Engel*; 2. *Stehe still*; 3. *Im Treibhaus*; 4. *Schmerzen*; 5. *Träume*. Nos. 3 and 5 were studies for *Tristan*, also written under the influence of Mathilde W. (Her influence on other comps. was not strong; a poem about cremation sent to Brahms was swiftly incinerated by him.)

Wesley, English family of musicians.

1. Charles W. (b Bristol, 11 Dec 1757; d London, 23 May 1834), English organist and composer. Pupil of Kelway and Boyce in London and later organist at var. churches and chapels. He also appeared in public as harpsichordist.

Works incl. incid. music for Mason's *Caractacus*; concerto grosso; 6 org. or harpsichord concertos; 6 string 4tets (1776); anthems, hymns, harpsichord pieces; songs.

2. Samuel W. (b Bristol, 24 Feb 1766; d London, 11 Oct 1837), English organist, composer and conductor, brother of prec. and nephew of John W. Like his brother he showed precocious musical gifts at a very early age. At 6 he was taught by the organist of the church of St James, Barton, Bristol, at 8 he finished the oratorio *Ruth* and soon after appeared at the org. as a prodigy. In 1784 injured his head in an accident, with the result that he periodically fell into strange behaviour for the rest of his life. He did much to spread a knowledge of Bach in Eng. and ed. some of his works. He cond. the Birmingham Festival in 1811, lectured at the Royal Institution and gave frequent org. recitals, but had periodically to retire for several years. Shortly before his death he met Mendelssohn and they played the org. to each other.

Works incl. oratorios *Ruth* (1774) and *The Death of Abel* (1779); 4 Masses, numerous Lat. and Eng. anthems incl. *In exitu Israel, Exultate Deo, Dixit Dominus, All go unto one place, Behold how good, Hear, O thou shepherd* (some with org.), Morning and Evening Service in F maj. and other church music; Ode on St Cecilia's Day; 4 symphs. (1784–1802), and 5 overtures; org. and vln. concertos; 2 string 4tets and other chamber music; org. fugues, voluntaries, etc.; numerous pf. works; glees, songs and duets.

3. Samuel Sebastian W. (b London, 14 Aug 1810; d Gloucester, 19 Apr 1876), English organist and composer, illegitimate son of prec. Pupil of his father and choir-boy in the Chapel Royal from 1820. In 1826 he was app. organist of a London church and by 1830 he held similar posts at 2 more. In 1832 he became organist of Hereford Cathedral, in 1835 (when he married) of Exeter Cathedral; in 1842–9 he was organist of Leeds Parish Church, in 1849–65 of Winchester Cathedral and then, until his death, of Gloucester Cathedral. He took the D.Mus. at Oxford in 1839 and became org. prof. at the RAM in London in 1850.

Works incl. 5 services. 24 anthems, Psalm c, 2 settings of *By the waters of Babylon* with sop. and with contralto solo, chants and hymn tunes; org. works; *Ode to Labour* and *The Praise of Music* for chorus; 3 glees; 9 songs (2 with cello *ad lib.*); pf. pieces.

Wessely, Carl Bernhard (b Berlin, 1 Sep 1768; d Potsdam, 11 Jul 1826), German

composer and conductor. Pupil of J.A.P. Schulz. He was cond. at the Berlin Nat. Theatre, 1788–95, and in 1796–1802 at Prince Heinrich's private theatre at Rheinsberg. After the prince's death he became a civil servant at Potsdam, where he founded a society for the perf. of classical music.

Works incl. operas *Psyché* (1789), *Louis IX* (1797); *Herbstes* (1789); ballet *Die Wahl des Helden* (1788); incid. music to Shakespeare's *Tempest*, Kotzebue's *Sonnenjungfrau* and other plays; cantatas on the deaths of Moses Mendelssohn and Prince Henry of Prussia (1802); string 4tets; songs.

Westrup, Jack (Allan) (b London, 26 Jul 1904; d Headley, 21 Apr 1975), English musicologist, critic, composer and conductor. Educ. at Dulwich Coll. and Balliol Coll., Oxford, where as an undergraduate he ed. Monteverdi's *Orfeo* and *Incoronazione di Poppea* for perf. by the Oxford Univ. Opera Club. He taught classics at Dulwich Coll. from 1928 to 1934, and was an asst. music critic on the *Daily Telegraph* from 1934 to 1940. From 1941 to 1944 he was lecturer in music at King's Coll., Newcastle upon Tyne, from 1944 to 1946 prof. of music at Birmingham Univ. and from 1947 to 1971 prof. at Oxford. He cond. *Idomeneo* and *Les Troyens*, the fp of Wellesz's *Incognita* and the 1st Brit. perfs. of *Hans Heiling* and *L'Enfant et les sortilèges*. He was chairman of the ed. board of the *New Oxford History of Music* and ed. of vol. VI. Ed. of *Music and Letters* from 1959. Other literary work incl. a book on Purcell and the 4th and 5th eds. of this dictionary (1962 and 1971). Knighted 1961.

Works incl. motet *When Israel came out of Egypt* for unaccomp. double chorus; part-song *Weathers*; passacaglia for orch.; 3 Shakespeare songs.

Wettergren, Gertrud (b Eslöv, 17 Feb 1897), Swedish contralto. Debut Stockholm, Royal Opera, 1922 as Cherubino; remained with the co. until 1952 as Eboli, Marfa, Kostelnička and in operas by Schreker, Boito and Britten. NY Met debut 1935, as Amneris; CG 1936–9. Other roles incl. Carmen, Azucena and Fricka.

Wetzler, Hermann (Hans) (b Frankfurt am Main, 8 Sep 1870; d New York, 29 May 1943), German, later American composer and conductor. Spent his childhood in the USA, but in 1882 went to study at the Hoch Cons. at Frankfurt under Scholz, Knorr, Humperdinck, Clara Schumann and others. In 1897–1901 he was organist at a NY church. In 1903 he organized symph. concerts there, but in 1905 returned to Ger. and became cond. at var. opera houses. About 1930 he retired to Ascona, Switz., and in 1940 settled in USA.

Works incl. opera *The Basque Venus* (after Mérimée, 1928); incid. music to Shakespeare's *As You Like It* (1917); Magnificat for sop., chorus and org. (1936); *Symph. Fantasy, Visions, Assisi* for orch. (1924); *Symphonie concertante* for vln. and orch. (1932); Easter music for wind insts. and org.; vars. for ob., clar. and strings; *Scot. Songs* and 6 other op. nos. of songs.

Wexford Festival. Season of three operas held each autumn at town in Eire, established 1951. A feature of festival has been the revival of neglected French works (Thomas' *Mignon*, 1986) and the encouragement of young singers (Kathleen Kuhlmann as Rossini's *Tancredi*, 1986). Elaine Padmore has been dir. since 1982.

Weyse, Christoph Ernst Friedrich (b Altona, 5 Mar 1774; d Copenhagen, 8 Oct 1842), German-Danish pianist and composer. Pupil of J.A.P. Schulz at Copenhagen from 1789. He settled there as organist and music teacher. He also collected and ed. Dan. folksongs.

Works incl. operas *The Sleeping-Draught* (1804), *Faruk*, *The Cave of Adullam* (1816), *An Adventure in Rosenborg Gardens* (1827), *Floribella*, *The Feast at Kenilworth* (after Scott), operettas; 7 symphs.; c 30 cantatas; org. and pf. works; Dan. folksongs, etc.

When Lilacs Last in the Dooryard Bloom'd, American Requiem for mezzo, bar., chorus and orch. by Hindemith (text by W. Whitman); fp NY, 14 May 1946, cond. Robert Shaw. Written in memory of Roosevelt and US war dead.

Whettham, Graham (Dudley) (b Swindon, 7 Sep 1927), English composer. Largely self-taught, he writes in a fairly conservative style: more honoured abroad then in his own country, he has pub. his works himself from 1970.

Works incl. opera *The Chef who Wanted to Rule the World* (1969), ballet *The Masque of the Red Death* (after Poe, 1968); concertos for ob., clar. and vln., 4 symphs., *Sinfonietta stravagante* (1964), Sinfonia concertante (1966), ; *Hymnos* for strings (1978); 2 ob. 4tets (1960, 1973), 3 string 4tets (1967, 1978, 1980), horn trio (1976), concerto for 10 wind (1979); choral music, songs; music for brass band and for organ.

Whitaker, John (b 1776; d London, 4 Dec 1847), English composer, organist and pub-

lisher. He was organist at the church of St Clement, Eastcheap, in London and a partner in the music pub. firm of Button and W. He was in request as a comp. of music for the Sadler's Wells Theatre pantomimes, incl. the song 'Hot Codlins' sung by the clown Grimaldi.

Works incl. stage pieces *The Outside Passenger* (with Corri and Reeves), *A Chip of the Old Block*, *A Friend Indeed*, *Three Miles from Paris*, *A Figure of Fun*, *The Apprentice's Opera*, *The Rake's Progress* and others; songs for a stage adaptation of Scott's *Guy Mannering*; anthems and other sacred music; settings of Eng. transs. of Anacreon's Odes and Aesop's Fables; 12 pedal exercises for org.

Whitbroke, William (*fl.* 1520–50), English cleric and composer. He was educ. at Cardinal Coll. (later Christ Church), Oxford, where he was ordained priest in 1529. In 1531 he was app. sub-dean at St Paul's Cathedral in London and soon afterwards also vicar of All Saints' Church at Stanton, Suffolk, where he may have retired on leaving St Paul's in 1535.

Works incl. Mass for 4 voices, Magnificat and other church music.

White, Eric Walter (b Bristol, 10 Sep 1905; d London, 13 Sep 1985), English writer on music. Studied at Balliol Coll., Oxford. He was active in various non-musical posts, in 1946 becoming a member of the Arts Council for Great Britain. He wrote books on Stravinsky, Britten, Tippett and Eng. opera (1982).

White, Paul (b Bangor, Maine, 22 Aug 1859; d Rochester, NY, 31 May 1973), American composer, conductor and violinist. Studied at the New Eng. Cons., also comp. with Chadwick, vln. with E. Ysaÿe and cond. with Goossens, whose orch. at Cincinnati he joined. Later became cond. of the Civic and Eastman School orchs. at Rochester, NY, and in 1938 became a member of the faculty of the Eastman School.

Works incl. *Voyage of the Mayflower* for chorus and orch.; symph. in E min., *Lyric Overture*; string 4tet.

White (or Whyte), Robert (b c 1538; d London, Nov 1574), English composer. He was prob. the son of a London org. builder, also named Robert W., and took the Mus.B. degree at Cambridge in 1560. In 1561 he succeeded Tye as choirmaster at Ely Cathedral. He married Tye's daughter Ellen in 1565 and left Ely in 1566 (he was succeeded by John Farrant) to become choirmaster of Chester Cathedral until c 1570, when he went to London to take up a similar post at Westminster Abbey. Along with nearly the whole of his family, he succumbed to the plague of 1574.

Works incl. 19 Lat. motets etc.; Eng. anthems; In Nomines for viols; hexachord fantasia for keyboard.

White, Willard (b St Catherine, Jamaica, 10 Oct 1946), West Indian bass. He studied at the Juilliard School and made his debut at the NY City Opera in 1974, as Colline. After engagements on the Continent he sang Monteverdi's Seneca with ENO in 1976; returned as Hunding in 1983. Glyndebourne from 1978, as the Speaker, Osmin, the King in *Love for Three Oranges* (1982) and Gershwin's Porgy (1986). He has been heard in concert in works by Shostakovich and Elgar.

Whitehill, Clarence (Eugene) (b Marengo, Iowa, 5 Nov 1871; d New York, 19 Dec 1932), American bass-baritone. Studied at Chicago and Paris and made his 1st stage appearance at Brussels in 1898, as Donner. After 1st singing in NY in 1900 he studied further with Stockhausen at Frankfurt and learnt Wagnerian parts with Cosima Wagner at Bayreuth; sang there 1904–9 as Wolfram, Amfortas and Gunther. He created Delius's Koanga (Elberfeld, 1904) and in 1908 sang Wotan under Richter at CG. NY Met 1909–32 as Sachs, Amfortas and Golaud.

Whitehouse, W(illiam) E(dward) (b London, 20 May 1859; d London, 12 Jan 1935), English cellist. Studied at the RAM in London, Piatti being among his masters, and joined the teaching-staff there in 1882. He travelled with Joachim and became a member of several chamber-music organizations.

Whithorn, an early English instrument of the oboe type, also called May-horn, made of willow bark with a double reed of material from the same tree. It was formerly used in Oxfordshire for the Whit-Monday hunt.

Whitlock, Percy (William) (b Chatham, 1 Jun 1903; d Bournemouth, 1 May 1946), English organist and composer. Learnt music as a choir-boy at Rochester Cathedral and later studied at the GSM and the RCM in London. Asst. organist at Rochester Cathedral, 1921–30 and organist at Chatham and Borstal; from 1932 borough organist at Bournemouth.

Works incl. services, anthems, motets and hymn-tunes; music for a Rochester pageant; symph. for organ and orch.; sonata in C min., *Plymouth Suite* and other works for org.

Whitman, Walt(er) (1819–92), American

poet. *See* **Bacon** (songs with orch.), **Brian** (*For Valour*), **Carpenter** (*Sea Drift*), **Carter** (*Warble for Lilac Time*), **Coleridge-Taylor** (*Sea Drift*), **Converse** (*Mystic Trumpeter* and *Night and Day*), **Farewell** (symbolistic study), **Harris (R.)** (suite), **Harty** (*Mystic Trumpeter*), **Henze** (chamber cantata), **Holst** (*Ode to Death*), **Kelley** (*My Captain*), **Loeffler** (*Beat! Beat! Drums!*), **Morning Heroes** (Bliss), **Mystic Trumpeter** (Holst), **Schoeck** (*Trommelschläge*), **Sea Drift** (Delius), **Sea Symphony** (Vaughan Williams), **Sessions** (*Turn, O Libertad*), **Vaughan Williams** (*Toward the Unknown Region*), **When Lilacs Last in the Dooryard Bloom'd** (Hindemith), **Wood (C.)** (*Dirge for 2 Veterans*).

Whittaker, W(illiam) G(illies) (b Newcastle upon Tyne, 23 Jul 1876; d Orkney Isles, 5 Jul 1944), English educationist, conductor, editor and composer. Taught and cond. choirs at Armstrong and King's Colls., Newcastle upon Tyne, and founded a Bach Choir there. In 1929 he was app. prof. of music at Glasgow Univ. and principal of the Scot. Acad. of Music there. He ed. much early music, incl. Byrd's Great Service (perf. Newcastle, Westminster and Oxford, 1924). Pub. miscellaneous essays and a book on Bach's cantatas.

Works incl. overture and choruses for Aeschylus' *Choreophorae, A Lykewake Dirge* for chorus and orch.; pf. 5tet *Among the Northumbrian Hills*; part-songs and folksong arrs.

Who is Silvia?, song by Schubert from Shakespeare's *Two Gentlemen of Verona,* trans. by E. von Bauernfeld as *An Silvia* and comp. 1826.

Whole-tone Scale, a musical scale progressing by steps of nothing but whole tones. Only 2 such scales are possible, i.e.:

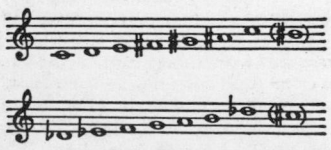

but they can of course begin at any point, there being no feeling of tonality or of any keynote; neither is there, consequently, any possibility of modulation, and the possibilities of harmonizing whole-tone music are limited. The accidentals may, of course, be equally well written as sharps or flats.

Whyte, Robert. *See* **White.**

Whythorne, Thomas (b Ilminster, 1528; d

London, c 31 Jul 1596), English composer. He travelled in It. and elsewhere on the Continent and pub. his 1st book of music in 1571 and his 2nd in 1590; the 2nd vol. contains the earlier printed Eng. inst. music. His autobiog. was pub. in 1961.

Works incl. psalms and secular songs for 2–5 voices or solo voice with insts.

Wich, Günther (b Bamberg, 23 May 1928), German conductor. Debut Freiburg, 1952; cond. opera there until 1959, then worked at Graz, Hanover and Duisburg/Düsseldorf (1965–80). Cond. *Die Zauberflöte* at CG in 1968. Often heard in modern music, he gave the Brit. première of Zimmermann's *Die Soldaten* (1972) and has been heard in *Moses und Aron* and all three 1-act operas by Schoenberg. He has recorded in the Baroque rep.

Widdop, Walter (b Norland nr. Halifax., 19 Apr 1892; d London, 6 Sep 1949), English tenor. He appeared as a Wagnerian singer with the BNOC in the 1920s and was almost alone among Eng. tenors to fill heroic parts of this kind; CG 1924–38, as Siegfried, Siegmund and Tristan. He appeared at Barcelona (1927), in Hol. and Ger., also sang in oratorio.

Widerspänstigen Zähmung, Der (*The Taming of the Shrew*), opera by Götz (lib. by J.V. Widmann, after Shakespeare), prod. Mannheim, 11 Oct 1874.

Widmann, Erasmus (b Schwäbisch Hall, bap. 15 Sep 1572; d Rothenburg ob der Tauber, 31 Oct 1634), German organist and composer. He wrote Lat. and sacred works and secular Ger. songs, and dance music, *canzone*, etc. for insts.

Widor, Charles-Marie-(Jean-Albert) (b Lyons, 21 Feb 1844; d Paris, 12 Mar 1937), French organist, teacher and composer. Studied under his father, an organist at Lyons, and later with Lemmens and Fétis in Brussels. In 1870 he became organist of the church of Saint-Sulpice in Paris, and in 1890 succeeded Franck as org. prof. at the Cons. He became prof. of comp. in succession to Dubois in 1896.

Works incl. operas *Maître Ambros* (1886), *Les Pêcheurs de Saint-Jean* (1905), *Nerto* (after Mistral); ballet *La Korrigane*; pantomime *Jeanne d'Arc*; incid. music to *Conte d'Avril* (adaptation of Shakespeare's *Twelfth Night*) and Coppée's *Les Jacobites*; Mass for double chorus and 2 orgs., Psalm cxii for chorus, orch. and org.

2 symphs. (1870, 1886), symph. poem *Une Nuit de Valpurgis*; symph. for org. and orch., 2 concertos for pf. (1876 and 1906)

and 1 for cello (1882); pf. 5tet, pf. trio; vln. and pf. sonata, suite for fl. and pf.; 6 duets for pf. and org.; 10 symphs. (1876–1900) and pieces for org.; pf. works; songs.

Wieck, Clara. *See* **Schumann.**

Wieck, Friedrich (b Pretzsch nr. Torgau, 18 Aug 1785; d Dresden, 6 Oct 1873), German pianist and teacher of his instrument, father of Clara Schumann. Taught at Leipzig and Dresden, and has Schumann and Bülow among his pupils. Toured with Clara as soloist. He was violently opposed to her marriage with Schumann.

Wiedemann, Hermann (b 1879; d Berlin, 2 Jul 1944), German baritone. Debut Elberfeld, 1905. His early career was in Brno, Hamburg and Berlin; created Raffaele in Wolf-Ferrari's *The Jewels of the Madonna*, 1911. From 1916 until his death he was a member of the Vienna Opera and he sang at Salzburg 1922–41 as Guglielmo and Beckmesser (1936, under Toscanini). He appeared at CG in 1933 and 1938, and at Munich and Buenos Aires was heard as Donner and Alberich in the *Ring*.

Wiegenlied (Ger. = cradle song), a title often given by German composers to vocal lullabies or to instrumental pieces in their manner.

Wiemann, Ernst (b Stapelberg, 21 Dec 1919; d Hamburg, 17 May 1980), German bass. After study in Hamburg and Munich he made his debut at Kiel in 1938. He sang in Berlin and Nuremberg after the war and in 1957 joined the Hamburg Staatsoper. During the 1960s he was successful at the NY Met (debut 1961, as King Henry). He was heard widely in Eur. and N. Amer. in the Wagner bass rep. (Met 1961–9) and in operas by Mozart and Verdi; sang Gurnemanz at CG (1971) and was much admired as Sachs, Philip II, Osmin, Rocco and Arkel.

Wiener, Otto (b Vienna, 13 Feb 1913), German baritone. He sang 1st with the Vienna Boys' Choir; concert singer from 1939. He continued in concert after the war and made his stage debut at Graz (Boccanegra, 1953). Düsseldorf 1956–9, Vienna from 1957, Munich from 1960. At Bayreuth, 1957–63, he sang Sachs, Wotan, Gunther and the Dutchman. He appeared as guest in London and Milan and sang in Klemperer's 1st recording of the *Missa Solemnis*.

Wieniawski, Henryk (b Lublin, 10 Jul 1835; d Moscow, 31 Mar 1880), Polish violinist and composer, father of Poldowski. Was sent to the Paris Cons. at the age of 8 and in 1846 allowed to make his 1st tour, in Pol. and Rus. From 1850 he travelled with his brother Józef and in 1860 was app. solo violinist to the Tsar, living in St Petersburg most of his time until 1872, when he toured the USA with A. Rubinstein. In 1875 he succeeded Vieuxtemps as 1st vln. prof. at the Brussels Cons. But he travelled again towards the end of his life, in spite of serious ill-health, which caused his sudden death in Rus.

Works incl. 2 vln. concertos (1853, 1862); *Souvenir de Moscou*, *Le Carnaval russe*, *Légende* and numerous other pieces, fantasies and studies for vln.

Wieniawski, Józef (b Lublin, 23 May 1837; d Brussels, 11 Nov 1912), Polish pianist and composer, brother of prec. Studied at the Paris Cons. He began to tour Eur. with his brother Henry, in 1850 and became prof. of pf. successively at Moscow and Brussels.

Works incl. chamber music and pf. pieces.

Wihan, Hanuš (b Police u Broumova, 5 Jun 1855; d Prague, 1 May 1920), Czech cellist. Studied at the Prague Cons. and made his 1st appearance in Berlin, 1876. Solo cellist in the Munich court orch., 1880, and prof. at Prague Cons., 1888. Founded the Cz. String 4tet in 1892. Dvořák's cello concerto is ded. to him. Met Wagner and Liszt. Strauss wrote his cello sonata for him (fp Nuremberg, 8 Dec 1883).

Wihtol, Joseph (b Wolmar, 26 Jul 1863; d Lübeck, 24 Apr 1948), Latvian composer. Studied with Rimsky-Korsakov and others at the St Petersburg Cons., where in 1886 he returned to Latvia and took an important share in its musical independence as a separate nation, becoming director of the Nat. Opera at Riga and director of the Latvian Cons.

Works incl. music for fairy play *King Brussubard*; symph., symph. poem *The Feast of Ligo*, Latvian overture *Spriditis*, dramatic overture for orch.; fantasy on Latvian folksongs for cello and orch.

Wilbye, John (b Diss, Norfolk, bap. 7 Mar 1574; d Colchester, c Sep 1638), English composer. His father, a tanner and landowner, seems to have given him a good educ. He was patronized by the Cornwallis family at Brome Hall and c 1595 went into the service of their son-in-law, Sir Thomas Kytson, at Hengrave Hall nr. Bury St Edmunds, and was frequently in London with the family. After the death of his patron he remained in the service of his widow, who died in 1628, whereupon he went to Colchester to join the household of her daughter, Lady Rivers. He never married and was well-to-do, having been granted a lease of a sheep-

farm by Kytson and gradually acquiring property at Diss, Bury St Edmunds and elsewhere.

Works incl. 2 sacred vocal pieces contrib. to Leighton's *Teares and Lamentacions*; 2 books of 64 madrigals (1598, 1609), madrigal *The Lady Oriana* contrib. to *The Triumphes of Oriana*; 5 sacred works; 3 fantasies for viols (incomplete), lute lessons (lost).

Wild, Earl (b Pittsburgh, 26 Nov 1915), American pianist. He studied with Egon Petri and appeared with Toscanini and the NBC SO in 1942; soon became widely known in USA in late Romantic repertory and commissioned concertos by Paul Creston and David Levy. London debut 1973.

Wildbrunn, Helene (b Vienna, 8 Apr 1882; d Vienna, 10 Apr 1972), Austrian soprano. She sang at Dortmund as a contralto, 1907–14, as Ortrud, Amneris and Dalila; Stuttgart 1914–18, when her voice changed to soprano. She appeared in Berlin and Vienna 1916–32 and at Buenos Aires from 1922 was heard as Brünnhilde, Isolde and the Marschallin. CG, 1927, as Leonore. Other roles incl. Kundry (La Scala, 1922), Fricka and Donna Anna.

Wilder, Philip van (b ? Flanders, c 1500; d London, 24 Feb 1553), Flemish lutenist and composer. App. lutenist to Henry VIII in 1538 and later became gentleman of the privy chamber to Edward VI. Comp. motets, *chansons*, etc.

Wildschütz, Der, oder Die Stimme der Natur (*The Poacher, or The Voice of Nature*), opera by Lortzing (lib. by comp. based on a play by Kotzebue), prod. Leipzig, 31 Dec 1842.

Wilhelm, Carl (b Schmalkalden, 5 Sep 1815; d Schmalkalden, 26 Aug 1873), German conductor and composer. He cond. a male-voice choral society at Crefeld in 1840–65, and in 1854 set the words of Max Schneckenburger's *Die Wacht am Rhein* as a patriotic song, for which Bismark granted him a pension in 1871.

Wilhelmj, August (Emil Daniel Ferdinand Viktor) (b Usingen, Nassau, 21 Sep 1845; d London, 22 Jan 1908), German violinist. Made his 1st public appearance in 1854 and in 1861 was sent by Liszt to Leipzig to study with David at the Cons. In 1865 he began to travel and in 1866 1st visited London, where in 1894 he settled as vln. prof. at the GSM.

Wilkinson, Robert (b c 1450; d ? Eton, 1515 or later), English composer. Comp. 2 settings of *Salve Regina* for 5 and 9 voices, *Credo in Deum/Jesus autem* for 13 voices in canon, 4 incomplete works (all in Eton Choirbook).

Wilkinson, ? Thomas (*fl.* ? 1579–96), English composer. He may have been a singer at King's College, Cambridge, and he contrib. 3 anthems to Myriell's *Tristitiae remedium* in 1616.

Works incl. services, 12 verse anthems, 3 pavans for viols.

Willaert, Adrian (b ? Bruges, *c* 1490; d Venice, 17 Dec 1562), Flemish composer and probably the most influential musician of the mid-16th cent. Trained in law but studied music with Mouton in Paris. Singer for members of the d'Este family at Rome, Ferrara and Esztergom, 1515–27; then *maestro di cappella* at St Mark's, Venice, where his pupils included Cipriano de Rore, Nicola Vicentino, Andrea Gabrieli, Gioseffe Zarlino and Costanzo Porta. He revisited Flanders in 1542 and 1556–7.

Works incl. Masses, hymns, psalms, motets, madrigals, *chansons* and inst. ens. pieces. They mark him as the most versatile and one of the most prolific comps. of his generation.

Willan, Healey (b London, 12 Oct 1880; d Toronto, 16 Feb 1968), English–Canadian organist and composer. Began his career as church organist in London, but emigrated to Toronto where he became lecturer at the univ. in 1914 and music director to the Hart House Players in 1919. He became vice-principal of the Cons. in 1920 and later prof. at the univ.

Works incl. incid. music to plays; church music, war elegy *Why they so softly sleep*, *Apostrophe to the Heavenly Hosts* and *Coronation* Te Deum for chorus and orch. (1953); 2 symphs. (1936, 1948); *Marche solennelle* for orch.; preludes and fugues, *Epilogue, Introduction, Passacaglia and Fugue* and other works for org.; songs to words by Yeats and others.

Willcocks, (Sir) David (Valentine) (b Newquay, 30 Dec 1919), English conductor, organist and teacher. He studied at the RCM and King's College, Cambridge. Organist at Salisbury then Worcester Cathedrals 1947–57, and of King's College 1957–74; many tours and successful recordings with the chapel choir. He conducted the Bach Choir from 1960 in annual perfs. of Bach's *St Matthew Passion* and in works by Fricker, Crosse and Hamilton. Director of RCM, 1974–84. Knighted 1977.

Willer, Luise (b Seeshaupt, Bavaria, 1888; d Munich, 27 Apr 1970), German contralto. Debut Munich 1910, as Mozart's Annius;

remained with co. until 1955 and took part in the fps of Pfitzner's *Palestrina* (1917) and *Das Herz* (1931). CG 1926 and 1931 as Erda, Waltraute and Brangaene. At Salzburg she was heard as Gluck's Clytemnestra and Strauss's Adelaide. Retired 1955, after singing Erda at Munich.

William Ratcliff. Opera by Cui (lib. by A.N. Pleshtcheiev, based on Heine's drama), prod. St Petersburg, 26 Feb 1869. *See also* **Guglielmo Ratcliff.**

William Tell. *See* **Guillaume Tell.**

Williams, Alberto (b Buenos Aires, 23 Nov 1862; d Buenos Aires, 17 Jun 1952), Argentine pianist, conductor, poet and composer of English and Basque descent. Studied at the Buenos Aires Cons. and later in Paris, where he studied pf. with Chopin's pupil Mathias, harmony with Durand, counterpoint with Guiraud and comp. with Franck. In 1889 he returned home, where he gave pf. recitals, cond. symph. concerts and founded the Buenos Aires Cons.

Works incl. 9 symphs. (1907–39, no. 2 *La bruja de las montanas*) and other orch. works; choruses; works for vln. and pf. and cello and pf.; *El rancho abandonado* and other pieces; songs.

Williams, Anna (b London, 6 Aug 1845; d London, 3 Sep 1924), English soprano. Studied in London, took a prize at the Crystal Palace in 1872, went to Naples to finish her studies with Scafati and in 1874 made her 1st important appearance in London.

Williams, Grace (Mary) (b Barry, Glam., 19 Feb 1906; d Barry, 10 Feb 1977), Welsh composer. Educ. at Cardiff Univ., where she took the B.Mus. in 1926; studied with Vaughan Williams at the RCM 1926–30 and with Wellesz in Vienna, 1930–1.

Works incl. opera *The Parlour* (1961); *Hymn of Praise* (*Gogonedawg Arglwydd*, from 12th-cent. Black Book of Carmarthen) for chorus and orch. (1939); Welsh overture *Hen Walia*, legend *Rhiannon*, *Fantasy on Welsh Nursery Rhymes*, symph. impressions *Owen Glendower* (after Shakespeare's *1 Henry IV*), *Penillion* (1955); vln. concerto (1950); 2 psalms for sop. and orch., *The Song of Mary* (Magnificat) for sop. and orch.; *Sinfonia concertante* for pf. and orch. (1941); elegy and *Sea Sketches* for string orch.; songs to words by Herrick, Byron, Belloc, D.H. Lawrence, etc.; arrs. of Welsh folksongs.

Williams, John (b Melbourne, 24 Apr 1942), Australian guitarist. London debut 1955; studied with Segovia from 1957. Prof.

at RCM, 1960–73. Plays a wide rep.; André Previn has written for him.

Williams, Ralph Vaughan. *See* **Vaughan Williams.**

Williamson, Malcolm (Benjamin Graham Christopher) (b Sydney, 21 Nov 1931), Australian-born British composer. Studied with Eugene Goossens at the Sydney Cons. and with Lutyens in London, where he later became an organist. Master of the Queen's Music from 1975.

Works incl. operas *English Eccentrics* (1964), *Our Man in Havana* (1965), *The Violins of St Jacques* (1966), *Lucky Peter's Journey* (1969); concerto for org. and orch., 3 pf. concertos (1957–62), vln. concerto (1965), 5 symphs. (1957–80); *Santiago de Espada*, overture for orch.; *Mass of Christ the King*, for soloists, chorus and orch. (1975–8); many vocal works; chamber music; pf. and org. works.

Wilm, (Peter) Nikolai von (b Riga, 4 Mar 1834; d Wiesbaden, 20 Feb 1911). Latvian composer. Studied at the Leipzig Cons. In 1857 became 2nd cond. at the Riga municipal theatre and in 1860 went to St Petersburg as prof. at the Nikolai Inst. He lived at Dresden in 1875–8 and then at Wiesbaden.

Works incl. motets; string 4tet, string 6tet; 2 sonatas and 2 suites for vln. and pf., sonata for cello and pf.; numerous pf. pieces; songs; part-songs.

Wilson, John (b Faversham, 5 Apr 1595; d London, 22 Feb 1674), English lutenist, singer and composer. Contrib., (?) with Coperario and Lanier, to *The Maske of Flowers*, perf. at Whitehall in 1614. He became one of the king's musicians in 1635. Lived at Oxford during the Civil War and took the D.Mus. there in 1645; soon afterwards was in private service in Oxfordshire, but in 1656–61 was prof. of music at Oxford Univ.; then returned to London to be at or near the restored court and became a Gentleman of the Chapel Royal in 1662 in succession to H. Lawes.

Works incl. music for Brome's *The Northern Lass* (1629), songs for *The Maske of Flowers*; anthem *Hearken, O God*; *Psalterium Carolinum* for 3 voices and continuo; elegy on the death of W. Lawes; *Cheerful Ayres* for 3 voices; airs and dialogues with lute; songs incl. Shakespeare's 'Take, O take those lips away' and 'Lawn as white as driven snow'; catches.

Wilson, (James) Steuart (b Bristol, 21 Jul 1889; d Petersfield, 18 Dec 1966), English tenor and administrator. He sang Tamino at Cambridge in 1910 and the following year

sang *On Wenlock Edge* by Vaughan Williams, who wrote for him *Four Hymns* (1914), of which Wilson gave the première (Cardiff, 1920). He suffered lung damage in the war, but studied with Jean de Reszke and pursued a successful career in concert (oratorios by Bach and Elgar) and in operas by Mozart and Boughton (following successful libel action against a schoolmaster who had questioned his vocal technique he financed and cond. a prod. of Boughton's *The Lily Maid* in 1939). After teaching at the Curtis Institute during the war he held appts. with the BBC and the Arts Council and was deputy general administrator at CG, 1949–55. Many Lieder trans. Knighted 1948.

Wilson, Thomas (Brendan) (b Trinidad, Colorado, 10 Oct 1927), Scottish composer. He studied at Glasgow Univ.; lecturer there from 1927), His works have employed serial technique and include the operas *The Charcoal Burners* (1968) and *Confessions of a Justified Sinner* (1976); 3 symphs. (1956, 1965, 1982), *Touchstone*, 'portrait for orch.' (1967), concerto for orch. (1967), pf. concerto (1984); 4 string 4tets, pf trio (1966), cello sonata (1973); 3 Masses, Te Deum and other church music; pf sonata and sonatina.

Wind Machine (Aeoliphone), a stage property used e.g. by R. Strauss in *Don Quixote*, Ravel in *Daphnis et Chloé*, Vaughan Williams in *Sinfonia antartica* and Tippett in his 4th symph. It is a barrel covered with silk, the friction of which on being turned prod. a sound like a whistling wind.

Windgassen, Wolfgang (b Andemasse, 26 Jun 1914; d Stuttgart, 5 Sep 1974), German tenor. Studied with his father and at the Hochschule für Musik in Stuttgart. From 1941 he sang in Pforzheim (debut as Alvaro) and from 1951 was a member of the Stuttgart Opera. Windgassen was the leading heroic tenor of the post-war years, excelling in Wagnerian roles; Bayreuth 1951–71 as Parsifal, Siegmund, Loge, Lohengrin and Walther. CG 1955–66 as Tristan and Siegfried. Other roles incl. Adolar, the Emperor and Otello.

Winkelmann, Hermann (b Brunswick, 8 Mar 1849; d Vienna, 18 Jan 1912), German tenor. After his 1875 debut at Sonderhausen, as Manrico, he moved to Hamburg and in 1879 created the title role in Rubinstein's *Nero*. He sang in Vienna from 1881; impressed Richter as Lohengrin, and sang under him at Drury Lane, London, in 1882 as the 1st London Tristan and Walther. Later the same summer Winkelmann created Parsifal; remained at Bayreuth until 1891 in this role and as Tannhäuser and Walther. He toured the USA in 1884 and was successful at Vienna until 1907 as Tristan, Otello and Kienzl's Evangelist.

Winter Journey (Schubert). See **Winterreise.**

Winter, Peter (von) (b Mannheim, bap. 28 Aug 1754; d Munich, 17 Oct 1825), German composer. Played as a boy in the court orch. at Mannheim, where he was a pupil of Vogler and met Mozart in 1778. Moved with the court to Munich, but went to Vienna 1780–81 and studied with Salieri. On his return to Munich he prod. the first of his many operas, *Helena und Paris*, became vice-*Kapellmeister* to the court in 1787 and *Kapellmeister* in 1798, but was periodically absent on tour.

Works incl. operas etc. *Helena und Paris* (1782), *Der Bettelstudent* (1785), *I fratelli rivali* (1793), *Das unterbrochene Opferfest* (1796), *Das Labyrinth* (sequel to Mozart's *Magic Flute*, 1798), *Maria von Montelban* (1800), *Tamerlan* (1802), *La grotta di Calipso* (1803), *Il trionfo dell' amor fraterno*, *Il ratto di Proserpina* (1804), *Zaira*, *Colmal* (1809), *Maometto II* (1817), *Scherz, List und Rache* and *Jery und Bätely* (both libs. by Goethe) and *c* 20 others; ballets *Heinrich IV* (1779), *Inez de Castro*, *La Mort d'Hector* and 6 others.

Masses and other church music; oratorios *Der Sterbende Jesus*, *La Betulia liberata* and others; cantata *Timoteo, o Gli effetti della musica* and others; 3 symphs, *Schlachtsymphonie* and overtures; concerted pieces for var. insts.; songs, part-songs.

'Winter Wind' Study, the nickname sometimes given to Chopin's pf. Study in A min., op. 25 no. 11.

Winter Words, song cycle to poems by Thomas Hardy for high voice and pf. by Britten; fp Harewood House, Leeds, 8 Oct 1953, by Peter Pears. The titles of the songs are 1. 'At Day-close in November'; 2. 'Midnight on the Great Western'; 3. 'Wagtail and Baby'; 4. 'The Little Old Table'; 5. 'The Choirmaster's Burial'; 6. 'Proud Songsters'; 7. 'At the Railway Station'; 8. 'Before Life and After'.

Wintermärchen, Ein (*A Winter's Tale*), opera by Goldmark (lib. by A.M. Willner, after Shakespeare), prod. Vienna, Opera, 2 Jan 1908.

Winterreise (*The Winter Journey*), song cycle by Schubert (poems by Wilhelm Müller), comp. Part i, Feb 1827; Part ii, Oct 1827. The 24 songs are 1. *Gute Nacht*; 2. *Die Wetterfahne*; 3. *Gefrorne Tränen*; 4. *Erstar-*

rung; 5. *Der Lindenbaum*; 6. *Wasserflut*; 7. *Auf dem Flusse*; 8. *Rückblick*; 9. *Irrlicht*; 10. *Rast*; 11. *Frühlingstraum*; 12. *Einsamkeit*; 13. *Die Post*; 14. *Der greise Kopf*; 15. *Die Krähe*; 16. *Letzte Hoffnung*; 17. *Im Dorfe*; 18. *Der stürmische Morgen*; 19. *Täuschung*; 20. *Der Wegweiser*; 21. *Das Wirtshaus*; 22. *Mut*; 23. *Die Nebensonnen*; 24. *Der Leiermann*.

Winter's Tale. See **Hermione**; **Wintermärchen.**

Wipo (Wigbert) (b Solothurn, *c* 995; d in the Bavar. Forest, *c* 1050), German poet and priest, who ended his life as a hermit. He is the reputed author (and perhaps adaptor of the music) of the sequence *Victimae paschali*.

Wirén, Dag (Ivar) (b Striberg, Närke, 15 Oct 1905; d Stockholm, 19 Apr 1986), Swedish composer and critic. Studied at the Stockholm Cons. In 1932 he received a stage grant and continued his studies with Sabaneiev in Paris. On his return he became a music critic at Stockholm.

Works incl. 5 symphs. (1932–64), sinfonietta; serenade for strings; cello concerto, vln. concerto, pf. concerto; 5 string 4tets (1930–70), 2 pf. trios, 2 sonatinas for cello and pf; pf pieces; songs.

Wise, Michael (b ? Salisbury, *c* 1647; d Salisbury, 24 Aug 1687), English organist and composer. Choir-boy at the Chapel Royal in London in 1660. In 1663 he became a lay-clerk at St George's Chapel, Windsor, and in 1668 organist and choirmaster of Salisbury Cathedral. He was admitted a Gentleman of the Chapel Royal in 1676, but retained his post at Salisbury until 1685. At the time of the coronation of James II he was suspended from the Chapel Royal, probably because of characteristically difficult conduct. In 1687 he became almoner and choirmaster at St Paul's Cathedral in London, but he still visited Salisbury, where his wife had remained. After a dispute with her at night he left the house and was killed in a quarrel with a watchman.

Works incl. services and anthems (incl. *The Ways of Zion Mourn*); songs and catches.

Wishart, Peter (b Crowborough, 25 Jun 1921; d Frome, 14 Aug 1984), English composer. He studied with Boulanger and at Birmingham Univ; lecturer there 1950–59. King's College, London, 1972–7, prof. Reading Univ. 1977–84. His music was influenced by Stravinsky and Orff.

Works incl. operas *Two in the Bush*

(1956), *The Captive* (1960), *The Clandestine Marriage* (1971) and *Clytemnestra* (1973); ballets *Beowulf* and *Persephone* (1957); 2 symphs. (1953, 1973), 2 vln. concertos (1951, 1968), concerto for orch. (1957); Te Deum (1952) and much other choral music; string 4tet (1954); org. sonata.

Witt, Christian Friedrich (b Altenburg, *c* 1660; d Altenburg or Gotha, 13 Apr 1716), German composer. Court music director at Altenburg.

Works incl. *Psalmodia sacra*, cantatas; Fr. overtures and suites for orch.; org. and harpsichord works.

Witte, Erich (b Graudenz, 19 Mar 1911), German tenor. After his 1932 debut at Bremen he sang in Wiesbaden and Breslau and in 1938–9 was heard at the NY Met as Froh and Mime. He sang David at Bayreuth during the war and was admired there and at CG during the 1950s as Loge; produced *Meistersinger* at CG in 1957 and sang Walther. He appeared at the Berlin Staatsoper until 1960 and was producer there from 1964. Other roles incl. Otello, Florestan and Peter Grimes.

Wittgenstein, Paul (b Vienna, 5 Nov 1887; d Manhasset, NY, 3 Mar 1961), Austrian pianist. He was a pupil of Leschetizky in Vienna and gave his 1st recital in 1913. He lost his right arm in the 1914–18 war and devoted the rest of his career to playing works for the left hand only. Among the comps. who wrote works for him were Strauss (*Parergon zur Symphonia domestica*), Ravel (concerto in D maj.), Korngold (concerto in C♯ maj.), Schmidt (*Vars. on a Theme of Beethoven*), and Britten (*Diversions on a Theme*).

Wittich, Marie (b Giessen, 27 May 1868; d Dresden, 4 Aug 1931), German soprano. Debut Magdeburg, 1882, as Azucena. She sang at Dresden 1889–1914 and in 1905 created Salome there. Bayreuth 1901–9, as Sieglinde, Kundry and Isolde. CG 1905–6, as Elsa, Elisabeth and Brünnhilde.

Wixell, Ingvar (b Luleå 7 May 1931), Swedish baritone. He sang Papageno at the Royal Opera, Stockholm, in 1955 and was heard as Ruggiero in *Alcina* when the co. visited CG (1960). Glyndebourne 1962, Guglielmo. At the 1966 Salzburg Festival he sang Mozart's Count and the following year he joined the Deutsche Oper, Berlin. Regular visitor to CG from 1970 where he has sung Boccanegra, Scarpia, Mandryka and Mozart's Count. US debut Chicago, 1967, as Belcore; NY Met debut Jan 1973, as Rigoletto.

Bayreuth from 1971. Other roles incl. Pizarro and Don Giovanni.

Woelfl, Joseph (b Salzburg, 24 Dec 1773; d London, 21 May 1812), Austrian pianist and composer. Pupil of L. Mozart and M. Haydn at Salzburg, where he was a choirboy at the cathedral. In 1790 he went to Vienna and *c* 1792 made his 1st public appearance, at Warsaw. He soon made his name as a virtuoso and after prod. some stage works in Vienna married the actress Therese Klemm in 1798 and went on a long tour in Boh. and Ger. He lived from 1801–5 in Paris, where he prod. 2 more operas, and then settled in London.

Works incl. operas *Der Höllenberg* (1795), *Das schöne Milchmädchen* (1797), *Der Kopf ohne Mann* (1798), *Liebe macht kurzen Prozess* (with others), *L'Amour romanesque* (1804), *Fernanda, ou Les Maures* (1805); ballets *La Surprise de Diane* and *Alzire* (on Voltaire's play); symph.; *Le calme* and other pf. concertos; chamber music; *Non plus ultra* and other pf. sonatas, var. pf. works.

Wohltemperierte Clavier, Das (*The Welltempered Clavier; see also* **Weber, B.C.**). Two sets of preludes and fugues by Bach for keyboard (not exclusively clavichord, as has sometimes been inferred from a misunderstanding of the title), finished in 1722 and 1744 respectively. Each set consists of a cycle of 24 preludes and fugues in all the maj. and min. keys in ascending order. The 2 books together are commonly known in Eng. as 'The 48'.

Wolf, a technical term for a jarring sound prod. between certain intervals on keyboard insts. tuned in meantone temperament or on string insts. by defective vibration on a certain note or notes.

Wolf, Ernst Wilhelm (b Grossgehringen nr. Gotha, bap. 25 Feb 1735; d Weimar, Nov 1792), German composer. He was leader and from 1768 court cond. at Weimar.

Works incl. operas *Die Dorfdeputierten* (after Goldoni, 1772), *Das grosse Los* (1774), *Der Zauberirrungen* (after Shakespeare's *Midsummer Night's Dream*), *Erwin und Elmire* (Goethe) and others; monodrama *Polyxena*; cantata *Seraphina* (Wieland, 1775); church music; oratorios, Easter cantatas (Herder); symphs.; string 4tets and other chamber music; songs.

Wolf-Ferrari, Ermanno (b Venice, 12 Jan 1876; d Venice, 21 Jan 1948), German–Italian composer. He was sent to Rome to study art by his Ger. father, a painter, but turned to music and studied with Rheinberger at Munich. In 1899 he sent to Venice and succeeded in having his oratorio perf. and in 1900 brought out his 1st opera, after which his stage successes were frequently repeated. Many of his operas were 1st prod. in Ger. In 1902–12 he was director of the Liceo Benedetto Marcello at Venice.

Works incl. operas *Cenerentola* (1900), *Le donne curiose* (1903), *I quattro rusteghi* (1906), *Il segreto di Susanna* (1909), *I gioielli della Madonna* (1911), *Amor medico* (after Molière, 1913), *Gli amanti sposi* (1925), *Das Himmelskleid* (1927), *Sly* (after Shakespeare's *Taming of the Shrew*, 1927), *La vedova scaltra* (1931), *Il campiello* (1936), *La dama boba* (after Lope de Vega, 1939), *Gli dei a Tebe* (1943).

Cantatas *La Sulamita* and *La vita nuova* (after Dante, 1903); vln. concerto, chamber symph. for strings, woodwind, pf. and horn (1901); pf. 5tet, pf. trio, 2 vln. and pf. sonatas; org. pieces; cello pieces; *Rispetti* for sop. and pf.

Wolf, Hugo (Filipp Jakob) (b Windischgraz [now Slovenj Gradec], 13 Mar 1860; d Vienna, 22 Feb 1903), Austrian composer. His father, a leather merchant, encouraged his early gifts by teaching him pf. and vln. After visiting var. schools, he was allowed to enter the Vienna Cons. in 1875, but left it the following year, preferring to pick up his own instruction where he could. From 1877, his father having incurred great losses in business, he was obliged to earn his own living by teaching. He often lived in great poverty, but when his pride would allow, he was befriended by var. musical families, while Schalk and Mottl took a professional interest in him. In 1881 he was engaged as 2nd cond. at Salzburg under Muck, but was found to be temperamentally so unfitted for the post that the engagement was terminated within 3 months. From 1884 to 1887 he was music critic for the Vienna *Salonblatt*, but here again he offended many people by his irascibility and intolerance (which saw no fault in Wagner and no good in Brahms). He had contracted syphilis, and in 1897 his mind became unhinged. He was sent to a sanatorium. Discharged as cured in Jan 1898, he had a relapse and was taken to an asylum in a hopeless condition in December, remaining there until his death.

Works incl. operas *Der Corregidor* (1886) and *Manuel Venegas* (unfinished); incid. music to Ibsen's *The Feast at Solhaug* (1891); 48 early songs, 53 songs to words by Mörike (1888); 20 to words by Eichendorff (1880–88), 51 to words by Goethe (1888–9), *Ita-*

lienisches Liederbuch (46 songs, 1890–91), *Spanisches Liederbuch* (44 songs, 1889–90), 31 songs to words by var. poets, incl. 6 by G. Keller and 3 sonnets by Michelangelo (1897).

Symph. poem *Penthesilea* (after Kleist, 1883); *Italian Serenade* for string 4tet or small orch. (1887, 1892); string 4tet in D min. (1880); *Christnacht* for solo voices, chorus and orch., *Elfenlied* from Shakespeare's *Midsummer Night's Dream* for sop., chorus and orch. (1890), *Der Feuerreiter* and *Dem Vaterland* for chorus and orch.; 6 part-songs.

Wolf, Johannes (b Berlin, 17 Apr 1869; d Munich, 25 May 1947), German musicologist. Studied with Spitta in Berlin and took a doctor's degree at Leipzig in 1893. In 1908 he became prof. of music at Berlin Univ. and in 1915 librarian of the music section of the Prus. State Library, where he succeeded Altmann as director in 1928. He specialized in and wrote on early music, treatises and notations.

Wolff, Albert (Louis) (b Paris, 19 Jan 1884; d Paris, 20 Feb 1970), French conductor and composer. Studied at the Paris Cons., became chorus master at the Opéra-Comique in 1908 and cond. in 1911, succeeded Messager as chief cond. in 1922. In 1928–34 he cond. the Lamoureux concerts and later the Pasdeloup concerts. Cond. of the Paris Opéra from 1949. He cond. the fps of Roussel's 4th symph. (1935) and Poulenc's *Les mamelles de Terésias* (1947).

Works incl. opera *L'Oiseau bleu* (after Maeterlinck; NY Met, 1919).

Wolff, Christian (b Nice, 8 Mar 1934), French-born American composer who came to the USA in 1941. Studied with Cage, and also classical languages at Harvard Univ., obtaining his Ph.D., and in 1962 becoming a lecturer there in classics. His music makes use of a strictly mathematical basis, particularly as regards rhythms and rests, while also including chance elements.

Works incl. *Nine* for 9 insts. (1951), *For 6 or 7 players*, *Summer* for string 4tet, *In Between Pieces* for 3 players, *For 5 or 10 Players* (1962), *For 1, 2 or 3 people*, 7tet for any insts. (1964), *For Pianist*, *For Piano I, II*, *Duo for Pianists I and II*, *Duet I* for pf. (4 hands), *Duet II* for horn and pf., *You Blew It* for chorus (1971).

Wolff, Fritz (b Munich, 28 Oct 1894; d Munich, 18 Jan 1957), German tenor. After study in Wurzburg he sang Loge at the 1925 Bayreuth Festival; returned until 1941 in this role and as Parsifal and Walther. He sang at the Berlin Staatsoper from 1928 and took part in the fp of Schreker's *Der Sing-ende Teufel*. He was admired in Wagner at CG (1929–38), and was heard in Chicago and Cleveland 1934–5.

Wolfram von Eschenbach (b *c* 1170, d *c* 1220), German Minnesinger. He took part in a singing contest at Wartburg in 1207. Seven lyric poems survive, without music, though two tunes are ascribed to him. He wrote an epic, *Parzival*, which was the prin. source for Wagner's *Parsifal*.

Wolfrum, Philipp (b Schwarzenbach, Bavaria, 17 Dec 1854; d Samaden, Switzerland, 8 May 1919), German composer and organist. Studied at Munich with Rheinberger and others, later became organist and music director to Heidelberg Univ., and also cond. choral perfs.

Works incl. oratorio *Weihnachtsmysterium* (1899), *Das grosse Hallelujah* (Klopstock, 1886) for male chorus, hymns *Der evangelische Kirchenchor* for chorus, *Festmusik* for bar. and male chorus (1903); string 4tet, 5tet, string trio, cello and pf. sonata; 3 sonatas, 57 preludes, 3 *Tondichtungen* for org.; pf. pieces; songs.

Wolkenstein, Oswald von (b Schöneck Castle, Tyrol, *c* 1377; d Meran, 2 Aug 1445), Austrian Minnesinger and politician. Led a very adventurous life, travelled much, even as far as Asia and Africa. From 1415 he was in the service of King (later Emperor) Sigismund and was sent to Spain and Por. on diplomatic missions. In 1421–7 he involved himself in much strife and was twice imprisoned in his endeavour to extend his land by encroaching on that of his neighbours.

Works incl. songs of love, spring, travel, etc. for 1–3 voices (to his own words).

Wolpe, Stefan (b Verlin, 25 Aug 1902; d New York, 4 Apr 1972), American composer of Russian and Austrian parentage. Studied with Juon and Schreker in Berlin and in 1933–34 with Webern, after which he went to Palestine and in 1938 settled in the USA.

Works incl. operas *Schöne Geschichten* and *Zeus und Elida*; ballet *The Man from Midian* (1942); symph., symph. for 21 insts. (1956), *Passacaglia* and 2 *Fugues* for orch.; cantatas *The Passion of Man*, *On the Education of Man*, *About Sport* (1932), *Unnamed Lands*, *Israel and his Land*; chamber music.

Wolstenholme, William (b Blackburn, 24 Feb 1865; d London, 23 Jul 1931), English organist and composer. Precociously gifted, although blind, he was trained in music at the Coll. for the Blind at Worcester, where Elgar taught him the vln. He cultivated the org. and pf. especially, became church

organist at Blackburn in 1887 and at var. churches in London from 1902. In 1908 he toured the USA as a recitalist.

Works incl. church music; orch. and military band works; chamber music; *c* 100 works for org., incl. sonatas, fantasy, prelude and fugue; pf. pieces.

Wolzogen, Ernst von (b Breslau, 23 Apr 1855; d Munich, 30 Jul 1934), German writer. Studied at the Univs. of Strasbourg and Leipzig. WIth O.J. Bierbaum and F. Wedekind he estab. the satirical cabaret *Das Überbrettl* in Berlin in 1901, for which Zemlinsky, O. Straus and Schoenberg provided some of the music. The cabaret lasted two successful years, before finally closing. He was the author of the lib. of R. Strauss's *Feuersnot*.

Wolzogen, Hans (Paul) von (b Potsdam, 13 Nov 1848; d Bayreuth, 2 Jun 1938), German writer on music, half-brother of prec. He was called to Bayreuth by Wagner in 1877 to become ed. of the *Bayreuther Blätter*, and wrote several works of analysis and propaganda on Wagner's music dramas.

Woman's Love and Life (Schumann). *See* **Frauenliebe und -leben.**

Wood, Anthony (à) (b Oxford, 17 Dec 1632; d Oxford, 29 Nov 1695), English antiquarian. Educ. at Merton Coll., Oxford, where he took the M.A. in 1655. He wrote several works on the hist. of Oxford and compiled biog. particulars of musicians. He was expelled from the university in 1693 for libelling the Earl of Clarendon.

Wood, Charles (b Armagh, 15 Jun 1886; d Cambridge, 12 Jul 1926), Irish music scholar, teacher and composer. Learnt music from the organist of Armagh Cathedral, where his father was lay vicar, and in 1883–7 studied at the RCM in London, where he became prof. in 1888. From 1888 to 1894 he cond. the Univ. Music Society at Cambridge, where he took the Mus. D. in 1894. In 1897 he became music lecturer to the Univ. and in 1924 succeeded Stanford of prof. of music.

Works incl. opera *The Pickwick Papers* (after Dickens, 1922); incid. music to Euripides' *Ion* and *Iphigenia in Tauris*; *Ode to the West Wind* (1890) and *The Song of the Tempest* for solo voices, chorus and orch.; *Ode on Music* (Swinburne, 1894), *Ode on Time* (Milton, 1898), *Dirge for Two Veterans* (Whitman), *Ballad of Dundee* for chorus and orch.; *Passion according to St Mark*; 8 string 4tets.

Wood, Haydn (b Slaithwaite, Yorks., 25 Mar 1882; d London, 11 Mar 1959), English violinist and composer. Having appeared as a child prodigy, he studied vln. with Arbós and comp. with Stanford at the RCM in London, the former also with Thomson in Brussels.

Works incl. cantata *Lochinvar* (from Scott's *Marmion*); rhapsodies, overtures, picturesque suites, vars. and other works for orch.; concertos for vln. and for pf.; fantasy string 4tet; inst. pieces; over 200 songs.

Wood, Henry J(oseph) (b London, 3 Mar 1869; d Hitchin, Herts., 19 Aug 1944), English conductor. He showed precocious gifts, esp. as an organist, and gave recitals and held church appts. as a boy. In 1889 he had his 1st experience as a cond., in opera, in which he toured for the next few years. In 1895 he was engaged by Robert Newman to take charge of the Promenade Concerts at the newly built Queen's Hall, and he remained in charge of them for 50 years to the end of his life, celebrating their half-century just before his death. He began modestly with popular programmes, but soon incl. many of the latest foreign and English novelties as they appeared; gave the fp of Schoenberg's 5 orch. pieces (1912) and 1st Brit. perfs. of Mahler's 1st, 4th, 7th and 8th symphs. He also cond. many music festivals and gave the fps of works by Delius and Vaughan Williams (*Serenade to Music*, 1938). In 1898 he married the Rus. sop. Olga Urussov (who died in 1909) and in 1911 Muriel Greatorex. Knighted 1911.

Wood, Hugh (b Parbold, Lancs., 27 Jun 1932), English composer. Studied comp. with A. Milner, I. Hamilton and Seiber. Taught at Morley College from 1959 to 1962, and then at the RAM; Liverpool Univ. 1971–3; Cambridge from 1976.

Works incl. *Scenes from Comus* for sop., tenor and orch. (1965); cello concerto (1969), chamber concerto (1971), vln. concerto (1972), symph. (1982); 4 string 4tets (1959–70), 5tet for clar., horn and pf. trio (1967), pf. trio (1984); songs to texts by Logue, Hughes, Muir and Neruda.

Wooden Prince, The (*A fából faragott királyfi*), ballet in 1 act by Bartók (scenario by Bela Balazs); comp. 1914–16, prod. Budapest, 12 May 1917, cond. Tango. Orch. suite (1931) perf. Budapest, 23 Nov 1931, cond. Ernö Dohnányi.

Woods, Michael (*fl.* 1568–73), English organist and composer. Was organist of Chichester Cathedral in the middle of the cent. and wrote motets.

Woodson, Leonard (b Winchester, *c* 1565; d ? Eton, ? 1641), English organist, singer and composer. He was in the choir at St

George's Chapel, Windsor, early in the 17th cent. and became organist of Eton Coll. in 1615.

Works incl. Te Deum and other church music; music for viols; songs.

Woodson, Thomas, English 16th–17th cent. composer. In 1581 he became a member of the Chapel Royal, his place being taken by William West in 1605. Comp. 40 canonic settings of the plainsong *Miserere* for keyboard, only 20 of which survive.

Woodward, Richard (b ? 1743; d Dublin, 22 Nov 1777), Irish organist and composer. Learnt music as a choir-boy at Christ Church Cathedral, Dublin, where his father, Richard W., was vicar-choral; in 1765 he was app. organist there. He took the Mus. D. at Trinity Coll., Dublin, in 1771.

Works incl. services, anthems, chants and other church music; catches and canons; songs.

Woodward, Roger (b Sydney, 20 Dec 1942), Australian pianist. He studied at the Sydney Cons. 1952–62 and moved to London 1964 (where he has lived since 1971); studied further in Poland and won the 1968 Chopin Competition, Warsaw. London debut 1967; he took part in the 1972 fp of Stockhausen's *Intervall* for pf. duo and has given frequent perfs. of works by Penderecki, Bussotti, Boulez, Cage and Barraqué. In 1986 he gave the NY fp of *Keqrops*, for pf. and orch., by Xenakis. OBE 1980.

Wooldridge, H(arry) E(llis) (b Winchester, 28 Mar 1845; d London, 13 Feb 1917), English painter and music scholar. He was Slade Prof. of Fine Arts at Oxford from 1895–1904, but made a special study of medieval music. His chief works were the 1st 2 vols. of the *Oxford History of Music*.

Wordsworth, William B(rocklesby) (b London, 17 Dec 1908), English composer, a direct descendant of the poet's brother. He became interested in music as a child, but did not begin to study seriously until he was 20. Finding work for the Mus.D. fruitless, he became a pupil of Tovey in 1935. During the 1939–45 war he took to farming, but after that devoted himself entirely to comp.

Works incl. oratorio *Dies Domini* (1944); *The Houseless Dead* (D.H. Lawrence) for bar. chorus and orch., *Hymn of Dedication* (Chesterton) for chorus and orch.; 8 symph. (1944–86), theme and vars., *3 Pastoral Sketches* for orch., *Sinfonia* and *Canzone and Ballade* for strings; pf. concerto, cello concerto.

6 string 4tets (1941–64); string trio; 2 sonatas for vln. and pf., 2 sonatas for cello

and pf.; sonata and suite for pf.; 3 hymn-tune preludes for org.; *4 Sacred Sonnets* (Donne, 1944) and other songs; rounds for several voices.

Worgan, John (b London, 1724; d London, 24 Aug 1790), English organist and composer. Pupil of T. Roseingrave. App. organist of the church of St Andrew Undershaft *c* 1749 and of Vauxhall Gardens *c* 1751 in succession to his brother James W. (*c* 1715–53), to which he was also attached as comp. until 1761, and again in 1770–74. He took the Mus.D. in 1775. He became famous as an org. recitalist.

Works incl. oratorios *The Chief of Maon, Hannah* (1764), *Manasseh* (1766) and *Gioas* (unfinished); anthem for a victory, psalm-tunes; serenata *The Royal Voyage*, dirge in memory of Frederick, Prince of Wales; ode on the rebellion of 1745; org. pieces; harpsichord lessons; glees; songs.

Working-out (or Development), the 2nd section of a movement in sonata form, following the exposition, where thematic material is subjected to var. developments, according to the comp.'s fancy. The usual procedure is to develop the 1st or 2nd subjects or both, but subsidiaries may be used as well, or instead, and new matter may be intro. at will.

Worldes Blis, work for orch. by Peter Maxwell Davies, fp London, 28 Aug 1968; although not well received by older members of the Promenade audience, the work established Davies with the younger set as a leading comp..

Wormser, André (Alphonse Toussaint) (b Paris 1 Nov 1851; d Paris, 4 Nov 1926), French composer. Studied at the Paris Cons. and obtained the Prix de Rome in 1875.

Works incl. operas *Adèle de Ponthieu* and *Rivoli*; pantomimes *L'Enfant prodigue* and *L'Idéal*; ballet *L'Etoile*; cantata *Clytemnestre*; symph. poems *Lupercale* and *Diane et Endymion, Suite tzigane* for orch.; songs.

Worshipful Company of Musicians of London, The, an assoc. dating back to the Middle Ages, but not formally incorporated by royal charter until 1604, under James I, though minstrels had already been allowed to form themselves into guilds by Edward IV in 1469. Among its present functions is the award of prizes and scholarships.

Wotquenne, Alfred (Camille) (b Lobbes, Hainault, 25 Jan 1867; d Antibes, 25 Sep 1939), Belgian music bibliographer. Studied at the Brussels Cons. and became its librarian in 1894. He pub. its catalogue, bibliogs.

of C.P.E. Bach, Galuppi, Gluck and Luigi Rossi.

Woyrsch, Felix (b Troppau, 8 Oct 1860; d Altona, 20 Mar 1944), German–Czech composer and conductor. He was self-taught in music and went to Altona in 1887 as chorus and orch. cond.

Works incl. operas *Der Pfarrer von Meudon* (1886), *Der Weiberkrieg* (1896), *Wikingerfahrt* (1896); incid. music to Moreto's *Donna Diana;* motets and other church music; Passion oratorio; works for male chorus and orch.; 6 symphs. (1908–33), prologue to Dante's *Divina commedia, Böcklin* suite, theme and variations, overture to Shakespeare's *Hamlet* for orch. (1913), vln. concerto; 5 string 4tets (1909–40), string 6tet, pf. 5tet, 2 pf. trios and other chamber music; org. and pf. pieces; numerous songs.

Woytowicz, Bolesław (b Dunajowce, Podolia, 5 Dec 1899; d Katowice, 11 Jul 1980), Polish pianist and composer. Began by studying mathematics and philosophy at Kiev Univ. and law at Warsaw Univ., but coming of a musical family, turned to the pf., which he studied at the Chopin High School at Warsaw, where he later became a teacher. He next took to comp., studying 1st with Szopski, Maliszewski and others, and in 1930 with Nadia Boulanger in Paris.

Works incl. concertino, concert suite, *Poème funèbre* on the death of Pilsudski, 3 symphs. (1926–63), vars. in the form of a symph. for orch.; pf. concerto; 2 string 4tets, trio for fl., clar. and bassoon, *Cradle Song* for sop.; clar. bassoon and harp. (1931); vars. and other works for pf.

Wozzeck, opera by A. Berg (lib. by comp. from G. Büchner's drama of 1836), prod. Berlin, Opera, 14 Dec 1925.

Opera by M. Gurlitt (lib. do.), prod. Bremen, 22 Apr 1926.

Wranitzky, Anton (b Nová Říše, 13 Jun 1761; d Vienna, 6 Aug 1820), Moravian violinist and composer. Pupil of Haydn, Mozart and Albrechtsberger, he was *Kapellmeister* to Prince Lobkowitz from 1797, and from 1814 music director at the Theater an der Wien in Vienna. He was a friend of Beethoven and arr. Haydn's *Creation* for string 4tet.

Works incl. symphs., concertos, serenades; string 4tets, 5tets, 6tets, and other chamber music.

Wranitzky, Paul (b Nová Říše, 30 Dec 1756; d Vienna, 26 Sep 1808), Moravian violinist and composer, brother of prec. Pupil of J.M. Kraus and Haydn in Vienna, in the 1780s he was in the service of Count Esterházy (not Prince E., Haydn's employer) and from *c* 1790 leader of the court opera orch. in Vienna.

Works incl. operas and *Singspiele*, e.g. *Oberon, König der Elfen* (1789), *Das Fest der Lazzaroni* (1794), *Der Schreiner* (1799), etc.; ballet divertissements *Das Waldmädchen* (1796), *Die Weinlese* (1794), *Zemire und Azore, Das Urteil von Paris* (1801); 51 symphs.; *c* 100 string 4tets and 5tets; pf. 4tets; vln. sonatas and large numbers of other inst. works; over 200 canons; vocal duets, trios, etc.; church music.

Wrest (noun), the old English term for a tuning-key, from the verb meaning to twist or wrench. The tuning-pins of the pf. are still called wrest-pins and the board into which they are inserted is the wrest-plank.

Wryght, Thomas, English 16th-cent. composer. He was a member of the Chapel Royal. 1547–8; his *Nesciens mater* is in the 'Gyffard' part-books (*q.v.*).

Wührer, Friedrich (b Vienna, 29 Jun 1900; d Mannheim, 27 Dec 1975), Austrian pianist and teacher. He studied at the Vienna Academy with Franz Schmidt and Löwe, and taught there 1922–32, 1939–45. Other teaching posts at Mannheim, the Salzburg Mozarteum and Munich (1955–68). His concert career began in 1923; toured Eur. and USA, usually incl. works by Bartók, Hindemith, Prokofiev and members of the Second Viennese School.

Wüllner, Franz (b Münster, 28 Jan 1832; d Braunfels, 7 Sep 1902), German conductor, composer and pianist. Studied at home and at Frankfurt, and appeared as pianist at Brussels in 1852–3, where he enlarged his experience by meeting Fétis, Kufferath and other musicians. He then made a tour in Ger., settled at Munich in 1854 and in 1856 became pf. prof. at the Cons. In 1858–64 he was music director at Aachen, where he did much choral and orch. cond., but he returned to Munich as court music director, reorganized the court church music and became cond. of the court opera in 1869 in succession to Bülow. Against Wagner's wishes he gave the fps of *Das Rheingold* (1869) and *Die Walküre* (1870). In 1877–82 he was court music director at Dresden, succeeding Rietz, and from 1884 director of the cons. at Cologne in succession to F. Hiller and cond. of the Gürzenich concerts; gave there the fps of Strauss's *Till Eulenspiegel* (1895) and *Don Quixote* (1898). Wrote church and chamber music. His son **Ludwig** (1858–1938) was a tenor and bar.;

well known as Elgar's Gerontius and sang *Kindertotenlieder* under Mahler in NY, 1910.

Wunderlich, Fritz (b Kusel, 26 Sep 1930; d Heidelberg, 17 Sep 1966), German tenor. He studied at Freiburg and made his debut at Stuttgart as Tamino in 1955. He moved to Frankfurt in 1959 and later sang at Munich and Vienna; sang Tiresias in the 1959 fp of Orff's *Oedipus der Tyrann* (Stuttgart) and Henry in *Die Schweigsame Frau* at Salzburg the same year. His Don Ottavio at CG (1966) will long be remembered. The ease, elegance and expressive power of his voice are well displayed in his recording of *Das Lied von der Erde* with Klemperer. He sang Tamino at the Edinburgh Festival shortly before his accidental death. Still regarded as a lyric tenor beyond compare. Other roles incl. Belmonte, Leukippos and Palestrina.

Wuorinen, Charles (b New York, 9 Jun 1938), American composer, conductor and pianist. He studied at Columbia Univ., and taught there 1964–71. His early works are tonal but he was later influenced by Varèse, Babbitt and serial technique.

Masque *The Politics of Harmony* (1967), 'baroque burlesque' *The Whore of Babylon* (1975); 3 symphs. (1958–9), 4 chamber concertos (1957–9), *Evolutio transcripta* for orch. (1961), 2 pf. concertos (1966, 1974), *Contrafactum* for orch. (1969), concerto for amplified vln. and orch. (1971), *Percussion Symph.* (1976), *Bamboula Squared* for orch. (1983); *Dr Faustus Lights the Light* for narrator and insts. (1957), octet (1962), string trio (1968), chamber concerto (1970), wind 5tet (1977), horn trio (1981); *Symphonia sacra* for vocal soloists and inst. ens. (1961), *The Prayer of Jonah* for voices and string 5tet (1962), *The Celestial Sphere,* sacred oratorio for chorus and orch. (1979); electronic music.

Wyk, Arnold van (b nr. Calvinia, Cape Province, 26 Apr 1916; d Cape Town, 27 May 1983), S. African composer. Began to learn the pf. at 12 and, after working in an insurance office at Cape Town, entered Stellenbosch Univ. in 1936. In 1937 he was commissioned to write music for the centenary of the Voortrekkers and in 1938 he went to live in London, having gained the Performing Right Society's scholarship. He studied comp. with Theodore Holland and pf. with Harold Craxton at the RAM, joined the BBC for a short time and later devoted himself to comp.

Works incl. 2 symphs. (1944, 1952), suite for small orch. on African tunes *Southern*

Cross (1943); *Saudade* for vln. and orch.; string 4tet, 5 elegies for string 4tet (1941); 3 improvisations on a Dutch folksong for pf. duet.

Wylde, John (*fl. c* 1425–50), English music theorist, precentor of Waltham Abbey nr. London. He wrote a summary of Guido d'Arezzo's theoret. work, entitled *Musica Gwydonis monachi*. This stands at the head of a collection compiled by him (Brit. Lib., Lansdowne MS. 763) which later belonged to Tallis, whose signature it bears.

Wynne, David (b Penderyn, Glam., 2 Jun 1900; d Pencoed, Glam., 23 Mar 1983), Welsh composer. He worked as a coalminer during adolescence but studied at Univ. College, Cardiff, from 1925; was active in the promotion of Welsh music.

Works incl. operas *Jack and Jill* (1975) and *Night and Cold Peace* (1979); 5 symphs. (1952–80), 2 rhapsody concertos, *Octade* for orch. (1978); 5 string 4tets (1944–80);

sextet for pf. and orch. (1977); song cycles and choral music.

Wynslate, Richard (d Winchester, buried 15 Dec 1572), English composer. He was a singer at St Mary-at-Hill, London, 1537–40, and master of the choristers, Winchester Cathedral, 1540–72. An org. piece, *Lucem tuam*, has survived.

Wyzewa (orig. Wyzewski), **Théodore de** (b Kalusik, 12 Sep 1862; d Paris, 17 Apr 1917), French musicologist of Polish parentage. He lived in France from 1869. In 1884 he founded the *Revue Wagnérienne* with Édouard Dujardin and in 1901 the Société Mozart with Boschot. He became a political and literary journalist, but also wrote articles on music and trans. var. lit. works from Eng. and Rus. His chief work is his study of Mozart, of which he completed 2 vols. in collaboration with Georges de Saint-Foix. He was a friend of Renoir and Mallarmé.

X

Xenakis, Iannis (b Braïla, 29 May 1922), Greek composer. First studied engineering and worked for some years as an architect with Le Corbusier, at the latter's invitation, in Paris; his musical structures have been of higher quality than the buildings of his mentor. He also studied music with Honegger, Milhaud and Messiaen, and evolved a method of comp. using the mathematics of chance and probability and also employing computers (sometimes referred to as 'stochastic' music. His ideas have exercised considerable influence on other comps.

Works incl. *Metastasis* for orch. (1954), *Pithoprakta* for string orch. (1956), *Achorripsis* for 21 insts. (1957), *Syrmos* for 18 strings (1959); *Akrata* for 16 wind (1965), *Polytope* for small orchs. (1967), *Synaphai* for pf. and orch. (1969), *Noomena* for orch. (1975), *Palimpsest* for pf. and ens. (1982), *Keqrops* for pf. and orch. (1986); electronic comps. incl. *Diamorphosis* (1958), *Orient-Occident* (1960); *Morsima-Amorsima* (1) for 4 players (1956–62), (2) for 10 players (1962); ballets *Kraanerg* for orch. and tape (1969) and *Antikhton* (1971); *Oresteia* for chorus and chamber ens. (1966); chamber works *Atrées* (1962), *Anaktoria* (1969), *Auroura* (1971), *Phlegra* (1975), *Retours-Windungen* (1976), *Tetras* for string 4tet (1983); *Akanthos* for sop. and ens. (1977).

Xerse (*Xerxes*). *See also* **Serse.**
Opera by Cavalli (lib. by N. Minato), prod. Venice, Teatro dei SS. Giovanni e Paolo, 12 Jan 1654.

Xylophone (from Gk. *xulon*, wood, and *phōnē*, sound), a percussion instrument with a series of wooden bars suspended over resonators and tuned in a chromatic scale. It is played with hammers and makes a dry, rattling but perfectly clear and richly sonorous sound. It is made in var. sizes

Xylorimba, a percussion instrument, a small Marimba made in Amer.

Xyndas, Spyridon (b Corfu, 8 Jun 1814; d Athens, 25 Nov 1896), Greek composer.

Works incl. It. operas *Anna Winter* (1855), *I due rivali* (1878), *Il Conte Giuliano, Il candidato al parlamento* (1867) and others; pf. pieces; many songs.

Y

Yan Tan Tethera, opera by Harrison Birtwistle; (text by T. Harrison). Written 1983–4 for TV, fp London, 5 Aug 1986.

Yansons, Arvid (b Leipaja, 24 Oct 1914; d Manchester, 21 Nov 1984), Latvian conductor. Debut Riga Opera, 1944. Leningrad PO from 1952. Chief guest cond. Hallé Orch. from 1964. His son **Mariss** (b Riga, 14 Jan 1943) studied at the Leningrad Cons. and has been chief cond. of the Oslo PO from 1979.

Year 1812, The, festival overture by Tchaikovsky, op. 49, written for the commemoration of the 70th anniversary of Napoleon's retreat from Moscow and 1st perf. during the Moscow Arts and Industrial Exhibition, 20 Aug 1882, at the consecration of the Cathedral of the Redeemer in the Kremlin.

Yellow Cake Review, The, work by Maxwell Davies for singers and pf. (text by comp. describes threat to Orkneys posed by uranium mining), fp Kirkwall, Orkney, 21 Jun 1980.

Yeomen of the Guard, The, or The Merryman and his Maid, operetta by Sullivan (lib. by W.S. Gilbert), prod. London, Savoy Theatre, 3 Oct 1888.

Yodel, an elaborate form of song in Switz., Tyrol, Styria, etc., usually sung by men in Falsetto, with rapid changes to chest voice, very free in rhythm and metre and using as a rule the restricted scale of the natural harmonics of insts. like the Alphorn. The yodel is thus very prob. derived or copied from the Ranz des Vaches.

Yonge, Nicholas (b ? Lewes; d London, buried 23 Oct 1619), English singer and music editor. Worked in London and pub. in 1588 a vol. of It. madrigals with Eng. trans. entitled *Musica transalpina*.

Yorkshire Feast Song, The, an ode or cantata by Purcell, 'Of old when heroes', for 2 altos, tenor, 2 basses, 5-part chorus, recorders, obs. tpts. and strings, words by Thomas Durfey, written in 1690 for the annual reunion of Yorkshiremen in London, intended to be held that year on 14 Feb but postponed to 27 Mar owing to parliamentary elections.

Youll, Henry English 16th–17th-cent. composer. Pub. a book of canzonets and balletts for 3 voices in 1608.

Young Apollo, work by Britten for pf., string 4tet and string orch. (1939, fp Toronto, 27 Aug 1939; withdrawn until 1979).

Young, (Basil) Alexander (b London, 18 Oct 1920), English tenor. Studied in London, Naples and Vienna. After singing in the Glyndebourne chorus and some small parts, he became one of the leading Eng. operatic and concert singers. One of his best-known roles is that of Tom Rakewell in *The Rake's Progress*, which he recorded under the comp.'s baton. CG, 1955–70 as Vašek, Matteo and Lysander; SW as Count Ory, Almaviva and Belmonte. Other roles incl. Orpheus (Gluck and Monteverdi) and many in Handel.

Young, Cecilia (b London, 1711; d London, 1 Oct 1789), English soprano, daughter of Charles Y., organist of All Hallows, Barking in London, married Arne in 1737.

Young, Douglas (b London, 18 Jun 1947), English composer and pianist. He studied at the RCM with Anthony Milner; several of his comps. are open-ended 'works in progress' influenced by Boulez.

Works incl. ballets *Pasipae* (1969), *Charlotte Brontë – Portrait* (1973) and *Ludwig, Fragments of a Puzzle* (1986); sinfonietta (1970), *Aubade* for orch. (1973), pf. concertino (1974); *The Listeners*, cantata-ballet for speaker, voices and orch. (1967), *Sir Patrick Spens*, ballad for voices and orch. (1970); *Not Waving but Drowning*, song cycle to poems by Stevie Smith (1970); *Realities* (Yeats) for sop., tenor and ens. (1974); sonata for string trio (1968), *Essay* for string 4tet (1971), *Chamber Music* (James Joyce) for sop. and guitar (1976–82); *The Hunting of the Snark* for chorus, pf. and orch. (1982).

Young, La Monte (b Bern, Idaho, 14 Oct 1935), American composer. Studied at Univ. of California, Los Angeles, 1956–7 and at Berkeley 1957–60. In 1959 he also studied with Stockhausen, and then lectured for a time on guerrilla warfare at the NY School for Social Research: the direction on one of his works is 'urinate'.

Works incl. *The Tortoise Droning Selected Pitches from the Holy Numbers for the Two Black Tigers, the Green Tiger and the Hermit* (1964); *The Tortoise Recalling the Drone of the Holy Numbers as they were Revealed in the Dreams of the Whirlwind and the Obsidian Gong, Illuminated by the Sawmill, the Green Sawtooth Ocelot and the High-Tension Line Stepdown Transformer* (both works staged with voice, gong and strings, 1964); pf. music.

Young, Percy M(arshall) (b Northwich, Ches., 17 May 1912), English music educationist, conductor and writer on music. Educ. at Christ's Hospital and Cambridge, where he was org. scholar at Selwyn Coll. and took the M.A. and Mus.B. degrees. Mus.D. at Trinity Coll., Dublin. In 1934 he became dir. of music at the Teachers' Training Coll., Belfast, in 1945 dir. of music studies at Wolverhampton Technical Coll. Pub. part-songs and var. collections for children, articles in music periodicals and a large number of books: subjects incl. Elgar, Handel, Sullivan and Vaughan Williams.

Young, Polly(or **Mary)** (b London, 1749; d London, 20 Sep 1799), English singer, niece of Cecilia Y. She appeared in opera in London and married Barthélemon in 1766.

Young, Thomas (b Canterbury, 1809; d London, 12 Aug 1872), English alto. Educ. as a choir-boy at Canterbury Cathedral where he became an alto in 1831. In 1836 he went to London to join the choir at Westminster Abbey and in 1848 he became 1st alto at the Temple Church. He also frequently sang at the concerts.

Young, William (d Innsbruck, 23 Apr 1662), English violist, violinist, flautist and composer. He was in the service of the Archduke Ferdinand Karl (probably in the Netherlands), but returned to England to join the king's band in 1660. From 1664 he and others were also allowed to play for Killigrew at the theatre. Visited Innsbruck 1655 and played for Queen Christina of Sweden.

Works incl. 21 sonatas for 3–5 insts. with appended dances, 3-part fantasies for viols, pieces for lyra viol and for vla. da gamba; airs for 2 treble viols and bass.

Yradier, Sebastian (b Sauciego, Álava, 20 Jan 1809; d Vitoria, 6 Dec 1865), Spanish composer. He was in Paris for a time as singing-master to the Empress Eugénie and later lived in Cuba for some years. Wrote popular Spanish songs, incl. *La Paloma* and the melody which formed the basis of the habañera in Bizet's *Carmen*.

Ysaÿe, Eugène(-Auguste) (b Liège, 16 Jul 1858; d Brussels, 12 May 1931), Belgian violinist, conductor and composer. Studied with his father, Nicolas Y., then at the Liège Cons. and later with Wieniawski and Vieuxtemps. Having already appeared in public in 1865, he played at Pauline Lucca's concerts at Cologne and Aachen, where he met F. Hiller and Joachim, and later, at Frankfurt, he came into touch with Raff and Clara Schumann. In 1886–98 he was vln. prof. at the Brussels Cons. and founded and cond. orch. concerts in the Belg. capital. He toured extensively, 1st visiting Eng. in 1889 and the USA in 1894.

Works incl. opera *Piére li Houïeu* (in Walloon dialect, 1931); 8 vln. concertos; *Poème élégiaque*, mazurkas and other pieces for vln. and pf.

Ysaÿe, Théo(phile) (b Verviers, 22 Mar 1865; d Nice, 24 Mar 1918), Belgian pianist and conductor, brother of prec. Studied at the Liège Cons., with Kullak in Berlin and with Franck in Paris. He often appeared at concerts with his brother and also gave recitals of his own.

Works incl. Requiem; symph., symph. poems, fantasy, *Suite wallonne* for orch.; pf. concerto; pf. 5tet.

Yun, Isang (b Tong-yong, 17 Sep 1917), Korean-born composer of W. German nationality. He studied in Korea and Japan, and with Blacher and Rufer in Berlin. An espousal of serial techniques led to withdrawal of works written before 1959. In 1967 he was kidnapped from W. Berlin by S. Korean agents and charged with sedition; after release became prof. at Hochschule für Musik, Berlin, in 1970.

Works incl. operas *Der Traum des Liu-Tung* (Berlin, 1965), *Die Witwe des Schmetterlings* (Berlin, 1967), *Geisterliebe* (Kiel, 1971), *Sim Tjong* (Munich, 1972); *Colloïdes sonores* for string orch. (1961), *Dimensionen* for orch. (1971), cello concerto (1976), fl. concerto (1977); *Om Mani padame hum*, cycle for sop., bar., chorus and orch. (1964), *Der weise Mann*, for bar., chorus and small orch. (1977); string 4tet (1959), pf. trio (1975), *Pièce concertante* for chamber ens. (1977).

Yvain, Maurice (Pierre Paul) (b Paris, 12 Feb 1891; d Paris, 28 Jul 1965), French composer. Studied at the Paris Cons. He served in the army during the 1914–18 war. Resuming his studies later, he devoted his whole attention to the comp. of operettas, the 1st of which, *Ta bouche*, was an immediate success in 1921. It was followed by many others, as well as a ballet, *Vent*.

Z

Zabaleta, Nicanor (b San Sebastián, 7 Jan 1907), Basque harpist. He studied in Madrid and Paris; debut Paris, 1925. He has been the foremost interpreter of 18th-cent. harp. music. Ginastera, Milhaud, Piston and Joseph Tal have written concertos for him.

Zacar (*fl. c* 1400), 2 or possibly 3 composers active in Italy, apparently divisible as follows:

1. Antonio Zacara da Teramo (*fl.* 1391–*c* 1420), active in the Papal chapel and perhaps in the Veneto. Works, found in MSS from many parts of Europe and evidently very influential, incl. Mass movements and It. and Fr. songs.

2. Nicola Zacharie of Brindisi (*fl.* 1420–34), documented in Florence. Works: perhaps only one It. song, one motet and one Mass movement.

Zaccaria, Nicola (Angelo) (b Piraeus, 9 Mar 1923), Greek bass. He sang in Athens from 1949 and appeared at La Scala, Milan, in 1953; remained until 1974. CG 1957 and 1959 as Oroveso and Creon; both roles opposite Callas, with whom he joined in recordings of operas by Verdi, Bellini and Rossini. He took part in the 1958 Scala fp of Pizzetti's *Assassinio nella cattedrale* and was heard at Salzburg from 1967. Other roles incl. Zaccaria, Silva, Bartolo, Sarastro and Marke.

Zacconi, Lodovico (b Pesaro, 11 Jun 1555; d Fiorenzuola di Focara, nr. Pesaro, 23 Mar 1627), Italian priest and music theorist. He went to live at Venice, joined the monastic order of St Augustine and was *maestro di cappella* at its church. In 1593, at the invitation of the Archduke Charles, he went to Vienna, where he became court music director and remained until 1619, when he returned to Venice. He wrote a large treatise in 4 vols., *Prattica di musica* (1592–1622).

Zach, Jan (b Čelákovice nr. Prague, bap. 13 Nov 1699; d Ellwangen, 24 May 1773), Bohemian organist and composer. Worked as a violinist and organist in Prague, where he came under the influence of Černohorský; later left for Ger. and in 1745 was app. *Kapellmeister* to the Electoral court in Mainz. Dismissed *c* 1757, he spent the rest of his life travelling, without permanent employment.

Works incl. 33 Masses, 3 Requiems; *Sta-*

bat Mater and other church music; symphs. and partitas for orch.; chamber music; organ music.

Zachau, Friedrich Wilhelm (b Leipzig, bap. 14 Nov 1663; d Halle, 7 Aug 1712), German organist and composer. Pupil of his father, a town musician, under whom he learnt to play all the current instruments. The family moved to Eilenburg in 1676 and in 1684 he was app. organist at the church of Our Lady of Halle, where Handel in due course became his pupil.

Works incl. church cantatas, org. pieces.

Zadok the Priest, 1st of 4 anthems comp. 1727 by Handel for coronation of George II; given at all subsequent coronations.

Zádor, Jenö (b Bátaszék, 5 Nov 1894; d Hollywood, 4 Apr 1977), Hungarian composer. Studied with Heuberger in Vienna and Reger at Leipzig, also took a course in musicology and graduated with the Ph.D. in 1921. In 1921 he became prof. at the new Vienna Cons. and in 1934 at the Budapest Acad. of Music. In 1939 he settled in the USA and devoted himself largely to the orchestration of film music by other composers.

Works incl. operas *Diana* (1923), *The Island of the Dead* (1928), *Asra* (1936) and others; romantic symph., dance symph., vars. on a Hung. folksong, carnival suite, Hung. carpiccio, etc.; chamber music; pf. works; songs.

Zagrosek, Lothar (b Waging, 13 Nov 1942), German conductor and composer. Studied in Vienna with Swarowsky and with Karajan and Maderna. Appts. in Salzburg, Kiel and Darmstadt 1967–73. From 1978 has often cond. the London Sinfonietta, in music by Ligeti, Messiaen, Weill and Stravinsky; also guest cond. with BBC SO. USA (San Diego and Seattle) from 1984. Music dir. Paris Opéra from 1986. Glyndebourne debut 1987, *Così fan tutte*.

Zaide, unfinished opera by Mozart (lib., in Ger., by J.A. Schachtner), begun 1779, 1st prod. Frankfurt, 27 Jan 1886.

Zaïs, *ballet héroïque* in a prologue and 4 acts by Rameau (lib. by L. de Cahusac), prod. Paris, Opéra, 29 Feb 1748.

Zajc, Ivan (also known as Giovanni von Zaytz) (b Rijeka [Fiumel], 3 Aug 1832; d Zagreb, 16 Dec 1914), Croatian composer and conductor. Pupil of his father, a bandmaster in the Aus. army and of Lauro Rossi at the Milan Cons. He lived at Fiume and Vienna and was from 1870 cond. at the theatre and director of the Cons. at Zagreb.

Works incl. 15 Croatian operas, It. opera

Amelia (after Schiller's *Räuber*, 1860) and others, 15 Ger. and Croatian operettas incl. *Sonnambula* (prod. Vienna, 1868); oratorio *The Fall of Man*; church music incl. 19 Masses and 4 requiems; songs.

Žak, Benedict. *See* **Schack.**

Zamboni, Luigi (b Bologna, 1767; d Florence, 28 Feb 1837), Italian bass. Debut Ravenna, 1791, in Cimarosa's *Il fanatico burlato*; was widely known in comic operas by Fioravanti and Paisiello and created Rossini's Figaro (Rome, 1816).

Zamboni, Maria (b Peschiera, 25 Jul 1895; d Verona, 25 Mar 1976), Italian soprano. She studied at Parma and made her debut at Piacenza in 1921, as Marguerite. She sang at La Scala 1924–31 and created Liù there in 1926. In 1930 she took part in the Rome fp of Pizzetti's *Lo straniero*. She was well known in S. Amer. and at Buenos Aires, Rio, Sao Paulo and Santiago was admired as Orpheus, Elsa, Eva, Mimi and Manon.

Zampa, ou La Fiancée de marbre (*Z., or The Marble Betrothed*), opera by Hérold (lib. by A.H.J. Mélesville), prod. Paris, Opéra-Comique, 3 May 1831.

Zandonai, Riccardo (b Sacco, Trentino, 30 May 1883; d Pesaro, 5 Jun 1944), Italian composer. Studied at Roveredo and later at the Liceo Musicale of Pesaro, where Mascagni was director. He left in 1902 and at Milan met Boito, who intro. him to the pub. Ricordi, by whom his 1st opera was commissioned.

Works incl. operas *Il grillo sul focolare* (after Dickens's *Cricket on the Hearth*, 1908), *Conchita* (after Louÿs's *La Femme et le pantin*, 1911), *Melenis* (1912), *La via della finestra*, *Francesca da Rimini* (on d'Annunzio's play, 1914), *Giuletta e Romeo* (after Shakespeare, 1922), *I cavalieri di Ekebù* (after Selma Lagerlöf, 1925), *Giuliano* (1928), *La farsa amorosa* (1933), *Una partitia*.

Film music for *Princess Tarakanova*; Requiem (1915), *Pater noster* for chorus, org. and orch.; *Ballata eroica*, *Fra gli alberghi delle Dolomiti*, *Quadri di Segantini* (1931), *Rapsodia trentina*, overture *Colombina* for orch.; *Concerto romantico* for vln. and orch. (1919); serenade and *Concerto andaluso* for cello and orch.; string 4tet; songs.

Zandt, Marie van (b New York, 8 Oct 1861; d Cannes, 31 Dec 1919), American soprano. Debut Turin, 1879, as Zerlina. She sang Amina at Her Majesty's, London, the same year and from 1880 was successful at the Paris Opéra-Comique, as Mignon, Rosina and Cherubino. She created Lakmé (1883)

and repeated the role in London 2 years later. NY Met 1891–2 and 1896.

Zanelli, Renato (b Valparaiso, 1 Apr 1892; d Santiago, 25 Mar 1935), Chilean tenor, formerly baritone. Debut Santiago, 1916, as Valentine; sang Amonasro at the NY Met in 1919 and studied further in It., appearing at Naples in the tenor roles of Raoul and Alfredo. His best role was Otello, which he sang at CG in 1928; he was widely known in It. as Lohengrin, Siegmund and Tristan.

Zannetti, Francesco (b Volterra, 28 Mar 1737; d Perugia, 31 Jan 1788), Italian composer. Pupil of Clari in Pisa, he became *maestro di cappella* at Perugia Cathedral in 1760, remaining there till his death.

Works incl. 7 operas incl. *L'Antigono* (1765) *La Didone abbandonata* (1766) and *Artaserse* (1782); Masses, Requiems and other church music; string 5tets, string trios, trio sonatas.

Zanotti, Camillo (b Cesana, c 1545; d Prague, 4 Feb 1591), Italian composer. Worked as vice-*Kapellmeister* at court of Rudolf II in Prague from Aug 1587. 4 books of madrigals were pub. 1587–90.

Zanotti, Giovanni (b Bologna, 14 Oct 1738; d Bologna, 1 Nov 1817), Italian composer. He was *maestro di cappella* at San Petronia, Bologna, 1774–89, wrote opera *L'Olimpiade* (1767); his *Dixit* (1770) was admired by Burney.

Zar lässt sich photographieren, Der (*The Czar has his photograph taken*), opera in 1 act by Weill (lib. by Kaiser), prod. Leipzig, 18 Feb 1928.

Zar und Zimmermann, oder Die zwei Peter (*Csar and Carpenter, or the Two Peters*), opera by Lortzing (lib. by comp. based on a Fr. play by A.H.J. Mélesville, J. T. Merle and E. Cantiran de Boirie), prod. Leipzig, 22 Dec 1837.

See also **Borgomastro di Saardam.**

Zarathustra (R. Strauss). *See* **Also sprach Zarathustra.**

Zareska, Eugenia (b Rava Ruska nr. Lwów, 9 Nov 1910; d Paris, 5 Oct 1979), Ukrainian, later British, mezzo. She studied with Bahr-Mildenburg; made her stage debut in 1939 and sang Dorabella at La Scala, Milan, 1941, repeating the role at Glyndebourne, 1948. Her London debut was as Rosina (Cambridge Theatre, 1947) and the following year she sang Carmen at CG. She sang Berg's Countess Geschwitz in 1949 at Venice and in 1952 settled in England, appearing as guest on the Continent and returning to CG until 1958. Other roles incl. Marina and Monteverdi's Ottavia.

Zarlino, Gioseffe (b Chioggia, 31 Jan 1517; d Venice, 4 Feb 1590), Italian theorist and composer. Studied theology and received minor orders in 1539, but was learned also in philosophy, sciences and languages. He settled in Venice in 1541, became a fellow-student with Rore under Willaert and in 1565 became 1st *maestro di cappella* at St Mark's. In 1583 he was offered the bishopric of Chioggia, but declined it, preferring to remain at St Mark's. He wrote 2 large treatises, the 3-vol. *Istitutioni armoniche* (1558) and *Dimostrationi armoniche* (1571), for which he was attacked by V. Galilei, whereupon he issued another vol., *Sopplimenti musicali* (1588), a 4th, non-musical, being added to the complete ed. later. He sought to summarise and develop the musical theory of the Greeks.

Works incl. Mass for the foundation of the church of Santa Maria della Salute and other church music; pageant for the victory of Lepanto.

Zarzuela (Span.), a light Spanish musical stage play or comic opera, usually in 1 act but sometimes in 2, generally of a satirical but occasionally tragic nature, and often a skit on a spoken play. The music is as a rule strongly nationalist. The libs. have spoken dialogue and allow improvised interpolations, in which the audience sometimes joins.

Zauberflöte, Die, opera by Mozart (lib. by E. Schikaneder, ? with the aid of K.L. Giesecke), prod. Vienna, Theater auf der Wieden, 30 Sep 1791. Winter's opera *Das Labyrinth* is a sequel to it. There is also an unfinished lib. by Goethe intended for a sequel.

Zauberharfe, Die (*The Magic Harp*), magic play with music by Schubert (lib. by G.E. von Hofmann), prod. Vienna, Theater an der Wien, 19 Aug 1820).

Zauberoper (Ger.). *See* Magic Opera.

Zauberzither, Die, oder Caspar der Fagottist (*The Magic Zither, or Jasper the Bassoonist*), *Singspiel* by Wenzel Müller, prod. Vienna, Leopoldstadt Theatre, 8 Jun 1791. The plot shows close resemblances to that of Schikaneder's lib. for Mozart's *Zauberflöte*, which may have been borrowed from it or based on the same source.

Zdravitsa (*Hail to Stalin*), cantata for chorus and orch. on folk texts by Prokofiev, op. 85; comp. 1939, fp Moscow, 21 Dec 1939. 1st Brit. perf. BBC, 21 Dec 1944, cond. Boult: the perf. has been scheduled for a Prom concert in Aug 1944 but was cancelled owing to the threat of flying bombs.

Zeani, Virginia (b Solovastru, 21 Oct 1928), Rumanian soprano. She sang Violetta at her Bologna, 1948, debut and repeated the role in London, Paris, NY (Met, 1966) and at the Bolshoy. She sang at La Scala from 1956 as Handel's Cleopatra, Rossini's Desdemona and Blanche in the 1957 fp of Poulenc's *Carmélites*. She was successful as Lucia, Alzira and Maria di Rohan, and later sang Verdi's Desdemona, Leonora (*Forza*) and Aida, as well as Puccini's Manon and Tosca. Indiana Univ., Bloomington, from 1980.

Zednik, Heinz (b Vienna, 21 Feb 1940), Austrian tenor. He has sung at the Vienna Opera since 1965 in such character roles as Pedrillo, Jacquino and Monostatos. Bayreuth debut 1970; Loge and Mime in the 1976 Chéreau–Boulez centennial *Ring*: in the same year he took part in the fp of Einem's *Kabale und Liebe* (Vienna). He has appeared as guest in Paris, Moscow and Montreal. Other roles incl. Berg's Painter, David and Lortzing's Czar Peter.

Zeffirelli (Corsi), Franco (b Florence, 12 Feb 1923), Italian producer and designer. After an early career as an actor he became asst. to Visconti and prod. *La Cenerentola* at La Scala (1953) followed by *Il Turco in Italia* and *Don Pasquale*. His prods. of *Lucia di Lammermoor*, *Pagliacci* and *Cavalleria rusticana* (CG 1959) revealed a taste for opulent Romantic realism. He returned to London for *Don Giovanni* and *Alcina* (1962) and *Tosca* (1964). His *Falstaff* has been seen at CG and at the Met; returned to NY for Barber's *Antony and Cleopatra* (1966), in a prod. which inaugurated the Met co. at Lincoln Center. In an age of austerity, his major work is now confined to film: *La Traviata* (1983) and *Otello* (1986).

Zehme, Albertine (b Vienna, 7 Jan 1857; d Naumburg, 11 May 1946), Austrian actress and soprano. After performing in plays by Schiller and Shakespeare at Leipzig she studied with Cosima Wagner at Bayreuth (1891–3); learnt the roles of Venus, Brünnhilde and Kundry and returned to Leipzig, becoming successful in Ibsen's plays and in recitations. In Jan 1912 she commissioned Schoenberg to write a cycle of recitations based on Albert Giraud's poems from *Pierrot lunaire*. After frequent consultations with Schoenberg, Zehme gave the work's fp in Berlin (12 Oct 1912) and toured widely with it in Eur.: Munich, Stuttgart, Vienna, Prague. At Leipzig in 1914 she gave the recitation in the 1st Ger. perf. of the *Gurrelieder*.

Zeitlin, Zvi (b Dubrovnia, 21 Feb 1923), American violinist of Russian birth. He studied at Juilliard and in Jerusalem; debut there 1940. His US debut was in 1951 and London debut 1961. From 1967 he has been on the faculty of Eastman School, Rochester. An authority on Nardini but is best known for his perfs. of modern works: the leading exponent of Schoenberg's concerto (recorded with Kubelik, 1971).

Zeitmasze, work by Stockhausen for fl., ob., horn, clar. and bassoon; comp. 1955–6, fp Paris, 15 Dec 1956, cond. Boulez.

Zelenka, Jan Dismas (b Lounovice, 16 Oct 1679; d Dresden, 23 Dec 1745), Bohemian composer. Studied at Prague, was double bass player in the court band at Dresden from 1710 and went to Vienna to study under Fux in 1716; then went to It. but returned to Dresden to collaborate with Heinichen, whom he succeeded as director of the church music in 1735.

Works incl. Lat. *Melodrama de Sancto Wenceslao* (1723); oratorios *I penitenti al sepolcro* (1736), *Il serpente di bronzo* (1730) and *Gesù al Calvario* (1735); 20 Masses, motets, psalms and other church music; Lat. cantatas.

Zeleński, Władysław (b Grodkowice, 6 Jul 1837; d Kraków, 23 Jan 1921), Polish teacher and composer. Studied at Prague Univ., also music (with Krejci) there and later in Paris. He became prof. at the Warsaw Cons. in 1872 and director of the Kraków Cons. in 1881.

Works incl. operas *Konrad Wallenrod* (1885), *Goplana* (1896), *Janek* (1900), *Balandina* and *An Old Story* (1907); Masses and motets; cantatas; 2 symphs. (1871, 1912), *Woodland Echoes*, concert overture *In the Tatra* and other orch. works; pf. concerto; 4 string 4tets, pf. 4tet, vars. for string 4tet, 6tet for strings and pf., pf. trio; vln. and pf. sonata; pf. pieces.

Zeller, Carl (Johann Adam) (b St Peter-in-der-Au, 19 Jun 1842; d Baden nr. Vienna, 17 Aug 1898), Austrian composer. He was a choir-boy in the Imp. chapel in Vienna and studied law at the univ. He also had counterpoint lessons from Sechter. He made his career in the civil service but was continuously active as a comp.

Works incl. operettas *Der Vogelhändler* (1891), *Der Obersteiger* (1894), *Der Vagabund* (1886) and many others.

Zelmira, opera by Rossini (lib. by A.L. Tottola, based on a Fr. tragedy by P.L.B. de Belloy), prod. Naples, Teatro San Carlo, 16 Feb 1822.

Zelter, Carl Friedrich (b Berlin, 11 Dec 1758; d Berlin, 15 May 1832), German con-

ductor, teacher and composer. Having completed his training as a master mason he joined his father's firm, and abandoned the trade completely only in 1815, but meanwhile was active as a musician. Pupil of Schultz and Fasch, he succeeded the latter as cond. of the Berlin Singakademie in 1800, founded the Berliner Liedertafel in 1809, the same year became prof. at the acad., and in 1822 founded the Royal Inst. of Church Music. Among his pupils were Nicolai, Loewe, Meyerbeer and Mendelssohn, whose plans to revive Bach's *St Matthew Passion* in 1829 he at first opposed but later approved. In the Singakademie he had himself done much to revive interest in Bach's music. He was a personal friend of Goethe, many of whose poems he set; he rejected Schubert's Lieder. Wrote principally songs, also church music, cantatas, inst. music.

Zémire et Azore, opera by Grétry (lib. by Marmontel), prod. Fontainebleau, at court, 9 Nov 1771; 1st Paris perf., Théâtre Italien, 16 Dec 1771.

Zemire und Azor, opera by Spohr (lib. by J.J. Ihlee, based on that by Marmontel) prod. Frankfurt, 4 Apr 1819. The familiar song 'Rose, softly blooming' is in this work.

Zemlinsky, Alexander von (b Vienna, 14 Oct 1871; d Larchmont, NY, 15 Mar 1942), Austrian composer and conductor. Studied at the Vienna Cons. He became cond. at the Vienna Volksoper in 1906 and at the Hofoper in 1908, later at Prague, where he cond. the Ger. Opera and the 1924 fp of Schoenberg's monodrama *Erwartung*; finally in 1927–31, he was one of the conds. at the Berlin State Opera and at the Kroll Opera, where he gave the 1st local perf. of *Erwartung*. He returned to Vienna in 1933 and later emigrated to the USA. Schoenberg was among his pupils and married his sister.

Works incl. operas *Sarema* (1897), *Es war einmal* (1900), *Kleider machen Leute* (G. Keller, 1908, prod. 1922), *Eine florentinische Tragödie, Der Zwerg* (both after O. Wilde, 1917, 1922), *Der Kreidekreis* (after Klabund, 1933), *Der Traumgörge* (1906, prod. 1980), ballet *Das gläserne Herz* (after Hofmannsthal, 1903), incid. music for *Cymbeline* (1914).

2 symphs. (1892, 1897), suite for orch. (1894), *Die Seejungfrau* for orch. (1903), sinfonietta (1934), *Lyric Symph.* for sop., bar. and orch. (1923), *Symphonische Gesänge* for voice and orch. (1926).

String 5tet (1895), trio for clar., cello and pf. (1895), 4 string 4tets (1895–1936); Lieder to texts by Heine and Eichendorff.

Zenatello, Giovanni (b Verona, 22 Feb 1876; d New York, 11 Feb 1949), Italian tenor, 1st appeared as a baritone at Naples, but changed to tenor. He then studied at Milan, appeared in It., S. Amer. and the USA, and 1st in London in 1905, as Riccardo. NY 1907–28, as Otello, Don José and Radames. He created the role of Pinkerton in P·.ccini's *Madama Butterfly*. He married Maria Gay in 1913.

Zender, Hans (b Wiesbaden, 22 Nov 1936), German conductor and composer. He studied at Frankfurt and Freiburg and in Rome under B.A. Zimmermann, whose works he has frequently cond. He worked at opera houses in Freiburg, Bonn and Kiel and became music dir. of Hamburg Opera in 1984 (Prin. cond. from 1977).

Works incl. pf. concerto (1956), *Zeitströme* for orch. (1974), cantata *Der Mann von La Mancha* for voices and Moog synthesizer (1969), *Continuum and Fragments* for chorus, *Cantos I–V* for voices and insts. and elec. works.

Zeno, Apostolo (b Venice, 11 Dec 1668; d Venice, 11 Nov 1750), Italian poet and librettist. Operas on his libs. *See* **Alessandro Severo** (Lotti), **Ambleto** (Gasparini and D. Scarlatti), **Astarto** (G.B. Bononcini), **Feramondo** (Handel), **Ifigenia in Aulide** (Caldara), **Lucio Papiro** (do. and Hasse), **Lucio Vero** (Pollarolo and Sacchini), **Merope** (Gasparini, Jommelli and Terradellas), **Scipione** (Handel), **Temistocle** (Porpora and J.C. Bach).

Zerr, Anna (b Baden-Baden, 26 Jul 1822; d Winterbach, 14 Nov 1881), German soprano. She sang at Karlsruhe 1839–46; joined the Kärntertortheater in 1846 and the following year created Flotow's Martha there. She visited London 1851–2, singing the Queen of Night, and Rosa in the fp of the rev. version of Spohr's *Faust* (CG, 4 Apr 1852).

Ziani, Marc' Antonio (b Venice, c 1653; d Vienna, 22 Jan 1715), Italian composer. *Maestro di cappella* at the church of Santa Barbara and cond. at the theatre at Mantua in 1686. He went to Vienna, where he became vice-music director in 1700 and 1st music director in 1711.

Works incl. operas *Alessandro magno in Sidone* (1679), *Damira placata* (1680), *Meleagro* (1706), *Chilonida* (1709) and 41 others; Masses, motets and other church music; oratorios, cantatas.

Ziani, Pietro Andrea (b Venice, c 1620; d Naples, 12 Feb 1684), Italian composer, uncle of prec. He was organist at Venice,

then at Santa Maria Maggiore, Bergamo, visited Vienna and Dresden in 1660–67 and became orgaist at St Mark's, Venice, in succession to Cavalli in 1669. He went to Naples on failing to be app. *maestro di cappella* in 1676, becoming a teacher at the Cons. di Sant' Onofrio and in 1680 royal *maestro di cappella*.

Works incl. operas *Le fortune di Rodope e di Damira* (1657), *L'Antigona delusa da Alceste* (1660) and 21 others; Masses, psalms, oratorios; inst. sonatas; org. pieces.

Zich, Otakar (b Králové Městec, 25 Mar 1879; d Ouběnice nr. Benešov, 9 Jul 1934), Czech composer. He was at 1st a secondary schoolmaster, but took a degree at the Univ. of Brno and was app. prof. of aesthetics there. He also collected folksongs.

Works incl. operas *The Painter's Whim* (1910), *The Sin* (1922) and *Les Précieuses ridicules* (after Molière, 1926); *The ill-fated Marriage* and *Polka Rides* for chorus and orch.; songs.

Zichy, Géza, Count (b Sztára Castle, 22 Jul 1849; d Budapest, 14 Jan 1924), Hungarian pianist, poet and composer. Pupil of Volkmann and Liszt at Budapest. He lost his right arm as a boy of 14 in a hunting accident and wrote much pf. music for the left hand. He became president of the Hung. Acad. of Music and the Nat. Cons. As Intendant from 1891 of the Budapest Opera, he sacked Mahler.

Works incl. operas *Castle Story*, *Alár* (1896), *Master Roland* (1899), trilogy *Rákóczi* (*Nemo*, *Rákóczi/Ferenc* and *Rodostó*, 1905–12); ballet *Gemma*; pf. concerto for the left hand; sonata, 6 studies, etc. for the left hand and other pf. music.

Žídek, Ivo (b Kravaře, 4 Jun 1926), Czech tenor. He sang Werther at Ostrava in 1944 and sang at the National Theatre, Prague, from 1948; appeared as guest at Vienna from 1956 and visited Edinburgh with the Prague co. in 1964 and 1970 (1st Brit. perf. of Janáček's *Mr Brouček*). He was well known as Smetana's Jeník and Janáček's Gregor and also appeared in operas by Verdi, Bizet and Mozart.

Zieleński, Mikołaj (b 1550, d 1615), Polish 17th-cent. organist and composer. Comp. offertories and communions for the service of the whole year. In service of Archbishop of Gniezno 1608–15 and studied with Gabrieli in It.

Zigeunerbaron, Der (*The Gypsy Baron*), operetta by J. Strauss, jun. (lib. by I. Schnitzer, based on author by M. Jókai founded on his own story *Saffi*), prod. Vienna, Theater an der Wien, 24 Oct 1885.

Zilcher, Hermann (b Frankfurt, 18 Aug 1881; d Würzburg, 1 Jan 1948), German composer. Studied at the Hoch Cons. at Frankfurt, became prof. at the Acad. of Music at Munich in 1908 and in 1920 director of the Würzburg Cons.

Works incl. opera *Doktor Eisenbart* (1922); incid. music for plays by Shakespeare, Dehmel's children's play *Fitzbutze* (1903) and Hauptmann's *Die goldene Harfe*; oratorio *Liebesmesse*; 5 symphs., *Tanzphantasie* and other works for orch.; pieces for solo insts. and orch.; chamber music.

Ziliani, Alessandro (b Busseto, 3 Jun 1907; d Milan, 18 Feb 1977), Italian tenor. Debut Milan, 1928, as Pinkerton; La Scala 1932– 47 (debut as Enzo, took part in the 1st It. perf. of Respighi's *Maria Egiziaca*, 1934). He also sang in early perfs. of works by Wolf-Ferrari, Busoni (*Turandot*) and Mascagni (*Pinotta*, written 1880 but not prod. until 1932).

Zilli, Emma (b Fagnana, Udine, 11 Nov 1864; d Havana, Jan 1901), Italian soprano. Debut Ferrara, 1887, in Donizetti's *Poliuto*. She appeared widely throughout Eur. and in 1893 created Alice Ford in *Falstaff*; repeated the role at CG in May 1894. She was successful in Puccini roles; died of fever while on tour in Central and S. Amer.

Zillig, Winfried (b Würzburg, 1 Apr 1905; d Hamburg, 18 Dec 1963), German composer and conductor. Studied with Schoenberg in Vienna and from 1927 to 1928 was asst. to Kleiber at the Berlin Staatsoper. From 1928 to 1947 he cond. in various Ger. theatres, becoming director of music at the radio station, 1st in Frankfurt and then in Hamburg. He also made a performing version of Schoenberg's unfinished oratorio *Die Jakobsleiter* (perf. Vienna, 1961).

Works incl. operas *Die Windesbraut* (1941), *Troilus und Cressida* (1951), *Das Opfer*, TV opera *Bauernpassion* (1955), radio opera *Die Verlobung von St Domingo* (1956); vln. and cello concertos; 4 serenades for various inst. groups; choral music; songs.

Ziloti, Alexander. *See* **Siloti.**

Zimbalist, Efrem (b Rostov on the Don, 21 Apr 1889; d Reno, Nev., 22 Feb 1985), American violinist and composer of Russian birth. Studied first with his father and then with L. Auer at the St Petersburg Cons. from 1901 to 1907, making his debut in Berlin in 1907. In 1911 he emigrated to the USA,

where he married the singer Alma Gluck (1914) and in 1941 became director of the Curtis Inst. in Philadelphia, which had been founded by his 2nd wife. He gave the 1952 fp of Menotti's concerto (Philadelphia).

Works incl. opera *Landara* (1956); *Amer. Rhapsody* for orch.; concerto and 3 Slavonic Dances for vln. and orch.; string 4tet; vln. sonata.

Zimerman, Krystian (b Zaorze, 5 Dec 1956), Polish pianist. He studied at Katowice and won the 1975 Chopin Competition, Warsaw. He has had successful engagements in Munich, Paris and London with the late Romantic rep., and in 1976 appeared with Karajan and the Berlin PO. US debut 1979, with the NY PO.

Zimmerman, Franklin B(ershir) (b Wauneta, Kansas, 20 Jun 1923), American musicologist. He studied in California and at Oxford, where his teachers incl. Egon Wellesz and Jack Westrup. He has taught at NY, Dartmouth and the Univs. of Kentucky and Pennsylvania; best known for his research on Baroque music and Purcell. His Purcell thematic catalogue (1963) gives the definitive numbering for the composer's works.

Zimmermann, Bernd Alois (b Bliesheim nr. Cologne, 20 Mar 1918; d Grosskönigsdorf, 10 Aug 1970), German composer. Studied in Cologne with Lemacher and P. Jarnach, and also studied linguistics and philosophy at the Univs. of Bonn, Cologne and Berlin. From 1950 to 1952 he taught at Cologne Univ. and from 1958 at the Hochschule für Musik in Cologne. He committed suicide.

Works incl. opera *Die Soldaten* (1965); ballets *Kontraste* (1953) and *Alagoana* (1955); cantata *Lob der Torheit* (1948); symph.; concertos for vln., ob. and cello; concerto for string orch. (1948): *Photoptosis*, prelude for orch. (1968), *Seille und Umkehr*, sketches for orch. (1970); *Die Soldaten*, vocal symph. from opera (1959); *Requiem for a Young Poet* (1969).

Zimmermann, Erich (b Meissen, 29 Nov 1892; d Berlin, 24 Feb 1968), German tenor. After his 1918 Dresden debut he had engagements in Munich, Vienna and Hamburg; retired 1951, as a member of the Berlin Städtische Oper. Bayreuth 1935–44, as David, Mime and Loge. He sang at CG before and after the war as Jacquino and Mime. At Salzburg (1930–32) he was heard in operas by Mozart and Strauss.

Zimmermann, Udo (b Dresden, 6 Oct 1943), German composer. He founded the Studio for New Music, Dresden, in 1974 and has worked in experimental music there.

Comp. and prod. at the Dresden Opera from 1970.

Works incl. operas *Die Weisse Rose* (1967), *Die zweite Entscheidung* (1970), *Levins Mühle* (1973), *Der Schuhe und die fliegende Prinzessin* (1975), *Die Wundersame Schustersfrau* (1982); *Music for Strings* (1967), *Sieh, meine Augen* for chamber orch. (1970), *Mutazioni* for orch. (1972); *Der Mensch*, cantata for sop. and 13 insts. (1969), *Psalm der Nacht* for chorus, perc. and organ (1973), *Pax questousa* for 5 soloists, 3 choruses and orch. (1980); *Choreographieren nach Edgar Degas* for 21 insts. (1974).

Zingara, La (*The Gypsy*), intermezzo by Rinaldo di Capua, prod. Académie Royale de Musique, 19 Jun 1753.

Zingarelli, Nicola Antonio (b Naples, 4 Apr 1752; d Torre del Greco, 5 May 1837), Italian composer. Studied at the Con. S. Maria di Loreto in Naples, where his intermezzo *I quattro pazzi* was prod. in 1768. Leaving the Cons. in 1772 he at 1st worked as an organist, but with *Montezuma* (Naples, 1781) began his career as an opera comp., and 1785–1803 prod. works in all the main It. cities and also in Paris. He was app. *maestro di cappella* at the cathedral in Milan in 1793, Loreto 1794, and in 1804 succeeded Guglielmi at St Peter's, Rome, from about this time onwards devoting himself chiefly to church music. He became director of the Real Collegio di Musica in Naples in 1813, and *maestro di cappella* of the cathedral there in 1816.

Works incl. 37 operas, e.g. *Montezuma* (1781), *Armida* (1786), *Antigono, Ifigenia in Aulide* (1787), *Antigone* (1790), *Il mercato di Monfregoso* (1792), *Artaserse, Quinto Fabio, Gli Orazi e Curazi, Giulietta e Romeo* (after Shakespeare, 1796), *Andromeda, La morte di Mitridate* (1797), *I veri amici* (1798), *Il ratto delle Sabine* (1799), *Edipo a Colono* (after Sophocles, 1802), *Berenice, regina d'Armenia* and *c* 20 others.

Oratorios *La Passione* (1787), *Gerusalemme distrutta* (1812), *La medificazione di Gerusalemme* and others; many cantatas; 23 Masses, Requiems and other church music, incl. 55 Magnificats; canon for 8 voices; *partimenti* and *solfeggi* for vocal exercise.

Zingaresa (It. noun) } words used to
Zingarese (It. adj.) describe music in, or supposed to be in, a gypsy manner; e.g. the finale of Brahms's vln. concerto. The adj. is used in the form of *alla z.*

Zingari, Gli (*The Gypsies*), opera by Leoncavallo (lib. by E. Cavacchioli and G. Emanuel, after Pushkin), prod. London, Hippodrome, 16 Sep 1912.

Zinman, David (b New York, 9 Jul 1936), American conductor. He studied at Tanglewood and was Pierre Monteux's asst. 1961–4. Music dir. Netherlands Chamber Orch. 1956–77; Rotterdam PO 1979–82. Chief cond. Rochester PO from 1974, prin. guest cond. Baltimore SO from 1983.

Zipoli, Domenico (b Prato, 16 Oct 1688; d Córdoba, Arg., 2 Jan 1726), Italian composer. Pupil (?) of A. Scarlatti in Naples and Pasquini in Rome, where he became organist of the Jesuit church, he entered the Jesuit Order and in 1717 went to S. Amer. as a missionary.

Works incl. 3 oratorios (music lost); church music; keyboard music (2 vols. of *Sonate d'intavolatura* pub. in 1716).

Zítek, Vilém (b Prague, 9 Sep 1890; d Prague, 11 Aug 1956), Czech bass. He sang at Prague 1911–47 as Kečal, Gremin, Boris and Mozart's Figaro. In the 1920s he appeared at La Scala, often under Toscanini, as Hunding, Fafner and the Commendatore. He sang as guest in Paris, Berlin and the USSR; often compared with Shalyapin. Other roles incl. Don Quichotte, Philip II and parts in operas by Dvořák and Smetana.

Zither (Ger. from Gk. *kithara*), a string instrument of the Dulcimer type, although etymologically connected with the Cittern, which it does not resemble. It has many strings (27–40) stretched over a flat soundbox, and is played with the tips of the finger, the bass strings alone being struck with a plectrum fixed to the thumb by a ring.

Zoghby, Linda (b Mobile, Ala., 17 Aug 1949), American soprano. She sang Donna Elvira with Houston Opera in 1975 and the following year Bellini's Giulietta at Dallas. At Glyndebourne she appeared as Mimi (1978) and repeated the role at her 1982 NY Met debut. She is well known as Pamina, Fiordiligi and Marguerite and has recorded Haydn's *L'isola disabitata* and *L'incontro improvviso*; *La fedeltà premiata* at Glyndebourne, 1980.

Zoilo, Annibale (b Rome, *c* 1537; d Loreto, 30 Jun 1592), Italian singer and composer. *Maestro di cappella* at the churches of St John Lateran and San Luigi in Rome, singer in the Papal Chapel from 1570 to *c* 1582, and *maestro di cappella* of the Santa Casa at Loreto in 1584–92. He worked with Palestrina on a rev. ed. of the *Graduale*.

Works incl. Masses, madrigals and songs.

Zoilo, Cesare (b Rome, *c* 1584; d after 1622), Italian composer, (?) son of prec. Wrote motets, madrigals, etc.

Zöllner, Heinrich (b Leipzig, 4 Jul 1854; d Freiburg, 4 May 1941), German composer, son of the comp. Carl Friedrich Z. (1800–60). Studied at the Leipzig Cons. App. teacher at Dorpat Univ. (Tartu, Estonia) in 1878, cond. at Cologne, lived in USA in 1890–98, became music director of Leipzig Univ. in succession to Kretzschmar until 1906, cond. the Flem. Opera at Antwerp from 1907 and retired to Freiburg in 1914.

Works incl. operas *Frithjof* (after Tegnér), *Faust* (on part of Goethe's orig. text, 1887), *Der Überfall* (on a story by Wildenbruch, 1895), *Die versunkene Glocke* (on Hauptmann's play, 1899) and others; festival cantata *The New World* and others; 5 symphs. (1883–1928), overture *Under the Starry Banner*.

Zopfstil (Ger., lit. 'pigtail style'), derogatory term sometimes applied to the formal courtly style of the later 18th cent.

Zoppa (It. = limp), a strong accent on a 2nd note off the beat or a long note following a short one, as in the Scotch snap. The motion of a musical piece in such a rhythm is called *alla zoppa*.

Zoraida di Granata, opera seria by Donizetti (lib. by B. Merelli after F. Gonzales), prod. Rome, Teatro Argentina, 28 Jan 1822.

Zorian, Olive (b Manchester, 16 Mar 1916; d London, 17 May 1965), English violinist. She studied at the RMCM and the RAM; formed her own string 4tet which gave works by Bliss and Bartók; the fps of Tippett's 2nd and 3rd 4tets (1943, 1946), of the rev. version of his 1st 4tet (1944), and of Britten's 2nd 4tet (1945). She was active as a soloist and led the Alan Bush chamber orch. and the EOG orch. (1952–7). She was married to the writer and broadcaster John Amis (1948–55).

Zoroastre, opera by Rameau (lib. by L. de Cahusac) prod. Paris Opéra, 5 Dec 1749.

Zottmayr, Georg (b Munich, 24 Jan 1869; d Dresden, 11 Dec 1941), German bass. He sang first in concert then appeared at the Vienna Hofoper, 1906–9, under Mahler. From 1910 he was popular at Dresden as Gurnemanz, Daland, Sarastro, Pogner and Marke: his father **Ludwig** had created Marke at Munich in 1865.

Zukerman, Pinchas (b Tel-Aviv, 16 Jul 1948), Israeli violinist, violist and conductor. He studied at Juilliard and won the 1967 Leventritt Competition; appeared with the NY PO and at Brighton in 1969. Many perfs. of chamber music with Stern and Barenboim. Debut as cond. London, 1974; music dir. St Paul Chamber Orch. from 1980; guest cond. in NY, Los Angeles and Boston. Well known as soloist in standard rep. and esp. Elgar's concerto.

Zukovsky, Paul (b Brooklyn, 22 Oct 1943), American violinist. He studied at Juilliard and in 1969 started a series of concerts, 'Music for the 20th Century Violin': he perfs. sonatas by Ives and concertos by Schuman and Sessions; in 1972 at Tanglewood, with the Boston SO, he gave the fp of the concerto for amplified vln. and orch. by Charles Wuorinen.

Zumpe, Hermann (b Oppach, 9 Apr 1850; d Munich, 4 Sep 1903), German composer and conductor. Educ. at a seminary at Bautzen to become a schoolmaster, but he was so taken up with music that he went to Leipzig in 1871, where he taught in a school and studied with A. Tottmann. In 1872–6 he asst. Wagner at Bayreuth and then succeeded in securing one post after another as theatre cond. until in 1891 he became court music director at Stuttgart. In 1895–7 he cond. the Kaim orch. at Munich; he then became court cond. at Schwerin, from 1901 at Munich. Cond. Wagner at CG (1898).

Works incl. operas *Anahra* (1881), *Die verwunschene Prinzess*, *Das Gespenst von Horodin* (1910) and *Sawitri* (from the Mahabharata, unfinished; prod. 1907), operettas *Farinelli* (1886), *Karin* (1888) and *Polnische Wirtschaft* (1889).

Zumsteeg, Johann Rudolf (b Sachsenflur, Baden, 10 Jan 1760; d Stuttgart, 27 Jan 1802), German composer. Fellow-pupil and friend of Schiller at the Karlschule in Stuttgart, he entered the service of the court there as a cellist in 1781, becoming *Konzertmeister* in 1792. His extended ballads were esp. influential, some later being used as models by Schubert.

Works incl. operas *Das Tartarische Gesetz* (1780), *Le delizie campestri, o Ippolito e Atricia* (1782), *Armida* (1785), *Die Geisterinsel* (after *The Tempest*, 1798), *Das Pfauenfest* and others; melodrama *Tamira*; incid. music to *Hamlet* (1785), *Macbeth*, Schiller's *Räuber* and other plays; cantatas; Masses and other church music; 10 cello concertos (1777–92), songs and ballads *Lenore* (Bürger), *Colma* (Ossian), *Die Büssende, Ritter Toggenburg* (Schiller), *Die Entführung*.

Zur Mühlen, Raimund von (b Livonia, 10 Nov 1854; d Steyning, Sussex, 9 Dec 1931),

German tenor. Educ. in Ger. he began to learn singing at the Hochschule für Musik in Berlin, later went to Stockhausen at Frankfurt and Bussine in Paris. He 1st visited London in 1882, frequently returned and finally settled in Eng., where he was much sought after as a teacher of singing.

Zusammenschlag (Ger. = hit together), Acciaccatura or Mordent.

Zweig, Fritz (b Olomouc, 8 Sep 1893; d Los Angeles, 28 Feb 1984), Bohemian-born American conductor. After study with Schoenberg, he worked at opera houses in Mannheim and Elberfeld; moved to Berlin 1923, working with Bruno Walter at the Städtische Oper. At the Kroll Opera, 1927–31, he was Klemperer's asst. and gave there operas by Gounod, Auber and Gluck, and the 1st German perf. of Janáček's *From the House of the Dead*. With the rise of the Nazis Zweig fled from one centre to another: Berlin Staatsoper, German Opera (Prague) and Paris. In 1938 he cond. *Rosenkavalier* at CG; moved to the USA in 1940 and taught at Los Angeles.

Zweig, Stefan (1881–1942), Austrian novelist and dramatist. *See* **Schweigsame Frau** (R. Strauss), **Toch** (*Heilige aus USA*).

He collaborated with Strauss from 1932; *Die Schweigsame Frau* was prod. at Dresden (1935) but soon proscribed because of Zweig's Jewishness. Zweig intended to write the lib. for Strauss's *Friedenstag*, suggested to him by Joseph Gregor; but the Nazi régime making his appearance on any Ger. stage impossible after 1935, this was afterwards undertaken by Gregor himself.

Zwerg, Der (*The Dwarf*), opera in 1 act by Zemlinsky (lib. by G.C. Klaren, after Wilde's *The Birthday of the Infanta*); 1920–21, fp Cologne, 28 May 1922, cond. Klemperer. At Edinburgh and at CG the work has been given in a prod. by the Hamburg Opera, under the new title *The Birthday of the Infanta*, with new lib. by A. Dresen.

Zwillingsbrüder, Die (*The Twin Brothers*), play with music by Schubert (lib. by G.E. von Hofmann), prod. Vienna, Kärntnertortheater, 14 Jun 1820.

Zwingburg, scenic cantata by Krenek (lib. by F. Werfel), comp. 1922, fp Berlin, Staatsoper, 21 Oct 1924; Krenek's 1st work for the stage.

Zwischenspiel (Ger.) = Interlude.

Zwyssig, (Johann) Joseph (Father Alberik) (b Bauen, Uri, 17 Nov 1808; d Mehrerau nr. Bregenz, 18 Nov 1854), Swiss priest, organist and composer. Educ. at the monastery school of Wettingen, ordained priest and became music teacher and cathedral organist and cond. After the dissolution of the monastery he led a precarious existence, but was in demand as an authority on the org.

Works incl. Masses, offertories and other church music; choruses, e.g. the patriotic *Schweizerpsalm* 'Trittst im Morgenrot daher' (1841); songs.

Zyklus, work for percussion by Stockhausen, involving random choice and improvisation; fp Darmstadt, 25 Aug 1959.

Zylis-Gara, Teresa (b Landvarov, 23 Jan 1935), Polish soprano. She studied at Łódź and sang Halka at Katowice in 1956. From the early 1960s she appeared in W. Ger. as Poppea and Butterfly. Glyndebourne 1965 as Octavian; CG 1968 and 1976 as Elvira and Violetta. Elvira was the role of her Salzburg and NY Met debuts (1968) and she has been widely admired as Anna Bolena, Desdemona, Fiordiligi and the Marschallin.

Żywny, Wojciech (b Bohemia, 13 May 1756; d Warsaw, 21 Feb 1842), Polish piano teacher and composer. He studied with Jan Kuchar and worked at the Polish court of Stanisław August during the 1780s. Later moved to Warsaw and was Chopin's piano teacher 1816–22. Works incl. pf. pieces, overtures and songs.

LIST OF OPERATIC ROLES

This list is intended as a guide to roles mentioned in the dictionary.

ROLE	OPERA	COMPOSER
Abigaille	*Nabucco*	Verdi
Acis	*Acis and Galatea*	Handel
Adalgisa	*Norma*	Bellini
Adèle	*Le Comte Ory*	Rossini
Adina	*L'Elisir d'Amore*	Donizetti
Admète	*Alceste*	Gluck
Adolar	*Euryanthe*	Weber
Adriana Lecouvreur	*Adriana Lecouvreur*	Cilea
Adriano	*Rienzi*	Wagner
Aegisthus	*Elektra*	R. Strauss
Aeneas	*Dido and Aeneas*	Purcell
Aennchen ⎫ Agathe ⎭	*Der Freischütz*	Weber
Agrippina	*Agrippina*	Handel
Aida	*Aida*	Verdi
Alberich	*Rheingold, Siegfried*	Wagner
Alceste	*Alceste*	Gluck
Alfonso (*see* Don Alfonso)		
Alfredo	*La Traviata*	Verdi
Alice	*Robert le Diable*	Meyerbeer
Alice Ford	*Falstaff*	Verdi
Alkmene	*Alkmene*	Klebe
Almaviva (tenor)	*Il Barbiere di Siviglia*	Rossini
Almaviva (baritone)	*Le Nozze di Figaro*	Mozart
Alphonse	*La Favorite*	Donizetti
Alvaro (*see* Don Alvaro)		
Alvise	*La Gioconda*	Ponchielli
Alwa	*Lulu*	Berg
Amadis	*Amadis*	Massenet
Amelia Boccanegra	*Simon Boccanegra*	Verdi
Amelia	*Un Ballo in Maschera*	Verdi
Amfortas	*Parsifal*	Wagner
Amina	*La Sonnambula*	Bellini
Aminta	*Il Rè Pastore*	Mozart
Aminta	*Die schweigsame Frau*	R. Strauss
Amneris ⎫ Amonasro ⎭	*Aida*	Verdi
Amor	*Orfeo ed Euridice*	Gluck
Andrea Chénier	*Andrea Chénier*	Giordano
Andromaca	*Andromaca*	Nasolini
Anna Bolena	*Anna Bolena*	Donizetti
Anne Trulove	*The Rake's Progress*	Stravinsky
Annius	*La Clemenza di Tito*	Mozart
Antigonae	*Antigonae*	Orff
Antonia	*Les Contes d'Hoffmann*	Offenbach
Antonida	*A Life for the Czar*	Glinka

ROLE	OPERA	COMPOSER
Antony	*Antony and Cleopatra*	Barber
Apollo	*Daphne*	R. Strauss
Arabella	*Arabella*	R. Strauss
Archibaldo	*L'Amore dei Tre Re*	Montemezzi
Ariadne	*Ariadne auf Naxos*	R. Strauss
Aricie	*Hippolyte et Aricie*	Rameau
Ariodante	*Ariodante*	Handel
Arkel	*Pelléas et Mélisande*	Debussy
Armida	*Armida*	Rossini
Armide	*Armide*	Gluck
Arnold	*Guillaume Tell*	Rossini
Aron	*Moses und Aron*	Schoenberg
Arsace/Arsaces	*Semiramide*	Rossini
Arturo	*Lucia di Lammermoor*	Donizetti
Arturo	*I Puritani*	Bellini
Ascanio	*Benvenuto Cellini*	Berlioz
Aschenbach	*Death in Venice*	Britten
Assad	*Die Königin von Saba*	Goldmark
Assur	*Semiramide*	Rossini
Athanaël	*Thaïs*	Massenet
Attila	*Attila*	Verdi
Azucena	*Il Trovatore*	Verdi
Baba the Turk	*The Rakes's Progress*	Stravinsky
Babinski	*Shvanda the Bagpiper*	Weinberger
Bacchus	*Ariadne auf Naxos*	R. Strauss
Balstrode	*Peter Grimes*	Britten
Banquo	*Macbeth*	Verdi
Barak	*Die Frau ohne Schatten*	R. Strauss
Bardolf	*Falstaff*	Verdi
Barnaba	*La Gioconda*	Ponchielli
Baron Ochs (*see* Ochs)		
Bartolo	*Le Nozze di Figaro*	Mozart
Bartolo	*Il Barbiere di Siviglia*	Rossini
Basilio	*Le Nozze di Figaro*	Mozart
Basilio	*Il Barbiere di Sivigilia*	Rossini
Baucis	*Philémon et Baucis*	Gounod
Beatrice	*Beatrice di Tenda*	Bellini
Béatrice	*Béatrice et Bénédict*	Berlioz
Beckmesser	*Die Meistersinger*	Wagner
Belfagor	*Belfagor*	Respighi
Belcore	*L'Elisir d'Amore*	Donizetti
Belinda	*Dido and Aeneas*	Purcell
Bella	*The Midsummer Marriage*	Tippett
Benoit	*La Bohème*	Puccini
Benvenuto Cellini	*Benvenuto Cellini*	Berlioz
Beppe	*Pagliacci*	Leoncavallo
Billy Budd	*Billy Budd*	Britten
Biterolf	*Tannhäuser*	Wagner
Blondchen/Blonde	*Die Entführung*	Mozart
Bluebeard	*Duke Bluebeard's Castle*	Bartók
Boccanegra	*Simon Boccanegra*	Verdi

ROLE	OPERA	COMPOSER
Boris Godunov	*Boris Godunov*	Mussorgsky
Borromeo	*Palestrina*	Pfitzner
Brangaene	*Tristan und Isolde*	Wagner
Brünehild	*Sigurd*	Reyer
Brünnhilde	*Die Walküre, Siegfried, Götterdämmerung*	Wagner
Butterfly	*Madama Butterfly*	Puccini
Caesar (see Giulio Cesare)		
Calaf	*Turandot*	Puccini
Calisto	*La Calisto*	Cavalli
Canio	*Pagliacci*	Leoncavallo
Captain	*Wozzeck*	Berg
Cardillac	*Cardillac*	Hindemith
Carmen	*Carmen*	Bizet
Carolina	*Il Matrimonio Segreto*	Cimarosa
Cassandre	*Les Troyens*	Berlioz
Castor	*Castor et Pollux*	Rameau
Cavaradossi	*Tosca*	Puccini
Cenerentola (Angelina)	*La Cenerentola*	Rossini
Ceres	*Il Ratto di Proserpina*	Winter
Chapelou	*Le Postillon de Lonjumeau*	Adam
Charlotte	*Werther*	Massenet
Chérubin	*Chérubin*	Massenet
Cherubino	*Le Nozze di Figaro*	Mozart
Child	*L'Enfant et les Sortilèges*	Ravel
Christine	*Intermezzo*	R. Strauss
Chrysothemis	*Elektra*	R. Strauss
Cio-Cio-San (*see* Butterfly)		
Claggart	*Billy Budd*	Britten
Cleopatra	*Giulio Cesare*	Handel
Clytemnestra	*Elektra*	R. Strauss
Clytemnestra	*Iphigénie en Aulide*	Gluck
Colline	*La Bohème*	Puccini
Commendatore	*Don Giovanni*	Mozart
Composer	*Ariadne auf Naxos*	R. Strauss
Concepcion	*L'Heure Espagnole*	Ravel
Constanze	*Die Entführung*	Mozart
Cornelia	*Giulio Cesare*	Handel
Cortez	*Fernand Cortez*	Spontini
Count (Mozart; *see* Almaviva)		
Count Ory	*Le Comte Ory*	Rossini
Countess	*The Queen of Spades*	Tchaikovsky
Countess Almaviva	*Le Nozze di Figaro*	Mozart
Countess Geschwitz	*Lulu*	Berg
Countess Madeleine	*Capriccio*	R. Strauss
Creon	*Médée*	Cherubini
Czar Peter	*Zar and Zimmermann*	Lortzing
Daland	*Der fliegende Holländer*	Wagner
Dalibor	*Dalibor*	Smetana
Dalila	*Samson et Dalila*	Saint-Saëns

ROLE	OPERA	COMPOSER
Danae	*Die Liebe der Danae*	Strauss
Dandini	*La Cenerentola*	Rossini
Danton	*Dantons Tod*	Einem
Dapertutto	*Les Contes d'Hoffmann*	Offenbach
Daphne	*Daphne*	R. Strauss
Dardanus	*Dardanus*	Rameau
David	*Die Meistersinger*	Wagner
Demetrius	*A Midsummer Night's Dream*	Britten
Demon	*The Demon*	Rubinstein
Des Grieux	*Manon*	Massenet
Des Grieux	*Manon Lescaut*	Puccini
Desdemona	*Otello*	Rossini
Desdemona	*Otello*	Verdi
Despina	*Così fan Tutte*	Mozart
Diana	*La Calisto*	Cavalli
Dick Johnson	*La Fanciulla del West*	Puccini
Dido	*Dido and Aeneas*	Purcell
Didon	*Les Troyens*	Berlioz
Dimitri	*Boris Godunov*	Mussorgsky
Dinorah	*Dinorah*	Meyerbeer
Djamileh	*Djamileh*	Bizet
Doctor	*Wozzeck*	Berg
Don Alfonso	*Così fan Tutte*	Mozart
Don Alvaro	*La Forza del Destino*	Verdi
Don Carlo	*Ernani*	Verdi
Don Carlo	*La Forza del Destino*	Verdi
Don Carlos	*Don Carlos*	Verdi
Don Fernando	*Fidelio*	Beethoven
Don Giovanni	*Don Giovanni*	Mozart
Don José	*Carmen*	Bizet
Don Magnifico	*La Cenerentola*	Rossini
Don Ottavio	*Don Giovanni*	Mozart
Don Pasquale	*Don Pasquale*	Donizetti
Don Quichotte	*Don Quichotte*	Massenet
Don Ramiro	*La Cenerentola*	Rossini
Don Rodrigo	*Don Rodrigo*	Ginastera
Donna Anna ⎫ Donna Elvira ⎭	*Don Giovanni*	Mozart
Donner	*Das Rheingold*	Wagner
Dorabella	*Così fan Tutte*	Mozart
Dosifey	*Khovanshchina*	Mussorgsky
Dr Schön	*Lulu*	Berg
Drum Major	*Wozzeck*	Berg
Drusilla	*L'Incoronazione di Poppea*	Monteverdi
Dubrovsky	*Dubrovsky*	Nápravník
Duke of Mantua	*Rigoletto*	Verdi
Dulcamara	*L'Elisir d'Amore*	Donizetti
Dutchman	*Der fliegende Holländer*	Wagner
Dyer's Wife	*Die Frau ohne Schatten*	R. Strauss
Earl of Nottingham	*Roberto Devereux*	Donizetti
Eboli	*Don Carlos*	Verdi

ROLE	OPERA	COMPOSER
Edgardo	*Lucia di Lammermoor*	Donizetti
Eglantine	*Euryanthe*	Weber
Eisenstein	*Die Fledermaus*	J. Strauss
Electra	*Idomeneo*	Mozart
Elektra	*Elektra*	R. Strauss
Elena	*Mefistofele*	Boito
Elisabeth	*Tannhäuser*	Wagner
Elisabeth de Valois	*Don Carlos*	Verdi
Elisabetta	*Elisabetta, Regina d'Inghilterra*	Rossini
Elizabeth I	*Maria Stuarda*	Donizetti
Elizabeth Zimmer	*Elegy for Young Lovers*	Henze
Ellen Orford	*Peter Grimes*	Britten
Elsa	*Lohengrin*	Wagner
Elvino	*La Sonnambula*	Bellini
Elvira	*Ernani*	Verdi
Elvira	*I Puritani*	Bellini
Emilia Marty	*The Makropoulos Case*	Janáček
Emma	*Khovanshchina*	Mussorgsky
Emperor ⎫ Empress ⎭	*Die Frau ohne Schatten*	R. Strauss
Enée	*Les Troyens*	Berlioz
Enobarbus	*Antony and Cleopatra*	Barber
Ernani	*Ernani*	Verdi
Enrico	*Lucia di Lammermoor*	Donizetti
Enzo	*La Gioconda*	Ponchielli
Erda	*Das Rheingold, Siegfried*	Wagner
Erik	*Der fliegende Holländer*	Wagner
Ernesto	*Don Pasquale*	Donizetti
Escamillo	*Carmen*	Bizet
Eugene Onegin	*Eugene Onegin*	Tchaikovsky
Euridice	*Favola d'Orfeo*	Monteverdi
Euridice	*Orfeo ed Euridice*	Gluck
Euryanthe	*Euryanthe*	Weber
Eva	*Die Meistersinger*	Wagner
Evangelist	*Der Evangelimann*	Kienzl
Fafner	*Das Rheingold, Siegfried*	Wagner
Falke	*Die Fledermaus*	J. Strauss
Falstaff	*Falstaff*	Verdi
Faninal	*Der Rosenkavalier*	R. Strauss
Fasolt	*Das Rheingold*	Wagner
Fatima	*Oberon*	Weber
Faust	*Doktor Faust*	Busoni
Faust	*Faust*	Gounod
Faust	*Mefistofele*	Boito
Fedora	*Fedora*	Giordano
Female Chorus	*The Rape of Lucretia*	Britten
Fenena	*Nabucco*	Verdi
Fenton	*Falstaff*	Verdi
Fenton	*Die Lustigen Weiber von Windsor*	Nicolai
Fernand	*La Favorite*	Donizetti

ROLE	OPERA	COMPOSER
Ferrando	*Così fan Tutte*	Mozart
Fides	*Le Prophète*	Meyerbeer
Fiesco	*Simon Boccanegra*	Verdi
Figaro	*Il Barbiere di Siviglia*	Rossini
Figaro	*Le Nozze di Figaro*	Mozart
Fiordiligi	*Così fan Tutte*	Mozart
Fiorilla	*Il Turco in Italia*	Rossini
Flamand	*Capriccio*	R. Strauss
Florestan	*Fidelio*	Beethoven
Ford	*Falstaff*	Verdi
Forester	*The Cunning Little Vixen*	Janáček
Francesca da Rimini	*Francesca da Rimini*	Zandonai
Frasquita	*Carmen*	Bizet
Frau Fluth	*Die lustigen Weiber von Windsor*	Nicolai
Freia	*Das Rheingold*	Wagner
Frère Laurent	*Roméo et Juliette*	Gounod
Fricka	*Das Rheingold, Die Walküre*	Wagner
Fritz	*L'Amico Fritz*	Mascagni
Froh	*Das Rheingold*	Wagner
Gabriele Adorno	*Simon Boccanegra*	Verdi
Geneviève	*Pelléas et Mélisande*	Debussy
Gennaro	*Lucrezia Borgia*	Donizetti
Genoveva	*Genoveva*	Schumann
Gerald	*Lakmé*	Delibes
Gérard	*Andrea Chénier*	Giordano
Germont	*La Traviata*	Verdi
Gertrude	*Hamlet*	Thomas
Gianetto	*La Gazza Ladra*	Rossini
Gianni Schicchi	*Gianni Schicchi*	Puccini
Gilda	*Rigoletto*	Verdi
Gioconda	*La Gioconda*	Ponchielli
Giovanna d'Arco	*Giovanna d'Arco*	Verdi
Giselda	*I Lombardi*	Verdi
Giuditta	*Giuditta*	Léhar
Giulietta	*I Capuleti e i Montecchi*	Bellini
Giulietta	*Les Contes d'Hoffmann*	Offenbach
Giulio Cesare	*Giulio Cesare*	Handel
Gloriana	*Gloriana*	Britten
Golaud	*Pelléas et Mélisande*	Debussy
Golitsin	*Khovanshchina*	Mussorgsky
Gonzalve	*L'Heure Espagnole*	Ravel
Grand Inquisitor	*Don Carlos*	Verdi
Gregor	*The Makropoulos Case*	Janáček
Gremin	*Eugene Onegin*	Tchaikovsky
Grigory (*see* Dimitri)		
Grisélidis	*Gresélidis*	Massenet
Guglielmo	*Così fan Tutte*	Mozart
Guillaume Tell	*Guillaume Tell*	Rossini
Gunther	*Götterdämmerung*	Wagner
Gurnemanz	*Parsifal*	Wagner

ROLE	OPERA	COMPOSER
Gutrune	*Götterdämmerung*	Wagner
Gwendoline	*Gwendoline*	Chabrier
Hagen	*Götterdämmerung*	Wagner
Halka	*Halka*	Moniusko
Hamlet	*Hamlet*	Thomas
Hans Sachs	*Die Meistersinger*	Wagner
Helen	*Ägyptische Helena*	R. Strauss
Helen	*War and Peace*	Prokofiev
Helena	*A Midsummer Night's Dream*	Britten
Hélène	*Les Vêpres Siciliennes*	Verdi
Henry Morosus	*Die schweigsame Frau*	R. Strauss
Henry VIII	*Anna Bolena*	Donizetti
Hermann	*The Queen of Spades*	Tchaikovsky
Herod	*Salome*	R. Strauss
Hérodiade	*Hérodiade*	Massenet
Herodias	*Salome*	R. Strauss
Hoffmann	*Les Contes d'Hoffmann*	Offenbach
Hunding	*Die Walküre*	Wagner
Huon	*Oberon*	Weber
Iago	*Otello*	Rossini
Iago	*Otello*	Verdi
Idamante ⎫ Idomeneo ⎬	*Idomeneo*	Mozart
Ighino	*Palestrina*	Pfitzner
Ilia	*Idomeneo*	Mozart
Imogene	*Il Pirata*	Bellini
Ines	*L'Africaine*	Meyerbeer
Ino	*Semele*	Handel
Iolanta	*Iolanta*	Tchaikovsky
Iphigénie ⎫ Iphigénie ⎬	*Iphigénie en Aulide* *Iphigénie en Tauride*	Gluck
Iris	*Iris*	Mascagni
Isabeau	*Isabeau*	Mascagni
Isabella	*L'Italiana in Algeri*	Rossini
Ismaele	*Nabucco*	Verdi
Isolde	*Tristan und Isolde*	Wagner
Ivan the Terrible	*Pskovitianka*	Rimsky-Korsakov
Ivanhoe	*Ivanhoe*	Sullivan
Jack	*The Midsummer Marriage*	Tippett
Jack Rance	*La Fanciulla del West*	Puccini
Jean de Paris	*Jean de Paris*	Boieldieu
Jenifer	*The Midsummer Marriage*	Tippett
Jeník	*The Bartered Bride*	Smetana
Jenůfa	*Jenůfa*	Janáček
Jochanaan	*Salome*	R. Strauss
Judith	*Duke Bluebeard's Castle*	Bartók
Julien	*Julien*	Charpentier
Juliette	*Roméo et Juliette*	Gounod
Jocasta	*Oedipus der Tyrann*	Orff

ROLE	OPERA	COMPOSER
Jocasta	*Oedipus Rex*	Stravinsky
Juno	*La Calisto*	Cavalli
Jupiter	*Die Liebe der Danae*	R. Strauss
Katerina Ismailova	*Lady Macbeth of the Mtsensk District*	Shostakovich
Katya Kabanová	*Katya Kabanová*	Janáček
Kecal	*The Bartered Bride*	Smetana
Khovansky	*Khovanshchina*	Mussorgsky
King Fisher	*The Midsummer Marriage*	Tippett
King Henry	*Lohengrin*	Wagner
King Marke (*see* Marke)		
King Priam	*King Priam*	Tippett
Klingsor	*Parsifal*	Wagner
Koanga	*Koanga*	Delius
Konchak	*Prince Igor*	Borodin
Kostelnička	*Jenůfa*	Janáček
Kothner	*Die Meistersinger*	Wagner
Kundry	*Parsifal*	Wagner
Kurwenal	*Tristan und Isolde*	Wagner
La Cieca	*La Gioconda*	Ponchielli
Lača	*Jenůfa*	Janáček
Lady Billows	*Albert Herring*	Britten
Lakmé	*Lakmé*	Delibes
Landgrave	*Tannhäuser*	Wagner
Lady Macbeth	*Macbeth*	Wagner
Laura	*La Gioconda*	Ponchielli
Lauretta	*Gianni Schicchi*	Puccini
Le Cid	*Le Cid*	Massenet
Leila	*Les Pêcheurs de Perles*	Bizet
Lensky	*Eugene Onegin*	Tchaikovsky
Leonora	*La Favorite*	Donizetti
Leonora	*La Forza del Destino*	Verdi
Leonora	*Oberto*	Verdi
Leonora	*Il Trovatore*	Verdi
Leonore	*Fidelio*	Beethoven
Leporello	*Don Giovanni*	Mozart
Lescaut	*Manon*	Massenet
Lescaut	*Manon Lescaut*	Puccini
Leukippos	*Daphne*	R. Strauss
Libuše	*Libuše*	Smetana
Linda di Chamounix	*Linda di Chamounix*	Donizetti
Lindoro	*L'Italiana in Algeri*	Rossini
Lionel	*Martha*	Flotow
Lisa	*The Queen of Spades*	Tchaikovsky
Liù	*Turandot*	Puccini
Lodoïska	*Lodoïska*	Cherubini
Lodoletta	*Lodoletta*	Mascagni
Loge	*Das Rheingold*	Wagner
Lohengrin	*Lohengrin*	Wagner
Lola	*Cavalleria Rusticana*	Mascagni

ROLE	OPERA	COMPOSER
Lord Percy	*Anna Bolena*	Donizetti
Loreley	*Loreley*	Catalani
Loris	*Fedora*	Girodano
Louise	*Louise*	Charpentier
Lucia	*Lucia di Lammermoor*	Donizetti
Lucio Silla	*Lucio Silla*	Mozart
Lucrezia Borgia	*Lucrezia Borgia*	Donizetti
Ludmila	*Ruslan and Ludmila*	Glinka
Luigi	*Il Tabarro*	Puccini
Luisa Miller	*Luisa Miller*	Verdi
Lulu	*Lulu*	Berg
Luna	*Il Trovatore*	Verdi
Lysander	*A Midsummer Night's Dream*	Britten
Lysiart	*Euryanthe*	Weber
Macbeth ⎤	*Macbeth*	Verdi
Macduff ⎦		
Maddalena	*Andrea Chénier*	Giordano
Maddalena	*Rigoletto*	Verdi
Magdalene	*Die Meistersinger*	Wagner
Malatesta	*Don Pasquale*	Donizetti
Malcolm	*La Donna del Lago*	Rossini
Maliella	*I Gioelli della Madonna*	Wolf-Ferrari
Mandryka	*Arabella*	R. Strauss
Manon	*Manon*	Massenet
Manon Lescaut	*Manon Lescaut*	Puccini
Manrico	*Il Trovatore*	Verdi
Marcellina	*Le Nozze di Figaro*	Mozart
Marcello	*La Bohème*	Puccini
Mařenka	*The Bartered Bride*	Smetana
Marfa	*Khovanshchina*	Mussorgsky
Margherita	*Mefistofele*	Boito
Marguerite	*Faust*	Gounod
Marguerite de Valois	*Les Huguenots*	Meyerbeer
Maria Stuarda	*Maria Stuarda*	Donizetti
Marie	*La Fille du Régiment*	Donizetti
Marie	*Wozzeck*	Berg
Marietta	*Die Tote Stadt*	Korngold
Marion Delorme	*Marion Delorme*	Ponchielli
Marina	*Boris Godunov*	Mussorgsky
Mark	*The Midsummer Marriage*	Tippett
Marke	*Tristan und Isolde*	Wagner
Mârouf	*Mârouf*	Rabaud
Marschallin	*Der Rosenkavalier*	R. Strauss
Martha	*Martha*	Flotow
Marzelline	*Fidelio*	Beethoven
Masaniello	*La Muette di Portici*	Auber
Masetto	*Don Giovanni*	Mozart
Mathilde	*Guillaume Tell*	Rossini
Mathis	*Mathis der Maler*	Hindemith
Mazeppa	*Mazeppa*	Tchaikovsky
Medea/Médée	*Médée*	Cherubini

ROLE	OPERA	COMPOSER
Mefistofele	*Mefistofele*	Boito
Meg Page	*Falstaff*	Verdi
Mélisande	*Pelléas et Mélisande*	Debussy
Melitone	*La Forza del Destino*	Verdi
Menelaos	*Die Ägyptische Helena*	R. Strauss
Méphistophélès	*Faust*	Gounod
Mercédès ⎱ Micaela ⎰	*Carmen*	Bizet
Micah	*Samson*	Handel
Michele	*Il Tabarro*	Puccini
Mignon	*Mignon*	Thomas
Milada	*Dalibor*	Smetana
Miller	*Luisa Miller*	Verdi
Miller	*Russalka* .	Dargomizhsky
Mime	*Das Rheingold, Siegfried*	Wagner
Mimi	*La Bohème*	Puccini
Minnie	*La Fanciulla del West*	Puccini
Mireille	*Mireille*	Gounod
Miss Jessel	*The Turn of the Screw*	Britten
Mistress Quickly	*Falstaff*	Verdi
Mittenhofer	*Elegy for Young Lovers*	Henze
Monostatos	*Die Zauberflöte*	Mozart
Montfort	*Les Vêpres Siciliennes*	Verdi
Mosè	*Mosè in Egitto*	Rossini
Moses	*Moses und Aron*	Schoenberg
Mrs Grose	*The Turn of the Screw*	Britten
Mrs Wingrave	*Owen Wingrave*	Britten
Musetta	*La Bohème*	Puccini
Mustafà	*L'Italiana in Algeri*	Rossini
Nabucco	*Nabucco*	Verdi
Nadir	*Les Pêcheurs de Perles*	Bizet
Nannetta	*Falstaff*	Verdi
Natasha	*War and Peace*	Prokofiev
Nedda	*Pagliacci*	Leoncavallo
Nelusko	*L'Africaine*	Meyerbeer
Nemorino	*L'Elisir d'Amore*	Donizetti
Neptune	*Il Ritorno d'Ulisse*	Monteverdi
Nerone	*Nerone*	Boito
Nerone	*Nerone*	Mascagni
Nevers	*Les Huguenots*	Meyerbeer
Nick Shadow	*The Rake's Progress*	Stravinsky
Nicklausse	*Les Contes d'Hoffmann*	Offenbach
Nightingale	*The Nightingale*	Stravinsky
Ninetta	*La Gazza Ladra*	Rossini
Norina	*L'Elisir d'Amore*	Donizetti
Norma	*Norma*	Bellini
Nurse	*Die Frau ohne Schatten*	R. Strauss
Oberon	*A Midsummer Night's Dream*	Britten
Oberon	*Oberon*	Weber

ROLE	OPERA	COMPOSER
Ochs } Octavian	Der Rosenkavalier	R. Strauss
Odabella	Attila	Verdi
Oedipus	Oedipus der Tyrann	Orff
Oedipus	Oedipus Rex	Stravinsky
Olivier	Capriccio	R. Strauss
Olympia	Les Contes d'Hoffmann	Offenbach
Ophelia	Hamlet	Thomas
Orestes	Elektra	R. Strauss
Orestes	Iphigénie en Tauride	Gluck
Orlofsky	Die Fledermaus	J. Strauss
Orontea	Orontea	Cesti
Oroveso	Norma	Bellini
Orfeo	Favola d'Orfeo	Monteverdi
Orfeo	Orfeo ed Euridice	Gluck
Ortrud	Lohengrin	Wagner
Oscar	Un Ballo in Maschera	Verdi
Osmin	Die Entführung	Mozart
Otello	Otello	Rossini
Otello	Otello	Verdi
Ottavia } Ottone	L'Incoronazione di Poppea	Monteverdi
Ottavio (see Don Ottavio)		
Owen Wingrave	Owen Wingrave	Britten
Padmâvatî	Padmâvatî	Roussel
Painter	Lulu	Berg
Palestrina	Palestrina	Pfitzner
Pamina } Papagena } Papageno	Die Zauberflöte	Mozart
Paolo	Simon Boccanegra	Verdi
Paris	Paride ed Elena	Gluck
Parsifal	Parsifal	Wagner
Paul	Die Tote Stadt	Korngold
Pedrillo	Die Entführung	Mozart
Peer Gynt	Peer Gynt	Egk
Pelléas	Pelléas et Mélisande	Debussy
Penelope	Il Ritorno d'Ulisse	Monteverdi
Pénélope	Pénélope	Fauré
Peter Grimes	Peter Grimes	Britten
Phébé	Castor et Pollux	Rameau
Philip II	Don Carlos	Verdi
Pimen	Boris Godunov	Mussorgsky
Pinkerton	Madama Butterfly	Puccini
Pistol	Falstaff	Verdi
Pizarro	Fidelio	Beethoven
Platée	Platée	Rameau
Plunkett	Martha	Flotow
Pluto	Orfeo ed Euridice	Haydn
Pogner	Die Meistersinger	Wagner
Pollione	Norma	Bellini

ROLE	OPERA	COMPOSER
Polly Peachum	*The Beggar's Opera*	Gay/Pepush
Poppea	*L'Incoronazione di Poppea*	Monteverdi
Porgy	*Porgy and Bess*	Gershwin
Posa	*Don Carlos*	Verdi
Preziosilla	*La Forza del Destino*	Verdi
Prince Igor	*Prince Igor*	Borodin
Princesse de Bouillon	*Adriana Lecouvreur*	Cilea
Procida	*Les Vêpres Siciliennes*	Verdi
Proserpine	*Il Ratto di Proserpina*	Winter
Puck	*Oberon*	Weber
Pylades	*Iphigénie en Tauride*	Gluck
Queen of Night	*Die Zauberflöte*	Mozart
Queen of Sheba	*Die Königin von Saba*	Goldmark
Queen of Sheba	*La Reine de Saba*	Gounod
Queen of Shemakha	*The Golden Cockerel*	Rimsky-Korsakov
Rachel	*La Juive*	Halévy
Radames	*Aida*	Verdi
Radamisto	*Radamisto*	Handel
Raimbaud	*Le Comte Ory*	Rossini
Raimondo	*Lucia di Lammermoor*	Donizetti
Ramfis	*Aida*	Verdi
Ramiro	*La Cenerentola*	Rossini
Raoul	*Les Huguenots*	Meyerbeer
Reiza	*Oberon*	Weber
Renata	*The Fiery Angel*	Prokofiev
Renato ⎫ Riccardo ⎭	*Un Ballo in Maschera*	Verdi
Riccardo	*I Puritani*	Bellini
Rienzi	*Rienzi*	Wagner
Rigoletto	*Rigoletto*	Verdi
Rinaldo	*Rinaldo*	Handel
Robert	*Robert le Diable*	Meyerbeer
Rocco	*Fidelio*	Beethoven
Rodelinda	*Rodelinda*	Handel
Rodolfo	*Luisa Miller*	Verdi
Rodolfo	*La Sonnambula*	Bellini
Romeo	*I Capuleti e i Montecchi*	Bellini
Romeo	*Giulietta e Romeo*	Zandonai
Roméo	*Roméo et Juliette*	Gounod
Rosalinde	*Die Fledermaus*	J. Strauss
Rosina	*Il Barbiere di Siviglia*	Rossini
Ruslan	*Ruslan and Ludmila*	Glinka
Russalka	*Russalka*	Dvořák
Sachs (see Hans Sachs)		
Sadko	*Sadko*	Rimsky-Korsakov
Saffo	*Saffo*	Paccini
Salomé	*Hérodiade*	Massenet
Salome	*Salome*	R. Strauss

ROLE	OPERA	COMPOSER
Salammbô	Salammbô	Reyer
Samson	Samson et Dalila	Saint-Saëns
Sancho Panza	Don Quichotte	Massenet
Santuzza	Cavalleria Rusticana	Mascagni
Sapho	Sapho	Massenet
Sarastro	Die Zauberflöte	Mozart
Saul	Saul and David	Nielsen
Scaramucchio	Ariadne auf Naxos	R. Strauss
Scaramucchio	Arlecchino	Busoni
Scarpia	Tosca	Puccini
Schaunard	La Bohème	Puccini
Schigolch	Lulu	Berg
Shvanda	Shvanda the Bagpiper	Weinberger
Scipione	Scipione	Handel
Selika	L'Africaine	Meyerbeer
Selim	Il Turo in Italia	Rossini
Sellem	The Rake's Progress	Stravinsky
Semele	Semele	Handel
Semiramide	Semiramide	Rossini
Seneca	L'Incoronazione di Poppea	Monteverdi
Senta	Der fliegende Holländer	Wagner
Sergei	Lady Macbeth of the Mtsensk District	Shostakovich
Servilia ⎱ Sextus ⎰	La Clemenza di Tito	Mozart
Sharpless	Madama Butterfly	Puccini
Siebel	Faust	Gounod
Sieglinde ⎱ Siegmund ⎰	Die Walküre	Wagner
Silva	Ernani	Verdi
Silvio	Pagliacci	Leoncavallo
Sinaide	Mosè in Egitto	Rossini
Snow Maiden	The Snow Maiden	Rimsky-Korsakov
Sobinin	A Life for the Tsar	Glinka
Sophie	Der Rosenkavalier	R. Strauss
Sophie	Werther	Massenet
Sparafucile	Rigoletto	Verdi
Speaker	Die Zauberflöte	Mozart
Števa	Jenůfa	Janáček
Storch	Intermezzo	R. Strauss
Suor Angelica	Suor Angelica	Puccini
Susanna	Le Nozze di Figaro	Mozart
Suzuki	Madama Butterfly	Puccini
Tamerlano	Tamerlano	Handel
Tamino	Die Zauberflöte	Mozart
Tancredi	Tancredi	Rossini
Tannhäuser	Tannhäuser	Wagner
Tatyana	Eugene Onegin	Tchaikovsky
Telramund	Lohengrin	Wagner
Teresa	Benvenuto Cellini	Berlioz
Thaïs	Thaïs	Massenet

ROLE	OPERA	COMPOSER
Thea	*The Knot Garden*	Tippett
Titania	*Oberon*	Weber
Titus	*La Clemenza di Tito*	Mozart
Tom Rakewell	*The Rake's Progress*	Stravinsky
Tonio	*La Fille du Régiment*	Donizetti
Tonio	*Pagliacci*	Leoncavallo
Tosca	*Tosca*	Puccini
Tristan	*Tristan und Isolde*	Wagner
Trulove	*The Rake's Progress*	Stravinsky
Turandot	*Turandot*	Puccini
Turridu	*Cavalleria Rusticana*	Mascagni
Tytania	*A Midsummer Night's Dream*	Britten
Ulisse	*Il Ritorno d'Ulisse*	Monteverdi
Ulrica	*Un Ballo in Maschera*	Verdi
Urbain	*Les Huguenots*	Meyerbeer
Vakula	*Vakula the Smith*	Tchaikovsky
Valentin	*Faust*	Gounod
Valentine	*Les Huguenots*	Meyerbeer
Varlaam	*Boris Godunov*	Mussorgsky
Vasco da Gama	*L'Africaine*	Meyerbeer
Venus	*Tannhäuser*	Wagner
Violetta	*La Traviata*	Verdi
Vitellia	*La Clemenza di Tito*	Mozart
Vixen	*The Cunning Little Vixen*	Janáček
Vreli	*A Village Romeo and Juliet*	Delius
Wally	*La Wally*	Catalani
Walther	*Die Meistersinger*	Wagner
Waltraute	*Götterdämmerung*	Wagner
Wanderer (Wotan)	*Siegfried*	Wagner
Werther	*Werther*	Massenet
Wilhelm Meister	*Mignon*	Thomas
Wolfram	*Tannhäuser*	Wagner
Wotan	*Rheingold, Walküre, Siegfried*	Wagner
Wozzeck	*Wozzeck*	Berg
Wurm	*Luisa Miller*	Verdi
Xerxes	*Serse*	Handel
Yriold	*Pelléas et Mélisande*	Debussy
Zaccaria	*Nabucco*	Verdi
Zaïde	*Zaïde*	Mozart
Zazà	*Zazà*	Zandonai
Zdenka	*Arabella*	R. Strauss
Zerbinetta	*Ariadne auf Naxos*	R. Strauss
Zerlina	*Don Giovanni*	Mozart
Zurga	*Les Pêcheurs de Perles*	Bizet